P9-EEB-635

WITHDRAWN
UTSA LIBRARIES

HANDBOOK OF COMPUTER NETWORKS

HANDBOOK OF COMPUTER NETWORKS

LANs, MANs, WANs, The Internet, and Global, Cellular, and Wireless Networks

Volume 2

Hossein Bidgoli
Editor-in-Chief
California State University
Bakersfield, California

John Wiley & Sons, Inc.

This book is printed on acid-free paper. ♾

Published by John Wiley & Sons, Inc., Hoboken, New Jersey
Published simultaneously in Canada

Library of Congress Cataloging-in-Publication Data:

Handbook of computer networks / edited by Hossein Bidgoli.
3 v. cm.
ISBN 978-0-471-78458-6 (cloth vol 1 : alk. paper)
ISBN 978-0-471-78459-3 (cloth vol 2 : alk. paper)
ISBN 978-0-471-78460-9 (cloth vol 3 : alk. paper)
ISBN 978-0-471-78461-6 (cloth set : alk. paper)
1. Computer networks Handbooks, manuals, etc. I. Bidgoli, Hossein.
TK5105.5.H32 2008
004.6–dc22

2007012619

Printed in the United States of America

10 9 8 7 6 5 4 3 2 1

To so many fine memories of my mother Ashraf, my father Mohammad, and my brother Mohsen, for their uncompromising belief in the power of education.

About the Editor-in-Chief

Hossein Bidgoli, Ph.D., is professor of Management Information Systems at California State University. Dr. Bidgoli helped set up the first PC lab in the United States. He is the author of 43 textbooks, 27 manuals, and over five dozen technical articles and papers on various aspects of computer applications, information systems and network security, e-commerce, and decision support systems published and presented throughout the world. Dr. Bidgoli also serves as the editor-in-chief of *The Internet Encyclopedia, The Handbook of Information Security,* and *The Encyclopedia of Information Systems.*

The Encyclopedia of Information Systems was the recipient of one of the Library Journal's Best Reference Sources for 2002 and *The Internet Encyclopedia* was recipient of one of the PSP Awards (Professional and Scholarly Publishing), 2004. Dr. Bidgoli was selected as the California State University, Bakersfield's 2001–2002 Professor of the Year.

Editorial Board

Contents

Part 3: Digital and Optical Networks

Volume II: LANs, MANs, WANs, The Internet, and Global, Cellular, and Wireless Networks

Part 1: LANs, MANs, and WANs

Part 2: The Internet, Global Networks, and VoIP

Part 3: Cellular and Wireless Networks

Volume III: Distributed Networks, Network Planning, Control, Management, and New Trends and Applications

Part 1: Distributed Networks

Part 2: Network Planning, Control, and Management

Part 3: Computer Network Popular Applications and Future Directions

Contributors

Tarek F. Abdelzhaer
University of Illinois, Urbana-Champaign
Mo Adda
University of Portsmouth, United Kingdom
Kemal Akkaya
Southern Illinois University, Carbondale
Fatih Alagöz
Bogazici University, Turkey
Omar Al-Bayari
Al-Balqa' Applied University, Jordan
Ala Al-Fuqaha
Western Michigan University, Kalamazoo
Jamal N. Al-Karaki
The Hashemite University, Jordan
Nirwan Ansari
New Jersey Institute of Technology
Ismail Ari
Hewlett-Packard Laboratories, Palo Alto, CA
Manuel Arriaga
New York University
Vijay Atluri
Rutgers University
Mark Baker
University of Reading, United Kingdom
Mario Baldi
Politecnico di Torino, Italy
Xiaoyi Bao
University of Ottawa, Canada
Valmir C. Barbosa
Universidade Federal do Rio de Janeiro, Brazil
Elyes Ben Ali Bdira
University of Sharjah, UAE
Keren Bergman
Columbia University
Larry A. Bergman
Jet Propulsion Laboratory (JPL), California Institute of Technology
Bhagyavati
DeSales University
Qi Bi
Bell Laboratory, Alcatel-Lucent Technologies Inc.
Hossein Bidgoli
California State University, Bakersfield
David Blockus
Independent Consultant
Fernando Boavida
University of Coimbra, Portugal
Benjamin Bock
Secure Business Austria
Noureddine Boudriga
University of the 7th of November, Tunisia
Nicholas David Bowman
Michigan State University
Thomas C. Bressoud
Denison University
Linda Bruenjes
Lasell College
Stephen F. Bush
GE Global Research
Werner Bux
IBM Corporation, Switzerland
Rajkumar Buyya
The University of Melbourne, Australia
John Cameron
University of Ottawa, Canada
Lillian N. Cassel
Villanova University
Tom S. Chan
Southern NH University
Kavitha Chandra
University of Massachusetts, Lowell
Hsiao-Hwa Chen
National Sun Yat-Sen University, Taiwan
Liang Chen
University of Ottawa, Canada
Thomas M.Chen
Southern Methodist University
Zhuojun Joyce Chen
University of Northern Iowa
Jau Ming Chew
University of Portsmouth, United Kingdom
Jaehak Chung
Inha University, Republic of Korea
Song Ci
University of Nebraska, Lincoln
Tim Collins
University of Birmingham, United Kingdom
Marco Conti
Institute of Informatics and Telematics (IIT), Italian National Research Council (CNR), Italy
David Coquil
University of Passau, Germany
Luís Cordeiro
University of Coimbra, Portugal
Marco Cremonini
University of Milan, Italy
Marilia Curado
University of Coimbra, Portugal
Leslie L. Daigle
Cisco Systems, Herndon, Virginia
Pragati Dalal
Canisius College
Marcos Dias de Assunção
The University of Melbourne, Australia
Serge Demidenko
Massey University, New Zealand, and Monash University, Malaysia
Hans-Peter Dommel
Santa Clara University

Kais Dridi
Université de Moncton, Canada
Arjan Durresi
Louisiana State University
Akihiro Enomoto
University of California, Irvine
Patrick J. Fahy
Athabasca University, Canada
Guangbin Fan
Intel Corporation
Farid Farahmand
Central Connecticut State University
Clayton Ferner
University of North Carolina at Wilmington
Daniel R. Fesenmaier
Temple University
Frank H.P. Fitzek
Aalborg University, Denmark
Sara Foresti
University of Milan, Italy
Dario Forte
University of Milano, Crema, Italy
Immanuel Freedman
Independent Consultant, Harleysville, Pennsylvania
Keita Fujii
University of California, Irvine
Muneo Fukaishi
NEC Corporation, Japan
Bruce Garrison
University of Miami
Z. Ghassemlooy
Northumbria University, United Kingdom
Filippo Giannetti
University of Pisa, Italy
William R. Gillis
WSU Center to Bridge the Digital Divide
James E. Goldman
Purdue University
Ulrike Gretzel
Texas A&M University
Qijun Gu
Texas State University
Xiaoyuan Gu
Technical University of Braunschweig, Germany
Mohsen Guizani
Western Michigan University
Sghaier Guizani
University of Quebec, Canada
Hong Guo
LLRC, Ontario Public Service, Canada
Mohamed A. Haleem
Stevens Institute of Technology
Habib Hamam
Universite de Moncton, Canada
Mohamed Hamdi
University of 7th of November, Carthage, Tunisia
Jon Hamkins
Jet Propulsion Laboratory, Pasadena, California
Omar M. Hammouri
University of Mississippi
Raymond A. Hansen
Purdue University
Shinsuke Hara
Osaka City University, Japan
David Harley
Small Blue-Green World, United Kingdom
Muhannad Harrim
Western Michigan University, Kalamazoo
Robert W. Heath
The University of Texas, Austin
Hamid Hemmati
Jet Propulsion Laboratory, California Institute of Technology
Murad Hizlan
Cleveland State University
Chengdu Haung
University of Illinois, Urbana-Champaign
Yuheng Huang
Qualcomm Inc.
James M. Hudson
PayPal, an eBay, Inc. Company
Gurdeep Singh Hura
University of Maryland, Eastern Shore
Hassan Ibrahim
The University of Maryland, College Park
François Ingelrest
IRCICA/LIFL University, France
Tariq Jadoon
Lahore University of Management Sciences (LUMS), Pakistan
Raj Jain
Washington University, St. Louis
Sushil Jajodia
George Mason University
Abbas Jamalipour
University of Sydney, Australia
Krishna Jayakar
Penn State University
Bandula Jayatilaka
Binghamton University, SUNY
Tao Jiang
University of Michigan, Dearborn
Stefan Joe-Yen
Northrup Grumman Corporation
Ari Juels
RSA Laboratories
Stella Kafetzoglou
National Technical University of Athens, Greece
Joonhyuk Kang
Information and Communications University (ICU), South Korea
Heather Kanuka
Athabasca University, Canada
Katz Marcos
Aalborg University, Denmark
Rick Kazman
University of Hawaii, Manoa
Azhar M. Khayrattee
Florida Institute of Technology
Yassine Khlifi
Carthage University, Tunisia
Chang-Su Kim
Korea University, Seoul

Nancy J. King
Oregon State University
David Klappholz
Stevens Institute of Technology
Markus Klemen
Vienna University of Technology, Austria
Harald Kosch
University of Passau, Germany
Jim Krause
Indiana University, Bloomington
Prashant Krishnamurthy
University of Pittsburgh
Peter Kroon
LSI, Pennsylvania
C.C. Jay Kuo
University of Southern California
Stan Kurkovsky
Central Connecticut State University
Yu-Kwong Kwok
The University of Hong Kong, Hong Kong
Amor Lazzez
CN&S Research Lab., University of the 7th of November at Carthage, Tunisia
Allen H. Levesque
Worcester Polytechnic Institute
Matthew Liotine
University of Illinois, Chicago
Natalia M. Litchinitser
University of Michigan, Ann Arbor
Jingxuan Liu
Frostburg State University
Mei-Ling L. Liu
Cal Poly San Luis Obispo
Peng Liu
Penn State University
Qingchong John Liu
Oakland University
Xiang Liu
Bell Laboratories, Lucent Technologies
Zhu Liu
AT&T Laboratories, Middletown, NJ
Asim Loan
University of Management and Technology, Lahore, Pakistan
David G. Loomis
Illinois State University, Normal
Robert D. Love
LAN Connect Consultants
Albert Lozano-Nieto
Pennsylvania State University
Ying Lu
University of Nebraska, Lincoln
Xuming Lu
University at Buffalo, SUNY
Michele Luglio
University of Rome Tor Vergata, Italy
Marco Luise
University of Pisa, Italy
Yuanqiu Luo
New Jersey Institute of Technology
Aarne Mämmelä
VTT Technical Research Centre of Finland
Konstantinos Markantonakis
Royal Holloway, University of London, United Kingdom
Manish Marwah
University of Colorado, Boulder
Mustafa M. Matalgah
University of Mississippi
Prabhaker Mateti
Wright State University
Emilio Matricciani
Dipartimento di Elettronica e Informazione Politecnico di Milano, Italy
Ketan Mayer-Patel
The University of North Carolina at Chapel Hill
Keith Mayes
Royal Holloway, University of London, United Kingdom
Cavan McCarthy
Louisiana State University
Patrick McDaniel
Pennsylvania State University
Daniel McFarland
Rowan University
Matthew K. McGowan
Bradley University
Amel Meddeb
University of the 7th of November at Carthage, Tunisia
Alfred Mertins
University of Lübeck, Germany
M. Farooque Mesiya
Rensselaer Polytechnic Institute
Marcus Messner
Virginia Commonwealth University
Mark Michael
Research in Motion Limited, Canada
Brent A. Miller
IBM Corporation
Milos Milosevic
Schlumberger Wireline Acquisition and Control Systems
Mário Minami
University of São Paulo, Brazil
Shivakant Mishra
University of Colorado, Boulder
Jelena Mišić
University of Manitoba, Canada
Vojislav B. Mišić
University of Manitoba, Canada
Shaheed N. Mohammed
Marist College
Edmundo Monteiro
University of Coimbra, Portugal
Michael Moore
University of California, Irvine
Syed H. Murshid
Florida Institute of Technology
Arun Srinivasa Murthy
Villanova University
B. Muthukumaran
Gemini Communication Limited, India
Tadashi Nakano
University of California, Irvine

Keivan Navaie
Tarbiat Modares University, Iran
Amiya Nayak
University of Ottawa, Canada
Thomas Neubauer
Vienna University of Technology, Austria
Darren B. Nicholson
Rowan University
Jennifer Nicholson
Rowan University
Richard Nieporent
Johns Hopkins University
Peng Ning
North Carolina State University
Paul W. Nutter
University of Manchester, United Kingdom
Mohammad S. Obaidat
Monmouth University
S. Obeidat
Arizona State University
Yoram Ofek
University of Trento, Italy
Yutaka Okaie
University of California, Irvine
Hong Ong
Oak Ridge National Laboratory, Tennessee
Priscilla Oppenheimer
Southern Oregon University
Raymond R. Panko
University of Hawaii, Manoa
G.I. Papadimitriou
Aristotle University, Thessaloniki, Greece
Symeon Papavassiliou
National Technical University of Athens, Greece
C. Papazoglou
Aristotle University, Thessaloniki, Greece
Stefano Paraboschi
University of Bergamo, Italy
Amanda Peart
University of Portsmouth, United Kingdom
Kenneth Pedrotti
University of California, Santa Cruz
Stephan Pfletschinger
Centre Tecnològic de Telecomunicacions de Catalunya (CTTC), Barcelona, Spain
Ronnie J. Phillips
Colorado State University
Thomas L. Pigg
Jackson State Community College
Martin Placek
The University of Melbourne, Australia
A.S. Pomportsis
Aristotle University, Greece
Dan Port
University of Hawaii, Manoa
G.N. Prezerakos
Technological Education Institute of Piraeus, Greece
Eddie Rabinovitch
ECI Technology
Miguel Arjona Ramírez
University of São Paulo, Brazil
Jeremy L. Rasmussen
Sypris Electronics
Indrajit Ray
Colorado State University
Mustapha Razzak
Université de Moncton, Canada
David R. Reavis
Texas A&M University, Texarkana
Slim Rekhis
CNAS Research Lab., University of Carthage, Tunisia
Jian Ren
Michigan State University, East Lansing
Vladimir V. Riabov
Rivier College
James A. Ritcey
University of Washington
Emilia Rosti
Università degli Studi di Milano, Italy
Liam Rourke
Nanyang Technological University, Singapore
Balqies Sadoun
Al-Balqa' Applied University, Jordan
Antonio Saitto
Telespazio, Italy
Hamidreza Saligheh
Harvard University
Atul A. Salvekar
Intel Corporation
Pierangela Samarati
University of Milan, Italy
Nabil J. Sarhan
Wayne State University
Damien Sauveron
University of Limoges, France
Michel Savoie
Communications Research Center (CRC), Canada
Mark Schaefer
OnStar Corporation
Chadwick Sessions
Northrup Grumman Corporation
Mark Shacklette
The University of Chicago
William A. Shay
University of Wisconsin, Green Bay
John Lucas Sherry
Michigan State University
Carolyn Siccama
University of Massachusetts, Lowell
Douglas C. Sicker
University of Colorado, Boulder
Farhan Siddiqui
Wayne State University
David Simplot-Ryl
Université de Lille, France
Robert Slade
Independent Consultant, Canada
Robert Slagter
Telematica Instituut, The Netherlands
Benjamin A. Small
Columbia University
Anthony H. Smith
Purdue University
Min Song
Old Dominion University

Hideyuki Sotobayashi
National Institute of Information and Communications Technology, Japan
Lee Sproull
New York University
William Stallings
Independent Consultant
Mark Stamp
San Jose State University
Charles Steinfield
Michigan State University
Ivan Stojmenovic
University of Birmingham, UK and University of Ottawa, Canada
Norman C. Strole
IBM Corporation
Koduvayur P. Subbalakshmi
Stevens Institute of Technology
Tatsuya Suda
University of California, Irvine
Anthony Sulistio
The University of Melbourne, Australia
Wayne C. Summers
Columbus State University
Vahid Tarokh
Harvard University
Colleen Taugher
WSU Center to Bridge the Digital Divide
Marvi Teixeira
Polytechnic University of Puerto Rico
Vassilis Tsaoussidis
Democritos University of Thrace, Xanthi, Greece
Michael Tunstall
University College Cork, Ireland
Okechukwu C. Ugweje
University of Akron
Zartash Afzal Uzmi
Lahore University of Management Sciences (LUMS), Pakistan
Shahrokh Valaee
University of Toronto, Canada
I.S. Venieris
National Technical University of Athens, Greece
Srikumar Venugopal
The University of Melbourne, Australia
Sabrina De Capitani di Vimercati
University of Milan, Italy
Linda Volonino
Canisius College
Mohamed El-Wakil
Western Michigan University, Kalamazoo
Youcheng Wang
University of Central Florida
James. L. Wayman
San Jose State University
Troy Weingart
University of Colorado, Boulder
Edgar R. Weippl
Vienna University of Technology, Austria
Stephen A. Weis
Google
Risto Wichman
Helsinki University of Technology, Finland
Barry Wilkinson
University of North Carolina, at Charlotte
Tin Win
Monash University, Malaysia
Raymond F. Wisman
Indiana University Southeast
Paul L. Witt
Texas Christian University
Albert K.S. Wong
Hong Kong University of Science and Technology, Hong Kong
Michael Workman
Florida Institute of Technology
Jing Wu
Communications Research Centre (CRC), Canada
Geoffrey G. Xie
Naval Postgraduate School
Jiang Xie
University of North Carolina, Charlotte
Xu Yan
Hong Kong University of Science and Technology, Hong Kong
Wei Ye
University of Southern California
Chee Shin Yeo
The University of Melbourne, Australia
Si Yin
New Jersey Institute of Technology
Jia Yu
The University of Melbourne, Australia
Viktor Zaharov
Polytechnic University of Puerto Rico
Faouzi Zarai
University of the 7th of November, Tunisia
S. Zeadally
University of the District of Columbia
Jingyuan Zhang
University of Alabama
Nan Zhang
Hong Kong University of Science and Technology, Hong Kong
Qinqing Zhang
Bell Laboratory, Alcatel-Lucent Technologies Inc.
Qiong (Jo) Zhang
Arizona State University, West Campus
Jiying Zhao
University of Ottawa, Canada
Mingshan Zhao
Dalian University of Technology, People's Republic of China
Wen-De Zhong
Nanyang Technological University, Singapore
Chi Zhou
Illinois Institute of Technology
Jin Zhu
University of Northern Iowa
Junaid Ahmed Zubairi
State University of New York, Fredonia

Preface

The Handbook of Computer Networks is the first comprehensive examination of the core topics in the computer network field. *The Handbook of Computer Networks,* a 3-volume reference work, with 202 chapters, 3400+ pages, is a comprehensive coverage of the computer network field with coverage of the core topics.

The primary audience is the libraries of 2-year and 4-year colleges and universities with Computer Science, Computer Engineering, Network Engineering, Telecommunications, Data Communications, MIS, CIS, IT, IS, Data Processing, and Business departments, public and private libraries and corporate libraries throughout the world, and educators and practitioners in the networking and telecommunications fields.

The secondary audience is a variety of professionals and a diverse group of academic and professional courses for the individual volumes.

Among industries expected to become increasingly dependent upon the computer networks and telecommunications and active in understanding the many issues surrounding this important and fast-growing field are: government agencies, military, education, libraries, health, medical, law enforcement, accounting firms, law firms, justice, manufacturing, financial services, insurance, communications, transportation, aerospace, energy, biotechnology, retail, and utilities.

Each volume incorporates state-of-the-art core information and computer networks and telecommunications topics, practical applications, and coverage of the emerging issues in the computer networks field.

This definitive 3-volume *Handbook* offers coverage of both established and cutting-edge theories and developments in the computer networks and telecommunications fields. The *Handbook* contains chapters from global experts in academia and industry. The *Handbook* offers the following unique features:

1. Each chapter follows a unique format including Title and Author, Outline, Introduction, Body, Conclusion, Glossary, Cross-References, and References. This unique format assists the readers to pick and choose various sections of a chapter. It also creates consistency throughout the entire series.
2. The *Handbook* has been written by more than 270 experts and reviewed by more than 1000 academics and practitioners chosen from around the world. These diverse collections of expertise have created the most definitive coverage of established and cutting-edge theories and applications of this fast-growing field.
3. Each chapter has been rigorously peer reviewed. This review process assures the accuracy and completeness of each topic.
4. Each chapter provides extensive online and off-line references for additional reading. This will enable the readers to go further with their understanding of a given topic.
5. More than 1000 illustrations and tables throughout the series highlight complex topics and assist further understanding.
6. Each chapter provides extensive cross-references. This helps the readers to read other chapters related to a particular topic, providing a one-stop knowledge base for a given topic.
7. More than 2500 glossary items define new terms and buzzwords throughout the series, assisting in understanding of concepts and applications.
8. The *Handbook* includes a complete table of contents and index sections for easy access to various parts of the series.
9. The series emphasizes both technical as well as managerial issues. This approach provides researchers, educators, students, and practitioners with a balanced understanding and the necessary background to deal with problems related to understanding computer networks and telecommunications issues and to be able to design a sound computer and telecommunications system.
10. The series has been developed based on the current core course materials in several leading universities around the world and current practices in leading computer, telecommunications, and networking corporations. This format should appeal to a diverse group of educators and researchers in the networking and telecommunications fields.

We chose to concentrate on fields and supporting technologies that have widespread applications in academic and business worlds. To develop this *Handbook,* we carefully reviewed current academic research in the networking field in leading universities and research institutions around the world.

Computer networks and telecommunications, network security, management information systems, network design and management, computer information systems (CIS), and electronic commerce curriculums, recommended by the Association of Information Technology Professionals (AITP) and the Association for Computing Management (ACM) were carefully investigated. We also researched the current practices in the networking field carried out by leading networking and telecommunications corporations. Our work assisted us in defining the boundaries and contents of this project. Its chapters address technical as well as managerial issues in the networking and telecommunications fields.

TOPIC CATEGORIES

Based on our research, we identified nine major topic areas for the Handbook:

- Key Concepts
- Hardware, Media, and Data Transmission
- Digital and Optical Networks
- LANs, MANs, and WANs
- The Internet, Global Networks, and VoIP
- Cellular and Wireless Networks
- Distributed Networks
- Network Planning, Control, and Management
- Computer Network Popular Applications and Future Directions

Although these nine categories are interrelated, each addresses one major dimension of the computer networks and telecommunications fields. The chapters in each category are also interrelated and complementary, enabling readers to compare, contrast, and draw conclusions that might not otherwise be possible.

Though the entries have been arranged logically, the light they shed knows no bounds. The *Handbook* provides unmatched coverage of fundamental topics and issues for successful design and implementation of a computer network and telecommunications systems. Its chapters can serve as material for a wide spectrum of courses such as:

Grid Computing
Distributed Intelligent Networks
Multimedia Networking
Peer-to-Peer Networks
Cluster Computing
Voice over IP
Storage Area Networks
Network Backup and Recovery Systems
Digital Networks
Optical Networks
Cellular Networks
Wireless Networks
Telecommunications Systems
Computer Network Management

Successful design and implementation of a sound computer network and telecommunications systems requires a thorough knowledge of several technologies, theories, and supporting disciplines. Networking researchers and practitioners have had to consult many resources to find answers. Some of these sources concentrate on technologies and infrastructures, some on applications and implementation issues, and some on managerial concerns. This *Handbook* provides all of this relevant information in a comprehensive three-volume set with a lively format.

Each volume incorporates core networking and telecommunications topics, practical applications, and coverage of the emerging issues in the networking and telecommunications fields. Written by scholars and practitioners from around the world, the chapters fall into nine major subject areas:

Key Concepts

Chapters in this group examine a broad range of topics. Fundamental theories, concepts, technologies, and applications related to computer networks, data communications, and telecommunications are discussed. These chapters explain the OSI reference model and then discuss various types of compression techniques including data, image, video, speech, and audio compression. This part concludes with a discussion of multimedia streaming and high definition television (HDTV) as their applications are on the rise. The chapters in this part provide a solid foundation for the rest of the Handbook.

Hardware, Media, and Data Transmission

Chapters in this group concentrate on the important types of hardware used in network and telecommunications environments and then examine popular media used in data communications including wired and wireless media. The chapters in this part explain different types of modulation techniques for both digital and optical networks and conclude with coverage of various types of multiplexing techniques that are being used to improve the efficiency and effectiveness of commutations media.

Digital and Optical Networks

Chapters in this group discuss important digital and optical technologies that are being used in modern communication and computer networks. Different optical switching techniques, optical devices, optical memories, SONET, and SDH networks are explained.

LANs, MANs, and WANs

This group of chapters examines major types of computer reworks including local, metropolitan, and wide area networks. Popular types of operating systems used in a LAN environment are discussed, including Windows and Linux. The chapters also examine various types of switching techniques including packet, circuit, and message switching. The chapters discuss broadband network applications and technologies and conclude with a discussion of multimedia networking.

The Internet, Global Networks, and VoIP

Chapters in this group explore a broad range of topics. They review the Internet fundamentals, history, domain name systems, and Internet2. The architecture and functions of the Internet and important protocols including TCP/IP, SMPT, and IP multicast are discussed. The chapters in this group also explain the network and end-system quality of service and then discuss VoIP and its various components, protocols, and applications.

Cellular and Wireless Networks

Chapters in this group explain cellular and wireless networks. Major standards, protocols, and applications in the cellar environment are discussed. This includes a detailed coverage of GSM, GPRS, UMTS, CDMA, and TDMA. The chapters in this group explore satellite communications principles, technologies, protocols, and applications in detail. The chapters conclude with coverage of wireless wide area networks and wireless broadband access.

Distributed Networks

The chapters in this group investigate distributed networks, their fundamentals, architectures, and applications. Grid computing, cluster computing, and peer-to-peer networks are discussed in detailed. These chapters also explore storage area networks, fiber channels, and fault tolerant systems. This part concludes with a discussion of distributed algorithms and distributed databases.

Network Planning, Control, and Management

The chapters in this group discuss theories, methodologies, and technologies that enhance successful network planning, control, and management. After discussion of network capacity planning and network modeling, the chapters concentrate on the identification of threats and vulnerabilities in a network environment. The chapters then present a number of tools and technologies that if properly utilized could significantly improve the integrity of data resources and computer networks by keeping hackers and crackers at bay. This part concludes with a discussion of business continuity planning, e-mail, and Internet use policies, and computer network management.

Computer Network Popular Applications and Future Directions

Chapters in this group present several popular applications of computer networks and telecommunications systems. These applications could not have been successfully utilized without a sound computer network and telecommunications system. Some of these applications include conferencing, banking, electronic commerce, travel and tourism, and Web-based training and education. This part concludes with a discussion of future trends in computer networking including biologically inspired networking, active networks, and molecular communication.

Specialists have written the *Handbook* for experienced and not so experienced readers. It is to these contributors that I am especially grateful. This remarkable collection of scholars and practitioners have distilled their knowledge into a fascinating and enlightening one-stop knowledge base in computer networks and telecommunications that "talks" to readers. This has been a massive effort, but one of the most rewarding experiences I have ever had. So many people have played a role that it is difficult to know where to begin.

I should like to thank the members of the editorial board for participating in the project and for their expert advice on help with the selection of topics, recommendations for authors, and reviewing the materials. Many thanks to more than 1000 reviewers who devoted their time by providing advice to me and the authors for improving the coverage, accuracy, and comprehensiveness of these materials.

I thank my senior editor Matt Holt, who initiated the idea of the *Handbook*. Through a dozen drafts and many reviews, the project got off the ground and then was managed flawlessly by Matt and his professional team. Matt and his team made many recommendations for keeping the project focused and maintaining its lively coverage.

Jessica Campilango, our editorial coordinator, assisted our authors and me during the many phases of its development. I am grateful for all her support. When it came to the production phase, the superb Wiley production team took over. Particularly I want to thank Deborah Schindlar and Miriam Palmer-Sherman, our production editors. I am grateful for all their hard work. I also want to thank Lynn Lustberg, our project manager from ICC Macmillan Inc. Her thoroughness made it easier to complete the project. I am grateful to all her efforts. I thank Kim Dayman and Christine Kim, our marketing team, for their impressive marketing campaign launched on behalf of the *Handbook*.

Last, but not least, I want to thank my wonderful wife, Nooshin, and my two children, Mohsen and Morvareed, for being so patient during this venture. They provided a pleasant environment that expedited the completion of this project. Mohsen and Morvareed assisted me in sending out thousands of e-mail messages to our authors and reviewers. Nooshin was a great help in designing and maintaining the authors' and reviewers' databases. Their efforts are greatly appreciated. Also, my two sisters, Azam and Akram, provided moral support throughout my life. To this family, any expression of thanks is insufficient.

Hossein Bidgoli
California State University, Bakersfield

Guide to The Handbook of Computer Networks

The Handbook of Computer Networks is a comprehensive coverage of the relatively new and very important field of computer networks and telecommunications systems. This reference work consists of three separate volumes and 202 different chapters on various aspects of this field. Each chapter in the Handbook provides a comprehensive overview of the selected topic, intended to inform a broad spectrum of readers, ranging from computer network professionals and academicians to students to the general business community.

In order that you, the reader, will derive the greatest possible benefit from *The Handbook of Computer Networks*, we have provided this Guide. It explains how the information within it can be located.

Organization

The Handbook of Computer Networks is organized to provide the maximum ease of use for its readers. All of the chapters are arranged logically in these three volumes. Individual volumes could be used independently. However, the greatest benefit is derived if all three volumes are investigated.

Table of Contents

A complete table of contents of the entire Handbook appears at the front of each volume. This list of chapter titles represents topics that have been carefully selected by the editor-in-chief, Dr. Hossein Bidgoli, and his colleagues on the Editorial Board.

Index

A Subject Index for each individual volume is located at the end of each volume. This index is the most convenient way to locate a desired topic within the Handbook. The subjects in the index are listed alphabetically and indicate the page number where information on this topic can be found.

Chapters

The author's name and affiliation are displayed at the beginning of the chapter. All chapters in the Handbook are organized according to a standard format as follow:

Title and Author
Outline
Introduction
Body
Conclusion
Glossary
Cross References
References

Outline

Each chapter begins with an outline indicating the content of the chapter to come. This outline provides a brief overview of the chapter, so that the reader can get a sense of what is contained there without having to leaf through the pages. It also serves to highlight important subtopics that will be discussed within the chapter. For example, the chapter "The Internet Fundamentals" includes sections for Information Superhighway and the World Wide Web, Domain Name Systems, Navigational Tools, Search Engines, and Directories.

The Outline is intended as an overview and thus it lists only the major headings of the chapter. In addition, second-level and third-level headings will be found within the chapter.

Introduction

The text of each chapter begins with an introductory section that defines the topic under discussion and summarizes the content of the chapter. By reading this section the readers get a general idea regarding a specific chapter.

Body

The body of each chapter discusses the items that were listed in the outline section of each chapter.

Conclusion

The conclusion section provides a summary of the materials discussed in a particular chapter. This section leaves the readers with the most important issues and concepts discussed in a particular chapter.

Glossary

The glossary contains terms that are important to an understanding of the chapter and that may be unfamiliar to the reader. Each term is defined in the context of the particular chapter in which it is used. Thus, the same term may be defined in two or more chapters with the detail of the definition varying slightly from one chapter to another. The Handbook includes approximately 2700 glossary terms. For example, the chapter "The Internet Fundamentals" includes the following glossary entries:

Extranet A secure network that uses the Internet and Web technology to connect two or more intranets of trusted business partners, enabling business-to-business, business-to-consumer, consumer-to-consumer, and consumer-to-business communications.

Intranet A network within the organization that uses Web technologies (TCP/IP, HTTP, FTP, SMTP, HTML, XML, and its variations) for collecting, storing, and disseminating useful information throughout the organization.

Cross References

All the chapters in the Handbook have cross references to other chapters. These appear at the end of the chapter, following the chapter text and preceding the References. The cross references indicate related chapters that can be consulted for further information on the same topic. The Handbook contains more than 2000 cross references in all. For example, the chapter "The Internet Fundamentals" has the following cross references:

Electronic Commerce, Electronic Data Interchange (EDI), Electronic Payment Systems, History of the Internet, Internet2, Internet Domain Name System, Information Retrieval on the Internet.

References

The References appears as the last element in a chapter. It lists recent secondary sources to aid the reader in locating more detailed or technical information. Review articles and research papers that are important to an understanding of the topic are also listed. The References in this Handbook are for the benefit of the reader, to provide references for further research on the given topic. Thus, they typically consist of a dozen to two dozen entries. They are not intended to represent a complete listing of all materials consulted by the author in preparing the chapter.

PART 1

LANs, MANs, and WANs

Local Area Networks

Wayne C. Summers, *Columbus State University*

INTRODUCTION TO LOCAL AREA NETWORKS

A network is a collection of two or more devices linked together. Typically the connection is a physical connection using wires or cables, although wireless connections are also possible for networks. In addition to the hardware required for this connection, there is communication software necessary to allow the communications to occur. Networks facilitate the sharing of resources including hardware, software, and data as well as providing a mechanism for enhancing communications between computers and users of computers.

Networks can be primarily classified as local area networks (LANs) and wide area networks (WANs). Traditionally the distinction between these classifications of networks has been the size or radius of the network. A LAN is a network where the computers are physically close together. This may mean that the computers are in the same room, the same building, or even at the same site. Computers in a WAN are often distributed beyond metropolitan areas. WANs are made up of multiple LANs as in the case of the Internet. Other classifications of networks may include personal area networks (PANs), metro area networks (MANs), and storage area networks (SANs). Networks can also be classified by the network protocols at the physical/data-link layers of the network. Often the distinction between LANs and WANs depends on who controls the network. WANs are typically controlled by the Internet service provider (ISP), whereas LANs are more often controlled by the local network administrator.

Why Do We Want to Network Computers?

In the early days of computing, there were a small number of computers, which could be used by only one person at a time. With the emergence of time-sharing linking terminals to mainframe computers in the 1960s, individual computers were able to be used by more than one user simultaneously. This significantly expanded the functionality of computers, but had several limitations. Chief among the limitations was that as more users connected to the shared computer, the amount of resources available for each user's transaction diminished. In the late 1970s and early 1980s, the personal computer (PC) resulted in the return of one computer—one user (Figure 1). Finally, in the 1990s, hardware and software became available to network multiple PCs (Figure 2). Before LANs, copies of data needed to be kept by every user of the data on each computer and copies of software or application programs used by each user had to be installed on each computer. Printing a document required that every computer needed its own printer or the user walked to the computer with the attached printer and loaded the document on that computer. Networking computers alleviates some of this need for redundancy, although there will still be some redundancy needed for backup purposes.

Figure 1: Before networks

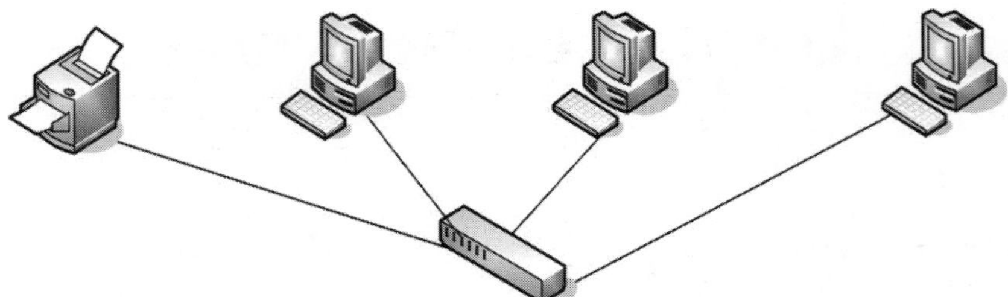

Figure 2: Networked computers

Data in a networked environment can be shared. Each user can access the data from other computers via the network. This feature of networks helped speed the transition from mainframe computing to networked computing. Networked computers allow important information to be shared among different computer users. Rather than keeping copies of data on each computer, one copy of the data is kept on a server and accessed remotely via the network. Changes to the data are made once, and then accessed by all.

Rather than installing software on every computer, software can be shared in a network environment. Application programs can be stored on one computer and run remotely from another computer. In an office configured with multiple non-networked computers, each computer must have installed a copy of each application program that is used. In addition to the need to purchase copies of the software for each computer, the software must be installed and maintained on each computer. Network versions of many application programs can be purchased. A networked version of software is typically much cheaper than purchasing large numbers of a particular piece of software. Network software only needs to be installed once on a server allowing users on the other computers to access the software. When it is time to upgrade the software, it only needs to be done once on the server, instead of on all of the computers. Installing software on multiple computers simultaneously can be facilitated using networked computers with the software residing on the server.

Networks facilitate the sharing of hardware. Hardware can be installed in one location and accessed over the network from other computers. Printers and scanners can be networked so that multiple users can share the same printer or other hardware device. Other peripheral devices might include CD-ROMs, DVD-ROMs, and other shared devices.

Before LANs, computer users that needed to communicate with others had to use traditional methods such as a physical visit to another user, a telephone call, or a letter delivered to the other person. Communications have been enhanced tremendously with e-mail and instant messaging (IM) facilitated by the use of LANs.

TYPES OF LANs

Computers that can access a network are often referred to as networked workstations or hosts. Any device (workstation, printer, modem) that connects to a network is called a node.

Many of the networks in the early 1980s only allowed the sharing of resources directly between PCs. These types of networks are called peer-to-peer networks. Each computer has the same potential for sharing files and hardware devices. A peer-to-peer network is easy to design and maintain, but is limited in its capabilities and in capacity.

Most networks today are classified as client/server networks. In a client/server network, one or more of the computers function as servers, whereas the remainder of the computers functions as clients. A server is a computer that provides a service, whereas a client computer makes use of the service provided. Examples of servers include print servers, file servers, mail servers, and Web servers. A print server (Figure 3) is a computer or peripheral device that provides access to one or more printers across the network. Print servers were among the earliest type of servers. A file server provides a repository for files that can be accessed by other computers over the network. Mail or communication servers manage the flow of incoming and outgoing electronic mail for users accessing the server from client workstations. Web servers are computers running software that provides access to World Wide Web documents.

Computers on a network can run more than one type of server software and can function as multiple types of servers. For example, a computer can have both Web server and e-mail server software installed and function as both a Web server and a communications server. A workstation can function both as a server and simultaneously as a client for another server. For example, a computer can be a Web server running Web server software, but print through the network using another computer that functions as a print server. It is generally not recommended that one computer function as more than one server. Doing so increases the likelihood of one point of attack on the network. However, using a separate computer for each server results in more potentially vulnerable computers and increased administration costs. This increases the points of attack and needs to be taken into consideration. Running only one main service (e.g., e-mail) can significantly increase the reliability of the network, because instability and maintenance associated with that service will typically not affect other services running on separate servers.

Similarly, it is recommended that servers not function as clients. Using a server as a client increases the

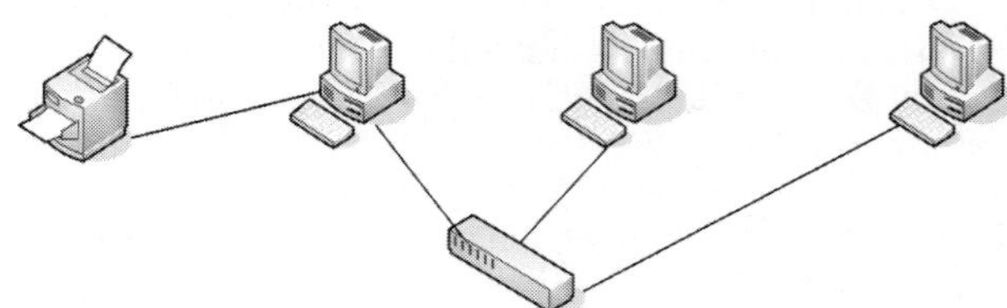

Figure 3: Print server

opportunity for introducing security vulnerabilities that might compromise the security of the server.

Difference Between LANs and WANs

As mentioned earlier, one distinction between LANs and WANs is the radius of the network. A LAN is a network where the nodes are physically close together. Typically, the nodes are in the same room, but they can be in the same building or in nearby buildings. In today's networks, the nodes are often scattered across the organization. Historically, networks with a radius greater than a kilometer or two are typically classified as WANs. Other ways of distinguishing between LANs and WANs include transmission speed and ownership. LANs are typically faster networks with speeds of at least 10 Mbps to 10 Gbps. WANs are generally significantly slower, with most WANs operating at speeds around 1.54 Mbps (T1/DS1) or 45 Mbps (T3/DS3). Today very high-speed WANs exist that approach LAN speeds. LANs are owned by the organization where the network is used. WANs generally use hardware that is owned and operated by a network provider, although there are public agencies that do own and operate their own WANs. A final distinction is with the difference in technologies used by LANs and WANs. The next section describes two of the technologies (Ethernet and token ring) used by LANs.WANs typically use different technologies, including Frame Relay, ATM, and X.25. Recently, Ethernet has started to be deployed in WANs as Metro Ethernet. These distinctions have continued to blur significantly over the last several years as WANs get faster and LANs get larger.

LAN Topology

LANs can be organized in a variety of ways. One way to classify networks is by their electrical configuration or logical topology. This is often called the signal topology and is determined by how the nodes communicate with each other. This is basically the way the data is transmitted between nodes. The two main logical topologies are bus and ring.

In a traditional bus network, the data is broadcast from one node to all other nodes in the LAN even though the data may be intended for only one node. Each of the nodes receives the data, but it is only "read" by the node where the data is intended. The data includes an address for the destination node or nodes. Ethernet is the primary technology that supports the bus logical topology.

In a ring network, the data is sent from one node to the next in sequential order in a circular fashion. Each node inspects the destination address of the data packet to determine if the data is meant for it. If the data is not meant for the node, the data packet is passed along to the next node in the logical ring.

LANs can also be classified by the physical layout of the network. The way that the nodes are physically connected to the network is known as the physical topology. The physical topology of the network can have a significant influence on a LAN's performance and reliability. The three main physical topologies are bus, ring, and star. There are also hybrid networks including star-bus and star-ring, which incorporate parts of both types of networks. These "mixed" topologies are more common implementations.

In a bus topology (Figure 4), the nodes are arranged in a linear fashion, with terminators (Figure 5) on each end. The nodes are connected to the "bus" with connectors. Bus networks are easy to install but not very reliable. Any break in the connection, or a loose connection, will bring down a portion of the network and possibly the entire network. This is old technology rarely used in modern LANs.

In a ring topology (Figure 6), each connected node is an active participant in the ring network. Each data packet is received by a node, and, if it is not intended for the node, it is passed along the ring to the next node. If one of the nodes or its network card malfunctions, the network stops functioning.

In a star network (Figure 7) each connected node is attached to a central device. Typically this device is a hub or a switched hub, but it could also be other devices, including a multistation access unit. Star networks are more economical and easier to troubleshoot. Star networks do require an additional hardware device like a hub or switch, and additional cable. Because each node is independently connected to the central device, a failure

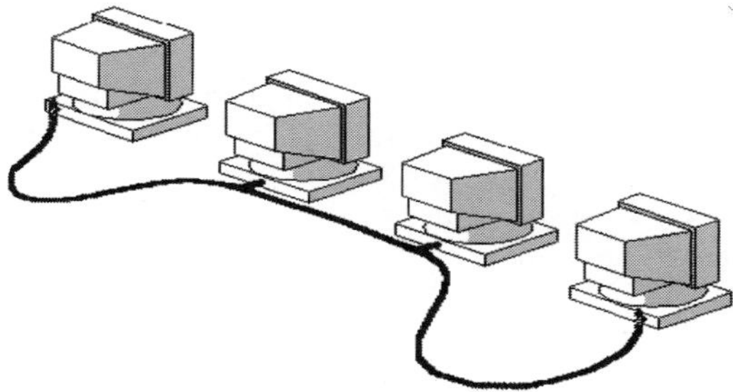

Figure 4: Bus network

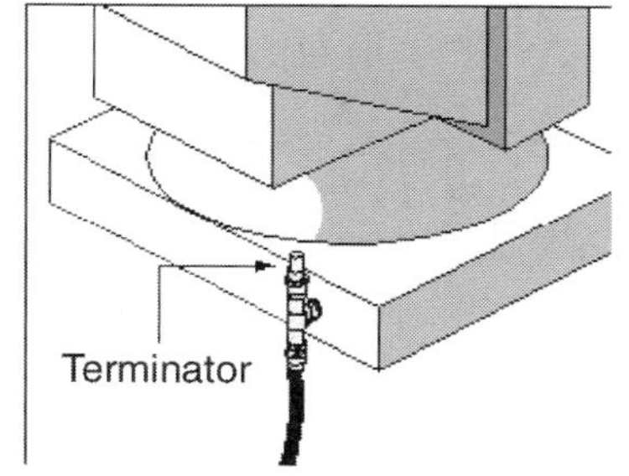

Figure 5: Terminator and BNC T-connector

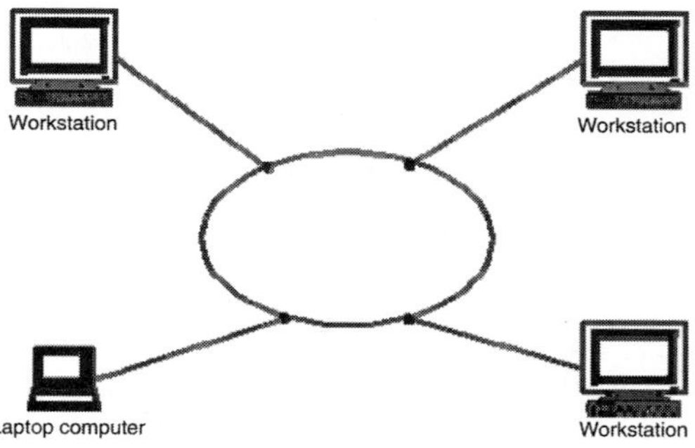

Figure 6: Ring network

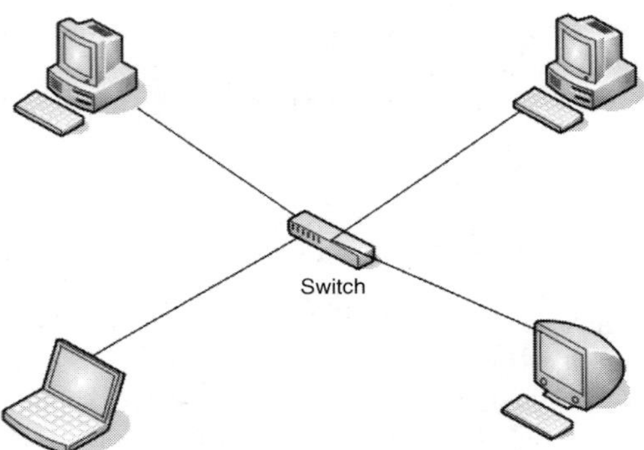

Figure 7: Star physical network

only affects the single node. Of course if the central device fails, the entire network fails.

A network's physical and logical topologies are not necessarily the same. For example, a twisted-pair Ethernet network using a hub is physically arranged with a star topology, although the data is transmitted via a bus topology.

LAN Architecture

The most dominant network architecture for LANs today is Ethernet. Ethernet was developed by Robert Metcalfe and others at the Palo Alto Research Center (PARC) in the mid-1970s (Metcalfe and Boggs, 1976).

Ethernet uses the carrier sense multiple access with collision detection (CSMA/CD) access method. Carrier sense refers to each node being able to "listen" for other users using the network, only attempting to use the network if it is not being used. Multiple access means that any node on the network may use the network without requiring further permission. Collision detection lets the node know if a message was not delivered and controls the mechanism for retransmitting the data packet. CSMA/CD is most efficient when there are a limited number of nodes requesting access to the network. As the radius of the network and number of nodes on the network increases, the likelihood of collisions increases.

In 1981, the first Ethernet standard was developed by a consortium comprised of Digital, Intel, and Xerox. This was followed by a second Ethernet standard in 1982, called Ethernet II. Ethernet II (Figure 8) had the following characteristics:

- bus topology
- coaxial cable using baseband signaling
- 10 Mbit/sec data rate
- maximum station separation of 2.8 kilometers
- 1024 maximum number of stations

In addition, the Institute of Electrical and Electronics Engineers (IEEE) developed a standard, also often referred to as Ethernet, called the IEEE 802.3 standard (Figure 9). The two standards are very similar and have similar frame layouts as shown. Although Ethernet has continued to evolve over the past 25 years, the main concepts have remained.

Ethernet can run over a variety of media types including several types of coax cable, twisted pair cable, and fiber optic cable, as well as wireless formats, including radio signals and infrared. Table 1 lists several of these media types. The first number indicates the speed in megabits, the "base" refers to baseband transmission meaning that the entire bandwidth is dedicated to just one data channel, and the last number or letter indicates the approximate maximum segment length or the media type.

A second network architecture, Token Ring or IEEE 802.5 (Figure 10), was developed in early 1970s by IBM. A Token Ring network is often preferred for time-sensitive and mission-critical applications. Token Ring networks use the token passing access method. Only the computer that has the 24-bit packet of data called the token may use the network. This token is generated by a designated computer called the active monitor and passed around the ring until one of the computers wishes to use the network. When a computer wants to use the network, it seizes the token, changes the status of the token to busy, inserts its data frame onto the network, and only releases the token when it receives a confirmation that the data packet has been received. A Token Ring network uses a sequential

Preamble 8 octets	Destination MAC Address 6 octets	Source MAC Address 6 octets	Type 2 octets	Data Unit and Padding 46–1500 bytes	Frame Check Sequence 4 octets

Figure 8: Ethernet II frame layout

Preamble 7 octets	SFD 1 octet	Destination MAC Address 6 octets	Source MAC Address 6 octets	Length 2 octets	Logical Link Control IEEE 802.2 Data and Pad 46–1500 bytes	Frame Check Sequence 4 octets

Figure 9: IEEE 802.3 frame layout

Table 1: Types of Network Media

Standard	Popular Name	Speed	Media	Maximum Segment Length
10Base2	Thinnet; cheapnet	10 Mbps	Thin coaxial cable RG-58	185 meters
10Base5	Thicknet, yellow hose	10 Mbps	Thick coaxial cable RG-8 or RG-11	500 meters
10BaseT	10BaseT twisted pair Ethernet UTP	10 Mbps	Unshielded twisted pair CAT3, CAT5	100 meters
10BaseFL	Fiber Ethernet FOIRL	10 Mbps	Multimode fiber-optic cable	1000 meters
100BaseT4	Fast Ethernet	100 Mbps	4 pair telephone grade cable	100 meters
100BaseTX	Fast Ethernet	100 Mbps	2 pair data grade cable	100 meters
100BaseFX	Fast Ethernet	100 Mbps	2 strands fiber cable	400 meters
1000BaseT	Gigabit Ethernet	1 Gbps	4 pair Cat5e	100 meters
1000BaseLX/LH	Long haul Gigabit Ethernet	1 Gbps	Multimode fiber	10 kilometers
1000BaseZX	Extended Gigabit Ethernet	1 Gbps	Single-mode fiber	100 kilometers
10GBase	10 Gigabit Ethernet	10 Gbps	Fiber	300 meters
10GBaseLX4	Long haul 10 GB Ethernet	10 Gbps	Single-mode fiber	10 kilometers

Starting Delimiter 1 octet	Access Control 1 octet	Frame Control 1 octet	Destination Address 6 octets	Source Address 6 octets	Optional Routing Information Field Up to 18 octets	Optional LLC Fields 3 or 4 octets	DATA Unlimited size	Frame Check Sequence 4 octets	Ending Delimiter 1 octet	Frame Status 1 octet

Figure 10: IEEE 802.5 token frame layout

logical topology, which was traditionally a ring physical topology but now is typically a star topology. IBM specified two architectures that operated at 4 and 16 Mbps. Token Ring networks are no longer widely supported. Ethernet and Token Ring standards are typically associated with the data-link layer of the Open Systems Interconnection Basic Reference (OSI) Model, in particular the Media Access Control (MAC) sub-layer that defines the access method and framing format corresponding to the LAN protocol.

In the mid-1980s, the American National Standards Institute (ANSI) X3T9.5 standards committee released a standard for data communications in a local area network called Fiber Distributed Data Interface (FDDI). FDDI is similar to token ring, using dual counter-rotating rings. The primary ring is used for data transmission with the main function of the secondary ring for backup. FDDI can extend the range of a local area network up to 100 kilometers at 100 Mbps. FDDI uses optical fiber as the transmission media. A similar architecture uses copper and is called Copper Distributed Data Interface (CDDI).

LAN HARDWARE AND MEDIA

There are a variety of media choices for connecting computers to a local area network. Early networks used copper wires—either coaxial or twisted pair. The standards detailing the LAN hardware and media are associated with the physical layer of the OSI Model.

Copper Wire

Coaxial cable consists of a center wire surrounded by insulation and then a grounded shield of braided wire. The shield minimizes electrical and radio frequency interference. A coaxial cable was typically referred to as either thinnet or thicknet. Thicknet (Figure 11) was the original standard for Ethernet and is defined by the IEEE 10Base-5 standard and uses 50 ohm coaxial cable (RG-8 or RG-11 A/U) with maximum lengths of 500 meters. Thinnet (Figure 12) is defined by the IEEE 10Base-2 standard and uses 50 ohm coaxial cable (RG-58 A/U) with maximum lengths of 185 meters. RG-58 is similar to the coaxial cable

Figure 11: RG-58 coaxial cable

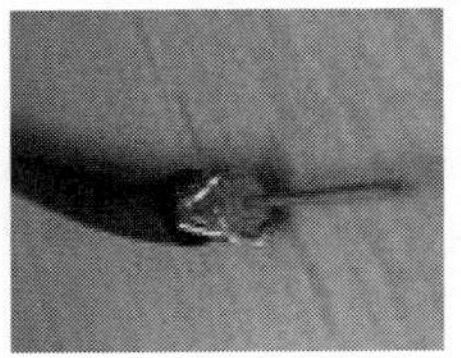

Figure 12: RG-8 coaxial cable

Figure 13: BNC connector

Figure 14: CAT5 patch cable

Figure 15: CAT6 twisted pairs of wires

used with cable TVs. Cables in the 10Base-2 system connect to other devices with BNC connectors (Figure 13).

Twisted pair networking cable also has two different forms—UTP (unshielded twisted-pair) and STP (shielded twisted-pair). Both types of cable consist of either two or four pairs of wire. Each pair is twisted together. Shielded twisted-pair cable has an additional layer of conducting material surrounding the twisted-pairs of wires. Unshielded twisted-pair cable does not have the additional layer. Telephone companies use UTP cable with two twisted-pairs of wires. UTP is the most common and least expensive method for networking computers (Figure 14). There are seven categories of unshielded twisted-pair cabling ranging from Category 1 (CAT1), which is ordinary telephone cable used to carry voice, to Category 7 (CAT7) (Figure 15), which is designed for high-speed networks. CAT6 and CAT7 use 23 AWG copper as opposed to the 24 AWG used in CAT5/CAT5e and lower, therefore the signal attenuates (loses signal strength) less with speed and distance. CAT6 also uses a tighter twist ratio that cuts down on internal crosstalk. CAT7 uses individually foil-shielded twisted-pairs to minimize crosstalk. UTP and STP use RJ45 connectors (Figure 16) to plug into the different networking devices.

Fiber Wire

Fiber-optic cable (Figure 17) has become more common as demand increases for higher transmission speeds. Fiber-optic cable transmits data using pulsating laser light instead of electricity. Fiber-optic cable consists of a thin glass or plastic filament protected by thick plastic padding and an external plastic sheath. A light signal allows the data to travel faster, farther, more reliably, and more securely than electricity. Fiber cable can send reliable signals at speeds of 100 GB/s as far as 40 kilometers. Unfortunately, fiber-optic cable is expensive to buy, install, and maintain. Although not impossible, it is more difficult to intercept data carried by fiber-optic cable. Fiber-optic cable is less susceptible to "noise" and interference.

Wireless

Wireless LANs have become commonplace in businesses and homes. WLANs are often referred to as WiFi or 802.11 networks. Early wireless LANs were light-based using infrared light to transmit the data. Wireless LANs that are light-based require line of sight for all devices on the network. Because of this limitation and the slow data speed, there are only a few light-based infrared wireless LANs.

Most wireless LANs use radio waves to transmit the data. Each device in a wireless network requires an antenna to receive and transmit the radio signals. Wireless LANs can be peer-to-peer or ad-hoc networks (Figure 18), which only requires that each device be equipped with a wireless network card that contains the antenna, or a more complete network called an infrastructure network that requires an access point (Figure 19). The access point

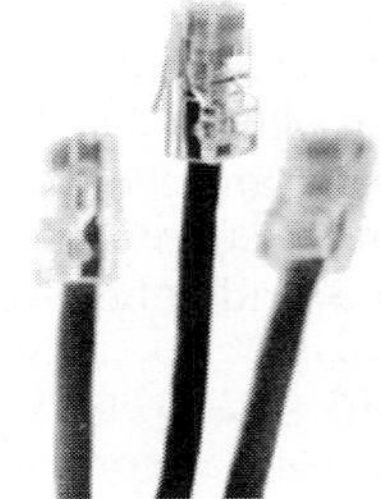

Figure 16: RJ45 connector

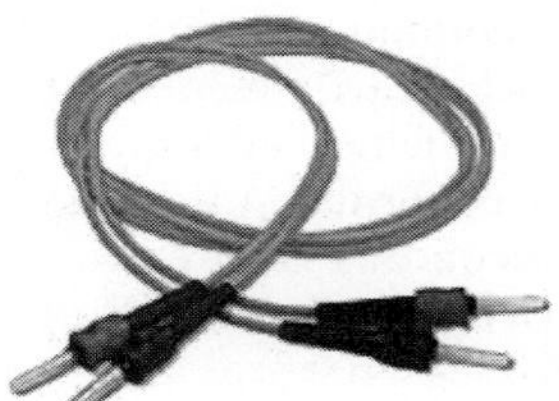

Figure 17: Fiber-optic cable

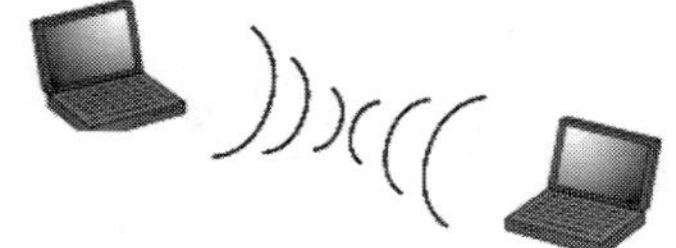

Figure 18: Peer-to-peer wireless network

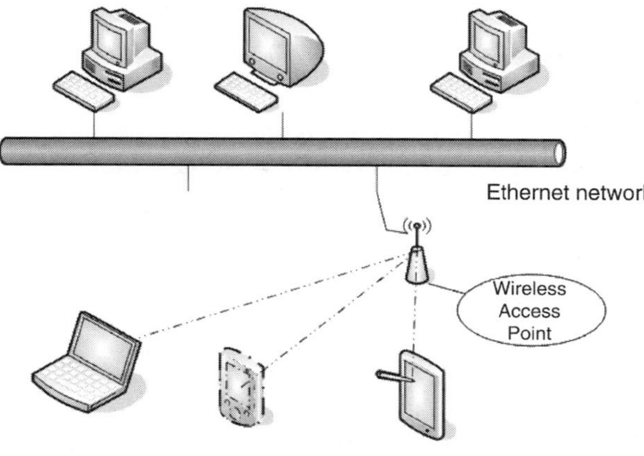

Figure 19: Wireless network with access point

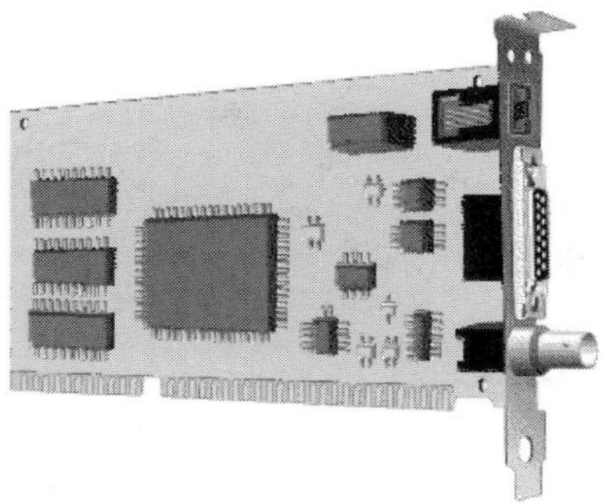

Figure 20: Network interface card (NIC) with RJ45, BNC, and AUI connections

contains an antenna, a radio transmitter, and a wired network interface, typically an RJ45 port. The access point acts as a base station (similar to a hub) for the wireless network and also as a bridge between the wireless and wired networks.

Regardless of whether the network is wired or wireless, every device on the network must be connected to the network with a network adapter or network interface card (NIC) (Figures 20, 21, and 22). The card must be physically connected to the device, either installed directly into a slot in the computer or connected via a port like a USB port. Most laptops and tablet PCs manufactured after 2004 have both wired and wireless interfaces built-in. The network card provides the interface between the node on the network and the network media. Because communication in a wireless network occurs through the air, it is easier for the signal to be intercepted. As wireless becomes more pervasive, security has become a significant issue.

Figure 21: Network interface card with RJ45 connection

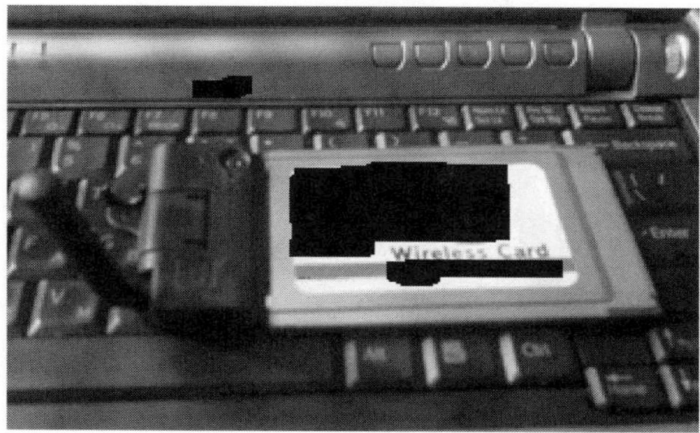

Figure 22: PCMCIA wireless NIC

Hardware Devices

Several factors limit the radius of a local area network. The farther a signal travels along the wire or through the air, the more likely it is to be degraded by noise. As the signal travels, it loses energy and becomes weaker, thus becoming difficult to read. As the network radius increases, it becomes more likely that two or more machines will transmit at the same time, causing a "collision." It will take longer for the machines to detect the collision. There are several ways to increase the radius of a network.

The simplest device to use is a repeater. A repeater (Figure 23) is an electronic device used to extend the distance of a network by amplifying the signal and reducing the electrical interference within the network. The repeater relays the data from one segment of the network to another without inspecting or modifying the data. Repeaters can also be used to connect segments of the network that use different cable media. Repeaters operate at the physical layer of the network.

A hub (Figure 24) is a multiport repeater that allows the distance of the network to be extended as well as allowing multiple devices to connect to the LAN. A hub is a device that brings all of the connections together (Figure 25). Like a repeater, the hub does not inspect or modify the data. Ethernet networks with only hubs and repeaters are constrained by the 5-4-3 rule that limits the connections between two nodes to no more than five segments each with no more than four repeaters where no more than three of the repeaters connect additional active nodes.

Figure 23: Repeater

Figure 24: Four-port hub

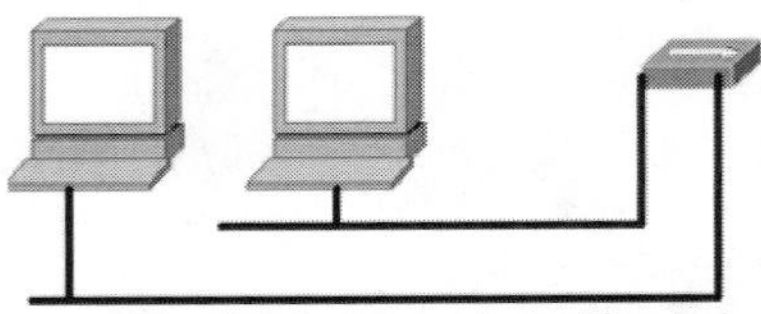

Two hosts connected with a hub.

Figure 25: Hub connecting two hosts

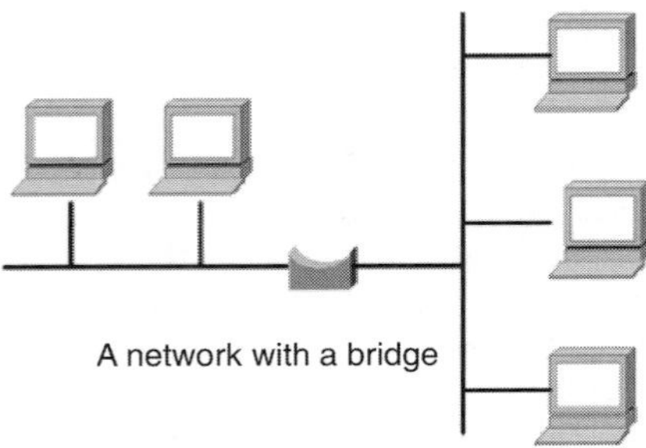

A network with a bridge

Figure 26: Bridges

Repeaters and hubs boost the signals on a network, but don't solve problems involving collisions. Other devices, however, alleviate this problem by limiting traffic on the network. A bridge (Figure 26) is an electronic device that connects two or more networks typically running the same network protocols. It allows the isolation of the different networks. The different networks may have different topologies. Bridges are used to increase the efficiency of a network by limiting the collision domain to "one side" of the bridge. By doing this, networks can be expanded without a significant increase of traffic. Bridges operate at the physical and data-link layers and make use of the physical addresses associated with the network cards. Segmenting can also improve LAN traffic by isolating workstations that pass large files or data set between them.

A switch (Figure 27) is a multiport bridge. Switches are often referred to as switching hubs. A switch combines the appearance and functionality of a hub with the

Eight-port switch

Figure 27: Switches

additional functionality of a bridge. Switches provide full duplex transmission between nodes eliminating collisions and enhancing the performance of the networks. Switches have typically replaced hubs in most local area network installations. A specialized type of bridge or switch called a "translating bridge" or gateway can be used to connect two or more networks using different protocols, for example Ethernet and token ring.

Although typically not part of a LAN, routers provide the interface between a LAN and WAN, or between different LANs. Routers route the traffic between different networks by maintaining tables of networks and their addresses. Routers forward layer 3 IP packets between different layer 2 domains. Routers are more sophisticated than switches and bridges and work at a higher level of the network.

LAN SOFTWARE

LAN software can be classified into three categories, network operating systems, network utilities, and network applications software. Not too many years ago, operating systems and network operating systems were distinct. Today almost all operating systems have the client functionality of a network operating system built in. In other words, you do not need to add any additional software to the operating system to get the computer to function on a network. All of today's popular operating systems including all recent versions of Microsoft Windows, all versions of Linux and UNIX, and all versions of the Macintosh OS support the connection of a computer to a network right out of the box. In addition to the usual computing tasks performed by an operating system, a network operating system also:

- manages the network connection
- manages data traffic between the computer and the network
- manages the flow of data between the different devices
- manages communication and messages between the network users
- provides for security of the data and other resources available on the network

The network operating system provides the interface between the LAN hardware and the applications running on the host.

Included with most of the network operating systems are specific network utilities like ping, ARP, and traceroute, which provides network control/management functions. Ping sends an Internet Control Message Protocol

(ICMP) ECHO_REQUEST packet to another device and waits for an ECHO_REPLY packet of data from the other device. This gives an indication of the time it takes to reach the target machine. Ping is a useful utility for troubleshooting networking problems. Address resolution protocol (ARP) is used to map the physical address of a networked device to the corresponding network IP address that has been assigned to the device. Traceroute uses the ping utility to map the route packets of data take from a source to a destination machine. Network operating systems typically include drivers for most network adapters so that the adapter can be plugged into the computer and the computer can be functioning on the network without too much additional configuration.

Network application software includes client front end software that is specific for use by client computers. This would include programs like Web browsers and e-mail software clients that would be run when needed. Hosts functioning as servers would have server software that would be constantly running waiting for connections from clients. Web servers and e-mail servers would be examples of this. Other types of network application software would include database client and server software as well as groupware software.

ROLE AND APPLICATIONS OF LANs

One of the major uses of LANs is to facilitate connections by users to the Internet. This requires the connection of the LAN to the Internet either via a dial-up telephone connection, a broadband connection, or a leased line. A dial-up connection requires a modem that converts the network's serial digital signal to the phone line's analog signal. A broadband connection typically requires a digital subscriber line (DSL), Integrated Services Digital Network (ISDN), or cable modem and a router and hub. Most commercial off-the-shelf devices include the functionality of a router, a hub, and often a wireless access point. A leased line connection requires a router that is then connected to another hardware device called a channel service unit/data service unit (CSU/DSU). The CSU/DSU in turn connects the network's router to the end of the leased line (e.g., T1 or T3) and converts the network's serial data signal to and from the leased line's digital signal. The leased line provides a high-speed Internet connection for the organization owning the LAN. The leased line is typically leased from a telecom provider through an ISP. The ISP maintains the actual connection to the Internet using its own router.

Connecting a LAN to the Internet requires that the devices on the LAN support the TCP/IP suite of protocols that provide the foundation of the Internet. At a minimum a computer accessing the Internet must have or be assigned an IP address, subnet mask, and default gateway. These protocols are necessary for computers on the LAN to be able to communicate with devices in other parts of the Internet. The TCP/IP suite of protocols include

- Transmission Control Protocol (TCP) [RFC 793]—establishes and maintains the Internet connection
- Internet Protocol (IP) [RFC 791]—handles the routing of packets of data across the Internet
- Simple Mail Transfer Protocol (SMTP) [RFC 821]—handles the transferring of e-mail messages
- Post Office Protocol (POP/POP3) [RFC1939]—facilitates e-mail drop services
- HyperText Transfer Protocol (HTTP) [RFC 2616]—facilitates the delivery of Web documents
- File Transfer Protocol (FTP) [RFC 959]—transfers files
- Telnet [RFC 854]—allows users to remotely connect to other computers over the Internet
- Secure shell (ssh) [RFC 4250]—allows users to securely connect to other computers over the Internet

Many organizations have set up their own internal Internet called an intranet. An intranet is a private network that uses the same protocols as the Internet. An intranet appears to the user like the Internet, but it is typically not open to anyone outside the organization. An intranet is not a replacement for a LAN, but rather runs within a LAN and supports many of the same applications as the Internet, typically Web servers and browsers, e-mail servers and clients, as well as additional groupware software. The core of most intranets is the Web site, which typically contains most of the internal documents that need to be disseminated among the organization's members. Setting up an intranet site on an organization's LAN requires a lot of organization and planning in selecting the hardware, software, and data needed to create a functional intranet.

Some organizations have taken the intranet concept one step further and link to external partners of the organization through the Internet via an extranet. An extranet is basically an intranet that may include access by customers, suppliers, and trusted partners.

WIRELESS LOCAL AREA NETWORKS

Wireless local area networks (WLANs) are rapidly becoming ubiquitous in both offices and homes. WLANs provide the freedom to access data without being tethered to the network with wires. WLANs enable users to take laptops and handheld computers anywhere, anytime and still be able to access the network. This is becoming more important in today's world of information.

Wireless networks are easier and less expensive to install. Most laptop and other portable devices can be purchased with a built-in WiFi card (wireless NIC). WiFi cards and USB WiFi devices can be installed with older laptops and desktop computers. Wireless networks require spending less money on cable and not needing to spend additional money and time installing the cable. Wireless access points and NICs have become more affordable in the past several years. Installing a wireless network involves turning on the access points, installing the software for the access points and NICs, and identifying the access points to which the NICs connect. Modifying a wireless network is easier, but does have its issues. There is no need to remove and/or relocate cable. There is no longer a concern for network cable failure.

Companies are using WLANs for keeping track of inventory in warehouses. Workers that need to be constantly in contact with their network are more frequently using wireless LANs. WLAN devices have become commonplace among workers in the health care industry. One area where WLANs are beginning to have a great impact is in education. Students and faculty no longer need to find wired computer labs to communicate and work. With wireless devices, students and faculty can access the networks in any building where wireless access points have been installed.

Wireless networks still have some drawbacks. Chief among these drawbacks are the limitations on distance and bandwidth. The radius of a WLAN can be extended by adding additional access points and radiofrequency (RF) repeaters to the network. Adding additional access points on the same channel can also help optimize the use of the limited bandwidth of the WLAN. There are also standards and associated wireless devices that support increased bandwidth. Both standards 802.11b and 802.11g use the unlicensed 2.4 GHz ISM band, and support transmission speeds up to 11 Mbps and 54 Mbps respectively. The 2.4 GHz ISM band is also used by many cordless phones and other electronic home devices that can cause interference. A third standard—802.11a—uses the 5 GHz UNII band and supports transmission speeds up to 54 Mbps. If these devices are unable to communicate at the preferred speed, the devices will drop the speeds to optimize the communications. This often happens when there is interference in the communications from other devices. Changing the channels can often overcome this problem.

Several new standards are emerging that will increase the communications for WiFi networks. One of these is 802.11n. It is expected to replace current WiFi devices with ones that will be able to communicate at up to 250 Mbps. The standard 802.11n is based on multiple-input multiple-output (MIMO) technology where two or more radio antennas allow increased communications speeds.

The other major drawback for WLANs is security. A WLAN transmits radio signals over a broad area. This allows an intruder to lurk anywhere and intercept the signals from the wireless network. One way of inhibiting access to wireless network is to turn on encryption. By default, most wireless networks use Wired Equivalent Privacy (WEP). WEP relies on a secret key that is shared between a mobile station and the access point. The secret key is used to encrypt packets before they are transmitted, and an integrity check is used to ensure that packets are not modified in transit. WEP is easily compromised. Better security can be obtained by using WiFi Protected Access (WPA and WPA2) which uses a passphrase as a seed for the encryption. There are a variety of additional security measures that should be implemented to better secure the wireless network.

LAN INSTALLATION

Before a LAN is installed, a lot of planning needs to take place. The process can typically be broken down into seven steps:

- Needs analysis
- Site analysis
- Equipment selection
- Site design
- Server configuration
- Installation schedule
- Installation

Needs Analysis

The first aspect of installing a LAN is determining the needs of the organization and the users. Is a LAN needed? What aspects of the network are needed? Who will be using the network? What will they be using the network for? Will a LAN help the bottom line of the organization?

Reasons for installing a local area network might include:

- Need for improved communication
- Need for centralizing data
- Need for sharing hardware
- Need for application sharing
- Need for automating work flow
- Need for enhanced security of data

Site Analysis

Once a need has been established, it is necessary to determine where the LAN will be installed. What parts of the organization's site will be networked? Where will the servers be located? A site plan will need to be drawn. If a fire escape plan is available, it can be used as a template for the building and location of rooms and doors. It is best if the architectural plans can be found. The site plan (Figure 28) is a map of the location where the network is installed and should include:

- The dimensions of the site, including the location of each employee
- The location of all immovable objects, including doors and windows
- The current location of all moveable objects
- The location of heating, ventilation, and air conditioning systems and ducts
- The location of electrical outlets and the current wiring scheme
- The current location of all computer equipment and the planned location for any additional devices

Equipment Selection

As the site plan is developed, an inventory of equipment on hand needs to be conducted. An inventory of equipment will identify the capabilities of the equipment incorporated into the proposed network. This will identify which equipment will be obsolete once the network is installed and which equipment will require modification. Older workstations may still be useful as print servers. Table 2 shows a table of the features to be noted in the equipment survey.

Once the current equipment has been inventoried, it is now time to identify new equipment that will need to be

Figure 28: Sample site plan

Table 2: Equipment Inventory Form

Serial Number	xxxxxxxxxxx
Processor	Pentium® 4 Processor 630 3.0 GHz, 800 MHz FSB
RAM size and configuration	2 GB DDR2 Non-ECC SDRAM 533 MHz
Hard disk	160 GB SATA 7200 RPM
Other drives	One 3.5″, 1.44 MB
CD-ROM	48X CD-ROM Drive
Monitor	17″ Flat Panel
Warranty information	Expires Jan. 2008

purchased. This list should be correlated with the user needs identified earlier. Once this list is prepared, vendors can be contacted, soliciting their recommendations for meeting the hardware and software needs. Be sure to consider any infrastructure constraints including electrical power and distances. Table 3 is an example of a form that could be used to compare different vendor proposals.

An important consideration is whether the network is completely wired, completely wireless, or a hybrid of the two. This will depend on the site analysis and the needs of the organization.

Site Design

Once the site plan from the site analysis has been completed and the equipment lists have been completed, it is time to create a working site design (Figure 29). This design will include details of where all devices including networking devices will be located. The location for all network connections must be indicated. The location of all network cable, patch panels, and riser backbone must be delineated.

Server Configuration

Once the computers arrive that will be installed as servers, they need to be configured. Server software needs to be installed and the directory structure of the server needs to be organized. The directory structure begins with the root directory with all other directories within it and the files and subdirectories within those. Typically, you will have directories for the network operating system, separate directories for each server application, and directories for the clients who will be connecting to the server. Network information including MAC and IP addresses for all devices needs to be recorded.

Installation Schedule

Networks take a considerable amount of time to install. It is important to have an installation schedule. There will be times when employees' computers will need to be turned off and possibly moved. Disruption needs to be minimized wherever possible. Be sure to include in the installation schedule the possibility for shipping delays on the equipment that has been ordered. Be sure to read

Table 3: Vendor Worksheet

	Vendor 1			Vendor 2			Vendor 3		
	Model	**Quan.**	**Price**	**Model**	**Quan.**	**Price**	**Model**	**Quan.**	**Price**
Server									
Hardware									
Software									
Workstations									
Hardware									
Software									
NIC									
Switches/hubs									
Bridges									
Access points									
Routers									
Cabling									
Other									
TOTAL COST:									

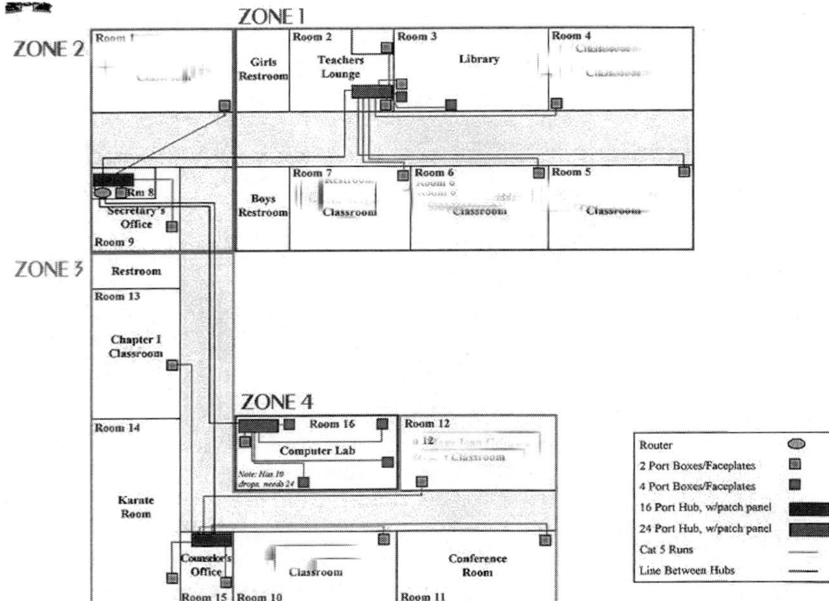

Figure 29: Sample site design

the manuals before the installation begins so that there will not be any surprises once the installation starts. Also prepare the site before the installation begins. This may involve moving furniture, installing new outlets, and removing equipment that will no longer be used. Don't forget to back up any data that is on systems that will be affected by the move.

Installation

Before the installation begins, it is best to discuss everything with someone who has been through a LAN installation before. Have this person look over the designs, schedules, and forms to ensure that nothing was forgotten. Depending on the size of the installation, it may take anywhere from a couple hours to a couple of days. Be prepared for delays. If this is a wired network, conduit may need to be installed and the cable media will need to be pulled. This is the part that typically takes the longest time. While the cable media is being pulled or shortly thereafter, the remaining components will need to be installed. This would typically include the patch panels in the communications rooms and the wall outlets for each device that will be networked (Figure 30). Once

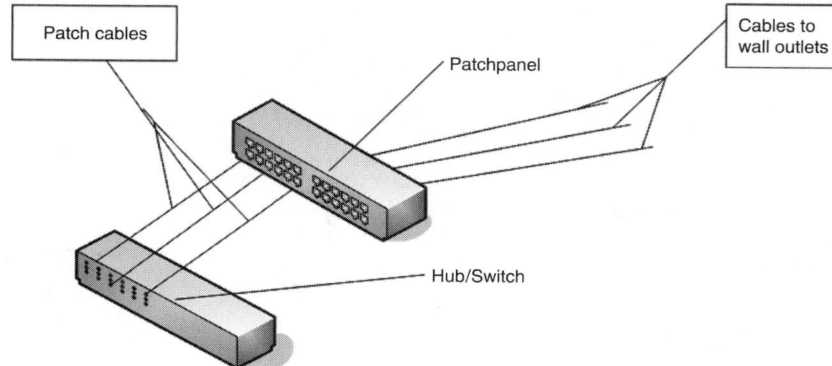

Figure 30: Configuration of wiring closet

this is completed, the electronic devices (hubs, switches, etc.) will need to be installed. If network cards need to be installed in the older computers, this will be done next. Finally, the software for the network cards will need to be installed on each workstation and server if it hasn't already been done. Be sure to install the appropriate network software.

The final two stages of the installation are the testing and training. Every device will need to be tested to ensure that its network connection works. This should be done before any of the users access the network. Be sure to test all of the network devices and the networked printers. Applications, service, and end-to-end testing must be performed. It is imperative that the security analysis of the network, including the wireless components, be conducted. The final phase is training. Users will need to be trained in the procedures they will need to follow to use the network.

LAN ADMINISTRATION

Once the LAN has been installed, there are several key aspects of administering the network.

Configuration List

Using the equipment inventory forms developed during the installation along with similar documentation for the new devices, a set of configuration lists needs to be developed. These would include a list of all computers similar to the equipment inventory form, directory lists for each server that is installed, a list of all server users, a list of all printers and other shared devices. It is also very important to keep copies of the network plans developed for the installation of the network.

System Log

The system log is documentation for the network. It provides a detailed history of the network's hardware, software, and configuration features. As changes are made to the network, these changes need to be documented in the system log. As problems arise with the network, these also need to be documented in the system log. This log needs to be maintained from the beginning. The system log should include all hardware and software warranties, hardware and software information, current setup structure, backup and recovery plan, backup logs, and error/downtime logs.

Training

Training doesn't end after the network has been installed. The network is a dynamic part of an organization's computing system. As changes are made, employees will need additional training.

Backup

As more and more data is kept on networked servers and shared by more than one user, it becomes critical that a procedure be established for backing up critical data. This may be the most important task for a network administrator. Hardware and software can be replaced. New employees can be hired. But it is difficult to recreate large amounts of data. The network administrator must establish a schedule for backing up all critical data. Separate storage area network (SAN) or networked attached storage (NAS) may be needed to provide added storage protection. Critical software may not necessarily be replaced and should be backed up as well. Configuration files on all servers should be backed up.

Security

Once computers become accessible to other individuals, security issues need to be considered. In a networked environment, users will need user IDs and passwords. If security is extremely important, then encryption of data might also need to be implemented. If the local area network is attached to another network, then a firewall may be necessary to control access to critical data between the two networks.

LAN SECURITY

In today's world of ubiquitous local area networks, security is of the utmost importance. This is true whether the LAN is a peer-to-peer or client/server network. Security is all about confidentiality, integrity, and availability. Where necessary, information should be confidential. The information should be only available to those who are authorized to access it. The integrity of the information must be maintained. We need to be assured that the information has not been altered. The availability of the information must be preserved. Authorized users need to be able to access the information and computing resources when needed.

Securing a LAN requires a multilayered approach. One of the main themes in security is "defense in depth" where multiple layers of technology and multiple procedures need to be implemented to minimize the threats to the local area network.

Physical Security

"I touch it, I own it!" Without physical security, there is no security. Having physical access to the devices and computers on a network is the greatest vulnerability in network security. No matter how strong other facets of security, if an attacker can physically access computers and other devices, the LAN can be easily compromised.

All LAN servers must be locked in a physically secure area. Network devices and cable need to be protected from intentional and unintentional disruption. To avoid inadvertent compromises, servers should not be used as client workstations. It is too easy for client-based vulnerabilities to be compromised and affect the server software running on the same computer. Securing a LAN includes more than preventing attacks. An inadvertent loss of power to the computers and network devices can be catastrophic. All devices should be protected by surge protectors. Power to servers and other critical hardware needs to be stabilized using uninterruptible power supplies (UPS). The UPS battery needs to be checked regularly. An alternate power supply, such as a generator or second utility grid should be available for mission-critical LANs.

Access Security

The first line of defense is access control. Access to servers and the data needs to be controlled. This can be implemented by instituting controls at the network level as well as individual controls at the directory and file levels. Connections to all servers and the network should be controlled through authentication procedures. All users must be registered and authenticated. There should be no guest accounts. Minimally the use of user IDs and passwords should be required for all connections to the network. All users need to use nontrivial passwords that are difficult to "guess." This includes using passwords that are sufficiently long and not using words that would be found in dictionaries or other wordlists. These passwords should be frequently changed and checked. Unfortunately, too many passwords can create operational issues. Often times, users will forget their passwords. A mechanism needs to be in place to address this problem. All default passwords for servers, operating systems, and applications must be changed immediately. All obsolete user accounts need to be terminated immediately. It may also be necessary to restrict user access to certain days and times to better control access to sensitive data.

There should be several levels of access to directories and files. These typically would include read, write, and execute. Users need to be given the minimum privileges to access all their files and directories. All data must be protected from access by unauthorized users. It is important that authorization is carefully planned. Audit logs of successful and unsuccessful access to systems and files may need to be kept to allow for tracking of problems that arise.

Data Security

Where necessary, critical data needs to be protected. In addition to those mechanisms discussed above, additional layers of security may be necessary. In the case of databases, views need to be provided to permit users to access only the minimum that is necessary.

Data confidentiality is especially important. Where necessary, encryption software needs to be used to protect confidential and sensitive data. Controls need to be implemented to protect all confidential and sensitive data stored and/or processed on the LAN. These controls should include any removable media associated with the LAN. It is important that all confidential and sensitive data be removed before disposing of the media that the data resides on. Remember that simply deleting a file that contains the data may not be enough. Be sure to delete any copies of the files stored on backup media and "empty the trash."

Backup procedures need to be implemented. All files servers need to be automatically backed up on a regularly scheduled basis. The backup media needs to be kept onsite for immediate recovery. Copies of the backup media need to be kept off-site in case the onsite backups are compromised. Both sets of backups need to be tested and audited to ensure recovery.

Network Security

There are two major approaches to securing a local area network: host-based security and network-based security. Typically, both approaches are combined to provide multiple levels of security.

In host-based security, selected hosts are separately protected. This could range from installing antivirus software and personal firewalls on each computer in the network, to installing a host-based intrusion detection system on each server. Minimally, every server should be protected with antivirus software and a personal firewall. If possible, the important servers should also be shielded by a host-based intrusion detection system.

Network-based security is equally important. Hardware-based security devices such as firewalls and intrusion detection devices can be placed at the perimeter of the network, typically inside the router where they can monitor all traffic coming in and out of the local area network. Intrusion detection and intrusion protection devices can also be set up with agents installed on those hosts needing the most protection. These agents can then be monitored and managed from a central location. In more secure environments, there may be layers of network-based security both at the perimeter of the LAN as well as internal to the network. One layer of security is the placement of a firewall device (Figure 31) between the LAN (trusted network) and the outside (untrusted networks).

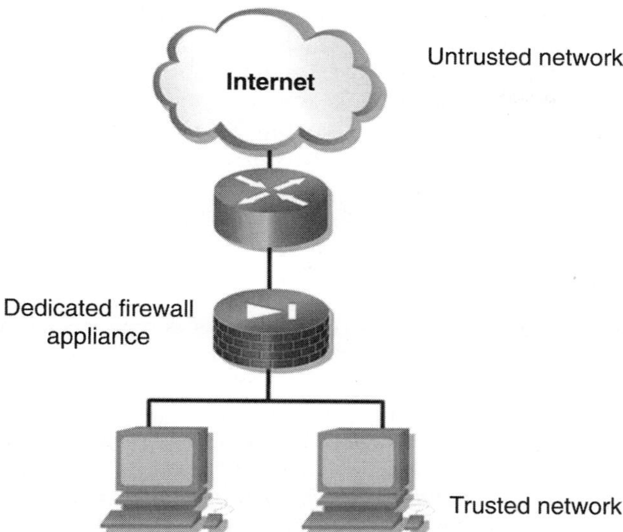

Figure 31: Placement of a firewall

The network should be audited for illicit use of inappropriate software (e.g., sniffers, traffic monitors.) No unauthorized connections to the network should be permitted. This would include rogue wireless access points and modems connections.

Malware

Malware includes programs like viruses, worms, and spyware. To protect against most malware attacks, antivirus software needs to be installed on all servers and clients. It is imperative that this software be kept up to date on all computers. Most antivirus software vendors have procedures for automatically updating the software. The auto-update feature should be configured to the shortest time that is tolerable by the users. All foreign media and all files downloaded from the Internet must be scanned for malware. The antivirus software needs to be running continuously. In addition to updating the antivirus software, it is mandatory that all operating systems and applications running on all computers in the network be patched. "Patching host software is probably the single most important thing companies can do to improve their security" (Panko, 2004). Software vulnerabilities are constantly being exposed. Threats that exploit these vulnerabilities are rapidly developed and can best be prevented from compromising the system's security by downloading security patches as soon as the patches are available. Users should be trained in how to disconnect their device from the network in the event of a virus attack to isolate their host. One vulnerability in an operating system or application can destroy the entire network of computers.

Policy, Procedures, and Awareness

"Security is not a product, it's a process" (Schneier, 1999). Using any security product without understanding what it does, and what it does not protect against is a recipe for disaster. Keep in mind that added security features tend to increase the complexity of the system and may decrease the degree of usability of the systems. Usability needs to be balanced with the increased need for security.

Any organization implementing or using a LAN must have a well-documented security policy. The policy should incorporate physical security procedures, email, Internet acceptable usage, and network usage procedures. The policy should include procedures for incident response and a LAN risk analysis. The policy should include a focus on software use to ensure compliance with license agreements. All unauthorized copies of software should be removed from workstations and servers. The policy needs to outline what additional response is necessary when unauthorized software is discovered.

The policy must include procedures for ensuring that all software is patched on a regular basis. This is especially important for all security software including antivirus software and any intrusion detection and prevention software protecting the LAN and its resources.

As mentioned earlier, audit logs need to be invoked. These logs should not only document successful and unsuccessful access to resources on the LAN, but should record any and all anomalies. These audit logs must be reviewed regularly with procedures in place for addressing any security alerts or identified anomalies. All attacks and breaches of security need to be investigated immediately and followed up with appropriate responses.

"The most potent tool in any security arsenal isn't a powerful firewall or a sophisticated intrusion detection system. When it comes to security, knowledge is the most effective tool..." (Schweizer, 2003). There needs to be a regular training program for administration and users. Administrators need to be trained on their responsibilities in managing the security of the LAN and its components. Regular security awareness sessions need to be scheduled and required for all employees including training against social engineering attacks. An important policy is to train before deploying any component in the network.

CONCLUSION

LANs play a very important role in providing computer resources to large numbers of users. They allow users to share hardware, software, and most importantly data. They also provide access to the Internet as well as organization intranets and extranets. With the emergence of WANs, the applications of LANs will continue to expand. It is imperative that we secure the LANs to ensure confidentiality, integrity, and availability of the data.

GLOSSARY

Access point: is a hardware device consisting of one or more antennae, a radio transmitter, and a wired network interface. Used as a bridge between a wireless network and a wired network. The access point acts a hub for the wireless network.

Attenuation: is a loss of energy from a signal as a result of resistance in the medium.

Bridge: is a network device for connecting two or more local area networks that typically use different media but the same network protocol.

Bus network: refers to a network where the nodes are connected to the same wire. Data is broadcast from one node to all other nodes in the LAN even though the data may be intended for only one node.

Ethernet: is a common data-link layer technology for networking computers in a LAN using the CSMA/CD access method.

Extranet: is a private portion of the Internet treated as an extension of an organization's intranet and allowing access to the organization's data by the organization's partners, customers, and so on.

Fiber-Distributed Data Interface (FDDI): data-link layer standard based on token ring for extended data communications using optical fiber.

Hub: is the central device in a star network for connecting multiple nodes to a network. It functions as a multiple point repeater.

IEEE 802.3: is a collection of standards for CSMA/CD (Ethernet)-based LANs.

IEEE 802.5: is a collection of standards for token ring–based LANs.

IEEE 802.11: is a collection of standards for wireless-based LANs.

Internet: is a worldwide collection of networks linked together and built around the TCP/IP suite of protocols. It was originally conceived in 1969 by the Advanced Research Projects Agency (ARPA) of the U.S. government.

Intranet: is an organization's private internal network based on the TCP/IP suite of protocols.

Local area network (LAN): is a data communication network of computers, peripheral devices, and other network devices allowing data to be communicated at high speeds over short distances.

Logical topology: or electrical topology is based on how the devices of the network are electrically configured.

Network: is an interconnection of two or more computers or devices.

Network interface card (NIC): is an adapter for connecting a computer or device to the network media.

Personal area network (PAN): is a communication network of computing devices within close proximity of a person typically a few meters.

Physical topology: is based on the way the nodes are physically configured in the network.

Repeater: is a network device that retransmits the communication signal and is used for extending the radius of a network. It operates at the OSI physical layer.

Ring network: refers to a network where the nodes are arranged in a closed loop where each device is connected directly to two adjacent devices.

Router: is a special-purpose network device that connects two or more networks at the OSI network layer.

Social engineering: is the process of compromising a computer system and/or its data by manipulating the users.

Star network: has the nodes arranged so that each device is connected to a central device, typically a hub or a switch.

Switch: is a network device operating at the OSI data-link layer that connects multiple network segments. It functions as a multiport bridge, allowing two devices to communicate only with each other at that moment.

Wide area network (WAN): is a data communication network spanning geographically dispersed areas.

CROSS REFERENCES

See *Ethernet LANs; Optical Fiber LANs; Token Ring LANs.*

REFERENCES

Metcalfe, R., and R. Boggs. 1976. Ethernet: Distributed Packet Switching for Local Computer Networks. *Communications of the ACM*, 19(5): 395–404.

Panko, R. 2004. *Corporate Computer and Network Security*. City, ST: Prentice-Hall.

Schneier, B. 1999. *Crypto-Gram Newsletter*. http://www.schneier.com/crypto-gram-9912.html (accessed September 17, 2006).

Schweizer, D. 2003. *The State of Network Security*. http://www.processor.com (accessed August 22, 2003).

Ethernet LANs

William Stallings, *Independent Consultant*

TRADITIONAL ETHERNET

The original commercial Ethernet, as well as the original Institute of Electrical and Electronics Engineers (IEEE) 802.3 standard, operated at 10 Mbps, and there are still a number of 10-Mbps Ethernet LANs in use. In recent years, standards have been developed for 802.3 systems operating at 100 Mbps, 1 Gbps, and 10 Gbps. Before looking at these high-speed LANs, we provide a brief overview of the original 10-Mbps Ethernet and introduce the concept of switched LANs.

Classical Ethernet operates at 10 Mbps over a bus topology LAN using the CSMA/CD media access control protocol. In this section, we introduce the concepts of bus LANs and CSMA/CD operation, and then briefly discuss transmission medium options.

Bus Topology LAN

In a bus topology LAN, all stations attach, through appropriate hardware interfacing known as a tap, directly to a linear transmission medium, or bus. Full-duplex operation between the station and the tap allows data to be transmitted onto the bus and received from the bus. A transmission from any station propagates the length of the medium in both directions and can be received by all other stations. At each end of the bus is a terminator, which absorbs any signal, removing it from the bus.

Two problems present themselves in this arrangement. First, because a transmission from any one station can be received by all other stations, there needs to be some way of indicating for whom the transmission is intended. Second, a mechanism is needed to regulate transmission. To see the reason for this, consider that if two stations on the bus attempt to transmit at the same time, their signals will overlap and become garbled. Or consider that one station decides to transmit continuously for a long period of time, blocking the access of other users.

To solve these problems, stations transmit data in small blocks, known as frames. Each frame consists of a portion of the data that a station wishes to transmit, plus a frame header that contains control information. Each station on the bus is assigned a unique address, or identifier, and the destination address for a frame is included in its header.

Figure 1 illustrates the scheme. In this example, station C wishes to transmit a frame of data to A. The frame header includes A's address. As the frame propagates along the bus, it passes B. B observes the address and ignores the frame. A, on the other hand, sees that the frame is addressed to itself and therefore copies the data from the frame as it goes by.

So the frame structure solves the first problem mentioned previously: It provides a mechanism for indicating the intended recipient of the data. It also provides the basic tool for solving the second problem, the regulation of access. In particular, the stations take turns sending frames in some cooperative fashion, as explained in the next subsection.

Media Access Control

For CSMA/CD, a station wishing to transmit first listens to the medium to determine if another transmission is in progress (carrier sense). If the medium is idle, the station may transmit. It may happen that two or more stations attempt to transmit at about the same time. If this happens, there will be a collision; the data from both transmissions will be garbled and not received successfully. The following procedure specifies what a station should do if the medium is found busy and what it should do if a collision occurs:

1. If the medium is idle, transmit; otherwise, go to step 2.
2. If the medium is busy, continue to listen until it is idle, then transmit immediately.
3. If a collision is detected during transmission, transmit a brief jamming signal to assure that all stations know that there has been a collision and then cease transmission.
4. After transmitting the jamming signal, wait a random amount of time, referred to as the backoff, then attempt to transmit again (repeat from step 1).

Figure 2 illustrates the technique. The upper part of the figure shows a bus LAN layout. The remainder of the figure depicts activity on the bus at four successive instants in time. At time t0, station A begins transmitting a packet addressed to D. At t1, both B and C are ready to transmit. B senses a transmission and so defers. C, however, is still unaware of A's transmission and begins its own transmission. When A's transmission reaches C, at t2, C detects the collision and ceases transmission. The effect of the collision propagates back to A, where it is detected some time later, t3, at which time A ceases transmission.

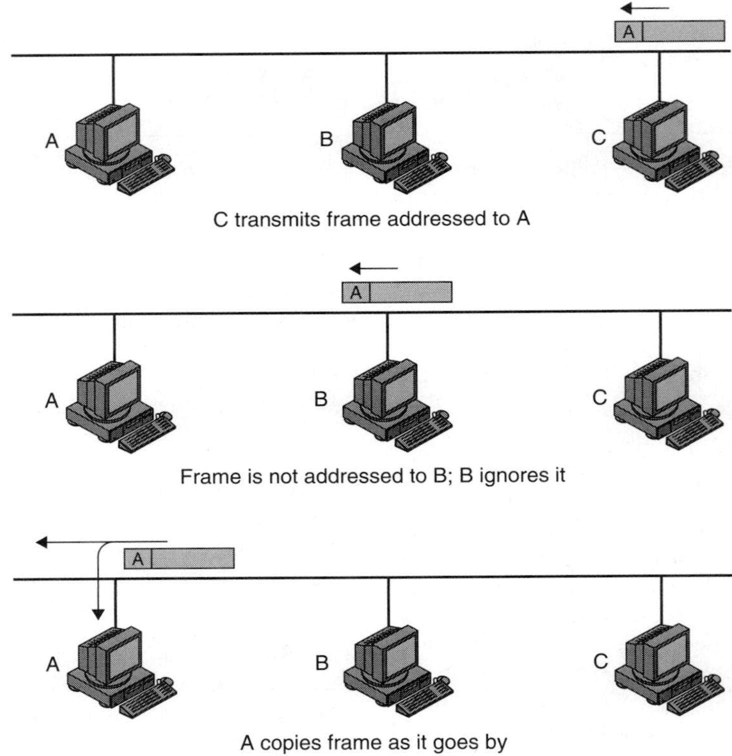

Figure 1: Frame transmission on a bus LAN

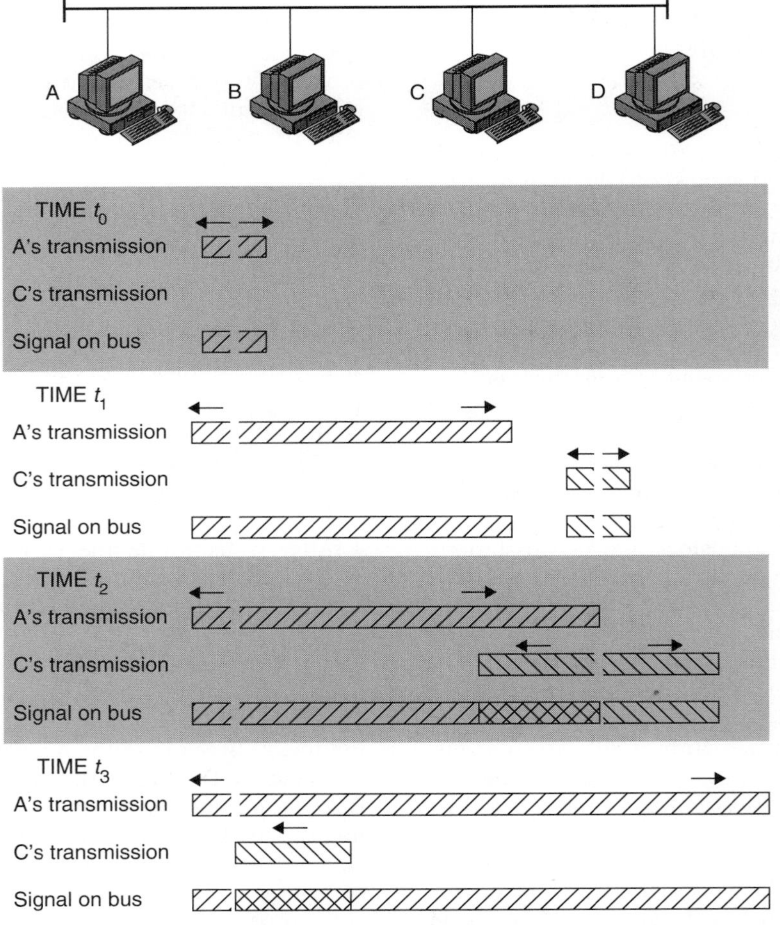

Figure 2: CSMA/CD operation

When a collision occurs, IEEE 802.3 systems use an algorithm called binary exponential backoff to calculate the random amount of time the sender must wait before attempting to retransmit the frame. For each of the retransmissions, the algorithm doubles the range of the random delay. Thus, after n collisions, the system will wait for a random amount of time, in the range from 0 to 2n to 1 units of time before attempting to retransmit the frame.

The advantage of CSMA/CD is its simplicity. It is easy to implement the logic required for this protocol. Furthermore, there is little to go wrong in the execution of the protocol. For example, if for some reason a station fails to detect a collision, the worst that can happen is that it continues to transmit its frame, wasting some time on the medium. Once the transmission is over, the algorithm continues to function as before.

MAC Frame

Figure 3 depicts the frame format for the 802.3 protocol. It consists of the following fields:

- Preamble: A 7-octet pattern of alternating 0s and 1s used by the receiver to establish bit synchronization.
- Start Frame Delimiter (SFD): The sequence 10101011, which indicates the actual start of the frame and enables the receiver to locate the first bit of the rest of the frame.
- Destination Address (DA): Specifies the station(s) for which the frame is intended. It may be a unique physical address, a group address, or a global address.
- Source Address (SA): Specifies the station that sent the frame.
- Length: Length of Logical Link Control (LLC) data field in octets. The maximum frame size, excluding the Preamble and SFD, is 1518 octets.
- LLC Data: Data unit supplied by LLC.
- Pad: Octets added to ensure that the frame is long enough for proper CD operation.
- Frame Check Sequence (FCS): A 32-bit cyclic redundancy check (CRC), based on all fields except preamble, SFD, and FCS.

IEEE 802.3 Medium Options at 10 Mbps

The IEEE 802.3 committee has defined a number of alternative physical configurations. This is both good and bad. On the good side, the standard has been responsive to evolving technology. On the bad side, the customer, not to mention the potential vendor, is faced with a bewildering array of options. However, the committee has been at pains to ensure that the various options can be easily integrated into a configuration that satisfies a variety of needs. Thus, the user who has a complex set of requirements may find the flexibility and variety of the 802.3 standard to be an asset.

To distinguish the various implementations that are available, the committee has developed a concise notation:

<data rate in Mbps> <signaling method><maximum segment length in hundreds of meters>

The defined alternatives are:

- 10BASE5: Specifies the use of 50-ohm coaxial cable and Manchester digital signaling. The maximum length of a cable segment is set at 500 meters (m). The length of the network can be extended by the use of repeaters. A repeater is transparent to the media access control MAC level; as it does no buffering, it does not isolate one segment from another. So, for example, if two stations on different segments attempt to transmit at the same time, their transmissions will collide. To avoid looping, only one path of segments and repeaters is allowed between any two stations. The standard allows a maximum of four repeaters in the path between any two stations, extending the effective length of the medium to 2.5 kilometers (km).
- 10BASE2: Similar to 10BASE5 but uses a thinner cable, which supports fewer taps over a shorter distance than the 10BASE5 cable. This is a lower-cost alternative to 10BASE5.
- 10BASE-T: Uses unshielded twisted pair in a star-shaped topology. Because of the high data rate and the poor transmission qualities of unshielded twisted pair, the length of a link is limited to 100 m. As an alternative, an optical fiber link may be used. In this case, the maximum length is 500 m.
- 10BASE-F: Contains three specifications: a passive-star topology for interconnecting stations and repeaters with up to 1 km per segment; a point-to-point link that can be used to connect stations or repeaters at up to 2 km; a point-to-point link that can be used to connect repeaters at up to 2 km.

Note that 10BASE-T and 10BASE-F do not quite follow the notation: "T" stands for twisted pair and "F" stands

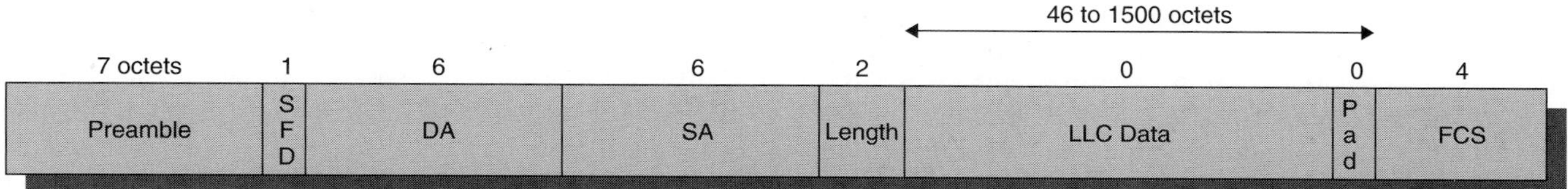

Figure 3: IEEE 802.3 frame format

Table 1: IEEE 802.3 10-Mbps physical layer medium alternatives

	10BASE5	10BASE2	10BASE-T	10BASE-FP
Transmission medium	Coaxial Cable (50 ohm)	Coaxial Cable (50 ohm)	Unshielded twisted pair	850-nm optical fiber pair
Signaling technique	Baseband (Manchester)	Baseband (Manchester)	Baseband (Manchester)	Manchester/On-off
Topology	Bus	Bus	Star	Star
Maximum segment length (m)	500	185	100	500
Nodes per segment	100	30	—	33
Cable diameter (mm)	10	5	0.4 to 0.6	62.5/125 μm

for optical fiber. Table 1 summarizes the preceding options. All of the alternatives listed in the table specify a data rate of 10 Mbps. In addition to these alternatives, there are versions that operate at 100 Mbps, 1 Gbps, and 10 Gbps; these are covered later in this section.

HIGH-SPEED ETHERNET

Fast Ethernet

If one were to design a high-speed (100 Mbps or more) LAN from scratch, one would not choose CSMA/CD as the basis for the design. CSMA/CD is simple to implement and robust in the face of faults. However, it does not scale well. As the load on a bus increases, the number of collisions increases, degrading performance. Furthermore, as the data rate for a given system increases, performance also decreases. The reason for this is that at a higher data rate, a station can transmit more bits before it recognizes a collision, and therefore more wasted bits are transmitted.

These problems can be overcome. To accommodate higher loads, a system can be designed to have a number of different segments, interconnected with hubs. The hubs can act as barriers, separating the LAN into collision domains, so that a collision in one domain does not spread to other domains. The use of switched Ethernet hubs in effect eliminates collisions, further increasing efficiency.

At this point, we need a brief digression to explain the difference between a simple (dumb) hub and a switching hub. In both cases, multiple end systems are attached to the hub. In the case of a simple hub, a transmission from any one station is received by the hub and retransmitted on all of the outgoing lines. Therefore, to avoid collisions, only one station should transmit at a time. In the case of a switching hub, the central hub acts as a switch, similar to a packet switch. An incoming frame from a particular station is switched to the appropriate output line to be delivered to the intended destination. At the same time, other unused lines can be used for switching other traffic.

Despite some drawbacks to its use, Ethernet-style LANs have been developed that operate at 100 Mbps, 1 Gbps, and 10 Gbps. The reasons for this are instructive. From the vendor's point of view, the CSMA/CD protocol is well understood and vendors have experience building the hardware, firmware, and software for such systems. Scaling the system up to 100 Mbps or more may be easier than implementing an alternative protocol and topology. From the customer's point of view, it is relatively easy to integrate older systems running at 10 Mbps with newer systems running at higher speeds if all the systems use the same frame format and the same access protocol. In other words, the continued use of Ethernet-style systems is attractive because Ethernet is already there. This same situation is encountered in other areas of data communications. Vendors and customers do not always, or even in the majority of cases, choose the technically superior solution. Cost, ease of management, and other factors relating to the already-existing base of equipment are more important factors in the selection. This is the reason that Ethernet-style systems continue to dominate the LAN market long after most observers predicted the demise of Ethernet.

Fast Ethernet refers to a set of specifications developed by the IEEE 802.3 committee to provide a low-cost, Ethernet-compatible LAN operating at 100 Mbps. The blanket designation for these standards is 100BASE-T. The committee defined a number of alternatives to be used with different transmission media.

Table 2 summarizes key characteristics of the 100-BASE-T options. All of the 100BASE-T options use the IEEE 802.3 MAC protocol and frame format. 100BASE-X refers to a set of options that use the physical medium specifications. All of the 100BASE-X schemes use two physical links between nodes; one for transmission and one for reception. 100BASE-TX makes use of shielded twisted pair (STP) or high-quality (Category 5) unshielded twisted pair (UTP). 100BASE-FX uses optical fiber; this option is being phased out in favor of faster fiber-based technologies.

In many buildings, any of the 100BASE-X options requires the installation of new cable. For such cases, 100BASE-T4 defines a lower-cost alternative that can use Category 3, voice-grade UTP in addition to the higher-quality Category 5 UTP. To achieve the 100-Mbps data rate over lower-quality cable, 100BASE-T4 dictates the use of four twisted-pair lines between nodes, with the data transmission making use of three pairs in one direction at a time. This option is rarely used.

For all of the 100BASE-T options, the topology is similar to that of 10BASE-T, namely a star-wire topology.

Table 2: IEEE 802.3 100BASE-T physical layer medium alternatives

	100BASE-TX		100BASE-FX	100BASE-T4
Transmission medium	2 pair, STP	2 pair, Category 5 UTP	2 optical fibers	4 pair, Category 3, 4, or 5 UTP
Signaling technique	MLT-3	MLT-3	4B5B, NRZI	8B6T, NRZ
Data rate	100 Mbps	100 Mbps	100 Mbps	100 Mbps
Maximum segment length	100 m	100 m	100 m	100 m
Network span	200 m	200 m	400 m	200 m

100BASE-X

For all of the transmission media specified under 100BASE-X, a unidirectional data rate of 100 Mbps is achieved transmitting over a single link (single twisted pair, single optical fiber). For all of these media, an efficient and effective signal encoding scheme is required. The one chosen is referred to as 4B/5B-NRZI. This scheme is further modified for each option.

The 100BASE-X designation includes two physical medium specifications, one for twisted pair, known as 100BASE-TX, and one for optical fiber, known as 100BASE-FX.

100BASE-TX makes use of two pairs of twisted-pair cable, one pair used for transmission and one for reception. Both STP and Category 5 UTP are allowed. The MTL-3 signaling scheme is used.

100BASE-FX makes use of two optical fiber cables, one for transmission and one for reception. With 100BASE-FX, a means is needed to convert the 4B/5B-NRZI code group stream into optical signals. The technique used is known as intensity modulation. A binary 1 is represented by a burst or pulse of light; a binary 0 is represented by either the absence of a light pulse, or a light pulse at very low intensity.

100BASE-T4

100BASE-T4 is designed to produce a 100-Mbps data rate over lower-quality Category 3 cable, thus taking advantage of the large installed base of Category 3 cable in office buildings. The specification also indicates that the use of Category 5 cable is optional. 100BASE-T4 does not transmit a continuous signal between packets, which makes it useful in battery-powered applications.

For 100BASE-T4 using voice-grade Category 3 cable, it is not reasonable to expect to achieve 100 Mbps on a single twisted pair. Instead, 100BASE-T4 specifies that the data stream to be transmitted is split up into three separate data streams, each with an effective data rate of 33.5 Mbps. Four twisted pairs are used. Data are transmitted using three pairs and received using three pairs. Thus, two of the pairs must be configured for bidirectional transmission.

As with 100BASE-X, a simple NRZ encoding scheme is not used for 100BASE-T4. This would require a signaling rate of 33 Mbps on each twisted pair and does not provide synchronization. Instead, a ternary signaling scheme known as 8B6T is used.

Full-Duplex Operation

A traditional Ethernet is half duplex: a station can either transmit or receive a frame, but it cannot do both simultaneously. With full-duplex operation, a station can transmit and receive simultaneously. If a 100-Mbps Ethernet ran in full-duplex mode, the theoretical transfer rate becomes 200 Mbps.

Several changes are needed to operate in full-duplex mode. The attached stations must have full-duplex rather than half-duplex adapter cards. The central point in the star wire cannot be a simple multiport repeater but rather must be a switching hub. In this case each station constitutes a separate collision domain. In fact, there are no collisions and the CSMA/CD algorithm is no longer needed. However, the same 802.3 MAC frame format is used and the attached stations can continue to execute the CSMA/CD algorithm, even though no collisions can ever be detected.

Mixed Configuration

One of the strengths of the Fast Ethernet approach is that it readily supports a mixture of existing 10-Mbps LANs and newer 100-Mbps LANs. For example, the 100-Mbps technology can be used as a backbone LAN to support a number of 10-Mbps hubs. Many of the stations attach to 10-Mbps hubs using the 10BASE-T standard. These hubs are in turn connected to switching hubs that conform to 100BASE-T and that can support both 10-Mbps and 100-Mbps links. Additional high-capacity workstations and servers attach directly to these 10/100 switches. These mixed-capacity switches are in turn connected to 100-Mbps hubs using 100-Mbps links. The 100-Mbps hubs provide a building backbone and are also connected to a router that provides connection to an outside WAN.

Gigabit Ethernet

In late 1995, the IEEE 802.3 committee formed a High-Speed Study Group to investigate means for conveying packets in Ethernet format at speeds in the gigabits per second range. A set of 1000-Mbps standards has since been issued. There are many forces driving demand for greater transmission capacity to the desktop. Gigabit Ethernet is moving to the desktop as demands for streaming multimedia, remote processing, videogaming, videoconferencing with concurrent video streams, and multitasking processes demand increased bandwidth.

The strategy for Gigabit Ethernet is the same as that for Fast Ethernet. Although defining a new medium and transmission specification, Gigabit Ethernet retains the CSMA/CD protocol and frame format of its 10-Mbps and 100-Mbps predecessors. It is compatible with 100BASE-T and 10BASE-T, preserving a smooth migration path. As more organizations move to 100BASE-T, putting huge traffic loads on backbone networks, demand for Gigabit Ethernet has intensified.

Media Access Layer

The 1000-Mbps specification calls for the same CSMA/CD frame format and MAC protocol as used in the 10-Mbps and 100-Mbps version of IEEE 802.3. For shared-medium hub operation, there are two enhancements to the basic CSMA/CD scheme:

- Carrier extension: Carrier extension appends a set of special symbols to the end of short MAC frames so that the resulting block is at least 4096 bit-times in duration, up from the minimum 512 bit-times imposed at 10 and 100 Mbps. This is so that the frame length of a transmission is longer than the propagation time at 1 Gbps.
- Frame bursting: This feature allows for multiple short frames to be transmitted consecutively, up to a limit, without relinquishing control for CSMA/CD between frames. Frame bursting avoids the overhead of carrier extension when a single station has a number of small frames ready to send.

With a switching hub, which provides dedicated access to the medium, the carrier extension and frame bursting features are not needed. This is because data transmission and reception at a station can occur simultaneously without interference and with no contention for a shared medium.

Physical Layer

The current 1-Gbps specification for IEEE 802.3 includes the following physical layer alternatives (Figure 4):

- 1000BASE-SX: This short-wavelength option supports duplex links of up to 275 m using 62.5-μm multimode or up to 550 m using 50-μm multimode fiber. Wavelengths are in the range of 770 to 860 nm.
- 1000BASE-LX: This long-wavelength option supports duplex links of up to 550 m of 62.5-μm or 50-μm multimode fiber or 5 km of 10-μm single-mode fiber. Wavelengths are in the range of 1270 to 1355 nm.
- 1000BASE-CX: This option supports 1-Gbps links among devices located within a single room or equipment rack, using copper jumpers (specialized STP cable that spans no more than 25 m). Each link is composed of a separate STP running in each direction.
- 1000BASE-T: This option makes use of four pairs of Category 5 UTP to support devices over a range of up to 100 m.

The signal encoding scheme used for the first three Gigabit Ethernet options just listed is 8B/10B. The signal encoding scheme used for 1000BASE-T is 4D-PAM5, a relatively complicated scheme whose description is beyond our scope.

10-Gbps Ethernet

With gigabit products still fairly new, attention has turned in the past several years to a 10-Gbps Ethernet capability. The principal driving requirement for 10-Gigabit Ethernet is the increase in Internet and intranet

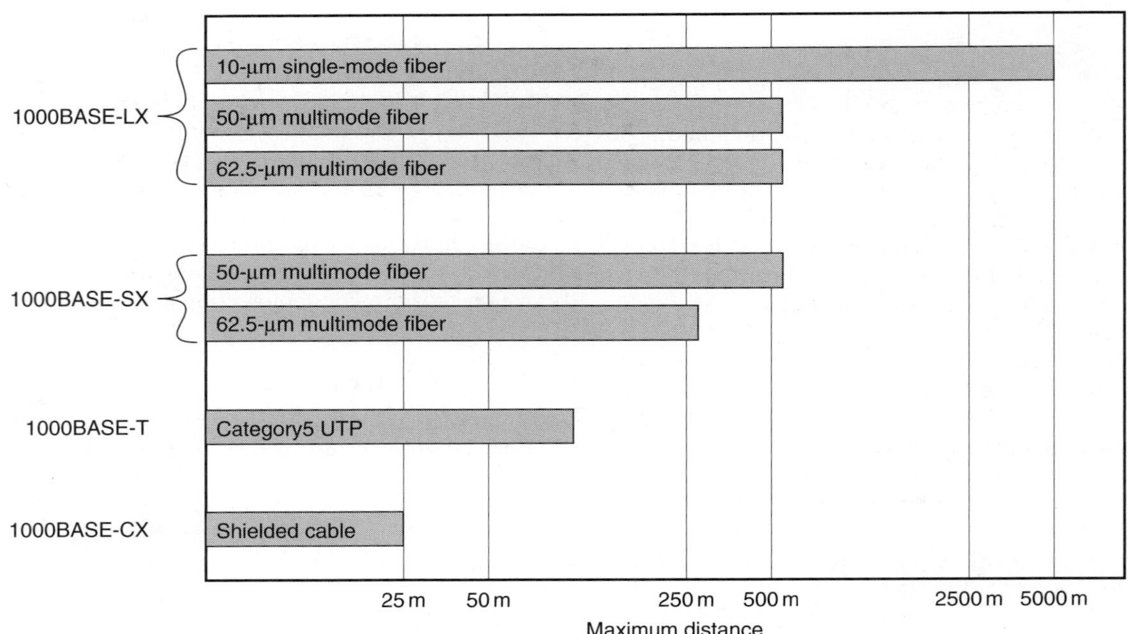

Figure 4: Gigabit Ethernet medium options (log scale)

traffic. A number of factors contribute to the explosive growth in both Internet and intranet traffic:

- An increase in the number of network connections
- An increase in the connection speed of each end-station (e.g., 10-Mbps users moving to 100 Mbps, analog 56-kbps users moving to DSL and cable modems)
- An increase in the deployment of bandwidth-intensive applications such as high-quality video
- An increase in Web hosting and application hosting traffic

Initially, network managers will use 10-Gbps Ethernet to provide high-speed, local backbone interconnection between large-capacity switches. As the demand for bandwidth increases, 10-Gbps Ethernet will be deployed throughout the entire network and will include server farm, backbone, and campus-wide connectivity. This technology enables Internet service providers (ISPs) and network service providers (NSPs) to create very high-speed links at a low cost, between co-located, carrier-class switches and routers.

The technology also allows the construction of metropolitan area networks (MANs) and WANs that connect geographically dispersed LANs between campuses or points of presence (PoPs). Thus, Ethernet begins to compete with asynchronous transfer mode (ATM) and other wide area transmission and networking technologies. In most cases where the customer requirement is data and TCP/IP transport, 10-Gbps Ethernet provides substantial value over ATM transport for both network end users and service providers:

- No expensive, bandwidth-consuming conversion between Ethernet packets and ATM cells is required; the network is Ethernet, end to end.
- The combination of IP and Ethernet offers quality of service and traffic policing capabilities that approach those provided by ATM, so that advanced traffic engineering technologies are available to users and providers.
- A wide variety of standard optical interfaces (wavelengths and link distances) have been specified for 10-Gbps Ethernet, optimizing its operation and cost for LAN, MAN, or WAN applications.

The goal for maximum link distances encompasses a range of applications: from 300 m to 40 km. The links operate in full-duplex mode only, using a variety of optical fiber physical media.

Four physical layer options are defined for 10-Gbps Ethernet (Figure 5). The first three of these have two suboptions: an "R" suboption and a "W" suboption. The R designation refers to a family of physical layer implementations that use a signal encoding technique known as 64B/66B. The R implementations are designed for use over dark fiber, meaning a fiber-optic cable that is not in use and that is not connected to any other equipment. The W designation refers to a family of physical layer implementations that also use 64B/66B signaling but that are then encapsulated to connect to SONET equipment.

The four physical layer options are:

- 10GBASE-S (short): Designed for 850-nm transmission on multimode fiber. This medium can achieve distances up to 300 m. There are 10GBASE-SR and 10GBASE-SW versions.
- 10GBASE-L (long): Designed for 1310-nm transmission on single-mode fiber. This medium can achieve distances up to 10 km. There are 10GBASE-LR and 10GBASE-LW versions.
- 10GBASE-E (extended): Designed for 1550-nm transmission on single-mode fiber. This medium can achieve distances up to 40 km. There are 10GBASE-ER and 10GBASE-EW versions.
- 10GBASE-LX4: Designed for 1310-nm transmission on single-mode or multimode fiber. This medium can

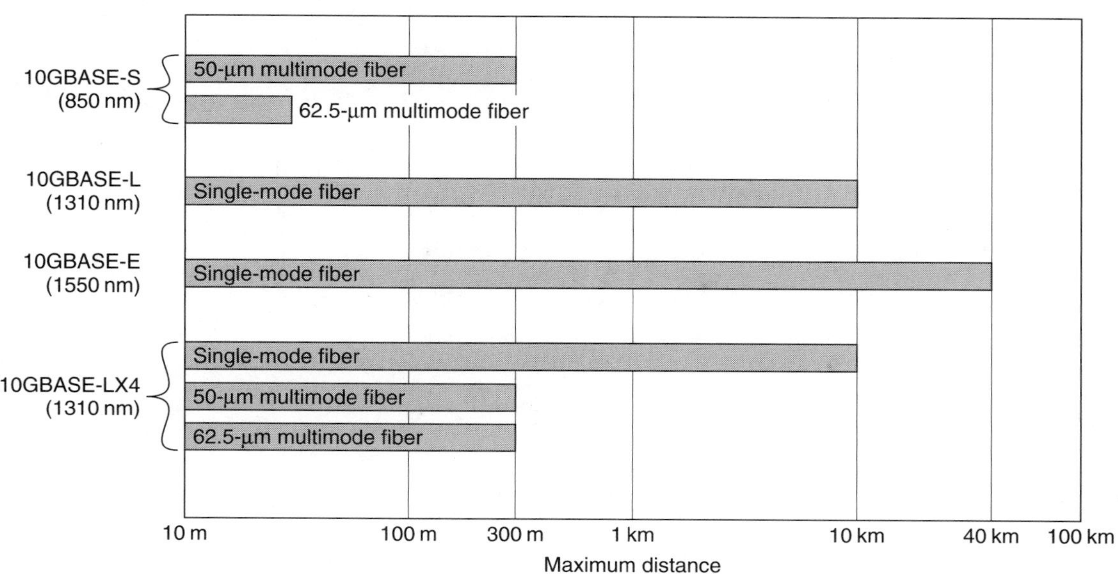

Figure 5: 10-Gbps Ethernet distance options (log scale)

achieve distances up to 10 km. This medium uses wavelength-division multiplexing (WDM) to multiplex the bit stream across four light waves. LX-4 can transmit 10 Gbps over legacy or existing 1-Gbps multimode fiber and single-mode fiber infrastructure. In fact, installations of LX4 are possible over installed 100 Mbps fiber. This can prove to be an excellent upgrade value.

The success of fast Ethernet, Gigabit Ethernet, and 10-Gbps Ethernet highlights the importance of network management concerns in choosing a network technology. Both ATM and fiber channel, explored later, may be technically superior choices for a high-speed backbone, because of their flexibility and scalability. However, the Ethernet alternatives offer compatibility with existing installed LANs, network management software, and applications. This compatibility has accounted for the survival of a nearly 30-year-old technology (CSMA/CD) in today's fast-evolving network environment.

GLOSSARY

Carrier sense multiple access (CSMA): A media access control technique for multiple-access transmission media. A station wishing to transmit first senses the medium and transmits only if the medium is idle.

Carrier sense multiple access with collision detection (CSMA/CD): A refinement of CSMA in which a station ceases transmission if it detects a collision.

Collision: A condition in which two packets are being transmitted over a medium at the same time. Their interference makes both unintelligible.

Ethernet: The name given to a family of local area network standards developed by the IEEE 802.3 committee.

Hub: A LAN connection device. A hub acts as a multiport repeater, to which multiple stations attach, each on a point-to-point link. A transmission on any one link from a station to the hub is repeated on all other links.

Layer 2 switch: A LAN connection device that operates somewhat like a multiport bridge. Typically, a LAN switch offers full-duplex operation so that multiple stations may be transmitting at one time.

Local area network (LAN): A communications network that encompasses a small area, typically a single building or cluster of buildings, used to connect various data processing devices, including PCs, workstations, and servers.

Media access control (MAC): The method of determining which device has access to the transmission medium at any time.

CROSS REFERENCES

See *Local Area Networks; Optical Fiber LANs; Token Ring LANs*.

FURTHER READING

Charles Spurgeon's Ethernet Web Site2007. http://www.ethermanage.com/ethernet/ethernet.html (accessed 18 April 2007)

Frazier, H., and Johnson, H. (1999). Gigabit Ethernet: From 100 to 1,000 Mbps. *IEEE Internet Computing*, 3, 24–31.

IEEE 802.3 10-Gbps Ethernet Task Force 2007. http://grouper.ieee.org/groups/802/3/ae/index.html(accessed 18 April 2007)

Kadambi, J., Crayford, I., and Kalkunte, M. (1998). *Gigabit Ethernet*. Upper Saddle River, NJ: Prentice Hall.

Seifert, R. (1998). *Gigabit Ethernet*. Reading, MA: Addison-Wesley.

Spurgeon, C. (2000). *Ethernet: The definitive guide*. Cambridge, MA: O'Reilly and Associates.

University of New Hampshire 2007. Interoperability Lab. http://www.iol.unh.edu (accessed 18 April 2007)

Token Ring LANs

Norman C. Strole, *IBM Corporation*, Werner Bux, *IBM Corporation, Switzerland*, and Robert D. Love, *LAN Connect Consultants*

INTRODUCTION

Local area networks (LANs) have evolved since the late 1970s to become central elements in corporate networks around the world. Many of today's LANs are based upon one or more of the network technologies that originated as one of the early standards developed within the Institute of Electrical and Electronic Engineer's (IEEE's) Project 802. The Token Ring Working Group, IEEE 802.5, which produced a family of token ring standards throughout the 1980s and 1990s, played a central role in the evolution of one highly popular LAN technology, particularly in commercial environments. Both the IEEE 802.5 and the ANSI X3T9.5 FDDI token ring standards were developed through the collaboration of many individuals representing a broad segment of the network industry. These token ring standards were subsequently endorsed as worldwide standards by the International Organization for Standardization (ISO).

BRIEF HISTORY OF RING NETWORKS[1]

A token ring network is distinguished from other networks by a combination of network topology and an access method that allows hundreds of devices to reliably share the total available bandwidth. Token ring and the predecessor networks were based on evolving time division multiple access (TDMA) schemes where a common media was used for both transmit and receive operations by tens or hundred of devices. Researchers continued their quest for the ideal protocol that was both efficient and reliable. The loop systems of the 1970s were important precursors to ring systems. In both systems, network nodes are interconnected in a serial fashion forming a closed loop (or ring) on which encoded digital information flows in one direction. Loop and ring systems can be distinguished by their respective access control schemes. Loops operate in a master/slave fashion in which access to the media is governed by a single master control node via the periodic issuance of a special control message known as the poll. Upon receipt of the poll, selected network nodes are permitted to send data to the master control node. In contrast, all nodes on a ring system are peers and autonomously determine when to transmit, based on the state of the ring. Early token ring prototypes also demonstrated that data transmission rates of 1 megabit per second (Mbps) and greater were achievable, representing a significant advancement over the 56 kilobits per second (kbps) link rates that were prevalent at the time.

One of the first accounts of a ring-based communication system was presented by Farmer and Newhall (1963); other significant ring networks include the Distributed Computing System (DCS) (Farber, Feldman, Heinrich, Hopwood, Larson, Loomis, and Rowe, 1973), the Pierce ring (Pierce, 1972), the ring built at MIT (Saltzer and Pogran, 1979), the Cambridge ring (Hopper, 1977), and the ring network at the IBM Zurich Research Laboratory (Bux, Closs, Janson, Kümmerle, Müller, and Rothauser, 1981).

Both the Pierce ring and the Cambridge ring utilized a slotted-ring technique where multiple fixed-length data slots continuously circulate around the ring. Any node can place a data packet (or a packet fragment) in one of the empty slots, along with the appropriate address information. Each node examines the address information and copies those slot contents destined to that node.

In a second type of ring system, the buffer or register insertion ring, contention between data ready to be transmitted by a node and the data stream flowing on the ring is resolved by allowing the transmitting node to dynamically insert sufficient buffer space into the ring to avoid loss of data (Hafner, Nenadal, and Tschanz, 1974; Reames and Liu, 1975).

[1]This paper is an updated revision of a previously published paper by Werner Bux and Norman Strole. 1999. "Token Ring Networks," *Wiley Encyclopedia of Electrical and Electronics Engineering*, Vol 22, edited by John G. Webster, pp. 274–80. Reprinted with permission of John Wiley & Sons, Inc.

A third scheme known as token-access control was first implemented in the DCS and the Massachusetts Institute of Technology (MIT) rings, and was the basis for the ring system built at the IBM Zurich Research Laboratory. It also underlies two important LAN standards, the IEEE 802.5 Token Ring (ISO/IEC 8802-5, 1998) and the American National Standards Institute (ANSI) X3T9.5 fiber distributed data interface (FDDI) (ISO 9314-1,2 & 3, 1989/90). In a token ring, access to the transmission medium is controlled by passing a unique digital signal, the permission token, around the ring. Each time the ring is initialized, a designated node generates a token that travels around the ring until a node with data to transmit captures the token and transmits its data. At the end of its transmission, the node passes the access opportunity to the next node downstream by generating a new token.

Standardization has played an important role in the evolution of the various LAN technologies. LAN standards have been developed primarily by the IEEE, the European Computer Manufacturers Association (ECMA), and ANSI. Token ring standardization was pursued by the IEEE 802.5 committee, which produced its first standard in 1984. ANSI ratified it as an American National Standard in 1985 and forwarded it to ISO in 1985, which approved it as an International Standard (IS) in 1986. In Europe, ECMA issued its first token ring standard, ECMA-89, in 1982.

The IEEE 802.5 Token Ring Standard was to a considerable extent based on contributions from IBM Corporation, which in the late 1970s had investigated various LAN techniques in its Zurich Research Laboratory. The token ring topology and protocol was found to be particularly applicable to commercial applications, with a number of advantages over other LANs. Performance studies showed that the token protocol was more efficient as the network load increased and that a token ring was not subject to the same distance constraints as collision-based access protocols (Bux, 1981). IBM's research also represented an advancement beyond earlier ring concepts in an effort to define a system architecture that was reliable, easily deployed, and relatively simple to recover from errors or faults. One important innovation was the introduction of a central wiring concentrator unit and the star-ring topology. Robustness of the token ring was improved through the concept of a backup ring path that would permit self-healing when a break in the primary ring occurred. A method to ensure that there was always a token on the ring was introduced with the development of the token monitor concept. The design of a priority access mechanism provided the basis needed to support real-time applications such as voice (Bux et al., 1981) and (Bux, Closs, Kümmerle, Keller, and Müller, 1983).

The first network adapter and concentrator products to support the IEEE standard were shipped by IBM and Texas Instruments in 1985. Several other companies joined them to provide a wide range of token ring products throughout the 1990s. IEEE standard-based token ring deployment declined, and in many instances, was replaced by higher-speed 100-Mbps and 1-Gbps switched Ethernet products in the early 2000s. However, the original IBM Cabling System remains in use as the transmission media for these 100-Mbps and 1-Gbps systems over 20 years after it was initially deployed for 4-Mbps LANs.

IEEE 802.5 Standards Evolution

IBM's technical contribution to the IEEE Project 802 committee in March, 1982 formed the basis for the initial IEEE 802.5 Token Ring Standard. This standard incorporates both the Physical (PHY) and Media Access Control (MAC) layers, which are Layers 1 and 2 of the Open Systems Interconnection (OSI) reference model (Strole, 1983). Token ring was initially standardized at the PHY layer as a 4-Mbps data transmit rate over 150-ohm shielded twisted pair (STP) cables known as the IBM Cabling System. Shortly after the issuance of that standard, subsequent releases expanded the cabling options to include 100 ohm unshielded twisted pair (UTP) cabling (i.e., telephone grade wire), and optical fiber. These were followed by standards for 16-Mbps token ring, first on 150-ohm STP cabling and optical fiber and later on 100-ohm UTP. Support of the 100 ohm UTP cabling required the introduction of active concentrators. The migration from a shared-ring to a dedicated, switched link per station, known as dedicated token ring (DTR), provided a transition path for 16-Mbps operation as well as for 100-Mbps token ring operation. With each of these changes, the frame format remained the same so that any token ring formatted frame could be easily and economically bridged between token ring segments operating at different speeds.

TOKEN RING TECHNOLOGY

Basic Protocol

Information on a token ring is transferred sequentially from one node to the next. The token is a control signal composed of a unique signaling sequence that any node may capture (Figure 1a). The node having control of the token, and thus sole access to the medium, transmits information onto the ring (Node A in Figure 1b). For IEEE 802.5 operation, capturing the token is accomplished by simply modifying a single bit on-the-fly to form a start-of-frame sequence, and then appending appropriate control information, address fields, the user information, frame-check sequence, and a frame-ending delimiter. All other nodes repeat, and thus redrive, each bit received. The addressed destination node copies the information from the ring as it passes (Node C in Figure 1b). After completion of its information transfer and after checking for the correct return of its frame header, the sending node generates a new token which provides other nodes with the opportunity to gain access to the ring (Node A in Figure 1c). The transmitting node keeps the ring open by transmitting idle characters until its complete frame has returned to be removed. The transmit opportunity passes with the token to all other nodes on the ring before a node can seize the token again to send additional data.

The maximum frame size is bounded by the maximum transmit time when a token is captured. The IEEE 802.5 standard defines this time as 9.1 milliseconds (e.g., 0.0091 seconds). Because the number of 8-bit octets transmitted in a fixed time period is dependent upon the data transmit rate, the upper limit becomes 4550 octets at 4 Mbps and

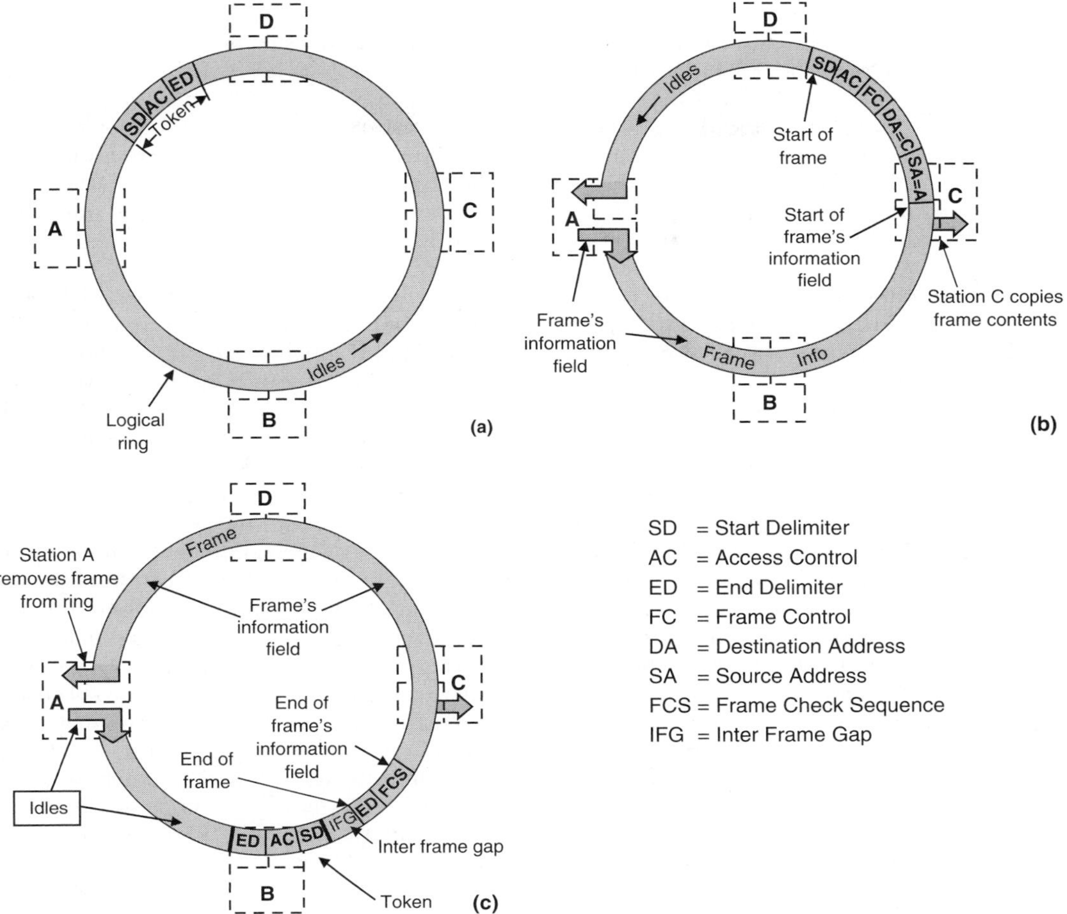

Figure 1: Token protocol overview. Reproduced by permission from James T. Carlo, Robert D. Love, Michael S. Siegel, Kenneth T. Wilson, *Understanding Token Ring Protocols and Standards,* 1998. © 1998 by Artech House, Inc.

18,200 octets at 16 Mbps (Carlo, Love, Siegel, and Wilson, 1998).

An important and unique characteristic of ring networks is that each node becomes an active participant in all ring communications, because each node must forward or retransmit the data signal to the next downstream node. This fundamental property is reflected in the wiring and transmission techniques that have been chosen for token rings, as described below.

Star Wiring

Because information flows sequentially from node to node around the ring, a failure in a single node can disrupt the operation of the entire ring. This potential problem is addressed by the star-wiring topology in which each node is wired to a so-called wiring concentrator or multistation access unit, although the wiring concentrators are interconnected with point-to-point links (Figure 2). Wiring lobes, consisting of two distinct send and receive signal paths, radiate from the wiring concentrators to the various network interface points, typically wall outlets, in a building. The wall outlets provide physical interfaces to the network to allow fast, reliable, and convenient attachment or relocation of workstations or servers.

The lobes are physically interconnected within the concentrators via electromechanical relays to form a

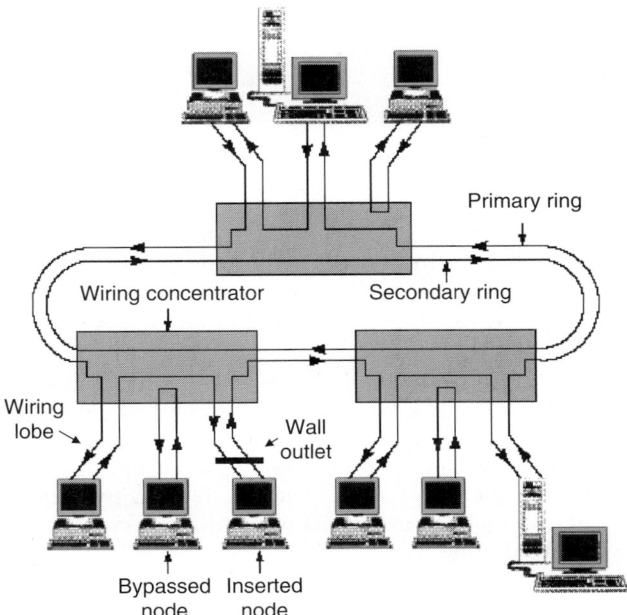

Figure 2: Star-wiring topology with dual ring example. Reproduced by permission from James T. Carlo, Robert D. Love, Michael S. Siegel, Kenneth T. Wilson, *Understanding Token Ring Protocols and Standards,* 1998. © 1998 by Artech House, Inc.

serial link. A lobe is only included in the ring path when the node is active; otherwise the bypass mechanism in the wiring concentrator causes that lobe to be skipped. If the bypass mechanism were positioned at the node itself, the inactive lobe would cause an undesirable increase in the distance between the active nodes on the ring. The wiring concentrators can be completely passive, that is, contain relays but no active elements, such as processing logic or power supplies, and require only enough power from an attached node to activate the relays when a node needs to get inserted into the ring. The concentrator design and interconnect scheme also provides an alternate ring path that can be used to bypass a break or disruption in the primary ring path (Figure 2).

As an alternative to the simple passive wiring concentrators, active concentrators or "hubs" later became very popular among users who required more stringent availability and manageability features. Active concentrators incorporate additional processing capability and contain either one or two complete token ring nodes, that is, they represent addressable entities, which enable them to provide powerful management, security, and reconfiguration functions. Furthermore, active concentrators may be combined with a bridging function to other rings or a high-speed "up-link" to a LAN switch.

When optical fibers are used to interconnect wiring concentrators and the nodes, insertion/removal signaling is accomplished via optical rather than electrical signals. The control information for ring insertion can be carried by special MAC control frames or unused code symbols; an alternative is to use out-of-band signaling with a suitable form of multiplexing. Wiring concentrators need to be active in this case.

Pre-cabling an office area or building with star wiring is practiced for most LAN installations and has a number of additional advantages:

1. It provides centralized points for reconfiguration management.
2. Workstations can easily be moved from one location to another without requiring installation of a new cable.
3. The wiring is segmented at the wiring concentrators rather than being a continuous cable, thus permitting the intermixing of transmission media. For example, twisted-pair wire can be used to interconnect the wiring concentrators and nodes, whereas optical fiber is employed for the transmission links between wiring concentrators.
4. As long as a node is in passive state (i.e., not inserted in the ring), its lobe is wrapped around in the wiring concentrator (Figure 2). This enables the node to perform a self-check before inserting itself into the ring. Should an active node detect a fault within either its own components or its wiring lobe, it can remove itself from the ring.

Transmission Media

When token ring was initially under development in the early 1980s, it was thought that telephone-grade unshielded twisted pair cabling was incapable of carrying high speed (4 Mbps) signals for sufficient distances to be practical for commercial LAN applications. Therefore, a specially designed STP cabling was simultaneously developed by IBM. In 1984 the IBM Cabling System using 150 ohm STP copper media for deployment in a star topology was introduced. Commercial customers embraced the star-wired topology but were unsatisfied with the large diameter of the 150 ohm cabling and subsequent cable expense. In that same time frame, the telephony industry was looking at ways to use thinner telephone wiring for high-speed data transmission and realized that to do so telephone wire would have to be substantially improved. Those improvements had not reached the market when the first token ring products became available in 1985. At that time complex wiring rules were published for robust operation of the token ring protocol over large networks spanning multiple wiring closets and containing up to 260 devices (Carlo et al., 1998, 64–9). As a result of customer demand to use existing telephone wires, alternate rules were also published for more modest networks of up to 100 nodes, all cabled to the same wiring closet (Carlo et al, 1998). Minimum requirements were placed on the telephone wire, which was dubbed "Type 3 media." During this time frame the telephony industry was also developing and standardizing improved telephone wiring and connectors for the express purpose of carrying high-speed LAN data for both token ring and Ethernet applications, first in North America under the auspices of TIA, and later internationally, under JTC/1 SC25/WG3. The North American Standard for telecommunication grade cabling was TIA/EIA 568. The first edition of that standard included the 150 ohm cabling of the IBM Cabling System, and a more rigorous standard for data grade telephone wire called Category 3 cabling. Later editions of that standard specified a Category 5 (and later Category 5e) telephone wiring, which was crucial for supporting token ring's next generation of hardware operating at 16 Mbps and later at 100 Mbps. The international standard, IS11801, specified the 150-ohm IBM data grade cable, as well as both Category 3 and Category 5 twisted pair cabling. Category 5 (and later Category 5e) cabling was more advanced, with better transmission characteristics and became the de facto twisted pair data cable. As token ring increased its operating speed, first from 4 to 16 Mbps and then to 100 Mbps, the requirement to operate over Category 5 cabling at distances of up to 100 meters had to be addressed. The solution at 16 Mbps was to require the concentrators to be active devices, repeating the signal between each pair of wiring concentrators but not between the nodes themselves. The solution at 100 Mbps was to use a more efficient line coding and to operate in DTR mode where each signal received by the concentrator from any of its attachment ports was regenerated and retransmitted to the next lobe. DTR design required one active device in the concentrator for each end station that attached to it. These topology and signal reclocking changes were required to overcome the signal attenuation that occurs over the copper media as the signal clock rate increases, thus decreasing the maximum distance before the signal must be reclocked.

Although there were two principle choices for cabling from the wiring closet to the active devices in the offices and within the wiring closet, the requirement to be able to transmit over multi-100 meter lengths between wiring closets and between buildings was addressed with optical fiber transmission media. Although optical fiber media could have been used to attach devices located in offices, it never gained significant market share for that application as a result of attachment and media cost.

Advances in signal processing technology have allowed transmission rates to increase from 100 Mbps to over 1000 Mbps while maintaining a clock rate that allows the 100-meter length to be maintained. Subsequent advances in the copper cable design and digital encoding schemes since the 1990s have resulted in transmission capacities of up to 10 gigabits per second (Gbps) over short distances (up to 15 meters), with the promise of longer distances in the future. Much of this increase in transmission capacity over copper media can be attributed to the advancements in Application Specific Integrated Circuit (ASIC) technology and digital encoding schemes.

Line Coding

The data generated by a node must be encoded for transmission over a ring network. The IEEE 802.5 standard specifies differential Manchester encoding for both the 4- and 16-Mbps token ring transmission rates (Figure 3a). Differential Manchester encoding is characterized by the transmission of two line signal elements per bit, resulting in a link clock rate that is double the bit transmission rate. In the case of a binary one or zero, a signal element of one polarity is transmitted for one half-bit time, followed by the transmission of a signal element of the opposite polarity. This line coding has two advantages: 1) The resulting signal has no DC component and can readily be inductively coupled, and 2) the mid-bit transition conveys inherent timing information. The ones are different from the zeros at the leading bit boundary; a value of one has no signal transition at the bit boundary, whereas a value of zero does. In decoding the signal, only the presence or absence of the signal transition and not the actual polarity is detected, thus interchanging the two wires of the twisted pair introduces no data errors. A code violation results if no signal transition occurs at the half-bit position. Code violations can be intentionally created to form a unique non-data signal pattern that can be distinguished from normal data (Figure 3b). These so-called J/K signals can be inserted to mark the start or end of a valid data frame. The J/K code violations are used in pairs to maintain the DC balance of the Manchester signaling.

Manchester coding is a very simple and robust technology, but, at the same time, is also very bandwidth inefficient and therefore not suitable for transmission rates significantly higher than 16 Mbps. For example, in FDDI,

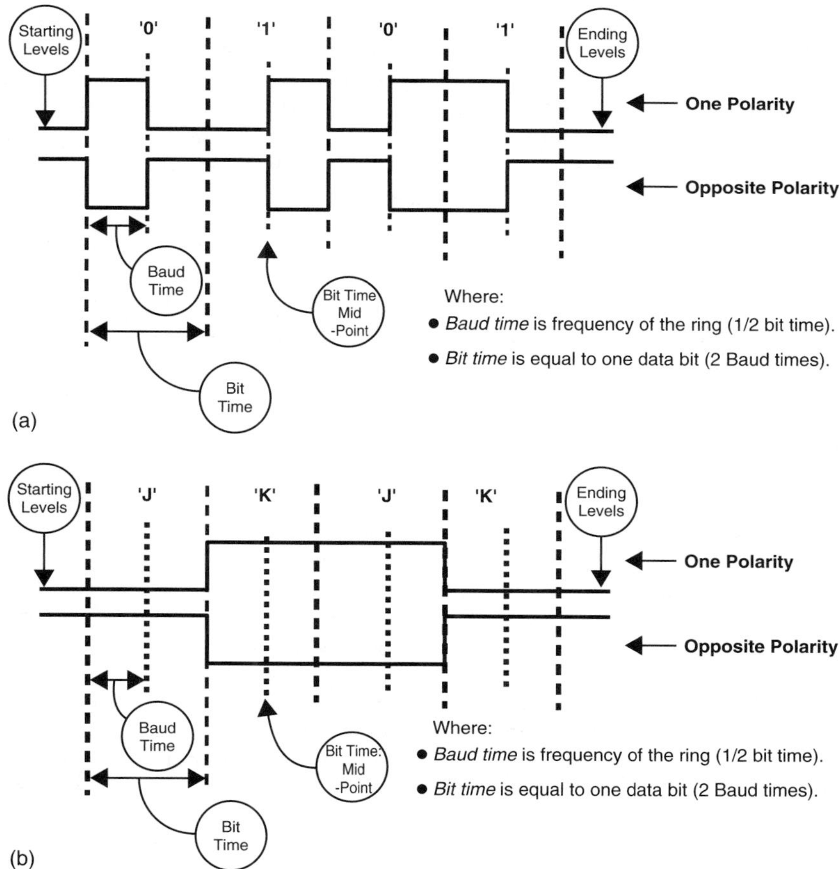

Figure 3: Differential manchester encoding. Reproduced by permission from James T. Carlo, Robert D. Love, Michael S. Siegel, Kenneth T. Wilson, *Understanding Token Ring Protocols and Standards,* 1998. © 1998 by Artech House, Inc.

information on the medium is transmitted in a 4-out-of-5 group code (4B/5B) with each 5-bit code group, called a symbol, used to represent 4 bits of data. The symbols are transmitted in a Non-Return to Zero Inverted (NRZI) line transmission format (ISO/IEC 9314-3, 1990). NRZI is distinguished from Manchester in that

1. There are no transitions at the half-bit boundary.
2. Transitions occur at the beginning of a binary "1," and
3. No transition occurs at the beginning of a binary "0."
4. The 4B/5B encoding scheme has excess code groups that can be used as nondata symbols to distinguish the start and end of a valid data frame.

Synchronization

Synchronization of the link clocking among stations is a key technical problem in the design of any ring system. Rings built according to the IEEE 802.5 standard employ a centralized clocking technique. In normal operation, one node on the ring is automatically designated as the active monitor during ring initialization. The monitor plays a crucial role in the supervision of the ring, as will be described below. In addition, it provides the ring master clock. All other nodes on the ring are frequency and phase-locked to the monitor. They extract timing from the received data by means of a phase-locked loop while redriving the digital signal to reach the next node. Each port of an active concentrator can also reclock and redrive the signal as well.

Although the mean transmission rate on the ring is controlled by the active monitor node, segments of the ring can, instantaneously, operate at rates slightly different from the frequency of the master oscillator. The cumulative effect of such rate variations are sufficient to cause variations of a few bits in the latency of a ring. Unless the latency of the ring remains constant, bits would have to be either dropped or added. To maintain a constant ring latency, an elastic buffer is provided in the monitor. If the received signal at the active monitor node is slightly faster than the master oscillator, the buffer will fill up to avoid dropping bits. If the received signal is slow, the buffer will be emptied to avoid adding bits to the repeated bit stream. Detailed discussion and analysis of this clocking scheme are given in (Müller, Keller, and Meyr, 1983) and (Carlo et al., 1998).

A major advantage of the centralized clocking approach is that it minimizes the total latency of the ring and thus allows use of the IEEE 802.5 protocol, which, for optimum performance, requires the ring latency to be small. An alternative synchronization technique that introduces greater latency but is easier to implement at high transmission rates is employed in FDDI, where information is transmitted between nodes asynchronously; that is, each node uses its own autonomous clock source to transmit or repeat information on the ring (ISO 9314-1, 1989). This type of operation requires the use of an elastic buffer at every node. Information is clocked into the buffer at the clock rate recovered from the incoming bit stream, but is clocked out of the buffer at the autonomous fixed clock rate of the node. A preamble that precedes each frame enables the buffer to be reset to its midpoint prior to frame reception. The reset operation increases, or decreases, the length of the preamble. For the IEEE 802.5 100-Mbps token ring operation, the issue of ring latency was sidestepped by defining only a switched token ring operation with one active repeater node in the wiring closet for each attached station. With this configuration, the attached station and its active repeater form a two-station ring. The active repeater acts like a bridge sending information onto this two-station ring, and broadcasting information received from the attached station to the other direct-attached stations.

TOKEN RING ACCESS PROTOCOL, MONITORING, AND RECOVERY

Data Frame Format

Figure 4 shows the token format and the general format for transmitting information on the ring, called a frame. A token contains only the access control (AC) subfield and the starting and ending delimiters (Figure 4a). The one-byte AC field includes a one-bit token (T) indicator that indicates whether this is a token (0) or a frame (1). A token priority mode that uses the priority reservation indicators provides different priority levels of access to the ring (see below). The monitor (M) bit is used in connection with the token monitor function to maintain the validity of the token.

The "data" portion of the frame is variable in length and contains the information that the sender is transferring to the receiver. The information (INFO) field is preceded by a header, which contains several subfields (Figure 4b). The first is a starting delimiter (SD) that identifies the start of the frame. The starting delimiter is a unique signal pattern that includes pairs of code violations of the differential Manchester encoding scheme as described earlier (Figure 3b). Next, the AC subfield, with the token bit (T) set to 1, is defined for controlling transmit access to the shared media as described above. The frame control (FC) subfield contains a two-bit frame format (FF) and a three-bit frame priority subfield. The frame format enables the receiving node to determine if the information within the data field of the frame contains media access control (MAC) information (FF = 00) or user data (FF = 01). MAC frames may optionally include frame status information within the control indicator subfield. Finally, the header includes the source address (SA) of the node that originated the information and the destination address (DA) of the node (or nodes) destined to receive the information. Both address fields contain six bytes, with the first two bits of the DA designating that the address is intended for multiple destination nodes (group bit) or that the address has been assigned by the user (local administered address bit). Use of the routing information field (RIF) will be described in the section on multiring networks.

The information field is followed by a trailer that is composed of three subfields. The first portion of the trailer contains a 4-byte frame check sequence (FCS) that is calculated by the source node and used by downstream nodes for detecting bit errors that may occur within the frame

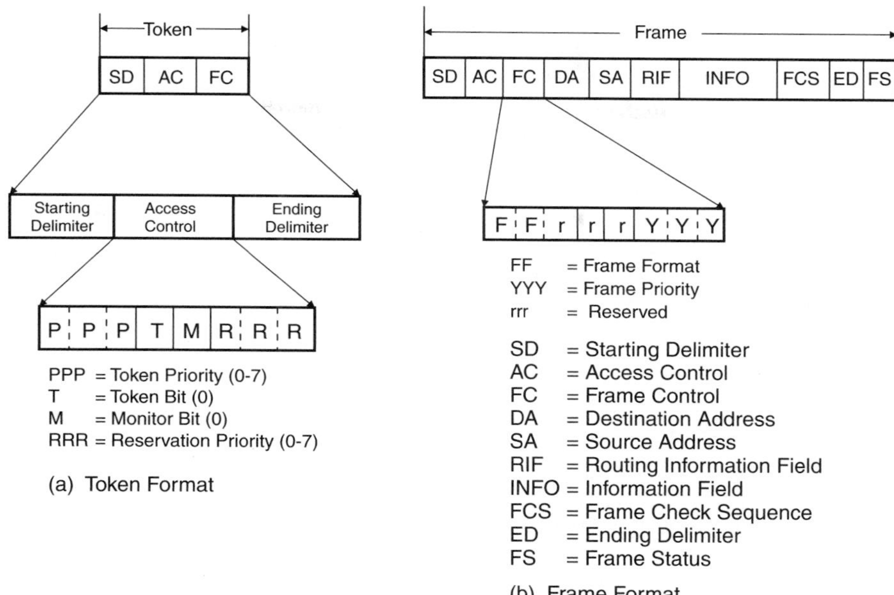

Figure 4: Token and frame formats. Reproduced by permission from James T. Carlo, Robert D. Love, Michael S. Siegel, Kenneth T. Wilson, *Understanding Token Ring Protocols and Standards,* 1998. © 1998 by Artech House, Inc.

during transmission bounded by the FC subfield and the last bit of the information field. Next, an ending delimiter (ED) is provided to identify the end of the frame. This delimiter also contains a unique, although slightly different, bit combination along with pairs of code violations as were found in the starting delimiter. The last bit of the ending delimiter is designated as the error-detected indicator (EDI). This indicator will always be zero during error-free ring operation. The ending delimiter is followed by a one-byte frame status (FS) field. The FS field contains bits that can be modified while the frame is traversing the ring by nodes that match the destination address and/or copy the frame. The FS field is therefore not included in the calculation of the FCS character. For this reason, these bits are defined as pairs to avoid erroneous conditions as a result of single-bit errors on the wire.

Priority Protocol

In some applications, it may be necessary for selected nodes to gain priority access to the ring. A priority scheme was designed specifically for the token ring protocol that was initially one of the distinguishing features versus other access control schemes. The priority (PPP) and reservation (RRR) indicators in the access control (AC) field are used to facilitate this access scheme (Figure 4b). Various nodes may be assigned priority levels for gaining access to the ring, with the lowest priority being "000" and the highest being "111." This allows up to eight protocol levels to be defined. A selected node can seize any token that has a priority setting (bits 0-3) equal to or lower than its assigned priority. The requesting node can set its priority request in the AC reservation field (bits 5-7) of a frame as it is being repeated if that node's priority is higher than any current reservation request. The current transmitting node must examine the reservation request in the returning frame and release the next token with the new priority indication (bits 0-3), but retain the previous priority level within its MAC state information for later release. A requesting node uses the priority token and releases the new token at the same priority so that any other nodes assigned that priority can also have an opportunity to transmit. When the node that originally released the priority token recognizes a token at that priority, it then releases a new token at the level that was interrupted by the original request. Thus, the lower priority token resumes circulation at the point of interruption.

In 1995, the IEEE 802.5 standard committee published a set of guidelines for the use of previously reserved priority levels 5 and 6. Priority 5 is recommended for delay sensitive, high-bandwidth data streams such as video applications. Priority 6 is recommended for delay sensitive, low-bandwidth data streams, such as interactive voice communication. Priority 7 is reserved for ring management and error recovery frames. Priority 4 is generally recognized for bridge access.

Token Protocol Performance Issues

From a performance point of view, token rings have two distinct advantages over other access protocols:

1. As a result of the cyclic operation (also sometimes referred to as "round robin") enforced by the rotating token, all users of the ring are serviced in a perfectly fair fashion within a given priority class. The priority mechanism, however, may be used to give a subset of the users preferential service as described above.
2. As a result of its deterministic behavior, the token protocol scales better with respect to network latency than random access protocols such as CSMA/CD.

However, the original IEEE 802.5 protocol is not totally insensitive to ring latency because it requires that idle characters be inserted by a transmitting node until it has recognized its source address in the header of the returning frame. This leads to improved error robustness of the operation and is required for a higher priority token to be released, but results in decreased efficiency as the physical ring length, number of active nodes, and/or the ring speed increase.

Ring protocol efficiency can be maximized at very high speeds and/or long ring lengths if nodes release the token immediately after finishing frame transmission. In 1987, the IEEE 802.5 standard was enhanced by an early token release (ETR) option that allows a transmitting node to release a new token as soon as it has completed frame transmission, whether or not the frame header has returned to that node. This enhancement was necessary to allow the support of 16-Mbps operation over large campus networks. One impact of ETR is that priority reservations applied to "short" frames are lost until the circulation of a subsequent frame that exceeds the ring length. This trade-off was shown to be acceptable for typical campus-wide 16-Mbps rings. A detailed discussion of token ring performance issues can be found in (Bux, 1989).

Ring Monitor Function

In token ring networks, error detection and recovery mechanisms are provided to restore network operation in the event that transmission errors or medium transients, for example, those resulting from node insertion or removal, cause the ring to deviate from normal operation. The IEEE 802.5 token rings utilize a network monitoring function that is performed in a specific token monitor node with backup capability in all other nodes attached to the ring. The monitoring function is based on the scheme developed by the IBM research team in Zurich (Bux Closs, Kümmerle, Keller, and Müller, 1983). Through an arbitration process, the nodes on the ring select one node to be the active monitor. As described above, this is also the node providing the master clock for the ring. The remaining nodes function as standby monitors. The active monitor keeps watch over the health of ring and token, activating recovery procedures when necessary.

Ring errors can be quickly isolated to a specific ring segment if an accurate map of the ring stations is maintained. Periodically, the active monitor will issue a broadcast frame called an active monitor present (AMP) frame. The first active node downstream from the monitor node will set the address recognized indicator (ARI) bits in the FS subfield and save the source address. Other nodes on the ring will ignore this particular broadcast frame when the ARI bits are set. The node that received the AMP frame will then issue a standby monitor present (SMP) frame containing its own source address whenever a token is observed. This frame is recognized and copied by the next downstream active node. This process continues around the ring until the active monitor receives the SMP frame without the address-recognized flag set. At that time, each node will have the specific address of the adjacent node immediately upstream. This is known as the nearest active upstream neighbor (NAUN). The NAUN information is transmitted with all beacon frames and soft error report frames, thereby allowing a network management node to log the logical location of the fault. The AMP and SMP frames are transmitted at the highest ring priority to insure that the process completes in the least amount of time, even during periods of peak ring utilization.

Ring Fault Detection and Isolation

The topological structure of a star-ring configuration, in conjunction with the token-access control protocol, permitted the development of additional protocols for rapid detection and isolation of network faults (Strole, 1983) and (Carlo et al., 1998). The unidirectional propagation of information (electrical signals and data frames) from node to node provides a basis for detecting certain types of network faults. Network faults can be categorized into two types: hard faults and soft faults.

A hard fault occurs when there is a complete break in the ring wiring between two adjacent nodes or wiring concentrators or a failure in the transmitter or receiver elements of a node. A node that detects loss of signal at its receiver will begin transmitting a unique series of contiguous MAC frames. Such a transmit state is called "beaconing." A hard fault may initially cause more than one node to enter the beacon state, but eventually all nodes but the one immediately adjacent to and downstream of the fault will exit the beacon state as they begin receiving beacon frames from their upstream neighbors. Thus, the location of the fault will be isolated to the particular ring segment and the last known NAUN that is immediately upstream from the node that is transmitting beacon type frames.

A soft fault is characterized by a high frame error rate, usually caused by a degradation in the electrical signal or environmental electromagnetic interference. The frame check sequence (FCS) of all frames is calculated and verified by all intermediate nodes as the frames are repeated. The first node on the ring that detects an FCS error sets the error detected indicator (EDI) in the ending delimiter field as an indication to all other nodes that the error has been logged. If a predetermined threshold of FCS errors is reached over a given time interval, an indication of the condition can be reported to a network management application. The location of the soft fault can be readily determined from the information in the error report message and isolated to the ring segment immediately upstream of the reporting node.

Once the location of a fault (hard or soft) has been determined, several options are available for eliminating the faulty segment(s) from the ring so that normal operation can resume. The wiring concentrators provide concentration points for bypassing such faults, as was discussed earlier with lobe bypass. Also, alternate backup links are normally available between the wiring concentrators in parallel with the principal links. If a fault occurs in the ring segment between two wiring concentrators or if a concentrator failure occurs, wrapping of the principal ring to the alternate ring within the two wiring concentrators on either side of the fault will restore the physical path of the ring (Figure 5). This wrapping

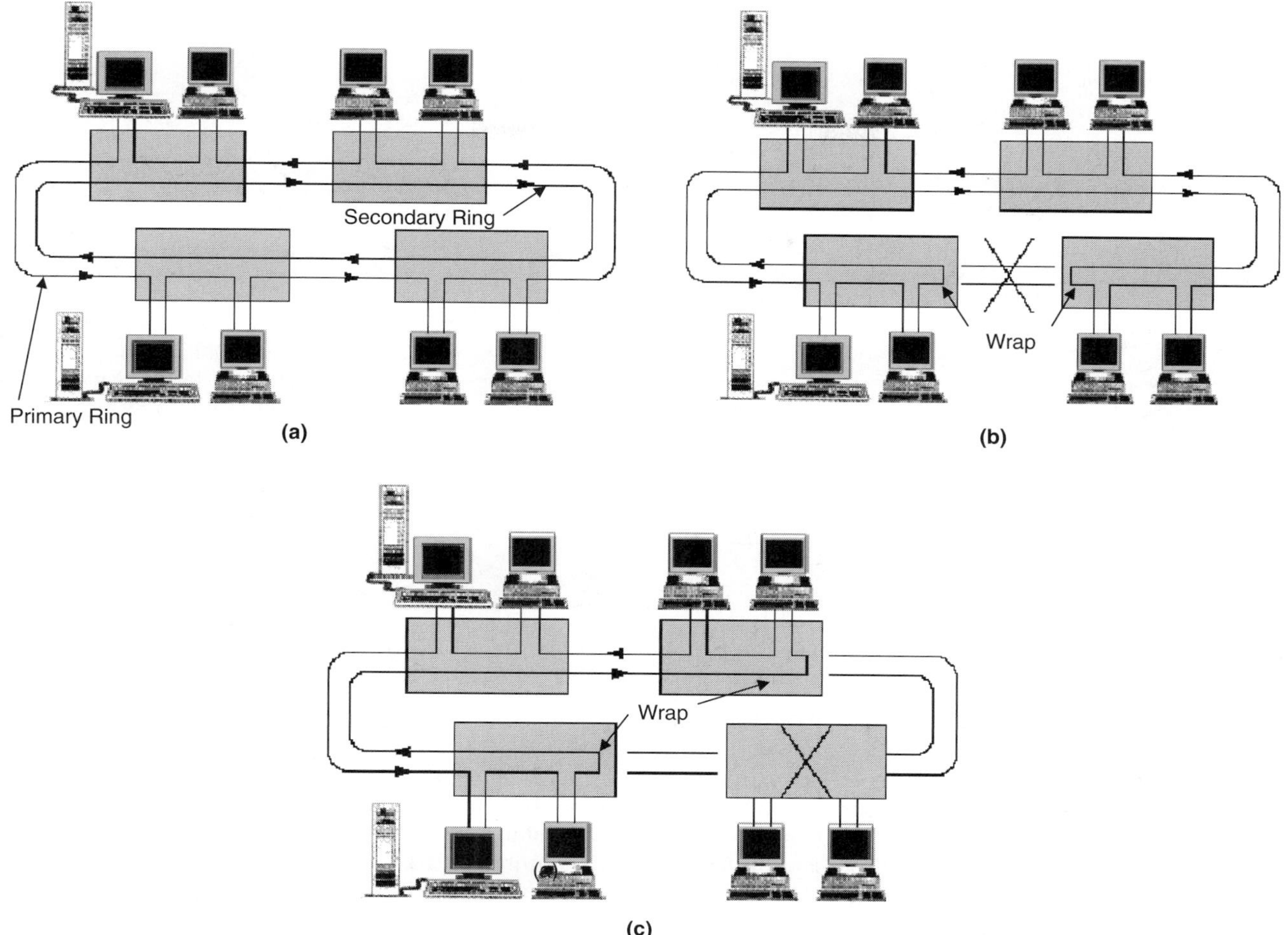

Figure 5: Fault detection and isolation with wiring concentrators. Reproduced by permission from James T. Carlo, Robert D. Love, Michael S. Siegel, Kenneth T. Wilson, *Understanding Token Ring Protocols and Standards,* 1998. © 1998 by Artech House, Inc.

function, like the lobe bypass function, is automatic in active concentrators. Figure 5 shows four wiring concentrators as they would be configured with both a principal and an alternate ring. The signals on the alternate ring are propagated in the direction opposite to those on the principal ring, thus maintaining the logical order of the nodes on the ring.

MULTIRING NETWORKS

Multiple rings are required in a campus or building LAN when the aggregate data transfer requirements or total number of stations exceed the capacity of a single ring or when a large number of attached nodes are spread over a broad area (Strole, 1983). Two rings can be linked together by a high-speed interconnect mechanism known as a bridge (Figure 6). A bridge is capable of providing a logical forwarding of frames between the rings based on the SA, DA, and/or RIF inserted by the source node. An additional capability of the bridge is to perform transmission speed changes from one ring to another. Each ring retains its individual identity and token mechanism, and could therefore stand alone in the event the bridge or another ring was to be disrupted. The bridge interface to a ring is the same as any other node, except that it must recognize and copy frames with a destination address or RIF subfield for one of the other rings within the network. Also, several frames may be temporarily buffered in the bridge while awaiting transfer to the next ring.

The local network can be further expanded to meet larger data capacity requirements by interconnecting multiple bridges, resulting in a hierarchical network in which multiple rings are interconnected via bridges and multiple bridges are interconnected via a separate high-speed link known as a backbone (Figure 6). The backbone itself may be a high-speed ring, such as FDDI, or it may be another network type, such as an asynchronous transfer mode (ATM) network.

Most token ring and FDDI network devices support a MAC-level bridging scheme known as source route bridging (SRB). With this scheme, intermediate bridges, switches, or routers and the associated ring segments that form the path between a source and destination node are uniquely and explicitly identified within the RIF within the frame header (Figure 4b). The RIF is created via a discovery protocol at the beginning of a session that allows the source node to designate a unique path to the destination node, enumerated as a sequence of bridge and ring segment IDs (Carlo et al., 1998). This scheme simplifies the bridge processing that is required at each intermediate device, whereas also

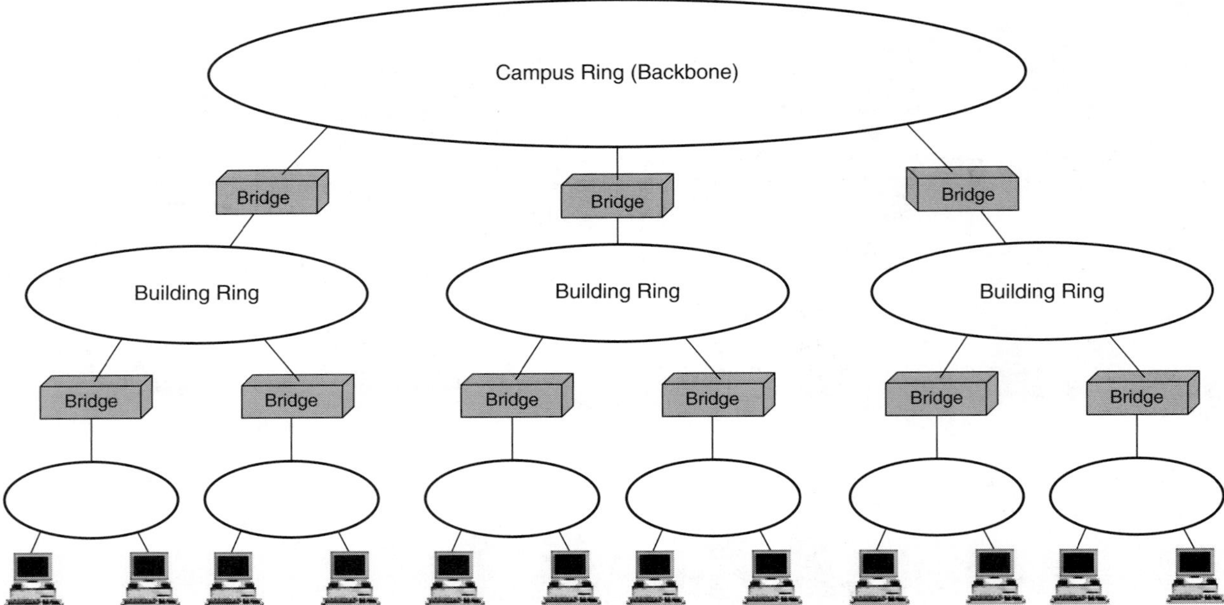

Figure 6: Multiring network topology. Reproduced by permission from James T. Carlo, Robert D. Love, Michael S. Siegel, Kenneth T. Wilson, *Understanding Token Ring Protocols and Standards,* 1998. © 1998 by Artech House, Inc.

providing a mechanism that allows multiple active data paths between two points of the network.

The IEEE 802.1 committee developed standards for LAN bridging. This committee developed an alternate scheme, known as transparent bridging (TB) that required the bridge devices to create and maintain bridge tables to determine which frames to forward (or drop). This scheme was more applicable to the existing IEEE 802.3 Ethernet standard-based products, without requiring changes to the existing adapter hardware and could also be applied to token rings as well. The IEEE 802.1 bridge standard incorporated the criteria for a combination TB/SRB bridge a few years later.

Traditional bridged networks were gradually replaced by switched networks beginning in 1995 (Christensen, Haas, Noel, and Strole, 1995). Fewer nodes per ring segment allow individual nodes access to more of the bandwidth. Dedicated switched links allow one node to use all of the available bandwidth without contention with other nodes.

DEDICATED ("SWITCHED") TOKEN RINGS

As long as a token ring is operated as a shared medium, the total transmission capacity available to all users can obviously not exceed the ring's transmission rate. FDDI extended token ring speed to 100 Mbps by using a different token-based media access protocol and different frame format in a separate standard effort that was completed in the late 1980s (ISO 9314-1,2 & 3, 1989/90). The IEEE 802.5 protocol could have been extended to 100 Mbps, but this was not considered to be a commercially viable option with the completion of the FDDI standard.

Overcoming the limitations of a shared-media protocol required the introduction of a high-speed switching function which became technically and economically possible in the early 1990s with the advancement of ASIC technology. In 1993, the IEEE 802.5 standard committee began looking at options to extend the token ring standard to meet the demand for additional bandwidth. As a result, the DTR standard was completed in 1997. DTR increased the number of ring segments with the introduction of the DTR concentrator by allowing a ring segment to contain one or more stations supported by one active node in the wiring concentrator and introduced the concept of full-duplex operation for directly attached stations (Carlo et al., 1998).

One catalyst for the DTR effort was to leverage the beacon transmit mode that was already present in the hardware design of millions of token ring adapters. In this mode, the node adapter is simultaneously transmitting the beacon frame and receiving frames on the inbound side in order to determine if it is the station nearest to the fault. The existing token ring adapter firmware was modified to create the new full-duplex mode defined by the DTR standard, thus allowing existing adapters to migrate to the new mode with a firmware update combined with the introduction of a multiport token ring packet switch to replace the classic wiring concentrator. DTR also allowed a node to be the only station on a ring shared with the DTR port as the other station. In this case, no change to the station interface is required. The DTR standard and technology was expanded in 1998 to enable 100-Mbps token ring to use Category 5 data cabling, which had become standard in many commercial businesses.

With DTR, a token ring node is allocated the full bandwidth via a dedicated segment between the node and the DTR concentrator (Figure 7) (Carlo et al., 1998). A new mode, full-duplex operation, is also supported. With the full-duplex mode, the token is no longer required. Instead, two dedicated parallel paths are established between the two nodes. For 100-Mbps token ring, up to 200 Mbps of data transfer (100 transmit and 100 receive) can be achieved per link. For 16-Mbps operation, up to 32 Mbps

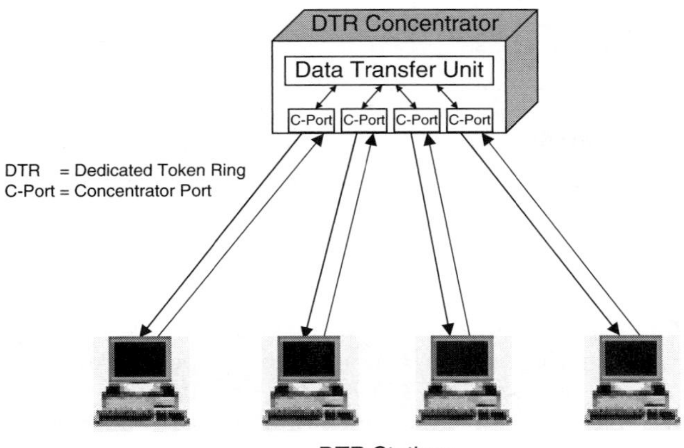

Figure 7: Dedicated token ring example. Reproduced by permission from James T. Carlo, Robert D. Love, Michael S. Siegel, Kenneth T. Wilson, *Understanding Token Ring Protocols and Standards,* 1998. © 1998 by Artech House, Inc.

of data transfer (16 transmit, 16 receive) can be achieved per link. Data frames are forwarded among the dedicated segments by a high-speed data transfer unit within a DTR (Figure 7) or a packet switch (Christensen et al., 1995). For commercial applications, the token ring switch utilizes the existing RIF within the frame header to accelerate the packet forwarding. The effective aggregate bandwidth of the DTR system is determined by the switch capacity rather than the clock speed of the shared media, thus providing much greater bandwidth than the shared-media configuration. Devices attached to a dedicated link have access to the full-duplex bandwidth, thereby providing significantly more application growth potential than with a shared-media access control scheme.

FDDI TOKEN PROTOCOL

A discussion of token ring would not be complete without a more detailed discussion of the FDDI token protocol, which is significantly different from the IEEE 802.5 operation in several fundamental areas (Ross, 1986). Unlike the IEEE 802.5 standard, FDDI defines two classes of data traffic, synchronous and asynchronous (ISO 9314-2, 1989). The synchronous class is applicable to traffic that requires regular intervals between consecutive frame transmissions, such as real-time voice or video for example. Synchronous traffic is given the highest priority and the protocol is designed to guarantee frames of this class a transmit opportunity on each revolution of the token within predetermined bounds on the transmit intervals. Stations requiring synchronous access are assigned reserved bandwidth in advance via a distributed control scheme. Asynchronous frames have up to eight priority levels or thresholds but with no guaranteed access. The protocol allocates asynchronous bandwidth based upon the priority after synchronous demand has been satisfied.

FDDI Token Timers and Operation

Unlike the IEEE 802.5 protocol, control of the FDDI ring under normal operation is decentralized; that is, there is no master station. The algorithm that each station executes allocates use of the ring based on a fixed value that is the same for all MAC entities on the ring, and on the contents of two timers present in every MAC (ISO 9314-2, 1989). The fixed value is the target token rotation time (TTRT), and the timers are the token rotation timer (TRT) and the token hold timer (THT).

As the network load increases, the TTRT defines the average time for the token to complete one rotation around the ring which, in turn, determines the response time that the network's users need for their synchronous traffic. The stations determine the value for TTRT during ring initialization. The FDDI protocol guarantees that the maximum token wait time for any station on the ring will never exceed 2 times the TTRT value.

One of the timers present in every station's MAC entity is the TRT. In conjunction with a counter called Late_Ct (the "late counter"), it indicates the amount of time that has elapsed since the station last received a token. By examining its TRT and Late_Ct, a station knows whether the token is taking more or less than the TTRT to complete a rotation. Stations can transmit asynchronous traffic only if the token is received when the Late_Ct is zero.

The Late_Ct is set to zero by the MAC each time the token is received and the TRT is initialized to the TTRT value each time the token is received early. TRT is a decrementing counter that measures the time required for the token to circulate around the ring. If the TRT expires before the token returns, the Late_Ct is incremented and TRT is reset to TTRT and continues to decrement. A late token, or one that arrives when Late_Ct = 1, does no reset the TRT, but allows it to continue decrementing, thus carrying forward the lateness of the current token rotation into the next token rotation time. This may restrict a station's ability to transmit asynchronous data frames for multiple successive token rotations. If the TRT expires again while Late_Ct = 1, an error condition recovery procedure is initiated by that station.

The second timer used in bandwidth allocation is the THT. Each THT indicates the amount of time that the MAC may use for asynchronous frame transmission. The value of THT for each station will vary from one token revolution to the next, depending upon the network load.

A station may use a "late" token only for synchronous transmission, because the token has taken more than TTRT to complete a rotation. However, if Late_Ct equals zero when the station receives the token, the station may transmit asynchronous frames as well. In this case, the THT will determine the amount of time the station may transmit asynchronous frames. A station transmits all pending synchronous frames first. The time required for synchronous transmission has already been factored into the TTRT value and is thus not subject to THT limits. THT is initialized as the residual value of the TRT (e.g., as the difference between TTRT and the amount of time that the early token took to rotate). THT is decremented by the MAC only during the transmission of asynchronous frames. A station may transmit multiple asynchronous frames until the THT expires.

The FDDI priority scheme is based on an array of priority threshold values called T_Pri. These values indicate the length of time that the station may transmit frames at a given priority. A station can only begin transmitting frames at a given priority if the remaining THT is greater than the threshold value for that priority. Thus, under elevated ring loads, it is possible that a given station will be allowed to transmit synchronous frames and only a few of the higher priority asynchronous frames, but will then need to wait additional token rotations to transmit the lower priority asynchronous frames. Dykeman and Bux (1988) provide an in-depth analysis of the FDDI token-access and priority schemes.

Additional details regarding FDDI operation can be found in referenced FDDI standard documentation (ISO 9314-1, 2, & 3, 1989/90).

LAN EVOLUTION

The full-duplex, star configuration continued to evolve from the early 1990s, but the basic principals remained the same. The current generation of LAN switches provides in excess of 100-Gbps internal switch capacity, with the Ethernet packet format being the most widely deployed. These advances are enabled by high-speed ASIC switch technology that allows high-density 1-Gbps and 10-Gbps ports on a single chip. Fiber media is also more pervasive now than in the past and the fiber connector technology has improved significantly. As pointed out in the Transmission Media section, dedicated link speeds of 1 and 10 Gbps are possible today on high-quality copper media as well.

CONCLUSION

This chapter provides both a historical perspective and in-depth technical review of the IEEE and ANSI token ring LAN protocols that emerged in the 1980s. Interested readers are encouraged to refer to (Carlo et al., 1998) as the most comprehensive source on the IEEE 802.5 token ring that is still available today.

GLOSSARY

ANSI: American National Standards Institute, sponsor of the FDDI X3T9.5 standard committee (www.ansi.org).

Bridge: An intermediate device that links two or more network segments together, usually forwarding only those data frames one from link to the other that are required for nodes on the separate links to communicate.

Code violation: A representation of a nondata bit (neither 1 nor 0) in the differential Manchester encoding scheme that can be used to identify the start and/or end of a valid data packet or frame.

Data frame: A variable length packet of information with a predetermined format that usually includes a start of packet delimiter, source and destination addresses, the frame information or payload, and the ending packet delimiter. The frame format varies depending upon the media access protocol (e.g., Token Ring, Ethernet, FDDI).

Data rate: The rate at which data is transmitted on the media, usually in millions of bits (megabits) or billions of bits (gigbits) per second. The effective data rate is usually lower than the actual clock rate on the media.

Dedicated token ring (DTR): An advancement in the token ring operation that allows a single node to utilize all of the link bandwidth without contention with another node.

Early token release: A node releases the token immediately after completing frame transmission and before the beginning of the frame has made a complete pass around the ring. This improves the ring efficiency for very high-speed or extremely long rings by eliminating wasted time.

Fiber distributed data interface (FDDI): A 100-Mbps token ring network standard developed in the mid-1980s by the ANSI X3T9.5 standards body.

Institute of Electrical and Electronics Engineering (IEEE): An affiliation of technical professionals from around the world. The IEEE sponsors international standards development projects, such as the IEEE 802.5 Token Ring Standard (www.ieee.org).

Line coding: The technique used to represent binary information (e.g., 1's and 0's) on the physical media. Differential Manchester and Non-Return To Zero are two example schemes that are used in token ring LANs.

Local area network (LAN): A network that usually spans a confined geographic area, such as an office building or university campus.

Media access control (MAC): The protocol or scheme that is defined for allowing multiple nodes to share access to a common transmission media, usually designed to minimize loss of information and to provide fair access to all of the nodes.

Nearest active upstream neighbor (NAUN): A means to identify the upstream node from a given node. If all NAUNs are known, an accurate ring map can be maintained for problem isolation.

Node: A device or station that is an active element in the network and shares access to the communication media with similar devices or stations.

Physical (PHY): The physical media and interface circuitry that handles the end-to-end signaling via the transmission media.

Token: A predefined, fixed-length packet that circulates on a ring. A node that has data to transmit must hold the token while it is transmitting. This prevents other stations from transmitting at the same time, thus avoiding "data collisions" on the ring.

Token monitor: A designated node on the IEEE 802.5 ring that monitors the health of the token. If the token is lost or damaged, the token monitor must release a new token.

Twisted-pair cable: A copper media used in LAN and telephony applications. Two pairs of copper wires are required for a bi-directional link (transmit and receive). Thus, cables usually have multiple pairs for additional capacity. The copper pairs may be shielded with a foil shield to reduce electromagnetic emissions.

Star wiring: The topology that results when wiring lobes traverse a building from a central wiring concentrator to various locations (offices, work stations, etc.).

Wiring concentrator: A device that allows multiple wiring lobes to terminate at a central point, thus creating a star configuration as the lobes radiate from the wiring concentrator to the various node locations.

Wiring lobe: The cable link between a node and a wiring concentrator, usually consisting of two pairs of copper media or a single pair of fiber media.

CROSS REFERENCES

See *Ethernet LANs; Local Area Networks; Optical Fiber LANs.*

REFERENCES

Bux, W. (1981). Local-area subnetworks: a performance comparison. *IEEE Transactions on Communications*, 29(10):1465–73.

Bux, W. (1989). Token-ring local-area networks and their performance. *Proceedings of the IEEE*, 77(2):238–56.

Bux, W., F. Closs, P. A. Janson, et al. 1981. A reliable token ring system for local-area communication. *Conference Record NTC*, Vol.1, IEEE, Piscataway, NJ (Nov. 1981), A.2.2.1–2.6.

Bux, W., F. Closs, K. Kümmerle, et al. 1983. A reliable token ring for local communications. *IEEE Journal on Select Areas of Communication*, SAC-1:756–65.

Carlo, J. T., R. D. Love, M. S. Siegel, and K. T. Wilson. 1998. *Understanding Token Ring Protocols and Standards*. Norwood, MA: Artech House, Inc.

Christensen, K. J., L. C. Haas, F. E. Noel, and N. C. Strole. 1995. Local area networks: Evolving from shared to switched access. *IBM Systems Journal*, 34(3):347–74.

Dykeman, D., and W. Bux. 1988. Analysis and tuning of the FDDI media access control protocol. *IEEE Journal on Selected Areas in Communications*, 6(6): 997–1010.

Farber, D. J., J. Feldman, F. R. Heinrich, et al. 1973. The distributed computing system. Proceedings of the Seventh Annual *IEEE Computer Society International Conference*, San Francisco, pp. 31–4.

Farmer, W. D., and E. E. Newhall. 1963. An experimental distributed switching system to handle bursty computer traffic. Proceedings of the ACM Symposium on Problems in the Optimization of Data Communications (Pine Mountain, GA), pp. 31–4.

Hafner, E. R., Z. Nenadal, and M. Tschanz. 1974. A digital loop communications system. *IEEE Transactions on Communications*, COM-22:877–81.

Hopper, A. 1977. *Data ring at computer laboratory, University of Cambridge, in computer science and technology: Local area networking*. NBS Special Pub 500-31. Washington, DC: National Bureau Standard, pp. 11–6.

ISO 9314-1:1989. Information Processing Systems—Fibre Distributed Data Interface (FDDI)—Part 1: Token Ring Physical Layer Protocol (PHY), www.iso.org.

ISO 9314-2:1989. Information Processing Systems—Fibre Distributed Data Interface (FDDI)—Part 2: Token Ring Media Access Control (MAC), www.iso.org.

ISO/IEC 9314-3:1990. Information Processing Systems—Fibre Distributed Data Interface (FDDI)—Part 3: Physical Layer Medium Dependent (PMD), www.iso.org.

ISO/IEC 8802-5:1998. Part 5. Token Ring Access Method and Physical Layer Specifications, www.iso.org.

Müller, H. R., H. Keller, and H. Meyr. 1983. Transmission design criteria for a synchronous token ring. *IEEE Journal on Select Areas of Communication*, SAC-1:721–33.

Pierce, J. R. 1972. Network for block switching of data. *Bell System Technical Journal*, 51:1133–45.

Reames, C. C., and M. T. Liu. 1975. A loop network for simultaneous transmission of variable length messages. Proceedings of the 2nd Annual Symposium on Computer Architecture, Houston, Texas, pp. 7–12, New York: ACM Press, http://doi.acm.org/10.1145/642089.642091

Ross, F. E. 1986. FDDI—A tutorial. *IEEE Communications Magazine*, 24(5):10–7.

Saltzer, J. H. and K. T. Pogran. 1979. A star-shaped ring network with high maintainability. Proceedings of the Local Area Communications Network Symposium, Boston, pp. 179–89, reprinted in *Computer Networks*, 4(5), October 1980, pp. 239–244, http://web.mit.edu/Saltzer/www/publications/starring/starring.html

Strole, N. C. 1983. A local communications network based on interconnected token access rings: A tutorial. *IBM Journal of Research and Development*, 27:481–96.

Optical Fiber LANs

Mo Adda, Amanda Peart, and Jau Ming Chew, *University of Portsmouth, UK*

INTRODUCTION

The 1960s saw the advent of digital communications and electromagnetic waves as the primary means for information transmission. There are currently constant demands for increased carrier frequency and larger bandwidth in order to accommodate the increasing volume of processed information (Kolimbiris, 2000). Conventional metallic or coaxial cable often suffer from attenuation as a result of spatial dispersion and heat, noise/interference, and bandwidth constraints, as the energy of higher frequency signals are lost, usually as heat, in traversing the transmission medium where higher frequencies are attenuated as the distance of cable increases (Schneider, 1999). These limitations have sparked the need for new ways to increase the carrier frequencies and the information-carrying bandwidth. As a consequence, a great interest in fiber optics was triggered.

History

The use of light has been an integral part in the development of human communication methods, from early communication signals using light to current optical fiber systems that enable us to cover greater distances. Early systems generally had the constraints of sunlight availability, low information capacity, or distance as in the communication system utilized by sailors who used lamplight to communicate with other ships or the shore in darkness.

Communication systems utilizing light can be traced back to 1880, when Alexander Graham Bell invented the Photophone (Forrest, 1980). The Photophone (see Figure 1) provided the means for Bell to transmit the first wireless telephone message. This was achieved by transmitting sound on a beam of light; the communication process was similar to that of the telephone except that this relied on light instead of electricity as the medium of transmission. The sender utilized sunlight as the light source reflected onto a voice-modulated mirror to carry speech. At the receiver side, the modulated sunlight fell on a photoconducting selenium cell that converted the message into electrical current, and a telephone receiver produced the sound.

As with many early prototype inventions it was not without its faults, hence the significance of the Photophone was never realized until fiber-optic cables had been developed.

Today's optical fibers are flexible silica glass fibers although not to the extent of creating right angles without breaking. The flexibility is accomplished by carefully encasing the glass in plastic jackets for support while bending. Light is sent along the fiber and a light-sensitive diode detects the light pulses at the receiver. Optical fiber communication has several advantages (Comer, 2001). Optical fibers can carry more information (channels) over longer distances with fewer repeaters. They are much lighter than copper, therefore, they occupy less volume in underground cabling ducts. They are immune against electrical interferences, and difficult to tap into without

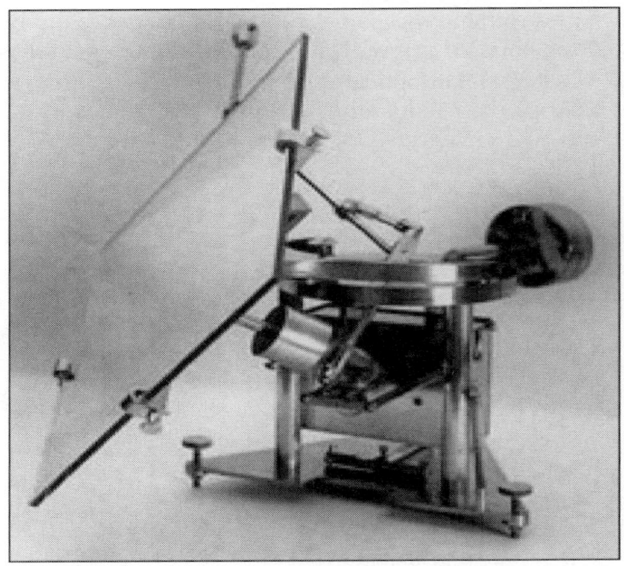

Figure 1: Alexander Graham Bell's Photophone

causing detection. For the same bandwidth, copper-wired systems consume more power, even more for wire pairs, to carry the signal than the optical fibers counter part. Therefore they keep the running cost of the system low. Despite all that, optical fibers have some disadvantages. Optical fibers are more expensive per meter than copper wires, although the sand is cheaper and abundant. However, the same fiber can carry far more information than the copper and fewer repeaters would be required for longer distance communications, keeping the overall cost at a minimum. Other drawbacks involve the difficulties in joining fibers together and finding breaks. This requires special equipment and training.

Evolution

Originally, the light sources were narrow bands of optic radiations in the form of a laser, which provided high-capacity optical communication. The lasers were not guided like today's fiber-optic cables and suffered similar problems encountered by Bell's Photophone atmospheric interference. A clear line of sight was required between transmitter and receiver for successful transmission. However, the lasers produce an invisible beam that if shone into the human eye could cause damage.

This new development inspired developers to continue to research the technological constraints. The major limitation to overcome was the need to guide the light while providing the ability to actually bend it away from the straight line. Another drawback of this early optical technology was the opaqueness of the glass, which hindered research from possible longer distance communication (Palias, 2005).

The first low-loss fibers were introduced in 1970 (Palias, 2005); this accomplishment triggered the rapid development of fiber-optic communication, leading to the rapid conversion of communication systems that previously relied on copper-wired technology to the faster and more efficient fiber-optic systems.

Today's technology is breaking communication barriers that were originally believed unfeasible. Initially the optical LANs were only expected to connect buildings to create a larger LAN. The first optical Ethernet standard specified a single 2 km optical repeater, but their spans were limited by the maximum delay that could be allowed on an Ethernet LAN while still detecting collision. The switched Ethernet LANs were further expanded by bridging the gap between two or more individual buildings. As optical links terminated at the switch ports, network performance was enhanced providing better network traffic control. To necessitate this process, the spanning-tree protocol (802.1D) was developed, which implemented path protection. Optical fiber technology could now enhance full-duplex transmission, which instantly doubled the bandwidth available. However, optical fiber LANs were only constrained by the distance that the lasers (light-emitting diodes) could reach.

In the next sections, we will examine different LANs expansions and connections based on optical communication. The following section gives an overview on the nature and properties of light when used in fiber-optic cables.

THE NATURE OF LIGHT

Light is often interpreted in different ways when dealing with different experiments. Sometimes it behaves like a wave and other times it behaves as a particle. In the context of this chapter we will look at light as being an electromagnetic wave with very high frequency and very short wavelength. The range of electromagnetic frequency is shown in Figure 2 (Nave, 2006).

The light frequency spectrum can be divided into three general bands:

infrared: wavelength is too long and is invisible to the human eye,

visible: wavelength is visible to the human eye,

ultraviolet: wavelength is too short and is invisible to the human eye.

For fiber-optic communications, the carrier frequency range from about 200THz to 370THz, which falls within the infrared spectrum. It is more common to measure higher frequency spectrums such as light in terms of wavelengths. A wavelength is the distance between repeating units of a wave pattern. The length of the wave depends on the frequency as well as the velocity of light, $\lambda = c/f$, where λ is the wavelength (meters), c is the speed of light and f is the frequency (Hz).

Light Characteristics

The light travels in the free space with the speed of 3 × 108 m/s. However its velocity is reduced when it crosses substances with higher densities (refraction index) than

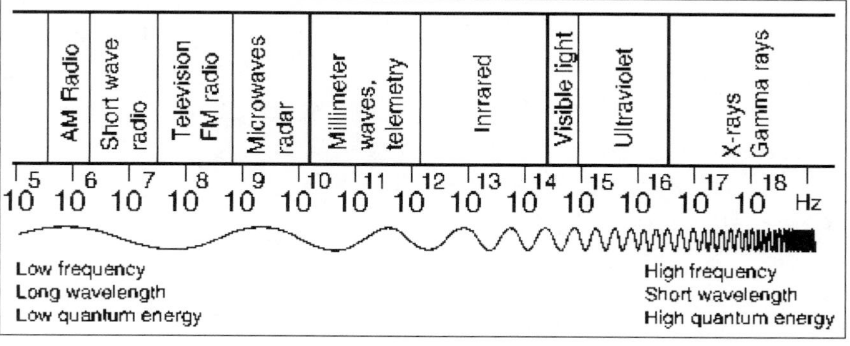

Figure 2: Electromagnetic spectrum (Nave, 2006)

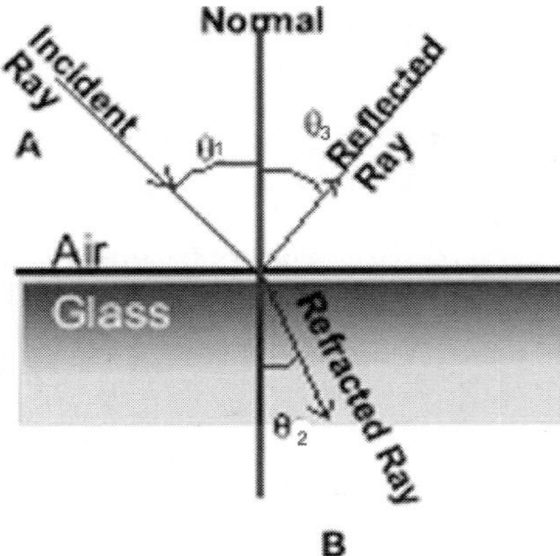

Figure 3: Reflection and refraction

the free space, causing the light rays to be distorted (Tomasi, 2001). The speed of light in a given medium can be evaluated as $c_m = c/n$, where n is the refraction index of the medium and c is the speed of light in the free space.

Reflection: The law of reflection specifies that when a light ray is impinging upon a reflective surface at the angle of incident θ1, it will be reflected from that surface with the same angle, θ1 = θ3, as shown in Figure 3.

Refraction: When a light ray passes from a material of a given density to another material with higher density, it bends toward the norm. Conversely, if it travels to a material with lower density it bends away from the norm (Tanenbaum, 2004, 94). Snell's law computes the angle of refraction for a given incident angle. The critical incident angle is defined as the angle that causes a 90-degree refracted ray from the norm, $\theta 1 = \sin^{-1}(n2/n1)$. This will only occur when the incident ray travels from a higher refraction index to a lower refraction index media, $n2 < n1$. Optical fibers operate on the principle of the total internal reflection of light. The light travels along the walls of the fiber, hits the wall at an angle larger than the critical angle and is reflected off the wall throughout the transmission.

Fiber-Optic Cable

A fiber-optic cable, as illustrated in Figure 4 (Tanenbaum, 2004), consists of four parts:

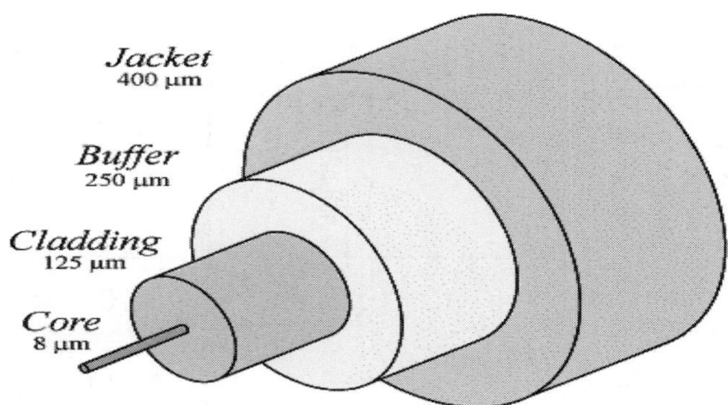

Figure 4: The structure of a fiber-optic cable

core: thin glass center of the fiber in which light travels in a zigzag mode using the cladding as the reflecting medium, with a total internal refraction,

cladding: outer optical material surrounding the core that reflects the light back into the core,

buffer: coating: a protective layer, which prevents the fiber from damage and moisture,

jacket: a protective layer made of PVC or Teflon to protect one or a bundle of fibers against moisture, abrasion, crushing and so on.

Classification of Optical Fibers

Optical fibers are classified into two categories: single-mode fibers and multimode fibers. The modes refer to the propagation characteristics of an electromagnetic wave as it travels through a particular type of fiber. In a single mode, rays of light travel in one direction along the center of the fiber. In multimode, rays of light travel in many directions through a number of paths. The single mode fiber is usually used in long-distance transmission such as telephony and multichannel broadcast systems, whereas the multimode fiber is best for short-distance transmission such as LAN systems and video surveillance (Fiber Optics, 2005).

Single-mode fiber: The single-mode fibers (see Figure 5) have a smaller diameter (6–8mm) and lower density than that of multimode fibers. As a result, the critical angle of the light beam is closer to 90 degrees making the propagation of different light beams almost horizontal, thus lowering the signal distortion by minimizing its dispersion (Forouzan, 2007). Usually, laser diodes are employed as the source of light to cover distances reaching up to 50 km.

Multimode fiber: The multimode fibers have larger diameters (50–1,000 μm), which allow multiple beams from a light source to travel through the core in different paths, resulting in different arrival times at the end of the fibers. Multimode fiber is further divided into two categories: step-index fiber and graded-index fiber.

Step-index fiber: In step-index fiber, the refraction indexes of the core and cladding are uniformly distributed over the whole substance. The core's index is higher than that of the cladding hence causing a total internal reflection when the light enters the core at an angle greater than the critical angle.

In Figure 6, three rays of light waves travel in different direction down the core. The first travels straight down the center of the core, the second travels in a steep angle, which is reflected back and forth, and the third one is refracted into the cladding. The second ray travels a longer distance than the first one, thus both arrive at the destination at different times. This phenomenon is known as the

Figure 5: Single-mode fiber

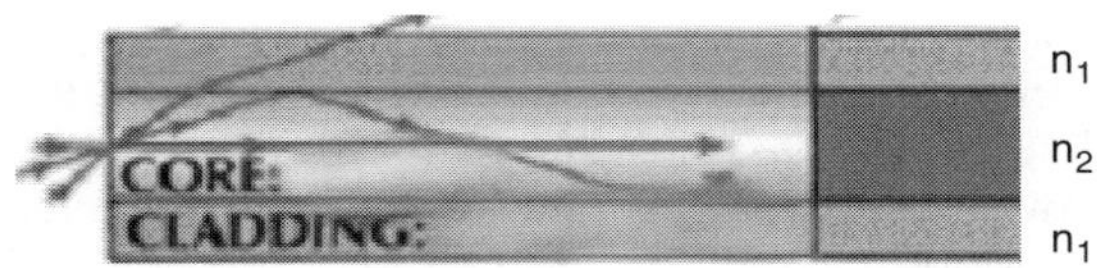

Figure 6: Total internal reflection in multimode step-index fiber

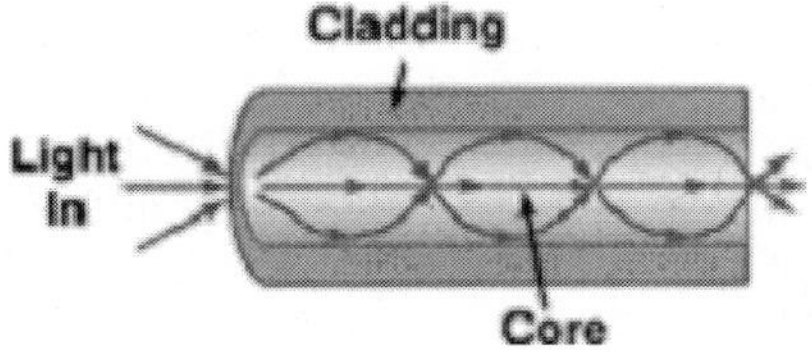

Figure 7: Multimode graded-index fiber

modal dispersion, which causes a signal distortion at the receiving end and therefore, limits the transmission rate.

Graded-index fiber: Graded-index fiber is manufactured in such a way that the refraction index of the core gradually decreases from the center of the core toward the cladding. This design speeds up the rays traveling away from the center as they travel through reduced refraction indexes. It therefore permits most rays to arrive at the receiver at the same time. Figure 7 depicts the light rays following a serpentine path. It gradually bends back toward the center by the continuously declining refraction index, hence reducing the pulse spread. In reality, the optical source of light emits several different wavelengths that travel at different speeds. The graded index at the core, similar to the single mode, causes a different pulse spreading called chromatic dispersion. Lasers are monochromatic sources of light which, when utilized, reduce the effect of chromatic dispersion.

Losses in Fiber-Optic Cables

There are several factors that complicate the transmission in optical fibers. These can be classified as linear and nonlinear effects. The linear effects increase with the length of the fiber. It includes the attenuation, the dispersion and the polarization.

Attenuation: Attenuation is result of the progressive amplitude reduction, loss in power, of the light ray traveling through the fiber. Attenuation is caused by absorption and scattering of light by the impurities. Absorption is also caused by the presence of Hydroxyl molecule (OH-) found in the glass during the manufacturing process. Figure 8 shows the lowest attenuation in the silica measured in various wavelengths (Refi, 1999). There are three regions in the diagram, which are highlighted in grey; these regions are referred as the principle "window." There are also several peaks that can be seen in the wavelength near 950 nm, 1200 nm, and 1380 nm where these peaks indicates the highest number of OH- impurities, possibly caused by excess water remnants during the manufacturing process or humidity of the surrounding environment, which causes attenuation to occur.

The first window represents the 850 nm wavelength. This window was first utilized in step index multimode fibers. However, as a result of the problems of high optical loss of 3 dB/km, the transmission distance was shortened to about a kilometer as signals beyond that distance are distorted and unreadable. As such, the graded-index fiber is introduced where it utilizes the second window with a wavelength of 1300 nm and offers lower optical loss of around 0.5 dB/km. The performance of fiber is improved as waves on the longer mode travel faster than that of a shorter mode. Thus they arrive at the receiver at around the same time, which greatly reduces the effect of modal dispersion (Greenfield, 2002). The third window was later discovered by Nippon Telegraph and Telephone (NTT) in late 1977, which utilizes wavelengths of 1550 nm and is used in single mode fibers that supports higher bandwidth as well as lower optical loss of about 0.2 dB/km. As a result, fiber of this type is usually used for long haul transmission, whereas multimode fiber is used for short-range transmission, usually within or between buildings.

Absorption happens when lights are absorbed by impurities found in the glass fiber and are converted into heat or vibration. Compared to scattering, absorption accounts for a very low percentage of the overall attenuation problem, 3% to 5%, and can be improved by reducing the number of impurities in the fiber. In the 1380 nm region the OH- peak was successfully eliminated resulting

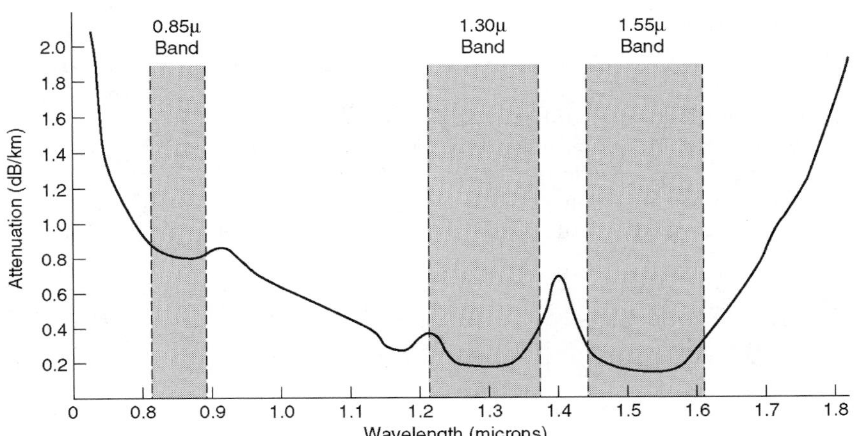

Figure 8: Attenuation (dB/km) in a silica-based optical fiber (Tanenbaum, 2004, 95)

in a zero-water-peak-fiber (ZWPF). On the other hand, wavelength over 1700 nm cannot be implemented in optical fiber communication as it suffers from high losses from infrared absorption (Alwayn, 2004).

Unlike absorption, Rayleigh scattering is a problem where light is diverted from its original angle while traveling along the fiber core as it interacts with the silica molecules in the fiber. In the event where the light is scattered, it will be diverted in a backward direction or out of the fiber core. Such an event contributes to 96% of the attenuation problem. Only when the light is diverted in an angle that supports forward traveling can attenuation be avoided. Short wavelengths experience higher scattering than long wavelengths; this can be seen in Figure 8. Notice that wavelengths shorter than 800 nm are having higher attenuation. This is because wavelengths below 800 nm suffer high scattering and therefore cannot be used in optical fiber communication.

Dispersion: Dispersion is because of the arrival of multiple wavelengths to the receiver at different times causing a spreading in the pulse and hence reducing the transmission rate. In single-mode fiber, a pulse containing several wavelengths broadens itself at the receiver producing an effect called inter-symbol interference. This phenomenon is referred as chromatic dispersion. The refraction index difference in the fiber also causes different traveling speeds among the wavelengths; this is referred to as material dispersion. The core has a higher refraction index than the cladding to ensure that light is to be reflected within the core. However, some of the lights might be propagated in the cladding and this will result in the broadening of the pulse as light in the cladding travels slower than that in the core as a result of lower refraction index. This phenomenon is known as waveguide dispersion. Modal dispersion is caused by delay differences among wavelengths traveling in different paths in a multimode fiber.

Polarization mode dispersion: A fiber core is generally seen as a cylindrical waveguide with a constant diameter. However, in actual fact a fiber core can have a different refraction index, geometric irregularity, temperature difference and stress placed upon the fiber. All these factors can cause two orthogonal polarization (vertical and horizontal) modes travelling at different speeds through the fiber, thus causing a difference in propagation time as one is travelling faster than the other. This phenomenon is referred to as differential group delay (DGD), which is measured in picoseconds.

In short, all these can be referred to as polarization mode dispersion (PMD), which according to Vivek Alwayn, is the result of "asymmetric distortions to the fiber from a perfect cylindrical geometry" (Alwayn, 2004). Polarization mode dispersion usually affects high-speed optical networks with a bit rate higher than 5 Gbps, which is used in long haul transmission (Lefebvre, 2001). Finally, nonlinear effects are problems caused by the optical signal power. For instance, scattering and four-wave mixing are such examples.

Fiber-Optic Communication System

A general fiber-optic system (see Figure 9), similar to other communication infrastructures, has several components. The information source produces various types of information such as voice, data, and video. The encoder encodes the information into different formats indicated by the underlying technology and then passes them to the transmitter. The transmitter serves as a light source, which launches the light into the fiber optic cable as well as a modulator that performs either analogue or digital modulation, for modulating light to represent the binary data that it receives from the source. The light source is either a light emitting diode (LED) or a laser diode (LD). Both LD and LED share the same characteristics. They emit light precisely within a small area, they have a long lifespan and they can be modulated at high speed. However, they differ in many instances. LD has a smaller spectral width compared to LED, hence it is able to couple more source power into the fiber and subsequently reduce attenuation. As such, LED can only be used in multimode fiber, whereas LD can be implemented in both multimode and single mode fibers. LD is more expensive than LED (Schneider, 2004).

A channel coupler feeds power into the information channel, before the light is transmitted into the fiber-optic cable, and then couples the emitted light. The information channel is made up of either glass or plastic fiber optics, which guide the light waves from the transmitter to the relay nodes and from the relay nodes to the receiver. The relay nodes may consist of optical amplifiers, repeaters, or switches (transparent or opaque) (Greenfield, 2002) that route and regenerate the signals in long distance transmission, if required. The receiver is either a PIN (p-type-intrinsic-n-type) diode or an avalanche photodiode (APD) where both sense light and convert it into an electrical current. However, the optical signal from the fiber optic cable and the resulting electrical current will have suffered losses. Consequently, the photodiode circuitry must be followed by one or more amplification stages. There may even be filters and equalizers to shape and improve the information-bearing electrical signal. The decoding part turns the modulated signal into binary form and delivers it to the information receiver.

OPTICAL LANs

The emergence of new high bandwidth-intensive multimedia applications make effective bandwidth allocation

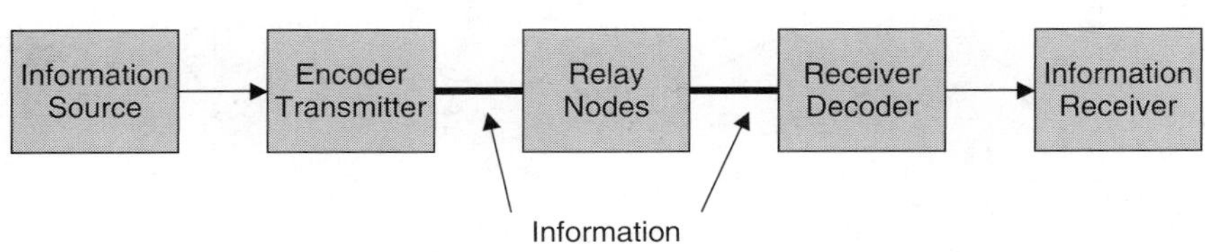

Figure 9: Components of a fiber-optic communication system

in LANs an increasingly important issue. Optical fiber technology provides the bandwidth necessary to support such applications. Optical local area networks (optical LANs) transmit data to stations within a limited region that are in the same geographical space, for example in the same building. Shorter transmission distances decrease the error rates, for example when transmitting to stations within the same room; the error rates are approximately 10 to 12 (Palais, 2005). The signal within the optical LAN is split to accommodate all stations within the network; each station will receive a fraction of the power of the signal.

Single-Hop LANs

In the bus topology (see Figure 10) the signal transmitted by each station is coupled into the bus, and splits to supply each receiver. A disadvantage to this topology is the power asymmetries. For instance, the signal reaching a terminal from its predecessor terminal is stronger than the signal reaching it from the first terminal (Chapman, 1989).

LANs adopting a star topology (see Figure 11) use the power more efficiently, and facilitate a shared medium optical LAN. The star coupler combines the signals from the transmitters and splits it into n signals sent to each receiver (Walrand and Varaiya, 2000). Perhaps the constraint of this topology is the size and the number of ports of the coupler. This is a serious issue with network scalability.

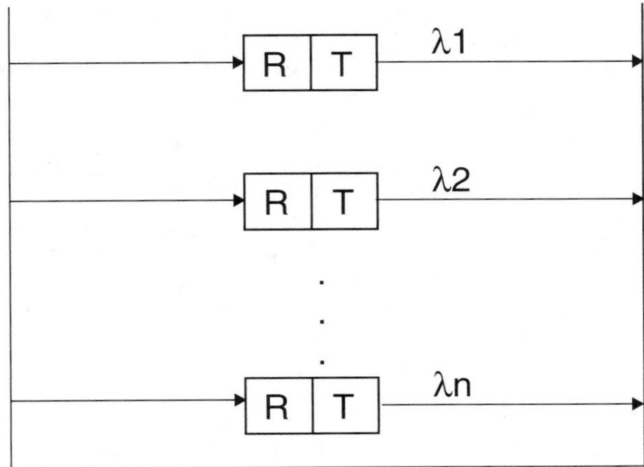

Figure 10: Optical LAN, bus topology

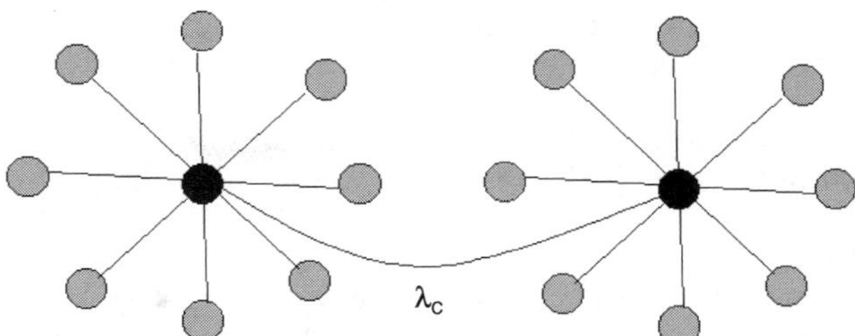

Figure 12: Interconnected star topologies

Fortunately, cascading couplers on specific wavelengths, as shown in Figure 12, permit the network to expand further and cover a larger number of distributed stations.

An interconnection between two stations lasting for the length of a data packet is set up on the control channel, by the transmitting station that informs the receiving user where to tune in to receive the data packet. If the optical star is operated with a single wavelength then it operates at the same level as an Ethernet. All the stations hear all the traffic and pick off only those addressed to them.

In both topologies the signal from all the transmitters will broadcast to all the receivers. Each station transmits on one wavelength but receives all the wavelengths, therefore requiring a tunable transmitter or receiver to select the desired wavelength. The introduction of a control channel where any stations wishing to communicate are required to request resources provides a more powerful, although complex, network configuration.

Multihop LANs

Single-hop LANs do not scale easily and require tunable receivers, whereas the multihop configuration utilizes a fixed receiver and transmitter wavelength and are scalable. The eight-station shuffle network configures each station to receive and transmit two wavelengths. The assumption is that the wavelength conversion is possible at each station and can be used simultaneously on two different hops.

OPTICAL ETHERNET

Brief Review on the Ethernet

The classical Ethernet, operating on a speed of 10 Mbps, works on a bus topology under the control of the CSMA/CD

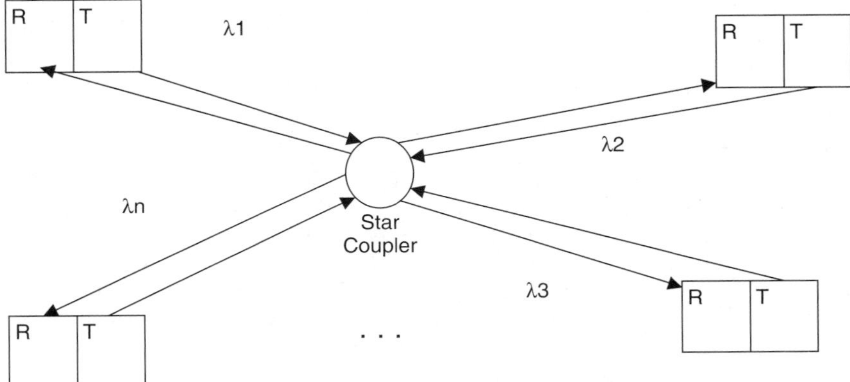

Figure 11: Optical LAN, star topology

protocol located in the MAC sub-layer. Stations are tapped to the coaxial cable with transceivers. At both ends of the bus are terminators that remove the signal preventing it from reflecting back and hence interfering with the transmitting stations. The bus spans a maximum distance of 200 m or 500 m depending on cable type. CheaperNet or 10BASE2 expands to 200 m, and ThickerNet or 10BASE5 expands to 500 m, at which point the signal degrades to a level where repeaters are required to boost the power into the signal.

Stations asynchronously compete for the line—cable—to transmit their frames. The contention mechanism is based on the carrier sense multiple access with collision detection (CSMA/CD). When a station receives a packet to transmit, the circuitry of the network interface card (NIC) senses the line. If the line is busy—a transmission is in progress with bit transitions occurring in the medium—the station waits until it becomes idle. When the line is idle, the station transmits the frame. There are several variants to this protocol regarding the behavior of the sending station after the line is detected idle. In the Ethernet, the station immediately transmits when the line is available after a predefined inter-frame gap. It may happen that two or more stations attempt a transmission at the same time. If this is the case, a collision occurs. The protocol has the capability to detect collisions and force the stations involved in the collision to back off for random times before attempting a retransmission.

Bus, Star, Mesh, and Hierarchical Topologies

Ethernet has adopted various interconnections, including the star topologies with the hub or the switch at the center connected to all the stations via a RJ-45 connector. To scale and expand the LAN further, multiple switches with possibly different speeds and levels of routing—layer 3 switching—are interconnected in mesh configurations. Such topologies have to be carefully planned, possibly adopting a virtual LAN (VLAN), to achieve the maximum bandwidth and manageability. Hubs or switches can be connected in tree configuration forming a deep hierarchy of switches or hubs with stations located at the leaves.

Although electrical cables link most Ethernet LANs, fibers offer other advantages. Fibers are electrically noiseless, less dense than wires, therefore easy to put in building conduit, are more highly secure, and support much higher speeds and distances than copper.

In the remaining subsections we trace briefly the evolution of the fiber Ethernet and its interconnection from half to full duplexes.

10BASE-F: The dominating technology based on 10BASE is the twisted-pair copper. However, several fiber standards—10BASE-FL (fiber link), 10BASE-FB (fiber backbone), 10BASE-FP (fiber passive), and FOIRL (fiber optic inter-repeater link)—have been developed to target different market needs. Perhaps the success of the twisted pair was because of the unused bandwidth of the fiber, as the signaling rate of 10 Mbps occupied a smaller fraction of it. Another reason would be the cost of the optical equipment.

Fiber connections require two separate lines, one for transmission and the other for reception. For link integrity, an active idle signal of 1 MHz (in FL) or 2.5 MHz (in FB), depending on the standard, is monitored. If the medium attachment unit fails to detect this signal, it declares the link as failed and prevents the station or the repeater from transmitting. Nowadays, many vendors optionally supply a link light on the medium attachments unit to give a visual indication of the link integrity status. Fibers for the 10BASE-F rely on multimode transmissions with core and cladding diameters of 62.5 μm and 125 μm respectively (Kadambi, Crawford, and Kalkunte, 1998). Although vendors have produced many methods to connect the fiber to the medium attachments unit, the Bayonet Fiber Optical connector, BFOC, and the ST are the most commonly used (Shah and Ramakrishnan, 1993).

In general 10BASE-F segments can span up to 2 km if used exclusively with 10BASE-FL and up to 1 km if used with the FOIRL. 10BASE-FB is mainly used to connect additional hubs or repeaters as it has the ability, in its design as oppose to FL, to signal remote faults between the two hubs. The maximum distance that this fiber extends to is about 2 km, although when used with other standards, it would span up to 1 km. Finally, 10BASE-FP implements a rather different topology. The stations are connected to a passive hub forming a star topology, similar to Figure 11. The passive hub is convenient in places where electrical powers are hazardous and impractical in some areas. The hub floods the light pulses on all its ports without converting them to electrical signals. Hence, if many light pulses occur simultaneously at the hub, the signals interfere, causing collisions. Figure 13 depicts a possible mixed topology with all the optical connections following the IEEE restriction on the fiber length. It must be noted that the collision domain rather than the attenuation constraints limits the length of the fiber.

The collision detection capability is a function of the bus length, D, and the Ethernet frame length, L, at the NIC transmission rate of R Mbps, and the speed of the wave in the medium (cm = c/n),

$$\frac{L}{R} \geq \frac{2Dn}{c} + \varepsilon \qquad (1)$$

in which c is the speed of light, n is the refraction index of the core, and ε in μsec is the latency associated with all repeaters or hubs and stations along the link. Lmin/R refers to the collision domain, which defines the minimum frame size to be transmitted to detect a collision. Two or more transmissions occurring within the collision window (left hand side of the inequality (1)) will indisputably result in a collision. The minimum frame size for a 2,500-m bus, or five ThickNet segments, with four repeaters at the transmission speed of 10 Mbps is about 512 bits, which on the worst-case scenario permits a station to detect a collision effectively (Stallings, 2002). This indication permits the fiber links to span a maximum distance of 2 km with the same safety margin indicated in inequality (1).

100BASE-F: To satisfy applications demanding higher bandwidth, Ethernet has been driven into two complementary directions. One is the switched Ethernet where a

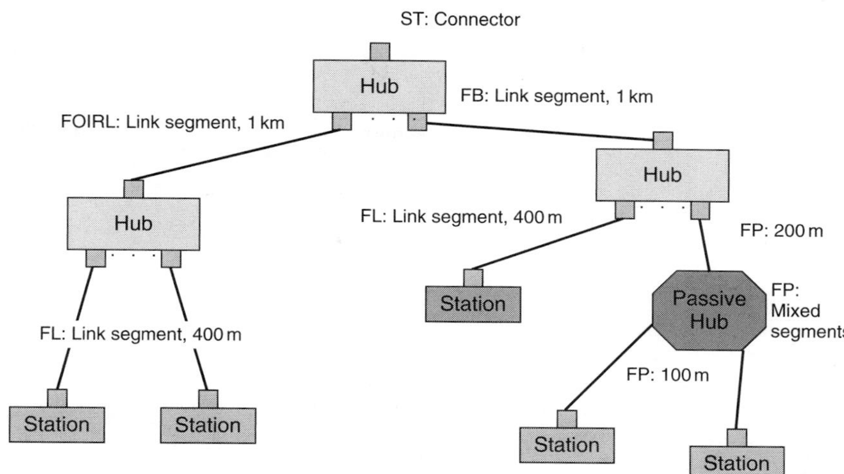

Figure 13: Mixed optical LAN with 10BASE-F connections

switch replaces the central hub, and therefore provides a full-duplex connection without a collision, and the other one is the faster Ethernet, where the clock or the speed of the NIC is increased by a factor of 10, yielding 100-Mbps transmission. In the former, restrictions on the length of the fiber are only imposed by the attenuation factors, and therefore larger topologies can be supported. In general, it is used in long-haul communications such as establishing connections between buildings. In the latter, the increase of speed to 100 Mbps requires a decrease in the fiber length by a factor of 10. Although the fiber connections based on switched Ethernet are desirable, there are design areas where mixtures of topologies have been configured. 100BASE-FX, the only standard in this class, has a much smaller geographical limit, a maximum length of 400 m. It is noted that with a mixed topology, using class I hubs, the maximum span of the fiber would be 130 m to 160 m (Kadambi, Crayford, and Kalkunte, 1998). 100BASE-FX uses two strands of graded-index multimode over a pair of fibers, 50/100 μm, or 62.5/125 μm.

The signaling speed in 10BASE is 20 MHz with Manchester encoding. However with 100BASE the same encoding technique would have required a clock of 200 MHz. Instead, 100BASE-FX, similar to 100BASE-TX, adopts the 4B/5B-encoding scheme, as shown in the simplified diagram in Figure 14. With this code four data nibbles are converted into 5 binary codes, chosen out of the 32 codes.

Two classes of hubs have been designed to permit interconnections with 100BASE media types.

Class I hub supports all 100BASE media types. This flexibility comes at the price of high latency that is induced when the hub converts from one code to another, and therefore reduces the length of the cable or the fiber. For instance, 100BASE-TX and 100BASE-FX use 4B/5B-coding scheme, 100BASE-T2 uses PAM 5X5 codes, and 100BASE-T4 uses 8B/6T codes. When 100BASE-FX is deployed with a class I hub within the mixed topology of 100BASE-T2 and 100BASE-T4, the maximum length of the fiber, limited by the collision domain, refer to inequality (1), would be 130 m. Whereas, when the class I hub connects only 100BASE-TX and/ or 100BASE-FX, the length of the fiber can be extended to 160 m.

Class II hubs are a two-hub topology with a 5-m separation between the hubs. It supports only 100BASE-TX and 100BASE-FX, therefore eliminating the code conversion process. This reduction gains extra spanning, and allows the fiber to extend up to 200 m, from the station to the hub. Figure 15 illustrates a mixed topology of 100BASE-TX and 100BASE-FX with class I hub and class II hub, and the switches operating on full and half duplex. Manufacturers usually design hubs, and switches with different delays; these have to be taken into consideration when designing mixed optical LANs.

1000BASE-F: Increasing the speed to 1000 Mbps will result in a decrease of 100 times in the length of the segment. Theoretically, the length of the segment in a half-duplex connection would be 20 m (Tanenbaum, 2004). This limitation is unacceptable for such a high transmission rate technology, especially when used with fiber-optics.

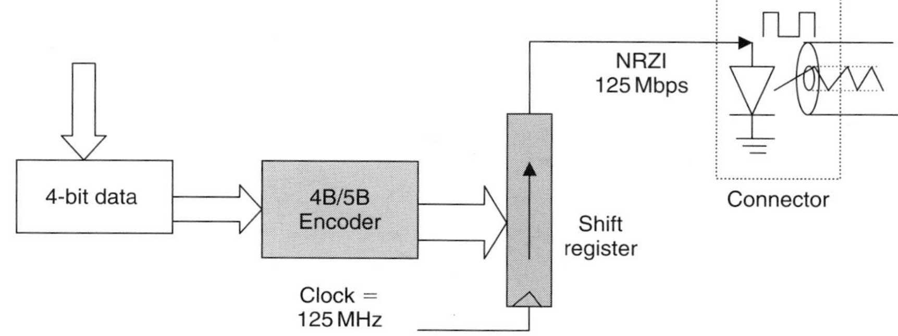

Figure 14: Encoding sequence for 100BASE-FX, which adopts the 4B/5B-encoding scheme

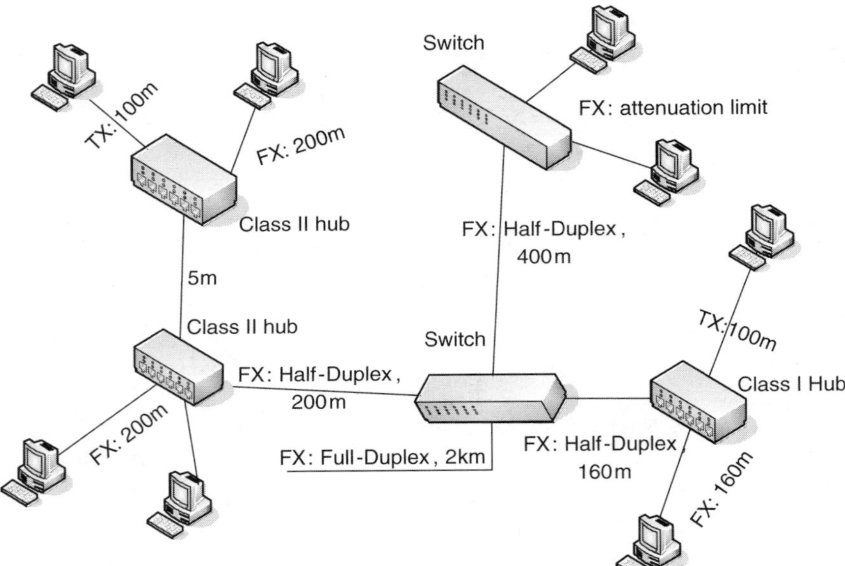

Figure 15: Mixed topology with 100BASE-FX length restrictions

Several design mechanisms have been deployed to overcome these limitations while maintaining the compatibility with predecessors, 10BASE and 100BASE standards. The efforts of the IEEE 802.3z task force went with the proposal of a carrier extension. This scheme involves changing the collision domain (time slot) from 512 bits to 512 bytes (4096) to maintain a segment of 8 times longer. The approach requires that frames of less than 512 bytes in size have to be padded by extra bytes, called extensions with special codes. Certainly, these extra overheads would reduce the efficiency of the Gig Ethernet to 12% (Haddock, 1996). Several approaches have been proposed to increase the efficiency to 76% (Molle, 1997) at least to match the 100BASE efficiency. Mainly, the frame bursting that involves sending several frames within a burst limit (65536bits) has been approved and adopted by the IEEE 802.3z task force (Haddock, 1996; Kalkunte, 1996).

The simplest approach would be to abolish the half duplex completely and connect stations to switches, thus removing the collision domain restrictions. This approach is becoming more popular as the prices of the switches are dropping. Furthermore, an adoption of fiber solutions with cheaper switches would be a more realistic and popular solution. With full-duplex connections, the worst-case normalized efficiency would be 76% for an interframe gap (IGP) of 96 bits and a minimum frame size of 512 bits. However, the major problem with full-duplex switched fast Ethernet is the congestion. Substantial losses of frames would lead to poor link efficiency. To overcome these challenges, the switching mechanism adopts one of the many control flow schemes to minimize frame loss, and hence avoid significant drops in the links efficiency.

One simple approach is for the switch to insert a carrier in the congested links forcing senders to wait until the congestion is over. More formally, IEEE 802.3x defines a PAUSE frame that indicates how long a sender will back off before attending a new transmission.

One of the key issues to the control flow is when to initiate and how long to wait for the control flow. With fiber links running at 1000 Mbps, significant buffering capacity would be required at the senders end, as several frames might be on transit before a PAUSE frame is received. The current technology designs switches with faster processing time to return the PAUSE frame immediately, and hence keep buffering capacity to a minimum.

Watermarks flow control is a technique that initiates the PAUSE frame when the number of frames received by the switch exceeds the low-watermark threshold, providing a safeguard to receive additional frames while the PAUSE frame is in transit. The credit-based control on the other hand, similar to ATM, assigns a number of credits for each sender. Upon congestion, the switch signals the senders with a smaller number credit to regulate their transmissions. The most interesting control flow is the rate-based flow. Upon receiving a control flow frame, the sending station adjusts its IGP to slow down the transmission. The new value of the IGP is part of the control flow frame (e.g., PAUSE frame), this approach smoothes the traffic through the switch, even at a higher rate.

At the physical layer, 1000BASE relies on fiber channel (FC) technology for connecting high-speed devices. The coding sub-layer of the physical layer, that implements Manchester encoding in 10BASE and 4B/5B encoding in 100BASE-TX, supports IBM 8B/10B code, which has an effective performance (Widmer and Franaszek, 1983). A very simple implementation of the code is to partition it into 5B/6B and 3B/4B subordinate coders. Furthermore, the physical medium dependent sub-layer relies entirely on FC0, fiber channel layer 0, dealing with connectors, and optical interfaces.

1000BASE supports two different media types: namely 1000BASE-SX (short wavelength laser) and 1000BASE-LX (long wavelength laser). 1000BASE-SX uses short wavelength laser in the region of 850 nm over a multimode fiber 50/62.5 μm. 1000Base-LX uses long wavelength laser 1300 nm over multimode fiber 50/62.5 μm and

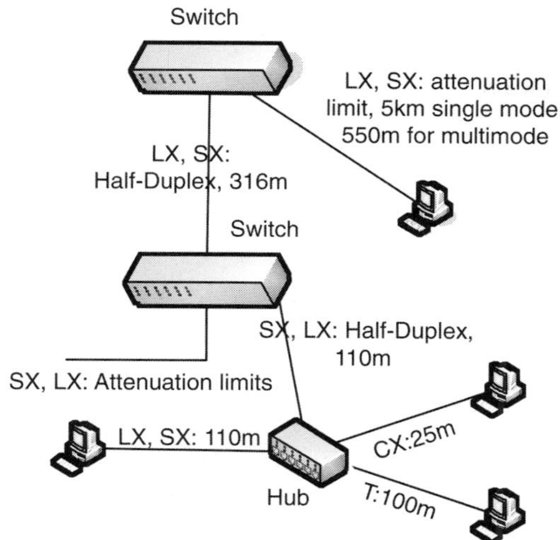

Figure 16: Mixture of 1000BASE cabling

single-mode fiber 2/10 μm. The multimode covers a distance from 220m to 550m, whereas the single mode spans over distances of 5km. Figure 16 depicts a possible network topology of 1000BASE-SX and 1000BASE-LX.

10GBASE-F: Although this technology may not be deployed now for LANs, except for parallel systems and high-speed servers, it is more attractive and appealing in the market of carrier networks. The speed of 10Gig Ethernet is about SONET, SDH, and OTN. It is worth mentioning that the success of Ethernet is its simplicity and low cost. These features would be carried over to the WAN, where the 10Gig Ethernet will play a major role. Ethernet equipment would be able to connect network premises to network carriers at no additional cost, induced by the use of SONET or SDH interfaces. It is expected that 10Gig Ethernet will interconnect LANs, MANs, and WANs.

The design of 10Gig Ethernet and possibly 100Gig Ethernet rely on full-duplex operation, with connections to switches (e.g., layer-3 switching) or routers. The optical fiber segments would only be limited by the attenuation factors. Currently, the technology permits 10Gig Ethernet single mode optical fibers to span a distance of up to 40 km.

Although 10Gig Ethernet was intended to be entirely supported by optical fibers, IEEE802.3 committee has proposed two standards for 10Gig Ethernet over cable. 10GBASE-CX4 operates over limited distances from 15 m to 30 m over 4-pairs of TWINAX cable each running at the data rate of 3.125 Gbps. With the 8B/10B encoding, this standard gives the required 10 Gbps. The goal of this standard is to support low cost inter-rack solutions.

10GBASE-T operates at full duplex with Category 6 (class E) and Category 7 (class F) for up to 100 m with four twisted-pair copper. Category 7 is adequately specified for this bandwidth; however, Category 6 would require performance characteristics beyond 250 MHz to 450 MHz. 10GBASE-T achieves the 10Gig speed by deploying 10-level PAM signaling with 3-bit per level, over four lanes of 833 Mbps, yielding an aggregate transmission rate of 10 Gbps. This technology offers cheaper installation over fibers. The market would target data centers and horizontal enterprise networks.

Although 10GBASE is similar in every way to its predecessors to maintain compatibility with the reconciliation sub-layer, it differs in the physical layer, as it is meant for different purposes. The encoding techniques utilized in the PCS, physical coding sub-layer, are the 8B/10B, similar to 1000BASE, and the 64B/66B. The IEEE 802.3 task force has used the suffix "X" to refer to the 8B/10B-encoding scheme. On the other hand, the physical layer implements different wavelengths and fiber modes. For instance, the suffix "S" refers to 850 nm wavelength with a serial transceiver on two multimode fibers. The suffix "L" refers to 1310-nm-long wavelength with a serial transceiver on two single-mode fibers. The suffix "L4" refers to 1310-nm-long wavelength with four wave division multiplexing, WDM—the interested readers may refer to other chapters of this handbook for more details about WDM—on a two multimode or two single-mode fibers. Finally, the suffix "E" refers to 1550-nm extra-long wavelength with a serial transceiver on two single-mode fibers. These standards can be combined to create several media types for the optical 10GBASE Ethernet.

10GBASE-LX4 or simply 10GBASE-X utilizes 8B/10B-encoding scheme at the PCS sub-layer, with four WDM and a long wavelength, 1310 nm, over distances of 300 m (multimode fibers) to 10 km (single-mode fibers). This would be a possible candidate for MANs, when the entire infrastructure is Ethernet-based to avoid any protocols or framing conversions. 10GBASE- SR, -LR, and -ER or simply 10GBASE-R uses 64B/66B encoding schemes. They deploy short wavelength, 850 nm, on multimode fibers, long wavelength, 1310 nm, on single-mode fiber, and extra-long wavelength, 1550 nm, on single-mode fibers over distances 65 m, 10 km, and 40 km respectively. This technology is intended for LANs and WANs where the infrastructure is all Ethernet-based. Finally, 10GBASE-SW, -LW, and -EW, or simply 10GBASE-W uses the same technology as 10GBASE-R with the exception of an additional sub-layer, called the WAN interface sub-layer (WIS). This sub-layer permits 10GBASE-W to connect to SONET, which dominates the WAN market today. Most vendors believe that 10GBASE-W and the future versions will dominate the carrier networks rending the entire public network a large optical Ethernet LAN. Figure 17 depicts a possible connection with the mixed interconnections of all the 10GBASE classes while maintaining the segments length restrictions. In full duplex, the length of the segment is only restricted by the attenuation that is proportional to the speed o f the transmission and the distance of the fiber. For instance, LX4 spans a distance of 300 m at the rate of 500 MHz per km.

OPTICAL RING

Fiber distributed data interface (FDDI) has been the LAN standard operating at the speed of 100 Mbps long before the 100BASE Ethernet was designed (Ross, 1986, 1989). It specifies a transmission over dual ring optical fiber primary and secondary rings, using token passing access protocol. Both multimode and single-mode fibers are

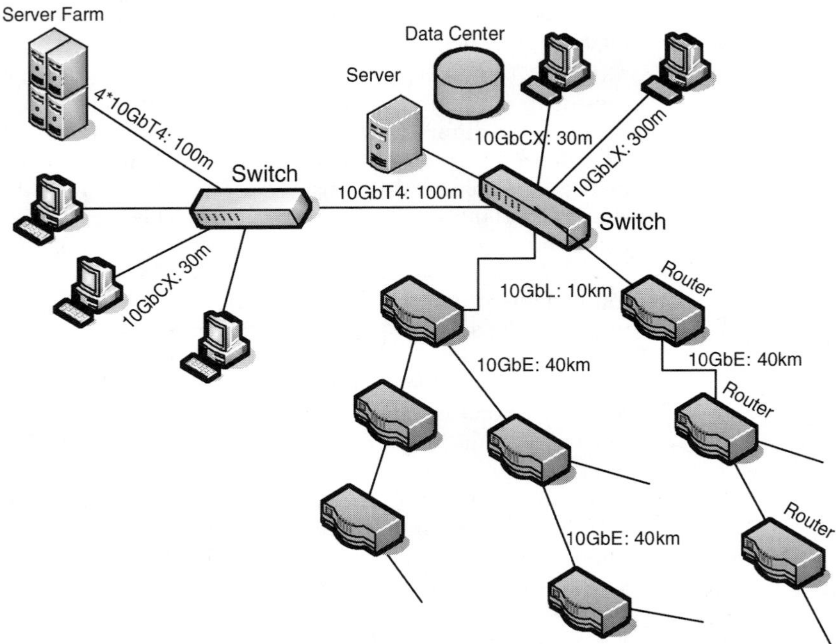

Figure 17: A network with mixed interconnections of all the 10GBASE classes

deployed to span longer distances. Similar to 100BASE Ethernet, FDDI relies on the 4B/5B encoding/decoding technique to provide transmissions with synchronization and clocking. Although FDDI, similar to copper distributed data interface (CDDI), can be utilized for LAN to attach workstations and servers, its speed made it a favorable candidate for backbone networks, where stations could be switches or bridges. Figure 18 shows FDDI wiring and connections to different stations using patch panels and concentrators. Single stations (SAS), are attached to the ring concentrator and mainly inject and remove traffic from the primary ring. Dual stations (DAS) are connected to the secondary and primary rings. The ring has some degree of fault tolerance. If the DAS or the optical fiber fails, the ring wraps itself by connecting the secondary to the primary rings, hence isolating the faulty cable or station. Further optical bypass (internal mirrors) can be used to reflect the light and hence bypass faulty stations, as shown in the DAS of Figure 18. With critical devices such as routers and servers, dual homing is used to provide additional redundancy and help maintain the ring operation by attaching critical devices to many concentrators.

FDDI standards for ring management: All FDDI standards reside on the physical and data link layer of the OSI model. Physical medium dependent (PMD) and physical layer protocol (PHY) fit into the physical layer, media access control (MAC) and logical link control (LLC) resides on the data link layer, whereas station management fits into both layers.

Station management: FDDI station management is the layer that maintains the overall ring operation including error reporting and fault isolation. Station management is also responsible for initialization, insertion, and deletion of nodes in the ring. Information of each node is stored in the management information base (MIB). A MIB includes the things like the unique station identifier, the station management version, the station configuration information, the available paths, and the number of MACs in the staion, the current port configuration, and the status report frames that are queued. Every node in the ring communicates with others by exchanging information using the station management frames. Listed below are different types of frames with their unique functionality:

Connection management (CMT) specifies the physical connection status between two neighboring stations on whether they are OFF, ON, ACTIVE, or CONNECT.

Configuration management (CFM) manages information of MAC connection and defines PHY and MAC parts in a station.

SMT entity coordination management (ECM) manages the operation of CFM and PCM by controlling the trace and optical bypass relays.

Ring management (RMT) informs the LLC on whether the MAC layer is ready to detect duplicate addresses and stuck beacons in the link.

Neighbor information frames (NIF) provides information of a node to its neighboring node from the management information base (MIB) every 2 to 30 seconds while detecting duplicated MAC address in a ring.

Status information frames (SIF) provides configuration and operation information to the neighboring nodes from the MIB.

Parameter management frames (PMF) provides remote access capabilities to a station attribute. The PMF-get is used to read the value of any parameters of a remote station while PMF-write writes value into a remote station.

Status report frames (SRF) are sent via a SRF multicast address whenever there is a change in the ring configuration.

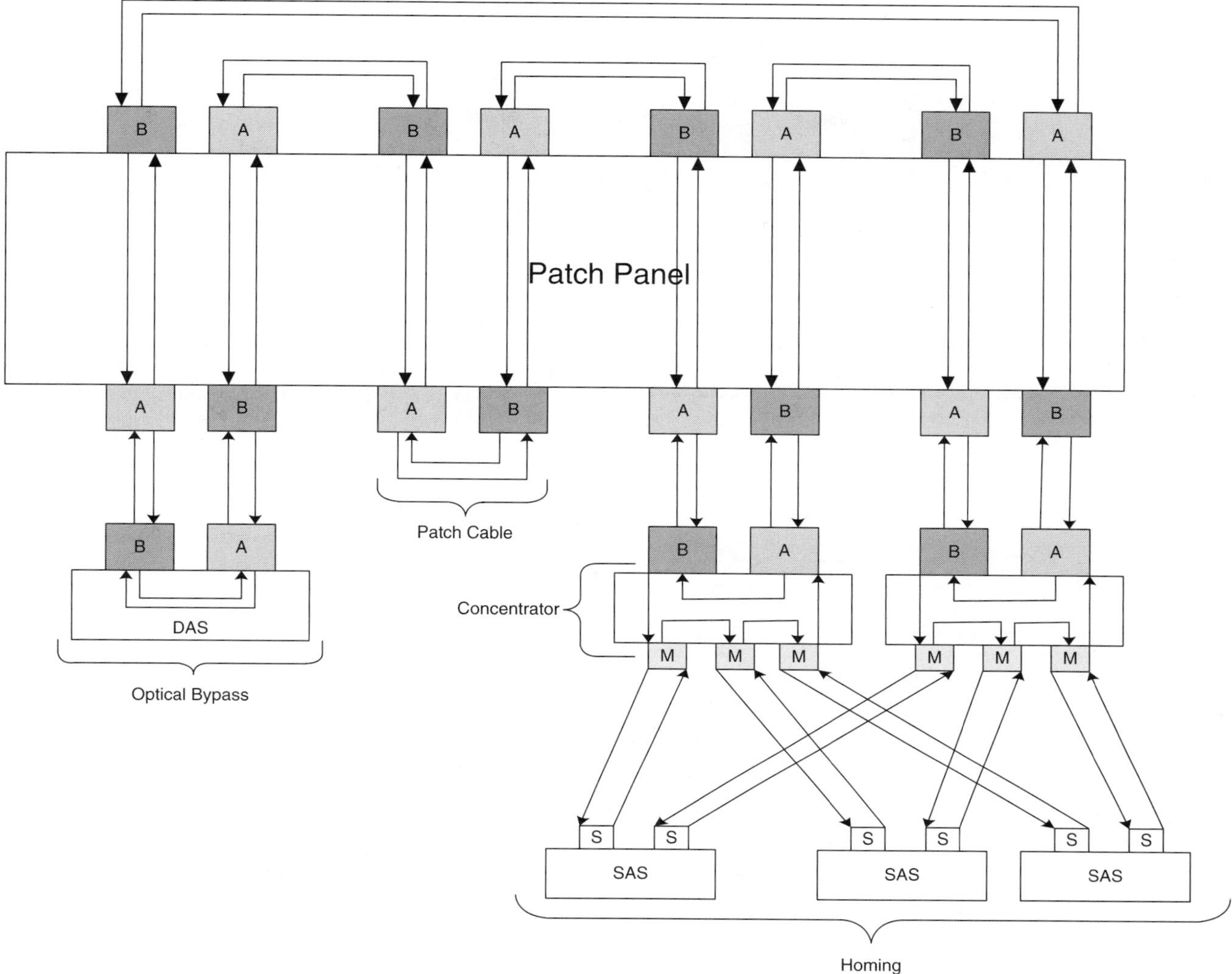

Figure 18: FDDI wiring connections, the connectors A, B, M, and S are different types to provide proper connections to the ring

To implement the access to the ring, FDDI deploys the same principle as the token ring. The management station plays an important role in maintaining a fair and efficient access to the ring. Both synchronous and asynchronous traffics can be supported at the same time (Joshi 1986). In particular, FDDI-II has optimal features in the MAC layer to provide QoS for delay-sensitive applications.

In general, FDDI uses timed token rotation protocol, which presets a defined value called target token rotation time (TTRT). The manager station adjusts this counter and broadcasts it to all stations sharing the ring. The counter (TTRT) plays an important role in the performance of the ring. Upon receipt of the token, a station transmits queued frames up to the time hold timer (THT), and then passes the token to the next station in turn. In this case, each station based on the actual traffic dynamically calculates the value of THT, which is utilized to maintain a fair access to the ring by all the stations, and hence defines the performance of the ring.

As shown in Figure 19, the maximum throughput of the ring increases with the target token rotation protocol. However, the maximum access delay also increases, refer to Figure 20. A minimum value for the TTRT (4ms) can offer a good ring performance. In general, the maximum standard value for the TTRT can go as high as 165ms, producing a very high access delay.

THE INTERFACE BETWEEN FIBER AND COAXIAL

The growing impetus of broadband prompted the upgrade of the cable system to high-bandwidth fiber. This meant that the central core is fiber with coaxial cable connecting residential properties to the system; this model is termed the hybrid fiber coax (HCF). The electro and optical elements of the system are interfaced via an electro-optical converter called "fiber nodes." These are "dumb" devices in that they do not interpret the signals and only provide an interface between the two media. The bandwidth of the fiber would then feed multiple coaxial cables via the

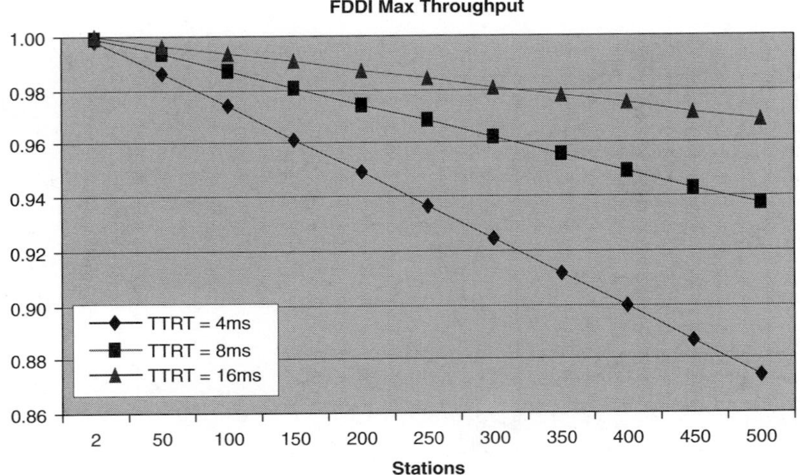

Figure 19: The maximum throughput attainable by the FDDI ring for a fiber of 500 m as a function of the number of attached stations for various TTRT

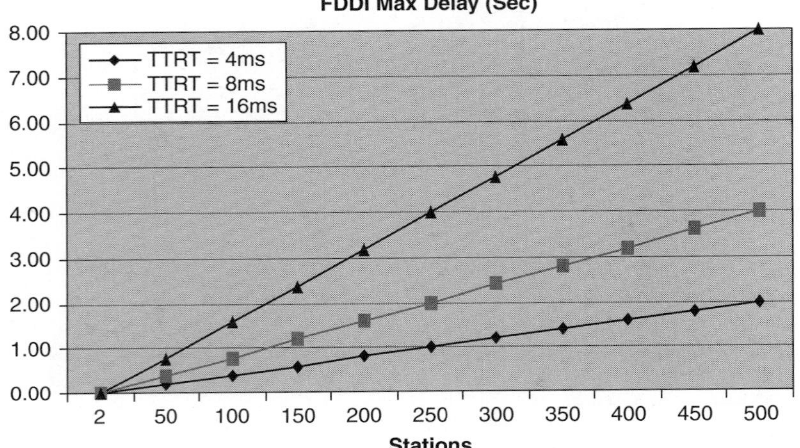

Figure 20: The maximum access delay attainable by the FDDI ring for a fiber of 500 m as a function of the number of attached stations for various TTRT

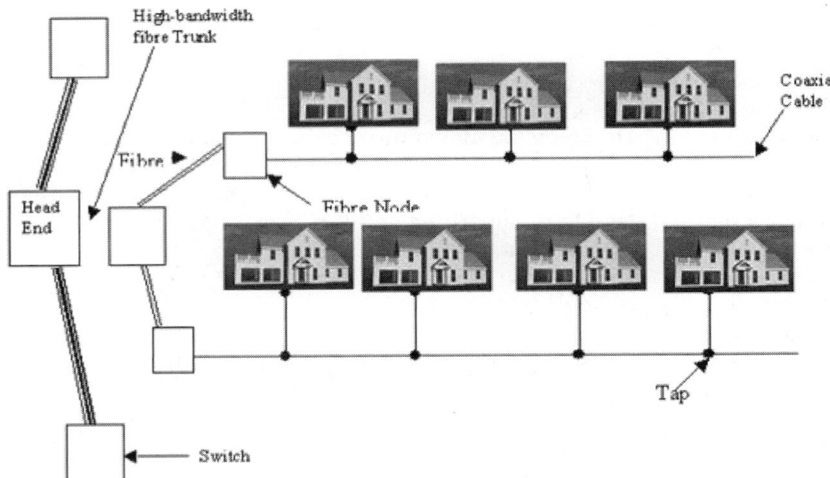

Figure 21: Broadband cable network for television using HCF

fiber nodes. By using frequency division multiplexing, an HFC network may carry a variety of services, including analog TV, digital TV (standard definition and HDTV), video on demand, telephony, and high-speed data. The fiber-optic cables connect the optical node to a distant headend (Figure 21).

OPTICAL INTERNET, MPLS, AND GMPLS

MPLS

The realization of an optical Internet depends on the synthesis and standardization of protocols that work in a multivendor environment. "The number of carriers

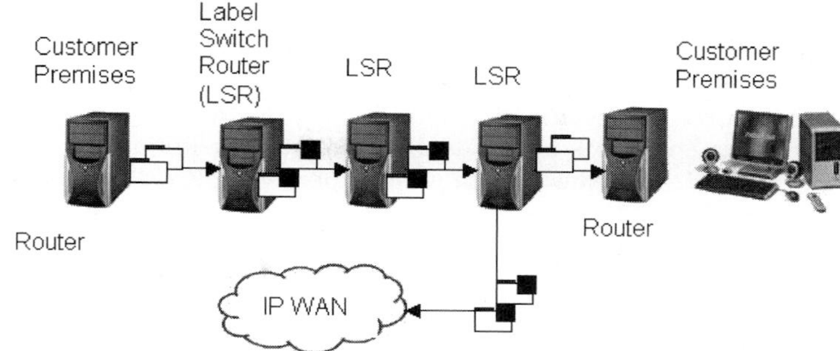

Figure 22: Multiprotocol label switching (MPLS)

deploying new MPLS-based metro Ethernet equipment doubled between 2005 and 2006, from 42 percent to 84 percent" (Campbell, 2006).

Research in the IP community integrated the IP protocol into connection-oriented technology, with the aim to improve QoS providing a virtual circuit to support end-to-end packet transfer. Using a virtual path promotes efficient allocation of network resources via statistical multiplexing, enabling QoS assurances to be made as opposed to the " best effort" service provided by IP.

Multiprotocol label switching (MPLS) (Figure 22) is a suite of standard routing and signaling protocols that supports a variable length stack of four-octet labels at the beginning of an IP packet. It is the first of these labels that help the label switching router (LSR), utilizing the label-forwarding table, to determine the packet output port or the label-switch path (LSP). Connections established using MPLS build on current protocols, such as OSPF and intermediate system to intermediate system (IS-IS), to exchange link-state topology (Basak and Siket, 2000). MPLS can provide rapid restoration of packets in an IP network at the point of failure by rerouting to another LSP.

The label switching and packet forwarding processes are completely decoupled from how the LSPs are created and destroyed. The MPLS paradigm is much simpler than traditional IP routing allowing much larger numbers of packets per second to be processed (Ramaswami and Sivarajan, 2002). The major benefit of decoupling these functions in any optimization of packet forwarding will be autonomous of label-switch, which is not the case in IP routers.

There are synergies between MPLS, LSR, and optical cross-connects (OXCs) and the MPLS, LSP, and optical channel trail. Similar to MPLS, OXCs need routing protocols, such as OSPF and IS-IS, to establish optical resource availability for path computation. Also, similar signaling protocols such as RSVP and LDP are used to configure OXCs to establish optical channel trails. The Internet Engineering Task Force (IETF) has proposed MPLS as the model to adapt for optical devices. OXCs are emerging as the fundamental building block of a seamless optical transport network.

GMPLS

As explained previously, MPLS is used for label switched path (LSP) to provide traffic engineering and levels of quality of service (QoS). GMPLS extends the functions of the MPLS to connect devices that may switch on packets (IP), cells (ATM), time (TDM/SONET), wavelength (DWDM), and physical space (OXC). It also adds capabilities for provisioning and managing networks at a low cost. The most apparent features of the GMPLS for optical networks are connections and flexibility at the physical layer, the way labels are distributed and acquired, the way capacity is allocated to overcome congestions and bottlenecks, and the way networks failures are handled and reported.

GMPLS operates in two modes: overlay and peer models. In the overlay model, the physical light path is determined by the optical domain and not by the routers. The edge routers do not participate into routing protocol that runs among the core routers. The core routers apply their own protocols, possibly within the optical domain. On the other hand, in peer models, the IP routers determine the full path of the end-to-end connection. The edge routers interact with the core routers deploying the same protocols and routing. For more details, the reader may refer to RFC 3471 (Berger, 2003). For instance, as shown in Figure 23, to establish a path between LSR1 and LSR2,

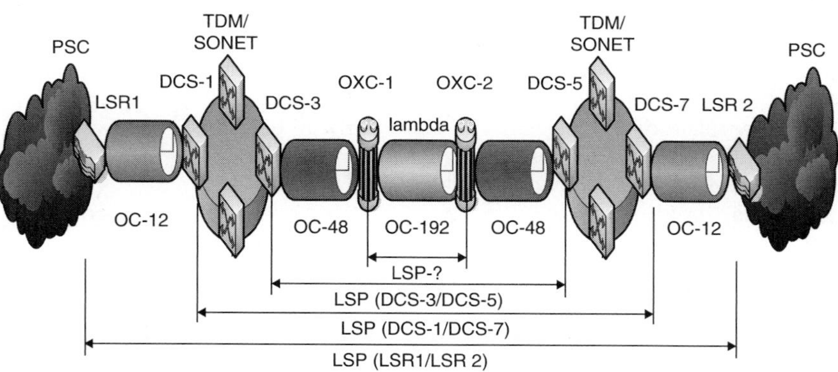

Figure 23: A path is established between peer devices, using downstream hierarchy

tunneling is applied in the lower hierarchy. The path is formed, by first having the sender node to transmit a PATH/LABEL request message holding specific parameters required for the intended network. The downstream node then sends back a RESV/LABEL. When the initiator receives it, it creates a path with its peer via a RSVP/PATH message.

Finally, GMPLS has two planes: the data and the control planes. They might be physically or logically separated. For instance, the control plane might direct the control information via ETHENET, X.25 connection, or use a slice of STS-1 (synchronous transport signal).

CONCLUSION

The demand for greater bandwidths is accelerating the distribution of fiber-optic communication systems. Fiber-optic cables have been successfully used in long-distance communication; with over 8% of the world's telecommunication systems now utilizing fiber-optic cables (Bellis, n.d.).

Telecommunication and cable companies have merged resources to distribute their services via fiber-optic cable to the home. This has lead to standards being defined; these incorporate five key criteria.

- Ability to carry multiple protocols
- Maintain architectural flexibility
- Provide good diagnostic capabilities for signal quality and fault management
- Transparent data transport protocols
- Compatibility with data transfer methodologies

Although the increased performance and greater bandwidth has been attractive for LANs, economic considerations have limited its development in this area. With today's demands forever increasing bandwidth, coupled with the diminishing cost, fiber-optic LANs are becoming very popular in areas where copper connections have limitations. Fiber-optic cables are implemented in areas that have an electrically noisy environment or systems that carry sensitive data. There are also minimal issues with building regulations when implementing an optical fiber network as opposed to an electric cabled one.

Optical communication has migrated from the WAN and MAN to the LAN across many technologies: Ethernet, ring, and fiber channels. Such a leap might reach the internal architectures of the servers and the PCs. Instead of electricity, the stations will operate entirely by optics/photons hence breaking the barriers of speed and bandwidth limitations imposed by the electrons. Furthermore, optical wireless is an interesting domain that will be well accepted by the ad hoc network infrastructure, especially in large-scale ad hoc networks (Adda et al., 2005; Owen and Adda, 2005).

GLOSSARY

10 gigabit Ethernet: Ethernet at 10 billion bits per second over optical fiber. Multimode fiber supports distances up to 300 m; single mode fiber supports distances up to 40 km.

1000BASE-LX: A fiber-optic gigabit Ethernet standard, using a long wavelength laser. Can work over a distance of up to 2 km over 9 μm single-mode fiber.

1000BASE-SX: A fiber-optic gigabit Ethernet standard, that operates over multimode fiber using a 0.85-micrometer near infrared light wavelength. The specification allows for a maximum distance between endpoints of 220 m over 62.5/125-μm fiber, although can usually work over significantly longer distances.

100BASE-FX: The IEEE Fast Ethernet standard for 100-Mbps Ethernet over fiber-optic cabling. It uses two strands of multimode optical fiber for receive and transmit.

100BASE-T2: 100-Mbps Ethernet over Category 3 cabling. Supports full duplex, and use only two pairs. It is functionally equivalent to 100BASE-TX.

100BASE-T4: The IEEE Fast Ethernet standard for 100-Mbps Ethernet over Category 3 UTP/STP. The IEEE Fast Ethernet standard for 100-Mbps Ethernet over Category 3 UTP/STP.

100BASE-TX: The IEEE Fast Ethernet standard for 100-Mbps Ethernet over Category 5 UTP/STP.

10BASE-F: 10-Mbps baseband Ethernet over optical fiber.

10BASE-FB: 10-Mbps baseband Ethernet over two multimode optical fibers using a synchronous active hub.

10BASE-FL: The implementation of the 802.3 standard designed to operate over fiber-optic cable at 10 Mbps.

10BASE-FP: A passive star network that requires no repeater.

Bandwidth: The data-carrying capacity of a transmission medium measured in bits per second (bps) or in cycles per second (cps) or Hertz (Hz).

Bridge: A networking device that connects local or wide area networks using the same or different data-link layer.

CDDI: Copper distributed data interface. Copper cable based implementation of FDDI.

CSMA/CD: Carrier senses multiple access with collision detection. The network access method used by Ethernet networks.

DAS: DAS is storage that is directly connected to a server by connectivity media such as parallel SCSI cables.

DCS: Digital cross-connect systems. It is software controlled and uses time-slot interchange to transfer slots between input and output lines.

Encoder: Encodes the information and passes them to the transmitter.

Ethernet: A 10-megabit per second (Mbps) baseband-type network that uses the contention-based CSMA/CD media access method. Invented by Robert Metcalfe at Xerox's Palo Alto Research Center in the mid-1970s.

FDDI: Fiber distributed data interface is a media access (transmission) control-level protocol with token-ring architecture, a communication bandwidth of 100 Mbps and supported on a fiber network medium.

Fiber-optic detectors: Can be either a PIN (p-type-intrinsic-n-type) diode or an APD (avalanche photodiode) where both senses light and converts it into an electrical current.

FOIRL (Fiber-optic inter repeater link): An early implementation of a subset of the 802.3 10Base-FL standard designed to connect fiber-optic repeaters at 10 Mbps.

FSPF: Fabric shortest path first is a routing protocol used in fiber channel networks. It calculates the best path between switches, establishes routes across the fabric, and calculates alternate routes in event of a failure or topology change.

GBIC: Gigabit interface converter; a fiber channel optical or copper transceiver that is easily swapped to offer a flexible choice of copper or fiber-optic media.

HBA: Host bus adapter, that plugs into a host enabling the host to communicate with a SCSI device.

IEFT: The Internet Engineering Task Force is charged with developing and promoting Internet standards.

IS-IS: Intermediate system-intermediate system is an International Organization for Standardization (ISO) dynamic routing specification.

LAN: Local area network is a computer network covering a local area, like a home, office or small group of buildings.

LD (laser diode): Similar to LED but can be used in both single and multimode fiber as it has a smaller spectral width.

LED (light-emitting diode): Converts the electrical signal into a corresponding light signal that can be transmitted in the fiber. More reliable than lasers, but both sources will degrade over time because of heat and uneven current. Has a larger spectral width compared to LD hence can only be used in multimode fiber.

LSP: Label switched paths are often also referred to as tunnels. LSPs are used to transport data, such as IP packets, across an MPLS network.

LSR: A node that resides inside the MPLS domain boundary and does no IP forwarding.

MAN (metropolitan area network): A data network designed for a town or city. MANs are larger than LANs, but smaller than WANs.

Media access unit: An Ethernet transceiver.

MPLS: MPLS is a widely supported method of speeding up data communication over combined IP/ATM networks.

Multimode fiber: The most common type of fiber-optic cabling used in network installations. Typically, multimode has a core diameter of 62.5 microns and an outer cladding diameter of 125 microns. Nearly all fiber-based networking hardware (repeaters, switches, LAN cards) are multimode.

Multimode graded index fiber: The refractive index of the core gradually decreases from the center of the core toward the cladding. This reduces the problem of dispersion as most light rays arrive at the receiver at the same time. Usually used in short distance transmission, such as a LAN.

Multimode step index fiber: A sharp difference in the refractive index of the core and cladding causing total internal reflection as light moves along the cable. This suffers from dispersion as light rays travels along different path hence arrive on the receiver at different times. Usually used in medium distance transmission, such as a MAN.

Network interface card (NIC): An adapter card providing the physical connection between a computer and the network medium.

Optical amplifiers: To strengthen the signals in a long-haul transmission to reduce the effect of dispersion and attenuation.

Optical fiber: Translucent fiber that can transmit beams of laser light. Ideal for reliable high speed LANs and backbones.

Optical fiber connectors: A mechanical or optical device that provides a demountable connection between two fibers or a fibers and a source or detector.

OSPF: Open shortest path first is a protocol used by routers on an IP network.

OTN: Open transport network.

OXC: Optical cross-connects, connects optical networks providing versatility and is reconfigurable.

Photophone: A wireless communication device using light to transmit signals through air, patented by Alexander Graham Bell.

PSC: Packet switch capable.

Receiver: A device that gets the packets from the communication network.

Router: A device that provides intelligent connections between networks. Routers operate at the network layer of the OSI model and are responsible for making decisions about which paths through a network the transmitted data will use.

SAS: Single stations are attached to the ring concentrator and mainly inject and remove traffic from the primary ring.

SDH: Synchronous digital hierarchy, the international standard for transmitting digital information over optical networks.

Single-mode fiber: A type of fiber that uses a single path for light transmission (i.e., the light is not reflected within the core). Single-mode fiber may support distances between 2 km up to 20 km.

SONET: Synchronous optical network, an international standard for high-speed communication over fiber-optic networks.

Spanning-tree protocol: The spanning-tree protocol is used to interconnect network switches.

Switch: A network device that selects a path or circuit for sending a unit of data to its next destination.

TCP: Transmission control protocol—A connection orientation transport protocol.

UDP: User datagram protocol—A connectionless orientated transport protocol. UDP is the transport protocol used by SNMP.

VLAN: Virtual LAN, a network of computers that behave as if they are connected to the same wire even though they may actually be physically located on different segments of a LAN.

WAN: Wide area networks, a computer network that spans a wider area than does a local area network.

WDM: For fiber channels, a variation of frequency division multiplexing is called wavelength division multiplexing.

CROSS REFERENCES

See *Ethernet LANs; Local Area Networks; Optical Fiber Communications; Token Ring LANs.*

REFERENCES

Adda, M., G. Owen, and M. Kassassbeh, et al. 2005. *Communication issues in large scale wireless ad hoc networks*. Athens, GA: ATINER, pp. 299–313.

Alwayn, V. 2004. *Optical network design and implementation*. Cisco Press.

Basak, D., and J. Siket. 2000. *The role of MPLS in the next-gen optical Internet. Telecommunications*. Norwood, MA: Horizon House Publication, Inc.

Bellis, M. n.d. inventors.about.com/od/pstartinventions/a/photophone.htm (accessed December 14, 2005).

Berger, L. 2003. Generalized MPLS signalling functional description. *RFC* 3471.

Campbell, C. A. 2006. IP/MPLS, MetroE, broadband are hot investment areas as carriers converge networks, *Market Wire*, November 1, 2006. http://www.market-wire.com/mw/release_html_b1?release_id=105957 (accessed January 14, 2006).

Chapman, D. A. 1989. Comment on 'using spread spectrum in a high capacity fiber-optic local network'. *Journal of Lightwave Technology*, LT-7:747.

Comer, D. E. 2001. *Computer networks and Internets with Internet applications*, 3rd ed. Upper Saddle River, NJ: Prentice Hall.

Fiber Optics. 2005. Illustrated Fiber Optic Glossary, http://www.fiber-optics.info/glossary-d.htm#Dispersion (accessed December 12, 2005).

Forrest, M. Mims III. 1980. Alexander Graham Bell and the Photophone: The centennial of the invention of light-waves communications 1880–1980. *Opt News* 6(1):8–16.

Forouzan, B. A. 2007. *Data communications and networking*. New York: McGraw-Hill.

Greenfield, D. 2002. *The essential guide to optical networks*. Upper Saddle River, NJ: Prentice Hall.

Haddock, S. 1996. Carrier extension issues. IEEE 802.3 High-Speed Study Group Plenary Meeting, Enschede NL.

Joshi, S. P. 1986. High-performance networks. Journal IEEE Micro. 6(3): 8–14.

Kadambi, J., L. Crayford, and M. Kalkunte. 1998. *Gigabit Ethernet*. Upper Saddle River, NJ: Prentice-Hall.

Kalkunte, M., and J. Kadambi. 1996. Packet packing and mTBEB simulation results. IEEE 802.3 High-Speed Study Group Plenary Meeting, Enschede NL.

Kolimbiris, H. 2000. *Digital communications systems with satellite and fiber optics application*. Upper Saddle River, NJ: Prentice Hall.

Lefebvre, K. 2001. *Environmental effects on chromatic and polarization mode dispersions*. Utica, NY: NetTest.

Molle, M., Kelkunte, M., and J. Kadambi. 1997. Frame bursting: a technique for scaling CSMA/CD to gigabit Ethernet. IEEE Network. 11(4):6–15.

Nave, R. 2006. The electromagnetic spectrum. http://hyperphysics.phy-astr.gsu.edu/hbase/ems1.html (accessed January 12, 2006).

Owen, G., and M. Adda. 2005. *Feasibility of geographically static data storage in ad hoc networks*, IADAT-tcn, Telecommunications and Computer Networks conference proceedings, Portsmouth, UK, September 7–9, pp. 172–7.

Palias, J. C. 2005. *Fiber optic communication*, 5th ed. Upper Saddle River, NJ: Prentice Hall.

Ramaswami, R. and K. Sivarajan. 2002. *Optical networks, a practical perspective*, 2nd ed. San Francisco: Morgan Kaufman Publishers.

Refi, J. 1999. Optical fibers for optical networking. *Bell Labs Technical Journal*, 4(1):24626.

Ross, J. E. 1986. FDDI: A tutorial. *IEEE Communications*, 24:10–5.

Ross, J. E. 1989. An overview of the FDDI—the fiber distributed data interface. *IEEE Journal on Selected Areas of Communications*, 7(7):1043–51.

Schneider, K. S. 2004. Fiber optic communications for the premises environment. http://www.telebyteusa.com/foprimer/foch1.htm#1.6 (accessed December 10, 2005).

Shah, A. and G. Ramakrishnan. 1993. *FDDI—A high speed network*. Englewood Cliffs, NJ: Prentice Hall.

Stallings, W. 2002. *High-speed networks and Internet*. Upper Saddle River, NJ: Prentice Hall.

Tanenbaum, A. S. 2004. *Computer networks*, 4th ed. Upper Saddle River, NJ: Prentice Hall.

Tomasi, W. 2001. *Advanced electronic communications Systems*, 5th ed. Englewood Cliffs, NJ: Prentice Hall.

Walrand, J. and P. Varaiya. 2000. *High-performance communication networks*, 2nd ed. San Francisco: Morgan Kaufmann Publishers.

Widmer, A. X. and P. A. Franaszek. 1983. A DC-balanced, partitioned-block 8B/10B transmission code. *IBM Journal of Research and Development*, 20(5):440.

Windows 2000 Operating System

Dario Forte, *University of Milano, Crema, Italy*

HOW WINDOWS 2000 MANAGES INTERNET PROTOCOL: IP AND DHCP

Although the basic architecture of the Windows 2000 OS is based on components that were already widely in use at the time of its debut, it did introduce a number of new features. One example is its support for the dynamic host configuration protocol (DHCP), a consolidated standard that greatly simplifies administration of networks based on TCP/IP protocols. DHCP nicely resolves a series of very important practical problems, although there are a number of "collateral" aspects that require careful attention. In this chapter we address technical and implementation issues as well as security aspects.

Every computer connected to a TCP/IP network must have a single, unambiguous Internet protocol (IP) address. This address may be provided manually or automatically by the system administrator. Although the former option allows greater control and even an extra layer of security (especially regarding event traceability), the latter is incontestably the option of choice for large, dynamic networks where manual operations cannot possibly play a structural role.

To address this situation, Microsoft has been working to develop the DHCP. DHCP architecture and functions are addressed by the RFCs 2131 and 2132. According to these documents, DHCP allows the automatic attribution of an IP address to a given machine as soon as it boots up or connects to the network. It also allows certain settings to be modified while the host is connected to the network.

DHCP is based on a series of components making up a central database of IP addresses, which—together with configuration information such as subnet masks, DNS, and default gateways—allow rapid and functional connection to the public network. As suggested above, the larger the network, the greater the advantages offered by DHCP. And as Microsoft says, this protocol also enhances Microsoft-based systems, which have the following characteristics:

Dynamic modification of configurations coming from a central location

In Windows 2000 Server, DHCP can interact with the DNS servers, thus avoiding the duplication of transiting information, enhancing both performance and security

Again, in Windows 2000, the implementation of DHCP contains an advanced monitoring tool with customizable reporting features. This operating system has a series of security features such as multicast address allocation control, recognition of unauthorized or "fake" DHCP servers, clustering, and so forth.

Windows 2000 and DHCP: A Few Details

Windows 2000 added specific features into its architecture on the basis of Internet Engineering Task Force (IETF) recommendations. These features interact dynamically with DNS servers. In particular, given the fact that the IETF indications are not fully definitive in this regard, Windows 2000 can register pointers (PTR) and addresses (A) for its clients on a DNS server. In theory, this would provide stable visibility to DHCP clients even on public DNSs, obviously ones based on dynamic DNS (DDNS).

Put simply, this feature allows a Windows 2000-based DHCP server to act as a proxy for its clients, which are in turn based on other Microsoft operating systems. Looking at this in detail, DHCP servers based on Windows 2000 server are able to distinguish between the different types of clients, including those using Windows 2000, which are able to interact dynamically with DDNS servers. Here we should point out that static DNS and DHCP cannot interact on a basic level. Thus, it is not possible to ensure that name-address mapping is conserved. This could cause problems unless, as Microsoft recommends, using WINS lookup, which should be queried by the DHCP clients when they get configured. Here is what the official Microsoft literature suggests:

If WINS servers are used on a network, enable WINS lookup for DHCP clients that use NetBIOS.

Assign IP address reservations with an infinite lease duration for DHCP clients that use DNS only and do not support NetBIOS.

Wherever possible, upgrade or replace older static DNS servers with DNS servers supporting dynamic DNS service. Dynamic DNS service is supported by the Microsoft DNS server included in Windows 2000 Server.

Installation of DHCP in Company Networks

One of the first things to do when you decide to implement DHCP is to find out how many DHCP servers are necessary for your network structure. In a modest-sized local network with only a physical subnet and no routing, a single DHCP server may be enough. If you add physical routers you will have to increase the number of DHCP servers proportionally.

Although in theory there is no limit to the number of clients that can connect to a DHCP server, there is a maximum number of connections that can be handled practically. This relates mainly to factors such as machine processing power, network speed, disk capacity, and so on. One parameter not related to processing power is the speed of network links. A slow link or, as an extreme, a dialup connection, requires a DHCP server on both sides. Additionally, many counsel the use of a multiple DHCP server with multicast functionality to ensure request coverage, even if one or more specific servers cannot be contacted.

Although every client computer has to have the right software to dialog with a DHCP machine running Windows 2000 Server, another factor to keep in mind is that of "scopes."

According to Microsoft, a scope is an administrative grouping of computers into a subnet using the DHCP service. Administrators create a scope for each physical subnet, which is then used to define parameters used by clients for this subnet. Scopes can be created based on the needs of particular groups of users, with appropriate lease durations for each scope. A DHCP scope consists of a pool of IP addresses on a subnet, such as 10.223.223.1 to 10.223.223.200, that the DHCP server can lease to DHCP clients. Each physical network can have only one DHCP scope or a superscope with one or more ranges of IP addresses. Prior to actual deployment, every administrator has to define the scopes. This is a rather important task that also has security ramifications.

DHCP Server Authorization

Another DHCP server function under Windows 2000 is that of "authorizing" DHCP servers. Practically speaking, this amounts to a sort of access/authenticity control list, whose basic purpose is to prevent access by nonauthorized DCHP servers. In addition to ensuring against duplication during IP address allocation, it also limits problems related to hijacking and the like. The authorization process is carried out by the group of domain administrators specifically delegated to DHCP management.

Authorization is managed by active directory (AD), which is used here to keep a registry of authorized DHCP servers. AD also provides information on the status of each server so that requests may also be redirected to something other than the default resource.

Microsoft's instructions on setting up the resources are very clear: The list of authorized servers can be created in the AD through the DHCP snap-in. When it first comes up, the DHCP server tries to find out if it is part of the directory domain. If it is, it tries to contact the directory to see if it is on the list of authorized servers. If it succeeds, it sends out DHCPINFORM to find out if there are other directory services running and makes sure that it is valid in others as well. If it cannot connect to the directory, it assumes that it is not authorized and does not respond to client requests. Likewise, if it does reach the directory but does not find itself on the authorized list, it does not respond to clients. If it finds itself on the authorized list, it starts to service client requests.

There is a well defined procedure for checking authorization requisites. When a DHCP server that is not a member server of the domain (such as a member of a workgroup) comes up, the resource itself broadcasts a DHCPINFORM message on the network. Any other server that receives this message responds with a DHCPACK message and provides the name of the directory domain to which it belongs. If a workgroup DHCP server detects another member DHCP server of a domain on the network, the workgroup DHCP server assumes that it is unauthorized on that network and does not service requests. If the workgroup DHCP server detects the presence of another workgroup server, it ignores it; this means that there can be multiple workgroup servers active at the same time, as long as there is no directory service. Even when a workgroup server comes up and finds itself allowed to run (because no other domain member server or workgroup server is on the network), it continues to probe DHCPINFORM every five minutes. If an authorized domain member DHCP server comes up later, the workgroup server becomes unauthorized and stops servicing.

This is a rather attractive feature, especially if you do not plan to invest in external tools or supplementary control architecture such as those based on network access control (NAC).

Security and the DHCP Audit

The Windows 2000 DHCP server has a number of fundamentally important auditing tools for those dealing with security and incident response. In the configuration step you will have to indicate the directory path where the system log files will be stored and specify the maximum size of the log files. The audit is not performed in real time, but on a scheduled basis. The administrator indicates how many times the DHCP server will have to write events before checking to see if the disk quota has been reached. From the DHCP console you can select the DHCP server to monitor: choose properties from the action menu, click the "advanced" tab and edit the audit log file pathway, if necessary. You can customize other settings on the configuration registry level.

IMPLEMENTING NAME RESOLUTION IN WINDOWS 2000 USING DNS

Windows 2000 vs. DNS: An Introduction

As described in the previous section, the Windows 2000 name resolution architecture is fundamentally compliant with RFC-2131 and RFC-2132. This means there is total compatibility with other systems of the same type, and also with DNS.

Although not actually calling it obligatory, Microsoft naturally recommends the use of a DNS under Windows 2000. Even though this might seem motivated purely by commercial motives, the reason is actually practical. Windows 2000 allows interaction with AD, something that offers important advantages, partly because AD uses the multimaster replication engine, which ensures, among other things, faster propagation. Regarding interaction with the clients (excluding the outdated Windows NT 3.5 and 3.51, Windows NT 4.0, Windows 95, and Windows 98, which rely on NetBIOS that can use NBNS (WINS), broadcast, or flat LmHosts files), because DNS as implemented in Windows 2000 is Windows Internet Name Services (WINS)-ware, a combination of both DNS and WINS can be used in a mixed environment to achieve maximum efficiency in locating various network services and resources.

In this section it is assumed that a description of DNS is not necessary. However, the Table 1 helps clarify the way the database for this type of service is structured, keeping in mind that a DNS database consists of resource records (RRs). Each RR identifies a particular resource within the database. There are various types of RRs in DNS.

The structure of the DNS databases is described in the reference RFCs. There is an updated list (June 2006) of RFCs relating to the domain name system at http://www.dns.net/dnsrd/rfc/. Nevertheless, an overview of how to manage the database, with special reference to replication, might still be useful here.

As noted, a DNS database can be subdivided into multiple zones by a method known as partitioning. A zone is a portion of the DNS database that contains the resource records with the owner names that belong to the contiguous portion of the DNS namespace. Zone files are maintained on DNS servers. A single DNS server can be configured to host zero, one, or multiple zones.

The role of the root domain, the domain name to which a particular zone is associated and bound, is very important in this case. Starting from the premise that a zone contains information about all names that end with the zone's root domain name, a DNS server is considered

Table 1: DNS vs. RR

Description	Class	TTL	Type	Data
Start of Authority	Internet (IN)	Default TTL is 60 minutes	SOA	Owner Name, Primary Name Server DNS Name, Serial Number, Refresh Interval, Retry Interval, Expire Time, Minimum TTL
Host	Internet (IN)	Zone (start of authority [SOA]) TTL	A	Owner Name (Host DNS Name), Host IP Address
Name Server	Internet (IN)	Zone (SOA) TTL	NS	Owner Name, Name Server DNS Name
Mail Exchanger	Internet (IN)	Zone (SOA) TTL	MX	Owner Name, Mail Exchange Server DNS Name, Preference Number
Canonical Name (an alias)	Internet (IN)	Zone (SOA) TTL	CNAME	Owner Name (Alias Name), Host DNS Name

authoritative for a name if it loads the zone containing that name. The first record in any zone file is a start of authority (SoA) RR. The SoA RR identifies a primary DNS name server for the zone as the best source of information for the data within that zone and as an entity processing the updates for the zone. However, there are cases where certain domain names that should be part of a given zone are delegated to other zones. There may be many reasons for this, including a need to delegate management of a DNS domain to a number of organizations or departments within an organization, or a need to distribute the load of maintaining one large DNS database among multiple name servers to improve the name resolution performance as well as create a DNS fault-tolerant environment. However, this might open up some well defined security issues, such as those associated with what is called "DNS Zone Transfer." Hence, "delegating" management must be carried out with extreme care. At any rate, the above-mentioned NS RRs facilitate delegation by identifying DNS servers for each zone. They appear in all forward and reverse look-up zones. Whenever a DNS server needs to cross a delegation, it will refer to the NS RRs for DNS servers in the target zone. Furthermore, according to Microsoft, if multiple NS records exist for a delegated zone identifying multiple DNS servers available for querying, the Windows 2000 DNS server will be able to select the closest DNS server based on the round trip intervals measured over time for every DNS server.

A number of advanced DNS-management features have been introduced into Windows 2000. Among these is support for AD-based replication. Known also as AD storage and replication integration, in addition to supporting a conventional way of maintaining and replicating DNS zone files, the Microsoft Windows 2000 DNS service has the option of using the AD services as the data storage and replication engine. This way, DNS replication will be performed by the AD service, so there is no need for other support. AD service replication provides per-property replication granularity, and AD service replication is more secure. The reader is urged to take a look at the features of the AD service database. The database is x500 compliant, operates in a tree-like hierarchical manner, and is managed at the domain controller level. The portion of the database that has authorization functions usually resides physically in the same machine that hosts the domain controller. In AD, each resource is identified as an object. Each object can either be a container (which can contain other containers and leaf objects) or a Leaf, that is, a specific resource in the AD tree.

Every object has an attribute that defines its characteristics. Both the classes of object and their attributes are defined in the AD service diagram. Examples of objects contained therein are users, groups, OU (organizational units), and DNS (zone and node). The node contains a DNS record multivalued attribute with an instance of a value for every record associated with the object's name.

Managing Replication and Synchronization Between DNS

As a result of the direct interaction between DNS and AD, all updates affect AD. It is thus AD that deals with record replication on all the DNSs in a certain domain and subsequently on the other domain controllers. This method is called the multi-master replication model. Particular attention should be paid to the update sequence. This could generate conflicts which are by default resolved in favor of the last one to update. The problem remains of a possibly divergent resolution in the event of a dispute. Practically speaking, the same rule is applied in the case where two or more nodes with the same name are created on two or more DNS servers. Until the conflict is resolved and the DNS server containing an invalid update polls the valid data from the directory service (DS), it is possible that requests for the same object made to two different DNS servers will be resolved differently. This is why the AD service (ADS) database is called loosely consistent.

Managing Zones

The DNS zones can be converted, that is, they can modify their roles. They can transform, for example, from a zone integrated into the DS (AD) to one that is not. Such a modification has to be followed by a series of deletions from AD in order to avoid replicating nonupdated zones. The security of these operations is ensured by secure dynamic DNS updates. The DS maintains the access control lists (ACL) specifying groups or users who are allowed to modify the DS-integrated zones.

This is a principle that is included in the domain name system security extensions (DNSSEC) specifications. In particular, DNS server supports the secure dynamic updates for the DS-integrated zones and Windows 2000 implementation provides even finer granularity allowing per-name ACL specification.

Managing Queries

Here we provide a description of the DNS query procedure. A request of this type is sent by a client (resolver) to a DNS server (a name server), or between two name servers. It is a rather simple process, at least on the conceptual level. A query is merely a request for records of a specified type with a specified name. For example, a query can request all host RRs with a particular name.

There are two types of queries that can be made to a DNS server: recursive and iterative. Some feel that recursive queries inherently compromise performance, especially in distributed environments. A recursive query forces a DNS server to respond to a request with either a fail or success response. Resolvers typically make recursive queries. With a recursive query, the DNS server contacts other DNS servers to help it resolve the request. When it receives a successful response from another DNS server (or servers) it sends a response to the client. Although a recursive query system may have its disadvantages, we cannot simply eliminate it. A recursive query is necessary if a given zone does not contain the requested information. In this case the resolution procedure is delegated to a root DNS, whose information is contained in the cache of every DNS that adheres to the specific RFC. For more information in this regard, visit http://rs.internic.net/domain/named.cache.

Iterative queries should be "smarter" than their recursive cousins in that they should be able to provide the best information (also known as referral if the server is not authoritative for the name) based on what the server knows from local zone files or from caching. If a name server does not have any information to answer the query, it simply sends a negative response. Hence there is no interaction with external DNS roots.

Configuring DNS Client

The official Microsoft literature provides an exhaustive description of client configuration, based in any case on a rather common condition: a DNS installed on a domain controller. Granted that this is not the only possible condition, we will begin by describing this scenario. If the server is the first and only domain controller that the administrator installs in the domain, and the server has DNS, the DNS client settings that point to that first server's IP address should be configured.

Regarding a domain controller with DNS installed, that is, a domain controller that also acts as a DNS server, Microsoft recommends that you configure the domain controller's DNS client settings according to these specifications: if the server is the first and only domain controller that you install in the domain, and the server runs DNS, the DNS client should be configured to point to that first server's IP address. DNSs other than the one specified above should not be pointed at by the client.

Furthermore, special attention should be dedicated to the DCPromo process, which promotes or demotes the domain controllers. Granted that in almost all cases a DC/DNS is used together with AD, you have to be careful to concatenate the various DNS servers (and also the various domains) in order to avoid loops and other errors. You can find more information on this at http://www.microsoft.com/windows2000/techinfo/planning/activedirectory/branchoffice/default.asp.

On the client side, to check for the availability of the right DNS you first have to key in ipconfig to check which DNS the client is pointing at. In particular it will be necessary to set up the DNS registered in AD as the first DNS (if present).

There is also the condition where the domain controller referred to by the client does not have DNS installed. In this case the client will have to point to a DNS having authority over the zone in question, hence, to a local DNS that is RFC compliant. If this is not available, establish a link to a DNS external to your domain but still within the company LAN/ wide area network (WAN). At any rate, Microsoft discourages pointing directly at an external DNS, for example, one on an ISP; it should always be an internal DNS. The same holds for Windows 2000 Server and Windows 2003 Server member servers. It is a different story however if you have servers that are not configured to be part of the domain. In this case you can still configure them to use AD-integrated DNS servers as their primary and secondary DNS servers. If you have nonmember servers in your environment that use AD-integrated DNS, they do not dynamically register their DNS records to a zone that is configured to accept only secure updates (see the verification of authorized DNS servers mentioned above). Again, according to Microsoft, if you do not use AD-integrated DNS, and you want to configure the nonmember servers for both internal and external DNS resolution, configure the DNS client settings to point to an internal DNS server that forwards to the Internet. Lastly, it may be possible that DNS is needed only to resolve Internet addresses. In this case it will be possible to point directly from the client to an external DNS, for example, that of an ISP.

IMPLEMENTING NAME RESOLUTION BY USING WINS

WINS (Windows Internet Name Service) developed alongside Windows Server systems. WINS provides a distributed database for registering and querying dynamic computer name-to-IP address mapping in a routed network environment.

In Windows 2000 the service was made even more advanced than what had been planned for Windows NT. Its salient features are advanced mapping of NetBIOS addresses, improvement in configurations on the client level, and improvements in management. One of the aspects of this last factor is a distributed database that can handle dynamic queries, also in conjunction with DHCP services to provide easy configuration and administration of Windows-based TCP/IP networks.

One of the most recurrent problems in the previous version of WINS was the resolution of NetBIOS names via IP broadcasts. There was also the need to relieve network administrators of the burden of having to do an excessive number of "manual" operations for updating static mapping files, such as LMHOST files. The WINS implementation under Windows 2000, which is compliant with the NetBIOS Name Server (NBNS) (RFCs 1001/1002), also automatically updates the WINS database when dynamic addressing through DHCP results in new IP addresses for computers that move between subnets. Additionally, the export command can be used to place WINS data into a comma-delimited text file that can be imported into Microsoft Excel, reporting tools, or scripting applications for analysis and reporting.

Under the client side, WINS clients can now re-register without rebooting the server, and they have better fault tolerance because they can query against more than two WINS servers.

The Windows 2000 version of the WINS service has the following new features:

Persistent connections
Manual tombstoning
Improved management tool
Enhanced filtering and record searching
Dynamic record deletion and multiselect
Record verification and version number validation
Export function
Increased fault tolerance
Dynamic re-registration

The most immediate is the improved management system with a graphic user interface (GUI) known as the

Microsoft management console (MMC), which greatly facilitates use. The MMC provides network managers with the consistency of using the console itself for all of their administrative tasks. With MMC, multiple WINS manager windows can be opened at once.

MMC provides better performance thanks to a multithreaded user interface (UI), which allows background tasks to take place while a foreground task is being performed, providing much faster response. This permits a network manager to run multiple UI tasks simultaneously. A manager can select the active registration node to display the database, and then—rather than waiting for the complete database to be displayed—can select the node of another server, change the configuration of replication partners, or perform other tasks.

It is also possible to use list views. This provides a flexible, Internet Explorer-like function for sorting information according to column type. This means network managers can sort data according to record name, type, IP address, and so on with a simple click of the mouse.

Using PKI for Security Management

Windows 2000 was introduced at a time when public key infrastructures (PKI) had reached a sort of peak and were much touted by vendors—mainly for marketing reasons, as many analysts would comment. Nevertheless we have to take our hats off to the engineers for their farsightedness in coupling Windows 2000 with a real use of public key cryptography.

According to the Redmond Software Producer, like other enabling technologies, public key cryptography requires an infrastructure to deliver its benefits. However, the PKI is not a physical object or software process; instead, it is a set of services provided by a collection of interconnected components. These components work together to provide public key–based security services to applications and users.

Understanding Public Key Cryptography

Public key cryptography differs from single key cryptography by the use of two separate keys, one of which can be—or rather must be—distributed publicly. There are a number of well known PK cryptographic algorithms. Some, such as RSA (Rivest-Shamir-Adleman) and ECC (elliptic curve cryptography), are general purpose in the sense they can support many security operations. Below we mention a few of them that are used massively by Windows 2000 PKI.

One of the most common (and important) aspects of public key cryptography is that of creating and validating digital signatures. This is based on a mathematical transform that combines the private key with the data to be "signed" to such that only someone possessing the private key could have created the digital signature. Anyone with access to the corresponding public key can verify the digital signature. Any modification to the signed data (even changing only a single bit in a large file) invalidates the digital signature. Digital signatures are themselves just data, so they can be transported. The use of digital signatures can be further improved by the use of authentication, by means of which it is possible to authenticate keys and their possessors by verifying the credentials given to the public keys. This attribution of "identity" is otherwise accomplished via the attribution of a digital certificate, which are what the PKIs are based on.

Certificates provide a mechanism for gaining confidence in the relationship between a public key and the entity owning the corresponding private key. A certificate is a particular type of digitally signed statement; the subject of the certificate is a particular subject public key and the certificate is signed by its issuer (holding another pair of private and public keys). Typically, certificates also contain other information related to the subject public key, such as identity information about the entity that has access to the corresponding private key. Thus, when issuing a certificate the issuer is attesting to the validity of the binding between the subject public key and the subject identity information.

Certificates are created, managed, and validated by a certification authority (CA), an entity often having legal status that deals with validating the match between the real and the virtual entity (the latter accompanied by keys and certificates). The CAs are hierarchical and may refer back to root systems called root CA.

Managing Clients

Windows 2000 clients are fundamentally interoperable with the PKIs. To tell the truth they already were way back in days of Windows NT 4.0, Windows 98, and Windows 95. At any rate, one of the most important characteristics of the implementation under Windows 2000 is integration with the domain administration and policy model, which dramatically simplifies application management within the enterprise.

With Windows 2000 it becomes simpler to generate and manage keys for one or more PK algorithms. Microsoft's CryptoAPI supports installable cryptographic service providers (CSP) supporting key generation and management for a variety of cryptographic algorithms. The CryptoAPI defines standard interfaces for generating and managing keys that are the same for all CSPs.

Keys can be stored in a number of ways. Mechanisms for storing key material are dependent on the selected CSP. The Microsoft-provided software CSPs (or base CSPs) store key material in an encrypted form on a per-user or per-machine basis. Other CSPs may implement different mechanisms. For example, smart card CSPs store the public-key pair in the smart card tamper-resistant hardware and generally require entry of a PIN code to access operations involving the private key. These "protection" mechanisms are transparent to an application, which references all key pairs via a key-set name unique in the context of a CSP. This is a rather important feature which, especially in the current historical timeframe, is used a great deal by banks.

We mentioned certification authorities above. Practically speaking, the PKIs under Windows 2000 are able to manage Microsoft or third party PKIs; they just need to be compatible with the standard. Microsoft also reminds us that support for PKCS-10 and PKCS-7 messages is provided by a Microsoft-supplied enrollment control

(Xenroll.dll) which can be scripted for Web-based enrollment or called programmatically to support other transport mechanisms such as RPC, DCOM, and e-mail. This control allows the calling application to specify the attributes included in the PKCS-10 message and allows use of an existing key pair or generation of a new key pair.

The PKI supports multiple enrollment methods including Web-based enrollment, an enrollment wizard, and policy-driven "auto-enrollment," which occurs as part of a user's logon processing. Subsequently, Microsoft decided to evolve the certificate enrollment process in a manner consistent with the certificate request syntax (CRS) document created in the IETF PKIX working group.

Certificates can be renewed. Certificate renewal is conceptually similar to enrollment, but takes advantage of the trust relationship inherent in an existing certificate. Renewal assumes the requesting entity wants a new certificate with the same attributes as an existing, valid certificate, but with extended validity dates. A renewal may use the existing public key or a new public key.

Renewal is of advantage primarily to the CA. A renewal request can presumably be processed more efficiently since one need not re-verify the existing certificate attributes. Renewal is currently supported in the Windows 2000 PKI for automatically enrolled certificates. For other mechanisms, a renewal is treated as a new enrollment request.

Industry-standard message protocols for certificate renewal are not overall accepted, but are included in the IETF PKIX CRS standards.

MORE SECURITY WITH IPSEC

One of a server's most important defensive tools against outside attacks is the use of access control devices (switches, routers, and firewalls) that should be configured to block all undesired traffic to the TCP and UDP ports corresponding to the network services that cannot, for whatever reason or choice, be deactivated. Furthermore, beyond issues related to the installation and configuration of these devices, it is always wise, especially when hardening a Web server, to implement additional connection filtering policies, even on the single host level. This ensures the presence of an extra layer of security which may help if one of the perimeter control devices ends up being bypassed by an attacker. The Windows 2000 operating system offers two tools for the implementation of connection filters: TCP/IP filters and IPSec filters.

TCP/IP Filters

This function is identical to the one in the Windows NT 4 operating system and it can be accessed via the properties menu of the local network connection by selecting Internet Protocol (TCP/IP) | Properties | Advanced | Options | TCP/IP Filtering | Properties.

In spite of the apparent benefits of filtering on the TCP/IP level, there are a number of drawbacks:

The rules created are applied in a monolithic fashion to all network cards

New settings have no effect whatsoever on existing connections and require a system reboot

There are a few functional problems: specifically, the filters appear not to fully comprehend the IP portion relating to the type of protocol (for example, although only TCP traffic corresponding to protocol number 6 is allowed, ICMP traffic will still not be blocked)

The filters can only be managed at the local level, which means more work for the administrator

The lack of granularity in connection control makes the tool rather inflexible and poorly suited to real use

The use of these functions is thus discouraged for these and other reasons, not least of which is the fact that more flexible tools are now available such as IPSec filters.

IPSec Filters

IPSec filters represent one of the advantages deriving from Windows 2000's full support for the IPSec protocol. IP Security is an extension of the IP protocol (it is an option with IPv4 and native with IPv6) defined by the Internet Engineering Task Force (IEFT) (RFC 2401-2411) and aimed at resolving the natural insecurity of IP-based networks through a nucleus of integrated services guaranteeing authentication, integrity control, and traffic confidence by using well known cryptographic algorithms. In addition to these, IPSec also offers "minor" functions, including the possibility of defining filtering rules for single host connections. The Windows 2000 components that ensure support for IPSec are IPSec policy agent and IPSec driver. The former is a bona fide system service that acquires policies as they are developed and distributes them to the various mechanisms. The latter is a driver that is loaded during system bootup and it is responsible for filter operation and connection maintenance. The driver thus directly uses the defined filters to determine which packets have to be blocked and which are acceptable.

IPSec filters have a series of advantageous characteristics such as:

Speed and efficiency in processing received datagrams

The possibility of being applied at individual network interfaces

Sufficient specificity in the type of managed and recognized protocols

Immediate operativity without system reboot

Creating Policies

The whole IPSec mechanism revolves around the concept of policies. A policy is an abstraction, a sort of virtual container that assembles various types of rules. These rules may encompass one or more lists of filters, each of which is assigned specific actions (e.g., accept or block). The first step in creating filters is the definition of a new policy. Proceed as follows:

Right click on IP Security Policies on Local Machine, which you can find via Programs | Administrative Tools | Local Security Settings.

Select the menu item Create IP Security Policy and follow the wizard. Give a name to the policy (for example, Web Server Security) and write a brief description.

In the next window, uncheck the Activate the default response rule box, click Next, leave the Edit box active, click Finish, and close the next properties window that pops up automatically.

Creating Filters

After having created a new policy and given it a name, you need to associate it with the appropriate list of filters.

Right click on IP Security Policies on Local Machine in the Local Security Settings window and select the menu item Manage IP filter lists and filter actions.

In the next window click Add from the Manage IP Filter Lists tab and give a name and brief description to the new list (e.g., Web server consented traffic).

Then click the Add button and add two new filters that will allow, for example, TCP connections only through the Web server ports 80 (http) and 443 (https).

We do not have to define a specific action for this list because it should already exist at the system level (and if we go to the Manage filter actions tab we should notice an action called Permit).

Proceeding in a similar fashion we also have to create a list of filters to block all nonconsented traffic (calling it, for example, Web Server Non-Consented Traffic). For this list we have to define a preset action as follows:

Select the Manage filter actions tab, unselect the Use Add Wizard box and click on the Add button.

In the next window, select Block in the Security Methods tab, give a name to the type of block (for example, Web Traffic Block) in the General tab and close the window by clicking OK.

Associating Filters and the Policy

Once the policy and the various list of filters with their associated actions have been determined, you will have to link them together. Here's how to do it:

Right click on the new policy in the Local Security Settings window and choose Properties.

In the next window unselect the Use Add Wizard checkbox and click on the Add button.

Then, on the Manage IP filters tab, select the list of access filters and go to the Manage filter actions tab.

Select Permit and close the window by clicking OK.

Do the same thing to associate the block-traffic list with its associated action.

Assigning the Policy to a Network Interface

The last step in making the whole mechanism operative is to assign the policy to a network interface (in the case of a Web server with two network cards, this would naturally be the public interface).

In the properties window of the specific local network connection, select Internet Protocol (TCP/IP) | Properties.

On the General tab, click Advanced and go to the Options tab.

Select IP filter | Properties, activate Use following rules and select the previously created policy from the list.

This way the filters become immediately operative without having to reboot the system.

THE TCP/IP STACK IN WINDOWS 2000

The TCP/IP stack in the Microsoft Windows 2000 family of operating systems introduces a number of improvements with respect to earlier implementations, including:

Increase in default size of TCP windows and the introduction of new algorithms to improve high congestion and high delay connections as well as the overall performance of the stack

Full compliance with RFC 1323 regarding scalable TCP window size

Full support for the selective acknowledgements (SACK) mechanism

A fast TCP packet retransmission mechanism

Improvements in round trip time (RTT) and retransmission timeout (RTO) algorithms

Improvements in management of a large number of connections

Furthermore, support is also guaranteed for other characteristics such as Internet protocol security (IPSEC), network address translation (NAT), quality of service (QoS), layer tunneling protocol (L2TP), and others.

Stack Security Parameters

The suite of TCP/IP protocols in Windows 2000 gets all the information for their proper function from the system registry to which they are written by the installation program and, in certain cases, by the DHCP client service, if used. Generally the default settings are good enough for a large variety of environments. However, in some circumstances (for example, in the case of a Web server) it may be opportune to manually reconfigure certain parameters to improve the robustness of the TCP/IP stack and the overall level of security.

However, modifications made manually to the system registry can make the whole system unstable. So before you go monkeying around, you should back up all your data and also the configuration registry. It is also strongly recommended to verify the new setup on test systems before replicating any modification on "working" systems.

Thanks to the management experience acquired by the Win2000test.com laboratories, Microsoft has succeeded in adding to the configuration registry a set of keys that can be set to "calibrated" settings to increase system resistance especially regarding certain types of attacks (e.g., denial of service). The parameters in question are found under the registry key.

HKEY_LOCAL_MACHINESYSTEMCurrentControlSetServicesTcpipParameters and are the following:

SynAttackProtect (REG_DWORD—valid settings: 0,1,2): the correct setup of this key reduces the attempts to retransmit SYN-ACK signals, reducing the time that the resources associated with the connections have to remain allocated. In order for this protection mechanism to operate effectively the maximum set values for the TcpMaxHalfOpen and TcpMaxHalfOpenRetried keys have to be exceeded. The default setting for the key is 0 (no protection) but a value of 2 is generally recommended. This offers the best protection because resource allocation is delayed until the three-way handshake has been completed. Nevertheless, this setting may at times cause connectivity problems especially for users who use remote connections with long response times. You should also remember that when the key is set to 2, certain stack functions cannot be used (specifically the scalable windows mechanism, window size, and the initial RTT);

TcpMaxHalfOpen (REG_DWORD—valid settings: 100 - 0xFFFF): this sets the maximum number of connections in the SYN_RCVD-permitted state before the SynAttackProtect key protection kicks in (the default value is 100 for the Windows 2000 Professional and Server systems and 500 for Advanced Server systems). The most opportune value depends on the environment but even more so on the volume of traffic that the server normally has to handle;

TcpMaxHalfOpenRetried (REG_DWORD—valid settings: 80 - 0xFFFF): this sets the maximum number of connections in the SYN_RCVD state for which there has been at least one retransmission of a SYN-permitted signal before the SynAttackProtect key protection kicks in (the default value is 80 for the Windows 2000 Professional and Server systems and 400 for Advanced Server systems). Here too, the most opportune value depends on the environment but even more so on the volume of traffic that the server normally has to handle;

EnablePMTUDiscovery (REG_DWORD—Boolean - valid settings: 0,1): this parameter affects the behavior of the TCP/IP stack in determining the maximum transmission unit (MTU), that is, the maximum size of network packets. A default value of 1 limits their size to a previously selected value. This translates into a lower probability of packet fragmentation by routers along the pathway with a lower MTU value. In spite of the advantages deriving from this setting, a value of 0 (false) is generally recommended because a fixed value of 576 bytes is used for all connections not directed to local network hosts, thus blocking all attempts to force the MTU down to low values to overload the stack;

EnableDeadGWDetect (REG_DWORD—Boolean - valid settings: 0,1): when this parameter is set to 1 (default) the TCP stack is able to use the "dead gateway" recognition function. With this mechanism, when a connection through the default gateway sends a TCP packet without received a response from the target for a certain number of times (half the value set for the TcpMaxDataRetransmission key) the routing path cache is overwritten so as to set up a secondary gateway for this connection provided that it has been defined in the network setup. The recommended setting for the key is 0 because this prevents an attacker from forcing connections to go through undesired gateways;

KeepAliveTime (REG_DWORD—valid settings: 1 - 0xFFFFFFFF): this parameter indicates the frequency (in milliseconds) of the attempts with which the stack verifies that an inactive connection is still established by sending a keep-alive packet. The default value is 7,200,000 milliseconds (2 hours), but a setting of 300,000 (5 minutes) is recommended.

There are also two other system registry keys that have an influence on network security. One of them is located on the pathway

HKEY_LOCAL_MACHINESYSTEMCurrentControlSetServices TcpipParametersInterfaces <interface no.>:

PerformRouterDiscovery (REG_DWORD—valid settings: 0,1,2): this parameter monitors whether the operating system attempts to detect the router applying RFC 1256. The recommended value is 0 because this prevents attempted attacks based on creating a counterfeit router. The default value is generally 2 if a DHCP service is used, or else 0,

whereas the other is found under

HKEY_LOCAL_MACHINESYSTEMCurrentControlSetServices NetBTParametersInterfaces <interface no.>:

NoNameReleaseOnDemand (REG_DWORD—Boolean - valid settings: 0,1): this parameter specifies whether the machine releases its NetBIOS name when it receives a name-release request from the network. The default setting is 0, whereas a setting of 1 is recommended, because this protects against attacks that try to get the name (Microsoft Security Bulletin MS00-047). However, you should bear in mind that this setting may have no effect at all for a network interface where the NetBIOS/SMB/CIFS services have been disabled (as it should be for the external network interface of a Web server).

Preliminary Remarks About Windows 2000 Server Remote Access

The Windows 2000 Server remote access, which is part of the integrated routing and remote access service, makes it possible to connect remote or mobile users to the networks of organizations. Remote users can work as if their computers were physically connected to the network.

The users run the remote access software and send a connection to the remote access server. The remote access server, which is a computer running Windows 2000 Server and the routing and remote access service, authenticates the user sessions and services until they are closed by the user or the network administrator. All services generally available to users connected to a LAN, such as file and printer sharing, access to the Web server, or messaging, are activated via the remote access connection.

The remote access clients use standard tools to access resources. A computer running Windows 2000 allows clients to use file manager to connect to storage devices and printers. The connections are permanent. Users do not have to re-establish connections to network resources during the remote access sessions. Given that the drive letters and the universal name convention (UNC) names are supported by remote access, most applications on the market, even when customized, run without need for any modifications.

A remote access server running Windows 2000 provides two different kinds of remote access connectivity:

Remote connection. This is established when a remote access client makes a nonpermanent remote access connection to a physical port on a remote access server using a telecommunications provider service, for example an analog telephone line or ISDN. The best example of remote connection is a remote connection client who dials the telephone number of one of the remote access server ports. A remote connection on an analog or ISDN telephone line is represented by a direct physical connection between the remote connection server and the client. Data sent over the connection can be encrypted even though it is not a virtual private network (VPN).

Virtual private network (VPN). A VPN comprises protected point-to-point connections through a private or public network such as the Internet. A VPN client uses special TCP/IP protocols known as tunneling protocols to make a virtual call to a virtual port on a VPN server. The best example of a VPN is a VPN client who makes a VPN connection to a remote access server connected to the Internet. The remote access server responds to the virtual call, authenticates the caller, and transfers data between the VPN client and the company network.

Unlike remote connection, the VPN is always an indirect logical connection between the VPN client and the VPN server. In order to guarantee privacy, the data sent over the connection have to be encrypted.

Remote Access Functions in Windows 2000 Server

Remote access under the Windows 2000 server offers a number of new functions:

Integration with Windows 2000 AD. A remote access server running Windows 2000 and part of a Windows 2000 domain registered in AD can access the user remote access settings memorized in AD, such as remote access authorizations and recall options. Once the server is registered in AD, it is possible to display and manage the contents of the remote access server using AD-based tools such as routing and remote access.

MS-CHAP version 2. Microsoft challenge handshake authentication protocol (MS-CHAP) version 2 significantly increases protection for transfer of protection credentials and for the generation of encryption keys during the negotiation of a remote access connection. MS-CHAP version 2 is specifically designed to authenticate VPN connections.

Extensible authentication protocol (EAP). With EAP it is possible to use new authentication methods with remote access. This is an important feature especially for the distribution of protection based on smart cards. EAP represents the interface that allows other authentication modules to connect to the Windows 2000 remote access PPP implementation. Windows 2000 supports EAP-MD5 CHAP, EAP-TLS (used for smart cards and authentication based on certificates), and the transmission of EAP messages to a RADIUS server.

Bandwidth allocation protocol (BAP). Thanks to BAP and bandwidth allocation control protocol (BACP), the multilink PPP protocol is made more efficient with the addition or deletion (depending on the case) of additional connections for managing changes in traffic flow. BAP is useful especially for operations where the number of simultaneous lines is based on the use of bandwidth. In Windows 2000 the BAP criteria can be set via remote access criteria. For example, a network administrator can set up a system so that a supplemental line will be cut off if use of the connection falls below 50% for more than 10 seconds. BAP offers a very effective mechanism for controlling connection costs while seeking the optimal bandwidth.

Remote access criteria. These criteria represent a series of connection settings that provide greater flexibility to network administrators in setting up remote access authorizations and connection attributes. Remote access criteria allow administrators to authorize incoming calls on the basis of date and time, the remote connection user's Windows 2000 group, or requested connection type, including remote connection or virtual private connection. Connection settings include limitations on maximum session time, authentication and encryption type, BAP criteria, and IP packet filtering.

RADIUS client. The Windows 2000 remote access server can act as a remote authentication dial-on user service (RADIUS) client on a RADIUS server. Windows 2000 provides RADIUS server functions through the Internet authentication service (IAS). An IAS server can offer authentication, authorization, and centralized accounting functions, as well as a central position for setting remote access criteria.

Layer two tunneling protocol (L2TP). In addition to the point-to-point tunneling protocol (PPTP), a remote access server running Windows 2000 includes the industrial standard layer two tunneling protocol (L2TP), which is used together with the IPSec to create protected VPN connections.

Support for AppleTalk Macintosh remote access clients. Windows 2000 remote access now supports the remote connections of Apple Macintosh remote access clients who use the AppleTalk protocol together with the point-to-point protocol (PPP).

IP multicast support. Thanks to the use of the Windows 2000 IGMP routing protocol, a remote access server can relay IP multicast traffic between connected remote access clients and the Internet or company network.

Account blocking. This is a protection function that blocks access after a set number of failed authentication attempts. Account blocking is designed to help prevent illicit connection attempts. By this we mean when an unauthorized user attempts to connect using an unknown username and a list of common words as passwords. Account blocking is disabled in the default setting.

Operations Improving Remote Access Management

Here is an important list of operations to carry out to ensure correct implementation and configuration of the remote access server:

Use DHCP to obtain IP addresses. If a DHCP server is installed, set up the remote access server so that DHCP is used to obtain IP addresses for remote access clients. If no DHCP server is installed, set up the remote access server with a static IP address pool that contains a subset of addresses from a subnet to which the remote access server is connected.

Use detailed authentication.

Do not use passwords based on names or words. Use advanced passwords that are more than eight characters long and that contain a combination of uppercase and lowercase letters, numbers, and acceptable punctuation. This prevents unauthorized users from hitting on the right passwords by sending commonly used names or words.

Even though the EAP-TLS protocol functions with certificates based on the system registry, for security reasons it is advisable to use EAP-TLS with smart cards.

If you are using MS-CHAP, use the version 2. You can request from Microsoft the most updated version of MS-CHAP for Windows NT version 4.0, Windows 98, or Windows 95, or for remote access clients running Windows NT.

Use automatic IPX network ID allocation.

Configure the remote access server so that the same IPX network ID is automatically allocated to all remote access clients.

Avoid setting up different remote access criteria for the same user.

If a user makes an incoming call using a multiple connection, all the connections must be made using the same remote access criterion as the first connection.

A Number of Detailed Procedures for Enabling the Routing and Remote Access Service

The routing service of Microsoft Windows 2000 Server offers multiprotocol routing services: LAN-to-LAN, LAN-to-WAN, VPN, and network address translation (NAT). Windows 2000 Server routing should be used by system administrators who are familiar with routing protocols and services, as well as with routable protocols such as TCP/IP, IPX, and AppleTalk.

You have to have administrator access to install and set up the Windows 2000 router. But first all the necessary hardware has to be installed correctly:

LAN or WAN card with a certified NDIS (network driver interface specification).

One or more compatible modems and a free COM port.

A multiport card to achieve adequate performance in multiple remote connections.

An ISDN card (if you use an ISDN line).

Check the Microsoft Windows Hardware Compatibility List on the Microsoft Web site to verify the compatibility of the hardware components of a computer running Windows 2000 Server.

Before proceeding with the installation and configuration of this complex of services, you should make sure you have done the following:

For a new network, decide which routing characteristics and protocols for the Windows 2000 router you want to use. For an existing network, determine which routing characteristics and protocols for the Windows 2000 router have to be activated.

Install and configure the protocols.

Activate and configure the routing and remote access service.

(Optional) Develop and distribute static IP routing.

(Optional) Develop and distribute the RIP routing protocol for IP.

(Optional) Add and configure the DHCP relay agent.

(Optional) Configure IP multicast support.

(Optional) Develop and distribute network address translation (NAT).

(Optional) Configure the appropriate IP or IPX packet filters.[1]

(Optional) Develop and distribute on-demand routing.

If you are not a domain administrator and if the server is a member of the Windows 2000 Active Directory domain, the domain administrator will have to add the server computer account to the RAS and IAS server security group in the server's domain. The domain administrator can add the computer account to the RAS and IAS server security group using users and computers in AD or else by using the command netsh ras add registered server.

Open Routing and Remote Access.

In the default setting, the local computer is listed as a server.

To add another server, right click on server status in the console, then choose add server.

In the add server dialog box, click the applicable option and then hit OK.

In the console, right click on the server you want to enable and then select configure and enable routing and remote access.

Follow the instructions in the routing and remote access wizard.

Note: To open routing and remote access, click on Start, choose Programs, then Administrative Tools, and then Routing and Remote Access.

Addition and Removal of Routing Protocols

To add an IP routing protocol

Open Routing and Remote Access.

In the console select General.

[1] IPX and SPX are very rarely used anymore; we have mentioned them here for the sake of completeness.

Pathway

Routing and Remote Access

Server name

IP Routing

General

Right click on General, then choose New routing protocol.

In the Routing protocols box, select the protocol you want to add, then hit OK.

If necessary, complete the configuration dialog windows for the protocol.

Note: To open Routing and Remote Access, click on Start, choose Programs, then Administrative Tools, and then Routing and Remote Access.

To delete an IP routing protocol.

Open Routing and Remote Access

In the console select an IP routing protocol.

Pathway:

Routing and Remote Access

server name

IP Routing

IP routing protocol

Right click on the IP routing protocol you want to eliminate and then choose delete.

Note: To open Routing and Remote Access, click on Start, choose Programs, then Administrative Tools, and then Routing and Remote Access.

Static Route Management

To add a static route

Open Routing and Remote Access.

In the console, select Static routes.

Pathway

Routing and Remote Access

server name

IP Routing or IPX Routing

Static Routes

Right click on Static routes, then do one of the following:

For a static IP route, click on New static route.

For a static IPX route, click on New Route.

In the Static route dialog box do one of the following:

For a static IP route, in the Interface, Destination, Network mask, Gateway, and Metric boxes, enter the interface, the destination, the network mask, the gateway, and the metric. If it is an on-demand connection interface, the Gateway box will not be available. You will also be able to select Use this route for on-demand connections for on-demand call-up connections for traffic on the route.

For a static IPX route, in Network number (hexadecimal), Next MAC hop Address (hexadecimal), Tick count, Hop count and Interface, enter the network number, the next MAC hop address, the tick count, the hop count, and the interface.

Note: To open Routing and Remote Access, click on Start, choose Programs, then Administrative Tools, and then Routing and Remote Access.

To delete a static route

Open Routing and Remote Access.

In the console select Static routes.

Pathway

Routing and Remote Access

server name

IP Routing or IPX Routing

Static routes

In the details box right click on the static route that you want to delete and then choose Delete.

You can also perform operations on default static IP routes.

To add a default static IP route

Open Routing and Remote Access.

In the console select Static routes.

Pathway

Routing and Remote Access

server name

IP Routing

Static routes

Right click on Static routes, then choose New static route.

In the Interface box, choose the interface that you want to use for the default route.

In the Destination box type 0.0.0.0.

In the Network mask box type 0.0.0.0.

In the Gateway box do one of the following:

If it is an on-demand connection interface, Gateway is not available. Select Use this route for on-demand connections for on-demand call-up connections for traffic on the route.

If the interface for this route is a LAN connection such as Ethernet or Token Ring, type in the IP address of the router interface on the same network segment as the LAN interface.

In the Metric box, type 1.

THE USE OF NAT FOR "SHARED" INTERNET CONNECTIONS

With the network address translation in Windows 2000 it is possible to configure the home or small business network so as to share a single connection to the Internet. NAT includes the following components:

Translation component

The NAT-enabled Windows 2000 router, henceforth called "NAT computer," functions as a network address translator, translating the IP addresses and the TCP/UDP port numbers of packets relayed between the private network and the Internet.

Addressing component

The NAT computer provides configuration information of the IP addresses to other computers in the private network. The addressing component is a simplified DHCP server that assigns an IP address, a subnet mask, a default gateway, the IP address of a DNS server, and the IP address of a WINS server. In order to automatically receive the IP configuration, the computers in the private network have to be configured as DHCP clients. The TCP/IP configuration of computers running Windows 2000, Windows NT, Windows 98, and Windows 95 is analogous to a DHCP client.

Name resolution component

The NAT computer becomes the DNS server and the WINS server for the other computers in the private network. When the NAT computer receives name resolution requests, it relays those requests to the DNS and WINS servers on the Internet for which it is configured, and returns the responses to the computer in the private network.

In planning this sort of implementation, please bear in mind the following: because NAT includes an addressing component and a name resolution component provided by the DHCP, WINS, and DNS services to the hosts on the private network, it is not possible to use the DHCP service or the DHCP relay agent if NAT addressing is enabled or the DNS service if NAT TCP/IP network name resolution is enabled.

How NAT Works in Practical Terms

If a network ID 10.10.0.0 is used for the intranet of a small company and if the use of the public address w1.x1.y1.z1 was granted by the Internet service provider (ISP), all the private addresses on 192.168.0.0 will be translated into the IP address w1.x1.y1.z1 by NAT. If several private addresses are translated into the same public address, NAT will use certain TCP and UDP ports in a dynamic fashion to distinguish one intranet position from another.

The addresses w1.x1.y1.z1 and w2.x2.y2.z2 represent the valid public IP addresses allocated by the Internet network information center (InterNIC) or by an ISP.

In the following illustration we have an example of using NAT to connect an intranet to the Internet in a transparent fashion.

If a private user at the address 10.10.0.10 uses a Web browser to connect to the Web server at the address w2.x2.y2.z2, an IP packet containing the following information will be created on the user's computer:

Destination IP address: w2.x2.y2.z2

Origin IP address: 10.10.0.10

Destination port: TCP 80

Origin port: TCP 1025

This IP packet is then sent to the NAT protocol, which translates the outgoing packet addresses into the following information:

Destination IP address: w2.x2.y2.z2

Origin IP address: w1.x1.y1.z1

Destination port: TCP 80

Origin port: TCP 5000

The NAT protocol keeps the mapping between the address {10.10.0.10, TCP 1025} and the address {w1.x1.y1.z1, TCP 5000} in a table.

The translated IP packet is sent via Internet. The response is sent back to the origin and received by the NAT protocol. The arriving packet contains the following public address information:

Destination IP address: w1.x1.y1.z1

Origin IP address: w2.x2.y2.z2

Destination port: TCP 5000

Origin port: TCP 80

The NAT protocol checks the translation table, maps the public addresses to the private ones and relays the packets to the computer whose address is 10.10.0.10. The relayed packet contains the following address information:

Destination IP address: 10.10.0.10

Origin IP address: w2.x2.y2.z2

Destination port: TCP 1025

Origin port: TCP 80

For outbound packets from the NAT protocol, the origin IP address (private address) is translated to the address allocated by the ISP (public address), and the TCP/UDP port numbers are translated to different TCP/UDP port numbers.

For inbound packets to the NAT protocol, the destination IP address (public address) is translated to the original intranet address (private address), and the TCP/UDP port numbers are translated to the original TCP/UDP port.

It should be pointed out that packets that contain the IP address only in the IP heading are translated appropriately by NAT. Packets that contain the IP address in the IP payload may not be translated correctly by NAT.

An important function is also provided by the Windows 2000 NAT Editor. The normal translation of network addresses is based on the translation of the following elements:

The IP addresses in the IP heading.

The TCP port numbers in the TCP heading.

The UDP port numbers in the UDP heading.

Any translation of elements other than the above requires additional processing and additional software components called NAT editors. A NAT editor modifies the IP packet beyond just translating the IP address in the IP heading, the TCP port in the TCP heading, and the UDP port in the UDP heading.

HTTP (hypertext transfer protocol) traffic on the Internet does not need, for example, a NAT editor because this type of traffic implies only the translation of the IP address in the IP heading and the TCP port in the TCP heading.

Below we illustrate two situations where NAT editors are required:

The IP address, the TCP port, or the UDP port is memorized in the payload.

The file transfer protocol (FTP) memorizes, for example, the numerical representation of the IP addresses in the FTP heading for the PORT FTP command. If NAT does not correctly translate the IP address in the FTP heading and regulate the flow of data, there may be connectivity problems.

The TCP or UDP port will not be used to identify the data flow.

Data using the point-to-point tunneling protocol (PPTP) do not use a TCP or UDP heading. Instead they use a generic routing encapsulation (GRE), and the tunnel ID memorized in that heading identifies the flow of data. If NAT does not correctly translate the IP tunnel in the GRE heading, there may be connectivity problems.

NAT editors are integrated into Windows 2000 for the following protocols:

FTP

ICMP

PPTP

NetBIOS on TCP/IP

The NAT routing protocol also includes proxy software for the following protocols:

H.323

Direct Play

LDAP-based ILS

RPC

We remind you that it is not possible to manage IPSec under Windows 2000 with the incorporated NAT editor.

Using IIS: From the Installation to the Administration

The information provided in this section refers to IIS version 5.0. For information on later versions of IIS, consult the documentation provided with the setup program.

Internet information services (IIS) 5.0 is installed by default with Windows 2000 Server. You can remove IIS or add new components using Add/Remove Programs in the control panel.

To Install IIS

Click Start, Settings, Control Panel, and then double click on Add/Remove Programs.

Select Add/Remove Windows Components, then the Components button, and then follow the instructions of installing, removing, or adding components to IIS.

NB:

If you upgrade to Windows 2000, IIS 5.0 will be installed with the default settings only if it was already installed on the previous version of Windows.

Software Checklist

Before you install IIS make sure the following are installed on your computer:

TCP/IP protocol and Windows connectivity utilities. If information is published on the Internet, your ISP will provide the IP address of the server, the subnet mask, and the IP address of the default gateway. The default gateway is the ISP computer through which your computer's exchanges with the Internet are routed.

We also recommend installing the following optional components:

The DNS service should be installed on a computer in the intranet. If your intranet is small you can use the hosts or Lmhosts files on all the computers in the network. Although it is optional, this allows users to use names in text format instead of IP addresses. Internet sites often use the DNS service. To connect to a site that is registered under a domain name, users can enter the domain name into the browser.

For security reasons, Microsoft recommends NTFS formatting of all the units used with IIS.

Microsoft FrontPage to create or edit HTML pages of a Web site. FrontPage is a what-you-see-is-what-you-get (WYSIWYG) editor with a user-friendly graphic user interface (GUI) for operations such as inserting tables, graphics, or text.

Microsoft Visual InterDev to create and develop interactive Web applications.

Related Notes

If IIS is already installed, you can get additional information from the online IIS documentation by typing http://localhost/iisHelp/ into your browser's address bar and hitting return.

Complete IIS documentation is available at http://windows.microsoft.com/windows2000/en/server/iis/.

Troubleshooting

If you have problems with the Web server, use the information provided in this section to resolve the problems described below.

Installation check

Once installation has been completed, you can check that it was done correctly using Internet Explorer to view the files in the home directory.

To check the installation of a Web site on the Internet

Make sure there are HTML files in the wwwroot folder of the Web server.

Start a Web browser, such as Internet Explorer, on a computer with an active Internet connection. You can do this on the computer you are checking, but it is preferable to use another computer in the network.

Type in the URL of the home directory of the new Web site.

The URL will be composed of "http://" followed by the name of the Web site, followed in turn by the pathway of the file you want to see. Please note the use of the slash. If your site is registered in DNS as "examples.microsoft.

com" and you want to view the file homepage.htm, which is located in the main directory of the home directory, type the following into the address bar: http://examples.microsoft.com/homepage.htm and hit return. You will see the home page.

To check the installation of a Web site on an intranet

Make sure the computer you are using has an active network connection and that the WINS server service is running or some other name resolution method.

Launch a Web browser such as Microsoft Internet Explorer.

Type in the URL of the home directory of the new server.

The URL will be composed of "http://" followed by the name of the server on the Windows network, followed in turn by by the pathway of the file you want to see. Please note the use of the slash. If your site is registered in the WINS server as "Admin1" and you want to see the file homepage.htm, which is located in the main directory of the home directory, type the following into the address bar: http://admin1/homepage.htm and hit return. You will see the home page.

Related Topics

If IIS is already installed, you can get additional information from the online IIS documentation by typing http://localhost/iisHelp/ into your browser's address bar and hitting return. Complete IIS documentation is available at http://windows.microsoft.com/windows2000/it/server/iis/.

At any rate, IIS is currently one of the most widely used Web servers. The Version 5.0 has been substantially reworked architecturally to the point where it has become a closely integrated component of Windows 2000 Advanced Server, Server, and—albeit with some limitations—Professional OS.

The main consequence of such a great success is that this system has drawn special attention from hackers and is thus very sensitive in terms of information security.

In this section we will look at aspects regarding the installation, configuration, and administration of IIS 5.0, dedicating particular attention to precautions to use in order to ensure an adequate level of security for the system.

In addition to the WWW service, other standard services generally associated with the IIS server include FTP, SMTP, and NNTP, and others that we will not be dealing with in this article, such as certificate server, index server, and Microsoft transaction server. Taken together, these services constitute a complete and integrated platform for e-business applications.

IIS: More Tips About Installation

It is a common (and misguided) notion that information security consists solely in the implementation of suitable measures to protect against external attacks. Actually it is impossible to know with any certainty or precision what it is you have to protect yourself against and what means you should use to do so unless you have carefully analyzed the situation, something which is of great help in avoiding poor choices that you will later rue.

The same is true, albeit in modified form, for the installation of software components, in particular those that may have an impact on the intrinsic security of an operating system such as a Web server. To simplify matters, we have listed below the steps to take in order to install IIS 5.0 correctly:

Carefully read the "Windows 2000 Security Guide" and the documentation provided with the server. You cannot expect to make a system secure without first finding out all you can about it. If this is the first installation it might not even be a bad idea to do a trial installation;

Carefully review the security policies regarding the filesystem, the configuration registry, password management, user rights, and all other aspects that have a direct or indirect relation with system security;

Review the documentation on all vulnerabilities that have affected IIS 5 in the past and download the patches provided by Microsoft;

Make sure the hardware on which IIS will be installed is truly adequate for the criticality of the service. This means computing power (CPU, RAM), data safeguarding (backup systems, RAID), and service continuity (UPS, clusters). After having resolved these issues, you will have to decide where to install your Web server;

Do not overlook the logistics aspects, which also have to be correlated to the criticality of the service. As a rule, it is preferable to have a temperature-controlled room with a fire protection system and limited access in order to exclude nonauthorized persons;

Choose the most suitable OS configuration. This means using servers configured in standalone mode that are not part of a Windows 2000 domain and that thus do not have trusted relations with other servers. This precaution helps prevent certain types of attacks based on privilege escalation or on exploiting trust;

In addition to the WWW and perhaps the FTP services, only run the other services that are truly necessary (link to the service configuration section);

Make sure that IP routing has been disabled to prevent undesired access to the intranet from the Internet and remove at the operating system level all protocols that are not absolutely necessary, with the sole exception of TCP/IP;

If you install IIS on a system that is directly accessible from the Internet, block all incoming traffic with a firewall or router and enable traffic again only after completing the configuration. This trick is very important since before all the necessary defenses have been set up, the server could be easily compromised.

IIS: Configuration and Administration

After you have installed the system you will have to perform the initial configuration and then administer it once it is up and running. In this case as well for clarity of exposition we will describe the steps to follow to render secure a standard installation of IIS 5.0:

Configure the user for the anonymous access created automatically during installation. The name is usually

IUSR_computername where the computer name is the name of the machine hosting IIS. This user has to have the minimum possible privilege level. You also have to make sure that on the properties tab the checkboxes User Cannot Change Password and Password Never Expires are ticked. Furthermore, the account has to be a local user and not require rights such as access this computer from network or log on as a batch job. If the Web site does not contemplate allowing anonymous access the best thing to do is to disable the IUSR_computername account;

Create at least two new groups of users to use with IIS. The first group will include users with system administrator functions. If the server handles a number of Web sites and/or services (WWW, FTP, etc.) it will be necessary to create an administrative account for each site or service. The second group will include users with nonadministrative privileges and will be the one held in consideration for the definition of NTFS authorization. In any case, the user IUSR_computername has to be associated exclusively with the second group and thus removed from the guest group, to which it is associated automatically by default;

Disable via the administration control panel the default site created during the installation. This operation has to be done not for to the WWW service, but also for all of the others (FTP, SMTP, NNTP);

Create, using the wizard, a new site that is different from the default site. Here you will have to choose the name, IP address, and the listening port, and define the root directory which should preferably reside in a partition different from that accommodating the operating system. It is also important that the minimal access level be set for this directory;

Edit the authorizations regarding the installation directory so that neither the everyone and guests groups nor the guest account have access privileges. Do not forget that after installation the everyone group automatically has full control privileges to the default home directory (for example C:Inetpub) and this could lead to the situation where the users in this group are used as vehicles for unwanted access;

Delete or move all directories containing example scripts that are generally installed automatically (even though there is an option not to install the examples). Although access to the examples is limited to the loopback address (localhost Â– 127.0.0.1), it is still preferable to delete or move the specified directories. If you should choose not to adopt this solution, then opportune authorizations have to be imposed that are only granted to administrative users. Table 2 presents the recommended authorizations for the various IIS directories.

Configure the auditing functions necessary for proper system monitoring. IIS memorizes all HTTP/FTP/SMTP events in incoming and outgoing server traffic while a general Â logging—which cannot be extended Â logging—is offered for the NNTP service.

Carefully choose the type of data to register in the log files so that important information may be obtained by examining them:

- a series of failed commands executed in sequence
- attempts to download/upload particular files from/to directories containing executables

Table 2: Recommended Authorizations for the Various IIS Directories

Type	Example Directory	Example Data	NTFS Authorizations	IIS 5 Authorizations
Static content	Inetpubwwwroothome Inetpubwwwrootimages Inetpubftprootftpfiles	HTML, images, download FTP	Administrators (Full Control); System (Full Control); WebAdmins (Read & Execute, Write, Modify); Authenticated Users (Read & Execute); Anonymous (Read & Execute);	Read
FTP upload	Inetpubftprootdropbox	Directory used as a place for users to store documents for review prior to the Admin making them available to everyone	Administrators (Full Control); WebAdmins or FTPAdmins (Read & Execute, Write, Modify); Specified Users (Write)	Write
Script	Inetpubwwwrootscripts	.asp	Administrators (Full Control); System (Full Control); WebAdmins(Read & Execute, Write, Modify); Anonymous (Read & Execute)	Read & Script
Other executables and include files	Inetpubwwwroot executables Inetpubwwwrootinclude	.exe, .dll, .cmd, .pl .inc, .shtml, .shtm	Administrators (Full Control); System (Full Control);	Read & Scripts, Executables

attempts to access internal files with the extension .bat or .cmd

requests coming from an identical IP address with characteristics indicating attempts at a Denial of Service (DoS) attack

Logging is enabled by default but you should still:

Change the pathway and name of the log file to hamper any attempts at altering it to mask illicit activities

Allow complete access to the log file directory only to administrative users

Monitor via Windows 2000 auditing the following types of events: Create Files / Write Data, Create Folders / Append Data, Delete Subfolders and Files, Delete, Change Permissions, or Take Ownership, which have their critical aspects for a Web server

Develop opportune log rotation rules on the basis of real needs (for example, a new file each day). It might also be useful to extend the information memorized in the file using the Extended Logging Properties function.

Delete all ISAPI extensions that are not strictly necessary. The mechanism provided by these extension is particularly powerful and flexible since it acts in such a way that different Web resources are managed in a completely transparent manner using different applications (in practice these are dll libraries or dynamic connections). However, in certain cases these applications have revealed specific vulnerabilities (buffer overflows). Hence, when they have no real use it is recommended to disable the associated extension in order to nip those risks in the bud. The Table 3 contains a list of typical ISAPI extensions in IIS with information on their field of application.

Download and use the tools available on the Microsoft Web site that may be helpful during the IIS configuration and/or startup phase (iisperm, hisecweb.inf, iislock).

BACKUP

Every information system is characterized by information having varying degrees of sensitivity. The nature of these data obviously varies depending on the role of the system, but nevertheless their importance implies the need to deploy suitable measures to prevent any harm from coming to them, and—and since there are no 100% guarantees in this respect—to allow them to be restored quickly if anything does happen so as to prevent negative consequences, be they economic or legal, or simply a question of image.

To this end, planned periodic backup procedures allow administrators easily to cope with all those situations, whatever the reason or nature (virus, hardware failure, malicious attacks), when an immediate recovery of data is necessary.

Naturally, for a backup policy to be truly effective it has to be well designed and engineered with respect to the system that is being protected.

In this section we will address the salient aspects of this theme, examining at some length the tool ntbackup available with the Windows 2000 operating system.

Table 3: List of Typical ISAPI Extensions in IIS with Information on Their Field of Application

Extension Type	Function
.htr	Web Password Reset
.idc	Internet Database Connector
.stm,.shtm,.shtml	Server Side Include
.printer	Internet printing
.cer	Represents a certificate
.cdx	Active Channel File Definition
.asa	Active Server Application
.htw,.ida,.idq	Index Server

Identifying Data

The first concrete necessity is to identify which data you are going to protect by means of backup. It would be inconceivable to back up every disk on the server every time you perform a backup, and hence the data especially requiring protection have to be singled out (for a Web server, as in our case, a considerable part of these data are the html pages, the scripts, and everything else that is part of the server resources). Additionally, but at greater time intervals, it is also a good idea to take a snapshot of the state of the system (startup and configuration files, configuration registry), and to create an emergency boot disk to be used should the system ever be unable to boot up on its own.

Choice of Support

The choice of support for backing up data will depend on the quantity of data to be copied and on the length of time that they will need to be kept. Fortunately there is currently a vast range of products on the market with prices and characteristics to satisfy a great variety of requirements. The most important thing is to make a decision keeping in mind not only your needs but also all aspects related to security (for example, opt for removable supports that can be kept in a safe place and/or write-once-read-many supports that are intrinsically more secure).

Scheduling

The time intervals between the data backup operations have to be calibrated on the basis of concrete needs, the speed at which the saved data are modified, and their importance.

Using ntBackup

This operating system utility meets data copying and restoration needs in a more than satisfactory fashion either using its GUI or through commands on the prompt line (although with some limitations in this latter case). Although there are certainly more sophisticated software products on the market, the ability to rely on an application already integrated into the operating system is nothing to turn your nose up at. Essentially, the application allows you to carry out the following operations:

Backup of files or directories on removable or non-removable supports
Data restore
Backup of data regarding system state
Restoration of data regarding system state
Creation of an emergency boot disk

To back up files or folders you have to be the owner with authorization to read, read/run, or edit, or be a local system administrator or backup operator. Clearly the best thing to do from the security standpoint is to create a special user and assign it to the backup operators. It is also a good idea to limit access to the backup files by ticking the checkbox Owner or administrator backup data access only in the dialog box Information on backup process.

Backing Up Your Data

To run backup using the graphic user interface you will have to:

Select the files, directories, and drives to be backed up
Select the backup support or pathway
Select the options
Launch the process or else schedule it for a later time

There are five different types of backup to choose from:

normal: A normal backup copies all selected files and marks each file as having been backed up (in other words, the archive attribute is cleared). With normal backups, you need only the most recent copy of the backup file or tape to restore all of the files. You usually perform a normal backup the first time you create a backup set;

copy: A copy backup copies all selected files but does not mark each file as having been backed up (in other words, the archive attribute is not cleared). Copying is useful if you want to back up files between normal and incremental backups because copying does not affect these other backup operations;

daily: A daily backup copies all selected files that have been modified the day the daily backup is performed. The backed-up files are not marked as having been backed up (in other words, the archive attribute is not cleared);

differential: A differential backup copies files created or changed since the last normal or incremental backup. It does not mark files as having been backed up (in other words, the archive attribute is not cleared). If you are performing a combination of normal and differential backups, restoring files and folders requires that you have the last normal as well as the last differential backup;

incremental: An incremental backup backs up only those files created or changed since the last normal or incremental backup. It marks files as having been backed up (in other words, the archive attribute is cleared). If you use a combination of normal and incremental backups, you will need to have the last normal backup set as well as all incremental backup sets in order to restore your data;

The combination of normal and incremental backup requires a minimum amount of memory and is thus the fastest method. However, because backup data can be archived on different disks or tapes, the restore operation is relatively complex and time consuming. Conversely, the combination of normal and differential backup takes longer, especially if the data are frequently modified, but it is easier to restore the data since the backup set resides on just a few disks or tapes.

Restoring Data

In order to restore data you will need to:

Select the files you want to restore from the catalog
Select the destination for the files and/or folders
Select the options
Launch the restore process
Use the command line

The utility ntbackup can be run from the command prompt or a batch file without having to use the graphic interface but this involves two principal limitations:

You can only back up entire folders and not single files. You can get around this by indicating a .bks file containing a complete list of files to back up (however, you will need to use the GUI to create the .bks file)

Wildcard characters are not supported

A complete list of the command line parameters can be found in the online guide.

HARDENING AND SECURITY MEASURES

Mechanisms that make it possible to identify changes at the filesystem level may be considered an integral part of any self-respecting security strategy. The reason is very simple. When a host is compromised by a malicious attack, one of the first things that the attacker does is to install "trojanized" versions of a number of important system executables, edit essential configuration files, or install other programs to open back doors in the system.

In this section we will examine the function of one of the best-known tools for verifying the integrity of the filesystem. It is known as Tripwire, and here we will be looking at version 2.2.1 for Windows NT/2000.

Tripwire was originally developed for the UNIX platform by Gene Kim and Eugene Spafford in the early 1990s but was later adapted to other platforms. The software is sold commercially by Tripwire Inc. (http://www.tripwire.com or http://www.tripwiresecurity.com).

Tripwire is a fully fledged member of the host-based intrusion detection systems (HIDS) because it is normally installed on the host it is supposed to protect. It focuses on the filesystem and not on network connections or the TCP/IP layer.

The application acquires a snapshot of the files selected for monitoring and catalogs them by getting a digital fingerprint for each. The fingerprint is a one-way hash that allows Tripwire to detect changes to any of the files at any time.

When changes occur that do not correspond to particular conditions, these changes are reported to the administrator in various ways (reports, email). The administrator can then confirm the changes, updating the internal signatures database, or else realize that they are unauthorized modifications and seek to restore the previous situation.

Installing Tripwire

There are no particular difficulties in installing the software because it is sold in the form of an archive with its own setup procedure.

During the setup process the user is asked to make choices regarding the configuration, which can be modified at any point. Most importantly, the user is asked to specify a "passphrase" that the software will use to digitally sign the files used by the application.

Function of Tripwire

Tripwire uses an architecture based on a set of files, each of which performs a specific task:

Policy file: this contains a series of rules specifying which elements of the filesystem and Windows registry to monitor, the data that have to be collected for each of them, and perhaps the email address for notification of any suspicious activity

Database files: Together, these represent the snapshot of the system. Obviously this snapshot has to be taken when you are 100% sure about the integrity of the system. Every time there is a system integrity check, this snapshot is compared with the current state of the objects in order to highlight all the possible differences or changes

Report files: these contain the information deriving from a check of filesystem integrity and display any anomalies found

Configuration file: this contains specific information for Tripwire operations and is initially written during the setup procedure

Key files: these files contain the public and private keys used to encrypt the files used by the application in order to prevent them from being modified in undesired ways. The keys, in turn, are encrypted by means of a secret passphrase

Before beginning it is absolutely necessary to modify the policies file. Here you can look at the file twpol.txt, which is installed with the software and contains a set of rather general rules.

The policies file has to be edited using any text editor so that its rules will be specific to the needs of the server to be protected (consult the exhaustive online manual for an explanation of the meaning of the various rule properties and attributes). The modifications can be saved in another text file (with a well-chosen name) and has to be digitally signed and installed as the new policies file before initializing the internal database. In order to do this you have to open a prompt window and type in the following command: twadmin --create-polfile <name of policies text file>

The new file will be installed in the folder indicated as the destination in the configuration file. After this it is possible to initialize the internal database by typing the command: tripwire --init-verbose

A signatures database will then be created in the folder indicated by the DBFILE variable in the configuration file.

Database Integrity Checks and Updates

Given the importance of the filesystem, it is opportune that its integrity be checked on a regular basis. The scheduling will depend on the real needs, but as a rule of thumb, a daily check is advisable to prevent any unpleasant surprises. The process can be launched in a prompt window (or using a batch file) with the following command: "tripwire --check"

With this instruction, the software checks the integrity of the filesystem on the basis of the specially created policies. It prints to screen a list of any anomalies and saves a copy of the report in binary format in the folder indicated by the variable REPORTFILE in the configuration file. It is also possible to carry out checks rule by rule, or by severity level of the anomalies, or for a specific section of the policies file (check the user's manual).

If and when anomalies are found, the internal database has to be updated so that it reflects the current state of the system and so that "normal" modifications will not be reported in the future as critical situations: "tripwire --update --twrfile <name of file report>"

The database can also be updated immediately after the check when the check is initiated by the command: "tripwire --check –interactive"

Synchronization has to be carried out in the event of changes to the policies file when:

It is necessary to add new objects to the list of monitored system components;

It is necessary to modify the rules because they are causing too many false positives;

You want to change the recipient of the email notifications or the way the rules are grouped;

In all these cases you have to take the following steps:

Create an ASCII version of the policies file via the command twadmin --print-polfile > <name of text file>

Edit the text file as desired

Instruct the software to accommodate the modifications via the command tripwire --update-policy <name of text file>

As a default setting the update process is carried out with a high level of security level in that it launches a simultaneous integrity check according to the new rules and displays any violation of old policy rules that is also covered by the new rules. Since the database is not updated if anomalies are found you have to make sure that the reported events are in fact normal, and if so, proceed with the update launching the process at a low security level via the command: tripwire --update-policy --secure-mode low <name of the policies text file>

FORENSIC ACQUISITION UTILITIES

Although security is not the main topic in this chapter, we might mention here some free utilities for carrying out initial incident response procedures in the event of an attack. The forensic acquisition utilities (FAUs) are a collection of utilities and libraries to manage digital investigations in a Windows environment. These utilities are widely used in information security to sterilize media for forensic duplication, discovering the position of logical volume information, verifying evidence integrity, and so forth. FAU should be used with a hardware write blocker. These utilities represent a very useful set of tools that includes the most up-to-date versions of the most widely used open-source digital forensics utilities.

FAU is available from the Web site http://users.erols.com/gmgarner/forensics/ and includes a modified version of Ulrich Drepper's MD5 checksum implementation in Windows DLL format. FAU is compatible with Windows 2000 and subsequent versions of Windows.

CONCLUSION

In this chapter we have sought to blend a high level description of the Windows 2000 operating system with some introductory technical guidelines and tips for people who have had to reckon, willingly or unwillingly, with the world of Windows. The platform is still widely used and deserves a bit of attention, even though on the formal level, Microsoft's support for this system is being phased out. But there are still so many sites based on Windows 2000 that it is almost impossible to avoid them. Our goal here has been to provide a number of basic operational guidelines to ensure the correct use of this operating system and to lay out the groundwork for the development of a new platform.

GLOSSARY

Active directory (AD): Active directory is Microsoft's trademarked directory service, an integral part of the Windows 2000 architecture.

Digital signature: An electronic signature that can be used to authenticate the identity of the sender of a message or the signer of a document, and possibly to ensure that the original content of the message or document that has been sent is unchanged.

DNS SECurity: A set of extensions to the DNS system that are designed to prevent attacks agains the DNS system as well as DNS hijacking, which directs the user to an erroneous Web site. DNSSec uses a digital signature to ensure that the correct IP address is used. For more information, visit www.dnssec.org.

Dynamic host configuration protocol (DHCP): A consolidated standard that greatly simplifies administration of networks based on TCP/IP protocols.

Elliptical curve cryptography (ECC): A public-key encryption technique based on elliptic curve theory that can be used to create faster, smaller, and more efficient cryptographic keys.

Fault tolerance: The ability of a system or component to continue normal operation despite the presence of hardware or software faults.

Multithreading: Multitasking within a single program. It allows multiple streams of execution to take place concurrently within the same program, each stream processing a different transaction or message. In order for a multithreaded program to achieve true performance gains, it must be run in a multitasking or multiprocessing environment, which allows multiple operations to take place.

NetBIOS: An acronym for Network Basic Input/Output System. The NetBIOS API allows applications on separate computers to communicate over a local area network. In modern networks, it normally runs over TCP/IP (NBT), giving each computer in the network both a NetBIOS name and an IP address corresponding to a (possibly different) host name. Older operating systems ran NetBIOS over NetBEUI. NetBIOS provides services related to the session layer of the OSI model.

Partitioning: The purpose of partitioning is to create a logical file structure for the operating system to access and to divide a portion of the disk drive to be used by more than one disk operating system.

PKI (public key infrastructure): A framework for creating a secure method for exchanging information based on public-key cryptography.

Tombstoning: Refers to a discrete component (resistor, capacitor) that has turned straight up instead of laying flat as it goes through the soldering process. It can be caused by uneven amounts of soldering paste at different ends of the component or by shadows on the board causing different temperatures at the ends.

WINS: Windows Internet Naming Service (WINS) is Microsoft's implementation of NetBIOS name server (NBNS) on Windows, a name server and service for NetBIOS computer names.

CROSS REFERENCES

See *Ethernet LANs; Linux Operating System; Local Area Networks; Optical Fiber LANs; Token Ring LANs.*

FURTHER READING

Asche, R. 1995a. Using the Windows NT custom driver wizard. Redmond, WA: Microsoft Corporation.

Asche, R. 1995b. Wizards simplify Windows NT kernel-mode driver design. Redmond, WA: Microsoft Corporation.

Baker, A. 1997. The Windows NT device driver book. A guide for programmers. Upper Saddle River, NJ: Prentice Hall PTR.

Booth, R. 1997. Inner loops: A sourcebook for fast 32-bit software development. Reading, MA: Addison-Wesley Developers Press.

Brelsford, H. M. 2000. Windows 2000 server secrets. Foster City, CA: IDG Books Worldwide, Inc.

Brown, R. and J. Kyle. 1991. PC interrupts: A programmer's reference to BIOS, DOS, and third-party calls Second Edition. Reading, MA: Addison-Wesley Publishing Company.

Brown, R. and J. Kyle. 1993. PC Interrupts: A programmer's reference to BIOS, DOS, and third-party calls Second Edition. Reading, MA: Addison-Wesley Publishing Company.

Brown, R. and J. Kyle. 1994. Network Interrupts: A programmer's reference to network APIs. Reading, MA: Addison-Wesley Publishing Company.

Chappell, D. 1999. Understanding Windows 2000 distributed services. Redmond, WA: Microsoft Press.

Chappell, G. 1994. DOS internals. Reading, MA: Addison-Wesley Publishing Company.

Custer, H. 1993. Inside Windows NT. Redmond, WA: Microsoft Press.

Custer, H. 1994. Inside the Windows NT file system. Redmond, WA: Microsoft Press.

Dabak, P., S. Phadke, and M. Borate. 1999. Undocumented Windows NT. Foster City, CA: IDG Books Worldwide.

Dekker, E. N., and J. M. Newcomer. 1999. Developing Windows NT device drivers: A programmer's handbook. Reading, MA: Addison Wesley Longman.

Gardinier, K. and C. Amaris. 2001. Windows 2000 performance tuning and optimization. San Francisco: Osborne/McGraw Hill.

Microsoft Corporation. 1999. Microsoft Windows 2000 server resource kit. Redmond, WA: Microsoft Press.

Russel, C., S. Crawford, and J. Gerend. 2002. Microsoft Windows 2000 server administrator's companion, 2nd edition. Redmond, WA: Microsoft Press.

Savill, J. 1999. The Windows NT and Windows 2000 answer book: A complete resource from the desktop to the enterprise. Upper Saddle River, NJ: Pearson Education.

Sjouwerman, S., B. Shilmover, and J. M. Stewart. 2000. Windows 2000 system administrator's black book: The systems administrator's essential guide to installing, configuring, operating, and troubleshooting a Windows 2000 network. Coriolis Group Books.

Smith, B. M., D. Toombs, M. Minasi, and C. Anderson. 2002. Mastering Windows 2000 server, 4th edition. Berkeley, CA: Sybex.

Solomon, D. A., and M. Russinovich. 2000. Inside Microsoft Windows 2000. Redmond, WA: Microsoft Press.

Linux Operating System

Mark Shacklette, *The University of Chicago*

INTRODUCTION

Linux is a free operating system (OS) originated by Linus Torvalds (cf. http://en.wikipedia.org/wiki/Linus_Torvalds) and further developed by thousands of others interested in the success of the free operating system. Although Linus originally contributed the initial kernel for what has become known as the Linux OS, he has overseen the continued development of the kernel, as well as the growth of what has become known as the Linux OS, often referred to simply as Linux. Linux benefits from the inclusion of free software from other sources, including most notably GNU software provided by Richard Stallman's Free Software Foundation (FSF). So although Linus originally contributed the kernel and still manages it, all the supporting standard Unix utilities (such as grep, tar, emacs, make, sed, and most notably the C compiler and symbolic debugger) are provided by the FSF. The graphical user interface for Linux, known as X Windows, is currently provided by the X.Org Foundation. The Linux OS is an open-source system developed under the GNU Public License, which stipulates that the source code may be freely copied and compiled, with the only stipulation that one cannot at any point take away the free right to copy, and any additions to the source also become public and freely available under the GNU License. Begun in 1991, Linux has grown from the interest of a very few highly-focused software developers to an industrial-strength OS deployed on millions of computers, from small portable devices to large mainframes.

HISTORICAL CONTEXT: UNIX OPERATING SYSTEMS PRIOR TO LINUX

AT&T Unix

Ken Thompson and his associates at AT&T Bell Labs delivered the first release of their Unix OS in November of 1971. The Unix OS was one of the world's first multiuser, multiprocessing operating systems, meaning that multiple users could be logged on to the same computer each running different programs, and the operating system could handle the load efficiently either by swapping the various users' programs onto a single processor, very quickly so that it would appear that the users' programs were actually running at the same time (a strategy known as "task swapping").

Because AT&T was prohibited from engaging in any business activity that did not directly deal with the delivery of phone service as a result of an antitrust decree handed down in the 1950s to AT&T and Western Electric Company, it decided to license the source code of its new Unix operating system to educational institutions for a minimal licensing fee (as low as 50 dollars). The power and flexibility of Unix made it an immediate hit, and the fact that the source code was easily available meant that the user community could contribute to the ongoing development of the operating system, by submitting bug fixes and enhancements back to AT&T Bell Labs for their incorporation.

In the fall of 1975, Ken Thompson, Unix's original creator (along with several others, including Rudd Canaday and Dennis Ritchie) was invited to visit the University of California, Berkeley, and offer a course in operating systems. He brought Unix along with him to demonstrate. Several individuals at Berkeley were impressed (many had already been using various versions of Unix by that time), and Ken helped to port one of the releases of Unix over onto Berkeley's Digital Equipment Company PDP computer (the PDP 11/70). One of Ken Thompson's students at Berkeley was Bill Joy, who ported Unix to DEC's new computer, the VAX 11/780. The versions of Unix developed at Berkeley under Bill Joy's direction came to be known as BSD Unix, which stood for Berkeley Software Distribution. BSD Unix came to be an important alternative to AT&T Unix.

Prior to 1976, Unix computers were stand-alone, meaning that they were not networked, although multiple users could be logged into the computer at the same time. This changed when Mike Lesk of AT&T developed a program called UUCP (for Unix to Unix Copy), which allowed two Unix computers that were networked together to be able to copy files back and forth between them.

Another important late 1970s event took place in 1978, when Eric Schmidt, working at Berkeley on his master's thesis, developed a networking program for BSD Unix that he called "Berknet," which allowed up to 26 different Unix computers to be interconnected together over a network. Berknet provided numerous capabilities including file transfer as well as email. By 1983, partly through the funding support of the U.S. Department of Defense Advanced Research Projects Agency (DARPA), Berkeley BSD version 4.2 was released in September of 1983 and supported the Berkeley socket interface. The Berkeley socket interface has since been adopted as the backbone of the Internet, and is supported by all networked computers, including Microsoft Windows OS as well as, of course, Linux (Stevens, 1990).

The Unix Divorce

By the late 1970s, AT&T realized that it had a valuable product in Unix, but the 1956 antitrust decision still prohibited AT&T from profiting from it. However, in 1982 AT&T was forced by another antitrust decision to dissolve into multiple "Baby Bells." The immediate effect of this dissolution of AT&T was that Unix now for the first time was considered intellectual property owned by AT&T, and no one was allowed to publish the source code in any form. Now, instead of being able to obtain Unix (along with the source code for modification) for a licensing fee under 100 dollars, corporations had to pay license prices skyrocketed in 1993 to sums as high as 200,000 dollars for a single source license (Salus, 1994, 222). AT&T threatened to sue any individual or organization that infringed on its copyright and it did so. Individuals as well as some institutions could no longer afford to license Unix on the scale and with the freedom that they had been able to previously. BSD Unix had also gone commercial in the form of Sun Microsystem's SunOS (Sun was started by former Berkeley student Bill Joy). Eventually other companies started selling their own versions of Unix, including IBM (AIX), Hewlett-Packard (HPUX), Silicon Graphics (IRIX), and Digital Equipment Corporation (Digital Unix). There were dozens of other offerings as well.

Richard Stallman and the GNU Project

The commercialization of Unix prompted outrage and resentment in the academic world, because students had become used to having a wonderful platform on which to develop and work, not to mention the creative opportunities to work together to enhance a "community" OS effort. One of the individuals severely bothered by the commercialization of Unix was an MIT researcher by the name of Richard Stallman. In 1984, Stallman responded by creating the Free Software Foundation (FSF) and the GNU Public License (GPL). "GNU" is a recursive anagram for "GNU is Not Unix"—indicating that Unix had by that time become a "four-letter-word." The GPL was designed, unlike most copyright licenses, not to prohibit reuse of licensed software, but rather, precisely to perpetually protect the free use of the licensed software, so that it would forever be free and no one could revoke that freedom and claim it as proprietary by not releasing source code along with binary code. This does not mean that software released under the GPL becomes "public domain," but rather that any software obtained under the GPL can be freely copied, compiled, used, republished, and cannot at any point in the future be made proprietary. Code under the GPL must always remain free and available as source code—it cannot be redistributed purely as binary code. Stallman began an effort to create Unix-like software and publish it under the GPL. Central to this effort was the creation of the GNU C compiler, a number of core Unix utilities, and a user interface or shell known as Bash (Bourne Again Shell—a play on words of the original Unix shell written by Stephen Bourne at AT&T, known simply as "sh"). A goal of the GNU effort was to create a truly free Unix-based operating system, which Stallman dubbed GNU Hurd. The development of Hurd began in earnest in 1990. It was and is a microkernel-based operating system (see the discussion of Minix below) based mainly on the CMU (Carnegie Mellon University) Mach code base now known as gnumach. Mach helps to form the core of several Unix-like operating systems, including Hurd as well as Apple's popular MAC OS X operating system.

Early development of Hurd was slow, partially because of Mach's complexity and partly because of licensing issues related to Carnegie Mellon University and the release of Mach under the GPL. Although discussions about Hurd had been progressing for over five years, there was still no operational GNU operating system as the 1980s ended and the 1990s began. There was a vacuum begging to be filled.

Minix

In 1987 Andrew Tanenbaum, an American by birth teaching in Amsterdam, Netherlands, at the Vrije Universiteit, published a book titled *Operating Systems: Design and Implementation*. A large part of the book is dedicated to the discussion of a microkernel, a concept that incarnates Antoine de St. Exupery's idea that perfection is achieved not when there is nothing left to add, but rather, when there is nothing left to take away. A microkernel is a minimalist operating system kernel that provides only the most basic of system services, such as memory and thread management, along with basic interprocess communication. All other common operating system features, such as device drivers, file management, networking, and so on are delivered as modules (called "servers") that run as any other user program on top of the microkernel. The advantages of a microkernel include the ability to "plug and play" different filesystems, devices, networking services, and so on, without burdening the core operating system kernel with the overhead. A "monolithic" kernel, on the other hand, incorporates many services into the kernel itself, thus making the kernel itself larger but also faster and easier to manage and develop. In order to elucidate the concepts of microkernels in his textbook, Tanenbaum included in an appendix the source code for a Unix-based microkernel implementation that he called (punning on the minimalist concepts of microkernels) "minix."

During his undergraduate studies at the University of Helsinki, Linus Torvalds studied Tanenbaum's textbook and started playing with the ideas and the code. The problem was that Minix (at the time) could not be altered by the public—in the sense that no one but Tanenbaum himself was allowed to make changes to the source code and then redistribute those changes. This lack of freedom is primarily what prompted Linus to begin, in April of 1991, to write the basics of a new operating system kernel. The initial development of the kernel which eventually came to be known as "Linux" (Linus had originally wanted to call it "freax") was done using the GNU C compiler running on Minix. Other factors that enabled Linux to succeed include an effort initiated by the Institute of Electrical and Electronics Engineers (IEEE) to form a committee in 1986 to define a formal standard for Unix-based operating systems, to try and regain some compatibility among a multitude of competing Unix systems. This standard was called POSIX, which stands for portable operating systems interface based on Unix.

Another critical success factor for the success of Linux was an announcement by AT&T, in 1987, to purchase shares in Sun Microsystems, which resulted in a powerful marriage between the BSD and AT&T versions. The first major result of this new relationship was the integration of SVR3 and 4BSD into a new operating system offering from Sun, called Solaris. The second result of this marriage between AT&T and Sun was the creation of the Open Software Foundation (OSF), a group formed by the "other" Unix vendors, who did not want to be left out in the cold. This group included Digital, IBM, and Hewlett-Packard, among others. Without the POSIX and OSF efforts it is doubtful that Linux (or any other Unix operating system) would have had the success that it has had (Tanenbaum, 2001).

LINUX DEVELOPMENT

The Early Years: 1991–1995

On August 25th, 1991, Linus Torvalds posted a now-famous post on the Usenix newsgroup comp.os.minix

(http://groups.google.com/group/comp.os.minix/msg/b813d52cbc5a044b?output=gplain). It read:

> Hello everybody out there using minix -
>
> I'm doing a (free) operating system (just a hobby, won't be big and
>
> professional like gnu) for 386(486) AT clones. This has been brewing
>
> since april, and is starting to get ready. I'd like any feedback on
>
> things people like/dislike in minix, as my OS resembles it somewhat
>
> (same physical layout of the file-system (due to practical reasons)
>
> among other things).
>
> I've currently ported bash(1.08) and gcc(1.40), and things seem to work.
>
> This implies that I'll get something practical within a few months, and
>
> I'd like to know what features most people would want. Any suggestions
>
> are welcome, but I won't promise I'll implement them :-)
>
> Linus (torva...@kruuna.helsinki.fi)
>
> PS. Yes - it's free of any minix code, and it has a multi-threaded fs.
>
> It is NOT protable [sic] (uses 386 task switching etc), and it probably never
>
> will support anything other than AT-harddisks, as that's all I have :-(.

The interesting thing to note here is that in the four months between April and August of 1991, Linus had created, from scratch, a "minix-lookalike" kernel that was capable of running the GNU C compiler. In September of 1991, version 0.01 of Linux was released, which included over 10,000 lines of code. It also sported the GNU bash shell (Bourne Again Shell). People rushed to compile the entire GNU FSF corpus of utilities onto the new Linux kernel. Thus Linux grew substantially by standing on the shoulders of existing code provided by the FSF and others.

At this early stage, Linux had no networking capability, ran only on an Intel 80386 processor, and had limited support for external devices such as tape drives. The early 1991 releases of Linux still required Minix to compile the system, and used a Minix filesystem (which had significant restrictions—including 14-character filename and 64 megabyte filesystem limits). Early Linux was not a stand-alone system, in the sense that it could be built and installed by itself. This changed with the December 1991 release of Linux 0.11, the first stand-alone version of Linux in the sense that it could be compiled under itself. In January of 1992 postings about Linux were no longer going to the comp.os.minix newsgroup. Instead, they were going to alt.os.linux, with the comp.os.linux newsgroup being created later in March of that year.

Two things principally distinguished this fledgling operating system from its Minix predecessor. First, the kernel was a monolithic kernel rather than a microkernel like Minix. Second, Linux was soon released under the GPL, which made it "free" for modification and republication as long as any new enhancements were also released under the GPL. Another thing that distinguished Linux from Minix was release 0.95 in March of 1992. This was the first release that supported the X Windows graphical interface. This was a huge step forward in the acceptance of Linux, as it promised for the first time the ability to run a windowing interface on top of the text-based shell. In contrast, Minix did not add X Windows support until 14 years later, in the 3.1.2 version of Minix that was released in March of 2006.

For the next two years, Linux hovered at various minor releases of 0.99, slowly growing in capability and extent and size. The first official release of Linux 1.0.0, in March of 1994, marked the growth of the code base to 17 times its original size, partly as a result of the inclusion of TCP/IP networking and Berkeley sockets into the kernel. Also included in the 1.0 release was support for multiple filesystems, SCSI storage devices, and running IP over a network (for modem-based network connections). It was also at this time that the versioning patterns for Linux were created. Kernels with odd-numbered minor releases (1.1, 1.3, 1.5) were designated as developer-targeted kernels, whereas kernels with even-numbered minor releases (1.0, 1.2, 1.4, 1.6) were designated as stable user-targeted kernels suitable for inclusion into released distributions. By the kernel 1.2 release in March of 1995, one year after the release of 1.0, Linux's size had almost doubled once again to over 175,000 lines of code. Along with the 1.2 release was the beginning of the move from a strict Intel-only platform, with code becoming available for Sparc-, Alpha-, and MIPS-based systems. Along with each new release came significantly increased capabilities. In June of 1996, Linux 2.0 was released, which included a fully functional 64-bit implementation for the Alpha and support for multiprocessor-based systems. Improvements were also delivered to memory management, TCP/IP networking, kernel threads, and support for loadable modules.

Since 1991, over 10,000 individuals across the world have contributed in some way or another to the development of Linux, either to the kernel itself or its myriad utilities and supporting environments. There are an estimated 20 to 30 million users of Linux throughout the world. Much of the reason for this is the development of easy to install packages, or distributions, that have been made available over the years. A distribution combines a default release of the Linux kernel, along with X Windows, graphical environments including Gnome and KDE, packaged into an easily installed and configured installation, complete with versioning of existing components. The first major advance in this distribution effort was made by Patrick Volkerding who released a packaging of Linux he called Slackware on July 16th, 1993. Other distributions followed on as companies provided copies of source trees on CDs. These included Yggdrasil and Walnut Creek. Today, there are over a hundred Linux distributions. The most recognized include SUSE Linux, Mandrake Linux, Debian Linux and Gentoo Linux, and RedHat, some of which are backed by public corporations. As an example of the extraordinary development effort that went into Linux during its first three years of existence, at the 1994 Comdex Conference on computing in Las Vegas, the staff of Yggdrasil demonstrated an example of the Windows game Solitaire running on a Linux system under WINE (the Windows Emulator for Linux) (cf. http://www.linuxjournal.com/article/0045).

In March of 1994, *The Linux Journal*, the premier journal devoted to all things Linux, began publication. It featured a comparison of Linux and OS2 in its first issue, and included an interview with Linus Torvalds. Over the past 12 years, *The Linux Journal*, along with other print magazines and online magazines, including *Linux Magazine* and *Linux Gazette* (an online publication that began in July of 1995), have aided in communicating information for Linux users across the world. In addition to journals, Matt Welsh, who originally managed the Linux Documentation Project (http://www.tldp.org/), wrote (with Lar Kaufman) one of the first books published on Linux in 1995 titled *Running Linux*.

The Open-Source Revolution

The powerful combination of the already-existing GNU tools and compilers, combined in 1991 with a GPL-based operating system kernel in the form of Linux, catapulted the adoption of free software into the fast lane. Although throughout the 1990s Linux was just catching on, by the late 1990s it had proven itself a viable free platform, and with a couple of other key successes in the open-source world, such as the Apache Web Server, which accounted for almost 70 percent of the Web server market by 2000, and by 2000 was running almost one-third of the world's Internet servers (http://www.leb.net/hzo/ioscount/). A 2004 *Information Week* survey found that roughly 67 percent of the companies questioned use open source or free software products, with an additional 16 percent planning to begin using it by 2005, and only 17 percent of those polled having little or no intention of incorporating open-source products into their environments over the near future (cf. http://www.informationweek.com/story/showArticle.jhtml?articleID=51201599&tid=5979). Although most successful open-source products, including Sendmail, PHP, OpenSSH, MySQL, to name a few, are not dependent on Linux, all these open-source products run on Linux and other Unix variants. The success of Linux has had a fundamental legitimizing effect in the further worldwide corporate adoption of other open-source products.

Linux in the 21st Century

As of August 21, 2006, Linux was 15 years old. In Internet years, that's a long time. Linux is still firmly grounded in its original philosophy as interpreted by Linus Torvalds and based in fundamental Unix principles. Linux development continues through the efforts of thousands of individuals who volunteer and provide their time and resources in order to improve "their" operating system. Today, the Linux kernel (2.6.17) has 6.9 million lines of code supporting close to two dozen different target architectures. As new hardware devices come into the market, new device drivers are written for the drivers and are incorporated into the Linux kernel. When Linus began developing Linux in 1991, he did not have to worry about high-speed networks, USB flash drives, wireless networks, or Bluetooth devices. As these and other new technologies have come into play, new Linux drivers have been written to support them. Linux continues to grow as a solid operating platform based on the sound fundamental principles that gave it its birth.

Today, Linux has the support of numerous major corporations, including IBM, Hewlett Packard, Sun, and almost every major corporation with the exception of Microsoft. Commercial and open-source databases targeting Linux include Oracle, DB2, MySQL, Sybase, Informix, PostgreSQL, Ingres, to name a few, almost every major DBMS in the world, with the exception of Microsoft SQL Server. Development environments supporting the GNU development tools are highly available as well. Whether Linux can sustain itself amidst all this growth in interest in terms of support, and keep its core integrity in terms of reliability, is yet to be seen.

OPERATING SYSTEM STRUCTURE

Fundamental Structure

The structure of Linux resembles other Unix-like OS (for more detailed information on Unix structure, see Shacklette 2004). This includes the typical Unix hierarchical filesystem, files and directories and permissions on each, hard and symbolic file links, individual user accounts and home directory, login processing and security, an online help system in the form of "man," pipes and filters, fundamental utilities such as ls, tar, cp, mv, etc., common editors including vi and emacs, and the notion of a user interface known as a shell, which itself supports redirection, command history, aliases, functions, job control, shell scripts and variables, along with command line editing and completion. Anyone with experience on any other Unix-like system will feel perfectly at home on a Linux system. Berkeley-derivative users, such as those who might have used Digital Unix or any of the BSD variants, might find the filesystem naming convention different, or the system startup process different from what they are used to (Linux uses System V init), or might find certain commands different in terms of their options (e.g., ps). But by-and-large, any Unix user will feel perfectly at home on a Linux system.

Figure 1 shows a screenshot of a typical Linux system running on an IBM Thinkpad laptop:

Again, with Mozilla Firefox, Gimp, Emacs, Smalltalk, and a Terminal, this screen looks familiar to any Unix user.

The Linux operating system supports the fundamentals of Unix philosophy, namely, using small utility programs that are designed to do one thing and do them well. It also supports the idea that these small utility programs, known as "filters," should be able to be "strung" together to form pipelines, so that data can be moved from one to the other in a stream, and each program can act as a filter to modulate or transform the data in one way or another. Unix requires a common text data format in order for these pipelines to function, and Linux as a Unix system supports text as its fundamental data format.

As an example of a pipeline, let's take the Unix utility echo, which is a standard Unix utility that "echoes" the contents of a file or stream of data to the screen. Another utility, named gawk, which is the GNU version of a venerable old Unix command called AWK, named after three of the individuals highly involved in the early versions of AT&T Unix, takes input from a stream of data, formats in some way, and then prints out the modified stream of data to the screen. What a pipe does is change the default paths of input and output. Instead of printing to the screen, a pipe will redirect the stream of output that would normally have gone to the screen, so some other destination, like another program. As an example, consider the command:

$ echo "Now, sir, a war is never even, sir, a war is won" | gawk '{print $4,$6,$10}' |tr 'w' 'W'

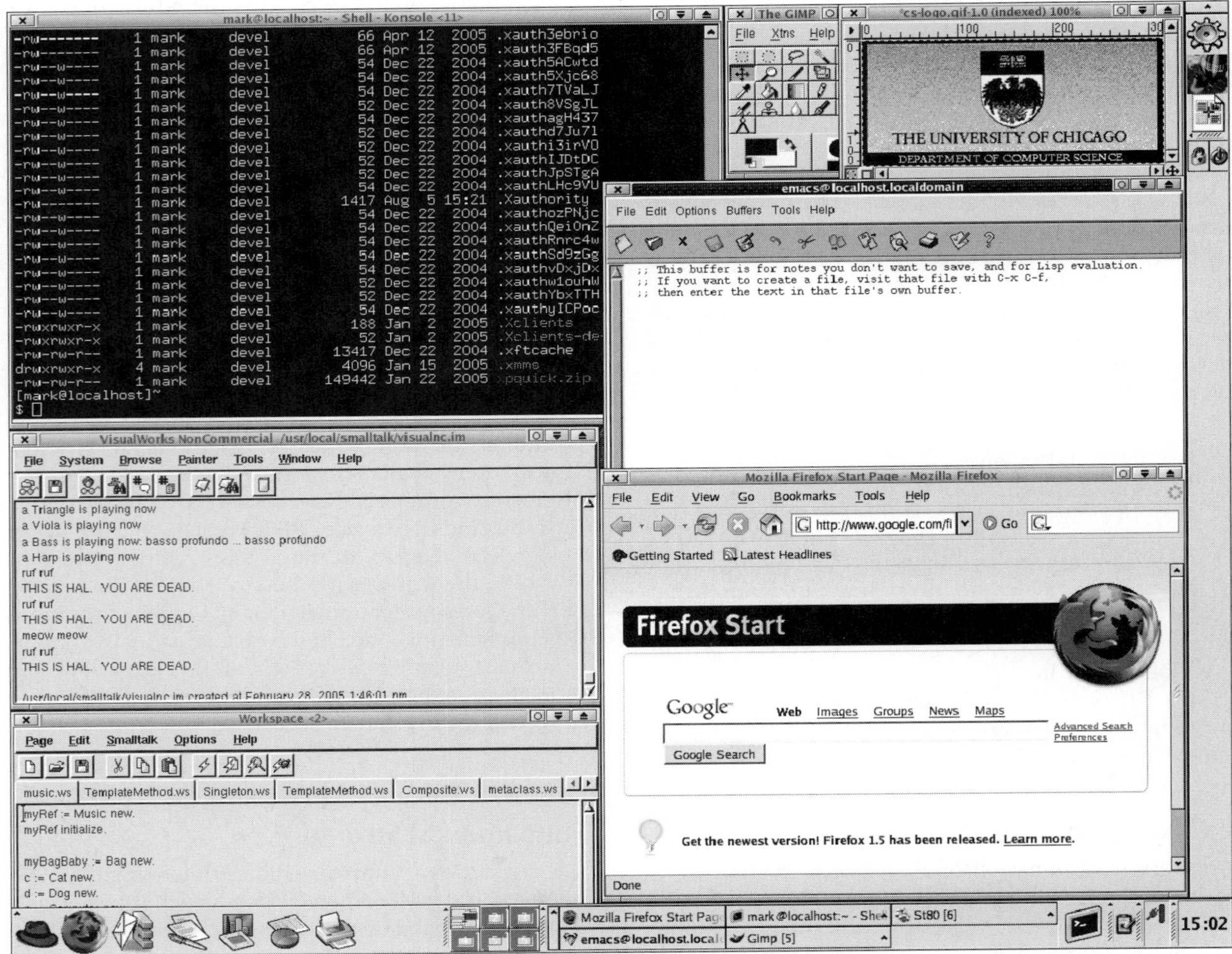

Figure 1: Typical Linux system screenshot

War never War

The "$" is the standard shell prompt (for Bourne shell derivatives). We are echoing a famous palindrome, and the output of the echo command, which would simply be to reproduce the same text to the screen, is redirected by the pipe (the "|" symbol) to become the input to the gawk command. The result is that gawk takes in that string from echo, and prints out the fourth, sixth, and tenth words or "fields" of the string (only), ignoring punctuation. That yields the output stream "war never war," drawn straight from the original. Then, this output from gawk is again piped (via the "|" symbol) to yet another utility, called "tr" (translate), and it replaces all instances of the "w" character with its capital form, "W." The result of the pipeline of filters is "War never War."

In Linux, as in other Unix systems, most everything is manipulated as a "file." This means that as far as the programmer is concerned, a socket is just another file, the screen is just another a file, a tape device is just another file, a modem device is just another file, and all files are manipulated using just a few fundamental system calls such as open(), creat(), read(), write(), and close(). This Unix consistency is continued in Linux.

Fundamental common Unix priorities, such as portability, simplicity, consistency, and empowerment of the user are all exhibited in the Linux OS. Consistency and simplicity are already seen in the common Unix way of dealing with different devices—they are all seen and manipulated as "files." Linux is written primarily in C, with only a small amount of native assembler, making Linux highly portable. This is the reason Linux has shown up on so many different hardware devices, because of its continuation of the Unix tradition of portability.

Finally, Linux, like other Unix operating systems, does not try to shield its users from the power of its operating system (or for that matter, try to shield its brittle operating system from its users). Instead, it lays it all out and opens up safe and controlled but open avenues so that the operating system can be manipulated, managed, and leveraged. Linux assumes its users are competent, resourceful human beings who can be trusted. This is not to say that controls and security are not in place to prohibit voluntary and involuntary malfeasance, but rather, the Linux philosophy is one of trust, access, and openness. Even the bugs known in Linux are advertised in the Linux man pages (another Unix tradition) (Gancarz, 1995).

Kernel Architecture

The kernel is the piece of the operating system that is loaded first—it's the fundamental part of the operating system, the part that manages all the other parts. The kernel does two things primarily. First, it provides a communication gateway to the hardware of the computer, controlling software access to hardware and acting to some degree as a "traffic cop." Second, the kernel provides an execution environment that can run multiple users' programs while at the same time keeping these programs safe and functioning in a cooperative overall system.

The Linux kernel is a monolithic kernel as opposed to a microkernel such as exists in Minix or GNU Mach. This means that many features are resident within the kernel, including a single kernel memory space including all data structures. All kernel features, including device drivers, filesystems and networking code, all run within the single address space of the kernel. When the kernel is running, it runs in kernel mode only, never in user mode. This means that no user-mode code is ever running within the kernel. System calls go through a call-gate that shifts the processor into execution in kernel mode for the length of the system call. Once the system call returns, the user code begins again running in user mode.

Linux's process model is Unix-based, providing a fundamental fork and exec model. Linux contains all the standard features one would expect in a Unix-like operating system, including virtual memory management, virtual filesystem support, lightweight processes, signals, System V interprocess communication, as well as symmetric multiprocessing. Linux (version 2.6) offers a fully pre-emptive kernel, meaning that the kernel can manage and manipulate multiple lightweight processes (LWPs) by managing the "time slices" or quantums that are given to each LWP as well as interrupting ones currently running but blocked (say waiting on some I/O) and put others onto the processor for temporary execution.

Linux can run on computers that have more than one physical processing unit or CPU. It can easily manage multiple users' processes onto any number of multiple CPUs, a capability known as symmetric multiprocessing (SMP).

The Linux kernel is said to be "reentrant," meaning that several programs can be in "kernel mode" at the same time on multiple physical processors, and in that sense, we can say that the kernel has been "entered more than once—by multiple processes at once." A kernel can be reentered even on a single processor, if one process is blocked in kernel mode waiting on I/O and another process enters kernel mode while the first process is waiting. A reentrant kernel has to be more robust than a non-reentrant kernel, because as more kernel threads are active within the kernel, there is greater complexity and greater potential for conflict. On the other hand, having a solid reentrant kernel such as Linux provides the means for a significant performance boost for the overall operation of the system.

Processes and Threads

A process is a "cradle" of sorts in which a user program executes—it is the execution environment for a user program. A process is a place to store the current state of an executing program, including the stack, the heap, signal mask. But a process is not what "executes." Rather, the process is the environment in which a program is executed, and it is a thread that actually does the "execution" of the program code. Thus, Linux allows for processes to have multiple threads that each may be scheduled onto a given physical processor, so that a single program can have multiple threads that are executing on its behalf simultaneously.

The OS ensures that user programs running in different processes are protected from each other. It would be a shame if one user is running a chess program and another is running a word processing program and the latter attempts to type some text while the first user moves her queen and she sees the phrase "Be4xd5 Bishop takes Queen" appear on the term paper she is writing. Linux manages processes so that they are protected from one another, that there is no possibility that one process's memory could become corrupted by the activity of some other process. The same management applies to the data written out to disk, information passed over a modem or socket.

Memory Allocation

Linux's memory handling is a complex topic, but the central concept is that as in all Unix-like systems, Linux manages memory abstractly using something known as virtual memory. Basically, virtual memory is a logical construct that allows the physical memory to be (a) hidden and (b) appear much larger than it actually is. The net result of this abstraction is that multiple processes can be talking to the virtual memory abstraction simultaneously; processes can still execute even when not all of their memory is physically available; programs can be relocated in physical memory without the process needing to worry about that fact; and finally, programs can "think" they have much more memory than they actually have, which is managed by the virtual memory manager. In fact, a program can be loaded into a process with very little of its actual memory being physically allocated at load time. Only when specific memory is requested which is not there (known as a page fault), is that data actually physically loaded and then logically mapped, a process known as on demand paging. This allows many more programs to exist in memory than would otherwise physically be possible. Linux has a robust memory abstraction layer and is quite efficient at handling multiple programs manipulating virtual memory. The Linux memory handling layer allows for speedy caching of disk data as well.

I/O and the Virtual Filesystem

Linux uses object-oriented abstraction principles to handle multiple filesystems. Let's address this using an example: one approach Linux could have taken was to hard code in the kernel the exact method by which a write would be conducted on say, an NTFS filesystem. We could call that ntfs-write. Then, in order to implement a method by which a write could be conducted on a DOS FAT filesystem, another version of write would be implemented in the kernel, say "dos-write." The problem here is that in order to support the vast number of different filesystems, Linux would have dozens of multiple write-like functions to have to implement and manage. And then there is the problem that in Linux "everything is a file"—thus, you'd have to have a modem-write and a socket-write and a terminal-write and on and on and on.

Instead, Linux uses a virtual filesystem approach. What does that mean? It means it has a single write. One. It's called write(). But, the single write "interface" has many different forms of implementation, many different methods by which write may be accomplished—all depending on the type of device being written to. Thus, each device implements its own version of write. The operating system just associates a driver with a particular device, and just calls write() on it. The implementation of write() in each driver actually manages the writing, regardless of whether the target device is a network, a tape drive, a terminal screen, a modem device, a physical file on a Macintosh HFS filesystem or a UFS file on a NEXTSTEP filesystem, a Unix pipe, an ISO9660 CD-ROM drive, or whatever.

By virtualizing filesystem access, the programming interface (the API) can remain simple, and drivers supporting the myriad methods by which that API can be implemented can be written and loaded on demand (see Loadable Modules).

Scheduling

Part of the responsibility of the kernel is to make sure that all processes play fairly. This means that in a pre-emptive multitasking operating system like Linux, a system scheduler exists that measures the time each process (a program runs in what is known as a "process") is allowed to run on a given physical processor. When one process's time allotment is up (this is called a "quantum," and is usually on the order of about a quarter of a second), the scheduler will have the kernel save the runtime state of that process and then move some other process onto the processor so it gets a chance to run (for its quantum). Now, certain processes have a higher priority than others, and for these special processes, they get a little advantage in their processor allocation. But by acting as a kind of fair-minded traffic cop, the scheduler still ensures that all processes get a chance to run in an equitable environment.

Loadable Modules

The Linux kernel can load "additions" to itself dynamically at runtime, through its loadable module capability. This means that support for additional devices (new CD/DVD drives, tape drives), filesystems (NTFS, HPFS), and networks (such as AppleTalk, ISDN) can be dynamically added to the Linux kernel at runtime. These additional modules still become part of the runtime kernel, but they do not have to be statically compiled into the kernel. This has several advantages. One, it keeps the default size of the kernel down, as well as giving users the ability to load additions to the kernel on an as-needed basis. If you do not have your DVD drive plugged in, you do not have to have the driver loaded into the kernel and taking up memory space. Linux's loadable module capability comes with support for the management of modules, the registration of drivers, and a conflict resolution strategy for different drivers wanting to manage the same hardware device. Loadable modules are available for all sorts of different devices, including device drivers for printers, monitors, mice, disk drives, and network interfaces, as well as support for multiple filesystems and networking protocols. Loadable modules are highly useful in Linux, and enable the Linux monolithic kernel to be able to be squeezed onto a single 1.44 MB floppy disk, and still boot and run a computer.

System Architecture

Filesystem

The Linux filesystem is a hierarchical composite of directories and files, starting with a base directory called root.

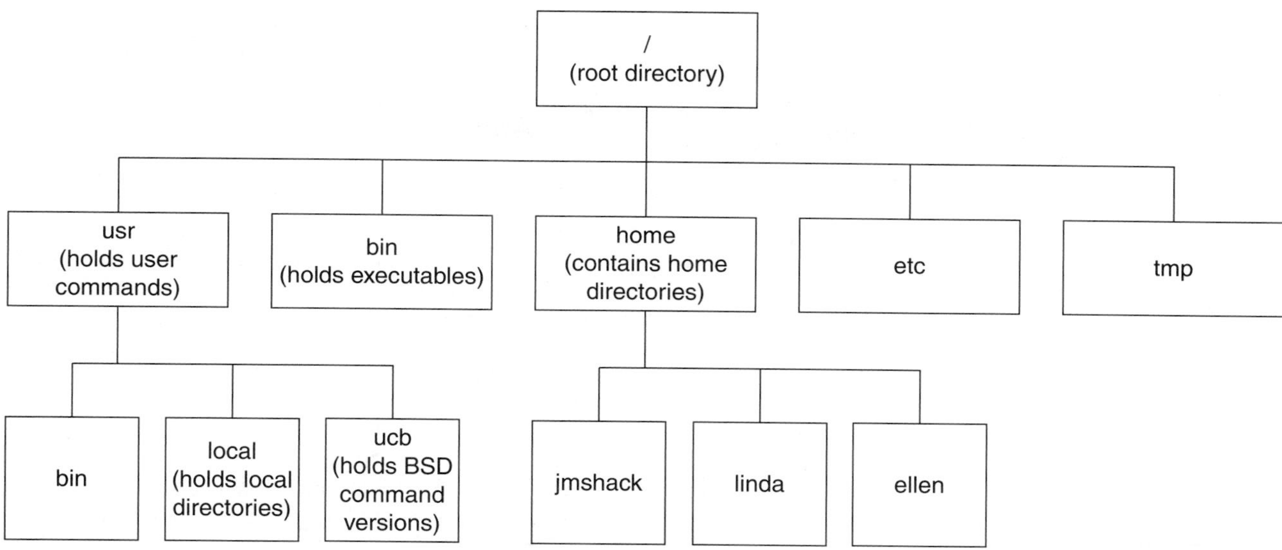

Figure 2: Typical Unix filesystem layout

Every directory in the filesystem, with the exception of the root directory, has a parent directory. All files on the system belong to a particular directory. Figure 2 shows a typical layout of a hierarchical Unix filesystem.

Table 1 gives the main directories and their functions on a typical Linux system.

The /home directory is significant because most users on a Linux system are assigned a default home directory, and this directory is stored under the /home directory. Therefore, a user with the username joe would usually have a home directory under /home/joe. A user's home directory is the current working directory immediately after the user logs in, and it is the place where each user can store personal files.

Table 1: Standard Filesystem Directories

/(root)	The base directory of all other directories
/boot	The directory that holds the kernel and startup configuration for booting the Linux operating system
/bin	The directory that holds system binaries
/lib	The top-level library directory, which holds the static and shared libraries required to run the operating system.
/usr	The directory that contains user commands
/mnt	The directory that forms the default base mount point for mounting external filesystems, such as NFS directories, CDROM devices, etc.
/etc	The directory that contains system configuration files, including the files involved in system initialization
/tmp	A world-writable directory for storing temporary files (deleted periodically)
/home	The base directory for all users' home directories

Each file in the system is associated with a structure known as an inode. An inode (known as an information node) contains information relative to that particular file in the filesystem. The inode contains information about each file in the filesystem including the file name, the current size on disk in bytes, the type of file (regular file, directory, link, device), the number of hard links to the file, information indicating the user and group associated with the file, an identifier for the filesystem the file belongs to, and some timestamps representing when the file's contents were last read, modified, and when the inode structure itself was last modified. Most significantly, the inode contains pointers to the physical location of the file's data on the actual hard disk (Vahalia, 1996).

Networking

Linux comes with vast protocol support for many different networking options, including base TCP/IP (including IPv6), Microsoft Windows SMB, Novell IPX/SPX, Apple Talk, WAN Networking including X.25, Frame-relay support, ISDN, PPP, SLIP, and PLIP, amateur radio, and ATM. It also comes along with support for more hardware than any other Unix-based operating system in existence.

Linux also supports enterprise computing including high availability solutions, RAID support, and redundancy, and, of course, standard Unix networking support if available, including support for Berkeley sockets, SUN NFS, NIS, NIS+, MMAP, SNMP, and so on. Linux can interoperate with a variety of network layers, in addition to Ethernet, including Fast Ethernet, FDDI, HIPPI, ireless LAN (802.11b and 802.11g), and Bluetooth (IEEE 802.15). An example of the overall architecture is seen in Figure 3.

This array of choices presents the Linux user with at once a great gift of variety, but it also comes with a liability in that most versions of Linux require some knowledge and industry on the part of the user in terms of

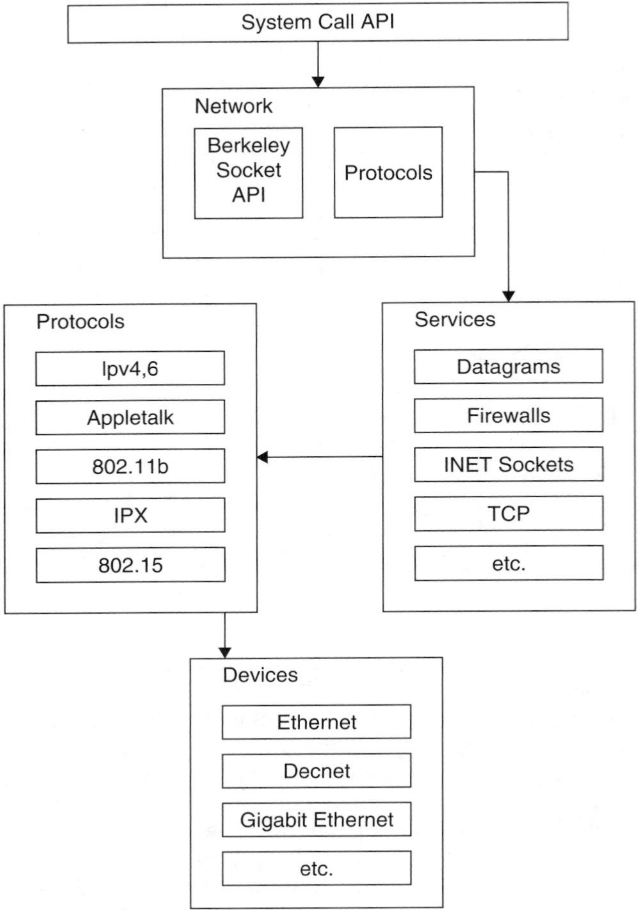

Figure 3: Network architecture

setting up and installing support for certain extensions. For example, although Linux supports wireless LAN, knowing what package to install, and then what configuration files to modify, and how to modify those files, is a bit daunting to the Linux newcomer. Linux does have a documentation project that attempts to keep up with a set of instructions for managing Linux, nevertheless, saying that Linux supports wireless LAN is one thing and successfully enhancing the kernel to support it and running it successfully is another. In addition, because Linux has to run on such a wide variety of hardware platforms (which, say Mac OS X does not), problems specific to a particular laptop or desktop system can always arise, and the answers can often take a while to resolve.

In addition, Linux extends its compatibility with other operating systems in that it can directly mount filesystems for a number of other operating systems, including MSDOS, Microsoft Windows, OS/2, Mac OS X, Solaris, SunOS, various BSD variants including FreeBSD.

Linux supports NFS and NIS/NIS+, with the standard configurations, so that Linux can mount NFS filesystems from other Unix systems, as well as offer its own filesystems as mountable, in addition to providing for centralized user management. Linux, through Samba, offers SMB compatibility so that users of Microsoft Windows can mount Linux file systems, allowing Linux to act as an SMB file server, and participate in Windows domains and workgroups as a file server. Samba also offers SMB client capabilities, which offers command line utilities for browsing Windows directories from Linux. Linux can also act as a print server through various protocols, allowing it to publish printers to a given network.

Security

Linux security is based on standard Unix security metaphors, including user accounts, login security with secure passwords, filesystem protection, and file permissions. But Linux also supports data encryption and secure networking strategies (for example OpenSSH and secure shell), the use of smart cards and firewalls, packet filtering and TCP Wrappers, and Kerberos, just to name a few areas of security support in Linux.

One of the key advantages of Linux over certain other operating systems, such as Microsoft Windows systems, is its security. Instead of trying to be all things to all people who might wish to buy your product, instead, Linux tries and succeeds in offering a secure platform on which to run any number of different types of applications. On of the key enablers in terms of security include the new Security-Enhanced Linux (SELinux) offerings. SELinux is a version of Linux produced by the efforts of the Information Assurance Research Group, part of the National Security Agency (NSA) of the federal government, and the Secure Computing Corporation (SCC). SELinux provides, among other things, access control policies that confine user programs (including those run as the superuser) and system servers to the minimum amount of privilege they require to do their specific work. The result is a Linux system that protects information from access by other programs that should not be accessing that information.

User Interface

The default user interface in Linux is a shell known as bash, which stands for the Bourne Again Shell, a pun on the name of Stephen Bourne, who wrote the first user shell known as the Bourne Shell. The bash shell provides a command line environment for users to interact with the operating system, including running programs and managing user files. As part of the choices available in Linux, users are not stuck with the bash shell but can use any number of other shells, including the korn shell (ksh), the Z shell (zsh), the C shell (csh), and tcsh (DuBois, 1995; Rosenblatt, 1993). The different shells have different capabilities, but most modern shells offer a number of capabilities, including an interface for redirection, a facility for remembering and reproducing and editing recent commands. Users can even use commands from their favorite text editor (such as vi or emacs) in the editing of command lines previously executed. Also supported is command line completion, which allows the user to type some part of a file specification, and then hit a key, such as the tab key, which will prompt the shell to look for files that match the beginning specification. If the shell finds such a match, it will automatically complete the name.

Users can also specify alias names for commands, which can make certain commands easier to execute, or provide default options for certain commands. For example, if you find yourself often typing a command such as:

/usr/bin/emacs –fn 6x13 –fg black –bg cyan –cr blue –ms white filename.txt

which will set the default font and colors for an emacs section, you can transform this into an alias in bash by entering the following command:

alias myemacs="/usr/bin/emacs –fn 6x13 –fg black –bg cyan –cr blue –ms white"

This allows the user to simply type "myemacs filename.txt" and emacs will then lauch with the font and colors specified in the alias.

Shells also allow the user to create variables in memory and also provide a small programming language for writing shell scripts, which are commands contained in a file that the shell will execute on after another. Additionally, most shells on Linux support job control, which provides an interface into the multitasking capability of the operating system. A user can, from the shell prompt, issue a command and direct the shell to run the command "in the background." This is done by attaching an ampersand "&" to the end of the command line. Once done, the user does not have to wait for the command to finish, but is instead presented with another prompt to enter another command. Jobs in the shell can be managed, in that a user can recall to the forefront any command that has been sent to the background, as well as kill any of the jobs using the kill command.

ADVANTAGES OF LINUX

Linux is one of several open-source Unix-like operating systems (others include FreeBSD) that can be obtained and used for very little cost. In fact, if you want, you can go online to www.kernel.org and download the Linux kernel for free. If you want to obtain a more easily managed Linux installation, you can go to any number of online providers and get a full Linux system (including X Windows, package management), still for no cost other than your time (for a site full of options, visit http://distrowatch.com/ for any number of different and flexible options for Linux). There are no necessary initial purchase fees with Linux, and there is no necessary annual maintenance or licensing fee associated either. If you want to obtain, install, and manage Linux at no cost other than your time, you are free to do so. However, you are "on your own" as they say in terms of the management and maintenance of your Linux installation. If you should wish to have support, you have several options. First, you can buy a packaged solution for Linux, say, from RedHat, and through paying a nominal charge (29 dollars to several hundred dollars), you get a short period of time (usually three months to a year) of online and or phone support to help you get along. Should you wish something more substantial in terms of support, there are several companies that provide different levels of maintenance support, everything from offering email support to on-site hand-holding. Obviously, the more on-site handholding required, the higher your annual maintenance costs will be. But again, these costs are manageable and optional. Further, there are numerous online sites for support (in terms of usergroups) that are dedicated to various aspects of working with Linux, everything from administration issues, development issues, hardware issues, networking issues, security issues, as well as vendor-specific questions (like questions specific to RedHat for example). All of these groups can be found under comp.os.linux.*.

Linux has probably the best array of device support of any Unix system in the world. Part of the reason for this is derived from its open-source advantage. Because Linux is nonproprietary, as opposed to Apple's OS X or Sun's Solaris operating system, more hardware options exist for Linux and this is because Linux is not restricted to one or two specific hardware configurations (such as PowerBooks and iMacs and MacBook Pros). Having said this, it is often more difficult to connect a given device (say a digital camera for example) to a Linux system precisely because the supporting driver may be buggy or unavailable, as distinguished from a digital camera that can be plugged into a Mac Powerbook Pro and work "out of the box." Because Linux is "open" and untied to any specific vendor or hardware architecture, there are a myriad of devices that can be attached to a Linux system, but often not without some work and effort on your part.

Linux runs on a variety of different hardware platforms, including tiny devices with limited memory such as the Linux Wristwatch created at IBM Watson Laboratories (http://www.eecs.utoledo.edu/_ewing/ieee/meetings/notices/25sep2002.pdf). Of course it can run on the full array of Intel-based computers also. It can just as easily run on an old 80386 machine with as little as 4 megabytes of memory or be embedded on tiny hardware platforms such as cell phones and PDAs. Linux was the operating system of choice on the original TiVo® digital video recorder. In addition, Linux can also run on Sun Sparc hardware as well as on the IBM 390 mainframe (cf. the "Iron Penguin" at Princeton University and http://linuxvm.org/index.html). It can run on a PowerPC along side of the Mac OS. Today, Linux can be built to run on Alpha, Motorola 68000, PowerPC, 32-bit and 64-bit Sparc, Mips, and many other architectures. Although it can run on a wristwatch, Linux also supports the TeraGrid (coordinated through the Grid Infrastructure Group [GIG] at the University of Chicago) and Linux NetworX Evolocity at Lawrence Livermore Laboratories. Evolocity was designed to run on approximately 2000 multiprocessors running at 2.4 GHz with a theoretical peak of 9,200,000,000,000 (9.2 trillion) calculations per second (by contrast this is approximately 27 trillion times faster than the original IBM PC introduced in the early 1980s).

Linux is solid and powerful. It tends to function well and not crash as often as some other proprietary operating systems. The average uptime of the average Linux computer is significantly longer than say the average uptime of a Microsoft Windows XP computer. The reasons for this are many, but suffice it to say that Linux is simply a solid and durable system. Linux is also fast and efficient. Developers working on some aspect of Linux number in the tens of thousands, and the core programmers are extremely talented and the intellectual capital at your

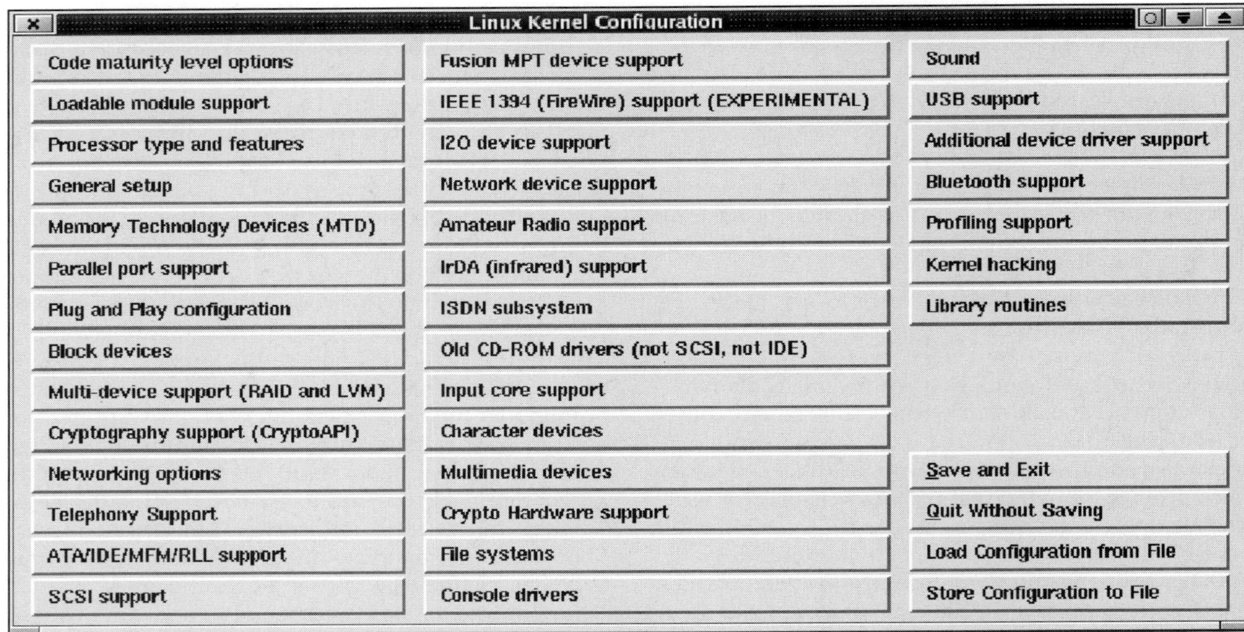

Figure 4: Screenshot of build configuration main screen

disposal on the Linux front simply is not available from any particular proprietary vendor, no matter what the resources of that vendor. Further, since the source code is open and freely available, when bugs exist, they tend not to exist for very long, because so many eyes are looking at the code. Linux is supposed to have once said that given enough eyes, all bugs are shallow. This means that if you have enough talented people working on a problem, a best-of-breed solution should be readily available.

Linux is also compatible with other systems. This is partly because it had to be—it started that way. The original Linux kernel was built on another system (Minix) and actually used its filesystem (minix). Since then, Linux was dual-booted on many Microsoft Windows systems, so, from the beginning, it had to be a good cooperative computational citizen. This means that Linux systems can directly mount and share files with a variety of other systems, including Microsoft Windows NT, OS/2, SVR4, Mac OS X, Solaris, SunOS, NEXTSTEP, FreeBSD, OpenBSD, and so on. Linux is also able to communicate over the network with these different filesystems over various protocols. For example, a Linux system can store and retrieve files on a Windows XP machine because of an add-on product called Samba that provides the Windows SMB protocol for Linux. Linux can also act as a file server for many other operating systems.

Linux, even more than most Unix operating systems, wants to give its users choices. As for user interfaces into the operating system, the text-based shells available by default as options for users to choose include the default bash shell, csh, tcsh, ksh, pdksh, zsh, and ash, just to name a few. As for graphical interfaces and window managers that run on top of X Windows, we can choose from Gnome, KDE, WindowMaker, Enlightenment, ICEwm, BlackBox, and Sawfish, just to name a few of the dozens available.

Figure 4 shows the main configuration screen for Linux and gives some hint as to the level of configuration that is available on Linux.

Note that the depth of options behind each one of these buttons is itself vast. For instance, just a drive into the "SCSI support" configuration would reveal further options including disk, tape, CDROM, and lower level drivers could be chosen from a list that includes standard SCSI drivers such as Adaptec, AMI MegaRAID, Buslogic, Compaq, Future Domain, Intel, IOMEGA, NCR, Qlogic, Seagate, UltraStor, just to name a few. Additionally, PCMCIA-based SCSI can be selected from vendors including Adaptec, Future Domain, NinjaSCSI, and Qlogic.

CONCLUSION

Linux is a solid, dependable, multiuser, multitasking operating system based on the Unix philosophical tradition. It is open source, meaning that you may obtain it, compile it, and run it at no monetary cost. It is freely available to all, and is modifiable by the community of users (with some coordinating restrictions), which in turn enriches the overall system available to all. It has given wind to the sails of the open-source movement, and has provided a solid, dependable platform on which much scientific work has been conducted. It has shown, like Unix, that much can come from hard work and a little bit of brilliance in a single individual who has nothing much else to do for a few months.

There are, however, problems associated with managing so much choice and so many configurations. Precisely because there is a driver for just about every new technology and hardware device that comes onto the market, the availability of hardware support in Linux is substantial. But this ubiquitous support comes at a cost. It is difficult for established Linux vendors to offer easy configuration tools for the variety of hardware and technology options available. Further, because of the way the kernel is structured, adding a new device often requires recompilation of the kernel itself. Although this is not terribly difficult, it can be daunting for the average or first time user. There are former Linux users who have switched to other operating systems, including Microsoft Windows and Mac OS X and free BSD derivatives, from Linux, precisely because of the complexities centered around managing and configuring a Linux system. It can be difficult to install a version of Linux onto a specific laptop, and expect that the laptop's modem, wireless LAN, Bluetooth, and even recovering from sleep when the laptop lid is closed and re-opened, will all work flawlessly the first time. This is in many cases unlikely. With a system such as Mac OS X running on, say, an Apple PowerBook, this is trivial stuff that requires little if any management or configuration. Not so with Linux. Some Linux distributions, for example, Gentoo Linux, have made the move to automated updating of the OS, so that the user can just "leave it running" and the OS would download updates as they become available. This is nothing new, Microsoft Windows does the same thing now, and Redhat at least for its distribution has been providing a similar service. Nevertheless, there is a substantial onus on Linux users to be "up to the task" of configuring and maintaining their free OS.

In the end, Linux is a highly capable free OS that provides its users with a variety of choices in terms of hardware and software. It can interoperate with other systems, both from a filesystem standpoint as well as from a networking standpoint. It is fast, reliable, and has support that allows it to act as a print server as well as a file server to other systems. Although it is far from perfect, it nevertheless has been instrumental in offering a cost-effective alternative to commercial software, and it has advanced the cause as well as the acceptance of free, open-source software, in the corporate world as well as in academia.

GLOSSARY

API: Application programmer interface. A library of functions that are callable as routines.

Bit: The smallest unit of information on a digital computer, standing for binary digit. A bit can have the value 1 or 0, meaning on or off.

Boot: The process of initializing the operating system on a computer by initializing hardware and establishing a sane environment in which users can work on the system.

BSD: Berkeley Software Distribution. One of the two major variants in Unix, begun during the mid-1970s by the Computer Systems Research Group at the University of California, Berkeley.

Byte: Eight bits of data on a digital computer. A byte generally contains a single character (like the character "a") or a small integer (generally less than 128 or 256).

Command substitution: The ability of a shell to execute a command and substitute the output of that command in another command.

Filter: A special type of program written to take its input from standard input files and write its output to standard output. Filters may be linked together using pipes. Grep and sort are two types of filters.

Function: A routine that is callable in a procedural programming language, such as C. A function promotes the concept of modularity in program design.

Inode: A fundamental data structure that holds information pertaining to a particular logical file on the filesystem. An inode holds information about the file such as its size in bytes, modification dates, security and access information, type of file, and the location of the data on the physical device.

Job control: An ability of the shell to run multiple programs at the same time, and a facility to manage multiple programs running in the background and foreground.

Kernel: The main "brain" of an operating system, providing an interface between the hardware itself and providing resource allocation services to the rest of the user system.

MMAP: Sun's memory mapped access protocol

Multitasking: The ability of an operating system to run more than one process at the same time, either on multiple physical processors or by quickly swapping tasks on and off of a single processor, giving the illusion of running multiple processes simultaneously.

Multiuser: The ability of an operating system to support more than one user at a given time.

NFS: Sun Microsystem's network filesystem. A set of services that allows users to access files on separate filesystems.

NIS: Sun Microsystem's network information services. A set of services to centrally manage users on a network.

Operating system: The fundamental control program on a computer, which provides a functional environment in which users can interact with the computer.

Pipe: A special connector that passes through a stream of text from one end to another. Special programs known as filters can connect their various inputs and outputs to a pipe, and therefore communicate over the pipe.

Process: A structure that provides an execution context for a given program, providing memory resources, terminal IO support, process state, file descriptors.

Program: A compiled and linked executable file that runs natively on the operating system, in order to execute some capability on behalf of the user.

Prompt: An indicator from a shell (usually in the form of "$" or "%") that it is ready and waiting for input.

Quantum: A period of time, usually in milliseconds, during which the scheduler runs a program on a processor.

Regular expression: A string composed of literal characters and special symbols that can represent a potentially larger domain of possible resolutions.

Shell: The primary user interface in a Unix system, allowing the user to interact with the computer by issuing consecutive commands.

Signal: A brief message that one process may use to contact another process.

Socket: A BSD-defined standard interface that allows two computers to communicate over a network. The standard interface for connecting to the Internet.

System call: A function in the kernel's API that offers user programs the ability to request services from a running kernel.

CROSS REFERENCES

See *Ethernet LANs; Local Area Networks; Optical Fiber LANs; Token Ring LANs; Windows 2000 Operating System.*

REFERENCES

DuBois, P. 1995. *Using csh & tcsh*. Scbastopol, CA: O'Reilly & Associates.

Gancarz, M. 1995. *The Unix Philosophy*. Boston: Digital Press.

Rosenblatt, B. 1993. *Learning the Korn Shell*. Sebastopol, CA: O'Reilly & Associates.

Salus, P. 1994. *A Quarter Century of UNIX*. Reading, MA: Addison-Wesley.

Shacklette, M. 2004. The unix operating system. *The internet encyclopedia*, v. 3. Bidgoli et al., editors. Hoboken, NJ: John Wiley & Sons.

Silberschatz, A., and P. Galvin. 1998. *Operating System Concepts*, 5th ed. Reading, MA: Addison-Wesley.

Stevens, W. R. 1990. *UNIX Network Programming*. Englewood Cliffs, NJ: Prentice Hall.

Tanenbaum, A. 2001. *Modern Operating Systems*. Upper Saddle River, NJ: Prentice Hall.

Vahalia, U. 1996. *UNIX Internals: The New Frontiers*. Upper Saddle River, NJ: Prentice Hall.

ONLINE RESOURCES

www.linux.org

www.kernel.org

www.linuxjournal.com

www.tldp.org

http://distrowatch.com/

www.linuxtoday.com/

Metropolitan Area Networks

Richard J. Nieporent, *Johns Hopkins University*

INTRODUCTION

Metropolitan area networks (MANs) were developed to meet the need for a very high-speed networking capability that would fill the technology void that existed between the availability of high speed local area networks (LANs) in the enterprise and wide area networks (WANs). WANs consist of common carrier circuits and switches. Originally these circuits were low-speed voice-grade communications channels that were used to transmit data from a terminal to a remote computer. Later, these voice-grade circuits were replaced first by digital and then by optical circuits that enabled high-speed communications to take place between remote computers.

LANs were developed to provide high-speed communications within a user's facility. They enabled an organization to link together all its computers at a site to support such applications as file sharing and printing. In addition, LANs enabled an organization to be able to access external networks through a single interface. By attaching a router to the LAN, an organization could communicate over the Internet or use a WAN to transfer data to its offices in different cities, states, or countries. What was missing from this scenario was the ability for an organization to communicate efficiently between its offices in a city. MANs were developed to fill this need for a high-speed network within a metropolitan area.

Just as the IEEE 802.3 and 802.5 Working Groups had taken the lead in the development of standards for Ethernet and token ring LANs in the early 1980s, the IEEE 802.6 Working Group developed the first MAN standard in 1987 (Institute of Electrical and Electronics Engineers, 1990). The IEEE 802.6 standard specified the media access control (MAC) and the physical layer (PHY) for a distributed queue dual bus (DQDB) MAN. In order to be able to support very high-speed communications, the 802.6 PHY specified the use of optical fiber for the communications medium. The DQDB MAN was the basis for the switched multimegabit data service (SMDS) that was developed by the telephone companies (telcos) (BellSouth Telecommunications, 1994). SMDS provided a high-speed communications service for LAN connectivity within a metropolitan area.

An enormous amount of optical fiber cable was laid by the telcos to provide the high-speed communications circuits needed to implement MANs. With the development in 1988 of the Synchronous Optical Network (SONET) standard by the American National Standards Institute (ANSI) in the United States (American National Standards Institute, 1995) and the similar Synchronous Digital Hierarchy (SDH) standard in Europe by the International Telecommunications Union Telecommunications Standardization Sector (ITU-T) (International Telecommunications Union, 2000), there now existed a common specification for multiplexing lower speed T1/E1 telephone network circuits onto a high-speed optical fiber circuit. Dual-ring SONET/SDH-based MANs were used to carry LAN and other broadband data traffic within a metropolitan area. The data were either carried directly in the SONET/SDH payload or the asynchronous transfer mode (ATM) protocol was used to carry the data over the SONET/SDH network. To provide the ever-increasing need for more bandwidth, dense wave division multiplexing (DWDM) was developed during the mid-1990s that enabled the data-carrying capacity of optical fiber cables to be increased by a factor of 80 or more (Fujitsu Network Communications, Inc., 2002).

Starting in the late 1990s, the IEEE 802 committee began the development of two new wireless standards for MANs. IEEE 802.16 is a high-speed wireless standard (dubbed WirelessMAN) that uses both the licensed and the license-exempt portions of the gigahertz (GHz) radio frequency (RF) spectrum. The 802.16 standard supports point-to-point, point-to-multipoint and mesh configurations. The initial IEEE 802.16 standard was approved in 2001. It covers the frequency spectrum from 10–66 GHz and provides line-of-sight (LOS) communications between a user site and a network hub. An addendum to the standard, approved in 2003, provides for non–line-of-sight (NLOS) communications in the 2–11 GHz portion of the RF spectrum (Institute of Electrical and Electronics Engineers, 2004a). The IEEE 802.16e standard, approved in 2005, adds a mobile capability to the Wireless MAN standards for subscribers moving at vehicular speeds (Institute of Electrical and Electronics Engineers, 2005). The IEEE 802.20 working group is also developing a wireless standard for mobile users at vehicular speeds up to 250 km/hr for the transport of IP data (Klerer, 2003).

Wireless MAN standards similar to IEEE 802.16, called HIPERACCESS and HIPERMAN, are being developed within the Broadband Radio Access Networks (BRAN) project of the European Telecommunications Standards Institute (ETSI). The HIPERACCESS standard was originally published in 2002 (European Telecommunications Standards Institute, 2002). It addresses the higher portion of the frequency spectrum above 11 GHz. The HIPERMAN standard, published in 2005, is being developed to provide an interoperable broadband fixed wireless access network in the 2–11 GHz RF spectrum (European Telecommunications Standards Institute, 2005). Both HIPERMAN and HIPERACCESS are being harmonized with the IEEE 802.16 standards to provide a worldwide standard for wireless MANs.

Another new standard being developed by IEEE is the 802.17 Resilient Packet Ring (RPR) MAN that was approved in 2004 (Institute of Electrical and Electronics Engineers, 2004b). RPR employs optical fiber circuits in a dual counter-rotating ring configuration that is optimized for packet transmission. However, unlike other dual ring MANs, the IEEE 802.17 RPR uses both rings for communications. It provides for efficient communications through the use of concurrent transmission, bandwidth reclamation, bandwidth reallocation, spatial and temporal bandwidth reuse, and traffic prioritization.

In addition to the standardization work being done by the IEEE 802 Working Groups, a number of industry forums have been formed to promote the development and implementation of these standards. The Worldwide Interoperability for Microwave Access (WiMAX) forum was formed in June of 2001 for the purpose of promoting the development of the 802.16 WirelessMAN standards (WiMAX Forum, 2006). The Metro Ethernet Forum was formed in September of 2003 to promote the use of high-speed Ethernet MANs (Metro Ethernet Forum, 2006). The Metro Ethernet forum has developed a number of specifications for implementing Gigabit and 10 Gigabit Ethernet MANs using either a point-to-point or a multipoint-to-multipoint configuration.

MAN FUNDAMENTALS

The principal technology alternatives that determine the nature of a MAN are its transmission media, topology, and the communications technology that it uses to transmit data. The transmission media is the physical path between the transmitter and receiver in a communications network. The topology of a network refers to the physical configuration of the communications media that interconnects the communicating devices. The communications technologies are the protocols that are used to transmit the user data over the network.

LANs vs. MANs vs. WANs

A local area network (LAN) is a communications network that provides a direct interconnection for a variety of computing devices. The distinguishing features of a LAN are its size and its speed. A LAN covers a small geographical area; in most cases it is limited to a diameter of 200 meters. The data rate of the LAN can be anywhere from 10 Megabits per second (Mbps) to 10 Gigabits per second (Gbps). Other characteristics of a LAN are its low bit error rate (from 10^{-9} to 10^{-12}) and its inexpensive interfaces. Finally, unlike WANs and MANs, the LAN is owned by a single private organization. Thus no recurring communications costs are incurred when using the LAN.

A metropolitan area network (MAN) is a high-speed communications network that provides a means for interconnecting LANs over an area as large as a small city. A MAN covers a much larger geographical area that a LAN; it has a maximum diameter of 100 to 150 kilometers. The data rate of a MAN can range from 155 Mbps (STM-1) to 10 Gbps (STM-64). Because the communications circuits that comprise the MAN are optical fiber, it has a very low bit error rate (from 10^{-11} to 10^{-12}). However, the cost to interface devices to a MAN is higher than that of a LAN. Finally, because of its large geographical coverage, MANs are owned by telcos as opposed to a private organization. Thus the cost to use a MAN will be higher than that of a LAN because usage charges must be paid to the network provider.

A wide area network (WAN) provides the means for interconnecting LANs and MANs over a very large area. The geographical extent of the WAN is essentially unlimited; it can be national or international in size. A WAN consists of a group of routers and/or switches that are connected together by public switched telephone network (PSTN) circuits. Depending on the type of circuits used, a WAN can support data rates from 64 Kbps (DS0 circuits) to 10 Gbps (SONET OC-192/STM-64 optical circuits) or more. As is the case with MANs, WAN circuits are provided by the telcos. The WAN bit error rate ranges from 10^{-6} to 10^{-12} depending on the type of circuits used and the technology employed to construct the WAN. The cost to use the WAN will depend on the extent of the WAN and the technology used. However, the cost will be higher than a LAN because usage charges must be paid to the network provider. Figure 1 shows examples of LAN, MAN, and WAN topologies.

MAN Media

As a result of the requirement for very high data rates, the media used to construct a MAN are limited to those with very large bandwidths. Therefore, optical fiber cable and the Gigahertz (GHz) portion of the radio frequency (RF) spectrum are the only two alternatives that are used. An optical fiber cable consists of a thin glass core that is

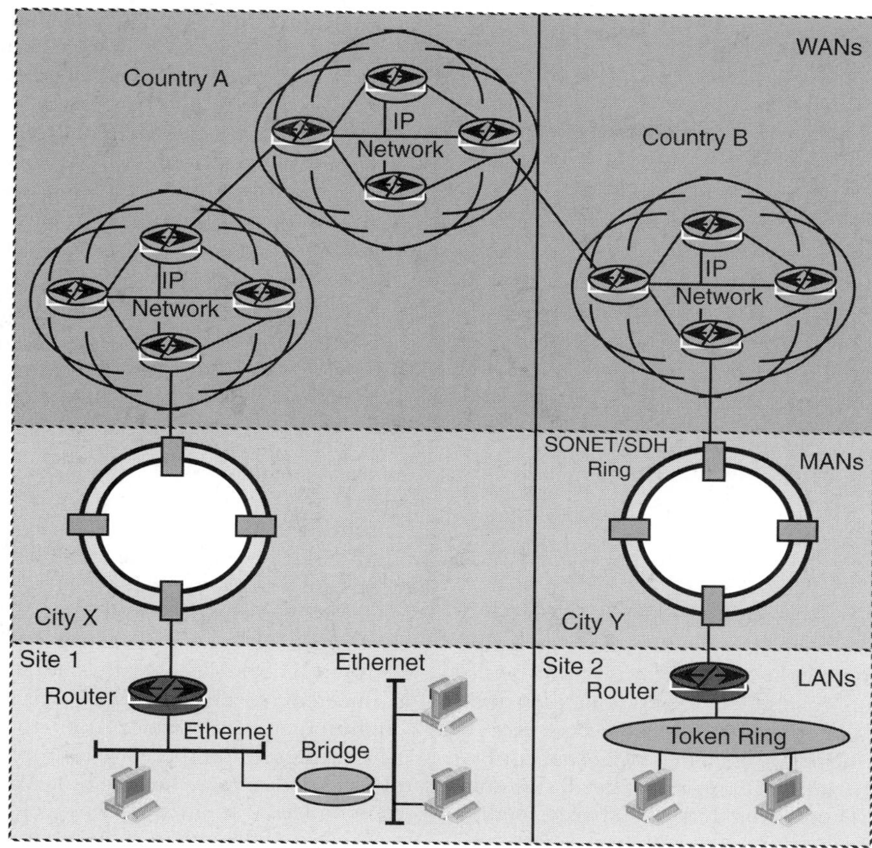

Figure 1: LAN, MAN, and WAN topologies

surrounded by another glass material (called cladding) with a lower index of refraction where the index of refraction, n, is a measure of the speed of light in free space, c, divided by the speed of light in the glass material. Because c is the maximum obtainable speed, the index of refraction is a number greater than 1.

The phenomenon of total internal reflection is used to transmit the light signal through the optical fiber medium. As shown in Figure 2 (ray 1), light going from a dense (higher index of refraction) medium to a less dense (lower index of refraction) medium will bend away from the normal (a line perpendicular to the medium). As the angle of incidence increases, the angle of refraction approaches 90 degrees (ray 2). The critical angle occurs when the angle of refraction equals 90 degrees (ray 3). Light transmitted at an angle greater than the critical angle experiences total internal reflection (ray 4). The light pulses are confined to the medium and the angle of incidence equals the angle of reflection. These light pulses can travel very large distances with very little attenuation. Because light consists of electromagnetic waves in the frequency range of 10^{14}–10^{15} Hz, an optical fiber cable has a very large bandwidth. Thus an optical fiber cable is capable of supporting extremely high data rates (10 Gbps to 40 Gbps and higher).

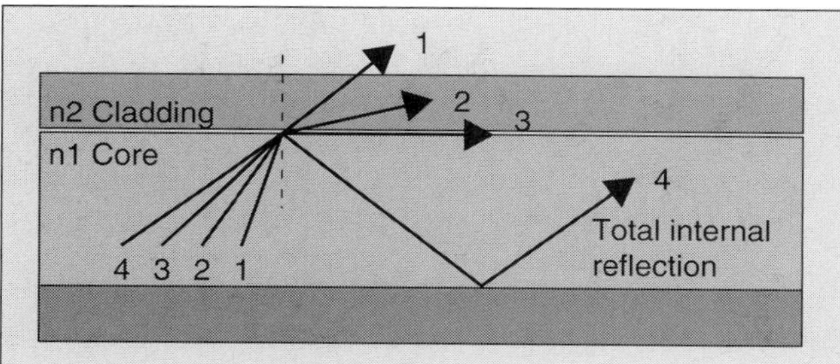

Figure 2: Total internal reflection

Unguided media (i.e., free space) can transport electromagnetic waves without the use of a physical conductor. The electromagnetic spectrum that is used for communications extends from very low frequencies (3 KHz) to extremely high frequencies (30 GHz to 300 GHz). The lower end of the frequency spectrum is called radio waves. The upper end of the frequency spectrum is called microwaves. By modulating the frequency, amplitude, and/or phase of an electromagnetic wave (Figure 3), it can be used to carry information through free space. Because the bandwidth used in the microwave portion of the frequency spectrum can be made very large, data can be transmitted at very high data rates (100 Mbps and higher).

MAN Topologies

The topology of a network refers to the physical configuration of the communications media that interconnects the communicating devices. There are four main topologies that are used in MANs: ring, point-to-point, point-to-multipoint, and mesh. A ring network consists of a closed loop of nodes (Figure 4d). Each node is connected to the

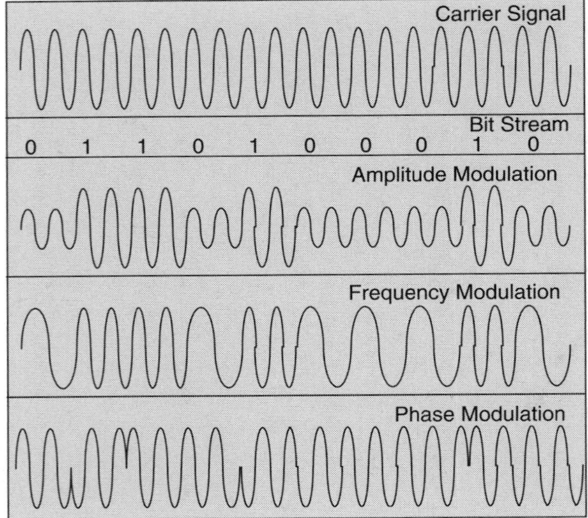

Figure 3: Amplitude, frequency, and phase modulation

previous node and the next node by a point-to-point link. Data circulates around the ring from node to node in either a clockwise or a counterclockwise direction. With a dual-ring configuration data travels clockwise on one path and counterclockwise on the other path. Because data circulates past each of the nodes on the ring, a packet sent by one station attached to the ring can be seen by all stations attached to the ring. Thus a ring acts as a shared media broadcast network. Dual-ring configurations are used for reliability. If one of the rings fails, the other ring can be used for backup.

A point-to-point (P-P) topology consists of a communications circuit that connects two fixed nodes (see Figure 4a).The P-P topology provides a user at a site with a fixed bandwidth with which to communicate with a network hub. This enables the user to have a guaranteed bit rate for communications. In a wireless network, the P-P link provides line of site communications between the user and the network hub.

A point-to-multipoint (P-MP) topology consists of a star configuration in which a number of users communicate with a central hub (see Figure 4b). The users must send data through the hub to communicate with each other or with other users attached to external networks. The hub acts as a repeater to pass traffic from one user to another user. A switch or a router is used to communicate with users on external networks.

A P-MP configuration can be directly implemented in a fixed wireless network. The network base station transmits data in the downstream direction to a number of subscriber locations. A modulation technique is used to assign a portion of the frequency bandwidth to each of the subscriber locations so that only the appropriate subscriber station will receive the data being sent to it. In the upstream direction, the P-MP network multiplexes the individual user transmissions into a high data rate channel for transmission over the external network.

A mesh network consists of a number of nodes that are connected to each other through P-P links. Each note can communicate with two or more nodes, so that unlike the ring configuration there are multiple paths between each of the nodes (see Figure 4c). With a mesh network each node acts as a repeater as well as a user interface. In a wireless environment a mesh network enables any node to communicate with any other node in the mesh network through one or more hops. The mesh topology solves the problem of communicating between nodes when there is no direct line of site (LOS) communicates path between the nodes.

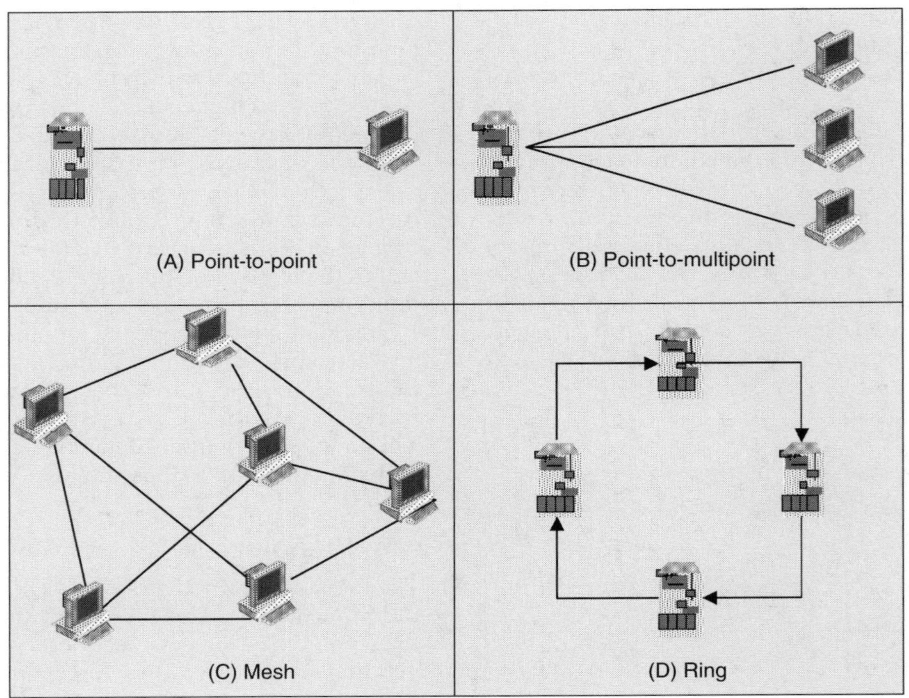

Figure 4: MAN topologies

MAN Communications Technologies

A number of communications technologies have been used to implement MANs including SONET/SDH, ATM, DWDM, and Ethernet. SONET/SDH was the initial technology used. It was originally developed as an optical transport technology to provide higher capacity circuits than the existing T1/E1 digital circuits. SONET/SDH provides a multiplexing scheme for combining data streams at multiples of the synchronous transport signal (STS) level 1 data rate of 51.84 Mbps. In a similar manner SDH multiplexes data streams at multiples of the synchronous transport module (STM) level 1 data rate of 155.52 Mbps. The SDH multiplexing scheme is exactly three times the rate of the SONET multiplexing scheme. Both the SONET and the SDH standards specify the method for multiplexing T1/E1 data streams within the basic STS-1/STM-1 frame (Goralski, 2002).

Because SONET/SDH was originally designed to carry circuit switched traffic, it was not optimized for transporting packet data. Thus the ITU-T specified that ATM was to be used to carry packet data. ATM provides a mechanism for partitioning packet data into 53 byte cells that consist of a 5-byte header and a 48-byte payload. An ATM adaptation layer (AAL) specifies how the packet data is to be encapsulation and segmented to fit into the ATM cells.

DWDM is used for transmitting multiple data streams over a single optical fiber. DWDM makes use of the fact that a light pulse is made up of a large number of wavelengths. Each wavelength can be used to transmit a separate data stream over a single optical fiber. Thus, by using DWDM it is possible to simultaneously carry 80 or more SONET/SDH data streams over an optical fiber.

Ethernet has become the dominant technology for LANs in the enterprise environment. Originally Ethernet had a data rate of 10 Mbps. As more and more traffic was being sent over LANs, higher speed versions of Ethernet were specified. With the development of Gigabit and 10-Gigabit Ethernet, the data rate was now fast enough for Ethernet to be used as a MAN technology. Because these high-speed versions of Ethernet were designed to run over optical fiber cables it was possible to transmit Ethernet over the much longer distances needed for MANs than the 200-meter limit of twisted-wire pair. Also, the 10-Gigabit Ethernet standard specified the use of SONET STS-192/SDH STM-64 circuits to transport the Ethernet frames.

DATA TRANSPORT OVER MANs

An encapsulation technique is used to enable SONET/SDH to carry packet data. The packet data is carried within the SONET/SDH synchronous payload envelope (SPE). With normal SONET multiplexing, a SONET STS-N frame is composed of N STS-1 frames. Thus an STS-3 frame contains three separate STS-1 frames that are time division multiplexed together a byte at a time. For the encapsulation technique to work efficiently, it is therefore necessary to replace the individual SONET/SDH payloads with a concatenated payload.

Continuous Concatenation

In order to have a signal that supports the full data rate of an STS-N, SONET allows for the combining of the SPEs from lower speed SONET circuits into a single high-speed SPE. The mechanism for doing this is called contiguous concatenation (Kartalopoulos, 2004). With contiguous concatenation the payload of an STS-3 frame is treated as a contiguous group of bytes as opposed to three separate STS-1 SPEs (Figure 5). Instead of having 3 separate STS-1 51.84 Mbps data streams carried in an STS-3, the concatenated STS-3 is a single 155.52 Mbps data stream.

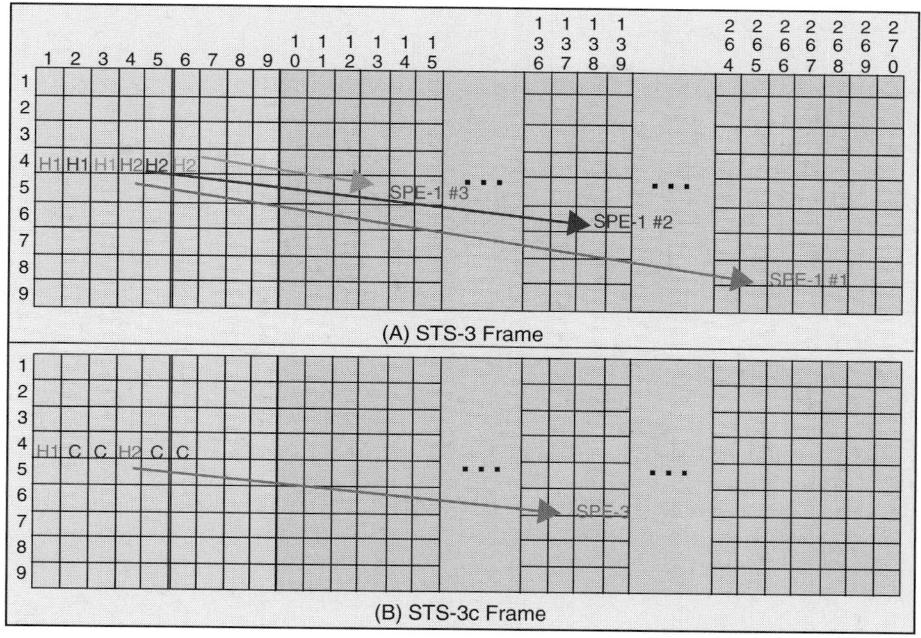

Figure 5: Multiplexed vs. contiguous concatenation frame

This concatenated frame is called STS-3c to distinguish it from a normal multiplexed STS-3 frame.

ITU-T specified the use of contiguous concatenation to transmit ATM cells over SONET/SDH. Data from an application is fragmented to fit into each ATM cell and reassembled at the destination. The SONET/SDH circuit transparently carries the ATM cells from the source to the destination node. ATM can provide different levels of QoS for each of the data streams it is transporting.

Virtual Concatenation

Contiguous concatenation was developed to provide an efficient procedure for transporting packet data over SONET/SDH. However, unless the data rate of the packet data matches the data rate of the SONET/SDH channel, it is necessary to send the packet data over a higher rate SONET/SDH channel. This led to an inefficient use of the SONET/SDH bandwidth. For example, sending 10-Mbps Ethernet over an STS-1c channel uses less than 20% of the STS-1c bandwidth. To enable packet data to be efficiently sent over a SONET/SDH channel, the technique of virtual concatenation (VC) was developed. VC enables SONET/SDH to match the bit rate of the packet data by using multiple slower speed SONET/SDH channels (Cavendish et al., 2002).

VC, in combination with the Generic Framing Procedure (see Generic Framing Procedures) allows the efficient mapping of packet data over SONET/SDH. VC allows a high data rate packet channel to be segmented and transmitted over multiple lower rate SONET/SDH channels. Each lower channel can be transported independently using different SONET/SDH payloads. At the destination node, the original packet data is reassembled from the independent SONET/SDH payloads.

The lower speed channels that comprise the high data rate stream are specified in SONET as STS-n-Xv, where n is the STS signaling level (1, 3, 12, etc.) and X is the number of these channels that are being used. (SDH uses the terminology STM-1-Xv to identify the number of STM-1 payloads that are being used for virtual concatenation.) For example, using STS-3c-7v, a 1-Gbps Ethernet data stream is partitioned into seven STS-3c channels that have a total data rate of 1.09 Gbps (Cavendish et al., 2002).

In addition to VC, a new capability, called the link capacity adjustment scheme (LCAS), has been developed to allow the dynamic adjustment of the size of a virtual concatenated SONET/SDH channel to meet periodic changes in user bandwidth requirements. LCAS provides a control mechanism to dynamically increase or decrease the number of VC channels assigned to a user to meet changing bandwidth needs. LCAS uses the H4 byte in the SONET/SDH header to pass the control information needed to reconfigure the link (Cavendish et al., 2002).

Classical IP over ATM

A number of framing procedures have been specified for carrying IP packet data over SONET/SDH. A straightforward solution is to first encapsulate the IP datagram in ATM cells and then have the SONET/SDH frame carry the ATM cells. Request for Comment (RFC) 1577, Classical IP over ATM, specifies the method of encapsulating IP in ATM cells (Lauback, 1994).

The ATM Adaptation Layer Type 5 (AAL5) is used to adapt the IP datagram to the ATM format (Figure 6). An 8-byte header is prepended to the IP datagram. The header contains the logical link control (LLC) and the subnetwork access protocol (SNAP) frames that identify the content of the SNAP protocol as IP data. A pad and an 8-byte AAL5 trailer are appended to the IP datagram. The pad is used to make the complete AAL5 frame an exact multiple of the 48-byte ATM payload so that the AAL5 trailer can be located within the ATM cell payload. The trailer contains the length of the IP datagram and a CRC that is used to determine if the reassembled IP datagram contains

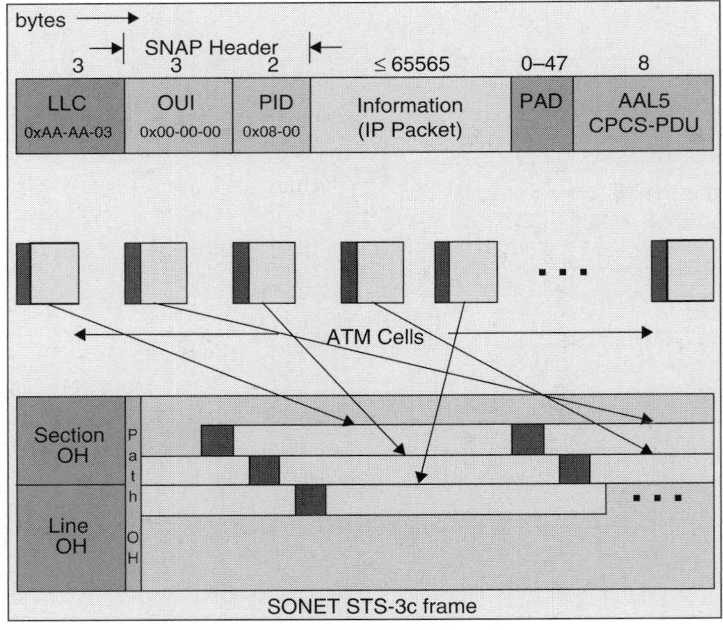

Figure 6: Classical IP over ATM

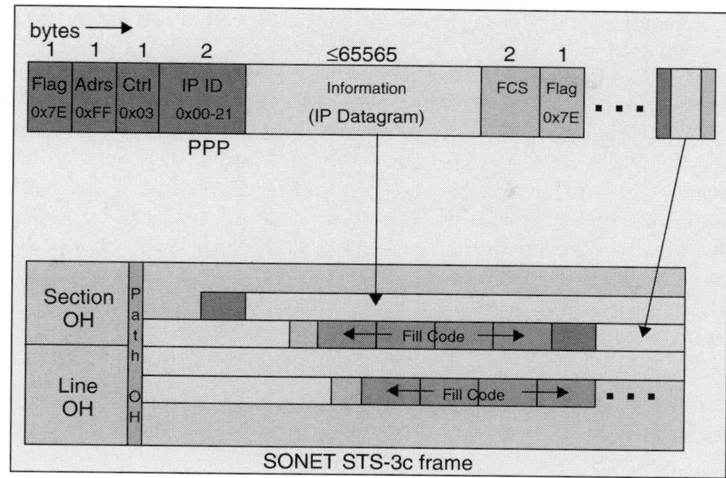

Figure 7: IP over SONET

any errors. The complete AAL5 frame is then fragmented into 48 byte segments that are placed in the payload of the ATM cells. Finally the ATM cells are mapped into the concatenated SONET/SDH payload for transfer over the network (Bonenfant and Rodriguez-Moral, 2001; Grossman and Heinanen, 1999).

IP/PPP over SONET/SDH

By using ATM to carry IP datagrams, it is possible to provide QoS for the transfer of the data; however, this procedure incurs a penalty of a significant increase in the size of the frame overhead (up to 25%). Packet over SONET/SDH (POS) is used to get around this problem. The ATM encapsulation is removed and the IP datagram is sent directly over the SONET/SDH circuit. RFC 2615 and ITU-T standard G.707 specify the use of the point-to-point protocol (PPP) over SONET/SDH to carry IP traffic (Figure 7) (Malis and Simpson, 1999; International Telecommunication Union, 2000).

The IP datagrams are first encapsulated inside PPP. The PPP header field is one or two octets long. A value of 0x0021 indicates that the PPP information field is carrying IP data. The high-level data link control (HDLC) protocol is used to frame the PPP encapsulated IP datagram. The flag field (0x7F) at the start of the HDLC frame enables PPP encapsulated IP datagrams to be delineated on the synchronous transport link. The cyclic redundancy check (CRC) in the HDLC frame FCS field provides error detection. The HDLC frame is then mapped byte synchronously into the SONET/SDH SPE.

To avoid frame misalignment, byte stuffing is used to prevent random bytes in the data from mimicking the HDLC flag field. When a flag field appears in the data, it is exclusive or'd with 0x20 and the escape sequence 0x7D is inserted in front of it. The same procedure is carried out when the escape sequence 0x7D appears in the data. Thus, 0x7E is encoded as 0x7D 0x5E and 0x7D is encoded as 0x7D 0x5D. However, byte stuffing has the undesired effect of increasing the overhead in the data stream (Scholten et al., 2002).

IP over DWDM

With the exponential growth of the Internet during the 1990s, the type of data being sent over MANs went from mostly circuit switched voice traffic to a preponderance of IP packet data. The telcos were thus faced with the problem of carrying huge amounts of IP packet data over their SONET/SDH networks. However with the development of WDM technology during this same time period there was a potential solution to this IP problem. The use of DWDM technology was able to increase the capacity of the telcos optical fiber cables by two orders of magnitude. A number of architectures were proposed to enable the existing SONET/SDH infrastructure to carry the IP packet data (Metz, 2000).

Initially, a four-layer IP over ATM over SONET/SDH over DWDM architecture was used. ATM equipment was employed to carry the IP traffic (Figure 8a). The ATM cells were sent inside the SONET/SDH frame. Then the SONET/SDH frame was mapped into one of the DWDM wavelengths. However this solution was inefficient for a number of reasons. First the 5-octet ATM cell header adds overhead to the transmitted data. In addition, the bursty IP traffic may not fully utilize the SONET payload. Finally, this approach requires four separate management layers.

The second architecture (see Figure 8b) does away with the ATM layer by having the SONET payload directly carry IP datagrams that have been encapsulated by PPP in HDLC encoding. However, this approach requires the use of byte stuffing to enable the receiver to detect the

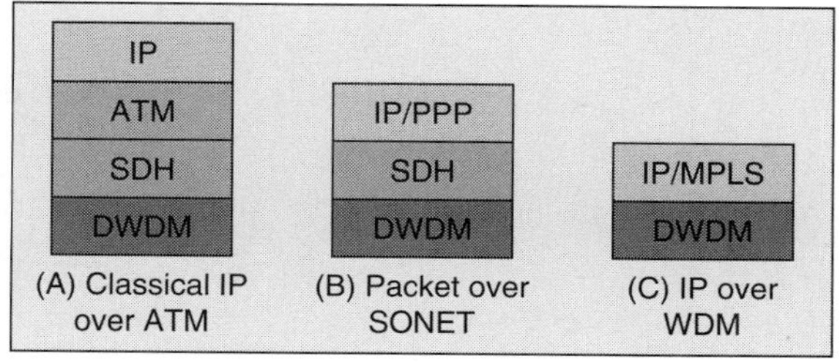

Figure 8: Multilayer network architectures

start of the HDLC frame. In addition, it requires the use of three separate management layers.

The best approach is to do away with the SONET layer completely and send the IP data directly over the DWDM optical layer (see Figure 8c). Thus, only two management layers are needed. Multiprotocol Label Switching (MPLS) is used as the adaptation layer between the IP and the optical layer to provide traffic engineering. By using wavelengths in place of labels, the IP traffic can be routed over the DWDM infrastructure. An extension to MPLS, called generalized MPLS (GMPLS) has been developed to support such a capability (see Generalized Multiprotocol Label Switching) (Gallaher, 2002).

Generic Framing Procedure

Two new encapsulation approaches for carry packet data over a SONET/SDH network have been developed by the ITU-T: generic framing procedure (GFP) and G.709. GFP (ITU G.7041/Y.1303) provides a generalized mechanism for enabling SONET/SDH networks to carry any type of packet data (Bonenfant and Rodriguez-Moral, 2002; International Telecommunication Union, 2005; Scholten et al., 2002). GFP specifies an efficient procedure for mapping both framed packet data such as IP in PPP and Ethernet, and block code oriented data such as enterprise system connect (ESCON), fiber connection (FICON), and fiber channel (FC) onto multiple concatenated STS-1 SPEs in a SONET/SDH frame. GFP also supports the multiplexing of diverse client data traffic over a DWDM wavelength.

The GFP frame format consists of a core header, a payload header, the client payload data, and a payload CRC (Figure 9). The core header contains a two-byte payload length and a two-byte core header error control (cHEC) field. The cHEC is a 16-bit CRC that is used for header error detection. The core header is also used for frame boundary delineation (i.e., frame synchronization). GFP frame delineation requires the correct detection of two consecutive cHECs.

The payload header contains the payload type and type header error control (tHEC) fields. The payload type field specifies whether the payload field contains user data or management information. For user data, the user data identifier field indicates the specific data type being carried by the GFP frame.

GFP support two transport modes: frame mapped GFP (GFP-F) and transparent mapped GFP (GFP-T). GFP-F is optimized for packed switched data such as IP, PPP, Ethernet, and MPLS data. GFP-F supports rate adaptation and multiplexing at the packet level and aggregates the frames at the STS level. Because frames must be buffered, latency is introduced into the data stream.

The GFP-T mode is optimized for data traffic that is delay sensitive such as FC, FICON, and ESCON. GFP-T operates on fixed length frames in real time. Because there is no buffering of the data traffic, no latency is introduced into the data stream.

G.709

In 2003, the ITU-T specified the G.709 protocol to enable packet data to be transported reliably and efficiently over optical fiber networks. It is a more efficient protocol for carrying packet data than the voice-centric SONET/SDH standard. It enables the transparent transport of client signals. In addition, it adds an optical channel layer for managing all of the wavelengths on a fiber in a DWDM network by wrapping each wavelength in a digital envelope (Bonenfant and Rodriguez-Moral, 2001; International Telecommunication Union, 2003).

The G.709 digital envelope consists of a header in which the overhead bytes are carried and a trailer that contains forward error correction (FEC) bytes (Figure 10). The header provides operations, administration, maintenance and provisioning (OAM&P) data for managing the optical network. The FEC bytes are used to detect and correct errors in the payload. G.709 uses the FEC specified in the ITU-T G.975 standard. It provides up to 5.6 dB improvement in the signal to noise ratio (SNR). The use of FEC enables either a longer span length or a higher bit rate for a SONET/SDH network, or more wavelengths to be carried over a DWDM network.

The G.709 frame consists of 4080 columns by 4 rows of bytes for a total of 16320 bytes. Unlike SONET/SDH the frame size is fixed; higher data rates are realized by an increase in the data rate of the channel. Thus, G.709 is no

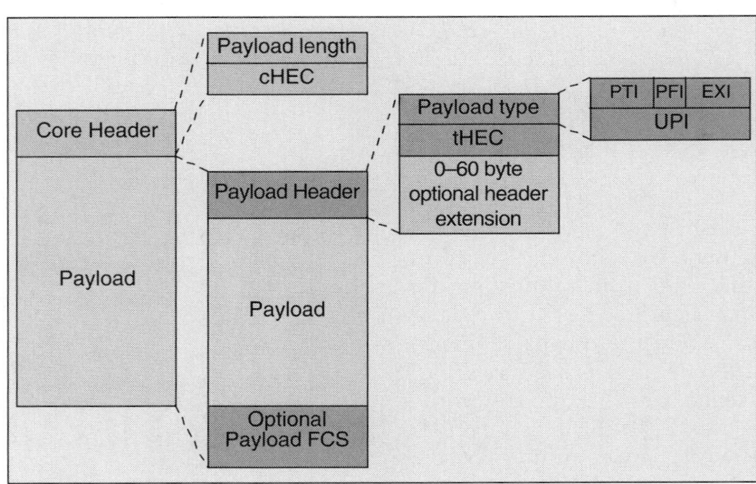

Figure 9: GFP frame format

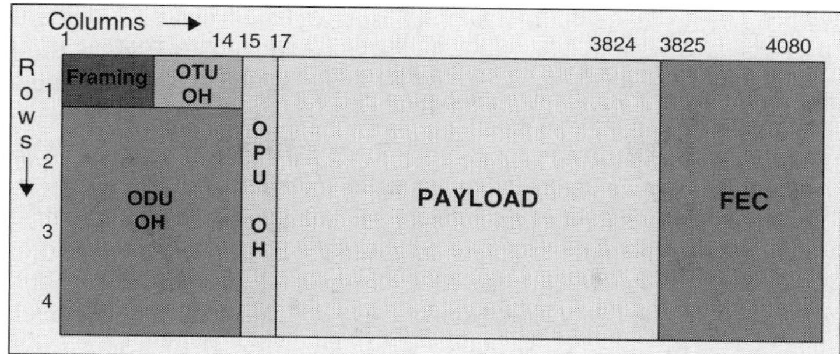

Figure 10: G.709 frame format

longer tied to the 8-KHz data rate used by SONET/SDH and other circuit switched protocols.

The G.709 frame header contains a frame alignment field, optical channel transport unit (OTU) overhead field, optical channel data unit (ODU) field and an optical channel payload unit (OPU) field. The frame trailer contains a Reed-Solomon (255,239) FEC. For every 239 bytes of data an additional 16 bytes of overhead is added for error detection and correction. The FEC can detect up to 16 symbols in error and correct up to eight symbol errors in the code.

G.709 defines three standard OTU interfaces that support data rates of 2.666, 10.709, and 43.018 Gbps for transporting STM-16, STM-64, and STM-256 payloads respectively. G.709 is protocol independent; the digital wrapper encapsulates a payload that can map SONET/SDH, Ethernet, ATM, IP, MPLS, and GFP protocols.

MAN STANDARDS

Initially, the IEEE 802 committee had limited its standardization efforts to LANs. The original IEEE 802 charter restricted the data rates for networks to a maximum of 20 Mbps. Beginning in 1980, the 802 committee developed standards for Ethernet (802.3), token bus (802.4), and token ring (802.5) LANs. However, the committee members soon saw a need for a network that provided higher speeds and spanned longer distances than LANs. Thus, the artificial restriction on speed was removed, and the 802 committee commenced the development of standards for MANs.

The initial standard for a fiber based distributed queue dual-bus MAN was developed by the 802.6 Working Group in 1987. Subsequently, the IEEE 802 committee developed two additional standards for MANs. In 1999, the 802.16 Working Group began the development of standards for fixed broadband wireless access MANs, and in 2001, the 802.17 Working Group commenced the development of a standard for a fiber-based resilient packet ring MAN.

IEEE 802.6 DQDB

In 1981 the IEEE 802.6 Working Group began the development of a high-speed MAN standard that would go beyond the boundaries of a LAN. The Working Group's requirement for a MAN was that it must support both voice and data; thus in addition to best effort packet transfer, it must provide a guaranteed bandwidth with a bounded delay. The resulting 802.6 standard for a distributed queue dual bus (DQDB) MAN was completed in 1987 (Institute of Electrical and Electronics Engineers, 1990).

A DQDB MAN consists of a head station, two unidirectional buses, access units, and an end station. The access units attach to both buses via read/write connections. The DQDB is implemented as a looped-bus topology that is physically a ring but acts logical as a bus. The end points are collocated so that one DQDB node serves as the master frame generator for both buses. Because data do not flow through the head point of the loop, it is not necessary to remove data from the medium as with a ring. Another benefit of the loop bus architecture is that it provides redundancy. If a node or a link fails, the network can close the data buses through the head point of the loop to enable the network to continue to function.

The basic unit of data transfer on a DQDB MAN is the 53-octet slot (Figure 11). A slot is the same size as an ATM cell. It consists of a 1-octet header called the access control (AC) field and a 52-octet segment field. The AC field contains the busy and request bits that control access to the medium.

DQDB Operation

The DQDB MAC protocol controls user access to the network. A single distributed queue is established for all of the nodes on each bus. Each node has a request (RQ) counter and a countdown (CD) counter. The node keeps track of the number of segments queued downstream from itself by counting the request (REQ) bits as they pass on the reverse bus. Each REQ passing on the reverse bus causes the RQ counter to be incremented. An empty segment that passes the node is used by a downstream node to transmit one of the segments that it has already queued. The RQ counter is decremented each time an empty slot passes on the forward bus. Thus the RQ counter keeps an exact count of the number of segments queued downstream.

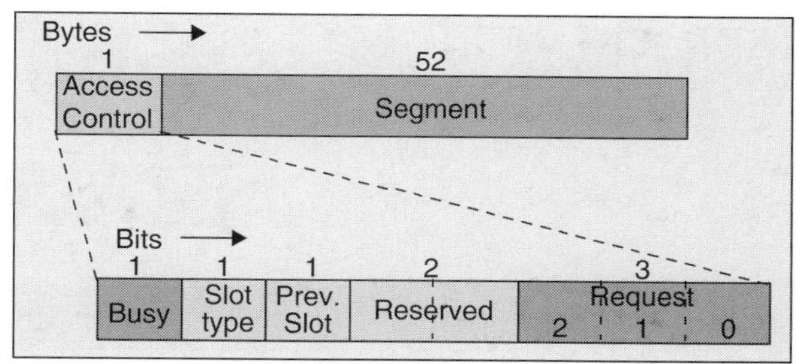

Figure 11: DQDB slot

To send data over the bus, the node transfers the current value of the RQ counter to its CD counter. The segment to be transferred is placed in the distributed queue by loading the CD counter with the number of downstream segments queued ahead of it (from the RQ counter), resetting the RQ counter, and sending a REQ over the reverse bus. The CD counter is decremented for every empty slot that passes on the forward bus. When the CD counter goes to zero, the node transmits its segment in the next empty slot that passes it. Any new requests received by the node after the CD counter is set are used to increment its RQ counter. Thus, the RQ counter tracks the current number of segments that have been queued by the downstream stations for its next transmission. Priority queuing is achieved by operating a separate distributed queue for each of the three levels of priority.

Data Transfer

In order to transfer data over a DQDB network using the connectionless MAC service, it is necessary to break the data into pieces that can fit into the DQDB slot. The MAC convergence function carries out the segmentation and reassembly of the data sent to it by the LLC layer. It accepts a MAC service data unit (SDU) from a DQDB user, segments it, and transmits it to the destination. The DQDB layer at the destination reassembles the segments into the original data and sends it to the user of the service. Before segmentation takes place, the MAC SDU is encapsulated with a header and a trailer to form an initial media access control protocol data unit (IMPDU). The IMPDU header contains the source and destination addresses of the data and a beginning-end tag that is matched against the beginning-end tag in the IMPDU trailer at the destination to check that all of the data was received (Figure 12).

The IMPDU is then divided into 44-byte segmentation units that are encapsulated with a two-byte header and a two-byte trailer to form a derived media access control protocol data unit (DMPDU). The DMPDU header consists of a 2-bit segmentation type, a 4-bit sequence number, and a 10-bit message identifier. The segmentation type indicates if the DMPDU is the first, middle, or last segment of the IMPDU. The sequence number is used to check for missing pieces of the data. The message identifier allows the destination station to separate fragments from multiple IMPDUs that are being sent at the same time.

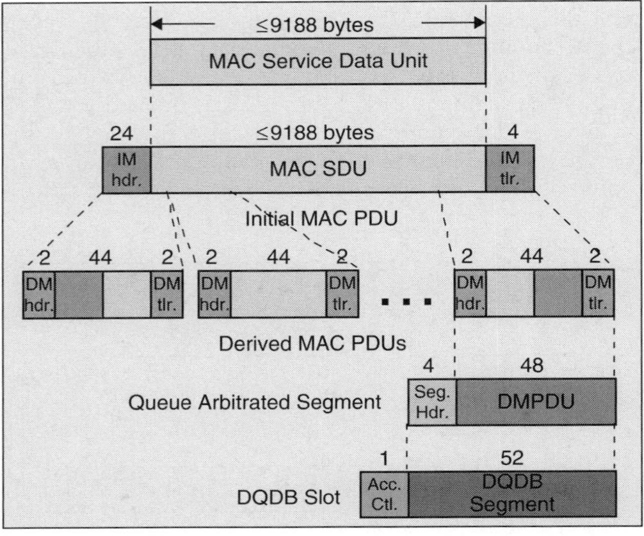

Figure 12: Data encapsulation and segmentation

The DMPDU trailer consists of a 6-bit payload length and a 10-bit payload cyclic redundancy check (CRC). The length field indicates the actual size of the data in the fixed size segment. The CRC checks for errors in the DMPDU.

The DQDB protocol provides excellent performance. If no segments are waiting, access to the bus is immediate. The node is able to transmit on the next empty segment that passes it. Also slots are never wasted if data is queued for transmission. The protocol guarantees a minimum access delay at all levels of loading right up to the maximum network utilization of 100%. The protocol also supports fair access to the bus. To prevent one node from grabbing all of the bandwidth, a node cannot make a second request until the first request is satisfied.

IEEE 802.17 Resilient Packet Ring

In 2003, the IEEE 802.17 Working Group completed the development of a new fiber-based standard for MANs. The resilient packet ring (RPR) is a high-speed network that is optimized for packet transmission (Institute of Electrical and Electronics Engineers, 2004b). As the name indicates, RPR is a ring-based network that comprises a dual set of counter-rotating rings. Each station on the ring is connected to its upstream and downstream neighbors by P-P links. The dual-ring architecture allows for resiliency; the network can recover from a break in one of the rings by wrapping the two rings together to bypass the failed link.

Unlike SONET/SDH rings, RPR provides a mechanism for using the full bandwidth of both rings for the transmission of data. SONET/SDH rings also consist of a dual counter-rotating ring configuration, but one of the rings is used solely for backup. With RPR it is not necessary to set aside half of the bandwidth for backup. In order to allow the full bandwidth to be used for data transmission, a fairness algorithm and a prioritization mechanism are specified so that higher priority data can be given preference. An auto-restoration capability is specified to enable the reconfiguration of the ring in the event of a link failure.

RPR Operation

RPR consists of two unidirectional counter-rotating rings. The outer ring is called ringlet 0 and the inner ring is called ringlet 1. Each station on the ring is given a standard 48-bit MAC address. The station with data to send to another station decides which of the two rings to use to send the data. Thus, RPR allows the shortest path between stations to be selected for the transmission of data. Each station on the path between the source and destination station forwards the frame to the next station (Yuan, Gambiroza, and Knightly, 2004).

Unlike the token ring protocol, when the destination station receives a unicast frame, it removes it completely from the ring rather than just copying it and sending it back to the source station. This technique enables the

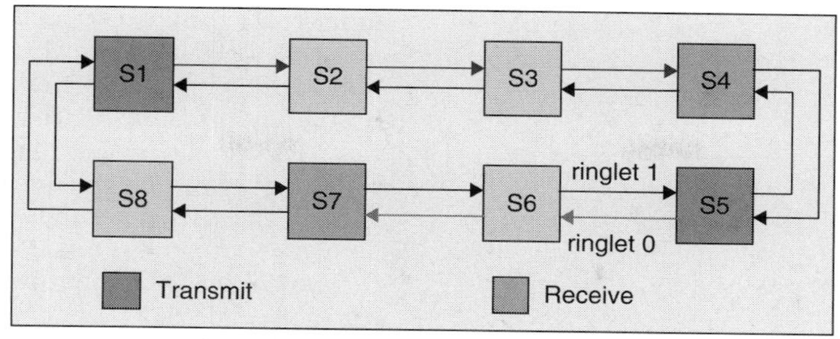

Figure 13: Spatial reuse in an RPR network

ring to be used more efficiently because it allows for spatial reuse of the bandwidth. The bandwidth that would have been used by the frame as it traveled back to the source station is now used by another station to send data. Thus, multiple stations can send data simultaneously over non-overlapping portions of the ring. This is called spatial reuse. As shown in Figure 13, station S1 is sending data to station S4 at the same time that station S5 is sending data to station S7.

To prevent a frame from circulating forever, a time to live (TTL) field is included in the frame header. The TTL is decremented each time the frame arrives at a station on the ring. When the TTL value goes to zero, the station removes the frame from the ring.

Like all of the IEEE 802 standards, RPR encompasses the data link and the physical layer of the ISO reference model. The data link layer comprises two parts: the logical link control (LLC) sublayer that is common to all IEEE 802 LAN and MAN protocols and the MAC sublayer that contains the control logic for the RPR protocol. The MAC sub-layer, in turn, contains two parts: MAC control and MAC data path. The MAC control sub-layer controls the transfer of data between the MAC and its LLC client. The MAC datapath sub-layer provides data transfer functions for each ringlet.

The physical layer contains a reconciliation sublayer and the physical layer protocol (PHY). Two Packet PHYs and a SONET/SDH PHY are specified in the RPR standard. The Packet PHYs are based on the 1 Gbps and the 10 Gbps-Ethernet PHYs. The SONET/SDH PHY supports data rates from 155 Mbps to 10 Gbps.

Classes of Service

The RPR data transfer service is controlled by two parameters: a committed information rate (CIR) and an excess information rate (EIR). RPR specifies three different service classes for data transfer. Class A service is for delay sensitive (real time) traffic. Class B service provides for the transfer of traffic with bounded delay (near real time). Class C provides a best effort data transfer service (see Table 1) (Davik et al., 2004).

Class A traffic is allocated with a CIR. It provides a guaranteed data rate and a low end-to-end delay and jitter. There is a maximum amount of Class A traffic that can be allocated; traffic above this allocated rate is rejected. Class A traffic has precedence over Class B and Class C traffic. Also, Class A traffic is not subject to the fairness algorithm; thus class A traffic will not be discarded by the RPR. Class A service consists of two subclasses: subclass A0 and subclass A1. Unused subclass A1 bandwidth can be reclaimed for use by class B-EIR and class C traffic.

Class B service also consists of two subclasses: Class B-CIR and Class B-EIR. Class B-CIR traffic is allocated with a CIR and provides bounded MAC end-to-end delay and jitter for the amount of traffic within the profile of the CIR. For data rates between CIR and EIR, Class B-EIR provides a best effort service.

Class C traffic provides a best-effort traffic service with no allocated or guaranteed data rate and no bounds on the end-to-end delay or jitter. Both Class B-EIR and Class C traffic is marked as fairness eligible. Fairness eligible traffic uses bandwidth that is available from the unallocated bandwidth and the unused reclaimable bandwidth. Thus Class A1 and Class B-CIR allocated bandwidth that is not being used can be reclaimed by a lower priority Class B-EIR or Class C station if it does not impact the service guarantee for the higher priority service class stations.

A weighted fairness algorithm is used to allocate bandwidth among the Class B-EIR and Class C stations. The fairness algorithm is used to prevent congestion on the

Table 1: RPR Classes of Service

Class of Service			Quality of Service				
Class	**Type of Use**	**Subclass**	**Guaranteed Bandwidth**	**Jitter**	**Type**	**SubType**	**Fairness Eligible**
A	real-time	SubclassA0	yes	low	allocated	reserved	no
		SubclassA1	yes	low	allocated	reclaimable	
B	near real-time	classB-CIR	yes	bounded			
		classB-EIR	no	unbounded	Opportunistic	reclaimable	yes
C	best effort	—					

ring. The algorithm calculates a fair rate for all of the stations with fairness eligible traffic.

G.709 with IEEE 802.16 WirelessMAN

The IEEE 802.16 Working Group is developing standards for fixed and mobile broadband wireless access (BWA) systems. The standards have been given the trademark name WirelessMAN by the 802.16 Working Group. The purpose of WirelessMAN is to provide an alternative to the fiber-based broadband access systems that have been implemented in metropolitan areas. The 802.16 standards support a point-to-multipoint topology in which a network base station (BS) communicates with a large number of subscriber stations (SSs). The network BS provides the SSs with connectivity to the wired public network.

The original 802.16 specification, published in April 2002, provided a LOS capability for fixed broadband wireless access in the licensed 10–66 GHz portion of the RF spectrum. Data rates of 120 Mbps or more can be achieve using channel bandwidths of 25–28 MHz. A revised version of the IEEE 802.16 air interface standard was published in 2004 (Institute of Electrical and Electronics Engineers, 2004a).

The 802.16 specification was followed by the 802.16a specification (published in April 2003), which added non-LOS BWA for both the licensed and the license-exempt bands in the 2-11 GHz portion of the RF spectrum. Changes were made to the 802.16 physical layer to support near-LOS and non-LOS (NLOS) signals. These changes include advanced power management techniques, interference mitigation, and the use of multiple antennas to process multipath signals.

The latest WirelessMAN standard, 802.16e, was published in December 2005. It adds a mobile capability to the WirelessMAN standard by allowing handovers to take place between BSs for SSs moving at vehicular speeds in the under 6 GHz licensed bands (Institute of Electrical and Electronics Engineers, 2005). The 802.16e standard specifies a system for a combined fixed and mobile BWA. It supports handovers between BSs managed by the same and different access control sites. In addition, it specifies an inter-technology mobility function that allows for handovers between IEEE 802.16e, WiFi, and 2.5G/3G networks.

MAC Functionality

The IEEE 802.16 standard specifies the MAC and PHY protocols for a high-speed wireless MAN. A common MAC protocol is specified across both frequency bands; however different PHYs are specified for each of the bands and for the licensed and unlicensed frequency bands. The MAC layer controls the transfer of data over the PHY and provides functions for authentication, association, and dissociation of the user devices. Both frequency division duplexing (FDD) and time division duplexing (TDD) are used to provide full duplex transmission for the uplink and downlink channels (Eklund et al., 2002).

The WirelessMAN MAC comprises three sublayers: the service-specific convergence sub-layer (CS), the MAC common parts sub-layer (CPS) and the security sub-layer. The CS maps external data formats into MAC service data units (SDUs) and associates the external SDUs to the proper MAC service flow identifier (SFID) and connection identifier (CID). In addition it may include payload header suppression (PHS). The CPS provides the basic MAC functionality of system access, bandwidth allocation, connection establishment and connection maintenance. The security sub-layer provides authentication, secure key exchange, and encryption.

Two CS specifications are provided: the asynchronous transfer mode (ATM) and the packet CS. The ATM CS accepts ATM cells from the ATM layer, classifies them, and if chosen, provides payload header suppression. The ATM CS PDU consists of an ATM CS PDU header and the ATM CS PDU payload. If no payload header suppression is being used then the ATM CS PDU header is the normal ATM cell header. The packet CS is used to transport all packet-based protocols including IP, PPP, and IEEE 802.3/Ethernet.

OFDM

The IEEE 802.16e standard specifies the use of both orthogonal frequency division multiplexing (OFDM) and orthogonal frequency division multiple access (OFDMA) technologies to transmit high-speed data over the air interface. OFDM is a form of frequency division multiplexing where a channel is divided into a large number of sub-channels and a portion of the data is sent over each of the sub-channels (Flarion Technologies, Inc., 2003). With OFDM, the frequencies used for each sub-channel are selected to be orthogonal. Orthogonal means that there is no interference between adjacent sub-channels because the main lobe of each carrier lies on the null of the other carriers (Figure 14). The orthogonal nature of OFDM allows the sub-channels to overlap, thus increasing the spectral efficiency of the channel. The 802.16e PHYs support 256, 1024, or 2048 sub-channels.

OFDM is an optimum solution for communicating in a NLOS environment where there is selective fading as a result of multipath propagation. The 802.16e standard specifies the use of quadrature phase shift keying (QPSK), 16-level quadrature amplitude modulation (16-QAM) or 64-QAM adaptive modulation techniques for the individual sub-channels to increase the spectral efficiency of these sub-channels. Up to 3.75 bps/Hz of bandwidth (2 bps/Hz average) can be achieved using this technique.

OFDMA

In order to share the bandwidth among the network subscribers, the 802.16e standard specifies the use of a scalable OFDMA scheme. OFDMA is a combination of a modulation and an FDMA and TDMA multiple access scheme. It divides the available OFDM sub-carriers into logical groups called sub-channels (Yaghoobi, 2004).

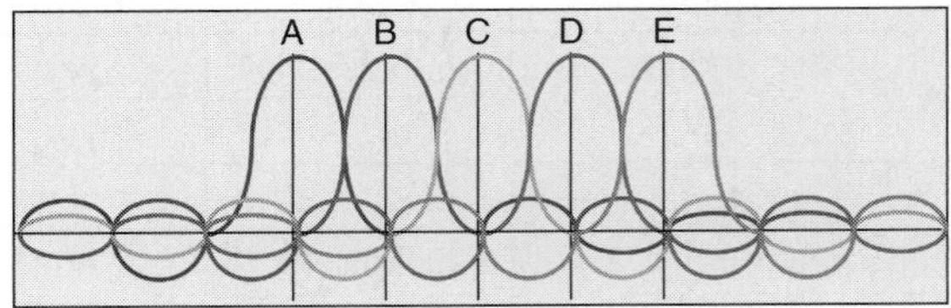

Figure 14: OFDM tones

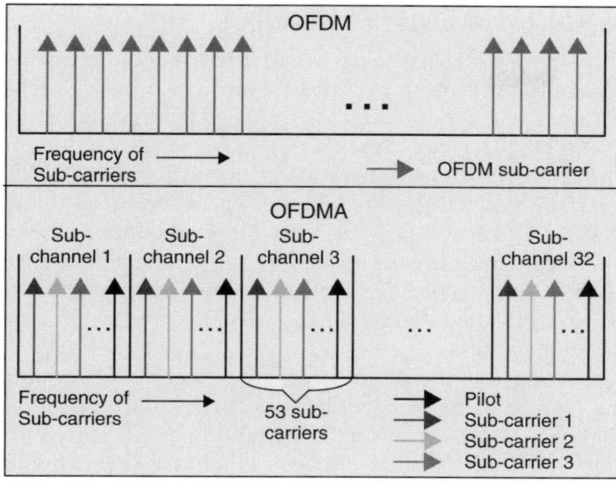

Figure 15: OFDMA channel partitioning scheme

For example, the 2048 sub-carrier uplink scheme specified in the 802.16e standard uses 1696 sub-carriers for data. The rest of the sub-carriers are used for guard bands and pilots. The 1696 sub-carriers are divided into 32 sub-channels that consist of 53 sub-carriers each (Figure 15). Coding, modulation, and amplitude can be separately set for each sub-channel to optimize the use of network resources. Multiple SSs can simultaneously access the channel by transmitting on different sub-channels. SSs are allocated one or more of the sub-channels for each transmission burst. By dynamically assigning the number of sub-channels, OFDMA provides a flexible means to allocate the capacity of the channel to the current SSs.

Because each SS concentrates its output power only on a portion of the channel bandwidth the signal to noise ratio (SNR) at the receiver is increased. If 32 SSs each transmit on one of the 32 sub-channels, there would be a 15-dB improvement in SNR on the channel. To provide support for asymmetric traffic rates for the upstream and downstream paths over the air interface, a time division duplex (TDD) scheme is specified. However, a frequency division duplex (FDD) scheme is also supported.

The 802.16e standard allows the bandwidth of the radio channel to be specified in multiples of 1.5 MHz (U.S.) or 1.75 MHz (Europe). To meet the needs of both urban and rural environments the standard supports variable bandwidth sizes between 1.5 and 20 MHz for NLOS operations. However, neither OFDM nor OFDMA (without scalability) can meet the performance requirements for all of these bandwidths for vehicular operation in a multipath fading environment without the use of a scalable OFDMA scheme. With scalable OFDMA, the fast Fourier transform (FFT) size scales with bandwidth to keep the sub-carrier spacing fixed. Scalable OFDMA enables the 802.16 standard to provide optimum performance for both a fixed and a portable/mobile communications environment.

It would appear that the 802.16e standard for mobile BWA duplicates capabilities provided by existing 2.5G/3G cellular standards and the draft IEEE 802.20 mobile broadband wireless access (MBWA) service. The optimistic view is that 802.16e will complement existing IP Internet access services provided by the 2.5G/3G cellular networks, WiFi, and the draft IEEE 802.20 MBWA service. A more realistic view is that it will compete with the existing and planned cellular network IP data services.

IEEE 802.20

In December 2002 the IEEE 802 committee approved the formation of the IEEE 802.20 MBWA Working Group (WG). The objective of the 802.20 WG is to develop a specification for the physical and medium access control layers of an air interface for a mobile broadband wireless access network that is optimized for the transport of IP based services. The air interface would operate in the licensed bands below 3.5 GHz and support peak data rates per user in excel of 1 Mbps at vehicular speeds up to 250 km/h in a MAN environment (Klerer, 2003).

The original intent of the 802 committee was for the 802.20 standard to fill the performance gap that existed between the 802.16 high data-rate low mobility services and the high mobility cellular networks. However that was before the 802.16 WG developed the 802.16e specification that added a mobile capability to the 802.16 standards.

Although both 802.16e and the cellular 2.5G/3G networks also support mobility, the 802.20 WG insists that 802.20 provides different capabilities than each of these networks. With respect to the cellular networks, the WG argues that 802.20 is being developed as a "pure IP" network that does not have the legacy issues of supporting circuit switched services. Also, because 802.20 is being designed to operate in the same frequency band as the 2.5G/3G cellular networks it will be able to coexist with the infrastructure of these cellular networks.

With respect to the 802.16e standard, the 802.20 WG argues that 802.20 was designed from the beginning for mobility and not as a mobile enhancement to a fixed broadband wireless network. In addition the WG states that 802.20 will supports higher vehicular speeds (250 km/h vs. 120 km/h) than the 802.16e standard and it will operate in the licensed frequency bands below 3.5 GHz as opposed to the 2 to 6 GHz frequency range for 802.16e.

At the time of the writing of this chapter (June 2006), the IEEE-SA Standards Board directed that all activities of the 802.20 WG be temporarily suspended. The reason given was to enable the board to deal with contention that had arisen among the members and "irregularities" in the operation of the 802.20 WG. The suspension will continue until October 1, 2006 to give the board time to address these problems.

European Standardization Activities

The European Telecommunications Standards Institute (ETSI) has commenced the broadband radio access network (BRAN) standardization effort for the purpose of developing broadband wireless access (BWA) standards. The BRAN standards will cover the physical and data link layers of the OSI 7-layer model for network communications. The BRAN Working Groups are focusing on standards for high-speed ($\geq$ 25 Mbps) broadband wireless communication that uses the GHz portion of the RF spectrum. In order to provide a set of standards that will be universally accepted, ETSI is working closely with the IEEE 802.16 Working Group to develop interoperable standards for BWA.

BRAN has developed two standards for the GHz portion of the RF spectrum. High performance radio access (HIPERACCESS) is a P-MP wireless access network that provides communications channels in the upper part of the millimeter portion of the RF spectrum (11–42 GHz). High performance radio metropolitan area network (HIPERMAN) is also a P-MP wireless access network that uses the 2–11 GHz portion of the RF spectrum.

HIPERACCESS

HIPERACCESS network deployments will consist of a number of cells. Each of the cells will cover a portion of a metropolitan area. The cells will have a P-MP topology in which a network base station communicates with multiple subscriber sites. The cell can be partitioned into a small number of sectors with a maximum of 256 subscriber sites per sector. As a result of the high frequencies used, LOS transmission is used and the distance covered is limited to a few kilometers. Either FDD or TDD duplex schemes can be used for the uplink and downlink paths (European Telecommunications Standards Institute, 2002).

The modulation scheme used for HIPERACCESS is QAM. A Reed-Solomon (R-S) code that is concatenated with a convolutional code, with no interleaving, is employed for forward error correction. In the downlink direction, data sent to different subscriber sites is multiplexed in the time domain. Because HIPERACCESS employs adaptive PHY modes, different TDM groupings can be assigned differentPHY modes.

In the uplink direction the subscriber stations use time division multiple access (TDMA) to share the RF channel. The channel spacing in both the uplink and downlink directions is 28 MHz with a maximum capacity of 60-Mbps downlink and 30-Mbps uplink.

HIPERMAN

The HIPERMAN standard is designed for fixed wireless access for small to medium size business and residential locations. HIPERMAN operates in the 2 and 11 GHz frequency spectrum. The communications environment is one in which there is NLOS communications; therefore HIPERMAN equipment must operate in the presence of multipath. HIPERMAN supports a P-MP topology and optionally a mesh topology. HIPERMAN was designed to be a subset of the IEEE 802.16a standard. It uses the 802.16a MAC layer; thus it supports the MAC layer QoS, packing, and fragmentation functions. HIPERMAN provides an aggregate throughput of 25 Mbps (European Telecommunications Standards Institute, 2005).

The PHY layer uses the OFDM modulation scheme with a 256-point transform. TDD is used for communications in the uplink and downlink directions. The HIPERMAN FEC scheme consists of an R-S outer code and a rate-compatible convolutional inner code. The channel bandwidths used can vary from 1.5 to 28 MHz. The standard is optimized for radio systems in the 3.4- to 4.2-GHz frequency band.

MAN IMPLEMENTATIONS

In response to the needs for a high-speed networking capability and more and more bandwidth in the metropolitan area, the local telcos installed a large number of SONET/SDH rings. SONET/SDH provided a means for multiplexing the existing slower speed telco T1/E1 digital circuit offerings onto a higher speed circuit. Although SONET/SDH was able to provide the bandwidth and reliability mechanisms needed to implement a high-speed MAN, it did not provide any native QoS features and provisioning of new customer circuits was a very slow and difficult process.

To address these problems the telcos implemented the standards-based switched multimegabit data service (SMDS). SMDS provides a capability to directly carry high-speed LAN traffic between customer sites. In addition, it provides a prioritization scheme based upon the IEEE 802.6 standard that enable the telcos to offer customers different levels of QoS.

Another approach taken by the telcos to meet the need for bandwidth in the metropolitan area was the use of DWDM to increase the capacity of existing and new fiber by two or more orders of magnitude. DWDM enabled the telcos to meet their customers' needs for bandwidth and QoS by providing them with an individual wavelength on the fiber that is dedicated to their data traffic.

An example of a DWDM MAN is the Komnet network in Berlin. As shown in Figure 16, the network consists of two dual DWDM rings. Each ring has a diameter of 60 km and contains 80 wavelengths. Access to the rings is through optical add-drop multiplexers. The rings are connected to Frankfurt by a long-haul WDM link. IP over WDM is used to transport Internet data over the DWDM rings. High-end users can use Gigabit Ethernet or SONET/SDH to transmit data onto the rings.

The latest approach taken by the telcos for implementing MANs is to provide their customers with a Metro Ethernet networking capability. Because Ethernet is the underlying communications technology for almost all data traffic at a customer's site, the idea is to simply provide a means to carry the Ethernet traffic directly over a MAN. However a major obstacle that must be overcome in order to make Metro Ethernet MANs as popular as Ethernet LANs is to be able to provide QoS mechanisms that are lacking in the Ethernet protocol.

SONET/SDH Rings

The Synchronous Optical Network (SONET) standard was developed by the T1 committee of the American National Standards Institute (ANSI). The initial SONET standard was complete in 1988. SONET was originally proposed by Belcore (now Telcordia) in the mid-80s to replace the existing PDH transport hierarchy for digital data (American National Standards Institute, 1995). Development of the Synchronous Digital Hierarchy (SDH) was carried out at the same time by the International Telephone and Telegraph Consultative Committee (CCITT; now the International Telecommunications Union-Telecommunications Standardization Sector [ITU-T]) (International Telecommunication Union, 2000). SONET and SDH are similar but not identical standards as a

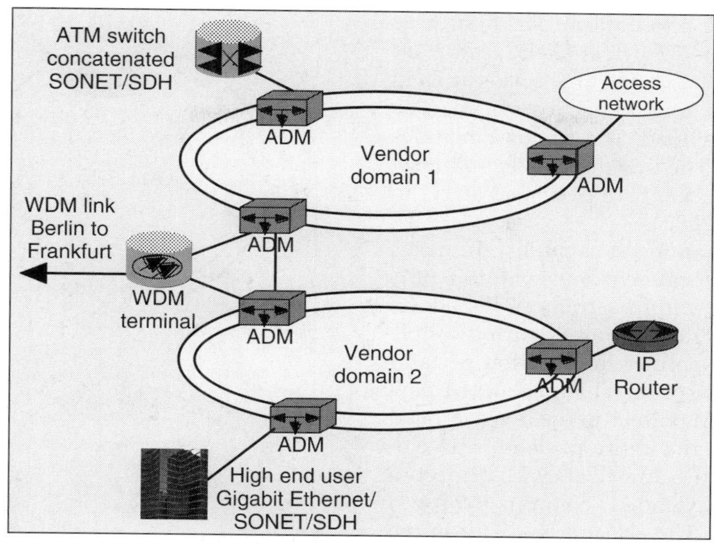

Figure 16: KomNet DWDM MAN

result of the need to accommodate the different digital data rate hierarchies that existed in the United States and Europe. However, the desire to have compatible worldwide optical standards led to a series of compromises that set the basic data rate of the SONET STS-1 circuit (51.84 Mbps) to be exactly one-third the rate of the SDH STM-1 circuit (155.52 Mbps).

Multiplexing Hierarchy

SONET/SDH is an interface specification for an optical transmission system. The specification defines the frame structure for carrying digital data and provides a standardized hierarchy of multiplexed digital transmission rates that accommodate existing North American and European data rates. It establishes an optical signal standard for interconnecting equipment from different suppliers along with extensive operational, administrative, maintenance, and procedural (OAM&P) functions to monitor and control the optical network.

The SONET specification defines an hierarchy of standardized digital data rates that are multiples of the basic synchronous transport signal level 1 (STS-1) rate of 51.84 Mbps. SDH defines a similar data rate structure based on multiples of the basic synchronous transport module 1 (STM-1) data rate of 155.52 Mbps (Table 2).

Table 2: SONET/SDH Multiplexing Hierarchy

SONET	SDH	Optical level	Line Rate (Mb/s)	Payload Rate (Mb/s)
STS-1	STM-0	OC-1	51.84	50.112
STS-3	STM-1	OC-3	155.52	150.336
STS-12	STM-4	OC-12	622.08	601.344
STS-48	STM-16	OC-48	2488.32	2405.376
STS-192	STM-64	OC-192	9953.28	9621.504
STS-768	STM-256	OC-768	39813.12	38486.016

The SONET/SDH standards also specify the method for multiplexing existing lower speed digital signals into a SONET/SDH frame. STM-1 is divided into a payload structure called virtual containers (virtual tributaries [VTs] in SONET). Three types are specified to support sub DS-3 (44.736 Mbps) data rates: VC-11 supports T-1 signals (1.544 Mbps), VC-12 supports E-1 signals (2.048 Mbps), and VC-2 supports DS-2 signals (6.312 Mbps). A set of rules specifies how these VCs and VTs can be packed into the STM-1 and STS-1 signals, respectively.

The basic SONET building block is the STS-1 frame (Figure 17). It consists of 810 bytes that are transmitted once every 125 μs (8000 Hz) for a data rate of 51.84 Mbps. (The basic STM-1 frame contains 2430 bytes.) The frame can be logically viewed as a matrix of 90 columns by 9 rows. Data transmission takes place one row at a

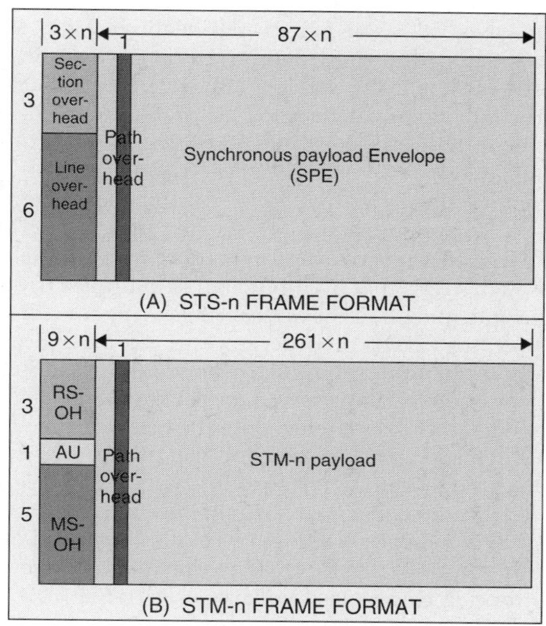

Figure 17: SONET and SDH frame format

time, from left to right and top to bottom. The first three columns (3 bytes × 9 rows = 27 bytes) of the frame are devoted to overhead bytes. Nine bytes are section-related overhead and 18 bytes are line-related overhead. The remainder of the frame is payload. The payload includes a column of path overhead. The line overhead contains a pointer that indicates where the path overhead starts in the payload field (Goralski, 2002).

SONET provides a drop and insert capability. It makes use of a set of pointers that locate channels within a payload and the entire payload within a frame. This allows data to be accessed, inserted, and removed with a simple adjustment of pointers. The pointer information pertaining to the multiplex structure of the channels in the payload is in the path overhead. A pointer in the line overhead serves the same purpose for the entire payload. The synchronous payload in an STS-1 frame floats with respect to the frame. Thus, the actual payload (87 columns × 9 rows) can cross a frame boundary. The H1 and H2 bytes in the line overhead are used to indicate the start of the payload.

Ring Topologies

A ring provides a simple mechanism for constructing a resilient network. A dual counter rotating SONETSDH ring architecture provides a fault tolerant and flexible transmission capability that is used to implement a self-healing network. If a break occurs in one of the rings, the traffic can be sent over the second ring to provide an automatic backup capability. Also if there is a break in both rings, a complete transmission path can be constructed by wrapping the rings together. This enables data to be sent to any node on the ring.

A SONET/SDH ring is constructed by connecting together a number of network nodes using P-P optical fiber links to form a closed path. The network nodes can be add-drop multiplexers (ADMs) or digital cross connects (DCSs). The ADMs allow traffic to be added and removed from the ring. The standards organizations have defined three types of SONET/SDH self-healing rings: a unidirectional path switched ring (UPSR), a two-fiber bidirectional line switched ring (BLSR2), and a four-fiber bidirectional line switched ring (BLSR4) (Goralski, 2002). Figure 18 shows the USPR, BLSR2, and BLSR4 ring topologies.

Each of these ring networks is composed of a set of nodes that are connected together by optical fiber links that form counter-rotating rings. Access to the network is through ADMs that multiplex and demultiplex tributary traffic onto and off of the optical rings using time division multiplexing (TDM). In order to restore communications rapidly in the event of a link or node failure, half of the capacity of the ring is reserved for backup. When a failure occurs the traffic is switched onto the reserved ring capacity. Switching can be done rapidly (on the order of 50 ms) because the automatic protection switching bytes in the SONET header can signal a ring failure in real time.

A USPR network (see Figure 18a) is composed of two counter-rotating rings, a working ring and a protect ring. The working ring is used to carry user traffic from node to node in one direction. The protect ring is also used to carry the same user traffic between the nodes in the other direction. Unless the protect ring has a better signal quality, only the working ring is used to transmit the data. If there is a link failure on the working ring, the protect ring is then used to transmit the data.

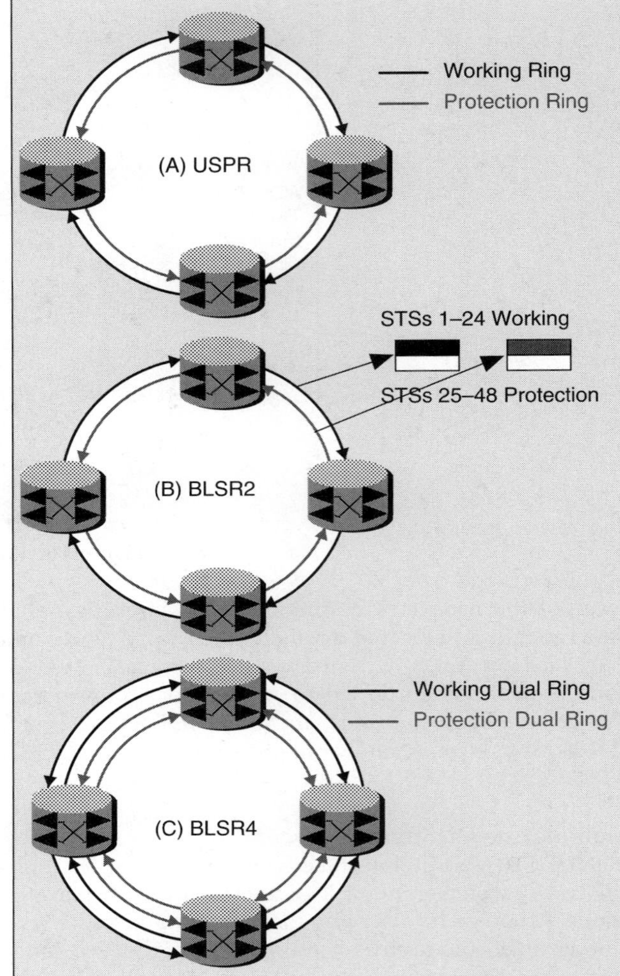

Figure 18: USPR, BLSR2, and BLSR4 SONET ring topologies

The BLSR2 network (see Figure 18b) also has two counter-rotating rings. Each fiber pair between two of the nodes is treated as a full-duplex link. However only half of the capacity of the fiber is used for transmitting data; the other half is used for protection. If there is a single link failure, the data is looped back around the ring using the protection bandwidth of the other links. The advantage of BLSR2 over USPR is that by having a full duplex path, the data can be sent over the shortest path between the nodes. Also, the bandwidth can be reused around the ring.

The BLSR4 network (see Figure 18c) has two pairs of counter-rotating rings. One pair is used for the transfer of working traffic and the other pair is used for protection. Thus, BLSR4 provides double the capacity of the BLSR2 and the USPR rings. BLSR4 increases the reliability and flexibility of traffic protection because it allows for both span switching and ring switching. Span switching occurs when a working span fails. The traffic is switched to the protect fibers only between those same pair of nodes. The traffic returns to the working fibers for the rest of the nodes. Ring switching occurs when both the working and protect link between a pair of nodes fails. To recover from a complete link failure, traffic is looped back through the protect fibers throughout the full ring.

Switched Multimegabit Data Service

Switched multimegabit data service (SMDS) was developed by Bell communications Research (Bellcore), the research arm of what was then the seven Bell Operating Companies (BOCs). Bellcore (now Telcordia) was formed as a result of the divestiture of the local phone companies from AT&T as part of the settlement of the 1984 antitrust lawsuit by the Justice Department. The SMDS service was aimed at supporting LAN interconnection and other data communications applications that require LAN-like performance across a metropolitan area. SMDS is based on the IEEE 802.6 MAN standard. It uses an underlying cell switching technology that is similar to ATM (both use a 53-octet cell) and the 802.6 DQDB media access control technique.

SMDS Operation

SMDS supports LAN interconnection through the encapsulation of LAN frames in SMDS packets. The encapsulation and decapsulation is performed by routers at the edges of the SMDS network. Because up to 9188 bytes can be sent in a single data transfer, SMDS provides the user with a high-speed subnet for the transparent transfer of any type of LAN data packets (e.g., Ethernet, token ring, FDDI).

User access to the SMDS network is over the SMDS subscriber network interface (SNI). To provide security, the SNI is limited to traffic from a single user; however, traffic from multiple users is multiplexed over the backbone SMDS transport network. The SMDS interface protocol (SIP) defines how the subscriber communicates with a SMDS network across the SNI (BellSouth Telecommunications, 1994).

SMDS traffic management is based on the concept called sustained information rate (SIR). It is similar to the frame relay committed information rate (CIR). SIR makes use of access classes over a DS3 access circuit. An access class places a limit on the amount of sustained information that the customer premise equipment (CPE) can send across the SNI interface. The access class also places a limit on the burstiness of the information transfer over the SNI. The SMDS edge router keeps track of the traffic from each user through a credit manager. If credit is not available, the router will not service the user payload.

SMDS Internetworking

SMDS is implemented as a public packet-switched service. It provides a connectionless (datagram) service to the user. Each unit of data must contain complete end-to-end (user) addressing information and transmission delivery is not guaranteed. End-to-end connectivity over SMDS is accomplished through the use of an internetwork protocol such as IP (Figure 19) (Piscitello and Lawrence, 1991).

LANs can be bridged or routed across an SMDS subnetwork. In order to bridge LAN traffic over an SMDS subnetwork, address resolution must be carried out between the 48-bit LAN MAC address and the 60-bit SMDS E.164 address. The MAC frame from the local LAN destined for a remote location is encapsulated by the 802 subnetwork access protocol (SNAP). SNAP contains the 24-bit organizationally unique identifier (OUI) value

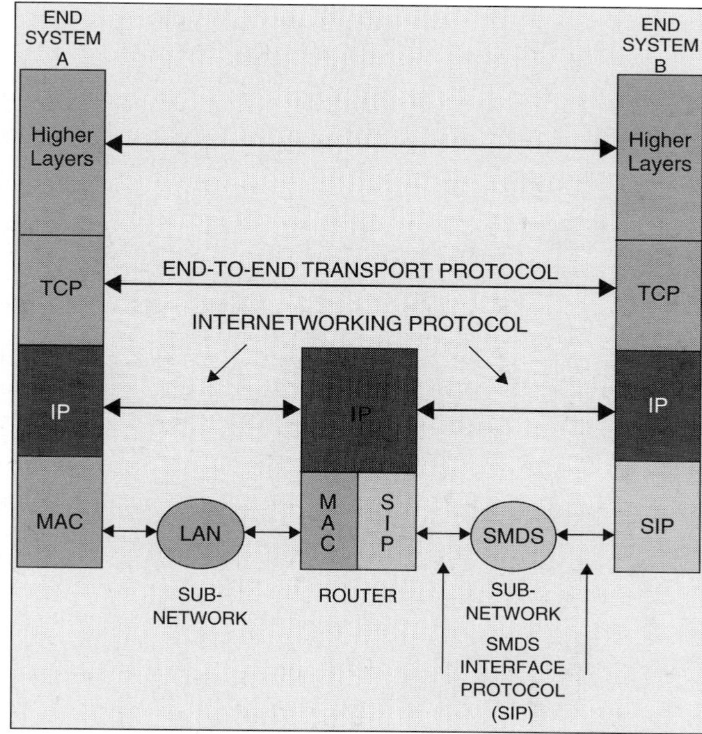

Figure 19: IP internetworking over an SMDS network

which identifies the organization and the 16-bit protocol ID (PID), which identifies the bridged MAC frame protocol. The SNAP protocol is then carried in a LLC frame. The resulting PDU is encapsulated in an 802.6 MAC frame (as an IMPDU). The IMPDU header contains the 60-bit E.164 SMDS address. Finally, the IMPDU is segmented into DMPDUs for transmission over the SMDS subnetwork to the remote bridge where the original MAC PDU is reconstructed and sent over the remote LAN.

DWDM Network

The two techniques that are used for multiplexing data over a communications channel are time division multiplexing (TDM) and frequency division multiplexing (FDM). TDM is a digital technique that divides a time interval into a number of time slots (Figure 20b). Each input data stream is assigned to one of the time slots. The bits from each time slot are interleaved and transmitted over the communications circuit as a single high-speed data stream at the aggregate speed of the individual data streams. Thus, the complete bandwidth of the communications circuit can be used to send the data. The reverse process is carried out at the receiver to recover the individual data streams.

FDM is an analog technique that partitions the bandwidth of a communications circuit into a group of subbands. Each input data stream is assigned to one of the subbands and is used to modulate the carrier frequency for that subband. The modulated signals from each subband are sent simultaneously over the communications circuit (see Figure 20a). Guard bands are used between the subbands to prevent the modulated signals on each subband from interfering with each other. At the receiver, the signals in each subband are separately demodulated to recover the original data streams.

Wave division multiplexing (WDM) is a technique for combining multiple individual optical subbands and simultaneously transmitting these subbands over a single fiber. Thus, WDM is a form of FDM. Different colors (wavelengths of light) are used to transmit individual data streams over the optical fiber cable. Each color used consists of a narrow band of wavelengths. Each data stream is assigned to one of the colors (wavelengths) and the wavelengths are simultaneously transmitted over the optical fiber cable. Since the combined signal contains different wavelengths of light, the wavelengths can be separated at the receiver and the individual data streams can be recovered (see Figure 21).

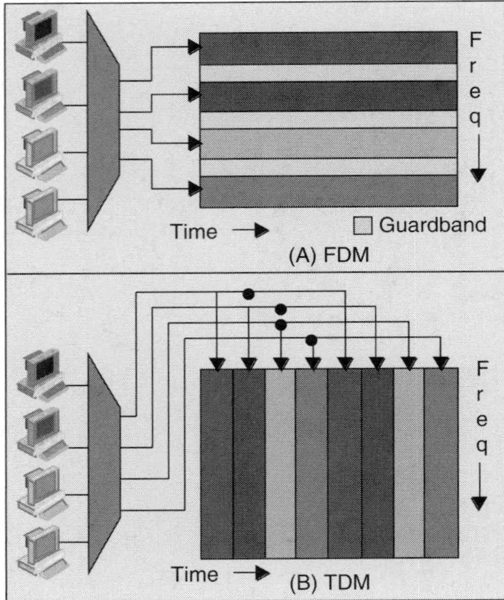

Figure 20: FDM vs. TDM

Dense wave division multiplexing (DWDM) is just WDM that uses a very narrow channel spacing (1 nanometer [nm] or less). With DWDM a single fiber can multiplex together 80 or more separate wavelengths of light, where each of the wavelengths is being used to transmit a bit stream at a data rate of from 2.5 Gbps to 10 Gbps (Fujitsu Network Communications, Inc., 2002). The ITU-T has issued recommendation G.694.1 for DWDM that specifies the operation in the optical S, C, and L bands for high-quality, high-rate MAN and WAN services. It specifies frequency spacing of 100 GHz to 12.5 GHz (0.8 nm to 0.1 nm) centered on the 1550 nm wavelength.

A DWDM network consists of P-P links between nodes. The links consist of a variety of passive and/or active devices to combine, amplify, distribute, add, and drop the optical wavelengths (Figure 22). Passive devices are used to split and combine optical signals. Active devices include tunable optical filters, add/drop multiplexers, switches, and amplifiers.

Both P-P and ring topologies are used in DWDM networks. Protection in P-P systems is provided by redundancy. Parallel links connect redundant equipment at each end of the link. A ring configuration can have a hub station and one or more optical add drop multiplexer (OADM) nodes (Figure 23). Traffic originates and terminates at the hub node. At the ADM nodes selective wavelengths are dropped and added. Protection in DWDM ring networks can be implemented using USPR or BLSR techniques (Gumaste and Antony, 2002).

In the early 1990s, SONET/SDH rings became the primary means for providing bandwidth for metropolitan areas. The SONET/SDH multiplexing hierarchy was designed to be able to efficiently carry the digitized circuit switched voice traffic that was being sent over the telcos T1/E1 digital circuits. However, as the amount of data traffic being sent over MANs increased and the type of traffic changed from primarily circuit switched voice data to mostly IP-based packet data, SONET/SDH circuits no longer provided the optimum means for carrying the data. In addition, with the exponential growth in IP-based packet data there was a need for more and more bandwidth in the metropolitan area.

DWDM provides the means to address both of these problems. The use of DWDM enables an optical fiber cable to carry 80 (or more) times the amount of data than it could by using only a single wavelength. In addition, DWDM is capable of transparently carrying any type of traffic so that both packet data and circuit switched data can be carried efficiently (Fujitsu Network Communications, Inc., 2002; Gumaste and Antony, 2002).

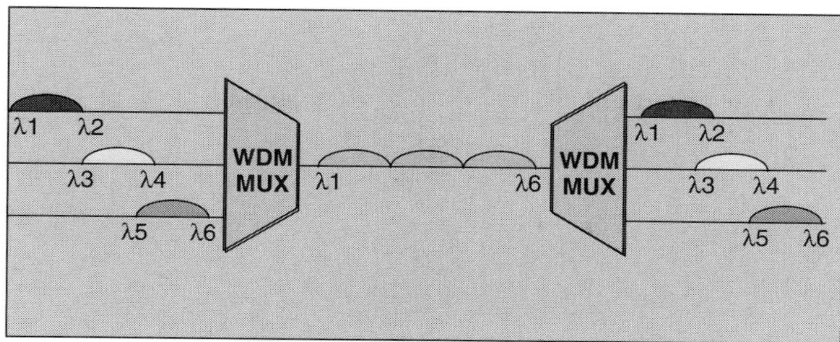

Figure 21: Wave division multiplexing

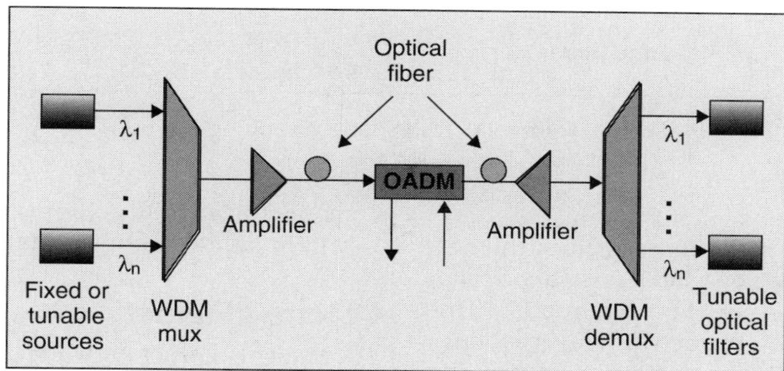

Figure 22: Components of a DWDM link

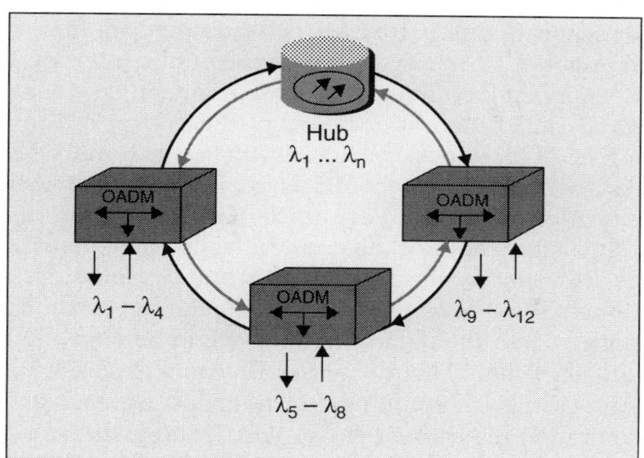

Figure 23: DWDM ring network

Data Transport over DWDM

Because the SONET/SDH multiplexing hierarchy was not efficient for carrying packet data, many MAN service providers favored the use of the asynchronous transfer mode (ATM) protocol to carry packet switched data. ATM is able to encapsulate different protocols and traffic types into a common format for transmission over a SONET/SDH network. However, the use of ATM over SONET/SDH adds another level of complexity to MANs. In addition, the use of ATM incurs a significant overhead penalty from the cell and segmentation headers. Finally, the packet segmentation and reassembly required for ATM cell transmission limit the speed at which one can transmit packet data over the SONET/SDH MAN (Metz, 2000).

Packet over SONET/SDH (POS) provides a means for efficiently transmitting packet data over a SONET/SDH network without the additional overhead, complexity and cost of ATM. However, POS still requires the use of SONET/SDH to transmit the packets over optical fiber links.

SONET/SDH can be done away with as a transport medium in DWDM MANs by directly transmitting the IP data over the optical transport. Because DWDM provides a large number of wavelengths, each wavelength can be used to carry a separate high-speed IP data stream. Thus there is no need for placing the IP data into an ATM or a SONET/SDH payload. However, existing IP over ATM over SONET/SDH and IP over SONET/SDH traffic can simultaneously be sent over the DWDM network by using separate wavelengths to carry these traffic types.

Multiprotocol Label Switching

The multiprotocol label switching (MPLS) protocol was developed to improve the performance of routing in an IP network by combining the datagram nature of IP with the label swapping hardware capability of switches. MPLS replaced the standard IP destination-based hop-by-hop forwarding paradigm with a label-swapping forwarding paradigm. Instead of using a longest match algorithm, label-swapping packet forwarding is based on a simple short-label exact match.

Routing protocol information is used to partition the entire forwarding space into forwarding equivalent classes (FECs). Each FEC is assigned a short, fixed-length, locally significant identifier known as a label. As packets enter a MPLS network, a conventional layer 3 lookup is performed and the next hop is determined. The label that is associated with the FEC is found and the packet is forwarded to the next hop with the assigned label.

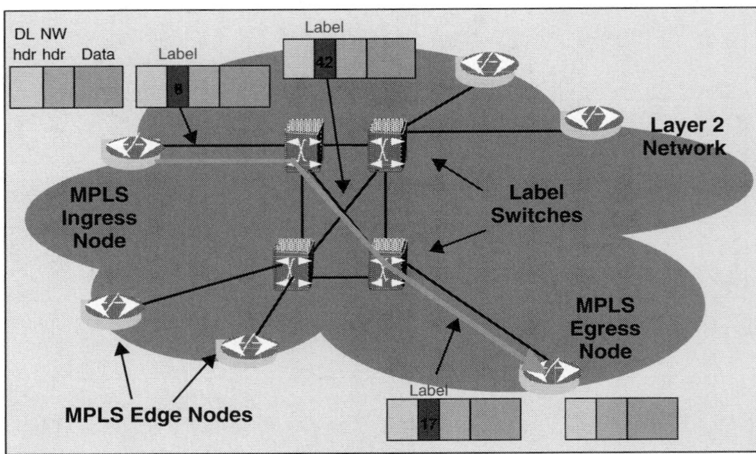

Figure 24: MPLS label swapping

At subsequent nodes label switch routers (LSRs) use the label as an index into a table that specifies the new outgoing label and next hop. The label is swapped and the packet is forward to the next hop (Figure 24). This procedure eliminates the need for network-layer lookups in all but the first node. Information from the routing protocols is used to assign and distribute labels to MPLS peers.

The label distribution is done via a label distribution protocol (LDP). An MPLS node receives an outgoing label mapping from the peer that is the next hop for the data stream and allocates and distributes incoming labels to upstream peers for this data stream. The labels are used to construct a switched path through the network as each MPLS node splices the incoming label to the outgoing label (Metz, 2000).

Generalized Multiprotocol Label Switching

In order to be able to transport IP over a DWDM network it is necessary for the IP network to establish optical connections through the optical transport network. The MPLS working group proposed extensions to MPLS to control optical cross connects. The initial effort was called multiprotocol lambda switching (MPλS). Further work on this capability was developed as part of the generalized multiprotocol label switching (GMPLS) standard (Gallaher, 2002).

The IP over DWDM model consists of IP routers attached to an optical core network. The optical core network comprises multiple optical cross-connects (OXCs) that are interconnected by optical links. GMPLS applies MPLS control plane techniques to optical switches and IP routing algorithms in order to manage light paths in an optical network.

Extensions to the open shortest first (OPSF) and the intermediate system to intermediate system (IS-IS) routing protocols are used to advertise characteristics of the optical connection. Extensions to the reservation protocol (RSVP) and the constraint-based routed label distribution protocol (CR-LDP) signaling protocols are used along with a link management protocol (LMP) to set up and manage the path. RSVP and CR-LDP convey label requests along an explicit path. LMP manages control channel availability, verifies connectivity of the component links and supports fault isolation.

Metro Ethernet

A Metro Ethernet network (MEN) is a network that uses high-speed Ethernet as the native transport protocol to provide connectivity services for broadband applications across a metropolitan area. A MEN connects geographically separate enterprise LANs within a metropolitan area and provides LAN users access to the public Internet. The MEN topology consists of point-to-point links that use Gigabit and 10-Gigabit Ethernet as the transport technology. The MEN nodes are either switches or routers. WAN links are used to connect MENs in different geographical areas (Metro Ethernet Forum, 2005a).

The fact that almost all data traffic on enterprise LANs uses Ethernet as the transport technology provides the rationale for a MEN. By extending Ethernet to the metropolitan area the data does not have to be converted to another format. This decreases the infrastructure costs because Ethernet equipment is much less expensive than the comparable frame relay or ATM equipment. In addition, bandwidth can be provisioned on demand from 1 Mbps to 1 Gbps.

The MEN is considered to be transport agnostic; it allows the use of other transport protocols to carry the Ethernet traffic such as SONET/SDH, WDM, or RPR. Thus, it is not necessary to replace existing infrastructure to implement a MEN. Instead it can be implemented over existing SONET/SDH and DWDM networks.

QoS

The major disadvantage for using Ethernet in the metropolitan area is that Ethernet has no built-in QoS capability. A requirement for a MAN is the ability to provide end-to-end QoS guarantees including connection admission, scheduling and policing, and prioritization of traffic. In addition there is a need for protection mechanisms that signal link failure and provide rapid reconfiguration of failed links as is done in a SONET/SDH network. In a standard Ethernet network recovery from link failure is done through the use of the spanning tree algorithm. However, it can take 10 or more seconds for reconfiguration to take place as opposed to the 50 ms recovery time for a SONET/SDH network.

A number of mechanisms have been proposed to provide resiliency and fast recovery in a MEN. The IEEE 802.1s standard, multiple spanning trees, allows the Ethernet network to have more than one loop-free path in a virtual LAN (VLAN) environment. This provides redundant paths for greater reliability. The IEEE 802.1w standard, rapid reconfiguration spanning tree, implements a faster convergence algorithm that takes 1 second as opposed to 10 or more seconds. Finally, the IEEE 802.3ad standard, link aggregation, provides sub-second failover on trunk groups.

Service Types

The Metro Ethernet Forum specifies the use of an Ethernet virtual connection (EVC) to access a MEN (Metro Ethernet Forum, 2005b). The EVC is an association of two (or more) user network interfaces (UNI) where the UNI is a standard Ethernet interface between the customer equipment and the service provider's MEN. Two types of EVCs are specified, point-to-point and multipoint-to-multipoint. These correspond to two Ethernet service types, Ethernet Line (E-Line) and Ethernet LAN (E-LAN). The E-Line service is P-P. It can provide either a best effort full duplex connection with no performance assurances (analogous to a frame relay PVC) or it can provide QoS guarantees with a committed information rate (CIR), committed burst rate (CBR) and excess information rate (EIR) (analogous to a TDM private line service).

The E-Line service is implemented as either an Ethernet Private line (EPL) or an Ethernet Virtual Private Line (EVPL) (Figure 25). An EPL consists of a P-P Ethernet connection that uses reserved, dedicated bandwidth. From the Ethernet client perspective, the transport network looks like a wire. An EVPL allows the sharing of network resources among multiple customers to enable the efficient use of those resources. Only a single UNI is needed to support all of the EVCs.

The E-LAN service is multipoint-to-multipoint. It provides multipoint connectivity between two or more UNIs. User data sent from one UNI can be received at one or more of the other UNIs. Like the E-Line service, the E-LAN service can provide either a best effort service with no performance guarantees or it can provide QoS guarantees.

As is the case of the E-Line service, the E-LAN service is implemented as either an Ethernet Private LAN (EPLAN) or an Ethernet Virtual Private LAN (EVPLAN). An EPLAN provides LAN-type connectivity between multiple customer sites through the use of dedicated channels. An EVPLAN can be considered to be a combination of an EVPL and a EPLAN. With an EVPLAN the transport channel bandwidth is shared among different customers.

ITU-T Study Groups 13 and 15 are working on developing standards for the Ethernet configurations documented in the Metro Ethernet Forum specifications. The Ethernet Service Framework is specified in ITU-T G.8011/Y.1307. The Ethernet Private Line Service and the Ethernet Virtual Private Line Service are specified in ITU-T G.8011.1/Y.1307.1 and ITU-T G.8011.2/Y.1307.2 respectively.

INDUSTRY FORUMS

In order to generate a market for new MAN products, companies that were instrumental in the development of new MAN standards and technologies have formed industry groups to promote the use of these technologies. The objective of these forums is to hasten the use of the technology by certifying products as conforming to the standards and carrying out interoperability testing of different vendors' products. Industry forums have been formed for both the WirelessMAN and the Ethernet MAN technologies.

WiMAX

The Worldwide Interoperability for Microwave Access (WiMAX) forum was formed in June of 2001 to promote the deployment of BWA through the use of a global standard (IEEE 802.16 and ETSI HIPERMAN) (WiMAX Forum,

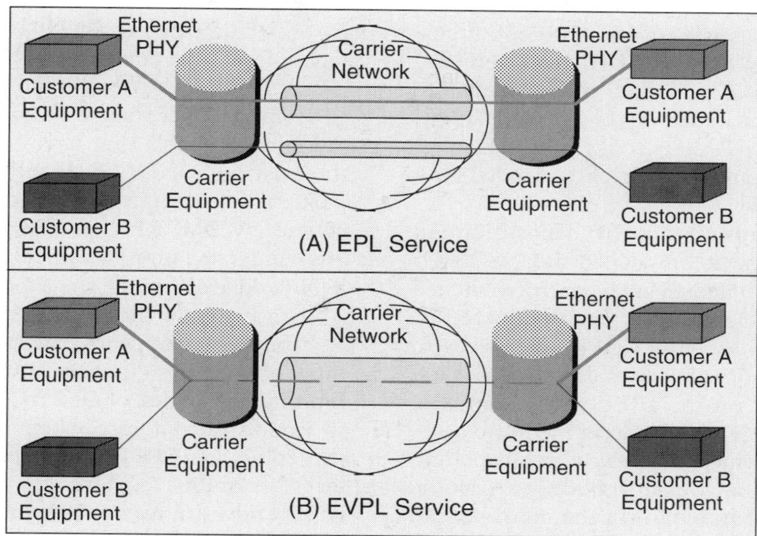

Figure 25: EPL and EVPL services

2005; WiMAX Forum, 2006). To facilitate the adoption of WirelessMANs networks, WiMAX has implemented a process for certifying the interoperability of products and technologies. A key function of the WiMAX forum is the definition of a set of profiles. These profiles specify a group of parameters that are to be used to enable interoperability to be achieved between system components. The WiMAX forum has implemented product certification testing to ensure radio link and protocol conformance to the 802.16 2004 standard. In addition, it is carrying out interoperability testing to guarantee that different vendor products will work with one another. The WiMAX forum issues a WiMAX certification to organizations that meet its profile requirements and pass its certification testing process.

Metro Ethernet Forum

The Metro Ethernet Forum (MEF) was formed in May of 2001 by a group of local exchange carriers to promote the use of high speed Ethernet technology for metropolitan area networks (Metro Ethernet Forum, 2006). MEF now includes chip manufacturers and equipment vendors. The rationale for using Ethernet is that it is easier to administer and cheaper to maintain than SONET/SDH networks. To foster the acceptance of Ethernet MANs, MEF has specified a set of standards for implementing Ethernet MANs. The standards encompass protection, hard QoS, TDM support, service management, and scalability.

MEF has implemented a certification program for carrier-class Ethernet. MEF defines carrier-class Ethernet as an Ethernet environment that provides the same reliability and QoS as SONET/SDH. MEF has instituted a testing program to implement the certification process.

THE FUTURE OF MANs

A vast amount of optical fiber cable has been laid in metropolitan areas. These optical fiber cables provide the infrastructure for the high-speed MAN technologies that have been implemented to meet the growing need for bandwidth to carry the ever-increasing amount of data traffic being generated by business and residential customers. In the early 1990s, SONET/SDH rings were employed by the local telcos to provide a robust means to transport their circuit switched traffic. SONET/SDH enabled lower speed T1/E1 circuits to be multiplexed together so that the data could be efficiently carried over the SONET/SDH rings.

With the change in the mix of traffic from mostly circuit switched data to mostly packet switched data, SONET/SDH MANs that were designed to carry circuit switched traffic were not able to efficiently carry packet data traffic. Thus, new technologies were employed by the telcos to handle the growing amounts of packet data traffic. First the SMDS service, based on the IEEE 802.6 standard, was implemented to provide a transparent means to carry LAN traffic between customer sites in the metropolitan area. Next DWDM technology was introduced to meet the need for more and more bandwidth in the metropolitan area. By multiplexing 80 or more wavelengths on a single optical fiber cable, DWDM enabled the existing fiber infrastructure to carry orders of magnitude more data.

Along with the use of new technologies, the development of new protocols allowed existing SONET/SDH MANs to better handle data traffic. Initially ATM was used to carry IP packet switched traffic over the SONET/SDH rings. However, ATM introduced its own inefficiencies, and IP/PPP over SONET/SDH was employed to reduce the overhead introduced by the use of ATM. Later IP/MPLS over DWDM was used to further reduce the overhead by allowing the SONET/SDH layer to be bypassed completely.

Changes were also made in SONET/SDH with the introduction of virtual concatenation and the use of the link capacity adjustment scheme. These changes enabled SONET/SDH to be able to carry packet data more efficiently. In addition, the GFP and the G.709 protocols were developed to transparently carry packet data over SONET/SDH rings and DWDM wavelengths.

With the development of the Gigabit and 10-Gigabit Ethernet standards, there has been a major effort to directly use Ethernet as a MAN technology. Because Ethernet is the dominant technology in the enterprise, it was natural to want to extend the use of Ethernet to the MAN environment. However, the benefit of using Ethernet as a MAN technology is somewhat mitigated by the fact that Ethernet does not provide a native QoS mechanism.

Recently two new MAN standards have been developed by the IEEE 802 committee to provide additional choices for implementing MANs. The 802.17 RPR standard provides a means to more efficiently use the dual ring fiber bandwidth by having both rings carry data. In addition, RPR supports a number of QoS mechanisms to provide customers with different classes of service for their data. The 802.16 WirelessMAN standard makes use of the 2–66 GHz portion of the RF spectrum to implement MANs using either P-MP or a mesh technology. The WirelessMAN technology enables a MAN to be implemented without the need to lay optical fiber cable.

Given the plethora of existing and new MAN technologies, it is clear that for the foreseeable future the marketplace will not converge on a single MAN technology. Unless it can be shown that cost savings can be realized by replacing existing SONET/SDH technology with new technology, the current SONET/SDH-based infrastructure will not be replaced in the near future. Thus, SONET/SDH optical fiber rings will continue to be used. However, the new protocols that have been developed will enable the existing SONET/SDH rings to more efficiently transport the ever-increasing amounts of IP packet data. Of course DWDM, RPR, and Metro Ethernet technologies are being used on new optical fiber infrastructure that is being added to handle the exponential growth in IP data.

As a result of the prevalence of Ethernet in the LAN environment, it appears that Metro Ethernet will gain significant market share as a MAN technology if its current limitations—a lack of QoS mechanisms and the inability to rapidly reconfigure when the network fails—can be overcome. Also, RPR should find at least a niche market given its ability to more efficiently use the optical fiber ring bandwidth and to provide the user with a range of service classes.

The most intriguing new MAN technology is the 802.16 WirelessMAN. It can be used to provide broadband infrastructure in developing nations where there is no existing infrastructure. However, that would not provide a major market for the technology. The other uses for this technology—to provide an alternative means of meeting the high-speed networking requirements of small business and residential customers and as a means of connecting WiFi hot spots and 3G cellular network to the Internet—is more interesting and more problematical. Whether there is a real need for such a capability and whether the 802.16 WirelessMAN can supply the needed bandwidth is still an open question. On the other hand, the 802.20 mobile wireless technology appears to be dead in the water. With the development of the mobile 802.16e standard and the problems being experienced by the 802.20 WG, it appears unlikely that there will be a market niche for 802.20. One thing is certain though. As new applications are developed that require additional bandwidth or new classes of service, there will be new MAN standards developed to meet those needs.

GLOSSARY

ATM: Asynchronous transfer mode is a cell-switching technology that provides QoS for the transfer of data and that is used to carry IP packet data over a SONET/SDH network.

BLSR2: A two-fiber bidirectional line switched ring that allows data to be sent over both of the fibers, but only uses half the bandwidth of each wire. In the event of a failure of the network the unused bandwidth can be used for backup.

BLSR4: A four-fiber bidirectional line switched ring that allows data to be sent over two of the fibers (clockwise on one and counterclockwise on the other). The other two fibers are used as a protect ring. In the event of a failure of the network the protect fibers are used for backup.

Contiguous concatenation: Combines the SPEs from lower speed SONET/SDH circuits into a single high-speed SPE. The payload of the higher speed frame is treated as a contiguous group of bytes.

DQDB: Distributed queue dual bus is a media access control technique for sending data over a dual fiber bus by constructing a single transmission queue for all stations attached to each bus.

DWDM: Dense wave division multiplexing is a form of frequency division multiplexing that uses different wavelengths on an optical fiber to transfer individual streams of data. DWDM uses closely spaced wavelengths so that an individual fiber can carry 80 or more separate data streams.

G.709: A ITU-T standard that uses a digital wrapper to carry packet data over an optical network. It uses an FEC technique to enable a longer span length and/or a higher bit rate for a SONET/SDH network or more wavelengths to be carried over a DWDM network.

HIPERACCESS: High performance radio access is an ETSI standard for a P-MP wireless access network that provides communications channels in the upper part of the millimeter portion of the RF spectrum (11 – 42 GHz).

HIPERMAN: High performance radio metropolitan area network is an ETSI standard for a P-MP wireless access network that uses the 2- to 11-GHz portion of the RF spectrum. It uses the OFDM modulation scheme to share the communications channel among the subscribers.

IP over ATM: A technique for encapsulating IP datagrams inside of ATM cell payloads in order to transfer the IP data over a SONET/SDH network. The IP datagrams are segmented to fit into the ATM payload and reassembled at the destination node.

IP over SONET/SDH: A technique for encapsulating IP datagrams directly inside of the SONET/SDH payload in order to transfer the IP data over a SONET/SDH network. The SONET/SDH payload uses contiguous concatenation to carry the IP datagram.

Metro Ethernet Network: A network that uses high-speed Ethernet (Gigabit/10 Gigabit Ethernet) as the native transport protocol to provide connectivity services for broadband applications across a metropolitan area.

OFDM: Orthogonal frequency division multiplexing is a form of frequency division multiplexing where a channel is divided into a large number of sub-channels and a portion of the data is sent over each of the sub-channels. With OFDM, the frequencies used for each sub-channel are selected to be orthogonal.

RPR: Resilient packet ring is a ring-based network that comprises a dual set of counter-rotating rings. RPR provides for efficient communications through the use of concurrent transmission, bandwidth reclamation, bandwidth reallocation and spatial and temporal bandwidth reuse. In addition, it provides for prioritization of the traffic through multiple classes of service and fairness though the use of a weighted fair access algorithm.

SMDS: Switched multimegabit data service is a service that is based on the IEEE 802.6 standard to provide a transparent means to carry LAN traffic between customer sites in a metropolitan area.

SOFDMA: Scalable orthogonal frequency division multiple access is a technique for sharing the OFDM bandwidth among the network subscribers by dynamically assigning a number of the sub-channels to each subscriber.

UPSR: Unidirectional path switched ring is composed of two counter-rotating rings: a working ring for data transfer and a protection ring for backup. In the event of a failure the data is switched to the protect ring.

Virtual concatenation: Uses multiple slower speed contiguously concatenated SONET/SDH channels so that the SONET/SDH payload matches the bit rate of the packet data.

WiMAX: The worldwide interoperability for microwave access (WiMAX) forum was formed in June of 2001 to promote the deployment of broadband wireless access systems in the 2–11 GHz portion of the RF spectrum through the use of the IEEE 802.16 and ETSI HiperMAN standards.

WirelessMAN™: The name given to the IEEE 802.16 standards that cover fixed broadband wireless access in the 2- to 11- and 10- to 66-GHz portion of the RF spectrum.

CROSS REFERENCES

See *Local Area Networks; SONET / SDH Networks; Terrestrial Wide Area Networks; Voice over MPLS and VoIP over MPLS; Wireless Wide Area Networks (WWANs).*

REFERENCES

American National Standards Institute. 1995. *Synchronous Optical Network (SONET) Basic Description including Multiplex Structure, Rates and Formats*. Washington, DC: American National Standards Institute, ANSI, T1.105.

BellSouth Telecommunications. 1994. SMDS Network Interface Specifications. Birmingham, AL: BellSouth Telecommunications, TR 73581 Issue A.

Bonenfant, Paul, and Antonio Rodriguez-Moral. 2001. Framing Techniques for IP over Fiber. *IEEE Network*, 15(4):12–8.

Bonenfant, Paul, and Antonio Rodriguez-Moral. 2002. Generic Framing Procedure (GFP): The Catalyst for Efficient Data over Transport. *IEEE Communications*, 40(5):72–9.

Cavendish, Dirceu, Kurenai Murakami, Su-Hun Yun, Osamu Matsuda, and Motoo Nishiara. 2002. New Transport Services for Next Generation SONET/SDH Systems. *IEEE Communications*, 40(5):80–7.

Davik, Fredrik, Mete Yilmax, Stein Gjessing, and Necdet Uzun. 2004. IEEE 802.17 Resilient Packet Ring Tutorial. *IEEE Communications*, 42(3):112–8.

Eklund, Carl, Roger Marks, Kenneth Stanwood, and Stanley Wang. 2002. IEEE Standard 802.16: A Technical Overview of the WirelessMAN™ Air Interface for Broadband Wireless Access. *IEEE Communications*, 40(6):98–107.

European Telecommunications Standards Institute. 2002. HIPERACESS; PHY protocol specification, Sophia Antipolis Cedex, France: European Telecommunications Standards Institute, ETSI TS 101 999 v1.1.1 (2002–04).

European Telecommunications Standards Institute. 2005. HIPERMAN Physical (PHY) layer. Sophia Antipolis Cedex, France: European Telecommunications Standards Institute, ETSI TS 102 178 v1.2.1 (2005–11).

Flarion Technologies, Inc. 2003. OFDM for Mobile Data Communications. Bedminister, NJ: Flarion Technologies, Inc.

Fujitsu Network Communications, Inc. 2002. Dense Wave Division Multiplexing (DWDM) Tutorial. Richardson, Texas: Fujitsu Network Communications, Inc. http://www.fujitsu.com/downloads/TEL/fnc/pdfservices/dwdm-prerequisite.pdf (accessed January 15, 2006).

Gallaher, Rick. 2002. Introduction to Multi-Protocol Lambda Switching (MpLS) and Generalized Multi-Protocol Label Switching (GMPLS). Converge! Network Digest. http://www.convergedigest.com/tutorials/mpls6/page1.asp (accessed January 12, 2006).

Goralski, Walter. 2002. SONET/SDH, 3rd edition. Berkeley, CA: McGraw-Hill.

Grossman, Dan, and Juha Heinanen. 1999. Multiprotocol Encapsulation over ATM Adaptation Layer 5. Reston, VA: Internet Society. IETF RFC 2684.

Gumaste, Ashwin, and Tony Antony. 2002. *DWDM Network Design and Engineering Solutions*. Indianapolis, Indiana: Cisco Press.

Institute of Electrical and Electronics Engineers. 1990. Distributed Queue Dual Bus (DQDB) Subnetwork of a Metropolitan Area Network (MAN). New York: Institute of Electrical and Electronics Engineers, IEEE Std. 802.6-1990.

Institute of Electrical and Electronics Engineers. 2004a. Part 16: Air Interface for Fixed Broadband Wireless Access Systems. New York: Institute of Electrical and Electronics Engineers, IEEE Std. 802.16-2004.

Institute of Electrical and Electronics Engineers. 2004b. Part 17: Resilient Packet Ring (RPR) Access methods and Physical Layer Specifications. New York: Institute of Electrical and Electronics Engineers, IEEE Std. 802.17-2004.

Institute of Electrical and Electronics Engineers. 2005. Part 16e: Physical and Medium Access Control Layers for Combined Fixed and Mobile Operation in Licensed Bands. New York: Institute of Electrical and Electronics Engineers, IEEE Std. 802.16e-2005.

International Telecommunication Union. 2003. Interfaces for the Optical Transport Network. Geneva, Switzerland: International Telecommunication Union, ITU-T Rec. G.709.

International Telecommunication Union. 2005. Generic Framing Procedure (GFP). Geneva, Switzerland: International Telecommunication Union, ITU-T Rec. G.7041/Y.1303.

International Telecommunication Union. 2000. Network Node Interfaces for the Synchronous Digital Hierarchy (SDH). Geneva, Switzerland: International Telecommunication Union, ITU-T, G.707.

Kartalopoulos, Stamatios. 2004. Next Generation SONET/SDH. Piscataway, NJ: IEEE Press.

Klerer, Mark. 2003. Introduction to IEEE 802.20. New York: Institute of Electrical and Electronics Engineers http://www.ieee802.org/20/P_Docs/IEEE%20802.20%20PD-04.pdf (accessed January 5, 2006).

Lauback, Mark. 1994. Classical IP and ARP over ATM. Reston, VA: Internet Society, IETF RFC 1577.

Malis, Andrew, and William Simpson. 1999. PPP over SONET/SDH. Reston, VA: Internet Society, IETF RFC 2615.

Metro Ethernet Forum. 2005a. Metro Ethernet Network Architecture Framework, Part 1: Generic Framework. Irvine, CA: Metro Ethernet Forum, Technical Specification (MEF 4).

Metro Ethernet Forum. 2005b. Metro Ethernet Network Architecture Framework, Part 2: Ethernet Services Layer. Irvine, CA: Metro Ethernet Forum, Technical Specification (MEF 12).

Metro Ethernet Forum. 2006. Irvine, CA: Metro Ethernet Forum. http://www.metroethernetforum.org (accessed January 20, 2006).

Metz, Chris. 2000. IP over Optical: From Packets to Photons. *IEEE Internet Computing*, 4(6):76–82.

Piscitello, Dave, and Joseph Lawrence. 1991. *The Transmission of IP Datagrams over the SMDS Service*. Reston, VA: Internet Society, IETF RFC 1209.

Scholten, Mike, Zhenyu Zhu, Enrique Hernandez-Valencia, and John Hawkins. 2002. Data Transport Applications Using GFP. *IEEE Communications*, 40(5): 96–103.

WiMAX Forum. 2005. Fixed, Nomadic, Portable and Mobile Applications for 802.16-2004 and 802.16e WiMAXNetworks. Mountain View, CA: WiMAX Forum. http://www.wimaxforum.org/news/downloads/Applications_for_802.16-2004_and_802.16e_WiMAX_networks_final.pdf (accessed January 10, 2006).

WiMAX Forum. 2006. Mountain View, CA: WiMAX Forum. http:// www.wimaxforum.org (accessed January 10, 2006).

Yaghoobi, Hassan. 2004. *Scalable OFDMA Physical Layer in IEEE 802.16 WirelessMAN. Intel Technology Journal*, 8(3): 201–12.

Yuan, Ping, Violeta Gambiroza, and Edward Knightly. 2004. The IEEE 802.17 Media Access Protocol for High-Speed Metropolitan Area Resilient Packet Rings. *IEEE Network*, 18(3):8–15.

Terrestrial Wide Area Networks

Gurdeep Singh Hura, *University of Maryland, Eastern Shore*

EVOLUTION OF NETWORKS

The computer network is usually defined as a set of autonomous computers interconnected (via different transmission media, e.g., twisted wires, coaxial cables, microwaves, satellite link, fiber optics, laser) together for exchange of information. It can also be defined as a model with associated protocols for different topologies, media access techniques, and signaling techniques that are required for communication between two remote nodes. The network finds its application in sharing of information processing resources (computers, printers, file servers) and bandwidth (frequency spectrum), distributed systems, exchange of multimedia information (video, images, audio, texts, graphics), accessing of remote information, and many other real-time applications. It has now become an integral part of organizations of any type like military, banking, air traffic, and other applications, which are solely dependent on the hardware (failure of which will collapse the whole system). The accessing of remote information includes: stock prices, airline schedules via public communication facilities, or dial-up for accessing our organization's databases. New applications like remote program, databases, and value-added communication facilities have been added economically. If we look at the evolution of data, we notice that in all these technologies, one of the main objectives was to define a high-speed with unlimited bandwidth network both for short and long distances that can transmit data, voice, video, and multimedia data.

CLASSES OF NETWORKS

There are mainly three classes of networks (based on the distance)—local area networks (LANs), metropolitan area networks (MANs), and wide area networks (WANs). LANs are primarily defined for short distance (few miles) applications within a single building typically using Ethernet technology, MANs are for a distance of a metropolitan area (about 50-100 miles) typically using optical fiber technology, whereas WANs or Internet cover a distance of thousands of miles within a country or between countries.

Local Area Network (LAN)

This is by far the most common type of data network that serves a local area (usually the area of a floor of a building, but in some cases spanning a distance of several miles). It finds its applications in industrial plants, office buildings, college or university campuses, or similar locations. In these locations, the LANs are owned by the organizations and as such we can install high-quality, high-speed communication links interconnecting nodes. Typical data transmission rates are 10 Mega (million) bits per second (Mbps) to 10 Giga (ten million) bits per second (Gbps) for resource sharing among the users within the organization.

Realizing the continuous trend of introducing LANs by different organizations for their applications, it was felt that these LANs have to be standardized by appropriate International Standards Organization (ISO) and as such IEEE 802 committee (grouper.ieee.org, 2006; standards.ieee.org, 2006) was formed to define standard LANs as 802.3 (Ethernet), 802.4 (token bus), 802.5 (token ring), and 802.11 (wireless). In order to avoid any technical and integration problems, ISO defined a uniform architecture known as Open System Interconnection (OSI) reference model standard that provides interoperability among these LANs. The IEEE 802 LAN model further partitioned the data-link layer into two sub-layers as logical link control (LLC) and media access control (MAC) (Figure 1).

The most widely used LAN is the Ethernet LAN developed by the Xerox Corporation. The first Ethernet LAN offered data rates of 10 Mbps Base-T and were extended to offer data rates of 100 Mbps, 1 Gbps. The Ethernet uses frame size of maximum 1500 bytes and in fact has been used in 10/100/1000-Mbps Ethernet devices. The Internet protocol version 4.0 (IPv4: currently being used) supports maximum size of 64 Kbytes, whereas Internet protocol version/new generation (IPv6 or IPng; currently being considered for the future) will support a packet of size of up to 4 Gbytes. The current 10-Gbps Ethernet (10GBASE-T) is being used efficiently on backbone connection end-to-end between networks. It uses the popular IEEE 802.3

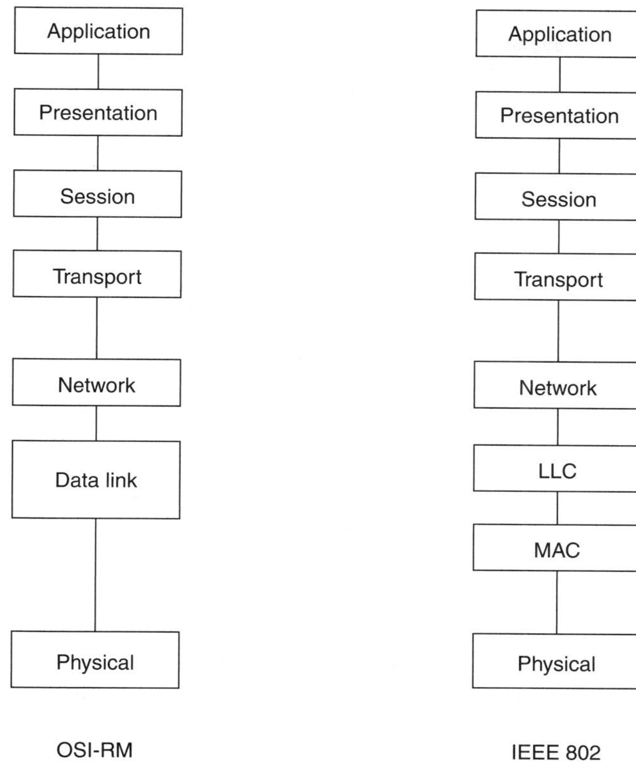

Figure 1: Comparison of OSI-RM and IEEE 802 model

Ethernet MAC protocol, its frame format, and size. Like Fast Ethernet and GB Ethernet, it also works on full-duplex transmission and covers a distance of 300 meters (m) (multimode fiber) and 40 kilometers (km) (single-mode fiber). It can replace existing networks that are using ATM and SONET multiplexers on OC-48 ring with a simpler network of 10-GB Ethernet switches for a data rates of 2.5 Mbps to 10 Gbps. It can also be used to interconnect LANs, MANs, and WANs. It is based on Ethernet media access control, its frame format, and size.

10-GB Ethernet has taken over fiber GB Ethernet, which offers data rates ten times greater than 10-GB Ethernet (IEEE). Meanwhile copper 10-GB Ethernet is expected to replace the twisted pair soon and in fact there are many commercially available adapters that provide connectivity between them. Ethernet over copper covers a distance of 15 meters. The GB Ethernet data-link layer encapsulates packets with a frame header (that included MAC addresses and other header control information) and 32-bit frame check sequence (FCS) before encoding to send across fiber or copper media. It supports optical fiber, twisted pair cable, and balanced copper cable (physical layer standards). IEEE 802.3z (grouper.ieee.org, 2006; standards.ieee.org, 2006) introduced the following standards: 1000BASE-SX transmission over multimode fiber (maximum distance of 220 meters, useful in large office buildings and carrier central internet exchanges), 1000BASE-LX over single mode fiber (2 km to 20 km), 1000BASE-CX for transmission over balanced copper (maximum distance of 25 km per segment, now obsolete), 1000BASE-T (also known as IEEE 802.3ab) standard over copper (maximum distance of 100/150 km). 1000 BASE-TX was created and proposed by the Telecommunication Industry Association and requires two pairs (commercial failure). These standards use 8B/10B encoding and support a data rates of 1000 Mbps to 1250 Mbps.

There are non-IEEE 802 LANs (proprietary) that can also be used for resource sharing. Interconnecting devices (i.e., repeaters, bridges, and switches) allow LANs to be connected together to form larger LANs. A LAN may also be connected to another LAN or to WANs and MANs using a router. A brief discussion on interconnecting devices is given below.

Internetworking Devices

The following section describes the functions of each of these interconnecting devices.

Repeater. It is used at the physical layer of OSI-RM that regenerates incoming electrical, wireless, or optical signals. The quality of data signals degrade or fade out after a limited distance in physical media like Ethernet or Wireless Fidelity (Wi-Fi) transmission used in wireless communication and repeater attempts to preserve signal integrity and extend the distance over which data can safely travel. Wi-Fi was primarily being used in place of 2.4 GHz 802.11b standard where the access point is being used as repeater only when it is operating in repeater mode. Now it refers to any type of 802.11 specifications (whether 802.11b, 802.11a, or dual-band) for interoperability as advocated by Wi-Fi Alliance as Wi-Fi Certified that works with any brand of access point with any other brand of client hardware. It was intended to be used for mobile computing devices like laptops and LANs, but now is being used in applications like Internet, VoIP phone access, gaming, TVs, DVD players, Intelligent Transportation Systems, and mobile commerce IEEE 802.11p (grouper.ieee.org, 2006; standards.ieee.org, 2006). It supports connectivity in peer-to-peer mode that enables devices to connect directly with each other.

Hub. A special type of network element that finds its applications in home and small business is known as a hub. A hub is a small rectangular box, often made of plastic that receives its power from an ordinary wall outlet. A hub joins multiple computers (or other network devices) together to form a single network segment. On this network segment, all computers can communicate directly with each other. Ethernet hubs are by far the most common type, but hubs for other types of networks such as USB also exist. This works at the physical layer of OSI-RM and cannot read any of the data passing through it and also is not aware of source or destination. Generally speaking, a hub receives incoming packets, amplifies the electrical signal, and broadcasts these packets out to all devices on the network including the one that originally sent the packet. There are three types of hubs: passive, active, and intelligent. Passive hubs (concentrator) do not amplify the electrical signal before broadcasting over the network. Active hubs (multiport repeater) amplify the signal (similar to repeater). Intelligent hubs add extra features to an active hub and are typically stackable (built in such a way that multiple units can be placed one on top of the other to conserve space). They include remote management capabilities via SNMP and Virtual LAN. A good five-port Ethernet hub can be purchased for less than 30 dollars, whereas a USB hub costs only a bit more.

Bridge. It is used for connecting and packet forwarding between identical networks (homogeneous networks) and operates at the data-link layer. Bridges are generally used to segment a LAN into a couple of smaller segments and have only a few ports for LAN connectivity. It is based on store-and-forward switching concept and does not provide any dedicated bandwidth to each segment. It forwards the frames b etween links. New bridges have been defined and standardized that can be used to interconnect different types of networks (heterogeneous).

MAC-layer bridge connects two Ethernets (IEEE 802.3) or token ring LANs (IEEE 802.5), whereas different types of LANs, such as Ethernet and token ring, can be connected by bridge (working at the data-link layer) as shown in Figure 2. Any frame coming out from Ethernet LAN host will be subjected to the same MAC sub-layer at bridge node. The mapping between frames of Ethernet and token LAN is performed by LLC sub-layer at bridge. The frame from bridge will have same frame format as that token ring host and as such will be interpreted as its frame. In the same way, the frame format mapping is done by LLC at bridge for frame coming out from token ring host to Ethernet host.

Switch. Switching technology is becoming an alternative to bridge-based interconnecting implementation as it offers better throughput performance, higher port density, lower cost for ports, and greater flexibility in configuration capability. It may soon replace the bridge-based interconnection and routing technologies. It is generally used to segment a large LAN into many smaller segments and have many ports. Small switches such as Cisco Catalyst 2924XL have 24 ports that can create 24 different network segments. Larger switches, such as Cisco Catalyst 6500, have hundreds of ports. LAN switch is used to interconnect multiple LAN segments. It provides dedicated, collision-free communication between network devices, with support for multiple simultaneous conversations. LAN switches are designed to switch data frames at high speeds.

Gateway. Heterogeneous networks are defined as a collection of different types of networks that have different protocols (from different vendors) at data-link and network layers. These networks (private or public) can communicate with each other through gateway, which operates at the network layer of OSI-RM. It maintains a routing table to provide internetworking addresses and offers compatibility between protocols of all three lower layers (physical, data, and network). It is also known as a router. Many gateways will require operation through all seven layers of OSI-RM. Examples would be the IBM LAN with bisynch and EBDIC connected to another type of LAN, such as Ethernet. 802.11a and 802.11b are standards. 802.11g standard offers wireless interface while 802.11n (emerging standard) is a transition at a frequency of 2.4GHz or 5GHz with data rates of 600MHz. 802.11b and 802.11g are compatible and devices can coexist in the same network.

Fiber Distributed Data Interface (FDDI)

It is 100-Mbps LAN, which uses optical fiber as a transmission medium and is mainly based on packet-switching approach for data communication. The FDDI protocol is based on token ring media access technique and uses ring topology that does not impose any restrictions on the number of stations and the length of links. The ring topology offers point-to-point communication and is being used by MANs as well. It offers features like reliability, availability serviceability, and maintainability even in the presence of broken link or failed node. The FDDI is being used as a backbone LAN in many corporations and universities.

The performance of ring topology can be improved by using two rings such that in case of a failed link or node, it can be reconfigured to bypass it and still offer same response without affecting the topology or the nodes. This finds its application in the implementation of MAN (IEEE 802.6) (grouper.ieee.org, 2006). The layers of FDDI node conform to both IEEE 802 and OSI-RM.

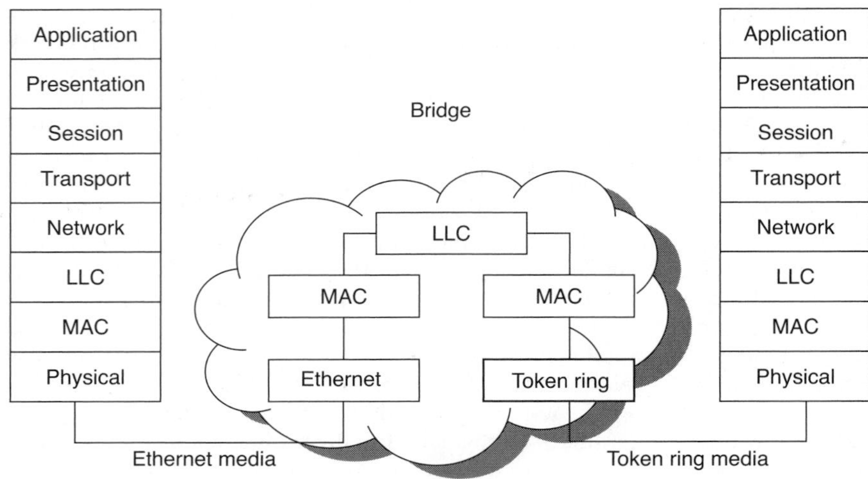

Figure 2: Bridge connectivity between different types of LANs

Fiber Distributed Data Interface-II (FDDI-II)

An enhanced version of FDDI known as FDDI-II was introduced that offers integrated services of packet switching and isochronous (requiring timing coordination for voice and digital video transmission) services at a bandwidth of 100 Mbps. It supports both packet switching and circuit switching for data transfer and as such the entire bandwidth can be allocated to both packet-switched circuit-switched data networks. The FDDI-II ring supports high-performance processors, high-performance workstations, mass storage system, distributed data base systems, and a switchable backbone LANs for a number of functions.

If FDDI-II ring network is working in a packet-switched mode, it may well be used as a backbone for interconnection devices (like gateways) to public data network. With packet-switched service, FDDI packets are of variable length and contain various control symbols, addresses, delimiters, for identifying the fields within packets.

If FDDI-II is working in circuit-switching mode, no addressing is required. Instead it establishes a connection upon request and requires the knowledge of time-slot and prior mutual agreement with the destination user node. In FDDI II, the synchronous operation typically works on packet-switching but can also operate on circuit-emulation (used in ATM networks). This emulation accepts all continuous bit rate information (generated by continuous bit rate [CBR]). The switching and multiplexing operations are always performed by higher layers (data-link layers network layers, and above layers), whereas transmission functions are performed by lower layer (physical).

FDDI-II handles three types of packets or traffic: 1) asynchronous: packets of different lengths arriving randomly, 2) synchronous: packets arrive at regular interval with pre-defined number and size defined, and 3) isochronous: packets are well defined in size, their arrival during time slots, the use of entire bandwidth, and other features and are well known in advance. An isochronous service is offered by wide band channel (WBC), which describes circuit-switched connections. A total bandwidth of 98.304 Mbps is available for a variety of applications. The isochronous bandwidth (WBC) may be allocated to different sub-channels supporting different virtual circuit services like (video, voice, image, control data, real-time data) within bandwidth of a WBC or more WBCs. The maximum length of a ring is about 200 km and supports up to 1000 users. The maximum distance between two nodes is 2 km.

Wireless Network Technology

Wireless networking technology offers wireless connection services across short distances for global voice and data communication. It uses infrared light, radio frequency and carrier currents media for wireless communication services via unlicensed frequencies of 10 Mbps. A variety of devices used for wireless networking include desktop computers, laptop computers, hand-held computers, personal digital assistants (PDAs), cellular phones, pagers, pen-based computers, and mobile computing. To lower the costs, ensure interoperability, and promote widespread adoption of wireless LANs, Electrical and Electronics Engineers (IEEE) working group 802.15 (standards.ieee.org, 2006), Internet Engineering Task Force (IETF), Wi-Fi Alliance: WFA (formerly known as Wireless Ethernet Compatibility Alliance: [WECA]) and International Telecommunication Union (ITU) are working on several standardization processes. Wireless networks can also be classified as wireless LANs, wireless MANs, and wireless WANs (Hura and Shinghal, 2001; grouper.ieee.org, 2006; standards.ieee.org, 2006).

Wireless technology has revolutionized a number of applications and market segments and encompasses a number of standards including:

Wi-Fi (802.11 a/b/g/n)
WiMAX (802.16)
Ultra Wide Band (UWB)
Bluetooth
ZigBee (802.15)
Near Field Communications (NFC)
Mesh
3G+

Out of these wireless technologies, Wi-Fi (802.11) has become more popular in laptops, communities, and cities. It poses some constraints in terms of performance flexibility, power consumption, and ease of use. In 1999, several industries formed a global, non-profit organization for adopting a single worldwide accepted standard for high-speed wireless local area networking (Wi-Fi Alliance). This alliance has over 3000 interoperable certified products.

Wireless Local Area Network (WLAN)

Wireless LANs can be used within corporations, buildings, and public areas such as an airport and as a temporary or supplement service for the users within building. Wireless LANs with a connection to Internet or any other similar network via digital subscriber line (DSL) is known as wireless DSL. It typically can be configured in two ways. It can define infrastructure where wireless nodes (radio network card or modem) are connected to wireless access point that provides bridge between nodes and existing network backbone. Alternatively, it can allow users within a conference room to form a temporary ad hoc network without any access points. IEEE approved 802.11 standards for wireless LAN (also known as wireless Ethernet or Wi-Fi) were previously known as Wireless Ethernet Compatibility Alliance and now known as Wi-Fi Alliance and offer a data rate of 1 to 2 Mbps.

Other ratified IEEE WLAN standards IEEE 802.b (11 Mbps over 2.4 Gigahertz frequency band within 50 to 100 meters), 802.11a (54 Mbps over 5-GHz frequency band), and 802.11g (54 Mbps over 2.44-GHz). WLAN link speed drops with a distance reaching out about 100 meters in open space. 802.11 offers quality of service (QoS) support for LAN applications (network card can be used in a new QoS Basic Service Set: QBSS) such as voice over wireless IP (VoWIP), high-speed Internet access with full motion video, high fidelity, audio and voice over IP, mobiles, and users of PDA and other bandwidth and delay-sensitive applications. It supports seamless interoperability between business, home, and public services like airports and hotels with multimedia capability.

It provides classes of services with managed levels of QoS for data, voice, and video. It supports two types of modes for managing different categories of traffic: enhanced distribution coordination function (EDCF) (based on carrier sense multiple access with collision avoidance) and hybrid coordination function (HCF). EDCF seems to be gaining more acceptance than HCF. It operates at radio frequencies between 2.400 and 2.4835 GHz (802.11b) or 5.725 to 5.850 GHz (802.11a). Enterprise WLAN is currently being deployed in small-scale applications like retail and health care systems and is slowly becoming popular for large-scale applications. A new evolving architecture is supposed to shift some key functions from AP to centralized WLAN switch/appliance is helping these large-scale applications by easing security and management concerns.

The following is a brief discussion on various 802.11 specifications (grouper.ieee.org, 2006; standards.ieee.org, 2006)

802.11—original WLAN standard, supports 1 Mbps to 2 Mbps in 2.4-GHz band using either frequency hopping spread spectrum (FHSS) or direct sequence spread spectrum (DSSS)

802.11a—extension of 802.11a, high-speed WLAN standard (5 GHz), supports 54 Mbps, uses orthogonal frequency division multiplexing encoding rather than FHSS or DSSS

802.11b—also known as 802.11 high rate or Wi-Fi, WLAN standard for 2.4 GHz, supports 11 Mbps (with a fallback to 5.5, 2 and 1 Mbps), uses only DSSS

802.11d—automatically configures devices to match local RF requirements, international roaming

802.11e—quality of service (QoS) specifications for all IEEE WLAN radio interfaces

802.11g—uses additional modulation for 2.4 GHz band and supports data rate of 54 Mbps

802.11h—explains the spectrum management of 5 GHz band

802.11i—approved standard that provides security for both authentication and encryption protocols, it encompasses 802.1X, temporal key integrity protocol (TKIP), advanced encryption standard (AES) protocol becomes the Wi-Fi WLAN technologies. AES is stronger than Wi-Fi protected access (WPA) mechanism

802.11n—supports higher throughput improvements, offers data rate of 500 Mbps.

Virtual LAN. This is another category of LAN where the connected devices do not have to be physically connected to the same segment (while these are needed in hubs, bridges or switches). It operates at the data-link layer of OSI-RM. It can also be configured to map directly to an IP network or subnet that may involve the network layer as well. The VLAN technology is based on broadcasting messages to all connected devices (end nodes) within VLAN without the need for a router and uses the management software that detects the port on a switch or any station without changing MAC or IP address. The 802.1Q specification supports the VLAM membership to be inserted into Ethernet frames with ability of setting profiles for each port by a central switch. The membership can be implemented in three different ways as port-based, MAC-based, and protocol-based. LAN emulation (LANE) software over ATM offers full support on existing LAN-based applications without any changes in backbone services.

Wireless Metropolitan Area Network (WMAN)

It provides users to establish connections between multiple locations within metropolitan area and can be used as a backup for wired networks. The data communication is based on either infrared wave or radio wave technologies. It offers high-speed access to Internet via broadband wireless access networks and uses either multichannel multipoint distribution service (MMDS) or local multipoint distribution service (LMDS). IEEE 802.16 (8,11) Working Group for broadband wireless access standards is still developing its specifications. It supports both fixed and mobile broadband wireless access and is concentrating on standardization of fixed BWA systems focusing on licensed spectrum near 30 GHz, but is intended to be broadly applicable from 10 to 66 GHz. A group World Inter-Operability for Microwave Access (WiMAX) supports 802.16a that provides broadband services at a rate of 4000 Mbps over a distance of 50 km. 802.20 (below licensed band of 3.5 Ghz) and IEEE 802.16e (in licensed band of 2 to 6 GHz) specify standards for mobile air interface for wireless broadband access (BWA) at data rate of 1 Mbps Internet services to mobile users up to 15 km or more. Carrier currents LAN use power lines for transport.

The industry trade group WiMAX Forum (http://www.winmaxforum.org) has defined WiMAX as a broadband wireless access alternative to cable modem service, telephone company, digital subscriber line (DSL), or T1/E1 service. It is an IEEE standard 802.16-2004 (fixed wireless applications and 802.16e-2005 (mobile wireless) (http://ieee.org). It has the potential to replace a number of existing telecommunication infrastructures. The fixed wireless standard can be used for telephone company's copper wire networks, cable TV's coaxial cable infrastructure while offering Internet service provider (ISP) services. The mobile wireless standard can be used for cellular networks. Many times we may get confused between Wi-Fi and WiMAX technologies. Wi-Fi technology provides limited security, QoS, and a throughput of 11 Mbps within a distance of 100 yards in one floor of the building or a home. WiMAX on other hand provides multilevel encryption, dynamic bandwidth allocation for voice and video and a throughput of 72 Mbps within a distance of six miles for a city with one base station. For data rates of different wireless architecture, visit http://www.bcr.com/architecture.

Wireless Wide Area Network (WWAN)

Wireless technology for WANs allows users to establish wireless connections with public or private networks. Wireless service providers use multiple antennas or satellite systems. The second-generation technology (limited roaming capability) uses global system for mobile communication (GSM), cellular digital packet data (CDPD), and code division multiple access (CDMA). The global standard for third-generation technology (global standard for global roaming capability) is under consideration by ITU.

Wireless Personal Area Network (WPANs)

This new class of wireless technology finds its use in establishing ad hoc wireless communication within PDAs, cellular phones, PCs, wireless printers, storage devices, pagers, or laptops within a distance of up to 10 m. Bluetooth and infrared technologies are being considered for this application by providing short-range wireless communications and simplified communication and synchronization. Both technologies eliminate wires and cables, and facilitate data and voice communication and possibility of ad hoc networks. Bluetooth uses radio waves for transmitting the data over a distance of 30 feet and in fact can go through walls and pockets. It uses a fast acknowledgement and frequency hopping scheme to make the link robust in noisy environment. It is based on globally available frequency band of 2.4GHz and provides compatibility to PCs, Apple computers, Palm OS-based handheld devices, mobile phones, and other peripherals within 30-feet range wirelessly. Infrared connection can be established for a small distance of one m or less. Bluetooth version 1.1 was ratified as IEEE 802.15 (standards.ieee.org, 2006) a long time ago. Bluetooth version 2.0 was completed in 2004 to increase link speed from 780 Kbps to 3 Mbps. Neither Bluetooth version is interoperable with 802.11 (i.e., Bluetooth devices cannot communicate with an 802.11 device). However, standard Bluetooth co-existence techniques have been defined, because Bluetooth and 802.11b//g use the same 2.4-GHz frequency band and thus would otherwise (and often do) generate radio interference. This technology is less complex, offers low power consumption, supports interoperability, and coexistence with 802.11 networks (For details read standards.ieee.org, 2006).

Wireless Local Loops (WLLs)

This new technology offers fixed wireless access (in addition to phone service) at several MHz of bandwidth for high-speed Internet access and data transfer and seems to be better than mobile access provided by cellular and PCS. It has become very popular among the users of local phone loops over fixed cellular networks.

Personal Communication Service (PCS)

PCS is similar to cellular, operates in 1900-MHz band and is based on three technologies in North America as GSM 1900, CDMA IS-95, and TDMA IS-136. Code division multiple access (CDMA) uses the same assigned frequency for transmitting a very wide signal as many other stations and does not offer any coordination between stations. Time division multiple access (TDMA) divides the frequency pair into several time slots and provides the frequency during that assigned time slot. Frequency division multiple access (FDMA) allocates its own specific radio frequency pair for entire duration of call. Local multipoint distribution systems (LMDS) is defined for fixed wireless access that can offer very high bandwidth and is based on line of sight. LMDS technology offers point-to-point and multipoint applications (e.g., high-speed Internet access, telephony, cable TV programming transmission) within a band of 28 to 31 GHz and is based on spread spectrum to support very high bit rates for two-way data transfer. IEEE 802.15 Working Group (standards.ieee.org, 2006) is developing standards for physical and MAC layer specifications for short distance (up to 10 m in all directions) wireless connectivity with fixed, portable, and moving devices within personal operating space (POS).

Mesh Network

A mesh network can be defined as a network that provides direct links to each other between all the nodes of the network. It works well when the nodes are located at scattered points that do not lie near a common line. The underlying topology can be either full mesh (all nodes are directly connected to each other) or partial mesh (some nodes are connected to all the other nodes and other nodes are connected to those nodes for exchange of data). If one node can no longer operate, all the rest can still communicate with each other, directly or through one or more intermediate nodes. Figure 3 shows full mesh topology. The connections can be wired or wireless. It is reliable and offers redundancy but is very expensive (as a result of a large number of connections).

Wireless mesh networks can offer a variety of applications and solutions securely and cost-effectively for both enterprises and end users. These networks are highly scalable and cost-effective and offer end users seamless broadband wireless access beyond traditional wireless boundaries and provide easy deployment in the areas that do not or can not support wired backhaul. Some of the applications of meshed wireless network include city governments and municipalities (residential areas, parks), which may benefit from enhanced employee safety, efficiency and improved business, campus environments (enterprise, universities), shopping centers, airports, manufacturing, military operations like disaster recovery, and public safety. The existing infrastructure such as installation of extensive Ethernet cabling in leased facilities can be used for wireless mesh networks to provide new opportunities for generating revenue, enhanced business productivity, and convenient services. The wireless mesh network can be used for both indoor and outdoor and will find its use where Ethernet cabling is prohibitive to install or leased backhaul needs to be minimized. This network is finding its use in all the WANs and mobile computing.

Metropolitan Area Network (MAN)

A metropolitan area network (MAN) is the second type of network that finds its applications in metropolitan area

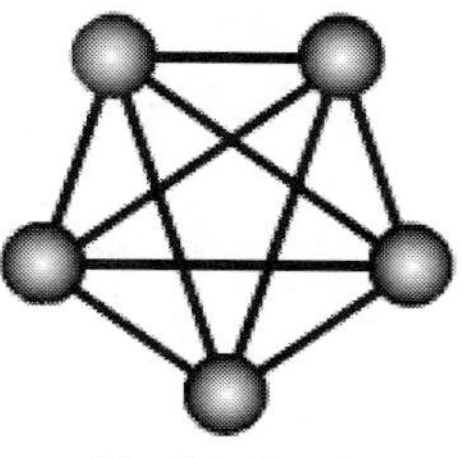

Mesh network

Figure 3: Topology of mesh network

(over 10 miles and less than 100 miles). It is a relatively new class of network and offers services through network service carrier in the same way as services offered by Internet service provider (ISP). It often uses fiber optic as transmission media for data communication. It is generally not owned by a single organization, but instead is owned by either consortium of users or by network providers (standards.ieee.org, 2006). IEEE 802.6 (standards.ieee.org, 2006) standard based on distributed queue dual bus (DQDB) has been defined. Figure 4 shows a typical MAN architecture that can be used to provide resource sharing (LAN) and shared access to WAN.

LANs provide resource sharing and groups of users, whereas MANs allow the users to share social, educational, and career challenges who are dispersed at large distance (over 10 miles, but less than WANs range). It can reach rural areas where the government agencies across a city or county can create a community network, but needs a substantial budget to lease or install fiber across the county and also digging of trenches. This problem can be alleviated by installing wireless communication over MAN that will provide point-to-point and point-to-multipoint links with higher bandwidth. Wireless MANs will be a lot cheaper in terms of expensive fiber infrastructures and leasing of lines from carrier companies.

Wide Area Network (WAN)

A WAN is a data communications network that covers thousands of miles and often uses transmission facilities provided by telephone carriers. Invariably, all WAN technologies focus on the lower three layers of the OSI-RM. Figure 5 shows the relationship between OSI-RM and

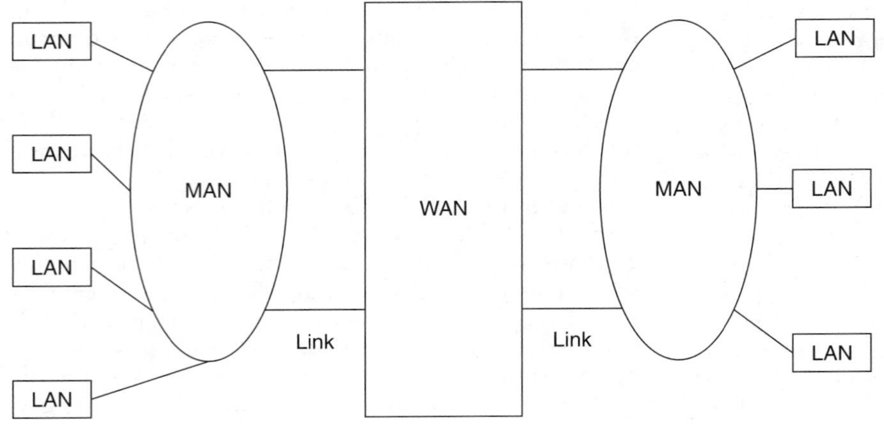

Figure 4: Typical MAN architecture

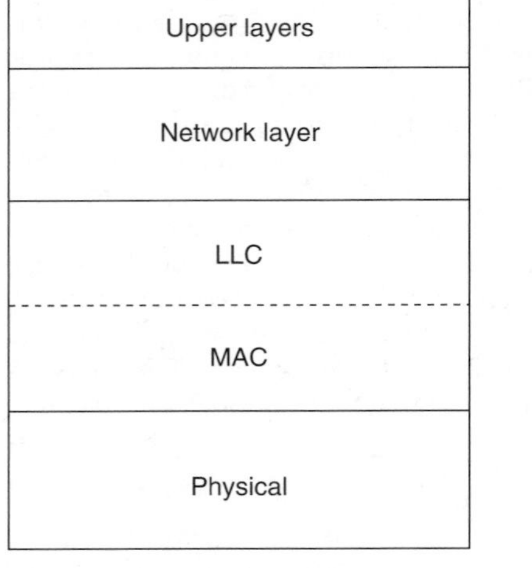

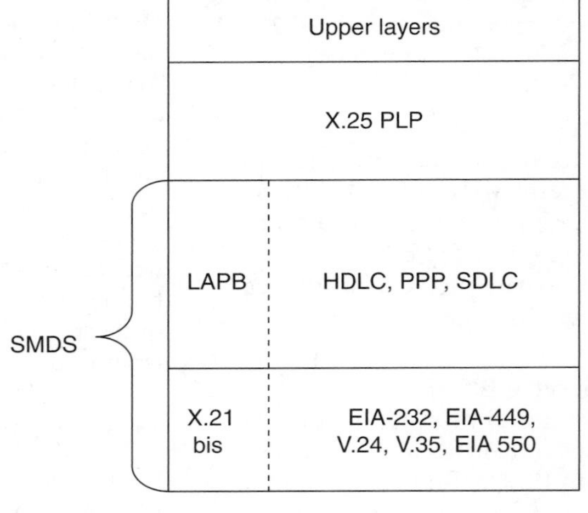

LLC: Logical Link Control

MAC: Media Access Control

PLP: Packet Layer Protocol

HDLC: High-level Data Link Control

SDLC: Synchronous Data Link Control

LAPB: Link Access Control-Balanced

EIA: Electronic Industries Association

SMDS: Switched Multimegabit Data Service

Figure 5: Relationship between OSI-RM and WAN model

WAN model of different technologies. The WAN protocols operate in these lower layers of the OSI model.

Point-to-point communication is being provided by a single, pre-established WAN logical circuits/links from the customer premises through a carrier network and is usually leased from a carrier as leased links. These circuits are generally priced based on bandwidth required and distance between the two connected points. In a packet-switching setup, networks have connections into the carrier's network, and many customers share the carrier's network. The carrier creates virtual circuits between customers' sites for the exchange of packets through the network.

NETWORK SWITCHING TECHNIQUES

The speed and capacity of any networks are highly influenced by the switching method used. A switch in networking can be considered the heart of the data communication (similar to engine in a car). Appropriate switches have to be used when a network (be it public or private) based on that switching technique (circuit or packet) is selected, although, we can get plug-in switches that can be used interchangeably on the networks. When the switches are used with different types of networks, different interfaces have to be provided by the switching equipment. The following section describes in brief the main features of these switching techniques.

Circuit Switching

In this technique, a circuit or link connection is established between source and destination users/nodes for the entire duration of the connection before sending any data and it supports end-to-end connection between the users. During the established connection, the entire bandwidth is allotted to the users/nodes. An unused bandwidth and resources by the user/node will be wasted and can not be used by other users/nodes or even by the network. It offers minimum delay and guarantees the delivery of the packets in order between nodes. The circuit switching supports different types of multiplexing techniques (space, time). For each of the circuits that are multiplexed, the same time slot with the frame is used during the entire duration of the connection. Similarly, a table describing the relationship between incoming and outgoing links along with time slots at each of the switching nodes is maintained. The time slots are fixed for both sides of switching for the duration of the connection. An initial set-up time in some applications may become a serious problem, for example, voice and video communications. It finds its use in N-ISDN for offering a fixed data rate and capacity network connection and is not suitable for bursty (irregular) traffic applications.

Fast Circuit Switching

This technique is a modified version of circuit switching in which the resources are allocated during the transmission of data and are released immediately after the transmission is completed. It is a form of connectionless packet switching in the sense that during the set-up of the connection time, a request for destination bandwidth for the connection is stored inside the switching system and allocates header for this data. The resources are allocated immediately after the source starts sending the information. One of the major drawbacks with this technique is its inability to allocate enough resources to unexpected bursty traffic.

Packet Switching

In this method, a fixed/variable size of packet (defined by the network) is transmitted over the network. Each intermediate node transmits packets to next node based on the availability of routes. An established logical link offers the entire bandwidth to the packets during its transmission. After the packets have been transmitted to the next node, the entire bandwidth of the link is released for other packets. In some packet-switched networks, all the packets are stored in main memory to reduce the accessing time of the packets, whereas other networks use other memory devices. As a result of this, the throughput offered by networks based on this switching can be improved.

Packet-switched networks allow the end nodes/users to share the media and its bandwidth. There are two methods of packet switching that have been used in networks The first method is based on a variable length packet where packets initiated from the source switch between segments of networks before reaching destination. It is usually used in efficient and variable data rate applications. The second method is based on statistical multiplexing where the bandwidth of media is used efficiently by grouping the packets together into one big packet.

Fast Packet Switching

The fast packet switch is based on the concept of T1 multiplexer, which executes the protocol at the physical layer only. The conventional T1 multiplexing carrier system generates 24 channels of 64 Kbps and uses time division multiplexing (TDM) technique. This technique suffers from wastage of bandwidth to other channels, and is not suitable for applications like bursty traffic or applications with variable and high data rates that require larger bandwidth.

WIDE AREA NETWORKS

Both types of networks (circuit- or packet-switched) are based on the concept of switching that is the backbone for any technologies for a high-speed WAN. The following is a brief description of each of these technologies for WANs.

Integrated Service Digital Network (ISDN)

This is a single digital network that transmits integrated voice and data information over the same transmission media. In most of the countries, the existing public switched telephone networks are being converted or replaced for full digital operations. It offers two types of interfaces (basic rate interface (popular in the United States) and primary rate interface (popular in Europe) and implements two types of networks (voice and data) within ISDN implementation. It offers two channels: bearer (B) and delta (D). The B channel has a bandwidth of 64 Kbps and can be configured either for circuit switching or packet switching connection. The D channel on the other hand is for signaling purposes and operates in packet-switched mode at a speed of 16 Kbps.

BRI offers 2B + D service at the rate of 144 Kbps (2X64Kbps + 16 Kbps), whereas PRI offers 23B + D service at the rate of 1.544 Mbps (23X64 + 64) (U.S.) and 30B + D service at the rate of 2.56 Mbps (23X64 + 64) (Europe).

Applications of ISDN: One of the earlier popular applications of ISDN has been videoconferencing and, in fact, became a standard service of ISDN. Recent years has seen a shift in ISDN services where it may not even include video conferencing as other technologies seem to be more appropriate for this application. In this service, the presentations, or seminars can be transmitted over TV screens anywhere around the globe if ISDN connection between them is available over T1/T3 or any other link. It offers two-way communications for both point-to-point and multipoint configurations between the users. Different conference places can be connected to receive point-to-point services and or multipoint (where small number of users can communicate with each other and discuss common documents, display the user's live pictures either one at a time or all of them together on the screen) services. All these options are usually handled by video service providers.

As a result of bandwidth limitations of ISDNs and basic rate interface of (2B + D) only, the TV signals (typically of 6 MHz bandwidth) cannot be transmitted over it. For transmitting uncompressed TV signals, a separate TV network may be required as ISDN supports only compressed TV signal. As a result of lower bandwidth, this network is also known as narrowband-ISDN (N-ISDN).

Broadband-ISDN (B-ISDN)

In order to extend the concept of ISDN's integration of voice and data into other types of services like video, multimedia, and images, a new unified network termed broadband-ISDN (B-ISDN) offering these services was introduced in the mid-80s. It is a service-independent network that transports these services by requiring transmission channels of supporting more data rates than PRI (1.544 Mbps) defined by N-ISDN and allows the users to share the resources of various networks for different services.

Optical transmission (based on fiber optics) is the main force for B-ISDN as it offers very high bandwidth and data rates over a longer distance. The diameter of fiber is very small and it offers low weight and volume. It is immune to electromagnetic fields and as such offers low transmission error probability. There is no cross talk between fibers and is very difficult to tap and offers virtually an unlimited bandwidth. The basic B-ISDN interface across broadband user-network interface offers 155 Mbps, whereas a second B-ISDN interface offers 622 Mbps. Big corporations, universities, and research laboratories extensively use B-ISDN interfaces, protocols, and reference models as a WAN at both national and international levels.

Synchronous Optical Network (SONET) and Synchronous Digital Hierarchy (SDH) Standards

The SONET is derived from Bellcore's (now known as Telecordia) Synchronous Optical NETwork. In the past few years, the telecommunication service carrier companies replaced the existing copper wires by the optical fiber (OF). The plesiochronous digital hierarchy (PDH) is a technology used in networks to transport large quantities of data over digital transport equipment, such as fiber optic and microwave radio systems. PDH allows transmission of data streams that are nominally running at the same rate, but allowing some variation on the speed around a nominal rate. The European and American versions of the PDH system differ slightly in the detail of their working, but the principles are the same. PDH is now being replaced by SDH equipment in most telecommunications networks. Synchronous Digital Hierarchy (SDH) standard includes all the functionalities of SONET. Both SONET and SDH were originally introduced for optical fiber transmission where SDH offers a network node interface (NNI) defined by CCITT/ITU-TS worldwide and is compatible with SONET.

SONET standard was defined by ANSI (American National Standards Institute), whereas SDH was introduced by ETSI (European Telecommunication Standards Institute). The specification and application of SDH and is now being used everywhere outside of North America and Japan. The Japanese version of SDH differs only in some details but is not significantly different than ETSI's. Both SDH and SONET are being used in public networks and offer data rates higher (over 40 Gbps). More detailed information on SONET can be found at the International Engineering Consortium (IEC) SONET Web ProForum (for more details, please refer to Hura and Singhal, 2001; Goldman, 2004).

X.25 Packet-Switched Network

In the early 1970s, there were many data communication networks (also known as public networks), which were owned by private companies, organizations, and governments agencies. Because those public networks were quite different internally, and the interconnection of networks was growing very fast, there was a need for a common network interface protocol. In 1976, X.25 was recommended as the desired protocol by the CCITT (now ITU). X.25 was originally approved in 1976 and subsequently revised in 1977, 1980, 1984, 1988, and 1992. It is currently (1996) one of the most widely used interfaces for data communication networks. Various WANs and also LANs use the capabilities offered by X.25 networks.

X.25 (Figure 6) is a packet-switched protocol architecture that defines an international recommendation for the exchange of data as well as controls information between a user device (host), called data terminal equipment (DTE) and a network node, called data circuit terminating equipment (DCE). It utilizes a connection-oriented service that ensures that packets are transmitted in order. X.25 comes with three levels based on the lower three layers of the OSI-RM. The physical level deals with the electrical, mechanical, procedural, and functional interface between the DTE and the DCE. It is specified by the X.21, X.21-bis,

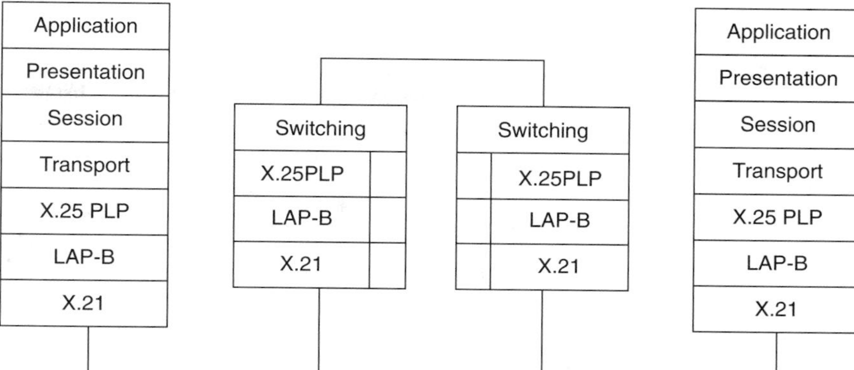

Figure 6: X.25 protocol architecture

and the V.24 recommendation for modems and interchange circuits. The link level (or frame level) ensures reliable transfer of data between the DTE and the DCE by transmitting the data as a sequence of frames (a frame is an individual data unit which contains address, control, information field, etc.). It uses link access protocol-balanced (LAP-B). The packet level (also known as network level) creates network data units called packets that route information and user data and uses packet layer protocol (PLP). In this network, the transport layer is expected to provide end-to-end connection (Clark and Hamilton, 1999; Hura and Singhal, 2001; Goldman, 2004).

Packet Level Protocol: X.25 evolved from standardization work of ISDN in a packet mode transmission service that minimizes the amount of error detection and error recovery within the network. This feature offers minimum delay, higher performance, greater efficiency, and higher throughput by defining a new streamlined communication process of user-to-network interface (UNI). This interface can connect LANs using WANs. The network-to-network interface (NNI) interface defines signaling and management functions between two frame relay networks. Both UNI and NNI are important in asynchronous transfer mode (ATM) model. X. 25 uses in-band signaling that forces both call control and data packets to be transmitted on the same channel as virtual circuit packets. The call control packet is used for setting up and clearing of virtual circuits (VCs). It only supports low-speed terminals at 19.2 Kbps and lower. A separate logical connection needs to be established for every data session.

Frame Relay: The frame relay can be considered as a streamlined version of X.25 and thus requires a close comparison with X.25 (as discussed above). Many of digital WANs offer their own error-correcting capabilities and thus, are not dependent on these capabilities of X.25 and even LANs. Frame relay is designed to overcome most of these drawbacks. It supports low speeds of 56 kbps to T1 (1.544 Mbps) or even T3 (45 Mbps). It uses statistical multiplexing interface for virtual connections at layer 2. It can handle multiple data sessions on a single logical connection. It does not provide any flow-control and error-control link-by-link or hoop-by-hop as it expects this to be provided by higher layers. It is based on the assumption that transmission and switching facilities are reliable. Figure 7 shows the lower three layers of frame relay.

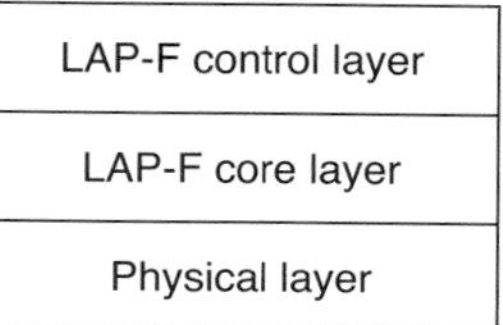

Figure 7: Frame relay

Link Access Protocol-Frame (LAP-F): Frame relay network offers two frame modes of services as frame relay and frame switching and both these modes use the same signaling procedures. Because frame switching requires the frame relay network to perform the error-control and flow-control, it offers minimum overhead. Further, the frame relay-based network performs multiplexing and routing at data-link layer as opposed to packet and link layers together performing these functions in X.25 networks. (See the frame relay forum at www.frforum.com or www.protocols.com.) Benefits of frame relay (according to the frame relay forum):

- Savings, greater bandwidth flexibility, greater reliability than private lines
- Allows the consolidation of LAN, SNA, voice, and packetized video
- Smooth migration to ATM
- Low overhead combined with high reliability
- Well-established, widely adopted standards that allow open architecture and plug-and-play

Frame Relay Services: The frame relay packet switching offers higher data rates and suffers very small overhead for communication. It allows multiple calls to different destinations to be handled at the same time by data-link layer. Thus, once a virtual circuit (path) has been established using D channel, a unique identifier is assigned to this circuit. This path is used for all the subsequent frames. This path identifier has a local significance and as such when the frames are traveling over different links is associated with virtual paths identifiers. When frames are received by the frame handler during data transfer phase, it checks the data link connection identifier and combines with all incoming numbers to determine the corresponding outgoing link and data link connection identifier. It assigns a new data link connection identifier and is forwarded to appropriate outgoing link. This maintains the order of arrival of frames and also the routing becomes faster. The only disadvantage with this switching is the congestion during heavy network traffic over the outgoing links.

Applications of Frame Relay: Frame relay finds its applications in block-interactive data applications (e.g., high-resolution graphics) file transfer, multiplexing of low-bit rate, character-interactive data applications (e.g., text editing), unpredictable, high-volume and bursty traffic applications (e.g., e-mail, computer-aided design/computer-aided manufacturing: CAD/CAM, client-server), and medium-to-large sized networks with mesh or star connectivity. This is not suitable for continuous traffic applications (e.g., co-development, multimedia, transfer of large files of 100 Mbps) and for providing connectivity between dumb terminals and mainframe.

Standardization of Frame Relay: The first specification for standardization of frame relay was introduced to Consultative Committee on International Telegraph and Telegraph (CCITT) in 1984. The frame relay did not get acceptance due to lack of interoperability and missing specifications for standardization. During the early 1980s, a consortium (Cisco, DEC, Northern Telecom, StrataCom) developed a specification that was based on CCITT's standard with added capabilities of complex internetworking environment and named as local management interface (LMI). ANSI (United States) and International Telecommunication Union-Telecommunication Standard section (ITU-T) have subsequently standardized their versions of LMI (www.frframe.com). The frame relay offers a connection-oriented link layer service known as frame relay bearer service (FRBS) (www.protocols.com).

Frame Relay Network: A typical frame relay network looks like as shown in Figure 8. It includes frame relay access equipment; frame relay switching equipment, and public frame relay services.

Access Equipment: This equipment converts data into frame relay packet and does not provide any routing. It is also known as customer premises equipment (CPE) that is being used by frame relay to send information over the network to data terminal equipment (DTE). This could be any device like terminal, PCs, bridge, router, packet switch, hosts or even frame relay packet assembly/disassembly (PAD) and other similar devices. This device may be used either with a private network frame relay switching equipment or with frame relay services.

Frame Relay Switching Equipment: These devices transport the frame relay frames generated by access equipment. These may be T1/E1 multiplexers, packet switches, or any other equipment that implements standard interface that is capable of switching and routing information received in frame relay format. Because the transmission of frame can be achieved either using variable length size (frames) or fixed length size (cells), the same equipment may be used for creating either private or public frame relay networks. Usually the public service providers (carriers) provide frame relay services by deploying frame relay switching equipment and also connectivity between access and switching equipments. They maintain access to network via standard frame relay interface.

Switched Multi-Megabit Data Service (SMDS)

It is a high-speed and performance, packet-switched, datagram-based WAN used for communication over public telecommunication carrier networks using fiber- or copper-based media and is service independent. It supports speeds of 1.544 Mbps over digital signal level 1 (DS-1) transmission facilities, or 44.736 Mbps (45 Mbps in United States) over digital signal level 3 (DS-3) and 155 Mbps transmission facilities. It allows easy transition from existing LAN interconnects arrangements into leased lines and private switched networks that offer a low transit delay. It has created enormous interest within the United States and Europe to accept this technology as a public service. In fact, British Telecommunication (BT) SMDS pilot project on SuperJANET (http://www.ja.net/sj5/history.html) is the preliminary step to the launch of a national SMDS service in the UK. Some of the materials presented here have been derived from Goldman, 2004.

Currently, the SMDS access is based on distributed queue dual bus (DQDB) standard MAN (IEEE 802.6). DQDB is based on fixed-length cells of 53 bytes and as such SMDS packet (variable length) must be broken into

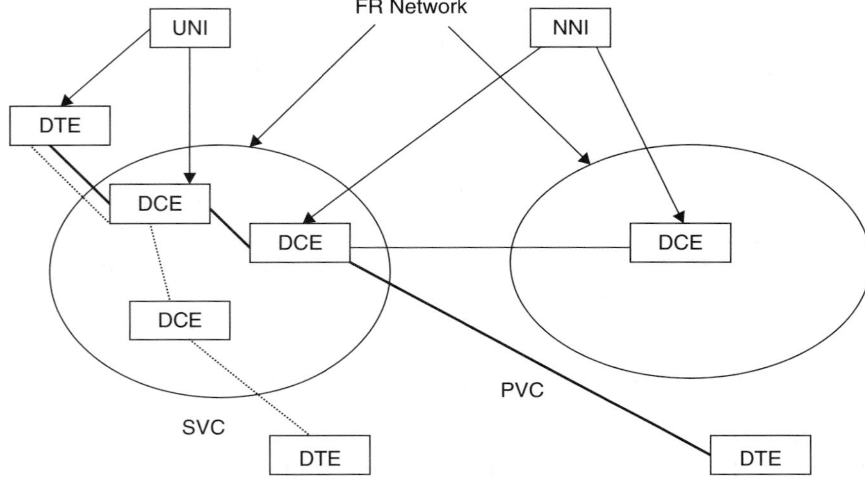

Figure 8: Typical frame relay network

these cells for its transmission over DQDB. The SMDS interface protocol (SIP) defines DQDB-compatible access from a customer site to a network switching site. The Data eXchange Interface (DXI) protocol supports the use of SMDS over serial links, particularly local attachments, and is based on high data link control (HDLC) framing. Both SIP and DXI have been used in a number of pilot projects (e.g., SuperJANET SMDS pilot network) and some attempts have been made to include ATM within SMDS network for offering broadband services.

Features of SMDS include:

1. Packet network reliability: In an Ethernet environment, under heavy traffic, packets have a higher rate of collision, and the ability to be lost. The reliability of packets (based on SMDS) for point to point transmission is much higher and is without error or collision.
2. SMDS security: Each destination node (CPE) is assigned with one of several address numbers that is specified in destination address field of PDU. The network keeps a multiple copies of PDU that are sent to all the members of group. When the packet is to be transmitted, it is associated with a given a destination address. This packet is then sent out over a nonspecific physical path. Each packet takes a different path to get to the destination. This means that there is much less chance for someone to catch all the packets that are sent. This makes SMDS more secure and offers data integrity. SMDS defines a number of nodes on SMDS that can transmit and receive the data and as such define LAN-like environment. It offers fully logical meshed connectivity that in turn supports fault tolerance, whereby a failure of one node does not affect the data transfer within the network. It implements security via address validation and address screening. The former ensures that PDU source address is accurately assigned to the SNI from which it was sent. It prevents address spoofing where illegal traffic assumes the source address of a valid device. The later allows the user to install a virtual private network that filters out the unwanted traffic. The data unit is not delivered if excludes if address is wrong or disallowed.

One of the main drawbacks of this network is that it does not offer any error-control (as a result of connectionless service), flow control, no guarantee of arrival of packets at the destination. Further enhanced overhead occurs for encapsulation that consumes considerable bandwidth as high as 75%.

Applications of SMDS: It found its applications in a limited business arena. One such application that uses SMDS for Internet access is CERFNet (www.cerfnet.com), a subsidiary of General Atomics. A case study was done over the company and their use of SMDS. The focus of the article was to demonstrate that SMDS gives full access to Internet and mail services, support of large usage and broadband requirements, multiple host connectivity, security, high-speed access, privacy, and functionality. Other service industries that are deploying SMDS include banking, insurance, finance, and others that use optical scanning methods for creating electronic file cabinets for increasing storage capacity and improved access mechanisms.

Standardization of SMDS: Bellcore (now Telecordia) defined the technical specifications of SMDS in the United States and has been adapted in Europe as well (European SMDS Interest Group [ESIG] and European Telecommunications Standards Institute [ETSI]). One of the aims of this specification was to provide a LAN-compatible connectionless (variable length of packets) data service between end users. It supports standard protocols and communication interfaces using the existing technology. Several organizations are active in supporting the development and use of SMDS. A European SMDS Interest Group was formed in October 1991 and SuperJANET is participating as an observer. The focus for SuperJANET SMDS work is the SMDS sub-committee set up by the IP Technical Advisory Group (IPTAG) (www.ja.net, 2006).

SMDS Network: It uses 53 octets (bytes) cell for transport and can accommodate maximum packet lengths of 9188 octets. In general SMDS network requires: Terminal equipment (computers), SMDS channel service unit (CSU)/data service unit (DSU) for SIP Protocol DS1 and DS3 or (1.17 Mbps to 34 Mbps), standard CSU/DSU for DXI DSO (56 kbps), router with SMDS protocol enabled, and network software.

Components of SMDS Network: It consists of customer premises equipment (CPE), carrier equipment, and the subscriber network interface (SNI). CPE includes end devices, such as terminals and personal computers, and intermediate nodes, such as routers, modems, and multiplexers. It is typically owned and maintained by the customer. Intermediate nodes, however, sometimes are provided by the SMDS carriers. Carrier equipment generally consists of high-speed WAN switches that must conform to certain network equipment specifications, such as those outlined by Bell Communications Research (Bellcore and currently known as Telecordia). These specifications define network operations, the interface between a local carrier network and a long-distance carrier network, and the interface between two switches inside a single carrier network. The SNI is the interface between CPE and carrier equipment (Figure 9). The function of the SNI is to offer the technology and operation of the carrier SMDS network transparent to the customer. For details, please

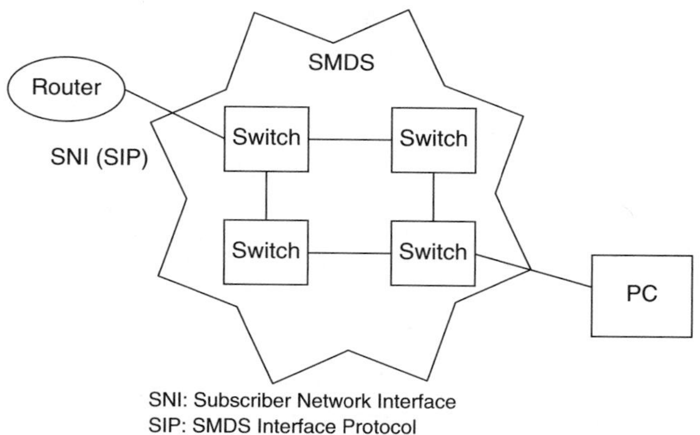

Figure 9: Components of SMDS network

visit www.alpeda.com, www.oreilly.com, www.pacebell.com, and www.cerf.net. It should be noted that the access class restrictions only apply to data transmitted into the network, not to data received from the network. The access class restrictions may result in packets being discarded; connectionless data networks do not guarantee to deliver the packets that are submitted to them and the communicating end systems are expected to be capable of detecting packet loss and recovering from it, for example, by re-sending the packets.

Internetworking of SMDS to LANs: Figure 10 shows how a LAN can be connected to SMDS network. The link between the network switching center and the customer site is provided by either a 2-Mbps megastream connection or a 34-Mbps optical fiber connection using the SIP standard. DXI supports the transmission of SMDS packet over local high-speed link, whereas SPI supports the transmission of SMDS packet in DQDB cell over optical fiber. DQDB (IEEE 802.DQDB) standard is a data-link layer communication protocol designed for use in MAN and consists of two unidirectional logical buses that interconnect multiple systems.

The optical fiber is terminated at each end by an optical line termination equipment (OLTE) providing an optical/electronic interface. On the customer's site, this interface is connected to a DSU, which in turn is connected to a router on a LAN via a high-speed serial media that uses the DXI protocol. The DSU provides conversion between DQDB on wide-area link side and HDLC on the router side. The interface between router and DSU allows routers to interface to a range of high-speed networking services via a standard hardware interface. Different DSUs are used to provide the specific interfacing requirements for the different services. A range of protocols can be routed over SMDS, including TCP/IP and widely used proprietary protocols. IP over SMDS is specified in RFC 1209.

Internetworking of SMDS to Internet: The Internet is composed of hosts or networks as nodes that provide the communications between end users. SMDS can also be considered as one of sub-networks similar to existing LANs (Ethernet, token ring). SMDS offers service at MAC level (OSI-RM) and as such IP datagram is treated similarly. In other words, both MAC and SMDS will receive the IP datagram that is included within IEEE 802.2 LLC type I (unnumbered information) and sub-network access protocol (SNAP). Customer's premises components include host, subnet (LAN), and gateway. The gateways offer both MAC and SIP protocols. SMDS network uses SMDS interface protocol (SIP) and defined clearly as the boundaries around SMDS (Figure 11).

SMDS does not enforce any minimum size of IP datagram and in fact is being supported by gateway and host. Gateway implementation must accept full-length of IP packets and should avoid fragmentation (if possible). Gateway will handle the address resolution for SMDS users (to be defined as permanent published bindings in a static table) in the same way as it does on X.25 public data networks. SMDS also allows the users to define their private network over Internet using screening features of SMDS. Assignment of unique SMDS group address for its use within IP network or sub-network has been discussed

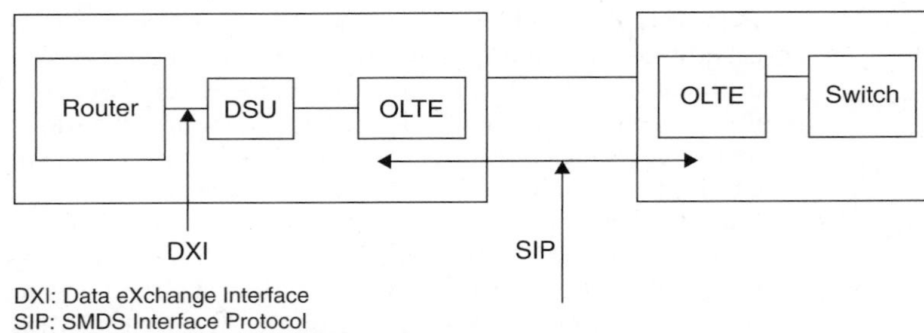

Figure 10: Internetworking of SMDS to LAN

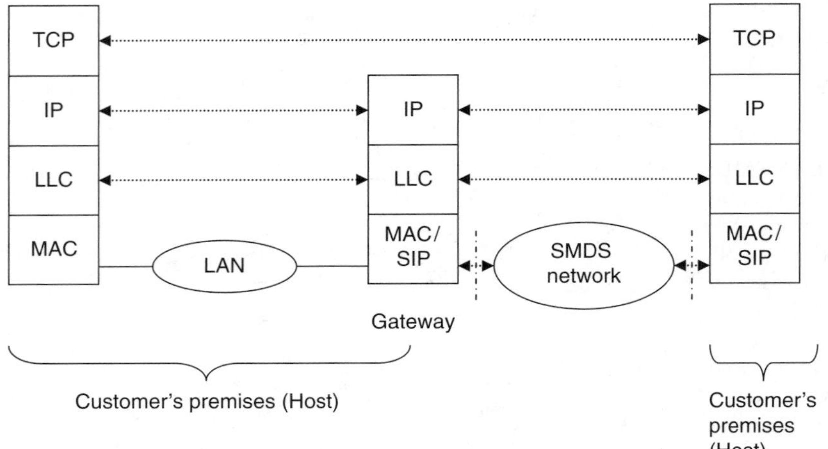

Figure 11: Internetworking of SMDS to Internet

in an SMDS interest group that has been formed within the Internet Engineering Task Force (IETF). SMDS network maintains the quality of service over metropolitan and wide area. It is hoped that the many of the features offered by SMDS will make it useful for a number of distributed processing and multimedia applications.

Asynchronous Transfer Mode (ATM)

One of the promising high-speed networks during 1993 and 1999 has been asynchronous transfer mode (ATM)-based network. This network does not distinguish between the types of networks and uses both circuit and packet switching methods. A fixed size of cell length of 53 bytes is defined, out of which 5 bytes is used for header (per CCITT's recommendations). It provides data rates of 25 Mbps to 155 Mbps and above to various types of application signals like data, voice, video, and images. This integrated switching technique in general is known as cell-based-switching technique and offers connection-oriented services to these applications. It offers a single link-by-link cell transfer capability, which is common to all applications. The higher layer information is mapped into ATM cell to provide service-specific adaptation function on end-to-end basis. It overshadowed DQDB technology around 1993.

The word asynchronous may be confusing. This concept refers to the multiplexing of ATM cells for different types of networks (data, voice, and video) and sends the data associated with these networks on same physical network only when there is a data to send. In other words, ATM is a service-independent network. It is flexible in terms of bandwidth and also efficient (same resources can be used for different types of networks). In contrast to this, in synchronous networks, a special bit packet known as idle must be sent over the channelized network during every time slot corresponding to the channel to keep both sending and receiving nodes synchronous. Further, every channel is assigned with a fixed bandwidth based on its position (time or frequency) and hence is service-dependent (Ginsburg, 1996; Hura and Singhal, 2001; McDysan and Spohn, 1998; Goralski, 1995; www.atmforum.org).

Applications of ATM: With the advent of ATM and its acceptance in B-ISDN high-speed networks, various applications have been developed including distributed multimedia (sales, engineering, and support organizations using multimedia applications over ATM), distance learning (video broadcasting of training sessions will be cheaper than existing satellite technology), video documentation (new CD-ROM technology documenting large volumes of video for sharing over high-speed and high bandwidth ATM networks), medical imaging (transmission, sorting, sharing data from medical imaging devices via high performance network within premises), which may be extended for WANs based on ATM networks.

ATM Cell: A fixed size of cell length of 53 bytes is defined, out of which 5 byte is used for header (Figure 12). It supports both types of data frames or traffic: continuous (PCM voice video applications), and bursty (data from LANs, subnets). It is important to know that ATM cell length is the smallest frame size of 64 byte in Ethernet LAN.

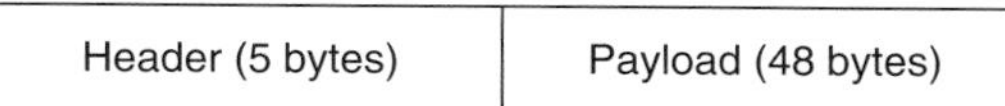

Figure 12: ATM cell

Payload typically contains data but may include some overhead bytes as well.

ATM Transmission: It defines a transfer mode where fixed length of information units with headers are multiplexed onto a transmission media. Each multiplexed channel is distinguished by the attached header. The ATM switching each channel does not have any limit on its speed other than the limit defined by the transmission media. It does not support error-control and flow-control and as such we do not have to synchronize the terminals with that of network for data communications. The ATM multiplexer, in general takes the data from the device (specific number or multiple cells), adds its 5-byte header, and transmits it. In some cases, ATM adaptation layer (AAL) processes the data and adds header and trailer and passes the frame to segmentation and reassembly (SAR). The SAR segments the data into data units, which are then sent to ATM.

The ATM addressing defines two identifiers as virtual path and virtual circuit. The virtual path defines multiple virtual channels to the same end points. The virtual channel is static to destination, whereas virtual paths are different at each node. The virtual path is predefined either through system administration or by signaling protocol. The ATM switching (packet or fast-packet) in fact provides translation of VCI and VPI at switching node or cross-connect node (ATM switching node). It also provides cell transportation between sets of input lines into dedicated output lines. A connection from end-user VCI to end-user VCI is defined as virtual channel connection, whereas end VPI to end VPI is defined as virtual path connection. The physical resources are used on demand and are available only when the data frame is to be transmitted. Each physical link can support a maximum of 256 VPIs at any node and each virtual path can support a maximum 64,000 virtual channels. On other side, NNI can support a maximum of 4096 VPIs.

The transmission of ATM cells through ATM networks goes through various ATM-based components like ATM multiplexers and cross-connect nodes. Obviously, we have to provide synchronization for proper communication for ATM cells. The transfer of ATM cells follows the following sequence of functions: generation of cells, transmission of cells, multiplexing, switching nodes, and switching of cells. The generation of cells mainly deals with the mapping between non-ATM information and ATM information. If the B-ISDN terminals are used, the information is inherently mapped onto ATM cell formats and hence no additional mapping is required.

ATM supports four basic classes of services with an option of offering other variant services around these basic classes as discussed below:

Class 1: Constant bit rate (CBR) service specifies connection-oriented service offering a constant bit rate. AAL0 specifies peak cell rate (PCR), pulse code modulation telephone systems, circuit emulation (transport of 2 Mbps or 45 Mbps) signals. Examples of this service include 64 Kbit/sec voice, fixed-rate uncompressed video, and leased lines for private data networks.

Class 2: Variable bit rate (VBR) service specifies an average cell rate that can peak at a certain level for a maximum time. AAL2 supports a connection-oriented service in which the bit rate is variable but requires a bounded delay for delivery. The requirement on bounded delay for delivery is necessary for the receiver to reconstruct the original uncompressed voice or video. It offers real-time and non-real-time variants and typically used for bursty traffic like compressed packetized video and audio.

Class 3: Connection-oriented data service specifies a minimum rate that is guaranteed for connection-oriented data communication. For connection-oriented file transfer and in general, data network applications where a connection is set up before data is transferred, this type of service has variable bit rate and does not require bounded delay for delivery. Two AAL3/4 protocols were defined to support this service class. But with its high complexity, the AAL5 protocol is often used to support this class of service.

Class 4: Connectionless data service allocates unused bandwidth after allocating bandwidth to other traffic, connectionless data. Examples of this service include datagram traffic and in general, data network applications where no connection is set up before data is transferred for unspecified bit rate (UBR). Either AAL3/4 or AAL5 can be used to support this class of service.

ATM Network: The networks based on ATM or fast packet-switching provide no flow-control or error-control and also no dynamics actions are defined for the lost packets. But, preventive actions for error-control are supported by these networks. This does not become a major drawback as these networks work on connection-oriented mode. The establishment of connection during set up phase is defined (based on the request received by networks) before the user data can be transmitted. After this phase, the user data will be transmitted only when the resources are available. After the user data transfer is over, the resources are released. All the networks are defined around some parameters of service and these parameters range from connectionless, connection-oriented, constant bit rate (CBR), variable bit rate (VBR), quality of service (QoS).

The ATM cell is transmitted as fixed-sized packet of bits at physical layer in contrast to defining a structure of 0s and 1s for a type of service in other existing networks. It integrates data, voice, video, images, and graphics for a higher bandwidth and LAN interconnectivity. This type of connection-oriented mode also provides an optional QOS and less probability of packet loss. The probability of losing a packet during the transmission is very low (typically 10-8 to 10-12) and also the allocation of resources is made available with an acceptable probability. A layered model for protocols handling these situations is shown in Figure 13.

Core Functions of AAL: The ATM adaptation layer (AAL) relays ATM cells between the ATM layer and the higher layer. When relaying information received from the higher layers, it segments the data into ATM cells in terms of packet data unit (PDU). When relaying information received from the ATM layer, it must reassemble the payloads into a format the higher layers can understand. This operation, which is called segmentation and reassembly (SAR), is the main task of AAL. Various services classes (1 through 4 as described above) supported by AAL PDU protocol are usually selected from the parameters of QOS and a particular service depends on the set of parameter(s) chosen and the service user. For example, if service user is LLC, the user has selected parameter of QOS for LLC and as such, this user service needs only segmentation and reassembly by AAL protocol (no error recovery as it is supported by LLC itself). But if the user service is X.25 PLP (packet-level protocol), then AAL protocol must provides these core functions: segmentation, reassembly, error detection, and error correction. In the case of user services other than LLC or X.25 PLP, all the functions of AAL are required for user services.

For any of the service users, AAL protocol defines a list of core functions (as discussed above) that will be used and other functions will be provided on the top of these core functions depending on the type of service user selected. The protocol reference model of ATM-based network

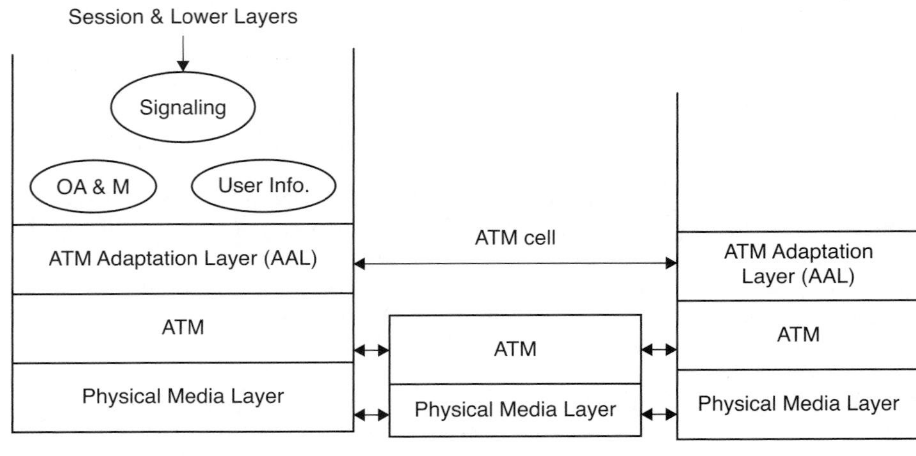

Figure 13: Layered ATM protocol architecture

follows the layered protocol reference model of OSI as shown in Figure 14.

Different AAL PDUs were defined in supporting different traffic or service that is expected to be used. The following section describes the main features of each of these PDUs along with steps required for the transmission of cells through ATM network.

ATM Adaptation Layer 0 (AAL0): AAL0, a connection-oriented service, is useful for applications of constant bit rate sources (CBR), such as voice and videoconferencing and class 1 service. Because AAL0 requires timing synchronization between the source and the destination, it depends on a medium, such as SONET, that supports clocking. AAL0 payload consists of 48 bytes without special field, is also referred to as raw cells.

The AAL0 requires three steps for the transmission of cells over the network. First, synchronous samples (for example, 1 byte of data at a sampling rate of 125 microseconds) are inserted into the payload field after the header. Second, sequence number (SN) and sequence number protection (SNP) fields are added to provide information that the receiving AAL0 uses to verify that it has received cells in the correct order. Third, the remainder of the payload field is filled with enough single bytes to equal 48 bytes.

ATM Adaptation Layer 2 (AAL2): This PDU is perfect for low-rate voice traffic, with compression, silent, and idle channel suppression mechanisms. It is subdivided into the common part sub-layer (CPS) and the service specific convergence sub-layer (SSCS). It handles the bursty traffic (timing requirements), which is also known as variable bit rate (VBR) traffic and class 2. It is suitable for VBR traffic and it uses 44 bytes of the cell payload for user data and reserves 4 bytes of the payload to support the AAL2 protocol. VBR traffic is characterized as either real-time (VBR-RT) or as non-real-time (VBR-NRT). AAL2 supports both types of VBR traffic.

ATM Adaptation Layer 3/4 (AAL3/4): AAL3/4 supports both connection-oriented and connectionless data and class 3 and 4 services. It was designed for network service providers and is closely aligned with switched multimegabit data service (SMDS). It requires four steps for cell transmission. First, the convergence sub-layer (CS) creates a protocol data unit (PDU) by attaching beginning and end fields at the header and appending the length field as a trailer in the frame. Second, the segmentation and reassembly (SAR) sub-layer fragments the PDU and attaches a header to it. Third, the SAR sub-layer attaches a CRC-10 trailer to each PDU fragment for error control. Fourth, the completed SAR PDU becomes the payload field of an ATM cell to which the ATM layer attaches the standard ATM header.

ATM Adaptation Layers 5 (AAL5): AAL5 is the primary AAL for data that supports both connection-oriented and connectionless data and AAL3/4 with limited error control. It supports error detection only without error recovery. It is used to transfer most non-SMDS data, such as classical IP over ATM and LAN emulation (LANE). It is also known as the simple and efficient adaptation layer (SEAL), because the SAR sub-layer simply accepts the CS-PDU and segments it into 48-octet SAR-PDUs without reserving any bytes in each cell and is used mostly for data traffic. It has no per-cell length or per-cell call CRC fields.

It requires three steps for cell transmission. First, the CS sub-layer attaches a variable-length PAD and an 8-byte trailer to a frame. Second, the SAR sub-layer segments the CS-PDU into 48-byte blocks. A header and trailer are not added (as is in AAL3/4), so messages cannot be interleaved. Third, the ATM layer places each block into the payload field of an ATM cell. For all cells except the last, a bit in the payload type identifier (PTI) field is set to 0 to indicate that the cell is not the last cell in a series that represents a single frame. For the last cell, the bit in the PT field is set to 1.

ATM-based LANs: In ATM-based LANs, the ATM switch sets up a point-to-point ATM communication between nodes and once ATM call is established between nodes, the full bandwidth of 100 Mbps can be used by them. ATM-based LAN may have ATM LAN switches with 16 to 68 connections, internal ATM interface cards for

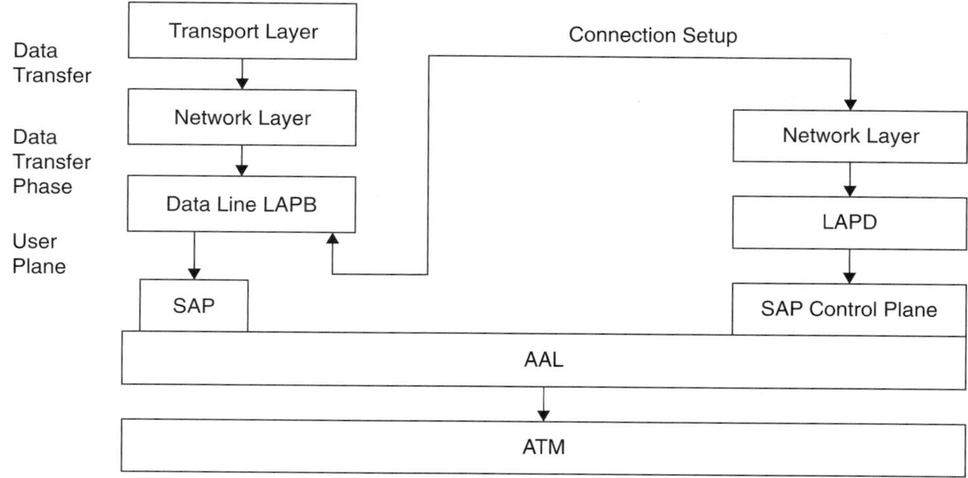

Figure 14: User and control planes for data transfer

nodes (PCs or workstations), and fiber optic transmission medium. The data rate for ATM LAN will be around 100 Mbps, which seems to be widely accepted among the members of the forum and may become a de facto standard. Each ATM interface card will provide a direct link between it and the switch and provides 100 Mbps full-duplex link between the nodes.

The private networks based on ATM switches can also be defined by defining ATM-based LANs. These LANs configure in the same way as other LANs do, for example, in Ethernet, token ring, token bus, and FDDI. The nodes (PCs or workstations) share the resources by sharing the LAN bandwidth. A typical ATM cell network is shown in Figure 15. In this network, nodes relay cells around the network and layer 2 is known as end-to-end layer and as such supports different types of LANs (802.3, 802.5, 802.4, or any other similar LANs). The network layer uses internetwork packet exchange (IPX) protocol (Novell Netware operating system) that offers datagram protocol for connectionless communication. This network seems to offer a better way for interconnectivity, but may not be practical as a result of the fact that the relationship between ATM and OSI-RM layers are still not defined clearly.

Wireless Asynchronous Transfer Mode: ATM has been traditionally used for high-speed applications as it prepares a packet of size (53 byte cell), transmits over network at very high speed. It seems obvious that wireless ATM (WATM) is an emerging and promising technology where ATM cells can also be transmitted over wireless channels. In this environment, part of ATM connection is being provided by wireless network. ATM provides seamless interconnection with backbone ATM networks, supports QoS of wireless and mobile users and small packets over wireless channel. Because ATM cells are transmitted over wireless links, a high rate of cell loss may occur. This cell loss may be reduced by use of forward error-correction algorithms, error-detection schemes (cyclic redundancy control). This may also require buffering, retransmission and re-sequencing of ATM cells. The ATM provides connection-oriented services and as such rerouting needs to be determined when a mobile user moves to new location. It may require setting up a new connection, providing multiple paths to mobile user, forwarding ATM cells or dynamically rerouting the connection. This information should be available to wireless ATM network and also any change in mobile user must be recorded in storage system, location database.

There are many factors that have not made wireless ATM popular and beneficial like cost, lack of standards, and complexity in implementation and amount of overhead. With increased radio bandwidth, emerging reliable and QoS-based protocols, and error-control protocols, it looks very promising that wireless ATM will support mobile users soon.

FUTURE DIRECTIONS

The introduction of a simple and cheap local area network (10 Mbps) solution has led to the development of many technologies dealing with customer premises environments like 100-Mbps and 10-Gbps IEEE LAN, switched Ethernet, and FDDI-II. A new LAN using the standard MAC protocol distributed queue dual bus (DQDB) for a metropolitan area was introduced as a MAN (IEEE 802.6). The evolution of ATM has gone through a number of phases and technologies. In the first phase we have seen 100-Mbps LAN, switched Ethernet, and FDDI-II. The second phase saw the emergence of MANs. A new switching technique known as packet switching was introduced for WANs. The last phase has seen a variety of public network services via technologies of SMDS and frame relay.

Wireless technology has introduced a new concept of networking in which a variety of hand-held devices can be connected. It also allows to be used in different types of networks (LANs, MANs, and WANs). It has also found its application in ATM-based WANs.

SMDS seems to be a matured technology and found its applications in limited business arena. One such application that uses SMDS for Internet access is CERF-Net (www.cerfnet.com), a subsidiary of General Atomics. A case study was done of the company and their use of SMDS and main focus was to demonstrate that SMDS gives full access to Internet and e-mail services, support of large usage and broadband requirements, multiple host connectivity, security, high-speed access, privacy, and functionality. CERFNet explained in the article that because SMDS is technology independent, it is a good way to provide service to customers that use frame relay, FDDI, ATM, and dedicated private lines. The company also felt that because SMDS is a broadband technology that can be compatible with whatever new speed rate is invented, that it would be a technology to stick with. Other service industries that are deploying SMDS include banking, insurance, finance, and others as these use

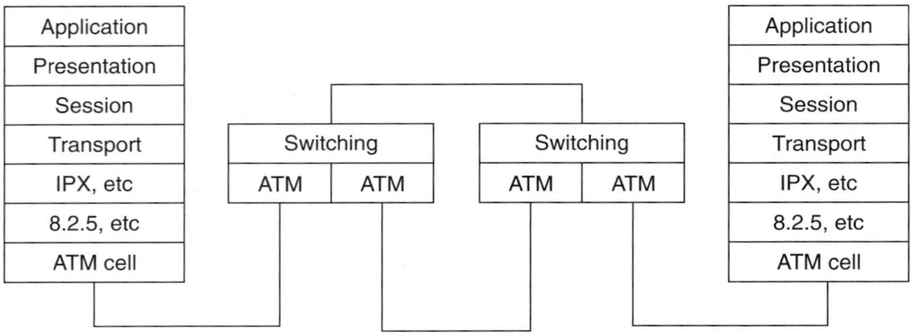

Figure 15: A typical ATM network

Table 1: Comparison of High-Speed Technologies

Parameters	FDDI	FDDI-II	ISDN	B-ISDN	X.25	Frame Relay	SMDS	ATM
Media access mechanism	Token ring	Token ring	Public Telephone network	Telephone network	Public data network	Public switched data network	Distribute Queue Dual Bus standard (IEEE 802.6)	ATM cell (53 byte)
Switching mechanism	Packet	Packet	Circuit	Circuit	Packet	Packet (frame)	Packet switched datagram over public data networks	Circuit and packet
Transmission media	Optical fiber	Optical fiber	Public telephone network	Optical transmission (fiber optics)	Public telephone network	Public telephone network	Optical fiber, copper	Fiber optics
Data rate	100 Mbps	100 Mbps	144 K–1.54 Mbps (U.S.) 2.56 Mbps (Europe)	155 Mbps (UNI), 622 Mbps (NNI)	Offers UNI and NNI, low-speed terminal at 19.2 Kbps	56 Kbps, T3, 100 Mbps	1.54 Mbps (DS-1)-44.736 Mbps (DS-3)-155 Mbps	25–155 Mbps
Features	As MAN, backbone in campus	High performance workstation		Higher bandwidth and data rate over a longer distance, immune to electromagnetic fields	Minimum delay, higher performance and throughput	Minimum overhead, error-control and flow-control	High speed and performance, no error and flow controls	Flexible bandwidth, multiplexing of ATM cells
Types of services	Point-to-point	isochronous	Integrated voice and data	Service independent network	Exchange of data and control between DTE and DCE	Streamlined control of X.25	Secured network version	End-to-end Service Independent
Network applications	As MAN	High performance processing	Video conferencing	Uses as a WAN	Connection-oriented services	Block interactive data and bursty traffic applications	Limited business like banks, finance, insurance	Distributed multi-media distance learning, video documentation, media imaging
Interconnectivity	LANs		Public switched data network		Lower layers of OSI-RM	Lower layers of OSI-RM	Public telephone networks	LAN/MAN/WAN
Standardization	IEEE 802 and OSI-RM		T1 (U.S.) 2.56 Mbps (Europe)		International standard	ANSI, ITU-T	U.S. and Europe	U.S., Europe

optical scanning methods for creating electronic file cabinets for increasing storage capacity and improved access mechanisms.

Both LAN technologies (100 Mbps and switched Ethernet) do not guarantee fixed delay for time-sensitive applications, but can deliver the variable length of frames where ATM is preferred for multimedia and video applications. With respect to services, both FDDI-II and ATM can be used, but FDDI-II would be cheaper than ATM. There is close relationship between ATM cell and DQDB slots. MANs are used as a public network for data and offer two advantages over private networks as ubiquity and reliability. The first advantage allows the users to send data to anyone that subscribes to public service (e.g., public voice telephone networks). ATM and SONET offer new technologies, whereas SMDS offers a service and in fact is public service extension of LAN and MAN services.

The Internet is still going strong for offering connections between remote computers and within a few years, these computing devices will be replaced by hand-held and mobile devices, which are expected to create a huge market for cellular phones and PDAs that offer a variety of services. A large amount of research is currently being done in the areas of wireless LANs, wireless PANs, satellite-based networks, wireless local loops (WLL), and wireless ATM, mobile computing, addressing and transport protocols for e-commerce, and GSM and PCS cellular phones.

In summary, it looks obvious that ATM networks can be used for providing LAN emulation, SDMS connectionless, and frame relay services all on the same network. Further, it also supports interconnectivity between these services. So why should we not build one network based on ATM? ATM uses the same procedures and protocols of LANs, MANs, and WANs and provides support for multimedia services. It offers these services at different media speeds and offers virtual connections as opposed to fixed physical channels in other networks. We can get the SMDS services over frame relay networks and vice versa.

ACKNOWLEDGMENT

I thank the following graduate students who helped me in writing this chapter—Jirafe Sameer, Kadri Ravi Kumar, Kifle Eyoel, Pranathi Yerragudi, and Susnerwala Abdul. I also express my sincere thanks to anonymous referees who have provided me with many positive and constructive suggestions/comments to improve the quality of this chapter.

GLOSSARY

Asynchronous Transfer Mode (ATM): This mode is defined for B-ISDN and supports different types of signals (data, voice, video, images).

ATM adaptation layer: This layer is above the ATM layer and provides interface between higher layers and ATM layer. It performs signaling, segmentation, and reassembly on ATM cell.

ATM cell: This interface can handle both types of traffic with unlimited bandwidth and high data rates.

Bridge: This interconnecting device provides interconnection between similar or different types of LANs and is connected at MAC sub-layer.

Broadband Integrated Service Digital Network (B-ISDN): This service independent network transports different types of services (asynchronous, synchronous, and isochronous traffic).

Bursty: An irregular signal distributed over time and denotes a type of noise.

Channel Service Units/Data Service Units (CSU/DSU): A pair of channels (CSU) and (DSU) is used to provide an interface between computer and digital switch of digital network.

Customer Premises equipment (CPE): CPE includes end devices, such as terminals and personal computers, and intermediate nodes, such as routers, modems, and multiplexers. It is typically owned and maintained by the customer.

Distributed Queue Dual Bus (DQDB): A standard MAC protocol for LAN/MAN and supports connection-oriented, connectionless, and isochronous simultaneously.

Ethernet: One of the most common and popular LANs.

Fiber Distributed Data Interface (FDDI): This is a high-speed LAN and is based on fiber optic supporting a data rate of 100 Mbps.

Gateway: This interconnecting device connects heterogeneous networks and works at lower three layers of OSI-RM.

Integrated Services Digital Network (ISDN): A digital network that transmits data, voice, and images together over the same link.

Link Access Protocol-B (LAP-B): This standard is a subset of HDLC that controls data exchange between DTE and public switched networks.

Metropolitan Area Network (MAN): This is a high-speed LAN that offers a data rate of over 100 Mbps within a metropolitan city (around 100 miles)

Plesiochronous Digital Hierarchy (PDH): The commonly used digital hierarchy for synchronous transmission networks and is very popular in Europe.

Switched Multi-megabit Data Services (SMDS): The network is based on concept of fast packet switching and offers broadband services to LANs and WANS.

Synchronous Digital Hierarchy (SDH): Two popular interface data rates for B-ISDN based on ATM are 155.520 and 622.080 Mbps.

Synchronous Optical Network (SONET): This standard is very popular in North America and is a new form compatible with the international SDH.

CROSS REFERENCES

See *ATM (Asynchronous Transfer Mode); BISDN (Broadband Integrated Services Digital Network); Digital Communications Basics; Frame Relay; Wireless Wide Area Networks (WWANs).*

REFERENCES

Clark, Kennedy, and Kevin Hamilton. 1999. *CCIE Professional Development: Cisco LAN Switching*. Indianapolis: Cisco Press.

Ginsburg, David. 1996. *ATM: Solutions for Enterprise Internetworking*. Boston: Addison-Wesley Publishing Co.

Goldman, James. 2004. *Applied Data Communication*. Hoboken, NJ: John Wiley and Sons.

Goralski, W. J. 1995. *Introduction to ATM Networking*. New York, NY: McGraw-Hill.

http://www.ja.net/sj5/history.html (accessed Dec 12, 2006)

http://univercd.cisco.com/cisintwk/into_doc/index.htm (accessed Dec 12, 2006)

http://grouper.ieee.org/groups/802/dots.html (accessed Dec 12, 2006)

http://www.dnsstuff.com/pages/rfc1694.htm (accessed Dec 12, 2006)

http://standards.ieee.org/getieee802/802.11html (accessed Dec 12, 2006)

http://standards.ieee.org/getieee802/802.15html (accessed Dec 12, 2006)

Hura, Gurdeep S. and Mukesh Singhal. 2001. *Data and Computer Communication: Networking and Internetworking*. Boca Raton, FL: CRC Press.

McDysan, David E., and Darren L. Spohn. 1998. *ATM Theory and Application*. New York: McGraw-Hill.

Packet Switching

Qinqing Zhang and Qi Bi, *Bell Laboratory, Alcatel-Lucent Technologies*

INTRODUCTION TO PACKET SWITCHING

Packet switching is the dominant communication technology in modern data networking and telecommunications. In previous chapters, the concepts of computer networks were introduced and different type of networks were described based on scale, connection method, functionality, topology, or services. The communication between computers or devices involves the term *switching,* which describes how information is exchanged between the input ports and output ports at each network element.

There have always been two fundamental and competing switching technologies in communications: *static allocation* and *dynamic allocation* of the transmission bandwidth. The public switched telephone network (PSTN) is a typical circuit-switched network, where a fixed bandwidth is pre-allocated for the duration of a call. The early radio system, that is the advanced mobile phone systems (AMPS), is also circuit-switched where the radio spectrum is pre-allocated during a mobile call. On the other hand, message, telegraph, and mail systems have been operated by dynamically allocating bandwidth or spaces after a message is received at the time. They never attempt to schedule bandwidth or space over the end-to-end source to destination path.

There are three major switching techniques, that is, *packet switching, circuit switching,* and *message switching*. In packet switching, packets (units of information block) are individually routed among nodes over data links that are shared by many other nodes in the data networks. In contrast with circuit switching that pre-allocates the transmission bandwidth for a user, packet switching allocates the transmission bandwidth dynamically, permitting many users to share the same transmission link previously required by one user. This improves the transmission efficiency especially when users transmit at variable bit rates. Packet switching optimizes the usage of the bandwidth available in a network and saves the transmission cost. It also improves the reliability and functional flexibility of packet delivery in communication networks. Packet switching has been so successful and become the exclusive communication paradigm in all the data networks built throughout the world. In this chapter, we describe the fundamentals, history and evolution, and key techniques of packet switching.

FUNDAMENTALS OF PACKET SWITCHING

Packets

A *packet* is a block of data that carries user information exchanged over a communication link. It usually consists of three elements: *header, payload,* and *trailer,* as shown in Figure 1. The first element, *header*, contains address and administrative information that allows the packet be delivered by the network nodes from the source to the destination. The second element, *payload*, contains the user information that needs to be exchanged in the network. The third element, *trailer*, usually contains information for error detection, allowing receivers to verify that packets do not have errors during transmission. (If errors occur during transmission and cannot be corrected, the packet is usually discarded.) Sometimes, a packet may not have a trailer. The payload together with the header contains all the information needed for packet delivery.

A packet is analogous to a letter (payload) sent through the mail (network) with the address (header) written on the envelope.

Unlike a message (in message switching), the length of a packet is limited and can vary between successive packets. Packets are usually transmitted via frames, which are either fixed-length or variable length data blocks transmitted over the actual physical links. Sometimes packets and frames are interchangeable in some places but they actually have different meaning. Packets are usually referred

Figure 1: The format of a packet

as the transmission unit at layer 3 or the network layer, in a layered network protocol stack, whereas frames are usually referred as the transmission unit at layer 1 or layer 2, the physical layer or the link layer (Tanenbaum 1981).

Nodes

A *node* is a physical device that is connected as part of a data network. Nodes can be personal computers, workstations or servers, specialized data processors, cell phones, personal digital assistants (PDAs), or various other network appliances. Depending on their functionalities, nodes can be characterized in different types. For example, in the SNA (systems network architecture) network architecture invented in early stages of computer networks (Cypser 1978), there are four type of nodes defined. Type I nodes are terminals. Type 2 nodes are controllers, machines that supervise the behaviors of terminals. Type 4 nodes are front-end processors, devices that relieve the main CPU of the processing and interrupt handling in data communications. Type 5 nodes are the main hosts themselves. There are no type 3 nodes. Nodes that route data for the other network devices as well as themselves are sometimes called super-nodes.

Packet Switching

Circuit Switching and Packet Switching

Computer-to-computer communication has some fundamentally differences from human-to-human communication. When you or your telephone places a telephone call, the switching equipment at the central office attempts to allocate a physical path all the way from the caller's telephone to the called telephone. This switching technique is called *circuit switching*. Figure 2 shows a simplified schematic model of circuit switching. In this example, there are multiple switching elements between the two telephones. Each switch has the same number of incoming lines and outgoing lines. When a call is placed through a switch, a physical connection is established between the incoming ports and outgoing ports. The dotted line shows the allocated physical path between the two end points. This dedicated link exists during the entire phone conversation. An important property of circuit switching is that it needs certain time to setup an end-to-end connection before any information can be sent. This is usually called the call setup time. Once the connection is established, the data transmission delay is only the propagation time, which is quite small.

In contrast to circuit switching, packet switching does not require any dedicated link or path be established in advance between sender and receiver. Instead, the user's overall message is broken up into a number of small packets, each of which is sent separately. Figure 3 shows a simplified schematic model of packet switching. Each packet of user information is labeled to identify its source and destination before it is sent. Each packet is stored at the receiving switching office and then forwarded later, one hop at a time. The receiving end re-assembles the packets in their proper order, with the assistance of the sequence number and other administrative information stored in the header and trailer fields. A network uses this *store-and-forward* technique and allocates the most efficient route available at the time for each packet.

Packet Switching and Message Switching

Yet another alternative switching technique is message switching. Message switching is very similar to packet switching, where there is no need to establish a physical path or link in advance between both ends. Compared to packet switching, message switching puts no restriction on the block size. In other words, the entire message is the transmission and switching unit at each switch. As a result, the switch needs to have large buffer or memory size to store and forward a large message, resulting in a longer queueing and transmission delay and reduced throughput. The advantage of message switching is that it maintains the complete message delivery from sender to receiver. Data networks are usually packet switched instead of message switched. More descriptions on message switching are provided in a subsequent chapter.

Circuit switching and packet switching differ in many respects. The key difference is that circuit switching statically reserves the required end-to-end bandwidth before any data can be sent. Any unused bandwidth on an allocated end-to-end circuit is just wasted. Packet switching acquires and releases the required bandwidth on a packet-by-packet basis. The unused bandwidth for a user's traffic may be utilized by packets from other unrelated users going to different destinations. Therefore,

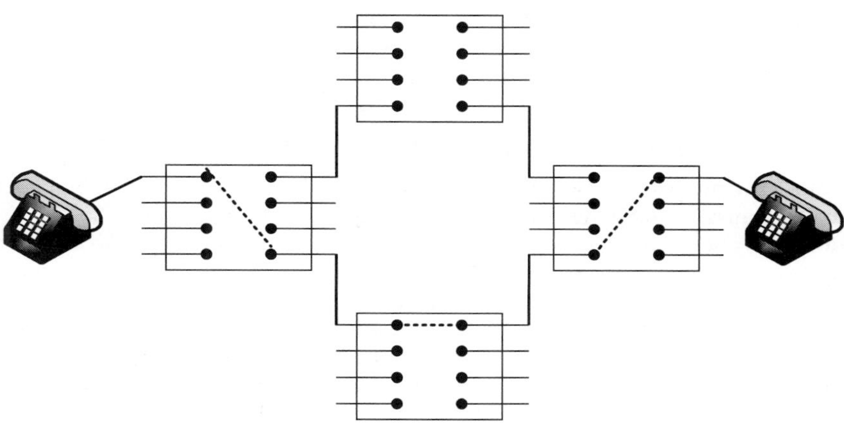

Figure 2: Circuit switching

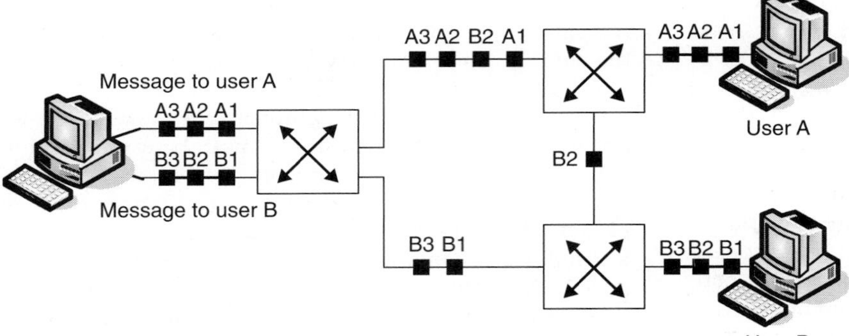

Figure 3: Packet switching

packet switching utilizes the network bandwidth more efficiently than circuit switching.

Because there is no dedicated circuit or path for a user's traffic, packets may be routed by each network node on different routes at the time. Packets may be delivered out of order to the destination with packet switching. Reordering of packets can never happen with circuit switching.

Transmission capacity between pairs of nodes in a packet-switched network is generally not split up into separately physical channels, each of which has a fixed bandwidth. Instead, the entire available bandwidth between pairs of nodes is treated as a single high bit-rate pipe and shared by all the packets sent on the link. In this way, individual packets are transported more quickly, that is, at full speed of the line rate, and bursts of transmission can be accommodated.

A problem occurs when more than one data sources try to send packets at the same time exceeding the bandwidth of the data link. This situation is accommodated by buffers at both sending and receiving ends of the connection between pairs of nodes. The use of buffers smoothes out the burstness of the traffic and improves the link utilization. This is achieved by *statistically multiplexing* the packets from different sources sharing the same link. The statistical average total bit-rate must be slightly lower than the link bit-rate so that there is no packet dropping as a result of buffer overflow.

The charging algorithms between the two switching technologies are different. In a circuit-switched network, carriers charge the clients based on the connection time and transmission distance. In a packet-switched network, carriers charge the clients based on both the time and number of bytes or packets carried. Transmission distance usually does not matter except when it involves the network layout internationally.

EVOLUTION OF PACKET SWITCHING

Before the modern advances in computer technology and digital signal processing, systems with dynamic allocation were necessarily limited to non-real time communications, because many manual sorting and routing decisions were required along the source to destination path of each message. In late 1960s, virtually all interactive data communication networks were circuit switched, the same as the telephone network. Interactive data traffic occurs in short bursts and thus 90% or more of the static allocated bandwidth is wasted. The rapid advances in technology evolution have made digital electronics with fast processing power inexpensive enough for a complete redesign of communication networks. The "packet-switching" concept was introduced to make the dynamic allocation systems superior to static allocation systems in terms of cost, connection time, transport efficiency, reliability, and flexibility. As a result, packet switching has become the dominant paradigm in modern communication networks and offered substantial economic and performance advantages over the conventional systems.

History of Packet Switching

Packet switching was evolved from the basic dynamic allocation technique used for conventional mail, telegraph, and paper tape switching systems. Bandwidth is allocated only when a block of data is ready to be sent, and only enough for that particular data block to be transferred over the data link at the time. Depending on the traffic characteristics of the data being transferred, packet switching is generally more efficient (3-100 times more) than static allocation approaches, because it can reduce the wasted available bandwidth resources. This is achieved by adding both processing power and buffer storage resources at each network switch along the path. The economic tradeoff between circuit switching and packet switching is obvious: if the bandwidth is cheap, use circuit switching; if computing is cheap, use packet switching.

The first published description of the so-called packet switching was an 11-volumn analysis, *On Distributed Communications*, written by Paul Baran of the Rand Corporation in August 1964 (Baran 1964). It proposed a fully distributed packet-switching system to provide for all military communications of data and voice. The RAND's proposed packet-switching system not only achieved the original goal but also projected superior economics for both voice and data communications.

Independently Donald Davies from the National Physical Laboratory (NPL) in the United Kingdom conducted detail design of a *store-and-forward* packet switching system. The first official publication of the NPL proposal was in October 1967. Davies' original proposal, developed in late 1965, was very similar to the actual networks being built today in almost all respects. His cost analysis demonstrated strong economic advantages for the packet-switching technique.

Baran's study had its influence to Robert Taylor and J. C. R. Licklider from the Advanced Research Projects Agency (ARPA). The interesting discussions motivated Lawrence Roberts to initiate the first two actual network projects. Merrill and Roberts (Roberts and Merrill 1966) did an experiment of connecting the TX-2 computer in Massachusetts to the Q-32 computer in California with a low-speed dial-up telephone line creating the first wide-area computer network. This experiment realized that time-shared computers could work together, running programs and retrieving data on the remote machine.

ARPANET is the creation of ARPA (now DARPA), the (Defense) Advanced Research Projects Agency of the U.S. Department of Defense. The design proposal, which was published in June 1967, consisted of a packet-switching network, with minicomputers at each computer site as the packet switches and interfacing devices, interconnected by 50 Kbps leased lines. The original ARPANET was an experimental four-node network that became operation in December 1969. Each minicomputer took blocks of data from the computers and terminals connected to it, subdivided the data into 128-byte packets and added a header specifying the source and destination addresses. The minicomputer used a dynamically updated routing table to send the packets over the most free line with the fastest route toward the destination. Upon receiving a packet, the next minicomputer would acknowledge it and conducted the same routing process independently from the previous node. Therefore, ARPANET (Roberts 1974; Roberts 1978) was a completely distributed network with a dynamic routing algorithm on a packet-by-packet basis. Much of our present knowledge of networking is a direct result of this pioneering work.

INTERCONNECTION IN PACKET-SWITCHED NETWORKS

Packet-switched network is a fully distributed system that dynamically routes the packets based on a continuous evaluation of the delay on the path, line availability, and queue length at the network node. The interconnection of numerous networks of different types or the connections within a network requires the physical devices that have different functionalities and purposes to serve the network.

Interconnection: Switches, Bridges, Routers, and Gateways

Switches

A switch is a computer networking device that channels incoming data from any of the multiple incoming physical ports to a specific output port toward its destination.

Switches are used in both circuit-switched networks and packet-switched networks. In the traditional circuit-switched telephone network, one or more switches are used to set up a dedicated connection or circuit for an exchange between two or more parties. A *telephone exchange* or *central office* houses equipment that is commonly known as simply a *switch*, which is a piece of equipment that connects phone calls. It makes phone calls "work" in the sense of making connections and relaying the speech information. In a packet-switched network, for example, in the Ethernet local area network (LAN), a switch examines the physical device's media access control or MAC address in each incoming packet and determines which output port to forward the packet. Figure 4 illustrates a simplified structure of a switch matrix in a central office. All the outgoing trunk circuits (numbered 1 to 4) may be accessed by any of the customer lines (marked A to D). Figure 5 illustrates a simplified internal structure of a packet switch device. It consists of a bus, or multiple buses, connecting together each of the incoming and outgoing ports. Packets received from any of the incoming ports are first stored in the buffers. The switching logic analyzes the address in the packet header and decides which outgoing port the packet is sent to.

A switch usually uses *store-and-forward*, or *cut-through* forwarding method. In store-and-forward method, the switch receives and buffers each frame entirely, typically performs a checksum on the frame, and then forwards it on the output port. In cut-through method, the switch only checks the frame's physical layer address and then forwards it to the output port. It does not do any error checking on the frame.

A switch only connects data from an incoming port to an output port. It does not monitor the traffic because each port is isolated, and only the sending and receiving ports are connected when they transmit the data. Two common methods, that is, *port mirroring* and *switch monitoring* (*SMON*), were specifically designed to allow

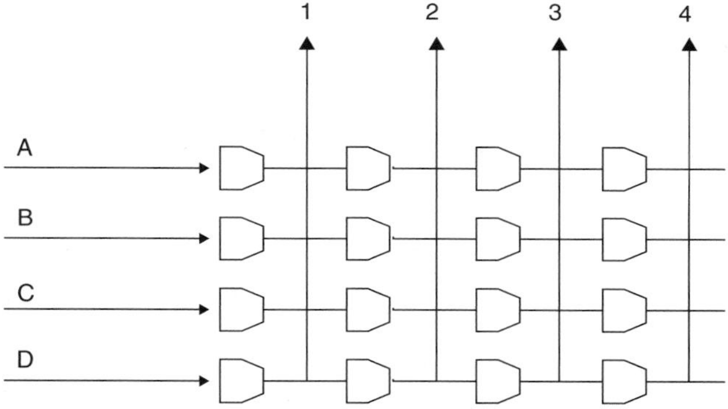

Figure 4: Switch matrix in an exchange office

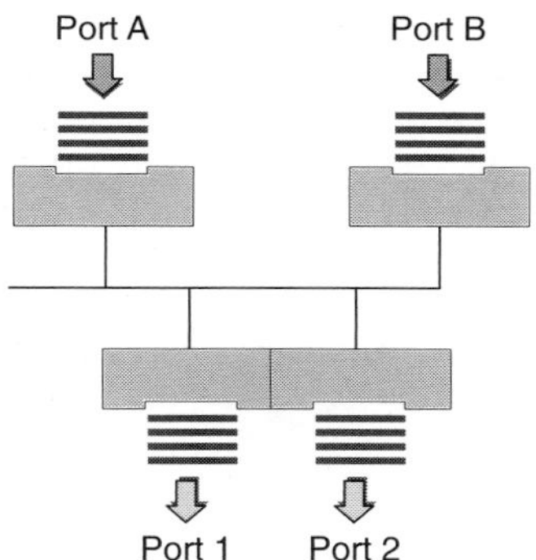

Figure 5: Packet switch internal structure

a network manager to monitor the traffic in a network with switches. In the port mirroring method, a switch sends a copy of network packets to a monitoring network connection so that the network manager can collect the information and monitor the traffic. The SMON (RFC 2613) is a protocol defined by the IETF RFC 2613 for controlling the interfaces and facilities between the switches and network managers for port mirroring.

Bridges

A bridge is a computer networking device that connects multiple network segments along the data link layer to operate as a single network. It works by using bridging as what its name entails, by connecting two sides of the adjacent networks. It forwards the traffic from one network to another network.

A bridge has intelligence built in the hardware to determine which packets should be transferred into another network. It examines the addresses (indicating a destination service access point and a source service access point) in the *logical link control* (LLC) header of each packet and transfers the relevant packets to the second network directly or via a second bridge. If the physical structure of the two networks is different, for example, one network is an Ethernet, the other is a token ring as shown in Figure 6, the bridge will transform the packet into the right format.

Primitive bridges are relatively cheap. They provide a very economic means for self-configurable interconnection. However, bridges have some limitations of their usage and functionalities. They do not limit the scope of broadcasts and do not scale to large networks. Bridges result in very complicated topologies that are extremely difficult to manage. Thus bridges are not recommended for large and complex networks. Instead, the *router* appears and is used to provide a more complex and intelligent functionality of interconnection in packet-switched networks.

Routers

A router is a computer networking device that forwards data packets across the network toward their destinations based on the routing algorithms. A router acts as a junction between two networks and transfers data packets between them (see Figure 7). Routers are more intelligent than switches and bridges. They are designed to "learn" the topology of complicated networks that are constantly changing and expanding and determine the "best route" for packets or packet flows to their destinations. The key design of routers is the routing algorithm. Routers can learn the network topology through experience, that is, the previous successful routes, and update the routing table accordingly.

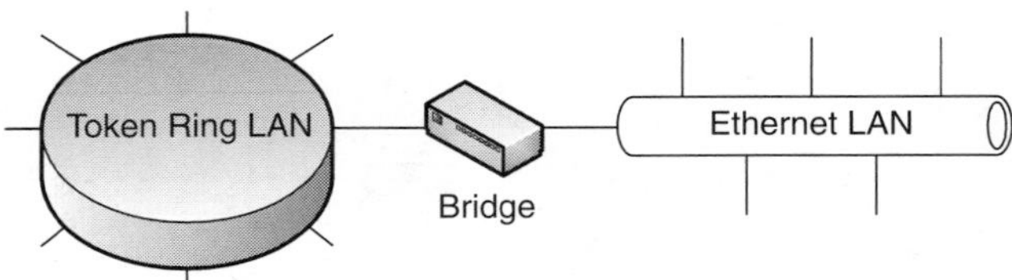

Figure 6: LAN bridge

There are different options when designing a network. One option is to put multiple segments into one bridged network. Another option is to divide the network into different sub-networks interconnected by routers. If a host moves between segments in a routed network, it has to get a new IP address and therefore break the transport layer connections, that is, TCP/IP connection. If the host moves in a bridged network, it does not have to reconfigure the packet format and thus is simpler and more economic. The drawback of a bridged network is that it lacks the intelligence and scalability in large and complex networks.

Gateways

A gateway is a computer networking device for interfacing with another network that uses different protocols. It is also called a protocol converter and can operate at any layer of the network model. The function of a gateway is much more complex than that of a router or switch. Typically, a gateway must convert one protocol stack into another.

A gateway may contain devices such as protocol translators, impedence matching devices, rate converters, fault isolators, or signal translators as necessary to provide system interoperability. It also requires the establishment of mutually acceptable administrative procedures between the two networks. A protocol translation/mapping gateway interconnects networks with different network protocol technologies by performing the required protocol conversions.

For example, a gateway may connect a local area network (LAN) or wireless LAN (WLAN) to the Internet or other wide area network (WAN). In this case the gateway connects an IPX/SPX (the LAN) to a TCP/IP network (the Internet), as shown in Figure 8.

Gateways that connect two IP-based networks, like TCP/IP, have two IP addresses, one on each network. An address like 192.168.1.xxx is an address in LAN, to which traffic is sent from the LAN. The other IP address is an

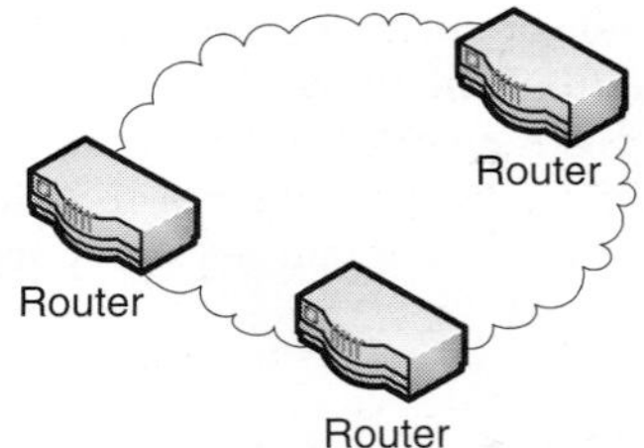

Figure 7: Network router

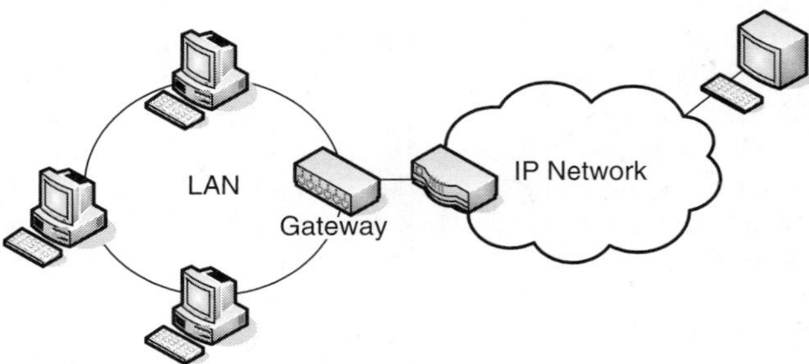

Figure 8: Gateway connecting two different networks

address in WAN, to which traffic is sent from the WAN. When talking about the gateway IP address, it commonly means the address of the gateway in LAN.

The addresses of computers connected to the LAN are hidden behind the gateway. This means that the WAN can only see the gateway's IP address. To regulate traffic between the WAN and the LAN, the gateway commonly performs network address translation (NAT), presenting all of the LAN traffic to the WAN as coming from the gateway's WAN IP address and doing packet sorting and distribution of return WAN traffic to the local area network.

MAIN TECHNIQUES IN PACKET SWITCHING

X.25

X.25 is the first international standard recommended by International Telecommunications Union (ITU) for packet-switched networks. It was developed in the early stages of packet networks evolution for the nations to agree on a standard user interface to the networks to facilitate network interconnection and permit easier user attachment. X.25 has been widely adopted and used in most packet switched networks.

The X.25 recommendation defines the protocols between a *data terminal equipment* (DTE), for example, personal computer or computer terminal controller, and a *data circuit terminating equipment* (DCE), for example, the connection point to a packet-switched network, as shown in Figure 9. It defines protocols corresponding to layer 1 (physical layer), layer 2 (link layer), and layer 3 (packet layer) in the International Standard Organization (ISO)'s Open System Interconnect (OSI) model.

The physical layer connection may either be X.21 for digital leased line or X.21 bis for V.24/V.28 modem in conjunction with an analogue leased line. The X.25 protocol provides for the data blocks for up to 4095 *virtual circuits* (VCs) on a single full-duplex leased line interface to the network. It includes all procedures for call setup and tear-down. One important feature of this interface is the notion of independent flow control on each VC. The flow control enables the network and the user to regulate the traffic on the flow to protect itself from congestion and overflow. In early networks like ARPANET that did not have the flow control capability, the network had to depend on the host to insure that no user transmitted more data to the network than the network could handle. The network had to shut off the entire host interface if congestion happened, which could be disastrous to other users communicating with the host or network.

Another significant aspect of X.25 is that it defines both layer 1, layer 2, and layer 3 protocol interfaces. These protocols are called the *link access procedures* (LAP) and the *packet level interface*. The link access procedure assures the correct delivery of data across the link connecting a DTE to an DCE for multiplexing of logical channels. The packet level interface guarantees the end-to-end delivery of data across the entire network.

The *link access procedures balanced* (LAPB) protocol provides for the balanced class of procedure and also allows making a single logical link using multiple physical circuits. The link access procedure uses the principles and terminology of *high-level data link control* (HDLC) as defined by ISO. HDLC provides error checksum and ensures the error-free transmission of data information across the link from a DTE to a DCE. However, it does not determine where the information should be forwarded by the DCE within the network, nor ensure its correct delivery at the destination in the packet network. This function is handled by the OSI layer 3 protocol, that is, the X.25 packet level interface.

After X.25 was adopted in March 1976, many additional standards have been agreed on and developed as well, all patterned around X.25. For example, X.31 has been adopted as the standard interface for physical layer connection between a DTE and DCE via an integrated services digital network (ISDN). X.32 specifies the use of dial-up connection for a packet mode connection via the telephone or ISDN network to an X.25 exchange. Finally, X.75 defines the standard protocol for connecting international networks.

Frame Relay

Frame relay is a standard protocol for fast packet switching in LAN. It has much less overhead than the earlier X.25 networks and operates more efficiently. Packets vary in length and are call frames for this protocol. Erroneous or bad frames are discarded instead of retransmitted and thus packets are switched more quickly. Frame relay began its commercial service in 1992 and is now widely deployed.

Standards for the frame relay protocol have been developed by American National Standards Institute (ANSI) and International telephone and telegraph consultative committee (CCITT), now known as ITU-T simultaneously.

Frame relay is essentially an enhancement of X.25, taking advantage of the widespread implementation of fiber optic communication links by long-distance carriers. Fiber is much less prone to introducing errors in a data stream. Therefore frame relay does not use the

Figure 9: X.25 data network structure

extensive error checking in X.25 at the switching nodes. The error-handling processes are instead completed by the sending and receiving devices.

The frame relay frame is transmitted to its destination using the concepts of virtual circuits as in X.25, that is, logical paths from an originating point in the network to a destination point. Virtual circuits may be permanent (PVCs) or switched (SVCs). PVCs are set up administratively by the network manager for a dedicated point-to-point connection. SVCs are set up dynamically on a call-by-call basis. Because virtual circuits consume bandwidth only when they are used to transport data, many virtual circuits can exist simultaneously across a given transmission line. In addition, each device can use more of the bandwidth as necessary, and thus operate at higher speeds. Frame relay is designed to operate at speeds up to 1.5 Mbps, and may be enhanced to operate at higher speeds.

Frame relay is particularly well-suited to the interconnection of LANs that generate bursty traffic consisting of variable-length frames of data. Frame relay accepts this traffic as is, adding only a wide area network address at the front and its own check sequence at the end of each frame. Frame relay interfaces for customer premise equipment such as routers, bridges, and hubs are available from a number of vendors.

Frame relay switches are also available, and numerous carriers offer public frame relay services. As the technology and standards are refined and carrier tariffs are clarified, frame relay networks are expected to replace many X.25 networks during the next several years. However, frame relay is not well-suited to the transmission of real-time voice or video, because of the variable delay allowed between frames.

ATM

ATM stands for asynchronous transfer mode. ATM is a high-speed advanced packet-switching scheme. ATM makes all its packets one length, i.e., the so called ATM *cells*. Each cell has 53 bytes, 48 bytes of data, and 5 bytes of header information. These uniformly small packets or cells let data flow smoothly. ATM also boasts improved error control compared to conventional packet switching, as well as numerous other features that make it a core technology of data networks.

ATM was initially designed to provide a single unified networking standard that could support both synchronous channel networking and packet-based networking (IP, frame relay, and so on), whilst supporting multiple levels of *quality of service* (QoS) for packet data. It was intended to resolve the conflict between circuit-switched networks and packet-switched networks by mapping both bit streams and packet streams onto a stream of small fixed-size cells tagged with virtual circuit identifiers. The cells are typically sent on demand within a synchronous time-slot pattern in a synchronous bit-stream. The asynchronous part here is the sending of the cells, which does not need to follow any synchronous pattern.

In its original conception, ATM was considered as the enabling technology of the broadband integrated services digital network (B-ISDN) that would replace the existing PSTN. The full suite of ATM standards provides definitions for layer 1 (physical connections), layer 2 (data link layer), and layer 3 (network) of the classical OSI seven-layer networking model. Standards that define ATM networks are established by two different organizations, the ITU and ATM Forum. ATM Forum is an industry consortium that is focused on ATM. The activities of this organization included setting of the technical standards for ATM networks and facilitating the market adoption of the ATM technology. Although the two organizations frequently use different terminology to describe the ATM systems, they present the same concepts of ATM.

ATM Transport and Switching

There are two layers relate to ATM functions and transport, that is, an ATM layer that handles packet transfer and switching capabilities, and an ATM adaptation layer (AAL) that handles specific services and mapping to ATM transport. The ATM layer defines the transmission of data in the format of cells and also the use of logical connections. The ATM layer is further divided into two switching levels supported in the network.

- Virtual channel (VC): A VC is a generic term representing the unidirectional transport of ATM cells. The cells carried over a specific VC are identified by a Virtual channel identifier (VCI).
- Virtual path (VP): A VP is used to describe a bundle of VCs. The VCs associated with a VP are transported over a transmission path within the network as a group. A VP is identified by a virtual path identifier (VPI).

The VPI and VCI values are carried in the header of an ATM cell, and are used for routing and switching the cell across the ATM network.

The ATM transport creates the need to define an adaptation layer to support specific services and map other transport protocols to ATM. The AAL maps higher-layer data to ATM cells and retrieve data from ATM cells for delivery to higher layers. The general services provided by AAL are: transmission error handling, segmentation and reassembly, flow control and timing control, handling of lost and misinserted cells. The AAL layer is further divided into two logical sub-layers.

- Convergence sublayer (CS): The CS provides the functions needed to support specific services and applications using the ATM transport. The CS is service and application dependant. Each user attaches to AAL at a service access point (SAP). The SAP is simply the address of the user application.
- Segmentation and reassembly sublayer (SAR): The SAR sublayer provides the functions of generating cells with the data received from CS and retrieving the data from the cells for delivery to CS.

There are five different protocol types defined for the class of services supported by ATM, that is, AAL Type 1, AAL Type 2, AAL Type 3//4, and AAL Type 5. Each protocol type supports specific class of service. For example, type 1 is used to support constant bit rate (CBR) service. Type 2 is used to support variable bit rate (VBR) service. For detailed descriptions of each protocol type and packet format, the readers can refer to the chapter on ATM.

ATM Switching Concept

As described earlier, the ATM layer consists of VC and VP sub-layers that form the basis of switching in ATM networks. There are correspondingly two levels of ATM connection:

- Virtual channel connection (VCC): A VCC extends between points where adaptation layer functionality is performed. The basic function of the adaptation layer is to format data for transport over an ATM connection on the sending end and extract data at the receiving end. These points are VC connection end points.
- Virtual path connection (VPC): A VPC extends from the point at which VCs are assigned with VCI values and associated with a VP, to the point where VCs are removed from the VP or have their VCI values modified. These end points are referred to as the VP connection end points.

VC and VP connections are established by the permanent VC (PVC) by a network operator manually, or the switched VC (SVC), established on demand by signaling procedures between the connection end points.

ATM provides a highly complex technology, with features intended for applications ranging from global telecommunication networks to private local area computer networks. ATM has been a partial success as a technology, with widespread deployment, but generally only used as a transport for IP traffic. Its goal of providing a single integrated technology for LANs, public networks, and user services has not been achieved.

TCP/IP

The Internet protocol suite is the set of communications protocols that implement the protocol stack on which the Internet and most commercial networks run. The TCP/IP protocol suite has the two most important protocols: the transmission control protocol (TCP) and the Internet protocol (IP).

TCP and IP were initially developed by a research project for the Department of Defense (DOD). The goal was to connect a number of different networks from different vendors into a network of networks (the so-called "Internet"). The Internet protocol suite includes not only lower-level specifications (such as TCP and IP), but also specifications for common applications such as electronic mail, terminal emulation, and file transfer. Several computers in a small department can use TCP/IP (along with other protocols) on a single LAN. The IP component provides routing from the department to the enterprise network, then to regional networks, and finally to the global Internet. A communication network needs to sustain damage on a battlefield. Therefore, the DOD designed TCP/IP a robust protocol suite that has the capability of automatically recovery from any node or phone line failure. This design allows the construction of very large networks with less central management. However, because of the automatic recovery, network problems can go undiagnosed and uncorrected for long periods of time.

TCP

TCP is a connection-oriented transport protocol that sends data as an unstructured stream of bytes. IETF RFC793 defines the transmission control protocol (TCP).

TCP provides a reliable stream delivery and virtual connection service to applications via the use of sequence numbers and acknowledgment messages. TCP can provide a sending node with delivery information about packets transmitted to a destination node. A three way handshake between the source and destination node in TCP sets up the protocol states properly. The retransmission protocol ensure that the data be delivered successfully to the destination. If data has been lost in transit from source to destination, TCP will retransmit the data until either a timeout condition is reached or successful delivery is achieved. TCP has the capability of detecting duplicate messages and discards them appropriately. TCP has a window-based flow control mechanism built in to regulate the data flow from source to destination. If the sending node is transmitting too fast for the receiving node, the flow control mechanism will take effect to slow down the data transfer. In addition to flow control, TCP also has a window-based congestion control mechanism built in to achieve congestion avoidance. When TCP detects any packet loss, the transmission window will be reduced to relieve the congestion along the path. Both flow control and congestion control make TCP very robust in different network environments.

IP

IP is the primary layer 3 protocol in the Internet suite. The main function of IP layer is to route packets in different network segments. In addition, IP provides fragmentation and reassembly of datagrams (that is, information units) for transmission over networks with different maximum transmission unit (MTU) sizes. IP represents the heart of the Internet protocol suite.

IP Addressing

IP address is a globally unique, 32-bit number assigned by the network information center and network administrator. Globally unique addresses permit IP networks anywhere in the world to communicate with each other. By convention, each byte in a 4-byte IP address is expressed as a decimal number (0 to 255) and separated with a period. For example, the IP address of my machine is 192.168.1.36.

An IP address is divided into two parts. The first part designates the network address; and the second part designates the host address. IP addressing supports three different network classes. Class A networks allocate 8 bits for the network address field and are intended mainly for use with a few very large networks. Class B networks allocate 16 bits and are intended for use with large networks. Class C networks allocate 24 bits for the network address field and are intended for use with small networks. Class C networks only provide 8 bits for the host field. Therefore

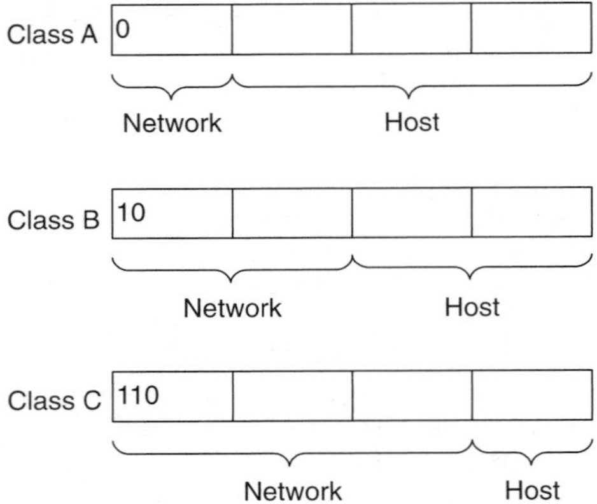

Figure 10: IP addresses for class A, B, C networks

the number of hosts per class C network may be a limiting factor. In all three cases, the left most bit(s) indicate the network class. Figure 10 shows the address formats for class A, B, and C IP networks.

It is convenient for most class A and class B networks to be internally managed as a much smaller and simpler version of the large network organizations. The two or three bytes available for host address are often divided into a *subnet* number and a workstation ID. Subnets provide extra flexibility for the network administrator. The administrator can subdivide the network into small units. This is done by "borrowing" bits from the host portion of the address and using them as a subnet field, as depicted in Figure 11.

The number of bits that can be borrowed for the subnet address varies. To specify how many bits are used and where they are located in the host field, IP provides subnet masks. Subnet masks use the same format and representation technique as IP addresses. Subnet masks have ones in all bits except those that specify the host field. For example, the subnet mask that specifies 8 bits of sub-netting for class A address 192.0.0.0 is 255.255.0.0. The subnet mask that specifies 16 bits of sub-netting for class A address 192.0.0.0 is 255.255.255.0. Subnet masks can be passed through a network on demand so that new nodes can learn how many bits of sub-netting are being used on the network.

IP Routing

An "internet" is a group of interconnected networks. The Internet is the collection of networks that permits communication between most research institutions, universities, and many other organizations around the world. Routing in IP networks is organized as a hierarchy structure. Some routers are used to move information through one particular group of networks under the same administrative authority and control. Such an entity is called an autonomous system. Routers used for information exchange within autonomous systems are called interior routers. They use a variety of interior gateway protocols (IGPs) to accomplish the task. Routers that move information between autonomous systems are called exterior routers. They use the exterior gateway protocol (EGP) or border gateway protocol (BGP). More details on hierarchical routings are described in other chapters.

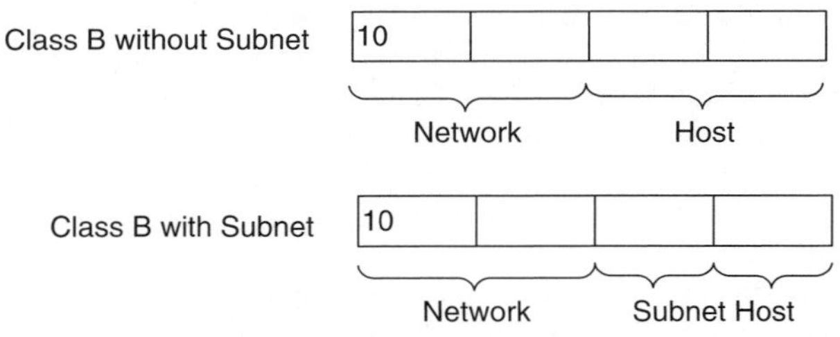

Figure 11: IP subnet addresses

Other Advanced Packet-Switching Networks

Packet-switching networks have experienced tremendous growth and development in recent years. IP network has become the dominating networking technology. Much research and development has been conducted in packet-switching networks. Particularly, advances in IP network routing, QoS managements, active queue management and congestion control, network traffic management, etc. have been made to design an efficient network supporting various applications and services.

In addition to layer 3 (such as IP) network development, the evolution in LAN has also gone through rapid changes. The most important LAN technologies are the fast Ethernet and Gigabit Ethernet, which are the extensions of the classical Ethernet with carrier sense multiple access with collision detection (CSMA/CD) to higher speeds.

Another important packet-switching technology is MPLS, that is, multiprotocol label switching. MPLS is defined by IETF as a base technology for using label switching and for implementation of label-switched paths over various link level technologies, such as frame relay, SONET, ATM, and Ethernet protocols, and so on. MPLS speeds up the traffic flow transmission by setting up a specific path for a given sequence of packets and saving the time needed for a router to route the packet. MPLS allows packets to be forwarded at the layer 2 (switching) level rather than at the layer 3 (routing) level. In addition to speeding up the network traffic, MPLS makes it easy to manage a network for quality of service (QoS). As a result of these reasons, MPLS technique has been rapidly adopted in today's networks carrying mixed traffic.

More detailed descriptions on Ethernet LAN, MPLS, and other advanced technologies are provided in other chapters.

GLOSSARY

ATM: asynchronous transmission mode. It is an advanced fast packet-switching technique. It provides quality of service for different applications.

Circuit switching: A switching technology used in conventional telephone networks. A dedicated circuit or connect is pre-allocated for an entire call.

Frame relay: An enhancement of X.25 for packet switching. It switches packets fast via eliminating the error checking procedures at the network nodes.

IP: Internet protocol.

ITU-T: International Telecommunication Union Telecommunication Sector. It is an international standards organization that provides recommendations in telecommunication technologies.

Packet switching: A switching technology used in modern data communication networks. Packets are individually allocated bandwidth dynamically and shared the transmission bandwidth with other users.

TCP: Transport control protocol.

X.25: The first international standards on packet switching. It defines the protocol interfaces between user terminals and the networks to facilitate network interconnection.

CROSS REFERENCES

See *ATM (Asynchronous Transfer Mode); Circuit Switching; Frame Relay; Message Switching; TCP/IP Suite.*

REFERENCES

ANSI T1-618. 1991. Core aspects of frame protocol for use with frame relay bearer service. Integrated Services Digital Network (ISDN).

Baran, P. 1964. On distributed communications: Introduction to distributed communications network. Memorandum RM-3420-PR. RAND Corporation. http://www.rand.org/publications/RM/baran.list.html.

Baran, P. 1964. On distributed communications networks, *IEEE Transactions on Communications*, 12(1), 1–9.

Clark, M. P. 1996. *ATM networks and principles*. New York: Wiley.

Clark, M. P. 1998. *Networks and telecommunications, design and operations, 2nd edition*. New York: Wiley. http://www.atmforum.com.

Cypser, R. J. 1978. *Communication architecture for distributed systems.* Reading, MA: Addison-Wesley.

IETF. 1981. Internet protocol (IP). RFC791. http://www.ietf.org.

IETF. 1981. Transmission control protocol (TCP). RFC 793. http://www.ietf.org.

Kleinrock, L. 1961. Information flow in large communication nets. *RLE Quarterly Progress Report.* July.

Kleinrock, L. 1964. *Communication nets: Stochastic message flow and delay*. New York: Mcgraw-Hill.

Kleinrock, L. and Opderbeck 1975. Throughput in the ARPANET—Protocols and measurement. *Proceedings of 4th Data Communications Symposium*. Quebec City. Canada. pp. 6–1 to 6–11, October.

Nakamura, R., F. Ishino, and M. Sasakoka. 1976. Some design aspects of a public packet switched network. *Proceedings of International Conference on Computers and Communications*. Toronto, Canada. pp. 317–22.

Roberts, L., and M. Merrill. 1966. Toward a cooperative network of time-shared computers. *Fall AFIPS Conference,* October.

Roberts, L. G. 1974. Data by the packet. *IEEE Spectrum*. 11(2), February.

Roberts, L. 1978. The evolution of packet switching. *Proceedings of the IEEE*. 66(1), November.

Tanenbaum, A. S. 1981. *Computer networks*. Englewood Cliffs, NJ: Prentice-Hall.

Circuit Switching

Farid Farahmand, *Central Connecticut State University*
Qiong (Jo) Zhang, *Arizona State University, West Campus*

INTRODUCTION

The fundamental purpose of a communication system is to exchange information between two or more devices. Such a system can be optimized for voice, data, or both. In its simplest form, a communication system can be established between two *nodes* (or *stations*) that are directly connected by some form of point-to-point transmission medium. A station may be a PC, telephone, fax machine, mainframe, or any other communicating device. This may, however, be impractical, if there are many geographically dispersed nodes or the communication requires dynamic connection between different nodes at various times.

An alternative method to a point-to-point connection is establishing a *communication network*. In a communication network, each communicating device (or station) is connected to a network node. The interconnected nodes are capable of transferring data between stations. Depending on the architecture and techniques used to transfer data, two basic categories of communication networks are *broadcast networks* and *switched networks*.

In broadcast networks, a single node transmits the information to all other nodes and hence, all stations will receive the data. A simple example of such network is a citizens' band (CB) radio system, in which all users tuned to the same channel can communicate with each other. Other examples of broadcast networks are satellite networks and Ethernet-based local area networks, where transmission by any station will propagate through the network and all other stations will receive the information.

In a switched network, the transmitted data is not passed on to the entire medium. Instead, data are transferred from source to destination through a series of intermediate nodes. Such nodes, often called *switching nodes*, are only concerned about how to move the data from one node to another until the data reaches its destination node. Switched communication networks can be categorized into different types such as the following:

- Circuit-switched networks.
- Packet-switched networks.
- Message-switched networks.
- Burst-switched networks.

In this chapter we focus on circuit-switched networks. In a circuit-switched network, also called line-switched network, a dedicated physical communication path is established between two stations through the switching nodes in the network. Hence, the end-to-end path from source to destination is a connected sequence of physical links between nodes and at each switching node the incoming data is switched to the appropriate outgoing link.

A circuit-switched communication system involves three phases: circuit establishment (setting up dedicated links between the source and destination); data transfer (transmitting the data between the source and destination); and circuit disconnect (removing the dedicated links). In circuit switching the connection path is established before data transmission begins. Therefore, the channel capacity must be reserved between the source and destination throughout the network and each node must have available internal switching capacity to handle the requested connection. Clearly, the switching nodes must have the intelligence to make proper allocations and to establish a route through the network.

The most common example of a circuit-switched network can be found in public telephone network (PTN) supporting services such as POTS (plain old telephone systems) and long-distance calls. Other examples of circuit-switched services are integrated services digital network (ISDN), and switched 56, 64, and 384 (Kbps) services. The majority of wireless application protocols (WAP)–enabled phones also operate on top of circuit-switched networks. Furthermore, many public networks dedicated to data transport also use circuit-switching techniques; an example of a network in Europe is circuit-switched public data network (CSPDN), which transports data on circuit-switched networks using the X.21 protocol. Circuit switching also has wide applications in optical networks including wavelength division multiplexed (WDM) systems and WDM SONET networks.

With tremendous growth in data communications and Internet traffic in the past few decades, circuit-switching technology may appear to have lost its importance and in fact, many believe that it will eventually be replaced by more residual competitors such as packet switching. Many major telephone companies have considered spending billions of dollars to upgrade their switches to support packet switching. However, the existing $100 billion investment in the public telephone network in the United States makes such migration non-trivial. In fact, there seems to be a renewed interest in implementing circuit switching in optical networks as a result of the ease of building very high-capacity optical circuit switches and rapid reconfiguration around failure. For example, many researchers have proposed using circuit switching instead of or in addition to packet switching at the core of the Internet where packet switching offers low link utilization.

In the remainder of this chapter we first examine the basic concepts of circuit switching networks and various switching technologies. Then, we look at different circuit-switched services. We briefly describe the general architecture of circuit-switched optical networks. We also investigate the performance of circuit-switched networks. Finally, we look at the future of circuit-switching technology and its position in future applications.

CIRCUIT-SWITCHED NETWORKS

In this section we describe the elements of a circuit-switched network and examine their basic functionalities. Figure 1 shows a circuit-switched network. Three basic elements in this network are end-stations (or terminals), transmission media, and switching nodes. Through one or more switching nodes, end-stations can be temporarily interconnected to each other. A switching node can simply provide a transmission path between other switches and it may not be connected to any terminals; this is the case with Node C in Figure 1. In general, switching nodes in circuit-switched networks are the most invisible elements to the users and yet represent the most important elements in terms of offering available services.

Depending on the transmission technology and the physical transmission media over which connections take place, a switching node can be based on electrical (analog or digital) or optical technology. In the following paragraphs we first describe the main building blocks of a generic switching node and then examine various switching technologies.

Switching Node Architecture

In general, a switching node provides the following basic functionalities:

- signaling
- control
- switching
- interfacing

The basic function of the signaling element in a switching node is to monitor the activity of the incoming lines and to forward appropriate status or control information to the control element of the switch. Signaling is also used to place control signals onto outgoing lines under the direction of the control element. The control element processes incoming signaling information and sets up connections accordingly. The switching function itself is provided by a switching matrix (or fabric), which is an array of selectable cross-points used to complete connections between input lines and output lines, as shown in Figure 2a. The switching fabric can operate in the electrical or optical domain. The network interface provides the hardware required to connect different devices, such as analog, digital TDM lines, optical fibers, etc. to the switch matrix. These basic components of a switching node are depicted in Figure 2b.

An important characteristic of a circuit-based switch is whether it is blocking or non-blocking (Stallings, 1999). Blocking occurs when the switching matrix does not allow some input lines to be connected to output lines. Consequently, at the network level, some stations will not be able to be connected together. A non-blocking switching node, on the other hand, allows all inputs to be connected

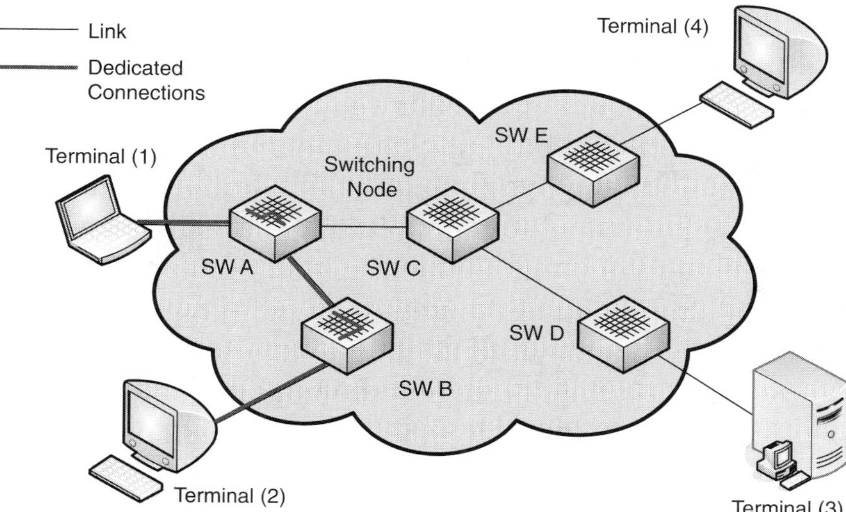

Figure 1: A circuit-switched network

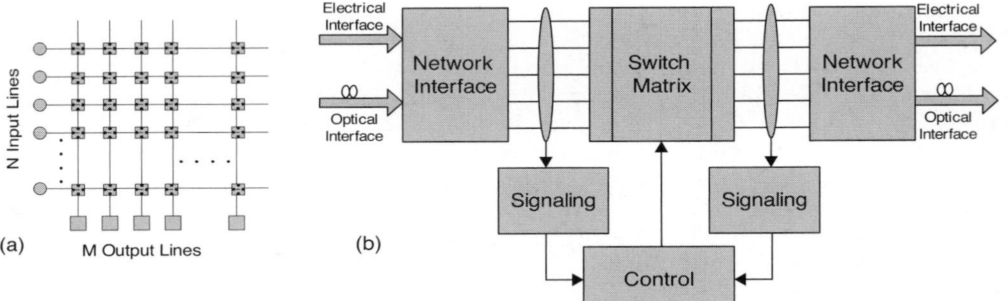

Figure 2: (a) An array of selectable cross-points, (b) switching node elements

to all outputs. As a result, a network with non-blocking switching nodes permits all stations to be connected (in pairs) at once and grants all possible connection requests as long as the destination node is free. Hence, it is desirable to have a non-blocking configuration, particularly in data communications. However, a major consideration is the high cost of non-blocking switching nodes. In fact, in many cases it is more practical to build blocking switches where the blocking probability is acceptable.

The switching function between the inputs and outputs in the matrix can be based on one or more of the following switching technologies:

- space-division
- time-division
- frequency-division
- wavelength-division

In the following sub-sections we briefly describe the characteristics of each switching technology.

Space-Division Switching

In space-division switching each input takes a different physical path in the switch matrix depending on the output. Hence, when a connection is established through a space switch matrix, a permanent physical contact is made on the matrix of cross-points. The connection will be maintained throughout the call duration. This technology can be primarily developed to accommodate analog transmission. Broadly speaking, space-division switching can be classified into three types: manual, electro-mechanical, and stored-program control.

Historically, circuit switching was designed for making standard telephone calls on the public telephone network. Hence, development of switching technology is traced back to the first commercial manual telephone switchboard used for public telephone network (the first manual switching machine started operating on January 2, 1878, in New Haven Connecticut, two years after the invention of the telephone, and it was only capable of supporting 21 subscribers (Bellamy, 2000). Every subscriber's line was terminated on the rear of the switchboard, while the front of the switchboard consisted of many loop jacks. Upon requesting a connection, the operator would manually connect the appropriate jacks using a loop cord with a loop plug on each end.

The second generation of space-division switching systems was electro-mechanical. Two common types of such systems were *step-by-step* (also known as the Strowger switch in honor of its inventor) and *crossbar* switches. Other types of electro-mechanical switches were All Relay, Panel, and X-Y systems; however, they were not as widely used.

A basic step-by-step switch has a single input terminal and multiple output terminals. Connection from the input terminal to the outputs is controlled by an internal rotary contact, or wiper. As the wiper rotates, it establishes a contact between the input and output terminals. Each time the user dials a rotary-dial digit, the rotary contact is advanced one position, and connects the input terminal to the next output terminal. This process continues until all digits are dialed (Chapuis, 1982; Clark, 1997). The principle of a step-by-step switch with a single input terminal and multiple output terminals is shown in Figure 3.

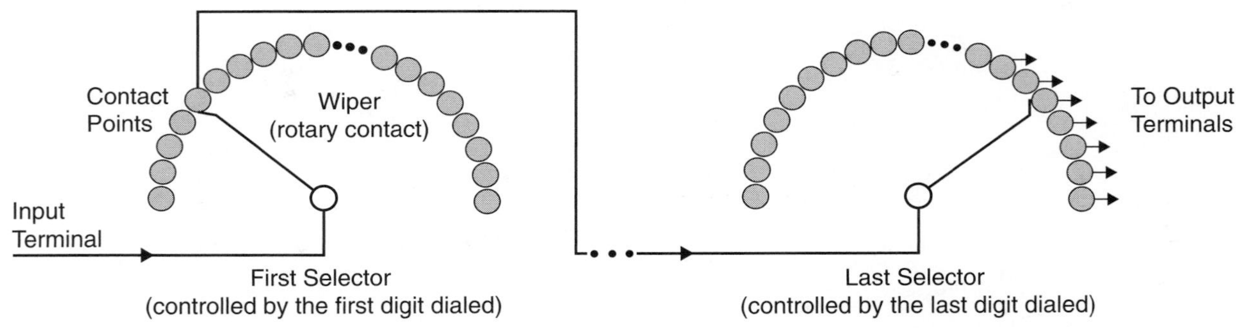

Figure 3: A step-by-step switch with a single input terminal and multiple output terminals

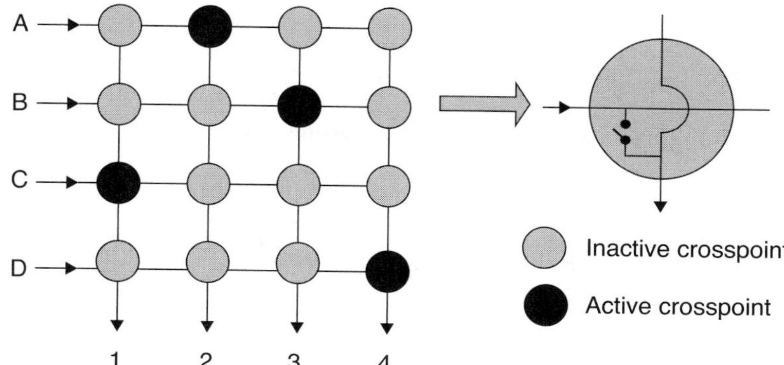

Figure 4: A crossbar switch with four incoming circuits, 4 outgoing circuits, and 16 switch cross-points

In a crossbar switch (also known as cross-point switch) as digits are dialed, the control element of the switch receives the entire address before processing it. The cross-points of the crossbar switch are mechanical contacts with magnets to setup and hold a connection. The term crossbar arises from the use of crossing horizontal and vertical bars to initially select the contacts on the cross-point. Once the circuit is established, the switching contacts are held by electromagnets energized with direct current passing through the established circuit. When the circuit is opened, the loss of current causes the cross-points to be released.

Figure 4 shows a crossbar switch with four incoming circuits, four outgoing circuits, and 16 switch cross-points, which may be active or inactive. Any of the incoming circuits can be interconnected to any one, and only one, of the outgoing circuits. The figure shows the simultaneous interconnections between the following circuits: A to 2, C to 1, D to 4, and B to 3. A typical internal design of the switch cross-point is also depicted in Figure 4.

Step-by-step and crossbar switching systems use electro-mechanical components for both switching matrix and control elements. In 1965, Bell Systems introduced the first computer-controlled switching system, known as No. 1 ESS (Electronics Switching System), which was used in the public telephone network (Martin, 1985). The electronic switching capability of No. 1 ESS was primarily referred to as the computer-controlled switching and not the nature of the switching matrix itself. In fact, the switching matrix was still using electro-mechanical reed relays (nickel-iron reeds sealed in a glass tube, which make contact as a result of magnetic field induced by coil around them). These switches were considered as the first stored-program control switch types used in the public telephone network.

Time-Division Switching

With the advents of digital technology and the development of pulse code modulation (PCM) both voice and data could be transmitted via digital signals. Digital technology led to a fundamental change in the design and architecture of switching systems. The need for time-division switching arises from the fact that digital signals are often carrying multiple individual circuits, or channels, in appropriate *timeslots* (TS). In such systems, when two different multiplexed channels are interconnected together through the switch matrix a *virtual circuit* is established. This is done by interchanging timeslots, each of which maintain partial contents of a particular channel. This operation is referred to as timeslot interchanging (TSI) (Stallings, 1999).

In a digital switch architecture, an incoming channel must be connected to a channel on any outgoing stream. A common architecture to achieve this utilizes both time-division switch capability, to shift channels between timeslots, and space-division switching capability, to enable a different physical outgoing line system to be selected. This architecture is referred to as time-space-time (TST).

Figure 5 shows a multistage time-space-time architecture to switch the timeslots of two digital line systems, each containing 24 time slots. The incoming signals are directly fed into the time switch, the output of which feeds the space switch in the middle. The output of the space switch feeds another time switch to which the outgoing

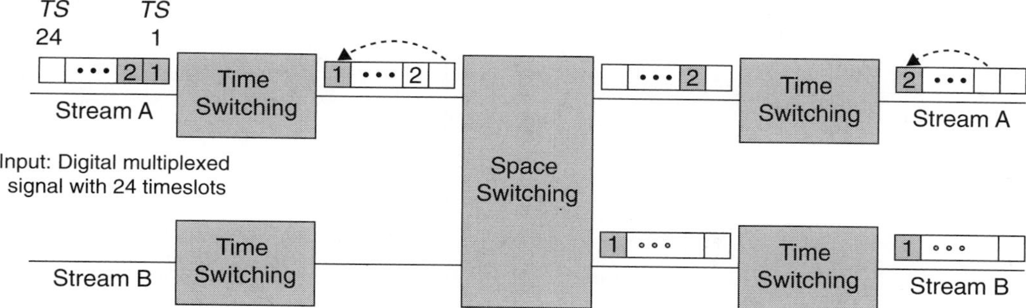

Figure 5: A time-space-time switch architecture, connecting channel 1 and 2 on incoming stream A to channel 24 on outgoing streams B and A, respectively

signals are connected. This figure shows timeslots (channels) 1 and 2 in incoming port (stream A) are switched to timeslot (channel) 24 in the outgoing stream B and A, respectively. Note that the second time switch stage is necessary to ensure that multiple timeslots in one incoming stream are not superimposed or blocked. Having more stages can further improve the switch performance. In addition to TST, some of the more common structures used in commercially available systems are TSSST, STS, SSTSS, TSTST.

The first time-division switching system deployed in the United States was the AT&T-designed No. 4 ESS, which was placed into service in 1976. The No. 4 ESS was considered as the first truly digital high-capacity switch adopted in the public telephone network. It implemented digital electronics in its control unit and switching matrix and was capable of serving a maximum of 53,760 circuits. Later, AT&T introduced No. 5 ESS, an improved version, handling 100,000 lines.

Frequency and Wavelength-Division Switching

Prior to full development of digital technology, telephone networks used frequency-division multiplexing (FDM) to carry several voice channels on a single physical circuit (e.g., a twisted cable). In these systems, multiple voice channels would be modulated onto carriers separated by some frequency spacing (e.g., 4 kHz). The composite signal, occupying the frequency range 60 to 108 kHz, was known as a group. In turn, five groups could themselves be multiplexed by a similar method into a super-group, containing 60 voice channels. Advances in FDM, allowed even higher levels of multiplexing, supporting transmission of hundreds of voice channels down a single connection.

Today, with the advances in optical networks, the same basic multiplexing principles used in FDM systems are being employed to optical signals. This is known as wavelength-division multiplexing (WDM). In fact, WDM is an analog multiplexing technique where the original signals are frequency shifted to occupy different portions of frequency spectrum of the transmission media. With the emergence of dense WDM (DWDM) system, 64 to 160 wavelengths (or channels) can be densely packed at 50 or 25 GHz intervals. Hence, the frequency and wavelength-division switching, in practice, are very similar. In the remainder of this section, we consider wavelength-division switching architecture (Toba, 1986).

WDM optical networks consist of optical switches, which are interconnected using WDM transmission systems. The basic functionality of the optical switch is to ensure that the data carried on any wavelength channel on any incoming optical link can be directed to any wavelength on any outgoing optical link. Based on the switching fabric technology, optical switches can be classified into two categories: *opaque* and *transparent* optical switches. An opaque optical switch, also called *optical cross-connect* (OXC), first, converts incoming optical signals to electrical signals, then, switches the electrical signals using an electronic switching fabric, and finally, converts the electrical signals back to optical signals at the output (Bernstein, 2003). A major disadvantage of such systems is that they need to perform multiple opto-electrical translations that can be both complex and expensive.

A transparent optical switch, also called *photonic cross-connect* (PXC), on the other hand, does not require any opto-electrical translation and switches incoming signals in optical domain. The photonic switch fabric can be developed using a variety of technologies, including opto-mechanical, electro-optic, acousto-optic, thermal, micro-mechanical, liquid crystal, and semiconductor switch technologies. In practice, these technologies differ based on their performance characteristics such as switching speed, power loss as optical signals are switched, and wavelength independency in which switching is independent of the specific wavelength being switched. Figure 6 depicts a typical multistage photonic switch equipped with wavelength converters.

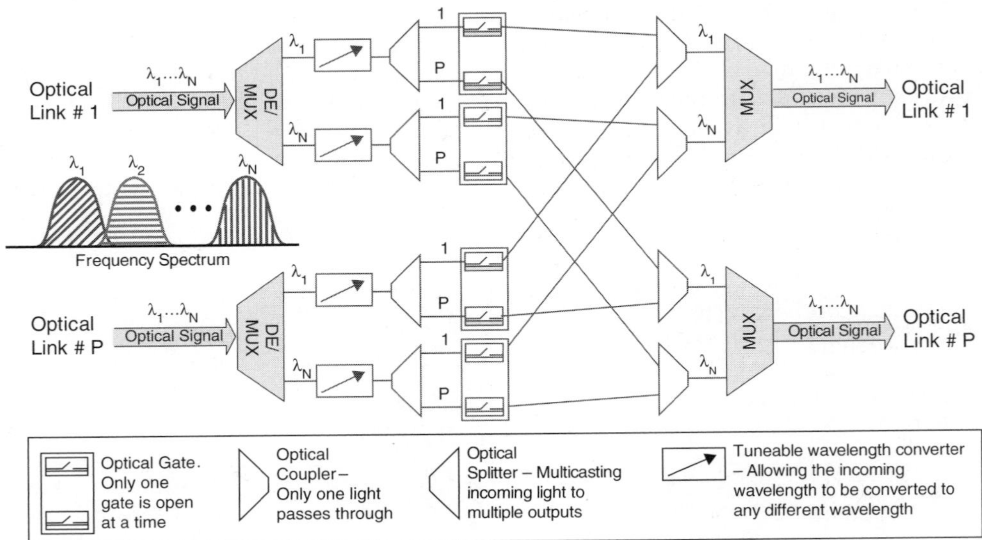

Figure 6: A typical optical switch architecture with wavelength converters, capable of supporting P incoming and outgoing optical links, each having N wavelength channels

Note that in this architecture, the photonic switch fabric is a matrix of optical gates. Similar architectures have been proposed and developed to eliminate the need for costly wavelength converters. With the current technology, control mechanism in the photonic switch fabrics is performed electronically.

Circuit-Switching Advantages and Disadvantages

Circuit switching was the dominant switching technology for more than 100 years. With such a long technological history, circuit switching is well understood, extremely well developed, and widely deployed in the form of the worldwide public telephone system. Furthermore, advances in solid-state technology and micro-processors have led to constant improvement of capabilities of circuit-switching technology and, consequently, its cost effectiveness. In addition, new switching techniques, including wavelength-division switching, as well as high-speed signaling between switches, such as *common channel signaling* (CCS), have reduced average circuit setup delay and provided numerous new features.

In spite of emergence of newer switching technologies, namely packet switching, circuit-switching technology remains an appropriate and easily used technique with many unique advantages. One of the major advantages of circuit switching is that it is an essentially transparent service with no storage requirement. Once the connection is established, constant-rate data is provided to the connected stations. An important consequence of transparency is that no buffer overhead is required to accommodate data bursts that can be created by store-and-forward packet switching. Furthermore, the analog or digital data is passed through as-is from source to destination. Clearly, upon establishing the switched path, the time delay in delivering the data is only that resulting from speed-of-light delays, which are typically small compared to buffer delays, allowing real-time interaction between stations.

Circuit-switching technology also has major drawbacks, which make it less desirable for certain applications. A major issue with circuit switching is that all resources must be available and dedicated through the network between terminals before the communication takes place. Otherwise, the communication request will be blocked. This can result in potential channel inefficiency. For example, consider a case in which channel capacity is dedicated for the entire duration of a connection, however, no data is actually being transferred. For voice communications, since the idle times are minimum, high utilization can be expected. However, for data communications, since the capacity may be idle during most of the time of the connection (e.g., when we are only reading a downloaded Web page), circuit switching can result in relatively low utilization.

Another major issue with circuit switching is that in order to setup circuits between end-stations, circuit-switching facilities must be capable of processing large signaling at high-speed. Hence, existing systems may not be efficient for *bursty* traffic with short message durations and sporadic transmissions.

CIRCUIT-SWITCHING SERVICES

Today, the public telephone network remains, by far, the largest circuit-switched network in the world. As more data communication applications and services are emerged, it becomes critical to develop a technology that creates general integrated voice and data network that can be available to all users. This led to the development of integrated services digital networks (ISDN). In the remaining of this section we briefly describe examples of circuit-switched services as listed in Table 1.

Plain Old Telephone Service (POTS)

Prior to the existence of new types of networks, all communication systems had to be built based on the existing telecommunications facilities, which were largely oriented to what the common carriers refer to as plain old telephone service, known as POTS. The original POTS telephone network was designed and implemented to transfer analog voice signals. Consequently, even today, in order to use POTS for data communications, it is necessary to use a modem to convert the data to a form

Table 1: Examples of Circuit-Switched Services

Type of service	Bandwidth	Features
POTS	$<$64 Kbps	Adequate for transmitting text and low quality video; it is a dial-up connection requiring modem; limited by 3 to 4 KHz bandwidth.
Switched 56	64 Kbps	Dial-up connection requiring DSU/CSU; sufficient for low-resolution video; also used as backup facilities.
Leased Lines	64 Kbps to 274 Mbps	Dedicated lines; expensive but dependable and offer high-quality connection. Typically, they are provisioned within the circuit-switched infrastructure for the duration of a lease.
ISDN	144 Kbps to 2 Mbps	End-to-end digital connectivity with different interfaces offering various bandwidths.
SONET	$N \times 51.84$ Mbps	Used with optical fibers; $N = 1,3,12,48,192,768$

suitable for voice-transmission media. Modem standards have been developed by ITU, formerly known as CCITT (*Comité Consultatif International Téléphonique et Télégraphique*), in the V-series Recommendations. Common examples of modem standards are V.32 (4.8 Kbps), V.34 (28.8 Kbps), V.42 (38.4 Kbps), and V.90 (56 Kbps).

The data transmission rate that can be obtained over a POTS connection is typically less than 64 Kbps. These rates are adequate for text and audio transmission. However, they are not sufficient for good quality video transmission in real-time. Video applications, such as video telephones, that operate over POTS often use small picture sizes in conjunction with image compression.

Switched 56 Service

Switched 56 service is a dial-up digital service provided by local and long distance telephone companies. For a connection, a data service unit/data channel unit (DSU/CSU) is used instead of a modem. Switched 56 service uses a 64 Kbps channel, but one bit per byte is used for band signaling, leaving 56 Kbps for data. This service allows the transmission of information over one or two twisted cable pairs to multiple points at a data rate of 56 Kpbs. Switched 56 service is ideally suited for use as a backup facility to leased lines where, if a break is detected in the leased line service, the data service unit (DSU) will automatically re-establish a connection using the switched 56 dial-up facility. This service is most cost-efficient for individuals and businesses that require moderate-volume file transfers, but do not need to have a permanent connection to all their locations.

Leased Lines

A leased line is a dedicated communication line that an individual or business can own and does not share with any other users. As a result, leased lines are highly dependable and offer high-quality connections. Leased lines are excellent for providing required quality of service (QoS) for the transmission of delay and bandwidth-sensitive applications such as multimedia information (Sharda, 1999). However, the main disadvantage of leased lines is the high cost. Leased lines can be analog or digital.

Analog Leased Lines

This type of access is often used for network usage with full-time connectivity requirement. An analog leased line does not require any dial-up procedure. In addition, it provides higher quality connection and higher signal-to-noise ratio, leading to higher data transmission rate as compared to those on dial-up lines.

Digital Leased Lines

The digital leased line access is often used for large networks serving many users and requiring a high level of reliability. The digital leased lines offer various bandwidths. Common examples of digital leased lines in the United States, Japan, and Korea are fractional T1 (FT1), T1, T2, T3, and T4. T1 is a dedicated connection supporting data rates of 1.544 Mbps. A T1 digital line consists of 24 individual channels, each of which supports 64 Kbps. Each 64-Kbps channel, referred to as DS0, can be configured to carry voice or data traffic. The framing specification used in transmitting digital signals in Europe is called E1, which operates at 2.108 Mbps and contains 32 DS0 channels. Other levels of digital transmission are T2, T3, etc., which allow digital transmission at higher line rates.

Table 2: Various Digital Leased Lines and Their Bandwidths

Line type	Bandwidth	Application
Switched 384	384 Kbps	High-quality video conferencing
T1	1.544 Mbps	Compressed video
T2	6.312 Mbps	Broadcast TV quality compressed video
T3	44.70 Mbps	HDVT-quality video transmission
T4	274.0 Mbps	Multiple video channels

In addition to the above rates, many telephone companies offer fractions of individual channels available in a standard T1 line, known as fractional T1 access. Bit rates offered by a fractional leased line can be 64 Kbps (one channel), 128 Kbps (2 channels), 256 Kbps (4 channels), 384 Kbps (6 channels), 512 Kbps (8 channels), and 768 Kbps (12 channels), with 384 Kbps (1/4 T1), and 768 Kbps (1/2 T1), also known as Switched 384 service and Switched 768 service, being the most common. Switched 384 service is particularly common for supporting high volumes of data and multimedia applications. Table 2 lists various digital leased lines along with their bandwidth and common multimedia applications.

Integrated Services Digital Network (ISDN)

The ISDN was designed in the 1980s to offer end-to-end digital connectivity, while providing the required QoS with data rates in the range of Kbps to Mbps over switched connections. ISDN also offers a more economical alternative to digital leased lines. In order to provide even higher data rates, the original ISDN was extended to broadband ISDN (BISDN) (Martin, 1985).

The ISDN services are provided to users as ISDN interfaces, each comprising a number of ISDN channels. Using 64-Kbps channels, called bearer or B channels, ISDN provides access to the digital network. ISDN provides lower error rate compared to typical voiceband modems and a relatively high bandwidth data channel. On the other hand, ISDN uses 16-Kbps or 64-Kbps signaling D channels to access the signaling network, which allows features such as accessing packet switching network, user-to-user message transfer, and simultaneous signal processing while having active connections. A very attractive application of signal accessing is to provide end-users the flexibility to dynamically reconfigure virtual private networks within the public network and have them interoperate with private facilities without a loss

Table 3: ISDN Interfaces

Interface type	Channels	Bandwidth	Application
Basic-rate interface	2B + D	144–192 Kbps	Digital voice and data
Primary-rate interface	23B + D or 30B + D	1.544 or 2.048 Mbps	Multimedia and LAN to LAN connection
Hybrid interface	A + C	Analog voice and 16 Kbps data	Hybrid connection for transition period

of features. Other ISDN channels are A and C, providing access to POTS and low-speed digital data transmission, respectively.

ISDN channels (A, B, C, D) are combined to provide standard interfaces: basic rate interface (BRI), primary rate interface (PRI), and hybrid interface. Table 3 lists these interfaces with their channels and common applications.

Basic Rate Interface (BRI): Basic rate access provides two clear 64-Kbps information channels and one 16-Kbps signaling channel (2B + D), given the total information rate of 144 Kbps. Each of the B channels can be used independently of the other, supporting simultaneous voice and digital data communications.

Primary Rate Interface (PRI): Primary rate interface gives an information transfer capability of 1.544 Mbps. The bandwidth can be configured in a variety of ways including having 23 B channels plus one D channel to connect a number of devices to an ISDN network via, for example, a PBX. PRI in Europe is available as a 2.048-Mbps connection with 30 B channels and one D channel.

Hybrid Interface: The hybrid interface allows connections that use a hybrid of analog and digital communications. This interface has been included in the ISDN systems to provide a transition path from the old POTS service to digital services.

Synchronous Optical Network (SONET)

The synchronous optical network (SONET) is a multiplexing system similar to conventional time-division multiplexing. However, SONET was developed to be used with optical fibers. SONET systems are common examples of optical circuit-switched networks, which offer high-speed communications (we will discuss these networks in the next section). The lowest level of SONET hierarchy is the basic SONET signal referred to as the synchronous transport signal level-1 (STS-1). STS-1 has a 51.84 Mbps synchronous frame structure compromised of 28 DS-1 signals. Each DS-1 signal is equivalent to a single 24-channel T1 digital line. Thus, one STS-1 system can carry 672 individual 64-Kbps voice or data channels (24x28). With STS-1, it is possible to extract or add individual DS-1 signals without completely disassembling the entire frame.

Higher level signals are referred to as STS-N signals. An STS-N signal is composed of N byte-interleaved STS-1 signals. The optical counterpart of each STS-N signal is an optical carrier level–N signal (OC-N). Although, the SONET specification is primarily concerned with OC-N interconnect standards, electrical signals within the SONET hierarchy are used for interconnecting network elements operating at lower rates. Common values of N are 1, 3, 12, 48, 192, and 768. An interesting feature of SONET frames is that they have constant period. That is, an OC-3 (155 Mbps) frame has the same 125 microsecond period as an OC-768 (40 Gbps) frame, although the OC-768 frame carries a much larger payload. This period corresponds to the 8-KHz sampling period (and clock rate) of the first PCM-based quasi-digital networks.

OPTICAL CIRCUIT SWITCHING

In early generations of circuit switching, circuits were established over copper wires and traversed a number of electronic circuit switching nodes. As the demand for network bandwidth increased, copper wire was (and continues to be) replaced by optical fiber, which provides significantly more bandwidth. The bandwidth of optical fiber can be further exploited through the use of WDM technology.

An optical circuit-switching network is similar to the example shown in Figure 1. In an optical network, however, transmission media are WDM links and switching nodes are optical (opaque or transparent). Using WDM transmission technology, the optical transmission spectrum is carved up into a number of over lapping wavelength bands. Each wavelength band can support a single communication channel operating at the peak electronic rate. Today, the majority of optical networks deployed in long-distance telecommunication networks are point-to-point DWDM SONET networks, where each node requires optical-electronic-optical (O-E-O) conversions and electronic switching.

As we mentioned before, in an optical network that utilizes photonic cross-connects (PXCs), all circuits over the network are established in the optical domain. End-to-end all-optical circuits offering bandwidth equivalent to the bandwidth provided by a single wavelength, are referred to as *lightpaths*. Such optical networks are called *wavelength-routed* WDM networks (Mukherjee, 2006; Ramaswami, 2001). If wavelengths cannot be converted from one wavelength to another at PXCs, then the same wavelength must be used on all links of a lightpath. This requirement is known as the *wavelength continuity constraint*. Figure 7 shows a wavelength-routed network with three lightpaths established. Lightpaths cannot share the same wavelength on the same link. Hence, the lightpath between source 1 and destination 1 and the lightpath

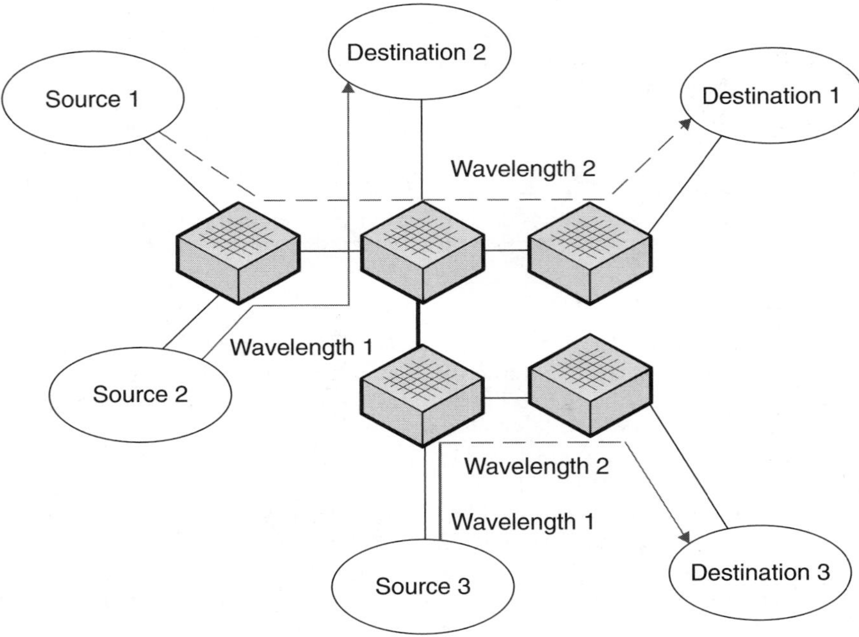

Figure 7: Wavelength-routed WDM network

between source 2 and destination 2 use different wavelengths. The lightpath between source destination 3 utilizes two different wavelengths without wavelength continuity constraint. This can be achieved using wavelength converters at intermediate nodes.

A key challenge in the practical implementation of optical networks is to develop efficient algorithms and protocols for establishing lightpaths (Zang, 2001). Such algorithms must select routes and assign wavelengths to all-optical circuits in a manner that efficiently utilizes network resources. Furthermore, signaling protocols must set up a lightpath in a timely manner, and must properly distribute control messages and network state information. In emerging optical networks, signaling and control for connection establishment may be implemented by one of three methods. First, it may be done within the generalized mulitprotocol label switching (GMPLS) framework. GMPLS defines the control architecture for establishing circuits, is based on MPLS in IP networks, and is primarily a construct supported by router vendors. A second approach uses the ASON ITU standards and has been put forward primarily within the carrier and telecom community. Finally, some research networks support a centralized control scheme that allows advanced reservation and scheduling of dedicated bandwidth.

CIRCUIT-SWITCHED NETWORK PERFORMANCE

When circuits are established, such as establishment of a phone call or a lightpath in a WDM network, the primary performance metrics of interest in circuit-switched networks are delay and blocking. Delay, or connection set-up time, refers to the time required to establish the circuit. Blocking occurs when there are insufficient resources along a given route to support an incoming circuit request. Blocking is often measured in terms of the blocking probability, which is the probability that an incoming call will be rejected due to the lack of resources.

Delay Analysis

Figure 8 depicts the transmission of data (a message) across four nodes in a circuit-switched network. The primary components of delay in circuit switching are the propagation delay of the signaling message on each link (D_p), the processing delay of the signaling message at each node (D_n), and the transmission delay of data traffic (D_t); for example it takes 0.1 second to transmit a 10,000 bit message onto a 100 Kbps line.

As shown in the figure, before the data (or message) is sent, a certain amount of elapsed time is required to setup the path. First, a setup message is sent through the network to setup a connection to the destination. Processing delay is the time spent at each node setting up the route of the connection.

Once the destination receives the call request, assuming the destination is not busy, it will return an acceptance message. On the return path, no processing delay at intermediate nodes will be required since the connections are already set up. This operation is referred to as *forward reservation*. In *reverse reservation*, however, the setup message will be directly sent to the destination and resource reservation at intermediate nodes occurs as the acceptance message is received; this is to avoid any resource reservation before ensuring that the end-to-end path is available. After the connection is set up, the message is sent as a single block, and the delay at the switching nodes will be negligible. Eventually, following the completion of data transmission, a release message will be sent requesting removal of all connections along the path.

Figure 8 also shows a case where an intermediate node (SW A) rejects a connection request. Note that in this case there is no need to propagate the setup message further to downstream nodes.

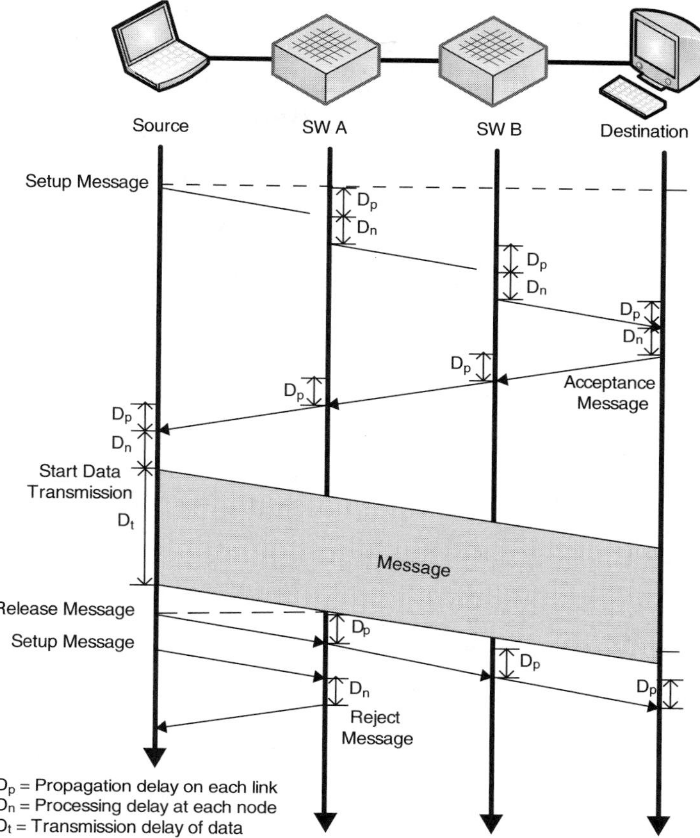

Figure 8: Event timing diagram in circuit-switched networks

The total delay prior to transmission of data, as shown in Figure 8, will be $h(2D_p + D_n) + Dn$, where h is the number of hops on the end-to-end path; in our example $h = 3$. This delay is referred to as circuit setup delay. If data transmission delay (D_t) is smaller or equal to the setup delay, circuit switching will not be efficient and it results in low utilization. However, if D_t is much larger than the setup delay, then circuit switching can offer high utilization.

Blocking Probability Analysis

In traditional telephony applications, blocking probability can be analyzed by using standard queuing theory techniques. The simplest model is one in which we evaluate a single link in the network and assume that the call arrival rate is Poisson and the call-holding time is exponentially distributed. The assumptions of Poisson arrivals and exponential holding times are standard in the analysis of telecommunications systems and have been found to accurately model the behavior of voice calls.

More complicated blocking models have been developed by evaluating the blocking probability along the entire path of a call rather than on a single link. In such models, there is some degree of statistical dependence among links in the network. It is often sufficient and much simpler to assume that the links along an end-to-end path are statistically independent of one another. The limitation of such an assumption is a less accurate estimation of the blocking probability.

Single Link Blocking Model

When analyzing the call blocking probability on a single communication link (e.g., the link between SW A and SW B in Figure 8), we assume that the link is capable of supporting C connections, simultaneously (in the case of WDM networks, C can be the number of wavelengths supported by each optical link). Furthermore, we assume that calls arrive (or lightpath requests) according to a Poisson process with rate λ calls per second, and the call holding time (or lightpath duration) is exponentially distributed with an average holding time of $1/\mu$ seconds. Calls are assumed to be independent of each other. Under these assumptions, the link may be modeled as an *M/M/C/C* queuing system (Schwartz, 1986) and the probability that there are n calls in progress is given by:

$$p(n) = \frac{\frac{1}{n!}\left(\frac{\lambda}{\mu}\right)^n}{\sum_{k=0}^{C}\left(\frac{1}{k!}\left(\frac{\lambda}{\mu}\right)^k\right)}.$$

An arriving request will be blocked if there are already C calls in progress. Thus, the probability that a call is blocked on the link is given by:

$$p(C) = \frac{\frac{1}{C!}\left(\frac{\lambda}{\mu}\right)^C}{\sum_{k=0}^{C}\left(\frac{1}{k!}\left(\frac{\lambda}{\mu}\right)^k\right)}.$$

This equation is referred to as the *Erlang B* formula.

Path Blocking Model

In addition to calculating the blocking probability on a given link, it is also possible to estimate the blocking probability of a given end-to-end connection request for a call traversing multiple links (e.g., the path from source to destination in Figure 8, passing through three links). One approach is to model each link in a path as an *M/M/C/C* system. We define the arrival rate of connection requests from source node s to destination node d as λ^{sd} calls per second, the arrival rate of connections on link (i, j) as λ_{ij} calls per second, and the route taken by a connection from s to d as $R(s, d)$.

The offered load on a given link, λ_{ij}, can be calculated by adding the traffic from all source-destination pairs that route traffic over link (i, j):

$$\lambda_{ij} = \sum_{s,d:(i,j)\epsilon R(s,d)} \lambda^{sd}.$$

To simplify the analysis, it is assumed that links are independent of one another. Furthermore, we assume call arrivals are Poisson and call holding times are exponentially distributed with an average holding time of $1/\mu$ seconds. In order for a connection request from s to d to succeed, spare capacity must be available on all links along the route. Alternatively, a connection will be blocked if at least one link in the connection's route has no available capacity. The blocking probability of a request from s to d can then be written as:

$$p(s,d) = 1 - \prod_{(i,j)\epsilon R(s,d)} (1 - p_{ij}(C)),$$

in which

$$p_{ij}(C) = \frac{\frac{1}{C!}\left(\frac{\lambda_{ij}}{\mu}\right)^C}{\sum_{k=0}^{C}\left(\frac{1}{k!}\left(\frac{\lambda_{ij}}{\mu}\right)^k\right)}.$$

We now consider a simple example in which we calculate the path blocking probability. In this example, we assume that an end-to-end connection traverses two links. The total load on each link is known. Using the single link blocking model, we can obtain the blocking probability on each link, say p_1 and p_2. Hence the path blocking probability for the connection will be $1-(1-p_1)(1-p_2)$.

In the above analysis, we assumed that a connection request on any one of the C channels of any incoming link can be connected to any channel on any outgoing link.When the switching operation is performed in the electrical domain, such an assumption is rather trivial. However, in optical networks with PXCs, wavelength converters are required to guarantee such an assumption. Additional analytical models have been developed to calculate blocking probability in optical networks when no wavelength conversion is utilized (Barry, 1996).

FUTURE OF CIRCUIT-SWITCHING TECHNOLOGY

The past half century, packet-switching technology has advanced tremendously and turned into a major competitor for circuit switching. In fact, packet switching has become the dominant technology for data networks, including the Internet. Not surprisingly, many telephone companies have been willing to spend billions of dollars to upgrade their networks to support packet switching, potentially phasing out their circuit-switched based equipments.

However, many researchers and engineers have been investigating the implementation of circuit switching technology in wide area networks (WAN) and optical networks. In fact, circuit-switching technology has been considered as the practical approach in deploying future optical WDM networks. This is mainly a result of the fact that development of all-optical packet switching networks still lacks reliable optical buffers and synchronization techniques. Today, with the current technology, circuit switching is seen as a viable solution to establish transparent optical paths (lightpaths) providing large amounts of bandwidth. The key challenge, however, is to ensure circuit switching can be made rapidly adaptive to traffic fluctuation and connection requests. While many issues related to circuit switching and lightpath establishment have been studied in detail, control plane techniques for setting up optical paths are still under active development.

In emerging core networks, applications are expected to have a wider range of QoS requirements than in existing networks. Bandwidth-intensive applications, such as video on demand, video conferencing, scheduled bulk-file transfer, and grid computing are expected to have strict transmission-completion requirements coupled with high bandwidth requirements. Telemedicine has both high bandwidth and extremely tight jitter requirements. For many such applications, best-effort packet-switched networks are incapable of providing the required services. Therefore, circuit switching in core networks (e.g., core of the Internet) may be expected not only to support static logical links for higher-layer packet switched protocols, but also provide resources directly to end users and applications. Hence, performance of the Internet where circuit switching is implemented at the core, the adaptability of circuit switching to existing Internet protocols, such as TCP/IP, and many other similar open issues require detailed study (Molinero-Fernández, 2003).

Furthermore, many in the telecommunications community strongly favor circuit switching over development of new packet-based services, due to existing huge investments in circuit-switched networks and their readiness. They question the wisdom of focusing on introducing new switching technologies and protocols, and consequently developing new expensive equipments. Instead, they argue that we must gain more in-depth technical knowledge and develop smarter encoding and transmission techniques, which will work just fine with our existing well-functioning circuit-switched networks (Cringely, 2004).

CONCLUSION

In this chapter, we described the basic principles of circuit-switching technology. We discussed the building blocks of circuit-switched networks and examined its characteristics. We looked at advantages and disadvantages of circuit-switched networks and briefly explained its applications in providing different services. We also examined the basic concepts of circuit-based optical networks and described their operations. Future applications of circuit-switching technology were also outlined in this chapter. We examined various view points and research proposals, which emphasize the importance of circuit-switching technology, particularly, in optical networks and core networks.

GLOSSARY

Bell System: This is an informal name given to the U.S. telecommunications company American Telephone & Telegraph Company (AT&T) before AT&T divested its local exchange telephone service operating companies on January 1, 1984.

CCITT: Short for Comité Consultatif International Téléphonique et Télégraphique, an organization based in Geneva, Switzerland, that sets international communications standards. CCITT changed its name to International Telecommunications Union (ITU), the parent organization, on March 1, 1993.

Citizens' Band Radio (CB): In the United States, it is a system of short-distance radio communication between individuals on a selection of 40 channels within the single 27 MHz (11 meter) band. CB does not require a license and unlike amateur radio can be used for commercial communications.

Common Channel Signaling (CCS): An out-of-band signaling method in which one channel of a communications link is used for carrying signaling for establishment and tear down of calls. The remaining channels are used entirely for the transmission of voice or data.

Data Service Unit/Data Channel Unit (DSU/CSU): A digital interface that provides the physical connection to the digital carrier network.

Frequency-Division Multiplexing (FDM): A scheme in which numerous signals are combined for transmission on a single communications line or channel. Each signal is assigned a different frequency (sub-channel) within the main channel.

Multi Protocol Label Switching (MPLS): A method used to increase the speed of network traffic flow by inserting information about a specific path the packet is taking to reach its destination. Hence, the router is no longer required to lookup the next node address. MPLS is multiprotocol in that it works with IP, ATM, and frame relay communications methods.

Protocol: A formal and pre-agreed set of rules that govern the communications between two or more entities. The protocol determines the meaning of specific values occurring in specific positions in the stream, the type of error checking to be used, the data compression method, how the sender will indicate that it has finished sending a message, and how the receiver will indicate that it has received a message.

Pulse Code Modulation (PCM): A way to convert sound or analog information to binary information (0s and 1s) by taking samples of the sound and recording the resulting number as binary information.

Quality of Service (QoS): It refers to the capability of a network to provide better service to selected network traffic over various technologies. The primary goal of QoS is to provide priority including dedicated bandwidth, controlled jitter and latency (required by some real-time and interactive traffic), and improved loss characteristics.

Time Division Multiplexing (TDM): A scheme in which numerous signals are combined for transmission on a single communications line or channel. Each signal is broken up into many segments, each having very short duration.

Wireless Application Protocol (WAP): A set of communication protocol standards to make accessing online services via handheld wireless devices such as mobile phones, pagers, two-way radios, Smartphones, and communicators.

CROSS REFERENCES

See *Message Switching; Packet Switching; SONET / SDH Networks; Wavelength Division Multiplexing (WDM).*

REFERENCES

Baroni, S. and P. Bayvel. 1997. Wavelength requirements in arbitrary connected wavelength-routed optical networks. *IEEE/OSA Journal of Lightwave Technology*, 15(2):242–51.

Barry, R. A. and P. A. Humblet. 1996. Models of blocking probability in all-optical networks with and without wavelength changers. *IEEE Journal on Selected Areas in Communications*, 14(5):858–67.

Bellamy, J. C. 2000. *Digital Telephony*, 3rd ed. New York: John Wiley & Sons.

Bernstein, G., B. Rajagopalan, and D. Saha. 2003. *Optical network control: Architecture, protocols, and standards*, 1st ed. Boston, MA: Addison-Wesley Professional.

Chapuis, R. J. 1982. *100 years of telephone switching (1878–1978), Part 1: Manual and electromechanical switching (1878–1960s)*. Amsterdam, Holland: North-Holland Publishing Company.

Clark, M. P. 1997. *Networks and telecommunications*, 2nd ed. New York, NY: John Wiley & Sons.

Cringely, R. X. 2004. Out of sight, out of mind: big old stupid telephone companies are throwing away their only real asset. http://www.pbs.org/cringely/pulpit/pulpit20040624.html (accessed April 27, 2007).

Martin, J. 1985. *Telecommunications and the computer*. Englewood Cliffs, NJ: Prentice-Hall.

Molinero-Fernández, P., and N. McKeown. 2003. The performance of circuit switching in the Internet. *OSA Journal of Optical Networking*, 2(4):83–96.

Mukherjee, B. 2005. *Optical wDM networks*, New York: Springer.

Ramaswami, R., and K. Sivarajan. 1995. Routing and wavelength assignment in all-optical networks. *IEEE/ACM Transactions on Networking*, 3(5):489–500.

Ramaswami, R., and K. Sivarajan. 2001. *Optical Networks: A Practical Perspective*, 2nd ed. San Francisco: Morgan Kaufmann.

Schwartz, M. 1986. *Telecommunication networks: protocols, modeling and analysis*. Boston, MA: Addison-Wesley Longman Publishing Co.

Sharda, N. 1999. Multimedia networks: Fundamentals and future directions. *Communications of the association for information systems*, 1. http://cais.isworld.org/articles/1-10/article.pdf (accessed April 27, 2007).

Stallings, W. 1999. *Data and computer communications*, 7th ed. Upper Saddle River, NJ: Prentice Hall.

Telephone Switch Timeline. http://www.dmine.com/phworld/switch/timeline.htm (accessed June 1, 2006)

Toba, H., K. Inoue, and K. Nosu. 1986. A conceptional design on optical frequency-division-multiplexing distribution systems with optical tunable filters. *IEEE Journal on Selected Areas in Communications*, 4(9):1458–67.

Tomasi, W. 2004. *Introduction to data communications and networking*. Upper Saddle River, NJ: Prentice Hall.

Zang, H., J. P. Jue, L. Sahasrabuddhe, R. Ramamurthy, and B. Mukherjee. 2001. Dynamic lightpath establishment in wavelength-routed WDM networks. *IEEE Communications Magazine*, 39(9):100–8.

FURTHER READING

Since the invention of telephone in 1876, circuit switching has been the dominant switching technology. With such long history, volumes of materials have been dedicated to understanding properties of circuit-switching technology, its architecture, and performance. A comprehensive description of circuit switching technology and its properties can be found in Stallings (1999), Bellamy (2000), and Chapuis (1982). Chapuis (1982) and Clark (1997) provide detail descriptions on switching node architecture and various technologies used in circuit switching nodes. Detailed discussions on frequency and wavelength-division multiplexing are provided in Toba (1986).

Various online articles, including Tomasi (2004), Martin (1985), and Telephone (2006), offer valuable information regarding development of public telephone network and POTs. Applications of circuit switching technology pertaining multimedia services are discussed in Sharda (1999). Tomasi (2004) and Martin (1985) offer excellent discussions on ISDN technology.

Abundant materials are available on optical networking, SONET, and WDM systems. Interested readers can refer to Bernstein (2003), Mukherjee (2006), and Ramaswami (2001) for a complete treatment of these topics. Good surveys describing more advanced topics, such as wavelength routing, and impact of wavelength continuity constraints, can be found in Zang (2001), Ramaswami (1995), and Baroni (1997).

A comprehensive treatment of circuit switching performance is provided in Schwartz (1986). Discussion regarding the performance of optical networks can be found in Barry (1996). Finally, interesting discussions regarding possibility of using circuit-switching technology at the core can be found in Molinero-Fernández (2003). Cringely (2004) provides a good argument as to why circuit switching must be maintained as the future switching technology for telephone companies.

Message Switching

Farid Farahmand, *Central Connecticut State University*

INTRODUCTION

A communication network consists of a collection of devices (or nodes) that wish to communicate and interconnect together. The primary objective in any communication network is simply moving information from one source to one or more destination nodes. Based on the techniques used to transfer data, communication networks can be categorized into broadcast and switched networks. In broadcast networks, data transmitted by one node is received by many, sometimes all, of the other nodes. In switched-communication networks, however, the data transferred from source to destination is routed through the switch nodes. The way in which the nodes switch data from one link to another as it is transmitted from source to destination node is referred to as a *switching technique*. Three common switching techniques are circuit switching, packet switching, and message switching.

In circuit switching, the end-users are interconnected using dedicated paths. The most common example of a circuit-switched communications network is the plain old telephone service (POTS) network. One major issue with circuit switching is that it can be rather inefficient, particularly in data communications (Stallings, 2004). This is because in a circuit-switched network the channel capacity is dedicated for the entire duration of a connection, even if no information is being transferred. Furthermore, in a circuit-switched network, the actual time to setup and tear down the path may in fact be longer than the data transfer time between end-users. Refer to "Circuit Switching" for a complete discussion on circuit switching.

In packet switching, data is divided into smaller units, called packets, and then transmitted through the network. The minimum length of the packet is determined by the network and varies from network to network. Packets are transported over the network between nodes. Each intermediate node queues the packet for a brief time while it determines the route the packet should take to reach the next node. For this reason, a packet-switched network is sometimes called *hold-and-forward* network (Tomasi, 2004). Please refer to "Packet Switching" for a complete discussion on packet-switched networks.

Prior to advances in packet switching, message switching was introduced as an effective alternative to circuit switching. In message switching, end-users communicate by sending each other a *message*, which contains the entire data being delivered from the source to destination node. As a message is routed from its source to its destination, each intermediate switch within the network stores the entire message, providing a very reliable service. In fact, when congestion occurs or all network resources are occupied, rather than discarding the traffic, the message-switched network will store and delay the traffic until sufficient resources are available for successful delivery of the message (Davis, 1973). The message storing capability can also lead to reducing the cost of transmission; for example, messages can be delivered at night when transmission costs are typically lower.

Message switching techniques were originally used in data communications. Early examples of message switching applications are paper tape relay systems and telex networks. Electronic mail (e-mail) and voice mail are also examples of message switching systems. Today, message switching is used in many networks, including ad hoc sensor networks, satellite communications networks, and military networks.

Basic Ideas in Message Switching

Message-switched data networks are hop-by-hop systems that support two distinct characteristics: store-and-forward and message delivery.

In a message-switched network, there is no direct connection between the source and destination nodes. In such networks, the intermediary nodes (switches) have the responsibility of conveying the received message from one node to another in the network. Therefore, each intermediary node within the network must store all messages before retransmitting them one at a time as proper resources become available. This characteristic is often referred to as *store-and-forward* (Stallings, 2004). In message-switching systems (also called store-and-forward systems), the responsibility of the message delivery is on the next hop, as the message travels through the path toward its destination. Hence, to ensure proper delivery, each intermediate switch may maintain a copy of the message until its delivery to the next hop is guaranteed. In case of message broadcasting, multiple copies may be stored for each individual destination node.

The store-and-forward property of message-switched networks is different from *queuing*, in which messages are simply stored until their preceding messages are processed. With store-and-forward capability, a message will only be delivered if the next hop and the link connecting to it are both available. Otherwise, the message is stored indefinitely. For example, consider a mail server that is disconnected from the network and cannot receive the messages directed to it. In this case, the intermediary server must store all messages until the mail server is connected and receives the e-mails. The store-and-forward technology is also different from admission control techniques implemented in packet-switched or circuit-switched networks. Using admission control, the data transmission can temporarily be delayed to avoid over-provisioning the resources. Hence, a message-switched network can also implement an admission control mechanism to reduce network's peak load.

The message delivery in message-switched networks includes wrapping the entire information in a single message and transferring it from the source to the destination node. The message size has no upper bound; although some messages can be as small as a simple database query, others can be very large. For example, messages obtained from a meteorological database center can contain several million bytes of binary data. Practical limitations in storage devices and switches, however, can enforce limits on message length.

Each message must be delivered with a header. The header often contains the message routing information, including the source and destination, priority level, expiration time. Figure 1 shows an example of a message datagram with possible information embedded in the message header.

It is worth mentioning that while a message is being stored at the source or any other intermediary node in the network, it can be bundled or aggregated with other messages going to the next node. This is known as *message interleaving*. One important advantage of message interleaving is that it can reduce the amount of overhead generated in the network, resulting in higher link utilization.

Message-Switching Characteristics

Message switching offers a number of attractive benefits, including efficient usage of network resources, traffic regulation, and message storage when messages cannot be delivered. However, there are several drawbacks associated with message-switching techniques. For example, since messages are entirely processed and stored indefinitely at each intermediate node, switches require large storage capacity (Davis, 1973).

In general, message-switched networks are relatively slow. This is because all messages must be entirely stored, processed, and retransmitted. This slow switching scheme may lead to poor performance, particularly in wide area networks (WANs). Although, using various scheduling techniques, time critical messages can be given higher transmission priority, it is always possible that a short message falls in line behind a very long one. Consequently, in message switching, messages initiated by different users can expect large delay variance.

Large overall delay and high delay variations make message-switched networks less suitable for real-time and interactive applications, such as voice communications or multimedia games. Instead, message-switched networks are very attractive for supporting applications which can tolerate high delays, yet very little loss. Furthermore, message switching can be an alternative solution for networks where continuous end-to-end connectivity cannot be guaranteed, such as ad hoc sensor networks. A detailed discussion on advantages and disadvantages of message switching compared to circuit switching and packet switching can be found in the subsection Comparison of Message, Packet, and Circuit Switching in this chapter.

MESSAGE-SWITCHED NETWORKS

In this section we first describe different elements of a message-switched network and examine their basic functionalities. Then we focus on store-and-forward switch node architecture and explain its building blocks.

Network Elements

Figure 2 shows a generic message-switched network allowing message transport from one end-user to another. This network consists of transmission links (channels), store-and-forward switch nodes, and end stations (Tomasi, 2004). The transmission links differ depending on the transmission technology and the physical transmission media over which the communications take place. The store-and-forward switch nodes provide end stations with access to transmission links and other switch nodes. They allow data storage and transport of messages from one node to another until they reach their destination

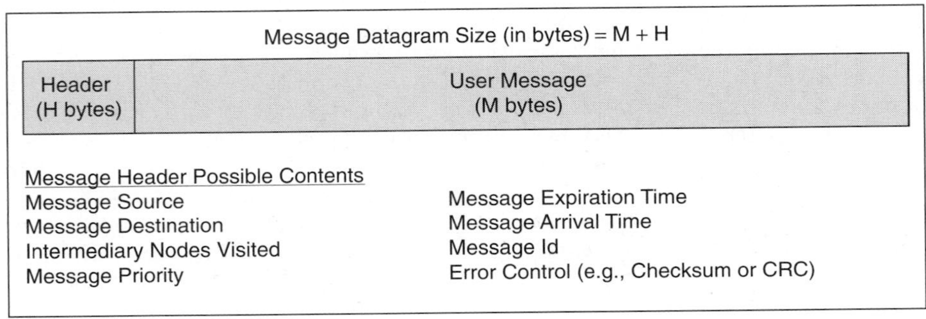

Figure 1: An example of a message datagram structure

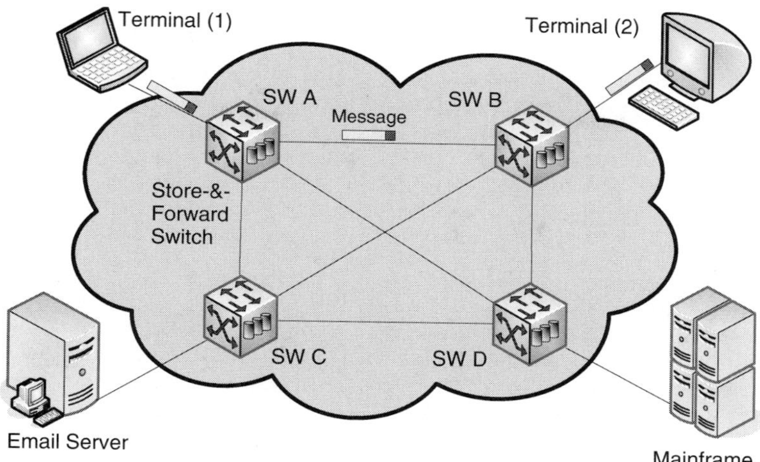

Figure 2: A message-switched network

nodes. The end stations can be individual computer terminals, servers, and mainframes. Many networks may be equipped with message gateways, which can convert one message protocol to another.

Store-and-Forward Switches

In general, a switch is a connectivity device that makes forwarding decisions. A store-and-forward switch performs forwarding functionalities similar to a switch in a packet-switched network. However, a store-and-forward switch forwards a message only if sufficient resources are available and the next hop is accepting new data. Hence, the switching strategy in store-and-forward switches is different from the common switching strategy used in packet-switched networks in which the incoming data is forwarded as soon as its destination address is determined.

Figure 3 shows the basic functional blocks of a generic store-and-forward switch node (Shafritz, 1964). In the following paragraphs we briefly outline the basic functionalities of each block.

The message received by a store-and-forward switch is first decoded and queued. When the input processing controller becomes available, it receives the message and analyzes its header for its destination, associated id, and priority level.

The input processing controller can also check for any errors in the message. Upon detection of any errors, it requests message retransmission. Examples of message errors include transmission errors and invalid addressing. Accepted messages with valid headers are stored in storage devices. Any stored message can be accessed or requested for retransmission using a specific id or serial number. After delivery, a copy of the message will be stored for future retransmission. These messages may be retained for many hours, days, or even weeks. The lookup table maintains the forwarding information and keeps track of which messages are waiting for delivery or have already been delivered.

When the output phase begins, the output processing controller retrieves the proper message from the storage device and after assigning a header, passes it to the output buffer queue and line coder block for appropriate formatting and transmission. The output buffer queue can be used to control the message transmission rate.

The output processing controller is also responsible for deciding how to forward the message to the next hop. In general, forwarding decisions used in message-switched networks are similar to routing schemes implemented in packet-switched networks. For example, forwarding decisions can be based on the least congested link, or shortest end-to-end path (Tanenbaum, 2002). A number of routing techniques in packet-switched networks are discussed in "Packet Switching".

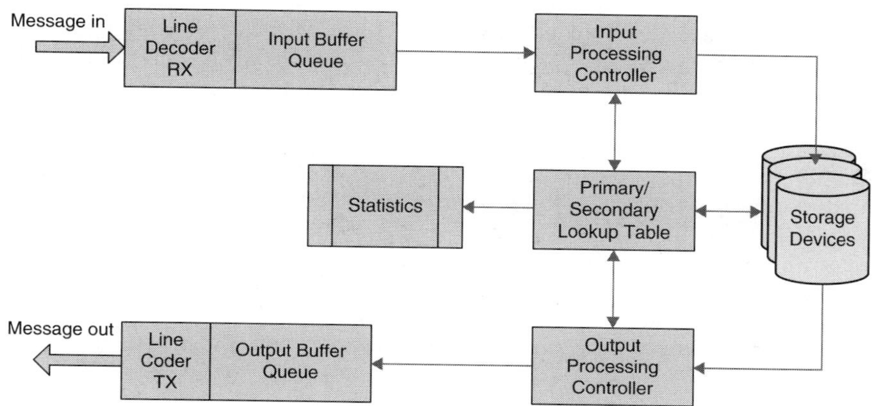

Figure 3: A generic store-and-forward switch node architecture

The exact characteristics of message-switched networks vary depending on features supported by the store-and-forward switch nodes in the network. In the following paragraphs, we elaborate on storage requirements and other features commonly provided by store-and-forward switch nodes.

The storage devices used in a store-and-forward switch node have large storage capacities. This is because messages delivered to each switch are often long and may be stored in the switch indefinitely until sufficient resources are available in order to forward them to the next node. In cases where a message has to be delivered to multiple destination nodes, multiple copies of the messages may be stored for a potentially long duration. A copy of the transmitted message may be stored for possible retransmission until message delivery to the next hop is confirmed. Moreover, the storage capacity must be large enough to avoid any types of data overflow and therefore data loss. The actual storage capacity of the switch is based on the desired performance and can be estimated through statistical analyses. Clearly, as the message arrival rate increases, the amount of data stored in the switch becomes greater, leading to larger storage requirement. Larger storage capacity, on the other hand, leads to requiring faster processors and more efficient search algorithms.

Each store-and-forward switch node is typically programmed to detect, report, and record any fault conditions, including presence of excessive noise, system tampering, and link failure. Switch nodes must also become aware of each other's status. For example, in order to notify its neighboring nodes that the node is *alive*, each node can periodically send each neighboring node the serial number of the last message it received from that node.

A common capability of store-and-forward switches is supporting message priority. Based on parameters such as delay (or loss) tolerance or message length, every message can have a particular priority level. Messages with higher priority must be treated first and forwarded in minimum time. Supporting message priority can add considerable complexity to message storage strategies, requiring separate listing for each priority group. Furthermore, the system must allow high-urgency messages to interrupt others during their transmission. The interrupted messages will be automatically retransmitted as soon as possible, with no further action by the sender. A system that does not support message priority can simply handle incoming messages on a first-in-first-out basis.

A store-and-forward switch can also perform various statistical analysis, billing operations, and status reports. For example, it can examine each message for its number of characters in order to charge the sending party. It may also analyze message headers to gather statistical information on various network links. The status report can include the status of facilities, error statistics, and message counts.

An important function of a store-and-forward switch is that it can intercept a message for various reasons. For example, if the destination node is temporarily unavailable, the switch can store the message until the destination is working again. The switch can also reroute the message to other alternative recipients acquiring the same message. Message interception can also be considered for cases where the destination node has moved and it is no longer in its previous location. In such cases, assuming the system can locate the user, the message will be redirected to the new location.

A store-and-forward switch that can also act as a message gateway is often called a *transactional switch* (Tomasi, 2004). In addition to storing messages and performing message routing, a transactional switch can change the message format and bit rate and then convert it to an entirely different form. Hence, through message reformatting, message switching can effectively allow for translating messages between dissimilar high-level applications and protocols.

Message-based Protocols and the OSI Model

In order to better understand functionalities of different message-based protocols, in this section we conform these protocols to the seven-layer Open Systems Interconnections/Reference Model (OSI/RM). Different layers of the OSI model are depicted in Figure 4. As we mentioned before, message transmission and message switching over the physical layer are performed one hop at a time. Each intermediate store-and-forward switch node receives the entire message, stores it, and forwards it to the next hop. A network using this technique is called a store-and-forward network.

Data-link layer protocols in message-switched networks deal with the algorithms (e.g., error detection and message flow regulation) for achieving reliable and efficient message passing between two neighboring store-and-forward switch nodes. Another important function of such protocols is providing proper services to the network layer (Tanenbaum, 2002). Such services include the following: (a) unacknowledged connection-less service (the sender sends the message randomly and expects no response back from the receiver); (b) acknowledged connection-less service (the sender sends the message randomly and expects some kind of response back from the receiver); (c) connection-oriented service (prior to sending the message, a direct circuit must be established between the two adjacent nodes).

Depending on the data-link protocol, different retransmission mechanisms, if any, may be implemented. A simple approach is to send an acknowledgement frame back to the sender. In this case, the sender can assume proper reception of the message by the downstream node and remove its copy of the message. In some networks the retransmission occurs when a negative acknowledgment or simply *nothing* is received.

The main functionality of the network layer in message switching is to provide routing algorithms, such as source routing and shortest-path routing. Based on the routing procedure, the intermediate store-and-forward node must determine the next hop and forward the message there. The network layer is also responsible for supporting message broadcasting and message multicasting.

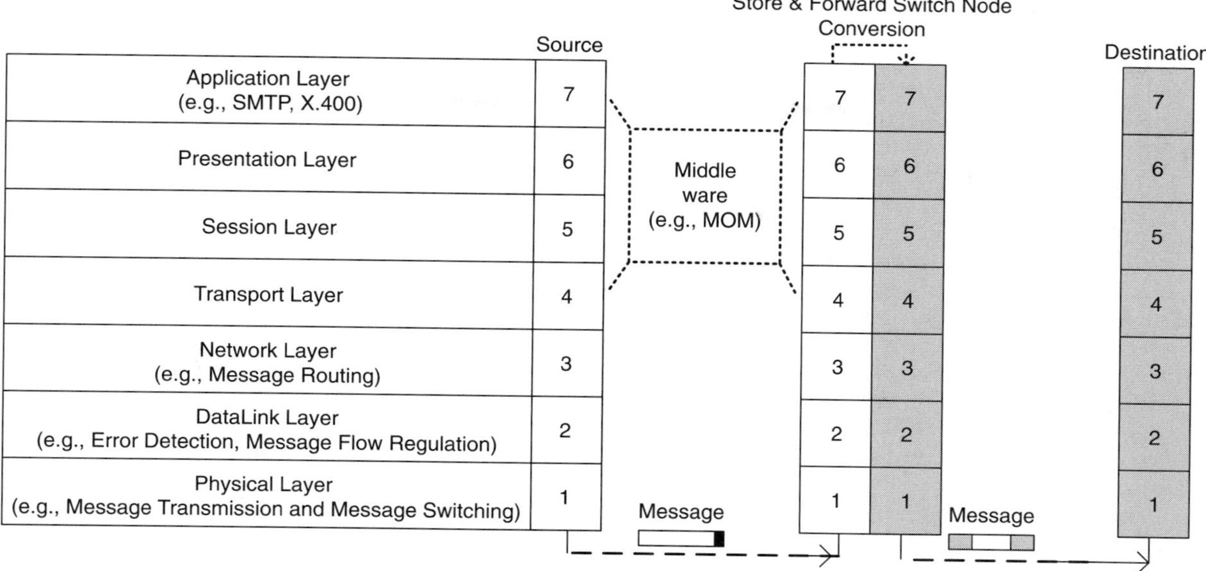

Figure 4: Store-and-forward technology can be implemented at different layers of the OSI model

In general, message-switched networks do not require an official transport protocol. In such networks, each pair of interconnected store-and-forward switch node can negotiate the use of any desired transport protocol (or none at all), as long as the underlying communication is reliable.

Because in message switching the entire message is delivered and stored at the next hop, message-based protocols can offer features beyond the transport layer. These protocols are typically application-aware and hence, they can operate in various transmission environments. For example, they are capable of tolerating temporary node unavailability or converting message format. Two common examples of message-based protocols are X.400 and SMTP, which will be discussed in Store-and-Forward Electronic Mail later in this chapter.

The store-and-forward technology can also be implemented in *middleware*. Middleware is a software that provides a translation mechanism, interconnecting application software across a network, such as a server/client network, and creating a single-system image. One category of middleware that utilizes store-and-forward technology and provides program-to-program communications by message passing is called Message-Oriented Middleware (MOM). We discuss MOM in Message-Based Client/Server Systems later in this chapter.

Figure 4 shows that an incoming message into the store-and-forward switch node can be entirely reformatted prior to its retransmission. In many systems a copy of each message will be stored until its reception by the next hop is acknowledged. Message storage can be performed at different layers, including the network layer or application layer. Data-link and possibly other higher layer protocols are responsible to provide message status information. Note that middleware mediates between top layers of the OSI reference model.

MESSAGE-SWITCHED NETWORKS AND THEIR APPLICATIONS

The basic concept of store-and-forward implemented in message switching has been around since the early use of smoke signals and beacons. The postal delivery system in the eighteenth century, which was not significantly different from the current postal system, also used store-and-forward techniques. In this system a piece of mail (e.g., a parcel) is dropped off at the local post office. The mail will be picked up and taken to the next post office closest to the destination when the delivery service becomes available. Eventually, the mail is delivered to the recipient or stored in the destination post office, waiting for pickup by the recipient. We should note that in the postal delivery system example, proper delivery to the next station is typically assumed.

In the late eighteenth century, semaphore networks became popular. These networks used visual signals (flags, lamps, heliographs) to convey messages between operators in towers. Each tower, in turn, would relay the message to the next until the message was delivered.

The store-and-forward method was also implemented in telegraph message switching centers, commonly known as torn-tape centers (Davis and Barber, 1973). In these centers operators tore message tapes from tape punches on incoming circuits and stored them in output baskets according to their outgoing address. Then, when the dispatcher clerk became available, the messages were keyed in an appropriate circuit to the next center. Telegraphy messages were also called telegrams or cable grams.

The development of mechanical teleprinters, also known as teletypewriters or teletypes, resulted in an increase in the message carrying capacity of telegraph lines. Furthermore, by using the teleprinter terminals the operators were no longer required to know special codes (e.g., Morse code). The telex, short for teleprinter exchange, was introduced as a public service using teleprinters connected through automatic exchanges (telex switching facilities). Using the telex network a subscriber can type out the telex number or code for the called party, wait for an acknowledgment from the called machine, and then transmit. The printed message is often stored at the other end even if the called teleprinter is not staffed.

Advancements in digital computers and digital storage devices made radical improvements in message switching systems. During the 1960s and 1970s, the store-and-forward technology was largely promoted by Western Union, which traditionally was a message carrying organization. Due to long distances between cities in the United States, Western Union primarily was focusing on store-and-forward techniques to maximize line utilization in order to offer telex and telegraph, as well as variety of computer-based services.

Today, although many major networks and systems are packet-switched or circuit switched networks, their delivery processes can be based on message switching. For example, in most electronic mail systems the delivery process is based on message switching, while the network is in fact either circuit-switched or packet-switched.

Store-and-Forward Networks

Message switching technology has been the forerunner of today's advanced data communications. It set the trends for packet switching technology and more sophisticated networks of the twenty-first century. In fact, many of the early data networks and communications services were actually built upon the message-switched concept and store-and-forward technology. In the remainder of this section, we first discuss a few of such networks, which are considered as major breakthroughs in development of current complex data communications networks. Then, we examine some of the common communications protocols that are designed based on store-and-forward technology.

AUTODIN Network

The Automatic Digital Network (AUTODIN), developed in the mid-1960s, is one of the largest and most complex message switching systems. Using store-and-forward switching technology, AUTODIN provided a message-based worldwide communication network for the U.S. military, handling the data communication needs for the Department of Defense and other Federal organizations (the alternative system to handle voice communications was AUTOVON) (FAS, 2003). AUTODIN has also been used by other major agencies including the NSA (National Security Agency), the DIA (Defense Intelligence Agency), and NATO (North Atlantic Treaty Organization).

AUTODIN was originally considered as a dedicated backbone network serving primarily for secret data transmission. All switches and routers in the network were controlled by a system called the AUTODIN Switching Center. The system was designed to run at 2400 bits-per-second (bps); however, speeds up to 9600 bps were possible.

The header of each message sent by AUTODIN included source, destination, security classification, priority statement, and a subject line. A very important aspect of AUTODIN was providing highly secure communications. Hence, all external connections to the network from telephone lines were subject to strong encryption techniques.

For the past several decades, AUTODIN has been regarded as a highly sophisticated message-switched network. It also had major contributions in advancing data communications. For example, in 1966 AUTODIN was one of the first systems that allowed electronic text messages to be transferred between users on different computers.

In 1982 an enhanced program, known as AUTODIN II, aiming to improve the system performance and security, was terminated in favor of using packet-based ARPANET technology. As of 2003, many AUTODIN switching sites have been shut down. The intention is to replace the old system with the Defense Message System (DMS). DMS is based on implementations of the OSI X.400 e-mail, which provides message services, through supporting multimedia messaging, directory services, and different grades of services, to all Department of Defense users.

SITA and AFTN Networks

Société Internationale de Télécommunications Aéronautiques (SITA) was originally established in 1949 by a group of airlines. The purpose of the project was to provide computer-based seat reservation service to facilitate the sale of seats on airplanes and exchange of operational information (Martin, 1985). SITA organized a common global service supported by a low-speed message switching network that was based on teletype message format generated by teleprinters.

Aeronautical Fixed Telecommunication Network (AFTN) is also another example of a worldwide message switching network. After World War II, following SITA experience, AFTN was introduced to support exchange of messages between aeronautical fixed stations and aircrafts. AFTN is composed of aviation entities, including aviation service providers, airport authorities, and government agencies. It exchanges vital information for aircraft operations such as urgency messages, flight safety messages, meteorological messages, flight regularity messages, and aeronautical administrative messages (Bush, 2003).

Today, the airline industry continues to use teletype messages over SITA and AFTN as a medium for communicating via messages. These teletype messages are machine-generated by automatic processes. The International Air Transport Association (IATA) is responsible for standardizing the message format throughout the airline industry. In the last several decades, however, as the packet switching has become the standard means of telecommunications, both SITA and AFTN networks have undergone major reengineering and their nodes have been replaced to support packet switching.

USENET Network

USENET (USEr NETwork) began in 1979 as a bulletin board between two universities in North Carolina. It is basically a public access network on the Internet and other TCP/IP-based networks that provides user news and group e-mail.

USENET provides a set of protocols for generating, storing, retrieving, and exchanging news articles among a widely distributed user group. The format of news messages and e-mail messages are structurally the same. Hence, USENET permits news messages to be carried the same way as e-mail messages. The only difference is the additional header fields indicating which newsgroups (a repository of articles posted by the users) the message belongs to.

USENET is considered as one of the first peer-to-peer applications. In this case the *peers* are the servers and can be accessed by the users. A major advantage of USENET is that it reduces network traffic and eliminates the need to store a copy of each article on every subscriber's system. This is done by putting all articles in a central database and allowing users to access the database to get the articles they need (Tanenbaum, 2002).

Originally, USENET relied on a message exchange system called UUCP (UNIX-to-UNIX Copy Program). UUCP is a *flood broadcast* mechanism. Hosts send news articles they receive to other hosts, which in turn forward the news on to other hosts that they feed. Usually, a host receives duplicates of articles and must discard those duplicates. This can be a time-consuming process, resulting in waste of bandwidth.

Today, message delivery in USENET is primarily handled by an Internet protocol called NNTP (network news transport protocol). NNTP uses an interactive command and response mechanism that lets hosts determine which articles are to be transmitted. A host acting as a client contacts a server host using NNTP, and then inquires if any new newsgroups have been created on any of the serving host systems.

Performance-Challenged Networks

Performance-challenged networks (or simply *challenged networks*) are interconnected networks in which end-to-end latency, bandwidth asymmetry, and/or path stability are substantially worse compared to typical Internet environments. Such network environments are particularly common in space or ocean (acoustic underwater) communications, sensor networks, and military tactical communications, all of which lack an infrastructure.

In challenged networks the signal propagation time is comparatively long as a result of either long physical separation of end nodes, as in space, or because of slow transmission speed, as in water. Consequently, the total transmission time in such networks can take literally hours or perhaps days. Protocols such as TCP/IP that expect acknowledgments may not be appropriate for such environments. This is mainly because too many timeouts can occur because of heavy congestions in the low capacity links. Another issue with challenged networks is path instability, which is generally the result of short node lifetime or mobility. For example, in sensor networks many of the sensors may run out of battery power after some period of time (Fall, 2003).

One approach to support interconnecting challenged networks and their interoperability is called delay tolerance networking (DTN), which is based on message switching. The use of message switching for these networks allows all the small request/responses to be aggregated, hence reducing the number of packets being routed through the network (Fall, 2002). Aggregated messages are often stored, scheduled, and eventually forwarded toward the destination node. The other benefit of implementing message switching is that it does not require pre-established end-to-end state of the network. Using store-and-forward technology, each node discovers its available neighboring nodes and forwards them the messages. Research in challenged networks is a relatively new area and is still being investigated.

Message-Switched Protocols

In this subsection we look at some of the most common protocols that are based on store-and-forward technology. As a result of their vast applications, we only focus on three specific systems: electronic mail systems, message-based client/server systems, and wireless messaging systems.

Store-and-Forward Electronic Mail

With the advancement in digital technology and digital data communications, sending electronic data, text messages, documents, as well as voice and images, collectively known as electronic mail (e-mail), became very popular. The first e-mail systems simply consisted of file transfer protocols. Over the years, many new protocols were developed for more ambitious e-mail systems. The majority of these protocols have been designed based on store-and-forward technology. In the following paragraphs, we briefly discuss two e-mail delivery protocols: X.400 and SMTP.

X.400. The main motivation in development of X.400 was to create a common standard that would allow different electronic mail systems to communicate together. X.400 (also referred to as message-oriented text interchange systems [MOTIS]) is a set of standards developed by ITU-T (the International Telecommunications Union-Telecommunications, formerly known as CCITT), which includes protocols dealing with message handling systems (MHS). These standards are designed to exchange messages (e-mails) between different store-and-forward servers and networks. In its original form, X.400 outlines a set of basic message-handling characteristics that establish functionalities including the following:

- Store-and-forward delivery of messages to multiple recipients
- Conversion of message content to allow message transfer between dissimilar sending and receiving devices (fax, telex, PC)
- Delivery-time control

X.400 was first published in 1984 (Red Book) and a substantially revised version, known as X.400/88, was published in 1988 (Blue Book). In 1992, new features and updates were added (White Book) (Betanov, 1992). Although X.400 was originally designed to accommodate OSI model transport services, today it is typically run over TCP/IP.

A network model defined by X.400 consists of a number of basic elements including user agent (UA), message transfer agent (MTA), and message store (MS), as shown in Figure 5. The UA is a program that allows the user to compose, send, and receive mail. The MTA is the electronic post office, accepting the e-mail from user agents and making sure it is delivered. MS, which often co-resides with MTA, maintains electronic mailboxes for each user. When a message is delivered, it may pass through multiple MTAs, each of which reads the message address and passes it to another message transfer agent, until the message reaches its destination. As indicated by Figure 5, messages can be transmitted directly by MTA to the UA recipient or, alternatively, they can be passed on to MS (the equivalent of a mailbox) which makes it possible to store the message. Incoming messages can be stored in these mailboxes until the user logs in. A collection of all message transfer agents cooperating to relay the messages until their destinations is called the message transfer system (MTS).

Figure 5 also shows some of main protocols of X.400. These are P1, defining the communication between MTAs; P3, standardizing the connection between the user agent and MTA; P2 standardizing the (virtual) protocol between the UAs; and P7, describing the interaction between the user agent and message store (Tanenbaum, 2002).

At its early development, X.400 was widely implemented, especially in Europe. However, as e-mails became more popular, many of X.400 features, such as structured addressing and central control, made it more complex for everyday usage. On the other hand, advances in the Internet-based e-mail protocols, in particular simple mail transfer protocol (SMTP), made X.400 less popular. Ironically, the same features which made X.400 less popular, made it attractive for special networks such as military and aviation. In fact, extended versions of X.400, such as military message handling systems (MMHS) and aviation message handling systems (AMHS), are still under research and development. These protocols employ integrated security capabilities, including message routing, password management, and provisioning of public key infrastructure (PKI).

SMTP. Simple mail transfer protocol (SMTP) is considered an application-level protocol, which runs over packet-based TCP/IP. SMTP was developed by IETF (Internet Engineering Task Force) and has become the de facto standard for mail transfer on the Internet. Virtually all e-mail systems that send mail via the Internet use SMTP to send their messages. SMTP is used for forwarding messages from one host to the other and writes them to a message store (e.g., mbox or Maildir). However, SMTP does not provide the functionality of allowing users to retrieve mail. The post office protocol (POP) has been developed for retrieving messages from the massage store.

Although SMTP is the most prevalent of the e-mail protocols, it lacks some of the rich features of X.400. A primary weakness of SMTP is the lack of support for non-text messages. Multipurpose Internet mail extensions (MIME) has been introduced to supplement SMTP allowing the encapsulation of multimedia (non-text) messages inside of a standard SMTP message (Parker, 2002).

X.400 and SMTP have similar features but also unique features in themselves. Generally speaking, X.400 is a more complex protocol and it makes it harder for users to fakee-mail addresses and contents, compared with the situation in SMTP. For a complete discussion on SMTP protocol, please refer to "SMPT (Simple Mail Transfer Protocol)".

Message-Based Client/Server Systems

Many client/server systems use middleware to exchange messages. Middleware is used to simplify the complexity of dealing with communication protocols and layers of software. Broadly speaking, middleware software is defined as the *glue* between software components or between software and the network or it is the *slash* in client/server (MRC, 2004). One category of middleware that provides program-to-program communication by message passing is called message-oriented middleware (MOM). MOM is based on message queuing and store-and-forward technology. MOM is a non-blocking asynchronous form of communication. Hence, every node in the system can randomly send message to the queue or

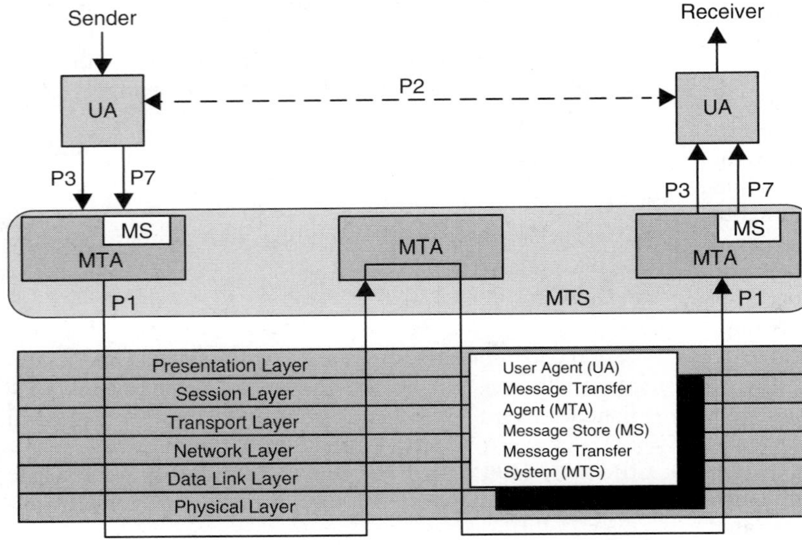

Figure 5: A general network model defined by X.400

taking message from queues. Note that the queue can be a part of the client or a dedicated server. Message storage and queuing can be persistent (logged on disk) or non-persistent (in memory). Persistent messages are slower but they can be recovered in case of power failures.

The message flow in MOM messaging products can have different types, including send-and-pray (no response about the message is required), send-and-nay (a response is required if there is something wrong with the message), and send-and-say (response is mandatory).

Store-and-Forward Wireless Messaging

Today, many wireless applications and services are based on store-and-forward technology in order to reliably transfer messages between end-users. A popular example is short message service (SMS). Although, SMS is being supported by many digital-based mobile communications systems, it was introduced as a datagram service in the GSM (global system for mobile communications) system. SMS is a text message service that enables short text messages (up to 160 characters in length) to be transmitted and received by a cell phone. Similar to e-mail, short messages are stored and forwarded at SMS centers, which means messages can be retrieved later if the user is not immediately available (MWR, 2004). SMS messages travel to the cell phone over out-of-band control channels, separated from voice channels. SMS has been broadly used in Europe and Asia for many years. In North America, SMS was made available initially on digital wireless networks built by early pioneers such as BellSouth Mobility, PrimeCo, and Nextel, among others.

Paging systems capable of storing and delivering messages (or pages) are also examples of store-and-forward wireless systems. A wireless pager receiver can be activated and alert its user via a tone or a vibrator. This is typically called a one-way paging system. Pager activation can be done using a telephone or a PC. In store-and-forward based paging systems, if the network cannot reach the user to deliver the message, it stores the message until the user can be reached (Taylor et al., 1996). Some paging systems have SMS capability and allow displaying small alphanumeric messages. Two-way paging systems include an acknowledgement feature that allows the user to acknowledge the receipt of the message.

Wireless sensor networks (WSN) also use store-and-forward technology. WSN are mesh networks of small sensor nodes communicating among themselves using RF communication. Sensor nodes can be deployed in large scale (from tens to thousands) to sense the physical world, for example, monitoring, tracking, and controlling. The data messages gathered by each sensor node will be periodically exchanged between nodes or passed on to intermediate nodes. Intermediate nodes can aggregate small data messages together prior to retransmitting them to the next node (Zhao and Guibas, 2005).

Store-and-forward technology has also been considered to be implemented in satellite communications systems in order to ensure higher reliability and network robustness. For example, message switching is recently being investigated for inter-satellite networks, where messages are transmitted between two communication satellites, as opposed to communications between a single satellite and Earth stations (Charles, 1999). Message switching is also being considered for interplanetary networks, a high-bandwidth infrastructure designed to link Earth's Internet to other parts of our solar system.

Research suggests that store-and-forward technology can also enhance the wireless range of low-cost short-range technologies, such as WiFi (IEEE 802.11). One approach is simply relaying the data between multiple wireless devices over long distance. A more cost-effective approach is to transmit data over short point-to-point links between mobile storage devices called mobile access points (MAP). Through the use of low-cost WiFi radio transceivers, the data carried by the MAP is automatically and wirelessly transferred at high-bandwidth for each point-to-point connection (Pentland, 2002). The motivation in utilizing this approach is providing a very low-cost and affordable solution to resolve the last mile connectivity problem, particularly in poor rural areas.

PERFORMANCE OF MESSAGE-SWITCHED NETWORKS

In this section we examine the performance of message-switched networks in terms of delay and peak traffic load.

Delay Performance

Figure 6 depicts the transmission of a message across four nodes. Three types of delays can be identified on the diagram: (a) propagation delay—the time it takes a signal to propagate from one node to the next; (b) transmission delay—the time it takes for a transmitter to send out a message (e.g., it takes 0.1 sec. to transmit a 10,000 bit message onto a 100 kbps line); (c) node delay—the time it takes for a node to perform the necessary processing as it switches data plus the message storage time. Hence, the total delay will be the sum of all propagation and transmission delays at each node plus the sum of node delays at each switch node (Rosner, 1981).

As Figure 6 indicates, prior to retransmission, the entire message must be received at each switch node. This results in a large end-to-end delay, particularly if the message size is very large. In fact, under heavy load, when the node delay is not negligible, the total delay using message switching can be significantly longer than for circuit switching, which requires time to setup and tear-down a connection.

Node Delay

An important factor impacting node delay is unavailability of the next hop or the destination node. The store-and-forward switches in a message-switched network avoid repeated attempts to send messages to the next hop. Hence, if the next node is not available, the message retransmission is simply delayed. Clearly, as the total number of messages in the network increases, the average node delay through the network will become longer until no storage resources are available and message dropping occurs. This is illustrated in Figure 7a.

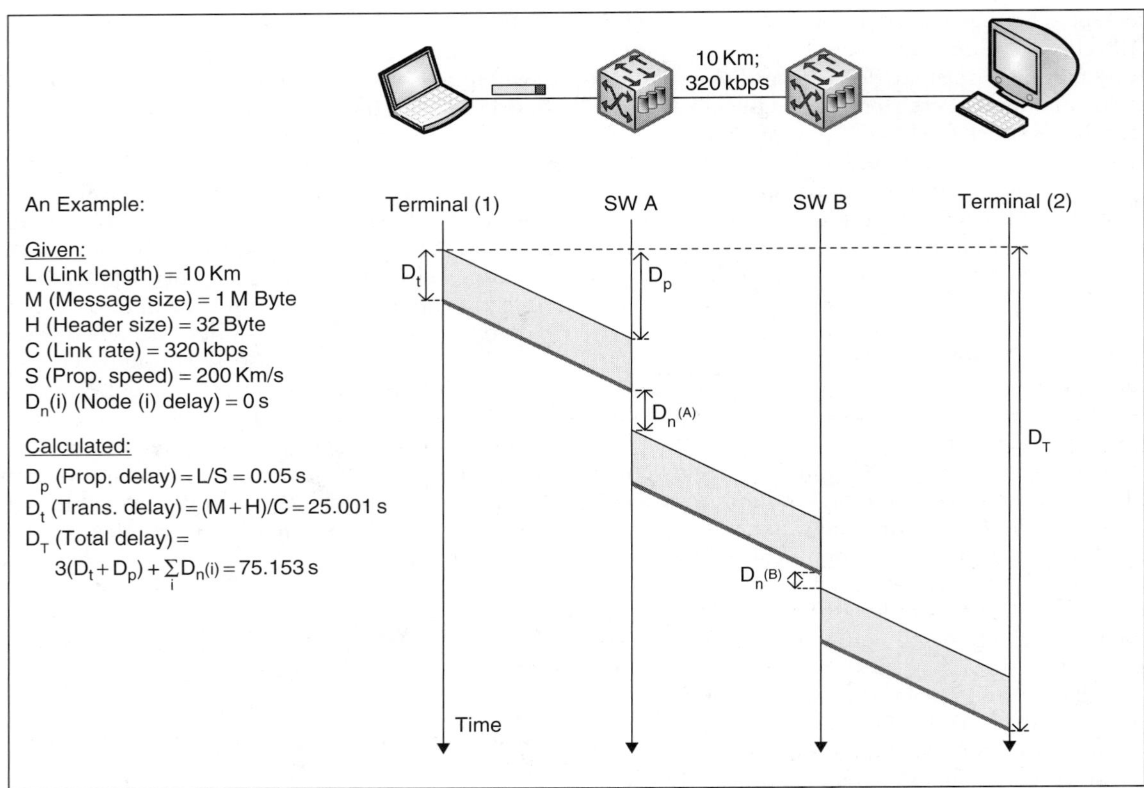

Figure 6: Event timing diagram in message-switched networks (the example assumes all the link speeds and lengths are the same; node delays are assumed to be negligible)

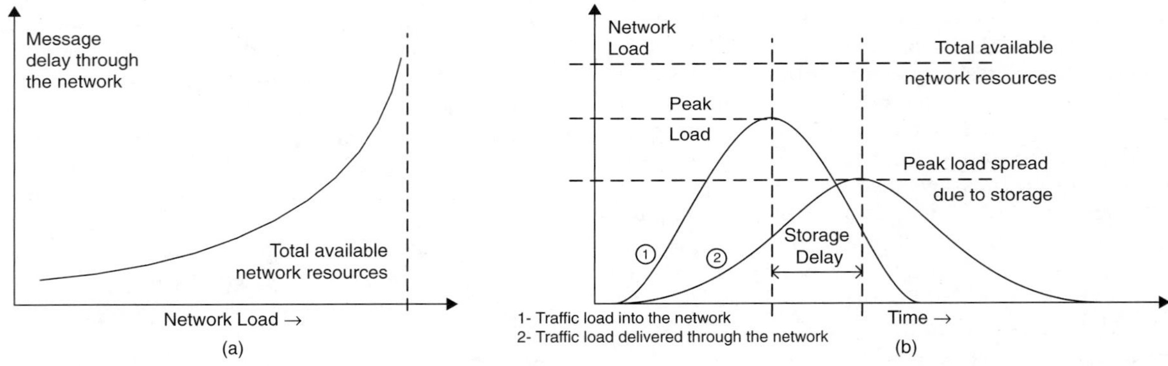

Figure 7: (a) Delay in message-switched networks as the load increases; (b) traffic characteristic as a result of store-and-forward switches

Another important factor affecting the node delay in a store-and-forward switch is network congestion. That is the case where switches cannot deliver as fast as messages are arriving. When congestion occurs, the system continues to accept new messages, as long as its storage capacity allows. In message switching new messages will be stored until free resources are available and the delivery is ensured; hence, no message blocking occurs as long as sufficient storage capacity is available. As the load of the network increases, more messages will have to wait for available processing resources and free links. The result is an increase in the message delivery time through the network.

Another way of looking at a network with store-and-forward switches is to regard it as a large distributed set of storage facilities, which gradually fill as the load on the network increases. Consequently, the peak load is shifted in time by an amount depending on the available storage (Davis et al., 1973). Figure 7b illustrates this point by showing how a peak load is reduced, but at the expense of being delayed. The area under each of the two curves represents the total number of messages delivered. Clearly, this area will be the same for both curves.

Comparison of Message, Packet, and Circuit Switching

Message-switched networks provide a number of advantages over circuit-switched networks. For example, message-switched networks provide more efficient use of network resources. This is a result of their inherent store-and-forward capability. As new information enters the network for future delivery, the message storage process creates a reservoir of traffic. This reservoir tends to remove the gaps between new message arrivals onto the network. In addition, it smoothes the peak network load, leading to some degree of traffic regulation over the network.

When traffic becomes heavy on a circuit-switched network, some connection requests are blocked; that is, the network refuses to accept any additional connection requests until the load on the network decreases. In a message-switched network, messages are still accepted as long as the storage capacity is available but delivery delay increases. As a result, message-switched networks translate potential message blocking into potential delay. As long as the total end-to-end message delay meets the user delay tolerance, message delaying can be far more convenient than message retransmission due to blocking.

Another attractive feature of message-switched networks is that in these networks each intermediary node can perform protocol translation. Since each intermediary node processes the entire message, it can perform any required line code, transmission speed, or protocol conversions between incompatible nodes. Therefore, message switching can be a potential solution for less robust communication environments. In circuit switching, protocol conversion is only possible through protocol gateways.

In message-switched networks, unlike circuit switching, simultaneous availability of sender and receiver is not required and the network can store the message pending the availability of the receiver. Moreover, features such as broadcasting, data auditing, and data rerouting can be supported by message-switched networks much more easily and typically require no major architectural modifications.

The difference between message switching and packet switching begins with the characteristics of messages and packets themselves. Messages are units of information with unrestricted lengths, whereas packets have maximum length size. Furthermore, in a message-switched network the network is responsible for the message and typically no responses or feedbacks exist. Consequently, in message switching, rather than minimizing transit time of the message, its guaranteed delivery is emphasized. On the other hand, packet-switched networks aim to deliver packets with minimum delay and do not hold packets for delayed delivery. Table 1 compares the main characteristics of message, packet, and circuit-switching technologies.

Figure 8 illustrates the transmission of data across four nodes using circuit-switched and packet-switched networks. An important characteristic of circuit switching

Table 1: Comparison of Message, Packet, and Circuit Switching (Stallings, 2004; Martin, 1985)

Circuit-Switched Networks	Message-Switched Networks	Packet-Switched Networks
Communication is performed through a dedicated path.	No dedicated path exists.	No dedicated path exists.
Provides real-time or continuous transmission of data.	Too slow for real-time or interactive data transmission.	Provides near real-time data transmission.
No data storing is required.	Messages are stored for later retrieval.	Packets are queued for delivery; they are not stored.
The switch path is established for the entire connection time.	The route is established for each message.	The route is established for each packet.
For small messages, the data transmission time is negligible compared to the time required to setup and tear-down the connection.	The message delivery time can be substantially long.	The packet delivery time is very short.
The connection is blocked if the end-user is busy or not available. Once the connection starts, no blocking may occur.	No message blocking can occur as long as the storage capacity is sufficiently large.	Packet blocking can occur, however, the blocked packets will be retransmitted to the end-user.
As the network load increases, more blocking can occur.	As the load increases, messages on average experience longer delivery delay.	As the load increases, packets on average experience longer queuing delay, although still very short compared to message switching.
The length of transmission is unlimited.	Messages have no theoretical maximum length and can be very long.	Packets have a maximum length.

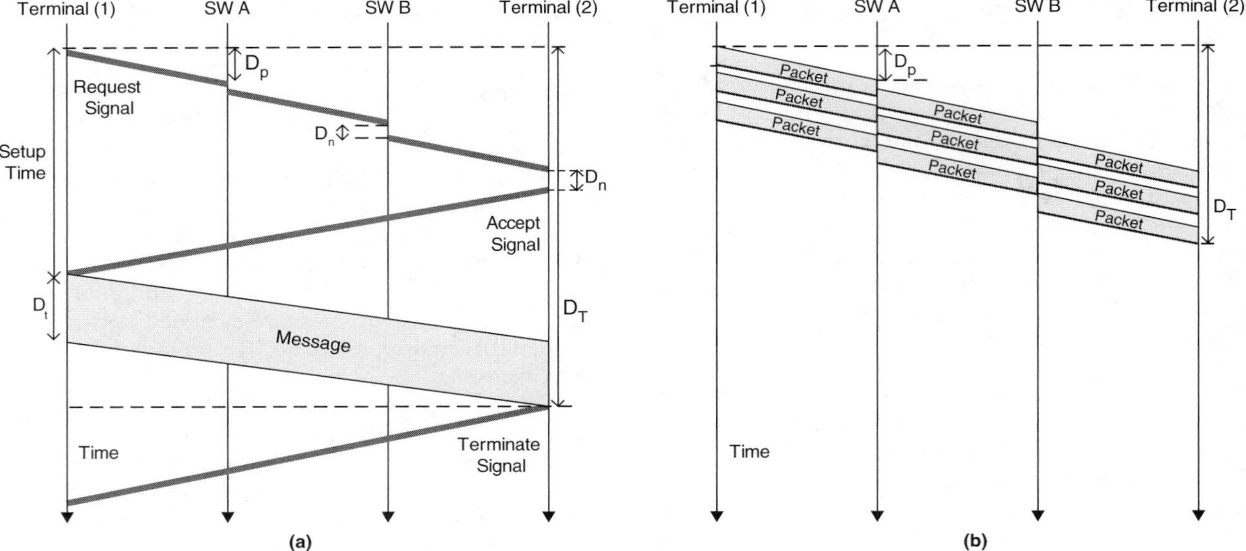

Figure 8: Event timing diagram in (a) a circuit-switched network and (b) a packet-switched network; we assume no loss of data occurs

is the need to setup an end-to-end path. During this time interval (setup time), depicted in Figure 8a, the system is ensuring path availability.

In packet switching, shown in Figure 8b, no physical path is established in advance between sender and receiver. Hence, unlike message switching (Figure 6), each node along the route may begin transmission of a packet as soon as it arrives.

CONCLUSION

In this chapter we examined the basic concepts of message-switched networks. We surveyed their advantages and disadvantages and demonstrated their applications. We also described different elements of a message-switched network and examined their basic functionalities. Although packet switching is becoming the dominant switching scheme, message switching is still considered for many dedicated networks.

GLOSSARY

ARPANET: The Advanced Research Project Agency Network created by the U.S. Department of Defense. This organization is credited with creating the Internet in 1969.

CCITT: Short for *Comité Consultatif International Téléphonique et Télégraphique*, an organization based in Geneva, Switzerland, that sets international communications standards. CCITT changed its name to International Telecommunications Union (ITU), the parent organization, on March 1, 1993.

Datagram: A sequence of bytes that constitutes the unit of transmission in the network layer.

Exchange: A room or building equipped with manual or automatic switching equipments that can interconnect incoming communication lines as required.

IETF: Internet Engineering Task Force is a large, open international community of network designers, operators, vendors, and researchers, which sets standards for the Internet. It is also responsible for much of the work done on TCP/IP.

Peer-to-Peer Architecture (P2P): It is a type of network architecture in which each workstation has equivalent capabilities and responsibilities.

Protocol: A formal and pre-agreed set of rules that govern the communications between two or more entities. The protocol determines the meaning of specific values occurring in specific positions in the stream, the type of error checking to be used, the data compression method, how the sender will indicate that it has finished sending a message, and how the receiver will indicate that it has received a message.

Telegram: A message transmitted by telegraph system.

Teleprinter: A typewriter-like terminal with a keyboard and built-in printer. It was used to communicate typed messages between terminals through a simple point-to-point electrical communication channel, often just a pair of wire. A teleprinter terminal is also called teletype or TTY machine.

CROSS REFERENCES

See *Circuit Switching; E-mail and Instant Messaging; Frame Relay; Packet Switching; SMTP (Simple Mail Transfer Protocol)*

REFERENCES

Betanov, C. 1992. *Introduction to X.400*. Norwood, MA: Artech House.

Bush, D. 2003. The AFTN message switch case study. http://www.ascolto.co.uk/Resources/ (accessed February 1, 2006).

Charles, J. 1999. Interplanetary network aims for the stars. *IEEE Computer Society*, 32(9):16–8, 21.

Davis, D. W., and D. L. Barber. 1973. *Communication networks for computers*. New York: John Wiley & Sons.

Fall, K. 2002. A message-switched architecture for challenged Internets. http://www.intel-research.net/Publications/Berkeley/120520021026_66.pdf (accessed December 1, 2006).

Fall, K. 2003. A delay tolerant networking architecture for challenged Internets. *Proc. SIGCOMM 2003*. August 25–29, 2003. pp. 27–34.

Federation of American Scientists (FAS). 2003. Automatic digital network (AUTODIN). http://www.fas.org (accessed March 1, 2006).

Martin, J. 1985. *Telecommunications and the computer*. Englewood Cliffs, NJ: Prentice Hall.

Middleware Resource Center (MRC). 2004. http://www.middleware.org/ (accessed December 1, 2006).

MobileIN Web Resources (MWR). 2004. http://www.mobilein.com /sms.htm (accessed January 1, 2007).

Parker, T., and K. B. Siyan. 2002. *TCP/IP unleashed (unleashed)*, 3rd ed. Indianapolis, IN: Sams.

Pentland, A. (Sandy), R. Fletcher, and A. A. Hasson. 2002. A road to universal broadband connectivity. http://www.itu.int/council/wsis/080_Annex4.pdf (accessed February 1, 2006).

Rosner, R. D. 1981. *Packet switching*. Belmont, CA: Lifetime Learning Pub.

Shafritz, A. B. 1964. The use of computers in message switching networks. *Proceedings of the 1964 19th ACM National Conference*, pp. 142.301–142.306.

Stallings, W. 2004. *Data and computer communications*, 7th ed. Upper Saddle River, NJ: Prentice Hall.

Tanenbaum, A. S (FAS). 2002. Computer networks, 4th ed. New York: Prentice Hall.

Taylor, M., M. Banan, and W. Waung. 1996. Internetwork mobility: The CDPD approach. Upper Saddle River, NJ: Prentice Hall.

Tomasi, W. 2004. *Introduction to data communications and networking*, 1st ed., Upper Saddle River, NJ: Prentice Hall.

Zhao, F., and L. Guibas. 2005. *Wireless sensor networks: An information processing approach*. San Francisco: Morgan Kaufmann.

FURTHER READING

Many of the original publications on message switching and store-and-forward technology belong to early 1960s and 1970s. Several comprehensive discussions on these topics are found in Davis et al. (1973) and Martin (1985). A basic analytical model for a message-switched network in terms of data loss and delay is provided by Rosner (1981). Stallings (2004), Tomasi (2004), and Martin (1985) offer a list of advantages and disadvantages of message switching and compare the performance between message, packet, and circuit switching. One of the first detailed tutorials on store-and-forward switch node functionalities can be found in Shafritz (1964).

Routing techniques in message-switched and packet-switched networks are very similar. Various routing techniques are described in Tanenbaum (2002).

Examples of message-switched networks, including SITA and AUTODIN, along with detailed discussions of their technical specifications and evolutions, are provided in Martin (1985). FAS (2003) is specifically dedicated to the history of AUTODIN. Bush (2003) offers background information on AFTN. Introductory information about USENET, including its commands and protocols, can be found in Tanenbaum (2002). Betanov (1992) and Parker and Siyan (2002) offer a comprehensive discussion on X.400 and SMTP protocols and their differences. More information about middleware and MOM can be found in MRC (2004).

Recent investigation on implementing message switching in challenged networks and satellite communications can be found in Fall (2003), Fall (2002), and Charles (1999). More information regarding the paging systems and wireless sensor networks can be found in Taylor (1996) and Zhao (2005), respectively. A number of books about short message services are listed in MWR (2004). Moreover, an interesting work demonstrating how store-and-forward technology can be used to provide a low-cost solution to resolve the last mile continuity problem in rural areas can be found in Pentland et al. (2002).

Frame Relay

Eddie Rabinovitch, *ECI Technology, Totowa, NJ*

INTRODUCTION

General Concepts

Frame relay is a connection-oriented end-to-end WAN protocol that operates at the two lowest layers of the OSI reference model—physical and data link layers. Developers of the protocol came up with its name "frame relay" as a result of the nature of the technology, where data is being transferred in "packets" or "frames" traversing the WAN. In fact, frame relay was developed as part of BISDN (Broadband Integrated Services Digital Network) described in "BISDN (Broadband Integrated Services Digital Network)," and is a classical implementation of a packet-switched technology described in this chapter. Packet-switched networks establish logical connections (virtual circuits) between devices as opposed to connecting them by dedicated leased lines (Peterson and Davie, 1996). This technology reduces the network complexity (and certainly price) required to connect multiple devices in a mesh network environment.

By implementing variable length packets, frame relay was designed with data networks in mind. Nevertheless, there were attempts by several vendors to use frame relay networks for transferring voice and even video. However, utilization of frame relay networks for voice or video transfer proved to be inefficient and short-lived. Therefore, today this technology is being used predominantly, if not exclusively, for data transfer only.

Historical Overview

As a successor of the original packet-switching X.25 technology, developers of frame relay monopolized on a more reliable digital network infrastructure emphasizing more efficient utilization of the network and deemphasizing packet integrity and error correction requirements. Thus, frame relay offers services at layers 1 and 2 of the OSI reference model, whether X.25 offers services at the network layer as well. Therefore, in frame relay networks error correction is performed at the end points offering superior performance and much better transmission efficiency than X.25.

Initial proposals for frame relay standard were presented in 1984 to the CCITT (Comité Consultatif International Téléphonique et Télégraphique)—now referred to by the name of its parent organization as ITU (International Telecommunication Union). The ITU was founded in 1865 and became a United Nations agency in 1947. Telecommunications standardization functions were formerly performed by the CCITT. However, after the 1992 reorganization of the ITU CCITT no longer exists as a separate entity.

Frame relay is a classical example of a technology developed from an existing protocol suite adopting to a modern environment and addressing the ever-growing needs for higher efficiency and network throughput. The original packet-switching technology X.25 was developed to allow cost-efficient connectivity of relatively unsophisticated computer systems over poor quality analog lines. Therefore, X.25 networks required error correction at many levels and nodes along the virtual circuit. Contrary to X.25 frame relay was developed in a more modern environment, with more sophisticated computer systems and higher quality digital telecommunications lines, enabling typically less expensive, but much more efficient and fast data transfer. In fact, frame relay is sometimes being referred to as fast packet switching.

The definition of frame relay in the so-called Blue Book, published in 1988 by CCITT is very vague. It indicates that on top of a BISDN network there may be various services, with frame-oriented service being one of them. In the early 1990s, this fairly vague definition was taken up by consortium of four companies Cisco Systems, Digital Equipment Corporation (now part of HP), Northern

Telecom, and Stratacom (now part of Cisco) and expanded by ANSI T1S1.2 subcommittee into a concrete interface definition, which subsequently became what we know today as the frame relay protocol (Malamud, 1992).

Indubitably, IBM's strong endorsement and support of the frame relay protocol had contributed to its dramatic success in the 1990s. By allowing encapsulation of its proprietary SNA (Systems Network Architecture) protocols into frame relay and wide implementation of this technology across IBM data communications family of products, that is, IBM 3174 terminal controllers, 3745 front-end communications controllers, and their 3172 LAN interconnect controllers, it allowed SNA users to take advantage of a low-cost multiplexed access network. Thus, frame relay networks quickly replaced the vast networks of multidrop SDLC leased lines used by SNA customers previously (Rabinovitch, 1995).

Frame Relay and the OSI Reference Model

Frame relay protocol specified in CCITT recommendations I.122 and Q.922 adds relay and routing functions to the data link-layer 2 of the OSI reference model.

Layer	Name	Function	Examples
...	...	...	
3	Network	Controls data transfers between computers	X.25, IP
2	Data link	Protocols for operating data communications lines	ISDN, ATM, frame relay
1	Physical	Physical medium for data transport	Connectors for copper wire, fiber optic cables, wireless

In contrast to X.25 that includes implementation of the network layer in OSI reference model with all the overhead associated with assembly/disassembly of packets and routing information, frame relay protocol has significantly lower overhead using a group of two octets only for data link control at layer 2. Frame relay performs simple and fast error checking, and if a frame is full of errors, it's being discarded.

PACKET SWITCHING AND NETWORK DESIGN CONSIDERATIONS

Protocol Description

Capitalizing on modern and more reliable network infrastructure frame relay developers aimed at an improved, faster, and more cost-efficient data transmission protocol than X.25. Thus, with frame relay data being sent in variable-size frames, error-correction, and retransmission requests are performed at the end nodes, which only speed up the transmission and reduce the sophistication requirements and obviously costs of the network devices.

Frame relay packet structure is based on the LAP-D (link access procedure–D-channel) protocol, which is a layer 2 protocol of the ISDN suite almost identical to LAP-B (link access protocol—balanced).

8 bits	16 bits	Variable	16 bits	8 bits
Flag	Address field	Information	FCS	Flag

Frame relay implementation of LAP-D incorporates the data link connection identifier (DLCI) and congestion bits in the address field. Consequently, the frame relay header is 2 bytes in length and has the following format:

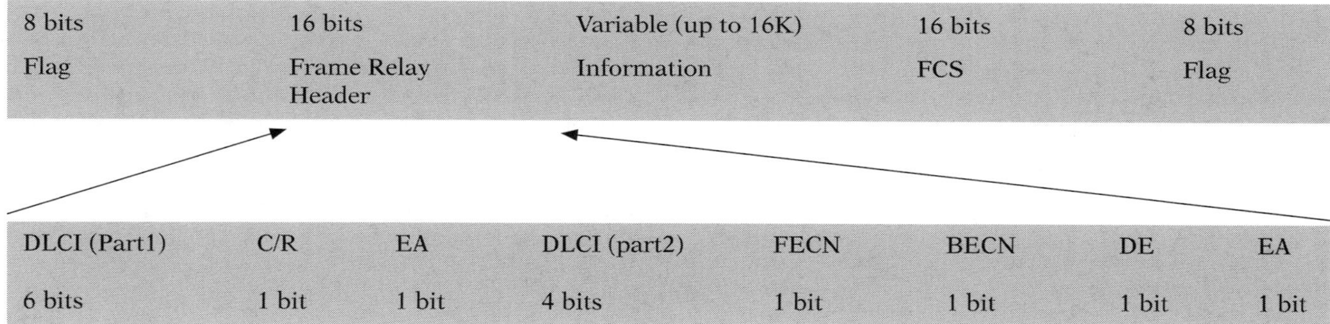

• Flag (X'7E') is the frame delimiter

DLCI is a multipart field that identifies virtual channel mapping onto the physical channel. Several virtual connections can be multiplexed over the same physical channel. And because DLCI values have local significance only devices at the different ends of a virtual channel may use different DLCIs for the same virtual channel. Valid values for DLCI are as follows:

- 0 – reserved for ANSI Annex D and ITU Annex A link management
- 1–15 – reserved
- 16 – 1007 any PVC
- 1008–1018 – reserved
- 1019 – 1022 reserved for LMI multicast
- 1023 – reserved for LMI link management

- EA (extended address) indicates if additional octets follow. EA=0 means more octets will follow. EA = 1 signifies the last octet of the header. Current frame relay implementations use a 2-octet DLCI, however, provisions for longer DLCIs managed by the EA bit are included in the protocol.
  - C/R (command/response)
  - FECN (forward explicit congestion notification)
  - BECN (backward explicit congestion notification)
  - DE (discard eligibility)

  Frame relay congestion handling mechanism is implemented by utilization of these last three bits in the frame relay header address field.
  - FCS (frame check sequence) based on the CRC algorithm allows frame integrity and error detection

As some of the definitions in the original frame relay specifications were quite vague, leaving room for interpretation by different vendors, interoperability "challenges" imposed a need for enhancement of the protocol. The consortium of the four companies, listed earlier in the historical overview section of this chapter (Cisco Systems, Digital Equipment Corporation [now part of HP], Northern Telecom, and Stratacom [now part of Cisco]) developed set of enhancement to the basic frame relay protocol called LMI (local management interface), which is a set of enhancements to the basic frame relay specification often called extensions.

Key LMI extensions include global addressing, virtual circuit status messages, and multicasting.

Below is an LMI frame format:

Flag	LMI DLCI	LAP-D Unnumbered Indicator	Protocol Discriminator	Call Reference	Message Type	Information	FCS	EA
1 octet	2 octets	1 octet	1 octet	1 octet	1 octet	Variable	2 octets	1 octet

New fields depicted in the above figure serve the following functions:

- LMI DLCI identifies the frame as an LMI frame as opposed to a basic frame relay frame. The LMI-specific DLCI value defined in the LMI consortium specification is DLCI = 1023 or DLCI = 0 defined by ANSI and ITU.
- LAP-D Unnumbered Indicator (X'03') sets the poll/final bit to zero.
- Protocol discriminator contains a value indicating that the frame is an LMI frame.
- Call reference (X'00') currently not in use.
- Message type identifies the frame as one of the following message types:
  - Status-inquiry message—device can inquire the status of the network.
  - Status message—response to status-inquiry messages, which includes report type, keepalives, and PVC status messages.

The LMI global addressing extension enables global DLCI values as opposed to values of local significance, where DLCIs were only significant to the physical channel they reside on. As a DLCI value can now be associated with DTE addresses that are unique in the frame relay WAN, the global addressing extension adds important functionality and manageability to frame relay networks. LMI virtual circuit status messages are used to periodically report on the status of PVCs, which in turn allows identification of non-existing PVCs and their removal from active circuits lists.

The LMI multicasting extension enables multicast group assignment that saves bandwidth by allowing routing updates and address-resolution messages to be sent only to specific groups of devices. With LMI multicasting a device sends a frame on a reserved DLCI known as a multicast group. The network replicates the relevant frame and delivers it to a predefined list of DLCIs: that is, multicasting a single frame to a collection of destinations in the group. The LMI multicast extension also transmits reports on the status of multicast groups in updatemessages.

Flow Control

To achieve high performance at a lower cost, designers of frame relay protocol decided to implement highly simplified flow control. To this extent, there is no link-by-link flow control as such in frame relay networks. Whenever network performance is being degraded as a result of congestion, it simply begins discarding frames that cannot be delivered, whereas end nodes handle all flow control and error correction functions.

One of the main parameters for pricing frame relay connections that is playing a major role in flow control is CIR (committed information rate). CIR, assigned to each DLCI, is usually based on the estimated volume of traffic and obviously cannot exceed the line speed. Frame relay protocol allows bursting above the CIR, but it is always a good idea to plan a frame relay connection according to the estimated bandwidth required for sustainable operations. Capacities of frame relay networks are designed so they can guarantee the CIR at any given point in time, whereas bursting above the CIR is only offered as "best effort" and is depending on conditions and the amount of traffic from other virtual circuits sharing the frame relay infrastructure. Frames entering the network above the CIR value are marked by the traffic originator with the DE bit. In other words, when the network is congested these frames may be dropped.

Some carriers are offering so called "zero" (0) CIR connections, meaning all frames entering the network over a "0 CIR" DLCI are marked with the DE bit and eventually may be dropped. "0 CIR" connections are obviously less expensive than CIRs with real values, but subscribing to such design is actually a business decision as there is a real possibility that at certain times most of the frames sent over "0 CIR" connections might be dropped. "0 CIR," however, have assumed great popularity because of the ability of higher layers (frame relay data terminal equipment) to selectively turn the DE-bit "on" or "off." This results in higher flexibility and ability to selectively send traffic over a "0 CIR" DLCI with the DE-bit turned off, when network conditions allow.

Performance and Congestion Management

Congestion management in frame relay networks includes the following functions:

- Admission control is the principle technique used in frame relay networks to guarantee allocation of required resources. Based on the characteristics of requested traffic and network capacity existing at a certain time the frame relay network decides whether a new connection is possible. Traffic descriptor is a set of parameters communicated to the switching nodes during virtual circuit setup based on statistical characteristics of the new connection. Traffic descriptor consists of the following three elements:
  - CIR: average rate at which frame relay network is capable of guaranteeing information transfer without oversubscription.
  - Committed burst size: maximum rate that can be transmitted during given time.
  - Excess burst size: maximum rate that the network will attempt to carry during given time.
- Explicit congestion notification is imbedded in the frame relay protocol as a congestion avoidance mechanism. When a virtual circuit is established in a frame relay network, the end nodes must monitor the traffic flow to ensure that the actual usage of network resources does not exceed this specification avoiding accumulation of undelivered data within the network.

According to the simple yet smart algorithm of frame relay networks, whenever the network becomes congested to a point where no new frames can be transmitted it simply begins discarding frames. However, as a result of requests from the higher layers of the ISO reference model the discarded frames eventually need to be retransmitted, which, in turn may cause even higher network congestion (Peterson and Davie 1996). To avoid this potentially dangerous network meltdown frame relay includes congestion management functionality. Frames with FECN value of 1 are sent downstream toward the destination location, when congestion occurs during data transmission, thus all downstream nodes including the egress device learn about congestion on the line. Similarly, BECN value is changed to 1 in frames traveling back toward the ingress device on congested paths warning the device to slow down transmission until the congestion situation is resolved. Thus, BECN = 1 has a more significant meaning from an operational stand point and it's very important making sure frame relay devices support it and know to act properly notifying the higher layers of the OSI Reference Model about the required slowdown in transmissions. FECN is generally implemented in FRDTEs with the following logic: if a frame arrives with FECN = 1, and the retry timer has not expired [within a certain arbitrary or configurable period], then no action is taken; if a frame arrives with FECN = 1, and the retry parameter has not expired, but the period is beyond the "allowable" value, the expiration timer is adjusted; if a frame arrives with FECN = 1, and the retry timer has expired, the expiration timer is adjusted, and retry is reset until the retry timer is exceeded once again (or a subsequent frame arrives with FECN = 1.)

DE bit in a frame relay network comes into play when a network is severely congested. Obviously, dropping discard-eligible frames will relieve congestion in the network so that frames not eligible for discard have a better chance of passing successfully through the network. It is the responsibility of the frame relay DTE to set the DE bits on so that the frame relay DCE (i.e., frame relay frame handler [FRFH]) knows which frames to discard in order to protect itself in case of severe congestion. However, if the FRFH's DLCI queue is full and the DTE continues sending frames with no DE set, the FRFH will mark all frames from that DTE as discard-eligible, notifying the DTE it has exceeded its committed burst. In a frame relay network handling different high-level application protocols, for example, legacy SNA and TCP/IP, during a mild congestion, most SNA applications will slow down by reducing the window size to avoid frame loss and the need to retransmit. However, typical TCP/IP applications ignore the mild congestion and continue to send frames until severe congestion occurs on their DLCI. Then, during severe congestion, FRFH discards TCP/IP frames so that frame loss will cause TCP/IP to slow. "Technically" speaking, response time for the "polite" SNA frame relay users will suffer during mild congestion; however, they are less likely to get into severe congestion trouble. "Impolite" TCP/IP users that cannot throttle down during mild congestion will definitely get into severe congestion trouble causing frame losses, and consequently, retransmissions (Lynch, Gray, and Rabinovitch 1997).

Split Horizon

Configuration of split horizon (Peterson and Davie 1996) is a very important characteristic to keep in mind, while designing partially meshed frame relay networks. By default, split horizon is disabled for frame relay networks, so routing updates can come in and out the same network interface. When the routers learn the DLCIs they need to use through LMI update messages they use inverse ARP for the remote IP address to create routing maps for local DLCIs to their respective remote IP addresses. However, because certain protocols require split horizon enabled, where a packet received on an interface cannot be transmitted out the same interface even if it is transmitted on different virtual circuits, partially meshed frame relay networks cannot be configured for protocols such as AppleTalk or IPX. To overcome such issues, frame relay sub-interfaces can be configured, whereby a single physical interface is now being treated as multiple virtual

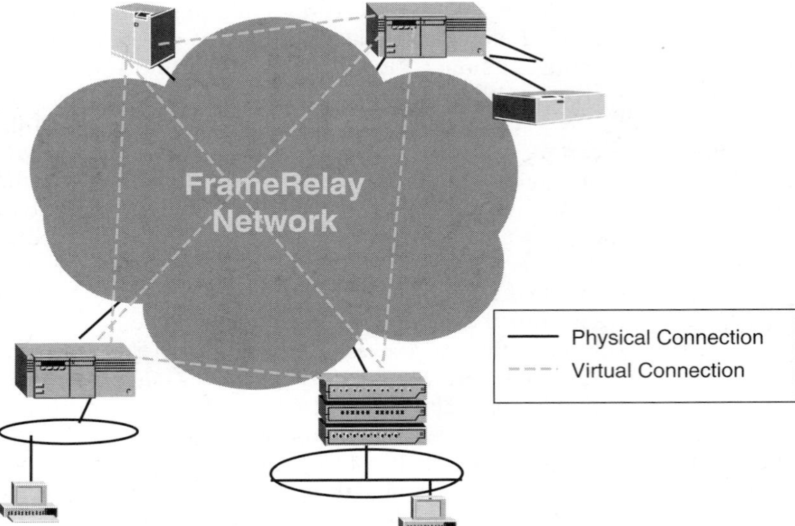

Figure 1: Frame relay network "cloud"

interfaces. This type of configuration allows overcoming split horizon rules for legacy protocols so packets received on one virtual interface will be forwarded out another virtual interface, even though both are configured over the same physical interface.

STANDARDS AND STANDARD BODIES

MFA Forum

To speed up the adoption and interoperability of frame relay technology among different vendors and carriers Frame Relay Forum was incorporated in May of 1991 as a non-profit organization. In April 2003, Frame Relay and MPLS forum merged into a new organization—MPLS & Frame Relay Alliance, which in April 2005 merged with the ATM Forum into a new organization currently known as the MFA Forum: www.mfaforum.org.

As it is known now: "The MFA Forum is an international, industry-wide, nonprofit association of telecommunications, networking, and other companies focused on advancing the deployment of multi-vendor, multi-service packet-based networks, associated applications, and interworking solutions. Through the efforts of the technical and marketing committees the forum encourages: (a) input to the development of standards throughout the various industry standards groups; (b) the creation of Specifications, based upon appropriate standards, on how to build and deliver MPLS, Frame Relay and ATM networks and services; (c) the definition of Interoperability test suites and coordination of Interoperability events to demonstrate the readiness of MPLS for network deployments; (d) the creation and delivery of educational programs to educate the industry about MPLS, Frame Relay and ATM technologies, services and solutions; and (e) building the awareness of MPLS as a technology ready for wide-scale deployment within service provider networks to deliver profitable services to the end-user community."

Some of the important specifications developed by what is known as the MFA Forum today include UNI (user-network interface), NNI (network-network interface), and FUNI (frame-based user-network interface). UNI/NNI interfaces define roles, transmission rates, service levels, and error recovery within the frame relay network. UNI defines interoperability between end points on the LAN and the end points of the frame relay network "cloud" (see Figure 1), whether NNI describes interconnection between frame relay network providers within the "cloud." In the mid-90s the original ATM Forum (MFA Forum now) had developed FUNI interworking specifications for ATM switches to frame relay devices offering packet delivery service that includes error detection, but not error correction—Greenstein (1995). It is also important to mention additional IWF (inter-working function) specifications developed by the Forum for connectivity between frame relay networks over ATM backbone. Additional information on ATM can be found in "ATM (Asynchronous Transfer Mode)."

Although, membership in the MFA Forum is required for access to specific programs or committees, a wealth of information is also available on their Web site for free and readers interested in frame relay, ATM, or MPLS technologies are strongly encouraged to use the MFA Forum Web site as a reference.

It is important to note, however, the MFA Forum does not develop standard specifications, but rather promotes and uses those specifications developed by the standard organizations, like ANSI, IEEE, IETF, ITU, and others.

ITU (International Telecommunications Union)

The ITU (www.itu.int) is part of the United Nations organization dealing with global telecommunications and service issues. ITU-T is a section within the ITU that was created on March 1, 1993, replacing the former CCITT organization) whose origins go back to 1865. CCITT (or the ITU-T now) has a very long history designing and promoting different telecommunications standards, with frame relay being one of such standards.

Recommendations and reference information for different frame relay standards handled by the ITU-T can be found on their Web site. Following is a list of these recommendations:

X.33: Access to packet-switched data transmission services via frame relaying data transmission services

X.36: Interface between data terminal equipment (DTE) and data circuit-terminating equipment (DCE) for public data networks providing frame relay data

X.37: Encapsulation in X.25 packets of various protocols including frame relay

X.76: Network-to-network interface between public networks providing PVC and/or SVC frame relay data transmission service

X.78: Interworking procedures between networks providing frame relay data transmission services via B-ISDN

X.84: Support of frame relay services over MPLS core networks

X.111: Principles for the routing of international frame relay traffic

X.124: Arrangements for the interworking of the E.164 and X.121 numbering plans for frame relay and ATM networks

X.125: Procedure for the notification of the assignment of international network identification codes for public frame relay data networks and ATM networks numbered under the E.164 numbering plan

X.142: Quality of service metrics for characterizing frame relay /ATM service interworking performance

X.144: User information transfer performance parameters for public frame relay data networks

X.145: Connection establishment and dis-engagement performance parameters for public frame relay data networks providing SVC services

X.146: Performance objectives and quality of service classes applicable to frame relay

X.147: Frame relay network availability

X.148: Procedures for the measurement of the performance of public data networks providing the international frame relay service

X.149: Performance of IP networks when supported by public frame relay data networks

X.151: Frame relay operations and maintenance—principles and functions

X.272: Data compression and privacy over frame relay networks

X.328: General arrangements for interworking between public data networks providing frame relay data transmission services and integrated services digital networks (ISDNs) for the provision of data transmission services

X.329: General arrangements for interworking between networks providing frame relay data transmission services and B-ISDN

IETF RFCs

Important standardization work for frame relay was also done by the IETF that also developed several RFCs for frame relay networks:

RFC 1293: Inverse Address Resolution Protocol (January 1992).

RFC 1586: Guidelines for running OSPF over frame relay networks (March 1994).

RFC 1973: PPP in frame relay (June 1996)

RFC 2115: Management information base for frame relay DTEs using SMIv2 (September 1997).

RFC 2427: Multiprotocol interconnect over frame relay (September 1998).

RFC 2590: Transmission of IPv6 packets over frame relay networks (May 1999).

RFC 2954: Definitions of managed objects for frame relay service (October 2000).

RFC 2955: Definitions of managed objects for monitoring and controlling the frame relay/ATM PVC service interworking function (October 2000).

RFC 3020: Definitions of managed objects for monitoring and controlling the UNI/NNI multilink frame relay function (December 2000).

RFC 3034: Use of label switching on frame relay networks specification (January 2001).

RFC 3070: Layer two tunneling protocol (L2TP) over frame relay (February 2001).

RFC 3133: Terminology for frame relay benchmarking (June 2001).

RFC 3202: Definitions of managed objects for frame relay service level definitions (January 2002).

In the section of this chapter dedicated to network management we will provide additional details on frame relay MIBs (RFC 2115 its predecessor 1315, 2954, 2955, 3020, and 3202). And in another section on frame relay in enterprise networks we will focus on one of the more important standards multiprotocol interconnects (RFC 2427 and its predecessors RFC 1294 and ARFC 1490) that played a significant role in transferring mission critical enterprise legacy protocols over frame relay WAN.

NETWORK MANAGEMENT

Troubleshooting

To get a practical perspective on frame relay network design and management techniques let's start with a description of the equipment, physical, and logical circuits comprising any frame relay network. Probably the most important devices at the heart of a frame relay network are the so-called FRADs (frame relay assembler/disassembler)—networking equipment that assembles and disassembles data frames. In fact, many networking devices that encapsulate other protocols into frame relay protocol are FRADs, that is, routers/switches encapsulating Ethernet, TCP/IP protocol, legacy protocols, and so on and performing frame assembly/disassembly are indeed FRADs. The same is true for devices performing encoding and encapsulation of voice and video streams into frame relay. Although, as we mentioned earlier, as a result of the nonhomogenous and bursty nature of frame relay networks, neither voice nor video implementation over frame relay became popular, occasionally we may still find such implementations here and there.

Because frame relay is a connection-oriented end-to-end protocol at any given point in time in a frame relay network, connections (or virtual circuits) exist between pair of devices utilizing the network. These virtual circuits provide bidirectional communications paths and are uniquely identified by DLCIs. Because multiple virtual circuits can be multiplexed over a single physical circuit, both network complexity and costs are significantly reduced in comparison with dedicated leased lines. And it's also very important to keep in mind the multiplexing logical over physical circuits capability of frame relay networks as well as the fact that a virtual circuit in frame relay network can pass through a large number of intermediate network switches. Thus, correlation between virtual circuits and their physical paths is extremely important for designing, managing, and troubleshooting the network.

One additional notable comment: originally designed as an end-to-end network topology, in the mid-1990s many frame relay networks had migrated to an ATM core further converting to MPLS in the late 1990s. And as was mentioned earlier, the MFA Forum played a very important role in enabling this transformation process by leading the effort and defining the UNI/NNI and NNI/NNI specifications for frame relay to ATM and frame relay to MPLS conversions.

There are two types of virtual circuits in frame relay networks: SVC (switched virtual circuit) and PVC (permanent virtual circuits).

An SVC is a temporary connection used when only sporadic data transfer between frame relay devices is required. SVC sessions consist of the following four states:

- **Call setup**—virtual circuit between two frame relay devices is established.
- **Data transfer**—data is actively being transferred between the devices.
- **Idle**—connection is active, but no actual data is being transferred. Typically, when the SVC stays idle a predefined period of time, the circuit will be terminated.
- **Call termination**—virtual circuit is being terminated.

A new SVC has to be created in order to transfer data after a virtual circuit has been terminated. Because frame relay was developed as part of BISDN standard setup, maintenance, and termination of SVC utilizes the same signaling protocols as defined in BISDN. It's important to note, though, that implementation of SVCs in frame relay network is very limited as most networks are using PVCs (permanent virtual circuits).

Contrary to SVCs, PVCs are permanently established connections used for frequent and consistent data transfers between devices across the frame relay network. Therefore, call setup and termination would only occur when a DLCI comes up or brought down either explicitly or because of restart as a result of error recovery circuit setup and termination. Hence, a PVC can only operate in one of the two following states:

- Data transfer—data is actively being transferred between the devices.
- Idle—connection is active, but no actual data is being transferred.

Because PVCs constitute permanent connections the virtual circuit will not be terminated regardless how long it was in an idle state.

One of the inherent mechanisms for examining and enforcing reliability of a frame relay network is the CRC algorithm used in FCS of frame relay packets. The CRC compares the calculated value with the value included in the FCS part of the frame to determine whether an error occurred during the transmission.

Let's describe some typical situations and techniques for troubleshooting frame relay connections. For purposes of description, let's use the terminology and examples from a popular frame relay device—Cisco router. Below are the different statuses a frame relay connection may be presented on a Cisco device:

- Both interface and line protocol are down: typically points to a physical connectivity problem. The first and simplest troubleshooting procedure at this point is testing the connection in a loopback mode.
- Interface is up while line protocol is down: at this point the router is receiving carrier signal from the CSU/DSU or modem. However, there is a problem with frame relay configuration settings. Make sure the carrier has activated their port and that the LMI settings match. Next step would be performing circuit integrity testing by using loopback tests at different points all the way from the port on the local device to the port on carrier's frame relay equipment. Another typical problem that may cause this situation is misconfiguration of DLCI numbers.
- Both the interface and line protocol are up: this typically means a reliable frame relay connection has been established. It's important to note that keepalive messages are necessary for frame relay networks, as this is the means for local frame relay devices to know which DLCIs have been provisioned.
- Using the debug mechanism on Cisco's equipment is a good way to monitor frame relay connections. Not as with other instances of using the debug function *"debug frame-relay lmi"* generates few messages only and is a good troubleshooting technique that can provide an answer to the following important questions:
  - Are we receiving full LMI status messages for the PVCs from the carrier?
  - Are the DLCIs correct?
  - Is the other end of the PVC up or down?

Problem Determination

Let's continue with more comprehensive problem determination scenario using our example of Cisco routers that can be used both as FRADs as well as carriers' frame relay switches. First, it's important to setup the keepalive on frame relay switches higher than it is on the FRADs. For problem determination, the following commands can be issued:

- On FRADs:
  show interface serial0 and/or *show frame-relay lmi* - confirming LMI is exchanged
  show frame-relay pvc—to check if FRAD knows about PVC
  show frame-relay map—to confirm DLCI is mapped to IP
- On the frame relay switch:
  show frame-relay route—to check how frames are switched

Designers of the frame relay had included multiple provisioning for network management and problem determination. Following are some the status information exchanges included in frame relay networks:

Link integrity verification timer: specifies how frequently the FRAD initiates a status inquiry message. The valid values are between 5 to 30 seconds, with the default value of 10 seconds.

Status information: is a standard inquiry from a frame relay device performed every time the link integrity verification timer expires. The status inquiry returns status information about the network. Also, by sending such inquiries the FRAD is confirming to the frame relay carrier equipment that it is in service. If a status inquiry is not sent, the network will generate an alarm.

Full status inquiry: also returns all of the active DLCI numbers. Its frequency ranges from 1 to 255, meaning full status inquiry will be the only inquiry sent by the FRAD (value = 1) or on each 254 status information inquiries one full status inquiry is sent (value-255). The default value is 6, which means the user equipment sends 5 regular status inquiries, then the full status inquiry.

Management Tools

A vast majority of the standard SNMP-based management tools have good interfaces for managing frame relay networks. Frame relay MIBs provide information that allows standard network management tools to obtain performance information, monitor status and configuration information. The MIB allows not just monitoring, but also implementation of certain operational and configuration commands: that is, adding, deleting, or modifying PVCs, turning selected PVCs on or off, and so on. Based on SNMP information received from different parts and devices in the frame relay network, a management tool can also obtain a detailed status of internal elements of the network, although not necessarily from the frame relay MIBs: that is, network cards and ports, routing tables, and so on (Stallings, 1997).

SNMP information can be obtained by issuing SNMP poll commands or from traps generated by the SNMP agents. Frame relay status inquiry information described in the previous section can also be obtained through SNMP polling. And because frame relay networks are typically shared between different service subscribers the MIBs support granularity necessary to provide only access to the relevant parts of the network, such as interfaces and PVCs to the eligible parties.

SNMP enables network management tools to gather important information from the frame relay MIBs that are composed of three groups. Samples of information obtained from frame relay networks by SNMP management tools include:

- Group for DLCI management interface offers port statistics, such as:
  - Signaling state
  - Signaling state downtime
  - Port unavailable time
- Group describing the circuits offers PVC statistics
  - Throughput (Tx/Rx, max/average)
  - Utilization (Tx/Rx, max/average)
  - Frame relay network delay (max/average)
- Group describing the errors

SUMMARY

Frame Relay—Current Status

In general, frame relay networks are provisioned by carriers (or service providers) offering services to different end users—that is, public frame relay service, whereas so-called private frame relay networks are deployed and maintained by enterprises. The vast majority of frame relay networks are public networks, whereas carriers' infrastructure and equipment is essentially shared by several end users. However, several typically large enterprises had also deployed private frame relay networks, where they own and maintain not just the peripheral equipment connecting to the frame relay "cloud" but also the "cloud" itself. In some cases private frame relay networks are also being implemented on "shared" equipment owned by an ISP. The SLA given by the service providers in such cases today is their commitment to map the PVC in the network core over exclusive LSPs (label switched paths). Additional information about label switching can be is provided in Chapter 92 dedicated to MPLS.

In the mid-1990s, market researcher Vertical Systems Group (Dedham, MA) predicted sales of frame relay access equipment to more than triple in the next three years from $171.8 million in 1995 to $613.4 million by 1998 (Rabinovitch, 1996). Obviously, given recent developments in WAN technologies, such a trend was not expected to continue. On the contrary, many market pundits predicted that frame relay was going to be displaced by the ATM technology. Surprisingly enough, frame relay technology proved to be so reliable and cost effective that this transition to ATM never really happened. And despite the fact users are migrating to newer technologies and the vast majority of new installations today are using MPLS or even Metro Ethernet, the total number of frame relay ports installed almost did not change and was estimated at more than 2 million ports in 2005, generating revenue in excess of $16B for the carriers.

The emerging trend, especially for public frame relay networks, is to migrate to so-called "hybrid" networks, where end-users are still using frame relay PVC connections, but instead of going end-to-end on a frame relay "cloud." frame relay PVCs are terminated in carriers' point of presence from where it's being carried over an MPLS network. In addition to new application requirements, such as voice over IP, video, and other multimedia applications requiring QoS differentiation cost is another major driver for migration from pure frame relay networks to MPLS networks. Because frame relay services are being priced according to the CIR and distance, long-haul PVCs are typically the first candidates for migration. And work performed by the MFA Forum described in the section above, assures smooth migration path to the newer technologies. In fact, migration of the core of the network to MPLS (with the PVCs terminating at the edge) had actually started in the early 2000s, when the major carriers started converging their dissimilar networks onto a single core topology, predominantly MPLS.

Enterprise Perspective

Popularity of frame relay networks in the 1990s introduced a new alternative for legacy network transport facilities in the form of multiprotocol interconnect over frame relay standard—RFC 2427. This standard allows transport of multiple protocols over the same access line and even the same DLCI. Although access devices allow separate queues for different protocols and a protocol-level prioritization scheme within the frame relay cloud, there are no provisions for legacy protocol prioritization. RFC 2427 supports protocol mixing for a single DLCI, in most implementations mission-critical legacy traffic is being separated from the less critical traffic on different DLCIs, with a higher CIR. So enterprises using frame relay networks for multiprotocol consolidation are always taking precautions to isolate mission-critical traffic from less critical applications.

Because of difference in behavior of different high-level protocols (i.e., legacy SNA and TCP/IP) as described in the section about Performance and Congestion Control above, "considerate" legacy SNA applications are reacting to mild congestions in frame relay networks by modifying the window size. "Inconsiderate" TCP/IP applications typically ignore mild congestion, instead increasing TCP window-size, and only reacting to severe congestion by eventually discarding frames (Lynch, Gray, and Rabinovitch, 1997). Therefore, capacity planning in a consolidated multiprotocol frame relay network becomes a challenging task sometimes resulting in over-provisioning.

Service Providers Perspective

Even though frame relay services are not as popular as they were a few years ago mainly because MPLS VPNs and even Metro Ethernet services are available in more and more places now, carriers are still offering frame relay services for new installations. Obviously, from a financial standpoint, it makes a lot of sense for service providers, because their edge frame switches are already depreciated, thus they can offer new circuits with minimal implementation costs, so the resulting revenues consist of almost pure profits. It's also important to mention, that if the original specifications for frame relay access were in the 56kbps to T1/E1 speed range, subsequently, T3/E3 speeds for frame relay access became available too. And in December of 1998, the Frame Relay Forum (now MFA Forum) ratified "Physical Layer Interface Implementation Agreement" FRF.14 for introducing support of OC3 and even OC12 access to frame relay services.

As was shown above frame relay remains an important source of revenue for service providers. However, with growing customer demand to accommodate multiprotocol and emerging multimedia applications at lower price points carriers are increasingly looking at deploying new but already proven technologies, such as MPLS VPNs or Metro Ethernet. Many carriers are already deploying both Metro Ethernet and MPLS VPN technologies in different locations all over the world, including North America, Europe, Central America, and Asia. In the United States, Metro Ethernet services are available not only from the major carriers but also the cable companies. An even a more important technology for WAN heavily lobbied by service providers is MPLS. Both MPLS tunneling (or MPLS at layer 2) and MPLS VPN (or MPLS at layer 3) are being aggressively pursued by service providers. Hybrid networks are integrating frame relay access with MPLS network cores, where DLCIs are being mapped to MPLS LSPs. Because MPLS tunneling is by nature a multiprotocol technology, it can natively support both IP and legacy traffic. The fact customers can still use their existing frame relay equipment while migrating to a hybrid network environment would also make such migration projects more affordable. And service providers can continue to support frame relay services while expanding their core infrastructure and positioning themselves for new Metro Ethernet and MPLS offerings.

CONCLUSION

Frame relay technology has been optimized for statistical multiplexing providing the same bandwidth-sharing and efficiency as its predecessor X.25. Statistical multiplexing means that no bandwidth is allocated to virtual circuits until actual data needs to be transmitted. Then, the bandwidth within the network is dynamically allocated on a frame-by-frame basis. If, for a short period of time, more data needs to be transmitted than the transmission facilities can accommodate, the switches within the network will buffer the data for later transmission. If this oversubscription persists, congestion control mechanisms are invoked.

Frame relay was developed based on experience gained from X.25, and took into account the modern digital physical network infrastructure, which became much more resilient and reliable. In comparison with X.25, frame relay eliminates much of the protocol processing done by the network, thereby reducing the portion of the transmission latency attributed to this processing. This simplification of the protocol is based on elimination of error recovery functions, utilizing functionality in the ingress and egress points of the network to guarantee error-free end-to-end transfer of frames. This protocol processing, which is still necessary to guarantee reliable data delivery is left to the higher layers of the OSI reference model implemented by the endpoint devices.

Frame relay interface specifications provide both signaling and data transfer mechanisms between endpoints and the network. This interface allows communication bandwidth to be shared among multiple users, creating instantaneous bandwidth allocation on demand. Each frame contains header information that is used to determine the routing of the data to the desired destination. This enables each endpoint to communicate with multiple destinations via a single access link to the network. Instead of fixed amounts of bandwidth allocated to the resource, frame relay traffic receives full bandwidth for short transaction bursts.

Let's briefly reiterate the main benefits of frame relay networks:

- Reduced internetworking costs,
- Increased performance with reduced network complexity, and
- Increased interoperability via international standards.

Reduced internetworking costs: when using a private frame relay network, statistically multiplexed traffic from multiple sources over private backbone networks can reduce the number of circuits and corresponding cost of bandwidth in the WAN. And public frame relay services always offer cost savings, when compared with the equivalent services over dedicated leased lines. Because frame relay provides multiple logical connections over a single physical connection, access costs are also reduced. Additionally, equipment costs may be lowered by reducing the number of ports required to access the network. For remote access devices, access line charges can also be lowered by reducing the number of physical circuits needed to reach the networks.

Increased performance with reduced network complexity: by reducing the amount of processing in comparison to X.25, and by efficiently utilizing high-speed digital transmission lines, frame relay can improve performance and response times of applications. Frame relay also reduces the complexity of the physical network without disrupting higher level network functions. In fact, it actually utilizes the existence of these higher layer protocols to its advantage. Frame relay also provides a common network transport for multiple traffic types while maintaining transparency to higher level protocols unique to the individual traffic types. Addressing information contained in the network frames enables the network to route them to the proper destination.

Increased interoperability via international standards: Frame relay is a well-established protocol accepted by networking vendors and service providers. Simplicity of the frame relay protocol accommodates quick and easy interoperability testing procedures between devices from different vendors, and the MFA Forum sponsors interoperability testing among different equipment manufacturers as well as between the different protocols it is responsible for: that is, frame relay, ATM, and MPLS.

Some industry pundits have labeled frame relay as an "interim technology." As a matter of fact, any technology is "interim," providing a basis for a better and improved technology in the future. The important question, however, is how long the "interim" technology will survive and is it going to offer return on investment? Obviously, based on the status of frame relay technology for over more than a decade, and its positioning today both by enterprises and service providers, frame relay is indeed a very interesting and successful "interim" technology that offered sizeable return on investment. Frame relay proved to be a reliable and cost-effective solution for WAN from the 1990s until today.

ACKNOWLEDGMENT

I would like to thank all the reviewers for their comments and suggestions that helped to improve this chapter making it more interesting and comprehensive. Especial thanks goes to a long time friend and colleague Robert Downing of IP Infusion, former President of the Frame Relay Forum, for his valuable feedback and remarks.

GLOSSARY

BECN: Backward explicit congestion notification is a header bit transmitted by the destination terminal requesting that the source terminal send data more slowly.

CIR: Committed information rate is bandwidth (in bits per second) associated with a logical connection in a permanent virtual circuit—see PVC.

DE: Discard eligibility is a header bit signifying the frame was sent above the CIR and, thus, is eligible for discard during network congestions.

DLCI: Data link connection identifier is a multipart field that identifies virtual channel mapping onto the physical channel.

FECN: Forward explicit congestion notification is a header bit transmitted by the source (sending) terminal requesting that the destination (receiving) terminal slow down its requests for data.

FRAD: Frame relay assembler/dissembler also sometimes referred to as frame relay access device is a box that encapsulates data packets and decapsulates (removes frame relay headers and trailers from) incoming packets.

Frame Relay Forum: Now part of the MFA (MPLS-Frame Relay-ATM) Forum is an international, industry-wide, nonprofit association of telecommunications, networking, and other companies focused on advancing the deployment of multi-vendor, multi-service packet-based networks, associated applications, and interworking solutions.

LMI: Local management interface is a set of enhancements to the basic frame relay specification often called extensions. Key LMI extensions include global addressing, virtual circuit status messages, and multicasting.

MIB for frame relay: (also see RFC 2115) Defines a portion of the management information base (MIB) for use with network management protocols in SNMP managed networks, which defines objects for managing frame relay interfaces on DTEs.

Multiprotocol over frame relay: (also see RFC 2427) Is a standard that allows transport of multiple protocols over the same access line and even the same DLCI. Although access devices allow separate queues for different protocols and a protocol-level prioritization scheme within the frame relay cloud there are no provisions for legacy protocol prioritization. RFC 2427 supports protocol mixing for a single DLCI, in most implementations mission-critical legacy traffic is being separated from the less critical traffic on different DLCIs, with a higher CIR.

PVC: Permanent virtual circuit is a software-defined logical connection in a frame relay network.

RFC 2115: (also see MIB for frame relay) Defines a portion of the management information base (MIB) for use with network management protocols in SNMP managed networks, which defines objects for managing frame relay interfaces on DTEs.

RFC 2427: (also see multiprotocol over frame relay) Is a standard that allows transport of multiple protocols over the same access line and even the same DLCI. Although access devices allow separate queues for different protocols and a protocol-level prioritization scheme within the frame relay cloud there are no provisions for legacy protocol prioritization. RFC 2427 supports protocol mixing for a single DLCI, in most implementations mission-critical legacy traffic is being separated from the less critical traffic on different DLCIs, with a higher CIR.

Split horizon: Is a method of preventing a routing loop in a network, whereby the information about routing for a particular frame is never sent back in the direction from which it was received.

SVC: Switched virtual circuit is a temporary virtual circuit that is established and maintained only for the duration of a data transfer session.

CROSS REFERENCES

See *BISDN (Broadband Integrated Services Digital Network); Packet Switching; Terrestrial Wide Area Networks.*

REFERENCES

Greenstein, L. 1995. Frame relay and frame-based ATM: A comparison of technologies. http://www.mfaforum.org/frame/Whitepaper/fratm/fratm.toc.shtml (accessed May 2, 2007).

Lynch, D., J. P. Gray, and E. Rabinovitch. 1997. *SNA and TCP/IP enterprise networking*. Greenwich, CT: Manning Publications, Co.

Malamud, C. 1992. *Stacks*. Englewood Cliffs, NJ: Prentice-Hall, Inc.

Peterson, L. L., and B. S. Davie, B.S. 1996. *Computer networks: A system approach*. San Francisco: Morgan Kaufman Publishers, Inc.

Rabinovitch, E. 1995. *IP over SNA with frame relay—How to?* Nashville, TN, Proceedings International Conference of the Computer Measurement Group (CMG). December 4–8, 1995.

Rabinovitch, E. 1996. (Barely) managing ATM, SunWorld Online. http://sunsite.uakom.sk/sunworldonline/swol-08-1996/swol-08-atm.html (accessed May 2, 2007).

Stallings, W. 1997. *SNMP, SNMPv2, and RMON: Practical network management*. Reading, MA: Addison Wesley Longman, Inc.

FURTHER READING

MFA Forum: Education: LEARN ABOUT FRAME RELAY—White Papers. http://www.mfaforum.org/frame/frfwhitepapers2.shtml (accessed May 2, 2007).

MFA Forum: Education: LEARN ABOUT FRAME RELAY—Tutorials & Presentations. http://mfaforum.org/frame/tutorials/4014.shtml (accessed May 2, 2007).

Asynchronous Transfer Mode (ATM)

Arjan Durresi, *Louisiana State University*
Raj Jain, *Washington University, St. Louis*

INTRODUCTION

The purpose of this chapter is to introduce the reader to the basic aspects of asynchronous transfer mode (ATM) networks. The length of this short chapter makes it impossible to cover all important aspects of ATM networks. Much of the material in this chapter is based on existing tutorials on ATM, including www.iec.org/online/tutorials/atm_fund/index.html, www.telecomspace.com/vop-atm.html, www.npac.syr.edu/users/mahesh/homepage/atm_tutorial/, www.mfaforum.org/education/downloads/CDNwhtpapr.final.pdf, www.mfaforum.org/education/downloads/Del.Vid.Final.pdf, www.corning.com/docs/opticalfiber/IEC%20FTTH%20101%20Tutorialv2.pdf, McDysan and Spohn (1999), Vetter (1995), Sackett and Metz (1997), Ibe (2001), Dobrowski and Grise (2001). The industrial momentum behind ATM technology and the intensive research interest in ATM has led to a vast and diversified literature in recent years. Most of the cited references are mainly review articles or documents of ATM and MFA Forums. Readers interested in further understanding of the individual topics are referred to the corresponding papers and the references therein.

Basic Principles

Various network applications are requiring increasingly higher bandwidth and generating a heterogeneous mix of network traffic. Existing networks cannot provide the transport facilities to efficiently support a diversity of traffic with various service requirements. ATM was designed to be potentially capable of supporting heterogeneous traffic (e.g., voice, video, data) in one transmission and switching fabric technology. It promised to provide greater integration of capabilities and services, more flexible access to the network, and more efficient and economical service.

ATM is a switching and multiplexing technology that employs small, fixed-length packets (called cells). Each cell has 5 bytes of header information and a 48-byte information field (payload). The reason for choosing a fixed-size packet was to ensure that the switching and multiplexing function could be carried out quickly, easily, and with least delay variation. The reason for choosing a small size cell was mainly a result of the need to support delay-intolerant interactive voice service (e.g., phone calls) with a a small packetization delay, i.e., the time needed to fill a cell with PCM (pulse code modulation) encoded voice samples arriving at the rate of 64 Kbps.

ATM is a connection-oriented technology in the sense that before two systems on the network can communicate, they should inform all intermediate switches about their service requirements and traffic parameters. This is similar to the telephone networks where a fixed path is set up from the calling party to the receiving party. In ATM networks, each connection is called a virtual circuit or virtual channel (VC), because it also allows the capacity of each link to be shared by connections using that link on a demand basis rather than by fixed allocations. The connections allow the network to guarantee the quality of service (QoS) by limiting the number of VCs. Typically, a user declares key service requirements at the time of connection setup, declares the traffic parameters, and may agree to control these parameters dynamically as demanded by the network.

ATM was intended to provide a single unified networking standard that could support both synchronous and asynchronous technologies and services, while offering multiple levels of quality of service for packet traffic.

ATM sought to resolve the conflict between circuit-switched networks and packet-switched networks by mapping both bit streams and packet streams onto a stream of small fixed-size "cells" tagged with virtual circuit identifiers. Cells are typically sent on demand within a synchronous time slot pattern in a synchronous bit stream: what is asynchronous here is the sending of the cells, not the low-level bitstream that carries them.

In its original conception, ATM was to be the enabling technology of the "broadband integrated services digital network" (B-ISDN) that would replace the existing narrowband "integrated services digital network (ISDN). The full suite of ATM standards provides definitions for layer 1 (physical connections), layer 2 (data link layer), and layer 3 (network) of the classical OSI seven-layer networking model. Because ATM is asynchronous, it provides true bandwidth-on-demand. Additionally, ATM is capable of handling any form of information (e.g., data, voice, video, audio, e-mail, faxes), moving this information quickly across a network with millions of virtual paths and channels between end-user equipment.

ATM allows the user to select the required level of service, provides guaranteed service quality, and makes reservations and preplans routes so those transmissions needing the most attention are given the best service.

The MFA Forum, ITU, and ANSI

With the objective of accelerating the convergence of standards and industry cooperation, an international consortium called the ATM Forum was founded to ensure interoperability between public and private ATM implementations and to promote the use of ATM products and services. Although it was not a standard body, the ATM Forum worked closely with standard organizations such as the International Telecommunications Union (ITU) and Internet Engineering Task Force (IETF) in developing the definitions for ATM standards. In 2005 the ATM Forum was merged in MPLS Frame Relay and ATM Forum—MFA Forum, which is an international, industry-wide, nonprofit association of telecommunications, networking, and other companies focused on advancing the deployment of multi-vendor, multi-service packet-based networks, associated applications, and interworking solutions.

The ITU is rooted in the International Telegraphy Union, founded in Paris in 1865. Its name changed in 1934, and in 1947 the ITU became an agency of the United Nations.The ITU works with public and private organizations to develop earth-linked and satellite communications, while developing standards for all types of telecommunication technology.

The ITU-Telecommunication Standardization Sector (ITU-T) is the leader in defining integrated services digital network (ISDN), B-ISDN, and ATM specifications. The American National Standards Institute (ANSI) is the formal standards body guiding the development of ATM in the United States.

New Developments

Numerous telcos have implemented wide-area ATM networks, and many ADSL implementations use ATM. However, ATM has failed to gain wide use as a LAN technology, and its great complexity has held back its full deployment as the single integrating network technology in the way that its inventors originally intended.

Many people, particularly in the Internet protocol-design community, considered this vision to be mistaken. Although there is a need for a unifying protocol at network layer, to be able to run over all existing and future link-layer technologies, ATM could not do this role. Conveniently, IP already plays the role of such an integrator in a more scalable, more flexible, less complex, and most importantly, less expensive way than ATM could do. Therefore, there was no point in implementing ATM as an integrator at the network layer.

In addition, the need for cells to reduce jitter has disappeared as transport speeds increased (see below), and improvements in voice over IP have made the integration of speech and data possible at the IP layer, again removing the incentive for ubiquitous deployment of ATM. Most telcos are now planning to integrate their voice network activities into their IP networks, rather than their IP networks into the voice infrastructure.

Many technically sound ideas from ATM were adopted by MPLS, a generic layer 2 packet switching protocol. ATM remains widely deployed, and is used as a multiplexing service in DSL networks, where its compromises fit DSL's low-data-rate needs well. In turn, DSL networks support IP (and IP services such as VoIP) via PPP over ATM.

ATM will remain deployed for some time in higher-speed interconnects where carriers have already committed themselves to existing ATM deployments; ATM is used here as a way of unifying PDH/SDH traffic and packet-switched traffic under a single infrastructure.

However, ATM is increasingly challenged by speed and traffic shaping requirements of converged networks. In particular, the complexity of SAR imposes a performance bottleneck, as the fastest SARs known run at 2.5 Gbps and have limited traffic shaping capabilities.

Currently it seems like Ethernet implementations (10-Gbit-Ethernet, Metro Ethernet) will replace ATM in many locations (http://standards.ieee.org/catalog/olis/lanman.html, www.metroethernetforum.org).

ATM PROTOCOL REFERENCE MODEL

The ATM protocol reference model is based on standards developed by the ITU. Communication from higher layers is adapted to the lower ATM defined layers, which in turn pass the information onto the physical layer for transmission over a selected physical medium. The protocol reference model is divided into three layers: the ATM adaptation layer (AAL), the ATM layer, and the physical layer, as shown in Figure 1. The three management planes—user/control plane, layer management and plane management, are shown in Figure 2.

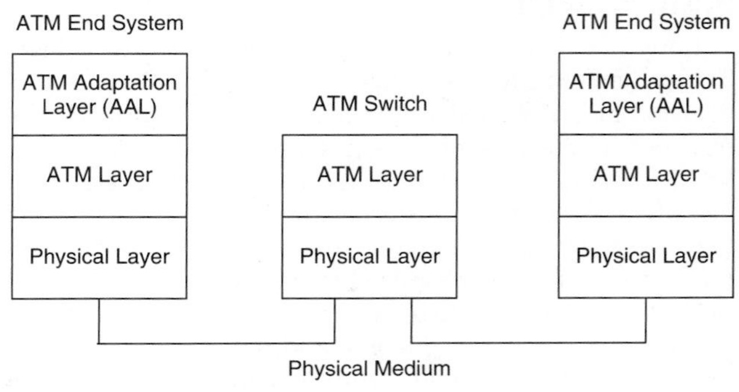

Figure 1: ATM protocol structure

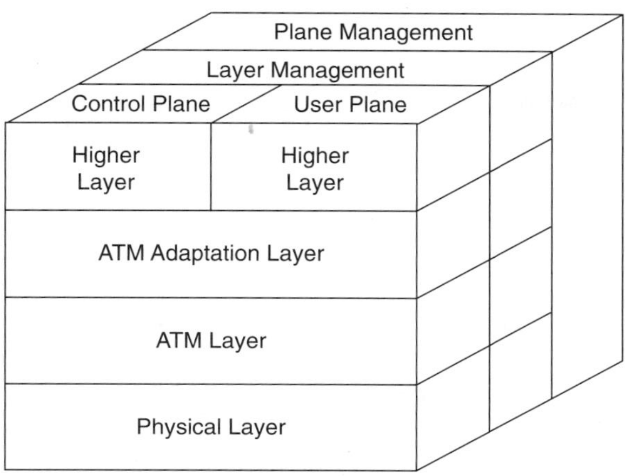

Figure 2: ATM model

The ATM Adaptation Layer

The ATM adaptation layer (AAL) interfaces the higher layer protocols to the ATM layer. It relays ATM cells both from the upper layers to the ATM layer and vice versa. When relaying information received from the higher layers to the ATM layer, the AAL segments the data into ATM cells. When relaying information received from the ATM layer to the higher layers, the AAL must take the cells and reassemble the payloads into a format that the higher layers can understand. This is called segmentation and reassembly (SAR).

Four types of AALs were proposed, each supporting a different type of traffic or service expected to be used on ATM networks. The service classes and the corresponding types of AALs are as follows:

- *AAL0:* AAL0 payload consists of 48 bytes without special field, is also referred to as raw cells.
- *AAL1:* AAL1 was designed to support constant bit rate applications. Examples of these types of applications include 64 Kbps voice, fixed-rate uncompressed video, and leased lines for private data networks.
- *AAL2:* AAL2 was initially conceived to support variable bit rate applications that require a bounded delay for delivery. One example of such applications is compressed packetized voice or video. The requirement on bounded delay for delivery is necessary for the receiver to reconstruct the original uncompressed voice or video. Although, AAL2 was conceived in early years of ATM development, it was not designed. So later when ATM designers needed an AAL for voice traffic, they first labeled it AAL6 and then quickly relabeled it as AAL2. So today, AAL2 is used for carrying voice traffic and allows several small compressed voice packets to be packed in a single 48-byte cell payload.
- *AAL3/4:* AAL3 and AAL4 were conceived for connection-oriented and connectionless data traffic that do not have delay constraints. Both these were to support variable bit rate data applications such as file transfer. However, designers quickly realized that there was little difference between the two types of traffic and so a single AAL called AAL 3/4 was designed. Because of the high complexity of AAL3/4 protocols, a simpler AAL called AAL5 was later proposed and is the common AAL used today. AAL 3/4 is no longer used.
- *AAL5:* AAL5 is designed for data traffic that do not have delay constraints. Examples of applications include IP traffic, LAN, FTP, and network management.

Although each AAL is optimized for a specific type of traffic, there is no stipulation in the standards that AALs designed for one class of traffic cannot be used for another. In fact, many vendors of ATM equipment currently manufacture products that use AAL5 to support all the above classes of traffic, and most activities at the ATM Forum were focused on AAL5. The AAL5 is also important in the internetworking of different networks and services. For more discussion on the issues in AAL5 design, see Suzuki (1994). AAL1 is also important, because it is used for streams and for circuit emulation (www.mfaforum.org/ftp/pub/approved-specs/af-arch-0204.000.pdf).

AAL5 places control information in an 8-octet trailer at the end of the packet. The AAL5 trailer contains a 16-bit length field, a 32-bit cyclic redundancy check (CRC) and two 8-bit fields labeled UU and CPI that are currently unused.

In AAL5, each higher layer packet is divided into an integral number of ATM cells. At the receiving end, these cells are reassembled into a packet before delivery to the receiving host. The last cell contains padding to ensure that the entire AAL5 protocol data unit (PDU) is a multiple of 48 octets long. The final cell contains up to 40 octets of data, followed by zero padding and the 8-octet trailer.

The ATM Layer

The ATM layer provides an interface between the AAL and the physical layer. This layer is responsible for relaying cells from the AAL to the physical layer for transmission and from the physical layer to the AAL for use at the end systems. When it is inside an end system, the ATM layer receives a stream of cells from the physical layer and transmits cells with new data. When it is inside a switch, the ATM layer determines where the incoming cells should be forwarded to, modifies the corresponding connection identifiers, and forwards the cells to the next link. Moreover, it buffers incoming and outgoing cells, and handles various traffic management functions such as cell loss priority marking, congestion indication, and generic flow control. It also monitors the transmission rate and conformance to the service contract (traffic policing). Traffic management was a hotly debated topic in the ATM Forum, and we shall address the important issues in more details later.

The fields in the ATM cell header define the functionality of the ATM layer. The format of the header for ATM cells has two different forms, one for use at the user-to -network interface (UNI) and the other for use internal to the network, the network-to-node interface (NNI), as shown in Figure 3 (www.mfaforum.org/ftp/pub/approved-specs/afarch-0193.000.pdf, www.mfaforum.org/ftp/pub/approved-specs/af-sig-0061.001.pdf). ATM user network interface (UNI) signaling specification version 4.1 was standardized in 2002. At the UNI, the header dedicates four bits to a function called generic flow control (GFC), which was originally designed to control the amount of

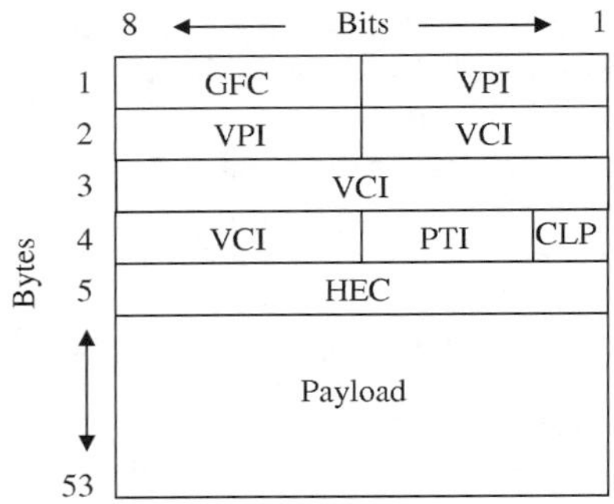

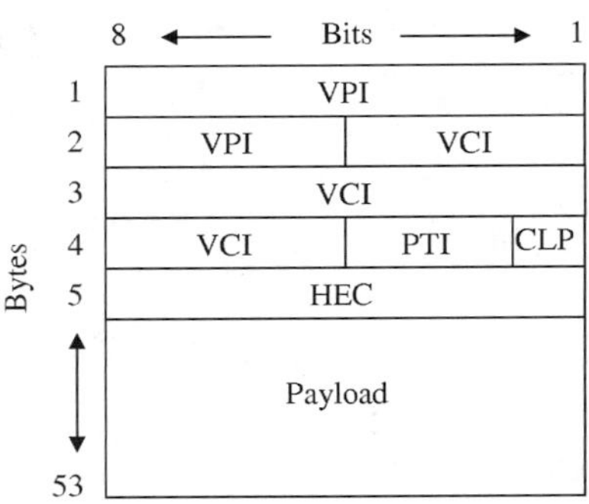

Figure 3: UNI (left) and NNI (right) ATM cell format

traffic entering the network. This allows the UNI to limit the amount of data entering the network during periods of congestion. At the NNI, these four bits are allocated to the virtual path identifier (VPI).

The ATM inter network interface (AINI) protocol was designed for use between ATM networks. AINI protocol is based on ATM Forum PNNI signaling (www.mfaforum org/ftp/pub/approved-specs-af-cs-0125.002.pdf, www.mfaforum.org/ftp/pub/approved-specs-af-pnni-0055.001.pdf). The networks on either side of the AINI may be running any protocol internally. However, the goal in defining this protocol was to facilitate interworking of two networks running PNNI internally in disjoint PNNI routing domains.

Figure 4 gives an illustration of ATM network interfaces.

The VPI and the virtual channel identifier (VCI) together, as shown in Figure 5, form the routing field, which associates each cell with a particular channel or circuit, see Figure 6. Each VCI identifies a single flow (channel); the VPI allows grouping of VCs with different VCIs that can be switched together as an entity. However, the VPIs and VCIs have significance only on the local link; the contents of the routing field will generally change as the cell traverses from link to link. For the UNI, the routing field contains 24 bits and thus the interface can support over 16 million concurrent sessions. At the NNI, the field contains 28 bits, allowing for over 268 million sessions to share a link within a subnet. We refer the readers to the discussion of important issues in private network-to-network interface (PNNI) routing to www.mfaforum.org/ftp/pub/approved-specs-af-pnni-0055.001.pdf and Lee (1995).

The payload type indicator (PTI) field is used to distinguish between cells carrying user data and cells containing control information. This allows control and signaling data to be transmitted on a different subchannel from user data and hence separation of user and control data. A particular bit is used by the AAL if the cell is a part of an AAL5 connection. Another bit is used to indicate that the cell has experienced congestion.

The cell loss priority (CLP) bit provides the network with a selective discard capability within each VPI/VCI. Cells with a CLP bit setting of 1 are discarded before cells with a CLP bit setting of 0. This bit could be set by a user to indicate lower-priority cells that could be discarded by the

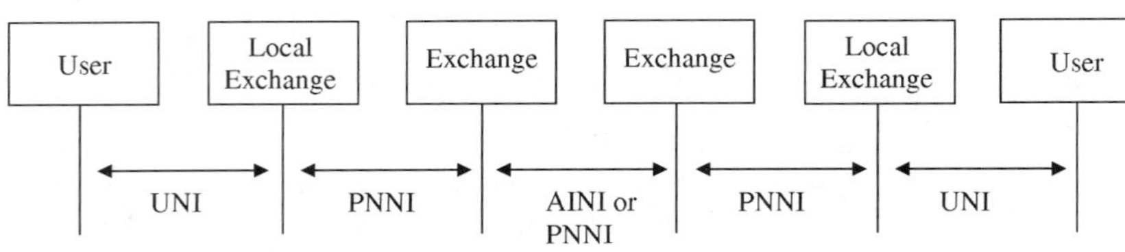

Figure 4: ATM network interfaces

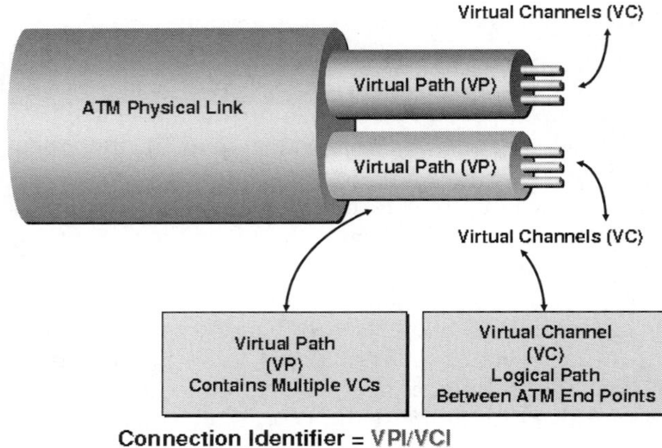

Figure 5: Virtual path and virtual channels

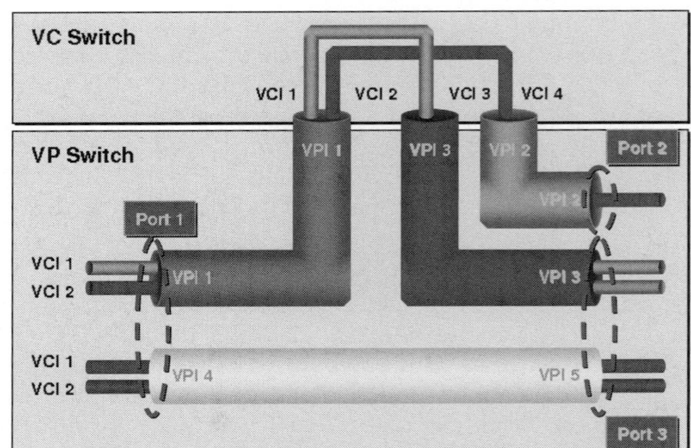

Figure 6: VP and VC switching

network during periods of congestion. Whereas data applications generally cannot suffer any cell loss without the need for retransmission, voice and video traffic, especially if not compressed, can tolerate minor cell loss. One could, therefore, code voice and video traffic such that some less important cells could be marked with CLP = 1 while other more important cells would be marked with CLP = 0. The CLP bit could also be used by the network to indicate cells that exceed the negotiated rate limit of a user.

The header error check (HEC) field is used to reduce errors in the header that cause a misrouting of the cell for one user into another user's data stream. This field contains the result of an 8-bit CRC checking on the ATM header (this does not include the payload). When a switch or an end system terminates the header, multiple-bit errors will be detected with a high probability. Moreover, a single-bit error can be corrected. This is desirable since ATM is intended for use on fiber optics link, where the error rate is less than 10^{-9} with current modulation techniques. Therefore, single-bit error correction is quite effective in removing most header errors.

The Physical Layer

The physical layer defines the bit timing and other characteristics for encoding and decoding the data into suitable electrical/optical waveforms for transmission and reception on the specific physical media used. In addition, it also provides cell delineation function, header error check (HEC) generation and processing, performance monitoring, and payload rate matching of the different transport formats used at this layer.

The Synchronous Optical Network (SONET), a synchronous transmission structure, is often used for framing and synchronization at the physical layer. In addition to the optical media and line rates defined for SONET, the ATM Forum has proposed a variety of physical layer standards, such as ATM over twisted-pair wire. This will accelerate the acceptance of ATM as a desktop connection technology since existing cabling plants can be retained and the cost per connection will be reduced. We refer the readers to Rao and Hatamian (1995) for a discussion on the ATM physical layer issues.

TRAFFIC MANAGEMENT

In order for ATM networks to deliver guaranteed quality of service (QoS) on demand while maximizing the utilization of available network resources, effective traffic management mechanisms are needed. Almost every aspect of ATM network operation, from signaling requests and routing to network resource allocation and policing, contains some traffic management mechanisms (www.mfa-forum.org/ftp/pub/approved-specs/af-tm-0121.000.pdf).

A set of six service categories are specified. For each one, a set of parameters is given to describe both the traffic presented to the network, and the QoS which is required of the network.

Generic Functions

To meet the QoS objectives, the following functions form a framework for managing and controlling traffic and congestion in ATM networks and may be used in appropriate combinations depending on the service category.

- *Network resource management:* is used in broadband networks to keep track of the way link resources are allocated to connections. The two primary resources that are tracked by network resource management are capacity (bandwidth) and connection identifiers. Network resource management keeps track of the capacity and controls the allocation of capacity to connections when requested as part of the connection setup process (Sexton and Reid 1997). In ATM, the service architecture allows logical separation of connections according to service characteristics. Although cell scheduling and resource provisioning are implementation and network specific, they can be utilized to provide appropriate isolation and access to resources. Virtual paths are a useful tool for resource management.
- *Traffic policing:* is monitoring network traffic for conformity with a traffic contract. An application that wishes to use the broadband network to transport traffic must first request a connection, which involves informing the network about the characteristics of the traffic and the quality of service (QOS) required by the application (Ferguson and Huston 1998). This information is stored in a traffic contract. If the connection request is accepted, the application is permitted to use the network to transport traffic.

  The main purpose of this function is to protect the network resources from malicious connections and to enforce the compliance of every connection to its negotiated traffic contract. The network also has the capability to discard non-conformant traffic in the network (using priority control). Traffic policing in ATM networks is known as usage parameter control (UPC) and network parameter control (NPC) (Saito 1993).
- *Traffic shaping*: provides a mechanism to control the volume of traffic being sent into a network (bandwidth throttling), and the rate at which the traffic is being sent (rate limiting). For this reason, traffic shaping schemes are commonly implemented at the network edges to control traffic entering the network. The objectives of this function are to achieve a better network efficiency while meeting the QoS objectives and/or to ensure connection traffic conformance at a subsequent interface. Simple traffic shaping schemes like leaky bucket and token bucket rely on shaping all traffic uniformly by rate.
- *Connection admission control (CAC): Admission control* is the simple practice of discriminating which traffic is admitted into a network in the first place (Ferguson and Huston 1998). Admission control in ATM networks is known as connection admission control (CAC) (Saito 1993).

  Connection admission control is defined as the set of actions taken by the network during the call set-up phase in order to determine whether a connection request can be accepted or should be rejected (or whether a request for re-allocation can be accommodated).
- *Feedback controls:* are defined as the set of actions taken by the network and by end-systems to regulate the traffic submitted on ATM connections according to the state

of network elements. This specification defines one network feedback control mechanism: the ABR flow control. The ABR flow control may be used to adaptively share the available bandwidth among participating users.

- *Usage parameter control (UPC):* is defined as the set of actions taken by the network to monitor traffic and enforce the traffic contract at the user network. Network parameter control (NPC) is a similarly defined set of actions at the Network Node Interface. The main purpose of UPC and NPC is to protect network resources from malicious as well as unintentional misbehavior, which can affect the QoS of other already established connections, by detecting violations of negotiated parameters and taking appropriate actions. Such actions may include cell discard and cell tagging.
- *Cell loss priority control:* For some service categories the end system may generate traffic flows of cells with cell loss priority (CLP) marking. The network may follow models which treat this marking as transparent or as significant. If treated as significant, the network may selectively discard cells marked with a low priority to protect, as far as possible, the QoS objectives of cells with high priority.
- *Frame discard:* A congested network that needs to discard cells may discard at the frame level rather than at the cell level.

Quality of Service Attributes

While setting up a connection on ATM networks, users can negotiate with the network the following parameters related to the desired quality of service:

- *Peak-to-peak cell delay variation (peak-to-peak CDV):* The delay experienced by a cell between network entry and exit points is called the cell transfer delay (CTD). It includes propagation delays, queueing delays at various intermediate switches, and service times at queueing points.

  The peak-to-peak CDV is the difference between the $(1 - \alpha)$ quantile of the CTD and the fixed CTD that could be experienced by any delivered cell on a connection during the entire connection holding time. The term "peak-to-peak" refers to the difference between the best and worst case of CTD, where the best case is equal to the fixed delay, and the worst case is equal to a value likely to be exceeded with probability no greater than α.
- *Maximum cell transfer delay (maxCTD):* Cell delay variation (CDV) is a measure of variance of CTD. High variation implies larger buffering for delay sensitive traffic such as voice and video.

  The maximum cell transfer delay (maxCTD) specified for a connection is the $(1 - \alpha)$ quantile of CTD. The CLR at connection request time is used to place an upper bound on α.
- *Cell loss ratio (CLR):* The percentage of cells that are lost in the network because of error or congestion and are not delivered to the destination, i.e.,

$$\text{CLR} = \frac{\#\,\text{Lost Cells}}{\#\,\text{Transmitted Cells}}$$

  Recall that each ATM cell has a cell loss priority (CLP) bit in the header. During periods of congestion, the network will first discard cells with CLP = 1. Because the loss of cells with CLP = 0 is more harmful to the operation of the application, CLR can be specified separately for cells with CLP = 1 and for those with CLP = 0.

All these parameters are described in details in the "Traffic Management Specification" document (www.mfaforum.org/ftp/pub/approved-specs/af-tm-0121.000.pdf).

Traffic Contract

To provide a guaranteed QoS, a traffic contract is established during connection setup, which contains a connection traffic descriptor and a conformance definition. However, it is not necessary for every ATM virtual connection to have a specified QoS. The reason for this is that if only specified QoS connections are supported by ATM, then a large percentage of the network resources will be wasted. This can happen when one or more connections are not utilizing the full capacity of their QoS contracts. Unspecified QoS contracts can be supported by an ATM network on a "best-effort" basis. Such best-effort services are sufficient for supporting most of the existing data applications.

In general, a traffic contract specifies one of the following six service categories:

- *Constant bit rate (CBR):* This service category is used for emulating circuit switching, where the bit rate is constant. Cell loss ratio is specified for cells with CLP = 0 and may or may not be specified for cells with CLP = 1.
- *Real-time variable bit rate (rt-VBR):* The real-time VBR service category is intended for real-time applications, i.e., those requiring tightly constrained delay and delay variation, as would be appropriate for voice and video applications. rt-VBR connections are characterized in terms of a peak cell rate (PCR), sustainable cell rate (SCR), and maximum burst size (MBS). Sources are expected to transmit at a rate that varies with time. Equivalently the source can be described as "bursty." Cells that are delayed beyond the value specified by maxCTD are assumed to be of significantly reduced value to the application. Real-time VBR service may support statistical multiplexing of real-time sources.
- *Non-real-time variable bit rate (nrt-VBR):* The non-real-time VBR service category is intended for non-real-time applications that have bursty traffic characteristics and which are characterized in terms of a PCR, SCR, and MBS. For those cells that are transferred within the traffic contract, the application expects a low cell loss ratio. Non-real-time VBR service may support statistical multiplexing of connections. No delay bounds are associated with this service category.
- *Available bit rate (ABR):* This service category is designed for normal data traffic such as file transfer and email. Although the standard does not require the cell transfer delay and cell loss ratio to be guaranteed, it is desirable for switches to minimize the delay and loss as much as possible. Depending upon the congestion state of the network, the source is required to control its rate. The users are allowed to declare a minimum cell rate (MCR), which is guaranteed to the VC by the

Table 1: ATM Service Category Attributes

<table>
<tr><th rowspan="2">Attribute</th><th colspan="6">ATM Layer Service Category</th></tr>
<tr><th>CBR</th><th>rt-VBR</th><th>nrt-VBR</th><th>UBR</th><th>ABR</th><th>GFR</th></tr>
<tr><td>Traffic Parameters</td><td colspan="6"></td></tr>
<tr><td>PCR and CDVT</td><td colspan="6">Specified</td></tr>
<tr><td>SCR, MBS, CDVT</td><td>n/a</td><td colspan="2">Specified</td><td colspan="3">n/a</td></tr>
<tr><td>MCR</td><td colspan="4">n/a</td><td>Specified</td><td>n/a</td></tr>
<tr><td>MCR, MBS, MFS CDVT</td><td colspan="5">n/a</td><td>Specified</td></tr>
<tr><td>QoS Parameters</td><td colspan="6"></td></tr>
<tr><td>Peak-to-peak CDV</td><td colspan="2">Specified</td><td colspan="4">Unspecified</td></tr>
<tr><td>MaxCTD</td><td colspan="2">Specified</td><td colspan="4">Unspecified</td></tr>
<tr><td>CLR</td><td colspan="3">Specified</td><td>Unspecified</td><td colspan="2">Network Specific</td></tr>
<tr><td>Feedback</td><td colspan="4">Unspecified</td><td>Specified</td><td>Unspecified</td></tr>
</table>

network. Most VCs will ask for an MCR of zero. Those with higher MCR may be denied connection if sufficient bandwidth is not available.

- *Unspecified bit rate (UBR):* This service category is designed for those data applications that want to use any left-over capacity and are not sensitive to cell loss or delay. Such connections are not rejected on the basis of bandwidth shortage (i.e., no connection admission control) and not policed for their usage behavior. During congestion, the cells are lost but the sources are not expected to reduce their cell rate. Instead, these applications may have their own higher-level cell loss recovery and retransmission mechanisms. Examples of applications that use this service are email and file transfer. Of course, these same applications can use the ABR service, if desired.
- *Guaranteed frame rate (GFR):* The GFR service category is intended to support non-real-time applications. It is designed for applications that may require a minimum rate guarantee and can benefit from accessing additional bandwidth dynamically available in the network. It does not require adherence to a flow control protocol. The service guarantee is based on AAL5 PDUs (frames) and, under congestion conditions, the network attempts to discard complete PDUs instead of discarding cells without reference to frame boundaries. On the establishment of a GFR connection, the end-system specifies a PCR, and a minimum cell rate (MCR) that is defined along with a maximum burst size (MBS) and a maximum frame size (MFS). The user may always send cells at a rate up to PCR, but the network only commits to carry cells in complete frames at MCR. Traffic beyond MCR will be delivered within the limits of available resources. There are no delay bounds associated with this service category.

These service categories relate traffic characteristics and QoS requirements to network behavior. Functions such as routing, CAC, and resource allocation are, in general, structured differently for each service category. Service categories are distinguished as being either real-time or non-real-time. For real-time traffic, there are two categories, CBR and rt-VBR, distinguished by whether the traffic descriptor contains only the peak cell rate (PCR) or both PCR and the sustainable cell rate (SCR) parameters. All service categories, except GFR, apply to both VCCs and VPCs. GFR is a frame-aware service that only applies to VCCs since frame delineation is not usually visible at the virtual path level.

ABR or UBR are usually specified in the traffic contract when the ATM network is providing a best-effort service. Thus, these two classes of traffic are sometimes referred to as best-effort traffic. The attributes for the above service categories are summarized in Table 1.

Congestion Control Techniques

Congestion control lies at the heart of the general problem of traffic management for ATM networks. In general, congestion arises when the incoming traffic to a specific link is more than the outgoing link capacity. The primary function of congestion control is to ensure good throughput and delay performance while maintaining a fair allocation of network resources to the users (Jain 1990). For unspecified QoS traffic such as ABR service, whose traffic patterns are often highly bursty and unpredictable, congestion control poses more challenges than for other services.

As described in Jain (1992), one way to classify congestion control schemes is based on the layer of ISO/OSI reference model at which the scheme operates. For example, there are data link, routing, and transport layer congestion control schemes. Typically, a combination of such schemes is used. The selection depends upon the severity and duration of congestion. Figure 7 shows how the duration of congestion affects the choice of the method.

One method to avoid network congestion is to accept a new ATM connection during connection setup phase only when sufficient network resources are available to provide the acceptable QoS. This is called connection admission control (CAC), which is needed for connections where the QoS must be guaranteed. The "busy" tone on

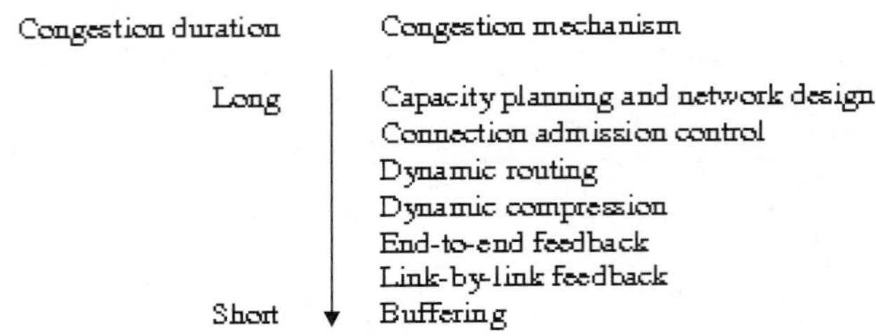

Figure 7: Congestion techniques for various congestion durations

telephone networks is an example of CAC. Mechanisms for CAC are currently not standardized and are at the discretion of the network operators.

In addition to CAC, Traffic Management Specification Version 4.1 also allows traffic shaping using a generic cell rate algorithm (GCRA) and binary explicit forward congestion indication (EFCI) feedback congestion control. These mechanisms are described next.

Generic Cell Rate Algorithm (GCRA)

The GCRA is also called the "leaky bucket" algorithm, which converts a bursty stream into a more regular pattern. This algorithm essentially works by putting all arriving cells into a bucket, which is drained at the sustained cell rate. If too many cells arrive at once, the bucket may overflow. The overflowing cells are called non-conforming and may or may not be admitted into the network. If admitted, the cell loss priority (CLP) bit of the non-conforming cells may be set so that they will be the first to be discarded in case of overload.

The leaky bucket algorithm is often used by the network to ensure that the input meets the pre-negotiated parameters such as the sustained and peak cell rates. Such "traffic shaping" algorithms are open loop in the sense that the parameters cannot be changed dynamically if congestion is detected after negotiation. In a closed-loop (feedback) scheme, however, sources are informed dynamically about the congestion state of the network and are asked to increase or decrease their input rate.

Feedback Congestion Control

As described earlier in Figure 3, four bits of the cell header at the user-network interface (UNI) are reserved for generic flow control (GFC). Originally, the plan was to use these bits to flow control the source. The discussions in ATM Forum eventually led to the development of end-to-end congestion control scheme instead of GFC.

An effective congestion control scheme must satisfy several key criteria. In addition to being able to maximally utilize available bandwidth, a good scheme must also provide fairness of network resources to users. Moreover, it must be scalable to a large number of nodes and links with various capacities, robust against slight mistuning of parameters and loss of control cells, as well as low in switch complexity and buffer requirement.

The ATM Forum initially considered the use of the explicit forward congestion indication (EFCI) bit in the ATM cell headers to mark congestion in the switches (Hluchyj et al. 1993). This scheme was to be based on DECbit scheme (Ramakrishnan and Jain 1990). The forum finally adopted an explicit rate-based indication scheme based on Charny et al. (1995).

The available bit rate (ABR) method of traffic management works as follows. The sources periodically send resource management (RM) cells, which indicate their current rate and the desired rate. The switches along the path adjust the desired rate down. The destination returns the RM cells to the sources. The sources then adjust their rate to that indicated in the RM cells. The algorithm for deciding the rate allocated by a switch is not specified and is left for the vendors to design. For examples of such algorithms, see Jain et al. (1995), Kalyanaraman et al. (2000), and Roberts (1994).

The rate-based congestion control approach and its development at the ATM Forum is described in more detail in www.mfaforum.org/ftp/pub/approved-specs/af-tm-0121.000.pdf. Other reference sources include the review papers of Jain (1996) and Bonomi and Fendick (1995).

SWITCH ARCHITECTURE

Perhaps the most developed aspect of ATM is the switch architecture. Over the past decade, a vast amount of research efforts have been made on studying and designing ATM switches. The field has now become a mature research area and a number of tutorial articles have appeared in the literature. The design of ATM switch architectures is at the discretion of switch vendors. Basic principles of switch design and examines the influence of traffic patterns on the design methodologies are discussed in Chen and Liu (2003), Awdeh and Mouftah (1995), and Simcoe and Pei (1995).

ATM switches are high-speed packet switches specialized to process and forward ATM cells (packets). Because ATM is a connection-oriented protocol, ATM switches must establish a virtual connection from one of its input ports to an output port before forwarding incoming ATM cells along that virtual connection.

A generic ATM switch architecture with N input ports and N output ports is shown in Figure 8. The functions of an ATM switching system may be divided broadly into the three planes as in Chen and Liu (2003).

- *User plane:* The main function of an ATM switch is to relay user data cells from input ports to the appropriate output ports. The switch processes only the cell headers and the payload is carried transparently. As soon as the cell comes in through the input port, the virtual path identifier/virtual channel identifier (VPI/VCI) information is derived and used to route the cells to the appropriate output ports. This function can be divided into three functional blocks: the input module at the input port, the cell switch fabric (sometimes referred to as switch matrix) that performs the actual routing, and the output modules at the output ports.
- *Control plane:* This plane represents functions related to the establishment and control of the VP/VC connections. Unlike the user data cells, information in the control cells payload is not transparent to the network. The switch identifies signaling cells, and even generates some itself. The connection admission control (CAC) carries out the major signaling functions required. Signaling information may/may not pass through the cell

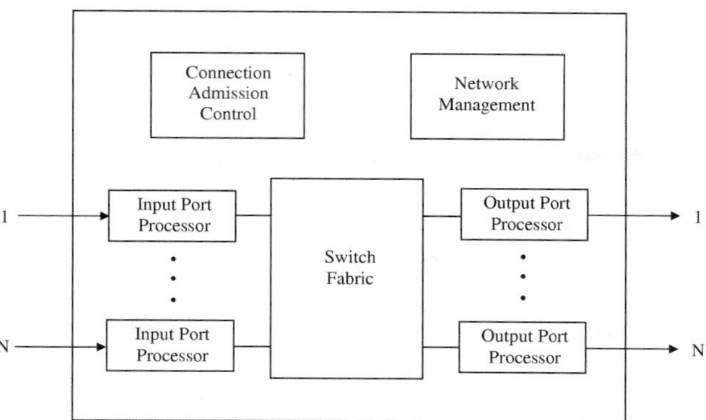

Figure 8: A generic ATM switch architecture

switch fabric, or may be exchanged through a signaling network such as SS7.

- *Management plane:* The management plane is concerned with monitoring the controlling the network to ensure its correct and efficient operation. These operations can be subdivided as fault management functions, performance management functions, configuration management functions, security management functions, accounting managements, and traffic management. These functions can be represented as being performed by the functional block switch management. The switch management is responsible for supporting the ATM layer operations and maintenance (OAM) procedures. OAM cells may be recognized and processed by the ATM switch. The switch must identify and process OAM cells, maybe resulting in generating OAM cells. As with signaling cells, OAM cells may/may not pass through cell switch fabric. Switch management also supports the interim local management interface (ILMI) of the UNI. The switch management contains, for each UNI, a UNI management entity (UME), which may use SNMP.

ATM cells containing user data are received at the input ports, and the input port processors prepare the cells for routing through the switch fabric. The fabric in the center of the switching system provides the interconnections between input port processors and output port processors. The output port processors prepare the outgoing user cells for transmission from the switch. User cell forwarding is characterized by parallelism and high-speed hardware processing. The ATM protocol was intentionally streamlined to allow incoming cells to be processed simultaneously in hardware and routed through the switch fabric in parallel. Thus, ATM switches have been able to realize high-end performance in terms of throughput and cell forwarding delay.

An ATM switch contains a set of input ports and output ports, through which it is interconnected to users, other switches, and other network elements. It might also have other interfaces to exchange control and management information with special purpose networks. Connection control, sometimes called the control plane, refers to the functions related to the establishment and termination of ATM virtual connections. Connection control functions generally encompass: exchange and processing of signaling information; participation in routing protocols; and decisions on admission or rejection of new connection requests.

The cell switch fabric is primarily responsible for routing of data cells and possibly signaling and management cells as well. Other possible functions include: cell buffering, traffic concentration and multiplexing redundancy for fault tolerance, multicasting or broadcasting, cell scheduling based on delay priorities, congestion monitoring, and activation of explicit forward congestion indication (EFCI). More details about switch fabrics can be found in Chen and Liu (2003) and Awdeh and Mouftah (1995).

Network management is currently carried out by SNMP (simple network management protocol), the standard protocol for managing data networks. ATM switches typically support an SNMP agent and an ATM MIB (management information base).

Switch Interface

Input Modules

The input module first terminates the incoming signal (for example a SONET signal) and extracts the ATM cell stream. This involves signal conversion and recovery, processing SONET overhead, and cell delineation and rate decoupling. After that, for each ATM cell the following functions should be performed:

- Error checking the header using the header error control (HEC) field
- Validation and translation of VPI/VCI values
- Determination of the destination output port
- Passing signaling cells to CAC and OAM cells to switch management
- UPC/UNC for each VPC/VCC
- Addition of an internal tag containing internal routing and performance monitoring information for use only within the switch

Output Modules

Output modules prepare the ATM cell streams for physical transmission by:

- Removing and processing the internal tag
- Possible translation of VPI/VCI values
- HEC field generation
- Possible mixing of cells from CAC and switch management with outgoing cell streams
- Cell rate decoupling
- Mapping cells to SONET payloads and generation of SONET overhead
- Conversion of the digital bitstream to an optical signal

Connection Admission Control (CAC)

CAC establishes, modifies and terminates virtual path/ channel connections. More specifically, it is responsible for:

- High-layer signaling protocols
- Signaling ATM adaptation layer (AAL) functions to interpret or generate signaling cells

- Interface with a signaling network
- Negotiation of traffic contracts with users requesting new VPCs/VCCs
- Renegotiation with users to change established VPCs/VCCs
- Allocation of switch resources for VPCs/VCCs, including route selection
- Admission/rejection decisions for requested VPCs/VCCs
- Generation of UPC/NPC parameters

If the CAC is centralized, a single processing unit would receives signaling cells from the input modules, interpret them, and perform admission decisions and resource allocation decisions for all the connections in the switch. CAC functions may be distributed to blocks of input modules where each CAC has a smaller number of input ports. This is much harder to implement, but solves the connection control processing bottleneck problem for large switch sizes, by dividing this job to be performed by parallel CACs. A lot of information must be communicated and coordinated among the various CACs (Chen and Liu 2003). Some of the distributed CAC functions can also be distributed among output modules which can handle encapsulation of high-layer control information into outgoing signaling cells.

Switch Management

Switch management physical layer OAM, ATM layer OAM, configuration management of switch components, security control for the switch database, usage measurements of the switch resources, traffic management, administration of a management information base, customer-network management, interface with operations systems and finally support of network management.

Switch management is difficult because management covers an extremely wide spectrum of activities. In addition, the level of management functions implemented in the switch can vary between minimal and complex.

Switch management must perform a few basic tasks. It must carry out specific management responsibilities, collect and administer management information, communicate with users and network managers, and supervise and coordinate all management activities. Management functions include fault management, performance management, configuration management, accounting management, security management, and traffic management. Carrying out these functions entails a lot of intraswitch communication between the switch management and other functional blocks.

A centralized switch management can be a performance bottleneck if it is overloaded by processing demands. Hence, switch management functions can be distributed among input modules, but a lot of coordination would be required. Each distributed input module switch management unit can monitor the incoming user data cell streams to perform accounting and performance measurement. Output module switch management units can also monitor outgoing cell streams (Chen and Liu 2003).

The Cell Switch Fabric

The cell switch fabric is primarily responsible for transferring cells between the other functional blocks (routing of data cells and possibly signaling and management cells as well). Other possible functions include:

- Cell buffering
- Traffic concentration and multiplexing
- Redundancy for fault tolerance multicasting or broadcasting
- Cell scheduling based on delay priorities
- Congestion monitoring and activation of explicit forward congestion indication (EFCI)

Concentration, Expansion, and Multiplexing

Traffic needs to be concentrated at the inputs of the switching fabric to better utilize the incoming link connected to the switch. The concentrator aggregates the lower variable bit rate traffic into higher bit rate for the switching matrix to perform the switch at standard interface speed. The concentration ratio is highly correlated with the traffic characteristics, so it needs to be dynamically configured. The concentrator can also aid in dynamic traffic distribution to multiple routing and buffering planes, and duplication of traffic for fault tolerance. At the outputs of the routing and buffering fabric, traffic can be expanded and redundant traffic can be combined.

Routing and Buffering

The routing and buffering functions are the two major functions performed by the cell switch fabric. The input module attaches a routing tag to each cell, and the switch fabric simply routes the arriving cells from its inputs to the appropriate outputs. Arriving cells may be aligned in time by means of single-cell buffers. Because cells may be addressed to the same output simultaneously, buffers are needed. Several routing and buffering switch designs have aided in setting the important switch design principles. All current approaches employ a high degree of parallelism, distributed control, and the routing function is performed at the hardware level.

Traditionally switching has been defined to encompass either space switching or time switching or combinations of both techniques. The classification adopted here is slightly different in the sense that it divides the design approaches under the following four broad categories: (1) shared memory, (2) shared medium, (3) fully interconnected, and (4) space division (Chen and Liu 2003).

Shared Memory Approach: Figure 9 illustrates the basic structure of a shared memory switch. Here incoming cells are converted from serial to parallel form, and written sequentially to a dual-port random access memory. A memory controller decides the order in which cells are read out of the memory, based on the cell headers with internal routing tags. Outgoing cells are demultiplexed to the outputs and converted from parallel to serial form.

This approach is an output queueing approach, where the output buffers all physically belong to a common buffer pool. The approach is attractive because it achieves 100 percent throughput under heavy load. The

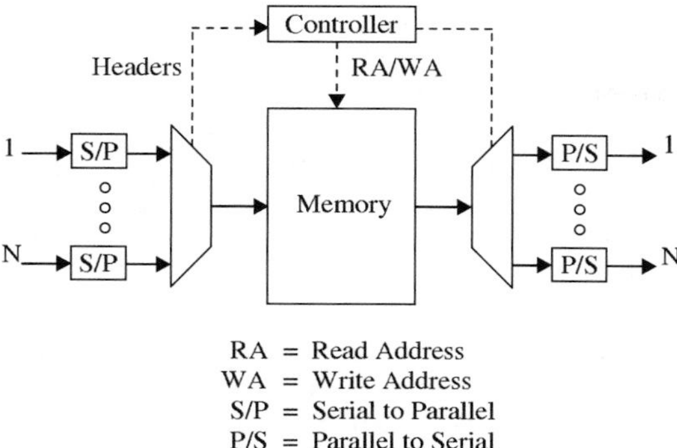

Figure 9: Basic structure of a shared-memory switch

buffer sharing minimizes the amount of buffers needed to achieve a specified cell loss rate. This is because if a large burst of traffic is directed to one output port, the shared memory can absorb as much as possible of it.

The approach, however, suffers from a few drawbacks. The shared memory must operate N times faster than the port speed because cells must be read and written one at a time. As the access time of memory is physically limited, the approach is not very scalable. The product of the number of ports times port speed (NV) is limited. In addition, the centralized memory controller must process cell headers and routing tags at the same rate as the memory. This is difficult for multiple priority classes, complicated cell scheduling, multicasting, and broadcasting.

Shared Medium Approach: Cells may be routed through a shared medium, like a ring, bus or dual bus. Time-division multiplexed buses are a popular example of this approach, and Figure 10 illustrates their structure. Arriving cells are sequentially broadcast on the TDM bus in a round-robin manner. At each output, address filters pass the appropriate cells to the output buffers, based on their routing tag. The bus speed must be at least NV for cells to eliminate input queueing.

The outputs are modular, which makes address filters and output buffers easy to implement. Also the broadcast-and-select nature of the approach makes multicasting and broadcasting straightforward. As a result, many such switches have been implemented, such as IBM's Packetized Automated Routing Integrated System (PARIS) and plaNET, NEC's ATM Output Buffer Modular Switch (ATOM), and Fore Systems' ForeRunner ASX-100 to mention a few (Onvural 1994). The Synchronous Composite

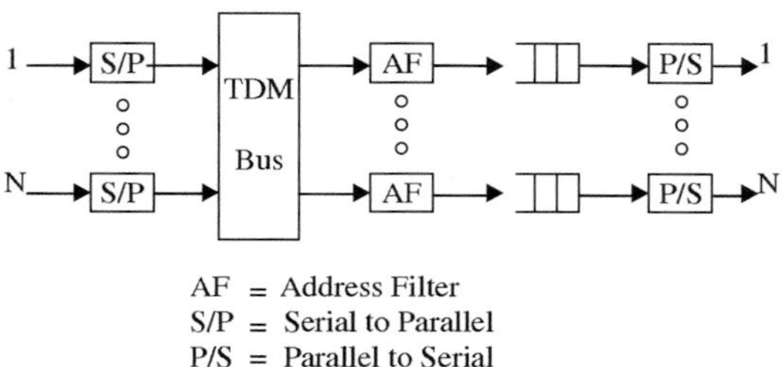

Figure 10: A shared bus switch (adapted from Chen and Liu 2003)

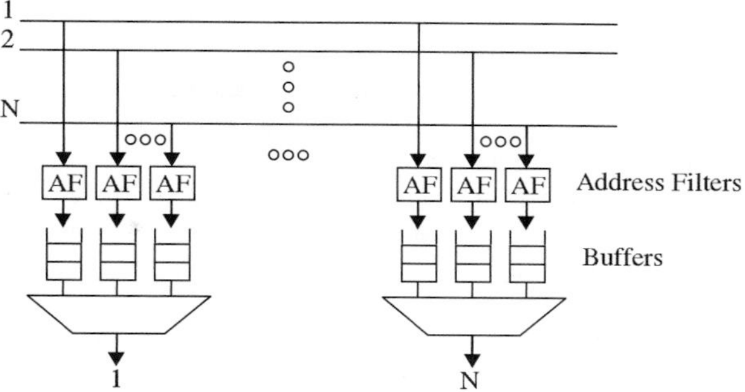

Figure 11: A fully interconnected switch (adapted from Chen and Liu 2003)

Packet Switching (SCPS), which uses multiple rings is also one of the most famous experiments of shared medium switches (Robertazzi 1993).

However, because the address filters and output buffers must operate at the shared medium speed, which is N times faster than the port speed, this places a physical limitation on the scalability of the approach. In addition, unlike the shared memory approach, output buffers are not shared, which requires more total amount of buffers for the same cell loss rate.

Fully Interconnected Approach: In this approach, independent paths exist between all N squared possible pairs of inputs and outputs. Hence arriving cells are broadcast on separate buses to all outputs and address filters pass the appropriate cells to the output queues. This architecture is illustrated in Figure 11.

This design has many advantages. As before, all queueing occurs at the outputs. In addition, multicasting and broadcasting are natural, like in the shared medium approach. Address filters and output buffers are simple to implement and only need to operate at the port speed. Because all of the hardware operates at the same speed, the approach is scalable to any size and speed. Fujitsu's bus matrix switch and GTE Government System's SPANet are examples of switches in which this design was adopted.

Unfortunately, the quadratic growth of buffers limits the number of output ports for practical reasons. However, the port speed is not limited except by the physical limitation on the speed of the address filters and output buffers.

The *Knockout* switch developed by AT&T was an early prototype where the amount of buffers was reduced at the cost of higher cell loss (Onvural 1994, Robertazzi 1993). Instead of N buffers at each output, it was proposed to use only a fixed number of buffers L for a total of NxL buffers. This technique was based on the observation that it is unlikely that more than L cells will arrive for any output at the same time. It was argued that selecting the L value of 8 was sufficient for achieving a cell loss rate of 1/1 million under uniform random traffic conditions for large values of N.

Space Division Approach: The *crossbar* switch is the simplest example of a matrix-like space division fabric that physically interconnects any of the N inputs to any of the N outputs. Multistage interconnection networks (MINs), which are more tree-like structures, were then developed to reduce the N squared crosspoints needed for circuit switching, multiprocessor interconnection and, more recently, packet switching.

One of the most common types of MINs is the banyan network. It is named for its resemblance to the roots of the Banyan tropical tree which crossover in complex patterns. The banyan network is constructed of an interconnection of stages of switching elements. A basic 2x2 switching element can route an incoming cell according to a control bit (output address). If the control bit is 0, the cell is routed to the upper port address, otherwise it is routed to the lower port address.

In general, to construct an NxN banyan network, the nth stage uses the nth bit of the output address to route the cell. For N = 2 to the power of n, the banyan will consist of n = log to the base 2 of N stages, each consisting of N/2 switching elements. A MIN is called self-routing when the output address completely specifies the route through the network (also called digit-controlled routing).

The banyan network technique is popular because switching is performed by simple switching elements, cells are routed in parallel, all elements operate at the same speed (so there is no additional restriction on the size N or speed V), and large switches can be easily constructed modularly and recursively and implemented in hardware.

It is clear that in a banyan network, there is exactly one path from any input to any output. Regular banyans use only one type of switching element, and SW-banyans are a subset of regular banyans, constructed recursively from LxM switching elements.

Delta networks are a subclass of SW-banyan networks, possessing the self-routing property. There are numerous types of delta networks, such as rectangular delta networks (where the switching elements have the same number of outputs as inputs), omega, flip, cube, shuffle-exchange (based on a perfect shuffle permutation), and baseline networks. A delta-b network of size NxN is constructed of bxb switching elements arranged in log to the base b of N stages, each stage consisting of N/b switching elements (Robertazzi 1993).

Unfortunately, since banyan networks have less than N squared crosspoints, routes of two cells addressed to two different outputs might conflict before the last stage. When this situation, called internal blocking, occurs, only one of the two cells contending for a link can be passed to the next stage, so overall throughput is reduced. A solution to this problem is to add a sort network (such as a Batcher bitonic sort network) to arrange the cells before the banyan network. This will be internally non-blocking for cells addressed to different outputs (Robertazzi 1993). However, if cells are addressed to the same output at the same time, the only solution to the problem is buffering. Buffers can be placed at the input of the Batcher network, but this can cause "head-of-line" blocking, where cells wait for a delayed cell at the head of the queue to go through, even if their own destination output ports are free. This situation can be remedied by First-In-Random-Out buffers, but these are quite complex to implement. Alternatively, buffers may be placed internally within the banyan switching elements. Thus if two cells simultaneously attempt to go to the same output link, one of them is buffered within the switching element. This internal buffering can also be used to implement a backpressure control mechanism, where queues in one stage of the banyan will hold up cells in the preceding stage by a feedback signal. The backpressure may eventually reach the first stage, and create queues at the banyan network inputs (Chen and Liu 2003). It is important to observe that internal buffering can cause head-of-line blocking at each switching element, and hence it does not achieve full throughput. Awdeh and Mouftah (1994) have designed a delta-based ATM switch with backpressure mechanism capable of achieving a high throughput, while significantly reducing the overall required memory size.

A third alternative is to use a recirculating buffer external to the switch fabric. This technique has been adopted in Bellcore's Sunshine and AT&T's Starlite wideband digital switch (Robertazzi 1993). Here output conflicts are detected after the Batcher sorter, and a trap network selects a cell to go through, and recirculates the others back to the inputs of the Batcher network. Unfortunately, this approach requires complicated priority control to maintain the sequential order of cells and increases the size of the Batcher network to accommodate the recirculating cells (Chen and Liu 2003).

As discussed before, output buffering is the most preferable approach. However, banyan networks cannot directly implement it since at most one cell per cell time is delivered to every output. Possible ways to work around this problem include:

- Increasing the speed of internal links
- Routing groups of links together
- Using multiple banyan planes in parallel
- Using multiple banyan planes in tandem or adding extra switching stages

Apart from banyan networks, many types of MINs with multiple paths between inputs and outputs exist. Classical examples include the non-blocking Benes and Clos networks, the cascaded banyan networks, and the randomized route banyan network with load distribution (which eliminates internal buffering). Combining a number of banyan planes in parallel can also be used to form multipath MINs. The multipath MINs achieve more uniform traffic distribution to minimize internal conflicts, and exhibit fault tolerance. However if cells can take independent paths with varying delays, a mechanism is needed to preserve the sequential ordering of cells of the same virtual connection at the output. Since this might involve considerable processing, it is better to select the path during connection setup and fix it during the connection. Special attention must be paid during path selection to prevent unnecessary blocking of subsequent calls.

Switch Design Principles

Internal Blocking

A fabric is said to be internally blocking if a set of N cells addressed to N different outputs can cause conflicts within the fabric. Internal blocking can reduce the maximum possible throughput. Banyan networks are blocking, whereas TDM buses where the bus operates at least N times faster than the port speed are internally nonblocking. By the same concept, shared memory switches which can read and write at the rate of NV cells per second are internally non-blocking, since if N cells arrive for N different outputs, no conflicts will occur. Hence, to prevent internal blocking, shared resources must operate at some factor greater than the port speed. Applying this to banyan networks, the internal links need to run square root of N times faster than the highest speed incoming link (Onvural 1994). This factor limits the scalability and throughput of the switch. Coppo et al. (1993) have developed a mathematical model for analyzing the optimal blocking probability versus complexity tradeoff.

Buffering Approaches

Buffering is necessary in all design approaches. For instance, in a banyan network, if two cells addressed to the same output successfully reach the last switching stage at the same time, output contention occurs and must be resolved by employing buffering. The location and size of buffers are important issues that must be decided (Onvural 1994).

There are four basic approaches to the placement of buffers. These basic approaches are illustrated in Figure 12. The literature abounds with comparative studies of these, augmented with numerous queueing analysis and simulation results. Uniform random traffic, as well as bursty traffic have been examined. Although each approach has its own merits and drawbacks, output queueing is the preferred technique so far.

Input Queueing: Buffers at the input of an internally nonblocking space division fabric (such as Batcher banyan network) illustrate this type of buffering. This approach suffers from head-of-the-line blocking. When two cells arrive at the same time and are destined to the same output, one of them must wait in the input buffers, preventing the cells behind it from being admitted. Thus capacity is wasted.

Several methods have been proposed to tackle the head-of-the-line blocking problem, but they all exhibit complex design. Increasing the internal speed of the space division fabric by a factor of four, or changing the first-in-first-out (FIFO) discipline are two examples of such methods.

Output Queueing: This type of buffering can be evident by examining the buffers at the output ports of a shared bus fabric. This approach is optimal in terms of throughput and delays, but it needs some means of delivering multiple cells per cell time to any output. Hence, either the output buffers must operate at some factor times the port speed, or there should be multiple buffers at each output. In both cases, the throughput and scalability are limited, either by the speedup factor or by the number of buffers.

Internal Queueing: Buffers can be placed within the switching elements in a space division fabric. For instance, in a banyan network, each switching element contains buffers at its inputs to store cells in the event of conflict. Again, head-of-the-line blocking might occur within the switching elements, and this significantly reduces throughput, especially in the case of small buffers or larger networks. Internal buffers also introduce random delays within the switch fabric, causing undesirable cell delay variation.

Recirculating Buffers: This technique allows cells to re-enter the internally nonblocking space division network. This is needed when more than one cell is addressed to the same output simultaneously, so the extra cells need to be routed to the inputs of the network through the recirculating buffers. Although this approach has the potential for achieving the optimal throughput and delay performance of output queueing, its implementation suffers from two major complexities. First, the switching network must be large enough to accommodate the recirculating cells. Second, a control mechanism is essential to sequentially order the cells.

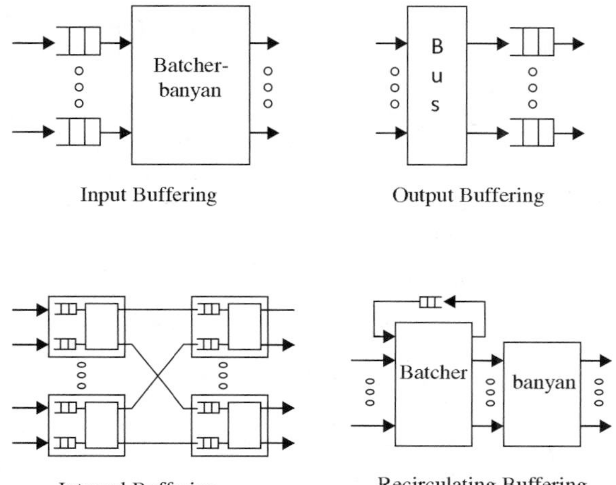

Figure 12: The various buffering approaches (combined from Chen and Liu 2003 and Onvural 1994)

Buffer Sharing

The number and size of buffers has a significant impact on switch design. In shared memory switches, the central buffer can take full advantage of statistical sharing, thus absorbing large traffic bursts to any output by giving it as much as is available of the shared buffer space. Hence, it requires the least total amount of buffering. For a random and uniform traffic and large values of N, a buffer space of only 12 N cells is required to achieve a cell loss rate of 1/10 to the power of 9, under a load of 0.9.

For a TDM bus fabric with N output buffers, and under the same traffic assumptions as before, the required buffer space is about 90 N cells. Also a large traffic burst to one output cannot be absorbed by the other output buffers, although each output buffer can statistically multiplex the traffic from the N inputs. Thus, buffering assumes that it is improbable that many input cells will be directed simultaneously to the same output.

Neither statistical multiplexing between outputs or at any output can be employed with fully interconnected fabrics with N squared output buffers. Buffer space grows exponentially in this case.

NEW DEVELOPMENTS

ATM could not fulfill the promise of providing a single integrated technology for LANs, public networks, and user services. IP was shown to provide such integration in a more flexible, more scalable, and less complex way than ATM. However, as it happens usually with technologies, the best ideas are borrowed by other solutions. In the case of ATM, various important concepts are inherited by other technologies, such as MPLS. Whereas other technologies, such as DSL, FTTP, and UMTS use ATM and AAL layers.

Multiprotocol Label Switching — (MPLS)

Multiprotocol label switching (MPLS) is a data-carrying mechanism which emulates some properties of a circuit-switched network over a packet-switched network (www.riverstonenet.com/support/mpls/intro_to_mpls.htm, www.ietf.org/html/charters/mpls/charter.html, and Rosen et al. 2001). MPLS has emerged as an elegant solution to meet the bandwidth-management and service requirements for next-generation Internet protocol (IP)–based backbone networks. MPLS addresses issues related to scalability and routing (based on QoS and service quality metrics) and can exist over existing asynchronous transfer mode (ATM) and frame-relay networks. MPLS is standardized by IETF in RFC 3031 (Rosen et al. 2001). For ATM-MPLS network interworking see www.mfaforum.org/ftp/pub/approved-specs/af-aic-0178.001.pdf.

Although the underlying protocols and technologies are different, both MPLS and ATM provide a connection-oriented service for transporting data across computer networks. In both technologies connections are signaled between endpoints, connection state is maintained at each node in the path and encapsulation techniques are used to carry data across the connection. Excluding differences in the signaling protocols (RSVP/LDP for MPLS and PNNI for ATM) there still remain significant differences in the behavior of the technologies.

The most significant difference is in the transport and encapsulation methods. MPLS is able to work with variable length packets whereas ATM transports fixed-length (53 byte) cells. Packets must be segmented, transported and re-assembled over an ATM network using an adaption layer, which adds significant complexity and overhead to the data stream. MPLS, on the other hand, simply adds a label to the head of each packet and transmits it on the network.

Differences exist, as well, in the nature of the connections. An MPLS connection (LSP) is unidirectional, allowing data to flow in only one direction between two endpoints. Establishing two-way communications between endpoints requires a pair of LSPs to be established. Because two LSPs are required for connectivity, data flowing in the forward direction may use a path different from data flowing in the reverse direction. ATM point-to-point connections (Virtual Circuits), on the other hand, are bi-directional, allowing data to flow in both directions over the same path (bi-directional are only SVC ATM connections; PVC ATM connections are uni-directional).

Both ATM and MPLS support tunneling of connections inside connections. MPLS uses label stacking to accomplish this while ATM uses virtual paths. MPLS can stack multiple labels to form tunnels within tunnels. The ATM virtual path indicator (VPI) and virtual circuit indicator (VCI) are both carried together in the cell header, limiting ATM to a single level of tunneling.

The biggest single advantage that MPLS has over ATM is that it was designed from the start to be complimentary to IP. Modern routers are able to support both MPLS and IP natively across a common interface allowing network operators great flexibility in network design and operation. ATM's incompatibilities with IP require complex adaptation making it largely unsuitable in today's predominantly IP networks.

Technologies Exploiting ATM and AAL Layers

DSL

DSL or xDSL is a family of technologies that provide digital data transmission over the wires of a local telephone network. DSL originally stood for digital subscriber loop, although in recent years, many have adopted digital subscriber line as a more marketing-friendly term for the most popular version of DSL, ADSL over UNE.

Typically, the download speed of DSL ranges from 128 kilobits per second (kbps) to 24,000 kbps depending on DSL technology and service level implemented. Upload speed is lower than download speed for asymmetric digital subscriber line (ADSL) and equal to download speed for symmetric digital subscriber line (SDSL).

Many DSL technologies implement an ATM layer over the low-level bitstream layer to enable the adaptation of a number of different technologies over the same link.

DSL implementations may create bridged or routed networks. In a bridged configuration, the group of subscriber computers effectively connect into a single subnet. The earliest implementations used DHCP to provide network details such as the IP address to the subscriber equipment, with authentication via MAC address or an assigned host name. Later implementations often use PPP over Ethernet (PPPoE) or ATM (PPPoA), while authenticating with a userid and password and using PPP mechanisms to provide network details (Mamakos et al. 1999, Kaycee et al. 1998).

PPPoA, Point-to-Point Protocol (PPP) over ATM, is a network protocol for encapsulating PPP frames in ATM AAL5. It is used mainly with cable modem, DSL, and ADSL services.

PPPoA offers standard PPP features such as authentication, encryption, and compression. If it is used as the connection encapsulation method on an ATM based network it can reduce overhead slightly (around 0.58 percent) in comparison to PPPoE (Mamakos et al. 1999). It also avoids the issues that PPPoE suffers from, related to having a MTU lower than that of standard ethernet transmission protocols. It also supports (as does PPPoE) the encapsulation types: VC-MUX and LLC based. PPPoA is specified in RFC 2364 (Kaycee et al. 1998).

Fiber to the Premises

Fiber to the premises (FTTP) or fiber to the home (FTTH) is a broadband telecommunications system based on fiber-optic cables and associated optical electronics for delivery of multiple advanced services such as the triple play of telephone, broadband Internet, and television all the way to the home or business.

Two competing FTTP technologies are active FTTP, also called active Ethernet, and passive optical network (PON) architectures.

Active FTTP networks utilize powered (i.e., "active") electronic equipment in neighborhoods, usually one equipment cabinet for every 400 to 500 subscribers. This neighborhood equipment performs layer 2/layer 3 switching and routing, offloading full layer 3 routing to the carrier's central office. The IEEE 802.3ah standard enables service providers to deliver up to 100 Mbps full-duplex over one single-mode optical fiber to the premises depending on the provider.

Passive optical network (PON) FTTP networks on the other hand avoid the placement of electronics in the field. PON networks use passive splitters to distribute fiber to individual homes. One fiber is optically split into 16, 32, or 64 fibers, depending on the manufacturer, which are then distributed to residential or business subscribers. In PON architectures, the switching and routing is done at the carrier's central office.

The International Telecommunications Union (ITU) has standardized on two generations of PON. The older ITU-T G.983 standard is based on ATM, and has therefore been referred to as APON (ATM PON) [7]. Further improvements to the original APON standard—as well as the gradual falling out of favor of ATM as a protocol—led to the full, final version of ITU-T G.983 being referred to more often as Broadband PON, or BPON. A typical APON/BPON provides 622 megabits per second (Mbps) of downstream bandwidth and 155 Mbps of upstream traffic, although the standard accommodates higher rates.

UMTS Core Network

ATM is also the data transmission method used within the universal mobile telecommunications system (UMTS) core network [24]. ATM adaptation layer type 2 (AAL2) handles circuit-switched connections. Packet connection protocol AAL5 is used for data delivery.

CONCLUSION

In this brief chapter, we have discussed several key aspects of ATM. ATM is a cell-oriented switching and multiplexing technology that uses fixed-length cells to carry various types of traffic, such as data, voice, video, multimedia, and so on through multiple classes of services.

ATM is a connection-oriented technology, in which a connection is established between the two endpoints before the actual data exchange begins.

The ATM protocol reference model is divided into three layers: the ATM adaptation layer (AAL), the ATM layer, and the physical layer, and three planes: user/control plane, layer management, and plane management. Four types of AALs were proposed, each supporting a different type of traffic or service that could be used on ATM networks.

ATM was designed to deliver guaranteed quality of service on demand while maximizing the utilization of available network resources. Therefore, effective traffic management mechanisms were specified.

ATM has been a partial success as a technology, with widespread deployment, but generally only used as a transport for IP traffic; its goal of providing a single integrated technology for LANs, public networks, and user services has largely failed. This role of integrator in today's networks in played by IP. However, various important ATM concepts are inherited by other technologies, such as MPLS, DSL, and FTTH. It is expected that the best ideas and lessons of ATM will be used in designing the next Internet.

GLOSSARY

AAL: ATM adaptation layer.
ABR: Available bit rate.
ANSI: American national standards institute.
ATM: Asynchronous transfer mode.
ATMF: ATM Forum.
B-ISDN: Broadband-integrated services digital network.
BT: Burst tolerance.
CAC: Connection admission control.
CBR: Constant bit rate.
CDV: Cell delay variation.
CDVT: Cell delay variation tolerance.
CLP: Cell loss priority.
CLR: Cell loss ratio.
CRC: Cyclic redundancy check.
CS: Convergence sublayer.
CTD: Cell transfer delay.
EFCI: Explicit forward congestion indication.
FTP: File transfer protocol.
GCRA: Generic cell rate algorithm.
GFC: Generic flow control.
HEC: Header error check.
IETF: Internet engineering task force.
ISDN: Integrated services digital network.
ITU: International telecommunications union.
LAN: Local area network.
LDP: Label distribution protocol.
MAC: Medium access control.
MBS: Maximum burst size.
MCR: Minimum cell rate.
MFA Forum: MPLS frame relay ATM Forum.
MIB: Management information base.
MPLS: Multi-protocol label switching.
NDIS: Network driver interface specification.
NNI: Network-to-node interface, or network to network interface.
nrt-VBR: non real-time VBR.
PCR: Peak cell rate.
PDH: Plesiochronous digital hierarchy.
PNNI: Private network-to-network interface.
PTI: Payload type identifier.
PVC: Permanent virtual circuit.
QoS: Quality of service.
rt-VBR: Real-time VBR.
RSVP: Resource reservation protocol.
SAR: Segmentation and reassembly.

SCR: Sustainable cell rate.
SDH: Synchronous digital hierarchy.
SONET: Synchronous optical network.
SSCOP: Service specific connection oriented protocol.
SVC: Switched virtual circuit.
VBR: Variable bit rate.
VC: Virtual channel.
VCC: Virtual channel connection.
VCI: Virtual channel identifier.
VPC: Virtual path connection.
VPI: Virtual path identifier.
UBR: Unspecified bit rate.
UNE: Unbundled network elements.
UMTS: Universal mobile telecommunication system.
UNI: User-to-network interface.

CROSS REFERENCES

See *BISDN (Broadband Integrated Services Digital Network); Frame Relay; Network Traffic Management; Packet Switching; Terrestrial Wide Area Networks.*

REFERENCES

Armitage, G. J. 1995. "Multicast and multiprotocol support for *ATM based Internets," ACM SIGCOMM Computer Communication Review*, 25(2): 34–46.

Awdeh, R. Y., and H. T. Mouftah. 1995. "Survey of ATM switch architectures," *Computer Networks,* 27(12): 1567–1613.

Awdeh, R.Y., and H. T. Mouftah. 1994."Design and performance analysis of input-output buffering delta-based ATM switch with backpressure mechanism," *IEE Proceedings: Communications,* 141(4): 255-264.

Badran, H., and H.T. Mouftah. 1994. "ATM switch architectures with input-output buffering: Effect of input traffic correlation, contention resolution policies, buffer allocation strategies and delay in backpressure signal," *Computer Networks and ISDN Systems*, 26: 1187–1213.

Bonomi, F., and K. W. Fendick. 1995. "The rate-based flow control framework for the available bit rate ATM service," *IEEE Network*, 9(2):25–39.

Charny, A., D. Clark, and R. Jain. 1995. "Congestion control with explicit rate indication," Proc. IEEE International Conference on Communications (ICC'95), 1954–1963.

Chen, T. M., and S. S. Liu. 2003. "ATM switching." *Wiley Encyclopedia of Telecommunications.*

Coppo, P., M. D'Ambrosio and R. Melen. 1993. "Optimal cost/performance design of ATM switches", *IEEE/ACM Transactions on Networking*, 1(5): 566–75.

De Prycker, M., R. Peschi, and T. Van Landegem. 1993. "B-ISDN and the OSI protocol reference model," *IEEE Network*, 7(2):10–18.

Dobrowski, G., and D. Grise. 2001. *"ATM and Sonet Basics,"* Redmond, WA: APDG Publishing.

Fahmy, S., "A Survey of ATM Switching Techniques," http://www.cs.wustl.edu/jain/cis788-95/atm_switching/index.html

Ferguson, P., and G. Huston. 1998. *"Quality of service: Delivering QoS on the Internet and in corporate networks," Hoboken, NJ: John Wiley & Sons.*

Henderson, T. R. 1995. "Design principles and performance analysis of SSCOP: A new ATM Adaptation Layer protocol," *ACM SIGCOMM Computer Communication Review*, 25(2): 47–59.

Hluchyj, M. et al. 1993. "Closed-loop rate-based traffic management," *ATM Forum Contribution* 94-0438R2.

Ibe, O. C. 2001."Converged network architectures: Delivering voice and data over IP, ATM, and frame relay," Hoboken, NJ: John Wiley & Sons.

Jain, R. 1996. "Congestion control and traffic management in ATM networks: Recent advances and a survey," *Computer Networks and ISDN Systems*, 28(13): 1723–1738.

Jain, R. 1990. "Congestion control in computer networks: Issues and trends," *IEEE Network*, 4(3):24–30.

Jain, R. 1992. "Myths about congestion management in high speed networks," *Internetworking: Research and Experience*, 3: 101–113.

Jain, R., S. Kalyanaraman, and R. Viswanathan. 1995. "The OSU scheme for congestion avoidance in ATM networks using explicit rate indication," Proceedings WATM'95 First Workshop on ATM Traffic Management, Paris.

Kalyanaraman, S., R. Jain, S. Fahmy, R. Goyal, and B. Vandalore. 2000. "The ERICA switch algorithm for ABR traffic management in ATM networks," *IEEE/ACM Transactions on Networking,* 8(1): 87–98.

Kaycee, M., A. Lin, A. Malis, and J. Stephens. 1998. "PPP over AAL5," *Request for Comments 2364 IETF.*

Lee, W. C. 1995. "Topology aggregation for hierarchical routing in ATM networks," *ACM SIGCOMM Computer Communication Review*, 25(2): 82–92.

Mamakos, L., K. Lidl, J. Evarts, D. Carrel, D. Simone, and R. Wheeler. 1999. "A method for transmitting PPP over Ethernet (PPPoE)," IETF Request for Comments: 2516.

McDysan, D., and D. Spohn. 1999. *"ATM theory and applications,"* McGraw-Hill, New York.

Onvural, R. O. 1994. *"Asynchronous transfer mode networks: performance issues,"* Boston: Artech House, Chapter 7, 207–252.

Ramakrishnan, K., and R. Jain. 1990. "A binary feedback scheme for congestion avoidance in computer networks with connectionless network layer," *ACM Transactions on Computer Systems,* 8(2): 158–181.

Rao, S. K., and M. Hatamian. 1995. "The ATM physical layer," *ACM SIGCOMM Computer Communication Review*, 25(2): 73–81.

Robertazzi, T. G. 1993. *"Performance evaluation of high speed switching fabrics and networks: ATM, broadband ISDN, and MAN technology,"* New York: IEEE Press.

Roberts, L. 1994. "Enhanced PRCA," *ATM Forum Contribution* 94-735R1.

Rosen, E., A. Viswanathan, and R. Callon. 2001. "Multiprotocol label switching architecture," *Request for Comments 3031 IETF.*

Sackett, G. C., and C. Metz. 1997. *"ATM and multiprotocol networking,"* McGraw-Hill, New York.

Saito, H. 1993. *"Teletraffic technologies in ATM networks,"* Artech House.

Sexton, M., and A. Reid. 1997. *"Broadband networking: ATM, SDH and SONET,"* Artech House.

Simcoe, R. J., and T.-B. Pei. 1995. "Perspectives on ATM switch architecture and the influence of traffic pattern assumptions on switch design," *ACM SIGCOMM Computer Communication Review*, 25(2): 93–105.

Stiller, B. 1995. "A survey of UNI signaling systems and protocols for ATM networks," *ACM SIGCOMM Computer Communication Review*, 25(2): 21–33.

Suzuki, T. 1994. "ATM adaptation layer protocol," *IEEE Communications Magazine*, 32(4): 80–83.

Vetter, R. J. 1995. "ATM concepts, architectures, and protocols," *Communications of the ACM*, 38(2): 30–38, 109.

Broadband Integrated Services Digital Network

B. Muthukumaran, *Gemini Communication Limited, India*

INTRODUCTION

Futuristic transmission systems will be based on fiber optic technology. Fiber optic network supports high-speed and low-delay data transfer required to meet the increasing demand for high bit-rate applications. A broadband service requires an information transfer rate exceeding the capacity of primary rate interface. Fiber optic network meets the bill of requirements for broadband service.

Narrow band-integrated services digital network (N-ISDN) (Kleinrock 1991) was the phoenix of the late 1990s. N-ISDN is a network providing end-to-end digital connectivity to support wide range of services. The basis of N-ISDN is a set of standards developed by CCITT. These standards were first issued in 1984. The N-ISDN standard is composed of two 64kbps B channel and a 16kbps signalling D channel. Each B channel can carry a separate telephone call and usually has its own telephone number called a directory number (DN). The B channels carry customer voice or data signals. The D channel carries signals between the ISDN equipment and the phone company's central office. The two bearer and one data channel are collectively called the basic rate interface (BRI).

The primary rate interface (PRI) is designed for businesses with larger data needs. The PRI offers 23 B channels for user information with one D channel operating at 64 kbps for user network signaling. It provides point-to-point connectivity between the network and a device requiring a significant amount of bandwidth. PRI is typically used as a trunk connection between the network and the PBX. PRI is capable of operating at 1.544 Mbps and 2.048 Mbps.

The N-ISDN physical layer is specified by the ITU I-series and G-series documents. The N-ISDN data link layer is specified by the ITU Q-series documents Q.920 through Q.923. Signaling on the D channel is defined in the Q.921 specification. N-ISDN builds upon the time division multiplexing (TDM) hierarchy. CCITT recommendation Q.931, defines a set of message types containing a number of information elements used to establish and release N-ISDN bearer connections.

N-ISDN was designed to switch fixed-rate channels. Switching channels at different rates requires different switching fabrics, each of which is designed to switch at a specific rate. Switching applications are concerned with point-to-point applications. N-ISDN was not designed to support switching and transmission rates at speeds necessary for services like high-speed data transport for business applications and distribution of high definition television (HDTV) signals. N-ISDN is not a panacea for all computer-to-computer communications. (Handel 1989; Kleinrock 1991).

CCITT defines broadband service as a service requiring transmission channels capable of supporting rates greater than 1.5 Mbps or primary rate in N-ISDN or T1 or DS1 in digital terminology (Handel 1989). Broadband ISDN is a network architecture that uses newer switching and transmission technique suitable for high-speed operation. The compatibility of a broadband packet network with the existing circuit switched network and with public switched network needs critical attention. The major advantage of the packet approach to B-ISDN is the high degree of service integration.

The primary objective of this chapter is to provide information on the evolution of B-ISDN, related protocols, and interface structures.

EVOLUTION OF BISDN

Recognizing the service limits of N-ISDN, BISDN was designed to extend the important concepts of ISDN to provide a universal, long-term transport capability for all services. The drivers of this technology are the advances in the field of fiber optics, desire of extending fiber networks into subscriber loop area, distributed processing requirements, and interest in HDTV.

The subscriber loops are divided into feeder loops and distribution loops. In the feeder loop high-speed transmission systems are used to link remote terminals (RT) to the central office (CO). The RTs are provided with simple multiplexing functions or line concentration functions for more efficient utilization of the feeder bandwidth. The distribution loops have separate fibers for each direction of transmission.

The final step toward integration of the network and service was done by using ATM. Although it was envisaged that B-ISDN would follow the circuit switching philosophy of N-ISDN, the use of ATM transport has pushed it the next generation. The adoption of ATM switching and transfer mechanism as the backbone provided B-ISDN with the capability to meet technology and market uncertainities with the flexibility unavailable in N-ISDN. For fiber in the loop (FITL) applications the emergence of ATM means that a single transmission fabric can support all current types of traffic including supervisory functions.

The Plenary assembly of CCITT (Consultative Committee for International Telegraph and Telephone) adopted the I series recommendations dealing with N-ISDN. The recommendations were proposed to satisfy the needs of services employing bit rates greater than 2Mbps. Some of the services visualized include broadband video telephony, video surveillance, high-speed unrestricted digital information transmission, high-speed file transfer, video document retrieval service, and so on. To provide broadband services, new attribute values supplement CCITT recommendation I.130.

Broadband ISDN Standards

The earlier section provided an overview of the evolution of B-ISDN. The need for high-speed data transfer were identified. This section outlines the basic standards of B-ISDN.

Broadband ISDN was designed to be a long-term solution for the variety of services identified. The need to standardize the proposed protocols both nationally and internationally was understood. Efforts from various forums like CCITT, ANSI, and so on to standardize the relevant aspects of B-ISDN were underway between 1990 and 1992 (Murano et al. 1990). The standards were developed to enable a service requiring both large and small bandwidths to operate in a cost effective manner. The standards define the protocols required to interface other network services (such as switched multimegabit data services).

Taking cue from earlier works, which defined networks as a set of layers, each offering a class of transparent service to the layer above, B-ISDN standardization opted for layered architecture. Each layer established a virtual communication (peer-to-peer) with an associated layer. The set of layers and the associated set of protocols define the architecture of B-ISDN.

The ITU-T recommendation I.320 provides a description for the protocol reference model. I.320 provides the concept of plane separation for the user, control, and management functions. ITU-T I.321, which is built on I.320, exploits the proposed layered approach. I.321 B-ISDN protocol model defines the physical and ATM layers that are the foundation for user, control, and management planes.

B-ISDN Architecture

The B-ISDN standards expressed in the earlier section outline the B-ISDN architecture (Kawarasaki and Jabbari 1991). The B-ISDN architecture was designed to offer access to bandwidths up to 155Mbps. The B-ISDN's reference model is consistent with the N-ISDN's reference architecture. The reference architecture does not imply a physical implementation. It identifies the principal functional units which make up the network and the interfaces between them.

A functional reference architecture model for the broadband network is the conceptual division of functions that must be performed in transporting information through the network. The perception of B-ISDN's development profile required the proposal of distinct protocol sets serving control, user, service, and transport functions (Byrne et al. 1989). The protocols were divided into the service layer, consisting of user plane (U plane) and control plane (C plane), the adaptation layer, and the transport layer spanning the ATM and transmission functions.

The user plane provides user information to flow along the path with its associated control fields for flow control and error recovery. (See Figure 1.)

The control plane includes all connection control functions required for setting up a connection (connection setup) supervision and release. The control plane and its relationship to ATM is best described through network functions. The user network interface (UNI) is the demarcation point between the network and subscriber domains. The network termination (NT) provides a bridge between the subscribers' internal network and the UNI. Here the functions of NT encompasses cell multiplexing, concentration, buffering, and switching. Separation and conversion of data streams into subscriber-specific service protocols is the principal role of NT. NT is also provided with operation and maintenance (OAM) functions to permit network initiated UNI testing. Network network interface (NNI) defines the interface between ATM networks and ATM nodes.

The management plane provides layer and plane management functions.

The functional architecture consists of broadband distant terminals (BDT), access nodes, service nodes, and transport nodes interconnected by broadband facilities.

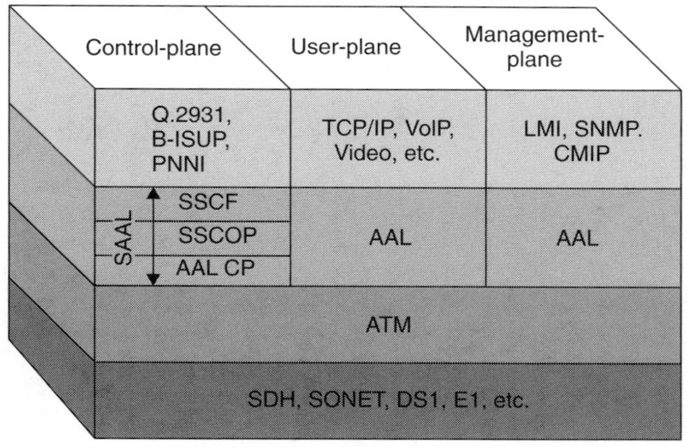

Figure 1: Protocol stack

BDT is positioned in the customer location and supports a variety of customer premises equipment (CPE) (Irvin 1990). Irvin has outlined the narrow band and broadband CPE directions. The functions of the BDT include media conversions, multiplexing and demultiplexing, signaling, and maintenance. BDT interfaces the customer terminal equipment with the fiber through the service or access nodes. It multiplexes information streams to the distribution fiber. It also demultiplexes the information streams, to various CPE (Irvin 1990). The distribution fiber uses SONET. The information carried over the broadband interface will vary both in terms of its service mix and the number of customers being served. The service nodes are interconnected through the transport network fibers. The transport nodes dynamically reroute traffic and cross connect fixed amount of bandwidth between service nodes. It provides a two-level transport hierarchy to interconnect service nodes. Light wave terminations, digital cross connects, add/drop multiplexing, and broadband packet cross connects are the functional components of the transport node.

B-ISDN Protocol Structure

Earlier the functional model of B-ISDN was discussed. This section provides an overview of the B-ISDN model of physical, ATM, and AAL layers. (Murano et al. 1990; Hac and Hasan 1989). (See Figure 2.)

The physical layer provides transmission of ATM cells over an electrical or optical physical transmission medium (Rider 1989). The physical layer is subdivided into two sublayers viz., the physical medium (PMD) sublayer and the transmission convergence (TC) sublayer.

PMD layer provides for the actual transmission of the bits in ATM cells. This layer interfaces with the electrical or optical transmission medium detecting the signals, transferring the bit stream and passing the bit stream to the transmission convergence (TC) sublayer.

The TC sublayer maps ATM cells from the TDM bit stream provided by the PMD sublayer. It provides five functions.

The TC sublayer takes care of generation and recovery of the transmission frame.

The transmission frame adaptation function adapts the received payload to the ATM cell structure. This layer transforms the flow of cells into a steady flow of bits and bytes for transmission over the physical medium such as DS1/E1, DS3/E3, or twisted-pair cabling within an office.

The cell delineation function enables the ATM receiver to recover cell boundaries. This is defined in ITU-T recommendation I.432.

The header error control (HEC) function is used prevent cells from reaching incorrect destinations when there are errors in the VCI or VPI fields.

The rate decoupling function inserts idle cells in the transmit direction to adapt the rate of ATM cells to the payload capacity of the transmission system.

The ATM layer performs multiplexing, switching, and control actions based on information in the ATM cell header and passes cells to AAL. The AAL layer is made up of segmentation and reassembly layer (SAR) and convergence sub-layer (CS). A common part (CP) component and a service specific component make up CS. The functions of AAL are described in ITU-T recommendation I.362.

Asynchronous Transfer Mode (ATM)

This section provides a brief overview of the concepts that make up ATM. ATM is a cell-based switching and multiplexing technology (Muthukumaran 2005). It is defined as an interface between the user and the network, and between networks. It takes the form of a network interface card, router, cross-connect, or an intelligent switch in the customer premises equipment. It is designed to switch any type of traffic over a common transmission medium. It offers service provider networks, the ability to simultaneously support video, voice, and data as an evolutionary successor to narrow band ISDN services.

ATM is a technology defined by protocols standardized by the ITU-T, ANSI, ETSI, and ATM forum. This is the technology of choice for the B-ISDN. This is considered to be the ground on which B-ISDN is built. ATM has the same basic characteristics of packet switching and delay of circuit switching.

Cell: ATM defines a mechanism to carry all traffic on a stream of fixed 53-byte packets. (See Figure 3.) The reasons

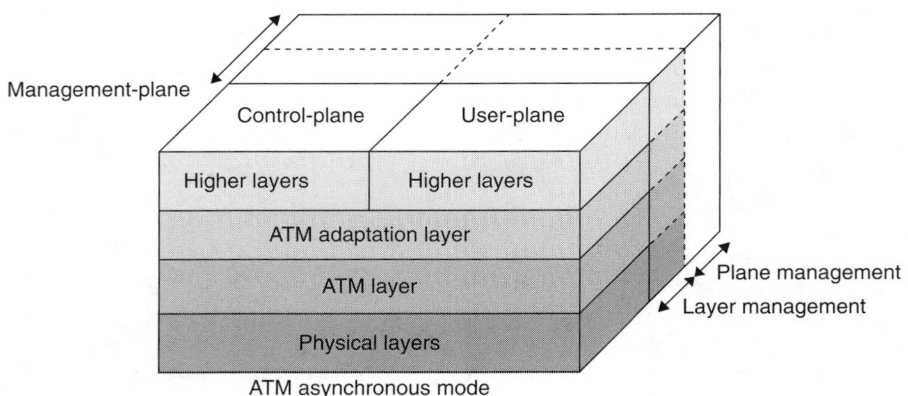

Figure 2: B-ISDN

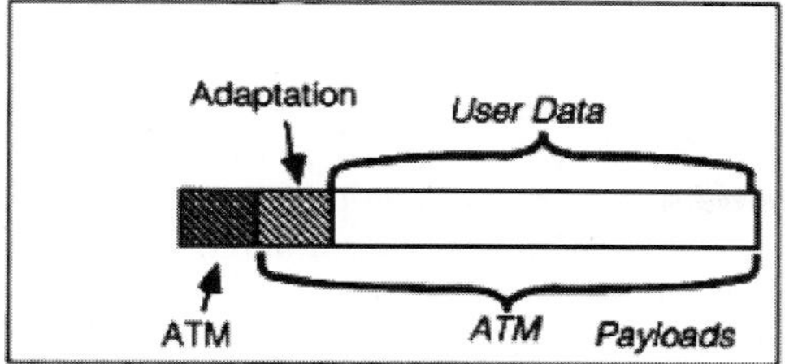

Figure 3: Cell structure

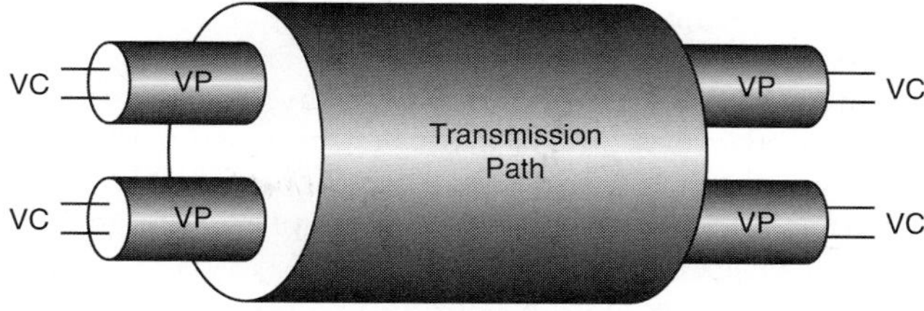

Figure 4: Transmission path

for fixing 53 bytes are discussed extensively by Prasanna (Zoccolillo and Prasana, 1989). These packets are called cells. According to ITU-T, a cell is a block of fixed length. It is identified at the ATM layer of B-ISDN. All packets in the network are of fixed length and hence are called cells.

The cell forms the basic element of the ATM layer. The ATM cell is made up of two parts: the header and the information (data). The data part is called the ATM payload. The cell header part is made up of 5-octets and the information part is made up of 48-octets giving a total of 53-octets. The job of the ATM header is to identify the characteristics of the virtual channel on a multiplex link. The information contained in the ATM header is designed to invoke functions that are internal and specific to the individual node. The header is made to carry only those attributes that define cell-by-cell variances. Attributes like traffic routing, data integrity and operations are required for connection maintenance.

The header is independent of service and transmission systems. The onus of service related attributes is given to the signalling system. Cell sequence identification in the ATM header is used to satisfy the requirements of cell ordering and cell loss.

Some of the functions contained in the cell header include:

- Generic flow control (GFC)
- A virtual path identifier (VPI)
- A virtual circuit identifier (VCI)
- A header error control (HEC)
- A payload type (PT)

The GFC exist in the UNI interface and is not present in the NNI interface. GFC is implemented to alleviate short term overload conditions that may occur. This implementation allows a terminal to achieve assured capacity or bandwidth allocated by the network to both VBR and CBR calls.

The B-ISDN interface between the customer and the network consists of ATM cells. The cells are multiplexed from several logical connections onto one physical interface.

ATM Virtual Channels and Paths

The ATM layer has two hierarchical levels, viz. a virtual channel and a virtual path level. A virtual channel is a bidirectional logical connection between the ends of a communication connection. A virtual channel is identified by the information carried in the header and by the attributes provided by the signaling protocol. There is a connection identifier in every cell header which explicitly associates a cell with a given virtual channel on a physical link. The connection identifier consists of two subfields, the virtual channel identifier (VCI) and the virtual path identifier (VPI). Coding for these levels is based on the use of VCI and VPI. The VCI is used to identify the logical channel connections and provides the basis for routing the cells. ATM standard specifies virtual channel connections (VCC) and virtual path connections (VPC). Together they are used in multiplexing, demultiplexing, and switching a cell through the network. When a virtual channel spans multiple links each link can potentially have a different VCI for the VC. The header contains at least one VCI.

The virtual path concept originated with concerns over the cost of controlling B-ISDN networks. A virtual path is bidirectional logical grouping of VCs that have the same destination. (See Figure 4.) Virtual paths are semi-permanent connections and the routing tables for the VP switch are preset by the network management functions. The plan was to group connections sharing common paths through the network into identifiable units. Network management actions including call set up, routing, failure management, bandwidth allocation, and so on, would then be applied to the smaller number of groups of paths instead of a larger number of individual connections (VCI).

The VPI is 8-bits at the user network interface and 12-bits at the network interface. The VP switch translates the VPI and VCI values. The VPI and the VCI together form the routing field, which associates each cell with a particular channel or circuit.

VP cross-connect is a network element which connects VP links. It translates VPI (not VCI) values and is directed by management plane functions and not by control plane functions. VC switch is a network element that connects VC links. It terminates VP connections, translates VCI values and is directed by control plane functions.

Adaptation Layers

Connection-oriented and connectionless, packet transfer services require an adaptation layer to provide segmentation and reassembly of the data packets into ATM cells. The efficient packing and reconstruction of services at ATM transport boundaries are essential to the successful utilization of ATM. ATM was not designed to be independent of the various communication services that may be using the network. ATM adaptation layer (AAL) was designed to achieve the complementary functions that make the data stream exchanged from end-to-end compatible with the requirements. The adaptation layer protocols remain transparent to ATM and lower layer protocols. The adaptation layer allows higher layer information of either the user plane or the control plane to be mapped to the ATM layer. The adaptation protocols provide alignment of service specific data structures with ATM cell payloads. CCITT recommendations I.362 and I.363 provide the definitions and specifications of AALs.

The AAL is organized in two logical sublayers, viz. convergence sublayer and segmentation and reassembly sublayer. The convergence sublayer generally provides the functions required to provide specific applications using AAL. The segmentation and reassembly sublayer is responsible for packaging the data received into cells for further transmission and unpacking the information at the other end. AAL layer provides the following services.

AAL-1 supports connection-oriented services that require constant bit rates and have specific timing and delay requirements. This is designed to carry voice and to emulate the characteristics of a TDM connection. This layer accepts a stream of incoming bytes.

AAL-2 provides for efficient transmission of variable length packets in delay sensitive applications and supports the transfer of time-sensitive constants as well as variable bit rate traffic. It consists of variable size packets encapsulated within the ATM payload. This was previously known as composite ATM or AAL-CU.

The AAL-3 and AAL4 specifications were originally almost identical in terms of PDU structure and functionality and hence were merged into AAL3/4. This layer provides connection oriented and connectionless variable bit rate services.

The AAL-5 layer supports connection-oriented variable bit rate data services. Message mode service and streaming mode service are two defined service modes. Message mode is used for framed data. Streaming mode is used for data separated in time.

Why were so many AAL layers designed when everything ends up packed into the 48-byte payload of ATM cells? We can answer this question based on the differences between key attributes supported by each AAL.

ATM implementations are based on switching and multiplexing technologies that induce very little delay in terms of the cell transmission time. They require very little variation in inter-cell delay to avoid "jitter" in voice applications. These systems utilize space division multiplexing also known as asynchronous time division multiplexing. The key characteristics of ATM are rate adaptation to support multimedia traffic and statistical multiplexing.

BROADBAND TRANSPORT

Traffic management is a set of network actions that monitor and control the flow of traffic (Amin-Salehi and Spears 1989). It is the act of managing network traffic, providing service guarantees to user connections, and ensuring optimal utilization of resources.

Basic traffic control functions of the ATM-based B-ISDN transport network are connection admission control (CAC) and usage parameter control (UPC). The main function of CAC is to accept or reject a connection request based on whether the available bandwidth in the network can satisfy the requirement of this connection. The bandwidth requirement of a connection can be expressed in terms of traffic descriptors such as peak rate, average rate, and burst length (Kawarasaki and Jabbari 1991). These traffic descriptors will then be monitored by the UPC function, and when the cells violating the negotiated parameter value are introduced to a network, these cells will be discarded or tagged by the network to ensure the negotiated performance of other existing connections.

Traffic characteristics of B-ISDN includes traffic parameters like call duration, bandwidth burstiness, and impairment. The traffic may consist of separate traffic streams that must be logically and physically bundled for integrated customer access but may be switched and processed separately in the network. Broadband network services require transmission medium for customer access and interoffice facilities. Optical fibers were preferred to be the optimal medium of transmission for broadband communications. Optical fibers provided low transmission loss, immunity from electromagnetic interference, and large information carrying capacity. Subscriber channels transported over optical fibers are multiplexed using SONET multiplexers.

SONET

B-ISDN transport architecture is based on the SONET protocol. It is used as physical interface for broadband services. Synchronous Optical NETwork (SONET) (Ballart and Ching 1989; Lee and Aprille 1991) is a North American standard for networking developed in the mid-1980's primarily by Bellcore and standardized by ANSI. It defines a digital hierarchy of synchronous signals including their formats and mappings of asynchronous signals (e.g., DS-1, DS-3) into these formats and defines the electrical and optical characteristics of the interface. This is byte interleaved synchronous digital hierarchy that consists of a family of standard electrical synchronous transport signals (STS).

SONET provides a set of standard transmission interfaces, interfaces for CPE, switches, interfaces, and interoffice transport systems. SONET frames allow for both voice channels and broadband services, and they carry framing overhead that is not embedded in the cell structure. Transport overhead is distributed throughout the frame. Each frame consists of 9 bytes of section overhead, 18 bytes of line overhead, 9 bytes of path overhead, and 774 bytes of payload transmitted in a pattern of 3 bytes of section/line overhead followed by 87 bytes of payload plus path overhead. An STS-N signal contains N copies of the section, line, and path overheads. If an STS-N signal is sent between two multiplexers with no intervening demultiplexing, it is permitted to send only one copy of the path overhead. SONET bit rates are integer multiples of 51.730 megabits per second. The base bit stream is made up of 125 microsecond frames of 810 bytes, where the bit rate is the integer part of the calculated bit rate. The B-ISDN user network interfaces will use two bit rates: 150 megabits per second and 600 megabits per second.

The basic SONET entity is the synchronous transport signal-1 (STS-1). It operates at 51.84 Mbps, of which 49.5 Mbpsec is usable payload and the rest is overhead. The

STS-1 frame structure is byte-oriented has 9 rows and 90 columns, four of which are used for overhead purposes. The frame rate is 8000/second (125 s/frame). Normally all SONET signals are bidirectional and run at the same rates in each direction. An STS-n signal (n > 1) is formed by byte-interleaving n STS-1's together.

Higher layer communication protocols will be based on the strengths of SONET. The bandwidth of ATM channel is determined by the rate at which cells are placed into the transmission stream. Explicit channel identification of fixed-length ATM cells facilitates implementation of flexible bandwidth allocation. The combined flexibility and capability of SONET, ATM, and photonic switching to serve adverse and demanding collection of various kinds of traffic opens up to final step to highspeed data traffic.

Traffic Descriptors

An ATM source sends ATM cell traffic to its corresponding ATM destination over the network. Traffic parameters are values that can specify the nature of the source traffic characteristics. A number of ATM attributes characterize the service categories. While setting up a connection on ATM networks, users can specify the parameters related to the desired quality of service. Traffic descriptors provide part of the connection related parameters like usage information, traffic type bandwidth requirement, and so on. The ATM forum has defined a number of descriptors that characterize the traffic pattern of ATM cells over an ATM connection.

The source characteristics of an ATM traffic flow are captured by the source traffic descriptor. This traffic descriptor describes the peak cell rate, sustainable cell rate, maximum burst size, and minimum cell rate. The maximum instantaneous rate at which the user will transmit is defined as peak cell rate (PCR). PCR is typically measured in cells per second. Sustainable cell rate is the average rate as measured over a long time interval. Maximum burst size (MBS) is a traffic parameter that specifies the maximum number of cells that can be transmitted at the ATM's PCR. MBS is a key measurement in capacity planning and network management. Burst tolerance (BT) determines the maximum burst size that can be sent at the peak rate conforming to the traffic contract. This is the measure of the time interval between consecutive bursts during which cells are sent at PCR. The characteristics of ATM flow over an ATM connection are captured in connection traffic descriptor.

Traffic Types

ATM is designed to handle a wide variety of traffic types. Several studies were conducted to address the issues of integrating different traffic sources. The B-ISDN traffic types can be categorized as follows.

Real Type Traffic

Traffic generated by voice and video sources have stringent performance requirements and are classified as type 0 traffic. The performance requirements are expressed in terms of delay, delay jitter, and cell loss.

Data Traffic

Traffic originating from data sources take the form of type 1, 2, or 3. A type 1 traffic is composed of low intensity traffic. This may consist of short burst of cells followed by long periods of relative inactivity. Type 2 traffic is made up of short file transfers between work stations and remote servers. Type 3 traffic moves large files between computers.

Service Categories

ATM virtual categories operate according to one of the following categories.

1. Constant bit rate
2. Variable bit rate
3. Unspecified bit rate
4. Available bit rate
5. Guaranteed frame rate

BROADBAND SIGNALING

Signaling is a technique whereby signals are used to exchange information or convey instructions to the remote machine. Signaling is used between a user and a network or between networks to exchange various control information. Signaling provides the functions such as the ability to establish point to multipoint connections, identification of virtual paths, recovery from network errors, and so on. The principal job of signaling is to establish, monitor, and release connections. The complexity of the signaling procedure depends on the flexibility provided by the network.

The year 1998 witnessed the emergence of signaling system seven (SS7) that provided the "out of band" common channel signaling capability. SS7 provided the signaling capability with which the users could specify quality of service (QoS) requirements. SS7 N-ISDN and B-ISDN are lower level capabilities that interconnect terminal equipment or service providers through local functional capabilities (ETSI 1998). SS7 provides out-of-band inter-exchange capabilities for telephony and N-ISDN. ATM SS7 interworking enables high-bandwidth ATM networks to integrate seamlessly with traditional circuit switched SS7 based digital telecommunications networks. Interworking between SS7 and ATM networks primarily involves signaling interworking, bearer service mapping, and traffic interworking, among other functions.

Signaling information traveling through the same virtual channel is called in-band signaling. Signaling information traveling through a different channel is called out-band signaling. The associated common channel signaling carries the signaling channels and the data paths through the same network elements. It is thus evident that the signaling channels closely follow the data paths. When the signaling channels do not share the same physical channel, it is then called as non-associated common channel signaling.

The control plane of B-ISDN handles all virtual connection related functions. This section provides an overview of B-ISDN UNI and NNI signaling protocols. Signaling over the B-ISDN UNI is specified by ITU-T recommendation Q.2931. The service specific coordination function (SSCF) is defined by ITU-T recommendation Q.2130. ITU-T Q.2110 specifies the service specific connection oriented protocol. B-ISUP (N-ISDN user part-ISUP) is defined in Q.2761 to Q.2767. This is used for signaling between networks at an NNI. In support of the deployment of large-scale public ATM networks, Bellcore has issued a document, entitled "broadband switching system SS7 requirements using the broadband integrated services Digital Network User Part (B-ISUP) (Chang et al. 1995) to describe procedures for using the B-ISUP of SS7 to establish and release switch-to-switch virtual connections based on the ITU recommendation Q.2761-2764.

The signaling channel operates on VPI-0 and VCI-5 on a physical interface. There are two types of signaling channel configurations viz., the associated signaling and non-associated signaling. The associated signaling is deployed by UNI3.1. The Q.2931 recommendation defines a virtual path connection identifier (VPCI), which associates a signaling VCC with one or more VPIs. UNI4.0 and UNI4.1 defines non-associated signaling based on Q.2931.

ATM provides elaborate signaling support for dynamic establishment and release of switched virtual circuits (SVC). It assumes a greater significance in ATM due to the extensive traffic contracting and CAC mechanisms. The signaling procedures for ATM are defined for user network interface and network-network interface. The signaling information includes QoS parameters. The UNI interface is implemented in one of the two ways. The UNI can be a continuous stream of ATM cells clocked at a bit rate of 155.520 Mbps, or 622.080 Mbps.

Meta Signaling

A different signaling technique is metasignaling. ITU-T draft recommendation Q.2120 describes the meta-signaling protocol. This is used for establishing, maintaining, and removing user network connections at the UNI. This is a part of the ATM layer and is located within the management plane.

In the ATM layer, the meta signaling protocol will be specified based on the terminal endpoint identifier (TEI) allocation procedure in LAP-D (Q.921).

Meta signaling refers to the process of establishing channels using signaling procedures. Meta signaling sets up three types of signaling channels, viz. point-to-point, general broadcast, and selective broadcast. The following procedures are used for the meta signaling protocol viz. assignment, check and removal. The assignment, checking, and removal procedures are independent of each other. The necessary relationship between them is performed via plane management. The assignment procedure is invoked by the user side sending an ASSIGN request to the network. The check procedure is initiated by the network sending a CHECK REQUEST message and waiting for CHECK RESPONSE. The removal procedure is initiated either by the network side or by the user side.

Signaling AAL

ITU-T recommendation Q.2100 specifies the protocol model for signaling AAL (SAAL). The SSCS portion of SAAL is made up of service specific coordination function (SSCF) and service specific connection oriented protocol (SSCOP). SSCF provides services to signaling AAL. Q.2130 defines the SSCF for UNI and Q.2140 defines SSCF for NNI. SSCF provides a mapping between the simple state machine for the user and the state machine employed by service specific connection oriented protocol (SSCOP). SSCOP is a peer-to-peer protocol. Q.2110 defines the SSCOP for UNI and NNI. (See Figure 5.)

The SSCOP of AAL provides mechanisms for the establishment and release of connections and the reliable exchange of signaling information between signaling entities. It performs the following functions.

It preserves sequence integrity by preserving the order of SSCOP-PDUs. It provides ordered delivery, error correction by retransmission, flow control, and error reporting to layer management entities. It generates status reports between peer entities. It helps two peer entities to remain in connection during prolonged absence of data transfer.

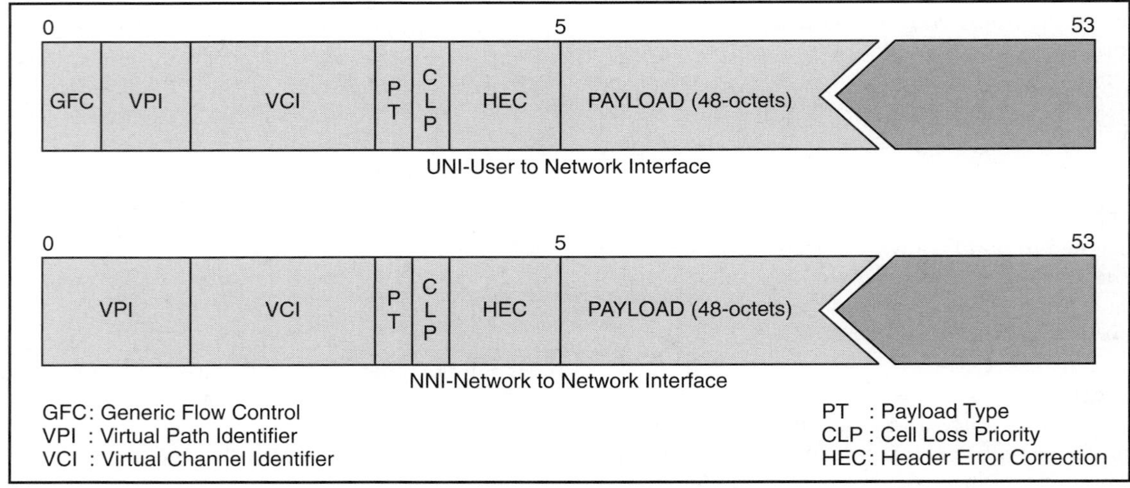

Figure 5: UNI-NNI

It provides local data retrieval, transfer of data, and link management functions. It is a fairly complicated protocol. The richness of SSCOP is in the assured data transfer mode. The SSCOP requires that the transmitter periodically poll the receiver as a keep alive action as well as a means to detect gaps in the sequence of successfully received frames.

Private Network Network Interface (PNNI)

PNNI protocol specifies interrelated routing and signaling protocols and functions to achieve the goal of controlling ATM connections established between nodes and connections. Version 1.0 of PNNI specification was released in 1996. PNNI is a routing protocol for ATM that allows for the exchange of routing information between ATM switches. Version 1.1 of the PNNI specification was released in 1996. It is an interesting standard and is less influenced by vendor competition. The PNNI protocol specifies interrelated and signaling protocols and functions to achieve the goal of controlling ATM connections established between nodes and networks. PNNI employs a recursive, hierarchical design that scales to huge networks. PNNI is the ATM routing protocol that enables switches to automatically discover the topology and characteristics of the links interconnecting the switches. PNNI uses UNI signaling to dynamically signal connection establishment and release request. PNNI identifiers uses the ATM end system address (AESA). AESA is derived from the international standards organization (ISO) defined in ISO/IEC8348 and specifies the formats, semantics, syntax, and coding of AESAs. The UNI specification specifies four AESA formats.

BROADBAND SERVICES

The services offered by telecommunications networks are increasingly diversified (Amin-Salehi et al. 1990). New service opportunities that address this trend in both residential and business environments extend beyond voice and low speed data applications. The service aspects of B-ISDN were jointly considered by CCITT SGI and SGXVIII. B-ISDN offers the flexibility to transport and switch a diverse range of services with bandwidth requirements from a few kbps to several Mbps. BISDN services are expected to have widely varying bandwidth, burstiness, and session length requirements. In response to the range of service requirements the B-ISDN design is based on high speed packet techniques. The broadband services are defined by ITU-T I.113 and I.211.

CCITT defines broadband service as a service requiring transmission channels capable of supporting rates greater than 1.5 Mbps or primary rate in N-ISDN or T1 or DS1 in digital terminology. Broadband and high-speed distribution services are characterized by long holding times and by constant bandwidth or constant bit rate.

Two families of data services are offered by ISDN (Day 1991). They are the circuit mode data services and packet mode data services. The circuit mode data services are offered by N-ISDN and accessed via the B channel based on the Q.931 setup and management procedures. The packet mode data services are further categorized as packet switched data services accessed via D or B channel and frame switched data services via the B channel. The B-ISDN with the ATM transfer technique, offers the cell relaying services on top of which other data services are offered. ITU-T differentiates the services into interactive and distributed services. Each service can again be divided into a number of sub-services.

Conversational services are basically end-to-end, real-time communications, between users or between a user and a service provider. This service supports the transfer of data, specific to user application. The additional bandwidth offered will allow services such as video telephony, video conferencing, video surveillance and high-volume, high-speed data transfer.

Messaging services are not real-time services. They provide user-to-user communication through storage units and store and forward mailboxes. Applications could include voice and video mail, as well as multimedia mail and traditional electronic mail. This places lesser demands on the network.

Retrieval services provide access to (public) information stores, and information is sent to the user on demand. This includes services like tele-shopping, videotex services, still and moving pictures, tele-software, and entertainment.

Distribution services are broadcast services, intended primarily for one-way interaction from a service provider to a user. The user has no control over the presentation of the information. Unlimited number of authorized receivers receive the information. This would be, for instance, a TV broadcast.

Business and residential services It is also possible to classify the B-ISDN services into business and residential services. Though there is a promise from B-ISDN to provide all the above-mentioned services, it is a lot more difficult to achieve the defined objectives.

Video Services

Two types of video services have emerged viz., entertainment distribution services targeting the residential customers and retrieval services targeting the business and residential customers. Switched access television service the delivery of entertainment video to residential customers over switched facilities is a good candidate for a representative B-ISDN application.

B-ISDN permits switched access television (SAT). This has several advantages over the traditional distribution networks. SAT provides higher quality signals with increased selectivity. SAT also requires significantly shorter setup delays than telephony. It eliminates the need for scrambling equipment. The most important capability requirement for this application is a high-bandwidth downstream digital channel. The transmission requirements between the user and the switch in order to handle switched access television are determined by the bit rate requirements for each video channel and for the number of video channels needed.

Broadband End User Applications

The set of applications can be grouped into general purpose applications and special purpose applications. The special purpose applications are the consumers of telecommunication bandwidth, super computers, high-speed workstations, and large data repositories interconnected for the purpose of processing medical images, molecular models, distributed CAD/CAM, geographical information services, and so on (Irvin 1993). As digital records are displacing paper records, applications such as backup and recovery, remote site storage, and distributed database update become increasingly important.

Connectionless services over ATM are being looked at with increasing interest and LAN to LAN interconnection. This service will be the first one to be offered in the B-ISDN together with the basic ATM bearer service, particularly in consideration of the fact that connectionless services may be offered efficiently over semi-permanent VP connections.

Another important class of application is multimedia combinations of text, image, speech, and music. This application includes distance learning, work-at-home, shop-at-home, electronic news paper, and electronic mail applications.

CONCLUSION

In the pre-ISDN era the data services available for PCs and PC network consist mainly of circuit switched data services and X.25 packet switched services. The development and standardization of B-ISDN, ATM, and signaling protocols for B-ISDN represent crucial elements in the evolution towards a multi service network. ATMs most important attribute is flexibility achieved through simplicity. N-ISDN and B-ISDN provide the overarching architecture for connecting CPE in a flexible, standard, and powerful manner. In a synergistic way, CPE and the public network are interlinked and each will provide an impetus for the other to evolve. Finally B-ISDN's ATM services meet the requirement of low-cost data transfer and connection time.

GLOSSARY

ATM Forum: The primary organization developing and defining ATM standards. Principal members participate in committees and vote on specifications

ATM layer: The layer of the ATM protocol stack that handles most of the processing and routing activities. These include building the ATM header, cell multiplexing, demultiplexing, cell reception and header validation, cell routing using VPIs/VCIs, payload-type identification, quality of service specification, and flow control and prioritization.

ATM management objects: (IETF RFC 1695) This specification defines objects used for managing ATM devices, networks, and services. ATM management objects allow net managers to consider groups of switches, virtual connections, interfaces, and services as discrete entities. The spec also specifies a MIB module for storing information about managed objects.

Constant bit rate (CBR): Digital information, such as video and digitized voice, must be represented by a continuous stream of bits. Such data gets transmitted through the network by committing traffic at a constant rate.

Guaranteed frame rate (GFR): A proposed standard from the Traffic Management subworking group of the ATM Forum. GFR lets users specify a connection-dependent minimum cell rate for transmissions.

Maximum burst size (MBS): A traffic parameter that specifies the maximum number of cells that can be transmitted at ATM's peak cell rate (PCR). MBS is a key measurement in capacity planning and network management.

Metasignaling: The technique employed by the ATM user-to-network interface (UNI) to establish a virtual circuit (VC) that conveys signaling information about switched virtual circuits (SVCs).

Multi protocol over ATM (MPOA): A proposed ATM Forum specification that defines how ATM traffic is routed from one virtual LAN to another.

Peak cell rate (PCR): The maximum rate at which cells can be transmitted across a virtual circuit, specified in cells per second and defined by the interval between the transmission of the last bit of one cell and the first bit of the next.

Physical layer (PHY): The bottom layer of the ATM protocol stack, which defines the interface between ATM traffic and the physical media.

Private network-to-network interface (PNNI): A routing information protocol that allows different vendors' ATM switches to be integrated in the same network.

Synchronous optical network (SONET): An international suite of standards for transmitting digital information over optical interfaces. "Synchronous" indicates that all component portions of the SONET signal can be tied to a single reference clock.

CROSS REFERENCES

See *ATM (Asynchronous Transfer Mode); Packet Switching; Terrestrial Wide Area Networks.*

REFERENCES

Amin-Salehi, B. and D. R. Spears. 1990. Support of transport services in BISDN. *IEEE*, 3: 1467–1472.

Amin-Salehi, B., G. D. Flinchbaugh, and L. R. Pate. 1990. Implications of new network services on BISDN Capabilties. *IEEE*, 3: 1038–1045.

Ballart, R. and Y-C Ching. 1989. Sonet: Now it's the standard optical network. *IEEE Communication Magazine*, 8–15.

Byrne, W. R., T. A. Kilm, B. L. Nelson, and M. D. Soneru. 1989. Broadband ISDN technology and architecture. *IEEE Network*, 23–28.

Chang, L. H., C. M. Hamilton, C. M. Liu, M. Rahman, and D. Y. Sze. 1995. ATM network signaling testing. *IEEE*, 1: 390–394.

Day, Andrew. 1991. International standardization of BISDN. *IEEE LTS*, 2(3): 13–20.

Eigen, D. J. 1990. Narrowband and Broadband ISDN CPE directions. *IEEE Communications Magazine*, 28 (4): 39–46.

EN301 029-9 V1.1.2 ETS I. 1998. Broadband ISDN signaling system no 7. *ETSI*, 1–5.

Hac, A. and H.B. Mutlu. 1989. Synchronous optical network and Broadband ISDN protocols. *IEEE Computer*, 22(11): 26–34.

Handel, R. 1989. Evolution of ISDN towards Broadband ISDN. *IEEE Network*, 3(1): 7–13.

Irvin, D. R. 1993. Making Broadband ISDN successful. *IEEE Network*, 7(1): 40–45.

Kawarasaki, M. and B. Jabbari. 1991. B-ISDN architecture and protocol. *IEEE Journal on Selected Areas in Communications*, 1405–1415.

Kleinrock, L. 1991. ISDN the path to broadband networks. *Proceedings of IEEE*, 112–117.

Lee, K. J. and T. J. Aprille. 1991. Sonet evolution. The challenges ahead. *IEEE GLOBECOM91*, 0736–0740.

Murano, K., K. Murakami, E. Iwabuchi, T. Katsuki, and H. Ogasawara. 1990. Technologies towards broadband ISDN. *IEEE Communications Magazine*, 28(4): 66–70.

Muthukumaran, B. 2005. *Introduction to high performance networks*. Chennai, Tamilnadu, Vijay Nicole Imprints.

Rider, M. J. 1989. Protocols for ATM access networks. *IEEE Network*, 17–22.

Zoccolillo, R., and P. K. Prasana. 1989. Discussion of emerging Broadband ISDN standards. *IEEE Transactions on Consumer Electronics*, 86–91.

DSL (Digital Subscriber Line)

Milos Milosevic, *Schlumberger Wireline Acquisition and Control Systems*

NEED FOR DIGITAL SUBSCRIBER LINE

What Is DSL?

The telephone network was originally designed to carry speech signals. The bandwidth needed for voice transmission is approximately 3.6 kHz from 0.406 to 4 kHz. Through various modulation techniques, it is possible to transmit data signals in the voice band. A number of standards ranging from V.21 to V.90 have been published dealing with data transmission over the voice band with each successive standard enabling a higher data rate.

Digital subscriber line (DSL) technologies use the bandwidth of the twisted-copper pair lines beyond the voice band (0.406–4 kHz) used by the voice telephone services. The DSL bridges what is commonly called the "last mile" (Goralski 1999) to the optical fiber deployed in the neighborhood by telecommunication companies. The DSL and voice band modems provide a dedicated link from the customer's premises to the central office, that is, a one-to-one connection. Although thought of as an interim solution until the full fiber deployment, DSL will be of interest for a number of years as the deployment of the direct optical fiber link has been slow and limited to urban areas (Henkel, Ölçer, Jacobsen, Saltzberg, and Bush 2002).

According to Mueller (2006), there were 209.3 million broadband subscribers worldwide at the end of 2005, which was an increase of 37% since the end of 2004. In the United States and China together, the number of DSL lines exceeded 40 million at the end of 2005. Adding the cable modem deployment numbers in those two countries brings total deployment to around 80 million at the end of 2005 (Mueller 2006). Mueller also finds that worldwide, the DSL share of broadband access stands at 66.2 percent, cable share at 24.29 percent, with the rest provided by the optical fiber. The largest number of lines is installed in the Asia-Pacific region (mostly China, South Korea, and Japan). The reason for the DSL success in Korea can be found in the high population density in urban centers collected around large apartment complexes. According to Lee and Lee (2003), the number of households with broadband access surpassed 70 percent and Korea Telecom alone has 5.4 million DSL users.

Broadband Access Model and Applications

Figure 1 shows the broadband access network model. Customer premises are connected to the network through a twisted-copper pair. At the customer premises, a splitter separates the broadband signal and the voice band. At the central office side, the voice service connects to the telephone network, whereas the broadband signal goes through the DSLAM (the figure is simplified as it does not show the multiplexing of many lines in the DSLAM module) and the ATM (or the IP router) switch to the Internet.

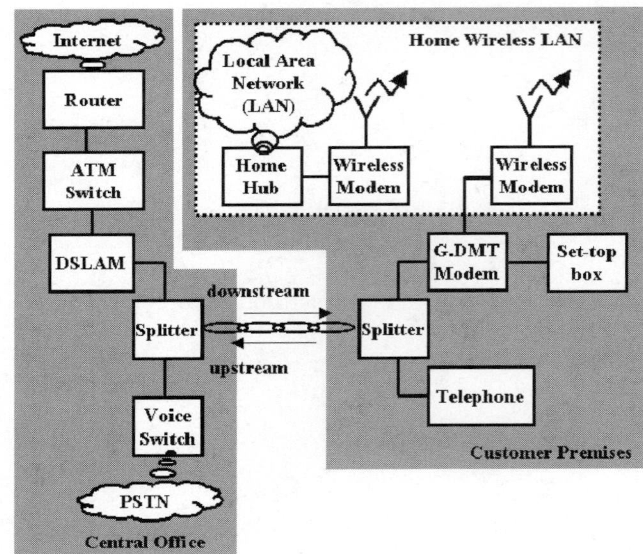

Figure 1: Block diagram of digital subscriber line broadband access (DSLAM, digital subscriber line access multiplexer, PSTN, public switched telephone network, DMT, discrete multitone modulation, ATM, asynchronous transfer mode, ISDN, integrated services digital network)

Table 1: Data Rate Requirements of Various Applications

Application	Downstream Rate(kb/s)	Upstream Rate (kb/s)	Demand Potential
Database Access	384	9	Medium
On line Directory; Yellow Pages	384	9	High
Video Phone	1,500	1,500	Medium
Home Shopping	1,500	64	Medium
Video Games	1,500	1,500	Medium
Internet	3,000	384	Medium
Broadcast Video	6,000	0	High
High Definition TV	24,000	0	Medium
Remote Office	6,000	1,500	Low
Office LAN	10,000	10,000	Medium
CAD	45,000	45,000	Low

Table 1 shows some of the applications driving the deployment of DSL technologies along with the data rates necessary to support their use. Although some DSL technologies are able to satisfy some of the data rate and loop reach requirements, none is able to satisfy all of them.

A survey of Internet access in Korea by the Korea Network Information Center (2003) notes that users primarily use email, games, Web surfing, and chatting. So, broadband access (nearly universal in Korea) allows faster use of these applications and does not, as of yet, facilitate high bandwidth applications such as streaming video or videophones.

DSL versus Other Technologies

Cable: *The Economist* (2003) writes that the U.S. local telephone carriers lose telephony customers at a rate of 5 percent to 6 percent per year to cable broadband access. Fitchard (2003) suggested that the market share for broadband services in the United States at the end of the third quarter of 2002 was 2:1 in favor of cable modem access over DSL. The number of United States households in 2001 with access to the cable network (not necessarily subscribers) was estimated at 99 million (Dutta-Roy 2001).

The coaxial cable TV infrastructure provided fertile ground for the development of a technology that multiplexes various types of content delivered over the same coaxial cable. Now cable providers offer cable TV services including TV interactive service, access to the Internet, VoIP, "always-on" service at connection speeds up to 5 Mbps, and video-on-demand. The disadvantage of cable is that it is a shared medium; that is, all users have to share the available bandwidth in contrast to a dedicated DSL line.

The Multimedia Cable Network System (MCNS) consortium began cable standardization in 1995 by producing Data Over Cable Service Interface Specification (DOCSIS) standards with versions 1.0 approved by the International Communications Union in 1998 and 1.1 approved in 1999. DOCSIS 1.1 improved upon DOCSIS 1.0 mainly in the area of quality of service (QoS) with the intent to enable VoIP (Lankford, Gameel, Boras, Cheema 2001). DOCSIS 2.0 was approved in December 2002 and adds greater upstream bandwidth, trellis-coded modulation (TCM) and an additional multiple access technology in code division multiple access (CDMA) besides time division multiple access (TDMA). The data rate available in DOCSIS 2.0 standard over a single downstream 6.4 MHz channel is approximately 30.7 Mbps (shared) and 1.5 Mbps upstream over a single upstream channel. Research based on statistical models cited in Dutta-Roy (2001) predicts that up to 400 households can be connected to a single 6.4 MHz channel without traffic congestion caused by the shared cable medium. The downstream is based on the 64-QAM modulation where each symbol carries 6 bits (optional TCM turns the 64-QAM into the 128-QAM to accommodate the extra bit for TCM). The upstream uses the 16-QAM where each symbol carries 4 bits. The choice of a smaller modulation signal set for upstream was dictated by the higher noise present in the upstream frequency band as a result of the interference from poorly terminated subscriber equipment, household appliances, and strong radio transmitters (Powell 1996). This was not of concern in the low data rate mode of interactive cable TV service using the upstream frequency band (Temple 1999; Hendry 1999). However, it has become a concern for the cable modem technology, which uses the upstream band at a much higher data rate.

Wireless: Wireless technologies are competing with DSL and cable for broadband access market. In 2005 Verizon Wireless begun a wireless broadband service based on 3G CDMA with access rates of 400 to 700 Kbps. This broadband service is available in major metropolitan areas in the United States and allows seamless switching between the Verizon's wireless broadband and cellular networks when the user leaves the broadband coverage area (Krakow 2004). Wireless broadband access offers VoIP and Internet access.

Table 2: DSL technologies (NA, North America; E, Europe; DS, downstream; US, upstream; Pairs, number of twisted-copper pairs; PAM, pulse amplitude modulation; 2B1Q; two bit per quaternary symbol; 3B1O, three bits per symbol; DMT, discrete multitone modulation)

DSL	Modulation	Data Rates	Bandwidth	Pairs	Distance
HDSL	2B1Q (4-PAM)	1544 kbps (NA) 2048 kbps (E)	193 Hz <580 kHz	2 3	12000 ft
G.991.2 SHDSL	3B1O (8-PAM) trellis-coded PAM	192 kbps 2312 kbps 4624 kbps	1.5 MHz	1 1 2	18000 ft
G.992.1 ADSL	DMT 256 tones	6144 (8192) kbps DS 786 (640) kbps US	1104 kHz	1	18000 ft
G.992.2 ADSL Lite	DMT 128 tones	1536 kbps DS 512 kbps US	552 kHz	1	25000 ft
G.992.3 ADSL2	DMT 256 tones	ADSL + 50 kbps Can group >1 pair	1104 kHz	1	18600 ft
G.992.5 ADSL2+	DMT 256 tones	25 Mbps DS 1 Mbps US	2208 kHz	1	3000 ft
G.993.1 VDSL	DMT 4096 tones	52 Mbps DS 3 Mbps US	12 MHz	1	3000 ft

The telephone companies are upgrading their telephone copper network to achieve higher data rates and enable services with higher entertainment value. DSL allows telephone companies to use their twisted-pair based network to offer VoIP, TV, and high-speed Internet access and to compete with the cable and wireless broadband access.

DSL STANDARDS

Overview

The predecessor of DSL is the physical layer of ISDN (integrated services digital network) developed in the 1980s for distances of up to 18,000 ft (ANSI 1992). ISDN offers two types of services: the basic rate interface (BRI) and the primary rate interface (PRI). The BRI has two B-channels (carrying user data at 64 kbps) and one D-channel (control signaling at 16 kbps) for a total of 144 kbps. The PRI has 24 B-channels and one D-channel (at 64 kbps) in Japan and North America for a total of 1.544 Mbps (with overhead bits), whereas other parts of the world offer 30 B-channels for a total of 2048 Mbps (with overhead bits). Following ISDN was the development of the high-bit-rate DSL (HDSL) (ITU-T 1998) at 1.544 kbps with the same signal processing techniques as ISDN. Single-pair HDSL (SHDSL) (ITU-T 2003b) is a version of HDSL over a single wire pair. Asymmetric DSL (ADSL) (ITU-T 1999) was standardized in 1995 and enjoys a rapid increase in worldwide deployment. ADSL uses the bandwidth of up to 1.1 MHz and achieves 6144 kbps downstream and 640 kbps upstream. ADSL2 (ITU-T 2002) improves on the reach and the rate adaptation of ADSL, whereas ADSL2plus (ITU-T 2003a) doubles the bandwidth used to 2.2 MHz. ADSL2 with the inverse multiplexing for ATM (IMA) standard allows bonding of several physical layer links from a single user thus, allowing multiplication of data rate (ADSL Forum 2003). A very-high-speed DSL (VDSL) (ITU-T 2004) is intended to bridge short copper access line lengths (shorter than 3000 ft) at high speeds ranging up to 22 Mbps from the network to the residential customer. Table 2 summarizes the specifics of different DSL technologies. Both the reach and the data rate vary as the technologies were developed for different applications.

Figure 2 shows the spectral allocation of different DSL services. Bandwidth allocated to different services is determined based on the desired data rate of the service, desired reach, and the presence of existing services and their mutual interference. For a detailed exposition on the DSL historical development, see Chen, 1998 and Starr, Cioffi, and Silverman, 1990.

SUBSCRIBER LOOP AND NOISE ENVIRONMENT

Bridge Taps and Loading Coils

The twisted-pair between the central office and the customer premises may have branching connections so that additional customers can be served or additional telephones can be connected at the customer premises. These branching connections are called "bridged taps" (Chen 1998, 20–21; Starr, Cioffi, and Silverman 1999, 57–58) and are connected to the cable on one end and usually un-terminated on the other. These branches cause attenuation and distortion as a result of the signal reflections from the un-terminated end. The distortion results from the spreading of the channel impulse response as a result of the multiple signal reflections. The attenuation is the result of signal cancellation caused by out-of-phase reflection from a bridge tap of a length matching the quarter-wavelength of a particular signal frequency. This results in deep

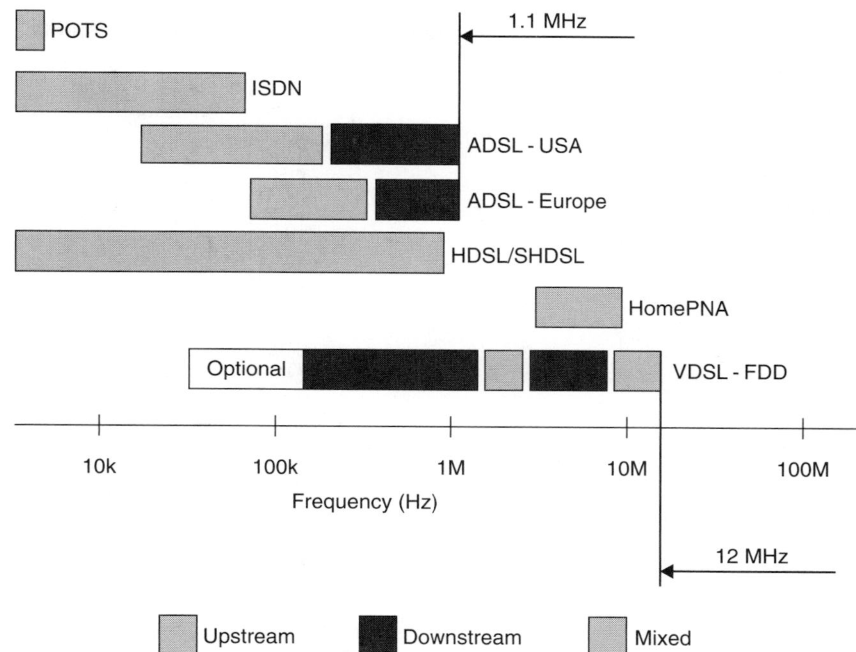

Figure 2: xDSL spectral allocation

notches in the frequency response of the system. These impairments are partly mitigated by the use of adaptive equalizers, echo cancellers, and time guard bands between symbol transmissions. Often, telephone lines in excess of 15,000 ft include loading coils. The coils decrease the attenuation in the voice band and extend the reach of voice service. However, these coils simultaneously increase the attenuation in the frequencies beyond the voice band and make it impossible to have a DSL connection. These coils have to be removed from the phone lines when a DSL connection is desired, thus, they have been removed in many countries as a result of the DSL deployment.

Transfer Function of the Twisted-Pair Transmission Channel

The twisted-pair lines can be modeled using the two-port ABCD matrix. The transfer function of a twisted-pair of any length can be calculated by cascading the appropriate number of unity cable sections that are represented using their ABCD parameters. The voltages and currents present at the cable are defined using the source (port 1) and load (port 2) impedances according to $\begin{bmatrix} V_1 \\ I_1 \end{bmatrix} = \begin{bmatrix} A & B \\ C & D \end{bmatrix} \begin{bmatrix} V_2 \\ I_2 \end{bmatrix}$ in which A is the open-load voltage ratio $A = \left.\frac{V_1}{V_2}\right|_{I_2=0}$, B is the short-load impedance $B = \left.\frac{V_1}{I_2}\right|_{V_2=0}$, C is the open-load admittance $C = \left.\frac{I_1}{V_2}\right|_{I_2=0}$, and D is the short-load current ratio $D = \left.\frac{I_1}{I_2}\right|_{V_2=0}$. For a detailed coverage of the ABCD modeling see Starr, Cioffi and Silverman, 1999 and Chen, 1998.

Noise Sources

The main source of crosstalk in DSL systems is the crosstalk from other DSL systems. Crosstalk is the current induced in neighboring wires by the electric and magnetic fields of the source. Twisted pairs are designed to minimize the electromagnetic coupling by twisting the wire so that currents of opposite directions cancel the induced signals. However, as a result of wiring imperfections, some energy leaks into the neighboring pairs as a source of noise. Figure 3 shows the near-end crosstalk (NEXT), far-end crosstalk (FEXT), and near-end echo. The NEXT is caused by a transmission of a signal traveling in the opposite direction compared to the desired signal. The NEXT transmitter is generally physically close to the receiver. A far-away transmitter transmits the FEXT, which travels in the same direction as the desired signal and traverses the length of the cable. In cases when a 4-to-2 wire interface (called hybrid circuit) is present and when a simultaneous transmission and receptions of signals on the same twisted pair is intended, the receiver may experience near-end echo. Echo is the signal from the local transmitter that leaks into the local receiver as a result of the imperfections of the hybrid circuit.

The FEXT power spectral density at the input to a DSL receiver is modeled by the $PSD_{FEXT}(f) = 9 \times 10^{-20} \times S(f) \left(\frac{N}{49}\right)^{0.6} d \times f^2$ in which $S(f)$ is the power spectral density of the noise source, d is the length of the cable in feet, f is frequency in Hz, and N is the number of disturbers. The PSD_{FEXT} grows with the square of the frequency but only linearly with the length. The PSD_{NEXT} at the input of a DSL receiver is modeled by the

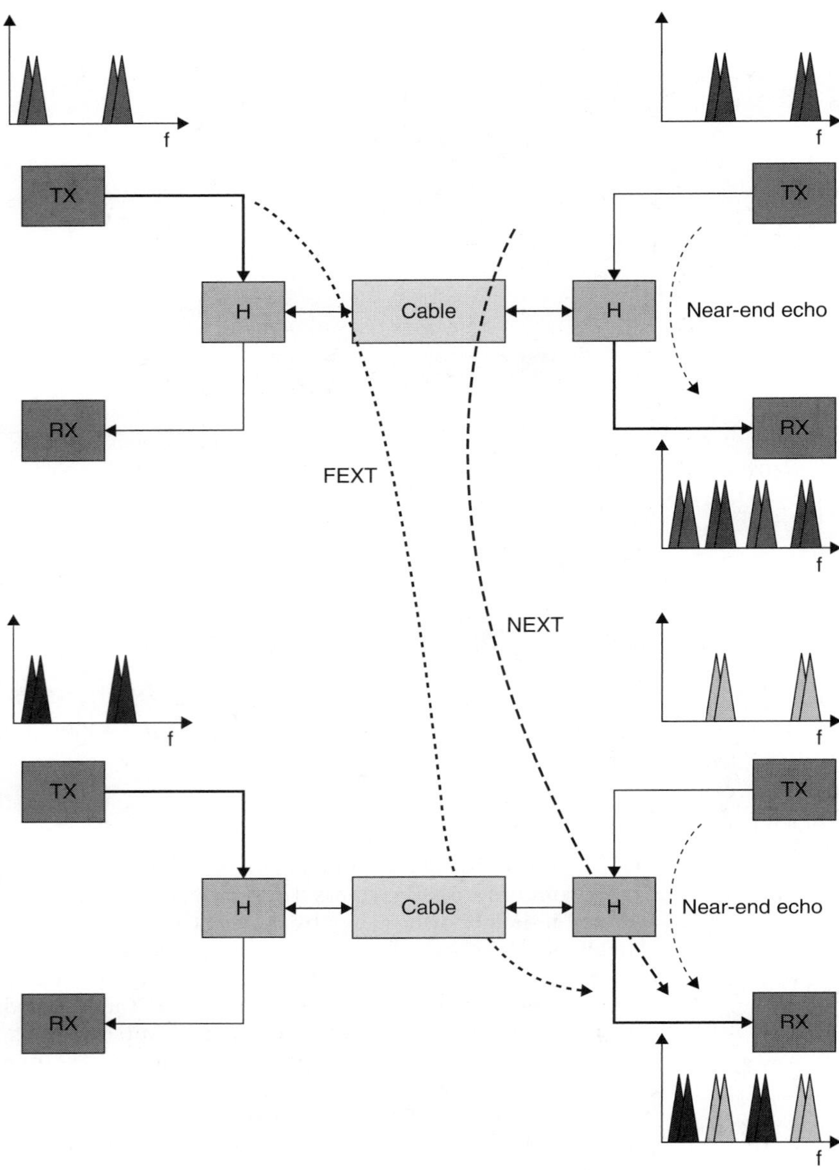

Figure 3: Near and far-end crosstalk

$PSD_{NEXT}(f) = S(f)\left(\frac{N}{49}\right)^{0.6} \frac{f^{1.5}}{1.134 \times 10^{13}}$ in which $S(f)$ is the power spectral density of the noise source, f is the frequency in Hz, and N is the number of disturbers.

HDSL

Applications

High bit rate DSL (HDSL) was developed as a replacement technology for the T1/E1 transmission systems. In October 1998 ITU approved G.991.1 (ITU-T 1998) HDSL modeled closely after the ETSI TM-03036. An amended version was approved in 2003. The second generation of HDSL, known as single-pair HDSL (SHDSL) (not to be confused with pre-standard implementations known as symmetric DSL) uses only one pair of wires instead of two to achieve variable 192 kbps to 2.312 Mbps payload. SHDSL reaches 18,000 ft without repeaters because its transmit power is 3 dB higher than the one for HDSL and the use of trellis-coded modulation. The improvement over HDSL is also found in the transmission spectral mask that was designed to reduce the crosstalk to other communication technologies.

HDSL is used to connect users requiring T1/E1-like data rates to central offices at a lower cost, with better reliability, and a higher maintainability than it is possible with T1/E1 systems. HDSL operates at 10^{-7} or better bit error rate. As Starr et al. (1999) mention, HDSL will operate at 10^{-7} under worst-case conditions, whereas 99 percent of the links operate at 10^{-9}or better. The T1/E1 systems were designed in the 1960s to carry traffic in between central offices (CO). The T1 achieves 1.544 Mbps using the alternate mark inversion (AMI) line code, whereas the E1 achieves 2.048 Mbps using HDB3. The T1/E1 systems are not used anymore as the high-speed links between central offices as fiber and microwave links have replaced them. The T1 systems are expensive to install because they require repeaters and they need to be congregated into binders where the lines carrying data to the customer are in one binder and the lines carrying data from the customer are in another (the T1 systems use four wires for communication). HDSL was developed as a low-cost alternative to the T1 as it did not require repeaters up to the loop length of 12,000 ft and no binding or loop conditioning apart from the elimination of loading coils. For the customers living beyond the 12,000 ft limit, HDSL systems are deployed using a single repeater to reach 24,000 ft or with two repeaters to reach up to 36,000 ft. HDSL also brought more advanced loop and traffic diagnostic capabilities compared to the older T1/E1 systems. As the HDSL was intended to replace the T1/E1 lines, it supports the communication over two or three pairs of wires for a data rate of 1.544 Mbps matching the T1 and 2.048 Mbps matching the E1. Each pair uses full-duplex communication with 784 kbps net and 768 kbps payload in each direction. It is common to use the term dual-duplex for two-pair HDSL and fractional-rate HDSL for each of the pairs. The dual-duplex uses echo cancellation to separate two directions of transmission, which occupy the same frequency band. The fractional-rate HDSL carries up to twelve DS0 (Digital Signal 0) channels and connects to a D4 channel bank, which multiplexes DS0 channels from multiple fractional-rate HDSL channels.

Line Code

The two-pair HDSL 3 dB bandwidth is 196 kHz and the symbol rate is 392 ksym/s, thus the data rate per wire pair is 784 kbps. HDSL uses a line code known as 2B1Q (4-PAM), which maps two bits of information into one quaternary symbol. SHDSL uses 3B1O modulation, which maps three bits of information into one symbol. The 2B1Q is a baseband code, that is, it contains a DC component. Figure 4 shows the HDSL time domain transmitted pulse mask.

The transmitted pulse is distorted by the transformers present in an HDSL circuit, which do not pass the DC and by the band-limited channel with varying frequency domain response over the transmission frequency band. The receiver uses equalizers to eliminate the effects of the channel. The mapping of two bits to symbols used in the 2B1Q is called Gray coding and it ensures that a decoding error would result in only one bit error.

ADSL

Applications

According to Chen (1999) the goal of arriving at the asymmetric digital subscriber loop (ADSL) standard was to promote the technology that was to serve economically subscribers at distances of up to 18,000 ft (from the CO) with the T1 rates of at least 1.544 Mbps over a single twisted-copper pair. Reusens et al. (2001) wrote that the original intent for the ADSL was video-on-demand (VoD); however, that application never succeeded as a result of a lack of a business case for it. Bingham (1990) argues that although the idea of multicarrier modulation has been present for many years, the signal processing power has enabled its use over telephone cables in the 1990s. The ADSL was standardized in the United States by the American National Standards Institute (ANSI) T1.413–1998 (1998), and internationally by the International Telecommunications Union G.DMT (G.992.1) (1999), G.Lite (G.992.2) (1999), ADSL2 G.992.3 (2005), and ADSL2 + G.992.5 (2005). The G.DMT reaches up to 18,000 ft and provides the uplink rate of up to 8,192 kbps and a downlink rate of up to 640 kbps.

Line Code

The G.992.1 ADSL is full duplex, that is, data simultaneously flows downstream from a central office to a remote terminal, and upstream in the opposite direction on a single twisted-wire pair. The ADSL uses discrete multitone (DMT) as a multicarrier modulation method in which the available bandwidth of a communication channel, such as twisted-pair copper media, is divided into numerous sub-channels or bins via a fast Fourier transform (FFT). In the G.992.1 ADSL standard, an FFT/IFFT block is used to generate up to 256 separate 4.3125 kHz wide

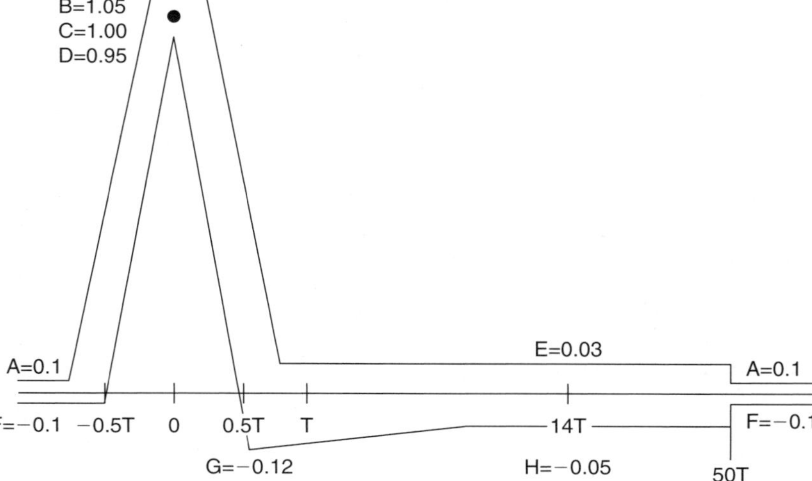

Figure 4: HDSL time domain transmit pulse (A, B, C, D, E, F, G, H are normalized signal levels where B maps to ±2.625V for the ±3 (10, 00) quaternary symbol and into ±0.875V for the ±1 (11, 01) quaternary symbol)

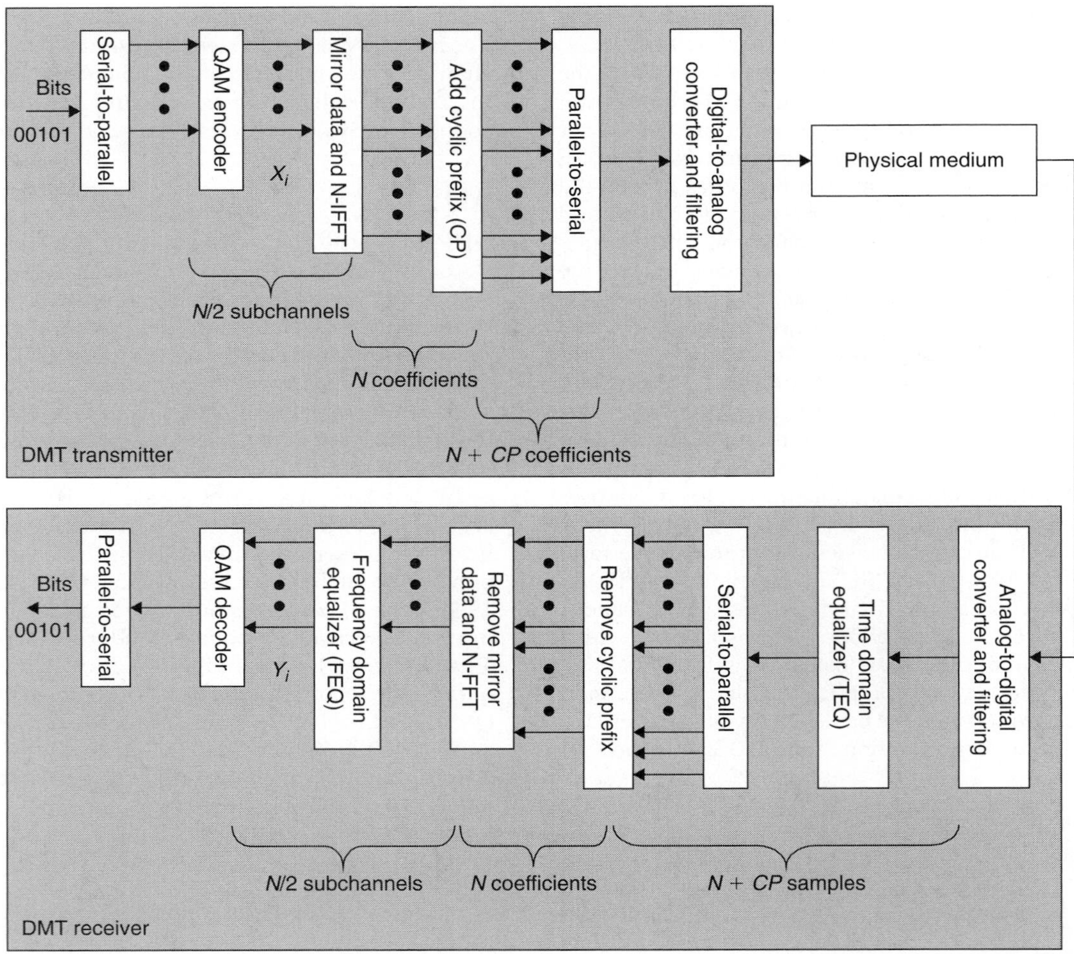

Figure 5: DMT transmitter and receiver

downstream sub-channels from 0 to 1.104 MHz. The ADSL uses the frequency band from 25.875 kHz to 1.104 MHz. Likewise, an FFT/IFFT block is used to generate 32 upstream sub-channels up to 138 kHz. Sub-channels in the range 0 to 25.875 kHz are not used in the ADSL so as not to interfere with the voiceband channel (0.406–4 kHz). The compatibility with the ISDN service is achieved by mandating lower transmission power in the frequency band 50 to 80 kHz for the 2B1Q ISDN or band 70 to 90 kHz for the 4B3T ISDN. Each DMT sub-channel is nearly independent of the other sub-channels and the degree of independence increases with the number of sub-channels (Cioffi 1991). Figure 5 shows a simplified block diagram of a DMT transceiver.

The input bit stream on the transmitter is mapped using quadrature amplitude modulation (QAM) into a $N/2 \times 1$ complex vector X_i at time i. The bit stream is partitioned, mapped into complex values and assigned to sub-channels based on the available SNR in each sub-channel and the desired bit error rate (10^{-7}). Vector X_i is mirrored into its conjugate-symmetric copy X_i^* and both are presented at the input of the IFFT block. An inverse fast Fourier transform (IFFT) block modulates each input entry into a different frequency band (sub-channel) with the carrier frequency lying in the center of the band.

The real-valued vector x of size N is defined using the IDFT as $x_k = \sum_{i=0}^{N-1} X_j e^{j\frac{2\pi ki}{N}}$ $k = 0, 1, \ldots N-1$. A guard period of CP samples is added before digital-to-analog (D/A) conversion and transmission. A spectrally shaped channel impulse response longer than $CP + 1$ causes inter-carrier interference (ICI) and inter-symbol interference (ISI). The ISI refers to the mixing of energy belonging to neighboring symbols during transmission, whereas the ICI refers to a similar process for the sub-channels. If the length of the channel impulse response is less than or equal to $CP + 1$, then adding a guard period of CP samples at the beginning of a DMT frame will prevent the occurrence of the ISI. If the guard period is chosen to be the copy of the last CP samples of a DMT frame and the length of the channel impulse response is less than or equal to $CP + 1$, then the ICI is eliminated as well. This choice of the guard period is also known as a cyclic prefix. This grouping of $N + CP$ samples is referred to as a frame. Frames are sent sequentially one after the other. The CP additional samples lower the data rate by a factor of $N/(N + CP)$.

For the ADSL downstream transmission, $N = 512$ and $CP = 32$ samples, whereas for the ADSL upstream transmission, $N = 64$ and $CP = 4$ samples. The receiver performs analog-to-digital (A/D) conversion, equalization using time-domain equalization (TEQ) using a finite impulse response (FIR) filter, CP elimination, FFT, QAM decoding, and error correction. The TEQ is designed during modem initialization and it shortens the impulse response to $CP + 1$ or less. A large number of research publications deals with the design of the TEQ; for a list of relevant publications see Milosevic, 2003.

The demodulation of the received DMT frame is done by the FFT block, after which the frequency domain equalizer (FEQ) completely removes the phase and frequency distortion of the channel. This fully equalized signal is then decoded using a QAM decoder resulting in an estimate of the transmitted complex symbol Y_i and further resolved into the corresponding bit stream. The data rate in bits per frame in the kth sub-channel is $b_k = \log_2\left(1 + \frac{SNR_k}{\Gamma}\right)$ in which the difference between channel capacity and the best achievable rate in practice can be characterized by the SNR gap $\Gamma = 9.8 + \gamma_m - \gamma_c$ in which in the G.DMT ADSL, typically, for the probability of error 10^{-7}, $\gamma_m = 6\,\text{dB}$, and $\gamma_c = 4.2\,\text{dB}$; hence, $\gamma = 11.6\,\text{dB}$ and SNR_k is the signal-to-noise power ratio in the subchannel k.

The major noise source faced by the ADSL is the crosstalk from other the T1/E1, the SHDSL, and the HDSL. Ouyang, Duvaut, Moreno, and Pierrugues (2003) state that the low frequencies of the upstream channel are impaired by the noise from the SHDSL. The noise from other ADSL lines becomes the dominant factor on lengthy connections because of the superior reach of the ADSL over other services (Ouyang et al. 2003).

VDSL

Applications

The need for the VDSL is driven by high-data rate applications such as high-speed Internet access with requirements for high download speeds, multi-user high bandwidth access, high-definition TV (HDTV), high-quality video conferencing, and video-on-demand. The VDSL could also aid more specialized activities such as remote publishing, movie editing, engineering using remote CAD connections, and remote medical procedures.

ITU-T Recommendation G.993.1 VDSL was prepared by the ITU-T Study Group 15 and approved in 2004. The VDSL uses copper wires previously designed for telephone voice traffic and it exploits the bandwidth of up to 12 MHz. G.993.1 is full duplex, that is, data simultaneously flows downstream from a central office to a remote terminal, and upstream in the opposite direction. Figure 6 shows the broadband access model of the VDSL in which the fiber from the service provider reaches into the neighborhood and terminates at the optical network unit (ONU).

This model is called "fiber-to-the-cabinet" and it allows the service provider to shorten the distance that the broadband signal will travel over the copper wires. The maximum distance that the signal will experience is up to 5,000 ft, which reduces the attenuation of the signal at the receiver compared to the ADSL and allows the VDSL to use the bandwidth of up to 12 MHz with correspondingly higher data rates compared to the ADSL (ADSL2), which uses up to 1.1 MHz (2.2 MHz). G.993.1 transceivers employ a frequency division duplexing (FDD) scheme to separate the upstream and downstream directions of transmissions. The G.993.1 FDD uses four bands starting from 138 kHz and ending at 12 MHz. The bands are denoted as optional, DS1, US1, DS2, and US2 with the spans shown in Figure 7 and Table 3.

The upstream and downstream bands are interlaced so that the VDSL connection can be established up to the specified length of the cable even though the attenuation of the cable may render bands DS2 and US2 unusable. The optional band usage and direction of transmission are determined during the initialization of the VDSL link. The start and end frequencies of the bands are determined by the bandplans specified in the standard. The bandplans are incorporated in the standard in order to accommodate regional specificities of national networks.

Line Code

The VDSL uses DMT as a multicarrier modulation method. The number of subcarriers will be equal to $N = 2^{n+8}$ in which $n = 0, 1, 2, 3,$or 4, thus the minimum number of tones is 256, whereas the maximum number is 4096. The exact number of tones used will be negotiated between the customer's modem (VTU-R) and the CO modem (VTU-C) during the initialization stage. The bandwidth occupied by each tone is 4.3125 kHz with the carrier centered in the middle of the tone band. Real-valued samples will be generated from complex-valued vector X of length $2N$ via the inverse discrete Fourier transform (IDFT), in whih the last N complex values are a conjugated mirrored image of the first N complex values. A value of zero is placed at the DC and at the Nyquist

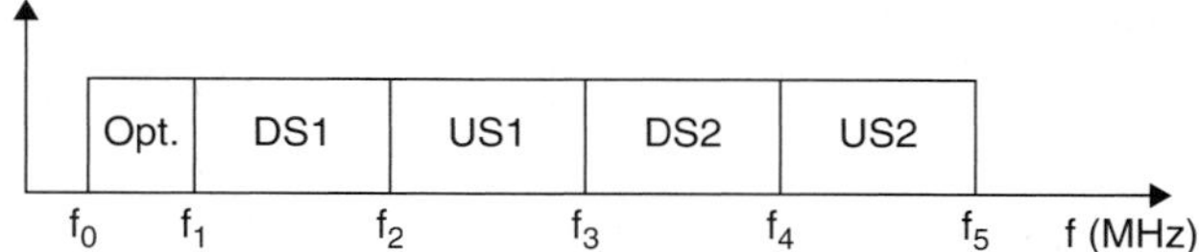

Figure 7: VDSL spectral allocation

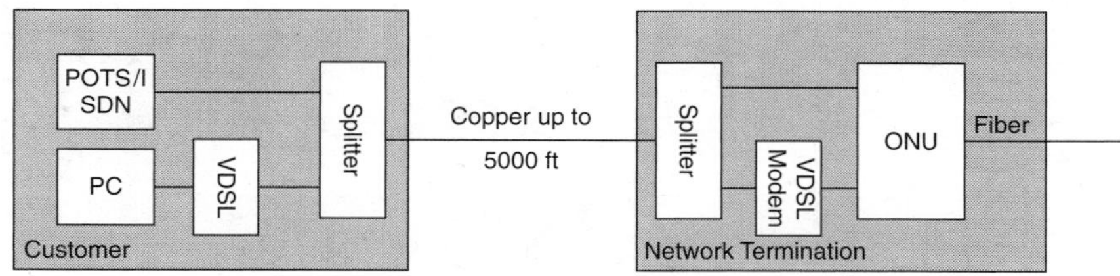

Figure 6: VDSL access network

Table 3: VDSL bandplans

	Bandplan (MHz)		
	A	B	C
Optional	0.025–0.138	0.025–0.138	0.025–0.138
DS1	0.138–3.75	0.138–3.0	0.138–2.5
US1	3.75–5.2	3.0–5.1	2.5–3.75
DS2	5.2–8.5	5.1–7.05	3.75–variable
US2	8.5–12	7.05–12	variable–12

frequency as no data is transmitted ever on those bands. The real-valued frame x of size $2N$ is defined using the IDFT as $x_k = \sum_{i=0}^{2N-1} X_i e^{j\frac{2\pi ki}{2N}}$ $k = 0, 1, \ldots 2N-1$.

The last L_{cp} samples of x are pre-pended to it as a cyclic prefix, whereas the first L_{cs} samples of x are appended to it as a cyclic suffix. The first B and the last B samples of the cyclic prefix and cyclic suffix are shaped (multiplied by a suitable window such as raised cosine), in which B is equal to 2^{n+4} where n is at most 3. The shaped portions of successive frames overlap. The sum of cyclic extensions is $L_{cp} + L_{cs} - B = m{*}2^{n+1}$ in which m is an integer. The purpose of pulse shaping is to reduce the leakage of energy from one frequency band to another (Isaksson and Mestdagh 1998). This reduces the self-NEXT where the crosstalking transmitters are not synchronized to the receiver DMT frames and it also reduces out-of-band energy into protected radio bands.

Although the uplink and the downlink transmissions are separated into different frequency bands, the fact that parts of successive self-NEXT frames are captured will lead to some leakage of downlink energy into the uplink band. This is because of the transition between the cyclic suffix of one frame and the cyclic prefix of another (Figure 8).

Thus, to make these transitions less rapid and reduce the out-of-band energy compared to the ADSL standard, the VDSL standard imposes the shaping of the first and last B samples of a frame. This offers protection against NEXT, but it also decreases the throughput and increases latency as a result of the additional samples. In addition, VDSL receiver designs also employ windowing of the received $2N$ samples of a DMT frame to reduce the radio-frequency ingress (Isaksson and Mestdagh 1998).

The VDSL standard makes optional synchronous operation where all transmitters in a bundle start the frames at the same time or asynchronous operation when that is not the case. The VDSL specifies that all modem pairs in the same binder in synchronous operation will have the same length of the non-overlapped cyclic suffix and that length will be equal to the one-way propagation delay of the longest line in the binder. Because the cyclic suffix of a self-NEXT frame last as long or longer than the one-way propagation delay of this particular transmitter-receiver, one and only one DMT frame from a NEXT transmitter is captured along with the far-end signal in the received frame (Figure 9).

This eases the removal of the self-NEXT as it remains orthogonal to the far-end signal because of the frequency division duplexing (FDD) scheme that makes upstream and downstream occupy different frequency bands.

The VDSL (and ADSL) uses Reed Solomon (RS) codes for forward error correction (FEC) coupled with interleaving. The VDSL distinguishes between the "fast" and "slow" channel. Both channel's data are protected using the RS code but the fast channel data is not interleaved, whereas the slow channel data is. The fast buffer gets its name because of its lower delay as a result of a lack of interleaving. The number of redundant bytes in the fast channel can be 0, 2, 4, or 16, whereas for the slow channel the value is set to 16. The VDSL encodes a stream of bits into symbols of constellations with 2^M points where $M = 1$ to 8 (15 in ADSL). The DMT modulation has a high peak-to-average ratio (PAR) and clipping is likely.

The fast buffer data is placed by into tones with lower signal-to-noise ratios (assigned smaller constellations), because impulse noise, for example, clipping noise, affects these tones less (the noise in these tones is already

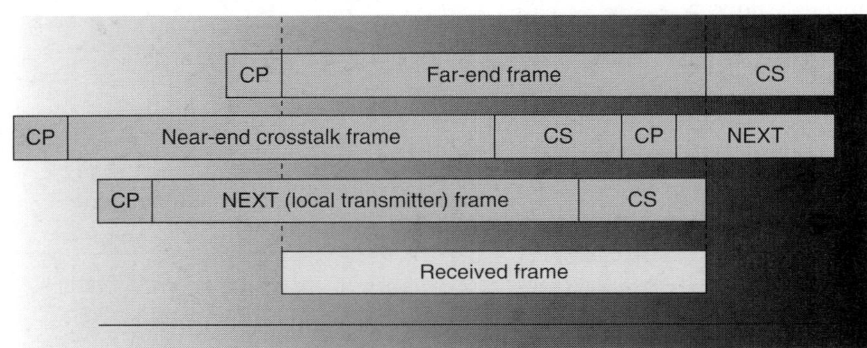

Figure 8: Misalignment of far-end and near-end DMT frames with more than one near-end crosstalk frame being captured at the receiver

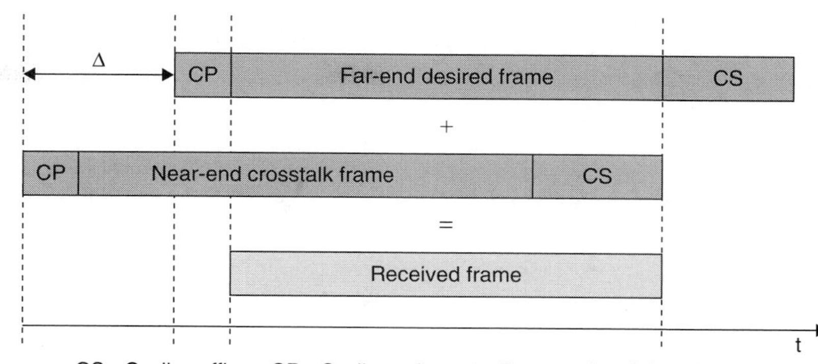

Figure 9: Misalignment of far-end and near-end DMT frames with only one near-end crosstalk frame being captured at the receiver

high). The slow buffer tones are put in higher signal-to-noise ratio sub-channels because they are protected against an impulse noise by the interleaved RS code. The bits at the receiver are reconstructed into fast and slow buffers thus, reversing the procedure. The VDSL introduces the concept of power back-off where the far-end upstream transmitters reduce the transmit power to allow the nearby downstream receivers to establish a link.

CONCLUSION AND FUTURE DEVELOPMENT

Telecommunications providers are striving to provide universal broadband connectivity 24/7, at home, at work, at school and on the road (i.e., via mobile phones). The highest data rates are provided by optical fiber technologies. However, fiber deployment is expensive and in the interim alternative technologies are useful. The xDSL has grown tremendously in popularity over the last few years. Along with the increase in computational power of digital signal processor, the telephony broadband access technology progressed from the ISDN to the HDSL, the ADSL, and the VDSL offering ever-increasing access data rates to the consumers. Today, telephone companies compete with cable and wireless broadband technologies to provide access to television, data, and voice services over DSL lines. The market share of xDSL will continue to depend on the data rates achieved, quality of service, and the number of services that the customers can get from a single provider.

GLOSSARY

ADSL: Asymmetric digital subscriber line; a type of telephony lines broadband technology; asymmetric data rates with upstream rates higher than downstream; standardized in 1999 by ITU-T G.992.1.

ADSL2+: A version of ADSL standardized in 2005 by ITU-T G.992.5; doubles the bandwidth used from ADSL's 1.1 MHz to 2.2 MHz.

ANSI: American National Standards Institute.

DFT: Discrete Fourier transform; used in signal processing to analyze spectral content of a sampled signal.

DMT: Discrete multitone modulation; used in ADSL and VDSL as a line code; modulates the information on 2^x simultaneously transmitted frequencies.

DOCSIS: Data over cable service interface specification; standardized by ITU-T in 1998 for cable transmission.

Downstream: Used in the telecommunications industry to describe transmission of data from the central office to the subscriber's premises.

DSLAM: A device residing in a central office that congregates the data from multiple DSL lines and multiplexes them onto the high-speed backbone.

ETSI: European Telecommunications Standards Institute; non-profit European telecommunications standardization agency.

FEXT: Far-end crosstalk; used in the telecommunications industry to describe electrical interference signal originating from a far-end transmitter; the interference signal travels the length of the cable.

HDSL: High bit rate DSL; developed as a replacement technology for the T1/E1 transmission systems; standardized in 1998 by ITU-T G.991.1 modeled closely after the ETSI TM-03036.

ISDN: Integrated services digital network; developed in the 1980s for distances of up to 18,000 ft; offers two types of services: the basic rate interface (BRI) and the primary rate interface (PRI).

ITU-T: International Telecommunication Union Standardization Sector; coordinates the work on international telecommunication standards.

NEXT: Near-end crosstalk; used in the telecommunications industry to describe electrical interference signal originating from an adjacent near-end transmitter.

POTS: Plain, old telephone service.

QAM: Quadrature amplitude modulation; modulates the information as the amplitude of two out-of-phase sinusoids.

SHDSL: Single-pair HDSL; a second generation HDSL technology reaching 18,000 ft without repeaters.

T1/E1: T1 is a telecommunication signaling technique used widely in North America and Japan; E1 is used in the rest of the world;

TCM: Trellis-coded modulation; coding technique used over bandlimited channels to increase the data rate.

Upstream: Used in the telecommunications industry to describe transmission of data from the subscriber's premises to the central office.

VDSL: A very-high-speed DSL; standardized by ITU-T in 2004; it is intended to bridge short copper access line lengths (shorter than 3,000 ft) at high speeds.

VoIP: Voice-over-Internet protocol; routes voice signals over an IP-based network.

xDSL: Used in telecommunications industry to describe a family of broadband access technologies.

CROSS REFERENCES

See *BISDN (Broadband Integrated Services Digital Network)*; *Cable Modems*; *Terrestrial Wide Area Networks*; *Wireless Broadband Access*.

REFERENCES

ADSL Forum. 2003. ADSL2 and ADSL2plus—The new ADSL standards. www.dslforum.org/aboutdsl/ADSL2_wp.pdf (accessed June 2006).

ANSI. 1992. Integrated service digital network (ISDN)-basic access interface for use on metallic loops for application on the network side of the NT (layer 1 specification) T1601-1992. *American National Standards Institute*.

Bingham, J. A. C. 1990. Multicarrier modulation for data transmission: an idea whose time has come. *IEEE Communications Magazine* 28:5–14.

Chen, W. Y. 1999. The development and standardization of asymmetric digital subscriber line. *IEEE Communications Magazine* 37: 68–72.

Chen, W. Y. 1998. DSL: *Simulation techniques and standards development for digital subscriber line systems*. Indianapolis: Macmillan Technical Publishing, pp. 9–12.

Cioffi, J. M. 1991. A multicarrier primer, T1E1.4/91-157. Amati Communication Corporation and Stanford University.

Dutta-Roy, A. 2001. An overview of cable modem technology and market perspectives. *IEEE Communication Magazine* 39:81–88.

Editorial. 2003. Crossed wires. *The Economist*, February:60.

Fitchard, Kevin 2002. Broadband deployment: cable is still king. http://telephonyonline.com/broadband/print/telecom_intelligence_broadband_economy_23/ (accessed May 9, 2006).

Goralski, W. 1999. DSL loop qualification and testing. *IEEE Communications Magazine* 37:79–83.

Henkel, W., S. Ölçer, K. S. Jacobsen, B. R. Saltzberg, and A. M. Bush. 2002. Guest editorial twisted pair transmission—ever increasing performances on ancient telephone wires. *IEEE Journal on Selected Areas in Communications* 20:877–80.

Isaksson, M., and D. Mestdagh. 1998. Spectral compatibility and asynchrony. T1E1.4/98-041.

ITU-T. 1998. High bit rate digital subscriber line (HDSL) transceivers, Recommendation G.991.1. *International Telecommunications Union*.

ITU-T. 1999. Asymmetrical digital subscriber line (ADSL) transceivers, Recommendation G.992.1. *International Telecommunications Union.*

ITU-T. 1999. Splitterless asymmetric digital subscriber line (ADSL) transceivers, Recommendation G.992.2. *International Telecommunications Union.*

ITU-T. 2002. Asymmetrical digital subscriber line (ADSL) transceivers, Recommendation G.992.3. *International Telecommunications Union*.

ITU-T. 2002. Asymmetrical digital subscriber line (ADSL) transceivers, Recommendation G.992.4. *International Telecommunications Union.*

ITU-T. 2003a. Asymmetrical digital subscriber line (ADSL) transceivers, Recommendation G.992.5. *International Telecommunications Union.*

ITU-T. 2003b. Single-pair high-speed digital subscriber line (SHDSL) transceivers. Recommendation G.991.2. *International Telecommunications Union.*

ITU-T. 2004. Very high speed digital subscriber line (VDSL) transceivers. Recommendation G.993.1. International Telecommunications Union.

ITU-T. 2005. Asymmetrical digital subscriber line (ADSL) transceivers 2. Recommendation G.992.3. *International Telecommunications Union*.

ITU-T. 2005. Asymmetrical digital subscriber line (ADSL) transceivers 2 Plus Recommendation G.992.4. *International Telecommunications Union*.

Korea Network Information Center. DATE. http://www.krnic.co.kr (accessed December 8, 2005).

Krakow, Gary 2004. http://www.msnbc.msn.com/id/6722931/ (accessed May 15, 2006).

Lankford, Daniel, E. Gameel, A. Boras, and S. Cheema. 2001. Why docsis over ieee 802.14. http://198.11.21.25/capstoneTest/Students/Papers/docs/Docsis39203.pdf (accessed December 20, 2003).

Lee, Yong-Kyung and D. Lee. 2003. Broadband access in Korea: Experience and future perspective. *IEEE Communications Magazine* 41:30–36.

Milosevic, Milos 2003. Maximizing data rate of discrete multitone systems using time domain equalization design. Ph.D. Dissertation. The University of Texas at Austin. www.ece.utexas.edu/~bevans (accessed May 10, 2006).

Ouyang, Feng, P. Duvaut, O. Moreno, and L. Pierrugues. 2003. The first step of long-reach ADSL: Smart DSL Technology, READSL. *IEEE Communications Magazine* 41:124–31.

Mueller, Katja 2006. *World Broadband Statistics: Q4 2005*. Point Source. http://www.point-topic.com/contentDownload/dslanalysis/world%20broadband%20statistics%20q4%2020.05.pdf (accessed April 26, 2006).

Powell, W. H. 1996. Developments and prospects for cable modems. *IEE Colloquium on Optical and Hybrid Access Networks* 16:1–5.

Reusens, P., D. Van Bruyssel, J. Sevenhans, S. Van Den Bergh, B. Van Nimmen, and P. Spruyt. 2001. A practical ADSL technology following a decade of effort. *IEEE Communications Magazine*, 39:45–51.

Starr, T., J. M. Cioffi, and P. Silverman. 1999. *Understanding digital subscriber line technology*. Upper Saddle River, NJ: Prentice-Hall, pp. 205–6.

Temple, S., and R. Hendry. 1999. Cable modems and their place in fast access technology. *IEE Seminar on Fast SoHo SME/Connectivity* 3:1–5.

Cable Modems

Shaheed N. Mohammed, *Marist College*

INTRODUCTION

Long before the Internet was publicly available, computer enthusiasts were using devices that changed binary data into sounds for transmission over telephone lines. The data were "modulated" into sound at the transmission end and were "demodulated" back into data at the receiving end—modem. For many years following the advent of Internet access to the general population, the telephone modem remained the primary source of connection to the network. However, it eventually became apparent that for many of the desired uses of the network, the dial-up connection (i.e., access to the network using regular telephone modems effectively limited to less than 56k transmission speeds) was insufficient.

Internet theorists have often expressed concern over a phenomenon known as the "last mile" problem (Cairncross, 2001; Drucker, 1999) "because it represents a bottleneck that constrains the benefits the consumer gets from the rest of a network..." (National Research Council Committee on Broadband Last Mile Technology, 2002, 45). As industry and e-businesses invested in technologies to deliver a wider range of content and services over the network, there was accompanying concern over the persistence of dial-up Internet access. The most sophisticated offerings, such as streaming video services, were simply infeasible with the limitations of telephone voiceband modem connections. This last link or "last mile" of the connection between provider and consumer was therefore a major barrier in the technical and economic expansion of the Internet— particularly at the level of the retail consumer. The introduction of broadband services to the consumer market has been seen as a signal of the elimination of the last mile problem and the development of the true potential of the network (Cairncross, 2001).

To date, the two primary broadband offerings to the consumer market have been DSL (digital subscriber line) and cable modem services. The former is offered by traditional telephone companies and utilizes existing telephone lines to transmit and receive network traffic. DSL involves dedicated connections to the provider network but is limited by distance from the provider's closest facility. The latter is offered by traditional cable television operations and uses existing coaxial cable infrastructure (or upgraded HFC or hybrid fiber/coaxial) to carry Internet traffic. Cable broadband access involves shared connections to the provider network.

Though there are wide variations in pricing and availability of these options worldwide, in North America DSL is often cheaper, offering somewhat lower bandwidth than cable modem service. Cable modem service costs more and can be limited by the capacity of the local cable franchises, but theoretically far surpasses the speeds available to DSL subscribers.

However, numerous factors complicate the comparisons, not the least of which is the fact that cable modem speeds can drop dramatically as more users crowd the cable system. Additionally, network conditions in both forms of access can vary tremendously from one point in time to the next and providers often employ some form of "capping" or reducing bandwidth to individual customers to maintain the speed of the network.

As more and more cable systems roll out both digital cable and modem services, however, DSL continues to remain a second choice generally lagging by a two to one margin (Wilson, 2005) except where there is limited or no availability of cable modem services. DSL is especially attractive in contexts outside of North America such as South Korea (Lee, 2005) and in other places where television delivery systems may not be as firmly rooted in the community antenna television (CATV) or "cable" model. Innovations from DSL providers may, of course, change this imbalance in the future as fully fiber-optic connections and various DSL improvements are developed and tested (Reed, 2005; Wilson, 2005).

MODEMS

The Modem Concept

Claude Shannon (1948) outlined the principles of information transmission in his paper entitled "A mathematical theory of communication." Shannon's model provided the basic foundation for much of modern information and communication theory. The model included the encoding of information at the source of transmission and subsequent decoding at the receiving end. Early attempts at data transmission over distance utilized these two concepts of encoding and decoding to convert (encode) bits of information into sound pulses for transmission over telephone lines and subsequently re-convert (decode) the sound pulses back into data bits at the receiving end.

The U.S. military first used modems for transmission of air defense information in the 1940s and 1950s. Commercially, Bell Labs began offering modems to corporate customers in 1958 (Wohleber, 2004). Modems began to evolve as popular tools with the development of the Usenet and electronic bulletin board systems (BBS) in the early 1980s. Combined with the increased adoption of personal computers and the introduction of information services in the 1980s, the modem became an important tool for connecting users. Demand and technological development saw rapid increases in consumer modem speeds into the early 1990s. Users in the mid- to late 1980s would usually have modems transmitting and receiving at 1200 or 2400 baud (a baud is equivalent to one bit per second under these low speed conditions). By 1996, the speed of so-called "voiceband" modems (which connected across traditional voice-carrying telephone lines) had risen to 56Kbits—a theoretical maximum speed never achieved in practice (Wohleber, 2004).

The term "bandwidth" refers to a technical measure of the amount of information that can be transmitted or received over a given communications channel. All else being equal, higher bandwidth is associated with a higher capacity for information transmission. Crandall (2005) pointed out that the "rapid diffusion" of the Internet into homes fuelled demand for more speed and greater bandwidth, leading to an increase in the variety of Web sites and the range of content offered "including recorded music, film clips, and electronic games" (Crandall, 2005, 110). He suggested that users became frustrated by the "worldwide wait" (a play on the term "World Wide Web") associated with dial-up connections and thus began to seek higher-speed connections. Often prompted by high-speed experiences in business and at colleges and universities, many consumers were able to satisfy this need for speed in the home by 1998 as broadband access to the home became available.

CABLE MODEM BASICS

What Is a Cable Modem?

The voiceband modem has been far surpassed by the speed of "broadband" alternatives with cable modems offering speeds ranging from 320 kbps to 10 Mbps (million bits per second) or up to about 200 times that of dial-up. The cable modem is a device that allows a user to access the Internet and other online services through a cable television network. Cable modems are 64/256 QAM (quadrature amplitude modulation) RF (radio frequency) devices that are capable of transmitting up to 40 Mbps (Cable Modems, 2005). QAM is a modulation scheme

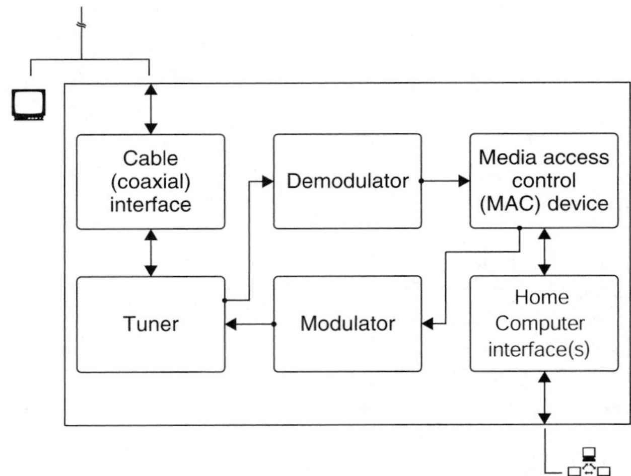

Figure 1: Main components of a cable modem

that utilizes amplitude modulation of two waves that are 90 degrees out of phase with each other. The choice of 64-QAM versus 256-QAM is one of speed versus reliability with the faster 256-QAM being more sensitive to interference from various sources. Figure 1 shows the basic operating components of a typical cable modem.

The cable modem connects on one end to the CATV system's coaxial cable feed and on the other to the user's computer or LAN (local area network). A tuner receives the modulated data signal that has been transmitted down the cable and passes it to the demodulator module. The demodulator extracts the data coded into the analog signal and converts it to a digital signal that it passes to the MAC (media access control). The MAC module, often in conjunction with a built in central processing unit (CPU), handles the exchange of upstream and downstream data and coordinates the various network protocols required for the process.

Despite advances in dial-up technologies featuring improved compression and caching, there remains little basis for comparison of speeds and services. Cable modems are faster than dial-up modems primarily because they operate on a system capable of greater bandwidth. Most cable systems today combine optical and legacy coaxial channels of distribution that allow for much greater capacity than the traditional wire networks of the telephone companies.

In principle, a cable modem performs the same basic function as a dial-up modem—converting information from one state to another for transmission and reception. However, in practice, the cable modem uses RF signals over a high bandwidth coaxial (or hybrid fiber coaxial/optical) network rather than voice signals over a simple copper network to achieve the data exchange. The result is a far superior data exchange rate and capacity with the cable modem compared to the dial-up connection. The fastest connections over the conventional telephone network are provided by digital subscriber line (DSL) services through the telephone companies. These connections, although generally cheaper than cable modem services, are sometimes slower. However, telephone companies are already touting next generation DSL technologies with speeds that exceed today's fastest cable modems (Research and Markets, 2004).

CABLE MODEM ROLLOUT

Diffusion/Adoption

As with all new and emerging technologies, the early cable modem rollout has followed a predictable pattern of adoption that features particular types of consumers (e.g., opinion leaders, the technologically savvy, well-educated and wealthy) among the early adopters. Chan-Olmsted et al. (2005), for example, pointed out that cable modem technology adoption is in keeping with the established patterns of diffusion of innovations literature. These patterns predict that early adopters will usually be relatively high in socioeconomic status, media ownership and media use, innovativeness, and information seeking.

Adoption patterns and statistics have, however, demonstrated market penetration well beyond the innovators and early adopters. Crandall (2005) noted that by mid-2004, there were 32.5 million "high-speed" lines in the United States. Of this number, 30.1 million were residential and small business lines. Cable television systems provided 57% of these lines, whereas DSL provided 35%.

Cable modem technology has also evidently crossed Rogers' (1998) "critical mass" of adopters beyond which a technology will "take off" in the market. Rogers and Scott (1997) described this "critical mass" as "the point at which enough individuals have adopted an innovation that the innovation's further rate of adoption becomes self-sustaining" (Rogers and Scott, 1997). Bass (1969) proposed three factors influencing such new technology adoption: 1) "market potential" (or total number of people who will eventually use the product), 2) the likelihood of someone adopting because of external influences such as media and 3) the likelihood of someone adopting because of the influence of other adopters.

According to M2 Presswire (2005), the number of cable modem subscribers in major markets such as North America, Asia, and Europe has increased steadily over recent years resulting in growth rates as high as 35% in some markets. This widespread adoption reflects numerous individual adoption decisions taken by individual customers. The work of Everett M. Rogers (1998) and others on the diffusion of innovations has focused on the reasons why consumers are likely to adopt certain products, services, or practices. This body of knowledge tells us that a consumer's decision to adopt a new technology is likely to be influenced by five principal factors:

1. Simplicity
2. Ease of trial
3. Relative advantage
4. Observability
5. Compatibility

In the case of cable modems the issue of simplicity (or, conversely, complexity) has two main dimensions: usage and installation. Using a cable modem is often simpler than using a traditional dial-up modem. For example, the "always-on" model removes the need for dialing in at the start of each session. Installation varies in complexity depending on the level of support from the local cable company. There is often a self-install option that allows users to save on installation fees by doing the cable modem installation themselves. This can make the installation a more complex undertaking, given that many computer systems come with dial-up modems already installed, and that software configuration is also necessary along with hardware installation. The non-technical user who opts for a service visit for the install may perceive little complexity associated with the process. However, standardization, such as is provided for by the DOCSIS standard makes the entire process easier than it would be with competing or noncompatible standards and equipment.

Ease of trial is related in some ways to the ease of installation and use cited above. Trying a cable modem service will usually involve calls to the cable company and arranging for equipment delivery or service calls. However, in most cases in United States markets, no annual contract is required. Trying cable modem service, then, is easier in some senses than either DSL or dial-up Internet access since both these alternatives tend to lean in favor of service term commitments (true for some time for DSL—only more recently a trend in dial-up whereby providers offer lower rates in exchange for a time period commitment). An often-overlooked element of the ease of trial is the extent to which consumers may "try out" high-speed Internet access through their use of high-speed connections at work or school.

In experiencing broadband access at school or work, consumers are exposed to the advantages of a cable modem compared to traditional dial-up. They may then be in a better position to evaluate the cost/benefit ratio (or relative advantage) of the move to broadband in general and the cable modem in particular with regard to factors such as usefulness, price, and convenience. Many consumers experience extremely high bandwidth and speeds on commercial/business or college-based T1 and T3 connections. This experience enables users to evaluate the DSL and cable modem services against prior high-speed experiences. This experience also gives users the ability to make more informed decisions regarding not only the relative advantage of broadband over dial-up, but also regarding the choice between DSL and cable modems with regard to price and speed differentials.

Observability refers to the question of the potential adopter being able to observe the consequences or benefits of the innovation. The difference between dial-up and cable modem access is quite clear and obvious. However, this is less the case with DSL service compared to cable modems. In such a comparison, a non-technically oriented user may not be able to observe the differences or to run relevant download comparisons or similar tests. Although the differences are clear in file downloads and other high-bandwidth processes, routine browsing and e-mail activities may not reveal observable differences.

The question of compatibility of an innovation is concerned with the extent to which the innovation is consistent with factors such as the cultural and social values, experiences, and needs of the potential adopters. It can also relate to technical compatibility and the extent to which an adopter may have to replace or upgrade existing technologies to adopt the innovation. Cable modem adopters generally do not need to perform any significant upgrades or changes in technology and find that the new technology integrates almost seamlessly with their existing technologies.

On the service side, there are compatibility issues with legacy software and systems. Dial-up subscribers, for example, often experience some dislocation when switching to cable modem service—some even opting to maintain their dial-up accounts after cable modem adoption to preserve not only e-mail addresses but also accustomed interfaces, services, and even concepts (such as "keywords"). Traditional dial-up providers, aware of this loyalty, even provide broadband portals to their former customers or those who are migrating to broadband. These portals are little more than an interface providing comfortable and familiar screens through which the new cable modem user accesses their new broadband connection, but their old e-mails and ancillary services.

CABLE MODEM TECHNOLOGY

Speeds and Standards

Cable modems typically offer consumers speeds in excess of 1 Mbps (million bits per second). In fact, by early 2006, some major cable providers in the United States had already upgraded their systems to offer 4 Mbps downstream and 384 Kbps (kilobits per second) upstream with premium offerings of 6 Mbps downstream and 786 Kbps upstream.

Yet, these speeds would be meaningless without standards-based interconnectivity and interoperability on the networks. Networks on the scale of those developed by the cable television providers for high-speed Internet access involve numerous technical components, often from different manufacturers. Without common specifications and standards, such networks would be difficult if not impossible to create and maintain.

To promote interoperability and stability on and across networks, the cable industry (through a grouping of major industry players, affiliates and partners known as the multimedia cable network system partners or "MCNS") introduced a set of standards in 1996 known as the "DOCSIS" or data over cable service interface specification. Laubach (2001) noted that: "The specifications were designed to be nonvendor-specific, allowing cross-manufacturer compatibility for high-speed data communications services over two-way hybrid fiber-coax (HFC) cable television systems" (Laubach, 2001, 38). The DOCSIS standard stipulated such specifics as modulation schemes and protocols for use on cable television data systems and was endorsed by major networking and computer players such as Microsoft and Cisco (DOCSIS, n.d.). According to Fellows and Jones (2001), the DOCSIS is the foundation for high-speed Internet access offered by North American cable operators. They also note that it facilitates interoperability and integration with computers as well as laying the foundation for voice, video, and data convergence along broadband lines provided by CATV systems.

Laubach (2001) identified emerging competition for broadband access in the late 1990s along with difficulties with manufacturers and a lack of development of various technical standards as the key factors prompting the move toward the eventual creation of the DOCSIS. The standard prevails today in North America and was adopted by the International Telecommunications Union in March of 1998. The DOCSIS has evolved into versions 1.1, and 2.0 with version 3.0 in development at the time of writing. The standard has also spread beyond North America and instructed development of networks in other regions (Cable Modem/DOCSIS, 2005). *Cablemodem.com* reports that three published versions of the DOCSIS specifications have been approved by major organizations such as the Society for Cable Telecommunications Engineers (SCTE), the European Telecommunications Standards Institute (ETSI), and the International Telecommunications Union (ITU)" (Cable Modems/DOCSIS, 2005).

Integration with Cable TV Networks

The DOCSIS standards have made the development of the cable-based Internet access networks easier, but they have not removed all the challenges facing cable providers who have become Internet service providers (ISPs). Significant investments in hardware and other technical improvements along with numerous technological challenges spell tremendous challenges for such operations. Among the main challenges has been the adaptation of the traditional cable network structure (a largely one-way affair) to the two-way demands of an Internet access network. Green (2002) identified the one-way nature of the conventional CATV network as a key impediment to the roll-out of new services delivered over cable, noting that the potential for increased revenue has led most operators to develop two-way capabilities and that some franchising authorities have compelled operators to develop such capabilities.

Bates (2002) noted that: "CATV has always been considered a one-way transmission system, designed to deliver TV and packaged entertainment to the residential marketplace" (Bates, 2002, 221). He suggested, further, that there was little impetus before the advent of the cable modem for any other form of network, because the coaxial cable infrastructure was traditionally sufficient to provide an acceptably large number of channels to the local subscriber. The situation of local monopoly and a generally fixed channel lineup (i.e., predictable bandwidth requirements) also meant that there was no impetus to challenge the capacity of the network or its fundamental operating principles.

Both competition from direct broadcast satellite (DBS) services and the demands of Internet access have spelled major challenges and changes for the traditional cable television networks. Somewhat ironically, it is this provision of broadband Internet access and related VOIP (voice over Internet protocol) service that now serve as a major selling point for cable providers in their battles against the dishes. This followed the commercial failure of early dish-based broadband services featuring one way downstream service from the satellite provider and upstream service via a telephone line in what is known as a TRI (telephony return interface) system. The one-way nature of the traditional cable television networks and the new bandwidth demands, however, have been major hurdles in the transition to Internet access.

Network Components and Structure

CATV systems were traditionally only able to manage small amounts of two-way data flow intended to facilitate such things as pay-per-view purchases. Bates (1999) noted that these systems "have historically carried a number of data services. These services have ranged from news and weather feeds, presented in alphanumeric form on single channels or as scrolling captions, to one-way transmission of data" (Bates 1999). The two-way nature of Internet access, however, has placed much higher demands on the CATV systems, requiring fundamental re-engineering and the addition of significant new components. The most important added component in an Internet-access/cable television network is the cable modem termination system (CMTS).

The CMTS provides the primary interface with the Internet, feeding data signals downstream into the headend transmitter (Figure 2). In such a system, the headend transmitter combines these data signals with the audio and video feeds from the cable provider and transmits the combined information to subscribers along a coaxial, fiber, optic, or (most commonly today) hybrid network. Similar to the cable system's ability to reference individual subscribers by unique addresses on their addressable cable boxes, the CMTS is able to communicate with individual cable modems on the network via their MAC addresses, and is therefore able to route data requests from individual modems to the Internet and deliver responses individually.

In cable data systems the CMTS is managed by an element management system (EMS) that administers day-to-day tasks. According to the IEC (2005), the operations tasks associated with the EMS include "provisioning, day-to-day administration, monitoring, alarms, and testing of various components of a CMTS" (online at http://www.iec.org/online/tutorials/cable_mod/topic01.html).

As the network structure becomes larger and more complex, added clients may be located farther and farther away from the headend and other key components.

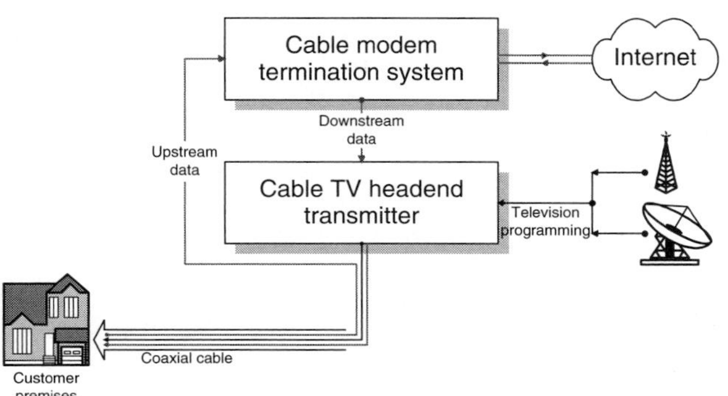

Figure 2: Cable modem integration into CATV system

In such cases attenuation becomes an issue with modems further from the headend facing longer hops for each packet sent upstream or downstream and greater potential for numerous types of interference along the way. Certain components of the network layers are designed to deal with this structural issue.

Network Layers

As in other computerized networks, data transmission and management as well as other functions in a cable modem network are arranged in a number of layers. The *physical layer* incorporates a downstream and an upstream data channel and translates data to and from digital form for use by upper layers of the network. Downstream data is transmitted as MPEG-2 frames in what is known as the *"transmission convergence layer"* or *"downstream convergence layer"* within the physical layer (Cisco Systems Inc, 2002). A MAC layer facilitates sharing of the upstream data channel by many modems and makes adjustments for variations in the distances of particular modems from the head end. The *network layer* uses Internet protocol (IP) with dynamic host configuration protocol (DHCP) that automates the assignment of IP addresses to clients on the network. These networks also feature a *transport layer* using transmission control protocol (TCP) and user datagram protocol (UDP), whereas an application layer supports various Internet program functions (IEC, 2005). Another important component of the network is the baseline privacy interface (BPI) data link encryption system that encrypts information between individual modems and the CMTS for user privacy.

Security

Within a given cable system, the cable modems in subscribers' homes are all connected to a single network. This shared architecture raises questions about the security of data and the privacy of individual connections. Truelove (2003), for example, warned of "inherent security risks" with cable modem broadband Internet access, pointing that communications among domestic local network elements such as PCs and printers are available to others on the network, whereas TCP/IP packets between the user's PC and the Internet may be particularly vulnerable to interception along shared segments on the network. However, Laubach (2001) noted that despite these vulnerabilities, cable modem systems if "properly administered" can be quite secure. The security of individual connections on the network is ensured by measures such as encryption of data between the CMTS and the subscriber's cable modem. Basic security precautions involving such encryption and the security of individual connections are provided within the DOCSIS standards.

Like so many other aspects of computer networking, these safeguards are rarely sufficient on their own and inadequate in the face of active interference. Among the threats to the cable modem network are actions by subscribers to subvert network regulations or protections. For example, Poulsen (2004) exposed the plans of a group of hackers to simplify a range of assaults on cable modem networks that would "topple long-held assumptions about the privacy of cable modem communications." This involved a downloadable program called Sigma that would automate processes involved in overriding network imposed limitations and security precautions, giving users "almost complete control of their cable modem—a privilege previously reserved for the service provider" Poulsen (2004) suggested that such actions violate service agreements and even the law when users change modem configuration files to uncap service limitations or even receive free service by running unregistered modems. Under the DOCSIS specifications, users are not allowed to adjust the configuration files even on modems that they own as this is a function reserved for the provider in order to control such things as bandwidth allocation.

Vulnerability within the network is one concern. Protection from outside attacks is another. Cable system-based Internet access providers face challenges similar to those faced by other networks and ISPs. Their security measures may include many of the same approaches as other major networks including firewalls, proxy servers, and the use of secure socket layer (SSL) connections for data collection functions.

However, there is another dimension of security concerns at the consumer end of the connection. The cable modem subscriber is faced with a connection to the Internet that is "always on." Whereas with a dial-up connection, the user made an active decision to log on to the Internet, with a cable modem connection the user is logged on every time their computer starts up. This leads to at least the perception (and, to some extent the reality) of greater risk. Laubach (2001), for example, suggested that the always-on connection is more susceptible to attacks. When this perception is coupled with the notion that a faster connection leads to more diverse online activities and downloads that may be almost instantaneous, the user is likely to perceive much greater risk from the broadband Internet connection than a dial-up connection. These dangers include the risks of infection by viruses and spyware, and the possibility of identity theft or falling victim to online scams and frauds. Some companies even trade on these fears, encouraging the idea that risks increase with broadband connections. An America Online press release (2005), for example, quoted a named company official as saying:

> A broadband connection is basically an open pipe to the Internet, which means that high speed users are particularly vulnerable to thousands of new viruses and spyware threats as they emerge.

Although it is certainly possible to argue that many of these same risks are equally true when applied to dial-up scenarios, it is easy to understand why the user who has embarked upon more diverse Web surfing activities made possible by a cable modem connection (Rappoport, Kridel & Taylor, 2003) might be concerned. The level of risk, of course, may have more to do with the surfing habits of the user than the speed of the connection, but certain risks are undoubtedly exacerbated by higher speed and greater bandwidth. Among the real concerns here are programs and pseudo-programs in the form of trojans, viruses, or spyware that may transmit personal data from the user's computer to be collected by unknown or nefarious elements for various purposes ranging from tracking surfing habits to (conceivably) perpetrating identity theft. The high speed of broadband connections may also mask the outward transfer of data in this case as any decline in speed due to that transfer becomes less perceptible.

Cathey and Wiggins (2002) argued that the persistent IP (Internet protocol) address associated with cable modems also increase risk. They point out that dial-up users are assigned different IP addresses at each login, but that broadband users who typically leave their cable modem or other appliance on all the time face risks associated with not periodically changing their IP address—particularly if an attacker identifies a persistent IP address and sets up a packet sniffer targeting the address. These persistent IP addresses allow a potential intruder multiple opportunities to attack a single target. Such risks, however, are not necessarily inherent in the system and pose little additional threat since an attacker could just as easily target a range of IP addresses issued by an ISP—whether dial-up or cable—accessing the packets of the random users who match the targeted addresses. The specific case of an attacker targeting a known IP address would probably involve more than just random hacking and intrusion. Cable modem providers and other industry players have been actively pursuing measures including IP randomization to correct for this weakness.

LEGAL AND BUSINESS ISSUES

The diversification of the cable television provider into a provider of Internet access and other services such as telephony has raised a number of legal issues—particularly surrounding the identity of these companies. Among the concerns in the United States is the question of whether these former cable providers can now be categorized as either ISPs or telephone companies or both. There are implications here not only for taxes and public policy, but also for competition in the marketplace.

Rulings have centered on issues such as the definition of cable modem Internet access as an "information service" but not a "cable service"—the latter being subject to certain fees that do not apply to the former (Tantono, Porcelli, Bagner, and Sonu 2002; Leanza, 2004) as well as issues of open access to cable infrastructure by competitors. Related to these questions is the debate over what is termed *asymmetric regulation* (Hausman, 2003)—with particular regard to whether cable providers of Internet access should be subject to the same rules of access and inter-accessibility as operators of more traditional public networks such as the terrestrial conventional telephone system. The argument for such similar regulation is based in part on the perception that the cable modem providers provides similar services as and even usurp the business of the traditional telcos.

VOIP

Consider for example, the former cable television provider that develops both Internet access and telephony offerings. The cable system provides telephone service via the Internet using what is known as voice over Internet protocol (VOIP). More recent cable modem models feature a built-in telephone port to enable the customer to plug a conventional telephone appliance directly into the modem for VOIP service. When a VOIP customer calls another VOIP customer, the call is routed entirely along the Internet, though at the user end the process is completely transparent and for all intents and purposes it is simply a telephone call. No computer is directly involved in the user experience. If the VOIP customer calls a traditional telephone, the call is routed along the Internet up to the closest local exchange of the destination telephone. All of this results in much lower calling costs with reductions even on international calls.

One of the problems with this scenario is that the cable company is not subject to the same regulations as the telephone companies. To complicate matters further, the cable based VOIP providers are also in direct competition with the telephone companies on another front, that of Internet access. The provision of VOIP service with Internet access all via a cable modem not only removes the need for a telephone line from the traditional telephone company, but also effectively removes the possibility of DSL services from a traditional telephone company.

A further issue with regard to VOIP provision over cable modem networks is that of emergency or 911 calling. The Federal Communications Commission (FCC)/National Association of Regulatory Utility Commissioners (NARUC) Joint Task Force on VoIP/E911 (2006) has noted in an FCC consumer advisory what it called a "critical public safety gap" associated with VOIP services. Factors such as the subscriber's ability to use a VOIP device from any broadband connection contribute to difficulties in locating callers in emergency situations. The FCC has therefore required interconnected VOIP services (that use the public switched telephone network to route portions of their calls) to take certain measures to protect consumers. These measures include mandatory provision of 911 service, obtaining the customer's residential address before activation, and obtaining acknowledgments from customers stating that they are aware of the limitations of 911 services provided via VOIP.

Cable Modems and File Sharing

For many users, the cable modem makes the practice of file sharing possible. File sharing is a valid and important technology that stands to enable researchers, scientists, and others to make important files available to others. The controversy over file sharing has to do with what music and film industry interests characterize as illegal exchanges of copyright material. Ongoing legal disputes have included huge multinational corporations suing private individuals over the practice of sharing music and video files. For most, file sharing is difficult and impractical, if not impossible, without a broadband connection. The increasing reach of broadband has also send further developments in file sharing technologies such as the emergence of torrent style sharing that marks a technological advance over traditional peer-to-peer sharing.

Commercial File Delivery

New products and services have become available or feasible because broadband access (led by the popularity and speed of cable modems). Chief among these is the slew of "legal" or commercially endorsed music purchase systems. These range from streaming audio services to downloadable music. Even more dependent on the speed and bandwidth of the cable modem is the provision of streaming and downloadable video on the World Wide Web. Software producers also take advantage of the availability of the high speed and bandwidth by providing their products for direct download. Customers at many commercial software sites can now download not just updates and fixes but also full versions of software after paying the appropriate fees. Cairncross (2001) would describe these transactions as representing trade in what she identified as completely "digital products," because they never need to occupy a physical form like traditional products.

E-commerce Developments

Other benefits to e-commerce beyond file delivery include the possibility of delivering more complex and detailed product descriptions and interfaces to customers across the Web. These include multimedia animations and even interactive three dimensional displays of products that were hitherto impractical without broadband. Less obvious elements of e-commerce are also aided by the cable modem, including the commercial provision of distance education and the feasibility of more sophisticated financial services online. Limitations remain, however, on the spread of these benefits into the international market despite the global reach of the Internet. Among these limitations are traditional barriers such as language differences and emerging barriers such as the discrepancy in the spread of broadband technologies in many countries.

Telecommuting

The cable modem with its high-speed capabilities, reliable connections and wide availability creates greater potential for telecommuting. Although the benefits and costs of telecommuting are still hotly debated, the possibilities of richer connections that are more readily available generally enhance the chances for successful telecommuting arrangements. Laughbach (2001, 256) notes, however, that this same broadband advantage also "increases the vulnerability of home computing equipment and, subsequently, threat to electronic commerce and telecommuting in the United States."

Telecommuting (or telework) and its variants have seen strong levels of adoption boosted by the power of broadband connections to facilitate such services as video-conferencing. However, barriers to adoption remain in place despite fast connections. Among these are reluctance from management to provide the facility, concerns about security and employee concerns about being marginalized or otherwise displaced from the workplace (U.S. Office of Personnel Management, 2003).

CONCLUSION

The advent and diffusion of cable modem technology at both the consumer and provider levels has marked a quantum leap into the world of broadband access for many in the United States and, increasingly, in other regions and countries. The successful deployment of this group of technologies has come as a result of astute technical planning (including negotiations with manufacturers and alliances among industry players). It has also benefited from the fortuitous pre-existence of successful and widely diffused cable television technology. Consumer familiarity with the concept of cable connections and the relative ease of connection and use of cable modem technology have aided the diffusion of the technologies, as has the increasingly widespread availability of broadband access of various types at businesses and educational institutions.

The transformation to cable modem Internet access has meant significant investments and technical improvements for cable providers and the emergence of associated services such as VOIP has raised serious regulatory and business-related issues. However, the lower costs and integration of services (e.g., cable television, Internet access, and voice) are proving attractive to the consumer market.

Consumers have benefited from competition between cable modem and DSL providers that keep prices low and raise the stakes for provision of higher speeds. The strengths and weaknesses of each type of broadband connection provide different benefits and risks to the consumer in terms of speeds and security. This situation is likely to continue in the short to medium term, spurring both technical development and further diffusion of broadband.

The long run prospects for cable modem technology appear to be quite positive—particularly in light of the robust networks that exist, the investments in infrastructure being made by the industry, the development and continual improvement of widely accepted standards, and the provision of cost-effective and feasible services. Legal disputes and regulatory questions notwithstanding, the technology is placed to spread even more widely and even to further diversify its consumer offerings in the medium to long term.

GLOSSARY

Bandwidth: A measure of the capacity of a transmission medium to carry data in terms of the number of wave frequencies transmitted. High bandwidth is associated with high rates and capacities for data flow.

Broadband: Describes electronic data exchanges or channels that allow for fast transmission of large amounts of data. Particularly common in distinguishing higher bandwidth systems from dial-up modem connections of the past.

Cable Modem: A device that allows digital signals to be transmitted and received through radio frequency (RF) modulation and demodulation on a coaxial CATV system.

CATV: Community antenna television—original and technical terminology for cable television systems.

CMTS: Cable modem termination system—a system to which all *cable modems* in a CATV-based Internet access system are connected. The CMTS interfaces between the modems and the Internet and routes data to and from specific modems on the system.

DOCSIS: Data over cable service interface specification—a set of standards established through industry consultation providing rules, procedures, and specifications to ensure equipment and systems conformation and interoperability for the delivery of Internet access over coaxial cable television networks.

DSL: Digital subscriber line—a system of modulation over the conventional telephone network utilizing specialized modems to provide broadband access.

EMS: Element management system—a network management and operations system used to control one or more *CMTS* and associated subscriber connections.

Encryption: The process of coding messages into forms that obscure their meanings—usually until such messages are received by an intended recipient capable of decoding the meaning—often by use of some type of decoding instrument or "key." Used in computer data transmission to protect data from interception by unintended parties.

Internet: A global network of interconnected network of computer networks using a common system of rules for data exchange.

IP address: Internet protocol address—a number assigned to a particular Internet connection or device to enable routing of messages on an appropriate network.

ISP: Internet service provider—any of a number of different types of services that enable users to connect their computers to the Internet.

Modem: Modulator demodulator—a device that encodes messages into a particular sequence for transmission over a communications channel, and decodes similarly encoded sequences that are received.

Spyware: Any of a range of different types of software that enable the (usually unauthorized) transmission of data from a user's computer and/or track various user activities such as browsing histories, passwords, and user IDs. The general term "malware" has come to encompass various types of spyware, as well as Trojans (programs that infiltrate users' computers without their knowledge) and viruses (programs that intentionally wreak harmful or destructive effects on users' computers).

SSL: Secure socket layer—a system of secure connections commonly used in e-commerce and other high-security transactions over computer networks.

VOIP: Voice over Internet protocol—a system for delivery of telephony services over computer networks.

CROSS REFERENCES

See *BISDN (Broadband Integrated Services Digital Network); DSL (Digital Subscriber Line); Modems; Terrestrial Wide Area Networks.*

REFERENCES

AOL Launches Comprehensive New Security Suite To Help Protect Members From Viruses, Spyware, Identity Theft. 2005. http://media.timewarner.com/media/newmedia/cb_press_view.cfm?release_num=55254487 (accessed December 2, 2005).

Bass, F. M. 1969. A new product growth model for consumer durables. *Management Science* 15:215–27.

Bates, R. J. 1999. *Broadband Telecommunications Handbook*. Blacklick, OH: McGraw-Hill Professional.

Bates, R. J. 2002. *Cable TV Systems and Modem Systems and Technology*. Blacklick, OH: McGraw-Hill Professional.

Cable Modems. 2005. http://www.iec.org/online/tutorials/cable_mod/topic01.html (accessed January 2, 2006).

Cable Modems/DOCSIS Project Primer. 2005. http://www.cablemodem.com/primer/ (accessed January 20, 2005).

Cairncross, F. 2001. The Death of Distance 2.0: *How the Communications Revolution Will Change Our Lives*. London: Texere.

Cathey, J. M., and C. E. Wiggins. 2002. Broadband: New speeds, new risks. *Strategic Finance* 83:38–44.

Chan-Olmsted, S.M, J. Li, and J. Jung. 2005. The profiling of cable modem broadband consumers: Characteristics, perceptions and satisfaction. *Journal of Targeting, Measurement and Analysis for Marketing* 13:327–45.

Cisco Systems Inc. 2002. Cable Access Technologies. http://www.cisco.com/univercd/cc/td/doc/cisintwk/ito_doc/cable.htm (accessed September 19, 2006).

Crandall, R. W. 2005. *Competition and Chaos: U.S. Telecommunications since the 1996 Telecom Act*. Washington: Brookings Institution Press.

DOCSIS. n.d. http://searchnetworking.techtarget.com/sDefinition/0,,sid7_gci213909,00.html (accessed December 30, 2005).

Drucker, P. F. 1999. Beyond the information revolution. *The Atlantic Monthly* 284:47–57.

FCC/NARUC Joint Task Force on VoIP/E911. 2006. FCC Consumer Advisory: VOIP and 911 Service. http://www.fcc.gov/cgb/consumerfacts/voip911.html (accessed September 19, 2006).

Fellows, D., and D. Jones. 2001. DOCSIS[TM] cable modem technology. *IEEE Communications Magazine* 39:202–9.

Green, J. H. 2002. Access Technologies: *DSL and Cable*. Blacklick, OH: McGraw-Hill.

Hausman, J. 2003. Internet-related services: The results of asymmetric regulation. In *Broadband: Should We Regulate High-Speed Internet Access?* edited by R. W. Crandall, pp. 129–56. Washington: Brookings Institution Press.

IEC Cable Modems. 2005. http://www.iec.org/online/tutorials/cable_mod/ (accessed October 31, 2005).

Laubach, M. 2001. *Delivering Internet Connections Over Cable: Breaking the Access Barrier*. New York: John Wiley & Sons.

Leanza, C. 2005. U.S. Supreme Court hears arguments in cable modem case. *Nation's Cities Weekly*, 28:4.

Lee, B. J. 2005. Wired, at Any Price; South Korea presents a paradox. It leads in high-speed connections. But profits are another matter. *Newsweek* 146:36.

M2 PRESSWIRE. AUGUST 4, 2005. Press release. *Research and Markets: Research and Markets: Cable Modem offerings now control some 63 percent of the residential and small-business broadband market.* http://www.m2.com (accessed May 11, 2007).

Mitchell, B. 2006. DSL vs. Cable: Broadband Internet Speed Comparison. http://wireless.about.com (accessed May 15, 2006).

National Research Council Committee on Broadband Last Mile Technology (CB) 2002. *Broadband: Bringing Home the Bits*. Washington: National Academies Press.

Poulsen, K. 2004. Cable modem hackers conquer the co-ax: Uncap in hand. The Register. http://www.theregister.co.uk/2004/02/05/cable_modem_hackers_conquer/ (accessed January 5, 2005).

Rappoport, P. N., D. J. Kridel, and L. T. Taylor. 2003. The demand for broadband: access, content, and the value of time. In *Broadband: Should We Regulate High-Speed Internet Access?* edited by R. W. Crandall, pp 57–82. Washington: Brookings Institution Press.

Reed, K. 2005. Verizon tests super-fast DSL as it also rolls out fiber optics. *Boston Globe*, D1.

Research and markets: Extending the broadband market opportunity: new technologies in xDSL. 2004. http://www.internetadsales.com/modules/news/article.php?storyid=662 (May 15, 2006).

Rogers, E. M. 1998. *Diffusion of Innovations*. New York: Free Press.

Rogers, E. M., and K. Scott. 1997. The diffusion of innovations model and outreach from the national network of libraries of medicine to Native American communities. http://nnlm.gov/pnr/eval/rogers.html (accessed January 5, 2006).

Shannon, C. E. 1948. A mathematical theory of communication. *Bell System Technical Journal* 27:379–423.

Tantono, W., N. Porcelli, J. Bagner, and C. Sonu. 2002. FCC declares cable companies are information service providers. *Intellectual Property & Technology Law Journal* 14:28.

Truelove, J. 2003. Security for broadband Internet access users. In *Information Security Management Handbook*, edited by H. F. Tipton. Boca Raton: Auerbach Publishers, Inc.

U.S. Office of Personnel Management. 2003. The Status of Telework in the Federal Government. Washington, DC: General Services Administration.

Wilson, C. 2005. Question remains whether Telcos will surpass cable. *Telephony* 246:12.

Wohleber, C. 2004. The Modem. It began as a work-around and survived to usher in the Internet. http://inventionandtechnology.com/xml/2004/3/it_2004_3_dept_obj-lessons.xml (accessed January 12, 2006).

FURTHER READING

Crandall, R. W. 2003. *Broadband: Should We Regulate High-Speed Internet Access?* Washington: Brookings Institution Press.

IEC 2006. Cable Modems. http://www.iec.org/online/tutorials/cable_mod/ (accessed February 9, 2006).

Ostergaard Rolf V. 2006. The Cable Modem Reference Guide http://www.cable-modems.org/tutorial/ (accessed January 12, 2006).

Rogers, E. M. 1998. *Diffusion of Innovations*. New York: Free Press.

Home Networking

Sherali Zeadally, *University of the District of Columbia*

INTRODUCTION

Home networks facilitate communication among appliances, home systems, entertainment products, and information devices in a home so that they can work cooperatively and share information. A device connected to a home network gains the capabilities of other networked devices, and as a result the device can provide a service or function that it would have otherwise been incapable of providing alone (Rose 2001). Several factors are pushing for the wide development and adoption of home networks. These include the advancement in telecommunications technologies, the wide proliferation of personal computers, and the decreasing costs of smart devices that allow users to control and monitor events in consumer-based appliances, and consumer demand for content-rich applications.

In the last few years, we have experienced a growing interest to advance state-of-the-art technologies to ease the adoption and deployment of home networks. In recent years, networks are being increasingly used in home environments. Information appliances such as digital TVs, videocassette recorders (VCR), set-top-boxes, personal computers (PCs), and mobile devices, such as personal digital assistants (PDAs) and cellular phones, can all be connected. Many of these appliances can be classified into two broad categories namely, those with high computational resources and capabilities (including processing power, memory, disk space) and those devices (PDAs, cellular phones) with little computing power.

The home networking industry is currently made up of various companies, organizations, vendors including Internet service providers, networking vendors, international standardization bodies, PC manufacturers, semiconductor manufacturers, home appliance developers, telecommunication providers, consumer electronics vendors, and middleware (including software) vendors. All of them are fueling the growth of home control and automation products have grown to 9.2 billion worldwide in 2006 (compared to 1.4 billion in 2001) (Cahners In-Stat Group 1999). Driven by compelling applications, decreasing hardware/software prices, and easier configurations, home networking is expected to penetrate 27 percent of U.S. households by 2008 (Greenspan 2003). As shown in Table 1, a recent report (IDC 2004) forecasts that worldwide households with home networks are expected to grow by 25 percent by the year 2008.

Most home networks deployed recently are typically made up of one or all of the following subnetworks (as shown in Figure 1) including:

- A *computing network*: this connects mainly the various PCs in the home to share files, printers, and broadband connections. This network also carries multimedia data such as audio, video, and images for applications such as video conferencing and voice over IP (VoIP). File transfer traffic, interactive traffic (generated by applications such as Telnet and secure shell) as well as Web traffic (browsing data) are also delivered through the network.
- A *home automation network*: this connects devices such as lamps, heaters, security devices responsible for home users comfort and security. Security traffic, originating from home network devices such as security camera,

Table 1: Forecast of home networks adoption by United States and worldwide households (Shaw 2004)

	2004 (millions)	2008 (millions)	Projected Increase (%)
Worldwide households with home networks	89	111	25
US households with home networks	13.5	36.6	171
US households with wireless access points, gateways, routers	10.1	35.1	247

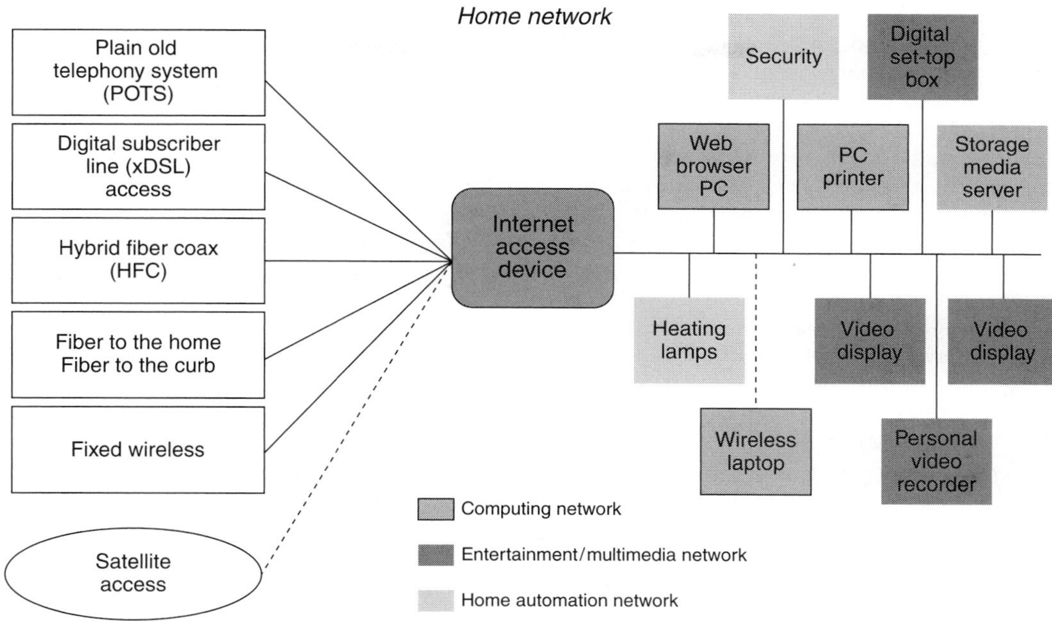

Figure 1: Remote Internet access to heterogeneous home network devices

and home device control traffic consisting of mainly control signals used by home devices are generated by the home automation network.

- An *entertainment network*: this connects devices such as digital set-top-boxes to personal video recorders[1] (such as TiVo or Replay TV) to stream video using standard-based Internet protocols and are often part of some system connected to a cable or satellite provider.

FACTORS INFLUENCING THE GROWTH OF HOME NETWORKS

Market for home networking and devices connected to home networks will grow from $14 billion in 2005 to more than $85 billion by 2011 according to recent ABI forecasts (ABI 2006). Various factors have been contributing to the dramatic growth and adoption of home networks. These home networking market drivers include:

- *Multiple PCs per household*: the decreasing costs of hardware/software and Internet access are enabling home users to acquire multiple PCs.
- *High-speed broadband Internet access*: in the last few years, many last mile high bandwidth Internet access solutions such as cable and digital subscriber lines (DSL) have been accessible to home users at low costs. Many of the broadband access technologies provide high-speed Internet data transfers with "always-on" connectivity. Consequently, many Internet applications such as video streaming, new streaming, games can now be supported with little impact on their quality (in contrast to past Internet connections based on dial-up access lines which significantly reduce connection performance).

[1]A consumer video device that allows users to capture telelvision programming to internal hard disk storage for later viewing.

- *Decreasing costs of communication devices and peripherals*: the cost of many networking devices such as hubs and switches along with peripherals such as cameras, scanners, and printers have been declining very rapidly in recent years making them more affordable to home users.
- *Widespread use of handheld devices and other smart devices*: many handheld devices have emerged recently ranging from personal digital assistants to cell phones most of which are often equipped with full Internet access enabling anytime, anywhere connectivity. Handheld users often need to communicate with other devices in the home environment for tasks such as backup, storage, and Internet connectivity. These tasks can be achieved transparently with a home network.
- *Impact of telecommuting*: we have witnessed a growing number of employees who are opting to work from home whenever possible. In fact, IDC Corporation predicts that there will be an estimated 9.9 million telecommuters in the United States by 2009.This has led to an increase in the number of small office home offices (SOHOs). To enable the convenience of office users, home networks are being deployed to provide access to computing and network resources to telecommuters (IDC 2006).
- *Emergence of Internet appliances*: many Internet appliances (typically used to describe non-PC devices that allow access to Internet content) have emerged on the market in recent years. Common examples include the Honeywell WebPAD, Microsoft's WebTV, Netpliance's I-Opener, Compaq's iPaq Home Internet Appliance, or the Sony PlayStation 2. These appliances are being connected to the Internet. Their ubiquity, deployment, and management in homes are being enabled by home networks (Das and Cook 2004; Zhaohui et al. 2004; Eckel et al. 2003).

- *Home automation*: from a consumer perspective, a home network facilitates communication among appliances, home systems, entertainment products, and information devices in a home, and enables them to work cooperatively and share information. This allows users to get information about the home condition and to remotely control home systems and appliances, as well as to gain access to information and entertainment resources from inside and outside the home. Home automation services including security, lighting, and heating are driving the need for home networking. It is also worthwhile pointing out that the capability to provide various monitoring services in the area of remote healthcare (through various sensing and monitoring devices) to elderly, sick or disabled people are also motivating the need for the deployment of home networks.
- *Consumer demand*: the demand for rich content and content-rich applications spawned the development of "convergence" products that combine the features of several consumer electronics products into a single device. Home networks have evolved into a "distributed convergence" model that is based on sharing content and functions among devices in the home. A device connected to a home network gains the capabilities of the other networked devices. Thus a networked device can provide a service or function that it is incapable of providing alone. Therefore, the home network provides the communications structure that allows the individual devices to operate as a larger cohesive unit (Marples and Moyer 2004).
- *Online gaming*: network (on local area networks) or Internet (across the Internet) gaming applications are increasingly being deployed in home networking environments. This trend continues to generate more money every year. For example, the Xbox 360 video gaming system, developed by Microsoft, is more than a just a new generation game console but is expected to become a centerpiece of future networked homes that provides both traditional and non-traditional gamers powerful gaming platforms in the comfort of their homes. Xbox's Ethernet connectivity support as well as wireless capabilities makes it well suited for home deployments at low costs. The portable gaming market is also experiencing significant competitions with the emergence of handheld game devices such as the Nintendo Dual-Screen (DS) and most recently the Sony Playstation Portable (PSP) with much larger widescreen displays and more powerful capabilities. All these developments in the gaming industry are becoming important drivers of home networking.

Cahners In-Stat Group (1999) reported on the main reasons that motivate home users (as consumers) of home networking products to deploy home networks. Some of most salient benefits encouraging home users to adopt home networks include:

- ***Shared Internet access***: home networks, in conjunction with devices called media gateways, allow different members of a family to simultaneously use a single, fast Internet access, thus saving money by having only one Internet Service Provider (ISP) account.
- ***Leverage existing investments***: home users want to leverage current investments in devices and appliances such as computers, set-top boxes, personal video recorders, digital cameras, and cable modems. Home networking technologies and networks enable the sharing of various hardware resources. For instance peripherals such as printers and scanners can be accessed by multiple computers reducing costs.
- ***File sharing***: users can easily share files, graphics, digital photographs, and other resources quickly through a home network compared to the use of other media such as disks, compact discs, etc. Exchange and distribution of large documents and media files such as video, MP3, and other digital content between information appliances can also be achieved more efficiently with home networking support.
- ***Evolving services***: home users want to have anywhere, anytime, in-home access to services such as voice over IP (VoIP), videophone, videoconferencing, remote monitoring, and multiplayer gaming, which can all be supported by an underlying home networking infrastructure.

HOME NETWORKING TECHNOLOGIES

As we mentioned previously, home networking has been receiving a lot of attention recently by home users, service providers, and consumer electronics manufacturers. Home networking initially started out as a way to connect multiple PCs in the home and having them simultaneously share a single Internet connection. This home networking trend has changed dramatically in the last few years with the emergence of the various applications and services (such as gaming, home control, distributed video, monitoring/security, and so on). Most of the efforts undertaken in the area of home networking by numerous consortia, standardization organizations, consumer electronics manufacturers, designers, developers, and researchers are being directed to three main areas:

- ***Connection technologies***: various competing technologies have been developed to help solve the issue of physical connection among home network devices. Many of the networking technologies (wired and wireless) now provide cost-effective ways to deploy a seamless network infrastructure in the home.
- ***Middleware technologies***: home networking has expanded to include a wide range of network-enabled products including digital audio/video servers, VoIP systems, Internet appliances, and many others. These new products add value and functionality to home networks but at the same time they have also made the management of home networks more complicated for consumers. The high heterogeneity of devices connected to the home network is pushing researchers and designers to explore middleware technologies that can be deployed to address the interoperability issue.
- ***Remote Internet access to home networks***: the traditional approach to home automation focused primarily on intuitive interfaces to simplify the management

and operation of networked homes. As a result, most home networking solutions have been exploiting wall-mounted keypads or tabletop touch panels through which a home user can synchronize, modify, and adjust setting for lighting, security, heating devices, and others. However, these interfaces only help users control their home devices while they are at home. The ubiquity of Internet access which enables anytime, anywhere access of information is also causing a shift in the way consumers want to access their home networks. The key is the provision of remote access to home networks. In a recent study by the Consumer Electronics Association on "Consumer Expectations of the Networked Home," almost 33 percent of consumers would want to exploit Internet access to monitor their homes, and 36 percent would want email notifications at work about events (delivery of a parcel, children arriving home, and so on) happening at home.

Connection Technologies

The various types of connection technologies that can be used in home networking environments can be classified according to the whether or not a new wiring of the home is needed to install the home network infrastructure. In addition, wired connection technologies can be distinguished from wireless ones. We present below a brief overview of some of the most popular wired and wireless technologies.

Various networking connection technologies are competing for the home market. These technologies can be broadly classified into three main categories: no new wiring, those technologies that require new wiring to be installed in the home, and connection technologies that are wireless (no wires).

No New Wiring

Phonelines. In 1998 the computer and semiconductor industries created the Home Phoneline Networking Alliance (HomePNA) (HomePNA 2006a) to select, promote, and standardize technologies for home phone line networking.

HomePNA initially introduced a first-generation (HomePNA 1.0) 1-Mbps technology (based on a system developed by Tut Systems Technology) followed by a second-generation (HomePNA 2.0) 10-Mbps technology (HomePNA 1999). Although HomePNA 2.0 quality of service-enabled (QoS-enabled) equipment manufacturers do provide priority support for voice traffic, HomePNA 2.0 was inadequate in its QoS support for high bandwidth audio/video streams. In 2003, HomePNA announced its third-generation (HomePNA 3.0) phone line technology that can support data rates up to 128 Mbps and, with optional extensions, data rates up to 240 Mbps. This third-generation technology addressed the QoS support inadequacy by having in-built, deterministic QoS support. HomePNA 3.0 can be used to meet the bandwidth requirements of emerging home multimedia networks that often need to deliver multiple, high-bandwidth digital audio and video streams simultaneously. HomePNA 3.0 has QoS support that allows it to deliver multimedia streams with QoS guarantees in the presence of on going best effort traffic. HomePNA technology uses 802.3 Ethernet framing and carrier sense multiple access with collision detection mechanism.

Phone line networking exploits existing phone lines wiring (no new wires need installation) in the home, is cheap and easy to maintain. Networking over the same phone line infrastructure suffers from several impairments such as high attenuation, reflections, impulse noise, and cross-talk. These issues need to be resolved in the future (HomePNA 2006b).

Powerlines. Powerline systems use electrical power lines to deliver high-speed voice and data services. Powerline carriers operate by transmitting high frequency data signals through the same powerline wired network used to deliver electrical power to homes. Devices outside the home (known as "outdoor devices") and devices inside the home (known as adapters) are used to handle the voice and data signals in the local transformers and filter the signals out to feed them into various home appliances respectively.

The principal benefit that is attributed to powerline systems is the wide availability of the wired infrastructure that is already in place. As a result there is no need for new wiring, and such systems are cheap and easy to maintain. However, powerline systems have several disadvantages: they can potentially cause interferences with other home devices and appliances such as radio, television, and telephones, they cannot bypass transformers, the maximum access speed of powerline systems is limited by the number of users simultaneous sharing the system (typical data rates offered by several powerline technologies range from 500 Kbits/s to 10 Mbps), no QoS support, and high voltages (hundreds of volts) need to be handled (Lonestarbroadband 2006).

It is worthwhile stressing that despite these disadvantages, the most serious drawback of powerline technologies are their use of proprietary protocols which makes interoperability very difficult ultimately impeding its acceptance by the home networking market. To address the proprietary issue the HomePlug Powerline Alliance (a non-profit industry association) (HomePlug 2006) was set up to promote an open specification for home networking products and services to leverage the worldwide pervasiveness of residential power lines. The HomePlug specification promises several benefits (cost-competitive, high-speed connectivity at Ethernet data rates) for home networks and the success of this standard will be known only in the future.

New Wires

The low cost of Ethernet makes it a popular local area network technology that is being widely deployed in home networks using either coaxial cable or twisted pair (connected to a hub to connect multiple computers). In recent years, new wiring technologies such as the universal serial bus (USB) (USB 2006) and the IEEE 1394 Firewire (IEEE 1394 2006) standards have also become available on the market. USB is widely covered in the literature already. In this work, we focus on IEEE 1394. These technologies can be used also to support a home networking infrastructure.

IEEE 1394. The IEEE 1394 (also known as the Firewire standard) is an international standard, low-cost digital interface developed by the IEEE 1394 working group, IEEE 1394. The Firewire interconnect technology was designed to connect computers and peripheral devices. Home networks can be designed using Firewire hardware/software technologies which support data rates up to 400 Mbps making it suitable for high-speed data and multimedia transfers. IEEE 1394 allows up to a maximum of 64 devices that can be connected on a single bus and up to 1024 individual buses can be connected.

Several design features of Firewire such as single-wire cabling for all devices, low cost, hot pluggable capability (allowing users to add or remove devices from the network without affecting the operation of other connected devices), flexible peer-to-peer topology (support of daisy chaining and branching for true peer-to-peer communication), ease of use (no need for terminators or complicated setup), non-proprietary, and its support for both asynchronous (the traditional computer memory-mapped load and store interface where data requests are sent to a specific address and an acknowledgment is returned) and isochronous (providing guaranteed data at a predefined rate, which is particularly important for multimedia transfers) data transfers.

Wireless Technologies

For some home users, large-scale rewiring of their homes is not affordable. For others, the installation of new wires in their home environments can be a cumbersome process. For both of these cases, the deployment of home networks becomes difficult. Competing technologies such as those based on wireless networking technologies can solve these issues (i.e., rewiring or new wires) and represent the "no-wires" solution (Zahariadis and Salkintzis 2003). In addition, wireless solutions also enable user mobility. Popular wireless networking technologies that have gained great popularity in home networks recently include wireless local area networks based 802.11 standards, Bluetooth, and HomeRF. Figure 2 shows a comparison of the adoption of wireless-based home networks compared to wired-based home networks in the last few years and estimated growth in the next few years.

A more in-depth review is given by Vaxevanakis et al. (2003).

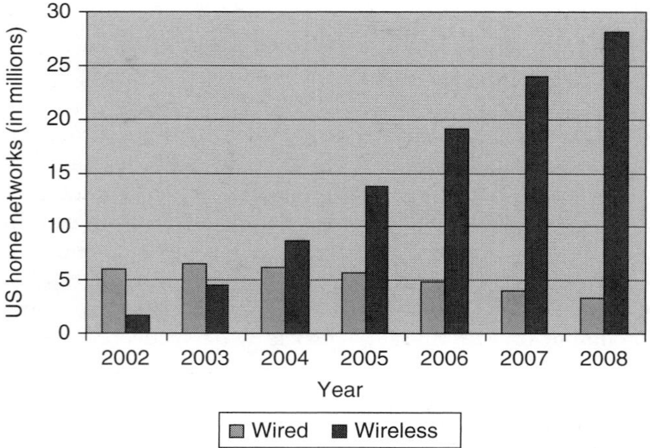

Figure 2: Growth of wired-based home networks compared with wireless-based home networks (Greenspan 2003)

Wireless Local Area Networks. The IEEE 802.11 project has set up several universal standards (IEEE Standard 802.11-1997, 1997), (IEEE Standard 802.11a–1999, 1999), (IEEE Standard 802.11b–1999, 1999) for wireless local area networks (WLANs) operating in the 2.4 GHz and 5 GHz bands. Table 2 gives a brief overview of the evolution of IEEE 802.11 standards in terms of frequency range, air access scheme, data rate, and compatibility with other technologies. In addition to these standards, we also include a European standard called higher performance radio LAN2 (HiperLAN2) (Ghazi-Moghadam 2001). HiperLAN2 was developed under the European Telecommunications Standardization Institute (ETSI) Broadband Radio Access Network (BRAN) project (Kruys 2006). HiperLAN2 is similar to IEEE 802.11a in that both use the 5-GHz band and OFDM. The 802.11 Study Group addresses the interoperability between 802.11a and HiperLAN. Wireless home networks can exploit any of the wireless communication technologies given in Table 2 depending on their bandwidth requirements.

Bluetooth. Bluetooth (Bluetooth 2002; Bisdikian 2001) enables the creation of ad-hoc networks based on the concept of master/slave devices and provides full-duplex transmissions using a slotted time division duplex (TDD) scheme. Master to slave transmissions always start in an even-numbered slot whereas slave to master transmission starts in an odd-numbered time slot. The master controls data transmission of up to 7 slaves using a polling mechanism. Slaves cannot communicate with each other in Bluetooth. Transmission is only between a slave and a master or vice versa. Slaves are allowed to transmit only after being polled. The device that initiates the connection is defined as the master. Three configurations are supported by Bluetooth: point-to-point connection, point-to-multipoint (known as a *piconet*), and multiple interconnected piconets with overlapping areas forming a *scatternet*. A Bluetooth unit can simultaneously be a slave of multiple piconets, but a master in only one, and can transmit and receive data in one piconet at a time. This implies that time division multiplexing is needed for participation in multiple piconets (Haarsten 1999). All these characteristics make Bluetooth a strong candidate for personal area networks which can be deployed within home networks.

HomeRF. The HomeRF Working Group (HRFWG) (HomeRF 2006) was formed to provide the foundation for a broad range of interoperable consumer devices by defining an open industry specification for wireless digital communication between PCs and consumer electronic devices anywhere in and around the home. The HomeRF group has developed a technology called the shared wireless access protocol (SWAP). Relying on FHSS technology, SWAP includes support for both carrier sense multiple access with collision avoidance (CSMA/CA) and time division multiple access (TDMA) to deliver data and voice services respectively. First-generation HomeRF products operate in the 2.4 GHz unlicensed bandwidth (the same band 802.11 and Bluetooth both use) to deliver services among PCs, cordless telephone handsets, and other consumer electronics products at a throughput of 1.6 Mbps. It is designed to operate throughout a

Table 2: IEEE 802.11 standards and HiperLAN2

	Frequency Range	Air Access Scheme	Data Rate (Mbps)	Compatibility
802.11	2.4 GHz	FHSS, DSSS, Ir	1 and 2	N/A
802.11b	2.4 to 2.4835 GHz	DSSS using CCK	Up to 11	Compatible with 802.11 DSSS 1 and 2 Mbps
802.11a	5.15 to 5.25 GHz (50 mW), 5.25 to 5.35 GHz (250 mW), 5.725 to 5.825 GHz (1 W)	OFDM	Up to 54	Not compatible with 802.11 and 802.11b
802.11g	2.4 to 2.4835 GHz	Mandatory CCK and OFDM, Optional PBCC and CCK/OFDM	Up to 54	Compatible with 802.11b; not compatible with 802.11 FHSS, Ir
HiperLAN2	5.15 to 5.35 GHz, 5.470 to 5.725 GHz	OFDM	Up to 54	Not compatible with 802.11, 802.11b, 802.11g

FHSS: Frequency Hoping Spread Spectrum
DSSS: Direct Sequence Spread Spectrum
Ir: Infrared
OFDM: Orthogonal Frequency Division Multiplexing
CCK: Complementary Code Keying
PBCC: Packet Binary Convolution Coding

home. The HRFWG argues that the open SWAP specification will: a) enable interoperability among many different consumer electronic devices available from a large number of manufacturers; b) provide the flexibility and mobility of a wireless solution. This flexibility factor is paramount to creating complete home networks in the future. The HRFWG-Japan subcommittee of HRFWG set up committees to plan future versions of SWAP that address the support of a variety of wireless multimedia applications being deployed at home (CEBus 2006).

Network Address Translation (NAT) Access Routers. The rapid growth of the Internet (including the adoption of numerous home and business networks) is causing IP addresses to be consumed at a fast pace. Prior to the advent of Internet protocol version 6 (IPv6) (which was designed to solve the shortage of IP addresses), the network address translation (NAT) (Egevang et al. 1994) technology was developed to conserve IP addresses. In recent years, NAT technology deployments have experienced an explosive growth and the NAT technology has been incorporated into various business and home broadband routers. A NAT-enabled router allows an entire non-routable range of network addresses to be hidden behind a single, unique routable "public" IP address (i.e., the address of the router itself). The NAT router is given two IP addresses: one non-routable IP address (that of the private local network) and one routable (for the public Internet assigned by an Internet service provider for example) (Dutcher 2001). In the context of a home network, NAT maps all private IP addresses of devices residing on the local home network to the single public IP address (supplied by an the Internet service provider) of the NAT router. All devices on the home network can therefore access the Internet simultaneously by sharing the Internet connection through the NAT-based router. In addition, because NAT works by snooping incoming and outgoing IP packets, it can enhance network security of the local home network by limiting access of external hosts to the private home network. External hosts can only communicate with those hosts residing behind a NAT router that have initiated sessions with them. Incoming network traffic to the NAT router without a prior outbound request made from a local host is simply ignored. NAT can support either fixed or dynamic mappings of one or more internal and external IP addresses and has been implemented in hardware products (such as routers) and software products (such as Microsoft's Internet Connection Sharing) (Microsoft 2006) that are being widely deployed in home networks.

Middleware Technologies

Several middleware technologies have emerged on the market recently. Most of them incorporate service discovery protocols and architectures to facilitate highly dynamic cooperation among devices/services with minimal administration and human intervention. Common features supported by various middleware technologies such as universal plug and play (UPnP), JoIN-In (JINI), and others include: the ability to announce device/service presence to the network, automatic discovery of devices in the neighborhood and those located remotely, the ability to describe device capabilities as well as query/understand the capabilities of other devices, seamless interoperability with other devices wherever possible, and self-configuration with minimal administrative intervention. All these features make middleware technology an important software substrate over which home networking users can run their applications independent of the underlying hardware platforms. We now present some popular middleware technologies that can be deployed in home networks.

Universal Plug and Play (UPnP)

UPnP (UPnP Forum 2000a) is an architecture for pervasive peer-to-peer network connectivity of intelligent appliances, wireless devices, and PCs of all form factors. UPnP is designed to bring easy-to-use, flexible, standards-based connectivity to ad-hoc or unmanaged networks whether in home, small businesses, public spaces, or connected to the Internet. UPnP is independent of any particular operating system, programming language, or physical medium. UPnP allows a device to dynamically join a network, obtain an IP address, convey its capabilities, and learn about the presence and capabilities of other devices. The addresses of the UPnP devices can be hardwired or obtained from a DHCP server, or devices can use Auto IP to assign an IP address. Auto IP is a new draft of the IETF (Internet Engineering Task Force) standard that allows dynamic configuration of IPv4 addresses. Auto IP permits a UPnP device to select an IP address from a range of nonroutable addresses.

UPnP is a distributed, open networking architecture that leverages transport control protocol/Internet protocol (TCP/IP) and the Web technologies to enable seamless proximity networking. In addition to supporting control and data transfer among networked devices, UPnP is designed to support zero-configuration and automatic discovery for a wide range of device categories possibly from different vendors.

UPnP devices have embedded functions called "services." Services can include turning off the device, scanning inputs for data, or similar functions. A UPnP network node can be a device, or a control point, or both. Devices have services that a control point can monitor or control. A control point in a UPnP network is capable of discovering and controlling other devices. After discovery, a control point could retrieve the device description and get a list of associated services, retrieve service descriptions for interesting services, invoke actions to control the service, and subscribe to the service's event source. Anytime the state of the service changes, the event server will send an event to the control point. Devices can incorporate control point functionality to enable true peer-to-peer networking.

UPnP-enabled devices or control points have six layers of functions (UPnP 2000b). Layers 0, 1, and 2 corresponding to addressing, discovery, and description respectively are fundamental; they exist in all devices and control points. Layers 3, 4, and 5 corresponding to control, eventing, and presentation respectively are optional. Control points can initiate an action on a device and send a control message using the definitions from the device-description document. To exchange information, the control layer uses a W3C (World Wide Web Consortium) draft standard, and the simple object access protocol (SOAP), which is a lightweight, eXtensible markup language-based (XML-based) protocol for exchange of information in a decentralized, distributed environment. The device completes the action and responds using SOAP.

The event-messaging layer relies on a basic push model in which control points listen for notifications of UPnP device state changes. To obtain event messages, control points subscribe to event messages for a specific service within a device. A network can contain multiple control points and multiple UPnP-enabled devices. A control point might want to listen to more than one network service but not all of them. By subscribing and unsubscribing to events, control points can be selective. When a service within a device has an event, it notifies all current subscribers. Consequently, all subscribers have current knowledge of the state of the device. Event messages use the general event notification architecture (GENA), an extension to the hypertext transfer protocol (HTTP) defined by the IETF draft standard. GENA is designed to send and receive notifications using HTTP over TCP and UDP. The presentation function presents information and control to the user. Presentation requires the completion of layers 0, 1, and 2: getting an address, discovering the device, and obtaining the device description. The description document provides the device URL for the presentation page for the device. A more in-depth discussion of the UPnP architecture can be found in (UPnP 2000a; UPnP 2000b; Lee and Helal 2002).

Join-in (JINI)

Jini (Sun Microsystems 2006a; Sun Microsystems 2006b), from Sun Microsystems, is a framework based on the idea of federating groups of users and the resources required by those users. The focus of the framework is to make the network a more dynamic entity that better reflects the dynamic nature of the workgroup by enabling the ability to add and delete services flexibly. Jini systems provide mechanisms for service construction, lookup, communication, and use in a distributed system. Examples of entities providing such services include devices such as printers, displays, or disks; software such as applications or utilities; information such as databases and files. The heart of the Jini system is a trio of protocols called discovery, join, and lookup. A pair of these protocols (discovery/join) occurs when a device is plugged in. Discovery occurs when a service is looking for a lookup service with which to register. Join takes place when a service has located a lookup service and wishes to join it, whereas lookup occurs when a client or a user needs to locate and invoke a service described by its interface type (written in the Java programming language) and possibly, other attributes. The following steps describe what interactions are needed among a client, a service provider, and a lookup service for a service to be used by the client in a Jini community (Sun Microsystems 2006b; Sun Microsystems 2006). First, a service provider locates a lookup service by multicasting a request on the local network or a remote lookup service known to it. Second, the service provider registers a service object and its service attributes with the lookup service. This service object includes methods that users and applications will invoke to execute the service, along with any other descriptive attributes. Third, a client requests a service by Java type and, perhaps, other service attributes. A copy of the service object is moved to the client. Finally, the client interacts directly with the service provider via the service object (Edwards 1999). Thus, Jini provides an infrastructure and a programming model that address the fundamental issues of how devices connect with each other to form an impromptu community. Jini is based on Java technology and exploits Java remote method invocation (RMI) protocol (which in turn rely on TCP/IP support) to move code around the network. Home networks can exploit Jini to support specific device communities (e.g., devices constituting an entertainment network in the home).

JetSend

JetSend (Meadows 2000; HP 1999) is a media-independent peer-to-peer information exchange protocol developed by Hewlett Packard to provide interoperability among various kinds of devices. Existing point-to-point protocols do not fully describe the content of the information being exchanged making the data transferred both machine and operating system dependent. The protocol allows devices to connect to each other, negotiate data types, and exchange information. JetSend can exchange information in its proper context without any product-specific knowledge or device drivers. This capability enables a variety of embedded devices such as digital cameras, cell phones, scanners, and so on to exchange data with each other without knowing about the protocol being used to transfer the data. Another strong motivation that is pushing the adoption of JetSend is its availability in many of the devices mentioned earlier. For instance, all Hewlett Packard's standalone printers and scanners support JetSend.

In JetSend, all information is stored as *electronic material* in areas called *surfaces*. Each surface object has a name, a description, and content. The description is similar to a file header and contains information about the type and content of the surface. The content may be null, data or a link to some other surface. The data contained in a surface is called electronic material (e-material) (Meadows 2000). JetSend devices exchange information with each other using versions of surfaces (i.e., impressions that are not necessarily identical copies of the original surface). The main benefit of JetSend is that impressions need not be exact copies of the original surface. Instead, the impressions can be changed to ensure device compatibility. An example would be a digital camera that may have a surface containing a picture. The digital camera would send the picture to the printer by sending an impression of the surface containing the picture to the printer device for printing. In contrast to JetSend (where the digital camera directly communicates with the digital printer), the traditional approach would have required a PC to be connected to the digital camera. The PC would then exploit some compatible digital camera application to receive the digital camera pictures and then prints the desired pictures using a compatible printer driver. The JetSend model removes the need of the PC and allows direct peer-to-peer connectivity between the digital camera and the printer.

To use JetSend to communicate, device-specific code must interact with an API composed of three main components namely, the *activity manager*, *interaction policies*, and *e-material routines*. The activity manager manages JetSend sessions between JetSend-enabled devices as well as the handling of events. Interaction policies control the type of interaction between devices using some types of policies. The e-material routines allow the device-specific code to format data to be communicated in a standard JetSend format for other JetSend-enabled devices to understand.

Home Audio Video interoperability (HAVi)

HAVi (HaVi 1999a; HAVi 1999b) is a digital audio/video (AV) networking initiative from several major consumer electronics companies, which is aimed at providing a home networking software specification for seamless interoperability among digital audio and video devices. Basically, HAVi allow functions of an audio or video device to be controlled from some other audio or video device regardless of the actual brands of these devices. Within a HAVi system, a device residing on the HAVi network is designed to have the capability of controlling other devices or being controlled by other devices. In other words, HAVi allows a device to be a controlling device and a controlled device simultaneously (there is no concept of a single master controller).

The HAVi platform running on HAVi devices is made up of several software modules that implement basic services such as network management, device abstraction, inter-device communication, and device user interface management. The HAVi specification defines a set of application programming interfaces (APIs) and system services to support the development of audio/video applications for the home network. The HAVi architecture is independent of any programming language, operating system, or CPU. This platform independence gives full flexibility to application developers and consumer electronics manufacturers to develop interoperable audio/video devices and applications. HAVi compliant devices automatically announce their presence and capabilities to other devices when they join the HAVi network without requiring any complex configuration and installation procedures—a featured often referred to as hot "plug-and-enjoy." HAVi-compliant devices' functionalities can be easily upgraded, via their dynamic device control modules, by simply downloading upgrades through the Internet. A device control module (DCM) is a software element that represents a single device on the HAVi network and makes available the device's HAVi-defined APIs. Whenever a device joins or leaves the HAVi network, the device's DCM is added or removed respectively by the DCM manager from the network (HAVi 1999b). Within a DCM, there are functional component modules (FCMs) responsible for each controllable function within the device. All HAVi software elements communicate using a message passing mechanism. It is worthwhile mentioning that it is not necessary to use PCs to deploy a HAVi-based network.

The interconnection technology used by HAVi is the digital IEEE-1394 network. The high bandwidth capacity of IEEE 1394 makes it suitable to simultaneously handle multiple digital audio/video streams around the home (HaVi 1999a). The 1394 communication media manager enables software elements of the HAVi architecture to perform asynchronous and isochronous transfers over the IEEE-1394 network.

Open Service Gateway Initiative (OSGi)

The Open Service Gateway initiative (OSGi 2003; Gong 2001) is an independent, nonprofit industry group working to define and promote an open standard to connect smart consumer and business appliances to Internet-based services (Gong 2001). The complex diversity of home networking architectures and device technologies need to be coordinated to enable home users to fully exploit and reap their benefits. As mentioned earlier, management of these network architectures and services can become overly complex for home users. The advent of OSGi simplifies the management of home networks composed of multiple heterogeneous communication technologies. OSGi defines a collection of APIs split into a set of *core APIs* and a set of *optional APIs*. The core APIs support service delivery, dependency and life cycle management, resource management, remote service administration, and equipment management. All of the core APIs are either contributed by a member of the OSGi alliance or developed by OSGi technical working groups. The optional set of APIs refine mechanisms for client interaction and data management. In addition, several existing Java APIs are included in the optional services. OSGi leverages existing Java standards such as Jini and Java database connectivity (JDBC). This includes JDBC and several other Java standards. OSGi technical working groups also focus on integrating non–Java-based standards into the OSGi framework (Condry et al. 1999). OSGi specifies a framework (similar in functionality to an application server) where it is possible to dynamically load and manage software components also known as *service bundles* (OSGi 2003). These bundles can be instantiated by OSGi to implement specific services required.

The ability for devices to self-configure is particularly important in home networks because most home users and consumers do not want and cannot be expected to manually configure and administer the home networked devices. Device and service discovery technologies, such as the UPnP, Jini, and HAVi discussed earlier, all enable automatic self-configuration of devices. However, each of these technologies assumes the use of its specific set of homogeneous protocols. For example, a Jini device can only communicate with another Jini device on the Jini network using the Jini device discovery protocol. It is not possible for a Jini device (residing on a Jini network) to communicate with a UPnP device residing on a UPnP network. OSGi can be used to serve as a platform to interconnect the Jini and the UPnP networks, thereby enabling the Jini device to seamlessly communicate with a UPnP network. By serving as the "glue" that allows various discovery protocols to interact with one another, OSGi promotes ease of use for the home network's end users, who need not be concerned with the underlying protocols supported by the devices in their home networks. Moreover, OSGi also allows device manufacturers to implement protocols that are most appropriate for their devices, because the OSGi discovery APIs allow devices to interact not only with other devices that support the same protocols, but also with devices that support different protocols (such as between Jini and UPnP).

The device access specification (DAS) of OSGi allows multiple devices to be discovered and their services advertised, thereby making these services available to other devices, services, and applications. Integration of discovery technologies with OSGi is based on an import/export model. Briefly, registered OSGi devices and services are exported out of the OSGi framework. For instance, an OSGi printing service can be exported to a Jini network to appear as a Jini printer. Similarly, devices and services found by native discovery techniques can also be imported into the OSGi framework to appear as valid OSGi entities and accessible to other OSGi entities. It is this importing/exporting feature that allows cross-technology discovery and promotes interoperability among multiple device types (Dobrev et al. 2002).

Some of the main benefits of OSGi can be summarized as follows (Marples and Kriens 2001):

a. *Platform and application independence*: The OSGi software environment can be implemented on different types of platforms and is applicable to different computing environments; this independence gives considerable freedom and flexibility to application developers and designers in their service offerings.
b. *Multiple service support*: OSGi environments allow multiple applications from different service providers to coexist on one single service platform.
c. *Service collaboration support*: OSGi services deployed can provide support to other OSGi services. Applications dynamically discover these services and can adapt their behavior based on the configuration of the environment and services that are present.
d. *Network choice*: OSGi does not require the use of any specific network technology for communication.
e. *Security*: OSGi has in-built security features that allow the concurrent support of services from different service providers to be supported. Many of these benefits of OSGi will simplify the management and deployment of home networks and services in terms of shared Internet access, energy management, security (alarm systems), remote healthcare, entertainment, and others.

Several software vendors have been developing OSGi-compliant products. Some of the prominent implementations that have emerged include the Gatespace Distributed Service Platform (Gatespace 2006), the service management framework (SMF) Micro Edition from IBM, mBedded server from Prosyst (Prosyst 2006), and lamp embedded server from Acronet (Chemishkian 2002).

Zero Configuration (ZeroConf) Technology

The IETF Zero Configuration Networking (Zeroconf) Working Group (IETF 2006) was chartered in September 1999. The goal of Zeroconf is to enable networking without requiring any configuration and administration. Zeroconf networking is particularly attractive for those environments where administration is impractical or impossible (Steinberg and Cheshire 2005). Common situations where Zeroconf technology can be of tremendous benefit include the home, embedded systems "plugged together" as in an automobile, or for impromptu networks such those set up between the devices of strangers with a view of collaborating with each other. There is tremendous potential for Zeroconf in the home networking area, because home owners often do not want to be burdened by configuration and administration tasks often associated with networked devices. It is worth noting that although one of the goals of Zeroconf networking is to make personal computer networking easier to use, the long-term objective is really to enable the creation of entirely new kinds of networked products, products that today would simply not be commercially viable because of the inconvenience and support costs involved in setting up, configuring, and maintaining a network to allow them to operate. AppleTalk users are already familiar with the benefits provided with such technology because the Mac operating system incorporates the Rendezvous technology to support zero configuration over standard IP protocol for automatic discovery of computers, devices, and services. Microsoft's NetBIOS software interface also provides similar capabilities over TCP/IP. Recent efforts of the IETF Working Group on Zeroconf (Zero Configuration Networking) have been focusing on standardization issues. Once Zeroconf protocols are standardized and implemented into commercial network products, they will play an important role in the future deployments of networked homes.

Remote Internet Access to Home Networks

Home networks enable users to get information about the home's condition, to remotely control home systems and appliances, and to gain access to information and entertainment resources both from inside (such as a computer hard drive) and outside the home (for instance, from the Internet) (Rose 2001). To provide these benefits to home consumers, different devices of the home network must be able to communicate with each other to provide services despite their implementation differences. This requires the management and coordination of discovery methods that work across heterogeneous device technologies and complex home networking architectures. To achieve this management and coordination transparently without user intervention is a complex task which, until now has been the major factor responsible for impeding the wide acceptance and delivery of advanced services into the home. A common solution is to exploit a central connection point often referred to as a ***residential gateway*** (Bull et al. 2004; Marples and Kriens 2001). The gateway manages the home network by hiding the complexity of various heterogeneous communication technologies (e.g., phoneline, powerline, HomeRF) from home users. The residential gateway also acts as a "bridge" between the wide area network (e.g., Internet) and the home network (as illustrated in Figure 3), thereby giving users access to home devices and control over the information exchanged among these devices.

Desired Characteristics of Residential Gateways

As mentioned previously, a residential gateway plays a central role in home networks in acting as a central coordination point for various home devices as well enabling remote access to the home network. The residential gateway also acts as a point of entry where services can be installed and managed by service providers. Since a residential gateway is responsible for many such crucial functions, it is important that the gateway device has some desired characteristics. We enumerate some of these desired features (Gong 2001; Condry et al. 1999; Tsai et al. 2004) below:

- **Platform and vendor independence:** residential gateways should be designed and programmed to be both platform and vendor independent so that service developers would not have to spend time porting their services. Achieving this independence requires gateway implementations from different vendors to exploit open,

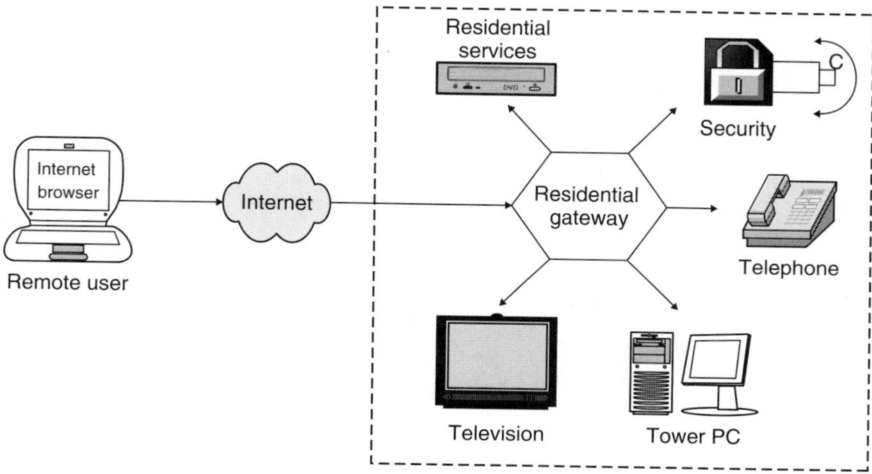

Figure 3: Residential gateway access to the home network

standard APIs so that the gateways can support services developed by different, independent software vendors.

- **Maintenance and upgradeability:** by conforming to some open standard (such as an API), home network users should not be required to change their residential gateways when their service providers change. It should be simple and easy to make dynamic upgrades of residential gateways to support new services or enhance existing services cost-effectively.
- **Integration and interoperability:** residential gateways should be capable of supporting heterogeneous network and device access technologies (for example, interoperability between a Jini-enabled camera and a UPnP-enabled display device) seamlessly.

Other typical residential gateway characteristics may include zero administration, limited memory and computation requirements (Condry et al. 1999).

Quality of Service-based (QoS-based) Residential Gateways. For several years, home networking users have been focusing primarily on computing-based applications using PCs and peripherals (printer, scanner). However, with the emergence of technologies such as HAVi and IEEE–1394, we have witnessed a shift towards entertainment-centric devices being installed and deployed over home networks. Most of these entertainment appliances and devices generate and handle high-quality, high-bandwidth audio/video streams over the home network.

To ensure the delivery of guaranteed performance over home networks for bandwidth-sensitive and delay-sensitive multimedia applications, we need efficient resource management techniques to be in place. These techniques should provide dynamic bandwidth allocation to devices and services based on their service requirement to deliver optimal performance to home users (Lei et al. 2002). It is worthwhile to mention two approaches that have recently been proposed to address the resource management issue in home networks:

- One approach is the adaptive resource management system (Okamura 2001) for home networks proposed by Okamura from Sony Laboratories Inc. Okamura's resource management approach (demonstrated by a prototype system called PPS/J) exploits dynamic adaptation mechanisms by allowing poor devices (for example, PDAs, cellular phones), with limited computational resources (such as memory, CPU power, and disk space), to borrow surplus of computational resources from rich devices (for example, PCs).
- Another approach proposed by Lei et al. (2002) exploits the notion of *Quality of Service-aware* (QoS-aware) *residential gateways* beneficial for both service providers and home consumers. From a service provider perspective, a QoS-aware residential gateway provides more attractive services in that the provider can charge home network users according to the quality level of the service delivered to actual home devices. Home network users also fully benefit from a QoS-aware residential gateway in the sense that the available home network bandwidth can be optimally distributed to different home networked devices according to their individual bandwidth requirements.

Web Access to Home Network Devices with Handheld Devices

To facilitate access to home network devices anytime, anywhere using small, portable handheld devices such as Web-enabled cellphones, PDAs, and other mobile handheld devices, the wireless application protocol (WAP) is often used. WAP defines the wireless markup language (WML) and WMLScript for mobile applications to display Web content by addressing the limitations of small screens in mobile clients. One of the key components of a WAP-based network is the WAP gateway (Ma and Irvine 2002) which is connected to the Web. The function of the WAP gateway is to provide operator specific services or to perform content and protocol translation between TCP/IP and the WAP stack. The WAP gateway also resolves domain names to IP addresses by performing all required domain name server (DNS) services, and translates Web pages into compact encoded formats that reduce the size and number of packets required to be transmitted over the wireless communications network. The result of these operations is to offload many TCP/IP functions from phones, and PDAs, enabling these devices to be smaller, less powerful, requiring less memory resulting in lower-cost of producing these devices. User interaction with the WAP gateway is initiated through the WAP browser. The terminal sends its request to the WAP gateway, which then requests the content from the Web server.

In the case of mobile Internet applications, data transfer speeds are low, and mobile handheld devices are much slower compared to computers connected to fixed, wired networks. Moreover, these devices typically have small screens and require that the Web content be displayed differently from the display on typical personal computers. WAP (Aust et al. 2002) is a protocol designed to specifically transmit Web-like content to mobile phones and other (usually wireless) devices with low bandwidth access (Saha et al. 2001).

A WAP-enabled handheld device can access Web sites similar to personal computers connected to the Internet by sending WAP requests to the WAP gateway. Using WAP, a small, portable device views Internet information that is presented in a format to suit the device's screen. Web browsing over the Internet uses HTTP to transport the Web pages and the language that defines the manner by which content is displayed is the hypertext markup language (HTML). Thus, to view the HTML pages associated with home network devices, we need to convert HTML pages to WML pages dynamically. By dynamically converting HTML to WML, we eliminate the need for having an HTML version and a WML version of the same Web site. Dynamic conversion of HTML to WML can be achieved using the following approaches:

- **WAP gateway** (Deri 2001): a plug-in at the WAP gateway can perform the necessary dynamic HTML to WML conversion. The WAP Gateway receives the request (in WML) from the WAP client for a particular HTML page. The gateway contacts the necessary Web server for that page using TCP/IP. After obtaining the HTML page, the WAP gateway runs a program (Perl or JavaScript) that converts the HTML to WML on-the-fly and forwards the converted WML file to the WAP client. The WAP gateway approach takes control away from Web content providers since they will have to rely on WAP gateways to provide this plug-in to make their Web sites accessible to small, portable, mobile devices. Alternatively, the content provider will have to provide a WML version of their site, which increases costs.

- **WAP browser:** a WAP Browser add-in that converts HTML to WML on-the-fly can also be used (Vantroys and Rouillard 2002). The disadvantage of this solution is that it increases resource demands on the small mobile devices that already lack resources. Thus, such a solution is ineffective.
- **Web server:** software such as the *mobile converters* could be added to Web servers (Christianson et al. 2002) to make the servers capable of distinguishing between requests from WAP and those from regular Web browsers. Depending on the source of the request, the Web server will either serve a WML or an HTML page. This solution is effective but it requires all Web servers to have the plug-in for it to be efficient. With this approach, the WAP gateway and Web server functionalities are merged together.

It is worthwhile noting that two common methods of implementing the dynamic conversion of HTML to WML include: a) *using Perl scripts* (Vanderdonckt et al. 2001): there are a few Perl scripts available that convert HTML to WML. The Perl script formats a WML page by ignoring tags in HTML that are allowed in WML and replaces those that are not with the corresponding WML tags (for instance, replacing the body tag in HTML with the card tag for WML); b) *using XSLT (eXtensible stylesheet language transformation)*—a language for transforming one XML document into another XML document. XSLT is designed for use as part of eXtensible stylesheet language (XSL), which is a style sheet for XML (Forstadius and Loytynoja, 2001). Given that an HTML document is not governed by strict standards and rules, it cannot be directly converted into a WML document. It has to be first parsed into an XHTML or XML document by using a tool such as tidy.exe and then converted into WML using XSLT. Tidy.exe is a HTML tool that was originally written by Dave Raggett of the World Wide Web Consortium (W3C). It is designed to fix mistakes in HTML, tidy up the layout, assist with web accessibility, and convert HTML to XHTML (Tsymbalenko and Munson 2001).

The various approaches discussed above can be used to convert HTML to WML to enable small portable device users to access and operate home network devices remotely. We argue that the most efficient solution is to place the HTML to WML converter at the WAP gateway. This approach yields two main benefits namely: a) it allows the converter to use gateway resources and will not place resource demands on the limited resources of small, portable handheld devices, and b) no changes are required by users of WAP-enabled devices and Web server administrators.

It is imperative that manufacturers of home control systems continue to develop Web-accessible home devices and appliances to enable home users to access their home networks locally or remotely via highly mobile devices such as PDAs and WAP-enabled phones. WebLink software, developed by Home Automation Inc. (HAI) (one of the first companies to exploit Web access to home networks), provides users home device functions displayed through Web pages.

RELATED WORK AND CHALLENGES OF HOME NETWORKS

Related Research

Many researchers are working on various components of home networks. Some of recent research efforts such as the PPS/J prototype system developed by Okumara (Okamura 2001) and the QoS-aware residential gateway developed by Lei et al. (2002) have already been discussed. Saif et al. (2001) discussed the design and implementation of a residential gateway in the context of the AutoHan project. As mentioned earlier, the OSGi expert group (OSGi 2003) is currently focusing on the development of drivers for all possible and probable protocols to be used in home networks. Several research groups have been exploiting OSGi technology to address many of the home networking challenges (such as interoperability, scalability). Dobrev et al. (2002) proposed a framework to extend the OSGi framework to enable redefining gateway services and to provide a smart querying technique for users and devices to look up services with particular attributes. The authors also addressed the interoperability feature and proposed implementing it through extensions of OSGi services. Wils and colleagues (Wils et al. 2002) proposes integration architectures for UPnP-based and Jini-based home network devices within an OSGi framework.

Rice University researchers recently proposed the Rice Everywhere NEtwork (RENE) (AAzhang et al. 2006) architecture to explore the integration of wireless code division multiple access (W-CDMA) cellular systems, high-speed wireless local area networks, and home wireless networks. Their goal is to develop a seamless multi-tier network interface card (mNIC) that can interact with various radio frequency units (AAzhang and Cavallaro 2001).

Challenges of Home Networks

Until recently, home networking was being deployed mainly to allow multiple PCs in the home to share a single Internet connection. This trend has changed significantly in the last decade. Home networks are expected to provide additional capabilities including network-enabled devices such as digital audio/video servers, VoIP systems, security services, and others. Although it is true that these new systems enhance the value of added services, they also make their management and maintenance by (most inexperienced) home users difficult as their complexities increase with new added features. As a result, we must ensure that such complexities do not overburden home users to the extent that they are discouraged from adopting home networks. It is therefore crucial that future home networks meet the following requirements:

- Home environments typically contain many heterogeneous devices and home users are unlikely to install significant new cabling to support a home network—lack of skills and the low desire to perform major network configuration or maintenance makes home networking deployment expensive. This means that configuring a home network and its maintenance should be simple and easy to do. A home network should support plug-and-work capabilities enabling new devices to join and leave the network without requiring any configuration whenever possible. Transparent mechanisms are needed to allow devices to advertise their services to other devices as well automatically discover other services from other home network devices.
- Seamless interoperability among devices remains a significant challenge in the deployment and operation of home networks. Open APIs and platform-independent representations need to be deployed to enable flexible modeling and optimal representations of devices, network states, device functions, and resource registration in the home network. Languages such as XML (W3C, 2006) and XSL (Adler 2000) can be deployed. Saif et al. (2001) discuss these issues in more depth in the Auto-Han project.
- Remote access to home networks is becoming an important feature. This trend is expected to continue with highly mobile users and the ubiquity of Internet access and the Web. Secure access to home networks will need to be implemented and deployed. A discussion of the security issues in home networks is beyond the scope of this work but is extensively covered in recent articles (Saif et al. 2001; Ellison 2002; Zhou et al. 2005).

The requirements above stem mainly from the fact that home network users have quite different expectations from traditional network environments. Many factors such as the ease of use of network, reliability, scalability, adherence to open standards, and cost will ultimately determine the adoption success and deployment of future home networks. Next generation home networks will be expected to support much higher resolution video terminals, networked appliances, different types of sensors, and various Internet terminals. To provide such support, novel home networking technologies (including network topology considerations, transmission medium, bandwidth control, residential gateway functionality and so on) need to be explored and developed (Seik 2004).

CONCLUSION

Over the last few years, we have experienced an explosive growth in the emergence of networking and computing technologies. The adoption and deployment of these technologies by end users are fueling new paradigms in our day-to-day activities in terms of the way we live, work, and communicate with each other. The home is one of the environments where we are currently witnessing the strong convergence of computing and communication. In this work, we focused on home networking—an area that has generated a lot of interest among consumers, service providers, and manufacturers of home networking products. We have presented many of the technologies that have become available and can be used to design, develop, and deploy sophisticated, highly dynamic home networks cost-effectively. The actual implementations of home networks may vary depending on the choice of the underlying connection technology, middleware, or residential gateway design. However, we argue that most home networks will still need to satisfy the following fundamental goals such as efficient sharing of resources (including sharing of Internet access and devices such as printers, playback, and storage devices) anywhere in the home, seamless connectivity of computing, home automation, and entertainment home network clusters, and strong interoperability among different home devices, and finally support remote access to home devices from anywhere inside and outside the home. Finally, to conclude, we argue that the success and deployment of digital networked homes will ultimately depend on value-added services that become available to home consumers and their associated costs.

ACKNOWLEDGMENT

Many colleagues provided their great support and contributions during the preparation of this chapter. We express our deepest gratitude to Mohammad Saklayen for his time and efforts in providing us some of the materials presented in this chapter. We express our thanks to Priya Kubher for her input and ideas on the WAP protocol. We thank Nadeem Ansari and Srivatsan Krishnamurthy for their help on OSGi interoperability features and recent home networking efforts respectively. This work was supported by grants from Sun Microsystems (Palo Alto) (EDUD–7824-000145–US), Microsoft Corporation (Seattle), and Ixia Corporation (Calabasas). We are grateful to Farhan Siddiqui and the anonymous reviewers for their suggestions and comments on early drafts of this chapter. We would also like to express our high appreciation to the editor-in-chief, Hossein Bidgoli, for his patience, encouragements, and kind support throughout the preparation of this chapter.

GLOSSARY

Extensible Hypertext Markup Language: Hybrid between HTML and XML specifically designed for networked device displays.

Extensible Markup Language: A specification (designed especially for Web documents) developed by the World Wide Web Consortium (W3C).

Extensible Stylesheet Language Transformation: The language used in XSL style sheets to transform XML documents into other XML documents.

Home Audio/Video Interoperability: A standard, developed by several leading electronics and computer manufacturers, that allows a number of different home entertainment and communication devices to operate from a single controller device such as a TV set.

Home Network: Home networks facilitate communication among appliances, home systems, entertainment products, and information devices in a home so that they can work cooperatively and share information.

HyperText Markup Language: The authoring language used to create World Wide Web documents.

HyperText Transfer Protocol: The underlying protocol used by the World Wide Web. HTTP defines how messages are formatted and transmitted and what actions Web servers and browsers should take in response to various commands.

Internet Protocol: The Internet Protocol (IP) is the method or protocol by which data is sent from one computer to another on the Internet.

Jini: Software from Sun Microsystems that seeks to simplify the connection and sharing of devices, such as printers and disk drives, on a network.

Middleware: A software layer residing between the operating system and applications. It is often used to support complex, distributed applications.

Network Address Translation (NAT): An IETF standard that enables a local area network (LAN) to use one set of IP addresses for internal traffic and a second set of addresses for external traffic.

Open Services Gateway Initiative: An industry plan for a standard way to connect devices such as home appliances and security systems to the Internet.

Residential Gateway: It a device that connects the home network to the Internet. It also enables access to services (such as telephony, cable TV) delivered to the home.

Service Discovery Protocol: The service discovery protocol provides a mechanism for client applications to discover the existence of services provided by server applications as well as the attributes of those services.

Universal Plug and Play: A standard that uses Internet and Web protocols to enable devices such as PCs, peripherals, intelligent appliances, and wireless devices to be plugged into a network and automatically know about each other.

Wide Area Network: A network that spans over large distances; usually connects many other networks together.

Wireless Application Protocol: A specification that allows users to access information instantly via handheld wireless devices such as mobile phones, pagers, two-way radios, smart phones, and communicators.

Wireless Markup Language: An XML language used to specify content and user interface for WAP devices.

CROSS REFERENCES

See *Network Middleware; Wireless Broadband Access; Wireless LANs (WLANs)*.

REFERENCES

AAzhang et al., 2006. Rice University, RENE project, http://cmc.rice.edu/researc/rene (accessed May 19, 2006).

AAzhang, B., and J. Cavallaro. 2001. *Multitier wireless communications, wireless personal communications*, Volume 7. Dortrecht, Netherlands: Kluwer Academic Publishers, pp. 323–330; http://cmc.rice.edu/docs/docs/Aaz2000Sep1MultitierW.pdf (accessed May 19, 2006).

Allied Business Intelligence (ABI). Report Code RR-HNET. 2006. http://abiresearch.com/products/market_research/Home_Networking_and_Connected_Home_Market_Analysis (accessed May 19, 2006).

Adler, S., et al. 2000. Extensible Stylesheet Language (XSL) Version 1.0. W3C candidate recommendation. http://www.w3.org/TR/xsl/ (accessed May 19, 2006).

Aust, S., N. Fikouras, and C. Gorg. 2002. Enabling mobile WAP gateways using Mobile IP. In Proceedings of European Wireless. Florence, Italy. http://docenti.ing.unipi.it/ew2002/proceedings/157.pdf (accessed May 19, 2006).

Bisdikian, C. 2001. An overview of the bluetooth wireless technology. *IEEE Communications Magazine* 39(12):86–94.

Bluetooth SIG. 2002. Specification of the Bluetooth system. Version 1.1.

Bull, P., P. Benyon, and P. Limb. 2002. Residential gateways. *BT Technology Journal* 20(2):73–81.

Cahners In-Stat Group. 1999. "Home networking: Markets, technologies, and vendors." Research Report, Report Number LN00-02MS.

CEBus Industry Council, Inc. 2006. http://www.cebus.org (accessed May 19, 2006).

Chemishkian, S.. 2002. Building smart services for smart home. In Proceedings of 4th International Workshop on Networked Appliances, pp. 215–224.

Christianson, L., K. Brown, and N. Tomar. 2002. Text reorganization for wireless Web devices. In Proceedings of Communications Systems, Networks, and Digital Signal Processing. Staffordshire, England: CSNDSP.

Condry, M., U. Gall, and P. Delisle. 1999. Open service gateway architecture overview. In Proceedings of the 25th Annual Conference of the Industrial Electronics Society (IECON '99), Vol. 2, pp. 735–742, December 1999.

Das, S., and D. Cook. 2004. Ongoing challenges and future directions. In *Smart Environments*, edited by A. Zomaya. New York: John Wiley & Sons.

Deri, L. 2001. Beyond the Web: Mobile WAP-based management. *Journal of Network and Systems Management* 9: 15–29.

Dobrev, P., et al. 2002. Device and service discovery in home networks with OSGi. *IEEE Communications Magazine* 40(8):86–92.

Dutcher, B. 2001. *The NAT handbook: Implementing and managing network address translation*. New York: Wiley Networking Council Series.

Eckel, C., G. Gaderer, and T. Sauter. 2003. Implementation requirements for Web-enabled appliances—a case study. In Proceedings of IEEE Conference on Emerging Technologies and Factory Automation (ETFA'03), 2:636–42.

Edwards, W. 1999. *Core Jini*. Upper Saddle River, NJ: Prentice Hall PTR.

Ellison, C. 2002. Home network security. *Intel Technology Journal* 6(4):37–48.

Egevang, K., C. Communications, P. Francis, and NTT. 1994. The IP Network Address Translator (NAT). RFC 1631.

Forstadius, J., and M. Loytynoja. 2001. XML in dynamic multimedia content management. In *Proceedings of 2001 Nordic Interactive Conference*, Copenhagen, Denmark. http://www.mediateam.oulu.fi/publications/pdf/80.pdf (accessed May 19, 2006).

Gatespace Networks Inc. 2006. http://www.gatespace.com/home/home.shtml (accessed May 19, 2006).

Ghazi-Moghadam, V. 2001. Performance results for SPW implementations of IEEE 802.11a and HIPERLAN/2 WLAN standards. In Proceedings of the 3rd IEEE Workshop on Wireless LANs.

Greenspan, R. 2003. Home is where the network is. Incisive Interactive Marketing LLC, http://www.clitz.com/stats/sectors/software/print.php/1301_3073431 (accessed May 19, 2006).

Gong, L. 2001. A software architecture for open service gateways. *IEEE Internet Computing* 5(1):64–70.

Haarsten, H., et al. 1998. Bluetooth: Vision, goals, and architecture. *Mobile and Computing Communications Review* 2(4):38–45.

The HAVi Consortium. 1999. HAVi, the A/V digital network revolution. http://www.havi.org/pdf/white.pdf (accessed May 19, 2006)

The HAVi Consortium. 1999. HAVi specification version 1.0. HAVi Specification Document.http://www.havi.org (accessed May 19, 2006).

HomePlug Alliance. n.d. www.homeplug.org (accessed May 19, 2006).

HomePNA. n.d. http://www.homepna.org (accessed May 19, 2006).

HomePNA. n.d. www.homepna.org/docs/paper500.pdf (accessed May 19, 2006).

HomePNA. 1999. Interface specification for homePNA 2.0. http://www.homepna.org (accessed May 19, 2006).

HomeRF. n.d. http://www.homerf.org (accessed May 19, 2006).

Hewlett Packard (HP). 1997. The JetSend protocol. Hewlett Packard white paper. http:///www.jetsend.hp.com/press/Whitepaper.html (accessed May 19, 2006).

IDC. 2004. Worldwide home networking 2004-2008 Forecast and Analysis. IDC1045162.

IDC. 2006. Technology profiles of small and medium-sized businesses with telecommuters. Doc # 201562.

IEEE 1394 Trade Association. n.d. http://www.1394ta.org/index.html (accessed May 19, 2006).

IEEE. 1997. Wireless LAN Medium Access Control (MAC) sublayer and physical layer specifications.

IEEE Standard 802.11a–1999. Part 11: Wireless LAN Medium Access Control (MAC) sublayer and physical layer specifications; High-speed physical layer in the 5 GHz band.

IEEE Standard 802.11b–1999. Part 11: Wireless LAN Medium Access Control (MAC) sublayer and physical layer specifications: Higher speed physical layer extension in the 2.4 GHz band.

IETF Zeroconf Working group. n.d. http://www.zeroconf.org/ (accessed September 24, 2006).

Kruys, J. 2000. The ETSI project broadband radio access networks. Nieuwegein, The Netherlands: Jan Kruys Technologies.

Lee, C., and S. Helal. 2002. Protocols for service discovery in dynamic and mobile network. *International Journal of Computer Research*11(1):1–12.

Lei, B., A. Ananda, and T. Teck. 2002. QoS-aware residential gateway. In Proceedings of the 27th Annual IEEE Conference on Local Computers Networks.

Lonestarbroadband. Powerline communications primer. 2006. http://www.lonestarbroadband.org/technology/powerlines.htm (accessed May 19, 2006).

Ma, I., and J. Irvine. 2002. Characteristics of WAP traffic. In Proceedings of European Wireless 2002, Florence, Italy. http://docenti.ing.unipi.it/ew2002/proceedings/168.pdf (accessed May 19, 2006).

Marples, D., and P. Kriens. 2001. The open services gateway initiative: An introductory overview. *IEEE Communications* 39(12):110–4.

Marples, D., and S. Moyer. 2004. Topics in consumer communications and networking. *IEEE Communications Magazine* 42(5):112–3.

Meadows, J. 2000. An introduction to the JetSend protocol. EmbeddedSystems. Internet Appliance Design http://www.embedded.com/2000/0001/0001ia2.htm (accessed September 5, 2006).

Microsoft Corporation. n.d. Description of Internet connection sharing in Windows XP. http://support.microsoft.com/kb/310563/ (accessed September 5, 2006).

Okamura, H. 2001. Adaptive resource management system for home-area networks. In Proceedings of 21st IEEE International Conference on Distributed Computing.

OSGi Forum. n.d. OSGi service-platform. Release 3. http://www.osgi.org/about/index.asp?section=1 (accessed September 24, 2006).

Prosyst. YEAR. http://www.prosyst.com/osgi.html (accessed May 19, 2006).

Rose, B. 2001. Home networks: A standards perspective. *IEEE Communications Magazine* 39(12):78–85.

Saha, S., M. Jamtgaard, and J. Villasenor. 2001. Bringing the wireless Internet to mobile devices. *IEEE Computer*34(6):54–8.

Saif, U., D. Gordon, and D. Greaves. 2001. Internet access to a home area network. *IEEE Internet Computing* 5(1):54–63.

Seik, K. 2004. Next generation home networking and relevant technologies. In Proceedings of Asia-Pacific Optical Communications Conference and Exhibition APOC'2004), SPIE Press, Beijing, China, November 2004.

Shaw, K. 2004. Home network predictions. Networkworld. http:/www.networkworld.com/net.worker/columnists/2004/1011shaw.html (accessed May 19, 2006).

Steinberg, D., and S. Cheshire. 2005. *Zero configuration networking: The definitive guide*. City, ST: O'Reilly Media.

Sun Microsystems. 2006a. Jini connection technology. http://wwws.sun.com/software/jini/ (accessed May 19, 2006).

Sun Microsystems. 2006b. Jini technology architectural overview. http://wwws.sun.com/software/jini/whitepapers/architecture.html (accessed May 19, 2006).

Sun Microsystems. 2006c. Jini specifications v1.2. http://wwws.sun.com/software/jini/specs/ (accessed May 19, 2006).

Tsai, P., C. Lei, and W. Wan. 2004. A remote control scheme for ubiquitous personal computing. *Proceedings of IEEE International Conference on Networking, Sensing and Control* 2:1020–5.

Tsymbalenko, Y., and E. Munson. 2001. Using HTML metadata to find relevant images on the World Wide Web. *Proceedings of Internet Computing*, pp. 842–8.

UPnP Device Architecture, Version 1.0. 2000a. http://www.upnp.org/download/UPnPDA10_20000613.htm (accessed May 19, 2006).

UPnP Forum. n.d. Understanding universal plug and play. http://www.upnp.org/download/UPNP_UnderstandingUPNP.doc (accessed May 19, 2006).

Universal Serial Bus. n.d. http://www.usb.org/home (accessed May 19, 2006). USB technical white papers can be found at: http://www.usb.org/developers/whitepapers.

Vanderdonckt, J., L. Bouillon, and N. Souchon. 2001. Flexible reverse engineering of Web pages with VAQUISTA. Proceedings of IEEE 8th Working Conference on Reverse Engineering, Stuttgart, October 2001, Los Alamitos, 2001.

Vantroys T., and J. Rouillard. 2002. Workflow and mobile devices in open distance learning. Proceedings of IEEE International Conference on Advanced Learning Technologies (ICALT 2002), Kazan, Russia, September 2002.

Vaxevanakis, K., T. Zahariadis, and N. Vogiatzis. 2003. A review on home wireless home network technologies. *Mobile Computing and Communications Review* 7(2):59–68.

Wang, Y., et al. 2000. A toolkit for building dependable and extensible home networking applications. Proceedings of 4th USENIX Windows Systems Symposium, August 2000.

Wils, A., F. Matthijs, Y. Berbers, T. Holvoet, and K. DeVlminck. 2002. Device discovery via residential gateways. *IEEE Transactions on Consumer Electronics* 48(3):478–83.

W3C recommendation. 2006. Extensible Markup Language (XML) 1.0 (2nd ed.). http://www.w3.org/TR/REC-xml/ (accessed May 19, 2006).

Zahariadis, T., and A. Salkintzis. 2003. Introduction to the special feature on wireless home networks. *Mobile Computing and Communications Review* 7(2):3–5.

Zhaohui, Y., J. Yindong, and S. Yang. 2004. Home automation network supporting Plug-and-Play. *IEEE Transactions on Consumer Electronics* 50(1):173–9.

Zhou, Y., et al. 2005. CPWCT: Making P2P home networking secure virtual multimedia service. IBM Research Report, RJ 10374 (C0505-002).

Multimedia Networking

Hans-Peter Dommel, *Santa Clara University*

INTRODUCTION

The field of multimedia networking is primarily concerned with the study of efficient audio and video transport through computer networks. Optimal digital transport of these media requires a thorough understanding of human perception and psychology at the end points of communication and the implied methods to effectively encode media into digital form. Encoding formats such as MP3 for music, or MPEG-4 and Quicktime (Apple 2007) for video are household words today, but the development of new standards to represent media content with the greatest fidelity, least amount of loss, and the most compact space requirements never ceases. Multimedia transport also requires an integral understanding of the complex interplay between network components, protocols, and performance factors. In particular, the Internet was originally not designed to store and forward continuous, time-sensitive, and bulky media. The diversity of devices and links in Internet transport infrastructure, from pocket-sized personal digital assistants to powerful multiprocessor machines communicating across phone, cable, or optical media in an amalgam of wired or wireless links, creates a complex spectrum of network interdependencies, across which multimedia transport has to be managed.

With its native best-effort service, the Internet does not inherently provide the end-to-end delay guarantees required for multimedia transport. Multimedia content is generally large in size, media storage and transmission costs are significant, and thus media generally must be compressed for effective storage and streaming. Newer devices blur the line between personal computing and home entertainment appliances. Similarly, next generation cell phones and "media pods" support television on-the-go and various modes of ad hoc multimedia information sharing. Along with these consumer market developments, network middleware for real-time transmission, media scaling, wireless media-supportive protocols, Quality-Of-Service (QoS), broadcasting or multicasting, and various forms of session support for small or large user groups are needed to augment the best-effort IP model and live up to the expectations associated with innovative networked media services. Recently, a complete redesign of the Internet to accommodate modern day communication requirements has been proposed (Clean Slate 2007).

This chapter discusses the principles of multimedia networking with focus on the network mechanics extending the Internet architecture to support the service requirements for multimedia through packet switching. Topics include human perception of multimedia content and their translation into network requirements for audio or video transport, packet-switching network service models for continuous and real-time media transmission, Quality-of-Service, streaming and synchronization protocols, multicast and content distribution, and the network middleware behind voice over IP and video over IP. Multimedia networking via asynchronous transfer mode (ATM, (see "ATM")) or other circuit-switched methods has lost much ground during the past decade to packet-switched solutions, mostly as a result of the fact that packet switching is simpler and less expensive to build upon and deploy. Details on circuit-switched multimedia delivery will hence be omitted. In addition, other topics such as authoring of documents, media servers and storage models, audio/video encoding and compression, error control in multimedia transport, wireless multimedia specifics, or security aspects in multimedia transport will

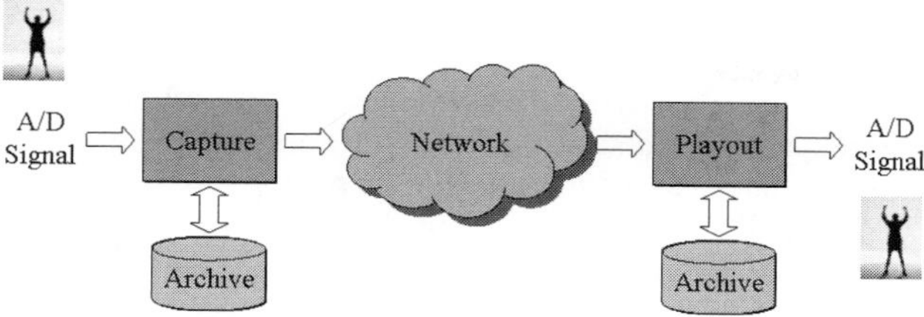

Figure 1: Basic multimedia networking architecture

not be discussed. The chapter concludes with an outlook on future developments.

MULTIMEDIA AND NETWORKING

"Multimedia" represents the integrated use of discrete (text, graphics, images, slides) and continuous (audio, video) forms of expression to convey digital information more fully than it would be possible through a single-medium representation alone. Multimedia networking is thus concerned with the control and transmission of integrated audiovisual content across communication channels, which today primarily means the Internet. "Medium" signifies the form through which the content is captured, processed, represented, and transported. Figure 1 shows a basic multimedia architecture with one or more capturing devices feeding analog input, either live or from server storage, in digital form into a network, which carries it to one or more receivers, where the content is played out at once or archived in media servers for later access.

Major efforts have been made during the past decades in Internet-based multimedia research to mimic and expand the use of conventional multimedia to enrich communication in fields such as medicine, sports, education and research, or entertainment. Telephony and television, movie recording and editing, music composition, e-learning, and the pervasive use of multimedia through mobile devices are examples for applications undergoing a fundamental facelift in the digital domain. The Internet's original purpose was to support data communication between computers. Today, the term "data" goes beyond early notions of discrete textual content, and encompasses multimedia in the widest sense. With increased computing power in network devices, greater bandwidth, and significant progress in network middleware (Duke and Herman 1998), the legacy Internet architecture is transforming into a federation of networks that natively encompass data, voice and video communications, reflecting the ITU-T definition of a next generation network (NGN) (ITU-T 2006). In contrast to classic data networking, multimedia networking incurs a much greater volume of data to be transferred. Network bandwidth, latency, media encoding, and device compatibility are a focal point in the development and deployment of networked multimedia applications.

Networking of multimedia can be supported in the network core with routers performing resource reservation and support for distinct media flows, in the transport layer with real-time supportive protocols, and at the network edge and in end-systems through overlay networks (Milic et al. 2005) and intelligent edge routers. Besides bandwidth, the most critical factor for multimedia networking is time, in contrast to legacy data networking which is foremost concerned with transmission errors. Bandwidth over-provisioning may not solve the need for timeliness guarantees. While packet loss can be compensated (Perkins et al. 1998; Feamster and Balakrishnan 2002), end-hosts cannot correct late packets. Furthermore, the processing and transport of multiple media demands much computing power, storage, and bandwidth. The sheer volume of data, synergy among all computation and communication components, and the integrated transport of traditional, discrete information and continuous media across the best-effort Internet have posed many research challenges. Multimedia networking hence relies on a variety of protocols and network topologies to provide users with media-rich content across networks and devices with varying capabilities.

Brief History of Multimedia Networking

The history of multimedia networking is intertwined with the history of real-time computing. However, where real-time computing is concerned with fault tolerance, scheduling and deadlines, multimedia networking adds bandwidth requirements and puts less weight on fault tolerance. The origins of this field can be traced back to the early developments in continuous media transmission, such as the AT & T Picturephone video conferencing systems (Lipartito 2003) in the late sixties, the network voice protocol (NVP) implemented in 1973 (RFC 741), early efforts on streaming with the ST-II protocol (RFC 1190), or the MIME extension format (RFC 1521) to attach multimedia content to e-mail. The ARPANET development of NVP laid the foundation for today's voice over IP (VoIP) technology: ". . . to demonstrate a digital high-quality, low-bandwidth, secure voice handling capability as part of the general military requirement for worldwide secure voice communication." (RFC 741) With the rapid improvement of personal computing and networking since the 1970s, information processing on computers has evolved from basic text-based representation to a rich mixture of media. The paradigm of standalone desktop computing has long been replaced by distributed computing and internetworking and traditional circuit-switched telecommunication is gradually displaced by packet-switching to transport images, voice and video across computer networks.

Traditionally, voice has been carried over telephone networks, video over cable networks, and data over computer networks. Early networking operated on a purely textual basis, but postal deregulation, private networking, the first digital PBXs and voice-mail innovations shifted networking into a voice-centric services model in the late 1970s and early 1980s. The first paper on speech compression for packet-switched transport was published in 1973 (Magill 1973) and in 1978, U.S. patent 4,100,377 was granted for "Packet Transmission of Speech." The late 1980s and early 1990s integrated data and voice communication with desktop computing, local area networking, public network data services, and commoditized voice technologies (Ziegler et al. 1989). In 1990, the ITU issued the G.764 recommendation for voice packetization and packetized voice protocols. Shortly thereafter the first IETF audio-cast over the multicast backbone (MBone) took place (Casner and Deering 1992). The MBone was built as an overlay network dedicated to IP multicast experiments. For greater scalability, IP multicast (see "IP Multicast") offers a solution to transmit a single stream across multicast-capable routers from one source to many receivers, where routers only replicate stream packets at junctures leading to downstream subscribers. In 1996, U.S. patent 5,526,353 was granted for a method to transmit packet audio over a computer network, offering a solution for temporal synchronization of data packets relative to their position in an audio stream. Although earlier experiments used special-purpose hardware and low-bit-rate encodings, new experimental interest for transmitting voice over packet networks arose after Sun Microsystems introduced the SPARCstation 1 with built-in μ-law audio codec.

The early 1990s also produced asynchronous transfer mode (ATM), a circuit-switching technology and connection-oriented network protocol encoding data into small fixed-sized (53 byte; 48 bytes of data and 5 bytes of header information) cells, developed in contrast to variable sized frames used in packet-switched networks. The most recent stage of multi-service network evolution brought innovation in integrated data, voice and video communication, more sophisticated Layer-3+ network services, virtual private networking and significant convergence of services in the industry. These developments mark a departure from traditional circuit-based communication to packet and cell-based infrastructures. Increasingly sophisticated convergence devices integrating telephone, TV, radio, and personal computing functions are constantly emerging in this marriage of multimedia, telecommunications, and computer networking technologies. With the World Wide Web as a platform for hyperlinked sharing of multimedia content, current research and development tackles PC-to-phone applications for scalable and low-cost voice communication, as well as video and TV applications through the Internet.

Despite these efforts to bring high-quality media distribution to user's fingertips, a common network-integrated multimedia infrastructure as shown in Figure 2, which allows seamless and scalable access to content across different platforms, whether mobile or desktop, small-scale or large, is still the focus of interdisciplinary research and development. Such complete integration of the multimedia PC with the smart home, house appliances, PDAs, laptops, digital photography, mobile music players, cell phones, recording devices, GPS, the home stereo and many other gizmos is the ultimate vision for a media-rich, network-augmented digital lifestyle.

Multimedia Characteristics

All media can be regarded as a special type of digital data. Transmission of graphics, music, photos, and video ultimately always results in a sequence of bits being carried across networks, however, the process and quality of multimedia networking is shaped by various factors:

- Perception: what senses are being used to perceive the media
- Representation: how are the media encoded
- Presentation: how are media recorded and formatted
- Storage: how and where are the media archived
- Transmission: what carrier type, distribution topology, and protocols are used for media transport

Media can be classified according to whether their representation is primarily a function of space or time, and whether they are created through recording or synthesis (Table 1.) Text or graphics are discrete media typically created on the computer, while photos are typically captured. For both media types, their spatial properties are critical for correct processing. Transmission of GIF and

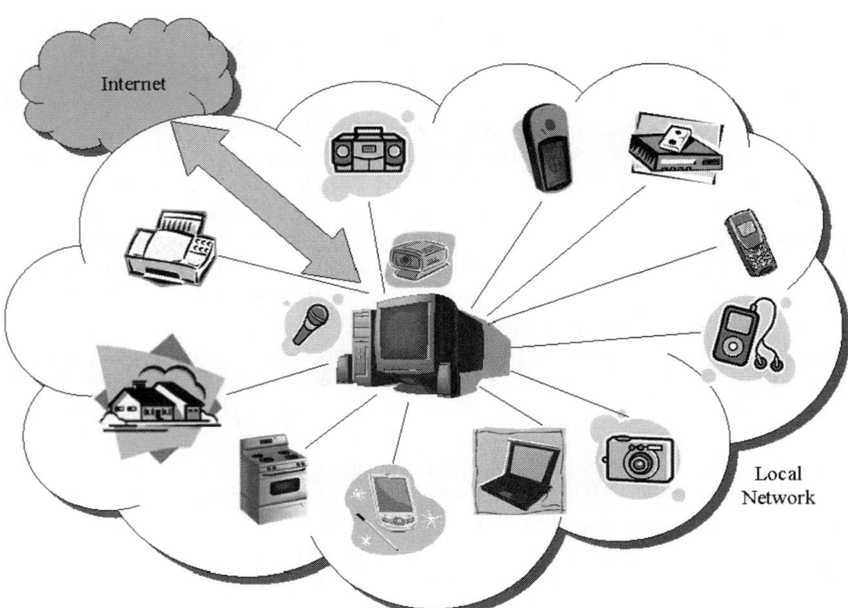

Figure 2: Integrated multimedia networking architecture

Table 1: Media Classification

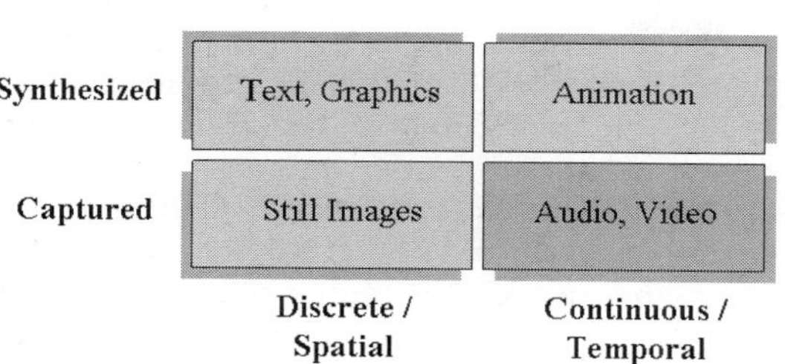

TIFF graphic files, or JPEG photos across networks is hence a matter of spatial representation and compression. As soon as the time of creation, mixing, or transmission becomes a critical factor in timely processing or reception, media can be categorized to be of temporal nature. This is the case for continuous media such as audio and video, which are captured and typically streamed, in contrast to animation, which is synthesized. Hybrids are possible, for example, when meta-data such as the creation date of a digital camera photo become important for network sharing, or when digital images are touched up with digital photography tools.

On the other hand, although numerous standards for continuous media encoding and compression (see "Image Compression," "Video Compression," and "Speech and Audio Compression") exist, such as MP3, Ogg, AAC, FLAC, or WMA for audio, or MPEG-1, MPEG-2, MPEG-4, DivX, or WMV for video, scalable and high-quality transmission of continuous media has been the core technical challenge in multimedia networking research since the inception of the field. The primary factor for multimedia transport beyond any encoding and compression technology, however, is simply network bandwidth. Bandwidth in the context of the Internet refers to the channel capacity or bit rate of a link (Crowcroft 2000). However, independent of technical capacities, the amount of bandwidth needed to transmit multimedia ultimately depends on processing and perception constraints, as well as quality expectations at the users' end. Table 2 contrasts data, pure voice, and mixed media traffic in terms of network characteristics. It shows that multimedia traffic has the highest complexity.

Human Perception and Multimedia Representation

Transmission constraints are dictated by the amount and quality of the media, and the perceptual constraints (Steinmetz 1996) of the human senses. Protocol design for real-time multimedia traffic should maximize the user-perceived quality in media transport while eliminating redundancy. Although the eyes respond to stronger signals or higher frequencies with cumulative reaction, the ears operate on a logarithmic scale. For audio, this means resolution in terms of sampling rate and quantization. The human ear, as a differentiating apparatus, perceives sound as a function of signal strength and frequency in the range of about 50 Hz to 20 kHz. Human speech and voice transport is limited to the 1 to 4 kHz range. Traditional copper wires were hence deployed for the purpose to carry baseband signals and "toll" speech quality audio with a bandwidth of 4 kHz. According to the Nyquist theorem, the sampling rate for voice is 8 kHz, and with 8 bits per sample, one voice conversation requires hence a minimum of 64 kbps. Two such conversations constitute the bandwidth of integrated services digital network (ISDN) connections.

The human eye on the other side is an integrating apparatus and sets video transmission constraints as a function of the resolution in pixels, bits per pixel, color space, and the frame rate. *Perceptual coding* exploits the strengths and flaws of the human auditory and visual system to filter out the relevant and mask the irrelevant. The resulting coding and compression schemes help to save bandwidth by filtering out information that contributes the least to the perceived quality of media by eliminating temporal redundancy and exploiting common patterns. For instance, knowledge of the threshold for audibility in the human ear for any frequency allows to mask weaker sounds in the shadow of stronger ones, or to omit sound from encoding if its falls below this audibility threshold. Once media are recorded and encoded observing perceptual qualities with a given frame rate, sampling frequency or quantization level or resolution, a certain minimum bandwidth is needed to carry the media across a network.

Table 2: Comparison of Traffic Types

	Data	Voice	Multimedia
Data Rate	Low	Low - Medium	High
Traffic Pattern	Bursty	Streamed	Streamed/Bursty
Loss Tolerance	None	Some	Some
Latency Constraints	None	Small (30ms)	Small
Connectivity	1-1	1-1	1-1, 1-n
Temporal	None	Synchronized	Synchronized
Service	Single Flow	Single Flow	Multiple Flows

The Role of the Multimedia Operating System

Integration of networked multimedia services with the operating system (OS) kernel is crucial for performance and interoperability. The multimedia OS (Steinmetz 1995) is quite similar to a real-time OS, because applications in both cases require predictable service and the ability to provide firm performance guarantees. However, the multimedia OS should operate from a *communication-oriented*, rather than computation-oriented perspective, offer *scalability* to facilitate among autonomous devices such as a networked camera, a set-top box controlling TV, and other home devices, and remain *extensible* to processor enhancements and future devices. In particular, the performance of the I/O subsystem is paramount for the massive amounts of data, as handled for example by multimedia servers (Gemmell et al. 1995). After various forerunners, such as the BeOS and NeXTstep, dominant operating systems of today such as Linux, Apple OS, and Windows come now with increasingly powerful, integrated multimedia capabilities.

Figure 3 shows the interplay between the various layers in a multimedia services stack, in correspondence to a network middleware model for multimedia applications. Networked devices interact with each other via the network layer, running media-centric applications to exchange content. This four layer model coarsely correlates with a TCP stack. The network middleware provides the glue between media and applications among two communicating devices, and includes codecs, component management, file management, media management, and an interface to network services such as sockets, enabling multimedia applications to interoperate.

Network Requirements for Multimedia Traffic

Network bandwidth is in constant need for growth as a result of the all-in-one convergence of data, voice, and video transport. The dimensions by which carrier systems are assessed in their capacity are rooted in the notion of how many voice flows can be routed through a data network. The stacked capacities of the T-carrier system in the United States and the European E-carrier system are based on the fact that one voice conversation through a digital medium requires a bandwidth of 64 kbps (Leon-Garcia 2001). In the T1 system, analog signals are sampled 8,000 times per second and each sample is digitized into 8-bit quanta. With 24 channels digitized in parallel, a 193-bit frame is hence transmitted, with one single bit as frame separator. The 192 bit frame multiplied by 8,000 and the additional 8,000 framing bits result in the T1's 1.544 Mbps data rate. The signaling bits are the least significant bits in each frame. An integrated T1 line can serve a different application on each channel. Higher capacity channels in the digital signaling hierarchy are multiples of T1 capacities. For instance, a T3 connection supports 672 conversation channels at a cumulative rate of 44.736 Mbps.

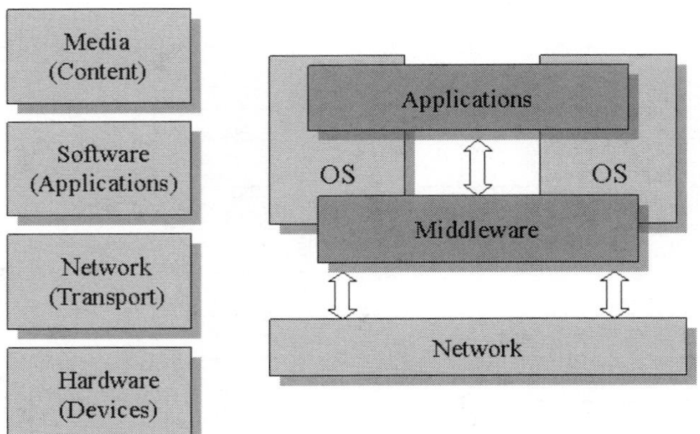

Figure 3: Multimedia stack and middleware abstraction

Table 3 compares the bandwidth requirements for common types of audio and video applications, from low-quality audio to tele-immersive applications. It shows that higher quality media distribution is currently only possible with powerful compression. The bit rate is a simple metric for required network bandwidth, but does not directly correlate with the actual quality of the transmitted media. For details on transmission requirements for other media types such as images and graphics, see Halsall (2000).

NETWORK SERVICES FOR MULTIMEDIA TRANSMISSION

Distribution of multimedia content entails media packetization for transport through datagram networks, multicast, content distribution networks, synchronization and scaling of media, Quality-of-Service, and the need for congestion control and fairness in transmitting multimedia alongside regular TCP connections.

Packetization

The raw digitized sound bit rate is not exactly the network bit rate, because packet headers add extra control bits to each packet. Packet headers for audio transport typically include the audio format, an identifier marking the conversation or flow that the packet belongs to, a timestamp and sequence number, and synchronization information. The realtime transport protocol (RTP) header typically adds 12 bytes to the packet, the UDP header adds 8 bytes for transport, and the IP header adds 20 bytes. For example, a raw G.711 stream of 64 Kbps effectively requires between 68 and 80 Kbps, but silence periods in speech can be used to compact the stream and decrease the nominal bit rate. Various ideas have been proposed to align application-layer semantics with IP packet processing for improved efficiency. The *application level framing (ALF)* principle (Clark and Tennenhouse 1990) states that networking mechanisms should be coordinated with application-level objectives, which is inherently difficult, since packet flows may incur inter-stream tradeoffs if they do not share a complete end-to-end path. ALF helps to coordinate the behavior of heterogeneous protocols distributed among various devices by incorporating knowledge to reflect the application-level semantics in

Table 3: Multimedia Transmission Characteristics

Media	Format	Uncompressed	Compressed
Telephone low	G.728 LD-CELP	16 Kbps	
Telephone standard	G.711 PCM	64 Kbps	
Telephone improved	G.722 SB-ADPCM	48–64 Kbps	
CD stereo	WAV	1410 Kbps	
CD surround (5.1)	MPEG-2, DTS		320 Kbps
DAT (Digital Audio Tape)	DAT	1636 Kbps	
Compressed music (MP3)	MP3, WMA, Ogg		128–384 Kbps
Internet radio	MP3, Real, etc.		<192 kbps
VCR-like TV	MPEG-1		1.2 Mbps
Broadcast-quality TV	MPEG-2		2–4 Mbps
Studio-quality TV	MPG-2, ITU-R 601	166 Mbps	3–8 Mbps
HDTV	MPEG-2, MPEG-4	Several Gbps	10–54 Mbps
Videoconference (H.xxx)	H.261, MPEG, Px64	64–1,536 Kbps	100 Kbps
Telepresence	Various	Several Gbps	100s of Mbps

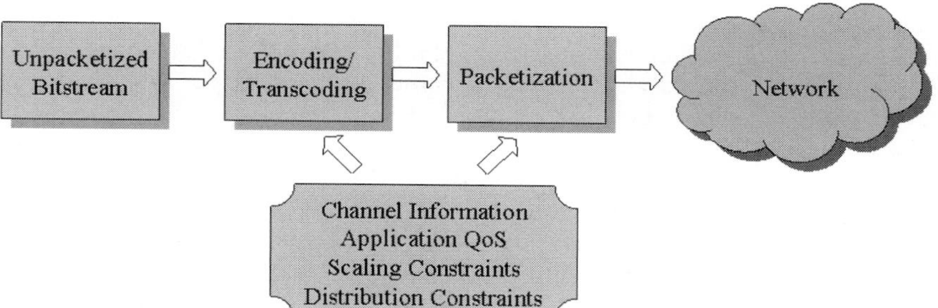

Figure 4: Media packetization process

the packetization process. Accordingly, IP packet boundaries align with video frame or audio sample boundaries rather than extending one video frame across two packets, which simplifies media-unit processing. Figure 4 depicts the simple steps in casting video and audio streams into packets, incorporation application-level information in the packetization process. The raw bitstream is encoded and packetized according to application, channel, and distribution constraints.

Media Distribution

Given the volume of multimedia content, it is paramount to use distribution methods that cause the least amount of traffic. Distributing content to clients is based either on unicast, network-native multicast, overlay multicast, also known as application-level multicast (Milic et al. 2005). With *unicast*, a separate copy of the media stream is sent from a server to each client. Broadcasting content to many receivers with repeat unicast hence causes massive data duplication. In contrast, *network multicast* sends only one copy of the media stream along the path between any two network routers, which multiplex the stream on all outgoing interfaces leading to stream subscribers. This paradigm uses network capacity more effectively, but is more complex to deploy, because routers at the network core must all be multicast-enabled and cooperate on stream forwarding. Multicast, as 1-*to*-k distribution, $k <= n$, where n is the entire receiver set, is the most general case of content distribution. With one receiver ($k = 1$) it becomes unicast, and with $k = n$ distribution it is equivalent to broadcast. *Anycast* is a special case, in which an especially qualified host from the set of k receivers is chosen, for example the fastest or least-loaded server, or the nearest cache. *Overlay multicast* is an edge-centric approach, where a network of servers instead routers perform stream forwarding, however, this paradigm incurs extra deployment cost, greater management overhead and application-level processing penalties. Although IP multicast as a rendition of network multicast lends itself to efficient and scalable distribution of live content to many receivers, current applications rather rely on repeat unicast of separate, identical streams due to multicast infrastructure deployment issues (Diot et al. 2000). Although IP multicast nowadays is available in routers of most networking vendors, it is often either deactivated or, across the mainstream Internet, blocked by firewalls. Universities and organizations running their own networks often use multicast for bandwidth-saving distribution of high-volume data and media and for research into more effective distribution methods. A significant portion of early research work on IP multicast and distributed multimedia applications was conducted in the multicast backbone (MBone) testbed (Kumar 1996; McCanne et al. 1997).

Accelerated media delivery to end users is the primary goal of *content delivery networks* (CDN) (Saroiu et al. 2002). The core idea is to bring content closer to the user by replicating it from an origin server into an overlay network of CDN nodes in multiple locations and over multiple backbones, and using application knowledge in *content routing* to match up media sources and clients. CDN nodes cooperate with each other transparently to shift content to locations with strong user demand and thus help to offload origin servers, reduce bandwidth costs, and give end users an optimized streaming or download experience. The choice of nodes is a function of latency, the number of hops, and the cost to serve content from a specific location. An interesting alternative to established content delivery mechanisms is BitTorrent (2006), an open-source, peer-based file distribution method and protocol often used for scalable media download, which fragments a file into smaller chunks of a few hundred KB to several MB. The BitTorrent protocol matches up peers requesting content, which download missing fragments from each other and reassemble them at reception into the entire file. BitTorrent achieves better throughput and robustness than monotlithic downloads in sharing large media files due to its highly distributed operation and sharing of smaller chunks of files.

Media Scaling

Audio and video transport requires computers to have sufficient processing power and bandwidth to support the required data rates, and low-latency interrupt paths in the OS kernel to prevent buffer under-run in clients. Content has hence to be adapted (Rejaie et al. 1999) according to receiver capabilities and the desired Quality of Service to scale media delivery to millions of heterogeneous receivers. Video can for example be scaled by reducing the number of bits per pixel, by reducing the display resolution, or by removing redundancy in image sequences. A cell phone user has different requirements and expectations for media delivery than a high-end desktop user. Through scaling of media, servers can hence adjust to different quality levels for media depending on fluctuating network conditions and end-host capabilities. Compression and layered encoding help servers to adapt streaming to the available bandwidth. The best quality level may be chosen with user input before streaming starts, or it may be negotiated before inception of delivery and automatically renegotiated and adjusted during delivery. Numerous solutions for media scaling have been proposed, such as layered coding or multiple description coding (Chakareski et al. 2003). *Layered coding* is based on the idea that a single sender transmits content in several layers of quality that progressively build on each other, where receivers join delivery channels according to their capabilities, receiving content asynchronously and at the quality they can handle. In *multiple description coding*, redundancy is added to data, which are broken into several streams. More bandwidth is consumed transmitting these redundant streams, but distorted streams can be reassembled under graceful degradation, which surpasses solutions based solely on compression.

Media Synchronization

Multimedia synchronization (Steinmetz 1991) is the ordering of messages in one-way or interactive media exchange by maintaining proper timing (or spatial) relationships in content presentation, from a single or multiple sources to a single or multiple destinations. Distributed applications using multimedia data depend on synchronization to assure temporal order of events at capture, transmission, mixing, and presentation, which may also affect their coordinated access to shared resources. Multipoint synchronization comprises both the definition and establishment of temporal relationships among distributed media such as video, voice, and graphics and fundamentally affects the Quality of Service, by which end-users perceive an application service. These relationships can exist within one media stream for intra-stream synchronization, or across several streams for inter-stream synchronization. Synchronization can target a single object in one stream needing to be synchronized with an object in another stream at one point in time, or handle stream synchronization continuously over a period of time. Timing information must be transmitted along with streams, either

- before the start of the presentation, which may cause a presentation delay,
- via a separate synchronization channel, where additional errors can occur, or
- by using multiplexed data streams, where cross-related synchronization information is delivered with media units, which is difficult to use for multiple sources.

The actual synchronization operation may be performed at the source, in routers along the path, or at the receiver, which consumes more bandwidth due to transmission of extra information. Intramedia synchronization handles the temporal relationship among the objects of one stream, whereas intermedia synchronization manages the temporal relationships between the objects of two or more parallel streams. Numerous models and solutions (Escobar et al. 1992) have been proposed for synchronization with or without external clocks, and in unicast and multicast contexts.

The synchronized multimedia integration language (SMIL, pronounced "smile") (W3C 2006) is an application-level tool to integrate timing and synchronization information into an XML-based language for composing interactive multimedia presentations. SMIL supports the description of temporal behavior in multimedia presentations in conjunction with layout and hyperlink association.

Quality-of-Service and Traffic Shaping

The concept of Quality-of-Service (QoS) for multimedia transport has a twofold purpose: to offer measurable quality criteria for multimedia traffic useful for fine-tuning network parameters and to give users tangible criteria for system evaluation, based on the fact that not all applications need or can claim the same performance in the networks they traverse. Thus, applications may specify certain requirements to the network to optimize the transmission and user experience. Meeting the QoS requirements of multimedia traffic is challenging in the current best-effort Internet. Network performance (Fitzek and Reisslein 2001) may be acceptable when demand does not exceed capacity but deteriorates rapidly otherwise. Numerous strategies have been suggested in the literature to add QoS on top of best-effort IP. Overprovisioning in networks for voice, video, and data traffic is a costly solution, because there is always a need for higher quality and scalability. The relevant service quality criteria are typically network performance parameters such as

- Throughput (bit rate)
- End-to-end delay
- Delay variation (jitter)
- Error rate

Throughput in applications such as streaming requires constant bit rate (CBR) transmission; however, not all networks are capable of carrying CBR traffic without noticeable loss, corruption, or delay. A private branch exchange (PBX) telephone conversation generates for example a constant bit rate equal to 64 kbps. In contrast, variable bit rate (VBR) applications are inherently bursty. *Delay* (Goyal et al. 1997) consists of the processing delay in a node, the transmission delay to place packets on the channel, the propagation delay across the channel, and the cumulative queuing delay in routers. Although the transport delay cannot be avoided due to the laws of physics, it can be shortened through caching, mirroring, and content routing. *Jitter* (Stone and Jaffey 1995), or delay variation, causes speech to quiver and video to become unsteady (Claypool and Tanner 1999), and occurs when networks cannot guarantee uniform delay for separate streams to each user as a result of traffic conditions and network imperfections. The essential method to avoid jitter is to buffer sufficiently so that delay variations can be equalized before surfacing in playout. The *error rate* represents three different types of errors: the bit error rate (BER) measuring the frequency of erroneous bits, the packet error rate (PER) measuring the frequency of lost, out-of-order, duplicated, or corrupt packets, and the packet loss rate (PLR), which specifically looks at the lost packets. Subjective measurements such as the mean opinion score (MOS) for voice quality evaluation may also be taken into account. QoS entails

- Admission control, testing if a requested QoS be met while honoring earlier QoS commitments to already accepted calls
- Traffic shaping/policing, making sure that a connection obeys its specified traffic once admitted
- Path selection via routing to satisfy a requested QoS
- Flow setup, communicating call requirements to intermediate routers to reserve necessary resources (buffers, bandwidth)
- Packet scheduling, managing the packets in the router queue to receive the requested service

QoS controls can be established from the network edge, or through the network core. The resource reservation protocol (RSVP) (Zhang et al. 1993) was a distinct approach for adding QoS to best-effort IP. "Network QoS" and "End-System QoS" discuss Quality-of-Service in more detail. Several principles to warrant service guarantees have been suggested (Kurose 2007), such as

- Packet marking to let routers distinguish between different service classes
- Policing and scheduling mechanisms to isolate one traffic class from another class and ensure efficient allocation for flows, for example, with weighted fair queuing, which sequences packets and allocates bandwidth to packet flows through various queues and weights determined by application needs and link capabilities
- Admission control to block unfitting flows

Media-Aware Congestion Control and Rate Control

The evolution to media-rich computing would not have been possible without major efforts in protocol standardization and cooperative deployment of services. Yet, although the market forces and customer interests are shifting towards media-integrated computing and networking, the existing infrastructure of the Internet was designed for non-continuous, bursty, and discrete data transfers under elastic time constraints. Despite concerted efforts in deploying helper protocols to leverage media-rich computing and networking, multimedia networking is still coming of age. This shows in particular when flash crowds and peak hours in Internet usage put heavy performance strains on a global network, where discrete data and continuous media transmissions must coexist in a fair manner. Although new technologies and trends in collaboration and communication leverage our collective abilities to work together, their bandwidth-intensive use poses a threat to the stability of the Internet, as they generally use non-congestion controlled transport protocols to satisfy timely delivery constraints. Some of the key components in network scalability are congestion avoidance and rate control for voice and video (Bolot and Vega Garcia 1996; Bolot and Turletti 1998), which in many variations of TCP implementations walk a fine line between network reliability and performance (Rhee and Xu 2005).

Currently implemented congestion control is oblivious of the semantics of packets carried, and does not cater to the specific transport characteristics of multimedia. Improving congestion control for multicast applications is still research matter, and networked multimedia systems are prone to unpredictable performance and low-grade quality both in delay and presentation as a result of a lack of sufficient capacity provisioning, and the fact that the underlying networking protocols have been designed primarily for a media-impoverished computing environment. Both unicast and multicast congestion control build on the notion of TCP fairness and friendliness to permit continuous and non-continuous media to coexist with reasonable allocation of bandwidth in the face of Quality-of-Service demands. Media-aware congestion control provides the backend support for interactive media flows, complementing TCP-friendly rate adaptation mechanisms in their support of one-directional streaming applications. In addition, continuous-media protocols should not use more than their "fair share" of network bandwidth. A flow is TCP-fair if its average rate matches what the average TCP rate would be on the same path, and TCP-friendly if its average rate is less than or equal to the TCP-fair rate. This results in the same transmission rate as TCP along the same data path, but with less rate variance, and hence, less oscillation, catering to the continuous playout requirement of media streams. Media awareness has the objective to make media-heavy applications operating under non-ideal network behavior more robust and effective.

NETWORK MIDDLEWARE AND PROTOCOLS

Multimedia Protocol Stack

The various protocols augmenting the Internet protocol stack to transport multimedia (Braun 1997) are shown in Figure 5. This suite of multimedia protocols adds middleware functionality to the Internet protocol stack to extend its best-effort service to time-aware, continuous media transport using the real-time transport protocol (RTP) and its helper protocols, RTSP and RTCP. Top-level protocols, for example HTTP or peer-to-peer protocols such as BitTorrent, feed their parameters into helper protocols mediating between applications and the transport layer. These protocols perform media transport with QoS (Aurrecoechea et al. 1998), using either TCP or UDP as transport service. At the bottom of the multimedia stack are link layer and physical services such as SONET, ATM, or Ethernet in local networks. The ATM adaptation layer (AAL) protocol or the point-to-point protocol provide the glue between network and physical layer services (Leon-Garcia 2001.)

Signaling and Session Control Protocols

The ITU-T H.323 standard is an umbrella recommendation for audio-visual communication services over packet networks, and is often used for voice over IP (VoIP) applications, IP telephony, and video conferencing. At the heart of the H.323 architecture is a gateway connecting the telephone network to the Internet, and a gatekeeper controlling the end points in its zone. H.323 adopted RTP as the first VoIP protocol for audio and video transport. Several protocols belong to the H.323 standard:

- The G.7xx protocol suite for speech encoding and decoding
- The real-time transport control protocol (RTCP) to control RTP channels
- The H.225 (RAS) registration/admission status protocol to manage the PC-gatekeeper channel
- The ITU Q.931 signaling protocol to establish and release connections, and to provide traditional phone functions such as the dial-tone
- The H.245 call control protocol for negotiating compression and bit rate of the link, and
- The RTP protocol for the actual data transport

During a H.323 session, five channels are accordingly open between caller and callee, dedicated to signaling, call control, upstream and downstream data channels, and a data control channel.

In response to the telco-steered H.323 standard, which was perceived as complex and inflexible, the Internet Engineering Task Force set off to create a simpler, lightweight and modular mechanism for VoIP. The Session Intiation Protocol (SIP) (RFC 2543, 3261) has been developed by the IETF MMUSIC working group to manage interactive sessions using multimedia, as with instant messaging, online gaming and, in particular, Internet phone applications. SIP is a text-based protocol modeled after HTTP, and clients use TCP and UDP port 5060 to connect to SIP servers to set up and tear down voice or video calls. The actual voice or video communication is handled over RTP. SIP components include the UAC (user agent client), the

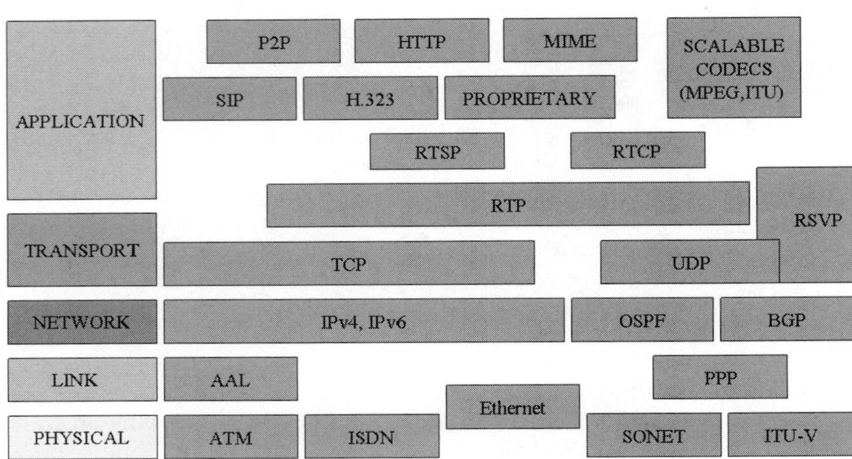

Figure 5: Internet multimedia protocol stack

UAS (user agent server), a SIP terminal, a proxy, a redirect server, and a location server. A connection is established, when a caller sends via TCP an INVITE message to the callee located with the help of a location server. The callee responds with a HTTP-type reply code to accept or deny the invitation. SIP is largely compatible with PSTN and modular, opposite to the monolithic protocol stack prescribed by H.323. SIP uses URLs for addressing, whereas H.323 uses host or telephone numbers.

SIP is only involved in the signaling portion of a communication session and acts as a carrier for the Session Description Protocol (SDP), which describes the media content of the session, such as the IP ports or codec being used. SDP (RFC 2327) provides short structured textual description of the name, port, and purpose of a session, the pertinent media, protocols, codec formats, timing and transport information required to decide whether a session is likely to be of interest and to know how to start media tools to participate in the session. SDP provides merely a format for session description and does not depend on a specific transport protocol.

The RTCP (Real-time Control Protocol), as a companion watchdog protocol for RTP, provides feedback on the reception quality of the distribution and helps to fine-tune RTP QoS. It delivers reports on receiver reception, sender performance and a source description to modify sender transmission rates and for diagnostics purposes. RTCP is a soft-state, announce-listen protocol, whose report frequency is adjusted to minimize network impact by limiting its traffic to 5 percent of a session bandwidth. The Real-Time Streaming Protocol (RTSP, RFC 2326) is an open-source application-layer protocol that allows the user to control a media bit stream in VCR-style remote control directly through a media player. The main protocol vocabulary of RTSP consists of directives to describe stream parameters, set up a logical control channel between a player and server, play, record, and pause streams, and tear down the connection at completion or user interrupt. Playback control, the choice between different quality levels, authentication and clip information are all conveyed via RTSP, which has been used for Quicktime, Realplayer, and Windows Media Player. RTSP may use RTP as underlying transport protocol for the actual transfer of audio and video information, or a proprietary transport mechanism such as the RealNetworks' RDT protocol (RealNetworks 2007). Besides RTSP, other streaming protocols such as Microsoft's Media Server Protocol (MMS) and RealNetworks' progressive networks audio (PNA) protocol have been proposed (Kuenkel 2003). Popular media players relieve the user from choosing a transport protocol and automatically attempt transmission first via RTSP/MMS and UDP, then RTSP/MMS and TCP, and, if streaming protocols are blocked, via HTTP as a last resort.

Quality-of-Service Protocols

Among the control protocols used to ensure QoS (Shenker 1995; Campbell et al. 1996) in media transmission, the RSVP (Resource Reservation Protocol) was designed for an integrated services (IntServ) approach (Clark et al. 1992) to request a specific QoS from the network on behalf of an application data stream. RSVP is receiver-initiated, handles unicast and multicast flows, and is decoupled from routing. As the routing changes, RSVP adapts its reservation to the new paths wherever reservations are in place. RSVP runs over IPv4 and IPv6 and provides opaque transport of traffic control and policy control messages. An RSVP request is carried from an end-host through the network, visiting each node that the network uses to carry the stream. At each node, RSVP attempts to make a resource reservation for the stream with RSVP daemon communicating with two local decision modules, admission control, and policy control. RSVP requires routers to carry a lot of state and is difficult to manage as a result of the potentially large number of flows.

The alternative differentiated services (DiffServ) approach (RFC 2638) provides simple functions in the network core and more complex functions at edge routers hosts, and does not define service classes, but rather enables router to distinguish traffic classes and queued packets accordingly through packet markers. As another alternative, Multi-Protocol Label Switching (MPLS) (RFC 3031) has been proposed to integrate QoS provision into routing. MPLS emulates properties of a circuit-switched network over a packet-switched network. MPLS labeled packets are switched according to a label lookup reflecting QoS choices instead of a routing table lookup, which can be done directly in the router fabric and not the CPU.

Media Transport Protocols

Real-time flows on the Internet are largely handled by the Real-time Transport Protocol (RTP) (Schulzrinne and Rosenberg 1999; RFC 1889). Other transport protocols such as XTP or the Tenet (Banerjea et al. 1996) protocol suite have been proposed before the introduction of RTP, which is a middleware protocol on top of end-to-end protocols such as UDP, TCP, or ST-II. It provides a standard packet header with media-specific timestamp information, payload specifics, and sequence numbers to transport packet flows for continuous media, carrying information for playout synchronization, demultiplexing of multimedia flows, quality-of-service monitoring, and media identification that other transport services would not specifically carry. Commonly, RTP flows are connectionless and packets are carried by UDP, which does not warrant against packet loss or corruption. Although RTP carries timing information, maintaining real-time constraints is not guaranteed with using RTP. Successful RTP media flows depend on sufficient capacity in the underlying traffic class, whose provision is a separate concern. The RTP header is 8 octets long and contains fields for the protocol version, a flow identifier, an options bit, a synchronization bit, a content type index, a packet sequence number, and a timestamp. More information on RTP is provided in "Multimedia Streaming".

IP MEDIA

Voice and Video over IP are sometimes subsumed under IP media, which includes all on-demand, streaming and subscriber-based content available over broadband Internet.

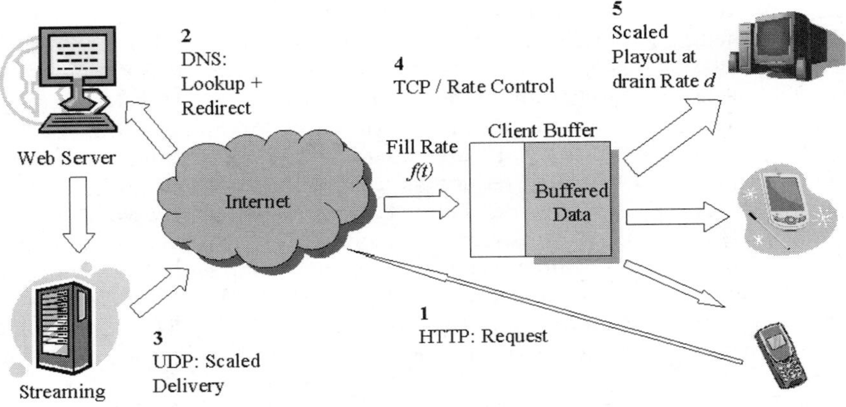

Figure 6: Streaming with media scaling

Streaming Protocols and Platforms

Before computer networks and end-hosts had the necessary capacity, multimedia were primarily distributed via non-streamed media such as CD-ROMs. Although traditional media delivery such as radio or television is inherently based on streamed delivery of content, the term streaming is now typically used for a distribution mechanism across computer networks, where media packets are being consumed during continuous delivery. Streaming (Wu et al. 2001) bypasses the need to download the entire file before playback and caters to limited storage and bandwidth capabilities of devices.

A typical streaming setup involves an audio or video source, a server or stream reflector, and a client where the stream is being played back. Figure 6 shows a setup with a cell phone, PDA, or desktop computer as clients, running a media player with a playout buffer; a Web server; and/or a streaming server. The content must be delivered in a coding format that the server has available and the client can understand. The media player manages the user interface, decompresses the incoming audio, handles transmission errors, and eliminates jitter through buffering.

First, one of these devices establishes a TCP connection and HTTP request from a browser or media player (both may be integrated) to a Web server orchestrating access to a media collection. The server might retrieve the media file locally or, through the domain name system, resolve to a streaming server, which retrieves a window of the requested media stream at a certain size or quality from its disk and responds to the client. Once the client knows the address of the streaming server, it will talk to the server directly. The streaming server may detect the capabilities of the client via protocol header information or by first testing the connection to the client, and scale its media stream accordingly to avoid that the client waits too long or receives a stream beyond its output capabilities. The stream data may also be cached along the path so that future requests can be satisfied more quickly. The media player in the client will start playout of the stream from the playout buffer once a sufficient amount of data is held in it. The client buffer is filled at rate $f(t)$ and emptied at rate d. Ideally, $f(t) = d$, that is, the server will fill the buffer at exactly the same rate it is being drained by the player. If the drain rate exceeds the fill rate, the buffer may underrun. If the media stream fills the buffer the buffer faster than the drain rate and beyond capacity, packets may get lost due to buffer overrun. In either case, a *gap problem* occurs, where video stops at the last available frame, or the audio stream stops in mid-play. By setting an upper and lower threshold, the server and client can communicate about throttling of the stream to calibrate toward the optimal speed.

Widespread deployment of media streaming hence raises scaling, Quality-of-Service, and service testing issues. For efficiency reasons, streaming is typically implemented on top of UDP, using RTP and companion protocols. It is possible to use HTTP for streaming with the benefit that HTTP flows easily pass through firewalls, however, as an application layer protocol designed for fast retrieval of static web objects it does not offer direct control of the bit stream. Furthermore, HTTP runs on top of TCP, which guarantees bit-wise correct delivery, however, timeouts and retransmissions for reliability make streaming via TCP more complex and slow. UDP on the other hand sends the media stream as a series of datagrams, but packets can be lost or corrupted in transit. Depending on the extent of the loss, the client may be able to recover the data with error correction techniques, may interpolate over the missing data, or may suffer a dropout. Firewalls are more likely to block UDP-based protocols.

Single stream servers are sooner or later overloaded and their operation is constrained by the available bandwidth, system availability and resources (storage, memory, CPU), and limitations in system software. Media streams may stall while the protocol handler detect data loss and retransmits the missing data, which necessitates more look-ahead buffering in clients defeating the intention of streamed content. In order to offload a single source server, media are often distributed in a server farm, or via splitters to other servers. Load balancing between servers is needed to assign encoding, splitting and serving to servers according to load and link usage, with the goal to maximize availability and response time. Splitting has two variants; in *pull splitting* an origin server contacts a splitter only for content replication when a client request the content from the splitter, which saves bandwidth for small audiences. In *push splitting*, a server by default forwards a freshly encoded stream to connected splitters for distribution.

Commercial Internet audio streaming was first introduced by RealNetworks in 1995 and expanded in 1997 to include video streaming with proprietary codecs, using the RTP and RTSP protocols. Today, numerous open-source and proprietary streaming solutions, including RealPlayer (RealNetworks 2007), iTunes with Quicktime (Apple 2007), and the Windows Media Player (Microsoft 2007) offer alternatives for end users to playback content from dedicated media servers or Web servers in various formats. Empirical studies with RealAudio traffic (Mena and Heidemann 2000) have shown that audio traffic is different from regular FTP, HTTP, or Telnet traffic. Audio sessions have longer duration, while user arrivals correlate with the time of day similar to regular web traffic. In addition, UDP audio flows, which can be identified by packet length and packet inter-departure time, are mostly unidirectional from the server. Similar studies have been conducted for RealVideo traffic (Wang et al. 2001).

Innovative streaming models are based on a peer-to-peer (P2P) architecture (Deshpande et al. 2001; Freecast et al. 2006), which links clients directly up for one-on-one media exchange. P2P streaming offloads dedicated media servers and the network, but raises other technical, business, and legal issues. Availability of streaming peers cannot always be guaranteed, users cannot be prevented from recording streamed content, and content distributors may use proprietary formats and encryption or rely on copyrights, patents, and license agreements to make local archival more difficult. It remains to be seen whether P2P video transport such as Joost (2007) will make its mark as Skype (Baset and Schulzrinne 2004) did for VoIP. "Multimedia Streaming" contains further details on video streaming.

Voice over IP

Voice over IP (VoIP) digitizes and packetizes voice (Bolot and Vega Garcia 1996) into discrete units sent across the Internet, rather than using legacy circuit-based mechanisms of the public switched telephone network (PSTN). Recent advances in such Internet telephony threaten to erode the market for legacy telecommunication services. A voice agent at the edge of the network converts information from a regular telephone into packets for Internet transmission, which may be subject to various levels of degradation at playout (Watson and Sasse 2000). The main issues in VoIP revolve around voice coding, signaling between parties, addressing between a PBX and IP host, port configuration, and error recovery (Boutremans et al. 2002). The latter is typically handled with retransmission, when possible, adding redundancy, interleaving of audio packets can be used to make streaming more robust against burst errors, so that a media layer can interpolate between missing samples, or with forward error correction. Advances in VoIP are steered by the VoIP Forum, a coalition of major networking vendors to promote the use of ITU-T H.323 as the standard for sending voice and video over IP across the public Internet and within intranets. VoIP protocols generally use RTP to ensure timely delivery of packets on top of best-effort Internet services. Directory services, emergency calling, and the use of touch-tone signals for automatic call distribution and voice mail are component services within VoIP. Typically, an organization places a VoIP box at a gateway, which receives packetized voice transmissions from users and routes them to other parts of an intranet or, using a T-carrier system or E-carrier interface, sends them over the public switched telephone network. Various open and proprietary solutions to improve call quality have been part of the VoIP evolution, for example the technique to ping all possible network gateway computers with access to the public network and choosing the fastest path before establishing a socket connection between end points. VoIP implementations use open standards such as SIP or H.323, or proprietary protocols (Baset and Schulzrinne 2004). VoIP is often synonymous with Internet telephony (Schulzrinne and Rosenberg 1999). For more information on Voice-over-IP and packet-based audio, see "Voice over IP (VoIP)".

Video over IP

Packet video (Bolot and Turletti 1998) finds its main incarnation in Internet TV, Web TV, and Webcasts, using Internet broadband connections or Web portals for digital broadcast. Typically Internet TV is based on Web-centric streaming of content. With improvements in broadband, the rising Internet user base, and decrease in connection cost, it is expected that video over IP will be a dominating market and new revenue opportunity for telecommunications providers, promising lower costs for operators and lower prices for consumers.

APPLICATIONS OF MULTIMEDIA NETWORKING

Applications for networked multimedia are manifold—examples are video-on-demand and multimedia-aided home shopping for residential services, video conferencing, and corporate training in business, distance education and use of digital libraries in education, distributed computation and collaborative data mining in the sciences, or distributed diagnosis and treatment in medicine. Networked multimedia applications, opposite to data-centric applications, stand out due to their delay sensitivity and loss tolerance. A media stream that arrives a few hundred milliseconds later at the receiver than an audio stream becomes useless, but a few lost packets in a stream will not harm the playout of a video stream significantly and can often be concealed.

Classes of Multimedia Applications

Multimedia applications can be differentiated according to the nature of the media (on demand, live, or interactive) (Kurose 2004), the type of devices (fixed or mobile), and the location and time of source and receiver (same or different time, same or different place.) On demand streams are stored on a server for a longer period of time, and are available to be transmitted at a user's request.

Table 4: Networked Multimedia Application Types

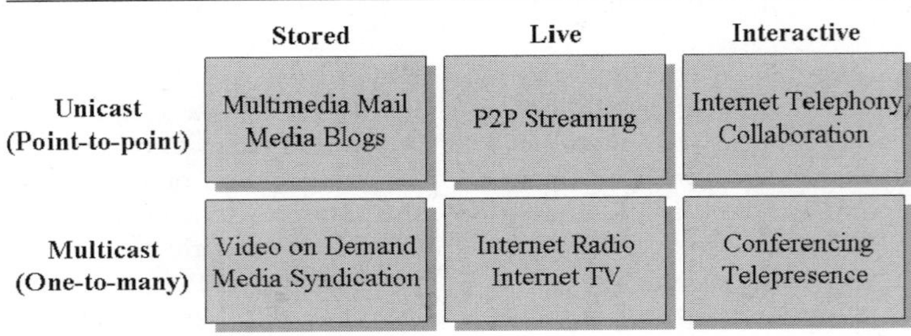

	Stored	Live	Interactive
Unicast (Point-to-point)	Multimedia Mail Media Blogs	P2P Streaming	Internet Telephony Collaboration
Multicast (One-to-many)	Video on Demand Media Syndication	Internet Radio Internet TV	Conferencing Telepresence

Live streams are only available at one particular time, as in a video stream of a live sporting event.

Table 4 categorizes various applications according to their distribution mode and freshness. One-to-many delivery may use network or end-system multicast. In particular,

- *Media on demand* delivers *stored* audio or video to end users, for example through video on demand
- *Live media* streaming brings real-time content to users, for example with Internet radio
- *Interactive media* deliver real-time audio or video, for example in IP telephony or video conferencing

The simplest type involves attachment of multimedia objects to regular data traffic such as MIME e-mail or weblogs. Video on demand or content syndication such as RSS may take advantage of multipoint delivery. Peer-based streaming applications are typically also point-to-point, and live. Live streaming applications such Internet radio broadcast or TV may benefit from multicast distribution. Interactive unicast or multicast cases are represented by Internet phone or collaboration applications, video conferencing and tele-immersive, virtual-reality systems. Notably, media encoding and transport may be quite different depending on whether the senders and receivers are stationary or mobile.

Media on Demand

Streaming of stored audio and video entails on-demand transmission of content from media servers, where users can pause, stop, forward, and rewind the presentation using a control protocol such as RTSP as with a traditional VCR or DVD player, albeit with a greater delay due to network latency. Content playout should adhere to the timing properties of the original recording and requires that the media server delivers each media unit in time for proper playout at the client. However, as long as packets are in the buffer when needed, it does not matter when they arrive or how substantial jitter is. End-to-end delay constraints are less stringent compared to live-casts or interactive applications such as teleconferencing. Video on demand (VoD) of archived material represents this class. In Internet-based VoD, users can watch selective video content accessible from a Web site or application as part of an interactive television system. VoD systems may stream or download content, the latter storing a program in its entirety into to a set-top box or the PC hard disk before viewing starts. A solution for greater scalability is Near Video On Demand (NVoD), where replicas of the same program are transmitted in regular time intervals, for example every 20 minutes, to aggregate streams and save bandwidth over individual on-demand broadcasts, while giving consumers some time flexibility to tune into a specific program. YouTube (2007) and similar video sharing services enable users to broadcast video materials on-the-fly and mark the transition into a new age of instant sharing of personal and dynamic multimedia content.

Live Media

Streaming of live audio and video resembles traditional broadcast, in which content is fed live into the Internet and distributed via reflector servers to various receivers around the globe. Opposite to media on demand delivery, which is typically point-to-point, live streaming targets large audiences. Live streams require also continuous playout where users can tolerate delays in tens of seconds. The live nature of content prohibits immediate stream control, although it is possible to couple such content playout with a digital video recorder (DVR) to allow later viewing and VCR-like manipulation.

Since its inception in 1995 with Internet Talk Radio on the MBone, streaming radio transmits live or stored content from a traditional radio station or an Internet radio station. Opposite to terrestrial radio, content can hence be created and accessed through the Internet anywhere, similar to the spirit of satellite radio. Instead of tuning into a traditional radio station, a Web search is used to find stations and streams of interest. Content is captured through an audio plugin, encoded in a media player, pushed on the Internet and stored or forwarded through a media server, which distributes it to a large number of TCP connections. Internet radio seems predestined for multicast, but TCP unicast is often used for radio flows, because RTP is blocked, whereas TCP is allowed through firewalls, and multicast is generally not available through ISPs. There is a trade-off between audience size and audio quality. Bandwidth is used more economically when more users with low grade connections can listen to stations transmitting at lower quality. At near CD quality, one T1 line can only handle under ten streams at 192 kbps. Hence streaming radio is often blocked in corporate settings to avoid bandwidth depletion. Podcasting is an asynchronous spin-off from Internet radio, where audio and video content similar to radio and TV content is published in various ways, including RSS feeds and peer-to-peer platforms. In contrast to Internet radio, pod casting is more a collaboration and sharing platform and allows media viewing independent of broadcast time.

Internet television is sometimes shortened to IPTV and may show exclusive content only found on the Internet, or content simulcast online and via traditional TV. It offers an alternative to legacy distribution via cable, terrestrial and satellite broadcast and is often coupled with video on demand. In contrast to traditional broadcast, IPTV allows for two-way, interactive transmissions and selective point-to-point transmission. Innovations such as the SlingBox (Sling Media 2007) allow forwarding home-subscribed TV to laptops on the road and bridge both worlds; PVRs complement these services and allow selective, simultaneous recording of multiple programs on home computers or specialized applicances; and existing pay-TV channels can be transmitted over the Internet to regular TV sets. As of January 2007, several thousand IPTV channels are available either free or fee-based. Online channels require only a broadband connection and a video-capable device, such as a set-top-box, PC, or HDTV, or a handheld such as an iPod or 3G cell phone for mobile TV. Video content comes in various formats such as MPEG-2 transport streams, DivX, MPEG-4, or H.264. IPTV has previously been implemented using the Internet group management protocol (IGMP) version 2 for live TV and RTSP for video on demand. The major bottlenecks for scalable, high-quality video distribution have been open and free encoding methods, streaming protocols, and available bandwidth to households. Similar to the peer-to-peer method used in Skype for Internet telephony, movie downloads via the Internet and Internet television (Joost 2007) are now available to the greater Internet community. Such highly scalable "disruptive" (Oram 2001) applications promise to revolutionize the way our global society is producing, sharing, and consuming digital media. In the long run these innovations will fundamentally change the media broadcast infrastructure. See "Peer-to-Peer Network Architecture" and "Peer-to-Peer Network Applications" for details on peer-to-peer systems.

Interactive Media and the World Wide Web

Interactive real-time audio and video (Noureddine and Tobagi 2002) imposes the most stringent delay constraints in the order of a few hundred milliseconds, because users interact with each other directly. In contrast to legacy circuit-switched interaction, call directories, larger-scale group communication, and integration with calendar and Web applications enhance the spectrum of available services through the Internet. This class of services is mostly represented by Internet phone applications, instant messaging tools, and conferencing applications (Turletti and Huitema 1996). Voice delay should be less than 150 ms to be unnoticeable to the listener, and must be less than 400 ms to yield acceptable conversation quality.

Pervasive audio and video, through wireless networks and nomadic devices, is destined to become a cornerstone in emerging communication services, and requires novel integrative approaches of signal processing and networking technology. Generally, these services are hidden from the user and concern low-bit rate, scalable, and multiple description encoding methods, error concealment and resilience measures, transcoding for interoperability across heterogeneous channels and platforms, quality measurements for mobile media distribution, as well as novel ways for user subscription and participation.

Currently the predominant interactive application is Internet telephony, where both server-based and peer-to-peer solutions compete for users. Video conferencing (see "Video Conferencing") and chat tools sometimes complement an Internet phone application, augmenting the instant exchange experience with text and personal presence. Voice-over-broadband companies such as Vonage (2006) require that customers acquire a phone adapter to enable their broadband router or modem to use the proprietary VoIP service. Speech packets to and from the Internet are processed by the phone adapter or integrated "VoIP router" and enable users to connect to regular telephones. An upload speed of 30-90 Kbps and a QoS optimized connection are necessary to make calls without substantial lag or jitter.

As an alternative to client-server solutions, peer-to-peer approaches may offer better scalability and robustness (Singh and Schulzrinne 2004). The Skype application and protocol uses a proprietary peer-to-peer based approach to establish voice and video calls among subscribers across an overlay network organized by supernodes. As a result of the decentralized peer-based approach, a Skype overlay network can scale easily to millions of users without a centralized, costly infrastructure and allows to traverse hosts with symmetric Network Address Translation (NAT) and firewalls. Skype allows users to both make PC-to-PC, phone-to-PC (SkypeIn), and PC-to-phone (SkypeOut) calls, with the latter two fee-based modes requiring routing across media gateways into a POTS network. Skype supposedly (Baset and Schulzrinne 2004) uses the STUN (simple traversal of UDP over NATs) protocol (RFC 3489) to create UDP communication between two hosts behind NAT routers. STUN allows media clients and servers to interconnect across firewalls, using client-server communication to find out the public IP address of a NAT, and its port to allow incoming traffic back in to the network.

Other media-rich, interactive applications have emerged in recent years on the World Wide Web. Blogs for rapid Web content authoring have replaced Usenet services, Wikis provide a platform for collaborative document creation, content syndication is used as a meta-tool to manage Web feeds for aggregated content sharing from Web sites, Web logs, and podcasts, and social computing provides a Web-based multimedia forum to deepen personal relations. Multimedia messaging via cell phones is based on the Synchronized Multimedia Integration Language (SMIL) as a recommendation by the World Wide Web Forum (W3C 2006) for describing multimedia presentations using XML (eXtensible Markup Language). SMIL is used in mobile communication for Multimedia Messaging Services (MMS) as an multimedia-rich version of Short Message Service (SMS), providing timing markup, media embedding and transitions, and media layout for Web content. Telepresence and collaboration through computer networks are the ultimate realization of networked, interactive workspaces, providing media-rich immersion in a mixture of real-world and virtual worlds.

CONCLUSION

Multimedia networking has become a pervasive and indispensable part of everyday personal and business interactions. Video conferencing, audio and video streaming, Internet telephony, media-rich Web content and mobile multimedia sharing through pod-casting and cell phones are now part of everyday interactions and the past few decades mark a shift from the age of discrete data processing to a new era of continuous media. The Internet-enabled home theater, Wi-Fi enabled pocket media players, media extenders forwarding video and audio streams from the PC to a traditional TV or stereo, cell phones with Internet TV capability, or Internet phone software for handhelds exemplify the wide spectrum of recent innovations in network-enabled multimedia consumer products.

This chapter discussed the principles of multimedia transmission through networks. Although the best-effort Internet is ill-prepared to transport time-critical media flows to the satisfaction of the millions of music, movie, and gaming consumers, numerous solutions have been proposed and implemented to fulfill these higher expectations. Protocols for multicasting, streaming, caching and content distribution, synchronization, real-time transport and control, and Quality-of-Service have been added to the Internet services repertoire to cater to the time-critical, loss-tolerant nature of multimedia distribution. Some of these services may change or completely disappear with the impending shift to IPv6.

What will the future hold for multimedia communications? With predicted increases in broadband capacity and user base, the near future promises greater diversity in services, in terms of interactivity and customized responses to user demands, mobility, immediacy and the quality in how users can create, access, and share multimedia content through networks. In particular, these advances entail improved representation and semantic metadata analysis of media, ubiquitous "anytime, anywhere" access to multimedia content, easy-to-use interfaces for all types of users, robust and safe connection together with diversified billing, seamless connectivity and interoperability between devices and encoding formats, user-tailored presentation, greater authoring and immediate sharing options for multimedia content across networks, linkage between TV-style appliances and the Web with near zero-delay availability of content (Paris et al. 1999), and, along with the evolution of high-speed networking, tele-immersive media use in everyday life with a greater sense of reality due to increased distribution quality. Social networking is also greatly boosted through the integrated use of multimedia applications.

Such services require technical progress in search and compression algorithms, metadata processing, media security, user interfaces and media handling, intelligent agents, media conversion, content production, multimedia service composition, and last but not least, network middleware. Service composition allows more efficient provisioning and improved reusability of components in the shift from data-driven to service-driven architectures, and from monolithic multimedia applications towards more flexible solutions, merging novel Web-based service oriented concepts and more sophisticated handling and processing of multimedia data. Continuous media carry an expressive power unmatched by words or static images. Multimedia networks enable new modalities of how people share information and express themselves, and their technical evolution will continue to have profound ripple effects on the social fabric, business, and governance.

GLOSSARY

ABR: Allocation of available bandwidth fairly according to resource consumption (primarily in ATM).

Admission control: Mechanism to control which traffic should be admitted to a network link.

ALF (Application-level framing): Protocol design principle stating that networking mechanisms such as packetization should be coordinated with application-level objectives.

ATM (Asynchronous Transfer Mode): Circuit-switching technology for telecommunications via computer networks.

Bursty traffic: Oscillating network traffic volume.

Codec: Coder-Decoder device or program for encoding and decoding of a signal or data stream.

DVP (Digital Video broadcast Protocol): Multimedia home platform (DVB-MHP) supporting the development of consumer video system applications under open standards for digital television.

E-carrier: European digital transmission format devised by the ITU-TS, equivalent of the North American T-carrier system, carrying data at a rate of 2.048 million bits per second with 32 channels of 64 Kbps each.

Gap problem: Lack of packets in audio or video stream leading to a visible or audible gap during playout.

H.263: Low-bit rate video codec by the ITU-T, designed for videoconferencing as replacement for H.261.

H.264: Advanced video coding standard (MPEG-4 Part 10) with very high data compression created by the ITU-T Video Coding Experts Group for videoconferencing and multimedia telephony.

ISDN (Integrated Services Digital Network): Circuit-switched telephone network system designed for digital transmission of voice and data over ordinary telephone copper wires with better quality than analog communication.

Jitter: Variability of packet delays within the same packet stream.

Lip synchronization: Method to keep audio and video frames in synchrony during playback.

MBone (Multicast Backbone): Dedicated testbed to deploy and evaluate IP multicast.

Media gateway: Translation unit between telecommunications networks (PSTN, 2G, 2.5G, 3G, PBX, NGN) to enable multimedia communication over multiple transport protocols.

MIME: (Multipurpose Internet Mail Extension) Extension of the Internet mail message format to carry non-US-ASCII textual messages, non-US-ASCII information, non-textual messages, and multipart message bodies.

MMS (Multimedia Message Service): Short message service for mobile devices with similarities to SMS, but with support for picture, audio, and video attachments.

Multicast: Allows sending just one message to reach a variable group of receivers through routers or servers replicating the message along the path to destinations at critical junctures leading to the receivers. It is more efficient and scalable than unicast to handle large messages and streams and hence particularly well-suited for multimedia transport.

Multimedia content: Various types and forms of multimedia information such as text, graphics, HTML, XML, dynamic Web pages, images, animations, sound or video, and files. Content differs not only in its semantics but also in how it is organized, delivered, and presented.

NGN (Next Generation Network): Packet-based network able to provide services including Telecommunication Services and able to make use of multiple broadband, Quality-of-Service–(QoS) enabled transport technologies and in which service-related functions are independent from underlying transport-related technologies.

NVP (Network Voice Protocol): Ancestor protocol of modern day VoIP technology (RFC 741).

Nyquist theorem (aka sampling theorem): States that discrete samples of a signal are a complete representation if the bandwidth is less than half the sampling rate, which is referred to as the Nyquist frequency.

PBX (Private Branch eXchange): Private telephone network used within an enterprise, sharing a certain number of outside lines for making telephone calls external to the PBX.

Policy: Rule assigned to a specific traffic class to determine how a single packet flow will be handled during bandwidth allocation.

QoS (Quality-of-Service): Measure of the performance of a network component against expectations. QoS parameters include jitter, skew, bandwidth, loss rate, and error rate.

Rate control: TCP-specific method to throttle traffic flow according to sender and receiver capabilities and in balance with other concurrent traffic flows.

RSVP (Resource Reservation Protocol): Reservation-based protocol to control receiver-initiated allocation of resources in an integrated services Internet for multicast or unicast data flows.

RTCP (Real-time Control Transport Protocol): Out-of-band watchdog protocol for RTP flows (RFC 3550).

RTP (Real-time Transport Protocol): Transmission protocol for audio and video over the Internet (RFC 1889).

RTSP (Real-time Streaming Protocol): Control protocol for time-based access to files on a streaming media server using VCR-like commands (RFC 2326).

SIP (Session Invitation Protocol): Control protocol to conduct interactive user sessions using multimedia data, often used for voice over IP along with H.323.

ST-II (Streaming Protocol version 2): IP-layer protocol to provide end-to-end service guarantees across the Internet (RFC 1190).

Streaming: Delivery of multimedia data without complete download and with playout during the delivery process.

T-carrier: Entirely digital North American carrier system introduced in 1960 using pulse code modulation (PCM) and time-division multiplexing (TDM) to support digitized voice transmission, with an original transmission rate of 1.544 Mbps for a T1 digital stream consisting of 24 64-Kbps multiplexed channels.

Traffic shaping: Bandwidth management directive to improve default bandwidth allocation by enforcing policies on traffic flows and aggregate flow partitions in a traffic class.

Near-VoD: Bandwidth-saving version of video on demand where video stream transmission is staggered and a new stream of the same content is transmitted at regular, announced time intervals for viewing of video content through networks.

VoIP (Voice over IP): IP telephony term for delivery services to carry voice information over the Internet, avoiding toll charges by ordinary telephone services.

CROSS REFERENCES

See *End-System QoS*; *Network QoS*; *The Internet Fundamentals*; *Voice over IP (VoIP)*; *Voice over MPLS and VoIP over MPLS*; *Multimedia Streaming, IP Multicast, Video Conferencing*.

REFERENCES

Apple. 2007. www.apple.com/quicktime (accessed April 10, 2007).

Aurrecoechea, C., Campbell, A. T., Hauw, L., 1998. A survey of QoS architectures, *Multimedia Systems Journal*, 6(3):138–151, May, 1998.

Banerjea, A., D. Ferrari, B. A. Mah, M. Moran, D. C. Verma, and H. Zhang. 1996. The Tenet real-time protocol suite: Design, implementation, and experiences. *IEEE/ACM Transactions on Networking* 4(1):1–10.

Baset, S. A., and H. Schulzrinne. 2004. An analysis of the Skype peer-to-peer Internet telephony protocol, Columbia University, TR CUCS-039-04.

BitTorrent. 2006. www.bittorrent.com (accessed April 20, 2006).

Bolot, J-C., and A. Vega Garcia. 1996. Control mechanisms for packet audio in the Internet. Proceedings IEEE INFOCOM, San Francisco, CA, March 1996, Vol. 1:232–239.

Bolot, J-C., and T. Turletti. 1998. Experience with control mechanisms for packet video in the Internet. proceedings ACM SIGCOMM, Vancouver, BC, January 1998.

Boutremans, C., G. Iannaccone, and C. Diot. 2002. Impact of link failures on VoIP performance. Proceedings NOSSDAV, Miami Beach, FL, May 2002, p. 63–71.

Braun, T. 1997. Internet protocols for multimedia communications, Part II: Resource reservation, transport, and application protocols. *IEEE MultiMedia* 4(4):74–82.

Casner, S., and S. Deering. 1992. First IETF Internet audiocast. *ACM Computer Communication Review* 22(3):92–7.

Chakareski, J., S. Han, and B. Girod. 2003. Layered coding vs. multiple descriptions for video streaming over multiple paths, *Multimedia Systems Journal,* 10(4):275–285, April 2003.

Clark, D. D., and D. L. Tennenhouse. 1990. Architectural considerations for a new generation of protocols. Proceedings ACM SIGCOMM, 200–8, Philadelphia, PA, September 1990.

Clark, D., S. Shenker, and L. Zhang. 1992. Supporting real-time applications in an integrated services packet network: Architecture and mechanism. Proceedings ACM SIGCOMM, 14–26, Baltimore, MD, August 1992.

Claypool, M., and J. Tanner. 1999. *The effects of jitter on the perceptual quality of video*, Volume 2:115–118, Orlando, FL: ACM Multimedia, Oct./Nov. 1999.

Clean Slate, 2007. www.100x100network.org, (accessed May 15, 2007).

Crowcroft, J., M. Handley, and I. Wakeman. 1999. *Internetworking multimedia*. San Francisco, CA: Morgan Kaufmann.

Deshpande, H., M. Bawa, and H. Garcia-Molina. 2001. Streaming live media over a peer-to-peer networks. Tech. Rep. 2001–31, CS Dept., Stanford University, CA, April 2001.

Diot, C., B. N. Levine, B. Lyles, H. Kassem, and D. Balensiefen. 2000. Deployment issues for the IP multicast service and architecture. *IEEE Network: Special Issue on Multicasting,* 14(1):78–88, January 2000.

Duke, D. J., and I. Herman. 1998. A standard for multimedia middleware. Proceedings ACM Multimedia, Bristol, UK, ACM Press, New York, NY, 381–90.

Escobar, J., D. Deutsch, and C. Patridge. 1992. Flow synchronization protocol. *IEEE/ACM Transactions on Networking* 2(2): 111–121, 1994.

Feamster, N., and H. Balakrishnan. 2002. Packet loss recovery for streaming video. Proceedings 12th International Packet Video Workshop, Pittsburgh, PA, April 2002.

Fitzek, F., and M. Reisslein. 2001. MPEG-4 and H-263 video traces for network performance evaluation, *IEEE Network* 15(6):40–54, November/December 2001.

Freecast 2006. Peer-to-peer streaming. http://www.freecast.org (accessed April 10, 2006).

Gemmell, J., H. M. Vin, D. D. Kandlur, and P. V. Rangan. 1995. Multimedia storage servers: A tutorial and survey. *IEEE Computer* 28(5):40–9.

Goyal, P., S. S. Lam, and H. M. Vin. 1997. Determining end-to-end delay in heterogeneous networks. *ACM Multimedia Systems* 5(3):157–63.

Halsall, F. 2000. *Multimedia communications: Applications, networks, protocols, and standards*. Edinburgh: Addison-Wesley.

ITU-T. 2006. Next Generation Network definition. www.itu.int/ITU-T/studygroups/com13/ngn2004/working_definition.html (accessed April 12, 2006).

Joost, 2007. www.joost.com (accessed May 15, 2007).

Kuenkel, T. 2003. Streaming media: Technologies, standards, applications. Chichester, UK: John Wiley and Sons.

Kumar, V. 1996. *MBone: Interactive multimedia on the Internet*. Indianapolis, IN: New Riders Publishing.

Kurose, J. F., and K. W. Ross. 2007. *Computer networking: A top-down approach featuring the Internet*, 3rd edition. Boston, MA: Addison-Wesley.

Leon-Garcia, A., and I. Widjaja. 2001. *Communication networks: Fundamental concepts and key architectures*. New York, NY: McGraw-Hill.

Lipartito, K. 2003. Picturephone and the information age—The social meaning of failure. *Technology and Culture,* 44(1):50–81, January 2003.

Magill, D. T. 1973. Adaptive speech compression for packet communication systems. Proceedings National Telecommunications Conference, Atlanta, GA, pp. 29D-1 to 29D-5, Nov. 1973,

McCanne, S., E. Brewer, and R. Katz. 1997. Toward a common infrastructure for multimedia-networking middleware. Proceedings of NOSSDAV, Washington University, St. Louis, MO, 39–49, May 1997.

Mena, A., and J. Heidemann. 2000. An empirical study of real audio traffic. Proceedings IEEE Infocom, Tel-Aviv, Israel, 101–110, March 2000.

Microsoft. 2007. www.microsoft.com/windows/windowsmedia (accessed April 12, 2007).

Milic, D., M. Brogle, and T. Braun. 2005. Video broadcasting using overlay multicast. Proceedings 7th IEEE International Symposium on Multimedia (ISM'05), 515–522, Irvine, CA, December 2005.

Noureddine, W., and F. Tobagi. 2002. Improving the performance of interactive TCP applications using service differentiation. Proceedings IEEE Infocom, New York, NY, June 2002.

Oram, A., 2001. *Peer-to-peer: Harnessing the power of disruptive technologies*. Sebastopol, CA: O'Reilly.

Paris, J., D. Long, and P. Mantey. 1999. Zero-delay broadcasting protocols for video-on-demand. Proceedings ACM Multimedia'99, Orlando, FL, 188–198, Oct./Nov. 1999.

Perkins, C., O. Hodson, and V. Hardman. 1998. A survey of packet-loss recovery techniques for streaming audio. *IEEE Network Magazine* 12(5):40–48.

RealNetworks. 2007. www.real.com (accessed April 20, 2007).

Rejaie, R., M. Handley, and D. Estrin. 1999. Quality adaptation for congestion controlled video playback over the Internet. Proceedings ACM SIGCOMM, Cambridge, MA, Aug./Sep. 1999.

Rhee, I., and L. Xu. 2005. Limitations of equation-based congestion control. Proceedings SIGCOMM '05, Philadelphia, Pennsylvania, USA, 49–60, August 2005.

Saroiu, S., K. P. Gummadi, R. J. Dunn, S. D. Gribble, and H. M. Levy. 2002. An analysis of Internet content delivery systems. *Operating Systems Review* 36:315–28.

Schulzrinne, H., and J. Rosenberg. 1999. Internet telephony: Architecture and protocols: An IETF perspective. *Computer Networks* 31(3):237–55.

Shenker, S. 1995. Fundamental design issues for the future Internet. *IEEE Journal of Selected Areas in Communication* 13(7):1176–88.

Singh, K., and H. Schulzrinne. 2004. Peer-to-peer Internet telephony using SIP. Proceedings International Workshop on Network and Operating System Proceedings (NOSSDAV) 2005, Washington, USA, 63–68, June 2005.

Sling Media. 2007, www.slingmedia.com (accessed May 25, 2007).

Steinmetz, R. 1991. Synchronization properties in multimedia systems. *IEEE Journal on Selected Areas in Communications* 8(3):401–11.

Steinmetz, R. 1995. Analyzing the multimedia operating system. *IEEE MultiMedia* 2(1):68–84.

Steinmetz, R. 1996. Human perception of jitter and media synchronization. *IEEE Journal of Selected Areas in Communications* 14(1):61–72.

Stone, D., and K. Jeffay. 1995. An empirical study of delay jitter management policies. *ACM Multimedia Systems* 2(6):267–79.

Turletti, T., and C. Huitema. 1996. Videoconferencing on the Internet. *IEEE/ACM Transactions on Networking* 4(3):340–51.

Vonage. 2007. www.vonage.com (accessed April 20, 2007).

Wang, Y., M. Claypool, and Z. Zuo. 2001. An empirical study of RealVideo performance across the Internet, Proceedings ACM SIGCOMM, Internet Measurement Workshop, San Francisco, CA, Nov. 2001.

Watson, A., and M. A. Sasse. 2000. The good, the bad, and the muffled: The impact of different degradations on Internet speech. Proceedings of the 8th ACM International Conference on Multimedia 2000, October 30–November 3, 2000, Los Angeles, CA.

Wu, D., Y. T., Hou, W. Zhu, Y.-Q. Zhang, and J.M. Peha. 2001. Streaming video over the Internet: Approaches and directions, *IEEE Transactions on Circuits and Systems for Video Technology* 11(1):1–20.

W3C. 2006. Synchronized multimedia integration language (SMIL). www.w3.org/AudioVideo (accessed April 20, 2006).

YouTube, 2007. www.youtube.com (accessed May, 17, 2007.)

Zhang, L., S. Deering, D. Estrin, S. Shenker, and D. Zappala. 1993. RSVP: A new resource reservation protocol, *IEEE Network* 7(5):8–18.

Ziegler, C., G. Weiss, and E. Friedman. 1989. Implementation mechanisms for packet switched voice conferencing. *IEEE Journal on Selected Areas in Communications* 7(5):698–706.

FURTHER READING

Fluckiger, F. 1996. *Understanding networked multimedia: Applications and technology*. London: Prentice Hall.

Irwin J., and C.-H. Wu. 1998. *Emerging multimedia computer communication technologies*. London: Prentice Hall.

Jeffay K., and H. Zhang. 2004. *Readings in multimedia computing and networking*. San Francisco, CA: Morgan Kaufmann.

Kuo, F., J. J. Garcia Luna-Aceves, and W. Effelsberg. 1998. *Multimedia communications: Protocols and applications*. London: Prentice Hall.

Raghavan, S. V., and S. Tripathi. 1998. *Networked multimedia systems: Concepts, architecture, and design*. London: Prentice Hall.

Sharda, N. 1999. *Multimedia information networking*. Upper Saddle River, NJ: Prentice Hall.

Shin, J., D. C. Lee, and C.-C. J. Kuo. 2004. *Quality of service for Internet multimedia*. London: Prentice Hall.

Steinmetz, R., and K. Nahrstedt. 2002. *Media coding and content processing*. London: Prentice Hall.

Part 2

The Internet, Global Networks, and VoIP

The Internet Fundamentals

Hossein Bidgoli, *California State University, Bakersfield*

INTRODUCTION

This chapter provides a basic introduction to the Internet and various Web technologies. It provides a brief history of the Internet and then explains domain name systems, navigational tools, and search engines. The chapter defines intranets and extranets and compares and contrasts them with the Internet. The chapter concludes with a brief survey of popular applications of the Internet in various industries and fields, including tourism and travel, publishing, higher education, real estate, employment, banking and brokerages, software distribution, healthcare, and politics. Other chapters throughout the *Handbook* discuss in more detail most of the topics presented here.

INFORMATION SUPERHIGHWAY AND THE WORLD WIDE WEB

The backbone of the information superhighway and electronic commerce (e-commerce) is the Internet. The Internet is a collection of millions of computers and networks of all sizes. Simply put, the Internet is the "network of networks." The information superhighway is also known as the Internet. No one actually owns or runs the Internet. Each network is locally administered and funded, in some cases by volunteers. Most countries throughout the world are directly or indirectly connected to the Internet making global e-commerce a reality.

The Internet started in 1969 as a United States Department of Defense project called ARPANET (Advanced Research Projects Agency Network). It served from 1969 through 1990 as the basis for early networking research and as a central backbone network during the development of the Internet. Since the Internet began, it has grown rapidly in size. ARPANET evolved into the NSFNET (National Science Foundation Network) in 1987. NSFNET is considered the initial Internet backbone. The term "Internet" was derived from the term "internetworking," which signified the connecting of networks. The physical network was established in 1969, connecting four nodes: University of California at Los Angeles, University of California at Santa Barbara, Stanford Research Institute (at Stanford), and University of Utah at Salt Lake City. The network was wired together via 50 Kbps circuits. Other nodes composed of computer networks from universities and government laboratories were subsequently added to the network. Taken together, these initial connections linked all existing networks in a three-level hierarchical structure:

- backbones
- regional networks
- local area networks (LANs)

Backbones provide connectivity to other international backbones. The NAPs (network access points) are a key component of the Internet backbones. NAP is a public network exchange facility where Internet service providers (ISPs) can connect with one another. The connections within NAPs determine how traffic is routed over the Internet and also are the focus of Internet congestion. Individual LANs became a standard connection interface through which computers could gain access to the Internet. Phone lines (twisted pair), coaxial cables, microwaves, satellites, and other communications media are used to connect LANs to regional networks. TCP/IP (transmission control protocol/Internet protocol) is the common language of the Internet that allows the disparate network systems to communicate with and understand each other. TCP/IP divides network traffic into individually addressed packets that are routed along different paths. Protocols are the conventions and rules that govern a data communications system. They cover error detection, message length, and transmission speed.

Protocols provide compatibility among different manufacturers' devices.

The National Science Foundation (NSF) and state governments have subsidized the creation of regional networks. NSFNET's acceptable use policy initially restricted the Internet to research and educational institutions; commercial use was not allowed. Because of increasing demand, additional backbones were eventually allowed to connect to NSFNET and commercial applications began.

The World Wide Web (WWW or the Web) changed the Internet by introducing a true graphical environment. It has been around since 1989, when it was proposed by Tim Berners-Lee at CERN. The WWW is an Internet service that organizes information using hypermedia. Each document can include embedded references to audio, text, images, full-motion video, or other documents. Comprised of billions of hypermedia documents, the WWW constitutes a large portion of the Internet. Hypermedia is an extension of hypertext. Hypertext allows a user to follow a desired path by clicking on highlighted text, called a "link," to follow a particular "thread" or topic. Hypermedia documents containing hypertext links allows users to access files, applications, and computers in a nonsequential fashion. It allows for combinations of text, images, sounds, and full-motion video all within the same document. It allows information retrieval with the click of a button. Hypertext is an approach to data management in which data are stored in a network of nodes connected by links. The nodes are designed to be accessed through an interactive browsing system. A hypertext document includes document links and supporting indexes for a particular topic. A hypertext document may include data, audio, and images. This type of document is called hypermedia. In hypertext documents, the physical and logical layouts are usually very different. This is not the case in a paper document. In a paper document, the author of the paper establishes the order and readers follow this pre-established path.

A hypertext system provides users to follow nonsequential paths to access information. This means that information does not have to be accessed sequentially, as in a book. A hypertext system allows the user to make any request that the author or designer of the hypertext provides through links. These link choices are similar to lists of indexes and allow the reader to choose a "custom path."

Any computer that stores hypermedia documents and makes them available to other computers on the Internet is called a server or a Web server. The computers that request these documents are called clients. A client can be a personal computer at home or a node in a LAN at a university or an organization. The most exciting feature of the Internet and the WWW is that these hypermedia documents can be stored anywhere in the world. A user can easily jump from a site in the United States to a site in Paris, France, all in a few milliseconds.

DOMAIN NAME SYSTEMS

Before a user can begin to navigate the Internet and use it for personal use or e-commerce applications, an understanding of domain name systems (DNS) (also called domain name servers) is essential. Domain names are unique identifiers of computer or network addresses on the Internet. The following are examples of domain names:

Netscape.com
Microsoft.com
UN.org
Whitehouse.gov

They come in two forms: English-like names and numeric or IP (Internet protocol) addresses. The Internet Corporation for Assigned Names and Numbers (ICANN) is the nonprofit corporation that assigns and keeps track of these addresses. This was previously performed under U.S. government contract by IANA (Internet Assigned Numbers Authority) and other entities.

IP addresses are less convenient because numbers are more difficult to remember. The English-like names are electronically converted to IP addresses for routing (transferring information from one network to another network). Domain names are used in URLs (uniform resource locator or universal resource locator) to identify a particular Web page. A URL is basically the address of a file or a site on the Internet. For example, in the URL http://www.csub.edu/~hbidgoli, the domain name is csub.edu. Every domain name has a suffix that indicates to which top-level domain (TLD) it belongs. In this example the suffix is edu, which stands for educational institutions. Combinations of the letters of the alphabet as well as the numerals 0 through 9 can be used in domain names. The hyphen is the only other character utilized; and spaces are not allowed.

The TLD is the data that comes after "www." It denotes the type of organization or country the address specifies. TLDs are divided into organizational (generic) and geographic (country code) domains (see Tables 1 through 3).

This system makes it easy to identify the type or location of the organization by looking at the last section of

Table 1: Organizational Domains (Generic Top-Level Domains, gTLD)

.com	Commercial organizations (e.g., Microsoft)
.edu	Education and academic organizations (e.g., California State University)
.int	International organizations (e.g., United Nations)
.mil	U.S. military organizations (e.g., U.S. Army)
.gov	U.S. government organizations (e.g., Internal Revenue Service)
.net	Backbone, regional, and commercial networks (e.g., the National Science Foundation's Internet Network Information Center)
.org	Other organizations such as research and nonprofit organizations (e.g., the Internet Town Hall)

Table 2: Examples of Proposed New Domain Names

.aero	For the aviation industry
.arts	For entities emphasizing cultural and entertainment activities
.biz	For businesses
.coop	For cooperative or cooperative service organizations
.firm	For businesses or firms
.inc	For corporations
.info	For entities providing information services
.law	For those in the legal profession
.museum	For a museum or professionally affiliated personnel
.name	For a noncommercial site associated with a private individual
.pro	For individuals or family names For a site associated with a certified professional or professional organization
.news	For news-related sites
.rec	For entities emphasizing recreation and entertainment activities
.shop	For businesses offering goods and commodities
.store	For electronic storefronts
.web	For entities emphasizing activities related to the WWW
.xxx	For adult content

the domain name. Organization, which is the second field from the right, refers to the name of the organization. A name for a small company is as easy as a large company name. The two leftmost fields of the domain name refer to the computer. This is relevant for large organizations with several levels of subdomains. An example of a relatively complete Internet address is the address of a document in the Web site of the editor-in-chief of the *Handbook*: http://www.csub.edu/~hbidgoli/books.htm
A brief explanation from left to right follows:

http—Means of access, hypertext transfer protocol. This is how the majority of Web documents are transferred.

www.csub.edu—This is the address of California State University. It is uniquely defined and differentiated from all other Web sites. WWW is an Internet service that organizes information using hypermedia.

Table 3: Sample Geographic Domains (Country Code Top-Level Domains, ccTLD)

.au	Australia
.br	Brazil
.ca	Canada
.fr	France
.de	Germany
.hk	Hong Kong
.il	Israel
.ir	Iran
.jp	Japan
.kr	Korea (Republic)
.ru	Russia
.es	Spain
.uk	United Kingdom
.us	United States
.va	Vatican City State
.zw	Zimbabwe

~hbidgoli—This is the name of the directory in which the file to be accessed is stored. A server may be divided into a series of directories for better organization.

books.htm—This is the document itself. The htm extension indicates that this is an HTML (hypertext markup language) document. It is the authoring language used to create hypermedia documents on the Web. HTML defines the structure and layout of a Web document by using a variety of tags and attributes. Most hypermedia documents are written in HTML format. Servers that do not support long extensions display “htm,” whereas other servers display “html.”

NAVIGATIONAL TOOLS, SEARCH ENGINES, AND DIRECTORIES

Navigational tools allow the user to surf the Internet and search engines provide access to various resources available on the Internet, such as those that provide library searches for writing a term paper or reservations for an airline ticket. Directories use indexes of information based on key words in the document. As will be discussed elsewhere in this chapter, Yahoo! is a popular directory on the Internet.

The original command language of the Internet was based on computer commands and was difficult to learn for most users. Character-based languages were used for tasks such as downloading files or sending e-mails. These languages are UNIX-based, which meant the user was required to know the specific syntax of many commands. Everything was communicated in plain text, and graphics, sound, and animation data were not available. The introduction of graphical browsers such as Netscape Navigator changed all of this. Microsoft Internet Explorer and Netscape Navigator are the best-known graphical browsers available for navigating the Internet. Each of these browsers combines powerful graphics, audio, and video capabilities. Each Web server has a "homepage" or a Web site that publishes information about the location. Using character-based browsers such as Lynx, a user will find this information in text form, whereas graphical browsers such as Microsoft Internet Explorer support multimedia information such as images and sound clips.

Navigational Tools

Microsoft Internet Explorer is the most popular graphical browser in the Internet world. With strong marketing support from Microsoft and improvement in its features, Internet Explorer (IE) has gained the lead in the browser market. Netscape Navigator is another graphical browser available for all major operating system platforms. Netscape, similar to IE, provides a true graphical environment that allows the user to surf the Internet using a mouse and the point-and-click technique. Similar to other Windows applications, both IE and Netscape Navigator feature a standard menu bar and toolbar buttons for frequently used commands.

Directories and Search Engines

There are several search engines and directories in use. Yahoo! is the most popular directory and Google, Excite, and Infoseek are three of the most popular search engines. These programs allow a user to scan the Internet and find information through the use of key words or phrases. A search could be for research for a term paper, finding an exotic antique for a personal collection, or anything in between. The following paragraphs briefly describe Yahoo!, Google, and Excite.

Jerry Yang and Dave Filo founded Yahoo! in April 1994. Yahoo! is one of the best-known directories on the Internet. A directory is a search service that classifies Web sites into a hierarchical, subject-based structure. For example, Yahoo! includes categories such as art, business, and entertainment. These categories are organized by topic. The user can go to a category and then navigate for specific information. Yahoo! also includes an internal search engine that can expedite the search process. Yahoo! soon expanded to offer other services and became a portal on the Internet. A portal or gateway for the WWW is an application that serves as an information search organizer. Portals provide a single-point integration and navigation through the system. Portals create an information community that can be customized for an individual or a corporation. Portals serve as the major starting sites for many individuals who are connecting to the Internet. Some of the services offered by Yahoo! include Yahoo! Travel, Yahoo! Classifieds, Yahoo! Pager, and Yahoo! Autos.

Excite, Inc. was founded in June 1994. Its basic mission is to provide a gateway to the Internet and to organize, aggregate, and deliver information to meet users' needs. The Excite Network, including the Excite and WebCrawler brands, contain a suite of specialized information services that combine proprietary search technology, editorial Web reviews, aggregated content from third parties, and bulletin boards. The Excite Network serves as a central place for consumers to gather and interact during each Web experience. Excite PAL is an instant paging service. By entering the names and e-mail addresses of friends, family, and colleagues into Excite PAL, a user can find them online.

Larry Page and Sergey Brin, two Stanford Ph.D. candidates, founded Google in 1998. Google helps its users find the information they are looking for with high levels of ease, accuracy, and relevancy. The company delivers its services to individuals and corporations through its own public site, http://www.google.com, and through co-branding its Web search services. To reach the Google Web site, the user simply types www.google.com (its URL) into the location box of the Web browser and presses the Enter key. At the initial Google screen, the user enters the desired search item(s), for example "computer viruses," and then again presses the Enter key or clicks on the "Google Search" button. In a few seconds, the items that closely match the search items will be displayed. Although the Web site's default language is English, the user can choose a different language if desired.

INTERNET SERVICES THAT SUPPORT ELECTRONIC COMMERCE

Electronic mail (e-mail), news and discussion groups, Internet relay chat (IRC), instant messaging, and the Internet phone are among the services offered by the Internet that could enhance a successful e-commerce program. Other chapters in the *Handbook* will provide a more in-depth discussion of these services. In this chapter a brief overview of these services is presented (Bidgoli 2002).

E-mail is one of the most popular services available on the Internet. Using e-mail, a user can create a message electronically and send it via the communications media. New products and services can be announced to customers using e-mail. Confirmations can be sent using e-mail and also many business communications can be effectively performed using e-mail. When a user sends an e-mail, the message usually stays in the recipient's e-mail server until the recipient reads it. In most e-mail systems, the receiver is able to store the e-mail message in an electronic folder for future reference. E-mail is fast and will get to the recipient's computer in a matter of seconds or minutes. All that is needed to send an e-mail message is the e-mail address of a recipient. A user can also send a single e-mail message to a group of people at the same time. A user can apply all the word processing tasks such as spell-checking and grammar correction before sending the e-mail message. Document files and/or multimedia files can be attached to an e-mail message and a user could ask for delivery notification. With e-mail, a user can usually establish various folders with different contents and send a particular e-mail to a specific group. Using e-mail enables a user to establish an effective message-distribution system for advertising products and services. (For detailed information on this topic, consult "E-mail and Instant Messaging".)

The Internet brings together people with diverse backgrounds and interests. Discussion groups exist to enable groups of people with common interests to share opinions and ideas. Each person in a discussion group can post messages or articles that can be accessed and read by others in the group. Newsgroups can be established for any topic or hobby and allow people to get together for fun and entertainment or for business purposes. For example, a user may join a newsgroup where the users are interested in ancient civilization, or a user may join a newsgroup that can help in writing and debugging a computer program in a specific programming language. Newsgroups can serve as an effective advertising medium in an e-commerce environment. For detailed information on this topic, consult "Online Communities".

Internet relay chat (IRC) enables a user to interactively communicate in written form with other users from all around the world. It is similar to a coffee shop where people sit around a table and start chatting. The three major differences between this electronic coffee shop and a real coffee shop are that there is no coffee, the user does not see the people that he/she is chatting with, and IRC leaves a "chat trail," which can be used later. However, a user is able to participate in many different discussions with people anywhere in the world who have the same interest. (For detailed information on this topic, consult "Internet Relay Chat (IRC)".)

Instant messaging (IM) is a communication service that enables a user to create a private chat room with another user. Different instant messenger applications offer different capabilities. They typically alert a user whenever someone on the user's private list comes online so that a user may initiate a chat session with that particular individual. (For detailed information on this topic consult "E-mail and Instant Messaging".)

Internet telephony is the use of the Internet rather than the traditional telephone-company infrastructure to exchange spoken or other audible information. Because access to the Internet is available at local phone connection rates, an international or other long-distance call will be much less expensive than through the traditional calling arrangement. This could be a major cost savings for an e-commerce site that offers hotline, help desk, and other services. (For detailed information on this topic, consult "Voice over IP (VoIP)".)

Three new services are now or will soon be available on the Internet:

1. The ability to make a normal voice phone call (despite whether the person called is immediately available; that is, the phone will ring at the location of the person called). In most of the technologies currently available, a "phone meeting" must be arranged in advance, and then both parties log onto the Internet at the same time to conduct the conversation.
2. The ability to send fax transmissions at very low cost (at local call prices) through a gateway point on the Internet in major cities.
3. The ability to leave voice mail at a called number.

Another recent application of the Internet for both personal as well as business use is called **blog** and **blogging**. Blog, short for Weblog, is a journal or newsletter that is frequently updated and intended for general public use. Blogs generally represent the personality and the interest of the author (creator) on the Web site itself. They usually include philosophical reflections, opinions on the Internet, and social or political issues. A blog also applies to Web sites dedicated to a particular topic and being updated with the latest news, views, and trends. They are becoming a popular source of online publication, especially regarding political information, opinions, and alternative news coverage. Automated tools have made the creation and maintenance of blogs an affordable and relatively easy task, making them available to individuals with minimum technical backgrounds. Blogs are now popular for business as well as personal uses. Blogs are sometimes used as a communications tool for small groups of people to keep in touch with each other. The activity of updating a blog is called "blogging" and the individual who keeps a blog is called a "blogger."

WHAT IS AN INTRANET?

The excitement created by the Internet has been transferred to another growing application called intranets. In simple terms, whatever a user can do with the Internet, a user should also be able to do with an organization's private network, or intranet.

An intranet provides users with easy-to-use access that can operate on any computer regardless of the operating system in use. Intranet technology helps companies disseminate information faster and more easily to both vendors and customers and can be of benefit to the internal operations of the organization. Although intranets are relatively new, they have attracted a lot of attention in a very short time (Bidgoli, 1999, 2002).

An intranet uses Internet and Web technologies to solve organizational problems traditionally solved by proprietary databases, groupware, scheduling, and workflow applications. An intranet is different from a LAN, MAN, (metropolitan area networks) or WAN (wide area network), although it uses the same physical connections. An intranet is an application or service (or set of applications or services) that uses the computer networks (the LANs, MANs, and WANs) of an organization, and that is how it is different from LANs, MANs, and WANs. The intranet is only logically internal to the organization. Intranets can physically span the globe, as long as access is specifically defined and limited to the specific organization's community of users behind a firewall or a series of firewalls.

In a typical intranet configuration, all users in the organization can access all the Web servers. The system administrator must define the degree of access for each user. They can constantly communicate with one another and post information on their departmental Web servers.

However, usually a firewall (or several firewalls) separates these internal networks from the Internet (the worldwide network).

Within these departmental Web servers, individual employees can have their own Web pages, divided by department. For example, the following departments each may include several Web pages as parts of the organization's intranet program:

finance
human resources
information services
manufacturing
marketing
sales

So what is an intranet? In simple terms, an intranet is a network within the organization that uses Internet technologies (TCP/IP, HTTP, FTP [file transfer protocol], SMTP [simple mail transfer protocol], HTML, and XML [extensible markup language]) for collecting, storing, and disseminating useful information throughout the organization. This information supports e-commerce activities such as sales, customer service, and marketing.

Employees can find internal information and they can bookmark important sites within the intranet. Furthermore, individual departments can create their own Web sites to educate or inform other employees about their departments by implementing intranet technology. For example, staff members in the marketing department can present the latest product information, and manufacturing staff members can post shipping schedules and new product designs. The human resources department can post new jobs, benefit information, new promotions, and information on the 401K plan. The finance and accounting departments can post cost information and other financial reports on their sites. The president's office might post information about the next company-wide gathering on its site. This information collectively supports a successful e-commerce program.

INTERNET VERSUS INTRANETS

The Internet is a public network. Any user can access the Internet, assuming the user has an active account with an ISP. The Internet is a worldwide network, whereas intranets are private and are not necessarily connected to the Web. Intranets are connected to a specific company's network, and usually the users are the company's employees. An intranet is separated from the Internet through the installation and use of a firewall (or several firewalls). Intranets usually have higher throughput and performance than the Internet and are usually more secure than the Internet.

Apart from these differences, the two have a lot in common. They both use the same network technology, TCP/IP, and they both use browsers for accessing information. They both use documents in HTML and XML formats, and both are capable of carrying documents with multimedia formats. Also, they both may use the Java programming (or its derivatives) language for developing applications.

Table 4: Internet versus Intranet

Key Feature	Internet	Intranet
User	Anybody	Employees only
Geographical scope	Unlimited	Limited to unlimited
Speed	Lower than that of an intranet	Usually higher than that of the Internet
Security	Lower than that of an intranet	Usually higher than that of the Internet
Technology used	TCP/IP	TCP/IP
Document format	HTML	HTML
Multimedia capability	Could be lower than that of an intranet	Could be higher than that of the Internet

Intranets may or may not use any of the technologies beyond HTML, that is, Java programming, JavaScript or VBScript, Active X, Dynamic HTML, or XML. One of the advantages of an intranet is that because the organization can control the browser used, it can specify a browser that will support the technologies in use. Beyond Web documents, the organization can also specify the use of the Internet phone, e-mail, video conferencing, and other Web technologies supported by the chosen browser. Table 4 summarizes the similarities and differences of these two technologies.

SELECTED APPLICATIONS OF AN INTRANET

A properly designed intranet can make the type of information listed in Table 5 available to the entire organization in a timely manner. This information directly or indirectly can improve the efficiency and effectiveness of an organization (Bidgoli, 1999, 2002).

Many internal applications in use today can be easily converted to an intranet or can be supported using an intranet. Human resources applications, such as job information, name and phone number lists, and medical benefits, can be securely displayed on a human resources intranet site. The finance site might present information on time cards, expense reports, or credit authorization. Employees can easily access the latest information on a server. With e-mail, e-mail distribution lists, and chat lines, employees can retrieve meeting minutes and much more.

Intranets also allow organizations to evolve from a "calendar-" or "schedule"-based publishing strategy to an "event-driven" or "needs-based" publishing strategy. In the

Table 5: Possible Information Provided by an Intranet

Human Resources Management
401K plans
Calendar events
Company mission statement and policies
Contest results
Department information
Employee classifieds
Employee stock options
Job postings
Job descriptions
Leave of absence and sabbatical news
Maps
Medical benefits
New-hire orientation materials
Online training
Telephone listings
Time cards
Training manuals
Training schedules
Travel authorization
Organizational charts
Meeting minutes
Personnel policy
Press releases
Salary ranges
Software program tutorials
Suggestion box
Upcoming functions
Employment applications
Security policies and procedures
Web usage and e-mail policies
Sales and Marketing
Call tracking
Data regarding the latest actions taken by the competitors
Customer information
Order tracking and placement
Newscast on demand to desktop, custom filtered to client profile

(*Continued*)

Table 5: (*Continued*)

Sales tips
Product information
Production and Operations
Equipment inventory
Facilities management
Industry news
New product offerings
Product catalog
Project information
Distribution of technical drawings
Accounting and Finance
Budget planning
Credit authorization
Expense report

past, companies published an employee handbook once a year. Traditionally, the handbooks would not be updated until the following year even though they may have been outdated as soon as they arrived on the users' desks. Some of these organizations sent a few loose pages as an update every so often. The employee is expected to add these pages to the binder. After a while, these materials become difficult to go through to retrieve specific information.

With an intranet publishing strategy, information can be updated instantly. If the organization adds a new mutual fund to the 401K programs, content on the benefits page can be updated immediately to reflect that change, and the company internal homepage can include a brief announcement about the change. Then, the employees have the new information at their desktops as soon as they look up the 401K programs.

Intranets dramatically reduce the costs and time of content development, duplication, distribution, and utilization. The traditional publication model includes a multistep process including

creation of content
production of the draft
revision of the draft
final draft preparation
migration of the content to the desktop publishing environment
duplication
distribution

However, intranet technology reduces the number of steps to only two (it eliminates the duplication and distribution steps):

creation of content
migration of content to the intranet environment

However, content still needs review and approval regardless of the medium used for delivery.

WHAT IS AN EXTRANET?

Interorganizational systems (IOSs) facilitate information exchange among business partners. Some of these systems, such as electronic funds transfer (EFT) and e-mail, have been used in traditional businesses as well as in the e-commerce environment. Among the most popular IOSs are electronic data interchange (EDI) and extranets. Both EDI and extranets provide a secure connection among business partners. Their roles in business-to-business e-commerce are on the rise. These systems create a seamless environment that expedites the transfer of information in a timely matter.

Some organizations allow customers and business partners to access their intranets for specific business purposes. For example, a supplier may want to check the inventory status or a customer may want to check account balances. These networks are referred to as extranets. It should be noted that an organization usually makes only a portion of its intranet accessible to these external parties. Also, comprehensive security measures must ensure that access is given only to authorized users and trusted business partners.

An extranet is defined as a secure network that uses Internet and Web technology to connect two or more intranets of business partners, enabling business-to-business, business-to-consumer, consumer-to-consumer, and consumer-to-business communications. Extranets are a network service that allows trusted business partners to secure access to useful information on another organization's intranet. Table 6 provides a comparison of the Internet, intranets, and extranets (Bidgoli, 2002; Fletcher, 1997).

There are numerous applications of extranets in the e-commerce world. Toshiba America Inc. is an example of a company that uses an extranet. Toshiba has designed an extranet for timely order-entry processing. Using this extranet, more than 300 dealers can place orders for parts until 5 p.m. for next-day delivery. Dealers can also check accounts receivable balances and pricing arrangements, read press releases, and much more. This secure system has resulted in significant cost savings and has improved customer service (Jones, 1998).

Table 6: Comparison of the Internet, Intranets, and Extranets

	Internet	Intranet	Extranet
Access	Public	Private	Private
Information	Fragmented	Proprietary	Proprietary
Users	Everybody	Members of an organization	Groups of closely related companies, users, or organizations

Another example of an extranet is the Federal Express Tracking System (http://www.fedex.com). Federal Express uses its extranet to collect information and make it available to its customers over the Internet. The FedEx Web site is one of the earliest and best-known examples of an extranet—an intranet that is opened to external users. The customer can access FedEx's public site, enter a package's tracking number, and locate any package still in the system. Using this system, a customer can enter all the information needed to prepare a shipping form, obtain a tracking number, print the form, and schedule a pickup.

Extranets provide very secure, temporary connections over public and private networks between an organization and a diverse group of business partners outside of the organization. These groups may include

customers
vendors
suppliers
consultants
distributors
resellers
outsourcers, such as claim processors, or those with whom the company is doing research and development (R&D) or other collaborative work, such as product design.

Extranets not only allow companies to reduce internetworking costs, they also provide companies with a competitive advantage, which may lead to increased profit. A successful extranet program requires a comprehensive security system and management control. The security system should provide comprehensive access control, user-based authentication, encryption capability, and comprehensive auditing and reporting capabilities.

An extranet offers an organization the same benefits that an intranet offers while also delivering the benefits that derive from being linked to the outside world. Some of the specific advantages of an extranet include (Bidgoli, 2002):

Coordination—An extranet allows for improved coordination among participating partners. This usually includes suppliers, distributors, and customers. Critical information from one partner can be made available so that another partner can make a decision without delay. For example, it is possible for a manufacturer to coordinate its production by checking the inventory status of a customer.

Feedback—An extranet enables an organization to receive instant feedback from its customers and other business partners. It gives consumers an opportunity to express their views about products or services before those products or services are even introduced to the market.

Customer satisfaction—An extranet links the customer to an organization. This provides the customer with more information about products, services, and the organization in general. This also makes ordering products or services as easy as a click of the mouse. Expediting business-to-business e-commerce is definitely one of the greatest benefits of an extranet.

Cost reduction—An extranet can reduce the inventory costs by providing timely information to the participants of a supply network program. Mobil Corporation, based in Fairfax, Virginia, designed an extranet application that allows distributors throughout the world to submit purchase orders. By doing this, the company significantly increases the efficiency of the operation. It also expedites the delivery of goods and services (Maloff, 1997).

Expedite communication—Extranets increase the efficiency and effectiveness of communication among business partners by linking intranets for immediate access to critical information. A traveling salesperson can receive the latest product information remotely before going to a sales meeting. A car dealer can provide the latest information to a customer on a new model without making several phone calls and going through different brochures and sales manuals.

SELECTED INTERNET APPLICATIONS

Several segments of service industries have significantly benefited from the Internet and its supporting technologies. The Internet has enabled these businesses to offer their services and products to a broad range of customers with more competitive prices and convenience. The Internet offers numerous tools and advantages to these businesses to sell their products and services all over the world. Table 7 lists popular Internet applications.

In the following pages, some of the major beneficiaries of the Internet and e-commerce will be reviewed.

Table 7: Popular Internet Applications

Popular Internet Applications
Marketing and advertising
Distance learning (e-learning, virtual learning)
Electronic conferencing
Electronic mail (e-mail)
Electronic posting
Healthcare management
Home shopping
Interactive games
Inventory management
News groups and discussions
News on demand
Online banking
Online employment
Online software distribution
Online training
Online politics (voting, participating in political forums, chat groups, and using the Internet for political fund raising)
Remote login
Sale of products and services
Telecommuting
Transferring files with FTP
Video on demand
Videophones
Online demonstrations of products and services throughout the world
Virtual reality games
Online request for proposal (RFP), request for quotes (RFQ), and request for information (RFI)

Tourism and Travel

Tourism and travel industries have significantly benefited from various Internet and e-commerce applications. As an example, the Tropical Island Vacation (http://www.tropicalislandvacation.com) homepage directs prospective vacationers to an appropriate online brochure after vacationers respond to a few brief questions about the type of vacation they would like to take. Customers simply point and click on appealing photographs or phrases to explore further. Another example is Zeus Tours (http://zeustours.com), which has been very effective at offering unique and exciting tours, cruises, and other travel packages online. Many Web sites allow customers to reserve tickets for planes, trains, buses, cruises, hotels, and resorts. Sites such as biztravel.com (http://biztravel.com) allow its business customers to plan a trip, book a vacation, gather information on many cities, gather weather information, and much more. Expedia.com, Travel.com, Travelocity.com, Priceline.com, hotels.com, and Yahoo! Travel are other examples of sites that offer all types of travel and tourism services.

Publishing

Many major textbook publishers in the United States and Europe have homepages. An interested individual can read the major features of forthcoming books or books in print before ordering them. The Web sites of some publishers include a sample chapter from specific books, or entire books that can be read online for free for 90 days, whereas others allow online customers to purchase portions of a book rather than the entire book. The Web site of John Wiley & Sons (http://wiley.com), publisher of *The Handbook of Computer Networks*, allows a prospective buyer to search the online catalog based on the author's name, the title of the book, and so forth. When the desired book is found, it can be ordered online.

Higher Education

Major universities also have homepages. An interested individual can go on a tour of a university and read about different departments, programs, faculty, and academic resources. Many universities throughout the world are creating virtual divisions that offer entire degree programs on the Internet. Many professional certificate programs are also offered through the Internet. These programs and courses provide a real opportunity and convenience for individuals in remote areas and individuals who cannot attend regular classes to enroll in these courses. They also provide a source of revenue for many colleges and universities that are facing enrollment decline in their service areas. They also allow renowned experts to teach courses to broad geographic audiences.

Real Estate

Numerous real estate Web sites provide millions of up-to-date listings of existing and new homes for sale throughout the world. These sites are devoted entirely to buying and selling real estate. The buyer or seller can review neighborhoods, schools, and local real estate prices. These sites allow the customer to find a realtor, find brokerage firms, and learn many home-buying tips. Some of these sites offer or will soon offer "virtual tours." These virtual tours enable a buyer to view a prospective property from distance. This is achieved by using virtual reality technologies. Some of the services offered by a typical real estate site are listed below:

appraisal services
buying
checking neighborhood profiles
checking schools profiles
financing
home improvement advice
obtaining credit reports
posting a free listing
renting services
selling advice, and much more

Table 8 lists examples of major real estate sites.

Employment

Employment service providers have established Web presences. Table 9 provides a listing of some of the popular sites to use for finding or recruiting for a job, especially if it involves information technology.

Banking and Brokerage Firms

Online banking is here. Many U.S. and Canadian banks and credit unions offer online banking services. Although online banking has not been fully accepted by customers, many banking-related resources are being utilized. For example, many banks use e-mail to communicate with their corporate customers. E-mail is a less expensive and more convenient alternative to a telephone call, especially for long distance communications. Financial reports for banks can be easily distributed via e-mail to mutual fund investors or customers.

The banking industry's ultimate goal is to carry out many of their transactions through the Internet. Consumer acceptance is the major factor that has kept this business from exploding. It is generally believed that a secure nationwide electronic banking system is almost in place. Soon people will be able to use their personal computers (PCs) and the Internet to do all types of banking activities.

Digital signatures are a key technology for the banking and brokerage industry because they provide an electronic means of guaranteeing the authenticity of the sending party and assurance that encrypted documents have not been changed during transmission. The current mergers and acquisitions taking place and the frequent downsizing within the financial industry are two reasons to support Internet banking. Table 10 lists some of the services available via the Internet for banking activities.

Many brokerage firms offer stock and other security transactions online. They provide quotations for stocks, bonds, and other securities. To encourage more customers to use these services, they may offer discounts.

Table 8: Examples of Online Real Estate Sites

Prudential California (http://www.prudential.com) provides wireless listing services and property data for agents.
ERA (http://www.era.com) is an Internet-based application with listing information for agents.
Century 21(http://www.century21.com) is an electronic system for tracking agent referrals worldwide and also offeres home buying, home selling, financing, and property listings.
Re/Max (http://www.remax.com) is a contact management tool for agents that interfaces with personal digital assistant (PDA) devices.
Homestore.com (http://www.homestore.com) provides a listing of properties throughout the United States.
Mortgage Expo.com (http://www.mortgageexpo.com) provides a listing of home lenders throughout the United States.

Table 9: Some of the Popular Sites to Use for Finding or Recruiting for a Job

http://www.careermosaic.com
http://www.hotjobs.com
http://www.monster.com
http://www.webhire.com
http://www.dice.com
http://www.guru.com

Software Distribution

Several major software vendors offer software on the Internet. Customers can view listings of available software, order, and designate an installation time. Nearly all

Table 10: Some of the Services Available via the Internet for Banking Activities

24/7 customer service by e-mail
Accessing current and old transactions
Categorizing transactions and producing reports
Exporting banking data to popular money management software
Obtaining online funding for checking accounts
Obtaining online mortgage and certificate of deposit applications
Obtaining written guarantee against frauds and late payments
Obtaining instant approval for personal loans
Obtaining interactive guides to aid selection of a proper banking product or service
Obtaining interactive tools for designing a savings plan, choosing a mortgage, and/or obtaining online insurance quotes all tied to applications
Obtaining online application for both checking and savings accounts
Obtaining online forms for ordering checks and issuing a stop payment
Obtaining free checks and free foreign ATM use
Obtaining IRA and brokerage account information
Obtaining loan status and credit card account information online
Paying bills
Paying credit card accounts
Transferring funds
Viewing digital copies of checks

hardware manufactures offer drivers and patches as updates on the Web. Microsoft and several other software companies already offer free software via the Internet. Routine downloading of the Netscape Navigator and Microsoft Internet Explorer browser applications are two good examples. Both are relatively small programs. In contrast is the Microsoft Office Suite, which would take significantly longer to download through an online application service provider. Given today's communications throughput and bandwidth limitations, program size definitely poses a challenge to online software distribution.

A successful application in this area is the distribution of antivirus programs over the Internet. Several of the vendors of this software application are already using the Internet to sell their software to prospective buyers. A major advantage of this method is the frequency of automatic updates that vendors provide for their customers. The Internet makes this process a cost-effective venture for both the vendors and the customers.

The development of online copyright-protection schemes continues to be a challenging problem. If users need an encryption code to "unlock" software, backups may not be possible. However, the odds are in favor of online software distribution because it provides an inexpensive, convenient, and speedy method of purchase and implementation (Cross, 1994; Hayes, 1995).

Healthcare

Electronic patient records on the Internet could provide complete medical information and allow physicians to order laboratory tests, admit patients to hospitals, refer patients to other physicians or specialists, and order prescriptions. Test and consultation results would be directed automatically to electronic patient records. The advantages of this approach include the fact that all patient information would be accessible from one central location. Another positive side of this application is that it would allow easy access to critical health information. Imagine a person who is far away from home and has a serious health problem because of injury or other causes. Any physician in any location will be able to download the complete medical history of this patient and prescribe a suitable treatment in a short period. However, these systems may offer disadvantages, such as potential problems with information privacy, accuracy, and currency.

Telemedicine (http://telemedtoday.com) may provide the medical profession with the ability to conduct remote consultation, diagnosis, and conferencing. This could result in major annual savings in travel costs and overhead for medical care professionals. As part of the information superhighway, a personal health information system (PHIS) could conceivably provide interactive medical tools to the public. Public kiosks located in shopping malls would be equipped with user-friendly computer equipment for Internet access. Patients would be prompted through the diagnosis procedure by a series of interview-like questions. Premature onset of disease could be minimized with this pre-emptive and proactive approach (Anonymous, 1994).

Virtual medicine on the Internet may allow specialists at major hospitals to operate on patients remotely. Telepresence surgery, as this is called, would allow surgeons to operate all over the world without physically traveling anywhere. A robot would perform the surgery based on the digitized information sent by the surgical specialist via the Internet. Robots would have stereoscopic cameras to create three-dimensional images for the surgeon's virtual reality goggles. Physicians would operate in a virtual operating room. Tactile sensors on the robot would provide position information to the surgeon so that he/she can feel what the robot feels. Already, prescription drugs are sold online and there are several Web sites that offer medical services (Bazzolo, 2000).

Politics

In the United States in recent years, the Internet has become a major promotional tool for all major political contenders in races for the White House, the House of Representatives and Senate, and other races. Political candidates use the Internet to announce the platforms that they are running on, their major differences with their opponents, their leadership styles, forthcoming debates, political events, and so forth. They even use the Internet for fund-raising.

The Internet may facilitate empowering voters and revitalizing democracy. Twenty-first century citizens may vote using a computer connected to the Internet, resulting in increased voter participation. Part-time legislators may have remote access to Washington and yet remain geographically close to the constituents they represent. Of course, an identification system would have to be in place, which could very likely use voice identification, face scan, finger image, hand geometry, or some other form of biometric verification technology. If such a system becomes available, then the security of the voting application, security of voting results, and counting accuracy must be carefully analyzed. Currently, the U.S. House of Representatives is attempting to put all pending legislation online. Presidential documents can be found on the Internet. Full-text versions of speeches, proclamations, executive orders, press briefings, daily schedules, the proposed federal budget, healthcare reform documents, and the Economic Report of the President are available. There are a number of repositories of this information that can be found using search engines.

CONCLUSION

This chapter reviewed the basics of the Internet and information superhighway. Navigational tools, search engines and directories were discussed and then the chapter explored intranets and extranets as two popular applications of the Internet that are being used in the e-commerce environment. The chapter concluded with a review of several popular applications of the Internet in selected fields of the service industry including tourism and travel, publishing, higher education, real estate, employment, banking and brokerage firms, software distribution, healthcare and politics.

GLOSSARY

ARPANET (Advanced Research Projects Agency Network): Started in 1969 and continued through 1990 as the basis for early networking research and as a central backbone network during development of the Internet.

Blog, short for weblog: A journal or newsletter that is frequently updated and intended for general public use.

Directories: An index of information based on key words in a document. Yahoo! is a popular directory on the Internet.

Domain name systems (or domain name servers, DNS): Unique identifiers of computer or network addresses on the Internet. Whitehouse.gov and csub.edu are two examples. The first one uniquely identifies the White House and the second identifies California State University in Bakersfield.

Extranet: A secure network that uses the Internet and Web technology to connect two or more intranets of trusted business partners, enabling business-to-business, business-to-consumer, consumer-to-consumer, and consumer-to-business communications.

Hypermedia: This allows links for combinations of text, images, sounds, and full-motion video in the same document. It allows information retrieval with a click of a button.

Hypertext: This provides users with nonsequential paths to access information whereby information does not have to be accessed sequentially, as in a book.

Internet: A collection of millions of computers and networks of all sizes. Simply put, the Internet is the "network of networks."

Intranet: A network within the organization that uses Web technologies (TCP/IP, HTTP, FTP, SMTP, HTML, XML, and its variations) for collecting, storing, and disseminating useful information throughout the organization.

Navigational tools: These allow the user to surf the Internet; Microsoft Internet Explorer and Netscape Navigator are two popular examples.

Search engines: These provide access to various resources available on the Internet, such as library searches for writing a term paper or resources for making a reservation for an airline ticket. Google.com is an example.

URL (uniform/universal resource locator): The address of a file or a site on the Internet used to identify a particular Web page.

CROSS REFERENCES

See *History of the Internet*; *Information Retrieval on the Internet*; *Internet Domain Name System*; *Internet2*.

REFERENCES

Anonymous. 1994. Heath care on the information superhighway poses advantages and challenges. *Employee Benefit Review* pp. 24–29.

Bazzolo, F. 2000. Putting patients at the center. *Internet Health Care Magazine*, 42–51.

Bidgoli, H. 1999. An integrated model for introducing intranets. *Information Systems Management* 16(3):78–87.

Bidgoli, H. 2002. Electronic Commerce: *Principles and Practice*. San Diego: Academic Press.

Cross, R. 1994. Internet: The missing marketing medium found. *Direct Marketing* pp. 20–23.

Fletcher, T. 1997. Intranet pays dividends in time and efficiency for investment giant. *InfoWorld*, p. 84.

Hayes, M. 1995. Online shopping for software. *Information Week* X:23–24.

Jones, K. 1998. Copier strategy as yet unduplicated. *Inter@ctive Week* 5(5):41.

Maloff, J. 1997. Extranets: Stretching the Net to boost efficiency. *NetGuide* 4:628.

FURTHER READING

Bayles Kalman, D. 2003a. Intranets. In *The Encyclopedia of Information Systems*, Volume 2, edited by H. Bidgoli, pp. 683–92. San Diego: Academic Press.

Bayles Kalman, D. 2003b. Extranets. In *The Encyclopedia of Information Systems*, Volume 2, edited by H. Bidgoli, pp. 301–12. San Diego: Academic Press.

Bidgoli, H. 2000. *Handbook of Business Data Communications: A Managerial Perspective*. San Diego: Academic Press.

Bidgoli, H. 2003. Electronic commerce. In *The Encyclopedia of Information Systems,* Volume 2, edited by H. Bidgoli, (pp. 15–28). San Diego: Academic Press.

Sullivan, D. 2001. Search engine sizes. http://searchenginewatch.com/reports/sizes.html (accessed May 1, 2007).

Sullivan, D. 2002. Jupiter Media Metrix search engine ratings. http://searchenginewatch.com/reports/mediametrix.html (accessed May 1, 2007).

Underdahl, B., and K. Underdahl. 2000. *Internet Bible*, 2nd edition. Hoboken: John Wiley & Sons.

History of the Internet

John Lucas Sherry and Nicholas David Bowman, *Michigan State University*

INTRODUCTION

In his prophetic and now famous 1945 *Atlantic Monthly* article, Vannevar Bush noted that inefficiencies in the exchange of new theory and discovery slowed scientific progress. He envisioned a system for rapid dissemination and organization of scientific information, instantly available to all who seek it, which he named the "memex." The memex was to be a "transparent platen" on which books, pictures, periodicals, newspapers, longhand notes, photographs, and other information would be provided to anyone who had access to the machine and knowledge of its indexing system. He foresaw scientists accessing information from around the world at unprecedented rates based on the same associational principles by which the human mind operates. Further, he saw scientists and professional data miners recording their journey through the data such that anyone who was interested could follow. A half century after the article appeared, his vision was realized in the form of the World Wide Web and related Internet technologies. This is the story of the inventors, ideas, and innovations that made Bush's vision a reality.

The Internet was created by a collection of visionaries and executed by hundreds of individuals whose contributions helped develop the technology (for a timeline, see Figure 1). The result is the technological and intellectual infrastructure of the Information Age, supporting the majority of the emerging economy for the 21st century. How did this marvel come to be? This chapter tells the story of the creation of the Internet and the World Wide Web. Guided by a unique vision of computer communication in a world of calculating machines and driven by the desire to solve a series of complex engineering problems, the Internet emerged as an open-architecture marvel of scientific and engineering cooperation. The principles that guided the creation of the Internet typify the finest realization of American cooperative scientific ideals. The Internet as we know it is the result of dedication to a set of core principles: that this communication system be the result of cooperation among interested parties, be open to new ideas, and be scalable. The vision was realized in a series of fits and starts, problems and solutions, ideas and the implementation of those ideas by engineers pushing the boundaries of current technology. It is the result of intellectual and political argumentation and compromise, funded by the military-industrial complex, but realized in the world of the academic. This chapter can hardly be called a history, though, because the open architecture of the Internet encourages further experimentation. Instead, this chapter can best be called a beginning.

A UNIQUE VISION

The Industrial Revolution of the nineteenth century brought about the development of technologies that allowed people, ideas, and products to travel across long distances in a short amount of time, facilitating exploration of scientific and technological frontiers (Moschovitis, Poole, Schuyler, and Senft 1999). Nineteenth-century scientific exploration laid the groundwork for the technological antecedents of modern computing and networking that came into popular use in the first half of the twentieth century, from the telephone to such early colossal computers as ENIAC. These early twentieth-century technologies were similarly dedicated to two goals: the desire to increase the ease of communication across distance and the desire to provide resources that assist humans in the efficient processing of information. However, it was the charged atmosphere surrounding the Cold War that provided the initial momentum to bring these two goals together as matters of national defense and pride.

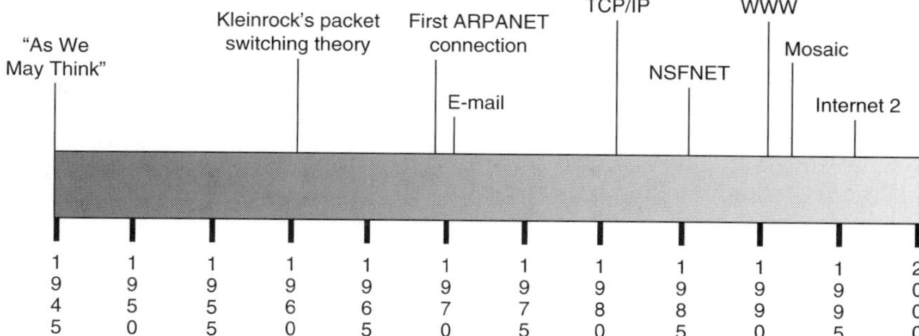

Figure 1: Timeline of major Internet events

The Marriage of Science and National Defense

By the late 1940s, the Soviet Union had long-range bombers and atomic capabilities. The Department of Defense, under President Harry Truman, enlisted the help of researchers at RAND and the Massachusetts Institute of Technology (MIT) Lincoln Laboratory to develop the Semi-Automated Ground Environment (SAGE) to detect and counteract Soviet airborne attacks (Segaller 1998). SAGE consisted of 23 direction centers linked back to a central computer; the first fully deployed data communication system between computers. It was at this time, the 1940s and early 1950s, that many of the graduate students and scientists at MIT and Lincoln gained the preliminary experience necessary to create networked computers, including connecting computers to phone lines, using computers to handle real-time data coming from antennas and submarines, digitizing communications, and developing and refining faster, more reliable computers (Segaller 1998).

On October 4, 1957, the Soviets launched Sputnik, the first human-made Earth satellite. The Eisenhower administration's fears of technological weakness came to the surface; the Soviet Union was leading the United States in space technology. Science and technology were instantly wed to national defense and the relationship was thrust into the social and political limelight as President Eisenhower, a supporter of science prior to Sputnik, ensured the public that he was committed to providing massive support for defense research. Eisenhower immediately convened a meeting of his Presidential Science Advisory Committee, and in November 1957, he appointed MIT president James Killian as the official presidential scientific advisor (Hafner & Lyon 1996).

ARPA Is Created

Working closely with President Eisenhower and the Secretary of Defense, Neil McElroy, Killian recommended that Congress create the Advanced Research Projects Agency (ARPA) within the Department of Defense (Zakon 2002). Congress quickly approved start-up funds of $520 million and an annual budget of $2 billion. In early 1958, ARPA was officially established as the U.S. government's sole research agency dedicated to the development of space-related military technology. The vigorous national commitment to beating the Soviets in defense and space technology had officially begun for the government and the American public. Although much of the computer-related funding by the mid-1960s came from the Department of Defense, many of the scientists involved with ARPA used the surge in governmental support as an opportunity to realize their academic pursuits (Abbate 1999). The intersection of military, governmental, academic, and public goals remains an integral part of the creation and maintenance of the modern Internet.

In 1958, the National Aeronautics and Space Administration (NASA) was split from the computer research section at ARPA in order to oversee all space exploration and missile research and to assure that this technology was developed in the civilian sector. ARPA was left with the relatively meager budget of about $150 million. However, the removal of space and missile research from ARPA's agenda allowed researchers to focus greater effort on the emerging fields of computer science and information processing. At this point, ARPA directly funded most of the top computer science researchers in the United States and at least partially funded projects at most of the research centers and universities engaged in high-tech endeavors (Hafner & Lyon 1996).

Networking Visions Emerge

In 1962, the first director of ARPA, Jack Ruina, hired mathematician, behavioral psychologist, and computer science connoisseur Joseph C. R. "Lick" Licklider to head ARPA's command and control division. In his groundbreaking essay "Man-Computer Symbiosis," Licklider (1960) had proposed the idea of interactive computing, an idea taken for granted by every personal computer user today. Inspired by the visionary works by Bush (1945) and Alan Turing (1950) on the use of computers to augment human intelligence, Licklider also prophesized that computers would become more than mere calculating tools. He envisioned that the relationship between humans and computers would evolve and result in cooperative decision making and problem solving in real time, that is, without the long delays that characterized computing in the 1950s (Licklider 1960).

In addition to envisioning the eventual state of interaction between human and computer, Licklider was the first to envision the linking of many computers at locations distant from each other. Nine years before it became a reality, he wrote: "It seems reasonable to envision . . . a 'thinking center' that will incorporate the functions of present-day libraries together with anticipated advances in information storage and retrieval. . . . The picture readily enlarges itself into a network of such centers, connected to one another by wide-band communication lines and to individual users by leased-wire services. In such a system, the speed of the computers would be balanced, and the cost of the gigantic memories and the sophisticated programs would be divided by the number of users" (Licklider 1960, 15).

Licklider expanded on the idea of a system of linked computers in a series of historically important memorandums written with Wesley Clark, entitled "On-Line Man Computer Communications" (Licklider and Clark 1962). They wrote of a "galactic network" where computers and information would be linked and accessible to everyone. MIT's Larry Roberts, a successor of Licklider's, commented that, "[t]he vision [of linking many computers together] was really Lick's originally. Lick saw this vision in the early sixties. He didn't have a clue how to build it. But he knew it was important" (Segaller 1998, 40).

Licklider's outline of an interactive network linking people and resources together was also seen as a possible solution to a practical problem surrounding computing in the early 1960s: stretched resources. In the 1950s and 1960s, ARPA had commissioned laboratories around the country to carry out a variety of projects in science and technology, providing each with large, expensive mainframe computers manufactured by different companies. Individual laboratories altered their computers, adding different applications, packages, and hardware, and each subsequent laboratory wanted the latest computing capabilities available. The enormous costs of building separate units for each project began to snowball.

In early 1966, Robert Taylor, director of the Information Processing Techniques Office (IPTO, the computing division of ARPA), proposed a remedy to the scarce resource problem that incorporated the latest research and developments: Build a system of electronic connections between research computers at different geographical locations across the country to allow convenient, quick, and inexpensive sharing of resources between many scientists (Hafner and Lyon 1996). The idea of networking was already being implemented on a smaller scale, for example linking two computers together (Marill and Roberts 1966), but nothing that approached the scale or complexity of Taylor's proposition had been attempted so far. The technology of the time did support such a notion. In 1958, communications engineers at Bell Laboratories had built the modulator-demodulator, or simply "modem" (Anderberg 2002). The modem made it possible to convert data from the digital computer format into the analog telephone line format, send it over existing phone lines, and translate it back to digital computer format. By using the long-distance infrastructure already in place, the task of linking many computers for the purpose of sharing resources was indeed an attractive and financially sound proposal. In 1966, Taylor pitched the idea to his boss, ARPA Director Charlie Hertzfeld, and received approval and financial support to build the experimental network. In 1967, Taylor enticed Larry Roberts to leave Lincoln Lab and join him at ARPA to begin planning the proposed computer network, which would soon become known as the ARPANET (Segaller 1998).

Networking: From Theory to Practice

Although Licklider imagined what a distributed, interactive computer network could accomplish and Taylor imagined what problems it could solve, Leonard Kleinrock had theorized in 1961 the new communication technology that could make such a network possible (Hafner and Lyon 1996). Two major obstacles to creating a long-distance computer network were (a) being able to receive and process data over existing phone lines fast enough to allow efficient, real-time processing, and (b) creating a network that could support the unique needs involved in the exchange of computer-generated data. While an MIT graduate student in 1961, Kleinrock proposed what would later be called "packet-switching" technology, the most efficient way to send data over a network (Kleinrock 1961, 1964). Two other researchers, Donald Davies at the British National Physical Laboratory (NPL) and Paul Baran at the RAND Corporation, were also investigating the idea of packet switching in unrelated research projects in the early 1960s (Baran 1964; Davis, Bartlett, Cantlebury, and Wilkinson 1967). Ultimately, Davies and his group of researchers at NPL would be the first to test a packet-switching network within a building, in Middlesex, England, in 1967 (Zakon 2002).

Packets, Queuing, Demand Access—The Theory of Networking

Packet switching involved chopping messages into packets, assigning each packet a number, sending the packets of data independently through the network, and reassembling the packets at the other end in the proper order in readable form (Hafner and Lyon 1996). The packets could queue up at nodes in the network until they were requested (demand access). In this fashion, network resources could be used as needed and not tied up with open circuits. Researchers hypothesized that packet switching would be a dramatic improvement over circuit-switched telephone networking because it avoided the inefficiency of a continuously open connection. In order to put packet-switching data transfer theory into action, however, ARPANET researchers had to address several key obstacles.

ARPANET planners were well aware that the computers that would be connected to the network were incompatible. Each ARPA-funded site had purchased different mainframe computers from different companies, using different operating systems and different languages (Segaller 1998). Moreover, each site research team was only familiar with the operation of the computer in their respective laboratory. How could these mainframe computers be connected, share data, and communicate with one another with a minimum of errors? Taylor called a meeting of ARPA-funded researchers at the University of Michigan in early 1967 to discuss this and other unresolved network design issues (Anderberg 2002).

Building on an idea proposed by Wesley Clark, a computer scientist at Washington University in St. Louis, the ARPA researchers envisioned a system of smaller, intermediate computers called interface message processors (IMPs) to solve the mainframe-to-mainframe incompatibility problem (Abbate 1999). Each IMP would act as an

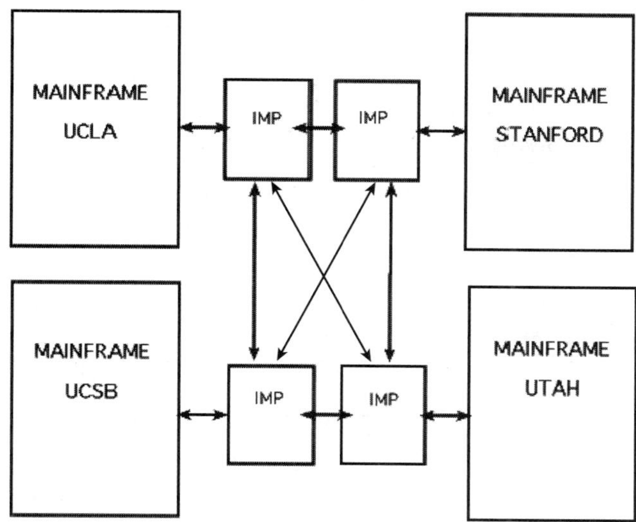

Figure 2: The interface message processing design

interface between the network and its mainframe computer (see Figure 2). Every mainframe had to send the same format packets to the IMPs and there was a standard interface all mainframes had to implement. NCP dealt with incompatibilities on an end-to-end basis. Each site's mainframe would communicate with its own IMP, and all IMPs would be designed to communicate with one another using the same operating system and speaking the same language. Roberts distributed a request for quotation (RFQ) to design and build the IMPs in July 1968 and received more than 100 proposals. He awarded the contract to Frank Heart and his team of computer scientists at Bolt, Benerak & Newman (BBN) in Cambridge, Massachusetts, in December 1968 (Anderberg 2002). The final step was deciding which sites would initially be connected to the network. Four sites, each with its own particular research specialties, were chosen: UCLA; the University of California, Santa Barbara (UCSB); Stanford Research Institute; and the University of Utah. The deadline for establishing the network at UCLA was set, somewhat arbitrarily according to Heart, for September 1, 1969, only nine months after the initial proposal was presented. Heart and his group would have $1 million and less than a year to turn theory into a working system (Hafner and Lyon 1996).

In the summer of 1968, IPTO organized a meeting for graduate students from the universities that would be the first sites connected to the network to discuss the technological aspects of the proposed network. The meeting gave rise to the Network Working Group (NWG), which solidified the collaborative nature of the ARPANET project (Abbate 1999). Rather than one single scientist taking charge of the direction of the group, the attendees recorded their thoughts and deliberations in a set of notes that Steve Crocker soon named request for comment (RFC). Crocker published the first RFC in April 1969, detailing the interface between the hosts and IMPs and asking for input on problems (Crocker 1969). The RFC became firmly established as a means of communicating information and seeking feedback about networking issues, and it was supported by all levels of researchers. This open manner of sharing ideas in the realm of scientific discovery remains in place to this day and, by many accounts, influenced the eventual spirit of community associated with the modern-day Internet (Internet Society 1999). The entire series of RFCs have been collected and cataloged by Jon Postel, the RFC editor for more than 30 years, and are available for viewing (RFC Editor Homepage, n.d.).

It is important to note that at this point, the number of researchers working on the development of ARPANET was relatively small. In fact, as news of the proposed network spread to scientific circles across the country, the idea was met with little enthusiasm. To the many ARPA-funded research teams, the idea of sharing resources across a network meant that "outsiders" would be meddling in their private computing centers and that their hard-earned computing equipment and power would be depleted. To researchers who still hoped that ARPA would fund their projects, the idea of a network meant that ARPA might not purchase new mainframes for them. Roberts, Taylor, and Licklider tried to win the support of the largely uninterested and skeptical ARPA-funded researchers, eventually resorting to subtle "blackmail" (Segaller 1998), reminding each site that as they were being supported by ARPA with hundreds of thousands, if not millions, of dollars a year, they should be just as enthusiastic about the project as the project managers were. Needless to say, ARPA-funded researchers started to come around, though most doubted the venture would work (Moschovitis, Poole, Schuyler, and Senft 1999).

ARPANET Comes Alive

By early 1969, the researchers at BBN were working around the clock to develop the IMPs by the deadline, whereas the research teams at each university were busy developing the custom software and hardware that would allow communication between their mainframe and the IMP. Significant challenges arose every day, all of which had to be resolved under the pressure of the looming deadline. To everyone's amazement, the UCLA IMP was delivered in time for the September 1 deadline and the IMP-mainframe connection was ready to go a few days later (Zakon 1993). The first test of the packet-switching technology, between the UCLA IMP and its mainframe, was a success. On September 2, 1969, the two machines began talking to each other. The second IMP arrived, at Stanford Research Institute, on schedule one month later and their first official test occurred on October 1, 1969 (Hafner and Lyon 1996).

The plan was to log-on from the UCLA host to the Stanford host by typing "LOG IN." An L was typed at UCLA and Stanford received an L. An O was typed at UCLA and Stanford received an O. A G was attempted and the system crashed. A couple of hours later, however, the system was up and running again, and the researchers successfully logged onto the network, performed some minimal operations, and logged off. The connection between UCLA and Stanford was a success, and the remaining two nodes, one at UCSB, and one at the University of Utah, were working by the end of the year (Zakon 1993). The technology of ARPANET proved that a long-distance packet-switching computer network was possible. Eventually, the ARPANET helped ARPA cut its computer budget by 30 percent and impressed the skeptics by providing them with more computing power and allowing researchers at different institutes to exchange papers, data, ideas, and software programs and upgrades.

GROWING THE NETWORK

The fifth ARPANET node was installed at BBN in March 1970, and over the next few years, Vint Cerf and Steve Crocker, under Kleinrock at UCLA, and Frank Heart and Bob Kahn, then at BBN, all worked to push the network to the limit, intentionally breaking the network in order to discover weaknesses in the design. They also formed the International Network Working Group in 1972 to coordinate standards. As the number of sites connected to the network steadily grew, moving from the West Coast to the East Coast, new technological innovations kept emerging, some expected and some surprising.

Electronic Mail: The "Killer" Application

In 1971, Ray Tomlinson, a computer engineer at BBN, devised an experimental program, called CPYNET, for sending files between computers. Tomlinson added an additional program to CPYNET for sending and receiving messages, called SNDMSG and READMAIL (Hafner and Lyon 1996). Within a few months, Tomlinson's application was being used to send messages over the network to machines in different geographical locations. Tomlinson paired each user's name with the user's host machine identification using the symbol "@" (meaning "at"), not knowing he was coining the universal symbol of the soon-to-be wired world (Hafner and Lyon 1996). The resulting application, "e-mail" for short, was the first killer application for the emerging network. The network e-mail capability spread rapidly, quickly becoming the most widespread use for the network in the early years. Kleinrock noted that "[a]s soon as e-mail came on, it took over the network. We said, 'Wow, that's interesting.' We should have noticed there was something going on here. There was a social phenomenon happening" (Segaller 1998, 105). The original purpose of the network, to share computing resources across distant geographical locations, was surpassed by its use as a communications tool. The instant popularity of e-mail among the scientists came as quite a surprise because the rationale for building the network was to share access to computers, not access to people (Abbate 1999). Other applications were soon developed that facilitated the creation of "virtual" work groups and news groups, firmly establishing the network as a "virtual community" (Moschovitis et al. 1999).

ARPANET Makes Its Public Debut

At this point, the use of ARPANET was almost exclusively confined to the networking branch of the computer science community, and the general public was unaware of the existence of it. Roberts knew that if the network was ever going to be widely adopted, it was time for a demonstration. Kahn and a small group of principle investigators were asked to devise a showcase of network capabilities. In 1972, ARPANET debuted to the public at the International Conference on Computer Communications (ICCC) in Washington, D.C. (Moschovitis et al. 1999). By that time, ARPANET had expanded to 15 nodes with 23 sites.

ARPANET's debut to computer vendors, university representatives, government officials, scientists from a variety of disciplines, and the press at ICCC was a success. The system crashed only once over the weekend conference, and oddly enough, this gave Kahn and his colleagues the opportunity to show that problems were fixable (Hafner and Lyon 1996). The conference attendees were astonished, curious, and anxious to become a part of the network; the buzz had officially begun. Although access to ARPANET was still under the tight control of ARPA and the U.S. Department of Defense, the demonstration at ICCC ignited curiosity and confidence in other networking projects. The early 1970s proved to be an intense period of network experimentation. Within three years of the first ARPANET transmission over telephone lines, different types of networks using packet-switching technology emerged. ARPANET remained under the control of the Department of Defense; thus, rather than expand the existing ARPANET, new networks were created. Networks that linked computers through radio connections, such as the ALOHAnet at the University of Hawaii, and ones that used satellites to link computers, such as SATnet, were popping up all over the world (Segaller 1998).

A NETWORK OF NETWORKS

The success at the ICCC conference swelled the ranks of computer scientists who were interested in packet-switching networks. But the 1972 conference revealed that there remained a significant obstacle to realizing Licklider's ultimate vision of "... a 'thinking center' that will incorporate the functions of present-day libraries together with anticipated advances in information storage and retrieval and the symbiotic functions." Although computers within a network could be used for time-sharing electronic communication and the sharing of files, these same options were not possible between networks. That is, a computer scientist working at the University of Utah (ARPANET) could not exchange files with a colleague at the University of Michigan (Merit). In order for the existing computer networks to become connected, there needed to be a new protocol so that computers on different networks could communicate with each other.

Robert Kahn began researching the internetworking problem at ARPA in 1973 (Kahn 1994). In many ways, the problem of inter networking was similar to the earlier problem of making dissimilar computers communicate that had been solved by using the IMPs. That is, each network used a different language to control the packet switching, preventing computers on different networks from being able to communicate with each other. Kahn decided that the network of networks needed an open architecture that would allow for innovation within networks, without requiring existing networks to abandon their software. The problem of connecting networks was solved similarly to the earlier problem of connecting computers in a network. Kahn's main collaborator, Vinton Cerf, proposed the idea of "gateways" between the networks that would employ a common language or protocol. These gateways would allow networks to interconnect in much the same way that the IMPs originally allowed computers to interconnect. Thus, Kahn and his team specified a set of four requirements for the internetwork:

> Each distinct network would have to stand on its own and no internal changes could be required to any such network to connect it to the Internet. Communications would be on a best effort basis. If a packet didn't make it to the final destination, it would shortly be retransmitted from the source. Black boxes would be used to connect the networks; these would later be called gateways and routers. There would be no information retained by the gateways about the individual flows of packets passing through them, thereby keeping them simple and avoiding complicated adaptation and recovery from various failure modes. There would be no global control at the operations level (Leiner et al. 1994).

A common language was needed to allow computers from different networks to communicate with one another. Network control protocol (NCP), the software used to oversee packet switching on the ARPANET, lacked end-to-end host error control because packets never traveled outside the ARPANET. Outside the United States, the UK National Physical Laboratory developed a standard called X.25, which subsequently garnered widespread acceptance in Europe and Japan. Meanwhile, Cerf and Kahn wrote the transmission control protocol/Internet protocol suite (TCP/IP) to implement the packet-switching process at gateways (Cerf and Kahn 1974). It took four incarnations before the final TCP/IP software was considered ready for deployment. TCP would be responsible for service features involved in the packet-switching process, including flow control and lost packet recovery, whereas the IP was used for the addressing and forwarding of individual packets. Standardized 32-bit IP addresses were assigned to each computer on the Internet; the first 8 bits signified the network and the other 24 bits designated the host on that network. Initially, TCP/IP protocol was used to connect the ARPANET (50 kbps) land lines, the Packet Radio Net (PRNET at 400/100 kbps), and the Packet Satellite Net (SATNET at 64 kbps; Kahn 1994). On January 1, 1983, the ARPANET made the transition from NCP to TCP/IP as the standard protocol for networking on ARPANET. Now, it was possible to interconnect networks and the *Internet* was born.

Standardization of the TCP/IP software led to the development of commercially available gateways and routers for industry workstations, minicomputers, and mainframes. As the number of local area networks (LANs) increased, so did potential engineering incompatibility problems. The Internet Activities Board (IAB) was founded in 1983 to oversee standardization of networks. For example, the IAB designated three network types based on the expansion of network interconnectivity: class A, which were large-scale national networks; class B regional networks; and class C local area networks. With increasing interconnection came difficulty in locating information on the Internet. IP addresses of all host computers were found in a distributed file called HOSTS.TXT. Eventually, the updating of this file became a bottleneck, so Paul Mockapetris of USC/ISI invented the domain name system (DNS) to alleviate this problem (1983a, 1983b). DNS assigns and tracks easy-to-remember names to IP addresses across the Internet (e.g., purdue.edu).

The ARPANET/MILNET Split

By 1984, the computer architecture in the United States for the Internet was in place, and a number of computer networks, both governmental and commercial, had emerged. Within a few years, there were a number of networks linking geographically proximate universities. Among these networks were the following.

ARPANET (1969)—UCLA, Stanford University, UCBS, University of Utah, BBN, MI T, RAND Corporation, SDC, Harvard University, MIT's Lincoln Laboratory, University of Illinois—Urbana/Champaign, Case Western Reserve University, Carnegie Mellon University, NASA/Ames.

Merit (1969)—University of Michigan, Michigan State University, Wayne State University.

THEORYNET (1977)—University of Wisconsin.

USENET (1979)—Duke University and University of North Carolina.

CSNET (1981)—University of Delaware, Purdue University, University of Wisconsin, RAND Corporation, and BBN.

BITNET (1981)—City University of New York and Yale University.

The expansion of the Internet to broader academic and commercial interests raised concerns about the security of Department of Defense information on the Internet. For that reason, the military component of the Internet was separated from the Internet, resulting in two networks: ARPANET and MILNET (the new military portion of the Internet). Computers on the MILNET would still be able to communicate with computers on the ARPANET, but the architecture was designed such that MILNET could be quickly disconnected from ARPANET in case of a threat of a security breach.

The NSFNet

Perceiving the advantage of the Internet for scientific research, the National Science Foundation (NSF) decided to expand use of the Internet beyond the limited number of computer scientists and defense contractors and make it available to all disciplines for research and education. Dennis Jennings was responsible for the initial decision to use TCP/IP to build a network linking the NSF sponsored super computer sites. In 1986, the NSF brought in Steven Wolff to oversee construction of a new research network (Leiner et al. 1994). Wolff was charged with developing a computer network that would facilitate cooperative research and that would eventually outgrow its need for NSF funding. In order to do this, Wolff created

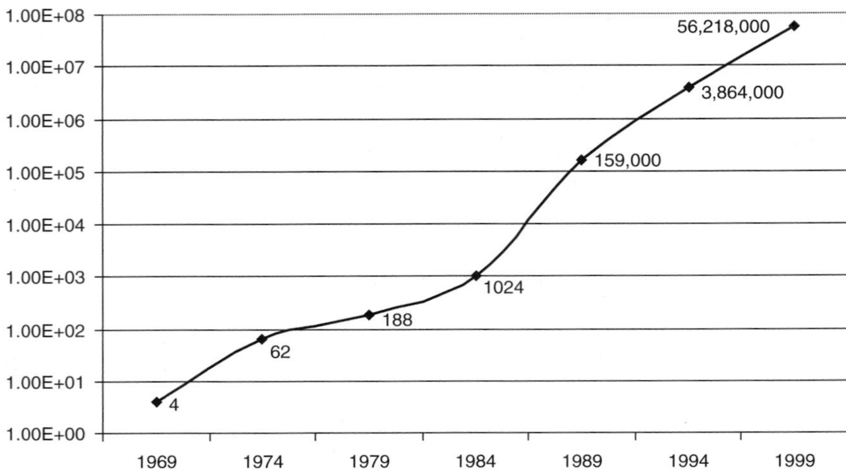

Figure 3: Exponential growth of Internet hosts

policy designed to encourage broad-based use of the Internet while encouraging the creation of separate, commercial, long-haul networks. The NSF required universities seeking funding for an Internet connection to make connections available to all qualified users on campus. Further, they encouraged growth of regional networks by urging regional networks to seek commercial, nonacademic customers in order to expand use of the networks, take advantage of increased economies of scale, and ultimately lower subscription costs. They also wrote the Acceptable Use Policy, which restricted use of the national NSF network to academic and research work (National Science Foundation 1986). It was believed that denying commercial users access to the national network would encourage creation of nationwide commercial networks. This strategy paid off when commercial Internet long-haul carriers UUNET and PSI opened.

In 1986, the NSF launched the NSFNET backbone, a high-speed (56 kbs) network connection between six supercomputer centers running across the United States. It was built by MCI, IBM, and MERIT (the University of Michigan). The supercomputer centers were at Princeton University, Cornell University, Carnegie-Melon University, the University of Illinois, the University of Colorado, and the University of California, San Diego. In under nine years, the NSFNET backbone grew from 6 nodes at 56 kbs to 21 nodes at 45 mbs, connecting 50,000 networks on all seven continents and in space.

FINDING OURSELVES IN VIRTUAL SPACE

A network with the breadth and reach of the Internet quickly surpassed users' ability to keep track of the location of information. With 50,000 networks, keeping track of files and IP addresses quickly became impossible. Soon computer scientists began writing software to help users find and transfer files. One of the most popular was Gopher, released in 1991 by Paul Lindner and Mark P. McCahill from the University of Minnesota. Gopher, and its descendents, allowed users to search through "Gopher space" for files to transfer via file transfer protocol (FTP). Gopher was an Internet protocol that provided menu-driven file-and-data retrieval from remote computer servers (Anklesaria et al. 1993). Gopher sites organized files for retrieval and were set up to be searched by users. Although they were text-based, these early versions of Internet searching software greatly simplified the problem of finding files on the Internet.

All this was soon to change. Desktop computers were becoming easier to use because of graphical user interfaces, developed at the Xerox Palo Alto Research Center (PARC), and the commercially distributed Apple Macintosh operating system, in 1984. One year after the introduction of the Macintosh operating system, Microsoft released the Windows 1.0 operating system in an attempt to replace MS-DOS text commands with an intuitive point-and-click graphical user interface similar to the Macintosh operating system, although the Windows operating system would not become commercially popular until the introduction of version 3.0 in 1990 (Microsoft 2002). Computing power that the early Internet pioneers could only dream of had found its way to business desktops, elementary school classrooms, and home recreation rooms. Access to the Internet was increasingly supplied to the general public through commercial gateways and public access points, such as Michigan's Merit network and Cleveland's Freenet. The number of hosts on the Internet had grown exponentially through the 1980s (see Figure 3). But the biggest change in the Internet was still to arrive.

The World Wide Web

In the late 1980s, Tim Berners-Lee was a research fellow at the European Laboratory for Particle Physics (CERN) in Switzerland. He had become intrigued with using computers to organize information via hyperlinked connections. As his ideas developed, his vision fixed on a scalable system for linking related documents via the Internet. It was important that such a system not use a central database to keep track of files, as updating the database would limit its speed and size to available resources (because of computer storage limits and the human resources needed for updating the database). Instead, Berners-Lee wanted all system users to be able to both find and contribute information. Administrators at CERN had a difficult time understanding what use they could make of Berners-Lee's invention and would not provide financial support for him to pursue the idea. Nonetheless, he persevered and finally received financial support in the form of a new NeXT computer.

Steve Jobs was forced out of Apple in 1985 and started up NeXT computers. Jobs felt his computers were the "next" great advance after the Macintosh for desktop computers. Berners-Lee found that much of what he needed to create his World Wide Web hyperlinking software was available on his NeXT computer. He developed an early prototype Web browser to make the CERN phone directory available online. From this modest success, he continued to promote the use of the Web both inside and outside of CERN. He traveled to the United States to display the Web at a conference of hypertext developers, posted information about the Web on Internet user groups, and provided telnet access to the browser on a server at CERN so that people could try it out.

Berners-Lee's (1999) vision was that the Web would maximize flexibility while accommodating standards that were already in play on the Internet. He wanted the Web to be open to existing Internet protocols, so he designed it to read FTP, Gopher, network news (NNTP), wide area information server (WAIS), and other documents. This was accomplished, in part, by specifying the protocol at the beginning of the link address or uniform resource indicator (URI). For example, links to FTP files began with "ftp://...," whereas links to Gopher sites began "gopher://...." His own protocol for linking hypertext documents is the now familiar hypertext transfer protocol (HTTP). This software provided instructions on how to download and connect hypertext documents via the Internet. Finally, Berners-Lee standardized the language that Web page designers would use, based on the earlier text and database publishing language SGML, called hypertext markup language (HTML).

The First Browsers and the Rise of Popular Internet

Despite the obvious advantages of the Web, which we see in retrospect, few in the computing world were eager to adopt this new technology (Berners-Lee 1999). Although Web browsers were developed for operating systems commonly used by computer programmers (e.g., UNIX), they were not available for the most commercially popular operating systems (PC, Mac), and Web editors were even more rare. Without a browser that was easy to install and without abundant content to discover, the Web was unlikely to take off. In 1993, Marc Andreessen and colleagues at the University of Illinois National Center for Supercomputing Applications (NCSA) released Mosaic, a Web browser that was eventually available for UNIX, Macintosh, and PC. The immediate advantage of Mosaic was that it was graphical, user friendly, and easy to install. Mosaic caught on quickly, thanks in part to an aggressive public relations campaign by the University of Illinois. Web use increased at a rate of over 340,000 percent in the first year. Soon new technologies proliferated on the Web. By the end of 1995, real-time audio streaming was made available by RealAudio, RT-FM had begun netcasting from Las Vegas, the Arizona law firm Canter & Siegel introduced "spam" to the Internet by mass e-mailing of advertising for immigration services, banner ads were introduced, Sun Microsystems introduced JAVA, and virtual reality markup language (VRML) made its appearance on the Web.

In 1994, Mark Andreessen left the NCSA to form Netscape Communications with Jim Clark. Netscape soon produced its own version of the Mosaic browser, making it available for free to educational institutions and for a small fee to others wanting the use the Web. Microsoft was slow to realize the potential of the Web but aggressively joined the Web when Bill Gates decided to bundle a Web browser with the new release of Windows 95. Rather than write their own code, Microsoft bought the rights to a NCSA spin-off browser from a small company called Spyglass for $2 million (Berners-Lee 1999). This marked the beginning of what became known as the "browser wars" between Netscape and Microsoft. Sensing competition in the market that it thought it controlled, Netscape urged the Justice Department to pursue antitrust action against Microsoft for bundling its browser with the most popular desktop operating system. Although this case, *US v. Microsoft*, demonstrated that Microsoft did use its market power to drive competitors out of the market, the settlement did nothing to relieve the harm done to the market. Netscape was forced out of business and was bought out by AOL. In protest of the decision, nine states and the District of Columbia withdrew from the case settlement stating that it was little more than a slap on the wrist.

In the years following 1995, the Internet, World Wide Web, and related technologies grew in the public consciousness. Magazines, newspapers, and television programs increased coverage of this new technology. Debates erupted on Capitol Hill in Washington, D.C., about what content could be allowed on the Web. Maybe most important for the continued development and commercialization of the Internet, Congress passed the Telecommunication Act of 1996, opening up media and telecommunications companies to increased competition. People became troubled by such security issues as "hacks" and "viruses" even as they slowly began purchasing products from "e-tail" outlets, such as Amazon.com, and auctions sites, such as eBay.com.

Google: A Web Necessity

As Web use expanded through the second half of the 1990s, it became necessary to have an application that would allow the user to more efficiently search for information. A number of companies offered search engines based on a variety of search strategies. Some early search engines required Web site administrators to register their site with the search engine, while others worked on algorithms to locate key search terms on Web sites. Out of the fray emerged the most popular and powerful search engine to date: Google. The advantage that Google offers users is that it calculated site importance based on the number of other sites that are linked to it. Thus, a Google search typically finds the most informative and pertinent Web sites—in relative rank order—for any search term.

Launched by two Stanford graduates in 1998, Google (which borrows its name from the mathematical term "googol," defined as a numeral one followed by 100 zeroes) quickly became most popular search engine, currently registering over 91 million unique searches per day (SearchEngineWatch 2006). The growing popularity of the Google search engine attracted many investors, and on August, 19, 2004, the company went public. By the end of the first day of trading, Google had received more than $1.67 billion, making it the largest initial public offering (IPO) in financial history.

Updates to Google allow users to track down images, newsgroups, news stories, items for sale, and directions and maps of most anywhere in the world via satellite imagery. In addition, two new Google programs—Gmail and Google Desktop— have been launched by Google that allow users to search their e-mail files and hard drives using Google's patented search technology. Recently, Google acquired the popular YouTube video delivery service. All of these features and programs are available to users at no cost.

However, Google has not been free of criticism. The Gmail program has been targeted by information privacy activists who are concerned because the program attaches customized advertisements to users' message when they are sent. For example, if one college student were to send a party invitation to another student and mentioned "beer" in the message, Google would attach a beer advertisement to the message. Copyright attorneys have repeatedly claimed that Google's search program makes it far too easy for individuals to steal images, text, and other proprietary information. Google's method of ranking search results has also been criticized, as it allows for corporations to purchase "paid-return" links, which will return specific links whenever a specific search term is entered. In a recent debate over electric cars, General Motors Company paid Google to include links to its Web site to combat negative publicity it was receiving from another Web site's blasting of GM's alleged anti-alternative energy policy; this type of paid-search return bothers many Web neutrality supporters who worry that this practice limits information sources to users.

The Semantic Web

Although Google is currently the most popular engine for navigating billions of Web pages available to the general public, it is still not the "gold standard" envisioned by Web pioneer Tim Berners-Lee. Berners-Lee and others at the World Wide Web Consortium continue to develop a more sophisticated mechanism for finding information on the Internet that allows machines to retrieve information based on semantic meaning. Sites on the semantic Web will have descriptive data included that will allow machines to read the meaning of information on the page. Included in this system are the resource description framework (RDF) that specifies information in a subject-predicate-object semantic expression, the Web ontology language (OWL) that provides additional vocabulary for describing properties and classes of information, and a new mark-up language called XML that provides the data descriptions used by RDF and OWL. Among other things, the semantic Web will allow computers to "talk to" each other, essentially creating a Web-based on machine intelligence in addition to human intelligence. Time-consuming tasks will be taken care of by computer agents on behalf of humans.

Web 2.0—The Present and Future of Activity on the Internet

Collectively, the browser wars, Google, and the semantic Web represent the events defining the core transition from the Internet of the past to the Internet of the future. The origins of the Internet were rooted in information-sharing and communication, with an emphasis on designing and selling applications, such as a Web browser. Some see the future of the Internet relying on delivery of powerful services, and providing the conduit though which information can be shared (e.g., peer-to-peer networks, wikis, and personal blog sites) and found (e.g., Google). This vision of the Internet has been dubbed Web 2.0.

The idea of Web 2.0 has been most enthusiastically advanced in a series of conferences hosted by computer science book publisher O-Reilly Media. Web 2.0 is envisioned as a qualitative shift to a new type of Web that attempts to leverage the collective intelligence of Internet users (Kelly 2005). This is accomplished via an impressive array of new activities one can engage in on the Web. Importantly, users provide the intellectual content; Internet companies provide access to and archiving of the enormous database that emerges. Unlike traditional media companies, new Internet companies won't necessarily require content experts as users provide much of the content.

One of the more impressive examples of user provided content has been Wikipedia. Launched in 2001 and based on wiki technology that allows users to add, remove, and edit content, Wikipedia has evolved into a large, decentralized and free online encyclopedia consisting of submissions and edits by Web users. Wikipedia claims to have over 5 million entries and is published in 250 languages. Alexa estimates that Wikipedia receives 55,000 hits per day, putting it in the top 20 most popular sites on the Web.

Currently, the most popular site on the Internet is another example of Web 2.0, MySpace. According to Hitwise (www.hitwise.com), MySpace accounts for 4.63 percent of Internet market share. MySpace began in 2003 as a social networking site modeled after friendster.com. It provides free searchable space for users to post photos, music files, and blogs, in addition to joining content-based groups. Importantly, sites on the service are networked by invitation, creating a massive collection of networked user-provided information. Portrayed as another hacker inspired Internet success story, MySpace is the actually the brainchild of viral marketing agent InterMix Media and is owned by Rupert Murdoch's News Corp.

Not all Web 2.0 have met with such wide acceptance. In 1999, college student Shawn Fanning released a simple application that allowed friends to share larger files more efficiently across the Internet. This application, Napster, was intended to be used to share MP3 music files among friends. However, soon the technology allowed for searching for MP3 files and the music industry, feeling its copyrights were under threat, fought to kill the service. Though successful in killing Napster, the industry hasn't been successful in killing off new versions of peer-to-peer sharing networks. Decentralized peer-sharing software, such as LimeWire, allow users to download free file-sharing software that gives them access to files and programs on other registered users' machines (LimeWire 2006). The legality of sharing copyrighted information via the Internet has been challenged, but these programs sill remain popular with Internet users. Although service providers such as LimeWire have been held harmless from civil lawsuits brought on by copyright holders (it has been established that file-sharing network providers are not responsible for the information contained on their public-access networks), individuals who illegally download copyrighted files and programs have been successfully prosecuted.

Internet and Media Convergence

Web 2.0 has not replaced traditional media content providers. Nearly every major news media outlet has a registered Web page that is updated throughout the day. Some news media sites offer exclusive content online that is not offered in the print or televised edition, and a select few no longer produce print or televised versions. For example, the Web site for *The New York Times,* the most popular print newspaper in America with a daily readership of nearly 5 million, registers nearly 1.1 million daily hits; in addition, the newspaper sends out over 3.3 million news alerts to registered users each day (New York Times 2005). Similar to the news media, several leading radio shows and cable stations, such as The Howard Stern Show (www.howardstern.com) and Comedy Central TV (www.comedycentral.com), now offer their content via the Internet, in addition to posting Web-exclusive content for registered users. Video games have taken advantage of this as well. Gamers can log on and play in each other in games ranging from chess and dominoes to Dungeons and Dragons simulators. Gambling and betting has also become a popular use of the Internet, especially for those users who don't live in areas where casinos are located or permitted. Some estimates claim that over $15 billion is wagered annually in online casinos, many of which are illegally registered (Lemke 2006).

Colleges and universities, traditional information providers, have started offering online classes to students. Community colleges and trade schools have also tapped into this growing trend, and some institutions, including the University of Phoenix (www.universityofphoenix-online.com) offer complete degree programs, including some graduate degrees, without ever requiring a visit to a college campus. Many of these programs cater to working adults and other "non-traditional" students who often don't have time to attend regular college classes.

A different type of information, product information, has become very popular on the Internet. E-commerce is a boon to today's economy, with billions of dollars in transactions annually on goods and services ranging from pizza delivery to an original Picasso (Pascale 2000). Just as many media outlets have included the Internet for part or all of their daily coverage and leading businesses now offer their goods and services for sale online. Research by the Boston Consulting Group showed that, by the end of 1999, online spending accounted for more than $44 billion (Pascale 2000). This trend was not lost on the mainstream retailers. In January 2000, Wal-Mart launched www.wal-mart.com, which offers over 1 million items for sale that can also be found on the shelves of their 5,000-plus store locations worldwide. And eBay, a popular auction house that allows users to buy and trade their personal items online similar to a virtual swap meet or garage sale, reports that over $15 billion annually is transacted on their site between some 42 million registered users (see http://pages.ebay.com/aboutebay.html).

From Personal Information to Personification

For a growing number of 'Net surfers, personal blogs and Web pages simply aren't personal enough. As technology improves, it is now possible for people to create personal characters, or avatars, that occupy virtual "worlds" in a three-dimensional, fully-interactive environment. Popular video game developer Blizzard Entertainment, owners of the Warcraft franchise, have capitalized on this phenomenon in their World of Warcraft game. This game, one of the first massively multiplayer online role-playing games (MMORPGs), boasts over 5 million active players from across the globe who pay a monthly subscription rate, typically around $30 per month, to live in the virtual land of Azeroth and accept the trials and tribulations that come with being a member of the warring factions of Hordes and Alliances (Blizzard 2006).

For users wanting a more "realistic" online living experience, Second Life (www.secondlife.com) offers residents a chance to buy property and live in a world that includes virtual shopping malls, space stations, vampire castles and movie theaters, among other "worldly" amenities. Unlike World of Warcraft, where the focus of the game is primarily challenge and competition, Second Life encourages users to adopt and experiment with an entirely new existence. As of 2006, the site boasts over 175,000 full-time residents who spend over $150,000 US, or $3.75 million Linden Dollars (the official currency of Second Life) daily on everything from virtual land and clothes to other users' characters. And the incentives for living online are appealing; allowances for basic account holders start at $50 Linden Dollars per week and increase with play time, and players who start virtual businesses and host virtual parties and events are rewarded with cash prizes, both in virtual and real dollars (Linden Labs 2006). To date, companies including Adidas, Reebok, Toyota, Nissan, IBM and Starwood Hotels have taken up residence in the Second Life world. Additionally, the news service Reuters has even opened a news bureau in Second Life.

A DIGITAL DIVIDE

As the Internet became more prevalent, an increasing number of public officials in the United States worried that a substantial portion of the population was being denied access to this newest form of telecommunication. In the mid-1990s, the U.S. Department of Commerce was concerned that this new technology was not achieving the goal of "universal service" that is the core of U.S. telecommunications policy (Department of Commerce 1995). In response to this perceived inequity, the Department of Commerce, in conjunction with the National Telecommunications and Information Administration, commissioned a series of reports to investigate the source of the problem. Their first report, released in July 1995, found that the rural poor—those living under the poverty line and away from urban centers—were at a significant "information disadvantage," as only 4.5 percent of these households had a computer, and less than 25 percent of these computers had the technology required for Internet access (i.e., modems and Web browsers). At the same time, urban poor were not doing much better, as less than 8 percent of these people had computers, about 45 percent of which had technology capable of accessing the Internet. Similar divides were found across age and education levels. These findings led to a series of reports on the newly discovered digital divide that appeared to separate the information "haves" from the information "have-nots."

A second report, released in July 1998, showed a significant nationwide increase in Internet access capability (i.e., households owning a computer with a modem). However, the report also identified the same pockets of "have-nots" as the first report, and policy discussions shifted to identifying why these people were still not connected. In November 1999, a third study released by the NTIA identified a promising trend: over one-third of all Americans were now connected to the Internet. For those people who did not have Internet access in the home, they were finding it easier to gain access by using public schools, libraries, and other community access centers. Also, their Internet usage was less recreational than the "haves," as they frequently used the Internet to enroll in college courses or to search for jobs.

By October 2000, a fourth study released by the NTIA showed that nearly 42 percent of Americans were logging onto the Internet, and the "have-nots" were experiencing the highest expansion and growth rates across all identified populations. Although an access gap still existed, the focus of the research had begun to shift to a more positive trend of identifying "digital inclusion" rates rather than a digital divide (Department of Commerce 2000). The final report of the NTIA, released February 2002, found that over 50 percent of the population readily identified as consistent Internet users, and that over 2 million new users sign on to the Internet every month (Department of Commerce 2002). An excerpt from the final page of the report proclaims:

> Our nation has passed a significant milestone now that the majority of Americans use computers and the Internet for their daily activities. This trend is enriching our world, facilitating our work lives, and providing a skill set needed for a growing economy.

Worldwide, the numbers are quite different. Currently, Internet use around the world is only at 16 percent penetration. The lowest penetration rates are in the most populated continents: Asia, representing 56 percent of the world's population, has an Internet penetration rate of only 11 percent. The second largest continent by population, Africa, is home to 14 percent of the world's population, but has an Internet penetration rate of only 4 percent. Compare these rates to Europe (12 percent of world population) and North America (5 percent of world population), which have 32 percent and 69 percent penetration respectively. Although the divide has reduced significantly in some areas of the world, the problem still remains a global issue.

Anybody's 'Net?

Positive trends in U.S. adoption of the Internet may point to issues that still need attention in developing nations. Data from the Pew Internet and American Life Project (2006) estimates that over 147 million U.S. citizens are now online; a number representing over 73 percent of the U.S. population. The report identified three factors that led to the shrinking divide in the United States.

1. Lower cost of access: In the mid-1990s, access to the Internet was not affordable to the average American. Internet Service Providers (ISPs) charged anywhere from \$20 to \$60 per month for subscription-based Internet access, which usually limited Web usage to a few dozen hours per month. Connection speeds were very slow, ranging between 9.6 and 14.4 kilobits per second (keep in mind that a one-page Microsoft Word text-only document is about 23 kb in size) and these connections were often unreliable. Today, a faster, more reliable Internet connection can be installed at home starting at \$6.95 per month for unlimited high-speed access.
2. Less computer knowledge required: Establishing Internet access in the mid-1990s could be difficult for the computer novice, as a working knowledge of networking jargon (e.g., TCP/IP protocol, modem settings, installing additional hardware) was necessary before one could surf the 'Net from home. Often, the monetary and opportunity costs of getting connected were too much for the average person, slowing diffusion (Rogers 2004). The process is much easier today, as ISPs routinely provide software free of charge to new subscribers and connecting the hardware is usually as simple as plugging a color-coded Ethernet or phone cable into the back of your machine and starting the appropriate Web browser program.
3. The Internet has become ubiquitous: Many advertisements in the United States refer the audience to a Web address for more information. Business associates and even men and women on the dating circuit often exchange their e-mail addresses along with (and sometimes in place of) phone numbers. As well, entire businesses, organizations, and communities exist wholly within cyberspace. There is a general assumption and understanding that the Internet is always there, and is readily accessible to meet our diverse information and entertainment needs.

CONCLUSION

The precursors of the Internet have outlived their usefulness. The ARPANET shut down in 1990 and the original NSFNET backbone followed in 1995.The NSF created the vBNS (very high performance backbone network service) through MCI in 1994 and it was used to link supercomputer centers sponsored by NSF. Nonetheless, there remains a place on the Internet restricted from trade and dedicated to researching and developing new communication technologies. Internet2, the very-high-speed backbone network, was created in 1996 and limited to research only. Internet2 is a project of the University Consortium for Advanced Internet Development (UCAID) and it uses both the vBNS network and the Abilene Network from QWEST to achieve desired flexibility. Internet2 continues to expand the horizons of new technologies, introducing richer communication experiences via three-dimensional immersive environments.

The Internet was born of the excitement of solving complex engineering problems in an open and collaborative manner. This led to an open-architecture design that has been flexible enough to support exponential growth in hosts and users as well as technological innovation in software. With a minimum of governance, the Internet has grown to be the information infrastructure for the twenty-first century, supporting the exchange of audio and video files, animations such as Shockwave Flash, three-dimensional interfaces such as VRML, media wrappers such as QuickTime, chat rooms, and instant messaging. Web 2.0 offers the vision of new user participation on the content end.

As the Internet has become more inclusive, it has grown to reflect the interests and ideas of a broad spectrum of people around the world. Despite tremendous expansion, it remains a forum for the exchange of ideas and information; what has changed is who is exchanging ideas. Truly an egalitarian forum, the Internet has expanded well beyond the technical details of engineers and scientists into the art and introspections of a great variety of people around the world. It is difficult to imagine where innovations on the Internet will take us, but it is clear we will never see the Internet in its final form. If future designers adhere to the simple rules of the Internet pioneers—an open architecture built through cooperation—we will likely never see the Internet stop evolving.

GLOSSARY

Advanced Research Projects Agency Network (ARPANET): Created by the U.S. Advanced Research Agency (ARPA) in 1969. ARPANET was a wide area network linking computers at various university research centers. ARPANET is considered the precursor to the modern-day Internet.

Analog: Electronic transmissions that represent data by continuous signals of varying frequency (versus being sent as an "on or off" data transmission; see *Digital*).

Circuit switching: A communication technology in which a dedicated path is established between the source and destination for the duration of the transmission. The telephone network is an example of a circuit-switching network.

Digital: Electronic transmissions that represent data in various combinations or strings of 1's and 0's, with 1 representing "on," or "positive, and 0 representing "off," or "nonpositive."

Host: A computer system containing data that is accessed by a user at a remote location.

Interface message processors (IMP): Smaller, intermediate computers connected to the mainframes involved in ARPANET. The IMPS were packet switches dedicated to the communications "subnet."

Internet: A vast system of linked computer networks, international in scope, that facilitates data transfer and communication services, such as remote log-in, file transfer (FTP), electronic mail (e-mail), newsgroups, and the World Wide Web (www); always capitalized.

Intranet: Internal network utilized within organizations allowing file sharing and collaboration. Intranets cannot (generally) be accessed from outside the organization.

IP address: A numeric address that identifies host computers on the Internet.

Local area network (LAN): A network that connects computers in a relatively small geographical area (generally no more than 2 miles). LANs are used in offices, buildings, or a set of buildings.

Network: A collection of two or more computers (and/or printers, routers, switches, or other devices) connected to one another allowing data to be shared and used over communication paths.

Network control protocol: The host-to-host protocol of the ARPANET that operated above the layer of packet switching implemented in the IMPs. Once ARPANET transitioned from NCP to TCP/IP, it was possible to connect to other independent networks.

Node: A connection point in a network, either for redistribution of data or as an end point for data transmissions.

Packet switching: Method used to efficiently move data around on a network. Data is divided into smaller pieces called packets, assigned a number and destination, sent independently through the network, and reassembled at the other end.

Protocol: Formal set of rules that govern how devices on a network exchange information; the "language" of a network.

Request for comment (RFC): Document series used among researchers as the primary means of communicating ideas and information about the Internet.

Router The device that forwards packets between networks.

Transmission control protocol/Internet protocol (TCP/IP): The common language that allows existing networks to be connected, or "inter-networked." TCP implements flow control and recovery in packet switching, and IP is used for addressing and forwarding individual packets. TCP runs over IP and the two form part of a layered protocol stack.

Uniform resource locator (URL): A character string describing the location and access method of a resource on the Internet.

World Wide Web: Invented in 1991 by Tim Berners-Lee, the World Wide Web is an application that facilitates exchange of documents via the Internet. It uses a variety of protocols including: HTTP, HTML, FTP, VRML, XML, and SSL.

CROSS REFERENCES

See *Internet Domain Name System*; *Internet2*; *The Internet Fundamentals*.

REFERENCES

Abbate, J. 1999. *Inventing the Internet*. Cambridge, MA: MIT Press.

Anderberg, A. 2002. History of the Internet and Web. http://www.anderbergfamily.net/ant/history (accessed August 1, 2002).

Anklesaria, F., M. McCahill, P. Lindner, D. Johnson, D. Torrey, and B. Alberti. 1993. *RFC 1436—The Internet Gopher protocol*. http://www.ietf.org/rfc/rfc 1436.txt (accessed August 30, 2002).

Baran, P. 1964. On distributed communications networks. http://www.rand.org/publications/RM/baran.list.html (accessed August 4, 2002).

Berners-Lee, T. 1999. *Weaving the Web: The original design and ultimate destiny of the World Wide Web by its inventor*. San Francisco: Harper.

Blizzard. 2006. Company profile. http://www.blizzard.com/inblizz/profile.shtml (accessed August 10, 2006).

Bush, V. 1945. As we may think. *The Atlantic Monthly* 176(1):101–8. http://www.theatlantic.com/unbound/flashbks/computer/bushf.htm (accessed August 14, 2002).

Cerf, V.G., and R.E. Kahn. 1974. A protocol for packet network interconnection. *IEEE Trans. Communication Technology* 5:627–41.

CNN. 2002. Netscape sues Microsoft. http://money.cnn.com/2002/01/22/technology/netscape (accessed August 14, 2002).

Crocker, S. 1969. Host software: Network working group request for comment 1. http://www.faqs.org/rfcs/rfc1.html (accessed August 6, 2002).

Davies, D. 1966. *Proposal for a digital communication network*. Unpublished manuscript.

Davies, D.W., K. Bartlett, R. Cantlebury, and P. Wilkinson. 1967. *A digital communications network for computers giving rapid response at remote terminals*. Paper presented at the Association for Computing Machinery Symposium on Operating Systems Principles, Gatlinburg, Tennessee, October 1-4, 1967.

Duffy, M. 2006. A Dad's encounter with The Vortex of Facebook. *Time*. 167(13):52–3. http://www.time.com/time/archive/preview/0,10987,1174704,00.html (accessed July 27, 2006).

Electronic Frontier Foundation. (n.d.). RIAA v. the people. http://www.eff.org/IP/P2P/riaa-v-thepeople.php (accessed April 10, 2006).

Family Safe Media. 2006. Pornography statistics. http://www.familysafemedia.com/pornography_statistics.html (accessed April 11, 2006).

Google. 2006. Google milestones. http://www.google.com/corporate/history.html (accessed April 10, 2006).

Hafner, K., and M. Lyon. 1996. *Where wizards stay up late: The origins of the Internet*. New York: Simon & Schuster.

Hagenbuch, S. 2006. MySpace: The music place. Elmira/Corning (NY) Star-Gazette. http://www.stargazette-news.com/apps/pbcs.dll/article?AID=/20060326/LIFE/603260335 (accessed April 11, 2006).

Hammonds, K. 2003. How Google Grows...and Grows...and Grows. Fast Company. http://www.fastcompany.com/magazine/69/google.html (accessed April 10, 2006).

Harris Interactive. 2003. The Harris Poll No. 8: Those with Internet access to continue to grow but at a slower rate. http://www.harrisinteractive.com/harris_poll/index.asp?PID=356 (April 10, 2006).

Internet Society. 1999. Request for comments 2555: 30 years of RFCs. ftp://ftp.isi.edu/in-notes/rfc2555.txt (accessed August 3, 2002).

Kahn, R.E. 1994. The role of the government in the evolution of the Internet. In *Revolution in the U.S. information infrastructure*. http://www.nap.edu/readingroom/books/newpath/chap2.html (accessed February 17, 2006).

Kelly, K. 2005. We are the web. *Wired* 13(8):43–48. http://www.wired.com/wired/archive/13.08/tech.html (accessed October 23, 2006).

Kleinrock, L. 1961. Information flow in large communication nets. Unpublished doctoral dissertation, Massachusetts Institute of Technology. http://www.lk.cs.ucla.edu/LK/Bib/REPORT/PhD/part1 (accessed February 17, 2005).

Kleinrock, L. 1964. *Communication nets: Stochastic message flow and delay*. New York: McGraw-Hill.

Kleinrock, L. 1976. *Queueing systems*, Volume II. New York: John Wiley & Sons.

Leiner, B.M., V.G. Cerf, D.D. Clark, R.E. Kahn, L. Kleinrock, D.C. Lynch, J. Postel, L.G. Roberts, and S. Wolff. 1994. A brief history of the Internet. http://www.isoc.org/internet/history/brief.shtml (accessed May 17, 2002).

Lemke, T. 2006. Odds favor Internet gambling. *The Washington Times*. http://washingtontimes.com/specialreport/20060319-010156-2817r.htm (accessed April 10, 2006).

Licklider, J.C.R 1960. Man-computer symbiosis. *IRE Transactions on Human Factors in Electronics* HFE-1:4–11. ftp://gatekeeper.research.compaq.com/pub/DEC/SRC/research-reports/SRC061.pdf (accessed May 10, 2002).

Licklider, J.C.R., and W.E. Clark. 1962. On-line man-computer communication. *Proceedings of the AFIPS SJCC* 21:113–128.

LimeWire. 2006. Company background. http://www.limewire.com/english/content/corporate.shtml (accessed April 10, 2006).

Linden Labs. 2006. What is Second Life? http://secondlife.com/whatis/ (accessed April 10, 2006).

Madden, M. 2006. Pew Internet and American Life Project: Internet penetration and impact. http://www.pewinternet.org/PPF/r/182/report_display.asp (accessed April 28, 2006).

Marill, T., and L.G. Roberts. 1966. Toward a cooperative network of timeshared computers. *AFIPS Conf Proc. FJCC* 29:425–32.

Microsoft. 2002. Windows operating systems family history. http://www.microsoft.com/windows/WinHistoryIntro.mspx (accessed August 30, 2002).

Mockapetris, P. 1983a. RFC 882—Domain names: Concepts and facilities. http://www.ietf.org/rfc/rfc882.txt (accessed August 30, 2002).

Mockapetris, P. 1983b. RFC 883—Domain names: Implementation and specification. http://www.ietf.org/rfc/rfc883.txt (accessed August 30, 2002).

Moschovitis, C.J.P., H. Poole, T. Schuyler, and T.M. Senft. 1999. *History of the Internet: A chronology, 1843 to present*. Santa Barbara, CA: ABC-CLIO.

National Science Foundation 1986. NSF network news. http://www.cni.org/docs/infopols/NSF.html (accessed August 30, 2002).

New York Times. 2005. Did you know: Facts about The New York Times 2005. http://www.nytco.com/pdf/didyouknow.pdf (accessed April 11, 2006).

Pascale, M. 2000. 4th annual electronic marketing survey—Online catalogers. Multichannel Merchant. http://multichannelmerchant.com/catalogage/mag/marketing_th_annual_electronic/index.html (accessed July 27, 2006).

Protect Kids. n.d. Internet dangers: Internet porn fact sheet. http://www.protectkids.com/dangers/stats.htm#cyberporn (accessed April 11, 2006).

RFC-Editor Homepage. n.d. The request for comments. http://www.rfc-editor.org (accessed August 2, 2002).

Segaller, S. 1998. *Nerds 2.0.1: A brief history of the Internet*. New York: TV Books.

Turing, A.M. 1950. Computing machinery and intelligence. *Mind* 59:433–460.

U.S. Department of Commerce. 1995. Falling through the 'Net: A survey of the "have nots" in rural and urban America. http://www.ntia.doc.gov/ntiahome/fallingthru.html (accessed April 10, 2006).

U.S. Department of Commerce. 1999. Falling through the 'Net: Defining the digital divide. http://www.ntia.doc.gov/ntiahome/fttn99/contents.html (accessed April 10, 2006).

U.S. Department of Commerce. 2000. Falling through the 'Net: Toward digital inclusion. http://www.ntia.doc.gov/ntiahome/fttn00/contents00.html (accessed April 10, 2006).

U.S. Department of Commerce. 2002. A nation online: Internet use in America. http://www.ntia.doc.gov/opadhome/digitalnation/index_2002.html (accessed April 10, 2006).

Zakon, R.H. 2002. Hobbes Internet timeline v. 5.6. http://www.zakon.org/robert/internet/timeline (accessed October 16, 2006).

Internet2®

Linda Bruenjes, *Lasell College*, Carolyn Siccama, *University of Massachusetts, Lowell*

INTRODUCTION

The Internet2 project was established in 1996 by a consortium of universities, corporations, and government agencies to support a variety of academic innovations requiring advanced networking capabilities. Currently, more than 200 universities, 60 corporations, and 40 affiliate members compose this "invitation-only" initiative, which serves an estimated 5 to 10 million people.

The mission of Internet2 is to improve scholarship and serve the needs of academics in universities, colleges, and schools with cutting-edge data processing solutions. The goals of the Internet2 consortium are to create a leading edge network capability for the national research community, to enable the development of revolutionary Internet applications, and to ensure the rapid transfer of new network services and applications to the broader Internet community. This next generation Internet promises to do what academics and researchers hoped the first generation Internet would do; that is, allow scholars to make use of its potential to collaborate with colleagues, researchers, and students around the world across a secure, uncongested, high-speed network.

SHORT HISTORY OF THE INTERNET

Origins

Rooted in the military culture of the cold war, the Internet's original ancestor was established at the Advanced Research Projects Agency (ARPA) of the U.S. Department of Defense. It was called ARPANET and was created out of the need for a robust, redundant system capable of carrying critical military data throughout a relatively small network of then-powerful computers. Serving as a critical element of military preparedness and civil defense, ARPANET was designed to function regardless of any kind of network disruption, no matter how cataclysmic. The original ARPANET has been replaced by a succession of bigger, faster, more powerful networked systems, leading to today's Internet. Sensing the potential of distributed computing for science discovery and application, the National Science Foundation (NSF) created a network dedicated to academic research and development based on the ARPA's Internet protocol. Operating from a system of regional computing systems interwoven by an Internet "backbone," the Internet offered researchers immediate access to colleagues and files throughout the world.

The Internet has grown into a loose amalgam of individual networks and computer systems, all operating according to agreed-upon network protocols allowing the worldwide transfer of information among systems built on a variety of operating platforms. As distinct from many of the well known commercial online network service providers (e.g., *America Online*, *AT&T Worldnet*), no individual, company, agency, or institution owns the Internet. It is a distributed system of interconnected computers and networks. This means that no single hyper computer or super network drives it. Rather, it is an enormous, electronic global neighborhood where some houses are bigger and more luxurious than others, but each one arranges its own furniture and landscaping.

The Internet's origin may be traced back to an American sense of shock and fear caused by the 1957 launch of Russia's first-ever space orbiting satellite, Sputnik. The earliest Internet-type operation was launched in 1969. At the time, this network was composed of four hosts (UCLA, Stanford, UC San Bernardino, and the University of Utah). By 1982, the Internet had grown to more than 200 hosts. By 1995, there were almost 6 million hosts, and at the end of 2005, the number had grown to more than 353 million.

Over 200 countries are now connected to the Internet (post-Taliban Afghanistan has recently become connected.) When we add other networks capable of interfacing with the Internet in some manner or other, the number of nations increases still further. As of December 2005, Zakon (2005) placed the number of Web servers at more than 70 million. Because most servers host multiple

Table 1: Internet Timeline

Year	Event
1957	First orbiting space satellite, Sputnik, launched by the former USSR
1963	First dial-up modem developed
1969	Four-node ARPANET established with network speed of 50 kpbs
1972	First e-mail message sent using the @ sign; first computer chat undertaken
1976	First Internet routers developed; Queen Elizabeth II sends e-mail
1977	First Transport Control Protocol (TCP) developed
1979	Emoticons ";-)" first appear in e-mail messages as antidote to dry text
1980	Accidental virus brings ARPANET temporarily to a halt
1982	TCP/IP protocol established as technical standard to drive Internet traffic
Mid-80s	Loose coalition of networks in ARPANET becomes known as Internet
1988	"Worm" infects 10 percent of all Internet hosts
1989	Creation of interconnected regional academic networks
1990	ARPANET decommissioned, leaving a loose network of networks, the Internet
1991	World Wide Web and Gopher are launched
1992	First Internet audio and video transmissions
1993	MOSAIC, the first GUI Web browser released; White House comes online
1994	First banner ads appear on the Web; first pizza ordered online
1995	Real-time audio streaming technology launched; Radio Hong Kong hits the Internet
1996	Internet becomes truly global; US Communications Decency Act (CDA) passed
1997	CDA ruled unconstitutional; Microsoft challenges Netscape with MSIE browser
1998	US Postal Service sells stamps for downloading and printing from the Web
1999	Securities fraud on Web raises a small company's stock price by 31percent in one day
2000	Catastrophic "denial of service" attacks launched against Amazon, eBay, and Yahoo
2001	Napster forced to suspend free service; resumes shakily as a subscription service
2002	Internet boasts more than 147,000,000 hosts (727,000 in 1992; 235 in 1982)
2003	Apple Computer introduces Apple iTunes music store; sells songs for .99 cents each
2004	Network Solutions begins offering 100 year domain registration
2005	"Podcast" is Word of the Year

Source: Public Broadcasting Service. 1997. "Life on the Internet: Timeline." http://www.pbs.org/internet/timeline/timeline-txt.html (accessed May 22, 2002); Zakon, R. H. 2005. "Hobbes' Internet Timeline." http://www.zakon.org/Robert/internet/timeline (accessed May 30, 2006); Verizon Corporation. 2001. "Who We Are: BBN Timeline." http://www.bbn.com/timeline (accessed May 22, 2002); Infoplease. 2006. "Internet Timeline." http://www.infoplease.com/ipa/A0193167.html (accessed May 30, 2006); Oxford University Press. 2006. "Podcast" is Word of the Year." http://www.us.oup.com/us/brochure/NOAD_podcast/?view=usa (accessed May 30, 2006).

Web sites, the number of sites would be in the hundreds of millions.

Some noteworthy Internet benchmarks are illustrated in Table 1.

With such growth has come a change in purpose and tone. In its earliest incarnation, the primary Internet purpose was military. As the Internet moved beyond military use, its function shifted to research and scholarship. At the dawn of the 1990s, the Web had neither entered the national lay consciousness nor had it become viable for commercial transaction. The 1990s changed all of that. In the industrially developed world, the Internet became an indispensable tool for all kinds of business, serving vendors, and consumers alike. As a result, the charitable camaraderie that characterized a relatively small number of Web users in the early 1990s has now become primarily a commercial marketplace, in which transactions for information, misinformation, financial services, transportation, products, education, romance, entertainment, culture, hate, and pornography are routinely carried out. From an earlier culture of open information sharing, a more defensive posture to protect commercial and personal interests has emerged. By the year 2000, the old neighborhood had changed for good.

With this change has appeared the ever-growing danger of mischief, intellectual property theft, and malicious destruction. Ever more devastating computer viruses and worms spring up faster than updated virus protection software can thwart them. Major institutional networks have been disabled for days at a time and sometimes longer by viruses such as *Melissa* (1999), *Love Letter* (2000), *Nimda* and *Code Red* (2001), *SQL Slammer* (2003), *and Kama Sutra* (2006). Network hackers have broken into the presumably secure private networks of major corporations (e.g., Microsoft), transportation services (e.g., British Rail), and the governments of several nations (e.g., the U.S. Senate). Predators have harmed children. Meanwhile, a passionate debate rages between those who advocate for legal restraints on putatively harmful Internet exploitation and those who value intellectual freedom above everything.

Globalization

Although a worldwide affiliation of groups vocally oppose economic and cultural globalization, Internet-based e-commerce has not only made common business transactions more accessible to global markets but has also created exponentially richer international choices in education, entertainment, and culture. For example, classical music buffs may choose from nearly 100 radio stations worldwide, many of them uninterrupted by annoying commercials. Such a shift in the network zeitgeist has created many employment opportunities and threatened others (e.g., travel agents). The Internet domain naming system, at one time limited to only six categories (*.com, .edu, .gov, .mil, .net,* and *.org*) has added several categories to accommodate growth (e.g., *.biz, . info, .name, .us, .tv, .museum* and *.aero*). Partly because of the inchoate spawning of commercial traffic, Internet2 represents an effort to regain the prominent place for research and education that formerly dominated the original Internet.

THE TRANSFORMATION: INTERNET TO INTERNET2®

The introduction of graphical user interface browsers forever changed the face of the Internet. Rather than a medium used only by those who understood how to navigate a text only protocol, the Internet became accessible to anyone who could operate a mouse and a keyboard thus creating congestion on a network that was not originally developed to handle this type of traffic.

Solutions to these network traffic problems, much like solutions to highway traffic problems, continue to be inadequate. At the same time that colleges and universities are trying to speed up and protect the delivery of data via the Internet with the addition of T1 and T3 lines, the demand for additional bandwidth has increased. The need to speed up the delivery of information has led to the creation of a new Internet protocol, IPv6 or Internet protocol version 6, which is currently being promoted and coordinated by the Internet2 IPv6 Working Group. IPv6 allows files to be transported as one packet to many locations and promotes the collaborative participation envisioned by the original designers of the Internet. High-capacity and high-speed delivery of data can be achieved once universities join the members-only Internet2 consortium.

THE INTERNET2® CONSORTIUM

This new generation high-speed network has been developed by the Internet2 consortium, which is a nonprofit research and development consortium that is currently led by over 200 universities in the United States. Member universities work in partnership with industry and government organizations to develop and deploy advanced Internet applications and technology (Internet2 2005a). The Internet2 consortium is governed by a board of trustees primarily composed of the presidents of the Internet2 university members. This board of trustees also governs the University Corporation for Advanced Internet Development (UCAID), which is the formal nonprofit organization that was formed to manage the activities, programs, dues, expenditures of Internet2.

The Vision

The essence of this new generation of network-based applications is to recreate the mission of the first generation Internet; that is, use advanced technology to support a variety of academic innovations that are designed to improve scholarship and allow for collaboration among colleagues and students around the world while serving the needs of academics in universities, colleges, and schools that require cutting-edge data processing solutions.

There is no doubt that the Internet has impacted teaching, learning, and research in a very important way. Interaction between faculty and students using online communication and course management tools have engaged students in learning experiences beyond the walls of the classroom. The Internet also provides the accessibility of online library materials any time of the day or night from computers located in coffee shops, airports, homes, and workplaces. Even while these advances are significant, Internet2 visionaries suggest that a new generation of network-based applications necessitates the need to build a unique environment that "will engender new possibilities for the synthesis of ideas that can ultimately lead to the creation of important new knowledge" (Wasley 1996). The current generation Internet cannot accommodate these needs.

Developing Tomorrow's Internet

Contrary to the unfettered growth of the first generation Internet, growth of the Internet2 has been controlled. Douglas E. Van Houweling, the current president and CEO of Internet2 works with a core staff of individuals who support the work of Internet2 members, overseeing three critical areas: 1) member and partner relations, 2) technology direction and development, and 3) deployment and infrastructure delivery. Their mission is to develop and deploy advanced network applications and technologies and then to transfer these new developments to the broader educational and network communities to create what is being called "tomorrow's Internet" (Internet2 2005a). Some of these new technologies such as IPv6, multicasting, and quality of service (QoS) will help to create a foundation upon which revolutionary network applications can be created. Completely new applications such as digital libraries, virtual laboratories, distance-independent learning and tele-immersion, inconceivable on the commodity Internet, have become a reality on the high-speed and high-capacity network associated with Internet2 (Internet2 2005d). Long-term, the goals of Internet2 are to accelerate the transfer and diffusion of these new developments into the commercial and public sectors, including K-12 educational environments and public libraries with a "focus on providing Internet2 capabilities to people with vision who have ideas how to use the network" (Van Houweling 2006).

The Partners

At the core of Internet2 collaborations are the partnerships. The partnerships between academia, industry, government and international organizations that existed when today's Internet was being created are being recreated to help develop and deploy Internet2 advanced networking technologies (Internet2 2005f). It is because of the close collaborations between Internet2 partners that research and development initiatives have been made possible.

Internet2 Government Partners

The United States government provides important support for Internet2 projects and initiatives. Internet2 and various United States government agencies have forged connections on many levels; however, the main role of Internet2 government partners has been to support innovation at the principal investigator or institutional level. The federal government also supports the link between Abilene and Internet2 international partners. Many federal agencies such as the National Science Foundation, United States Census Bureau, National Institutes of Health, the National Aeronautics and Space Administration, the National Oceanic and Atmospheric Administration, and the Library of Congress are Internet2 Affiliate members. Many Internet2 member universities work in partnerships with federal agencies to research new Internet technologies, and Internet2 is a key collaborator in many federally funded projects. On a policy level, Internet2 monitors, analyzes and advocates on federal Internet policy issues. The federal government has its own advanced Internet initiative, the Large Scale Networking Effort, and more recently, the National Science Foundation has created the Office of Cyberinfrastructure to stimulate advances in science and engineering research and education. To sustain and achieve both national and international goals for the advancement of Internet technologies, the United States government, along with international network organizations, are critical partners for Internet2.

National LambdaRail

At a national level within the United States, one new partnership is currently under negotiation between Internet2 and the National LambdaRail (NLR). In the summer of 2005, the Internet2 Board and the NLR Board voted to pursue discussions of a merger of the two consortiums. A consortium of leading U.S. research institutions and private sector technology companies, the NLR owns and operates a national fiber-optic network that covers 10,000 miles across the United States. According to Tracy Futhey (2005), chair of the NLR board of directors, "as long as the two organizations have a shared goal and can provide complementary benefits, they can find ways to harmoniously coexist, be that in the current organizational forms and with the existing services of each or in some modified organizational structure" (p. 81).

International Partners

Internationally, Internet2 has partnered with over 40 organizations in Latin America, South America, Canada, Asia, the Pacific Rim, Europe, and the Middle East. The link between Internet2 and their international counterparts is a memorandum of understanding (MoU), which allows the international advanced network organizations to participate in Internet2 activities and connect to Abilene via a NGIX (next generation Internet eXchange point), gigaPop, or a peer network (Internet2 2005g, 2005l). The goals of the international partnerships are critical for Internet2 to ensure global interoperability, to enable research and education on a global scale, and to enable global collaboration between faculty, researchers and students with their international colleagues (Internet2 2005k). Internet2 international partners are organizations that have similar and parallel goals to Internet2, however they are not Internet2 members and do not pay membership dues.

Membership in the Internet2 Consortium

Membership in the Internet2 consortium is open to U.S. universities, corporations, and nonprofit research-oriented organizations (Internet2 2005p). To become a member of Internet2 there is a very specific and structured application process for each of the four different types of membership options: university (or regular), corporate, affiliate, and association. Corporations have three options for membership, which include corporate partner, corporate sponsor, and corporate member. Setting these three options apart are the expectations of goods and services that corporations will contribute to university or affiliate members. Those applying for affiliate membership can apply as an affiliate member or affiliate members with collaboration site status (Internet2 2005m).

Members of Internet2 do not automatically become connected to the high-speed backbone of the Internet2, Abilene. Only university members, affiliate members with collaboration site status, or a corporate collaboration site can connect to Internet2 high-performance networks. As of January 1, 2007, the membership types eligible to become connected to Abilene pay annual dues of $30,000. In addition, they pay a $22,000 Abilene primary participation fee as well as Abilene connection fees. The Abilene connection fees are bandwidth dependent and can cost anywhere from $220,000 for OC12 SONET to $480,000 to 10 GigE (10 Gbps). Those membership types not eligible for Abilene connections pay according to their membership type with annual costs ranging from $2,700 to $12,000.

THE INFRASTRUCTURE

Presently, the underlying foundation of the Internet2 infrastructure is based on a series of simple to complex connections to a high-performance backbone network known as Abilene. Internet2 members may be connected to the backbone through universities, affiliate members, regional networks or gigaPOPs, which serve as network hubs or aggregation points. Abilene provides advanced network capabilities to Internet2 members in all fifty states as well as Puerto Rico and the District of Columbia. Internet2 connections are also available to Abilene sponsored participants such as community colleges, hospitals, museums, and colleges and universities as well as to Abilene Sponsored Education Group Participants (SEGPs).

Networks

In operation since 1999, the Abilene network was named after a railhead established in Kansas in 1880. Like its namesake, Abilene sees itself on the edge of a new frontier and has set its sights on providing an advanced network that will support innovative applications, advanced services not available on the commodity Internet, global connectivity to advance collaborative research efforts, and access to a rich source of data collections (Abilene 2006c). Currently, the Abilene network "is an OC-192c (10 Gbps) backbone employing optical transport technology and advanced high-performance routers" (Abilene 2006b, 1). Capable of providing speeds of 10 gigabits per second, the goal of the Internet2 Abilene dual-stack IPv4/IPv6 network is to "offer 100 megabits per second of connectivity between every Abilene connected desktop" (Abilene 2006a, 1). The transmission speed of Abilene, 10 Gbps, is more than 15,000 times faster than a typical home broadband connection (Pollak 2004).

The main concern with the standard Internet Protocol, IPv4, is that it has been deemed inadequate to handle the volume of addresses needed to connect wired and wireless computers, handheld devices, cell phones, and other mobile electronic devices to the Internet. On the other hand, IPv6, the upgraded Internet Protocol, promises to deliver an estimated 340 trillion trillion trillion addresses; a vast improvement over the 4 billion addresses currently available (Internet2 2006d). This enhanced Internet Protocol will offer improved security, efficiency, and quality of service.

> As IPv6 is deployed around the globe, more applications will be designed to use it, including high-quality streaming and interactive video that has become integral to the work of the research and education community. Internet2 members will be able to take advantage of IPv6 multicast connectivity not only within the Abilene network but also with their peers in Asia and Europe, where IPv6 deployment is progressing very quickly. (Rotman, L., personal communication, October 31, 2005)

One way to test the speeds and capabilities of new advanced networks is via the Internet2 Land Speed Record competition. The Internet2 Land Speed Record competition was inaugurated in 2000 by computer science pioneers Jim Gray and Gordon Bell who understood that "to realize Internet's full potential, end-to-end network performance needs to take a huge leap forward" (Internet2 2006b, 1). The first Land Speed Record for the highest bandwidth, end-to-end networks using IPv4 was set in March 2000 with a transmission rate of 751 megabits per second. In 2005, the Land Speed Record using IPv6 was set with an average throughput of 5.58 gigabits per second. This competition had led to some break through speeds culminating in April 2006 when an international team lead by the University of Tokyo transferred data using IPv6 at a rate of 6.96 Gbps and IPv4 at a rate of 8.80 Gbps. Although it is believed that the latest IPv4 record may be the last using 10Gbps networks, new networking techniques may mean increased performance for future IPv6 networks.

Current research is now pushing the standard infrastructure for network architecture. Both the standard internet protocol, IPv4, and the upgraded internet protocol, IPv6, use IP packet switches as the basis of their infrastructure. This is currently changing as new research in networking is currently being conducted. The Internet2 Hybrid Optical and Packet Infrastructure (HOPI) project is currently developing and testing an infrastructure that consists of a hybrid of packet and circuit switched optical networks. Tests and experiments on hybrid networks are currently using resources from both the Internet2 Abilene network and the National LambdaRail infrastructure. In early 2006 it is being reported that the experiments done so far have been "used to create dedicated transcontinental network circuits that reliably transmit terabytes of radioastronomy data" (HOPI 2006, 2). Critical to the reliable transmission of such vast quantities of data is the software, or middleware, that creates the link between the network and the application. Researchers are inventing new middleware that will facilitate the unprecedented sharing of intellectual resources.

Middleware

Middleware is Internet2's system of standardizing identification, authentication, authorization, directory, and security services to allow for a smooth and secure collaboration between members. To meet the mission of systemizing core services at Internet2 universities (Internet2 2006c), a number of core activities address the fundamental infrastructure in order to promote policies and best practices:

- Authentication of core identity
- Permissions for authenticated users
- Interoperability of databases
- Clarify identifier types, forms, and policies
- Address issues related to the use of certificates for individual authentication, email encryption, digital signatures, and access control

Additionally there are middleware development projects addressing unique issues related to healthcare education and practice, mailing-list services, and video conferencing. Essential to the operation and development of the Internet2 networks and middleware initiatives are the associated research and development initiatives focused on network security.

Security

Current approaches to network security on today's commercial Internet cannot meet the security requirements of high-performance and advanced networks. A few different affiliated, yet independent, organizations, and task forces have formed to collaborate on the challenges that exist relating to network security and Internet2. Internet2 security initiatives are advised by SALSA, a group of leading campus network security architects (Internet2 2005n) and is considered to be "future-oriented and state-of-the-art in nature, focusing on high performance and advanced networks" (Internet2 2005r, 1). Their task is to address the issues related to security architecture and how it interrelates with network performance, deployability, support, and protection. Working groups within SALSA have formed to look deeper at specific issues related to authorized network access, transit traffic, forensic support for investigation of abuse and the deployment of a pilot federated wireless network authentication system (EDUCAUSE 2005).

Internet2 security initiatives are also part of the Computer and Network Security Task Force. Various working groups within the Computer and Network Security Task Force work to pursue projects and initiatives related to four strategic goals: 1) education and awareness, 2) standards, policies, and procedures, 3) security architecture and tools, and 4) organization and information sharing. Such working groups and task forces are an integral part of the Internet2 community and serve to "provide intellectual capital and shared will to develop solutions" (Internet2 2006g, 1).

Development Activities

In early 2006, there were nineteen active working groups (WGs), sixteen special interest groups (SIGs), and ten advisory groups (AGs). WGs perform specific tasks, SIGs are mainly issue driven discussion groups, and AGs bring in a specific expertise to work with one or more working groups. Most of the groups have Web sites that specify their goals, purpose, members, and progress.

APPLICATIONS OF INTERNET2® TECHNOLOGIES

The applications being developed for Internet2 are so advanced that they are expected to significantly change and improve how we conduct research and engage in teaching and learning in higher education (Internet2 2005h). Attributes unique to Internet2 applications include such features as interactive collaboration, real-time access to remote resources, large scale, multisite computation and data mining, shared virtual reality, or any combination of these attributes (Internet2 2004). Once developed, these applications will not run on today's commercial Internet, because they require advanced networking features such as high bandwidth, low latency, and multicast (Internet2 2005h). The National Laboratory for Applied Network Research, via their Advanced Applications Database (AAD), and Pace University, via their Base^2 System, are two examples that provide Web-based searchable databases of advanced software applications developed and running on advanced networks such as Internet2 (Base2 2005; NLANR/DAST 2005).

Members of the Internet2 community who wish to keep abreast of Internet2 application priorities and initiatives can look to the Applications Strategy Council (ASC), Industry Strategy Council (ISC), and the Network Research Liaison Council (NRLC) for current information. Although each of these councils have specific goals, their missions are interrelated. The ASC advises on matters related to the design and development of applications for research and education (Internet2 2005b). The ISC provides a strategic vision related to advanced networking and applications development and helps focus technology transfer aspects of Internet2 initiatives (Internet2 2005e). The NRLC helps identify priorities related to adapting computer systems to fit the Internet2 infrastructure, including research, access, and prototype deployment (Internet2 2005q).

The development of Internet2 applications spans across a number of disciplines from science and engineering to the arts and humanities. The following sections provide insight into some of the Internet2 applications being developed in four broad disciplines.

Health Sciences

Current Internet2 health science applications include areas such as medical education, virtual reality, and telepathology all of which require advanced network capability (Internet2 2005j). The Department of Community Medicine at West Virginia University School of Medicine uses Internet2 technology to conduct their monthly Public Health Grand Rounds series allowing practitioners from around the world to participate in discussions of case histories related to public health concerns (*Public Health Grand Rounds WebCast* 2005). To promote use and understanding of advanced networks and their applications in healthcare, the National Library of Medicine is working with Internet2 to showcase their tutorial "Advanced Networks and Applications in Healthcare." Such tutorials are being developed as a way to inform health care providers about the advantages of high-performance networks in delivering healthcare (Internet2 2005o).

At the same time, doctors at Stanford University have created a Virtual Reality experience for medical students called Anatomy and Surgery Simulation Over the Internet project. The purpose of this project is to teach surgical techniques online. By having access to an anatomical database over Internet2, students can manipulate anatomical structures by seeing it in multiple dimensions as well as feel the anatomical structure with a new technology called haptics (Ackerman 2003).

Arts and Humanities

Innovative Internet2 applications in the arts and humanities include collaborative live performances, master classes, and remote auditions (Internet2 2005i). There are currently many different types of pilot music projects being conducted to test the capabilities and limitations of the advanced networks available today. Many of the Internet2 applications in the arts and humanities are using a medium called the Access Grid. The Access Grid allows users to interact simultaneously via multi-conferencing from up to fifty different sites around the world (Deal 2005) allowing for the broadcasting of productions from remote locations. For example, the *Cultivating Communities: Dance in the Digital Age* project conducted at the fall 2002 Internet2 member meeting featured a showcase of regional dance and music from the University of Southern California where live performers interacted remotely with performers from the University of Oklahoma, University of Illinois at Urbana—Champaign, New World Symphony in Miami, FL, Case Western University, and the Cleveland Institute of Music.

Additional exciting and relevant applications of this technology are also being used by museums and archeologists, as well as by foreign languages instructors (Doyle 2005). For example, the University of Pennsylvania Museum of Archeology and Anthropology recently used Internet2 to collaborate and consult with master Tlingit, fiber craftsman from Alaska, to examine 100-year-old textiles and baskets over a 3,000 mile distance. They employed Internet2 and DVDs to examine and discuss the pieces (Internet2 2005c).

Science and Engineering

Current Internet2 applications in science and engineering are centered on collaborative initiatives for data mining and data storage, multisite computation, real-time access to remote resources, and shared virtual reality (Internet2 2006f). For example, scientists from MIT have demonstrated how Internet2 can be applied to the field of radio astronomy in the electronic transmission of very long baseline interferometry (e-VLBI) data. As data was being transmitted from the Haystack Observatory in Massachusetts and NASA's Goddard Astromomical and Geophysical Observatory in Maryland, the data correlation was simultaneously being displayed in a 3D plot at a remote site in Pittsburg. This sharing of highly sophisticated instrumentation facilitates the collaboration of a scientific community separated by geography.

Another exciting application made possible by Internet2 is tele-immersion. Electronic Visualization Laboratory (EVL 2006) at the University of Illinois Chicago has been partnering with engineers and scientists across the nation to develop tele-immersion, which they define as:

> collaborative virtual reality over networks, an extension of the "human/computer interaction" paradigm to "human/computer/human collaboration," with the computer providing real-time data in shared, collaborative environments, to enable computational science and engineering researchers to interact with each other (the "tele-conferencing" paradigm) as well as their computational models, over distance.

This sophisticated technological process allows virtual excursions through the human body, machines, and buildings; virtual visits to historical sites; as well as "environments that explore truths about irony, humor, music, and levels of consciousness" (Lemley 2002, 1) in which one can experience virtual physical experiences such as jumping off a set of stairs. Taking advantage of national and international high-speed networks, EVL's goal is to move from the laboratory to the next generation Internet where they can "access distributed computing, storage and display resources more efficiently than ever" (EVL 2006).

Education

Educators and students at all educational levels are creating innovative ways to communicate, collaborate and learn. Examples of education applications range from a live high-quality multicast stream of Washington University's May 2005 commencement activities to a virtual studio space developed to enable simultaneous teaching and learning space for a viola maestro and student separated by continents. Communication students at Northwestern University connected with political candidates and staff via videoconferencing over Internet2 high-performance networks; students from Bradley University and California State University, Los Angeles, learned from professionals in a screen writing course; Manhattan School of Music collaborated with Columbia University to present a live jazz combo performance over Internet2's Abilene Network; and the University of Delaware is collaborating with teachers and students at the Delaware School for the Deaf to bring in specialized student tutors from remote sites across the United States.

Internet2 access has also provided the K-12 community opportunities to take advantage of its high-speed networks and video conferencing capabilities. In its third year, the Megaconference Jr. took place in May 2006 and provided an opportunity for elementary and secondary students from around the world to participate in learning activities designed to build international cultural awareness (Megaconference 2006). Additional Internet2 and K-12 partnerships have spawned programs such as Read Across America; re-enactment of the Lewis and Clark expedition for K-12 schools; the Jason Project, an inquiry based science learning adventure; and the Internet2 Jazz Concert, a collaboration between university and K-12 music programs. The following case studies provide further examples of how Internet2 technologies are being used in K-20 educational settings and beyond.

CASE STUDIES

School Children, High-Speed Networks, and New Educational Opportunities

The National K-20 initiative was prompted by the decision of the Internet2 technology community to bring together those who would use the services and tools with those who are creating the advanced network applications. The Sponsored Education Group Participant (SEGP) process enables members to sponsor organizations outside of Internet2, which means that entire state educational networks have the opportunity connect to Abilene. Through the SEGP, education innovators in K-12, community colleges, universities, libraries, and museums have been brought together to explore the ways that the advanced networking efforts developed by Internet2 can be used collaboratively to enhance teaching and learning (Internet2 2006a). Currently, there are 34 state education networks connected to Internet2.

Two Internet2 members sponsored by the Massachusetts K-20 Initiative, the University of Massachusetts Amherst and Worcester Polytechnic Institute, are connected to the Abilene backbone through the Northern Crossroads (NoX) gigaPoP. One part of this K-20 initiative is the Merrimack Education Center (MEC), which connects over 2/3 of the K-12 schools in Massachusetts, although not all at high speed.

There are a number of innovative educational projects designed to engage students in real-world applications. One such project was developed through the partnerhips of MEC Technology System (MECnet) and the Jason Project to bring interactive science and math curriculum to students in grades 4 through 9. Named after the mythical Greek adventure, Jason and the Argonauts, the Jason Project was founded by Dr. Robert Ballard, one of three scientists who discovered the Titanic. MECnet (2004, 1) describes the Jason Project as one that "combines genuine scientific expeditions around the world, standards-based science and math classroom curriculum and professional learning for teachers to deliver real adventures in learning and measurable gains in student achievement." This inquiry-based learning project is enhanced by online digital laboratories, probeware, online communications, and online assessments made possible by Internet2 technologies.

The Jason Project has also partnered with experts such as NASA to explore "Earth and Mars," ecologists and geologists to explore the "Disappearing Wetland," and anthropologists and entomologists to explore "Rainforests at the Crossroads." High bandwidth streams and videoconference events with scientists are made possible to schools with limited resources through the relationship with Internet2 organizations in the K-20 community.

Orchestras, Auditions, and Master Classes

On March 18 2004, the first ever National Internet2 Day, a jazz combo from the Manhattan School of Music used the Internet2 connection at Columbia University to broadcast a live music performance to a live audience in Ann Arbor, Michigan. Simultaneously, the performance was multicast to over thirty Internet2 members nationwide who were participating in National Internet2 Day. This is one example that demonstrates how the arts and humanities have been one of the greatest benefactors of Internet2 technologies. Although Internet2 will not and is not intended to replace or eliminate live, in-person music education, it provides opportunities for augmentation of traditional methods to music performance education (Shephard 2005).

Internet2 technologies are becoming so advanced that they are able to handle the elements critical in music performance education such as sound, rhythm, timing, visual imagery, and movement. Such technologies are able to support the requirements for high-quality audio and video over the Internet including low-latency, high-bandwidth transmissions of high-fidelity, stereo or multi-channel sound with accompanying full-motion video using broadcast quality standards (Orto 2004).

In the music world, master classes are music classes taught by, or consultations offered by, nationally or internationally acclaimed musicians. Mirabai Weishmehl, a student at New World Symphony, participated in a master class with Gordon Nikolitch, who is the London Symphony Concert Master. Both musicians were in geographically separate locations for the master class, however, as a result of Internet2 technologies they were able to experience high quality and clarity of sound with the immediacy of video presentation expected by a master musicians.

Conducting music performance education, including live performances, auditions, and master classes, over Internet2 is not without its challenges. Musicians who participate in such videoconferencing events rely on trained technologists to minimize echo in the transmission, to create high-quality full motion video and real time interactivity. In early 2005, Internet2 in collaboration with the New World Symphony offered a hands-on performance and master class production workshop. Such workshops have been established to train technology staff how to set up the equipment, maintain communication systems, and design the stages for interactive media events.

ENCOURAGING INNOVATIONS OF INTERNET2®

Exciting developments are constantly being innovated and deployed by Internet2 members. Such developments are enabling new collaborations, capabilities and experiments never before possible. Encouraging innovations of Internet2 are being seen across all spectrums of disciplines within higher education.

The NASA Research and Education Network (NREN) project will continue to use its Internet2 high-performance networking technologies to conduct advanced research and support collaborative applications. "A major goal of the NREN Project is to enable the fusion of emerging network technologies into NASA mission applications, resulting in new paradigms for conducting science across all NASA Enterprise Programs" (NREN 2006, 1). The NREN project has a number of ongoing applications such as the Virtual Collaborative Clinic (VCC), which involves key concepts such as telemedicine, virtual reality, and 3-D imaging with the long-term goal of introducing VCC to astronauts on the Space Station.

The Library of Congress plans to use its Internet2 membership "to collect and preserve the digital heritage of the nation" (Internet2 2006e, 1). The Library's National Digital Newspaper program plans to create a digital resource of newspapers from the United States and its territories published between 1836 and 1922.

The Motion Picture Association of America (MPAA) and the Recording Industry Association of America (RIAA) are among the newest corporate members of Internet2 who hope to take advantage of the research and academic collaborative in order to develop a secure environment for the distribution of their media. This is an important time for

RIAA to become an Internet2 member, especially after the legal issues that ensued in 2005 with i2hub, a file-sharing service that allowed college students to use Internet2 to share copyrighted materials.

Although still in its infancy, the National Health Information Network (NHIN) is working toward a common framework for standards, policies, and methods for creating a health information exchange. The goal for such an exchange is to improve patient care by allowing appropriate individuals to request and retrieve patient health records rapidly and accurately. Such innovations are endorsed by the Internet2 consortium.

Internet2 CEO, Douglas Van Houweling, warns that "it is only a matter of time before consumers will make the same capacity demands on the network in their day-to-day use of network applications that the research and education community has today" (Talbot 2005, 1).

THE "NEWNET"

In his address to the Internet2 Spring Member Meeting, Douglas Van Houweling (2006) talked about the challenges that lie ahead for Internet2. Chief among his concerns was the merger of Internet2 and National LambdaRail (NLR). Although negotiations about the merger had broken down in April 2006, he expressed the Internet2 commitment of moving the Abilene network to the NLR infrastructure. Such a merger will allow for a focus on use and innovation, rather than on maintenance. Larry Faulkner, Chairman of the Board of Trustees of Internet2 confers that to best meet the needs of higher education in the United States there needs to be "a single strong agile structure" and a "unified organization" that can handle the challenges that lie ahead (Faulkner 2006).

To emphasize the importance of working together, the Internet2 CEO introduced the term "newnet." Van Houweling stressed the importance of collaboration and looking to the future while building upon the heritage of the work and research that has already been accomplished. As a way to respond to the complex challenges inherent in building such advanced technologies, the governance structure of the Internet2 consortium is changing and attempting to create closer ties between national and regional infrastructures and federal agencies which will be a necessity if they are to serve the Internet2 member universities. Van Houweling acknowledged the importance of international partners and emphasized the continued need for global collaboration and integration, noting that the "best ideas are coming from all over our world" (Van Houweling 2006). Finally Van Houweling reiterated that the focus of Internet2 is to provide a network to the "people who have new visions for applications that can be enabled using this network," whereas at the same time reminds us that "we need to imagine a future that is yet to be invented."

GLOSSARY

Abilene: An advanced backbone network that connects regional aggregation points (gigaPoPs) and supports the work of Internet2 universities.

Gigabit point of presence (gigaPoP): A regional Internet working aggregation point used for accessing the Internet2 network.

Hybrid optical and packet infrastructure (HOPI): An Internet2 initiative that is designing and building a network that is a hybrid of packet- and circuit-switched optical network infrastructures.

Internet protocol version 6 (IPv6): Called the next version of the Internet protocol replacing Internet Protocol version 4, which is used by the current Internet.

Middleware: The layer of software between the application and Internet2 network which provides services such as identification, authentication, and security.

National LambdaRail (NRL): is a consortium of leading U.S. research universities and private sector technology companies that has deployed 10,000 miles of fiber optic cable across the United States.

Next generation Internet eXchange point (NGIX): A facility where federal research networks connect with each other and with other advanced networks.

University Corporation for Advanced Internet Development (UCAID): The nonprofit organization manages the activities, programs, dues, and expenditures of Internet2.

Sponsored Educational Group Participants (SEGP): A type of indirect Internet2 membership which enables members to sponsor organizations outside of Internet2.

CROSS REFERENCES

See *History of the Internet*; *Internet Domain Name System*; *TCP/IP Suite*; *The Internet Fundamentals*.

REFERENCES

Abilene. 2006a. Abilene. http://abilene.internet2.edu/ (accessed May 29, 2006).

Abilene. 2006b. Abilene network: Abilene.internet2.edu. http://www.internet2.edu/pubs/200502-IS-AN.pdf (accessed January 4, 2006).

Abilene. 2006c. About Abilene. http://abilene.internet2.edu/about/ (accessed January 4, 2006).

Ackerman, M. 2003. Anatomical and surgery simulation over the Internet. http://health.internet2.edu/files/surgery.wmv (accessed December 16, 2005).

Base2. 2005. Base2 system. https://base2.csis.pace.edu/index.php (accessed December 9, 2005).

Deal, S. 2005. Percussion on the Internet: Teaching and performing in cyberspace. *Percussive Notes* 43(2):74–7.

Doyle, A. 2005. Internet2 overview and arts and humanities initiatives. http://www.internet2.edu/presentations/20050124-Performance-Doyle3.htm (accessed December 16, 2005).

EDUCAUSE. 2005. Computer and network security task force. http://www.educase.edu/Elements/Attachments/security/flyer.pdf (accessed December 16, 2005).

EVL. 2006. Tele-immersion. http://www.evl.uic.edu/core.php?mod=2&type=1&cat=5 (accessed January 8, 2006).

Faulkner, L. 2006. The future of Internet2. http://events.internet2.edu/2006/spring-mm/sessionDetails.cfm?session=2576&event=242 (accessed May 28, 2006).

Futhey, T. 2005. Life of lambda. EDUCAUSE Review 40:80–1.

HOPI. 2006. HOPI: hybrid optical and packet infrastructure project. http://networks.internet2.edu/hopi/HOPI%20Infosheet%20FINAL.pdf (accessed May 30, 2006).

Infoplease. 2006. Internet timeline. http://www.infoplease.com/ipa/A0193167.html (accessed May 30, 2006).

Internet2. 2004. Applications 201. http://www.internet2.edu/presentations/fall04/20040927-Apps201-Yun.htm (accessed December 9, 2005).

Internet2. 2005a. About Internet2. http://www.internet2.edu/about/ (accessed December 9, 2005).

Internet2. 2005b. Applications Strategy Council. http://www.internet2.edu/about/asc.html (accessed December 9, 2005).

Internet2. 2005c. Bridging the ancient and modern: New ways of thinking a Archaeology and anthropology using Internet2. http://events.internet2.edu/2005/fall-mm/gala.html (accessed December 16, 2005).

Internet2. 2005d. The FAQs about Internet2. http://www.internet2.edu/about/faq.html (accessed December 9, 2005).

Internet2. 2005e. Industry Strategy Council. http://www.internet2.edu/about/isc.html (accessed December 9, 2005).

Internet2. 2005f. Internet2. http://www.internet2.edu/resources/Internet2Overview.htm (accessed December 9, 2005).

Internet2. 2005g. Internet2 and Abilene terms of affiliation. http://members.internet2.edu/terms-of-affiliation.html#MoU (accessed December 9, 2005).

Internet2. 2005h. Internet2 applications: frequently asked questions. http://apps.internet2.edu/faq.html (accessed December 9, 2005).

Internet2. 2005i. The Internet2 arts and humanities initiative. http://arts.internet2.edu/arts.html (accessed December 16, 2005).

Internet2. 2005j. Internet2 health sciences. http://www.internet2.edu/resources/infosheethealth.pdf (accessed December 9, 2005).

Internet2. 2005k. Internet2 international partner organizations and networks. http://international.internet2.edu/partners/ (accessed December 9, 2005).

Internet2. 2005l. Internet2 membership and Abilene network structure. http://members.internet2.edu/Internet2Diagrams.html# (accessed December 9, 2005).

Internet2. 2005m. Internet2 membership FAQ. http://members.internet2.edu/membershipfaq.html (accessed December 9, 2005).

Internet2. 2005n. Internet2 security. http://security.internet2.edu/ (accessed December 16, 2005).

Internet2. 2005o. Internet2/NLM infoRAD demos and tutorials at RSNA. http://apps.internet2.edu/rsna2005-demos.html (accessed December 16, 2005).

Internet2. 2005p. Membership in Internet2. http://members.internet2.edu/JoinInternet2.html (accessed December 9, 2005).

Internet2. 2005q. Network Research Liaison Council. http://www.internet2.edu/about/asc.html (accessed December 9, 2005).

Internet2. 2005r. SALSA. http://security.internet2.edu/salsa/ (accessed December 16, 2005).

Internet2. 2006a. Internet2 K20 initiative: Background. http://k20.internet2.edu/about/background.html (accessed January 9, 2006).

Internet2. 2006b. Internet2 land speed record. http://lsr.internet2.edu/ (accessed January 8, 2006).

Internet2. 2006c. Internet2 middleware initiative. http://middleware.internet2.edu/#core (accessed January 6, 2006).

Internet2. 2006d. IPv6. http://ipv6.internet2.edu/ (accessed January 7, 2006).

Internet2. 2006e. Library of Congress joins Internet2. https://mail.internet2.edu/wws/arc/i2-news/2005-05/msg00004.html (accessed January 13, 2006).

Internet2. 2006f. science.internet2.edu. http://science.internet2.edu/ (accessed January 8, 2006).

Internet2. 2006g. Working groups: Information. http://www.internet2.edu/wg/ (accessed May 26, 2006).

Lemley, B. 2002. Internet2: A supercharged new network with true tele-presence puts the needs of science first. http://www.discover.com/issues/may-02/features/featinternet2/ (accessed January 8, 2006).

MECnet. 2004. Internet2 more accessible to Massachusetts teachers. http://www.mecnet.net/other/pdfs/MECnet_Jason%20Academy%20Press%20Release.pdf (accessed January 12, 2006).

Megaconference. 2006. Megaconference Jr. 2006. http://megaconferencejr.org/id=overview&PHPSESSID=0fea02b60479da06281f19800a85e272\ (accessed January 9, 2006).

NLANR/DAST. 2005. The Advanced Applications Database. http://dast.nlanr.net/AAD/aad_main.html (accessed December 9, 2005).

NREN. 2006. NASA Research and Education Network: Tomorrow's networking applications today. http://www.nren.nasa.gov/apps/index.html (accessed January 13, 2006).

Orto, C. 2004. Video conferencing for music performance education at the Manhattan School. http://www.campus-technology.com/article.asp?id=8744 (accessed January 14, 2005).

Oxford University Press. 2006. "Podcast" is Word of the Year. http://www.us.oup.com/us/brochure/NOAD_podcast/?view=usa (accessed May 30, 2006).

Pollak, M. 2004. Abilene network upgrade to 10 Gbps complete. https://mail.internet2.edu/wws/arc/i2-news/2004-02/msg00001.html (accessed January 15, 2006).

Public Broadcasting Service. 1997. Life on the Internet: Timeline. http://www.pbs.org/internet/timeline/timeline-txt.html (accessed May 22, 2002).

Public Health Grand Rounds WebCast. 2005. http://www.hsc.wvu.edu/som/cmed/ophp/grandrounds.asp (accessed December 16, 2005).

Shephard, B. 2005. Teaching music through advanced network videoconferencing. rcf.usc.edu/~bkshepar/masterclass.html (accessed January 14, 2005).

Talbot, D. 2005. Next-generation networks: Today's Internet is like "second-class mail." http://www.technology-review.com/Infotech/15937/ (accessed May 17, 2007).

Van Houweling, D. 2006. The future of Internet2. http://events.internet2.edu/2006/spring-mm/sessionDetails.cfm?session=2576&event=242 (accessed May 28, 2006).

Verizon Corporation. 2001. Who we are: BBN timeline. http://www.bbn.com/timeline (accessed May 22, 2002).

Wasley. 1996. The focus of the Internet ii vision. http://www.bbn.com/timeline (accessed May 22, 2006).

Zakon, R. H. 2005. Hobbes' Internet Timeline v8.1. http://www.zakon.org/Robert/internet/timeline (accessed May 30, 2006).

Internet Domain Name System

Krishna Jayakar, *Penn State University*

INTRODUCTION

Any person who has used the Internet is familiar with the names of popular Web sites such as online bookstores (www.amazon.com), government departments and agencies (www.parliament.uk), business corporations (sony.co.jp), and news organizations (www.cnn.com). These easily remembered Web addresses, called domain names, are part of a two-part name-and-number addressing system that uniquely identifies every device connected to the Internet. The other part is 32-bit Internet protocol (IP) addresses, associated with each domain name. Together, this two-part naming system called the domain name system (DNS), makes all Internet communication possible.

A two-part addressing system is necessary in part to enable human users to interact with a computer network. If all Internet communications were between machines, unique IP addresses alone would have sufficed—for example, a network enabled printer connected to an office computer requires only an IP address. However, it would be impossible for human users to interact with a system based only on numerical addresses due to the obvious limitations of human memory recall. Though the advent of better search engine technologies have reduced the importance of domain names as mnemonic devices, users may still find it easier to remember the domain names of their most-visited Web sites, rather than strings of abstract numbers. A two-part naming system has other advantages as well: since external users only use the domain name, and never interact with the IP addresses, an organization can easily route traffic to multiple servers at high-traffic Web sites by mapping multiple IP addresses to the same domain name. Server shut down and maintenance is also facilitated by this system, because traffic can be rerouted internally without affecting the public presence of the organization. Thus, for multiple reasons, the DNS has become one of the key technical infrastructures of the Internet. This article discusses its technical, institutional, and policy aspects, in that order.

TECHNICAL DESCRIPTION

In the early days of the Internet, when the network connected only a few computers at government research labs and universities, the addressing system was contained in a simple text file called hosts.txt, that identified each host computer connected to the network by a simple name, and provided basic information about it including location and network address. Whenever new computers were added to the network, the hosts.txt file would be updated and a new version mailed out to all host computers. This simple system sufficed to take care of addressing needs for the first decade or so of the Internet's early history.

However, as the number of hosts on the Internet gradually grew, this early addressing system proved inadequate (National Research Council 2005). The system failed to scale because the hosts.txt file became enormously large as the number of computers increased. The traffic demands too grew exponentially as an updated file had to be sent out to the thousands of networked computers whenever a new one was added, or the particulars of an existing one changed. New hosts were effectively invisible to the rest of the network until an updated hosts.txt file was mailed out and installed on each computer. Naming conflicts were also inevitable because of the logistical problem of finding unique names for every host on the burgeoning Internet. It thus became inevitable that a new naming system had to be devised.

The current domain name system was organized in response to this pressing need. It envisions a hierarchical and distributed naming system organized in an inverted tree structure, beginning with the "root" server at the very top (see Figure 1 below). At each level a "name server" contains the authoritative listing of all domain name assignments in the layer immediately below. Under the "root" are a number of top-level domains (TLDs), classified as generic top-level domains (gTLDs) (also commonly called global top-level domains) and country-code top-level domains (ccTLDs). Name servers in each TLD contain the

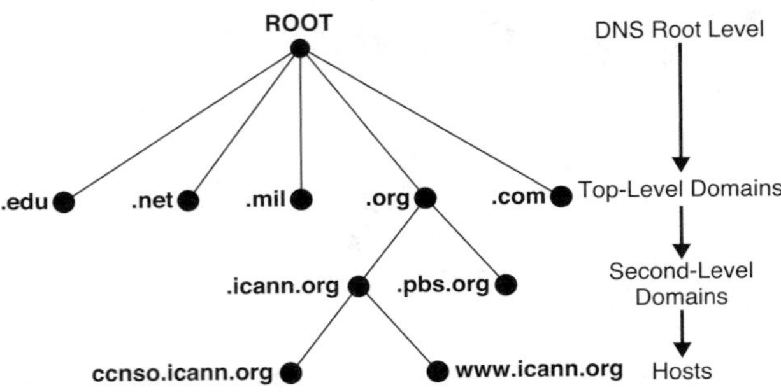

Figure 1: Inverted tree structure (partial) of the domain name system

list of all secondary level name assignments made within that top-level domain. The secondary level domains may in turn be sub-divided into further hierarchical layers. The paragraphs that follow provide additional information on the structural elements of the DNS.

The Root

In conformity to the inverted tree architecture of the domain name system, its highest level is called the root. The key root resource is the root server, that contains an exhaustive listing of all top-level domain assignments, that is, it identifies IP address for the authoritative name server (see below) for each top-level domain under the root. Since it is critical that access to the root server be available at all times, the DNS has duplicated the contents of the root on root servers located on different continents. Currently, there are thirteen root servers designated by the letters A to M (see Table 1). Each root server is maintained and operated by organizations called root server operators: these include private firms, universities, government research laboratories, and international consortia. While several of the root servers are located on single servers at one location, others (C, F, I, J, K, and M) are mirrored at dozens of sites around the world using a technology called *anycast*, that routes addressing queries to the nearest root server. This redundancy ensures that local outages, server failures, and so on would not deprive the Internet of one of its most essential resources.

Top-Level Domains

The name space under the root server is divided into a number of top-level domains. Generic TLDs (gTLDs) organize domain names into categories based on type of organization or subject interest. They include the popular '.com' space for commercial businesses, the '.gov' space for U.S. government Web sites and '.edu' for educational institutions (see Table 2 for a list of gTLDs as of end-2006). Some of the gTLDs are 'sponsored' and serve a narrow community of interest (for example, .aero), whereas others are unsponsored, with domain name assignments available to all users (for example, .com). Country-code TLDs (ccTLDs) are assigned to different countries, such as '.uk' for the United Kingdom. To avoid political controversy, ccTLD assignments are based strictly on the two-letter list of nations and sub-national regions maintained by the International Organization for Standardization (ISO), which in turn is based on United Nations sources. Currently, there are approximately 250 ccTLD designations in the DNS databases. In addition to gTLDs and ccTLDs, the DNS also contains a special purpose 'infrastructure' TLD, .arpa, used by the system for technical coordination purposes.

Each top-level domain has an authoritative TLD name server. Name servers are special computers that exhaustively list all domain names and IP addresses belonging to a section or subsection of the Internet, for which that name server is considered to be authoritative (Mockapetris 1983a). In addition, name servers are equipped with address resolution software such as the popular Berkeley Internet Name Domain (BIND) program that can identify the IP addresses associated with domain names in other zones when queried by users.

Domain Names

The domain names of the DNS comprise of two or more parts or labels, separated by dots. They are character strings set up according to a few simple, yet rigorously enforced rules. Domain names may be 1 to 63 characters long, and can use a limited subset of ASCII, namely the 26 alphabets, the 10 numerical digits, and the hyphen.

It may be worth pointing out the distinction between uniform resource locators (URLs) and domain names. An example will clarify this: Penn State University's Web site is located at the domain name www.psu.edu, accessible at the Web address, http://www.psu.edu. The arrangement of both the domain name and the Web address indicate the hierarchical levels to which they belong in reverse order, that is, right to left. The assignments are made within the .edu gTLD intended for educational establishments, within which the second-level domain name psu.edu is assigned by the DNS to Penn State University. The third-level assignment www.psu.edu is made internally by the host organization.

As mentioned before, not all Internet devices require domain names to be assigned. Domain names are required only where human users need to interact with the technical system.

IP Addresses

In addition to domain names, IP addresses are the second part of the name-and-number DNS system (this section is based on Hall 2000; see especially Appendix B, IP Addressing Fundamentals). IP addresses are number strings of fixed bit length: 32 bits in the common IP version 4 (IPv4) assignments, or 128 bits in IP version 6 (IPv6). IP addresses in IPv4 are commonly represented as four numbers between 0 and 255, separated by dots. For example, the Web site for the U.S. Congress, www.congress.gov, maps to 140.147.248.209. IPv6 addresses are represented in the hexadecimal (base 16) system, as eight number-letter strings separated by colons.

In IPv4, there are two sub-addresses as part of the IP address, the network prefix, and the host ID. The network prefix is assigned by a central authority to network

Table 1: Root Servers and Their Locations

Server	Operator	Locations	IP Address
A	VeriSign Naming and Directory Services	Dulles VA	198.41.0.4
B	Information Sciences Institute	Marina Del Rey CA	IPv4: 192.228.79.201 IPv6: 2001:478:65::53
C	Cogent Communications	Herndon VA; Los Angeles; New York City;	192.33.4.12
D	University of Maryland	Chicago College Park MD	128.8.10.90
E	NASA Ames Research Center	Mountain View CA	192.203.230.10
F	Internet Systems Consortium, Inc.	**40 sites:** Ottawa; Palo Alto; San Jose CA; New York City; San Francisco; Madrid; Hong Kong; Los Angeles; Rome; Auckland; Sao Paulo; Beijing; Seoul; Moscow; Taipei; Dubai; Paris; Singapore; Brisbane; Toronto; Monterrey; Lisbon; Johannesburg; Tel Aviv; Jakarta; Munich; Osaka; Prague; Amsterdam; Barcelona; Nairobi; Chennai; London; Santiago de Chile; Dhaka; Karachi; Torino; Chicago; Buenos Aires; Caracas	IPv4: 192.5.5.241 IPv6: 2001:500::1035
G	U.S. DOD Network Information Center	Columbus OH	192.112.36.4
H	U.S. Army Research Lab	Aberdeen MD	IPv4: 128.63.2.53 IPv6: 2001:500:1::803f:235
I	Autonomica/NORDUnet	**29 sites:** Stockholm; Helsinki; Milan; London; Geneva; Amsterdam; Oslo; Bangkok; Hong Kong; Brussels; Frankfurt; Chicago; Washington DC; Tokyo; Kuala Lumpur; Palo Alto; Jakarta; Wellington; Johannesburg; Perth; San Francisco; New York; Singapore; Miami; Ashburn (US); Mumbai; Beijing	192.36.148.17
J	VeriSign Naming and Directory Services	**22 sites:** Dulles VA (2 locations); Sterling VA (2 locations); Mountain View CA; Seattle WA; Atlanta GA; Los Angeles CA; Miami FL; Sunnyvale CA; Amsterdam; Stockholm; London; Dublin; Tokyo; Seoul; Singapore; Sydney; Sao Paulo, Brazil; Brasilia, Brazil; Toronto, Canada; Montreal, Canada	192.58.128.30
K	Reseaux IP Europeens - Network Coordination Centre	**17 sites:** London; Amsterdam; Frankfurt; Athens; Doha; Milan; Reykjavik; Helsinki; Geneva; Poznan; Budapest; Abu Dhabi; Tokyo; Brisbane; Miami; Delhi; Novosibirsk	IPv4: 193.0.14.129 IPv6: 2001:7fd::1
L	ICANN	Los Angeles	198.32.64.12
M	WIDE Project	Tokyo; Seoul; Paris; San Francisco, CA	IPv4: 202.12.27.33 IPv6: 2001:dc3::35

Source: http://www.root-servers.org

providers, who then assign the host IDs to machines on their networks. The length of the network prefix is identified by a separate 32-bit identifier called the subnet mask: the remaining part of the IP address then becomes the host ID.

When users type in domain names into their computer's browsers, the computer is able to "resolve" or identify the associated IP address. Domain names and IP addresses need not be mapped one to one. In some cases, for example when a manufacturer wants to promote multiple brand names, several domain names may point to the same IP address for the content server on which all of the company's Web-accessible information is stored. In other cases, a network administrator may want to have the same domain name associated with multiple content servers, to ensure access during periods of heavy usage.

Table 2: List of Generic Top-Level Domains (gTLDs) as of 2006

gTLD	Introduced	Available to:
.aero	2001	air transportation industry
.biz	2001	business; open to any registrant
.cat	2005	Web sites in the Catalan language
.com	1995	commercial; open to any registrant
.coop	2001	cooperative organizations
.edu	1995	educational institutions, mainly in the United States
.gov	1995	agencies and departments of the U.S. government
.info	2001	any type of information; open to any registrant
.int	2001	international agencies and organizations
.jobs	2005	human resource agencies
.mil	1995	U.S. military
.mobi	2005	mobile content providers and users
.museum	2001	museums
.name	2001	individuals
.net	1995	network providers; open to any registrant
.org	1995	organizations not included elsewhere; open to any registrant
.pro	2002	professionals such as lawyers, doctors etc
.tel	2006	Internet communications
.travel	2005	travel and tourism industry

Source: ICANN Registry Listing, available http://www. icann.org/registries/listing.html.

Traffic could be routed to whichever server that has spare capacity at that moment.

To facilitate communication between different networks, Internet routers have 'routing tables', which identify a pathway through the network from each network prefix to every other network prefix. Thus, the size of routing tables increases exponentially as the number of network IDs increases. Not all network prefixes have direct routes assigned in all routing tables, in which case they will be routed with extra "hops." Network prefixes with direct listings in the highest level routing tables (on the backbone) are the most valuable, because they can be reached with the fewest "hops."

Network prefixes were initially assigned in five 'sizes': classes A to E (Hall 2000; Mueller 2002). Class A networks use the first 8 bits for the network prefix, and the remaining part of the fixed-length IP address (32 bits) to identify the host ID. Since each network and host needed to be assigned a unique number, only a limited number of class A networks are available to be assigned: however, these networks could accommodate a large number of hosts. Class B networks used 16 bits for the network prefix, with the effect that there could be a larger number of class B networks, though they were smaller in size. The most common category is class C networks with less than 256 hosts. Class D networks are used for multicasting group addresses and E networks for experimental purposes. This system of fixed size networks is called "classful" addressing.

One of the pressing problems confronting the Internet today is IP address scarcity, caused by the enormous growth in the number of networks connected to the Internet. When TCP/IP was being designed in the 1980s, it was projected that the numbering protocols would need to support 100,000 networks sometime in the remote future: that number was reached and exceeded by 1996 (Bradner and Mankin 1995). The original IPv4, with a 32-bit addressing space, is capable of generating approximately 4.3 billion unique addresses: this proved to be inadequate, especially when new devices such as wireless phones and even home appliances need to be connected to the Internet. Address scarcity was compounded by the fact that address blocks could be assigned only in fixed sizes, leading to wastage of IP numbers and additional entries in routing tables: for example, a network with an estimated size of 300 hosts would require two Class C networks to be assigned, with some IP addresses remaining unused, and two separate entries in routing tables. This resulted in exponential growth in the number of entries in routing tables, imposing additional processing costs on Internet routers.

From 1994, a number of steps were taken to solve these problems. One of the most commonly used solutions is dynamic IP addressing. Instead of assigning a permanent "static" IP address to a node on its network, an Internet service provider may temporarily allocate an IP address from a common pool to a device using a protocol such as dynamic host configuration protocol (DHCP). These "dynamic" IP addresses are made available only for the duration of a session, and can be reassigned to other uses as they come online. Network address translation (NAT) was another technique that was promoted as a short-term solution to number scarcity, by enabling multiple nodes on a private network to share the same IP address (Egevang and Francis 1994). Each node on the private network is assigned a unique "inside local address" that the local NAT-enabled router recognizes, but is not transparent to the outside network. The router encodes outgoing messages with the common IP address, receives incoming data and redirects it to the appropriate machine. With NAT, a large number of private network nodes are able to share a limited number of "outside" IP addresses.

Another solution is classless inter-domain routing (CIDR) that allows flexible network prefix sizes, instead of the five standard classes that existed earlier (Fuller, Li, Yu, and Varadhan 1993). The length of the network prefix is easily modified by setting the subnet mask to the appropriate length. This enabled better utilization of the existing IP number space by increasing the number of network assignments that could be made, and tailoring the network sizes more closely to actual demand so that wastage could be limited. In effect, CIDR allows an Internet registry to divide up and allocate an address block in several different sizes to different organizations based on need. CIDR was also able to support hierarchical route aggregation, in which many traditional classful networks could be represented by a single entry in the routing tables. This checked for the time being the phenomenal growth in the number of entries in routing tables. Assignment policies were also tightened (Mueller 2002).

In spite of these measures, it was recognized that address exhaustion in the IPv4 space was eventually going to result. In response, the Internet Engineering Task Force (IETF) introduced a new numbering protocol called next generation Internet protocol or IPng (also called IP version 6, or IPv6), with a document titled *The Recommendation for the IP Next Generation Protocol* (RFC 1752) (Bradner and Mankin 1995). Detailed specifications were published in *Internet Protocol, Version 6 (IPv6) Specification* (RFC 2460) (Deering and Hinden 1998). The most important change in IPv6 was the expansion of the IP address size from 32 bits to 128 bits, increasing the total number of addresses that can be assigned to approximately 3.8 x 10E38. The IP addresses in IPv6 are expressed in the format X:X:X:X:X:X:X:X, where each X is a four-digit hexadecimal (base 16) integer (3Com 2001). Since each digit in a hexadecimal system needs four bits for representation, each integer X requires 16 bits (4 x 4) and the whole IP address of 8 integers 128 bits (4 x 4 x 8).

In addition to expanding the number space, IPv6 introduced a number of innovations relating to routing, addressing and security. First, it added more levels to the addressing hierarchy: Internet registries and large Internet service providers are top level aggregators (TLAs) with very large address blocks assigned to them; in turn, specific customer sites are next level aggregators (NLAs) to which smaller address chunks are assigned, and subnetworks within organizations are site level aggregators (SLAs) (3Com 2001). Each of these hierarchical levels is identified by a specific field within the IPv6 host address, so that traffic directed at user interfaces can be appropriately routed. This is similar to the route aggregation under CIDR. The advantage of this arrangement is that the number of entries in the global routing tables is kept to a minimum, with routers at each level directing traffic to the appropriate sub-hierarchical units. Smaller users would no longer be able to obtain address assignments directly from the registries under IPv6.

In terms of addressing, a significant innovation in IPv6 is the augmentation of addressing methods. As in IPv4, unicast addressing identifies a unique host interface as the recipient of a data transmission. In addition to this, IPv6 permits multicasting and anycasting as well (3Com 2001). Multicasting, where data is sent from one originating node to a group of packet recipients, is part of the basic protocol in IPv6 compared to IPv4 where it was optional. Anycasting enables a packet sent to an anycast address to be routed to the nearest or best of a group of interfaces, based upon network topology.

Another key improvement in IPv6 is enhanced support for privacy, and data security. The protocol includes extensions to support authentication and data integrity, as well as confidentiality through encryption. IPv6 allows the labeling of packets so that particular traffic flows such as "real time" services can be given special handling on the basis of sender requests. Finally, IPv6 allows server-less autoconfiguration, that enables any device to connect to the network without requiring the network administrator to assign an IP address using protocols such as dynamic host configuration (DHCP). The vastly expanded pool of available IP addresses in IPv6 allows all devices to be provided with "static" IP addresses, making the process of connecting to the network much simpler than before.

Address Resolution

One of the most important tasks performed by the DNS is address resolution, namely the matching of an IP address to the domain name typed into a browser or an e-mail program by a user. Originally, this was accomplished by looking up the corresponding IP address entry for the domain name in the hosts.txt file available on each computer. However, after the advent of the hierarchical and distributed DNS, there no longer exists a central repository of all domain name–IP address combinations. Address resolution therefore follows a multi-stage recursive process in which name servers at each hierarchical level of the DNS are successively queried, beginning with the root server. The discussion below is based on Mockapetris (1983b) and National Research Council (2005). Figure 1 illustrates the process diagrammatically.

The address resolution process begins when a user's application program initiates a domain name query to a software program called a resolver resident on the user's computer (Step 1 in Figure 2 below). Some resolvers are simple programs that only forward the query to a local name server belonging to the user's Internet service provider, and then wait for the system to respond—these types

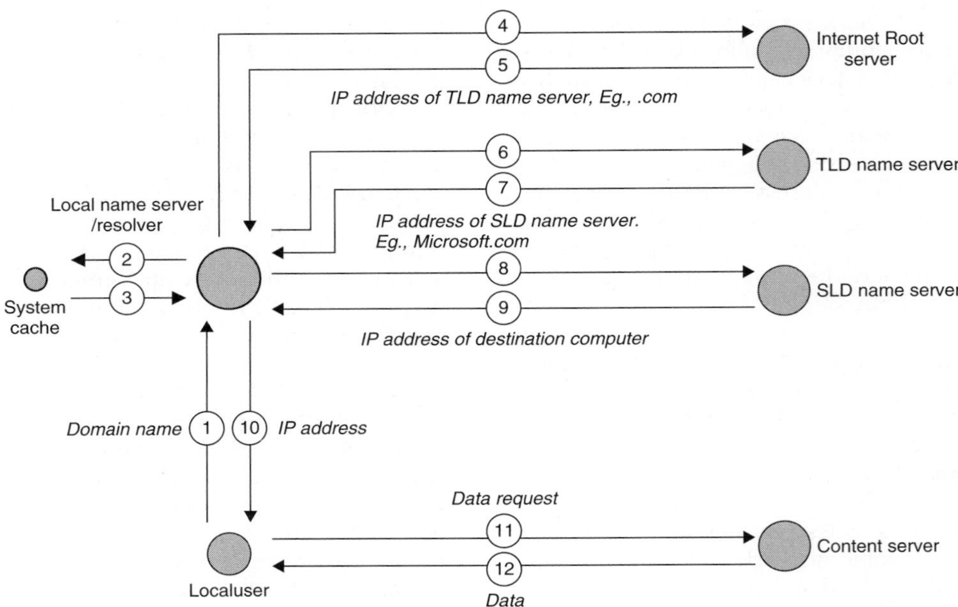

Figure 2: Steps in the address resolution process

of programs are called stub resolvers. More complex versions called iterative resolvers are capable of managing every stage of the resolution process themselves. Initially, the local name server checks its own resources to see if the IP address is available. For example, if the destination computer belongs to the same local network as the user, the local name server itself is authoritative for that space and will contain the needed IP address. In other cases, a local name server may maintain a cache, or memory of recent searches performed by local users. The cache is a feature put in place to reduce the enormous number of address resolution requests that are submitted to the DNS. If the search is available in the cache, the appropriate answer is delivered to the user's application program, and the resolution process is concluded (Steps 2-3 and 10). To maintain the cache at a manageable level, prior searches are retained in memory only for a specified period of time called the time to live (TTL).

If the destination computer is not local and a record of prior searches is unavailable in the cache, the next step for the local name server is to submit the request to the DNS. To do so, the local name server begins at the top of the DNS with the root server, and works its way down the hierarchy (Step 4). As mentioned above, there are 13 root servers distributed throughout the world, with several of these also mirrored at dozens of additional locations. The IP addresses for these root servers, called the root hints data, are manually entered into every computer and are constantly available. The local name server chooses one of these locations using a selection algorithm intended to minimize the response time, and submits the query. The root server examines the request and returns the IP address of the appropriate server at the next lower level, namely the top-level domains (Step 5). The resolver then sends a second query to the TLD name server requesting the IP address of the SLD name server, working its way progressively down the hierarchy until the IP address of the destination computer is located (Steps 6-7 and 8-9) and sent back to the user (Step 10). Finally, once the user's computer has the IP address for the destination computer, a data request is initiated (Step 11), in response to which the host's content server sends the requested data (Step 12).

Sometimes, the local name server's cache may be able to resolve the address partially, for example by identifying the local network to which the destination computer belongs. In this case, the resolution process bypasses the higher levels of the hierarchy, and directly communicates with name servers at the local network level; that is, the process moves directly from Step 1 to Step 8, in which the IP address of the content server is requested from the SLD name server. The remaining steps then proceed sequentially. These protocols have been put in place to minimize the query volumes on the DNS as much as possible.

INSTITUTIONAL STRUCTURE

The operations of the DNS described above require the performance of a number of different activities including the assignment of domain names and addresses, address resolution, technical standard-setting, the creation of new top-level domains, dispute resolution, coordination and communication, and so on. In keeping with the decentralized, public-private, international, and internetworked nature of the Internet itself, the management of these DNS activities is also diffused between several different agencies based in the private, public, and quasi-public spheres, cooperating through a complex set of institutional arrangements and relationships.

Historical Background

The current institutional framework for the DNS evolved out of a long and complicated sequence of events (see Froomkin 2000; Mueller 2002; Pare 2003 for a detailed chronicle of these events: unless otherwise stated, the discussion in this section is summarized from these sources). Initially, when the Internet was confined to a few government research laboratories and university departments, many of these management functions were performed by one individual, Jon Postel, functioning as the director of the Internet Assigned Numbers Authority (IANA). A researcher and professor at the Information Sciences Institute at the University of Southern California, Postel derived his authority from a contract with the U.S. Department of Defense, that had funded the early Internet infrastructures. As the director of IANA, Postel assigned domain names and IP addresses, created new top-level domains as demand arose, and edited the Request For Comment (RFC) document series that laid out the technical and policy principles underlying DNS management.

As the Internet grew, and with it the demands on domain name administration, this ad hoc system could no longer fulfill the demands placed on it. In its place, a number of institutions sprang up to handle various aspects of Internet management. In 1986, the Internet Engineering Task Force was created to develop standards and protocols that promote the interoperability of the Internet, with the aid of all-volunteer, specialized working groups. The Internet Research Task Force (IRTF) is active in the same field as the IETF, but with a longer-term focus. Both these organizations are overseen by the Internet Architecture Board or IAB (formerly known as the Internet Activities Board). In turn, the IAB reports to the Internet Society (ISOC), an umbrella organization formed in 1992 to coordinate between the various ad-hoc organizations active in the management of the Internet. It accepts membership from both individuals and organizations.

Over time, DNS management acquired significant participation from for-profit, private corporations as well. In 1992, a private company, Network Solutions was licensed by the National Science Foundation to accept domain name registrations for the Internet. In 1995, as the number of registrations exploded (especially in the .com TLD), Network Solutions was authorized to charge a fee for registering .com addresses. In the year 2000, Verisign Incorporated acquired Network Solutions along with its DNS related businesses. Verisign continues to operate the gTLD name servers for two of the most popular Internet domains, .com and .net.

By the mid-1990s, the Internet had become an enormously popular global medium. This explosive growth and the increasing commercial use of the Internet brought to the fore a number of issues such as allegations of trademark violations in domain name assignments, the formation of new top level domains, control over new country-code TLDs and the creation of alternative root server systems in competition with the DNS (see Froomkin 2002; Mueller 2002; Pare 2003). By 1996, it became clear that changes in the DNS governance structure were an unavoidable need and key stakeholders put forward competing proposals for reform. The Internet Society, through a new organization called the Internet Ad Hoc Committee (IAHC), initiated a set of reform proposals called the generic TLD-memorandum of understanding (gTLD-MoU). It drew significant international attention and participation, with ITU Secretary General Pekka Tarjanne (1997) hailing it as a new type of international organization, based on "voluntary multilateralism." Alarmed at the potential loss of DNS control to an international entity, the U.S. government put forward a competing proposal called the Green Paper in January 1998, around which a 'dominant coalition' was gradually assembled, including formerly warring sides—the technical community led by Jon Postel, the large corporations, trademark interests, and some foreign groups and governments ("Improvement of technical management of Internet names and addresses" 1998).

The outcome of this process was a White Paper in June 1998, calling for a new not-for-profit private corporation, headquartered in the United States to administer the name and numbers system ("Management of Internet names and addresses" 1998). To assuage international concerns, the White Paper specified that the new corporation would have an internationally representative board and a membership drawn from all major stakeholders such as "IP address registries, domain name registries and registrars, the technical community, ISPs, and users including commercial entities, non-commercial users and individuals" (Mueller 2002, p. 174). Accordingly, a non-profit public benefit corporation called the Internet Corporation Assigned Names and Numbers (ICANN) was formed, based in California. In a Memorandum of Understanding with the U.S. Department of Commerce (DOC), ICANN was ordered "to transition management of the domain name system (DNS) from the U.S. government to the global community" (online), as well as to ensure stability, promote competition, support private-sector leadership in DNS management and policy-making and make the decision-making process representative of the global Internet community (ICANN 2004). The DOC-ICANN MOU has been periodically amended: the most recent amendment in September 2006 reiterated the commitment to private sector leadership in managing the DNS, and to protecting the stability and security of the Internet (Modification to Joint Project Agreement 2006).

In the following paragraphs, we discuss the main institutions and agencies active in DNS management, beginning with ICANN.

ICANN Structure and Processes

ICANN came into existence pursuant to the White Paper's commitment to non-governmentalism, citing the greater flexibility and speed of private sector decision-making ("Management of Internet names and addresses" 1998, 31749). Accordingly in ICANN's structure, there was only a limited role for government: the main decision-making body of ICANN is the board of directors with fifteen members selected by a nominating committee comprised of various Internet stakeholders. Directors are appointed for three-year terms. The corporation's chief responsibilities include establishing the policies for the allocation of IP number blocks; overseeing the root server system; creating new top-level domains as required; and promoting standards and technical parameters that would ensure universal connectivity to the Internet (Memorandum of Understanding [MOU] 1998). Responsibility for IP number blocks and the root server system were originally

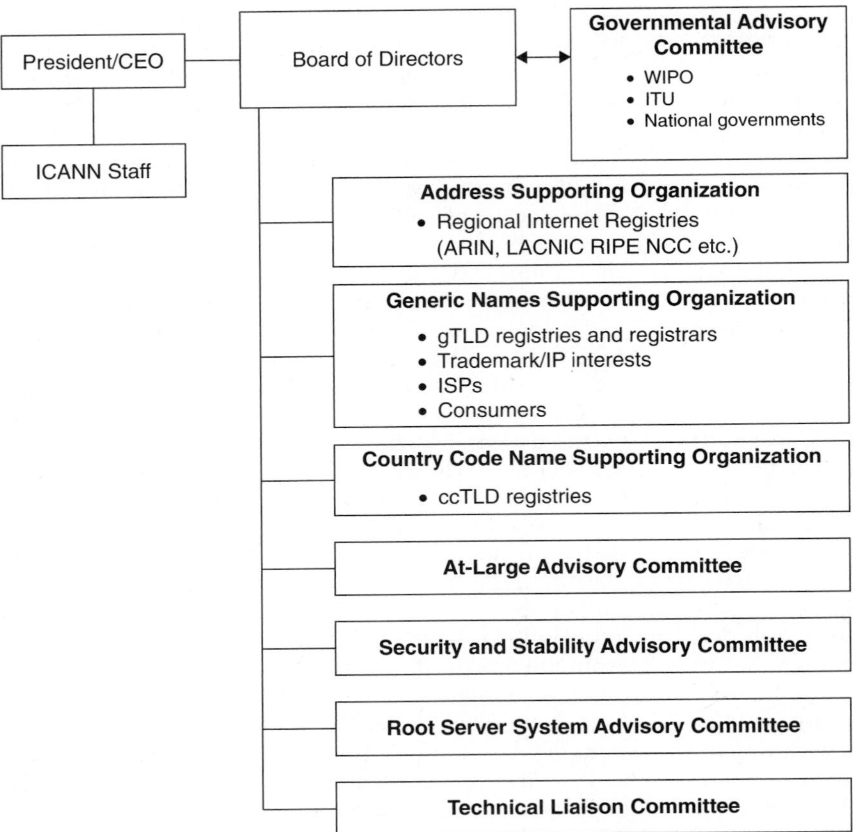

Figure 3: ICANN organizational chart

IANA responsibilities that were transferred to ICANN consequent to the MOU.

ICANN is aided by a number of supporting organizations and advisory committees, representing various Internet stakeholder groups (see Figure 3, adapted from organizational chart at ICANN, 2004 and Mueller 2002, p. 187). These include the Address Supporting Organization whose membership is drawn from the Regional Internet Registries, the Generic Names Supporting Organization (GNSO) representing various gTLD entities such as registries and registrars (see below), Internet service providers, users and intellectual property interests; the Country Code Name Supporting Organization, (CCNSO) representing the ccTLD managers; and the Technical Liaison Committee with membership drawn from the technical standards organizations, such as the European Telecommunications Standards Institute (ETSI), the International Telecommunications Union, the World Wide Web Consortium (W3C), and the Internet Architecture Board (IAB). In keeping with the private sector orientation of ICANN, national governments have no direct role in ICANN: they find a voice only on the Governmental Advisory Committee (GAC), The GAC would "consider and provide advice on the activities of ICANN as they relate to concerns of governments, particularly matters where there may be an interaction between ICANN's policies and various laws and international agreements or where they may affect public policy issues" (Art. IX, Section 2(1)(a), ICANN Bylaws). The GAC has only a purely advisory function, and no decision-making authority. This led some observers to herald ICANN as a new type of international organization, with a clear global mandate but no basis in multilateral treaty, and no role for national governments (Feld 2003; Mueller 2002).

Registries and Registrars

Until the formation of ICANN, Network Solutions, originally contracted by the U.S. Department of Defense in 1992 to accept domain name registrations, had exercised control over the operation of the root and important gTLDs such as .com, while continuing to offer retail registration services to customers. In a new agreement crafted with ICANN after the latter's formation, Network Solutions agreed to separate its registry and registrar businesses. Registry operations involve the administration of the root server and the gTLD servers, whereas the registrar business entails assigning second-level domain names within the TLDs such as .com and .org. Only one registry is authorized for each TLD, whereas there are multiple registrars in each TLD name space.

Each TLD would have a monopoly registry entrusted with the responsibility of maintaining the authoritative list of domain name assignments within that name space. In addition, they are expected to fulfill several conditions as part of their registry agreements with ICANN (see for example the .com Registry Agreement, 2001, between Verisign and ICANN). Chief among these obligations include providing registry services to the Internet community in a transparent and non-discriminatory fashion, upholding ICANN's dispute resolution policies in case of disputes about trademarks, and dealing only with ICANN-accredited registrars. In addition, registries are also required to financially support ICANN, through a complex system of a fixed registry level fee (a set amount each year, collected in equal installments quarterly), a registry level transaction fee (indexed to the annual increases in the number of new or renewal registrations, or inter-domain transfers in each TLD), and a variable registry level fee (with two sub-components, the first related to the total number of domain name registrations and the second to the number of registrars active in each TLD zone).

Within each TLD, many registrars offer retail second-level domain name registration services to customers. Registrars are required to fulfill a number of conditions relating to financial solvency, and would need accreditation from ICANN before Network Solutions and other registries will contract with them. Accredited registrars will pay a one-time fee to ICANN and an annual variable fee depending on the number of second-level domains they register. Registries are also authorized to collect an annual fee from each registrar offering domain name registrations in their zones, plus a fee for each name registration. Currently Verisign (a private corporation that acquired Network Solutions in the year 2000) serves as the registry for two of the most popular gTLDs, .com and .net, under a six-year renewable contract with ICANN and the U.S. Department of Commerce.

Regional Internet Registries

In addition to the procedures for administering domain names described in the previous paragraphs, a parallel system exists for IP addresses. It may be recalled that the allocation of IP addresses was one of the responsibilities of IANA, transferred to ICANN after the latter's creation. Currently, IP address allocations are handled by five Regional Internet registries (RIRs) formed in 1992: IANA allocates IP address blocks to the RIRs based on projections of need, as defined in the Global Addressing Policy (2005) document. The RIRs in turn assign IP number blocks to local Internet registries (LIRs) or Internet service providers.

Each of the five RIR has jurisdiction for a well-defined geographical region: the Asia-Pacific Network Information Center (APNIC) with jurisdiction over south, southeast, and east Asia and Australia; the African Network Information Center (AfriNIC) for Africa; the American Registry for Internet Numbers (ARIN) for North America excluding Mexico; the Latin American and Carribean IP Address Regional Registry (LACNIC) for Central and South America and the Carribean; and the Reseaux IP Europeens Network Coordination Center (RIPE NCC) for Europe, the former Soviet Union and central and west Asia (Internet Society 2005). The activities of these RIRs are coordinated through the Number Resources Organization (NRO), formed in 2003. The NRO liaises with the Address Support Organization of ICANN in matters related to the IP number management, such as framing the resource allocation policies, creating new RIRs if needed, and other policy questions.

DNS POLICY QUESTIONS

As is evident from the previous discussion, the domain name system is not only a technical but also an institutional system, in which multiple political, economic, and social objectives need to be reconciled. It is also a system with distinct international ramifications, due to the global nature of the Internet and its rising importance for trans-border information flows and commerce. It is therefore not surprising that DNS policy has been heavily contested, with multiple agencies and interest groups vying for influence. In this section, we discuss some of the policy questions that have attracted considerable attention in the past, and continue to in the current environment.

Property Rights in the DNS

Ever since 1994, when Network Solutions began accepting a registration fee for domain name registrations, it has been popularly regarded that registrants have some form of ownership rights in the domain names assigned to them. The fact that domain names can be bought and sold, or otherwise transferred, has reinforced this notion. However, the question of what specific property rights are inherent in domain names has led to numerous disputes, including some high-profile court cases. One such case was *Kremen v. Cohen* where the domain name sex.com, originally assigned to the plaintiff, was illegally appropriated by the defendant on the basis of a forged letter and developed into a multimillion dollar pornography Web site (Soares 2001). When the plaintiff sued to recover the domain name, the key question for the court was whether a domain name was tangible property or intangible property. The tort of conversion, in which one party wrongfully interferes with the right of possession of the other, has historically applied only to tangible property. Though the court ruled to return the registration to Kremen, it refused to identify domain names as tangible property subject to conversion, leaving it to the legislature to define the appropriate standards. In contrast, the Virginia Supreme Court ruled in another case, *Network Solutions, Inc. v. Umbro International*, that domain names were not property at all, but only a claim to a service provided by the domain name registrar. Therefore, a domain name was not subject to garnishment, because services provided by a third party could not be used to satisfy monetary claims against a defendant.

Property rights claims in other parts of the domain name system have also proved to be controversial. In *Verisign v. ICANN*, Verisign claimed that ICANN's attempt to prevent it from offering a service called Sitefinder was an unlawful restriction on its ability to do business (McGwire 2004; Jayakar 2004). Sitefinder was a service that would redirect an Internet user who mistypes a Web address to a site managed by itself, listing alternative Web sites for the user to choose. Verisign was able to offer this service due to its status as the registry for the .com and .net gTLDs, and therefore in charge of the authoritative TLD name servers. Implicit in this suit was Verisign's claim that the database of name registrations is also a registry's intellectual property, in which it has certain ownership rights. Network Solutions, Verisign's predecessor as the .com registry, had claimed in successive annual reports that the company had certain ownership rights in the database of information relating to customers in its registration business (Network Solutions 1998). The court dismissed the case citing insufficient evidence, but left the more fundamental question of property rights in registry lists unanswered.

All of these cases indicate the profound ambiguity surrounding the concept of property rights, as they are applied to domain names and registry lists. This question is likely to grow in importance with the increasing commercial value of domain names and other elements of the DNS. Some of these issues may need to be clarified by legislatures, and increasingly through international agreements. A question closely related to that of property rights is trademark policy.

Trademark Policy

Since the mid-1990s, a number of controversies have arisen over allegations by corporations that third-party registrants have registered trademarks belonging to them. Mueller (2002) has classified trademarks conflicts into several categories: character string conflicts (registration by a third party exactly matches a trademarked name); name speculation (deliberate registration of names to resell it at profit to trademark owner); typo-squatting (registering names close to that of a popular site, to benefit from mistyped addresses—e.g., yahooo); parody (registering a competitor's or opponent's name to suppress communication); and personality names (registering the names of celebrities).

Initially, the DNS had no policy to cover trademark disputes. RFC 1591, the document enunciating policies with respect to domain name allocations stated only that "In case of a dispute between domain name registrants as to the rights to a particular name, the registration authority shall have no role or responsibility other than to provide the contact information to both parties" (Section 4(1), Postel 1994). However, Network Solutions as the domain name registry was concerned that trademark disputes involving domain name allocations may create legal liabilities for itself: consequently, a dispute resolution policy was framed in 1995 that required registrants to certify that they intended to use the assigned name, and that the name did not violate the trademark of third parties (Mueller 2002). Also, Network Solutions reserved the right to take back a name assignment in case of a dispute when a prior trademark registration existed (previously, assignments were considered to be final). Network Solutions was trying to transfer liability to customers, and minimize legal costs—and ended up privileging large corporations over small users.

Soon after its formation, ICANN too came under pressure to frame a dispute resolution policy with regard to trademarks. The World Intellectual Property Organization (WIPO) representing the intellectual property industries presented a report to ICANN advocating several steps to protect trademarks (WIPO 1999). Incorporating some of the WIPO recommendations, ICANN eventually produced a Uniform Domain Name Dispute Resolution Policy (UDRP) that all registrars agree to implement as a formal requirement for accreditation (ICANN 1999). As was the case with the Network Solutions policy, registrants are held responsible for ensuring that domain name registrations did not violate any pre-existing trademarks: in addition, the UDRP framed administrative dispute-resolution procedures. Any third party may bring a dispute to ICANN if "a domain name is identical or confusingly similar to a trademark or service mark in which the complainant has rights; and the (current user) has no rights or legitimate interests in respect of the domain name; and/or (the) domain name has been registered and is being used in bad faith" (Section 4(a), ICANN 1999). The case will be referred to an administrative dispute-resolution service provider, which the complainant chooses from a list maintained by ICANN. If the complaint is sustained, the domain name registration may be cancelled or transferred to the complainant.

ICANN's UDRP has been generally welcomed by trademark and intellectual property interests, but it has also drawn a fair share of criticism. Froomkin (2002) for example has criticized the UDRP on both procedural and constitutional grounds: he argues that it tilts the process too much in favor of trademark interests and against individual users, and leads to the usurpation of the law-making function by a private corporation using its control over a vital Internet chokepoint. Geist (2002) examines cases arbitrated under the UDRP and finds considerable evidence of "forum shopping"—plaintiffs have used their right to choose the arbitration service provider to steer cases towards complainant-friendly courts, leading to a disproportionate number of judgments against registrants.

Creation of New Generic Top-Level Domains

One of the main responsibilities of ICANN as the custodian of the DNS root is to determine whether new generic TLDs need to be created, and to speedily create them whenever the need exists. However, attempts to add new gTLDs have repeatedly run into opposition from trademark interests who allege that new top-level domains increase the opportunity for unscrupulous third-parties to indulge in practices such as cybersquatting. To prevent such abuses, trademark interests have often registered their marks in multiple domains as a way of preempting malicious registrations—the addition of new TLDs, they allege, would impose additional costs of registration and monitoring on trademark holders. Thus, a recommendation against the creation of new gTLDs was a part of the WIPO Report submitted to ICANN in 1999 (WIPO 1999).

However, as several observers have argued (Mueller 2002; Pare 2003), restricting the number of new top-level domains creates an artificial scarcity in the domain name space that increase the value of existing registrations, and ironically provides an incentive for cybersquatting. But in spite of the increasing demand for new gTLDs, ICANN has expanded the original list only twice since 1998, the latest expansion bringing the total number to nineteen (see Table 1). Currently, ICANN is engaged in a public comment process to develop a policy framework for the introduction of new gTLDs: some of the questions under discussion include the framing of criteria to determine whether new gTLDs need to be added, procedures for the selection of TLD names, allocation methods to choose TLD registries, and the contractual obligations of ICANN and registries/registrars in the new domains.

Relationship with Country Code TLDs

Althogh ICANN was able to conclude registry agreements with Network Solutions/Verisign and other gTLD registries relatively easily with the backing of the U.S. government, it has faced more significant problems in bringing the ccTLDs within its sphere of oversight. The lack of any international treaty conferring legitimacy on ICANN, and the perception that it is a creature of the U.S. government has made international entities such as the ccTLD managers and the regional Internet registries (RIRs) managing IP address allocations less keen to submit themselves to ICANN oversight.

ICANN wanted ccTLD registries to be bound by the same responsibilities as the gTLDs under the registry agreements: however, country governments wanted to choose registries and registrars for their ccTLDs themselves, and to have policy authority over their own national Internet space. This conflict was especially acute when ccTLD registry functions needed to be transferred from one entity to the other. ICANN's original policy stated that ccTLD registry functions could be transferred only by consensus: "(IANA) must receive communications from both the old organization and the new organization that assure the IANA that the transfer is mutually agreed" (Section (e), Transfers and Disputes over Delegations, of ICANN policy document ICP-1 1999). However, national governments with coercive powers over their citizens have less need for consensus, and can take decisions unilaterally. As reported by Feld (2003), in South Africa, the government "acted unilaterally to assume control of its ccTLD, .za, through the expedient of making it a crime to operate the .za ccTLD except in a manner prescribed by the South African government" (p. 354).

Currently, an agreement crafted in ICANN's Government Advisory Committee (Principles and guidelines 2005), clearly establishes that the national government has the right to name the ccTLD registry: "ICANN should delegate the administration of a ccTLD only to an organization, enterprise or individual that has been designated by the relevant government or public authority" (Section 7.4). As of this writing, the vast majority of ccTLDs have not concluded a separate registry or sponsorship agreement with ICANN.

FUTURE OF THE DOMAIN NAME SYSTEM

So far in this article, the technical, institutional and policy aspects of the domain name system have been discussed. Though it is primarily a technical system, the importance of the DNS for the smooth functioning of the Internet has created tremendous public interest in its institutional and policy environment. Many aspects of the DNS are heavily contested politically, by both domestic and international interest groups and constituencies. A number of challenges remain to be overcome. Several initiatives now underway are likely to have a long term impact on the future of the DNS and by extension, the Internet.

Transition to IPv6

Policy documents on the IPv6 transition had intended the process to be simple, incremental and flexible by specifying four basic requirements (Bradner and Mankin 1995): that existing IPv4 hosts and routers should be upgradeable at any time without any other hosts or routers being upgraded; that new IPv6 hosts and routers could be installed at any time; that existing IPv4 hosts and routers may continue to use their existing addresses after being upgraded to IPv6; and that both upgrades and new IPv6 installations should be low cost, and involve little or no preparation work. In spite of these built-in precautions, IPv6 deployment has been slower than expected. A survey of local Internet registries (LIRs) to which IPv6 allocations have been made identified some of the reasons: absence of vendor support; low consumer demand, and lack of a "killer application" that requires the features available only in IPv6 (RIPE NCC 2002). Concerns about privacy may be a problem too: since the interface identifier portion of the IP address remains constant to enable autoconfiguration, it becomes possible to track the location and usage of a particular device (Euro6IX 2005). Cost is another factor—as one recent news report stated, the U.S. government alone may have to spend as much as $25 to $75 billion for a full transition to IPv6 (Kerner 2005).

In spite of the potential hurdles, it is evident that IPv6 deployment is only likely to accelerate as the problem of address scarcity becomes more acute. This is evident from the fact that more IPv6 prefixes have been allocated in Europe and Asia than in North America, including the United States (RIPE NCC 2006). Because proportionally more IPv4 address blocks were assigned in the United States in the early days of the Internet, the problem of address scarcity has been felt more quickly in Europe and Asia, resulting in quicker uptake of IPv6 address blocks.

Alternative Name Systems

Periodically, there have been attempts to set up competing domain name systems (called alt roots) in competition with the DNS, with their own root servers and top level domains. For example, several small Internet service providers came together to create the enhanced domain name service (eDNS) in 1997, with top-level domains such as .k12 for children, .npo for non-profit organizations, and .corp for corporations (Denninger 1997; Mueller 2002). Other alt roots include the Open Roots Server Confederation (ORSC) (www.open-rsc.org) and Open DNS (www.opendns.com). Most of these alternative root systems are now defunct.

A recent report (SSAC 2006) identified some of the reasons why alternative root systems continue to be attractive to some Internet stakeholders. Private name systems are sometimes set up by private networks for internal communications. Some commercial name system administrators may want to profit from registering names in new TLDs over which they have full control. Others may support alt root systems to signal dissatisfaction and to protest against the slow process of defining new TLDs by ICANN. National governments, distrustful of the U.S.-centered governance model embodied in ICANN, may want to support alt root systems to gain better control of the national domain name space, to remedy insufficient root server support in their territories, or to support domain names in local linguistic character sets. For example, official Chinese sources first announced (and later denied) that the Chinese government has set up its own top-level domains permitting the use of Chinese characters (Bray 2006a; 2006b). The reported reason was frustration at ICANN's lack of progress in creating non-Latin character domains.

Alternative root systems have major implications for interconnection and stability on the Internet. Because domain names listed with an alt root system would be invisible to the rest of the Internet unless listed in the dominant root system (the DNS) as well, the rise of alt root systems threaten to split the Internet. However, there are strong self-reinforcing "network externalities" inherent in root server systems—network administrators would "point" their name servers at the root system with a larger number of listings, and registrants would prefer root systems with more name servers pointing to them (Mueller 2002). This need to "see" and "be seen" would perpetuate the dominance of root systems with a larger number of domain name listings. It is very difficult for alternative systems to survive unless a critical mass of Internet stakeholders (registries, ISPs, users) simultaneously shift allegiance. Technically, alternative root systems may coexist with the dominant DNS if domain name registrants list their name in both the dominant DNS as well as in alt root systems; or if root systems "point" to one another to resolve unknown addresses. But dual registrations are unlikely because of the burden of registration fees and transaction costs, and cooperation between root systems is hindered by animosity and lack of trust. The emergence of an alternative system at present seems unlikely.

Althogh this appears to assure the continuing dominance of the DNS, there is a possibility that alternative root systems could be set up in the future especially if dissatisfaction with ICANN continues to mount. The root could be fragmented if, for example, an alliance of national governments, opposed to the special relationship of the U.S. government to ICANN, decides to promote up an alternative root system. Internationalizing domain name governance is thus a pressing priority.

Internationalizing Domain Name Governance

The Domain Name System enjoys a rather unique role as an emergent form of international cooperation. Traditionally, activities that span national borders have been conducted under the aegis of states, or of international organizations created through treaties between states. On the one hand, ICANN has been heralded as a new type of international organization, a path-breaking "private-public partnership" with global reach (ICANN 2004); an emergent "international regime" (Mueller 2002); "private ordering" (Schwarcz 2002), etc. On the other, ICANN has been criticized for the insularity and 'clubbiness' of its board of directors, the opacity of its decision-processes, the uncertainty about the values ICANN seeks (or should seek) to promote and the lack of meaningful outside appeal of its decisions (Froomkin 2002; Mueller 2002; Schwarcz 2002; Pare 2003; Weinberg 2000).

A recurrent theme of criticism is also that a decision-maker like ICANN whose influence spans the globe functions under a contract with the U.S. government. Though the U.S. government has often stated that its policy goal is to preserve private management of the DNS, several recent events have demonstrated that the U.S. government continues to exercise significant influence over ICANN's decision-making. In one such instance, ICANN in June 2005 initially approved a new TLD for adult content tentatively labeled .xxx (McCullagh 2005), but reversed itself in May 2006 by blocking it ("Internet agency nixes '.xxx' Web addresses", 2006). ICANN's Paul Twomey explained that the .xxx domain was rejected because ICANN did not want to become the enforcer of all national pornography laws. Though many foreign governments and private citizens too had objected to the new TLD for pornography, critics alleged that the main influence on ICANN was a letter from Michael Gallagher, assistant secretary in the U.S. Department of Commerce (Gallagher 2005).

It was for this reason that proposals like the gTLD-MOU have periodically surfaced to put Internet governance on a clearer international footing. The most recent of these initiatives is the dialog on Internet governance under the aegis of the World Summit on the Information Society (WSIS). The United Nations General Assembly resolved in 2001 to create an organization to promote a "people-centred, inclusive and development-oriented Information Society" (Section A(1), WSIS 2003). Accordingly, two summits of the WSIS were organized, the first at Geneva in December 2003, and the second at Tunis in November 2005. The issue of Internet governance gained prominence in the preparatory meetings to the Geneva WSIS summit: key concerns centered on the creation of a suitable international organization, support for a multilingual Internet and national sovereignty over each country's domain name space (Kleinwachter 2004). The final Declaration of Principles of the Geneva WSIS reflected these concerns calling for Internet management to be "multilateral, transparent and democratic, with full involvement of governments, the private sector, civil society and international organizations" (Art. 48); to be supportive of multilingualism (Art. 53); and to render assistance for developing countries (Art. 63) (WSIS 2003).

However, neither the Geneva Summit nor the parallel deliberations in the ITU Plenipotentiary Conference at Marrakech (1992) was able to bring about substantive changes in Internet governance: the final compromise was to agree to disagree, and to postpone the issue to the second WSIS in Tunis in 2005 (Kleinwachter 2004). To prepare a set of formal proposals for Tunis, a Working Group on Internet Governance was set up by the U.S. Secretary General. Its final report recommended that "no single government should have a pre-eminent role in relation to international Internet governance" (Section V, A(2), Working Group on Internet Governance 2005 p. 10). Four separate governance models were proposed for consideration, all involving a greater role for national governments in either an oversight or a policy-making capacity.

Meanwhile, the U.S. government, concerned about the internationalization of the DNS, produced a statement of principles asserting its intention to "maintain its historic role in authorizing changes or modifications to the authoritative root zone file" and supporting ICANN as "the appropriate technical manager of the Internet DNS" (NTIA 2005). This statement was seen by many as a preemptive shot-across-the-bow to forestall any moves at the WSIS or ITU to assert oversight over the DNS root. The same intention was also reflected in a "Sense of the Congress" resolution passed unanimously (423-0) in the U.S. House of Representatives (H. Con. Res. 268, passed November 16, 2005) stating that "the current structure of oversight and management of the Internet's domain name and addressing service works" and "therefore the authoritative root zone server should remain physically located in the United States and the Secretary of Commerce should maintain oversight of ICANN(.)" U.S. mainstream media too were generally supportive of the U.S. position: one national newspaper editorialized that the WSIS-ITU initiative was motivated only by anti-Americanism, a "reflexive" commitment to international governance, or Internet censorship (Puddington 2005). Though critics argued that the U.S. government's assertion of an "exceptional role as unilateral contracting and oversight authority for ICANN" (p. 2) was directly contradicting its own White Paper policy (Mueller et al., 2005), the overall consensus within that country was in favor of continued U.S. Department of Commerce control over ICANN.

These competing influences came to a head at the Tunis WSIS summit. Eventually, a compromise was negotiated preserving the status quo fundamentally unchanged, but authorizing the creation of an Internet Governance Forum with "no power beyond the ability to bring together all the 'stakeholders' in the Internet, from consumer groups to governments to private business" (Shannon 2005, p. 2). The structure, procedures, and policies of the forum are currently being debated (see for example, Mueller and Mathiason 2006).

The outcome of the WSIS debates on Internet governance was seen as a major victory for the U.S. position. But with the majority of Internet users now residing outside the United States, this victory may be temporary and calls for the internationalization of Internet governance are likely to recur in the future. Apace with the technical improvement of the system, the Internet community also needs improve the institutional and policy aspects of DNS management to make it more transparent, participative, fair, and internationally legitimate.

CROSS REFERENCES

See *History of the Internet; TCP/IP Suite; The Internet Fundamentals.*

REFERENCES

3Com. 2001. Understanding IP addressing: Everything you ever wanted to know. Santa Clara, CA: 3Com Corporation. http://www.3com.com/other/pdfs/infra/corpinfo/en_US/501302.pdf (accessed August 12, 2006).

Bradner, S., & A. Mankin. 1995. The recommendation for the IP next generation protocol. Request for comments (RCF) No. 1752. Network Working Group. http://tools.ietf.org/html/rfc1752 (accessed August 12, 2006).

Bray, H. 2006a, March 1. China creates own net domains: Bypass of U.S. control stirs fear of censorship. *Boston Globe*, p. 6.

Bray, H. 2006b, March 4. China denies launching Internet domain names. *Boston Globe*, p. 9.

.com Registry Agreement 2001. Marina del Rey, CA: ICANN. http://www.icann.org/tlds/agreements/verisign/registry-agmt-com-25may01.htm (accessed March 15, 2006).

Deering, S., & R. Hinden. 1998. Internet protocol, version 6 (IPv6) specification, request for comments (RCF) No. 2460. Network Working Group. http://tools.ietf.org/html/rfc2460 (accessed August 12, 2006).

Denninger, K. 1997. eDNS offers truly competitive Internet domain name registration (press release). http://www.iperdome.com/releases/970304.htm (accessed August 12, 2006).

Egevang, K., and P . Francis. 1994. The IP network address translator (NAT). (RCF) No. 1631. Network Working Group. http://tools.ietf.org/html/rfc1631

Euro6IX 2005. IPv6: Legal aspects of the new Internet protocol. Madrid, Spain. http: European IPv6 Internet Exchanges Backbone [Euro6IX]. http://www.ipv6tf.org/pdf/ipv6-legalaspects.pdf (accessed August 15, 2006).

Feld, H. 2003. Structured to fail: ICANN and the 'privatization' experiment. *Who rules the net? Internet governance and jurisdiction,* edited by, A. Thierer & C. W. Crews Jr. Washington, DC: Cato Institute, pp. 333–362.

Froomkin, A. M. 2000. Wrong turn in cyberspace: Using ICANN to route around the APA and the Constitution. *Duke Law Journal*, 50(1), 17–186.

Froomkin, A. M. 2002. ICANN's uniform dispute resolution policy: Causes and (partial) cures. *Brooklyn Law Review* 67(3), 605–718.

Fuller, V., T. Li., J. Yu. & K. Varadhan. (1993). Classless inter-domain routing (CIDR): An address assignment and aggregation strategy. RFC 1519. http://www.rfc-editor.org/rfcsearch.html

Gallagher, M. 2005. Letter from Michael Gallagher to Dr. Vinton Cerf, dated August 11, 2005. http://www.icann.org/correspondence/gallagher-to-cerf-15aug05.pdf (accessed November 28, 2006).

Geist, M. 2002. Fair.com?: An examination of the allegations of systematic unfairness in the ICANN UDRP. *Brooklyn Journal of International Law*, 27(3), 903–938.

Global Addressing Policy, ASO-001–2 2005. Marina del Rey, CA: ICANN. http://www.icann.org/general/allocation-IPv4-rirs.html (accessed March 12, 2006).

Hall, E. 2000. *Internet core protocols: The definitive guide: Help for network administrators*. Cambridge, MA: O'Reilly Media.

ICANN 1999. Uniform domain name dispute resolution policy. Marina del Rey, CA: ICANN. http://www.icann.org/udrp/udrp-policy-24oct99.htm (accessed, March 12, 2006).

ICANN. 2004, January 12. *Fact Sheet*. http://www.icann.org/general/fact-sheet.html (accessed March 12, 2006).

ICP-1, Internet domain name system structure and delegation: ccTLD administration and delegation 1999. Marina del Rey, CA: ICANN. http://www.icann.org/icp/icp-1.htm (accessed August 12, 2006).

"Improvement of technical management of Internet names and addresses" 63 Fed. Reg. 8825 1998 (to be codified at 15 CFR Chap. XXIII). http://www.ntia.doc.gov/ntiahome/domainname/dnsdrft.htm (accessed August 12, 2006).

Internet agency nixes '.xxx' Web addresses" 2006, May 10. msnbc.com. http://www.msnbc.msn.com/id/12728784/ (accessed July 17, 2007).

Internet Society 2005. The regional Internet registries. ISOC Member Briefing #21. Reston, VA: The Internet Society. http://www.isoc.org/briefings/021/briefing21.pdf (accessed August 7, 2006).

Jayakar, K. 2004. The Internet domain name system: Private property or public resource? Paper presented at the Telecommunications Policy Research Conference, Washington, DC.

Kerner, S.M. 2005. Could a U.S. shift to IPv6 cost $75B? Internetnews.com. http://www.Internetnews.com/infra/article.php/3570211 (accessed August 12, 2005).

Kleinwächter, Wolfgang 2004. Beyond ICANN vs. ITU: Will WSIS open new territory for Internet governance? In Don MacLean (Ed.) *Internet governance: A grand collaboration* (ICT Task Force Series 5). New York: United Nations ICT Task Force, pp. 31–52.

"Management of Internet names and addresses" 63 Fed. Reg. 31741 1998. http://www.ntia.doc.gov/ntiahome/domainname/6_5_98dns.htm (accessed June 12, 2006).

McCullagh, D. (2005, June 1). Porn-friendly '.xxx' domain approved. CNETnews.com. http://www.cnet.com (accessed November 29, 2006).

McGwire, D. 2004. Suit challenges the powers of key Internet authority. http://www.washingtonpost.com/wpdyn/technology/techpolicy/icann/ (accessed February 27, 2004).

Memorandum of understanding between the U.S. Department of Commerce and the Internet Corporation for Assigned Names and Numbers (1998). http://www.icann.org/general/icann-mou-25nov98.htm (accessed February 5, 2004).

Mockapetris, P. 1983a. Domain names: Concepts and facilities, RFC 882. Sterling, VA: Internet Engineering Task Force Secretariat. http://www.ietf.org/frfc/rfc882.txt (accessed November 29, 2006).

Mockapetris, P. (1983b). Domain names: Implementation and specification, RFC 883. Sterling, VA: Internet Engineering Task Force Secretariat. http://www.ietf.org/frfc/rfc883.txt (accessed November 29, 2006).

Modification to Joint Project Agreement, Affirmation of Responsibilities for ICANN Private Sector Management 2006, September 29. http://www.icann.org/general/JPA-29sep06.pdf (accessed November 29, 2006).

Mueller, M. 2002. *Ruling the root: Internet governance and the taming of cyberspace*. Cambridge, MA: MIT Press.

Mueller, M., J. Mathiason, L. McKnight, H. Klein, M. Holitscher. 2005. The future U.S. role in Internet governance: 7 points in response to the U.S. Commerce Department's 'Statement of Principles'. Syracuse, NY: Internet Governance Project. http://www.Internetgovernance.org/pdf/igp-usrole.pdf (accessed November 25, 2005).

Mueller, M., J. Mathiason. 2006. Building an Internet governance forum. Syracuse, NY: Internet Governance Project. http://www.Internetgovernance.org/pdf/igp-forum.pdf (accessed August 12, 2006).

National Research Council. 2005. *Signposts in cyberspace: The domain name system and Internet navigation*. Washington, DC: National Academies Press.

National Telecommunications and Information Administration (NTIA). 2005. U.S. principles on the Internet's domain name and addressing system. Washington, DC: NTIA. http://www.ntia.doc.gov/ntiahome/domainname/USDNSprinciples_06302005.htm (accessed January 5, 2006).

Network Solutions. 1998. Form 10-K annual report. Washington, DC: Securities and Exchange Commission.

Pare, D. M. 2003. *Internet governance in transition: Who is the master of this domain?* Lanham, MD: Rowman & Littlefield Publishers.

Postel, J. 1994. Domain name system structure and delegation. RFC 1591. http://www.faqs.org/rfcs/rfc1591.html (accessed November 16, 2006).

Principles and guidelines for the delegation and administration of country code top level domains. 2005. Government Advisory Committee. http://gac.icann.org/web/home/ccTLD_Principles.rtf (accessed August 12, 2006).

Puddington, A. 2005, November 12. Keep the Internet free. Washington Post, p. A25.

RIPE NCC. 2002. Survey of IPv6 Address Space Usage. http://www.ripe.net/rs/ipv6/index.html. (accessed August 15, 2006).

RIPE NCC. 2006. Total number of allocated IPv6 prefixes per RIR. http://www.ripe.net/rs/ipv6/stats/ (accessed August 15, 2006).

Schwarcz, S. L. 2002. Private ordering. *Northwestern University Law Review,* 97, 319.

Shannon, V. 2005, November 16. A compromise of sorts on Internet control. *New York Times,* p. C2.

Soares, V. 2001. Are domain names property? The sex.com controversy. *Duke Law and Technology Law* Review 0032. http://www.law.duke.edu/journals/dltr/articles/2001dltr0032.html (accessed August 9, 2006).

SSAC 2006. Alternative TLD name systems and roots: Conflict, control and consequences. SSAC Report SAC009. Marina del Rey, CA: Security and Stability Advisory Committee [SSAC], ICANN. http://www.icann.org/committees/security/alt-tlds-roots-report-31mar06.pdf (accessed August 15, 2006).

Tarjanne, P. 1997. Internet governance: Towards voluntary multilateralism. Keynote address at the Internet Domain Names Information session, Meeting of the Signatories and Potential Signatories of the Generic Top Level Domain Memorandum of Understanding (gTLD-MOU). Geneva: ITU. http://www.itu.int/newsarchive/projects/dns-meet/KeynoteAddress.html (accessed February 16, 2004).

Weinberg, J. 2000. ICANN and the problem of legitimacy. Duke Law Journal, 50(1), 187–260.

WIPO 1999. The management of Internet domain names and addresses: Intellectual property issues. Final Report of the WIPO Internet Domain Name Process. Geneva, Switzerland: WIPO. http://arbiter.wipo.int/processes/process1/report/pdf/report.pdf (accessed March 12, 2006).

Working Group on Internet Governance (2005). Report from the Working Group on Internet Governance, Doc. WSIS-II/PC-3/DOC/5-E. Geneva: World Summit on the Information Society.

World Summit on the Information Society [WSIS] 2003. Geneva Declaration of Principles, Doc.WSIS-03/GENEVA/DOC/4-E. Geneva: WSIS. http://www.itu.int/wsis/docs/geneva/official/dop.html (accessed August 17, 2006).

Information Retrieval on the Internet

Raymond F. Wisman, *Indiana University Southeast*

INTRODUCTION

Information retrieval research and development cuts across many disciplines that include cognitive science, human-computer interfacing, information science, and linguistics and has long been considered a fundamental part of computing. Through Web-based search engines, information retrieval has become a mass consumer item and a large and sometimes lucrative business. But what precisely is meant by information retrieval? For this chapter an appropriate dictionary definition of information is "knowledge acquired in any manner; facts, data; learning; lore" implying that information can take any form including the text, images, music, or multimedia content common to the Internet. Definitions of information retrieval are numerous and exist in part as a result of the shared interest by the many disciplines concerned with acquiring, storing, and discovering information. However, the term information retrieval has generally come to be applied to such content that lacks a predefined structure and must then be modeled (by keyword, color, rhythms, and so on) in order to determine the content relevant to a particular query.

Internet IR is distinguished by the connection of an unparalleled number of information sources. Internet technology has at a minimum changed the scale and scope of information retrieval but promises more fundamental outcomes. Information has played a critical role in human development, a role that has often been focused and magnified through technology. The importance of information technology cannot be overstated as historically technology has determined whether information has been limited to the few or many, whether spanning geography and time. Writing, as an information storage technology, gave those with the means access to information from those they might never directly meet. Writing provided long-term information storage and retrieval, books collected and stored information on related topics and libraries were established to systematize storage and retrieval of books. The printing press revolutionized society; by reducing book costs literacy rates increased to give an average person access to information outside their personal experience. The press did not produce any new information but merely encouraged sharing information by being more rapid, cheaper, and available than previous technologies, a technology that merely made information retrieval—in essence—easier.

Print and the Internet each support the collecting and sharing of information, but Internet technology provides two additional abilities. Where printing promoted literacy which increased the consumption of information, the Internet has made everyone a potential producer—where print created mostly disconnected islands of information, the Internet has created the potential of a single large collection. The intersection of these two capabilities make Internet information retrieval unique and important as for the first time in history a major portion of the world's information is instantly available to a large number of individuals. Although Internet technology creates the collective information pool, the challenge is locating the right information to retrieve.

This chapter is primarily about that challenge—how to find the right information—providing an overview of the approaches currently employed. The chapter focus is then Internet IR technology, meaning those systems that would not exist without the massive number of information sources the Internet provides. Those information types considered include the most common on the Internet—text, images, audio, music, video, and multimedia. Purposely limited from close examination are many important IR systems that happen to be accessed over the Internet, but do not effectively utilize the information collection created by the Internet structure. Such systems do not depend upon the high degree of interconnection or great number of potential information sources available through the Internet.

The Internet has been a remarkable vehicle for IR development. Because Internet IR depends upon such a large and diverse set of technologies that range from search algorithms to mobile devices to server architectures to user interfaces and beyond, some choice of topics and depth of coverage have been necessary in organizing the chapter. As the most familiar and successful contemporary example of an Internet IR system, the text search engine is discussed in some detail serving as a model for discussing IR of other media. Although IR for each media type will be examined, a short overview now of some key points will be helpful later.

IR system technology can be viewed as having two main parts, the interface used by the searcher to query the retrieval system and that part concerned with organizing and retrieving the information. In systems such as the text search engine the two parts are very loosely coupled and user control strictly limited. Text search engines and browser text boxes for queries form the predominant IR system of the Internet. But searching other media presents a very different set of problems that require very different retrieval techniques depending on whether the information form is text, images, audio, metadata, or some combination. User interfaces can also provide a richer set of tools to control search and assist in organizing the results into meaningful information.

One key characteristic possessed by text versus other media is semantics or that each individual word has meaning. Words are also easy to index, for users to create queries and for retrieval; users can also understand and use the results in refining their next query. Other media, such as images and audio, consist of many low-level features that only when combined and synthesized can be understood to have meaning. For example, at low-level, digital images may contain millions of differently colored pixels but at a higher-level, that of semantics, these pixels represent a friend or for a group of audio features, a song. Non-text media is also of much higher dimension, there are many features that define an image, such as color, texture, and shape, which must be distinctively encoded and indexed for efficient retrieval over large, Internet-size collections. Formulating queries in a non-text media has often been limited to low-level feature (e.g. colors) examples for retrieving similar media or text when semantics could be inferred from the media. Combined, these differences help explain why text IR is a key technology on the Internet while there are currently few Internet-scale non-text IR systems. Even though none have achieved the functional level of text search engines, research and development progress has been significant and continuing.

The chapter is organized as follows. As the most familiar, intuitive, and developed of IR systems, text search engines are examined first and most extensively while providing a foundation for separately exploring other media types and systems. Because IR systems are also tools for exploring information, user interfaces that support discovery of information are a critical part of the system. The retrieval technology and user interface will generally be reviewed in context as a complete IR system to better understand their interaction. However, exploratory search, a distinct search strategy of importance particularly for large information collections, will be examined separately. The reader should also be aware that Internet text IR as exemplified by the search engine is comparatively mature and commercially established but IR of other media and other approaches, although many examples exist, is still much in the realm of research.

TEXT INFORMATION RETRIEVAL

Text IR, as exemplified by search engine sites such as Google, is arguably the most common, economically successful and technically mature of the Internet IR. An examination of text IR and search engines can provide the fundamentals necessary to understanding Internet IR in general; hence, we will examine common text search engines first and in greater detail and apply those lessons to understanding other approaches and media.

What explains the success of search engines? For technical reasons examined later, text is simpler to search than other media such as audio or visuals. Much of Internet text IR is Web-based and involves three participants: the searcher, the search engine site, and the information source, a Web site. The Internet IR and Web development has been strongly influenced by business models based on text that is generally available for free as compared to commercial audio and visuals. Web sites generally post free text for self-promotional reasons, whereas audio and visuals are often produced at considerable cost for explicitly commercial reasons. One can argue that text search is successful to a large degree because a common interest is served where the information searcher, search engine, and Web sites each derives benefit. It is useful to keep in mind that the searcher is the only reason for Web sites and search engines to exist and is then in the interest of each to satisfy the searcher's needs.

The searcher, search engine, and Web site then comprise an IR system that to fully examine, we should and will consider each in turn. Examined first will be searcher issues that include the recognized types of search strategies and measures of performance followed by the workings of a typical search engine and concluding with the Web site holding the information, how to establish what search engines search, and how to manage or influence search engines to a Web site's benefit. Although IR has a strong technical element, IR serves human activities that are directly influenced by human perceptions; the discussion will necessarily include a mixture of technical and non-technical topics.

Developing a broad perspective of the text search process is useful before a detailed examination of individual components begins. Figure 1 illustrates the characteristic interaction between the three partners in information search and retrieval. First steps of the process typically begin by submitting the Web site's main page URL to the search engine or when the site is otherwise discovered. The typical search engine architecture (Arasu et al. 2001) consists of two main parts; one component called a spider (or crawler, robot) visits the Web site to retrieve pages linked from the main page much as a person using a browser would follow links to new pages. The spider follows links, indexing meaningful words from the retrieved pages which are stored along with the page's Web site location for later searches and retrievals. The second component of the search engine interacts with the searcher by providing a user interface for the searcher to query the search engine and receive back a list of relevant Web site page locations from which the searcher can select and retrieve pages directly from the Web site. Closing

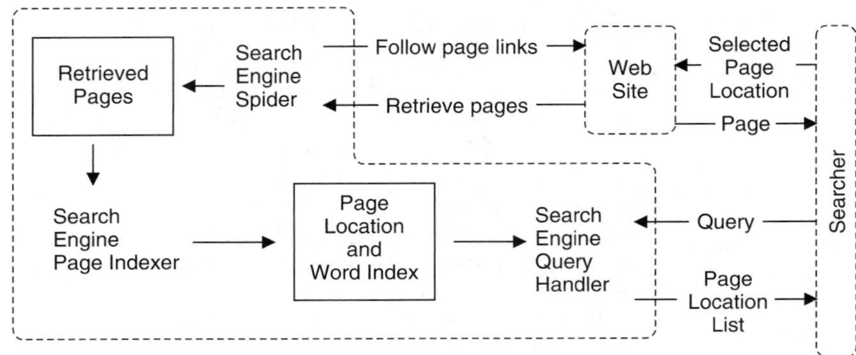

Figure 1: An overview of a search engine and its relation to Web sites and information searchers. The basic steps to Web search are as follows: a search engine spider visits a Web site to retrieve and index pages into a database for later searches; the searcher sends queries to the search engine; the search engine locates pages containing text similar to the query and sends the searcher a list of page locations; the searcher selects and retrieves pages from the Web site.

the information space between the searcher and Web site is then the primary purpose of the search engine.

The IR system implemented by a typical text search engine is relatively technically simple, but, unlike most non-Internet IR systems, involves three separate entities each with differing and sometimes conflicting goals for IR. To separate one from the other, the following sections examine this system from the three different points of view of the searcher, search engine, and Web site.

Searcher Issues

Why search? A simple answer is that the Web is too large and unorganized to find much useful information by simply employing a manual browsing strategy that follows links from one page to another. Describing the growth of the Internet and the Web would seem an exercise in hyperbole but for the fact that it is astounding. By 1999, public sites already contained about 800 million pages on about 3 million servers (Lawrence and Giles 1999), by 2005 it was estimated to have grown to 11.5 billion pages (Gulli and Signorini 2005). The number of Web sites exceeded 100 million in November 2006 (Netcraft.com 2006), an increase of over 30 million in a single year.

The purpose of the original Web design was simply to interconnect bits and pieces of scattered information with no plan to find information other than by manually browsing from one piece of information to another via connecting links. To some degree, search engine systems merely automate the process and move faster from one piece to the next than users do while collecting information along the way for later retrieval. Web site usability studies recognize search as one of the most important means for finding information (Nielsen 1997). Although Web pages generally provide specific navigation choices, more than half of all Web site visitors navigate predominately by search and use search as their first choice to find specific information. Many usability experts argue that search is so important it should be available from every single page on a Web site. Part of that rationale for search is that once visitors navigating connection links get lost they will need search and should not have to search for a search page.

Types of Search

Search often fails to some degree; even though the information may be available in the IR system, searcher strategies may not be compatible to produce optimal results. For the IR system designer interested in identifying good search strategies it is worthwhile to consider the different types of search and how search engines align with different strategies. Information retrieval experts (Rosenfield and Morville 1998) recognized four ways in which people search.

Known-item Search: A search engine is not always necessary. Searching a brokerage site for the latest stock quote is one example. The information sought is unique, is easily recognized when found, and often exists at known Web sites. Searching, if any, is short and direct and the answer immediately recognized. Search is unneeded if the information location remains fixed, even as the information changes. The search can be restricted to specific sites, reducing search time and improving the information quality.

Existence Search: Appropriate when prior knowledge of a subject exists. For example, existence search can easily discover cases of plagiarism, such as where some part of one site has been copied to another. However, consider the difficulty in searching for something that may not exist. Suppose that someone who needed to organize phone number lists, notes, and appointments had never heard of a personal digital assistant (PDA). The person would know the needed function but not where to look or that a PDA even existed. Search can meander as users discover and digest information; even recognizing the answer when found may be difficult. Web search engines are a natural choice for determining whether information exists because they attempt to find all available information on the Web. Entering a few well-chosen query words to a search engine will search millions of pages and can produce thousands of pieces of information. One gap in existence searching is that search engines cover only a fraction of the Web; the more obscure information can exist on parts of the Web never visited and hence unknown to the search engine.

Exploratory Search: An iterative process of acquiring subject knowledge by collecting and integrating information that leads to further exploration. This is the case when the user knows that the subject such as a PDA exists, but does not know exactly what a PDA can do and needs to learn more. Uncovering and comprehending the information may be long and circuitous; recognizing the answer may not be immediately possible due to the lack of subject knowledge. One productive search strategy is browsing information organized into subject lists with main subject areas and a breakdown into finer categories of related subjects.

Comprehensive Search: This type of search is best suited when users know the search subject, can recognize the answer when found, and need all available information on the subject. For someone with a general knowledge of PDAs, buying a PDA requires comprehensive information on several brands, models, and suppliers to make an informed decision. Web search engines work well for comprehensive searching of the entire Web but for broad subjects such as PDAs can produce an overwhelming volume of information.

Text IR as currently practiced on the Internet can be further lumped into the two broad types of analytical and exploratory search (Marchionini 2006). The common search engine supports analytical searches, those that are primarily a direct look up based on existing knowledge of the information sought. Exploratory search is not well supported by the search engine model. Exploratory search places the user more in control of the direction and pace of search, providing organization, cues, or other guidance to create an uninterrupted exploration guided by human participation. A variety of exploratory search models have been developed, many visually illustrate information relationships in spatial dimensions, and many include elements of text mining to reveal those relationships. Although search engines support only analytical search directly, alternative approaches often incorporate search engine results for implementing other forms of search and other media than text; several of these will be discussed in the following sections.

Information Sources

Most successful information searches fail to some degree on the first attempt. Other than the known-item search, most searches evolve to use several search strategies as one attempts to iteratively improve the relevancy of information retrieved. Though the term search engine is often applied to any Web-based information source, there are at least two main types of Web information sites: those that automatically organize information and those having human-organized lists. Many information sites provide a mixture of the two following approaches.

Lists: Catalogs, directories, and lists are similar examples of human-organized subject indexes of Web-based information. A list arranges subjects into a hierarchy that allow exploration from a general topic, such as "education," down to the more specific subtopic of "graduation poems." On most lists, humans index the subjects providing control and intelligence to the subject hierarchy organization, arguably yielding less but higher quality information than current automated cataloging systems. The hierarchical approach works well for exploratory search when one is familiar with the search subject and has a good sense of how the subject fits within the hierarchies of a larger subject.

Finding a subject in a hierarchical list can be difficult when the searcher's idea of subject organization differs from that of the person creating the list. For those cases, a keyword query can search the subject list as a way to pierce an opaque subject hierarchy; a query such as "graduation poems" will generally locate the same information as manually moving through the "education" subject hierarchy. If the query fails, many list services automatically send the query to a Web search engine.

Although information sites consisting mainly of human-organized lists or automated searches are often lumped together as search engines, how each gathers and represents information is quite different. Human-organized lists depend upon editors to first review Web site pages and organize the collected information into subject hierarchies. A searcher can then manually browse a subject hierarchy list to find information. Lists more accurately reflect true page content than automated searches because human editors do not review the parts of a page not normally seen by a reader and can ignore gratuitous or repetitive words used to attract a search engine. One weakness of lists is the effort required of the editors to perform the review. After a site review is completed, significant changes to the site content are unlikely to prompt another review, although most lists do accept site resubmissions.

Search Engine: A search engine essentially matches query words with words on Web pages and lists the pages containing the matching words. Entering the query word "zucchini" returns a list of pages containing the word "zucchini." In practice, Web search engines examine pages drawn from across the Internet to automatically calculate measures to rank pages in order of some specified information relevancy. Determining a meaningful page rank based on a few query words is challenging and sometimes produces completely irrelevant results. Entering the single word "zucchini" will find any page mentioning "zucchini," from gardening to cooking to diet; which "zucchini" page is important is ultimately in the mind of the searcher. Determining how to rank one document against thousands of others is a key point of competition between search engines and often the identical search on any two will produce different results, searchers may need to consult several to have confidence in the results. Metasearch engines automate searching on multiple sites by sending the search query to a number of search engines and creating a fusion of the results. Overall, search engines are best suited for existence and comprehensive types of analytical searches where the relative quantity of information retrieved is important.

Measuring Performance

Ideally, a search engine result includes all relevant documents, ranked in order of relevance. Search engine performance can therefore never be perfect as the Web is indexed incompletely and relevancy is highly subjective.

Several definitions of search performance common in the literature are: "relevancy," "recall," and "precision." Relevancy measures the usefulness of the references retrieved, is subjectively determined, and may vary as searching and knowledge acquisition of a subject evolve.

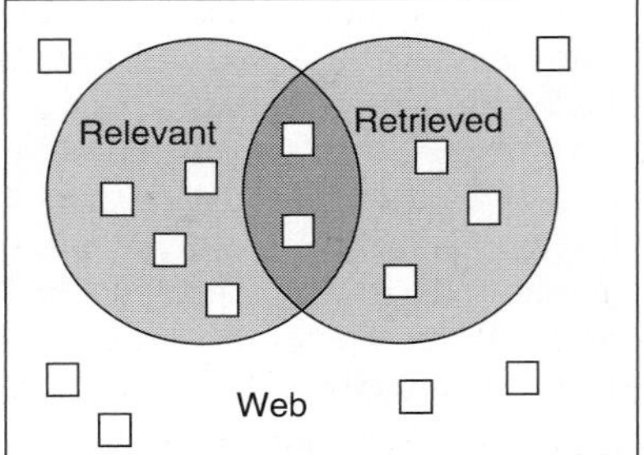

Figure 2: Retrieved versus relevant pages when searching the Web. The intersection of retrieved and relevant pages will likely be relatively small in part because only a fraction of the Web is indexed

Figure 2 illustrates three useful points: (1) that relevant references are generally a subset of all the references available; (2) that retrieved information generally includes some irrelevant references; and (3) that the intersection of retrieved and relevant references will often exclude references that are relevant (van Rijsbergen 1979). The following definitions of *recall* and *precision* complement the intuition illustrated in Figure 2:

$$recall = \frac{|retrieved \cap relevant|}{|relevant|}$$

$$precision = \frac{|retrieved \cap relevant|}{|retrieved|}$$

Recall is the percentage of relevant references retrieved. A recall of 50% means that only one-half of the relevant references were retrieved; retrieving every possible reference yields 100% recall but often includes many references that are irrelevant. Precision is the percentage of retrieved references that are relevant. Of the references retrieved, a precision of 50% means that only one-half of the references were relevant; returning only one relevant reference yields 100% precision but possibly very poor recall. A "weight loss" query can yield perfect recall by retrieving every Web page in existence but will likely produce many that are not relevant, so that precision is poor. Simultaneously achieving perfect recall and precision is nearly impossible even when searching carefully designed and constructed sets of known information.

Performance Measures

The three most common performance measures are recall, precision, and ranking. As discussed, *recall* is defined as the percentage of relevant pages found and *precision* as the percentage of pages found that are relevant. A search engine calculates *rank* to measure relative page relevancy, using individual page rank to order the pages from less to highly relevant. As a way to gauge individual search engine strengths and weaknesses, the following describes searches that provide observations of these three measures.

Recall: Searching for something one knows is on a Web site gives a rough estimate of recall. If a user's name appears in Web pages on his or her site, searching on that name should return results from the site and perhaps other sites as well. If recall is 100 percent, restricting the search to the user's specific site should return all pages on the site containing the user's name. For testing recall, the Google search engine query "vegetarian site: www.eatmorevegetables.com" should return all pages with the word "vegetarian" from the fictitious site "www.eatmorevegetables.com." Most search engines follow only a limited number of page links on a single site, stopping at some maximum number of links deep. Searching for pages several links deep from the site main page then measures the search engine's recall ability. If one-half of the relevant pages on a site are found, recall is 50 percent and indicates that the search engine spider stopped after following some arbitrary number of links from one page to the next.

Precision: Precision is difficult to mechanically quantify as it measures the number of relevant pages among those found and relevancy is by nature subjective. Because search engines generally list only pages that contain matching query words, precision is always arguably high. However, when users find thousands of pages and only a few are relevant to their needs, the challenge is to focus the search on more relevant and generally fewer pages. The searcher can influence the search precision by including or excluding query words, limiting the search to known sites, or using other search controls. Searching for a known page can test the degree of search control and precision afforded by a search engine. Most search engines provide sufficient control to limit the results to a single page. For example, on some search engines the query "vegetarian diet" would find all pages with "vegetarian diet" anywhere in the page whereas the query title: "vegetarian diet" would find only pages with that phrase in the page title. The more refinement afforded by the search controls, the better the search precision possible.

Rank: Rank reflects the calculated relevancy of a document. One key factor determining rank is the number of query words matched in a page; generally the more words matched the higher the rank. Matching rare words also increases the rank of the page. Search engines can also employ the structure of the Web to improve relevancy based on links to and from other pages to augment the ranking of pages. Pages with many links from other pages generally rank higher than pages of equal similarity to the query but with fewer links.

Page popularity and importance are two common ranking measures based on link structure. Popularity assigns a higher rank to pages having more references from other pages, under the assumption that a frequently referenced page is more relevant than a page with fewer references. However, a popular page is not automatically important. Page importance further assumes that pages or sites that mutually refer to one another form groups of importance or authority on a subject. The more references to a page from others in the group, the greater the importance and consequent rank of the page. The resulting groups are somewhat analogous to the subjects of a list service with the exception that humans organize subject lists and the interconnecting references organize a group. Automatic grouping can produce more focused and higher quality references but eschew the hierarchical organization that supports browsing of subjects by the searcher.

Which ranking approach produces the best result depends upon the user's search needs. Comprehensive search is the natural outcome of search based on word match ranking alone but yields no organization of the results. Existence and exploratory search can benefit from the reference-based ranking methods of popularity and importance. Popularity ranking anticipates that the information that many others reference represents common knowledge of a subject. Importance attempts to refine popularity ranking by organizing references into supporting groups. Grouping together documents that have common references will generally provide more homogeneous results and is best suited for exploratory search in which the subject is recognized.

Search Control

The user interface is a key component of any system involving humans, in the case of an IR system, the user interface provides the searcher the means of controlling the search process. User interfaces for the major search engines are a model of simplicity and appropriate for analytical searching. Text IR on the Internet, by almost any measure, has been a success in part as a result of this simplicity and intuitiveness in which the searcher and search engine interact through a straightforward turn-taking relationship of sending queries and receiving a linear ranking of results. Key is that the search model employs text to find text allowing the searcher to compose a simple example query in text to search for documents having matching text. This uncomplicated user interface is possible in large part because the searcher has a well-developed knowledge of the semantic value of the words used in the open-ended queries and in the returned results. It should be noted that although the searcher is keenly interested in the semantics of the query and results, as will be seen in the next section, the typical search engine makes little use of semantics.

An important element of IR user interfacing is feedback that indicates not only some measure of search success but also reflects an obvious relationship between the query and results. The feedback provided by the search engine is often a linear, ordered ranking of search results relating the query words with the text in which the words were matched. Because the search engine makes little if any use of query or document semantics, the results are strongly influenced by query word occurrence within the document. Given that search engines are tuned to achieve a high degree of precision for the first few page results and high recall for subsequent pages, result lists can consist of several thousands of matched documents. Although the feedback is critical to refining future queries, the feedback provided is often too great and not always clearly related to the initial query as to be helpful in refining future queries.

Fine control of search queries to yield higher quality references is possible in theory and is provided in some form by most search engines. The more common search controls include ones similar to those below.

Adding Search Terms: Adding search terms to the query can improve the precision of search results. The query "weight loss" produces millions of pages with each containing the word "weight," "loss," or both. Adding terms for "vegetarian weight loss diet" produces merely 10,000 but more focused references. Each page found still contains at least one or more of the query words. Because search engines generally rank pages higher that match more query terms, pages with fewer discriminating terms are effectively ignored.

Phrases: Queries consisting of phrases can yield more precise results than the same words when matched independently. A query of the phrases "vegetarian diet" "weight loss" produces only about 3,000 page references, of which the highest ranked pages contain both of the two phrases.

Inclusion and Exclusion: Query words prefixed with a "+" are words that must be included or found on a Web page, whereas words prefixed with a "−" must be excluded or not occur on the page. The query "+diet -vegetarian" then means that "diet" must be found on the page and "vegetarian" must not be found. The Boolean operators AND, NOT, AND NOT are often used alternatives to the "+" and "−" operators. The query "diet AND NOT vegetarian" is normally equivalent to our earlier query. The OR operator matches either term; "weight OR mass" matches "weight" interchangeably with "mass."

Proximity: Limiting matches to only words or phrases occurring within a close proximity to another assumes that nearness implies some relation between the words. The query "vegetarian NEAR diet" would find pages having "vegetarian" within a few words of "diet" but exclude pages having "diet" distanced from "vegetarian" by more than the proximity word limit.

Wildcard: An "*" at the end of a word or partial word expands the range and number of matching words. For example, the query "veget*" finds pages that include "vegetarian," "vegetable," and any other words starting with "veget."

Field: Limiting the search to a designated field of the Web page, such as considering only pages available on a specified Web site, can greatly narrow the search focus. As an example, title: "vegetarian diet" requires "vegetarian diet" to be part of the page title field, whereas "site:food.com" limits the search to the "food.com" Web site pages. The link control lists all pages with a reference link to a specified site; the query "link:food.com" will list all pages that link to pages on the "food.com" Web site.

As already noted, the common search engine supports analytical searches, those that are primarily a direct lookup based on existing knowledge of the information sought, but does not support browsing of information necessary for rapid exploration of a topic for which little is known. Ideally, the user interface complements IR, adapting to the changing needs of the user as their search for information evolves. However, the typical user interface strictly limits user choices and control of the interaction possible between the search engine and searcher. User interfacing is more of an issue for IR of media other than text and other search strategies than direct search; a more general user interface discussion will be delayed for inclusion with other media and strategies.

Basic Search Engine Implementation

Automated search engines have two main tasks: organizing selected words from each page into an index and answering search queries from that index. Web-based search engines owe a debt to the foundational work on traditional full-text IR systems, such as the SMART and SIRE systems discussed below (Salton and McGill 1983) to present a foundational and somewhat simpler perspective of their operation. In place of human editors to extract and index subject information from pages, such systems perform automatic indexing of complete pages into an inverted index database containing lists of words and the corresponding pages that contain each word. In answering queries, the search system compares query words to page words from the index, retrieving those pages that have a high calculated similarity to the query.

Indexing

Selected words of a page have a weight factor calculated based in part on word frequency. Weight measures may also give greater or lesser importance to words in different parts of the page; for example, title words generally receive more weight than regular text words. A word that occurs in few pages also has a higher weight, based on the proportion of times that the word occurs in a single page relative to all other pages. A word that occurs on only one page would have relatively high weight, whereas a word occurring on all pages would have low weight, the rationale being that a rare word is more useful in finding a specific page than a word common to many pages.

The same rationale applies to the removal of stop words such as conjunctions and pronouns that convey little meaning due to the high frequency of their use. Note that stop words may also be indexed for comparison with user queries consisting of phrases containing stop words such as "The Statue of Liberty." Stemming is an additional method used to minimize the number of unique words retained by converting all word forms to some base form. A simple stemming algorithm may only convert plural to singular form while a more aggressive stemming algorithm might additionally convert *vegetable* and *vegetarian* to a common stem of *vegeta*.

Conceptually, a simple two-dimensional matrix is constructed (commonly known as a term-document matrix) containing the calculated weight of each remaining word on each page; pages define one dimension and the other dimension defined by the words remaining in that page after stemming and stop word removal. In fact, an inverted index is often generated that contains all remaining words from all pages; included with each word is a list of all the pages that contain the word. For each page in the list, there is stored the frequency with which the word occurs in the page for weight calculation and the external location of the page for later retrieval.

A variety of methods exist to quantify the importance of a given word in a given document (page). Documents (pages) can be represented by a weighted vector of terms (words) as

$$D_i = <t_j, w_{ij}>$$

in which w_{ij} represents the weight of term t_j in document D_i and non-existent terms in a particular document have a weight of zero. Queries can be represented similarly as

$$Q_i = <t_j, w_{ij}>$$

The weight of each term depends upon its frequency of occurrence in the document and the number of documents in which it appears. The weight of a term is then given as

$$<w_{ij}> = tf_{ik} \times \mathrm{idf}_k$$

in which tf_{ik} is the number of occurrences or term frequency of term t_k in document i, and idf_k is the inverse document frequency of the term t_k in the collection of all documents. Among the simpler of the numerous inverse document frequency definitions is

$$\mathrm{idf}_k = \log(N/n_k)$$

in which N is the total number of documents in which n_k have occurrences of t_k.

Note that Web search engines must differ significantly from traditional search engines because of the large number of pages that are scattered across many thousands of Web sites and that each page can have connecting links to many other pages. To find pages and build the index, the indexing program must then visit Web sites as one would with a browser, starting at a page, visiting connected pages, and indexing each page as it goes. In the jargon of the Web, a spider, robot, or Web-crawler is the program that visits or crawls connected pages, indexing selected parts from the visited pages. The resulting index contains the word lists of traditional text searching and the unique location of the page for retrieval. For each page indexed, the connecting references to other Web pages are also included when link analysis to determine ranking by such measures as popularity or importance of pages is to be performed.

Retrieval

The traditional retrieval process produces a ranking of all pages that contain one or more query words entered by the searcher which serves to restrict the number of pages examined. The retrieval operation consists of converting the query words to the same representation as the pages, calculating some similarity measure between the query and each page in the collection, and retrieving pages from the collection ranked in order of high to low similarity.

Boolean logic forms the basis of the conceptually simplest retrieval approach. Queries are formed as combinations of search words and logic operators such as AND, OR, and NOT; simple retrieval is implemented as set intersection, union and difference respectively between the query and pages. For example, the query "diet AND vegetarian" is implemented by retrieving pages that contain the intersection of "diet" and "vegetarian."

Though search engines generally compute a ranking derived from multiple factors such as links, the cosine similarity measure is a classical full-text retrieval approach that allows an intuitive graphical representation used here for illustrative purposes. The similarity measure value is defined by the angle between the vectors representing words of the query and the words of individual pages. Determining the cosine similarity measure then requires representing the words of the query and pages as weighted vectors in a multidimensional word space where each axis corresponds to a different word drawn from the indexed pages.

Using the weighted vector space representation, documents similar to queries are located by finding document vectors in proximity to the query vector. A common similarity measure is the cosine of the angle between document and query vectors defined as

$$\text{Cosine}(D_i, Q_j) = \frac{\sum_{k=1}^{t}(D_{ik}, Q_{jk})}{\sqrt{\sum_{k=1}^{t}(D_{ik})^2 \times \sum_{k=1}^{t}(Q_{jk})^2}}$$

in which D_i and Q_j represent a document and query vector respectively, D_{ik} and Q_{jk} are the weights of term k in the document and query, and t is the total number of terms. The range of similarity measures is then commonly normalized to a value between 0 and 1 to avoid word count bias.

Notice that if the query exactly matches all the words of a page, the angle between the query and the page vector is zero and the similarity measure is one; having few words in common produces a greater angle and smaller similarity. Figure 3 illustrates the indexing of page 1 containing the word "weight" and page 2 the words "diet" and "loss" where each axis corresponds to one of the three words. Representing the pages and query as vectors in three-dimensional space, the query vector for "diet" has a smaller angle with respect to the "diet" and "loss" text of page 2 than with respect to the "weight" text of page 1. Intuitively, the "diet" query is somewhat similar to the "diet" and "loss" page and not at all similar to the "weight" page. Based strictly on similarity to the query "diet," the search engine would return a higher ranking for page 2 and a lower ranking for page 1.

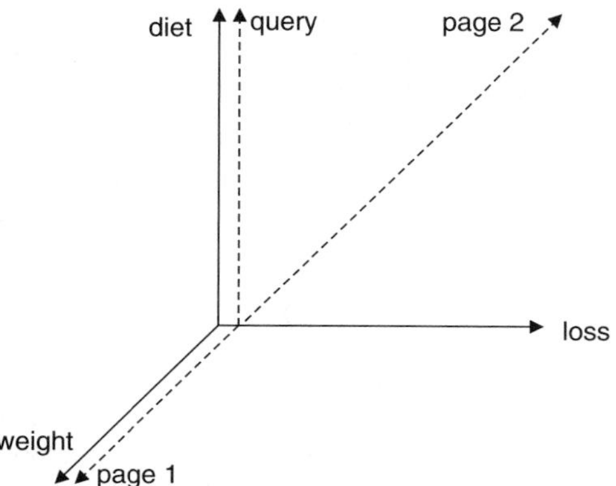

Figure 3: Two pages indexed on the words "weight," "loss," and "diet" where page 1 contains the word "weight" and page 2 contains the words "loss" and "diet." Similarity is measured as the cosine of the angle between a page and query vectors; the smaller angle corresponds to greater similarity. A query of "diet" would have some similarity to page 2 but no similarity to the "weight" page 1.

One computational weakness of the vector space model just described is high dimensionality; each word effectively increases the dimension of the space. As noted earlier, the document space, consisting of those pages located by the spider, can be represented by a term-document matrix. For Internet-scale IR the matrix size becomes unreasonably large as does the dimensionality of the corresponding vector-space representation, that of the number of words in the document space. One approach that can significantly reduce dimensionality is latent semantic indexing (Deerwester et al. 1990), which is based upon the conceptually simple notion that pages having words in common are semantically similar. One distinguishing characteristic of this approach is that pages need not share a specific word to be semantically similar which allows the discovery and ranking of pages that do not contain the query terms. Though the implementation details are beyond the scope of this chapter, the fundamental insights are accessible and worthwhile. Key to this method is reducing the dimensionality of the document space by the process known as singular value decomposition, which, by ignoring very small components, creates an approximate model in a smaller dimensional space. By reducing dimensionality, pages initially represented by somewhat different vectors can now be mapped to the same vector. Ranking can be then be performed for queries using the vector space methods.

Search engines can exploit special features of pages to further improve retrieval quality beyond that possible using query and page words alone. Specific elements of a page, such as title words or anchor text, can be weighted to reflect a lesser or greater relative importance in ranking. When a page is retrieved, a Web search engine generally returns the calculated ranking, designated parts of the page such as the title and a description of the page content, some text surrounding the word found, and most importantly, the location of the page to retrieve.

Web search engines often follow an approach that utilizes the additional features of Web pages such as the *in* and *out* degree of hypertext links to improve the performance quality of IR. Page popularity and importance measures utilize the natural links between Web pages to refine rank calculated on word matches alone. Popularity can be defined to assign a higher rank to pages having more references from other pages, under the assumption that a frequently referenced page is more relevant than a page with fewer references. Figure 4 illustrates the popularity of page A to be greater than that of either B or C, as more links or references are to A than to either B or C.

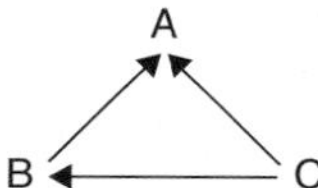

Figure 4: The number of links to a page measures its popularity. Two links confer on page A the greatest popularity, B the next, and C the least popularity. The ranking based on popularity would be ABC.

Link or citation analysis is the basis of the PageRank algorithm (Brin and Page 1998), used by the search engine Google in prioritizing search results. Although a complete discussion of the PageRank algorithm is beyond the scope of this chapter, the basic concept is relatively straightforward. The PageRank of page A or PR(A) can be calculated iteratively and is defined as:

$$PR(A) = (1 - d) + d(PR(T1)/C(T1)) + \ldots + PR(Tn)/C(Tn)$$

in which:

$PR(A)$ is the PageRank of page A,
d is a damping factor that limits the contribution of linking pages and usually set to 0.85,
$T1 \cdots Tn$ are the pages that link to page A, and
$C(Tn)$ is the number of links from page Tn to page A.

Note that the term $PR(Tn)/C(Tn)$, the PageRank of page Tn divided the number of page links from page Tn, reduces the ranking contribution of page as the number of links on the page increases. This fits one's intuition that a page with links to many, possibly loosely related pages should not contribute as much rank as a page that links to only a few, likely more closely related pages.

In practice, the algorithm ranks a page higher than an otherwise identical one if a large enough set of pages link to that same page. This characteristic of the algorithm has proven sensitive to manipulation by a relatively few cooperating Web sites. Called "Google bombing," pages on multiple Web sites are constructed to hold essentially the same phrase and links to the target page. As more Web sites add the manipulation page, the rank of the target page increases to the point where a matching search query returns a high ranking of the target page. After a successful bombing, the algorithm ranks the targeted page higher than the referring pages that contain the actual query words. A manipulation page could consist of only the HTML page linking tag <a href='http://www.eatmorevegetables.com'>bomb phrase</a>; after indexing enough sites containing the bomb page, Google will respond to the query "bomb phrase" by returning a highly ranked link to the target site www.eatmorevegetables.com. This particular manipulation method appears to have been first recognized by an individual (Mathes 2001) when searching for "internet rockstar" using Google.

A popular page as defined by the number of referring links is not automatically important. Importance of a page can be defined in terms of the number of links to the page and the importance of the linking sites. For example, a link from an Internal Revenue Service page to a page on taxes is intuitively more important and should confer greater rank than a link from a random individual to the same page. Authority ranking assumes that a page referring to another confers some measure of authority to the page. Authority and hub ranking utilize page links to identify authoritative pages on a subject and hub pages that link to many of these authoritative pages. The HITS (Hyper-text Induced Topic Selection) algorithm considers mutually referring pages to form authoritative groups on a subject (Kleinberg 1999), where the more links to a

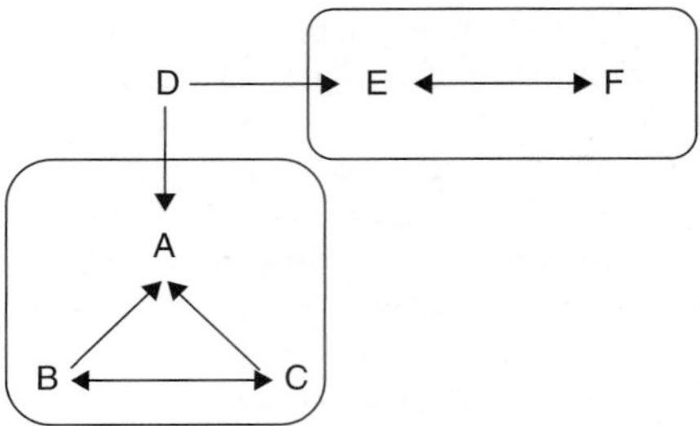

Figure 5: Pages ABC and EF define two separate authority groups connected by hub page D to form a common subject authority

page from others within the authority group, the higher consequent rank of the page. Figure 5 illustrates a simplistic method of forming groups through mutual B and C links and common BC links to A. Page D marginally contributes to the authority of A but is not included in the ABC group as no other group member references D.

Hub pages are defined to have extensive links to authority pages and serve to bring together authorities on a common subject to form a mutually self-referential community. In Figure 5, page D acts as a hub that connects two separate groups into a single community. The resulting community is somewhat analogous to a single subject within a list service except that humans organize subject lists and the interconnecting links organize a subject community. Automatic grouping can produce more focused and higher quality references than strict similarity ranking but eschew the hierarchical organization that requires subject knowledge on the part of the searcher.

Which ranking approach produces the best result depends upon the user's search needs. Comprehensive search is the natural outcome of search based on word match ranking alone but yields no organization of the results. Existence and exploratory search can benefit from the reference-based ranking methods of popularity and importance. Popularity ranking anticipates that the information that many others reference represents common knowledge of a subject. Importance attempts to refine popularity ranking by organizing references into supporting groups. Grouping together documents that have common references will generally provide more homogeneous results and is best suited for exploratory search when some initial subject knowledge exists.

What Search Engines Search

Web pages can be richer sources of search information than traditional documents such as books and journals because of the natural connections formed to related pages and the characteristics of the hypertext markup language (HTML) used for writing Web pages. Web search engines seek to improve upon traditional retrieval systems by extracting added information from the title, description, and keyword HTML tags and by analyzing the connecting links to and from a page.

Recognizing the parts of a Web page that attract the attention of indexing spiders is critical to Web site designers attempting to raise the visibility of the Web site. Ideally, a Web site designer could give instructions to visiting spiders on precisely how best to index the page to produce high-quality search results. Unfortunately, self-promoting Web sites generally have a history of hijacking spider indexing rules for their own benefit. In response to blatant self-promotion, few spiders observe a strict or stable protocol as to which page to index or which parts of the page are considered important. However, most spiders do observe the following common guidelines (Sonnenreich and Macinta 1998).

Content

The result of search is the page content that the searcher sees and reads. The readable text, as displayed by a browser in Figure 6, provides the bulk of the words indexed by the spider.

Characteristically, less common words increase the page rank but are valuable only if a searcher uses that word in a query. Using many different words in a page improves search breadth but the words must be obvious for a searcher to use in a query. Including important keywords in the title, increasing the frequency of a keyword in the text and placing keywords near the beginning of the page content can improve page rank on most search engines. Be aware that repeating a keyword multiple times in the title may gain a higher ranking but many search engines ban blatantly bogus attempts at manipulation and may reject the page or site entirely. The challenge to the page writer is to find the right keywords rare enough to stand out, descriptive of the content subject and that are familiar to the searcher. Bear in mind that indexing spiders may examine only the first few hundred words of content so it is important to provide descriptive keywords early in the content text.

Tags

HTML tags are not generally visible to the reader but do contain information important to the spider. Along with content keywords, spiders also extract the page location and may examine HTML tags when indexing a page. The Web site designer can influence the page rank and provide more descriptive results to the searcher through the tags. Figure 7 gives the source for the HTML page rendered in Figure 6 to illustrate the page content and use of the following tags.

Keyword: The HTML keyword meta-tag contains human-defined keywords to augment the automated indexing of the page content. One use of the tag is to provide alternative words or phases for those in the content, for example, using "PDA" in the content and "personal digital assistant" as keywords. Unfortunately, promoters have so often abused the keyword tag that many spiders generally ignore it. When search is limited to a trustworthy site, such as a university Web site, keywords can be valuable to the designer and searcher.

Description: The description meta-tag provides a short content summary for display when the search engine retrieves the page. Figure 8 illustrates how a search engine would display the description tag with other page information.

Title: Indexing the title tag independently allows explicit searches on the title; the search engine can also display

Automated Search Engines
Automated Web search engines have two main tasks; one of indexing the Web information, the second of answering search queries from the index. First, an indexing program visits a Web site much as you would with a browser, normally starting at the default homepage, visiting connected pages and indexing the site information (see Figure 6).

Figure 6: How the HTML of Figure 7 would appear in a browser

```
<html>
<head>
<meta name = "description" content = "Human lists and automated search engines.">
<meta name = "keywords" content = "search engine, indexing">
<title>How Search Engines Work</title>
</head>
<body>
<h1>Automated Search Engines</h1>
Automated Web search engines have two main tasks; one of indexing the Web information,
the second of answering search queries from the index. First, an indexing program visits a
Web site much as you would with a browser, normally starting at the default homepage,
visiting connected pages and indexing the site information (<a href = "Figure6.html">see
Figure 6</a>).
</body>
</html>
```

Figure 7: An HTML page contains visible parts displayed by the browser and hidden parts that can help spiders index the page more accurately, provide descriptive information to the searcher, and links to other HTML pages

How Search Engines Work
Human lists and automated search engines.
http://www.insearchof.org/how.htm

Figure 8: An example of how a search engine might respond to a query of "search engines." The word "indexing" is part of the keyword meta-tag and embedded in the text content. The title is "How Search Engines Work" and the description meta-tag is "Human lists and automated search engines." The document URL "www.insearchof.org/how.htm" and the title provide links to the complete document

the title as part of the page information, as in Figure 8. As previously mentioned, keywords placed in the title may also improve page rank.

Heading: The large print of headings catches the attention of the reader and also is important to an indexing spider. The influence of headings on rank generally follows the scale of the heading number, so that weight of the words of a level 1 heading is greater than the weight of the words of a level 2 heading.

Links: The spider follows link connections to other documents through the attribute and hypertext reference tag; for example, "<a href = 'Figure6.html'>" directs the spider to follow the link to the index page "Figure6.html." The popularity and importance methods would generally rank a page with many links from other pages relatively high. Influencing other sites to link to a site's pages is not easy, generally depending upon good content to attract recognition. However, cross-listing agreements to share mutual links with other sites are a technique that can provide a quicker start to that recognition. Link farms are commercial services to increase link-based rankings by creating artificial links to subscriber sites; however, search engine sites generally consider artificial manipulations to be adversarial and can remove offending sites from the search engine index.

Anchors: The text associated with an anchor can be used to describe the page that the link references. For example, "<a href='http://www.insearchof.org/how.htm'>Human lists and automated search engines.</a>" defines hypertext describing the contents of the page defined by the link address. The Google search engine considers anchor text of special importance (Brin and Page 1998) in providing an accurate description of the linked page and text for indexing of pages that have not been spidered.

What Search Engines Ignore

Can designers accidentally make their Web sites invisible to spiders? Are all spiders the same? Most spiders purposely ignore or cannot see large parts of a page that human readers might see and manipulate; certain page elements can hinder or prevent indexing. The most common spider problems and solutions are the following:

Frames: The purpose of frames is to visibly divide a browser screen into several parts, but unfortunately frames can stop an indexing spider and create confusion for visitors arriving from a search engine. At least three separate pages are needed for frames: a hidden frameset page that defines the frames and links visible pages into the frames, a second page for visible content, and a third that is often for navigation. A spider normally arrives at the hidden frameset page but must understand how to handle frames in order to follow links to the other, visible pages. Spiders that do not understand frames simply stop and never index further. For those spiders and browsers that do not understand frames, the remaining site pages may be unreachable. Because frames cause some spiders problems, the obvious solution is to avoid the use of frames entirely. However, when the Web site designer is forced to use frames, including the "noframes" tag exposes alternative text for navigation and content to frame-ignorant spiders and browsers. The "noframes" tag designates text to be displayed in place of the framed pages, effectively duplicating the page content and design effort. Spiders that understand frames create a different problem. Visitors can now arrive at a content page directly from the search engine rather than through the main frameset page as the Web site designer intended. Without the main frameset page there is no navigation page either; visitors can become wedged on a dead-end page and, without any navigation, forced to leave the site. One solution is to place a link to the main frameset or site home page in every navigation and content page to help keep the visitor on the site. Of course, another solution is to avoid frames altogether.

Scripts: Most spiders ignore script programs written in JavaScript or other scripting languages; others simply index the script program text. Spiders that index the script may also index only the first few hundred words of the document and possibly never reach the content. Place important content and keywords before scripts and, for pages that are mostly scripts, include title, keyword, and description tags.

Java Applets and Plug-Ins: To a spider, a Java applet, plug-in, or other browser-executed program is invisible. For indexing purposes, include descriptive content and tags within the page that contains the program reference.

Server-Generated Pages: Spiders may ignore any unusual link references, such as ones that do not end in "HTM" or "HTML." For example, a spider will follow the connecting link "<a href='mainpage.HTML'>" but may not follow the link to the Web server program of "<a href='mainpage.ASP'>" as a result of the ending "ASP." Generating the Web site main page with a server program could mean that some spiders ignore the complete site. One solution is to provide some HTML pages for the spider to index and navigation to guide the searcher to generated pages.

Forms: Collecting visitor information is one of the most important functions of many Web sites, but spiders do not know how to fill out forms; a site login form automatically stops a spider. Spiders that do index the content and links of the page containing the form create potential problems by leading visitors directly to the form page from a search engine rather than through pages intended to precede the form. An example would be an airline reservation system with forms for itinerary and payment. Visitors arriving directly at the payment form would obviously have problems; consider adding links back to a starting page.

Robot Exclusion: Forms represent one good reason to exclude spiders from indexing certain pages. Two standards exist that instruct well-behaved spiders on excluding specified pages. The recognized standard (Koster 1995) is the "robots.txt" file that lists a site's acceptable and unacceptable directories, pages, and robots (i.e., spiders). A single robot.txt file exists for the entire Web site, which only the site administrator can access, creating a maintenance bottleneck as multiple designers make changes to the site. A better but less accepted solution defines a special "robots" meta-tag to specify how to index each individual page. Options are that every spider or no spider should index the page, the page should be indexed or not, and the page links should be followed or not.

Images: Spiders may index the image location, image title, and alternate text but that is probably all. For searchers to find the image, include some additional information about the image in the page content and the HTML tags.

Deeply Linked Pages: Most spiders completely index only small sites, generally indexing only limited pages on each site. Spiders limit indexing to several connecting links deep, ignoring pages linked beyond that depth. As a rule, keep pages important in attracting visitors linked directly from the site home page.

Reorganization and Broken Links: Resist the urge to reorganize the site. Until all the spiders come again, the new greeting for visitors arriving from search engines to pages that have been renamed or otherwise permanently hidden may be "404 Not Found." Adding new pages to the site is fine; just leave existing page locations and names alone.

File encodings: Although many search engines translate certain specialized file encodings such as PowerPoint or PDF (Portable Document Format) to text for indexing, any file type that cannot be translated will be ignored. One simple solution is to provide a descriptive page for the spider to index with links to the encoded file.

Metasearch

As a result of different search algorithms, sites indexed and the type of search required, one search engine can never perform the best in all cases. Individual search engines produce results biased in ways that are unpredictable and often invisible to a searcher. Sending the same query to several search engines will obtain widely different results. One study on search engine bias (Mowshowitz and Kawaguchi 2002) demonstrated that querying nine popular search engines for information on "home refrigerators" produced 14 different brand names in the cumulative top 50 results of each engine. Reporting of the brands was unpredictable and uneven across search engines consulted; several brands were found by only a single search engine and no search engine found a majority of the 14 brands. And obviously there was no clue at all as to the brands not found.

Given that individual search engines index only a small fraction of the Web and the degree of index overlap among a group of search engines may be small, it makes sense to consult multiple search engines. Consulting several engines is intuitively appealing and nearly always improves recall. Using multiple search engines for a single search is one strategy for improving the likelihood of finding relevant information. Metasearch engines automate multiple searches by sending the query to several standard search engines and organizing the fusion of the results uniformly. Although increasing the number of information sources will generally improve recall, it is also likely that precision will suffer correspondingly. Balancing these conflicting goals is the key challenge in designing a metasearch engine.

The essential architecture of a metasearch engine (Dreilinger and Howe 1997) consists of a dispatch mechanism to determine which search engines receive a specific query; interface agents to contact and adapt the query and result formats of each search engine; and a display mechanism that creates and displays a uniform ranking of results after removing duplicates. By depending upon the direct results returned from regular search engines, metasearch engines cannot expand or improve upon the information sources. However, to a searcher, metasearch represents an obvious improvement over a single search engine by the simple increase in the number of search engines consulted and the corresponding increase in the fraction of the Web examined. Metasearch is also a commonly integrated into the text-mining applications discussed later.

Web Site Issues

Web site success requires the intersection of the goals of users and owners which have lead some researchers (Belanger et al. 2006) to develop site goal taxonomies to better measure when the site matches its planned purpose. One obvious site goal is to attract visitors and they most often find a new site via a search engine implying that building an easily found and searched Web site is critical. A study of search success (Spool 2001) illustrates the challenges of designing a Web site for search. After watching 30 searchers search different sites for content that was on the sites, the study concluded: "The more times the users searched, the less likely they were to find what they wanted." Single searches found the content 55 percent of the time, those searching twice found the content only 38 percent of the time, and those searching more than twice never found the content. Nearly 23 percent of the searchers received a "no results" response on their first searches, causing most to give up immediately. For those who continued to search, results only grew worse. Further compounding search problems is the prevalence of invalid links to pages that are no longer accessible; one study (Lawrence et al. 2000) gives the percentage of invalid links ranging from 23 percent of 1999 pages to 53 percent of 1993 pages. Although the study did not define the human or IR system problems with search, the collective message seems clear: design the site and pages for search and test that search works.

Web Site Discovery

How is a Web site discovered by a search engine? Given that any one search engine indexes only a small fraction of the Web (Lawrence and Giles 1999) and that fraction is declining, the answer is of critical importance to the Web site designer hoping to attract visitors. Most search engines accept free submissions for indexing all or part of the Web site and paid submission to multiple search engines is available through service companies. Links from other sites will also widen visibility and speed the discovery of a Web site; sites with few links have a lower probability of being indexed. The spiders of some search engines also identify new sites automatically using registered domain names as a starting point. The most certain and direct approach is to purchase keywords on a search engine; a query with a site's keyword is guaranteed to return the site, normally before those listed by the merit of rank. Once a Web site is discovered by search engines, the methods examined earlier to influence automated search become important, though often the best strategy is to develop and maintain high-quality content to attract and cultivate loyal visitors who link to your site. Where content quality or time is in shorter supply than money, the paid listing will guarantee that a site is highly ranked by at least the paid promotion search engine.

Measuring Search Success

How can a site's owner determine if efforts to attract search engine attention have been a success? Search engines represent the most obvious and direct means to check if and to what extent a specific search engine has indexed a site. Search engines generally provide searcher controls to limit search to a specific Web site; these same controls can also provide feedback to point out search problems with the Web site. Although tests with individual search engines will determine if and how a Web site has been indexed, it will not tell if, why, or how anyone visits. The site server holds the primary information on Web site success in the server access log file. The log holds details about every attempted or successful visit; Table 1 lists the information retained in the Web server access log following the Common Logfile Format. Free and commercial analysis software can produce detailed summaries and graphs of the log; however, the most telling information about search success is contained in the following three fields:

Client Request Line: Contains the page on the server the visitor requested. For visitors arriving from a search engine, this contains the link to the page indexed by the spider.

Server Status Code: Status codes starting with a 2 or 3 indicate success (3 indicates a redirect); those starting with 4 or 5 indicate an error (4 a client error, 5 a server error). In Table 1, the "mainpage.htm" page does not exist, earning the visitor a "404 Not Found" response from the Web site.

Referring Site: The visitor client reports the referring site address. In Table 1, the visitor arrived via a reference to "mainpage.htm" made by the hypothetical "www.insearchof.com" search engine.

Of what value is the access log? Examining the log entries can point out search errors and successes. Counting the number of visitor requests (i.e., client request line) to each page immediately grades pages on success in attracting visitors and, by their absence, identifies those pages that failed. Investigating the referrer list will show how visitors arrive at a Web site; search engines missing from the list have not indexed the Web site or rank its pages below others. A table of visitor page requests with the referring site will clearly show which search engines successfully found specific pages and can flag pages that create indexing problems for particular search engines. As discussed earlier, some spiders are stopped by frames, only index the first few content lines, or crawl a limited number of links on each site. Pages that are never accessed can indicate indexing problems for the spider or navigation problems for the visitor. Examining the access log file is a good starting point for finding these and other potential search engine and link problems.

Can the log tell us when a complete site or some part of the site is broken? Interpreting the three fields for client request line, server status code, and referring site from the Table 1 example tell us that the "www.insearchof.com" search engine referred a visitor via an indexed page link to "mainpage.htm" and that link is now broken, as reported by a "404 Not Found" message. A likely reason the link broke is the Web site was reorganized since the last visit by the "www.insearchof.com" spider or the page location on the site otherwise changed. Should we inform "www.insearchof.com" they now have a problem

Table 1: Server access log fields in Common Logfile Format

Access Log Field	Example
Client IP address	24.10.2.3
Client identity – unreliable	–
Authenticated client userid	–
Time request completed	[01/may/2006:17:57:03 −0400]
Client request line	"GET/mainpage.htm HTTP/1.1"
Server status code	404
Referring site	"http://www.insearchof.com/search.html"
client browser	"Mozilla/4.08 [en] (WinNT; I;Nav)"

and need to fix their link to point to the new page location? Un-reorganizing an active Web site is no solution because other search engines may have already indexed the new site organization. A limited solution is to redirect visitors requesting each old page to the new page location through the server configuration or an individual page redirection file for each page moved.

TEXT-MINING

Humans are masters of pattern recognition and the advantageous association of seemingly unrelated facts, no doubt an acquired survival skill. Although Internet text IR as characterized by search engines has proven valuable in directly locating sources of information about which one has some knowledge, queries often return thousands of potentially relevant documents, more than can be effectively managed. By design, the relationship on which search engine retrieval algorithms determine commonality among documents is that queries and text share common words rather than necessarily sharing common concepts. Text-mining represents a natural extension of text IR to extract higher-level information from unstructured data, often to determine underlying structure and relationships among a collection of information where none is apparent, serving to organize information into recognizable patterns. Text-mining of unstructured information shares comparable goals to that of data-mining applied to structured databases. The notion of information mining implies revealing information that is buried within non-obvious patterns requiring deeper analysis than commonly provided through search engine queries. Some common examples of text-mining include analysis of writing styles to establish authorship and the U.S. government's purported ECHELON intelligence gathering system. An early text-mining example (Swanson 1989) sought to establish an unpredicted connection between a disease (Raynaud's disease) with possible cures (fish oil) through a trial-and-error strategy connecting existing research literature on the disease and unrelated studies that might produce a cure. Clinical tests later demonstrated the validity of the disease and cure link.

Ideally, text-mining could be as simple as text searches and results measurably related to query requests. But where search has the one clear function of matching search queries with documents and measurable results (e.g., precision) text-mining, by attempting to extract information that may only be apparent through interconnected evidence, is at present complicated by the need for multiple approaches with a large degree of subjectivity as to performance results. Text-mining technologies (Fan et al. 2006) are based on elements of natural language processing, needed to analyze text and extract relevant features such as proper names and parts of speech. Individually, key technologies applicable to text-mining include information extraction, topic tracking, summarization, categorization, clustering, concept linkage, information visualization, and question answering. In each, the overriding goal is to automate some human approach to understanding unstructured text but at the speed and accuracy of a machine. Few are general or scalable enough to directly mine the text of the Internet but are useful tools for restricted domains such as a financial news feed. Finally, text-mining is still an area of very active research; production systems and support by major data mining vendors such as SPSS and SAS exist but few mature technologies are generally available. The following presents explanations of these technologies and some example systems.

Information extraction (IE) is generally a more sophisticated analysis than the word matching IR as supported by search engines. IE is able to recognize word usage in the context of other text but does not fully achieve text understanding. Further, separate documents are generally considered independent, meaning no attempt is made to relate elements of one document with another. The goal is to extract structured information from a targeted domain, such as building indexes of new product type and company name from financial news articles for subsequent use in structured IR databases. As with full-text IR, IE performs word stemming, thesaurus lookup and other operations but must also understand, from the earlier example, how to recognize a company and a new product. There are two basic approaches (Appelt and Israel 1999) in constructing an IE tool, either automatically by analyzing, perhaps statistically, a corpus of training examples or hand-engineering the grammars necessary for extraction in a particular application domain. In either case, the resulting IE tool operates in the restricted domain.

Topic tracking attempts to categorize new documents by detecting a shared feature with those of a training set, potentially predicting new documents of interest based on specified preferences or previous documents viewed and added to a profile of user preferences. Yahoo! (www.alerts.yahoo.com) and Google (www.google.com/alerts) offer limited topic-tracking services for Internet sources including news and Web pages. Services range from airfare price alerts to notification when a specified Web page becomes highly ranked. These services are essentially applications of text IR technology, for example, simply matching text to identify topics. The difficulty in a text matching approach is that different topics often use the same text and the same topic may use different text which produces no matches. In contrast, TopCat (Clifton et al. 2004) was designed to organize news geographically whether or not the geographic area was mentioned. The approach attempts to identify key language concepts such as people, places and organizations to determine those that tend to appear together for grouping as topics.

Summarization, such as that provided by Microsoft Word's AutoSummary tool, attempts to reduce a document to a few representative sentences. Strategies include statistically weighting document sentences based on word frequency to calculate the average relevance of each sentence (Neto et al. 2000) and heuristics that give higher weight to sentences based on location, such as the one following the introduction section. Summarization can be combined with other technologies such as topic-tracking and clustering to summarize all suggested or clustered documents to a single representative phrase.

Clustering technology groups those documents together that share a common topic. Each cluster of documents is characterized by keywords extracted from those

Software (32)
Resources (22)
Information Retrieval System (22)
Language (16)
Book (13)
Intelligent (12)
Information Retrieval Group (9)
Modern (12)
Images (8)
Project (12)

Figure 9: Clusters and number of members in each produced by the query "information retrieval"

documents allowing individual documents to be a member of multiple clusters. Rather than placing documents in predefined, static topic groups as in categorization, the clusters are constructed dynamically from a given document training set. Clustering would naturally group documents by language and disambiguate queries containing multiple use terms such as acronyms. A Web clustering application (www.clusty.com) powered by the Vivísimo Clustering Engine (Vivísimo 2006) retrieves documents by a normal query to multiple search engines and attempts to organize those documents into related clusters labeled by the dominant topic. Please refer to Figure 9 for an example of the clustering results; also produced by the query but not shown are the standard search engine individual page rankings.

Categorization generally implies placing documents into predefined groups, somewhat similar to clustering but the groups are static and the domain is restricted. Cookbooks are an example, often organized by grouping key ingredients in which dishes containing chicken are rarely categorized with desserts but may show up in other categories. Weaknesses of clustering addressed by categorization include the difficulty in accurately labeling groups automatically. Clustering must determine representative text to describe the group or list keywords used to form the group; categorization groups and labels are, of course, human defined. Categorization is obviously limited to restricted, predetermined domains.

Current search engine IR technology lacks the ability to organize any but superficial text patterns and the implied relationship defined by hyperlinks. Text-mining attempts to bring structure to unstructured text by understanding, at least parts, of the patterns in text. Mechanically finding and exploiting patterns as part of IR complements inherent human pattern matching skills; accurately and efficiently performed, large collections can be organized for effective information retrieval. Unfortunately, most current text-mining technology achieves neither the accuracy nor efficiency necessary for Internet-scale IR. Alternatives generally include elements of manual classification schemes in which human intelligence serves to define information features (e.g., subject, date, location) and annotate as metadata; essentially imposing a structure rather than discovering one. MPEG-7 and the Semantic Web, discussed later, are examples that utilize some elements of this approach.

EXPLORATORY SEARCH

Exploratory search can be an alternative to or complement a purely analytical strategy for exploring information. Exploratory search seeks to create an interactive IR system by placing the searcher more in control of the direction and pace of search, providing organization, cues, or other guidance to create an uninterrupted exploration with strong human participation. Hypertext browsing was recognized as a non-analytical search strategy (Marchionini and Shneiderman 1988) before the invention of the Web, an exploratory strategy invited by navigating the links connecting one document to another. Though browsing is not directly supported by the most common Web search engines, it is often performed ad hoc by the searcher seeking to locate further information by following navigation links from the ranked result list and those embedded within a retrieved page. The following will examine some of the variety of exploratory search methods that have been developed; many that visually illustrate information relationships in spatial dimensions and many that include elements of text mining to reveal those relationships.

As noted, search can be divided into the two broad types of analytical and exploratory (Marchionini 2006). Analytical search depends upon prior knowledge and is appropriate for retrieving facts, known-item search and existence verification. The search engine effectively supports analytical searches in which existing knowledge of the information sought is used in formulating a query and recognizing the relevancy of the results. Early IR researchers (van Rijsbergen, 1979) recognized that information discovery is an iterative process requiring different search strategies that produce repeated strategy transitions in between. Exploratory search is needed for learning or investigation of new information and is appropriate for knowledge acquisition, comparison, analysis, evaluation and discovery; tasks requiring a user interface that complements IR by adapting to the changing needs of the searcher as the search for information evolves. The ideal user interface combines multiple search strategies in a way that transitions occur smoothly and naturally to support the discovery process; this has led the IR community mindful of human limitations and strengths to incorporate human-computer interfacing developments to involve humans more actively in the search process.

An idea common in many exploratory search interfaces is the notion of browsing as a means to rapidly navigate and explore information and some form of feedback to focus further exploration. Browsing can exploit existing connections and those relationships determined between information sources based on methods such as those described in text-mining. Feedback describes the mechanism by which a system can improve future performance by taking into account results from past performance. In analytical search, the searcher considers the results (feedback from the search engine) of one query to modify the next; the search engine eschews feedback by considering each query as independent of others. Exploratory search uses feedback from the searcher and IR system. Search feedback can be obtained directly from the searcher, by requiring ranking of results positively or negatively for

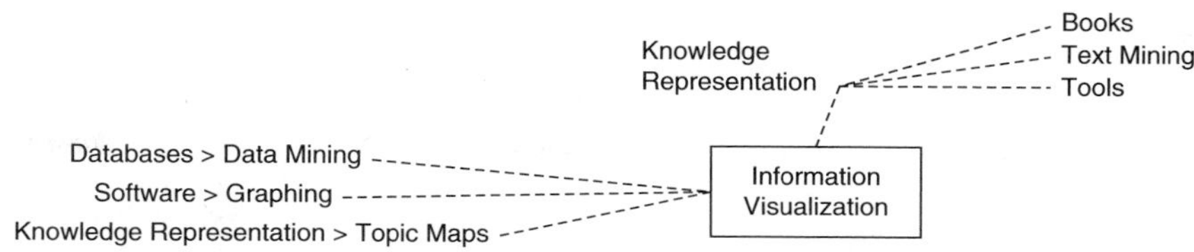

Figure 10: The graphical relationships and categories presented for further exploration by the WebBrain query of "information visualization"

use in the next retrieval round, or indirectly by presenting multiple navigation choices to explore further.

Browsing is intended to be rapid, requiring obvious, condensed choices for effective exploratory search. CiteSeer (citeseer.ist.psu.edu) promotes browsing of computer and information science research literature through concise textual cues to a paper's significance by ranking on the number of citations, indexed date, citations weighted by year indexed, et cetera and providing direct access to other publications associated through citation linkage for exploring further related research. A typical session begins with a subject related text query to generate a ranked list of documents; selecting one produces several navigation categories for browsing (i.e., bibliography, citations, similar documents based on text, and other documents located on same site) inviting exploratory search through several different information criteria groupings.

Discovering information seldom occurs along a predictable path or using a single strategy. Exploration is often over several dimensions whose importance changes as the user's investigation and knowledge of the domain evolves. Given the variety of dimensions on which to organize information, for music—by composer, genre, period, and so on, and the appropriateness of different search models at different points in the information discovery process, a Swiss-army knife approach to discovery tools is often necessary though integration difficult. One such example is mSpace (www.mSpace.fm) (Schraefel et al. 2006) which provides keyword search, dimensional views (e.g., music grouped by era), and audio clips. The user is able to dynamically control exploratory focus and direction by selecting items within a dimensional listing or by rearranging the hierarchy of the dimensions to change the exploration viewpoint. This is somewhat similar to sorting on the instances in multiple categories but changing the category hierarchy or the categories explored to achieve a different organization or view of the instance information. In this example, categories not only serve to organize related instance information, but also provide cues for further exploration; hovering over a category produces an exemplar of that grouping that may be based on expert recommendation, collaborative filtering or, surprisingly effective, random selection.

Visual text-mining (or information visualization) graphically presents relationships between documents to allow users to quickly comprehend and navigate the information groupings; a narrow definition of text-mining that focuses only on reasoning about document organization. Internet-scale implementations include Web-based WebBrain (www.webbrain.com); a metasearch engine that extracts topic clusters from metasearch results (K-Praxis 2003) and presents the relationship visually. WebBrain labels topic clusters by keywords extracted from the search results, supporting exploratory browsing by issuing new metasearch queries when the topic label is selected and reclustering the new results. An initial query on "information visualization," as illustrated in Figure 10, produces topics with labels that include "Databases>Data Mining" with "Text Mining" as a subtopic of "Knowledge Discovery." Browsing over the "Text Mining" label visually highlights the relationship connection to "Knowledge Discovery" and "Databases>Data Mining." Selection of the "Text Mining" category results in a new metasearch on text-mining and categorization, continuing the exploration process. Note that analytical search is also supported, though not shown in Figure 10, through an aggregated list of the metasearch ranking results.

Another Web-based example is the metasearch, information visualization engine, KartOO (www.kartoo.com). Information navigation is through a dynamically categorized topic list labeled by keyword and a graphical mapping of the information sources (i.e., Web site); the map includes spatial cues of category to site relation in the form proximity and quantity by font size; visual connections are drawn between topics to sites. Figure 11 illustrates how major category topics are overlaid within map contours to illustrate strength and proximity of topic relationship. Passing the mouse over a Web site displays topic links and a synopsis the site contents.

Basic elements of exploratory search are transitioning from research topics to standardized software components. Software vendors (Inxight, www.inxight.com) now provide development tools to implement user interfaces for navigating information sources available on an individual Web site, for example. A graphical interface displays hierarchical relationships between information groups in a connected format that allows the user to incrementally follow links from a parent to a child or skip over several generations at a time (Inxight 2006). Multiple parent and non-hierarchical cross links provide the ability to redirect focus in the direction determined by the user. Using such an interface, a Web site hosting a large bidding auction could then display the site auction items as a hierarchy graph showing "computers" as the parent of "hardware" and "software." Visual cues of link size and color can indicate the comparative strength of a relationship allowing the searcher to quickly assess the information direction to explore further.

MULTIMEDIA INFORMATION RETRIEVAL

Text-based IR as characterized by search engines certainly dominates Internet IR by almost any measure whether financial, by popularity, scale, or by technological maturity.

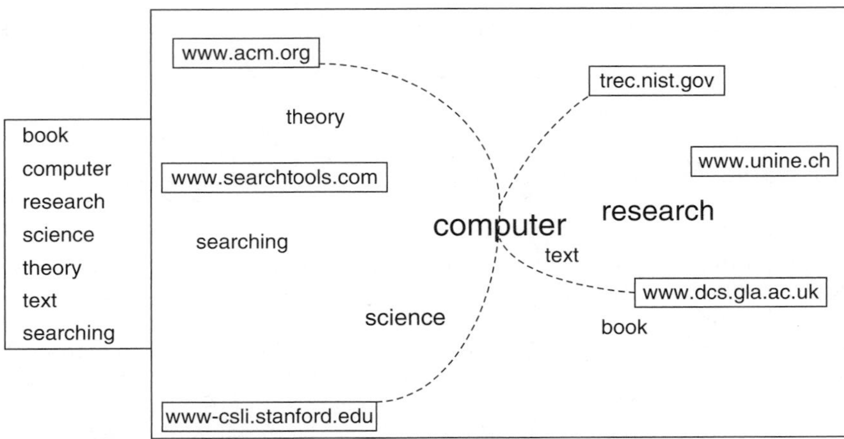

Figure 11: Information visualization of KartOO graphically displays an information map of Web sites in proximity to the related information category. Selecting a category dynamically connects all related sites; "computer" is connected to four related sites

Efficient algorithms for text indexing and retrieval provide a key advantage to search engines. However, the technology is limited to direct search only on text and not other media accessible on the Internet. As noted earlier, an understanding of text-based IR by search engines is a useful foundation for understanding other IR approaches and media. We will now see that search engines are in fact often directly incorporated with other schemes and that text is often used for IR on other media.

Visual

Visual information presents many challenges to IR. Where text exists in a domain formally defined by the language characters, common spellings and vocabulary, visuals have few formal constraints and far more variables, such as colors, texture, and motion. Visuals can be static as in photographs, cartoons and data graphs or temporally and spatially changing as in a movie. Visual information exists in many forms: as figures surrounded by related text, annotated pictures (static images) and video with audio, to name just a few of the many available on the Internet. Not surprisingly, a wide variety of IR methods have been developed to exploit one or more multimedia features.

Before examining visual IR in detail, we should first consider some of the key issues. Although methods of searching vary, the ultimate goal is generally to retrieve a relevant visual from among many available. In a text search, the query is submitted and a set of pages containing those words is returned; the query is essentially an example of text to be matched. The text query "flying horses" should produce a set of relevant pages that include the mythical Pegasus. A visual search can also use text queries that describe the visual sought, for example, the same text query "flying horses" should produce a set of relevant images that include Pegasus. Matching query words to visuals, however, requires a degree of understanding of the visual content. A visual search can also use examples of the visual sought as a query, an image of Pegasus should produce a set of relevant images that include other images of Pegasus. A purely visual search has many more possible dimensions for matching than does text, such as color and texture, providing distinct opportunities and challenges compared to text IR. Fundamental questions about visual search include: "how are queries expressed in a way that the user can understand and provides sufficient precision to produce relevant results?", "what component of a visual serves as an example for search?", and "are results understandable in a way that allows further queries to be refined?" The following section will provide an overview of the predominant general approaches with illustrative examples from specific cases.

Text to Retrieve Visuals

Librarians retrieve images by first annotating with keywords and possibly other metadata and subsequently retrieving images by the corresponding annotations. A similar, automated approach to retrieving visual information transforms the problem to one suited to existing text search engine technology. Since many visuals have some associated text such as the captions of Web page images and nearby surrounding text, the most simple of approaches assumes that any text near the visual describes the visual. This adjacent text-to-image association is used by a number of commercial image search engines such as Google (http://images.google.com/). Visual queries are then the same as text queries using essentially the same search engine technology. Although a close text-to-image association is an appropriate assumption in some domains such as captioned news photographs or figures in journals, such an assumption is not necessarily valid for all Internet visual IR. Obviously, this approach works only as well as the degree of implicit association of the text to the visual, producing satisfactory results for restricted visual collections such as art museums where the visual is professionally annotated with text.

Visual IR based on text searches require that either annotation exists or the annotation process be automated. One illustrative example that based retrieval on both existing text and visual features is *WebSeer* (Swain, Frankel, and Vassilis 1996) an image retrieval system utilizing surrounding HTML text and the classification of the image to restrict the search to a subset of images. The classification is based in part on known differences between photographs and drawings such as number of colors and the degree of color saturation. Further classifications could restrict the search to photographs with faces or cartoon drawings for example. Text queries could then be combined with visual classification information on whether the image sought was a drawing or photograph.

Text annotations can be generated directly from the visual itself in several ways. Visual features (such as predominant colors, texture, and shapes) can generally be determined from a still image; motion images (video) can be analyzed similarly while possessing other dimensions (time and motion) in combination with other media such as audio. The difficulty is capturing the semantic information of the visual for conversion to text. Image-to-word transformations often use some form of a learning algorithm (Mori et al. 1999). Hand annotated images generally serve as training examples from which categories of images and associated index words are formed. New images are then collected, analyzed and assigned one or more of the textually labeled categories determined from the training set. A text query would then return images with matching labels. However, a single label to describe an image forms too broad of categories to be useful. To improve precision, image-to-text systems commonly subdivide the image into regions and assign each region a label so that one image could have multiple labels for different regions; the image would then appear much as a text document to a search engine. Associating a characteristic region and label is a key problem. A somewhat intuitive approach (Pan et al. 2004) uses blob regions or parts of the image a human would generally describe as a distinct region such as sky, grass or an automobile; training data consists of images with blob regions and corresponding words. Blobs are represented by a vector of features including color, position, shape, and texture; when matched with blobs of new images, the new image is assigned the blob labels which can be indexed for image retrieval. Once again, the key idea is to transform the image into associated text that can then be used for indexing and retrieval.

Content-based video indexing and retrieval methods similarly attempt to create a text index of a video for text IR (Sebe, Lew, and Smeudlers 2003). In addition to visual information (e.g., color), video may contain captioning text, characteristic audio (such as a national anthem) and speech that can be extracted and converted to text for indexing. For example, speech can be directly converted into text and combined with associated segments through image analysis to construct an index to specific segments of a video. The image analysis consists of video segmentation, in major part detecting shot boundaries to segment the sequence of video frames into similar visual elements such as those contained in a movie scene; text from speech and other extracted scene components can then be associated temporally with the video segment and indexed for later retrieval.

Text searches against assigned annotations in media such as images remain the most successful approach to image retrieval. Text contains higher-level semantic information than features such as color or texture. But professional hand-labeling is in general prohibitively expensive and, except for iconic cases such as an image of the Statue of Liberty, often cannot be definitively classified for later retrieval by non-experts. Crowd-based approaches or *folksonomies* (Lew, Sebe, and Jain 2006) is an attempt to harness the collective wisdom of the crowd in assigning annotations. For example, multiple individuals may assign different annotations to the same image; each unique annotation provides a potentially different categorization while duplicates can reinforce or strengthen a categorization. Flickr.com and Del.icio.us are example sites that use the general notion of the collective crowd wisdom on the Web for creating text annotations of their media.

Static Visuals Without Text

Users generally want to retrieve photos by semantically describing objects in the image at a high-level, such as *bridge* or *train*, rather than by low-level image features, such as a color, texture or geometric constructs. A purely manual approach to visual retrieval might start with a mental query as in "find photographs of the Brooklyn Bridge." An individual, assuming they have seen the Brooklyn Bridge, transforms the query into retrieval by recalling the image and proceeding to match the mental image with photographs, possibly retrieving some other bridge pictures similar in appearance. For an automated system using text as queries for visual IR, either the retrieval system must conjure an image from the text and then match similar images or, standing the problem on its head, the system must extract semantic meaning as text from the visual collection and retrieve visuals based on the text (as described in the previous section). Either approach, for an unrestricted domain image collection is daunting.

Systems that retrieve visuals based on visual features alone must first be presented a query; the form may be words or an example visual. Word queries describing a visual by feature components such as color or texture (patterns) can produce high recall but generally low precision results. For example, the texture query of "red checkerboard" should retrieve visuals of a red checkerboard. Indexing visuals on predominant colors is straightforward but retrieving predominantly red visuals from the Internet would not be useful (however, for some applications, finding images with the predominant color of flesh may be). Querying in additional dimensions, such as texture, to improve precision results in explosive indexing growth and complicates the query interface with a shopping list of features; perhaps more importantly, users have difficulty associating image features presented by the user interface with an unseen, imaginary image. The difficulty in describing image components to produce high precision retrieval has effectively limited this approach to restricted domain, non-Internet image collections. One noteworthy example is the Query By Image Content (QBIC) system of IBM that powers image retrieval of the artwork presented at the Hermitage Art Museum in St. Petersburg, Russia (www.hermitagemuseum.org/fcgi-bin/db2www/qbicSearch.mac/qbic?selLang=English). Queries can be defined by selecting colors from a two dimensional chart and choosing a category such as painting or sculpture. Images of the original art matching the color and category are retrieved from the collection for viewing.

Visual examples used directly as a query offer an alternative to a text or image feature query. One approach is to present an example image as a query, somewhat as in the *query by example* (QBE) used in text searches, and search for images with similar features such as color and texture. After retrieval, the user can refine further queries by feedback that selects positive or negative examples that move closer to the desired image. This, however, leads to the *zero image* problem, how to generate the first image as the query. Solutions range from an initial text query to retrieve a first set of exemplar images, browsing an existing image catalog, to submitting the URL to a known example image.

In some cases, visual IR demands specific example images as queries. For applications where visual identification is the primary purpose, such as optical character recognition, trademark, or face identification, some initial training examples must be available along with the images that serve as queries. The queries, when correctly identified, can also provide feedback as additional training data. An Internet company, Riya (http://www.riya.com), exploits this approach. Given a set of training photos explicitly identifying individuals by name, Riya retrieves the names of those individuals from new photos. The new photos, when correctly identified, then serve as additional training data. As of this writing, Riya's search space is limited to those photos submitted directly to the site so is relatively small; plans have been announced to extend photo identification of individuals to the Web.

Text search engines are successful in part due to the relatively free and open-ended character of queries formulated by the user; the user can create the query without the need to locate an external source of a similar query. Although text queries possess aspects of QBE in that those documents with text matching the query will be retrieved, creating the query is relatively easy and retrieval feedback generally useful for refining the query. Creating an analogous image query would be challenging for most users so different approaches are required.

One weakness with a pure QBE approach is that user input and control is limited to existing examples. Providing users greater control to query representation was exemplified by *Blobworld* (Carson et al. 1999), which operated under the basic principle that users search for objects such as boats or bridges rather than features such as color or texture. Blobs generally correspond to an object that can be defined as a somewhat homogeneous region in terms of components such as color and texture; these components then serve as indexes, and new images can be added to the collection by automatically dividing the image into recognizable blob regions. Unlike most text search systems, the user interface is an important element of the search process. Queries begin with an example image, which is returned with objects automatically identified marked as blobs from which the user can select objects (blobs) to match. The process is then repeated as the user selects blobs from returned images to submit as refined queries.

Motion Visuals

Motion visuals, generally characterized simply as video, present a large, multidimensional information source for retrieval. Motion alone adds temporal and spatial dimensions to visual information as the images change position over time; audio and text are common additional components that can be exploited for retrieval.

Videos are generally organized as a hierarchical structure consisting of, at the lowest level, individual frames (Marchand-Maillet 2000). Contiguous frames from a continuous recording are grouped in temporal order to form shots or segments. Scenes consist of one or more segments grouped semantically where the component segments may not themselves be contiguous. Temporally ordered segments form the video. Segments often mark discrete boundaries and serve are one important unit for information extraction. Importantly, segments can be automatically determined by scene cut detection that recognizes the boundary defined by a significant image change between one or more frames. Such low-level, high-dimension features are not well suited for indexing and retrieval but are practical within the context of an exploratory search user interface. Representative individual images of segments are useful in rapidly browsing a video; by displaying single thumbnail images for each of many selected segments, the complete video can be visually summarized.

IR systems require a means for users to compose queries that relate in an understandable way to the information retrieved. The QBE method, as employed by text searches, provides feedback whereby entering a query word is expected to return results containing that word. QBE video queries, at the most basic level, consist of single frames for retrieving similar videos based on attributes such as color and texture. However, video retrieval can exploit dimensions unique to the media but require novel approaches to the user interface. Motion visual IR can measure object motion and duration over time in addition to the visual features available in static visuals (such as object color, shape, and texture) and associated audio and text. One QBE retrieval system, VideoQ (Chang et al. 1998), exploits spatial-temporal relations by capturing motion and time features from an animated sketch query to match features from a video collection. Videos are automatically segmented into scenes and indexed on attributes that include motion direction, spatial ordering, shape, color, and texture. The user sketches an example scene as a query for which retrieval returns shots from similar scenes from the collection.

The more traditional text IR is also possible on motion videos. The titling and closing segment can often provide textual data for indexing the entire video, whereas speech-to-text translation can provide text for indexing associated video segments.

Issues of Visual IR on the Internet

One analysis of visual IR on the Internet (Kherfi et al. 2004) concludes that it is not currently possible to index the visuals available on the World Wide Web as a result of the number of sources and diversity of media. While even text search engines are outpaced by the growth of the Web, indexing a smaller portion each year, indexing visuals face additional challenges.

The most cited issue facing visual IR, commonly referred to as the curse of dimensionality, stems from the number of visual features and their high dimension. For example, color is one feature but has other dimensions such as saturation and contrast. The need for a large number of visual descriptors is in part due to the variety of forms visuals take on that include data visualization figures, cartoons, and photographs. Increasing features and dimensionality allows greater discrimination but can quickly overwhelm current indexing techniques. Research has demonstrated (Weber et al. 1998) that sequential search outperforms any other index navigation method when dimension exceeds 10. Research to reduce dimensionality (Rui et al. 1999) suggests ways to eliminate redundant or features with low predictive value.

Audio

Audio IR can be broadly divided into that which has or does not contain speech. Speech provides an opportunity for speech recognition and translation to text, which, as in videos, creates another dimension for indexing and retrieval. When text can be associated temporally with audio, several types of retrieval are possible. The text can be used as a search engine style query to locate audios containing the corresponding speech and retrieve a complete audio much as one would retrieve text documents; at that point the searcher could listen to the audio. However, because speech is linear and inherently temporal, speeding up speech significantly causes listeners to miss content, so that browsing audio becomes problematic. But audio and video are often synchronized and the corresponding text can also serve to access audio in nonlinear patterns to facilitate audio browsing (Amir, Srinivasan, and Efrat 2003).

For audio that lacks speech such as music, features in the time and frequency domain must be exploited for retrieval. Applications include systems that identify audio with similar features and can retrieve the same song performed by different artists given a short example audio query. Purely audio IR is challenging in part as a result of the massive data requirements, one minute of stereo audio in 16-bit pulse code modulation form requires over 10 million data bytes, demanding data reduction and some form of indexing for efficient retrieval to be possible. Other problems are in matching two audio signals of different quality, such as that of a CD and that of a lossy compression. Approaches include some having similarities to text retrieval, in which processing segments of digitized audio features, such as volume, are transformed to code words to form an audio index (Ribbrock and Kurth 2002) for fast retrieval.

As in other media, purely audio queries depend upon existing examples or a means to create one. Musical fingerprinting is an example where the query must exactly match the sought-after recording, a query example from a different performance of the same tune would fail. Music presents a special case of audio having multiple representations that can be exploited for retrieval. For those with some musical expertise, *Meldex* (http://www.nzdl.org/fast-cgi-bin/music/musiclibrary) part of the New Zealand Digital Library Project at the University of Waikato (McNab et al. 1997), queries composed through a Web page by musical notation, keyboard, humming, or singing queries will return titles of songs containing similar note sequences. The melody database is in music notation and acoustical queries are automatically transcribed to music notation for matching. Matching transcribed tunes is analogous to string matching, a logarithmic time operation. However, deviations between the query and database transcriptions as a result of a performer's artistic style or a user's imprecise memory of the tune when sung or hummed preclude exact matching; therefore approximate string matching, a linear time search, is required. For Internet-size tune collections, search time would be prohibitive.

STRUCTURED APPROACHES

We have seen that for every media the lack of structure and the challenge of automatically extracting meaning from low-level features create serious problems for IR in general and, due to scale, Internet IR in particular. We have also seen that the most common approach for making non-text IR tractable is to add text annotation as a form of metadata to describe the actual object; Web-page image captioning is an example. Two fundamental limitations to this approach are that the annotation lacks a controlled vocabulary with which to describe the information and lacks a consistent structure in which to represent the added information; IR indexing and retrieval is then limited to simple text matching of the annotations.

Though many of these IR problems could be addressed by an Internet-scale database system, neither traditional database systems nor the document representations common to the Internet were designed for that task and are unacceptable for several key reasons. Traditional databases represent consistent collections of data having some intrinsic meaning which requires a centralized definition of the data, but a centralized definition of data is too restrictive and runs counter to the distributed nature of the Internet. And most Internet documents, including those written in HTML, lack the structure necessary to organize data in a coherent fashion. Finally, although HTML contains links to other documents, the relationship between the documents is not clearly defined and must be inferred.

Several solutions have been proposed that effectively create an Internet-wide shared database of which MPEG-7 and the Semantic Web are representative examples. Sharing data efficiently and accurately across networks requires a common language for representing information, the most prevalent language basis for data representation and interchange being the extensible markup language (XML).

XML

A common Internet-wide database model is one that is without central control of data definition, which is open to uncontrolled contributions of data, and for which data sources that can be formed ad-hoc as the need requires. The foundational specification and technologies on which most structured Internet IR approaches are based is XML; an application for which XML is well suited. XML itself imposes few syntactical restrictions, allowing new structured data definitions to be created; an important element for a decentralized database. The essential syntax of XML specifies that the data representation be *well-formed*, meaning that data be enclosed by a start and matching end tag. The following XML:

<Address>

<City>Chicago</City>

<State>IL</State>

</Address>

is well-formed; the example also illustrates the hierarchical structure of the data representation. An XML document can be further syntactically constrained through the definition of a grammar defined in document type definition (DTD) or XML Schema format; a parser can then determine if the XML syntax is well-formed and valid for the specified grammar. As an example, the grammar could specify that the <City> tag must occur and precede the <State> tag.

Technologies and specifications built upon the XML foundation provide the additional elements necessary for developing practical applications that can, as is XML, be network protocol and computer architecture neutral. It is notable that many commercial database systems can translate between internal representation and XML and that database contents represented as XML can be easily shared over the Internet as simple text files. The key contribution of XML to Internet IR and that exploited by the following structured approaches to Internet IR is as a standard of a common foundational language for data representation.

MPEG-7

The Moving Pictures Expert Group (MPEG) developed MPEG-7, an ISO/IEC standard (Martinez 2004), to provide standardized tools for describing multimedia content used in human and machine processing systems. The MPEG-7 goal most relevant to Internet IR is in providing a common basis for applications requiring multimedia content descriptions such as filtering, search, and browsing. The MPEG-7 standard only defines descriptors for multimedia features and does not define how those features are determined or used. However, the standard representation of descriptors does directly support indexing and retrieval of multimedia and data interchange for applications such as electronic program guides and automatic generation of descriptors.

The relevant elements of the MPEG-7 definition to IR are:

- use of reference links to Internet resources,
- feature syntax and semantics descriptors,
- component relationship structure and semantics,
- a description definition language (DDL) to create new or extend existing description schemes,
- coded representations of text and binary in formats for storage and transmission,
- management and protection of intellectual property in descriptions,
- content and descriptor synchronization,
- and multiplexing of descriptions with multimedia content.

The XML Schema language serves as the base of the DDL for MPEG-7 descriptors and description schemes allowing for interoperability with other metadata standards. Descriptors are designed to describe low-level features such as color or texture in visuals or frequency in audio media. Description schemes (DSs) are metadata structures for describing and annotating multimedia content regarding higher-level features such as segments, objects, and creation and production information such as author. Annotation tools assist in manually adding metadata to multimedia, for examples see IBM's MPEG-7 Annotation Tool (http://www.alphaworks.ibm.com/tech/videoannex). DSs will, in most cases, be created manually when describing high-level features while some low-level descriptors can be generated automatically; a Web site for automatically generating WAV file audio descriptors is at http://www.whisper.elec.uow.edu.au/mpeg7.

Semantic Web

Internet IR based on search engines is limited by the lack of understanding the information it attempts to retrieve. Text implicitly has some meaning, expressing and understanding semantics in other media is less obvious. Over unstructured collections IR is severely limited by the current difficulty in extracting precise semantics to establish an information structure, such as that needed to ascertain relationships between documents or disambiguate words. In multimedia, MPEG-7 was designed to standardize metadata description of low-level features, many of which are automatically extractable, and higher-level descriptions such as annotations, which most often must be created by humans. However, MPEG-7 was not designed for reasoning about metadata (Hunter 2001).

A framework for defining meaningful metadata and inferencing proposed by Tim Berners-Lee is the Semantic Web (Berners-Lee et al. 2001). The Semantic Web vision is a Web where information has an exact meaning and can be easily processed and integrated by machine. The primary goal is to add logic to the Web, expressed in a language for defining data and rules for reasoning about the data, and to answer questions—many of the same questions that text mining also seeks to answer. For example, a simple relationship might define two terms to be synonyms; the relationship might state that the somewhat exotic term of "lady fingers" ≅ "okra" term more commonly used by Americans. Ontologies, which can define relationships among entities, are central to automated data and logic exchange and integration into larger collections allowing, in this case, American recipes for "okra" to be internationalized through the synonym relationship.

The Semantic Web framework includes three key layers with the top layer of uniform resource identifiers (URI) to identify items on the Web and form the foundational syntactical element. A URI can identify anything locally or globally, for example, a uniform resource locator (URL) is a familiar form (e.g., http://eatmorevetables.com) of a URI that identifies a Web site and specifies a location.

A second layer supports an arbitrary data structure that can be defined by individuals using XML, whereas the meaning of the data can be expressed by the resource

```
<?xml version="1.0"?>
<rdf:RDF
      xmlns:rdf="http://www.w3.org/1999/02/22-rdf-syntax-ns#"
      xmlns:hasA="http://Family.Relations">
  <rdf:Description rdf:about="Alice">
    <hasA:daughter>Mary</hasA:daughter>
    <hasA:son>John</hasA:son>
  </rdf:Description>
</rdf:RDF>
```

Figure 12: The RDF statements defining the relationship "Alice has a son John" and "Alice has a daughter Mary"

description framework (RDF). In RDF one can make assertions that data has certain properties through URI triples defining a subject, predicate and object such as a certain person "is an author of" a Web page. With family relationships defined by assertions such as "has a daughter," one's family relationship could easily be inferred by a software agent, the data and logical inferences could then be expressed in RDF and XML and shared with other agents. Figure 12 gives the RDF code to define statements "Alice has a daughter Mary" and "Alice has a son John." The RDF statement consists of the triplet having subject "Alice," predicate "has a son" and object "John," each identified by a URI of shared resource located on the Web.

Ontologies form the third key layer to provide shared data structures for information exchange, explicit annotations and knowledge representation; ontologies can be expressed in the Web ontology language (OWL), which is defined as a layer above that of RDF. Ontologies are necessary to the Semantic Web in order to specify the concept of class (things), relationships among things and the properties of things. But how is IR improved? In our simple example, we defined the equivalency relation between "lady fingers" and "okra" that would allow a Semantic Web search engine to index on one term and retrieve on the other. A slightly more clever IR system might return links to the ontologies consulted along with search results so that the searcher could view the document with the ontology relations applied.

Standards are a key element to the Semantic Web's acceptance and the sharing of Semantic Web data and rules over the Internet; all the components are defined by the World Wide Web Consortium. A number of development tools are becoming available and applications based on the key technologies have been implemented. It is noteworthy in regard to sharing of resources that RFD is also commonly used by other Internet applications such as news aggregators for information interchange and publishing. Another example of an RDF database is The Open Directory Project (http://dmoz.org/); a human-edited directory of the Web constructed and maintained by volunteer editors. SWOOGLE is a research project implementation of a Semantic Web search engine (swoogle.umbc.edu). OntoWeb is an example of an ontology based portal (http://www.ontoweb.org/). Protégé (http://www.co-ode.org) is an interactive development environment for defining and verifying ontologies specified in OWL and other development frameworks are available commercially (http://www.altova.com) and as open-source (http://jena.sourceforge.net).

CONCLUSION

Ultimately IR must support reaching some conclusion based on understanding; whether directly by a simple existence verification as in copyright identification or an analytical insight based on logically connected information as in a medical diagnosis. For now, Internet IR is primarily defined by search engines and the unstructured text of the Web. Though search engines have brought a remarkable degree of order and access to otherwise unorganized and scattered information of the Internet they have serious limitations. Search engines lack understanding of the semantic relationship between the query and the information they are asked to retrieve leaving that to the searcher to establish. They do not naturally support multiple types of search strategies instead requiring analytical search for all types. They do not generally support multimedia IR except though text search. Finally, ranking methods are influenced more by the implied "Web wisdom" expressed as page links than by recognized expert knowledge. Clearly the future holds great opportunity for advances in these areas.

Some IR problems are a result of the scale of the Internet and may be addressed by distributed IR architectures. Current search engines, though consisting of multiple computers, operate as essentially centralized architectures in which machine resources and tasks are centrally defined. Performing IR of non-text media typically depends upon text IR exploiting either human or machine generated annotations; search engines retrieve images based on nearby text or captioning. Though progress has been made in some areas, such as speech-to-text translation, machine understanding of an image or audio from component features has proven a difficult and continuing problem. Feature extraction, indexing, query processing and retrieval based on low-level media features such as audio frequency or image color are computationally intensive and does not scale beyond restricted collections. Peer-to-peer (P2P) architectures offer the promise of distributing the resources for computational operations and data storage across computers on the Internet, particularly IR on the more challenging non-text media (Sia 2002). Although three standard P2P architectures are generally recognized (Lv et al. 2002), P2P networks can consist of any grouping of interconnected computers without imposing predefined restrictions on their organization or tasks. There are other applications for which P2P networks appear ideally suited, particularly those involving naturally distributed resources such as the shared databases of the Semantic Web (Arumugam, Sheth, and Arpinar 2002).

So what does the future hold for Internet IR? Barring some remarkable progress in machine intelligence, IR of purely text-based unstructured information will continue to be dominated by the current search engine model; though even the search engines will continue to fall further behind Internet growth. IR of other media will progress for specialized and limited applications but is likely to continue exploiting text annotations for indexing and retrieval of Internet-scale information as a result of the high dimensionality of non-text media. Given the recognized benefits, IR based on semantics will expand. Many Internet IR systems can already automatically share information defined within a common representation, eventually the Semantic Web or other coherent information representation structure will spread and grow to achieve a critical mass on the Internet, creating a large collection of information intentionally related. Exploratory search will play a more significant role when tailored to fit with specialized IR applications that enable the searcher to explore information in a more adaptive fashion.

In the not so distant early days of personal computing, each software application stood alone with no natural integration path, not even a clipboard for cut-and-paste operations; application software function took precedence over user interfaces and interaction. Fortunately improved technology and time allowed changes as market pressures forced improvements, particularly in usability. Ultimately, Internet IR will also evolve with other Internet and computer technologies to integrate different media and search strategies through user interfaces that support the essential human requirements in exploring information.

GLOSSARY

Common log format: A standard format for logging and analyzing Web server entries.

DDL: Description definition language provides for the definition syntactic of MPEG-7 description tools.

DTD: Document type definition, part of the XML specification, used to define grammars for restricting the valid syntax of XML documents.

Exploratory search: An iterative process of acquiring subject knowledge by collecting and integrating information that leads to further exploration.

Index: List of words extracted from pages and the location of each page where the word was extracted. Used for matching query words and locating the pages containing the matches.

Information retrieval: Information retrieval has come to be a generic term applied to the access and delivery of information from natural language databases by whatever method.

Latent semantic indexing: A method for reducing the dimensionality of a document space to establish a measure of semantic relationship among documents in that space.

Metasearch: The fusion of the results from multiple search engines simultaneously searching on the same query.

MPEG-7: A Moving Pictures Expert Group (MPEG) standard for describing multimedia content used in human and machine processing systems. Formally named the "Multimedia Content Description Interface."

OWL: The Web ontology language that defines Semantic Web ontologies.

Ontology: A document that defines the relations among terms.

PageRank: A system for ranking Web pages where a link from page A to page B increases the rank of page B.

Precision: The degree to which a search engine matches pages with a query. When all pages are relevant to the query, precision is 100 percent.

QBE: Query by example allows queries to be formulated by providing an example of the expected result.

RDF: Resource description framework, a standard representation used to express meaning through URI triples defining a subject, predicate and object.

Recall: The degree in which a search engine matches relevant pages. When all relevant pages are matched, recall is 100 percent.

Relevancy: The degree to which a page provides the desired information, as measured by the searcher.

Search engine: The software that searches an index of page words for query words and returns matches.

Semantic Web: A framework for knowledge representation and discovery.

Similarity: A measure of how closely the words of a query match the words of a document (page), one means of ranking documents for retrieval.

Spider: The software that locates pages for indexing by following links from one page to another.

Text-mining: Applying machine intelligence to extract the meaning of information from text.

URI: Universal resource identifier used to identify anything locally or globally on the Web, the URL "http://eatmorevegetables.com/ broccoli" is one example.

URL: Universal resource locator defines the unique location of a Web resource; see the URI definition for an example.

Vector space: A representation of each document as a weighted vector in a multidimensional space; the angle between vectors measures the similarity between documents.

XML: Extensible markup language, a foundational framework for the specification and representation of structured data.

XML Schema: Defines the grammar for restricting the valid syntax of XML documents.

CROSS REFERENCES

See *Internet Domain Name System*; *TCP/IP Suite*; *The Internet Fundamentals*; *Voice over MPLS and VoIP over MPLS*.

REFERENCES

Amir, A., S. Srinivasan, and A. Efrat. 2003. Search the audio, browse the video-a generic paradigm for video collections. *EURASIP Journal on Applied Signal Processing* 2:209–32.

Appelt, D., and D. Israel. 1999. Introduction to information extraction technology: A tutorial prepared for IJCAI-99. Artificial Intelligence Center, SRI International.

http://www.ai.sri.com/~appelt/ie-tutorial/IJCAI99.pdf (accessed September 23, 2006).

Arasu, A., J. Cho, H. Garcia-Molina, A. Paepcke, and S. Raghavan. 2001. Searching the Web. ACM *Transactions on Internet Technology* 1(1):2–43.

Arumugam, M., A. Sheth, and I. B. Arpinar. 2002. Towards peer-to-peer semantic web: a distributed environment for sharing semantic knowledge on the Web. International Workshop on Real World RDF and Semantic Web Applications, Hawaii, May 7, 2002. http://www.cs.rutgers.edu/~shklar/www11/final_submissions/paper1.pdf (accessed May 15, 2007).

Belanger, F., W. Fan, L. Schaupp, A. Krishen, J. Everhart, D. Poteet, and K. Nakamoto. 2006. Web site success metrics: addressing the duality of goals. *Communications of the ACM* 49(12):114–16.

Berners-Lee, T., J. Hendler, and O. Lassila. 2001. The semantic web. *Scientific American* 284(5):34–43.

Brin, S., and L. Page. 1998. The anatomy of a large-scale hypertextual Web search engine. Proceedings of the Seventh International Conference on World Wide Web 7, pp.107–17, April 14–18, 1998, Brisbane, Australia.

Carson, C., M. Thomas, S. Belongie, J. Hellerstein, and J. Malik. 1999. Blobworld: A system for region-based image indexing and retrieval. Third International Conference on Visual Information Systems. June 2–4, 1999, Amsterdam, The Netherlands.

Chang, S., W. Chen, and H. Sundaram. 1998. VideoQ: A fully automated video retrieval system using motion sketches. Proceedings Fourth IEEE Workshop on Applications of Computer Vision, pp. 270, Princeton, New Jersey, October 19–21, 1998.

Clifton, C., R. Cooley, and J. Rennie. 2004. TopCat: Data mining for topic identification in a text corpus. *IEEE Transactions on Knowledge and Data Engineering* 16(8):949–64.

Deerwester, S., S. T. Dumais, G. W. Furnas, T. K. Landauer, and R. Harshman. 1990. Indexing by latent semantic analysis. J*ournal of the American Society for Information Science* 41(6):391–407.

Dreilinger, D., and A. Howe. 1997. Experiences with selecting search engines using metasearch. *ACM Transactions on Information Systems* 15(3):195–222.

Fan, W., L. Wallace, S. Rich, and Z. Zhang. 2006. Tapping the power of text mining. *Communications of the ACM* 49(9):77–82.

Gulli, A., and A. Signorini. 2005. The indexable Web is more than 11.5 billion pages. In Poster Proceedings of the 14th International Conference on World Wide Web, pp. 902–903, Chiba, Japan, May 10–14, 2005. ACM Press.

Hunter, J. 2001. Adding multimedia to the Semantic Web – Building an MPEG-7 ontology. Proceedings of the First Semantic Web Working Symposium (SWWS), pp. 261–281, Stanford University, California, USA, July 30–August 1, 2001.

Inxight. 2006. Inxight StarTree illuminating relationships, networks and large information hierarchies. http://www.inxight.com/products/sdks/st/ (accessed October 10, 2006).

Kherfi, M., D. Ziou, and A. Bernardi. 2004. Image retrieval from the World Wide Web: Issues, techniques, and systems. *ACM Computing Surveys* 36(1):35–67.

Kleinberg, J. 1999. Authoritative sources in a hyperlinked environment. *Journal of the Association for Computing Machinery* 46(5):604–32.

Koster, M. 1995. A standard for robot exclusion. http://www.robotstxt.org/wc/norobots.html (accessed December 17, 2006).

Lawrence, S., F. Coetzee, E. Glover, G. Flake, D. Pennock, B. Krovetz, F. Nielsen, A. Kruger, and L. Giles. 2000. Persistence of information on the Web: Analyzing citations contained in research articles. In *Proceedings of the Ninth International Conference on Information and Knowledge Management*, edited by A. Agah, J. Callan, and E. Rundensteiner, pp. 235–42. New York: ACM Press.

Lawrence, S., and C. Giles. 1999. Accessibility of information on the Web. *Nature*, 400:107–9.

Lew, M., N. Sebe, and R. Jain. 2006. Content-based multimedia information retrieval: state of the art and challenges. *ACM Transactions on Multimedia Computing, Communications and Applications* 2(1):1–19.

Lv, Q., P. Cao, E. Cohen, K. Li, and S. Shenker. 2002. Search and replication in unstructured peer-to-peer networks. In Proceedings of the 16th Annual ACM International Conference on Supercomputing, New York City, New York, June 22–26, 2002.

Marchand-Maillet, S. 2000. Content-based video retrieval: An overview. Technical Report Vision. Geneva, Switzerland, Universitie de Geneve, Centre Universitaire d'Informatique Groupe Vision. October 1, 2000, No. 00.06.

Marchionini, G. 2006. Exploratory search: from finding to understanding. *Communications of the ACM* 49(4):46.

Marchionini, G., and B. Shneiderman. 1988. Finding facts vs. browsing knowledge in hypertext systems. *IEEE Computer* 21(1):70–80.

Martinez, J. 2004. MPEG-7 overview (Version 10). International Organization for Standardization. ISO/IEC JTC1/SC19/WG11. Coding for Moving Pictures and Audio. http://www.chiariglione.org/MPEG/standards/mpeg-7/mpeg-7.htm (accessed October 11, 2006).

Mathes, A. 2001. Filler friday: Google bombing. http://www.uber.nu/2001/04/06/ (accessed January 15, 2004).

McNab, R., L. Smith, D. Bainbridge, and I. Witten. 1997. The New Zealand Digital Library MELody index. D-Lib Magazine. http://www.dlib.org/dlib/may97/meldex/05witten.html (accessed October 6, 2006).

Mori, Y., H. Takahashi, and R. Oka. 1999. Image-to-word transformation based on dividing and vector quantizing with words. MISRM'99 First International Workshop on Multimedia Intelligent Storage and Retrieval Management, Orlando, Florida, October 30, 1999.

Mowshowitz, A., and A. Kawaguchi. 2002. Bias on the Web. *Communications of the ACM*, 45(9):56–60.

Neto, J., A. Santos, C. Kaestner, and A. Freitas. 2000. Document clustering and text summarization. Proceedings of the 4th International Conference on Practical Application of Knowledge Discovery and Data Mining, New York City, New York, August 27–31, 1998.

Netcraft.com. 2006. December 2006 Web server survey. http://news.netcraft.com/archives/web_server_survey.html (accessed December 11, 2006).

Nielsen, J. 2000. Is navigation useful. The alertbox: Current issues in Web usability. http://www.useit.com/alertbox/20000109.html (accessed October 13, 2006).

Pan, J., H. Yang, P. Duygulu, and C. Faloutsos. 2004. Automatic image captioning. Proceedings of the 2004 IEEE International Conference on Multimedia and Expo, Taipei, Taiwan, June 27–30, 2004, pp. 1987–1990.

Ribbrock, A., and F. Kurth. 2002. A full-text retrieval approach to content-based audio identification. Proceeding of the 5th IEEE Workshop on MMSP, St. Thomas, Virgin Islands, USA, November 30-December 4, 2002.

Rosenfield, L., and P. Morville. 1998. *Information architecture for the World Wide Web*. Sebastopol, CA: O'Reilly and Associates.

Rui, Y., T. S. Huang, and S.-F. Chang. 1999. Image retrieval: current techniques, promising directions and open issues. *Journal of Visual Communication and Image Representation,* Volume 10, Number 1, pp. 39–62.

Salton, G., and M. McGill. 1983. *Introduction to modern information retrieval*. New York: McGraw–Hill.

Schraefel, M., M. Wilson, A. Russell, and D. Smith. 2006. MSPACE: Improving information access to multimedia domains with multimodal exploratory search. *Communications of the ACM*. 49(9):47–9.

Sebe, N., M. Lew, and A. Smeudlers. 2003. Video retrieval and summarization. *Computer Vision and Image Understanding* 92(2-3):141–6.

Sia, K. 2002. P2P information retrieval: A self-organizing paradigm. Technical report. http://citeseer.ist.psu.edu/cache/papers/cs/27076/http:zSzzSzwww.cse.cuhk.edu.hkzSz~kcsiazSztp3.pdf/p-p-information-retrieval.pdf (accessed December 18, 2006).

Sonnenreich, W., and T. Macinta. 1998. *Guide to search Engines*. New York: Wiley.

Spool, J. 2001. Users don't learn to search better. UIEtips. http://web.archive.org/web/20041019224401/www.uie.com/articles/learn_to_search/ (accessed October 13, 2006).

Swain, M., C. Frankel, and A. Vassilis. 1996. *WebSeer: An image search engine for the World Wide Web*. Technical report TR-96-14, University of Chicago, Chicago, Illinois, USA. http://citeseer.ist.psu.edu/swain97webseer.html (accessed May 15, 2007).

Swanson, D. 1989. Online search for logically-related noninteractive medical literatures: a systematic trial-and-error strategy. *Journal of the American Society for Information Science* 40(5):356–58.

van Rijsbergen, C. J. 1979. Information retrieval. Newton, MA: Butterworth-Heinemann.

Vivísimo Cluster Engine. 2006. Making sense of information overload. http://vivisimo.com/html/vce (accessed October 8, 2006).

Weber, R., H.-J. Schek, and S. Bot. 1998. A quantitative analysis and performance study for similarity-search methods in high-dimensional spaces. In Proceedings of the 24th International Conference on Very Large Data Bases, New York, 194–205.

Internet Architecture

Geoffrey G. Xie, *Naval Postgraduate School*

INTRODUCTION

In this chapter, we explore the architectural design of the Internet. We believe that a historic perspective is essential for this exploration. Many important lessons about network design can be learned from the evolution of the Internet architecture. The Internet had a very modest start, borne out of an experimental network with a handful of nodes in the late 1960s. There was no comprehensive theory about packet network design in place at the time. It was not until a dozen or so years later, when the Internet had already become a network with about 100,000 nodes that the broad research community started to realize that several early design choices made for the Internet architecture, with an emphasis on *simplicity*, had played a crucial role in its growth and robustness. (Clark et al. 1988). In other words, it is not by accident that the basic elements of the Internet architecture have withstood the test of time for over three decades, creating the one and only global data networking infrastructure in the process; several architecturally profound design principles were at work. In the first half of the chapter, up to "Security," we will try to expose as many key points of these design principles as possible while describing nuts and bolts of the Internet architecture.

Examining the Internet architecture from a historic perspective would not be complete without pondering the future of the Internet architecture. In the second half of the chapter, we pose and try to answer the following question: Has the current Internet architecture reached the end of its historical role? To put the question another way: Is a clean-slate design of Internet architecture necessary in order to meet all emerging requirements? We first provide a holistic view of the current Internet architecture based on its division of core functionality into three planes: data, control, and management. We then discuss why the Internet control and management planes have fundamental limitations in coping with several emerging service requirements and why a completely new approach to network control and management may be required. Finally, we describe the 4D network architecture (Greenberg et al. 2005b), which is an instance of a clean slate design of Internet architecture.

For brevity, the discussion will be kept at a high level, with a focus on the fundamental trade-offs behind some of the most important network design choices embodied in the Internet architecture. No complete detail of an individual protocol or mechanism will be provided unless doing so is necessary for the discussion. Almost all important Internet protocols and mechanisms are specified in Internet request for comments (RFCs), a collection of documents that is maintained at the official Web site of the Internet Engineering Task Force (IETF). Interested readers are referred there for more information about a specific protocol or concept.

ORIGIN OF INTERNET ARCHITECTURE

The Internet is easily the largest computer system ever built, with tens of millions of nodes running hundreds of protocols. Examining its architecture is foremost about looking beyond the low-level system components and protocols and identifying the set of *core functionalities* that make it tick. The Internet is essentially a network for transporting digital data (i.e., bit streams) between computer processes. In the most abstract form, a network simply consists of nodes connected by links. In the Internet setting, the nodes are computers and the links are connections between computers. To help illustrate the set of necessary functionalities for providing communication services over the Internet, consider a typical computer communication scenario where process A running on one computer wants to transmit a file to process B running on another computer. For this transmission to be successful, the following functions are required:

- *Data Formatting*. A and B must agree on a common data format so that B can extract and reassemble the content of the file from the bit streams received.
- *Addressing*. Process A must have a means to both uniquely identify B from other processes and supply this identification, called B's address, to the network.
- *Routing*. Methods must be in place for determining a feasible path for moving bits from A to B, based on the addresses of A and B.

- *Forwarding*. Methods must be in place for actually moving bits from A to B, through a predetermined sequence of nodes.
- *Error recovery*. Because no physical transmission medium is perfect and bits may be inverted or lost in transit, algorithms are required to detect and correct these errors.

Equally important is the *division of work*, regarding both the creation of distinct node types and the placement of the aforementioned key functions among the nodes. In one design, the network may consist of homogenous nodes, all of which implement one identical set of functions. Although conceptually simple, this design may be inflexible and/or incur unnecessarily high cost. It is consideration of this kind of design trade-offs that has shaped the development of the Internet architecture.

In this section, we will introduce and briefly describe a set of design principles that have made the Internet architecture into what it is today. Because these design principles started as practical solutions to specific network design problems (Clark et al.1988), we first look back at history and ground our discussion by laying out the key enabling technologies and the key requirements faced by the architects of the early Internet.

The purpose of introducing the design principles *before* describing the detail of the Internet architecture is twofold. First, we believe that one may appreciate many subtleties of the Internet architecture *better* after having a solid grasp of the big-picture design philosophy of the Internet architecture. Second, as mentioned in the introduction, the focus of this chapter is on the fundamental design trade-offs and thus we would like to start the discussion at a 30,000 foot level.

Enabling Technologies

In the pre-Internet era, the communications technology was dominated by a circuit-based approach used by telephone networks. In circuit-switching the bandwidth of each communication link in the network is segmented into multiple smaller transmission channels called circuits, by utilizing either a frequency division multiplexing (FDM) or a time division multiplexing (TDM) technique (Kurose et al. 2005). Each circuit can only be allocated to one conversation at a time. Because the number of circuits in the network is finite, a call setup process is required before a conversation can start in order to ensure that there are adequate free circuits to form an end-to-end path between the calling parties.

The static allocation of circuits works well for telephony where the network traffic loads are well understood. However, circuit-switching would cause a significant waste of bandwidth when used to transport computer data traffic such as from a telnet session, which typically is very bursty with long periods of inactivity. This problem motivated people to seek an alternative approach to building networks for linking computer resources, which led to the invention of the *packet-switching* technique in the early sixties (Internet Histories 2006).

In the packet-switching approach, computer data (i.e., bit streams) are transported in small chunks called packets. The capacity of a communication link is not segmented; packets of different users take turns being transmitted at the full link rate. This form of dynamic sharing of the whole link capacity among different connections, termed *statistical multiplexing*, ensures no waste of link bandwidth as long as there are packets to be transmitted.

Statistical multiplexing requires the use of buffers to hold packets waiting for their turn to be transmitted. This type of buffering naturally led to the birth of a "store and forward" communication paradigm in which packets may be forwarded on a hop by hop basis toward their destinations. Under this paradigm, it is also very easy for intermediate nodes to independently adjust routes that packets take based on current network conditions. Such a dynamic routing capability was quickly recognized as a desirable function of a computer network for resisting link or node failures in the network even before the first packet network was ever built (Internet Histories 2006).

Driving Requirements

The Internet began as an experimental network called ARPAnet, which was sponsored by the U.S. Department of Defense (DoD) initially for testing the viability of packet switched computer networks and later for demonstrating ways of combining packet networks that use different link technologies (leased phone lines, satellite, radio, etc.) into one integrated data communications infrastructure for the military (Internet Histories 2006). High on the requirement list for the Internet project were:

1. Robustness: Because of the military sponsorship, an emphasis is put on the ability of the network to continue to operate in the presence of link or node failures.
2. Link heterogeneity: Also important to the military is the network's ability to rapidly assimilate different link technologies so the network can be quickly deployed and extended.

Other requirements for the Internet architecture included the support for multiple types of communications service and distributed management of network resources (Clark et al. 1988). Surprisingly, both network security and quality of services (i.e., performance guarantees) are not in the original list of requirements for the Internet. The reason is simple: ARPAnet was originally envisioned as a private data network for the U.S. military and, as such, security was considered more of a physical layer concern and quality of services deemed a non-issue with the assumption that traffic entering the network would be carefully planned resulting in a lightly loaded network at all times.

Design Principles

To meet the overriding requirements of robustness and link heterogeneity, the original architects of the Internet made two important design decisions regarding how to organize the core computer networking functionalities. First they recognized that a monolithic network architecture where each switching node can cope with all link technologies will not scale (Clark et al.1988). The concept of adding specialized packet switching nodes, called Internet message processors (IMPs), to the network architecture was developed to address that problem and to take advantage of the then new store-and-forward communication paradigm. Each IMP, which we call a gateway or router today, would be an intermediary linking two or more different packet networks. A three-part address format was defined: one for identifying a communicating process, another for identifying the process's host computer, and the last one for identifying the host network. A packet would carry both source and destination addresses in its header. A gateway would only need to inspect the network portion of the destination address when making packet forwarding decisions. Once a packet arrived at the destination network, that network would use the other parts of the destination address to deliver the packet to the receiving process (Cerf et al. 1974; Living Internet 2006).

The use of packet-switching gateways not only greatly *simplified* the task of establishing connectivity between independently managed networks with heterogeneous link technologies, but also enabled the store-and-forward paradigm, under which dynamic routing of packets in transit could be done transparent to the communicating processes. However, this design had a distinct performance disadvantage compared to a circuit-switched network: no guarantee of quality of service. Although aware of the disadvantage, the Internet architects made a conscious decision to choose simplicity over efficiency. This design choice since has become an overarching design philosophy for the Internet:

Simplicity over efficiency: *Whenever possible, trade efficiency for simplicity.*

The second far-reaching design choice made by early Internet architects can be thought of also as a practice of the "simplicity over efficiency" principle, although with a little twist. Initially, one "super" protocol that combines routing, packet forwarding, and end-to-end reliable delivery functionalities was developed to provide the communication service for all applications (Cerf et al. 1974). After closer examination, the Internet architects realized that reliable service may not be a good fit for some applications, for example, one that exchanges real-time voice traffic, to which timeliness is much more important and for which retransmissions are counterproductive by incurring extra latency. This observation inspired the concept of having the network core provide *minimal* packet level forwarding service, upon which different types of data communication services including reliable data transfer would be built at the end hosts of the network. Following this concept, the forwarding functionality was extracted out of the super protocol and made into an independent Internetworking Protocol (IP). Two types of end-to-end communication services were then defined over IP: (i) user datagram protocol (UDP) which provides just an end multiplexing point for IP packets of different application processes running on the same host; and (ii) transmission control protocol (TCP), which has added functionality to support reliable data transfer.

By treating packets independently and forwarding them based on their destination network address, the IP protocol does not require the gateways to maintain any connection state about application processes. This flexibility has greatly *simplified* the design of gateways, the main piece of the technology puzzle for connecting new networks into the Internet, and therefore should be considered one of the crucial factors for the rapid growth of the Internet. Throughout the years, the Internet architects have upheld this design choice of a "thin" Internetworking layer, resulting in the following design principle for division of functionalities required for building communication services over the Internet:

Datagram service: *Provide simple connectionless packet forwarding service in the network core.*

The minimalistic approach to gateway design was later justified and generalized into the so called end-to-end argument for placement of functions among modules of a distributed computer system (Saltzer et al. 1984). The argument can be stated succinctly as below (Saltzer et al. 1984):

End-to-end argument: *Functions placed at low levels of a system may be redundant or of little value when the cost of providing them at the low level is factored in.*

The Internet is a distributed system with two levels of functionality: the network subsystem at the lower level providing communication services to application clients at the upper level. Under the end-to-end argument or design principle, networking functions that deal with network anomalies such as bit errors, node crashes, packet duplications, buffer overflow, would be best implemented at the end hosts where application client processes reside, particularly when the occurrences of anomalies are too infrequent to make it cost effective to place corrective functions inside the network (Saltzer et al. 1984).

CURRENT INTERNET ARCHITECTURE

Today, the Internet has evolved from a U.S. military system prototype into an open, world-wide infrastructure over which a rich set of applications, including Web, E-business, voice over IP (VoIP), video broadcast, and online gaming, is deployed. These applications have imposed additional performance and security challenges on the network. New elements have been incorporated into the Internet architecture in an attempt to address these challenges. In this section, we delve into the major building blocks of the Internet architecture: describe their *current* functionality and trace their evolution path.

Data Formatting

In the Internet, all types of digital information are encapsulated in packets with a standard format defined by the IP protocol (RFC 791). At a minimum, a host needs to be able to send and receive packets in that format in order to be connected to the Internet. As discussed in

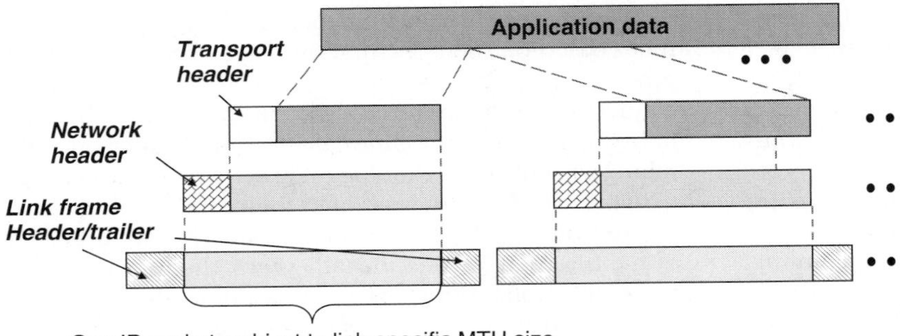

Figure 1: Packet encapsulation; from a router's perspective, all types of application data are encap sulated in IP packets; these packets are delivered using different link-layer technologies hop by hop

"Design Principles," two types of end-to-end communications service (or transport protocol), TCP and UDP, have been defined on top of IP. Moreover, each application has its own set of agreements on the message format and the method of exchanging these messages. For example, a Web browser uses the hypertext transfer protocol (HTTP) protocol (RFC 1945; RFC 261) to communicate with a Web server. Therefore, the packaging of application data into IP packets at an end host involves several layers of encapsulation, as described below.

Packet Encapsulation

Figure 1 illustrates the typical packet encapsulation process at an end host. The "Application data" box represents the sequence of bits for an application-specific message (e.g., an HTTP message requesting a Web page) that is to be sent from the host. In the first encapsulation step, the message is encapsulated in *one or more* transport-layer segments with the same TCP or UDP header (see RFC 793 and RFC 768, or a networking textbook such as Kurose et al. (2005), for details about TCP and UDP). In the next step, each transport-layer segment is encapsulated in an IP packet by prepending an IP header. In the final step, a link-layer frame is created by prepending an additional header and possibly a trailer. The link-layer frame format may vary from network to network, specific to the link layer technology used in each network. For example, the Ethernet format would be used here if the host were part of a local area Ethernet network. It should be noted that the link-layer header and trailer will be removed before the packet is passed to router modules that make routing and forwarding decisions.

Also, each link-layer technology defines its own maximum transfer unit (MTU) parameter: the maximum number of bytes that can be encapsulated in one frame. For example, the MTU size for the Ethernet protocol is 1500 bytes; therefore, the size of an IP packet cannot exceed 1500 bytes in an Ethernet environment. That's why the application message may have to be encapsulated in multiple transport layer segments.

Because there is not a standard MTU size across all link-layer technologies, it may also happen that an IP packet is forwarded to a network with an MTU smaller than the packet's size. Should the packet be discarded or fragmented into multiple packets of an appropriate size? We defer this topic to "Dynamic Routing" after we have a chance to inspect the IP header format.

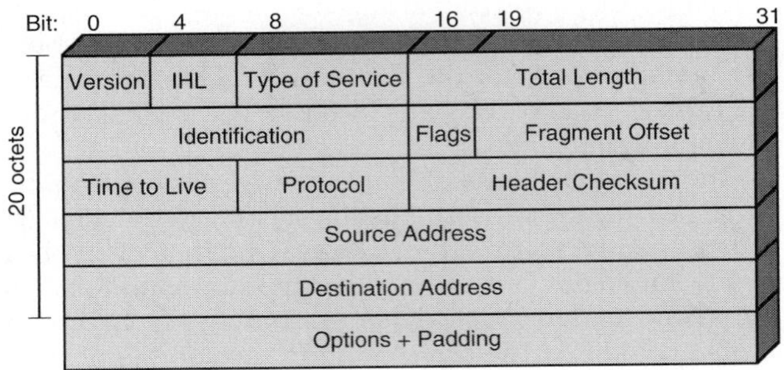

Figure 2: IP header format. [Figure 18.6 of Stalling04] Each row represents a 4 byte word. The total length is always a multiple of 4 bytes after possible padding

IP Header Format

Figure 2 shows the IP header format. The individual fields are defined as follows (RFC 791):

- *Version*: a 4-bit value indicating the version of the IP protocol used. Currently, we are at version 4, abbreviated as IPv4. Some experimental networks are running IP version 6 (IPv6). We will briefly discuss the features of IPv6 in "NAT and IPv6."
- *Internet Header Length (IHL)*: a 4-bit value indicating the length of the IP packet header (including all the option fields and padding), in 4-byte words. For example, a packet with a 24-byte long header would have this field set to 6.
- *Type of Service (ToS)*: an 8-bit value indicating the quality of service desired for the packet. This field had not been widely used until the differentiated service (DiffServ) model was introduced in the mid-1990s. We will briefly discuss DiffServ in "Integrated Services Model."
- *Total Length*: a 16-bit value indicating the total length of the IP packet in bytes, including the header and the data payload encapsulated in the packet.
- *Identification, Flags, and Fragment Offset*: These fields are used by the IPv4 fragmentation and assembly algorithm, which we will describe in the next subsection.
- *Time to Live (TTL)*: an 8-bit value representing an upper bound on the number hops (routers) that the packet can still traverse. Any router module that forwards packets must (i) decrement each packet's TTL field by at least one and (ii) discard a packet with a zero TTL value. The

intention is to cause undeliverable packets to be discarded, and to place an upper bound on the maximum packet lifetime. Upon discarding a packet with a zero TTL, the router will notify the sender of that packet of this action via the Internet Control Message Protocol (ICMP). (ICMP is defined in RFC 792.)

- *Protocol*: an 8-bit value identifying the next level protocol that is encapsulated. The id's for various protocols, called protocol numbers, are specified in RFC 790. For example, the protocol number for TCP is 6.
- *Header Checksum*: 16-bit one's complement of the 1's complement sum of all 16-bit half-words in the header. For purposes of computing the checksum, the value of the checksum field is zero.
- *Source Address and Destination Address*: 32-bit addresses for the source and destination network interfaces, respectively. The specifics of the IP addressing scheme will be examined in the next subsection. It should be noted that an end host may have multiple network interfaces; in that case, this host is said to be "multi-homed" and any one of the interfaces can be used to reach an application running on this host.
- *Options*: The field may specify the presence of optional IP functionality. One of the existing options is source routing, whereby a predetermined sequence of routers that must be traversed by the packet can be specified.

In summary, the IP header format is quite simple, reflecting the desire for imposing minimal requirements for connecting new hosts into the Internet. In accordance with the datagram service, no header fields are provided for recording session-specific state and each packet is required to carry destination address information.

Packet Fragmentation and Reassembly

The "Identification" field in the IP header is designed to give a unique identifier to each packet upon its generation at a host. Different host operating systems (Windows, Linux) may use different algorithms for setting this field. Most commonly, the value is derived from reading the host's system clock. When the packet encounters a network with an insufficient MTU size and thereby needs to be fragmented, that is, broken down into several smaller packets, the same identifier is inherited by all the fragments. Additionally, the 13-bit "Fragment Offset" field of each fragment packet is calculated based on where the first byte of the fragment is situated, in length of 8-byte double-words, relative to the start of the original packet. One of the bits of the "Flags" field, the More Fragments (MF) bit, is set for all fragments except the last one. This information allows the receiving host to identify and assemble the fragments back into the original packet. It is possible that these fragment packets need further fragmentation at another network with an even smaller MTU. However, reassembly is done only once for the packet at the receiver.

The IP protocol allows the fragmentation/reassembly feature to be turned off by setting another bit of the "Flags" field, the so-called Don't Fragment (DF) bit. When that bit is set, the packet would be dropped under the scenario described in the previous paragraph. Additionally, the router that dropped the packet would send an error notification message to the sender of the packet via ICMP.

The design of the IP fragmentation/reassembly functionality can be viewed as an application of the "Simplicity over Performance" principle. It certainly has a negative performance impact on the routers that have to perform the checking and the fragmentation. But it avoids imposing a standard MTU size on every link technology and thus removes a potential barrier for connecting a new type of network into the Internet. Instead, a minimum MTU is instituted, which is 576 bytes for the current version of IP (version 4) and 1280 bytes for IP version 6.

Addressing

The basic approach of the three-level hierarchical addressing scheme as described in "Design Principles" remains unchanged through the years. More specifically, the process portion of the address definition, called *port*, has been standardized as part of both TCP and UDP header formats, and the network and host portions of the address definition have been combined into one 32-bit value, called *IP address*, which should be globally unique. For ease of writing, an IP address is usually represented in the so-called dotted-decimal form, in which the 32 bits are partitioned into four bytes written in their decimal form and separated by a period (dot). For example, "192.128.10.168" is the IP address assigned to the network interface installed on the laptop that I have used to write this chapter.

Subnet and Subnet Mask

As shown in Figure 3, an IP address is composed of two continuous blocks of bits. The left block contains the "Network bits" and identifies the home network (or subnet) for the host. All network interfaces in one subnet should be assigned the same block of network bits, called the *subnet prefix*. The right block contains the "Host bits," which should be uniquely assigned to each network interface installed on a host in the subnet.

To reduce the size of the forwarding tables at routers, routing in the Internet is done based on matching subnet prefixes instead of matching the entire 32-bit addresses. Accordingly, one or more gateway routers should be attached to each subnet. The Internet routing and forwarding algorithms are only responsible for transporting packets to these gateways, which then deliver the packets to the receiving hosts (or more precisely, the network interfaces of these hosts) using a technology specific link protocol. Similarly, packets destined for a remote host (i.e., not in the same subnet as the sending host) also have to depart through the gateways.

Clearly, a method for determining the boundary between the network and host blocks of an IP address is required for extracting the right subnet prefix. For example,

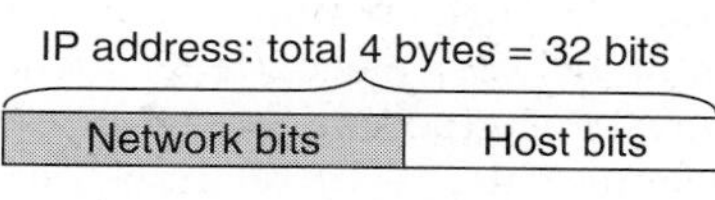

Figure 3: IP address layout

"192," "192.128," "192.128.10," are just a few of the possible subnet prefixes for the IP address "192.128.10.168." The original solution was to define several classes of network prefixes, each with a unique starting bit pattern, and then assigning a fixed number of network bits per class. Specifically, class A network prefixes start with binary "0" and always have 8 network bits. Therefore, there are a total of 128 possible class A networks, each with a total of $2^{32-8} - 2 = 16{,}777{,}214$ unique addresses to assign to its network interfaces. Class B network prefixes start with binary "10" and always have 16 network bits. Finally, class C network prefixes start with binary "110" and always have 24 network bits.

Later, the class-based network assignment was found to be inflexible and wasteful in terms of the percentage of addresses actually assigned per network. For example, a company with a dozen of employees would be unlikely to fully utilize even a class C network address space that contains $2^{32-24} - 2 = 254$ valid host addresses. The subtraction of 2 is needed because two special addresses are preconfigured for each subnet and not available as host address: one for broadcast, with all host bits set to 1, and the other being the subnet id, with all host bits set to zero. The current solution is to allow subnets of any size and to require each subnet to explicitly declare the exact number of network bits that it is assigned. For example, the subnet where my laptop is located has a prefix of "192.128.8.0/22." The "/22" notation indicates the prefix is made of 22 network bits. "192.128.8.0" is the *subnet id* and is obtained from zeroing out all the host bits (i.e., the rightmost 10 bits) in "192.128.10.168." The zeroing step can be easily accomplished by a bit-wise AND operation between "192.128.10.168" and a special address "255.255.252.0," which is obtained by setting all the network bits and clearing all the host bits. This special address is called the *subnet mask*. Under this scheme, a router can easily determine if a given destination address matches one of the network prefixes in its forwarding table: for every network prefix in the table, first calculate a subnet id value for the IP address using the prefix's subnet mask and then match it against the subnet id for that prefix.

DNS and DHCP

Even in the dotted decimal form, IP addresses are not easy for humans to remember. Also, *manually* configuring every network interface with the right combination of IP address, gateway address, and subnet mask can be a challenge for a large network with hundreds of hosts. Fortunately, two protocols have been developed to help us with these tasks.

The domain name service (DNS) protocol allows an application to refer to a host by its fully qualified domain name (FQDN), which is also in a dotted format, albeit with words in a string format, not decimal numbers. For example, the FQDN of my laptop has been set to be "xielap.cs.nps.navy.mil," which is a lot easier to remember than "192.128.10.168." "xielap" is the *host name* chosen by myself, whereas "cs.nps.navy.mil" is the name for the *network domain* of my work place: Department of Computer Science of Naval Postgraduate School. The "." operator in an FQDN denotes the *part-of* relationship: "cs.nps.navy.mil" is part of the "nps.navy.mil" domain, "nps.navy.mil" is part of "navy.mil," and so forth. All network domains can be thought of being part of a root domain. A network domain may contain multiple subnets and subnets of the same domain are typically administrated by one domain authority. Since the IP protocol does not recognize FQDNs, DNS provides applications a service that translates an FQDN into its IP address counterpart, and vice versa. Each domain authority is responsible for setting up a DNS server that maintains a mapping between the FQDNs and IP addresses of all local hosts in its domain and answers queries about the mapping from either an application running on a local host or a remote DNS server on behalf of a remote application. A detailed specification of the DNS protocol is given in RFC 1035.

The dynamic host configuration protocol (DHCP) supports auto-configuration of a network interface. To enable this feature on a subnet, one must set up a DHCP server and assign to it a pool of free IP addresses for that subnet. When a host in the subnet is booted up, it will use broadcast to reach, maybe via a relay agent, the DHCP server and request an IP address and other information required for configuring its network interface. In response, the server will typically remove an address from the free address pool and allocate it to the host for a fixed duration. The host will contact the server to renew the allocation periodically when it stays up for a long time. The host may also contact the server to explicitly return its address to the pool of free addresses, for example, when the host is being shut down. A detailed specification of DHCP can be found in RFC 951.

NAT and IPv6

In the mid-1990s, as a result of years of explosive growth of the Internet, a crisis of IP address shortage seemed looming. Theoretically, the 32-bit address space provides close to 4 billion unique addresses. However, even with classless network allocation, a significant percentage of allocated addresses are unused and thus wasted. Also, many addresses are reserved for special purposes: broadcast, multicast, private, and so on, and not available for hosts. Therefore, when people started to talk about connecting everything, from cell phones to toasters, to the Internet, it was perceivable that the pool of unallocated IP addresses could soon run dry. In response to this crisis, two major solutions were proposed. One was supposedly a near-term fix which requires no change of the current IP address format and the other was touted as a long-term solution which changes the address format to make it 128-bit long.

The near-term solution is called network address translation (NAT), specified in RFC 1631. In this scheme, a network's external connection must go through a NAT server. The server replaces the source address and source port pair of every outgoing packet with its own IP address and a "surrogate" source port that is unique to a specific source address and source port combination. In other words, there is a one-to-one mapping between a source address and source port combination to a "surrogate" port. The NAT server records such mappings in a hash table keyed by the value of the "surrogate" port. The server also inspects every incoming packet, uses the packet's destination port field as the key to find the right address mapping for the packet, overwrites the destination address and destination port fields with the ones obtained from the mapping, and finally forwards the packet on inside the network. Thus, it is not necessary to assign globally unique addresses to hosts inside the network. A common practice is to use private address ranges for these hosts. Only the NAT server needs to have a globally unique address, making NAT an effective solution for mitigating the address shortage problem.

The long-term solution requires upgrading the IP protocol (version number 4) to a new version, IP version 6 (IPv6). In addition to a drastically larger address space than IPv4, IPv6 also includes new features such as auto-configuration and a streamlined header structure. Interested readers are referred to RFC 2460 and (Davies 2002) for details about IPv6.

Dynamic Routing

Routing in the context of the Internet is about maintaining consistent forwarding tables at the routers, in accordance with the network's store and forward communicationparadigm. In the early days of the Internet, routing was not a major issue because of the small number of networks connected to it. Routing within a network was often done with a private protocol and routes between networks were static and manually set up (Clark et al. 1988). Later, as the size of the Internet grew, it was no longer possible to assume a static topology, and dynamic routing became necessary.

Before we delve into routing, let's briefly look at how forwarding is done given consistent forwarding tables at all routers. As mentioned in "Subnet and Subnet Mask," the forwarding is done by matching subnet prefixes. A typical forwarding table at a router, often referred to as the Forwarding Information Base (FIB) for the router, contains entries (i.e., routes) in the format of: <network prefix>, <next hop>, <metric>. <network prefix> is the subnet prefix of the destination network for this route, <next hop> the interface to use as part of this route to reach the destination, and <metric> a measure of goodness of this route. To forward a packet, the router first looks up its FIB with the packet's destination address and searches for subnet prefix matches using the method described in the end of "Subnet and Subnet Mask." When the packet's destination address matches multiple routes in the FIB, the router chooses the route with the *longest prefix match*, i.e., with the most matching network bits. If there are more than one longest prefix matches, the router uses the <metric> field to break the tie. After determining a route, the router forwards the packet to the output port as defined by that route's <next hop>.

Hierarchical Organization of Networks

To scale to millions of networks, a two-level routing hierarchy has been defined for the Internet, analogous to the "first state, then city, and finally street" way of delivering mail by the post offices. At the top level, routing is done among network domains. Each domain is designated as an autonomous system (AS) and assigned a unique 16-bit *AS number* for routing purposes. For example, my school's domain "nps.navy.mil" is also AS 257. Currently, there are about 30,000 active ASes in the Internet. At the bottom level, within an AS, routing is done between routers inside that AS. This "divide-and-conquer" approach ensures that each router only needs to maintain a relative small number of routes in its FIB. The largest FIB reported has about 200,000 entries, which is a lot smaller than the total number of subnets in the Internet.

Because ASes are independently administrated, different intra-domain routing protocols may be deployed in different ASes. This is not the case for inter-domain routing; all ASes must implement the same inter-domain routing protocol to achieve full interoperability.

Intra-Domain Routing

Typically, a single administrative authority has total control over all routers in an AS. Such control makes it possible to consider additional performance objectives when designing intra-domain routing protocols. The current generation of intra-domain routing protocols are designed to rank routes based on a distance metric defined as follows. First, each link connecting two subnets is given a cost metric. The distance of a route is the sum of the costs of all links traversed by that route. The simplest definition of link cost would be assigning a value of "1" to every link. In that case, the distance of a route would be its *hop count*, that is, the total number of links it traverses. In summary, an intra-domain routing protocol is about computing shortest paths between all pairs of subnets within an AS.

Two classes of protocols have been developed for dynamically computing shortest paths between routers: *distant vector* and *link state*. A distant vector protocol is totally distributed, based on *iterative* computation of shortest paths. A router only communicates with a direct neighbor and exchanges updates on each other's distance vector, that is, a table of current minimum distance to all known destinations. A neighbor's update message may trigger a new update at the router following the iterative Bellman-Ford algorithm. Much like human gossiping, the router will eventually know about every other router in the network, the correct minimum distance to it, and the neighboring router to use to achieve that minimum distance. Routing information protocol (RIP), one of the earliest dynamic routing protocols designed for the Internet and currently at version 2 (RFC 2453), is a primary example of distance vector routing protocols.

A link state protocol is centralized in the sense that each router will first obtain a *global* view of the network, including topology and link costs, through flooding of link state packets by all routers and then *independently* apply the Dijkstra's algorithm to compute the shortest paths. If all routers have the same global view, then the FIBs built by the routers will be consistent. Upon a change in the network topology or link cost, the affected router(s) will flood new link state packets to update the global view at each router and trigger new shortest path computation. Open shortest path first (OSPF) and intermediate system-intermediate system (IS-IS), specified in RFC 2328 and RFC 1142 respectively, are the two most prominent link state routing protocols.

Inter-Domain Routing

The AS-level topology is a mesh, with each AS having connectivity with one or more other ASes based on business agreements. Because ASes are independently managed, there is no uniform scale for the link cost metric across different ASes. So determining the distance between two ASes based on adding link costs is not very meaningful. Instead, policy is more important in interdomain routing. For example, an Internet Service Provider (ISP) may choose to avoid a particular AS (belonging to a competitor) in all its routes. To assist policy based routing, the Internet uses a *path vector* protocol called border gateway protocol (BGP) for inter-domain routing (RFC 4271). Each AS sets up one or more BGP border routers for exchanging path vectors, each of which is a full sequence of ASes to use to reach a specific destination network, with border routers of neighboring ASes. In general, an AS will advertise a route learned from one neighbor to other neighbors after appending its own AS number to that route. Policy-based actions may be specified in three stages of BGP operation at a border gateway. First, import filters may be placed to reject certain routes received from a neighboring AS. Second, policy may be defined regarding how multiple imported routes for the same destination are ranked. Third, export filters may be placed to restrict the scope of route advertisements to neighboring ASes.

Resource Allocation

Resource allocation did not receive serious consideration in the original design of the Internet architecture because of the datagram service principle. However, as the reach of the Internet extends and the access speed increases, latency or loss sensitive applications such as video phone start to be deployed. These applications require the network to provide some minimum level of performance guarantee with respect to throughput, packet delay, packet loss rate, and so on. A new catch phrase, quality of services (QoS), has since been coined by the networking community to refer to the level of performance guarantee a computer network provides.

Although some people still view over-provisioning, that is, making bandwidth so abundant that link congestion is unlikely, as a viable solution to all QoS problems, both the network research and operational communities have recently explored alternative solutions aimed at avoiding link congestion through elaborate resource allocation schemes. These efforts are described below.

Traffic Engineering

Traffic engineering involves adapting the flow of packets through the network based on a given set of performance objectives and the traffic matrix, that is, the observed *typical* volume of traffic from each ingress point to each egress point. Often, a network designer needs to deal with conflicting performance objectives, such as minimizing the maximum link utilization and bounding the propagation delay between each pair of routers. Satisfying them simultaneously for a dynamic network environment is very challenging under the current Internet architecture. A good commentary on the existing traffic engineering approaches is given in (Rexford et al. 2004), which we will quote below:

> "Early attempts to engineer the flow of traffic involved extending the routing protocols to compute load-sensitive routes in a distributed fashion. In these protocols, the cost of each link is computed as some (possibly smoothed) function of delay or utilization, in order to steer packets away from heavily-loaded links. However, routing oscillations and packet loss proved difficult to avoid, since routers were computing routes based on out-of-date information that changed rapidly, and the effort was eventually abandoned. To improve stability, the distributed algorithms were extended to compute a path for groups of related packets called *flows*. These load-sensitive routing protocols can have stability problems as well, unless the dynamic routing decisions are limited to aggregated or long-lived flows. Perhaps more importantly, the protocols require underlying support for signaling and distributed algorithms for optimizing paths for multiple metrics.
>
> Many existing IP networks have instead adopted a centralized approach for engineering the flow of traffic using traditional IP routing protocols (e.g., OSPF). In this scheme, the management plane collects measurement data to construct a network-wide view of the offered traffic and the network topology. Because the optimization of the OSPF weights is an NP-complete problem, the management plane conducts a local search through candidate settings of the link weights, looking for a solution that satisfies the various performance objectives. Considering additional performance metrics is as simple as changing the objective function used to evaluate the solutions. However, this approach has its limitations in satisfying different metrics for traffic to different destinations, and for avoiding disruptions during failures and planned maintenance. Ultimately, having a single integer weight on each link is not sufficiently expressive, though this approach has proven very useful in practice."

Integrated Services (IntServ) Model

In the early 1990s, the network research community made a serious attempt to extend the datagram service model and retrofit a QoS solution over the Internet. The effort was motivated by the seminal work of Parekh and Gallager, which shows that the end to end delay of one application's packets can be upper bounded regardless of the behaviors of other applications if an appropriate packet scheduling algorithm, such as packetized generalized processor sharing (P-GPS) or weighted fair queuing (WFQ), is used at every output link that the packets traverse. The new service model was named integrated services (IntServ) after its lofty goal to meet the QoS requirements of all types of application data including interactive audio and video (RFC 1633). The core of the service model is a new type of service called "guaranteed service," which provides a deterministic (i.e., for 100% of the packets) guarantee of performance, in terms of maximum end-to-end packet delay and minimum throughput, on a per application basis. All packets for an application that has subscribed to this service traverse the same set of links, and are referred to as a *flow*. The flow has a separate buffer at each output link and receives a guaranteed rate of service from the packet scheduling algorithm based on the flow's bandwidth requirement. Clearly, in order for the guaranteed service to work, the application must reserve network resources (link bandwidth, buffer) along a network path ahead of time. A protocol called RSVP (resource ReSerVation Protocol) has been developed to facilitate this task. RSVP is specified in RFC 2205.

Differentiated Services (DiffServ) Model

IntServ is elegant in theory. However, the research community soon realized that IntServ might not be able to scale to the size of the Internet because it requires per-flow state to be maintained at all routers, including the backbone routers which may have to deal with millions of flows concurrently. An alternative solution was quickly developed. The solution centers on a differentiated service (DiffServ) model, in which only inter-class *performance differentiations* are guaranteed over a small number of service classes. Neither per-flow nor absolute, quantitative service guarantees are provided. Three DiffServ service classes have been well defined, in the order of increased performance: default forwarding, which is the same as the default best-effort service offered by the Internet, assured forwarding, which ensures a sustained throughput, and expedited forwarding characterized by low loss, low delay, and low jitter. It is up to each network provider (ISP) to choose particular packet scheduling and queue management algorithms at each of its routers to support the required per-hop forwarding behaviors (PHBs) for the defined service classes.

DiffServ achieves scalability by implementing complex classification and conditioning functions (metering, marking, shaping, and policing) only at access routers at the edge of the Internet. These functions are carried out based on the service level agreements (SLAs) between network customers and providers. The core routers need to allocate buffer and bandwidth only on a per service class basis while applying PHBs to aggregates of traffic which have been appropriately conditioned and marked using the ToS field in the IP header by edge routers. The details of DiffServ can be found in RFC 2474 and RFC 2475.

Multi-Protocol Label Switching (MPLS)

MPLS is the latest attempt of the computer networking community to retrofit a connection-oriented forwarding service over the Internet. Such a forwarding service not only is conceptually appealing and but also streamlines resource allocation. Strictly speaking, MPLS is not a network layer protocol; it operates between the link and network layers and independently of the IP protocol. It is called "multi-protocol" because its 4-byte header format has been incorporated into the frame headers of different link technologies. For an Ethernet link, the header is simply appended to the front of an Ethernet frame. For an ATM link, the 32 bits of the ATM cell header fields, virtual path id (VPI) and virtual circuit id (VCI), are re-designated to carry the MPLS header fields. The MPLS header contains mainly a 20-bit "label" field, which serves as a connection ID and a 3-bit "class of service" (CoS) field for support of QoS differentiation. A label switching router (LSR), one that is able to process MPLS packets, will use this label to make the forwarding decision and bypass the IP header. The LSR will also overwrite the label with a new value that is anticipated by the downstream LSR. That is why the protocol has "label switching" in its name. All the label values are determined ahead of time as part of the MPLS connection (tunnel) set-up process performed by a label distribution protocol (LDP).

MPLS is mostly used by an ISP as a local traffic engineering solution, often combined with DiffServ mechanisms. Typically, a set of MPLS tunnels is preconfigured within the ISP's network. The ingress routers of the ISP classify all arriving packets based on their header fields, and insert corresponding MPLS header fields at the output link for those classified to be transported by one of the MPLS tunnels. More information about MPLS can be found in RFC 3031.

Security

For the reason explained in "Driving Requirements," security was not high on the original list of goals for the Internet. Today, with the Internet becoming an open infrastructure for e-commerce and e-government, security is one of the most pressing issues faced by the Internet community. Several security mechanisms such as firewall, virtual private network, transport layer security, secure email, and public key infrastructure (PKI), have been added to the Internet architecture with some level of successes. Two of them are described below.

Firewall

A firewall is a combination of specialized hardware and/or software acting as a network's *security gate* that can restrict types of communication between the network and the public Internet, mainly to prevent unauthorized access to the network's resources. Typically, a firewall administrator has configured the firewall with a set of packet filtering rules based on security policy. The firewall inspects the header fields of all packets that come in and out of the network and drops those matching the filtering rules. For example, a firewall may only allow Web traffic to come in the network by filtering out all packets that don't carry an HTTP payload. A firewall can also be *stateful* in that it will try to enforce certain communication patterns involving several packet exchanges. For example, a stateful firewall will deny a TCP connection response (so-called TCP SYN-ACK message) from coming in if it has not seen a corresponding connection request going out.

Virtual Private Network (VPN)

Often an organization spans multiple geographical locations. It's very expensive for this organization to build a private data network with leased lines to connect all its sites. An alternative approach is to use the public Internet for connectivity and rely on additional security protocols for data privacy, resulting in a virtual private network (VPN). Currently, most VPNs are built by setting up a VPN proxy between each site network and the Internet. The proxies run a tunneling protocol that allows packets for this VPN to be encrypted and encapsulated with additional headers at the proxy of the source site and then decrypted and de-capsulated at the proxy of the destination site. By treating the network core as a black box, VPN is a design based on the end-to-end argument. There are two types of VPN tunneling protocols: some, like L2TP, run at layer 2 (link layer), and the others, like IPsec, run at the layer 3 (IP layer). L2TP and IPsec are defined in RFC 3931 and RFC 4301, respectively.

In summary, the current security techniques for the Internet focus on establishing a security perimeter around a network and preventing unwanted traffic from coming in. Very little can be done to defend against attacks originated inside the security perimeter. It is also very difficult to verify if the security perimeter has been properly configured or if the security perimeter will hold in the event of link or node failures (Xie et al. 2005).

FUTURE OF INTERNET ARCHITECTURE

Starting from this section, we will look forward and examine the future of the Internet architecture. Several stirring proposals, such as Clark et al. (2003) and Greenberg et al. (2005b), have come out recently calling for a clean slate design of the Internet architecture. Regardless of whether they will stand the test of time, these proposals constitute serious efforts aimed at understanding the limitations of the current Internet architecture and seeking future directions in network design. As a result of space constraints, the rest of the discussion will be based mainly on one of them, called the 4D architecture (Greenberg et al. 2005b, 2005c).

The 4D architecture was conceived by a team of researchers from Carnegie Mellon, Princeton, AT&T Research, and Naval Postgraduate School, including the author of this chapter. The 4D architects argue that the current Internet architecture has reached the end of its historical role because it does not have intrinsic capacity to meet emerging QoS and security requirements and the bandage solutions such as presented in "Resource Allocation" and "Security" are creating an even bigger problem by inducing bewilderingly high network management complexity (Greenberg et al. 2005b).

To better understand this argument, let's introduce another abstraction of the Internet architecture based on the time scale of execution of its constituent functions. Specifically as described in Rexford et al. (2004), the current Internet architecture can be decomposed into three planes:

Data plane: The data plane is local to an individual router, or even a single interface card on the router, and operates at the speed of packet arrivals, *down to nanoseconds per packet*. For example, the data plane performs packet forwarding, including the longest-prefix match that identifies the outgoing link for each packet, as well as the access control lists (ACLs) that filter packets based on their header fields. The data plane also implements functions such as tunneling, queue management, and packet scheduling.

Control plane: The control plane consists of the network-wide distributed algorithms that compute parts of the state in the data plane. The convergence times of these algorithms *vary from seconds to minutes*. For example, the control plane includes BGP update messages and the BGP decision process, as well as the Interior Gateway Protocol (such as OSPF), its link-state advertisements (LSAs), and the Dijkstra's shortest-path algorithm. A primary job of the control plane is to compute routes between IP subnets, including combining information from each routing protocol's Routing Information Base (RIB) to construct a single Forwarding Information Base (FIB) that drives packet forwarding decisions. Currently, the control plane exhibits the classic symptom of an over-engineered yet *unstable* system: the decision logic (e.g., for controlling reachability) is spread across multiple independently configured protocols or mechanisms and a local configuration error may cause cascading network-wide failures.

Management plane: The management plane stores and analyzes measurement data from the network and generates the configuration state on the individual routers. For example, the management plane collects and combines Simple Network Management Protocol (SNMP) statistics, traffic flow records, OSPF LSAs, and information extracted from BGP update message streams. A tool that configures the OSPF link weights and BGP policies to satisfy traffic engineering goals would be part of the management plane. Similarly, a system that analyzes traffic measurements to detect denial-of-service attacks and configures ACLs to block offending traffic would be part of the management plane.

From this view of the Internet architecture, the 4D architects have identified the following problem: The management plane is currently the only place where decisions are made based on *network-wide* information to meet *network-level* performance objectives, but placing these control functionalities in the management plane suffers from two fundamental weaknesses. First, the time scale of their operation is too long for them to adapt to changing network conditions without causing noticeable periods of severe performance degradation. Second, the management plane does not have direct control over the data plane, or more precisely, the FIB entries at the routers. The decisions made at the management plane have to be carried out through setting specific protocol parameters (e.g., OSPF weights) in the control plane. However, determining the right protocol parameters is often an NP-hard problem, requiring complex modeling and inverting of the actions of the control plane. Furthermore, this type of indirect control creates a performance bottleneck since it is not conducive to an integrated view of different mechanisms and joint optimization of multiple metrics. Rexford et al. (2004) and Greenberg et al. (2005c) provide several detailed examples of this problem.

The 4D architects argue that network-level decision making at a faster time scale and direct control are necessary to meet stringent QoS and security requirements.

Continuing on the current evolution path by tweaking the management and control planes will not fundamentally address either of the issues. A revolutionary change to the Internet architecture is inevitable.

THE 4D ARCHITECTURE

The design of the 4D architecture centers on streamlining network-level decision making and execution. Conceptually, network control, and management functions are refactored into four planes: Decision, Dissemination, Discovery, and Data; thus the name 4D. Before we delve into the role of each plane in the 4D architecture, we follow the main theme of this chapter by first presenting three design principles behind the refactoring of functions.

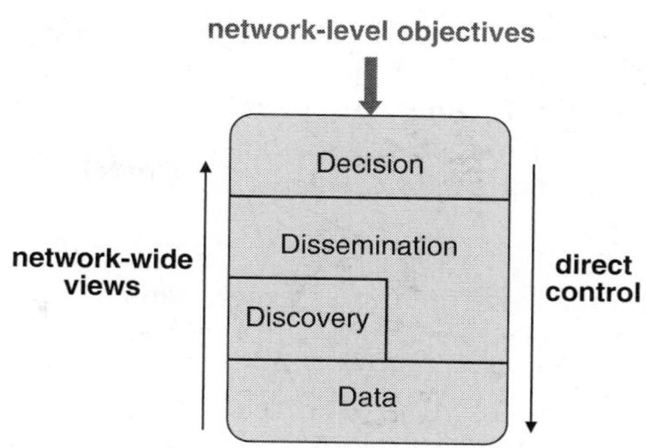

Figure 4: Four planes of 4D architecture with network level-objectives, network-wide views and direct control (Greenberg et al. 2005b)

New Design Principles for Network Control

The 4D designers carefully researched the root causes of some of the major problems plaguing the current Internet architecture, to identify the desirable features for a new approach to network control (Rexford et al. 2004; Greenberg et al. 2005c). The problems examined included reachability control, traffic engineering, and planned maintenance. The effort has led to the formulation of the following design principles for crafting a more robust network architecture (Greenberg et al. 2005c).

Network-level objectives: *A network should be configured via specification of the requirements and goals for its performance, which should be expressed separately from the low-level network elements.*

Network-wide views: *Timely, accurate, network-wide views of topology, traffic, and events are crucial for running a robust network.*

Direct control: *Satisfying network-level objectives is much easier with direct control over the configuration of the data plane. The control and management system should have both the ability and the sole responsibility for setting all the state in the data plane that directs packet forwarding.*

Refactoring of Network Control and Management Functions

Guided by the design principles above, the 4D proposal refactors network control and management functions into four planes, as illustrated in Figure 4. Below is a brief description of the main functions of each plane (Greenberg et al. 2005b).

Decision plane: The decision plane makes *all* decisions driving network control, including reachability, load balancing, access control, security, and interface configuration. Replacing today's management plane, the decision plane operates in real time on a network-wide view of the topology (e.g., layer-3 topology, as well as layer-2 and layer-1 inventory), the traffic (e.g., the traffic matrix), and the capabilities and resource limitations of the routers. The decision plane directly configures the data plane based on network-level objectives, such as a reachability matrix, load-balancing goals, survivability requirements, and planned maintenance events. The algorithms in the decision plane may be customized based on knowledge of the network structure (e.g., simple path-computation algorithms for a ring topology). In one extreme design point, the decision plane may be a logically centralized component, with its functionality replicated by multiple decision elements (DEs) that connect directly to the network for fast, reliable communication with the routers and switches.

Dissemination plane: The dissemination plane provides a robust and efficient communication substrate that connects routers/switches with decision elements. Although control information may traverse the same set of physical links as the data packets, the dissemination paths are maintained separately from the data paths so they can be operational without requiring configuration or successful establishment of paths in the data plane. In contrast, in today's networks, control and management data are carried over the data paths, which need to be established by routing protocols before use. The dissemination plane moves management information created by the decision plane to the data plane and state identified by the discovery plane to the decision plane, but does not create state itself.

Discovery plane: The discovery plane is responsible for discovering the physical components in the network and creating logical identifiers to represent them. The discovery plane defines the scope and persistence of the identifiers, and carries out the automatic discovery and management of the relationships between them. This includes box-level discovery (e.g., what interfaces are on this router? How many FIB entries can it hold?), neighbor discovery (e.g., what other routers does this interface connect to?), and discovery of lower-layer link characteristics (e.g., what is the capacity of the interface?). The decision plane uses the information learned from the discovery plane to construct network-wide views. In contrast, in today's IP networks, the only automatic mechanism is neighbor discovery between two preconfigured and adjacent IP interfaces; physical device discovery and associations between entities are driven by configuration commands and external inventory databases.

Data plane: The data plane handles individual packets based on the state that is *output* by the decision plane.

This state includes the forwarding table, packet filters, link-scheduling weights, and queue-management parameters, as well as tunnels and network address translation mappings. The data plane may also have fine-grain support for collecting measurements on behalf of the discovery plane.

The results from an initial experimental study of the 4D architecture have confirmed the potential of the 4D design to achieve more robust and more efficient network-level decision making than currently possible (Greenberg et al. 2005c). The same study also shows that a logically centralized decision plane, with decision functions and state replicated cross multiple DEs, is resilient in the event of link/router/DE failures or network partitions.

CONCLUSION

We have examined the Internet architecture from a historic perspective. Now it should be clear that the Internet is a success not purely because of economic forces; the network was built with a solid technology foundation which allows it to grow rapidly, foster innovations, and adapt to new application requirements. I hope you are also convinced that new thinking at the architecture level may be required in order to move forward and make the Internet become the integrated communications infrastructure of the future. This area of networking boasts a rich set of exciting research topics. For example, how to turn network configuration from an art, prone to human errors and cascading failures, into a science with precise abstractions and sound reasoning/checking frameworks (Maltz et al. 2004; Xie et al. 2005). A research agenda specific to the 4D architecture is outlined in Greenberg et al. (2005b).

ACKNOWLEDGMENT

I'd like to thank my colleagues Peter Denning and John Gibson for vetting early drafts of this writing and providing helpful feedback. I'd also like to thank five anonymous reviewers whose insights have led to significant improvements in both content and presentation.

GLOSSARY

Addressing: Means to uniquely identify source and destination of packets.

Data formatting: Means to convert application data into packets.

Firewall: Hardware device or software program which establishes a security perimeter around a network.

Forwarding: Means to move packets from input ports to output ports of a router.

Internet architecture: Communication services provided by the network, core building blocks for these services, and division of functionality among network elements.

IP: Internetworking protocol.

Network control and management: All functionality deployed for managing resources in the data plane.

Packet switching: Communication paradigm in which large messages are partitioned into multiple, self-contained packets.

Quality of service: Level of performance guarantee provided by a network, measured by packet delay, loss rate, throughput, etc.

Resource allocation: Techniques for dividing available network resources among traffic flows of different users.

Routing: Means to determine a suitable path from a given a source to a given destination.

Service model: Abstraction of communication services provided by a network.

TCP: Transmission control protocol, which provides reliable service.

Traffic engineering: Optimization of resource allocation for a given traffic matrix.

Tunneling: Encapsulating a packet within another packet.

UDP: User datagram protocol.

Virtual private network: A private network where nodes are connected via encrypted tunnels built over the public Internet.

CROSS REFERENCES

See *Internet Domain Name System*; *TCP/IP Suite*; *The Internet Fundamentals*.

REFERENCES

Cerf, V., and R. Kahn. 1974. A protocol for packet network intercommunication. *IEEE Trans. Communications* 22(5):627–641.

Clark, D. "The Design Philosophy of the DARPA Internet Protocol," in Proc. ACM SIGCOMM'88, August 1988.

Clark, D., K. Sollins, J. Wroclawski, D. Katabi, J. Kulik, X. Yang, R. Braden, T. Faber, A. Falk, V. Pingali, M. Handley, and N. Chiappa. 2003. New Arch: Future generation Internet architecture. White paper. http://www.isi.edu/newarch/ (accessed January 22, 2006).

Davies, J. 2002. *Understanding IPv6*. Seattle, WA: Microsoft Press.

Greenberg, A., G. Hjalmtysson, D. Maltz, A. Myers, J. Rexford, G. Xie, J. Zhan, H. Zhang, "A revolutionary 4D approach to network-wide control and management." Research Proposal Submitted to NSF, January 2005a.

Greenberg, A., G. Hjalmtysson, D. Maltz, A. Myers, J. Rexford, G. Xie, H. Yan, J. Zhan, and H. Zhang. 2005b. A clean slate 4D approach to network control and management. *ACM Computer Communications Review* 35(5):41–54.

Greenberg, A., G. Hjalmtysson, D. Maltz, A. Myers, J. Rexford, G. Xie, H. Yan, J. Zhan, and H. Zhang. 2005c. Refactoring network control and management: A case for the 4D architecture. Technical report CMU-CS-05-177, Carnegie Mellon University.

Internet Histories. http://www.isoc.org/internet/history (accessed March 28, 2006).

Kurose, J. F., and K. W. Ross. 2003. *Computer networking: A top-down approach featuring the Internet*, 3rd edition. Reading, MA: Addison-Wesley.

Living Internet. http://www.livinginternet.com (accessed January 22, 2006).

Maltz, D., G. Xie, J. Zhan, H. Zhang, A. Greenberg, and G. Hjalmtysson. Routing design in operational networks: A look from the inside, in Proc. ACM SIGCOMM'04, Portland, OR, August 2004.

Rexford, J., A. Greenberg, G. Hjalmtysson, D. Maltz, A. Myers, G. Xie, J. Zhan, and H. Zhang. 2004. Network-wide decision making: Toward a wafer-thin control plane, in Proc. ACM SIGCOMM HotNets'04, San Diego, CA, November 2004.

Saltzer, J. H., D. P. Reed, and D. D. Clark. 1984. End-to-end arguments in system design. *ACM Trans. Computer Systems* 2(4):277–88.

Stallings, W. 2004. *Data and computer communications*, 7th edition. Saddle River, NJ: Pearson Prentice Hall.

Xiao, X., and L. M. Ni. 1999. Internet QoS: A big picture. *IEEE Network* 13(2):8–18.

Xie, G., J. Zhan, D. Maltz, H. Zhang, A. Greenberg, G. Hjalmtysson, and J. Rexford. 2005. On static reachability analysis of IP networks. *Proc. IEEE INFOCOM'2005 Conference*, Miami, FL, March 2005.

TCP/IP Suite

Prabhaker Mateti, *Wright State University*

INTRODUCTION

It is difficult to imagine modern living without the Internet. It connects all kinds of computer systems from million dollar supercomputers to personal computers worth no more than a couple of hundred. The networks that connect them are varied, from wireless to wired, from copper to fiber. All of this is enabled by protocols and software collectively known as the *TCP/IP* suite or simply TCP/IP.

The two primary protocols in the suite are IP (Internet protocol) and TCP (transmission control protocol). IP delivers packets from machine to machine using Ethernet or other physical layers and routers. TCP, running on top of IP, reliably delivers packets from process to process. IP requires the support of the infrastructure protocols. ARP (address resolution protocol) maps addresses of the physical layer to IP addresses. ICMP (Internet control message protocol) informs of errors and controls packet traffic. UDP (user datagram protocol) is a thin layer over IP serving those applications where throughput is more important, and unreliability issues are secondary. The size of the Internet is so large that routing tables must be constructed with the help of routing protocols such as RIP (routing information protocol) OSPF (open shortest path first) and BGP (border gateway protocol). Domain name system (DNS) brings not only mnemonics but also indirectly stabilizes the association of services to IP addresses.

TCP/IP details constitute one or more university courses on computer networks. Entire textbooks have been written on the topic that this chapter is attempting to cover. Different views exist as to what should be included under the heading of TCP/IP suite. Our goal is to present the practical TCP/IP landscape as it is today. To limit this chapter to some thirty pages in print requires that certain protocols are treated only briefly, and several other protocols are barely mentioned.

This chapter describes the core protocols known as IP, TCP, UDP; infrastructure protocols named ARP, ICMP, DHCP (dynamic host configuration protocol), SNMP (simple network management protocol), and DNS; application protocols such as, HTTP, SMTP (simple mail transfer protocol), POP (post office protocol), IMAP (Internet messaging access protocol), FTP (file transfer protocol), and SSH (secure socket shell); and the next generation of TCP/IP. As we describe these protocols, we will point out any weaknesses. The definitions of several terms are collected at the end in the glossary.

Protocols

A computer system communicates with another system by sending messages. The Internet is a packet-switched network; messages are split up into *packets*, which are logically viewed as sequences of fields. A *field* is a grouping of certain consecutive bytes or bits from the packet. Depending on the protocol, a packet is retermed as a frame, a datagram, or a segment.

The communication of messages is actually between a process running on one system and one running on the other system. Many of these processes are standard components of an operating system (OS); others are invoked when necessary as independent programs.

The rules of the protocol govern the communications between two or more processes, and their behavior in terms of semantics, timing, and ordering. The protocol also determines the data compression method, how the sender will indicate that it has finished sending, and so on. A protocol describes not only the syntax or structure of the message, that is, of the various fields of a packet, but also the interrelationships of the fields, the type of error checking to be used, and validity conditions.

RFCs

TCP/IP is an open system. Its protocols are written up as technical reports known as RFC (Request for Comments) documents and receive wide scrutiny. RFCs are freely downloadable public documents archived at www.rfc-editor.org. In general, these are proposed designs and solutions published by researchers from universities and corporations soliciting feedback. Protocols evolve through many drafts and versions. Some of these become Internet standards. The Internet Standards Process is described in RFC 2026. The status of various RFCs as standards is currently (2007) described in RFC 3700. In this chapter, we cite only the latest and/or the most relevant RFC for each protocol.

RFCs depict a packet as stacked rows of adjacent rectangles, with tick marks for bits. The field names are written inside the rectangles. When the row is too long to fit in the page width, the row is folded into several 32-bit wide rows, as shown in Figure 1. The indices of the bits start from 00 at the left to 31 at the right. The unit digits of these bit indices are shown in the second row, and the tens digits are shown in the first row. Indices of the bytes start from top-left at 0 but are not shown.

Implementation Issues

In general, there are multiple implementations of each protocol. They have become interoperable; this is often attributed to the fact that many of the implementations of the protocols are open source. However, their behaviors do differ in performance, resource usage, and in other details, often omitted in the RFCs, for example, in dealing with invalid packets. Security attacks have often exploited these details. Packets containing "unexpected" values in some of the fields are illegal in the sense that a legitimate sender would not have constructed them. Software/firmware in the receiver ought to check for such illegal packets, but legacy software was not cautious. Attackers have written special programs that construct illegal packets and cause the receiving network hosts to crash or hang. All major OSs have made improvements in their implementations of the protocols.

An attacker wants to identify the exact version of an OS running on a targeted victim. Nuances in the TCP/

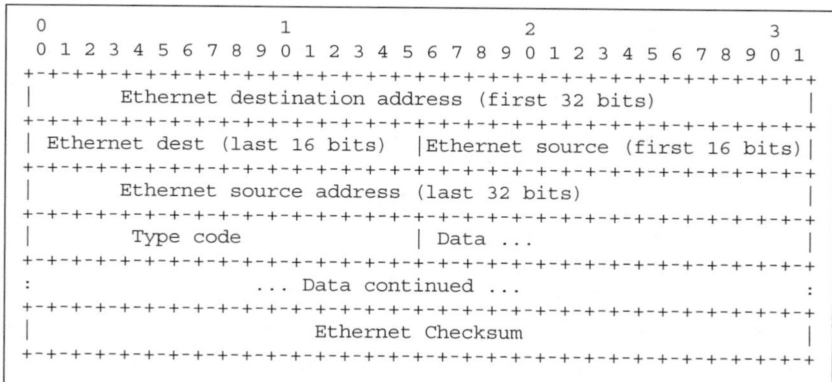

Figure 1: Ethernet (10- and 100 Mbps) frame

IP stacks implemented in the various OSs and versions of the same OS make it possible to remotely probe the victim host and identify the OS. Such probing deliberately constructs illegal packets, attempts to connect to each port, and observes the responses it gets.

A large number of TCP/IP server programs suffer from a class of programming errors known as buffer overflows. Many of these server programs run with the privileges of a superuser. Among the many servers that suffer from such bugs are several implementations of FTP servers, the ubiquitous DNS server program called `bind`, the popular mail server called `sendmail`, and the Web server IIS, to name a few. An attacker supplies cleverly constructed inputs to such programs causing them to transfer control to executable code he or she has supplied. A typical inputted "code" produces a shell that he can interact from a remote machine with all the privileges of the super user.

This chapter does not focus on vulnerabilities, but we do hint at the specifics of these issues. There are several chapters in this book that cover security issues, such as "Network Attacks," "Intrusion Detection Systems," "Virtual Private Networks," "Cryptography," "Authentication," and "Password Authentication."

LAYERS

Network protocols are easier to understand as a stack of layers, with each layer providing the functionality needed by the layer above it. In each layer, there are one or more protocols.

Encapsulation

The data unit of each layer is *encapsulated* by the layer below it (Figure 2), similarly to how sheets of paper are enclosed in an envelope. Each layer adds control information, typically prefixed to the data, before passing on to the lower layer. An application data unit [AP] is encapsulated by the TCP layer by computing a TCP header TCPH and prefixing it as [TCPH [AP]]. The IP layer encapsulates it as [IPH [TCPH [AP]]], where IPH is the IP header. Ethernet encapsulates it as [EH [IPH [TCPH [AP]]] FSC], where EH is the Ethernet header, and FSC is a frame check sequence generated by the Ethernet hardware.

The layers are used in both directions: receiving and sending. While sending, each layer encapsulates the data payload supplied by the above layer. While receiving, each layer strips off the headers and suffixes of the layer to produce the data payload for the layer above it.

Connections

We will be characterizing protocols as either connection-oriented or connectionless.

In the connection-oriented communication, there are three well-defined phases: (i) connection establishment, (ii) data transfer, and (iii) connection release. A client A initiates the negotiation for a connection with B. Based on resource considerations and other issues, B may or may not agree to connect. If it does, it allocates the resources for this virtual circuit. The data transfer can now happen and must always contain a connection identifier. There may be gaps of idle time when there is no data transfer even though the connection is not broken. When A or B realizes that there is nothing more to communicate, the connection is closed, releasing all the resources allocated to it.

In the connectionless communication, one process sends data to another without prior negotiation. The recipient does not acknowledge the receipt of the message, but for communication to be successful, it should be ever ready to receive. The sender has no guarantee that the message is indeed delivered. In general, connectionless service will be faster and less resource consuming than a corresponding connection-oriented service but at a cost of no guarantee of delivery, order, or duplication. Long (in terms of time), steady, and large (in terms of content size) transfers benefit from virtual

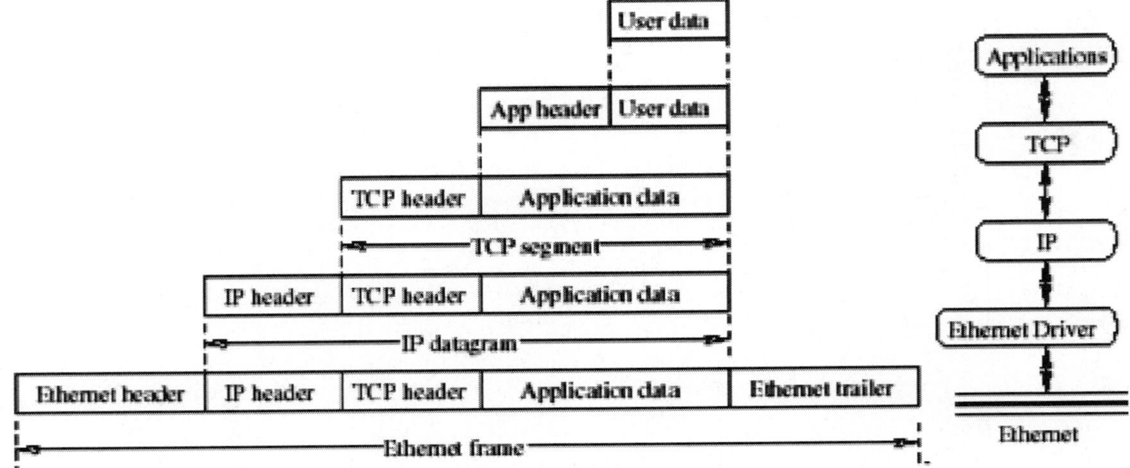

Figure 2: Encapsulations

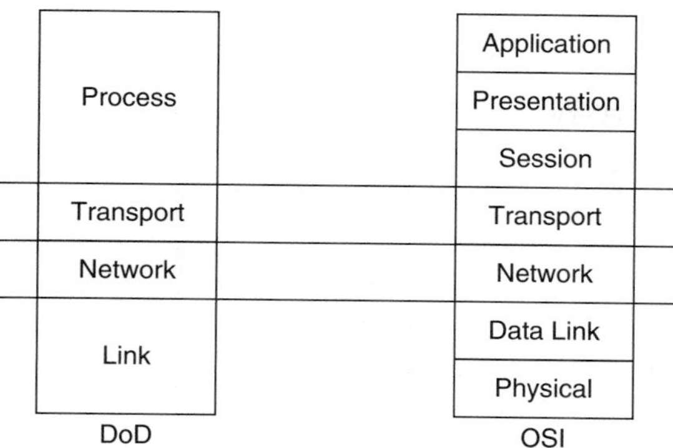

Figure 3: Comparison of DoD and OSI models

circuits. Infrequent and short transfers need only have the connectionless mode.

Models

There are three models of layers: the DoD (Department of Defense), the OSI (open system interconnection), and the "hourglass" models. All the models bring in the notion of layers based on overall functionality, not performance, resources, or even requirements. The DoD and OSI models are shown in Figure 3.

The DoD Model

This model is widely used but unofficially. It is referred to as (i) the TCP/IP model, (ii) the DoD (U.S. Department of Defense) model, or even more simply (iii) the Internet reference model. This model organizes networks into four layers. The location of various protocols in the layers is shown in Figure 4.

1. The *link* (or network access) layer deals with delivery over physical media. It defines the format of a data frame and physical addresses of the devices, and uses the physical and logical properties of the connection to transmit a frame.
2. The *network* (or Internet) layer deals with delivery between source and destination machines. The network layer accepts messages from the source host, converts them into packets of bytes, and sends them through the data link. This layer deals with how a route from the source to the destination is determined. This layer also deals with congestion control. IP, ARP (address resolution protocol), RARP (reverse ARP), ICMP (Internet control message protocol), RIP (routing information protocol), BGP (border gateway protocol), IGMP (Internet group management protocol), and so on belong to this layer.
3. The *transport* (or host-to-host) layer deals with connections, flow control, retransmission of lost data, and so on. TCP and UDP are in this layer.
4. The *application* (or process) layer deals with user-level services. This layer includes protocols such as SSH and SSL/TLS, in addition to those shown (FTP, HTTP, etc.) in Figure 4. This layer corresponds to the session, presentation and application layers of the OSI model (refer to Figure 3).

Note that in some literature, the DoD model is described as having five layers where the physical portion of the link layer is introduced as a separate layer at the bottom.

SCTP (stream control transmission protocol) is defined in RFC 2960 (2000), DCCP (datagram congestion control protocol) is defined in RFC 4340 (2006). Both are transport layer protocols. Both are on the IETF standards track. Because of space reasons and because these are yet to be deployed widely enough, we omit further discussion of these two protocols.

The OSI Model

The OSI (open systems interconnection) model of computer networks is officially recognized by the ISO (International Organization for Standardization). It has seven layers. The practical world of TCP/IP networking was in full use by the time the OSI model was formulated. The OSI model is influential for design purposes, but its

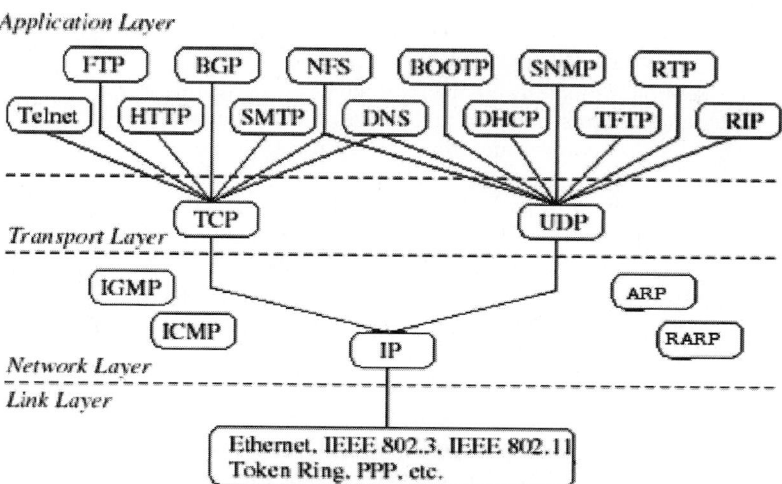

Figure 4: Protocol placement in the DoD model

protocols, developed alongside the OSI model, such as connectionless network protocol (CLNP), transport protocol class 0 (TP0), and common management information protocol (CMIP), are not widely deployed. We place the DoD protocols, rather than CLNP or TP0, as examples into the OSI seven layers. Note that some DoD protocols overlap multiple OSI layers.

1. The bottom most layer, known as the *physical layer*, provides the physical means of carrying the stream of bits. Ethernet, Wireless 802.11, T-carrier, and DSL (digital subscriber line) are examples of this layer. All media are considered functionally equivalent. The differences are in speed, convenience, and cost.
2. The *data link layer* structures the raw stream of bits of the physical layer and, using its encoding functionality, sends and receives a meaningful message unit called a *frame* and provides error detection functions. A frame includes checksum, source and destination addresses, and data. The frame boundaries are special patterns of bits. Software of this layer will retransmit a frame if it is damaged, for example, because of a burst of noise on the physical layer. This layer describes the specification of interface cards to specific types of networks (e.g., Ethernet, and token ring). The data link layer is divided into the media access control (MAC) sublayer, which controls how a computer on the network gains access to the data and permission to transmit it, and the logical link control (LLC) sublayer, which controls frame synchronization, flow control, and error checking. Example protocols from the TCP/IP suite that occupy this layer are SLIP (serial-line Internet protocol) and PPP (point-to-point protocol).
3. The *network layer* accepts messages from the source host, converts them into packets of bytes, and sends them through the data link. This layer deals with how a route from the source to the destination is determined. This layer also deals with congestion control. IP, ARP, RARP, ICMP, RIP, BGP, IGMP, and so on belong to this layer.
4. The *transport layer* transfers data and is responsible for host-to-host error recovery and flow control. TCP, SCTP, and UDP belong to this layer. UDP provides connectionless service, and TCP provides connection-oriented service (Iren et al. 1999).
5. The *session layer* establishes, manages, and terminates connections between the programs on the two hosts that are communicating. The concepts of ports and connections belong to this layer. SAP (session announcement protocol), NetBIOS, SDP (session description protocol), and so on belong to this layer.
6. The *presentation layer* provides independence from possibly different data representations, such as ASCII, little or big endian, MIDI, and MPEG. XDR (external data representation), SSL (secure sockets layer), TLS (transport-layer security), and so on belong to this layer.
7. The *application layer* supports the end-user invoked programs. HTTP, IMAP (Internet messaging access protocol), NTP (network time protocol), POP, FTP, telnet, rlogin (Remote Login), SMTP, SNMP, SOCKS, X-Window, NFS (network file system), Web services, and so on are part of this layer.

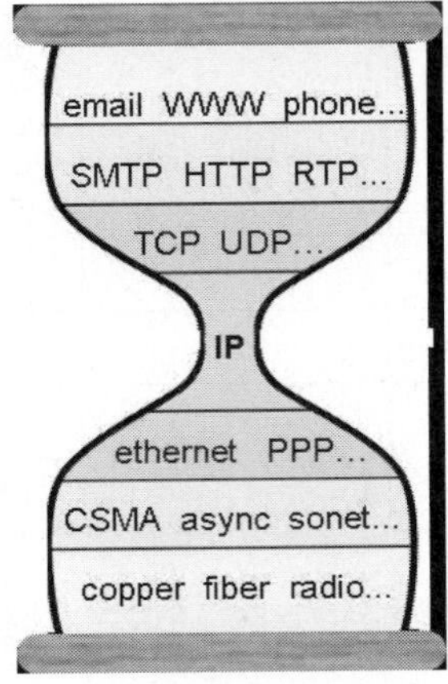

Figure 5: The hourglass model

The OSI model is discussed in most textbooks because of its pedagogical utility but is considered obsolete.

The Hourglass Model

Internet protocols can be described as following an hourglass model with IP at the neck of the hourglass (Figure 5). The hourglass illustrates dependencies among the underlying networks, IP, and the applications.

PHYSICAL AND LINK LAYERS

A few prominent entries from the physical and link layers are described in this section.

Ethernet

Ethernet has been standardized by the Institute of Electrical and Electronics Engineers as IEEE 802.3. There are variations of Ethernet, and the plain Ethernet now refers to 10-megabits-per-second (Mbps) transmission speed, Fast Ethernet refers to 100 Mbps, Gigabit Ethernet refers to 1000 Mbps, and 10GbE refers to 10 Gbps. The connecting media varieties include twisted pair (1000Base-T, 100Base-T, with RJ45 connectors), thick coaxial system (10base5), thin coaxial (10base2), and fiber-optic systems (10basesF).

Ethernet Frames

A frame describes the structure of a byte sequence that constitutes one unit on the physical medium. Every Ethernet controller is assigned a worldwide unique 48-bit MAC address by the factory. For communication among humans, the MAC address is written with each byte in hexadecimal, separating bytes with either a hyphen or a colon, as in `00-0A-E6-9B-27-AE`. Every Ethernet frame (refer to Figure 1) has a 14-byte header that begins with the 6-byte MAC addresses of the destination and source followed by a 2-byte-long type code. Ethernet can support IP and other protocols simultaneously. The type code identifies the protocol family (such as IP, ARP, and NetBEUI). The different frame types have different formats and maximum transmission unit (MTU) values but can coexist on the same physical medium. The data field is from 46 to 1500 bytes in length. Following the data, there is a 4-byte checksum (see Glossary) frame check sequence (FCS) computed by the Ethernet controller for the entire frame.

There are several types of Ethernet frames:

- Ethernet Version 2 frame (refer to Figure 1) was described previously.
- The Raw IEEE 802.3 frame is almost identical to the Ethernet Version 2 frame, except that the 2-byte Type Code field is now interpreted as the length of the data. Because the assigned type codes are greater than 1500 while the data length is at most 1500, there is no ambiguity.
- The IEEE 802.2 LLC frame inserts into the raw frame three 1-byte LLC fields destination service access point (DSAP), a source service access point (SSAP), and a Control field between the Frame Length and Data.
- IEEE 802.2 LLC/SNAP frame sets DSAP to 0xAA, SSAP to 0xAA, and Control field to 0x03, and inserts a 5-byte sub network access protocol (SNAP) field before the Data begins.

All the preceding four frames begin with synchronizing bits, called the preamble, which repeats the bit string 10101010 seven times, and a start frame delimiter 10101011; however, these 8 bytes are not counted in the frame length. These were omitted in Figure 1.

Every Ethernet device is expected to listen for frames containing its MAC address as the destination. All devices also listen for Ethernet frames with a wildcard destination address of FF-FF-FF-FF-FF-FF, called a broadcast address. When a packet is received by the Ethernet network interface card (NIC), it computes the checksum and throws the packet away if an error is detected by the checksum. If the type code is IP, the Ethernet device driver passes the data portion of the frame up to the IP layer of the OS.

Under OS control, the NIC can be put into a so-called promiscuous state wherein the NIC listens to all frames regardless of their destinations.

Unswitched Networks

In an unswitched network, such as when each host is connected to a hub or the obsolete thin cabled Ethernet, every NIC can see the frame being sent. All hosts on the network contend equally for the transmission opportunity. Access to the shared medium is governed by the MAC mechanism based on the carrier sense multiple access with collision detection (CSMA/CD) system. To send data, a host waits for the channel to become idle and then transmits its frame. If two or more devices do try to transmit at the same time, after transmit collisions were detected c times so far, each device chooses a random integer n from 0 to 2^{k-1}, $k = min(c, 10)$, and waits for a period equal to $n*s$, where s is a time period based on propagation delays, before trying to transmit again. This "exponential back off" ensures that access to the network channel is fair and that no single host can lock out other hosts.

Switched Networks

Switched networks use either twisted-pair or fiber-optic cabling, with separate conductors for sending and receiving data. Collision detection is not necessary because the station and the switch are the only devices that can access the medium. End stations and the switch can transmit at will, achieving a collision-free environment.

Unswitched Ethernet segments have all but disappeared. Switched Ethernets replace the shared medium of legacy Ethernet with a dedicated segment for each host and extend the bandwidth. Today, a typical end user connects to a full duplex switched Ethernet, instead of hubs to connect individual hosts or segments. Note that a *hub* is a physical layer device. It transmits the frames received from one port to all other ports it has. A *switch* is a link layer device. A *switch* builds ("learns") a table of ports and the MAC address it is connected to, reads the destination address of each frame, and forwards a frame it receives to only the port connected to the destination MAC address; the other ports do not see the frame.

Sniffing

Sniffing is eavesdropping on the network by a process, the sniffer, on a machine S that records copies of packets sent by machine A intended to be received by machine B. Such sniffing, strictly speaking, is not a TCP/IP problem, but it is enabled by the physical and data link layers. Sniffing can be used for monitoring the health of a network as well as capturing the passwords used in telnet, rlogin, and FTP connections.

In the normal mode, an NIC captures only those frames that match its own MAC address. In the promiscuous mode, an NIC captures all frames that pass by it. In an unswitched Ethernet segment, sniffing is therefore easy. The sniffer can be run on some other host in the same subnet as the victim. The volume of such frames makes it a real challenge for an attacker to either immediately process all such frames fast or clandestinely store them for later processing.

Switched Ethernets mitigate sniffing attacks. If the LAN segment is switched, a sniffer needs to be run either on the victim machine whose traffic is of interest, or on the router. However, switches can be "overwhelmed" into behaving as though they are hubs.

An attacker at large on the Internet has techniques that make it possible to remotely install a sniffer on the victim machine.

IEEE 802.11 a/b/g/n Wireless LANs

This section briefly describes wireless LANs known as the IEEE 802.11 family. For more detailed information, see Part 3 of this book. The 802.11a operates at a theoretical maximum speed of 54 Mbps, 802.11b at 11 Mbps, and 802.11g at 54 Mbps. Note that WiMAX (Worldwide Interoperability for Microwave Access, Inc.) is unrelated to 802.11.

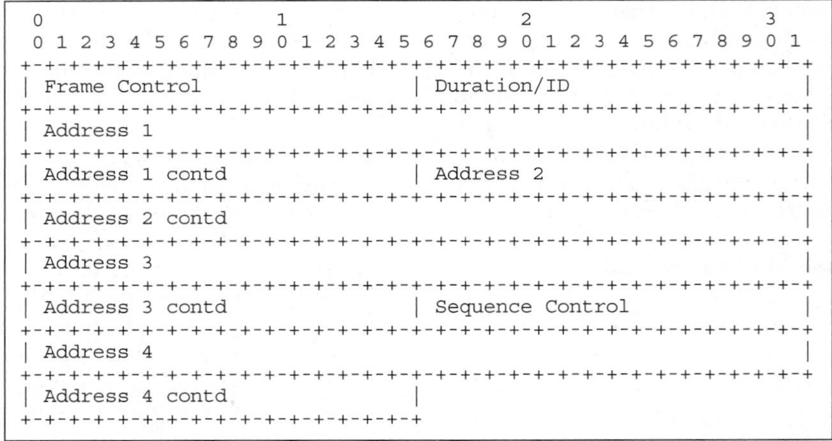

Figure 6: An IEEE 802.11 MAC header

Stations and Access Points

A wireless network *station* provides a radio link to another station. The station has a MAC address, a worldwide unique 48-bit number, assigned to it at the time of manufacture, just as wired network cards do. An *access point* (AP) is a station that provides frame distribution service to stations associated with it. Each AP has a 0- to 32-byte-long service set identifier (SSID) that is used to segment the airwaves for usage. The AP itself is typically connected by wire to a LAN.

Frames

A dot-11 frame consists of a MAC header (see Figure 6) followed by a frame body (payload) of 0 to 2312 bytes and an FCS.

There are three classes of frames. The *management* frames establish and maintain communications. The *control* frames help in the delivery of data. The *data* frames encapsulate the OSI network layer packets. These contain the source and destination MAC address, the BSSID (Basic Service Set Identifier), and the TCP/IP datagram.

Authentication and Association

Data can be exchanged between the station and AP only after a station is authenticated and associated with an AP. A station that is currently unauthenticated and unassociated listens for management frames known as *beacon* frames. The station and the AP mutually authenticate themselves by exchanging authentication management frames. After authentication, the station sends an association request frame, to which the AP responds with an association response frame that includes an association ID to the station. A station can be authenticated with several APs at the same time but associated with at most one AP at any time.

WEP and IEEE 802.11i

Wired equivalent privacy (WEP) is a shared-secret key system encrypting the payload part of the frames transmitted between an AP and a station. WEP is intended to protect wireless communication from eavesdropping and to prevent unauthorized access to a wireless network. Unfortunately, WEP is insecure.

Asynchronous Transfer Mode

Asynchronous transfer mode (ATM) is widely deployed as a backbone technology. ATM is connection-oriented. During the connection setup, the type of the flow, the quality of service (QoS), and so on are negotiated. A path between the end points and the needed resources to provide the QoS are allocated. Transfer of information is then begun. ATM uses fixed-length packets called *cells* for transport. Information is divided among these cells, transmitted, and then reassembled at their final destination. Each cell consists of a 48-byte payload and 5 bytes of additional information, referred to as overhead.

ATM itself consists of a series of layers. Its physical layer is based on various transmission media that range in speed from kilobits per second to gigabits per second. The layer known as the adaptation layer holds the bulk of the transmission converting between packets and cells. The ATM layer handles cell switching.

Frame Relay

Frame relay (FR) is a WAN (wide area network) protocol operating at the physical and data link layers. FR is less expensive but slower than ATM.

When a FR packet-switched network (PSN) is installed, several virtual circuits numbered with a data link connection identifier (DLCI) are established. A virtual circuit provides bidirectional communication between two stations. Virtual circuits may be permanent or switched. A switched virtual circuit is created for each data transfer and is terminated when the transfer is complete. A permanent virtual circuit is set up administratively by a network manager for a dedicated point-to-point connection and does not terminate when the transfer is complete.

Serial Line Internet Protocol

A serial network is a link between two computers over a serial line, which can be a dial-up connection over telephone lines or a direct connection between the serial ports of two computers. Serial line Internet protocol (SLIP; RFC 1055) defines the encapsulation protocol, just as an Ethernet frame envelops an IP packet. Unlike

Ethernet, SLIP supports only IP across a single link. The serial link is manually connected and configured, including the specification of the IP address. SLIP provides no mechanisms for address negotiation, error correction, or compression. However, many SLIP implementations record the states of TCP connections at each end of the link, and use header compression that reduces the size of the combined IP and TCP headers from 40 to 8 bytes.

Point-to-Point Protocol

Point-to-point protocol (PPP; RFC 1661, RFC 2153) replaces the older SLIP and is an encapsulating protocol for IP and other protocol datagrams over serial links. The encapsulation and framing adds 2-, 4-, or 8 bytes depending on the options chosen. PPP includes a link control protocol (LCP) that negotiates the encapsulation format, sizes of packets, authentication methods, and other configuration options. The CCP (compression control protocol) used by PPP negotiates encryption. The IP control protocol (IPCP) included in the PPP configures the IP address and enables the IP protocol on both ends of the point-to-point link.

Digital Subscriber Line

Digital subscriber line/loop (DSL) connects to the same wires as a regular telephone line via a DSL-modem that provides a higher-speed connection, than a typical modem does using either SLIP or PPP.

DSL creates 4.3125 kHz wide channels in the 10 kHz to 100 kHz bandwidth of the local loop, which is unused in plain old telephone service (POTS). The channels are then grouped into two: one for the upload bit stream and the other for the download bit stream.

There are many DSL technologies. Most homes have asymmetric DSL (ADSL) that divides up the available channels so that receiving speeds are much higher than sending speeds. An ATM layer can be built over the DSL. Early implementations of DSL used DHCP to provide network configuration details, where as current implementations often use PPP over Ethernet (PPPoE) or ATM (PPPoA).

INTERNET PROTOCOL

This section describes IP version 4 (RFC 791), which currently (2007) dominates the Internet. The next generation of TCP/IP, numbered v6, is described later.

IP delivers a sequence of bytes, called a *datagram*, from a source host S to a destination host D, even when the hosts are on different networks, geographically vastly separated. The IP layer forms an IP datagram from the byte sequence and the destination given by the upper layer during a send; the reverse of this happens during a receive.

The IP layer software discovers routes that the packet can take from S to various intermediate nodes, known as *routers*, ultimately arriving at D. Thus, IP is routable. Routing is described later in this chapter.

Each datagram travels independently, even when S wants to send several datagrams to D; each datagram is delivered independently of the previous ones. The route that each packet takes may change. Thus, IP is connectionless.

The IP layer is designed deliberately not to concern itself with guaranteed delivery (e.g., datagrams may be lost or duplicated), but instead it is a "best effort" system. ICMP, described later, aids in this effort.

IP Addresses

An OS, during boot-up, assigns a unique 32-bit number known as its IP v4 address to each NIC located in the host system. There is no rigid relationship between the MAC address and the IP address. The IP address is obtained either by looking it up in a configuration file or via dynamic host configuration protocol (DHCP). When a machine is moved from one network to another, we must reassign an IP address that belongs to the new network. This is one of the problems that mobile IP solves.

IP addresses are typically written in a dotted-quad notation, such as `i.j.k.l`, where `i` is the first byte, `j` the second, `k` the third, and `l` the fourth byte. The first `p` bits constitute the network ID/address, and the rest `32 - p` bits constitute the host ID. The number p is implicitly given by the IP address in the classful addressing scheme and identified externally in the classless scheme.

There are a few specific 32-bit numbers that are set aside for special usage. An IP address whose host ID portion is zero is the network address and is not the address of any host on that network. Occasionally, a network node X needs to discover certain information from other nodes, but the node X does not know the addresses of these others. In such situations, X broadcasts using special destination IP addresses. The direct broadcast address of X is the 32-bit number whose host ID portion is all ones and whose network address equals that of X. The limited broadcast address is 255.255.255.255.

Class A, B, and C Networks

Three address ranges known as class A, class B, and class C are of historical importance. In a class A address, the 0-th bit is always a 0, bits 1 through 7 identify the network, and bits 8 through 31 identify the host, permitting 2^{24} hosts on the network. In a class B address, the bit 0 is always a 1, bit 1 is always a 0, bits 2 through 15 identify the network, and bits 16 through 31 identify the host, permitting 2^{16} hosts on the network. In a class C address, bits 0 and 1 are both 1 always, bit 2 is a 0 always, bits 3 through 23 identify the network, and bits 24 through 31 identify the host, permitting 2^{8} hosts on the network. This classful addressing is self-identifying in that the subnet ID and the host ID can be computed by examining the first two bits.

An organization would be assigned one or more blocks from these classes. Class C, with a maximum of 254 host addresses, is too small, whereas class B is too large to be densely populated, and the few class A networks are sparsely populated.

Subnets and Masks

A subnet is a collection of hosts whose IP addresses match in several bits indicated by the ones in a sequence of 32 bits known as a subnet mask, also written in the dotted-quad notation. Thus, 255.255.255.0 is a mask of 24 ones followed by 8 zeroes. Because of this structure, the mask is also written as /24. Nodes and routers use the mask to identify the address of the network on which the specific host resides. The address of the network is the bitwise-AND of the IP address and the mask. The host ID is the bitwise-AND of the IP address and the complement of the mask.

CIDR and VLSM

The classless interdomain routing (CIDR) model (RFC 1518, 1993) solves the problems of efficient utilization of IP address space and reducing routing table sizes by using variable length subnet masking (VLSM). Instead of using class A, B, or C network identifiers of 8-, 16-, or 24 bits, CIDR replaces them with p bits, and the address is written as `a.b.c.d/p`. With CIDR, a single number a.b.c.d can designate many different hosts based on the prefix.

A single network (say of class B) can be divided into finer ranges of addresses with different prefix values. Organizations can be assigned a smaller range instead of an entire class B. An organization can further divide it internally into sub subnets, and so on using VLSM.

A CIDR block is a collection of addresses that have the same prefix. It is possible that these are collections of networks belonging to different organizations, and the collection is then called a supernet. Modern routing protocols reduce their table sizes by constructing large CIDR blocks through prefix aggregation and maintaining a single row per block.

Public and Private Address Ranges

The public IP addresses are carefully controlled worldwide. The IANA, Internet Assigned Numbers Authority (www.iana.org), assigns the public IP addresses to organizations and individuals upon application.

There are three blocks of the IP address space intended for private intranets: (i) 10.0.0.0 to 10.255.255.255 (10/8 prefix, class A), (ii) 172.16.0.0 to 172.31.255.255 (172.16/12 prefix), and (iii) 192.168.0.0 to 192.168.255.255 (192.168/16 prefix, class C).

Most operating systems are internally structured to depend on the presence of a network layer. To facilitate this, the address 127.0.0.1 is assigned as the address of the `localhost` (spelled as one word) and 127.0.0.0 as the `localnetwork` (spelled as one word). Packets sent to this address do not actually travel onto the external network. They simply appear as received on the local (artificial) device.

That is, on the Internet at large, there must only be IP packets whose source or destination addresses are assigned public addresses.

IP Header

An IP header is a sequence of bytes that the IP layer software prefixes to the data it receives from the higher layers. The resulting IP header plus the data (see Figure 7) is given to the lower layer (e.g., the Ethernet card device driver). Except for the IP Options field, all other fields are fixed in length as shown. Minimally (i.e., without options), the IP header is 20 bytes in length. With IP options, an IP header can be as long as 60 bytes. The maximum length of an IP datagram is 65535 bytes. (IP over Ethernet limits this to 1500.)

IPv is the version number of the protocol, which is currently 4. The value of IHL multiplied by 4 is the length of the IP header in bytes. The type of service field specifies the "relative urgency" or importance of the packet. Total length is a 2-byte field giving the length, in bytes, of the entire packet, including the header, options (if any), and the packet data. The identification field, flags, and fragment offset are used to keep track of the pieces when a datagram must be split up as it travels from one router to the next. IP fragmentation is discussed further next. The time to live (TTL) is a number that is decremented by 1 whenever the datagram passes through a router node. When it goes to 0, the datagram is discarded, and an error message is sent back to the source of this packet. The protocol field identifies the protocol of the data area. The header checksum field is a 1's complement arithmetic sum of the entire header viewed as a sequence of 16-bit integers. The source address is the datagram's sender IP address, and destination address is the IP address of the intended recipient.

```
 0                   1                   2                   3
 0 1 2 3 4 5 6 7 8 9 0 1 2 3 4 5 6 7 8 9 0 1 2 3 4 5 6 7 8 9 0 1
+-+-+-+-+-+-+-+-+-+-+-+-+-+-+-+-+-+-+-+-+-+-+-+-+-+-+-+-+-+-+-+-+
|  IPv  |  IHL  |Type of Service|          Total Length         |
+-+-+-+-+-+-+-+-+-+-+-+-+-+-+-+-+-+-+-+-+-+-+-+-+-+-+-+-+-+-+-+-+
|         Identification        |Flags|      Fragment Offset    |
+-+-+-+-+-+-+-+-+-+-+-+-+-+-+-+-+-+-+-+-+-+-+-+-+-+-+-+-+-+-+-+-+
|  Time to Live |    Protocol   |         Header Checksum       |
+-+-+-+-+-+-+-+-+-+-+-+-+-+-+-+-+-+-+-+-+-+-+-+-+-+-+-+-+-+-+-+-+
|                       Source Address                          |
+-+-+-+-+-+-+-+-+-+-+-+-+-+-+-+-+-+-+-+-+-+-+-+-+-+-+-+-+-+-+-+-+
|                    Destination Address                        |
+-+-+-+-+-+-+-+-+-+-+-+-+-+-+-+-+-+-+-+-+-+-+-+-+-+-+-+-+-+-+-+-+
.  IP Options (if any)                                          .
|  IP packet data ...                                           |
.  ...                                                          .
+-+-+-+-+-+-+-+-+-+-+-+-+-+-+-+-+-+-+-+-+-+-+-+-+-+-+-+-+-+-+-+-+
```

Figure 7: IPv4 datagram

IP Fragments

When datagrams are too large to be sent in a single IP packet, they are split up by an intermediate router unless prohibited by the Don't Fragment flag. IP fragmentation occurs when a router receives a packet larger than the maximum transmission unit (MTU) of the next network segment, usually determined by interface hardware limitations. All such fragments will have the same identification field value (refer to Figure 7). The fragment offset indicates the position of the current fragment in the context of the presplit-up packet. Intermediate routers are not expected to reassemble the fragments. The final destination will reassemble all the fragments into one IP datagram.

Mobile IP

As a mobile network host moves, its point of attachment may change, and yet to maintain existing transport-layer connections, it must keep its IP address the same.

The mobile node uses two IP addresses. The home address is static and is used to identify TCP connections. The care-of address changes at each new point of attachment. Whenever the mobile node moves, it registers its new care-of address with its home agent. The home agent redirects the packets to the current care-of address by constructing a new IP header that contains the care-of address as the destination IP address. This new header encapsulates the original packet, causing the home address to have no effect on the routing of the encapsulated packet until it arrives at the care-of address. When the packet arrives at the care-of address, the effect of this "tunneling" is reversed so that the packet once again appears to have the home address as the destination IP address. Mobile IP discovery of the care-of address uses an existing standard protocol called *router advertisement* (RFC 1256). A router advertisement carries information about default routers, and in addition carries further information about one or more care-of addresses. Home agents and care-of agents typically broadcast these advertisements at regular intervals (say, once every few seconds). A mobile node that needs a care-of address will multicast a router solicitation. An advertisement also informs the mobile node whether the agent is a home agent, a care-of agent, or both, and therefore whether it is on its home network or on a care-of network and about special features provided by care-of agents (for example, alternative encapsulation techniques).

The registration of the new care-of address begins when the mobile node, possibly with the assistance of the care-of agent, sends a registration request to the home address. The home agent typically updates its routing table. Registration requests contain parameters and flags that characterize the tunnel through which the home agent will deliver packets to the care-of address. The triplet of the home address, care-of address, and registration lifetime is called a binding for the mobile node. The home agent authenticates that the registration was originated by the mobile node.

Occasionally, a mobile node cannot contact its home agent. The mobile node tries to register with another home agent by using a directed broadcast IP address instead of the home agent's IP address as the target for the registration request.

Each mobile node and home agent compute an unforgeable digital signature using one-way hash algorithm MD5 (Message Digest 5; RFC 1321) with 128-bit keys on the registration message, which includes either a time stamp or a random number carefully generated.

IP Issues

Several aspects of IP design have become troubling issues as the mischievous elements began to use the Internet.

The typical IP layer of an OS does not check for anomalies in the header. For example, an IP packet should not have source address and port equaling the destination address and port. The 1997 attack tool called *land* exploited this vulnerability.

Covert channels can be set up using the ID field of IP packets, IP checksums, and so on (Rowland 1997).

IP Spoofing

The IP layer of the typical OS simply trusts that the IP source address is valid. It assumes that the packet it received was sent by the host officially assigned to that source address.

Replacing the true IP address of the sender (or, in rare cases, the destination) with a different address is known as *IP spoofing*. Because the IP layer of the OS normally adds these IP addresses to a data packet, a spoofer must circumvent the IP layer and talk directly to the raw network device. IP spoofing is used as a technique aiding an exploit on the target machine. Note that the attacker's machine cannot simply be assigned the IP address of another host T using `ifconfig` or a similar configuration tool. Other hosts, as well as T, will discover (through ARP, for example) that there are two machines with the same IP address.

IP spoofing is an integral part of many attacks. For example, an attacker can silence a host A from sending further packets to B by sending a spoofed packet announcing a window size of zero to A as though it originated from B.

IP Fragment Attacks

A well-behaving set of IP fragments is non overlapping. Malicious fragmentation involves fragments that have illegal offsets. For example, the fragments may be so crafted that the receiving host in its attempts to reassemble calculates a negative length for the second fragment. This value is passed to a function (such as `memcpy`) that copies from/to memory, which takes the negative number to be an enormous unsigned (positive) number. A pair of carefully crafted but malformed IP packets thus causes a server to "panic" and crash. The 1997 attack tool called *teardrop* exploited this vulnerability. The 2004 *Rose Attack* sent two small IP fragments of 32 bytes each, from a SYN segment, that do not form a complete packet. The first fragment was with zero-offset, and the second fragment was set to an offset of 64800 bytes into the datagram.

The RFCs require no intermediate router to reassemble fragmented packets. Obviously, the destination must reassemble. Many firewalls do not perform packet reassembly in the interest of efficiency. These only consider the fields of individual fragments. Attackers create artificially fragmented packets to fool such firewalls. In a so-called tiny fragment attack, two fragments are created where the first one is so small that it does not even include the destination port number. The second fragment contains the remainder of the TCP header, including the port number. A variation of this is to construct the second fragment packet with an offset value less than the length of the data in the first fragment so that upon packet reassembly, it overrides several bytes of the first fragment (e.g., if the first fragment was 24 bytes long, the second fragment may claim to have an offset of 20). Upon reassembly, the data in the second fragment overwrites the last 4 bytes of the data from the first fragment. If these were fragments of a TCP segment, the first fragment would contain the TCP destination port number, which is overwritten by the second fragment. Such techniques do not cause a crash or hang of a targeted system but can be used to bypass simple filtering done by some firewalls.

Fragmentation attacks are preventable. Unfortunately, in the IP layer implementations of nearly all OSs, there were/are bugs and naïve assumptions in the reassembly code.

ICMP

Internet control message protocol (RFC 792, 1981; RFC 950, 1985) is a required protocol that manages and controls the IP layer. In general, much of the best effort in delivering IP datagrams is associated with ICMP. The purpose of the ICMP messages is to provide feedback and suggestions about problems. The popular network utilities `ping` and `traceroute` use ICMP.

ICMP is in the network layer. But, an ICMP message is encapsulated as an IP datagram. These are treated like any other IP datagrams.

Message Format

Each ICMP message begins with a 1-byte ICMP type field, which determines the format of the remaining data, a one-byte code field, and a 2-byte checksum (Figure 8). ICMP messages are either error or query/reply messages.

Error Messages

ICMP is designed to report network errors, such as a host or entire portion of the network being unreachable or a packet being directed at a closed port. Error messages are reported to the original source on problems encountered by a router or the destination host in processing an IP datagram. However, ICMP is not designed to correct errors. To avoid infinite regress, no ICMP messages are sent about ICMP messages. Also ICMP messages are not sent about errors in handling (i) other than fragment zero of fragmented datagrams, (ii) multicast address, and (iii) addresses such as 127.0.0.0, or 0.0.0.0.

In an ICMP error message, the 4 bytes of Rest of Header is set to 0, and the data section is the first 8 bytes of the IP datagram causing the error.

A Destination Unreachable (Type = 3) error message is sent to the original source host when a datagram cannot reach its destination. The code field indicates the cause.

A Source Quench Message (Type = 4) is sent (i) if the gateway does not have the buffering capacity to forward a datagram, or (ii) if datagrams arrive too fast to be processed.

A router R1 sends a Redirect Message (Type = 5) to a source host S if datagrams to a destination D through R1 will make the next hop to another router R2 and S can send directly to router R2.

The Time-Exceeded (Type = 11) ICMP error messages are delivered when the TTL of a datagram is 0. The `traceroute` utility constructs IP datagrams with well-chosen TTL values and collects the time exceeded messages to map a route from the source to a destination IP address.

The Parameter Problem (Type = 12) message is sent if a router finds a problem with any of the parameters in an IP header that causes it to drop the datagram.

Request/Reply Messages

The Echo Request (Type = 8) and Echo Reply (Type = 0) query messages can identify network problems. The well-known `ping` (packet Internet groper) command sends several echo requests, captures their echo replies, and displays statistics about speed and datagram loss.

The Router Advertisement (Type = 9) and Router Solicitation (Type = 10) messages are periodically multicast by a router announcing its multicast addresses. Hosts can discover the addresses of their neighboring routers simply by listening to the advertisements. When a host starts up, it may multicast a Router Solicitation to ask for immediate advertisements, rather than waiting for the next periodic ones to arrive. Note that these router discovery messages do not indicate which router is best to reach a particular destination. A host choosing a poor first-hop router for a particular destination should receive an ICMP Redirect from that router.

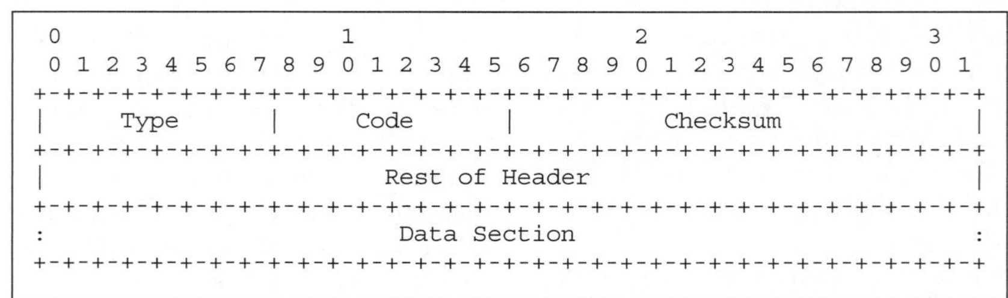

Figure 8: ICMP packet

A Timestamp Request (Type = 13) includes the time stamp, a 32-bit unsigned integer counting milliseconds since midnight UT, of the sender. A Timestamp Reply (Type = 14) Message includes the originate time stamp and the time stamp of the receiver. These can be used to estimate the round-trip time of a datagram or to synchronize clocks.

The Address Mask Request (Type = 17) and Address Mask Reply (Type = 18) messages enable a host to discover its address mask.

ICMP Issues

ICMP has been one of the easiest among the protocols to exploit. For example, the ICMP redirect message, intended to improve routing performance, has often been used maliciously.

ICMP scanning is a way to gather information regarding hosts on the Net (Arkin 2001). In the simplest form, Echo Request messages are sent, and the received Echo Replies are analyzed. The standard utility called `ping` does this with a single host. An attacker, however, uses a broadcast address and/or parallel sweeps.

The attack tool of 1997, called *smurf*, sends ICMP Echo Request messages. There are three hosts in smurfing: the attacker, the intermediary router, and the victim. The attacker sends to an intermediary an echo request packet with the IP broadcast address of the intermediary's network as the destination. The source address is spoofed by the attacker to be that of the intended victim. The intermediary puts it out on that network. Each machine on that network will send an echo reply packet to the source address. The victim is subjected to network congestion that could potentially make it unusable.

The so-called Ping of Death attack of 1996 sent an echo request packet that was larger than the maximum permissible length ($2^{16} - 1$).

ICMP echo request packets should have an 8-byte header and a 56-byte payload. ICMP echo requests should not be carrying any data. However, significantly larger ICMP packets can be generated carrying covert data in their payloads.

In addition to the exploits described here, ICMP has enabled several other exploits via reconnaissance and scanning.

USER DATAGRAM PROTOCOL

UDP (RFC 768, 1980) is a connectionless protocol belonging to the transport layer (OSI layer 4). It is a thin protocol on top of IP, providing high speed but low functionality. UDP does not guarantee the delivery of datagrams. Messages can be delivered out of order, delayed, or even lost. Datagrams may get duplicated without being detected. The UDP protocol is used mostly by application services where squeezing the best performance out of existing IP networks is necessary, such as Trivial File Transfer (TFTP), NFS, and DNS.

Port Numbers

IP delivers host-to-host. Port numbers are used by the transport layer to multiplex communication between several pairs of processes. To each message, this layer adds addresses, called port numbers. The port numbers are assigned by the OS. The UDP layer of an OS picks up the IP datagrams, examines the UDP payload, extracts the destination port number, and delivers the UDP data to the process that registered with the destination port.

The port numbers appearing in the UDP header are similar to the TCP port numbers (see next section), but the OS support required by UDP ports is much simpler and less resource consuming than that of TCP ports.

The ports 0 to 1023 are reserved for specific well-known services provided by privileged processes. These numbers are assigned by IANA. These are often called *well-known* ports. For example, HTTP officially uses port 80, telnet officially uses port 23, and DNS officially uses port 53. The ports in the range 1024 to 49151 are called *registered ports* because they are listed by the IANA for specific services, but on most systems, these ports can be used by unprivileged processes. The *dynamic* or *private* ports range from 49152 to 65535. Client processes and nonstandard services are assigned port numbers by the OS at run-time. On most computer systems, there is a list of these port numbers and service names in a file named `etc/services`. Almost always, the same port assignments are used with both UDP and TCP.

User Datagrams

UDP packets are called user datagrams. The source port is the port of the sending process (Figure 9). When not meaningful, this field is set to 0. The destination port is the UDP port on the receiving machine, whose IP address is supplied by the IP layer. Length is the number of bytes in the datagram, including the UDP header and the data. Checksum is the 16-bit 1 complement of the 1 complement sum of the UDP header, the source and destination IP addresses obtained from the IP header, and the data, padded with 0 bytes at the end (if necessary) to make a multiple of 2 bytes.

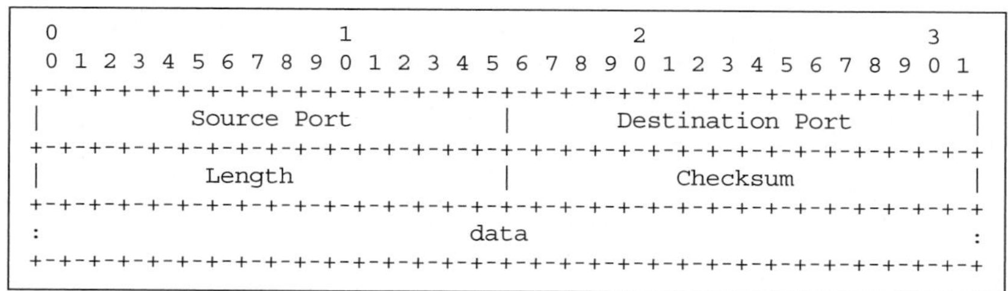
```
 0                   1                   2                   3
 0 1 2 3 4 5 6 7 8 9 0 1 2 3 4 5 6 7 8 9 0 1 2 3 4 5 6 7 8 9 0 1
+-+-+-+-+-+-+-+-+-+-+-+-+-+-+-+-+-+-+-+-+-+-+-+-+-+-+-+-+-+-+-+-+
|          Source Port          |        Destination Port       |
+-+-+-+-+-+-+-+-+-+-+-+-+-+-+-+-+-+-+-+-+-+-+-+-+-+-+-+-+-+-+-+-+
|            Length             |            Checksum           |
+-+-+-+-+-+-+-+-+-+-+-+-+-+-+-+-+-+-+-+-+-+-+-+-+-+-+-+-+-+-+-+-+
:                             data                              :
+-+-+-+-+-+-+-+-+-+-+-+-+-+-+-+-+-+-+-+-+-+-+-+-+-+-+-+-+-+-+-+-+
```

Figure 9: UDP packet

Connectionless Service

Each user datagram sent from a process to another is independent from others. UDP headers contain no information that specifies the order of individual datagrams, or that some were sent before. As a result, the sending and receiving processes have no way of deducing if datagrams have been lost or that they arrived out of order.

When a receiver detects an error using the checksum, there is no provision for requesting a retransmit. The datagram in error is simply discarded without informing any entity.

There is no flow control. A prolific sender process can overwhelm a receiver making its buffers overflow.

TCP

Transmission Control Protocol (RFC 793, 1981; RFC 3168, 2001) provides an end-to-end reliable service. TCP is a connection-oriented protocol belonging to the transport layer (OSI layer 4). It is a complex protocol on top of IP, providing lower speed than UDP but high functionality. It is the most dominant protocol of the TCP/IP suite. TCP guarantees the correct (both in content and in order) delivery of the data. TCP sends its message content over the IP layer and can detect and recover from errors. TCP, however, does not guarantee any speed of delivery, even though it offers congestion control.

TCP Header

TCP messages, called *segments*, are sent as one or more IP datagrams. A segment consists of a TCP header (Figure 10) followed by the data payload.

The Source Port and Destination Port are the port numbers of the sender and receiver. The port numbers are classified as in UDP. Both UDP and TCP ports coexist, and, to the extent possible, the same port assignments are used with both UDP and TCP. However, many protocols, such as HTTP (port number 80), use TCP exclusively.

The sequence number and the acknowledgment number are strongly coupled together and are explained in the next section. The 4-bit DATAX number multiplied by 4 specifies the number of bytes in the TCP header. This indicates where the data payload begins. TCP segments have a number of control flags letters |U|A|P|R|S|F| in the fourth row that have, collectively, a strong influence on how the segment is processed. These letters are abbreviated names for control bit flags further explained in the "Operation" section. Window size is described in later sections. Options, if any, are given at the end of the TCP header and are always a multiple of 8 bits in length. All options are included in the checksum. An option can be just a single byte, or it can be a byte of option-kind, followed by a byte of option-length and the actual option-data bytes. The option-length counts the 2 bytes of option-kind and option-length as well as the option-data bytes.

Operation

This section describes the typical operation without worrying about flow control, congestion control, and errors, which are discussed in later sections.

A connection needs to be established and kept alive between two processes, initiated by A and accepted by B, for them to communicate. The following data structures, together called TCB (transmission control block), exist per each connection at both hosts, A and B.

- Sequence Number (SEQN) is a 32-bit unsigned integer. It is initialized with carefully selected random number and is known as the Initial Sequence Number (ISN).
- Acknowledgement Number (ACKN) is a 32-bit unsigned integer. Its initial value is garbage. It is set equal to the sequence number of the next byte from B that A expects to receive.
- The send buffer SBUF of bytes, with has three indices set up on it: (i) the window left edge SWLE, (ii) next byte to be sent SWNX, and (iii) window right edge SWRE, buffer right edge SBRE. The section of the buffer from SWLE to SWRE is known as the sliding window.
- `The receive buffer RBUF of bytes, with has four indices set up on it: (i) buffer left edge RBLE, (ii) window left edge RWLE, (iii) window right edge RWRE, and (iv) buffer right edge RBRE. Between RWLE and RWRE is known as the receive window of this connection.
- `A state identifier represents the name of the state (see Figure 11 later in this section) that the TCP subsystem is in.

Imagine the bytes of the buffers to be indexed from 0 to infinity, even though only a finite subrange of 0 to infinity

```
 0                   1                   2                   3
 0 1 2 3 4 5 6 7 8 9 0 1 2 3 4 5 6 7 8 9 0 1 2 3 4 5 6 7 8 9 0 1
+-+-+-+-+-+-+-+-+-+-+-+-+-+-+-+-+-+-+-+-+-+-+-+-+-+-+-+-+-+-+-+-+
|          Source Port          |       Destination Port        |
+-+-+-+-+-+-+-+-+-+-+-+-+-+-+-+-+-+-+-+-+-+-+-+-+-+-+-+-+-+-+-+-+
|                        Sequence Number                        |
+-+-+-+-+-+-+-+-+-+-+-+-+-+-+-+-+-+-+-+-+-+-+-+-+-+-+-+-+-+-+-+-+
|                    Acknowledgment Number                      |
+-+-+-+-+-+-+-+-+-+-+-+-+-+-+-+-+-+-+-+-+-+-+-+-+-+-+-+-+-+-+-+-+
| DATAX | Reserved  |U|A|P|R|S|F|         Window  Size          |
+-+-+-+-+-+-+-+-+-+-+-+-+-+-+-+-+-+-+-+-+-+-+-+-+-+-+-+-+-+-+-+-+
|           Checksum            |         Urgent Pointer        |
+-+-+-+-+-+-+-+-+-+-+-+-+-+-+-+-+-+-+-+-+-+-+-+-+-+-+-+-+-+-+-+-+
|                    Options                    |    Padding    |
+-+-+-+-+-+-+-+-+-+-+-+-+-+-+-+-+-+-+-+-+-+-+-+-+-+-+-+-+-+-+-+-+
```

Figure 10: TCP header

is in use at any moment. Operating systems implement such buffers as cyclic buffers.

The TCP subsystem of the OS keeps track of the connection (that is, messages between the two processes of A and B) through SEQN and ACKN. TCP is full duplex; that is, A and B can send and receive segments at the same time. While continuing to send segments, A expects to receive segments from B that contain acknowledgement of its segments. This applies to B also. For compactness, the rest of this section is written from the perspective of one end of the connection at host A.

Acknowledgments are piggybacked on reply data. Each segment sent by B contains (i) the data payload that B wants to send to A, (ii) the SEQN of this payload, and (iii) the ACKN set equal to the *sequence* number of the next byte expected from A. Additionally, ACKN confirms to A that B has received all bytes numbered from ISN of A up to and including ACKN -1. Obviously, the very first segment from A to B, and vice versa, do not have a valid ACKN, and hence ACK = 0.

TCP has a number of control bit flags that have, when set to 1, the following meanings: Urgent pointer is valid when URG is 1. Its value is an offset from the sequence number in this segment. ACK, acknowledgment number is valid; PSH, push function is active; RST reset the connection; SYN synchronize sequence numbers; and FIN, sender is finished with this connection. In a typical segment, we expect only ACK = 1 and all others to be 0.

TCP is a *sliding window* protocol that performs the following repetitively. TCP at A computes the data payload size for the segment, which is the lesser of (i) available number of bytes and (ii) the receive buffer window size of B. If this is zero, it pauses. Otherwise, it sends a segment to B made of consecutive bytes starting from the index of the next byte to be sent, SWNX. The SEQN in the segment is set to ISN + SWNX. SWNX is incremented by the length of this data payload for the next segment. All the bytes of the send buffer to the left of SWLE have been acknowledged by B as successfully received. The number of available bytes to send is SWRE-SWNX. The window slides forward (i.e., both SWLE and SWRE are incremented by the same amount) as and when appropriate acknowledgements are received by A. SWRE is further considered in the sections on flow and congestion control. Note that the send buffer is filled by the local (i.e., at host A) process at its right edge.

A segment S received from B may or may not fall in the receive window of A as determined by the SEQN and segment length of S. The receive window is filled by the segments that do fall in this window. In between such filled sequences, there may be gaps because the corresponding segments are yet to be received. RWLE is moved to the beginning of the left most gap in the window. Note that TCP at A advertises the receive window size (RBRE - RWLE) in each segment it sends to B. The bytes between RBLE and RWLE-1 are for the local process, and as it consumes, RBLE byte index gets incremented. If RBLE = RWLE, the local process must pause.

State Diagram

A TCP server process starts its life by passively opening a port and listening to connection attempts from clients. This process causes a number of changes in the TCB data structures maintained by the TCP layer software. These transitions are described in a simplified manner by the state diagram shown in Figure 11. The boxes denote the states, and the arrows denote a state transition. Each transition has a label of the form input/output, which describes that while in the state U at the tail end of the arrow, if the event described by input occurs, the event described by output is caused, and a state transition to V occurs. We describe how to read this diagram further in the next few sections.

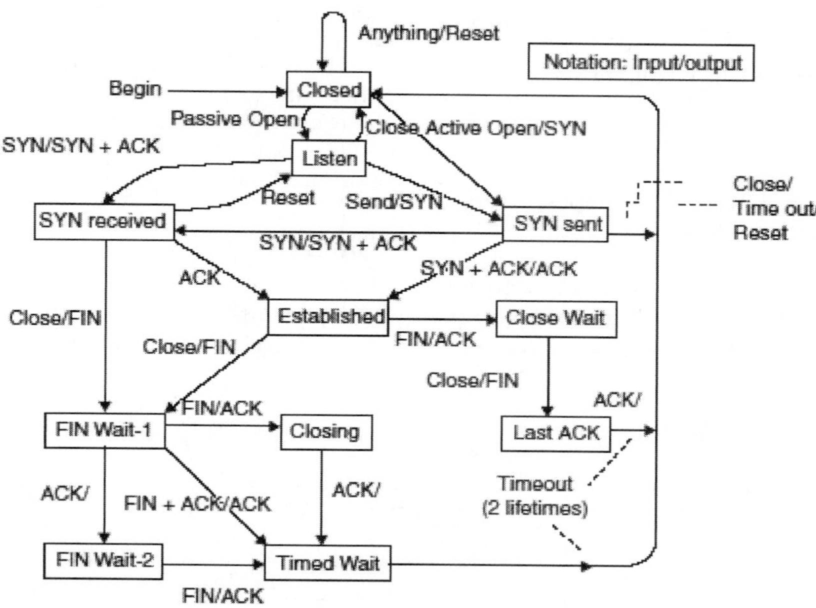

Figure 11: TCP state diagram

Connections

TCP establishes a connection (using the three-way handshake) between a client, say A, and a server, say B, transfers a continuous stream of bytes in each direction by packaging some number of bytes into segments, and in the end formally terminates (using the four-way handshake) the connection.

Establishment: Three-Way Handshake

A three-way handshake establishes a connection as follows:

- A: "I would like to talk to you, B." A sends to B a segment with ACK = 0, SYN = 1, and ISN chosen by A. This segment includes an initial window size advertisement. A was in the Listen state and now enters SYN-sent state. B was in the Listen state and on receiving this SYN-segment, enters the SYN-received state.
- B: "OK, let's talk." B replies with a SYN+ACK segment (i.e., SYN = 1 with SEQN to the ISN of B, and ACK = 1, ACKN = ISN of A + 1). At this point, B remains in the SYN-received state. The condition of the connection is known as *half-open*. If B was unwilling to talk, it would have responded with a RST = 1 segment refusing the request for service and would have moved into the Listen state.
- A: "Thanks for agreeing!" Having received the SYN+ACK segment from B, A sends a segment with ACK = 1, ACKN = ISN of B + 1, SYN = 0, SEQN = previous SEQN + 1. At this point, A is in the Established state. When B receives this segment, B also enters the Established state, and the connection is fully open and functional: A and B can continue to exchange messages. In these messages, ACK = 1 and SYN = 0.

The ISN can be a zero, but that is not secure, so the ISN is randomly chosen.

Here is an example (shown in Figure 12 as a ladder diagram and with the ACK numbers in Table 1) where the client is on port 1037 establishing a connection with a service on port 80.

The connection establishment results in the creation of the TCP data structures at both ends.

Closing: Four-Way Handshake

This gracefully terminates a previously established connection between A and B as follows:

- A: "No more data from me." A sends to B a segment with FIN = 1 and of course ACK = 1. The FIN flag is used when closing a connection down the normal way. Host A enters the FIN-Wait-1 state. The receiving host B enters the CLOSE WAIT state and starts the procedure of gracefully closing the connection. Each end of the connection sends a segment with the FIN = 1. The receiver is expected to acknowledge a received FIN segment by sending a FIN = 1 segment.
- B: "I acknowledge your FIN." B sends to A a segment with FIN = 0, ACK = 1, acknowledgment number = sequence number of A's FIN segment + 1. On receiving the ACK segment from B, host A enters the FIN-WAIT2 state.
- B: "No more data from me either." B sends to host A another segment but now with FIN = 1. B enters the Last-ACK state, and after two time-out periods, enters the CLOSED state.
- A: "I acknowledge your FIN too." On receiving the FIN segment from B, host A sends to B a segment with FIN = 0 and ACK = 1. Host A enters the TIMED-WAIT state, and after two time-out periods, enters the CLOSED state.

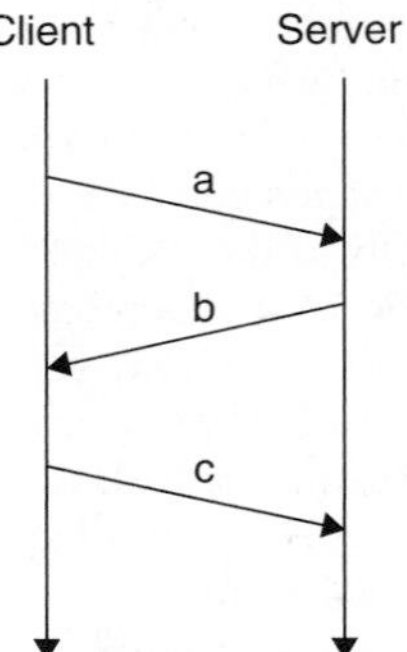

Figure 12: Three-way handshake steps in time

So, four segments are used to close a TCP connection in the normal situation. This is a teardown of two *half-closes*.

From the state diagram, it can be seen that the FIN and ACK packets from B can arrive in the reverse order to the preceding or even FIN+ACK together in one packet.

The preceding can be termed a graceful termination. There are two other ways that TCP connections terminate; see the section on "Connection Closing."

TCP data structures at both ends are deleted upon closing a connection.

Timers

TCP depends on many timers that the host must maintain per (attempted) connection as it follows the state diagram (refer to Figure 11).

Table 1: An Example Three-Way Handshake

Step	SYN	ACK	Source Port	Destination Port	Sequence number	Acknowledgement number
a	1	0	1037	80	102723769	0
b	1	1	80	1037	1527857206	102723770
c	0	1	1037	80	102723770	1527857207

1. The Connection Establishment Timer is started on receiving the first packet of the three-way handshake. A typical value of this timer is 75 seconds. If a time-out occurs, the connection is aborted.
2. A Retransmission Timer is started when a segment is sent. Its value, known as RTO (retransmission time-out), is dynamically computed (RFC 2988). If the timer expires before an ACK is received, the segment is resent, and the timer is restarted.
3. A Delayed-Acknowledgement Timer is set when data are received that do not need to be acknowledged immediately. If, after 200ms, the acknowledgement is still pending (i.e., it has been unable to piggy-back on an outgoing data segment), it is then sent.
4. The KEEP-ALIVE Timer lets us distinguish silences caused because there is no data to send from those caused by a broken connection. Setting a KEEP-ALIVE timer allows TCP to periodically probe the other end. The default value of this timer is 2 hours. After the expiration of the timer, probes are sent to the remote end. The connection is dropped if the remote does not respond.
5. A FIN-WAIT Timer is started when there is a transition from the FIN-WAIT-1 state to the FIN-WAIT-2 state. The initial value of this timer is 10 minutes. If a packet with FIN = 1 is received, the timer is canceled. On expiration of the 10 minutes, the timer is restarted with a value of 75 seconds. The connection is dropped if no FIN packet arrives within this period.
6. TIMED-WAIT Timer is started when the connection enters the TIMED-WAIT state. This is to allow all the segments in transit to be removed from the network. The value of the timer is usually set to 2 minutes. On expiration of the timer, the connection is terminated.
7. A Persistence Timer is used to detect if any window size updates were lost. The timer is set when the remote node advertises a window size of zero, thus preventing any data being sent. If the window has not been opened when the timer expires, 1 byte is sent in case the window update was lost.

Flow Control

Flow control prevents the sending process from overwhelming the receiving process. The size of the sliding window is dynamically adjusted because of flow or congestion issues. Each acknowledgment segment from B to A advertises *rwnd* (Window Size field of Figure 10), which is the number of bytes B has in its receiver buffer. If *rwnd* is larger than the current sliding window size, TCP at A can increase it by incrementing the right edge of the window, SWRE. If it is smaller, let Z = SWRE - *rwnd*, and there are two cases. If SWNX > Z, set SWRE to SWNX and pause; else, set SWRE to Z and keep sending.

Congestion Control

Congestion is a condition of significant delay caused by overload of datagrams at one or more routers. A congestion window size *cwnd* that limits the number of outstanding unacknowledged bytes that are allowed at any time is dynamically computed by the sender based on network congestion. The TCP sliding window size is the smaller of *rwnd* and *cwnd*. TCP improves throughput by avoiding congestion. When a segment loss is detected, TCP assumes that the loss is due to congestion. There are many variations on how *cwnd* should be adjusted.

TCP Slow-Start algorithm doubles *cwnd* until a slow-start threshold is reached. Then *cwnd* is increased by 1. When ACKs are not received, the slow-start threshold is set to half of *cwnd*, and the algorithm restarts.

TCP congestion control operates on two time scales. On round trip times (RTT) of the order of 10 to 100s of msec, TCP performs additive-increase, multiplicative-decrease (AIMD) control. At times of severe congestion, TCP operates on longer time scales of RTO. In an attempt to avoid congestion collapse, flows reduce their congestion window to one packet and wait for a period of RTO after which the packet is resent. Upon further loss, RTO doubles with each subsequent time-out. If a packet is successfully received, TCP reenters AIMD via slow start.

TCP congestion control has undergone major improvements in recent years resulting in many TCP variants that are soon to be adopted in actual implementations. For example, Linux 2.6 has TCP BIC and TCP CUBIC, and Windows Vista has TCP New Reno and Compound TCP.

Reliable Transmission

Recovery from data that is damaged, lost, duplicated, or delivered out of order is achieved using error control. Damage is handled by adding a checksum to each segment transmitted, checking it at the receiver, and discarding damaged segments. If the sender S does not receive an acknowledgment from the destination D within the RTO period, S retransmits the segment. The time-out period is continually adapted by TCP per connection by measuring the round-trip delay. At the receiver, the sequence numbers are used to correctly order segments that may be received out of order and to eliminate duplicates.

TCP Issues

This section briefly describes several TCP weaknesses. TCP has been in long and heavy use. Many of its implementations have made improvements that go beyond the prescriptions of its RFC. Nevertheless, there are several old issues with no clear solutions and new vulnerabilities are being discovered. For example, not all the control flags can be independently set or reset. The combinations of SYN FIN, SYN FIN PSH, SYN FIN RST, and SYN FIN RST PSH set to 1 are all illegal. Past implementations have accounted only for valid combinations, ignoring the invalid combinations as "will not happen." Covert channels can be set up using the TCP initial sequence numbers, and so on. The TCP time stamps option can allow malicious, off-path third parties to stall systems with persistent TCP connections. For example, CERT advisory VU#637934 (2005) notes that some TCP implementations may allow a remote attacker to arbitrarily modify host time stamp values, leading to a denial-of-service condition.

Sequence Number Prediction

TCP exploits are typically based on IP spoofing and sequence number prediction. In establishing a TCP connection, both the server and the client generate an initial sequence number (ISN) from which they will start counting the segments transmitted. Host Y accepts the segments from X only when correct SEQ/ACK numbers are used.

The ISN is (should be) generated at random and should be hard to predict. However, some implementations of the TCP/IP protocol make it rather easy to predict this sequence number. The attacker either sniffs the current SEQ+ACK of the connection or can algorithmically predict them.

Even when random numbers are used, there have been problems. CERT VU#498440 (2001) notes that using random increments to constantly increase TCP ISN values over time provides insufficient variance in the range of likely ISN values, allowing an attacker to exploit the statistical weakness to predict the ISN and disrupt or hijack existing TCP connections or spoof future connections. A related weakness in BGP is described in the section on "Route Spoofing."

Connection Closing

The four-way handshake described previously is not the only way to close a connection. Connections can be closed by sending a TCP segment with its RST flag set to 1, which indicates to the receiver that a reset should occur. The receiving host accepts the RST packet, provided the sequence number is correct, and enters the CLOSED state and frees any resource associated with this instance of the connection. The RST segment is not acknowledged. A host B sends a connection resetting the RST segment if host A requested a connection to a nonexistent port p on host B, or for whatever reason (idle for a long time, or an abnormal condition, etc.), the host B (client or the sever) want to close the connection. Resetting is unilateral. Any new incoming segments for that connection will be dropped.

The 2004 TCP reset attack led to severe concerns in the routing protocol BGP used in large routers. TCP (RFC 793) requires that sequence numbers are checked against the window size before accepting data or control flags as valid. It also specifies that RST control flags should be processed immediately, without waiting for out-sequence packets to arrive. Even though RFC 793 allows a TCP implementation to verify both sequence and acknowledgement numbers prior to accepting a RST control flag as valid, most TCP stack implementations check only that the sequence number is within the window. This allows connections to be reset with much less effort than previously believed. This risk is compounded by the easy prediction of source port selection used in TCP connections.

Connections can be closed by FIN also. The attacker constructs a spoofed FIN segment. It will have the correct SEQ numbers so that it is accepted by the targeted host. This host would believe the (spoofed) sender had no data left. Any segments that may follow from the legitimate sender would be ignored as bogus. The rest of the four-way handshake is also supplied by the attacker.

Connection Hijacking

Suppose X has initiated a TCP connection to Y. An attacker Z can take over this connection. Z can send segments to Y spoofing the source address as X, at a time when X was silent. Y would accept these data and update ACK numbers. X may subsequently continue to send its segments using old SEQ numbers, as it is unaware of the intervention of Z. As a result, subsequent segments from X are discarded by Y. The attacker Z is now effectively impersonating X, using "correct" SEQ/ACK numbers from the perspective of Y. As a result, Z has hijacked the connection: host X is confused, whereas Y thinks nothing is wrong as Z sends "correctly synchronized" segments to Y.

If the hijacked connection was running an interactive shell, Z can execute any arbitrary command that X could. Having accomplished his deed, a clever hijacker would bow out gracefully by monitoring the true X. He would cause the SEQ numbers of X to match the ACK numbers of Y by sending to X a segment that it generates of appropriate length, spoofing the sender as Y, using the ACK numbers that X would accept.

Floods and Storms

There have been several attacks that generate enormous numbers of packets rendering (portions of) a network ineffective. The attackers send source spoofed packets to intermediary machines. These amplify the numbers of packets into a "storm."

The SYN flood attack first occurred in 1996, and many systems in 2006 can be brought down. In the TCP protocol as designed, there is no limit set on the time to wait after receiving the SYN in the three-way handshake. An attacker initiates many connection requests with spoofed source addresses to the victim machine. The victim machine maintains data related to the connection being attempted in its memory. The SYN+ACK segments that the victim host sends are not replied to. Once the limit of such half-open connections is reached, the victim host will refuse further connection establishment attempts from any host until a partially opened connection in the queue is completed or times out. This effectively removes a host from the network for several seconds, making it useful at least as a stepping tool to other attacks, such as IP spoofing.

ACK storms are generated in the hijack technique described previously. A host Y, when it receives segments from X after a hijack has ended, will find the segments of X to be out of order. TCP requires that Y must send an immediate reply with an ACK number that it expects. The same behavior is expected of X. So, X and Y send each other ACK messages that may never end.

Legitimate applications or OS services can generate a storm of packets. On many systems, the standard services known as `chargen` that listens typically at port 19 and `echo` that listens typically at port 7 are enabled. `Chargen` sends an unending stream of characters intended to be used as test data for terminals. The `echo` service just echoes what it receives. It is intended to be used for testing reachability, identifying routing problems, and so on. An attacker sends a packet to the port 19 with the source address spoofed to a broadcast address and the source port spoofed to 7. The `chargen` stream is sent to the broadcast address and hence reaches many machines on port 7. Each of these machines will echo back to the victim's port 19. This ping-pong action generates a storm of packets.

Congestion Control Attacks

Simple attacks by misbehaving receivers that send spurious ACKs were described in 1999 that drive a standard TCP sender arbitrarily fast by defeating TCP congestion control without losing end-to-end reliability.

The so-called Shrew DoS Attacks (2003) are examples that exploit omissions of important details in the design of the congestion control algorithms. They attempt to deny band width to legitimate TCP flows while sending at sufficiently low average rate to elude detection. These low-rate TCP attacks send a periodic short burst of segments that exploits the homogeneity of the RTO and forces all affected TCP flows to back off and enter the retransmission time-out state. This attack is difficult to identify because attack patterns are many.

Attacks via ICMP

In 2005, several blind connection-reset, blind throughput-reduction, and blind performance-degrading attacks were reported. These were all based on malicious ICMP messages. Note that the RFC 792 of ICMP does not recommend any kind of validation checks on the received ICMP error messages. All these attacks can be performed even being off-path, and without the need to sniff the packets of the attacked TCP connection.

TCP/IP Traffic Scrubbing

Scrubbing refers to forcing the TCP/IP traffic to obey all the rules of the RFCs. Reserved fields can be set to a random value; illegal combinations of flags are checked, and so on. Scrubbing is expected to be done not only at the originating hosts but also on the routers and especially in firewalls. Scrubbing adds to the computational burden of the hosts. Unfortunately, scrubbing may disrupt interoperability because of hidden assumptions made by programs beyond the specifications of the RFCs.

ROUTING

When the source S and the destination D are on the same network, we have direct delivery of an IP datagram that does not involve routing. When the two hosts are not on the same network, there can be multiple paths, in general, between S and D. Because of failures, maintenance, and other reasons, the intermediate nodes, known as routers, may come on or off during the delivery of packets. Note that consecutive packets sent by S to D may have to travel entirely disjoint routes depending on how the network is connected at the moment.

Routing algorithms and protocols discover routes that the datagram can take from S to various routers ultimately arriving at D.

Routers

Routers are specialized computer systems whose primary function (often their sole function) is to route network traffic. The typical network host has only one NIC and hence is on only one network; sending and receiving of network traffic not intended for it is secondary to its main functionality. Routers have multiple NICs, each on a separate network. A router examines the destination IP address of a packet, consults its routing tables, and sends the packet on the network connected to the final destination or the next router.

Routers are network layer (OSI layer 3) devices. Note that a router may run several routing protocols simultaneously.

Routing Tables

Network hosts (including routers) have routing tables that record information regarding where to deliver a packet next so that definite progress is made in moving the packet closer to its final destination. It can be visualized as a table of just two columns: To send the packet to a destination given in column 1, send the packet to the *next hop* whose IP address is given in column 2. Such a table would have to list all possible destinations. Table 2 shows the actual routing table of a "simple" host that has three network cards named `eth0 ... eth2`.

Given the destination IP address `d` of a datagram, the routing module of the IP layer scans the rows of the table for a *match* where the Destination[r] value of that row r equals `d & Mask[r]`, the result of d bit-wise-ANDed with the mask in that row. The *next-hop* n is then Gateway[r]. If n is zero, the datagram is delivered direct; d and the source address are on the same network. If n is nonzero, the datagram is delivered to the IP address n. The last row has both mask and destination set to zero. This catch-all default row indicates the next hop IP address for any packet whose destination address does not match any other row. After the next-hop IP address is determined, the router uses the lower layer address (such as the Ethernet MAC) to deliver the packet to the next host.

The Flags (refer to Table 2) indicate whether the device of the row is Up or not, Gateway or not, and so on. The metric column shows a cost number for datagrams going

Table 2: Routing Table of a Simple Host with Three NICs

Mask	Destination	Gateway	Flags	Metric	Ref	Use	NIC
255.255.255.0	192.168.17.0	0.0.0.0	U	0	0	0	eth0
255.255.255.0	130.102.12.0	0.0.0.0	U	0	0	0	eth1
0.0.0.0	0.0.0.0	192.168.17.111	UG	0	0	0	eth2

through that row. The metric can quantify delay, throughput, and so on.

Routing Protocols

The routing tables of real routers are considerably more complex than the preceding. For example, they are structured to permit the use of longest CIDR prefix match, which can (i) override routes to large networks with more specific host or network routes, and (ii) aggregate routes to individual destinations into larger network addresses.

The routing table of an ordinary host is tiny and rarely changes from boot-up to shut down. The tables of routers on the Internet, however, are large (tens of thousands of rows) and must be dynamically adjustable to changing Internet conditions, perhaps by the millisecond. Routing protocols keep the routing tables up-to-date. The structure and content of the routing tables depend on the protocol.

Interior gateway protocols (IGP) maintain the routing tables within an *autonomous* system, that is, a network within the control of a corporation, university, or an ISP. Exterior gateway protocols (EGP) maintain the routing information among autonomous networks.

Globally consistent routing information is achieved by routing *arbiter* database of reachability information that is replicated by route servers at network access points where autonomous systems connect.

Interior Gateway Protocols: RIP and OSPF

Routing information protocol (RIP) and open shortest path first (OSPF) are examples of IGPs.

RIP (RFC 2453, 1998) is based on the *distance vector* routing method, which represents the internetwork as a graph G of nodes and edges, and computes shortest paths from the source node to other nodes. Hop count is the number of edges on a path to a destination. A path between two nodes S and D may be defined as the shortest among many paths from S to D based on hop count, minimum delay, and so on. RIP maintains the routing table with rows for each destination network it has encountered along with the hop count, and so on. obtained from G. RIP periodically propagates, as unsolicited responses, the contents of its table to neighboring routers. RIP-based routers receive these responses and update their own tables.

RIP messages are UDP transported.

RIP is easy to implement but does not scale well with the number of nodes. Route changes may result in tables not stabilizing, even forming routing loops, and some routers may have incorrect rows at any given time. Also, the number of RIP messages is proportional to the number of networks.

OSPF (RFC 2328, 1998) is based on *link states*. Two routers are said to be *linked* if they can communicate directly. The link is *up* if both are alive and reachable; otherwise, the link is *down*. An OSPF-based router periodically broadcasts the status of all its links. Link status messages propagate unchanged. OSPF-based routers listen to these messages, and recompute shortest paths whenever there is a link status change. OSPF messages are encapsulated in IP.

Each OSPF-router computes the status of links independently of other routers. Routing table updates will converge. The number of messages depends only on the number of links of a router, not on the number of networks. Thus, OSPF scales better than RIP.

Exterior Gateway Protocol: BGP

BGP4 (RFC 4271, 2006) is the most widely deployed of the exterior gateway protocols (Stewart 1999). Each autonomous system (AS) designates one router, typically at the border, on its behalf. BGP maintains routing information among these routers. BGP runs in two modes: Exterior BGP is run between different AS, and Interior BGP is run between BGP routers in the same AS. BGP messages are TCP transported.

BGP uses ideas from both distance vector and link status methods and extends them into path vectors described later. BGP routers collect routing information from other BGP routers, and from within their own autonomous systems through RIP and/or OSPF, and pass the combined information to their BGP router peers.

BGP has four message types. An OPEN message establishes a connection to a BGP peer, which also authenticates the sender. UPDATE messages communicate reachability information. KEEP-ALIVE messages actively test peer connectivity. NOTIFICATION messages both control and report on errors.

A BGP UPDATE message contains withdrawals of destinations that are now unreachable and *path attributes* to newly reachable destinations. The path attributes can specify seven types of information: (i) the origin of this information, (ii) list of autonomous systems that the path goes through, (iii) the next hop, (iv) multi-exit discriminator (MED) which suggests a preferred route into the AS that is advertising, (v) a local preference number that indicates preference for an exit point from the local AS that has many exits, (vi) ATOMIC_AGGREGATE, and (vii) AGGREGATOR. Full information is sent only once to a newly acquired peer, and later update messages carry only the incremental changes.

A BGP router R conceptually has three routing information tables/bases (RIB). All information received in UPDATE messages is entered into the RIB-IN table. RIB-LOCAL holds the routes that R has selected for use by R's own AS. R analyzes the data of RIB-IN in the context of policies set by its administrator and may or may not update RIB-LOCAL. Among the multiple advertisements that it receives for the same route, BGP selects one path as the best route and inserts it into RIB-LOCAL. Contents of RIB-OUT are extracted from RIB-LOCAL to be disseminated to peers.

The best route is chosen based on path attributes; delay, bandwidth, or latency does not matter. A typical selection is as follows. If the path specifies a next hop that is inaccessible, drop the update. Select the path with the largest local preference. If the local preferences are the same, prefer the path that was originated by BGP running on this router. If no route was originated, prefer the route that has the shortest AS path. If all paths have the same AS path length, prefer the path with the lowest origin type (where IGP < BGP < "incomplete"). If the origin codes are the same, prefer the path with the lowest MED.

If the paths have the same MED, prefer the external path over the internal path. If the paths are still the same, prefer the path through the closest IGP neighbor. As a final tie breaker, select the path with the lowest IP address, as specified by the BGP router ID.

IGPs may converge faster, but an IGP does not scale up. Also, through the path attributes, BGP has inherent support for routing policies.

Route Spoofing

Several routing spoofs have become known.

An attacker can send a specially crafted ICMP redirect packet with the source address set to the regular router. The packet also contains the "new" router to use. An ICMP route redirect is normally sent by the default router to indicate that there is a shorter route to a specific destination. A host adds a host-route entry to its routing table after some checking, all of which is ineffective. Unlike ARP cache entries, host route entries do not expire. Name servers are obvious targets for this attack.

RIP-based attacks work by broadcasting illegitimate routing information to passive RIP hosts and routers. In both of these cases, the redirection can be made to any host chosen by the attacker.

Source routing allows the sending host to choose a route that a packet must travel to get to its destination. Traffic coming back to that host will take the reverse route. The attacker designs a route so that the packets go through his site.

A compromised BGP router can modify, drop, or introduce fake updates. Also, there are several assumptions underlying the UPDATE messages, such as (i) each AS along the path is authorized by the preceding AS to advertise the prefixes, (ii) the first AS in the path is authorized to advertise the prefixes by the holder of the prefixes, and (iii) a route is withdrawn only by the neighbor AS that advertised it. When these assumptions are invalid, BGP is vulnerable to many forms of attack.

BGP relies on TCP to maintain persistent sessions (Butler et al. 2005). The ISN-related vulnerability in TCP allows remote attackers to terminate these sessions. CERT advisory VU#415294 (2004) notes that sustained exploitation of this vulnerability could lead to a denial-of-service condition affecting a large segment of the Internet.

INFRASTRUCTURE PROTOCOLS

In this section, we describe DNS, ARP, RARP, DHCP, and SNMP that can be considered "infrastructure" protocols. The primary purpose of these protocols is to support other protocols.

Domain Name Service (DNS)

Because of the mnemonic value, humans prefer to work with host names such as `gamma.cs.wright.edu`, rather than its IP address 130.108.2.22, where `gamma` is the name of the host, and `cs.wright.edu` is the name of the domain the host is in. The primary function of DNS is to map such a name into its IP address.

The DNS name space is a tree hierarchy (RFC 1035) as shown in Figure 13. The top most subtrees are the top-level domains such as `.com`, `.edu`, `.net`, and `.org`, and the country code domains such as `.us` and `.in`. Subtrees of these are known as sub domains. The leaves are the individual hosts. A *fully qualified domain name* is the sequence of labels, separated by a dot, on the path from a node to the root of the tree.

The top-level domains (2006) are `ac, ad, ae, aero, af, ag, ai, al, am, an, ao, aq, ar, arpa, as, at, au, aw, az, ba, bb, bd, be, bf, bg, bh, bi, biz, bj, bm, bn, bo, br, bs, bt, bv, bw, by, bz, ca, cat, cc, cd, cf, cg ch, ci, ck, cl, cm, cn, co, com, coop, cr, cu, cv, cx, cy, cz, de, dj, dk, dm, do, dz, ec edu, ee, eg, er, es, et, eu, fi, fj, fk, fm, fo, fr, ga, gb, gd, ge, gf, gg, gh, gi, gl, gm gn, gov, gp, gq, gr, gs, gt, gu, gw, gy, hk, hm, hn, hr, ht, hu, id, ie, il, im, in, info int, io, iq, ir, is, it, je, jm, jo, jobs, jp, ke, kg, kh, ki, km, kn, kr, kw, ky, kz, la lb, lc, li,`

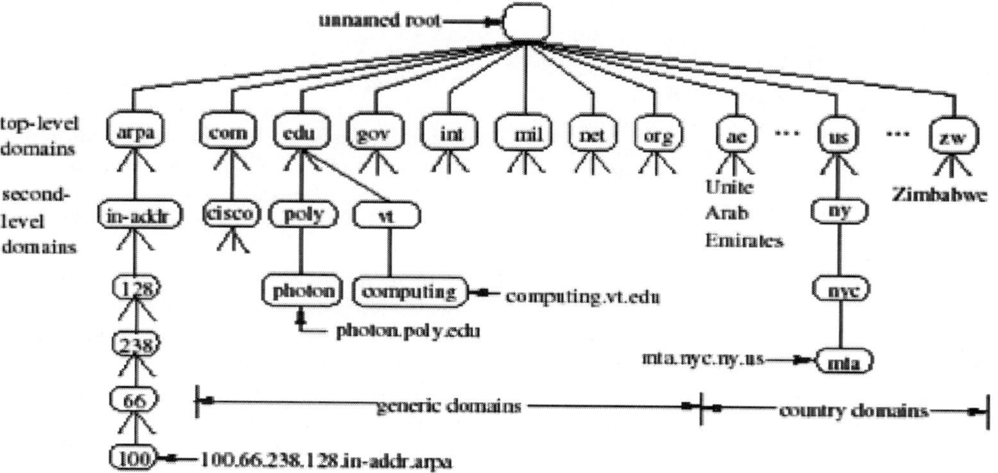

Figure 13: Domain name hierarchy

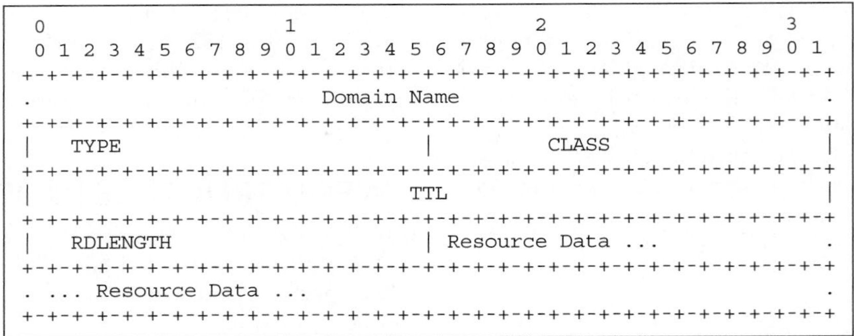

Figure14: Resource record

lk, lr, ls, lt, lu, lv, ly, ma, mc, md, mg, mh, mil, mk, ml, mm, mn, mo, mobi mp, mq, mr, ms, mt, mu, museum, mv, mw, mx, my, mz, na, name, nc, ne, net, nf, ng, ni, nl no, np, nr, nu, nz, om, org, pa, pe, pf, pg, ph, pk, pl, pm, pn, pr, pro, ps, pt, pw, py, qa re, ro, ru, rw, sa, sb, sc, sd, se, sg, sh, si, sj, sk, sl, sm, sn, so, sr, st, su, sv, sy, sz, tc, td, tf, tg, th, tj, tk, tl, tm, tn, to, tp, tr, travel, tt, tv, tw, tz, ua, ug, uk, um, us, uy, uz, va, vc, ve, vg, vi, vn, vu, wf, ws, ye, yt, yu, za, zm, and zw.

Of these, the two-letter names are country domains. The top-level domain arpa is an *inverse domain* used to map an IP address to its name.

The mapping of names to addresses is not one-to-one. It is possible to associate a name with multiple IP addresses, thus providing load distribution. A single IP address can be associated with multiple names, one being a *canonical* name and others perhaps more mnemonic, and thus providing host aliasing.

DNS Servers

The domain name space is maintained as a database distributed over several *domain name servers*. A server can delegate the maintenance of any subdomain to another server. A delegated subdomain in the DNS is called a *zone*. The parent server keeps track of such delegations. Each name server has authoritative information about one or more zones. It may also have cached, but non authoritative, data about other parts of the database. A name server marks its responses to queries as authoritative or not.

A server whose zone is the entire tree is known as a *root server*. There are 13 root servers (in 2006; visit www.root-servers.org) located in the United States and other countries.

Resource Records

The database is a collection of *resource records* (Figure 14), each of which contains a domain name and four attributes. (i) The *record type* identifies what is stored in the data value. (ii) The *class* attribute of the record is "IN" for Internet. (iii) The time-to-live (TTL) value indicates how long a nonauthoritative name server can cache the record.

Some record types are A, AAAA, MX, and PTR. The data of an A record type is an IP address, of an AAAA record is an IPv6 address, of an MX record is the canonical host name of the mail server and its IP address, and of a PTR record is a pointer used to map an IP address to a domain name.

Name Resolution

The DNS *resolver* is a piece of software. Every host is configured with at least one local name server N if it is to find hosts not listed in the etc/hosts file. Each host maintains a short cache table that maps fully qualified domain names to IP addresses. When a name is not found in either this file or this cache, the host enquires with N via the DNS protocol using the resolver. TCP is used for zone transfers, UDP is used for look-ups, connecting to server port 53. The protocol is stateless—all the information needed is contained in a single message.

The primary function of DNS is to answer a query to translate a fully qualified domain name into its IP address. This is done by retrieving the A record. A reverse look-up (also called an inverse query) is to find the host name given the IP address. This is done by retrieving the PTR record. Some network services use this to verify the identity of the client host.

An *iterative* DNS query to a name server D receives a reply with either the answer or the IP address of the next name server. If the name is in the local zone, the local name server N can respond to a query directly. Otherwise, N queries one of the root servers. The root server gives a *referral* with a list of name servers for the top-level domain of the query. N now queries a name server on this list and receives a list of name servers for the second-level domain name. The process repeats until N receives the address for the domain name. N then caches the record and returns the address or other DNS data to the querying host.

A *recursive* DNS query to D will make D obtain the requested mapping on behalf of the querying host. If D does not have the answer, it forwards the query to the next name server in the chain, and so on until either an answer is found or all servers are queried and hence returns an error code. Because recursive look-ups take longer and need to store many records, it is more efficient to provide a recursive DNS server for LAN users and an iterative server for Internet users.

Security of DNS

The DNS answers that a host receives may have come from an attacker who sniffs a query and answers it with misleading data faster than the legitimate name server answers. The attacked host may in fact be a DNS server. Such DNS spoofing results in DNS cache poisoning, and all the clients of this server will receive false answers.

DNS zone transfers help map the targeted network during the reconnaissance stage of an attack.

The DNS protocol is improved in the DNSSEC (DNS security extensions), which is expected to be deployed widely. DNSSEC provides (i) origin authentication of DNS data, (ii) data integrity, and (iii) authenticated denial of existence. The answers in DNSSEC are digitally signed. Note that DNSSEC does not provide confidentiality of data.

The BIND (bounding-interval-length–dependent) package is a widely deployed implementation of DNS. Unfortunately, this otherwise highly capable software, in many releases over the years, has had much vulnerability of its own that allowed remote attackers to launch denial-of-service attacks, hijack domain names, or use vulnerable DNS servers to gain access to other systems.

Address Resolution Protocol (ARP)

ARP (RFC 826, 1982) is typically used to determine the Ethernet MAC address of a device whose IP address is known. This needs to be done only for outgoing IP packets because IP datagrams must be Ethernet framed with the destination hardware address. The translation is performed with a table look-up.

Reverse ARP (RARP) (RFC 903) allows a host to discover its own IP address by broadcasting the Ethernet address and expecting a server to reply with the IP address.

ARP is a network layer (OSI layer 3) protocol, but it does not use an IP header. It has its own packet format as shown in Figure 15. The ARP request packet has 0s in the target hardware address fields. It is broadcast on the local LAN without needing to be routed. The destination host sends back an ARP reply with its hardware address

Table 3: A Small Portion of an ARP Cache

IP address	Ethernet address
130.108.2.23	08-00-69-05-28-99
130.108.2.1	00-10-2f-fe-c4-00
130.108.2.27	08-00-69-0d-99-12
130.108.2.20	08-00-69-11-cf-b9
130.108.2.10	00-60-cf-21-2c-4b
192.168.17.221	00-50-ba-5f-85-56
192.168.17.112	00-A0-C5-E5-7C-6E

so that the IP datagram can now be forwarded to it by the router. An ARP response packet has the sender/target field contents swapped as compared to the request.

ARP Cache

An OS maintains a table called the ARP cache (see Table 3). The cache accumulates as the host continues to network. If the ARP cache does not have an entry for an IP address, the outgoing IP packet is queued, and an ARP request packet that effectively requests "If your IP address matches this target IP address, then please let me know your Ethernet address" is broadcast. After the table is updated because of receiving a response, all the queued IP packets can be sent.

The entries in the table expire after a set time period in order to account for possible hardware address changes for the same IP address. This change may have happened, for example, because of the NIC being replaced.

ARP Poisoning

ARP poisoning is an attack technique that corrupts the ARP cache with wrong Ethernet addresses for some IP addresses. An attacker accomplishes this by sending an

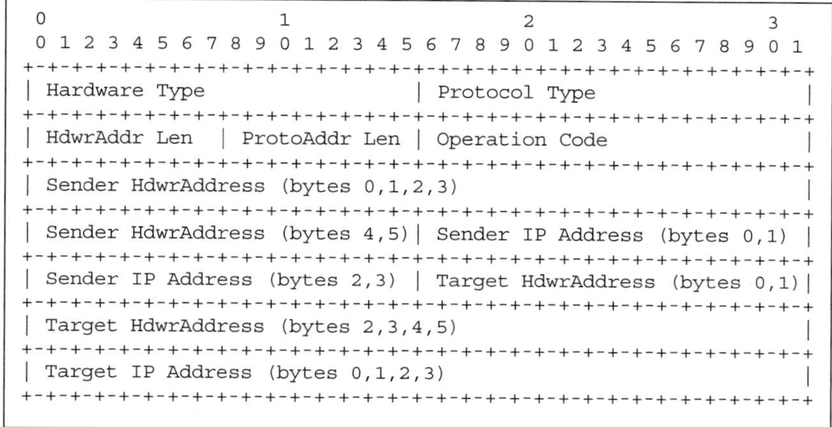
```
 0                   1                   2                   3
 0 1 2 3 4 5 6 7 8 9 0 1 2 3 4 5 6 7 8 9 0 1 2 3 4 5 6 7 8 9 0 1
+-+-+-+-+-+-+-+-+-+-+-+-+-+-+-+-+-+-+-+-+-+-+-+-+-+-+-+-+-+-+-+-+
| Hardware Type                 | Protocol Type                 |
+-+-+-+-+-+-+-+-+-+-+-+-+-+-+-+-+-+-+-+-+-+-+-+-+-+-+-+-+-+-+-+-+
| HdwrAddr Len  | ProtoAddr Len | Operation Code                |
+-+-+-+-+-+-+-+-+-+-+-+-+-+-+-+-+-+-+-+-+-+-+-+-+-+-+-+-+-+-+-+-+
| Sender HdwrAddress (bytes 0,1,2,3)                            |
+-+-+-+-+-+-+-+-+-+-+-+-+-+-+-+-+-+-+-+-+-+-+-+-+-+-+-+-+-+-+-+-+
| Sender HdwrAddress (bytes 4,5)| Sender IP Address (bytes 0,1) |
+-+-+-+-+-+-+-+-+-+-+-+-+-+-+-+-+-+-+-+-+-+-+-+-+-+-+-+-+-+-+-+-+
| Sender IP Address (bytes 2,3) | Target HdwrAddress (bytes 0,1)|
+-+-+-+-+-+-+-+-+-+-+-+-+-+-+-+-+-+-+-+-+-+-+-+-+-+-+-+-+-+-+-+-+
| Target HdwrAddress (bytes 2,3,4,5)                            |
+-+-+-+-+-+-+-+-+-+-+-+-+-+-+-+-+-+-+-+-+-+-+-+-+-+-+-+-+-+-+-+-+
| Target IP Address (bytes 0,1,2,3)                             |
+-+-+-+-+-+-+-+-+-+-+-+-+-+-+-+-+-+-+-+-+-+-+-+-+-+-+-+-+-+-+-+-+
```

Figure 15: An ARP request/response packet

ARP response packet that is deliberately constructed with a "wrong" MAC address. The ARP is a stateless protocol. Thus, a machine receiving an ARP response cannot determine if the response is because of a request it sent or not.

ARP poisoning enables the so-called man-in-the-middle attack that can defeat cryptographic communications such as SSH, SSL, and IPSec. An attacker on machine M inserts himself between two hosts A and B by (1) poisoning A so that B's IP address is associated with M's MAC address, (2) poisoning B so that A's address is associated with M's MAC address, and (3) relaying the packets M receives A from/to B.

ARP packets are not routed, and this makes it very rewarding to the attacker if a router can be ARP poisoned.

Dynamic Host Configuration Protocol (DHCP)

A typical host will invoke a DHCP (RFC 2131, 1997) client program soon after booting into the OS to configure its network. A DHCP server delivers host-specific configuration parameters, such as an IP address, a subnet mask, a list of default routers, TTL, and MTU. An OS utility then associates the IP address with a host name.

DHCP assumes that the IP layer software will pass the packets delivered to the NIC of the host even though it has not been assigned an IP address yet. A DHCP client broadcasts (i.e., the IP destination address is 255.255.255.255) a request in a UDP packet containing its own MAC address. A DHCP server process listens to such requests, and IP-broadcasts or hardware-unicasts a reply that contains the configuration parameters.

DHCP has three mechanisms for IP address allocation. In automatic allocation, DHCP assigns a permanent IP address to a client. In dynamic allocation, DHCP leases an IP address to a client for a limited period (or until the client explicitly relinquishes the address). In manual allocation, the IP address is assigned manually but is conveyed to the client via DHCP. Dynamic allocation is the only one of the three mechanisms that allows automatic reuse by a different host of an address that is no longer needed by the client to which it was assigned.

Simple Network Management Protocol (SNMP)

SNMP (RFC 3411) allows network managers to see how the network is functioning and control it. A management agent (MA) runs as a server process on each managed device. A network administrator invokes a management client (MC) program on his console. The MC can send queries as IP datagrams to the MA obtaining status information, or commands to alter the conditions in the managed device. Network devices that are simple enough to not run an agent are known as unmanaged devices.

All SNMP operations can be cast as a sequence of one or more of (i) retrieve the current value of a management information base (MIB) variable, or (ii) store a value for a variable. For example, an immediate reboot of a managed device can be caused by storing a 0 in the MIB variable that gives the time until the next reboot.

Transport Layer Security (SSL/TLS)

Transport layer security (RFC 4346, (2006) provides privacy and data integrity. Privacy refers to a third party being unable to get unencrypted versions of messages between two parties. Integrity refers to the receiver being able to rely that the messages have not been tampered with in transit. TLS was referred to as secure socket layer (SSL) before becoming a standard.

TLS is implemented as a layer above the TCP. Higher-level protocols can layer on top of the TLS transparently. Programs that used TCP can be readily rewritten to use TLS instead. HTTPS and modern implementations of such protocols as FTP, telnet, POP3S, and SMTP are based on TLS. The TLS standard, however, does not specify how other protocols add security with TLS; the decisions on how to initiate TLS handshaking and how to interpret the authentication certificates exchanged are left up to the judgment of the designers and implementers of protocols that run on top of TLS. For example, it is possible to switch to a new TLS connection on different ports, or initiate TLS service on the same connection by issuing a special command token such as STARTTLS done by Enhanced SMTP.

TLS is composed of Record and Handshake protocols. The Record protocol provides connections that are private by encrypting data using symmetric cryptography (Stallings 2005). The encryption keys are generated for each connection based on a secret negotiated by the TLS Handshake protocol. The connection is tamper-proof. Messages are integrity checked using a keyed message authentication code based on secure hash functions such as SHA and MD5.

The TLS Handshake protocol provides (i) authentication of the peer's identity using public key cryptography, such as RSA, and DSS; (ii) secure negotiation of a shared secret even if an attacker is present in the middle of the connection; and (iii) reliable negotiation messages that no attacker can modify without being detected by the parties to the communication.

Authentication Protocols

Authentication is the process of verifying the credentials of a user, a host (node), or a service. Authentication protocols enable such procedures by sending or receiving messages in encrypted form. Authentication without encryption is like having a paper-thin door to a house. Some well-known authentication protocols are Kerberos, RADIUS, PAP, and CHAP.

PAP and CHAP

PPP uses PAP or CHAP for authentication. PAP (password authentication protocol; RFC 1334) is a two-way handshake protocol. It sends the user name and password in plain text, obviously vulnerable to sniffing. CHAP (challenge handshake authentication protocol; RFC 1944) is a three-way handshake protocol. The CHAP server sends the user client a challenge, which is a randomly generated sequence of bytes unique to this authentication session. The client encrypts the challenge using a previously issued secret key that is shared by both the client and CHAP server. The result, called a response, is then returned to the CHAP server. The CHAP server performs the same operation on the challenge it sent with the shared secret key and compares its results, the expected response, with the response received from the client. If they are the same, the client is assumed authentic.

Radius

Remote authentication dial-in user service (RADIUS; RFC 2865) is a widely used protocol that provides authentication, authorization, and accounting services for managing access to resources, in particular wireless or dialup Internet access. The protocol itself is quite simple and has been implemented many times. A RADIUS client running on a network access server machine collects the user name and password and sends them as an access request to a server. The RADIUS server has a database of user names associated with their passwords through which it validates the user. The client and the RADIUS server have a shared secret that is used to encrypt portions of their messages.

APPLICATIONS

There are numerous applications are based on TCP/IP. In this section, we describe briefly several protocols and applications that belong in the applications (OSI 7) layer. Several chapters in this book are devoted to applications, for example, "Streaming Multimedia," "Virtual Private Networks," "Computer and Network Authentication," "Password Authentication," "Computer Network Management," and "E-mail and Instant Messaging."

Nearly all network applications are based on a client/server architecture where one process, the client, requests services from a second process, the server. Typically, the client and server processes are on different machines, but they need not be.

Virtual Private Networks (VPN)

Virtual private networks (VPN) enable secure communication through public networks using cryptographic channels. Point-to-point tunneling protocol (PPTP) is used in providing VPNs. After the initial PPP connection to a PPTP server, a PPTP tunnel (see Glossary), and a PPTP control connection are created. PPTP uses an enhanced generic routing encapsulation (GRE) mechanism to provide a flow- and congestion-controlled encapsulated datagram service for carrying PPP packets. See Chapter 181 for details on VPNs.

Network File System

NFS protocol (RFC 3530, 2003) makes the file volumes located on a file server available, using UDP or TCP, to client machines.

File volume mounting, file open, read, write, and close operations are standard system calls in OSs. The mount operation can detect an attempt at mounting a remote directory via NFS. Such a remote mount operation sends client machine information and the path name of a remote directory being requested to the NFS server process. The server returns a mount handle, assuming the file volume export permissions are positive for this client. File open, read, write, and close operations on the client machine specify path names relative to the mount point as if they are local.

File Transfer Protocol (FTP)

The primary function of FTP (RFC 959, 1985) is to place a copy of a local file on a remote machine (called PUT, popularly known as uploading) or bring a copy of a remote file (called GET, popularly known as downloading). Additionally, there are a few directory maintenance commands.

FTP uses two TCP connections, one called the *control* connection and the other the *data* connection. The FTP client opens a control connection to port 21 of the FTP server machine. On the control connection, the client can issue commands that change various settings of the FTP session. The GET command requests for the transfer of files that the server has, and the PUT command requests the server to receive and store the files that the client is about to send. All content transfer occurs on the data connection. This connection persists the entire session.

The data connection can be opened in one of two modes. In the active mode FTP, the server initiates a data connection as needed from its port 20 to a port whose number is supplied by the client on the control connection via the PORT command.

In the passive mode FTP, the server informs the client a port number higher than 1024 that the server has chosen, to which the client initiates a data connection. Passive FTP is useful in firewall setups that forbid initiation of a connection from an external host (the FTP server) to the internal network (the FTP client).

FTP is an insecure protocol. The messages between the client and the server over both the connections are in the clear text. In particular, the user name, password, and all file data are transmitted in the unencrypted form. This comment does not apply to SSL-based FTP.

Telnet

Telnet belongs to a class of programs called remote shells that provide a virtual terminal to a command line shell running on a remote machine.

Telnet (RFC 854, 1983) establishes a TCP connection with a telnet server on the reserved port 23 and passes the keystrokes of the telnet client to the server and accepts the output of the server as characters to be displayed on the client. The server presents these keystrokes as input received from a pseudo terminal to the OS hosting the telnet server.

Telnet defines a network virtual terminal (NVT) format as that which permits interoperability with machines that use different characters for common operations such as terminating a line and interrupting a run-away process. The telnet client typically maps the signal-generating keys of the keyboard to invoke the corresponding control functions of the NVT. The control functions are encoded as escape sequences of 2 bytes, the IAC (255), followed by the 1-byte code of the control function. Telnet uses the URGENT DATA mechanism of TCP to send control functions so that the telnet server can respond appropriately.

Telnet is an insecure protocol. User name, password, and all data in both directions are transmitted in the unencrypted form. This comment does not apply to SSL-based telnet.

rlogin

The rlogin protocol (RFC 1282) operates by opening a TCP connection on the rlogin server machine at port 513. It is widely used between UNIX hosts because it provides transport of more of the UNIX terminal environment semantics than does the telnet protocol and because on many UNIX hosts it can be configured not to require user entry of passwords when connections originate from trusted hosts.

Rlogin is an insecure protocol. User name, password, and all data in both directions are transmitted in the unencrypted form.

Secure Shell

SSH (RFC 4251, 2006) provides the functionality of FTP, telnet, and rlogin but with greater security. There was a version called SSH-1; the version as defined in RFC 4251 is called SSH-2.

FTP, telnet, and rlogin send authentication information and data in the clear (i.e., unencrypted) and hence are easily compromised by network sniffers. In addition, their authentication of the host is simply the IP address. Consequently, utilities based on these protocols should not be used in situations where security is a concern.

There are three primary advantages in using SSH. (i) Telnet and rlogin do not authenticate the remote machine; SSH does. (ii)The password that the user types as part of the login ritual is sent as clear text by telnet and rlogin; SSH sends it encrypted. (iii) The data being sent and received by telnet and rlogin is also sent as clear text; SSH sends and receives it in encrypted form.

The main disadvantages are the following. (i) Encryption and decryption consumes computing and elapsed time. (ii) If the remote system has been legitimately reinstalled, and the installer was not careful to use the same authentication keys for the host, a false alarm may be raised. (iii) SSH is susceptible to man-in-the-middle attack.

SSH Architecture

SSH-2 protocol is dependent on SSH authentication protocol (RFC 4252), SSH transport layer protocol (RFC 4253), and SSH connection protocol (RFC 4254).

The transport protocol (SSH-TRANS) handles the cryptographic initial key exchange and authenticates the server, and sets up encryption and compression. The transport layer also arranges for key re-exchange during a long session. The functionality of the transport layer is comparable to TLS.

The authentication protocol (SSH-USERAUTH) authenticates the user to the SSH server process. It provides for a number of authentication methods and runs over SSH-TRANS.

The connection protocol (SSH-CONNECT) provides interactive login sessions, remote execution of commands, forwarded TCP/IP connections, and forwarded X11 connections. SSH-CONNECT defines the concept of channels. A channel transfers data in both directions. A single SSH connection can simultaneously host multiple channels multiplexed into a single encrypted tunnel. Some channel types are (i) shell for terminal shells, `sftp`, `scp`, and execution of other commands; (ii) direct-tcpip for client-to-server forwarded connections; and (iii) tcpip-forward for server-to-client forwarded connections. SSH-CONNECT runs over SSH-TRANS and SSH-USERAUTH.

Host Authentication. During the first few steps of installing an OS on a machine, an authentication key pair for the host is generated using cryptographic algorithms. The pair consists of two rather large numbers that are coupled in the sense that any message encoded by one can be decoded by the other. Care should be taken to reuse this key pair whenever an OS is re-installed. The public key of the host is widely published. The private key is safe guarded.

The SSH client program verifies that it is talking to the real server by sending a message after encrypting using the public key of the SSH server machine. The server would decrypt using the private key it should have to obtain the original message.

The public key of the SSH server machine is obtained in one of two ways. (i) The client maintains a database of SSH server names and their public authentication keys that the server offers the first time an SSH session is opened to the server. Subsequent SSH sessions compare the authentication key offered by the server with that stored in the client database. (ii) The host name-to-key association is certified by a trusted certification authority (CA).

User Authentication. User authentication is client-driven. Several authentication methods are in wide use. (i) Password where the user types a password that is sent to the server through an encrypted channel. (ii) Public key, supporting at least DSA or RSA key pairs. (iii) Keyboard-interactive method (RFC 4256) where the server sends one or more prompts to enter information and the client displays them and sends back responses keyed in by the user. This is used in one-time password authentication, such as S/Key or SecurID.

Tunnels. The SSH-CONNECT protocol provides encrypted channels that can be used for setting up forwarding (tunneling) arbitrary TCP/IP ports and X11 connections. Suppose we have an SSH session for user U going between the client at host C and the server at host S. SSH can establish a tunnel to a host H connecting a TCP port i at C with a port j at H; that is, traffic sent to C:i will be delivered to H:j and vice versa. All traffic on this tunnel is encrypted.

Mail Protocols

Electronic mail existed "before Internet" but has become as common as the telephone due to it. E-mail now encompasses SMTP, POP, IMAP, and MIME. E-mail client programs such as Microsoft Outlook or Mozilla Thunderbird are made up of two components: a user agent (UA) and a mail transfer agent (MTA). A UA program accepts, from a user, mail memos to be sent. The mail is delivered to a server by an MTA program using SMTP. Mail is received using the protocols POP or IMAP.

Mail Message Format

An e-mail consists of a message body, headers, and an envelope that includes the FROM and TO headers. An optional header line is REPLY-TO. The message body consists of text and attachments. The mail headers adhere to the standard format of Internet messages (RFC 2822). The headers are plain text lines, each line made up of a keyword, a colon, and a value. Certain keywords must appear among the headers. For example, a TO address header is required. This specifies the e-mail address of the recipient in the form of `mbx@dnm`, where `mbx` is the name of a mail box on the local machine, and `dnm` is the domain name of the destination.

SMTP

Simple mail transfer protocol (RFC 2821, 2001) defines the commands and replies among mail transfer agent (MTA) clients and servers. An MTA client transfers the mail spooled on the local machine across the Internet to an MTA server. The transfer can occur in a single connection between the original mail-sender and the final mail-recipient, or may go through intermediary systems known as MTA relays.

SMTP is specified to require only a reliable ordered data stream channel. Modern e-mail clients use SSL/TLS as the transport.

POP

Post office protocol (POP) is used to send/receive e-mail from a server. POP2 requires SMTP to send messages. POP3 can be used with or without SMTP. POP downloads entire message bodies and can optionally keep the messages on the server. A user reading e-mail from multiple machines may not have a consistent view of his messages.

IMAP

Internet message access protocol (IMAP) is a protocol for accessing e-mail while it is sill located on the server. IMAP4 supports encrypted login mechanisms and SSL for the transport.

MIME

Multipurpose Internet mail extensions (MIME) defines the format of messages to allow for (i) textual message bodies in character sets other than US-ASCII, (ii) an extensible set of different formats for non-textual message bodies, (iii) multi-part message bodies, and (iv) textual header information in character sets other than US-ASCII.

Hypertext Transfer Protocol (HTTP)

HTTP (RFC 2616, 1999) is at the core of the World Wide Web. The Web browser on a user's machine and the Web server on a machine somewhere on the Internet communicate via HTTP using TCP usually at port 80. HTTPS (RFC 2660, 1999) is a secure version of HTTP. A Web browser displays a file of marked-up text with embedded commands following the syntactic requirements of the HTML. There are several ways of invoking these commands, the most common one being the mouse click. Most of the clickable commands displayed by a Web browser are the so-called links that associate a URL with a (visible piece of) text or graphic. URLs have the following syntax:

```
scheme://[userName[:password@]]serverMachineName[:port]/[path][/resource][?parm1=parma&parm2= parmb]
```

A simple example of the above is `www.cs.wright.edu/~pmateti/InternetSecurity` where the scheme chosen is `http`, and the port defaults to 80. A click on such a link generates a request message from the browser to the Web server process running on the remote machine www.cs.wright.edu, whose name is obtained from the link clicked. The Web server maps the path `~pmateti/InternetSecurity` to a local file according to the rules of the Web server. This may be a preexisting file or generated on the fly. The server transmits a copy of this local file. The browser then displays the page it receives from the server.

HTTP Message Format

The request and response are created according to the HTTP message format, which happens to be a sequence of human-readable lines of text. The first line identifies the message as a request or response. The subsequent lines are known as header lines until an empty line is reached. Following the empty line are lines that constitute the "entity body." Each header line can be divided into two parts, a left- and right-hand side, separated by a colon. The left-hand side names various parameters. The right-hand side provides their values.

The request line has three components: a method (one of GET, POST, or HEAD), a URL, and the version number of HTTP (either 1.0 or 1.1) that the client understands. The GET method requests the content of a Web page. The POST method is used when the client sends data obtained from a user-filled HTML form. The HEAD method is used in program development.

The response line also contains three components: HTTP/version-number, a status code (such as the infamous 404), and a phrase (such as Not Found, OK, or Bad Request). The entity body in a response message is the data, such as the content of a Web page or an image, which the server sends.

Cookies

HTTP is stateless in that the HTTP server does not act differently to a specific request based on previous requests. Occasionally, a Web service wants to maintain a minor amount of historical record of previous requests. Cookies (RFC 2965) create a stateful session with HTTP requests and responses.

The response from a server can contain a header line such as "Set-cookie: value." The browser then creates a cookie stored on the browser's storage. In subsequent requests sent to the same server, the browser includes the header line "Cookie: value." Depending on the browser, cookies are stored in a database or as small files of text.

The value of a cookie is not interpreted by the browser in any way. Cookie values often store user-specific information, such as a saved shopping cart, previous pages visited, user name and password, and previous advertisements shown.

Authentication

Web servers requiring user authentication send a `WWWAuthenticate:` header. The browser prompts the user for a user name and password, and sends this information in each of the subsequent request messages to the server.

NEXT GENERATION TCP/IP

The TCP/IP that is in wide use now (2006) is version 4. Version number 5 does not exist. Version 6 is available now but may take a few years to be widely deployed in place of v4. All U.S. federal agencies must deploy IPv6 by 2008. However, IPv4 is not expected to die even by 2010.

In TCP/IP v6 suite, IPv4 is replaced by IPv6, and ICMPv4 is replaced by ICMPv6. There is no TCP v6. The same UDP, TCP, and infrastructure protocols are implemented over IPv6.

IPv6

IPv6 (RFC 2460) has several improvements over IPv4, in areas such as IP address size, authentication and security, header format, flow labeling, extensions and options, auto configuration, and multicast routing. IPv6 was previously known as IPng (IP Next Generation).

IPv6 Header

The value of the Version field (Figure 16) is 6. The 20-bit Flow Label specifies special router handling from source to destination(s) for a sequence of packets. A flow is a sequence of packets that a specific source sends to a specific destination. The Payload Length is a 16-bit unsigned integer specifying the number of bytes of data that follow the IPv6 header. The 1-byte Next Header identifies the type of header that follows the IPv6 header. The header that follows will be either an extension header (if present), or the payload header such as TCP or ICMP. The 1-byte Hop Limit (cf. TTL of IPv4) is an unsigned integer. It is decremented by one by each node that forwards the packet. The packet is discarded if Hop Limit becomes zero.

IPv6 Addresses

IPv4 addresses are only 4 bytes long, and the address space is nearly exhausted. IPv6 addresses are 16 bytes long. This is sufficiently large that every cell phone and electronic device can be assigned a unique address. IPv6 uses CIDR.

When data is to be sent to a number of hosts simultaneously, a multicast address destination is used. In IPv6, each multicast address can have a different scope, allowing a transmission to be targeted to a wide or narrow range of hosts. With a so-called anycast destination, data is sent to any one in a group of hosts.

Extensions

IPv6 options are placed in separate extension headers located between the IPv6 header and the transport-layer header in a packet. Many of these IPv6 extension headers are skipped by intermediate routers until the packet arrives at its destination. This is a major improvement in router performance. In IPv4, the router examines all options. Current IPv6 extensions are extended routing, fragmentation and reassembly, integrity authentication and security, encapsulation and confidentiality, hop-by-hop, and destination options to be examined by the destination node.

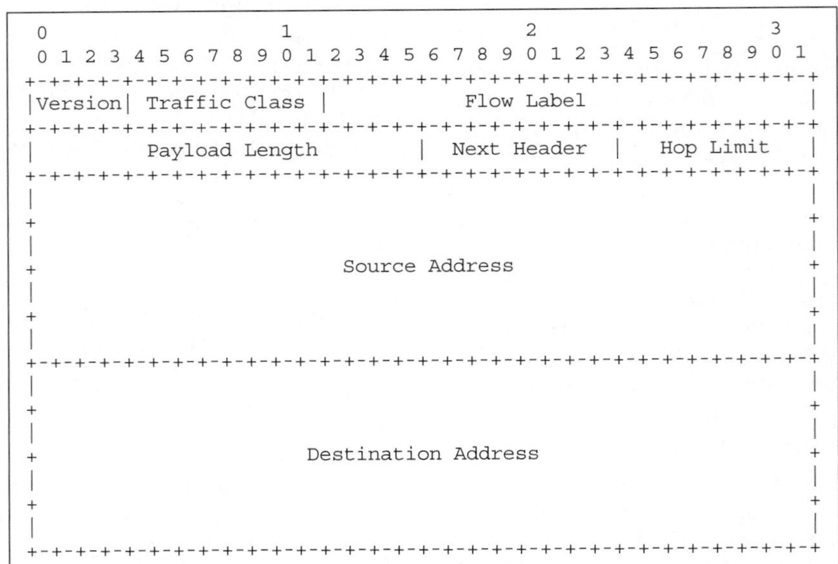

Figure 16: IPv6 header

Encrypted Security Payload

The encrypted security payload (ESP) is an extension for data confidentiality and the prevention of easy decodability of information obtained through eavesdropping. IPv4 sends all its payload and headers in clear text. A determined attacker can install remote sniffers along every path that a communication uses from host B to host C and assemble full messages being sent at the application level. The IPsec protocol adds authentication and encryption. The IPv6 includes IPsec. The cryptographic protocols of IPsec provide authentication, encrypt data, and guarantee message integrity. It also provides for a key exchange protocol, such as the IKE (Internet key exchange) protocol.

Other Improvements over IPv4

Note that the following fields of IPv4 header (refer to Figure 7) are dropped: IHL, Type of Service, Identification, Flag, Offset, and Header Checksum. The simpler header of IPv6 improves routing efficiency, performance, and forwarding rate.

An IPv6 host that wants to auto-configure sends a link-local request for its configuration parameters to which a router should respond with a router advertisement packet. A host can also use DHCPv6 or be configured manually.

The sending IPv6 host uses a path MTU discovery technique and does the fragmentation. Unlike IPv4, the IPv6 routers along the way do not (further) fragment. Removal of this task and the check summing task contributes to improved router performance.

IPv4 to IPv6 Transition

Many current systems (including personal computers and routers) are "dual stack"; that is, they support both IPv4 and IPv6 simultaneously.

A device capable of both IPv4 and v6 can have a regular IPv6 address and another IPv4 compatible IPv6 address by prefixing the `i.j.k.l` IPv4 address with 96 zero bits; for brevity, such an IPv6 address is written as `::i.j.k.l`. A device capable of only IPv4 is IPv6-addressable by having its IPv4 address prefixed with a string of 80 zeroes followed by 16 ones; for brevity, such an IPv6 address is written as `::FFFF:i.j.k.l`.

IPv6 network islands that do not have a path between them communicate through an IPv4 tunnel by encapsulating IPv6 datagrams within IPv4 at the head-end of a tunnel and decapsulate at the tail-end. This requires configuring the tunnels. Such isolated nodes and networks can also use the "6to4" mechanism (RFC 3056) with the addition of a 6to4 router at the borders. The IANA has permanently assigned 2002::/16 as a 6to4 prefix to IPv4 addresses, which provides a network prefix for the local IPv6 host or network. The IPv4 address is the endpoint for all external IPv4 connections. The 6to4 effectively uses a IPv4 network as a unicast point-to-point layer, requires no end-node reconfiguration, and requires minimal router configuration.

The 6bone was an IPv6 test bed to assist in the evolution and deployment of IPv6. It was phased out in June 2006.

ICMPv6

ICMPv6 (RFC 2463, 1998) is used by IPv6 to report errors encountered in processing packets, and to perform other network-layer functions. ICMPv6 is a required companion to IPv6. IGMP and ARP are merged into ICMPv6, and RARP is omitted.

Every ICMPv6 message (Figure 17) is preceded by an IPv6 header and zero or more IPv6 extension headers. ICMPv6 messages are either error messages or request/reply informational messages.

Error Messages

There are error messages in ICMPv6 corresponding to those in ICMPv4, except a source quench. The source-quench message is no longer needed because the `Traffic Class` Priority and `Flow Label` fields of IPv6 (Figure 16) are sufficient for congestion control purposes. Additionally, there is a new "Packet Too Big" message sent by a router when it receives an IPv6 datagram that is longer than the MTU of the outgoing link.

Request/Reply Messages

The Echo Request, Echo Reply, Router Advertisement, and Router Solicitation query messages are essentially as in ICMPv4. The ICMPv4 Timestamp Request and Address Mask Request messages are dropped.

Neighbor Discovery (ND)

ICMPv6 subsumes the functionality of ARP through the Neighbor Discovery (RFC 2461) protocol. ND uses ICMPv6 messages named Router Solicitation, Router Advertisement, Neighbor Solicitation, Neighbor Advertisement, and Redirect. Through these messages routers, next-hops, address prefixes, and parameters are discovered; IPv6 addresses are auto-configured; unreachability of neighbors and duplicate addresses are detected.

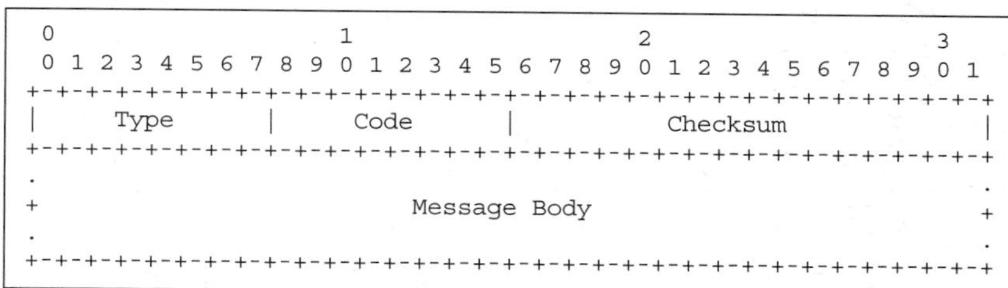

Figure 17: ICMPv6 packet

DHCPv6

The dynamic host configuration protocol for IPv6 (RFC 3315, 2003) is to IPv6 what DHCP was to IPv4. DHCPv6 enables DHCP servers to pass configuration parameters such as IPv6 network addresses to IPv6 nodes. It offers the capability of automatic allocation of reusable network addresses and additional configuration flexibility. This protocol is a stateful counterpart to IPv6 Stateless Address Auto Configuration (RFC 2462), and can be used separately or concurrently with the latter to obtain configuration parameters. With auto-configuration, every host that connects to the network can get an IPv6 address assigned and can use network resources.

Auto-configuration does not allow a network administrator to define admission control policies. Even in just assigning IPv6 addresses, auto-configuration is not appropriate in administrated infra structures, such as enterprise networks. In contrast, DHCPv6 servers provide means for securing access control to network resources by checking admission control policies. Note also that IPv6 auto-configuration does not cover information about further services in the network, for example, DNS. Many of the options commonly supported by DHCPv4 are supported also by DHCPv6.

A client obtains an IPv6 address and other parameters as follows. (i) Send a multicast Solicit message to find a DHCPv6 server and ask for a lease. (ii) Any server that can fulfill the client's request responds to it with an Advertise message. (iii) Choose one of the servers, and send a Request message asking to confirm the offered address and other parameters. (iv) The server responds with a Reply message to finalize the process. This four-message process can be reduced to two, where the client multicasts a Solicit message indicating that a server should respond back with a Reply message. A client who already has an IPv6 address multicasts an Information-Request message. A server with configuration information for the client sends back a Reply message. A DHCPv6 client renews its lease after a period of time by sending a Renew message.

CONCLUSION

The Internet and the World Wide Web are based on a suite of protocols and software collectively known as TCP/IP. It includes not only the transmission control protocol and Internet protocol but also other protocols such as UDP, ARP, DNS, and ICMP, and applications such as telnet, FTP, Secure Shell, and Web browsers and servers. We surveyed these topics starting from the four-layer Internet reference model to recent improvements in the implementations of the protocol stack and security.

GLOSSARY

Big Endian: A 32-bit integer is stored in four consecutively addressed bytes *a*, *a*+1, *a*+2, and *a*+3. In a big-endian system, the most significant byte of the integer is stored at *a*. In a little-endian system, the least significant byte is stored at *a*.

Byte: A byte is a sequence of 8 bits. Viewed as an unsigned number, it is in the range of 0 to 255. *See also octet.*

CERT: Advanced countries have a Computer Emergency Response Team that can assess network and computer security incidents and issue advisories. The site for USA is www.cert.org. It issues timely and authoritative alerts regarding computer exploits and has a comprehensive collection of guides on security.

Checksum: A checksum is a function of the sequence of bytes in a packet. It is used to detect errors that may have altered some of the numbers in the sequence. The IP checksum field is computed as the 16-bit 1 complement of the 1 complement sum of all 16-bit words in the header. For purposes of computing the checksum, the value of the checksum field is 0.

Client: The process that establishes connections for the purpose of sending requests.

Datagram: A sequence of bytes that constitutes the unit of transmission in the network layer (such as IP).

Frame: The unit of transmission at the data link layer, which may include a header and/or a trailer, along with some number of units of data.

Host: A device capable of sending and receiving data over a network. Often, it is a computer system with an NIC, but it can be a much simpler device.

Network: A collection of links in which the hosts are connected either directly or indirectly.

Network Applications: Programs that operate over a network.

Network Operating Systems: These systems have network software built in and are aware of byte order issues.

Node: A synonym for host.

Octet: An 8-bit quantity on older computer architectures where the smallest addressable unit of memory was a word (of sizes such as 36 or 60 bits) and not a byte.

Packet: A generic term used to designate any unit of data passed between communicating entities and is usually mapped to a frame.

Process: The dynamic entity that can be summarized as a "program during its execution on a computer system."

Program: A file of binary data in a certain rigid format that is specific to each platform, capable of being both a client and a server. Our use of these terms refers only to the role being performed by the program for a particular connection rather than to the program's capabilities in general.

Protocol: A formal and pre-agreed set of rules that govern the communications between two or more entities. The protocol determines the meaning of specific values occurring in specific positions in the stream, the type of error checking to be used, the data compression method, how the sender will indicate that it has finished sending a message, and how the receiver will indicate that it has received a message.

RFC: Request for Comments documents are Internet standards, proposed designs, and solutions published by researchers from universities and corporations soliciting feedback and archived at www.rfc-editor.org.

Server: A process that accepts connections to service requests by sending back responses. It is also called a daemon.

Spoofing: In IP spoofing, either the source or the destination is a fake address. In DNS spoofing, a query receives a fake response.

Tunneling: Sending packets of a certain protocol embedded in the packets of another protocol.

CROSS REFERENCES

See *Internet Architecture*; *The Internet Fundamentals*.

REFERENCES

Arkin, O. 2001. ICMP usage in scanning: The complete know-how. www.sys-security.com/html/projects/icmp.html (accessed December, 2003).

Butler, K., T. Farley, P. McDaniel, and J. Rexford. 2005. A survey of BGP security. www.patrickmcdaniel.org/pubs/td-5ugj33.pdf (accessed March, 2006).

Iren, S., P. D. Amer, and P. T. Conrad. 1999. The transport layer: Tutorial and survey. *ACM Computing Surveys*, 31: 360–404.

Rowland, C. H. 1997. Covert channels in the TCP/IP protocol suite. *First Monday*. www.firstmonday.dk (accessed December, 2003).

Stallings, W. 2005. *Cryptography and network security: Principles and practice*. 4th ed. Englewood Cliffs, NJ: Prentice Hall.

Stewart, J. W., III.\1999. *BGP4: Inter-domain routing in the Internet*. Reading, MA: Addison Wesley.

FURTHER READING

TCP/IP details are part of many university courses on computer networks. There are several textbooks. Of these, the three authoritative volumes of *Comer's Internetworking with TCP/IP* are classic technical references in the field aimed at the computer professional and the degree student. Volume I surveys TCP/IP and covers details of ARP, RARP, IP, TCP, UDP, RIP, DHCP, OSPF, and others. There are errata at www.cs.purdue.edu/homes/dec/tcpip1.errata.html. *The Internet Book: Everything You Need to Know about Computer Networking and How the Internet Works* is a gentler introduction. The books listed in the References section by Forouzan, Tanenbaum, and Kurose and Ross are also popular textbooks. The book by Stevens discusses from a programming point of view.

Routing protocols are discussed briefly in the aforementioned books. The books by Halabi and Doyle cover this topic extensively. BGP security is surveyed in the article by Butler et al.

HTTP and related issues are thoroughly discussed in the books of Krishnamurthy and Rexford, and Gourley and Totty.

The book by Denning and Denning is a high-level discussion of how the vulnerabilities in computer networks are affecting society. Mateti has an extensive Web site (www.cs.wright.edu/~pmateti/InternetSecurity) that has lab experiments and readings online. The book by Garfinkel and Spafford explores security from a practical UNIX systems view.

All the RFCs are archived at www.rfc-editor.org. The Usenet newsgroup `comp.protocols.tcp-ip` is an active group that maintains a frequently asked questions (FAQ) document that is worth reading. The Technical Committee on Computer Communications of the IEEE Web site (www.comsoc.org) maintains an extensive collection of conference listings. The *IEEE/ACM Transactions on Networking* is a peer-reviewed archival journal that publishes research articles.

Comer, D. 2006. *Internetworking with TCP/IP: Vol. 1. Principles, protocols, and architecture*. 5th ed. Englewood Cliffs, NJ: Prentice Hall.

——. 2007. *The Internet book: Everything you need to know about computer networking and how the Internet works*. 4th ed. Englewood Cliffs, NJ: Prentice Hall.

Denning, D. E., and P. J. Denning. 1998. *Internet besieged: Countering cyberspace scofflaws*. Reading, MA: Addison Wesley.

Doyle, J. 2005. *Routing TCP/IP*. Indianapolis, IN: Cisco Press.

Forouzan, Behrouz A. 2005. *TCP/IP protocol suite*. 3rd ed. Boston, MA: McGraw-Hill.

Garfinkel, S., G. Spafford, and A. Schwartz. 2003. *Practical UNIX and Internet security*. 3rd ed. Sebastapol, CA: O'Reilly.

Gourley, D., and B. Totty. 2002. *HTTP: The definitive guide*. Sebastapol, CA: O'Reilly.

Halabi, B. 2000. *Internet routing architectures*. Indianapolis, IN: Cisco Press.

Krishnamurthy, B., and J. Rexford. 2001. *Web protocols and practice: HTTP/1.1, networking protocols, caching, and traffic measurement*. Reading, MA: Addison Wesley.

Kurose, J. F., and K. W. Ross. 2003. *Computer networking: A top-down approach featuring the Internet*. 3rd ed. Reading, MA: Addison Wesley.

Mateti, P. 2006. Internet security class notes. www.cs.wright.edu/~pmateti/InternetSecurity (accessed February, 2006).

Stevens, W. R. 1993. *TCP/IP illustrated: Vol. 1. The protocols*. Reading, MA: Addison Wesley.

Tanenbaum, A. S. 2003. *Computer networks*. 4th ed. Englewood Cliffs, NJ: Prentice Hall.

SMTP (Simple Mail Transfer Protocol)

Vladimir V. Riabov, *Rivier College*

INTRODUCTION

Electronic mail (e-mail) is one of the most popular network services nowadays. Most e-mail systems that send mail over the Internet use simple mail transfer protocol (SMTP) to send messages from one server to another. The mail delivery is a two-stage process that provides for mail instances when the network connection or the remote machine has failed (Comer 2005). For example, when a user does not have a permanent Internet connection, it should have a mailbox on a computer that does have such a connection. That computer must run the SMTP server and be able to always receive incoming mail. The mail messages can then be retrieved by the user from the mailbox with an e-mail client (installed on the user's machine) using either post office protocol (POP) or Internet message access protocol (IMAP). The computer with the permanent mailbox must run two servers: SMTP for accepting mail and POP/IMAP for retrieving mail. SMTP is also generally used to send messages from a mail client to a mail server in "host-based" (or Unix-based) mail systems, where a simple mbox utility might be on the same system [or via network file system (NFS) provided by Novell] for access without POP or IMAP.

This chapter describes the fundamentals of SMTP, elements of its client–server architecture (user agent, mail transfer agent, ports), request–response mechanism, commands, mail transfer phases, SMTP messages, multipurpose Internet mail extensions (MIME) for non-ASCII (American Standard Code for Information Interchange) data, e-mail delivery cases, mail access protocols (POP3 and IMAP4), SMTP software, some vulnerability and security issues, standards, associations, and organizations.

SMTP FUNDAMENTALS

SMTP, an application layer protocol, is used as the common mechanism for transporting electronic mail among different hosts within the transmission control protocol/Internet protocol (TCP/IP) suite. The history of SMTP has been described by Kozierok (2006). Under SMTP, a client SMTP process opens a TCP connection to a server SMTP process on a remote host and attempts to send mail across the connection. The server SMTP listens for a TCP connection on a specific port (25), and the client SMTP process initiates a connection on that port (Cisco SMTP 2006). When the TCP connection is successful, the two processes execute a simple request–response dialogue, defined by the SMTP protocol (see RFC 2821 and RFC 821 for details), in which the client process transmits the mail addresses of the originator and the recipient(s) for a message. When the server process accepts these mail addresses, the client process transmits the e-mail message. The message must contain a message header and message text ("body") formatted in accordance with RFC 2822 and RFC 822.

In February 1993, the SMTP Service Extensions standard (RFC 1425), which describes a process for adding new capabilities to extend how SMTP works while maintaining backward-compatibility with existing systems, was published. The extended SMTP (ESMTP) standard (RFC 1425) was revised in RFC 1651 in July 1994 and then RFC 1869 in November 1995. Particular SMTP extensions, such as message size declaration (RFC 1653 and RFC 1870), authentication (RFC 2554), and pipelining (RFC 2920), were defined later. In April 2001, revisions of RFC 821 and RFC 822 were published, as RFCs 2821 and 2822 respectively. The current base standard protocol for

SMTP (RFC 2821) incorporates the base protocol description (RFC 821) and the latest SMTP extensions (RFC 1869) and updates the description of the e-mail communication model to reflect changes of TCP/IP networks, especially the e-mail features built into the domain name system (DNS) (Kozierok 2006).

Mail that arrives via SMTP is forwarded to a remote server, or it is delivered to mailboxes on the local server. POP3 or IMAP allow users to download mail that is stored on the local server. The delivery of e-mail to a user's mailbox typically takes place via a mail delivery agent (MDA). The MDA software accepts incoming e-mail messages and distributes them to recipients' individual mailboxes (if the destination account is on the local machine), or forwards back to an SMTP server (if the destination is on a remote server) (Wikipedia 2006). On UNIX systems, /bin/mail is the most popular MDA. Many mail transfer agents (MTAs) have basic MDA functionality built in, but a dedicated MDA like procmail can provide more sophistication.

Most mail programs such as Eudora allow the client to specify both an SMTP server and a POP server. On UNIX-based systems, Sendmail is the most widely used SMTP server for e-mail. Sendmail includes a POP3 server and also comes in a version for Windows NT ("What is SMTP?", 2006). The MIME protocol defines one way files can be attached to SMTP messages. Microsoft Outlook and Netscape/Mozilla Communicator are some popular mail-agent programs on Window-based systems. The other functional and capable method of file attachment includes uuencode and uudecode techniques that are no longer in widespread use.

The X.400 International Telecommunication Union standard (Tanenbaum 2003) that defines transfer protocols for sending electronic mail between mail servers is used in Europe as an alternative to SMTP. Also, the message handling service (MHS) developed by Novell is used for electronic mail on Netware networks ("What is SMTP?" 2006).

SMTP MODEL AND PROTOCOL

The SMTP model (RFC 821) supports both end-to-end (no intermediate message transfer agents [MTAs]) and store-and-forward mail delivery methods. The end-to-end method is used between organizations, and the store-and-forward method is chosen for operating within organizations that have TCP/IP and SMTP-based networks.

A SMTP client will contact the destination host's SMTP server directly to deliver the mail. It will keep the mail item being transmitted until it has been successfully copied to the recipient's SMTP server queue. This is different from the store-and-forward principle that is common in many other electronic mailing systems, in which the mail item may pass through a number of intermediate hosts in the same network on its way to the destination and where successful transmission from the sender only indicates that the mail item has reached the first intermediate hop ("Simple Mail Transfer Protocol" [SMTP] 2004).

The RFC 821 standard defines a client–server protocol. The client SMTP is the one, which initiates the session (that is, the sending SMTP) and the server is the one that responds (the receiving SMTP) to the session request. Because the client SMTP frequently acts as a server for a user-mailing program, however, it is often simpler to refer to the client as the sender-SMTP and to the server as the receiver-SMTP.

An SMTP-based process can transfer electronic mail to another process on the same network or to another network via a relay or gateway process accessible to both networks (Sheldon 2001). An e-mail message may pass through a number of intermediate relay or gateway hosts on its path from a sender to a recipient. A simple model of the components of the SMTP system is shown in Figure 1.

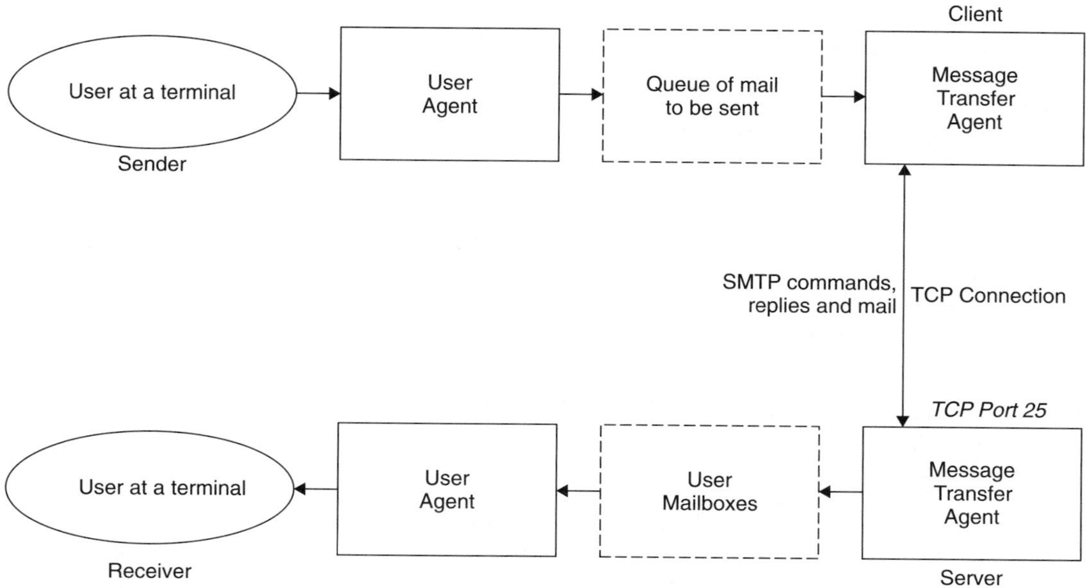

Figure 1: The basic simple mail transfer protocol (SMTP) model

Users deal with a user agent (UA). Popular user agents for UNIX include Berkeley Mail, Elm, MH, Pine, and Mutt. The user agents for Windows include Microsoft Outlook/Outlook Express and Netscape/Mozilla Communicator. The exchange of mail using TCP is performed by an MTA. The most common MTA for UNIX systems is Sendmail, and for Windows is Microsoft Exchange 2000/2003. In addition to stable host-based e-mail servers, Microsoft Corporation has developed LDAP/Active-directory servers and B2B-servers that enhance mail-delivery practices. Users normally do not deal with the MTA. It is the responsibility of the system administrator to set up the local MTA. Users often have a choice, however, for their user agent (Stevens 1993). The MTA maintains a mail queue so that it can schedule repeat delivery attempts in case a remote server is unable. Also the local MTA delivers mail to mailboxes, and the information can be downloaded by the UA (see Figure 1).

The RFC 821 standard specifies the SMTP protocol, which is a mechanism of communication between two MTAs across a single TCP connection. The RFC 822 standard specifies the format of the electronic mail message that is transmitted using the SMTP protocol (RFC 821) between the two MTAs. As a result of a user mail request, the sender-SMTP establishes a two-way connection with a receiver-SMTP. The receiver-SMTP can be either the ultimate destination or an intermediate one (known as a mail gateway). The sender-SMTP will generate commands, which are replied to by the receiver-SMTP (see Figure 1).

Both the SMTP client and server should have two basic components: UA and local MTA. There are few cases of sending electronic-mail messages across networks. In the first case of communication between the sender and the receiver across the network (see Figure 1), the sender's UA prepares the message, creates the envelope, and puts message in the envelope. The MTA transfers the mail across the network to the TCP-port 25 of the receiver's MTA. In the second case of communication between the sending host (client) and the receiving host (server), *relaying* could be involved (see Figure 2). In addition to one MTA at the sender site and one at the receiving site, other MTAs, acting as client or server, can relay the electronic mail across the network.

The most common way in the early days of SMTP was through a process called *relaying* (Kozierok 2006). SMTP routing information was included along with the e-mail address, to specify a sequence of SMTP servers that the mail should be relayed through to get to its destination. The system of relays allows sites that do not use the TCP/IP protocol suite to send electronic mail to users on other sites that may or may not use the TCP/IP protocol suite. This third scenario of communication between the sender and the receiver can be accomplished through the use of an e-mail gateway, which is a relay MTA that can receive electronic mail prepared by a protocol other than SMTP and transform it to the SMTP format before sending it. The e-mail gateway can also receive electronic mail in the SMTP format, change it to another format, and then send it to the MTA of the client that does not use the TCP/IP protocol suite (Forouzan 2005). In various implementations, there is the capability to exchange mail between the TCP/IP SMTP mailing system and the locally used mailing systems. These applications are called mail gateways or mail bridges. Sending mail through a mail gateway may alter the end-to-end delivery specification, because SMTP will only guarantee delivery to the mail-gateway host, not to the real destination host, which is located beyond the TCP/IP network. When a mail gateway is used, the SMTP end-to-end transmission is host-to-gateway, gateway-to-host or gateway-to-gateway; the behavior beyond the gateway is not defined by SMTP.

The creation of domain name system (DNS) radically changed the e-mail delivery approach. DNS includes support for a special *mail exchanger record* that allows easy mapping from the domain name in an e-mail address to the IP address of the SMTP server that handles mail for that domain (Kozierok 2006). The sending SMTP server uses DNS to find the mail exchanger record of the domain to which the e-mail is addressed. The sender uses this information for identifying the DNS name of the recipient's SMTP server and for resolving an IP address that can be used for a direct connection between the sender's SMTP server and the recipient's one to deliver the e-mail (RFC 2821).

USER AGENT

Introduced in RFC 821 and RFC 822, the SMTP defines user agent functionality, but not the implementation details. A survey of the SMTP implementations can be found in RFC 876. The UA is a program that is used to send and receive electronic mail. The most popular user agent programs for UNIX are Berkley Mail, Elm, MH, Mutt, Mush, and Zmail. Some UAs have an extra user interface (e.g., Eudora) that allows window-type interactions with the system. The user agents for Windows include Microsoft Outlook/Outlook Express and Netscape/Mozilla Communicator.

Sending E-Mail

Electronic mail is sent by a series of request–response transactions between a client and a server. An SMTP transaction consists of the envelope and message, which is composed of header (with From: and To: fields) and body (text after headers sent with the DATA command). The envelope is transmitted separately from the message itself using MAIL FROM and RCPT TO commands (see RFC 1123). A null line, that is, a line with nothing preceding the `<CRLF>` sequence, terminates the mail header. Some implementations (e.g., VM, which does not support zero-length records in files), however, may interpret this differently and accept a blank line as a terminator (SMTP 2004). Everything after the null (or blank) line is the message body, which is a sequence of lines containing ASCII characters. The message body contains the actual information that can be read by the recipient.

Mail Header Format

The header includes a number of key words and values that define the sending date, sender's address, where replies should go, and some other information.

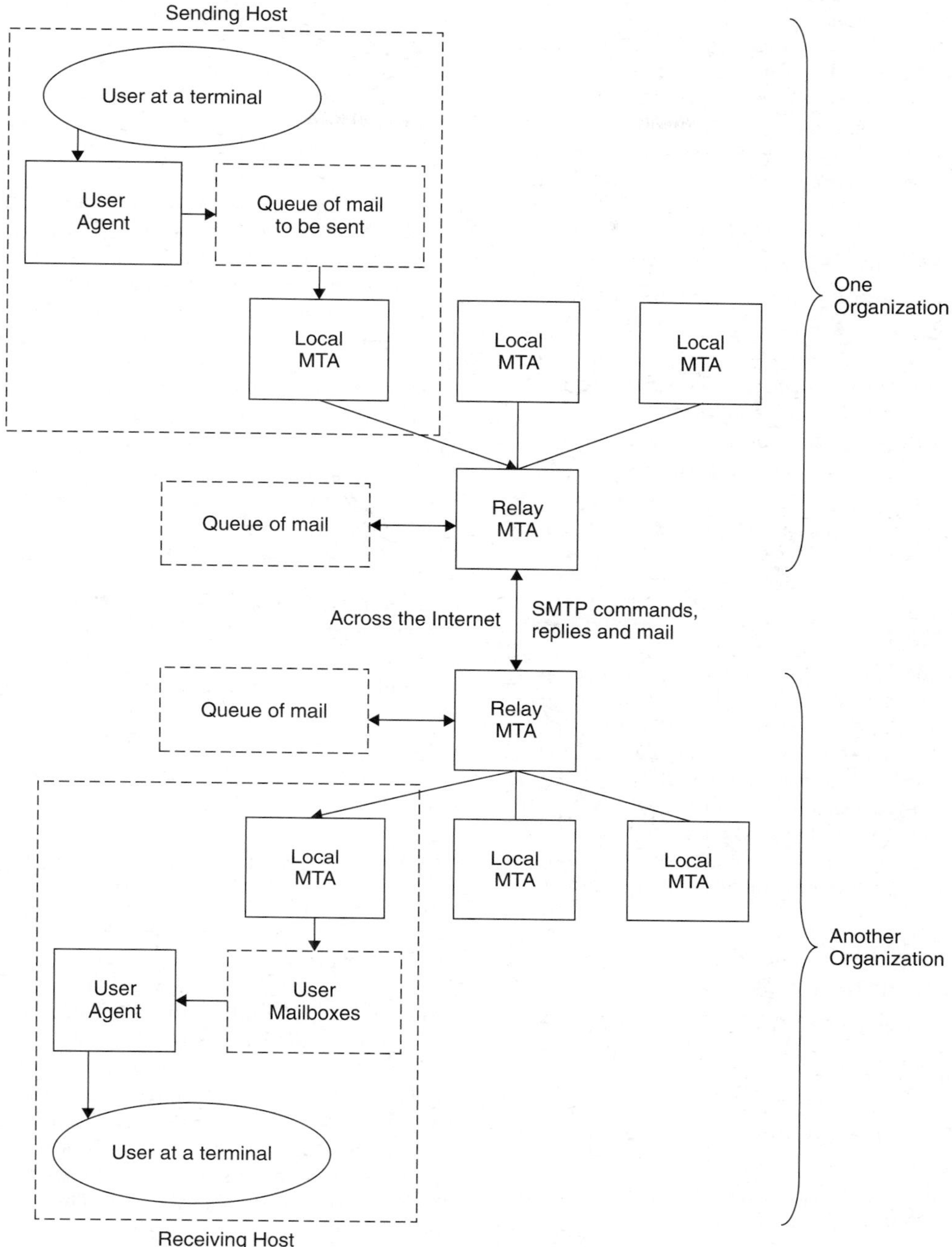

Figure 2: The simple mail transfer protocol (SMTP) model with relay mail transfer agents

The header is a list of lines, of the form (SMTP 2004):

field-name: field-value

Fields begin in column 1: Lines beginning with white space characters (SPACE or TAB) are continuation lines, which are unfolded to create a single line for each field in the canonical representation. Strings enclosed in ASCII quotation marks indicate single tokens within which special characters such as the colon are not significant. Many important field values (such as those for the "To" and "From" fields) are "mailboxes." The most common forms for these are the following:

- jsmith@mail.it.rivier.edu
- John Smith `<jsmith@mail.it.rivier.edu>`
- "John Smith" `<jsmith@mail.it.rivier.edu>`

The string "John Smith" is intended for human recipients and is the name of the mailbox owner. The string "jsmith@mail.it.rivier.edu" is the computer-readable address of the mailbox (the angle brackets are used to delimit the address but are not part of it). One can see that this form of addressing is closely related to the domain name system (DNS) concept (Internet Assigned Numbers Authority [IANA] 2006). In fact, the client SMTP uses the DNS to determine the IP address of the destination mailbox.

Some frequently used fields (key words) are the following:

- to Primary recipients of the message.
- cc Secondary ("carbon-copy") recipients of the message.
- from Identity of sender.
- reply-to The mailbox to which responses are to be sent. This field is added by the originator.
- return-path Address and route back to the originator. This field is added by the final transport system that delivers the mail.
- Subject Summary of the message. The user usually provides the summary.

Receiving E-Mail

The UA periodically checks the content of the mailboxes (see Figure 1). It informs the user about mail arrival by giving a special notice. When the user tries to read the mail, a list of arrived mail packages is displayed. Each line of the list contains a brief summary of the information about a particular package in the mailbox. The summary may include the sender mail address, the subject, and the time the mail was received or sent. By selecting any of the packages, the user can view its contents on the terminal display.

The SMTP Destination Address

The SMTP destination address (a mailbox address), in its general form *local-part@domain-name*, can take several forms (SMTP 2004):

- user@host—For a direct destination on the same TCP/IP network.
- user%remote-host@gateway-host—For a user on a non-SMTP destination remote-host, via the mail gateway gateway-host.
- @host-a,@host-b:user@host-c—For a relayed message. This form contains explicit routing information. The message will first be delivered to host-a, who will resend (relay) the message to host-b. Host-b will then forward the message to the real destination host-c. Note that the message is stored on each of the intermediate hosts; therefore, there is no end-to-end delivery in this case. This address form is obsolete and should not be used (see RFC 1123).

Delayed Delivery

The SMTP protocol allows delayed delivery, and the message can be delayed at the sender site, the receiver site, or the intermediate servers (Forouzan 2005).

In the case of delaying at the sender site, the client has to accommodate a spooling system, in which e-mail messages are stored before being sent. A message created by the user agent is delivered to the spool storage. The client mail transfer agent periodically (usually every 10 to 30 minutes) checks the spool to find the mail that can be sent. The mail will be sent only if the receiver is ready and the IP address of the server has been obtained though DNS. If a message cannot be delivered in the timeout period (usually about 3 to 5 days), the mail returns to the sender.

Upon receiving the message, the server-MTA stores it in the mailbox of the receiver (see Figure 1). In this case, the receiver can access the mailbox at any convenient time.

Finally, the SMTP standard procedures allow intermediate MTAs to serve as clients and servers. Both intermediate clients and servers can receive mail, store mail messages in their mailboxes and spools, and send them later to an appropriate destination.

Aliases

The SMTP mechanism allows one name, an alias, to represent several e-mail addresses (this feature is known as "one-to-many alias expansion"; Forouzan 2005). Additionally, a single user can also be defined by several e-mail addresses (this is called "many-to-one alias expansion"). The system can handle these expansions by including an alias expansion facility (connected to the alias databases) at both the sender and receiver sites.

MAIL TRANSFER AGENT (MTA)

MTAs transfer actual mail. The system must have the client MTA for sending e-mail and the server MTA for receiving mail (see Figure 1). The SMTP-related RFCs do not define a specific MTA. The UNIX-based MTA uses commonly the Sendmail utility. The most common MTA for Windows is Microsoft Exchange 2000/2003.

The "mta-name-type" and "address-type" parameters (e.g., dnc and rfc822 for the Internet mail, respectively) are defined for use in the SMTP delivery status notification document (see RFC1891). An identification of other mail systems can also be used. One of the identification methods has been described in "The COSINE and Internet X.500 Schema" (section 9.3.18) in the RFC1274 document. The mail system names listed here are used as the legal values in that schema under the "otherMailbox" attribute "mailboxType" type, which must be a PrintableString. The "Mapping between X.400 (1988)/ISO 10021 and RFC 822" is described in the section 4.2.2 of the RFC1327 document. The names listed here are used as the legal values in that schema under the "std-or-address" attribute "registered-dd-type" type, which must be a "key-string" (for details, see Mail Parameters 2006).

SMTP Mail Transaction Flow

The SMTP protocol (RFC 821) defines how commands and responses must be sent by the MTAs. The client sends commands to the server, and the server responds with numeric reply codes and optional human-readable strings.

There are a small number of commands (less than a dozen) that the client can send to the server. An example of sending a simple one-line message and an interpretation of the SMTP connection can be found in Stevens (1993).

Although mail commands and replies are rigidly defined (see "SMTP Commands" and "SMTP Responses" later in this chapter), the exchange can easily be followed in Figure 3.

In this scenario (Comer 2005; SMTP 2004), the user jsmith at host sun.it.rivier.edu sends a note to users darien, steve and bryan at host mail.unh.edu. Here the lines sent by the server (receiver) are preceded by S, and the lines sent by the client (sender) preceded by C. Note that the message header is part of the data being transmitted. All exchanged messages (commands, replies, and data) are text lines, delimited by a `<CRLF>`. All replies have a numeric code at the beginning of the line.

The scenario includes the following steps (SMTP 2004):

1. The client (sender-SMTP) establishes a TCP connection with the destination SMTP and then waits for the server to send a 220 Service ready message or a 421 Service not available message when the destination is temporarily unable to proceed.
2. The HELO command is sent, and the receiver is forced to identify himself by sending back its domain name. The client (sender-SMTP) can use this information to verify if it contacted the right destination SMTP. If the sender-SMTP supports SMTP service extensions as defined in the RFC 1651, it may substitute an EHLO command in place of the HELO command. A receiver-SMTP, which does not support service extensions, will respond with a 500 Syntax error, command unrecognized message. The client (sender-SMTP) should then retry with HELO, or if it cannot transmit the message without one or more service extensions, it should send a QUIT message. If a receiver-SMTP supports service extensions, it responds with a multiline 250 OK messages that include a list of service extensions, which it supports.
3. The client (sender) now initiates the start of a mail transaction by sending a MAIL command to the receiver. This command contains the reverse-path, which can be used to report errors. Note that a path can be more than just the *user-mailbox@host-domain-name* pair. In addition, it can contain a list of routing hosts. Examples of this are when the mail passes a mail bridge or when the user provides explicit routing information in the destination address. If accepted, the server (receiver) replies with a 250 OK message.
4. The second step of the actual mail exchange consists of providing the server SMTP with the destinations for the message (there can be more than one recipient). This is done by sending one or more RCPT TO:`<forward-path>` commands. Each of them will receive a 250 OK reply if the destination is known to the server or a 550 No such user here reply if it is not.

```
S: 220 mail.unh.edu Simple Mail Transfer Service Ready
C: HELO it.rivier.edu
S: 250 mail.unh.edu

C: MAIL FROM:<jsmith@it.rivier.edu>
S: 250 OK

C: RCPT TO:<darien@mail.unh.edu>
S: 250 OK

C: RCPT TO:<steve@mail.unh.edu>
S: 250 OK

C: RCPT TO:<bryan@mail.unh.edu>
S: 550 No such user here

C: DATA
S: 354 Start mail input, end with <CRLF>.<CRLF>
C: Date: 26 Jan 2004  11:02:34 EST
C: From: John Smith <jsmith@it.rivier.edu>
C: Subject: Important meeting
C: To:  <darien@mail.unh.edu>
C: To:  <steve@mail.unh.edu>
C: cc:  <bryan@mail.unh.edu>
C:
C: Best wishes
C: See you soon...
C: .
S: 250 OK

C: QUIT
S: 221 mail.unh.edu Service closing transmission channel
```

Figure 3: An example of the interactive session between the client ("sender" C) and the server ("receiver" S)

5. When all RCPT commands are sent, the client (sender) issues a DATA command to notify the server (receiver) that the message contents are following. The server replies with the 354 Start mail input, end with `<CRLF>.<CRLF>` message.
6. The client now sends the data line by line, ending with the sequence `<CRLF>.<CRLF>` line on which the receiver acknowledges with a 250 OK or an appropriate error message if anything went wrong.
7. The following actions (SMTP 2004) are possible after that:
   - The sender has no more messages to send; he will end the connection with a QUIT command, which will be answered with a 221 Service closing transmission channel reply (see Figure 3).
   - The client (sender) has another message to send and simply goes back to step 3 to send a new MAIL command.

In this description, only the most important commands that must be recognized in each SMTP implementation (see RFC821) have been mentioned. Other optional commands (the RFC 821 standard does not require them to be implemented everywhere) implement several important functions such as forwarding, relaying, mailing lists, and so on.

SMTP Commands

The commands formed with ASCII (text) are sent from the client to the server. The simple structure of the commands allows for building mail clients and servers on any platform. Table 1 lists commands and their description and formats. The command consists of a key word followed by zero or more arguments. Five commands (HELO, MAIL FROM, RCPT TO, DATA, and QUIT) are mandatory, and every implementation must support them. The EHLO command is strongly preferred to HELO when the server will accept the former (RFC 2821). Servers must continue to accept and process HELO in order to support older clients.

The other two commands (RSET and NOOP) are often used and highly recommended. The VRFY and EXPN commands are often disabled. This technique allows reducing spam validation of email addresses. The next five programs (TURN, HELP, SEND FROM, SOML FROM, and SAML FROM) are seldom used. The TURN command raises security issues (RFC 2821), because, in the absence of strong authentication of the host requesting that the client and server switch roles, it can easily be used to divert mail from its correct destination. SMTP systems should not use this command unless the server can authenticate the client. The SEND, SAML, and SOML commands were originally introduced in RFC 821 to provide additional, optional mechanism of delivering messages directly to the user's terminal screen. They were rarely implemented, and changes in workstation technology and the introduction of other protocols may have rendered them obsolete even where they are implemented (RFC 2821). SMTP clients should not provide SEND, SAML, or SOML as services.

For a full list of commands, see the RFC 821 "Simple Mail Transfer Protocol," RFC 1123 "Requirements for Internet Hosts—Application and Support," and RFC 2821 "Simple Mail Transfer Protocol." For details of SMTP service extensions, see the RFC 1651 "SMTP Service Extensions," RFC 1652 "SMTP Service Extension for 8bit-MIMEtransport," RFC 1653 "SMTP Service Extension for Message Size Declaration," and RFC 2554 "SMTP Service Extension for Authentication."

The commands normally progress in a sequence (one at a time). The advanced pipelining feature introduced in the RFC 2920 document allows multiple commands to be sent to a server in a single operation of the TCP-send type.

Mail Service Types

The set of services desired from a mail server are sometimes characterized by the "hello" key word. The various mail service types are as follows (Mail Parameters 2006):

- HELO for Simple Mail (see RFC821)
- EHLO for Mail Service Extensions (see RFC1869)
- LHLO for Local Mail (see RFC2033).

The EHLO key word has a numerical parameter SIZE for specifying the new format of e-mail messages (see RFC1870).

SMTP Service Extensions

SMTP (RFC821) specifies a set of commands or services for mail transfer. A general procedure for extending the set of services is defined in the STD11/RFC1869 document. The service extensions are identified by key words sent from the server to the client in response to the EHLO command (Mail Parameters 2006). The set of service extensions are as follows:

- SEND—Send as mail (see RFC821)
- SOML—Send as mail or to terminal (see RFC821)
- SAML—Send as mail and to terminal (see RFC821)
- EXPN—Expand the mailing list (see RFC821)
- HELP—Supply helpful information (see RFC821)
- TURN—Turn the operation around (see RFC821)
- 8BITMIME—Use 8-bit data; it defines support for the 8-bit content transfer encoding type in MIME (see RFC1652)
- AUTH—Use to implement an authorization mechanism for servers requiring enhanced security (see RFC2554)
- SIZE—Message size declaration, which allows information about the size of a message to be declared by an SMTP sender prior to transmitting it, so the SMTP receiver can decide if it wants the message or not (see RFC1870)
- CHUNKING—Chunking (see RFC3030)
- BINARYMIME—Binary MIME (see RFC3030)
- CHECKPOINT—Checkpoint/restart (see RFC1845)
- PIPELINING—Command pipelining, which allows multiple commands to be transmitted in batches from the SMTP sender to the receiver, rather than sending

Table 1: Simple Mail Transfer Protocol (SMTP) Commands. Adapted from SMTP Specifications 2006.

Command	Description	Format	References
ATRN	Authenticated TURN		RFC 2645
AUTH	Authentication		RFC 2554
BDAT	Binary data		RFC 3030
DATA	Data; used to send the actual message; all lines that follow the DATA command are treated as the e-mail message; the message is terminated by a line containing just a period	DATA Best wishes.	RFC 821, RFC 2821
EHLO	Extended Hello		RFC 1869, RFC 2821
ETRN	Extended TURN		RFC 1985
EXPN	Expand; asks the receiving host to expand the mailing list sent as the arguments and to return the mailbox addresses of the recipients that comprise the list	EXPN: a b c	RFC 821, RFC 2821
HELO	Hello; used by the client to identify itself	HELO: sun.it.rivier.edu	RFC 821, RFC 2821
HELP	Help; requests the recipient to send information about the command sent as the argument	HELP: mail	RFC 821, RFC 2821
MAIL FROM	Mail; used by the client to identify the sender of the message; the argument is the e-mail address of the sender	MAIL FROM: jsmith@ sun.it.rivier.edu	RFC 821, RFC 2821
NOOP	No operation; used by the client to check the status of the recipient; requires an answer from the recipient	NOOP	RFC 821, RFC 2821
QUIT	Quit; terminates the message	QUIT	RFC 821, RFC 2821
RCPT	Recipient; used by the client to identify the intended recipient of the message; if there are multiple recipients, the command is repeated	RCPT TO: steve@unh.edu	RFC 821, RFC 2821
RSET	Reset; aborts the current e-mail transaction; the stored information about the sender and recipient is deleted; the connection will be reset	RSET	RFC 821, RFC 2821
SAML	Send to the mailbox or terminal; specifies that the mail have to be delivered to the terminal or the mailbox of the recipient; the argument is the address of the sender	SAML FROM: jsmith@ sun.it.rivier.edu	RFC 821
SEND	Send; specifies that the mail is to be delivered to the terminal of the recipient and not the mailbox; if the recipient is not logged in, the mail is bounced back; the argument is the address of the sender	SEND FROM: jsmith@ sun.it.rivier.edu	RFC 821
SOML	Send to the mailbox or terminal; it specifies that the mail is to be delivered to the terminal or the mailbox of the recipient; the argument is the address of the sender	SOML FROM: jsmith@ sun.it.rivier.edu	RFC 821
STARTTLS	Extended Hello with transport layer security		RFC 3207
TURN	Turn; it lets the sender and the recipient switch positions whereby the sender becomes the recipient and vice versa (most SMTP implementations today do not support this feature; see RFC2821)	TURN	RFC 821
VRFY	Verify; it verifies the address of the recipient, which is sent as the argument; the sender can request the receiver to confirm that a name identifies a valid recipient	VRFY: steve@unh.edu	RFC 821, RFC 2821

one command at a time and waiting for a response code (see RFC2920)

- DSN—Delivery status notification, which allows an SMTP sender to request that the SMTP receiver notify if a problem occurs in delivering a message the sender gives to it (see RFC1891)
- ETRN—Extended turn (see RFC1985)
- ENHANCEDSTATUSCODES—Enhanced status codes; it extends the traditional 3-digit SMTP reply code format with extra codes that provide more information (see RFC2034 and RFC1893)
- STARTTLS—Start TLS (see RFC3207)

Some of these key words have parameters (for details, see Mail Parameters 2006).

SMTP Responses

Responses are sent from the server to the client. A response is a three-digit code that may be followed by additional textual information. The meanings of the first digit are as follows:

- 2bc—positive completion reply; the requested command has been successfully completed and a new command can be started.
- 3bc—positive intermediate reply; the requested command has been accepted, but the server needs some more information before completion can occur.
- 4ab—transient negative completion reply; the requested command has been rejected, but the error condition is temporary, and the command can be sent again.
- 5ab—permanent negative completion reply; the requested command has been rejected, and the command cannot be sent again (e.g., see RFC 1846).

The second (b) and the third (c) digits provide further details about the responses. Table 2 shows the list of typical reply codes and their descriptions.

SMTP SERVER

The SMTP server sends and receives mail from other Internet hosts using the SMTP. The SMTP server processes all incoming and outgoing mail. Outgoing mail is spooled until the SMTP server can confirm it has arrived at its destination; incoming mail is spooled until users access it by using a POP3 or IMAP4 mail client. Spooling allows the transfer from client and server to occur in the background. The instructions on how to configure the SMTP server in the Windows NT environment and how to set options to provide security for the SMTP server are described in "How to Set SMTP Security Options" (2006).

ON-DEMAND MAIL RELAY

On-demand mail relay (ODMR), also known as authenticated TURN (ATRN), is an e-mail service that allows a user to connect to an Internet service provider (ISP), authenticate, and request e-mail using a dynamic IP address (instead of static IP addresses used in a "traditional" SMTP model) from any Internet connection (see RFC 2645). The initial client and server roles are short-lived, because the point is to allow the intermittently connected host to request mail held for it by a service provider. The customer initiates a connection to the provider, authenticates, and requests its mail. The roles of client and server then reverse, and the normal SMTP scenario proceeds. The provider has an ODMR process listening for connections on the ODMR port 366 (SMTP Specifications 2006). On the server, this process implements the EHLO, AUTH, ATRN, and QUIT commands. Also, it has to be an SMTP client with access to the outgoing mail queues. An MTA normally has a mail client component, which processes the outgoing mail queues, attempting to send mail for particular domains, based on time or events, such as new mail being placed in the queue or receipt of an ETRN command by the SMTP server component. The ODMR service processes the outgoing queue on request. The ISP provider side has normal SMTP server responsibilities, including generation of delivery failure notices (SMTP Specifications 2006).

MULTIPURPOSE INTERNET MAIL EXTENSIONS (MIME)

The RFC 821/ STD 10 standard specifies that data sent via SMTP is 7-bit ASCII data, with the high-order bit cleared to zero. This is adequate in most instances for the transmission of English text messages but is inadequate for non-English text or nontextual data.

There are two approaches to overcoming these limitations. In the first approach, the multipurpose Internet mail extensions (MIME) supplementary protocol was defined in RFC 1521 and RFC 1522, which specify a mechanism for encoding text and binary data as 7-bit ASCII within the mail envelope defined by the RFC 822 standard. MIME is also described in SMTP (2006).

In the second approach, the SMTP service extensions (RFC 1651, RFC 1652, and RFC 1653) define a mechanism to extend the capabilities of SMTP beyond the limitations imposed by the RFC 821 standard. The RFC 1651 document introduces a standard for a receiver-SMTP to inform a sender-SMTP, which service extensions it supports. New procedures modifies the RFC 821 standard to allow a client SMTP agent to request that the server responds with a list of the service extensions that it supports at the start of an SMTP session. If the server SMTP does not support the RFC 1651, it will respond with an error and the client may either terminate the session or attempt to start a session according to the rules of the RFC 821 standard. If the server does support the RFC 1651, it may also respond with a list of the service extensions that it supports. A registry of services is maintained by the Internet Assigned Numbers Authority (IANA 2006); the initial list defined in the RFC 1651 document contains those commands listed in RFC 1123 as optional for SMTP servers.

Specific extensions are defined in RFC 1652 and RFC 1653. A protocol for 8-bit text transmission (RFC 1652) allows an SMTP server to indicate that it can accept data consisting of 8-bit bytes. A server, which reports that this

Table 2: Simple Mail Transfer Protocol (SMTP) Reply Codes. Adapted from SMTP Specifications 2006.

Code	Description
Positive Completion Reply	
211	System status or system help reply
214	Help message
220	*Domain* service ready; ready to start TLS
221	*Domain* service closing transmission channel
250	OK, queuing for node *node* started; requested command completed
251	OK, no messages waiting for node *node*; user not local, will forward to *forwardpath*
252	OK, pending messages for node *node* started; cannot VRFY user (e.g., information is not local) but will take message for this user and attempt delivery
253	OK, *messages* pending messages for node *node* started
Positive Intermediate Reply	
354	Start mail input; end with `<CRLF>.<CRLF>`
355	Octet-offset is the transaction offset
Transient Negative Completion Reply	
421	*Domain* service not available, closing transmission channel
432	A password transition is needed
450	Requested mail action not taken: mailbox unavailable; ATRN request refused
451	Requested action aborted: local error in processing; unable to process ATRN request now
452	Requested action not taken: insufficient system storage
453	You have no mail
454	TLS not available due to temporary reason; encryption required for requested authentication mechanism
458	Unable to queue messages for node *node*
459	Node *node* not allowed: *reason*
Permanent Negative Completion Reply	
500	Command not recognized: *command*; Syntax error
501	Syntax error in parameters or arguments; no parameters allowed
502	Command not implemented
503	Bad sequence of commands
504	Command parameter temporarily not implemented
521	*Machine* does not accept mail
530	Must issue a STARTTLS command first; encryption required for requested authentication mechanism
534	Authentication mechanism is too weak
538	Encryption required for requested authentication mechanism
550	Requested action not taken (command is not executed): mailbox unavailable
551	User not local; please try *forwardpath*
552	Requested mail action aborted: exceeded storage allocation
553	Requested action not taken: mailbox name not allowed
554	Transaction failed

extension is available to a client, must leave the high-order bit of bytes received in an SMTP message unchanged if requested to do so by the client.

The MIME and SMTP service extension approaches are complementary. Following their procedures (RFC 1652), nontraditional SMTP agents can transmit messages, which are declared as consisting of 8-bit data rather than 7-bit data, when both the client and the server conform to the RFC 1651 or RFC 1652 options (or both). Whenever a client SMTP attempts to send 8-bit data to a server, which does not support this extension, the client SMTP must either encode the message contents into a 7-bit representation compliant with the MIME standard or return a permanent error to the user.

The SMTP service extension has the limitation on maximum length of a line (only up to 1,000 characters as required by the RFC 821 standard). The service extension also limits the use of non-ASCII characters to message headers, which are prohibited by the RFC 822 regulations.

The RFC 1653 document introduces the protocol for message size declaration that allows a server to inform a client of the maximum size message it can accept. If both server and client support the message size declaration extension, the client may declare an estimated size of the message to be transferred, and the server will return an error if the message is too large. Each of these SMTP service extensions is a draft standard protocol and each has a status of elective.

The MIME can be considered as a set of software functions that transforms non-ASCII data to ASCII characters and vice versa, as shown in Figure 4.

The MIME protocols define five header lines that can be added to the original header section to define the transformation parameters: MIME-version, content-type, content-transfer-encoding, content-id, and content-description (see Figure 5). Each header line is described in detail in the following sections.

MIME-Version

The header line MIME-Version: 1.1 declares that the message was composed using the (current) version 1.1 of the MIME protocol.

Content-Type

The header line Content-Type:`<type/subtype; parameters>` defines the type of data used in the body of the message. The identifiers of the content type and the content subtype are separated by a slash. Depending on the subtype, the header may contain other parameters. The MIME standard allows seven basic content types of data, the valid subtypes for each, and transfer encodings, which are listed in Table 3. Examples of the content-type headers can be found in Forouzan (2005).

Content-Transfer-Encoding

The Content-Transfer-Encoding:`<type>` header line defines the method to encode the messages into a bit-stream

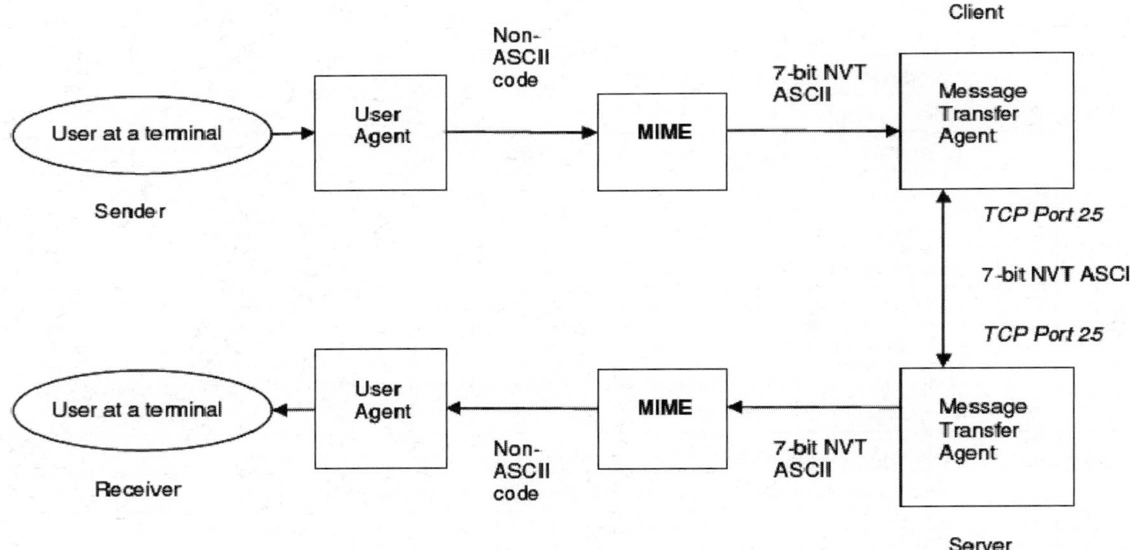

Figure 4: MIME functionality

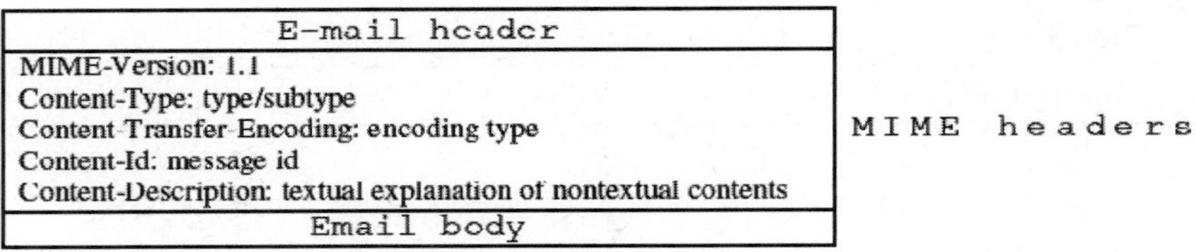

Figure 5: MIME header

Table 3: Data Types and Subtypes in a Multipurpose Internet Mail Extensions (MIME) Content-Type Header Declaration.

Type	Subtype	Description
Text	Plain	Unformatted 7-bit ASCII text; no transformation by MIME is needed
	HTML	HTML format
Multipart	Mixed	Body contains ordered parts of different data types
	Parallel	Body contains no-ordered parts of different data types
	Digest	Body contains ordered parts of different data types, but the default is message/RFC822
	Alternative	Parts are different versions of the same message
Message	RFC822	Body is an encapsulated message
	Partial	Body is a fragment of a bigger message
	External-Body	Body is a reference to another message
Image	JPEG	Image is in JPEG format
	GIF	Image is in GIF format
Video	MPEG	Video is in MPEG format
Audio	Basic	Single channel encoding of voice at 8 KHz
Application	PostScript	Adobe PostScript
	Octet-stream	General binary data (eight-bit bytes)

GIF = Graphics Interchange Format; HTML = Hypertext Markup Language; JPEG = Joint Photographic Experts Group; MPEG = Motion Picture Experts Group.

of 0s and 1s for transport. The five types of encoding are as follows:

- 7bit—for NVT ASCII characters and short lines of less than 1,000 characters.
- 8bit—for non-ASCII characters and short lines of less than 1,000 characters; the underlying SMTP protocol must be able to transfer 8-bit non-ASCII characters (this type is not recommended).
- binary—for non-ASCII characters with unlimited-length lines; this is 8-bit encoding. The underlying SMTP protocol must be able to transfer 8-bit non-ASCII characters (this type is not recommended).
- base64—for sending data made of bytes when the highest bit is not necessarily zero; 6-bit blocks of data are encoded into 8-bit printable ASCII characters (for details, see Tschabitscher 2006; Stevens 1993), which can then be sent as any type of character set supported by the underlying mail transfer mechanism.
- quoted-printable—for sending data that consist of mostly ASCII characters with a small non-ASCII portion; if a character is not ASCII, it is sent as three characters: the first character is the equal sign, and the next two are the hexadecimal representation of the byte.

Although the content type and encoding are independent, the RFC 1521 document recommends quoted-printable for text with non-ASCII data, and base64 for image, audio, video, and octet-stream application data. This allows maximum interoperability with RFC 821 conformant MTAs (Stevens, 1993).

Figure 6 shows an example of a multi-part message in MIME format with mixed subtypes.

Content-Id

The header line Content-Id: `id=<content-id>` uniquely identifies the whole message in a multiple message environment.

Content-Description

The header line Content-Description:`<description>` defines whether the body is image, audio, or video.

Security Scheme for MIME

The S/MIME is a security scheme for the MIME protocol. It was developed by RSA Security and is an alternative to the pretty good privacy (PGP) encryption and digital signature scheme that uses public-key cryptography. The S/MIME scheme was standardized by IETF. According to "Report of the IAB Security Architecture Workshop" (RFC 2316), the designated security mechanism for adding secured sections to MIME-encapsulated e-mail is security/multipart, as described in "Security Multiparts for MIME: Multipart/Signed and Multipart/Encrypted" (RFC 1847).

The S/MIME is widely used by large companies that need to standardize e-mail security for both interorganization and intraorganization mail exchange (Internet Engineering Task Force [IETF] SMIME, 2006). It requires establishing a public-key infrastructure either in-house or by using any of the public certificate authorities (Sheldon 2001).

```
From: "Smith, John" <jsmith@college.edu>
To: "Peter Adams" <peter_adams@hotmail.com>
Subject: CS Mid Term
Date: Fri, 3 Mar 2006 09:08:10 -0500
MIME-Version: 1.0
Content-Type: multipart/alternative;
        boundary="----_=_NextPart_001_01C3AF7F.35820A9B"

Received: from EXCHANGEMAIL.COLLEGE.EDU ([67.251.112.30]) by
bay0-mc10-f2.bay0.hotmail.com with Microsoft SMTPSVC(6.0.3790.211); Fri, 3
Mar 2006 06:08:12 -0800
X-Message-Info: JGTYoYF78jEHjJx36Oi8+Z3TmmkSEdPtfpLB7P/ybN8=
Content-class: urn:content-classes:message
X-MimeOLE: Produced By Microsoft Exchange V6.5.7226.0
X-MS-Has-Attach: X-MS-TNEF-Correlator: Thread-Topic: CS Mid Term
Thread-Index: AcY+qoksOm67V+jHSd+jwoRpQ5vCCwAICufp
References: <BAY108-F243FC3114EBD6165216203E9EA0@phx.gbl>
Return-Path: jsmith@college.edu
X-OriginalArrivalTime: 03 Mar 2006 14:08:12.0085 (UTC)
FILETIME=[E827E650:01C63ECB]

This is a multi-part message in MIME format.

------_=_NextPart_001_01C3AF7F.35820A9B
Content-Type: text/plain;
        charset="utf-8"
Content-Transfer-Encoding: base64

RGVhciBTdHVkZW50LA0KIA0KVG9uaWdodCBhZnRlciBvdXIgQ1M1NTMgY2xhc3MgKGF0IDc6MzAg
UE0pIHlvdSBhcmUgaW52aXRlZCB0byB2aXNpdCBvdXIgY29sbGVnZSBJVCBMQU4gQ2VudGVyIGxv
Y2F0ZWQgaW4gdGhlIFNUSCBidWlsZGluZyBvbiB0aGUgZmlyc3QgZmxvb3IgbmVhci==

------_=_NextPart_001_01C3AF7F.35820A9B
Content-Type: text/html;
        charset="utf-8"
Content-Transfer-Encoding: base64

PCFET0NUWVBFIEhUTUwgUFVCTElDICItLy9XM0MvL0RURCBIVE1MIDQuMCBUcmFuc2l0aW9uYWwv
L0VOIj48SFRNTD48SEVBRD48TUVUQSBIVFRQLUVRVUlWPSJDb250ZW50LVR5cGUiIENPTlRFT1Q9
InRleHQvaHRtbDsgY2hhcnNldD11dGYtOCI+PC9IRUFEPjxCT0RZPjxESVY+RGVhciBTdHVkZW50
LDwvREl=
```

Figure 6: An example of a multi-part message in MIME format with mixed subtypes

MAIL TRANSMISSION TYPES

The SMTP (RFC821) and the Standard for the Format of Advanced Research Project Agency (ARPA) Internet Text Messages (RFC822) specify that a set of "Received" lines will be prepended to the headers of electronic mail messages as they are transported through the Internet (Mail Parameters 2006). The received line may optionally include either or both a "via" phrase or a "with" phrase (or both). The legal value for the "via" phrase is intended to indicate the link or physical medium over which the message was transferred (e.g., the UUCP link type should be specified for the Unix-to-Unix Copy Program). The "with" phrase is intended to indicate the protocol or logical process that has been used to transfer the message (e.g., SMTP or ESMTP parameters are used respectively for SMTP [RFC821] or SMTP with service extensions [RFC1869] protocol types).

MAIL ACCESS MODES

To reach its final destination, an e-mail message should be handled by a mail server, the mail access protocol, and the mail client. A general concept of how these components work together is described in "Accessing Your Mail" (QUALCOMM 1997).

An Internet mail server (known as the mail transfer agent, described earlier) is the software responsible for transmitting and receiving e-mail across the Internet. The MTA software is run on a computer that has a connection to the Internet and is managed, monitored, and backed up by ISPs or a company's information services staff. Some mail servers store mail only until the user retrieves it, whereas others store user mail permanently. An e-mail user typically uses a mail client program to interact with the mail server (Rose 1993).

A mail client (known as the mail user agent, described earlier) is the software that a user employs to read, send, file, and otherwise process the electronic mail. Usually running on a user's desktop computer, the mail client also manages related e-mail data (address books, spelling dictionaries, and stationery). The mail client connects to a mail server to retrieve new mail. Some mail clients also use the mail server to store all e-mail (Rose 1993).

The communication between the mail client and mail server is regulated by the mail access protocol, a standardized set of transmitted commands and responses sent over many different types of network connections. The protocol commands (created for managing access to the Internet e-mail only) depend on a design approach that can significantly affect the manner, modes, characteristics, and capabilities of the interaction between the mail client and mail server (QUALCOMM 1997). The SMTP protocol handles the task of the actual sending of e-mail on the Internet.

A mail access protocol operates in three common modes that differ in where and how a user stores and processes his or her mail (QUALCOMM 1997):

- **Offline mode**—e-mail is downloaded from a temporary storage on the mail server to the user's computer. After download, the mail is deleted from the server.
- **Online mode**—user's e-mail, his or her inbox, and all filed mail remains permanently on the mail server. By connecting to the server and establishing an e-mail session, the user can download a temporary copy of his or her e-mail and read it, or send e-mail. Once the connection is finished, the copy is erased from user's computer, and only the original remains on the server.
- **Disconnected/resynchronization mode**—combines both offline and online modes. A copy of the user's e-mail is downloaded to his or her computer(s), and the original message remains on the mail server. The user can change a local copy of his or her e-mail on any computer, then resynchronize all copies, including the original e-mail message on the server and copies on additional computers.

All three modes offer multiplatform support. This includes support for existing platforms such as UNIX, Microsoft Windows, and Apple Macintosh, and future platforms such as Java Mail Service–based network computers. All three modes, including their advantages and disadvantages, are discussed in detail in "Accessing Your Mail" (QUALCOMM 1997). Two dedicated protocols (POP3 and IMAP4) of retrieving e-mail are considered in the next section.

Instead of using POP3 or IMAP4, on some systems it is possible for a user to have direct server access to e-mail. This is most commonly done on UNIX systems, where protocols like TELNET or NFS (Network File System) can give a user shared access to mailboxes on a server (TCP/IP Guide 2006). Being the oldest method of e-mail access, it provides the user (who must be on the Internet to read e-mail) with the most control over his or her mailbox, and is well-suited to those who must access mail from many locations.

MAIL ACCESS PROTOCOLS

POP3

POP is used on the Internet to retrieve e-mail from a mail server. There are two versions of POP. The first, known as POP2 (RFC 937), became a standard in the mid-1980s and requires SMTP to send messages. Nowadays it has a status of "not recommended." The newer version, POP3 (RFC 1725), can be used with or without SMTP.

POP was designed primarily to support the offline access mode (RFC 1939). Typically, e-mail arrives from the network and is placed in the user's inbox on the server. POP is then used to transfer the mail from the user's inbox on the server to the user's computer. POP is designed so that mail client software can determine which messages have been previously downloaded from the server. The mail client can then download only new messages. POP also provides the ability to selectively delete messages from the server. It can be used by a mail client to perform basic resynchronization of the inbox on the server and on the user's computers. The client can leave the most recent messages on the server after they have been downloaded. These messages can then be downloaded a second time to a second computer. Additionally, some POP implementations provide optional features, such as allowing users to download only headers at one session, to review the topics, and then download selected bodies and attachments in a subsequent session to minimize connection times over slow links (QUALCOMM 1997).

POP servers are widely available both commercially and as freeware on a number of operating systems. Moreover, there are almost no interoperability issues between POP servers and mail clients, and users can use any POP mail client with any POP server. All ISPs support and use POP.

In the end-to-end application related to SMTP, the server must be available whenever a client (sender) transmits mail. If the SMTP server resides on an end-user PC or workstation, that computer must be running the server when the client is trying to send mail. For some operating systems (e.g., when a server program is activated on the VM SMTP service virtual machine or the MAIL program on DOS), the server becomes unavailable and unreachable by the SMTP client (SMTP, 2004). The mail-sending process will fail in these cases. Especially, it is important for single-user systems that the client has an accessible mailbox on various types of server (RFC 1725).

One of the simplest approaches to resolve this problem is to allow the end user to run a client program, which communicates with a server program on a host. This server program acts as both a sender and a receiver SMTP (SMTP 2004). Here the end-user mailbox resides on the server, and the server system is capable of sending mail to other users.

In another approach, the SMTP server function has to be off-loaded from the end-user workstation, but not the SMTP client function. In this case, the user has a mailbox that resides on a server system, and he can send mail directly from the workstation. To collect mail from the mailbox, the user must connect to the mail server system.

The current post office protocol version 3 (RFC 1725) is a draft standard protocol, and its status is elective. POP3 extensions are described in RFC 2449. POP3 security options are introduced in RFC 2595. The RFC 1734 describes the optional AUTH command for indicating an authentication mechanism to the POP3 server, performing an authentication protocol exchange, and optionally negotiating a protection mechanism for subsequent protocol interactions (Sheldon 2001).

IMAP4

IMAP is a protocol for retrieving e-mail messages (RFC 1064). The IMAP4 version is similar to POP3 but supports some additional features. For example, with IMAP4, the user can search through his or her e-mail messages for key words while the messages are still on the mail server.

The user can then choose which messages to download to his or her machine.

IMAP uses SMTP as its transport mechanism. Following the simple analogy (Sheldon, 2001), IMAP servers are like post offices, whereas SMTP is like the postal carriers. IMAP uses TCP to take advantage of its reliable data delivery services, which are allocated on the TCP port 143. The latest IMAP version 4, revision 1 (IMAP4rev1) is defined in RFC 2060.

IMAP has many advanced features, such as the ability to address mail not by arrival number, but by using attributes (e.g., "Download the latest message from Smith"). This feature allows the mailbox to be structured more like a relational database system rather than a sequence of messages (Tanenbaum, 2003). Authentication mechanisms are described in RFC 1731. Security issues have been introduced in "IMAP4/POP Authorization for Simple Challenge/Response" (RFC 2195), "IMAP4 Login Referrals" (RFC 2221), and "IMAP4 Implementation and Best Practices" (RFC 2683).

SMTP VULNERABILITIES

The processes of retrieving e-mail from servers and managing data communication through the Internet are vulnerable to various attacks. A review of vulnerabilities can be found in "Vulnerability Tutorials" (2006) released by the Saint Corporation. The Common Vulnerabilities and Exposures (CVE) organization provides a list of standardized names for SMTP vulnerabilities (for both CVE entries and CAN candidates) and other information security exposures (CVE 2006). Summaries of major SMTP vulnerability problems are discussed in (Riabov 2006).

SMTP was designed in an era when security of the Internet was not an issue. As a result, the SMTP protocol includes no robust security mechanism. For example, someone can use the TELNET protocol to connect directly to an SMTP server on port 25. The SMTP commands and replies can all be sent as text, and, therefore, a person can manually perform a mail transaction. This is useful for debugging, but also makes abuse of a wide open SMTP server trivially easy. Since spammers often do not want to be identified, they employ spoofing techniques to make it more difficult to identify them (Kozierok 2006). Nowadays, most modern SMTP servers incorporate several security features to avoid vulnerability problems.

A security audit of selected SMTP problems has been provided by the U.S. Computer Emergency Readiness Team (CERT) Coordination Center operated by Carnegie Mellon University, and E-Soft. Detailed information about vulnerability problems, possible actions of an attacker or spammer, recommendations for downloading updated versions of software, examples of code modification, and test results can be found on the CERT (2006) and Security Space ("SMTP Problems," 2006) Web sites.

The vulnerability problems can be grouped into several general high-risk categories: buffer overflow; redirection attacks through the firewall; bounced "piping" attacks; and host-shell-gaining attacks. The medium-to-high risk category includes denial-of-service attacks. Low-to-medium-risk categories include mail relaying on the remote SMTP server, mail-queue manipulation attacks; debug-mode-leak category; and crashing antivirus-software attack ("SMTP Problems" 2006). Most SMTP-specific vulnerabilities occur from misapplied or unapplied patches related to Sendmail installations or misconfigured Sendmail daemons on the SMTP servers (Campbell et al. 2003).

ISPs restrict access to their outgoing mail servers to provide better service to their customers and prevent spam from being sent through their mail servers. There are several methods for establishing restrictions that could result in denying users' access to their outgoing mail server.

Originally (see RFC 821), e-mail servers (configured for SMTP relay) did not verify the claimed sender identity and would simply pass the mail on with whatever return address was specified. Bulk mailers have taken advantage of this to send huge volumes of mail with bogus return addresses. This results in slowing down servers.

To fix the problem, the origin of a spam e-mail should be identified. An e-mail message typically transports through a set of SMTP servers (including the sender's and receiver's servers) before reaching the destination host. Along this pass, messages get "stamped" by the intermediate SMTP servers. The stamps release tracking information that can be identified in the mail headers. Mismatches between the IP addresses and the domain names in the header could unveil the real source of spam mail. The real domain names that correspond to the indicated IP addresses can be found out by executing a reverse DNS lookup. Modern mail programs have incorporated this functionality, which generates a Received: header line that includes the identity of the attacker (see examples in Campbell et al. 2003).

Antispoofing measures are under active development. Mail Abuse Prevention System (MAPS) and Open Relay Behavior-Modification System (ORBS) provide testing, reporting and cataloging of e-mail servers configured for SMTP relay. These organizations maintain real-time blackhole lists (RBL) of mail servers with problematic histories. For protection and security purposes, companies may configure their SMTP servers and other e-mail service systems in such manner that any mail coming from RBL-blacklisted mail servers is automatically rejected (Campbell et al. 2003). Other initiatives for restricting the sender address spoofing include SPF, Hotmail domain cookies, and Microsoft's caller ID. The analysis of various SMTP security issues can be found in (Riabov 2006).

STANDARDS, ORGANIZATIONS, AND ASSOCIATIONS

Internet Assigned Numbers Authority

The IANA (2006) provides the central coordinating functions of the global Internet for the public needs. The IANA organization maintains a registry of the following services:

- Domain name services
- Database of indexes by Top-Level Domains code
- "Whois" service of domain name recognition
- IP address assignment services (for both IPv4 and IPv6)
- Protocol number assignment services

Internet Engineering Task Force Working Groups

Internet electronic mail was originally defined in the RFC821 standard as a part of the IETF project. Since August 1982, e-mail standards declared in this document were updated and revised by the IETF Detailed Revision/Update of Message Standards (DRUMS) Working Group. The group is also searching new directions in the electronic message communication through the Internet. The latest SMTP documents (including RFCs) can be found on the DRUMS Web site (IETF DRUMS 2006).

The IETF Message Tracking Protocol (MSGTRK) Working Group (IETF MSGTRK 2006) is designing diagnostic protocols that a sender can use to request information from servers about the submission, transport, and delivery of a message, regardless of its status. The "Deliver by SMTP Service Extension" document (RFC 2852) specifies extensions to define message delivery time for making a decision to drop the message if it is not delivered within a specific time period. For diagnostic purposes, the "diagnostic-type" parameter (e.g., smtp for the Internet Mail) is defined for use in the SMTP delivery status notification (see RFC1891).

The IETF S/MIME Mail Security (SMIME) Working Group is developing S/MIME security standards. The latest S/MIME documents (including RFCs) can be found on the SMIME Web site (IETF SMIME, 2006).

Internet Mail Consortium

The Internet Mail Consortium Web site (IMC 2006) publishes a complete list of electronic mail-related requests for comments documents (RFCs).

Mitre Corporation

The Mitre Corporation publishes a list of standardized names for all publicly known vulnerabilities and security exposures known as Common Vulnerabilities and Exposures (CVE 2006).

CONCLUSION

SMTP is an application protocol from the TCP/IP protocol suite that enables the support of e-mail on the Internet. Mail is sent by a series of request–response transactions between a client and a server. The transactions pass the message, which is composed of header and body, and the envelope (SMTP source and destination addresses). The header contains the mail address(es), which consists of two parts: a local address (also known as a "user mailbox") and a domain name. Both SMTP client and SMTP server require a user agent (UA) and a mail transfer agent (MTA). The MTA function is transferring the mail across the Internet. The command–response mechanism is used by SMTP to transfer messages between an MTA client and an MTA server in three stages: connection establishment, mail transfer, and connection termination. The envelope is transmitted separately from the message itself using the MAIL and RCPT commands. MIME, which is an extension of SMTP, allows the transfer of non-ASCII (multimedia) messages. POP3 and the IMAP 4 together with SMTP are used to receive mail by a mail server and hold it for hosts. The SMTP's lack of security is a problem for businesses. The security in the SMTP transactions can be supported by S/MIME and other methods.

GLOSSARY

Body: The text of an e-mail message. The body of a message follows the header information.

Client: Any application program used to retrieve information from a server. Internet clients include World Wide Web browsers, Usenet newsreaders, and e-mail programs.

Client–server: The relationship between two application programs. One program, the server, is responsible for servicing requests from the other program, the client.

Delivery status notification (DSN): An extended SMTP service that provides information about the delivery status of an e-mail message to the sender.

Disconnected–Resynchronization Mode: A mail-access mode in which mail is synchronized between a server and a client computer. By synchronizing mail on the server, users can access their own mail from any computer that has access to the server where the mail is stored.

Domain name system (DNS): A behind-the-scenes Internet service that translates Internet domain names to their corresponding IP addresses, and vice versa.

E-mail client: An application that runs on a personal computer or workstation and enables the sender to send, receive, and organize e-mail. It is called a client because e-mail systems are based on a client–server architecture. Mail is sent from many clients to a central server, which reroutes the mail to its intended destination.

Encapsulated address: This address provides a way to send the e-mail to a site acting as a gateway for another site while indicating the server to which the message eventually needs to be sent. An encapsulated address consists of an address within an address; the outer address directs the mail to the gateway, which uses the inner address to determine where to send the e-mail. Because the Exchange Internet Mail Service (IMS) uses SMTP as its e-mail protocol, mails sent to an IMS will use encapsulated SMTP as their addressing scheme.

Gateway: Software that translates data from the standards of one system to the standards of another. For example, a gateway might exchange and convert Internet e-mail to X.400 e-mail.

Header: Part of an e-mail message that precedes the body of the message and provides the message originator, date, and time.

Internet message access protocol (IMAP): An Internet protocol used by mail clients for retrieving e-mail messages stored on servers. The latest version, IMAP4, is similar to POP3 but supports some additional features; for example, a user can search through his e-mail messages for key words while the messages are still on mail server. The user can then choose which messages to download to his or her computer. While IMAP-based applications can operate in offline mode, they typically operate in online or disconnected–resynchronization mode.

Mail access protocol: A standardized set of commands and responses responsible for communication between the mail client and mail server.

Mailbox: A file where e-mail messages are stored.

Mail client: The software used to read, file, send, and otherwise process e-mail, typically running on a user's desktop computer.

Mail delivery agent (MDA): The software that runs mail-delivery processes on the machine where a users' mailbox is located. Often, that delivery is performed directly by the mail transfer agent (MTA), which then serves a secondary role as an MDA. Examples of separate mail delivery agents include Procmail, Deliver, and Cyrdeliver.

Mail relaying: A legitimate practice in which e-mail is routed to an intermediate mail server, which then delivers it to the recipient's mail server. For example, a company can have several servers and one of them is designated as a mail gateway to the Internet. Any e-mail sent to the company would arrive at the gateway server and then be relayed to the appropriate server for delivery to the recipient. Malicious users sometimes try to perform unauthorized mail relaying.

Mail server: A computer typically managed by an ISP or information services department that handles receipt and delivery of e-mail messages. It also may store mail for the user on a temporary or permanent basis.

Mail transfer agent (MTA): The software that is running on a mail server that relays, and delivers mail.

Mail user agent (MUA): The software (also known as the mail client) used to read, file, send, and process e-mail, typically running on a desktop computer.

Multipurpose Internet mail extensions (MIME): An Internet standard that provides the transfer of nontext information, such as sounds and graphics, and non-U.S. English (such as Cyrillic, Chinese, or Japanese) via e-mail.

Network virtual terminal (NVT): A set of facilities for establishing communication by using the TCP/IP protocols

On-demand mail relay (ODMR): A restricted profile of SMTP described in RFC 2645.

Port: In a software device, a port is a specific memory address that is mapped to a virtual networking cable. Ports allow multiple types of traffic to be transmitted to a single IP address. SMTP traditionally uses port 25 for e-mail communication.

Post office protocol (POP): A protocol used to retrieve e-mail from a mail server in offline mode. An e-mail client that implements the POP protocol downloads all new mail from a mail server, terminates the network connection, and processes all mail offline at the client computer. The current version, POP3 can be used with or without SMTP.

Server: A host computer that provides resources to client computers.

Simple mail transfer protocol (SMTP): A protocol widely used to exchange e-mail between e-mail servers on the Internet.

Spam: Undesired junk e-mail or junk postings offering dubious business deals.

User agent (UA): An SMTP component that prepares the message, creates the envelope, and puts the message in the envelope.

CROSS REFERENCES

See *E-mail and Instant Messaging*; *Internet Domain Name System*; *TCP/IP Suite*.

REFERENCES

Campbell, P., B. Calvert, and S. Boswell. 2003. *Security+ guide to network security fundamentals*. Boston: Cisco Learning Institute.

CERT Computer Emergency Readiness Team. 2006. Vulnerability database. http://www.cert.org/ (accessed March 11, 2006).

Cisco SMTP. 2006. http://www.cisco.com/univercd/cc/td/doc/product/software/ioss390/ios390ug/ugsmtp.htm (accessed March 11, 2006).

Comer, D. F. 2005. *Internetworking with TCP/IP, Vol. 1: Principles, protocols, and architecture*, 5th edition. Upper Saddle River, NJ: Prentice Hall.

CVE: Common vulnerabilities and exposures. 2006. Mitre Corporation. Retrieved March 11, 2006, from http://cve.mitre.org/ (accessed March 11, 2006).

Forouzan, B. A. 2005. *TCP/IP protocol suite*, 3rd edition. New York: McGraw-Hill.

How to set SMTP security options in Windows 2000. 2006. http://support.microsoft.com/default.aspx?scid=http://support.microsoft.com:80/support/kb/articles/Q303/7/76.ASP&NoWebContent=1 (accessed March 11, 2006).

IETF DRUMS. 2006. Internet Engineering Task Force Working Group: Detailed Revision/Update of Message Standards (DRUMS). http://www.ietf.org/html.chapters/OLD/drums-chapter.html (accessed March 11, 2006).

IETF MSGTRK. 2006. Internet Engineering Task Force Working Group. Message Tracking Protocol (MSGTRK). http://www.ietf.org/html.chapters/OLD/msgtrk-chapter.html (accessed March 11, 2006).

IETF SMIME. 2006. Internet Engineering Task Force Working Group. S/MIME Mail Security (SMIME). http://www.ietf.org/html.chapters/smime-chapter.html (accessed March 11, 2006).

Internet Assigned Numbers Authority (IANA). 2006. http://www.iana.org/ (accessed March 11, 2006).

Internet Mail Consortium (IMC). 2006. http://www.imc.org/rfcs.html (accessed March 11, 2006).

Kozierok, C. M. 2006. TCP/IP electronic mail delivery protocol: The simple mail transfer protocol (SMTP). http://www.tcpipguide.com/free/t_TCPIPElectronicMailDeliveryProtocolTheSimpleMailTr.htm (accessed March 11, 2006).

Mail Parameters. 2006. http://www.iana.org/assignments/mail-parameters (accessed March 11, 2006).

QUALCOMM. 1997. Accessing your mail when and where you want on the Internet. http://www.eudora.com/pdf_docs/primer.pdf (accessed March 11, 2006).

RFC821 (STD 10): Simple mail transfer protocol. 1982. http://www.ietf.org/rfc/rfc821.txt (accessed March 11, 2006).

RFC822 (STD 11): Standard for the format of ARPA—Internet Text Messages. 1982. http://www.ietf.org/rfc/rfc822.txt (accessed March 11, 2006).

RFC876. Survey of SMTP implementations. 1983. http://www.ietf.org/rfc/rfc876.txt (accessed March 11, 2006).

RFC937: Post office protocol—Version 2. 1985. http://www.ietf.org/rfc/rfc937.txt (accessed March 11, 2006).

RFC1064: Interactive mail access protocol—Version 2. 1988. http://www.ietf.org/rfc/rfc1064.txt (accessed March 11, 2006).

RFC1123: Requirements for Internet hosts—application and support. 1989. http://www.ietf.org/rfc/rfc1123.txt (accessed March 11, 2006).

RFC1274: The COSINE and Internet X.500 schema. 1991. http://www.ietf.org/rfc/rfc1274.txt (accessed March 11, 2006).

RFC1327: Mapping between X.400 (1988)/ISO10021 and RFC 822. 1992. http://www.ietf.org/rfc/rfc1327.txt (accessed March 11, 2006).

RFC1425: SMTP service extensions. 1993. http://www.ietf.org/rfc/rfc1425.txt (accessed March 11, 2006).

RFC1521: MIME (multipurpose internet mail extensions), part one: Mechanisms for specifying and describing the format of Internet message bodies. 1993. http://www.ietf.org/rfc/rfc1521.txt (accessed March 11, 2006).

RFC1522: MIME (multipurpose Internet mail extensions), part two: Message header extensions for non-ASCII Text. 1993. http://www.ietf.org/rfc/rfc1522.txt (accessed March 11, 2006).

RFC1651: SMTP service extensions. 1994. http://www.ietf.org/rfc/rfc1651.txt (accessed March 11, 2006).

RFC1652: SMTP service extension for 8bit-MIME transport. 1994. http://www.ietf.org/rfc/rfc1652.txt (accessed March 11, 2006).

RFC1653: SMTP Service extension for message size declaration. 1994. http://www.ietf.org/rfc/rfc1653.txt (accessed March 11, 2006).

RFC1725: Post office protocol—version 3, RFC 1725. 1994. http://www.ietf.org/rfc/rfc1725.txt (accessed March 11, 2006).

RFC1731: IMAP4 authentication mechanisms. 1994. http://www.ietf.org/rfc/rfc1731.txt (accessed March 11, 2006).

RFC1734: POP3 AUTHentication command. 1994. http://www.ietf.org/rfc/rfc1734.txt (accessed March 11, 2006).

RFC1845: SMTP service extension for Checkpoint/Restart. 1995. http://www.ietf.org/rfc/rfc1845.txt (accessed March 11, 2006).

RFC1846: SMTP 521 reply code. 1995. http://www.ietf.org/rfc/rfc1846.txt (accessed March 11, 2006).

RFC1847: Security multiparts for MIME: Multipart/signed and multipart/encrypted. 1995. http://www.ietf.org/rfc/rfc1847.txt (accessed March 11, 2006).

RFC1869: SMTP service extensions. 1995. http://www.ietf.org/rfc/rfc1869.txt (accessed March 11, 2006).

RFC1870: SMTP service extension for message size declaration. 1995. from http://www.ietf.org/rfc/rfc1870.txt (accessed March 11, 2006).

RFC1891: SMTP service extension for delivery status notification. 1996. http://www.ietf.org/rfc/rfc1891.txt (accessed March 11, 2006).

RFC1893: Enhanced mail system status codes. 1996. http://www.ietf.org/rfc/rfc1893.txt (accessed March 11, 2006).

RFC1939 (STD 53): Post office protocol, Version 3. 1996. http://www.ietf.org/rfc/rfc1939.txt (accessed March 11, 2006).

RFC1985: SMTP Service extension for remote message queue starting. 1996. http://www.ietf.org/rfc/rfc1985.txt (accessed March 11, 2006).

RFC2033: Local mail transfer protocol. 1996. http://www.ietf.org/rfc/rfc2033.txt (accessed March 11, 2006).

RFC2034: SMTP service extension for returning enhanced status codes. 1996. http://www.ietf.org/rfc/rfc2034.txt (accessed March 11, 2006).

RFC2060: Internet message access protocol, Version 4rev1. 1996. http://www.ietf.org/rfc/rfc2060.txt (accessed March 11, 2006).

RFC2195: IMAP/POP authorization for simple challenge/response. 1997. http://www.ietf.org/rfc/rfc2195.txt (accessed March 11, 2006).

RFC2221: IMAP4 login referrals. 1997. http://www.ietf.org/rfc/rfc2221.txt (accessed March 11, 2006).

RFC2316: Report of the IAB Security Architecture Workshop. 1998. http://www.ietf.org/rfc/rfc2316.txt (accessed March 11, 2006).

RFC2449: POP3 extension mechanism. 1998. http://www.ietf.org/rfc/rfc2449.txt (accessed March 11, 2006).

RFC2554: SMTP service extension for authentication. 1999. http://www.ietf.org/rfc/rfc2554.txt (accessed March 11, 2006).

RFC2595: Using TSL with IMAP, POP3 and ACAP. 1999. http://www.ietf.org/rfc/rfc2595.txt (accessed March 11, 2006).

RFC2645: On-demand mail relay (ODMR) SMTP with dynamic IP addresses. 1999. http://www.ietf.org/rfc/rfc2645.txt (accessed March 11, 2006).

RFC2683: IMAP4 implementation and best practices. 1999. http://www.ietf.org/rfc/rfc2683.txt (accessed March 11, 2006).

RFC2821: Simple mail transfer protocol. 2001. http://www.ietf.org/rfc/rfc2821.txt (accessed March 11, 2006).

RFC2822: Internet Message Format. 2001. http://www.ietf.org/rfc/rfc2822.txt (accessed March 11, 2006).

RFC2852: Deliver by SMTP service extension. 2000. http://www.ietf.org/rfc/rfc2852.txt (accessed March 11, 2006).

RFC2920: SMTP service extension for command pipelining. 2000. http://www.ietf.org/rfc/rfc2920.txt (accessed March 11, 2006).

RFC3030: SMTP service extensions for transmission of large and binary MIME messages. 2000. http://www.ietf.org/rfc/rfc3030.txt (accessed March 11, 2006).

RFC3207: SMTP service extension for secure SMTP over transport layer security. 2002. http://www.ietf.org/rfc/rfc3207.txt (accessed March 11, 2006).

Riabov, V. V. 2006. Simple mail transfer protocol. In: *Handbook on information security, volume 1: Key concepts, infrastructures, standards and protocols*, edited by Hossein Bidgoli. Hoboken, NJ: John Wiley & Sons, pp. 878–900.

Rose, M. T. 1993. *The Internet message, closing the book with electronic mail*. Upper Saddle River, NJ: Prentice Hall.

Sheldon, T. 2001. *McGraw-Hill encyclopedia of networking and telecommunications*. New York: McGraw-Hill.

Simple Mail Transfer Protocol (SMTP). (2004). http://ulla.mcgill.ca/arts150/arts150bs.htm (accessed September 24, 2004).

SMTP problems. (2006). E-Soft, Inc. http://www.securityspace.com/smysecure/catdescr.html?cat=SMTP+problems (accessed March 11, 2006).

SMTP specifications. 2006. http://www.networksorcery.com/enp/protocol/smtp.htm (accessed March 11, 2006).

Stevens, W. R. 1993. *TCP/IP illustrated: The protocols, volume I*. Boston, MA: Addison-Wesley.

Tanenbaum, A. S. 2003. *Computer Networks*, 4th edition. Upper Saddle River, NJ: Prentice Hall PTR.

TCP/IP Guide. 2006. TCP/IP electronic mail access and retrieval protocols and methods. http://www.tcpipguide.com/free/t_TCPIPElectronicMailAccessandRetrievalProtocolsandM.htm (accessed March 11, 2006).

Tschabitscher, H. 2006. How base64 encoding works. In: *Your guide to e-mail*. http://email.about.com/cs/standards/a/base64_encoding.htm (accessed March 11, 2006).

Vulnerability Tutorials. 2006. Saint Corporation. http://www.saintcorporation.com/demo/saint/vulnerability_tutorials.html (accessed March 11, 2006).

What is SMTP? 2006. http://whatis.techtarget.com/definition/0,289893,sid9_gci214219,00.html (accessed March 11, 2006).

Wikipedia. 2006. Mail delivery agent. http://en.wikipedia.org/wiki/Mail_Delivery_Agent (accessed March 11, 2006).

FURTHER READING

Antirelay Parse. 2006. Sendmail organization, antirelay rules. http://www.sendmail.org/antirelay.Parse0.txt (accessed March 11, 2006).

Authentication error in SMTP service could allow mail relaying. 2001. Microsoft Security Bulletin, MS01-037. http://www.microsoft.com/technet/security/bulletin/MS01-037.mspx (accessed March 11, 2006).

Bastille Linux Project. 2006. Open Source Development Network. http://sourceforge.net/projects/bastille-linux/

Bastille Project. 2006. http://www.bastille-linux.org/ (accessed March 11, 2006).

CA Vulnerability Information Center. 2000. @Work SmartServer3 SMTP vulnerability. http://www3.ca.com/securityadvisor/vulninfo/Vuln.aspx?ID=1972 (accessed March 11, 2006).

Fugatt, M. 2002. Blocking incoming mail using Microsoft Exchange 2000. Tutorials: Exchange 2000, Pentech Office Solutions. http://www.msexchange.org/tutorials/MF014.html (accessed March 11, 2006).

Fugatt, M. 2002. Understanding relaying and spam with Exchange 2000. Tutorials: Exchange 2000, Pentech Office Solutions. http://www.msexchange.org/tutorials/MF005.html (accessed March 11, 2006).

IMAP Information Center. 2006. http://www.washington.edu/imap/ (accessed March 11, 2006).

Microsoft Security Bulletins. 2006. http://www.microsoft.com/technet/security/bulletin/ (accessed March 11, 2006).

Raynal, F. 2000. Bastille Linux, MISC Magazine. http://www.security-labs.org/index.php3?page=103 (accessed March 11, 2006).

RFC1090: SMTP on X.25. 1989. http://www.ietf.org/rfc/rfc1090.txt (accessed March 11, 2006).

RFC1730: Internet message access protocol—Version 4. 1994. http://www.ietf.org/rfc/rfc1730.txt (accessed March 11, 2006).

RFC1733: Distributed electronic mail models in IMAP4. 1994. http://www.ietf.org/rfc/rfc1733.txt (accessed March 11, 2006).

RFC1830: SMTP service extensions for transmission of large and binary MIME messages.1995. http://www.ietf.org/rfc/rfc1830.txt (accessed March 11, 2006).

RFC2045: MIME, part one: Format of Internet message bodies. 1996. http://www.ietf.org/rfc/rfc2045.txt (accessed March 11, 2006).

RFC2046: MIME, part two: Media types. 1996. http://www.ietf.org/rfc/rfc2046.txt (accessed March 11, 2006).

RFC2047: MIME, part three: Message header extensions for non-ASCII text. 1996. http://www.ietf.org/rfc/rfc2047.txt (accessed March 11, 2006).

RFC2048: MIME, part four: Registration procedures. 1996. http://www.ietf.org/rfc/rfc2048.txt (accessed March 11, 2006).

RFC2049: MIME, part five: Conformance criteria and examples. 1996. http://www.ietf.org/rfc/rfc2049.txt (accessed March 11, 2006).

RFC2197: SMTP service extension for command pipelining. 1997. http://www.ietf.org/rfc/rfc2197.txt (accessed March 11, 2006).

RFC2442: The batch SMTP media type. 1998. http://www.ietf.org/rfc/rfc2442.txt (accessed March 11, 2006).

RFC2487: SMTP service extension for secure SMTP over TLS. 1999. http://www.ietf.org/rfc/rfc2487.txt (accessed March 11, 2006).

RFC2505: Anti-spam recommendations for SMTP MTAs. 1999. http://www.ietf.org/rfc/rfc2505.txt (accessed March 11, 2006).

RFC3461: Simple mail transfer protocol (SMTP) service extension for delivery status notifications (DSNs. 2003. http://www.ietf.org/rfc/rfc3461.txt (accessed March 11, 2006).

Setting SMTP Security. 2006. Texoma, Inc. http://help.texoma.net/imail/user/setting_smtp_security.htm (accessed March 11, 2006).

SMTP Tutorial at RAD Data Communications. (1998). http://www.rad.com/networks/1998/smtp/smtp.htm (accessed March 11, 2006).

The IMAP Connection. 2006. http://www.imap.org/ (accessed March 11, 2006).

What is SMTP Security? 2006. http://help.westelcom.com/faq/what_is_smtp.htm (accessed March 11, 2006).

IP Multicast

Emilia Rosti, *Università degli Studi di Milano, Italy*

INTRODUCTION

IP multicast is an internetwork service that provides efficient delivery of data from one or more sources to a set of recipients, commonly known as a group (Deering 1989). Live video/audio streaming (for example, videoconferencing and collaborative groupware, webcasting), distribution of large amounts of data (for example, software updates to a community of users and applications with shared data, such as whiteboards), periodic data distribution or data feeds (for example, newspaper/magazine distribution, and sport or stock quotes), Web server updates, pay-per-view services (for example, video on demand), and distributed videogames are examples of services that could take great advantage of multicast communication.

Multicast communication can be one-to-many, as in video streaming or webcasting, or many-to-many, as in multiparty computer games or conference calls. In both cases, its goal is to reduce sender transmission overhead, network bandwidth usage, and the latency observed by receivers. If the source can send only one IP multicast datagram, or packet as we interchangeably call it, containing, for example, video information, to multiple teleconference sites instead of one packet per site, network bandwidth is saved and time synchronization is closer to optimal. For this to be possible, special addresses are necessary, so that the source does not have to know who and how many the receivers are, nor it has to specify their address in the packet. Ad hoc routing schemes must also be devised in order to optimize the distribution of the minimum number of packets necessary to reach only all the intended recipients. Furthermore, group management protocols that define how a host may join or leave a multicast group, how a group is started and terminated, how a group address is selected, are also necessary. Because groups are likely to become larger and highly dynamic as multicast usage becomes widespread, membership changes will occur frequently. Therefore, the design of efficient and scalable group management protocols is crucial for the deployment of multicast services in real scenarios.

The first experiments with multicast date back to the early 1990s, when multicast traffic was encapsulated in traditional unicast datagrams thus defining a virtual network called Mbone (Almeroth and Ammar 1997). Multicast communication is now available by default in the TCP/IP stack. Routing protocols such as OSPF and IGRP use multicast addressing to distribute control messages. Yet, more than fifteen years later, only a limited number of autonomous systems support multicast at the time this chapter is written (see Multicast Technologies 2006), namely 2 percent of the autonomous systems as ranked by Caida (Caida 2006). Research and standardization efforts are still ongoing, however, because some areas have not reached a final development stage or still can be improved (e.g., IETF n.d.a; n.d.b; n.d.c; n.d.d).

Because of the limited deployment of multicast services at the IP layer, overlay multicast, that is, multicast at the application layer, has been proposed as an alternate approach (e.g., Quinn and Almeroth 2001; Birrer and Bustamante 2005; Chu, Rao, and Zhang 2000). Nodes of an overlay multicast group use the underlying unicast IP connections between them and implement all the multicast functionalities at the nodes rather than the routers. Although overlay multicast is easy to deploy and does not need any change in the existing architecture, it may introduce long latencies and packet duplication.

Another criticism moved to the original IP multicast model is its inefficiency when dealing with large numbers of groups with few members each. In this case, the overhead incurred by the network to deliver data to each group outweighs the advantage of a multicast distribution at IP level. A variety of proposals to overcome this problem have appeared in the literature. As an example, we recall here the Small Group Multicast (SGM; Boivie, Feldman, and Metz 2000), where the source knows the group members' addresses and explicitly lists them in the datagram, which is sent as a regular IP unicast packet. No multicast routing protocols are necessary, or group addressing or group management. Although the performance advantage over the IP multicast model is evident when the number of recipients is little, the SGM model radically departs from the IP multicast philosophy. Therefore, as in the case of overlay multicast, we will not investigate it any further.

In this chapter, we review the basic concepts of IP multicast for IPv4 with particular attention to addressing, group management, and routing protocols, as they embody the core of IP multicast. The aspect of reliability and the modifications introduced by IPv6 are also considered.

This chapter is organized as follows: the second section reviews the IP multicast architecture originally proposed by Deering, the third section illustrates multicast addressing, the fourth section focuses on group management, the fifth section describes multicast routing, the sixth section addresses the issues of reliable multicast, and the seventh section gives an overview of IPv6 multicast. Finally, the eighth section summarizes our contributions and concludes the chapter.

THE ORIGINAL MULTICAST MODEL

In this section, we illustrate the basic concepts of IP multicast within the IPv4 context as proposed in the original service model (Deering 1989). IP multicasting is the ability to send IP datagrams to multiple nodes in a logical group, in such a way as to minimize the number of packets. Datagrams are delivered according to the best-effort style of unicast IP. The group is identified by a special IP address, on the range from 224.0.0.0 to 239.255.255.255. Such addresses are statically assigned if the group is permanent, that is, it exists with any number of members, zero included, or dynamically assigned if the group is transient, in which case the group exists as long as there are members. Addresses of permanent groups are published in the "Assigned Numbers" (Reynolds and Postel 1994; Reynolds 2002).

Traffic forwarding is performed by multicast-enabled routers, which will forward the IP multicast datagram outside the local network if it has a time-to-live greater than 1 so that other routers may complete the packet distribution to other group members. No provisions are made for reliable delivery of the packets or for secure services such as encrypted data or closed groups. Figure 1 illustrates the transmission of a single multicast packet to a group of receivers by a source node S. Only multicast-enable routers (MR) handle the multicast packet.

Group membership is dynamic: hosts may join and leave a group at any time, with no limitations on their number and location. Groups are open and public. Any host can send to a group, although only group members may receive. As we will see, such a general service model makes the design of efficient protocols for routing traffic, managing groups, and assigning addresses quite challenging.

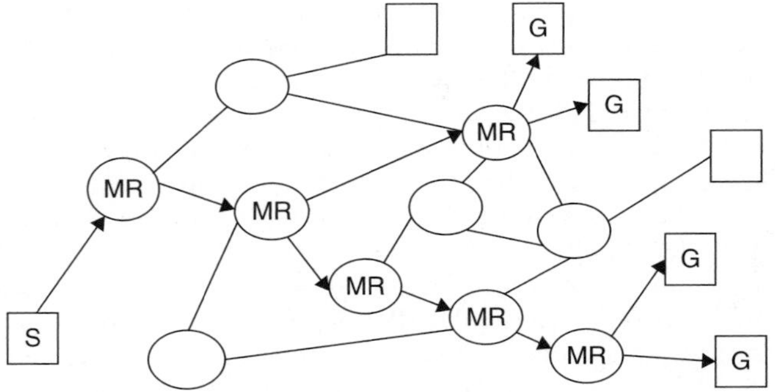

Figure 1: A typical scenario of multicast service: source S sends a multicast packet to the group members G. Multicast-enabled routers (MR) handle traffic forwarding to the receivers

In what follows, we review the addressing scheme and multicast routing protocols. We then describe how group management is performed and discuss the issues of reliable multicast communication.

ADDRESSING

A multicast group is identified by a particular address, G, which allows a source, S, to send a message simultaneously to all the hosts in the group. This way the source does not need to know the recipient identities and their individual IP addresses do not have to be listed in the IP datagram. Only the group address is necessary to transmit an IP multicast datagram. The notation (*,G) indicates all possible sources for group G, and (S,G) indicates the specific source S for group G. While specific sources are regular IP addresses, G's are multicast addresses only.

Address Allocation

By restricting multicast addresses to a specific range, routers can distinguish them from unicast addresses and handle them accordingly. For this purpose, the Internet Assigned Number Authority (IANA) has reserved class D address space, that is, addresses with the four high-order bits equal to 1110, covering the range 224.0.0.0–239.255.255.255 (Reynolds and Postel 1994). The remaining 28 bits of the address identify the group, for a total of about 268 million groups. Three main groups of addresses can be identified over the reserved range, namely those that are reserved for well-known groups, those that are reserved for Internet-wide communications (globally scoped), and those reserved for local multicast communications (administratively scoped). In each of these groups, some of the addresses may be assigned statically and some dynamically on a per-session basis and reclaimed when the session is terminated. In what follows, we will look at some of the well-known addresses and remind the reader to IANA (n.d.a), 2006 for a complete up to date list.

Although address 224.0.0.0 is not assigned to any group, the addresses in the range 224.0.0.1–224.0.0.255 are reserved for specific purposes and routers do not forward multicast packets with destination address in such a range. The local network segment and network protocols use these addresses for automatic router discovery and routing information exchange. In particular, 224.0.0.1 and 224.0.0.2 identify the permanent groups of all the IP hosts and all routers on the subnet, respectively. 224.0.0.4, 224.0.0.5, 224.0.0.9, and 224.0.0.10 are the sets of routers involved in specific protocols, namely DVMRP, OSPF, RIP2, and IGRP, respectively. Other well-known groups are 224.0.0.12 for DHCP and 224.0.0.22 for the IGMP protocol that reports on group membership.

The range of globally scoped addresses 224.0.1.0–238.255.255.255 is used to multicast data between organizations and across the Internet. Some of the addresses are statically assigned, e.g., 244.0.1.1 for the network time protocol, and the rest are assigned dynamically. The

Table 1: A subset of multicast address blocks assigned by IANA according to RFC 3171

Address range	Type	Usage
224.0.0.0–224.0.0.255	Reserved	Local network control
224.0.1.0–224.0.1.255	Globally scoped	Internetwork control
224.0.2.0–224.0.255.0		Ad-hoc
224.2.0.0–224.2.255.255		SDP/SAP
225.0.0.0–231.255.255.255		Reserved
232.0.0.0–232.255.255.255		Source-specific multicast
233.0.0.0–233.255.255.255		GLOP
234.0.0.0–238.255.255.255		Reserved
239.0.0.0–239.255.255.255	Administratively scoped	Internal distribution

so-called "ad-hoc group" spans the 224.0.2.0–224.0.255.0 range and is assigned to various projects. 224.2.0.0–224.2.255.255 is the range of the session description and session advertisement protocols, which the client uses to determine which group it wants to join. Among the set of dynamically assigned addresses, the range 232.0.0.0–232.255.255.255 is reserved for source-specific multicast (SSM) (Bhattacharya 2003; IETF, n.d.e.,), that is, one-to-many groups. This service model has been gaining popularity because it is simpler than the many-to-many or any-source multicast (ASM) of the original proposal and the majority of commercially viable applications, such as video on demand, news casting, and Web updates, are one-to-many. The greater complexity of the ASM model is due to the need for the network to discover all sources for a given group and deliver the traffic to the group members. On the contrary, with SSM, the future group member typically specifies the source when it contacts its router to join a group. In its request, the host specifies both the group and the sender, thus relieving the network from source discovery and simplifying multicast delivery. The statically assigned range 233.0.0.0–233.255.255.255 is known as the GLOP range and is reserved for organizations that already have an autonomous systems (AS) number (Meyer and Lotheberg 2001) and would like to set up a multicast group. Each AS can generate any of the addresses in the 233.X.Y.0–233.X.Y.255 range, where X.Y is the 16 bit sequence corresponding to the AS number, converted in the IP address style.

In order to allow routers to restrict packets distribution within an administrative domain, the address range 239.0.0.0–239.255.255.255 is reserved to internal multicast (Meyer 1998) and is therefore called "administratively scoped." Packets carrying those addresses are not to be propagated outside the borders of the administrative region. Unlike the globally scoped ones, the administratively scoped addresses do not have to be uniquely assigned, as they are not visible outside their domain. As a consequence, there is a saving in the address space consumption, because those addresses can be replicated in different regions. Another way to restrict the distribution of multicast packets is to use specific values in the time-to-live (TTL) field of the IP header. This is an inheritance of MBone but is now deprecated because of the ambiguity resulting from overloading the TTL with both packet lifetime and scope limitation semantic when reconfiguring a distribution tree. Table 1 summarizes a subset of the current address assignment by IANA according to RFC 3171 (Albanna, Almeroth, Meyer, and Schipper 2001).

Address Translation

Unicast Internet IP addresses are translated into link layer addresses by the ARP protocol (Plummer, 1982), which maps an IP address onto the MAC address of the host. Although MAC addresses are unique to each network card, a problem arises with multicast addresses as a single IP multicast address should be mapped onto multiple MAC addresses and it should be possible to differentiate between multicast groups. The IEEE LAN 802.3 (Ethernet) standard specifications define a direct mapping technique to resolve multicast addresses combined with the use of a specific bit, namely the 0-th of the first octet, to indicate a broadcast/multicast address. In order to allow IP multicast address mapping to Ethernet addresses, the IANA has reserved the block of Ethernet addresses 01:00:5E:00:00:00–01:00:5E:7F:FF:FF, that is, those with the high 24 bits set to 01:00:5E, (IANA n.d.b.). Thus, the low order 23 bits of the 28 bits of an IP multicast address replace the low order 23 bits of a 48 bit Ethernet address. It is evident that the mapping is not one-to-one, because 5 bits are not utilized. In fact, 32 different IP multicast addresses converge to the same Ethernet address. This requires that a host be able to filter out multicast packets for other groups with the same Ethernet address.

The reverse mapping, that is, from an Ethernet address to the IP address, is not really a mapping. When a multicast packet at IP level reaches the data-link layer, it becomes the payload of the Ethernet frame, whose address is built as discussed above. If the packet needs to be routed outside the LAN, the border router strips the Ethernet frame, recovering the original packet. Thus no address transformation is necessary.

Address Management Issues

The address assignment scheme described so far has some problems. No central authority exists that allocates multicast addresses upon request. Addresses are allocated in a distributed uncoordinated fashion, thus leading to possible clashes. The address space is limited and may be exhausted, as multicast becomes more popular, which would require address reuse when sessions terminate. The multicast address allocation architecture proposed by the former malloc working group of the IETF copes with these issues by defining a three-layer hierarchical approach to address allocation (IETF n.d.b.; Thaler, Handley, and Estrin 2000). The MADCAP, multicast address dynamic client allocation protocol, allows a host to dynamically request an address to a multicast address allocation server (MAAS) (Hanna, Patel, and Shah 1999). The server provides an address that is unique within its allocation domain, but not necessarily globally unique. Although such an approach provides for scalability and locality of group members, it does not guarantee address uniqueness across the Internet, due to the lack of a central address distribution authority. A partial solution to the problem is provided by the multicast address-set claim (MASC) protocol that allows a router to claim sets of addresses at interdomain level for the MAASs in their domain (Kumar et al. 1998; Radoslavov et al. 2000), although domains do not have to allocate an address set for hosts in the domain to be able to allocate group addresses. A module for managing multicast address allocation in a protocol-independent manner, as well as for managing specific protocols used in allocating multicast addresses, has also been defined (Thaler 2003). The module provides the ability to configure and monitor the status of multicast address allocation within the local domain, answering questions regarding how full a given scope is and who filled it up, who allocated a given address, and whether requests are being met.

GROUP MANAGEMENT

In the original model, multicast groups are public and open, that is, any node can be a source for any group, regardless of its membership in that group, and any node can join any group (Deering 1989). Group members ignore the other members' identity. Routers are in charge of filtering traffic for a given group and then forwarding it on their LAN. The Internet group management protocol (IGMP) defines how nodes join, leave, and interact with their local multicast router. It is used between a node and its immediately neighboring router. The original version of protocol was defined together with the overall architecture and later refined in two subsequent versions.

IGMPv1 and IGMPv2

According to IGMPv1, two types of message are possible: membership queries and membership reports (Deering 1989). Routers periodically query their attached networks to determine which groups have members on them. Hosts reply with a membership report only if they are interested in any of the advertised groups. A host that wants to join a group sends a membership report without waiting for the router query message. The router then adds the group to the membership list for the interface that received the report, unless it is already present, and begins forwarding the multicast traffic onto the network segment.

In IGMPv1 there are no explicit leave messages. If a host wants to leave a group, it simply does not reply to the router membership query and lets it time out. Because of time out expiration, leave latencies can be even in the order of minutes. In order to improve on leave latencies, explicit leave were added in IGMPv2 (Fenner 1997). Version 2 and version 1 are not interoperable. In case IMGPv1 messages are present, all routers must be configured to use version 1.

IGMPv3

Although IGMPv2 improves on version 1, the service model they both assume has some drawbacks. Because there is no control on sources nor is their location known, establishing a distribution tree is hard but flooding multicast groups is easy. Furthermore, address uniqueness is not guaranteed, as we saw in the Addressing section.

IGMPv3 (Cain et al. 2002) addresses these issues by allowing hosts to specify the list of sources from which they are willing to receive traffic and the list of sources from which they do not want any traffic. Unwanted traffic can be discarded at the network level, thus saving system resources. Specific (S,G) joins and leaves are also possible. The service model converges toward a source-specific paradigm, making distribution tree establishment, source identification, and address collision avoidance easier.

ROUTING

Routing multicast traffic requires that packets be delivered in a more efficient way than simply broadcasting them to the entire network or individually sending them as unicast messages to each receiver, in order to avoid wasting network bandwidth or overloading the sender. With multicast routing, the source sends only a single datagram and the routers replicate the packet along the branches of a distribution tree. The leaves of such a tree are the routers directly connected to the group members, which then deliver the packet to their local network. Building the distribution tree is not easy because routers do not necessarily know where the sender is or who the receivers are, given that groups are open and sources do not have to be part of the group. How the distribution tree is built and what information routers store and/or compute distinguishes the various routing protocols. They are classified as "dense" or "sparse" depending upon whether they are more efficient with densely populated groups, or sparsely populated ones, respectively. Initially the focus of multicast routing has been on intradomain protocols but later interdomain protocols have started to be developed. In this case the internetwork structure rather than the group density is the critical issue.

Dense Protocols

Dense mode protocols were proposed first. They build the spanning tree rooted at the source that connects all

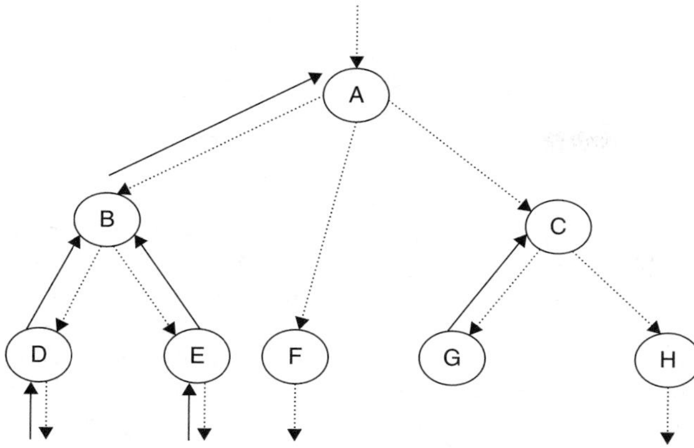

Figure 2: A simple example of "broadcast and prune" strategy. Dotted lines represent the broadcast message; solid lines represent the prune messages

the group member networks, by using the "broadcast and prune" strategy, which is the core of the reverse-path multicast (RPM; Deering and Cheriton 1983), illustrated in Figure 2. The reverse shortest path tree (RSPT; Dalal and Metcalfe 1978) rooted at the source is built by broadcasting a packet to the entire network (dotted lines in the figure) and then pruning all the interfaces toward subtrees that do not have any group members among their leaves. Routers whose domains contain no group members (e.g., G in Figure 2) send prune messages (solid lines) back to the root, which nodes upstream propagate if all of their downstream interfaces have received one (e.g., D, E, B). So, in Figure 2, at the end of the broadcast and prune phase, A will forward multicast traffic only to F and C.

The first multicast routing protocol proposed is a dense protocol based on the RPM approach, namely the distance vector multicast routing protocol (DVMRP; Waitzman, Partridge, and Deering 1988). It builds and maintains its own unicast routing table, regardless of the unicast routing protocol and corresponding tables. For each (S,G) pair, DVMRP builds a new RSPT rooted at the source and keeps state information for each source at every router in the network, regardless of whether there are group members downstream. Packet transmission is geographically scoped using the TTL, although such use is now deprecated, as we discussed in the Addressing section.

Another dense protocol is the protocol-independent multicast dense mode (PIM-DM; see Adams, Nicholas, and Siadak 2005 for the latest specification). PIM-DM uses the existing IP unicast routing protocol and routing tables to forward the multicast traffic. PIM-DM floods multicast traffic through the network and prunes the unwanted traffic, periodically. It supports only source trees rooted at the traffic source. Thus a new tree must be built for each source S transmitting in a given group G.

Sparse Protocols

When groups have few widely distributed members, the broadcasting and prune strategy to build the distribution tree is too heavy from a performance point of view. A more efficient approach is to have nodes that want to receive traffic from a given group send an explicit join message to

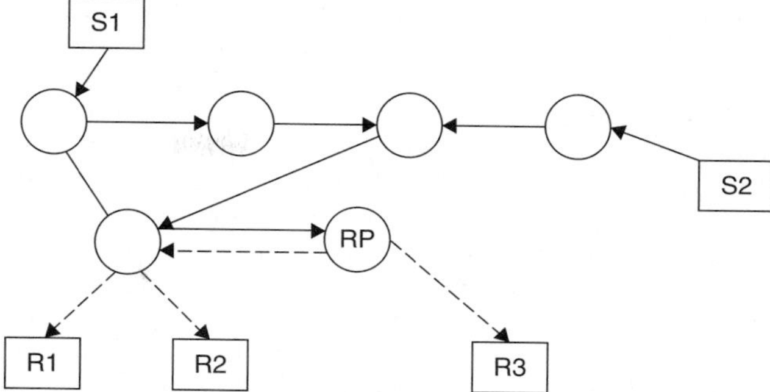

Figure 3: An example of shared tree rooted at the rendezvous point RP. Sources S1 and S2 send their traffic (solid lines) to the RP, which forwards it (dashed lines) to receivers R1, R2, R3

a designated router, known as the rendezvous point (RP) or core, as illustrated in Figure 3. "Sparse mode," or explicit join, protocols aim at optimizing multicast routing when members are widely distributed. They allow for a better network bandwidth usage, because multicast traffic only flows through links that have been explicitly added to the tree.

Distribution trees are rooted at the RP and are shared by all members of a group, regardless of the number of sources. Sources send packets to the RP, which forwards them to the registered members. Only routers along the distribution tree need to maintain state for each group, thus providing for better scalability with respect to dense mode protocols. However, scalability is limited by the RP, which can be a single point of failure and can easily become a performance bottleneck. Furthermore, it may force the use of less-than-optimal routes between the source and the receivers.

The core based tree (CBT; Ballardie, Francis, and Crowcroft 1993; Ballardie 1997) protocol addresses the drawbacks of DVMRP, in particular the large overhead routers incur when multiple sources and groups are present and the cost of the initial RPM phase when the network is big but few nodes participates in multicast groups. Nodes that are not yet part of the group can send a join request to the core router. The bootstrap router protocol performs RP discovery and selects a backup RP if the primary one fails. Shared distribution trees are updated dynamically as nodes join and leave. CBT uses bidirectional trees to limit the hot spot effect on the RP. Yet, traffic concentration on a single link may result from using a single shared tree for each multicast group, and the core based tree may not be the optimal path between sources and receivers in case of few high data rate sources.

PIM sparse mode (PIM-SM; Estrin et al. 1998) is the explicit join version of PIM-DM designed to overcome the limitations of CBT. Unlike CBT, it allows the system administrator to select different RPs for different groups, thus avoiding the traffic concentration issue and improving on the distribution latency with distribution trees that suits better the group. When a source starts transmitting data, it sends a register message to the RP for its group. The RP sends a join toward the source, which allows the intermediate routers to set up the path between the RP and the source. PIM-SM allows the RP to switch forwarding from the shared tree to the shortest path tree to a given leaf router depending on traffic conditions. Because of the flexibility in managing distribution trees, PIM-SM scales well to networks of any size. Furthermore, by means of the transport level Multicast Source Discovery protocol (MSDP, Fenner and Meyer 2003), the sources of a group can be known to various RPs. RPs operate as MSDP peers and exchange lists of sources over a TCP connection. They also announce sources within their domains using MSDP. If any of the receivers in a domain are interested in the multicast sources of other domains, data is delivered over the normal delivery mechanism in PIM-SM. When the first-hop router registers the first data packet from a source, before sending it down the shared distribution tree, it encapsulates it in a source-active (SA) message that forwards to all MSDP peers. The SA message contains the address of the source, of the group the source is sending to, and of the RP. Each MSDP peer receives and forwards the SA message to RPs farther away from the originator. SA message routing is performed using the currently available routing tables, whether from BGP or MBGP. When a peer that is an RP receives an SA message, if there is a member of the multicast group in its shared tree, it recovers the data from the SA message and forwards it down the distribution tree. By relying on the distributed nature of the various domains and their RPs, MSDP does not require global source multicast routing tables nor does it require global group membership advertisements by domains with only receivers, thus saving on memory and bandwidth.

Mixed Density Protocol

A different type of protocol is the multicast extensions to OSPF (MOSPF; Moy, 1994), which relies on the link-state routing paradigm of the OSPF unicast routing protocol to deliver multicast packets. MOSPF is considered a dense protocol with respect to control information, but it is a sparse one with respect to data. Each MOSPF router uses IGMP to keep track of group membership status and distribute updates by flooding a group membership link-state advertisement message to the entire domain. This way all routers have the same view of group membership and build the correct tree. On the contrary, data is sent only to receivers that explicitly requested it, thus reducing the protocol overhead.

Interdomain Routing

The routing protocols presented so far are typically employed within a domain, or autonomous system. Core based tree of sparse mode protocols or the amount of resources to maintain status information in routers not on the multicast distribution tree are not acceptable in global deployment. Hierarchical interdomain routing has been proposed to address such issues. The multiprotocol extensions to BGP (MBGP; Bates, Rekhter, Chandra, and Katz 2000) and the border gateway multicast protocol (BGMP; Kumar et al. 1998; IETF n.d.a.; Thaler 2004) are examples of interdomain protocols.

MBGP was the initial response to the need for interdomain routing. It extends BGP-4 with the ability to provide next-hop information between domains, to provide reachability and policy control for multicast routing, and to route various types of network traffic. BGMP was proposed as the long-term solution to wide-scale interdomain routing, in association with the multicast address-set claim (MASC) protocol for hierarchical address space allocation. It strongly relies on the existence of a domain-oriented address allocation scheme to avoid collisions. BGMP is independent of the intradomain multicast routing protocol. It builds a bidirectional, shared tree of domains using a domain as global root for the distribution tree. Choosing the root domain is a delicate operation in the interdomain case because of administrative issues regarding the ownership of the root domain and the effect on performance that the location of the root may have. BGMP selects the domain of the group initiator as the root domain, hoping that this domain will be the source of most of the traffic.

The complexity of the general nature of the ASM model, that is, any source sending traffic to any group of receivers without any previous notification, the inadequacy of the unicast financial charging scheme, the lack of access control, and its limited scalability are behind the proposal of the source-specific multicast model. As mentioned in the Addressing section, SSM captures the single-source nature of most commercially viable applications, such as file distribution and Internet TV. It simplifies routing significantly because sources are unique and well known, and allows for a new addressing scheme. With the EXPRESS multicast protocol (Holbrook and Cheriton 1999) groups are replaced by "channels," or <source, express destination address> pairs. This solves the problem of address collisions and address space scarcity. Nodes explicitly subscribe to channels, possibly also in an authenticated manner. This allows service providers to guarantee the channel owner exclusive use of the channel and subscribers to receive traffic only from a given channel. A single protocol supports both channel subscription and efficient collection of channel information such as subscriber count. Another proposal in this direction is represented by the simple multicast protocol (SM; Perlman et al. 1999). SM builds on the bidimensional address space proposed by EXPRESS and the shared bidirectional trees of CBT. It identifies groups with <core, multicast address> pairs, which are sent by an end node to the router, thus eliminating the need for core router advertisements. Thanks to its simplicity and scalability, SM is suitable both for intra- and interdomain routing.

RELIABLE MULTICAST

IP multicast is an unreliable service, as it is based on the IP protocol. Because multicast applications typically use UDP as a transport protocol, which is also unreliable, either the applications themselves implement the necessary services to add reliability, or ad hoc reliable multicast protocols are adopted. Military applications are typical users of reliable multicast, for example, "command and control" applications distributed across multiple possibly mobile platforms require a consistent information base to allow the officers in charge to make correct decisions.

To make multicast reliable, the problem of packet corruption and/or packet loss must be eliminated. The total, or partial, packet ordering should also be considered. Error control and possibly congestion control are the techniques adopted to provide reliability. Error control provides a solution to packet loss, whereas congestion control allows the system to maintain a smooth traffic flow.

Error control can be performed reactively, that is, by retransmitting packets when a packet loss is detected, or proactively, that is, by sending redundant data as part of the normal traffic flow. Although the former is more efficient when packets are lost, the latter is better suited for slightly lossy links, that is, links where packets are corrupted rather than lost. Because in this case parity checks and other error correcting codes are adopted, proactive or forward error correction has been considered as an add-on to reliable multicast protocol of the reactive type. Various reliable multicast protocols, such as the scalable reliable multicast (SRM; Floyd, Jacobson, Liu, McCanne, and Zhang 1995), the reliable multicast transport protocol (RMTP; Lin and Paul 1996), the pragmatic general multicast (PGM; Speakman et al. 2001), the light-weight multicast service (LMS; Papadopoulos, Parulkar, and Varghese 1998), or the NACK-Oriented Reliable Multicast protocol (NORM; Adamson, Bormann, Handley, and Macker 2004) have been proposed that follow the retransmission approach.

The way error detection and recovery are performed distinguishes the various protocols. The nature of the applications that requires reliable data transport determines which one is more suitable. When an error is detected, two approaches are possible. In one case, the source receives a negative acknowledgement, or NACK, meaning that at least one node lost a packet. In the other case, the source does not receive all of the expected ACKs confirming the reception of traffic from the receivers. SRM, PGM, LMS, and NORM are NACK-based protocols, whereas RMTP is ACK based. Protocols also differ on how control messages are propagated from a receiver to the source, regardless of their type. This affects the amount of state the source or the multicast routers may have to maintain, hence the protocol scalability, and the amount of bandwidth consumed. Suppression mechanisms are usually in place that eliminate redundant control messages in entire subtrees, to avoid flooding the sender (implosion).

Once errors have been detected, retransmission is required. The issues to be considered in this case are which nodes resend the lost packet and how they resend it. In particular, it can be the source that unicasts the lost packet to the requesting receivers, or nodes in the distribution tree, whether routers or end hosts, that multicast the lost packet to an entire subtree. The goal is to minimize traffic retransmission to nodes that did not request it (exposure). The error detection and recovery strategies affect the recovery latency, that is, the average amount of time it takes to receive a reply after detecting a loss, and the adaptability of the protocol to dynamic membership changes.

Whereas in SRM the source waits for the NACKs and every member may perform retransmission with retransmission suppression in place to minimize traffic duplication, RMTP channels ACKs through a hierarchy of statically designated "ACK processor" nodes. Such nodes merge ACKs from their subtrees and unicast a single ACK up to their parents. They are also in charge of retransmission, using unicast or multicast depending on the percentage of nodes requesting it. In PGM, each router along the distribution tree forwards only one NACK for every packet loss up to the source, thus reducing the NACK traffic at the source. Routers also selectively retransmit traffic only to the nodes that sent NACKs. In LMS, routers select a receiver in their subtree as their substitute and forward all the control messages to it and redistribute messages from it to the subtree. Thus, the burden that in PGM was on the router in LMS has been shifted to a receiver, thus maintaining the router load light. In NORM, typically adopted in military networks, NACKs are used for transport reliability and congestion control for bandwidth sharing with other transport protocols, for example, Transmission Control Protocol (TCP). Reliable multicast sessions may be set up with limited coordination among senders and receivers. Multicast routing can be reciprocal among senders and receivers or asymmetrical, with unicast return paths. Different types of applications or possibly other transport protocols may use NORM services.

IPV6 MULTICAST

Support for multicast in IPv6 has been made a requirement for the protocol (Hinden and Deering 2006) while it is optional in IPv4. Of the differences with respect to IPv4 multicast, we focus on the new address architecture. A brief overview of the impact of IPv6 on group management and routing is also given.

The IPv6 multicast address space is larger than the IPv4 one and structured using a subset of the bits, which define an address. Multicast addresses are identified by the high order octet with value 11111111, or hexadecimal value FF. The next octet is used for flags (4 bits) and scope definition (4 bits). The remaining 112 bits, of which the network prefix and actual group ID occupy the lower 64 and 32 bits, respectively, distinguish the various groups. Part of the information that in IPv4 is associated with a particular range of addresses is now specified by the combination of flag and scope values. In particular, the transient bit flag distinguishes between dynamically assigned, or transient, addresses, and permanent ones, that is, those statically assigned to well-known groups. Transient addresses are valid only within a given scope, namely node, link, site, organization, or global (Internet wide). On the contrary, permanent addresses are valid regardless of the scope value, that is, a version exists for each scope value. Thus, the same group ID (the low 112 bits) may be used at different locations for transient groups and as a permanent address, simultaneously. Like in IPv4, entire subsets of the address space are reserved by IANA, for example, the all node addresses or the all router addresses. IPv4 well-known groups have their IPv6 equivalent, for example, DVMRP routers are identified by FF02:0:0:0:0:0:0:4, RIP routers by FF02:0:0:0:0:0:0:9, and so on. For a complete list of the currently assigned addresses see IANA (n.d.a, n.d.c.).

The translation into Ethernet addresses is also different. Of the 6 bytes of an Ethernet address, the leading two are each set to 33, while the remaining 32 bits are set with the low order 32 bits of the IPv6 multicast address, that is, with the actual group ID. The problem of 1 to 32 mapping between Ethernet and IPv4 addresses does not exist anymore.

In IPv6 the multicast listener discovery protocol (MLD; Vida and Costa, 2004) replaces IGMP for group management. MLD is a subprotocol of ICMP and in its version 2 it is similar IGMPv3. Receivers interested in a particular group must join the group by signaling their local router using MLD, which in turn, routers use to learn whether members of a group are present in their subnets.

IPv6 does not support dense mode routing protocols, PIM-SM being the preferred protocol. Source discovery at interdomain level does not exist, as MSDP is no longer available. Embedded rendezvous points defined at address level are a possible solution for PIM-SM interoperability across various domains. Another alternative is source specific multicast.

CONCLUSION

IP multicast is a fundamental tool for efficient communication of one-to-many and many-to-many services, such as videoconferencing, collaborative work, and periodic data distribution. Its key components are address allocation, routing, and group management. Focusing on many-to-many communication, the original service model makes address allocation and routing complex and heavy for the underlying network. The greater generality of the original model and the intrinsic difficulties that it accounts for have somewhat hindered multicast deployment until recently. To have an idea of how much "experimental" multicast is still considered suffices to compare its diffusion with that of the almost equally as old http, which quickly conquered the world with the World Wide Web.

As a result of the complexity of the original model and the difficulty to force architectural change at network level, various trends have emerged that tend to move away from the original specification along different directions. One direction tends to shift the service paradigm toward easier-to-manage source-specific multicast, as one-to-many communication better suits commercially viable applications, such as video on demand or file distribution. Another direction moves the implementation of multicast services at the application layer, thus pushing the complexity to the edges of the network, according to the Internet philosophy. Along another direction, the popularity of small groups with single senders pushes toward unicast implementations under the sender control, which are more efficient at group level and scale well as the number of such small groups increases. Group management is also being adjusted to fit the less-general service model and allow for closed groups, possibly fee-based, which require restricted data distribution.

Although some of the issues of the IPv4 version have been addressed in the IPv6 version, multicast as an off-the-shelf network component is yet to come for few more years.

GLOSSARY

Addressing scheme: The collection of policies and mechanisms used to restrict access to and usage of system resources to authorized users only.

Group management: The practice of managing multicast group membership.

Multicast: The efficient delivery of information to a group of destinations simultaneously.

Reliability: From a network perspective, the guaranteed delivery of data to the intended recipient(s).

Routing: The means of forwarding logically addressed packets from their local subnetwork toward their final destination.

Scalability: The ability of a system to maintain quality performance or service under an increased system load.

Spanning tree: In graph theory, the tree that includes all the vertices of the graph.

CROSS REFERENCES

See *Internet Architecture*; *TCP/IP Suite*.

REFERENCES

Adams, A., J. Nicholas, and W. Siadak. 2005. Protocol independent multicast—dense mode (PIM-DM): Protocol specification (RFC 3973). http://www.ietf.org/rfc/rfc3973.txt (accessed May 19, 2006).

Adamson, B., C. Bormann, M. Handley, and D. Macker. 2004. Negative-acknowledgment (NACK)-Oriented Reliable Multicast (NORM) Protocol (RFC 3940). http://www.ietf.org/rfc/rfc3940.txt (accessed May 19, 2006).

Albanna, A., K. Almeroth, D. Meyer, and M. Schipper. 2001. Guidelines for IPv4 multicast address assignments (RFC 3171). http://www.ietf.org/rfc/rfc3171.txt (accessed May 19, 2006).

Almeroth, K., and M. Ammar. 1997. Multicast group behavior in the Internet's multicast backbone (MBone). *IEEE Communications Magazine* 35(6):124–9.

Ballardie, A. 1997. Core based tree (CRT version 2) multicast routing protocol specification (RFC 2189). http://www.ietf.org/rfc/rfc2189.txt (accessed May 19, 2006).

Ballardie, T., P. Francis, and J. Crowcroft. 1993. Core based trees. *ACM Computer Communication Review* 23(4):85–95.

Bates, T., Y. Rekhter, R. Chandra, and D. Katz. 2000. Multiprotocol extensions for BGP-4 (RFC 2858). http://www.ietf.org/rfc/rfc2858.txt (accessed May 25, 2004).

Bhattacharya, S. 2003. An overview of source-specific multicast (SSM) (RFC 3569). http://www.ietf.org/rfc/rfc3569.txt (accessed May 19, 2006).

Birrer, S., and F. Bustamante. 2005. Resilient peer-to-peer multicast without the cost. In *Proceedings of the 12th Annual Multimedia Computing and Networking Conference (MMCN'05)*, edited by S. Chandra and N. Venkatasubramanian, pp. 113–20, San Jose, CA.

Boivie, R., N. Feldman, and C. Metz. 2000. Small group multicast: A new solution for multicasting on the Internet. *IEEE Internet Computing* 4(3):75–9.

Caida. 2006. Autonomous system ranking. http://as-rank.caida.org/ (accessed May 19, 2006).

Cain, B., S. Deering, I. Kouvelas, B. Fenner, and A. Thyagarajan. 2002. Internet group management protocol, version 3 (RFC 3376). http://www.ietf.org/rfc/rfc3376.txt (accessed May 19, 2006).

Chu, Y., S. Rao, and H. Zhang. 2000. A case for end system multicast. In *Proceedings of the ACM SIGMETRICS 2000*, edited by A. Brandwajn, J. Kurose, and P. Nain, pp. 1–12. New York, NY: ACM Press.

Dalal, Y.K., and R. M. Metcalfe. 1978. Reverse path forwarding of broadcast packets. *Communication of the ACM* 21(12):1040–8.

Deering, S. E. 1989. Host extensions for IP multicast (RFC 1112). http://www.ietf.org/rfc/rfc1112.txt (accessed May 19, 2006).

Deering, S. E., and D. R. Cheriton. 1983. Multicast routing in datagram internetworks and extended LANs. *ACM Transactions on Computer Systems* 8(5): 85–110.

Estrin, D., D. Farinacci, A. Helmy, D. Thaler, S. Deering, M. Handley, V. Jacobson, C._G. Liu, P. Sharma, and L. Wei. 1998. Protocol independent multicast-sparse mode (PIM-SM): Protocol specification (RFC 2362). http://www.ietf.org/rfc/rfc2362.txt (accessed May 19, 2006).

Fenner, B. 1997. Internet group management protocol, version 2 (RFC 2236). http://www.ietf.org/rfc/rfc2236.txt (accessed May 19, 2006).

Fenner, B., and D. Meyer. 2003. Multicast source discovery protocol (MSDP) (RFC 3618). http://www.ietf.org/rfc/rfc3618.txt (accessed May 19, 2006).

Floyd, S., V. Jacobson, C.-G. Liu, S. McCanne, and L. Zhang. 1995. A reliable multicast framework for lightweight sessions and application level framing. In *Proceedings of the ACM SIGCOMM 1995*, edited by D. Oran, pp. 342–56. New York, NY: ACM Press.

Hanna, S., B. Patel, and M. Shah. 1999. Multicast address dynamic client allocation protocol (MADCAP) (RFC 2730). http://www.ietf.org/rfc/rfc.txt (accessed May 19, 2006).

Hinden, R., and S. Deering. 2006. IP version 6 addressing architecture (RFC 4291). http://www.ietf.org/rfc/rfc4291.txt (accessed May 19, 2006).

Holbrook, H. W., and D. R. Cheriton. 1999. IP multicast channels: EXPRESS support for large-scale single-source applications. In *Proceedings of the ACM SIGCOMM 1999*, edited by L. Chapin, J.P.G. Sterbenz, G. Parulkar, and J.S. Turner. pp. 65–78. New York, NY: ACM Press.

IANA. n.d.a. Internet multicast addresses. http://www.iana.org/assignments/multicast-addresses (accessed May 19, 2006).

IANA. n.d.b. Ethertypes. http://www.iana.org/assignments/ethernet-numbers (accessed May 19, 2006).

IANA. n.d.c. Internet Protocol Version 6 Multicast Address. http://www.iana.org/assignments/ipv6-multicast-addresses (accessed May 19, 2006).

IETF. n.d.a. Multicast & anycast group membership working group (magma), http://www.ietf.org/html.charters/magma-charter.html (accessed May 19, 2006).

IETF. n.d.b. Multicast-address allocation (malloc) working group. http://www.ietf.org/html.charters/OLD/malloc-charter.html (accessed May 19, 2006).

IETF. n.d.c. Multicast security working group (msec). http://www.ietf.org/html.charters/msec-charter.html (accessed May 19, 2006).

IETF. n.d.d. Protocol independent multicast working group (pim). http://www.ietf.org/html.charters/pim-charter.html (accessed May 19, 2006).

IETF. n.d.e. Source-specific multicast working group (ssm). http://www.ietf.org/html.charters/ssm-charter.html (accessed May 19, 2006).

Kumar, A., P. Radoslavov, E. Thaler, C. Alaettinoglu, E. Estrin, and M. Handley. 1998. The MASC/BGMP architecture for inter-domain muticast routing. In *Proceedings of the ACM SIGCOMM 1998*, edited by M. Steenstrup. pp. 93–104. New York, NY: ACM Press.

Lin, J. C., and S. Paul. 1996. RMTP: A reliable multicast transport protocol. In *Proceedings of the IEEE INFOCOM 1996*. Vol. 3, pp. 1414–1424. Los Alamitos, CA: IEEE Press.

Meyer, M. 1998. Administratively scoped IP multicast (RFC 2365). http://www.ietf.org/rfc/rfc2365.txt (accessed May 19, 2006).

Meyer, D., and P. Lotheberg, P. 2001. GLOP addressing in 233/8 (RFC 3180). http://www.ietf.org/rfc/rfc3180.txt (accessed May 19, 2006).

Moy, J. 1994. *Multicast extensions to OSPF* (RFC 1584). http://www.ietf.org/rfc/rfc1584.txt (accessed May 19, 2006).

Multicast Technologies. 2006. Active multicast autonomous system info. http://www.multicasttech.com/status/mbgp.sum (accessed May 19, 2006).

Papadopoulos, C., G. M. Parulkar, and G. Varghese. 1998. An error control scheme for large-scale multicast applications. In *Proceedings of the IEEE INFOCOM 1998*. Vol. 3, pp. 1188–1196. Los Alamitos, CA: IEEE Press.

Perlman, R., C-Y. Lee, A. Ballardie, J. Crowcroft, Z. Wang, T. Maufer, C. Diot, J. Thoo, and M. Green. 1999. Simple multicast: A design for simple, low-overhead multicast (IETF Internet Draft). http://tools.ietf.org/html/draft-perlman-simple-multicast-03 (accessed May 19, 2006).

Plummer, D. 1982. An Ethernet Address Resolution Protocol (RFC 826). http://www.ietf.org/rfc/rfc826.txt (accessed May 19, 2006).

Quinn, B., and K. Almeroth. 2001. IP Multicast applications: Challenges and solutions (RFC 3170). http://www.ietf.org/rfc/rfc3170.txt (accessed May 19, 2006).

Reynolds, J., and J. Postel. 1994. Assigned numbers (RFC 1700). http://www.ietf.org/rfc/rfc1700.txt (accessed May 19, 2006).

Reynolds, J. Ed. 2002. Assigned numbers: RFC 1700 is obsoleted by on-line database (RFC 3232). http://www.ietf.org/rfc/rfc3232.txt (accessed May 19, 2006).

Radoslavov, P., E. Estrin, R. Govindan, M. Handley, S. Kumar, and D. Thaler. 2000. The multicast address-set claim (MASC) protocol (RFC 2909). http://www.ietf.org/rfc/rfc2909.txt (accessed May 19, 2006).

Speakman, T., J. Crowcroft, J. Gemmell, D. Farinacci, S. Lin, D. Leshchiner, et al. 2001. PGM reliable transport protocol specification (RFC 3208). http://www.ietf.org/rfc/rfc3208.txt (accessed May 19, 2006).

Thaler, D., M. Handley, and D. Estrin. 2000. The Internet multicast address allocation architecture (RFC 2908).

http://www.ietf.org/rfc/rfc2908.txt (accessed May 19, 2006).

Thaler, D. 2003. Multicast address allocation MIB (RFC 3559). http://www.ietf.org/rfc/rfc3559.txt (accessed May 19, 2006).

Thaler, D. 2004. Border gateway multicast protocol (BGMP): Protocol specification (RFC 3913). http://www.ietf.org/rfc/rfc3913.txt (accessed May 19, 2006).

Vida, R., and L. Costa. 2004. Multicast Listener Discovery Version 2 (MLDv2) for IPv6 (RFC 3810). http://www.ietf.org/rfc/rfc3810.txt (accessed May 19, 2006).

Waitzman, D., C. Partridge, and S. Deering, S. 1988. Distance vector multicast routing protocol (RFC 1075). http://www.ietf.org/rfc/rfc1075.txt (accessed May 19, 2006).

FURTHER READING

Haberman, B., and D. Thaler. 2002. Unicast-prefix-based IPv6 multicast addresses (RFC 3306). http://www.ietf.org/rfc/rfc3306.txt (accessed May 19, 2006).

Haberman, B. 2002. Allocation guidelines for IPv6 multicast addresses (RFC 3306). http://www.ietf.org/rfc/rfc3307.txt (accessed May 19, 2006).

Network QoS

Ying Lu, *University of Nebraska, Lincoln*

INTRODUCTION

Quality of Service is defined as the capability to provide resource assurance and service differentiation in a network (Wang 2001). As the Internet becomes ubiquitous, network applications with varied requirements emerge. For applications such as checking emails or browsing the Web, reliable data delivery is their key requirement. Applications such as data backup and bulk file transfer need a certain amount of bandwidth. Although for teleconferencing or IP-telephone, they demand timely data delivery to function properly. To support diversified applications, network QoS for resource assurance and service differentiation is essential.

QoS is supported in an ATM network. It provides multiple service classes with deterministic performance. By adopting a circuit-based model, ATM also enables traffic engineering capabilities in ATM networks.

The Internet was originally designed for best effort service. When transmitting packets from their sources to destinations, the routers treat them in an undifferentiated way. Upon arriving at a router, a packet is put into a first-in first-out (FIFO) queue. The queuing delay experienced by the packet depends on the queue length at that time. When traffic is bursty, packets encounter unpredictable network delays and could even be dropped when a queue overflows. Therefore, new service classes are called upon to support QoS on the Internet. To enable such advanced services, routers need to support new forwarding behaviors. Instead of putting all traffic into a FIFO queue, a QoS-capable router should adopt proper classification, queuing and scheduling mechanisms for packet forwarding. In IntServ and DiffServ architectures, new service classes and forwarding behaviors are designed. To set up QoS-capable routers for desired forwarding behaviors and services, resource reservation and resource provisioning are respectively employed.

To satisfy QoS requirements of a large number of customers, service providers need to use their network resources optimally. Conventional IP shortest path routing does not guarantee optimal resource consumption and may sometimes even lead to congestion. Internet traffic engineering is concerned with performance optimization of IP networks. It helps service providers find optimal routes to transmit traffic across their networks. By enabling explicit non-shortest-path routing, MPLS facilitates the deployment of traffic engineering solutions. When combined together, MPLS and traffic engineering offer service providers powerful tools to better manage their network resources.

This chapter introduces network QoS, its requirements and the basic aspects of major QoS technologies. Much of the material in this chapter is based on related RFCs and existing papers on network QoS including (Kurose and Ross 2002; El-Gendy, Bose, and Shin 2003; Xiao and Ni 1999; Semeria 2000; Semeria 1999; Armitage 2000). Because the subject of network QoS is very complex, this chapter focuses the discussion on wired networks, omitting the QoS issues in wireless or mobile networks.

NETWORK QOS REQUIREMENTS

To obtain QoS, customers must state their service requirements that need to be met by the network. Common parameters used to describe QoS requirements are throughput, delay, jitter, and loss rate (El-Gendy, Bose and Shin 2003). Throughput is the effective rate at which data is transferred. It is measured in terms of how many bits have been transported per second (e.g., bits/sec). This parameter is usually used to specify bandwidth assurance. For example, bit rate guarantees for a flow could be specified in ATM, IntServ, and DiffServ architectures. In addition, bit rate could also be used to express a traffic profile entitled to a service. Delay is the time experienced by a packet while passing through a network, i.e., the time interval between the packet's departure from its source to the packet's arrival at its destination. Usually a maximum bound is used to specify the delay requirement. Jitter refers to the variation in packet delays. There are multiple ways to quantify jitter. For example, jitter can be calculated as the difference between delays of two successive packets in a flow. Packet loss rate is a ratio of the number of lost packets to the total number of transmitted packets. Similar to delay, maximum bounds are specified in QoS requirements for jitter and loss rate.

Besides using absolute values, QoS requirements could also be specified in a relative manner where desired service levels of multiple traffic classes are given according to their relative importance. DiffServ is purposely designed to support differentiated QoS requirements.

ATM

The development of asynchronous transfer mode (ATM) can be traced back to mid-1980s. It is a multiservice network technology designed for transporting multiple classes of traffic: data, voice, and video. ATM is one of the first frameworks that supports QoS. Its traffic is carried in fixed-size packets (called cells). Each cell has a 5-byte header and a 48-byte payload. The fixed-size cell facilitates high-speed switching. Compared to variable-size packet, the fixed-size cell makes scheduling, queuing and buffer management easier and consequently leads to more predictable behavior. ATM network uses virtual circuits (VCs). Before transmission, a VC needs to be setup between the sender and the receiver. The network layer decides the path for the VC and may also reserve resources along the patch for the VC. By careful planning, different levels of services can be provided on these VCs.

ATM provides the following four service models (Kurose and Ross 2002).

- Constant bit rate (CBR) service is used to provide fixed bit rates to connections. The connection is characterized by a peak cell rate (PCR) as the allocated transmission rate. The sender is expected to emit cells at or below this rate. It is ideal for real-time constant-bit-rate audio and video traffic. CBR service provides the applications quantitative guarantees on the end-to-end cell transfer delay (CTD), cell delay variation (CDV), and cell loss rate (CLR).
- Variable bit rate (VBR) service comes in two flavors: real-time VBR and non-real-time VBR. In VBR service, traffic is described using parameters like peak cell rate (PCR), sustainable cell rate (SCR), and maximum burst size (MBS). Traffic transmits at a variable rate that follows these parameters. Real-time VBR service, intended for time-sensitive applications, is ideal for bursty audio and video traffic. It specifies acceptable CTD, CDV and CLR. Same as CBR service, real-time VBR service guarantees quantitative QoS. Non–real-time VBR service is indented for bursty traffic with no tight constraints on delay and jitter. In the service, CTD and CLR are specified. It provides a cell loss rate guarantee.
- Available bit rate (ABR) service is designed for applications that have the ability to adapt their sending rates according to the bandwidth availability. This service is intended for data traffic like file transfer and email. Besides PCR, a user could specify a minimum cell rate (MCR), which is guaranteed to the VC. Depending upon the network congestion, the sender will control its rate between the MCR and the PCR. ABR service provides the application a minimum bandwidth guarantee and allows it to transmit data as fast as possible.
- Unspecified bit rate (UBR) service is a best effort service. No guarantees on rate, delay, jitter and loss are provided. In UBR service, applications could use any leftover bandwidth. Unlike ABR service, no congestion information is fed back to UBR application senders. UBR service is designed for non-interactive data transfer applications.

Despite ATM's sophisticated support for QoS, it is not successfully adopted by end-host applications. The main reason is that the Internet and its TCP/IP protocols have already been widely accepted: the most popular operating systems support TCP/IP and many applications have been developed on the Internet with TCP/IP. However, as a result of the high switching speed and the deterministic performance, ATM has found its way in the Internet backbone, where TCP/IP runs on top of ATM and views an entire ATM network as one link-layer network. Before the emergence of high-speed IP backbone routers and MPLS, IP-over-ATM model has once been a very popular overlay architecture used by ISPs to manage the operation of their networks. In the section on traffic engineering, IP-over-ATM will be discussed in detail.

INTSERV

The Internet was originally designed to provide best-effort data delivery. For having variable queuing delays and packet losses, the Internet could not support real-time applications well. To meet the growing need for real-time service, IETF proposed Integrated Services (IntServ) (Braden, Clark, and Shenker 1994) in 1994. IntServ was designed from the beginning for a multicast environment so that real-time applications such as teleconferencing and virtual reality could be supported.

Service Classes

As an extension to the Internet architecture and protocols, IntServ provides services where end-to-end packet delays could be controlled. Two new services are introduced to the Internet—the guaranteed service (Shenker, Partridge, and Guerin 1997) and the controlled load service (Wroclawski 1997b). The guaranteed service provides firm upper bounds on end-to-end delays. It is a service suitable for intolerant real-time applications that cannot function properly if delay bounds are violated. The controlled load service provides "a quality of service closely approximating the QoS that same flow would receive from an unloaded network element" (Wroclawski 1997b). It is intended for applications sensitive to overloaded conditions, such as adaptive real-time applications. Although delay bounds achieved by the controlled load service are fairly reliable, no quantitative guarantees are provided. Efficiency was the main incentive behind the controlled load service. By relaxing delay requirements, increased network utilization can be sustained.

In both services, to achieve QoS, an application must first reserve sufficient resources in the intermediate routers along its source-to-destination path. Applications should characterize their data flows and specify the desired QoS requirements. Every passing router must support admission control to determine whether a new data flow could be accepted. Adequate resources such as link bandwidth and buffer space are required from each of these routers to meet the flow's end-to-end QoS requirements. Each router should consider the amount of its resources that are already reserved and decide if it can grant the requested QoS to the flow without violating committed QoS guarantees. Once resources are reserved along the path, the application could start transmitting its data. When a router receives a packet, it classifies the packet and puts it into a corresponding queue. The packet is then scheduled for transmission, using the reserved resources for its flow. Following this procedure, the QoS services are enforced. Figure 1 illustrates the required modules in a router to support IntServ. In the management component of a router, reservation setup and admission control install flow state information for packet forwarding, while classifier, queuing mechanism and scheduler in the forwarding component are those that actually provide the desired forwarding behavior.

Reservation with RSVP

Having presented IntServ services and its enabling components in an IntServ router, next the use of the resource ReSerVation Protocol (RSVP) (Zhang et al. 2001; Wroclawski 1997a) with IntServ services will be illustrated. Same as IntServ model, RSVP was fundamentally designed for a multicast environment. It is receiver-oriented, where a data flow receiver initiates the resource reservation. This enables RSVP to accommodate heterogeneous receivers in a multicast group.

Figure 2 illustrates the use of RSVP resource reservation in IntServ services. The sender first sends a PATH message to receiver(s). In the message, an object, SENDER TSPEC, specifies the traffic that the application expects to generate. ADSPEC is another object included in a PATH message. As the message moves from the sender to the receiver(s), the ADSPEC is updated by intermediate routers to describe properties of the data path, such as the availability of specific QoS control services, and parameters required by those services to operate correctly. For example, C_{tot} and D_{tot}, respectively representing the accumulated rate-dependent and rate-independent queuing delays along a path, are parts of an ADSPEC object for the guaranteed service. Upon receiving a PATH message, the receiver uses the data in the SENDER TSPEC and the ADSPEC to guide its selection of resource reservation parameters. For example, C_{tot} and D_{tot} parameters could be used to calculate a bound on end-to-end packet delay when using the guaranteed

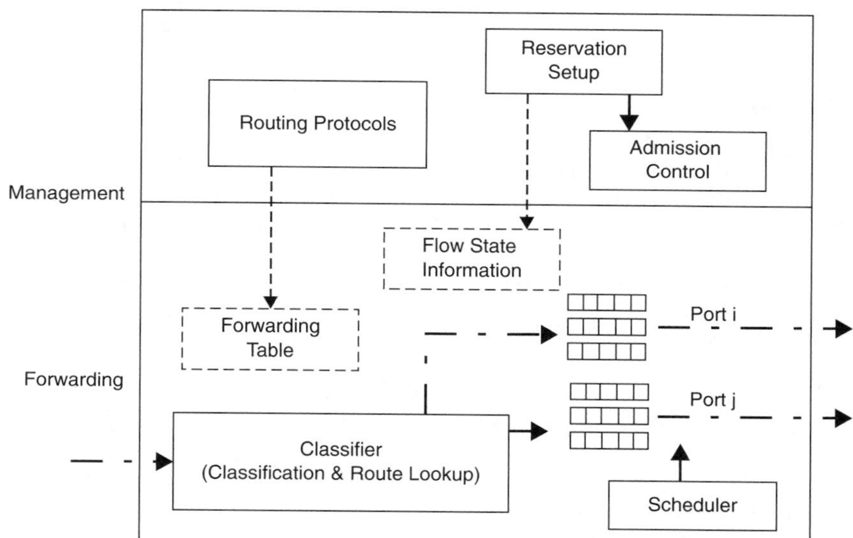

Figure 1: Functional blocks of an IntServ router

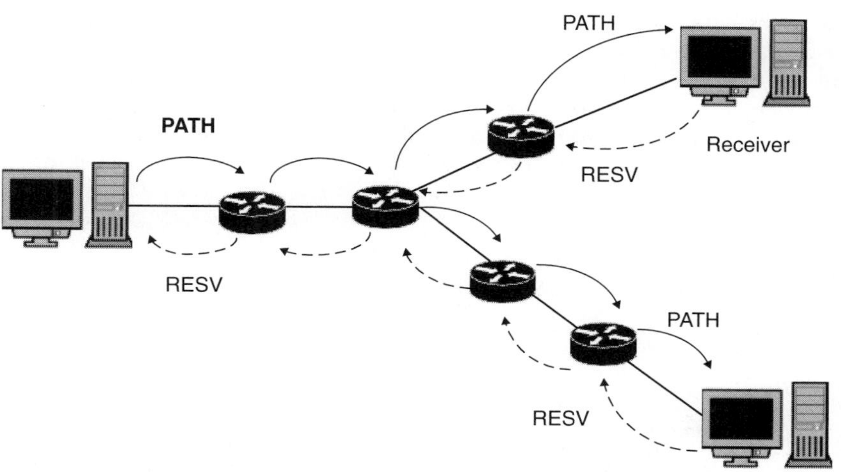

Figure 2: RSVP resource reservation

service (Shenker, Partridge, and Guerin 1997). To make resource reservation, a receiver replies back with a RESV message to the sender. In the message, a FLOWSPEC object carries information about the desired flow for the receiver. The desired QoS service (guaranteed or controlled load service) is specified. In addition, tailored to the receiver's individual capability, a receiver TSpec is included, characterizing the traffic flow the receiver could handle and for which resource reservation is requested. If it requires the guaranteed service, an RSpec parameter is used to describe the specific QoS being requested. For example, RSpec includes a required service rate R for all routers along the path to guarantee the end-to-end delay bound for the flow. Upon arrival of the RESV message, each of the intermediate routers carries out the admission control process locally. If the request is rejected by any of the routers, an error message is sent to the receiver and the resource reservation process is terminated. If the RESV message is accepted by all routers along the path, resources are allocated for the flow and corresponding flow state information is installed in each of the routers so that mechanisms for classifying, queuing, and scheduling the flow's packets are configured properly.

DIFFSERV

As described in the previous section, IntServ provides per-flow end-to-end QoS guarantees. Despite its flexibility in satisfying resource requirements of individual flows, IntServ model is not suitable for the Internet core due to its lack of scalability. IntServ requires each router to keep state information of every passing flow and to support resource reservation, admission control, and sophisticated multifield classification. These cause huge storage and processing overheads on the routers. Besides, only two very specific services, the guaranteed service and the controlled load service, are provided in IntServ framework. No services with different relative importance are supported. To overcome these limitations, IETF developed a more scalable QoS model: differentiated service (DiffServ) architecture (Blake et al. 1998).

To achieve scalability, DiffServ architecture pushes complex management operations to network edges and leaves only simple packet handling and forwarding within the network core. The architecture aggregates traffic into a limited number of service classes. Sophisticated classification, admission control, and traffic conditioning are only required at network boundaries where packets are classified and marked to receive a specific per-hop forwarding behavior in the network. Because resources are allocated to traffic aggregates and not to individual flows, only per-class state information and simple classification are required in the network core routers. Unlike IntServ, DiffServ architecture not only supports specific services, like the premium service and the assured service (Nichols, Jacobson, and Zhang 1999), but also provides building blocks upon which a wide variety of services can be constructed.

Service Classes

DiffServ can be traced back to RFC 2638 (Nichols, Jacobson, and Zhang 1999), where a two-bit differentiated services architecture is proposed. The document presents two new services: the premium service and the assured service. In the architecture, two bits are used to mark packets, a P-bit for the premium service and an A-bit for the assured service.

For the premium service (Nichols, Jacobson, and Zhang 1999), a small percentage of the total network capacity is allocated to its traffic to create a "virtual leased line." The contracted bandwidth is specified with a desired peak bit rate. The volume of the flow or the aggregated-flow entitled to the service is limited by the peak rate. When the traffic is sent, the availability of the contracted bandwidth will be guaranteed.

For the assured service (Clark and Wroclawski 1997), a traffic profile specifies expected traffic rate and burst size. The assurance is that traffic in the service is unlikely to be dropped as long as it stays within the expected traffic profile.

To provide the premium or the assured services in a network, appropriate packet marking is required at edge routers. Edge routers could use complicated multi-field classification to differentiate incoming packets. The packets will then be marked with a P-bit or an A-bit in their IP headers or left unmarked (e.g., for those best effort packets). Intermediate routers in the network will classify packets and treat them differently simply based on the single bit carried by their IP headers.

Edge routers are configured with traffic profiles for flows or flow aggregations. All arriving packets must be classified based on the content of their headers. If a header matches a configured value, the packet will be passed to the corresponding marker. In the marker, a token bucket has been constructed from the flow traffic profile. For the premium service, the token bucket is very small and can only hold one or two packets. It is filled at the specified peak rate. For the assured service, the token bucket is set by the profile's burst size. It is filled at the expected rate. Figure 3 illustrates how the edge marker works (Nichols, Jacobson, and Zhang 1999). Upon arriving at the premium-configured marker, the packet that sees a token present will be marked with a

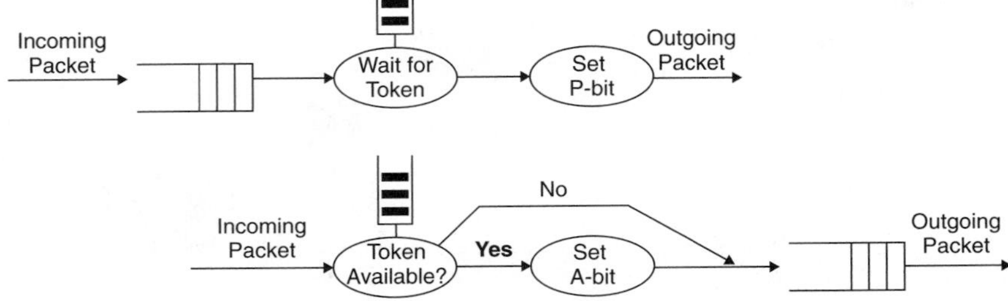

Figure 3: Edge router markers in the two-bit DS architecture

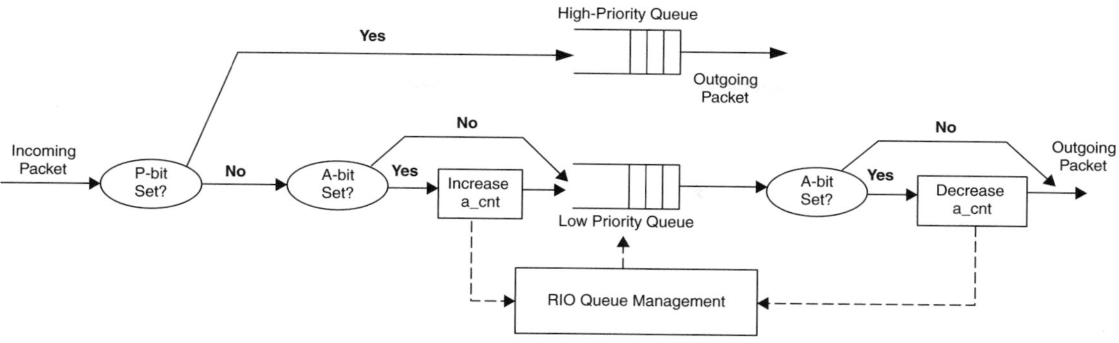

Figure 4: Edge router forwarding in the two-bit DS architecture

P-bit and forwarded. When no token is present, a premium packet is held until a token arrives. For the assured service, the packet will have its A-bit set to one if a token is present. Otherwise, the packet will be forwarded unmarked (i.e., the packet will be treated as best-effort traffic).

To provide different forwarding behaviors to different service classes, the forwarding components (Nichols, Jacobson, and Zhang 1999) of both edge and intermediate routers first put packets into their corresponding queues (Figure 4). If the packet is marked with a P-bit, it enters a high priority queue. Otherwise, the packet enters a low priority queue. The two queues are served by simple priority, with premium packets being forwarded first. As premium traffic flows are shaped, hard-limited to their provisioned peak rates and forwarded first, they will experience little jitter and queuing delay.

The low priority assured queue will be managed using RED in/out (RIO) algorithm (Clark and Wroclawski 1997). It is an extension of the random early detection (RED) scheme. RED manages a queue at a router by dropping packets randomly. This prevents the queue from overflowing, avoids the tail-drop behavior and therefore prevents TCP flows from decreasing and later increasing their rates simultaneously. RIO runs two RED algorithms, one for "in" packets, and one for "out" packets. Two thresholds are used to decide when to start dropping packets in these two RED algorithms. When a lower threshold, based on the total queue length, is exceeded, unmarked "out" packets from the best effort traffic or the out-of-profile traffic will be dropped randomly. The higher threshold, based on the count of the number of A-bit packets enqueued, is used for the "in" RED algorithm to drop assured packets. The "out" RED algorithm drops much more aggressively than the "in" algorithm. This forwarding behavior assures that compliant assured traffic experiences low loss rate even in case of congestion.

Architecture

This section presents the common building blocks of the DiffServ architecture. These building blocks can be used to construct the premium, assured services as well as a wide variety of other services. The discussion in this section focuses on a single DiffServ domain. Interested readers should refer to (Bernet et al. 2000; El-Gendy, Bose, and Shin 2003) for using bandwidth brokers and SLS for end-to-end services across multiple DiffServ domains.

In DiffServ architecture (Blake et al. 1998), traffic entering a DiffServ (DS) domain is classified and possibly conditioned at boundary nodes. Packets are assigned to different classes and will receive different per-hop forwarding behaviors. The class of traffic that experiences the same forwarding behavior at every node within a domain is called a behavior aggregate (BA). Each behavior aggregate is identified by a single DS codepoint in the packet IP header. Nodes will forward a packet according to the per-hop behavior (PHB) associated with its DS codepoint. The DS field in the IP header carries the DS codepoint. It coincides with the (former) IPV4 TOS or the (former) IPV6 traffic class octet (Grossman 2002). The first six bits of the field are used for the DS codepoint (DSCP), and the remaining two bits are currently unused (Figure 5) (Nichols et al. 1998).

- **Traffic Classification and Conditioning.** To receive the differentiated service, a customer must negotiate a service level agreement (SLA) with a service provider. Here a customer could be a user organization or another DS domain. The SLA specifies the service the customer should receive and the amount of traffic entitled to the service. A service provider configures and provisions its routers to meet these SLAs. For instance, a classifier and a traffic conditioner are configured at the edge router to map the customer traffic to appropriate service classes within the provider's DS domain.

  When a packet arrives at a boundary node, the classifier invokes either sophisticated multifield classification or simple BA classification to classify it. The packet is then steered to corresponding traffic conditioner for further processing. Because available resources are finite, only restrictive amount of traffic from a customer is entitled to the requested service level. Therefore, a traffic profile

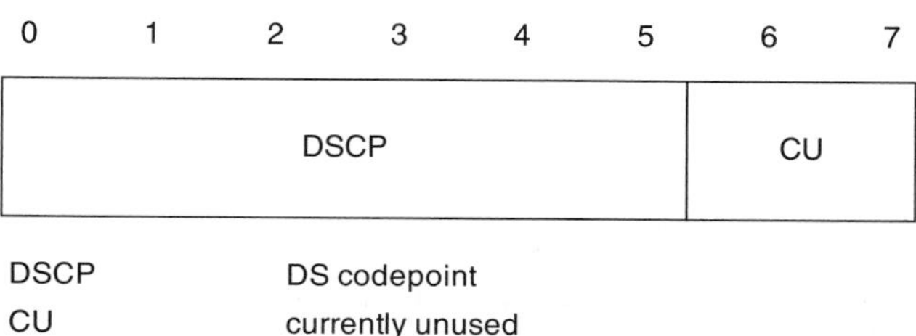

Figure 5: DS field structure

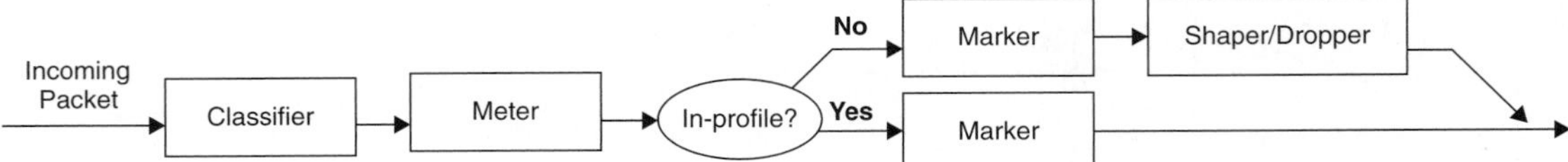

Figure 6: Logical view of a traffic conditioner

is included in a SLA, specifying the properties of a traffic stream like its rate and burst size. Only in-profile packets are allowed to receive the contracted service level. In the traffic conditioner (Figure 6), which is located in the forwarding component of a DS edge router, the packet is first metered against its traffic profile. The meter determines if the packet is in-profile or out-of-profile. An in-profile packet is marked with appropriate DS codepoint and is allowed to enter the DS domain without further conditioning. An out-of-profile packet may be directed to a shaper where it is queued until it is in-profile, to a dropper to be discarded, or to a marker to be marked with a new DS codepoint indicating an inferior service class. When the packet exits the traffic conditioner of the DS boundary node, DS codepoint of the packet is set to an appropriate value (Blake et al. 1998).

- **Per-Hop Behaviors.** Once being marked, the packet becomes part of a behavior aggregate. It will receive the same per-hop behavior as all other packets marked with the same DS codepoint. A per-hop behavior (PHB) is "a description of the externally observable forwarding behavior of a DS node applied to a particular DS behavior aggregate" (Blake et al. 1998). It is achieved by DS nodes properly allocating resources to behavior aggregates. Complimentary to the traffic classification and conditioning, this basic hop-by-hop resource allocation mechanism is the other key building block of the DiffServ architecture.

  A simple example of a PHB is one which guarantees that a behavior aggregate receives a minimal x% of a link bandwidth over some time interval. Another example is PHBs being specified, as a group (PHB group), in terms of relative priority of access to link resources. Two most well-known PHBs finalized by the DiffServ working group are: the expedited forwarding (EF) PHB (Davie et al. 2002) and the assured forwarding (AF) PHB group (Heinanen et al. 1999).

  EF PHB (Davie et al. 2002) is intended to provide a building block for low delay, low jitter, and low loss services. The dominant causes of packet delay in a network are fixed propagation delay and queuing delay. EF PHB ensures that EF packets usually encounter short or empty queues, thus experience low queuing delay and low jitter. The packet loss is minimized at the same time if queues are kept short relative to buffer spaces. Short queues are achieved by allocating resources to EF packets with a higher service rate than their arrival rate. It is guaranteed that EF packets receive service at or above a configured rate. Since this guarantee is made independently of the load of other classes, the low delay, low jitter and low loss EF PHB is protected from non-EF traffic. The DS codepoint allocated for EF PHB is 101110.

  AF PHB Group (Heinanen et al. 1999) is used to build services with controlled loss. It divides traffic into four independent AF classes. A DS node must allocate some minimum amount of forwarding resources to each class. Within an AF class, packets are further categorized into three different levels of drop precedence. In case of congestion, packet is discarded based on its drop precedence. As a result, at a DS node, the level of forwarding assurance for a packet depends on the amount of forwarding resources allocated to its AF class, the current load of the class, and when congestion happens within the class, the drop precedence of the packet. Figure 7 summarizes the DS codepoints allocated to AF PHB Group.

MPLS

This section describes multiprotocol label switching (MPLS). In an IP network, when a packet travels from one router to the next, each router makes an independent forwarding decision for the packet. That is, the router analyzes the packet's header and chooses a next hop for the packet. The process of choosing the next hop could be divided into two steps. In step one, the packet's header is checked to determine which forwarding equivalence class (FEC) it belongs to. FEC is defined as a group of IP packets that are forwarded over the same path and with the same forwarding behavior. Once the packet has been assigned to a FEC, its forwarding path is determined. Therefore, in the second step, the packet is forwarded to a next hop mapped to its FEC.

In conventional IP forwarding, a router considers two packets to be in the same FEC if their destination addresses map to the same "longest-match" IP address prefix in the forwarding table. This mapping procedure is repeated at every crossing router. The packet is reexamined, mapped to a FEC and then forwarded to a next hop. The forwarding table is constructed and updated using standard IP routing protocols such as open shortest path first (OSPF) protocol, for topology discovery and route determination.

Drop Precedence \ Class	Class1	Class2	Class3	Class4
Low	001010	010010	011010	100010
Medium	001100	010100	011100	100100
High	001110	010110	011110	100110

Figure 7: The recommended AF codepoint values

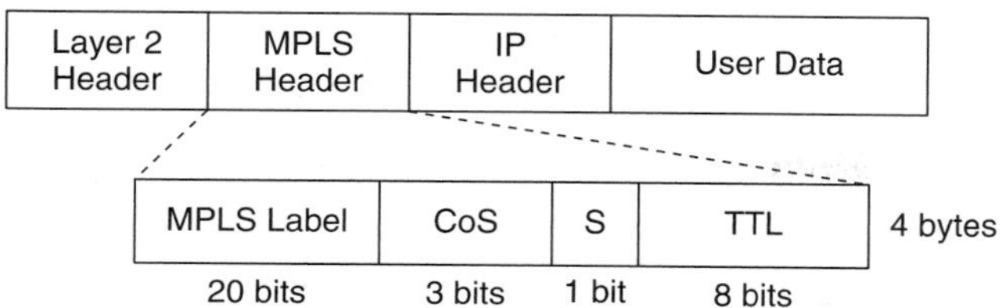

Figure 8: MPLS header

In MPLS, instead of repetitively mapping a packet to a FEC at each router, a packet only needs to be assigned to a FEC at an ingress router where the packet enters a MPLS network. A packet is then labeled with its FEC as it is forwarded. Subsequent routers do not need to further analyze the packet's network layer header. They forward the packet based on its FEC label.

Each MPLS packet has a header (Figure 8). It is positioned between the link layer (layer 2) and the network (IP) layer headers (Semeria 1999). The 32-bit header contains a 20-bit MPLS label field, a 3-bit class of service (CoS) field that can affect the forwarding behavior applied to the packet, a 1-bit stack field to support a hierarchical MPLS label stack and an 8-bit time-to-live (TTL) field to detect and discard packet looping.

A router that supports MPLS is called a label switching router (LSR). In the forwarding component of a LSR, a label-swapping forwarding algorithm, similar to that used in ATM, is applied. When a packet enters a MPLS domain, an ingress LSR examines the packet and inserts into it a MPLS header. The label carried in the MPLS header is used to identify the packet's FEC. There could be an unlimited number of ways to assign packets to FECs. The considerations could be very complicated but the complexity is isolated from the core LSRs that simply forward labeled packets. After being labeled, the packet is forwarded to the next hop on a label-switched path (LSP). A LSP, similar to a virtual circuit in ATM, defines a sequence of LSRs for a particular FEC. On the LSP, a core LSR uses the packet's input port number and MPLS label to index the forwarding table. The matched forwarding table entry includes information like the outgoing label, the outgoing interface, and the next-hop address. The LSR then swaps the packet's incoming label with the outgoing label and directs the packet to the outgoing interface for transmission to the next hop on the LSP. Before the labeled packet leaves a MPLS domain, its MPLS header is removed by an egress LSR and it will be forwarded thereafter using conventional IP forwarding.

To construct and update the forwarding table, MPLS applies a standard IP routing protocol and a label distribution protocol (LDP). The standard IP routing protocol is only used to obtain network topology information. After the topology discovery, a LDP is used to construct labeled paths between ingress and egress LSRs. Distinct LSPs are constructed for all FECs of the MPLS network. Figure 9 illustrates the differences between a conventional IP router and a LSR within the network core.

MPLS provides a solution that seamlessly integrates the control of IP routing with the simplicity of layer 2 switching. It provides a foundation that supports the deployment of advanced routing services. Compared to conventional hop-by-hop network layer routing, MPLS has the following benefits (Semeria 1999). First, it gives a service provider tremendous flexibility in the way that it assigns packets to FECs. Second, service providers can construct customized LSPs that support specific application requirements. Third, MPLS can take any type of user traffic, associate it with a FEC, and map the FEC to a LSP that has been specifically designed to satisfy the FEC's requirements.

By deploying MPLS in the network core, an ISP can obtain precise control over the flow of traffic in its network. This unprecedented level of control results in a network that operates more efficiently and provides a more predictable service.

Next, an example is used to illustrate the advantages of MPLS. Figure 10 shows how MPLS supports explicit non-shortest-path routing and thus improves applications' performance. Assume host A is transmitting packets to host C and host B is transmitting packets to host D. If the routers perform conventional OSPF routing protocol,

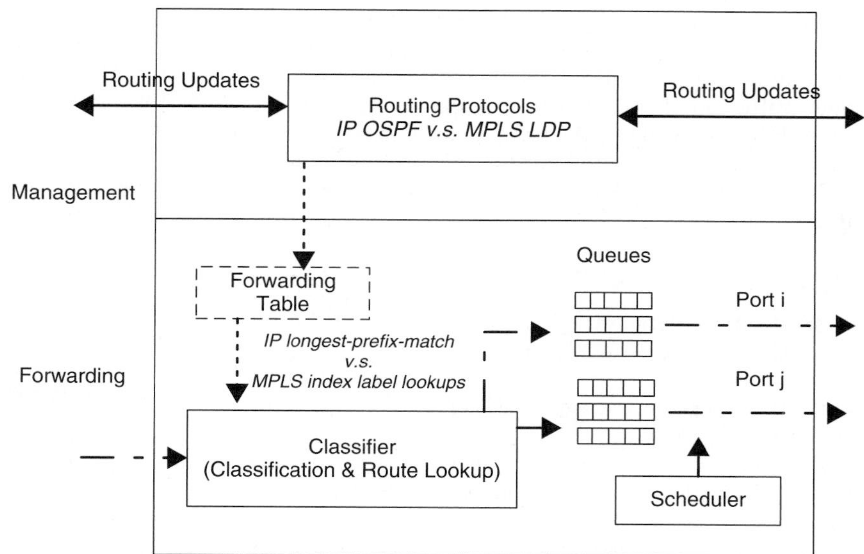

Figure 9: Routing functional components: conventional IP router vs. LSR

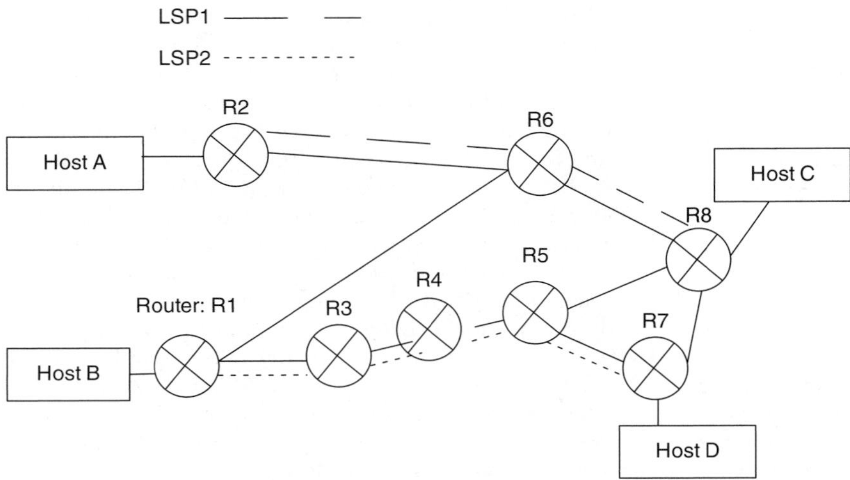

Figure 10: Explicit non-shortest-path routing

routes R2 → R6 → R8 and R1 → R6 → R8 → R7 will be followed for traffic streams from host A to host C and from host B to host D respectively because they are the shortest paths computed by the OSPF protocol. Suppose congestion is observed at router R8. One policy to reduce the congestion is to reroute some traffic load along different paths across the network. For example, let the traffic originated from host A to host C follow its shortest path, R2 → R6 → R8, and let the traffic from host B to host D follow a new path, R1 → R3 → R4 → R5 → R7. However, with conventional IP routing, it is difficult if not impossible to support this policy. On the other hand, if the routers support MPLS, it is easy to reduce the congestion at router R8. A LSP1 could be configured to follow route R2 → R6 → R8 and a LSP2 to follow route R1 → R3 → R4 → R5 → R7. The forwarding tables could be configured so that at router R2, traffic from host A to host C will be associated with a FEC and mapped to LSP1 while traffic from host B to host D will be placed on LSP2 at router R1. The ability to assign any FEC to a customized LSP gives ISPs precise control on how traffic flows through their networks. It provides a foundation that permits them to deliver new services. As another example, MPLS could be used to support service differentiation. An ISP could provision multiple LSPs between each pair of edge LSRs. With careful capacity planning, each LSP could provide different performance and bandwidth guarantees. The ingress router could then place traffic into different LSPs based on the traffic's priority, with high-priority traffic being placed on one LSP and low-priority traffic on another LSP. The three CoS bits carried in the MPLS header also facilitate forwarding service differentiation.

TRAFFIC ENGINEERING

As service providers struggle to keep pace with the ever-growing volume of Internet traffic, one major challenge for them is to provision and manage their network resources to support the committed services and to sustain high rates of growth.

Internet traffic engineering, concerned with performance optimization of operational IP networks, provides important tools for ISPs. The key objective of Internet traffic engineering is to simultaneously optimize network resource utilization and traffic performance. Its main function is to route and steer traffic through the network in the most effective way so that congestion will be reduced and network resource utilization will be improved.

Process Model

There are four phases in the traffic engineering process model (Awduche et al. 2002). The first phase is the definition of control policies. The control policy is determined by factors like the network cost structure, the operating constraints, and the utility model. The second phase applies a feedback mechanism to acquire measurement data from the network. It enables the network to adaptively optimize its performance in response to changes from inside and outside of the network. The third phase of the process model is traffic characterization and network performance analysis. Traffic characterization investigates the traffic distribution in the network and identifies the traffic workload characteristics. Performance analysis could be categorized into two types. Proactive performance analysis predicts potential problems that may occur in the future, while reactive performance analysis identifies existing problems and diagnoses their causes. Many quantitative and qualitative techniques, such as model-based analysis and simulation, could be applied in this stage. A traffic matrix may be constructed to be used for the network performance optimization. Other results such as identified performance bottlenecks could help guide network design, configuration and capacity planning. The forth phase is the network performance optimization. It chooses and implements optimization actions. Optimization actions manage either traffic or capacity. Examples include controlling traffic distribution across the network, adding additional links, increasing link capacity, and adjusting routing parameters.

Developments

This section first discusses the limitations of conventional IP technologies for traffic engineering. Then, the popular approach, IP-over-ATM, used by many ISPs to circumvent the limitations is presented. In the end, constrained-based routing and its combination with MPLS for traffic

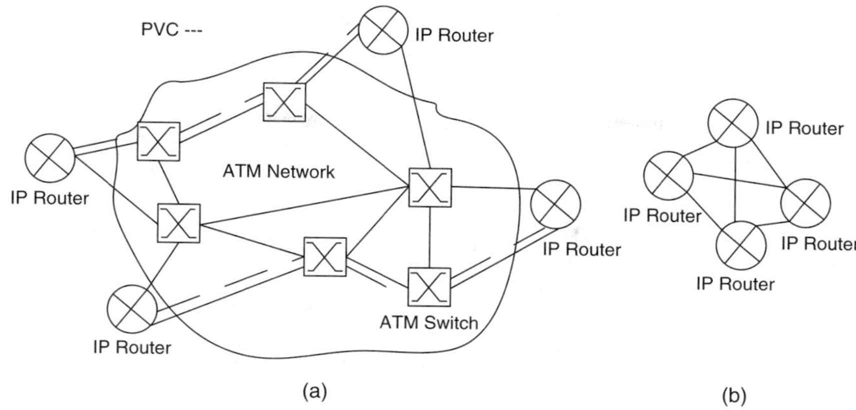

Figure 11: The IP-over-ATM model: (a) physical topology, (b) logical topology

engineering is described. Conventional IP routing is based on shortest path computation using simple additive link metric. When making routing decision, it does not take traffic characteristics and bandwidth constraints into consideration. As a result, conventional IP routing may lead to uneven distribution of traffic, causing congestion as illustrated by the example in the MPLS section. Congestion may also happen when a traffic stream requires more bandwidth than that available on its path. To circumvent these limitations and to have a better control of network performance, IP-over-ATM model has been adopted by many ISPs. It allows ISPs to support the traffic engineering process model in their networks.

Figure 11 shows an IP-over-ATM overlay model. In the ATM backbone, a permanent virtual circuit (PVC) is established between each pair of routers (for the sake of readability, only two PVCs are illustrated in the figure). By using PVCs, ATM cells are transmitted without the need to dynamically set up VCs. Router communicates with each other using PVCs. To the routers, PVCs appear as simple point-to-point links (Figure 11b). IP-over-ATM has been a popular technique adopted by many ISPs to overcome the limitations of conventional IP technologies for traffic engineering. ATM PVCs provide a powerful tool to control traffic across the ATM network precisely. By supporting explicit route of PVCs, traffic could be distributed across the network so that all the links are evenly utilized. This way, congestion caused by conventional shortest path first routing is avoided. In the overlay model, statistics on the PVCs could be used for traffic characterization, which could then be used to optimize PVCs' placement. For example, PVCs' placement could be adjusted dynamically to accommodate shifting traffic loads.

Because of ATM switches' high speed, deterministic performance and traffic engineering capabilities, IP-over-ATM has been widely adopted by ISPs and it permits ISPs to provide better services with lower costs to their customers.

However, there are a few fundamental drawbacks to the IP-over-ATM model. First, it requires the management of two separate networks. Second, it has the n-squared scalability problem. IP-over-ATM requires a full mesh of PVCs, that is, $n \times (n-1)$ PVCs for n routers. This is only feasible when the number of routers is relatively small. The difficulties of ATM SAR interfaces to reach very high speed (2.488-Gbps OC-48 speed) and the 20% cell tax only make the scalability problem worse. Third, this solution is not possible over a non-ATM infrastructure.

The emergence of high-speed Internet backbone routers and MPLS makes more integrated and scalable solutions possible for ISPs to successfully manage their networks. As a result, IP-over-ATM model has begun to lose its popularity.

Because MPLS can potentially provide most of the functionality available from IP-over-ATM model in an integrated manner, it plays a significant role for Internet traffic engineering. RFC 2702 (Awduche et al. 1999) listed seven factors that make MPLS attractive for traffic engineering such as lower overhead and supporting explicit LSPs. In the following, one of the MPLS benefits, how it facilitates constrained based routing, is explained.

In traffic engineering, constraint based routing is used to compute routes subject to multiple constraints. To determine a route, constraint based routing considers network topology, flow requirements, link available resources and other police-related factors. Thus, to do constraint based routing, routers need to distribute new link state information like topology update information and link bandwidth availability information. Such information is then used in constraint based routing to compute routes. When selecting routes, the constraint based routing aims to optimize certain metric such as hop-count, bandwidth, delay, jitter, reliability or cost. For example, the objective for constraint based routing could be to minimize the distance of a k-hop path P defined as $dist(P) = \sum_{i=1}^{k} \frac{1}{r_i}$, where r_i is the bandwidth of link i (Xiao and Ni 1999). Once the routes are computed, they will be placed in routers so that the traffic flows will follow them. LSRs could use extended IP routing protocol to exchange link state information. To facilitate route placement, MPLS uses LDP to set up LSPs. MPLS makes constraint based routing at the granularity of traffic trunk possible. Per-LSP statistics in MPLS provide constraint based routing with precise information about the traffic trunk. It helps constraint based routing improve its route optimization.

CONCLUSION AND FUTURE WORK

This chapter introduces major network QoS architectures and technologies. Despite ATM's strong support for QoS, it is not adopted by most network applications. To provide QoS on the Internet, IETF has proposed IntServ, DiffServ, MPLS, and traffic engineering. By properly addressing issues like packet forwarding and routing, these technologies provide service providers powerful tools to efficiently utilize their network resources as well as satisfy their customers' QoS requirements with lower costs.

As introduced in this chapter, there have been many efforts to provide network QoS. However, challenges remain to be addressed before we can easily deploy QoS technologies on the Internet. It is crucial when achieving the required QoS that the networks should still be kept simple, scalable, and manageable. To avoid the complexities associated with most QoS technologies, some service providers such as Sprint (Diot, Meyer, and Whiting 2001) would rather choose over-provisioning of their networks for QoS. Meanwhile, companies such as Cisco are proposing QoS toolset (AutoQoS) (*Service provider* 2003) to simplify QoS deployment. The other challenge that prevents the widely deployment of QoS technologies is their requirement that network elements implement QoS mechanisms. Research (Crowcroft and Oechslin 1998; Singh, Pradhan, and Francis 2004; Subramanian et al. 2004) has recently been conducted on providing network QoS without requiring support from IP routers, where (Singh, Pradhan, and Francis 2004; Subramanian et al. 2004) discuss overlay QoS services. In the future, the integration of network QoS and end-system QoS (see the chapter "End-System QoS") should also be investigated.

GLOSSARY

BA classification: The process of classifying packets based on the DS codepoint only.

Classifier: An entity which selects packets based on the content of packet headers according to defined rules.

Flow: A traffic stream with the same source IP address, source port number, destination IP address, destination port number, and protocol ID.

Multi-field classification: The process of classifying packets based on the content of multiple fields such as source address, destination address, DS field, protocol ID, source port number, and destination port number.

Policing: The process of discarding out of profile packets by a dropper.

Queue management: Controlling the packet queue length by dropping packets when necessary or appropriate.

Scheduling: The process of selecting queued packets for transmission.

Service Provisioning Policy: A policy which defines how traffic conditioners are configured on DS boundary nodes and how traffic streams are mapped to DS behavior aggregates to achieve a range of services.

Shaping: The process of delaying packets within a traffic stream to cause it to conform to some defined traffic profile.

Traffic trunk: An aggregation of flows with the same service class that can be put into a Label-Switched Path (LSP).

CROSS REFERENCES

See *ATM (Asynchronous Transfer Mode); End-System QoS; Network Traffic Management; Voice over MPLS and VoIP over MPLS.*

REFERENCES

Armitage, G. 2000. MPLS: The magic behind the myths. IEEE *Communications Magazine* 38(1):124–131.

Awduche, D., A. Chiu, A. Elwalid, I. Widjaja, and X. Xiao. 2002. Overview and principles of Internet traffic engineering. RFC 3272. http://www.ietf.org/rfc/rfc3272.txt (May 21, 2007).

Awduche, D., J. Malcolm, J. Agogbua, M. O'Dell, and J. McManus. 1999. Requirements for traffic engineering over MPLS. RFC 2702. http://www.ietf.org/rfc/rfc2702.txt (May 21,2007).

Bernet Y., P. Ford, R. Yavatkar, F. Baker, L. Zhang, M. Speer, R. Braden, B. Davie, J. Wroclawski, and E. Felstaine. 2000. A framework for integrated services operation over diffserv networks. IETF, RFC 2998. http://www.ietf.org/rfc/rfc2998.txt (May 21, 2007).

Blake, S., D. Black, M. Carlson, E. Davies, Z. Wang, and W. Weiss. 1998. An architecture for differentiated service. RFC 2475. http://www.ietf.org/rfc/rfc2998.txt (May 21, 2007).

Braden, R., D. Clark, and S. Shenker. Integrated services in the Internet architecture: An overview. 1994. RFC 1633. http://www.ietf.org/rfc/rfc1633.txt (May 21, 2007).

Clark, D., and J. Wroclawski. 1997. An approach to service allocation in the Internet. http://tools.ietf.org/id/draft-clark-diff-svc-alloc-00.txt (May 21, 2007).

Crowcroft, J., and P. Oechslin. 1998. Differentiated end-to-end Internet services using a weighted proportional fair sharing TCP. *ACM Computer Communication Review* 28(3):53–69.

Davie, B., A. Charny, J. Bennet, K. Benson, J. L. Boudec, W. Courtney, S. Davari, V. Firoiu, and D. Stiliadis. 2002. An expedited forwarding PHB (per-hop behavior). RFC 3246. http://www.ietf.org/rfc/rfc3246.txt (May 21, 2007).

Diot, C., D. Meyer, and P. Whiting. 2001. MPLS and the sprint Esolutions IP backbone network. http://whitepapers.zdnet.co.uk/0,1000000651,260079694p,00.htm?r=1 (May 21, 2007).

El-Gendy, M. A., A. Bose, and K. G. Shin. 2003. Evolution of the Internet QoS and support for soft real-time applications. *Proceedings of the IEEE* 91(7):1086–1104.

Grossman, D. 2002. New terminology and clarifications for diffServ, IETF RFC 3260. http://www.ietf.org/rfc/rfc3260.txt (May 21, 2007).

Heinanen, J., F. Baker, W. Weiss, and J. Wroclawski. 1999. Assured forwarding PHB group. RFC 2597. http://www.ietf.org/rfc/rfc2597.txt (May 21, 2007).

Kurose, J. F., and K. Ross. 2002. *Computer Networking: A Top-Down Approach Featuring the Internet*. Boston, MA: Addison-Wesley Longman Publishing Co., Inc.

Nichols, K., S. Blake, F. Baker, and D. Black. 1998. Definition of the differentiated services field (DS Field) in the IPv4 and IPv6 headers. RFC 2474. http://www.rfc-editor.org/rfc/rfc2474.txt (May 21, 2007).

Nichols, K., V. Jacobson, and L. Zhang. 1999. A two-bit differentiated services architecture for the Internet. RFC 2638. http://www.faqs.org/rfcs/rfc2638.html (May 21, 2007).

Semeria, C. 1999. Multiprotocol label switching: Enhancing routing in the new public network. http://www.urec.cnrs.fr/hd/MPLS/JUNIPER/routing_public_net.pdf (May 21, 2007).

Semeria, C. 2000. Traffic engineering for the new public network. http://www.juniper.net/solutions/literature/white_papers/200004.pdf (May 21, 2007).

Service provider quality-of-service overview. 2003. Cisco Systems. http://www.cisco.com/en/US/netsol/ns590/networking_solutions_white_paper09186a00801c796d.shtml (May 21, 2007).

Shenker, S., C. Partridge, and R. Guerin. 1997. Specification of guaranteed quality of service. RFC 2212. http://www.faqs.org/rfcs/rfc2212.html (May 21, 2007).

Singh, M., P. Pradhan, and P. Francis. 2004. MPAT: Aggregate TCP congestion management as a building block for Internet QoS. IEEE International Conference on Network Protocols, Berlin, Germany, October 5–8 2004.

Subramanian, L., I. Stoica, H. Balakrishnan, and R. Katz. 2004. OverQoS: An overlay based architecture for enhancing Internet QoS. USENIX First Symposium on Networked Systems Design and Implementation, San Francisco, CA, March 29–31, 2004.

Wang, Z. 2001. *Internet QoS: Architectures and Mechanisms for Quality of Service*. San Francisco, CA: Morgan Kaufmann Publishers Inc.

Wroclawski, J. 1997. The Use of RSVP with IETF integrated services. RFC 2210. http://www.ietf.org/rfc/rfc2210.txt (May 21, 2007).

Wroclawski, J. 1997. Specification of the controlled-load network element service. RFC 2211. http://www.ietf.org/rfc/rfc2211.txt (May 21, 2007).

Xiao, X., and L. M. Ni. 1999. Internet QoS: A big picture. *IEEE Network* 13(2):8–18.

Zhang, L., S. Deering, D. Estrin, S. Shenker, and D. Zappala. 2001. RSVP: A new resource reservation protocol. Readings in multimedia computing and networking, 624–634, San Francisco, CA: Morgan Kaufmann Publishers Inc.

Internet Security Standards

Raymond R. Panko, *University of Hawaii, Manoa*

INTRODUCTION

When the Internet was created, security was left out of its TCP/IP standards. At the time, the crude state of security knowledge may have made this lack of security necessary, and the low frequency of attacks made this lack of security reasonable.

Today, however, security expertise is more mature. In addition, the broad presence of security threats on the Internet means that security today must be addressed deliberately and aggressively. In 2004, between 5 and 12 percent of all sampled traffic moving across ISP (Internet service provider) networks was malicious (Legard 2004). This chapter describes two ways to add standards-based security to the Internet:

- The first is for users to add standards-based security to individual dialogues, that is, to two-way conversations between pairs of communicating processes. Today, this can be done largely through the use of virtual private networks (VPNs) using the IPsec, SSL/TLS, and PPTP protocols. This "security overlay" approach is not as desirable as good general Internet security standards, but it solves many current user needs.
- The second approach is to add more security to central Internet standards. In addition to the "core three" standards (IP, TCP, and UDP), these central Internet standards include supervisory standards (such as ICMP, DNS, DHCP, SNMP, LDAP, and dynamic routing protocols) and application standards (such as SMTP, HTTP, and FTP). A major effort to retrofit existing Internet standards to add security is underway in the Internet Engineering Task Force under the Danvers Doctrine, but this effort is far from complete.

In this chapter, we will look at these two broad approaches, in the order just presented.

This chapter will not look at security for single network standards, including Ethernet, wireless LANs, asynchronous transfer mode (ATM), frame relay, and the public switched telephone network (PSTN). These individual LANs and WANs operate at the physical and data link layers. As Figure 1 shows, the Internet is a collection of individual LANs and WANs connected by routers. Under normal circumstances, attackers can only send data link layer commands to hosts on their own LAN or WAN. Consequently, for attacks occurring over the Internet, only Internet, transport, and application layer attacks are possible. This chapter focuses on Internet security standards, so it will not discuss attacks on individual LANs and WANs.

This chapter focuses more specifically on TCP/IP internetworking, which is used on the Internet, rather than on IPX/SPX (internetwork packet exchange/sequenced packet exchange), SNA (systems network architecture), and other forms of internetworking, which cannot be used on the Internet. More formally, this chapter focuses on security in TCP/IP standards at the Internet, transport, and application layers.

SECURITY THREATS AND DEFENSES

Before looking at security in Internet standards, we need to consider major security threats and defenses. We will begin with types of attacks because IETF Internet security efforts have focused on one type of attack, namely attacks on dialogues.

Penetration Attacks

One set of threats against which networks must guard is attackers attempting to penetrate into networks and hosts

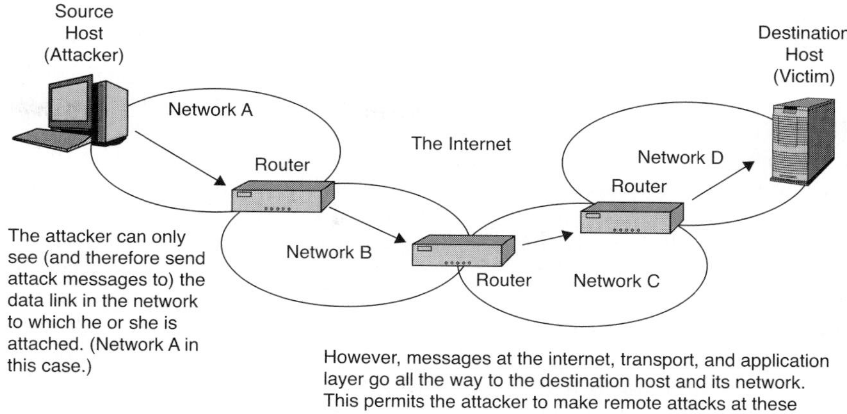
Source
Host
(Attacker)
Destination
Host
(Victim)
Network A
The Internet
Router
Network D
Router
The attacker can only see (and therefore send attack messages to) the data link in the network to which he or she is attached. (Network A in this case.)
Network B
Router
Network C
However, messages at the internet, transport, and application layer go all the way to the destination host and its network. This permits the attacker to make remote attacks at these layers.

Figure 1: The reason for focusing on Internet layer (and higher) security

by sending probe and break-in messages. These include the following:

- Hacking (when humans intentionally access systems without authorization or in excess of authorization)
- Attempting to conduct denial-of-service (DoS) attacks against networks or hosts by crashing them or overloading them to the point of being useless to their legitimate users
- Automated malware attacks using viruses, worms, spam, and other undesirable content

Attacks on Dialogues

Second, when two parties communicate, they normally engage in a dialogue, in which multiple messages are sent in both directions between two hosts. These dialogues must be secure against attackers who may want to read, delete, alter, add, or replay messages.

An IETF Focus on Dialogue Security

In general, dialogue security has been the main focus of IETF efforts to add security to Internet (TCP/IP) standards. Hacking, DoS attacks, and malware attacks are sometimes addressed, but this is comparatively uncommon. Consequently, we will focus on dialogue security in our discussion.

DIALOGUE SECURITY

In dialogue security, there are three major goals: confidentiality, authentication, and integrity. Confidentiality is relatively easy to provide, and integrity normally appears as a by-product of authentication. Authentication is the most difficult protection to apply, so we will focus the most attention on it.

Confidentiality

Confidentiality means that eavesdroppers who intercept messages en route over the Internet cannot read them. Encryption for confidentiality is the chief tool against unauthorized reading en route.

Encryption is relatively easy to do well if the security developer stays with strong and proven encryption algorithm. In the past, this meant DES and 3DES. Today, this means the advanced encryption standard (AES), which is strong and places a comparatively light processing and memory burden on the communicating devices. AES has also been strongly tested and has survived many attempts to break it. If a security designer does not specify AES, it is incumbent on them to provide a very strong reason for this deviation from good practice.

Authentication and Integrity

Authentication means that the receiver of messages (called the verifier) can verify the identity of the sender (called the applicant or supplicant) in order to ensure that the sender is not an impostor. There are two forms of authentication:

- *Initial authentication*: One side proves its identity to the other side at or near the beginning of a dialogue.
- *Message-by-message authentication*: The sender continues to identify itself with every message, much as parties exchanging letters sign each letter. Message-by-message authentication is crucial to good security.

Integrity means that if a message has been captured and changed en route, then the receiver will be able to detect that a change has occurred. All forms of message-by-message authentication provide message integrity as a by-product. If a message is changed during transmission, either deliberately or through transmission errors, authentication will fail, and the receiver will discard the message.

Initial Authentication

As discussed later, when cryptographic protection systems begin to operate, they usually do initial mutual authentication. Virtual private network (VPN) protocols, which add overlay protection on individual dialogues between hosts, tend to have well-developed initial authentication methods. All three major VPN standards—IPsec, SSL/TLS, and PPTP—have well-defined initial authentication stages.

However, when the IETF adds security to individual existing protocols, such as TCP, it usually implements message-by-message authentication but not initial authentication. Furthermore, it usually does this by providing HMAC (key-hashed message authentication code) authentication, which is discussed later. HMAC requires the two parties to have a shared secret key. Protocols that use HMACs usually are silent on how to distribute these secret keys. Although these keys can be distributed manually, this approach will not scale to large and complex networks.

One possibility for the future is to require protocols to use the extensible authentication protocol (EAP) (Blunk and Vollbrecht 1998), which uses public key authentication with digital certificates for at least one of the two parties. This would work well in many cases in which a server needs to work with multiple clients. Clients can use weaker authentication mechanisms if appropriate.

Kerberos authentication traditionally has used pre-shared master keys between computers and Kerberos authentication servers. Given the weaknesses of this approach, the IETF extended Kerberos to use public keys and digital certificates for initial authentication in 2006 (Zhu and Tung 2006).

Message-by-Message Authentication

Although initial authentication is important, the most complex authentication issues revolve around message-by-message authentication. Consequently, we will focus more specifically on this type of authentication. There are two common message-by-message authentication methods: HMACs and digital signatures. Both are described in more detail in the chapter on electronic and digital signatures. However, we need to discuss them briefly here.

Digital Signatures and Digital Certificates

As discussed in the chapter on electronic and digital signatures, when security uses digital signatures, a bit string called a digital signature is added to each outgoing message. More specifically, the sender creates a message digest by hashing the message and then encrypts this message digest with his or her own private key. Encrypting a message digest with the sender's private key is called signing the message digest. The sender transmits the digital signature along with the original message to the receiver.

As Figure 2 shows, to test the digital signature, the receiver (verifier) must know the public key of the *true party*—the party the sender claims to be. Normally, the receiver obtains the public key of the true party by obtaining the true party's digital certificate. The digital certificate, among other things, contains the name and public key of the true party. The receiver obtains the true party's digital certificate once and then uses the public key in the digital certificate to test the digital signature in each message.

The receiver must obtain the digital certificate from a trusted certificate authority (CA). One problem with digital certificates is that CAs are not regulated in most countries, leading to questions about their trustworthiness. Although European countries are planning to create regulated CAs, the United States and most other countries are trusting market forces to self-regulate CAs.

It is possible to obtain public keys without using CAs. pretty good privacy (PGP) offers one way to do so. Each user has a "key ring" of trusted public key/name pairs. If User A trusts User B, User A may trust User B's key ring, which may, of course, contain keys received through further distributed trust. If an impostor can dupe even one user, trust in the impostor can spread widely. This is not a good way to manage large public systems of routers, DNS (domain name system) hosts, and other sensitive devices.

Beyond these traditional approaches, efforts are now underway, as noted later in the "Web Services" section, to develop federated authentication methods that allow one-to-one and one-to-few exchanges of digital certificates and other ways to share public keys.

It is also possible to distribute public keys manually. This works well in small systems, but it does not scale well to very large systems.

HMACs

Another tool for message-by-message authentication is the key-hashed message authentication code (HMAC). For HMAC authentication, two parties share a secret key. To send a message, one of the parties appends the key to the message, hashes the combination, and adds this hash (the HMAC) to the outgoing message. To test an arriving message, the receiver also adds the key to the message and hashes the combination. This creates another HMAC. If the received and computed HMACs are the same, the sender knows the secret key, which only the other party should use.

HMACs require less processing power than digital signatures because HMACs only involve hashing, which is a fast process. In contrast, public key encryption and decryption, which are used in digital signatures, are extremely processing intensive.

However, a secret key for HMAC authentication needs to be created and distributed securely for *each pair* of

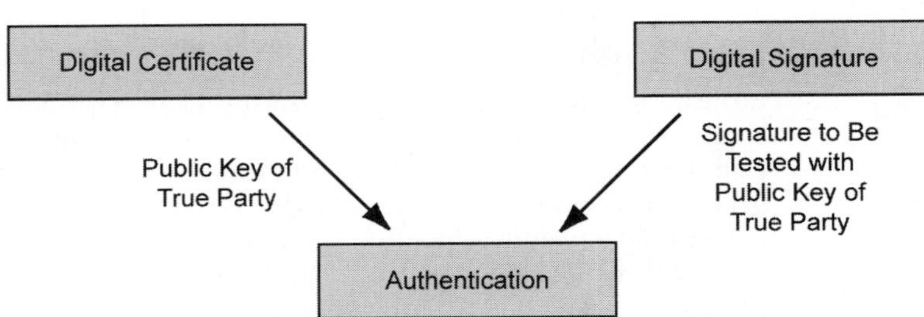

Figure 2: The need for digital certificates with digital signatures

communicating parties. In large systems of routers and hosts, this can be highly problematic. One approach to reduce this problem is to use public key authentication for initial authentication, and then use the Diffie-Hellman key agreement or public key distribution (using either the RSA or DSA [digital signature algorithm] protocol) to send the secret keys between pairs of communicating parties. However, these approaches only work if there is good initial authentication.

Another "solution" to the key distribution problems is to use community keys, which are shared by all communicating parties in a community. The problem here, of course, is that if a single member of the community is compromised, attackers reading its community key will be able to authenticate themselves to all other members of the community. In addition, community keys are rarely changed because of the need to coordinate the change among many users. When many users are communicating with a key that is rarely if ever changed, a large volume of communication is encrypted with the same key. With a large volume of communication, cryptanalysts often can crack the key. Using community strings for security is a very bad idea.

Another problem with HMACs is repudiation. In repudiation, a party that sent a message denies that they sent it. With digital signatures, repudiation is technically impossible because only the true party should know the true party's private key, so only the true party could have sent the message. Digital signatures provide nonrepudiation.

However, with HMACs, both sides know the shared secret key. So if the sender argues that the repudiated message was fabricated by the receiver, there is no possible technical counter-argument. HMACs do not provide nonrepudiation.

ADDING OVERLAY SECURITY TO INDIVIDUAL DIALOGUES

As noted previously, the first approach to creating standards-based security is for users to add security to individual existing dialogues. Effectively, this overlays security on the Internet for individual dialogues and works without requiring the creation of completely new Internet standards.

Cryptographic Protection Systems (CPSs)

Secure dialogues require that confidentiality, authentication, and integrity be protected. This is a somewhat complex process involving several phases.

Cryptographic Protection System Phases

Establishing a secure dialogue with a CPS typically involves four sequential phases (although the specific operations and the order of operations can vary among cryptographic protection systems). Figure 3 illustrates these phases. The first three are quick handshaking phases at the beginning of the dialogue. After the secure dialogue is established, the two parties usually engage in a long ongoing secure conversation.

1. The two parties must select security standard options within the range offered by a particular cryptographic protection system. For instance, in encryption for confidentiality, the system may offer the choice of a half dozen encryption methods. The communicating parties must select one to use in their subsequent exchanges. The chosen methodology may offer several options; these too must be negotiated.
2. The two parties must authenticate themselves to each other. Although initial authentication might seem like it should be the first step instead of the second, the two parties need the first phase to negotiate which authentication method they will use to authenticate themselves.
3. The two parties must exchange one or more secrets (keys are examples of secrets) securely. These secrets will be used in the ongoing dialogue phase that will take place after the initial three "hand-shaking" phases of the CPS are finished.
4. The security of the communication is now established. The two parties now engage in ongoing dialogue with message-by-message confidentiality, authentication, and integrity. Typically, nearly all communication takes place during this ongoing dialogue phase.

The User's Role

Few users have the training to select security options intelligently, much less handle authentication and other tasks. Consequently, cryptographic protection systems work automatically. The user selects a communication partner, and the systems of the two partners work through the four phases automatically.

At most, users may have to authenticate themselves to their own systems via password, an identification card, biometrics, or some other approach. This user authentication phase tends to be the weak link in CPSs because of poor security practices on the part of users, such as using weak passwords.

The Policy Role

Different security options have different implications for the strength of a cryptographic protection system's security. Users rarely are capable of selecting intelligently among options. Consequently, companies must be able to set policies for which methods and options will be

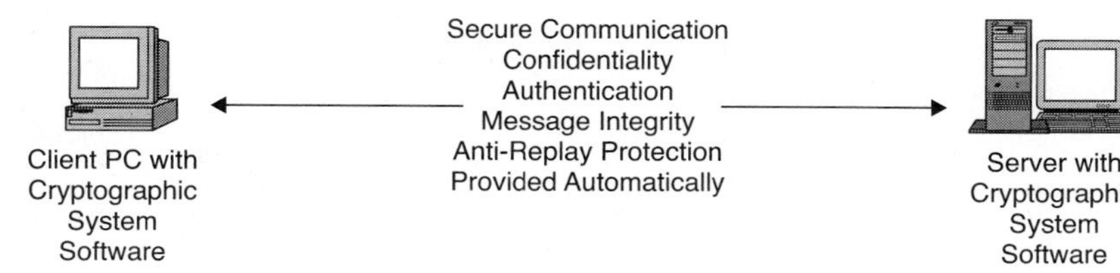

Figure 3: Cryptographic protection system (CPS)

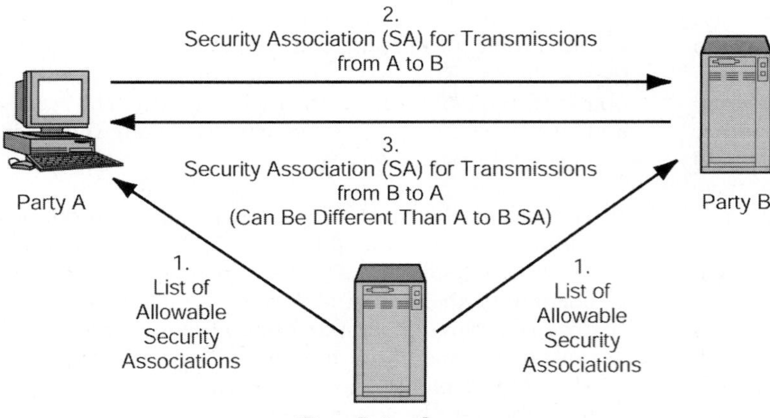

Figure 4: Policy-based security associations in IPsec

acceptable under different circumstances, and they must be able to support these policies by promulgating them and enforcing their use.

Figure 4 shows how policy guides security in IPsec, which we will see later. In IPsec, security often is handled by IPsec gateways. When two IPsec gateways begin to communicate, they establish security associations, which are contracts for how security will be done. A policy server can tell the IPsec gateways what security association parameters they may select or not select. This ensures that the IPsec gateways do not select security associations that are too weak for the traffic they will carry. This approach works with host computers as well as with IPsec gateways.

PPP and PPTP VPNs

Dial-Up Security and PPP at the Data Link Layer

Early computer systems used dial-up security. As Figure 5 shows, the user dialed into a server, generally using the point-to-point protocol (PPP) (Simpson 1994) at the data link layer. Later, companies added security to this approach by creating remote access servers (RASs) for sites. The user dialed into the RAS, authenticated himself or herself (usually with a password), and then received access to all servers at a site or to selected servers.

If a company has several RASs, it normally uses a RADIUS server or some other authentication server to store authentication information remotely, as Figure 5 shows. This way, all RASs use the same authentication data. Otherwise, if a firm has several RASs, their authentication data may be inconsistent. Adversaries may try different RASs until they find one that is configured incorrectly.

PPP can be used without security, but PPP offers moderately good encryption and several options for authentication ranging from nothing to very strong. Again, the dialogue partners must select the security options they want to employ.

Tunneling

Although PPP is secure, it is limited to a single data link because it operates at the data link layer, as Figure 6 illustrates. However, when a connection is made over the Internet, each connection between a host and a router or between two routers is a separate data link. PPP cannot function over the Internet.

Consequently, Internet-based data link layer security approaches must use tunneling. In tunneling, a data link layer frame is placed within the data field of a packet—the opposite of the usual situation. Placing a message within another message is called tunneling.

The packet is sent from the user computer to the RAS, across multiple links. Finally, the RAS receives and reads the tunneled (encapsulated) frame. Although this effect seems needlessly complex, it allows us to use traditional PPP user-RAS security over the Internet.

Again, when a message is placed inside another message—especially within a packet—this is called

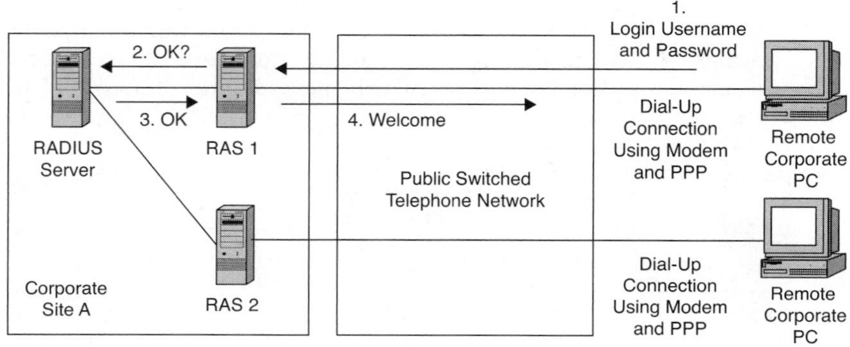

Figure 5: RADIUS authentication

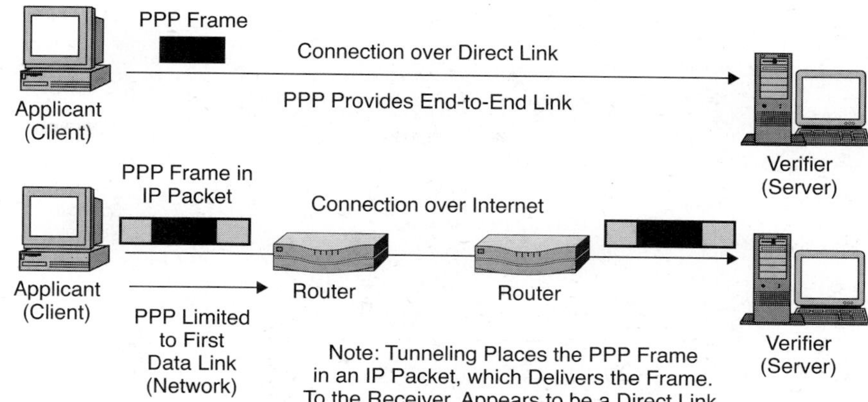

Figure 6: Tunneling PPP

tunneling. We will see later that IPsec also uses tunneling in one of its operating modes (tunneling mode, of course). Tunneling is a delivery technology, not a security technology (Panko 2004). Many security articles and even textbooks confuse the two.

PPTP

The main tunneling protocol for PPP is the point-to-point tunneling protocol (PPTP) (Hamzeh et al. 1999). As its name suggests, PPTP does not have its own security. Rather, PPTP is a way to tunnel PPP frames over the Internet. PPTP uses PPP security methods (encryption and authentication), extending them over an entire Internet connection instead of over a single dial-up data link. PPTP has a number of moderate security weaknesses, but it is good for low-threat or medium-threat environments.

L2TP

Although PPTP works and is attractive, it is limited to transmission over an IP network such as the Internet. The newer layer two tunneling protocol (L2TP) (Tonsley et al. 1999) can tunnel frames over a number of transmission mechanisms, including IP, frame relay, and ATM, to name just three (Tonsley et al. 1999).

However, L2TP does not offer security by itself. It requires users to rely on the IPsec protocol discussed next to provide security at the Internet layer during transit. L2TP is a pure tunneling protocol, not a security protocol at all.

IPsec VPNs

The Internet layer (the OSI network layer) is the core layer in TCP/IP internetworking. The Internet protocol (IP) is the main packet standard at this layer. IP comes in two versions—IP version 4 (IPv4) and IP version 6 (IPv6). IPv4 is the dominant version in use on the Internet today, but IPv6 is beginning to grow, especially in Asia, where relatively few IPv4 addresses were allocated when the Internet was first created.

The IPsec Effort

The Internet Engineering Task Force (IETF) has been working to retrofit IP to be more secure. Their effort has crystallized around a group of standards collectively called IPsec (IP security) (Thayer, Doraswamy, and Glenn 1998). Although IPsec was initially planned for IPv6, the IETF has developed it to work with IPv4 as well.

Encryption and Authentication

The dominant way to use IPsec is to employ the encapsulated security protocol (ESP) option, which offers both encryption and authentication. We will focus on ESP rather than on the authentication header (AH) option, which only provides authentication. AH is useful primarily when encryption is illegal; this is a rare situation.

Tunnel Mode

As Figure 7 shows, IPsec can operate in two modes: tunnel mode and transport mode. We will discuss tunnel mode first.

In tunnel mode, IPsec is handled by IPsec gateways at the two sites of the communicating parties, not by the computers of the communicating parties themselves. The packet to be delivered securely is tunneled by encapsulating it in another packet, encrypting the original packet, adding authentication, and sending the encapsulating packet from one IPsec gateway to the other. Although attackers can read the IP header of the encapsulating packet, they cannot read the secured packet; nor can they change the secured packet without the change being obvious.

Tunnel mode is attractive because it does not impose expensive installation and configuration burdens on each host. It does not require the individual hosts to have IPsec software on their computers or know how to configure the software. In fact, the users may not even be aware that IPsec is protecting their packets over the Internet. Even more importantly, it is not necessary to obtain a digital certificate for each host and install one on each host if tunnel mode is used; only the IPsec gateways need digital certificates.

The disadvantage of tunnel mode is that it does not provide any protection for the packet as it travels *within* the two sites. The focus is entirely on security during the Internet stage of transmission.

Transport Mode

In contrast, as Figure 7 also shows, IPsec's transport mode offers *end-to-end* encryption and authentication between

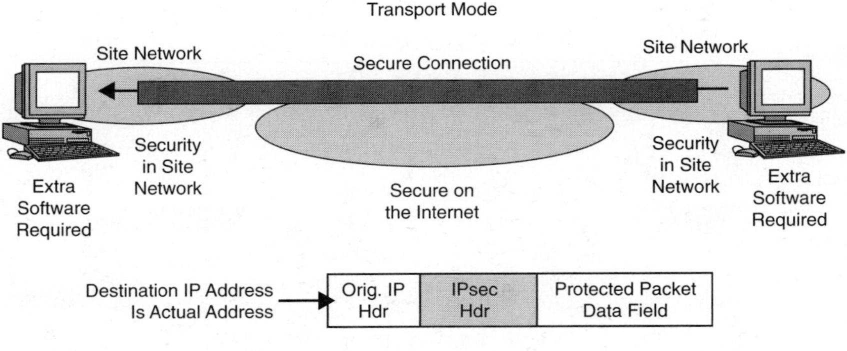

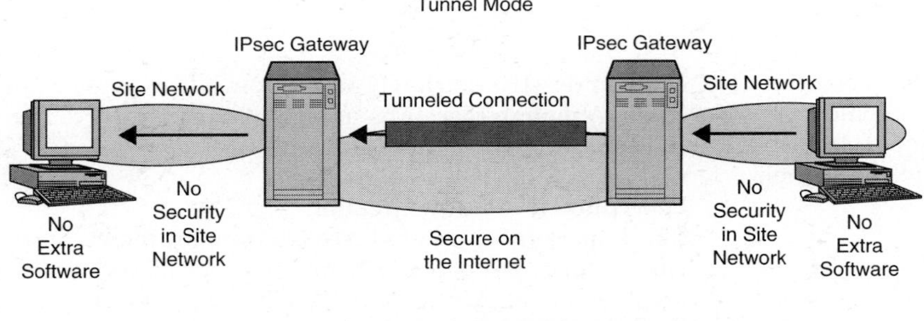

Figure 7: IPsec in tunnel mode and transport mode

the two computers in a dialogue. This approach provides security not only while packets travel through the Internet but also when the packets are passing through local site networks on their way to and from the Internet. Although the Internet exposes traffic to many attackers, there also are dangers within corporate networks. In fact, some of the worst attacks are made by corporate insiders working within corporate networks.

Although the end-to-end security of transport mode is attractive, it comes at a substantial price. Larger firms have thousands or even tens of thousands of PCs. Transport mode requires the configuration of IPsec software and a digital certificate on every PC to be protected. This is extremely expensive.

A more modest problem is that transport mode packets must have the IP address of the receiving computer in the destination address field of the packet header. If sniffers can be placed along the route of these packets, attackers will be able to learn the IP addresses of many corporate hosts. This is a first step in most types of Internet-based attacks. In contrast, tunnel mode packets only have the IP addresses of the receiving IPsec gateway in their destination address fields. This only tells attackers about the IP address of a single machine that usually is well hardened against attacks.

Combining Tunnel Mode and Transfer Mode

One solution to the relative weaknesses of the two modes is to use both. The user can use transport mode to provide end-to-end security but also to use IPsec in tunnel mode between sites to hide IP addresses.

IPsec in IPv4 and IPv6

As noted at the beginning of this section, IPsec can be used with both IPv4 and IPv6. However, with IPv6, the use of IPsec is *mandatory* (Microsoft 2004). With IPv4, however, IPsec is optional.

SSL/TLS VPNs

IPsec is a very complex security mechanism, but it has the advantage of transparency. This means that IPsec protects *all* higher-layer traffic at the transport and application layers automatically, without requiring higher-layer protocols to do any work or even be aware of this protection.

In some applications, dialogues are limited to World Wide Web or at most WWW and e-mail. Under these conditions, the costly burden of implementing IPsec is not justified, and many firms turn to a simpler protocol, transport layer security (TLS), which was originally created by Netscape as secure sockets layer (SSL) and was then renamed transport layer security (TLS) by the Internet Engineering Task Force when the IETF took over the standard's development (Dierks and Allen 1999). If your URL begins with "https," then you are using SSL/TLS.

Whereas IPsec provides a blanket of protection at the Internet layer, SSL/TLS creates a secure connection at the transport layer. This secure connection potentially can protect all application layer traffic. Unfortunately, SSL/TLS requires that applications be *SSL/TLS-compliant* to benefit from this protection. Although all browsers and WWW servers can use SSL/TLS, only some e-mail

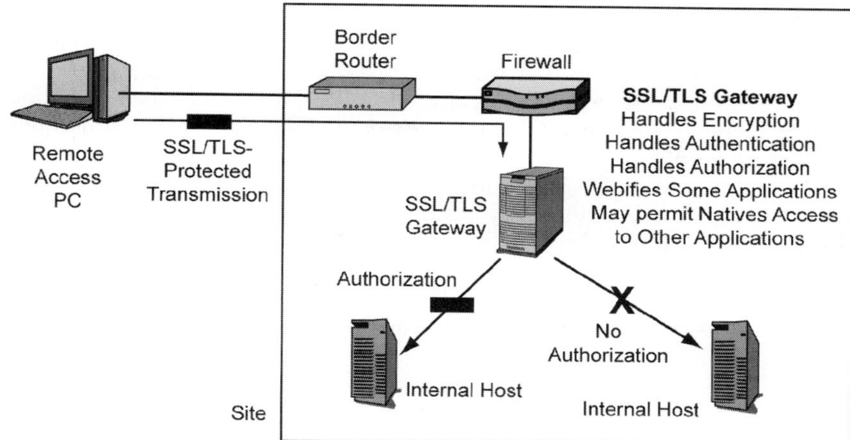

Figure 8: SSL/TLS using gateway operation

systems can use SSL/TLS, and few other applications can benefit from SSL/TLS protection at the transport layer.

SSL/TLS was created for e-commerce, in which a residential client PC communicates with a merchant server. SSL/TLS requires the merchant to authenticate itself to the client using digital certificates and digital signatures. However, few residential client PC owners have digital certificates. So while SSL/TLS permits client authentication using a digital certificate, it makes client authentication optional. This lack of mandatory client authentication is a major security vulnerability that is intolerable in many situations. If SSL is used in dialogue security, client authentication should be required.

Vendors have begun to create semiproprietary techniques to create remote access SSL/TLS VPNs for corporate use, and these techniques have become very popular. As Figure 8 shows, the user firm places an SSL/TLS gateway server at each site, and users have an SSL/VPN connection to this gateway server. The gateway server provides initial client PC authentication using passwords or some other proprietary mechanism. The gateway server then connects the user to internal servers.

SSL/TLS gateway servers can even get around the limitations of SSL/TLS's HTTP focus. Of course, they can protect HTTP traffic easily because SSL/TLS does this automatically.

In addition, most SSL/TLS gateways can "webify" non-HTTP applications such as Microsoft Outlook—sending screen images over HTTP. If the browser will accept a downloaded add-in, many SSL/TLS gateways can even give the user protected access to traditional applications. However, both webification and application access via browser downloads requires proprietary techniques.

The main attraction of SSL/TLS is that the user can use any PC that has a browser, including those in Internet cafes. Unfortunately, trace information from the user's session continues to reside on the PC after the session. Plug-in browser software to remove these traces can be added to the browser, but this requires operating system privileges that users are not likely to have when they work on PCs in Internet cafes.

Multilayer Security

As Figure 9 shows, security can be applied at several standards layers. A major principle of security is defense in depth. Vulnerabilities are discovered in almost all security protections from time to time. Until they are fixed, the attacker has free access—unless the attacker must break through two or more lines of defense. With multiple protections in place, the company will still be protected while it repairs a broken security countermeasure.

Consequently, companies would be better protected if they added dialogue security to more than one layer, say by implementing both IPsec and application security. However, this is expensive, so it is not common.

Dialogue Security and Firewalls

Although adding security to dialogues passing through the Internet is attractive, it creates problems for firewalls. Firewalls need to examine arriving and leaving packets. However, almost all cryptographic protection systems encrypt packets for confidentiality.

Unless these packets are decrypted before passing through the firewall, the firewalls cannot scan their packets for attack signatures. Consequently, companies that

Layer	Cryptographic Protection System
Application	Kerberos
Transport	SSL/TLS
Internet	IPsec
Data Link	PPP, PPTP
Physical	Not applicable. No messages are sent at this layer—only individual bits.

Figure 9: Multilayer Security

buy added security by implementing cryptographic protection systems (CPSs) tend to lose some scanning security. This places a heavier burden on end stations to do scanning, and many end stations are client PCs whose owners lack the willingness, much less the knowledge, to do packet scanning.

One solution is to decrypt all incoming packets before they reach the border firewall, by placing a cryptographic gateway between the border firewall and the border router. However, this leaves the cryptographic gateway unprotected from Internet attacks. If the cryptographic gateway is taken over by attackers, the results can be disastrous.

ADDING SECURITY TO INDIVIDUAL INTERNET STANDARDS

Although adding dialogue security to individual dialogues works, it would be better for Internet standards themselves to offer high security. For instance, if DNS servers are disabled so that clients cannot find application servers, dialogue security will do little good.

When the Internet was first created, none of its standards offered any security. Today, several TCP/IP standards offer security. Unfortunately, the closer you examine their security features, the less adequate many appear. Fortunately, the IETF has a program to add security to a broad range of existing Internet standards individually.

A Broad IETF Commitment

The IETF efforts we have discussed so far are not isolated actions. The IRTF has a broad programmatic commitment to increasing the security of its standards.

The Danvers Doctrine

In 1995, a meeting of the IETF in Danvers, Massachusetts, reached a consensus that the IETF should develop strong security for all of its protocols (Schiller 2002). Originally, the consensus was limited to a decision to use strong encryption keys rather than weak encryption keys that met existing export restrictions. Soon, however, this Danvers Doctrine expanded into a consensus to develop strong security for all TCP/IP protocols. As a first step, all RFCs are now required to include a section on security considerations. As we will now see, considerable progress has also been made in adding security to individual TCP/IP standards.

User Choice

Although all TCP/IP standards are to be given strong security, the IETF decided that it should be the option of individual organizations whether or not to implement security in individual protocols. In part, this decision reflects a desire not to force security on anyone. In part, it also reflects the fact that some networks are in protected environments that do not require security. However, an important consequence of the decision to leave security up to organizations is that organizations must decide which security options to use or not use.

There are five broad layers of functionality in networking—physical, data link, Internet, transport, and applications. Implementing security at all layers would be horrendously expensive and generally unnecessary.

Consequently, many organizations will only want to implement security at one layer. Although this would provide security, individual security technologies often are found to have vulnerabilities. To maintain protection during these periods of vulnerabilities, organizations probably will want to implement security in the protocols at two layers at least, as noted earlier.

Security and Vulnerabilities

Security in Protocols

In discussing the security of Internet protocols, there are two issues. One is whether security has been built into the protocol at all and to what degree it has been placed in the protocol. This is the aspect of Internet protocol security we focus on in this chapter.

Protocol and Implementation Vulnerabilities

Another aspect of Internet protocol security is whether the protocol or its implementation has vulnerabilities that attackers can exploit. In some cases, the protocols themselves are exploitable because of design oversights. In more cases, vendor implementations cause problems. For instance, both the BIND program, which is dominant for Domain Name System servers, and the Sendmail program, which is dominant on UNIX SMTP servers, have had long and troubled histories of security vulnerabilities.

Implementation vulnerabilities are especially dangerous when the same flaw is discovered in multiple vendor code bases. (For example, in February 2001, two major vulnerabilities were found in the simple network management protocol [SNMP] version 1 programs of multiple vendors.) This too can result in Internet-scale disruptions.

The worst-case scenario is a serious vulnerability in a protocol itself because this will affect all products and may take some time to change. In 2003, for example, the TCP Reset vulnerability was discovered. It is difficult to insert messages into a TCP segment stream because TCP uses 32-bit sequence numbers. This gives more than four billion possible sequence numbers. An attacker normally must guess the precise next sequence number that the receiver is expecting. However, TCP acknowledgements contain a Window field. In an odd choice, the TCP standard specifies that if a TCP segment has its RST (reset) bit set, then the receiver will accept *any* sequence number within the Window range. This greatly reduces the number of sequence numbers an attacker must try to cause the target to accept a RST message, which will break its connection with its communication partner. This is a DoS attack. BGP (border gateway protocol), which has long sessions and uses large Window size values, is especially vulnerable to this attack. This is disturbing because BGP is critical for exchanging routing information between Internet core routers and between corporate border routers and Internet core routers. As discussed in the section on BGP later in this chapter, using TCP authentication can reduce the TCP Reset danger.

Lack of Code Diversity

For some protocols, a single code base is used by most or all vendor implementations. For instance, most DNS servers use BIND. In e-mail, use is dominated by Sendmail on UNIX systems and Exchange on Microsoft mail servers. This means that if a vulnerability is found, an attack can produce Internet-scale disruptions. This is called the "potato famine" problem because the Irish potato famine was caused by a lack of genetic diversity in the Irish potato crop. The failure of many systems due to the same problem is also called a common mode failure.

Tardy Patching

In addition, when vendors release patches for vulnerabilities, many firms fail to install patches quickly or at all. This makes some vulnerabilities exploitable for weeks, months, or even years after they are discovered. All too often, firms only patch vulnerabilities in earnest when a virus or hackers create widespread damage.

Perspective

Although protocol and implementation vulnerabilities are important, they are situation-specific. This chapter focuses on security within Internet standards themselves.

The Core Three: IP, TCP, and UDP

There are three core standards at the heart of the Internet: IP, TCP, and UDP.

IP

The main job of the Internet protocol (IP) (Postel, RFC 791, 1981) is to move packets from the source host to the destination host across the Internet, which consists of thousands of networks connected by routers. IP is a hop-by-hop protocol designed to govern how each router handles each IP packet it receives.

A packet may travel over one to two dozen routers as it passes from the source host to the destination host. Many core routers in the Internet backbone handle so much traffic that they can barely keep up with demand. To reduce the work done on each router, IP was designed as a simple, unreliable, and connectionless protocol. Although packet losses on the Internet are modest, IP is a "best effort" protocol that offers no guarantee that packets will arrive at all, much less arrive in order. Given this minimalist vision for IP, it is hardly surprising that security was completely left out of IP's core design. Given continuing router overload, it would be difficult to make IP secure throughout the Internet.

IPsec was created to add security to IP, making IPsec at least somewhat more than a security overlay method. However, IPsec cannot achieve its promise without a truly worldwide system of certificate authorities.

TCP

To compensate for IP's unreliability at the Internet layer, TCP/IP was given a reliable sibling protocol, the transmission control protocol (TCP) (Information Sciences Institute 1981) at the transport layer. However, TCP was not created with security. When TCP was created in the early 1980s, security technology was far too immature to be implemented. Today, there are no plans to add security to TCP given the IETF's focus on IPsec and IPsec's capability to provide security for higher-layer protocols. Later, however, we will see that TCP does have an authentication option, but it is only used in BGP.

UDP

When transport layer error correction is not required or is not practical, applications specify the user datagram protocol (UDP) (Postel 1980) at the transport layer. Like TCP, UDP was created without security and is also is not likely to receive security extensions because of the IETF's reliance on IPsec to protect UDP.

Administrative Standards

The "core three" Internet standards do most of the work of the Internet. However, several other administrative protocols are needed to keep the Internet functioning. We will look at security in the most important of these standards.

ICMP

IP merely delivers packets. It does not define any Internet layer supervisory messages. To compensate for this lack, the IETF created the Internet control message protocol (ICMP) (Postel, RFC 792, 1981) to carry supervisory information at the Internet layer. ICMP messages are carried in the data fields of IP packets. ICMP messages allow hosts to determine if other hosts are active (by "pinging" them). ICMP also allow hosts to send error messages to other hosts and allows hosts to tell other hosts or routers to act differently than they have been acting. ICMP is a powerful tool for network managers.

Unfortunately, this power also makes ICMP a popular tool for hackers. Making ICMP less useful to hackers would also tend to make it less useful to network administrators, so the IETF has done nothing to implement ICMP security. For this reason, most corporate firewalls block all ICMP traffic except for outgoing pings (echo messages) and returning pongs (echo reply messages).

If ICMP were given good authentication, however, corporations might be more willing to allow it through firewalls. In addition, authenticated ICMP would protect against attacks generated within the firewalls at individual sites. However, there are no current IETF activities to add authentication and other security to ICMP. The reason may be that ICMP messages are carried in the data fields of IP packets, which can be protected by IPsec, including the authentication of the sending ICMP process.

Domain Name System (DNS)

Richard Clarke, former National Coordinator for Security, Infrastructure Protection, and Counter-Terrorism for the President of the United States, has characterized the domain name system (DNS) as one of the two greatest danger points on the Internet. (Later we will look at the second item on Clarke's list, BGP.)

In a sense, DNS is the telephone directory of the Internet. The DNS allows a source host to find the IP addresses of a target host if the source host only knows the target host's host name (Mockapetris 1987).

The domain name system has multiple servers organized in a hierarchy. These are called DNS servers, or, sometimes, name servers.

There are two likely attacks on DNS servers. First, attackers may be able to "poison" the databases in DNS servers. When user computers send DNS request messages to poisoned servers, they will get incorrect IP addresses that send users to pornography sites, to sites containing Trojan horses, and to other undesirable sites. Companies can even poison their competitor's DNS listing so that all e-mail messages go first to the attacking company before being relayed to the victim's mail servers.

DNS poisoning is not just a theoretical concern. As long ago as 1997, users trying to reach InterNIC.com twice found themselves redirected to a competitor, alterNIC.com. The redirection episodes only stopped when a judge ordered alterNIC.com to stop the redirection. At the time, InterNIC.com was the only registrar for .com, .edu, .org, and .net. There have been many other instances of DNS poisoning since then. DNS poisoning is also known as DNS spoofing.

To address problems with DNS poisoning attacks, the IETF DNSSEC (DNS security extensions) Working Group is developing an authentication approach based on public key encryption with digital signatures (Rose 2002). There are a (relatively) limited number of high-level DNS servers, so giving each a public key and a private key is not too daunting a challenge. As long as DNS servers do not get taken over so that their private keys can be stolen, authentication should be very good. Complicating matters somewhat, in mid-2004, the DNSSEC Working Group created *bis* versions of most of its RFCs to make DNSSEC somewhat weaker but easier to implement. Although DNSSEC is incomplete, a number of DNS servers now support its main elements. For more information, go to www.dnssec.net.

In addition to poisoning attacks, there is the possibility that attackers will use DoS attacks to make DNS servers unavailable to users. Most client users only know the host names of the servers they use. Consequently, if the DNS were to fail for some period of time, clients could no longer reach servers.

As noted earlier, DNS is hierarchical, and if all DNS servers at the highest level are subjected to successful DoS attacks, clients would soon begin to lose the ability to access many servers. At the top level of the DNS server hierarchy, there are only thirteen root DNS top-level domain (TLD) servers run by ten different organizations; one of them periodically feeds changes to the others. Nearly all of these servers, furthermore, use the BIND DNS server program, which has a long history of vulnerability.

Although these root DNS hosts are geographically distributed, most use the same software, leaving them open to common mode attacks if vulnerabilities are found. Also, geographical distribution is not strong protection when there are only thirteen targets to attack. In late 2002, a brief DoS attack degraded the service given by nine of the thirteen root DNS hosts. Had this attack been more intense, and had it continued over many hours or even some days, service disruption would have begun across the Internet.

The threat raised by such concentrated DNS resources is very real. The root DNS servers are well protected with both technical and human protections. However, below the root servers are top-level domain (TLD) DNS servers for the various generic (.com, .edu, etc.) and national (.jp, .ca., etc.) TLDs. The degree to which the DNS servers of these TLDs are distributed and have code diversity is unknown.

In addition, there are literally tens of thousands of corporate second-level domain DNS servers. Firms are required to have two and preferably three DNS servers. However, if these two or three servers are attacked, corporate communication will stop.

In traditional DNS, only the host names and IP addresses of servers are recorded. However, DNS has been extended by the IETF to dynamic DNS (DDNS). In this newer protocol, clients that receive temporary IP addresses from DHCP (dynamic host configuration protocol) servers can register their temporary IP addresses with the firm's DNS server. This is very good because it extends the usefulness of DNS. However, it raises obvious poisoning security concerns that have not been addressed by the IETF.

In addition to protecting DNS, the IETF has moved toward making DNS records a place to store security keying information. (RFC 4025 described how to do this in IPsec, and RFC 4225 did the same for SSH.)

Simple Network Management Protocol (SNMP)

The goal of the simple network management protocol (SNMP) is to allow a central administrative computer (the manager) to manage many individual managed devices. Figure 10 shows that the manager talks to an agent on each device. The manager does this by sending the managed devices Get messages (which ask for information on the device's status) or Set messages (which tell the managed device's configuration).

Obviously, SNMP is a powerful management tool. Unfortunately, it also is a golden opportunity for attackers. It potentially allows attackers to learn a great deal of information about target networks through Get commands. It also allows them to inflict an endless amount of damage through the malicious use of the Set command to create misconfigurations on large numbers of devices. These misconfigurations can make the devices unusable or can even make the devices interfere with the operation of other devices.

SNMP version 1 had no security at all, making the protocol extremely dangerous given its power. SNMPv2 was supposed to add security, but an inability to settle differences within the IETF prevented full security from being built into SNMP.

Version 2 did receive one authentication advance. To send SNMP messages to a version 2 SNMP agent, a manager would have to know the agent's "community string," which is like a password. In practice, most firms have all of their agents use the same community string. In fact, many do not even change the vendor's default community string, which often is "public." In any case, SNMPv2 sends community strings in messages without encryption, so attackers with sniffers can quickly learn community strings.

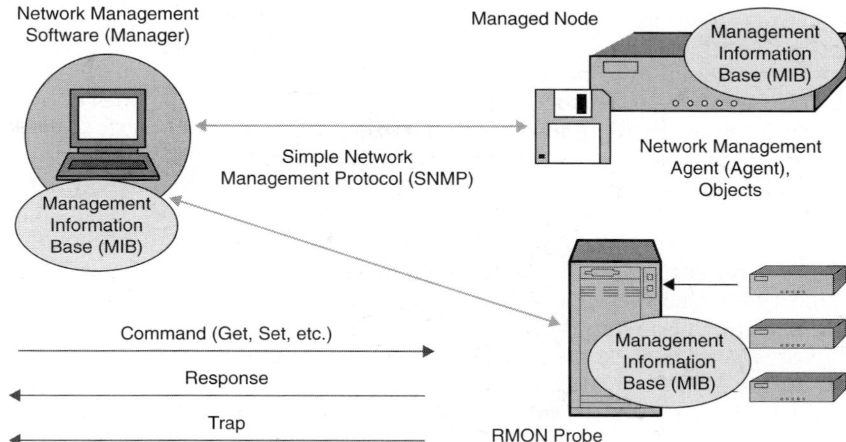

Figure 10: Simple network management protocol (SNMP)

There actually are four different possible community strings for manager-agent communication: read-only access to device agents, read/write access, read/write/all (which allows the modification of device settings), and trap (trap messages are warnings of problems sent by agents on managed devices) (Beckenhauer 2002). Given the dangers inherent in writing and modification, many firms only set the read-only community string, and many products only set the read-only community string by default.

Only in version 3 (www.snmplink.org/SNMPv3.html) did security get built into SNMP extensively. Version 3 offered confidentiality (optional), message-by-message authentication, message integrity, and time stamps to guard against replay attacks. It also offers the possibility of giving different devices different access to MIB (management information base) data based on security restrictions.

Unfortunately, SNMPv3 authentication and message integrity is based on HMACs, which require the network administrator to know a secret bit string that is different for each managed device. This difficult situation could be alleviated if the standard specified the use of digital certificates for managers. Authentication and integrity would then only require that managed devices know the manager's public key, and there is no problem with shared public keys. In addition, public key encryption would allow the secure exchange of symmetric keys for bulk encryption for confidentiality. However, the large number of devices involved and the desire to keep processing loads on managed devices low (public key encryption is highly processing-intensive) has made public key authentication and integrity unattractive to standards makers.

For more information about SNMP security, read Blumenthal and Wijen (1998).

LDAP

Increasingly, companies store security information and other critical corporate information in central repositories called directory servers. To query data in a directory server, devices commonly use the lightweight directory access protocol (LDAP), which governs search request and responses.

The IETF has long understood the importance of creating good security for LDAP in light of the extreme importance of information contained in the directory. The core security focus of LDAP must be authentication because successful impostors could learn large amounts of damaging information about a firm if they could get wide access to this data by claiming to be a party with broad authorization to retrieve data. They could also do extensive damage by "poisoning" the directory with bad data.

The first version of the standard, LDAPv1, had no security. LDAPv2 provided authentication options for the first time. It permitted initial anonymous, simple, and Kerberos 4 authentication. All of these were fairly weak. In 2006, the IETF extended LDAP security through a flurry of security-focused LDAP RFCs.

LDAPv3 also supports the simple authentication security layer (SASL) (Myers 1997). This method allows the searcher and the directory server to authenticate each other in several ways, including Kerberos 5, HMACs, and external authentication. External authentication means that the parties can do authentication any way they want, essentially taking authentication outside the LDAP process. For instance, if the searcher and directory server create an SSL/TLS connection at the transport layer, the authentication that takes place at that layer may be sufficient. SASL is extremely flexible, but companies using it must ensure that a sufficiently strong authentication option is selected. Later, LDAP security was extended considerably. This included the use of public key authentication for initial authentication in 2006.

LDAPv3 makes encryption for confidentiality optional. This may seem odd, but many firms use SSL/TLS at the transport layer to protect LDAP traffic. SSL/TLS does encryption for confidentiality, and many firms feel that also encrypting LDAP traffic at the application layer as well would be needlessly expensive.

Address Resolution Protocol (ARP)

When a router receives a packet, it looks at the packet's destination IP address. Based on this destination IP address, the router sends the packet back out another interface (port), to the destination host or to a next-hop router (NHR) that will next handle the packet. We will use the term "target" for the destination host or NHR.

The destination IP address in the packet gives the target's IP address. However, to deliver the packet, the router must encapsulate the packet in a data link layer frame and deliver the frame to the target. This requires the router to know the data link layer address of the target, for instance, the target's Ethernet MAC (media access control) address.

If the router does not know the target's data link layer address on an Ethernet network, the router must use the address resolution protocol (ARP) (Wahl, Howes, and Kille 1997). The router first broadcasts an ARP request message to all hosts on the subnet connected to the port out of which the packet is to be sent. In an Ethernet network, the broadcast MAC destination address is forty-eight 1s. Switches on the subnet will deliver frames with this address to all hosts on the subnet. All hosts on the subnet, furthermore, will accept frames with all-1s destination addresses.

Within a broadcast frame, the router sends an ARP request message. The ARP request message contains the IP address of the target. All hosts except the target ignore this message. The target, however, recognizes its IP address and sends an ARP reply message back to the router. This message tells the router the target's data link layer address.

Now that the router knows the target's data link layer address, the router takes the IP packet it has been holding and places it in a frame with the target's data link layer address in the destination address field. The router sends this frame to the target.

To handle future packets to the same destination IP address, the router also places the target's IP address and data link layer address in the router's ARP cache. When the next packet addressed to this IP address arrives, the router will not have to do ARP. It will simply look up the data link layer address in the ARP cache.

The ARP assumes that all hosts are trustworthy. However, an attacker host can use this trust to make an attack. Specifically, an attacker's host can send ARP reply messages with the attacker's data link layer address and all possible IP addresses on its subnet. Due to the fact that ARP is stateless, routers should accept ARP response messages even if the router did not send an ARP request message. This approach will poison the ARP cache, causing the router to send all messages intended for most hosts on the subnet to be sent to the attacker.

In some cases, after reading frames, the attacker passes them on to the intended destination host. It may also be able to relay traffic going in the opposite direction. In this man-in-the-middle attack, the two sides are unaware that their traffic is being read and perhaps added to.

The widely available arpsniff program implements a man-in-the-middle attack with extreme ease. However, the computer in the middle has to be on the same broadcast or ring subnet as the other two communicating partners for it to work. This makes ARP spoofing difficult to implement. However, if a computer on a subnet is hacked remotely, the attacker does not have to be on the victims' subnet.

Currently, there are only preliminary efforts within the IETF to add authentication to the ARP, under the ARPsec label.

ARP only works on Ethernet and other broadcast networks. Other protocols for finding host data link layer addresses associated with IP addresses are used for other types of nonbroadcast network technologies. These generally suffer the same security exposures that ARP does.

Dynamic Host Communication Protocol (DHCP)

It is possible to manually configure a client PC by typing in its IP address and other configuration parameters needed to communicate over the Internet or a corporate internet. Servers typically are configured manually. However, client PCs normally are configured automatically by getting these configuration parameters from a dynamic host configuration protocol (DHCP) host (Droms 1997).

When a client PC boots up, it realizes that it has no IP address. It broadcasts a DHCPDISCOVER message to learn what DHCP servers are reachable. Each DHCP server that receives the discover message sends back a DHCPOFFER message that gives an offer specifying what IP address it will provide, a lease time (how long the client may keep the IP address), and other configuration information.

The client PC selects one offer and sends a DHCPREQUEST to the selected server. The DHCP server sends back a DHCPACK message acknowledging the acceptance and providing configuration parameters, including an IP address, subnet masks, DNS addresses, and other information. The client PC is now configured.

DHCP is built on connectionless UDP, which makes adding security difficult in general. More specifically, DHCP does not authenticate the client or the DHCP server, and this allows several possible attacks. For an example, an attacker posing as a client PC can repeatedly request DHCP service, each time accepting an IP address. Within a few seconds, the DHCP server will be drained of available IP addresses. If a legitimate client then requests configuration service, it will not be able to get an IP address and so will not be able to use the Internet or an internal corporate internet.

The attacker also can impersonate a DHCP server. The attacker will then respond to all DHCPDISCOVER messages with a very attractive offer (long lease duration and so forth). If a client accepts this configuration information, this information may cause the client to send packets that cannot be delivered or to act in other ways that harm itself or other hosts.

The IETF is now working on DHCP authentication. RFC 3118 (Droms and Arbaugh 2001), which defines two authentication options for DHCP. The first involves a key that is shared by the client PC and by the DHCP server. This key, however, is transmitted in the clear. This easily-read transmission approach is only useful for protecting the client against a host that *accidentally* installed a DHCP server.

The second option requires each client to use a pair-shared secret key with each DHCP server. Only the DHCP server and the client will know this key. The client and server use this pair-shared secret to add a key-hashed message authentication code (HMAC) to each message. If companies adopt this option, they can have fairly strong authentication, although the authentication will not be as strong as it would be if digital signatures and digital certificates were used.

Dynamic Routing Protocols

Operation. When a packet arrives at a router, the router compares the packet's destination IP address with the rows in its routing table. Each row represents a route to a subnet, network, or larger cluster of IP addresses that contains the destination IP address. The router finds all matches, selects the best match, and sends the packet back out according to instructions found in the best-match row.

How do routers get the information in their routing table? Quite simply, they talk to each other frequently, exchanging data on what they know, especially about recent changes. This communication is governed by dynamic routing protocols. These protocols specify both message exchanges and the types of information that will be exchanged.

Security Concerns. Dynamic routing protocols are dangerous because spoofed messages can seriously poison routing tables and therefore can cause routers to black hole or misdeliver most or all traffic. They can even cause a router to deliver all packets to a single target destination, creating an intense DoS attack. Unfortunately, dynamic routing protocols traditionally have not used cryptographic authentication or other protections.

IETF Efforts. Several routing protocols are in common use, including OSPF (open shortest path first), BGP, EIGRP (enhanced interior gateway routing protocol), and IS-IS (intermediate system to intermediate system). Historically, each of these standards evolved separately, including security features. Today, however, the IETF has a working group on Routing Protocol Security Requirements (rpsec). As we will see, all current IETF routing protocols at least have HMAC authentication.

RIP. For communication within small firms, the IETF created a simple routing protocol called the routing information protocol (RIP). Due to its simplicity, RIP has three main constraints (Panko 2004).

First, RIP selects routes on the basis of the number of hops between routers to get to a destination network or subnet. Selecting the route with the least number of hops generally works well in simple networks but works poorly in large networks. Large networks usually have a mix of LAN and WAN links with widely different costs and speeds. Sending data over a WAN link is much more expensive than sending data over a LAN link, but RIP does not consider these costs or other factors.

Second, RIP only works in networks with a maximum of sixteen hops. In effect, it can only count to sixteen because its hop count field only has four bits. Again, this is not a problem in small networks.

Third, RIP does not scale well. Every minute or so, depending on configuration parameters, each router broadcasts its routing table to all routers on its subnet and also to all hosts on its subnet. With large routing tables, the disruptions caused by this intrusive broadcasting would create serious host and network performance problems. Again, however, RIP is for small networks.

Just as it has a simple general design, RIP initially had no security. RIPv2 (Malkin 1998), however, brought RIP security up to date. Most notably, RIPv2 has three authentication modes:

- *Null authentication (RFC 1583)*: No authentication at all.
- *Simple password authentication (RFC 1583)*: The password is sent in the clear in every packet. This method is useful for systems that are accidentally set up as RIP routers.
- *MD5 HMAC authentication (RFC 2328)*: This method uses HMACs. RIP broadcasts to all other routers out each interface, so all routers connected to a subnet must share the same subnet secret. Looked at another way, a router must have a different secret on each interface.

As in most other standards, there is no digital signature authentication. RIPv2 does have HMAC authentication, but this uses a community secret compared to a pair-shared secret.

The rpsec's publications discuss other problems with RIPv2's authentication and various ways to address them.

OSPF. For larger networks, most firms use the open shortest path first (OSPF) dynamic routing protocol. This is a more sophisticated protocol for three reasons (Panko 2004). First, it gives routers richer information about possible routes, so that routers can select best-match rows with greater effectiveness. Second, OSPF can serve large networks. Third, OSPF scales well because it only sends messages when there are changes and because selected area routers can centralize communication in a hub-and-spoke topology instead of sending messages in a dense mesh. OSPF should be used in all but the simplest networks.

OSPFv2 (Moy 1998) has the same authentication options as RIP. This includes the weakness of using group-shared HMAC secrets among all OSPF routers in an area. Jones and Le Moigne (2004) discuss other security vulnerabilities in OSPF. These vulnerabilities can lead to some attacks even if HMAC authentication is used. OSPFv3 is used with IPv3.

BGP. Both RIP and OSPF are interior dynamic routing protocols that are only used within the networks of individual corporations. However, firms need an exterior dynamic routing protocol to communicate with their ISP's router. In addition, ISPs need an exterior dynamic routing protocol to communicate with one another.

On the Internet, a single exterior dynamic routing protocol is dominant: the border gateway protocol (BGP). *Gateway* is the old term for *router*, so BGP is a protocol for communication between border routers at the edges of their networks.

Richard Clarke, former National Coordinator for Security, Infrastructure Protection, and Counter-Terrorism for the President of the United States, has labeled BGP as one of the two greatest dangers on the Internet. As noted earlier, Clarke's other nomination is DNS. DNS is dangerous because it potentially could be forced to redirect all Internet traffic in harmful ways. BGP is dangerous because if it is compromised, traffic over the Internet could be redirected in harmful ways by the routers that actually move traffic. The DNS danger is like vandals removing or switching around road signs. The BGP danger is like vandals blowing up bridges.

The most recent version of BGP, BGPv4 (Rekhter and Lo 1995), has been in use for more than a decade and is used almost universally on the Internet, although it was updated several times in 2006, especially in RFC 4271.

Despite its critical importance to the Internet, BGPv4 has no cryptographic security at all. However, BGP runs over TCP on port 179, and a large number of BGP users employ an authentication mechanism in TCP (Stewart 1999). This mechanism, described in RFC 2385 (Heffernan 1998), uses a pair-shared HMAC using MD5 (message digest algorithm 5) (although the RFC calls it an MD5 digital signature). If a BGP messages is contained in a TCP segment with an improper HMAC, the transport layer discards the message before BGP even sees it.

Dialogues protected with MD5 HMACs are difficult to hijack. Attackers must not only guess TCP sequence numbers, but they must also guess or learn the secret shared by the two routers being connected via TCP.

For stronger security, the two routers exchanging BGP messages can connect via IPsec with at least initial public key authentication. They could also connect via SSL/TLS. In either case, the two routers would need to have public and private keys. In addition, the routers would have to be fast enough to handle the large amount of additional work needed for IPsec or SSL/TLS. This approach does not work for other routing protocols, which use broadcasting (RIP) or multicasting (OSPF).

BGP routers have many options, which have varying levels of security and vulnerability. Windowsecurity.com (2002) has developed a template for securing BGP on the Cisco routers that dominate corporate and Internet use.

In 2006, RFC 4278 formally proposed to allow BGP to continue using weak security methods while a fuller analysis was done on BGP security. It was argued that in BGP's limited environment, external threats were weak enough to justify the continuation of weak security.

EIGRP and IS-IS. There are two other dynamic routing protocols to mention. For interior routing, many firms use Cisco's proprietary EIGRP interior dynamic routing protocol, which can handle the packets of multiple standards architectures in an integrated way. (RIP and OSPF are limited to IP packets.) In addition, OSI offers IS-IS, which would at least provide security by obscurity (not recommended). However, this chapter is about Internet security standards, and Internet transmission requires IP transmission.

Dynamic Routing Protocol Security: Perspective. To date, the focus on dynamic routing protocol security has been authentication. Unless IPsec or SSL/TLS are used to transmit BGPv4 messages, the highest level of authentication for BGP4 is MD5 HMACs with pair-shared secrets. In addition, for interior routing, the highest level of security for RIP and OSPF is MD5 HMACs with group-shared secrets.

Another issue is that authentication assumes trust. If an attacker gets inside an organization managing a router or somehow compromises a router, they will be able to send poisoned routing information to other routers, and these other routers are likely to trust the information.

One way to reduce the danger of spurious trust is to block all incoming packets containing dynamic routing protocol information at the firm's border firewall—or at least, to limit incoming packets containing such information to one or two specific external routers.

Application Layer Standards

To users, the Internet is attractive because of its application standards for the WWW, e-mail, and other popular services. While decent security is present for some application standards, many application standards continue to have only weak security—if they have any at all.

Hypertext Transfer Protocol (HTTP) over SSL/TLS

To communicate with a WWW server, a browser uses HTTP version 1.1 (Fielding et al. 1999). HTTP is a simple protocol that offers no security by itself. However, all browser and WWW server programs support SSL/TLS security, and the use of SSL/TLS in e-commerce applications and other sensitive applications is overwhelming. HTTP over SSL/TLS uses port 443 rather than HTTP's normal port 80.

SSL/TLS allows both the browser and the Web server to authenticate each other using digital signatures and digital certificates. However, only the server is *required* to use a digital signature to authenticate itself. This is done because few PCs running browsers have digital certificates. Obviously, not requiring client authentication is a serious problem for protecting Web servers against attack.

E-Mail Security

Security for e-mail is perhaps the great scandal in IETF history. Competing cliques within the IETF have consistently simply refused to cooperate in selecting security standards for e-mail. Consequently, companies that want to implement e-mail security have to use a nonstandard method to do so.

Not surprisingly, sending application layer e-mail traffic over a secure SSL/TLS transport connection is the most popular way to secure e-mail in organizations today. SSL/TLS is well understood, offers consumer-grade security, and has been widely used for HTTP security for several years. Most e-mail programs support SSL/TLS security. SSL/TLS only encrypts e-mail between clients and e-mail servers, not all the way between clients. This only requires a digital certificate on the mail server. However, it requires trust in the e-mail server and in downstream parts of the system (other clients, mail servers, and Internet links).

Another approach, S/MIME (Ramsdell 1999) encrypts e-mail all the way between two clients. This provides end-to-end security. However, it also prevents e-mail servers and firewalls from scanning e-mail messages for malware, and it requires each client to have a digital certificate.

A third approach, pretty good privacy (PGP) (Atkins, Stallings, and Zimmerman 1996), is used primarily by individuals. Organizations have tended to stay away from PGP because PGP uses user-based transitive trust. (If User A trusts User B, and if User B trusts User C, User A may trust User C.) As noted earlier, this is not a good security policy. If a single user mistakenly trusts an impostor, others may unwittingly trust the impostor as well. PGP by itself is a commercial product. Many mail programs actually implement the OpenPGP standard.

Remote Access Protocols: Telnet, Rlogin, Rsh, and SSH

The first ARPANET (Advanced Research Projects Agency Network) application was Telnet (Postel and Reynolds 1983), which allows a user to log into a remote computer and execute commands there as if the user was a local user. This allows ordinary users to access remote services. It also allows system administrators to manage servers and routers remotely. This use of remote administration is attractive, but it must be done carefully or hackers will end up "managing" corporate servers and routers.

Unfortunately, Telnet has poor security. For example, Telnet does not encrypt host usernames and passwords. Sniffers can intercept usernames and passwords, allowing hackers to log in as these users with all of the privileges of these users.

Telnet should never be used for remote administration because hackers intercepting root passwords would be able to execute any commands on the compromised machine. Telnet is not alone in this respect. In the UNIX world, rlogin and rsh do not even require passwords to gain access to a computer, although other conditions must apply.

For remote administration, some organizations turn to the secure socket shell (SSH) protocol, which offers good authentication, integrity, and authentication (Ylonen et al. 2002). Unfortunately, SSH version 1 had security flaws, and although these have been fixed in SSH version 2, some version 2 implementations will also permit version 1 connections, thus leaving the system open to attack. In 2006, the IETF began an intensive effort to improve SSH security.

File Transfer Protocol (FTP) and Trivial File Transfer Protocol (TFTP)

Another early ARPANET service that continues to be popular on the Internet is file transfer protocol (FTP) (Postel and Reynolds 1985), which allows a user to download files from a remote computer to his or her local computer and sometimes to upload files from his or her local computer to the remote computer. Unfortunately, FTP also sends usernames and passwords in the clear, making it very dangerous. In addition, while the use of Telnet has declined to the point where quite a few companies simply stop all Telnet traffic at their firewalls, FTP is still widely used. The FTPEXT Working Group is considering security for FTP. In addition, FTP can be protected by sending it over SSL/TLS if the FTP program allows this.

FTP has a simpler sibling, the trivial file transfer protocol (TFTP) (Sollins 1992). TFTP does not even require usernames and passwords, making it a darling of hackers who often use TFTP after taking over a computer to download their rootkits (collections of hacker programs) to automate their exploitation of the computer they now "own."

Web Services

An important emerging application class is Web services. Web service protocols allow programs on different computers to interact in a standardized way. Web services are creating a new level of interoperability between programs on different computers.

The figure shows that Web service interactions often are "chained," meaning that a single Web service message may initiate a series of other Web service messages.

Web services have only been operational since about 2000, and Web services standards are still rather embryonic. The three main Web service standards are SOAP (simple object access protocol), which governs the format of messages, UDDI (universal description, discovery, and integration), which is like a yellow pages and white pages for finding Web services relevant to a firm's need, and WSDL (Web Services Description Language), which tells a firm exactly how to work with a specific Web service. However, many other standards need to be set before Web services can be used with confidence.

As in many other applications, security was an afterthought for Web services standardization. Consequently, Web service security standards are even more embryonic than Web service standards in general. Worse yet, Web service security standards have suffered from conflicts among vendors.

The initial security standards for Web services (SOAP, UDDI, and WSDL) were created by the World Wide Web Consortium (W3C). However, Microsoft, which had been a major driving force behind the first three standards, pulled its support from W3C. Rumor suggests that Microsoft did this because W3C only creates standards if the technology is not encumbered by patents (Koch 2003). Microsoft, according to the rumor, wanted to preserve its intellectual property rights.

Whatever its motivation, Microsoft and its main partners, IBM and VeriSign, moved their standards development efforts to OASIS (the Organization for the Advancement of Structured Information Standards). Their efforts were based on the Microsoft/IBM/VeriSign standards efforts called WS- (because all standards begin with WS and a dash).

Sun Microsystems and its allies initially supported a different family of standards, ebXML. In fact, it has been suggested that the IETF gave the WS- standards a cold reception at the 2000 IETF meeting because Sun had the chair role (Newcomer 2003). However, when the ebXML effort fell apart, Sun threw its weight behind the WS-standards efforts at OASIS.

To confuse matters even further, Microsoft and its allies created a new standards organization, WS-I, where the I stands for interoperability. Initially, WS-I's purpose is to develop implementation profiles built from various Web services standards. Sun was excluded from WS-I but was eventually allowed to join as a board member.

In 2004, there was a major breakthrough when OASIS ratified the WS-Security standard submitted by Microsoft, IBM, and VeriSign in 2002. WS-Security, in a move toward openness, adopted several standards from W3C, including standards for encryption and digital signatures. In the near future, WS-Security should be extended to work with the OASIS SAML (Security Assertions Markup

Language) standard, which specifies how organizations can exchange authentication information.

Unfortunately, WS-Security is only part of the framework created for Web service security by Microsoft, IBM, and VeriSign. To be effective, six more elements are needed: WS-Policy, WS-Trust, WS-Privacy, WS-Secure Conversation, WS-Federation, and WS-Authorization. Microsoft and its allies have not submitted these additional elements to OASIS, making the standardization of WS-Security a limited development.

Authentication is a complex issue for Web services standards. WS-Security does not have complete authentication, and Sun and its partners have developed a major authentication system under the auspices of the Sun-led Liberty Alliance. Although Sun has endorsed the Microsoft standards efforts, Microsoft has not done the same for the Liberty Alliance standards, probably because Microsoft has a competing authentication product, Passport.

Especially interesting aspects of the W3C standards are its XML Encryption and XML Signature standards, which are part of WS-Security. Obviously, these standards provide for encryption for confidentiality and digital signing. What makes them interesting is not their cryptographic methods but the fact that they can be applied to *parts* of a message as well as to the entire message. The capability to encrypt and sign parts of messages is important because some Web service messages go to more than one party, and only some parts of the message are relevant to (or should be read by) each party.

Web services security protocols have a long way to go before they are ready for use with confidence. In addition, the protocols that do exist still are subject to DoS attacks and other dangers.

However, if a Web service interaction will only take place between two parties, it may be sufficient to protect and authenticate the communication using SSL/TLS. However, not having protection and authentication *within* messages via XML Encryption and XML Signature leaves Web services open to certain attacks.

Other Applications

There are many other Internet applications, and their standards vary widely in their degree of security. VoIP (voice over IP) security is a particularly sensitive emerging standards application issue. In addition, database applications and many other applications are not even standards-based.

Unfortunately, many operating system installations automatically turn on quite a few applications without the knowledge of the systems administrators or users. For example, when SNMP vulnerabilities were found in 2002, it was discovered that many vulnerable machines should not have been running SNMP at all. An important rule in hardening clients and servers against attack is to turn off all applications that are not absolutely needed to run the computer.

CONCLUSION: THE STATE OF INTERNET SECURITY STANDARDS

Today, if two communication partners want to communicate securely, they can do so by adding dialogue security on top of the nonsecure Internet transmission. For lightweight needs, they can turn to PPTP or SSL/TLS. For industrial-strength security, they can use IPsec.

General Insecurity

More generally, however, under the Danvers Doctrine, the standards that the Internet needs for message delivery (IP, TCP, and UDP), Internet supervisory standards (ICMP, DNS, SNMP, LDAP, etc.), and Internet application standards (WWW, e-mail, etc.) vary widely in security from none to semi-adequate. Consequently, the Internet today is rather fragile and open to seriously damaging attacks. Given the pace of security implementation in individual standards, the fragility of the Internet is not likely to change radically in the next two or three years. Even after more secure standards are developed, it will take several years for them to be widely adopted.

The Broad IETF Program

At the same time, there is an extremely broad concern with security across the IETF. Although some standards have better security than others, standards working groups appear to be playing leapfrog in their efforts to improve security across a broad spectrum of Internet standards.

The Authentication Problem

Digital Certificates

The most difficult problem in Internet security standards is authentication. Most Internet standards today from the IETF offer a maximum of HMAC message-by-message authentication.

However, unless authentication uses public key authentication (such as digital signatures) coupled with digital certificates managed by a reliable and well-regulated network of CAs, authentication strength will only be moderate. However, creating large public key infrastructures will take years, and while European countries are moving to manage and regulate CAs, the United States has adopted the let-the-market-do-it philosophy that has worked so well recently in the energy industry and in corporate financial reporting.

One option is to use public key authentication with digital certificates and then use HMACs for message-by-message authentication. Although this would lose nonrepudiation for individual messages, it would decrease the processing intensiveness of VPNs and other CPSs. However, this still requires an infrastructure for managing public/private key pairs and digital certificates.

Distributed Authentication

Another problem is distributed authentication. There is unlikely to be a single global authentication authority. Consequently, multiple authentication authorities must be able to work together. Most importantly, there must be mechanisms for implementing transitive trust, in which an authentication authority trusts credentials provided by another authentication authority. In public key authentication, there has long been the concept of a hierarchy of certificate authorities, but no single CA tree is likely to emerge across the world.

More federated one-to-one and one-to-few horizontal trust systems are now under development, especially for Web services. These include the Liberty Alliance, IBM and Microsoft (WS-* security) standards, and OASIS standards.

The Primary Authentication Problem

One broad and deep problem in authentication is the primary authentication problem—proving the identity of a person or organization in the first place, say to give them a digital certificate or accept them as an employee. Identity theft has long allowed impostors to obtain fraudulent drivers' licenses and other authentication instruments. Even within closed systems, such as corporate networks, the prime authentication problem can be daunting. For consumer authentication and other large communities, the technical and operational problems for credible initial authentication are extremely daunting.

Protection from Denial-of-Service (DoS) Attacks

One security threat that has barely been faced so far is the prospect of DoS attacks. Although a few standards have taken some steps to reduce DoS attack risks, this is an area of little general development within the IETF.

Internet Forensics Standards

One area that we did not look at in this chapter is standards to make the Internet forensic, that is, able to collect and analyze traffic data in a way that would make the prosecution of attacks possible. Without forensics standards, it will continue to be nearly impossible to find and prosecute attackers.

The IETF to date has shown no interest in developing forensics standards. In fact, in 1999, the IETF polled its members about whether the IETF should develop protocols to support law enforcement requirements for wiretapping voice conversations carried over the Internet. There was a strong preponderance of comments against developing standards for implementing wiretapping (Macavinta 1999).

GLOSSARY

Community Key or Community Secret: Secret shared by multiple devices within a network.

Cryptographic Protection System (CPS): Standards-based system for automatically providing multiple protections in a dialogue between two parties.

Danvers Doctrine: An IETF decision to add security to all or nearly all TCP/IP protocols.

Denial-of-Service (DoS) Attacks: Attacks that attempt to render a computer or network useless to its user; not addressed in most Internet security efforts.

Dialogue: The transmission of multiple messages in both directions between two hosts.

Dialogue Security: Security applied to a dialogue (ongoing message exchange between two parties); often added on top of nonsecure Internet transmission.

Digital Signature: Message-by-message authentication system based on public key encryption. To work very well, the parties should have digital certificates from trusted certificate authorities.

Dynamic Routing Protocol: A protocol that routers use to communicate with one another to exchange information for their routing tables.

HMAC: See Key-Hashed Message Authentication Code.

Internet Engineering Task Force (IETF): The body that creates TCP/IP standards for the Internet. Now engaged in a broad effort to add security to Internet standards.

In the Clear: When a message is transmitted without encryption for confidentiality or other cryptographic protections.

IPsec: Family of standards for adding security to both IPv4 and IPv6 transmission dialogues.

Kerberos Server: Authentication system in which a central server gives out authentication and authorization information.

Key-Hashed Message Authentication Code (HMAC): Message-by-message authentication system based on a secret key shared by two parties.

Multilayer Security: Providing security at multiple standards layers in order to provide defense in depth.

Password Authentication: Authentication in which the two sides know a password consisting of keyboard characters.

Point-to-Point Protocol (PPP): Secure protocol for communicating over a point-to-point data link.

Point-to-Point Tunneling Protocol (PPTP): Protocol that extends PPP transmissions over an internet; extends PPP security over the route.

Policy Server: In a security system, a server that tells devices how they must implement security.

Remote Authentication Dial-On User Service (RADIUS) server: A server that stores authentication data so that access servers can apply authentication criteria consistently.

Remote Access Server (RAS): Security server at a site that terminates and manages a PPP connection or PPTP connection over the Internet.

Secure Sockets Layer (SSL)/Transport Layer Security (TLS): General standard for adding security at the transport layer. Formerly called Secure Sockets Layer (SSL) and still widely known by that name. Also called HTTPS because URLs beginning with "https" are requesting SSL/TLS security.

Virtual Private Network (VPN): Family of standards for adding security to a dialogue over an untrusted network, most commonly the Internet. Includes PPTP, IPsec, and SSL/TLS.

CROSS REFERENCES

See *Cryptography; Internet Architecture; TCP/IP Suite.*

REFERENCES

Note: In selecting RFCs, an attempt has been made to give the definitive base version of the standard. However, the IETF frequently updates standards, giving a new base version of the standard.

Atkins, D., W. Stallings, and P. Zimmerman. 1996. *PGP message exchange formats*. RFC 1991, August.

Barabasi, A. L. 2003. Scale-free networks. *Scientific American*, May, pp. 50–59.

Beckenhauer, B. 2002. SNMP alert 2002: What is it all about? www.sans.org/rr/protocols/SNMP_alert.php (accessed February 21, 2002).

Blumenthal, U., and B. Wijen. 1998. *User-Based Security Model (USM) for Version 3 of the Simple Network Management protocol (SNMPv3)* 1998.

Blunk, L. and J. Vollbrecht. 1998. *PPP Extensible Authentication Protocol (EAP)*. RFC 2284, March.

Dierks, T., and C. Allen. 1999. *The TLS Protocol Version 1.0*. RFC 2246, January.

Dierks, T., and Rescorla, E. 2006. *The Transport Layer Security (TLS) Protocol Version 1.1*. RFC 4346, April.

Droms, R. 1997. *Dynamic Host Configuration Protocol*. RFC 2131, March.

Droms, R., and W. Arbaugh. 2001. *Authentication for DHCP messages*. RFC 3118, June.

Fielding, R., J. Gettys, J. Mogul, H. Frystyk, L. Masinter, P. Leach, and T. Berners-Lee. 1999. *Hypertext Transfer Protocol – HTTP 1/1*. RFC 2616, June.

Hamzeh, K., G. Pall, W. Verthein, J. Taarud, W. Little, and G. Zorn. 1999. *Point-to-Point Tunneling Protocol (PPTP)*. RFC 2637, July.

Heffernan, J. 1998. *Protection of BGP Sessions via the TCP MD5 Signature Option*. RFC 2385, August.

Information Sciences Institute. 1981. *Transmission Control Protocol DARPA Internet Program Protocol Specification*. RFC 793, September.

Jones, E., and O. Le Moigne. 2004. OSPF security vulnerabilities analysis. draft-ietf-rpsec-ospf-vuln-00.txt, IETF, May 2004.

Koch, C. 2003. *The battle for Web services, CIO Magazine*. www.cio.com/archive/100103/standards.html (accessed February 21, 2002).

Legard, D. 2004. Analyst digest: Worms carry heavy cost. *Network World Fusion*. www.nwfusion.com/news/2004/0601analydiges.html (accessed June 1, 2004).

Malkin, G. 1998. *RIP Version 2*. RFC 2453, November.

Macavinta, C. 1999. Internet protocol proposal raises privacy concerns. *CNET News.com*. http://news.com.com/2100-12-231403.html (accessed October 14, 1999).

Microsoft. 2004. *Introduction to IP Version 6*. www.microsoft.com/technet/itsolutions/network/security/ipvers6.mspx (updated March 31, 2004).

Mockapetris, P. 1987. *Domain names: Concepts and facilities*. RFC 1034, November.

Moy, J. 1994. *OSPF Version 2*. RFC 1583, March.

Moy, J. 1998. *OSPF Version 2*. STD 54, RFC 2328, April.

Myers, J. 1997. *Simple Authentication and Security Layer (SASL)*. RFC 2222, October.

Newcomer, E. 2003. The Web services standards mess. *WebServices.org*. www.mywebservices.org/index.php/article/articleview/1202/1/24 (accessed December, 2003).

Panko, R. 2004. *Business computer and network security*. Upper Saddle River, NJ: Prentice-Hall.

Plummer, D. C. 1982. *An address resolution protocol*. RFC 826, November.

Postel, J. 1980. *User Datagram Protocol*. RFC 768, August.

Postel, J., ed. 1981. *Internet Protocol: DARPA Internet Program Protocol Specification*. RFC 791, September.

Postel, J., ed. 1981. *Internet Control Message Protocol DARPA Internet Program Protocol Specification*. RFC 792, September.

Postel, J., and J. Reynolds. 1983. *Telnet Protocol specification*. RFC 854, May. (Actually, Telnet was developed in the early 1970s for the ARPANET; this RFC specifies the TCP/IP version Telnet.)

Postel, J., and J. Reynolds. 1985. *File Transfer Protocol (FTP)*. RFC 959, October. (Actually, FTP was created in the 1970s for the ARPANET. This RFC is the specification for TCP/IP.)

Ramsdell, B., 1999. *S/MIME Version 3 Message Specification*. RFC 2633, June.

Rekhter, Y., and T. Lo. 1995. *A Border Gateway Protocol 4 (BGP-4)*. RFC 1771, March.

Rose, S. (2002). DNS security document roadmap. draft-ietf-dnsext-dnssec-roadmap-06, IETF, September 5, 2002.

Schiller, J. 2002. *Strong security recommendations for Internet Engineering Task Force standard protocols*. RFC 3365, August.

Sermersheim, J. 2006. *Lightweight Directory Access Protocol (LDAP): The Protocol*. RFC 4511, June.

Simpson, W. 1994. *The Point-to-Point Protocol (PPP)*. RFC 1661, STD 51, July.

Sollins, K. 1992. *The TFTP Protocol (Revision 2)*. RFC 1350, July. (The original version was RFC 783, which was published in 1981.)

Stewart, J. W. III. 1999. *BGP4: Inter-domain routing on the Internet*. Addison-Wesley.

Thayer, R., N. Doraswamy, and R. Glenn. 1998. *IP security document roadmap*. RFC 2411, November.

Thomas, S. A. 2002. *IP switching and routing essentials*. New York: Wiley.

Tonsley, W., A. Valencia, A. Rubens, G. Pall, G. Zorn, and B. Palter, B., 1999. *Layer Two Tunneling Protocol "L2TP"*. RFC 2661, August.

Wahl, M., T. Howes, and S. Kille. 1997. *Lightweight Directory Access Protocol (v3)*. RFC 2251, December.

Wagner, M. 2002. Increased Internet centralization threatens reliability. *InternetWeek*. www.internetwk.com/story/INW20021202S0004 (accessed December 2, 2002).

Windowsecurity.com. 2002. Secure BGP template version 2.0. www.windowsecurity.com/whitepapers/Secure_BGP_Template_Version_20.html (accessed October 16, 2002).

Ylonen, T., T. Kivinen, M. Saarinen, T. Rinne, and S. Lehtinen. 2002. SSH authentication protocol. Internet Draft, IETF, September 20, 2002.

Zhu, L., and B. Tung. 2006. *Public Key Cryptography for Initial Authentication in Kerberos (PKINIT)*. RFC 4556, June.

Technology and Standards for Low-Bit-Rate Vocoding Methods

Miguel Arjona Ramírez and Mário Minami, *University of São Paulo, Brazil*

INTRODUCTION

Speech coding is about representing a speech signal with as few bits as possible provided that only acceptable distortion is introduced when the speech signal is reconstructed from the bit stream. Or else, given a bit rate, the speech coder designed for lowest distortion is sought. In actual practice, other requirements have to be satisfied. A certain product may be envisaged, imposing requirements on power consumption and restricting the possibilities for processor selection and memory resources that will be made available. Even when a powerful processor is available in a media gateway, for instance, system resources may have to be shared among a large number of simultaneous users.

For two-party communications, which is the rule for vocoding, delay has to be constrained so that dialog conditions may prevail. This may restrict coder delay depending on the communication links between encoder and decoder. Moreover, in the recent and expanding domain of packet communications, variable delay must be tolerated and the coder must behave nicely when packets get lost or are delayed on their way. This adds requirements of robustness on top of usual care for single-bit error correction and frame erasure concealment. The latter mostly affects wireless communications.

Speech-coding techniques range from companded (compressing-expanding law) sample quantization in pulse code modulation (PCM) and differential signal coding with adaptive quantization in differential PCM (DPCM) to differential signal coding with additional adaptive prediction in adaptive DPCM (ADPCM) for waveform coders. These techniques are directly linked in the text to ITU-T (Telecommunication Standardization Sector of the International Telecommunication Union) recommendations for wireline telephony, which are the strictest in requirements of speech quality and communication links or tandeming between communicating parties.

Next, the important set of linear prediction (LP) techniques is introduced in a parametric vocoding context. This paves the way to the discussion of code-excited LP (CELP) coding with its important notions of an analysis-by-synthesis loop and an excitation search driven by the speech signal reconstruction error. In the ITU-T evolution line, the introduction of a CELP coding recommendation marks the overcoming of a resistance to the acceptance of a delayed speech coder, albeit to a moderate degree, with the adoption of low-delay CELP (LD-CELP). In addition, the increment in coder complexity prompts the adoption of a new style of "executable" standards where a reference coder implementation in C language comes along with the classical written recommendation. Eventually, a bit-exact fixed-point reference implementation is provided.

In general, an ITU-T speech-coding project goes through the following phases:

- Establishment of the Terms of Reference.
- Selection of one candidate. If more than one candidate fulfill the requirements, then a compromise solution is found.
- Optimization of the selected candidate.
- Characterization.

Evolutions in speech coding were adopted after intensive tests in the next recommendation for vocoding at 8 kbit/s by means of conjugate-structure algebraic CELP (CS-ACELP) with its capability of both delivering high-quality speech and allowing for efficient search algorithms. This combination of features, besides fulfilling the ITU-T requirements for certain types of multimedia communications over wireline telephone connections, has prompted a wave of new digital cellular standards for operation at 8 kbit/s and below and even for operation at variable bit rate.

New developments of CELP coding in its combination with parametric coding, mainly for variable bit rate mobile and packet communications, including wideband codecs, are outlined as well as the move of parametric vocoding to higher-quality speech coders in secure communications, albeit without reaching strict toll quality. Also, as a guide to techniques that may eventually play important roles in the development of future speech coding standards, sinusoidal coding and waveform interpolation (WI) techniques are presented in connection with research topics in speech analysis and very low-bit-rate vocoders.

SPEECH CODER ATTRIBUTES

Speech coders are supposed to provide a compact representation of the speech signal from which it can be reconstructed. Therefore, bit rate and distortion are important attributes in the design and selection of a speech coder. Additionally, complexity is an important issue in the design and portability of the codec, and delay is a characteristic that impacts its applications over communication channels.

Bit Rate and Distortion

A speech coder may be functionally divided into an encoder and a decoder. The encoder analyzes the speech signal $s(n)$ whose relevant features are encoded into the bit stream $c(n)$, to be transmitted through the channel to the decoder as shown in Figure 1. In turn, on its propagation through the channel, a distorted bit stream $c'(n)$ reaches the decoder, which decodes it and delivers a reconstructed speech signal $\tilde{s}(n)$.

As an input to the coder, the speech signal is supposed to be given by a sequence of samples. Table 1 provides a description of various classes of speech and audio signals, relating their bandwidths, sampling rates, amplitude resolution, and bit rates. This chapter will be mostly concerned with narrowband (NB) and wideband (WB) speech signals.

The speech encoder is supposed to represent the speech signal by a set of parameters, which in turn it codes into codewords whose bits are joined and transmitted sequentially. This output binary signal is the bit stream, and the bit rate, usually measured in bit/s, is just its rate of binary symbols. In rate-distortion theory, the rate is usually measured in bits per sample of the original signal waveform (Jayant and Noll 1984).

Rate and distortion are inextricably related. The most popular measure related to distortion is the signal-to-noise ratio (SNR). Actually, the SNR is a measure of similarity or fidelity, which is the reciprocal ratio or the reverse of a distortion depending on whether SNR is measured as a linear ratio or logarithmically in decibels (dB). As a matter of fact, we should say signal-to-quantization-error ratio instead of SNR as no actual noise is involved in the process of coding, but the treatment of quantization error as a noise source has proven a very powerful mathematical construct.

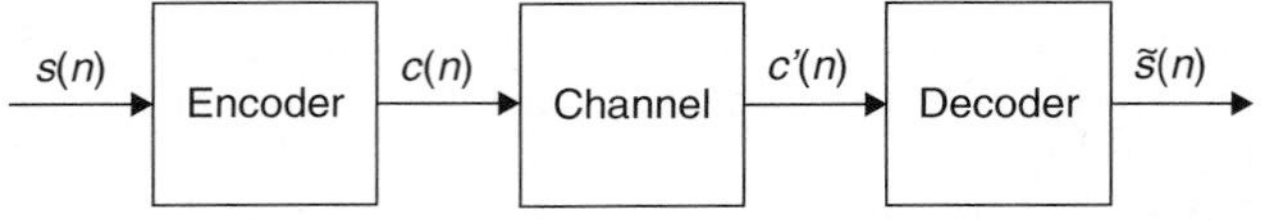

Figure 1: Major blocks for speech coding

In lossy coding, if the rate is increased while keeping other conditions constant, distortion may not increase and is likely to decrease. That is, rate and distortion vary inversely. When quality is measured instead of distortion, a rate increase is likely to cause an increase in quality as shown for two complexity levels in Figure 2, where subjective quality is measured by the mean opinion score (MOS) explained next. The relative positions of some selected standard coders in this figure should be considered indicative only because the data have been extracted from different tests. In rate-distortion theory, the condition is that, when given a rate, the minimum possible distortion or bound is tabulated for the corresponding distortion. Likewise, given a distortion, the minimum possible rate is assigned as the corresponding rate. But this theory is not concerned with the implementation of the coder that would actually realize that rate for the given distortion or, conversely, that causes that distortion for the given rate. In practice, we have to be concerned with the actual coder at hand. Then, two additional coder attributes come in our way, complexity and delay, as will be discussed in the following subsections.

A meaningful and practical measure of distortion may not be trivial to find or define. Even for waveform coders, the SNR may not reflect adequately our hearing perception because weak signal segments do not influence SNR calculation, which is dominated by the louder segments. This situation is ameliorated by evaluating each SNR over a signal segment in dB and taking an average over the number of segments in the signal. This measure is the segmental SNR (SNRSEG), which is typically evaluated for segments 16 ms long (Jayant and Noll 1984).

Ultimately, subjective opinions collected in listening tests are the most appropriate to assess actual coder performance but are prohibitive while the coder is in development due to the cost and schedule delays incurred. So, objective measures that simulate subjective opinion are an important tool during coder development. There are various methods for subjective testing (ITU-T 1996c; Kroon 1995), but the most widely used is by far the mean

Table 1: Bit Rates for Typical Digitization of Audio Signals

Description	Bandwidth	Sampling Frequency	Bits per Sample	Bit Rate
Narrowband (NB) speech	300 Hz–3.4 kHz	8.0 kHz	16	128 kbit/s
Wideband (WB) speech	50 Hz–7.0 kHz	16.0 kHz	16	256 kbit/s
Super-wideband speech	50 Hz–14.0 kHz	32.0 kHz	16	512 kbit/s
Audio (CD format)	10 Hz–20.0 kHz	44.1 kHz	16	706 kbit/s
Audio (DAT format)	10 Hz–20.0 kHz	48.0 kHz	16	768 kbit/s

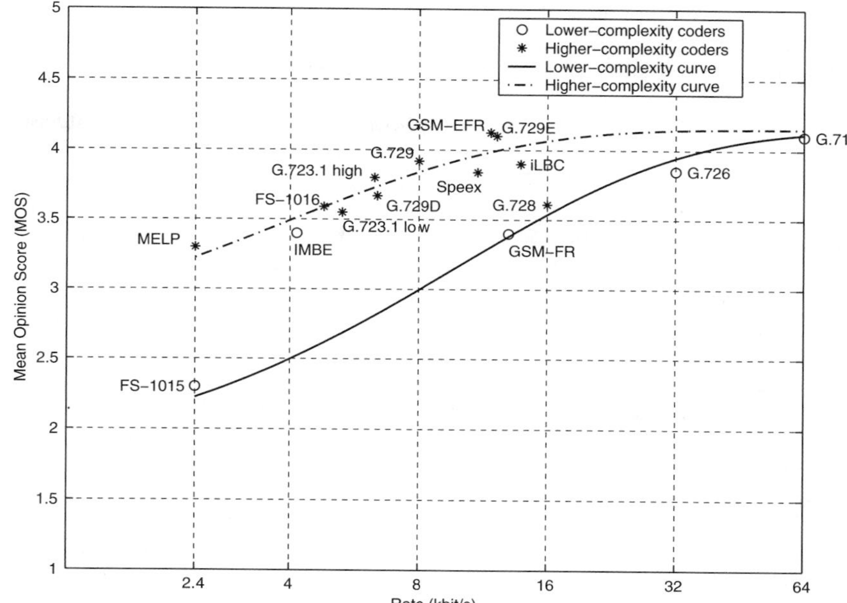

Figure 2: Subjective quality for narrowband speech coders over a range of bit rates for two illustrative complexity level curves

Table 2: Quality Rating Scales Referred to Quality and Impairment for Use in Absolute Category Rating (ACR) Tests and Degradation Category Rating (DCR) Tests, Respectively

Quality-Based Description	Impairment-Based Description	Quality Rating
Excellent	Imperceptible	5
Good	Perceptible but not annoying	4
Fair	Perceptible and slightly annoying	3
Poor	Annoying but not objectionable	2
Bad	Very annoying or objectionable	1

opinion score (MOS) where each listener is asked to evaluate the whole quality of reconstructed speech absolutely in an adjectival scale that ranges from bad to excellent. Then opinions are mapped to numerical indices from 1 to 5, respectively, and the final MOS is the average of the indices taken over all listeners, talkers, and samples in the test. The description and an illustrative range of MOS rating are displayed in Table 2 and Figure 2, respectively.

The MOS is an absolute category rating (ACR) test where listeners are presented only to a single speech sample at a time. For degradation discrimination, both the original and the degraded speech signal are presented to the listeners in what is called a degradation category rating (DCR) test. Its rating scale is also 5-point but the adjectival descriptions are focused on the perceived degradation as shown in Table 2. A more precise impairment discrimination may be achieved by comparison category rating (CCR) tests where the listeners are asked to identify which stimulus is the original one by means of a two-sided scale as given by Table 3. Also, the modified CCR (Mod CCR) method uses processed reference speech samples but with no noise suppression, whereas the pure CCR method uses unprocessed reference samples. Besides, pair-comparison or A-B preference tests are binary comparison tests where just a preference is asked from the listener. The binary nature of these tests, however, does not preclude the derivation of nonbinary ratings as long as possible coder pairs are compared.

Table 3: Quality Rating Scales Referred to Relative Quality for Use in Comparison Category Rating (CCR)

Description	Quality Rating
Much better	3
Better	2
Slightly better	1
About the same	0
Slightly worse	−1
Worse	−2
Much worse	−3

Although it is not wise to dispense with listening tests altogether, the development of objective perceptual measures of speech quality has been fruitful in recent years. Most illustrative of these advancements is the sequential development of the perceptual speech quality measure (PSQM) (ITU-T 1996d) and the perceptual evaluation of speech quality (PESQ) (ITU-T 2001). Most notably, PESQ measurements correlate well with subjective opinions even when delay and variable delay intervene between the original and the reconstructed signals, although some limitations still apply (ITU-T 2005a, 2005b). In addition, the wideband PESQ (ITU-T 2005d) is intended for wideband codec evaluation but it should be used only for relative rating because its MOS values are much lower than expected (Gibson 2005).

Actually, the PESQ is the first objective measure of speech quality that is capable of testing network impairments (Rix 2004). However, the PESQ is an intrusive measure in the sense that it uses the original signal as a reference. A nonintrusive algorithm for objective quality assessment is provided by the P.563 Recommendation (ITU-T 2004) to be used at network nodes.

Complexity

The operational complexity of a coder implementation is usually considered to involve the processing speed and the read-write memory (RAM) necessary for running variables (Kroon 1995). However, a comprehensive quality measure should also include read-only memory (ROM) for both data and program usage. Fixed-point arithmetic is especially convenient for bit-exact measurements, and its importance accrues as most implementations of speech coders run in mobile devices that are capable of fixed-point arithmetic only for lower power consumption reasons among others.

For a specific digital signal processor (DSP) architecture, the measure of processing speed is million instructions per second (MIPS). But, during algorithmic development, the final DSP to be chosen is not usually known; in fact, various platforms may be contemplated in the development of a reference coder for a standard, for instance. Therefore, the important step has been taken by ETSI to establish a virtual basic DSP for speech coding through a library of basic operations (BASOPs) to be used in simulated fixed-point C language speech coder implementations. Extensions to this library have been made available by ITU-T through Recommendation G.191 on "Software Tools for Speech and Audio Coding Standards." Each BASOP has an individual complexity weight, which is unity for simple operations like addition, multiplication, and multiply-accumulate (MAC) and is correspondingly larger for more complex operations. The per-second average operation count obtained in a statistically significant coding session is the weighted million operations per second (WMOPS) measure.

This primary set of basic operators uses 16- and 32-bit variables and a 32-bit accumulator. More recently, an alternative set of basic operators with a 40-bit accumulator has been developed for use in 3GPP2 and standardized in the 2005 revision of ITU-T G.191 (STL2005).

Delay

Delay or the time lag between the production and reception of sound is the attribute of a speech coder that may have the most disruptive effect on interactive communication. Nonetheless, for VoIP, it is reported that in a conversation, packet losses are a more severe impairment than delay (James, Bing Vhen, and Garrison 2004).

For the design and deployment of speech communication systems, it is important to break down the total delay into components that may be attributed to functional system elements. An inherent component of delay is called *algorithmic delay*, which comes about as a consequence of signal acquisition and buffering and is directly related to block length. Sometimes algorithmic delay has to include look-ahead buffering, which may be used for smoothing the evolution of some coder parameters such as pitch and in the analysis of short-term LP coefficients. However efficient the implementation, algorithmic delay is irreducible because it is an attribute of the algorithms used themselves, the processor notwithstanding.

Another component of delay is actual signal processing, which is the time it takes the processor to analyze the buffered signal to be encoded and to reconstruct the signal from the decoded parameters. This component depends on the processing speed provided by the processor and memory used. As a major component of delay, algorithmic delay and processing delay are jointly referred to as one-way codec delay (Cox and Kroon 1996).

The third component of delay includes bit stream buffering, multiplexing, and transmission delay. This component depends on propagation and other properties of the channel. In particular, in packet communications, transmission delay is variable and is further decomposed into fixed delay and a jitter. As a general rule of thumb, a rough estimate of delay is three times the frame length plus signal processing delay, including any look-ahead. To enable interactive voice communications, total delay should be below 200 ms in the absence of echoes. If echoes are present, total delay should not exceed 25 ms (Cox and Kroon 1996). This underlines the importance of echo cancellation and the need for low-delay coders in some applications as typified by the G.728 coder in the "Vocoding Standards" section later in this chapter.

In VoIP applications, additional delay occurs because the packet usually contains more than one frame. For instance, G.711 is generally packetized in 10 ms, 20 ms, or even larger blocks.

TRANSMISSION IMPAIRMENTS

The medium across the speech encoder and the speech decoder may harm the bit stream as indicated earlier in Figure 1. In store-and-forward systems, the damage usually affects isolated bits while they are stored. Similarly, in wireline communications, single-bit toggling can occur due to impulse noise. On the other hand, in mobile communications, burst errors usually affect whole frames of code causing frame erasures. Likewise, in packet communications, whole packets may be lost or be received out of order. When a speech coder is tested for a given transmission channel, sensitivity to an error in each bit is evaluated by the magnitude of the degradation incurred, and groups of bits are formed for different sensitivity levels so that even different channel coders may be used for different groups (Steele 1993).

The more complex speech coding standards such as G.728 and G.729 that use CELP models have provisions for frame erasure concealment by extending the application of model parameters for previous good frames to the erased frames. On the other hand, for simple, one codeword per sample coders such as G.711, no model parameters are available for working out any signal extension to bridge across the missing frames. Therefore, the packet loss concealment (PLC) algorithm itself maintains a memory of past samples, organized as pitch periods for voiced speech, which are repeated with progressive attenuation. However, pitch periods may be repeated out of their order of occurrence in the original signal if the loss is rather long. To prevent artificial enhancement of periodicity, the synthetic speech signal is modified. Such a PLC algorithm was recommended as ITU-T Recommendation G.711 Appendix I (09/99) and also in ANSI Standard T1.521-1999 (Cox, Malah, and Kapilow 2004).

For operation in the public switched telephone network (PSTN), a codec should be robust to asynchronous tandem encodings with itself and with other codecs in the network. In this respect, the G.711 codec is remarkable for its MOS will still be above 4.0 after 8 asynchronous tandems with itself, down from an MOS of about 4.4 for a single encoding (Gibson 2005). On the other hand, the G.726 codec drops to an MOS of about 3.0 after 4 asynchronous tandems with itself when for a single encoding an MOS of about 4.0 is obtained.

The connection of two speech codecs usually involves decoding and reencoding, causing a loss of quality. If the codecs use the same technology, a direct mapping of their parameters could be done without ever having to reconstruct the speech signal. This is called intelligent or smart transcoding (Kang, Kim, and Cox 2003).

TECHNIQUES FOR SPEECH CODING

The very basic technique in signal coding is entropy coding, which is lossless; that is, the signal waveform may be exactly recovered from the code sequence or bit stream. In other words, entropy coding exploits only information redundancy in the signal or sample sequence. But the compression ratio that may be attained for speech signals is really low, and lossy coding is always used. The hub of lossy coding is quantization, which is essentially irreversible. The proper use of this technique will remove only irrelevant information. The definition of irrelevance, to be sure, rests upon human auditory perception. And, actually, approximate loudness discrimination was the feature initially used in speech quantization as mentioned later in the "Vocoding Standards" section.

The quality and efficiency of vocoding rests upon the isolation of irrelevance and the ease or difficulty in its removal. Rather, based on the characteristics of the human speech production process, an efficient collection of methods called linear prediction has been developed that is very effective in isolating much of the redundancy in the speech signal to be extracted during encoding and later reinstated when decoding. Then, anticipating what will happen in the listening process, the coder uses the masking properties of human listening in the identification and removal of irrelevance by proper quantization methods.

Waveform Coding

Waveform coding involves the quantization of some signal or waveform. In its simplest form, the waveform used is the original speech signal, and quantization levels are nonuniformly distributed over the amplitude range. These are said to be PCM (pulse code modulation) coders.

Higher complexity waveform coders use the difference signal $d(n)$ for quantization by an adaptive uniform quantizer. This signal is generated inside a quantizer-predictor loop as the difference between the original speech signal $s(n)$ and the predicted speech signal $\hat{s}(n)$ as represented in Figure 3. Therefore, it is a prediction error signal. Quantizer $Q(\cdot)$ approximates $d(n)$ by its nearest code level $\tilde{d}(n)$, which is added to the predicted speech sample $\hat{s}(n)$ to come up with the reconstructed sample $\tilde{s}(n)$. Finally, the reconstructed sample is input to predictor $P(z)$, which delivers the predicted speech signal $\hat{s}(n)$, so closing the loop.

The predictor may be fixed, and the coder is said to be a differential PCM (DPCM) coder. A special case of DPCM is delta modulation (DM) whose quantizer codes at the rate of 1 bit/sample. In fact, adaptive DM (ADM) has a fixed predictor and an adaptive quantizer, which is generally adapted by either of two algorithms: continuously variable slope delta modulation (CVSD) or the Jayant multiplier algorithm (Jayant and Noll 1984). Actually, it has been widely used by the military and also for avionic

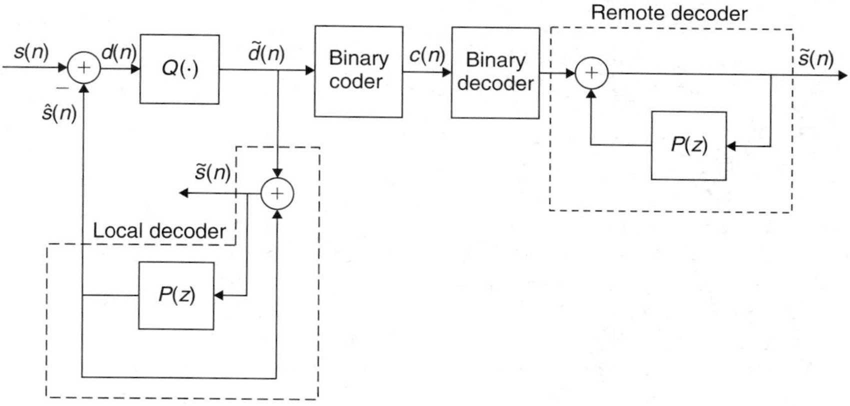

Figure 3: Quantizer-predictor feedback loop in a differential PCM coder and associated decoder

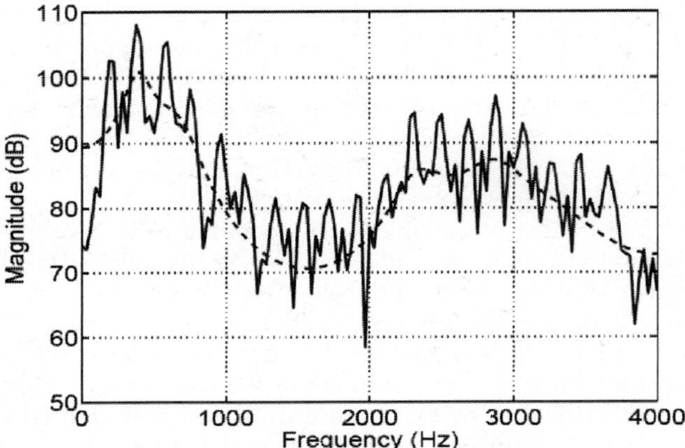

Figure 4: Power spectral density of a voiced speech segment (solid line) extracted at 0.75 s from the signal in Figure 10 and its corresponding 10th-order LP spectral envelope (dashed line)

communications and private communications due to its robustness to transmission errors, low cost, low delay, and low power consumption. However, ADPCM, discussed later, delivers higher-quality speech in error-free conditions (Steele 1993).

For higher performance, the predictor coefficients are adapted on a sample basis for adaptive DPCM (ADPCM) coders or on a block basis for adaptive predictive coders (APCs). In adaptive predictive coding, LP analysis techniques are employed.

Linear Prediction (LP)

The greater part of the redundancy in a speech signal may be represented by an LP model. Its spectral representation is a smoothed version of the speech signal spectrum, corresponding to a kind of spectral envelope as shown in Figure 4 for a voiced speech signal segment also represented by a vertical slice at 0.75 s in Figure 10 later in this chapter, where the gain in the model has been adjusted to match the signal's integrated power spectrum. The remaining fine details in the signal spectrum may be captured as the prediction residual spectrum, whose corresponding waveform is shown in Figure 5.

In the synthesis phase, a coded version of the prediction residual signal feeds the synthesis filter that shapes its spectral envelope. This constitutes a simplified yet powerful model of speech production, schematically represented in Figure 6. In linear predictive coding (LPC), the residual signal is modeled as a linear combination of a periodic pulse train for the periodic or voiced component of speech and a pseudorandom noise sequence for its unvoiced component. A greater simplification of the model consists of using only the major voiced or unvoiced component. For determining the excitation, LP analysis is a very helpful aid for the residual signal waveform displays enhanced peaks as compared to the original speech signal waveform (see Figure 5). Besides, the reader should not be misled by scale normalization and notice that the amplitude range of the residual signal is much lower.

Further analysis of the residual signal waveform in Figure 5 reveals that because it is periodic just as its

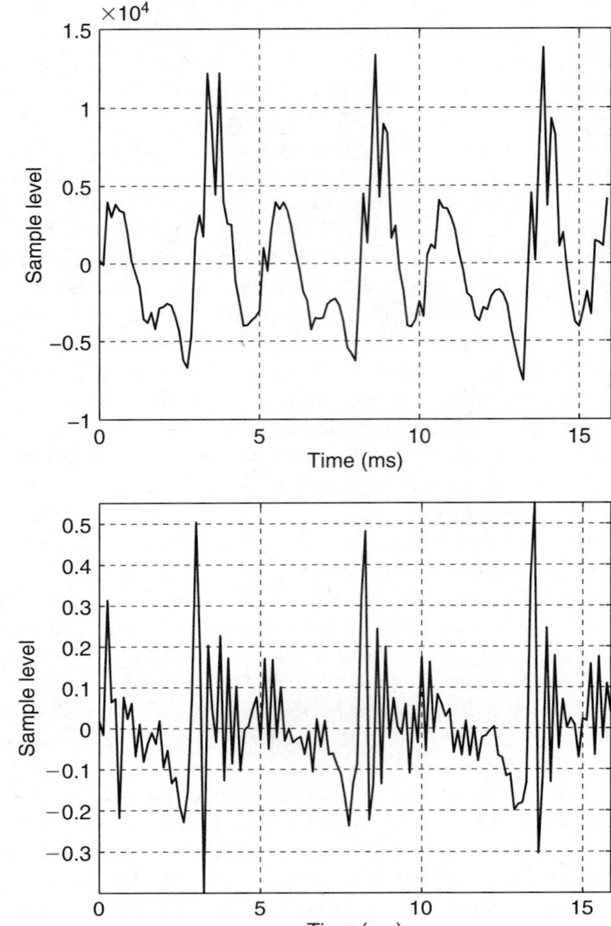

Figure 5: Waveform of a voiced speech signal segment (top) extracted at 0.75 s from the signal in Figure 10 and its corresponding 10th-order LP residual signal waveform (bottom)

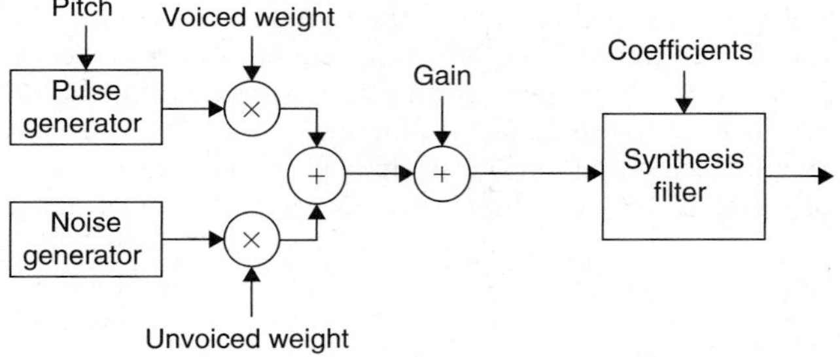

Figure 6: Source-filter model of speech production where excitation type may be a linear combination of pseudorandom noise or periodic pulses whose fundamental frequency should be further specified. The amplitude of both types of excitation must be adjusted by their weights and common gain factor. Filter coefficients may be controlled

corresponding speech signal segment, it may be linearly predicted as well. In this case, the LP analysis uses an autocorrelation lag range of the order of a pitch period so that the predictor obtained is called a long-term predictor (LTP) as opposed to the sample period predictor discussed previously, which is called a short-term predictor (STP). Lower prediction orders, such as first- or third order, are more usual for the LTP. The pitch period or pitch lag ranges from about 20 to 147 samples for NB speech and from about 30 to 230 samples for WB speech for a fundamental frequency range from about 55 Hz to 400 Hz. The LTP replaces the LPC pulse generator with advantage because it is less sensitive to pitch detection and can additionally shape the excitation signal.

Linear prediction analysis algorithms usually deliver a set of prediction coefficients a_i, $i = 1,2,\ldots, p$, where p is the prediction order, which define a synthesis filter

$$H(z) = \frac{1}{1+\sum_{i=1}^{p} a_i z^{-i}}. \tag{1}$$

Usually, $p = 10$ for most NB codecs. The prediction coefficients are not suitable for quantization because their range can't be easily determined and the stability of the synthesis filter in Eq. (1) cannot be guaranteed when using quantized and interpolated prediction coefficients. On the contrary, the partial correlation (PARCOR) or reflection coefficients are bounded like

$$|k_m| < 1 \tag{2}$$

for $m = 1,2,\ldots, p$ when the synthesis filter is stable. Prediction coefficients can be converted to reflection coefficients and back to prediction coefficients by step-down and step-up relations, respectively (Markel and Gray, Jr. 1976). Still, the spectral sensitivity of PARCOR coefficients to quantization is different around ± 1 and around 0 (Furui 1985). Fortunately, some transformations yield more efficient parameters. The two most important sets of such parameters are θ_m, the arcsine of reflection coefficients (ASRC), for $m = 1,2,\ldots, p$ and the log area ratio (LAR) coefficients

$$o_m = \log\frac{1-k_m}{1+k_m} \tag{3}$$

for $m = 1,2,\ldots, p$. These parameters may be quantized uniformly.

For low sensitivity to interpolation as well, the parameters of choice are the line spectral pair (LSP) or line spectral frequency (LSF) coefficients (Itakura 1975; Furui 1985) or the immitance spectral pair (ISP) representation (Bistritz and Peller 1993). These sets of coefficients and the set of prediction coefficients are convertible to and from one another. For a stable pth-order synthesis filter, the LSFs must satisfy the relations

$$0 < w_1 < w_2 < \cdots < w_{p-1} < w_p < \pi. \tag{4}$$

The ISP representation includes the immitance spectral frequencies (ISFs), which are the LSFs for the embedded p-1st-order LP component of the synthesis filter and k_p, the pth-order reflection coefficient, so that the conditions for stability of the synthesis filter include the relations

$$0 < w_{I,1} < w_{I,2} < \cdots < w_{I,p-2} < w_{I,p-1} < \pi \tag{5}$$

coupled with the additional relation $|k_p| < 1$. The ISP representation incurs in lower quantization distortion in differential scalar quantization (Bistritz and Peller 1993; So and Paliwal 2007) and is used for coding the predictor coefficients in the 3GPP and ITU-T G.722.2 AMR-WB coder in split-multistage vector quantization (S-MSVQ) (Bessete et al. 2002).

For higher-quality signal reconstruction, more complex speech excitation models are used. Yet, basically the same LP analysis is done by the encoder and the same synthesis filter is used by the decoder. The first such speech coder to consider is the APC (Atal and Schroeder 1970), which features frame rate LP analysis for reestimation of the predictor coefficients, whereas the ADPCM coder uses sample rate predictor adaptation.

Code-Excited LP (CELP)

In the previous section, LP analysis techniques were presented that are quite efficient in determining the coefficients for the filter in the source-filter synthesis model in Figure 6. The configuration of the source or generator, however, has only been sketched for LPC to involve the determination of a pitch period for a periodic pulse train excitation and also a gain factor, or simply a gain factor should the excitation be random. The next step in coding these parameters is their quantization.

The analysis and coding just described for LPC is open-loop because all the parameters for the synthesis model are determined straight from the speech signal. Alternatively, a loop may be closed around a comparator between the original speech signal and a reconstructed speech signal generated by feeding the synthesis model with quantized parameter codevectors. Conceptually, in this so-called analysis-by-synthesis procedure, each quantization codevector is used to generate its corresponding reconstructed signal, and its overall reconstruction error is stored if below the current minimum value. This allows the selection of the quantization codevector causing the minimum overall error.

For CELP, the information that most clearly warrants an analysis-by-synthesis quantization is the excitation waveshape, and the "code" in the name stands for the selected waveshape quantization code. The analysis-by-synthesis search procedure through one codebook in a CELP coder is illustrated in Figure 7. Filter coefficients are quantized open-loop, and excitation gain is usually quantized in an analysis-by-synthesis loop. Original waveshapes for the codebook were drawn from an independent and identically distributed zero-mean, unit-variance Gaussian source (Schroeder and Atal 1985), segmented as 1024 codevectors containing 40 samples each. Accordingly, a 10-bit codeword was used to identify a 40-sample waveshape for a 5 ms excitation subframe.

As the search through stochastic codebooks is very computation-intensive, sparse codebooks were developed whose large amount of zero samples ease the processor. Coders such as QCELP8, IS-96 digital cellular standard (Yang, Fischer, Kang et al. 1995), and secure CELP FS-1016

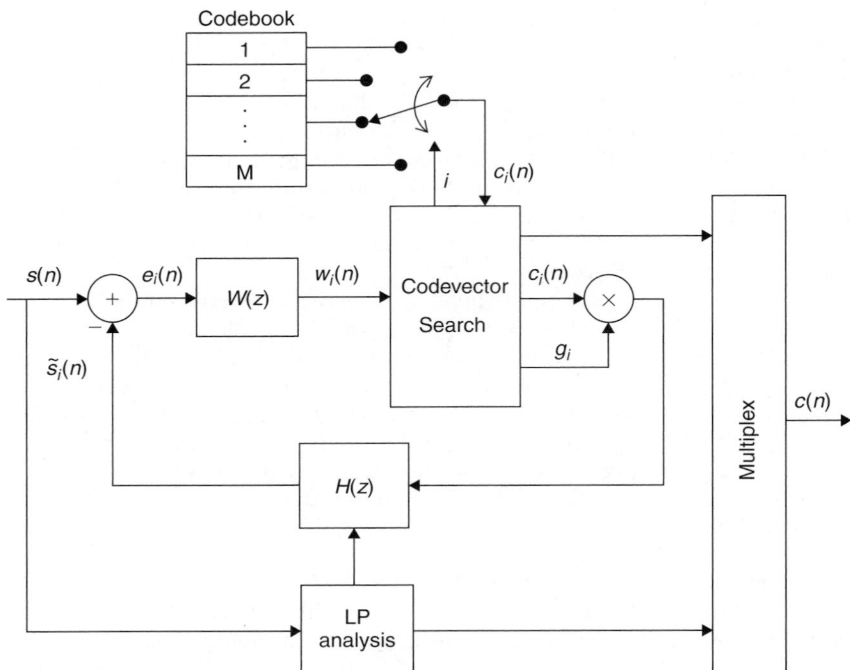

Figure 7: CELP coder encodes signal $s(n)$ into bit stream $c(n)$. Coder includes analysis-by-synthesis loop driven by the reconstruction error signal $e_i(n)$

(Campbell Jr., Tremain, and Welch 1991) use sparse stochastic codebooks. Search complexity can also be reduced with focused search algorithms, which avoid testing unlikely codevectors.

The reconstruction error spectrum is shaped by the weighting filter $W(z)$ that lets less error power spread over frequency regions where the signal power density is low and allows most of the error power to appear where the signal power density is large enough to mask the error. The effect of the weighting filter upon the spectrum of the final reconstruction error signal $e_i(n)$ (see Figure 7) can be seen in Figure 8. The spectral envelope of the reconstruction error (dashed line) stays below the spectral envelope of the speech signal (solid line) when the weighting filter $W(z)$ is in the analysis-by-synthesis loop (top plot); whereas it may rise above the speech envelope (bottom plot) when $W(z)$ is not in place (bottom plot), particularly in interformant regions such as the frequency band extending from about 900 Hz to 2100 Hz. In addition, it should be noticed that the reconstruction error spectrum follows more closely the speech signal spectrum when W(z) is used.

The weighting filter is adapted as a function of the synthesis filter like

$$W(z) = \frac{H(z/\gamma_2)}{H(z/\gamma_1)}, \tag{6}$$

where γ_1 and γ_2 are bandwidth expansion factors lying between 0 and 1. A usual solution is to set $\gamma_1 = 1$ and $\gamma_2 = 0.8$, but the bandwidth expansion factors for the G.729 coder are adapted according to the shape of the spectral envelope of the speech signal (Salami et al. 1998). By means of the first two LAR coefficients of the synthesis filter, the spectral shape is detected to be flat or tilted. For a flat spectrum, the factors are set to $\gamma_1 = 0.94$ and $\gamma_2 = 0.6$, while for a tilted spectrum, γ_1 is set to 0.98, and γ_2 is set to a value

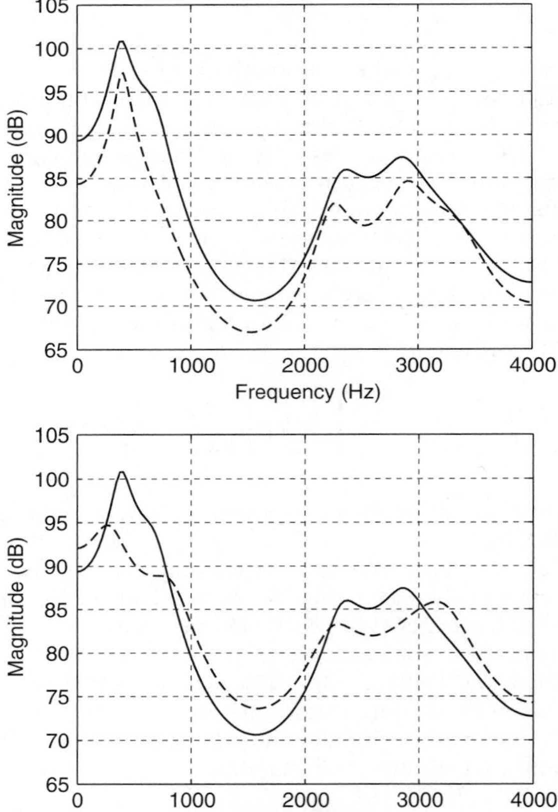

Figure 8: Spectral envelopes of speech signal (solid lines on top and bottom plots) segment extracted at 0.75 s from the signal in Figure 10, reconstruction error signal at the input of the weighting filter (dashed line on top plot) in a CELP coder, and reconstruction error without weighting filter (dashed line on bottom plot)

between 0.4 and 0.7 depending on resonance strength detected by minimum LSF separation.

A strong resonance pushes γ_2 towards 0.7. Still, for WB speech, the spectral tilt is stronger so that, in order to handle it, the AMR-WB codec (Bessette et al. 2002) performs the LP analysis on the speech preemphasized by $P(z) = 1 - 0.68z^{-1}$ while using the following weighting filter

$$W(z) = \frac{1}{P(z)H(z/\gamma_1)}, \quad (7)$$

where $\gamma_1 = 0.9$.

In addition to the fixed codebook (FCB), CELP coders have a second adaptive codebook (ACB), which is an implementation of an LTP using segments of the composite excitation prior to the subframe under analysis as codevectors. The composite excitation is the linear combination of the adaptive and the fixed codevector scaled by their respective gain factors. After computing the composite excitation for the current subframe, the past excitation samples in the adaptive codebook are updated.

Usually, the lag range used in the adaptive codebook search is reduced by focusing around a delay value determined by an open-loop pitch detector. In particular, the AMR-WB codec, following the G.729 and AMR codecs, refines the lag in three stages. The second stage determines an integer value for the lag in a search around the first-stage open-loop pitch estimate, while the third stage searches for the fractional lag refinement around the optimum integer value with quarter-sample resolution at the finest time scale (Bessette et al. 2002).

For lags larger than the subframe length, the adaptive codebook is equivalent to an LTP filter, while for shorter lags, the available excitation memory is replicated. The ACB introduced previously operates out of one tap located on the past excitation memory at the pitch lag with a single gain, corresponding to a single-tap pitch prediction

$$P_h(z) = b_0 z^{-T}, \quad (8)$$

where b_0 is the ACB gain, and T is the pitch lag. Multitap ACBs may be used with taps at unit sample spacing around sample $n - T$ at one pitch lag T behind. Therefore, multitap ACBs require an odd number of gain factors, determined by crosscorrelation analysis around the pitch lag. The corresponding pitch predictor now has the form

$$P_h(z) = \sum_{i=-(p_h-1)/2}^{(P_h-1)/2} b_i z^{-(T+i)}, \quad (9)$$

where b_i for $i = -(p_h - 1)/2,\ldots,(p_h - 1)/2$ are the gain factors, and p_h is the pitch prediction order. For instance, the G.723.1 coder features a five-tap ACB (ITU-T 1996b), that is, $p_h = 5$. Integer lag multitap ACBs provide additional periodicity fit over integer lag single-tap ACBs, allowing greater amplitude adjustment among harmonics, whereas fractional lag ACBs allow finer frequency resolution while providing a flat harmonic spectrum.

The noise masking effect of human hearing also applies to the harmonic component of the speech spectrum. Therefore, a harmonic weighting filter $W_h(z)$ may be defined for the open-loop pitch prediction error filter $A_{ho}(z) = 1 - P_{ho}(z)$ as

$$W_h(z) = 1 - \gamma_h P_{ho}(z), \quad (10)$$

where γ_h is a gain weighting factor constrained to be between 0 and 1 but usually lying between 0.3 and 0.4 (ITU-T 1996b; Gerson and Jasiuk 1991). The open-loop pitch predictor $P_{ho}(z)$ is usually a single-tap filter even though it may operate in a subsample time scale. For a coder with a harmonic weighting filter $W_h(z)$, filter $W(z)$ may be referred to as the formant weighting filter. Then, the resulting weighting filter will be $W(z)\, W_h(z)$.

The analysis-by-synthesis method used in CELP coders inherits most of its features from multipulse excitation (MPE) coders (Atal and Remde 1982). In these speech coders, the excitation for the synthesis filter consists of

$$x(n) = \sum_{k=0}^{K-1} A_k \delta(n - m_k), \quad n = 0,1,\ldots,L-1 \quad (11)$$

for a subframe of length L and K pulses whose amplitudes and locations are A_k and m_k, respectively, for $k = 0,1,\ldots, K - 1$. The original proposal suggests $K = 8$ and $L = 80$ and outlines an efficient algorithm that determines pulse positions one at a time using analysis-by-synthesis, while the final pulse amplitudes are determined at the end. A more efficient search procedure came along when pulse locations were restricted to be equidistant, that is, $m_k = kS + l$, where S is the regular pulse spacing, and $l = m_0$ is the position of the first pulse or the phase of the regular pulse excitation (RPE). Therefore, regular pulse positions have to be searched only for phases $l = 0,1,\ldots, K - 1$, bringing about a substantial reduction in complexity over MPE search (Kroon, Deprettere, and Sluyter 1986). The GSM (Global System for Mobile Communications) full-rate standard coder employs RPE with long-term predictor (RPE-LTP) (Hellwig et al. 1989).

Another form of deterministic sparse excitation is algebraic CELP (ACELP) excitation

$$x(n) = G\sum_{k=0}^{K-1} a_k \delta(n - m_k), \quad n = 0,1,\ldots,L-1 \quad (12)$$

where individual pulse amplitudes α_k take on values of 1 or -1, and a common gain factor G affects all pulses. Furthermore, pulse positions are taken from tracks related by interleaved single-pulse permutations (ISPP). This means that all the positions in a subframe are distributed over K tracks so that positions on a track are equidistant, and positions on adjacent tracks are shifted. In general, just one pulse position per track will be assigned. For instance, the position grid for the G.729 coder is shown in Table 4 where one position is drawn from each of the first three tracks, and just one position is drawn from the last two tracks taken together. Therefore, 3 bits are necessary for coding each position on the first three tracks, while

Table 4: ACELP Position Grid for the G.729 40-Sample Subframe

Track	Positions							
0	0	5	10	15	20	25	30	35
1	1	6	11	16	21	26	31	36
2	2	7	12	17	22	27	32	37
3	3	8	13	18	23	28	33	38
	4	9	14	19	24	29	34	39

4 bits are needed for coding the position on the last double track. Adding on the 4 bits for coding the four pulse amplitudes, this makes for a 17-bit codebook index or a codebook holding 2^{17} waveshapes. This ACELP codebook is 128 times larger than the original stochastic CELP codebook, but its search is much more efficient due to its structured organization. Some coders assign more than one pulse position per track, such as the G.729E, EFR, and AMR coders, and the AMR-WB coder at high rates.

The gains for the FCB and ACB excitation components have to be vector quantized for low-bit-rate vocoding as a bit-rate savings measure. For instance, the G.729 coder applies VQ in the log gain domain in an analysis-by-synthesis loop while keeping the fixed and adaptive codevectors constant. Furthermore, the FCB gain is predicted by an MA (moving-average) predictor, and a correction factor is coded so that the prediction error might be decoded. This predictor removes a great deal of intersubframe gain redundancy, reducing its dynamic range and decreasing its dependence on input speech power variation (Salami et al. 1998). Also, its MA structure reduces the propagation of transmission errors.

There is more to perceptual processing than formant and harmonic weighting, which are applied to both the original and the reconstructed speech signals. Still, it has been found perceptually beneficial to include a so-called postfilter to apply on the reconstructed speech for formant, spectral tilt, and harmonic open-loop weighting. However, this postfiltering tends to degrade the codec performance under tandem connection conditions.

Finally, the lowpass nature of speech signals may cause serious numerical processing errors, mainly for fixed-point implementations. As a prevention measure, preemphasis as a preprocessing stage reduces the spectral dynamic range of the signal. This has already been mentioned in connection to WB speech preprocessing. Generally, even for NB speech, some highpass filtering is beneficial to attenuate the low-frequency power in the speech as well as to reinforce its high-frequency components. Another reason for this prefiltering is to block DC offset and attenuate additive interference such as power line induction. For instance, the G.729 reference implementation includes a second-order IIR highpass prefilter with a cutoff frequency of 140 Hz (ITU-T 1996a).

Subband and Transform Coding

Subband coding (SBC) is based on an analysis filterbank that decomposes the full-band speech signal into several NB subband signals that may then be downsampled for independent coding by PCM, ADPCM, or analysis-by-synthesis techniques. Perceptual modeling is used for bit allocation among the subbands. In the decoder, each subband is decoded, and the full-band signal is reconstructed by the synthesis filterbank.

Practical subband filters will partially overlap causing aliasing distortion in each individual subband since critical sampling is used. Fortunately, the collective action of the analysis and synthesis filterbanks combining all the subbands after upsampling can manage to virtually cancel the aliasing distortion. The two-subband quadrature mirror filterbank (QMF) is the smallest structure capable of this cancellation effect. In fact, it is the core signal processing component in the ITU-T G.722 codec (ITU-T 1998), the first one from the ITU-T to handle WB speech, intended to be used in videoconferencing. In addition, it is one of the standard codecs in the H.323 videoconferencing protocol suite besides being a common option for VoIP systems.

The G.722 codec operates at the three bit rates of 64-, 56-, and 48 kbit/s by separating the signal into two subbands for independent ADPCM coding as shown in Figure 9a.

Conceptually, in transform coding (TC), each coefficient evolving in time may be viewed as a subband signal in SBC. In this equivalence, TC block length equals SBC subsampling factor, so constraining the impulse response of TC subband filters to be this long. Since SBC subband filters are not constrained this way, SBC includes TC as a special case. Accordingly, the design of transform coders is primarily concerned with windows and block length so that blocking artifacts constitutes an important distortion to be controlled.

More sophisticated techniques combine subband filterbanks with transform decomposition. These techniques are employed by high-quality audio coders and by the ITU-T G.722.1 speech coder, which implements a modulated lapped transform (MLT). This codec operates at 32- and 24 kbit/s and uses a categorization procedure to determine quantizer stepsizes and parameters for regions of the MLT output as schematized in Figure 9b. The ACELP coder in Figure 9c will be explained later in the "Multirate and Variable-Rate Codecs" section in connection with the G.722.2 speech coder, also know as the AMR-WB codec. It is further noted in that section that the upper layers of the G.729.1 codec employ a TC technique.

The G.722.1 codec (ITU-T 2005c) delivers good quality music while performing not so well for speech since filterbank techniques are more suited to general audio coding (Gibson 2005).

LOSS RECOVERY FOR GRACEFUL DEGRADATION

Generally, frame erasure or packet loss recovery procedures can be divided into two classes: those that use frame redundancy and those that reduce interframe dependence. Usually, speech coder recommendations such as the G.723.1 codec (ITU-T 1996b) and the AMR codec (ETSI 2004b) incorporate error concealment strategies to be applied upon

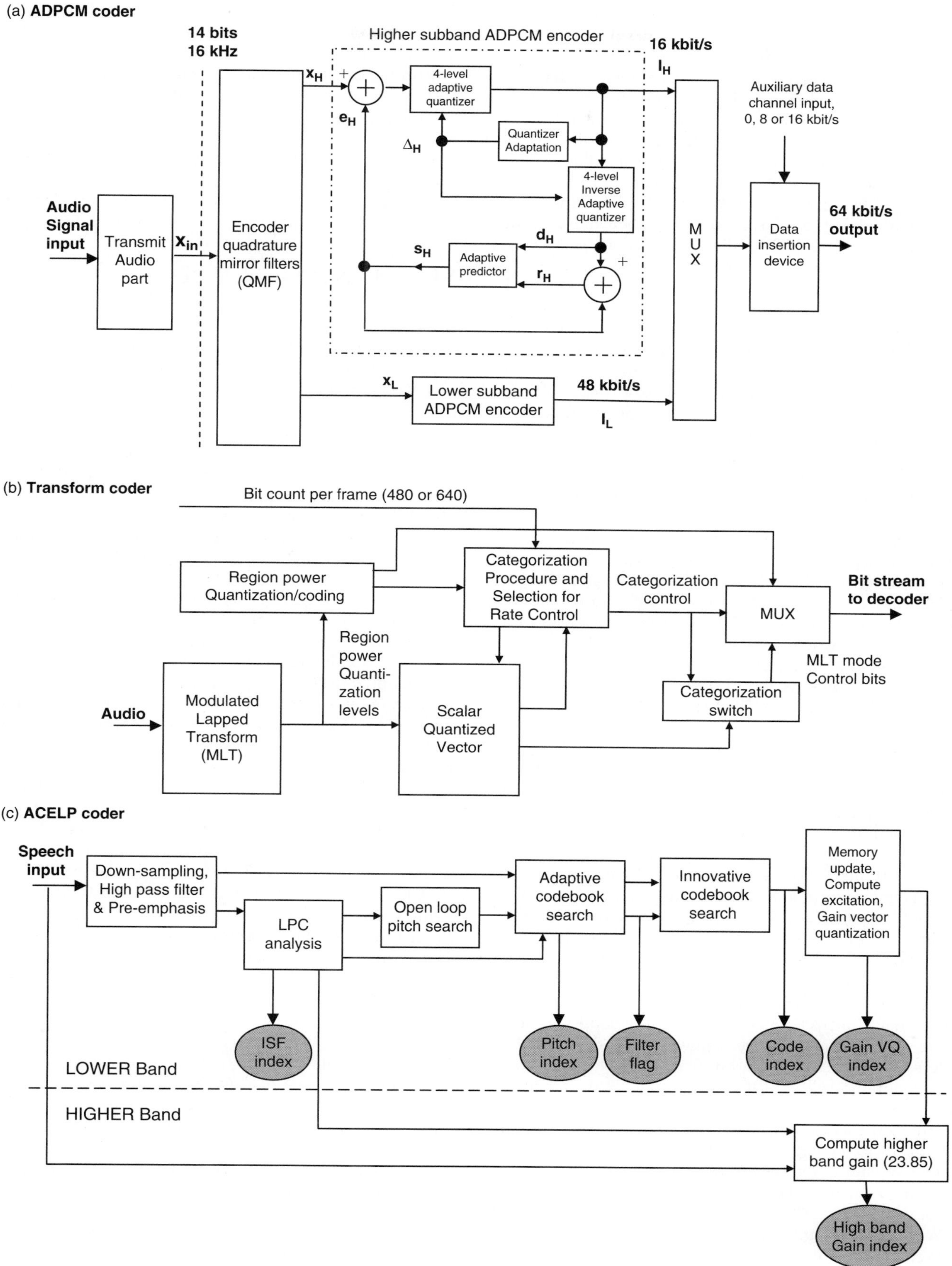

Figure 9: Three ITU-T wideband speech coders: (a) G.722, (b) G.722.1, and (c) G.722.2

detection of frame erasure occurrences. These strategies apply different combinations of last good frame repetition with progressive attenuation. Their implementation may be rather sophisticated as for the AMR codec reference (ETSI 2004a), which is based on a seven-state finite state machine that counts bad frames up to six. Fixed codebook and adaptive codebook gains are adapted according to different sequences of attenuation factors depending on the value of a moving median filter. Line spectral frequencies are updated by an exponentially windowed moving average filter. Pitch lags are largely based on their most recent good values, whereas FCB indices are used as received or generated randomly if they are lost.

Even when a frame is missing when it should be played out, if it arrives while the next frame is being decoded, it may be useful in driving the inner states of the coder to where they would be in case the late frame had arrived in time (Gournay, Rousseau, and Lefebvre 2003).

The 3GPP2 VMR-WB codec conceals a frame loss after a good voiced speech frame by estimating separately the excitation frame and its envelope. Loss recovery is completed when normal frame decoding is resumed, and this may involve the construction of an artificial voiced onset that can only be done if the first good frame after the frame erasure is full-rate generic because only such frames contain all the parameters needed for recovery. But this poses no further restriction because voiced onsets are coded as full-rate generic (Jelínek et al. 2004).

Alternatively, a parameter set for a reduced resolution vocoding model may be estimated from the past good frames. In cases when no modeling is done by the encoder, the decoder itself makes a simple model by organizing previous good samples as the PLC algorithm for the G.711 coder, which is presented in the "Transmission Impairments" section.

Similar to this last strategy, a number of techniques using frame redundancy actually transmit alternate lower-resolution vocoding model parameters along the main coding stream for alternate signal reconstruction depending on the severity of the transmission impairment.

For VoIP applications, a recent development in vocoding techniques capable of graceful degradation is the Internet Low Bit Rate Codec (iLBC), which is a kind of modified CELP vocoder specified by RFC 3951 (Andersen et al. 2004) for 30 ms frames and 20 ms frames with payload rates of 13.33 kbit/s and 15.20 kbit/s, respectively. The modification breaks the main mechanism of propagation of the effects of packet losses through the adaptive codebook, which happens to be a powerful device in CELP coders. To prevent degradation from propagating across frame boundaries, the iLBC codec initializes the adaptive codebook within each frame with a start state vector that is extended forward through the end of the frame and backwards to the beginning of the frame. This process of predictive coding forward in time and then backward in time has come to be known as FB-LPC (Cable Television Laboratories, Inc. 2005).

While there is certainly a bit rate penalty to be traded in exchange for the additional robustness, it is remarkable that the iLBC coder can operate without excessive degradation for packet loss rates up to about 20 percent (Andersen et al. 2002), while coders for mobile communications are often tested for maximum frame erasure rates of 3 percent or 5 percent (Cox and Kroon 1996).

Another development for VoIP and voice over cable and DSL applications includes BroadVoice®16, a low complexity, low delay PacketCable 1.5 mandatory 16 kbit/s NB speech codec and BroadVoice®32 WB speech codec. They implement two-stage noise feedback coding and excitation VQ with just 5 ms algorithmic delay for total complexities of 12- and 17 MIPS for BroadVoice®16 and BroadVoice®32, respectively (Chen 2007).

VOCODING STANDARDS

The most basic standard for vocoding is G.711 (ITU-T 1989) 64 kbit/s PCM, which uses waveform sampling, analog-to-digital conversion, and nonuniform amplitude coding. Its nonuniform quantizer operates at 8 bit/sample and 8000 sample/s according to a compressing-expanding law, or "companding" law for short. Actually, two companding laws are supported by the standard, namely, A-law companding that is used in Europe, South America, Africa, and Australia, and μ-law companding that is typically used in North America and Japan (Jayant and Noll 1984). The G.711 companded PCM coder was introduced in first-generation public digital telephony and its sampling frequency of 8 kHz has become standard for NB speech. However, new enhancements to vocoding such as WB speech coding are pushing the sampling frequency upwards (Cox et al. 2004).

Next in compression rate comes G.726 ADPCM at 40-, 32-, 24-, 16 kbit/s based on the use of adaptive predictor and quantizer (ITU-T 1990). It was originally established as Recommendation G.721 in 1982 by CCITT, the forerunner of ITU-T, for operation at 32 kbit/s. At this rate, it came to be used in CT2 and DECT cordless telephones. This rate accommodates 4 bit/sample of the difference signal, and both the quantizer and the predictor are backward-adapted at the sample rate from the codes delivered by the quantizer. On its upgrade to G.726, the Recommendation was extended to the three additional rates by using quantizers at 5-, 3-, and 2 bit/sample, respectively.

A further extension is Recommendation G.727, which defines an embedded coder whose quantizer levels for lower rates are exact subsets of those for the higher rates. It was intended for packet circuit multiplication equipment (PCME) (Cox 1995) as specified in Recommendation G.765 and, therefore, for packetized speech systems (Bellamy 2000) operating according to the packetized voice protocol (PVP) defined in Recommendation G.764. This protocol allows silence to be suppressed and replaced by its duration while packets are required to be sequence numbered, and nodal delay may be added to the time stamp. Additionally, G.727 classifies its bit stream into core bits, which provide for a base quality equivalent to a 16 kbit/s rate, and multiple level enhanced service bits such that each level provides for an 8 kbit/s rate enhancement. This functionality makes it possible for nodes to drop enhanced service bits in speech packets en route according to network traffic conditions.

The standardization process for a universal 16 kbit/s toll quality speech coder at ITU-T as Recommendation

G.728 was the start of a more active era in the process of defining a standard as well as in its application. First, in addition to the written recommendation, a pseudocode was provided as a reference. Further on, a bit-exact fixed-point reference implementation was also provided along with test vectors for testing compliance to the recommendation, so allowing the verification of strict compliance to the recommendation even though comparisons involving floating point implementations require the allowance of some tolerance. This new kind of "live" operational standard also motivated the provision of a floating-point reference implementation for the G.726 ADPCM coder as part of the G.191 Software Tools Library.

Since ADPCM is unable to deliver toll quality speech at 16 kbit/s, CELP was acknowledged as the vocoding technique of choice. But the algorithmic delay incurred by usual CELP coders was around 10 ms, whereas Recommendations G.711 and G.726 can be implemented with 0.125 ms of delay. So a concession was yielded by calling for a maximum one-way codec delay of 5 ms and a desirable delay below 2 ms. Actually, the winning candidate that became Recommendation G.728 has an algorithmic buffering delay of just 0.625 ms, as shown in Table 5, for a total one-way codec delay of less than 2 ms (Chen, Cox, Lin, et al. 1992; ITU-T 1992). This was achieved in a rather unusual way since this coder is backward-adapted; that is, the only code transmitted is the index to the five-sample codevector. But, unlike usual predictor adaptation such as that used in the G.726 coder, this coder uses a 50th-order LP predictor that is estimated from reconstructed speech samples in a block basis. Also, this high-order predictor can make up for the adaptive codebook in yet another distinguishing feature from a usual CELP coder.

The following ITU-T speech coder recommendation, G.729, was meant to be applied in digital cellular communications and also in digital simultaneous voice and data (DSVD) multimedia communications where the data-bearing signal to be transmitted along with the speech signal could be related to file sharing or a fax message. In this case, low delay was not such a stringent requirement due to the inherent delay incurred by the data modems. However, toll quality remained a target, meaning quality equivalent to that of the G.726 standard.

The coder that finally met the G.729 specification (ITU-T 1996a) is the conjugate-structure algebraic CELP (CS-ACELP) coder (Salami et al. 1998). It has a deterministic sparse fixed codebook whose codevectors are composed of four signed unit pulses positioned along the forty-sample long subframe as described in the "Code-Excited LP (CELP)" section. This ACELP structure allows for efficient codebook search algorithms such as the focused search proposed for the reference coder. In this algorithm, the computation of the correlation between the codevector and a backward-filtered version of the target vector

Table 5: Operational Data for Selected Speech Coders

Coder	Algorithm	Bit Rates (kbit/s)	Frame Size + Look Ahead (ms)	Complexity (MIPS/ kword[a])
G.711[2]	Comp. PCM	64	0.125 + 0	<<1/0.001
G.726[1]	ADPCM	40, 32, 24, 16	0.125 + 0	7.2[c]/ < 0.050[b]
G.727[2]	ADPCM	40, 32, 24, 16	0.125 + 0	7.2/<0.050
G.728[2]	LD-CELP	16	0.625 + 0	30/2.0[b]
G.723.1[2]	ACELP	5.3	30 + 7.5	20[d]/2.2[e]
	MP-MLQ	6.3	30 + 7.5	28[d]/2.2[e]
G.729[3]	CS-ACELP	8, 6.4, 11.8	10 + 5	22, 20, 27/2.6[f]
G.729A	CS-ACELP	8	10 + 5	10.8/1.9[g]
iLBC[4]	FB-LPC	15.2, 13.3	20 + 5, 30 + 10	15, 18/4[f]
AMR[5]	ACELP	12.2, 10.2, 7.95, 7.40, 6.70, 5.90, 5.15, 4.75	20 + 5	15–20/4[h]

[a]16-bit words.
[b]Extracted from (Cox 1995).
[c]Extracted from (VOCAL Technologies, Ltd. 2004) for an implementation on the ADSP-2181 digital signal processor (DSP).
[d]Extracted from (VOCAL Technologies, Ltd. 2004a) for an implementation on the ADSP-2181 DSP.
[e]Extracted from (Cox and Kroon 1996).
[f]Extracted from (Cable Television Laboratories, Inc. 2005) for implementation on TMS320C54x DSPs.
[g]Extracted from (VOCAL Technologies, Ltd. 1998) for an implementation on the ADSP-2181 DSP.
[h]Extracted from (VoiceAge Corporation 2005).
[1]ITU-T coder, toll quality at 32 kbit/s and 40 kbit/s.
[2]ITU-T coder.
[3]ITU-T coder, toll quality at 8 kbit and 11.8 kbit/s (Annex E) and lower than toll quality at 6.4 kbit/s (Annex D).
[4]IETF coder.
[5]ETSI/3GPP coder, toll quality at 7.40 kbit/s and higher rates.

proceeds to the fourth pulse only if the joint contribution of the first three pulses exceeds a threshold. Also the computation of the energy of the reconstructed vector is terminated shortly if this intermediate condition is not met, thus saving a lot of computation.

An even lower complexity version of the G.729 coder is defined in the Annex A to the Recommendation. This G.729A coder uses an ACELP codebook search algorithm that is less complex than the focused search, as shown in Table 5, and was originally targeted to DSVD communications but is widely used for VoIP and media gateways. Also, lower average system bit rates are possible by using voice activity detection (VAD) for deciding about switching to a noise coding model for which a comfort noise generator (CNG) has to be used by the decoder and a discontinuous transmission (DTX) mode has to be understood by both the encoder and the decoder. These three features are provided by Annex B. In GSM, the DTX mechanism allows the radio transmitter to be switched off during most of the length of speech pauses, when VAD switches the codec to a lower rate noise coding mode that transmits discontinuously (Bessette et al. 2002).

Strictly speaking, DTX is a minimum source controlled rate (SCR) operation that sends comfort noise (CN) parameters during silence periods. More advanced SCR operation is performed in multimode codecs, which are discussed in the "Multirate and Variable-Rate Codecs" section. For packet voice applications such as VoIP and streaming, IETF has defined the real-time transport protocol (RTP) payload formats that include a DTX bit to support DTX operation for 3GPP AMR and AMR-WB codecs (Sjoberg, Westerlund, Lakaniemi, et al. 2002) and also for the 3GPP2 VMR-WB codec (Ahmadi 2006).

A lower-rate version at 6.4 kbit/s and a higher-rate version at 11.8 kbit/s are specified in G.729 Annex D and Annex E, respectively. Actually, G.729E is a two-mode CS-ACELP coder, where the forward-adaptive mode uses 18 bits to code the LP filter parameters for each 10 ms frame, and the backward-adaptive mode uses a 30th-order backward-adaptive synthesis filter that needs no coding bits. This latter mode is better for music, and its complexity is higher. The 18 bits freed up in the backward-adaptive mode are used to increase the excitation codes from 35 bits to 44 bits for each 5 ms subframe (ITU-T 1998). Still another interoperable codec recommendation is G.729.1, which is discussed in the "Multirate and Variable-Rate Codecs" section.

In the ITU-T collection of toll-quality speech coder recommendations, G.729 is the lowest rate one. Intensive work has been expended in defining and testing lower-rate coders, but their recommendation for toll quality has not yet been achieved. However, a lot of near toll quality coders have been deployed employing the ACELP technology used by G.729 for digital cellular applications, including all the major systems like the GSM enhanced full-rate (EFR) codec, the TIA EFR codec for the NA TDMA system, and the GSM/3GPP adaptive multirate (AMR) codec.

The GSM full-rate (FR) codec is based on RPE and LTP and operates at the speech bit rate of 13 kbit/s for a gross channel bit rate of 22.8 kbit/s (Hellwig et al. 1989). The 5.6 kbit/s half-rate (HR) GSM codec operates at the gross channel rate of 11.4 kbit/s (Gerson and Jasiuk 1993) providing the same clean speech quality as the FR coder. The first GSM codec to provide toll quality speech was the 12.2 kbit/s ACELP enhanced full-rate (EFR) codec (Järvinen et al. 1997).

At lower rates, most of all, voiced segments have to be closely represented, and their periodicity cannot be overemphasized. One solution to this requirement is the mixed excitation linear prediction (MELP) vocoder, which meets speech quality of service for secure communications. The excitation signal has voicing determined for five frequency bands along with the first ten pitch harmonics. The degree of periodicity in the excitation may be further controlled by pulse position jitter within the period (McCree and Barnwell III 1995). The MELP codec was selected for a 2.4 kbit/s DoD Digital Voice Processing Consortium (DDVPC) standard replacement to the FS-1015 LPC-10 in 1996 (Supplee, Cohn, Collura, et al. 1997; Spanias 1994). Later the standard was extended for operation at 1.2 kbit/s.

An enhanced MELP (MELPe) coder operating at 2.4- and 1.2 kbit/s has become the NATO STANAG 4591 standard (Wang, Koishida, Cuperman, et al. 2002). The operation at 1.2 kbit/s exploits interframe redundancy by jointly quantizing the parameters for three consecutive 22.5 ms frames into what is called a superframe.

Further, there are two established implementations of sinusoidal models (McAulay and Quatieri 1995). One of them is the sinusoidal transform coding (STC) model, which does not impose harmonic relations between the oscillator frequencies, in principle, and has a voicing cutoff frequency above which the oscillator phases become random. The other one is the multiband excitation (MBE) coding model that imposes harmonic relations between the oscillator frequencies and has a voiced/unvoiced switch for each harmonic frequency band. As the Improved MBE (IMBE) codec (Kondoz 2004), a coder based on this model has been standardized for Inmarsat-M system (INMARSAT 1991).

For coders designed for voice over packet communications, refer to the "Loss Recovery for Graceful Degradation" section or the "Multirate and Variable Codecs" section, where their main features are highlighted.

Multirate and Variable-Rate Codecs

Multirate coders are capable of operating at various constant bit rates (CBRs). This enables communication in various channel traffic conditions by reducing the instantaneous bit rate when they are more stringent either because of more severe noise or when additional subscribers start sessions as usual in CDMA digital cellular communications. On the other hand, when the channel supports a higher bit rate, higher-quality speech may be delivered. This is particularly well handled by multimode coders that can control their bit rate according to the class of speech sounds being uttered. Usually, speech is classified as voiced, unvoiced, or transient voiced besides silence when voice activity is not detected.

As an example of a simple multirate coder, the G.726 codec operates at four bit rates. In addition, if the quantization levels for the lower rates are subsets of the higher rate ones, the multirate coder is said to be embedded. Simple embedded coders may be easily driven to lower rates by bit dropping as the G.727 codec discussed earlier.

As an enhanced embedded coder, the G.729-based embedded variable bit rate codec, G.729.1, is targeted at packet voice applications. Its bit rate will adapt to the network starting from a core layer at 8 kbit/s and the next one at 12 kbit/s, both for NB speech, and then stepping up in 2 kbit/s steps until a maximum rate of 32 kbit/s for WB speech for a total of 12 layers (ITU-T 2006). The coding structure consists of three algorithms that are activated in corresponding stages. The first two stages provide bandwidth scalability with an embedded CELP coding stage that operates on the lower narrow band (50-4000 Hz) for generating layer 1 and a time-domain bandwidth extension (TDBWE) parametric coding stage for the higher band (4000-7000 Hz) of the speech signal and the weighted CELP coding error signal in the lower band, comprising layer 2. The third stage is activated in layers above the second one for enhancing the full-band WB signal by applying a time-domain aliasing cancellation (TDAC), which is a predictive transform coding technique. The G.729.1 codec operates on 20-ms frames, which are actually two-frame superframes for layers 1 and 2, thereby ensuring interoperability with the base G.729 codec (Ragot et al. 2007).

Additionally, the G.729 series of recommendations includes a floating point implementation as Annex C+, integrating the base G.729 coder with its Annexes B, D, and E for provision of CS-ACELP at 6.4-, 8-, and 11.8 kbit/s with DTX functionality.

The G.723.1 ACELP/MP-MLQ codec is a dual rate speech coder for multimedia communications transmitting at 5.3- and 6.3 kbit/s. Switching between the two rates is allowed at any frame boundary. Variable rate operation may be implemented with DTX functionality, and Annex A provides VAD/CNG for higher system compression. The G.723.1 codec is included in ITU-T H.323 and H.324 Recommendations for wireline audio and videoconferencing and telephony and is also used in media gateways.

The evolution of the GSM EFR coder for NB speech and multimedia messaging services over GSM and evolved GSM (WCDMA, GPRS, and EDGE) networks is the 3GPP adaptive multirate (AMR) codec. This ACELP coder operates at 12.2 kbit/s at the same quality level as the GSM EFR codec, while its operation at 7.4 kbit/s is equivalent to the NA TDMA EFR codec (TIA/EIA 1997) and at 6.7 kbit/s, it is equivalent to the Japanese personal digital cellular (PDC) EFR (ETSI 2004b). Starting at 7.4 kbit/s, AMR provides toll quality speech while delivering near toll quality reproduction at lower rates (VoiceAge Corporation 2005). The AMR codec can operate at 8-bit rates: 4.75, 5.15, 5.9, 6.7, 7.4, 7.95, 10.2, and 12.2 kbit/s. Additionally, CN generation operates at the silence indicator (SID) rate of 1.80 kbit/s (ETSI 2004b). Bit rate switching is controlled by network conditions.

WB speech services are provided within 3GPP for GSM and the third generation WCDMA system by the Adaptive Multirate Wideband (AMR-WB) speech codec, also selected by ITU-T under Recommendation G.722.2 for WB speech coding around 16 kbit/s. It is a multirate ACELP coder operating at the nine speech coding rates of 23.85, 23.05, 19.85, 18.25, 15.85, 14.25, 12.65, 8.85, and 6.60 kbit/s. It also has a 1.75 kbit/s rate for coding CN to be used in DTX operation in GSM.

Starting from 12.65 kbit/s upward, all operating rates provide good-quality WB speech. In particular, at 23.05 kbit/s, its quality reaches that of G.722 at 64 kbit/s. Consistent with its LP base, G.722.2 performs better for speech than for music (Gibson 2005). The two lowest rates are intended to be used only under severe radio channel conditions or during network congestion (Bessette et al. 2002). Since the G.722.2 codec already includes PLC, it should be considered for VoIP applications.

The AMR-WB codec splits the full-band WB speech signal into two bands. The lower band from 50 to 6400 Hz is most perceptually important. Only the 23.85 kbit/s mode encodes the higher band gain as shown in Figure 9c.

A multimode codec is capable of operating at an average bit rate (ABR) that characterizes each mode of operation. The ABR is the result of a source-driven mixture of CBRs. The collection of CBRs is referred to as a rate set. In CDMA systems, the component CBRs are called full rate (FR), half rate (HF), quarter rate (QR), and eighth rate (ER). A mode establishes a quality of service (QoS) for speech reproduction, and rate selection depends on characteristics of the speech signal within bounds set by the established quality level.

Two rate sets are supported in CDMA systems. In Rate Set II, a variable rate codec may operate at the source coding bit rates of 13.3 (FR), 6.2 (HR), 2.7 (QR), and 1.0 (ER) kbit/s. The 3GPP2 variable-rate multimode wideband (VMR-WB) speech codec operates in four modes (Jelínek et al. 2004):

- *Premium mode*: ABR specified to be equivalent to that of QCELP13 (IS-733), was designed to be equivalent to AMR-WB at 14.85 kbit/s.
- *Standard mode*: ABR specified to be the average of those of QCELP13 and EVRC (IS-127), was designed to be equivalent to AMR-WB at 12.65 kbit/s.
- *Economy mode*: ABR specified to be equivalent to that of EVRC, was designed to be equivalent to AMR-WB at 8.85 kbit/s.
- *Interoperable FR*: Still, VMR-WB may operate at a fourth mode for compatibility at 12.65 kbit/s with systems using the AMR-WB codec. This mode includes 13 extra bits in the frame to fit the 13.3 kbit/s full rate.

For packet voice applications, two payloads for assembling packets for the VMR-WB codec bit stream are specified in IETF RFC 4348 (Ahmadi 2006; Ahmadi and Jelínek 2006). In particular, the header-free payload format provides for rate efficiency and low latency in VoIP applications although it is not compatible with AMR-WB RTP payload.

Rate determination for the VMR-WB codec is done in stages (Jelínek et al. 2004). At first, VAD classifies speech and silence. Active speech frames are classified as unvoiced and voiced. Voiced frames are further classified for stability by means of a signal modification procedure. If declared stable voiced, the frame is handed to the Voiced HR encoder. Finally, if the frame is not classified as stable voiced, it is deemed likely to contain an onset or a voiced transition and set to be encoded as an FR type. But, frame energy may override this classification if it does not reach a given threshold. Then, the frame is encoded as Generic HR.

The signal modification procedure used in the VMR-WB codec to classify voiced frames (Tammi, Jelínek, and Ruoppila 2005) incorporates a very important technique called generalized analysis-by-synthesis (Bastiaan Kleijn, Ramachandran, and Kroon 1992) or relaxed CELP (RCELP). It involves the modification of the original signal to a perceptually equivalent version that is better suited to the encoding algorithm. It often consists of a variable time warping that reduces the encoding rate of the ACB in a CELP coder.

Previously, two other variable-rate codec standards have incorporated the RCELP technique. They operate at Rate Set I, including the source coding bit rates of 8.55 (FR), 4.0 (HR), 2.0 (QR), and 0.8 kbit/s (ER). The 3GPP2 Selectable Mode Vocoder (SMV) coding technique is dubbed extended CELP (eX-CELP) and it operates in modes 0, 1, and 2 at ABRs of 7.3, 5.1, and 4.1 kbit/s, respectively (Gao et al. 2001). In mode 1, the SMV was designed to perform similar to IS-127. The TIA IS-127 Enhanced Variable-Rate Coder (EVRC) (TIA/EIA 1996) is an RCELP/ACELP codec whose rate determination algorithm lacks flexibility since it does not use the quarter rate at all and hardly uses the half rate (Gao et al. 2001).

At the same quality level, the EVRC was designed to operate at a lower bit rate than TIA IS-733 codec, also known as QCELP13 since it operates at Rate Set II and employs the Qualcomm CELP (QCELP) coding technique.

A codec functionality provided by enhanced embedded coding is scalability. A scalable codec issues several bit streams, referred to as a core bit stream and enhancement bit streams. The core bit stream provides a complete description for a minimum resolution signal reconstruction. Enhancement bit streams provide finer reconstruction if received by the decoder.

Scalable coders may have SNR or bit rate scalability and also bandwidth scalability. In bandwidth scalable coding, the enhancement bit streams provide parameters for reconstructing extended frequency bands. An example consists of a core bit stream for NB coding and an enhancement bit stream such that the combination of both bit streams will provide for WB coding as mentioned previously in connection with the G.729.1 codec.

Another example of scalable coding is the MPEG-4 natural audio coding toolbox (Brandenburg, Kunz, and Sugiyama 2000). For lower bit rates of 2 kbit/s and 4 kbit/s, it provides for NB speech the harmonic vector excitation coder (HVXC), which performs preliminary pitch estimation and LP analysis of the speech signal whose residual signal is Fourier transformed to the frequency domain where detailed pitch analysis and envelope VQ is performed for voiced speech. For unvoiced speech, the excitation is searched from a codebook in the time domain. The HVXC coder is the association of the LSP VQ tool and the harmonic VQ tool. Higher bit rates and 3.85 kbit/s are handled by the CELP coder, which may be selected from a set of 28 bit rates for NB speech up to 12.2 kbit/s and 30 bit rates from 10.9 kbit/s to 23.8 kbit/s for WB speech. The CELP coder consists of the LSP VQ tool coupled to the MPE tool or the RPE tool. The latter is used just for WB speech for lower complexity.

Targeted at packet voice communications, Speex is an open-source multirate embedded speech coder. Additionally, it features source-controlled variable rate coding, VAD and DTX operation, besides variable search complexity. The LSF coefficients are the only parameters coded at the 20 ms frame period by means of nonpredictive VQ for packet loss resilience. Speex can code NB speech at bit rates from 2.15 kbit/s to 24.6 kbit/s. For WB speech coding, a QMF splits the signal into two subbands, which are CELP coded using a subband CELP (SB-CELP) technique where the lower band is coded by the NB CELP encoder, while the higher-band CELP encoder neglects pitch period information. In the latter case, pitch is not used because the periodicity in the higher band is said to be severely affected by the aliasing caused by the filterbank. Speex rates for WB speech range from 3.95 kbit/s to 42.2 kbit/s (Valin and Montgomery 2006).

Multiple description coding is another diversity-based communication strategy. Multiple description coders send bit streams with independent complete and complementary descriptions of the signal so that with any number of arriving descriptions, the decoder will reconstruct the signal at a partial resolution level.

TRENDS IN LOW-BIT-RATE CODING

In general, lower bit rate vocoders are bound to track the speech signal in a time-frequency domain where they should identify a pattern change in either the time or the frequency domain or even in both. We can loosely identify such changes with speech events that could lead to the ultimate low-bit-rate coder if they could be reliably identified and coded.

We can use the spectrogram as a guide; the spectrogram is a powerful instrumental representation of speech signals that has aided phonetic research ever since its invention in the 1940s (Koenig, Dunn, and Lacey 1946). The two usual operating modes to take a spectrogram are wideband and narrowband and both are exemplified in Figure 10. A wideband spectrogram displays the formant structure in its pattern of frequency bands, whereas the periodicity shows in the pattern of time striations. On the other hand, a narrowband spectrogram displays the periodicity as a set of thin frequency tracks. In other words, a wideband spectrogram has larger time resolution, and a narrowband spectrogram has larger frequency resolution.

From a vocoding standpoint, there are two rather different models of harmonic coders that are roughly analogous to the two modes of taking spectrograms. A sinusoidal model is a set of narrowband oscillators that can be driven by a kind of narrowband spectrographic analysis. On the other hand, a WI coder extracts pitch-length cycles during voiced speech and arbitrary length waveform segments during unvoiced speech. All extracted cycles and segments are stretched to a common length and laid out sideways to the time evolution axis in a two-dimensional arrangement (Bastiaan Kleijn and Haagen 1995). Their Fourier-series coefficients or other transform coefficients are usually employed instead of the cycles themselves.

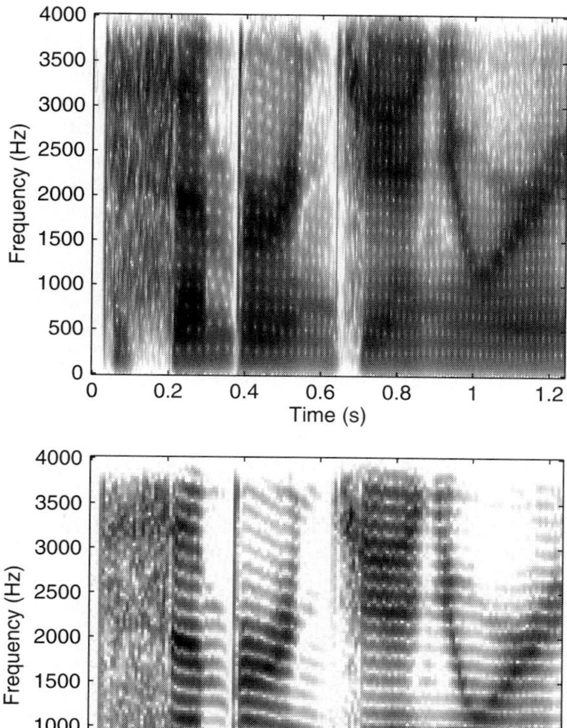

Figure 10: Spectrograms in two resolutions, wideband spectrogram (top) and narrowband spectrogram (bottom), for the truncated phrase "December and January…", uttered by a female speaker

The characteristic waveform (CW) surface so obtained is lowpass filtered along the evolution axis to uncover the slowly evolving waveforms (SEWs), which also define the rapidly evolving waveforms (REWs) when subtracted from the CWs. Both can be efficiently coded since SEWs can be coarsely interpolated in time but require fine resolution in frequency, whereas REWs require almost no frequency resolution but have to be interpolated rather frequently in time.

Speech coders based on codebooks of sequences of speech subunits with properly defined distortion measures will also play an important role in advancing the toll quality frontier into the bit-rate range below 1 kbit/s (Arjona Ramírez and Minami 2003). Codebooks of speech subunits are used by concatenative synthesizers and may be used in a speech coding structure under some constraints for prosody modification (Lee and Cox 2001).

The idea of speech events may be implemented in different ways. Temporal decomposition (TD) is based on the notion that parameter tracks could be composed with localized interpolation functions, each located where an event occurs and fading when going away from it. Essentially, the parameter values at event locations only are coded along with a coarse representation of the interpolation functions. Events then behave as targets and interpolation functions are the weights that allow the reconstruction of the parameter tracks. This decomposition was proposed by Bishnu Atal to be used with LAR tracks (1983). It has been applied to LSF tracks, which are the most popular LP representation in speech coding (Nguyen and Akagi 2002) and has also been proposed for excitation parameters as well (Nandasena and Akagi 1998).

Temporal decomposition may be used to find a representation of speech parameters for a speech recognizer to chop the signal in segments. The recognizer may be trained automatically in the case of a segment vocoder (Černocký, Baudoin, and Chollet 1998). Speech segments for segment vocoders may be represented by their waveform and only be parameterized for time scale and pitch scale modifications (Roucos and Wilgus 1985). Coding rates around 300 bit/s may be obtained by segment vocoding.

If the speech recognizer, usually based on Hidden Markov Models (HMMs), in a segment vocoder is trained on phonetic units and concatenated phonetic units, then a phonetic vocoder is obtained. These vocoders can operate at around 100 bit/s (Tokuda, Masuko, Hiroi, et al. 1998).

The evolution of these techniques to higher speech quality is bound to increase the range of communication services supported by speech coding. But, these source coding techniques for low-rate speech coding also find application in enhancements to normal NB communication services such as bandwidth extension (BWE) to provide greater phoneme identification and speaker recognition (Jax and Vary 2006). Of course, BWE depends on some additional information about the signal that may be added by a system previously trained with true WB speech and its NB version.

True WB speech is better if available through the communications network even though BWE is still useful in connecting to NB terminals. As discussed before, the development of the AMR codec ushered in a great evolution in WB speech coding, continued with the AMR-WB and VMR-WB codecs.

Wider bandwidths up more than 19 kHz are supported by the 3GPP Extended AMR-WB (AMR-WB+) codec specified in 2004 for high-quality audio on mobile services (Salami et al. 2006). It is based on a hybrid ACELP and transform coded excitation (TCX) technology operating at several bit rates between 6 and 48 kbit/s. The use of ACELP allows good performance for speech signals at the lower rates.

More recently, a super-wideband (14 kHz bandwidth and 32 kHz sampling rate, refer to Table 1) codec has been specified as Annex C to the ITU-T G.722.1 Recommendation (ITU-T 2005c). It is a low complexity MLT codec operating at 24-, 32-, and 48 kbit/s with 20 ms frames, intended for videoconferencing, teleconferencing, and Internet streaming applications. A fixed-point reference source code and a series of test vectors is provided along with the Recommendation.

To cope with the increasing trend toward widespread multimedia applications, codec designers will have to wield the potential of different strategies such as scalable and multiple description coding. This will take a lot of hard work in research and development of vocoding technologies.

CONCLUSION

The selection of a speech codec involves many considerations, precluding a single solution. Besides the basic operational dimensions of bit rate, distortion or quality, complexity and delay, system constraints and connections with different networks have to be given due attention.

In some cases, the availability of a suite of codecs using the same technology or complying to some standard for interoperability may provide a wide-ranging solution. This happens to be the case for the ITU-T G.726/G.727 ADPCM coders; the ITU-T G.729 CS-ACELP codec and its Annexes, also including Recommendation G.729.1; and the ETSI/3GPP AMR codecs, including multiple ACELP coding rates.

However, other constraints such as low complexity, low power, and low delay may restrict the offer of speech codecs available for the task and call for new developments.

New challenges in multimedia communications will require the concerted application of multiple technologies. These efforts will eventually lead to new technologies drawing from evolving research in source coding and communications. In turn, research efforts are expected to increase.

GLOSSARY

3GPP: The 3rd Generation Partnership Project is a collaboration agreement that was established in December 1998. It brings together a number of telecommunication standards bodies, including ETSI.

ABR: Average bit rate for a speech quality level is the average data rate that the codec will keep by switching between coding algorithms or layers for different types of speech sounds.

ACELP: Algebraic CELP refers to a CELP codec whose fixed codevectors are a sum of a few positive or negative unit pulses.

ADM: Adaptive delta modulation is a differential speech coding technique that uses a two-level backward-adaptive quantizer and a fixed predictor. The stepsize is adapted, and the one-bit codeword is interpreted as the algebraic sign that affects the current stepsize.

ADPCM: Adaptive differential PCM is a speech coder that uses a backward-adaptive PCM quantizer to code the difference signal sample that results when the predicted sample is subtracted from the speech sample. In turn, the predicted sample is generated by the backward-adaptive predictor from previous quantized samples. More specifically, ADPCM may refer to ITU-T Recommendation G.726/G.727.

AMR: ETSI GSM/3GPP adaptive multirate codec consists of integrated ACELP codecs that operate at eight bit rates from 12.2 kbit/s to 4.75 kbit/s. The highest rate codec is the same as GSM EFR (enhanced full-rate) codec.

Analysis-by-Synthesis: In a CELP encoder involves the use of an exact replica of the decoder for generating the reconstructed speech vector in the process of excitation codevector search. This procedure ensures that the encoder will track the decoder in the absence of transmission errors.

ANSI: The American National Standards Institute is a private, nonprofit organization that administers and coordinates the U.S. voluntary standardization and conformity assessment system.

APC: Adaptive predictive coding is a technique used in a type of adaptive differential PCM codecs whose quantizer and predictor are forward-adaptive; that is, their parameters are adapted based on a block of original speech signal samples at the frame rate.

Bit Rate: is the rate of serialized coder output. It may be a time rate measured in bit/s or referred to the signal sampling when measured in bit/sample.

Bit Stream: A sequence of bits generated by the ordered serialization and concatenation of the codewords for all encoder parameters.

CBR: Constant bit rate refers to the data rate for a codec based on fixed-length framing.

CCITT: Comité Consultatif International Téléphonique et Télégraphique, international organization that set communications standards until 1993. Now known as ITU.

CELP: Code-excited linear prediction is a speech coding technique that uses a codebook of codevectors to be input to a synthesis filter capable of producing a near match to a block of speech signal samples. The selection of codevector is carried out in an analysis-by-synthesis loop. CELP codecs are usually distinguished by their codebook structures and their codevector search algorithms.

Channel: The medium for communication between encoder and decoder. It may be modeled as a two-port component that adds noise and delays to the data-bearing signal, besides causing incidental phase distortion. Alternatively, the channel may be described by its capacity, or maximum bit rate, and the statistical bit error rates observed at the decoder. It is interesting to note that a store-and-forward system may also be modeled as a channel whose longer delay is not usually an application issue.

EIA: Electronic Industries Alliance is a national trade organization that includes the full spectrum of U.S. manufacturers. The Alliance is a partnership of electronic and high-tech associations and companies.

ETSI: European Telecommunications Standards Institute.

GSM: Global System for Mobile Communications.

G.XXX: It stands for all ITU-T recommendations with prefix G. See http://www.itu.int/publications/publications.aspx?lang=en&parent=T-L&selection=2§or=2. ITU-T Recommendations for "Transmission systems and media, digital systems and networks."

H.XXX: It stands for all ITU-T recommendations with prefix H. See http://www.itu.int/publications/publications.aspx?lang=en&parent=T-L&selection=2§or=2. ITU-T Recommendations for "Audiovisual and multimedia systems."

ITU-T: Telecommunication Standardization Sector of the International Telecommunication Union (ITU), which is an international organization within the United Nations System.

LP: Linear prediction is the process that generates a match to a speech signal sample by a linear combination of past samples. The weights in this combination are adjusted to make a block of predicted samples match the original block of samples in the mean-square sense, and this estimation is what LP often stands for.

LPC: Linear predictive coding is a parametric vocoding technique that uses a synthesis filter determined by LP analysis, and its excitation is either a periodic pulse train whose repetition rate and amplitude may be adjusted or a pseudorandom sequence whose power may be adjusted. Some LPC vocoders may combine both excitation sources.

NB: Narrowband speech is a signal in the frequency band ranging from 300 Hz to 3.4 kHz sampled at 8.0 kHz.

PCM: Pulse code modulation originally refers to the transmission of a bit stream by a sequence of pulses where each one of them is associated to a bit. In source coding, PCM stands for the quantization process that generates the codewords in the bit stream from the speech signal samples.

TIA: Telecommunications Industry Association represents the communications sector of EIA.

WB: Wideband speech is a signal in the frequency band ranging from 50 Hz to 7.0 kHz sampled at 16.0 kHz.

CROSS REFERENCES

See *Speech and Audio Compression*; *Voice over IP (VoIP)*; *Voice over MPLS and VoIP over MPLS*.

REFERENCES

Ahmadi, S. 2006. *Real-time transport protocol (RTP) payload format for the variable-rate multimode wideband (VMR-WB) audio codec*. www.ietf.org/rfc/rfc4348.txt (accessed July 21, 2006).

Ahmadi, S., and M. Jelínek 2006, May. On the architecture, operation, and applications of VMR-WB: The new cdma2000 wideband speech coding standard. *IEEE Commun. Mag. 44*(5): 74–81.

Andersen, S. V., W. Bastiaan Kleijn , R. Hagen, J. Linden, M. N. Murthi, and J. Skoglund. 2002. iLBC: A linear predictive coder with robustness to packet losses. In 2002 *IEEE Speech Coding Workshop Proceedings*, Tsukuba, October, pp. 23–25.

Andersen, S. V., A. Duric, H. Astrom, R. Hagen, W. Bastiaan Kleijn, and J. Linden. 2004, December. *Internet low bit rate codec*. www.ietf.org/rfc/rfc3951.txt (accessed October 13, 2005).

Arjona Ramírez, M., and M. Minami. 2003. Low bit rate speech coding. In *The Wiley Encyclopedia of Telecommunications*, edited by J. G. Proakis. (Vol. 3, pp. 1299–1308). New York: Wiley.

Atal, B. S. 1983. Efficient coding of LPC parameters by temporal decomposition. In *Proceedings of IEEE Int. Conf. Acoust., Speech, Signal Processing, Boston*, April, Vol. 1, pp. 81–84.

Atal, B. S., and J. R. Remde. 1982. A new model of LPC excitation for producing natural-sounding speech at low bit rates. In *Proceedings of IEEE Int. Conf. Acoust., Speech, Signal Processing, Paris*, May, Vol. 1, pp. 614–617.

Atal, B. S., and M. R. Schroeder. 1970, October. Adaptive predictive coding of speech signals. *Bell Syst. Tech. J.* 49(8), 1973–1986.

Bastiaan Kleijn, W., and J. Haagen. 1995. Waveform interpolation for coding and synthesis. In *Speech coding and synthesis* (pp. 175-207) edited by W. Bastiaan Kleijn and K. K. Paliwal. Amsterdam: Elsevier Science.

Bastiaan Kleijn, W., R. P. Ramachandran, and P. Kroon. 1992. Generalized analysis-by-synthesis coding and its application to pitch prediction. In *Proceedings of IEEE Int. Conf. Acoust., Speech, Signal Processing*, San Francisco, March, Vol. 1, pp. 337–340.

Bellamy, J. C. 2000. *Digital telephony*. 3rd ed. New York: John Wiley & Sons.

Bessette, B., R. Salami, R. Lefebvre, M. Jelínek, J. Rotola-Pukkila, J. Vainio, et al. 2002, Nov. The adaptive multirate wideband speech codec (AMR-WB). *IEEE Trans. Speech Audio Processing* 10(8): 620–636.

Bistritz, Y., and S. Peller. 1993. Immitance spectral pairs (ISP) for speech encoding. In *Proceedings of IEEE Int. Conf. Acoust., Speech, Signal Processing, Minneapolis*, April, (Vol. 2, pp. 9–12).

Brandenburg, K., O. Kunz, and A. Sugiyama. 2000, January. MPEG-4 natural audio coding. *Signal Processing: Image Communication* 15: 423–444.

Cable Television Laboratories, Inc. 2005. *PacketCable(TM) Audio/Video Codecs Specification PKT-SPCODEC 1.5-I01*-050128. www.packetcable.com/downloads/specs/PKT-SP-CODEC1.5-I01-050128.pdf (accessed January 14, 2006).

Campbell Jr., J. P., T. E. Tremain, and V. C. Welch. 1991. The DoD 4.8 kbps standard (Proposed Federal Standard 1016). In *Advances in Speech Coding* edited by B. S. Atal, V. Cuperman, and A. Gersho (pp. 121–133). Amsterdam: Kluwer.

Černocký, J., G. Baudoin, and G. Chollet. 1998. Segmental vocoder—Going beyond the phonetic approach. In *Proceedings of IEEE Int. Conf. Acoust., Speech Signal Processing, Seattle*, May, Vol. 2, pp. 605–608.

Chen, J.-H., and J. Thyssen 2007. The BroadVoice speech coding algorithm. In *Proceedings of IEEE Int. Conf. Acoust., Speech, Signal Processing, Honolulu*, April, Vol. 4, pp. 537–540.

Chen, J.-H., R. V. Cox, Y.-C. Lin, N. Jayant, and M. J. Melchner. 1992, June. A low-delay CELP coder for the CCITT 16 kb/s speech coding standard. *IEEE J. Select. Areas Commun*. 10(5): 830–849.

Cox, R. V. 1995. Speech coding standards. In *Speech coding and synthesis* edited by W. Bastiaan Kleijn and K. K. Paliwal (pp. 49–78). Amsterdam: Elsevier Science.

Cox, R. V., and P. Kroon. 1996, December. Low bit-rate speech coders for multimedia communication. *IEEE Commun. Mag.*, 34(12): 34–41.

Cox, R. V., D. Malah, and D. Kapilow. 2004. Improving upon toll quality speech for VoIP. In *Conference record of the thirty-eighth Asilomar Conf. Signals, Systems and Computers*, Asilomar, November, Vol. 1, pp. 405–409.

ETSI. 2004a. AMR speech codec; error concealment of lost frames. 3GPP TS 26.091 version 6.0.0 release 6. Sophia Antipolis.

ETSI. 2004b. AMR speech codec; transcoding functions. 3GPP TS 26.090 version 6.0.0 release 6. Sophia Antipolis.

Furui, S. 1985. *Digital speech processing, synthesis, and recognition*. New York: Marcel Dekker.

Gao, Y., E. Shlomot, A. Benyassine, J. Thyssen, H. Su, and C. Murgia. 2001. The SMV algorithm selected by TIA and 3GPP2 for CDMA applications. In *Proceedings of IEEE Int. Conf. Acoust., Speech, Signal Processing, Salt Lake City*, May, Vol. 2, pp. 709–712.

Gerson, I. A., and M. A. Jasiuk. (1991). Techniques for improving the performance of CELP type speech coders. In *Proceedings of IEEE Int. Conf. Acoust., Speech, Signal Processing*, Toronto, May, Vol. 1, pp. 205–208.

Gerson, I. A., and M. A. Jasuik. 1993. A 5600 bps VSELP speech coder candidate for half-rate GSM. In *Proceedings of IEEE Workshop on Speech Coding for Telecommunications, Sainte-*Adèle, Québec, October, pp. 43–44.

Gibson, J. D. 2005, 4th quarter. Speech coding methods, standards, and applications. *IEEE Circuits Syst. Mag.* 30–49.

Gournay, P., F. Rousseau, and R. Lefebvre. 2003. Improved packet loss recovery using late frames for prediction-based speech coders. In *Proceedings of IEEE Int. Conf. Acoust., Speech, Signal Processing*, Hong Kong, April, Vol. 1, pp. 108–111.

Hellwig, K., P. Vary, D. Massaloux, J. P. Petit, C. Galand, and M. Rosso. 1989. Speech coding for the European mobile radio system. In *Proceedings of IEEE GLOBECOM* Dallas, November, (Vol. 4, pp. 1065–1069).

INMARSAT. 1991, November. INMARSAT SATELLITE COMMUNICATIONS SERVICES Inmarsat-M System Definition. Issue 3.0, Module 1.

Itakura, F. 1975, April. Line spectral representation of linear predictor coefficients of speech signals. *J. Acoust. Soc. Am.* 57(S1): S35.

ITU-T. 1988, November. 7 kHz audio-coding within 64 kbit/s. Recommendation G.722. Geneva.

ITU-T. 1989. Pulse code modulation (PCM) of voice frequencies. Recommendation G.711. Geneva.

ITU-T. 1990. 40, 32, 24, 16 kbit/s adaptive differential pulse code modulation (ADPCM). Recommendation G.726. Geneva.

ITU-T. 1992, September. Coding of speech at 16 kbit/s using low-delay code excited linear prediction. Recommendation G.728. Geneva.

ITU-T. 1996a, March 19. Coding of speech at 8 kbit/s using Conjugate-Structure Algebraic-Code-Excited Linear-Prediction (CS-ACELP). Recommendation G.729. Geneva.

ITU-T. 1996b, March 19. Dual rate speech coder for multimedia applications transmitting at 5.3 and 6.3 kbit/s. Recommendation G.723.1. Geneva.

ITU-T. 1996c, August. Methods for subjective determination of transmission quality. Recommendation P.800. Geneva.

ITU-T. 1996d, August 30. Objective quality measurement of telephone-band (300 - 3400 Hz) speech codecs. Recommendation P.861. Geneva.

ITU-T. 1998, September. 11.8 kbit/s CS-ACELP speech coding algorithm. Recommendation G.729 Annex E. Geneva.

ITU-T. 2001, February. Perceptual evaluation of speech quality (PESQ), an objective method for end-to-end speech quality assessment of narrowband telephone networks and speech codecs. Recommendation P.862. Geneva.

ITU-T. 2004, May. Single ended method for objective speech quality assessment in narrowband telephony applications. Recommendation P.563. Geneva.

ITU-T. 2005a, October. Application guide for objective quality measurement based on Recommendations P.862, P.862.1, and P.862.2. LC-Text: Recommendation P.862.3. Geneva.

ITU-T. 2005b, October. Application guide for objective quality measurement based on Recommendations P.862, P.862.1 and P.862.2. LC-Summary: Recommendation P.862.3. Geneva.

ITU-T. 2005c, May. Low-complexity coding at 24 and 32 kbit/s for hands-free operation in systems with low frame loss. Recommendation G.722.1. Geneva.

ITU-T. 2005d, November. Wideband extension to Recommendation P.862 for the assessment of wideband telephone networks and speech codecs. Recommendation P.862.2. Geneva.

ITU-T. 2006, May. G.729 based embedded variable bit-rate coder: An 8-32 kbit/s scalable wideband coder bitstream interoperable with G.729. Recommendation G.729.1. Geneva.

James, J. H., C. Bing, and L. Garrison. 2004, July. Implementing VoIP: A voice transmission performance progress report. *IEEE Commun. Mag.* 42(7): 36–41.

Järvinen, K., J. Vainio, P. Kapanen, T. Honkanen, P. Haavisto, R. Salami, et al. 1997. GSM enhanced full rate speech codec. In *Proceedings of IEEE Int. Conf. Acoust., Speech, Signal Processing*, Munich, April, Vol. 2, pp. 771–774.

Jax, P., and P. Vary. 2006, May. Bandwidth extension of speech signals: A catalyst for the introduction of wideband speech coding? *IEEE Commun. Mag.* 44(5): 106–111.

Jayant, N. S., and P. Noll. 1984. *Digital coding of waveforms*. Englewood Cliffs: Prentice-Hall.

Jelínek, M., R. Salami, S. Ahmadi, B. Bessette, P. Gournay, and C. Laflamme. 2004. On the architecture of the CDMA2000® variable-rate multimode wideband (VMR-WB) speech coding standard. In *Proceedings of IEEE Int. Conf. Acoust., Speech, Signal Processing*, Montreal, May, Vol. 1, pp. 281–284.

Kang, H.-G., H. K. Kim, and R. V. Cox. 2003, March. Improving the transcoding capability of speech coders. *IEEE Trans. Multimedia* 5(1): 24–33.

Koenig, W., H. K. Dunn, and L. Y. Lacey. 1946. The sound spectrograph. *J. Acoust. Soc. Am.* 18: 19–49.

Kondoz, A. M. 2004. *Digital speech coding for low bit rate communication systems.* 2nd ed. Chichester: John Wiley & Sons.

Kroon, P. 1995. Evaluation of speech coders. In *Speech coding and synthesis* edited by W. Bastiaan Kleijn and K. K. Paliwal (p. 467–494). Amsterdam: Elsevier Science.

Kroon, P., E. F. Deprettere, and R. J. Sluyter. 1986, October. Regular-Pulse Excitation: A novel approach to effective and efficient multipulse coding of speech.

IEEE Trans. Acoust., Speech, Signal Processing 34(5): 1054–1063.

Lee, K.-S., and R. V. Cox. 2001, July. A very low bit rate speech coder based on a recognition/synthesis paradigm. *IEEE Trans. Speech Audio Processing* 9(5): 482–491.

Markel, J. D., and A. H. Gray, Jr. 1976. *Linear prediction of speech*. Berlin: Springer.

McAulay, R. J., and J. F. Quatieri. 1995. Sinusoidal coding. In *Speech coding and synthesis* edited by W. Bastiaan Kleijn and K. K. Paliwal (pp. 121–173). Amsterdam: Elsevier Science.

McCree, A., and T. P. Barnwell III. 1995, July. A mixed excitation LPC vocoder model for low bit rate speech coding. *IEEE Trans. Speech Audio Processing* 3(4): 242–250.

Nandasena, A. C. R., and M. Akagi. 1998. Spectral stability based event localizing temporal decomposition. In *Proceedings of IEEE Int. Conf. Acoust., Speech, Signal Processing*, Seattle, May, Vol. 2, pp. 957–960.

Nguyen, P. C., and M. Akagi. 2002. Improvement of restricted temporal decomposition method for line spectral frequency parameters. In *Proceedings of IEEE Int. Conf. Acoust., Speech, Signal Processing*, Orlando, May, Vol. 1, pp. 265–268.

Ragot, S., B. Kövesi, R. Trilling, D. Virette, N. Duc, D. Massaloux et al. 2007. An 8-32 kbit/s scalable coder interoperable with G.729 for wideband telephony and voice over IP. In *Proceedings of IEEE Int. Conf. Acoust., Speech, Signal Processing*, Honolulu, *April*, Vol. 4, pp. 529–532.

Rix, A. W. 2004. Perceptual speech quality assessment: A review. In *Proceedings of IEEE Int. Conf. Acoust., Speech, Signal Processing*, Montreal, May, Vol. 3, pp. 1056–1059.

Roucos, S., and A. M. Wilgus. 1985. The waveform segment vocoder: A new approach for very-low-rate speech coding. In *Proceedings of IEEE Int. Conf. Acoust., Speech, Signal Processing*, Tampa, April, Vol. 7, pp. 236–239.

Salami, R., C. Laflamme, J.-P. Adoul, A. Kataoka, S. Hayashi, T. Moriya, et al. 1998, March. Design and description of CS-ACELP, a toll quality 8 kb/s speech coder. *IEEE Trans. Speech Audio Processing* 6(2): 116–130.

Salami, R., R. Lefebvre, A. Lakaniemi, K. Kontola, S. Bruhn, and A. Taleb 2006, May. Extended AMR-WB for high-quality audio on mobile devices. *IEEE Commun. Mag.* 44(5): 90–97.

Schroeder, M. R., and B. S. Atal. 1985. Code-excited linear prediction (CELP): High quality speech at very low bit rates. In *Proceedings of IEEE Int. Conf. Acoust., Speech, Signal Processing*, Tampa, March, Vol. 2, pp. 437–440.

Sjoberg, J., M. Westerlund, A. Lakaniemi, and Q. Xie. 2002, June. *Real-time transport protocol (RTP) payload format and file storage format for the adaptive multi-rate (AMR) and adaptive multi-rate wideband (AMR-WB) audio codecs*. www.ietf.org/rfc/rfc3267.txt (accessed July 21, 2006).

So, S., and K. K. Paliwal. 2007, January. A comparative study of LPC parameter representations and quantisation schemes for wideband speech coding. Digital Signal Processing 17(1): 114–137.

Spanias, A. S. 1994, October. Speech coding: A tutorial review. *Proc IEEE* 82(10): 1541–1582.

Steele, R. 1993, November. Speech codecs for personal communication. *IEEE Commun. Mag.* 31(11): 76–83.

Supplee, L., M., R. P. Cohn, J. S. Collura, and A. V. McCree. 1997. MELP: The new federal standard at 2400 bps. In *Proceedings of IEEE Int. Conf. Acoust., Speech, Signal Processing*, Munich, April, Vol. 2, pp. 1591–1594.

Tammi, M., M. Jelínek, and V. T. Ruoppila. 2005, September. Signal modification method for variable bit rate wide-band speech coding. *IEEE Trans. Speech Audio Processing* 13(5): 799–810.

TIA/EIA. 1996, July 19. Enhanced Variable Rate Codec, Speech Service Option 3 for Wideband Spread Spectrum Digital Systems. Arlington.

TIA/EIA. 1997, September 17. IS-641-A TDMA Cellular/PCS: Radio Interface Enhanced Full-Rate Voice Codec, Revision A. TR45.

Tokuda, K., T. Masuko, J. Hiroi, T. Kobayashi, and T. Kitamura. 1998. A very low bit rate speech coder using HMM-based speech recognition/synthesis techniques. In *Proceedings of IEEE Int. Conf. Acoust., Speech, Signal Processing*, Seattle, May, Vol. 2, pp. 609–612.

Valin, J.-M., and C. Montgomery. 2006. Improved noise weighting in CELP coding of speech: Applying the Vorbis psychoacoustic model to Speex. In *Audio Engineering Society Preprints, Audio Engineering Society (AES) 120th convention*, Paris, May, Vol. Convention Paper 6746, pp.1–9.

VOCAL Technologies, Ltd. 1998. *G.729/G.729 Annex A Speech Compression*. www.vocal.com/datasheets/full/g729.html (accessed December 12, 2005).

VOCAL Technologies, Ltd. 2004. *G.726 40, 32, 24, 16 kbit/s Adaptive Differential Pulse Code Modulation (ADPCM)*. www.vocal.com/data sheets/g726.html (accessed December 12, 2005).

VOCAL Technologies, Ltd. 2004a. *G.723.1 Dual rate speech coder*. www.vocal.com/data sheets/full/g723.html (accessed June 18, 2007).

VoiceAge Corporation. 2005. *AMR Speech Codec*. www.voiceage.com/prodamr.php (accessed December 29, 2005).

Wang, T., H. Koishida, V. Cuperman, A. Gersho, and J. S. Collura. (2002). A 1200/2400 bps coding suite based on MELP. In *2002 IEEE Speech Coding Workshop Proceedings*, Tsukuba, October, pp. 90–92.

Yang, L., T. R. Fischer, S. Kang, and I. Lee. 1995. Codebook optimization in variable-rate CELP coders with sparse codebooks. In *1995 IEEE Workshop on Speech Coding for Telecommunications Proceedings*, Annapolis, September, pp. 85–86.

Voice Over Internet Protocol

Sherali Zeadally, *University of the District of Columbia*
Farhan Siddiqui, *Wayne State University*

INTRODUCTION

Recent years have seen a growing interest in the transmission of voice using packet-based protocols. Voice over Internet protocol (VoIP) is a rapidly growing technology that enables the transport of voice over data networks such as the public Internet. VoIP has been discussed since the early 1970s (Varshney et al. 2002), when the idea and technology were developed. At that time, however, VoIP did not find wide acceptance and deployment among users or telecommunication providers. This was mainly due to the lack of IP infrastructure and the fact that circuit-switched calling was still a much more reliable alternative, especially with regard to the poor quality of early VoIP calls. However, following the rapid growth of the Internet in the mid-1990s, and large investments in the IP networking infrastructure by businesses, vendors, and carriers, VoIP increasingly became a viable alternative to sending voice over public switched telephone networks (PSTNs).

The basic idea behind VoIP involves the transmission of voice as data packets using IP. The user's voice is converted from an analog form into a digital signal, compressed (or uncompressed), and is then broken down into a series of packets (packetization). These packets are routed through public or private IP networks—from one user to another—and are reassembled and decoded (if compressed) at the receiving end, as shown in Figure 1.

VOIP BACKGROUND

VoIP Growth

VoIP was first used as a simple way to provide point-to-point voice transport between two IP hosts, primarily to replace expensive international phone calls. However, the growing interest in providing integrated voice, data, and video services has expanded its scope; IP telephony now encompasses a range of services. These include traditional conferencing, call-control supplementary services,

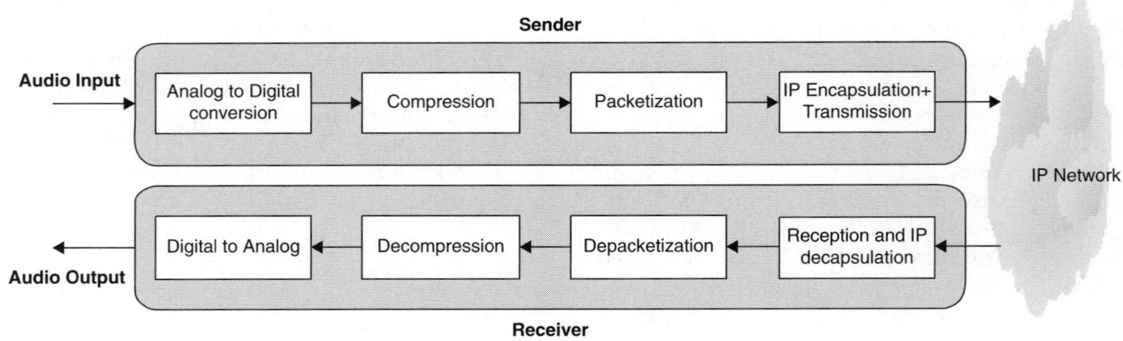

Figure 1: Basic operations in a VoIP system

multimedia transport, and mobility, as well as new services that integrate Web, e-mail, presence, and instant messaging applications with telephony. Furthermore, it is generally accepted that IP telephony and traditional circuit-switched telephony will coexist for quite some time, requiring gateways (nodes that interconnect data networks such as the Internet and wide area networks [WANs] with the plain old telephone system [POTS] networks) between the two worlds.

Voice has been transmitted over PSTNs for almost over a century; in the United States, the long-distance voice market has grown to about $100 billion a year in business and residential demand. The desire of businesses and consumers to reduce this cost, along with substantial investments over recent decades in IP-based networks—both public and private—has generated substantial interests in delivering VoIPs (Varshney et al. 2002). Several recent industry surveys and projections estimate that VoIP could account for over 10 percent of all voice calls in the United States by 2006. In fact, VoIP is likely to be used first in places with significant IP infrastructure or where cost savings are significant. One example would be a company with multiple sites worldwide connected through a private or public IP network.

The Asia Pacific region is also expected to be one of the leading markets for VoIP services. Asia registered a volume of about 175.2 billion minutes of VoIP calls in 2004, and the total VoIP calling minutes are expected to reach 484.2 billion by 2009. During the same period, VoIP service revenue is expected to rise from $5.5 billion to $10.8 billion (Asia Networking/Telecom 2006). The rapid proliferation of VoIP services in the Asia Pacific region can be attributed to the existence, until recently, of monopolies in the telecommunications sector in most markets. In most cases, prices have been set considerably higher than in other regions. As a result of high price sensitivity, customers from the Asia Pacific region would be more willing to switch to cheaper VoIP services.

BENEFITS OF VOIP

Several factors influence the adoption of VoIP technology (Varshney et al. 2002). Some of the major ones include:

- Cost savings: The cost of a packet-switched network for VoIP could be as little as half that of a traditional circuit-switched network (e.g., the PSTN) for voice transmission. This expected cost savings is the result of a more efficient use of bandwidth requiring fewer long-distance trunks between switches. The price of a VoIP phone line is a fraction of the cost of a traditional telephone line; long-distance calls are much less expensive if they are made via a VoIP provider, and applicable taxes are far lower with VoIP phone service than with a traditional phone service. For example, some phone service providers offer a phone line for around $9 per month and will charge between one and three cents per minute per call, depending on the provider. Most VoIP phone providers offer a bundled service that includes unlimited incoming calls and unlimited long distance calls to anyone in the United States or Canada for one small fee. VoIP also enables low taxes. Governments have thus far taken a hands-off approach to VoIP service providers: because calls are carried over the Internet, governments have not heavily taxed VoIP phone services.

  At present, the only tax users can expect to see on a VoIP phone service provider's bill is a federal excise tax, which accounts for only 3 percent of the cost of the service (for example, if a user chooses a $19.95 unlimited calling plan, the federal excise tax would equal 3 percent of $19.95, or sixty cents). This cost is much lower than taxes on a local telephone bill, resulting in significant savings. Moreover, most VoIP phone providers include features such as free voicemail, call forwarding, caller ID, call waiting, call waiting ID, three-way calling, and speed dialing for a minimal monthly fee, compared to traditional phone companies that have significantly higher charges for similar services.
- Improved network utilization: The traditional circuit-switched networks have to dedicate a full duplex 64 kbits/s channel for the duration of a single call, whereas, with VoIP networks, the bandwidth is used only when something has to be transmitted. More efficient use of bandwidth enables more calls to be carried over a single link without requiring the carrier to install new lines or further augment network capacity.
- Opportunities for value-added services: VoIP offers other features, including caller ID and call forwarding, that can be added to VoIP networks at minimal extra costs.
- Integrated infrastructure: VoIP allows Internet access and voice traffic simultaneously over a single phone line, potentially eliminating the need for two phone lines in a home (one for data and one for voice).
- Progressive deployment (Varshney et al. 2002): IP telephony is an additive to today's communications networks because it can be easily integrated with existing PSTN infrastructure and networks. One area of concern with VoIP that remains is connectivity with the 911 service (i.e., emergency services).

RECENT TRENDS IN VOIP

There are expected to be approximately 19.2 million residential VoIP lines in use by the end of 2007, as shown in Figure 2 (eMarketer 2005). The low cost, efficiency, and flexible nature of VoIP are leading to its increasing

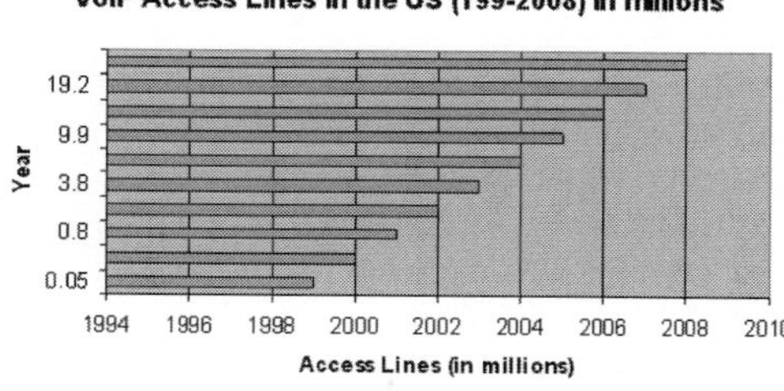

Figure 2: VoIP access lines in the United States (eMarketer 2005)

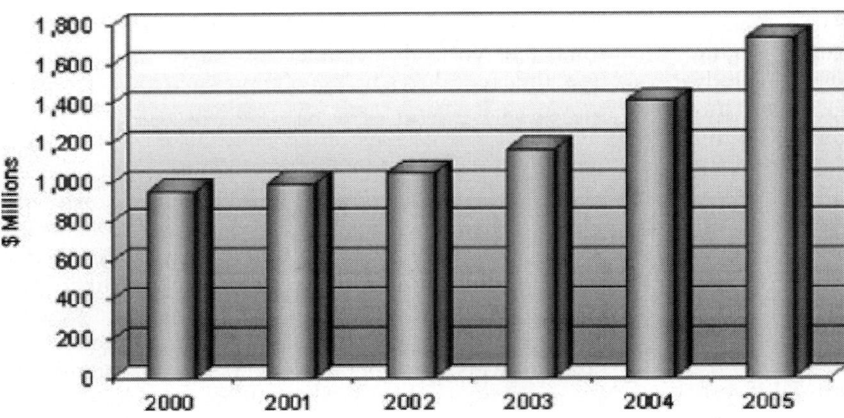

Figure 3: Growth of VoIP products (eMarketer 2005)

acceptance in the marketplace. In fact, as the telecom industry regains momentum from its 2002 decline, and large service providers complete depreciation of their legacy investments, more bundled offerings are emerging on the market—many of which integrate voice and data capabilities. Moreover, as Figure 3 illustrates, the growth of VoIP products over the five-year forecast is strongly skewed toward the later years.

HARDWARE-BASED RESIDENTIAL VOIP SERVICES IN THE UNITED STATES

A wide variety of VoIP products and services are available on the market today. Some of these different types of VoIP products are described as follows.

Gateways: Allow analog and digital voice/fax communications over IP networks or the Internet. They can be used for origination and/or termination. They are the backbone of most VoIP networks and service providers, and they support H.323 and/or SIP.

Gatekeepers: Allow centralized control of gateway administration and call routing. They also allow load balancing and a single IP address for multiple gateways.

Advanced gateway options: For VoIP applications requiring advanced functionality and higher performance, these specialized products provide features not normally found in standard gateways or gatekeepers.

Digital phone sets to VoIP: VoIP gateways that allow most popular private branch exchange (PBX) digital phone sets to retain their full functionality across an IP network or the Internet. Popular PBXs include Nortel, Avaya, Definity, Alcatel, Panasonic, Toshiba, and more.

Cellular to VoIP: In many countries, cellular global system for mobile (GSM) telecommunications, code division multiple access (CDMA), or time division multiple access (TDMA) may be the only cost-effective choices for voice communications. These systems allow VoIP transmissions to terminate on standard GSM and/or CDMA/TDMA networks.

VoIP billing: Allows service providers and organizations to extract data about voice and fax calls from VoIP gateways or gatekeepers. This allows full control of VoIP networks that support services such as prepaid, post-paid, or wholesale.

Gateway channel banks: Many digital VoIP gateways with E1, T1, or primary rate interface (PRI) voice ports may require access to analog PSTN phone lines. With these devices we can convert E1, T1, or PRI voice interfaces from most gateways to either foreign exchange subscriber (FXS) or foreign exchange office (FXO) interfaces (the two most common interfaces found in analog telephony environments).

Table 1 provides a snapshot of prices and features for some of the major hardware-based residential VoIP services in the United States. New VoIP services are continuously emerging on the market, and prices and features change rapidly. Many more providers, especially the established cable and phone companies, are entering the VoIP market (Tripos Corporation 2005).

A COMPARISON OF VOIP AND VOICE OVER PUBLIC SWITCHED TELEPHONE NETWORK

The PSTN has served the needs of businesses and consumers worldwide for more than 100 years and has gone through major technological advances, including resilient and robust long-distance networks based on technologies such as synchronous optical network (SONET), intelligent networking, Signaling System No. 7 (SS7)-based signaling, and a high degree of redundancy in telephone switches. All of these advanced features and components have considerably increased the reliability of PSTN, which is today operational 99.999% of the time (Wright 2001) and offers low latency rates and very high quality during voice transmissions.

IP-based networks are now ubiquitous and are being used to provide integrated voice-data communications. As a result, conventional PSTN carriers realize they have to respond to this competitive capability (handling of integrated voice-data transmissions) of IP technology. For example, Telcordia (formally Bellcore) has developed a Voice over Packet (VoP) architecture and has initiated an

Table 1: VoIP Service Providers in the United States

VoIP Service Provider	Cost per Month	Features
AT&T CallVantage	$30	Voicemail to e-mail, speed dialing, call logs, Do Not Disturb, a flexible call-forwarding feature called "Locate Me," and a conferencing system for up to nine users. AT&T also offers number portability and 911 service.
BroadVoice	$20	Selective call forward and blocking, lets customers choose their own session initiation protocol (SIP)-compatible devices.
Broadvox Direct	$20	Do Not Disturb, contact management, Find Me, and Follow Me.
EarthLink Unlimited Voice	$30	911 emergency service, 411 directory assistance, multiple lines and virtual numbers, personalized voicemail, and a $10/month fax line. There is also a bandwidth-saver feature for those with limited upstream broadband speeds, letting them adjust their voice quality based on available bandwidth.
Net2Phone	$35	Toll-free plans, flexible pay-as-you-go plans, and add-on options offering minutes to particular international regions and countries. Other features include call blocking and the ability to make local and long-distance calls.
Packet8	$20	Voicemail to email; 911 service for $3 a month; and a videophone plan that provides unlimited phone and videoconferencing calling for $30 a month plus a $30 activation fee.
Time Warner Cable Digital Phone	$40	911 service, voicemail, and the ability to rewire all existing phones through regular phone jacks to the cable modem router.
Verizon VoiceWing	$35	911 service, address books with click-to-dial settings, enhanced call forwarding, and speed dialing.
VoiceGlo	$30	Voicemail and customized call following.
VoicePulse	$35	Call blocking, Do Not Disturb, multi-ring, contact management, and a sophisticated customized call following feature. Directory assistance is available at extra cost.
Vonage	$25	911 access, voicemail with access available via e-mail or the Web, number portability, 411 directory assistance, additional voice and fax lines, and a PC-based soft-phone version of Vonage.

industry-wide effort to develop generic requirement documents; the documents are expected to allow local and interexchange carriers, vendors, and other stakeholders to address interoperability issues associated with networks, services, protocols, and equipment. These initiatives recognize that distinct networks cannot cost-effectively offer bundled services, and there is therefore a strong need to identify a migration path for PSTN carriers to preserve their investments in circuit-switched technology and services. This migration path is supposed to allow PSTN carriers to modify and add only some components to existing networks to offer multiple services, including VoIP (Varshney et al. 2002). As mentioned previously, VoIP offers end users a great deal of features and cost savings compared to the traditional PSTN. Table 2 presents a comparison of the main features of Voice over PSTN and Voice over IP technologies.

VoIP IMPLEMENTATION CONFIGURATIONS

The overall technology requirements of an IP telephony solution can be split into four categories: signaling, encoding, transport, and gateway control. The purpose of the signaling protocol is to create and manage connections between endpoints, as well as to create and manage calls. Next, when the conversation starts, the analog signal produced by the microphone from the human voice needs to be encoded in a digital format suitable for transmission across an IP network. The IP network then transports the real-time voice content across the available media and needs to maintain an acceptable level of voice quality. In some cases, the IP telephony system may also need a gateway (also known as a VoIP gateway) to convert from the digital format to another format—either for interoperability with a different IP-based multimedia scheme or because the call needs to be placed on PSTN.

VoIP Hardware Configurations

PC-to-PC Configuration

The PC-to-PC configuration is the simplest VoIP design because the conversion from voice to data and back is performed on a PC using a sound card and the appropriate software. As Figure 4 shows, calls can only be made within the data network (in this case, within the Internet).

Table 2: A Comparison of Voice over PSTN and Voice over IP Features

Feature	Voice over PSTN	Voice over IP
Switching	Circuit switched (end-to-end dedicated circuit set up by circuit switches)	Packet switched (statistical multiplexing of several connections over links)
Latency	Less than 100 milliseconds	200–700 milliseconds (depending on the traffic on the IP network)
Bandwidth	Dedicated	Dynamically allocated
Equipment	Dumb terminal (cheap); intelligence in the network	Integrated, smart, programmable terminal (expensive); intelligence not in the network
Quality of Service (QoS)	High (extremely low loss)	Low and variable; QoS depends on the amount of traffic, packet loss, and delay experienced
Network Availability	99.99% uptime	Level of reliability is unknown
Electrical Power Failure	Not a problem; powered by a separate source from the telephone company	May have problems with equipment being down
Security	High level of security because one line is dedicated to one call	Possible eavesdropping at routers
Standards/ Status	Mature (simplified internetworking between equipment of different vendors)	Emerging; possible problems in internetworking
Carrier Lines	Dedicated lines required from the telecommunication companies	All voice channels can be transmitted over one Internet connection
Bandwidth	Each analogue telephone line uses 64 kbits/s in each direction	Using compression, VoIP can use as little as ~10 kbits/s in each direction; further bandwidth can be saved by using silence suppression (not transmitting when the person is not speaking)
Advanced Features (e.g., call waiting, caller ID, conferencing, on hold, etc.)	Often available at an extra cost	Generally available for free
Remote Private Automatic Branch Exchange (PABX) Extensions for Teleworkers and Branch Offices	Very costly and require dedicated lines for each remote extension	Remote extensions are a standard feature
Expansion and Upgrade	Complex: can require significant hardware additions, provisioning of new lines, etc.	Often just requires more Internet bandwidth and software upgrades
Choice of Companies to Terminate Calls	Each line is provisioned by a single telecommunication company, meaning there is very limited least-cost routing	Hundreds of VoIP providers to choose from to terminate calls
Typical Business Line Rental	$40 per month	$11 per month
Free Calls	None	To other VoIP users of the same gateway

Source: Varshney et al. (2002)

Such a configuration requires that both users be online during a conversation. This implies that users have to plan their calls in advance, or one of them must call the other using a standard phone (PSTN phone) in advance. Only then can the users start a VoIP conversation. This makes a call very time consuming, especially when both users are connected to the Internet via a modem connection.

PC-to-POTS Configuration

The next step in the VoIP evolution was to exploit a VoIP gateway. A gateway is a node that interconnects data

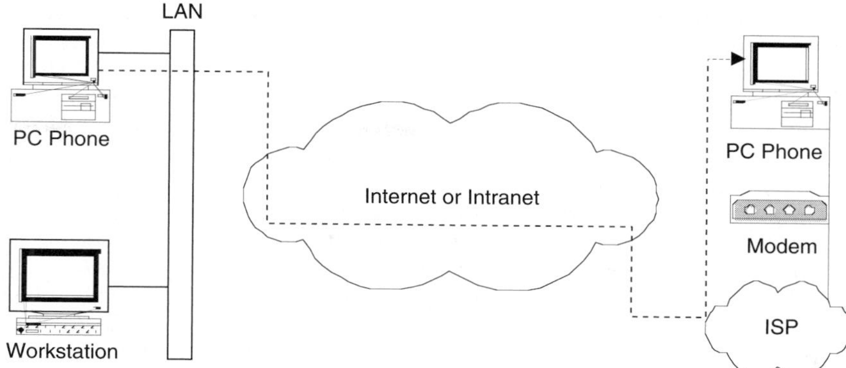

Figure 4: PC-to-PC VoIP scenario

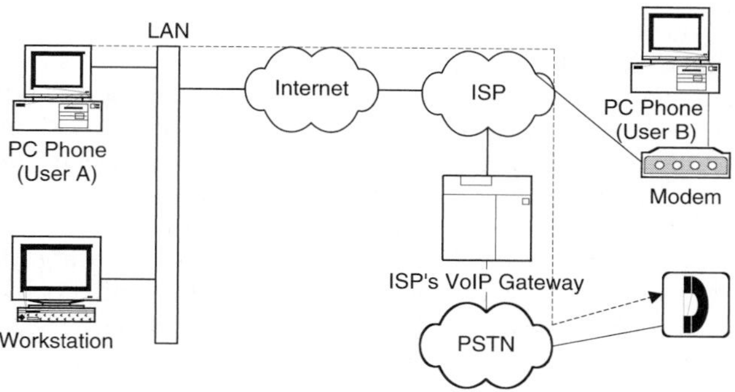

Figure 5: PC-to-POTS VoIP scenario

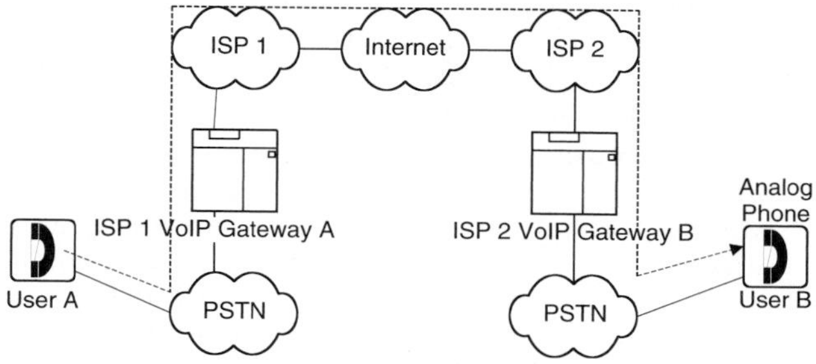

Figure 6: Phone to phone via IP

networks (e.g., local area network [LAN], Internet, WAN) and POTS networks. Some Internet service providers (ISPs) offered new services for IP telephony via gateways. Now users could call the other party from their PC to POTS telephones.

As shown in Figure 5, the VoIP gateway performs the conversion from a packet data stream into an analog voice signal. This enables users to dial telephone numbers in the gateway's domain. Program solutions such as VocalTec, MediaRing Talk, and others are capable of calling someone outside the IP world. A voice call from User A travels through the Internet to the gateway nearest to User B. This is important because User A pays for a call from the gateway to User B's destination, as well as for the gateway services and his Internet connection.

Phone-to-Phone Configuration

The next step in VoIP evolution was to exploit VoIP gateways at both ends for bidirectional calls. Using such a gateway, users can call each other from analog telephones via IP. If the ISP offers such a service, User A (Figure 6) first dials the ISP's service telephone number, followed by the telephone number of User B. Gateway A translates this number to the IP address of gateway B (the one nearest to User B) and forwards the call. Such a service is particularly appealing to those users who make many expensive international calls and would like to reduce their phone expenses. The price of such a conversation can be very low, at least until ISPs offer quality of service (QoS), in which case they may start charging customers higher amounts.

To make phone calls using the configuration shown in Figure 6, individuals make use of IP phones that provide considerable benefits. The most important benefit is a reduction in costs in implementing, managing, and maintaining only one network only instead of two. Consider a large company with Intranet implemented on a LAN and with geographically dispersed offices connected through a WAN via leased links. Because leased lines are quite expensive and mostly unoccupied, the transmission of voice over these lines enhances traffic throughput.

VoIP Gateways

Different types of VoIP gateways are being deployed to support VoIP. Some of the popular are described as follows.

PBX-based gateways: Leading manufacturers of PBX equipment are introducing their own solutions to address the VoIP challenge. The drawback is that these vendors have minimal experience in IP-centric data networking. However, the biggest disadvantage of the PBX-based approach is that it is tied so directly to highly proprietary PBX platforms. Leading PBX vendors have no demonstrable track record in either defining or adopting the types of open technical standards that have accelerated adoption of the Internet over the past decade.

Router-based gateways: Manufacturers of routers and other data networking hardware are also getting actively involved in the VoIP market. Unfortunately, router vendors' unfamiliarity with voice technology and call management continues to hamper their abilities to deliver corporate-class telephony solutions. Many of the router-based gateway vendors are steering their customers to end-to-end solutions, which require a single manufacturer's equipment across the edge and core of the network. This approach is precisely the type of lock-in that most technology managers would prefer to avoid during the early stages of their VoIP plans.

PC-based gateways: Several vendors are also bringing stand-alone PC-based gateways to the market. These commercial products offer a router/PBX-independent solution, since they are not tied to a particular manufacturer's platform. However, stand-alone gateways are also typically based on the PC platform, which may not be inherently reliable.

Intelligent multipath switching gateways: A fourth alternative to the gateways discussed above that has recently been introduced on the market is the multipath switch gateway. This device has been designed to address issues not addressed by previous VoIP gateway designs—namely, voice quality, network reliability, and vendor independence.

Multipath voice/data switch: A multipath voice/data switch resides between the corporate PBX and both the PSTN and the corporate IP data network. Its most prominent distinguishing characteristic is its ability to continuously monitor the condition of the data network and to route voice traffic accordingly. This intelligent switching capability is the key to its value for safe, controlled migration to VoIP. If conditions on the corporate network are sufficient to support the required level of voice quality, the gateway switches voice traffic to the appropriate router. If conditions on the corporate network deteriorate for some reason, the switch automatically and transparently redirects voice traffic over the public switched network. Intelligent multipath switching addresses the foremost concerns of both business and technology managers who are considering a first-stage implementation of VoIP.

Voice Coders/Decoders

A coder-decoder (codec) is usually implemented in a digital signal processor (DSP) at a voice gateway or in software running on a desktop computer. The voice codec performs conversions between analog voice and the compressed digital representation of the voice. Coding is done at the entry point to a packet network, and decoding is done at the exit point of the packet network. The voice codec used must be the same at each end of the communication link. Gateways that transport voice over a packet backbone network negotiate with one another via standardized signaling messages to decide on the common codec they will be use. Several factors must be taken into account to evaluate the best voice codec (where "best" refers to the trade-off between optimal quality and bandwidth usage).

Criteria for Voice Codec Selection

The bit rate of current narrowband codecs using today's technology ranges from 1.2 to 64 kbits/s. The most efficient codec available today allows quasi-toll quality (where toll quality is equal to a PSTN telephone conversation). Manufacturers must pay royalty fees to implement some codecs into their VoIP products. This can sometimes lead a vendor's VoIP application to use an inefficient codec that may be cheaper to license. Hence, the issue of royalties is another aspect that needs to be considered when evaluating voice coders in terms of the trade-off between cost and performance. Most narrowband codecs compress voice in chunks (frames) and need look-ahead information; in other words, these codecs require information about the samples immediately following the samples they are currently encoding. The minimal delay introduced by a coding-decoding sequence is the frame length plus the look-ahead size (algorithmic delay). Codecs with a small frame length have a smaller delay than those with longer frame lengths, but they introduce a large overhead. Most implementations choose to send multiple frames per packet; the real frame length to take into account is the sum of all frames stacked in a single IP packet. Another factor that must be considered in selecting a voice codec is packet loss handling. IP does not handle packet loss; if this happens, it affects the operation of the codec. Packet loss can be further exacerbated on the Internet, where several consecutive packets may be lost or dropped. Thus, implementing packet loss recovery may not be productive if the algorithm only protects against intermittent packet loss. Forward error correction (FEC) redundancy can be used to recover from serious loss conditions, but at the expense of delay. Alternatively, multiple send redundancy can be utilized, but it would transmit more packets; if router congestion were the cause, using this technique would not be beneficial. Finally, it is worth pointing out that most codecs used today can only multicast voice at a single level of quality (bit rate). Therefore, it would not be possible to transmit the same data at different quality rates to multiple listeners without sending individual VoIP streams.

The following three International Telecommunications Union (ITU)-based audio codecs are frequently used in VoIP applications:

- G.711: The G.711 codec describes a relatively simple way to digitize analog data by using pulse code modulation (PCM). Its goal is to increase the resolution for small signals, whereas large signals are treated proportionally. The encoded stream is 64 kbits/s, consisting of 8 KHz sampling of 8-bit signals.
- G.723.1: The G.723.1 codec has been selected as the baseline codec for narrowband H.323 communications by the International Multimedia Telecommunications Consortium (MTC) VoIP forum. G.723.1 is a coded representation that can be used to compress the speech component of multimedia services at a low bit rate (compared to 64 kbits/s for the G.711). The voice coder has two bit rates associated with it—5.3 and 6.3 kbits/s—whose modes of operation can change dynamically at each frame. The frame length is 30 milliseconds; however, another 7.5-millisecond delay is necessary for its

Table 3: Characteristics of Voice Codecs

Codec Type	Algorithm	Frame Size (milliseconds)	Rate (kbits/s)	Mean Opinion Score (MOS)
G.711	PCM[1]	0.125	64	4.1
G.726	ADPCM[2]	0.125	32	3.9
G.728	LD-CELP[3]	0.625	16	3.6
G.729A	CS-ACELP[4]	10	8	3.7
G.729e	Hybrid CELP	10	11.8	3.92
G.723.1	MPC-MLQ[5]	30	6.3	3.9
G.723.1	ACELP	30	5.3	3.65
AMR[6]	ACELP	20	4.75-12.2	

1. PCM: pulse code modulation
2. ADPCM: adaptive differential pulse code modulation
3. LD-CELP: low delay code excited linear prediction
4. CS-ACELP: conjugate-structured algebraic code-excited linear prediction
5. MPC-MLQ: Multi-pulse code-maximum likelihood quantization
6. AMR: adaptive multi-rate

Source: ITU-T (1998)

look-ahead buffer, resulting in a total algorithmic delay of 37.5 milliseconds. The G.723.1 voice coder encodes speech in frames using linear predictive analysis-by-synthesis coding. The high-rate voice coder uses multi-pulse-maximum likelihood quantization (MP-MLQ), whereas the low-rate coder uses algebraic code-excited linear prediction (ACELP).

- G.729A: The G.729/G.729A voice coder uses conjugate-structured algebraic code-excited linear prediction (CS-ACELP) coding technique (Udani and Mehta 2001). It produces a speech rate of 8 kbits/s, with an algorithmic delay of 15 milliseconds (10 milliseconds of frame length and 5 milliseconds of look-ahead time). G.729A is the reduced-complexity version of the original version of G.729.

A summary of the different types of codecs available for VoIP applications is given in Table 3. The quality of a voice call through a codec is often measured by subjective testing under controlled conditions using a large number of listeners to determine a mean opinion score (MOS). The general order of fixed rate codecs, from best to worst in tandem, is G.711, G.726, G.729e, G.728, G.729, and G.723.1 (Wright 2001).

Performance Metrics for Assessing Voice Quality

Conditions in the PSTN are totally different from those in packet-based networks. The circuit-switched PSTN network provides a separate connection for each voice connection, with stable delay and noise level conditions. However, in a packet-based network, links are shared between different connections, resulting in the interaction between various traffic types. Hence, voice connections over best-effort IP networks are subject to unstable conditions, including unpredictable delays, delay jitter, and packet loss.

Some of the metrics used are described as follows:

- Mean opinion score: this technique uses human judges and perceptual speech quality measurement (PSQM) to evaluate human hearing (Lakaniemi, Rosti, and Raisanen 2001).
- Latency: The end-to-end delay of voice between the source and the destination is an important metric that determines the ultimate quality of voice delivered. A summary of different delay values and their acceptability or unacceptability when compared to delays associated with the delivery of traditional voice over PSTN will be discussed. To ensure good voice quality, latency for voice communications should not exceed 400 milliseconds, as shown in Figure 7 (Goode 2002).

Many processing components add delays during the capture and delivery of the voice to the destination user. The various delay components that constitute the end-to-end delay are shown in Table 4. The "Internet delivery" delay takes into account the delays incurred (e.g., due to network devices such as routers become overloaded, congestions over communication links, packets taking more hops than normal and thereby increasing the travel time over the network) as packets are transported through the Internet. It is important to point out that high end-to-end delays lead to echoes; the greater the delay, the more offensive the echoes become, and the more important it is to deal with them effectively. If packets containing voice do not arrive within a reasonable time, they are dropped and a condition known as *clipping* (the cutting off of the first or final syllables in a conversation) occurs.

To overcome the effects of high latency, a class of service (CoS) or QoS can be assigned to various applications running over the network. For instance, voice and other multimedia applications can be recognized as time sensitive and therefore take priority over other, less time-sensitive media types. QoS over the Internet and corporate

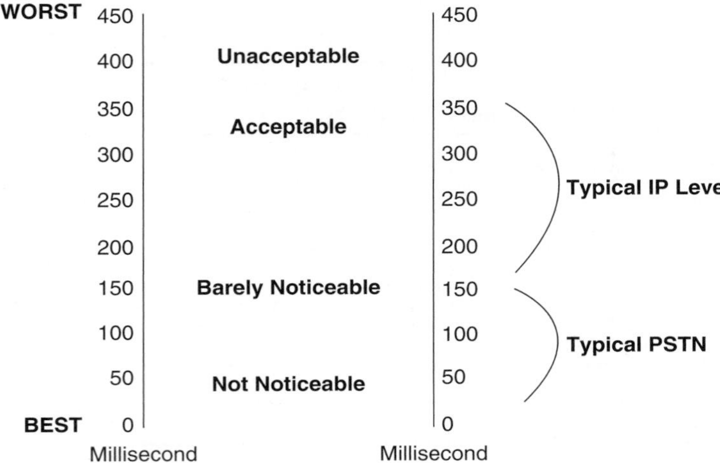

Figure 7: Voice delay levels (milliseconds)

Table 4: End-to-End VoIP Packet Delay

Processing Delay	Delay (milliseconds)
Recording	10–40
Encoding	5–10
Compression	5–10
Internet Delivery	70–120
Jitter Buffer	50–200
Decompression	5–10
Decode	5–10
Average end-to-end delay (sum of all individual delay components)	150–400

Source: Kampichler and Goeschka (2001)

intranets is handled by routers and switches that implement various resource reservation (e.g., bandwidth) techniques: IntServ, Diffserv, and multiprotocol label switching (MPLS; Mahadevan and Sivalingam 1999; Rouhana and Horlait, 2000). Currently, QoS is easier to apply on corporate intranets in which a single company has complete end-to-end control over the network. Applying QoS over the public Internet is a lot harder because it requires the cooperation of many ISPs, which do not all have QoS-enabled routers and switches. Therefore, we are still relying on best-effort delivery provided by the Internet for most delay-sensitive media types such as voice and video.

- Delay jitter: IP networks do not guarantee the delivery time of data packets (or their order), so data may arrive at inconsistent rates. The variation in interpacket arrival rate is known as *jitter*, which is introduced by variable transmission delays over the network. Jitter buffers can be used to remove the packet-delay variation that each packet is subjected to as it travels through the network.
- Packet loss: For VoIP, packet loss leads to lost portions of speech that results in poor voice quality. The total packet loss experienced by the receiver in the case of wired networks has two components: packet loss occurring in the network because of congestion at some intermediate node(s), and at the receiver because of packets arriving later than their scheduled playback times. However, in the case of wireless environments, packet losses may occur as a result of several other causes such as handoffs, interference, fading of wireless signals, and so forth. Some packet loss is tolerable; for example, many voice encoders can handle up to 1 percent packet loss (Wright 2001). Since the emergence of the concept of packetized voice in the late 1970s, extensive work has been undertaken to reduce packet loss and its effects.
- Coding distortion: Before voice is transmitted over an IP network, the voice signal must be encoded to fit into the available bandwidth. Voice codecs such as G.723.1 and G.729 are the most commonly used. These algorithms are efficient in keeping the bandwidth consumed by a voice call to a minimum. However, the quality of voice generally degrades when high compression ratios are used. Some algorithms are better at maintaining voice quality than others. For example, the ITU's G.711 algorithm provides toll-quality voice by converting a 16-bit linear code to an 8-bit U-law or A-law code. However, G.711 uses 64 kbits/s of channel capacity, which is considered too much for a VoIP system. New algorithms such as G.723 and G.729 consume much lower bandwidth but reduce voice quality to some extent. Efforts are constantly under way to find algorithms that can boost compression ratio while maintaining high voice quality.

VoIP Protocols and Standards

VoIP requires a connection between users—in the case of VoIP, a virtual connection. As mentioned earlier, a VoIP architecture includes many components. First, a signaling protocol is needed to set up individual sessions for voice connections between users. Once a session is established, a transport protocol can be used to send the data packets. Directory access protocols are another important part of VoIP, providing routing and switching information for connecting calls. A signaling protocol handles user location, session establishment, session negotiation, call participant management, and feature invocation. Session establishment is invoked when a user is located, allowing the call recipient to accept, reject, or forward the call. Session negotiation helps to manage different types of media, such as voice and video, transmitted at the same time. Call participant management helps to control users who are active on the call, allowing for the addition and subtraction of users. A signaling protocol also involves feature invocation and call features such as hold, transfer, and mute. Various signaling protocols recently developed can also be used to support VoIP transmissions. Two of the most popular signaling protocols are discussed as follows.

H.323

The H.323 standard (Glasmann and Keller 2001) is the ITU's standard with which vendors need to comply when providing VoIP services. The standard was originally developed for multimedia conferencing over LANs but was later extended to cover VoIP. The first version was released in 1996, and the second version of H.323 came into effect in January 1998. The standard encompasses both point-to-point communications and multipoint conferences. The products and applications of different vendors can interoperate if they abide by the H.323 specification. H.323 defines four logical components: terminals, gateways, gatekeepers, and multipoint control units (MCUs; these provide the capability for three or more terminals and gateways to participate in a multipoint conference). Terminals, gateways, and MCUs are known as end points.

Session Initiation Protocol

Session initiation protocol (SIP) is an application-layer control protocol that can establish, modify, and terminate multimedia sessions such as multimedia conferences, Internet telephony calls, and similar applications with one or more participants (Handley et al. 1999). The basic role of SIP is to locate and invite participants to a multimedia session that could range from a VoIP call to text chat, application sharing, video, and so forth. A participant in an SIP session could be a human user or an automaton, such as a media server, or even a gateway to some other network, such as the PSTN. SIP also provides a rich framework of other telephony services including user location, forward, transfer, multiparty, mute, and hold. It also supports certain advanced features such as interactive voice response systems and a form of mobility. The architecture of SIP follows the client-server model and is similar to that of HTTP with requests issued by the client and responses returned by the server. With regard to VoIP calls, the caller acts as the client and the callee as the server. A single call may involve several servers and clients because the requests may be forwarded. SIP supports the following features that enable the establishment and teardown of VoIP calls:

- User location: discovery of the location of the end system from which the user wishes to communicate
- User availability: determination of the willingness of the called party to engage in communications
- User capabilities: negotiation and determination of the various media parameters to be used by the caller and the callee
- Call setup: establishment of call parameters and flow of media streams
- Call handling: termination of call sessions, transfer of calls, and invocation of other services

SIP is text based and works independently of the underlying transport and network layer protocols. SIP uses a simple signaling scheme to handle only the basic requirements such as the creation, modification, and termination of sessions. This simplicity helps in the rapid call-setup, which is crucial for high QoS.

SIP message types. An SIP message—the basic unit of SIP communication—is either a request from a client to a server or a response status code from a server to the client. Six methods exist by which SIP requests can be made:

- INVITE: indicates that a user or service is being invited to participate in a session
- ACK: confirms that the client has received a final response to an INVITE request; provided for reliable exchange of invitation messages
- BYE: used by the user agent client (UAC) to indicate to the server that it wishes to release the call; may be issued by either the caller or the callee, and is basically used to terminate a connection between the two end points
- OPTIONS: solicits information about a user's capabilities
- REGISTER: gives information about the location of a user to the SIP registration server; used by an SIP client to register its address with the registration server
- CANCEL: used to cancel a pending request; may be issued by the user agent client or the proxy client

Related Works on SIP-Based VoIP Systems

Efforts to implement SIP features for VoIP services have been under way for the past few years. Hyun, Huh, and Kang (2002) address the design and implementation of SIP server components such as proxy and registrar server. Their implementation supports call forking, authentication, and a stateful proxy nature. Huh et al. (2002) describe the implementation of a user agent system for voice services; the features supported include call establishment, termination, registration, and capability negotiation. Zou et al. (2000) present a Java-based implementation of SIP components that focuses primarily on PC-to-PC communication within the context of a virtual private network (VPN) service. As VoIP continues to compete with the PSTN in providing advanced voice communication features, implementing high-level features in IP-based voice service architecture that would further enhance its usability and make it a viable alternative to circuit-switched calling is desirable.

The authors have developed an SIP-based VoIP system that: 1) supports a point-to-point VoIP call with the added

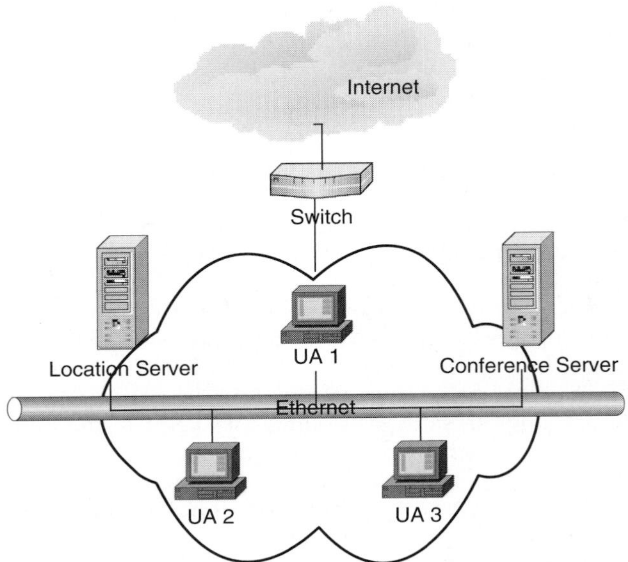

Figure 8: General architecture of the SIP-based VoIP system

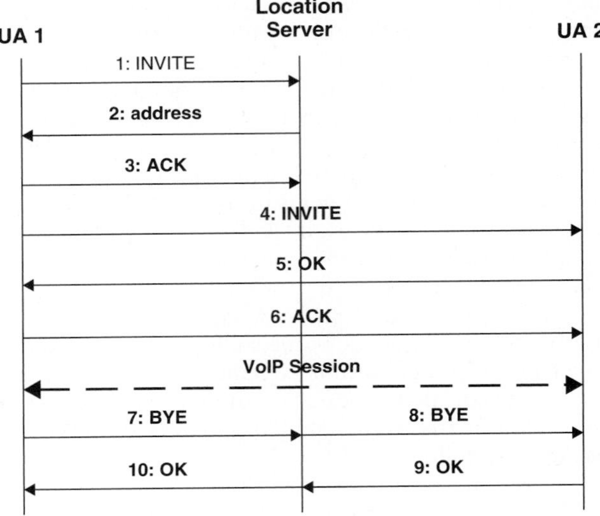

Figure 9: Call flow for a two-participant VoIP call

capability of transitioning to a multipoint conference; 2) provides a rich set of extensible call-related features using the lightweight SIP protocol; 3) and supports call-related features such as call muting and call-hold facility as well as personal mobility. Personal mobility provides users with the freedom to move and still be able to access the telecommunication services regardless of the terminal or the network.

Our implementation differs from past SIP-based VoIP systems in that our design further extends the SIP component capabilities to support multiparty user interaction compared to only two-participant calls supported by previous efforts. In addition, our prototype SIP-based VoIP implementation provides support for personal mobility and offers additional features, which include multiple audio encoding formats (e.g., G.711 U-law [CCITT 1972], G.726-7 adaptive differential pulse code modulation [ADPCM], and linear PCM).

Implementation of an SIP-Based VoIP Architecture

Our SIP-based VoIP architecture, shown in Figure 8, is implemented and deployed on Sun Ultra-10 workstations running Solaris 8 and connected to a 100 mbits/sec ethernet LAN. The main components of our implementation constitute user agents (UAs) and SIP network servers:

User agents: Each UA consists of a user agent client (UAC) and a user agent server (UAS). The UAC is a logical entity for creating new SIP requests. The UAS is responsible for receiving SIP requests and sending the corresponding responses, along with suitable processing of those SIP requests. In addition, the UAS is capable of functioning either as a caller or a callee.

SIP network servers: These include the registrar server and a proxy/redirect server. The registrar server receives updates from users about their current addresses and sends an appropriate response message back to the user after the registration process. The registrar server thus maintains the current location of each user in the form of a database. The proxy/redirect servers are responsible for routing SIP messages. Our software implements a single location server that collectively implements the functions of the aforementioned servers.

Conference server: Has been implemented to provide multipoint communication support. Our prototype implementation allows point-to-point and multipoint real-time audio interaction between two or more SIP UAs. In addition, our architecture supports all basic communication handling features such as inviting users for call setup, acknowledging requests, canceling pending invitations, and call teardown messages. Additional functionalities such as personal mobility of clients, multiparty conference support, message retransmission, and authentication are also supported.

Figures 9 and 10 briefly demonstrate call flow establishment in our implementation for a two-participant call and a multiparticipant, respectively. The location server implements the functions of the SIP network servers.

Software components of the SIP-based VoIP architecture. Each UA in our implementation consists of several modules that interact with one another through well-defined interfaces. Figure 11 shows the architecture of the UA system.

UDP is used to transfer SIP messages through configured UDP ports. Each outgoing message is associated with a timer value, the expiration of which triggers a retransmission. UDP is also used to deliver audio packets during a voice call. When an SIP message is received, the parser module parses it and the values interpreted are passed to the UA server for an appropriate response. An outgoing message is composed by the message generator and transmitted using UDP. An audio codec module has also been implemented to compress and decompress voice packets. The audio codec supports different types of compressions (e.g., G.711 U-law, G.726 ADPCM, and

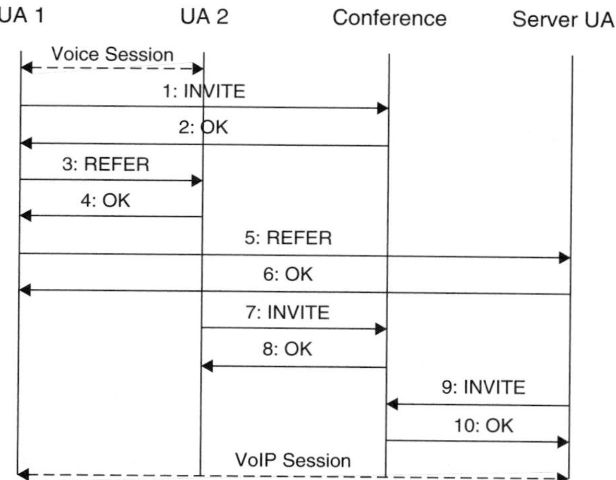

Figure 10: Multiple participant conferencing using the ad hoc centralized conference during a VoIP session

User Interface	
User Agent Server	User Agent Client
Audio CODEC	SIP Message Parser/Generator
UDP	

Figure 11: UA modules implemented

linear PCM). The UAS is a continuously running thread that waits for incoming SIP messages. Each request received is handled by the creation of a new thread, thereby making the user agent capable of concurrent processing. Finally, the user interface enables a user to log into the system and make choices to initiate, accept, or reject calls.

The proxy/location server consists of a server thread that listens to incoming requests from other SIP entities. Upon receipt of an SIP message, the SIP parser function is called to interpret the message for processing. This component has been designed to support the functions of registering new users, retrieving current user locations by querying the associated database, and signaling call teardown to participating users.

Multiple-participant VoIP conference support. Our implementation also supports multiparty audio interaction among users (Rosenberg and Schulzrinne 2000). This feature allows the addition of further participants during an ongoing two-participant session. To accomplish this, the ad hoc centralized conferencing model has been exploited in our design.

The first step toward the transition is the discovery of a conference server. In this implementation, the conference server's address is specified in the user-agent source code. This allows any participant of an ongoing call to invite a new participant to join a session. The caller first sends an INVITE message to the conference server. The server replies with an OK message and sends a new conference identifier assigned to the new session (involving the additional participant). The inviter then issues REFER messages (containing the new conference identifier) directly to the other participants. These participants in turn send INVITE messages to the conference server. When each participant receives the acknowledgement from the conference server, a voice conference session is established.

The conference server supports two main functions. First, it maintains a list of conferences and their corresponding participants. Second, it performs redistribution of incoming audio data to each participant. For a centralized conferencing model such as the one adopted in our prototype, the conference server receives voice packets from n participants and retransmits $(n-1)$ streams to each user; it does not retransmit a source's own packets back to itself again. Figure 12 shows the underlying idea of the centralized conference server. When a user wishes to leave a conference, it issues a BYE message and quits. The conference session is terminated when the last participant leaves.

Our architecture differs from other centralized audio conferencing schemes (Wang, Zhang, and Li 2000) previously implemented in its support for personal mobility through registration and redirection services performed by the location server.

Personal mobility. Personal mobility provides users with the freedom to move and yet be able to access the telecommunication services regardless of the terminal or the network. To support personal mobility, our implementation uses a combination of a user's personal identity and location tracking performed by the location server.

A location server is used to keep track of the location of each user (i.e., from which terminal a user is working). From a user's perspective, personal mobility is obtained by logging on to the network through some terminal (using a designated personal identity, which is assigned the first time the user accesses the service) and then being able to make and receive calls from the terminal from which he is logged on. When a user on any terminal logs on to a network, SIP messages are sent to the location server, which records the IP address from which the entry was made. Thus, each time the user signs into the system through the UA, an SIP message is immediately sent to the location server to register its current location into the database for future lookup requests by potential callers. The user location is purged from the list after disconnecting from the service and reentered if the user registers again from a new location. This feature makes the application independent

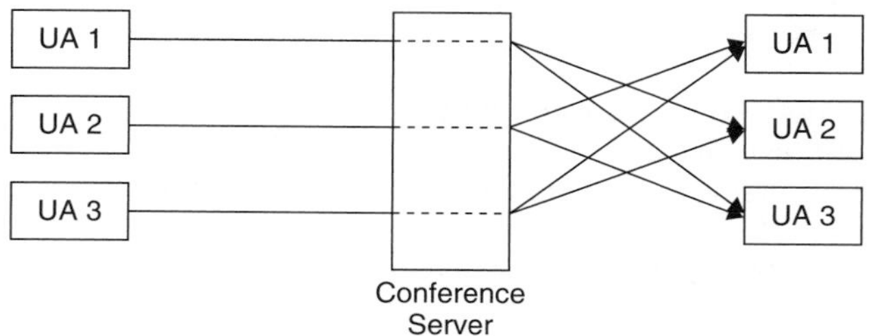

Figure 12: Packet redistribution by a conference server

Table 5: Variation of Interarrival Packet Delays

Encoding Format	Variation of Interarrival Packet Delays (milliseconds) with Number of Participants		
	2	3	4
U-law	64	158	169
ADPCM	16	52	77
Linear PCM (uncompressed)	8	28	51

of the IP address of the participating users' terminals, allowing the user to access the service independent of the location.

The use of a personal identity in our implementation is further complemented by a password corresponding to each identity, thereby making the service accessible to authenticated users only.

Performance with SIP. The impact of increasing numbers of participants and different types of voice-encoding formats on interarrival VoIP packet delays (as shown in Table 5) were measured. The encoding formats used include linear PCM, ADPCM, and U-law. Linear PCM is an uncompressed audio format in which each audio sample is stored using 16 bits, thereby requiring 128 kbits/s of bandwidth (16 bits/sample × 8000 samples/sec). With regard to U-law, voice is compressed to 8-bit samples, thereby reducing the bandwidth to 64 kbits/s. A further reduction in the bandwidth requirement was obtained by using the International Multimedia Association (IMA)-ADPCM algorithm, which compresses linear PCM samples into 4-bit quantization levels. Each ADPCM sample represents a 16-bit audio sample providing a compression ratio of 4:1 and yielding a bit rate of 32 kbits/s. The interarrival delay was calculated as the difference in arrival times of two consecutive packets at the receiver host. The measurements were taken for one-way transmissions and repeated several times for each participant, and average values were recorded.

As observed from the values recorded, the interarrival packet delay is lowest for a two-participant session and increases almost linearly with the increasing number of participants. The transition from a two-participant session to a multiparticipant session causes a slightly higher increase in delay because packets need to go through the conference server to the destination (in the latter case). Lower packet-arrival delays were obtained using the linear PCM and ADPCM formats as compared to the U-law encoding format. However, the linear PCM format has a higher bandwidth requirement than the ADPCM and U-law formats.

Benefits of SIP Compared to H.323

SIP provides a set of services similar to H.323. However, SIP offers major benefits over H.323 in terms of lower complexity, rich extensibility, and better scalability (Schulzrinne and Rosenberg 1998):

- Complexity: H.323 is a rather complex protocol. The sum total of the base specifications alone is over 700 pages; SIP, on the other hand, even with its call control extensions and session description protocols totals merely 128 pages. H.323 also defines several hundreds of elements, whereas SIP has only 37 headers, each with a small number of values and parameters that contain more information. H.323 uses a binary representation for its messages, based on ASN.1 and the packed encoding rules (PERs). ASN.1 generally requires special code generators to parse. SIP encodes its messages as text, similar to HTTP, which leads to simple parsing and generation. H.323's complexity also stems from its use of several protocol components. There is no clean separation of these components; many services require interactions between several of them. SIP, on the other hand, uses a single request that contains all necessary information.
- Extensibility: With regard to H.323, adding new elements, features, and headers and managing compatibility across different versions is not easily done. A critical issue involves audio and video codecs; SIP uses the session description protocol (SDP) to convey the codecs supported by an end point in a session and is capable of working with any codec. H.323, however, can only work with a small number of standardized ITU speech and video codecs.
- Modularity: SIP is a reasonably modular protocol compared to H.323. It encompasses basic call signaling features such as user location and registration. Advanced features such as directory accesses, service discovery, session content description, and so forth are orthogonal and reside in separate protocols. Conversely, H.323 defines a vertically integrated protocol suite for a single application. The mix of services provided by the H.323 components is intertwined within the various subprotocols it contains, thereby making H.323 less modular.
- Scalability: H.323 is not very scalable because it was originally designed for use on a single LAN; as a result, it has certain problems in scaling (newer versions have suggested techniques to get around the problem). H.323 is still limited when performing loop detection in complex multidomain searches. It can be done statefully by storing messages, but this technique is not very scalable. SIP uses a loop detection method by checking the history of the message in the header fields, which can be done in a stateless manner.

Other Supporting Protocols

SIP can be used with other IETF protocols to build a complete multimedia architecture, though a discussion of such protocols is beyond the scope of this chapter. Some of these protocols include: resource reservation protocol (RSVP; Komolafe and Sventek 2005), real-time transport protocol (RTP) and real-time control transport protocol (RTCP; Ping, Wenjuan, and Haifeng 2005), real-time streaming protocol (RTSP; Schulzrinne, Rao, and Lanphier 1998), session announcement protocol (SAP), and session description protocol (SDP). RSVP is used for reserving resources, RTP/RTCP for transporting real-time data, RTSP for controlled delivery of streams, SAP for advertising multimedia sessions, and SDP for describing multimedia sessions. H.323 also works in conjunction with RTP and RTCP.

EMPIRICAL VOIP RESULTS

In this section, we present some empirical VoIP performance results of a simple VoIP system we have designed and implemented.

Experimental Setup

The implemented VoIP software (shown in Figure 13) allows the use of compressed or uncompressed voice on the Solaris 8 operating system running on Ultra SPARC workstations (each with an Ultra SPARC- II i440 MHz processor and 512 MB RAM). The machines were connected through an IP network, and VoIP connections were set up in a real networking environment.

On the sender's side, analog voice was given as input through a microphone. This was sampled at a rate of 8 KHz. Voice was then transmitted in UDP packets over the network, in both uncompressed (linear PCM) and compressed (G.711 U-law and G.726-7 ADPCM) formats. On the receiver's side, the voice samples were retrieved from the UDP packets, decompressed (in the case of compressed samples), and put in the playout buffer of the sound card, which was played back and listened to by the end user through a headset connected to the receiving host.

Measurement Procedures

We used two identical machines with the configurations described above for all experiments performed to eliminate variance in delays that may occur as a result of hardware differences. The implemented VoIP software was executed at the sender and receiver hosts. All real-time VoIP tests were conducted during daytime hours. The packet size used in the VoIP transmission tests was 200 bytes. Experimental tests measured the following metrics that affect the ultimate quality of voice delivered to the end user:

- End-to-end delay: For the VoIP system, this was calculated by the sum of all delays contributed by each individual component (recording, compression, transmission, decompression, and playback). Measuring the delay introduced by the different components in the end-to-end delay path identified components that introduce high delays and bottleneck areas. The network transmission delay was measured by sending a voice packet from the sender to the receiver and making the receiver echo it back to the sending host. Time was recorded before transmission and after reception at the sending host. The time difference yields the round-trip time (RTT), which—when halved—gives the one-way transmission delay.
- Interarrival packet delay: This was calculated in terms of differences in the arrival times of two consecutive packets at the receiver host. Each voice packet received at the receiver node was immediately time stamped (T_i); the difference between two consecutive time stamps of two consecutive packets gives the interarrival packet delay of $D_i = T_i - T_{(i-1)}$.
- Jitter: This was calculated as the difference between the average of the interarrival delay (D_{AVE}) and the individual interarrival delay (D_i).

End-to-End Delay Performance

Influence of Delay Components on End-to-End Performance

The total end-to-end delay between the source and destination consists of different delay components: recording, compression, transmission delay (includes packetization and network delays), decompression, and playback. As the results in Table 6 illustrate, ADPCM yields end-to-end delays close to uncompressed (PCM) voice; this is because the compression delay introduced by ADPCM is very small (approximately 0.13 to 0.23 milliseconds, depending on the packet size used). In addition, with ADPCM,

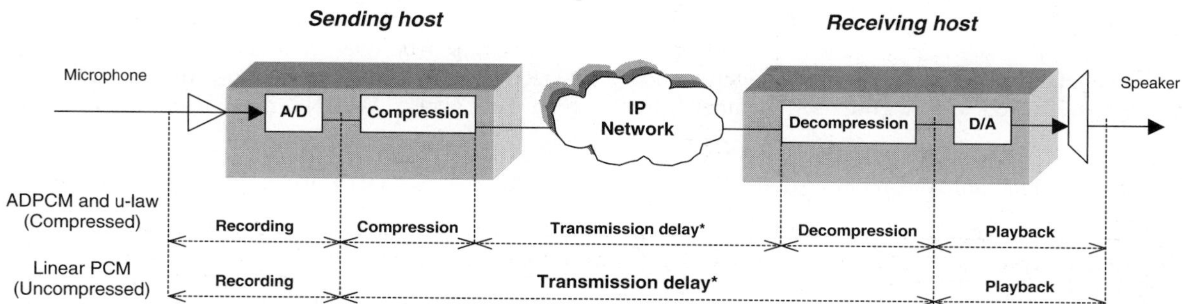

Figure 13: Delay components of our implemented VoIP system. The transmission delay includes the delay involved in transferring the packet between the voice application and the physical network (at sender and receiver) and the network delay

Table 6: A Breakdown of the End-to-End Delay Components with VoIP Packets of Size 200 Bytes[1]

Delay Component	Linear PCM	ADPCM	U-Law
	Time (milliseconds)	Time (milliseconds)	Time (milliseconds)
Recording	12.5	12.5	12.5
Compression	0 (0%)	0.20 (1.20%)	12.4 (42.5%)
Transmission	3.99	4.04	4.05
Decompression	0 (0%)	0.13 (0.76%)	0.08 (0.30%)
Playback	0.13	0.13	0.13
Total End-to-End Delay	16.62	17.0	29.16

[1] The transmission delay includes the delay involved in transferring the packet between the voice application and the physical network (at sender and receiver) and the network delay. The percentage of the delay overhead of the total end-to-end delay due to compression and decompression is also shown in parentheses.

the compression delays and decompression delays are almost the same, though the compression delays are slightly higher. Compression and decompression delays with ADPCM account for 1.2 percent and 0.76 percent of the end-to-end delay, respectively. However, with U-law compression, compression delays (42.5 percent of the end-to-end delay) were much higher than decompression delays (0.30 percent).

U-law not only gives higher compression-decompression delays but also yields a higher bit rate (64 kbits/s per voice channel) than the bit rate that results from ADPCM (32 kbits/s per voice channel). One may wonder why U-law should still be used at all if ADPCM is preferable in these two respects. However, although the voice quality of both is acceptable in these cases, in terms of output speech quality, MOS scores from previous experiments (Hagsand, Hanson, and Marsh 1999) found that a slightly better voice quality is obtained with U-law than with ADPCM; the compression-decompression process performed by ADPCM causes a slightly larger voice distortion than does U-law.

Interarrival Packet Delay

Figure 14 shows the variation of mean interarrival packet delays with packet sizes. The results show that linear PCM yields on average the lowest interarrival delay and U-law the highest. In contrast to the close end-to-end delay values obtained for PCM and ADPCM, the results for interarrival packet delays for ADPCM on average tend to be slightly higher than those with PCM.

Jitter

Table 7 shows the jitter obtained at the receiver host when voice is delivered to the end user. A mean jitter of approximately 7 to 9 milliseconds was obtained for ADPCM and μ-law (twice the mean jitter obtained with PCM).

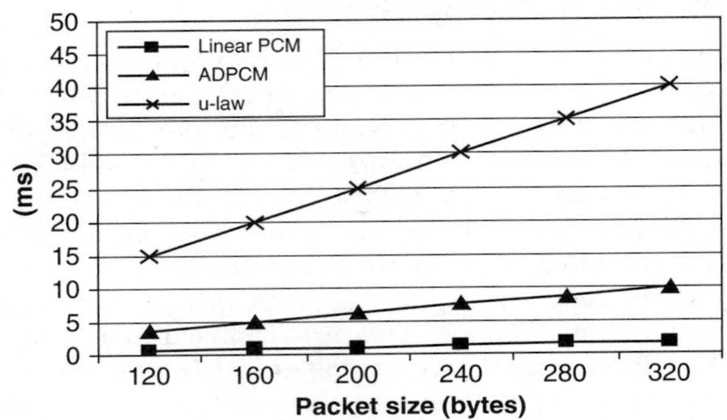

Figure 14: Variation of interarrival packet delay with voice packet size using linear PCM, ADPCM, and μ-law

VOIP OVER WIRELESS LOCAL AREA NETWORKS

Wireless Local Area Networks (WLANs) are frequently used as extensions to the wired Internet. Internet applications that have traditionally been deployed and executed on the wired infrastructure are increasingly being deployed over WLANs (IEEE 802.11a/b/g) as well because of WLANs' convenience in terms of mobility and wireless access. WLAN represents an important trend for

Table 7: Minimum, Maximum, and Mean Jitter Values at the Receiver Using a Voice Packet Size of 200 Bytes

CODEC Type	Minimum (milliseconds)	Maximum (milliseconds)	Mean (milliseconds)
PCM	0.08	20.3	3.4
ADPCM	2.9	32.7	8.2
μ-law	4.7	17.4	7.5

"last-mile" Internet access (Wang, Chang, and Li 2005) and will be expected to support popular Internet applications such as VoIP. In fact, the convergence of VoIP and WLAN technologies has led to the creation of an important Internet application called Voice over WLAN (VoWLAN). However, before a standard VoWLAN solution can be completely deployed, several technical issues including system capacity, voice quality, roaming latency, and security need to be addressed.

VoIP Transmission Schemes over WLANs

Different methods can be used for voice transmissions over a WLAN (Prasad 1999):

- Distributed coordination function (DCF): DCF is a contention-based access method. A station (client) that is ready to transmit a frame will sense the medium; if the medium is busy, it will wait for an additional predetermined time period of DCF interframe space (DIFS) length. During the contention window period, WLAN stations calculate the random back-off time by multiplying the time slot picked up in the window by a random number. A WLAN station ticks down the random back-off time, checking if the medium is busy. The station with the shortest time gains access to the medium first and transmits its frame. The collisions can now occur only when two or more stations select the same time slot to transmit. These stations will have to reenter the contention procedure to select new time slots to transmit the collided frames (Wang et al. 2005).
- Point coordination function (PCF): PCF is specified in the 802.11 standard as an optional protocol framing method. PCF was designed to accommodate those services requiring both voice and data transactions. The frame-slotting structure of PCF is viewed as a master-slave infrastructure network. The access point (AP) is the point coordinator (PC) for a given coverage area. The coverage area is commonly referred to as basic service area (BSA). The AP is the master controller and the stations are the slave radios in a BSA. The PC maps a prioritizing scheme and determines which radio has the right to transmit. The access priority given by the PCF is used to create the contention-free (CF) period. At the beginning of the CF period, the AP transmits a beacon frame that contains the maximum duration of the contention-free period (CFPMaxDuration). All stations receiving the beacon set the network allocation vector (NAV) to the maximum duration to lock out DCF-based access to the wireless medium. During this period, all slave radios are polled in a slotted fashion. At the beginning of the CF period a beacon is broadcast to the slave radios, assigning priorities. The radio with the highest priority is polled first. The slave radio responds with the data "piggyback" of a special acknowledgement (ACK) just after a short inter-frame space (SIFS) timeout. Each slave radio is polled in priority until the NAV and CF period has expired. The timing of the slave radios is synchronized by resetting the NAV timer located in the media access control (MAC) layer; this is set at the beginning of each CF interval. The CF interval polling process is repeated from then onward. All transmissions in the CF period are generally separated by the SIFS. To ensure that the point coordinator retains control of the medium, it may send to the next station on its polling list if no response is received after an elapsed PIFS (Prasad 1999).
- Priority queuing: Priority queuing is a scheme that gives voice packets priority over data packets within a system. The channel access process remains the same as in a WLAN except that the random back-off value is varied for voice and data transmissions.
- Blackburst: Blackburst is a multiple-access scheme for voice communication that can be overlaid on an IEEE 802.11 implementation. This scheme uses carrier sense capability, as in IEEE 802.11, and only requires the ability to jam the channel with pulses of energy of specified duration. Using this process the voice stations appear to access the channel in a time division multiplexed fashion, which is perturbed and repositioned by data packet transmission. Mixed populations of data and voice stations share a common radio channel in the Blackburst design. The data stations regulate their access to the channel according to the carrier sense multiple access with collision avoidance (CSMA/CA) protocol, and the voice stations follow a variation of CSMA/CA that will give them priority over data stations.

VoIP over WLAN Issues

Impact of WLANs on VoIP Transmissions

The convergence of voice and data networks enables new applications as well as saving benefits. However, there are several restraining factors that make the delivery of voice over WLANs particularly challenging. Some of those factors are as follows:

- Excessive latency, jitter, and degraded voice quality: One of the major differences between VoIP applications and data applications is the sensitivity to latency (transmission delays). Data applications (e.g., Web, e-mail, file transfers) are much less sensitive to latency than reduced throughput. A delay of seconds in receiving a data file is normally acceptable; however, a latency of tens of milliseconds in a voice call is very noticeable, annoying, and typically intolerable. As a comparison, TCP/IP has a maximum latency of 120 seconds (Wang et al. 2005), whereas the ITU G.114 recommends a maximum one-way latency of 150 milliseconds for voice calls.
- Another difference between VoIP applications and data applications is the sensitivity to jitter. Jitter refers to random variations in latency. Jitter in a voice call is readily audible as clicks, pauses, or unintelligible speech. Jitter buffers are used to overcome the effects by turning jitter into a longer constant latency; this is accomplished by buffering received voice packets and delaying their decoding. The jitter buffer adds delay according to the slowest packet (largest latency), creating substantial additional latency. Every transmitting and receiving node in the network, such as the AP in a WLAN, typically buffers incoming and outgoing packets. This causes latency and jitter. The overheads of roaming, security mechanisms, retransmissions, and data and voice convergence add latency and jitter in WLAN environments. These factors are discussed as follows.

- Poor coverage: One of the advantages of VoIP over WLANs is that no wiring is required, thereby providing the freedom of mobility. To enable callers to move around the enterprise freely, however, their connections must be maintained without interruption. That is, to have true mobility, coverage must be ubiquitous and continuous throughout the enterprise. Traditional topologies based on cell planning cannot provide continuous coverage at the maximum data rate. The limited numbers of channels result in limited overlap between cells, creating shadows, or "black holes" (areas of poor or no coverage). In addition, interference and obstructions make it difficult to provide uninterrupted voice service even in a single cell.
- Roaming latency and interruptions in voice service: Traditional WLAN topology uses cell planning to achieve coverage. As mobile users move from one cell to another, handoffs between access points (also known as inter-AP handoffs) are required. As the cell size decreases to provide capacity, inter-AP handoffs occur more frequently. A handoff requires several steps, including AP discovery, re-association, security measures, and higher-level protocol exchanges. AP discovery typically takes 150–400 milliseconds and introduces 40–100 milliseconds of jitter in 802.11b and 802.11g, which exceeds acceptable voice latency. AP discovery latency and jitter in 802.11a or in multimode networks may be twice as high or more (Wang et al. 2005).

A reassociation consists of several steps, including station-to-AP handshake, inter-AP protocol, inter-access point protocol (IAPP) exchanges, and bridge notification. Each step introduces additional latency and jitter, and security measures introduce even more. Higher-level protocol exchanges can also introduce several seconds of latency and result in temporary disruption of service. The exact amount of latency depends on network configuration.

Traditional topologies place the burden of inter-AP handoffs on the client. Clients who are unaware of the network topology frequently make the wrong choices. A WLAN client requires a long time to select an AP and tends to remain with an AP, even if it is far away. Because the handoff is controlled by the client, new solutions that provide AP topology awareness only marginally improve the described latency and jitter. Slow handoffs, or handing off to a nonoptimal AP, result in rate adaptation, which introduces more latency and jitter, reduces capacity, and increases power consumption. Packets buffered in the previous access point may be dropped, degrading the voice quality.

Recent research efforts have begun to focus on reducing inter-access point handoff delays. In particular, IEEE has finalized the IAPP for inter-access point communication. The IAPP, as standardized in IEEE standard 802.11f (2003), enables (fast) link layer reassociation at a new access point in the same hotspot. On the network layer, similar efforts are ongoing in the IETF Seamoby group, which defines different protocols to reduce network discovery and reconfiguration delays.

Security Issues for VoIP over WLANs

Wired equivalent privacy (WEP; Majistor 2003), the original security protocol for 802.11 wireless networks, is now considered flawed by the industry. The IEEE 802.11i standard introduced newer security standards for WLANs. The interim WiFi protected access (WPA; Majistor 2003) includes temporal key integrity protocol (TKIP), message integrity checks (MIC), and strong authentication through the extensible authentication protocol (EAP), thereby addressing several of the security problems of WEP. Although WPA is necessary to provide adequate security, it introduces an additional overhead for each inter-AP handoff. WPA requires strong authentication mechanisms, along with exchange of pair-wise (AP to station) keys. These processes typically introduce a latency of 500–1500 milliseconds (Wang et al. 2005), potentially resulting in disrupted services. Until better solutions are introduced, voice over WLAN deployments are typically without any security at all. This lack of VoIP security may be responsible for the reluctance of VoIP adoption for an enterprise deployment.

Retransmissions and Dropped Packets over WLANs

Data applications do not tolerate dropped packets; TCP/IP retransmits erroneous or missing packets to avoid data corruption. However, due to TCP/IP's slow start mechanisms, a drop rate of 1 percent or above will result in a severe degradation of throughput. Unlike data, voice can tolerate some packet dropping, typically around 4 to 5 percent (Prasad 1999), as long as the dropped packets are not consecutive. The wireless medium can be quite unreliable; as a result, the WLAN standard includes a retransmission mechanism to avoid dropped packets. Unfortunately, although this is a good solution for data, it results in a significant amount of jitter and latency for voice applications that require timely arrival of packets. To minimize retransmissions in voice applications, a low drop rate is required. This is impossible using traditional network topologies: large distances from APs, temporary and random interference, obstructions, and co-channel interference caused by neighboring cells all cause poor reception of packets with these topologies. Radio frequency (RF) technologies at neighboring organizations or sites may add another source of interference, which may also lead to poor packet reception. Without retransmissions, a large drop rate and consecutive dropped packets occur. With retransmissions, significant latency and jitter are experienced, and the capacity is greatly reduced. In either case, voice quality can be severely affected and require solutions that address the issues mentioned previously.

Low Capacity, Reduced Number of VoIP Calls

Although the major requirements for voice are low latency and jitter, the need for adequate capacity is also important. Capacity determines the number of concurrent calls that can be supported. Given that VoIP typically uses small packets with large overheads, the usual methods of measuring network capacity do not apply to voice. A more relevant measure of capacity for voice applications is the number of packets per second (PPS) that can be transferred. Several factors limit the PPS over a WLAN, the most important of which are contention windows, acknowledgment packets, retransmissions, and rate adaptation. The proposed IEEE 802.11e standard reintroduces contention-free access (scheduled access), termed the hybrid coordination function (HCF). Similar to the original 802.11 PCF, HCF replaces client competition for airtime with centralized client polling. By avoiding contention, contention-free access methods typically utilize 75 percent of the maximum bandwidth (compared with 37 percent for contention-based access methods; Wang et al. 2005). Contention-free access provides a higher PPS, resulting in an increased number of voice calls that can be supported. Unfortunately, PCF was never supported by mobile clients, and client support for HCF is not yet available. Even if scheduled access will be supported (which is not yet certain), multiple co-channel APs are bound to cause interference, making it difficult to use scheduled access in cell-planning–based topologies. Acknowledgement packets are one the most significant causes of PPS reduction for voice over WLAN applications, and can account for 30 to 40 percent of the airtime used in a single VoIP packet transfer (Wang et al. 2005). If retransmissions can be avoided and a low drop rate maintained, the need for ACK packets can be eliminated. Unfortunately, retransmissions and the resulting lower-network PPS are unavoidable in traditional topologies. All the restrictions mentioned earlier limit the number of voice calls that can be simultaneously supported over an IEEE 802.11b network (typically five to seven voice calls; Wang et al. 2005).

Quality of Service for Voice and Data Convergence

Converged voice and data networks pose additional challenges to the deployment of voice over WLANs. Although voice applications consume low bandwidth per call, they do require very low latency and jitter. When the network load is high, data packets (typically much larger than voice packets) may use up a significantly high amount of airtime, causing sharp increases in latency and jitter for the voice packets. Typical deployments will prefer good voice quality even if it means lower bandwidth for data. The 802.11e task group has proposed QoS extensions to the 802.11 standard to provide a mechanism for giving higher priority to voice packets over the shared wireless medium. Until the standard is ratified, a subset of the standard, WiFi multimedia (WMM), is being tested. The proposed mechanisms are required in converged voice and data networks to provide acceptable voice quality. However, for such mechanisms to be truly effective, all clients in the WLAN need to support these extensions.

IEEE 802.11e

IEEE 802.11e (2006), as of late 2005, has been approved as a standard that defines a set of QoS enhancements for LAN applications, in particular the 802.11 WiFi standard. The standard is considered of critical importance for delay-sensitive applications, including voice over wireless IP (VoWIP) and streaming multimedia. The protocol enhances the IEEE 802.11 MAC layer.

The 802.11e enhances the DCF and PCF through a new coordination function: the HCF. Within the HCF are two methods of channel access similar to those defined in the legacy 802.11 MAC: HCF controlled channel access (HCCA) and enhanced DCF channel access (EDCA). Both EDCA and HCCA define traffic classes (TCs). For example, e-mails could be assigned to a low-priority class, and VoWIP could be assigned to a high-priority class.

- EDCA: High-priority traffic has a better chance of being sent than low priority traffic; a station with high-priority traffic waits a little less time before it sends its packet, on average, than a station with low-priority traffic. In addition, each priority level is assigned a transmit opportunity (TXOP), a window of time that a given station (STA) or AP has to send as many frames as possible. This helps minimize the problem of low-rate stations gaining an inordinate amount of channel time in the legacy 802.11 DCF MAC. WMM-certified APs must be enabled for EDCA and TXOP. All other enhancements of the 802.11e amendment are optional.
- HCCA: HCCA is similar to PCF: the interval between two beacon frames is divided into two periods, the CFP and the CP. During the CFP, the hybrid coordinator (HC)—which is also the AP—controls the access to the medium. During the CP, all stations function in EDCA. The main difference with PCF is that TCs are defined; moreover, the HC can coordinate the traffic in any fashion it chooses, not just round robin. Stations provide information about the lengths of their queues for each TC. The HC can use this information to award priority to one station over another. Another difference is that stations are given a TXOP: they may send multiple packets in a row for a given time period selected by the HC. During the CP, the HC allows stations to send data by sending CF-poll frames.

HCCA is generally considered the most advanced (and complex) coordination function. With the HCCA, QoS can be configured with great precision. QoS-enabled stations have the ability to request specific transmission parameters (e.g., data rate, jitter, etc.), which should allow advanced applications like VoIP and video streaming to work more effectively on a WiFi network.

HCCA support is not mandatory for 802.11e APs. In fact, few (if any) APs currently available are enabled for HCCA. The WiFi Alliance has a forthcoming certification (WMM scheduled cccess) that will allow network integrators to easily distinguish APs that allow HCCA.

Other 802.11e Specifications

In addition to HCCA, EDCA, and TXOP, 802.11e specifies additional optional protocols for enhanced 802.11 MAC layer QoS:

- Automatic power save delivery (APSD): A more efficient power management method than legacy 802.11 power save polling. Most newer 802.11 STAs already support a power management mechanism similar to APSD.
- APSD is very useful for a VoIP phone because data rates are roughly the same in both directions. Whenever voice data are sent to the access point, the access point is triggered to send the buffered voice data in the other direction. The voice over IP phone then enters a doze state until the next voice data have to be sent to the access point.
- Block acknowledgements (BAs): Allow an entire TXOP to be acknowledged in a single frame. This provides lower protocol overheads when longer TXOPs are specified.

- NoAck: In QoS mode, service classes for outgoing frames can have two values: QosAck and QosNoAck. Frames with QosNoAck are not acknowledged, which avoids retransmissions of highly time-critical data.
- Direct link setup (DLS): Allows direct STA-to-STA frame transfer within a BSS. This is designed for consumer use, where STA-to-STA transfer is more frequent.

Limitations of IEEE 802.11 in Supporting Voice

Recent research has shown that neither DCF nor EDCA is effective or efficient in supporting delay-sensitive voice traffic. Their contention-based natures and binary exponential back-off mechanisms cannot guarantee that a voice packet will be successfully delivered within the required delay bound. In addition, the time to transmit the payload of a voice packet is only a very small portion of the total time to transmit the packet, as a result of overheads such as the RTP/UDP/IP headers, MAC header, and physical (PHY) preamble. Subsequently, the capacity to accommodate voice traffic in DCF or EDCA is very limited. Active research efforts are focusing on enhancing the performance of voice services using IEEE 802.11e (Wang, Jiang, and Zhuang 2006).

CONCLUSION

VoIP is one of the fastest growing Internet applications today. Given the significant cost savings and benefits that can be achieved with VoIP, interest in this technology continues to grow. Many emerging VoIP solutions and products are exploiting packet-switched networks of the Internet to carry voice traffic using IP. This chapter has presented an overview of VoIP technology and some of its recent growth trends, and has discussed fundamental concepts of VoIP as well as the hardware, software, and protocol support required to deploy it. However, several issues still need to be resolved before VoIP becomes truly ubiquitous. One of these issues, which recently has garnered a lot of attention, is VoIP over WLANs. The major obstacles that can degrade VoIP performance over WLANs—and make VoIP unusable because of significant delay, jitter, or packet loss—have been introduced. Innovative techniques need to be investigated that will efficiently support VoIP transmissions over WLANs. Only with the advent of such techniques will a true end-to-end VoIP solution (spanning both wired and wireless networks) become feasible and pave the way for wide deployments of VoIP over both wired and wireless IP-based infrastructures.

ACKNOWLEDGMENT

This work was supported by grants from Sun Microsystems (Palo Alto) (EDUD-7824-000145-US), Microsoft Corporation (Seattle), and Ixia Corporation (Calabasas). We thank the anonymous reviewers for their comments and suggestions, which helped to improve the quality of this chapter. We would also like to thank the following colleagues for their help and support during the preparation of this article: Joe Oravec, Cassandra Daugherty, Mustafa Siddiqui, Scott Fowler, Aarti Kumar, and Zhaoming Zhu. We express our sincere gratitude to the editor-in-chief, Hossein Bidgoli, for his patience, encouragement, and kind support throughout the preparation of this chapter.

GLOSSARY

Codec: An acronym for coder-decoder. A codec performs conversions between analog voice and the compressed digital representation of the voice. Coding is done at the entry point to a packet network, and decoding is done at the exit point of the packet network.

Compression: The reduction in size of data in order to save space or transmission time.

H.323: A standard approved by the International Telecommunications Union (ITU) in 1996 to promote compatibility in videoconference transmissions over IP networks.

Jitter: In VoIP, the variation in the time between packets arriving; caused by network congestion, timing drift, or route changes.

Latency: A synonym for *delay*; is an expression of how much time it takes for a packet of data to get from one designated point to another. In some cases, latency is measured by sending a packet that is returned to the sender; the round-trip time is considered the latency.

Mean Opinion Score (MOS): In voice communications, particularly Internet telephony, this provides a numerical measure of the quality of human speech at the destination end of the circuit. The scheme uses subjective tests (opinionated scores) that are mathematically averaged to obtain a quantitative indicator of the system performance.

Public Switched Telephone Network (PSTN): The world's collection of interconnected voice-oriented public telephone networks, both commercial and government owned; also referred to as the plain old telephone service (POTS).

Quality of Service (QoS): On the Internet and in other networks, this is the idea that transmission rates, error rates, and other characteristics can be measured, improved, and, to some extent, guaranteed in advance. QoS is of particular concern with regard to the continuous transmission of high-bandwidth video and delay-sensitive multimedia information.

Session Initiation Protocol (SIP): An Internet Engineering Task Force (IETF) standard protocol for initiating an interactive user session that involves multimedia elements such as video, voice, chat, gaming, and virtual reality.

VoIP (Voice over IP): An IP telephony term for a set of facilities used to manage the delivery of voice information over the Internet. VoIP involves sending voice information in digital form in discrete packets rather than using the traditional circuit-committed protocols of the public switched telephone network (PSTN).

VoWLAN (Voice over WLAN): A method for sending voice information in digital form over a wireless broadband network. Essentially, VoWLAN is VoIP delivered via wireless technologies.

Wired Equivalent Privacy (WEP): A security protocol, specified in the IEEE wireless fidelity (WiFi) standard, 802.11b, that is designed to provide a wireless local area network (WLAN) with a level of security and privacy comparable to what is usually expected of a wired local area network (LAN).

CROSS REFERENCES

See *Speech and Audio Compression*; *Voice over MPLS and VoIP over MPLS*; *Wireless LANs (WLANs)*.

REFERENCES

Asia Networking/Telecom. 2006. 2006 Research. *In-Stat*. http://www.instat.com/catalog/ncatalogue.asp?ID=238&year=2006#IN0502395ANT (accessed June 22, 2006).

CCITT. 1972. Recommendation G.711. *Pulse code modulation (PCM) of voice frequencies*. Geneva: International Telecommunications Union.

eMarketer, Inc. 2005. VoIP: Spending and trends. http://www.emarketer.com/Report.aspx?voip_jun05 (accessed June 22, 2006).

Glasmann, J., and W. Kellerer. 2001. Service development and deployment in H.323 and SIP. In *Proceedings of Sixth IEEE Symposium on Computers and Communications, Tunisia, July*, pp. 378–385.

Goode, B. 2002. Voice over Internet protocol. In *Proceedings of the IEEE*, September, pp. 1495–1517.

Hagsand, O., K. Hanson, and I. Marsh. 1999. Measuring Internet telephony quality: Where are we today? In *Proceedings of IEEE GLOBECOM*, pp. 838–1842.

Handley, M., H. Schulzrinne, E. Schooler, and J. Rosenberg. 1999. SIP: Session initiation protocol. In *IETF RFC 2543*, March.

Huh, M., W. Hyun, S. Kang, & D. Kim. 2002. Call management mechanism for Internet phone services based on SIP. In *Proceedings of the Fifth International Conference on High Speed Networks and Multimedia Communication*, pp. 66–70.

Hyun, W., M. Huh, & S. Kang, 2002. An implementation of SIP servers for Internet telephony. In *Proceedings of the Fifth International Conference on High Speed Networks and Multimedia Communication*, pp. 61–65.

IEEE 802.11e. 2006. *Wikipedia*. http://en.wikipedia.org/wiki/802.11e (accessed June 22, 2006).

IEEE. 2003. IEEE trial-use recommended practice for multivendor access point interoperability via an inter-access point protocol across distribution systems supporting IEEE 802.11 operation. *IEEE Computer Society Journal*, pp. 1–67.

ITU-T. 1998. Recommendation P.861. *Objective quality measurement of telephone-band speech codecs*, February.

Kampichler, K., and K. Goeschka. 2001. Plain end-to-end measurement for local area network voice transmission feasibility. In *Proceedings of the Ninth International Symposium on Modeling, Analysis, and Simulation of Computer and Telecommunication Systems*, Cincinnati, Ohio, August, pp. 235–240.

Komolafe, O., and J. Sventek. 2005. RSVP performance evaluation using multiobjective evolutionary optimization. In *Proceedings of the Twenty-Fourth IEEE Annual Joint Conference of the IEEE Computer and Communications*, Miami, Florida, March, pp. 2447–2457.

Lakaniemi, A., J. Rosti, and V. Raisanen. 2001. Subjective VoIP speech quality evaluation based on network measurements. *IEEE Communications* 3: 748–752.

Mahadevan, L., and M. Sivalingam. 1999. Quality of service architectures for wireless networks: IntServ and DiffServ models. In *Proceedings of the Fourth International Symposium on Parallel Architectures, Algorithms, and Networks*, Perth, Australia, June, pp. 420–425.

Majistor, F. 2003. WLAN security threats and solutions. In *Proceedings of the Twenty-Eighth Annual IEEE International Conference on Local Computer Networks*, October, p. 650.

Ping, L., L. Wenjuan, and W. Haifeng. 2005. The characteristics of the transmission delay via Internet and analysis of the real-time protocol design. In *Proceedings of the IEEE Conference on Networking, Sensing, and Control*, Tucson, Arizona, March, pp. 1005–1008.

Prasad, A. 1999. Performance comparison of voice over IEEE 802.11 schemes. In *Proceedings of IEEE VTC*, Texas, September, pp. 2636–40.

Rosenberg, J., and H. Schulzrinne. 2000. Models for multiparty conferencing in SIP. Internet Draft, IETF, November.

Rouhana, N., and E. Horlait. 2000. Differentiated services and integrated services use of MPLS. In *Proceedings of the Fourth IEEE Symposium on Computers and Communications*, Red Sea, Egypt, July, pp. 194–199.

Schulzrinne, H., and J. Rosenberg, J. 1998. A comparison of SIP and H.323 for Internet telephony. In *Proceedings of International Workshop on Network and Operating System Support for Digital Audio and Video (NOSSDAV)*, Cambridge, England, July.

Schulzrinne, H., A. Rao, and R. Lanphier. 1998. RFC 2326, Real-time streaming protocol (RTSP), April.

Tripos Corporation. 2005. Voice over Internet protocol. http://www.tripos.com.au/newsletter_March05.html (accessed June 22, 2006).

Udani, S., and P. Mehta. 2001. *Overview of VoIP*. Report MS-CIS-01-31, Department of Computer Information Science, University of Pennsylvania, February.

Varshney, U., A. Snow, M. McGivern, and C. Howard. 2002. Voice over IP. *Communications of the ACM* 45(1): 89–96.

Wang P., H. Jiang, and W. Zhuang. 2006. IEEE 802.11e enhancements for voice service. *IEEE Wireless Communications* 13(1): 30–35.

Wang, W., S. Chang, and V. Li. 2005. Solutions to performance problems in VoIP over 802.11 wireless LAN. *IEEE Transactions on Vehicular Technology* 54(1): 366–84.

Wang, Y., X. Zhang, and W. Li. 2000. Audio multimedia conferencing system based on the technology of speech recognition. In *Proceedings of IEEE Asia-Pacific Conference on Circuits and Systems*, Tianjin, China, December, pp. 771–774.

Wright, D. 2001. *Voice over packet networks*. West Sussex, UK: Wiley.

Zou, H., K. Wang, W. Mao, B. Wang, S. Focant, K. Handekyn, D. Chantrain, and N. Marly. 2000. Prototyping SIP-based VoIP services in Java. In *Proceedings of WCC-ICCT International Conference on Communication Technology*, pp. 1395–99.

Signaling Approaches

Edmundo Monteiro, Fernando Boavida, Marilia Curado,
and Luis Cordeiro, *University of Coimbra, Portugal*

INTRODUCTION

As Internet Protocol (IP) networking evolves to support all kinds of applications, signaling becomes an essential part of networks and applications, providing the means for many functions, including resource management and control, security support, service announcement and initiation, and capabilities negotiation. This chapter addresses the main signaling approaches in use or being proposed for the current, highly heterogeneous Internet. Signaling in the Internet is quite different from the traditional networks, in which a separate path was used for management and signaling. IP-based networks utilize the data, management, and control planes over a single channel.

OBJECTIVES AND ORGANIZATION

The Objectives of Signaling

Signaling can be defined as the exchange of data needed among network elements and end systems to support the setup, maintenance, and release of the network services. In IP based networks, signaling is needed at the application, transport, and network levels. At the application layer, signaling is needed to manage application sessions (e.g., VoIP or videoconferencing session) and to negotiate service parameters between the applications. At the transport level, signaling is needed to set up and tear down connections between the end systems, and to perform flow, congestion, error, and synchronization control in the active connections. Signaling also is needed at the network level to support mobility or for dynamic discrimination of flows (or flow aggregates) to give these flows a treatment different from the normal flows (e.g., different route, priority, delay, or security treatment).

Signaling always has been a controversial issue when the Internet is concerned. Ideally, signaling on the Internet should be reduced to a minimum and should be performed by end-systems, to keep the network as simple as possible. Reality has shown that this is not possible.

Although the current Internet is still data-driven—as opposed to the signaling-driven nature of, for instance, the telephone network—signaling is present in virtually all its components, for network operations support, quality of service support, management, and application/user support.

IP companion protocols such as ICMP (Internet Control Message Protocol), ARP (Address Resolution Protocol) and DHCP (Dynamic Host Configuration Protocol) perform network operation signaling. Routing protocols such as OSPF (Open Shortest Path First) and BGP (Border Gateway Protocol) can carry signaling information used for network signaling operations. RSVP (Resource Reservation Protocol), MPLS (Multi-Protocol Label Switching) signaling extensions and NSIS (Next Steps in Signaling) are examples of signaling protocols that support quality of service and resource control. SNMP (Simple Network Management Protocol) and COPS (Common Open Policy Service) are examples of management protocols.

SIP (Session Initiation Protocol) and H.323 are examples of application/user support signaling protocols. Session and transport protocols such as TCP (Transmission Control Protocol), RTSP (Real Time Streaming Protocol), and RTCP (Real Time Control Protocol) also include signaling mechanisms for application/user support, to ensure end-to-end connectivity with flow, error, and synchronization control.

All of the above protocols and mechanisms have the common objective of providing some form of control and support of user traffic and communication services. Thus, they contribute to the good operation of the network.

Signaling mechanisms can be on-path or off-path. When signaling messages follow the same path as data messages, it is said that on-path signaling is being performed (also mentioned as path-coupled or in-band signaling). Sometimes, however, entities that are not on the data path have to be signaled. Signaling protocols that allow the signaling of entities that are not on the data path are called off-path signaling protocols (also mentioned as path-decoupled or out-band signaling). Hybrid signaling solutions using on-path signaling inside each domain and off-path signaling between domains also are possible. The EuQoS project signaling approach described later in this chapter is an example of hybrid signaling.

Signaling also can be explicit or implicit. Explicit signaling is achieved through explicit messages that can be carried together with user data, in specific packet fields, as in TCP header fields, or in separate signaling packets, as in RSVP and NSIS. Implicit signaling information can be extracted from the normal application flow to trigger reservation mechanisms in network devices. Some signaling solutions, such as the EuQoS project approach, combine implicit signaling near the end-systems (to reduce the complexity of end-systems) and explicit signaling inside the network.

Signaling is closely related to the amount of state information stored in the network elements. State information can be stored per flow or per flow aggregates. State information can be maintained until explicitly released (hard-state) or expire after a given time limit if not refreshed before (soft-state). If state information is needed per flow, signaling also has to be performed on a per-flow basis; otherwise signaling is needed only to manage the flow aggregates. In soft-state approaches, signaling has to be issued periodically to refresh the state information. In hard-state approaches signaling is needed only for the establishment and release of state information.

The definition of a signaling scheme is a trade-off between the application needs and the complexity introduced in the network. Best effort applications need basic signaling mechanisms for flow, error, and congestion control like the ones included in TCP. Multimedia applications, with quality of service requirements, can operate smoothly if the network is over-provisioned. In a limited resource environment they will require per flow or aggregated signaling to support resource reservation and traffic differentiation mechanisms. Thus, there is also a trade-off between the amount of signaling and network resources.

Overall, the definition of the signaling mechanisms for the support of real-time applications over the global Internet with quality and security is still an open issue. The solution is expected to emerge from the signaling proposals being discussed and standardized at the Internet Engineering Task Force (IETF) and considering the settlement of the above trade-offs.

This chapter describes the main signaling protocols and mechanisms for IP networks. The focus is on signaling protocols for network operation and quality of service support. Signaling mechanisms embedded in routing and transport protocols will be mentioned only briefly because these protocols are covered in specific chapters in this book. For each signaling protocol described, the main advantages, limitations, and deployment trade-offs are discussed.

Organization of the Chapter

The main on-path and off-path signaling protocols for IP networks are presented in this chapter. The first section is dedicated to the Resource Reservation Protocol (RSVP), an important signaling protocol for quality-of-service provision in Integrated Services environments. This protocol has inspired the emerging IETF's Next Steps In Signaling (NSIS) framework, which is addressed in the second section of the chapter. The third section is devoted to the two main signaling protocols for voice, video and multimedia support: SIP and H.323.

Other relevant signaling protocols and approaches are presented later of which Common Open Policy Service (COPS) and Multi-Protocol Label Switching (MPLS) signaling extension are the most important. The chapter ends with a brief presentation of a case study—the EuQoS project—in which various signaling protocols and approaches are combined to provide end-to-end quality of service over heterogeneous networks.

RESOURCE RESERVATION PROTOCOL

Background

Resource reservation is a preventive way to provide quality-of-service guarantees. By reserving resources along a given path, the flows are protected from congestion situations and get the contractually agreed service level no matter what the network usage level is. This is good, of course, from the user perspective but may be not as good from the network operator perspective, as resources are reserved and cannot be used by other flows even if the respective flows are not using them.

The Resource Reservation Protocol (RSVP) originally was defined in RFC 2205 (Braden et al. 1997), later updated by RFC 2750 (Herzog 2000), and provides ways to perform resource reservation in Internet-like environments. The basic idea behind RSVP is that receivers identify their quality of service needs and send signaling messages upstream (i.e., toward the sources) that will be used by routers along the path to reserve the necessary resources. RSVP was designed to overcome the limitations of the Internet Stream Protocol Version 2, ST2 (Delgrossi and Berger 1995).

RSVP is the signaling protocol used by the Integrated Services (IntServ) QoS architecture, as specified in RFC 2210 (Wroclawski 1997), for the support of multiple traffic types, including data traffic, audio traffic, and video traffic. In IntServ, resources are reserved at network elements on an individual flow basis, through the use of RSVP. This

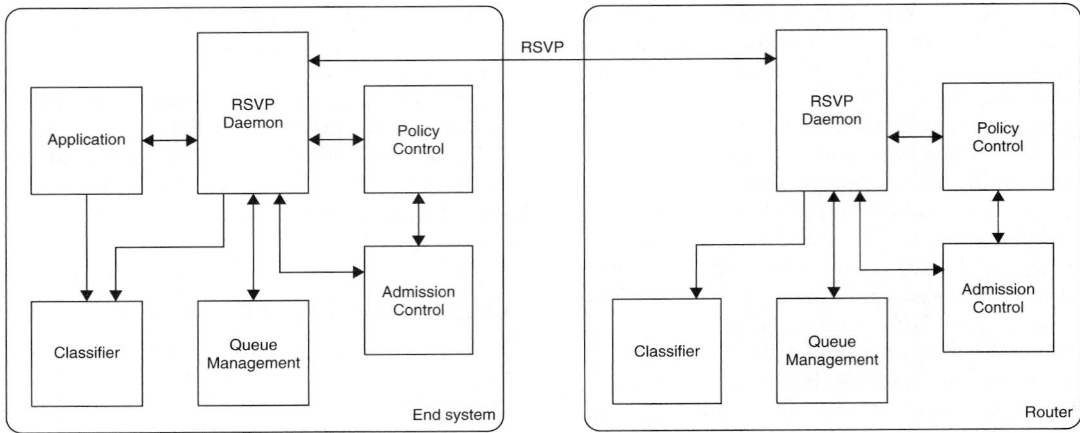

Figure 1: IntServ architecture

approach supports what is called the fine-grained QoS provision, as routers must be aware of the QoS needs of each of the existing flows. With this approach, the IntServ architecture provides three classes of service: best effort (the Internet's default service), controlled load (similar to best effort in an uncongested network), and guaranteed service (assured bandwidth, no losses, and bounded delay service).

In addition to signaling, which is based on RSVP, IntServ requires a set of other supporting functions to provide quality-of-service guarantees—namely, policing, shaping, admission control, packet classification, and queue management. Figure 1 presents the general IntServ architecture.

Although resource reservation has clear advantages in some cases, it is not feasible in a large network or service provider environment because of the high signaling overhead. RSVP messages pertain to individual flows and must be refreshed periodically. This leads to scalability problems and precludes the use of IntServ in core networks, where the number of flows may be extremely high.

Main Characteristics of RSVP

RSVP was designed to support both unicast and multicast operation—meaning that it supports reservations for unicast and multicast flows. Resources are reserved based on the individual requirements of multicast members. In addition, RSVP dynamically adapts itself to changing group membership and to changing routes.

RSVP has a simple mode of operation. Reservations are made for unidirectional data flows. Bidirectional flows require two separate reservations. This is tied to the fact that resource reservations are receiver-initiated, which, in turn, results from the fact that different members (receivers) of a multicast group may have different QoS requirements and, thus, may require dissimilar resources.

Another important characteristic of RSVP is that it is a soft-state protocol. IP is a stateless, connectionless-oriented protocol. Thus, one of the major concerns of the RSVP developers was to avoid connection-oriented operation. The way to do this was to cause reservations (i.e., state kept in the routers) to expire unless receivers were to regularly refresh them. This has some drawbacks and some advantages. On one hand, it leads to higher communication overhead, as reservation messages continue to be generated and sent over the network. On the other hand, if a receiver leaves a multicast group or if a route changes, the reservations for the unused route expire, without the need for any further action.

A key aspect of RSVP is the aggregation of reservation requests. As reservation requests flow from receivers to sources, routers along the way can aggregate resource requests (e.g., bandwidth requests) whenever possible, thereby optimizing the use of Internet resources. There are several forms of aggregating reservation requests for the same multicast group, depending on the reservation style used by the receivers. This will be explained later in this chapter. Figure 2 illustrates the aggregation of reservation requests for a given multicast group. In this figure, requests from Hosts 1 and 2 are merged at Router 3. This merged reservation request, in turn, is merged with that from Host 3 at Router 1.

RSVP Data Flows

RSVP data flows are called sessions. A session is characterized by the session identification, a flow specification, and a filter specification. The session identification is composed of the destination IP address (unicast or multicast), the IP user-protocol identifier (e.g., TCP, UDP), and the destination port. The flow specification, FlowSpec, determines the desired quality of service and is composed of the following sub-parameters: Service class, which identifies the requested type of service; Reservation specification, Rspec, which defines the desired QoS; and Traffic specification, Tspec, which describes the data flow. The filter specification, FilterSpec, determines the packets the reservation applies to. The FilterSpec parameters consist of the source address and/or the TCP/UDP source port.

Figure 3 illustrates the handling of packets in a session. First the FilterSpec is checked. On the one hand, the packets that do not pass the filter get a best-effort service. On the other hand, the packets that pass the filter specification get the service determined by the flow specification.

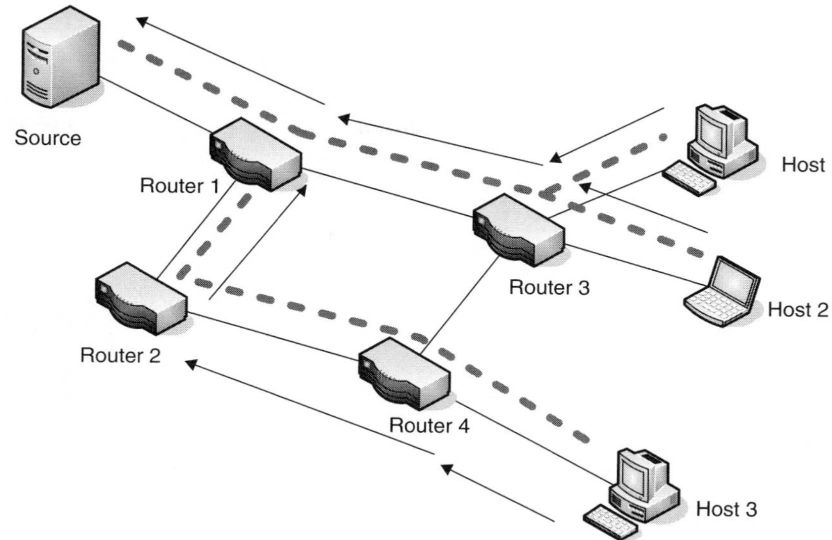

Figure 2: Aggregation of reservation requests

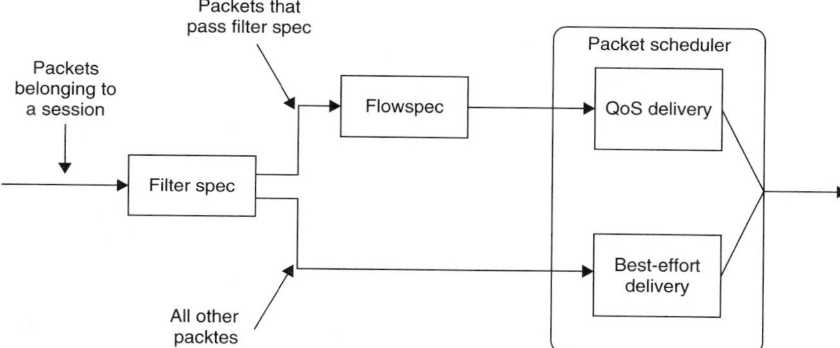

Figure 3: Handling of packets in an RSVP session

RSVP Protocol Operation

The RSVP protocol relies on two basic message types: RESV and PATH. RESV messages are originated by unicast or multicast group receivers requesting resource reservation for packet flows from one or more sources. These messages propagate upstream through the distribution tree, and the respective resource requests can be merged when appropriate at each node (router) along the way. RESV messages create soft states within the routers of the distribution tree, and they must be reissued periodically to maintain the resource reservation.

PATH messages are generated by sources to announce themselves as multicast group sources. These messages are transmitted downstream through the distribution tree to all multicast destinations. Each router along the way creates a path state that indicates the reverse hop to be used for the corresponding source. Similarly, each destination host creates a path state that indicates the reverse hop to be used for the corresponding source. This path state allows hosts and routers to route RESV messages.

The RSVP signaling protocol basic operation sequence can be described as follows:

1. A receiver joins a multicast group, by using the general group management mechanism, i.e., by sending an IGMP Join message to a multicast router in its network.
2. A source issues a PATH message to the multicast group.
3. The receiver receives the PATH message identifying the source.
4. The receiver uses the reverse path information to send RESV messages, specifying the desired QoS.
5. The RESV message propagates upstream, is merged with other RESV messages from other receivers, and is delivered to the source.
6. The source starts sending data packets.
7. The receiver starts receiving data packets.

This basic operation is illustrated in Figure 4.

Other RSVP messages include: teardown, error, and confirmation messages. Teardown messages remove the path and reservation state without waiting for the cleanup timeout period. These messages can be generated by a receiver, or an intermediate router as the result of a state timeout. Reservation-request teardown messages delete the reservation state, travel upstream toward all senders from the point of teardown initiation, and are routed like reservation-request messages. To add reliability to the requests, RSVP

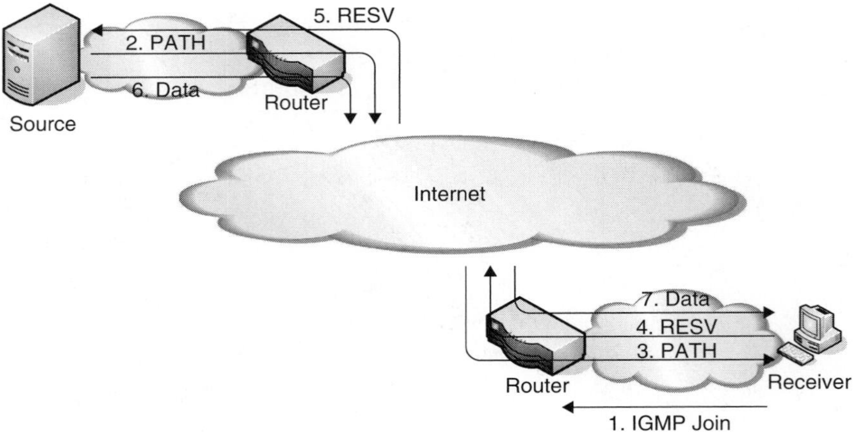

Figure 4: RSVP protocol operation sequence

Table 1: RSVP reservation styles

	Distinct Reservation Attribute	Shared Reservation Attribute
Explicit Sender Selection	Fixed-Filter (FF)	Shared-Explicit (SE)
Wild-card Sender Selection	---	Wild-card Filter (WF)

contains three error and confirmation messages: path-error messages, reservation-request error messages, and reservation-request acknowledgment messages.

Reservation Styles

Reservation styles determine the way in which resource requirements are aggregated at each router. The three reservation styles are determined by a combination of two options: the reservation attribute and the sender selection. The former can specify a distinct reservation for each sender or, alternatively, a shared reservation applicable to groups of senders. The latter can specify an explicit list of sources or all sources (wild-card). The combinations that lead to the three reservation styles—wild-card filter (WF), shared-explicit (SE) filter, and fixed filter (FF)—are identified in Table 1.

In the wild-card filter reservation style, reservations are made irrespective of the senders and, thus, are applicable to all senders of the group. This is the simplest reservation style, and the one with more potential in terms of request aggregation, as any resource request is valid to all senders of the group. A wild-card filter reservation style scenario is illustrated in Figure 5. In this figure, bandwidth reservation is requested by the sources in multiples of B bandwidth units. For each link, the router simply propagates upstream the highest bandwidth request received from the downstream links.

In the shared-explicit filter reservation style, receivers provide an explicit list of sources, but the reservations may be shared by several sources. This scenario is illustrated in Figure 6.

In the case of the fixed-filter reservation style, receivers perform a distinct reservation for each sender and, thus, requests can be aggregated at routers only if they pertain to the same source. This scenario is illustrated in Figure 7.

RSVP Traffic Engineering Extensions

RSVP was extended to establish Label-Switched Paths (LSPs) in MPLS (Multi-Protocol Label Switching). These extensions, called RSVP-TE extensions, enable the creation of MPLS Traffic Engineering (TE) tunnels to handle specific traffic aggregates. Tunnels can be created automatically to circumvent network failures, congestion, and bottlenecks.

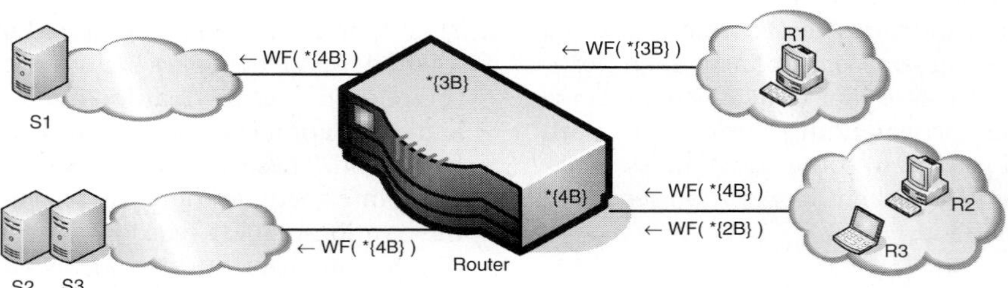

Figure 5: Wild-card filter reservation style

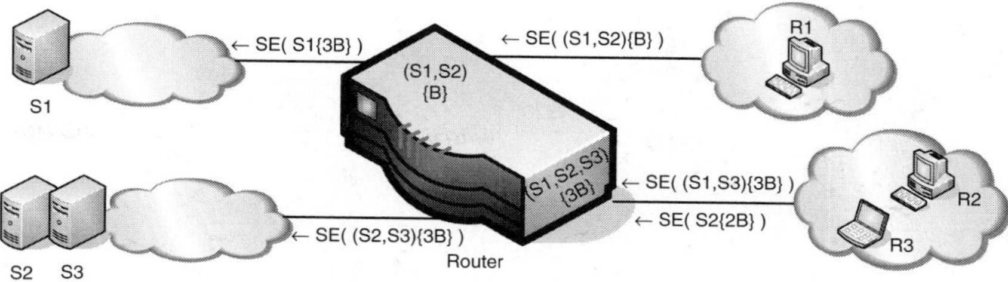

Figure 6: Shared-explicit filter reservation style

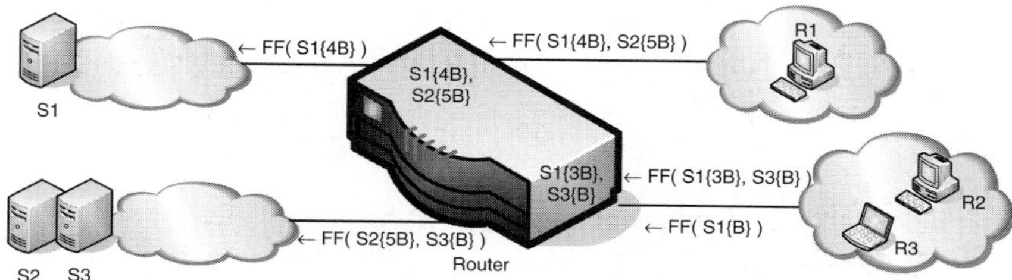

Figure 7: Fixed-filter reservation style

Operation of RSVP-TE with MPLS is described below, together with the description of the MPLS signaling extensions.

RSVP Security Mechanisms

RSVP includes mechanisms for information integrity and authentication. Confidentiality, however is not supported by RSVP. The security operation is supported by establishing security associations between RSVP entities and by the exchange of AUTH_DATA and INTEGRITY objects.

The AUTH_DATA object is used to authenticate RSVP PATH or RESV messages. The INTEGRITY object is used to provide integrity and authentication of the content of the signaling message exchange between two RSVP entities (two routers or a router and a host).

The Integrity Handshake protocol allows an RSVP entity to recover, after a failure, the sequence numbers used for reply attack protection.

RSVP security properties are summarized in RFC 4230 (Tschofenig et al. 2005).

NEXT STEPS IN SIGNALING

Background

Next Steps In Signaling (NSIS) is a signaling framework being developed by the Internet Engineering Task Force (IETF) in the context of the NSIS Working Group (Hancock et al. 2005) for the purpose of installing and maintaining flow states in the network. NSIS is based on various signaling protocols, the main one being RSVP. The intention is to reuse RSVP mechanisms whenever possible, because these mechanisms already have been widely tested, leaving out all unnecessary complexity (e.g., multicast support). Thus, it is a simpler and more scalable approach to resource reservation, when compared to RSVP.

By using a two-layer signaling architecture, signaling transport is separated from signaling applications. This architecture opens the way to develop several emerging signaling applications, of which quality of service signaling is the first-use case to be implemented.

Initial requirements of NSIS include support for the independence of application signaling and network control mechanisms, ability to place NSIS initiators, forwarders, and responders anywhere in the network through on-path and off-path signaling, transparent signaling through the network (the signaling message are opaque for the signaling transport), grouping of signaling for several microflows, flow aggregation, scalability, flexibility, and security.

NSIS Characteristics

Although NSIS can work on a per-flow basis, it allows flow aggregation based on the use of the DSCP field or tunnels. In addition, it works on a hop-by-hop basis, between NSIS-aware nodes (NSIS Entities, NE, also referred to as NSIS hops). Nodes not supporting NSIS are transparent, which means that there is no need for deployment of NSIS in every network entity. This is illustrated in Figure 8, where the end-systems and two of the routers support NSIS Entities that exchange signaling messages related to the data flow.

NSIS allows signaling to hosts, network elements, and proxies. Proxies allow the existence of NSIS-unaware hosts, by carrying out signaling on their behalf, as illustrated in Figure 9.

As stated before, NSIS supports both on-path and off-path signaling. In the case of path-coupled signaling, signaling messages are routed through NSIS entities on the data path only, although between adjacent NEs, the route taken by signaling and data might diverge. In the case of path-decoupled signaling, messages are routed to NEs, which are not assumed to be on the data path but which are aware of it (NEs have to know the path topology). In this case, the signaling endpoints may have no relation at all to the ultimate data sender or receiver.

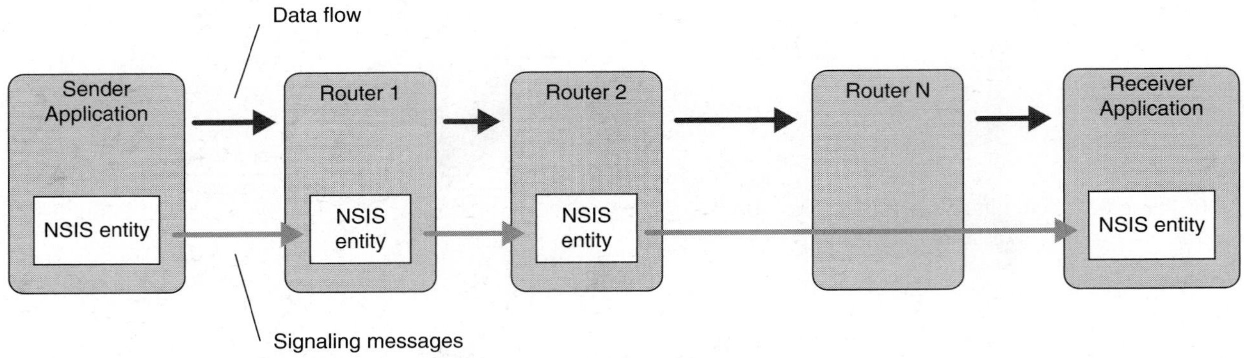

Figure 8: Simple NSIS scenario

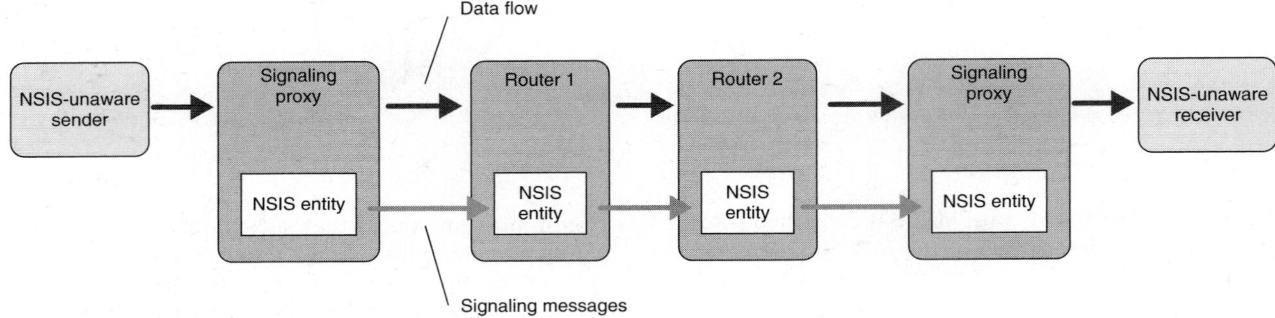

Figure 9: Signaling proxies

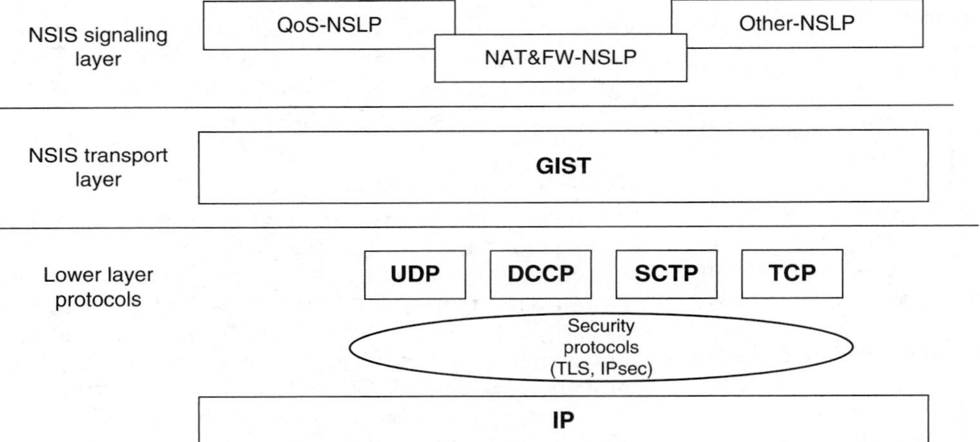

Figure 10: NSIS two-layer architecture

NSIS Architecture

NSIS is being developed as a two-layer modular architecture, comprising an NSIS transport layer and an NSIS signaling layer. The NSIS transport layer protocol, known as General Internet Signaling Transport (GIST), is responsible for the transport of signaling messages between network entities. The signaling layer contains specific functionality of signaling applications and may have several NSIS signaling layer protocols, generically known as NSLPs. With this approach, illustrated in Figure 10, the transport of the signaling messages and the signaling application are separate, which allows the use of the same signaling transport protocol for the support of all signaling applications. Examples of signaling protocols are the QoS-NSLP (Manner and Fu 2005) and the Network Address Translation (NAT) and Firewall (FW) NSLP (Stiemerling et al. 2006).

GIST

The GIST layer is responsible for the transport of signaling messages. When a signaling message is ready to be sent, it is passed to the GIST layer along with flow information details associated with it. Then it is up to the GIST layer to get the message to the next NSIS Entity (NE) along the path, downstream in the flow direction from the source to

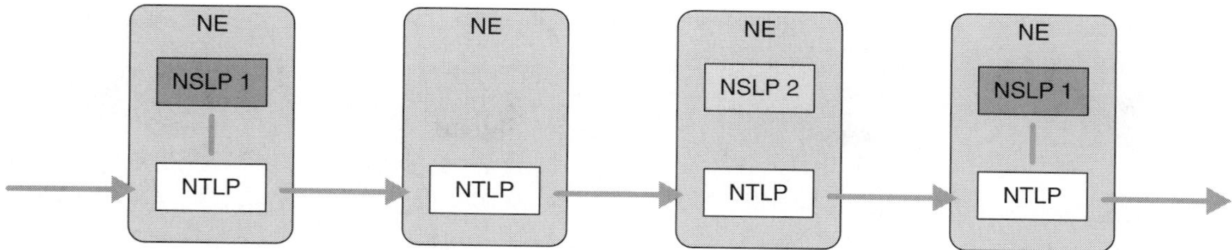

Figure 11: Example of GIST transport between NSIS entities

the destination, or upstream in the direction opposite to the flow, from the destination to the source. In the receiving NE, GIST either forwards the message directly to the next hop or, if there is an appropriate signaling application, passes it upward for further processing. The signaling application then can generate another message to be sent via GIST. Figure 11 illustrates this behavior, showing two different signaling applications and how NEs handle the signaling messages accordingly.

GIST allows two modes of operation, Datagram mode (D-mode) and Connection mode (C-mode). D-mode uses UDP to encapsulate messages and is used for small and infrequent messages. The C-mode uses TCP or any other stream or message-oriented transport protocol (currently only Stream Control Transmission Protocol, SCTP, is being considered in addition to TCP), which allows GIST to provide reliability and security (for example, using Transport Layer Security, TLS, over TCP) in the message transport. In addition, GIST defines a three-way handshake connection setup between adjacent peers, composed of a Query, a Response, and an optional Confirm message.

GIST was designed as a soft-state protocol to manage all the messages and associations. Each time a state is entered or updated, a timer is set up or restarted. GIST has two main state tables: Message Routing State (MRS) and Message Association State (MAS). The MRS is responsible for managing individual flows and the MAS is responsible for managing associations between individual peers. When a timer expires (if no message is received for the corresponding flow or association), the state is automatically removed from the state tables. If a state is required again, a new handshake is needed and a new association must be created.

QoS-NSLP

To be able to establish and maintain resource reservations, QoS-NSLP (Karagiannis and McDonald 2006) defines four message types: RESERVE, QUERY, RESPONSE, and NOTIFY. Each message contains three parts: Control information, QoS specification (QSPEC), and Policy objects.

The RESERVE message is used to create, refresh, modify and remove states. RESERVE messages are the only messages that manipulate states, and if received more than once, the result is the same. The QUERY message is used to probe the network without installing or changing any state. The result of a QUERY message can be used to configure subsequent messages. The RESPONSE message is used to provide feedback from previous messages. The NOTIFY message is similar to the RESPONSE message but is an asynchronous message that can be generated without any previous message. Usually the NOTIFY messages report error conditions.

Figure 12 illustrates the use of QoS-NSLP in a basic reservation scenario. The figure shows the signaling messages exchanged with time (time elapses from the top to bottom). This example represents a receiver-initiated reservation, in which the data sender probes the network by means of a QUERY message that gathers information on the network capability. When this message arrives at the receiver, it triggers the start of the reservation. The receiver, which in this case plays the role of QoS NSLP Initiatior, QNI, starts the reservation by sending a RESERVE message to the QoS NSLP Responder, QNR. This message will install the request in the network. In all NSIS entities along the data path for which the QoS NSLP is available, the message is processed (in this case in the two QNEs) and the reservations are made if possible. After the request is installed

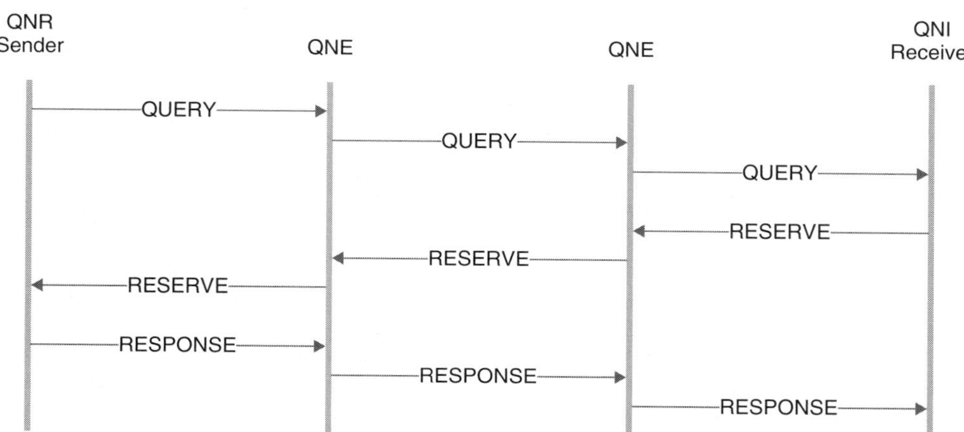

Figure 12: QoS NSLP basic reservation scenario

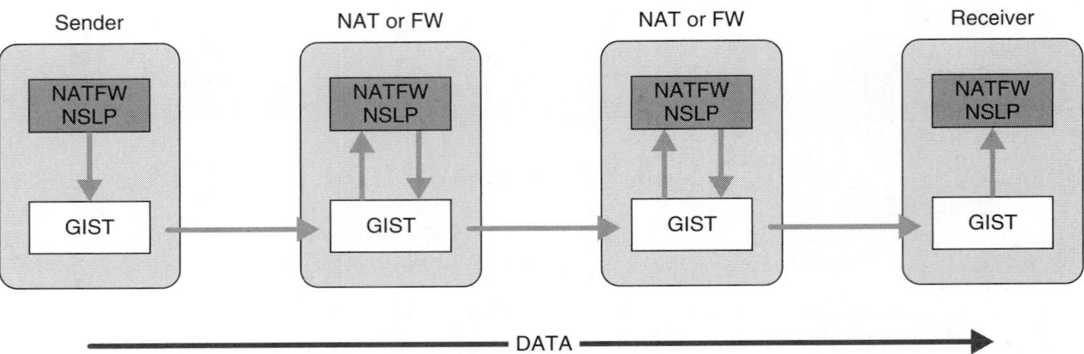

Figure 13: NATFW NSLP scenario

in the QNR, the QoS-NSLP generates a RESPONSE message. This message is sent to the QNI along with the result of the RESERVE message. When this message arrives at the QNI, the procedure is complete.

NAT and Firewall NSLP

The NAT and Firewall (NATFW) NSIS Signaling Layer Protocol (Stiemerling et al. 2006) is being defined in the NSIS IETF Working Group to provide dynamic configuration of NAT and firewall devices along the data path of a specific flow. These types of devices may create obstacles to applications such as IP telephony and peer-to-peer application unless appropriate firewall rules or NAT bindings are in place.

Figure 13 illustrates a simple example of NATFW NSLP use between a sender and a receiver, with two middleboxes network elements (NAT or firewall devices). The source host (sender) generates a NATFW NSLP signaling message and sends it to the destination host (receiver). This message traverses the data path, and hence every NSIS entity having NATFW NSLP functionality will process it. Based on the message-processing outcome, the NATFW NSLP triggers configuration changes of the middleboxes network elements accordingly and forwards the message to the receiver. Middleboxes are configured for the specific flow and the data flow can start.

NATFW NSLP signaling messages contain general information (such as IP address, ports, protocol) and policy rules. Policy rules are abstractions of actual network equipment policy rules. The request initiator generates the abstract policy rules, and in each NATFW NSLP along the path, these rules must be mapped to the specific NAT or firewall rules. This mapping is vendor- and model-dependent.

NATFW NSLP defines five message types: CREATE, RESERVE-EXTERNALADDRESS(REA), TRACE, NOTIFY, and RESPONSE. The CREATE message creates, changes, refreshes and deletes NATFW NSLP sessions on the data path between the sender and the destination. The REA message is forwarded from the receiver to the edge NAT to allow inbound CREATE messages to be forwarded to the receiver. This message reserves an external address (and a port number if needed) in the edge router and requests the configuration of all intermediate middleboxes (between the receiver and the edge NAT). The TRACE message gathers information from all NATFW NSLP on the data path. The NOTIFY message is an asynchronous message used by NSLP to notify upstream peers of specific events. The RESPONSE message is a response to CREATE, REA, and TRACE messages.

NSIS Security Mechanisms

The security mechanisms of the NSIS framework are supported by the Generic Internet Signaling Transport (GIST) protocol that provides the basic signaling transport services to the application signaling protocols. GIST can use available security mechanisms (alone or combined) to ensure authentication, integrity, and confidentiality, namely: Transport Layer Security (TLS) with X.509 PKI; Extensible Authentication Protocol (EAP); and 3GPP (3rd Generation Partnership Project) Generic Bootstrapping Architecture (GBA).

TLS and X.509 PKI certificates can be used to protect GIST message exchange over TCP connections.

EAP used in AAA (Authentication, Authorization, and Accounting) infrastructure can also be used for authenticating of NSIS messages.

The 3GPP GBA key distribution mechanisms can also be used for authorization between NEs.

The discussion about NSIS security mechanisms is ongoing. The Internet-Draft draft-tschofenig-nsis-gist-security-01.txt (Tschofenig and Eronen 2006) summarizes the proposals currently being discussed.

SIP AND H.323

With the advent of multimedia and QoS-demanding applications, the need for application signaling in the Internet became imperative. Applications requiring QoS guarantees include: IP telephony, videoconferencing, multimedia conferencing, and GRID computing.

The two basic types of approaches to application signaling are: data-driven and signaling-driven. The former is the approach typically used on the Internet. The latter has its origin in the traditional telecommunications networks, for which separate signaling and data networks were common. With the convergence of the Internet and the telecommunication communities, both types of approaches can be found in current IP networks.

This section presents the two main application signaling approaches used nowadays: SIP, an Internet-originated approach to application signaling; and H.323, a telecommunications-originated approach. Other application signaling protocols, such as MGCP or MEGACO, will not be addressed, as they are historic only or their installed base is rapidly decreasing in favor of SIP.

Session Initiation Protocol

This subsection is dedicated to the Session Initiation Protocol (SIP), covering the origin, objectives, elements, addressing, message types, and dialogue organization of SIP.

Origin and Objectives

SIP is a text-based application layer control protocol developed by the IETF. It is based on HTTP and, thus, it inherited the message header format from RFC 822 (Crocker 1982). SIP is defined in several RFCs, of which RFC 3261 (Rosenberg et al. 2002) contains the core specification.

SIP is used for multimedia session control—namely, session creation, session modification, and session termination. SIP sessions consist of sets of senders, receivers, and associated states. Telephone calls, multimedia conferences, and distributed computer games are examples of SIP sessions.

SIP provides the mechanisms for establishing point-to-point and point-to-multipoint calls, caller and called authentication, call forwarding and transfer, call forking, terminal capability negotiation, and location-independent addressing.

By itself, SIP is not enough to make the communication possible. It requires some companion protocols—namely, the Session Description Protocol, SDP (Handley and Jacobson 1998) and the Real-Time Protocol Real-Time Control Protocol, RTP/RTCP (Schulzrinne et al. 2003). SDP is necessary for the description of multimedia sessions (e.g., media types, time characteristics), while RTP/RTCP carries the real-time multimedia data over the network.

SIP Elements

SIP relies on the use of several different types of elements—namely, user agents, proxies, registrars, and redirect servers. Some of these may be logical entities residing in the same system.

User agents (UA) are session endpoints. They negotiate session characteristics and are logically divided into User Agent Clients (UAC), which send requests and receive responses, and User Agent Servers (UAS), which receive requests and send responses.

Proxy servers route session invitations according to the current location of the called party. In addition, they perform user authentication and accounting. Session invitations may traverse several proxies until they reach the remote UA. Proxy servers may be stateless or stateful. The former are simple message forwarders, do not take care of transactions (messages are usually organized into transactions), are faster than stateful proxies, and do not perform forking (for multiparty communication). The latter keep track of ongoing transactions, may perform forking, keep track of retransmissions and can perform call redirection.

Figure 14 illustrates a session establishment between two users from different organizations. Each organization may have its own proxy server. These proxy servers are used to route the session invitation (unless the organizations use hosted service providers).

Registrars usually are co-located with proxy servers. They receive registrations from users and keep track of their current location (namely username, IP address, and port number). User location information is stored in a

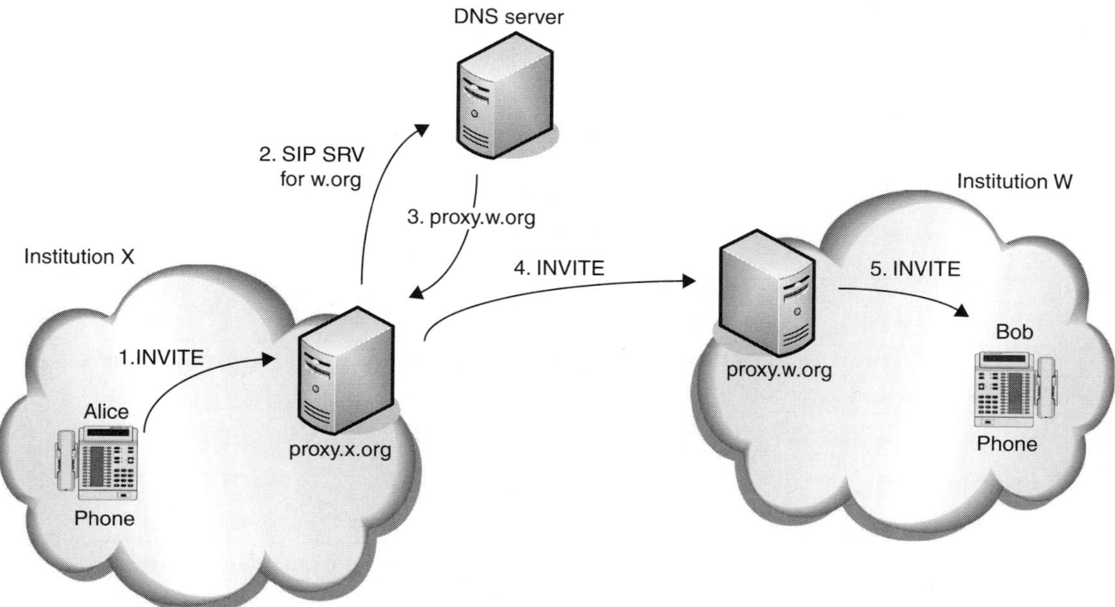

Figure 14: Example of SIP session establishment

location database. Because user registrations have a limited life span, user agents must refresh their registration periodically. If a registration is not refreshed, it expires and the user becomes unavailable.

Redirect servers are also usually co-located with proxy servers. They receive location requests and return a list of the current locations of users.

Addresses

SIP entities are identified through Uniform Resource Identifiers (URI), which are similar to e-mail addresses. A SIP URI consists of a username part and a domain part, with the following format: sip:username@domain. This is convenient, as it is thus possible to use the same URI for e-mail and SIP communication, and to use the omnipresent DNS service to find the network location of SIP users and corresponding servers. A SIP URI includes a user phone number and a user IP address or a user Web address.

Although SIP addressing works well on the Internet, it is being adapted to other environments, such as the telephone network. With the advent of IP telephony, for which SIP is being used widely as signaling protocol, it is extremely important to find a way to map traditional telephone numbers (unique numerical addresses administered by the International Telecommunications Union (ITU-T) according to Recommendation E.164) into DNS query strings and, consequently, into SIP addresses. This mapping is provided by ENUM (Electronic Numbering), defined in RFC 3761 (Faltstrom and Mealling 2004).

Messages

The two types of SIP messages are requests and responses. Requests are used to initiate actions. The main types of requests are: INVITE, ACK, OPTIONS, BYE, CANCEL, and REGISTER. Responses, also named replies, are used to confirm that a request has been received and processed. These include a status code that conveys the result of the corresponding request processing. All requests must be replied to, with the exception of the ACK request.

The INVITE message is the first message the calling party sends in the call establishment cycle. It contains endpoint IDs and call ID, among other parameters. The ACK message indicates that the calling party has received confirmation (a 200 OK response) to an INVITE request. The OPTIONS message is sent to query the capabilities of a call agent—namely, to determine which media types a remote user supports. The BYE message is used to release a call. The sending endpoint terminates the media flow and considers the call terminated. The CANCEL message cancels a request in progress but has no effect if no requests are in progress. The REGISTER message is used by a user agent to register with a local server on start-up. This message is sent to the well-known "all SIP servers" multicast address 224.0.1.75.

Responses convey a status code, suitable to be processed by machines, and a reason phrase, that is, a human-readable message. Both of them describe the result of the processing of the associated request. The SIP responses for defined status code ranges are identified in Table 2.

Transactions, Dialogues, and Calls

SIP messages normally are arranged into transactions, dialogues, and calls. A transaction is a sequence of one request message and all subsequent responses to that request. A request may have zero or more provisional responses and one or more final responses. A dialogue is a sequence of transactions that are related somehow and that persist for some time. Dialogues facilitate the sequencing of messages and can be viewed as peer-to-peer SIP relationships between two user agents. By contrast, a call consists of one or more dialogues and may involve multiple user agents. Each responding user agent establishes a separate dialogue with the calling party.

Figure 15 illustrates a SIP dialogue between two user agents and the constituent transactions.

Figure 16 shows a SIP messages exchange between a calling party and a called party, through a proxy server, for the purpose of establishing a session. The figure illustrates the use of two types of requests (INVITE and ACK) and of provisional responses (100 Trying and 180 Ringing), as well as the positive final response 200 OK. After establishing the session, RTP carries the data streams.

Table 2: SIP Responses

Status code	Description
1xx	Informational (code range 100-199). Proceeding with the execution of the request
2xx	Success (code 200). The request was successfully parsed and executed by the called party
3xx	Redirection (code range 300-399). The call needs more processing by the calling party in order to be completed
4xx	Client request failure (code range 400-499). The request cannot be parsed by the server or cannot be serviced
5xx	Server failures (code range 500-599). The server cannot execute the request
6xx	Global failures (code range 600-699). The user request cannot be serviced by any server

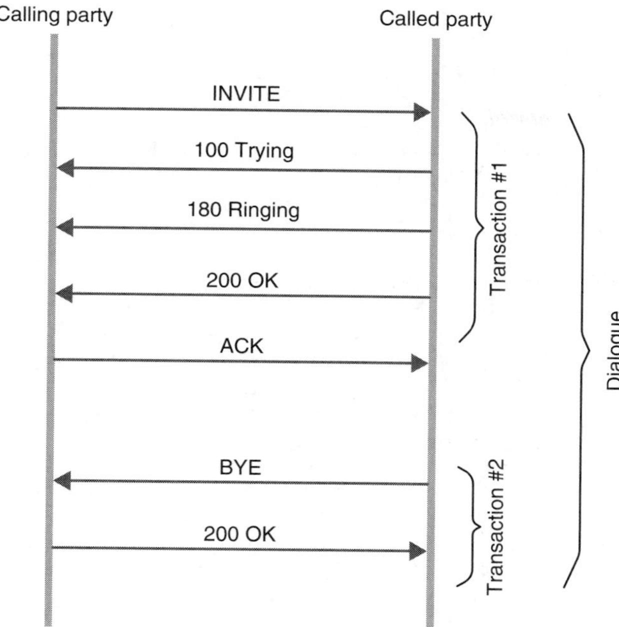

Figure 15: SIP dialogue

SIP Security Mechanisms

As with NSIS, SIP reuses common security protocols to provide security, namely: IP Security protocol (IPSec) and Transport Layer Security (TLS) security with X.509 certificates. TLS security and X.509 certificates of a public key infrastructure (PKI) are used for authentication, integrity, and confidentiality signaling transactions carried by HTTP. IPSec can be used to complement TLS security and provide protection for specific ports and sensitive applications.

RFC 3329 (Arkko et al. 2003) describes the use of TLS and IPSec to provide security to SIP signaling functions.

H.323

This sub-section introduces the ITU-T Recommendation H.323 (ITU-T H.323, 2003), by identifying its origin and objectives, components, protocol architecture, signaling models, and communication phases.

Origin and Objectives

ITU-T Recommendation H.323 is part of a series of recommendations on video telephony and multimedia conferencing services. The first versions of these recommendations were developed in the mid-1990s, addressing the support of the referred services over a variety of network technologies—namely ISDN (H.320), ATM (H.310, H.321), PSTN (H.324), Isochronous Ethernet (H.323), and LANs (H.323).

With the widespread use of LANs, IP protocols, and the Internet in general, the developers quickly arrived at the conclusion that the original H.323 recommendation scope could be extended to Internet-wide deployment, not just LANs. Nowadays, H.323 plays an important role as an application signaling technology, with a large installed base. Nevertheless, because of its complexity and overhead, it is being precluded in favor of SIP. This also is related to the fact that H.323 uses a signaling paradigm that is highly similar to the one used in the telephone network (which is consistent with the fact that it originated in the telecommunications community), as opposed to SIP, which originated in the Internet community.

Components

Figure 17 illustrates the basic components of H.323: terminals, gateways, gatekeepers, and multipoint control units.

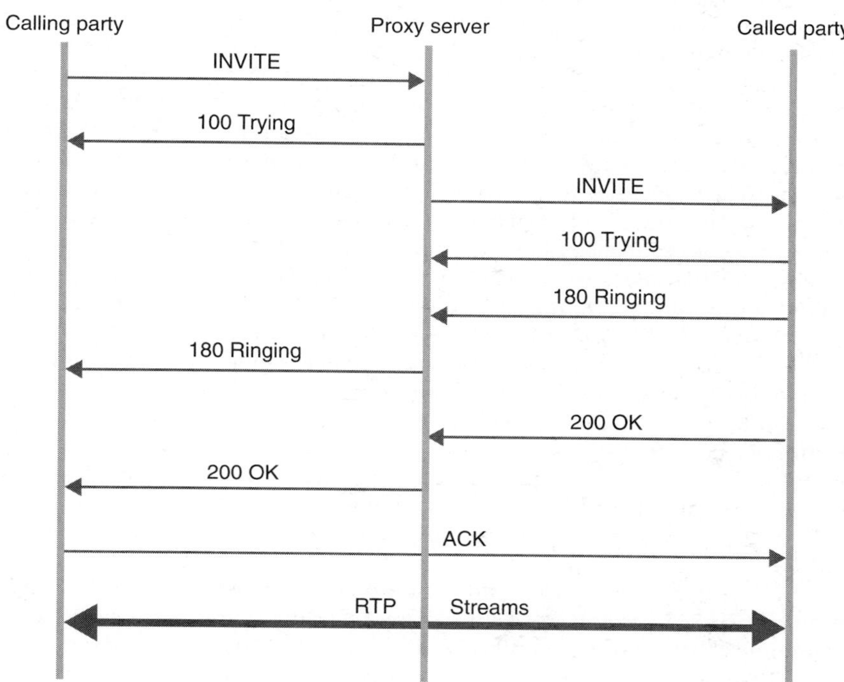

Figure 16: SIP invitation example

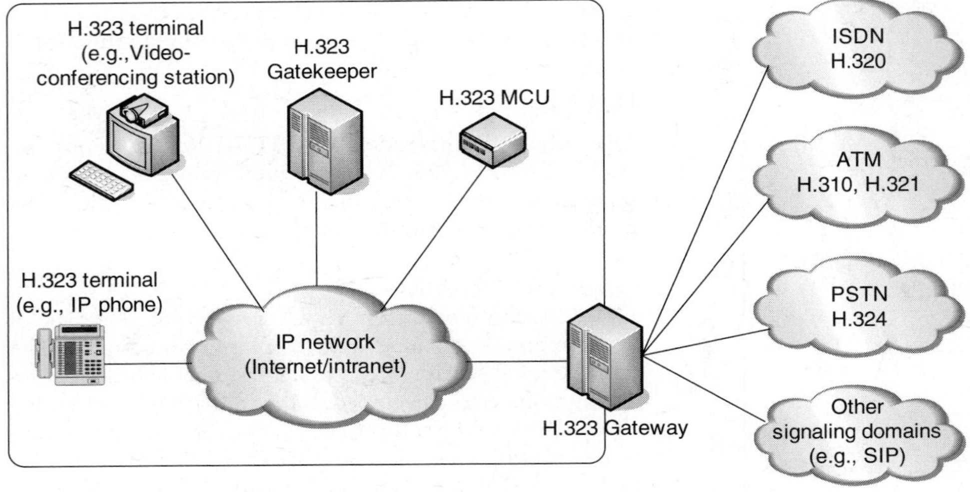

Figure 17: H.323 components

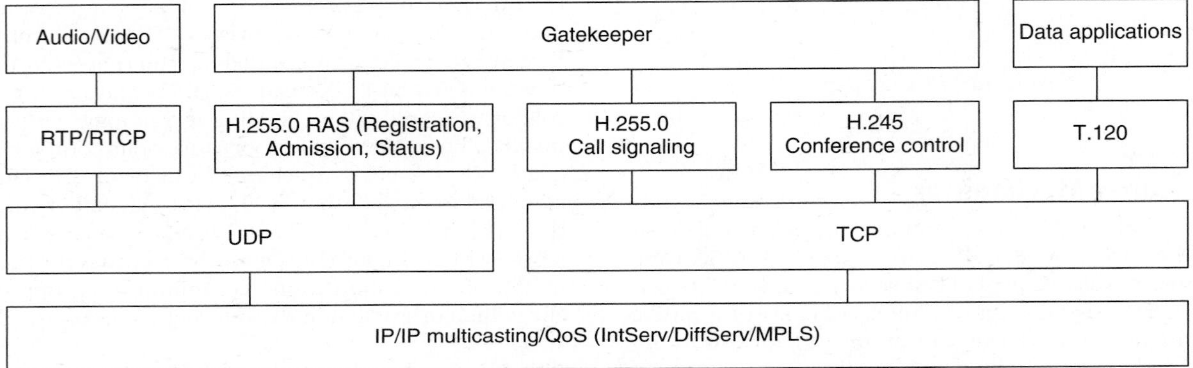

Figure 18: H.323 protocol architecture

Terminals are H.323-capable endpoints, implemented in software or hardware, and with one or more identifiers (URI and/or telephone number). Gateways interconnect H.323 entities with other network and/or protocol environments. Gatekeepers are central management entities of zones. They perform access control, address resolution, call management, and provide basic and supplementary services. They can also act as proxies for security, QoS, or accounting purposes. Thus, in terms of functionality, H.323 gatekeepers are equivalent to SIP proxies. Multipoint Control Units (MCUs) perform multipoint control, i.e., call signaling and conference control of two or more H.323 entities belonging to the same call, and multipoint processing, such as the combination of media streams from individual endpoints belonging to a multipoint call.

Protocol Architecture

H.323 specifies a complex protocol architecture, represented in Figure 18. This includes signaling protocols, data transport protocols, and audio/video transport protocols.

The H.225.0 RAS (Registration, Admission, Status) protocol is used for gatekeeper discovery by endpoints, endpoint registration, endpoint location, endpoint admission requests (authentication/authorization), bandwidth requests, information on the state of endpoints, and resource availability checks.

The H.225.0 Call Signaling protocol was derived from ISDN call signaling and, in fact, is a simplified version of the Q.931 protocol. It is used for conveying information on call setup intention, call setup progress, call setup success, call setup failure, call release, and call status.

H.245 is used for conference control—namely, for the establishment and control of two-party calls and multi-party conferences, negotiation of modes for media exchange according to terminal capabilities, and configuration of media streams. It is a complex, heavy-weight protocol inherited from other network technologies—namely ATM and the PSTN.

Signaling Models

As mentioned before, H.323 is a complex protocol. The complexity derives from its extensive functionality and modes of operation. The richness of H.323 also is apparent in the signaling models that it uses. These are:

1. *Direct signaling*. In this case, only H.225.0 RAS messages are routed through the gatekeeper. Other signaling messages are exchanged directly between the two endpoints.

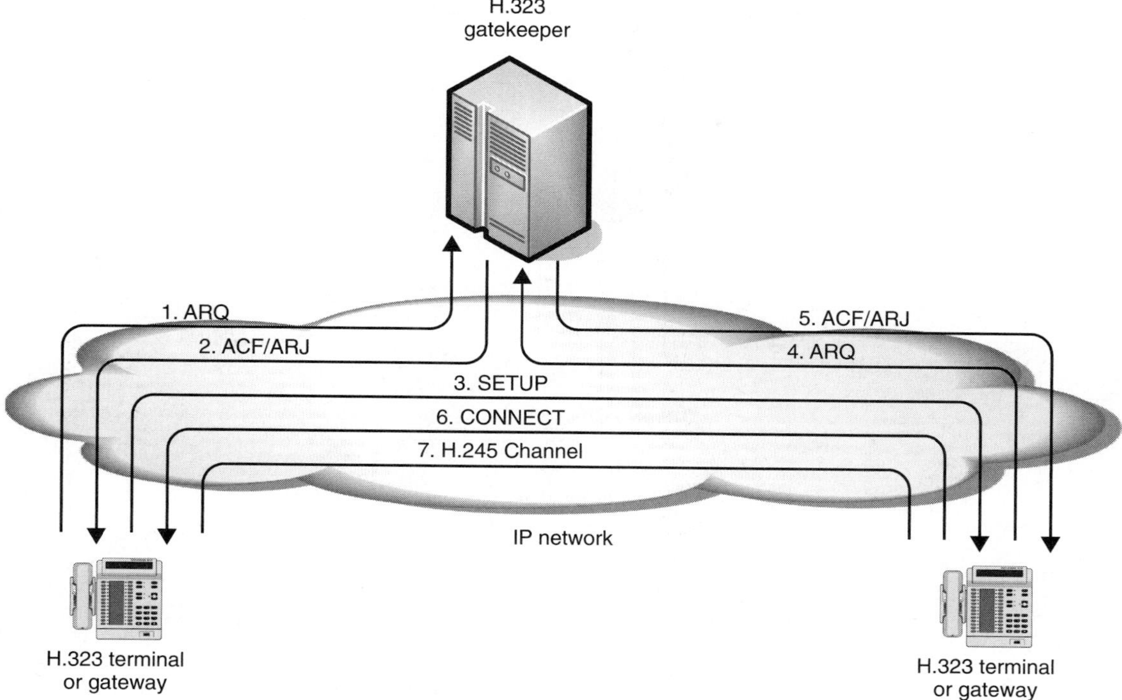

Figure 19 (a): Direct signaling

2. *Gatekeeper-routed call signaling*. In this case, H.225.0 RAS and H.225.0 call signaling messages are routed through the gatekeeper. H.245 conference control messages are exchanged directly between the two endpoints.
3. *Gatekeeper-routed H.245 control, RAS, and call signaling*. All signaling messages are routed through the gatekeeper. Only media streams are exchanged directly between the two endpoints.

Figures 19 (a), (b), and (c) illustrate the three H.323 signaling models described above.

Examples of Call Setup

Some H.323 call setup examples follow. Call setup is only the first phase of the several phases in H.323 calls. The various phases are:

1. *Call setup*. Establishment of point-to-point or multipoint calls between parties.
2. *Initial communication and capability exchange*. Role determination (master, slave); terminal capabilities determination.
3. *Establishment of audiovisual communication*. Opening of logical channels for the various information streams.
4. *Call services*. Request/establishment of additional services (e.g., bandwidth changes).
5. *Call termination*.

Figure 20 illustrates a call setup according to the direct signaling model.

Figure 21 illustrates a call setup, now according to the gatekeeper-routed call signaling model.

In addition to the basic services, such as call establishment and termination, H.323 includes several other services, such as multipoint tightly-coupled conferences for which access control and synchronization are performed by an MCU, broadcast loosely coupled conferencing (Mbone style), and supplementary services such as call transfer, call diversion, call hold, and message waiting indication, among other services.

OTHER SIGNALING PROTOCOLS AND APPROACHES

YESSIR and Boomerang

YESSIR (Pan and Schulzrinne 1998) and Boomerang (Manner and Fu 2005) were designed as an attempt to simplify RSVP. YESSIR is an extension to the Real Time Transport Control Protocol, RTCP (Schulzrinne et al. 2003), which reduces the processing overhead to a minimum, uses soft state to maintain reservation states, supports shared reservations, and is able to merge different flow reservations. Boomerang has only one type of message and a single signaling loop for reservation setup and teardown, and it has no requirements on the far-end node. The flow initiator is responsible for all of the protocol management. This protocol supports sender- and receiver-initiated requests.

None of these on-path signaling protocols registered a significant deployment base because of their limitations. Being an extension of RTCP, YESSIR requires support from applications, and routers have to unpack packets

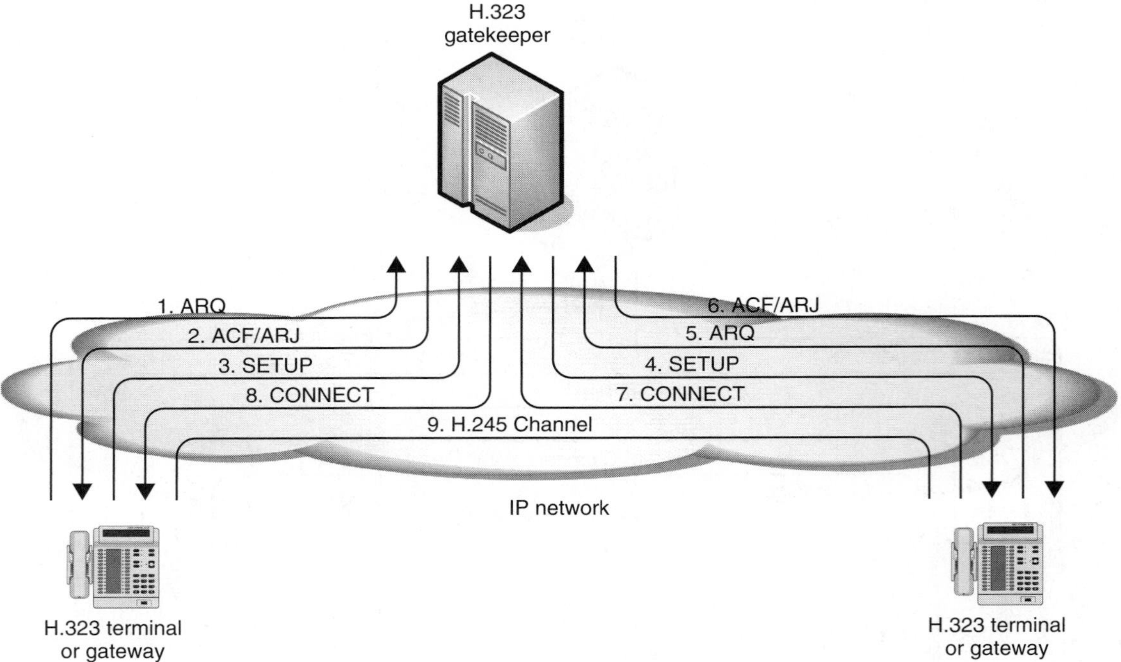

Figure 19(b): Gatekeeper-routed call signaling

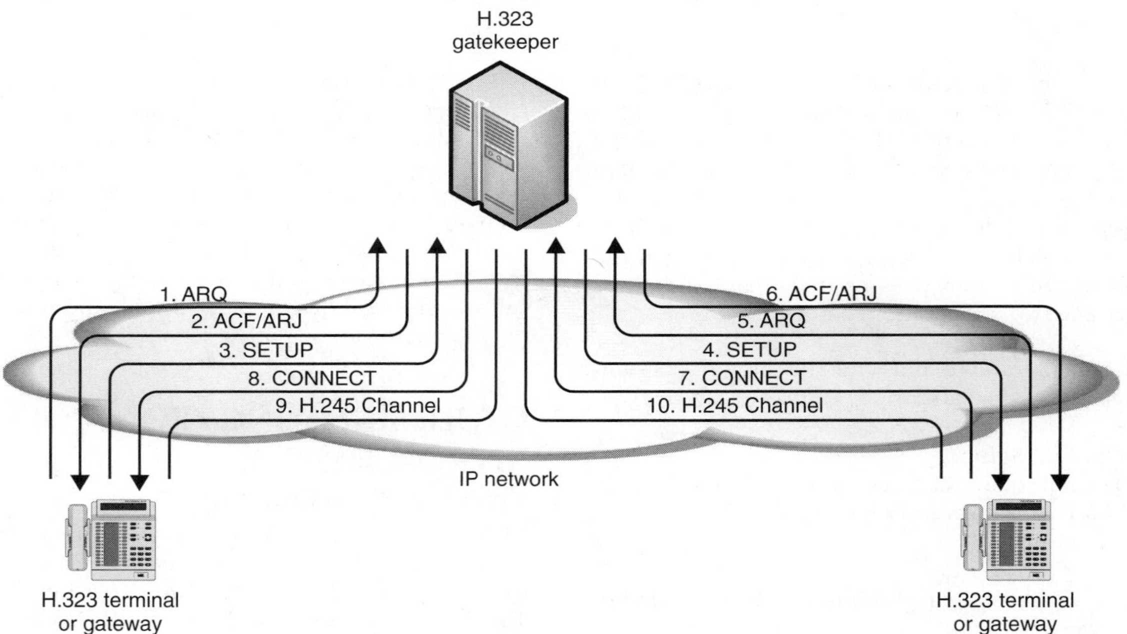

Figure 19(c): Gatekeeper-routed H.245 control, RAS, and call signaling

and analyze the RTCP data. Boomerang is so light that it misses important functionality such as security and multicast.

SIBBS

The Simple Inter-domain Bandwidth Broker Protocol, SIBBS, was defined by the QBone Signaling Design Team, available at http://qbone.internet2.edu/bb/ (date of access: January 2, 2007), for use in DiffServ bandwidth-broker-based domains. SIBBS is a simple protocol to be used between Bandwidth Brokers (BB) for resource negotiation between different domains, which uses TCP for reliability. It is composed of two main protocol data units (PDU): Resource Allocation Request (RAR) and Resource Allocation Answer (RAA).

The RAR message includes a globally well-known service identifier, information related to the QoS request

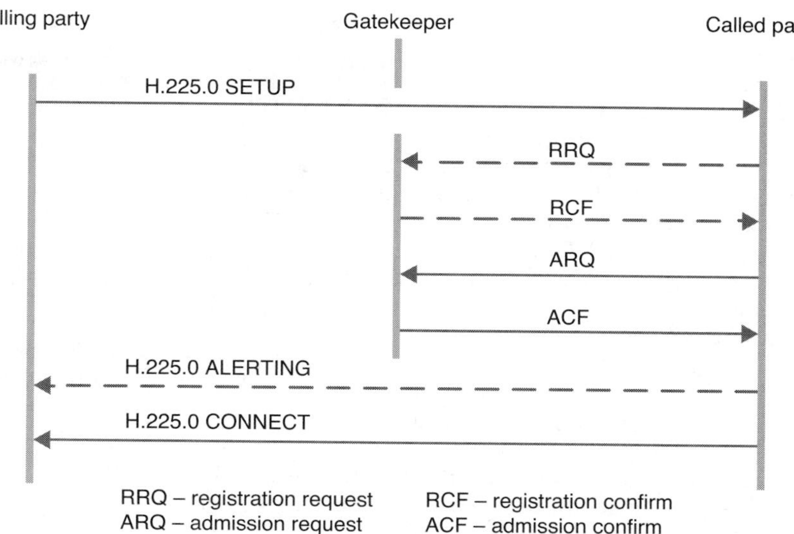

Figure 20: Call setup using the direct signaling model

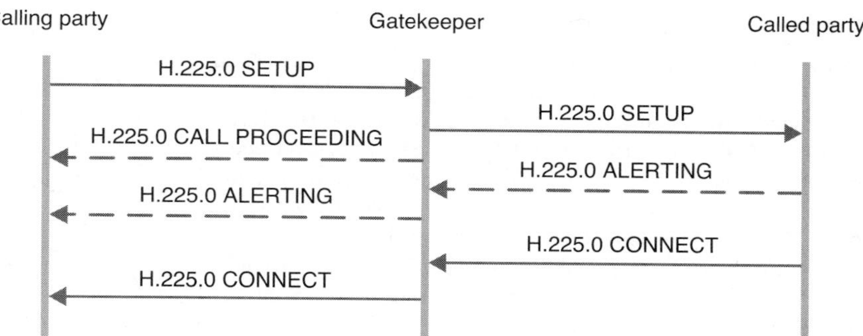

Figure 21: Call setup using the gatekeeper-routed call signaling model

(classes of service and bandwidth), a destination IP address, a source IP address, an authentication field, and other parameters of the service. The sender can be a client host, a BB, or a proxy. The RAA message contains the answer to an RAR PDU.

When a bandwidth broker receives an RAR message, it checks the authenticity, determines the egress router (interface) from its (inter-domain) routing tables, checks that the requested resources fall within the Service Level Specification (SLS), ensures that the domain has sufficient resources within it to support the flow, and determines whether the flow can or cannot be accepted according to the policies of the domain. If all of these constraints are met, the request is propagated recursively through the inter-domain path to the last BB. This last BB returns an RAA message to its BB immediately upstream, and the process continues until reaching the originating BB. Resources are confirmed by means of periodically sent refresh messages.

To configure border routers, bandwidth brokers must have access to them. SIBBS does not specify a particular protocol for this purpose, but it can use protocols such as DIAMETER (Calhoun et al. 2003), Simple Network Management Protocol (Case et al. 1990), or Common Open Policy Service (Boyle 2000).

COPS

The Common Open Policy Service, COPS, is a client/server protocol designed for policy-based network management. The basic model of COPS is presented in Figure 22.

The Policy Decision Point (PDP) is a central management entity, in charge of making policy decisions.

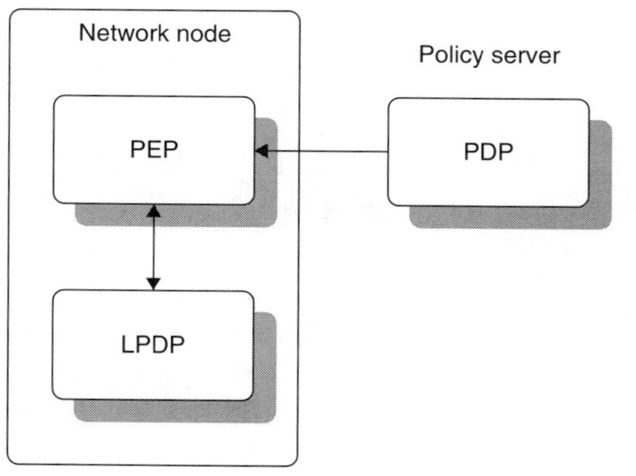

Figure 22: COPS basic model

The Policy Enforcement Point (PEP) is the point where the policies are applied, such as a router. The device can use the optional Local Policy Decision Point (LPDP) to make local policy decisions in the absence of a PDP.

COPS is a request/response protocol that allows a PEP (router) to interrogate its PDP about the action to perform once an event has occurred (for instance, if a signaling message arrived). COPS-SLS (Nguyen et al. 2002) is an extension to the COPS protocol for SLS management in a multi-domain environment. COPS-SLS basically has the same behavior as SIBBS: A request is propagated from one BB to the other in each domain on the data path. Each BB has a dual role: PDP role for its domain, and PEP role for the next domain BB.

Compared to SIBBS, COPS-SLS adds some features to the protocol, such as renegotiation of classes of service in case of failure of admission control. The COPS-PR protocol assures communication between BB and border routers (Chan et al. 2001). The discussion of bandwidth brokers and border routers is outside the scope of COPS-SLS.

MPLS Signaling Extensions

Multi-Protocol Label Switching (MPLS) originated in the mid 1990s to explore the performance of ATM switches in IP environments and now is standardized by the IETF in RFC 3031 (Rosen et al. 2001). Some of its predecessor protocols are IP switching (developed by Ipsilon), Tag switching (developed by Cisco Systems) and Aggregate route-based IP switching (developed by IBM).

Although, strictly speaking, MPLS is not a signaling protocol, it is an alternative approach to QoS-oriented signaling and, thus, it is included in this section. The main objective of MPLS is the support of quality of service through the use of predefined paths and adequate allocation of resources.

Main Characteristics

MPLS provides connection-oriented-equivalent QoS support by efficiently routing packets through preestablished paths, to which resources can be allocated based on service-level agreements and service-level specifications (SLA/SLS). By labeling packets and associating them with given paths, MPLS leads to a reduction in the amount of per-packet processing at each router. In addition, it eases traffic engineering, optimizes network utilization, and provides flow-based dynamic routing.

Basic Operation

MPLS-enabled routers (label-switching routers, LSR) switch and route packets based on a label appended to each packet. This clearly is simpler and quicker than IP routing. Labels define a unicast or multicast flow of packets, called Forwarding Equivalent Classes (FEC). Each FEC is allocated to a specific path consisting of a sequence of LSRs. Each FEC has a traffic characterization that defines the QoS requirements for the flow. A particular per-hop behavior can be defined at each LSR for a given FEC.

Prior to the beginning of a flow, a Label Switched Path (LSP) must be defined, either manually or by using an interior routing protocol (e.g., OSPF). Labels must be assigned for the various links that make up the path. Labels have local significance: Incoming packets with a given label are, in the general case, forwarded to the next link with a different label.

Figure 23 illustrates the basic operation of MPLS. This figure shows two FECs.

Labels

MPLS is said to be a Layer 2.5 technology because MPLS protocol control information (i.e., labels) are placed between layer 2 and layer 3 headers. MPLS labels are

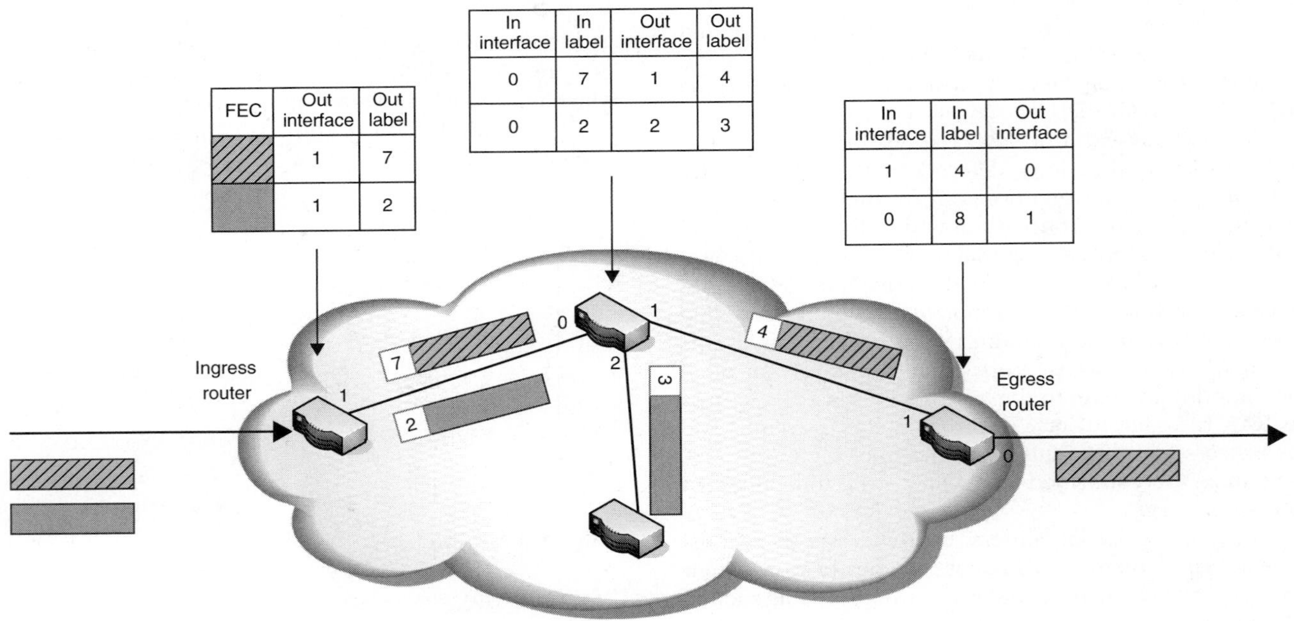

Figure 23: MPLS basic operation

stackable. A packet may carry an unlimited number of labels, organized as a last-in-first-out (LIFO) stack. MPLS processing at LSRs is always based on the top label. Label stacking allows aggregation of LSPs into a single LSPs for portions of the route.

Each LSR in an LSP must assign a label to the LSP so packets belonging to the corresponding FEC can be recognized, inform upstream LSRs of the label assigned by this LSR to this FEC, and determine the next hop for the FEC and learn the label that the downstream LSR has assigned to this FEC.

Labels can be manually configured at each LSR or distributed using a label distribution protocol. Label distribution protocols establish a correspondence between FECs and LSPs and inform LSRs of label/FEC bindings. In addition, they negotiate LSR forms of interaction and advertise/negotiate MPLS capabilities.

Label distribution protocols are either extensions to existing protocol, e.g., extensions to BGP (Rekhter and Rosen 2001) or to RSVP, or specially developed protocols such as the Label Distribution Protocol, LDP (Andersson et al. 2001) or the Constraint Routed LDP, CR-LDP (Andersson et al. 2002).

CASE STUDY—EUQOS

The EuQoS Project

The EuQoS Project is a European IST FP6 Integrated Project, involving 24 partners (5 network providers, 5 corporations, 5 SMEs, and 9 research institutes). The motivation for the project is the increasing shift to the Internet Protocol in the vast majority of networks and the desire of telecommunications service providers to offer new added-value services to their customers. In this context, there is the need to coordinate the delivery of end-to-end quality of service driven by customer applications so providers may offer services that can respond directly to these application needs.

The general objective of the EuQoS project was to solve design issues associated with the delivery of end-to-end QoS service across heterogeneous networks. The main result of the project was the so-called EuQoS system, which supports the delivery of end-to-end quality of service, and encompasses network technologies, protocols, applications, and management.

The end-to-end QoS provision is achieved not only by end-to-end mechanisms and functions at the application layer but also at network-technology-independent and at network-technology-dependent layers. This requires the cooperation of a range of system features and functions that reside on end systems and on servers/network elements.

The Role of Signaling in EuQoS

The EuQoS project has a key central objective: end-to-end quality of service. Also, the project scope outlines several mechanisms, components, and approaches to be able to achieve this aim.

The basic mechanisms for end-to-end QoS provision are signaling and resource reservation. Signaling is carried out at various levels: end-to-end, at application level through the use of SIP; hop-by-hop, at the inter-domain level through the use of NSIS complemented by routing and/or traffic engineering; locally, at the intra-domain level for resource management and provision through the use of COPS and technology-dependent mechanisms.

The EuQoS architecture is made up of a series of components that cooperate to achieve the end-to-end QoS provision goal. These components, called features and functions, make use of the mechanisms referred above in order to negotiate, manage and provide the required quality of service on an end-to-end basis. For example, the Signaling and Service Negotiation (SSN) function coordinates the use of the various signaling mechanisms (end-to-end, hop-by-hop, local) to support the establishment of QoS-enabled end-to-end sessions between user applications.

In the scope of EuQoS, two basic approaches for end-to-end quality of service provision are being proposed, developed, and studied: hard-model and loose-model approaches. The hard-model approach relies on inter-domain MPLS-based traffic engineering to accommodate traffic demands. This model is more appropriate for situations in which traffic needs are reasonably predictable and quite stable over time. The loose-model relies on the use of BGP routing, allowing for more flexible traffic support and being subject to possible constraints of resource availability.

Thus, it can be said that EuQoS addresses the end-to-end QoS problem in several dimensions, using a comprehensive methodology that explores complementarities and cooperation signaling mechanisms at various levels, system components cooperation, and inter-domain routing and traffic engineering.

Signaling and Service Negotiation

The main purpose of SSN is to provide the means for establishing end-to-end sessions according to user requirements. This requires a variety of signaling protocols in the various levels that make up the EuQoS control plane.

In EuQoS, the QoS provision is achieved by complex resource management and resource allocation, involving inter-domain and intra-domain signaling interactions. The EuQoS architecture has four different "signaling levels," as illustrated in Figure 24.

The first signaling level pertains to applications. To establish, maintain, and release sessions with the required QoS levels, applications must express their needs and interact with the communication system, with the objectives of guaranteeing that these needs will be fulfilled, of adapting to network conditions whenever the available resources do not allow the initially requested level of QoS to be met, and of releasing the resources when sessions end. Application signaling uses the SIP protocol. SDP also is used to support session characterization.

To enable interactions between Level 1 signaling functions and Resource Managers (RMs), vertical interactions are needed. EuQoS-aware application proxies interact with RMs for technology-independent connection admission control and trigger Level 2 signaling for resource reservation. These interactions can be bidirectional, and RMs also can notify proxies of changes in network conditions.

The main objective of the Level 2 signaling functions is the support of resource reservation and management along

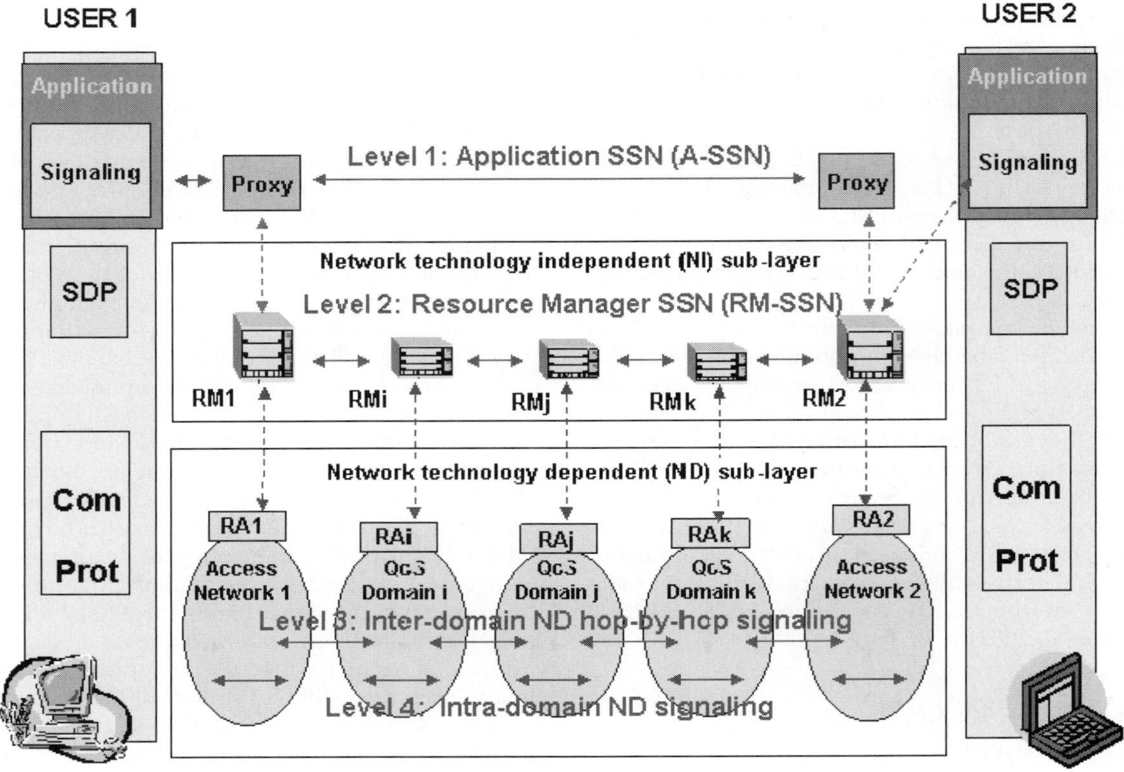

Figure 24: High-level view of the EuQoS signaling architecture

the data path across the various network domains. To enable domain administrative independence, Level 2 signaling functions operate on a hop-by-hop basis, between Resource Managers of adjacent administrative domains.

Level 2 signaling in EuQoS is based on NSIS. The vertical interactions between RMs and resource allocators (RAs) are supported on the COPS protocol.

Level 3 of signaling in the EuQoS architecture is the network technology-dependent (NTD) hop-by-hop inter-domain signaling. NTD hop-by-hop inter-domain signaling is commonly carried out by BGP (Border Gateway Protocol), which provides mechanisms for inter-domain traffic routing and enables the use of routing policies to control the exchange of routing information between different administrative domains (Autonomous Systems, ASs).

The definition of signaling mechanisms to be used at intra-domain level (the fourth signaling level) in the network technology-dependent layers is also in the scope of the EuQoS project. Knowledge about specific network-dependent signaling mechanisms has to be included in the domain's Resource Allocator to enable intra-domain resource management and QoS control.

Examples of intra-domain NTD signaling that RAs can use to configure network resources include RSVP and specific access network mechanisms such as ADSL bandwidth management, 3GPP, and Ethernet and Wi-Fi priorities. NSIS path-coupled also can be used for this level of signaling.

CONCLUSION

To avoid complexity inside the network, the Internet has been developed according to a data-driven approach—i.e., avoiding signaling as much as possible. Nevertheless, even the core Internet protocols, such as IP and TCP, do not work without some form of signaling functionality. ICMP is an IP-companion protocol that can be considered a signaling protocol. Many of the control mechanisms of TCP are signaling mechanisms.

Nowadays, the Internet is used for the support of countless applications with varying needs and characteristics. Internet elements must be managed, data flows must be secured, and quality of service must be provided to applications according to service-level agreements. All of this must be provided in a highly heterogeneous environment, as dynamically as possible. In this environment the original paradigm of keeping the network simple and free from signaling is not possible any more.

Signaling is indispensable for providing quality of service because QoS requires control over the existing resources. It also is indispensable for security, having an impact on NAT boxes and firewalls. With the advent of VoIP and of multimedia conferencing applications, in multipoint environments, signaling has become a key element of the current Internet.

In this chapter we have looked into the main signaling approaches and solutions for signaling. RSVP was developed as the supporting protocol for the Integrated

Services architecture for QoS provision. The Differentiated Service QoS architecture also requires some form of signaling, and this has also been dealt with here. Because of the growing need for signaling, the IETF is developing a comprehensive signaling framework, called NSIS, that has the potential to support the signaling needs of an unrestricted number of application areas, of which QoS and NAT/Firewall are the first cases. For voice, video, and multimedia applications, however, H.323 and, especially, SIP/SDP are the main solutions to session-oriented signaling. The future of signaling on the Internet certainly will include all of these.

GLOSSARY

COPS: Common Open Policy Service. COPS allows vertical signaling between Policy Decision Points (PDPs) and Policy Enforcement Points (PEPs).

GIST: General Internet Signaling Transport. GIST is a NSIS framework protocol for signaling transport between NSIS entities.

IETF: Internet Engineering Task Force. This is the organization responsible for the definition of Internet standards.

MPLS: Multi-Protocol Label Switching. MPLS is a protocol that supports traffic engineering (TE) using RSVP-TE extensions.

NATFW NSLP: NAT and Firewall NSIS Signaling Layer Protocol. This is the NSIS signaling protocol for NAT (Network Address Translation) and firewall transversal.

Network signaling: This is the exchange of data among network elements and end systems to support setup, maintenance, and release of network services.

NSIS: Next Steps in Signaling. This is the new signaling framework being standardized at the IETF.

RSVP: Resource Reservation Protocol. RSVP provides signaling for resource reservation in Integrated Services (IntServ) networks.

RTCP: Real Time Control Protocol. This signaling protocol enables synchronization of RTP (Real Time Protocol) flows.

SIP: Session Initiation Protocol. This is a signaling protocol for negotiation and maintenance of multimedia sessions.

CROSS REFERENCES

See *End-System QoS*; *Network QoS*; *TCP/IP Suite*; *Voice over MPLS and VoIP over MPLS*.

REFERENCES

Andersson, L. et al. 2001. *RFC 3036—LDP specification*. Internet Engineering Task Force.

Andersson, L. et al. 2002. *RFC 3212—Constraint-based LSP setup using LDP*, edited by B. Jamoussi. Internet Engineering Task Force.

Arkko, J. et al. 2003. *RFC 3329—Security mechanism agreement for the Session initiation Protocol (SIP)*. Internet Engineering Task Force.

Braden, R. et al. 1997. *RFC 2205—Resource ReSerVation Protocol (RSVP)—Version 1 functional specification*. Internet Engineering Task Force.

Calhoun, P. et al. 2003. *RFC 3588—Diameter base protocol*. Internet Engineering Task Force.

Case, J. D. et al. 1990. *RFC 1157—Simple Network Management Protocol (SNMP)*. Internet Engineering Task Force.

Chan, K. et al. 2001. *RFC 3084—COPS Usage for Policy Provisioning (COPS-PR)*. Internet Engineering Task Force.

Crocker, D. 1982. *RFC 822—Standard for the format of ARPA Internet text messages*. Internet Engineering Task Force.

Delgrossi, L., and L. Berger. 1995. *RFC 1819—Internet Stream Protocol Version 2 (ST2) protocol specification—Version ST2+*. Internet Engineering Task Force.

Faltstrom, P., and M. Mealling. 2004. *RFC 3761—The E.164 to Uniform Resource Identifiers (URI) Dynamic Delegation Discovery System (DDDS) application (ENUM)*. Internet Engineering Task Force.

Hancock, R. et al. 2005. *RFC 4080—Next Steps in Signaling (NSIS): Framework*. Internet Engineering Task Force.

Handley, M., and V. Jacobson 1998. *RFC 2327-SDP: Session Description Protocol*. Internet Engineering Task Force.

Herzog, S. 2000. *RFC 2750—RSVP extensions for policy control*. Internet Engineering Task Force.

ITU-T H.323. 2003. *Series H: Audiovisual and multimedia systems*. International Telecommunications Union.

Karagiannis, G., and A. McDonald. 2006. *NSLP for quality-of-service signaling*, <draft-ietf-nsis-qos-nslp-12.txt>, edited by J. Manner. Internet Engineering Task Force.

Manner, J., and X. Fu. 2005. *RFC 4094—Analysis of existing quality-of-service signaling protocols*. Internet Engineering Task Force.

Nguyen, T. et al. 2002. COPS-SLS: A service level negotiation protocol for the Internet, *IEEE Communication Magazine*, 40(5).

Pan, P., and H. Schulzrinne. 1998. YESSIR: A simple reservation mechanism for the Internet. *Computer Communication Review* 29(2). [ACM SIGCOMM].

Rekhter, Y., and E. Rosen. 2001. *RFC 3107—Carrying label information in BGP-4*. Internet Engineering Task Force.

Rosen, E., A. Viswanathan, and R. Callon. 2001. *RFC 3031—Multiprotocol label switching architecture*. Internet Engineering Task Force.

Rosenberg, J. et al. 2002. *RFC 3261—SIP: Session Initiation Protocol*. Internet Engineering Task Force.

Schulzrinne, H. et al. 2003. *RFC 3550—RTP: A transport protocol for real-time applications*, Internet Engineering Task Force.

Stiemerling, M. et al. 2006. *NAT/Firewall NSIS Signaling Layer Protocol (NSLP)*. <draft-ietf-nsis-nslp-natfw-13.txt>. Internet Engineering Task Force.

Tschofenig, H. et al. 2005. *RFC 4230—RSVP security properties*. Internet Engineering Task Force.

Tschofenig, H., and P. Eronen, P. 2006. Analysis of options for securing the Generic Internet Signaling Transport (GIST), Internet—Draft. Internet Engineering Task Force.

Wroclawski, J. 1997. *RFC 2210—The use of RSVP with IETF integrated services*. Internet Engineering Task Force.

FURTHER READING

Brandl, M. et al. 2004. *IP telephony cookbook*. TERENA Report, Terena, Amsterdam, The Netherlands.

Chowdhury, D. 2000. *High-speed LAN technology handbook*. Heidelberg, Germany: Springer-Verlag.

Douskalis, B. 2000. *IP telephony*. Upper Saddle River, NJ: Prentice Hall.

Hassan, M., and R. Jain, R. 2004. *High performance TCP/IP networking—Concepts, issues and solutions*. Upper Saddle River, NJ: Pearson Prentice Hall.

Johnston, A. et al. 2003. *RFC 3665—Session Initiation Protocol (SIP) basic call flow examples*. Internet Engineering Task Force.

Stallings, W. 2002. *High-speed networks and internets—Performance and quality of service*, 2nd edition. Englewood Cliffs, NJ: Prentice Hall.

Voice over MPLS and VoIP over MPLS

Junaid Ahmed Zubairi, *State University of New York, Fredonia*

INTRODUCTION

For the past few years, we have witnessed an increased deployment of multimedia traffic over the Internet. The triple play (voice, video, and data) services are taking shape using MPLS (multiprotocol label switching) as the core technology for integration. The standards and protocols for voice over MPLS have been developed by IETF (Internet Engineering Task Force), MFA Forum (formerly MPLS Forum) and the ITU-T (Telecommunication Standardization Sector of the International Telecommunication Union).

In this chapter, we focus on the deployment of voice over MPLS (VoMPLS) and VoIP (voice over IP) over MPLS (VoIPoMPLS). Voice and speech traffic is service sensitive because the packets delayed beyond the threshold time become unusable. Delays exceeding 400 ms are unacceptable, and the recommended maximum delay is 150 ms as per ITU-T recommendation G.114. On the other hand, some packet loss can be tolerated using redundant data to recover lost content and silence intervals to recover from problems. Since the TCP/IP network cannot guarantee the delay bounds of service-aware traffic, new protocols are developed that ensure the provisioning of required QoS (quality of service) using bandwidth allocation, traffic management, and fault handling. In the next section, we define the MPLS protocol as the core integration technology enabling QoS and traffic engineering in the network. The key concepts of MPLS are described and traffic treatment in an MPLS domain is discussed. MPLS serves as an enabling technology for QoS, and it works with DiffServ for prioritized handling of the QoS traffic. DiffServ is introduced, and the interworking of the MPLS-DiffServ network is explained.

Real-time VoIP and VoMPLS traffic has stringent requirements on the network, including zero packet loss, minimum delay, minimum jitter, and near zero call completion rate change (MFA 2004). In case of link or node failure, the network should recover within milliseconds to avoid any loss of communications. We discuss some of the protection schemes designed to meet these requirements and then look at the protocols and standards developed for VoIPoMPLS and VoMPLS. The enabling technologies, including codecs, signaling protocols, and transport protocols, are defined. The last section covers the issues and challenges and the future for packetized voice.

MPLS AND DIFFSERV PROTOCOLS

Since IP routers work with statistical multiplexing, the datagrams do not follow a fixed path and may arrive at the destination out of order and with large variations of end-to-end delay under congested network conditions. These problems make conventional IP networks largely unsuitable for connection-oriented applications such as interactive real-time voice. MPLS (Rosen 2001) has emerged as the key integration technology for carrying voice, video, and data traffic over the same network. In an MPLS-enabled network, LSPs are installed from an ingress node to an egress node prior to start of transmission. Therefore, the connection-oriented applications can take advantage of the "virtual connections" set by MPLS. There may be several ingress-egress pairs in an MPLS domain resulting in a complex management challenge. Since the LSPs are stackable, traffic from different flows sharing some common characteristics can be aggregated on an LSP. These characteristics may include common egress and identical QoS and protection requirements. "Stackable" refers to the fact that each packet is treated as per the topmost label in the label stack. Therefore, two LSPs can be merged together by pushing the same label on top of the label stack for packets belonging to both LSPs. Various LSPs may also be aggregated and segregated based on the loading and the status of the network links. For example, in case of link failure, the Fast Reroute (FRR) protection trigger would reroute the traffic around the faulty link and merge with the original path forward of the downstream node of the faulty link. In this case, the downstream node would act as the PML (Protection Merge LSR) for the rerouted traffic, and it would swap labels to ensure that the rerouted traffic is handled transparently after the fault location.

MPLS operates by defining labels for the packets that belong to LSPs installed in the domain. An MPLS "shim header" is placed on the packet between the layer-2 and layer-3 headers. The 32-bit shim header is organized as shown in Figure 1.

MPLS Label (20 bits)	EXP (3 bits)	S (1 bit)	TTL (8 bits)

Figure 1: MPLS header fields

The MPLS header fields include an unstructured 20-bit label that identifies the LSP to which this packet belongs. The label is assigned based on the FEC (forwarding equivalency class) of the traffic trunk. It is followed by 3 bits EXP (experimental) field and 1 bit indicating whether this is the bottom of the label stack. The TTL (Time to Live) field has the same usage as the TTL field in an IP header.

MPLS network runs constrained routing against traffic demands to find the most suitable LSP. Constrained routing involves computing the shortest path after pruning the network links that do not meet the requirements that may include reliability, bandwidth availability, cost, and delay. Constrained routing requires extended interior gateway protocols (IGP) such as open shortest path first–traffic engineering extensions (OSPF-TE) or intermediate system to intermediate system protocol–traffic engineering extensions (ISIS-TE). This capability to find the routes other than IGP shortest paths is known as MPLS-TE (MPLS traffic engineering) (Awduche et al. 1999). MPLS-TE achieves uniform distribution of traffic across the whole network, resulting in optimized utilization of the network. Once an LSP is installed, its minimum bandwidth is guaranteed on original and protection paths, and the status of all the links in the network is updated to reflect the bandwidth booking by the new LSP. LSPs are installed using label distribution protocol (LDP) or traffic engineering extensions of resource reservation protocol (RSVP-TE) defined by IETF. MPLS allows seamless integration with conventional IP networks because the MPLS header is removed by the egress router before forwarding the packet to the conventional IP network. The scalability offered by LSPs is unmatched even by asynchronous transfer mode (ATM) network because ATM offers only two levels of hierarchy as opposed to arbitrary number of levels in MPLS.

LSPs may carry different types of traffic, including e-mail messages, real-time stock quotes and bids, real-time biomedical data, real-time voice packets, FTP (file transfer protocol) packets, streaming video frames, and Web postings. In general, traffic can be categorized as elastic best effort and inelastic QoS traffic. The best effort traffic does not need any bandwidth, delay, and loss guarantees. On the other hand, QoS-sensitive traffic such as VoIP has certain minimum bandwidth and delay requirements. Therefore, the core routers should offer appropriate services based on the type of traffic involved. Class based queuing (CBQ) can be invoked on routers that implement the differentiated services (DiffServ) protocol. DiffServ is defined by IETF in various Request for Comments (RFC) standard documents. CBQ allows routers to create separate queues for each outgoing link based on the class of traffic. The QoS traffic is placed in a high-priority queue and serviced first.

DiffServ divides the traffic into expedited forwarding (EF) and assured forwarding (AF) per-hop behaviors (PHBs). EF is the premium service offered under DiffServ. It is suitable for low latency and low jitter flows that maintain almost constant rate. EF flows receive a minimum guaranteed bandwidth even under most congested conditions. AF PHB is subdivided into four classes, each receiving a minimum bandwidth and each class getting subdivided into three drop preferences. The packets in microflows falling into one of the subclasses cannot be reordered where a microflow refers to an individual user application generated traffic. The router can choose to discard packets based on their drop preferences. Best effort traffic receives default forwarding (DF) behavior from the network without any bandwidth or delay guarantees. Each packet carries a PHB identifier that is used by the router to place the packet in an appropriate queue, and each queue is serviced as per its priority. DiffServ provides a mechanism to control the amount of traffic per PHB entering a domain through the use of shaper, marker, and dropper entities operating within the ingress node. The core routers identify the packet PHB and offer appropriate service accordingly. The type of service (ToS) field in an IP packet header is modified to carry the DiffServ class information as shown in the Figure 2.

Differentiated services codepoint (DSCP) is a field in the IP packet header for classifying the packet in one of the DiffServ PHBs. As seen in Figure 2, DSCP extends to 6 bits, allowing a total of 64 PHBs to be defined. However, practically, only 14 PHBs have been defined because of varying drop precedences with one EF, one DF and twelve AF subclasses. To indicate drop precedences, DSCP field is subdivided into PHB Scheduling class (PSC) and Drop precedence. The two ECN bits are for explicit congestion notification. With two ECN bits, only four values are possible for congestion notification. Values 10 and 01 are set by the sender to indicate ECN-capability. The value 00 indicates that the packet is not using the ECN mechanism, and the value 11 is used by a router to indicate congestion to the end nodes (Ramakrishnan et al. 2001). The DiffServ protocol follows the Internet model of keeping the network core simple. The core routers only determine

DiffServ codepoint (DSCP) 6 bits	ECN 1 bit	ECN 1 bits

Figure 2: DiffServ mapping in IPv4 ToS field

the DSCP and serve each packet according to the PHB to which it belongs. The complex functions of admission control, shaping, marking, and dropping are pushed to the edge routers.

In an MPLS-DiffServ network, the routers jointly implement various MPLS and DiffServ functions. The ingress router is responsible for determining an LSP for a new flow request. The QoS requirements of the new flow can be translated into DiffServ class assignment at the ingress. For this purpose, the EXP field in the MPLS shim header is used. As the EXP field is 3 bits in length, it can represent only eight different scheduling and drop precedences. Under MPLS-DiffServ (Le Faucheur et al. 2002), two types of LSPs are defined. E-LSP interprets the label field of MPLS shim header as the egress identifier and the EXP field as the DiffServ PSC (PHB scheduling class) combined with the drop precedence. On the other hand, L-LSP interprets the label field as the DiffServ scheduling priority and the destination. The EXP field in L-LSP is used to indicate only the drop precedence of the packet. The main difference between E-LSP and L-LSP is the aggregation feature in E-LSP resulting in scalability; however, some PSCs in an E-LSP may suffer because the bandwidth is reserved for the whole LSP (Fineberg 2003).

When the transmission starts, the packets belonging to an assigned flow are marked as per the DiffServ PSC (PHB Scheduling class) and labeled as per the LSP installed. When a core router receives a packet belonging to this LSP, the LSP label is swapped based on the pre-installed label table, and the packet is placed in an appropriate outgoing queue as per the DiffServ PSC identifier found in the packet. Figure 3 shows the placement of the DiffServ class identifier and MPLS label for an E-LSP.

Priority flows must be protected against link and node failures. In an MPLS domain, protection schemes are implemented to provide backup paths. The next section discusses some MPLS protection schemes. Another requirement is security and portability that can be ensured by using MPLS-based VPN (virtual private network) tunnels.

In summary, MPLS-DiffServ networks offer the following services that are of particular importance to VoIP and VoMPLS:

- Advance reservation of bandwidth through installation of LSPs
- Aggregation (Multiplexing) of similar flows by the use of stackable LSPs
- Priority handling through the use of DiffServ identifiers and CBQ on routers
- Fast and efficient fault handling by the use of MPLS-based protection schemes
- Security and portability through the use of MPLS-based VPN tunnels

MPLS PROTECTION SCHEMES

To guard against failures, a number of protection and restoration techniques have been proposed for MPLS networks. Protection and restoration are separate techniques that yield different results. *Restoration* reacts to a failure by computing the path around the failed node or link after the failure has occurred. On the other hand, *protection* is a proactive technique that precomputes and installs backup paths for the high-priority LSPs. In most cases, the protection paths may be utilized by best effort traffic that can be preempted if the original high-priority path fails. In case of extremely sensitive high-priority traffic, protection paths can be used to carry duplicate streams (1+1) so that the communication is assured even if one of the original LSPs fails. The other proposals include 1:1 (one backup LSP for each primary LSP), 1:N (one backup LSP for a group of primary LSPs), M:1 (a group of backup LSPs for one primary LSP), and M:N (a group of backup LSPs for a group of primary LSPs).

MPLS labels are stackable, so traffic can be switched from the primary LSP to the backup LSP or backup segment LSP by a simple push of a label. Because each LSP is destined toward a specific node, any link failures that occur before the egress can be resolved by the FRR (fast reroute) technique, which creates a bypass tunnel around the fault. The bypass tunnel would resolve the local failures without involving L3 (Layer 3 or network layer). If the bypass tunnel rejoins the primary tunnel at the next hop, it only protects against link failures. If the bypass tunnel does not join the primary tunnel until after several hops, the PML is configured to identify and remove the backup label so that the original tunnel is identified at the primary egress node. Issues pertaining to the bypass tunnel include the scope of the label space and modification of forwarding information base (FIB) entries. To avoid signaling for label exchange, global label space should be used for the domain. In case of failure, FIB entries in the router are modified to push the bypass tunnel first hop label on each packet carrying the primary tunnel label and to point to the new interface through which the traffic would pass (Suwala 2004).

In addition to FRR, protection paths in MPLS can be installed on a per link basis (SLB) or per path basis (DP). In SLB (Single Link Basis) protection, each link of the primary LSP is protected by a backup LSP that is computed after pruning the original link from the tree. Thus it results in comprehensive protection of all the links that are members of an LSP. In DP (Disjoint Path) based protection, each LSP is protected by a link disjoint global backup LSP that reaches the same egress as the original LSP (Conte et al. 2002). The SLB scheme is computation intensive as it installs "L" backup paths for an LSP consisting of "L" links.

MPLS Label (20 bits) (FEC Destination)	EXP (3 bits) (DiffServ PSC) 3 bits	S (1 bit)	TTL (8 bits)

Figure 3: DiffServ PSC placement in MPLS E-LSP header

In MPLS, a global backup path may be established for a working path; however, the fault indication may be implemented with simple path continuity tests. Thus, it may result in larger recovery time. Using reverse backup (RB) can speed up recovery in the following way (Marzo et al. 2003). When an outgoing link goes down, the current node can utilize a reverse backup LSP to direct the traffic back to the ingress of the working path. This node can also propagate the fault indication signal (FIS) to the ingress in addition to the traffic that can now be directed through the global backup path. Thus no packets are lost, and the FIS is propagated to the ingress within the shortest possible time. The RB scheme is most suitable for loss-intolerant applications, and it protects against multiple failures. It may also help in achieving a better performance in a Voice over Packet (VoP) network where loss bursts can render the service unsatisfactory.

VOMPLS AND VOIPOMPLS MECHANISMS

VoIP is implemented with RTP. Voice segments are packetized with RTP headers and placed in UDP segments for onward transmission through the IP/MPLS network. On the other hand, VoMPLS (MFA 2001) removes the overhead associated with the protocol stack of VoIP and carries voice directly over MPLS. Figure 4 shows the comparison of protocol stacks in both schemes. VoIP has the clear advantage of providing end-to-end connectivity because the user-to-network interface (UNI) definition for bringing users in direct contact with MPLS networks is still not mature, and its specification was released only recently (ITU-T 2002). VoIP protocol stack results in large headers that can be compressed to reduce the overhead. VoMPLS is currently more suitable for core network where a number of voice calls can be multiplexed and carried directly over the MPLS.

In both VoIP and VoMPLS, it is required to convert the voice into digital format using any of the several codecs proposed. Signaling is also needed to establish, maintain, and terminate a call. Transporting the digitized voice requires special protocols that can handle the real-time characteristics of the speech traffic. The next sections discuss the signaling and conversion standards, transport protocols, and VoIP over MPLS and VoMPLS issues.

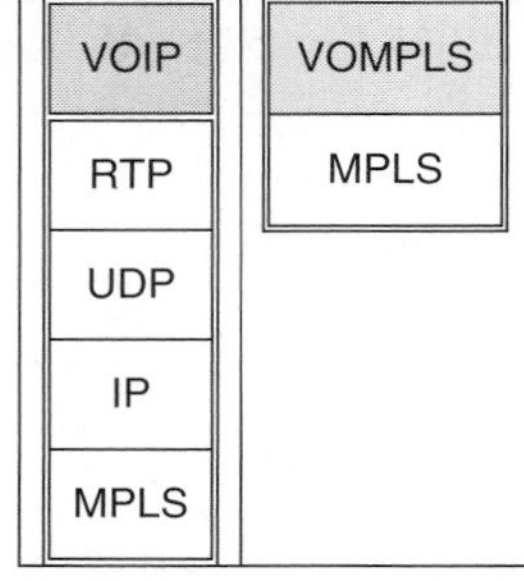

Figure 4: VoIPoMPLS and VoMPLS protocol stacks

Codecs

Several codecs have been proposed for encoding voice, including the pulse code modulation (PCM) based G.711, G.721, G.722, G.726, and G.727, and the code excited linear prediction (CELP) based G.729 (ITU-T, G.729.1). PCM-based codecs digitize voice samples for rates reaching up to 64 kbps. However, G.726 and G.727 can also work with variable rates. On the other hand, G.723.1 uses voice samples of 30 ms duration to produce 20 to 24 bytes, resulting in rates of 5.3 kbps to 6.4 kbps. High-complexity coder G.729 is based on conjugate structure algebraic code excited linear prediction (CS-ACELP) algorithm, and it has a coding rate of 8 kbps with 80 bits every 10ms. The code-excited codecs take advantage of the properties of the human conversation to produce a much lower bit rate.

High bit rate codecs, such as G.711, G.726, and G.728, are found to produce very good mean opinion score (MOS) values meaning low voice degradation (Duysburgh et al. 2001) even in loaded best effort network conditions. It was determined through experiments that compressed adaptive differential pulse code modulation (ADPCM) codecs (G.721, G.722, G.726, G.727) yield end-to-end delays close to uncompressed PCM delays. The G.711 u-law codec has a higher compression/decompression delay and higher bit rates as compared to ADPCM codecs making it unattractive. However, the MOS scores for u-law codecs are better than those for ADPCM codecs (Zeadally et al. 2004). It is argued that uncompressed voice may be suitable in the intranet where higher bandwidth connections are available to save on the extra compression and decompression processing. In wide area VoIP implementations, G.729 has generated considerable interest because of its good quality and low bit rate. As opposed to PCM high bit rate codecs used in PSTN, G.729 is capable of taking advantage of the 60 percent silence periods in a conversation to reduce its effective rate to about 3.2 kbps (Scheets et al. 2004). This reduction in bandwidth is made possible by detecting voice presence or absence in a sample and not transmitting during silence periods. The receiver fills in comfort noise during the periods when G.729 transmitter is not sending any samples to avoid the dead line effect. However, this reduction in bandwidth turns the constant bit rate flow into variable rate flow.

SIP and H.323

H.323 is a comprehensive protocol introduced by ITU-T to allow real-time multimedia conferencing on the Internet. H.323 is a collection of various standards and protocols that allow the end users to choose the codecs, connect and register with the gatekeepers, route to the PSTN network through gateways, and encapsulate and transmit media by using RTP over the Internet. H.323 includes the following:

- H.225 registration, admission and status (RAS) protocol for registration with the gatekeeper
- H.225.0 for data transportation
- H.245 for connection management
- Q.931 signaling channel
- Optional video support through H.261

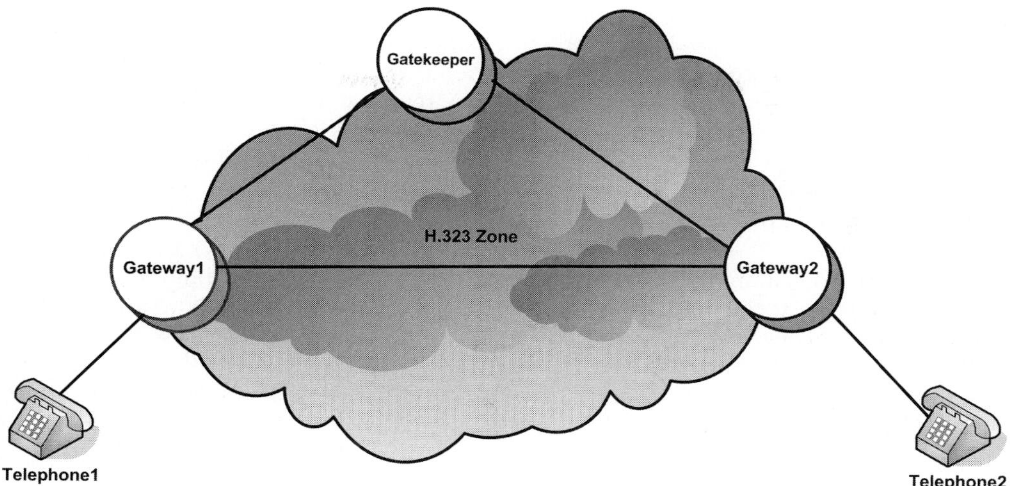

Figure 5: H.323 devices

H.323 zone gatekeeper is an entity on the network that translates H.323 IDs and PSTN phone numbers into IP addresses. It coordinates the admission of end points into the H.323 network by using the RAS protocol. RAS messages are exchanged between gateways and gatekeeper using UDP. The gateways are the interface between the PSTN and the IP network. The gatekeeper also performs bandwidth management and control, and it may reject calls when the appropriate bandwidth is not available. Call control and setup signaling is carried out between gateways via the gatekeeper or directly using Q.931 signaling messages. Following are some example steps in the H.323 call setup process, which are based on H.323 working descriptions (Cisco, ID5244). The devices mentioned in the explanation are illustrated in Figure 5. It is assumed that the call is being placed between two PSTN phones namely Telephone1 and Telephone2. Telephone1 is connected through Gateway 1 (GW1) to the H.323 zone, and Telephone2 is connected through Gateway2 (GW2) to the H.323 zone.

1. The gateways periodically attempt to discover the zone gatekeeper. After the gatekeeper is discovered, gateways register with an e-mail address or a phone number.
2. A new phone call across the H.323 network originates from Telephone1, and it touches GW1 first, which forwards it for acceptance to the gatekeeper.
3. The gatekeeper looks up the destination in its tables and consults peer gatekeepers in other zones until the destination is determined. Some vendors implement a centralized directory gatekeeper to keep the architecture scalable. In this example, the call is intra-zone, and the gatekeeper finds the destination gateway, which is GW2, in its tables.
4. The gatekeeper informs the origin gateway GW1 about the coordinates of the destination gateway GW2.
5. The origin gateway GW1 sends a call setup request to the destination gateway GW2.
6. The destination gateway GW2 requests clearance of the new call from the gatekeeper of its zone.
7. On receiving clearance, the destination gateway GW2 places a call to the destination PSTN phone Telephone2.
8. On connecting to the destination phone, the destination gateway GW2 sends a connection confirmation message to the origin gateway GW1.
9. When one of the parties hangs up, the related gateway sends a control message to the gatekeeper of its zone and another control message to the other gateway. For example, if Telephone1 hangs up, GW1 will send control messages to the gatekeeper of this zone and GW2.
10. The other gateway informs the gatekeeper of its zone about the call termination and sends a call disconnect signal to the other party through the PSTN network. Continuing the example of disconnection initiated by Telephone1, GW2 will inform the gatekeeper about call termination and indicate call disconnection to Telephone2.

SIP (Session Initiation Protocol) is a signaling protocol introduced by IETF (Rosenberg et al. 2002) for real-time multimedia communications over the Internet. SIP has a limited scope as compared to H.323. SIP specifies the call initiation, management, and termination mechanisms and does not mandate the use of any specific transmission protocols or codecs. Two primary categories of devices in SIP are servers and user agents. A SIP registrar is equivalent to an H.323 gatekeeper in functionality as it registers each SIP user and provides coordinates of a user when a call request is received (Kurose and Ross 2005). The SIP proxy server manages signaling and works in conjunction with the SIP registrar to return the appropriate response to the caller. SIP does not provide direct support for interfacing to PSTN as opposed to H.323. SIP commands are text based, thus making it easy to develop SIP-based applications. Both H.323 and SIP allow selection of any codec, and both communicating parties need not use the same codec. Following are some steps in registering SIP clients and using SIP to establish voice calls with other SIP users:

1. On initiation, a SIP device (user agent) sends its coordinates to the SIP registrar and periodically refreshes this registration information.
2. When a SIP device wants to call another SIP device, the caller is termed as user agent client, and the called party is termed as user agent server. The caller sends the INVITE request to the SIP proxy server.
3. The SIP proxy server returns the most recent coordinates of the called party as obtained from the SIP registrar.
4. Using the location as returned by the proxy, the caller establishes direct connection to the called party for exchanging media bytes.
5. Any of the parties engaged in a call can terminate the call by sending a call termination request that is acknowledged by the other party.

VoIPoMPLS and VoIP Issues

VoIPoMPLS involves encapsulating the coded voice bytes into the RTP packets and transmitting over the UDP/IP/MPLS protocol stack. The combined count of header bytes for RTP, UDP, and IP is 40 bytes. Figure 6 shows the voice data together with L3 and above headers. For MPLS VPN transporting voice, this overhead reaches 48 bytes and exceeds the payload size. Therefore, it is very important to multiplex different voice packets and to compress the header. Voice packets that belong to the same connection can be multiplexed together in one MPLS frame. However, it would require extra wait time at the sender side before transmitting the multiplexed frame. Thus, this option has to be carefully exercised given the delay budget of VoIP. Various header compression techniques have been proposed, including compressed RTP, enhanced compressed RTP, and robust header compression. Also, composite IP (CIP) and lightweight IP encapsulation (LIPE) concatenate voice packets together (Vázquez 2004). With RFC 2508 (Casner et al. 1999) compression of RTP/UDP/IP headers, the header length reduces to 2-4 bytes. Other issues in VoIP include jitter removal, silence suppression, echo cancellation, serialization delay, and loss recovery. We discuss each issue briefly and point out the solutions proposed.

Jitter

Jitter is the unwanted variation in end-to-end delay that results from indeterministic queuing delays in routers. Jitter can cause the VoIP service to fail. Jitter can be smoothed out by using a jitter buffer, but the jitter buffer tends to increase the overall end-to-end delay. Jitter can be removed by service-aware routing, assigning highest priority to speech traffic and bandwidth allocation through the use of MPLS and DiffServ.

Silence Suppression

Silence suppression seeks to save on the network bandwidth by not transmitting the voice packets during the silence intervals. However, to avoid the "dead line" effect, it is important to use CNG (comfort noise generation) when the receiver does not get any voice samples from the sender. The sender deploys VAD (voice activity detection) to scan each sample and determine if voice is present or not.

Echo

Echo is an annoying effect in conversation, and it may be caused in VoIP by coupling between a microphone and a speaker and line cross-talk (Scheets et al. 2004). The most difficult type of echo is the one produced by the use of independent microphone and speaker in VoIP conversations as done by most PC users today. Echo can be controlled and reduced by the use of echo canceller filters that detect and filter out the copies of the original signal. Such filters can be programmed into codecs that digitize the voice. Increased end-to-end delay causes the perceived echo signal level to increase, and thus the filters may not work correctly. Noise reduction and automatic level control techniques are part of the G.169 standard (ITU-T 1999) for alleviating these problems. Noise reduction techniques work on suppressing nonvarying noise by learning the spectral frequencies of the noise and filtering out the same. ALC (Automatic Level Control) involves keeping the transmitted signal at a predetermined level by adjusting the gain and loss.

Serialization Delay

Serialization delay is caused by the placement of packets on the serial network path. On the receiving end, the bits on the serial line are then captured and converted back to packets. Faster hardware has evolved reducing this type of delay.

Speech Traffic Loss

Finally, it is not critical for speech traffic to arrive without any loss because up to 10 percent loss in the original uncompressed data is reported to have no effect on the perceived quality of speech (Kostas et al. 1998) provided that the data is not highly compressed. However, loss burst may affect the conversation in an adverse way. Loss bursts of a small number of packets may be corrected

IP Header (20 bytes)	UDP Header (8 bytes)	RTP Header (12 bytes) plus optional RTP mux	Voice Data (40 bytes for G.711 at 64 kbps)

Figure 6: L3 and above uncompressed headers for VoIPoMPLS

Payload Type (one byte)	Sequence Number (2 bytes)	Time Stamp (4 bytes)	SSRC (4 bytes)	Miscellaneous (one byte)

Figure 7: Some header fields for RTP

Channel Identifier (8 bits)	Payload Type (8 bits)	Counter (8 bits)	Payload Length (6 bits)	Pad Length (2 bits)

Figure 8: VoMPLS (MFA 1.0) primary frame header fields

by the use of the forward error correction (FEC) techniques that add redundant information to packets or perform interleaving to reduce the burst errors. In case of holes in the received stream, FEC techniques can plug the holes with reduced quality speech recovered from FEC chunks in the packets.

RTP and RTCP

RTP (Schulzrinne et al. 2003) and RTCP (Real Time Control Protocol) (Schulzrinne et al. 2003) have been developed to facilitate the transmission of time-sensitive traffic over the Internet. RTP is the actual transmission protocol that works above UDP.

The voice data at the sending side is concatenated with a header that identifies the codec used and specifies the time stamp and sequence number. Some of the fields in the RTP header are shown in Figure 7 and explained here:

- The Payload Type field identifies the encoder used for VoIP out of various codecs discussed earlier.
- Each RTP segment is numbered sequentially, and the number is placed in the Sequence Number field.
- The time stamp is taken from the sender clock, and it reflects the time at which the first byte in the voice data was sampled.
- Synchronization source identifier (SSRC) is a random number generated and attached to a stream when a new stream starts to get transmitted. Optionally, contributing source identifier (CSRC) can be added ahead of SSRC if multiplexing of various streams is performed.
- Extra information can be attached using the next field, and possibly an extension header can be added by the application using RTP.

RTCP is a protocol that works in conjunction with RTP to provide valuable feedback to each participant. RTCP opens a port numbered one higher than the RTP port and periodically allows the receiver to send statistics of the session to the RTP sender and vice versa. RTP sender can use the information from the receiver to readjust the rate in order to decrease the losses. The RTCP packets contain statistics of packets sent/received and lost as well as jitter for a particular session identified by SSRC. To contain the amount of control traffic to a minimum, RTCP limits the frequency of its packets so that the overall bandwidth usage is less than or equal to 5 percent of the total bandwidth used by the session.

VoMPLS

VoMPLS refers to the scenario in which the voice packets are directly transported over the MPLS without the use of RTP/UDP/IP protocol stack. As seen earlier in Figure 4, the VoMPLS protocol stack is more compact as compared to VoIP. Two types of frames are defined in VoMPLS: primary and control frames. The VoMPLS primary frame header is shown (MFA 2001) in Figure 8.

VoMPLS primary frame header is 4 bytes long and includes 5 fields:

- Channel Identifier uniquely identifies the voice channel that is the source of the payload. Thus, a total of 248 different voice calls can be multiplexed into a single LSP.
- Payload Type identifies the encoding scheme used as well as silence removal/insertion descriptors. A value equal to or above 224 indicates control payload (part of the control frame) that would allow DTMF (dual tone multi frequency) dialed digits as well as signaling for the channel to be carried (Fjellskål 2002).
- The revolving Counter field is set at the first sample or frame and keeps incrementing for each additional frame.
- Payload Length is read in conjunction with the pad length to keep the payload a multiple of 4 bytes.

Multiple LSPs can be aggregated with the use of optional inner MPLS labels in addition to one mandatory outer MPLS label. The VoMPLS control frame header is also 4 bytes in length, and the fields in the header are shown in Figure 9.

The Payload Type field distinguishes between dialed digits and the channel related signaling. Time Stamp is relative to the first randomized time stamp. The Redundancy field is very important to ensure the receipt of the control frames. If the Redundancy field is set to 0, 1, or 2, the control packet is repeated that many times.

Another solution for VoMPLS reuses ATM Adaptation Layer 2 (AAL2) components but replaces ATM by MPLS (ITU-T 2002) (MFA 2003), thus eliminating the ATM cell overhead. The MFA 5.0 implementation agreement

Channel Identifier (8 bits)	Payload Type (8 bits)	Time Stamp (16 bits)	Redundancy (8 bits)

Figure 9: VoMPLS control frame header format

MPLS Label Stack	A2oMPLS Header			CPS Packet Header			
	Reserved	Length	S No	CID	LI	UUI	HEC

Figure 10: A2oMPLS and CPS header in MPLS frame

proposes voice trunking over MPLS by directly encapsulating AAL2 common part sublayer (CPS) packets into MPLS (A2oMPLS). The gateway to the MPLS network should be able to function as an AAL2 switch. Multiple A2oMPLS connections can be multiplexed into a single LSP. One MPLS frame may carry multiple CPS packets. The detailed header fields are shown in Figure 10.

The following fields are included in the A2oMPLS header:

- Reserved (10 bits) currently ignored.
- Length (6 bits) used for padding length. It is set to 0 if A2oMPLS packet length exceeds 64 bytes.
- Sequence Number (S No) (16 bits) used if guaranteed ordered packet delivery is required. Sequence number of 0 indicates otherwise.

The following fields are inside the CPS packet header; several CPS packets may be packed in one MPLS frame.

- CID (8 bits) identifies the A2oMPLS connection carried. Thus a total of 248 connections (8 to 255) can be multiplexed into a single LSP.
- LI (6 bits) identifies the length of the CPS packet.
- UUI (5 bits) is used for user-to-user indication (0 to 27 for users, 30-31 for layer management, and above 31 reserved).
- HEC (5 bits) (header error control) uses CRC checksum. However, this field may not be used in the MPLS environment.

The AAL2 is suitable for transport of streams for which the bit rate may be variable, but they require bounded delay guarantees. Examples are the compressed voice and video streams. Several streams of AAL2 can be multiplexed into a single MPLS LSP using the A2oMPLS implementation agreement.

THE ROAD AHEAD FOR VOIP AND VOMPLS

VoP (Voice over Packet) is emerging as the most preferred method of transporting voice calls. Packetized voice is flexible as different voice calls can be multiplexed in the core and encrypted to ensure privacy. The service providers can use most of the deployed bandwidth for profit and the users pay only for the services that they use. Traditional Internet was unable to support the voice traffic with QoS guarantees. VoIP had to work under the best effort scenario, utilizing dejitter buffers to minimize jitter and put packets in order. Loss recovery was implemented using interleaving and adding redundant information to the packets. Even with these corrective measures, the user-perceived quality was poor. With the introduction of new protocols such as DiffServ, MPLS, and MPLS-TE, it has become possible to achieve performance closer to the toll quality voice as in PSTN.

Industry is converging on MPLS as the protocol of choice for voice, video, and data transmission over the Internet. MPLS is adaptable to various QoS demands and allows stacking of LSPs for scalability and aggregated treatment. VoIPoMPLS deploys voice over the RTP/UDP/IP protocol stack, which uses MPLS tunnels. VoMPLS runs voice directly over MPLS, reducing the protocol tax. VoIPoMPLS with compressed headers is a viable option for providing the Internet telephony to the end users as the overhead reduces to a minimum. VoMPLS is well suited for multiplexing in the core and carrying the bulk of voice calls through the MPLS domain. If the MPLS user-to-network interface (UNI) is implemented widely in the near future to allow the users to connect directly with the MPLS network, it may take VoMPLS to the end users with new possibilities. An important consideration is to segregate the best effort traffic and QoS traffic in the core of the network to reduce the possible delays and loss due to the congestion resulting from data bursts on shared links. Work has been done to automate the segregation of traffic in an MPLS-DiffServ domain (Zubairi 2002), and further enhancements are needed to fully automate the segregated allocation of bandwidth to the MPLS tunnels.

Some of the challenging issues in implementing VoIP include the suppression of echo, location-aware E911 emergency services, uninterrupted power for VoIP phones, making VoIP intruder safe, and porting numbers. We discuss some of these issues here:

- The VoIP security threats include fraud related to billing and unauthorized usage by stealing the service. WLAN-based telephony gives rise to major security problems because WLAN is mostly open and unencrypted.

MPLS-based VPNs can be used to ensure security and privacy for VoIP calls.

- The FCC had mandated the E-911 service (FCC 2005) for VoIP phones by November 2005, but this deadline is now pushed back by four years because of problems in implementing the user location detection in VoIP phones.
- Because VoIP phones are operated with utility power, blackouts and brownouts may leave customers disconnected. Therefore, efforts are under way to ensure uninterrupted service for VoIP.

The efforts to provide uninterrupted power can benefit from the recent interest in extending MPLS into the wireless network and especially 3G UMTS (universal mobile telephone service). It is expected that in the near term, there will be an increased VoIP implementation in the cellular network. The IMS (IP multimedia subsystem) specification has generated a lot of activity for enabling quad play services, making video phone calls a closer target that can be achieved with increased bandwidth in wireless networks. IMS is a modular platform that is based on IP and SIP. If the quad play continues to grow, the traffic mix in future networks would change to mostly delay bounded VBR (variable bit rate) streams, causing the interest in MFA IA 5.0 (MFA 2003) and similar standards to increase. MFA IA 5.0 is specified by MFA Forum as a standard for voice trunking over MPLS. It is believed that the next generation interactive telephony will be based on MPLS, and it will allow transparent connectivity through landline and mobile networks. The user will be able to continue the conversation while changing the connection from landline network to mobile network. The VoP phones would be flexible and allow all the functionality of current PSTN phones. The most significant new functionality would include multiway audio and text conference calling, videoconferencing, and several options for security and encryption.

GLOSSARY

IETF: Internet Engineering Task Force is an open volunteer organization that develops Internet protocols and standards.

IMS: IP multimedia subsystem is a SIP-based standardized architecture developed to merge multimedia services in IP and cellular networks.

ITU-T: International Telecommunications Union-Telecommunication Standardization Sector is a body that produces telecommunication standards for ITU.

MFA Forum: MPLS and Frame Relay Alliance Forum is an international association of telecom and networking companies advancing deployment of multiservice packet-based networks.

MPLS: Multiprotocol label switching is a mechanism to implement connection oriented and regulated services over the connectionless TCP/IP-based Internet. IETF and MFA Forum are responsible for advancing MPLS standards.

QoS: Quality of service is the probability of meeting the goals of reliability, timeliness, and delivery of packets in a network.

RTP: Real time protocol is a standard format for delivering multimedia over the Internet.

SIP: Session initiation protocol is a signaling protocol for multimedia conferencing over the Internet.

VoIP: Voice over IP is the routing of voice phone calls over the Internet fully or partly.

VoMPLS: Voice directly over MPLS is the routing of voice calls over MPLS instead of voice over IP over MPLS.

VoP: Voice over Packet is a general term that covers VoIP,VoIPoMPLS, and VoMPLS.

VPN: Virtual private network is a private network configured over the public Internet. It allows remote users to connect to their corporate network as if they were local users.

WLAN: Wi-Fi (IEEE 802.11) based wireless local area network that allows users within the range of radio waves to connect to the network.

CROSS REFERENCES

See *End-System QoS; Network QoS; Network Traffic Management; Voice over IP (VoIP).*

REFERENCES

Awduche, D. et al. 1999. *Requirements for traffic engineering over MPLS*. RFC 2702.

Casner, S. et al. 1999. *Compressing IP/UDP/RTP headers for low-speed serial links*. RFC 2508.

Cisco. ID5244. Understanding H.323 gatekeepers, Document ID 5244. www.cisco.com/warp/public/788/voip/understand-gatekeepers.html (accessed January 16th, 2006).

Conte, G. et al. 2002. Strategy for protection and restoration of optical paths in WDM backbone networks for next-generation Internet infrastructures. *Journal of Lightwave Technology* 20(8): 1264–1276.

Duysburgh, B. et al. 2001. On the influence of best-effort network conditions on the perceived speech quality of VoIP connections. Proceedings of 10th ICCCN, Oct '01, Scottsdale, Arizona, 334–339.

FCC Consumer Advisory. 2005. *VoIP and 911 service*. www.fcc.gov/cgb/consumerfacts/voip911.html (accessed January 15, 2006).

Fineberg, V. 2003. QoS Support in MPLS networks. MFA Forum white paper.

Fjellskål, E., and S. Solberg. 2002. Evaluation of Voice over MPLS (VoMPLS) compared to Voice over IP (VoIP) (masters thesis, Agder Univ College).

Halsall, F. 2001. *Multimedia communications*. Boston: Addison Wesley. ISBN 0-201-39818-4.

ITU-T. 1999. Recommendation G.169. *Automatic Level Control Devices*.

ITU-T. 2002. Recommendation Y.1261. *Service requirements and architecture for voice services over MPLS*.

ITU-T. 2006. Recommendation G.729.1. An 8-32 Kbit/S scalable coder interoperable with G.729 for wideband telephony and voice over IP. *ITU-T standards for speech compression and decompression*.

Kostas, T. et al. 1998. Real-time Voice over Packet-switched networks. *IEEE Network* 1-2: 18–27.

Kurose, J., and K. Ross. 2005. *Computer networking*. 3rd ed. Boston: Addison Wesley. ISBN 0-321-22735-2.

Le Faucheur, F. et al. 2002. *MPLS support of differentiated services*. RFC 3270.

Marzo, J. et al. 2003. QoS online routing and MPLS multilevel protection: A survey. *IEEE Communications Magazine*, 126–132.

MFA. 2001. Voice over MPLS: Bearer Transport Implementation Agreement (MFA IA 1.0). MFA Forum.

MFA. 2003. Voice trunking format over MPLS. MPLS/FR 5.0.0. I.366.2. MFA Forum.

MFA. 2004. MPLS ready to serve the enterprise. MPLS Frame Relay Alliance Forum white paper. www.mfaforum.org/tech/superdemo_2004.pdf (accessed January 14, 2006).

Ramakrishnan, K. et al. 2001.*The addition of explicit congestion notification (ECN) to IP*. RFC 3168.

Rosen, E. et al. 2001. *Multiprotocol Label Switching Architecture*. RFC 3031.

Rosenberg, J. et al. 2002. *SIP: Session Initiation Protocol. RFC 3261*.

Scheets, G. et al. 2004. Voice over the Internet: A tutorial discussing problems and solutions associated with alternative transport. *IEEE Communications Surveys and Tutorials* 6(2): 22–31.

Schulzrinne H. et al. 2003. RTP: A transport protocol for real-time applications. RFC 3550. (RFC1889 defines RTCP also).

Suwala, G. et al. 2004. SONET/SDH like resiliency for IP networks: A survey of traffic protection mechanisms. *IEEE Network* 3-4, 20–25.

Vázquez, E. 2004. Network convergence over MPLS. In *Lecture Notes in Computer Science*, Vol. 3079: High Speed Networks and Multimedia Communications. New York: Springer Verlag.

Zeadally, S. et al. 2004. Voice over IP in intranet and Internet environments. *IEE Proc.-Commun*. 151–3, 263–269.

Zubairi, J. 2002. An automated traffic engineering algorithm for MPLS-DiffServ domain. In *Proceedings Advanced Telecommuncations Sympsoium02*, April '02, San Diego, CA.

Telephone Number Mapping (ENUM)

Leslie L. Daigle, *Cisco Systems, Herndon, Virginia*

INTRODUCTION

Depending on whom you ask, "ENUM" is short for "tElephone NUmber Mapping," "E164 NUmber Mapping," or "Electronic NUMbering." Although the name may have multiple interpretations, ENUM is clearly defined as a use of the *domain name system* (DNS) for storage of telephone numbers to identify available services connected to one telephone number.

The advent of Internet services has broadened the range of possibilities for routing communications as well as brought an explosion in the number of common contact service types. Anyone who uses the Internet is likely to have more than one e-mail address, instant messaging identity, telephone number, and so on. To make matters more complicated, most Internet users will not have addresses for every contact service type. This leads to a basic challenge of discovering what services are available for a given user so that a mutually agreeable contact form can be used for any given communication. ENUM provides that discovery service by giving end users the ability to use one reference to locate several types of (current) contact information. ENUM serves its purpose by tying an existing, globally deployed contact identifier to other related contact identifiers in a way that is globally accessible and usable by communications systems software. In other words, given a person's telephone number, ENUM enables a user's desktop software to find the appropriate instant messaging or e-mail coordinates to connect with another person using the appropriate services. Figure 1 illustrates a sample scenario.

Generally speaking, ENUM uses DNS to store information within the network so that coordinates for one or more contact services are globally accessible for each telephone number.

ENUM is not unique for using the DNS for mapping from identifiers to resources other than traditional host names to *Internet protocol* (IP) addresses. For example, *uniform resource names* (URNs) (Moats 1997) use DNS to map non–host name identifiers to network-accessible resources. ENUM leverages DNS technology that was originally developed for URNs. ENUM is not even the first effort to map telephone numbers into DNS: tcp.int was established in the early 1990s "to provide transparent mapping between general-purpose computers on the Internet and special-purpose devices directly connected to the telephone network" (Malamud and Rose 1993). ENUM is a particular mapping proposal designed to address, in ways not answered by any existing technology, the motivations of several interests that converged in the late 1990s.

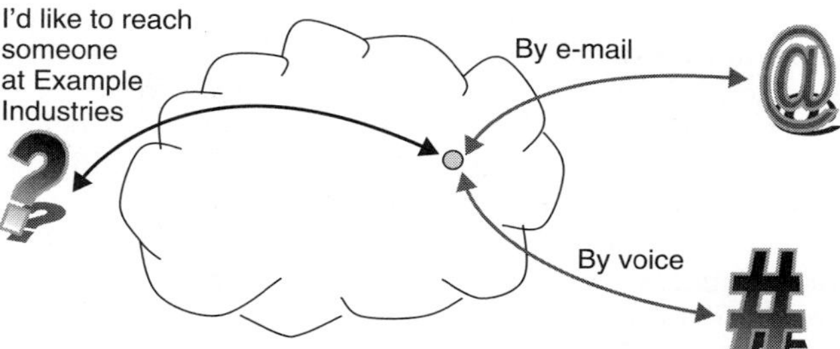

Figure 1: Generally speaking, ENUM uses DNS to store information within the network so that coordinates for one or more contact services are globally accessible for each telephone number

After a brief review of motivations for ENUM, this chapter will outline the details of the ENUM specification. Although the basic ENUM technology is straightforward in its specification, there is a lot of latitude in configuring and deploying it. To be able to achieve the desired effect, it is important to understand what is intended in the technology and how the pieces fit together. The reader will obtain a working understanding of the technology; advanced readers will obtain further insight into the specifics of the technology usage. The chapter will further discuss ENUM deployment realities from an operational and case history perspective. Finally, some insight into the future development of ENUM is provided in the closing section.

ENUM MOTIVATIONS

Just as there are multiple interpretations of the name "ENUM," there are different, largely compatible, motivations for the application of the technology. Two classes of motivations are described below.

Managing in a World of Multiple Contact Services

One of the most ubiquitous pieces of modern technology is the telephone. From a young age, we learn to recognize phone numbers and know that all we have to do is pick up a phone, dial the digits, and expect to speak to the person or service associated with the number. In our daily lives, other means of communication continue to become ever more prevalent: e-mail, instant messaging, and so on. Each new technology form brings a new address to remember. How can we manage all of these addresses, providing our own contact data as well as knowing where to reach people for each communication medium?

The ENUM standard provides the facility to associate and look up communication services associated with any given telephone number. Specifically, telephone numbers are mapped into DNS names. The corresponding DNS records hold data about specific services and uniform resource identifiers (URIs) to access them.

Specifically, ENUM supports the mapping telephone numbers to contact service URIs, allowing multiple contact coordinates (of different service types) to be associated with any number (see Figure 2).

In the late 1990s, when ENUM work was started, there was still a general desire for some form of standardized, widespread information infrastructure services. However, even though "spam" was not yet a debilitating problem, most of the world had given up hope for the possibility of creating a "global white pages service" to search for a person's e-mail address or other coordinates. Deploying new infrastructure information services was perceived as being challenging at best, minimally requiring a strong

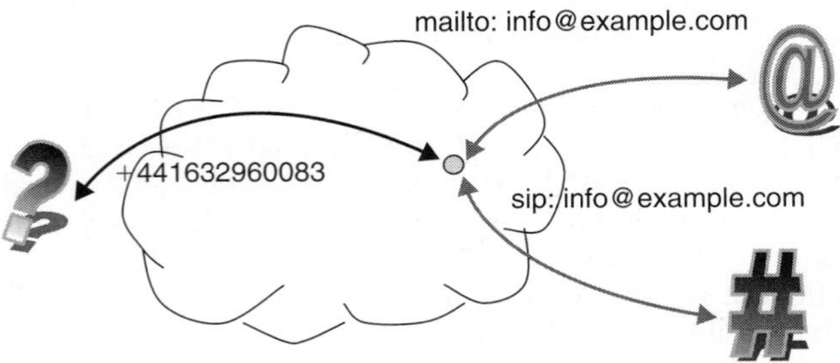

Figure 2: Specifically, ENUM supports the mapping of telephone numbers to contact service URIs, allowing multiple contact coordinates (of different service types) to be associated with any number

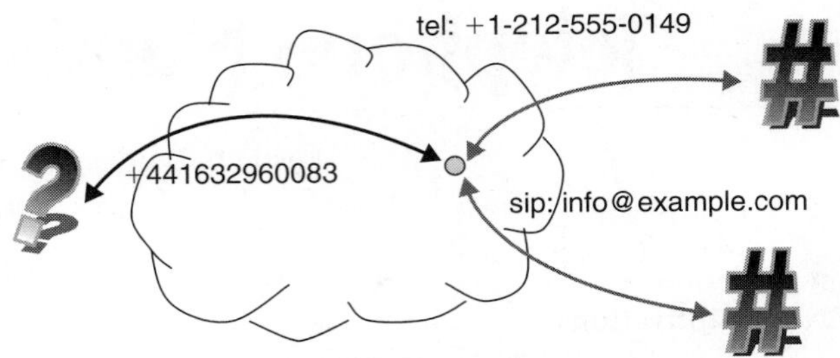

Figure 3: With ENUM, it is possible to publish one telephone number and yet be reached through a variety of voice communication mechanisms. This example illustrates support for connections via telephony at a different telephone number (in a different country), or using SIP-supported voice over IP

corporate interest (which tended to be at cross-purposes with the desire for global interoperability).

ENUM was never designed as "the global whitepages service," but it had to address the same challenges as it sought to enable global dynamic discovery and retrieval of service contact point information associated with identifiers assigned to individuals or organizations. Therefore, ENUM leveraged two established, deployed, and managed global infrastructures: international telephone numbers and the domain name system.

Routing Telephony in the Internet Age

The discussion above treads lightly around the subject of telephony. One of the more obvious motivations to pursue ENUM is to facilitate the mapping between telephone numbers (dynamic number portability); another is to support *voice over IP* (VoIP).

With ENUM, it is possible to publish one telephone number and yet be reached through a variety of voice communications mechanisms (see Figure 3). This example illustrates support for connections via telephony at a different telephone number (in a different country), or using *session initiation protocol* (SIP) supported VoIP.

Discussion of VoIP brings to light another facet of ENUM: It has application beyond a user's desktop. An ENUM client could equally be used by telephony gateway software or other VoIP network infrastructure elements.

With this, ENUM brings the world of VoIP and traditional telephony together in ways that challenge established business models and mechanisms for managing or controlling call routing. This makes ENUM a matter of considerable interest to carriers as well as national regulators and the International Telecommunications Union.

ENUM TECHNOLOGY

The preceding sections outlined the goal and motivation for the ENUM technology. Engineers began discussing possible approaches in Internet Engineering Task Force (IETF) meetings in 1998 and formed the ENUM Working Group in 1999. Its job was to develop a standard specification for the technology; to achieve global deployment and accessibility, open specifications and interoperability are required.

This section will outline the explicit and implied requirements identified for the ENUM technology and then describe the technology framework and the standard developed by the ENUM Working Group.

Requirements and Applicability

ENUM does not set out to be the only solution in managing multiple contact coordinates. It started from some specific implicit and explicit requirements that are important to understand in order to determine its ultimate applicability. These are detailed as follows.

Software Accessibility: ENUM is intended to provide a service to communications software. This requires structured data exchanges as opposed to a Web interface to do searches.

Public Use: The data provided in ENUM is public and for public use. Any constraints on access (to the contact services, for example) are provided by the contact services rather than by restricting the ENUM access for determining the contact addresses.

Contact Look-Up but Not Updating: The emphasis in ENUM is in providing the ability to look up contact information. Although it must be possible to update the contact information in a reasonable time frame (e.g., minutes not weeks), ENUM does not specifically address how information updating is done.

Global Identifier: The identifier used as the key in ENUM must be global in scope—that is, whatever identifier is used must be usable everywhere in the world.

Global Accessibility: It must be possible to carry out an ENUM lookup from anywhere in the Internet, and the set of results (list of contact service information) should be the same from all points of the Internet. In that vein, any ENUM result set should be uniformly interpretable—in a standards-based form—to support the interoperability of software and services. Note, however, that the contact services returned by an ENUM query may vary in terms of reachability (for privacy or other reasons).

Dynamic Data: It must be possible to update the identified contact services independently of distributing the ENUM identifier. In other words, the identifier itself in no way constrains the set of possible contact services that are available at one point in time or the next.

Distributed Management: It must be possible to delegate the management and administration of ENUM and contact services for identifiers or groups of identifiers. The goal is to allow management of the ENUM responses to occur as close to the owner of the identifier as reasonably possible. It must also be possible to delegate the management of portions of the whole set of identifiers to different groups if partitioning of the space is needed to meet different legal and social requirements.

Unconstrained Contact Services: It must be possible to use ENUM to connect to a wide range of contact services: not just VoIP, voice over landlines, or e-mail. And it must be possible to add new contact services as technologies are developed and deployed.

Solution Framework

All that is needed to appreciate the ENUM technology is an understanding of three things:

1. ENUM is all about mapping one globally unique identifier (international telephone numbers) onto an Internet infrastructure system that is designed to manage and serve up data for hierarchical, globally unique identifiers (the domain name system);
2. what data can be stored within the DNS to provide pointers to associated contact services; and
3. how the telephone number and the DNS hierarchical resolution and management structure allow distributed control of the ENUM infrastructure to keep data in the hands of the appropriate owners.

This section will discuss those points in general, and the next will provide more specific technical details.

Telephone Number DNS Mapping

It is important to see the similarities and differences between telephone numbers and domain names in order to understand ENUM's chosen mapping between them.

International telephone numbers are defined by ITU-T recommendation E.164 (International Telecommunications Union 1997). The first one to three digits represent the country codes (top of the hierarchy). The organization of the remaining digits into area codes (where used) and exchange identifiers depends on rules established for each country or operating body. This structure is generally opaque to the common telephone user. The important points to note about the number are:

- the top of the hierarchy is at the left-hand side of the string of digits;
- the E.164 number does not explicitly indicate the separation of components in the hierarchy (country, area code if used, and exchange); and
- the separation varies from one country code to another, so there is no single general way to parse an E.164 number without knowing the rules specific to the country code.

By contrast, domain names are explicitly organized by hierarchical components, and the top of the hierarchy is expressed in the right-most component: the top-level domain (e.g., "com" or "org"). So,

- the top of the hierarchy is at the right of the domain name component sequence;
- the domain name does explicitly indicate the separation of components (with a period or "dot"); and
- although there are different approaches to assigning domain names from one top-level domain to the next, it is possible to write a single generic parser of domain name components.

Therefore, to map E.164 telephone numbers onto domain names, the direction of hierarchy had to be matched and something had to be done to allow the variable length (administrative) components to be preserved within the E.164 number. To achieve this mapping, all nondigit characters (except "+") are removed from the E.164 number string, the resulting string is reversed, and each digit is represented as a separate domain component in the domain name. All such domain names are rooted at "e164.arpa."

For example, the E.164 number

```
+44-163-296-0083
```

is converted to the domain name

```
3.8.0.0.6.9.2.3.6.1.4.4.e164.arpa.
```

ENUM Contact Service Information

With the mapping between E.164 number and DNS name in hand, the next step is to look at how ENUM uses the DNS to store contact service information.

ENUM maps telephone numbers onto DNS names for the purpose of using the DNS to retrieve contact service information associated with the telephone number. As described in Chapter 81 of this volume, information is retrieved using the DNS by resolving the domain name and getting a set of structured *resource records* (RRs) as a response. Therefore, an important part of the ENUM standard is specifying how contact service information can be stored in DNS RRs.

ENUM makes use of a particular DNS RR type: the *naming authority pointer* (NAPTR). As described in more detail in the section below titled "The ENUM Standard," each NAPTR RR associated with the name being resolved includes a "service" field that indicates which contact services' coordinates are provided from the NAPTR record. For example, one NAPTR record might provide directions to a number's SIP contact service. Another, for the same number, might provide the coordinates for e-mail contact. At any given time, there is a fixed set of these service types. They are specified publicly and listed with the *Internet Assigned Numbers Authority* (IANA) to ensure interoperability and compatibility between software implementations (clients and servers). The purpose of the IANA registry is to allow orderly extension of the set of accepted types.

In the most typical case, the NAPTR record provides the coordinates for a service by directly including a mapping to the relevant URI for the service. For example, a NAPTR record for "3.8.0.0.6.9.2.3.6.1.4.4.e164.arpa." might provide the URI "sip:info@example.com" for the "SIP" ENUM service type. Another NAPTR record for the same name might provide the URI "mailto:contact@example.com" for the "email:mailto" ENUM service type.

Making Use of the DNS Infrastructure

There is more value to using the DNS infrastructure for storing and retrieving contact service information than simply mapping from one global namespace (E.164) to another (DNS) and storing data in structured DNS resource records. An obvious benefit is the fact that the DNS infrastructure is already deployed, and it has demonstrated its stability and ability scale to the needs of the Internet. An architecturally sound reason is that the distributed nature of the DNS infrastructure aligns reasonably closely with the locality of responsibility and management of the various forms of Internet contact services.

With the mapped telephone number translated into one domain component per digit, the flexibility of DNS delegation allows distribution of control at appropriate levels of the hierarchy. Countries can directly manage the ENUM-related DNS delegations for their own country code telephone numbers. This does not mean that all the country's telephone numbers must be managed out of a single DNS server. Quite the contrary: Any given country may elect to delegate portions of its ENUM DNS space to other organizations (based on the existing structure of the E.164 number) and ultimately down to the level of the individual E.164 number subscriber. This is described in more detail below in the section on ENUM deployment.

The ENUM Standard

This section will build on the preceding one to give more specific detail from the ENUM standards documentation. The goal here is to give a comprehensive and accurate overview of the technology without distracting detail. Therefore, the reader is referred to the ENUM specification RFC 3761 (Faltstrom and Mealling 2004) and related standards documents to obtain a complete and authoritative understanding of how to implement or operate ENUM-related services.

Mapping System: Dynamic Delegation Discovery System

RFC 3761 defines the mapping of E.164 numbers onto domain names for the purpose of enabling the storage and look-up of contact service coordinates associated with a given telephone number. To do this, it uses an existing DNS-based mapping system: the *dynamic delegation discovery system* (DDDS), which is defined in RFC 3401 (Mealling 2002a). ENUM does not simply specify the use of a particular DNS RR type; instead, it is defined as an "application" of DDDS, which already leverages the DNS. As noted above, DDDS was developed for an entirely different application: uniform resource naming. It is designed to support any number of applications, of which ENUM is just one.

The essential purpose of DDDS is to start from a string defined by an application and successively retrieve and apply transformation rules until a terminating rule is reached and the final location information is determined. This process is called *resolution*. The first string is defined by the application and is the *application unique string*.

DDDS is dynamic in that the transformation rules are stored in the network. They can be updated as appropriate at any time by entities that are authorized to maintain them. This means they may change between users' retrieval actions, but that eventuality is managed by appropriate implementation of the DDDS algorithm—that is, client software should expect such changes to occur. The DDDS specification provides a specification for the one currently existing DDDS implementation, which uses the domain name system.

In this case, ENUM is the DDDS application and the application unique string is a fully qualified E.164 number minus any nondigit characters except for the plus sign (+) character that appears at the beginning of the number. For example, the E.164 number could start out as +44-116-496-0348. To ensure there is no ambiguity in transcribing numbers, all other E.164-related syntactic elements such as "-" are removed and all nondigits except for "+" are removed, yielding +441164960348.

To use this application unique string within DNS, the following process takes place:

1. The "+" is dropped:

```
441164960348
```

2. A "." is placed between each digit:

```
4.4.1.1.6.4.9.6.0.3.4.8
```

3. The string is reversed:

```
8.4.3.0.6.9.4.6.1.1.4.4
```

4. Finally, ".e164.arpa." is appended:

```
8.4.3.0.6.9.4.6.1.1.4.4.e164.arpa.
```

This yields a fully qualified domain name, which is the key that is used for the series of DNS look-ups required to obtain the contact service references stored for the telephone number.

ENUM's Use of DNS Resource Records

To appreciate the breadth and depth of the possible deployment uses of ENUM, it is necessary to understand some of the details of ENUM's use of DNS NAPTR records and the ENUM resolution algorithm.

Once the key has been obtained as outlined above, the first step in ENUM resolution is to retrieve all available NAPTR resource records (Mealling 2002b) for that key. Those NAPTR RRs contain information pertaining to all ENUM-related services associated with that E.164 number. The information contained in the NAPTR records may provide the contact service information directly in the form of a URI or it may provide direction for subsequent DNS look-ups or other actions.

It should be clear that there may be several NAPTR records available for the key, and the ENUM client must review them to find the applicable next step. This is done by sorting the NAPTR RRs, selecting the preferred RR that matches for the desired target service, and determining the appropriate next action based on the RR's contents.

Sorting the NAPTR RRs. NAPTR RRs have an ORDER field that is used to sort the NAPTR RRs into the sequence intended by the DNS administrator for the service because the DNS itself does not guarantee any particular delivery order of result records. ENUM clients are required to review NAPTR records in this order. Note that two or more records may have the same value for ORDER; that means that any of the records are equally applicable and the client will select the most appropriate for its needs (if any).

Selecting the Preferred RR. Three fields of the NAPTR records are used for distinguishing which records are applicable for defining the client's next steps: REGEXP or REPLACEMENT (exactly one can have a value in any given NAPTR RR), SERVICE, and PREFERENCE.

If the REGEXP field is not empty, it contains a POSIX regular expression that, if it matches the key, derives from it the string to be used for the next step. If the regular expression is applied to the key and no match is made, then the next NAPTR RR of the same order is considered. In practice, most ENUM regular expressions are complete rewrites of the key (i.e., they match any input string).

If the REPLACEMENT field is not empty, then it is considered an automatic "match" for the key in this part of the ENUM processing.

Once the client has a NAPTR RR for which the REGEXP matches or there is a REPLACEMENT value, then the SERVICE and PREFERENCE fields are to be considered.

The SERVICE field includes a list of NAPTR service descriptors. For ENUM, these begin with "E2U" and may contain any number of "+`<enumservice>`" descriptors. The `<enumservice>` descriptor might in turn consist of a service and subservice, separated with a colon. For example, `<enumservice>` could be "SIP," "PRES," or any of the other IANA-registered ENUM services. An ENUM client will be looking for NAPTR RRs containing one or more specific ENUM services of interest and expects to find them here. If not, the next record is considered until all possibilities have been exhausted.

The PREFERENCE field indicates which NAPTR record includes the information for the services the registrant would prefer the client to use (in order). Unlike the ORDER field, the ENUM client is permitted to use this as guidance only and override the PREFERENCE ordering at its discretion.

Using these fields, it is the ENUM client's responsibility to find a record for which the REGEXP matches the key (or there is a REPLACEMENT value), and the SERVICE field contains the token for the ENUM service the client is seeking. The client starts with all the NAPTR records at the lowest ORDER and reviews them to find an applicable record. Only if no applicable record at a given ORDER is found does the client proceed to review all of the records at the next ORDER.

Determining the Next Action. Assuming it has found an applicable NAPTR RR, the ENUM client's next action is governed by the value of the FLAG field in the selected NAPTR record as well as by the result of applying the REGEXP to the key or using the value in the REPLACEMENT field for the new key (transformed key).

At this time, only one flag is defined for ENUM, so the FLAG field can have one of two possible states: It may be empty or it may have the value "U."

If the FLAG field has the value "U," then the NAPTR RR is considered "terminal"; this represents the termination of the DDDS processing for the ENUM look-up. The NAPTR RR must include a REGEXP, not a REPLACEMENT value, because the REPLACEMENT field must contain fully qualified domain names and thus cannot include a URI. The point of the "U" flag is that the transformed key is a URI for the service indicated in the SERVICE field, and this result is the final output of the ENUM resolution.

If the FLAG field is empty, then the NAPTR RR is called *nonterminal*, and, per the DDDS algorithm, the transformed key is used to do another NAPTR lookup, and the whole process begins again. Note that any REGEXP in this next round is applied again to the original, not the transformed, key.

Theory and Practice. By far the most common current practice is to have a single NAPTR RR set look-up that yields terminal NAPTR records (with "U" flags and REGEXPs).

There is discussion of the best application of the use of nonterminal NAPTR records, and whether they should be allowed in ENUM deployments. This chapter takes no particular stand on that issue, but, where applicable, describes how nonterminal NAPTR records would be used in ways that are consistent with the ENUM and DDDS published standards.

Target Contact Services

To achieve maximum flexibility for use and future evolution, the ENUM specification itself does not enumerate the set of contact services that can be located using ENUM resolution. Instead, there is a standard process for defining such services and the necessary tokens for the ENUM standard. These definitions and tokens are registered with the IANA.

These services are defined and registered to ensure uniqueness, allowing the creation of interoperable clients and resolution services. ENUM defines these services in terms of *type* and *subtype*. Any given type may have several subtypes; together they uniquely identify a particular service.

The definition of the ENUM service type (and subtype) includes the intended function of the service and the expected URI schemes to be included as the target for the service. Although it is reasonable to expect an ENUM service type SIP to use the "sip:" URI scheme, there is no inherent requirement that the URI scheme name match the ENUM service type. For example, the ENUM SMS service type allows the "mailto:" URI scheme. Any given type may have a number of subtypes registered for it.

Example ENUM Service: SIP

The ENUM SIP service registration is contained in RFC 3764 (Peterson 2004). URIs in NAPTR records advertising this service are expected to be of the "sip:" or "sips:" scheme.

Clearly, the intention of this ENUM service is to provide mapping from a traditional telephone number to some SIP voice over IP or other media service. It is important to note that RFC 3764 specifically indicates that any URIs registered in NAPTR records for this service should include SIP "address of record" URIs as opposed to any general SIP contact URIs. The intention here is to use ENUM to find the "logical" address of the service and continue to use SIP's more refined capabilities for determining the current contact address of the targeted party.

Example ENUM Service: Web

RFC 4002 (Brandner et al. 2005) defines the ENUM service "web" with two subtypes: "http" and "https." The respective URI schemes associated with the types are "http:" and "https:".

The purpose of this ENUM service is to indicate that the resource identified by the associated URI scheme is capable of being a source of information. Ultimately, connecting to the resource may yield a descriptive document, or it may launch some other form of interactive service. The "web" service definition is intentionally vague on that point, leaving much to the discretion of implementers and system developers.

Current Registered ENUM Services

The list of validly registered ENUM services is maintained and updated by IANA, based on specifications developed within the IETF (per the process defined in RFC 3761).

Table 1 enumerates some of the services that are registered at the time of this writing; see Internet Assigned Numbers Authority (2004) for the complete and official list of registered services.

Practical Examples

Following from the illustrations above, an entry for +44 1632960083 offering both "sip" and "web" ENUM services might have the following NAPTR DNS RR set:

```
$ORIGIN 3.8.0.0.6.9.2.3.6.1.4.4.e164.arpa.
  NAPTR 100 100 "u" "E2U+sip" "!^.*$!sip:
        frontdoor@example.com!"
  NAPTR 100 102 "u" "E2U+web:http"
  "!^.*$!http://www.example.com!"
```

Table 1: A Sampling of IANA-Registered ENUM Services

Type	Subtype	URI scheme
H323		h323:
SIP		sip:, sips:
IFAX	mailto	mailto:
PRES		pres:
WEB	http	http:
WEB	https	https:
FT	ftp	ftp:
EMAIL	mailto	mailto:
FAX	tel	tel:
SMS	tel	tel:
SMS	mailto	mailto:
VPIM	mailto	mailto:
VPIM	ldap	ldap:
VOICE	tel	tel:

This NAPTR RR set indicates:

- equal ordering among the NAPTR RRs ("100"), so all must be considered;
- "sip" ENUM service is provided at the SIP address frontdoor@example.com;
- "web" ENUM service is provided at http://www.example.com; and
- both of these NAPTR RRs have the "u" flag, and therefore these are terminal look-ups (there are no further steps in the resolution).

Note that the regular expression will always match the key: It matches every character in the key string ("^.*$"), so it is always successful.

There is some concern that an E.164 number with many contact services and highly refined expression of preference between services would have a NAPTR RR set that was too large (for a standard DNS response). There are no agreed-on solutions for this potential situation as yet, but one approach that illustrates the potential extended use of DNS here is as follows:

```
$ORIGIN 3.8.0.0.6.9.2.3.6.1.4.4.e164.arpa.
NAPTR 100 100 "" "E2U+sip" "!^.*$!sip.enum.
              example.com.!".
NAPTR 100 102 "" "E2U+web:http" "" web.
            enum.example.com.
```

Note that the flag field is empty—meaning that this is not a terminal look-up. If the first record matches (i.e., the client is looking for the "E2U+sip" service), then the regular expression provides the replacement that is used to look up another NAPTR RR set. Because the regular expression matches any key and uses none of it in the rewrite, it is clear the transformed key is "sip.enum.example.com." If the second record matches, then the REPLACEMENT field value provides the transformed key: "web.enum.example.com."

That NAPTR RR set can then be used to provide the refined level of preference expression. For example,

```
$ORIGIN sip.enum.example.com.
NAPTR 100 100 "u" "E2U+sip" "!^.*$!sip:
        frontdoor@example.com!"
NAPTR 100 101 "u" "E2U+sip" "!^.*$!sip:
        sidedoor@example.com!"
NAPTR 100 103 "u" "E2U+sip" "!^.*$!sip:
        backdoor@example.com!"
```

Note that these are all terminal look-ups.

Putting It All Together

This section started with a discussion of requirements and then described the technology that has been developed to meet those requirements and expectations. These pieces fit together as follows.

Software Accessibility: The ENUM standard defines a technology that is based on providing structured DNS queries and responses; as such, it is fully software-accessible.

Public Use: By its nature, the DNS infrastructure is publicly accessible. As part of the design choices, however, the only data that are stored in the DNS pertain to contact services the end user wishes to advertise for use (as opposed to requiring the exposure of personally identifying data such as name or address).

Contact Look-Up but Not Updating: DNS is uniquely a look-up protocol. There are tools and systems that have been built up to support the *provisioning*, or management, of DNS data, and they can equally be employed for ENUM-related DNS data.

Global Identifier: The E.164 telephone number is the identifier chosen for ENUM. By definition and design, it is global in scope.

Global Accessibility: ENUM makes use of the existing global DNS infrastructure. For the Internet to work, DNS name servers must be globally accessible, providing consistent answers from and to all parts of the network.

Dynamic Data: ENUM stores the contact service identifiers within the DNS resource records that are associated with E.164 numbers. If contact service particulars change for a given E.164 number, then the DNS resource record is deleted or modified as appropriate. This is transparent to users of ENUM: The DNS always provides the contact service identifiers that are available at the time of look-up.

Distributed Management: The DNS infrastructure is highly distributed. A primary concept of DNS is that of *delegations*, or allowing different entities to be responsible for separate parts of the hierarchical tree. The sections below, describing ENUM's deployment, provide more detail on how ENUM makes extensive use of DNS delegation.

Unconstrained Contact Services: ENUM's only requirement for contact services is that it is possible to represent them by some form of URI scheme. New URI schemes are being developed regularly, so this is not a closed set of communication service types.

Security Issues

The sections above describe how ENUM does or should work. However, no technology is perfectly resistant to attack from sources that are intent on breaking systems or bending them to their own purposes. The security issues of ENUM are well elaborated in RFC 3761. This section simply describes the key classes of potential security issues and mitigating strategies.

DNS-Specific Security Issues

In its current form, DNS is a completely open protocol, and it has long been known that there is the potential for many forms of attack to be launched against DNS servers and unsuspecting clients. For this reason, *domain name system security protocol* (DNSSEC) has been developed (Arends et al. 2005).

Irrespective of the form of the attack—for example, "man in the middle" packet interception attacks or cache poisoning—the biggest concern is whether the data the client receives for its DNS query is, in fact, authentic.

For example, in ENUM, are the NAPTR records retrieved for a given E.164 number the actual ones the end user registered? Or are they forgeries, pointing the ENUM client to connect to bogus SIP, e-mail, or other contact services?

DNSSEC is designed to address such issues by providing the means to sign and therefore authenticate DNS responses. By carrying out proper authentication of the data, the ENUM client can be assured that the DNS data retrieved are, in fact, the data the E.164 number's name server intended to provide.

As noted above, DNSSEC was developed to address many of these issues (for DNS generally, not just for ENUM). Unfortunately, deployment of DNSSEC is proceeding more slowly than recognition of the problems, and this is likely to remain an operational concern for some time to come.

Note also that DNSSEC can only ensure that the DNS data that are retrieved are what was intended.

Potential Security Issues Related to Contact Services

Even if the ENUM client can authenticate the results from the DNS query—and therefore have confidence that the correct contact service URIs have been retrieved—bad actors may still prevent the ENUM client from connecting to the desired communications service.

The process of resolving target URIs and connecting to a remote server is also potentially subject to attack. The ENUM standard requires that individual URI schemes registered for ENUM services elaborate any appropriate means for mitigating security threats. If the application protocol associated with the URI scheme supports some form of (server) authentication, then it is important to use it.

DEPLOYMENT

Having completed the discussion of the theory of ENUM—what it is trying to achieve and how the technology is designed—it is now time to review how ENUM can and does work in practice.

There are three key components to deploying ENUM:

1. the clients who build software that makes use of the data in the infrastructure;
2. the infrastructure, which establishes the authoritative registry of E.164 numbers mapped to DNS entries; and
3. data maintenance, or creating and managing the DNS resources for each number.

All three components must be functional, at least to some degree, before ENUM can be said to be deployed and useful. To a certain extent, there is a chicken-and-egg situation: Without populated infrastructure, there is no motivation to build clients; without clients, there is no motivation to populate the infrastructure.

The rest of this section will review these components in greater detail, discussing the general requirements for each and describing what exists today.

ENUM and the End User: ENUM Clients

One immediate measure of the success of ENUM is its utility to end users: It succeeds in solving the contact information problem if people can use it to advertise their contact services and make contact with other people. The last few sections have outlined the technology for how ENUM supports that. The question remains: "How do I, as an end user, access that information?"

The general assumption that drove the design of ENUM is that support for ENUM would be absorbed into a variety of communications-supporting software. This is happening in certain instances, although there is not yet a single general approach to using ENUM. Examples of what has been done so far are detailed below.

Software Using ENUM

The most obvious way to use ENUM is to incorporate its use directly into some or all forms of communication software. This software might be used directly by a user or it might be some software acting on behalf of a user to effect a communication link.

"Softphones" are software programs with telephone functionality. Notably, SIP softphones use the SIP protocol to establish voice calls. It is natural to expect that softphones would incorporate ENUM functions directly, so that the best connection can be made for any telephone number entered into the softphone. One softphone that supports ENUM today is the ENUM RTC phone, available from http://www.enum.at/index.php?id=softphone

However, not only client software might make use of ENUM but also various forms of server software. For example, SIP proxy servers might take a phone number from a client softphone and use ENUM to look for an appropriate SIP connection (rather than routing immediately to the public switched telephone network). For instance, the *SIP express router* (SER) server software has an ENUM module that will incorporate ENUM lookup functionality into the SER server.

Direct Lookup of ENUM Data

Another approach to making use of ENUM is to use a specialized client or a Web browser to look it up directly.

For example, the Japan Registry Service developed a software client that will allow a user to perform ENUM look-ups (see http://jprs.co.jp/enum/software/software.html).

This can also be achieved using special-purpose Web sites that are portals to ENUM and provide look-up services. For example, http://enum.nic.at/ provides the ability to enter a phone number and find the ENUM results in the Austrian ENUM service.

Also, http://www.enum-trial.de/index_frame_ie.html provides a German portal to look up ENUM resources: For an E.164 number (directly or mapped into an ENUM key), it will provide contents of available NAPTR and other DNS resource records for the ENUM key.

More directly, because it is now common to use the Web browser bar to do all manner of search, there are browser plug-ins that enable ENUM lookups. For example, the ENUMapper plug-in for Firefox (available from http://falb.at/enum4firefox/enummapper-0.1.0.xpi) allows a user to enter a string such as "enum:+441632960083" in the Web browser and see the result of the ENUM look-up.

Command-Line Tools

Of course, it is always possible to look up ENUM information from a computer's command-line interface, making use of a standard DNS look-up tool. For example, it is possible to look up all of the NAPTR records associated with a telephone number by doing the ENUM mapping to the domain name and using a tool like "host" to query the DNS.

For example,

```
host -t NAPTR 3.8.0.0.6.9.2.3.6.1.4.4.
              e164.arpa.
```

might yield something like:

```
3.8.0.0.6.9.2.3.6.1.4.4.e164.arpa NAPTR 100
   10 "u" "E2U+sip" "!^.*$!sip:custserv@
               example.net!"
```

This is hardly expected to be the widespread access method for ENUM, but it is useful for debugging and potentially for writing basic scripts.

Building More ENUM-Enabled Tools

If none of the above tools is sufficient, then it is always possible to develop new software to make use of ENUM. This can be done using standard DNS libraries and implementing the ENUM DDDS application directly. Software development kits also have been made available to facilitate the creation of new ENUM software (or for retrofitting ENUM capability into existing software). For example, see http://jprs.co.jp/enum/software/software.html.

Is Anybody Out There? ENUM Infrastructure

Before it is possible to look anything up using any of the tools and techniques mentioned above, there must be populated ENUM infrastructure. Although ENUM is defined to provide services to and for the telephone number end user, it is designed to leverage the distributed nature of the DNS by following the hierarchy of the telephone number assignment established with E.164. Therefore, individual E.164 numbers are not registered directly into a centrally managed database; instead, each country must establish its ENUM infrastructure, and end-user ENUM resources can be managed within the national context and available services.

There are four general classes of ENUM DNS infrastructure to review: (1) the root of the end-user ENUM DNS, (2) per-country code registries, (3) within-country ENUM providers, and (4) within-country code registrars. These are described in more detail below.

The Root of All ENUM: e164.arpa

To provide a stable point of reference for ENUM resolution, the ENUM standard defines an authoritative root of the ENUM DNS hierarchy in which individual country codes are registered: e164.arpa. This is often referred to as "tier 0" of ENUM.

This is a key point at which the DNS infrastructure for ENUM is aligned with the administration of E.164 numbers. As part of the IETF ENUM standard, the Internet Architecture Board has established instructions to ensure that the ITU-T TSB authenticates each request for registration of country codes in e164.arpa. This, in turn, ensures that the roles and responsibilities for ENUM E.164-based DNS is aligned with those for E.164 numbers.

In terms of DNS, an approved request is implemented by inserting *name server* (NS) records for the appropriate subzone of e164.arpa for each registered country code to direct queries to the services established by its national administrator.

For example, the current registration for country code 49 (Germany) is as follows:

host -t NS 9.4.e164.arpa.

9.4.e164.arpa name server enum3.denic.de.

9.4.e164.arpa name server enum1.denic.de.

9.4.e164.arpa name server enum2.denic.de.

Note that, if no request has been made or a request has been made but not authenticated, then there will be no DNS resource records for that country code in e164.arpa., and no telephone number within that country code can make use of ENUM.

Table 2 shows the country codes that have been registered at the time of this writing. See RIPE NCC (undated) for current information.

Country Code Registries

Before making a request to register a country code, the administrator of the E.164 numbers of that country code must establish policies and infrastructure to support ENUM. While remaining consistent with implementing ENUM per the standard, the final form of infrastructure can vary from one country code to another, depending on regional requirements. In all cases, provision must be made to register the country code's telephone numbers in DNS. The country code registry is often referred to as "tier 1" of ENUM service.

In principle, the ENUM DNS infrastructure for a given country code could be constructed to directly contain the NAPTR records for all of the country code's E.164 numbers (this is called the "thick tier 1" model). However, that works against the purpose of DNS architecture and established administration best practices. It creates a great separation between the entity with the operational data for each domain (E.164 number) and the administration of the DNS. In addition, it would either constrain the ability to have dynamic ENUM updates or create a DNS zone that was in a constant state of flux.

Instead, more DNS delegations are usually made ("thin tier 1" model). This is done by inserting appropriate NS records along the lines of hierarchy within the E.164 number. In country codes that have explicit area codes, each area code could be delegated to other DNS servers. Commonly, though, the country code's ENUM DNS server simply holds the NS records for each registered E.164 number.

Table 2: Current Country Code Registrations Approved for Delegations in e164.arpa

Country code	Delegee, country	Date of ITU TSB approval (dd-mm-yyy)
+1	CC1 ENUM LLC, shared country code	15-02-2006
+30	Hellenic Telecommunications and Post Commission (EETT)	06-02-2006
+31	Ministry, the Netherlands	23-05-2002
+33	DiGITIP (Government), France	28-03-2003
+36	CHIP/ISzT, Hungary	15-07-2002
+39	Ministerio delle Communicazioni , Italy	02-11-2005
+40	MinCom, Romania	10-12-2002
+41	OFCOM, Switzerland	01-10-2003
+43	Regulator, Austria	11-06-2002
+44	DTI/Nominum, United Kingdom	16-05-2002
+46	NPTA, Sweden	10-12-2002
+47	Norwegian Post and Telecommunications Authority, Norway	16-03-2005
+48	NASK, Poland Registry Whois	18-07-2002
+49	DENIC, Germany	16-05-2002
+55	Brazilian Internet Registry, Brazil	19-07-2002
+61	Dept of Communications, Information Technology and the Arts, Australia	17-01-2005
+63	Commission on Information and Communications Technology, Philippines	29-09-2005
+65	IDA (Government), Singapore	04-06-2003
+66	CAT Telecom, Thailand	22-06-2005
+81	Ministry of Internal Affairs and Communications, Japan	15-11-2005
+82	NIDA (National Internet Development Agency of Korea), Republic of Korea	06-05-2005
+86	CNNIC, China	02-09-2002
+246	Government, Diego Garcia	12-08-2002
+247	Government, Ascension Island	12-08-2002
+290	Government, Saint Helena	12-08-2002
+350	Gibraltar Regulatory Authority	31-10-2005
+353	Commission for Communications Regulation, Ireland	25-05-2004
+354	Post and Telecom Administration, Iceland	28-02-2005
+358	Finnish Communications Regulatory Authority STET	26-02-2003
+359	ISOC, Bulgaria	12-04-2006
+374	Arminco Ltd, Armenia	
+420	Ministry of Informatics, Czech Republic	24-06-2003
+421	Ministry of Transport, Post and Telecommunications, Slovak Republic	04-06-2003
+423	SWITCH, Liechtenstein	
+971	Etisalat, United Arab Emirates	13-01-2003

The country code's set policies must further define the conditions under which E.164 numbers are added to the registry or otherwise modified.

ENUM Providers

As the country code's ENUM registry does not contain the NAPTR records for each E.164 number, there must be DNS servers to which the NS records in the registry refer to complete the DNS resolution of each ENUM domain. These are operated by organizations generically referred to as "ENUM [service] providers," or "tier 2" of ENUM.

ENUM providers' DNS servers offer the current set of NAPTR records for each E.164 number.

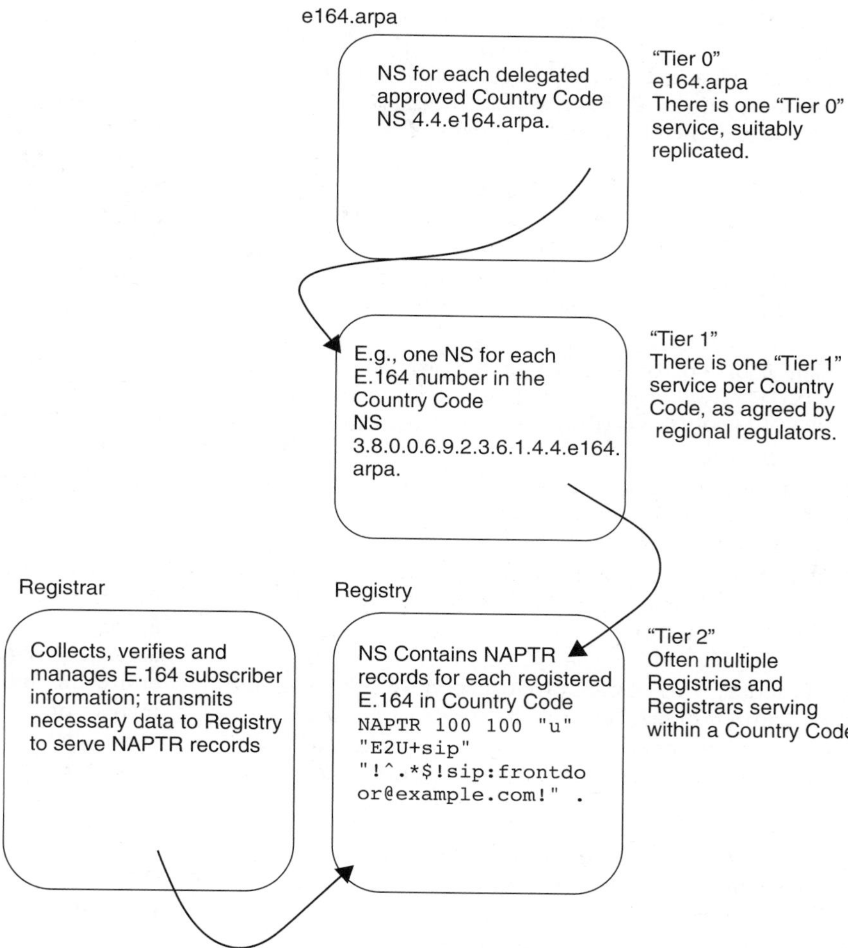
e164.arpa
NS for each delegated approved Country Code NS 4.4.e164.arpa.
"Tier 0" e164.arpa There is one "Tier 0" service, suitably replicated.
E.g., one NS for each E.164 number in the Country Code NS 3.8.0.0.6.9.2.3.6.1.4.4.e164.arpa.
"Tier 1" There is one "Tier 1" service per Country Code, as agreed by regional regulators.
Registrar
Registry
Collects, verifies and manages E.164 subscriber information; transmits necessary data to Registry to serve NAPTR records
NS Contains NAPTR records for each registered E.164 in Country Code NAPTR 100 100 "u" "E2U+sip" "!^.*$!sip:frontdoor@example.com!" .
"Tier 2" Often multiple Registries and Registrars serving within a Country Code

Figure 4: A view of one possible flow for distributing the tiers of ENUM DNS data management

ENUM Registrars

The registry and ENUM providers above provide the operational support for ENUM resolution. However, for ENUM to work for end users, a user-facing component of infrastructure is required. "Registrars" carry out the work of managing the creation, modification, and deletion of entries in the registry. The registrars' duties generally include the following data management duties.

Collection: Registrars work directly with E.164 end users and collect the current information about the end user's ENUM provider (for the NS record in the registry) as well as available contact service information and any other information about the registration required by the country code's established policies.

Verification: Registrars work to verify the authenticity of registration requests. Minimally, it must be clear that the request is coming from an entity that has current appropriate authority for the E.164 number (i.e., the current end user).

Publishing: NS records for verified requests must be put into the country code's registry. The registry must also be updated in the case of modifications to the data or deletion if ENUM support for the E.164 number is withdrawn.

Related data: The country code's policies will indicate what other information the registrar must gather and retain from each request. For example, it is general practice to maintain address information for DNS registration contacts, and these include DNS entries for ENUM.

The details of information gathered, relationships with the country code's ENUM registry, and ENUM service providers, as well as other organizations responsible for the administration of E.164 numbers within the country code do vary significantly from region to region.

Pictorially

As noted above, specific choices for balancing responsibility and organization of DNS administration for ENUM may vary from region to region based on the decisions of local regulators and service providers. Figure 4 shows one possible implementation. The illustration is intentionally simplified to reduce clutter; refer to the preceding paragraphs for further detail.

End-User Data in End-User ENUM

Of course, for there to be ENUM results for those clients to retrieve, there must be data stored and maintained in the ENUM infrastructure. The ENUM standard is directed specifically at end users—that is, it is end users who have the right and responsibility to make their contact information available (or not) using ENUM.

The European Telecommunications Standards Institute has published a technical specification on "ENUM administration in Europe" (TS 102 051) (European Telecommunications Standards Institute 2002), and it includes the following for end user registration:

1. ENUM users shall be able to choose the ENUM tier 2 nameserver provider and ENUM registrar they want to use for a given E.164 number.
2. ENUM users may decide to delegate the provisioning and management of NAPTR RRs to a third party (e.g., ASP).
3. The choice of application service provider for a given ENUM-based application shall not be constrained by the choice of ENUM registrar or ENUM tier 2 nameserver provider.
4. ENUM users have the right to decide whether their assigned E.164 numbers are inserted or withdrawn within the ENUM database.
5. ENUM users have full control over the provision and content of the NAPTR resource records in the ENUM tier 2 nameserver.

In practice, this means that everything begins and ends with end users' choices to register one or more of their E.164 numbers in the ENUM infrastructure. For each E.164, end users choose to make available in ENUM, they must

- identify contact services to be included in their ENUM registration of the E.164 number (e.g., which SIP addresses, Web sites, etc.);
- ensure those contact services are operational, whether the end user is providing them directly or obtaining the service from some other entity;
- select and establish a relationship with an ENUM provider to create and serve the appropriate NAPTR RRs for those contact services from the ENUM provider's nameserver; and
- contact an ENUM registrar to request that the E.164 number be appropriately registered in the ENUM registry (i.e., have DNS NS records point to the selected ENUM provider).

The ENUM registrar then has the responsibilities outlined above, with respect to verifying and publishing the DNS data.

If end users wish to withdraw E.164 numbers from the ENUM infrastructure, they must contact their registrars. For any changes related to changing information about contact service information, priorities, or other data in the NAPTR RRs, end users will work with their ENUM providers.

RELATED TOPICS AND FUTURE DIRECTIONS

The previous sections have outlined the ENUM standard and technology in some depth. Of course, end user ENUM does not exist in a vacuum. This section provides a taste of other related topics with a view to inspiring the reader to continue the exploration of this topic.

Related Topics

Managing ENUM Entries

As noted earlier, the ENUM standard is focused on providing a look-up service, not specifying updates. However, this is generally true of the DNS, and the *extensible provisioning protocol* (EPP) was defined to provide a standard registry-registrar communications protocol for generic domain name registration processes. EPP is XML-based, and intentionally extensible.

An extension of EPP has been specified in RFC 4114 (Hollenbeck 2005) to accommodate ENUM services: the specification of content for NAPTR resource records, as well as the required service interactions to create, delete, renew registrations, and so on.

Information about ENUM Registrants

Another carryover from general DNS infrastructure management is the desire to have accessible information about the registrants of the ENUM (DNS) entries. Generally, this has been useful for contacting operators and owners of DNS services in the case of network issues or other operational problems.

The IETF defined an XML-based protocol for providing access to registry information—IRIS (RFC 3981) (Newton and Sanz 2005)—and there is an IRIS service, EREG, that is specifically designed for ENUM defined in RFC 4414 (Newton 2006). EREG provides the capability of storing registrant information particular to ENUM in a standardized service while providing managed access to that information, encryption, and authentication.

Privacy

As ENUM development and deployment as advanced, concerns about privacy have been voiced. Although privacy was not originally a driving requirement for the development of ENUM, there have been discussions about the implications of exposing (personal) data in the global DNS and the infrastructure systems that have been built to support ENUM.

At the level of basic ENUM technology, it must be recognized that the purpose of ENUM was to provide global, unbiased access to mapping telephone numbers to contact coordinates. Therefore, the only way to ensure that personally sensitive information is not available through ENUM resolution is "simply" not to store it in the NAPTR records associated with one's telephone number. "Simple" gets a little more complex when considering the technological and regulatory aspects.

Most of the contact service types supported by ENUM provide some means of "aliasing" contact addresses. Therefore, it is not necessary to store a personal e-mail address in a NAPTR record; one could instead list an anonymized alias and configure that alias's service to forward any received mail to one's personal account. Some contact services also provide end-user control over connections. For example, one can publish SIP address in a NAPTR record and still only accept connections from known callers. That places the burden of filtering unwanted communications on the communication technology itself.

On the regulatory front, as countries establish ENUM services in trial or deployment form, much care and consideration has gone into determining the right balance of providing a uniform service (all telephone number subscribers) while protecting personal privacy rights. Most people favor a balance that ensures that no subscriber is required to participate, and all subscribers have control over the contact service information that is (or is not) stored in NAPTR records associated with their telephone numbers.

The Future: Beyond End-User ENUM

This chapter has focused on ENUM as originally designed for the use of individual telephone subscribers, or end users. There have been many discussions about other possible uses and extensions of ENUM for other purposes—for example, within enterprises or between telephony networks.

One such proposal is for an "infrastructure" or "carrier" ENUM to facilitate the interconnection of networks providing E.164 number services. The purpose would be to provide a means for the E.164 number's "carrier of record" to advertise its point of connection for (voice over IP) services for that number. The important difference between this and the end-user ENUM described in this chapter is that the carrier ENUM registrations would be managed by and for the carrier and its services, as opposed to holding the URIs that end users specifically designate as their specific points of contact.

Nothing is yet standardized within the IETF's ENUM Working Group, and discussions continue to evaluate the merits of the overall proposal.

CONCLUSION

This chapter has provided a brief tour of ENUM from inception through current deployment reality and directions for growth. The designers of ENUM set out to provide easy access to several communications technologies by providing a robust, dynamic, and distributed system that associates contact service information with existing telephone numbers. ENUM is being actively deployed, as is witnessed by the number of E.164 country codes that have been registered and for which operational services are available. The story is not finished; more services will be defined to use and support ENUM, and new directions are still unfolding within the IETF's ENUM Working Group.

GLOSSARY

Dynamic Delegation Discovery System (DDDS): A generic framework for managing mapping and discovery services across the global Internet.

E.164 Number: The ITU-defined standard for global telephone numbers.

International Telecommunications Union (ITU): The international organization within the United Nations system where governments and the private sector coordinate global telecom networks and services.

Internet Engineering Task Force (IETF): The organization responsible for the creation and maintenance of standards that define many of the core protocols of the Internet, including the ENUM standard.

Naming Authority Pointer (NAPTR): A particular DNS resource record type defined for use in DDDS applications.

Session Initiation Protocol (SIP): An IETF-defined protocol for IP-based media services, including Voice over IP.

Voice over Internet Protocol (VoIP): A general class of applications that carry voice communications over the Internet rather than through traditional telephony networks.

CROSS REFERENCES

See *Public Switched Telephone Network (PSTN)*; *Voice over IP (VoIP)*.

REFERENCES

Arends, R., et al. 2005. Protocol modifications for the DNS security extensions. RFC 4035, March.

Brandner, R., et al. 2005. IANA registration for enumservice "web" and "ft." RFC 4002, February.

European Telecommunications Standards Institute (ETSI). 2002. ENUM administration in Europe. ETSI Technical Specification 102 051, July.

Faltstrom, P., and M. Mealling. 2004. The E.164 to uniform resource identifiers (URI) dynamic delegation discovery system (DDDS) application (ENUM). RFC 3761, April.

Hollenbeck, S. 2005. E.164 number mapping for the extensible provisioning protocol (EPP). RFC 4114, June.

International Telecommunications Union (ITU-T). 1997. The international public telecommunication number plan. Recommendation E.164, May.

Internet Assigned Numbers Authority (IANA). 2004. Enumservice registrations (retrieved from www.iana.org/assignments/enum-services).

Malamud, C., and M. Rose. 1993. Principles of operation for the TPC.INT subdomain: General principles and policy. RFC 1530, October.

Mealling, M. 2002a. Dynamic delegation discovery system (DDDS)—Part one: The comprehensive DDDS. RFC 3401, October.

———. 2002b. Dynamic delegation discovery system (DDDS)—Part three: The domain name system (DNS) database. RFC 3403, October.

Moats, R. 1997. URN syntax. RFC 2141, May.

Newton, A. 2006. An ENUM registry type for the Internet Registry Information Service (IRIS). RFC 4414, February.

Newton, A., and M. Sanz. 2005. IRIS: The Internet Registry Information Service (IRIS) core protocol. RFC 3981, January.

Peterson, J. 2004. Enumservice registration for session initiation protocol (SIP) addresses-of-record. RFC 3764, April.

RIPE NCC. Undated. ENUM request archives (retrieved from www.ripe.net/enum/request-archives/).

Web Hosting

Thomas C. Bressoud, *Denison University*

INTRODUCTION

Web hosting is an arrangement by which a company that specializes in the ongoing management of the technology and resources to run a Web site provides such a service for another company, organization, or individual. A typical Web hosting provider offers such services for many clients. Web hosting is not about the *creation* of an organization's Web site; it is about taking an organization's Web site and placing it on one or more servers, making it available on the Internet, and maintaining the Web site's operations on behalf of the client organization.

Web hosting is a rapidly growing and changing area. Hosting service providers and the types of services they offer change week by week and month by month. Likewise, the platforms and specific software employed are also subject to rapid change. With this in mind, the goal of this chapter is to focus on the technical aspects of Web hosting, seeking the conceptual core that will persist even amongst the constant change that we must expect to continue.

The subject of Web hosting must be viewed from two perspectives—the perspective of the provider and the perspective of the client. From the perspective of the client, Web hosting is about the business decision to outsource the day-to-day operational concerns of running their Web site and the technical issues that must be considered in making such a decision. The client must also decide what service components they require from the provider among a myriad of choices. From the perspective of the provider, Web hosting involves the integration and composition of many of the networking topics addressed in other chapters of this book. Web hosting is a vertical slice from the network stack, and the provider must select from alternatives at each level, resulting in a large number of possible combinations.

In the remainder of this introduction, the client perspective will be discussed as we explore the central idea of outsourcing and its advantages and disadvantages. We then describe in the section entitled "Provider Models" each of the provider service models that predominate in the industry. This is in part a client perspective and in part a provider perspective. The models section continues by differentiating the provider models of Web hosting from those of application service providers. In the section entitled "Architectural Issues," we introduce the service component hierarchy, allowing an integration of the provider models. The issue of fault tolerance, which has aspects in all of the levels of the service component hierarchy, is also introduced. The service component hierarchy will serve as a framework for the rest of the chapter, in which it will be used as a vehicle to discuss the various network issues and decisions that form the technical basis of Web hosting in the section entitled "Physical Infrastructure," the section entitled "Network Connectivity and DNS," and the section entitled "Web Site Architectures." The presentation will also serve to relate the service components back to the provider models.

Outsourcing is the decision to contract services with an external company instead of providing those services within an organization. In the case of Web hosting, this refers to the outsourcing of information technology (IT) expertise, Internet connectivity, data center operation, domain name service management, Web servers, and affiliated software for the operation of the organization's Web site.

Two issues are core to the genesis of the rapidly growing Web hosting industry. First, for almost every business, large or small, and almost every organization, large or small, the presence of the organization on the Web has become a mandatory and critical element. Second, and corollary to the first, there has been a transition in the types of organizations with a Web presence. In the early days of the Web, the organizations with a Web presence were dominated by high-tech companies and research organizations, wherein networking and computer services were a core competency. As the Web has evolved into the primary face of marketing for any type of business, the domain of expertise has shifted, and it is now the exception that networking and computer services are a core competency of the organization.

Given these two central issues, the advantages of outsourcing Web hosting can be summarized into the areas of competency, reliability, time, and cost.

- *Competency:* Web hosting providers specialize in the infrastructure and networking issues that are required to operate and maintain availability of a Web site. When the domain of expertise of an organization is not aligned with this networking competency, outsourcing Web hosting allows the organization to focus on the strengths and mission of the organization.
- *Reliability:* An organization's Web site has become the "store front' by which interested parties (existing or potential customers, organization members, etc.) interact with the organization. In many respects, the Web presence becomes a proxy for the organization itself. As such, the Web site has become a business-critical resource and any lack of availability or decrease in reliability (actual or perceived) becomes costly to the organization. Web hosting providers, in addition to the networking competency, are (or should be) experts in fault tolerance and in increasing the availability and reliability of the Web sites they host.
- *Time:* Web hosting services can greatly reduce the time required to make a Web site for an organization available on the Internet. Web hosting providers have all of the infrastructure and servers already in place, along with many tools for rapid development and deployment of a Web site. Particularly for small Web sites, the site can be up and running and available on the Internet almost immediately.
- *Cost:* The issue of cost is at the heart of many of the previously cited advantages of outsourcing. The Web hosting provider can amortize all the associated costs of running a Web site, from building and supporting a data center with fault-tolerant data and control, to security, to support staff and operators on site around the clock, over many clients and Web sites. In addition to reducing the cost per client, this also serves to reduce risk among the set of clients.

The disadvantages of outsourcing the Web site operations for an organization revolve around the issues of (i) control; (ii) cost, if the outsourcing is a duplication of expertise you require in-house for other reasons; and (iii) recourse when something goes wrong. Whenever a decision is made to outsource, the organization is giving up control of the operational aspects of its Web site. This is primarily a concern when existing IT staff have made a significant investment in time and effort for current Web site operations. Likewise, if the organization is an Internet-based enterprise for which Web technologies are already a core competency, outsourcing may mean duplication of resources and expertise and thus may mean additional cost over what is already required for in-house purposes. Finally, the issue of how often things go awry with a Web hosting provider and how quickly the problem is resolved can be a disadvantage. For the client, the best protection is through contracted service level agreements with the Web hosting provider. Since the purpose of this chapter is to detail the technical and networking issues of Web hosting, such business-level issues will not be addressed further.

Corollary to the issue of the loss of control is the issue of privacy. In Web hosting, the service provider has access to the information and raw data of the client organization, creating an inherent set of privacy concerns. The client organization must assess to what degree the provider can be trusted to protect its information.

PROVIDER MODELS

Web hosting services may be packaged and assembled in numerous ways, corresponding to the wide range of requirements different types of customers may have. Over time, the sets of services have converged to a handful of *provider models* agreed upon within the industry. A brief look at these models will allow a categorization of vendor offerings and will give a starting point from which to discuss the service component hierarchy in the third section of the chapter and then to proceed level by level up that hierarchy in the sections that follow.

COLOCATION

One of the most fundamental (and earliest) provider models is that of *colocation*. In colocation, the client is simply contracting for two things: the physical facilities in which to house their Web servers, and the Internet access required for data to and from those Web servers. The client provides its own server hardware, Web server software, and expertise for operations of its Web site. The vendor provides the data center real estate sufficient for the client's server hardware and the intra-data center networking and Internet access.

Colocation offers clients control and in-house expertise over their Web site operations. High-quality Internet data center facilities are costly, and sharing good facilities with other clients while maintaining control and/or unique configurations of a Web site is a reasonable alternative for some organizations. Also, colocation facilities may be combined with Managed Services, discussed in the section entitled "Managed Service Providers."

SHARED SERVERS

For a client organization, the least expensive entry in Web hosting is the *shared server* model. This is the predominant model in use at the present time. The use of the word *shared* refers to the fact that clients' software Web servers are, in fact, virtual, and multiple Web servers are executed on the same physical server (see Figure 1a). In this model, the provider is responsible for the Internet data center and also owns and maintains the server hardware. The client rents its portion of the physical server and publishes its Web site by transferring the Web site to the server.

The client typically has a registered domain name, and the mapping from the client's domain name (or a subdomain thereof) resolves to an IP address of the physical server. Multiple IP addresses can map to the same physical server, meaning that multiple Web sites can be

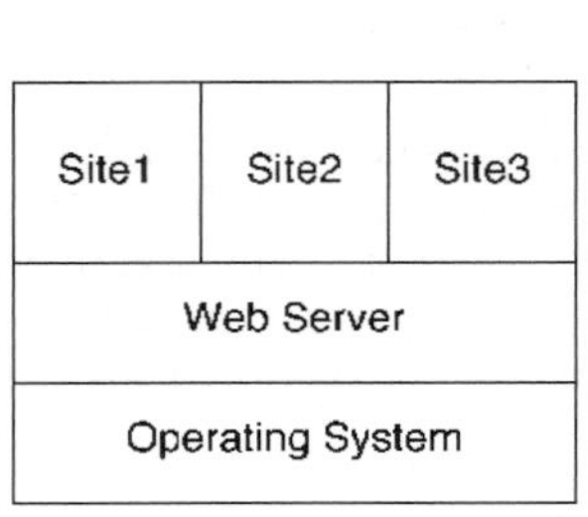

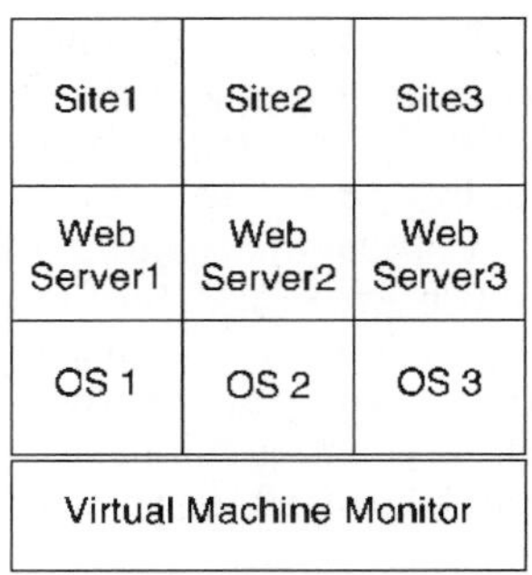

(a) Shared Server (b) Virtual Private Servers

Figure 1: Shared server alternatives

supported on the same machine. Once traffic (in particular, HTML traffic) is directed to the correct machine, this becomes a function of the Web server software on the server. See the chapter entitled "Domain Name Systems," for more information on mapping from a domain to an IP address.

Depending on a number of factors, tens to hundreds of clients may be shared on a server. The implication is that they are sharing CPU, memory, and bandwidth, as well as the operating system software and other layers of software up to the point at which traffic is split among virtual Web servers. A variant of this provider model is known as *virtual private servers*. In this variant, the server is partitioned into *virtual machines* (not virtual Web servers). As depicted in Figure 1b, each virtual machine is capable of running its own (and perhaps different) operating system along with any desired support software. Although CPU and memory are still shared, resource allocation may be tightly controlled with no single virtual machine able to usurp more than its share of resources. This also serves to build a security barrier between virtual machines and their associated clients.

Under the shared server model, it is still possible to define a Web site that utilizes database and/or interactive or scripting capabilities. This depends on the vendor and the tools and facilities that they provide. If the shared server is not a virtual private server, the set of tools are likely to be prescribed and controlled by the vendor (such as type of database and tools for interacting with the database).

An extreme point in the spectrum of shared servers is that of *free hosting* service providers. These Web hosting providers host the Web sites of client organizations, typically with many client Web sites on the same physical server. Such free hosting providers do not charge the client organization for the hosting service. The business model may realize revenue through alternative channels such as the appearance of forced advertising integrated into the client Web site, or through potential future revenue by offering management and customization when the client organization moves into a higher tier of service. This would then become a managed service provider model as discussed in the section entitled "Managed Service Providers." Often in this free hosting arrangement, client organizations may not have their own registered domain names; instead, they have a subdivision of the provider's domain. This style of Web hosting is made cost effective by limiting client capabilities through prescribed templates and Web site building tools, resulting in Web sites that may be created and maintained with little human system administration.

The shared server provider model is appropriate for small to midsized Web sites.

Dedicated Servers

The *dedicated server* model, as its name implies, involves no sharing of a physical server between multiple clients. The server hardware is provided by the vendor but is under the complete control of the client, who is leasing the entire machine. The provider is also still responsible for the physical infrastructure and Internet data center. This solution offers more capacity, more flexibility, and better security. As a result, it is also a more expensive alternative.

For a single Web site on the server machine, the mapping of domain/subdomain to the IP address of the server is simplified, but it still involves appropriate domain name system (DNS) translation to the IP address on the physical server at the provider's data center.

The dedicated server provider model is appropriate for midsized to large Web sites, and for Web sites with unique configurations and/or the need for custom software. A single client with multiple Web sites might also find this an attractive model, as it could place these Web sites onto the dedicated server.

Managed Service Providers

For organizations that require high levels of configuration and customization for their Web site but lack the in-house expertise that a dedicated server solution would require, the *managed service provider* may offer an appropriate solution. In this model, the provider is responsible for building a complete solution, including the design, configuration, and customization of the server hardware and software. In this model, the vendor often does *not* provide the physical infrastructure and Internet connectivity. This may occur independently through a colocation vendor, or a managed service provider and a colocation vendor may enter into a partnership agreement, in which the data center choice is predetermined.

Since managed service providers specialize in custom solutions, often targeted at high-end Web site requirements, the exact set of services included is difficult to pin down. Managed service providers range over a spectrum from extremely flexible providers who build very custom solutions, to those with a more rigid set of a la carte choices that they have vetted and are compatible with one another.

HYBRID AND SPECIALIZED MODELS

It should be clear from the preceding discussion that these provider models are rough categorizations, and many permutations are possible, resulting in many *hybrid models*. A managed service provider may be coupled with a colocation provider. A managed service provider may provide the configuration and customization but use a dedicated server provider for the data center and server hardware. A vendor providing colocation services may also offer managed services that are tied to its locations.

Specialized Web hosting providers are those providers that may host a subset of their client organizations' Web site content. A popular class of specialized Web hosting provider is that of media content providers. In this example, client organizations may already maintain their own Web site, or may have a general Web hosting provider for their main Web site content, but the storage and bandwidth performance issues associated may make providing it in-house infeasible. The media content providers host just the streaming media on their streaming servers, and typically will have customized the storage and network bandwidth infrastructure to more efficiently provide this type of content.

Another type of specialization also deserves description. Instead of hosting a traditional Web site, or a subset thereof, one could host specialized content that appears in prescribed form and with a limited set of potential elements. One form of this specialization is that of *profile hosting*, such as that provided by organizations such as MySpace (Anderson 2006) or Facebook (Zuckerberg 2006). Members, profiles may be tailored and customized according to the clients' interests and share many qualities of personal Web sites. Another form of this specialization is *blog hosting*, in which the focus is the exchange and sharing of information (news, journals, photos) through Web logs (blogs). These types of specialization may also be categorized as shared server providers. In these cases, the number of individual clients hosted on a physical server may be quite large. As a consequence, the request/reply traffic to the physical server could differ substantially from a traditional Web site.

Differentiating from Application Service Providers

The purview of *application service providers* (ASPs) is the application software, such as human resource software, or software for the management of business processes. These applications are critical business elements and most often execute within a company's intranet.

Whereas many of the applications that are supported by ASPs have Web-based interfaces, this means that they require the support that Web hosting solutions provide, not that they supplant nor subsume Web hosting. ASPs are not infrastructure providers and typically do not share the same expertise as that required by Web hosting providers in designing and operating a high-quality Internet data center. Because of the complex requirements and configurations ASPs need to support the intranet applications, ASPs may often be clients of managed service providers. See the chapter entitled "Application Service Providers" for more information on ASPs.

ARCHITECTURAL ISSUES

Service Component Hierarchy

The *service component hierarchy* in Figure 2 is used to illustrate the components of Web hosting and their relationships. It is composed similarly to a network stack

Application
Web Server and Database
Operating System and Script Support
Server Hardware
Load Balancing
Support Services
Network Connectivity and DNS
Physical Infrastructure

Figure 2: Service component hierarchy

with each layer supporting the layers above it, and each layer depending on the layers below.

The three lowest levels of the service—component hierarchy—physical infrastructure, network connectivity, and support services—are services provided by colocation providers, shared server providers, and dedicated server providers. The support services level is intended to capture the need for providing backup and recovery mechanisms for client organizations as well as the ability to reboot server machines in the event of a failure. Given that many Web hosting providers have limited physical access by the client organizations, these types of remote services are commonplace. The sections entitled "Physical Infrastructure" and "Network Connectivity and DNS" will describe the lowest two levels of the service component hierarchy in detail.

Depending on the particulars of the service offerings, the next three to four levels of the service component hierarchy, namely the load balancing, server hardware, operating system and script support, and Web server and database, are provided by shared server providers, dedicated server providers, and managed services providers. These levels in aggregate define the Web site architecture, and are described together in the section entitled "Web Site Architectures." Managed service providers specialize in more variations of Web server and database configurations, whereas shared and dedicated server providers have more constrained support in these levels. The application level, and the content that is encompassed by the application level, is the responsibility of the organization or may be provided through an ASP.

Fault Tolerance

As the discussion continues in the next set of sections of this chapter, we shall repeatedly discuss the issue of fault tolerance at many of the levels of the service component hierarchy. It is worthwhile at this juncture to describe some of the common principles of fault tolerance, as we will be applying these principles throughout the remainder of the chapter.

At the heart of any fault-tolerant design, be it for physical infrastructure or for networks or for services, is the guiding principle of using redundant, failure-independent elements, so that the failure of any individual element does not cause a system-level failure. System-level failures translate into a lack of availability of services. Through the use of redundant paths and network and computing elements, and based on the assurance that these elements fail independently, the probability of a system failure is the product of the probability of the failure of the elements.

When there is no redundant path, network element, or software service, this constitutes a *single point of failure*. The probability of failure of the system is simply the probability of failure of this nonredundant element. It should also be noted from the above characterization that redundancy alone is not sufficient to get a fault-tolerant benefit. The key is that failures must be *independent*. Nonindependent failures are called *common-mode* failures and tend to be the result of elements having a common root cause for a failure.

Security

We noted in the introduction that privacy concerns must be assessed when a client organization considers outsourcing its Web site. In addition, the overall security of an organization's Web site crosses the boundaries of most of the service component hierarchy levels. This issue is not specific to Web hosting, as the same security issues must be addressed whether the Web site is hosted in-house, or is hosted by a Web hosting provider.

Physical security must be addressed in the physical infrastructure level, including limiting access to the facilities and securing the infrastructure discussed in that section. In the network connectivity level, data as transmitted between browsers and Web servers must be confidential and protected against both eavesdropping and manipulation. Encryption techniques are typically employed through the use of the HTTPS protocol and certification of servers. In the support services level, backup and recovery contribute to the security of the Web hosting solution. Above this level, within the Web site architecture, additional protection may be provided through the use of firewalls and intrusion detection systems. Furthermore, load balancing can be used to provide some protection against denial of service attacks.

Detailing all the possible security issues and their solutions is beyond the scope of the present chapter. Within Volume 3 of this handbook, the section on networking planning, control, and management dedicates a number of chapters to various security issues, including the chapters entitled "Social Engineering," "Intrusion Detection Systems," "Network Attacks," "Denial of Service Attacks," "Cryptography," and "Firewalls."

PHYSICAL INFRASTRUCTURE

At the lowest level of the service component hierarchy is the *physical infrastructure* layer. This level includes the physical plant, such as the building in which physical servers are stored; the utilities to power, air condition, and heat the facility; security to limit access to the facility; power distribution within the facility; and racks and cages used for the installation of server hardware. When the physical infrastructure is combined with the next level of network connectivity, these facilities are known as Internet data centers (IDCs).

Whether the provider model is colocation, shared server, or dedicated server, a Web host provider must design and provision a quality physical infrastructure. For a colocation provider, this, along with network connectivity and DNS (the next layer up), is the primary service provided. For shared and dedicated server providers, this physical infrastructure is needed to assure reliability for the servers at the facility. The physical infrastructure design should encompass goals of adequate power requirements for current and anticipated growth of hosted servers, physical security, and fault tolerance.

Physical infrastructure includes the following elements:

- Building
- Electrical power (including generator or battery backup)
- Other utilities, such as natural gas and telecommunications
- Air conditioning
- Fire suppression
- Physical security
- Physical connection to the Internet service provider (ISP) of the facility
- Internal equipment racks, cabinets, or cage

Considerations for these elements can be divided into concerns from *within* the facility, and, for those with external connections, the *point of entry* of the physical infrastructure element.

Point of Entry

The physical infrastructure elements of electrical power, natural gas, telecommunications, and physical Internet connection must all originate from suppliers outside the facility and have some point of entry into the facility. Likewise, a generator providing backup electrical power may be outside the facility and require a power line entering the facility.

For all of the above, this point of entry constitutes a single point of failure, and to provide fault tolerance at the physical infrastructure level, a Web hosting provider must provision redundant points of entry for all such entering utilities. This kind of fault-tolerance design is often to guard against so-called *backhoe* failures, in which a construction-site backhoe can inadvertently cut through electrical or fiber-optic paths entering a facility. To be effective, multiple points of entry should be on opposite (and hopefully failure-independent) sides of the facility, and the paths to utilities must remain independent all the way to the source. When multiple points of entry rejoin at the next power substation or telecommunications central office, these represent common-mode failures, and the fault-tolerance benefit is lost.

Note that there is a difference between providing fault-tolerant paths for electrical power and natural gas from that of the fiber-optic bundles used for the physical Internet connection. In the former, the utilities are commodity, and one point of entry is equivalent to another. In the latter, failure independence argues for physical connection to at least two different Internet service providers. When the failure of one occurs, the network routing from anywhere on the Internet must be able to handle a change in routing through a different ISP to access the Web server addresses that will be housed in the Internet Data Center. This issue is not part of the physical infrastructure and will be addressed in the section entitled "Inter-Domain Routing."

Intra-Facility

The point-of-entry discussion implies the requirement of redundant power (including generators), natural gas, telecommunications, and physical Internet connection. Within the facility, redundancy is also required.

Air conditioning is required to keep servers, which generate a great deal of heat, from overheating, particularly when servers are packed together to maximize computing power per building square area. Data centers should provide redundant air conditioning. If a facility requires n air conditioning systems for current requirements, they should employ $n + 2$ or $n + 3$ to provide the additional redundancy.

Redundant power supply from the grid was cited earlier as a requirement, but good data centers also provide generators and battery backup. For generators, sufficient fuel should also be provisioned. For greater reliability, many modern data centers maintain contracts with separate fuel suppliers to ensure deliveries in the case of a regional natural disaster.

Another issue within the facility is the layout and utilization of space required for servers, routers, storage subsystems, and other Web site hardware components. Since colocation vendors must provide access to the staff from their client organizations, cages can be used to create individual data centers. Servers may also be configured in locked cabinets and/or standard-form racks.

A final issue for the physical infrastructure layer is that of physical security. The Web host provider must limit access to the data center and may incorporate alarm and locking systems and biometric security devices. This becomes increasingly important for colocation providers and dedicated server providers in which the IT staff of the organization may require access to the servers.

NETWORK CONNECTIVITY AND DNS

One of the most basic requirements of Web hosting is that end users, whose locations may be anywhere on the Internet, must be able to access a hosted Web site of the client organization, given a logical name. The end users are the customers, members, or general visitors of the company or organization that is responsible for the content of the site. The logical name is a fully qualified domain name, such as `www.company.com` or `www.organization.org`. This accessibility is encompassed by the term *network connectivity* and refers to the two-way flow of traffic between end users and the Web site. The translation from the logical name into the IP address(es) of the Web site is handled by the DNS. These, then, are the topics of this section.

For the purposes of this discussion, the problem is divided into three parts:

1. Inter-domain routing: routing between the IP address of an end user and the physical facility that houses the Web site.
2. Intra-domain routing: routing within the data center.
3. DNS: mapping the logical name known to the end user into an IP address. In an end user access timeline, this step would be accomplished before inter-domain routing would begin.

As a starting point, we assume that the IP address(es) involved have been allocated and assigned. Either the Web hosting provider owns its own set of IP addresses (which it may have received through its own Internet service provider 0 and apportions them out to the client, or the client owns its own IP addresses. A client coming in with its own IP addresses is not common, and is more likely with a colocation provider client than a dedicated or shared server provider client.

We will first discuss the two parts of the IP routing problem, assuming that the logical name of the end user maps to one of the IP addresses of the Web server. The logical name to IP address mapping is relatively independent of the routing issues, and will be discussed in the section that follows.

We have allowed that multiple IP addresses can resolve to the same physical server, both to support virtual servers in the shared server case, and to support multiple Web sites for a single client in the dedicated server case. This may be accomplished by a combination of multiple network interfaces, and by the ability to assign multiple IP addresses to a single network interface.

Inter-Domain Routing

As described in the chapters entitled "The Internet Fundamentals" and "The Internet Architecture," the Internet is partitioned into a set of autonomous systems (ASs), which defines an area of network infrastructure under a single technical and administrative control. Every public IP address must belong to at most one AS; typically, an ISP is associated with a single AS. Most end users' IP addresses belong to the AS of their ISP, whereas larger organizations may define their own AS, as opposed to the AS of their ISP. ASs interconnect via dedicated links and public network access points, and exchange routing reachability information through an exchange between border routers of the connected ASs using the border gateway protocol (BGP).

BGP (currently version 4) is the standard used for inter-domain routing in the Internet. The unit of routability provided by BGP is the *network prefix*, which is an aggregation of IP addresses in a contiguous block. BGP peering sessions between ASs convey to one another information about these sets of addresses that they know about, and the path through a set of ASs by which those addresses may be reached. BGP is a path vector protocol and its default routing for a given IP address is to use the shortest AS path to the network prefix that includes that specific IP address.

Suppose that an end user initiates an interaction with a target Web server at an IP address, x. Each AS will, in turn, look at the destination IP address and determine what network prefix, p, it belongs to. Through the information collected in BGP peering sessions, the current AS can determine the next-hop neighbor AS in the AS path for p, as well as the border router r that connects that next-hop neighbor AS with the current AS. The current AS will then route packets with target address x across its own AS to r, where they will proceed to the next AS.

Note that calling the role of BGP *inter-domain routing* is, in fact, a misnomer; it is really inter AS routing. This becomes evident in Web hosting, where the Web hosting provider defines an AS that end users need to route to for access to the Web server of their organization, but the logical domains/subdomains of many organizations are within the umbrella of the single Web hosting provider AS.

We argued in the "Physical Infrastructure" section that, for reliability and fault-tolerance, an Internet data center should be connected to at least two different ISPs. When a Web hosting provider is connected to the rest of the Internet through a single ISP, there is only one BGP AS-path route to the AS of the Web hosting provider. When a Web hosting provider is connected to two different ISPs, the supporting inter-domain routing can be configured in two ways: *failover* and *multihomed*.

In a failover configuration, one of the ISP connections serves as the primary one. If no failure has occurred, *all* of the Internet traffic to and from the Web hosting provider occurs through the primary ISP. The BGP information is the same as if there were only one connection. If the connection to the primary ISP fails, a recovery action takes place and all traffic occurs through the backup ISP. The path through the backup ISP is not advertised through BGP peering exchanges until the failure occurs or exchanges effect the BGP metrics so that the backup will not be selected if the primary is viable.

In a multihomed configuration, paths through multiple ISPs are active and available for the routing of traffic to the Web hosting provider. Because of limited mechanisms for controlling BGP, this method is complex and it can be exceedingly difficult to balance the IP traffic load between the multiple ISPs. The traffic associated with a network prefix can have great variability. When configured well, however, this configuration offers the possibility of greater traffic balance in the absence of failures, and this can translate to better performance in terms of latency and jitter between an end user and the target Web site. When a failure occurs, all network prefixes of the Web hosting AS must be advertised through BGP at the surviving ISP connection.

ISP Relationships: Peering and Transit

Another issue that requires consideration when a Web hosting provider connects to multiple ISPs is the business relationship between the Web hosting provider and their ISPs (and between ISPs in general). Just as an individual can pay for Internet access through his or her ISP, a Web hosting provider or a local ISP can pay for upstream access through another ISP. This type of relationship is called *transit*, and, in exchange for the payment, the ISP guarantees to accept packets bound for any host on the Internet and to provide a return path for packets bound for the customer. At the backbone of the Internet, and sometimes at regional levels as well, ISPs (or, more precisely, ASs) may agree to exchange traffic without a corresponding payment. This is called a *peering* relationship and is generally established for the mutual benefit of two comparably sized ASs. A peering relationship will always route traffic to the transit customers of the peering partner. It may not, however, route traffic coming in from one peering partner, route within the AS, and exit the AS through *another* peering partner. This type of routing uses the resources of the AS without any corresponding revenue.

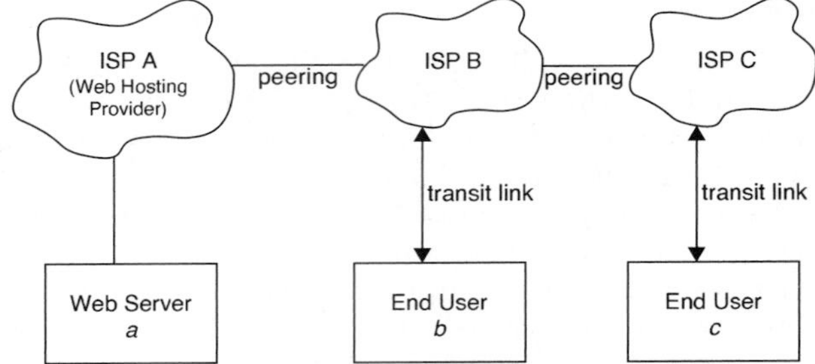

Figure 3: Peering/transit example

What this means for Web hosting is that, if the Web hosting provider has multiple ISPs and is in a peering relationship with one or more of these ISPs, there is a possibility that an end user may be precluded from accessing a hosted Web site. Consider the example depicted in Figure 3. Suppose for this example that the Web hosting provider is itself an ISP labeled A in the figure. As such, it may have a peering relationship with ISP B. Assume a Web site named *a* is hosted by this provider. Further suppose that we have two end users: end user *b* is a transit customer of ISP B, and end user *c* is a transit customer of ISP C. ISP C and ISP B may also have a peering relationship, as depicted in this example. End user *b* is guaranteed accessibility to *c* through the transit relationship with *B*, and, when B routes to A, A will route to the Web server at *a*. End user *c*, however, is not guaranteed accessibility. End user *c* uses transit routing to ISP C, and ISP C will use the peering relationship with ISP B to pass traffic to this next AS in line. However, since ISP A is not in a transit relationship with ISP B, ISP B has no obligation to pass traffic across its AS from C to A. So, for end user *c*, the Web site *a* may be inaccessible.

To preclude such reachability problems, a Web hosting provider should establish a transit relationship with at least two of its connecting ISPs.

Satellite Data Centers

This subsection on inter-domain routing and the connections of a Web hosting provider to multiple ISPs concludes with a matter that occurs in practice, the connectivity architecture when a Web hosting provider establishes *satellite data centers*. Satellite data centers are typically the result of the growth of a Web hosting provider beyond its current facilities, and its needs to create an additional data center in the same regional area. If a Web hosting provider has existing business relationships with two ISPs, the resultant connectivity with a satellite data center could take a number of forms. Figure 4 illustrates three basic possibilities.

In Figure 4a the existing data center and the satellite data center both have independent connections to both ISP A and ISP B. The fault tolerance of the system has not been diminished by adding the satellite data center. In Figure 4b the satellite data center is not connected to any ISP and receives all traffic through the existing data center. This link constitutes a single point of failure, and fault tolerance suffers. In Figure 4c each data center is connected to one ISP, but not to both. Here the two data

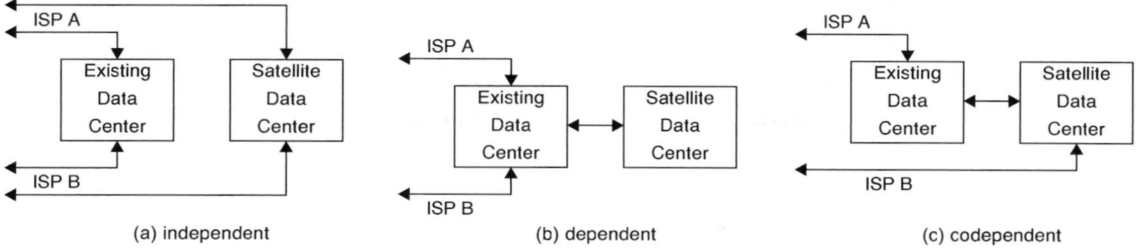

Figure 4: Satellite data center/ISP connectivity

centers are codependent, and, although there is no single point of failure, the links in the absence of failures will act in a failover mode of operation, and traffic load may not be balanced.

Intra-Domain Routing

Once traffic can be routed between end users and the AS of the Web hosting provider, traffic within the AS still needs to be routed from the border router(s) to the physical server of the Web site. Intra-domain routing protocols at the network protocol stack level define the process to determine, hop to hop, the route packets take within the AS. These protocols are described elsewhere in the chapter entitled "Network Layer Protocols." These protocols support multiple paths between source and destination, and dynamically adapt to changing conditions, such as a path becoming inviable, perhaps due to failure.

The concern for Web hosting providers is again one of reliability. To eliminate single points of failure, the intraAS network of the Web hosting provider must include multiple paths through redundant routers between border gateways and the server hardware. These issues must be considered from the initial design of the internal network of the Web hosting provider.

DNS

With respect to Web hosting, the basic requirement of DNS is to translate a logical Web site name, such as `www.client.org`, to the IP address of the appropriate server at the data center of the Web hosting provider. In this example, the `www` is the name of the host, and `client.org` is the *second-level domain*. Together, the host part and the second-level domain part constitute a fully qualified domain name.

Recall the steps of the translation process, described more fully in the chapter entitled "Domain Name Systems." The end user begins with a DNS query with the fully qualified domain name. This query is sent to a root name server, which returns a top-level name server. This top-level name server has translation mappings from all second-level domain names under its top level (client.orgunder.org, in this example) to the authoritative name servers for the second-level domain. These name servers are returned through DNS to the end user, who continues by then making a query to these name servers for therequested host (`www`). The authoritative name servers for `client.org` then provide an IP address for `www` in the `client.org` second-level domain.

The issue in the context of Web hosting involve two levels of the DNS translation process and how (or by whom) the content is maintained. At the lower level, the authoritative name servers for the client organization's second-level domain must have entries for the IP addresses of the Web site's servers. At the higher level, whenever there is a change of second-level domain name servers for the client organization, the top-level name servers must be updated to reflect the new name servers.

Improper management of DNS entries is an extremely common source of failure preventing an end user from accessing the Web site of a client organization. As such, the Web hosting provider, for whom reliability should be paramount, has great incentive to control the second-level domain name servers. Control of the name servers also gives the Web hosting provider flexibility in making changes in physical server IP addresses. The client organization, however, also desires control of these name servers, because they also must provide mappings for all the other DNS-resolvable hosts of the client organization. These could include mail servers, internal hosts, or hosts of an extranet defined by the organization.

For shared server providers, the name servers are almost always under the control of the Web hosting provider. To allow for other (non-Web site) hosts to be resolved by the name server, the provider typically offers a *control panel* with which the client organization can add additional entries. The capabilities and level of DNS control offered by these control panels can vary widely.

For colocation and dedicated server providers, wherein the client organization is typically larger and involves more non-Web site hosts that must be managed, a common solution is for the public name servers to be owned by the provider, but for these to be slaves to a master name server that is maintained behind the firewall of the client organization. The master can perform a transfer of the non-Web site hosts from the master to the slave in a DNS operation called a *zone transfer*.

Another solution is possible that provides a clear distinction between the Web site hosts and the non-Web site hosts—this solution involves creating a subdomain for the Web site hosts. A subdomain would be a third-level domain and would translate a DNS query for the third-level domain into the name server for the subdomain. This name server could be used for just the Web site hosts and could be owned by the Web hosting provider. For this solution to work, a DNS alias would be required that would map a request for `www.client.org` into `www.subdomain.client.org`. The alias (a DNS *CNAME* entry) would be translated and require the third level of name server lookup. This third level would resolve to the name server of the Web hosting provider. All other DNS queries would resolve at the second level, which would be maintained by a name server controlled by the client organization.

For acceptable performance, DNS entries are cached wherever and whenever possible. This includes the IP addresses of top-level and second-level name servers, and caching can occur both at the end user and at name servers. Cached entries expire after a fixed amount of time, known as the time to live (TTL). The translation entries for second-level name servers are controlled by the domain registrar of the client organization and typically have an expiration time set between twenty-four and forty-eight hours. If a client organization contracts for a new Web hosting provider or changes Web hosting provider, this often involves changing the second-level name servers through the domain registrar. For end users and top-level name servers that have cached the IP address of the second-level name server, such changes will not be visible until after the expiration of the cached entry. This is why a propagation delay is incurred from the time of a name server change to the time when end users can access the Web site through the new DNS entries.

WEB SITE ARCHITECTURES

As we examine the next set of levels in the service component hierarchy (again, see Figure 2), the levels of load balancing, server hardware, operating system, and Web server/database together form the architecture of the Web site. For this reason, we address all four levels in this section on Web site architectures.

At this point, we have moved beyond the services that a colocation provider might offer and are within the realm of the shared server, dedicated server, and managed services provider models. For a shared server, the set of Web site architectures are limited, although fault tolerance and reliability through load balancing may still be achieved. For dedicated server providers and managed services providers, a full range of Web site architectures is possible. It is clear, though, that regardless of the type of provider, the level of sophistication of the client organization's Web site continues to grow, and Web hosting providers must continue to expand the architectures they support to meet this growing expectation.

A Web site architecture governs the set of hardware servers, their interconnection, and what software components run on what servers. Goals in the design of the Web site architecture include issues of capacity, scalability, reliability, and performance. This section will begin by describing one- and two-tier architectures, followed by the issues of fault tolerance, load balancing, and more advanced architectures.

One and Two-Tier Models

As depicted in Figure 5, the simplest Web architecture consists of a Web server, such as Apache or Microsoft IIS, executing on a physical server and utilizing a host-accessible storage system. This architecture could also incorporate elements such as common gateway interface (CGI)-based scripting in various interpreted programming languages such as Perl, Python, TCL, JavaScript, and server-side technologies such as PHP and Java Servlets. It is beyond the scope of this chapter to investigate the many possibilities entailed. Note also from the figure that the storage could either be directly attached, as in Figure 5a, or it could be separated from the server, as in Figure 5b, such as that enabled by network attached storage or using a proprietary storage area network (SAN, described in the chapter entitled "Storage Area Networks").

When a Web site becomes more dynamic, it often incorporates on-the-fly creation of Web pages using scripting techniques coupled with data contents obtained from a database. This results in the two-tier application model are also shown in Figure 5. As Figure 5c shows, the database software may execute on the same physical server as the Web server, or, as in Figure 5d, it may execute on a second server. When executing on the same server, the Web server software and the database software will be competing for resources. Shared-server providers must be particularly careful because multiple sites share the same Web server and now, in the two-tier model, the same

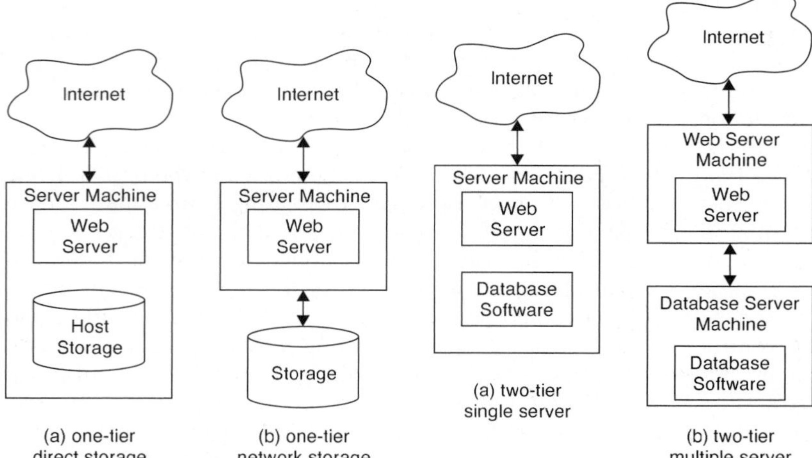

Figure 5: One and two-tier Web architectures

database software as well. In large configurations, the Web and database servers are almost always placed on different physical servers so that these servers may be configured and tuned to meet the performance requirements specific to serving Web pages or to executing a database.

Fault Tolerance

Two approaches may be taken to incorporate greater reliability and fault tolerance in the one-and two-tier architectures. The first is adding redundancy *within* the server. Although a failure of the server hardware could cause a system failure, that possibility can be mitigated by replicating some of the more failure-prone elements of the server. For instance, the Web hosting provider could employ redundant power supplies. Likewise, servers can be configured using Redundant Array of Inexpensive Disks (RAID). This isolates the failure of an individual disk drive and keeps the individual failure from bringing down an entire system or site. Some other intraserver redundancy strategies include replication of the network interface cards (NICs) either in an active/passive failover mode, or in a configuration in which both interfaces are used to transmit traffic, and use of redundant memories and/or ROM for the physical server. A database server might employ a battery backed write cache on the RAID controller. Additionally, server vendors offer options for hot-pluggable components, such as disk drives and other peripheral equipment, so that they can be replaced on the fly while the server continues operation.

The second approach to incorporate greater reliability and fault tolerance is to add redundancy *across* servers. This implies the incorporation of redundant servers for hosting the Web server and/or for hosting the database software. Database redundancy will be discussed further in the forthcoming section entitled "Database Redundancy."

When using redundant Web servers, two styles of fault tolerance are possible. First, one physical server could be the designated *primary;* in the absence of failures, all interaction between an end user and the Web server occurs through the Web server on the primary. When a failure occurs, all new interaction is directed to another machine designated as the *backup*. Upon a failure, the backup must take over the IP address of the primary, or end users must issue subsequent requests using the IP address of the backup. With a Web server, this simple primary/backup solution works because most end user interactions are *stateless*, with no dependence between one interaction and a subsequent interaction. When a set of end user interactions is grouped together into a session, a failure becomes visible to the end user because the Web server taking over has lost the prior history of the session.

The second style of fault-tolerance actively uses all of the redundant server hardware during the time when no failures have occurred. When done carefully, this redundancy provides benefits of additional scalability and capacity as well. It also requires the use of a new architectural element, the *load balancer*, which serves to distribute load across the set of servers. Although combining this style of active replication with load balancing has the potential to increase fault tolerance, the reality depends on the style of load balancing, which will be discussed next.

Load Balancing

Given a set of interactions between multiple end users and the Web site of a client organization, the function of load balancing for Web site servers is to apportion these interactions among a set of equivalent Web sites. Load balancing involves directing end user traffic to a particular physical server for a Web site. For a single given end user, this interaction may involve multiple request/reply exchanges that are dependent on one another. Thus, for an individual end user, traffic should be directed to the *same* physical server for the duration of the interaction.

Figure 6 shows two examples of load balancing one-tier Web site architectures. Figure 6a depicts a shared server provider scenario, in which the set of Web servers shared on a single machine is replicated on a second server. Figure 6b depicts a dedicated server provider using load balancing between a set of three servers. Note that, in the figure, neither the operating system nor the storage of the Web site content is depicted. The same Web site content must be available to all of the actual Web servers behind the load balancer. For static content, this may be accomplished by mirroring the content between direct host storage. Another alternative is enabled through network storage, whereby the multiple Web site servers could access the same storage.

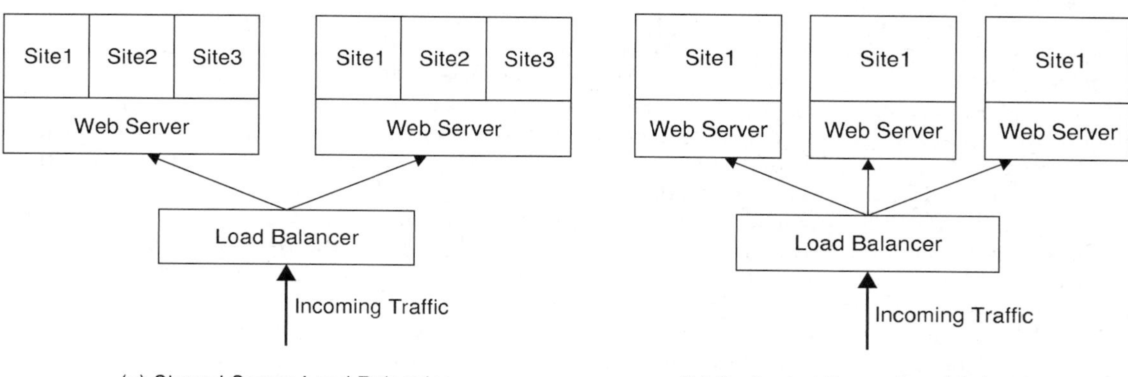

Figure 6: Load-balancing architectures

Two types of load balancing are common: DNS-based load balancing and layer 4/7 switching based load balancing. These load-balancing techniques and more are covered in detail in the chapter entitled "Load Balancing on the Internet." A brief overview will be presented here.

One of the facilities of DNS is to allow a *set* of IP addresses associated with the resolution of a fully qualified domain name. DNS responds to a request with one of the several translations, and a given DNS name server will rotate through the multiple translations in round-robin fashion. Using this facility, DNS can itself provide load balancing. A given end user performs a DNS operation to resolve the Web site name and receives one IP address, which it uses for the duration of the interaction. Another end user may get a different IP address, and its interaction will be directed to another Web server.

DNS load balancing, however, does not support fault tolerance. In addition to distributing load, we would like our Web architecture to allow that, when a physical server fails, interactions with the failed server cease and subsequent interactions are directed to nonfailed servers. The failure of an individual server does not cause its IP address to be removed from the DNS name server. Thus, end users will continue to be given the IP address of the failed server, and the failure of the server will be apparent.

By way of contrast, layer 4/7 switching load balancing more accurately corresponds to the depiction in Figure 6. An actual hardware device exists, the load balancer, with an associated IP address, that sits between end users and the set of server hardware. The IP address of the load balancer is placed in the DNS name server as the address of the Web site and can be considered the *virtual* address of the Web site. End users initiate interactions with this IP address, and, when connections are received at the load balancer, it translates the virtual IP address to the real IP address of one of the servers, effectively splicing the network connection between the end user and a particular physical server. All subsequent traffic from the same end user during a given connection or session is directed to the same server.

In this load-balancing technique, failures can be handled much more effectively. The load balancer can monitor the health (through heartbeats and/or network activity) and the load on each of the physical servers. When a failure occurs, or when load on a server gets too high, new connection/session requests from end users can be directed to healthy and/or lightly loaded servers.

Layer 4/7 switching load balancing can be accomplished either through hardware or software solutions. Hardware solutions include entries from Cisco Systems (2006), Nortel Networks (2006), Radware Ltd. (2006), and others. A popular software approach creates a load balancer using a Linux server and extending the TCP/IP stack in the kernel. This work has been gathered together under the name Linux Virtual Server (LVS; 2006), and includes layer 4 switch load balancing through the kernel module IP virtual server (IPVS) and layer 7 application level load balancing through the kernel TCP virtual server (KTCPVS).

Modern load balancers are capable of significant intelligence in performing their function. They can route requests for specific URLs to a single or a small set of servers. They can also make decisions based on protocol, so that HTTPS requests may be directed differently than HTTP requests.

The distinction between layer 4 and layer 7 switches involves what protocol-level information is used to determine a correspondence between an end user and a physical server. At layer 4, the correspondence is determined by a TCP connection, and all packets within the same connection are directed between the same end user/server pair. At layer 4, different TCP connections from the same end user can be directed to different servers. At layer 4, higher-level session information is used to determine the correspondence so that multiple TCP connections that are within a higher-level session are still directed between the same end user/server pair.

Advanced Architectures

As Web sites become more complex, the set of architectural variants can become quite numerous. In this subsection, we will highlight a few of the directions that Web site architectures can progress, and note some of the implications on Web hosting.

Two-tier Web site architectures employ the combination of the database and scripting techniques to define the operation of database-driven Web applications. As the load to the Web site increases, this architecture can suffer in performance. Each interaction between end user and Web site is separate, and, when scripting and making requests of the database are involved, each interaction results in a separate process. This implies many short-lived processes along with a lack of ability to maintain state over a set of interactions. An alternative is to extend the architecture with another element known as the *application server*, as depicted in Figure 7. The application server can maintain state and a single logical connection with the database and respond to a set of individual interactions from the Web server. In the three-tier model, the application server can also be replicated for additional fault tolerance. An example redundant three-tier architecture is also depicted in Figure 7.

Geographic Distribution

Geographic distribution refers to the redundancy of Web servers at multiple geographically distributed locations. This level of redundancy offers protection against natural disasters or Internet routing problems that can potentially make an entire single data center unavailable. It does so, however, at additional complexity and cost.

Database Redundancy

Databases are more complex to replicate than are Web servers. Consistency of data through atomicity of updates is a requirements of databases, and the addition of redundant copies of the database must be handled with care. All of the examples shown thus far have only included a single copy of the database. The subject of database redundancy is beyond the scope of this chapter.

Caching and Content Delivery Networks

Performance is an issue of great concern to client organizations. Some of the Web site architectures we have examined, particularly those that employ load balancing,

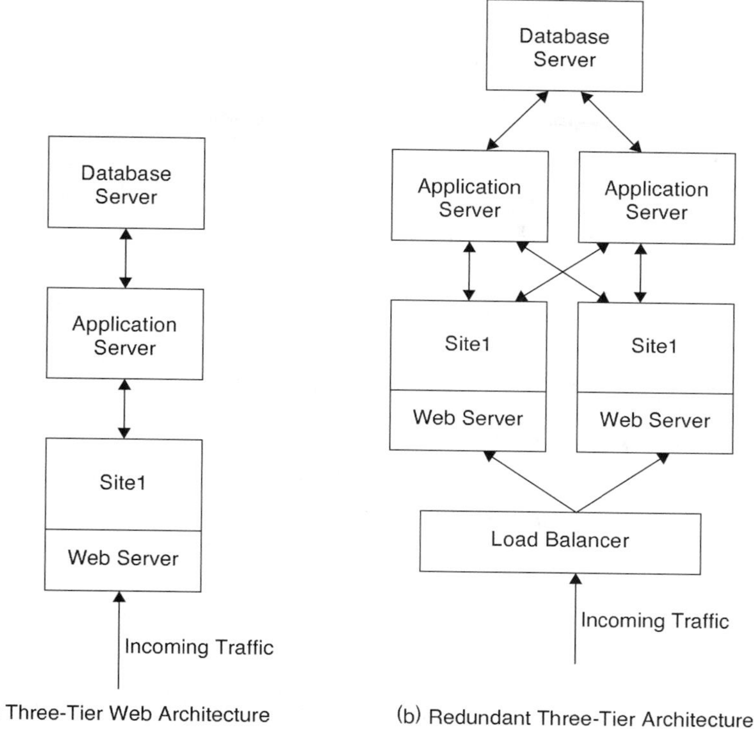

Figure 7: Three-tier architectures

can improve the scalability and the end user performance of the Web site.

Another common technique used to improve performance is that of caching of Web site contents. Caching distributes Web site contents, such as Web pages and images, and places them at locations closer to the end user. End users make requests for Web pages and images, when these requests are received by a cache, and if the cache has stored the requested elements, the request can be serviced immediately, and does not continue to the Web server.

Caching of Web site content occurs on many levels, from within the browser and file system of the end user, to corporate and organizational level proxies. Most caching has little impact on Web hosting because it occurs at locations closer to the end user. The effect on Web hosting is indirect, because successful caching reduces the volume of requests that are directed to the web site at the web hosting provider data center. This results in reduced revenue for the Web host vendor because request bandwidth and storage are the two primary metrics used by Web host providers to determine the price associated with hosting a Web site.

Another form of caching that also has the effect of reducing traffic volume to the hosted Web site is known as *content distribution networks* (CDNs). In this case, end users are directed through DNS lookups to one of a distributed set of sites caching content for a given Web site. These cache locations are placed at *edge devices*, whose network location may be closer to end users. The end user then interacts with the CDN cache instead of interacting with the original Web site.

The topics of caching and content distribution networks are described in much greater detail in the chapter entitled "Load Balancing on the Internet."

CONCLUSION

This chapter has described the topic of Web hosting, an arrangement by which an outsourcing organization, specializing in Web site infrastructure and management, provides this Web site hosting and management for a client organization. This is typically a many-to-one relationship, with potentially many client organizations being served by a single Web hosting provider.

The chapter has examined the two dimensions in the organization of such a relationship. The first dimension includes the provider models by which multiple clients may be supported, along with the services that may be provided by the outsourcing organization. Central to the provider model design and the support of a multiplicity of clients, the network issues are a primary focus of the chapter. The second dimension includes the Web site architectures that may be required of different client organizations and how the Web hosting provider may support those architectures. It is the merging of these two dimensions into a coherent whole that really defines a particular Web hosting solution.

GLOSSARY

Colocation Model: A Web hosting provider model in which the services provided are limited to the physical facilities and Internet access.

Dedicated Server Model: A Web hosting provider model in which a client organization's Web site is placed on one or more dedicated physical servers of the provider.

Fault Tolerance: The ability of a system to provide availability of operation in the presence of hardware or software failures of individual components.

Internet Data Center (IDC): The physical infrastructure for Web site servers including physical plant, power, air conditioning, and Internet connectivity.

Load Balancing: The partitioning and apportioning (directing) of a set of network interactions between end users and a set of physical servers.

Managed Service Provider: A Web hosting provider model in which the services include customized design of the Web site architecture to meet advanced requirements of the client organization.

Outsourcing: The contracting of services with an external provider instead of providing the services within an organization.

Profile Hosting: A form of shared server hosting in which a specialized form of user Web site, the *member profile,* is hosted for large numbers of users.

Satellite Data Center: An additional IDC serving as an adjunct to a primary IDC.

Service Component Hierarchy: The layered architecture of services offered by Web hosting providers.

Shared Server Model: A Web hosting provider model in which multiple Web sites are placed on the same physical server owned by the provider.

Virtual Private Servers: A variant of the shared server provider model in which each client organization is allocated a virtual machine to provide greater isolation between Web sites.

Web Hosting: An arrangement by which a company that specializes in the ongoing management of the technology and resources to run a Web site provides such a service for another company, organization, or individual.

CROSS REFERENCES

See *Application Service Providers (ASPs)*; *Fault Tolerant Systems*; *Network QoS*; *TCP/IP Suite.*

REFERENCES

Anderson, T. 2006. MySpace, owned by News Corporation. http://www.myspace.com/ (accessed September 18, 2006).

Cisco Systems. 2006. Cisco Systems catalyst switch series. http://www.cisco.com/ (accessed September 18, 2006).

Linux Virtual Server. 2006. http://www.linuxvirtualserver.com/ (accessed September 20, 2006).

Nortel Networks. 2006. Nortel application switches. http://www.nortel.com/ (accessed September 21, 2006).

Radware Ltd. 2006. Radware AppDirector. http://www.radware.com/ (accessed September 20, 2006).

Zuckerberg, M. 2006. Facebook. http://www.facebook.com/ (accessed September 19, 2006).

FURTHER READING

Albitz, P., and C. Liu. 2001. *DNS and bind*. 7th ed. O'Reilly & Associates.

Apache Software Foundation. 2006. Apache Web server. http://www.apache.org/ (accessed March 4, 2006).

Brisco, T. 1995. *DNS support for load balancing*. RFC 1794, Network Working Group.

Burnham, C. 2001. *Web hosting: A complete strategy for delivering high-quality Web hosting services*. New York: McGraw-Hill/Osborne.

Cisco Systems. 2000. Cisco content routing protocols. White paper. http://www.cisco.com/warp/public/cc/pd/cxsr/cxrt/tech/ccrp_wp.pdf (accessed July 31, 2007).

FindMyHosting. 2006. Guide to Web hosting. http://www.findmyhosting.com/webhosting-guide.htm (accessed March 4, 2006).

Foundry Networks. 2006. Foundry Networks ServerIron. http://www.foundrynet.com/ (accessed September 18, 2006).

Hostcompare. 2006. Comparisons of Web hosting vendors. http://www.hostcompare.com/ (accessed March 4, 2006).

Kalyanakrishnan, M., R. Iyer, and J. Patel. 1999. Reliability of Internet hosts: A case study from the end users, perpective. *Computer Networks* 31(1–2):47–57.

Kaye, D. 2002. *Strategies for Web hosting and managed services*. New York: John Wiley & Sons.

Long, D. D. E., A. Muir, and R. A. Golding. 1995. A longitudinal survey of Internet host reliability. In *Proceeding of the Symposium on Reliable Distributed Systems (SRDS)*, pp. 2–9.

Oppenheimer, D., A. Ganapathi, and D. Patterson. 2003. Why do Internet services fail, and what can be done about it? In *Proc. 4th USENIX Symp. on Internet Technologies and Systems (USITS)*, pp. 1–16. Seattle, WA: USENIX Association.

Qiu, L., V. N. Padmanabhan, and G. M. Voelker. 2001. On the placement of Web server replicas. In *INFOCOM 2001, Proceedings of the Twentieth Annual Joint Conference of the IEEE Computer and Communication Societies, Vol. 3*, pp. 1587–1596.

Rekhter, Y., and P. Gross. 1991. *Application of the border gateway protocol in the Internet*. RFC 1268, Network Working Group.

Saroiu, S., K. Gummadi, R. Dunn, S. Gribble, and H. Levy. 2002. An analysis of Internet content delivery systems. In *Proceeding of the Fifth Symposium on Operating Systems Design and Implementation*, Boston, December.

Stevens, R. 1994. *TCP/IP illustrated, Volume 1: The protocols*. Reading, MA: Addison-Wesley.

Stewart, J. W. 1999. *BGP4: Inter-domain routing in the Internet*. Reading, MA: Addison-Wesley Longman, Inc.

Subramanian, L., S. Agarwal, J. Rexford, and R. H. Katz. 2002. Characterizing the Internet hierarchy from multiple vantage points. In *Proceedings of IEEE INFOCOM 2002*, New York. Vol. 2, pp. 618–627.

W3Schools. 2006. W3Schools Web hosting tutorial. http://www.w3schools.com/hosting/ (accessed March 5, 2006).

End-System QoS

Tarek F. Abdelzhaer and Chengdu Huang, *University of Illinois, Urbana-Champaign*

INTRODUCTION TO END-SYSTEM QOS

The Internet has become a mainstream medium for distributed applications with various demands for reliability, availability, security, privacy, timeliness, and network bandwidth. These properties are often called *quality of service* dimensions. The new demands call for both network and end-system architectures for performance guarantees to satisfy quality of service. Deployment of QoS architectures at the application layer has been much more successful than at the network layer. The lack of support for network-layer architectures such as int-serv, RSVP, and diff-serv is attributed in part to the lack of a good pricing model for network QoS, the lack of appropriate enforcement, and the lack of an end-to-end solution that spans multiple administrative domains and is upheld by all Internet service providers (ISPs) on the path of a client's packet. In the absence of an agreed-upon end-to-end solution, incremental deployment of QoS mechanisms by a subset of ISPs is not enough to guarantee QoS and does not encourage client buy-in. In contrast, end-system solutions can be implemented and priced entirely within a single administrative domain, which explains their recent success. In this chapter, we first review the main components of the Internet service architecture and describe the protocols that govern their interaction. We then discuss how this architecture and these protocols are affected by QoS considerations, and explore the different performance considerations that emerge specifically in QoS-aware end-systems.

Generally, research on end-system QoS focused on three major directions. The first and most widely explored direction was developed in the context of multimedia applications (Jin and Nahrstedt 2004). With the proliferation of audio and video streaming, much work focused on end-system approaches to improve multimedia quality. This work can be partitioned into server-side approaches and client-side approaches. On the server side, operating system support was developed to provide QoS-aware services to multimedia flows. This includes real-time extensions to common operating systems, resource management extensions to expedite handling more urgent flows, transcoding and distillation work that transforms multimedia quality depending on channel conditions and client-side limitations, and mechanisms for differentiated access to resources such as virtual memory and I/O. On the client side, multimedia research focused on operating system support for real-time playback of received flows, including support for resource reservation and application-aware prioritization.

A second important direction in QoS research concerns itself with peer-to-peer systems and applications. One thread under this category is to use P2P networks for application-level routing in a way that achieves better perceived network performance for premium flows (Rakotoarivelo et al. 2005). QoS-aware overlay topologies received much attention (Subramanian et al. 2004). Another important category addresses download speeds in P2P file distribution networks. Mechanisms are developed to ensure QoS in the presence of topological changes and neighbor turnover (Bindal and Cao 2006). Yet another important direction considers wireless networks (Zhu et al. 2004), where additional challenges arise because of lack of structure and frequent changes in the underlying physical topology and resource availability. Recently, some approaches focused on achieving QoS by jointly considering coding techniques and P2P data distribution. For example, erasure coding was proposed in P2P networks to improve transfer throughput (Dairaine et al. 2005).

Finally, much QoS research addressed the performance of the Web infrastructure. This direction focused on extensions to Web servers and Web proxies to provide acceptable content access latency to clients. The current chapter focuses on this last direction. We do not focus on multimedia applications and networks because these are covered elsewhere in the book (e.g., see "Multimedia Streaming," "Internet Domain Name System," and "Mobile Commerce").

Many of these approaches rely on network or operating system extensions that are covered elsewhere (see "Telephone Number Mapping (ENUM)" for network QoS and "Packet Switching," and "Circuit Switching" for operating system coverage). We also do not cover peer-to-peer issues because these are discussed in much detail in Part 1 of Volume III (for example, see "Network Capacity Planning"and "Network Traffic Modeling"). We concentrate in this chapter on wired networks. Wireless network issues are described at length in Part 3 of Volume II (wireless and cellular).

In addressing QoS assurances in the rest of this chapter, we focus on time-related metrics such as latency. Time-related metrics are key attributes of system performance, but are not the only ones. QoS research broadly covers other attributes as well such as reliability and security. These are covered elsewhere in this book. For security issues, please see "Web Hosting," "Computer Conferencing: Protocols and Applications," and "Telecommuting and Telework." For reliability, see "Firewalls." In general, research on time-related metrics can be partitioned into hard real-time and soft real-time assurances. The former is typical to military systems, avionics, and other applications where missing timing requirements can have catastrophic consequences. Because current Internet applications do not fall in this category, this chapter focuses on soft real-time assurances, where correct temporal behavior is desirable but some flexibility exists.

End System Architecture and QoS Implications

The questions this chapter addresses are why end-system QoS emerged as a new challenge area, and what makes this challenge important. Today, many critical business, personal, and entertainment transactions use the Internet. Improving the performance of such transactions, therefore, has dramatic global effects. Efforts to improve performance come in two flavors. First, infrastructure improvements are pursued, such as realizing higher bandwidth, faster servers, and better last-mile technologies. This is largely a cost and capacity provisioning problem that motivates development of lower cost facilities and higher capacity switches and routers. Concurrently, a substantial amount of research is done to make Internet performance more *predictable*. Performance is said to be predictable when its quality can be *guaranteed* in advance. Many societal and commercial forces contribute to this need. In particular, the commercialization of the Internet and the pricing of many Internet services play a significant role in elevating the idea of performance guarantees from a value-added option to a primary concern driven by contractual obligations.

In traditional commercial products, commercial users have grown to take quality guarantees for granted. Vendors have contractual obligations to accept returns of defective products or products that do not perform as advertised. Similarly, paying consumers of Internet-based services expect a performance guarantee or a money-back statement. Much as with other services, it will be important that clients and service providers be able to negotiate mutually acceptable quality levels in the service contract for a corresponding price. QoS-violations can therefore result in monetary losses to online business.

This relation between performance guarantees and revenue is manifested today in several domains. For example, ISPs often sign mutual service level agreements (SLAs), which among other things describe the performance that the traffic of one ISP should receive in the network of the other and the corresponding fee. Closer to the end user, online trading services sometimes tie their commission fees to performance in executing the trades. The fee is waived for trades that are delayed by more than a specified amount of time. In view of this emphasis on performance as a contractual obligation, a significant amount of research has been spent on architectures that enforce quality of service guarantees on end systems. These include mechanisms and policies for QoS provisioning, QoS negotiation, and utility optimization as well as means for protection against QoS violations.

The Need for QoS Support

Most popular QoS attributes of importance from an end-system perspective revolve around some notion of time. For example, guarantees may be needed on delay, or on the number of requests served per unit of time. We call such metrics, *temporal*. A significant body of literature has addressed the issue of guaranteeing temporal QoS attributes in the absence of adequate prior knowledge of operating service conditions such as load and resource capacity. Until recently, the current state of the art in providing acceptable temporal performance to the users has been over-design. Throwing money and hardware at a performance problem eventually ensures that there are enough resources to service incoming requests sufficiently fast. This approach, however, is inadequate for several reasons. First, it is rather expensive, because more resources are expended than is strictly necessary. Second, it provides the same service to all clients. In many cases, however, a service provider might want to use performance differentiation as a tool to entice clients to subscribe to a "better" (and more expensive) service. Third, the server provides only a best-effort service in that there are no bounds on worst-case performance. It is sometimes advantageous to be able to quantitatively state a performance guarantee for which users can be commensurately charged.

In this chapter, we describe performance guarantee mechanisms for server end systems with an emphasis on enforcement considerations that prevent QoS violations. As a running application example, consider a server farm that hosts multiple services (e.g., data retrieval services in a data center) on behalf of different content providers. Software and data service hosting is a large business in which major investments are made by companies such as Intel, IBM, and Hewlett Packard. We discuss the type of performance guarantees required, the parties to whom the guarantees are made, and the mechanisms used to enforce these guarantees in the face of denial-of-QoS attacks. The server farm example provides a context for describing the general classes of server performance challenges and helps illustrate solutions needed when resources are shared among multiple parties with different QoS requirements.

A server farm end system interacts with at least three different parties: (i) end users who access the hosted content; (ii) content providers who own the content, services, or software exported for hosting; and (iii) network providers who provide Internet connectivity to the hosting farm. End users are typically interested in a fast response time; content providers care more about throughput, which translates into total capacity dedicated to their hosted sites; and network providers care primarily about network bandwidth consumed by the hosting installation.

In general, the mechanisms to provide these guarantees lie either on servers (i.e., on the end system) or inside the network. Many QoS mechanisms inside network such like IntServ and DiffServ have been proposed in the past 15 years. These technologies usually require network users to make "reservations" so that different types of network service (traffic) will receive different qualities in terms of delay, packet drop ratio, and so forth. While these QoS mechanisms on the network layer are vital for successful end-to-end QoS guarantees, their widespread deployment is yet to be realized. On the other hand, QoS guarantee mechanisms on the end system have been widely adopted by various operating system kernels and commercial application server products. In the following sections, we describe several approaches for end-system QoS guarantees in more detail with emphasis on Web applications.

Example: The World Wide Web

Several middleware components such as SOAP may be used to build and interface myriads of distributed services for client applications. Such services may deal with content distribution, information retrieval, content processing, or data storage. QoS in component architectures has, in fact, become an interesting research area. Different applications would typically use their own special-purpose service components, accessed by application clients. These components will be hosted by third-party hosting providers. Popular protocols, such as HTTP/1.1 (Mogul 1995) govern data exchange with clients.

In addition, because much of the Internet architecture is geared for content retrieval, an important general class of services is that of content distribution and caching. To improve service access delays and reduce backbone traffic, caching and content distribution services have gradually emerged. These services attempt to redistribute content around the network backbone so that it is closer to the clients who access it. The difference between caching and content distribution lies in a data-pull versus a data-push model. Whereas caches store content locally in response to user requests, content distribution proxies proactively get copies of the content in advance.

In this chapter, we take the architecture of the World Wide Web as a running example, and use this architecture to describe QoS concepts. In the Web architecture, there are generally three types of caches, namely proxy caches, client caches, and server caches. Proxy caches, shown in Figure 1, are typically installed by the ISPs at the interface to the network backbone. They intercept service requests originating from the ISP's clients and save copies of the requested pages when replies are received from the contacted servers. This process is called page

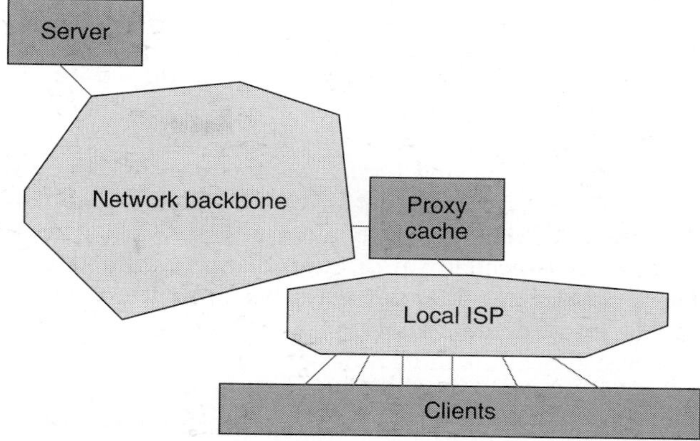

Figure 1: Web proxy caching

caching. A request to a page that is already cached can be served directly from the proxy, thereby improving client-side latency, reducing server load, and minimizing backbone traffic for which the ISP is responsible to the backbone provider. An important question is what to do when the cache becomes full. To optimize its impact, a full cache retains only the most recently requested results, replacing those that have not been used the longest. This is known as the least-recently-used replacement policy. Several variations and generalizations of this policy have been proposed, e.g., to account for page size, cost of a page miss, and the importance of the client.

To improve performance further, client application software (e.g., browsers) locally caches the most recently requested pages. Finally, some server installations use server-side caches (also known as reverse proxies) to reduce the load on the server. The caching infrastructure significantly affects the user-perceived service performance. Arlitt, Friedrich, and Jin (1999) compare the effects of different replacement policies on cache performance. Recent research efforts address developing caches that provide some form of performance differentiation or QoS guarantees. A proxy cache, for example, can offer preferential treatment to content requested by a certain subset of clients or content belonging to a certain subset of providers. This mechanism will be described in later sections.

Content Distribution Networks (CDN) are another technology that enables scalable content delivery from content providers to clients. Compared to caches, CDNs have the advantage that content can be pre-populated to the proxies based on the business relationships between CDN providers and content providers. Next, we describe the types of performance guarantees needed in the services described above.

PERFORMANCE ISOLATION

The most basic guarantee needed among multiple traffic classes is that of performance isolation. Informally, the guarantee states that the performance seen by any particular class of clients should be independent of the load imposed by any other class. For example, consider an end system that hosts two services, A and B. Unless proper action is taken, an overload on B may slow down the entire server, preventing the clients of A from accessing the server as well. Performance isolation mechanisms resolve the problem by imposing limits that prevent (clients of) any one hosted service such as B from monopolizing the server. Hence, performance isolation localizes the effects of denial-of-QoS attacks. It acts as a fault-containment mechanism in fault-tolerant architectures. There are several different ways performance isolation may be implemented. They typically rely on some form of resource allocation and admission control. In the following subsections, we discuss some of the most important mechanisms for performance isolation in the operating system, middleware, and application layer.

Operating Systems Solutions

The core mechanism for performance isolation is resource reservation. Each service must be allocated its own resource quota on the end system. Requests for that service are allowed to consume only those computing resources that are within its quota. Excess load on one service should not be allowed to divert resources dedicated to others. Traditionally, resource allocation and management is the responsibility of operating systems. Hence, the most fundamental solutions to performance isolation are operating system solutions.

Generally speaking, in a shared computing system, such as a server farm shared by multiple cohosted services, common resource sharing can be categorized into two different types; sharing in time and sharing in space. Predominantly space-shared resources include, for example, memory and disk space. Different processes may own different subsets of the resource concurrently and be denied access to resources owned by others. Space-sharing implies that the resource can be partitioned. Some resources, however, are indivisible. The prime example is the CPU. Indivisible resources can only be allocated in their entirety to one process at a time. However, they can be given to different processes at different time, and therefore time-shared. Clients are queued up on the time-shared resource. The queuing order and duration of resource access allowed by each client decide how the resource is shared.

Traditional operating systems such as UNIX implement a time-sharing scheduling policy, which allocates the processor one quantum at a time in a round-robin fashion among the waiting processes. This policy is inadequate for performance isolation in that it allows one class to affect performance of others. Consider our server farm example, where it is desired to isolate requests for different services cohosted on the same platform. The CPU capacity available to one service under the UNIX time-sharing scheduling policy is roughly proportional to the number of processes serving the corresponding service clients at a given time. This number is in turn proportional to the client request rate. A very popular service will have a large request rate which generates a large number of processes to serve these requests. It can monopolize the CPU.

To ensure performance isolation, many researchers have addressed the problem of reservation of time-shared resources. The first effort on this subject came from the Real-Time Mach project at Carnegie Mellon University and is called *processor capacity reserves*. The idea of processor capacity reserves is to implement separate accounting entities (the reserves), which keep track of the processing budgets allocated to abstract CPU activities. For example, a programmer can associate a budget with each separate service on the hosting server. The budget specifies the percentage of time that the CPU is allowed to spend on the corresponding site (e.g., 4ms every 30ms). The budget is replenished periodically. To enforce performance isolation, when a server end-system receives a request, the request is classified and the corresponding budget is charged for the time it takes to serve the request. If the reserve is exhausted before the end of the period, the budget is said to have expired. When a budget expires, processes charged to that budget are blocked until the next replenishment period. Hence, these processes cannot jointly exceed the CPU allocation specified for the service they implement.

One limitation of the aforementioned technique is the way accounting is done in the operating system. The party that the CPU is working for at any given time is identified in the operating system as either the kernel or a particular user process. Hence, only total kernel execution time and the total execution time of any single process can be measured. In particular, kernel execution time is not properly broken into independent activities. For example, the kernel-processing time of incoming requests is not properly attributed to the site for which the requests are destined and is thus not charged properly to the correct reserve. The problem is exacerbated by the inability to differentiate connections until they have been processed by the TCP/IP stack. To address the aforementioned accounting problem, resource containers (Banga, Druschel, and Mogul 1999) have been proposed as a new operating system abstraction for resource reservation and performance isolation in monolithic kernels running server end systems. The authors of this approach make the observation that the accounting problem arises from the fact that in traditional operating systems the resource principal (i.e., the system entity capable of owning resources) is generally associated with a protection domain (such as a process). In server end-systems, this association is not appropriate. The logical resource principal could be a user or a content provider. Depending on the server architecture, multiple processes can serve the same principal, or a single process can serve multiple principals. The resource principals should be charged for processing that occurs both on the kernel level and in user space. Banga et al. (1999) propose the abstraction of resource containers to resolve the dichotomy. In this approach, packet filters are placed at the lowest level of the end-system protocol stack. These filters demultiplex incoming traffic into distinct categories (e.g., by IP address). All kernel and user-level processing of traffic in each category is charged to the corresponding resource container. As before, when the container is exhausted, the operating system stops processing the corresponding traffic type until the container is replenished. The approach has been shown to provide excellent isolation. It is also very efficient in isolating denial-of-QoS attacks. For example, if the identity of the attackers is known, all traffic from them can be isolated and associated with a separate resource container of zero capacity. This traffic will thus be dropped, causing no negative effects on the rest of the system.

The need for early demultiplexing presents several challenges of its own. Such demultiplexing is typically performed based on fields in the TCP or IP headers. Unfortunately, in many cases, client classification is a little more complex (Menasce et al. 2000). Designing general-purpose mechanisms to express such classification constraints at the operating system level is a challenging task, unless one is willing to sacrifice the application-independent nature of general-purpose operating systems.

Another complication is that packets arriving at the bottom of the protocol stack (e.g., IP fragments) may not always have an application-layer header, which contains the information necessary for classification. These headers would be reconstructed higher in the communication protocol stack, which makes early classification more challenging. Construction of efficient packet filters for early classification based on application-specific information is therefore an important research challenge.

Middleware Approaches

When client classes are defined in an application-specific manner, a different solution to performance isolation is to develop middleware that augments generic operating system support with application-specific middleware policies. The operating system approach, described in the previous section, is perhaps the most efficient approach for fine-grained performance isolation. However, it suffers from the lack of generality and the lack of portability. The former refers to the difficulty of incorporating application-specific classification policies into the kernel. The latter (i.e., portability) stems from the fact that support for time-multiplexed resource reservation described above is still far from being a standard operating system feature. Thus, performance isolation solutions that do not *require* this support in the operating system are often preferred. These considerations lead to middleware solutions.

Middleware refers to any software layer that runs below the application and above the operating system. Generally, there are two types of middleware; that which is transparent to the application and that which requires application modification to adhere to a new interface. The former is more general in that it does not require access to application source code. Hence, a hosting service, for example, can develop in-house middleware components even when the source code for the Web server and the operating system is not available. Similarly, a middleware vendor can develop its software independently to interoperate with multiple application and operating system products without the need to modify their code.

An important challenge in designing transparent middleware support is to architect the (transparent) interaction with the server software. Such interaction is usually implemented by instrumenting standard dynamic shared libraries used by the server. Dynamic shared libraries are those loaded by the server at run time, as opposed to being precompiled together with server code. This feature is made possible due to late binding, supported by most operating systems today. In late binding, references to called library functions are not resolved until the call is made at run time and the corresponding library is dynamically loaded into the server's memory. It is therefore possible to make changes to the shared library without having to recompile or relink the server software. Once the server makes the standard library call, the new (modified) library gets invoked. In the case of middleware for performance isolation, the modified shared library may implement accounting functions that approximate resource containers.

One of the most obvious libraries to instrument is the socket library. Hewlett Packard Labs researchers (Bhatti and Friedrich 1999) were the first to suggest architectures where the socket library is replaced with a QoS-sensitive version, which implements performance isolation. In the context of regular socket calls, the QoS-sensitive library dequeues service requests from the server's well-known port and classifies them into per-class queues. The accept() or read() socket calls are modified so that no connections are accepted from a given per-class queue unless the budget of the corresponding class (maintained by the modified library) is nonzero. The scheme, shown in Figure 2, implements approximate performance isolation. It has been successfully integrated into a server platform sold by Hewlett Packard, called WebQoS.

A frequently encountered problem with middleware approaches to performance isolation is their larger overhead. All requests (regardless of their importance and regardless of server load) have to be processed by the operating system before reaching the middleware layer where they are classified and handled in accordance with their class. Hence, in cases of severe end-system overload, the number of incoming requests may become large enough that their operating system processing overhead alone is sufficient to saturate server resources. The server, therefore, performs no useful work since application-layer software never gets to run. This is called live-lock. It is a price paid for the convenience of implementation and generality of the mechanisms.

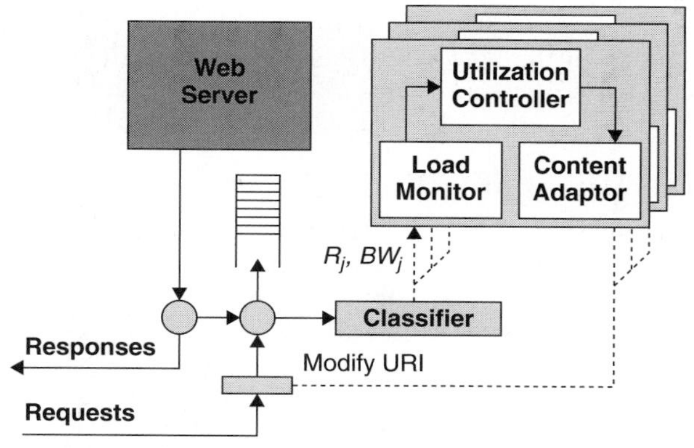

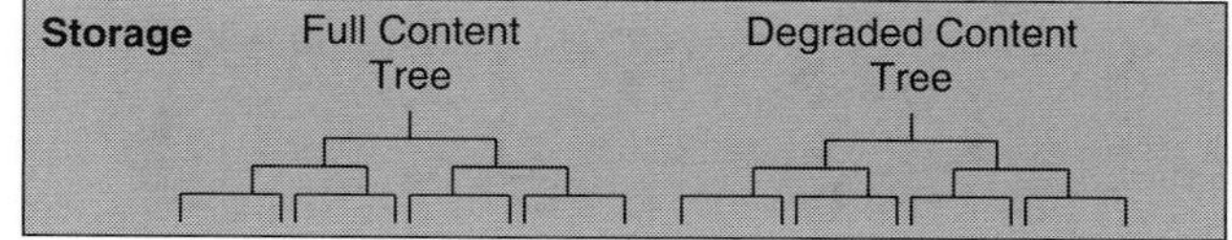

Figure 2: A middleware architecture for Web QoS

An interesting new direction in middleware-based QoS is to add QoS-awareness to component-based architectures such as CORBA, DCOM, and .NET. If the individual components are QoS-sensitive, their composition may satisfy certain QoS guarantees. This class of middleware is sometimes referred to as DRE systems. Models for composition (Xiao and Boutaba 2005) and adaptation (Schantz et al. 2006) of performance properties are therefore needed. These models are often very hard to obtain. On the surface, the composition problem is simple. For example, end-to-end throughput of multiple component is the throughput of the bottleneck. End-to-end delay is the sum of delays of the individual components. The problem arises due to unexpected interactions among the components. For example, adding components on a given machine may eventually run into physical memory limitations, leading to thrashing which increases delay disproportionately. Synchronization and use of semaphores can also cause unpredictable effects on delay when components are put together. In large systems, it is very difficult to model and predict how components compose, making distributed component-based architecture an important QoS topic.

Application-Layer Mechanisms

Current state-of-the-art application servers, such as the Apache Web Server (the most widespread Web server today), maintain a single process pool for all incoming requests. The single-pool architecture significantly complicates QoS provisioning because all requests are treated alike in the server. Hence, a popular class can send a large number of requests to the server until the entire process pool is consumed, thereby denying QoS guarantees to other client classes. In a multi-class server, attainment of performance isolation can be significantly simplified if the server is designed with QoS guarantees in mind. The single main feature that provides the most impact is to maintain a separate pool of processes for each traffic class. Once the server identifies an incoming request as belonging to a particular class, it is queued up for the corresponding process pool. Hence, it is possible for clients to continue to use their quota of server processes regardless of load on other classes. Several examples of this architecture have been proposed in the literature. QoS provisioning amounts to controlling the resource allocation of each separate pool.

SERVICE DIFFERENTIATION

An important second category of QoS guarantees is service differentiation. The goal of performance isolation, discussed above, is to logically *partition* the resource so that each class of clients would get its own independent portion. Competition among classes is *eliminated* by giving each exclusive ownership over a subset of resources. Faults and overload are localized to individual resource partitions and hence are conveniently contained. In contrast, service differentiation policies do not attempt to partition the resource. The resource is *shared*. When the resource is in demand by multiple classes, the differentiation policy *resolves* the competition in a way that favors some class over others. Service differentiation policies are classified depending on what it means to "favor" a particular class. Informally, to borrow travel metaphors, performance isolation is analogous to a timeshare in which your contract guarantees, say, three weeks per year. You can always redeem up to three weeks regardless of who else has a contract for the premises. Indeed, the resource is "shared" but each principal has its own guaranteed quota. In contrast, service differentiation is analogous to airline "waitlists." When room is available, it is assigned in some competitive manner. Your chances of getting the resource (e.g., getting on the plane) depend on your priority (or the differentiation policy in general) and the available resource supply.

Some authentication mechanisms are needed to make sure that selfish or malicious clients cannot impersonate an important client class and send unauthorized requests that degrade service to authorized clients. Authentication refers to the act of verifying client identity to prevent identity theft. A server should not treat a client preferentially until the server has determined that this client is entitled to the preferential service. In the following sections, we describe the most common examples of service differentiation and their enforcement mechanisms.

Prioritization

The simplest method to provide differentiation is prioritization. Consider a situation where a service is accessed by two classes of clients: paying customers and nonmembers. The server offers two types of service; premium and basic. Assume that a dedicated authentication server exists that ensures that only authorized (i.e., paying) clients can get premium service. In contemporary service architecture, paying customers are usually allowed access to protected service functions that are inaccessible to nonpaying users. In other words, differentiation among class is typically in terms of available service functionality. This type of differentiation, however, is often inadequate. It is equally important to differentiate in terms of service performance as well. For example, if the end system is overloaded, all functionality will degrade in no relation to the client class unless provisions are made to degrade performance of lower-class (e.g., nonpaying) clients before that of higher-class (e.g., paying) clients. Performance isolation can be applied between paying and nonpaying users, but it suffers the problem of having to decide on the relative sizes of the respective resource partitions, which typically depend on the current load. One approach to circumventing this problem is to serve clients in absolute priority order. In this scheme all client requests are queued up in a single priority queue for server access. Under overload, the queue overflows. Clients at the tail of the queue are dropped. These clients, by construction of the queuing policy, are the lower-priority ones. The mechanism ensures that nonpaying clients cannot degrade the performance of paying clients.

The problem with prioritization alone is that it fails to provide meaningful performance guarantees to the low-priority clients. The top priority class receives the best service, but very little can be predicted about the performance received by other classes. Prioritization, however, becomes an extremely useful analyzable tool once combined with admission control techniques discussed below.

Absolute Delay Guarantees

Prioritization, in conjunction with admission control, allows providing customizable absolute delay guarantees to an arbitrary number of client classes. Consider a case where there are N classes of paying clients. To recover a fee, the server end-system is contractually obligated to serve each class within a maximum time delay specified in the corresponding QoS contract signed with that class. For example, in an online trading server, first-class clients may be guaranteed a maximum response time of 2 s, whereas economy clients are guaranteed a maximum response time of 10 s. Failure to execute the trade within the guaranteed response time results in a commission waiver. Alternatively, in a content hosting service, the content provider of each hosted site might have a QoS contract with the host that specifies a target service time and a fee paid to the host per request served within the agreed-upon delay. Hence, an overloaded hosting server, which consistently fails to meet the delay constraints, will recover no revenue from the content providers.

Because, in these examples, a host does not derive revenue from requests that miss their deadlines, admission control may be used against clients who are unlikely to meet their timing constraints. The rationale for such admission control is that scarce server capacity should not be wasted on clients who are unable to make revenue. Although theoretically, admission control refers to a choice between acceptance and rejection, it is more realistic to choose between acceptance and *background service*. In other words, for the purposes of the following discussion, a rejected client is put in a separate lowest-priority queue to be served if resources permit.

Admission control has received much attention in QoS literature. Admission control algorithms may be classified into optimistic and pessimistic. The former type may admit clients optimistically even when they may miss their deadlines. The latter may reject them unnecessarily. Note that absence of admission control can be thought of as the extreme of optimistic admission control tests. Recent results (Abdelzaher and Lu 2001) have shown that in a server with randomly arriving requests, it is possible to use a constant-time admission control test to distinguish clients who will meet their deadlines from those who may not. The test is based on a running counter, which maintains a utilization-like metric. The counter is updated by a constant-time operation upon request arrivals and departures. If a request arrives while the counter is below a certain high-water mark, it is guaranteed to meet its deadline. Otherwise, the deadline may be missed and the request is served at the lowest priority level. Recent evaluation results of this admission control algorithm show that it rarely errs in the sense of unnecessarily rejecting requests. The test is shown to improve revenue at overload, not only by eliminating resource consumption wasted on requests that miss their deadlines but also by favoring smaller requests (all other factors being equal) and hence improving server throughput. The derivation of the high-water mark representing the client admission threshold assumes that clients are served in a priority order such that more urgent requests are served first. A generalization of this test has later been proposed for FIFO scheduling.

When priority-driven scheduling is used to meet deadlines, priority should be set proportional to urgency. There are two ways urgency can be defined. In the first, clients with shorter per-class response times are considered more urgent. The resulting priority assignment is called deadline-monotonic (or rate-monotonic if requests are strictly periodic). In the second, urgency is defined by absolute deadline. The resulting priority assignment is called earliest-deadline-first (EDF). For example, consider a request arriving at time 0 with a maximum response time constraint of 10 s. At time $t = 9$, a second request arrives of a different class with a maximum response time constraints of 2 s. According to the deadline-monotonic priority assignment, the second request should receive higher priority because its maximum response time constraint, 2, is tighter than 10. According to EDF the first request should receive higher priority because its absolute deadline is $0 + 10 = 10$, which is before the absolute deadline of the second request, $9 + 2 = 11$.

EDF has been proven to be the optimal priority-driven scheduling policy. Deadline-monotonic scheduling is optimal among time-independent scheduling policies (i.e., those where priorities are assigned independent of absolute request arrival times). Optimality, here, is defined in terms of the ability to meet a larger number of deadlines. EDF can meet deadlines when deadline-monotonic scheduling fails because it takes arrival times into account. For instance, in the above example, if the first request has an execution time of 9.5 s, and the second request has an execution time of 1.5 s, both requests meet their deadlines under EDF, but not under deadline-monotonic scheduling. A problem with EDF is that it is less commonly implemented on standard operating systems, with the exception of embedded real-time operating systems where application timing is of prime importance. Deadline-monotonic scheduling is therefore a good compromise.

Statistical Delay Guarantees

An entirely different line of reasoning is to provide statistical guarantees on delays and deadline misses. Statistical guarantees require queuing analysis of the end system. This analysis makes two types of assumptions. First, it must make assumptions regarding the queuing structure of the server. Second, it must make assumptions regarding the request arrival process. In the following, we outline the most important challenges underlying the statistical approach to QoS guarantees on end systems.

Consider the first challenge, namely, deriving the queuing structure of the end system. This queuing structure depends on the service protocol used. Consider a typical multithreaded (or multiprocess) Web server. Packets arrive from the network, causing hardware and software interrupts that, respectively, read the packets from network interface cards and deposit them into a kernel-level input queue called the *IP queue*. In between interrupts, packets in the IP queue are processed by the kernel and queued for the particular application ports for which they are destined. These ports are often called sockets. Each socket is associated with an input queue, called the *listen queue*, where incoming connection requests are queued. Independently schedulable entities in the server end system, called *worker threads*, are blocked for data to be deposited at the listen queue. These threads are unblocked by request arrivals to execute the arriving requests. Each thread implements a loop that processes each incoming request and generates a response. Worker threads that have been unblocked by request arrival become runnable.

Multiple runnable threads may exist at a given time. The order in which such threads get the CPU to execute a request is determined by the CPU scheduling policy. This policy maintains a priority queue called the *ready queue*. The thread at the top of this queue executes for a particular time quantum or until it is blocked. Request processing by a worker thread typically entails access to one or more auxiliary server resources, the most notable being disk I/O. Access to auxiliary resources blocks the calling thread, at which time it is queued for I/O until the awaited resource becomes available. Each resource usually has a queue, which determines the order in which accesses are served. We call it the *I/O queue*. The resource is made available to the thread at the top of the queue, at which time the corresponding thread becomes runnable again and re-enters the CPU ready queue. When request processing is done, the worker thread sends a response back to the client. Sending the response entails queuing data into the *outgoing packet queue* for transmission on the network.

The above discussion identifies five different queues involved in the server's queuing structure: namely, the IP queue, the listen queue, the ready queue, the I/O queue (assuming a single I/O resource, such as, disk), and the outgoing packet queue. The interconnection of these queues creates a queuing network with loops and other dependencies. For example, threads that repeatedly read and process disk data essentially loop between the ready queue and the I/O queue. Moreover, when the number of threads is fixed, dequeuing from the listen queue is synchronized with progress in the ready queue in that new requests are dequeued from the former only when some runnable thread has finished serving a request or has blocked. These factors make accurate analysis of the server's queuing structure difficult. Instead, many approximations are possible. For example, it is possible to consider only the queue for the bottleneck resource. The general idea is that a service request is likely to spend most of its time waiting in the bottleneck queue.

The second challenge in providing statistical guarantees on end-system services is to identify the stochastic nature of the service request arrival process. Many queuing theory results assume a continuous Poisson arrival process. This process is characterized by an exponential distribution of interarrival times. This assumption does not hold for several classes of Internet traffic. For example, research on Web traffic characterization has identified that arrival of Web requests is generally modeled by a heavy tailed distribution (Crovella and Bestavros 1997). One distribution that is commonly used to model request interarrival times and request execution times is the Pareto distribution. Breslau et al. (1999) also determined that URL popularity follows a Zipf-like distribution. This information is important for studies of service performance because it helps quantify the effects of caching. To experiment with Web performance in laboratory testbeds, Barford and Crovella (1998) developed a synthetic Web workload generator that faithfully reproduces the characteristics of realistic Web traffic, including its heavy-tailed distribution, URL popularity, and reference locality characteristics. The problem of providing queuing-theoretic performance predictions for traffic arriving at a server modeled by the queuing structure outlined above is still an open research topic. Moreover, serving Web requests is only one example of an end-system service. Other services may have distinctly different request patterns that need to be analyzed, understood, and properly modeled.

Relative Guarantees

From queuing theory we know that delay experienced by a request is a function of server load. Ultimately, the only way one can reduce delay to meet deadline guarantees is to keep the load low enough. This implies denying service to some requests under high load to improve performance. In many cases, however, it is preferred that *all* clients receive service when capacity permits. One QoS-provisioning paradigm that subscribes to this model is *proportional relative differentiated services*.

Proportional relative differentiation was first proposed in the networking community in the context of delay differentiation in routers. It was since extended to server end systems. In the relative differentiated services model, it is desired that the ratio between the performance levels of different classes of traffic be fixed; e.g., it may be that the delays of two traffic classes in a network router should be fixed at a ratio of 3:1. In general, if there are multiple traffic classes in the system, and if H_i is the measured performance of class i, the relative guarantee specifies that H_1: H_2:...: $H_n = C_1$: C_2:...: C_n, where C_i is the weight of class i. Hence, only relative delay between any pair of classes is specified. The absolute delay can take any value. When the system approaches overload, the delay of all classes increases, although some classes see a larger delay increase than others, in accordance with the relative delay guarantee. At present, mechanisms for providing relative delay differentiation are well understood, but not yet deployed.

Relative delay guarantees make the most sense under moderate server load. When the load is light, all classes see identically good service (no delay). When the load is very high, all classes suffer unacceptable delays and timeouts. In general, it is useful to combine relative delay guarantees with absolute delay guarantees in a single framework. The combined architecture bounds the maximum delay of different classes in addition to providing the correct delay ratio when the bound has not been reached. The architecture allows specifying a partial order on absolute and relative time constraints that determines which constraints should be relaxed first when network conditions make the combination unrealizable. Typically, the relative constraints should be relaxed first, hence breaking the performance dependency among the different classes. The performance of more important classes (bound by absolute delay constraints) is then enforced.

Convergence Guarantees

In an environment in which unpredictable traffic conditions make it impossible to satisfy absolute constraints, an alternative type of performance guarantees has recently been defined. This guarantee views QoS provisioning as a convergence problem and employs control theory to ensure stability and timeliness of convergence of system performance to the right specification (Abdelzaher, Shin, and Bhatti 2002). The statement of the guarantee is that a performance metric, R, will converge within a specified exponentially decaying envelope to a fixed value, called the *set point*, and that the maximum deviation from the set point will be bounded at all times.

The absolute convergence guarantee is translated into a control loop such as those used in industrial control plants. The loop samples the measured performance metric (e.g., delay), compares it to the set point, and uses the difference to induce changes in resource allocation and load. Typically, it performs admission control to reduce load, and reallocates resources to alleviate the bottlenecks.

The use of control theory to control the performance of software processes has gained much popularity in recent years. Traditionally, control theory was used to model and control industrial processes described by difference equations. The intuitive reason that such a theory would be applicable to server performance control is that input load on a server resembles input flow into a water tank. The fill level of the server queue resembles the tank fill level. Admission control resembles a valve on the input flow pipe. Hence, the delay dynamics of a Web server are similar to flow and level control dynamics in a physical plant. The latter are well understood and can be described by difference equations. The second reason that control theory is becoming popular for server control is that feedback control loops are very robust to modeling errors. Hence, accurate models of software dynamics are not needed.

In the context of time-related performance metrics, it is interesting to classify the convergence guarantee loops depending on the performance variable being controlled. As is the case with physical plants, the controlled output of interest affects the model of the system and whether the control loop is linear or not. Because most of control theory was developed for linear processes, the ability to satisfy the convergence guarantee is often contingent on the ability to approximate the server well by a linear model.

To a first approximation, rate metrics and queue length are easiest to control because they result in linear feedback loops. Rate can be controlled in much the same way physical flow is controlled in pipes. Queue length is simply the integral of rate, and therefore is also linear. Delay guarantees are more difficult to provide. This is because delay is inversely proportional to flow. If a request arrives at a queue of length Q, with a constant dequeueing rate of r, the queuing delay, d, of the request is $d = Q/r$. The inverse relation between the manipulated variable (rate) and the delay makes the control loop nonlinear. At present, providing convergence guarantees on delay remains an active research topic.

COMMON CHALLENGES

In the previous section we outlined the semantics of the most important types of performance guarantees and corresponding enforcement mechanisms. Next we summarize the challenges that are common to achieving these guarantees on end systems.

Admission Control

A common enforcement mechanism of many QoS guarantee types in end systems is client admission control. An important decision in the design of an admission controller is to choose the entity being admitted or rejected. In a typical Internet service, admission control can operate on individual requests, individual TCP connections, or individual client sessions.

Per-request admission control is the simplest to implement, but has serious limitations. Consider an overloaded server operating at 300% capacity. Statistically, this means that two out of three requests must be rejected on average. For simplicity assume that all clients belong to the same class. Client transactions typically feature interactions with multiple requests over the duration of the client's session with the server. Per-request admission control will uniformly cause each client to encounter failures in two thirds of the accesses. All transactions will therefore be affected. Such service will virtually be unusable. In addition to affecting all transactions, per-request admission control discriminates against longer sessions. This has very negative implications, especially from an e-commerce perspective. For example, it has been shown in many studies that those e-shoppers who eventually complete a purchase from an online server typically have longer sessions with the server than occasional visitors who do not buy. Hence, discriminating against longer sessions gives a lower QoS precisely to those users who are more likely to generate revenue.

A better admission control scheme is to select a consistent subset of clients to admit. Those clients are admitted as long as they continue to send requests to the server within a specified time interval. The rest are consistently rejected. This scheme succeeds in making the service usable by at least some consistent subset of clients. It is also more meaningful in the context of addressing attacks on the server, as malicious clients may be tagged for rejection. This scheme is commonly called *session-based admission control*. It was first analyzed at length for Web servers by Cherkasova and Phaal (1999) and continues to be an important research topic (Chen and Mohapatra 2002). Session-based admission control is more difficult than per-request admission control because at the time a session is admitted the server has no knowledge of the future load that it may impose, and whether the client is indeed malicious. Hence, it is difficult to decide how many and which sessions can be admitted. Different clients can impose substantially different load demands. For example, if the admitted client is a Web crawler, it may impose a much larger load than a human user. A mechanism is needed to identify malicious clients. The admission controller must continuously refine the subset of clients to be admitted based on measurements of resulting load and outcomes of authentication.

Rejection Cost

Another issue tightly related to admission control is the cost of rejecting an incoming request. If admission control is based on client identity (such as his or her encrypted signature) a connection cannot be classified early inside the kernel. Instead, all requests have to reach the application layer, where the server process can interpret the signature and identify the client as belonging to a particular client or class. Now imagine an overloaded server, which decides to admit all requests of class A and reject all requests of class B. Because the kernel cannot tell the two classes apart, all requests are forwarded to the application layer after being processed in the kernel. Kernel processing, as mentioned before, takes a nonnegligible overhead. This overhead is incurred whether the request is accepted or not. In particular, it is incurred for each rejected request. It is therefore called *rejection cost*. For short requests, the rejection cost of the request can be more than half the cost of processing the request successfully. Hence, at overload, a significant portion of server capacity is wasted on request rejection. Rejection cost is therefore one of the primary challenges in improving overload behavior of a server.

Consistent Prioritization

Many guarantee types, such as absolute delay guarantees, usually rely on priority-driven scheduling. Prioritization imposes a significant challenge in most mainstream operating systems. To be effective, all resource queues should be *identically* prioritized. Unfortunately, CPU priorities, which can be set explicitly in many operating systems, control only the order of the ready queue. It has been shown in recent studies that this queue is often not the bottleneck. In a previous section, we have identified at least five resource queues involved in a typical end system. In many cases, the largest queue on the end system is the operating system's listen queue where requests wait on the application server's well-known port. This queue is maintained in the TCP layer and is handled in FIFO order. Correct prioritization would imply prioritizing the socket listen queues as well. In I/O intensive servers, the I/O queue may be the bottleneck. Hence, disk access should be prioritized. Moreover, in a server implementing data structures protected by semaphores, it must be ensured that processes queued on a semaphore are awakened in consistent priority order. Unless all queues are consistently prioritized, it is possible to overload a nonprioritized resource, making that resource the performance bottleneck. Such a load pattern will circumvent any priority differentiation mechanisms employed by other resources to protect high-priority clients, because prioritizing access to non-bottleneck resources has only a marginal effect on performance. For example, if access to disk is not prioritized, a disk-intensive workload may cause high-priority threads to block on disk I/O in a FIFO manner behind a large number of malicious low-priority ones.

Communicating priority information among multiple resources is a nontrivial undertaking. Proper operating system support must exist for priority inheritance across different resources. This support is complicated by the fact that blocking over nonpreemptive resources may cause involuntary priority inversion. The classical example of that is the case of two requests, A and B, where A is of higher priority. Let request B arrive first at some server and be blocked on a nonpreemptive resource such as a shared data structure protected by a semaphore. Request A arrives later and is blocked waiting for B to release the lock. Meanwhile, the progress of B may be interrupted by an arbitrary number of requests of intermediate priority. In this scenario, A is forced to wait for an arbitrary number of lower priority requests, even when all resource queues (including the semaphore queue) are correctly prioritized. The problem may be solved by the *priority ceiling protocol* developed at CMU, which bounds priority inversion. Unfortunately, current mainstream operating systems neither enforce resource priorities nor implement mechanisms for bounding priority inversion, such as the priority ceiling protocol. Thus, the current state of deployment is far from adequate for the purposes of implementing priority-based QoS support on end systems.

QoS Adaptation

The forgoing discussion focused on controlling load to provide time-related guarantees. The underlying assumption is that service must be provided by the deadline. There are no intermediate compromises. In the following, we present a case for QoS adaptation algorithms, which can negotiate intermediate performance levels within a predefined range deemed acceptable by the user. We describe mechanisms that implement adaptation in end systems.

The Case for QoS Adaptation

Most QoS-sensitive applications have a certain degree of flexibility in terms of resource requirements. For example, JPEG images can be adapted to bandwidth limitations by lossy compression or resolution reduction. Dynamically generated pages can be replaced by approximate static versions to save execution time. Thus, when the server is overloaded, an alternative to rejection of further requests would be to adapt the quality of responses such that the load on the server is reduced. Many leading news and sports sites adopt this policy. For example, the appearance of the Cable News Network Web site www.cnn.com is often significantly simplified upon important breaking news to absorb the higher request rate. An instance of that was the great reduction in CNN site content during the first hours after the attack on the World Trade Center on September 11, 2001.

Content degradation is preferred to service outage for obvious reasons. One is that it maintains service to all clients, albeit at a degraded quality, which is preferred to interruption of service. Another is that it does not incur rejection cost because service is not denied. As mentioned before, rejection cost can be considerable when user-level admission control is used.

To express the flexibility of adaptive applications, an expanded QoS-contract model is proposed. It assumes that the service exports multiple QoS levels with different resource requirements and utility to the user. The lowest level, by default, corresponds to request rejection. Its resource requirements are equal to the rejection cost, and it has no utility to the user. The objective is to choose a QoS level delivered to each user class such that utility is maximized under resource constraints. QoS adaptation should be used with great care because malicious clients can take advantage of it to artificially degrade server performance to a lower QoS level. Several content adaptation architectures have been proposed in the QoS literature. They can be roughly classified into two general types, depending on the reason for adaptation, namely, adaptation to network/client limitations and adaptation to server load. These two types are described below.

Adaptation to Network and Client Limitations

In the first type, adaptation is performed online and is sometimes called dynamic distillation or online transcoding. For example, see the work of Chandra, Ellis, and Vahdat (2000). The reason for such adaptation is to cope with reduced network bandwidth, or client-side limitations. Note that the dynamic distillation algorithm itself will in fact increase the load on the server. In effect, the algorithm implements a trade-off where extra computing capacity on the server is used to compress content on the fly to conform to reduced network bandwidth. Alternatively, transcoding or distillation proxies may be introduced into the network. For example, a transcoding proxy can identify a client as a wireless PDA device and convert a requested HTML page into WML for display on the client's limited screen.

Adaptation to client-side limitations can also be done using layered services. In this paradigm, content delivery is broken into multiple layers. The first has very limited bandwidth requirements and produces a rough version of the content. Subsequent layers refine the content iteratively, each requiring progressively more resources. JPEG images, for example, can be delivered in this manner. An adaptive service could control the number of layers delivered to a client depending on the client's available bandwidth. A client with a limited bandwidth may receive a fraction of the layers only. The determination of the number of layers to send to the client can be done either by the server or by the client itself. For example, consider an online video presentation being multicast to the participants of a conference call. The server encodes the transmitted video into multiple layers and creates a multicast group for each layer. Each client then subscribes to receive a fraction of the layers as permitted by its resource capacity and network connectivity. Such adaptation architectures have initially been proposed in the context of streaming media.

Adaptation to Server Load

In the second type of adaptation, content is adapted to reduce server load. In this case, dynamic distillation or compression cannot be used because the server itself is the bottleneck. Instead, content must be preprocessed a priori. At run time, the server merely chooses which version to send out to which client. The server in such an architecture has multiple content trees, each of a different quality. For example, a content server can have a full content tree (where data is generated from live database queries), a reduced content tree where some data has been abbreviated or replaced with stale values from caches, and a low-quality tree that has minimal information. A transparent middleware solution has been described that features a software layer interposed between the server processes and the communication subsystem. The layer has access to the service requests received and the responses sent. It intercepts each request and directs it to the "right" content tree from which it is served. This redirection occurs in accordance with load conditions. To decide on the "right" content tree for each client the interposed content adaptation layer measures the current degree of server utilization and decides on the extent of adaptation that will prevent underutilization or overload.

An interesting question is whether or not load can be adapted in a continuous range when only a small finite number of different content versions (trees) are available. Such continuous adaptation is possible when the number of clients is large. To illustrate this point, consider a server with M discrete service levels (e.g., content trees), where M is a small integer. These levels are numbered $1, \dots, M$ from lowest quality to highest quality. The level 0 is added to denote the special case of request rejection. The admission control algorithm is generalized, so that instead of making a binary decision, it determines a continuous value m, in the range $[0,M]$, which we call the degree of degradation. This value modulates server load in a continuous range. In this case, $m = 0$ means rejecting all requests (minimum load), and $m = M$ means serving all requests at the highest quality (maximum load). In general, when m happens to be an integer, it uniquely determines the service level (i.e., tree) to be offered to all clients. If m is a fractional number, composed of an integral part I and a fraction F (such that $m = I + F$), the two integers nearest to m (namely, I and $I+1$) determine the two most appropriate service levels at which clients must be served. The fractional part F determines the fraction of clients served at each of the two levels. In effect, m is interpreted to mean that a fraction $1\text{-}F$ of clients must be served at level I, and a fraction F at level $I+1$. The policy can be accurately implemented when the number of clients is large. It ensures that load can be controlled in a continuous range by fractional degradation and offers fine-grained control of delay and server utilization. Figure 3 shows an example of content (an image) with two service levels; regular (Figure 3-a) and degraded (Figure 3-b). In this example, the storage requirements of the degraded image are roughly an order of magnitude less than the requirements of the regular image.

DISTRIBUTED QOS CONSIDERATIONS

Most Internet services are concerned with some form of content or information retrieval. Service performance can therefore be significantly improved by employing proxy servers. A word is thus in order on improving the perceived end-system performance by interjecting proxy services. Proxy servers are intermediaries between the clients and the accessed end-system servers. They are the main performance acceleration mechanism of content retrieval services, which makes their study very important. Interjecting a proxy makes the service distributed. The performance of the service becomes a function of

Figure 3: Example of content degradation (a) regular content (b) degraded content

mechanisms that run both on the origin servers and added proxies. QoS architectures should consider the effects proxy servers have on user-perceived service performance and make use of them to satisfy client QoS requirements. Proxies may be used for caching, transcoding, or content distribution. A proxy intercepts incoming requests and attempts to serve them locally. If the requested content is not locally available the proxy may forward the request to another server (e.g., content distribution proxies), contact the origin server and save the response (proxy caches), or contact the origin server, transcode the response, and forward it to the client (transcoding proxy). Although current proxy servers typically treat all clients alike, there has been much talk on making them QoS-aware. For example, the proxy may offer preferential treatment to some classes of clients or classes of content. QoS considerations that arise in the new distributed architecture of services and their proxies are described below.

Several research efforts have looked at biased replacement policies in proxy caches (Kelly, Chan, Jamin, & Mackie-Mason 1999). Such policies attempt to maximize a weighted hit ratio, where weights are set in accordance with content importance. For example, content fetched from the preferred providers can have a higher weight and therefore a lower likelihood of being replaced. Another research direction is to determine dynamically the disk space allocation of a cache or a content distribution proxy such that content of preferred providers receives a higher hit ratio. In this approach, the "performance distance" between different content types can be controlled (Lu, Saxena, & Abdelzaher 2001). For example, one can specify that preferred content is to receive twice the hit ratio of regular content. The underlying adaptive disk allocation policy uses feedback control to translate this specification into a dynamic disk space allocation that satisfies the specified requirement in the presence of dynamically changing load patterns.

Content distribution networks composed of multiple proxy servers situated around the Internet backbone bring another degree of freedom in distributed QoS provisioning. The distribution provider may make agreements with content providers to distribute their content preferentially for a corresponding fee. Alternatively, the distribution provider may make agreements with certain ISPs to improve the quality of service to their clients by virtue of the content distribution network. An example of such a network is that introduced by Akamai. When a content provider authorizes a CDN provider to host its content, the CDN could create more than one replica of the content provider's Web objects on the CDN's servers. Obviously, the more replicas there are, the better average client access latency can be achieved because chances are clients' requests can be redirected to a replica closer than the origin server. The actual number of CDN servers hosting a content object is decided by its popularity, the workload conditions of the CDN, and the QoS SLA between the CDN provider and the content provider. Supporting secure content distribution is an attractive feature of CDNs. It is envisioned that in the near future not only content but also "computation" of content providers will be distributed to CDNs. Security concerns have to be carefully addressed before content providers are willing to authorize CDN providers to distribute their sensitive information, such as private data and applications.

CONCLUSION AND FUTURE TRENDS

In this chapter, we briefly introduced the most important issues and mechanisms for providing quality of service in the modern end systems. The topic of providing quality of service guarantees is becoming increasingly important with the pricing of Internet services, and with the tendency to include performance requirements within the contractual obligations of service providers. The need for performance guarantees makes computing systems more vulnerable to attack, since impairing a system's ability to meet its performance requirements now constitutes a violation of its "proper" functionality. This gives rise to a multitude of QoS mechanisms that must be in place to enforce QoS requirements. In this chapter, some of the most common QoS requirements were reviewed, as well as mechanisms that can be used to enforce them. The chapter also touched on performance considerations that arise in content distribution networks, as well as mechanisms for improving the performance of some essential components of any QoS infrastructure. A particularly good reference for further readings on Web architecture, performance, QoS, and security issues is the recent book by Krishnamurthy and Rexford (2001).

GLOSSARY

Authentication: The act of verifying client identity.

Backbone provider: A party that owns the communication fabric of an Internet backbone. Examples of backbone providers include AT&T, Sprint, MCI, and UUNET.

Cache server: A network server that acts as a cache of popular Web content and is able to serve it on behalf of the original servers.

Content distribution network: A network of server platforms whose sole purpose is efficient content dissemination around the Internet backbone.

Cookies: Small text files that servers put on the client's hard drive to save client and session information needed for future access.

Data pull model: A data communication model in which the client explicitly asks the server for data each time the data are needed.

Data push model: A data communication model in which servers unilaterally push data to the client without being asked. The model is a good optimization when future client requests can be accurately predicted.

Demultiplexing: Separating an incoming packet flow into multiple segregated flows. For example, demultiplexing must occur upon the arrival of a packet at a server, in order to queue the packet for the right recipient.

Differentiated services: A framework for classifying network traffic and defining different policies for handling each traffic class, such that some classes receive better service than others.

EDF: Earliest-deadline-first scheduling policy. As the name suggests, it schedules the task with the earliest deadline first.

HTML: Hypertext markup language, a language for defining the content and appearance of Web pages.

HTTP: Hypertext transfer protocol. It is the protocol used for Web access in the current Internet. Currently, it has two popular versions, HTTP 1.0 and HTTP 1.1.

IP (Internet protocol): It is the glue that connects the computer subnetworks of which the Internet is composed and is responsible for packet addressing and routing between Internet senders and receivers.

IP fragment: Part of an IP-layer message after fragmentation.

Kernel: The core part of the operating system, typically responsible for scheduling and basic interprocess communication.

Microkernel: An operating system architecture where most operating system functions are delegated to user-level processes, keeping the kernel small.

QoS: Quality of service, a term used in quantifying different performance aspects of Web access such as timeliness and throughput.

Packet: A unit of data transfer across a network.

Persistent connections: Communication abstraction implemented by HTTP 1.1. It allows the same TCP connection to be reused by multiple Web requests to the same server. This is a main departure from the traditional "one request per connection" model of HTTP 1.0.

Proxy server: A specialized server that performs an auxiliary Web content management function such as content replication, caching, or transcoding.

Semaphore: An operating system construct used for synchronization.

Sockets: The main interprocess communication abstraction, originally introduced in UNIX. A socket represents a connection endpoint. The connection is between two processes on the same or different machines.

TCP: Transmission control protocol, the transport protocol used for reliable data communication on the Internet.

Threads: The smallest schedulable entities in multithreaded operating systems.

Transcoding: The process of converting content on the fly from the server's format to a format more suitable to the client, or more appropriate for network load conditions.

Web hosting: The business of providing resources (servers, disk space, etc.) to serving customers' Web pages. Typically, Web-hosting companies build large server installations of hundreds of machines for serving the Web sites. These installations are called server farms.

CROSS REFERENCES

See *Network Middleware*; *Network QoS*.

REFERENCES

Abdelzaher, T.F., and C. Lu. 2001. Schedulability analysis and utilization bounds for highly scalable real-time services. In *IEEE Real-Time Technology and Applications Symposium*, Taipei, Taiwan.

Abdelzaher, T.F., K. G. Shin, and N. Bhatti. 2002. Performance guarantees for Web server end-systems: A control-theoretical approach. *IEEE Transactions on Parallel and Distributed Systems*, 13(1), 80–96.

Arlitt, M., R. Friedrich, and T. Jin. 2000. Performance evaluation of Web proxy cache replacement policies. *Performance Evaluation*, 39(1–4), 149–164.

Banga, G., P. Druschel, and J.C. Mogul. 1999. Resource containers: A new facility for resource management in server systems. In *Symposium on Operating Systems Design and Implementation* (pp. 45–58). New Orleans, LA.

Barford, P. and M. Crovella. 1998. Generating representative Web workloads for network and server performance evaluation. In *Proceedings of the ACM SIGMETRICS '98 Conference*.

Bhatti, N. and R. Friedrich. 1999. Web server support for tiered services. *IEEE Network*, September/October.

Bindal, R. and P. Cao. 2006. Can self-organizing P2P file distribution provide QoS guarantees? *Operating Systems Review*. 40(3), 22–30.

Breslau, L., P. Cao, L. Fan, G. Phillips, and S. Shenker. 1999. Web caching and Zipf-like distributions: Evidence and implications. In *Proceedings of the IEEE Infocom '99 Conference* (pp. 126–134), New York. IEEE. Piscataway, NJ.

Chandra, S., C.S. Ellis, and A. Vahdat. 2000. Application-level differentiated multimedia Web services using quality aware transcoding. *IEEE Journal on Selected Areas in Communication*, 18(12), 2544–2465.

Chen, H., and P. Mohapatra. 2002. Session-based overload control in QoS-aware Web servers. In *Proceedings of the IEEE Infocom 2002 Conference* (pp. 516–524), New York. IEEE. Piscataway, NJ.

Cherkasova, L., and P. Phaal. 1999. Session based admission control—A mechanism for improving performance of commercial Web sites. In *Proceedings of the International Workshop on Quality of Service* (pp. 226–235), London. IEEE. Piscataway, NJ.

Crovella, M., & Bestavros, A. 1997. Self-similarity in World Wide Web traffic: Evidence and possible causes. *IEEE/ACM Transactions on Networking*, 5(6), 835–846.

Dairaine, L., J. Lacan, L. Lancerica, and J. Fimes. 2005. Content-access QoS in peer-to-peer networks using a fast MDS erasure code. *Computer Communications*. 28(15). 1778–90.

Denial of Service Attacks. http://www.cert.org/tech_tips/denial_of_service.html, CERT, 1999.

Jin, J. and K. Nahrstedt. 2004. QoS specification languages for distributed multimedia applications: A survey and taxonomy. *IEEE Multimedia*, 11(3), 74–87.

Kelly, T., Y. Chan, S. Jamin, and J. Mackie-Mason, J. 1999. Biased replacement policies for Web caches: Differential quality-of-service and aggregate user value. In *Proceedings of the 4th International Web Caching Workshop*, San Diego, CA.

Krishnamurthy, B. and J. Rexford. (2001). *Web protocols and practice: HTTP/1.1, networking protocols, caching, and traffic measurement*. Reading, MA: Addison-Wesley.

Lu, Y., A. Sexana, and T. Abdelzaher, T. 2001. Differentiated caching services: A control-theoretical approach. In *Proceedings of the 21st International Conference on Distributed Computing Systems* (pp. 615–622), Phoenix. IEEE. Los Alamitos, CA.

Menasce, D.A., V. Almeida, R. Fonseca, and M.A. Mendes. 2000. Business-oriented resource management policies for e-commerce servers. *Performance Evaluation*, 42(2–3), 223–239.

Mogul, J.C. 1995. The case for persistent-connection HTTP. *ACM Computer Communications Review*, 25(4), October 1995, pp. 299–313.

Moore, D., G.M. Voelker, and S. Savage. 2001. Inferring Internet denial-of-service sctivity, In *Proceedings of the 10th USENIX Security Symposium*.

Rakotoarivelo, T., P. Senac, A. Seneviratne, and M. Diaz. 2005. A structured peer-to-peer method to discover QoS enhanced alternate paths. *Third International Conference on Information Technology and Applications*, (pp. 671–676), Sydney, Australia, IEEE. Los Alamitos, CA.

Schantz, R.E., J. P. Loyal, C. Rodrigues, and D.C. Schmidt. 2006. Controlling quality-of-service in distributed real-time and embedded systems via adaptive middleware. *Software Practice and Experience*, 36(11–12): 1189–1208.

Subramanian, L., I. Stoica, H. Balakrishnan, and R.H. Katz. 2004. OverQoS: An overlay based architecture for enhancing Internet QoS. *First Symposium on Networked Systems Design and Implementation*, (pp. 71–84), San Francisco, CA. USENIX, Berkeley, CA.

Xiao, J. and R. Boutaba. 2005. QoS-aware service composition and adaptation in autonomic communication. *IEEE Journal on Selected Areas in Communications*, 23(12), 2344–2360.

Zhu, H., M. Li, I. Chlamtac, and B. Prabhakaran. 2004. A survey of quality of service in IEEE 802.11 networks. *IEEE Wireless Communications* 11(4): 6–14.

Web Services

Mei-Ling L. Liu, *Cal Poly San Luis Obispo*

INTRODUCTION

Web services refers to an instance of the network services model for distributed computing (Liu 2001). In the network service model (Figure 1), a network application performs all or some of its tasks by making use of ready-made services available on the network.

In such an application, network services can be integrated dynamically, on an as-needed basis. Service providers register themselves with a directory. An application desiring a particular service contacts the directory server at run-time and, if the service is available, will be provided a reference to the service. Using the reference, the application interacts with the service. Java's Jini technology is an example technology that implements this model (Sun Microsystems 2000). This model has been extended to Web services (Figure 2), a technology that initially emerged in 1998 and received public attention by 2002. The World Wide Web Consortium (http://www.w3.org/) created the Web services Architecture, Description, and Coordination Groups in January of that year.

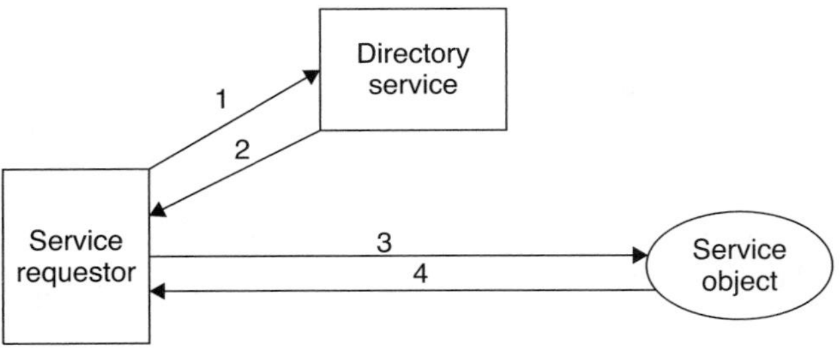
Directory service
1
2
Service requestor
3
4
Service object
1. Service requestor looks up service object.
2. Directory service returns a reference to requestor.
3. Service requestor accesses the service object.
4. Service object provides a response to the request.

Figure 1: The network services model of distributed computing

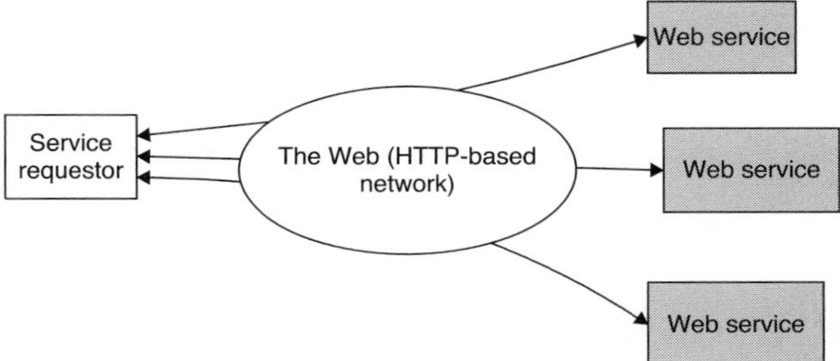
Service requestor
The Web (HTTP-based network)
Web service
Web service
Web service

Figure 2: The conceptual model of Web services

The popularity of Web services technologies has given rise to the term *service-oriented architecture* (SOA; Channabasavaiah et al. 2003; Weerawarana et al. 2005; Erl 2005) for a software architecture that makes use of reusable services to support the requirements of software users. The implementation of an SOA is typically comprised of individual network-accessible services that are assembled into composite applications. In principle, services in an SOA can be built using any network-access technology. However, open Web services standards that meet cross-platform interoperability requirements for service-oriented computing, such as Web Services Description Language (WSDL), simple object access protocol (SOAP), and universal description, discovery, and integration (UDDI), have gained broad industry acceptance.

The Web services technology provides network services over the World Wide Web, commonly using as transport the basic protocol that is at the heart of the Web: HTTP. The technology has been promoted as a new way to build network applications from distributed components (represented as services), in a language- and platform-independent manner. Since its emergence, the

Web services technology has received widespread attention from the industry, and protocols and tools in support of the technology have proliferated.

WEB SERVICES PROTOCOL HIERARCHY

A Web service is provided by a server object and is accessed by a client. The server and client exchange messages in accordance with standard protocols developed for Web services. Figure 3 depicts the conceptual protocol hierarchy. Logically, the server and client exchange messages at the application layer. Physically, a series of protocols is required to support the message exchange. A service discovery protocol allows the service to be registered and located. The functionalities provided at the service description layer allow a service to be described to the directory. The messaging layer supports the mechanisms for interprocess communication, including the functionalities for data marshaling, and the transport layer delivers the messages. Finally, the network layer represents the network protocol hierarchy for the physical transmission and routing of data packets.

Figure 4 illustrates the typical protocols used for Web services. The standard for service discovery is UDDI, and it includes alternatives such as Web Services Inspection Language (WSIL). The syntax and semantics for services are described using WSDL. The service policy negotiation layer allows the client and the service to reach an agreement on which of the various security and messaging options will be employed for the service. The service policy is described using Web Services Policy (WS-Policy) and associated domain-specific policy assertion standards. At the message layer, XML-encoded messages are exchanged according to SOAP. At the transport layer, HTTP transmits the requests and responses; simple mail transfer protocol (SMTP) or Jabber (an instant messaging protocol) transmits messages; and transmission control protocol (TCP) transmits the data. Finally, Internet protocol (IP) serves as the network layer protocol.

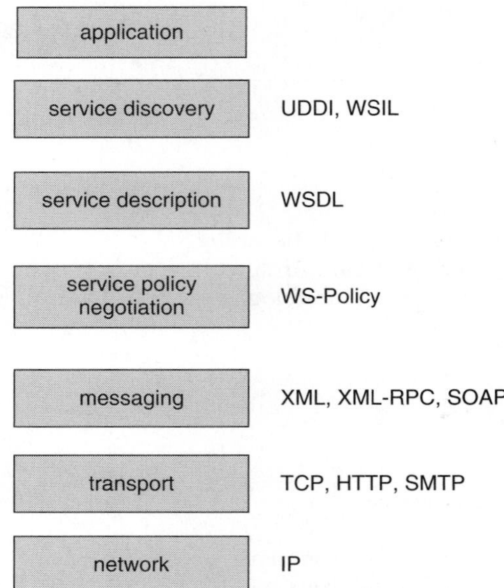

Figure 4: Key Web service protocols

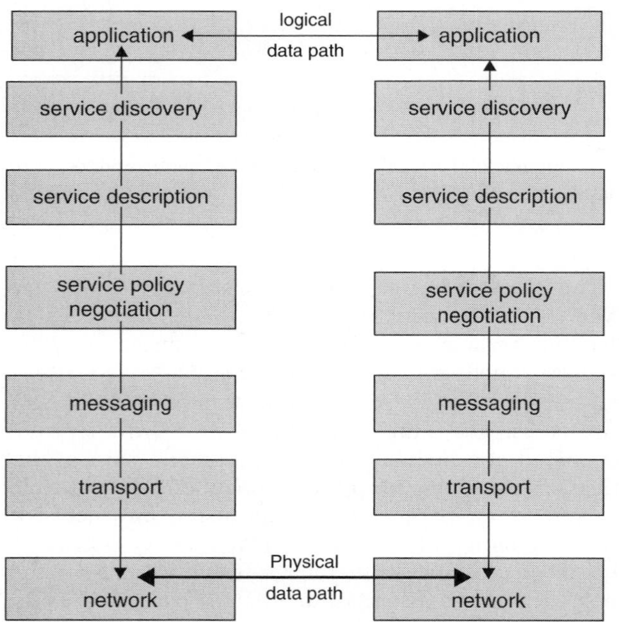

Figure 3: Web service protocol hierarchy

WEB SERVICES SOFTWARE ARCHITECTURE

Figure 5 illustrates the software architecture for a Web service. A service listener on the server host listens for service requests transmitted over the Web. When a request is received, it is forwarded to a proxy for the service. The proxy invokes the application logic in the service object and relays the return value to the caller.

Using the Web services architecture, the World Wide Web represents a networked information system hosting resources accessible by service proxy agents. Resources, identified using uniform resource identifiers (URIs), are described, represented, and accessed using a set of standard data formats and protocols.

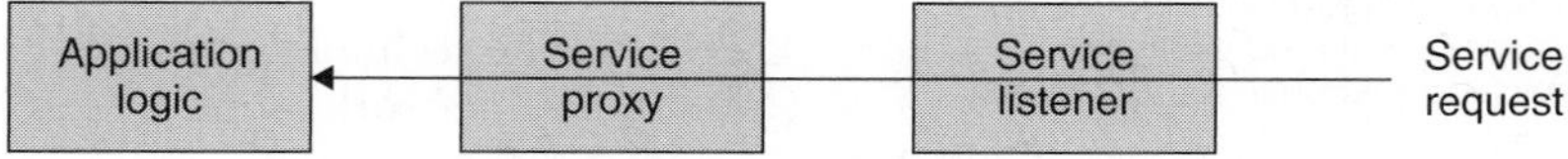

Figure 5: Web service software architecture

KEY WEB SERVICES TECHNOLOGIES

Following is an overview of some of the key technologies that support Web services. Many recent books investigate these technologies in detail (see Weerawarana et al. 2005; Erl 2005).

XML

XML is a data description language for data sharing among applications, primarily Internet applications, using syntax similar to hypertext markup language (HTML), the language used for composing Web pages. XML allows the use of customized tags (e.g., *message*, *to*, and *from* in Figure 6) to enclose and specify a unit of data contents. XML can be used to facilitate data interchange among heterogeneous systems, to segregate the data content of a Web page (written in XML) from the display syntax (written in HTML), and to allow the data to be shared among applications. Since its introduction in 1998, XML has gained considerable attention and is now widely employed in computer applications

In its basic form, XML is composed of elements, each of which starts with a beginning tag (e.g., <ELEMENT1>) that specifies the element name (ELEMENT1, in this case) and a corresponding closing tag (e.g., </ELEMENT1>). Many XML-related standards exist, including the XML schema. An XML schema defines the structure, content, and semantics of XML documents, including a hierarchy of elements, attributes, data types, and default values that can appear in a document (W3C Working Group 2004). The use of an XML schema allows XML contents to be validated without requiring a computer application to enforce data compliance. Within the context of Web services, XML is used extensively for service invocations and data sharing.

XML-RPC

XML-RPC is a remote procedure call protocol adapted to the Internet. In XML-RPC, XML-formatted messages are exchanged using the POST request of HTTP. Messages may contain a procedure invocation, a return value, or an error notification.

An example of an XML-RPC request, excerpted from XML-RPC (2006), is presented in Figure 7. An example of an XML-RPC response is presented in Figure 8.

In the procedure call, as well as in the return values, parameters may be data types that include integer, Boolean, string, double, base64, struct, or array. If a procedure call is erroneous, a message containing one or more error codes is returned instead of the return values, as shown in the example in Figure 9.

```
<message>
   <to>MaryJ@BigU.edu</to>
   <from>JohnL@OpenU.edu</from>
   <subject>Interprocess Communications</subject>
   <text>IPC is the backbone of distributed computing ...</text>
<message>
```

Figure 6: A sample XML file

SOAP

SOAP allows messages to be exchanged using object method invocations. Compared to XML-RPC, SOAP is more sophisticated: message composition is constrained by the XML schema, and message validation can be enforced.

The description that follows is a simplified presentation of SOAP messages (W3C Working Group 2004). The protocol is presented in relative detail to illustrate how Web services protocols relate to HTTP.

Figure 10 illustrates the model for SOAP. A Web client issues an HTTP request, whose body contains a message specially formatted for SOAP, which represents a method call to a service object. The request is transmitted to a Web server, which forwards the method call to the named method. The method is invoked. Upon its completion, the value returned by the method is sent to the Web server and then transmitted to the Web client in the body of the HTTP response.

Each SOAP message has a simple format, as depicted in Figure 11.

Each SOAP request is carried in an HTTP request or response, as will be explained in the following section.

A SOAP Request

Figure 12 illustrates the syntax of an HTTP request that carries a SOAP request. The elements of the request are described as follows. Figure 13 highlights the SOAP request extracted from the HTTP request presented in Figure 12. (The example presented in these figures uses a namespace identifier of "m.")

HTTP Header Lines

The URI in the first line of the HTTP header should specify the object to which the remote method call is directed. In the preceding example, the remote object is */examples*. The User-Agent and Host header lines must be specified.

The Content-Type should be specified as *text/xml*. The charset is a specification of the character representation employed; the default is *US-ASCII*, but another acceptable charset specification is unicode transformation format (UTF). As of SOAP 1.2, the Content-Type can also be application/soap+xml. The SOAP-ENV namespace should be mentioned so that it is clear that the SOAP-ENV prefix is bound to the SOAP namespace that defines the XML schema for SOAP messaging. The Content-Length, if specified, should be the byte length of the request body.

The SOAPAction header line specifies the remote object to which the request is to be directed. The interpretation of this header element is up to the program. In most cases, the URI (specified in the first header line) and the SOAPAction header will have the same value.

HTTP Body

The HTTP body contains a SOAP envelope. Each SOAP envelope in turn contains an optional SOAP header and a required SOAP body.

SOAP envelope. The SOAP envelope is defined with the *<SOAP-ENV:Envelope>* element, which contains a set of required attributes. These attributes specify the encoding

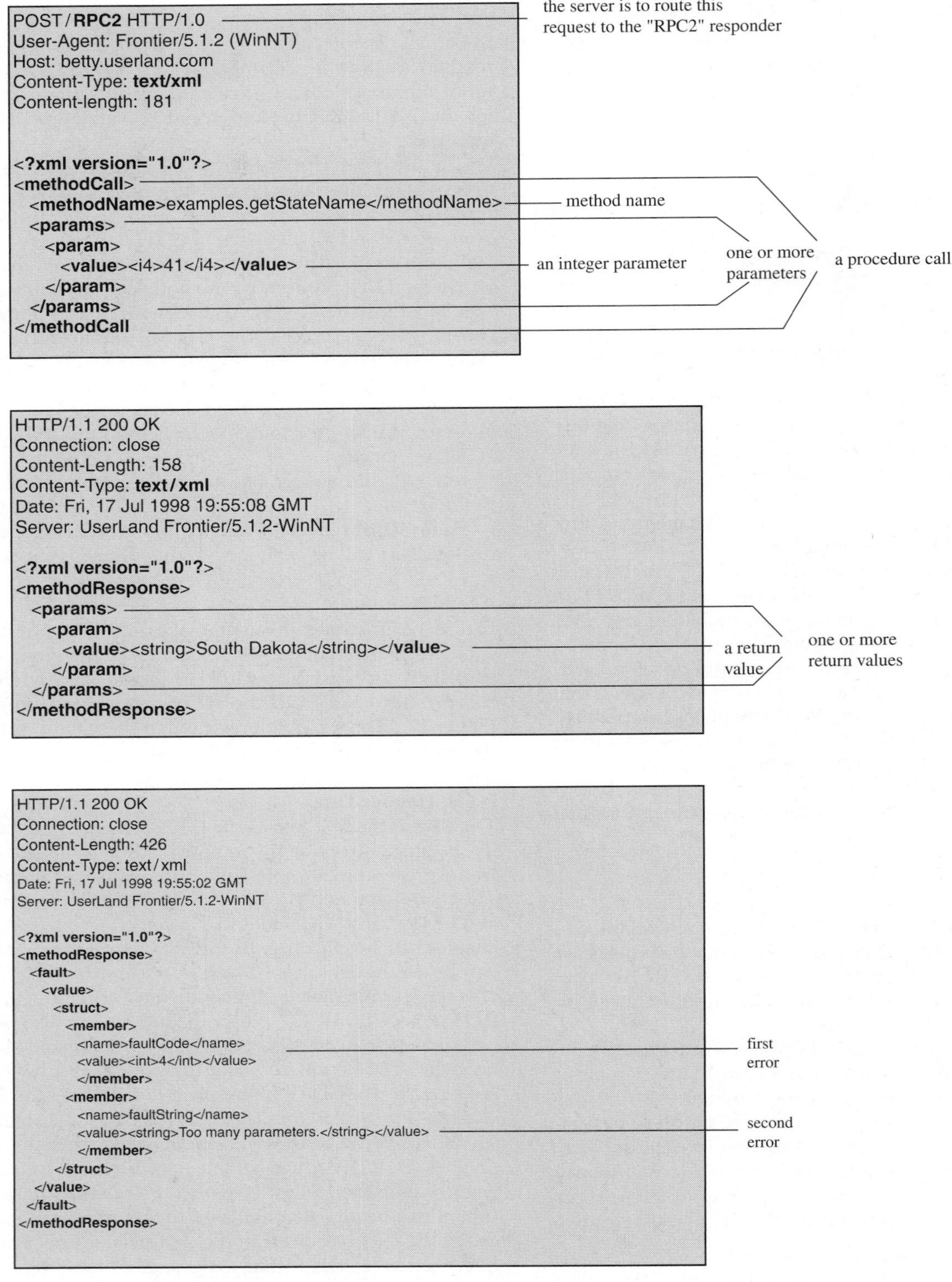
POST / RPC2 HTTP/1.0
User-Agent: Frontier/5.1.2 (WinNT)
Host: betty.userland.com
Content-Type: text/xml
Content-length: 181
<?xml version="1.0"?>
<methodCall>
<methodName>examples.getStateName</methodName>
<params>
<param>
<value><i4>41</i4></value>
</param>
</params>
</methodCall
the server is to route this request to the "RPC2" responder
method name
an integer parameter
one or more parameters
a procedure call
HTTP/1.1 200 OK
Connection: close
Content-Length: 158
Content-Type: text / xml
Date: Fri, 17 Jul 1998 19:55:08 GMT
Server: UserLand Frontier/5.1.2-WinNT
<?xml version="1.0"?>
<methodResponse>
<params>
<param>
<value><string>South Dakota</string></value>
</param>
</params>
</methodResponse>
a return value
one or more return values
HTTP/1.1 200 OK
Connection: close
Content-Length: 426
Content-Type: text / xml
Date: Fri, 17 Jul 1998 19:55:02 GMT
Server: UserLand Frontier/5.1.2-WinNT
<?xml version="1.0"?>
<methodResponse>
<fault>
<value>
<struct>
<member>
<name>faultCode</name>
<value><int>4</int></value>
</member>
<member>
<name>faultString</name>
<value><string>Too many parameters.</string></value>
</member>
</struct>
</value>
</fault>
</methodResponse>
first error
second error

Figure 7: An example XML-RPC procedure call message (XML.RPC 2006)

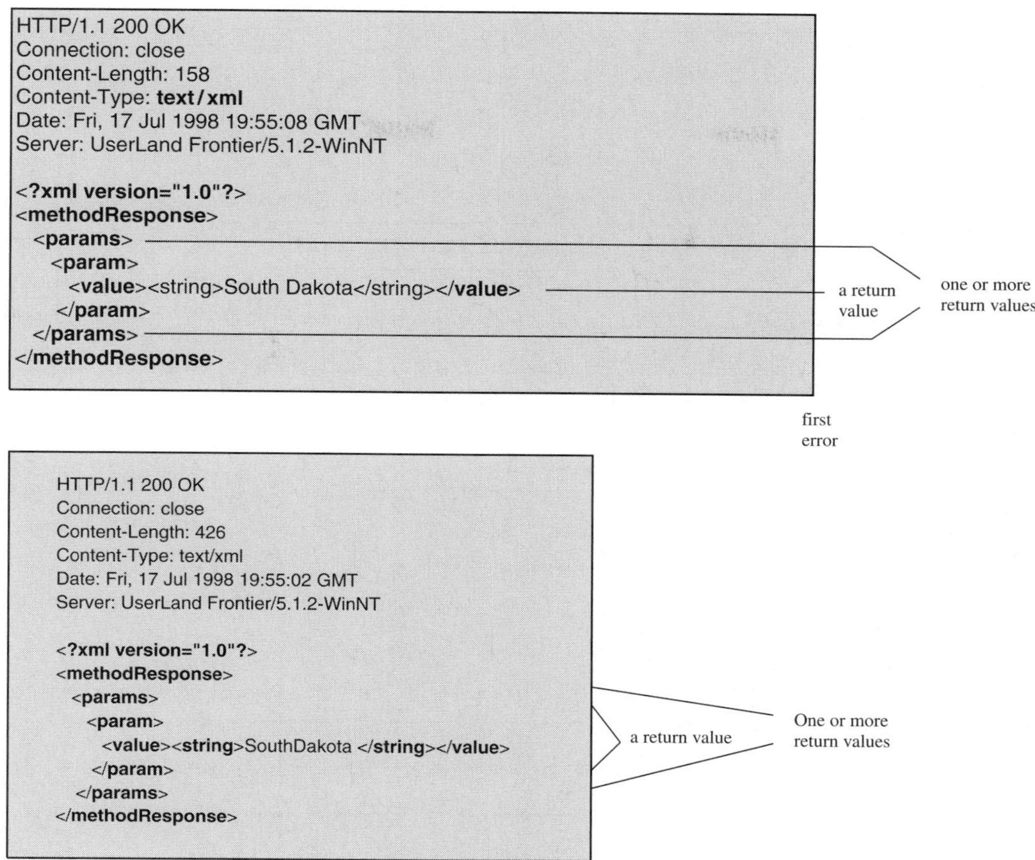
HTTP/1.1 200 OK
Connection: close
Content-Length: 158
Content-Type: text/xml
Date: Fri, 17 Jul 1998 19:55:08 GMT
Server: UserLand Frontier/5.1.2-WinNT
<?xml version="1.0"?>
<methodResponse>
<params>
<param>
<value><string>South Dakota</string></value>
</param>
</params>
</methodResponse>
a return value
one or more return values
first error
HTTP/1.1 200 OK
Connection: close
Content-Length: 426
Content-Type: text/xml
Date: Fri, 17 Jul 1998 19:55:02 GMT
Server: UserLand Frontier/5.1.2-WinNT
<?xml version="1.0"?>
<methodResponse>
<params>
<param>
<value><string>SouthDakota </string></value>
</param>
</params>
</methodResponse>
a return value
One or more return values

Figure 8: An example XML-RPC return values message (XML.RPC 2006)

scheme and envelope style; the syntax is not dependent upon the method call.The *xmlns:soap-env* attribute specifies the namespace that defines the XML schema for SOAP messaging.

SOAP header. The SOAP header is optional. It is defined with the *<SOAP-ENV:Header>* element. The header element provides metainformation specific to the request. Examples of such information include:

- Protocols that the server is expected to understand
- A digital signature for the body of the message
- A schema for the XML application used in the body
- Credit card information to pay for the processing of the request
- A public key to be used to encrypt the response

SOAP body. The SOAP body is defined with the *<SOAP-ENV:Body>* element. The SOAP body contains a single element, which represents the procedure call. The name of the procedure is the name of this element (e.g., *getStateName*). The elements contained within the procedure call are the parameters to the procedure, if any exist. The names of the parameters are significant, but the order of the parameters is not. Parameter data type is indicated by the *xsi:type* attribute, which will be described later on in the chapter.

Data Types

SOAP contains a rich set of language-independent data types that are based on XML schema data types. The table in Figure 14 summarizes a subset of the key scalar data types supported by SOAP 1.1; nonscalar data types including structs, arrays, objects, vectors, and enumerations are also supported in SOAP.

SOAP response. Figure 15 shows an HTTP response that contains a successful SOAP response. The header follows the usual format. Note that the content type is *text/xml*.

Figure 16 highlights the SOAP response extracted from the HTTP response presented in Figure 15. As with the SOAP request, the response is composed of two parts: the envelope and the body. (The example presented in these figures uses a namespace identifier of "m.") The syntax for the envelope is the same as for the request. The syntax for the body, highlighted in Figure 16, is also analogous to that of the request.

The single element contained in the *<SOAP-ENV:Body>* has a name that must match the name of the method that was called, with *"Response"* attached to the end of the method name. The data type and value of the returned value are contained in the Result subelement.

A SOAP method call may fail, perhaps due to an erroneous method name or a bad parameter passed. When a method call cannot be completed successfully, the HTTP

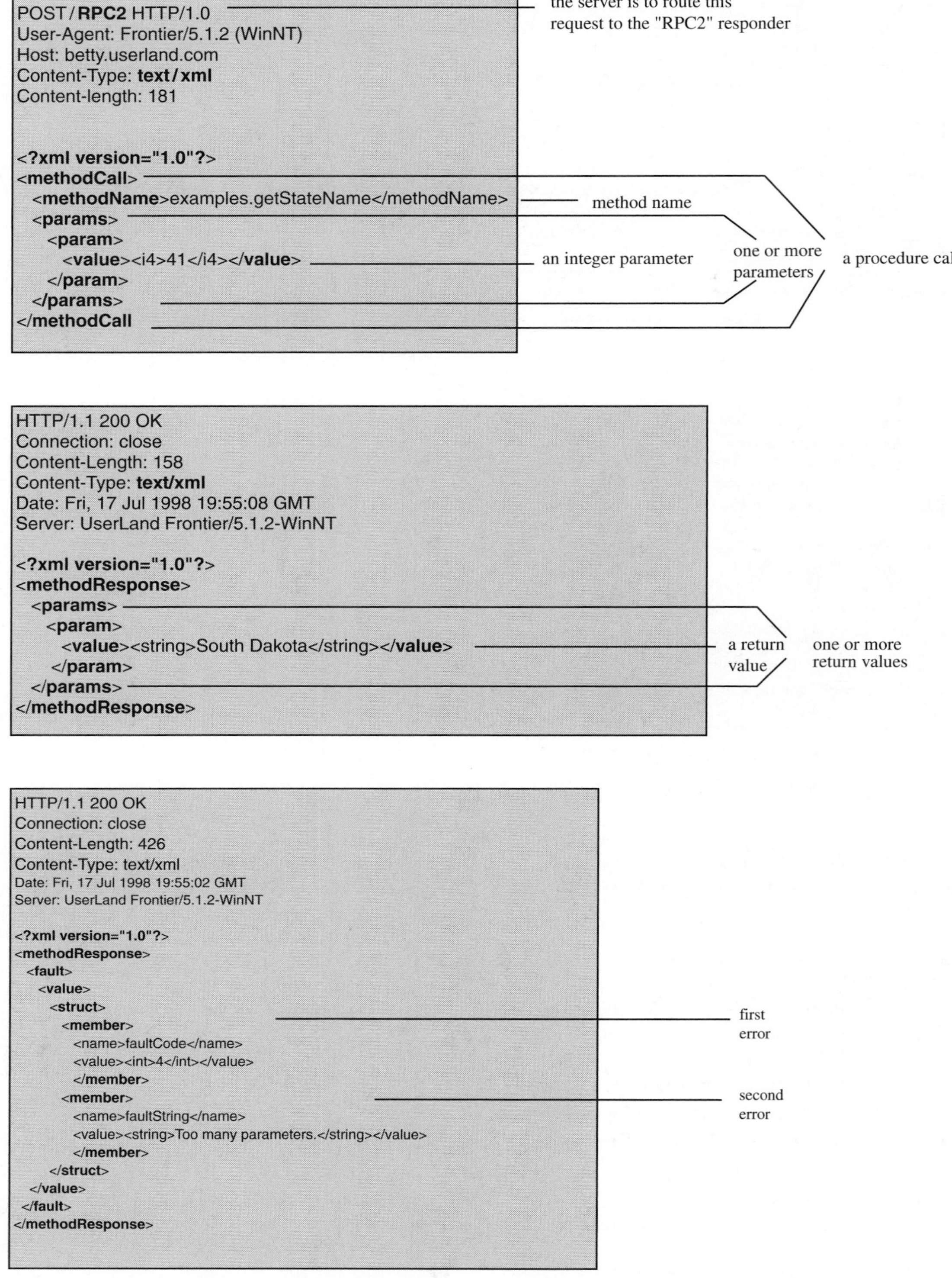
POST / RPC2 HTTP/1.0
User-Agent: Frontier/5.1.2 (WinNT)
Host: betty.userland.com
Content-Type: text / xml
Content-length: 181
<?xml version="1.0"?>
<methodCall>
<methodName>examples.getStateName</methodName>
<params>
<param>
<value><i4>41</i4></value>
</param>
</params>
</methodCall>
the server is to route this request to the "RPC2" responder
method name
an integer parameter
one or more parameters
a procedure call
HTTP/1.1 200 OK
Connection: close
Content-Length: 158
Content-Type: text/xml
Date: Fri, 17 Jul 1998 19:55:08 GMT
Server: UserLand Frontier/5.1.2-WinNT
<?xml version="1.0"?>
<methodResponse>
<params>
<param>
<value><string>South Dakota</string></value>
</param>
</params>
</methodResponse>
a return value
one or more return values
HTTP/1.1 200 OK
Connection: close
Content-Length: 426
Content-Type: text/xml
Date: Fri, 17 Jul 1998 19:55:02 GMT
Server: UserLand Frontier/5.1.2-WinNT
<?xml version="1.0"?>
<methodResponse>
<fault>
<value>
<struct>
<member>
<name>faultCode</name>
<value><int>4</int></value>
</member>
<member>
<name>faultString</name>
<value><string>Too many parameters.</string></value>
</member>
</struct>
</value>
</fault>
</methodResponse>
first error
second error

Figure 9: An example XML-RPC procedure call fault response (XML.RPC 2006)

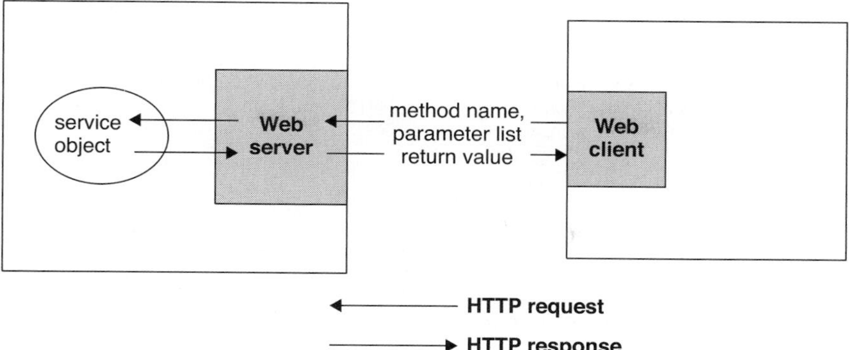

Figure 10: The SOAP model

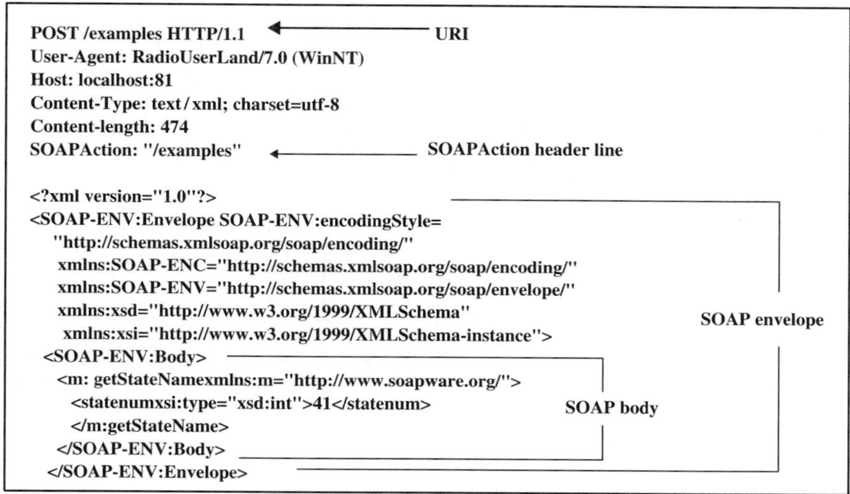

Figure 11: The layout of a SOAP request message

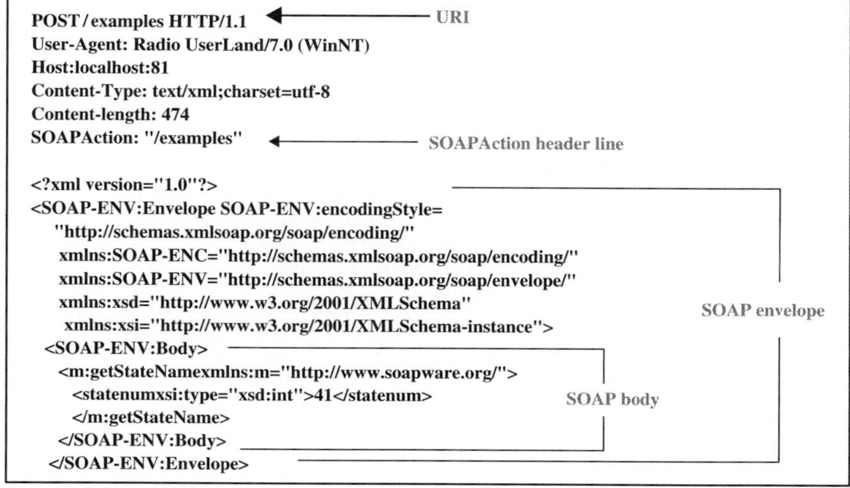

Figure 12 A SOAP request embedded in an HTTP request (Winer and Savin 2001)

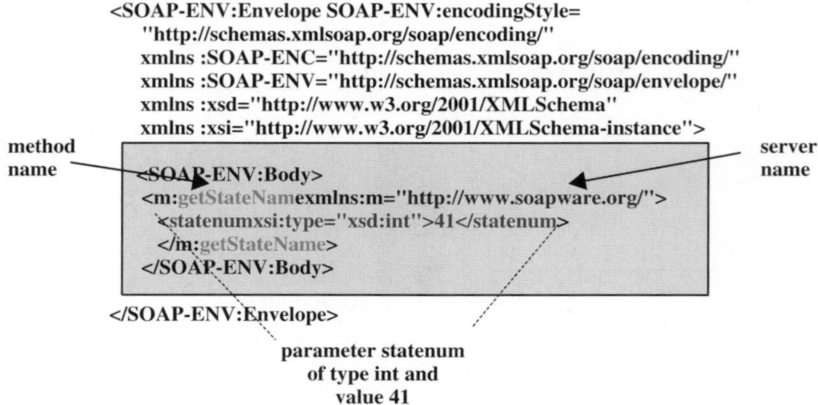

Figure 13: A SOAP request body (Winer and Savin 2001)

Attribute value	Type	Example
xsd:int	32-bit signed integer	-12
xsd:boolean	a boolean value, 1 or 0	1
xsd:string	string of characters	hello world
xsd:float or xsd:double	signed floating point number	-12.214
xsd:timeInstant	date/time	2001-03-27T00:00:01-08:00
SOAP-ENC:base64	base64-encoded binary	eW91IGNhbid0IHJlYWQgdGhpcyE=

Figure 14: Scalar XML schema data types (Winer and Savin 2001)

```
HTTP/1.1 200 OK
Connection: close
Content-Length: 499
Content-Type: text/xml
Date: Wed, 28 Mar 2001 05:05:04 GMT
Server: UserLand Frontier/7.0-WinNT

<?xml version="1.0"?>
<SOAP-ENV:Envelope SOAP-ENV:
    encodingStyle="http://schemas.xmlsoap.org/soap/encoding/"
    xmlns:SOAP-ENC="http://schemas.xmlsoap.org/soap/encoding/"
    xmlns:SOAP-ENV="http://schemas.xmlsoap.org/soap/envelope/"
    xmlns:xsd="http://www.w3.org/2001/XMLSchema"
    xmlns:xsi="http://www.w3.org/2001/XMLSchema-instance">
  <SOAP-ENV:Body>
    <m:getStateNameResponsexmlns:m="http://www.soapware.org/">
      <Result  xsi:type="xsd:string">South Dakota</Result>
    </m:  getStateNameResponse>
  </SOAP-ENV:Body>
</SOAP-ENV:Envelope>
```

procedure name

name of server

returned value

Figure 15: A SOAP request (Winer and Savin 2001)

```
<?xml version="1.0"?>
<SOAP-ENV:Envelope SOAP-ENV:
    encodingStyle="http://schemas.xmlsoap.org/soap/encoding/"
    xmlns:SOAP-ENC="http://schemas.xmlsoap.org/soap/encoding/"
    xmlns:SOAP-ENV="http://schemas.xmlsoap.org/soap/envelope/"
    xmlns:xsd="http://www.w3.org/2001/XMLSchema"
    xmlns:xsi="http://www.w3.org/2001/XMLSchema-instance">
  <SOAP- ENV:Body>
    <m: getStateNameResponsexmlns:m="http://www.soapware.org/">
      <Result xsi:type="xsd:string">South Dakota</Result>
    </m: getStateNameResponse>
  </SOAP-ENV:Body>
</SOAP-ENV:Envelope>
```


Figure 16: A SOAP response (Winer and Savin 2001)

response (see Figure 17) contains a SOAP body that defines a fault code and a fault string. The fault code (SOAP-ENV: Client) identifies the fault, and the fault string provides a description of the fault.

REST

Representational state transfer (REST) is an architectural style for distributed hypermedia systems (Fielding 2000) that has received wide acceptance among Web application developers. REST focuses on the nature and state of a system's data elements. These data elements have a shared understanding of data types (using metadata) but limit the scope of what is revealed to a standardized interface. REST components communicate by transferring a representation of a resource, such as a Web service, in a format selected dynamically based on the capabilities or desires of the recipient and the nature of the resource. Using REST, each procedure or method call of remote procedure call (RPC) and SOAP may instead be represented as a separate resource identified by its own URL, resulting in a simplified user interface for accessing the service. REST has been touted as the technology for second-generation Web services (Prescod 2002).

```
HTTP/1.1 500 Server Error
Connection: close
Content-Length: 511
Content-Type: text/xml;charset=utf-8
Date: Wed, 28 Mar 2001 05:06:32 GMT
Server:UserLand Frontier/7.0-WinNT

<?xml version="1.0"?>
<SOAP-ENV:Envelope SOAP-ENV:
    encodingStyle="http://schemas.xmlsoap.org/soap/encoding/"
    xmlns:SOAP-ENV="http://schemas.xmlsoap.org/soap/envelope/"
    xmlns:xsd="http://www.w3.org/2001/XMLSchema"
    xmlns:xsi="http://www.w3.org/2001/XMLSchema-instance">
  <SOAP-ENV:Body>
    <SOAP-ENV:Fault>
      <faultcode>SOAP-ENV:Client</faultcode>
      <faultstring>
        Can't call get State Name because there are
        too many parameters.
      </faultstring>
    </SOAP-ENV:Fault>
  </SOAP-ENV:Body>
</SOAP-ENV:Envelope>
```

Figure 17: An HTTP response that contains a failed SOAP method call (Winer and Savin 2001)

WSDL

WSDL 2.0 (W3C Working Group 2004) is a language used to describe Web services. For each service, WSDL can be used to describe the messages that are exchanged between the requester and provider, and the operations exposed for accessing the service.

Web service definitions can be mapped to any implementation language, platform, object model, or messaging system, as long as both the service requester and the service provider agree on the service description. This provision allows Web services to be implemented for interaction via browsers, or directly within an application implemented using any language/technology that understands WSDL.

Figure 18 presents a sample WSDL file that describes a Web service for hotel reservations. A detailed explanation of the WSDL syntax and semantics is available from the W3C Working Group (2004).

UDDI

The UDDI protocol was set forth by OASIS (UDDI 2006; OASIS 2004); it defines a standard for publishing and discovering the network-based software components of a service-oriented architecture. UDDI creates a standard interoperable platform that enables Web clients to dynamically discover and make use of Web services, and it allows service directories to be maintained independent of the purposes and contexts of diverse applications.

The UDDI protocol makes use of XML, HTTP, domain name system (DNS), and XML protocol messaging. Detailed description of the protocol and an explanation of its usage can be found in Chappell and Jewell (2002).

```
<?xml version="1.0" encoding="UTF-8"?>
<definitions name="HelloService"
  targetNamespace="http://www.ecerami.com/wsdl/HelloService.wsdl"
  xmlns="http://schemas.xmlsoap.org/wsdl/"
  xmlns:soap="http://schemas.xmlsoap.org/wsdl/soap/"
  xmlns:tns="http://www.ecerami.com/wsdl/HelloService.wsdl"
  xmlns:xsd="http://www.w3.org/2001/XMLSchema">

 <message name="SayHelloRequest">
   <part name="firstName" type="xsd:string"/>
 </message>
 <message name="SayHelloResponse">
   <part name="greeting" type="xsd:string"/>
 </message>
```

Message(s) used in the service

```
 <portType name="Hello_PortType">
   <operation name="sayHello">
     <input message="tns:SayHelloRequest"/>
     <output message="tns:SayHelloResponse"/>
   </operation>
 </portType>
```

The operation(s) performed by the service

```
 <binding name="Hello_Binding" type="tns:Hello_PortType">
   <soap:binding style="rpc"
     transport="http://schemas.xmlsoap.org/soap/http"/>
   <operation name="sayHello">
     <soap:operationsoapAction="sayHello"/>
     <input>
       <soap:body
          encodingStyle="http://schemas.xmlsoap.org/soap/encoding/"
         namespace="urn:examples:helloservice"
         use="encoded"/>
     </input>
     <output>
       <soap:body
          encodingStyle="http://schemas.xmlsoap.org/soap/encoding/"
         namespace="urn:examples:helloservice"
         use="encoded"/>
     </output>
   </operation>
 </binding>
```

The communication protocols used by the service

```
 <service name="Hello_Service">
   <documentation>WSDL File for HelloService</documentation>
   <port binding="tns:Hello_Binding" name="Hello_Port">
     <soap:address
       location="http://localhost:8080/soap/servlet/rpcrouter"/>
   </port>
 </service>
</definitions>
```

Service name and location

Figure 18: A sample service description in WSDL (W3C 2004)

USING WEB SERVICES

Steps

The World Wide Web Consortium (W3C Working Group 2004) specifies four steps involved in the process of engaging a Web service:

1. The service requester and provider entities make contact with each other. In a typical case, the requester initiates the interaction in one of two ways: (1) the requester obtains the provider's address directly from the provider entity; or (2) the requester may use a discovery service to obtain the address of a suitable service description. The discovery may be manual or through autonomous selection, and it is accomplished using a functional description of the service.

   Less typically, the provider initiates the interaction by obtaining the address of the requester in some way.

2. The requester and provider reach an agreement on a policy alternative per WS-Policy.
3. The requester and provider implicitly or explicitly reach an agreement on the description and semantics of the service in one of the following ways:
   - The requester and provider may communicate directly with each other to explicitly agree on the service description and semantics.
   - The provider may publish the service description and semantics.
   - The service description and semantics (except the network address of the particular service) may be defined as a standard by an industry organization.
   - The service description and semantics may be defined and published by the requester entity and offered to a potential provider as a solicitation for the service.

4. The requester and provider implement the service and exchanges according to its description and semantics. The implementation may be carried out in many ways, including:
   - A service may be hard coded to implement a specific, static service description and semantics.
   - A service may be coded in a general way that allows the desired service description and/or semantics to be input dynamically.
   - The service description and/or semantics may be generated dynamically by an agent created to provide the service.
5. The requester and provider exchange requests and responses for the service.

Development Environments

A large number of tools and systems have been developed by a multitude of organizations to facilitate the building of Web services and clients. These tools and systems provide abstractions to allow a developer to focus on the logic at the highest layer of the protocol stack. Following is a list of such tools and systems. (Note: this list is not comprehensive.)

- The Apache Software Foundation (http://www.apache.org/) has a Web services Project that provides a toolkit for XML-RPC. The Apache XML-RPC toolkit features a set of Java classes for Web service servers and clients.
- The Apache Software Foundation has another product known as Apache Axis (http://ws.apache.org/axis/), which supports SOAP-based Web service servers and clients written in Java.
- The Java Web services Developer Pack (Java WSDP) by Sun MicroSystems, now dubbed the Java XML Web services (JAX-WS) open-source project, provides a Java application programming interface (API) that supports Web services (Sun Microsystems 2006).
- The IBM Web services toolkit (WSTK), now known as the Emerging Technologies Toolkit (ETTK) for Web services and Autonomic Computing (ETTK-WS), also provides an API for Web services development (alphaWorks 2006).
- Microsoft's .NET Framework provides Web services support (Shodjai 2006) via Visual Studio.
- The Web services interoperability (WSI) site, http://www.ws-i.org/, provides implementation guidelines for how related Web services specifications should be used together for best interoperability. It also provides testing tools and sample Web services applications.
- SoapClient (http://www.soapclient.com/) is a site that hosts links to a repertoire of useful resources, including (1) a generic SOAP client that allows one to execute SOAP services using a Web browser, and (2) a SOAP interoperability test that defines a set of standard methods that can be invoked for testing interoperability of Web services.
- Xmethods (http://xmethods.net/) provides a repository that houses Web services contributed from third parties and available for free access. The site also includes links to tools and tutorials of interest to software developers.

WEB SERVICES STANDARDS

Because interoperability is an inherent goal for Web services, the architecture has prompted intense efforts in standardization.

Standards Organizations

Industry vendors have participated in the Web services standardization process under the sponsorship of various consortia, including the following three key organizations:

1. The World Wide Web Consortium (W3C; http://www.w3.org/): The W3C released XML 1.0 in 1998 and is the originator of the specifications of HTTP, HTML, SOAP, and WSDL. The W3C is also responsible for a number of XML-based specifications: XML encryption, XML XSL (extensible stylesheet language), XSL transformations (XSLT), XPath, and XQuery. Currently, WS-Policy and WS-PolicyAttachment are being standardized by the W3C.
2. The Organization for the Advancement of Structured Information Standards (OASIS; www.oasis-open.org): OASIS specifies standards that enable specific business or IT functionality, including standards that cover business aspects (e.g., security, transaction support, and management). Standards developed by OASIS relevant to Web services include UDDI, WS-ReliableMessaging (WS-RM), Web services resource framework (WSRF), Web services security (WS-security) and Web services transaction (WS-TX).
3. The Web Services Interoperability Organization (WS-I; www.ws-i.org): WS-I promotes interoperability between Web services product implementations. WS-I is best known for its guidelines of interoperability specifications for the core set of Web services standards: WSDL, UDDI, and SOAP. The best known of such guidelines is WS-I BasicProfile. WS-I has also released a variety of tools for conformance testing.

WS-* Standards and Proposals

A plethora of WS-prefixed standards and proposals have been developed by the aforementioned standard organizations and other entities. These specifications are in a state of flux. Following is a nonexhaustive enumeration of these standards and proposals:

- WS-Addressing: used to address Web services and messages
- WS-Agreement: used for service-level agreements between Web services in a grid environment
- WS-AtomicTransaction: provides the definition of the atomic transaction coordination type that is to be used with the extensible coordination framework described in the WS-Coordination specification

- WS-Attachments: encapsulates a SOAP message and zero or more attachments; this work has been rendered obsolete by the SOAP message transmission optimization mechanism (MTOM) specified by the W3C
- WS-BusinessActivity: provides the definition of the business activity coordination type that is to be used with the extensible coordination framework described in the WS-Coordination specification
- WS-Coordination: provides protocols that coordinate the actions of distributed applications
- WS-Discovery: defines a multicast discovery protocol to locate services
- WS-Enumeration: extends the single-request/single-reply in basic SOAP to allow a data source to provide a session abstraction, called an enumeration context, to a consumer
- WS-Eventing: allows a Web service to receive messages when events occur in other services and applications
- WS-Federation: defines mechanisms to allow different security realms to federate using different or like mechanisms by allowing and brokering trust of identities, attributes, and authentication between participating Web services
- WS-Inspection: specification provides an XML format for assisting in the inspection of a site for available services and a set of rules for how inspection-related information should be made available for consumption
- WS-Manageability: defines the manageability interface for the Web services end point based on the general concepts of a manageability model in terms of manageability topics (identification, configuration, state, metrics, and relationships) and the aspects (properties, operations, and events) used to define them.
- WS-MetadataExchange: defines a standard mechanism for metadata-driven message exchange
- WS-Notification/WS-Topics: define a standard approach to notification using a topic-based publish/subscribe pattern
- WS-Policy: provides a general purpose model and syntax for expressing the capabilities, requirements, and general characteristics of entities in an XML Web services-based system
- WS-Provisioning: describes the APIs and schemas necessary to facilitate interoperability between provisioning systems and to allow software vendors to provide provisioning facilities in a consistent way
- WS-ReliableMessaging: describes a protocol that allows messages to be delivered reliably between distributed applications in the presence of software component, system, or network failures
- WS-ReliableMessaging Policy: defines policy assertion formats for reliable messaging in conjunction with WS-Policy
- WS-Resource Framework: defines a family of specifications for accessing stateful resources using Web services
- WS-SecureConversation: defines secure conversation assertion formats for security in conjunction with WS-Policy
- WS-Security: describes enhancements to SOAP messaging to provide quality of protection through message integrity, message confidentiality, and single message authentication
- WS-SecurityPolicy: defines policy assertion formats for security in conjunction with WS-Policy
- WS-Transfer: defines a mechanism for acquiring XML-based representations of entities using the Web service infrastructure

WEB SERVICES SECURITY

The interoperable nature of Web services gives rise to special concerns about security. Security threats involve the systems that host Web services, the applications that deploy the services, and the underlying network infrastructure.

Security Requirements

The W3C Working Group (2004) lists the following requirements for providing end-to-end security for Web services:

- Authentication mechanisms for verifying the identities of the requester and provider agents.
- Authorization mechanisms for controlling requester access to appropriate system resources. Policies based on the principle of least privilege access may be used to determine the access rights of a requester to systems and their components.
- Data integrity mechanisms to ensure that information has not been altered during transmission. Data confidentiality ensures that the data are only accessible by the intended parties. Data encryption and digital signatures are techniques that can be used to implement these mechanisms.
- Integrity of transactions and communications mechanisms to ensure that the business process and work flow conducted on behalf of the Web service is performed properly.
- Nonrepudiation mechanisms that provide evidence about the occurrence of a transaction. This protects a party to a transaction against false denial of the occurrence of that transaction by another party.
- End-to-end integrity and confidentiality of messages must be ensured even in the presence of intermediaries.
- Audit trails to allow tracing of user access and behavior, and to ensure system integrity through verification.
- Distributed enforcement of security policies across various platforms with varying privileges.

Security Consideration of the Web Services Architecture

The W3C Working Group (2004) further specifies the following Security Consideration of the architecture for Web services:

> Organizations that implement Web services must be able to conduct business in a secure fashion. All aspects of Web services, including routing,

management, publication, and discovery, should be performed in a secure manner. Web services implementers must be able to utilize security services such as authentication, authorization, encryption, and auditing.

Web services messages can flow through firewalls and can be tunneled through existing ports and protocols. Web services security requires the use of appropriate corporate-wide policies that may need to be integrated with external cross-enterprise policy and trust resolution. Organizations may need to implement capabilities that include:

- Cross-domain identities: Requester and provider agents may communicate with each other using various identity verification schemes from different security domains. It is important for Web services to be able to support the mapping of identities across multiple domains and even within a single domain.
- Distributed policies: Security policies should be available to define the access privileges of requests and responses between parties.
- Trust policies: Trust policies should be available to allow the requester to trust the environment of a service and the provider to trust the environment of the requester entity.
- Secure discovery mechanism: Secure discovery mechanism should be in place to enforce policies that govern the publication and discovery of a service, thus allowing a service to selectively provide an identity only to trusted requesters.
- Trust and discovery: Provisions should be made to allow a judgement to be made by a requester with respect to whether a service discovered can be trusted.
- Secure messaging: Secure nessaging ensures privacy, confidentiality, and integrity of interactions. The digital signatures techniques can be used to help ensure nonrepudiation. Techniques that ensure channel security can be used for securing messages. Message security techniques such as encryption and signing of the message payload can be used in routing and reliable messaging.

Web Services Security Technologies

Web services technologies are based on the aforementioned WS-Security standard. The W3C Working Group (2004) cites the following technologies available for Web services security:

XML-Signature: XML-Signature, jointly developed by W3C and the Internet Engineering Task Force (IETF), is designed for use in XML transactions. This standard defines a schema for capturing the result of a digital signature operation applied to arbitrary data and their processing. XML-Signature has the ability to sign only specific portions of the XML tree rather than the complete document, thus allowing a single XML document to be signed multiple times by a single or multiple parties. This flexibility can ensure the integrity of certain portions of an XML document while leaving open the possibility for other portions of the document to change.

XML-Encryption: XML-Encryption specifies a process for encrypting data and representing the result in XML. The data may be arbitrary data (e.g., an XML document), an XML element, or XML element content.

Web Services Security: Web Services Security (WSS) defines a SOAP extension that provides message integrity, confidentiality, and authentication.

WSS provides a general mechanism for associating security tokens with messages. The specification defines an end-to-end security framework that provides support for intermediary security processing. Message integrity is provided by using XML-Signature in conjunction with security tokens to ensure that messages are transmitted without modifications. The integrity mechanisms can support multiple signatures, possibly by multiple actors. The techniques are extensible such that they can support additional signature formats. Message confidentiality is granted by using XML-Encryption in conjunction with security tokens to keep portions of SOAP messages confidential.

XML Key Management Specification: The XML Key Management Specification (XKMS) is an XML-based way of managing the public key infrastructure (PKI), a system that uses public key cryptography for encrypting, signing, authorizing, and verifying the authenticity of information on the Internet. It specifies protocols for distributing and registering public keys, suitable for use in conjunction with the proposed standard for XML-Signature and XML-Encryption.

XKMS allows implementers to outsource the task of key registration and validation to a "trust" utility. This simplifies implementation because the actual work of managing public and private key pairs and other PKI details is done by a third party.

An XKMS trust utility works with any PKI system, passing the information back and forth between it and the Web service. Because the trust utility does the work, the Web service itself can be kept simple. XKMS is a W3C specification.

Security assertion markup language: Security assertion markup language (SAML) is an XML-based standard for exchanging authentication and authorization data between a service provider and a client. SAML is useful for providing single sign-on.

The three basic SAML components are assertions, protocol, and binding. An assertion can be one of many types, including authentication, attribute, and authorization. Authentication assertion validates the identity of the user; the attribute assertion contains specific information about the user; and the authorization assertion identifies what the user is authorized to do.

Extensible access control markup language: Extensible access control markup language (XACML) is an XML-based technology for supporting distributed access control polices.

XACML includes an access control language along with a request/response language that allows policies to be written to control users' access. XACML has been integrated with SAML so that the SAML query and response protocol can be used with an XACML policy engine consuming XACML policies, and SAML can be used to transmit XACML artifacts (e.g., requests, responses, policies, attributes) securely over the Web.

Identity federation: Federated network identity is the notion that businesses or organizations can be affiliated into circles of trust and trust relationships.

The Liberty Alliance (http://www.projectliberty.org/) project was established to develop an open standard for federated network identity through open technical specifications. The Liberty specifications make extensive use of XML, including the use of SAML for simplified sign-on. Their work is grouped into three categories: identity federation framework (ID-FF), identity Web services framework (ID-WSF), and identity service instance specifications (ID-SIS; Liberty Alliance Project 2006).

ID-FF focuses on human-to-application interactions and has been integrated with SAML 2.0; ID-WSF focuses on application-to-application interactions in a Web services environment; and ID-SIS specifies particular identity-based services. Following is a summary of the three categories.

A separate effort in identify federation is WS-Federation by IBM and Microsoft, created as part of their proposal for a Web services security framework (WS-Security). The WS-Federation framework includes three components: (1) the Web Services Federation Language, which defines how different security domains broker identities, user attributes, and authentication between Web services; (2) Passive Requestor Profile, which describes how a federation provides identity services to Web browsers, Web-enabled cell phones, and devices; and (3) Active Requestor Profile, which describes how a federation provides identity services to applications such as those based on SOAP (Network World 2006).

INDUSTRIAL ACCEPTANCE OF WEB SERVICES

The concept of Web services has strong appeal to the industry. Major companies, including Microsoft, IBM, and Sun Microsystems, have promoted Web services. Microsoft in particular has significant involvements in the development of Web services standards and at one time had an ambitious plan for delivering consumer Web services. Although the industry shows interest in expanding Web services, the research firm IDC reported in 2002 that full-scale adoption could be at least a decade away (Dignan 2002). A somewhat recent ComputerWorld article (2004) stated that Web services have yet to enjoy their predicted widespread adoption, and Web services technology has yet to be embraced by the broader IT and economic climate because its deployment does not generally reduce costs.

Gartner Research (Cantara 2006) reported that, based on surveys conducted at SOA conferences held in 2005 and 2006, "spending on SOA and Web Services as a percent of IT Budget . . . increased from 11% in spring 2005 to 18% in June 2006. Conference attendees expect to spend 22% of their IT budgets on SOA, Web Services, and Web 2.0 in 2007."

Web services are now employed by many enterprises to link internal business systems and exchange data with other companies. Online sites now commonly make use of Web services offered by major companies, such as those listed below, to provide customer support (e.g., price comparison and shipment tracking).

Amazon.com (2006): The online bookseller has provided a Web service that allows client applications to browse its product catalog and place orders.

FedEx (2006): The shipping company has provided a FedEx API Client Libraries interface for Windows, Solaris UNIX, and LINUX clients to issue a remote procedure call as a FedExAPI transaction to the FedEx Internet server. Using the mechanism, a client may retrieve tracking information for packages.

eBay (2006): eBay supports Web services that provide easy access to the eBay marketplace. The Web services support communication directly with the eBay business logic and database, allowing customized applications for item sales management, inventory systems, item search, user account management systems, partner item listings, and buyer's managing of listings of interest. According to Chappelle (2004), in 2004 over 40 percent of eBay's listings came through the E-Bay Web services API calls.

eBay provides multiple software developer kits (SDKs) for using the API, allowing applications to be developed in most popular languages.

Google (2006): The search engine provider is giving developers direct access to its search database, bypassing its Web site and allowing them to design their own ways to use Google's search engine technology. Google supplies a downloadable developer's kit that allows developers to use Google's service to "query billions of Web pages directly from their own computer programs" (Google 2006). A sample Java program and .NET program that make use of the service can be found on the download site at http://www.google.com/apis/download.html.

Microsoft (2006): Microsoft offers a MapPoint Web service for use by enterprises and independent software developers to "integrate location-based services, such as maps, driving directions and proximity searches, into software applications and business processes" (Microsoft 2006). According to Microsoft, the MapPoint Web service currently supports more than 15 million transactions daily.

WEB SERVICES ACCESS FROM MOBILE DEVICES

A promising growth area for Web services is applications deployed on mobile platforms. However, mobile devices such as cell phones typically do not come with built-in Web services support for processing HTTP commands and XML requests. Even if they do, performance is a concern. A proxy may be used to serve as an intermediary between the mobile device and the Web service provider (Elkarra 2003).

Some of the most promising technologies in this arena are described as follows.

Java ME

The Java Micro Edition (Java ME) is one of the most widely used application platforms for mobile devices such as mobile phones, personal digital assistants (PDAs), TV set-top boxes, and printers. The Web services API (WSA) for Java ME comprises two optional packages:

- The XML processing package is based on the Java API for XMP Processing (JAXP) and on the Simple API for XML (SAX).
- The API for remote Web services invocation is a subset of the Java API for XML-Based RPC (JAX-RPC) specification.

To support platform independence, WSA uses a stub as a proxy between the application and the mobile service provider interface. The architecture is depicted in Figure 19.

VoiceXML

VoiceXML (W3C Working Group 2000) is an extensible markup language with which Web services can be provided to customers with voice interfaces on devices such as the telephone, specifically cell phones.

Accessing Web services with VoiceXML (2006) is facilitated by the use of tools such as BeVocal's JavaScript SOAP API (2006). The BeVocal Cafe offers a phone number that a user can call to access a voice-interfaced Web service.

The Tellme Networks Inc. (2006) offers a Tellme service that provides, among other things, voiced driving directions using Microsoft's MapPoint Web service (Microsoft 2006). Tellme Inc's Studio also offers a development environment for developing VoiceXML applications. Tellme does not support RPC directly but can be coupled with a Web service to generate VoiceXML output to the client. For example, Tellme's Notifier service allows a VoiceXML application to initiate phone calls to clients. The Notifier service can also be used to deliver reminders of appointments and other voice messages.

Microsoft's .NET Compact Framework

The .NET Compact Framework provides an environment for developing mobile applications using the traditional Microsoft point-and-click interface.

The .NET Compact Framework is a subset of the .NET Framework and is designed specifically to provide support for Web services. The .NET Compact Framework is available for devices running the Microsoft Windows CE operating system. Compact Framework applications can be developed using Visual Studio.NET, VB.NET, and C#. A sample Web service and client can be found in Microsoft (2003).

RELATED TECHNOLOGIES

The following technologies, though noteworthy, are beyond the scope of this article:

1. Web service interaction protocols: One of the most promising applications of Web services is their use to support business processes that involve complex interactions. A host of Web services standards have been created to support such business processes (e.g., WS-transaction, Business Process Execution Language [BPEL], and Web Service Choreography Description Language [WSCDL]). Readers are referred to Weerawarana (2005) for details.
2. The application of semantic Web: Semantic tagging of the Web promises to bring dramatic changes to the cyber world. Once the semantics of Web services descriptions can be interpreted and understood by computers, the automatic discovery and composition of Web services will be much more powerful than the current approach (e.g., UDDI). Among the noteworthy emerging semantic Web services description protocols is the Ontology Web Language—Service (OWL-S)

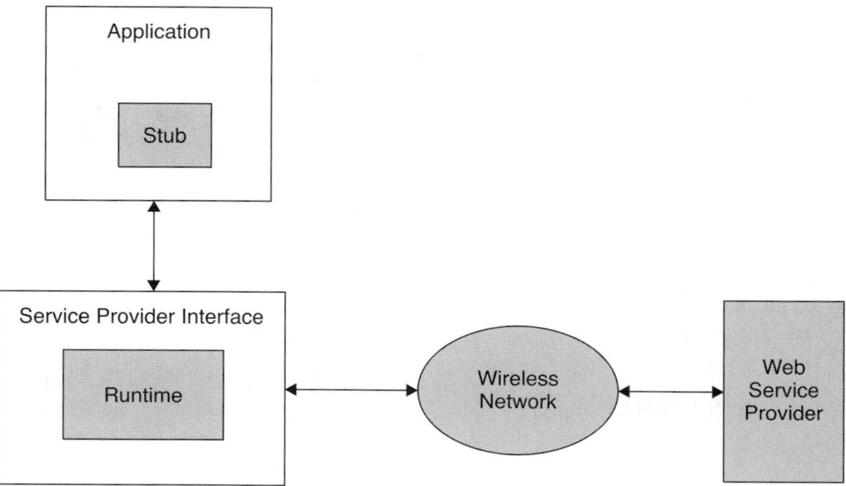

Figure 19: The Architecture of Web Services APIs (WSA) for Java ME

ontology standard. Readers are referred to Alesso and Smith (2004) for details.

CONCLUSION

The service-oriented architecture in general and Web services in particular hold great promise for networked applications.

Web services technology has received widespread attention from the information technologies (IT) community and computing industries, and has spawned a plethora of protocols and supporting technologies.

This chapter has provided an overview of the Web services technology and its underlying architectures and protocols. The key supporting protocols, including XML, XML-RPC, SOAP, WSDL, and UDDI, were presented, and the steps and tools for deploying Web services were explained. Also presented were the standards, the security concerns and technologies, and the current state of industrial acceptance of Web services.

Although Web services technology has attracted widespread attention, it has yet to fulfill its promise as a mainstream IT technology. Some of the major hurdles that the technology must overcome include security concerns, reliability, and performance. The overwhelming number of standards that have been developed by diverse organizations poses another challenge: sorting out these standards and ensuring their interoperability is a daunting task.

For now, the technology has found acceptance in Web-based commercial sites such as eBay, Amazon, and Google, which support direct access by the customer to the organization's business logic and database. The technology has also made headway on mobile platforms.

GLOSSARY

HTTP: Hypertext transfer protocol, the basic protocol that supports the transport of data over the World Wide Web.

OASIS: Organization for the Advancement of Structured Information Standards (www.oasis-open.org).

Service-Oriented Architecture (SOA): Software architecture that makes use of reusable services to support the requirements of software users.

SOAP: Simple object access protocol.

UDDI: Universal description, discovery, and integration.

W3C: The World Wide Web Consortium (http://www.w3.org/).

Web Services: Network services provided over HTTP.

WSDL: Web Services Description Language

WS-I: The Web Services Interoperability Organization (www.ws-i.org).

XML: Extensible markup language

XML-RPC: a remote procedure call protocol adapted to the Internet

CROSS REFERENCES

See *Application Service Providers (ASPs); Cryptography; TCP/IP Suite.*

REFERENCES

Alesso, and Smith. 2004. Developing semantic Web services. Wellesley, MA: A. K. Peters.

alphaWorks. 2006. ETTK for Web service: Overview. http://www.alphaworks.ibm.com/tech/ettkws (accessed August 1, 2006).

Amazon. 2006. http://www.amazon.com (accessed August 1, 2006).

BeVocal. 2006. VoiceXML 2.0. http://cafe.bevocal.com (accessed August 8, 2006).

Cantara, M. 2006. The SOA reality show: Insights from user survey analysis. http://blog.gartner.com/blog/index.php?blogid=34&archive=2006-12 (accessed August 8, 2006).

Channabasavaiah, K., K. Holley, and E. Tuggle Jr. 2003. Migrating to a service-oriented architecture. *IBM*. http://www-128.ibm.com/developerworks/library/ws-migratesoa/.

Chappell, D. A., and T. Jewell. 2002. *Java Web services*. Sebastopol, CA: O'Reilly Press.

Chappelle, R. 2004. Build a marketplace with the eBay SDK and Web services. *IBM*. http://www-128.ibm.com/developerworks/webservices/library/ws-buildebay/ (accessed August 8, 2006).

ComputerWorld. 2004. Web services hurdles. http://www.computerworld.com/developmenttopics/development/webservices/story/0,10801,95201,00.html (accessed July 18, 2007).

Dignan, L. 2002. Web services a decade away. CNET News. http://news.com.com/2100-1001-963179.html (accessed July 18, 2007).

eBay. 2006. My eBay Web services: eBay developers program. http://developer.ebay.com (accessed August 10, 2006).

Elkarra, N. 2003. A Web services strategy for mobile phones. http://webservices.xml.com/lpt/a/ws/2003/08/19/mobile.html (accessed July 18, 2007).

Erl, T. 2005. *Service-oriented architecture (SOA): Concepts, technology, and design*. Upper Saddle River, NJ: Prentice Hall.

FedEx. 2006. FedEx Web: Web integration—FedEx Shipping Tracking. http://fedex.com/us/solutions/wis/index.html (accessed July 23, 2006).

Fielding, R. 2000. Architectural styles and the design of network-based software architectures (dissertation, University of California, Irvine).

Google. 2006. SOAP search API—Home (beta). http://www.google.com/apis (accessed July 23, 2006).

Liberty Alliance Project. 2006. http://www.projectliberty.org/ (accessed July 18, 2007).

Liu, M. L. 2001. On the power of abstraction: A look at the paradigms and technologies in distributed applications. *Proceedings of the International Conference of Parallel and Distributed Processing Techniques and Applications*, Las Vegas, Nevada, June.

Microsoft. 2006. Microsoft Mappoint Web service. http://www.Microsoft.com/mappoint/products/webservice/default.mspx (accessed August 3, 2006).

Microsoft. 2003 .NET Compact Framework QuickStart tutorial. http://samples.gotdotnet.com/quickstart/CompactFramework/doc/xmlwebservice.aspx (accessed August 3, 2006).

Network World. 2006. WS-Federation. http://www.networkworld.com/details/6284.html (accessed July 18, 2007).

OASIS. 2004. UDDI executive overview: Enabling service-oriented architecture. (accessed August 3, 2006).

Prescod, P. 2002. Second generation Web services. *XML.com*. http://webservices.xml.com/pub/a/ws/2002/02/06/rest.html (accessed August 3, 2006).

Shodjai, P. 2006. Web services and the Microsoft platform. http://msdn.microsoft.com/webservices/default.aspx (accessed August 3, 2006).

Sun Microsystems. 2000. Jini network technology. http://www.sun.com/software/jini/ (accessed September 1, 2000).

———. 2006. The Java API for XML Web services (JAX-WS). http://java.sun.com/webservices/jaxws (accessed August 5, 2006).

Tellme Networks Inc. 2006. Studio. https://studio.tellme.com (accessed August 8, 2006).

Universal Description, Discovery, and Integration (UDDI). 2006. http://www.uddi.org/ (accessed August 8, 2006).

VoiceXML. 2006. Forum. http://www.voicexml.org (accessed August 9, 2006).

W3C Working Group. 2000. Voice extensible markup language (VoiceXML). http://www.w3.org/TR/voicexml/ (accessed August 3, 2006).

———. 2004. W3C Working Group note: Web services architecture. http://www.w3.org/TR/ws-arch (accessed August 3, 2006).

Weerawarana, S., Francisco, C., Leymann, F., Storey, T., and Ferguson, D. 2005. *Web services platform architecture: SOAP, WSDL, WS-Policy, WS-Addressing, WS-BPEL, WS-Reliable Messaging, and more*. Upper Saddle River, NJ: Prentice Hall.

Winer, D., and J. Savin. 2001. A busy developer's guide to SOAP 1.1. *SoapWare.org*. http://www.soapware.org/bdg (accessed August 3, 2006).

XML-RPC. 2006. http://www.xmlrpc.com (accessed August 4, 2006).

PART 3

Cellular and Wireless Networks

Cellular Communications Channels

Aarne Mämmelä, *VTT Technical Research Centre of Finland, Finland*
Risto Wichman, *Helsinki University of Technology, Finland*

INTRODUCTION

A mobile cellular system (Jakes 1974; Rappaport 2002) consists of base stations and mobile stations; the latter are also called *terminals*. The mobile stations communicate with each other through the base stations. Each mobile station uses a two-way wireless radio channel dedicated to it. The base stations usually communicate with each other through optical fibers. The area around a base station where communications with the base station are possible is called a *cell*. Thus, a set of base stations forms a *cellular system*, which ideally covers the whole world. The cells are partially overlapping so that continuous communications are possible when a mobile station moves from one cell to another. A handover is made when the cell is changed.

We will present an introduction to the cellular communications channels between a base station and a mobile station. The link between a base station to a mobile station is called a *downlink*. The link between a mobile station to a base station is called an *uplink*. Usually, the downlink and uplink are separated by using different frequencies. Nearby base stations must also use different frequencies to avoid interference. Frequencies for cellular systems are a scarce resource that must be efficiently used and the frequencies must be reused. In a typical reuse cluster, there are seven approximately hexagonal cells: the cell of interest and its six surrounding cells. All cells in the same cluster use different frequencies, and the corresponding cells in the other clusters reuse the same frequencies. The reuse is possible because the radio waves are attenuated when they are broadcasted in many directions and partially absorbed by the intervening medium. The interference can be further reduced if in a base station a cell is split into three sectors by using narrow-beam antennae.

Cellular communications channels are fundamentally different from wired ones. The quality of the channels changes rapidly as a function of time, frequency, and location or space when the users of the mobile stations are moving. These changes in quality propagate to higher protocol layers—that is, to the data-link layer and the network layer. Understanding the characteristics of the channels is paramount to the successful design of wireless networks.

The main emphasis in this chapter is on channel models for radio wave propagation in terrestrial outdoor mobile cellular systems in either microcells or macrocells. Most contemporary cellular systems, such as the *global system for mobile communications* (GSM), *enhanced data rates for GSM evolution* (commonly referred to as EDGE), cdmaOne, CDMA2000, and *universal mobile telecommunications system* (UMTS), typically work in the frequency range from approximately 1 GHz to 2 GHz with the corresponding wavelengths between 0.3 m and 0.15 m (the abbreviation CDMA refers to *code division multiple access*). The bandwidth of the transmitted signals is on the order of 100 kHz to 5 MHz. The fourth-generation systems that will be used in the 2010s are envisioned to use carrier frequencies as high as 5 GHz and 10-MHz to 100-MHz signal bandwidths. The velocity of a terminal can vary from the walking speed of approximately 5 km/h up to the maximum speed of trains, or from 250 km/h to 500 km/h.

The location of the base station antenna has a significant effect on channel modeling. In *microcells*, the cell radius is approximately 0.1 km to 1 km, and the base station antenna is below the rooftop level of the surrounding buildings. On the other hand, in *macrocells* the base station antenna is above the rooftop level, and the cell radius is approximately 1 km to 30 km. The area types are usually divided into *urban, suburban*, and *rural*, each of which may be nonhilly or hilly.

A radio channel is almost always linear (Bello 1963) (see Figure 1). Because of mobility, the channel is also time variant. The received signal is attenuated because of the path loss from the radio waves propagating in all directions and being partially absorbed by the intervening medium. Fading can be caused by shadowing when the propagation environment is changing significantly so that the path loss is changed randomly. This fading is typically much slower than the multipath fading caused by multipath propagation. Modem design is mainly affected by the faster multipath fading (Stein 1987), which can be normally assumed to be locally *wide sense stationary* (WSS).

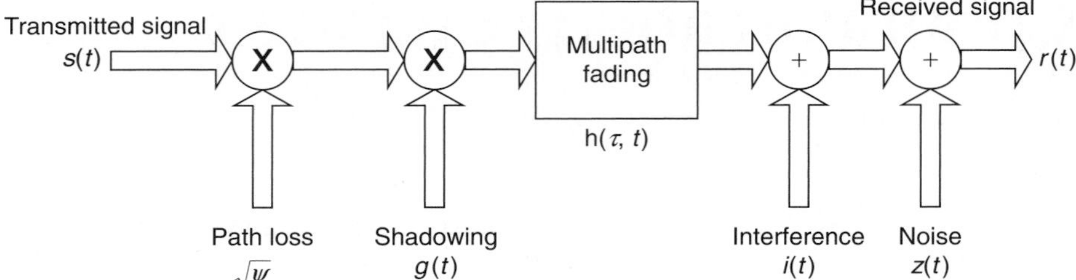

Figure 1: Several parts of the channel model

Thus, in many cases, only the multipath fading needs to be analyzed or simulated. The signal is also corrupted by additive noise and interference.

The chapter is organized as follows. First, we present the complex envelope of real bandpass signals. Second, we give a statistical description of one- and two-dimensional channel models. Third, we summarize the methods by which the channel is measured. Fourth, we describe widely available simulation models, and then we conclude by noticing recent trends in cellular communications channels. More extensive reviews are included in Pahlavan and Levesque (1995) and Rappaport (2002) for the one-dimensional models and in Ertel et al. (1998) for two-dimensional models. Models for indoor communications are summarized in Hashemi (1993). Much of the theory is valid also for outdoor communications. Our list of references is not exhaustive, and important work has been left out because of space limitations. Additional references can be found from the books and papers cited. We assume that the reader knows the basics of linear systems including the Fourier transform. All of the necessary information can be found from Haykin (1983).

COMPLEX ENVELOPE MODEL OF REAL BANDPASS SIGNALS

All signals that appear in nature are real. To make mathematical equations compact and simulations efficient, we use the *complex envelope* (Haykin 1983; Proakis 2001) or the low-pass equivalent model $s(t)$ of the actual real bandpass signal $s_B(t)$, which are both functions of time t. A bandpass signal $s_B(t)$, whose bandwidth is assumed to be $W < f_c$ where f_c is the carrier frequency, can be represented in two equivalent forms:

$$\begin{aligned} s_B(t) &= a(t)\cos[2\pi f_c t + \theta(t)] \\ &= s_{B,c}(t)\cos(2\pi f_c t) - s_{B,s}(t)\sin(2\pi f_c t) \end{aligned}$$

where $a(t) \geq 0$ and $\theta(t)$ are the amplitude or envelope and the phase of the signal $s_B(t)$, respectively. The phase $\theta(t)$ is measured with respect to the carrier $\cos(2\pi f_c t)$. The signals $s_{B,c}(t)$ and $s_{B,s}(t)$ are the in-phase and quadrature components of the signal $s_B(t)$, respectively, also measured with respect to the carrier $\cos(2\pi f_c t)$. The complex envelope is a complex-valued signal that includes all of the information about both the amplitude and phase modulation of the bandpass signal. A complex-valued signal, an ordered pair of two real signals, is an extension of the concept of a complex number.

It is easiest to understand the complex envelope concept in the frequency domain. When defining the complex envelope, we need the Hilbert transform $\hat{s}_B(t)$ of the original signal $s_B(t)$, or

$$\hat{s}_B(t) = \frac{1}{\pi}\int_{-\infty}^{\infty}\frac{s_B(t)}{t-\tau}d\tau \longleftrightarrow \hat{S}_B(f) = \begin{cases} -jS_B(f), f > 0 \\ +jS_B(f), f < 0 \end{cases}$$

where $\longleftrightarrow$ refers to a Fourier transform pair, τ is the delay, $S_B(f) = \int_{-\infty}^{\infty} s_B(t)\exp(-j2\pi ft)dt$ is the Fourier transform or spectrum of $s_B(t)$, j is the imaginary unit, and exp refers to a power of e ($e = 2.718\ldots$) so that $\exp(x) = e^x$. The Hilbert transformer shifts positive frequencies by $-\pi/2$ radians (rad) and negative frequencies by $+\pi/2$ rad ($j = e^{j\pi/2}$ and $j^2 = e^{j\pi} = -1$). We also note that for real signals the Fourier transform is symmetric, or $S_B(-f) = S_B^*(f)$, where the asterisk (*) refers to a complex conjugate. The complex envelope is defined to be

$$\begin{aligned} s(t) &= [s_B(t) + j\hat{s}_B(t)]\exp(-j2\pi f_c t) \longleftrightarrow S(f) \\ &= \begin{cases} 2S_B(f+f_c), f > -f_c \\ 0, f < -f_c. \end{cases} \end{aligned}$$

Because of the symmetry $S_B(-f) = S_B^*(f)$, no information is lost and the original bandpass signal can be computed from

$$\begin{aligned} s_B(t) &= \mathrm{Re}[s(t)\exp(j2\pi f_c t)] \leftrightarrow \\ S_B(f) &= \frac{1}{2}S^*(-f-f_c) + \frac{1}{2}S(f-f_c) \end{aligned}$$

where Re denotes the real part. For a complex number z, $\mathrm{Re}(z) = (1/2)(z^* + z)$. The complex envelope $s(t)$ is up-converted to the carrier frequency, and the spectrum at positive and negative frequencies divided by two appears when the real part of the signal is taken. The imaginary part includes the Hilbert transform of the original signal, or $\hat{s}_B(t) = \mathrm{Im}[s(t)\exp(j2\pi f_c t)]$.

We next derive the complex envelope for the bandpass signal $s_B(t) = s_{B,c}(t)\cos(2\pi f_c t) - s_{B,s}(t)\sin(2\pi f_c t)$ with $W < f_c$ (Haykin 1983). We first note that $\cos(x) = (1/2)[\exp(jx) + \exp(-jx)]$, $\sin(x) = (1/2j)[\exp(jx) - \exp(-jx)]$, and $\hat{s}_B(t) = s_{B,c}(t)\sin(2\pi f_c t) + s_{B,s}(t)\cos(2\pi f_c t)$ (Haykin 1983). Therefore, we obtain by direct substitution $s(t) = [s_B(t) + j\hat{s}_B(t)]\exp(-j2\pi f_c t) = s_{B,c}(t) + js_{B,s}(t)$, a surprisingly simple result that is valid when $W < f_c$ or the spectra $S^*(-f-f_c)$ and $S(f-f_c)$ at negative and positive frequencies do not overlap. Thus, the in-phase and quadrature components of the original signal are $s_{B,c}(t) = \mathrm{Re}[s(t)]$ and $s_{B,s}(t) = \mathrm{Im}[s(t)]$, respectively. In a similar way the magnitude of the complex envelope is the envelope of the original signal or $a(t) = |s(t)|$, and the phase is $\theta(t) = \arg[s(t)]$, where arg refers to the phase of $s(t)$. Each operation made for the complex envelope has a corresponding operation for the bandpass signal. In simulations, all of the signals are time-discrete and complex, but it is convenient to express the equations in a time-continuous form.

ADDITIVE NOISE AND INTERFERENCE

We assume that the noise $z(t) = z_c(t) + jz_s(t)$ is additive and WSS (Proakis 2001), usually added at the output of the channel model to the received signal (Figure 1). Here $z_c(t)$ and $z_s(t)$ are the real and imaginary parts of $z(t)$, respectively. According to the central limit theorem, the sum of many independent zero mean complex noise sources is approximately Gaussian, or its bivariate probability density function has the form

$$\begin{aligned} p_z(z) &= p_{z_c,z_s}(z_c,z_s) = p_{z_c}(z_c)p_{z_s}(z_s) \\ &= \frac{1}{2\pi\sigma^2}\exp[-(z_c^2+z_s^2)/2\sigma^2] \end{aligned}$$

where σ^2 is the variance of both $z_c(t)$ and $z_s(t)$, which are assumed to be uncorrelated. Thus, the probability density function is obtained by multiplying the marginal probability density functions $p_{z_c}(z_c)$ and $p_{z_s}(z_s)$.

We usually assume that the noise has an ideal autocorrelation function $\varphi_{zz}(t)$ or

$$\phi_{zz}(\tau) = E\{z(t+\tau)z^*(t)\} = N_0\delta(\tau) \longleftrightarrow \Phi_{zz}(f) = N_0$$

where τ is the delay, E denotes statistical mean, the asterisk (*) refers to complex conjugation, N_0 is a real nonnegative constant, $\delta(t)$ is the unit impulse function, and $\Phi_{zz}(f)$ is the noise power spectral density, which is uniform. The noise is called *white noise* with the power spectral density of N_0. We have used the Wiener-Khinchine relation, according to which the autocorrelation function and the power spectral density of a random signal form a Fourier transform pair.

Complex Gaussian noise $z(t)$ is easy to analyze because such noise will remain Gaussian in a linear system. White noise is not always Gaussian. The term *white* refers only to the form of the spectrum, not to the amplitude distribution. On the other hand, Gaussian noise can also be nonwhite or colored. No physical noise source can have an infinite bandwidth, which would imply an infinite variance or power. However, it is enough that the noise is white within the signal bandwidth because the noise outside the signal bandwidth is usually filtered. Thermal noise is approximately *additive white Gaussian noise* (AWGN). According to the information theory, AWGN is the most detrimental additive noise. Therefore, AWGN is by far the most common noise model.

In digital transmission, the channel model is usually normalized in such a way that the average received energy per bit E_b divided by the noise power spectral density N_0 obtains a reasonable value. The ratio E_b/N_0 must be above ln 2 or $10\lg(\ln 2) \approx -1.6$ decibels (dB), which is the Shannon limit (ln refers to natural logarithm of base e and lg refers to Brigg's logarithm of base 10). Below the Shannon limit it is not possible to obtain error-free transmission even in theory. The ratio E_b/N_0 cannot be made arbitrarily large in cellular communications systems because the transmitted energy is finite and users would interfere with each other. There are also safety reasons to limit the transmitted energy. Usually the ratio is below, say, 30 dB to 40 dB (Proakis 2001).

Cellular communications systems are also subject to impulsive noise such as automotive ignition noise and atmospheric noise. However, such noise types are usually not considered important in performance studies at the large frequencies of interest. In addition, the received signal usually includes some additive *multiple access interference* (MAI), $i(t)$, from other users of the channel (Rappaport 2002) (see Figure 1). In cellular systems, the same frequencies are used again at a distance where the channel path loss is large enough. Also, the filters in the system are never ideal. Thus, the MAI can be either co-channel or adjacent channel interference. Modeling of the interference is complicated because of the many parameters involved. For example, each interference source has its own channel model.

PATH LOSS AND SHADOWING

The radio waves are distributed to all directions from the transmitter antenna. In addition, in the signal path there are obstacles where the signal is further attenuated because of absorption. The total attenuation includes a mean that we call *path loss* and slow random changes that we call *shadowing*. We neglect multipath propagation for the time being. The received signal $r(t)$ without noise and multipath fading has the form (Proakis 2001)

$$r(t) = \sqrt{\psi}\,g(t)s(t)$$

where $\psi = P_r/P_t$ represents the path loss, P_t is the average transmitted power, P_r is the average received power at a given distance d from the base station, $g(t)$ is the shadowing, and $s(t)$ is the transmitted signal represented by the complex envelope (Figure 1).

Path Loss

There are several path loss models summarized in the literature (Rappaport 2002). For our purposes, it is enough to present the simplified path loss model (Goldsmith 2005):

$$\Psi = \frac{P_r}{P_t} = K\left(\frac{d_0}{d}\right)^{\gamma}$$

where $K < 1$ is a unitless constant that depends on the antenna characteristics and the average channel attenuation, d_0 is a reference distance for the antenna far field (typically 10 m to 100 m outdoors), d is the distance between the transmitter and the receiver ($d > d_0$), and γ is the path loss exponent. The constants K, d_0, and γ are usually determined from empirical measurements.

In free space, the path loss exponent is $\gamma = 2$. In urban microcells, the path loss exponent is 2.7 to 3.5; in urban macrocells, it is 3.7 to 6.5 (Goldsmith 2005).

Shadowing

The path loss depends not only on the distance but also on the objects in the signal path. The received power at a given distance is random. If the attenuation is expressed in decibels, then it is normally or Gaussian-distributed. Thus, a typical model for shadowing is log-normal with the probability density function $p_g(g)$ in the linear scale (Coulson, Williamson, and Vaughan 1998; Goldsmith 2005)

$$p_g(g) = \frac{\xi}{\sqrt{2\pi}\sigma_s g} \exp[-[\xi \ln(g) - \mu_s]^2/2\sigma_s^2], \; g \geq 0$$

where μ_s is the path loss (dB) averaged in decibels, σ_s is the standard deviation (dB) of the path loss averaged in decibels, and $\xi = 10/\ln 10$. Typically σ_s ranges from 4 dB to 13 dB in outdoor channels (Goldsmith 2005).

The attenuation resulting from shadowing is assumed to be a product of positive, random, and independent attenuation factors coming from the obstacles between the transmitter and the receiver. The logarithm of the product of several random variables is the sum of the logarithms of the random variables, and thus we can apply the central limit theorem to the sum, which is normally distributed. The product itself is therefore log-normally distributed.

Because of the nonlinearity of the logarithm function in the definition of decibels, the actual path loss averaged in the linear scale and presented in decibels is

$$\rho_s = 10 \lg \psi = \mu_s + \frac{\sigma_s^2}{2\xi}$$

It is the common practice that the path loss is averaged in the linear scale (Rappaport 2002).

Shadowing is typically caused by large objects in the signal path. For example, when a receiver is moving, a tall building may enter between the transmitter and the receiver, increasing the attenuation of the received signal. The receiver continues to move and, after some time, the building is no longer in the signal path and the power of the received signal increases again. Shadowing is essentially frequency-nonselective fading such that it affects all frequencies of the signal in a similar manner.

MULTIPATH FADING

A linear multipath fading channel is fully described by its time-variant impulse response $h(\tau, t)$ where τ is the delay and t is the time (Bello 1963; Proakis 2001). Early important work on WSS fading multipath channel models in a more general framework came from Turin, Kailath, and Bello in the 1950s and 1960s (Bello 1963; Kailath 1963; Turin 1980). The channel is equivalently characterized by its time-variant transfer function $H(f,t) = \int_{-\infty}^{\infty} h(\tau,t) \exp(-j2\pi f t)d\tau$, which is the Fourier transform of the impulse response with respect to the delay parameter (f is the frequency).

If the transmitted signal is denoted by $s(t)$, then the received signal $r(t)$, without path loss, shadowing, and interference and noise, is given by the convolution integral $r(t) = \int_{-\infty}^{\infty} s(t-\tau)\, h(t,\tau)d\tau$.

Alternatively, the received signal is $r(t) = \int_{-\infty}^{\infty} S(f)\, H(f,t)\, \exp(j2\pi f t)df$. We emphasize that the Fourier transform $R(f)$ of $r(t)$ is *not* $S(f)\, H(f,t)$ in time-variant systems: $R(f)$ is time-invariant, but $S(f)\, H(f,t)$ is time-variant. To compute $R(f)$, we need first to compute $r(t)$ and then find its Fourier transform. In general, the channel is frequency-selective, implying that different frequencies are affected differently. Frequency selectivity comes from the memory of the impulse response on the delay axis. If $H(f,t)$ depends only on time t and not on frequency f, the then channel is frequency-nonselective and we denote its transfer function by $H(t)$. In that case, we find that $r(t) = \int_{-\infty}^{\infty} S(f)\, H(t)\, \exp(j2\pi f t)df = H(t)s(t)$. Therefore, a special case of convolution is multiplication.

The magnitude $|H(f,t)|$ of the transfer function at a given frequency f is changing randomly in time, and we say that the mobile radio channel is a *fading* channel. The phase $\arg[H(f,t)]$ is also a random function of time. Multipath fading is caused by multipath propagation resulting from reflection, scattering, and diffraction of the radio waves from nearby objects such as buildings, vehicles, hills, and mountains.

In the following discussion, we neglect the amplitude changes of the multipath components themselves for simplicity. Multipath fading is easiest to understand when an unmodulated carrier $\cos(2\pi f t)$ at a certain frequency $f = c/\lambda$ is used as a test signal where λ is the wavelength and c is the velocity of the radio waves. When the mobile station is moved, the path length $d(t)$ of each multipath component changes randomly, and therefore the delay $\tau(t) = d(t)/c$ is changed. Thus, the received signal is a sum of attenuated carriers of the form $\cos[2\pi f[t - \tau(t)]] = \cos[2\pi f t + \varphi(t,f)]$, whose phases $\varphi(t,f) = -2\pi f \tau(t)$ are randomly changing.

There can be additional phase changes—for example, in reflections—but we neglect them for the time being. Multipath fading is a result from addition of such carriers with randomly and independently changing phases, which can cause either constructive or destructive fading when the carriers are added in the same phase or in the opposite phase, respectively.

If the delay $\tau(t)$ is changed only by $\lambda/2$, then the phase $\varphi(t,f)$ at a given frequency is changed by $-\pi$ rad. This means that the mobile station needs to be changed only a few tens of centimeters, and the fading may change from constructive to destructive or vice versa. We say that the fading channel is *time-selective*—that is, the attenuation depends on time. The phases $\varphi(t,f)$ depend on frequency for the same delay $\tau(t)$, and thus the channel is in general also frequency-selective—that is, the attenuation depends on frequency. For a given delay $\tau(t)$ at a certain time t, the phase $\varphi(t,f)$ is changed by $-\pi$ rad if the frequency

f is changed by $1/2\tau(t)$. With respect to a stationary base station, multipath propagation creates a random frequency-dependent standing wave pattern through which the mobile station moves (Stein 1987).

The changing delays also cause a Doppler effect. For simplicity, let us consider only the *line-of-sight* (LOS) component coming directly from the base station. A similar phenomenon occurs for all multipath components. The velocity of the mobile station v is assumed to be constant. The delay is linearly changing according to $\tau(t) = \tau_0 - vt \cos \alpha_v/c$, where τ_0 is the initial delay, and α_v is the angle between the half line from the mobile station toward the base station and the velocity vector. The received carrier has the form $\cos\{2\pi f[t - \tau(t)]\} = \cos[2\pi (f + f_m \cos\alpha_v)t + \varphi_0]$, where $f_m = (v/c)f_c$ is the Doppler frequency—that is, the maximum frequency shift when $\alpha_v = 0$ and $\varphi_0 = -2\pi f\tau_0$ is the initial phase. The frequency shift resulting from the Doppler effect in this case is $\Delta f = f_m \cos \alpha_v$. It is positive when the delay τ is decreasing ($|\alpha_v| < \pi/2$). It is negative when the delay is increasing.

Some modern systems use directive antennae to direct the antenna beam toward the desired transmitter or receiver and to reject the interfering signals. Another way to use multiple antennae is to place them far enough from each other so that transmitted and received signals experience independent fading channels. These antenna arrays provide *diversity* and *spatial multiplexing* gain, but antenna patterns do not have directional interpretation. Conventionally, only horizontal directions are taken into account. In such systems, the direction of arrival of the received signals as well as the azimuthal power gain of the antenna are important concepts, and the models are *two-dimensional* (2D). The two dimensions are the delay and the azimuth, whereas in *one-dimensional* (1D) models the only dimension is the delay. All of the models are dependent on time, but in this case time is not counted as a dimension. Important early work on 2D models has been done by Clarke in the 1960s (Ertel et al. 1998). However, elevation is important in single-frequency networks as in the UMTS, where intercell interference and cell coverage can be effectively controlled by tilting base station antennae mechanically or electronically (Laiho, Wacker, and Novosad 2002). In CDMA systems, all of the cells can use the same frequencies because of the immunity of CDMA receivers to interference.

The channel models are used for performance analysis and simulations of mobile systems. The models can also be used for simplified measurements in a controlled environment to guarantee repeatability and to avoid the expensive measurements in the field because only the statistical parameters of the model need to be measured. However, any model is only an approximation of the actual propagation in the field. For measurements, the average received *signal-to-noise ratio* (SNR) must be defined. It is estimated by making a link power budget (Proakis 2001) that includes the transmitter power, distance-dependent attenuation of the channel, antenna gains in the transmitter and receiver, and various loss factors and margins. It depends on the system designer whether a margin for fading is taken into account or whether the performance simulations or measurements with the channel model will include fading. The power of additive noise is also estimated for modeling purposes.

One-Dimensional Models

The multipath fading model is either one-dimensional or two-dimensional. We will first consider 1D models, which are described by the time-variant impulse response and transfer function (Bello 1963; Proakis 2001). If the transmitted signal has a bandwidth of W, then the delay resolution of the measurement is approximately $1/W$, which means that the receiver cannot resolve delay differences smaller than $1/W$. We define such unresolved multipath components as clusters on the delay axis (Turin 1980). The receiver can resolve multipath components whose delay differences are larger than $1/W$. We will apply the central limit theorem for the clusters.

The impulse response has the general form $h(\tau,t) = \sum_{l=0}^{L-1} h_l\ (t)\ \delta(\tau - \tau_l)$, where L is the number of resolvable clusters whose complex amplitudes are $h_l(t)$ and delays are τ_l. Because the channel is random, we need a stochastic description for it. The delays of the clusters are usually assumed to be constant in channel models because they are changing slowly compared to the time interval $1/W$, but it must be noted that fading is mainly caused by the randomly changing delays, which change the relative phase shift between the multipath components within the clusters.

If several multipath signals caused by scattering with approximately equal amplitudes, or alternatively with random amplitudes, are added at random phases, then the resultant has a complex Gaussian distribution with a zero mean. The amplitude of such a cluster is Rayleigh distributed and the phase is uniformly distributed. The channel is then said to be a *Rayleigh fading channel*. Alternatively, if in addition to the scattered components, the received signal includes a strong component, which is either an LOS signal coming directly from the transmitter or from a specular reflection, the impulse response at that delay will have a Gaussian distribution with a nonzero mean, and the amplitude is Ricean distributed. In this case, the channel is a *Ricean fading channel*. In both Rayleigh and Ricean fading channels, only the first- and second-order statistics, including the mean and autocorrelation functions, are needed to fully describe them. A more general description is the covariance matrix of a discretized impulse response.

For multipath fading, a widely used model is a *wide sense stationary uncorrelated scattering* (WSSUS) model (Bello 1963). It is WSS with respect to the time variable. *Uncorrelated scattering* means that the autocorrelation function of the WSS Rayleigh fading impulse response has the form $E[h^*(\tau,t)\ h(\tau + \Delta\tau, t + \Delta t)] = P_h(\tau, \Delta t)\ \delta(\Delta\tau)$, or there is no correlation on the τ axis but some correlation may exist on the time axis. The function $P_h(\tau, \Delta t)$ is the autocorrelation of the impulse response at the delay τ with the time difference Δt. With the time difference $\Delta t = 0$, we obtain the average power density $P_h(\tau, 0) = P_h(\tau) = E\,[|h\ (\tau, t)|^2]$ of the impulse response at the delay τ, and the average is taken over time t. Therefore, the function $P_h(\tau)$ is called the *delay power spectrum* of the channel. The impulse response is nonstationary white noise in the delay variable. It can be shown that in a WSSUS channel the transfer function is WSS also with respect to the frequency variable (Bello 1963).

The Fourier transform of $P_h(\tau, \Delta t)$ with respect of the time difference Δt is the *scattering function* $S(\tau, \Delta f)$ of the channel (Bello 1963; Proakis 2001), or $S(\tau, \Delta f) = \int_{-\infty}^{\infty} P_h(\tau, \Delta t) \exp(-j2\pi\Delta f\, \Delta t)d\Delta t$, where Δf is the frequency shift. For a given delay τ, the scattering function as a function of Δf is the power spectral density of the impulse response. The function $S(\tau, \Delta f)$ is thus a measure of the average power density as a function of the time delay τ and the frequency shift Δf. The delay power spectrum is $P_h(\tau) = \int_{-\infty}^{\infty} S(\tau, \Delta f)d\Delta f$. If we transmit several times a narrow pulse through the multipath channel with a large enough spacing so that the received responses are not overlapping and then average the received power density on the delay axis, the result has approximately the form of the delay power spectrum. The *Doppler power spectrum* is $S_H(\Delta f) = \int_{-\infty}^{\infty} S(\tau, \Delta f)d\tau$. If we transmit an unmodulated carrier through the fading channel, the carrier is modulated by the channel, and the received power spectral density has approximately the form of the Doppler power spectrum.

The width of the delay power spectrum is referred to as the *multipath spread*, and the width of the Doppler power spectrum is referred to as the *Doppler spread*. A suitable engineering definition is used for the width. The channel is frequency-nonselective or flat fading if the signal bandwidth W is much smaller than the inverse of the multipath spread, or the coherence bandwidth; otherwise the channel is frequency-selective. The Doppler spread and its inverse, or the coherence time, are measures of the rapidity of fading.

A typical approximation for the delay power spectrum is exponential with respect to the delay variable τ. A typical approximation for the Doppler power spectrum is $S_H(\Delta f) = (1/\pi f_m)[1 - (\Delta f/f_m)^2]^{-1/2}$, where $f_m = (v/c)f_c$ is the Doppler frequency, v is the velocity of the mobile station, and f_c is the carrier frequency. This Doppler power spectrum is based on the assumption that the multipath components arrive at the omnidirectional antenna uniformly from all horizontal directions. It is often referred to as *Jakes's Doppler power spectrum* (Jakes 1974) even though it was derived earlier by Clarke (Rappaport 2002). This is a reasonable approximation in cellular communications systems where scatterers are located close to mobile stations.

At any time instant, the multipath components arrive from distinct directions, but when the mobile station is moving in the scattering environment and the received directions are averaged over time, the average received direction becomes uniformly distributed. Conversely, scatterers are located far away from high-elevated base station antennae, especially in macrocells, and the azimuthal power spectrum of the received signal can be parameterized by Laplacian distribution (Pedersen, Mogensen, and Fleury 2000). In *wireless local area networks* (WLANs), transmitters and receivers are stationary and Doppler power spectrum is caused by moving objects, such as people and vehicles, in the propagation environment. Thus, characteristics of Doppler power spectrum in WLANs are different from those in cellular systems.

In addition to Rayleigh and Ricean distributions, a useful amplitude distribution for the multipath fading is a *Nakagami-m distribution* (Proakis 2001), which is, in fact, a form of the generalized Rayleigh distribution. When selecting a suitable distribution, one should note that for system performance, the most notable effect has the distribution at small amplitudes (Stein 1987).

Two-Dimensional Models

Fourth-generation research targets to wide bandwidths and peak throughputs as high as 1 Gbit/s. Although bandwidths as high as 100 MHz are envisioned, the proposed data rate target is especially challenging because it assumes spectral efficiency as high as 10 bit/s/Hz; current cellular systems achieve the spectral efficiency of 0.05 bit/s/Hz to 2 bit/s/Hz. Multiantenna transceivers are generally considered as one of the most efficient options to increase the spectral efficiency, and 2D and even 3D channel models are needed to develop and analyze such transceivers.

The most attractive feature of *multiple-input multiple-output* (MIMO) channels using many antennae in the transmitter or receiver is that the capacity of these channels increases linearly as a function of the number of transmitter or receiver antennae. If the numbers of antennae in the transmitter and receiver are different, then we use the smaller of the two numbers. The increase of the capacity in MIMO systems is remarkable because the capacity of *single-input single-output* (SISO) channels increases only logarithmically as a function of SNR (Proakis 2001). This seriously limits the spectral efficiency of SISO systems in cellular communications channels because large transmitter powers create large interference in cellular systems.

The high spectral efficiency of MIMO systems results from their capability of spatial multiplexing in the case of rich scattering environment. This is illustrated in Figure 2 by using the angular domain decomposition (Sayeed 2002) of MIMO channels and the clustering phenomenon (Saleh and Valenzuela 1987) of multipath components. Channel measurements have shown that multipath components tend to arrive in clusters, with each cluster of signal paths resulting from a group of scattering objects in the propagation environment. Such a group can consist of, for example, nearby walls in an office.

The resolution of the antenna arrays in the angular domain determines how many signal paths can be separated in the receiver. This is analogous to the resolvability of band-limited signals in the time domain where the receiver is not able to resolve delay differences shorter than $1/W$. In the same vein, an antenna array of length L is not able to separate signals whose directional cosines with respect to the antenna array differ less than $1/L$. This is illustrated in Figure 2 where the receiver antenna array has four different angular sectors numbered from 1 to 4. All sectors of the receiver antenna array are excited by signal components resulting from different clusters of scatterers. In contrast, if there were only one cluster of scatterers, then all signal paths would arrive in the same sector. Signals that arrive from the same angular sector cannot be separated in the receiver; in Figure 2, these signal components are scattered from the same cluster of scatterers. Thus, the performance of the MIMO system depends intimately on the structure of the scattering environment and the resolution of the antenna arrays.

Examples for possible structures of MIMO channels are depicted in the bottom part of Figure 2, where the

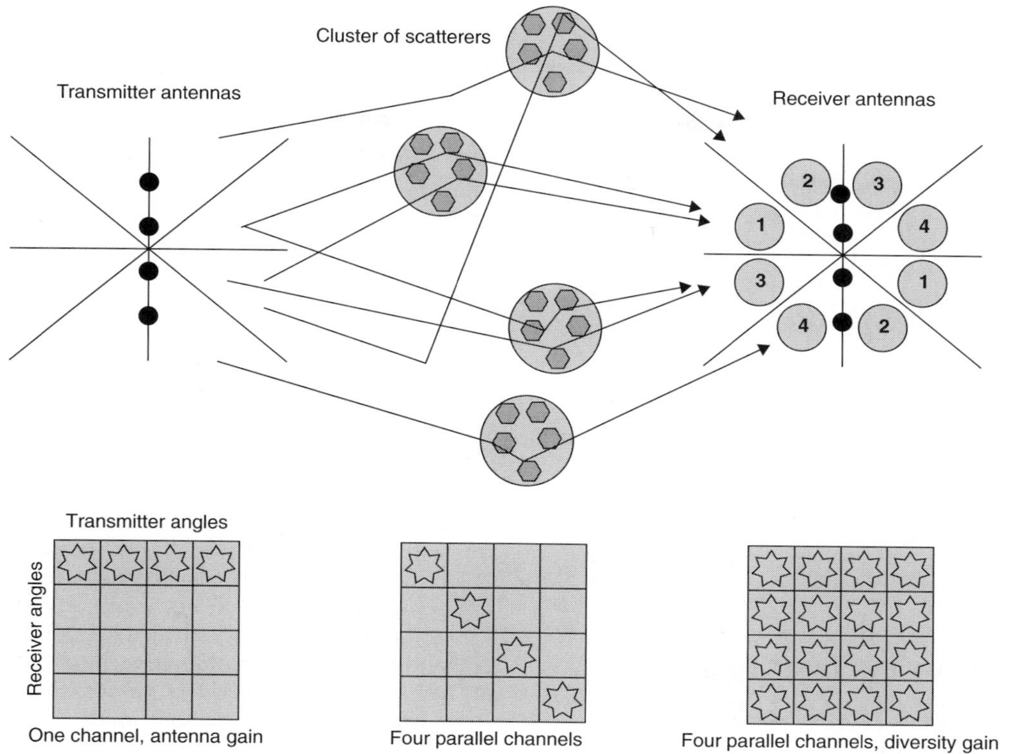

Figure 2: Schematic representation of a MIMO channel in angular domain and examples of coupling between transmitter and receiver angles

stars indicate that corresponding received and angular sectors are connected by a cluster of scatterers. In the leftmost case, the transmission is received by one angular sector, and the received signal has a clear direction. Spatial multiplexing is not possible, and the capacity increases logarithmically, but the system obtains an SNR gain. In the central box, one transmitter sector is connected to exactly one receiver sector. Now a MIMO system can set up four parallel channels that do not interfere with each other. Medium access control could then acknowledge that the transceiver is able to support four parallel links. However, this case is highly improbable in wireless channels unless the transmitter knows the forward channel, which enables it to form four orthogonal transmitter beams. The rightmost case corresponds to a situation in which all angular transmitter sectors contribute to all receiver sectors. This is the case in rich scattering environment where the capacity of MIMO system increases linearly as a function of the number of transceiver antennae even when the transmitter has no information on the forward channel (Telatar 1999). A lot of research have been devoted to modeling the structure of the 2D scattering environment and its effect on the performance of MIMO systems.

The 1D WSSUS model can be generalized to the 2D case as follows. The azimuth or the angle of arrival relative to the velocity vector of the mobile station is denoted by α. As previously, the multipath components are combined into clusters in space with a delay resolution of $1/W$ and with an angular resolution $\Delta\alpha$ of the receiver antenna. Each cluster has a Rayleigh or Ricean fading amplitude. Each complex gain of the impulse response has now the general form $h_l(t) = \sum_{n=0}^{N-1} a_{ln} \exp[j(\varphi_{ln} + 2\pi f_m t\cos(\alpha_{ln}))]$, where α_{ln} is the azimuth of arrival, φ_{ln} is the phase of the nth component in the lth delay, and N is the number of components in the model at the lth delay. As a generalization of the delay power spectrum, we can define an *azimuthal delay power spectrum* that shows the distribution of the received power versus azimuth and delay.

For a given velocity and direction of the mobile station, and for a given azimuthal power gain of the antenna, the azimuthal delay power spectrum corresponds to a certain scattering function of the WSSUS channel (see Figure 3).

The scattering function is an aliased form of the azimuthal delay power spectrum because two different azimuths α_{ln} and $-\alpha_{ln}$ of arriving clusters create the same frequency shift because of the cosine function in $h_l(t)$. Given a uniform distribution $p_\alpha(\alpha)$ for the received power in mobile station, we obtain Clarke's Doppler power spectrum given earlier; because of the reciprocity of the channel, the Doppler power spectrum is the same in the base station as well. However, azimuthal power spectra in the base station and the mobile station are in general different because the signal received by the high elevated base station antennae has a clear mean direction of arrival. Azimuthal spectrum does not affect the Doppler power spectrum in the base station because the Doppler power spectrum is generated by scatterers around the mobile station. Angular domain decomposition as sketched in Figure 2 further

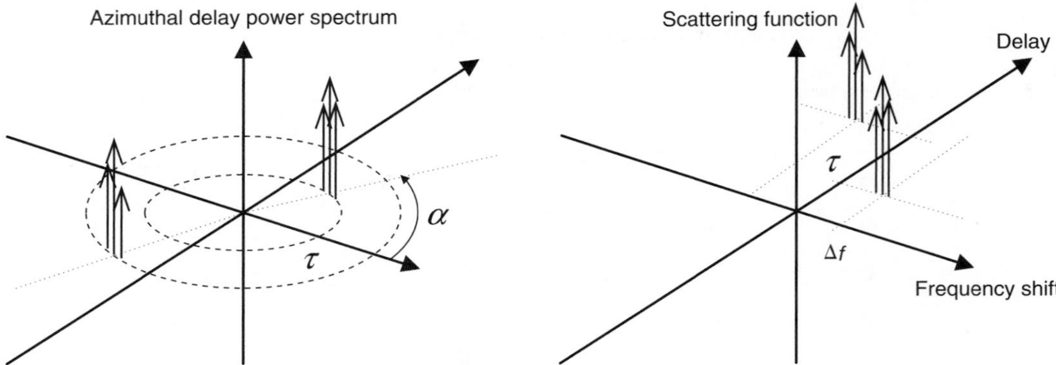

Figure 3: Azimuthal delay power spectrum and scattering function of the channel

increases the detail level in 2D models aiming to resolve the channel as $h_l(t, \alpha, \beta)$, where β refers to the azimuth of departure—that is, each receiver angle is mapped to the corresponding transmitter angle.

MEASUREMENT OF LINEAR TIME-VARIANT CHANNELS

Channel measurements can be divided into narrowband and wideband measurements. Wideband measurements use measurement signals, which have about the same bandwidth as the intended information signal. Unlike narrowband measurements, which use a single unmodulated carrier as a measurement signal, wideband measurements provide information on the multipath propagation as well as frequency selectivity of the channel. Therefore, only wideband measurements are discussed here. The measurements can also be divided into measurement of (1) instantaneous values of the impulse response and (2) the average parameters of the channel. The average parameters include first- and second-order statistics, or the mean and the autocorrelation function of the impulse response, and the scattering function of the channel. Several ways to perform systematic measurements have been listed in Hewitt and Vilar (1988) and Pahlavan and Levesque (1995).

The problem of the measurement of system functions of time-variant channels differs from that of the time-invariant case. Even in the absence of noise, the system function of a time-variant channel may be unmeasurable. The condition on the measurability of a linear time-varying WSSUS channel was first presented by Kailath (1963) and later extended in Bello (1969). It turns out that the channel measurability depends on the value of the area spread factor, which is the area of region where the scattering function is effectively nonzero. If the area spread factor is less than or equal to a threshold, then the channel impulse response could be measured unambiguously (Bello 1969). The value of the threshold is on the order of unity. The channels for which the area spread factor fulfills the criterion mentioned above are called *underspread;* otherwise, they are called *overspread*. If the channel is overspread, then it is not possible to measure the instantaneous values of the impulse response, even in the absence of the noise. Fortunately, most physical channels are underspread. The average parameters can be determined either from the instantaneous values of the channel impulse response or by cross-correlation methods. Because the statistical averages contain much less information than the instantaneous values, the channel need not always be underspread before the average parameters could be measured.

Two practical methods to measure the impulse response of the underspread cellular channel can be identified (Hewitt and Vilar 1988). One method is to transmit an extremely short impulse-like pulse to the channel and observe the multiple pulses received. To follow the time variation of the channel, the pulses need to be transmitted periodically. The short pulses result in a high ratio of peak to average transmission power, which could be undesirable. Another, more efficient method to measure the impulse response is the use of direct sequence spread-spectrum signals (Pahlavan and Levesque 1995). A pseudonoise sequence is used to modulate the carrier. *Maximal length sequences* (m sequences) are widely used because of their excellent periodic autocorrelation properties.

The receiver is based on a correlation principle. It can be implemented by a matched filter or a sliding correlator (Hewitt and Vilar 1988). Nowadays, high-speed digital signal-processing techniques can be employed to implement real-time matched filter channel sounders. In a WSSUS channel, time averaging can be used to obtain the autocorrelation function of the measured impulse response. An estimate of the scattering function can then be computed by the Fourier transform (Braun and Dersch 1991; Dersch and Zollinger 1994). Angle of arrival measurements can be conducted by using directional or array antennae at the receiver (Ertel et al. 1998). To some extent, angle of arrival can be deduced from the estimated scattering function (Braun and Dersch 1991). The number of samples in the spatial domain is strictly limited by the number of receiver antennae, and therefore high-resolution estimation techniques such as *multiple signal classification* and *space-alternating generalized expectation maximization* are often applied to estimate azimuthal directions.

One of the earliest measurement results of the impulse response of the cellular channel in urban and suburban areas by using short pulses were reported by Turin et al. in 1972 (Turin 1980). The delay, amplitude, and phase of multipath components were measured at three different frequencies simultaneously. It was found that spatial correlation distances of these variables at neighboring geographical points varied considerably. They ranged from less than a wavelength for the phases, through tens of wavelengths for the amplitudes and delays, to hundreds of wavelengths for the means and variances, or powers, of the amplitudes.

More recent measurement studies have used almost exclusively the direct sequence spread-spectrum signals with m-sequences to measure the channel. Wideband macrocell measurements conducted at 1 GHz show that in typical urban areas the multipath spread from 1 μs to 2 μs is characteristic. In suburban areas, multipath spreads from 10 μs to 20 μs are typical. The longest multipath spreads occur in mountainous environments where multipath spreads from 100 μs to 150 μs have been encountered. In open areas, the multipath spread is practically nonexistent and the received signal consists of the directly propagated LOS component only (Braun and Dersch 1991). Wideband measurements in urban microcell environments at 2 GHz have been reported in Dersch and Zollinger (1994). The delay power spectrum, average normalized correlation functions, and scattering functions have been computed from the measured impulse response. Under LOS conditions, the direct component with unresolvable specular reflections dominated the propagation. Some resolvable specular reflections existed at multipath spreads of as much as 1.5 μs.

In non-LOS situations, the powers of the strongest received signals were more than 15 dB below the LOS components that resulted in nearby locations. The propagation process was found to be dominated by multiple reflections and scattering along the streets, not by diffraction (Dersch and Zollinger 1994).

Several results on spatial channel measurements have been published in recent years. Some results have been summarized in Ertel et al. (1998). Measurements conducted at 2 GHz with a 10 MHz bandwidth, by using a rotating azimuth beam directional antenna at the receiver, have shown that delay and angle of arrival spreads are small in rural, suburban, and even many urban environments. Measurements in urban areas have shown that most of the major features of the delay and angle of arrival spectra can be accounted for by considering the large buildings in the environment. Finally, the variation in the spatial characteristics with both time and frequency have been measured. The results indicate that the uplink spatial characteristics cannot be directly applied for downlink beam forming in most current cellular and personal communication systems that have 45 MHz and 80 MHz of separation between the uplink and downlink frequencies, respectively (Ertel et al. 1998).

True spatio-temporal measurements of the time-varying channel would require multichannel sounders, which are complex and expensive. To this end, simpler measurement techniques have been developed in which the location of a single receiver antenna is altered with a predetermined pattern or a receiver is connected to one element of an antenna array at a time using a fast switch at the radio frequency (Kalliola et al. 2003). Finding the coupling between transmitter and receiver angles requires a large number of parameters to be estimated and fitting measurements to a deterministic model becomes cumbersome when the number of antennae in the model is increasing. The number of estimated parameters can be reduced by using stochastic channel models.

SIMULATION MODELS

Simulation models are divided into link and system level models. Both of them are considered in this section.

Link-Level Simulation Models

The evolution of channel simulation models has been parallel to that of cellular systems. The early models considered only the signal amplitude level distributions and Doppler spreads of the received signals. Frequency selectivity was later added to the channel models. In addition to those, modern channel models include also such concepts as angle of arrival and adaptive array antenna geometries. The signal parameters that need to be simulated in these models for each multipath component are the amplitude, carrier phase shift, time delay, angle of arrival, and frequency shift. In general, all of these parameters are time varying, causing Doppler spread in addition to multipath spread (Ertel et al. 1998).

The channel simulators can be categorized into three classes according to the way the channel impulse response is modeled: stored channel impulse response, ray tracing models, and stochastic parametric models for the channel impulse response. The stored channel impulse responses are based on selected measurements, which are then stored for later use. Although this method provides actual information from the channel, the proper selection criteria for the measurements may be difficult to identify. Also, the large amount of data needed to store the measurement results could be difficult to handle. However, some models have been proposed in Ertel et al. (1998) and Fleury and Leuthold (1996). The ray tracing models are deterministic. They are based on geometric propagation theory and reflection, diffraction, and scattering models. Accurate channel models are possible using this method. However, the high computational burden and lack of detailed terrain and building databases make these models difficult to use (Ertel et al. 1998).

By far the most popular channel simulation models are stochastic parametric models. In this approach, the channel impulse response is characterized by a set of deterministic and random parameters. The values of the parameters and the probability distributions governing their behavior are selected according to measurements. Such models are easy to use and fast when compared to ray tracing. The remaining challenge is to develop models that exhaustively reproduce the propagation scenarios accounted in reality (Fleury and Leuthold 1996). A recommended summary of stochastic channel models can be found in Fleury and Leuthold (1996). Spatial or 2D stochastic channel models are summarized in Ertel et al. (1998) and Yu and Ottersten (2002).

Usually, discrete-time channel impulse responses in the form of transversal filters are used in the stochastic channel simulators. The transversal filter model allows the simulators to be implemented either by software or hardware. The time-varying complex coefficients and delays of the transversal filter are generated according to the statistics associated with the different parameters. In 2D models, the filter taps are matrices instead of scalars as in 1D models. The matrices capture the spatial structure of each delay tap. The amplitudes are usually assumed to be Rayleigh or Ricean distributed because of multipath fading. A uniform and Poisson distribution is usually assumed for the phases and delays, respectively. However, in a Ricean fading channel, the phase is concentrated around the phase of the strong component unless there is a frequency shift in it.

As mentioned earlier, the delay power spectrum is typically approximated by an exponential function. There are several methods to simulate the angles of arrival. For example, in Olmos et al. (1999), they are modeled as normally distributed random variables. Other methods have been summarized in Ertel et al. (1998). Rayleigh and Ricean processes needed to simulate the amplitudes can be generated by using filtered complex Gaussian noise processes. Typically, the Doppler power spectrum by Clarke is used, but its limitations mentioned earlier should be noted. Several alternative Doppler power spectra are listed in Simon and Alouini (2005), including rectangular, Gaussian, and first- and second-order Butterworth spectra.

A well-known method to produce colored Gaussian noise processes is to filter WGN with a filter having a transfer function of the square root of the Doppler power spectrum. Another method is based on Rice's sum of sinusoids. In this case, a colored Gaussian noise process is approximated by a finite sum of weighted and properly designed sinusoids (Pätzold 2002). The long-term variations in the channel impulse response can be modeled by making the delays drift with time and by using an attenuation filter to model the log-normal fading caused by shadowing or transitions between different environments (Fleury and Leuthold 1996).

An exponential function is used to approximate the autocorrelation function of the shadowing as a function of distance (Gudmundson 1991), corresponding to the first-order Butterworth filter in a simulation model (Simon and Alouini 2005). A correlation distance on the order of 10 m is typically used for microcells. For macrocells, much larger correlation distances on the order of 100 m should be used. This implies that shadowing tends to be faster in microcells than in macrocells at the same terminal velocity. Because the wavelength is at most a few tens of centimeters, this also implies that shadowing is much slower than multipath fading for which the correlation distance is usually less than the wavelength. A model useful for multiple cells is presented in Viterbi (1995). In a hardware implementation, digitally controllable attenuators can be used to simulate the attenuation caused by the shadowing (Olmos et al. 1999).

Different standardization organizations are actively defining channel models as a part of the specifications of new mobile cellular systems. Their motivation is to specify the operational environment of the system and provide test parameters for manufacturers. The channel models for the second-generation digital advanced mobile phone system and the GSM mobile cellular systems were specified by the Telecommunications Industry Association in the United States and by the European Telecommunications Standards Institute in Europe. For the third-generation cellular systems, a global standard has been defined as the International Mobile Telecommunications 2000 (IMT2000) proposal by the International Telecommunication Union. For a more thorough discussion, see Pahlavan and Levesque (1995). Lately, the standardization work of the third-generation systems has been shifted to the international 3rd Generation Partnership Project (3GPP) and 3GPP2 in the United States.

The channel models have also been developed by different research consortia in international research programs. In Europe, the Cooperation in the Field of Scientific and Technical Research (COST) projects have been extremely influential when the GSM and digital communication system at 1800 MHz (DCS 1800) systems were developed. The achievements in the COST 259 project partly stimulated the UMTS Code-Division Testbed (CODIT) project within the Research and Development in Advanced Communication Technologies in Europe II (RACE II) program. The CODIT 2D channel models are directional models with multiple antennae in the base station and a single antenna in the mobile station. Recent channel models developed in COST 273 and in the Intelligent MultiElement Transmit and Receive Antennae (I-METRA) and Wireless World Initiative New Radio (WINNER) projects, funded also by the European Union, concentrate on MIMO models. Two-dimensional channel models have also been developed within IEEE 802.11n and IEEE 802.16e standardization.

System-Level Simulation Models

Link-level simulations are not enough to assess the performance of cellular communication system, but system-level simulations are required. Detailed modeling of cellular communications systems is still too demanding computationally, which gives rise to simplified approaches. According to the two-stage approach described in Holma and Toskala (2002), link-level simulations in the resolution defined by the signal bandwidth are first performed to obtain required quality-of-service (QoS) values for different services and mobile classes. This information is further compressed to radio frame resolution and used as an input for a system simulator. The resolution in time drops from 1/3.84 MHz in link-level simulations to 1/1.5 kHz in system-level simulations.

Multidimensional MIMO channels cannot be described with a single QoS value, and large downsampling ratios in the time domain would lose important information on MIMO links. The *spatial channel model* (SCM) introduced in the 3GPP forum (3GPP 2003) divides into link-level and system-level models in which the link-level model is used for calibration purposes. The computational burden in the system-level simulation is reduced by adopting a quasi-static approach. The network is simulated in snapshots (or *drops* in 3GPP parlance), and the performance metrics are averaged over several drops. Large-scale characteristics such as the positions of mobile stations are randomly generated at the beginning of each drop, and they remain fixed within the drop. Small-scale characteristics such as wireless channel and MAI for each mobile station are evolving during a drop. A software implementation of SCM and its extension have been described in Baum, Hansen, and Salo (2005).

CONCLUSION

Channel modeling for cellular communications is a rapidly changing area, and the models are becoming more and more accurate. Some of the recent trends are summarized here. Higher frequencies as high as approximately 60 GHz will be used in the future. The cell size is made smaller because the channel attenuation is larger at higher frequencies. Frequencies above approximately 10 GHz are also affected more by air molecules and rain. Consequently, the highest frequencies can only be used in indoor environments. Also, with the increasing data rates, the bandwidths are becoming larger, approaching 10 MHz to 100 MHz. 3D channel models are important in macrocells—for example, in urban and mountainous areas where the base station antenna is much higher than the mobile station antenna. The 3D models take into account the elevation angle of the arriving waves in addition to the azimuthal angle and the delay.

Various nonstationary models are often used. In addition to the log-normal distribution, shadowing effects are modeled with birth-death processes in which some delays suddenly appear and disappear, simulating rapid changes as in street corners and in tunnels (Chong et al. 2005). In some models, the delays are time-variant to test the delay tracking ability of the receiver. Furthermore, the models are becoming more comprehensive in the sense that they will have multiple inputs and outputs. In this way, the models can be used to simulate diversity systems with many users. Even handoffs between base stations should be simulated. Correlation and cross talk between the multiple channels are important effects in such systems. An example of cross talk is the co-channel and adjacent channel interference between the various users of the same frequency band in the same geographical region.

ACKNOWLEDGMENT

This work was partially supported by the Advanced Wireless Communication Systems project of the Academy of Finland.

GLOSSARY

Azimuthal Delay Power Spectrum: The average power density at the output of a fading channel as a function of the azimuth and delay.

Complex Envelope: A low-pass equivalent of a real bandpass signal or system.

Delay Power Spectrum: The average power density at the output of a fading channel as a function of the delay.

Diversity: Use of multiple channels to combat fading using different antennae, times, frequencies, or polarizations.

Doppler Power Spectrum: The power density at the output of a fading channel as a function of the frequency shift.

Doppler Spread: The range of values of the frequency shift over which the Doppler power spectrum is essentially nonzero.

Fading: Random changes in the received signal amplitude because of, for example, multipath propagation or shadowing.

Macrocell: In cellular systems, macrocells provide large area coverage in, for example, rural areas.

Microcell: Microcells cover smaller areas than macrocells, and they are typically used in areas with high user population densities and traffic volumes.

Multipath Propagation: Multiple transmission paths because of the reflection, scattering, and diffraction of radio waves.

Multipath Spread: The range of values of the delay over which the delay power spectrum is essentially nonzero.

Multiple-Input Multiple-Output (MIMO) System: A system model in which several antennae are used in the transmitter or receiver to obtain beam forming, diversity, or spatial multiplexing.

Scattering Function: The average power density at the output of a fading channel as a function of the delay and frequency shift.

Shadowing: Random fading because of blockage from objects in the signal path.

Spatial Multiplexing: Multiplexing that is based on the use of several antennae in the transmitter and receiver.

Wide Sense Stationary (WSS) Process: A process whose mean and autocorrelation function are time-invariant.

CROSS REFERENCES

See *Cellular Communications Channels; Cellular Telephony; Wireless Channels*.

REFERENCES

3GPP. 2003. Technical report TR 25.996: Spatial channel model for multiple input multiple output (MIMO) simulations (release 6) (retrieved from www.3gpp.org).

Baum, D. S., J. Hansen, and J. Salo. 2005. An interim channel model for beyond 3G systems: Extending the 3GPP spatial channel model (SCM). In *Proceedings of the IEEE Sixty-First Semiannual Vehicular Technology Conference* (VTC2005-Spring), May 30–June 1, Stockholm. Pp. 3132–6.

Bello, P. A. 1963. Characterization of randomly time-variant linear channels. *IEEE Transactions on Communication Systems*, 11: 360–93.

———. 1969. Measurement of random time-variant linear channels. *IEEE Transactions on Information Theory*, 15: 469–75.

Braun, W. R., and U. Dersch. 1991. A physical mobile radio channel model. *IEEE Transactions on Vehicular Technology*, 40: 427–82.

Chong, C. C., C. M. Tan, D. I. Laurenson, S. McLaughlin, M. A. Beach, and A. R. Nix. 2005. A novel wideband dynamic directional indoor channel model based on a Markov process. *IEEE Transactions on Wireless Communications*, 4: 1539–52.

Coulson, A. J., A. G. Williamson, and R. G. Vaughan. 1998. A statistical basis for lognormal shadowing effects in multipath fading channels. *IEEE Transactions on Communications*, 46: 494–502.

Dersch, U., and E. Zollinger. 1994. Physical characteristics of urban microcellular propagation. *IEEE Transactions on Antennas and Propagation*, 42: 1528–39.

Ertel, R. B., P. Cardieri, K. W. Sowerby, T. S. Rappaport, and J. H. Reed. 1998. Overview of spatial channel models for antenna array communication systems. *IEEE Personal Communications*, 5(1): 10–22.

Fleury, B. H., and P. E. Leuthold. 1996. Radiowave propagation in mobile communications: An overview of European research. *IEEE Communications Magazine*, 34(2): 70–81.

Goldsmith, A. 2005. *Wireless communications*. New York: Cambridge University Press.

Gudmundson, M. 1991. Correlation model for shadow fading in mobile radio systems. *Electronics Letters*, 27: 2145–6.

Hashemi, H. 1993. The indoor radio propagation channel. *Proceedings of the IEEE*, 81: 943–68.

Haykin, S. 1983. *Communication systems*. 2nd ed. New York: John Wiley & Sons.

Hewitt, A., and E. Vilar. 1988. Selective fading on LOS microwave links: classical and spread-spectrum measurement techniques. *IEEE Transactions on Communications*, 36: 789–96.

Holma, H., and A. Toskala, eds. 2002. *WCDMA for UMTS*. New York: John Wiley & Sons.

Jakes, W. C., ed. 1974. *Microwave mobile communications*. New York: John Wiley & Sons.

Kailath, T. 1963. Time-variant communication channels. *IEEE Transactions on Information Theory*, 9: 233–237.

Kalliola, K., H. Laitinen, P. Vainikainen, M. Toeltsch, J. Laurila, and E. Bonek. 2003. 3D double-directional radio channel characterization for urban macrocellular applications. *IEEE Transactions on Antennas and Propagation*, 51: 3122–33.

Laiho, J., A. Wacker, and T. Novosad, Eds. 2002. *Radio network planning and optimization for UMTS*. New York: John Wiley & Sons.

Olmos, J. J., A. Gelonch, F. J. Casadevall, and G. Femenias. 1999. Design and implementation of a wideband real-time mobile channel emulator. *IEEE Transactions on Vehicular Technology*, 48: 746–64.

Pahlavan, K., and A. H. Levesque. 1995. *Wireless information networks*. New York: John Wiley & Sons.

Pätzold, M. 2002. *Mobile fading channels*. New York: John Wiley & Sons.

Pedersen, K. I., P. E. Mogensen, and B. H. Fleury. 2000. A stochastic model of the temporal and azimuthal dispersion seen at the base station in outdoor propagation environments. *IEEE Transactions on Vehicular Technology*, 49: 437–47.

Proakis, J. G. 2001. *Digital communications*. 4th ed. New York: McGraw-Hill.

Rappaport, T. S. 2002. *Wireless communications: Principles and practice*. 2nd ed. Upper Saddle River, NJ: Prentice Hall.

Saleh, A. A. M., and R. A. Valenzuela. 1987. A statistical model for indoor multipath propagation. *IEEE Journal on Selected Areas in Communications*, 5: 128–37.

Sayeed, A. M. 2002. Deconstructing multiantenna fading channels. *IEEE Transactions on Signal Processing*, 50: 2563–79.

Simon, M. K., and M. S. Alouini. 2005. *Digital communication over fading channels*. 2nd ed. New York: Wiley-IEEE Press.

Stein, S. 1987. Fading channel issues in system engineering. *IEEE Journal on Selected Areas in Communications*, 5: 68–89.

Telatar, E. 1999. Capacity of multiantenna Gaussian channels. *European Transactions on Telecommunications*, 10: 585–95.

Turin, G. L. 1980. Introduction to spread-spectrum antimultipath techniques and their application to urban digital radio. *Proceedings of the IEEE*, 68: 328–53.

Viterbi, A. J. 1995. *CDMA: Principles of spread spectrum communications*. Reading, MA: Addison Wesley.

Yu, K., and B. Ottersten. 2002. Models for MIMO propagation channels: A review. *Journal on Wireless Communications and Mobile Computing*, 7: 653–66.

FURTHER READING

Correia, L. M., ed. 2001. *Wireless flexible personalised communications. COST 259: European co-operation in mobile radio research*. Chichester, UK: John Wiley & Sons.

———. 2006. *Mobile broadband multimedia networks: Techniques, models and tools for 4G*. San Diego: Academic Press.

Jeruchim, M. C., P. Balaban, and K. S. Shanmugan. 2000. *Simulation of communication systems: Modeling, methodology, and techniques*. 2nd ed. New York: Kluwer.

Kay, S. M. 1993. *Fundamentals of statistical signal processing: Estimation theory*. Englewood Cliffs, NJ: Prentice Hall.

Krim, H., and M. Viberg. 1996. Two decades of array signal processing research: The parametric approach. *IEEE Signal Processing Magazine*, 13(4): 67–94.

Oppenheim, A. V., R. W. Schafer, and J. R. Buck. 1999. *Discrete-time signal processing*. 2nd ed. Englewood Cliffs, NJ: Prentice Hall.

Papoulis, A. 1991. *Probability, random variables, and stochastic processes*. 3rd ed. New York: McGraw-Hill.

Sarkar, T. K., Z. Ji, K. Kim, A. Medouri, and M. Salazar-Palma. 2003. A survey of various propagation models for mobile communication. *IEEE Antennas and Propagation Magazine*, 45(3): 51–82.

Schwartz, M., W. R. Bennett, and S. Stein. 1966. *Communication systems and techniques*. New York: McGraw-Hill.

Tse, D., and P. Viswanath. 2005. *Fundamentals of wireless communication*. New York: Cambridge University Press.

Cellular Telephony

Elyes Ben Ali Bdira, *University of Sharjah, UAE*

INTRODUCTION

Mobile communications has been around since the beginning of the twentieth century (Black 1998, Rappaport 2001, Schwartz 2005) with experimental service attempted by the maritime industry as early as 1919. Ships were pioneers in using wireless communication because their big size allowed them to carry the big antennas and heavy equipment that were then required. Commercial amplitude modulation (AM) service immediately followed in the 1920s. However, the development of portable mobile cellular devices, the next important step toward enabling individuals to communicate from almost anywhere, took another fifty years. In 1971, Bell Labs introduced the first cellular system. However, it was not commercially deployed until 1983, two years after a Nordic European consortium introduced a similar system Nordic mobile telephone (NMT). Both systems had the main advantages that made cellular communication possible: frequency reuse and handoff (or handover) between multiple base stations (BSs) that had limited coverage areas. Advanced mobile phone service (AMPS) was among the first generation of cellular systems that were introduced throughout the developed world in the early eighties. The mobile industry was then about to take off, amid the many issues that challenged the global proliferation of mobile phones. However, despite immediate demand for the first-generation systems, the industry faced limited capacity, initial high cost, and high power consumption by mobile stations (MSs). It was only after the introduction of the three main second-generation (2G) digital cellular systems (IS-95 cdmaOne, GSM, and IS-54/IS-136, which will be explained shortly in the next section) that the mobile industry took off and never looked back. The boom of data service in the late nineties along with the emergence of the Internet as the dominant information technology application driver has motivated the telecommunication industry to follow suit and work toward convergence of mobile and wireless networks in a *data-centric* environment and become a reliable provider of multimedia service. An intermediate step in that direction was the *data-friendly* third generation (3G), which came in different flavors (UMTS and cdma2000 being the main ones). The commercialization of 3G systems is, however, taking longer than expected, as the third-generation cellular was competitively weak compared to many wireless access alternatives such as wireless local area networks (WLANs) and wireless digital subscriber line (DSL). Furthermore, implementation of 3G technologies was sluggish and was not helped by the particular global economic and geopolitical situation in the last five years. It is hoped that the fourth generation or an intermediate 3.5 generation might have a better chance to become more economically viable. In the meantime, some 3.5G standards with higher data capabilities (e.g., high-speed downlink packet access, or HSDLPA) are already introduced as a companion technology or an upgrade to 3G in many countries. The recent advent of the mobile worldwide interoperability for microwave access (WiMax) standard (also known as IEEE602.16e) as a potential competitor to the cellular technologies is also not to be overlooked. Actually, this technology has a potential to be the immediate solution for seamless first-mile wireless high-speed access (WiMax 2006a, 2006b).

With all these quickly changing standards, and despite the constant evolution of services and network architectures and protocols, the general perspective and the overall picture of cellular system design did not change much. Many features of cellular systems are getting more and more complicated, though. The air interface with its traffic and control channels now needs a media access control (MAC) layer similar to what is used in computer networks. There is also a need for more advanced mobility, location, and resource management. More advanced power control is also required.

The reader will find in the following section a more technical overview of how the cellular industry has evolved from a voice-only service (analog AMPS) to the current UMTS system, with a look ahead to future generations. In the following sections, more technical detail is given on the architecture, services, and interfaces of a second-generation (2G) cellular system. Then, principles of cellular system design, including cell planning and transceiver design, are discussed (including some expected 3G and 4G improvements). Second-generation GSM and IS-95 systems are used as the main platforms to illustrate concepts, and any differences that arise with other systems are specified when they are encountered.

OVERVIEW OF CELLULAR TELEPHONY STANDARDS

Introduction

This section introduces the key highlights of the technical standards of the first three generations of cellular systems. The main key features of these systems are shown in Table 1 (Rappaport 2001, Holma and Toskala 2001).

Intermediate generations such as general packet radio service (GPRS) and enhanced data rates for GSM evolution (EDGE) have not been included in this table due to space constraints. However, major aspects of these technologies are discussed briefly in the section entitled "Data Service in 2.5 Generation."

The reader can refer to the glossary of abbreviations and terms at the end of the chapter for a brief explanation of some of the terms used in the table. Some subjects and related technical terms that are central to cellular system design are treated in detail in the following sections. Readers who are less familiar with communication system design concepts may want to consult the sections entitled "Principles of Cellular System Design" and "Physical Layer Transceiver Technologies" for some of the technical background details.

Table 1: Survey of Technology Features for the Cellular Standards Currently in Use

	AMPS	GSM	IS-136	IS-95	UMTS (FDD)
Year of introduction	1983	1990	1991–1993	1993	1999
Frequency bands	824–894 MHz	890–960 MHz, 1.8 GHz, and PCS band: 1.9–2 GHz	824–894 MHz and PCS band 1.9–2.0 GHz	824–894 MHz and PCS band in 1.9–2.0 GHz	1.9–2.170 GHz
Spreading factor	NA	1	1	64	Variable up to 512
Multiple access/duplexing	FDMA/FDD	TDMA/FDD	FDMA/TDMA FDD	CDMA FDD	CDMA FDD/ TDD (China)
Modulation	FSK	GMSK, BT = 0.3	?/4DQPSK	QPSK/BPSK	Dual Channel QPSK
Carrier separation	30 kHz	200 kHz	30 kHz	1.25 MHz	5 MHz
Voice channels/ carrier frequency	1	8	3	Theoretical maximum: 63	Theoretical maximum: 255 in Reverse link.
Channel data rate	NA	270.833 kbps	48.6 kbps	1.228 Mcps	3.84 Mcps
Power control frequency	Low	Around 2 Hz		800 Hz	1500 Hz
Diversity exploitation	None	Frequency diversity (slow hopping)	None	Rake receiver "path diversity"	Path diversity (rake) and transmit diversity
Vocoder type and rate	NA	RPE-LPT at 13 kbps	VSELP at 7.95 kbps	CELP at 13 kbps also Enhanced VRC at 8 kbps	RPE-LPT at 13 kbps
Data service	NA	9.6 kbps	9.6 kbps	9.6 kbps	144 kbps– 384 kbps (2 Mbps goal)

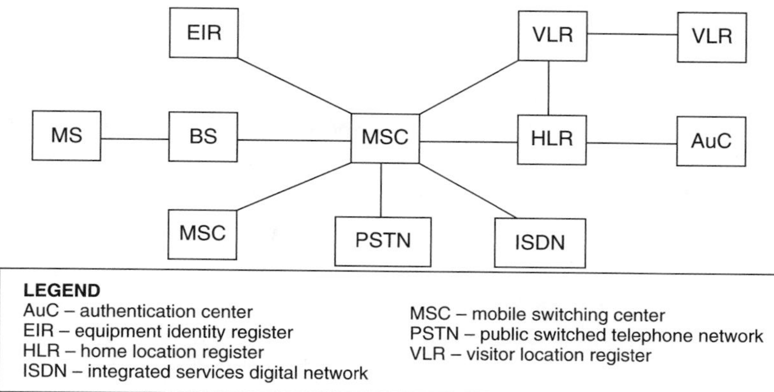

Figure 1: ANSI-41 architecture

First-Generation Cellular Systems: AMPS

First-generation systems did not consist of AMPS only. European systems also had their own versions of analog systems using frequency division multiple access (FDMA) and analog frequency modulation (FM), the first of which, as was mentioned earlier, was the NMT system. First-generation systems were incompatible and it was impossible to roam (get service across networks) between systems in different countries, especially within Europe. The need for a "global" second-generation technology was the motivation behind the introduction of a backward-incompatible GSM and the main reason why the first generation systems died out quickly in Europe whereas AMPS survived for more than two decades in geographically isolated and backward-compatibility–conscious North America, where 50 percent of mobile sales were still analog in the year 2000. It is for this reason that the discussion of first-generation systems is limited to the AMPS system here. A quick account of frequency allocations for AMPS is given in the following section, followed by a an overview of the main aspects of call processing including registration, roaming, and handoff, along with an introduction to initial network architecture and signaling standards.

AMPS Architecture

AMPS was designed to support voice communication and thus all of its architecture is geared towards this service. The main elements of this architecture are the mobile station (MS), which has all the functions needed to support voice calls as a subscriber unit; the base stations (BSs), also known as the base transceiver system (BTS), which provide the air interface to the MSs and relay signals to the rest of the network; and the mobile switching center (MSC), which provides the networking functions needed to connect the calls to other networks. A customized signaling standard called ANSI-41 is used by AMPS and all generations of North American cellular carriers. Figure 1 shows the reference model for the ANSI-41 architecture. The reader is referred to the glossary at the end for further explanation of some of the terms. The other units shown in this figure are databases that will be revisited in more detail in our discussion of second-generation systems.

AMPS Physical Layer Aspects

Table 2 lists the frequency allocations of AMPS. BS transmitter and receiver channels are separated by 45 MHz. Two cellular service providers are authorized and allocated a total of 416 channels in bands A and B, respectively. These channels can be used for voice traffic as forward or reverse voice channels (FVC and RVC, respectively), or they can be reserved as control channels (to be discussed briefly in the section entitled "AMPS Control Channels"). More detail can be found in Black (1998).

Note that frequency bands A', B', and A" are expansions of the original systems to provide more capacity. Normally, 312 of the channels (Channels: 1–312 for System A and 354–666 for System B) are used for voice traffic. The other 21 channels in each original unexpanded system are used for control traffic, and each network is free to choose which channels to use as control channels. Generally each control channel is assigned to a given set of voice channels.

Table 2: AMPS Channels

Frequency Band	Channel Number	Reverse Link Freq. (MHz)	Forward Link Freq. (MHz)
A″	991–1023	824.04–825	869.04–870
A	1–333	825.03–834.99	870.03–879.99
B	334–666	835.02–844.98	880.02–889.98
A′	667–717	845.01–846.48	890.01–891.48
B′	718–799	846.51–848.97	889.51–883.97

AMPS Identification and Information Parameters

The following three parameters are used for subscriber and mobile identification in AMPS:

1. An electronic serial number (ESN) is required by the Federal Communication Commission (FCC). In AMPS, the ESN is made of 32 bits including an 8-bit manufacturer code.
2. A 15-bit system identification (SID) to identify the cellular operator. It includes a 2-bit international code and a 13-bit system number.
3. A mobile identification number (MIN), which is a 34-bit sequence that contains the MS's ten-digit telephone number. It includes MIN1 (24 bits corresponding to the seven-digit number without area code) and MIN2 (10 bits corresponding to a three-digit area code).

One more parameter used in AMPS control channels is the station class mark (SCM). It is used for the following purposes:

1. It conveys information on MS's maximum deliverable effective radiated power (ERP). Each of the eight power levels is coded in a three-bit sequence mobile attenuation code (MAC).
2. It tells whether discontinuous transmission (DTX) is used; that is, if a mobile can use voice activity detection (VAD) to switch to a lower power level during idle periods.
3. It provides information on bandwidth (BW) utilization by the MS.

AMPS Control Channels

Stand-alone control channels: An AMPS mobile when not in *active* conversation mode is required to monitor a forward control channel (FOCC) for any possible orders coming from the base station, including paging signals (calls coming from the network). The MS also can use a reverse control channel (RECC) if it has to communicate control information while it is in idle mode. This channel is shared with other MSs using random access. Both control channels operate at 10 kbps.

The FOCC includes streams of control data multiplexed in time division multiplexing (TDM) fashion: channel A, channel B, and a busy/idle channel. Note that A and B are just labels; these channels are unrelated to frequency bands A and B mentioned earlier. An MS will use either channel A or B depending on the least significant bit (LSB) of its MIN. The busy/idle channel indicates whether the RECC is being used. This helps to avoid collisions in this channel.

Tone channels: In addition to the dedicated control channels, AMPS uses tones for control purposes, namely a supervisory audio tone (SAT) and a signaling tone (ST). The SAT is added to each FVC, and the MS uses this same tone on the RVC. It provides a handshake mechanism between the MS and BS to confirm that the MS is tuned to the right channel, especially during handoff. The ST signal, on the other hand, has many purposes: it is used to request to send data from the keypad during conversation, to indicate that an MS has been alerted and is not yet responding during call pages, and to initiate termination of calls from users. Furthermore, the ST is also used during handoff for confirmation purposes.

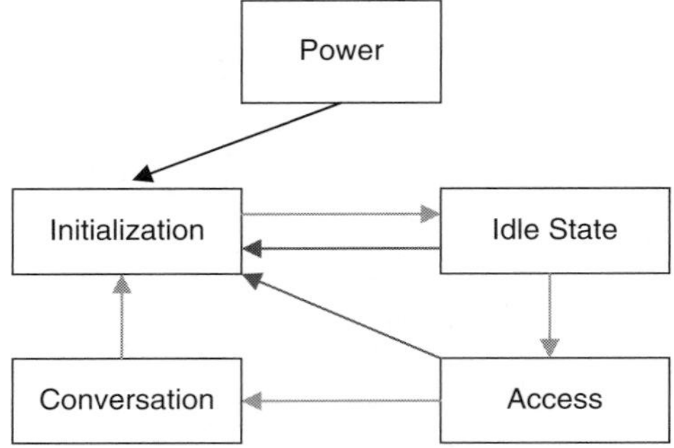

Figure 2: MS state transition diagram

Associated control channels: In addition to these dedicated control channels, the analog FVC and RVC may be "blanked" and used by an associated control channel labeled appropriately *blank and burst* channel. This is a digital channel transmitted at 10 kbps and using frequency shift keying (FSK). To allow the receiver to recognize and synchronize with the data burst, a *dotting sequence* (a sequence of alternating ones and zeros) is transmitted first, followed by a synchronization preamble that precedes the real control data.

AMPS Call-Processing Procedures

A mobile needs to register with the system as soon as it powers up or arrives in a new system.

This procedure is called autonomous mobile registration. The following steps summarize the actions of an MS and a BS during this initialization stage. Note that call processing procedures are similar in most cellular systems; only details of the control channels used differ from one system to another. The general idea of call processing is the same and will not be revisited when other standards are discussed. Figure 2 shows the state transition of a mobile upon power-up. Note that the access state is a transition state after which the MS must go into conversation mode; otherwise, it goes back to initialization.

Initialization

1. Upon power-up, the MSenters the *receive system parameter* state and determines whether system A or B is going to be used.
2. The MS scans all twenty-one forward control channels, tunes to the channel with the strongest signal, and receives and updates operating parameters and SID. It also identifies which service provider and paging channels will be used.
3. The MS uses the RECC to identify itself to the network, and registers in the network by sending its MIN, ESN, and SID.
4. Upon reception of FOCC message verifying registration information, the MS enters the *idle state*.
5. In idle state, the MS monitors the FOCC for any paging messages and uses this channel as well as the RECC to

keep it synchronized with the system, and to inform the network of its mobility parameters.

Call initiation and reception. When idle, the MS can have a call connected either after being paged by the BS, or when the user originates a call. The call origination state is entered when the user dials a number and presses the send button, in which case the MS goes into the following call processing steps. These steps are a summary of a detailed enumeration by Black (1998).

1. The MS sends an origination message containing its own MIN and ESN and the destination's MIN to BS using the RECC control channel.
2. Using ANSI-41 protocols, the BS, via Base Station Controller, passes the MS's request for connection to the MSC, which relays it to the external network.
3. The BS uses the FOCC control channel to order the MS to tune to some specific RVC and FVC.
4. The BS and the MS both switch to their respective voice channels.
5. The BS sends an SAT signal on the FVC.
6. The MS responds with an SAT signal on the RVC.
7. An answer from the network is received and the conversation starts.

A page signal that is coming from the BS means that a call is generally coming from an external switch and is requesting a connection with the MS using ANSI-41. Similar steps are followed in this case, with one difference: the BS pages the MS on the FOCC, the MS responds with a page response on the RECC, and then the BS switches to FVC and asks the MS to tune to the specific FVC and RVC channels. Then SAT signals are exchanged until the user responds to the rings and starts the call.

Call termination. Upon call termination, the MS goes back to initialization state. Call termination is a procedure that can be triggered by many events including the user, the called party, or the network. Successful call termination has always been an issue in cellular design because it affects customer billing. It may be as important as service parameters such as probability of successful connection. Call termination can be triggered by the serving MSC as a result of one of the following events: called party busy, no page response, no answer, not reachable, or routing failure. Termination can also be triggered by the originating MSC upon incoming call redirection. More information about this issue can be found in the ANSI-41 standard (ANSI/TIA/EIA, 1995).

Second-Generation Cellular Systems: IS-54/IS-136, IS-95, and GSM

The main difference between the first- and second-generation cellular systems is that the first generation was based on analog signals using FDMA, whereas the second-generation and third-generation systems use digital signals for voice, data, and control. 2G and 3G systems also use a combination of one or more of time division multiple access (TDMA), FDMA, and code division multiple access (CDMA) as multiple access methods. This allowed the second-generation systems to manipulate digital data in ways that were not possible with analog signals. These included:

- Encryption of data for privacy
- Channel coding to correct errors
- Source coding to take advantage of redundancy and minimize bandwidth requirements
- Spreading the spectrum to combat interference and fading
- Other newly introduced methods that increased efficiency and capacity and decreased the cost of communication.

Despite the declared goal of global interconnectivity, the second generation still suffered from a number of competing incompatible systems, all of which eventually had to coexist. The main second-generation standards currently in use are

1. One standard based on spread spectrum: CDMA, known as cdmaOne or IS-95
2. Two different TDMA standards: IS-136 (for North America and other niche markets) and GSM (for most of the globe)

In the mid-1990s an intense battle raged between the respective proponents of IS-95 could GSM as to whether IS-95 could deliver its initial declared capacity goals, which are ten to forty times stronger than the three-times capacity initially specified by international organizations. A decade later, a few arguments still remain regarding which system is better, but the reality "on the ground" perhaps proves these to be moot. None of the systems were as ideal as advertised, and all three standards required major enhancements and improvements to the initial versions, either in the physical layer or in voice coding, to achieve acceptable capacity and voice quality. It is, however, undeniable that CDMA and orthogonal frequency division multiple access (OFDMA) are ideally superior technologies if their theoretical capacity limits are reached. The arguments of the opponents of IS-95 did not contradict this. They merely stated that IS-95 was not mature enough for a second generation and that it would have been better to wait and introduce it as a third generation.

The section entitled "Principles of Cellular System Design" emphasizes the GSM TDMA standard as the main example of 2G cellular systems. However, IS-136 (also using TDMA) and IS-95 (using CDMA) have many differences, which are listed in the following two subsections.

IS-136 (North American Digital Cellular)

IS-136 was an evolution of the D-AMPS system that was adopted in 1991 as the IS-54 standard, but did not really take off in many markets. IS-136 can use the personal communication system (PCS) band in North America (1900 MHz) as well as the traditional cellular band (800 MHz).

Table 3: Logical Control Channels of IS-136

Logical Channel	Function	Physical Channel
FDTC/RDTC	Forward/reverse digital traffic channel: user information and signaling	Digital traffic channel (DTC)
FACCH	Fast associated control channel: burst short-term signaling	DTC
SACCH	Slow associated control channel: long-term continuous signaling	DTC
RACH	Random access channel: used by MS to gain access to system	Dedicated control channel (DCCH)
PCH	Paging channel: used by BS to page the MS	DCCH
ARCH	Access response channel: used after access request by MS	DCCH
SMSCH	Short message service channel: used for SMS on DCCH	DCCH
F-BCCH, E-BCCH, S-BCCH	Fast, extended, and SMS broadcast control channel: control channel broadcast by BS to all MS for various purposes	DCCH
SCF	Shared channel feedback: used by BS to control RACH access	DCCH

Table 3 lists the logical channels used by IS-136 and their use.

The physical layer of IS-136 also differs from that of GSM or IS-95 in the modulation schemes, channel coding, and many other aspects, even though the same general concepts are used. In particular, the following features are noted:

- Frequency division: IS-136 assumes the same carrier frequencies and the same carrier separation as AMPS; however, each frequency is potentially shared by six users (half-rate vocoders) or three users (full-rate vocoders) using TDMA.
- Time division: channels are divided into six time slots and a full-rate user is assigned to either slots 1 and 4, or 2 and 5, or 3 and 6.
- Channel coding: Voice traffic uses two layers of error protection: CRC for the 12 most important bits (Class I) and a convolutional encoder for these bits and the 77 next most important bits. The least important 82 bits do not have any error protection. This approach results in the generation of 260 bits for every 159 *source bits*. These bearer channel bits are then transmitted in the assigned time slots.

IS-95 cdmaOne Basics

In this section, an overview is presented of the IS-95 physical layer details for traffic and control data, including block diagrams of the reverse and forward traffic channels. The reader is referred to Schwartz (2005) and Steele, Lee, and Gould (2001) for more detail. The physical layer design of CDMA-based systems is very different from that of TDMA systems and is quite elaborate. More details about the concepts used by CDMA physical layer technology are found in the sections entitled "Physical Layer Transceiver Technologies" and "GSM Network Architectures, Services, and Interfaces." Here, we simply highlight the main features of CDMA technology and contrast them with the other 2G systems. Readers who are unfamiliar with the concepts such as channel coding, rake receivers, fading, and so forth are advised to read those tutorial sections in parallel.

The concept of spread spectrum. The IS-95 standard uses direct sequence spreading: each bit sequence, with a bit period T_b, is modulated by a pseudo-noise (PN) sequence running at a much higher rate, the *chip* rate = $1/T_c$. The processing gain (PG) is the bandwidth spreading ratio and is equal to T_b/T_c.

PN sequences are named this way because they are "almost" random. They actually are generated using feedback shift-registers, which generate periodic sequences that would look random for a receiver that does not have the same code used by the shift registers in the transmitter. Different PN sequences are *pseudo-orthogonal* (almost orthogonal); in other words, demodulation of the received spread signal using anything but the correct PN code used in the transmitted will result in an output signal that is close to zero (if it is exactly zero, the codes are called orthogonal).

Initially introduced in the military, spread spectrum had obvious benefits only in applications in which there was no limitation on bandwidth and a bigger need for jamming and interference avoidance. CDMA became feasible as a multiple access scheme for cellular systems primarily because IS-95 introduced a few tricks to increase its capacity. These tricks include closed-loop power control (see the section entitled "Physical Layer Transceiver Technologies"), and a significant amount of coding and spreading activity, as well as a relatively complicated rake receiver. This is a customized equalizer-type receiver with diversity combining that takes advantage of, rather than suffering passively from, multipath. One more feature of IS-95 that was not possible with TDMA-based systems is the use of *soft* handoff, a handoff procedure in which the MS gets connected with two or more BSs and combines the signals it receives from all of them, thus achieving better reception in the weak coverage areas at the edge of the cells. More technical details about such physical layer features of IS-95 are covered in the following two sections.

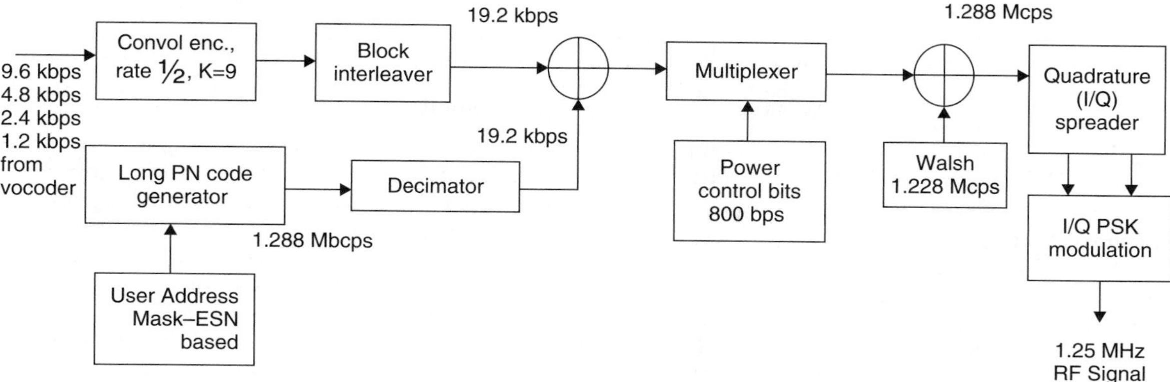

Figure 3: Forward link block diagram of IS-95 (Note that input bits are already partially CRC–encoded and have a variable bit rate according to voice activity; only the maximum data rate is shown here)

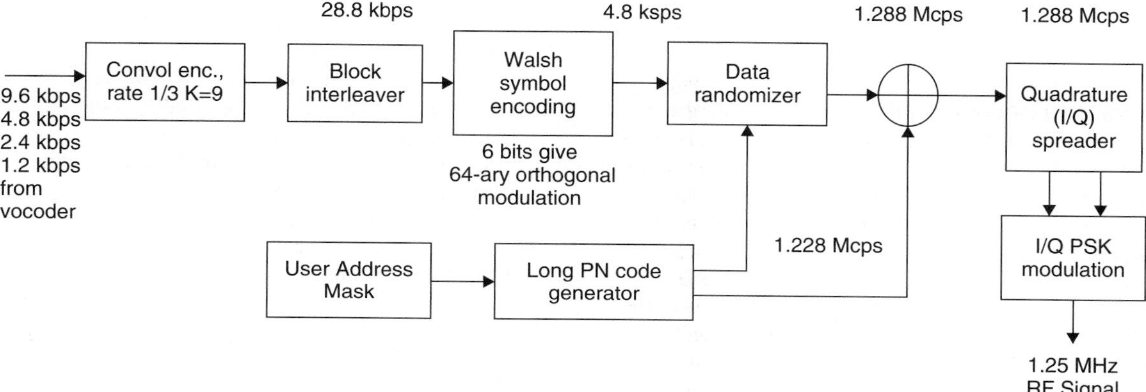

Figure 4: Reverse link block diagram of IS-95 (Note that input bits are already partially CRC–encoded and have a variable bit rate according to voice activity; only the maximum data rate is shown here. For explanation of symbols and terms, refer to the section entitled "Physical Layer Transceiver Technologies" and the text in this section.)

Block diagram of the physical layer of IS-95 traffic channels. Figures 3 and 4 show a block diagram of the main functions of the IS-95 transmitters in the forward and reverse links. They also include some major technical details of the major transmitter and receiver stages (for details, please consult Schwartz 2005; Steele and Hanzo 1999). Some technical details of the major transmitter and receiver stages are included in these figures. A brief explanation of the different stages follows.

Vocoder output. The data rate coming from the vocoder and going into the channel encoder (convolutional encoder) is augmented by a 12-bit/frame cyclic redundancy check (CRC) and an 8-bit tail sequence. The CRC redundancy is used for error detection, and the tail bits are needed for the nine-stage shift registers used by the convolutional encoder and are discarded after decoding in the receiver. This makes the 8.6 kbps original data stream a 9.6 kbps channel. Note that this corresponds to only one vocoder rate (Rate Set 1). There is also a higher vocoder rate (Rate Set 2), which gives an output bit rate of 14.4 kbps instead of 9.6 kbps.

Convolutional encoder. A rate 1/3 coding means that three output bits are generated for every input bit. K=9 is the constraint length, which signifies how far back in the bit sequence the encoder must go to generate the current bit. It is basically the number of shift register stages used. After convolutional coding, some relatively unorthodox methods are used in the forward link to make the higher rate data fit into the same 19.2 kbps channel bit rate, namely, a severe *symbol puncturing* where one-third of the symbols are eliminated! In the reverse link, rate 1/2 encoding is simply used instead of rate 1/3 encoding, thus achieving a bit rate of 19.2 kbps after this stage. It should be noted that this puncturing does not necessarily result in loss of data because the channel-coded symbols carry a lot of redundancy.

Block interleaver. Most channel coding schemes are not able to correct errors that come in bursts, so separating the errors into different blocks of data makes it easier for the decoder to eliminate those errors. The block interleaver shown in the figure achieves this function. This is a device that enters the bits into an 32 x 18 matrix (one column at a time) and outputs them one row at a time, thus uniformly spreading out each block of 32 consecutive bits in a larger block of 576 bits. Thus, if some bursts of errors occur in the channel, they are separated in the receiver after de-interleaving and before error correction.

Power control bit multiplexing. Power control bits are inserted instead of information bits at a rate of 800 bits per second. This is done just before the Walsh function spreading. These power control bits tell the MS to either raise or lower its transmitting power by 0.5 db or 1 dB. For information on how and where the bits are multiplexed, see pages 225–231 in Steele, Lee, and Gould (2001).

Long and short PN code generation.

1. A long PN sequence of period 2^{42} is used in many steps in the forward and reverse link. One such use in the reverse link is the DS spreading and user identity. Another use in the forward link is to generate a decimated sequence that would be added to the bit sequence for scrambling purposes.
2. A short PN sequence of length 2^{15} is used in quadrature spreading, and an offset is introduced in every sequence that is unique for every BS in a cluster, thus minimizing interference from neighboring base stations.

Use of Walsh functions. Walsh functions are periodic and orthogonal functions of time, values of which are generated using rows in a Hadamard matrix of variable ranks (see Viterbi 1995). Orthogonal Walsh functions are used in different ways depending on which direction the traffic is going.

- In the reverse link, the sixty-four orthogonal functions are used as an orthogonal M-ary Modulation tool, generating 4.8 ksps with a pre-DS spreading channel chip rate of 307.2 kcps.
- In the forward link, Walsh functions are used for DS spreading and user identification.

Direct sequence versus quadrature spreading. The term *quadrature spreading* might be thought of as a misnomer due to the fact that the chip rate stays practically the same after this step. However, it is very important in the forward link to reduce interference between signals from nearby BSs that might end up with the same Walsh codes. A different offset between the short-code PN sequences will ensure they are pseudo-orthogonal even if the Walsh sequence was the same. In the reverse link, in addition to the use of quadrature spreading for similar reasons, the long code is used for DS spreading of the 64-ary symbol sequences. Different offsets of this long code determine the user identity, and the ESNs of the mobile units are used to generate these offsets.

Control channels used in IS-95. Table 4 lists the major reverse and forward control channels in CDMA. The use of the control channels is very similar to GSM or IS-136. A pilot channel, however, is needed to achieve code acquisition and phase synchronization. No channel encoding is used for this channel because the information sent is already known (all zeros). Paging channels are usually limited to one or two, but any of the first seven Walsh functions can be used by a paging channel. Note that control channels such as the paging channel have lower information bit rate than voice channels, but the same channel bit rate is used eventually. This allows some extra redundancy to achieve higher link reliability for control data.

Data Service in 2.5 Generation: GPRS and EDGE

The 2.5G standards were introduced to allow second-generation systems to have more efficient and higher bit

Table 4: Overview of Control Channels Used in IS-95 and Their Physical Layer Properties

	Channel Type	Code Used	Data Rate	Channel Encoder
Forward Link BS to MS	Pilot channel	Walsh function W0	All 0s	None
	Synch channel	Walsh function W32	1200 bps	Conv. encoder rate 1/2, K = 9 Symbol repetition and interleaving
	Paging channel	Up to seven channels Wl to W7	4.8 kbps or 9.6 kbps	Conv. encoder rate 1/2, K = 9 Symbol repetition (for 4.8 kbps) and interleaving
	Traffic-signaling and pilot channels	Up to sixty-three traffic channels, W1–W63, but normally sixty-one is the maximum	800 bps pilot channel, signaling	Same as voice traffic (see the section entitled "GSM Network Architectures, Services, and Interfaces" for details)
Reverse Link MS to BS	Access channel Up to thirty-two channels	PN sequence direct spreading	4800 bps	Conv. encoder, rate 1/3, K = 9, symbol repetition, interleaver, Walsh encoding, PN sequence quadrature spreading
	Traffic channel signaling	PN sequence direct spreading; number is interference-limited	Variable (0 to 168 bits out of each 172 bits	Same as voice traffic (see the section entitled "GSM Network Architectures, Services, and Interfaces" for details)

Table 5: 2.5G Main Features and Upgrade Requirements Compared to 3G (W-CDMA)

	Channel Bandwidth	Data Service	New Hardware Requirement	New Software Requirement
HSCSD	200 KHz	Up to 57.6 kbps	None	At BTS
GPRS	200 KHz	Up to 171.2 kbps	Routers and gateways	Routing SW in MSC
EDGE	200 KHz	Up to 384 kbps	New transceiver at BTS	BSC and BTS upgrade
W-CDMA	5 MHz	Up to 2 Mbps	Completely new BTS	Completely different SW

rate data service than earlier standards. One first attempt at higher data rate was the introduction of high-speed circuit-switched data (HSCSD), which merely increased the connection bit rate in GSM by assigning more than one time slot to each user. The calls remained circuit-switched, with all of the inefficiencies resulting from circuit switching for bursty data traffic. The two main 2.5 generation data service standards that made it past the hypothetical standard development stage and into full commercialization are GPRS and EDGE. The next two paragraphs give a very brief overview of these two intermediate standards. Table 5 shows the main features of 2.5 generation systems, and the extent of hardware and software changes needed to upgrade to it from 2G compared to the features and requirements of 3G.

General Packet Radio Service (GPRS)

GPRS uses packet switching that employs the MSC as a routing switch. Figure 5 shows the protocol stack of GPRS. The fact that the physical layer used in GSM is not affected ensures that no new hardware is needed in the base station, although routing software and hardware are needed in the switch.

The main innovation introduced in this standard other than packet switching, requiring the MSC to be a router (labeled SGS in Figure 5), is multiple data classes with various quality of service (QoS) requirements. These classes range from 1 (with mean delay less than 0.5 s and 95 percentile delay less than 1.5 s) to 4 (best-effort traffic with unspecified delay). Note that delay here accounts for the time it takes the data to traverse the mobile network only, not the external networks. Other QoS parameters are data integrity (BER) and requested throughput. To ensure that these Quality of Service (QoS) parameters are satisfied and that correct priority is given to the correct classes of traffic, some second-layer protocols are introduced. The second layer of the protocol stack in the GPRS architecture (data link layer) is divided into three sublayers: logical link control (LLC), radio link control (RLC), and MAC. The last two layers are specific to the radio interface, and they are primarily tasked with allocating channels and maintaining link integrity between MS and BS (see Schwartz 2005 for details). Principles of communication protocol stacks are discussed in more detail in other chapters of this handbook.

Enhanced Data Rates for GSM Evolution (EDGE)

EDGE is proposed as an enhancement on GPRS and IS-136 to achieve higher data rates not possible with GPRS. Minor changes in the physical layer are introduced, such as the use of 8-PSK modulation instead of Gaussian minimum shift keying (GMSK), thus increasing the possible bit rate by a factor of three. An EDGE time slot has the same length as that of GSM—namely, 0.577 ms. However, 116 symbols are transmitted, carrying the equivalent of 69.6 kbps per time slot. If eight time slots are allocated for one connection, the maximum data rate achievable is 557 kbps. This is within a comparable range of values for 3G. However, in practice EDGE might not allocate

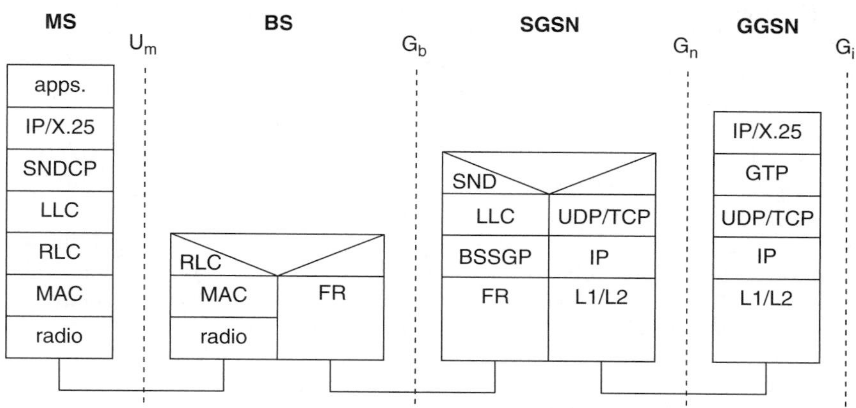

Legend of New Terms (for general networking terms, refer to other networking chapters)
LLC: logical link control
BSSGP: BS subsystem GPRS packet
FR: frame relay
RLC: radio link control
SGSN: serving GPRS support node, the gateway between the radio network and the core network.
GGSN: gateway GPRS support node; the gateway between a cellular network and an IP network.
U_m, G_b, G_n, and G_i: interfaces between MS, BS, SGSN, and GGSN, respectively, as shown.

Figure 5: Suggested protocol stack for GPRS

more than 384 kbps for static users and 144 kbps for mobile users.

3G Systems: The UMTS Example

3G Evolution and Standards

Despite efforts to develop a *universal 3G* system that is accepted globally, 3G systems could not be unified. 3G systems were adopted and were practically incompatible unless mobile units were designed to have practically three phones in one. Ironically, all third-generation standards adopted very similar technologies based on direct spreading of CDMA. In North America, the CDMA2000 standard development activity under the 3G Partnership Project (3GPP2) organization initially split into two backward-compatible technologies, 1xRTT and 3xRTT. Having evolved from IS-95, their standardization work was initially under the label of IS-95C. 1xRTT later evolved into 1xEV-DO. According to the 3GPP2 Web site (2006), as of the year 2006, CDMA2000 is "the most widely deployed 3G technology with 51 CDMA2000 1xEV-DO systems, serving more than 300 million subscribers."

In Europe and much of the world, however, a new wideband CDMA technology that is incompatible with previous North American standards has been introduced: universal mobile telecommunication system (UMTS). Unlike CDMA2000, it uses a 5 MHz bandwidth and is totally incompatible with IS-95. Signaling based on GSM MAP and a network architecture evolving from it has also been adopted for this standard. The 3GPP organization has been using protocols similar to GSM, with a major difference in issues that are particular to third-generation data service, such as radio resource management (RRM) and security (see 3GPP 2001, 2004, 2005). The major aspects of the UMTS physical layer are described in the next two subsections (more details can be found in Holma and Toskala [2001] and in the 3GPP documentation).

The third version of 3G is TD-CDMA, or UMTS-TDD, which has been recently introduced in many countries including Japan, Great Britain, Australia, and South Africa, among others. It differs from the standard UMTS in using TDD instead of FDD to duplex between the forward and reverse links, which allows for variable asymmetric traffic between the directions (UMTS TDD Alliance 2006).

Due to space constraints, only UMTS will be discussed here.

UMTS Physical Layer Features

The following features are introduced with UMTS:

1. UMTS uses the wideband code division multiple access (W-CDMA) standard, which uses direct sequence spread spectrum (DSSS) modulation with a chip rate of 3.84 Mcps (mega chips per second, which is the spread sequence chip rate discussed earlier the chapter).
2. The channel bandwidth is 5 MHz, with benefits such as higher data rates and improved multipath resolution.
3. Error control coding options include rate 1/2 and 1/3 convolutional coding as well as rate 1/3 turbo coding.
4. The supported data rates range from a few kb/s to 2 Mb/s.
5. The physical layer supports two modes of operation: FDD and TDD (mainly in China).

Table 6 lists some of the UMTS/FDD physical layer specifications (see Korhonen [2003] for an extensive treatment on 3G systems).

It is noted that the variable bit rate of UMTS is achieved by using a variable spreading factor using Walsh functions with variable chip period.

UMTS Channels

In UMTS systems, transport channels (channels transporting higher-layer information) are mapped into one or more physical bearer channels. There are also physical channels that carry only physical layer information and do not get mapped to any transport channels.

Forward Link Channels

The UMTS physical layer has variable bit rate transport channels and is designed to offer *bandwidth on demand.* As is the case in second-generation cellular systems, two types of transport bearer channels are supported by UMTS: dedicated channels and shared channels.

Only one type of dedicated transport channel is specified: *the dedicated channel* (DCH). The physical channels treat all information in the DCH equally, whether it is control information (carried in the dedicated physical control channel [DPCCH]) or actual user data (carried in the dedicated physical data channel [DPDCH]). Variable bit rate capability and service multiplexing make these channels the only channels needed for speech, control data, measurements, or even handoff information. These dedicated channels benefit from many physical layer enhancements such as fast power control, data rate change from frame to frame, soft handoffs, and adaptive smart antenna systems.

The following common transport channels are specified:

1. The common pilot channel (CPICH): a continuous downlink pilot signal that is used by the mobile terminal (MT; nomenclature used in 3G instead of MS) as a reference signal for carrier synchronization and channel estimation.
2. The common control physical channel (CCPCH): used to carry several upper-layer transport channels, as well as the forward access channel (FACH) and the paging channel.
3. The synchronization channel (SCH): the first channel that an MT looks for upon start-up; it is a channel that helps the MT receive a sequence used for synchronization.

Reverse Link Channels

1. The DPDCH carries data dedicated for one user. For example, this channel could be used to carry voice traffic as well as audio/video data from a specific user. There can be up to six DPDCH channels.
2. The DPCCH is used to carry physical layer control information associated with the DPDCH. Pilot bits are carried on the DPCCH to aid the base station with

Table 6: UMTS/FDD Features

Frequency band:	1920 MHz–1980 MHz and 2110 MHz–2170 MHz (Frequency Division Duplex) UL and DL
Minimum frequency band required:	~2x5 MHz, Frequency re-use: 1, Carrier Spacing: 4.4 MHz–5.2 MHz
Physical layer spreading factors:	4 … 256 UL, 4 … 512 DL
Maximum number of (voice) channels on 2 x 5 MHz:	~196 (spreading factor 256 UL, with Voice coding at 7.95 kbps)
Data type:	Packet and circuit switch
Channel coding:	Convolutional coding, turbo code for high rate data
Receiver:	Rake, modulation: QPSK, pulse shaping: raised cosine roll-off = 0.22
Chip rate:	3.84 Mcps
Maximum user data rate (physical interference limited.	2 Mbps (spreading factor 4, parallel codes (3 DL / 6 UL), 1/2 rate coding), but
Frame length:	10 ms. Number of slots / frame: 15
Handovers:	Soft, Softer, (= interfrequency hard handoff)
Power control period:	Time slot = 1500 Hz rate, power control step size: 0.5, 1, 1.5 and 2 dB (variable), power control range: UL 80 dB, DL 30 dB
Mobile peak power:	Power class 1: +33 dBm (+1 dB/-3 dB) = 2W; class 2 +27 dBm, class 3 +24 dBm, class 4 +21 dBm
Number of unique base station identification codes:	512 / frequency

channel estimation and carrier recovery for the DPDCH. Channel estimation procedures, which are essential for adaptive receivers, aim at identifying channel effects on the signal. Carrier phase recovery is needed for coherent detection in the receiver (coherent detection is a term that means detection based on knowledge of the phase and/or the frequency of the received signal). Regardless of the number of DPDCH channels, there is always only one DPCCH.

3. The physical random access channel (PRACH) is used to carry random access transmissions. For example, random access transmissions are used when the MT wishes to set up a connection with the base station in order to place an outgoing call.
4. The physical common packet channel (PCPCH) is a shared channel that carries packet-based data transmissions using carrier sense multiple access with collision detection (CSMA/CD), a protocol in which the MT first senses the medium to see if it is available before transmitting, and retransmits the packet after a random delay when "collision" occurs. This is how Ethernet transmissions operate as well.

3.5G, 4G, and Evolution Path of Cellular Telephony

3G had a very slow start, mainly because it did not offer significant improvements in data rates compared to GPRS and EDGE, and especially when compared with the competing broadband wireless and wireline access technologies. The wireless industry is less interested in producing a new fourth-generation (4G) standard than in really transforming mobile cellular services. Table 7 shows the lofty goals that 4G aims to achieve compared to 3G (LeFevre and Okrah 2001).

Note that the above parameters are just ballpark figures; the cellular industry is careful not to promise any exact figures. However, many technologists see the goals in Table 7 as reasonable expectations in an eventual fourth generation that may take time to be implemented (Schmitz 2005).

In the meantime, the 3GPP standard group has produced some enhanced standards that many people call 3.5G or even 3.75G. These standards are asymmetric (designed for either the downlink or the forward link) and are geared toward better data service. Two intermediate standards have emerged recently high-speed downlink packet access (HSDPA) and high-speed uplink packet access (HSUPA). They are briefly discussed in the following subsections.

HSDPA

HSDPA is a new cellular telephony protocol that is referred to as a 3.5G technology because it extends W-CDMA capabilities and provides a smooth evolutionary path for UMTS networks, allowing higher data capacity in the downlink (up to 14.4 Mbit/s). HSDPA introduces a new W-CDMA channel, the high-speed downlink shared channel (HS-DSCH), which operates in a different way from existing W-CDMA channels, but is only used for downlink communication to the mobile terminal. Along with the HS-DSCH channel, two new physical channels are also introduced. One is the signaling control channel, which informs the user about the data to be sent on HS-DSCH. The second

Table 7: 4G versus 3G (UMTS) Features

Parameter	3G	4G
Frequency band	1.8–2.5 GHz	2–8 GHz
Core network	IP-intranet, mobile IP support	Integrated mobile Internet backbone
Bandwidth	5–20 MHz	5–20 MHz
Smart antennas and space time coding	limited	standard
Data rate	Up to 2 Mbps (384 kbps deployed)	Up to 20–100 Mbps
Access	W-CDMA	MC-CDMA or OFDM (TDMA)
Forward error correction	Convolutional rate 1/2, 1/3	Concatenated coding scheme
Traffic switching (voice/data)	Circuit/packet	Packet only
Control traffic	Wireless transport channels	IP traffic
Multi-user detection (MUD)	No	Yes

one is a reverse channel, which carries acknowledgements and current channel quality information.

The first phase of HSDPA was specified in 3GPP release 5. Phase one is aimed at achieving peak data rates of 14.4 Mbps. HS-DSCH and the use of adaptive modulation are introduced in this phase. This technology has already been deployed in many countries. The second phase of HSDPA is currently being specified in 3GPP release 6 and is aimed to achieve data rates of up to 28.8 Mbps. It will introduce advanced antenna array technologies using multiple-input multiple-output (MIMO).

HSUPA

HSUPA is a very high-speed data access protocol for the uplink of mobile phone networks, with upload speeds that can reach up to 5.76 Mbps. Unlike HSDPA, it is sometimes considered a 3.75G.

The specifications for HSUPA are also included in the UMTS release 6 standard published by 3GPP. Although HSDPA relies on higher modulation schemes to achieve higher data rates, HSUPA cannot use these schemes because of the power constraints on the mobiles. Thus, a fixed QPSK modulation may be used with higher-rate multiple code multiplexing. HSUPA has already been demonstrated successfully in some countries.

PRINCIPLES OF CELLULAR SYSTEM DESIGN

Concepts of Mobile Channel Fading and Path Loss

Radio propagation results in three main distortions of the RF signal:

1. Large-scale and relatively slow shadowing and path loss: These are big variations in received signal power that are caused by randomly varying attenuation of the signal as most of the radio energy is dissipated elsewhere and only a small part reaches the receiver's antenna. This type of distortion, since it is slowly varying, can be easily managed with power control. However, severe shadowing of many users in one cell affects overall system capacity, as interference from different BSs limits the power each BS can transmit.
2. Short-term multipath signal fading: This phenomenon results from the self-destructive interference of multiple copies of the same signal traveling in different paths, due to reflections, diffractions, and scattering. This random distortion of the signal may cause severe dispersion of the pulses used, and intersymbol interference may be destructive by limiting the bit rate and increasing the BER. This phenomenon is more difficult to counter than shadowing and path loss. Equalization is normally used to reverse it, if possible. However, modulation methods immune to this type of fading (e.g., as spread spectrum) may be unavoidable when high bit rate transmissions in a mobile environment are needed.
3. The time-varying nature of the channel behavior: Randomly varying Doppler frequency spread caused by the mobility of the MS and/or the surrounding environment makes the communication channel characteristics time vary. An optimal receiver has to adjust to these variations.

Long-Term Shadowing and Path Loss Models

Free space propagation loss. In wireless propagation environments, the signal-received power is affected by the propagation of radiated power in all directions, but the receiver only receives the power captured by its antenna. Path loss from free space propagation is shown to be

$$\left(\frac{P_t}{P_r}\right)_{dB} = -10\log\left[\frac{\lambda^2}{(4\pi^2)d^2}\right] \quad (1)$$

where λ is the wavelength and d is the distance between transmitter (P_t) and receiver (P_r). The equation assumes omnidirectional propagation. Signals from directional antennas also obey the equation, but the gain introduced by these antennas would vary with the propagation angle.

General path loss formula based on log-normal shadowing model. In reality, free space propagation is not possible in cellular systems because there are always two or more paths between the transmitter and the receiver (one direct and one reflected). Actually, a study of a two-ray model shows that the loss in this case is already proportional to d^4 rather than d^2 (Mark and Zhuang 2003). The random addition of many paths with varying attenuations is modeled often as a *log-normal* distribution for the received power with a path loss exponent n, (the power of d in the formula, between 2 and 4 and even larger for indoor propagation). The model assumes the following equation for path loss $L_p(d)$:

$$L_p(d)(dB) = \overline{L_p(d_0)} + 10n \log\left(\frac{d}{d_0}\right) + X_\sigma \tag{2}$$

where d_0 is the minimum distance between the transmitter and the receiver, X_σ is assumed to be a Gaussian random variable with variance σ, and n is assumed to be a fixed number to be determined along with σ using measurements of transmitted and received power and minimum mean square (MMS) estimation.

Link budget and cell coverage. Link budget planning is a part of the network planning process that helps predict the required coverage, capacity and quality of service requirement in the network. In the forward link direction (the direction from the BS to the MS), the available capacity of a cell is limited by the BTS transmission power (typically 20–40 W), which has to be shared by signals transmitted to all users. The objective of the link budget design is to calculate the maximum cell size under some given criteria such as cell coverage. The above path loss model allows us to compute the probability that the received power is above any value, and thus allows us to determine percentage coverage of a cell of any given size, as will be seen in the section entitled "Coverage and Capacity of Cellular Systems."

Multipath Fading Models

Due to propagation effects such as multiple reflections of the same signal on stationary or moving objects (scattering and diffractions), multiple images of the same communication signal arrive at the receiving antenna with generally random amplitudes, phases, and delays. The received modulated symbol can thus be modeled as a sum of a random number of such images. In addition, the channel is time varying due to the potential mobility of both the MS and its environment. This means that the random parameters affecting the signal propagation may change in value in any given instant.

Probability density function of received envelope. In the receiver, matched filters are used to maximize the signal-to-noise ratio and detect which signal was received. Matched filters generally are optimal in the presence of additive white Gaussian noise (AWGN) environments, but not in channels suffering from multipath distortions. The performance of the receiver must be assessed after a new probability density function is found for the resulting multipath signal envelope. It can be easily shown using the central limit theorem (Mark and Zhuang 2003) that the received envelope has either a Rician distribution, when there is a strong line-of-sight component corresponding to a direct path, or a Rayleigh distribution, when no such direct path exists. The performance of various modulation schemes used in mobile communication is then assessed assuming such distributions for the received signal amplitude (see the next section).

Delay profile and time dispersion. A *delay profile* of the channel can be estimated by *sounding* it, which means transmitting multiple narrow pulses (approximations of impulses) and then estimating the average received power at different delays for the same transmitted pulse. The mean delay and mean square delay are then used to estimate how much dispersion the signal suffers. Note that the delay profile could be modeled as a continuous or discrete profile. In the first case, we have a discrete number of possible delays τ_k with average powers of $P(\tau_k)$, where k is between 1 and N, which is now a deterministic number; in the second case, we have an average power $P(\tau)$ defined for all positive τ. In the discrete case, one can compute some statistical parameters for the delay spread:

The mean and mean square delay spread are $\overline{\tau} = \frac{\sum_{k=1}^{N} P(\tau_k)\tau_k}{\sum_{k=1}^{N} P(\tau_k)}$ and $\overline{\tau^2} = \frac{\sum_{k=1}^{N} P(\tau_k)\tau_k^2}{\sum_{k=1}^{N} P(\tau_k)}$, respectively, while the root mean square delay is the standard deviation of the delay,

$$\sigma_\tau = \sqrt{\overline{\tau^2} - \overline{(\tau)}^2} \tag{3}$$

In the continuous time delay case, the sums above become integrals since $P(\tau)$ is in continuous time.

Note that $P(\tau)$ is a statistical average power density profile over all delays τ. It should not be confused with probability, although a normalized power density profile can be interpreted as an estimate of the probability density function of the delay.

Doppler frequency shifts. As a mobile moves, its speed relative to the BS antenna changes. This causes the speed of the electromagnetic wave that travels between the two antennas to change, which affects the received frequency of the signal. This phenomenon is called the "Doppler shift." In general, a simple formula can illustrate this concept:

$$\Delta f = \frac{1}{2\pi}\frac{d\varphi}{dt} = \frac{f}{\lambda}\cos\theta, \tag{4}$$

where f is the frequency of the signal, ϕ is its phase, and θ is the angle between the direction to the BS and the direction of the velocity of the mobile as illustrated in Figure 6.

Note that Δf is a random variable since both the angle and speed of the mobile are random numbers in general.

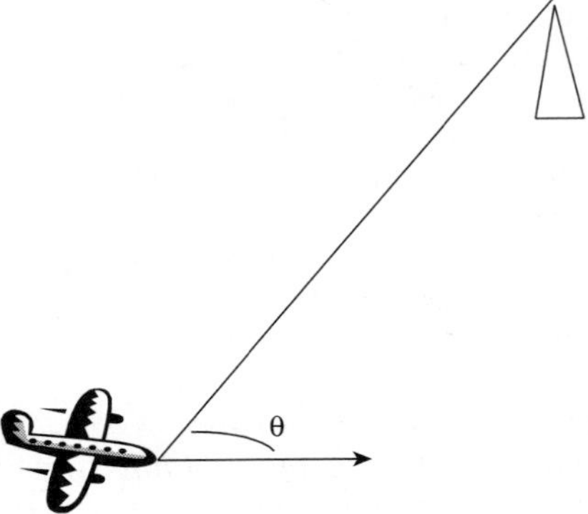

Figure 6: An illustration of velocity of a mobile relative to base station antenna

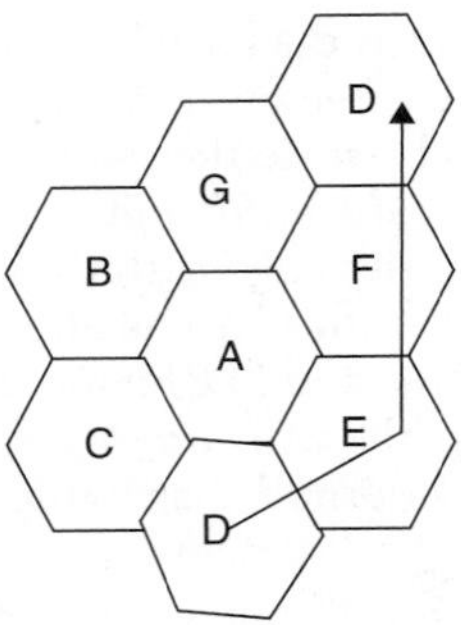

Figure 7: An example of hexagonal cell frequency reuse (A cluster of seven is shown; A frequency set assigned to cell D can be assigned again following the direction of the arrow)

This causes a random frequency error at the receiver, which is changing as fast as the mobile velocity changes.

Coherence bandwidth and coherence time. These are the two most important parameters that affect the performance of a channel-estimating receiver at the input. We define an x-coherence bandwidth as the bandwidth at which the signal preserves an x correlation (e.g., a 0.9-coherence BW means that the signal at this bandwidth still preserves some 90 percent correlation). Generally we specify at least 50 percent coherence BW. Qualitatively, channel coherence time is the time it takes the channel characteristics to change. Quantitatively, it is shown to be inversely proportional to the Doppler spread, Δf. It has also been shown (Mark and Zhuang 2003; Rappaport 2001) that a good approximation of the channel coherence time is $T_c = 0.423/\Delta f$, whereas 90 percent coherence BW is around $0.02/\sigma_\tau$.

Coverage and Capacity of Cellular Systems

This section gives a brief overview of the main cellular system design methods, including:

- Cell planning using frequency reuse to maximize capacity per square kilometer. Frequency reuse, as the name might suggest, is the process of using the same carrier frequencies in different cells that are separated by a distance large enough to minimize interference between signals coming from these two cells.
- Cell coverage determination.
- Capacity utilization versus grade of service (GoS), which is the QoS metric used for circuit switching, as will be shown shortly.

Frequency Reuse and Cell Planning

Co-channel interference coming from neighboring cells is a major problem that limits the capacity of a cellular system. This is the interference that comes from unwanted signals using the same carrier frequency. Normally a frequency once used in one cell cannot be reused in a neighboring cell if pure FDMA is used. The distance that must separate two co-channel base stations divided by the cell radius is entitled frequency reuse ratio (Q). A hexagonal cellular system, in which each base station is surrounded by six neighboring base stations in a hexagonally shaped grid, as shown in Figure 7, is used in cellular systems.

In a hexagonal cellular system, one must organize frequency assignment in such a way that the signal-to-interference ratio (SIR) resulting from co-channel interference is minimized for all users. One simple way is to use the hexagonal structure to uniformly allocate N different frequencies in each cluster of cells. This can be done by setting $N = i^2 + ij + j^2$, where i and j are positive integers. Then one can reuse the same frequency set used in a specific cell again in another cell if it is located using the following procedure: moving i cells the direction of the six surrounding base stations, then turning 60 degrees to the left and moving j cells in that direction. It can be shown using simple geometry that the frequency reuse ratio Q is given by the following formula: $Q = \frac{D}{R} = \sqrt{3N}$.

An example of frequency reuse of a set of $N = 7$ frequencies is shown in Figure 1.

In the forward link, the SIR can be written in terms of the signal power S, and the interfering signals arriving from all co-channel base stations, as follows:

$$SIR = \frac{S}{\sum_{i=1}^{i_0} I_i}, \tag{5}$$

where I_i is the power received from the i'th interferer, and i_0 is the number of co-channel interferers.

When only the first tier of interferers is considered, neglecting interference coming from second and third layers of interferers due to significant path loss, the SIR can be approximated as:

$$SIR = \frac{Q^n}{6}, \tag{6}$$

where n is the path loss exponent. This equation means that the higher the frequency reuse ratio, the higher the signal-to-noise ratio. However, we should also note that the higher N is, the lower the channel capacity per cell. In CDMA systems, for example, a frequency reuse of $N = 1$ can be used because all cells can use the same frequencies.

However, the number of channels per frequency can be very limited due to SIR resulting from nonorthogonal codes between users. As was mentioned briefly earlier in the chapter, nonorthogonal PN codes result in interference from signals other than the wanted signal.

Note that Equation 5 can be used in conjunction with Equation 2 to compute the statistics of SIR levels for mobiles in all locations in a cell. Frequency reuse can then be designed based on worst-case scenarios (MS in the edge of the cell) based on average scenarios or based on an estimate of the average outage probability, where the outage probability is the probability that a mobile has a smaller SIR than the minimum required.

Cell Coverage

The probability that the power received is less than a specific threshold, P_{th}(dB), follows directly from Equation (2) for log-normal shadowing:

$$\Pr[P(d) < P_{th}] = Q\left(\frac{\overline{P(d)} - P_{th}}{\sigma}\right) \tag{7}$$

where $\overline{P(d)}$ is the mean received power at distance d, which is computed by assuming $X\sigma$ averaging to zero in Equation 2, and $Q(x)$ is the Q function that results from integrating the Gaussian density function.

Given a required received power threshold, the average area of the cell in which mobiles get a received signal power over this threshold can then be computed (Rappaport 2001).

Channel Trunking Capacity and GoS

The concept of trunking and GoS. The concept of *trunking* allows a large number of users to share a discrete number of channels, for example, in a cell where each user is allocated a channel among those available on a per-call basis. In a trunked cellular system, when a particular user requests service while all channels (frequencies, time slots, or codes) are already in use, the user is blocked and gets a busy signal. Alternatively, users are allowed to wait for a channel to become free, and then they are blocked after a specific maximum time. In the first case, the Erlang B formula (Mark and Zhuang 2003; Schwartz 2005) is used to determine the relationship between traffic intensity, capacity, and the probability of blocking, which in this case is the designated GoS. Here, traffic intensity is a result of the average projected subscriber activity assigned to the specific cell or sector in question, and capacity is the number of channels assigned to that cell/sector. Generally, the GoS is a requirement on the system based on service provider judgment (which is generally made after studies of customer expectations).

The second queuing scheme can be analyzed using the Erlang C formula, which gives a relationship between capacity, traffic intensity, and the probability of being queued (see Mark and Zhuang [2003] and Rappaport [2001]) for details on assumptions and trunking capacity analysis using these formulas). The main GoS in this case is the probability of finding all channels busy, and the probability that the call is rejected after being queued for a given amount of time.

Cell planning versus trunking capacity. The relationship implied above between a required GoS, the average traffic intensity per cell (or per sector), and the number of traffic channels available per cell (or sector) is an important factor considered in cell planning and channel assignment. Given a GoS and a number of channels, the network planners need to set limits with regard to the number of users in the system, and to manage radio resources optimally to avoid having cells with low GOS and others with idle channels. The reduction of cell sizes to achieve the required capacity per square kilometer may be the only choice if the system as a whole cannot guarantee the required GoS for some cells due to a high density of users.

Channel Assignment Strategies

The previous analysis assumed rigid assignment of channels or frequencies to each cell or sector. In reality, channel assignment strategies are more flexible. Other factors affect channel assignments than frequency reuse and required GoS of new or handoff calls. The choice of channel assignment strategy impacts the performance of the system, particularly the way calls are managed when an MS is handed off from one BS to another.

In a fixed channel assignment strategy, the call is blocked and the subscriber does not receive service if all channels in that cell are occupied. Several variations of the fixed assignment strategy exist. In one approach, called the borrowing strategy, a cell is allowed to *borrow* channels from a neighboring cell if all of its own channels are already occupied.

In a *dynamic* channel assignment strategy, voice channels are not allocated to different cells permanently. Instead, each time a call request is made, the serving base station requests a channel from the MSC. The switch then allocates a channel to the requested cell following an algorithm that takes into account the *likelihood of future blocking within the cell*, the frequency of use of the *candidate channel*, the *reuse distance of the channel*, and other cost functions.

Handoff also needs to get priority in channel assignment since it cannot be queued for long; neither can it be allowed to be dropped often during conversation. Most systems have *reserved capacity* for handoffs (channels that are exclusively used for handoff) in addition to the priority given to handoff calls in the assignment of the other channels.

Techniques to Improve Cell Capacity and Coverage

Cell sectoring. With this approach, the co-channel interference potential is reduced by using three or six directional antennas per base station to divide the cells into three or six geographic sectors. It also increases capacity by reducing the number of cells required in a cluster. However, increasing the number of sectors reduces the trunking efficiency because channels are not generally shared by sectors in the same cell. This implies that there should be a net gain from sectoring for it to make sense.

Cell splitting. Cell splitting is the process of subdividing a congested cell into smaller cells, each with its own base station and a corresponding reduction in antenna height and transmitter power.

Cell splitting allows a system to increase its capacity per square kilometer by replacing large cells with smaller cells while not affecting the channel allocation scheme required to maintain the minimum co-channel reuse ratio Q, a very tricky task.

As an example, cell splitting may make cells smaller by reducing the power transmitted by a cluster of base stations and inserting base stations in such a way that the radius of each new microcell is half that of the original cells. The transmit power of the new cells can be found by setting the received power at the new and old cell boundaries to be equal, and finding the new required transmit power.

Repeaters. Repeaters are used to cover hard-to-reach areas. They are bidirectional (i.e., they receive and transmit signals to either direction and relay them to further points). This reduces the need to add power in transmitters that would cause more interference to nearby cells. This also improves the percentage of the cell coverage.

Umbrella cells. These are larger cells that are covered by BSs with higher antennas and larger transmission power that coexist in the same geographical region as smaller microcells covered by base stations with shorter antennas and low transmitting power. This has many benefits, the most obvious of which is having faster-moving users (such as mobiles in cars) covered by the umbrella cells to reduce the rate of handoffs, while more numerous but slower-moving users are covered by the more dense network of micro-base stations.

PHYSICAL LAYER TRANSCEIVER TECHNOLOGIES

Modulation and Detection Methods

In second generation systems, various digital modulation schemes are used with variable modulation efficiencies. The main modulation methods that are used in 2G and 3G cellular systems are GMSK and M-PSK, (M = 2 gives BPSK, M = 4 gives QPSK, and M = 8 gives 8-PSK). Multiple quadrature amplitude modulation (M-QAM), a combination of amplitude and phase shift keying, also is used in more recent systems.

The main figures of merit for any digital modulation scheme are bandwidth efficiency (the ratio of channel bit rate to occupied RF bandwidth in b/s/Hz) and energy efficiency (the needed energy per bit to achieve a certain level of bit error rate, given a particular noise and interference level). Both of these factors are analyzed by Rappaport (2001), Goldsmith (2005), and Mark and Zhuang (2003). In the following section, only an overview is given of recent results that are or will be used to improve performance in the physical layer.

Comparing Energy Efficiency of Digital Modulation Schemes

The main modulation schemes used in second-generation cellular are QPSK and GMSK. Energy efficiency is determined by the probability of bit error given E_b/N_0 the ratio of bit energy to noise. Noise here can be a combination of interference and thermal noise. In the following formulae, coherent detection is assumed (i.e., is that the carrier phase is completely known to the receiver).

QPSK. Note that in QPSK we use four different phases, and one of four signals are sent each carrying one of four possible combinations of two bits.

$$s_i(t) = \sqrt{\frac{2E_b}{T_b}}\cos\left(2\pi f_c t + (i-1)\frac{\pi}{2}\right) \quad 0 \le t \le T_b \tag{8}$$

The following equation describe the relationship between E_b/N_0 and the bit error probability for QPSK (Mark and Zhuang 2003; Rappaport 2001).

$$P_b(error) = Q\left(\sqrt{\frac{2E_b}{N_o}}\right) \tag{9}$$

QPSK has the same BER as BPSK and sends two bits for every symbol. It is therefore one of the better modulation schemes in energy efficiency.

GMSK. GMSK is a special kind of minimum shift keying (MSK) that uses a Gaussian pulse-shaping filter to reduce the BW of the transmitted signal; this is used in GSM. Comparing GMSK efficiency with QPSK may be disadvantageous to GMSK. Its BER performance is hard to compute analytically and is estimated in Equation 10 (Rappaport 2001).

$$P_{b,GMSK}(error) = Q\left(\sqrt{\frac{2\gamma Eb}{N_o}}\right) \text{ where} \quad \gamma = \begin{cases} 0.68 & BT = 0.25 \\ 0.85 & BT = \infty \; noG-filter \end{cases} \tag{10}$$

On the other hand, in terms of BW efficiency, GMSK does have an advantage due to the narrow Gaussian filter used.

Higher M-QAM modulation schemes. Higher modulation rates for M-QAM use multiples phases and multiple amplitudes to achieve a much higher modulation rate (bits per symbol). The BER for M-QAM can be approximated as:

$$P_{b,M-QAM}(error) = \frac{4}{\log_2 M} Q\left(\sqrt{\frac{3(\log_2 M)E_b}{(M-1)N_o}}\right) \text{ where } M > 4 \tag{11}$$

It obviously has weaker energy efficiency than QPSK (i.e., it needs more signal energy to get the same error rate). However, the gain in bandwidth efficiency makes this an attractive choice when lower signal-to-noise ratios can be allowed.

Bandwidth Analysis of QPSK, M-QAM, and GMSK

For QPSK, with proper pulse shaping, the 90 percent energy BW used (bandwidth in which 90 percent of the signal energy resides) can be around 1.5 times the symbol rate, resulting in a bandwidth efficiency of 1.33 bps/Hz. Comparatively, GMSK depends on the BW of the filter and can have a 90 percent BW of around 0.57 times the bit rate, thus having a BW efficiency of 1.75 bps/Hz. In reality, the modulation technique used in GSM achieves 1.35 bps/Hz, and the one used by IS-95 has BW efficiency of less than 1 before spreading.

Performance in Fading

The formulae shown in the section entitled "Comparing Energy Efficiency of Digital Modulation Schemes" not only assumed coherent detection, it assumed only Gaussian-type noise or interference affecting the signal. This is not the case with Rayleigh fading, and, in reality, the BER versus. E_b/N_0 relationship becomes very erratic and random. On average, it becomes less than exponential in nature (geometric or worse), achieving a plateau beyond which any increase in E_b/N_0 will not improve the performance. (Goldsmith [2005] and [2003] provide a detailed analysis on computing the average probability of error in a fading channel, and the reader is referred to these textbooks for the details). In general, fading channels may result in unacceptable performance if not countered by diversity combining (to be discussed next), interleaving (an example of which was discussed earlier in the chapter), or other burst error correction methods.

Diversity Combining Methods

Future cellular systems are expected to achieve a much better BW efficiency and much lower required E_b/N_0 by using transmitter and receiver diversity techniques to overcome interference, fading, and noise. Two examples of such advances are discussed.

Antenna Arrays and Microdiversity

Using multiple antenna arrays, in which the elements of arrays are separated in space, achieves *space diversity*. This assumes that the Rayleigh or Rician fading observed in received signals coming from different antennas is uncorrelated. Combining the signals coming from multiple antennas allows us to take advantage of the independence between the paths to achieve higher performance.

The main diversity combining techniques are:

1. Selective diversity uses the branch with the highest SNR after detecting the signal through each of the diversity branches. A simple procedure, but not fast or optimal.
2. Equal gain combining (EGC) combines all signals equally. Since the SNR is an average of all branches, a sole good branch will be affected by the others. Simplest and quickest of all, yet far from optimal.
3. Maximal ratio combining (MRC) multiplies each of the signals by a variable gain to maximize the SNR. This is the best procedure, but it is iterative and complicated.
4. Scanning (or threshold) diversity combining: sets an SNR threshold and uses the first diversity branch that achieves that threshold or higher. This is a compromise on selective diversity to achieve quicker detection. Variations of these methods would choose the first n diversity branches out of N that would combine to the required SNR using either MRC or EGC.

Distributed Antennas and Macrodiversity

The cited methods are normally used to combine signals that are suffering Rayleigh multipath fading. However, the distance between antennas is in this case assumed to be small (in the order of a fraction of a wavelength). This implies that such multiple antenna systems may still suffer from correlated shadowing and thus any diversity combining might not help increase capacity. Having distributed antennas that are spaced away from the center of the cell allows the signals from different antennas to experience uncorrelated shadowing. This level of diversity (called *macrodiversity*) can achieve much higher capacity levels for 3G CDMA systems in urban environments (Bdira and Mermelstein 1999). Its drawback is the cost involved in distancing the antennas. In microcellular urban environments, however, this scheme may be very feasible due to the smaller size of the cells.

Space-Time Coding and MIMO Systems

In MIMO systems, m transmit antennas and n receive antennas are used to achieve much higher BER performance (Yaun, Chen, and Vucetic 2003). They can also be used to increase data rate through multiplexing, thus achieving very high spectral efficiency gains. The added complexity at the transmitter and the receiver can be prohibitive, though. It is actually equivalent in complexity to an nxm space diversity system if the channel can be known to the transmitter in *space-only* diversity (Giannakis et al. 2001). A theoretical analysis of space-time codes using MIMO systems can be found in Chapter 10 of Goldsmith (2005).

CDMA Power Control and the Rake Receiver

CDMA is a particular system in which power control accuracy affects capacity, and also in which multipath diversity can be used to increase performance. A brief overview of the peculiarities of CDMA transceivers follows. For readers unfamiliar with spread spectrum, this section should be read in parallel with the section entitled "IS-95 cdmaOne Basics."

CDMA Channel Model and Rake Receiver

Due to the properties of PN sequences used in spread-spectrum CDMA systems, interference coming from a signal that is modulated using a different PN sequence, or from the same PN sequence shifted in time by more than one chip period, becomes attenuated at the output of the correlator. As a result, the interference power is divided by the processing gain (Viterbi 1995).

The rake receiver takes advantage of this property when frequency selective fading occurs. The chip period in this case is smaller than the multipath spread, so images of the received signal exist in more than one chip and

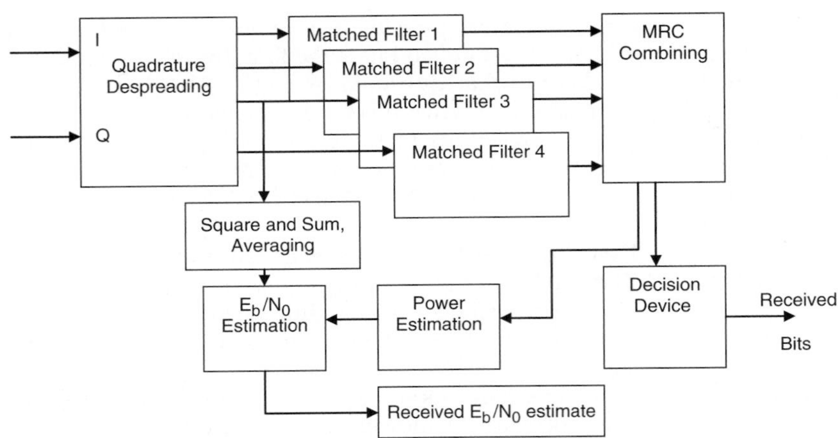

Figure 8: A diagram of a rake receiver with four decorrelators (or matched filters) and E_b/N_0 estimation

thus can be treated as uncorrelated, attenuated versions of the same signal. This allows the signal images to be combined using maxim MRC or EGC. This is done by having multiple decorrelators (or matched filters) using the same PN sequence used by the transmitter, but shifted in time by multiples of a chip period.

Figure 8 shows a simplified block diagram of a rake receiver using four *fingers*. This figure illustrates two concepts.

1. The use of multipath in a diversity combining multiple outputs of four mathed filters
2. The estimation of received SNR that is done in parallel, and is used for both power control and to channel estimation in order to achieve optimal combining of the diversity paths

Note that using the central limit theorem, the interference resulting from other users can be modeled as AWGN. This allows the average signal-to-noise ratio after maximal ratio combining to have a *diversity gain* in addition to the processing gain. In Figure 8, two stages in the estimations of SNR can be seen. In the first stage, the four outputs of the despreaders are squared and summed to estimate the energy plus noise, before the match filters, and in a second stage the power estimate is computed at the output of the combiner and fed back to be used for the SNR computation.

One example of how diversity combining coupled with MRC combining with distributed transmitting antenna systems in the downlink is presented in a simplified form here. Assuming uncorrelated path losses L(k) from the k'th paths, SNR(k) being the SNR seen at the k'th branch, P_s the power of the received signal, and P(i) the total power transmitted by the i'th interfering base station, ignoring other system and synchronization losses, the total SNR seen after MRC combining can be given by the following simplified equations (Bdira and Mermelstein 1999):

$$SNR = \sum_k SNR(k), \text{ where}$$
$$SNR(k) = \frac{P_s L(k) PG}{\sum_{n\neq k} P(n)L(n) + \sum_m \sum_n P(m)L(n)} \qquad (12)$$

PG is the processing gain. Note that as the number of diversity paths increases, the average received SNR after using MRC increases. In the rake receiver, all signal images from paths other than the path of interest to the particular matched filter (or *finger* of the rake) look like Gaussian white noise and are treated as such in the preceding equation. In Equation 12 the first sum in the denominator corresponds to interference coming from signals transmitted to other users in the same cell, and the second sum corresponds to interference coming from other base stations.

Estimation of Received Power and E_b/N_0 in Rake Receivers

Figure 8 shows how the received power and E_b/N_0 can be estimated in the receiver in two stages. Before the matched filters, the signal and noise are squared and averaged to estimate the received power. After the matched filters and the combiner, at which point ideally the signals is emphasized and noise is deemphasized, the output is fed back to the SNR estimator to compute an estimate of the SNR. With MRC, the weights of the different filters are adjusted to achieve a maximum of the SNR.

The following clarifications need to be made, however:

1. Estimation of E_b/N_0 is crucial for proper operation of both downlinks and forward links. First, it is used in power control decisions, as we will see in the next paragraph. Second, it can be used in mobile assisted handoff (MAHO). With MAHO, the MSC/BSC uses the MS's reports of SNR measurements of signals coming from neighboring BSs to make handoff/soft handoff decisions.
2. E_b/N_0 is estimated by collecting measurements of the signal before matched filtering (i.e., before the noise and interference levels are reduced) and after filtering, and this may be done with or without the aid of a training sequence to help with channel estimation.

Power Control Schemes

Power control schemes for CDMA depend on which link (forward or reverse) the signal is traveling.

1. In the forward direction, *open-loop power control* is used in IS-95 to assign power levels unilaterally by the

BS for each signal depending on the information the BS has about each connection in its cell. The BS does power estimation and E_b/N_0 estimation on its side and may use information coming from the MS about the link performance.

2. In the reverse link, a more accurate closed-loop power control is adopted using a power control bit every 1.25 ms (every 0.67 ms for UMTS) in the forward channel. This bit tells the MS to either increase or decrease its power by a fixed or variable power level. A variable (adaptive) power control step size does not necessarily need extra information exchange with the BS. The MS itself may act unilaterally and vary its step size based on statistics of the previous power control bits. Consecutive zeros or ones may suggest that the step size needs to be increased to keep up with rapidly increasing or decreasing received power, whereas alternating ones and zeros may suggest that the step size needs to be decreased to reduce power control errors. A detailed analysis of power control is found in (Steele and Hanzo 1999).

Equalization

An equalizer's goal is to reverse the effect of a multipath channel. In general, equalizers have three categories:

1. Linear zero-forcing equalizers. These equalizers use the discrete impulse response of the channel ($h(k)$) to design a discrete N-tap filter $b(k)$ such that $h(k)*b(k) = 1$ for $k = 0$ and 0 elsewhere around 0. Due to the finite length of the equalizer, only a finite number of time shifts can be equalized.
2. Nonlinear decision feedback equalizers. This type of equalizers has two stages. One stage is similar to the linear equalizer, and the second stage feeds back the output of the decision of the *maximum likelihood detection* device to be used in an N-tap feedback filter to correct any errors in the channel estimation done by the first stage.
3. Adaptive equalizers (linear or with decision feedback). These use variable filter coefficients that adjust with channel variations. Mark and Zhuang (2003) and Goldfield (2005) can be consulted for detail on the fundamentals of equalizer design.

Channel Coding and Turbo Codes

Channel coding in cellular telephony is an essential step to achieve the required BER performance. Unlike optical channels where one could get by with one bit parity check per byte, error protection is much more sophisticated in wireless systems. Second- and third-generation systems use concatenated coding (cascaded codes), hybrid codes combining forward error correction (FEC) with retransmissions (ARQ), and multiple classes of data. The main channel-coding techniques used are as follows:

1. Cyclic redundancy checks (CRC) using BCH and Reed-Solomon(RS) block codes. These are generally (n,k) codes that take each block of k *information* bits (or nonbinary symbols for RS codes) and generate from it a block of n *code* bits (or symbols). BCH block codes are often used as CRC codes to provide extra protection to the most important class of data, whereas FEC is used for for this class and a second class of important bits. A third, less important class of bits may be transmitted even without FEC.
2. FEC often uses convolutional codes of various constraint lengths and coding rates. Convolution codes use feedback shift registers to sequentially generate output bits that are higher in number and more interdependent than the input bits. A lot of work has been done on these codes in the previous three decades to show their superior performance in error correction. If a code is well designed, the higher the coding rate of a convolutional encoder (output bits vs. input bits), the better its performance. One can also use puncturing with these codes, in which some of the output symbols are *sacrificed* to reduce channel bit rate and still achieve better performance than in the case where the coding rate is lower and no puncturing is done.
3. Turbo coding. This is an advanced parallel concatenated coding technique that also uses interleaving and recursion (the output is fed back to the input). Theoretical bounds on channel capacity can be approached with some turbo codes. However, the receiver for such encoders can get quite complicated, with multiple interleaving/de-interleaving stages and more than one detector stage (Schwartz 2005).

Multi-User Detection Methods

So far, a CDMA receiver was assumed not to know of the interfering signal in a CDMA system and that the sum of all interfering signals can be assumed to be AWGN. With multi-user detection (MUD), receivers know of the interfering sequences and use this knowledge to cancel the interference coming from the other users. The BS in particular can detect all uplink signals simultaneously, thus optimizing interference cancellation and maximizing capacity. An optimal MUD receiver can be prohibitively complex. However, close-to-optimal receivers with reduced complexity can be designed. A comprehensive overview of MUD techniques is presented by one of the pioneers of this field in Verdu (1998).

GSM NETWORK ARCHITECTURES, SERVICES, AND INTERFACES

Introduction

The previous three sections have emphasized physical layer standards and concepts, which are often viewed as the main domains of innovation that allow wireless technology to succeed in its goals. However, issues such as hardware, software, and network architectures are central to cellular system design. This section presents some typical cellular components, interfaces, network architectures, and protocols using GSM as an example.

Mobile Station Elements and Functions

A mobile station (MS) is the user access device to the mobile network and the only user interface for all mobile

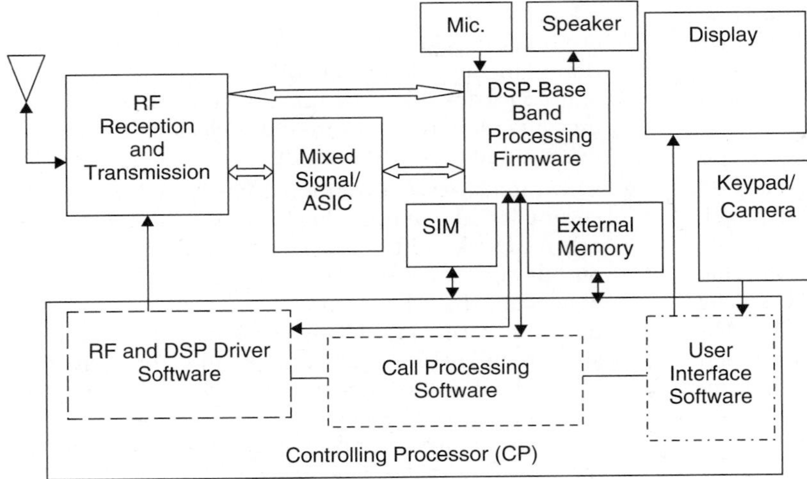

Figure 9: Illustration of the main functions of a mobile phone

applications. It needs to implement all mobile applications and interoperate with any compatible system to ensure that the user obtains access to the promised services. The MS must actually have the counterpart of all functions that are in the BS, MSC, and other network entities. OSI layers supported by these network entities in the data plane, and in the radio-interface control plane, need to be supported by the MS. To do this, the MS typically has the main parts shown in Figure 9 and explained in the following subsections. Sauter (2006) can be consulted on details.

Smart Card (SIM)

The subscriber identity module (SIM) is a smart-chip card that contains a microprocessor chip that stores unique information about the user. Subscribers activate their phones upon insertion of SIM cards.

This detachable module provided by the service provider supports all the terminal/user-specific network interface information (identity, billing, etc.), and the rest of the MS comprises all hardware and software needed for the user interface (UI) and radio interface.

A GSM MS has the following identity parameters stored in the SIM, which is exchanged with the network when necessary:

1. International mobile subscriber identity (IMSI): Stored in the SIM, assigned to an MS at the time of purchase, uniquely identifies a given MS. It contains fifteen digits and includes the following: mobile country code (MCC), mobile network code (MNC), mobile subscriber identification number (MSIN), and national mobile subscriber identity (NMSI).
2. Other parameters are as follows: Authentication key, access control class, cipher key, TMSI, additional GSM services, location area identity (LAI), and forbidden PLMN. These are parameters used for authentication, during registration with home or remote network, and for roaming purposes.

RF, DSP, and Mixed Signal Units

As illustrated in Figure 9, these parts manage most of the physical layer functions in the mobile station. Including Digital signal processing (DSP), analog RF modulation/demodulation, filtering and amplification (RF board/module), and any steps in between that are hardwired in application-specific integrated circuit (ASIC) chips. Many newer mobile units integrate most of these functions within a single chip.

Controlling Processor Functions

This is the *brain* of the phone, so to speak, and thus exerts all the *intelligent* functions, such as decoding all the upper-layer control and user information, hardware control via drivers, user interface control and response, and overall control of all phone parts and functions to set them to sleep and initiate wake-up, for example. As services using mobile cellular become increasingly data-centric, the processor is required to exert much more effort in upper-layer functions, including security procedures, mobile IP tasks, and application layer tasks.

User Interface Units

User interface functions are becoming more varied and demanding. Initially a phone had a microphone, a speaker, and a simple display/keypad combination to help set up calls and configure the phone. Now, a camera is an input device often added to a cellular phone, and the display is becoming more sophisticated with video graphic array (VGA) video display and Internet browsing requirements. Actually, the user interface is often the limiting factor on the size of the phone. The user interface software functions are dedicated to responding and controlling all the input and output devices of the phone. Unlike call processing, most user interface specifications are not standardized and are left to the manufacturer because they do not affect interoperability between different systems.

Base Station Elements and Functions

The base station transceiver system (BTS) was originally a relaying entity that mainly had RF and DSP transceivers but did not contain many intelligent or upper-layer functions, which are managed by the MSC. It also did not do any source coding or decoding, which are normally done at the BSC or even at the user's end.

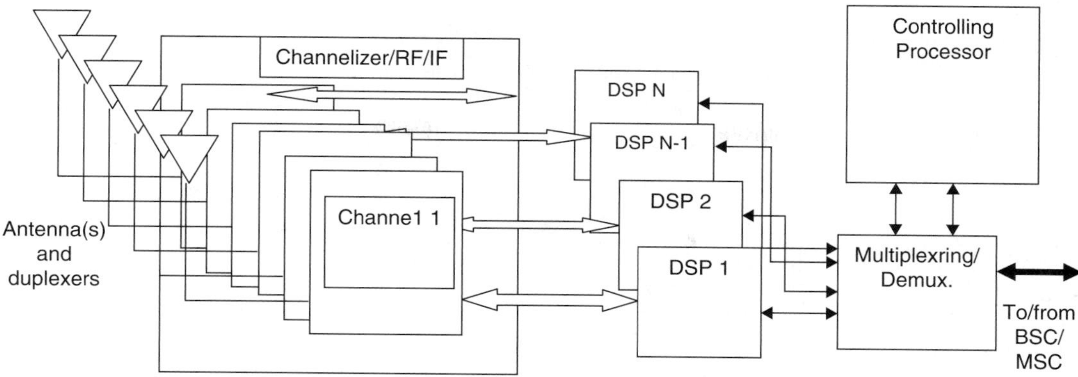

Figure 10: Typical base station transceiver elements

Figure 10 shows a high-level block diagram of a base station. The main components are as follows:

1. The antennas and duplexers at the front end, which receive and transmit signals in both directions. These antennas can either be directional to divide the cells into three or six sectors or omni directional to transmit diversity (see previous sections on cellular system design and diversity). Duplexers are used to provide isolation between the transmitted and received signals in the RF front end.
2. A channelizer is a set of demodulators that separate the received signals from different users into separate baseband channels that are sent to separate DSPs.
3. DSPs are modules that accomplish all the processing needed in the baseband.
4. The controlling processor and associated chips are the intelligent part of the base station because they control all the action and decode any upper-layer messages that are meant for the BS.
5. Multiplexing and demultiplexing of DS0 lines is done also to convert all voice channels into DS0 circuits and back.

Note that in future-generation systems, the BSC functionality may be moved to the BTS. A channelizer may have a different RF receiver for each channel or, in the CDMA case, one or more PN sequence codes for each channel, with a common RF front end.

GSM Land Mobile Network Architecture

Goals of the Land Mobile Network

Some of the goals of the GSM land mobile network are:

1. To provide subscriber services that are compatible with those offered by existing networks (e.g., PSTN, ISDN)
2. To provide these services with various MS types including vehicle-mounted stations, portable stations, and handheld stations
3. To allow connection to the external networks regardless of the location of the MS, including the use of foreign networks (roaming)
4. To allow for a low-cost infrastructure and terminal and to keep cost of service low

Public Land Mobile Network Architecture, GSM Example

It may be ironic that a cellular network is connected with mostly fixed land-based interfaces, and the only wireless interface is the air-interface between the MS and BS (called the U_m interface). The interfaces shown in Figure 11 are all based on wired or fiber interfaces using TDM to multiplex data coming from all channels (data or control traffic) in either a DS1 circuit, an E1 circuit, or other multiplexing standards.

Other than the BTS and MS, the other entities introduced in Figure 11 have the following functions:

The base station subsystem (BSS). The BSS consists of the control function carried out by the BS controller (BSC) and a transmitting function performed by the BTS. A BSS can serve several cells because it can have multiple BTSs. The interface between the BTS and its BSC is called the A_{bis} interface.

The networking and switching subsystem (NSS). The NSS is the functionality that takes care of routing calls to external networks so they get properly connected, in addition to all the networking functions necessary to maintain the security, availability, and quality of service. The entities that are part of this subsystem are the mobile switching center (MSC), the main processing entity of the mobile network, and some specialized databases connected to it: the home location register (HLR) and the visitor location register (VLR), already covered in the overview section. There is also the AUC, a database that stores authentication and cipher keys, and the EIR, which stores information about mobiles including faulty or fraudulent equipments.

The operation and maintenance subsystem (OMS). The OMS is in charge of remote operation and maintenance functions of the PLMN. It may have one or more network management centers (NMCs) to centralize PLMN control. The operational and maintenance center (OMC) is used by the service provider to monitor and control the

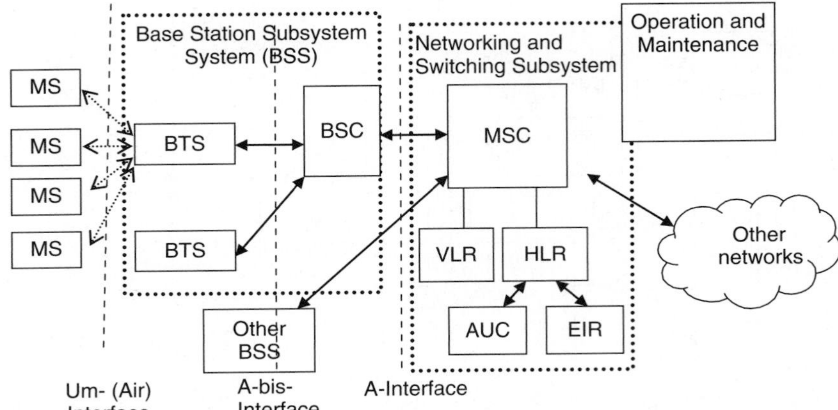

Figure 11: Illustration of a PLMN architecture using the GSM example

system. It is a single point through which the entire system (even multiple MSCs) can be maintained.

More detail about the functions and protocols of all of these entities can be found in the GSM chapter, as well as in *Principle and Application of GSM* by Garg and Wilkes (1999).

Air Interface Protocols: The GSM Example

Introduction

This section gives a brief overview of the protocol stack used for data communication in the air interface. Figure 12 gives a simplified protocol stack for voice and data service in GSM.

GSM Protocol Layers

The U_m interface is the most important interface in mobile communication because it is the only one that is special to wireless communication. Further more, it is usually the bottleneck in the connection to the rest of the world due to the specific constraints that wireless channels impose on transmission bit rates. This interface has its own protocol stack that includes a physical layer, a link layer usually including a MAC and an LLC, and a radio resource management sublayer, in addition to the other layers or sublayers needed for each specific connection (control, data, voice, or SMS).

The physical layer—interfaces to the data link layer (L2) and radio resource management sublayer (L2) in the MS and BS and to other functional units in the MS, BSS, and MSC to support traffic channels. The physical interface uses a set of physical channels (using an FDMA/TDMA combination). Each physical channel supports a number of logical channels for user traffic and signaling. The physical layer simply takes care of the transmission and reception of bits.

The data link layer role—is multiplexing, error detection and correction, flow control, and segmentation to allow for long messages on the upper layers. A link

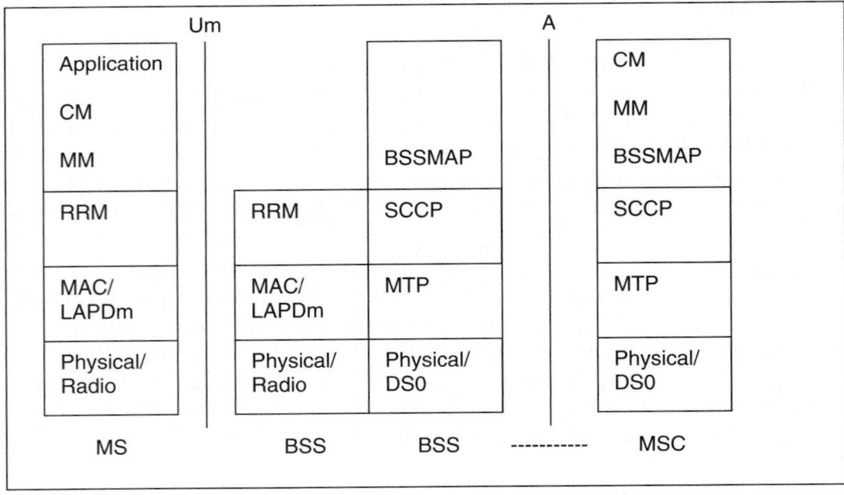

Figure 12: Simplified GSM protocol stack

access protocol is also supported on Dm channel (LAPDm).

The radio resource layer—ensures communication between the MS and BSS concerning the management of the radio connection, including connection establishment and control, call release, and handoff requirements.

The mobility management layer—supports location update, authentication, and encryption management in a mobile environment.

The connection management layer includes:

1. The call control entity, which controls end-to end call management.
2. The supplementary service entity, which supports the management of supplementary services.
3. The SMS protocol, which supports the high-level functions related to the transfer and management of short message services.

GSM Logical Channels

The following is a brief list of the logical channels used by GSM. All logical channels in the air interface use the same physical channels, given by the absolute radio frequency channel number (ARFCN) and time slots TS0–TS7. A physical channel is one of eight time slots in a single frequency.

1. Speech traffic channels (TCH): full-rate TCH (TCH/F), half-rate TCH (TCH/H).
2. Broadcast channels (BCCH): frequency correction channel (FCCH), synchronization channel (SCH), broadcast control channel (BCCH). These channels usually multiplex within the same slot in a designated frequency. The SCH and FCCH are the first channels the MS looks at when it attempts to register to a new wireless network.
3. Common control channels (CCCH): paging channel (PCH), random access channel (RACH), access grant channel (AGCH), similar to the ones covered in the earlier section entitled "Overview of Cellular Telephony Standards" for other standards.
4. Cell broadcast channel (CBCH), which uses the same physical channel as the DCCH.
5. Dedicated control channels (DCCH): Stand-alone dedicated control channel (SDCCH), slow associated control channel (SACCH), and fast associated control channel (FACCH). The last two are channels used to communicate control information while a call is in progress.

SOURCE CODING FOR VOICE

Source coding aims to represent the source information using a digital sequence that has the lowest bit rate possible while achieving the best possible voice quality. This is done by exploiting the redundancy that naturally exists in most multimedia signals including voice, video, and some data files. JPEG and MPEG standards are known algorithms that achieve very big compression ratios for still and moving pictures, respectively. With voice, many algorithms have been developed and many standards adopted.

Note that source coders are only one subset of the general group of speech coders, which includes vocoders and waveform coders (see Chapter 8 of Rappaport [2001] and the other references that it cites).

Following are the three general families of vocoders used in second-generation cellular; they are all linear predictive coders (LPC). (See Steele and Hanzo [1999] for a detailed description and analysis of these codecs).

1. Vector-sum excited linear prediction codec), which is used by IS-136. (See Steele [1993] for details).
2. QCELP, a variation of CELP produced by Qualcomm for IS-95 (Wang 1999).
3. LPC-RPE, adopted by GSM after comparisons between many algorithms using a subjective testing study.

UMTS uses the same vocoder as GSM. However, there are many studies suggesting the use of voice over IP, especially for future generations, as wireless networking becomes dominated by IP traffic.

CONCLUSION

This chapter has presented an overview of cellular telephony and the state-of-the-art-technology available as of the printing of this handbook. Some tutorial sections on the principles of cellular system design are included for novice readers. There was no attempt to cover other wireless technologies such as fixed wireless access technologies, wireless LANs and PANs, and the newly evolving mobile broadband access. Other chapters in this handbook can be consulted on such subjects.

GLOSSARY

ARFCN: Absolute radio frequency channel number: GSM carrier frequency number.

AUC: Authentication center. A database used by the MSC for encrypting and authentication purposes.

BCCH: Broadcast control channel: A logical channel used by the BS to broadcast control messages to all mobiles.

BER: Bit error rate: The probability of error in the detection of a bit.

BS/BTS: Base station/base transceiver system: The equipment used in each cell to transmit and receive signals to and from the mobiles and relay them to and from the rest of the network (MSC, etc.).

CDMA: Code division multiple access: A multiple-access scheme in which users are identified via codes.

CRC: Cyclic Redundancy Check.

D-AMPS: Digital AMPS: Same as IS-136/54: North AmericanTDMA-based standard.

DCCH: Digital control channel: A channel used to transmit bits that carry control messages.

ESN: Electronic serial number: A sequence of bits stored in memory in the phone and embedded in the IMSI that is unique to every mobile phone.

FACCH: Fast associated control channel: Control bits that are transmitted by taking over whole time slots that are originally allocated to voice traffic. Used when immediate information needs to be sent (e.g., handoff).

FCCH: Frequency correction channel: A control channel used for frequency correction.

FDD: Frequency division duplex: Full duplex system in which the forward link uses one frequency band and the reverse link uses another.

FDMA: Frequency division multiple access: Distributed users sharing a medium by using different frequency bands.

FEC: Forward error correction: A redundancy scheme that allows some errors to be corrected at the receiver without need for retransmission.

FVC: Forward voice channel: A logical channel that carries voice bits in the forward direction (BS to MS).

GPRS: General packet radio service: A 2.5-generation packet data service that uses the same physical layer as GSM but with modifications in upper layers to allow packet switching in the MSC.

GSM: Global system for mobile communication, initially "Groupe Spécial Mobile." Second-generation TDMA-based digital cellular system.

HLR: Home location register: A database containing information about local subscriber MS's and their main "care of" address used in routing calls when away from their home network.

HSDPA: High-speed downlink packet access. A 3.5-generation cellular enhancement allowing higher data rates in the downlink.

HSUPA: High-speed uplink packet access. A 3.5-generation cellular enhancement allowing higher data rates in the uplink.

IMSI: International mobile subscriber identity: A permanent number assigned to a subscriber mobile and stored in the SIM that includes its MIN and other crucial information used to authorize connections.

MAC: Medium access control: A second layer protocol providing logical channel access.

MAHO: Mobile assisted handoff: A protocol in which mobiles are active in the handoff process, providing information used by the MSC to decide on handoff.

MRC: Maximum ratio combining: A diversity combining method that maximizes SNR.

MSC: Mobile switching center: The main switching and networking entity and the "brain" behind it all in PLMN decisions related to call processing, channel assignment, handoffs, location and mobility management resource management, routing ... you name it!

PN: Pseudo-noise: Digital sequence that is usually generated using a sequence of shift registers. It is periodic but its period is long enough to consider the output sequence almost random, thus the word *pseudo-random*. Used in CDMA and any instances that require use of a recoverable random sequence.

QPSK: Quadrature phase shift keying: A digital modulation scheme that uses four different phases. Variations include π/4-QPSK, DQPSK (differential QPSK), OQPSK (offset-QPSK),and π/4-DQPSK (Used in IS136).

RACH: Random access channel: A reverse control channel used by all mobiles to request a connection. Random access (ALOHA) is used as the multiple-access mechanism.

RVC: Reverse voice channel: A logical channel that carries voice bits in the reverse direction (MS to BS).

SACCH: Slow associated control channel: Control bits associated with the voice connection (bits in the same slot as voice bits) carrying less urgent information than FACCH.

SCH: Synchronization channel: One of the control channels used for synchronization purposes.

SIM: Subscriber interface module (or subscriber identity module): A small unit containing information such as IMSI and subscriber information used by the phone to call authorization and billing.

TCH: Traffic channels: As opposed to control channels, all channels carrying user data.

TDD: Time-division duplexing: Full duplex system in which the forward link uses one time slot and the reverse link uses another.

TDMA: Time-division multiple access: Distributed users sharing a medium by using different slots.

TMSI: Temporary subscriber identifier: Temporary identity assigned by a host network via its VLR.

UMTS: Universal mobile telecommunications system: 3G cellular system using CDMA that has packet switching for data up to 2 Mbps.

VLR: Visitor location register: Stores temporary local copy of subscriber information of all mobiles registered to its associated MSC(s).

CROSS REFERENCES

See *Cellular Communications Channels*; *Code Division Multiple Access (CDMA)*; *Universal Mobile Telecommunications System (UMTS)*; *Wireless Channels*.

REFERENCES

3GPP Technical Specification Group Service and System Aspects. 2001. Third generation partnership project; 3G security; Security threats and requirements. 3GPP TS 21.133. http://www.3gpp.org/ftp/Specs/html-info/21133.htm (accessed December 20, 2005).

3GPP Technical Specification Group Services and System Aspects. 2004. General UMTS architecture. TS 23.101. version 3.0.1. http://www.3gpp.org/ftp/Specs/html-info/23101.htm (accessed July 27, 2007).

3GPP Technical Specification Group Services and System Aspects. 2005. Radio interface protocol architecture (Release 7). http://www.3pgg.org/ftp/Specs/archive/25_series/25.301/ (accessed July 27, 2007).

3GPP2 Specifications. 2006. http://www.3gpp2.org/public_html/specs/index.cfm (accessed December 15, 2006).

ANSI/TIA/EIA. 1995 IS-41 Rev. C. http://ansi.org.

Bdira, E. B., and P. Mermelstein. 1999. Exploiting macrodiversity with distributed antennas in microcellular CDMA. *Wireless personal Communication* 9(2): 178–96.

Black, U. 1998 1. *Second generation mobile and wireless networks*. Upper Saddle River, NJ: Prentice Hall.

Garg, V. K., and J. E. Wilkes. 1999. *Principles and applications of GSM*. Upper Saddle River, NJ: Prentice Hall.

Giannakis, G. B., Y. Hua, P. Stoica, and L. Tong. 2001. *Signal processing advances in wireless and mobile communications, Volume 2: Trends in single-user and multiuser systems*. Upper Saddle River, NJ: Prentice Hall.

Goldsmith, A. 2005. *Wireless communications*. Cambridge, UK: Cambridge University Press.

Haykin, S. and M. Moher. 2005. *Modern wireless communications*. Upper Saddle River, NJ: Prentice Hall.

Holma, H. and A. Toskala, eds. 2001. *WCDMA for UMTS, Radio Access for Third Generation Mobile Communications*. Hoboken, NJ: John Wiley & Sons.

Korhonen, J. 2003. *Introduction to 3G mobile communications*. Norwood, MA: Artech House.

LeFevre, M. and P. Okrah. 2001. Making the leap to 4G wireless. *CommsDesign*. http://www.commsdesign.com/showArticle.jhtml?articleID=16503085, (accessed July 27, 2007).

Mark, J. W., and W. Zhuang. 2003. *Wireless communications and networking*. Upper Saddle River, NJ: Prentice Hall.

Ojanperä, T. and R. Prasad, eds. 1998. *Wideband CDMA for third generation mobile communications*. Norwood, MA: Artech House.

Rappaport, T. S. 2001. *Wireless communications, principles and practice*. 2nd ed. Upper Saddle River, NJ: Prentice Hall.

Rysavy, P. Undated. Voice capacity enhancements for GSM evolution towards UMTS. http://www.rysavy.com/Articles/GSM_voice_capacity_71802.pdf (accessed July 27, 2007).

Sauter, M. 2006. *Communications systems for the mobile information society*. Hoboken, NJ: John Wiley & Sons.

Schmitz, N. 2005. The path to 4G will take many turns: Emerging standards, intensive research, and powerful enabling technologies make for an interesting race to 4G mobile broadband. *Wireless Systems Design*. http://www.wsdmag.com/Articles/ArticleID/10001/10001.html, (accessed July 27, 2007).

Schwartz, M. 2005. *Wireless networks*. Cambridge, UK: Cambridge University Press.

Simon, M. K., and M.-S. Alouini. 2000. *Digital communication over fading channels: A unified approach to performance analysis*. Hoboken, NJ: John Wiley & Sons.

Stallings, W. 2005. *Wireless communications and networks*. 2nd ed. Upper Saddle River, NJ: Prentice Hall.

Steele, R. 1993. Speech codecs for personal communications. *IEEE Communications* November, pp. 76–83.

Steele, R. and L. Hanzo, eds. 1999. *Mobile radio communications*. Hoboken, NJ: John Wiley & Sons.

Steele, R., C.-C. Lee, and P. Gould. 2001. *GSM, cdmaOne, and 3G systems*. Hoboken, NJ: John Wiley & Sons.

Stüber, G. L., 2001. *Principles of mobile communications*. 2nd ed. New York: Kluwer Academic Publishers.

UMTS TDD Alliance. Undated. http://www.umtstdd.org.

Verdu, S. 1998. *Multiuser detection*. Cambridge, UK: Cambridge University Press.

Viterbi, A. J. 1995. *CDMA—Principles of spread spectrum communication*. Reading MA: Addison-Wesley.

Wang, D. Q. 1999 QCELP vocoders in CDMA systems design. *CommsDesign*. http://www.commsdesign.com/main/1999/04/9904feat3.htm (accessed February 17, 2006).

WiMAX Forum. 2006a. Mobile WiMAX—Part I: A technical overview and performance evaluation. http://www.wimaxforum.org/news/downloads/Mobile_WiMAX_Part1_Overview_and_Performance.pdf (accessed November 20, 2006).

WiMAX Forum. 2006b. Mobile WiMAX—Part II: A comparative analysis. June 2006. Available in http://www.wimaxforum.org/news/downloads/Mobile_WiMAX_Part2_Comparative_Analysis.pdf (accessed November 20, 2006).

Yaun, J. Z. Chen, and B. Vucetic. 2003. Performance and design of space-time coding in fading channels, *IEEE Transactions on Communications*, December, pp. 1991–1996.

Zeng, Q-A., and D. P. Agrawal. 2002. Handoff in wireless mobile network. In *Handbook of wireless networks and mobile computing*, edited by Ivan Stojmenovic. Hoboken, NJ: John Wiley & Sons.

FURTHER READING

A good reference on all cellular and wireless standards is Sauter (2006).

For more details on GPRS, refer to Chapter 10.3 in Schwartz (2005) as well all the references quoted in it, especially Kaldren et al. (2000) and Koodli and Punskari (2001).

For more details on GSM and all the first- and second-generation cellular systems, refer to Black (1998) and Rysavy (n.d.).

Goldsmith (2005), Simon and Alouini (2002), and Mark and Zhuang (2003) are very good references on mobile channel characterization and theory of cellular system design. They are quite advanced and are meant for readers familiar with communication theory.

Steele and Hanzo (1999) and Steele, Lee, and Gould (2001) present a comprehensive in-depth study and analysis of second-and early third-generations cellular systems.

A detailed description of 3G systems can be found in Korhonen 2003.

For an advanced treatment of the physical layer including modulation performance in fading, diversity combining, multi-user detection, multi-carrier modulation, and MIMO systems, see Goldsmith (2005) and Stuber (2001).

Haykin and Moher (2005) and Stallings (2005) provide general wireless system coverage that requires little background.

Zeng and Agrawal (2002) is a good reference for handoff procedures and algorithms.

Mobile Radio Communications

Chi Zhou, *Illinois Institute of Technology*

INTRODUCTION

Wireless communications has experienced explosive growth over the last few decades, especially the cellular communications (for details, see "Cellular Telephony"). The first-generation cellular systems emerged in the 1980s, and the systems were analogue and voice centric. Those systems were typically limited in capacity. The second-generation cellular systems appeared about 10 years later with improved capacity, and were digital and voice centric with limited data capacities. Because the second-generation systems were not capable of supporting high bandwidth applications, third-generation systems were developed to support multimedia services such as audio, video, real time video conferencing, and high-speed Internet connections (for details, see "Evolution of Mobile Cellular Networks"). In addition to cellular networks, other wireless networks have also emerged, such as Wireless Local Area Networks (WLANs) (for details, see "Wireless LANs (WLANs)"), Wireless Wide Area Networks (WWANs) (for details, refer to "Wireless Wide Area Networks (WWANs)," wireless ad hoc systems, wireless sensor networks (for details see, "Principles and Applications of Ad Hoc and Sensor Networks"), etc. Next-generation communications systems are expected to integrate various communications networks, support fully integrated services, and provide full coverage and ubiquitous mobile access.

Mobile radio communications refers to transferring information through electromagnetic signals over a wireless radio channel between mobile users. In contrast to the wireline channel, the wireless channel is random and time-varying. As a signal is propagated over the air, the signal may get reflected, diffracted, or scattered. Therefore, the received signal at the receiver usually consists of multiple components corresponding to each distinct path. Because each multipath component has different attenuation gain and delay, the addition of multipath components may contribute constructive or destructive interference, which makes the received signal unpredictable. In addition, when the transmitter, the receiver, or the surrounding objects move, the multipath changes over time, which makes the wireless channel random and time-varying. Due to the nature of wireless channels, the design of wireless systems is fundamentally different from that of wireline systems. (For more details about wireless channels, see "Wireless Channels" and "Cellular Communications Channels.")

The basic elements of mobile radio communications systems are shown in Figure 1. Most communications systems today are digital systems. The digital signals may come directly from digital sources or may be converted from analog signals through the Analog/Digital converter. The source encoder aims to remove redundancy of the

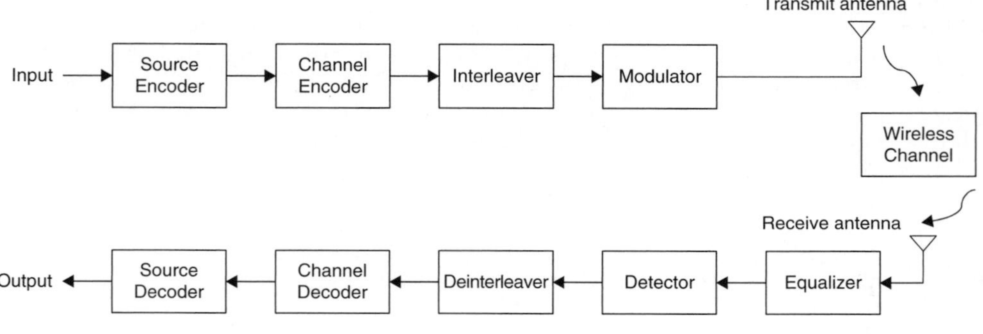

Figure 1: Basic elements of a mobile radio communications system

input signal and represent the signal in an efficient way. Because the channel is unavoidably noisy, the transmit signal becomes corrupted, which leads to error at reception. The purpose of channel encoding is to add redundant bits to the information in a controlled manner in order to reduce reception error. To overcome deep fading of the wireless channel, interleaver is usually added in wireless communications systems to scramble the bits before modulation. The modulator modulates the discrete bits into continuous waveforms that can be sent via a transmit antenna through the wireless channel. On the receiver side, the receive antenna usually receives a distorted signal due to the additive noise and wireless fading channel. To compensate for the distortion of the wireless multipath channel, an equalizer may be employed at the receiver, though multicarrier modulation has been used instead in many current 3G systems. The detector performs some signal processing techniques on the received distorted signals and makes the decision about transmit signals according to certain predefined decision rules. One example of this is matched filter detector. The rest blocks at the receiver are just the counter blocks of each component at the transmitter. The deinterleaver, performing the inverse function of the interleaver, puts the bits into the original order. The channel decoder removes the redundant bits added by the channel encoder. The source decoder maps the coded bits into the information message.

Mobile radio communications includes a broad range of topics, each of which needs a separate chapter in order to provide detailed discussion. Because a single chapter cannot fully cover it all, we aim to provide an overview of some major components and try to avoid mathematical details as much as possible due to the page limit. The remaining sections of this chapter are organized as follows: "Antennas" discusses the antenna configuration used in mobile radio communications systems today and what is currently evolving. In "Speech Coding," speech coding is presented with the different options and challenges of speech compression. Next, "Channel Coding" describes channel coding and includes some examples. "Digital Modulation for Fading Channel" and "Equalization" discuss digital modulation for fading channel and equalization. MIMO systems are described in "MIMO Systems." Lastly, "Conclusion" provides a summative conclusion of the previous sections.

ANTENNAS

The antenna is a device that radiates signal energy over radio frequency (RF) from transmitter to outside and receives RF energy from outside to the receiver (Okamoto, 2002). Because the antenna transfers information through an RF signal, it is crucial for any communications system. The design of antennas has a big influence on spectrum efficiency and quality of services (QoS). Traditionally, there are two major types of antennas, omnidirectional and directional. The omni-directional antenna radiates or receives energy equally well in all directions, while the directional antenna transmits or receives signal energy in some specific direction. The communication mode can be classified as either half duplex or duplex. In half duplex mode, the transmitter and receiver are generally connected to the same antenna. When a transmitter transmits, the receiver has to keep silent, and vice versa. The transmission and reception are controlled by an electronic switch, which prevents the transmitter output from damaging the receiver. In half duplex mode, the transmission and reception may or may not be done on the same frequency. In duplex mode, the transmitter and receiver are attached to different antennas, so that transmission and reception happen simultaneously. The two antennas usually operate at two frequencies considerably separated so that the transmission does not interfere with reception.

Antennas for Base Station

In cellular networks, the purpose of a base station is to transfer signals between mobile users and the core network through a radio link in microwave frequency ranging from several hundred MHz to several GHz (e.g., AMPS [Advanced Mobile Phone System] operates at 806 – 902 MHz, and PCS [Personal Communications Service] operates at 1.85 – 1.99 GHz). In general, a base station consists of antenna boxes, an equipment cabinet, and a mast. The equipment cabinet contains a power supply and the actual transmitter cables, which provide the energy and transfer the signal between the antennas. Depending on the coverage area, the antennas may be mounted on a free-standing mast with height between 20 and 35 meters for wide rural areas, on the roof of a building or outer wall for urban or rural populated areas, or on the wall close to the ceiling within a building.

Many types of antennas are being used for base stations, among which two dominant types of antennas are omni-directional and directional antennas. The omni-directional antenna radiates or receives energy equally well in all directions, as shown in Figure 2(a). This type of antenna provides the simplest solution for mobile telecommunications systems, although the gain of an omni-directional antenna is low because most of the radiated energy is wasted and interference is generated in all directions. On the other hand, the directional antenna transmits or receives energy signals in some specific direction, as shown in Figure 2(b). A base station needs to employ multiple directional antennas to provide full coverage. Compared with the omni-directional antenna, the directional antenna has a higher gain, because it receives signals in only one direction, which reduces the received interference from other mobile users.

The exposure to the radiofrequency radiation from wireless communications, such as antennas, raises health concerns in the public (Health Council of the Netherlands, 2004). Many national and international organizations have instituted safety guidelines for exposure of the public to the RF energy produced by base station antennas. The most widely accepted standards include the Institute of Electrical and Electronics Engineers and American National Standards Institute (ANSI/IEEE), the International Commission on Non-Ionizing Radiation Protection (ICNIRP), and the National Council on Radiation Protection and Measurements (NCRP). For instance, for base stations that operate in the 1800-2000 MHz range, the ANSI/IEEE exposure standard for the general public is 1.2 mW/cm-sq. For antennas that operate around 900 MHz, the ANSI/

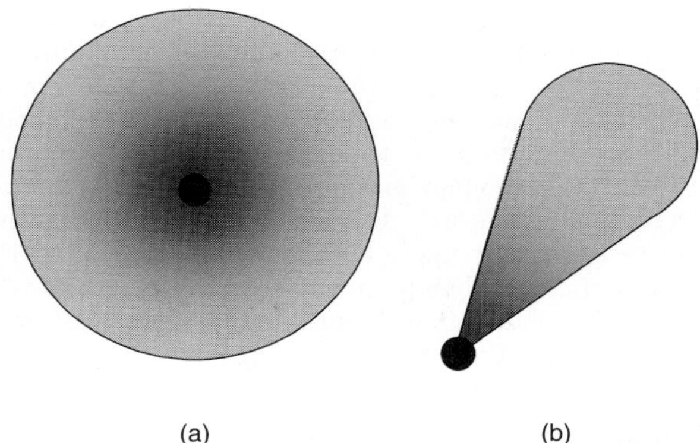

Figure 2: Radiation pattern for (a) omni-directional antenna (b) directional antenna

IEEE exposure standard for the general public is 0.57 mW/cm-sq (Moulder 2005).

Smart Antennas

A smart antenna is an array of antenna elements connected to a digital signal processor, which enables the system to optimize the radiation and reception based on the location of users (Chryssomallis 2000). These antennas can automatically adjust the antenna direction and reception pattern according to the movement of mobile users and the surrounding environment. The use of these antennas can improve the signal quality and dramatically increase the capacity of a wireless link due to array gain, diversity gain, and interference suppression (Ingram 2000).

The two types of smart antennas are switched beam antennas and adaptive array antennas, as shown in Figure 3. Switched beam antenna systems form multiple predetermined beams with heightened sensitivity in particular directions. For a mobile user within the sector, the switched-beam antennas detect the user's signal strength according to some predetermined scanning pattern, then choose one predetermined fixed beam for best reception quality and switch the beam from one to another as the user changes position. On the other hand, the adaptive array antennas use a variety of signal processing algorithms to dynamically locate and track various types of signals to minimize interference and maximize intended signal reception.

Smart antennas have been developed to achieve Space-Division Multiple Access (SDMA) technique in multi-user environments to complement major multiple access schemes, such as Frequency Division Multiple Access (FDMA), Time Division Multiple Access (TDMA) (for details, see "Time Division Multiple Access"), or Code Division Multiple Access (CDMA) (for details, see "Code Division Multiple Access (CDMA)"). SDMA enables multiple users within the same cell but separated by some distance to use the same radio channel such as frequency, time slot, or code. In the smart antenna system, each antenna element can identify each propagation pattern so that multiple users can be differentiated within a certain resolution. With the channel reuse, SDMA can increase the system capacity significantly.

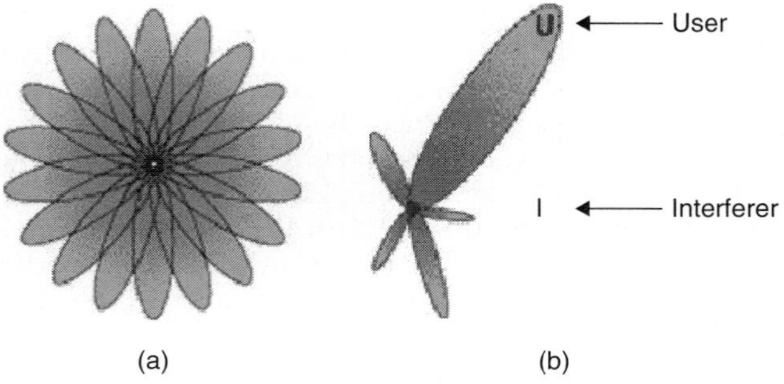

Figure 3: Smart antenna (a) switched beam antennas, (b) adaptive array antennas

In summary, smart antenna systems can increase signal gain by combining inputs from multiple antennas, reduce the interference by automatically adjusting the radiation and reception pattern to suppress the interference, and significantly increase the system capacity by exploiting SDMA. However, the great challenge for smart antenna implementation is complexity. The complicated signal processing algorithms have to be executed in real time. It is expected that in the near future, advancement in computer technologies will make smart antenna systems possible for commercial communications systems.

SPEECH CODING

With increasing demand for cellular service, service providers are continuously facing the challenge of accommodating more and more users within limited bandwidth. Low bit-rate speech coding, which aims to transmit speech with the high quality but small channel capacity (Rappaport, 2002), provides a solution to this challenge. Speech coding is a technique for audio signal and speech processing, in which speech is compressed into a code for transmission with speech codecs (coder-decoder). The voice for telephone applications is frequency limited between 200 Hz and a little under 4 kHz. For a band-limited speech signal, a sample of the waveform at a particular rate can be extracted and the signal can be reconstructed with those samples. Speech coding is also referred to as lossy coding (Lucent Technologies 2000). The lower the bit rate at which the coder can deliver speech, the more voice users it can support within a given bandwidth. However, there are tradeoffs in speech compression. To deliver low bit rate, complex algorithms need to be used, which lead to higher processing and computation delays. (For more information, see "Speech and Audio Compression.")

Most speech coders can be classified into two categories: waveform coders and source coders. Waveform coders are designed to replicate and reconstruct the original waveform (after quantization) as much as possible. On the other hand, source coders measure certain parameters from the original speech waveform, and send these parameters to the receiver to reconstruct the waveform using those parameters. In general, waveform coders provide excellent speech quality with low complexity and high robustness. Consequently, they produce a moderate to high bit rate of 32 to 64 kbps. Meanwhile, source coders, using highly complex algorithms, produce low bit rates (less than 32kbps) but they are less robust than waveform coders. In addition, the performance of source

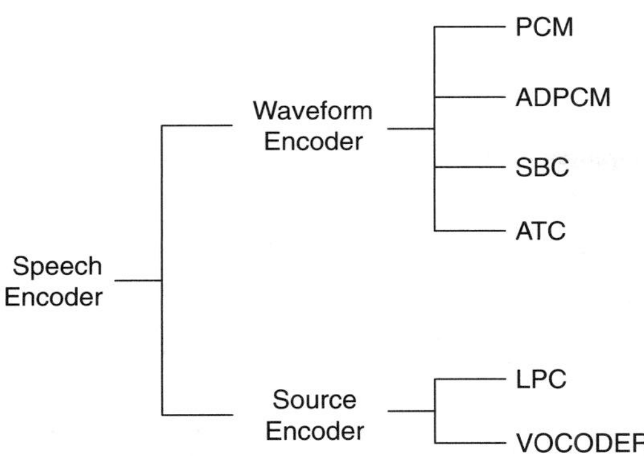

Figure 4: Types of speech coders

coders relies heavily on the speaker. Figure 4 below shows the types of some commonly used speech coders.

Waveform Coders

Pulse Code Modulation (PCM), invented by the British engineer Alec Reeves in 1937 while working for the International Telephone and Telegraph in France, was deployed in the United States Public Switched Telephone Network in 1962 (Hall 1996). A PCM encoder executes three operations on the input signal: filtering, sampling, and quantization. The purpose of the front-end filter is to limit the bandwidth of the input signal so that the signal bandwidth is less than one half of the sampling frequency. A non-uniform quantizer is used to represent the amplitude of each sample as an eight-bit binary codeword. PCM encoder produces an output of a 64 kbps DSO (Digital Signal 0) bit stream corresponding to each voice channel.

Adaptive Differential Pulse Code Modulation (ADPCM) is a differential waveform coder in the time domain, as shown in Figure 5 (Zilog 2005). The speech waveforms are highly correlated; thus, the variances of their differences are very small. Rather than using original quantized and adjacent samples of a speech waveform, the ADPCM coder uses a linear predictor to predict the next sample. The predictor samples are then subtracted from the quantized values of the original speech waveform. Then the difference is encoded for transmission and sent over the transmission line. This difference between the predicted and actual sample is called the prediction error. Both uniform and non-uniform quantizers can be used in ADPCM coder to quantize values of the original speech waveform (Robinson 2001). The receiver takes a succession of these adjacent sample differences, decodes the samples, and put them together in piecewise fashion in order to reconstruct the original speech waveform. Because encoding the small prediction errors uses less bits, ADPCM can encode speech at a bit rate of 32kbps, which is half the standard 64kbps PCM, while still maintaining the same voice quality as PCM.

Sub-band coding (SBC) is a waveform coding scheme in the frequency domain that works by exploring the statistics of the speech signal. In these coders, speech frequency is divided into a number of sub-bands by a bank of band-pass filters and then the signal in each band is encoded using a different number of bits. For example, in speech, the lower frequency bands contain critical information about pitch and formant; thus more bits are usually allotted in those frequency bands than higher bands in order to preserve the critical information. The design of the filter bank is very important in the SBC design. The filter bandwidth may be equal or unequal. Once the output of each filter is sampled and encoded, the codes are sent over the transmission line. At the receiver side, the receiver has the signals de-multiplexed, decoded, demodulated, and then summed to reconstruct the signal. Sub-band coding can produce the speech coding at bit rates in the range of 9.6 to 32 kbps. In this range, speech quality is roughly equivalent to that of ADPCM at an equivalent bit rate. In addition, its low complexity and relative good speech quality at low bit rates make it particularly advantageous for coding below 16 kbps (Rappaport 2002). SBC has been adopted by the CD-900 cellular telephone system for speech compression.

Adaptive Transform Coding (ATC) is another waveform speech coder in the frequency domain. The ATC transform coder transforms signals into some transform components according to a particular unitary transform and the corresponding inverse-transform is performed at the receiver. Because the unitary transforms tend to

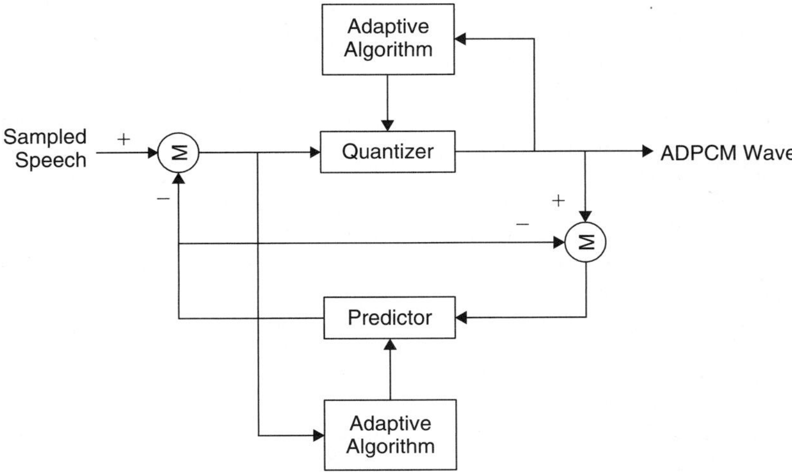

Figure 5: Adaptive differential pulse code modulation encoder

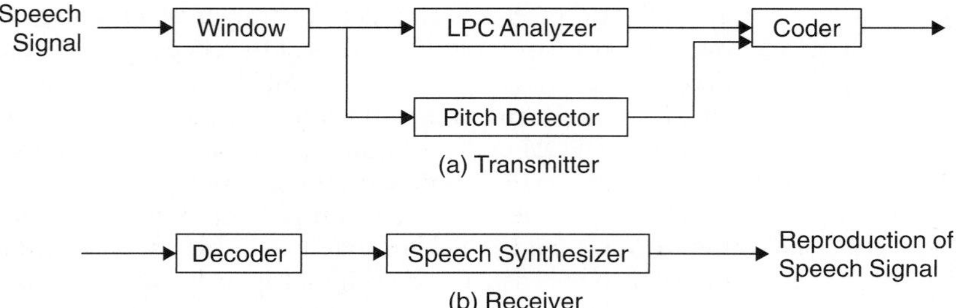

Figure 6: LPC vocoder (a) transmitter, (b) receiver

generate near-uncorrelated transform components that can be coded independently (Spanias 1994), the ATC coder has the potential to reduce the bit rate. In general, ATC can outperform ADPCM by about 6 dB gain at 16 kbps. Although perceptual distortion tends to be small for rates as low as 12 kbps or lower, ATC suffers from the "low-pass filtering" effect, which is a consequence of the fact that only high-energy components are coded (Spanias 1994).

Source Coders

The vocoder (voice coder) is a speech analyzer and synthesizer. Though vocoders were originally developed in 1930s, they were never taken seriously in telecommunications until the late 1970s. Since then, most vocoders have been implemented using linear prediction, whereby the target signal's spectral envelope or formant is estimated by an all-pole IIR (infinite impulse response) filter. In linear prediction coding, the IIR filter is used at the encoder to whiten the signal (i.e., flatten the spectrum) and correspondingly, the decoder at the receiver re-applies the spectral shape of the target speech signal. All vocoder systems attempt to model the generation of the speech process as a dynamic system and try to quantify certain physical limits of the system. Vocoders tend to be much more complex and rigorous than waveform coders, but they can achieve very high economy in terms of the transmission bit rate.

The channel vocoder was the first among the analysis-synthesis systems of speech demonstrated in practice. Channel vocoders are the vocoders in frequency domain that determine the envelope of the speech signal for a number of frequency bands and then sample, encode and multiplex these samples with the encoded output of the other filters. The sampling is done synchronously every 10 to 30 ms. Along with the energy information about each band, the voice/unvoiced decision and the pitch frequency for voiced speech are transmitted.

The formant vocoder is similar to the channel vocoder but theoretically can operate at lower bit rates because fewer control signals are used. Rather than sending samples of the power spectrum envelope, the formant vocoder attempts to transmit the peak positions of the spectral envelope. To represent the speech sounds, a formant vocoder should be able to identify at least three formants. In addition, the intensities of the formants must also be controlled. Formant coders are able to reach bit rates of 12kbps.

The cepstrum vocoder separates the excitation and vocal tract spectrum by using the Inverse Fourier Transform of the log magnitude spectrum in order to produce the cepstrum of the signal. The low frequency coefficients in the cepstrum correspond to the vocal tract spectral envelope and the high frequency excitation coefficients form a periodic pulse train at multiples of the sampling period. Linear filtering is performed to separate the vocal tract cepstral coefficients from the excitation coefficients. In the receiver, the vocal tract cepstral coefficients are transformed by Fourier Transform to produce the vocal tract impulse response. By convolving the impulse response with a synthetic excitation signal, the original speech is reconstructed.

Voice excited vocoders are a hybrid that combines the PCM and channel vocoder. Specifically, PCM transmission is used in low-frequency bands of speech and channel vocoding is used in high-frequency bands in order to eliminate the need for pitch extraction of speech waveforms. A pitch signal is generated at the synthesizer by rectifying, band-pass filtering, and clipping the base band signal. This creates a spectrally flat signal with energy at pitch harmonics. Voice excited vocoders have been designed for operation at 7.2kbps and their quality is usually superior to any general pitch excited vocoder.

Unlike the vocoders, Linear Predictive Coding (LPC) concerns the time domain, as shown in Figure 6 (Zilog 2005). These vocoders strive to extract the significant features of speech from the time waveform. The coefficients of the all pole filter are obtained in the time domain using linear prediction techniques. Specifically, the current sample can be expressed as a linear sum of all the past samples. The predictor coefficients are calculated because the average in the error signal, that represents the difference between the predicted and actual speech amplitude, needs to be minimized. LPCs are similar to ADPCM except that instead of sending differential samples from the transmitter to the receiver, LPCs send selected characteristics of the error signal. These parameters include gain factor, pitch information, and the voiced/unvoiced decision information. Then, the receiver takes the error signal information and uses the error signal itself as the excitation. By using LPCs, it is possible to transmit good quality voice at 4.8kbps and poorer qualities at even lower rates (Rappaport 2002).

CHANNEL CODING

Data signals transmitted over a channel are inevitably exposed to natural and man-made electromagnetic interferences. The detector at the receiver cannot detect the signal correctly when the received signal is severely distorted.

The situation get worse in wireless radio communications. The wireless channel is random and time-varying; thus, it is more prone to errors. When a wireless channel experiences deep fading, bursts of data bits may be lost. Therefore, data signals must be protected to reduce the errors. Channel coding is a technique to control errors through adding redundancy in a controlled manner. The code rate is defined as the number of message bits over the number of total encoded bits. Channel coding may have either error-detection capability or error-correction capability. Error-detection channel codes can detect transmission errors. Once an error is detected, the receiver sends a request to the transmitter for retransmission. On the other hand, error-correction channel codes have the capability of correcting a certain amount of errors without retransmission. Adding more redundant bits leads to a lower code rate, but in general can increase the error correction capability. If more errors can be corrected, the communications system can operate with a lower transmitted power, can transmit over larger distances, can tolerate more interference, and can use smaller antennas and transmit at higher data rate. However, the cost of low code rates is large bandwidth consumption.

In 1948, Claude Shannon commenced error control coding with his famous publication "A Mathematical Theory of Information" (Shannon 1948). Shannon showed that it was possible to design a communications system with any small probability of error desired whenever the rate of transmission is smaller than the capacity of the channel. In 1950, the first single-error-correcting codes were introduced. In the late 1950s and 1960s, Reed-Solomon Codes and Convolutional codes appeared. Since then, many channel coding techniques have been developed. In this section, three techniques which are widely used in cellular networks are discussed: cyclic codes, convolutional codes, and turbo codes. In addition, interleaving is discussed as a technique to overcome the deep fading in wireless radio communications.

Cyclic Codes

A cyclic code exhibits two fundamental properties, linearity and cyclic properties. A cyclic code is a linear code; that is, the sum of any two code words is also a code word. In addition, any cyclic shift of a code word is also a code word. Cyclic code is usually generated by using a generator polynomial $g(D)$ of degree $(n - k)$ in a (n, k) block, where k is the number of information bits in a block, n is the number of bits in a code word, and $(n - k)$ bits are the redundant parity bits introduced for error control. For instance, the Global System for Mobile Communications (GSM) uses a (53, 50) cyclic code where a block of 50 information bits is coded into a codeword of 53 code bits by adding 3 parity bits (Grech 1999) (for details, see "Global System for Mobile Communications (GSM)"). Encoding for a cyclic code is usually performed by a linear feedback shift register based on either the generator or parity polynomial. For a cyclic code only capable of error detection, the detector at the receiver divides the received discrete data by the chosen parity-check polynomial. If the remainder of the division is not zero, this indicates that an error has occurred and the data block is discarded. On the other hand, if the remainder is not zero, this indicates that the transmission is error-free. For a cyclic code capable of error correction, syndrome decoding technique can be used for detection.

The popularity of cyclic codes is mainly due to their efficient error-detection capability. As an example, Cyclic Redundancy Check (CRC) codes (Lin and Csotello 1983) are cyclic codes typically used in automatic repeat request (ARQ) systems for error detection (Lin, Costello, and Miller 1984). Though some cyclic codes have no error-correction capability, they can be combined with another error-correcting code to improve performance. For example, GSM uses the combination of cyclic codes and convolutional codes for channel coding.

Convolutional Codes

In contrast to block codes, in which information bits are grouped into blocks and codewords are generated on a block-by-block basis, convolutional codes encode the incoming message sequence continuously in a serial manner (Pless 1998). A convolutional code consists of a K-stage shift register and n additional operators. Each stage in the shift register holds k bits. The information bits pass through the shift register k bits at a time. Each additional operator takes the bits from the shift register to generate an output bit. Therefore, k-bit input is encoded into n-bit output and the rate of the code is $R=k/n$. Figure 7 shows the block diagram for the convolutional coder, where the shift register has $K = 5$ stages, each stage holds $k = 1$ bit, and the number of additional operator is $n = 2$. Thus, $R = 1/2$ is the code rate; that is, the output bit rate is twice the input rate. Each output bit depends on the state of the registers and on the actual input, providing a kind of prediction capability to the detector in order to determine incorrect transitions on the received coded data.

If no errors occur, the received message can easily be related back to the original bit stream, given the initial condition. With the aid of the Trellis diagram (Proakis 2001), a received message can be decoded according to maximum likelihood method when the received data contains errors. However, maximum likelihood decoding

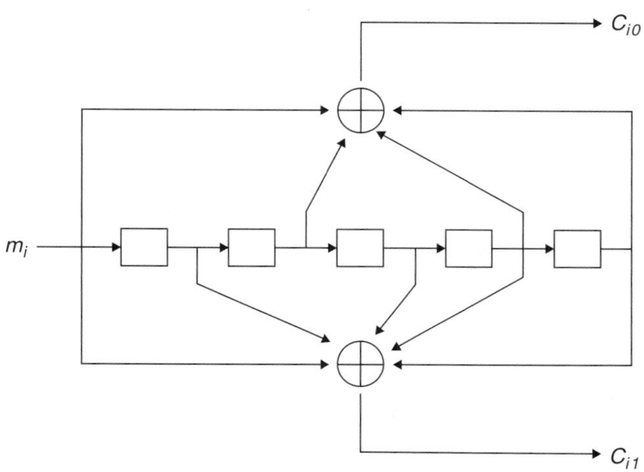

Figure 7: Convolutional encoder

results in a high load of computation work. Thus, some systematic procedure is required to reduce the computation complexity, especially when the error location of the frame is unknown or when more than one error occurs. One widely used algorithm is the Viterbi algorithm (Viterbi 1967; Forney 1973). Exploring the structure of the path metric computation, the Viterbi algorithm only considers the paths that can reach the highest path metric and discards the rest. Both computation and required memory are reduced significantly, compared to the maximum-likelihood decoding.

Convolutional codes provide error tolerance and error correction capability. In addition, they permit a transmitter to transmit with low power. Convolutional codes have been adopted in both GSM and IS-95 systems for error control. In many applications where the noise is predominantly Gaussian, the better solution is obtained when block and convolutional codes are jointly used in series. To improve performance in wireless fading channel, convolutional codes are commonly used with interleaving (a detailed discussion of interleaving is provided later in the chapter). This type of interleaver, usually referred as a *convolutional interleaver*, is designed both to smear the error bursts and to work well with the incremental nature of convolutional code generation (Forney 1971).

Turbo Codes

Turbo codes are a class of powerful error correction codes that were introduced in 1993 by a group of researchers from France: Berrou, Glavieux, and Thitimajshima, along with a practical decoding algorithm (Berrou et al. 1993). Turbo codes have large coding gains and allow a wireless communications link to come amazingly close to the theoretical limit specified by Shannon Capacity Theorem. In order to achieve low-power performance, the turbo encoder deals with large-size blocks of message bits. Because of the long latency involved in such large block codes, turbo codes did not gain much attention at the beginning. With the use of widespread spectrum in 3G cellular networks, turbo codes became applicable and started to gain a lot of attentions. Turbo codes have been used for low-power applications such as deep-space and satellite communications, as well as for interference-limited applications such as PCS systems. In addition, turbo codes have been adopted by Wideband CDMA (WCDMA) interface for third-generation cellular systems.

The basic block diagram for a turbo code encoder is shown in Figure 8. A turbo code encoder consists of two (or more) systematic recursive convolutional encoders separated by an interleaver that performs a scrambling

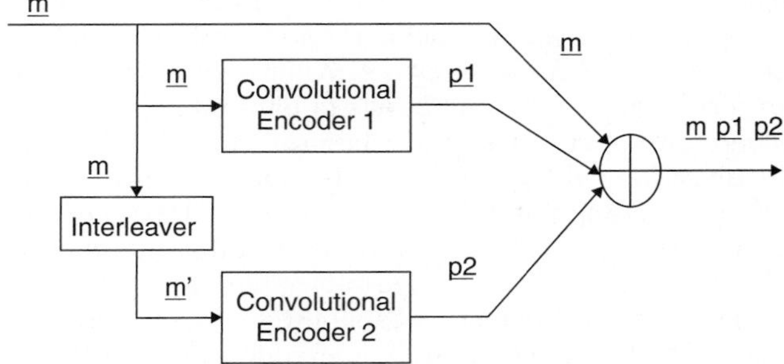

Figure 8: Turbo encoder

operation on the input message sequence. The two convolutional encoders generate two different sets of parity bits, p_1 and p_2. Using two encoders can achieve considerable coding gains in spite of the iterative soft decoding schemes whose complexity is only twice of a single convolutional decoder.

The complete encoded sequence is formed by three sub-blocks. The first one is the sequence itself, that is, the k-bit input sequence m. The second sub-block is the encoder 1 output, which corresponds to $n/2$ parity bits obtained from the sequence passed to a convolutional encoder. The third sequence is another $n/2$ parity bits obtained from passing a pseudo randomly interleaved copy of m to a second convolutional coder. Therefore, the encoded output sequence has $N = n/2 + n/2 + k = (n+k)$ bits. Then the code rate is the k-bit input over the N output bits, i.e., $R = \dfrac{k}{k+n}$.

The iterative decoding algorithm is based on simple decoders individually matched to the simple constituent codes. Each constituent decoder sends an estimated posteriori likelihood of the decoded bits to the other decoder, and uses the corresponding estimates from the other decoder as a priori likelihood. The received bits, corrupted by the noisy channel, are available to each decoder to initialize the a priori likelihoods. The decoders may use the soft output Viterbi Algorithm (SOVA) or a Maximum a-Posteriori decoding algorithm (MAP). The turbo decoder iterates between the outputs of the constituent decoders until reaching satisfactory convergence. The final output is a hard quantized version of the likelihood estimates of either of the decoders. The decoder block diagram is shown in Figure 9. The dotted lines show the iterative path. Note that the turbo decoding algorithms may not converge and in general six iterations can provide satisfactory performance.

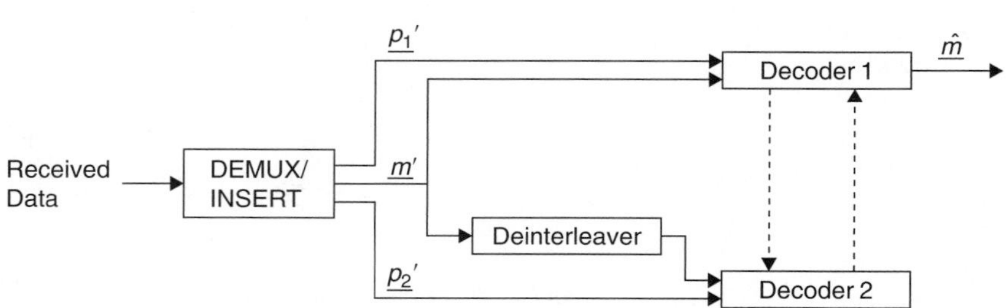

Figure 9: Turbo decoder block diagram

Though turbo codes allow a communications link to closely approach closely the Shannon limit, they exhibit an error floor phenomenon (Perez, Seghers, and Costello 1996), which results in a relatively high bit-error rate (BER). One solution to the problem is concatenating turbo codes with another type of code. Low-Density Parity-Check codes (LDPC) are a good choice. LDPC codes were originally invented by Gallager (Gallager 1962), and then revisited by Mackey (Mackay and Neal 1996). LDPC codes are linear block codes with a low-density parity check matrix. They can come near to the Shannon limit with relatively low decoding complexity. The concatenated LDPC-turbo code, which uses LDPC code as an outer code and turbo code as an inner code, can achieve very low BER and improve the performance of turbo codes (Kou, Lin, and Fossorier 2001).

Interleaving

Though many channel codes have the error-correction capability, the number of errors within a single codeword that can be corrected is limited. In another word, channel codes usually cannot correct burst of errors. When a wireless channel exhibits deep fading for a certain time period, all the bits transmitted during this period may get lost, and in general, those errors cannot be corrected. Interleaving is a technique in combination with channel coding to improve performance in a fading channel. The main function of interleaving is to spread out bursts of error bits in time over multiple codewords so that if a deep fade or noise burst occurs, the errors can still be corrected by channel codes. In the spatial analogy, the interleaver pushes the points farther apart in space, which decreases the probability of error. In turbo code encoder, the interleaver scrambles bits in a pseudo random predetermined fashion to bring more diversity to the codewords.

A variety of interleaving approaches is possible. Conceptually, the simplest approach is block interleaving, in which the interleaver memory is viewed as a rectangular array of storage locations. Block codes are usually combined with block interleavers so that the error bursts can be spread out across multiple codewords. For convolutional codes, in which the notion of codeword does not exist, the convolutional interleavers are designed in a slightly different way. A block interleaver is used to illustrate the general operations. The block interleaver operation is shown in Figure 10 (a). The data are written in memory by columns. When the memory array is full, the stored data are read out by rows. Block deinterleavers perform the inverse operation by writing the received data into the rows of a similar memory array and reading them out by columns after the array is full, as shown in Figure 10 (b). The size of the interleaver depends on the fading characteristics of wireless channel. Slow fading channel in general needs large interleavers so that all the bits in a received codeword are rather independent.

Though interleaving can improve the performance in terms of probability of error, especially in deep fading channel, it introduces additional delays. In block interleaving, the read-out operation for both interleaver and deinterleaver can only be performed when the memory array is full. Interleavers of large size generate large delays.

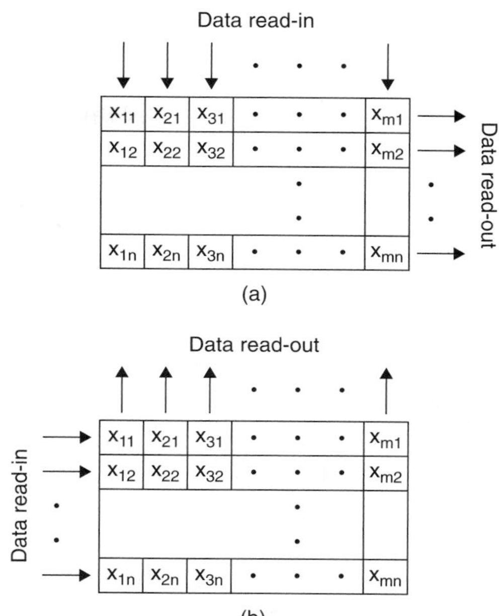

Figure 10: (a) Block interleaver, (b) block deinterleaver

Moreover, interleaving basically removes the correlation of fading, which information may be used for optimum maximum likelihood decoding. Therefore, coding combined with interleaving may cause a decrease in the channel capacity (Goldsmith and Varaiya 1996).

DIGITAL MODULATION FOR FADING CHANNEL

Modulation is a process of conveying information through electronic signals. In general, the information or message-bearing signals are superimposed upon a carrier signal for transmission. Sinusoidal signal is the typical carrier signal. Because various modulation techniques are discussed in detail in Part 2 of Volume I, this section provides a general overview of various modulation schemes, followed by detailed discussions of adaptive modulation.

Overview of Modulation Schemes

Modulation can be classified as analog modulation and digital modulation. In analog modulation, a carrier signal is varied continuously in phase, frequency, or amplitude. Analog modulation includes Phase Modulation (PM), and Frequency Modulation (FM) (for more details, see "Frequency and Phase Modulation"), and Amplitude Modulation (AM) (for more details, see "Pulse Amplitude Modulation"). PM is not widely used, because it tends to require more complex receiving hardware and there can be ambiguity problems in detection. FM is commonly used at VHF radio frequencies for high-fidelity broad casts of music and speech. AM is commonly used at radio frequencies.

Over the years a major transition has occurred from analog modulation to digital modulation, which converts an information-bearing discrete-time symbol sequence into continuous waveform. Digital modulation mainly includes Amplitude Shift Key (ASK), Frequency Shift Key (FSK), and Phase Shift Key (PSK) (for more details, see, "Digital Phase Modulation and Demodulation"). ASK changes the amplitude of a carrier wave to represent digital data. This technique is used in optical fiber communications. FSK shifts the output frequency to achieve distinct waveforms. FSK may be used for high-frequency radio communications or used in Local Area Networks (LAN) that use coaxial cable as media. PSK is a digital modulation scheme that conveys data by changing or modulating the phase of a sinusodial signal. Examples of PSK modulation techniques include BPSK, QPSK, Offset QPSK, Π/4-QPSK, and DPSK. Because symbol signals are distinct by their phases, phase needs to be aligned between transmitter and receiver so that the detector can perform the decision making. In addition, hybrid modulation techniques have also been developed, such as Quadrature Amplitude Modulation (QAM) that varies both phase and amplitude. QAM can represent multiple bits per symbol, and can thus deliver high data rate. QAM and its derivatives are used in both mobile radio and satellite communication systems.

In general, PSK and FSK are considered to be lower order modulation techniques, because each distinct signal represents fewer bits. Therefore, the system capacity is low. On the other hand, 16QAM, 64QAM, etc., are referred to as higher order modulation techniques, because each signal represents more bits. High data rate can be achieved by applying higher order modulation techniques. However, applying higher order modulation requires good channel condition in order to maintain certain bit error rate performance. The choice of modulation scheme depends on various factors, such as spectral efficiency, BER performance, power efficiency, cost and ease of implementation, channel condition (e.g., carrier-to-interference ratio), robustness to the multipath effect, etc. Some applications of digital modulation techniques are given in Table 1 (Fitton 2003).

In traditional communications systems, the radio transmission method is designed to cope with channel variations in a worst-case manner. For wireless systems, this implies the use of a simple modulation scheme, and

Table 1: Modulation Schemes for Various Applications

Modulation Format	Application
BPSK	Deep space telemetry, cable modems
QPSK	Satellite, CDMA, DVB-S, cable modems
OQPSK	CDMA, stellite
MSK, GMSK	CDPD, GSM
FSK, GFSK	DECT, paging, AMPS, CT2
8PSK	Satellite, aircraft
16 QAM	Microwave digital radio, modems
32 QAM	Terrestrial microwave, DVB-T

a complex error-correcting code. When the coding fails to compensate for temporary bad conditions, higher layers in the protocol ensure that the information is correctly and completely transmitted by requiring a retransmission of the erroneous data. Though simple, the traditional modulation setup is inefficient as it is designed for the worse-case scenario and cannot adapt to the time-varying channel condition.

Adaptive Modulation

Adaptive modulation, or link adaptation, is a powerful technique for improving the spectral efficiency in wireless transmissions over fading channels. The idea is to make efficient use of the bits: Whenever the channel conditions are adequate, transmission of redundant bits should be avoided (Ericsson 1999). To also achieve a high throughput over fading channels, the modulation parameters—such as signal constellation size, transmitted power level, and data rate—should be adjusted according to the channel conditions. The adaptation can also take into account requirements of different traffic classes and services such as required bit error rates. (Falahati et al. 2002).

Higher order modulations allow users to send more bits per symbol and thus achieve higher throughputs. However, higher order modulations require higher signal-to-noise ratios (SNRs) to overcome any interference and maintain a certain BER. The use of adaptive modulation allows a wireless system to choose the highest order modulation depending on the channel conditions. When the channel condition is good (e.g., mobile is close to the transmitter), the user receives higher SNR and thus can utilize higher order modulations like 64-QAM to increase throughput. As the mobile moves away from the transmitter (i.e., the channel is getting bad), the received SNR is decreased and the user has to step down to lower modulations (e.g., BPSK) in order to maintain certain BER. In addition, adaptive modulation allows the system to overcome fading and other interference.

Adaptive modulation is sensitive to measurement error and delay. To select appropriate modulation, the system must be aware of the channel quality. Errors in the channel estimate cause wrong modulation selection. It is well known that turbo codes are specified as the channel coding technique for packet data in the 3G standards. Even a small prediction error in channel SNR can result in a large degradation in BER. Therefore, it is essential to take into account the possible prediction errors when designing an adaptive modulation system where turbo codes are employed (Yang et al. 2002). Delay of channel measurement also reduces the reliability of channel quality estimate. Furthermore, changes in the interference add to the measurement errors.

Conventionally, the threshold method is used to determine which modulation scheme should be used in adaptive modulation. The threshold values for the average channel SNR values are denoted by $\{-\infty, \gamma_1, , , , \gamma_{n-1}, \infty\}$. These threshold points partition the range of SNR into n regions, denoted by $[\gamma_i, \gamma_i+_1)$ for $i = 0...n-1$. One modulation scheme is assigned for each SNR region. One example is shown in Table 2 (IEEE Standard 802.16 Working Group 2004).

Table 2: Adaptive Modulation for 802.16d

Modulation	BPSK	QPSK	16 QAM	64 QAM
SNR threshold (dB)	6.2 – 8.2	9.4 – 11.2	16.4 – 18.2	22.7 – 24.4

Table 3: Modulation and Coding Schemes for IEEE 802.16d

Rate ID	Modulation rate	Coding	Information bits/symbol	Information bits/ OFDM symbol	Peak data rate in 5Mhz (Mbps)
0	BPSK	1/2	0.5	88	1.89
1	QPSK	1/2	1	84	3.95
2	QPSK	3/4	1.5	280	6.00
3	16 QAM	1/2	2	376	8.06
4	16 QAM	3/4	3	568	12.18
5	64 QAM	2/3	4	760	16.30
6	64 QAM	3/4	4.5	854	18.36

The first version of IEEE standard 802.16, completed in October 2001, defines the air interface and medium access control (MAC) protocol for a wireless metropolitan area network (WMAN™), intended for providing high-bandwidth wireless voice and data for residential and enterprise use. This is the first industry-wide standard that can be used for fixed wireless access with substantially higher bandwidth than most cellular networks. The IEEE 802.16 standard, often referred to as WiMax, heralds the entry of broadband wireless access as a major new tool in the effort to link homes and businesses to core telecommunications networks worldwide. Adaptive Modulation and Coding (AMC) is adopted by IEEE 802.16 standard. Specifically, the 802.l6a/d standard defines seven combinations of modulation and coding rate that can be used to achieve various trade-offs of data rate and robustness, depending on channel and interference conditions. These possible combinations, shown in Table 3, follow a pattern similar to the modulation/coding pairs available in the IEEE 802.11 a/g standard for wireless LANs (IEEE Standard 802.16 Working Group, 2004).

The allowed modulation schemes in the downlink (DL) and uplink (UL) are BPSK, QPSK, 16-QAM, and 64-QAM. A total of eight pilot sub-carriers are inserted into each data burst in order to constitute the OFDM symbol, and they are modulated according to their carrier locations within the OFDM symbol. Additionally, known preambles are used in 802.16d to aid the receiver with synchronization and channel estimation. In the DL, a "long preamble" of two OFDM symbols is sent at the first 184 bits of each frame. In the UL, a "short preamble" of one OFDM symbol is sent by the SS at the beginning of every frame.

EQUALIZATION

Time dispersion in radio channel due to multipath propagation may cause Inter-Symbol Interference (ISI), in which a given transmit signal is distorted by other transmit symbols, causing bit errors at the receiver (for details see "Wireless Channels" and "Cellular Communications Channels"). ISI is one of the major obstacles to high speed data transmission over wireless channels. Generally speaking, equalization refers to any signal processing technique used at the receiver to reduce the ISI. Signal processing techniques can also be employed at the transmitter to combat the delay spread, such as spread spectrum. (For details, see "Spread Spectrum") and multicarrier modulation. This section focuses on equalization only.

Introduction to Equalization

The concept of equalization is shown in the frequency domain in Figure 11. Suppose the channel does not have equal gain over the spectrum due to multipath propagation. Equalizer is designed to have frequency response equal to the inverse of channel frequency response. In this way, the combined filters provide a unity gain over the complete spectrum. In the time domain, this means that convolution of the channel impulse response and the equalizer impulse response is equal to one at the center tap and has nulls at the other sample points within the filter span. Equalization techniques are classified into two categories: linear and nonlinear. Some examples of equalizers are described later in this section.

Because the radio fading channel is random and time-varying, an equalizer should be adaptive so that it can track the time of varying characteristics of the mobile channel and self-adjust to the unknown environment to provide reliable performance (Rappaport 2002). In other words, adaptive equalization does not require any prior information about the channel and the transmitted data. An array of adaptive equalizers can also be used in flat fading applications to perform diverse combinations to enhance signal level. The general operations of

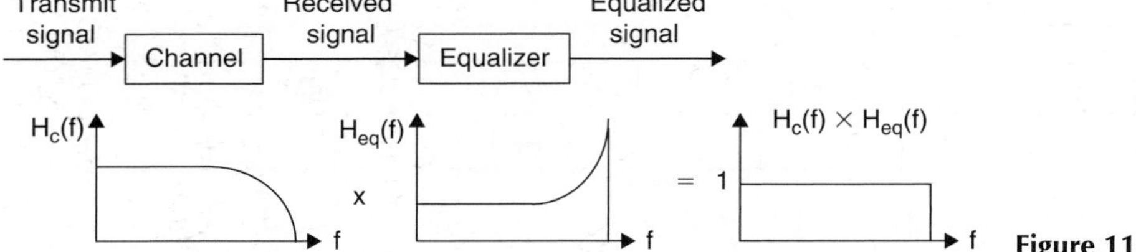

Figure 11: Equalized channel

an adaptive equalizer include training and tracking. First, a known, fixed-length training sequence is sent by the transmitter so that the receiver's equalizer may adapt to a proper setting for minimum BER detection. The training sequence is typically a pseudorandom binary signal or a fixed, prescribed bit pattern. Immediately following this training sequence, the data is sent, and the adaptive equalizer at the receiver uses a recursive algorithm to evaluate the channel and estimate filter coefficients in order to compensate for the distortion created by multipath in the channel (Rappaport 2002).

Linear Equalization

Linear equalizers typically compare a received time-domain reference signal to a stored copy of the undistorted training signal. With a comparison of the two, a time-domain error signal is determined that may be used to calculate the coefficient of an inverse filter. The formulation of this inverse filter may be accomplished strictly in the time domain (e.g., zero-forcing equalization and least mean square equalization), or converted in spectral representation. A spectral inverse response can be calculated to compensate for the channel response. This inverse spectrum is then converted back to a time-domain representation so that filter tap weights may be extracted.

The zero-forcing equalization (ZFE) technique is a simple method to form an inverse filter. To formulate a set of FIR inverse filter coefficients, a training signal consisting of an impulse is transmitted over the channel. By solving N simultaneous equations based on the received sample values, a set of coefficients can be determined to force all but the center tap of the filtered response to zero. This means, the $(N - 1)$ samples surrounding the center tap do not contribute ISI. The main advantage of this technique is that the solution to the set of equations is reduced to a matrix inversion. The major drawback of ZFE is that the channel response may often exhibit attenuation at high frequencies around one-half the sampling rate (the folding frequency). Because the ZFE is simply an inverse filter, it applies high gain to these upper frequencies, which tends to exaggerate noise. A second problem is that the training signal, an impulse, is a low-energy signal, which results in a much lower received signal-to-noise ratio than could be provided by other training signal types (Qureshi 1992).

The least mean squared (LMS) equalizer is a more general approach (Proakis 2001). In contrast to the ZFE that solves a set of N simultaneous equations, LMS iteratively adjusts the coefficients during each sample period in the training sequence and eventually converges to a set of optimal coefficients. These coefficients minimize the error between the equalized signal and the reference signal stored in the equalizer. Only one parameter, the adaptation size, needs to be adjusted. There is a tradeoff in the choice of step size between speed of convergence and residual steady-state error. If step size is set too large, the filter converges rapidly but stops at some coefficients around the optimal ones with some error. It is shown that the LMS equalizer has better noise performance than the ZFE. Another major advantage of LMS equalizer is that any arbitrary sequence can serve as a training sequence. In general, it is desirable to use a high-energy signal to improve the received signal-to-noise ratio of the training sequence. Typical training sequences employed for LMS equalization include pseudorandom noise sequences and chirp-type signals.

Nonlinear Equalization

On the other hand, nonlinear equalizers attempt to minimize an error signal based on the difference between the output of the equalizer and the *estimate* of the transmitted signal, which is generated by a decision device. In other words, the equalizer filter outputs a sample and the predictor or decision device determines what value is most likely transmitted. The adaptation logic endeavors to keep the difference small between the two. The main idea is that the receiver takes advantage of the knowledge of the discrete levels possible in the transmitted pulses. When the decision device quantizes the equalizer output, it is essentially throwing away received noise. Typically, training is used to make a filter converge at startup as part of the initialization overhead. Adaptation techniques can then be employed to track and compensate for minor variations in channel response on the fly using the detected version of its output signal. This equalization is called the decision-directed equalization, as shown in Figure 12. When the adapted filter is perfect, the filter produces the actual transmit symbol value and the error of the decision device would be zero. In practice, the error can never be zero. However, if the adapted filter is near perfect, the predictor is able to remove significant received noise, leading to perfect decisions. The coefficient update can be performed similar to that for the LMS equalizer.

Decision-feedback equalization (DFE) is another nonlinear adaptive equalizer, in which a feedback filter structure is used to achieve the post-cursor ISI removal. When the decision device makes a decision on the current symbol, the decided sequence is then fed back through a feedback filter to calculate the ISI by subtracting the decided symbol value from the received signal (Svensson 1989). Because the same amount of ISI tends to occur

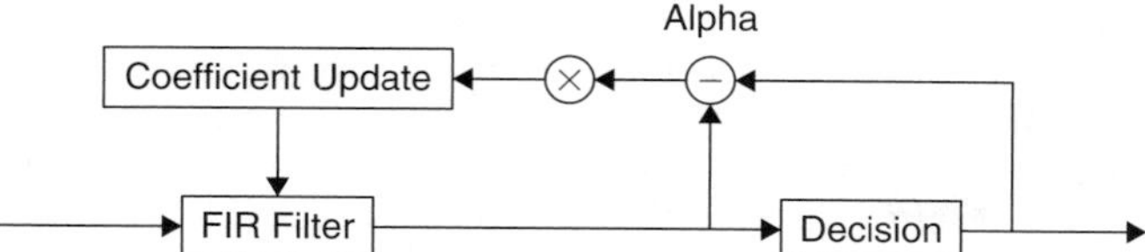

Figure 12: Decision-directed equalization

in subsequent transmission, the current ISI value is used to compensate the input to the decision device for the next symbol detection. DFE is the most common nonlinear equalizer due to its simple implementation and fairly good performance. However, when channels are noisy, DFE tends to propagate errors and consequently causes performance degradation.

MIMO SYSTEMS

Multiple-input-multiple-output (MIMO) communications systems refer to the systems that use multiple antennas at both the transmitter and the receiver. By deploying multiple antennas, MIMO systems establish many multi-path fading paths between each transmit and receive antenna pair. In high scattering environments, these multiple fading paths can be assumed independent. When the multiple transmit antennas transmit the same symbol simultaneously, MIMO systems create spatial diversity and consequently improve performance in terms of probability of error. On the other hand, when each transmit antenna transmits an independent symbol, MIMO systems achieve significant capacity gains through multiplexing.

A spatial multiplexing MIMO system with N transmit antennas and M receive antennas is shown in Figure 13. The transmit antennas transmit independent data on different transmit antennas simultaneously in multiplexing. Let x denote the independent transmit signals at the transmitter, y denote the received signals at the receiver, and H denote the channel matrix. The received signal can be expressed as,

$$y = Hx + n$$

where n is the noise. Channel matrix H is a M x N matrix,

$$\mathbf{H} = \begin{bmatrix} \mathbf{h}_{11} & \mathbf{h}_{12} & \mathbf{h}_{13} & \cdots & \mathbf{h}_{1N} \\ \mathbf{h}_{21} & \mathbf{h}_{22} & \mathbf{h}_{23} & \cdots & \mathbf{h}_{2N} \\ \cdots & \cdots & \cdots & \cdots & \cdots \\ \mathbf{h}_{M1} & \mathbf{h}_{M2} & \mathbf{h}_{M3} & \cdots & \mathbf{h}_{MN} \end{bmatrix}$$

When the channel is wireless fading channel, the gains h_{ij} are random.

For wireless fading channel, the capacity of multiplexing MIMO systems depends on whether or not the transmitter and/or receiver know the channel matrix. When both the transmitter and receiver know the channel matrix perfectly, the transmitter can adaptively adjust power allocation according to channel fading. When the power allocation is optimized, the capacity equals the average channel matrix realization. However, most commonly the channel matrix is known only by the receiver and the transmitter is not aware of the channel fading. In this case, the transmitter can only decide a transmission strategy based on the distribution of channel matrix H, and the channel capacity can be formulated as

$$C = \log_2[\det(I_M + \frac{\rho}{N} HH^H)]$$

where ρ is the average signal-to-noise-ratio per transmit antenna, and I_M is an identical M x M matrix. It is shown that the capacity grows linearly with $min(M, N)$ rather than logarithmically (Foschini and Gans 1995; Telatar 1995).

To reduce the decoding complexity, a linear receiver can be employed at the front ends to separate the transmitted data streams and then independently decode each stream. Examples of linear receivers include the zero-forcing receiver and minimum-mean square error receiver. Some nonlinear receivers may also be used, such as the maximum likelihood receiver and successive interference cancellation receiver. MIMO systems employ various space-time coding schemes to offer a significant diversity advantage over traditional wireless communications systems (Gesbert et al. 2003). The space-time codes (STC) are designed to explore both the space domain (over multiple antennas) and the time domain (over multiple time slots). Some STCs, such as Space-Time Block codes, can only provide the diversity gains, while some STCs, such as Space-Time Trellis codes, can provide not only diversity

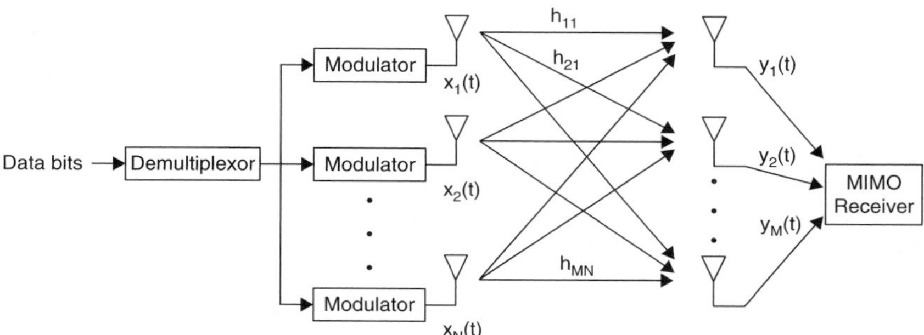

Figure 13: MIMO spatial multiplexing systems

gain but also coding gain. These benefits have made MIMO technology promising for next-generation communications systems.

MIMO systems deliver greater performance, but with additional cost of deploying multiple antennas and additional power consumption to operate those antennas and perform multidimensional signal processing. Competition of consumer markets imposes pressure on the cost, while limited battery life constrains the tolerable power consumption in wireless portable devices. One low-cost solution is the high system-level integration of CPUs and other peripherals (Diouris 2005). To achieve highest performance, the antennas need to be placed far apart, yet small user devices like cell phones requires antennas to be close to each other. One way to solve this problem is to employ antennas with different polarization and radiation patterns for minimal overlapping.

CONCLUSION

This chapter examines major components of mobile radio communications, including antennas, speech coding, channel coding, digital modulation, equalization, and MIMO systems. Antennas are crucial for any communications system. The most common are the omni-directional antenna and directional antenna. The smart antenna, one type of directional antenna, has emerged as a promising antenna technique. Speech coding is an audio signal and speech processing technique in which speech is compressed into a code for transmission. Two major categories of speech codes are discussed: waveform coders and source coders.

In mobile radio communications, transmitted data signals are exposed to natural and man-made electromagnetic interferences. Channel coding aims to control these errors by adding redundancy. Three widely used channel codes are presented: cyclic codes, convolutional codes, and turbo codes. In addition, the interleaving technique is introduced. Its function is to spread out successive bits produced from speech coders, so that the lost bits due to deep fading can be recovered through channel coding.

Modulation techniques, also discussed in this chapter, are a process of representing information by varying carrier signals. In this chapter, the focus is on the adaptive modulation technique specifically for mobile radio communications, although modulation techniques are covered in other chapters in this book. Equalization is used to compensate for the distorted wireless channel so that the bit error rate is reduced. Lastly, MIMO systems are discussed. By employing multiple antennas at both the transmitter and receiver, MIMO systems can either increase system capacity through multiplexing or improve performance through diversity.

Because the broad range of topics in mobile radio communications cannot be covered in a single chapter, we only provide an overview of some major components. Though some omissions are unavoidable, fortunately other chapters in this book, especially in Part 3 of Volume II provide complementary discussions. For instance, specific cellular networks are discussed in "Global System for Mobile Communication (GSM)," "General Packet Radio Service (GPRS)," "Universal Mobile Telecommunication System (UMTS)," and "IMT-2000 (International Mobile Telecommunications-2000) and 3G Wireless Systems." (Please refer to the table of contents for complete coverage). As the communications systems move to the next generation, which will require high speed and ubiquitous access, new technologies will be developed to provide various applications with different QoS supports.

GLOSSARY

Antenna: A device that radiates signal energy over radio frequency from transmitter to outside and receives radio frequency energy from outside to the receiver.

Channel coding: A technique to control errors by adding redundancy bits in a controlled manner.

Equalization: Signal processing technique used at the receiver to reduce the Inter-Symbol Interference.

Interleaving: A technique used to spread out bursts of error bits to improve performance in a fading channel.

Mobile radio communications: Transferring information through the electromagnetic signal over wireless radio channel between mobile users.

Modulation: A process of conveying information through electronic signals.

Multiple-input-multiple-output (MIMO) systems: Systems that use multiple antennas at both the transmitter and the receiver.

Smart antenna: An array of antenna elements connected to a digital signal processor which enables the system to optimize the radiation and reception based on the location of users.

Speech coding: An audio signal processing and speech processing technique in which the speech is compressed into a code for transmission.

CROSS REFERENCES

See *Cellular Telephony*; *Digital Radio Broadcasting*; *Frequency and Phase Modulation*; *Speech and Audio Compression*; *Wireless Channels*.

REFERENCES

Berrou, C., A. Glavieux, and P. Thitimajshima. 1993. Near Shannon Limit error–correcting coding and decoding: Turbo codes. *Proceedings of* ICC, pp 1064–1070, 1993.

Chryssomallis, M. 2000. Smart antennas, *IEEE Antennas and Propagation Magazine*, 42 (3)(June):129–136.

Diouris, J. F. 2005. MIMO Systems-Application of antenna processing to wireless communications. Available at http://med-hoc-net2005.lri.fr/slides/slides-diouris-05mimo.pdf (Date of access: December 18, 2005).

Ericsson, N. C. 1999. Adaptive modulation and scheduling for fading channels. *IEEE GLOBECOM* (December), Rio de Janeiro, Brazil.

Falahati, S., A. Svensson, T. Ekman and M. Sternad. 2002. Effect of prediction errors on adaptive modulation systems for wireless channels. *RVK02* (June), Stockholm.

Fitton, M. 2003. Digital modulation: Current wireless techniques. Available at http://wireless.ictp.trieste.it/school_2005/lectures/ermanno/Mobile_communications_Fitton_2004.pdf (accessed December 15, 2005).

Forney Jr., G. D. 1971. Burst error correction codes for the classics bursty channel. *IEEE Trans. Commun. Tech.*, (October), 772–781.

Forney Jr., G. D. 1973. The Viterbi algorithm. *Proceedings of the IEEE*, 61(3)(March): 268–278.

Foschini, G. J. and M. J. Gans. 1995. On limits of wireless communications in a fading environment when using multiple antennas. *Wireless Personal Communications*, 6: 311–335.

Gallager, R.G. 1962. Low-density parity-check code. *IRE Trans. Inform.Theory*, 8 (January): 21–28.

Gesbert, D., M. Shafi, D. S. Shiu, P. J., Smith, and A. Naguib. 2003. From theory to practice: An overview of MIMO space-time coded wireless systems. *IEEE Journal on Selected Areas in Communications*, 21: 281–302.

Goldsmith, J. J., and P. P. Varaiya. 1996. Capacity, mutual information, and coding for finite-state Markov channels. *IEEE Trans. Info. Theory*, (May): 868–886.

Grech, S. 1999. Channel coding standards in mobile communications. Available at http://www.tml.hut.fi/Studies/Tik-110.300/1999/Wireless/channel_1.html (accessed December 10, 2005).

Hall, J. 1996. A brief history of data communications. Available at http://www.k12.hi.us/~telecom/datahistory.html (accessed December 9, 2005).

Health Council of the Netherlands 2004. TNO study on the effects of GSM and UMTS signals on well-being and cognition. The Hague: Health Council of the Netherlands, 2004; publication no. 2004/13E.

IEEE Standard 802.16 Working Group 2004. IEEE standard for local and metropolitan area networks part 16: Air interface for fixed broadband wireless access systems.

Ingram, Mary A. 2000. Tutorial: What is a smart antenna? Smart Antenna Research Laboratory. Georgia Institute of Technology. Available at http://users.ece.gatech.edu/~mai/tutorial_sa_def.htm (accessed December 15, 2005).

Kou, Y., S. Lin, and M.P.C. Fossorier. 2001. Low-density parity-check codes based on finite geometrics: A rediscovery and new results. *IEEE Trans. Inform. Theory*, 47, (7) (November): pp. 2711–2736.

Lin, S., D. J. Costello Jr., and M.J. Miller. 1984. Automatic-repeat-request error control schemes. *IEEE Communications Magazine*, 22 (12)(December): pp. 5–16.

Lin, S. and D. J. Costello Jr. 1983. Error control coding: Fundamentals and applications. Englewood Cliffs, NJ: Prentice-Hall, Inc.

Lucent Technologies 2000. Speech and audio coding. http://www.bell-labs.com/org/1133/Research/SpeechAudioCoding/ (accessed December 8, 2005).

Mackay, D. J. C. and R. M. Neal. 1996. Near Shannon limit performance of low density parity check codes. *Electron. Lett.*, (August): 1645.

Moulder, J. 2005. Mobile Phone (Cell Phone) Base Stations and Human Health. Available at http://mcw.edu/gcrc/cop/cell-phone-health-FAQ/toc.html (accessed December 20, 2005).

Okamoto, G. T. 2002. *Smart antenna systems and wireless LAN*, New York: Kluwer Academic Publishers.

Perez, L. C., J. Seghers, and D. J. Costello. 1996. A distance spectrum interpretation of turbo codes. *IEEE Trans. Inform. Theory*, 42 (6)(November):1698–1709.

Pless, V. 1998. *Introduction to the theory of error-correcting codes*. 3rd edition, New York: John Wiley and Sons.

Proakis, J. G. 2001. *Digital communications*. 4th edition, New York: McGraw-Hill.

Qureshi, S. 1992. Adaptive equalization. *IEEE Communications Magazine*, (March): pp. 9–16.

Rappaport, T. S. 2002. *Wireless communications: Principles and practice.* 2nd edition. Upper Saddle River, NJ: Prentice Hall.

Robinson, T. 2001. Speech coding. Available at http://svr-www.eng.cam.ac.uk/~ajr/SA95/node78.html (accessed December 8, 2005).

Shannon, C. E. 1948. A mathematical theory of information. *The Bell System Technical Journal*, 27: 379–423, 623–656, July, October, 1948.

Spanias, A. S. 1994. Speech coding: A tutorial review. Available at http://www.eas.asu.edu/~spanias/papers/review.ps (accessed December 9, 2005).

Svensson, L. 1989. Channel equalizer for a digital mobile telephone using narrow-band TDMA transmission. *39th IEEE Vehicular Technology Conference*, 1 pp. 155–158.

Telatar, E. 1995. Capacity of multi-antenna Gaussian channels. AT&T Bell Laboratories, Technical Memorandum.

Viterbi, A. J. 1967. Error bounds for convolutional codes and asymptotically optimum decoding algorithms. *IEEE Trans. Inform. Theory*, (April): pp. 260–269.

Yang, J., A. K., Khandani, A. and N. Tin. 2002. Adaptive modulation and coding in 3G wireless systems. Report of University of Waterloo, Technical Report UW-E&CE#2002–15, August 2002.

Zilog. 2005. Adaptive filtering application explained. Technical Report AN008001–0301. December 2005.

Evolution of Mobile Cellular Networks

Jiang Xie, *University of North Carolina, Charlotte*
Xiaoyuan Gu, *Technical University of Braunschweig, Germany*

INTRODUCTION

The use of cellular telephony has expanded dramatically worldwide within the past two decades. According to an International Telecommunications Union (ITU; n.d.) report, the number of mobile phones worldwide has outnumbered fixed-line phones. Several technical innovations have contributed to the success of mobile phones. In particular, cellular telephony systems can now be deployed much more economically; the handsets have become smaller and lighter, battery life has increased, digital technology has improved reception, and the costs associated with mobile telephones have been decreasing. In addition, newer generation devices, with access to the Internet and built-in digital cameras, are becoming the mainstream in many countries in Europe and Asia. New types of wireless services, such as Web access, instant messaging, e-mail, and location-dependent services, have helped to further increase the popularity of mobile phones.

In the history of cellular network evolution, the first thirty years of cellular telephony saw little market penetration due to high cost and the technological challenges involved (Rappaport 2002). The forerunner of cellular network was policy radio systems. By 1934, fifty-eight state police stations had adopted amplitude modulation (AM) mobile communication systems for public safety in the United States, serving more than 5,000 radio-equipped police cars (Rappaport 2002). The theory and techniques of cellular telephony were developed by AT&T Bell Laboratories and other telecommunication companies during the 1950s and 1960s. In 1968, AT&T proposed the concept of cellular telephony to the Federal Communications Commission (FCC). The proposed cellular concept divides the service area into many small regions known as cells, each served by a low-power transmitter with moderate antenna height known as a base station (BS). Frequency channels are assigned for data transmission between a BS and mobile phones inside the radio coverage area of the BS. Frequency channels are not reused in adjacent cells to avoid interference. Cells using different frequency channels form a cell cluster. Channels are only reused in different clusters and when there is sufficient distance between the transmitters (MacDonald 1979).

The technology to implement the concept of cellular telephony was not available until the late 1970s. In 1979, Nippon Telephone & Telegraph (NT&T) introduced the first cellular system in Japan (Agrawal and Zeng 2003; Chandran and Valenti 2001). The microprocessing technology revolution in the 1980s helped to easily implement wireless communication protocols, and the digital control link between mobile telephones and the BS helped to realize the cellular concept. In 1983, the advanced mobile phone system (AMPS) was deployed in Chicago, Illinois. AMPS was the first U.S. cellular telephone system and relied on frequency division multiple access (FDMA) to maximize system capacity.

In Europe, several first-generation cellular systems were introduced in different countries. The Nordic mobile telephone (NMT) system was first developed in 1981 and operated in the 450 MHz frequency band. The European total access cellular system (ETACS) was deployed in 1985 and was virtually identical to the U.S. AMPS system. In the same year, the C-450 cellular standard was introduced in Germany. These cellular systems were not compatible with each other because of the different frequencies and communication protocols used. In addition, the digital transmission technique had become more mature and economical. In 1990, the pan-European digital cellular standard, Group Special Mobile (GSM), which uses the digital transmission technique to transmit digital signals, was deployed to replace those incompatible first-generation cellular systems. Group Special Mobile was founded in 1982 by the Conference of European Posts and Telegraphs. Later, the European Telecommunications Standards Institute (ETSI) assigned new meanings to the standard GSM letters, resulting in today's global system for mobile communications. The GSM system supports roaming in Europe and is currently accepted worldwide in more than 210 countries.

In the United States, the AMPS system was gradually replaced by the U.S. digital cellular (USDC) system, a second-generation cellular system, in the 1990s. The USDC standard (Electronic Industry Association Interim Standard IS-54 and, later, IS-136) uses time division multiple access (TDMA) together with FDMA and increases the system capacity threefold. In 1993, a new cellular system based on code division multiple access (CDMA) was proposed by Qualcomm, Inc. The concept of the CDMA system was later standardized by the Telecommunications Industry Association (TIA; n.d.) as an interim standard (IS-95). The CDMA system can use the same set of frequencies in every cell, which greatly improves the system capacity.

The increasing demand of supporting multimedia services over wireless systems triggered the design of new wireless systems and improvements of the GSM system. Several wideband wireless systems with higher data rates have been proposed since 2000, such as high-speed circuit-switched data (HSCSD), general packet radio service (GPRS), and enhanced data rates for GSM evolution (EDGE). In 2000, the GPRS system had its first trial. The GPRS system is an overlay system on top of the GSM network entities. It uses the same radio channels as GSM but with higher data rates. In order to harmonize global telecommunications, the design specifications of GSM successors began in 1998. International Mobile Telecommunications-2000 (IMT-2000) was proposed by the ITU, the United Nations organization responsible for global telecommunications. The objectives of IMT-2000 are to support multimedia applications over a family of wireless systems globally, standardize as many interfaces as possible, and provide compatibility to services within the IMT-2000 system (ITU n.d.). In 2001, the universal mobile telecommunications system (UMTS) was agreed upon as the European system for IMT-2000. UMTS was proposed by the 3rd-Generation Partnership Project (3GPP; n.d.) as a wideband, circuit- and packet-based transmission systems of text, digitized voice, video, and multimedia with data rates up to 2 Mbps (UMTS Forum n.d.). Currently, several third-generation wireless systems exist worldwide that provide both voice and data services.

Multiple Access: FDMA, TDMA, and CDMA

Multiple-access techniques provide a means of sharing the available bandwidth in the wireless system among multiple mobile users. Three major multiple-access techniques have been proposed for mobile cellular networks: FDMA, TDMA, and CDMA.

FDMA systems divide the available radio spectrum into multiple frequency bands. The width of each frequency band is a portion of the total available bandwidth. Different channels are assigned different frequency bands, as shown in Figure 1. Each user is allocated, on demand,

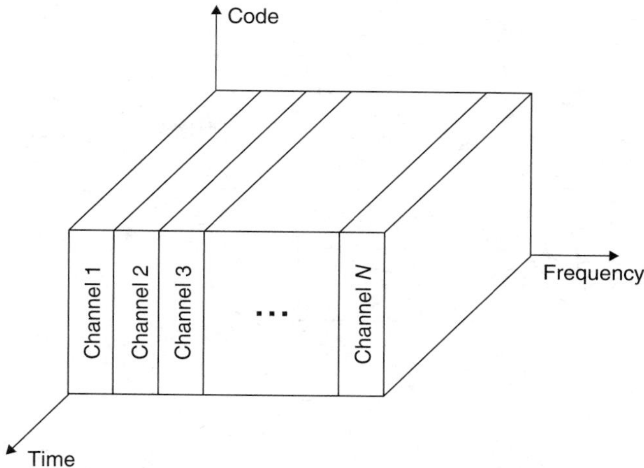

Figure 1: Frequency division multiple access (FDMA)

a unique frequency band or channel by the corresponding BS. During the period of the call, no other user can share the same channel. Multiple users inside the same cell must use different channels at the same time.

TDMA systems divide the available radio spectrum into multiple time slots. In each time slot, only one user is allowed to either transmit or receive. A physical channel is considered a particular time slot that reoccurs every frame, as shown in Figure 2, where N time slots comprise a frame. A TDMA frame is the basic unit of logic channels. Each user is allocated a unique time slot. Thus, the transmission of a user is noncontinuous, occupying a cyclically repeating time slot in every frame. TDMA shares a single-carrier frequency with multiple users, in which each user takes turns to use the nonoverlapping time slots.

In a CDMA system, all users may transmit simultaneously using the same carrier frequency, as shown in Figure 3. The narrowband signal from each user is multiplied by a very large bandwidth signal called spreading signal. Since the bandwidth of the spreading signal is much

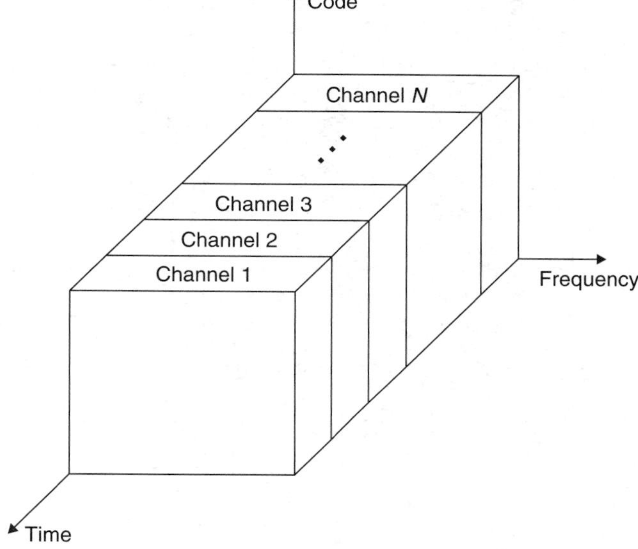

Figure 2: Time division multiple access (TDMA)

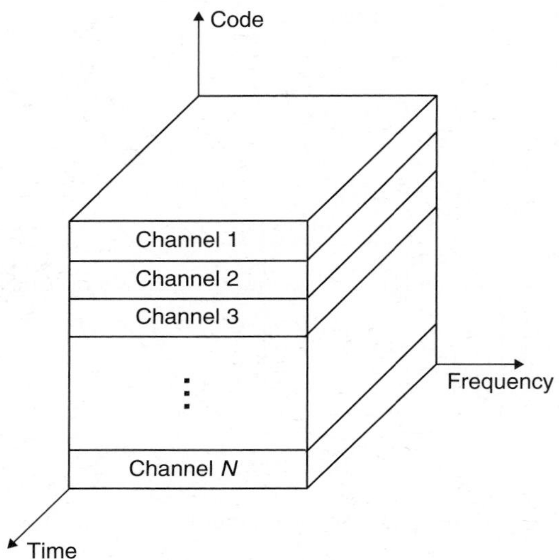

Figure 3: Code division multiple access (CDMA)

larger than the bandwidth of the original information-bearing signal, the encoding process is known as spread-spectrum modulation and the resulting signal is also called a spread-spectrum signal. The spreading signal is a pseudo-random code sequence. Each user has its own pseudo-random code word, which is approximately orthogonal to all other code words. The receiver knows the code word used by the transmitter. Because of the existence of the orthogonal code words, the receiver can decode the desired signal correctly by performing a time correlation operation. All other code words appear as noise due to decorrelation. CDMA provides anti-jamming capability, privacy, resilience to interference, low probability of interception, and protection against multipath interference (Prasad and Ojanpera 1998).

Different Generations of Mobile Cellular Networks

First-generation (1G) cellular networks use analog transmission techniques to transmit analog voice signals. FDMA is adopted as the multiple-access technique for multiple users sharing the system-available bandwidth. Two separate frequency bands are assigned to each user for transmissions from the BS to the mobile phone (forward link or downlink) and from the mobile phone to the BS (reverse link or uplink). The second-generation (2G) cellular networks use the digital transmission technique to transmit digital signals. TDMA or CDMA are adopted together with frequency division as the multiple-access techniques, which greatly increase the system capacity. Most of the 1G and 2G cellular networks are connected to the public switched telephone network (PSTN) to provide access to wireline telephones. The voice service is the major supported service of 1G and 2G cellular networks. Third-generation (3G) cellular networks are designed with the objective of supporting both voice and data services with higher data rates and quality. Wireless networks are connected to the PSTN for voice connections (circuit-switched services) and the Internet for data connections (packet-switched services). Second-and-a-half generation (2.5G) cellular networks, such as GPRS systems, use evolutionary technologies toward 3G by adding packet-switched entities to the existing circuit-switched domain of 2G in order to support both voice and data services. 2.5G can be considered a stepping stone between 2G and 3G wireless technologies.

Table 1 provides a mapping of various standards to different generations of cellular networks. The standards listed in the table will be explained in the following sections.

FIRST-GENERATION (1G) CELLULAR NETWORKS

First-generation cellular networks were widely deployed in the world in the 1980s. They were based on analog cellular standards (i.e., the radio signals of 1G cellular networks were analog). Frequency modulation (FM) was used to modulate analog voice signals to the carrier frequency for transmissions.

Major standards of 1G cellular networks include:

- AMPS, mainly used in the United States
- NMT, mainly used in northern Europe, eastern Europe, and Russia
- ETACS, used in the United Kingdom
- C-450, used in Germany, Portugal, and South Africa
- Radicom 2000, used in France

Advanced Mobile Phone System (AMPS)

AMPS was the first U.S. analog cellular system. It was developed by Bell Labs in the 1970s and considered a revolutionary accomplishment. From 1974 to 1978, a

Table 1: Standards for Different Generations of Cellular Networks

1G Cellular	2G Cellular	2.5G Cellular	3G Cellular
AMPS NMT-450 NMT-900 TACS ETACS C-450 Radicom 2000	GSM IS-54/IS-136 PDC IS-95/cdmaOne	HSCSD GPRS EDGE IS-95B	W-CDMA (UMTS) cdma2000 TD-SCDMA

large-scale AMPS trial was conducted in Chicago, and commercial AMPS service has been available since 1983. A total of 50 MHz in the 824–849 MHz and 869–894 MHz bands was allocated for AMPS. This spectrum was divided into 832 full-duplex channels (i.e., 832 for downlink and 832 for uplink), with a bandwidth of 30 kHz for each channel. Voice channels are assigned to radio frequencies using the FDMA technology; twenty-one channels are allocated for control. The control channels are data channels that operate at 10 kbps. The voice channels carry the conversation in analog using frequency modulation.

During the period of a call, each user is assigned a pair of duplex frequency channels with a 45 MHz split: one channel as the downlink and the other channel as the uplink. The simultaneous radio transmission and reception between a user and a BS is achieved by assigning a pair of duplex channels to each user. This is called frequency division duplexing (FDD). Simultaneous users are accommodated by giving each user a unique duplex channel. Therefore, AMPS is based on FDMA-FDD. When a call is completed, or when a handoff (the process of transferring an ongoing call from one channel to another; Akyildiz et al. 1999) occurs, the corresponding duplex channel is released so that other users may use it. Cells using different frequency channels form a cell cluster. The same set of frequencies is reused by cells in different clusters. In AMPS, the typical frequency reuse plan is either a twelve-cell cluster using omnidirectional antennas or a seven-cell cluster using three sectors per BS.

The coverage radius of one BS ranges from 2 kilometers to 20 kilometers. A signal-to-interference-ratio of 18 dB is required for satisfactory system performance. Table 2 lists the major parameters used in AMPS (Stallings 2005).

AMPS was widely deployed in the United States, Australia, the Philippines, and several other countries. However, the market share for AMPS continues to decline as digital systems become more prevalent (Rogers and Edwards 2003).

Table 2: AMPS Parameters

Base station transmission band	869–894 MHz
Mobile unit transmission band	824–849 MHz
Spacing between downlink and uplink	45 MHz
Channel bandwidth	30 kHz
Number of full-duplex voice channels	790
Number of full-duplex control channels	42
Mobile unit maximum power	3 watts
Cell radius	2–20 km
Modulation, voice channel	FM, 12-kHz peak deviation
Modulation, control channel	FSK, 8-kHz peak deviation
Data transmission rate	10 kbps
Error control coding	BCH (48, 36, 5) and (40, 28, 5)

Nordic Mobile Telephone (NMT)

The NMT system was a 1G cellular network developed by Ericsson and deployed in the Nordic countries. It has been widely recognized as the first commercial cellular system in the world. The NMT system has two variants: NMT-450 and NMT-900. The NMT-450 system opened for service in Sweden and Norway in 1981, in Denmark and Finland in 1982, and in Iceland in 1986. It was optimized for use in areas of low population density. NMT-450 operated in the 450–470 MHz frequency bands with a 25 kHz channel bandwidth; the total number of duplex channels was 180. The NMT-900 system was introduced in 1986 with the operating frequency bands in 890–960 MHz and had been deployed for higher population density areas. The total number of duplex channels was 1,999, with a 12.5 kHz channel bandwidth. Both NMT-450 and NMT-900 systems used the FDMA technique for multiple access and frequency modulation for analog signal transmission. The cell sizes in an NMT system ranged from 2 kilometers to 30 kilometers. The NMT system was fully replaced by the GSM system in Europe except for limited use in rural areas. However, there are several initiatives to reopen the 450 MHz frequency band for 3G wireless services. In 2003, the NMT Association (NMTA; n.d.) reorganized and changed its name to the International 450 Association (IA450; n.d.) in order to reflect the focus on promoting the use of the frequency band 400 to 500 MHz for IMT-2000 digital wireless services.

Total Access Communications System (TACS) and European Total Access Communications System (ETAC)

TACS was the European version of AMPS. ETACS was an extended version of TACS with more channels and was mainly deployed in the United Kingdom. TACS was first introduced in 1982, operating in the 900 MHz frequency band. The channel bandwidth of TACS and ETACS was 25 kHz; the total number of duplex channels was 1,000 in TACS and 1,240 in ETACS. TACS and ETACS are now obsolete in Europe, having been replaced by the GSM system. In the United Kingdom, the ETACS service was discontinued in 2001.

Comparison of Major Standards

Table 3 gives a comparison of the major standards for 1G cellular networks using initialization year, frequency band, channel bandwidth, number of channels, and adopted countries (Rappaport 2002).

SECOND-GENERATION (2G) CELLULAR NETWORKS

2G cellular networks were first introduced in the early 1990s. In many countries, they were designed and deployed

Table 3: Comparison of IG Analog Cellular Standards

Standard	Introduction on Year	Multiple Access	Modulation	Frequency Band (MHz)	Channel Bandwidth	# of Channels	Region
AMPS	1983	FDMA	FM	824–894	30 kHz	832	United States
NMT-450	1981	FDMA	FM	450–470	25 kHz	180	Europe
NMT-900	1986	FDMA	FM	890–960	12.5 kHz	1999	Europe
TACS	1982	FDMA	FM	890–960	25 kHz	1000	Europe
ETACS	1985	FDMA	FM	872–950	25 kHz	1240	United Kingdom
C-450	1985	FDMA	FM	450–465	10 kHz	573	Germany Portugal
Radicom 2000	1985	FDMA	FM	192–207 207–233 165–173 414–428	12.5 kHz	560 640 256 256	France

for conventional mobile telephone services as a high-capacity replacement for existing 1G cellular telephone networks. The main difference between 1G and 2G cellular networks is that the radio signals of 1G cellular networks are analog, whereas those of 2G cellular networks are digital. In 2G networks, the acoustic analog voice signals are first converted into digital signals. In order to use bandwidth more efficiently, compression is used to reduce the amount of digital information required to represent a digital voice signal. After that, digital transmission is used for transmitting the digital signal to the destination. Digital transmission is less susceptible to noise, compared to the analog transmission technique. The inherent benefits of using digital voice include that digital voice quality is independent of distance and it can be multiplexed into one channel, thus reducing cost. Hence, unlike 1G cellular networks that relied exclusively on FDMA/FDD and analog frequency modulation, 2G networks use digital modulations and TDMA/FDD and CDMA/FDD multiple-access techniques. 2G technologies offer at least a threefold increase in spectrum efficiency, so the system capacity is increased at least three time, compared to 1G analog technologies. Therefore, the number of customers supported by a 2G cellular system grows significantly.

2G standards can be divided into TDMA-based and CDMA-based standards depending on the type of multiple-access techniques used (Black 1999). The three major TDMA-based 2G standards and one CDMA-based 2G standard are:

- GSM (TDMA-based), originally from Europe, but used worldwide
- IS-136 or D-AMPS (TDMA-based, commonly referred as simply TDMA in the United States), used in the Americas
- PDC (TDMA-based), used exclusively in Japan
- IS-95 or cdmaOne (CDMA-based, commonly referred as simply CDMA in the United States), used in the Americas and parts of Asia

2G services are frequently referred to as a personal communications service (PCS) in the United States.

Global System for Mobile (GSM)

GSM is a pan-European digital cellular standard developed by ETSI (n.d.) and now maintained by the 3GPP. An important goal of the GSM development process was to offer compatibility of cellular services among European countries by providing a single unified standard. The GSM development process was similar to that of AMPS, except that no large-scale trial was conducted. The intellectual property rights of the GSM radio system from all vendors were waived, making GSM hugely popular.

Because there were many different first-generation systems in Europe, it was necessary to allocate a new frequency band for GSM. Most GSM networks operate in the 900 MHz or 1800 MHz frequency bands. Some countries in the Americas (including the Unietd States and Canada) use the 850 MHz and 1900 MHz frequency bands because the 900 and 1800 MHz frequency bands were already allocated. In the 900 MHz band, the uplink frequency band is 890–915 MHz and the downlink frequency band is 935–960 MHz. This 25 MHz bandwidth is subdivided into 124 carrier frequency channels, each spaced 200 kHz apart. GSM combines both TDMA and FDMA. In GSM, a frequency carrier is divided into eight time slots, and the eight time slots are grouped into a TDMA frame. In a GSM BS, every pair of radio transceiver-receivers supports eight voice channels, whereas an AMPS BS needs one such pair for every voice channel. The channel data rate is 270.833 kbps and the TDMA frame duration is 4.615 ms (Goodman 1997; Garg and Wilkes 1999). There are four different cell sizes in a GSM network: macro, micro, pico, and umbrella cells. The coverage area of each cell varies according to the implementation environment. Macro cells are the cells in which the BS antenna is installed on a building above average rooftop level. Micro cells are the cells in which antenna height is under average rooftop level. Both types of cells are typically used in urban areas. Pico cells are small cells whose diameter is a few dozen meters; they are mainly used indoors. Umbrella cells are used to cover shadowed regions of smaller cells and to fill gaps in coverage between larger cells. The longest cell radius the GSM specification supports in practical use is 35 kilometers.

The transmission power in mobile phones is limited to a maximum of 2 watts in GSM850/900 and 1 watt in GSM1800/1900. GSM mobile phones control their output power to maintain interference at low levels. In addition, GSM introduced a subscriber identification module (SIM), which plugs into a card slot in the GSM handset and provides handset identification and additional security protection (ETSI/TC 1994a, 1997).

GSM is the most popular standard for mobile telephony in the world. GSM services are used by over 2 billion people across more than 210 countries (GSM World n.d.). The ubiquity of the GSM standard makes international roaming very common between mobile phone operators, enabling subscribers to use their phones in many parts of the world. The GSM roaming management protocol is specified by the GSM mobile application part (MAP), supporting handoff, paging, and location management (Rahnema 1993; Akyildiz et al. 1999; ETSI/TC 1994b).

In addition to connection-oriented voice services, GSM also provides the short message service (SMS), a connectionless transfer of messages with low-capacity and short-duration performance. In December 1992, the first short message sent from a personal computer to a mobile phone was delivered in the Vodafone GSM network in the United Kingdom (Lin and Chlamtac 2001). The SMS operates similar to the paging service. Short messages up to 140 octets are transported on the GSM stand-alone dedicated control channel (SDCCH) signaling channel and can be received while the mobile users are in conversation. Both the broadcast service, which periodically delivers short messages to all subscribers in a given area, and the point-to-point service (ETSI/TC 1994c), which delivers short messages to a specific user, are supported by GSM. Due to the potential for revenue, cellular providers have opened their networks to a number of additional services designed to increase SMS messaging volume. These additional services, such as e-mail, allow users across the Internet to contact mobile subscribers through SMS messaging without the use of a cell phone. However, the connections between the Internet and cellular networks introduce open functionality that detrimentally affects the fidelity of a cellular provider's service. The security impact of Internet-originated text messages on cellular voice and SMS services was discussed and evaluated in Enck et al. (2005).

IS-54/IS-136/D-AMPS

The Electronic Industries Alliance (EIA; n.d.) and TIA Interim Standard IS-136 is also referred to as digital advanced mobile phone system (D-AMPS), American digital cellular (ADC), or North American TDMA (NA-TDMA), the successor to IS-54. It is used throughout the Americas, particularly in the United States and Canada. IS-136 supports TDMA, which is similar to GSM and is considered as an evolutionary technology.

IS-136 is a digital extension of, and backward compatible with, AMPS. The IS-136 system operates in the same spectrum (824–849 and 869–894 MHz) with the same frequency spacing (30 kHz) used by the existing AMPS system. It allows smooth transition between digital and analog systems in the same area. Using TDMA, every IS-136 frequency carrier is divided into three time slots and supports three voice channels; thus, the IS-136 capacity is approximately three times greater than that of AMPS. The channel transmission bit rate for digitally modulating the carrier is 48.6 kbps. IS-136 uses the IS-41 standard (EIA/TIA 1991) for mobility management, which provides similar functionality to GSM MAP.

Personal Digital Cellular (PDC)

The personal digital cellular (PDC) standard is developed and used exclusively in Japan. As with D-AMPS and GSM, PDC systems also use the TDMA technology. The standard was defined in 1991 and launched in 1993 by NTT DoCoMo.

PDC systems are implemented in the 800 MHz frequency band (810–830 MHz for uplink and 940–960 MHz for downlink) as well as the 1.5 GHz frequency band (1429–1453 MHz for uplink and 1477–1501 MHz for downlink). The channel bandwidth is 25 kHz, and each carrier frequency is divided into three time slots. NEC and Ericsson are the major network equipment manufacturers.

In early 2005 PDC had about 56 million subscribers, following a peak of nearly 80 million (Yamauchi, Chen, and Wei 2005). It is slowly being replaced by 3G technologies such as W-CDMA and cdma2000.

Table 4 provides a comparison of the three major TDMA-based 2G digital cellular standards: GSM, IS-136, and PDC.

Table 4: Comparison of 2G Digital TDMA-Based Cellular Standards

Standard	Introduction Year	Multiple Access	Frequency Band	Channel Bandwidth	Channel Data Rate	# of Voice Channels	Regions
GSM	1990	TDMA/ FDMA/ FDD	890–960 MHz	200 kHz	270.833 kbps	1000	Worldwide
IS-136	1991	TDMA/ FDMA/ FDD	824–894 MHz	30 kHz	48.6 kbps	2500	The Americas
PDC	1993	TDMA/ FDMA/ FDD	810–960 or 1429–1501 MHz	25 kHz	42 kbps	3000	Japan

IS-95/cdmaOne

The EIA/TIA IS-95 (1993) digital cellular system was introduced by the TR45.5 subcommittee of the TIA in 1993 and has been operating in the United States since 1996. The brand name for IS-95 is cdmaOne. IS-95 is based on the CDMA technology that supports wideband signaling and offers increased capacity. The advantages of CDMA—such as multipath resistance, resilience to signal jamming, and privacy—make it especially attractive to military applications.

Similar to IS-136, IS-95 operates in the same frequency bands as AMPS (i.e., 824–849 MHz frequency bands for downlink and 869–894 MHz frequency bands for uplink). The channel bandwidth used by IS-95 is 1.25 MHz. This bandwidth is relatively narrow for a CDMA system, which makes the service migrations from analog to digital within an existing network more difficult than with AMPS and D-AMPS. The capacity of an IS-95 system is estimated to be ten times that of AMPS. Similar to AMPS, IS-95 uses the IS-41 standard for mobility management. Soft handoffs, during which a mobile phone is temporarily connected to more than one base station simultaneously, can be supported by the CDMA system.

IS-95 is currently used in the United States, South Korea, Canada, Mexico, India, Israel, Australia, Venezuela, and China.

SECOND-AND-A-HALF GENERATION (2.5G) CELLULAR NETWORKS

A 2G system is a digital mobile phone system and primarily transmits voice signals based on circuit-switched technologies, but it can also be used for circuit-switched data services as well (Black 1999). This circuit-switched data transmission limits data users to a single circuit-switched voice channel, and the data rate is limited to the voice channel data rate, which is too low for e-mail and Internet browsing applications. A 3G system is a mobile phone system that provides both packet-switched data services and circuit-switched voice services. Therefore, the term *second-and-a-half generation* (2.5G) is used to describe 2G systems that have implemented a packet-switched domain in addition to the existing circuit-switched domain. 2.5G can be considered a stepping stone between 2G and 3G wireless technologies.

2.5G standards are data-centric standards that can be overlaid upon existing 2G technologies. These standards allow existing 2G equipment to be modified and supplemented with new BS add-ons and subscriber unit software upgrades to support higher data rate transmissions for Web browsing and e-mail traffic. The 2.5G technologies also support a new Web browsing application using wireless application protocol (WAP), which allows standard Web pages to be viewed in a compressed format specifically designed for small and portable handheld wireless devices.

A wide range of 2.5G standards have been developed to allow each of the major 2G technologies (GSM, IS-136, and IS-95) to be upgraded incrementally for faster Internet data rates. Following are the three major TDMA upgrade options:

- High-speed circuit-switched data
- General packet radio services
- Enhanced data rates for GSM evolution

High-Speed Circuit-Switched Data (HSCSD)

HSCSD is an enhancement to circuit-switched data, the original data transmission mechanism of the GSM system. It uses multiple time slots and/or different coding methods to increase data throughput. HSCSD allows individual data users to use multiple consecutive time slots in order to obtain higher-speed data access on the GSM network. It also allows different error-correction methods to be used for data transfer. HSCSD provides different levels of possible error correction that can be used according to the quality of the radio link. This means that under the best conditions, 14.4 kbps can be achieved through a single time slot, as compared to the original 9.6 kbps in the GSM specification. By using four consecutive time slots, HSCSD can provide a transmission rate of up to 57.6 kbps to individual users (four times 14.4 kbps). By combining up to eight GSM time slots, the capacity can be increased to 115 kbps (Rappaport 2002).

HSCSD requires the time slots being used to be fully reserved to a single user. However, voice calls have higher priority than HSCSD users. HSCSD users are typically charged based on the total period of time that a data connection is active, which is at a rate higher than a normal phone call (e.g., by the number of time slots allocated). This makes HSCSD relatively expensive in many GSM networks, because even during times when no data is being transferred, the bandwidth is unavailable to other potential users. This is one of the reasons that packet-switched GPRS, which typically has lower pricing (based on the amount of data transferred rather than the duration of the connection), has become more common than HSCSD.

General Packet Radio Services (GPRS)

GPRS is a packet-based data network for non-real–time Internet usage. It provides a packet network on dedicated GSM or IS-136 radio channels. GPRS retains the original modulation formats specified in the 2G TDMA standards but uses a redefined air interface in order to better handle packet data access (Rappaport 2002). Unlike HSCSD, which dedicates circuit-switched channels to specific users, GPRS supports multi-user network sharing of individual radio channels and time slots. This means that the total available bandwidth can be immediately dedicated to those users who are actually sending at any given moment, providing higher utilization. Therefore, GPRS can support many more users than HSCSD. Moreover, GPRS subscriber units are automatically instructed to tune to dedicated GPRS radio channels and particular time slots for "always-on" access to the network.

Packet-switched data under GPRS is achieved by allocating unused cell bandwidth to transmit data. When dedicated voice channels are set up by phones, the bandwidth available for packet-switched data reduces.

Hence, packet-switched data has a poor bit rate in busy cells.

Usually, GPRS data is billed per kilobytes of information transmitted. By using appropriate encoding schemes, GPRS can achieve a peak data rate of 21.4 kbps per channel per time slot. When all eight time slots of a GSM radio channel are dedicated to GPRS, an individual user is able to achieve as much as 171.2 kbps (eight times 21.4 kbps; ETSI/TC 1998a, 1998b).

Enhanced Data Rates for GSM Evolution (EDGE)

EDGE was first introduced to GSM networks around the world in 2003, initially in North America. EDGE is a more advanced upgrade to the GSM and IS-136 standards. It requires the addition of new hardware and software at existing BSs. EDGE introduces a new digital modulation technique, octal phase shift keying (8-PSK), which is used in addition to the GSM Gaussian minimum shift keying (GMSK) modulation. When EDGE uses 8-PSK modulation and all eight time slots of a GSM radio channel are dedicated to a single user, a raw peak data rate of 547.2 kbps can be achieved. In practice, the practical raw data rate is about 384 kbps for a single dedicated user on a single GSM channel (Furuskar et al. 1999). By combining the capacity of different radio channels, EDGE can provide up to several megabits per second of peak data rate to individual data users.

Whether EDGE is 2G or 3G depends on its implementation. EDGE can qualify as 3G services (because it can provide a data rate of above 144 kbps) but is considered by most to be a 2.5G service because the practical data rates are several times lower than true 3G services. Hence, EDGE is sometimes referred to as a 2.75G technology.

THIRD-GENERATION (3G) CELLULAR NETWORKS

Both 1G and 2G systems have been designed primarily for speech with low-bit-rate data services. The increasing number of Internet and multimedia applications is a major factor driving the third-generation wideband wireless technology. 3G mobile phone systems support 144 kbps data rate for users with high-speed mobility (e.g., in vehicles), 384 kbps for pedestrian users, and 2 Mbps for stationary users. The services include high-quality voice, wireless Internet access, and wireless multimedia services, which include audio, video, images, and data (3GPP 1999). 3G systems provide both a packet-switched and a circuit-switched domain from the beginning.

Work on 3G started around 1992, when the ITU formulated a plan to implement a global frequency band in the 2,000 MHz range that would support a single, ubiquitous wireless communication standard for all countries throughout the world. The new standard needed to be able to support a wide variety of mobile environments and have the flexibility to allow the introduction of new services and technologies (Zeng, Annamalai, and Bhargava 2000). This plan was renamed International Mobile Telecommunications-2000 (IMT-2000) in 1996. Figure 4 illustrates the ITU's view of a 3G system integrating disjoint networks and offering seamless services. In 1996, NTT and Ericsson initiated 3G development; in 1997, the U.S. TIA chose the CDMA technology for 3G; and in 1998, ETSI also selected the CDMA technology for 3G. In the same year, wideband CDMA (W-CDMA), cdma2000, and 3G time division duplexing (TDD) were proposed and developed by ETSI, the TIA TR45.5 subcommittee, and China/Europe, respectively.

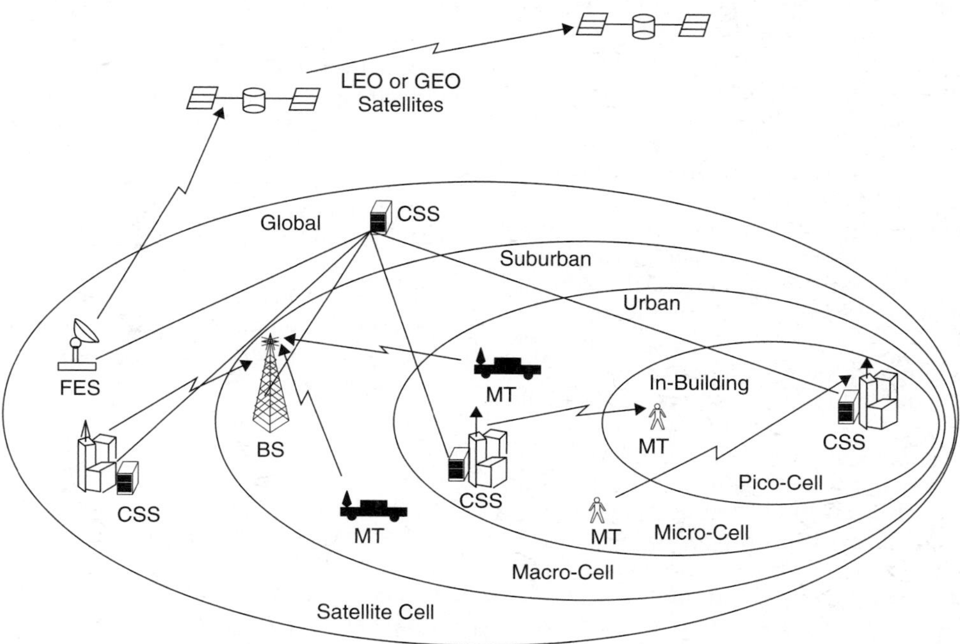

Figure 4: IMT-2000 integrated networks and services

Due to cost and complexity, the rollout of 3G has been much slower than anticipated. The spectrum licensing fees of 3G were collected many years before any income could be expected from 3G business. In addition, 3G requires a new access network, different from that already available in 2G systems. Hence, enormous investments are necessary to build the 3G networks. Therefore, many telecommunication operators encountered significant financial difficulties, which greatly delayed the 3G rollout in all countries except Japan and South Korea, where the spectrum licensing fees were avoided because priority was focused on national information technology (IT) infrastructure development.

The first country that introduced 3G on a large commercial scale was Japan. In 2005, about 40 percent of subscribers used 3G networks only, and currently 2G is on the way out in Japan. It is expected that the transition from 2G to 3G will be largely completed in Japan very soon, and upgrades to the next 3.5G stage with 3 Mbps data rates are under way.

The CDMA-based 3G standards selected from numerous proposals to ITU have become the major stream for IMT-2000. In particular, W-CDMA and cdma2000 are major 3G radio standards. W-CDMA was first developed by NTT DoCoMo, the predominant mobile phone operator in Japan, and later selected as the air interface for UMTS. The eventual 3G evolution for GSM, IS-136, and PDC systems leads to W-CDMA, whereas the eventual 3G evolution for 2G CDMA systems (i.e., IS-95) leads to cdma2000, a direct successor of IS-95. Several variants of cdma2000 are being developed, but all are based on the fundamentals of the IS-95 technology.

3G W-CDMA

In late 1996, ETSI developed the early versions of UMTS as a competitive open air-interface standard for 3G wireless telecommunications. In 1998, UMTS was submitted by ETSI to the ITU for consideration as a world standard for IMT-2000. W-CDMA is the technology behind the 3G UMTS standard (Ojanpera and Prasad 1998).

W-CDMA is a wideband spread-spectrum 3G mobile telecommunication air interface that utilizes code division multiple access. It is a complete set of specifications that includes a detailed protocol defining how a mobile phone communicates with the BS, how signals are modulated, and how datagrams are structured. In addition, system interfaces are specified to allow free competition on technology elements. The 3GPP standards body is developing W-CDMA for both wide-area mobile cellular coverage (using FDD) and indoor cordless type applications (using TDD).

W-CDMA is based on the direct spread CDMA technique. It requires a pair of a minimum spectrum allocation of 5 MHz, which is an important distinction from the other 3G standards. W-CDMA supports variable data rates up to 144 kbps for mobile vehicular data rate, up to 384 kbps for pedestrian data rate, and up to 2 Mbps for fixed data rate. Although W-CDMA is designed to provide backward compatibility and interoperability for all 2G and 2.5 G TDMA equipment and applications, the wider air-interface bandwidth of W-CDMA requires a change of the RF equipment at each BS. Therefore, the installation of W-CDMA will likely be slow and gradual throughout the world.

3G cdma2000

Based on the original IS-95 (cdmaOne) CDMA standard, the cdma2000 3G standard allows wireless carriers to introduce a family of new high-data–rate Internet access capabilities in a gradual manner within existing systems, while assuring backward compatibility with existing cdmaOne subscriber equipment. Thus, current CDMA operators may seamlessly and selectively introduce 3G capabilities in each cell without having to change BSs.

The cdma2000 standard is being developed under the TIA working group 45 and involves the participation of 3GPP2. It is being developed for both FDD (mobile radio) and TDD (in-building cordless) applications. The first 3G CDMA air interface is cdma2000 1xRTT. It can support a typical data rate of up to 144 kbps per user and up to twice as many voice users as the 2G CDMA standard. When upgrading from 2G CDMA to cdma2000 1xRTT, only new backbone software and new channel cards at the BS need to be purchased. There is no need to change any RF system components at the BSs.

The cdma2000 1xEV is an evolutionary advancement for CDMA and has been adopted by many CDMA mobile phone service providers. It is standardized by 3GPP2 as part of the CDMA family of standards. The initial design of cdma2000 1xEV was developed by Qualcomm in 1999 to meet the IMT-2000 requirements as a high-data–rate packet standard to be overlaid on existing IS-95 networks. In August 2001, the ITU recognized cdma2000 1xEV as part of IMT-2000. The cdma2000 1xEV has two options for radio channels with data only (cdma 2000 1xEV-DO), and with data and voice (cdma 2000 1xEV-DV). Originally, 1xEV-DO referred to *1x evolution-data only* because it was a direct evolution of the 1xRTT air-interface standard, with its channels carrying only data traffic. Later, it was changed to mean *1x evolution-data optimized*.

Using cdma2000 1xEV technology, individual 1.25 MHz channels may be installed in CDMA BSs to provide high-speed data access within selected cells. Compared to the 1xRTT standard or the GPRS and EDGE networks, 1xEV-DO is significantly faster, supporting a data rate of greater than 2.4 Mbps per user (Bi et al. 2003). Only terminals with 1xEV-DO chipsets can take advantages of the higher speeds. The cdma2000 1xEV-DV supports both voice and data users with data rate up to 144 kbps and twice as many voice channels as IS-95.

3G TD-SCDMA

Time division-synchronous code division multiple access (TD-SCDMA) is a 3G standard being developed in China. In 1998, the China Academy of Telecommunications Technology (CATT) and Siemens Corporation jointly submitted an IMT-2000 3G standard proposal. This proposal was adopted by the ITU as one of the 3G options in late 1999. On January 20, 2006, the Ministry of Information

Industry of China formally announced TD-SCDMA as the country's standard of 3G mobile telecommunications.

TD-SCDMA relies on the existing core GSM infrastructure and allows a 3G network to evolve through the addition of high-data–rate equipment at each GSM BS. TD-SCDMA combines TDMA and TDD techniques to provide a data-only overlay in an existing GSM network (Li et al. 2005). TD-SCDMA supports a data rate of up to 384 kbps, and its radio channel bandwidth is 1.6 MHz. TD-SCDMA uses TDD, in contrast to the FDD scheme used by W-CDMA. With TDD, different time slots within a single frame on a single-carrier frequency are used to provide both downlink and uplink channel transmissions. By dynamically adjusting the number of timeslots used for downlink and uplink, the system can more easily accommodate asymmetric traffic with different data-rate requirements than FDD schemes. Because it does not require paired spectrum for downlink and uplink, spectrum allocation flexibility is also increased. In addition, the uplink signals are synchronized at the BS receiver, achieved by continuous timing adjustments. This reduces the interference between users of the same time slot using different codes. Therefore, the system capacity is increased, but at the cost of some hardware complexity in achieving uplink synchronization.

RECENT ADVANCES IN THE CELLULAR WORLD

3G and Beyond (B3G) Systems

In order to predict and define the next generation wireless system after 3G, shortcomings of 3G and necessary improvements need to be identified first. The first shortcoming is related to data rates. Current 3G systems can only support data rates up to 2 Mbps and limited multimedia services. No matter how fast the data rates a system can provide now, it will be a very slow system in ten years' time. According to the current 3G specifications, the realistic UMTS data rate is around 384 kbps. The 2 Mbps data rate can only be provided to low-mobility users in pico cells. For real-time multimedia services such as live high-definition video and music, more bandwidth and higher data rates are needed to deliver the service to mobile phones. Second, the FDD mode adopted by W-CDMA does not support asymmetric data connections very well. The FDD spectrum is paired and the same amount of spectrum is allocated for both directions. For services like Web surfing, multimedia applications, and e-shopping, traffic along the downlink will be much heavier than along the uplink. Therefore, using the FDD scheme, the downlink capacity will be in short supply but the uplink capacity will remain underused.

Several enhancements for 3G technologies, such as high-speed downlink packet access (HSDPA; included in UMTS standard release 5 published by 3GPP) and high-speed uplink packet access (HSUPA; included in UMTS standard release 6 published by 3GPP) were recently developed. HSDPA and HSUPA, often jointly referred to as HSxPA, provide a smooth evolutionary path for UMTS-based 3G networks supporting higher data transfer speeds. Current HSDPA deployments support 1.8 Mbps or 3.6 Mbps in downlink, whereas HSUPA supports 5.76 Mbps for uplink. Under the HSDPA protocol, a new W-CDMA channel is defined: a high-speed downlink shared channel (HS-DSCH) that operates in a different way from existing W-CDMA channels. HSDPA achieves the increase in the data transfer speeds through adaptive modulation and coding, fast packet scheduling, and fast retransmissions (also known as hybrid automatic repeat request, or HARQ; 3GPP 2006). Similarly, HSUPA uses a new W-CDMA uplink channel, the enhanced dedicated channel (E-DCH), and employs similar link adaptation methods (adaptive modulation and fast scheduling) and HARQ to make retransmissions more effective. In addition, 3GPP is currently working on further advancing data rates. The UMTS terrestrial radio access network long-term evolution (UTRAN LTE), 3GPP's long-term evolution upgrade path for 3G systems, is expected to support 100 Mbps for downlink and 50 Mbps for uplink.

Fourth generation (4G) is often referred to as the successor wireless access technology to 3G. The Institute of Electrical and Electronics Engineers' (IEEE) official name for 4G is "3G and Beyond (B3G)." B3G is expected to provide users with on-demand, high-quality video and audio. B3G may use orthogonal frequency division multiplexing (OFDM) and orthogonal frequency division multiple access (OFDMA) to better allocate network resources to multiple users. B3G devices may use cognitive-radio-enabled or multimode receivers, which allow for better use of available bandwidth and use of multiple channels simultaneously. Unlike the 3G networks that include both circuit-switched and packet-switched networks, B3G will be based on packet switching only. This will allow low-latency data transmission.

The B3G technology will involve a collection of different kinds of multiple-access networks, such as 2G/3G cellular networks, wireless local area networks (WLANs), and Worldwide Interoperability for Microwave Access (WiMAX) networks (WiMAX Forum n.d.), from which a user can access the Internet by the most appropriate means. These networks must cooperate seamlessly and provide transparent applications to users. Both the network and the mobile devices will be able to configure themselves to adapt to different physical environments and transmission requirements. This includes software downloads for mobile devices to reconfigure themselves and the adaptability of networking protocols. Seamless vertical handoffs between different access networks will be supported for mobile devices to choose the best service provider and technology.

The major difference between 3G and B3G will be the all-packet–switched domain in B3G. The Internet will be the major backbone network connecting all kinds of wireless access networks for both voice and data services. Therefore, a B3G system is often referred to as an all-IP–based wireless system. The killer application of B3G is not clear, but consumers would expect from their mobile devices to receive all the multimedia applications they can receive from landline access, such as Internet access, voice over IP, music downloading, images, games, video, and mobile TV. However, since mobile phones are battery-constrained devices, power constraints have become a major concern for the newer-generation devices requesting multimedia services.

CONCLUSION

In this chapter, different generations of cellular networks—1G, 2G, 2.5G, 3G, and B3G—were reviewed. The historical evolution and main technical features of each generation were briefly introduced. The main difference between 1G and 2G cellular networks is that the radio signals of 1G cellular networks are analog, whereas those of 2G cellular networks are digital. The driving force of evolution from 2G to 2.5G, 3G, and B3G is the demand for mobile wireless access of data and multimedia applications. In addition, possible new features for the next-generation wireless system are also summarized in this chapter. This chapter aims to provide an overall picture of the evolution of the cellular technology. More technical details of some of the technologies mentioned in this chapter will be covered in the following chapters.

GLOSSARY

3GPP: 3rd-Generation Partnership Project.
AM: Amplitude modulation.
AMPS: Advanced mobile phone system.
CDMA: Code division multiple access.
EDGE: Enhanced data rates for GSM evolution.
ETACS: European total access cellular system.
ETSI: European Telecommunications Standard Institute.
FDD: Frequency division duplexing.
FDMA: Frequency division multiple access.
GPRS: General packet radio service.
GSM: Group Special Mobile/global system for mobile communications.
HSCSD: High-speed circuit-switched data.
HSDPA: High-speed downlink packet access.
HSUPA: High-speed uplink packet access.
IMT-2000: International Mobile Telecommunications-2000.
ITU: International Telecommunications Union.
NMT: Nordic mobile telephone.
OFDM: Orthogonal frequency division multiplexing.
OFDMA: Orthogonal frequency division multiple access.
PCS: Personal communications service.
PSTN: Public switched telephone network.
SIM: Subscriber identification module.
SDCCH: Stand-alone dedicated control channel.
SMS: Short message service.
TDD: Time division duplexing.
TDMA: Time division multiple access.
UMTS: Universal mobile telecommunications system.

CROSS REFERENCES

See *Cellular Communications Channels*; *Circuit Switching*; *Code Division Multiple Access (CDMA)*; *Frequency Division Multiplexing (FDM)*; *Packet Switching*; *Time Division Multiple Access (TDMA)*.

REFERENCES

3rd Generation Partnership Project (3GPP). 1999. *Technical specification group services and system aspects QoS concept*. Technical report 3G TR 23.907, version 1.2.0.

3rd Generation Partnership Project (3GPP). 2006. *Technical specification high-speed downlink packet access (HSDPA): Overall description, stage 2*. Technical report 3G TR 25.855, version 7.0.0.

3rd Generation Partnership Project (3GPP). Undated. http://www.3gpp.org/.

Agrawal, D. P., and Zeng, Q.-A. 2005. *Introduction to wireless and mobile systems*. 2nd ed. Toronto: Thomson Engineering.

Akyildiz, I. F., J. McNair, J. S. M. Ho, H. Uzunalioglu, and W. Wang. 1999. Mobility management in next generation wireless systems. *Proceedings of the IEEE* 87(8): 1347–84.

Bi, Q., R. R. Brown, D. Cui, A. D. Gandhi, C.-Y. Huang, and S. Vitebsky. 2003. Performance of 1xEV-DO third-generation wireless high-speed data systems. *Bell Labs Technical Journal* 7(3): 97–107.

Black, U. 1999. *Second-generation mobile and wireless networks*. Upper Saddle River, NJ: Prentice Hall.

Chandran, N., and M. C. Valenti. 2001. Three generations of cellular wireless systems. *IEEE Potentials* 20(1): 32–5.

Electronic Industries Alliance (EIA). Undated. http://www.eia.org/.

Enck, W., P. Traynor, P. McDaniel, and T. La Porta. 2005. Exploiting open functionality in SMS-capable cellular networks. *Proceedings of the Twelfth ACM Conference on Computer and Communications Security*, Washington, DC, November, pp. 393–404.

EIA/TIA. 1991. *Data communications*. Technical report IS-41.5-B.

———. 1993. *Mobile station-base station compatibility standard for dual-mode wideband spread-spectrum cellular system*. Technical report IS-95.

ETSI/TC. 1994a. *Security management*. Technical report recommendation GSM 12.03.

ETSI/TC. 1994b. *Mobile application part (MAP) specification, version 4.8.0*. Technical report recommendation GSM 09.02.

ETSI/TC. 1994c. *Point-to-point (PP) short message service (SMS) support on mobile radio interface, version 4.5.0*. Technical report recommendation GSM 04.11.

ETSI/TC. 1997. *Specification of the SIM application toolkit for the subscriber identity module-mobile equipment (SIM-ME) interface*. Technical report recommendation GSM 11.14, version 6.3.0.

ETSI/TC. 1998a. *GPRS service description, stage 1*. Technical report recommendation GSM 02.60, version 7.0.0.

ETSI/TC. 1998b. *GPRS service description, stage 2*. Technical report recommendation GSM 03.60, version 7.0.0 (Phase 2+).

European Telecommunications Standards Institute (ETSI). Undated. http://www.etsi.org/.

Furuskar, A., S. Mazur, F. Muller, and H. Olofsson. 1999. EDGE: Enhanced data rates for GSM and TDMA/136 evolution. *IEEE Personal Communications* 6(3): 56–66.

Garg, V., and J. Wilkes. 1999. *Principles and applications of GSM*. Upper Saddle River, NJ: Prentice Hall.

Goodman, D. J. 1997. *Wireless personal communications systems*. Reading, MA: Addison-Wesley.

GSM World. Undated. www.gsmworld.com/about/index.shtml.

International 450 Association. Undated. http://www.450world.org/.

International Telecommunications Union (ITU). Undated. Activities on IMT-2000. http://www.itu.int/home/imt.html.

———. Undated. World telecommunication indicators. http://www.itu.int/ITU-D/ict/statistics/.

Li, B., D. Xie, S. Cheng, J. Chen, P. Zhang, W. Zhu, and B. Li. 2005. Recent advances on TD-SCDMA in China. *IEEE Communications, January*, pp. 30–7.

Lin, Y.-B., and I. Chlamtac. 2001. *Wireless and mobile network architectures*. Hoboken, NJ: John Wiley & Sons.

MacDonald, V. H. 1979. Advanced mobile phone service: The cellular concept. *Bell System Technical Journal* 58(1): 15–41.

NMT Association (NMTA). Undated. http://www.nmt-world.org/.

Ojanpera, T., and R. Prasad. 1998. *Wideband CDMA for third generation mobile communications*. Boston, MA: Artech House.

Prasad, R., and T. Ojanpera. 1998. An overview of CDMA evolution toward wideband CDMA. *IEEE Communications Surveys* 1(1): 2–29.

Rahnema, M. 1993. Overview of the GSM system and protocol architecture. *IEEE Communications*, April, pp. 92–100.

Rappaport, T. S. 2002. *Wireless communications: Principles and practice*. 2nd ed. Upper Saddle River, NJ: Prentice Hall.

Rogers, G. S., and J. Edwards. 2003. *An introduction to wireless technology*. Upper Saddle River, NJ: Prentice Hall.

Stallings, W. 2005. *Wireless communications and networks*. 2nd ed. Upper Saddle River, NJ: Prentice Hall.

Telecommunications Industry Association (TIA). Undated. http://www.tiaonline.org/.

UMTS Forum. Undated. http://www.umts-forum.org/.

WiMAX Forum. Undated. http://www.wimaxforum.org/.

Yamauchi, K., W. Chen, and D. Wei. 2005. 3G mobile phone applications in telemedicine: A survey. *Proceedings of the Fifth International Conference on Computer and Information Technology*, Shanghai, China, September, pp. 956–60.

Zeng, M., A. Annamalai, and V. Bhargava. 2000. Harmonization of global third-generation mobile systems. *IEEE Communications*, December, pp. 94–104.

Global System for Mobile Communications

Mohamed A. Haleem and Koduvayur P. Subbalakshmi, *Stevens Institute of Technology*

INTRODUCTION

The *global system for mobile* (GSM) communications is the world's first cellular system to specify digital modulation and to have digital technology for both signaling and speech channels. Therefore, it is considered a *second-generation* (2G) mobile phone system. Nevertheless, GSM has undergone evolutions of twenty-one 2G and *third-generation* (3G) enhancements from *general packet radio services* (GPRS), *enhanced data rates for GSM evolution* (EDGE), to *universal mobile telecommunications system* (UMTS). These subsequent advancements are backward-compatible with GSM while adding new capabilities. The release 1997 version added packet data capabilities with GPRS. In 1998, the *3rd Generation Partnership Project* (3GPP) was formed. Originally, it was intended only to produce the specifications of the third generation of mobile networks. However, 3GPP also took over the maintenance and development of the GSM specification. Higher speeds were added using EDGE in release 1999. In this introduction, we provide a brief history of GSM's development.

During the early evolution of cellular mobile communication, systems were developed without paying much attention to standardized specifications. In 1982, a committee was formed with the French name *Groupe Spéciale Mobile* (GSM) under the umbrella of the *Conference of European Posts and Telegraphs* (CEPT). The purpose has been to define a new standard for mobile communications in the 900-MHz range. This was to serve as the standard for pan-European cellular service. In 1991, the acronym GSM changed to stand for global system for mobile communications; this was the year the first GSM system was ready for user-friendly operation. CEPT has now evolved into the organization called the *European Telecommunications Standards Institute* (ETSI).

The proposed system had to meet a set of criteria including subjective speech quality, low terminal and service cost, support for international roaming, the ability to support handheld terminals, support for range of new services and facilities, spectral efficiency, and *integrated services digital network* (ISDN) compatibility.

Following the discussions during 1982 to 1985, a digital system was adopted for GSM. The technical fundamentals of the GSM system were defined in 1987. This included the choice of the narrowband *time-division multiple access* (TDMA) as the multiple access technique. In 1989, ETSI took over control, and by 1990 the first GSM specification amounting to more than 6000 pages of text was completed. Phase 1 GSM 900 specifications were also frozen that year. The variation of GSM system named *Digital Cellular System 1800* (DCS 1800), operating in the 1800-MHz frequency range, also was finalized this year to be used in the United Kingdom. DCS 1800 was adapted to operate in the 1900-MHz band in the United States, where it is called *Personal Communication System 1900* (PCS 1900).

By 1992, many European countries had operational networks based on GSM and started to have worldwide penetration. The first GSM network operator was Oy Radiolinja Ab in Finland in January 1992. Following the success of GSM in Europe in 1992, the first demonstration in Africa took place in 1993 at Telkom 1993 in Cape Town, and the first GSM network in Africa was launched in South Africa in 1994. During 1993 to 1997, more and more countries and regions around the world adopted GSM. The first PCS 1900 network went live "on air" in the United States, and the U.S. Federal Communications Commission auctioned off PCS licenses. In an industry conference, Telecom 1995, in Geneva, Nokia showed 33.6-kbps multimedia data transmission via GSM. The phase 2 of the standard was completed in 1995, and the fax, data, and *short message service* (SMS) roaming also were included that year.

In 1996, the 8-K subscriber identity module was launched, and prepaid GSM SIM cards were available. A SIM is a smart card that securely stores the key that identifies a mobile phone service subscriber as well as subscription information, preferences, and text messages. The SIM stores network state information such as its current *location area identity* (LAI). If the handset is turned off and back on again, it will take data off the SIM and search for the LAI it was in. Each SIM is uniquely identified by its international circuit card ID. SIM cards identify users uniquely by holding an *international mobile subscriber identity* (IMSI). SIM is further discussed below under "Mobile Station Subsystem." The first dual-band GSM 900-1900 phone was launched in 1997. In 1998, Vodacom introduced free voicemail.

Market Penetration of GSM

As this chapter is written, GSM service is used by more than 1.6 billion people across more than 210 countries and territories. Originally developed to serve as the pan-European cellular service, GSM is now the world's most popular standard for cellular radio and personal communication services. The growth was rapid. In December 1992, there were thirteen networks on the air in seven areas, and the GSM world congress in Berlin consisted of 630 participants. By December 1993, there were thirty-two networks on the air in eighteen areas, and there were 760 participants in the GSM world congress in Lisbon. There were 780 participants in the GSM world congress in Athens. By December 1994, there were sixty-nine networks on the air in forty-three areas. In 1995, the world congress in Madrid has had 1400 participants; by December, there were 117 networks in sixty-nine areas. In December 1996, there were 120 networks on the air in eighty-four areas. By December 1998, there were 125 million GSM 900, 1800, and 1900 users worldwide. This number grew to 165 million in 1999, 480 million in 2000, and 500 million in 2001. By 2001, there were 500 million GSM users (CellularOne, undated).

The widespread use of the GSM standard makes international roaming possible, and the subscribers are able to use the same mobile communication devices in different parts of the world with ease. GSM is an open standard that is currently developed by the 3GPP. More than 1.6 billion people used GSM phones as of 2005, making GSM the dominant mobile phone system worldwide with approximately 78 percent of the world's digital mobile market and 75 percent of the world's wireless market (GSM World, undated). GSM's main competitor, cdmaOne, is used primarily in North America and parts of Asia (Heine 1998). cdmaOne also benefited from increased radio spectrum efficiencies compared with the more common GSM networks. Roaming with GSM phones is a major advantage over the competing technology because roaming across CDMA networks with different operators is difficult, depending on the handsets and operators concerned. However, as pointed out in the sections to follow, there are limitations to the level of roaming in terms of geographical areas and regions because of commercial and licensing reasons. Furthermore, the standards do not fully specify some elements and different implementations by different vendors which may hinder interoperability. Another major reason for the growth in GSM usage, particularly between 1998 and 2002, was the availability of prepaid calling from mobile phone operators. This allows people who are either unable or unwilling to enter into a contract with an operator to have mobile phones. For example, students and teenagers can get prepaid accounts that they can manage themselves without needing parents to manage and sign for contracted accounts. It also allows some operators to offer solutions for infrequent users who are likely to spend less per month on prepaid accounts than on minimum basic service plans. Prepaid accounts also enabled the rapid expansion of GSM in many developing countries where large sections of the population do not have access to banks or bank accounts and countries where there are no effective credit rating agencies. (In many developed countries, starting a non-prepaid contract with a cellular phone operator is almost always subject to credit verification through personal information provided by credit rating agencies).

GSM was also the first to have SMS text messaging, which proved extremely popular with the teenage market.

Factors Contributing to the Success of GSM

The major factors that have contributed to the commercial success of GSM systems manufacturers and network operators are:

- the liberation of the monopoly of telecommunications in Europe during the 1990s, which led to competition and hence lower prices;
- the knowledge base and professional approach within the GSM committee and the active cooperation of the industry; and
- the lack of competitions from other parts of the world at the time of GSM was being developed.

The GSM specifications define the functions and interface requirements in detail but do not address the hardware. The reason for this is to not limit designers yet still make it possible for operators to buy equipment from different suppliers. Further, it is the first standard to specify the network-level architecture and services for mobile communication systems.

From the point of view of the consumer, the key advantage of GSM systems has been higher digital voice quality and low-cost alternatives to making calls such as text messaging. The advantage for network operators has been that the vendors can address a large market, allowing easy interoperability. Also, the open standards have allowed network operators to offer roaming services, which means subscribers can use their phones all over the world.

GSM SERVICES

GSM services can be grouped into three categories: *teleservices* (TS), *bearer services* (BS), and *supplementary services* (SS). In essence, TS is telephony, BS the data transmission, and SS the value-added features.

Teleservices

TS includes bidirectional telephony, emergency calls, and voice messaging. An emergency call feature allows the mobile subscriber to contact a nearby emergency service, such as police, by dialing a unique number. Voice messaging permits a message to be in the voice mailbox when the called party is not reachable.

Bearer Services

BS includes data services (with data terminals or computers connected to the mobile devices), short message service, cell broadcasting, and local features. Rates as high as 9.6 kbit/s are supported. With a suitable data terminal or computer connected directly to the mobile apparatus, data may be sent through circuit-switched or packet-switched networks. For SMS (as many as 160 alphanumeric characters), a message center is involved. The broadcast mode is used to send a message to all subscribers in a given geographic area. This service also can be used for short messages of as many as ninety-three characters. Local features of the mobile terminal include abbreviated dialing, editing of short messages, and repetition of failed calls.

Supplementary Services

Some of the SS are as follows:

- advice of any charges (i.e., the cost of a call in progress);
- blocking of all outgoing calls;
- blocking of incoming or outgoing international calls as a whole or only those associated with a specific basic service as desired;
- blocking of roaming calls (e.g., all incoming roaming calls or only those associated with a specific service);
- call forwarding of all incoming calls, or only those associated with a specific basic service, to another directory number (forwarding may be unconditional or be set to take place when the mobile subscriber is busy, there is no reply, the mobile subscriber is not reachable, or there is radio congestion);
- call holding, or allowing interruption of an existing call with subsequent reestablishment of the call permitted;
- call waiting, or allowing the notification of an incoming call when the mobile subscriber is busy;
- call transfer, which permits an established incoming or outgoing call to be transferred to a third party;
- call completion to busy subscribers, which allows notification when a busy called subscriber becomes free and call reinitiation if desired;
- closed user group, which allows a group of subscribers to communicate only among themselves;
- calling number identification presentation or restriction, which permits or restricts the presentation of the calling party;
- SS identification number (or additional address information);
- connected number identification presentation, which indicates that the phone number that has been reached;
- free-phone service, which allocates a number to a mobile subscriber, with all calls to that number free of charge for the calling party;
- malicious call identification, which permits the registration of malicious, nuisance, and obscene incoming calls; and
- three-party service, which permits the establishment of conference calls.

The GSM project embraces an ambitious set of targets—namely, international roaming, open architecture, high degree of flexibility, easy installation, interoperation with ISDN, the *circuit-switched public data network* (CSPDN), the *packet-switched public data network* (PSPDN), and the *public switched telephone network* (PSTN), high-quality signal and link integrity, good spectral efficiency, low-cost infrastructure, small terminals, and security features. These objectives have been gradually achieved, and a broad collection of services are provided.

NETWORK ARCHITECTURE

GSM uses the cellular communication structure in which a geographical area to be served is partitioned into subareas called *cells*. A *mobile station* (MS) within a cell achieves connectivity to the network via a *base transceiver station* (BTS) with limited transmission range. The frequency spectrum available to an operator is divided into narrow band frequency channels. Each cell is assigned a subset of the set of channels according to a frequency plan. The frequency plan achieves good reuse of channels to control the co-channel interference and maximize the capacity with a given set of cells. As the demand for service is increased, the cells are split into smaller cells, thus increasing the network capacity. Another technique is to divide the cells into sectors with one transceiver for each sector. The transceivers for all of the sectors in a cell can be co-located and therefore can be part of the same base station. Figure 1 illustrates cellular structure, frequency reuse, and cell splitting.

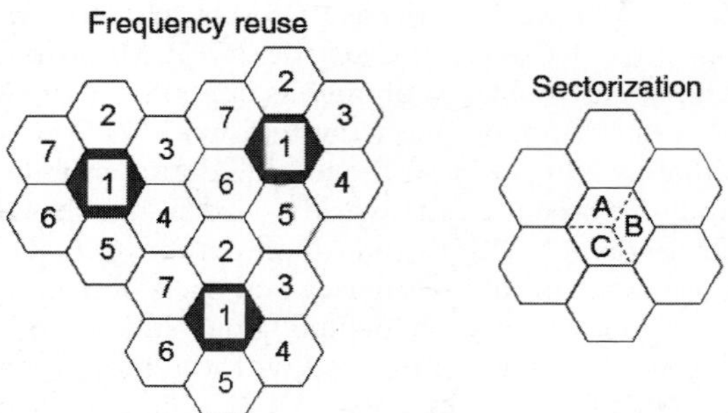

Figure 1: Cellular structure, frequency reuse, and cell splitting

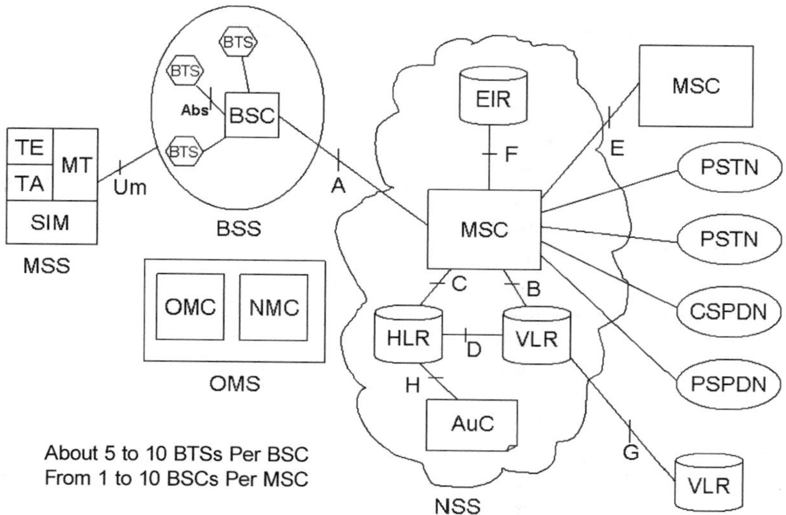

Figure 2: The GSM networks architecture

A mobile station in a cell establishes connection to another MS within the same cell, an MS in another cell, or to a wired telephone via the base station covering the cell. As the mobile station moves from one cell to another, a handover process is invoked and the connection is made via the base station in the new cell. This process as well many other network-related communication overheads are handled in GSM with a modular and hierarchical network structure. The required computations and communications are performed with distributed computer systems as opposed to a central computer.

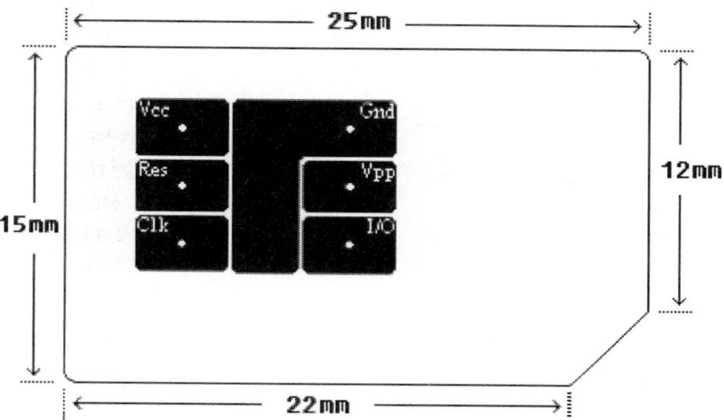

Figure 3: The GSM plug-in SIM

GSM Subsystems

A GSM network is made up of the *mobile station subsystem* (MSS), the *base station subsystem* (BSS), the *network and switching subsystem* (NSS), and the *operation and support subsystem* (OSS). All of these entities form a *public land mobile network* (PLMN). Figure 2 describes schematically the various subsystems and the components of subsystems of a GSM PLMN. Also shown are the various interfaces to be described later. The components of each subsystem are described here.

Mobile Station Subsystem

The MSS includes the *terminal equipment* (TE), the *terminal adapter* (TA), the *mobile termination* (MT), and a *subscriber identity module* (SIM). TE, TA, and MT compose the *mobile equipment* (ME), and SIM enables its use. A device such as a fax or a computer may be considered a TE. An MT incorporates the standard GSM mobile terminal functions. A TA works as an interface between the TE and the MT.

GSM Recommendation 02.07 describes in detail the mandatory and optional functionalities of mobile equipment. The most important features are *dual tone multifrequency* (DTMF) capability, SMS capability, availability of the ciphering algorithms A5/1 and A5/2, display capability for short messages, dialed numbers, available PLMN, support for emergency calls (without SIM), and an *international mobile equipment identifier* (IMEI). These devices may be fully or partially integrated into one piece. In addition to its IMEI, the mobile equipment is identified through its classmark, which includes the revision level, encryption capability, frequency capability, short message capability, and *radio frequency* (RF) power capability. There are five MSS classes in GSM 900 based on the maximum RF power. The maximum RF power levels for classes I, II, III, IV, and V are 20, 8, 5, 2, and 0.8 watts, respectively. Class I GSM 900 devices are no longer used. DCS 1800 and PCS 1900 have power levels of 1 and 0.25 watts for classes I and II, respectively. Class III DCS 1800 has a power level of 4 watts, whereas a class III PCS 1900 has a power level of 2 watts.

In GSM, the mobile station is distinguished from mobile equipment by the SIM. The GSM allows the use of mobile phone (mobile equipment) without SIM only for emergency calls. The mobile equipment and SIM together form the MS (see Figure 3). SIM is a microchip planted in one of the two forms, the check card (ID-1 SIM), which is the size of a credit card and can be inserted into larger equipment such as a car phone or the smaller (approximately 2.5 cm × 1.5 cm) plug-in SIM (Rappaport 1996). Both versions are functionally same.

The SIM holds various data related to the subscriber as described in Table 1.

Part of data are subscriber information such as the international mobile subscriber identity. Parameters such as *personal identification number* (PIN) and *PIN unblocking key* (PUK) are needed for administrative tasks. Others

Table 1: Data on a SIM

Purpose	Parameters	Description
Administrative	PIN/PIN2 PUK/PUK2 SIM service table Last dialed number Charging meter Language	Personal identification number PIN unblocking key Optional functionality Redial Charges, increments Prompts by the mobile station
Security	Algorithm A3 and A8 Key K_i Key K_c CKSN	Authentication to find K_c Only on SIM and HLR Ciphering key sequence number
Subscriber data	IMSI (international mobile subscriber identity) MSISDN (mobile subscriber ISDN) Access control class(es)	Directory number of a subscriber For control of network access
Roaming data	TMSI T3212 Location updating status LAI Network color codes (NCCs) of restricted PLMNs NCCs of preferred PLMNs	Temporary mobile subscriber identity For location updating Is location updating required? Location area information
PLMN data	NCC, mobile country code (MCC) Mobile network code (MNC) of the home PLMN Absolute radio frequency channel numbers (ARFCNs) of home PLMN	 Network identifier Frequencies for which the home PLMN is licensed

are used in functionalities related to security and roaming. As for the security-related parameters, the key K_i is subscriber-specific and is only on SIMs and *home location registers* (HLRs). The key K_c is the result of algorithm A8, K_i, and a *random number* (RAND).

Base Station Subsystem

The BSS is responsible for the radio coverage of a given geographic region and for appropriate signal processing. As the MS moves from one cell to another, the connection is transferred to the next BTS (i.e., the handover). The BSS consists of one or more base transceiver stations, a *base station controller* (BSC), and a transcoding rate and adaptation unit. Although the size of a BTS has diminished over time, the functionalities remains more or less the same as in the original systems. A BTS contains one or more *transmitter and receiver* (TRX) modules, an *operation and maintenance* (O&M) module with a clock module, and input-output filters. GSM recommendation allows as many as sixteen TRXs. The O&M module of a BTS is directly connected to the BSC, which allows this module to process the commands from the BSC or the *mobile switching center* (MSC) directly into the BTS and to report the results. It also includes a human–machine interface for local control of BTS. The internal clock of GSM BST is required for testing in a stand-alone environment or when the connection to BSC's pulse code modulation clock is not available. All of the TRXs of a BTS are required to use the same clock signal. The required accuracy of the clock is defined to be 0.05 parts per million. This translates to ±0.5Hz at a clock speed of 10 MHz. The input-output filters limit the bandwidth of the receiver-transmitter signals. The input filters on the uplink (MS to BTS) are fixed wideband filters designed to pass GSM 900, DCS 1800, or PCS 1900 frequencies. On the downlink (BTS to MS), the output filters have bandwidths of 200 kHz and are remotely controllable by the operation and maintenance center (OMC).

Network and Switching Subsystem

The NSS carries out the GSM switching procedures and the manipulation of the databases for mobility management of the subscribers. Its functions include coordination of call setup, paging, resource allocation, location registration, encryption, interfacing with other networks, handover control, billing, and synchronization, among others. The NSS consists of the MSC, the HLR, the *visitor location register* (VLR), the *authentication center* (AuC), and the *equipment identity register* (EIR).

The MSC performs the switching functions and coordinates all of the calls and routing procedures within GSM. In general, an MSC controls several BSSs. Thus, it is responsible for traffic management and the radio coverage of a given geographic area—the MSC area. A GSM network may have one or more MSCs, depending on the traffic to be controlled. An MSC is responsible for several functions such as paging, coordination of call setup, allocation of resources, interworking with other networks, handover management, billing, encryption, echo canceling, control, and synchronization with BSSs, among others. It interfaces the GSM PLMN with the external networks such as PSTN, ISDN, CSPDN, and PSPDN. Such interfacing may be carried out through a gateway MSC connected to a serving MSC.

The HLR is a database that contains a list of those subscribers who belong to one or more MSC areas within which they have originally been registered. An HLR, therefore, defines the subscription area. In the HLR, these subscribers are associated with information records that are relevant to call management. Both permanent and temporary data are held within the HLR. The permanent data constitute data that are modified only for administrative reasons and are kept for every call. The temporary data are modified to accommodate the transient status of the subscribers' parameters and can be changed from call to call. The permanent data include IMSI, MS-ISDN, information on roaming restriction, permitted supplementary services, and an authentication key for security procedures. The temporary data consist of MSRN, data related to ciphering, the VLR address, the MSC address, and information on roaming restrictions. An HLR is usually centralized, but it can also be distributed within the network, with the configuration chosen in accordance with the operator's needs.

The VLR is a database that contains a list of those subscribers belonging to another subscription area but who are now in roaming condition within this MSC area. In the VLR, these roaming subscribers are associated with information records relevant to the call management. In essence, the VLR contains the same information associated with the HLR. In fact, when a subscriber roams into another MSC area, the relevant data belonging to this subscriber stored in the HLR are transferred to the corresponding VLR. The data of the roaming subscriber, retrieved from the HLR, remain in the respective VLR as long as the subscriber is found in a roaming condition. A VLR is usually co-located with the MSC.

The AuC is a functional entity that manipulates the authentication functions and encryption keys for each subscriber within the system. An authentication key, kept in the SIM card and in the AuC, is provided for each subscriber in the system and is never transmitted over the air. Instead, a random challenge and the response to this challenge are transmitted (to be detailed later). The random challenge and the respective response are based on authentication keys and ciphering algorithms. Note that the contents of the information exchanged in such a procedure may change for each call. In conjunction with the *temporary mobile subscriber identity* (TMSI), this constitutes an interesting procedure that renders GSM robust with respect to unauthorized accesses. On the other hand, vulnerability is present when the authentication key must be transmitted from an HLR to a VLR in a roaming situation. The EIR is a database that contains the IMEIs of all subscribers. The IMEIs are grouped into three categories:

1. a white list, which contains the IMEIs known to belong to equipment with no problems;
2. a black list, which contains the IMEIs of equipment that has been reported stolen; and
3. a gray list, which contains the IMEIs of equipment with problems that are not substantial enough to warrant barring.

Operation and Support Subsystem

The OSS performs the operation and maintenance functions through two entities, namely, the OMC and the *network management center* (NMC). The GSM standards do not fully specify these elements. Therefore, different manufacturers may have different implementations, which may be a problem for interoperability between different GSM systems. The NSS uses lines leased on the PSTN or other fixed networks to communicate with the GSM entities. Protocols used for data transfer are SS7 and X.25. In general, the O&M functions performed by the OSS include alarm handling, fault management, performance management, configuration control, and traffic data acquisition, among others. In many circumstances, the actions may be taken remotely and automatically and, on detection of an abnormal operation, tests, diagnoses, and fault removal can be carried out to place the system back in service.

The network resources may be activated or deactivated via the OMC functions. There may be one or several OMCs, depending on the size of the network. An OMC is a regional entity used for daily maintenance activities. The NMC serves the entire network. It performs a centralized network management and is used for long-term planning.

INTERFACES

Several interfaces are defined in GSM standards for communication between different components of the GSM network as shown in Figure 2. They are called *open interfaces* and allow the choice of equipment from different vendors. Eight of these interfaces are named by uppercase letters A through H. There are two others—namely, Abis-interface and Um-interface. Each interface is briefly described here.

A-interface is the interface between BSC and MSC. It supports signaling and traffic (voice and data) information transmitted by means of one or more 2.048-Mbit/s transmission systems. The Abis-interface is defined for the communication between BTS and BSC. It handles common control functions within a BTS. It is physically supported by a digital link using the *link access protocol for the ISDN D-channel* (LAPD). The Um-interface, or air interface, defines the standards for the interface between MSS and BSS. The physical and logical channel structure as well as the frame hierarchy are part of the definitions of this interface. The remaining interfaces are as follows.

- B: between MSC and VLR.
- C: between MSC and HLR.
- D: between HLR and VLR.
- E: between MSCs.
- F: between MSC and EIR.
- G: between VLRs.
- H: between HLR and AuC.

The great majority of the GSM interfaces make use of well-consolidated protocols such as SS7, X.25, and LAPD (the ISDN data-link layer). The 2.048-Mbit/s E1 digital links are used to interconnect the several GSM elements and external elements. For example, E1 is used to interconnect MSC and PSTN, MSC and MSC, and BSC and MSC. Each E1 channel is then used to convey payload information or control information. The control information may use protocols such as SS7, LAPD, and X.25.

SPECTRAL EFFICIENCY

In this section, we discuss the techniques used in the physical and radio link layers to optimize spectral efficiency. This includes signal processing, the transmitter-receiver chain, equalization, frequency hopping, discontinuous transmission with speech activity detection, and power control.

Signal-Processing Functions

As a fully digital system, GSM mobile equipment employs analog-to-digital conversion at transmission on the uplink and digital-to-analog conversion at reception on the downlink. To this end, GSM adopts a sampling rate of 8 kHz and uniform quantization with thirteen bits per sample leading to a row rate of $8 \times 13 = 104$ kbit/s. This rate is reduced to 13 kbit/s using a speech coding algorithm—namely, regular pulse excitation and long-term prediction linear prediction coding. This is followed by a forward error-correction code block and an interleaver to minimize burst errors. In particular a 1/2 rate convolution code is used. Following this process, a channel rate of 270.833 kbit/s is achieved. The resulting binary bit stream is carrier modulated using *Gaussian minimum shift keying* (GMSK) scheme and is transmitted through the wireless channel. The receiver chain on the uplink at the base station consists of a demodulator, a deinterleaver, an error-correction block, and a decoder to convert 13-bit uniform to 8-bit A law, leading to a raw bit rate of 64 kbit/s. The bit stream is then transmitted to MSC. For the downlink direction, the signal processing functions take place in the reverse order and ends with a digital-to-analog conversion at the mobile station.

Multipath Equalization

RF signals in the 900-MHz band are reflected or refracted from objects in the environment such as buildings, cars, and hills. Many such reflected signals, each with a different phase, can superimpose constructively and destructively at the receiver antenna, leading to multipath fading phenomena. *Equalization* refers to signal processing used to undo the distortion introduced by this effect. It works by finding out how a known transmitted signal is modified by multipath fading and then constructing an inverse filter to extract the rest of the desired signal. This known signal is the 26-bit training sequence transmitted in the middle of every time-slot burst. The actual implementation of the equalizer is not specified in the GSM specifications.

Frequency Hopping

To further improve frequency reuse planning, GSM uses *frequency hopping* (FH) and slow FH in particular. Although FH is available in all GSM mobile equipment, its use is up to the operator. With slow FH, the transmission in a given time slot moves from one GSM frequency carrier to another, according to a hopping pattern. The hopping takes place for each frame of duration 4.615 ms. As the number of frequencies utilized increases, the probability of encountering more than one faded frequency at the same time diminishes. Therefore, with FH, the transmission becomes less vulnerable to fading. Further, if the co-channel cells are assigned different hopping sequences, then the co-channel interference may reduce. The hopping can take place on any carrier in the GSM band except the standard broadcast carrier (base channel). To achieve these desired results, the signals within a group of cells are required to use mutually orthogonal hopping sequences. This, in turn, requires coordination among all of the signals. Both the uplink and the downlink operate with the same FH sequence. When a terminal is to use FH, it is informed by the network on the available set of hopping channels and the hopping sequence number.

Discontinuous Transmission

In a normal conversation, the voice activity factor is less than 60 percent on average. Therefore, switching the transmitter off during the inactive period can significantly save battery power and also help reduce interference (thereby increasing the user capacity). To achieve this, GSM equipment is designed for *discontinuous transmission* (DTx). The implementation includes a *voice activity detector* (VAD), which plays a decisive role in transmission performance. When it detects voice (in the presence of noise) or noise, the VAD outputs a signal to control a transmitter switch. A decision in favor of a wrong detection will produce annoying effects in the transmission such as a clipping in speech. As the transmitter is switched off between talkspurts, at the receiving end the background acoustic noise present during the conversation abruptly disappears. It has been observed that this also can be annoying to the listener. To minimize the effect of such a noise "modulation," a synthetic signal known as a *comfort noise signal* (CNS), which has characteristics that match those of the background noise, is introduced at the receiver. It tries to conform with the characteristics of the background noise of the current transmission. To accomplish this, the noise parameters are computed at the transmit end during a time span of four frames after the VAD detects the end of a talkspurt. These parameters are sent to recompose the noise at the receiver. In addition to VAD and CNS, the DTx implementation includes *speech frame extrapolation* (SFE) function. The SFE aims to replace a speech frame that has been badly corrupted by error with a preceding uncorrupted speech frame. This replacement is based on the fact that consecutive speech frames are highly correlated. The use of SFE improves the signal quality (i.e., improves mean opinion score).

Power Control

Power control can be used to reduce co-channel interference and increase battery life. The GSM standard allows power control at both uplink and downlink. Power control requires periodic feedback signaling from the receiver to transmitter. In GSM, the mobile power can be adjusted in steps of 2 dB from a minimum of 13 dBm (20 mW) to as high as 30 dB, resulting in sixteen power levels. Power adjustment can take place for every 60 ms corresponding to thirteen frames. In comparison to CDMA, where the power control resolution is 1dB or lower, this appears to be coarse.

Spectral Efficiency of GSM

Efficient signal-processing stages used in GSM such as adaptive equalization, error-correction codes, GMSK modulation, and SFE makes it possible to operate at low carrier to interference ratio and therefore allows small frequency reuse clusters of three or four cells. The spectral efficiency in terms of users per cell per MHz for a typical scenario can be calculated as follows. In GSM 900, for instance, there are 50 MHz of spectrum and 124 pairs of frequency channels. Because each frequency channel has eight time slots, there are $8 \times 124 = 992$ combinations of frequency channels and time slots, allowing that many simultaneous users. With a frequency reuse cluster size of four and thus a spectral efficiency of $992 = (3 \times 50) = 4.96$ users/cell/MHz is achievable. Similarly, for a cluster size of 3, 6.61 users/cell/MHz is achieved.

BURSTS, CHANNELS, DUPLEXING, AND FRAME STRUCTURE

Physical Channels

GSM is a fully digital system with a multiple-access architecture based on the narrowband frequency division multiple access, TDMA, and *frequency division duplexing* (FDD) technology. The carrier spacing is 200 kHz in GSM 900, *extended GSM* (EGSM), DCS 1800, and PCS 1900. A channel consists of a pair of 200-kHz frequency segments, one for uplink and one for downlink. The separation between uplink and downlink varies, depending on the GSM version. Table 2 shows the parameters of GSM channels. In EGSM, the original GSM 900 operating band is extended, and lower-power terminals and smaller serving areas (microcells) are specified. In all versions of GSM systems, a frequency channel is divided into eight time slots (0 to 7) per frame, allowing simultaneous use of the channel using time sharing. The duration of a GSM frame is 4.615 ms and therefore a time slot has a duration of 577 μs.

Although the 25-MHz spectrum per direction for GSM 900 admits 125 200-kHz carriers, in order to allow for 100-kHz of guard bands at both edges of the spectrum, only 124 carriers are used.

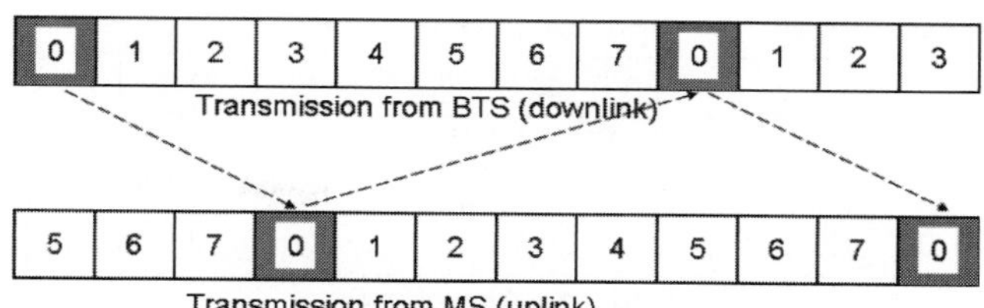

Figure 4: Time division duplexing in GSM

Duplexing

In the communication via radio channel, the interference between uplink and downlink transmissions is avoided with one of two duplexing techniques—namely, frequency division duplexing and *time division duplexing* (TDD). Both modes are specified in the GSM standard. In the FDD mode, two filters called *duplexers* at the transceiver attenuate the operating frequency of the complementary functions. This keeps the transmitter's energy out of the receiver's input. Thus, a single common antenna could be used with such a filter system. This allows the use of the channel in full duplex mode. In TDD mode, on the other hand, different time slots are used for uplink and downlink; therefore, the channel operates in half-duplex mode in some sense. In GSM TDD mode, the uplink and downlink transmission takes place with an offset of three time slots. Figure 4 shows the uplink-downlink time-slot structure. The eight time slots numbered from 0 to 7 are assigned to eight different users.

Slot Formats

As already described, a time slot in GSM with duration contains 156.25 bits. GSM specifies five different time slot formats, or burst formats that are used for various functions: normal, synchronization, frequency correction, access, and dummy burst. Furthermore, these bursts are used in different logical channels based on the tasks.

1. The *normal burst* carries user information or network control information.
2. A *synchronization burst* performs time synchronization of the terminal operations with the base station.
3. The *frequency correction burst* synchronizes the terminal with the base station. During this burst, the BTS transmits a signal that has a frequency 67.7 kHz above that of the carrier.

Table 2: Channels in GSM Bands

System	Uplink (MHz)	Downlink (MHz)	Number of duplex channels	Uplink–downlink spacing (MHz)
GSM 900	890–915	935–960	125	45
EGSM	880–915	925–960	175	45
DCS 1800	1710–1785	1805–1880	375	95
PCS 1900	1850–1910	1930–1990	300	80

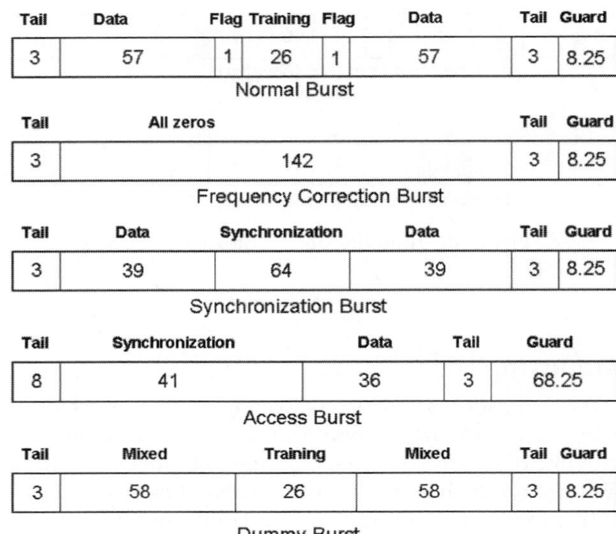

Figure 5: The GSM burst (time-slot) structure

4. An *access burst* initiates a dialog with the system through a signaling protocol.
5. The *dummy burst* carries no information and is transmitted by the BTS.

Figure 5 shows the format of each of these bursts with respect to the use of bits. All of the burst types have a tail field entirely of zero bits to indicate the start and end of the burst. These bits are also used by the adaptive equalizer. All of the burst types use the first three bits to indicate the start of a burst except for the access burst, which uses the first eight bits for this purpose. In all of the burst types, the last 8.25 bits are used for the guard field except for the access burst, which uses the last 68.25 bits for the guard field. The guard bits avoid overlaps between slots. The access burst is allocated a large guard to allow for uplink transmissions from different areas of a cell to arrive at the BTS within a time-slot duration. The guard field also allows the transmitter to turn off at the end of a time slot and to turn on at the start of the next. The three bits just before the guard bits are used for the ending tail field. The normal and the synchronization bursts have two data fields, one following the start tail field and another before the end tail field. These fields are fifty-seven and thirty-nine bits long, respectively, for the normal burst and the synchronization burst. The access burst includes one data field before the ending tail and is thirty-six bits. The data field in a normal burst may be used for user information or network control information. In other bursts, it is used for network control information. The normal burst includes a single bit flag just after the first data field and another single bit flag just before the second data field. These flags indicate weather the transmitted information is user information or network information. The training bits carry the training sequence used in adaptive equalization. As seen in Figure 5, this is used in normal burst and the dummy burst. The synchronization field present in the synchronization burst and the access burst contains a known bit pattern (synchronization sequence) to be used in time synchronization.

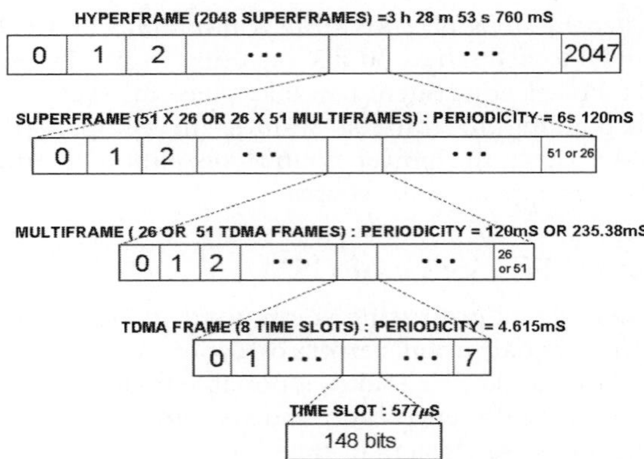

Figure 6: The GSM frame hierarchy

The Frame Hierarchy

In the frame hierarchy of GSM, the largest frame—namely, the *hyperframe*—has a duration of 3h, 28m, 53s, and 760 ms. Down the hierarchy, there are *superframes, multiframes, frames*, and *slots*. A hyperframe includes multiple superframes. There are two formats for superframes with fifty-one or twenty-six multiframes. Each multiframe in turn consists of multiple frames. Again, there are two formats for multiframes. Nevertheless, the duration of a superframe is 6s, 120ms in both formats. This is achieved by having twenty-six frames per superframe in the case of fifty-one multiframes or a superframe and vice versa. Each frame consists of eight time slots and therefore has a duration of 4.615 ms. The hierarchy and timing are shown in Figure 6.

Logical Channels

Several logical channels are defined in GSM. The definitions are based on the tasks. Figure 7 shows the categorizations and subcategorizations of these channels. There are two major types: (1) traffic channels used for speech and data and (2) signaling channels for control signaling. As seen in the figure, for speech there are full rate and half-rate traffic channels (TCH/F and TCH/H, respectively). There are three types of traffic channels with varying data rates. Numbers indicated are in kbits/s.

There are three groups of signaling channels: (1) broadcast, (2) common control, and (3) dedicated control channels. Broadcast channels and common control channels are one-way channels and occupy time slot 0 on standard broadcast carriers. The common control channels may also use slots 2, 4, and 6 of this carrier. Dedicated control channels are two-way channels and may use any time slot of the frame and of any carrier except slot 0 of the standard broadcast carrier.

Broadcast channels are of three types: (1) the *frequency correction channel* (FCCH), (2) the *synchronization channel* (SCH), and (3) the *broadcast control channel* (BCCH). The following are three common types: (1) the *paging channel* (PCH), (2) the *access grant channel* (AGCH), and (3) the *random-access channel* (RACH).

There are three types of dedicated control channels: (1) the *stand-alone dedicated control channel* (SDCCH),

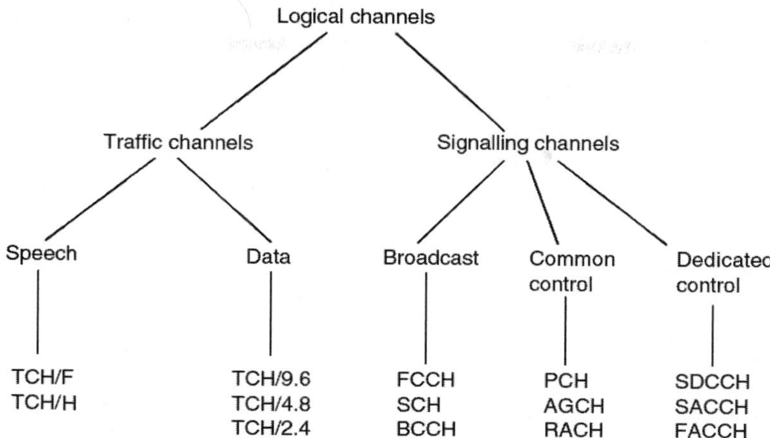

Figure 7: The logical channels in GSM

(2) the *slow associated control channel* (SACCH), and (3) the *fast associated control channel* (FACCH). These channels will be detailed later in this chapter. The logical channels are related to the frame hierarchy.

FUNCTIONS AND MESSAGES

In this section, we discuss different functions defined in the GSM standards and describe the related messages passed between different entities.

Call Management

Among the call management procedures are mobile initialization, location update, authentication, ciphering, mobile station termination, mobile station origination, handover, and call clearing. Mobile initialization procedure includes frequency synchronization, timing synchronization, and overhead information acquisition.

When a mobile terminal is switched on, the following sequence of events takes place. First, the terminal scans the available GSM RF channels and performs operations such as estimating signal strengths using several readings of power levels. Starting with the channel with the highest level, the terminal then searches for the frequency correction burst on the BCCH. When a burst is found, the terminal then synchronizes its local oscillator with the frequency reference of the base station transceiver. Once the frequency synchronization has been achieved, the terminal will search for the synchronization burst for the timing information present on the SCH. If it is not successful, it then moves to the channel with next highest signal level and repeats the process starting from the frequency synchronization procedure until it is successful. Once the time synchronization is achieved, the terminal moves to the BCCH to acquire overhead system information. If the BCCH information does not include the current BCCH number, then the terminal will restart the mobile initialization procedure. If successful in finding the information, the terminal will have acquired (from the BCCH and through the system information message present on the BCCH) information such as country code, network code, location area code, cell identity, adjacent cell list, BCCH location, and minimum received signal strength. Next, the terminal checks to see if the acquired identification codes coincide with those in the SIM card. In a successful event, it will maintain the link and monitor the PCH. Otherwise, it will start a location update procedure. A location update procedure is carried out also in the event of moving into an area different from that currently registered or when there is no activity for a certain amount of time. Location reports are used in the paging procedure as well. The time span between location reports constitutes a system parameter whose value is indicated on the BCCH, varying in accordance with the network loading.

Mobile Station Termination

After the mobile initialization procedure, the terminal locks onto the PCH. It eventually detects a paging request message conveying its TMSI. This causes the terminal to access the RACH to transmit a channel request message. An immediate assignment with the SDCCH number is sent by the network on the AGCH. The terminal moves to SDCCH and then transmits a paging response message indicating that the response is to a paging. Next, an authentication procedure is carried out. The authentication procedure is described in "Authentication" below. If the authentication is successful, a ciphering procedure is accomplished. The base station then sends a setup message. The terminal responds with a call confirmed message followed by an alerting message to indicate that the subscriber is being alerted. At the subscriber's call acceptance, the terminal sends a connect message and removes the alerting tone. The network responds with an assignment command message indicating the traffic channel number to be used for the conversation. The subscriber, still on the SDCCH, responds with an assignment acknowledgment message and moves to the traffic channel that has been assigned. The network confirms the acceptance of the call by the other party by means of a connect acknowledgment message on the FACCH of the assigned TCH. And the conversation proceeds on the TCH.

Mobile Station Origination

The terminal detects a user-originated call. It then accesses the RACH to send a channel request message.

An immediate assignment with the SD-CCH number is sent by the network on the AGCH. The terminal moves to this channel and transmits a paging response message indicating that the message is for call setup. The base station responds with an unnumbered acknowledgment message. As will be described below, an authentication procedure is carried out. If authentication is successful, then a ciphering procedure is performed. The terminal then sends a setup message. The base station responds with a call confirmed message followed by an alerting message in which case the terminal applies the ring-back tone. At the called party's call acceptance, the network sends an assignment command message informing the traffic channel number to be used for the conversation. The subscriber, still on the SDCCH, responds with an assignment acknowledgment message and moves to the traffic channel that has been assigned. The network confirms the acceptance of the call by the other party by means of a connect acknowledgment message on the FACCH of the assigned TCH. And the conversation proceeds on the TCH.

Handover

The handover process in a GSM is termed *mobile-assisted handover* because the mobile terminal plays a major roll in the process. Using the traffic channel, the mobile monitors the signal levels on the channel used by the terminal itself as well as the channels used within a cluster of six cells, including the cell in which the terminal is located. The measurements are then reported to the base station on an SACCH. Concerning the control of the process, handovers may occur within the same BTS, between BTSs controlled by the same BSC, between different BSCs controlled by the same MSC, between different BSCs controlled by different MSCs, or between different BSCs controlled by different MSCs belonging to different PLMNs.

Furthermore, there are two modes of handovers in GSM: synchronous and asynchronous. In the *synchronous* mode, the origin cell and the destination cell are synchronized. By measuring the time difference between their respective time slots, the mobile may compute the timing advance by itself. This is used to adjust its transmissions on the new channel, therefore speeding up the handover process. In the *asynchronous* mode, the origin cell and the destination cell are not synchronized. In this case, the timing advance must be acquired by means of a procedure involving the terminal and the new BTS, as follows. The mobile terminal sends a series of access bursts with a zero timing advance through several handover access messages. The BTS then computes the required timing advance using the messages round-trip time delay. On the average, the handover processing time in the asynchronous mode is twice as long as that of the synchronous mode (200 ms versus 100 ms).

A simple asynchronous handover procedure occurring between BTSs of the same BSC is described. While in conversation on a TCH, the terminal monitors the signal levels of several channels. These measurements are reported to the base station on a periodic basis by means of the measurement report message running on the SACCH. Whenever suitable, the base sends a handover command message on the FACCH, indicating that a handover is to take place. The number of the new TCH is included within the message. The terminal then moves to this new channel and sends a series of handover access messages so that the base may compute the timing advance to be transmitted to the terminal. This is done in the physical information message transmitted to the terminal on the FACCH. The timing adjustment is carried out, and the terminal responds with a handover complete message.

Call Clearing

The call clearing process may be initiated either by the network or by the mobile. In either case, the channel used for the exchange of information is the BCCH. Assuming that the network initiates the clearing, the base sends a disconnect message to the terminal. The terminal responds with a release message. The base replies with a release complete message. If the terminal initiates the clearing, then the same messages flow in the opposite direction.

Mobility and Roaming Location-Based Services

Regional Roaming

Regional roaming refers to the ability to move from one region to another region inside national coverage of the mobile operator. This is only allowed if a mobile operator grants a user this right in the user's subscription. In the first ages of GSM, operators made commercial offers restricted to a region (sometimes to a town). Because of GSM's widespread success and the decrease in cost usage, regional roaming is no longer offered to clients unless in wide geographical areas such as large countries (e.g., the United States, Russia, and India). In this last case, regional roaming is more related to national roaming.

National Roaming

National roaming refers to the ability to move from a mobile operator to another mobile operator in the same country. As an example, consider subscribers of T-Mobile US. They would have national roaming rights if they were allowed to roam inside Cingular's wireless coverage. For commercial and license reasons, this type of roaming is not allowed unless under specific circumstances and under regulator scrutiny. As an example, the first 3G operators (like Hutchinson subsidiaries) had little coverage compared to 2G operators. For fair competition, regulators (e.g., in the United Kingdom and in Italy) granted rights for these operators to make national roaming agreements with one of the 2G operators. These agreements were limited in space to geographical areas and in time.

International Roaming

International roaming refers to the ability to move onto other foreign mobile operators from a national subscription. By now, as stated before, *roaming* now commonly refers to international roaming.

Security

The known problems in GSM's analog counterparts included phone fraud by cloning, making calls at an owner's expense, and intercepting phone calls. The GSM system includes strong authentication between MS and MSC. Furthermore, there is strong data encryption for transmission through wireless channel from MS and BTS. The GSM specifications were developed in secrecy and were distributed on a need-to-know basis to the manufacturers and network operators. The security algorithms for GSM were developed by the *Security Algorithm Group of Experts* (SAGE). Although the specifications were supposed to be closed to the public, information on the algorithms leaked in the mid-1990. SAGE's security mechanisms for GSM are implemented in three different elements—namely, the SIM, ME, and the network. The SIM contains the IMSI, K_i, algorithm A8 (for cipher key generation), algorithm A3 (for authentication), and the PIN. The ME contains the ciphering algorithm A5. The three algorithms A3, A5, and A8 are present in the network. The AuC contains a database of identification and authentication information for subscribers. It includes the IMSI and K_i of each subscriber as well as the algorithms A3 and A8.

The elements of GSM security are subscriber identity authentication, user and signaling data confidentiality, and subscriber identity confidentiality.

Authentication

The IMSI and the authentication key, K_i constitute the a subscriber's identity credentials. These bits of information are never transmitted over the radio channels. Instead the TMSI is used by the MS to identify itself to the network. The authentication is performed with a challenge–response mechanism that avoids sending the key K_i over the air.

The authentication procedure starts when the network sends an authentication request message to the terminal; the message conveys a 128-bit RAND. The terminal uses the RAND, the secret key K_i stored at SIM, and the encryption algorithm (referred to as *A3*) to compute a 32-bit number, which is referred to as a *signed response* (SRES). The 64-bit ciphering key, K_c also is computed using another encryption algorithm, referred to as *A8*. The K_c parameter is later used in the ciphering procedure. After these computations, the terminal responds with an authentication response message, which contains the SRES. The network uses the same parameters and the same algorithm to compute another SRES. The terminal SRES and the network SRES are then compared with each other. If a match occurs, the network then accepts the user as an authorized subscriber. Otherwise, the authentication is rejected.

The TMSI update process is as follows. The network knows the association between the TMSI and IMSI. The MS identifies itself to the network by sending the TMSI. Following the authentication process, the new TMSI generated by the network is sent to the MS encrypted with the cipher key K_c. The MS replaces the old TMSI with the new one.

Ciphering

Ciphering (or *encryption*) is usually required for user transactions over the RF link after authentication has been successful. The network transmits a ciphering mode message to the terminal that indicates whether encryption is to be applied. If ciphering is to be performed, the secret key K_c (64 bits), which was generated previously in the authentication procedure, the frame number (22 bits), and an encryption algorithm (referred to as *A5*) are used to compute a 114-bit encryption mask. This mask is modulo-2 added to the $2 \times 57 = 114$ bits of the data fields in the bursts. Deciphering is obtained at the base station by performing the same procedure. The terminal answers with a ciphering mode acknowledgment message. Note that the ciphering to be used is continuously changing (on a frame-by-frame basis) because it depends on the current frame number. Note that the key K_c is temporary.

Attacks on GSM Security

Although the security algorithms were originally kept secret, they later became public knowledge. The security research community now widely accepts that keeping the algorithms secret is not the way to achieve security. Communication between BS and BSC is often established with microwave links, which are not encrypted in general. This is one of the vulnerabilities in GSM networks. Some operators implement lower-layer bulk encryption for protection against this vulnerability. Another known vulnerability exists in the COMP128 algorithm that combines A3 and A8 into a single algorithm and generates both SRES and the key K_c on one run. COMP128 takes the 128-bit RAND and the 128-bit K_i as input and generates a 128-bit output of which the first thirty-two bits are SRES and the last fifty-four bits are the session key, K_c. The session key is appended by zeros to produce a 64-bit key. Nevertheless, the effective key length is fifty-four bits. In 1998, the Smart Card Developer Association and the Internet Security, Applications, Authentication and Cryptography security research group showed that it is possible to retrieve the secret key K_i with 160,000 chosen RAND-SRES pairs. With faster SIM, this could be achieved in approximately 2.5 hours. It is also possible to use a false BS to send the RAND over the air interface.

Another possible attack uses the side channels such as those used in the computation of power consumption and timing operations. With physical access to the SIM card, it is possible to extract secret key K_i by a partition attack approach developed by IBM researchers.

Messages

The signaling channels, with the exception of FCCH, RACH, and SCH, use the *link access protocol on the Dm channel* (LAPDm) format to transmit information. The LAPDm protocol in the mobile network is equivalent to the LAPD protocol in the fixed network. The messages are transmitted in segments of 184 bits. In general, the messages fit into a single segment and the 184 bits of raw information are processed to yield 456 bits. These 456 bits are then transmitted through four time slots. Apart from the length indicator field, which appears in every message, the presence of the other fields will depend on the message itself. For example, there may be messages with zero length; in this case, with the exception of the eight-bit length indicator field, all of the other fields (176 bits) are filled with 1's.

Six of the bits in the length indicator field denote the number of octets in the variable length information field. Another bit in the length indicator field determines whether the current message segment is the final segment in the corresponding message. The address field contains the following fields: One bit indicates whether the message is a command or a response; three bits indicate the current version of the GSM protocol; one bit is an extension of the address (set to 0 in the initial version of GSM); and three bits indicate network management messages or SMS messages. The control field contains three bits to indicate the sequence number of the current message and another three bits to indicate the sequence number of the last message received by the entity that is sending the current message. In case the complete message encompasses fewer than 184 bits, the fill field is stuffed with 1's.

Several network management messages are specified in GSM. According to their specific functions, the messages can be of three types: *supervisory* (S), *unnumbered* (U), or *information* (I). The S and U messages precede or follow the I messages to control the flow of messages between terminals and base stations. The I messages perform the main tasks concerning network management. An S message may request (re)transmission or may suspend transmission of I messages. An U message may initiate or terminate a transfer of I messages, or it may confirm a command. The S and U messages are layer 2 messages and, more specifically, *data-link control* (DLC) messages. The I messages are layer 3 messages. More specifically, they carry out the network management operations such as *radio resources management* (RRM), *mobility management* (MM), and *call management* (CM). The RRM messages involve interactions between mobile station, base station, and mobile switching center. The MM and CM messages use the base station as a relay node between mobile stations and the MSC, where they are effectively treated.

The next subsections summarize the main GSM messages.

Data-Link Control Messages

The main DLC messages and their respective purposes are listed below.

- Set asynchronous balanced mode: This is a U command message that initiates a transfer of I messages.
- Disconnect: This U command message terminates a transfer of I messages.
- Unnumbered acknowledgment: This U response message confirms a command.
- Receive ready: This S command or S response message requests transmission of an I message.
- Receive not ready: This S command or S response message requests retransmission of an I message.
- Reject: This S command or S response message suspends transmission of I messages.

Radio Resources Management Messages

The main RRM messages and their respective purposes are listed below.

- Sync channel information: This is a downlink message running on the SCH. It conveys the base station identifier and the frame number, the latter allowing the terminal to achieve time synchronization.
- System information: This downlink message running on the BCCH contains the location area identifier, the number of the physical channel carrying signaling information, the parameters of the random access protocols, and the radio frequency carriers active in the neighboring cells.
- System information: This downlink message running on the SACCH provides local system information to those active terminals that are moving away from the cell where the call was originated.
- Channel request: This uplink message running on the RACH is used to respond to a page, to set up a call, to update the location, to attach the IMSI, and to detach the IMSI.
- Paging request: This downlink message running on the PCH sets up a call to a terminal.
- Immediate assignment. This downlink message running on the AGCH assigns an SDCCH to a terminal at the setup procedure as a result of a channel request message.
- Immediate assignment extended: This downlink message running on the AGCH assigns two terminals to two different physical channels.
- Immediate assignment reject: This downlink message running on the AFCH is utilized as a response to channel request messages from as many as five terminals when the system is not able to provide these terminals with dedicated channels.
- Assignment command: This downlink message running on the SDCCH is used at the end of the setup call process to move the terminal to a TCH.
- Additional assignment: This downlink message running on the FACCH assigns another TCH to a terminal already operating on a TCH.
- Paging response: This uplink message running on the SDCCH is used to respond to a page with the aim of identifying the terminal and causing initiation of the authentication procedure.
- Measurement report: This uplink message running on the SACCH indicates the signal level of the terminal and the signal quality of the active physical channel and of the channels of the surrounding cells for intracell or intercell handover purposes.
- Handover command: This downlink message running on the FACCH is used to move a call from one physical channel to another physical channel. It is also used by the terminal to adjust its timing advance.
- Handover access: This uplink message running on the TCH provides the base station with the necessary information so that the base can instruct the terminal on the timing adjustment needed in a handover process.
- Physical information: This downlink message running on the FACCH transmits the timing adjustment required by the terminal in a handover process.
- Handover complete: This uplink message running on the FACCH is utilized after the terminal has adjusted its

transmission time within the newly assigned physical channel.

- Ciphering mode: This downlink message running on the FACCH indicates whether user information is to be encrypted.
- Channel release: This downlink message running on the FACCH informs the terminal that a given channel is to be released.
- Frequency redefinition: This downlink message running on both the SACCH and the FACCH informs the terminal about the new hopping pattern to be used.
- Classmark change: This uplink message running on both the SACCH and the FACCH informs the network about the terminal's new class of transmission power. This message occurs, for example, when a phone is plugged in or removed from an external apparatus with high power.
- Channel mode modify: This downlink message running on the FACCH commands the terminal to change from one channel mode (speech or data) to another. The channel mode defines the specific source coder (for speech) or the data speed (for data).
- RR status: This two-way message running on both the FACCH and the SACCH reports the error conditions of the *radio resource* (RR).

Call Management Messages

The main CM messages and their respective purposes are listed below.

- Setup: This two-way message running on the SDCCH is used to initiate a call.
- Emergency setup: This uplink message running on the SDCCH is used to initiate a call.
- Call proceeding: This downlink message running on the SDCCH is used as a response to a setup message.
- Progress: This downlink message running on the SDCCH informs the calling party, through an audible tone, that the call is being transferred to a different network (e.g., from a public to a private one).
- Call confirmed: This uplink message running on the SDCCH is used as a response to a setup message.
- Alerting: This two-way message running on the SDCCH indicates to the calling party that the called party is being alerted.
- Connect: This two-way message running on the SDCCH indicates that the call is being accepted.
- Start DTMF. This uplink message running on the FACCH is used to indicate that a button of the phone keypad has been pressed. This causes the network to send a dual-tone multiple frequency to the terminal.
- Stop DTMF: This uplink message running on the FACCH indicates that a button of the phone keypad has been released. This causes the network to turn off a dual-tone multiple frequency.
- Modify: This two-way message running on the FACCH indicates that the nature of the transmission is being modified (e.g., from speech to facsimile).
- User information: This two-way message running on the FACCH is used, for example, to carry user-to-user information as part of GSM supplementary services.
- Disconnect, release, release complete: This two-way message running on the FACCH is used to end a call. For example, if the terminal is concluding a call, it sends a disconnect message to the network, which responds with a release message; this causes the terminal to send a release complete message to the network. The same sequence of messages flow in the opposite direction if the other party terminates the call.
- Disconnect: This two-way message running on the FACCH indicates that a call is terminating.
- Release: This two-way message running on the FACCH is used as a response to a disconnect message.
- Release complete: This two-way message running on the FACCH is used as a response to a release message.
- Status: This two-way message running on the FACCH is used as a response to a status enquiry message to describe error conditions.
- Status enquiry: This two-way message running on the FACCH causes the network element (either the terminal or the base) to respond with a status message.
- Congestion control: This two-way message running on the FACCH initiates a flow control procedure, in which case the flow of call management messages is retarded.

The CM messages occur at different stages of a call. At the beginning of a call, the following messages run on the SDCCH: setup, emergency setup, call proceeding, progress, call confirm, alerting, and connect.

During a call, the following messages run on the FACCH of the assigned channel: start DTMF, stop DTMF, modify, and user information.

At the end of a call, the following messages run on the FACCH of the assigned channel: disconnect, release, and release complete.

During abnormal conditions, the following messages run on the FACCH of the assigned channel: status, status enquiry, and congestion control.

Mobility Management Messages

The MM messages travel on the SDCCH. The MM messages and their respective purposes are listed below.

- Authentication request: This downlink message sends a 128-bit RAND to the terminal, which, by means of an encryption algorithm, computes a 32-bit number to be sent to and checked at the base.
- Authentication response: This uplink message is used as a response to an authentication request message, conveying the 32-bit number generated from the encryption algorithm.
- Authentication reject: This downlink message aborts the communication between the terminal and the network as a result of an unsuccessful authentication.
- Identity request: This downlink message is used to request any of the three identifiers: the IMSI (stored on the

SIM), the IMEI (stored in the terminal), and the TMSI (assigned by the network to a visiting terminal).

- Identity response: This uplink message is used as a response to the identity request message.
- TMSI reallocation command: This downlink message assigns a new TMSI to the terminal.
- Location updating request: This uplink message is used by the terminal to register its location.
- Location updating accept: This downlink message is used to accept a location registration.
- Location updating reject: This downlink message is used to reject a location registration. A location updating may be rejected in any of the following events: unknown subscriber, unknown location area, roaming not allowed, or system failure.
- IMSI detach indication: This uplink message cancels the terminal registration when the terminal is switched off.
- CM service request: This uplink message initiates an MM operation. As a consequence, one or more MM messages will follow.
- CM reestablishment request: This uplink message reinitiates an MM operation that has been interrupted.
- MM status: This two-way message reports error conditions.

RESOURCES

This section provides information on various resources related to GSM. These include standards organizations and forums. The inception of GSM in the early 1980s started with the Conference of European Posts and Telegraphs, which later evolved into the European Telecommunications Standards Institute. Currently, ETSI supports GSM and UMTS standardization activities. The International Telecommunications Union's Telecommunication (ITU-T) and its Standardization Sector is another organization that is coordinating cellular standardization activities. The ITU's Development Sector has contributed to promoting GSM. The Global Mobile Suppliers Association is another contributor to the development of GSM standards. The GSM Association (GSMA), is a consortium of second- and third-generation mobile operators, manufacturers, and suppliers. GSMA promotes triband GSM networks and equipment. The GSM Roaming Forum is an organization that promotes platforms and mobile equipment for seamless roaming across national boundaries and frequency bands. The GSM Alliance, the Mobile Data Association, and the Mobile Data Initiative Next-Generation Consortium are among other players.

CONCLUSION

GSM has emerged as a digital solution to the incompatible analog air interfaces of the differing cellular networks operating in Europe. Among the set of ambitious targets to be pursued, full roaming was indeed an extremely important one. In addition, a large number of open interfaces have been specified within the GSM architecture. Open interfaces favor market competition with operators able to choose equipment from different vendors. GSM was the first system to stimulate the incorporation of the personal communication services philosophy into a cellular network. These and other innovative features rendered GSM networks, either in the original GSM conception or as an evolution of it, a highly successful project with worldwide acceptance. GSM systems are found operating in frequency bands around 900 MHz (GSM 900), 1.8 GHz (GSM 1800), and 1.9 GHz (GSM 1900). A new revision of the GSM specifications defines an EGSM that extends the original GSM 900 operation band and stipulates lower power terminals and smaller serving areas.

GLOSSARY

Access Grant Channel (AGCH): A downlink channel (base to mobile) used by a base station to tell the mobile station which dedicated control channel to use.

Authentication Center (AuC): A function to authenticate each subscriber identification module.

Base Station Controller (BSC): The functional entity that is responsible for radio resource allocation to a mobile station, frequency administration, and handover between base transceiver station.

Base Station Subsystem (BSS): A term given to a base station controller and the base transceiver station associated with it.

Base Transceiver Station (BTS): The equipment that facilitates the wireless communication between user equipments and the network.

Bearer Service (BS): Typically, data transmission instead of voice. Fax and short message services are examples.

Broadcast Control Channel (BCCH): The channel by which the mobile station is informed of the specific system parameters needed to identify the network or gain access.

Burst: The signal transmitted during a GSM time slot.

Conference of European Posts and Telegraphs (CEPT): The main European body for telecommunications standardization.

Digital Cellular System 1800 (DCS 1800): The U.K. Department of Trade and Industry defined *personal communications network* to consist of GSM operating in the 1.8-GHz band.

Discontinuous Transmission (DTx): A method that takes advantage of the silences in voice to increase the utilization of the channels.

Equipment Identity Register (EIR): Database employed within mobile networks to hold records of mobiles.

European Telecommunications Standards Institute (ETSI): An independent, not-for-profit, standardization organization of the telecommunications industry in Europe.

Frequency Correction Channel (FCCH): The logical channel in GSM systems used to transmit a frequency correction data burst of all zeros.

Frequency Division Duplexing (FDD): Radio technology using a paired spectrum for two-way communication.

Frequency Hopping (FH): Method of transmitting radio signals by rapidly switching a carrier among many frequency channels.

Home Location Register (HLR): Central database that contains details of each mobile.

International Mobile Equipment Identifier (IMEI): A unique fifteen-digit number that serves as the serial number of the GSM handset.

International Mobile Subscriber Identity (IMSI): Unique number associated with all GSM and universal mobile telecommunications system (UMTS) network mobile phone users.

Link Access Protocol for the ISDN D-channel (LAPD): Protocol providing error-free transmission between the BSC and MSC.

Mobile-Assisted Handover: Handoff technique involving feedback from the mobile station as part of the handoff process.

Mobile Station (MS): All user equipment and software needed for communication with a wireless telephone network.

Mobile Station Subsystem (MSS): Section of a traditional cellular telephone network responsible for handling traffic and signaling between a mobile phone and the network switching subsystem.

Mobile Subscriber ISDN (MSISDN): Telephone number of a mobile subscriber.

Mobile Switching Center (MSC): An ISDN switch coordinating and setting up calls to and from mobile stations.

Network and Switching Subsystem (NSS): Component of a GSM system that manages the communications between mobile phones and the public switched telephone network.

Operation and Support Subsystem (OSS): Functional entity from which the network operator monitors and controls the system.

Paging Channel (PCH): Base to mobile channel used to alert a mobile to a call originating from the network.

Personal Communication System 1900 (PCS 1900): Digital network working on a frequency of 1900 MHz; used in the United States and Canada.

Personal Identification Number (PIN): Four-digit secret number built into the subscriber identity module that should be entered to enable mobile use.

PIN Unblocking Key (PUK): Eight-digit personal unblocking key required when a wrong personal identification number is entered three times.

Random-Access Channel (RACH): Channel used by mobiles to gain access to the system when first attaching to it.

Security Algorithm Group of Experts (SAGE): With ETSI approval, carries out work for other organizations (e.g., for GSM by request of the GSM MOU).

Short Message Service (SMS): Often called *text messaging*; a means of sending short messages to and from mobile phones.

Slow Associated Control Channel (SACCH): Signaling channel that provides a relatively slow signaling connection.

Stand-Alone Dedicated Control Channel (SDCCH): This channel is used in the GSM system to provide a reliable connection for signaling and SMS.

Subscriber Identity Module (SIM): Smart card that provides mobile equipment with an identity.

Supplementary Services (SS): Services that complement and support telephony and data services such as call forwarding, call holding, and call waiting.

Synchronization Channel (SCH): Supplies the mobile station with the training sequence needed for the demodulation of information from the base station.

Teleservices (TS): Includes videotex, teletex, and advanced message handling.

Temporary Mobile Subscriber Identity (TMSI): Issued by the network and may be changed periodically (i.e., during handoffs) for additional security.

Terminal Adapter (TA): Part of the mobile station handling authentication requests from the GSM network.

Terminal Equipment (TE): Equipment in mobile that handles various functions such as control signaling and signal processing.

Time Division Duplexing (TDD): Radio technology for use in unpaired spectrum by applying time division multiplexing to separate outward and return signals.

Time Division Multiple Access (TDMA): Technique for multiplexing multiple users onto a single channel on a single carrier by splitting the carrier into time slots and allocating these on an as-needed basis.

Traffic Channel (TCH): Channels reserved for user data.

Visitor Location Register (VLR): Contains relevant data of all mobiles currently located in a serving mobile switching center.

Voice Activity Detector (VAD): Procedure to determine the presence or absence of speech.

CROSS REFERENCES

See *Cellular Communications Channels*; *Time Division Multiple Access (TDMA)*; *Wireless Channels*.

REFERENCES

GSM World. Undated. http://www.gsmworld.com/index.shtml,(accessed September 6, 2007).

Heine, G. 1998. *GSM networks: Protocols, terminology, and implementation*. Norwood, MA: Artech House Publishers.

Rappaport, T. S. 1996. Wireless communications: Principles and practice. Upper Saddle River, NJ: Prentice Hall.

General Packet Radio Service

Allen H. Levesque, *Worcester Polytechnic Institute*

INTRODUCTION

The GSM cellular system, described in the chapter entitled "Global System for Mobile Communications," was designed to support both digital voice traffic and user data traffic to and from mobile subscribers (Mouly and Pautet 1992; Haug 1994; GSM World n.d.). However, the data services provided by the initial GSM system are *circuit-switched services* in which, when a user invokes a data service, a data traffic channel is assigned and held in place until the call is terminated. This is analogous to using a dialup modem in the public telephone network. The user data rates for GSM circuit-switched data were limited to a maximum of 19.6 kbits/s (Heine 1999). The GSM system does include provisions for wireless access to public switched packet data networks (PSPDNs); however, this form of access simply carries packet-formatted data traffic over a circuit-switched traffic channel for the full duration of a call connection. In cases of discontinuous traffic, such as Internet and Web access, circuit-switched access can result in very inefficient use of wireless spectrum. Thus, the use of true *packet-switched data service* on the GSM radio channels can provide better utilization of wireless network capacity.

Another issue for the evolution of GSM data services was the customer demand for substantially higher data rates than could be supported in the early GSM networks. This led to the specification in Phase 2+ of the GSM development of *high-speed circuit-switched data* (HSCSD), in which a mobile station can access up to four time slots in each *time-division multiple access* (TDMA) frame, thereby achieving uplink data rates up to 57.6 kbits/sec (ETSI 1997a). Another important Phase 2+ element in the evolution of data services in GSM is general packet radio service (GPRS), which is the subject of this chapter. The GSM designation Phase 2+ denotes the fact that these services are built upon the Phase 2 GSM architecture while providing some of the capabilities envisioned for a subsequent third generation (3G) of wireless systems. A section near the end of this chapter provides further discussion of 3G objectives.

Stated briefly, GPRS overlays true packet-switched data service onto a GSM network in a way that maintains strict separation between radio subsystem and the network system, with the advantage that no modifications to *mobile switching centers* (MSCs) are required (Steele, Lee, and Gould 2001). GPRS provisioning does require some enhancements and modifications to GSM infrastructure and mobile stations (MSs). In GPRS, the allocation of the eight time slots on one radio frequency (RF) channel is flexible, and various combinations of uplink and downlink time slots can be assigned depending upon the capabilities of the MS, the customer's service subscription, and the number of channels dedicated by the network operator to packet data service. The capacity of an underlying GSM service network can be shared dynamically between circuit-switched and packet data services, according to observed traffic demands. The theoretical upper limit on GPRS data rate is 171.2 kb/s, achieved by assigning all eight time slots in a GSM radio channel to a single user (Halonen, Romero, and Melero 2003). However, as a practical matter, GPRS mobile terminals operate at rates in the range of 30 to 80 kilobits/sec, using at most four time slots in one direction. As a related point, it is important to note that not all of the capabilities defined in the GPRS specifications have been implemented by equipment manufacturers and network operators.

Before discussing the details of GPRS, it is useful to review the differences between circuit-switched and packet-switched data services.

Circuit-Switched versus Packet-Switched Data Service

The key characteristic of GPRS is that it provides packet-switched data service rather than circuit-switched data service, and this technique makes much more efficient use of the available capacity of the cellular network. This efficiency improvement comes from the fact that most data transfers are interactive and occur in a bursty fashion. Typical data transfers occur in short bundles, interspersed with longer intervals when there is little or no activity. The original GSM specification was developed to support primarily voice services, in which an end-to-end circuit connection is set up through the network and stays in place for the full duration of the call session. This is known as a circuit-switched service, and the services of the original GSM system provided exactly the same form of connection for data and fax transmissions, much like support of dialup modems and fax machines in the public switched telephone network (PSTN). Given the bursty nature of typical data transfers, the circuit-switched mode of service does not make the most efficient use of transmission capacity in the network.

To provide more efficient use of transmission resources, the overall capacity can be shared among multiple users. To achieve this the data stream to be transmitted is segmented into packets, and tags are inserted into the packets to provide destination addressing and other information. When one user's packet has been transmitted, the channel is made available for another user's packets. Packets from multiple sources can then be interspersed and transmitted over the channel. As it is unlikely that the data bursts for different users will occur all at the same time, by sharing the overall resource in this manner, the channel—or combined channels—can be used far more efficiently. This approach is known as *packet switching* (Tanenbaum 2003), and it is at the core of the GPRS design. The chapters entitled "Circuit Switching" and "Packet Switching" in this handbook deal with these switching technologies in detail.

Readers familiar with Internet technology (see the chapter entitled "Internet Fundamentals") know that traffic is relayed across the Internet by way of *routers*, which function as packet-switching nodes. Though the user may typically access the Internet by way of a circuit-switched PSTN connection to an Internet service provider (ISP), the user's message stream is then handled as data and transported across the network in segments called Internet protocol (IP) *datagrams*—the datagrams being directed individually by the network routers. In fact, given the widespread use of the Internet, the reader will appreciate that data traffic carried over public networks today is predominantly packet oriented. Our later discussion of the GPRS network architecture will explain how GPRS separates the mobile user's data traffic from voice traffic, transporting the data using packet switching and the digital voice traffic using circuit switching in the underlying GSM network.

Evolution of Cellular Data Services

Data support over first-generation (1G) wireless networks began with the use of modems and facsimile terminals over advanced mobile phone service (AMPS) circuit-switched analog cellular telephone channels (DeRose 1999). In this form of data communication, the mobile user simply accessed a cellular channel just as he would in making an ordinary voice call over the cellular network. The customer attached a cellular modem—much like a dialup wireline modem, but designed to operate on the AMPS radio interface—to a data terminal, a facsimile device, or a laptop computer. In this form of data communication, the cellular network was not actually providing a data service but simply a voice link over which the data modem or fax terminal could interoperate with a corresponding data modem or fax terminal in the office or service center (Pahlavan and Levesque 1995). Typical users of this mode of data communication included service technicians, real estate agents, traveling salespeople, and public safety personnel.

In another early form of mobile data service, the mobile subscriber used a portable modem or fax terminal as already described but accessed a modem installed by the cellular service provider as part of a *modem pool*, which was connected to the MSC. The user dialed into the modem pool using dedicated telephone numbers. The modem pool sometimes provided the customer with a choice of several standard modem types (Muller 1995). The call connection from the modem pool to the office or service center might be supported by any of a number of public packet data networks (PDNs), such as X.25 networks. Here, the cellular operator provided a special service in the form of modem pool access, and this service typically carried a higher tariff than did standard cellular voice service, due to the operator's added investment in the modem pools. In this form of service, however, the user in the office or service center did not require a modem but instead had a direct digital data connection to a desktop or host computer.

Each of the early types of wireless data communication just described was in effect an appliqué onto an underlying analog cellular telephone service and, therefore, suffered limitations imposed by the characteristics of the underlying voice-circuit connection. That is, the cellular segment of the call connection was a circuit-mode service, which might have been cost effective if the user needed to send long file transfers or fax transmissions, but relatively costly if only short messages were to be transferred. This is because the subscriber was being charged for a connection that remained in place throughout the duration of the communication session, even when only intermittent short message exchanges were needed.

The need for systems capable of providing more cost-effective communication of relatively short message exchanges led to the development of wireless packet-switched systems, including the first cellular packet data system: *cellular digital packet data* (CDPD). CDPD, developed by IBM in collaboration with the major cellular network carriers, allowed any cellular carrier owning a license for AMPS service to implement a cellular data service without need for further licensing (Muller 1995; Pahlavan and Levesque 1995). The basic concept of the CDPD system was to provide packet data service on a noninterfering basis along with the existing analog cellular voice service using the same 30 kHz radio channels. This was accomplished by devoting one or a few AMPS channels in each cell site to the transmission of packet-formatted data at data rates up to 19.2 kbits/sec.

The provision of CDPD service in an existing AMPS service network did not require modification of any of the AMPS network elements but did require the addition of *mobile data base stations* (MDBSs) and packet-switching equipment. The MDBS implements the functions needed to support communication with the mobile user terminals, including modulation and demodulation of traffic data bits and support of the multiple-access protocol, over the RF channels reserved for CDPD traffic. The MDBSs are physically located at the service provider's cell sites, and each MDBS in effect relays mobile user data traffic between the mobile device and a key CDPD network element called a *mobile data intermediate system* (MD-IS). The MD-IS is responsible for most of the mobility management functions in the CDPD service network, tracking the current access point (an MDBS) for each mobile device active within the network. On its network side, the MD-IS serves as a routing node, communicating with outside packet data networks using standard packet-networking protocols. In a CDPD service network, the MD-IS is physically located at the MSC, which provides connections for analog voice traffic to and from the PSTN. Thus, in CDPD, we see data traffic being separated from voice traffic at the MSC level of the network architecture. Later, we will see a somewhat different configuration in the GPRS network architecture.

For a number of reasons, CDPD has not been successful in the marketplace and has been supplanted by data services designed into the second-generation (2G) cellular systems, as well as by GPRS, the subject of this chapter.

Data Services in GSM Networks

The first phase of the GSM specification, adopted in 1987, provided basic data transfer capabilities for the support of circuit-oriented data services, with maximum data rate initially limited to 9.6 kbits/s on one time slot in an eight-slot radio channel. During the development of the GSM specifications and the early deployment of GSM services, the customer demand for mobile access to the Internet had not been envisioned, and thus work was started on more advanced forms of data service. GSM Phase 2+, in Release '96, specified HSCSD, which significantly increased achievable data rates in the GSM system (ETSI 1997a). The maximum radio interface bit rate of an HSCSD service with 14.4 kbits/s channel coding is 115.2 kbits/sec, that is, up to eight times the bit rate of the single-slot full-rate traffic channel. In practice, the maximum data rate is limited to 64 kbits/sec owing to limitations in the GSM network (Hakaste, Nikula, and Hamiti 2003). Further evolution of cellular data services includes *enhanced data for global evolution* (EDGE), which builds upon the GPRS architecture, and other improved data services envisioned for the universal mobile telecommunications system (UMTS; 3rd-Generation Partnership Project [3GPP] n.d.). More is said about the future evolution near the end of the chapter.

From its inception, the GSM specification included short message service (SMS) in addition to the data transport services summarized earlier. SMS is a bidirectional service for transferring short (up to 160 bytes) alphanumeric messages with a store-and-forward protocol. Although SMS was conceived initially as supporting incoming-message alerts and perhaps some telemetry applications, users and service providers soon recognized the potential usefulness of SMS for text messaging, which has become very popular. In addition to point-to-point messaging, SMS also provides a cell-broadcast mode for distributing messages such as traffic reports and news updates. SMS messages can be stored in the subscriber identity module (SIM) card of a GSM mobile phone for later retrieval. The great popularity of SMS service led (in 2.5G) to the specification of GPRS in GSM and to packet data service in the CDMA cellular system as well (Brasche and Walke 1997; Cai and Goodman 1997; Bates 2002).

Mobile messaging has now evolved beyond SMS text messaging with the introduction of multimedia messaging service (MMS), which allows delivery of personalized multimedia content such as images, audio, text, and video, as well as combinations of these.

Soon after the first GSM networks became operational in the early 1990s and customers gained experience with the GSM data services, it became evident that the circuit-switched bearer services were not particularly well suited for certain types of applications in which data traffic was discontinuous. The circuit-switched data services, although satisfactory for long file transfers, were not cost effective for the customer using the service for connections to the Internet or corporate networks, applications of growing importance in the business world. Similarly, from the service provider's perspective, the use of circuit-switched connections for carrying packet-formatted traffic did not make efficient use of cellular network capacity. At the same time, customer demand for higher-rate data grew steadily as new software applications for mobile users entered the marketplace. The development of GPRS, begun in 1994 as part of the GSM Phase 2+ specification, was an important step toward satisfying the evolving needs of mobile customers and cellular service providers as well. The primary GPRS specifications were approved by 1997.

The GPRS system brings packet-switched data services to the existing GSM system, providing the customer many advantages not afforded by the earlier GSM circuit-switched data services. In the GPRS system, mobile users can access public data networks directly using their standard protocol addresses, such as IP or X.25. The GPRS mobile station can use between one and eight traffic channels over the radio link. Depending on the MS capabilities, those channels are dynamically allocated to the MS when there are packets to be sent or received. In the GPRS network, uplink and downlink channels are reserved separately, making it possible to have MSs with various uplink and downlink capabilities. The resource allocation in the GPRS network is dynamic and dependent on demand and resource availability. Packets can also be sent in idle periods between speech calls, and the system supports SMS and MMS services. The theoretical maximum throughput in the GPRS system is 160 kbits/sec per MS using all eight channels without error correction coding redundancy (Hakaste et al. 2003).

GPRS facilitates new applications that have not been available in legacy GSM networks due to the speed limitations of circuit-switch data services and the message-length limitation of SMS. GPRS now fully enables users to access Internet applications that they are accustomed to using on their desktop computers, but in mobile environments. For personal applications, GPRS is being used to download mobile ringtones, real-time news and weather reports, stock prices, games, and movie trailers, and to make ticket purchases and restaurant reservations.

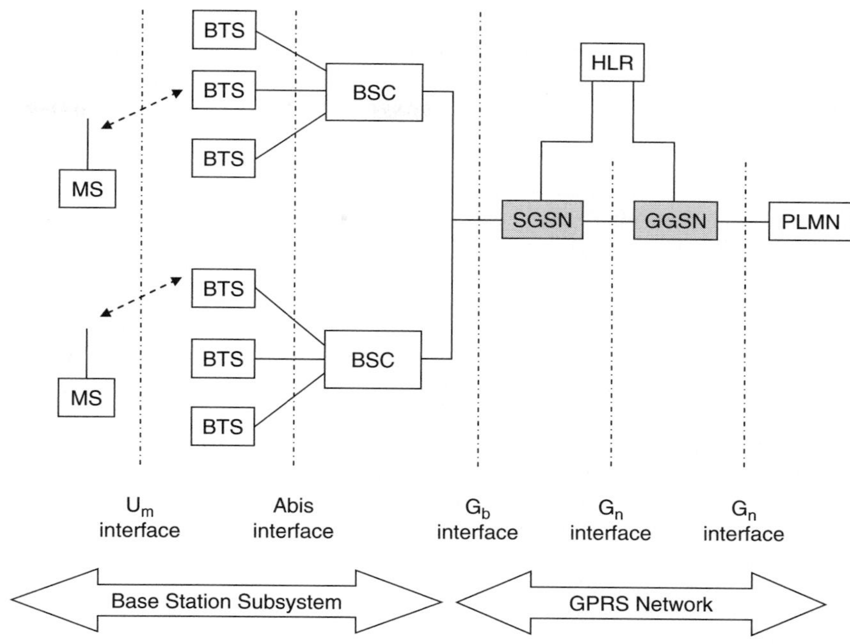

Figure 1: GPRS network architecture

Business applications include Web browsing, e-mail, file transfer, collaborative document preparation, job dispatch, and tech support. Industry observers envision increasing use of wireless data service for transfer of moving images, which can support a host of new applications such as emergency medical service, remote vehicle positioning, stolen-vehicle tracking, and various home automation and security applications. GPRS provides an efficient communication medium for all such applications.

GPRS ARCHITECTURE AND NETWORK ELEMENTS

Some of the GPRS network elements are the same as GSM elements, but GPRS adds certain elements to the underlying GSM architecture. In addition, some software changes must be made in certain GSM network elements in order to support GPRS services. Figure 1 provides a simplified diagram of the GPRS network architecture, with underlying GSM network elements shown unshaded and GPRS-required changes more heavily shaded.

The network elements that are part of the underlying GSM network are as follows:

- MS: mobile station
- BTS: base transceiver station
- BSC: base station controller
- HLR: home location register
- PLMN: public land mobile network

The network elements that must be added or modified in order to enable GPRS service in the GSM network are as follows:

- GPRS-capable mobile station (MS)
- Software upgrade in the BTS
- Software upgrade in the HLR
- SGSN: serving GPRS support node
- GGSN: gateway GPRS support node

The main interfaces for GPRS data transmission, shown in the figure, are:

- Um: air interface or radio interface
- Gb: interface between the BSC and SGSN
- Gn: interface between all SGSNs and also to the GGSN
- Gi: interface between the GSSN and a PLMN

The figure also shows two signaling interfaces toward the GPRS-enhanced HLR from the SGSN and GGSN, respectively.

In the GPRS architecture, the packet-mode traffic is separated from the GSM circuit-mode traffic at the BSC using a packet control unit (PCU), not shown in the figure, which is the principal modification to the BTS for support of GPRS traffic.

As is usually done when describing the legacy GSM system architecture, it is useful to distinguish three broad categories of elements in a GPRS-equipped system: (1) mobile stations, the wireless terminals that customers use; (2) the base station subsystem, which controls the radio links; and (3) the network subsystem, which handles the switching of calls between mobile subscribers and fixed networks, as well as calls between mobile subscribers in the same cellular service network or in different cellular networks. The MSs supporting GPRS service have, of course, considerably increased functionality relative to GMS mobiles, and several classes of GPRS mobile device have been defined, each with different capabilities for supporting data services.

The BSS comprises the base transceiver station, which supports the radio interface, and the base station controller, which controls the assignment of each individual call connection to an appropriate BTS according to the current location of the mobile subscriber. In any GSM network, each BSC connects to a number of BTSs. In the GPRS upgrade of a GSM network, some software changes must be made to the BTS and the BSC, the changes being concerned mainly with the use of the radio interface for packet-formatted data rather than circuit-oriented data. In addition, some new hardware must be added to the BSC for control of packet data traffic.

Integration of GPRS into the standard GSM architecture also requires the addition of two new network elements shown in the figure: *support nodes*, called the *serving GPRS support node* and the *gateway GPRS support node* (GGSN). An SGSN is connected to the BSS and transfers data packets to and from the MSs within its service area. It performs packet routing and transfer, attachment and detachment of MSs, authentication functions, and logical link management. Associated with each SGSN is a location register, the SLR, not shown in the figure, which stores location information and user profiles for all users registered with that SGSN. The SGSN in turn connects to the GGSN, which provides an interface between an external packet data network, such as the Internet, and the GSM network supporting GPRS service. The GGSN stores information needed to route incoming data packets to the SGSN that is serving a particular mobile. In general, a GGSN can be the interface to an external packet network for several SGSNs, and an SGSN may route its packets to different GGSNs (Eberspächer, Vogel, and Bettstetter 2001; Steele et al. 2001; Bates 2002).

In any communications service network, essential ancillary functions include charging and billing, and the packet nature of GPRS service has a significant influence on the way these functions are implemented. Thus, the GPRS specification provides for a charging gateway function (CGF), which controls the collection of charging data records from the SGNSs and GGSNs. The GPRS specification stipulates the minimum amount of charging information that must be collected, but network operators have considerable latitude in how they implement the CGF function in their networks. Detailed discussion of GPRS billing systems can be found in Bates (2002) and Hoffman (2003).

The following sections describe the main characteristics of the GPRS network elements, with emphasis on their differences relative to the underlying GSM network elements. Detailed information on the GPRS standards can be found in the GPRS specifications, published by the 3GPP standardization group. The specifications can be downloaded from the 3GPP Web site, www.3gpp.org.

GPRS Mobile Stations

In order to have access to GPRS services, the customer must use an entirely new type of mobile station, though these new terminals are backward compatible with traditional GSM voice services. The new MSs are required because existing GSM terminals cannot handle the upgraded radio interface introduced with GPRS. Different GPRS mobiles are designed to provide different levels of service. The GPRS specifications have defined three classes of device, each having its own distinct characteristics. In order for a device to access GPRS services, it must support at least one of the defined classes. The actual handset implementation will determine whether the class of service is preassigned by the manufacturer, or if the user can change the service class (Bates 2002). The three service classes have been designated as Classes A, B, and C. In discussing these classes of handsets, it is useful to think of the GPRS-overlaid GSM network as a two-branch network (branches splitting at the BSC) capable of serving a single wireless user device. One branch supports circuit-switched connections with the public telephone network, and the other supports connections to packet-switched data networks such as the Internet or business intranets (Lischetzki 2003).

Class A: Class A GPRS devices have the greatest functionality among the three classes. This class of device can connect simultaneously to GPRS and GSM services. The user can access voice and data services at the same time, each service being carried in a single time slot on the radio interface. A Class A device has to support at least two active time slots in both the uplink and downlink directions. The device can access additional time slots to increase the supported data rate.

The Class A device allows the user to transfer data over the packet-switched GPRS branch of the network while simultaneously carrying on a voice call over the circuit-switched GSM branch. Furthermore, the user can initiate and terminate GPRS data sessions and GSM voice calls independently.

The implementation of GPRS Class A services places some significant demands on the network as a whole. In the handsets, clearly, both GSM voice and GPRS data functions must operate in parallel. On the network side, sufficient capacity must be provided to support uninterrupted voice service while also supporting a range of data rates that users will require for a variety of applications. Additionally, in call handoff situations, the receiving cell must be able to provide at least two time slots to handle both voice and data traffic to and from the mobile device.

Class B: A Class B device is able to access both GPRS and GSM services but not simultaneously as in a Class A device. In a Class B device, voice calls and GPRS data sessions are supported sequentially rather than in parallel. When a Class B terminal attaches to the network but has not initiated a GPRS data session, the device operates as a standard GSM voice terminal, initiating and receiving voice calls exactly as it would in a GSM-only network. In this mode, SMS messages can also be transferred. If the user initiates a voice call, GPRS data service is not possible until the voice call has been terminated. During a GPRS data session, the Class B device uses *suspend* and *resume* functions to park data sessions for the duration of voice calls. When a voice call comes in, the user can either continue with the data session, diverting the voice call to voicemail, or suspend (park) the data session for the duration of the voice call. In the latter case, the user may resume the data session after the voice call is completed. A Class B device requires at least one time slot in each direction, uplink and downlink, which can be used for either voice or data service. Additional time slots can be accessed to increase the data service transfer rate (Lischetzki 2003).

Class C: In contrast with Class A and B devices, a Class C device allows registration on only one service, either voice (with SMS supported) or GPRS data. The GPRS specification has defined three types of Class C devices: Class CC, Class CG, and a combination of the two.

Class CC devices provide only circuit-switched GSM services. These devices function as legacy GSM handsets, supporting voice, SMS, and circuit-switched data services.

Class CG devices support only GPRS services. Legacy GSM circuit-switched voice and data services cannot be supported with these devices.

As a third option, the handset manufacturers can provide devices that allow the user to switch manually between classes CC and CG.

GPRS Multislot Classes

GPRS mobile devices are also categorized by the data rates they can support. Within GSM there are eight time slots on each radio frequency carrier, and each uplink RF carrier is always paired with a corresponding downlink RF carrier. In a legacy GSM network, a circuit-switch service utilizes only one slot in each direction, but in GPRS it is possible to use more than one slot, allowing higher data rates to be achieved when the extra slots are available. The different GPRS data rate capabilities of the devices, referred to as *multislot classes*, are dependent upon the number of slots that can be used in either direction.

GPRS specifies a total of twenty-nine multislot classes, and Table 1 shows those that are most commonly implemented. For each class, the table gives the maximum number of downlink and uplink slots the mobile can support, and the right-hand column gives the upper limit on the combined number of downlink and uplink slots. For example, if a Class 12 mobile is assigned four downlink slots, it can be assigned no more than one uplink slot, since the maximum sum for Class 12 is five slots. Note also that since the specified numbers of slots are maximum numbers, a given mobile device might be able to support more than one multislot class. For example, a Class 8 terminal can also support classes 1, 2, and 4. The permitted multislot configuration also depends on the mobile type: Type 1 mobiles cannot transmit and receive simultaneously, whereas Type 2 mobiles can, and thus can support more time slots. Multislot classes 13 to 29, not included in the table, can be supported only by Type 2 mobile terminals. To date, only one Type 2 device has appeared in the market.

More extensive discussions of the GPRS multislot classes can be found in Bates (2002) and Sanders et al. (2003), and the GPRS specifications appear on the 3GPP Web site, www.3Gpp.org.

Location Registers

The home location register, already an element in any GSM network, must be enhanced to support GPRS services. As in a legacy GSM service network, the HLR serves as the principal database for the network, storing the information related to all subscribers connected to the network and keeping track of the location of each mobile in the network, including the corresponding SGSN for a GPRS mobile. In support of GPRS services, the HLR handles GPRS subscription data, including subscribed quality of service (QoS), and also handles data-packet addressing and mobile roaming (Bates 2002; Bilgic et al. 1999; Priggouris, Hadjiefthymiades, and Merakos 2000).

As in a legacy GSM service network, a visitor location register (VLR) associated with each MSC keeps a temporary database of the subscribers who have roamed into the area served by that MSC. Although the VLR holds information similar to that held in the HLR, it holds information for only those mobiles in the areas being served by its MSC, and a mobile moving out of its serving area is dropped from the VLR's database.

Base Station Subsystem

In the GSM architecture, the base station subsystem comprises the base transceiver station, which handles the radio interface with mobile devices, and the base station controller, which manages the connection of each call between the wired network and the BTS handling the particular RF link connection (Mouly and Pautet 1992; Heine 1999; Eberspächer et al. 2001). In the overlay of GPRS services onto a GSM network, some changes are required in both the BTS and the BSC, but there is greater impact on the BSC than on the BTS. For the BTS, some software upgrades are required to accommodate the changes in the radio interface needed to support packet-formatted traffic. However, the BTS requires no hardware modifications

Table 1: Selected GPRS Multislot Classes

Multislot Class	Downlink Slots	Uplink Slots	Maximum Sum
1	1	1	2
2	2	1	3
4	3	1	4
6	3	2	4
8	4	1	5
12	4	4	5

because the GPRS traffic is carried in the same eight-slot time-multiplexed RF channels that support GSM circuit-switched services. The BSC, however, requires both software upgrades and hardware modifications.

In order to implement GPRS services in a GSM network, the BSC requires a new piece of hardware called a *packet control unit*, which directs the packet data traffic to and from the GPRS network. Each BSC requires installation of one or more PCUs along with a software upgrade. The PCU provides a physical and logical data interface at the BSS for packet data traffic (Bates 2002). When either circuit-switched voice or packet data traffic is sent from the mobile device, it is carried over the radio interface to the BTS, and from the BTS to the BSC, just as in a standard GSM call. However, at the output of the BSC, the traffic is separated—the voice traffic going to the MSC as in standard GSM, and packet data traffic going via the PCU over a frame-relay interface to a new network element called the serving GPRS support node.

Serving GPRS Support Node

In a GPRS network, the SGSN serves as a packet version of a combination of the MSC and the VLR. Not surprisingly, the SGSN employs packet switching, in effect functioning as a router, passing data packets in both directions between the mobile terminal and a public packet data network (e.g., the Internet). In addition to its packet-switching function, the SGSN also handles some of the functions that the BSS handles in a legacy GSM network and is effectively the end point of communication with the mobile device in its GPRS data mode. The SGSN performs the following primary functions:

- Mobility management, including session management, state control, and data packet routing and location tracking on the downlink (toward the mobile)
- Authentication and encryption
- Compression, including TCP/IP header compression and data compression (using V.42 *bis*)

Mobility management is a particularly critical function because customers will expect data sessions to be kept intact as they move about the GPRS service area. The same handoff capability afforded in circuit-switched voice service must be supported reliably in packet data service. This is accomplished in GPRS by defining *routing areas*, which are tracked by the SGSN. Each routing area comprises a number of cells, each cell defined by the signal coverage area of a BTS. As a mobile station moves about a routing area, the SGSN will locate it to a cell and send data packets to it. When the mobile is in active state, the SGSN can track its location to the cell level and promptly deliver arriving data packets. (See the section entitled "Packet Data Handling.")

Authentication and encryption are essential functions that must be provided in GPRS to prevent intrusion into the network and to protect the privacy of data transferred over the radio interface. These security functions are discussed in the section entitled "Security Procedures."

In order to make data transfer over the radio interface as efficient as possible, IP packets are compressed before being encrypted and transmitted. The compression occurs between the MS and the SGSN and is performed by the sub-network dependent convergence protocol (SNDCP) layer of the protocol stack. The compression involves, for example, minimizing the long strings of consecutive ones and zeros in the packet data stream. The compression and expansion are done in a way that ensures the exact reconstruction of the original bit sequence. The SNDCP protocol is specified in 3GPP TS 04.65 (n.d.).

Gateway GPRS Support Node

Although the SGSN supports GPRS data traffic by routing data packets to and from mobile devices, it does not perform all the functions needed to interface that traffic with external packet data networks. The gateway GPRS support node provides this additional functionality. Because users of GPRS services will typically want to access the Internet, each registered user must be provided an IP address for receipt of IP datagrams. Similarly, data originating in an MS must be appropriately addressed for delivery to the intended destination on the Internet. These address resolution functions are performed in the GGSN (Bates 2002; Watts and Wright 2003).

In common networking terminology, a *gateway* is a node that interfaces two networks using different protocols, and this is exactly what the GGSN does in the GPRS architecture. On its GPRS side, the GGSN connects to the SGSN, and on its other side it connects to external packet networks such as the Internet, corporate intranets, and X.25 networks. As seen from the external networks' perspective, the GGSN is simply a router to some subnetwork, because the GGSN conceals the GPRS network infrastructure from the external networks. When the GGSN receives data addressed to a particular GPRS user, it forwards the data to the SGSN currently serving the user's mobile. Data packets originated by the mobile are routed by the GGSN to the appropriate data network. One can see from this discussion that the GGSN performs a function similar to that of the gateway MSC (GMSC) in the GSM architecture. In addition, with respect to handling of IP traffic, its function is much like that of a router.

The GGSN has a mobile-tracking function corresponding to that in the SGSN. If a mobile's location changes beyond the routing area, it can reconnect to a local SGSN, and the GGSN will find it, though data stored in the old SGSN buffers may be lost and have to be retransmitted (e. g., by the transport-layer protocol [TLP]). Data traffic originating in a public packet data network, intended for a GPRS data user, must be directed to a single point of contact; that point of contact is the GGSN. For this reason, the GGSN performs what is sometimes described as the *anchor function* in the GPRS system.

As we have just seen, packet data handling within a GPRS network involves moving packets among SGSNs by way of a GGSN. The delivery of data packets between external data networks and GPRS mobiles is based on the packet handling procedures known as *mobile IP* (Perkins 1998; Mobile IP n.d.). The interconnected subnetwork of support nodes is called the *GPRS backbone*. Within this backbone, the packet data traffic is transported and protected using a protocol called the *GPRS tunneling protocol*

(GTP). In data networking terminology, a tunneling protocol encapsulates one data protocol within another to provide delivery of the encapsulated protocol data units over a network that could not otherwise support that protocol (Leon-Garcia and Widjaja 2000; Tanenbaum 2003). Within the GPRS backbone, the GTP is used to encapsulate IP and X.25 packets, making the underlying transport network invisible to the user data. The GGSN handles the encapsulated packets as follows:

- In the upstream direction, from the mobile to the external packet network, the GGSN removes the GTP and lower-layer headers, and then delivers the IP or X.25 packet in its native form to the external network.
- In the downstream direction, the GGSN performs the opposite operation, adding GTP and lower-layer headers, and transporting the packet to the appropriate SGSN.

PACKET DATA HANDLING

The central purpose of a GPRS network is to transfer packet data between a GPRS mobile terminal and external packet data networks, such as the Internet. There are two essential aspects of the required procedures: *data-packet routing* and *mobility management* (MM). The packet-routing function in GPRS is fundamentally the same as must be performed in any packet-data network. A data packet arrives as a network node, and a routing function in the node determines the node to which the packet should next be sent in order to eventually reach the intended destination. The packet is forwarded to the next node, where the process is repeated. However, in GPRS the packet routing function is complicated by the fact that data packets may be carried across several different networks in order to reach their intended destination (Sanders et al. 2003). The problem here is that the different networks might not use the same form of packet addressing.

The second aspect of GPRS data handling is mobility management. Although MM has been an essential part of all mobile networks, there are some MM features in GPRS that differ from those in circuit-switched network services such as legacy GSM. Since data packets are routed across the network individually, and the MS may be located in different cell areas as individual packets are being routed, the GPRS MM procedure is designed to make optimum use of transmission resources, such as unassigned time slots, in the underlying GSM network.

Before data packets can be transferred between an MS and an external data network, three key steps must be performed:

- The MS must attach itself to the GPRS network. This is phrased purposefully, since the procedure for accomplishing this, called *GPRS attach*, is always initiated by the MS. This is a logical interaction between the MS and the SGSN, taking note of the current location of the MS. Storing and updating the MS location is particularly important for downlink (SGSN to MS) data transfer since this information enables the GPRS network to locate the MS.
- In the next step, called *activation of a PDP context*, a connection is set up between the MS and the GGSN, providing a path for IP packets to traverse inside the GPRS network. When this step has been accomplished, each node in the GPRS network knows how to forward IP packets to the intended MS.
- Finally, the path between the MS and the external data network is set up, enabling transfer of IP packets through the GPRS network to the intended destination.

These procedures are discussed in further detail in the following paragraphs.

GPRS Attach

GPRS attach is a GPRS MM procedure initiated by the MS. Depending upon the settings in the MS, the attach procedure may be performed each time the MS is powered on, or it may be initiated manually by the mobile user. The request for a GPRS attach is made by the MS to the current SGSN by a procedure that is transparent to the BTS and BSC currently serving the MS. First the MS identifies itself and sends its old *routing area identity* (RAI) and desired attach type. The latter indicates to the SGSN whether it wants to attach as a GPRS device, a GSM device, or both. The SGSN then attaches the MS and informs the HLR if there has been a change in the routing area. If the desired attach type is both GPRS and GSM, the SGSN will also update the MS location with the VLR. Once the MS is attached to the SGSN, it remains attached until instructed to detach, thus accounting for the phrase "always on" often used in characterizing GPRS capability.

The result of the GPRS attach procedure is that the current SGSN knows that the MS has activated GPRS. If the MS was already registered with another SGSN, the new SGSN updates the HLR so that the HLR knows the identity of the current SGSN. The HLR then sends the GPRS-specific data for the MS to the current SGSN. The GPRS-specific data corresponds to the different packet data protocol (PDP) contexts that are set up for this specific MS (see next subsection). A PDP context describes the GPRS data connection for an MS. The information describing such a context consists of:

- The *access point name* (APN), a logical name for the desired outside data network. The APN might be a specific Internet address or the address of an Internet service provider.
- The quality of service—including priorities, delays, reliability, and throughput—for the intended application (voice, Web browsing, video, music downloads, etc.).
- The PDP protocol to be used between the MS and the external data network, usually IP.
- The permanent address of the MS, if it has a permanent address.

Several PDP contexts can be set up for an MS such that the MS can reach several IP networks (i.e., several APNs) with different QoS specifications. With respect to QoS, it is worth noting here that some implementations have diverged to varying degrees from the GPRS specifications.

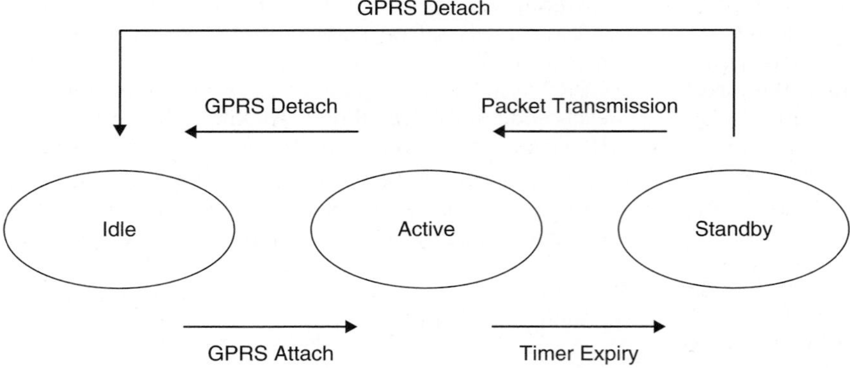

Figure 2: Mobility management states

The messages passed between the MS and the SGSN concerning the GPRS attach procedure are part of the *GPRS mobility management* (GMM) protocol. Other examples of GMM procedures include the updating of MS location (routing area), switching off the MS (GPRS detach), authentication, and GPRS paging.

The final step in enabling the MS to transmit and receive data is activation of a communication session using a packet data protocol context, described next.

PDP Context Activation

A mobile user wanting to start a GPRS service session must activate a *PDP context*, which is in effect a data destination address. A PDP context is used for routing data packets through the GPRS network, between the MS and a GGSN, allowing the MS to exchange data with an external packet data network. The activation procedure begins with the MS sending an activation request to the SGSN. The SGSN then selects a GGSN based on information (APN, QoS, PDP protocol) provided by the MS, and requests the GGSN to provide a context for the MS. Next, the GGSN replies to the SGSN with a tunnel ID (TID), and maps the TID and the SGSN IP addresses to the particular MS associated with them. Finally, the SGSN informs the MS that a PDP context has been activated, and it also updates its information tables with the TID and GGSN IP address with which it has established the protocol tunnel for the MS. (See the section entitled "Gateway GPRS Support Node" for discussion of protocol tunneling in GPRS.) At this point, the entire GPRS network is able to route data packets in either direction between the MS and an external data network.

The preceding paragraph outlined the procedure for mobile-initiated PDP context activation. However, if data arrives at a GGSN for a GPRS mobile user, a PDP context activation can be initiated by that GGSN (Bates 2002).

Once a PDP context is activated, transmission resources are assigned to the communication session until data transfer ceases for a specified interval of time.

Data Packet Transfer

Once the PDP context to an APN selected by the MS has been activated, a logical path is in place between the MS and an external IP network, and packet data transfer can begin. The GGSN has updated routing information supplied by the SGSN about the current location of the MS, and, as packets arrive from the external network, they are encapsulated using the GTP protocol (see the section entitled "Gateway GPRS Support Node") for transfer over the GPRS backbone to the SGSN currently serving the MS. The GGSN also undoes the encapsulation of MS-originated packets and forwards them to the appropriate external data network.

GPRS Mobility Management

Mobility management is an essential aspect of all mobile communications networks, allowing mobile users to maintain reliable communications sessions while moving about a service network or even roaming from one service network to another. In the case of a GPRS network, the underlying GSM circuit-switched network already has MM protocols in place, but GPRS adds certain MM features that are appropriate for packet-switched traffic while minimizing the required signaling traffic across the network.

Figure 2 depicts the three different states of a GPRS MS: idle, standby, and active. A GSM mobile has two states, idle and active, whereas GPRS adds the standby state to address the packet nature of GPRS traffic.

In the *idle state*, the MS does not have a GPRS context activated or any outside packet network addresses allocated. In this state, the MS is effectively unknown to the GPRS network, and it cannot receive any messages from external data networks; it can only receive those multicast messages that can be received by any GRPS mobile. In the idle state, if the GPRS MS is also a GSM mobile, rather than a GPRS-dedicated mobile, it will be known to the VLR and will make location updates while switched on. However, the GPRS network will not hold any location information for the MS.

In the *standby state*, the MS and the SGSN have established an MM context so that the SGSN location register knows the current routing area of the MS, which can comprise one or more cells within a GSM location area. The MS performs routing area updates as it moves across routing area borders. When the SGSN has to send a packet to an MS that is in standby state, the mobile must first be paged. Because the SGSN knows the routing area in which the MS is currently located, a packet-paging message is sent to that routing area. Upon receiving the paging message, the MS provides its cell location to the SGSN, and the active state is then established. The use of packet-paging messages simplifies the process of receiving downlink packets. The MS has to listen to only the packet-paging messages, rather than all the data packets being carried in the downlink channels, thus conserving battery power in the mobile.

Once the MS has been paged and responds, it switches to the *active state*, sometimes termed the *ready state*. Additionally, in the SGSN, the MM context is switched to the active state, and packet delivery to the MS begins. In the active state, the SGSN knows the exact location of the MS. Because of the discontinuous nature of GPRS data traffic, the cell selection and reselection are usually performed by the MS; that is, the MS monitors the surrounding cells and decides for itself which one to use. Requests from the MS to use a particular cell may be accepted, or the SGSN may instruct the MS to use a different cell.

When an MS has data packets to be transmitted, access to an uplink channel is needed. The uplink channel is shared by a number of MSs, and its use is allocated by the BSS (BSC and BTS) currently serving the mobile. The MS requests use of the channel with a packet random-access message, using the slotted-Aloha protocol. The BSS allocates an available channel to the MS and sends a packet-access grant message to the mobile. The packet-access grant message includes a description (i.e., one or more time slots) of the allocated channel.

Transition from the active state to the standby state usually occurs upon expiration of the ready timer in the SGSN. This occurs if the MS has not sent or received any data within a period of time set in the timer.

When the subscriber wishes to terminate the GPRS connection, the *GPRS detach* procedure is used. The detach procedure includes transitions either from active to idle or from standby to idle. Such a transition is usually initiated by a detach request from the MS. Upon detachment, the SGSN places the MS in idle state, indicating that the MS is disconnected from GPRS.

More detailed descriptions of GPRS data-handling procedures and MM functions can be found in Halonen et al. (2003), Sanders et al. (2003), Bates (2002), and the GPRS specifications.

Security Procedures

As is the case with any wireless communications service, the radio transmission medium is vulnerable to interception techniques. Thus, to prevent unauthorized intervention in the GPRS system, two primary techniques are employed: authentication and encryption (also termed ciphering). These security procedures are fundamentally the same as those performed in legacy GSM networks, though there are some differences in implementation.

The security procedures utilize information stored both in the mobile terminal's SIM card and in the authentication center (AC). This information includes: (1) an identification key, K_i, which serves as the subscriber's password; (2) an encryption key, K_c, which is calculated anew for each connection; and (3) two algorithms for calculating, respectively, an *authentication key* and an *encryption key*.

Before any GPRS mobile terminal is allowed to have access to the network, it must be authenticated. This procedure insures that the user attempting to initiate a network connection has an authentic SIM card with a valid identification key, K_i. The AC is responsible for generating a set of variables called a *triplet*. A triplet consists of: (1) a *random number*, RAND; (2), a *signed response*, SRES; and (3) an *encryption key*, K_c. The first two variables are used in a challenge-response interchange, initiated and controlled by the SGSN, to authenticate the mobile's SIM card and its identification key K_i. The authentication algorithm is designed to make it extremely difficult for an intruder to calculate the subscriber's identification key K_i (128 bits long), even if he intercepts the RAND and SRES variables on the radio interface.

Once the MS has been authenticated, the calculated encryption key K_c is used to encrypt all the data transferred between the MS and the SGSN. Further details of the GPRS security procedures can be found in Sanders et al. (2003).

GPRS RADIO INTERFACE

The transmission formatting for GPRS is based upon much the same underlying structure as found in GSM; however, there are important differences between the two (ETSI 1997b). As in the GSM specification, each radio channel carries TDMA frames of duration 4.615 ms, each frame containing eight time slots. Also, as in GSM, physical channels are each defined by a combination of frequency channel and time slot for the uplink and downlink, and logical channels are mapped onto physical channels for carrying data traffic and for carrying signaling and control information. However, a number of new logical channels were defined for the GPRS standard. Additionally, many changes in channel structure were made relative to the channel structure defined for GSM circuit-switched services. These changes include a longer multiframe length (described below), new channel-coding schemes, new power-control algorithms, and a link adaptation scheme designed to change the channel-coding scheme according to conditions on the radio channel. The following paragraphs describe how physical and logical channels are assigned to an MS, followed by a brief description of channel coding for GPRS traffic and control channels.

Radio Resource Management

As noted earlier, in a legacy GSM network, a physical channel—which is a time slot in sequentially transmitted TDMA frames—is assigned to an MS throughout the call session, whether information is being transmitted or not. Furthermore, a time slot is assigned in both the uplink and the downlink. In contrast, GPRS assigns time slots in a more flexible manner that is better suited to the transmission of discontinuous data packets. A GPRS MS can transmit on multiple time slots in the same TDMA frame; this is termed *multislot operation*. The number of time slots assigned to an MS corresponds to the multislot class, as discussed in the section entitled "GPRS Multislot Classes." In a further contrast with legacy GSM, the numbers of uplink and downlink time slots are assigned separately, which enables efficient use of radio resources in cases of asymmetric traffic, such as Web-browsing applications.

In a GPRS-equipped GSM network, the radio resources of each cell are to be shared among all MSs, both standard GSM and GPRS, currently located in the cell's signal coverage area. In GPRS, the assignment of physical channels to either circuit-switched GSM service or packet-switched GPRS service can be done dynamically. A physical channel allocated for GPRS data transmission is termed a packet data channel (PDCH), and the number of PDCHs can be adjusted in response to the current traffic demand. Physical channels not currently needed for circuit-switched GSM calls can be assigned as PDCHs, for example, enabling faster delivery of GPRS packet data traffic. Similarly, if there is increased demand for GSM traffic, PDCHs can be deallocated.

The ability of GPRS to dynamically assign multiple time slots to packet data traffic is particularly valuable given the real-world characteristics of wireless data transmission. Under some conditions, received signal quality can be degraded; GPRS deals with this in the *radio link control* (RLC) layer of the protocol stack using error-detection and *automatic repeat request* retransmission of erroneous data. Under very poor signal conditions, large numbers of retransmissions can significantly slow the delivery of data across the radio interface, and the ability to dynamically assign multiple time slots for data delivery can help to offset the effects of high retransmission rate. More detailed discussion of the RLC layer can be found in Eberspächer et al. (2001).

When a particular MS has finished transmitting or receiving its data packets, its assigned PDCHs are released. In this way, multiple MSs can share a physical channel, enabling the efficient use of the radio resources.

Management of Logical Channels

Here we briefly describe the process of allocating transmission resources to an MS for transfer of GPRS data. As in legacy GSM, logical channels in GPRS are divided into two categories, traffic channels and control channels. The *packet data traffic channel* (PDTCH) is used for the transfer of user data. The control channels comprise three categories: the *packet broadcast channel* (PBCCH), four *packet common control channels* (PCCCHs), and two *packet dedicated control channels* (PDCCHs). To provide a simple example of channel allocation, assume that an MS has data packets to transfer to some destination through the GPRS service network. The MS requests a traffic channel by sending a packet channel request on the *packet random access channel* (PRACH), which is one of the four PCCCHs. Alternatively, the request may be sent on the *random access channel* (RACH) of the underlying GSM network. The BSS responds on the *packet access grant channel* (PAGCH), which is another of the four PCCCHs. If the MS made its channel request on the GSM RACH, the BSS responds on the GSM *access grant channel* (AGCH).

Once the MS's channel request is granted, a *temporary block flow* (TBF) is established between the MS and the BSS. The TBF is a physical connection for transfer of *packet data units* (PDUs) in one direction over the radio interface. If bidirectional data transfer is needed, two TBFs are established, one uplink and one downlink. When data packets arrive from the network intended for a particular MS, the BSS pages the MS with a *packet paging request*, and the MS initiates the channel allocation with a packet channel request, as in the MS-initiating example.

There is at most one TBF established per MS per direction, but each TBF can be mapped onto multiple PDCHs. TBFs established for different MSs can share the same PDCH or a group of common PDCHs. As its name implies, TBF is a temporary connection maintained only for the duration of data transfer; when all of the PDUs have been transferred, the PDCHs are released, making them available for other data transfers.

It is important to point out that data transfer over the GPRS radio interface will have characteristics much different from the familiar situation of data communication using modems on the public telephone network. Wireless communication sessions will invariably exhibit intervals of poor signal quality with the potential of imposing errors on the transferred data. GPRS accommodates these situations by providing for the optional use of acknowledge (ACK) mode operation, with retransmission, in the *radio link control* (RLC) layer of the system. The retransmission of erroneous RLC blocks under degraded signal conditions has a direct effect upon *data throughput*, that is, the amount of data delivered successfully to the user per unit of time. Correspondingly, there is a direct impact on the delay characteristics of the delivered data packets. In addition, the throughput and delay characteristics of GPRS data transfer will be affected by the traffic load on the network, along with the availability of traffic channels as each channel request is made. Detailed treatments of TBF throughput and delay characteristics can be found in Halonen et al. (2003) and other references cited therein.

It is beyond the scope of this chapter to describe all of the details of the GPRS radio interface and the management of its radio resources, but the reader may find these details in a number of recent texts (see Halonen et al. 2003; Seurre, Savelli, and Pietri 2003; Steele et al. 2001). The following subsection describes the multiframe structure of a GPRS physical channel.

Multiframe Structure

Figure 3 shows the structure of a 240-ms GPRS multiframe, which contains fifty-two TDMA frames, each with eight time slots. A GPRS multiframe has the same duration as two GSM multiframes, each containing twenty-six TDMA frames. The GPRS multiframe contains twelve blocks (B0–B11) of four consecutive TDMA frames plus four idle frames. A physical channel is referred to as a packet data channel, fully defined by a frequency channel together with one uplink time slot and one downlink time slot. On any given PDCH, blocks of four bursts, called radio blocks, form the logical channels, carrying either user data or signaling information. Each radio block consists of 456 bits. The packet data logical channels are mapped dynamically onto the radio blocks B0–B11 of the multiframe. The mapping can change from one radio block to another, controlled by parameters broadcast on a packet

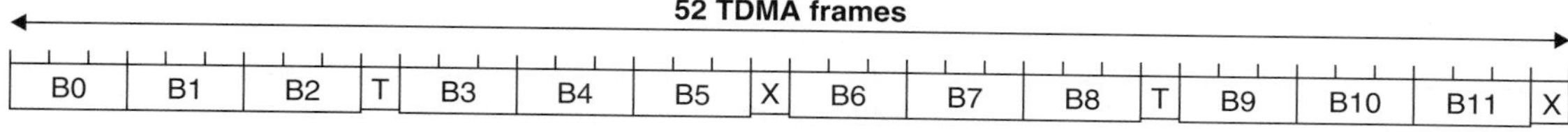

Figure 3: GPRS multiframe structure

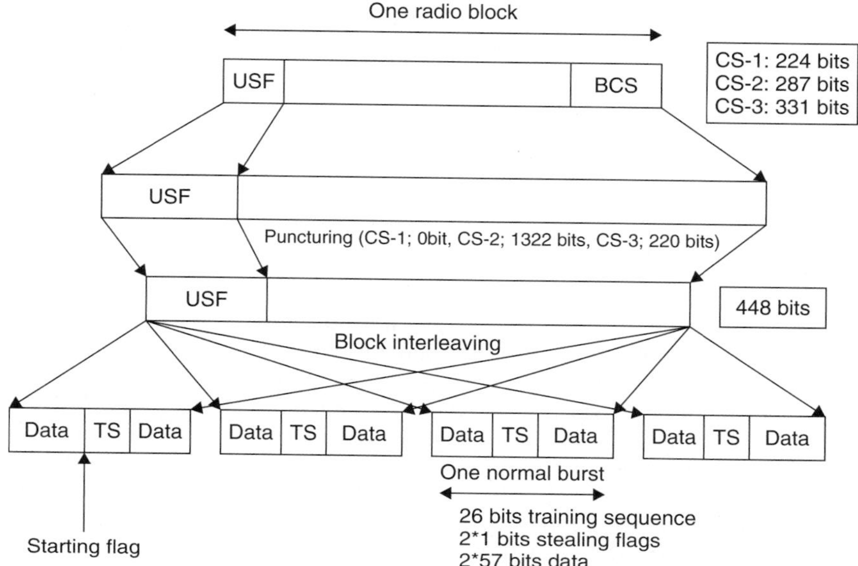

Figure 4: Radio block encoding for three GPRS coding schemes (CSs)

broadcast control channel. This dynamic mapping function allows the system to adapt to the traffic load by allocating or releasing resources as needed (Seurre et al. 2003).

An important feature of the GPRS specification is the provision of four *coding systems* (CSs) providing different degrees of error protection. The lowest coding rate (greatest redundancy) is provided by CS-1 and the highest rate (no redundancy) by CS-4. The coding uses a cyclic redundancy check (CRC) code together with convolutional channel coding for CS-1, CS-2, and CS-3. For CS-4, only CRC coding is used, providing error detection without error correction. Code puncturing (selective removal of parity bits) is applied to the convolutional encoding output to adjust the transmitted bit sequence to the radio block length. To illustrate the channel-coding scheme, Figure 4 shows the encoding of one radio block for coding systems CS-1 to CS-3.

The GPRS specification includes a link adaptation procedure for choosing the coding system in accordance with the measured radio transmission environment. However, link adaptation has generally not been implemented in deployed equipment, and, as a practical matter, CS-1 is typically used for signaling and CS-2 for packet data transfer.

ENHANCED DATA FOR GLOBAL EVOLUTION

Soon after the introduction of GPRS in 2000, network operators perceived that GSM-based networks would have to provide even higher data rates. The need for higher rates has grown out of the market demand for an expanding menu of services, such as multimedia transmission. In response to this market demand, the European Telecommunications Standards Institute (ETSI) defined a new family of data services, built upon the existing structure of GPRS. This new family of data services was initially named enhanced data Rates for GSM evolution and was subsequently renamed *enhanced data for global evolution* (EDGE). Although the primary motivation for the EDGE development was enhancement of data services in GSM/GPRS networks, EDGE can also be introduced into networks built to the IS-136 (U.S. digital cellular) standard (Furuskar et al. 1999). In Europe, EDGE is considered a 2.5-generation (2.5G) standard, providing a transition between 2G and 3G systems. As is the case with GPRS, a GSM network operator requires no new license to implement EDGE services in its network, since the 200 kHz RF channel organization of conventional GSM is reused with a different organization of logical channels within each RF channel. This section describes the implementation of EDGE in GSM/GPRS networks.

EDGE enhances data service performance over GPRS in two ways. First, it replaces the GMSK radio link modulation used in GSM with an eight-PSK modulation scheme capable of tripling the data rate on a single radio channel. Second, EDGE provides more reliable transmission of data using link adaptation, which dynamically chooses a *modulation and coding scheme* (MCS) in accordance with the current transmission conditions on the radio channel. The EDGE link adaptation mechanism is

Table 2: EGPRS Modulation and Coding Parameters

Modulation and Coding Scheme	Code Rate	Modulation Type	Data Rate per) Time Slot (kb/s)	MCS Family
MCS-9	1.00	8-PSK	59.2	A
MCS-8	0.92	8-PSK	54.4	A
MCS-7	0.76	8-PSK	44.8	B
MCS-6	0.49	8-PSK	29.6	A
MCS-5	0.37	8-PSK	22.4	B
MCS-4	1.00	GMSK	17.6	C
MCS-3	0.80	GMSK	14.8	A
MCS-2	0.66	GMSK	11.2	B
MCS-1	0.53	GMSK	8.8	C

an enhanced version of the link adaptation mechanism introduced and specified in GPRS (Halonen et al. 2003; Seurre et al. 2003). EDGE also improves upon GPRS by incorporating a new hybrid ARQ technique called *incremental redundancy* (IR). In the IR scheme, when an RLC data block is received with detected errors and must be retransmitted, reception of each retransmission of that block combines information from previous transmissions in order to increase the probability of an eventual error-free reception of the block.

EDGE provides two forms of enhanced data service for GSM networks: *enhanced circuit-switched data* (ECSD) for circuit-switched services and *enhanced GPRS* (EGPRS) for packet-switched services. In each form of EDGE data service, there are provisions for combining logical channels (time slots) in the GSM transmission format to provide a wide menu of achievable data rates.

The major impact that EDGE has on the GSM/GPRS protocol structure is at the physical layer of the radio interface, and there is only minor impact on medium-access control (MAC) and radio link control (RLC) layers (Halonen et al. 2003). The EDGE RF specification and definition of burst structures are common to EGPRS and ECSD. A major modification in EGPRS, relative to GPRS, is the *link quality control* (LQC) function, which provides a wider array of link error-control schemes than exist in conventional GSM or in GPRS. The LQC function provides nine different modulation and coding schemes, MCS-1 to MCS-9, as well as related signaling and adaptation procedures for switching between MCSs in response to radio link conditions. Table 2 summarizes the nine MCSs used in EGPRS and shows the data throughput provided by each MCS. The EGPRS modulation and coding schemes are organized into three families, A to C, according to their RLC block sizes. For example, in Family A, MCS-9 carries 1,184 payload bits in two RLC data blocks during one EGPRS radio block of four consecutive bursts (radio blocks). MCS-6 carries 592 payload bits in one RLC frame, and MC-3 carries 296 payload bits within the RLC block. In each family, the numbers of payload bits carried in the lower-rate coding schemes are submultiples of the payloads at higher rates. This feature enables efficient retransmission of negatively acknowledged RLC blocks when this functionality is needed following a sudden change in radio channel conditions. For a detailed discussion of EGPRS link adaptation and analysis of its performance, see Halonen et al. (2003).

The ECSD service is built upon the HSCSD service standardized in the GSM Phase 2+ specification. Although the user data rates provided by ECSD (up to 64 kb/s) are not higher than those in HSCSD, the same data rates are achieved in ECSD by using smaller numbers of time slots and simpler implementation in the mobile terminals (Halonen et al. 2003). As was the case with HSCSD, ECSD provides both *transparent* (T) and *non-transparent* (NT) services. Transparent data service employs forward-error correction and is characterized by a fixed time delay in data delivery. Generally speaking, transparent service cannot assure a specified level of accuracy in delivered data. Non-transparent data service uses a *radio link protocol* (RLP) that includes error detection and retransmission, termed *automatic repeat request* (ARQ), to assure that the error rate in delivered data will be maintained below some specified level (Lin and Costello 2004). The use of retransmission results in variable time delay in the delivered data. Table 3 shows the data rates provided by ECSD service in EDGE.

THE EVOLUTION GOES ON

In the last few decades, the telecommunications industry has become very responsive to market demands for new services and capabilities. This has been particularly true of the wireless segment of the industry, which has seen vigorous growth from cordless phones and first-generation analog cellular networks through 2G digital networks, low-speed mobile data networks, paging systems, and now 3G technologies that provide improved voice quality and the integration of voice and data services. Two dominant themes have been discernable throughout this wireless evolution: the growing dependence on mobility, and the increasing importance of data services in the mobile environment (see Pahlavan and Levesque 2005).

Table 3: ECSD Service Data Rates in EDGE

Coding Scheme	Code Rate	Modulation Type	Gross Rate (kb/s)	Radio Interface	User Rate (kb/s)
TCH/28.8 (NT/T)	0.419	8-PSK	69.2	29.0	28.8
TCH/32.0 (T)	0.462	8-PSK	69.2	32.0	32.0
TCH/43.2 (NT)	0.629	8-PSK	69.2	43.5	43.2

NT = non-transparent Service; T = transparent service

The earliest cellular networks were driven by the voice service market, that is, "cutting the telephone cord" and allowing the customer to have untethered access to the public telephone network for standard voice calls. Consequently, the early cellular networks were designed as circuit-switched networks, simply adding user mobility to traditional dialup phone service. With the introduction of digital transmission in the 2G cellular networks, data services were provided, but data calls were circuit switched as were traditional voice calls, and the available data rates were modest. For a number of years, this was considered a satisfactory way of supporting cellular data service, since early demand for mobile data service was limited, and service providers were concerned primarily with meeting the rapidly growing market for cellular voice service. However, the market for mobile data services, slow to emerge, began to take on increasing importance. Today, the terms "mobile office," "road warrior," and "M-commerce" are familiar references to the increasing use of wireless data communications as part of everyday business.

A major driver in the growth of demand for mobile data was the tremendous expansion in use of the Internet and the World Wide Web and the growth in popularity of new applications requiring data service. The traveling business or professional person is increasingly dependent upon wireless access to e-mail, FTP file transfers, Web site access, and even video teleconferences. Other applications have also emerged for handling financial transactions, traffic inquiries, fleet management, alarm notification, and many other functions. These emerging applications and markets have produced a growing demand for wireless data services, and, as users gain familiarity with the use of these services, their levels of expectation continually rise. SMS is a prominent example; since its inception, SMS has become extremely popular as a means for rapidly exchanging alphanumeric text messages, and this has led to a demand for wireless exchange of digital images and even multimedia video clips using MMS. Another phenomenon is the increasingly popular use of wireless communications to download music files, games, ringtones, and custom screens from the Web.

As the demand for wireless data services grew, the limitations of the circuit-switched architecture became obvious. Every cellular service network operates within a fixed spectrum allocation, perhaps licensed at a high capital cost, and frequency channels allocated to circuit-switched data service are not available for voice service, creating a capacity problem as demand for both voice and data services grows. Furthermore, since most data applications are discontinuous in nature, packet-switched data service is well suited to those applications, and the GPRS architecture, by overlaying packet-switching onto legacy GSM networks, provided a nondisruptive solution. However, as wireless data service grows in acceptance and popularity, the demand for ever-higher data rates continues. The EDGE service, summarized in the previous section, addresses the data rate requirement by changing the physical-layer modulation scheme, allowing more data to be transmitted in each time slot of the underlying GSM transmission format.

The next stage of the GSM evolution is the 3G standardization initiative, intended to combine and gradually replace 2G digital cellular voice and data services. The 3G systems are expected to improve voice quality, expand network capacity, and increase the data rates of wireless data services. The primary set of requirements for 3G systems is referred to as *International Mobile Telecommunications Beyond the Year 2000* (IMT-2000). Although the 3G initiative was originally envisioned to result in a single, unified, worldwide standard, in reality several approaches have been pursued. The two leading approaches are as follows.

- Universal mobile telephone system, which is based on W-CDMA technology, will also incorporate GPRS and EDGE services in areas in which the highest data rates provided by W-CDMA are not needed. Thus, the UMTS approach is attractive to service providers that already have major capital investments in GSM-based networks. With respect to its high-speed data services, UMTS provides rates up to 144 kbits/s for vehicular users, up to 384 kbits/s for pedestrian users, and up to 2 Mbits/s for indoor users. However, the achievable performance will in reality depend upon a number of factors, including network engineering and the traffic loads experienced in the service networks.
- The CDMA-2000 system, which builds upon the earlier CDMA systems, IS-95 and cdmaOne (Viterbi 1995; Steele et al. 2001). CDMA-2000 supports data rates ranging from 144 kbits/s to over 3 Mbits/s.

Looking beyond 3G, several developments are under way, including *high-speed downlink packet access* (HSDPA), a variation of 3G also called 3.5G. HSDPA utilizes versions of link adaptation and IR, techniques already employed in EDGE. It is seen by some industry observers as a strong candidate to succeed 3G in GSM-based networks. In December 2005, Cingular announced availability of HSDPA in sixteen U.S. cities, with average data speeds of 400–700 kbps, under the brand name "BroadbandConnect."

High-speed uplink packet access (HSUPA) is a data access protocol similar to HSDPA, also utilizing link adaptation and IR, with upload speeds up to 5.8 Mbit/s (Holma and Toskala 2006). HSUPA is being referred to as 3.75G or sometimes 4G technology. The specifications for HSUPA are still under development and will be included in UMTS Release 6.

At this writing, the vision for enhancements of 3G networks and for evolution of 4G wireless networks is still being formulated. Indeed, the term *4G* is being used with somewhat different meanings; an alternative term, perhaps more appropriate, is "beyond 3G"—a broader designation encompassing a number of different but overlapping technologies.

Although the designation for the wireless generation beyond 3G is not settled, the technical objectives are being formulated. The data service rates for 4G are planned to be up to 20 Mbps for high vehicular speeds and 100 Mbps under stationary conditions. Network capacity will be at least ten times greater than in 3G networks, and seamless connectivity and global roaming will be provided across multiple networks. Some observers foresee an all-IP architecture for 4G, based entirely on packet-switched networking, eventually enhanced by the promulgation of the IPv6 network-layer standard.

An important 4G application is projected to be high-quality streamed video. Some observers believe, however, that transferring music files will be a "killer application," a belief based on the enormous market success of the iPod. At present, using 3G services, only very short music clips can be downloaded. 4G is likely to enable the download of full-length songs or music selections, which may change the market response dramatically.

Though the overall market for cellular services continues to be dominated by voice service, the demand for cellular data services grows steadily and is paralleled by the growth in use of wireless data transport in other technical regimes, such as wireless fidelity (WiFi) and Worldwide Interoperability for Microwave Access (WiMax). Many people in the telecommunications industry have long observed that customers pay for services, not technology, and this has been particularly true in the case of wireless data, where customer use of the technology has been shaped not by the technical capabilities of the service networks but rather by the steady evolution of new uses and applications.

Today we see such uses as music and video downloading, multiplayer gaming, and location-based services, applications that were not even envisioned when early wireless data systems were being conceived and standardized. It is safe to assume that as the wireless data industry continues to evolve, there will be customer demand for constantly higher data rates, and the industry will respond with new approaches to meeting these demands while also finding ways to increase efficiency in use of spectrum, which in the final analysis is always limited. Along with demands for steadily higher data rates, many industry observers also foresee a pattern of convergence, not only in integrated use of voice and data services but in intermingled use of data drawn from diverse sources. As always, customers will shape the market, and the technology will follow.

CONCLUSION

This chapter describes the basic concepts of GPRS, the mobile services it provides, and its relationship to the underlying GSM network architecture. The development of the GPRS system has enabled GSM network operators to leverage their considerable infrastructure investments by adding packet-switched data services to legacy networks designed originally for strictly circuit-switched digital voice and data services. The packet nature of GPRS is much better suited than is circuit-switched service to mobile data applications that generate inherently bursty traffic, enabling GPRS-equipped networks to achieve considerable efficiency improvements in the use of valuable spectrum radio spectrum. Another significant benefit yielded by GPRS, EDGE, and the evolving new generations of mobile data services is the enhancement of capabilities for digital communications across diverse networks. This becomes increasingly important as we see the steady progress toward convergence of network technologies, particularly wireless networks and the Internet, and the growing popularity of mobile Internet service, mobile TV, and mobile multimedia services.

GLOSSARY

1G: First-generation mobile wireless technology, employing analog signal modulation. Prominent examples included AMPS, deployed in North America, and TACS, deployed in many parts of Europe.

2G: Second-generation mobile wireless technology, employing digital voice coding, digital modulation, and providing both voice and data services.

3GPP: 3rd-Generation Partnership Project, an international cooperative agreement established in 1998 to produce a global 3G mobile phone system specification. 3GPP is a project under the aegis of the European Telecommunications Standards Institute (ETSI).

BSC: Base station controller, a GSM network element that controls traffic between an MSC and one or more BTSs. A BSC controls the handover of call connections from one BTS to another as a mobile user moves around a service network.

BSS: Base station subsystem, an entity defined in the GSM architecture, comprising the BSC and the BTS.

BTS: Base transceiver station, the GSM network element that supports radio coverage for mobile users within a limited geographical area. A BTS will typically include a number of radio transceivers, power amplifiers, and antennas, as well as signal processing elements.

CS-1, -2, -3, -4: Coding systems that provide different levels of error protection in GPRS data services.

EDGE: Enhanced data for global evolution, a service that builds upon the GPRS architecture and other improved data services envisioned for the Universal Mobile Telecommunication System (UMTS).

EGPRS: Enhanced GPRS, a service that allows combining time slots in the GSM transmission format to provide a wide menu of achievable data rates.

HSCSD: High-speed circuit-switched data, a service that allows a mobile station to access up to four time slots in each TDMA frame on a GSM channel.

IP: Internet protocol, the network-layer protocol implemented throughout the Internet.

MS: Mobile station, the wireless terminal used by a cellular service customer.

MSC: Mobile switching center, the GSM network element that provides the interface between wired public networks and the wireless network.

PCU: Packet control unit, a hardware element added to a BSC to handle GPRS data traffic.

PDCH: Packet data channel, a physical transmission channel defined by a frequency channel together with an uplink and a downlink time slot.

Phase 2+: A version of the GSM specification incorporating several new data services, including HSCSD and GPRS.

PSTN: Public switched telephone network, the legacy wired telephone network, providing traditional analog voice service as well as support for dialup modems and fax machines.

QoS: Quality of service, a profile of data-transfer attributes, which may be selected by the user on a per-call basis. The user may have different requirements relating to time delay and data reliability for different data applications.

SGSN: Serving GPRS support node, a network element added to a GSM network to route data packets in both directions between a GPRS handset and packet data networks, such as the Internet and X.25 networks.

SMS: Short message service, a bidirectional GSM service for transferring short alphanumeric messages, with a store-and-forward capability.

SNDCP: Sub-network dependent convergence protocol, a mapping and compression function residing between the network layer and lower layers of the GPRS protocol stack. It also performs segmentation, reassembly, and multiplexing.

Support nodes: A term that encompasses the SGSN and GGSN, network elements added to a GSM network in order to support packet data services.

TDMA: Time-division multiple access, a transmission scheme in which multiple users share a frequency channel, each user being given access to one or more repetitive time slots in the transmitted bit stream.

UMTS: Universal mobile telecommunications system, one of the 3G mobile phone technologies, standardized by 3GPP. It uses wideband CDMA as the underlying standard. To distinguish UMTS from competing network technologies, UMTS is sometimes called 3GSM, emphasizing the combination of the 3G nature of the technology and the GSM standard that it was designed to succeed.

CROSS REFERENCES

See *Cellular Communications Channels*; *Cellular Telephony*; *Network QoS*; *Universal Mobile Telecommunications System (UMTS)*.

REFERENCES

3rd-Generation Partnership Project (3GPP). Undated. http://www.3gpp.org.

3GPP TS 04.65. Undated. GPRS subnetwork dependent convergence protocol (SNDCP), 3rd Generation Partnership Project; echnical Specification Group GERAN.

Bates, R. J. 2002. *GPRS: General packet radiosService*. New York: McGraw-Hill.

Bilgic, M., K. Essigmann, T. Holston, M. Lord, M. Renschler, H. Traven, and E. Westerberg. 1999. Quality of service in general packet radio service. Paper presented at the 1999 IEEE International Workshop on Mobile Multimedia Communications, Colorado Springs, Colorado.

Brasche, G., and G. Walke. 1997. Concepts, services, and protocols of the new GSM Phase 2+ general packet radio service. *IEEE Communications*, August, pp. 94–104.

Cai, J., and D. J. Goodman. 1997. General packet radio service in GSM. *IEEE Communications*, October, pp. 122–31.

DeRose, J. F. 1999. *The wireless data handbook*. 4th ed. New York: John Wiley & Sons.

Eberspächer, J., H.-J. Vogel, and C. Bettstetter. 2001. *GSM switching, services, and protocols*. 2nd ed. Chichester, UK: John Wiley & Sons.

ETSI (TS 101 038 Version 5.0.1). 1997a. Digital cellular telecommunications system (Phase 2+); High-speed circuit-switched data (HSCSD)—Stage 2 (GSM 03.34).

ETSI (TS 03 64 Version 5.1.0). 1997b. Digital cellular telecommunications system (Phase 2+); General packet radio service (GPRS); Overall description of the GPRS radio interface—Stage 2 (GSM 03.64).

Furuskar, A., S. Mazur, F. Muller, and H. Olofsson. 1999. EDGE: Enhanced data rates for GSM and TDMA/136 evolution. *IEEE Personal Communications* June: pp. 56–66.

GSM World. Undated. http://www.gsmworld.com.

Hakaste, M., E. Nikula, and S. Hamiti. 2003. GSM/EDGE standards evolution (up to Release 4). In *GSM, GPRS, and EDGE performance* (2nd ed.), edited by T. Halonen, J. Romero, and J. Melero, 3–56. Chichester, UK: John Wiley & Sons.

Halonen, T., J. Romero, and J. Melero, eds. 2003. *GSM, GPRS, and EDGE performance*. Chichester, UK: John Wiley & Sons.

Haug, T. 1994. Overview of GSM: Philosophy and results. *International Journal of Wireless Information Networks* 1: 7–16.

Heine, G. 1999. *GSM Networks: Protocols, terminology, and implementation*. Norwood, MA: Artech House.

Hoffman, J., ed. 2003. *GPRS demystified*. New York: McGraw-Hill.

Holma, H., and A. Toskala. 2006. *HSDPA/HSUPA for UMTS*. Hoboken, NJ: John Wiley & Sons.

Leon-Garcia, A., and I. Widjaja. 2000. *Communication networks: Fundamental concepts and key architectures*. New York: McGraw-Hill.

Lin, S., and D. J. Costello. 2004. *Error control coding: Fundamentals and applications*. 2nd ed. Upper Saddle River, NJ: Prentice Hall.

Lischetzki, R. 2003. GPRS devices. In *GPRS demystified*, edited by J. Hoffman, 331–48. New York: McGraw-Hill.

Mobile IP. Undated. http://www.mobileip.org.

Mouly, M., and M.-B. Pautet. 1992. *The GSM system for mobile communications*. ISBN 2–9507190–0-7, privately printed.

Muller, N. J. 1995. *Wireless data networking*. Norwood, MA: Artech House.

Pahlavan, K., and A. Levesque. 1995. *Wireless information networks*. New York: John Wiley & Sons.

Pahlavan, K., and A. Levesque. 2005. *Wireless information networks* 2nd ed. Hoboken, NJ: John Wiley & Sons.

Perkins, C. E. 1998. *Mobile IP—Design principles and practices*. Reading, MA: Addison-Wesley.

Priggouris, S., L. Hadjiefthymiades, and L. Merakos. 2000. Supporting IP QoS in the general packet radio service. *IEEE Network*, September/October, pp. 8–17.

Sanders, G., L. Thorens, M. Reisky, O. Rulik, and S. Deylitz. 2003. *GPRS networks*. Chichester, UK: John Wiley & Sons.

Seurre, E., P. Savelli, and P.-J. Pietri. 2003. *EDGE for mobile Internet*. Norwood, MA: Artech House.

Steele, S., C.-C. Lee, and P. Gould. 2001. *GSM, cdmaOne, and 3G systems*. Chichester, UK: John Wiley & Sons.

Tanenbaum, A. S. 2003. *Computer networks*. 4th ed. Upper Saddle River, NJ: Prentice Hall.

Viterbi, A. J. 1995. *CDMA: Principles of spread spectrum communication*. Reading, MA: Addison-Wesley.

Watts, C., and G. Wright. 2003. Implementation and testing. In *GPRS demystified*, edited by J. Hoffman, 129–50. New York: McGraw-Hill.

Location Management in Personal Communication Systems

Jingyuan Zhang, *University of Alabama*
Ivan Stojmenovic, *University of Birmingham, UK and University of Ottawa, Canada*

INTRODUCTION

Cellular communication allows subscribers to make and receive calls from anywhere. In the United States, cellular communication was first deployed at the 800MHz band. In order to accommodate more subscribers, the FCC (Federal Communications Commission) allocated the 1900MHz band for PCSs. PCS uses a cellular network as its infrastructure. In a cellular network, a service coverage area is divided into smaller areas called cells, each of which is served by a base station (Black 1996; Rappaport 2002). Mobile terminals (also known as mobile stations) such as cell phones within a cell can be reached wirelessly through the corresponding base station. In order to reach a mobile terminal, the cellular network needs to know the cell in which the mobile terminal is located. Location management deals with how to find the cell location of a mobile terminal that is not in a call.

There are two operations in location management: location update and paging. The cellular network performs the paging operation. The goal of this operation is to find the cell in which the mobile terminal is located when an incoming call arrives for it. Once the mobile terminal is located, the incoming call can be routed to the corresponding base station. The location update operation is performed by the mobile terminal. When performing the location update operation, the mobile station sends to the network its current cell location and other related information depending on the specific location management scheme. The number of cells to be paged in the paging operation usually depends on how frequently the location update operation is performed.

The current cellular network uses the location areas location management scheme (Rahnema 1993). In this scheme, the service coverage area is divided into location areas, each of which consists of contiguous cells. When a mobile terminal enters a new location area, it needs to update its location (i.e., the new location area) with the network. When an incoming call arrives for the mobile terminal, the network pages all the cells within the location area last reported by the mobile terminal. The location areas scheme is global in the sense that all mobile terminals update their locations in the same set of cells, and it is static in the sense that the location areas in the network are fixed (Bar-Noy, Kessler and Sidi 1995; Ramanathan and Streenstrup 1996). In contrast, a location management scheme is individualized if each individual terminal can decide when and where to update its location, and it is dynamic if a mobile terminal can update its location in any cell instead of in a pre-defined set of cells. In this chapter, individualized and dynamic schemes as well as global and static schemes will be described.

The call arrival rate and the mobility of mobile terminals can greatly affect the design of a location management scheme. If the call arrival time to a mobile terminal is known beforehand, the mobile terminal can update its location just before the call arrives. In this way, the number of location updates and the scale of paging (i.e., the number of cells to be paged) will be minimized. Similarly, if the mobility of a mobile terminal is known or can be predicted, only the cells on the predicted or known mobility path need to be paged. This will also reduce the number of locate updates and the scale of paging. In this chapter, the location management schemes that take advantage of the call arrival rate and the mobility of mobile terminals will be discussed.

In the location areas scheme, no matter how well the location areas are designed, there is a ping-pong location update effect when a mobile terminal moves back and forth between two neighboring location areas. This chapter presents several location management schemes proposed to reduce or eliminate the ping-pong effect, thereby effectively reducing the number of location updates. In the location areas scheme, all the cells in the last-reported location area are paged simultaneously. If a paging delay is allowed, the paging task can be divided into multiple rounds and the most probable set of cells will be paged first. This will greatly reduce the number of cells to be paged to locate the mobile terminal. In this chapter, we will also discuss selective paging schemes that minimize the number of cells to be paged within a constrained paging delay.

This chapter introduces location management in PCS networks. It does not offer an exhaustive description of all location management schemes. Its focus is the location areas scheme currently used in PCS networks.

(For detailed classification of location management methods, the reader is referred to a recent article in Kyamakya and Jobmann 2005.) Specifically, this chapter introduces the location areas scheme, discusses its weak points, and presents some advanced schemes to overcome these weak points. The rest of this chapter is organized as follows: The Current Location Areas Scheme describes the location areas scheme, Global and Static Schemes deals with global and static schemes, while Individualized and Dynamic Schemes discusses individualized and dynamic schemes. Call-Arrival-Rate and Mobility-Based Schemes presents several location management schemes that take advantage of the call arrival rate and the mobility of mobile subscribers. Ping-Pong-Effect Reduction Schemes discusses the location update schemes that can reduce or eliminate the ping-pong effect, and Selective Paging Schemes presents selective paging schemes. Finally, Conclusion provides a summary.

THE CURRENT LOCATION AREAS SCHEME

The location areas scheme is used in current cellular networks. In the location areas scheme, the whole service coverage area is divided into location areas, each of which consists of contiguous cells. The base station of each cell broadcasts the ID of the location area to which the cell belongs, in addition to its cell ID. Listening to the control channels of the base stations, a mobile terminal knows whether it is moving out of (or into) a cell as well as a location area. The base stations in a location area are connected to a mobile switching center (MSC). An MSC is connected to the PSTN (Public Switched Telephone Network) and the PSPDN (Packet Switched Public Data Network) in a personal communication system.

Figure 1 illustrates a typical cellular network for a personal communication system in which each cell is represented by a hexagon, and each base station is represented by a triangle. Each mobile subscriber or terminal is associated with a home MSC. (The terms subscriber and terminal will be used interchangeably hereafter.) A mobile subscriber considers an MSC as the home if the mobile subscriber has subscribed for wireless services from the MSC. Each MSC has two main databases: HLR (Home Location Register) and VLR (Visitor Location Register). HLR contains information about each mobile subscriber that considers the MSC as the home. VLR contains information about the visiting mobile subscribers that are currently located in the location area covered by the MSC.

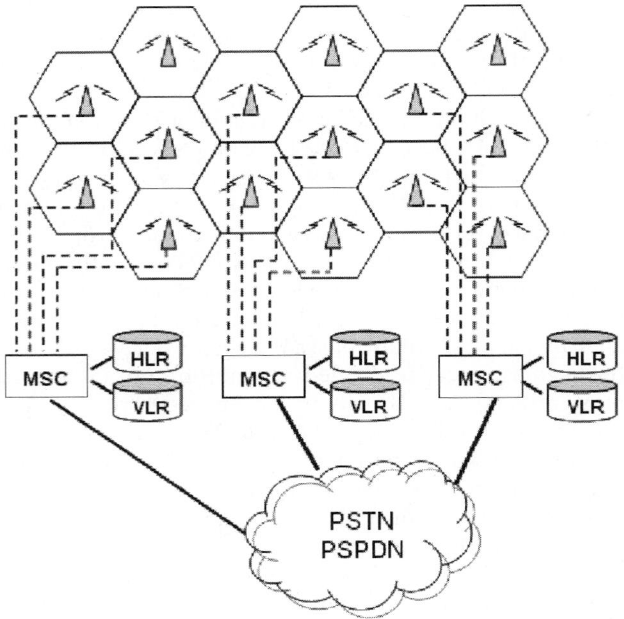

Figure 1: A typical PCS cellular network

When an incoming call arrives for a mobile terminal, it is first routed to the home MSC of the mobile terminal. The current location area of the mobile terminal in HLR is checked to determine whether the mobile terminal is located within the home MSC or within another MSC called the visited MSC (to be explained later). If the mobile terminal is located within a visited MSC, the call will be routed to the visited MSC. The visited MSC or the home MSC will be responsible for locating the mobile terminal in the corresponding location area. This process is called paging.

When a mobile terminal moves out of the location area covered by the home MSC, it enters a neighboring location area. The MSC in charge of the location area that the mobile terminal just entered is called the visited MSC, and the mobile terminal needs to register with the visited MSC. The visited MSC will record the fact that the mobile terminal is located within its location area in its VLR and will notify the mobile terminal's home MSC of the current location area. The home MSC will record the mobile terminal's current location area in its HLR. If the mobile terminal enters the visited MSC from another visited MSC, the home MSC also needs to notify the old visited MSC, and the old visited MSC removes the record about the mobile terminal from its VLR. This process is called location update.

Location update and paging are two operations of a location management scheme. The location management cost is the sum of the location update cost and the paging cost. As shown in the previous two paragraphs, in both location update and paging operations, there are a lot of signaling activities over the wireline part and the wireless part of the cellular network. Each signaling activity has a cost. However, only the wireless signaling cost is usually considered. This is mainly because the radio frequency bandwidth is limited and is not readily expandable. In contrast, the bandwidth of the wireline network is easily expandable. Therefore the paging cost is in proportion to the total number of cells paged by the cellular network, and the location update cost is in proportion to the total number of location updates made by mobile terminals.

There is a trade-off between the location update cost and the paging cost. Consider two extreme cases for the location areas scheme, namely the Never-Update and Always-Update cases (Bar-Noy, Kessler, and Sidi 1995). In the Never-Update case, there is only one location area for the whole service area; therefore no location updates are necessary and no location update cost is incurred. In this case, the paging cost will reach the maximum because the cellular network needs to page all the cells to locate a mobile terminal. In the Always-Update case, each cell forms a location area. In that case, the maximum location update cost will be incurred because a mobile terminal needs to update its location whenever it enters a cell. However, the cellular network knows exactly which cell a mobile terminal is in. When an incoming call arrives for a mobile terminal, the call can be directly routed to the cell last reported by the mobile terminal without paging. Therefore the paging cost is kept to the minimum. In general, if a mobile terminal updates its location more frequently, the location update cost will be higher. However, the cellular network will usually better know the location of the mobile terminal. Therefore the paging cost will be lower when an incoming call arrives for the mobile terminal.

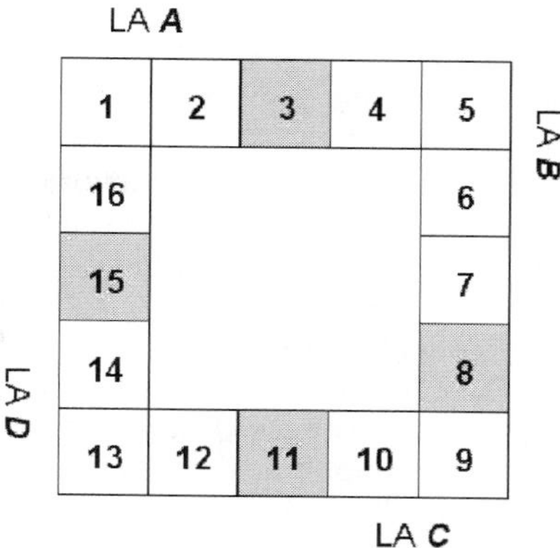

Figure 2: Relationship between reporting cells and location areas

GLOBAL AND STATIC SCHEMES

A location management scheme can be either global or individualized (Bar-Noy, Kessler, and Sidi 1995; Ramanathan and Steenstrup 1996). A location management scheme is global if all the mobile terminals update their locations at the same set of cells, and it is individualized if an individual terminal is allowed to decide when and where to perform its location update. A location management scheme can also be classified as either static or dynamic (Bar-Noy, Kessler, and Sidi 1995; Ramanathan and Steenstrup 1996). A location management scheme is static if a mobile terminal needs to perform location updates at a fixed set of cells, and it is dynamic if a mobile terminal can perform its location update at any cell, mainly because of its mobility. Usually a global scheme is static, and a good individualized scheme is dynamic. The location areas scheme used in the current system is global because all mobile terminals update their locations in the same set of cells, and it is static because the location areas are fixed. The division of location areas is usually determined by the aggregate mobility behavior and call statistics. In principle, a division should be made such that the total location management cost is minimized.

Use of reporting cells, also known as reporting centers, is another popular global and static scheme (Bar-Noy and Kessler 1993; Hae and Zhou 1997). In the reporting cells scheme, a subset of cells is designated as reporting, and the others non-reporting. A mobile terminal needs to update its location when it enters a new reporting cell. When an incoming call arrives for a mobile terminal, the cellular network pages all cells within the vicinity of the reporting cell last reported by the mobile terminal. The vicinity of a reporting cell is defined as the set of all non-reporting cells that are reachable from the reporting cell without crossing another reporting cell. For simplicity's sake, a reporting cell belongs to its own vicinity. Figure 2 illustrates four reporting cells (shown in shade) in a one dimensional cellular network. The vicinity of a reporting cell, say cell 8, consists of cells 4, 5, 6, 7, 9, 10, and 8 itself. The reporting cells scheme is global because all mobile terminals perform their location updates in the same set of reporting cells, and it is static because the reporting cells are fixed. The set of reporting cells should be selected such that the total location management cost is minimized. Many methods have been proposed to find the set of reporting cells. In Subrata and Zomaya 2003, the authors proposed three artificial life techniques including genetic algorithm, tabu search, and ant colony algorithm to identify the set of reporting cells.

Although the location areas scheme seems completely different from the reporting cells scheme, a method is proposed to derive the location areas from a set of reporting cells (Wang, Fan, and Zhang 2002; Wang and Zhang 2005). Figure 2 shows four location areas *A*, *B*, *C*, and *D* derived from four reporting cells. Basically, all the contiguous non-reporting cells form a location area. A reporting cell can form a location area by itself or can belong to a neighboring location area, depending on the amount of traffic going in and out the reporting cell. It is also observed that the location update cost difference is small between the original reporting cells scheme and the derived location areas scheme, whereas the paging cost in the original reporting cells scheme is larger than that in the derived location areas scheme. This is mainly because there is no overlapping between two location areas, and yet the vicinity of one reporting cell could overlap with vicinity of another reporting cell. Simulation has been done to verify the observation in both aggregate and individualized mobility models.

INDIVIDUALIZED AND DYNAMIC SCHEMES

A global scheme is usually static. In a global and static scheme, a subset of cells bears the burden of all location update signaling. For example, in the location areas scheme, all location updates are performed in the boundary cells between two location areas and no location updates occur in an interior cell. This causes disparity among cells in terms of location update signaling. To address this issue, many individualized and dynamic schemes have been proposed. The most classical ones are time-, movement-, and distance-based (Bar-Noy, Kessler, and Sidi 1995). In the time-based scheme, a mobile terminal updates its location every T units of time for a given time threshold T. In this way, location updates can occur in any cell. The corresponding paging strategy for the one-dimensional network topology is described as follows (Bar-Noy, Kessler, and Sidi 1995): when a call arrives for a mobile terminal, the cellular network first searches the cell last reported by the mobile terminal, say i. If the mobile terminal is not found there, the network searches the cells at distances j from i, with j starting with 1 and the process continues until the mobile terminal is found.

In the movement-based scheme, each mobile terminal maintains a counter that keeps track of the number of cell boundaries it has crossed since its last location update. The counter is initialized to zero after each location update. Whenever the mobile terminal moves out of the current cell and enters a neighboring cell, it increases the counter by one. When the counter exceeds a predefined threshold, say M, the mobile terminal updates its location and reset the counter to zero. When an incoming call arrives for a mobile terminal, the cellular network will page all the cells within a distance of M from the last-reported cell. Figure 3 illustrates the movement-based scheme with $M = 3$. It is assumed that the mobile terminal updates its location and resets the movement counter to zero at cell O. When the mobile terminal moves from cell O $\rightarrow$ A $\rightarrow$ B $\rightarrow$ C $\rightarrow$ D, its movement counter increases from $0 \rightarrow 1 \rightarrow 2 \rightarrow 3 \rightarrow 4$. Therefore when the mobile terminal enters cell D, it needs to report cell D as its current location, reset the movement counter to zero, and start a new iteration. If there is a phone call for the mobile terminal before it enters cell D, all the cells in the figure have to be paged. In Casares-Giner and Mataix-Oltra 1998, the authors enhanced the movement-based scheme by resetting the counter to zero when a mobile terminal moves back to the last-reported cell. It is shown that the enhanced version reduces the location update cost significantly with a slightly increased paging cost.

In the distance-based scheme, a mobile terminal keeps track of the distance between the current cell and the last-reported cell. The distance between two cells is the minimal number of cell boundaries that need to be crossed from the source cell to reach the destination cell. When the distance exceeds a predefined threshold, say D, the mobile terminal updates its location. When an incoming call arrives for a mobile terminal, the cellular network pages the mobile terminal in all the cells that are within a distance of D from the last-reported cell. The distance-based scheme with $D=3$ is illustrated in Figure 3; again it

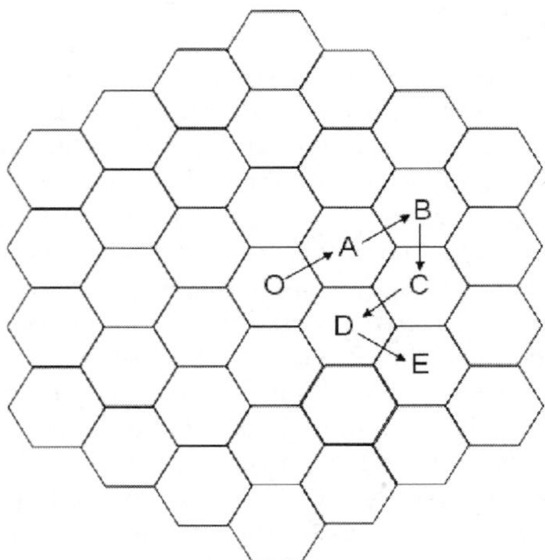

Figure 3: Comparison of movement- and distance-based schemes

is assumed that the mobile terminal updates its location at cell O. Unlike the movement-based scheme, a mobile terminal does not need to update its location as long as it stays within the cells in the figure. As with the movement-based scheme, if there is an incoming call for the mobile terminal before a new location update, all the cells in the figure have to be paged. It seems intuitive to think that the distance-based scheme would perform better than the movement-based scheme. In Bar-Noy, Kessler, and Sidi (1995), the authors have shown that the distance-based scheme performs significantly better than the time-based and movement-based schemes in both memoryless and Markovian memory movement patterns. However, it has been claimed that it is hard to compute the distance between two cells or that it requires a lot of storage to maintain the distance information among all cells (Akyildiz, Ho, and Lin 1996; Li, Kameda, and Li 2000). In Nocetti, Stojmenovic, and Zhang 2002, it is shown that, if the cell IDs can be assigned properly, the distance between two cells can be computed very easily. Specifically, the authors proposed two three-component cell address forms, i.e., the shortest-path form and the zero-positive form.

In the time-based scheme, sequential paging is used. If the simultaneous paging is required, the cellular network has to know the paging radius. To address this issue, the time-based scheme is extended in Zhang 2000. In addition to keeping the elapsed time, the scheme in Zhang 2000 also keeps track of the maximal distance traveled since last update. When it is time for location update, the mobile terminal reports both its current cell and the traveled maximal distance that can be used later as the paging radius. A mobile terminal performs its location update either when the timer expires or when the traveled maximal distance exceeds the last-reported maximal distance. The scheme is a combination of the time-based and distance-based schemes.

The dynamic location management scheme proposed in Naor 2000 is also based on both time and distance. Specifically, both the cellular network and the mobile terminal keep a look-up table that consists of a distance row D_1, $D_2, \ldots, D_k$ and a time row $T_1, T_2, \ldots, T_k$. The table describes the relationship between the distance and the time: the distance decreases while the time increases. That is, $D_1 > D_2 > \ldots > D_k$ and $T_1 < T_2 < \ldots < T_k$. A mobile terminal updates its location if the distance it has traveled exceeds Di, when time T_i has elapsed since the last update. Therefore, if a mobile terminal has not performed any location update when time T_i has elapsed, the mobile terminal is within a distance of D_i from the last-reported cell. In this case, when an incoming call arrives for the mobile terminal, the cellular network only needs to page the mobile terminal in all the cells that are within a distance of D_i from the last-reported cell. The nice feature of this scheme is that, if the mobile terminal has not updated its location when time elapses, the paging area for the mobile terminal automatically becomes smaller. Therefore, the paging cost is reduced without any additional location update cost. Performance analysis shows that the look-up table based scheme performs better than the time-based, distance-based, and location areas scheme.

The look-up table based scheme in Naor 2000 works very well with a mobile terminal traveling at a low speed.

At a low speed, a mobile terminal cannot travel the corresponding distance when a specified time elapses. In this case, the mobile terminal does not need to update its location, and the paging area will be small when there is an incoming call for the mobile terminal. However, the scheme does not perform well when the incoming call arrival rate is high or when the traveling speed of a mobile terminal is high. To address these two issues, the authors in Wang and Zhang 2002 proposed to use an enhanced look-up table that consists of two parts. The distance in the first part increases while the time increases, and as in the original look-up table, the distance in the second part decreases with increasing time. By introducing the first part of the table, the paging cost for a call arriving shortly after a location update will be greatly reduced. Numerical simulation shows that the enhanced look-up table based scheme performs well for mobile users traveling at a high speed as well as for those traveling at a low speed.

CALL-ARRIVAL-RATE AND MOBILITY-BASED SCHEMES

In the location areas scheme, when an incoming call arrives for a mobile terminal, the cellular network will page for the mobile terminal within its last-reported location area. However, a location area is usually large, and a mobile terminal normally moves only among a fraction of cells in the location area (Rose and Yates 1995). If the mobility of a mobile terminal is known, there is no need to page all the cells in the location area; this leads to reduction in the paging cost. Similarly, the call arrival rate can affect the design of a location management scheme. If the probability is low that a mobile terminal will receive a call, it is a waste of wireless bandwidth to ask the mobile terminal to keep updating its locations. Therefore, a good location management scheme should take advantage of the mobility and the call arrival rate of individual subscribers.

The call arrival rate and mobility of a subscriber are used to dynamically decide the size of location areas for that individual subscriber in Xie, Tabbane and Goodman 1993. Analysis results show that the proposed dynamic scheme uses significantly less signaling bandwidth than the fixed location areas scheme when the call arrival rates are user-variant or time-variant. Furthermore, without fixed borders of location areas, the proposed scheme allocates the signaling burden of location updates more evenly. In Akyildiz and Ho 1995, the mobility pattern and the incoming call arrival probability of a mobile terminal are used to decide whether it needs to update its location. Whenever a mobile terminal enters a new cell, it computes the paging cost if it does not perform a location update. The weighted paging cost, i.e., the paging cost multiplied by the call arrival probability, will be compared with the cost of one location update. A location update will be performed if the weighted paging cost is more than the cost of one location update.

A selective location update strategy was introduced into the location areas scheme in Sen, Bhattacharya, and Das (1999). The idea is that if a mobile terminal has little chance of receiving a call while within a location area either because it remains there for a very short time or it has an extremely low probability of receiving a call, then wireless bandwidth would be wasted by performing a location update. In the scheme presented by Sen, Bhattacharya, and Das, a mobile terminal updates its location only at a subset of location areas, called update areas. The corresponding paging cost will be higher because the cellular network needs to track down a mobile terminal's current location area from the last-reported location area. To determine the update areas, a genetic algorithm is used to optimize the total location management cost.

Semi-real-time velocity information about a mobile terminal is used in Wan and Lin 1999 with either the movement- or distance-based scheme to dynamically compute the paging zone for an incoming call. If only the magnitude of the velocity is used, the resulting paging zone is a smaller circular area; if both magnitude and direction are used, then the resulting paging zone is an even smaller sector. The analysis and simulation results of Wan and Lin show that their schemes have a significantly lower cost than the standard location areas scheme.

In the distance-based scheme, the cellular network locates a mobile terminal by paging the cells around the last-reported cell. This works well if the mobile terminal follows the random walk mobility model. In Liang and Haas 1999, the authors argued that the Gauss-Markov mobility model is more realistic than the random walk mobility model. The Gauss-Markov mobility model is then used to predict the future cell of a mobile terminal. The mobile terminal updates its location if it reaches some threshold distance away from the predicted cell. When an incoming call arrives for the mobile terminal, the cellular network pages the cells around the predicted cell instead of the last reported cell. The simulations demonstrate the performance advantage of the predictive distance-based scheme over the regular distance-based scheme. In Tsai and Jan 1999, the authors proposed a look-ahead strategy to be used with the distance-based scheme. The look-ahead strategy uses a multi-scale, straight-oriented mobility model, referred to as normal walk, to compute the optimal future cell. The optimal future cell is reported at location update instead of the current cell. The analysis of Tsai and Jan shows that the look-ahead strategy effectively reduces the tracking cost for mobile subscribers with large mobility scales.

A subscriber profile is used to dynamically create location areas for each subscriber (Scourias and Knuz 1997). A subscriber profile describes the subscriber's average duration of stay in each cell, and the number of transitions the subscriber has made from cell to cell. When a mobile terminal enters a cell that is not in its current location area, a location update is performed and a new location area is created from the new cell and the profile. First, the new cell will be in the new location area. Then the cells that were visited frequently from the new cell, referred to as the neighbor ring of the new cell, will be added to the new location area in order of decreasing frequency. Once the first neighbor ring of the new cell has been added, the above process is repeated using the newly added cells, and the process is repeated again until the location area is full or there are no more cells to be added. When an incoming call arrives for the mobile terminal, cells in the current location area with above-average duration of stay will be paged first. If the first attempt fails, all the cells in the current location area will be paged. Their experiments using an activity based mobility model show that the the profile-based dynamic location area scheme significantly outperforms the fixed location areas scheme.

In the LeZi-Update scheme proposed in Bhattacharya and Das (1999), a mobile terminal reports a new path of location areas traveled instead of a new location area, and a dictionary is used to store all the traveled paths. The dictionary, in fact, is the subscriber profile maintained by both the subscriber and the cellular network. Initially, the dictionary is empty, and a path will be reported if and only if there is no such path in the dictionary. Therefore, every proper prefix of the reported path is in the dictionary. The dictionary is stored as a trie, and the path to be reported can be encoded as the index of the largest proper prefix plus the last location area. Therefore, the location update cost is not significantly increased compared to the location areas scheme. When an incoming call arrives for the mobile terminal, the cellular network will use the trie and the last-reported path to figure out all possible paths and therefore all possible location areas for the mobile terminal. A blending weight vector is used to compute the blended probability of every possible location area. Those location areas can then be paged in order of decreasing blended probability.

PING-PONG-EFFECT REDUCTION SCHEMES

In the location areas scheme, location areas are fixed. If a mobile subscriber lives near the boundary between two location areas, there will be excessive location updates when the mobile subscriber moves back and forth between two neighboring location areas. This phenomenon is called the ping-pong effect. Besides the regular ping-pong effect, there is another kind of ping-pong effect, referred to as the generalized ping-pong effect that occurs around a corner. A corner is the intersection of three different cells that belong to three different location areas. When mobile terminals move around a corner, excessive location updates also occur. Figure 4 illustrates regular and generalized ping-pong effects. In the left figure, the regular ping-pong effect happens when a mobile terminal keeps moving between *A* and *B* that belong to two different location areas. In the right figure, the generalized ping-pong effect occurs when a mobile terminal moves around *A*, *B*, and *C* that belong to three different location areas. In Fan, Stojmenovic, and Zhang 2002, it is shown that this regular ping-pong effect could account for 14% of the total location update cost, and the generalized ping-pong effect could account for 7% of the total location update cost. Several location management schemes have been proposed to reduce or eliminate the ping-pong effect. Some of them are also able to reduce or eliminate the generalized ping-pong effect.

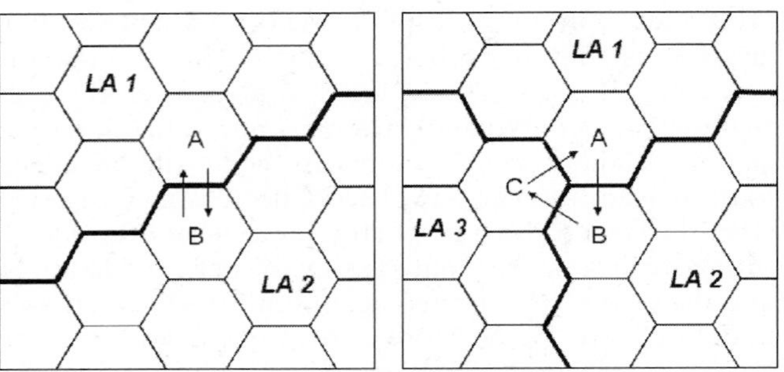

Figure 4: Regular and generalized ping-pong effects

In the location areas scheme, the most recently visited location area is recorded in a mobile terminal. In the two location scheme, a mobile terminal memorizes two most recently visited location areas instead of one (Lin 1997). When the mobile terminal enters a new location area, it checks whether the new location area is in the memory. If the new location is in the memory, no location update is necessary. Otherwise, the most recently visited location area will be kept and the other location area will be replaced by the new location area. Consequently, a location update is needed to report such a change to the cellular network. When a mobile terminal moves back and forth between two location areas, both location areas are memorized and no location updates are needed. Therefore the regular ping-pong effect has been eliminated. However, the two location scheme cannot eliminate the generalized ping-pong effect because the mobile terminal cannot memorize all three location areas around a corner. To eliminate the generalized ping-pong effect, something like a three location area scheme is needed.

In the location areas scheme, two location areas are non-overlapping in terms of cells. In the overlapping location area scheme (Gu and Rappaport 1999), two neighboring location areas can be overlapping, and the boundary cells of a location area can belong to more than one location area. Assume a mobile terminal moves out of cell *A* and enters cell *B* that belongs to a new location area. Due to the overlapping nature of the location areas, cell *B* is not a boundary cell of the new location area. If the mobile terminal moves back to cell *A* from cell *B*, it is still in the new location area. Therefore no location update is needed, and the regular ping-pong effect is eliminated. However, if the degree of overlapping between two location areas is small and the mobile terminal moves back multiple cells, a location update is still possible. One solution is to make the area of overlapping large, which also eliminates the generalized ping-pong effect. To make the area of overlapping large, the location areas themselves must be large, which leads to a high paging cost.

To reduce the ping-pong effect, the authors in Chung, Choo and Youn (2001) proposed a location update scheme using a virtual layer, referred to as the virtual layer scheme. The scheme places a virtual layer of location areas on the original location area layer such that each original location area will be covered by three virtual location areas, and vice versa. In the scheme, each cell belongs to two location areas. One is in the original layer and the other is in the virtual layer. If a mobile terminal leaves a location area in the original layer by moving from cell *A* to cell *B*, it will enter a new location area in the virtual layer instead of the original layer. The placement of the two layers guarantees that cell *B* will not be at the boundary of the new location area in the virtual layer. When the

Table 1: Ping-Pong-Effect Reduction Schemes

Scheme	Regular Ping-Pong Effects	Generalized Ping-Pong Effects
Two Location (Lin 1997)	Eliminated	
Overlapping Location Area (Gu and Rappaport 1999)	Eliminated	Eliminated if overlapping is large
Virtual Layer (Chung, Choo, and Youn 2001)	Reduced	
Triple-layer (Fan, Stojmenovic, and Zhang 2002)	Eliminated	Eliminated
Multiple-layer (Fan and Zhang 2004)	Eliminated	Eliminated

mobile terminal moves back to cell A from cell B, it is still in the same location area of the virtual layer. Therefore, no location update is needed. It is shown that the virtual layer scheme can significantly reduce the regular ping-pong effect. However, the virtual layer scheme cannot completely eliminate the regular ping-pong location updates. Sometimes it may introduce more ping-pong location updates at the intersection point made by the two boundaries from two different layers. The intersection point cannot be completely covered by a third location area. The virtual layer scheme is not able to eliminate the generalized ping-pong effect either.

To eliminate both the regular and generalized ping-pong effects, a triple-layer location management scheme is proposed in Fan, Stojmenovic and Zhang (2002). Three layers of location areas are placed properly such that any boundary or corner in one layer will be completely covered by a location area of another layer. In the triple layer scheme, each cell belongs to three location areas in three different layers. If a mobile terminal moves out of the location area of the current layer, it could register with any of two location areas in the other two layers. The mobile terminal chooses the layer whose corresponding location area center is closer to the mobile terminal. Therefore, location update will not be immediate. Simulation results have shown that the triple-layer scheme performs better than the two location scheme, the overlapping scheme, and the virtual layer scheme in reducing ping-pong effects.

A multi-layer location management scheme is a generalization of the triple-layer scheme (Fan and Zhang 2004). A multi-layer scheme is referred to as the k-layer scheme if a total of k layers are employed. In the k-layer scheme, any cell belongs to k location areas, each of which is in a different layer. If a mobile terminal moves out of the location area of the current layer, it could register with any of the other k-1 location areas of the corresponding k-1 layers. To keep the mobile terminal away from the boundary in the new location area, the mobile terminal will choose the layer whose corresponding location area center is closer to the mobile terminal. It is shown the multi-layer scheme bridges the static location area scheme and the dynamic distance-based scheme. Although increasing the number of layers reduces the location update cost, the difference will be very small after the saturated number of layers is reached. Table 1 summarizes how these schemes eliminate or reduce the regular and generalized ping-pong effects.

SELECTIVE PAGING SCHEMES

In the current location areas scheme, to locate a mobile terminal within a location area, all the cells within the location area are paged simultaneously. The paging cost will be the maximum, and it is in proportion to the number of cells in the location area. If the paging delay is not constrained, the cells in the location can be paged sequentially until the mobile terminal is found. This will greatly reduce the number of cells to be paged, thereby reducing the paging cost. It is obvious that the paging strategy mentioned earlier in the time-based scheme (Bar-Noy, Kessler, and Sidi 1995) has no constrained paging delay.

The paging delay is an important QOS (Quality of Service) metric in location management. The paging delay cannot be arbitrarily large. If the paging delay is large, the caller may perceive the delay. In addition, if the paging delay is large, a mobile terminal may move out of the current cell or even the current location area during the paging process. In general, there is a trade-off between the paging cost and the paging delay. If all the cells have to be paged simultaneously, the paging cost reaches the maximum, whereas the paging delay is the minimum. On the other hand, if there is no constraint on the paging delay, the cells can be paged sequentially in order of decreasing probability, which leads to the minimal paging cost. Therefore, many researchers proposed selective paging schemes to minimize the paging cost under an acceptable delay constraint. Figure 5 illustrates paging with no delay and with a constrained delay. In the left figure, no delay is allowed and all the cells have to be paged simultaneously. In the right figure, four page cycles are allowed, and all the cells are divided into four rings named from Ring 0 through Ring 3. A cell is in Ring n if and only if the cell has a distance of n from the last reported cell. The four rings will be paged sequentially, and the paging process stops whenever the mobile terminal is located.

Given a probability distribution on user location, the relationship between the paging delay and the paging cost were formally studied in Rose and Yates 1995. It is shown that the optimal paging strategy that minimizes

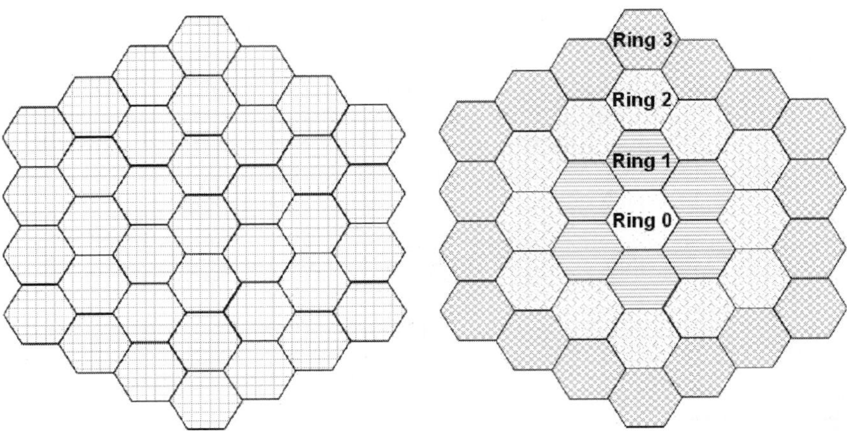

Figure 5: Paging with no delay and with a constrained delay

the expected number of locations paged is to page each location sequentially in order of decreasing probability. Because the paging delay resulting from sequential paging can be unacceptably large, Rose and Yates also consider the problem of minimizing the paging cost under constraints of the paging delay. It is also shown that if a moderate average paging delay is acceptable, the average paging cost to locate a mobile user can still be significantly reduced.

A dynamic selective paging strategy was introduced into the location areas scheme in Abutaleb and Li (1997). The goal is also to minimize the paging cost, subject to a constraint on the paging delay. If m is an acceptable paging delay, a location area will be partitioned into m partitions. Based on the mobility pattern and call arrival rate of the mobile subscriber, the partitions of the location area are computed such that the average number of cells paged are minimized. When an incoming call arrives, the cellular network pages the partitions sequentially until the mobile subscriber is located.

The selective paging strategy was studied with the movement-based scheme (Akyildiz, Ho, and Lin 1995). In the movement-based scheme, when an incoming call arrives, the cellular network pages the called mobile terminal within its residing area, i.e., all the cells that have a distance below the movement-threshold to the last-reported cell by the mobile terminal. That is, the paging is done within one polling cycle. However, if more than one paging cycle is allowed, the authors propose to apply a selective paging strategy in which the residing area of the called terminal is partitioned into a number of subareas, and then each subarea is polled, one after another, in order of decreasing probability until the called mobile terminal is located. It is shown that if the paging delay is increased from one to three polling cycles, the total location update and paging cost is reduced to the midpoint between the maximum and the minimum. It is shown that although increasing the allowable paging delay reduces the total cost, a large paging delay does not necessarily translate into a significant total cost reduction. Similarly, the selective paging strategy was applied to the distance-based scheme (Ho and Akyildiz 1995). The result shows that the reduction in the total cost of location update and paging is significant even for a maximum paging delay of two polling cycles. It is also shown that in most cases, the average total costs are very close to the minimum when a maximum paging delay of three polling cycles is used.

In the predictive distance-based scheme (Liang and Haas 1999), the future cell of a mobile terminal is predicted, and the mobile terminal performs a location update whenever it reaches some threshold distance (referred to as the update distance) from the predicted cell. When an incoming call arrives, the cellular network pages the mobile terminal starting from the predicted cell outwards, in a shortest-distance-first order, until the mobile is located. The scheme does not deal with the paging delay. If the paging delay is imposed, it is not hard to evenly divide all possible rings around the predicted cell, and page the divisions from the inside outwards.

CONCLUSION

The personal communication system uses a cellular network as its infrastructure. In a cellular network, a service coverage area is divided into cells, each of which is served by a base station. When an incoming call arrives for a mobile terminal, the network needs to know the exact cell location of the mobile terminal so the call can be routed to the corresponding base station. Location management keeps track of mobile terminals. This is accomplished using two basic operations: location update and paging. When an incoming call arrives for the mobile terminal, the network performs the paging operation to find the cell in which the mobile terminal is located. The number of cells to be paged usually depends on how frequently the mobile terminal performs the location update operation.

The current cellular network uses the location areas location management scheme. Although simple, the location areas scheme has a lot of weak points. This chapter identified these weak points and discussed the schemes to eliminate or reduced these weak points. The location areas scheme is global and static. In a global and static scheme, a subset of cells bears the burden of all location update signaling. This chapter has reviewed several individualized and dynamic schemes that are able to more evenly distribute the signaling burden of location updates. In the location areas scheme, a location update is performed whenever the mobile terminal enters a new location area, regardless of the call arrival rate of the mobile terminal, and all the cells in the last-reported location area need to be paged regardless of the mobility of the mobile terminal. This chapter introduced some mobility and call arrival rate based location management schemes. In the location areas scheme, the ping-pong effect (i.e., an excessive number of location updates) exists when mobile terminals move back and forth between two neighboring location areas. This chapter discussed several location update schemes to eliminate or reduce the ping-pong effects. Again in the location areas scheme, all the cells in the last-reported location area are paged simultaneously. This chapter discussed selective paging schemes that minimize the number of cells to be paged within a constrained paging delay.

ACKNOWLEDGMENT

The authors thank Professor Hossein Bidgoli and five anonymous referees for their constructive comments and suggestions that greatly improved the quality of this chapter. The authors also thank Li Gao of the University of Alabama for drawing the figures in this chapter. This research is partially supported by NSERC.

GLOSSARY

BS (Base Station): A fixed station in the cellular network that connects mobile stations to the backbone network, such as the public switched telephone network.

Call-arrival-rate: The number of phone calls received per unit of time.

Cell: The area covered by a base station.

Cellular Network: A network that divides a geographic area into cells to reuse the radio frequency allocated for cellular communications.

HLR (Home Location Register): An MSC database that stores information about the users who consider the area covered by the MSC as their home.

Location Areas: A location management scheme that divides the coverage area into location areas, each of which consists of contiguous cells.

Location Management: A subject that deals with how to track a mobile station when the mobile station is not in a call.

Location Update: Signals sent by a mobile terminal to the personal communication system to report its current location.

MS (Mobile Station): A station in the cellular network that can communicate with base stations via radio even if it is in motion. It is also called a mobile terminal.

MSC (Mobile Switching Center): The switching center that interconnects cellular phones with the land telephone network.

PCS (Personal communication systems): The system designed for wireless communications using the 1900MHz band.

PSPDN (Packet Switched Public Data Network): A network that divides the data into packets to be transported individually within the network.

PSTN (Public Switched Telephone Network): The regular wireline telephone network.

Paging: Signals sent from the personal communication system to locate a mobile terminal when a phone call is made to it.

Ping-pong-effect: A phenomenon of excessive location updates when the mobile subscriber moves back and forth between two neighboring location areas.

Selective Paging: A strategy to divide a paging area into several regions based on a certain criterion and to page these regions sequentially or selectively instead of simultaneously to reduce the paging cost.

VLR (Visitor Location Register): An MSC database to temporarily store information about the subscribers who are visiting the area covered by the MSC.

CROSS REFERENCES

See *Cellular Communications Channels*; *Cellular Telephony*.

REFERENCES

Abutaleb, A. and V. O. K. Li. 1997. Paging strategy optimization in personal communication systems, *Wireless Networks*, 3: 195–204.

Akyildiz, I.F. and J. S. M. Ho. 1995. Dynamic mobile user location update for wireless PCS networks, *Wireless Networks*, 1: 187–196.

Akyildiz, I. F., J. S. M. Ho, and Y.-B. Lin. 1996. Movement-based location update and selective paging for PCS networks, *IEEE/ACM Transactions on Networking*, 4 (4): 629–638.

Bar-Noy, A. and I. Kessler. 1993. Tracking mobile users in wireless communications networks, *IEEE Transactions on Information Theory*, 39 (6): 1877-1886.

Bar-Noy, A., I. Kessler, and M. Sidi. 1995. Mobile users: To update or not to update? *Wireless Networks*, 1: 175–185.

Black, U. 1996. *Mobile and wireless networks*, Upper Saddle River, NJ: Prentice Hall.

Bhattacharya, A. and S. K. Das. 1999. LeZi-Update: An information-theoretic approach to track mobile users in PCS networks, MOBICOM'99, Seattle, WA, 1999, 1–12.

Casares-Giner, V. and J. Mataix-Oltra. 1998. On movement-based mobility tracking strategy: An enhanced version, *IEEE Communications Letters*, 2 (2): 45–47.

Chung, D., H. Choo, and H. Y. Youn. 2001. Reduction of location update traffic using virtual layer in PCS, *Proceedings of the 30th Annual International Conference on Parallel Processing*, Valencia, Spain, (September 2001): 331–338.

Fan, G., I. Stojmenovic, and J. Zhang. 2002. A triple layer location management strategy for wireless cellular networks, *Proceedings of the 11th International Conference on Computer Communications and Networks*, Miami, FL, (October 2002): 489–492.

Fan, G. and J. Zhang. 2004. A multi-layer location management scheme that bridges the best static scheme and the best dynamic scheme, *Proceedings of the Fifth International Conference on Mobile Data Management*, Berkeley, CA, (January 2004), 125–132.

Gu, D. and S. S. Rappaport. 1999. Mobile user registration in cellular systems with overlapping location areas, *Proceedings of the 50th Vehicular Technology Conference*, (May 1999): 802–806.

Hac, A. and X. Zhou. 1997. Locating strategies for personal communication networks: A novel tracking strategy, *IEEE Journal on Selected Areas in Communications*, 15 (8): 1425–1436.

Ho, J.S.M., and I. F. Akyildiz. 1995. Mobile user location update and paging under delay constraints, *Wireless Networks*, 1: 413–425.

Kyamakya, K. and K. Jobmann. 2005. Location management in cellular networks: Classification of the most important paradigms, realistic simulation framework, and relative performance analysis, *IEEE Transactions on Vehicular Technology*, 54 (2): 687–708.

Li, J., H. Kameda, and K. Li. 2000. Optimal dynamic mobility management for PCS networks, *IEEE/ACM Transactions on Networking*, 8(3): 319–327.

Liang, B. and Z. J. Haas. 1999. Predictive distance-based mobility management for PCS networks, INFOCOM'99, New York City, NY, (March 1999): 1377–1384.

Lin, Y.-B. 1997. Reducing location update cost in a PCS network, *IEEE/ACM Transactions on Networking*, 5, (1): 25–33.

Naor, Z. 2000. Tracking mobile users with uncertain parameters, MobiCom'00, Boston, MA, (August 2000): 110–119.

Nocetti, F. G., I. Stojmenovic, and J. Zhang. 2002. Addressing and routing in hexagonal networks with applications for tracking mobile users and connection rerouting in cellular networks, *IEEE Transactions on Parallel and Distributed Systems*, 13 (9): 963–971.

Rahnema, M. 1993. Overview of the GSM system and protocol architecture, *IEEE Communications Magazine*, 31 (4): 92–100.

Ramanathan, S. and M. Steenstrup. 1996. A survey of routing techniques for mobile communication networks, *Mobile Networks and Applications*, 1: 89–104.

Rappaport, T. S., 2002. *Wireless communications: Principles and practice*, Upper Saddle River, NJ: Prentice Hall.

Rose, C. and R. Yates. 1995. Minimizing the average cost of paging under delay constraints, *Wireless Networks*, 1: 211–219.

Scourias, J. and T. Knuz. 1997. A dynamic individualized location management algorithm, *Proceedings of the 8th IEEE International Symposium on Personal, Indoor, and Mobile Radio Communications*, Helsinki, Finland, (September 1997): 1004–1008.

Sen, S. K., A. Bhattacharya, and S. K. Das. 1999. A selective location update strategy for PCS users, *Wireless Networks*, 5: 313–326.

Subrata, R. and A. Y. Zomaya. 2003. A comparison of three artificial life techniques for reporting cell planning in mobile computing, *IEEE Transactions on Parallel and Distributed Systems*, 14, (2): 142–153.

Tsai, I.-F., and R.-H. Jan. 1999. The lookahead strategy for distance-based location tracking in wireless cellular networks, *ACM Mobile Computing and Communications Review*, 3(4): 27–38.

Wan, G. and E. Lin. 1999. Cost reduction in location management using semi-realtime movement information, *Wireless Networks*, 5: 245–256.

Wang, H., G. Fan and J. Zhang. 2002. Performance comparison of location areas and reporting centers under aggregate movement behavior mobility models, *Proceedings of the 31st Annual International Conference on Parallel Processing*, Vancouver, Canada, August 2002, 445–352.

Wang, H. and J. Zhang. 2005. Performance comparison of location areas and reporting centres under individualized mobility models, *International Journal of High Performance Computing and Networking*, 3(5/6): 405–416.

Wang, Z. and J. Zhang. 2002. A speed-adaptive location management scheme, *Proceedings of the 9th International Conference on Parallel and Distributed Systems*, Taiwan, December 2002, 597–602.

Xie, H., S. Tabbane, and D. J. Goodman. 1993. Dynamic location area management and performance analysis, *Proceedings of the 43rd IEEE Vehicular Technology Conference, Secaucus*, NJ, (May):536–539.

Zhang, J. 2000. A cell ID assignment scheme and its applications, *Proc. ICPP Workshop on Wireless Networks and Mobile Computing, Toronto, Canada*, (August), 507–512.

Mobility Management in Heterogeneous Networks

Guangbin Fan, *Intel Corporation*
Xuming Lu, *University at Buffalo, SUNY*
Song Ci, *University of Nebraska, Lincoln*

INTRODUCTION

As a result of the development of communication technologies, a variety of wireless networks have been deployed worldwide. The third-generation (3G) networks, including code division multiple access 2000 (CDMA2000) and the universal mobile telecommunications system (UMTS), support both voice and data traffic from 144 kbps to 2.4 Mbps. They constitute the backbone of future wide area networks (WANs). In the meantime, technologies coming along the evolutionary path (e.g., global system for mobile communications [GSM], interim standard 95 [IS-95], general packet radio service [GPRS], and code division multiple access 1x [CDMA1x]) will coexist for a long time. The Institute of Electrical and Electronics Engineers (IEEE) 802.16 Working Group creates standards for broadband wireless access, Worldwide Interoperability for Microwave Access (WiMAX), in metropolitan area networks (MANs) with a scalable solution to extend fiber optic backbones. IEEE 802.16 supports point-to-multipoint data transmission at rates up to 134 Mbps.

The interest in wireless local area network (WLAN) technology has surged in recent years due to its low cost and high data rates. WLAN systems are widely deployed in hotspot locations, such as airports, hotels, and coffee shops, as well as in business enterprises and homes. WLAN has developed many versions, including 802.11a, 802.11b, 802.11h, 802.11i, 802.11n, and so forth. These technologies can provide relatively high-speed communication (up to 540 Mbps in 802.11n) but limited coverage area. The UWB 802.15 family technologies can even provide Gbps speed in personal area networks (PANs). These networks may have overlapping coverage areas and different cell sizes, ranging from a few meters to tens of kilometers as shown in Figure 1. Some technologies complement one another and may compete for market shares. This naturally calls for integration in terms of authentication, billing,

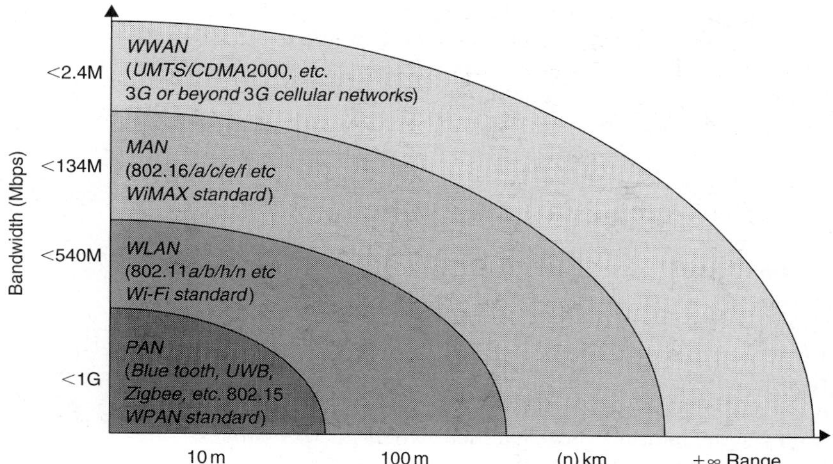

Figure 1: Wireless networks range-to-speed plot

roaming, mobility, and quality of service (QoS) among all of these technologies. Mobility management issues in such a heterogeneous environment have become a hot research topic, aiming to enable users to move around while staying connected and receiving calls, data streams, and other services.

The mobility issue is accompanied by the development of wireless local area networks. In 1971, the first WLAN prototype, composed of seven computers, was deployed by the University of Hawaii. In 1990, following three generations of development, the IEEE 802 Executive Committee established the 802.11 Working Group to standardize the WLAN. In the meantime, in the early 1990s, GSM/CDMA offered a 9.6 kbps data-service standard. The vertical mobility concept was first introduced by the BARWAN project at the University of California–Berkeley to deal with global roaming. Since then, the research and development of mobility management schemes has been very active. Currently, intensive efforts are being made to address the mobility issues among some specific interfaces. Mobility issues will be raised mainly in the following three circumstances:

Network availability—The network situation changes from time to time as a result of interference, equipment noise, and multipath loss factors. The serving access point (AP) may fall out of service due to certain errors. The terminal should have the ability to transit connections in overlay networks.

Client moving—The mobile node (MN) moves away from an AP and enters into a new AP, or roams from one network to another network in overlay networks.

Load balancing—MN may be switched to a neighboring AP in order to reduce the load on the current AP and guarantee QoS.

Terminal devices must be capable of automatically detecting multiple-access networks in order to support seamless transition from one network to another. Mobility management has two major functions: location management and handoff management (Akyildiz et al. 1999). Location management keeps track of the position information of the MN through the registration and paging processes. Authentication is usually done in the registration process. The paging area depends on the network topology and design. The size of the paging cluster should not be too large or too small, to avoid unnecessary system overhead. The handoff management process allows the MN to stay connected while moving around the overlay networks. These two functions will interact instead of standing alone in modern mobility management schemes; for example, the location process can assist handoff decisions.

There are two types of handoff mechanisms: horizontal handoff and vertical handoff. The former refers to the movement among different access points in the same network interface, which is also called intra-system handoff. Horizontal handoff is theoretically easier to handle. Vertical handoff often refers to the movement under different technologies or network systems, which is also called intersystem handoff. For instance, when an MN moves from a WLAN hotspot to 3G networks, vertical handoff takes place to support seamless service transition. For the purposes of our discussion, a domain refers to a cluster of certain subnetwork elements. Micromobility essentially involves intradomain handoffs in which the MN is handled without external coordination. Macromobility involves moving between two domains that may belong to different types of networks or organizations.

In comparison to macro- and micromobility, the terminology of *horizontal* and *vertical* reflects the wireless access network technology change instead of the domain-based subnetwork change. Therefore, there are subclasses such as vertical macromobility, horizontal vertical macromobility, vertical micromobility, and horizontal micromobility (Akyildiz, Xie, and Mohanty 2004). Regardless of the mobility model, the handoff decision can be made on either the terminal or network side. If the handoff is totally decided by the terminal side, it is called mobile-controlled handoff; if the handoff is decided by the network side, it is called network-controlled handoff. In some systems, the terminal provides some measurements to the network, and the network executes the handoff. This is called a mobile-assisted handoff mechanism.

Many mobility solutions have been proposed to support both macro- and micromobility, either in homogeneous or heterogeneous circumstances. The idea is to achieve a trade-off between QoS, efficiency, and latency requirements. The issue of cost in terms of additional network infrastructure to implement these solutions will also affect the application of these protocols. The handoff latency should be reduced to as small as possible. Once the handoff begins, the process is expected to complete efficiently. Here, efficiency refers to less signaling traffic and fewer unnecessary handoffs. The quality of service is becoming a more and more important factor that needs to be evaluated with the development of multimedia applications. It is, of course, ideal to meet all criteria for a scheme; in reality, these factors must usually balance against one another. For example, the tolerance of short interruption will lead to lower latency and higher efficiency. Figure 2 illustrates the trade-off among the influencing factors. Compromised solutions are generally looked for inside the

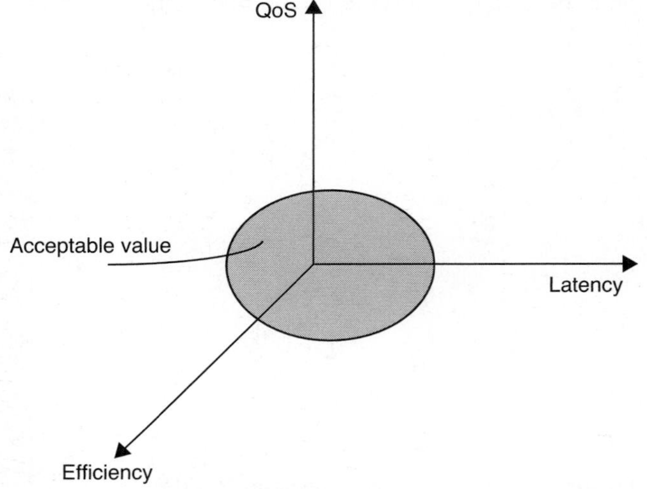

Figure 2: Influencing factors tradeoff

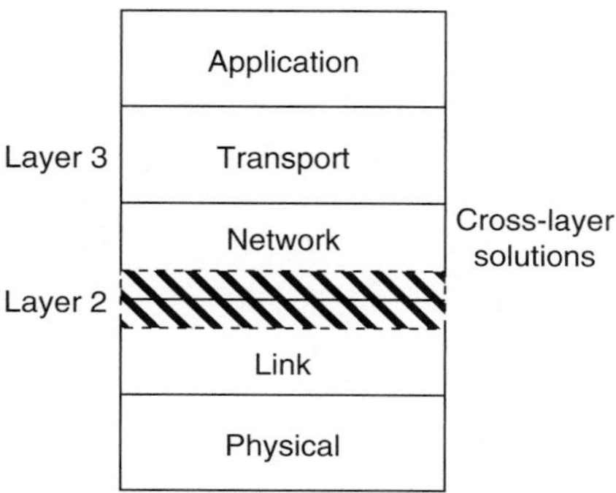

Figure 3: Network layers for mobility

gray area, which can satisfy all the criterias of QoS, latency, and efficiency.

Currently there are various mobility management schemes aimed at different network layers, including the data-link layer, network layer, and transport layer. Eddy (2004) attempts to answer the question of which layer should handle mobility, focusing on the properties of the layers themselves instead of a particular mobility scheme. Figure 3 presents the general five-layered architecture for wireless networks. The link layer reports link status (e.g., link up and link down) and channel conditions to upper layers, which in some cases are used to help layer-three handoff. The network layer mainly supports terminal mobility, in terms of using mobile Internet protocol (IP) techniques. The application layer supports various types of applications and interacts with lower layers. Session initiation protocol (SIP) is an application-layer solution that has been enhanced to support mobility. Based on the layers in which mobility functions reside, mobility solutions can be classified as link-layer protocols, network-layer protocols, transport-layer protocols, application-layer protocols, and cross-layer protocols. This chapter will introduce each of these layers in a bottom-up manner.

The rest of the chapter is organized as follows: The following three sections present mobility management solutions based on their functioning layers. Most of the schemes have particular advantages and disadvantages. Cross-layer solutions, including multiprotocol label switching (MPLS) and media-independent handover (MIH) solutions are then discussed. The section that follows discusses the challenges of designing mobility management solutions, which are the principle aspects that need to be addressed in future networks. Finally, the chapter contents are summarized.

LINK-LAYER SOLUTIONS

Link-layer mobility management solutions focus on the issues related to intersystem roaming between heterogeneous access networks with different radio technologies and different network management techniques (e.g., mobility management in UMTS/WLAN or CDMA2000/WLAN interfaces). These solutions are designed to gain seamless communications in various mobility models. As a result, they are correlated to specific wireless network interfaces.

Link-layer mobility management solutions rely on the link properties of various network interfaces. These solutions focus on access network management instead of routing issues. Therefore, these solutions are usually tightly coupled with specific networks. The main target is to provide seamless, lower-latency vertical handoffs while guaranteeing the application's QoS. Seamless handover describes the capability of vertical handoffs between different networks without service interruption. A typical handoff scenario between WLAN and 3G networks is illustrated in Figure 4. The process usually includes new agent detection, authentication, registration and acknowledgement, and more. Parikh et al. (2003) proposed a seamless handoff solution from WLAN to CDMA2000 network; this scheme splits the whole handoff process

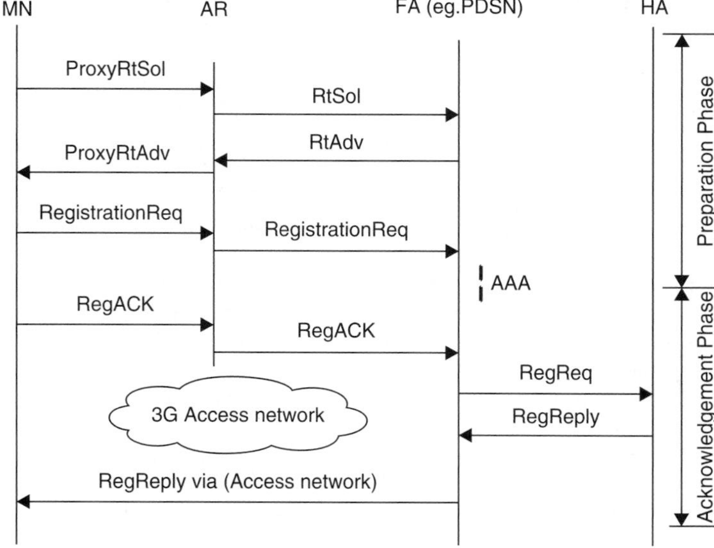

Figure 4: A typical handoff scenario between WLAN and 3G networks

into two phases—the preparation phase and the acknowledgement phase—and proactively executes the preparation phase when coming to border areas. The preparation phase includes processes of network detection, authorization to neighboring networks, getting QoS information of the applications, and so forth. This solution reaches a lower handoff latency (90 ms) than do brute force and other seamless solutions (Parikh et al. 2003). A link-layer handoff scheme needs to address two aspects of handoff issues: triggers and execution. The former refers to when to start the handoff, and the latter refers to how to execute the handoff process efficiently. G. Fan et al. (2005) further proposed a three-phased handoff scheme by introducing a pending phase to handle the gaps across WLAN hotspots. This scheme improved the handoff triggers and execution processes by differentiating the service types and considering the QoS requirements besides the receiving signal strength (RSS).

In policy-based handoff schemes (Murry, Mathur, and Pesch 2003; Wang, Katz, and Giese 1999), a set of predefined rules are used to optimize the vertical handoff trigger. A network policy engine and a client policy engine are resided on the network side and the terminal side respectively. The policy rules are like a black box whose inputs are outside events and outputs are handoff triggers. The input events may include link drop, worsening signal-to-noise ratio, QoS status change, and so forth. The inside of the box could be as simple as a priority list or as complicated as complex fuzzy logic algorithms (Vanem, Svaet, and Paint 2003; Tenhunen and Sauvola 2003). Making the policy more intelligent and adaptive based on the run-time feedback is an important research topic.

To achieve low latency, a number of fast handoff schemes have been proposed. The planning of the delay budget for seamless mobility is discussed in Alimian and Aboba (2004). The handoff delay usually comprises detection time, configuration time, and registration time (Chakravorty et al. 2003, 2004). One common idea of the fast handoff schemes is to optimize the handoff decision point by executing some preparation steps proactively prior to handover. The preregistration post-registration handover methods are proactive handoff schemes to reduce handoff latency (Network Working Group 2007). The preregistration method allows the mobile terminal to communicate with the new foreign agent (FA) while still connected to the old foreign agent. The mobile host can perform a layer-3 handover before it completes the layer-2 handover because L2 trigger is used to trigger layer-3 handoff; L2 trigger is the information from L2 that informs L3 of particular events before and after L2 handoff. The post-registration method provides data delivery to the mobile node at the new FA even before the formal registration process has completed because there is a bidirectional or unidirectional tunnel between the old FA and the new FA that allows the mobile host to continue using its old FA while on the new FA's network. A combination of the two methods has been proposed (e.g., fast router advertisement handoff, router advertisement caching, and so forth; Vidales et al. 2004). In Ylianttila et al. (2001), the proactive execution of the detection phase greatly reduced the detection and configuration time. However, the proactive execution may also result in unnecessary overhead signaling. When to start the proactive steps is an issue to be carefully considered. In some special cases (e.g., a fast-moving terminal in a complicated electronic circumstance), spurious handoffs should be reduced to an acceptable percentage. This is called ping-pong effect, which causes unnecessary signaling traffic and even service disruptions. QoS requirements can be used to filter these redundant handoffs. In a QoS-assisted scheme, the QoS requirements (besides RSS) are taken into consideration. Another method to overcome ping-pong effect is to use Dwell Timer (Ylianttila et al. 2001). The signal strength must carry over the threshold within this timer before a handoff can take place. Thus, it can reduce the unnecessary handoffs caused by signal fading or a client's frequent moving. The timer should be adapted to the specific network implementation. If the timer is too long, the service may disrupt before handoff completion; if the timer is too short, it will leak spurious handoffs. Although the use of such techniques may not filter all redundant handoffs, a good design should balance these two factors and use appropriate values, as shown in Figure 5.

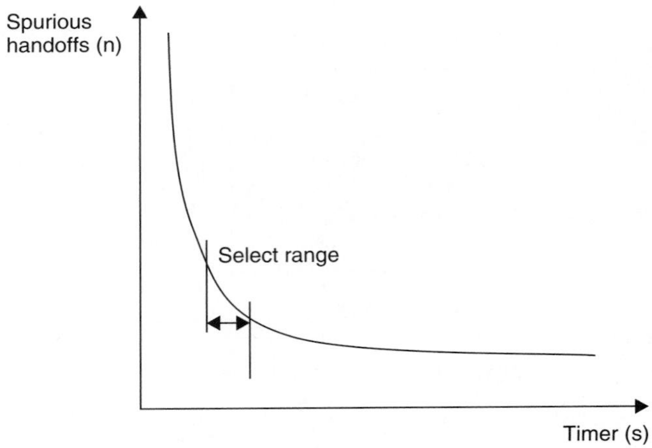

Figure 5: Spurious handoff with Dwell Timer

NETWORK-LAYER SOLUTIONS

Network-layer solutions are usually called layer-3 solutions, in which the mobility model is integrated in the IP layer. Mobile IP (MIP) technologies are used to support macromobility, which is defined in RFC3344 for IPv4 (Perkins 2002), and in RFC3775 for Mobile IPv6 (Perkins, Johnson, and Arkko 2003). Both versions can provide mobility management and data forwarding. In mobile IP networks, each mobile host has a permanent IP address (home address) and a care-of address (foreign address) when roaming in a foreign location. Tunnels are established between the home agent and the foreign agent; the incoming data can be routed to the correct address through this tunnel. Many MIP extended solutions are proposed to support micromobility more effectively, such as cellular IP, Hawaii, and hierarchical mobile IP (HMIP). The common goal among all of the architectures is to ensure that all packets can be routed correctly with lower latency, which can be summarized by two design principles: correctness and efficiency. More detail on those protocols will be covered in the following sections.

Mobile IP

A packet is transmitted from the source to the destination depending on the destination address in the IP header. As a mobile host moves to another subnet, it must acquire a new IP address along with other necessary information. This changing of IP address usually results in interruption of services. Mobile IP was first introduced to support mobility of various wireless applications and has become an underlying technology. It allows seamless handover for mobile data applications and wireless computing.

In a mobile-IP–enabled network, there are usually four components. A mobile node (MN) is a terminal device that roams in the wireless network. The home agent (HA) is a router on the home network, which records the permanent address of an MN. The foreign agent (FA) is a router that records the MN's care of address (CoA) when it roams in a foreign network. The current MN communicates with the corresponding node (CN) through the mobile IP network. A tunnel is established between the HA and the FA. Data to the MN in a visited network are delivered via tunnel from the permanent address (HA) to the CoA. However, the basic mobile IP may result in routing inefficiencies. Packets from the mobile node are first routed to HA and then rerouted to FA through the existing tunnel in a process called triangle routing. Triangle routing leads to routing inefficiencies and aggregates the load of HA. When MN moves between different FAs, there is no direct link between those FAs. This also introduces long delays in packet delivery. Because the tunnel should be established between the FA and HA before rerouting, it cannot support high-mobility situations.

FMIPv6 (Dommety 2005) reduces latency packet loss by providing fast IP connectivity as soon as a new link is established. FMIPv6 provides preconfiguration of link information (e.g., the subnet prefix) in the new subnet while the MN is still attached to the old subnet; therefore, MN can quickly detect and connect the new subnet. This reduces the preconfiguration time in the new subnet. In addition, FMIPv6 improves the packet forwarding success rate by fixing up the routing during link configuration and binding update, so that packets delivered to the old CoA are forwarded to the new address.

Hierarchical Mobile IP

Hierarchical mobile IP (HMIP) aims to minimize the aforementioned problems in basic mobile IP technologies and improve the micromobility performance (see Gustafsson, Jonsson, and Perkins 2000; Soliman et al. 2003, 2004; Haverinen and Malinen 2000). The FAs are organized into a hierarchical structure, as illustrated in Figure 6. A mobility anchor point (MAP) is introduced for regional registration; MAP is a router in the hierarchy tree that can mimic the function of HA inside a MAP subnet. A connection is established between MAP and HA through initial registration to handle the macromobility between MAP subnets. The mobile node only needs to conduct reregistration to the MAP while moving inside the

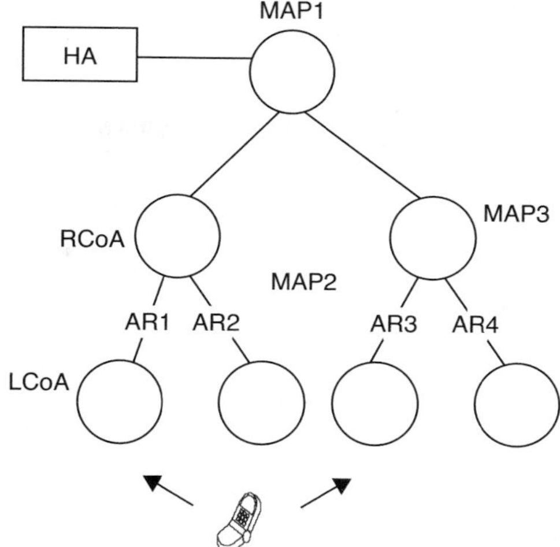

Figure 6: HMIP architecture

domain. If all the routers are directly connected to the MAP, this is called a two-level hierarchical structure. Otherwise, one MAP connects to a root MAP in a subnet that is called a multiple-level hierarchical structure. There are two types of care-of addresses: regional care-of address (RCoA) and local care-of address (LCoA). RCoA is the MAP address, and LCoA is the local AR address. Packets can be correctly forwarded to MN only using LCoA inside the subnet. Changing an attachment within a subnet will not affect RCoA. When the MN moves to a neighboring MAP subnet, the MN needs to update both the LCoA and the RCoA. The packets intercepted by the HA are first sent to corresponding MAPs using RCoA. As we can expect, the handover latency is reduced because mobility is managed locally in micromobility scenarios. The load of HA is greatly reduced because no signaling traffic exists in case of an intra-domain handover.

This hierarchical structure is also used in MIPv6 to handle micromobility issues. HMIPv6 (Soliman et al. 2003) shares the same design principle as HMIP. MAP is used to reduce the amount and latency of signaling between an MN, the HA, and the CN. The MAP acts as a local HA for the visiting mobile node by limiting the amount of signaling required outside the MAP's domain. The disadvantage of the hierarchical version of MIP is that it improves the handoff performance through scarifying routing optimization. HMIPv6 can be used together with FMIPv6 to reduce or eliminate signaling overhead and handoff delays in mobile IPv6.

Cellular IP

Cellular IP was mainly developed for mobility management in cellular networks. It inherits a number of cellular features such as paging, seamless handoff, and security management. It was first developed by Columbia University and Ericsson (Campbell et al. 2000; Valkó 1999). Each base station (BS) acts as an access point and IP router. A gateway is used to connect the cellular network to the common IP network, and the address of the gateway is used as the MN's CoA. Therefore, the incoming packets are first routed to the gateway router and then to the MN using cellular IP function. During the routing, the location update and handoff management function are integrated in order to minimize the message overhead. The path of packets is cached so that it can be used for later forwarding. Cellular IP supports both hard handoff and soft handoff. In a soft handoff, the MN can receive messages from old BSs and new BSs simultaneously. The new connection is established before the old connection is lost so that latency and packet loss are greatly reduced. The paging function is similar to normal cellular networks; base stations are organized geographically into paging clusters. Before the first packet can be routed to the MN, the network pages the MN within the area of the paging cluster. Such a mechanism can minimize the signaling overhead and save power consumption. Cellular IP represents a new approach to IP host mobility that incorporates a number of important cellular system features such as passive connectivity, paging, seamless handoff, and so forth. For mobility between different cellular IP networks, cellular IP can work with MIP to provide macromobility capability.

Hawaii

Hawaii (handover aware wireless access Internet infrastructure; Ramjee et al. 2000, 2002) is another domain-based mobility protocol, proposed by Lucent Technologies. It extends mobile IP and addresses its limitations. Each domain has a domain root router, which is a gateway to other domains. The interdomain and intra-domain mobility are handled differently. Intra-domain mobility is handled by Hawaii, but interdomain mobility needs MIP support. Like mobile IP, each MN has a home domain and a foreign domain. When packets are sent out by a CN, they are intercepted by HA and then tunneled to the corresponding domain root router. The foreign domain root router forwards the packets to the correct path by checking the cached path entries. The mobility management function is handled by the domain root router in an intra-domain handover without interacting with HA. The domain root router updates the routing path in its cache using a path-update message. Thus, the latency and signaling overhead can be minimized for intra-domain handover. The address of the domain root router is assigned as the MN's CoA. Obviously, HA needs to update its CoA only if the MN moves to a new domain. Hawaii also differentiates the MN's idle status and active status by introducing the paging function as cellular IP. The idea behind Hawaii is not very different than cellular IP protocols.

TRANSPORT-LAYER SOLUTIONS

Transport-layer mobility is a very promising scheme with regard to overcoming various limitations imposed by network-layer schemes such as MIP. Compared with other mobility management schemes, transport-layer–based schemes have several unique advantages that motivate researchers to study them to manage mobility at the transport layer.

A great deal of research has been done on transport-layer mobility schemes (Eddy 2004; Henderson 2003; Maitz and Bhagwat 1998; Atiquzzaman and Reaz 2005; Aydin, Seok, and Shen 2003; Chakravorty et al. 2004; Gurtov and Korhonen 2004; Huang and Cai 2005; Sarolahti et al. 2006; Schutz et al. 2005; Manner and Kojo 2004), all of which is built on a common assumption: an MN should be able to use a connection without any requirement for reconnection with the end node. As the transport layer establishes an end-to-end connection between communicating nodes, mobility schemes at this layer put the notion of mobility at the end nodes. A complete mobility management scheme consists of handoff, connection migration, and location management. In this section, the transport-layer mobility management schemes are classified and compared. The evaluation criteria include handoff, packet loss and delay, change in network infrastructure, mobility type, support for IP diversity, and more.

Mobility management in data networks involves changing the point of attachment as well as the IP addresses of an MN. A change in IP address gives rise to the challenges in maintaining an uninterrupted data flow while the MN is changing its address, minimizing loss of packets, maintaining security, identifying the newer location, and so forth. When an MN decides to detach itself from one subnet and connect to another one based on the signal strength of neighboring subnets, the MN obtains a new IP address from the new subnet. The data already in transit to the MN's old IP address may be lost, resulting in increased delay due to retransmission of the lost packets. The change in point of attachment may be confined to a single subnet or to a group of neighboring subnets. The handoff may require applications running on MN and CN to be aware of mobility, thereby reducing application transparency. Additionally, handoff between subnets—known as vertical handoff—may result in conflicts with standard network security solutions and may require additional hardware/software to be deployed in the existing network infrastructure. Based on the approach toward mobility, the current transport-layer mobility management schemes may be classified into the following categories.

Proxy-Based Protocols

A third-party device, called a proxy or gateway, is introduced and divides the TCP connection between MN and CN into two parts: MN to proxy and proxy to CN. Usually the connection between the proxy and the CN is fixed while allowing the MN to roam and change its connection with the proxy. MSOCKS (Maitz and Bhagwat 1998) uses TCP Splice for connection migration and supports multiple IP addresses for multiple interfaces. The MSOCK architecture allows mobile nodes to control which network interfaces are used for different kinds of data leaving from and arriving to the mobile nodes when changing point of attachment. Other typical methods include I-TCP, M-TCP, M-UDP, BARWAN, and so forth (Atiquzzaman and Reaz 2005).

Enhanced TCP Protocols

These protocols enhance the original TCP protocol and aim to reduce transmission delay, reduce data loss, or protect the unbroken connection. They can also add new mechanisms to provide more complete end-to-end mobility management. Migrate and SIGMA use domain name system (DNS) for location management; Freeze-TCP and TCP-R allow a connection to be stopped and restarted before and after a handoff (Atiquzzaman and Reaz 2005). In recent years, with the increasing interest in heterogeneous network interconnection, vertical handoff has been the focus of much research effort. In general, a vertical handoff in a heterogeneous mobile wireless environment can be classified into two types: break-before-make and make-before-break (Manner and Kojo 2004). However, both approaches have their own pros and cons under different mobile scenarios. When an MN roams through different networks with various available bandwidth, the performance of TCP protocol can be highly dynamic, causing longer handoff delays due to unnecessary TCP congestions and inefficient loss-recovery processes that then make QoS provisioning in the mobile wireless environment very difficult. Therefore, several TCP enhancements for supporting vertical handoff have been proposed to tackle this problem (Chakravorty et al. 2004; Gurtov and Korhonen 2004; Huang and Cai 2005; Sarolahti et al. 2006; Schutz et al. 2005; Manner and Kojo 2004).

Other Transport-Layer Based Approaches

Stream control transmission protocol (SCTP) is a reliable message-based transport protocol developed by the Internet Engineering Task Force (IETF) that could replace TCP in some applications. SCTP allows end points to have multiple IP addresses for the purposes of fault tolerance. Some extensions based on SCTP are used for transport-layer mobility management. Mobile SCTP (mSCTP; Atiquzzaman and Reaz 2005) supports IP diversity and soft handoff. Cellular SCTP (cSCTP; Aydin, Seok, and Chen 2003) uses two primary addresses in parallel to duplicate the packet transmissions (while halving the transmission rate) during handoff to provide soft handover. R2CP and MMSP (Atiquzzaman and Reaz 2005) also belong to this category.

APPLICATION-LAYER SOLUTION

Session initiation protocol (SIP) is a signaling protocol to support real-time multimedia applications of roaming users. SIP is an application-layer control protocol that transparently supports name mapping and service redirection. Users can maintain a single externally visible identifier (e.g., an -mail address) regardless of their network location. SIP can be used to provide means of personal, terminal, and session mobility in a mobile Internet (IETF SIP Working Group 2002). Terminal mobility is the ability of a terminal to access the network while changing its location. Personal mobility is the ability of a user to reach any available network through a per-user level ID of any type of terminal belonging to this ID. Session mobility refers to the ability of a user to maintain the same session while changing its supporting terminals.

Entities in SIP include user agents (UAs) and SIP servers. User agents are end-user devices—such as cell phones, PCs, laptops, personal digital assistants (PDAs), and so forth—that initiate SIP sessions. SIP servers enable network operators to install routing and security policies, authenticate users, and manage user locations. There are three types of session servers: proxy server, redirection server, and registrar server. A user is identified using an email-like address: "user@host." The session remains active when a user moves or changes communication terminals. SIP registrar servers are databases that contain the locations of all user agents within a domain. Each time the MN changes its location, the server needs to update its location information, as shown in Figure 7. This resembles the function of the home agent in MIP. If the mobile node moves during a session, it must send a new INVITE message to the CN using the same call identifier as in the original call setup. The MN tells the CN of its new IP addresses in the INVITE message. During the registration, the MN also notifies the CN of other terminal addresses for this user. When the session is moved from one terminal to another, the CN can find the correct mapping information from the registrar server; thus, the session can be correctly routed to the new terminal.

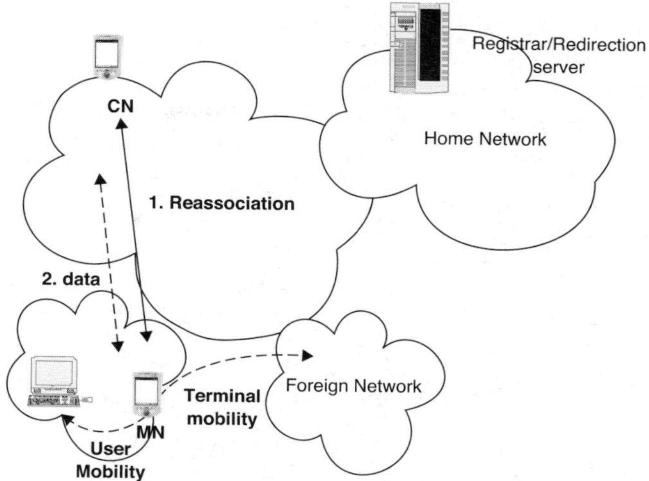

Figure 7: SIP network model

The SIP supports personal mobility in the application layer; however, the seamless and low latency requirements may not be satisfied in some cases. The SIP could be complementary techniques acting with network and link-layer mobility solutions. In order to reduce the handoff latency, the media-independent pre-authentication (MPA) scheme is proposed in Dutta et al. (2005). MPA is a mobile-assisted, secure handover scheme that works over different link-layer and network-layer protocols. Thus, it is an optimization scheme in the application layer. It shares the common motivation of fast handoff schemes to perform discovery or authentication proactively. A great deal of related research has been conducted on coordinating the SIP and MIP protocols to support the terminal mobility, personal mobility, and session mobility simultaneously (Nakajima et al. 2003; Wang, Abu-Rgheff, and Akram 2004). Interested readers can refer to related documents on the detailed implementation of these various SIP variations.

CROSS-LAYER SOLUTIONS

Multiprotocol label switching (MPLS) is a packet-forwarding technology that integrates the label-swapping paradigm with network-layer routing (Rosen, Viswanathan, and Callon 2001). In MPLS-enabled networks, each packet is assigned a label through which it can be routed by label-switching routers (LSRs) in an MPLS domain. MPLS operates between layer 2 and layer 3 in the protocol stack; thus, it is referred to as a layer-2.5 protocol. The mapping between IP and a label-switched path (LSP) is done by a forwarding equivalence class (FEC) function in each LSP. MPLS can also be integrated with mobile IP. Some variations of MPLS protocols can be used to support macro- and micromobility; these variations will be discussed later in the chapter.

Media-independent handover (MIH) is a new layer designed to support handoff in a variety of access technologies. The IEEE 802.21 Working Group is standardizing the media-access–independent mechanism in heterogeneous networks, focusing on 802 families and cellular systems. The purpose is "to improve the user experience of the mobile devices by facilitating handover whether or not they are of different media types, including both wired and wireless, where handover is not otherwise defined and to make it possible for mobile devices to perform seamless handover where the network environment supports it" (IEEE 2005). The 802.21 Working Group officially began work in this area in March 2004. A separate MIH layer between layer 2 and layer 3 is designed to support handoff in a variety of access technologies, such as 802.3, 802.11, 802.16, 3rd-Generation Partnership Project (3GPP), and 3GPP2 networks. The MIH should be supported in both the mobile terminal and the network to enable the layer-2.5 platform. A series of procedures is used to communicate between the MIH layer and data-link layers/IP layers.

MPLS Solutions

MPLS stands for multiprotocol label switching because its techniques are applicable to any network-layer protocols (Rosen et al. 2001). Each router independently chooses a next hop for the packet based on its analysis of the packet's header and the results of running the routing algorithm. A router that supports MPLS is known as an LSR, and the edge routers that assign labels to the packets are called label edge routers (LERs; Dutta et al. 2005) Several MPLS-based mobility schemes have been proposed in Kompella and Rekhter (2002), Sethom et al. (2004), Doria and Worster (2000), Choi, Kang, and Choi (2003), Kim et al. (2001), Nguyen, Li, and Xie (2003), Guo, Antoniou, and Dixit (2002), Chiussi, Khotimsky, and Krishnan (2002), Zhong et al. (2001), and Xie, Wong, and Leung (2003). The MPLS Working Group is responsible for standardizing the use of label switching and the implementation of label-switched paths over various packet-based link-level technologies, such as Packet-over-Sonet, Frame Relay, asynchronous transfer mode (ATM), and local area network (LAN) technologies. To improve scalability of generalized MPLS, it may be useful to aggregate LSPs by creating a hierarchy. Several methods for creating hierarchical MPLS structures can be found in Kompella and Rekhter (2002). The assignment of a particular packet to an FEC is made only once as the packet enters the MPLS domain. This ensures that once a packet is assigned an FEC, subsequent routers do not need to analyze the header again.

General Switching Management Protocol

General switching management protocol (GSMP) controls MPLS-based networks (Doria and Worster 2000; Choi, Kang, and Choi 2003). Each GSMP domain consists of a GSMP controller and many MPLS routers as slaves. GSMP allows a controller to establish and release connections across the switch, add and delete leaves on a multicast connection, manage switch ports, request configuration information, request and delete reservation of switch resources, and request statistics (Doria and Worster 2000). The GSMP slaves can inform the GSMP controller of the attachment or detachment of an MN or events like link up and link down. Usually, multiple routers are controlled by a single controller. The GSMP controller stores all of the information such as routing tables, MN connection status, LSP connection information, and so forth. When a handover occurs inside the subnet, this event can be detected by the controller via LSP slaves. The controller can easily inform the old LSP to release and the new LSP to establish the path. As shown in Figure 8, when the MN moves from LSR-8 to LSR-6, the GSMP controller2 will let the LSP1 switch to LSP2 and informs LSR-7 and LSR-8 to release the connection. The HA is not involved in the handoff process; thus, the latency can be reduced. In order to support cross-controller mobility, an interface is established between the GSMP controllers. The interdomain handover can be handled using this interface. The main difference between GSMP and common MPLS networks is that the GSMP needs a third-party controller for each subnet. GSMP is a centralized, domain-based micromobility solution, whereas common MPLS is a decentralized, hop-by-hop routing mechanism.

Mobile IP and MPLS Integration

The integration of mobile IP and MPLS is important because these two roaming protocols are expected to coexist over the long term. Some selected LSRs are set up as HAs and FAs for integration purposes. Many studies have been carried out toward integration issues (see Nguyen, Li, and Xie 2003; Guo, Antoniou, and Dixit 2002; Chiussi, Khotimsky, and Krishnan 2002; Zhong et al. 2001; Xie, Wong, and Leung 2003). Nguyen, Li, and Xie (2003) propose a new framework of hierarchical IP/MPLS integration model for 3G radio access networks. The DiffServ model is chosen for the QoS differentiation model integrated with MPLS as the underlying forwarding scheme for micromobility. This common framework aims to achieve continuous QoS with efficient micromobility support. Label edge mobility agent (LEMA) is introduced to support chained LSP redirection in Chiussi, Khotimsky, and Krishnan (2002). The major advantage of this scheme is scalability because the hierarchy of the agents is created by the mobile itself based on factors such as available bandwidth, mobility pattern, and so forth. Integration schemes of mobile IP and MPLS have been proposed in Zhong et al. (2001) and Xie, Wong, and

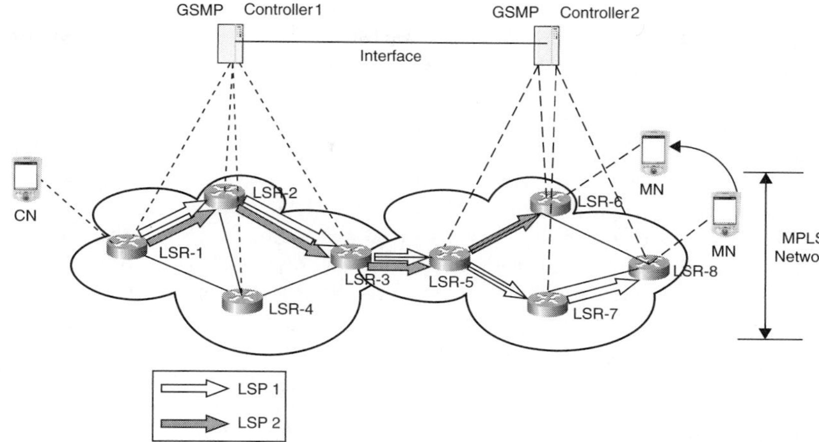

Figure 8: GSMP network architecture

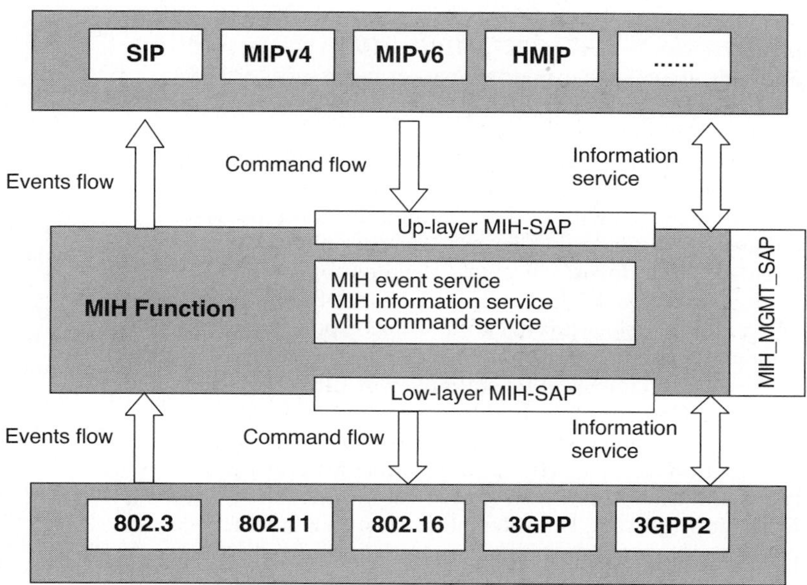

Figure 9: 802.21 reference model

Leung (2003) to improve the efficiency of mobile IP mobility support with the enhancement of features in MPLS. The HAs are freed of the burden of micromobility with MPLS-enabled gateways. Special attention is given to reduce packet loss due to handoffs in Xie, Wong, and Leung (2003) with the assistance of a MAC layer packet-recovery scheme. Each AP has a buffer through which packets can be forwarded from the old AP to the new AP. The key concept for designing the integration schemes is to establish new label-switching paths timely and efficiently with continuous QoS support, either with or without (without is usually preferable) the intervention of HAs in case of micromobility. Interested readers may refer to the corresponding literature for each of these integration models.

Media-Independent Common Platform

Existing schemes provide diverse mechanisms for detection and selection of network policies. In order to provide a common interface for supporting various mobility schemes in heterogeneous wireless networks, the 802.21 Working Group is standardizing the media-access–independent mechanism in heterogeneous networks.

The purpose of the IEEE 802.21 standard is to develop specifications that provide the upper layers with relevant network information in order to perform and optimize the handover between different heterogeneous media (IEEE 2005) The specifications include 802.3, 802.11, 802.16, 3GPP, 3GPP2, and more. MIH is a new layer that resides between the network layer (layer 3) and lower layers: MAC and physical layer protocol (PHY) or radio resource control (RRC) and link access control (LAC). Thus, it is referred to as layer-2.5 solution. This means that each existing protocol stack, both for the 802 families and the 3GPP cellular protocols, should be added with a media-independent function layer (see 3GPP TS 2006a, 2006b). The 802.21 reference model is illustrated in Figure 9. Handover occurs due to the change of user environment (e.g., a gap in radio coverage, another network is more attractive, etc.), and it is based on triggers and measurements provided by link layers of terminals (e.g., signal quality, transmission error rates, etc.). When a handoff is going to occur, the media-independent handover function (MIHF) collects the lower-layer information and informs the upper layer, which can be used to improve or assist layer-3 handover performance.

The IEEE 802.21 architecture includes the media-independent event service (MIES), the media-independent information service (MIIS), and the media-independent command service (MICS). The MIH protocol defines the format of the messages that are exchanged between MIH entities and other layer entities. The selection of the transport mechanism depends on the access technology that connects the MN to the network. Service access points (SAPs) are collections of well-defined application programming interfaces (APIs), through which messages can be exchanged between the MIH layer and adjacent layers. The upper layers make handover decisions between heterogeneous networks (3G cellular networks, wired and wireless media in IEEE 802) by exchanging information through these SAPs. The existing upper-layer protocols can be SIP, MIPv4, MIPv6, HMIP, and so forth, and they are easy to expend whenever necessary.

The MIES provides a set of events and triggers from local and remote interfaces. The events or triggers could come from local lower layers or from peer-to-peer remote MIH functions. Events can indicate changes in state and transmission behavior of the L2 data links or predict state changes of the data-link layers. For example, the events could be "link down," "link up," "configuration change," "link event rollback," "pre-trigger (L2 handoff imminent)," and so forth. Upper layers can take corresponding action upon receiving these events.

The MIIS collects information from different access networks and provides the MIH users network information to make effective handovers. MIIS provides a set of information elements (IEs), information structure and its representation, and a query/response mechanism for information transfer. The information may include service provider information, available network information, access network information, neighbor graphs, link access parameters, location information, user authorization information, and more. The information could be stored in a separate server or in combination with other servers.

MICS refers to the commands sent from the higher layers to the lower layers in the reference model. The higher layers can use MICS to control the actions of lower layers. MICS includes the commands from the upper layer to MIH and from MIH to the lower layer, as well as commands from a peer MIH entity. These commands mainly carry the upper-layer decisions to the lower layers on local device entity or at remote entity, and thus control the behavior of lower layers. The commands are classified into two categories, MIH commands and link commands, which deal with incoming commands (from upper layer) and outgoing commands (to lower layer), respectively.

The IEEE 802.21 MIH function assists in handover decision making. Upper layers make handover decisions and link selections based on inputs and context from the MIH function. The MIH function offers a unified interface to upper layers. The service primitives exposed by the MIH function are independent of the technology-specific protocol entities of the multiple-access networks. The standard provides architecture to support transparent service continuity between heterogeneous link layer technologies. To take advantage of the MIH function, the MN is assumed to support various access technologies, and the MIH protocol stack resides both in the network and in the terminal.

Before the end of this section, the existing schemes within various aspects (e.g., functioning layer, registration process, complexity, and standards) are compared and summarized in Table 1. The common characteristic of the techniques is that they all rely on IP technologies, which are the backbone of future networks.

CHALLENGES OF MOBILITY DESIGN

Mobility management is a key issue in providing seamless roaming in the future. We have discussed most of the major mobility management techniques in the previous sections. However, some challenges still exist with regard to the following aspects:

Smooth evolution: A wide variety of access network technologies, including cellular (2G, 2.5G, 3G), wireless local area technologies (802.3, 802.11, 802.15, 802.16, etc.) and wired access technologies, have been developed or are in development. Roaming from one access network to any other access network with different capabilities, supporting both upward smooth handoff (2G-3G-4G) and downward handoff (4G-3G-2G), is a big challenges when it comes to designing mobility management schemes. Those handoffs also require compatibility between different mobility management algorithms and modules.

Security: A user may move across different access networks; in this case, the same level of security should be guaranteed. The security management level is quite varied for different access networks with regard to authentication, authorization, and key management aspects. Mechanisms and policies, such as security mapping and separate solutions from access technologies, are needed to secure roaming on different networks.

QoS: The QoS measurements vary among different technologies. Most of them address latency, handover processing time, overhead, throughput, packet error rate, and other common characteristics. The QoS level is expected to be maintained in different mobility scenarios. QoS requirements for signaling across different network environments, such as across technology domains, are documented in Brunner (2004). However, the QoS model in heterogeneous networks is far from being solved.

Standardization: Many efforts have been made to standardize the handover interface and improve intersystem roaming capability. The 3GPP TSG SA Working Group (2006) has issued six releases toward integration, security, roaming, and framework for services issues. The IEEE 802.21 Working Group (2006) is standardizing the common cross-layer media-independent solution. IEEE 802.21 is a developing standard to enable handover and interoperability between heterogeneous network types, including both 802 and non-802 interfaces. A draft was originally released in July 2005 and

Table 1: Summary of Mobility Solutions

	SIP	M-TCP	MSOCKS	Mobile SCTP	MIP	HMIP	Cellular IP	Hawaii	W-MPLS	GSMP	Mobility-Aware MPLS	Integrated MIP/ MPLS	802.21
Function Layer	Application	Transport	Transport	Transport	Layer 3	Layer 3	Layer 3	Layer 3	Layer 2.5	Layer 2.5	Layer 2.5	Layer 2.5	Layer 2.5
Switching Node	Mobile	DHCP	proxy	Mobile	HA	MAP	BS-Intra-domain HA-Interdomain	Router-Intra-domain HA-Interdomain	Router Gateway	GSMP Controller	Home GW-Interdomain Visiting GW-Intra-domain	MPLS Gateway	Depend on design
Registration	SIP Server	DNS	proxy	AR/DHCP	HA/FA	HA/FA	HA & gateway	HA & router	Router Gateway	GSMP Controller	Gateway	Gateway	Probably HA
Personal Mobility	Yes	Yes	Yes	Yes	Yes	Yes	No	No	Yes	Yes	Yes	Yes	Yes
Vertical Handover	Yes	Yes	Yes	No	Yes	Yes	No	No	Yes	Yes	Yes	Yes	Yes
Extra Infrastructure	SIP Server	Dynamic DNS	Proxy	No	No	No	Gateway	Root Router	No	GSMP Controller	Gateway	Gateway	Depend on design
Macro-mobility	Yes	Yes	No	No	Yes	Yes	Yes,	yes	Yes	Yes	Yes	Yes	Yes
Macro-mobility Latency	High	Low	N.A	N.A	High	High	High	high	Low	Low	High	High	Low
Micro-mobility	Yes	Yes	Yes	Yes	Yes	Yes	Yes	Yes	Yes	Yes	Yes	Yes	Yes
Micro-mobility Latency	High	Low	High	High	High	Low	Low	Low	Low	Depend on Hops	Low	High	Low
Standardization	IETF SIP WG	No	No	IETF	IETF MIP WG	IETF MIP WG	MIP WG	MIP WG	No	IETF MPLS WG	No	No	802.21 WG

is still under revision. The IETF SEAMOBY Working Group (2006) is focusing on special issues such as context transfer, handoff candidate discovery, and dormant mode host alerting, among others.

CONCLUSION

A main feature of future communication is that it will need to support various types of services and seamless roaming, anytime and anywhere. Mobility management is a key issue toward this goal. Great efforts have been expended on this research topic, and a number of mobility management models have recently been proposed. This chapter gives an overview on the mobility management issues in heterogeneous networks across different layers. The mobility solutions are organized in categories based on their functioning layers. SIP is a new technology that handles session mobility in the application layer. The transport-layer approaches can be used to support mobility in heterogeneous environments for TCP and user datagram protocol (UDP) connections without adding extra infrastructure. Network-layer solutions have been developed to improve handover and registration efficiency both for micro- and macromobility. The concept of domain is widely adopted in these solutions, despite the diversity of network topology. A number of link-layer solutions aim to solve the specific seamless roaming in access networks. To improve the compatibility of mobility in heterogeneous networks, cross-layer solutions (e.g., MPLS and MIH) have been explained. Finally, we discussed the challenges for mobility management and summarized important issues for future mobility design.

GLOSSARY

GSMP: General switching management protocol; controls MPLS-based networks.

Horizontal handoff: Handoffs that take place when mobile users move under different access points of the same network interface.

MAN: Metropolitan area network.

MIH: Media-independent handover; an IEEE 802.21 standard that handles the handoff in heterogeneous networks.

MIP: Mobile IP; an Internet engineering task force (IETF) standard communications protocol that is designed to allow mobile device users to move from one network to another while maintaining their permanent IP address.

Mobility management: The assigning and controlling of wireless links for terminal network connections under various kinds of mobility models. MPLS: Multiprotocol label switching; a standard from the IETF for including routing information in the packets of an IP network.

PAN: Personal area network.

SIP: Session initiation protocol; a signaling protocol for Internet conferencing, telephony, presence, events notification, and instant messaging.

Vertical handoff: Handoffs that take place when mobile users move under different access points in different network interfaces.

WLAN: Wireless local area network.

WWAN: Wireless wide area network.

CROSS REFERENCES

See *Network QoS*; *TCP/IP Suite*.

REFERENCES

3GPP TS. 2006a. 23.002. *Network architecture*. http://www.3gpp.org/ftp/Specs/html-info/23002.htm (accessed October 1, 2006).

3GPP TS. 2006b. 23.234. *3GPP system to wireless local area network (WLAN) inter-working: System description*.

3GPP TSG SA Working Group. 2006. http://www.3gpp.org/tb/SA/SA1/SA1.html (accessed October 1, 2006).

Akyildiz, I. F., J. McNair, J. Ho, H. Uzunalioglu, and W. Wang. 1999. Mobility management for next-generation wireless systems. *Proceedings of the IEEE* 87(8): 1347–84.

Akyildiz, I. F., J. Xie, and S. Mohanty. 2004. A survey of mobility management in next-generation all-IP-based wireless systems. *IEEE Wireless Communications*, August, pp. 16–28.

Alimian, A., and B. Aboba. 2004. *Analysis of roaming techniques*. IEEE 80211-04/0377r1. http://www-ieee802org/11/Documents (accessed October 1, 2006).

Atiquzzaman, M., and A. S. Reaz. 2005. Survey and classification of transport layer mobility management schemes. In *Proceedings of Personal, Indoor, and Mobile Radio Communications* (PIMRC), Berlin, Germany, September, pp. 2109–2115.

Aydin, I., W. Seok, and C. C. Shen. 2003. Cellular SCTP: A transport-layer approach to Internet mobility. *Proceedings of the Twelfth International Conference on Computer Communications and Networks*, Dallas, Texas, October, pp. 285–90.

Brunner, M. 2004. *Requirements for QoS signaling protocols*. RFC 3726, April.

Campbell, A. T., J. Gomez, S. Kim, Z. Turanyi, C.-Y. Wan, and A. Valko. 2000. Design, implementation, and evaluation of cellular IP. *IEEE Personal Communications*, August, pp. 42–9.

Chakravorty, R., P. Vidales, L. Patanapongpibul, K. Subramanian, I. Pratt, and J. Crowcroft. 2003. *On inter-network handover performance using mobile IPv6*. Technical Report, University of Cambridge Computer Laboratory.

Chakravorty, R., P. Vidales, I. Pratt, and J. Crowcroft. 2004. Performance issues with vertical handovers: Experiences from GPRS cellular and WLAN hotspot integration. In *Proceedings of the IEEE Pervasive Communications and Computing Conference*, Orlando, Florida, March, pp. 155–64.

Chiussi, F. M., D. A. Khotimsky, and S. Krishnan. 2002. A network architecture for MPLS-based micromobility. In *Proceedings of IEEE Wireless Communications and Networking Conference* (Vol. 2), Orlando, Florida, March, pp. 549–55.

Choi, S. G., H. J. Kang, and J. K. Choi. 2003. An efficient handover mechanism using the general switch management protocol on a multi-protocol label switching network. *ETRI Journal* 25(5): 369–78.

Dommety, G. 2005. *Fast handovers for mobile IPv6*. RFC 4068, July.

Doria, A., and T. Worster. 2000. *General switch management protocol*. Internet draft. http://www.ietf.org/html.charters/gsmp-charter.html (accessed October 1, 2006).

Dutta, A., T. Zhang, Y. Ohba, K. Taniuchi, and H. Shulzrinne. 2005. MPA-assisted optimized proactive handoff scheme. In *Proceedings of IEEE International Conference on Mobile and Ubiquitous Systems (MobiQuitous)*, San Diego, California, July, pp. 155–65.

Eddy, W. M. 2004. At what layer does mobility belong? *IEEE Communications* 42(10): 155–59.

Fan, G., and X. Lu. 2005. Novel service-oriented handoffs in heterogeneous wireless networks. In *Proceedings of QShine 05*, Orlando, Florida, August, pp. 38–44.

Guo, Y., Z. Antoniou, and S. Dixit. 2002. IP transport in 3G radio access networks: MPLS-based approach. In *Proceedings of IEEE Wireless Communications and Networking Conference* (Vol. 1), Orlando, Florida, March, pp. 11–17.

Gurtov, A., and J. Korhonen. 2004. Effect of vertical handovers on performance of TCP-friendly rate control. *ACM Mobile Computing and Communications Review* 8(3): 73–87.

Gustafsson, E., A. Jonsson, and C. Perkins. 2000. *Mobile IP regional registration*. Internet draft. draft-ietfmobileip-reg-tunnel-03 (accessed October 1, 2006).

Haverinen, H., and J. Malinen. 2000. Mobile IP regional paging. Internet draft (in progress). draft-haverinen-mobileip-reg-paging-00.txt (accessed October 1, 2006).

Henderson, T. R. 2003. Host mobility for IP networks: A comparison. *IEEE Network* 17(6): 18–26.

Huang, H., and J. Cai. 2005. Improving TCP performance during soft vertical handoff. In *Proceedings of the Nineteenth International Conference on Advanced Information Networking and Applications* (Vol. 2), Taipei, March, pp. 329–32.

IEEE. 2005. IEEE P802.21/D00.01. Draft IEEE standard for local and metropolitan area networks: Media independent handover services.

IEEE 802.21 Working Group. 2006. http://www.ieee802.org/21/ (accessed October 1, 2006).

IETF SEAMOBY Working Group. 2006. http://www.ietf.org/html.charters/OLD/seamoby-charter.html (accessed October 1, 2006).

IETF SIP Working Group. 2002. SIP: *Session initiation protocol*. RFC 3261, June.

Kim, H., K.-S. D. Wong, W. Chen, and C. L. Lau. 2001. Mobility-aware MPLS in IP-based wireless access networks. *Proceedings of IEEE Globecom'01* (Vol. 6), San Antonio, Texas, November, pp. 3444–48.

Kompella, K., and Y. Rekhter. 2002. *Hierarchy with generalized MPLS TE*. Internet draft. draft-ietf-mpls-lsp-hierarchy-08.txt (accessed October 1, 2006).

Maitz, D. A., and P. Bhagwat. 1998. MSOCKS: An architecture for transport layer mobility. *Proceedings of IEEE INFOCOM*, San Francisco, March/April, pp. 1037–45.

Manner, J., and M. Kojo. 2004. *Mobility-related terminology*. RFC 753, June.

Murry, K., R. Mathur, and D. Pesch. 2003. Intelligent access and mobility management in heterogeneous wireless networks using policy. In *Proceedings of the First International Symposium on Information and Communication Technologies*, Dublin, Ireland, September, pp. 181–86.

Nakajima, N., A. Dutta, S. Das, and H. Schulzrinne. 2003. Handoff delay analysis and measurement for SIP-based mobility in IPv6. In *Proceedings of the IEEE International Conference on Communications* (Vol. 2), Seattle, Washington, May, pp.1085–89.

Network Working Group. 2007. *Low latency handoffs in mobile IPv4m*, edited by K. El Malki.

Nguyen, H. M., F. Li, and Q. Xie. 2003. Integration of micro-mobility with QoS in IP/MPLS-based radio access networks. In *Proceedings of the IEEE Vehicular Technology Conference*, Location, Month, pp. 2261–65.

Parikh et al. 2003. Seamless handoff of mobile terminal from WLAN to cdma2000 network. In *Proceedings of IEEE 3G Wireless*, San Francisco, May.

Perkins, C., ed. 2002. *IP mobility support for IPv4*. RFC 3344, August.

Perkins, C., D. Johnson, and J. Arkko. 2004. *Mobility support in IPv6*. RFC 3775, June.

Ramjee, R., T. LaPorta, S. Thuel, and K. Varadhan. 2000. IP micro-mobility support using HAWAII. Internet engineering task force. draft-ramjee-micro-mobility-hawaii-00.txt (accessed October 1, 2006).

Ramjee, R., F. Thomas, L. Porta, S. Thuel, K. Varadhan, and S. Y. Wang. 2002. HAWAII: A domain-based approach for supporting mobility in wide-area wireless networks. *IEEE/ACM Transactions on Networking* 10(3): 396–410.

Rosen, E., Y. Rekhter, D. Tappan, G. Fedorkow, D. Farinacci, T. Li, and A. Conta. 2001. *MPLS label stack encoding*. RFC 3032, January.

Rosen, E., A. Viswanathan, and R. Callon. 2001. *Multiprotocol label-switching architecture*. RFC 3031, January.

Sarolahti, P., J. Korhonen, L. Daniel, and M. Kojo. 2006. Using quick-start to improve TCP performance with vertical handoff. In *Proceedings of the Thirty-First IEEE Conference on Local Computer Networks*, November, pp. 897–904.

Schutz, S., L. Eggert, S. Schmid, and M. Brunner. 2005. Protocol enhancements for intermittently connected hosts. *ACM SIGCOMM Computer Communication Review* 35(2): 5–18.

Sethom, K. et al. 2004. Wireless MPLS: A new layer 2.5 micro-mobility scheme. In *Proceedings of Mobiwac'04*, Philadelphia, October, pp. 64–72.

Soliman, H., C. Castelluccia, K. El-Malki, and L. Bellier. 2003. *Hierarchical mobile IPv6 mobility management (HMIPv6)*. Internet draft. draft-ietf-mobileip-hmipv6-07.txt (accessed October 1,2006).

Soliman, H., C. Castelluccia, K. El-Malki, and L. Bellier. 2004. *Hierarchical MIPv6 mobility management*. Internet draft.

Sun J., J. Tenhunen, and J. Sauvola. 2003. CME: A middleware architecture for network-aware adaptive applications. In *Proceedings of the Fourteenth IEEE*

International Symposium on Personal Indoor and Mobile Radio Communications, Beijing, China, September, pp. 839–43.

Valkó, A. 1999. Cellular IP: A new approach to Internet host mobility. *ACM SIGCOMM Computer Communication Review* 29(1): 50–65.

Vanem E., S. Svaet, and F. Paint. 2003. Effects of multiple-access alternatives in heterogeneous wireless networks. In *Proceedings of the IEEE Wireless Communications and Networking Conference* (Vol. 3), New Orleans, Louisiana, March, pp. 1696–1700.

Vidales, V. P., L. Patanapongpibul, G. Mapp, and A. Hopper. 2004. Experiences with heterogeneous wireless networks: Unveiling the challenges. In *Proceedings of the Second International Working Conference on Performance Modeling and Evaluation of Heterogeneous Networks*, Ilkley, UK, July.

Wang, H. J., R. H. Katz, and J. Giese. 1999. Policy-enabled handoffs across heterogeneous wireless networks. In *Proceedings of the Second IEEE Workshop on Mobile Computing Systems and Applications*, New Orleans, Louisiana, February, p. 51.

Wang, Q., M.A. Abu-Rgheff, and A. Akram. 2004. Design and evaluation of an integrated mobile IP and SIP framework for advanced handoff management. In *Proceedings of the IEEE International Conference on Communications* (Vol. 7), Paris, June 2004, pp. 3921–25.

Xie, K., V. Wong, and V. C. M Leung. 2003. Support of micro-mobility in MPLS-based wireless access networks. In *Proceedings of IEEE WCNC'03*, New Orleans, Louisiana, March, pp. 1242–47.

Ylianttila, M., M. Pande, J. Makela, and P. Mahonen. 2001. Optimization scheme for mobile users performing vertical handoffs between IEEE 802.11 and GPRS/EDGE networks. *IEEE GLOBECOM* (Vol. 6), November, pp. 3439–43.

Zhong, R., C. K. Tham, C. C. Foo, and C. C. Ko. 2001. Integration of mobile IP and multi-protocol label switching. In *Proceedings of IEEE International Conference on Communications* (Vol. 7), Helsinki, Finland, June, pp. 2123–27.

Universal Mobile Telecommunications System

Faouzi Zarai and Noureddine Boudriga, *University of the 7th of November, Tunisia*
Mohammad S. Obaidat, *Monmouth University*

INTRODUCTION

The evolution of telecommunication networks can be characterized by an increase in mobility functions and a solid support for a growing number of sophisticated services. The first-generation mobile wireless systems were based on analog transmission technologies with voice transmission as a unique available service. With the *second generation* (2G), digital wireless systems replaced analog systems. Digital communication not only results in better spectrum efficiency and higher quality of voice but also enables users to take advantage of new services such as *short messaging services* (SMS). The 2.5G wireless networks such as *general packet radio service* (GPRS) appeared to enhance the 2G wireless networks with best-effort packet-switched data services. However, with 2.5G wireless systems, data rates are limited to approximately 115 kbps. The goals of the *third-generation* (3G) wireless networks are to solve problems of 2G and 2.5G systems and offer wireless Internet services at a wide scale, extending the scope of 2G wireless networks from simple voice telephony to complex data applications including *voice over Internet protocol* (VoIP), video conferencing over IP, Web browsing, and multimedia services (3GPP 2001, "3G security"; Nicopolitidis et al. 2003).

Universal mobile telecommunications system (UMTS), a major 3G wireless technology, offers mobile users a large set of advantages, including: (1) new radio spectra; (2) more bandwidth; (3) security and reliability; (4) fixed, asymmetric, and variable data rate; (5) backward compatibility of devices with existing networks; and (6) enhanced multimedia services.

The *fourth-generation* (4G) systems will enable users to dynamically switch between various wireless accessing technologies to the IP-based core network. Users are expected to use different interfaces transparently and simultaneously to access the network. Therefore, system integration is the most important enabler to the evolutionary step from 3G to 4G wireless systems.

The purpose of this chapter is to present the basics of UMTS systems, analyze their features (especially their security features), and discuss their limits. The chapter begins with a discussion of the evolution process from the *global system for mobile communications* (GSM) to UMTS. It also presents the characteristics and the architecture components of UMTS. Then it presents its *quality-of-service* (QoS) and security mechanisms. Finally, the chapter discusses the evolution toward 4G.

EVOLUTION TO 3G

GSM, a major 2G network, is evolving into 3G networks starting with the *UMTS terrestrial radio access network* (UTRA NETWORK), which is built on a 2G core network. The air interface has been changed from a system based on *time division multiple access* (TDMA) to an air interface based on *wideband code division multiple access* (W-CDMA). This modification was required to achieve 2 Mbits/s data rate connections for assignment to mobile users. UMTS offers the potential to enhance services to end users through increased bandwidth and enables the provision of more advanced data services compared to the current systems (such as SMS and multimedia messaging service). In addition to the increased bandwidth, other features in the UMTS architecture make it more attractive, including enhanced capabilities in terms of security and quality of service (Nicopolitidis et al. 2003).

In this section, we first show an evolutionary migration path from GSM to UMTS. We then compare and contrast 3G wireless technologies, focusing on their requirements and features.

UMTS Requirements

3G communication systems will enhance and extend mobility by providing anytime and anywhere accessibility, IP mobility, privacy, security of communication, and diversity of services while keeping low cost. The UMTS requirements, which were identified by the International Telecommunications Union, focus on the following items: interoperability, flexibility, service, packet-based network, fixed wireless access, fast and seamless handoff, and security.

Interoperability

UMTS must be designed to interoperate with GSM in order to facilitate the evolution from GSM to UMTS networks. Only minor modifications would be needed to enable network operators to benefit from the improved cost efficiency of UMTS while protecting their GSM infrastructures. Existing GSM and GPRS networks elements should, however, be extended to adopt UMTS QoS requirements.

Flexibility

The architecture of UMTS must be flexible to support multiple systems that are capable of offering large access to broadband mobile services anytime and anywhere. The integration of *wireless local area networks* (WLANs) to UMTS should become possible and make the heterogeneity of networks transparent.

Service

The UMTS will offer unlimited mobility and support high data rates and services with variable bandwidths and symmetric and asymmetric data transfer. This large set of services will be provided to mobile users while supporting load balancing, connection priorities, and guaranteed quality-of-service classes.

Packet-Based Network

2G wireless networks are *circuit-switched,* meaning that separate connections (or circuits) must be set up for each voice call. Packet-based networks, on the other hand, enable "always on" connections and allow multiple subscribers to receive data traffic simultaneously over the same network segment. UMTS reserves a large place to IP.

Fixed Wireless Access

UMTS network should support all types of fixed wireless access services and should be utilized for interconnecting and supplementing capacity to the fixed wired network.

Fast and Seamless Handoff

The handoff operations should be quick enough to ensure that the mobile station can receive IP packets at its new location within a reasonable period of time and so reduce the packet delay as much as possible. It also should be seamless to the mobile user and at the same time achieve efficient usage of the network resources. *Seamless* means smooth transition, such that a user does not perceive any delay or interruption of service.

Security

The mobility scheme provided by UMTS should support different levels of security requirements. In fact, security elements that have shown to be robust and useful in 2G systems should be adopted while real and perceived weaknesses must be corrected or dropped.

UMTS Key Characteristics

UMTS wireless technology is a proposed standard as a part of 3rd-Generation Partnership Project (3GPP) solutions to satisfy the International Mobile Telecommunications 2000 requirements. It is based on W-CDMA technology. The UMTS terrestrial radio access provides two modes: (1) W-CDMA FDD (*frequency division duplexing*) and (2) W-CDMA TDD (*time division duplexing*).

The specific frequencies used for UMTS are as follow.

- W-CDMA FDD: 1920–1980 MHz (uplink)
- W-CDMA FDD: 2110–2170 MHz (downlink)
- W-CDMA TDD: 1900–1920 MHz as well as 2010–2025 MHz bands

UMTS operates using 2 × 60 MHz bands as opposed to 2 × 25 MHz bands used for GSM operation (see Figure 1). One significant difference, however, is that W-CDMA has a carrier spacing of 5 MHz (resulting in just twelve carrier frequencies in each direction) as opposed to GSM, which has a carrier spacing of 200 KHz (giving it 125 different carrier frequencies). The larger bandwidth of 5 MHz is needed to support higher bit rates; the lower number of carrier frequencies is not a drawback on its capacity because each W-CDMA user is allocated the entire 5-MHz band.

The first release of UMTS specifications published by 3GPP was known as 3GPP release 99 because of a naming scheme used with GSM specifications that were released on a yearly basis. This release provides specifications concerning the UTRA NETWORK radio access network, based on the UTRA radio interface and enhancements to GSM and GPRS core networks. The following release was originally called 3GPP release 2000, but the new changes

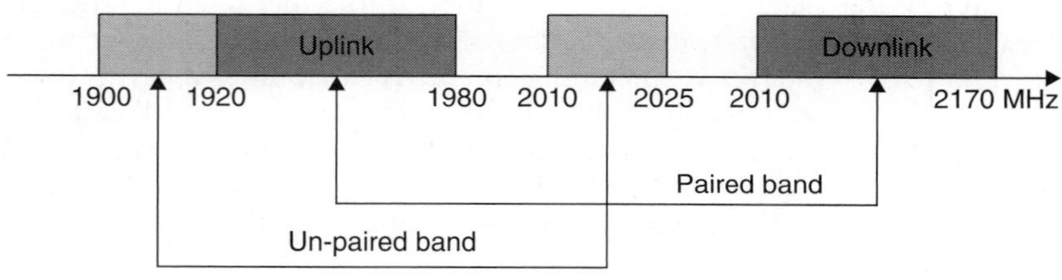

Figure 1: UMTS spectrum

were too significant to be totally included in a single release. Consequently, release 2000 was divided into release 4, 5, 6, and 7. One key feature defined in UMTS releases 5 and 6 is high-speed downlink packet access, which offers considerably higher data capacity and data-user speeds on the downlink compared to release 99 of UMTS. This is possible through the use of a new downlink shared transport channel and a set of smart mechanisms such as a dynamic adaptive modulation and coding, a rapid scheduler, and fast retransmissions based on hybrid automatic request techniques.

In addition to the increased bandwidth, the following features planned in UMTS architecture provide enhanced capabilities in terms of quality of service and security:

- UMTS offers full coverage and mobility for 144 Kb/s, preferably 384 Kb/s for limited coverage and mobility for 2 Mbps connections. This accommodates high-speed wireless audio and video systems.
- UMTS supports the provision of innovative services such as Web browsing, instant messaging, mobile payment, and multimedia content delivery.
- UMTS provides mobile users with IP multimedia services with a guaranteed end-to-end quality of service.
- UMTS allows internetworking with GSM and GPRS systems and WLANs. Coexistence of GSM, GPRS, UMTS, and intersystem handoffs for coverage enhancements and load balancing are possible.
- UMTS allows mobile users and applications to negotiate bearer QoS characteristics.

UMTS builds on the success of the GSM system (see "UMTS Security" below). One factor that contributed to the success of GSM has been its security features. The new services introduced in UMTS require new security features to protect them. In addition, the shortcomings of GSM security need to be addressed in UMTS. The security key characteristics of UMTS are as follow.

Mutual Authentication

The mobile user and the serving network authenticate each other. In fact, each entity must prove to the other that it knows its password without actually revealing or transmitting it. In GSM, only the network can initiate authentication, which is an optional procedure, and only the mobile user is authenticated.

Signaling Data Integrity

In UMTS, signaling messages between mobile stations and a *radio network controller* (RNC) are protected by integrity code. This security feature has no equivalent in GSM. It provides protection against false base station attacks as the origin of signaling messages required to set up a communication with a mobile can now be authenticated by the mobile.

Network to Network Security

To secure communication between serving networks, *Internet protocol security* (IPsec) can be used to provide confidentiality and integrity of communication at the IP layer. In GSM, communications in the fixed network portion are not protected.

Wider Security Scope

Security is based within the RNC rather than the base station. The confidentiality protection in GSM is located at the link layer and is always initiated by the network.

Secure International Mobile Subscriber Identity Usage

After call admission, the user is assigned a temporary *international mobile subscriber identity* (IMSI) by the serving network. This feature is the same as in GSM.

UMTS ARCHITECTURE

Wireless network evolution can be characterized by an increase in functionality and its support for a growing number of services. However, this also means that networks are becoming increasingly complex in terms of architecture. The goal of this section is to identify the key elements of the UMTS architecture and explain their interfaces.

The basic architecture of a UMTS network is divided into three components as depicted in Figure 2. These are (1) the *mobile station* (MS), (2) the *access network* (UTRA NETWORK), and (3) the *core network* (CN) (Corbett and Everit 2003). The UTRA NETWORK handles all of the functions related to radio resources and air-interface management, while the core network performs switching functions and interfaces to external networks such as the Internet or a *public switched telephone network* (PSTN).

Radio connection with mobile stations is established by means of the UMTS *Uu interface,* which is actually the W-CDMA–based UTRA radio interface. The UTRA NETWORK is connected to the transport network using the *Iu interface;* its most important feature is enabling the user to interact both with circuits and packet-based connections.

Satellite-UMTS (S-UMTS) is expected to play a complementary role to the terrestrial UMTS. In addition to its fast service deployment and coverage extension capability, S-UMTS—as a direct consequence of its broadcast nature and ubiquitous coverage—offers a natural way

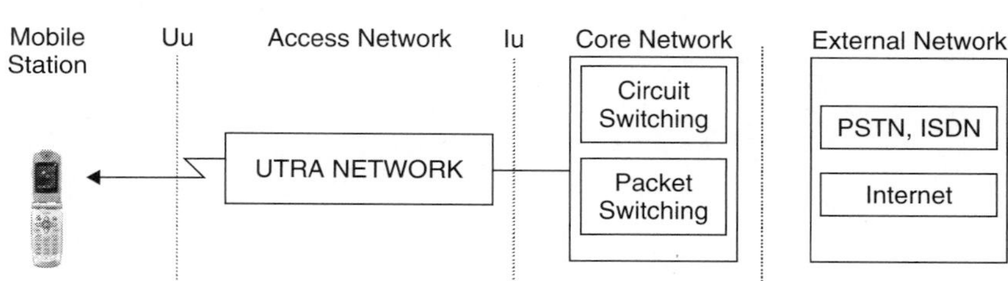

Figure 2: UMTS architecture

to provide multicast and broadcast services in the most cost-efficient manner.

Mobile Station

An MS is defined as a device allowing a user access to network services and the *universal subscriber identity module* (USIM). It is involved in every major UMTS procedure: call setup and management, handoff procedures, and mobility management. The USIM contains the functions and data needed to identify and authenticate users, as well as a copy of the user's service profile and the security parameters needed for confidentiality and integrity services. A mobile station has many different types of identities. Most of these UMTS identity types are taken directly from GSM specifications and include the following.

- The international mobile subscriber identity represents the permanent user identity as stored in the USIM secure component.
- The *temporary mobile subscriber identity* (TMSI) is a temporary identifier in the local network in which a user is registered. It is used to avoid user traceability, which may lead to the compromise of user identity confidentiality. The temporary identities are changed regularly.
- The *packet temporary mobile subscriber identity* (P-TMSI) replaces the TMSI in the packet-switched domain.
- The *mobile subscriber integrated services digital network* (MSISDN) represents the user phone number.
- The *international mobile station equipment identity* (IMEI) represents the mobile equipment serial number and can be used for fraud prevention.
- The *international mobile station equipment identity and software number* (IMEISV) is similar to the IMEI and addresses both hardware and software identity.

UMTS mobile stations can operate using one of the three modes: (1) simultaneous packet and circuit switching, (2) packet switching, or (3) circuit switching.

In the combined *packet-switching* (PS) and *circuit-switching* (CS) mode of operation, the MS is attached to both the PS and CS domains. Therefore, the MS is capable of simultaneously operating PS services and CS services.

In the PS mode of operation, the MS is only attached to the PS domain and may only operate services of the PS domain. However, this does not prevent CS-like services to be offered over the PS domain.

In the CS mode of operation, the MS is only attached to the CS domain and can only operate services of the CS domain.

UMTS Terrestrial Radio Access Network Architecture

The UTRAN consists of a radio network subsystem connected to the core network through the Iu interface (3GPP 2004, "General"). It is responsible for handling the radio functions of the system (3GPP 2002, "UTRAN"). As depicted in Figure 3, the UTRAN consists of node B's and several RNCs, which play roughly equivalent roles to these performed in GSM by the base transceiver stations and base station controller, respectively.

Node B

Node B in UMTS is the physical unit for radio transmission and reception with cells. In fact, its main role is to perform physical layer functions (e.g., modulation and demodulation, coding, interleaving, spreading, etc.). The main tasks of node B are the air-interface transmission and reception and *code division multiple access* (CDMA) physical channel coding. It also measures quality and the strength of the connections and determines the frame error rate. It transmits these data to the RNC as a measurement report for handoff and macrodiversity. In addition, the node B also participates in power control because it enables the MS to adjust its power.

Radio Network Controller

The RNC is one of the key elements of the UTRAN. It connects node B to the transport network. It is responsible for handoff decisions that require signaling to the MS. Node B's resources are controlled by the RNC. Typically, the functions of RNC are:

- radio resource control, admission control, and channel allocation;
- power control settings, handoff control, and macrodiversity;
- encryption;
- segmentation and reassembly;
- broadcast signaling; and
- open-loop power control.

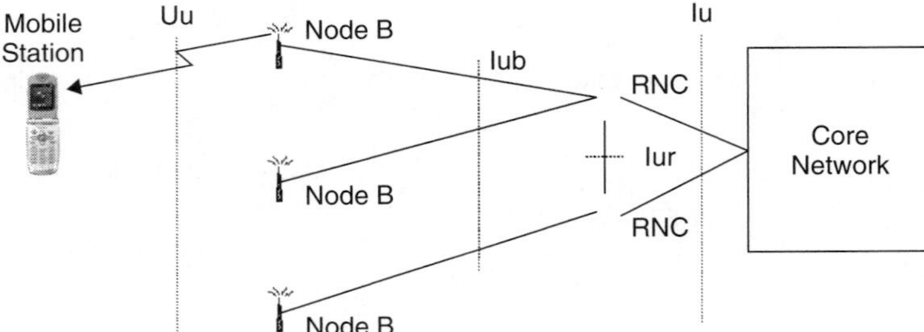

Figure 3: UTRAN architecture

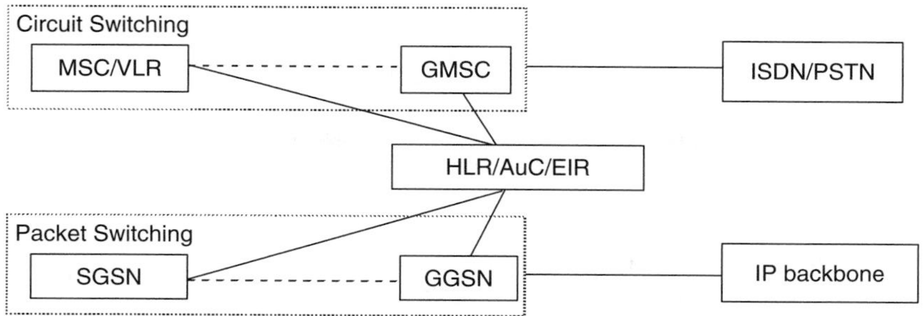

Figure 4: UMTS release 99 core network architecture

Core Network Architecture

The CN is responsible for such major communication functions as call establishment and handling, data transmission, mobility management, and traffic management. In core networks, two layers are defined: (1) the radio network layer and (2) the transport network layer. Figure 4 shows a block diagram of a typical CN that has basically circuit-switched and packet-switched building blocks. The major circuit-switched components are the mobile services switching center, the visitor location register, and the gateway mobile services switching center.

The *mobile services switching center* (MSC) is the interface between the cellular network and external fixed circuit-switched telephone networks such as the PSTN. This component performs the routing of calls from an external network to an individual mobile station and all of the switching and signaling functions for mobile stations located in a geographical area designated as the MSC area. Additional functions include carrying out the procedures required for location registration, handover, and encryption parameter management.

The *visitor location register* (VLR) component is generally implemented in connection with an MSC. It holds information related to every mobile station that roams into the area serviced by the associated MSC. Thus, the VLR contains information about the active subscribers in its network, even from those to whom this network is their home network. As subscribers register with different networks, the information in their *home location registers* (HLRs) is copied to the VLR in every network visited and discarded when the subscribers leave those networks.

The *gateway MSC* (GMSC) plays the role of gateway to external networks.

Packet-switched components are of two types: (1) serving GPRS support node and (2) gateway GPRS support node.

The *serving GPRS support node* (SGSN) component is responsible for mobility management and IP packet session management. It routes user packet traffic from the radio access network to the appropriate *gateway GPRS support node* (GGSN), or the gateway between the cellular network that uses UMTS and external packet data networks such as the Internet and corporate intranets.

The network elements shared by both domains (CS and PS) are the following:

- The *home location register* stores data related to each subscriber of the services provided by the mobile network. This information is entered when a user subscribes to the network.
- For each subscriber, the *authentication center* (AuC) stores an authentication key (K) as well as the corresponding IMSI, which are permanent data entered at subscription time.
- The *equipment identity register* (EIR) checks to see whether a mobile device is valid.

UMTS Interfaces

Three interfaces are used in UMTS: Iu, Iur, and Iub. The service provided by each is as follows.

- The Iu interface connects UTRAN to the transport network. It is logically divided into two entities: (1) the Iu-CS, through which an RNC is connected to the CN circuit-switched domain; and (2) Iu-PS, through which an RNC is connected to the CN packet-switched domain.
- The Iur is the interface between two RNCs (3GPP undated, TS 25.421). Using this interface, RNCs can communicate during handoff with the serving RNC.
- The Iub interface connects an RNC and a node B and allows an RNC a node B to negotiate the radio resources (for example, they can negotiate adding or deleting cells controlled by node B) to support communication of the dedicated connection between an MS and a serving radio network subsystem (3GPP Services and System Aspects, TS 25.431).

UMTS LAYERS

The radio interface is layered into three protocol layers, as depicted in Figure 5. Each layer plays an important role as described below:

Layer 1 comprises the W-CDMA physical layer.

Layer 2 comprises the *medium access control* (MAC), the *radio link control* (RLC), the *packet data convergence protocol* (PDCP), and the *broadcast and multicast control* (BMC).

Layer 3, the network layer, is divided into the *radio resource control* (RRC), the *mobility management* (MM), and the *connection management* (CM) sublayers.

UMTS Physical Layer

The physical layer defines the access to the transmission media, the physical and electrical properties, and how to

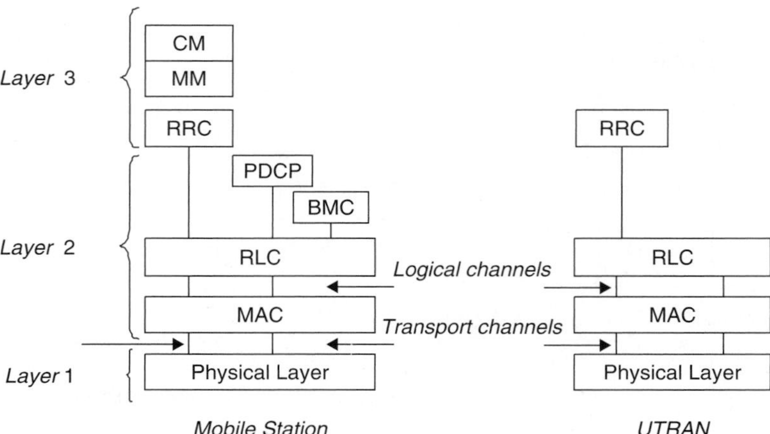

Figure 5: Radio interface protocol architecture

activate and deactivate a connection. It offers data transport services to higher layers. The main functions performed by this layer are multiplexing of transport channels and demultiplexing of coded composite transport channels, error detection, modulation and demodulation, spreading and despreading of physical channels, measurements and indication to higher layers [e.g., frame error rate, *signal-to-interference ratio* (SIR), interference power, transmit power], macrodiversity distribution and combining, soft handover execution, frequency and time synchronization, and power control.

W-CDMA scheme allows mobile and network systems to transmit over a single, widely spread frequency band and different transmitters. The user data sequence is multiplied with a so-called spreading sequence, whose symbol or chip rate is much higher than the user data rate. This spreads the user data signal to a wider frequency band. The relation between user data rate and chip rate is called a *spreading factor*. The chip rate in W-CDMA is 3.84 Mcps, and spreading factors are in the range of 4 to 512; therefore, the user net bit rates supported by one code channel are in the range of 1 to 936 kbps in the downlink. As many as three parallel codes can be used for one user, giving bit rates as high as 2.3 Mbps. In the uplink, data rates are half of these figures because of modulation differences.

The W-CDMA standard includes two modes of operation:

1. The W-CDMA FDD mode is utilized to perform an efficient use of the paired and unpaired band of the allocation spectrum (as depicted by Figure 1).
2. The W-CDMA TDD mode is intended for applications in macrocell and microcell environments with medium data rates and high mobility. The W-CDMA TDD mode is particularly well suited for environments with high traffic density and indoor coverage, where client applications require high data rates.

W-CDMA TDD and W-CDMA FDD differ in the physical layer of UTRA protocol layers because they use different duplex and different multiple access techniques. All other protocols and system components are nearly the same.

The W-CDMA transmission is split into 10-ms radio frames, each of which consists of fifteen time slots of 666 ms (2560 chips). The bit rate and channel coding can be changed in every 10-ms frame, offering highly flexible control of the user data rate. Every time slot has bits reserved for pilot signal, power control, and, if necessary, transmission diversity. *Diversity* is a method to combat noise and fading (Pedersen et al. 1999). It provides the receiver with multiple copies of signals generated by the same underlying data.

UMTS Link Layer

The data-link layer contains four sublayers: (1) the MAC layer, (2) the RLC layer, (3) the PDCP, and (4) the BMC. The PDPC enables the independence of layer 3 and lower layers by making possible their independent development. The main functions of BMC are the scheduling and delivery of cell broadcast and multicast messages.

UMTS MAC Layer

The MAC layer is located on top of the physical layer. It is responsible for mapping logical channels used for communication with the higher layers into physical ones. It is also used for priority handling of users' equipment and the data flows of MS, traffic monitoring, ciphering, and multiplexing processes.

UMTS RLC Layer

The RLC layer is responsible for the acknowledgement and unacknowledgement of data transfer, establishment connections, QoS settings, and ciphering. There is one RLC connection per radio carrier. Management addresses the following tasks:

- Communication management includes functions and procedures that are related to user connections.
- MM includes functions and procedures that are related to mobility and security.
- Radio resource management includes algorithms that are related to the radio resource.

UMTS Network Layer

UMTS RRC Layer

The radio resource control sublayer constitutes the split of layer 3 in the radio interface. It handles the control plane signaling between the mobile station and the UTRAN (3GPP 2005). Some of the functions offered by the RRC include the following:

- broadcasting information provided by the core network;
- management of connections between the mobile station and the UTRAN, including their establishment, reestablishment, maintenance, and release;
- management of the radio bearers, including their establishment, maintenance, release, and corresponding connection mobility;
- RRC connection mobility functions;
- paging and notification;
- control of requested quality of service;
- mobile station measurement reporting and control of the reporting;
- control of the encryption;
- timing advance control;
- configuration of the MAC and RLC; and
- controlling packet data size to be sent on transport channels.

Channel Structure

The MAC can support multiple channel types: The transport channels are depicted between MAC and layer 1, and the logical channels are depicted between MAC and RLC.

Transport Channels

These channels are resources that are divided among all or a group of users in a cell. They include the following different types:

- A *random access channel* is used on the uplink from the MS to the network to request a *dedicated traffic channel* (DCCH).
- A *forward access channel* carries downlink control information to terminals known to be located in the cell under control. It is further used to transmit a small amount of downlink packet data.
- A *downlink shared channel* carries dedicated user data or control information and can be shared in time between several users. It is considered as a pure data channel and is always associated with a downlink dedicated channel.
- A *common packet channel* carries uplink packet-based user data. It supports uplink inner loop power control with the aid of a downlink dedicated physical control channel.
- An *uplink shared channel* is used for *time division duplexing* (TDD) operation only.
- The *broadcast channel* is used to transmit specific information to the UTRAN or to a given cell (e.g., random access codes, cell access slots, cell type transmit diversity methods, etc.)
- The *paging channel* carries data that are relevant to the paging procedure. The paging message can be transmitted in a single or several cells, according to the system configuration.

Logical Channels

The MAC layer provides data transfer services on logical channels. A set of logical channel types is defined for different kinds of data transfer services as offered by MAC. The control channels used for transfer of control plane information are the broadcast control channel, the paging control channel, the common control channel, the DCCH, and the shared channel control channel.

The traffic channels are used for the transfer of user plane information only using the dedicated traffic channel and the common traffic channel.

MOBILITY MANAGEMENT

MM is the essential technology that enables networks to support mobile users, allowing them to move, while simultaneously offering incoming calls, data packets, and other services. It is concerned with location procedures and handoff management. It enables communication networks to locate roaming terminals in order to deliver data packets and maintain connections.

Location Management

Location management is concerned with the procedures that enable the system to discover the current attachment point (or current location) of the mobile user for call delivery. It contains two processes: *location registration* and *service delivery.*

In location registration, the mobile terminal periodically notifies the network of its new access point, allowing the network to authenticate the user and revise the user's location profile. With service delivery, the network can be queried for the user's location profile; the current position of the mobile host is then found.

The UMTS scheme consists of a two-level hierarchy of location registers (the home location and the visitor location registers) that are used to track mobile registration. Information about each user (such as the types of services subscribed) and location information are stored in a user profile located at the HLR. Each VLR stores the information of the mobile station (downloaded from the HLR) visiting its associated area.

Location Registration

To correctly deliver calls, the system must keep track of each mobile's location. As described previously, the databases HLR and VLR are used to store the location information. As the mobiles move around the network coverage area, this information may no longer be accurate. To ensure that calls can be delivered successfully, the databases are periodically updated through a process called *location registration.* The registration steps are given as follows (see Figure 6).

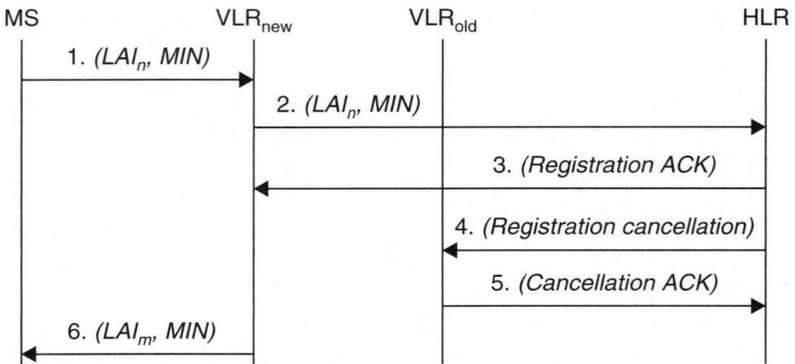

Figure 6: Location registration

- The MS enters a new local area and transmits a location update message containing the *local area identity* and *mobile identification number* (LAI_n, MIN) to the new VLR (VLR_{new}). This is formally denoted by:

$$MS \rightarrow VLR_{new} \qquad (LAI_n,\ MIN)$$

- If the new local area belongs to a different VLR, then the VLR_{new} determines the address of the HLR of the MS from its MIN. Otherwise, location registration is complete:

$$VLR_{new} \rightarrow HLR \qquad (LAI_n,\ MIN)$$

- The HLR performs the required procedures to authenticate the MS and records the ID of the VLR_{new} of the MS. The HLR then sends a registration *acknowledgment* (ACK) message to the VLR_{new}.

$$HLR \rightarrow VLR_{new} \qquad (\text{registration ACK})$$

- The HLR sends a registration cancellation message to the VLR_{old}:

$$HLR \rightarrow VLR_{old} \qquad (\text{registration cancellation})$$

- The VLR_{old} removes the record of the MS and returns a cancellation acknowledgment message to the HLR:

$$HLR \rightarrow VLR_{old} \qquad (\text{cancellation ACK})$$

- The VLR_{new} sends to the MS the new local area identity (LAI_m),

$$VLR_{new} \rightarrow MS \qquad (LAI_m,\ MIN)$$

Service Delivery

The call delivery procedures locate the mobile terminal based on the information available in the HLR and the VLR when a call for a mobile terminal is initiated. Two major steps are involved in call delivery: (1) determining the serving VLR of the called mobile station, and (2) locating the visiting cell of the called mobile terminal. Locating the serving VLR of the MS involves the following database lookup procedure (Figure 7 depicts the steps and messages involved in this process):

- The calling mobile terminal sends a call initiation signal to the serving MSC of the mobile terminal through a nearby base station.
- The MSC determines the address of the HLR of the called mobile terminal by global title translation and sends a location request message to the HLR.
- The HLR determines the serving VLR of the called mobile terminal and sends a route request message to the VLR. The VLR then forwards the message to the MSC serving the mobile terminal.
- The MSC allocates a temporary identifier called the *temporary local directory number* (TLDN) to the mobile terminal and sends a reply to the HLR together with the TLDN.
- The HLR forwards this information to the MSC of the calling mobile terminal.
- The calling MSC requests a call setup to the called MSC through the *signaling system 7* (SS7) network.

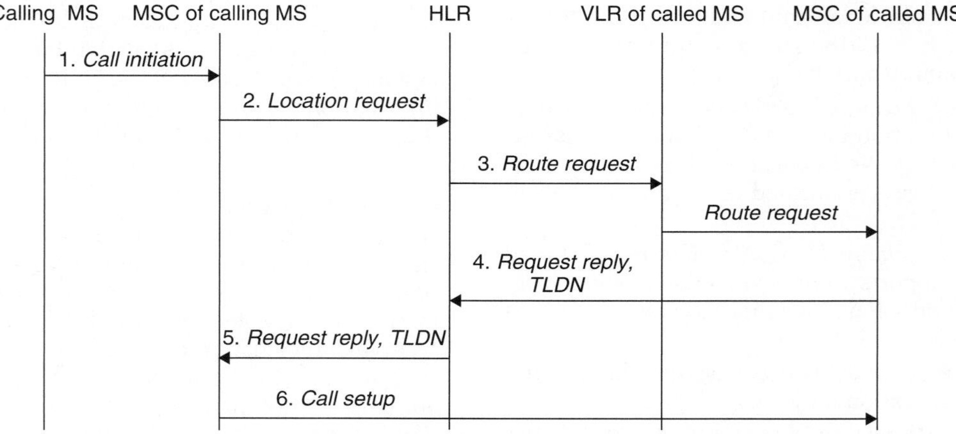

Figure 7: Service delivery

Handoff Management

The ability to make and receive calls anywhere at any time, creating a totally new dimension in human communications, has frequently been advertised as the main advantage of new wireless systems. Handoffs are a key concept in providing this mobility. It enables the user to move within the network while in a call and involves the reconfiguration of the communication channels. Handoff management is the process of initiating and ensuring a seamless and lossless handoff of a mobile station from the region covered by one node to another. It consists of three operations: handoff decision, network connection, and data flow control.

Requirements of Handoff

To achieve a high level of efficiency while providing acceptable guarantees for quality of service, the handoff performed by UMTS should satisfy the following requirements.

- *Latency* is the time required to perform the handoff; it should be appropriate to the rate of mobility of the terminal and the nature of data transferred.
- With *scalability,* the handoff procedure should support handoffs within the same cell and between different base stations in the same or in different networks.
- Minimal drop-off and fast recovery.
- The quality of service should be maintained or renegotiated after the handoff process if needed.
- Minimal additional signaling, or the reduction of control signals, has been the fundamental design consideration. In fact, handoff signaling should have a minimal impact on networking performance and quality.

Handoff Decision

The handoff decision needs the monitoring of the current network connections, recognizing the need for handoff and subsequently initiating it. In most technologies, the conventional criteria used to reflect the state of the current network connection are the received signal strength, SIR, coverage area, *bit error rate* (BER), and *block error rate* (BLER). In addition to these criteria, UMTS takes into consideration other factors such as the status of neighboring base stations and different radio link measurements. Two basic criteria for measurements reporting are used: *periodic reporting* and *event-triggered reporting.* The different types of air-interface measurements, performed at every cell, are classified into the following six categories.

- Intrafrequency measurements: These are measurements on downlink physical channels made at the frequency used by the active set.
- Interfrequency measurements: These are measurements on downlink physical channels at frequencies that differ from the frequency used by the active set.
- Inter-RAT (i.e., *radio access technology*) measurements: These are measurements on downlink physical channels belonging to another radio access technology than UTRA network such as GSM.
- Traffic volume measurements: These measurements control the uplink traffic volume.
- Quality measurements: These measurements report on downlink quality parameters such as the downlink transport block error rate. A measurement object corresponds to one transport channel in case of BLER. Performed on a time slot, in case of SIR, it is used with the TDD mode only.
- MS-internal measurements: These measurements report on MS transmission power and MS received signal level.
- MS positioning measurements: These measurements track the MS position.

Handoff Types

UMTS provides mobile users four types of handoff: softer, soft, hard, and intertechnology.

Softer Handoff. A *softer handoff* is also called an *intersector handoff.* It occurs when the mobile station is in the overlapping coverage area of two adjacent sectors belonging to the same node B serving one cell as shown by Figure 8, where the MS is connected to two adjacent sectors (1 and 2). One important advantage of softer handoff is the shorter service interruption caused by handoff. A disadvantage is, however, observed with a softer handoff: data duplication during the softer handoff phase may degrade the total system throughput.

Soft Handoff. *Soft handoff* means that the radio links are added and removed in a way that the MS always keeps at least one radio link to the UTRA network. A soft handoff occurs when the mobile station is in the overlapping coverage area of two or more adjacent cells (as shown in Figure 9). The user has two or more simultaneous connections to the UTRA network as part of the network using different air-interface channels concurrently. Normally, soft handoff can be used when cells that operate on the same frequency are changed.

A key benefit of soft handoff is the path diversity on the forward and reverse traffic channels. Diversity gain is obtained because less power is required on the forward and reverse links. This gain implies that the total system interference is reduced. As a result, the average system capacity is improved.

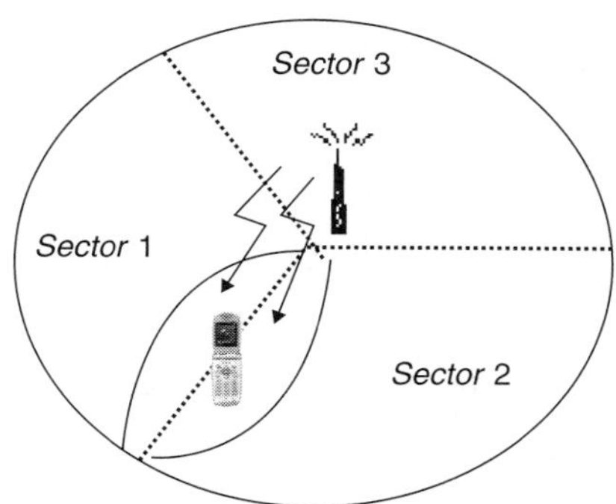

Figure 8: Softer handoff

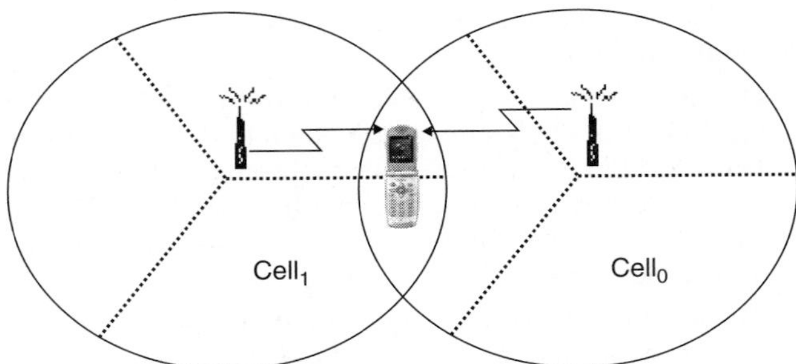

Figure 9: Soft handoff

Hard Handoff. *Hard handoff* is different from the soft handoff process. It means that a connection is broken before a new radio connection is established between the user equipment and the radio access network. Hard handoff can be seamless or nonseamless. *Seamless* hard handoff means that the handoff is not perceptible to the user. In practice, a handoff that requires a change of carrier frequency (i.e., interfrequency handoff) is always performed as a hard handoff.

The main problem observed with hard handoffs is characterized by the blocking probability experienced by users entering a new cell. This probability can be reduced by giving priority to handoff users over new users. This can be done, for example, by reserving a certain part of the capacity in each cell for users with ongoing communication.

Intertechnology Handoff. From the technical point of view, one can distinguish between intrasystem and intersystem handoffs. For UMTS, the following types of *intersystem* handoff are specified:

- In an intersystem *FDD* or *TDD handoff,* the calls are transferred from FDD access mode to TDD.
- In an intersystem *TDD* or *FDD handoff,* the calls are transferred from TDD access mode to FDD.
- In an intersystem *UMTS-2G handoff,* a call is transferred from one UMTS cell to a 2G cell (e.g., handoff from UMTS to GSM).
- In an intersystem *2G-UMTS handoff,* a call is transferred from one 2G cell to a UMTS cell (e.g., handoff from GSM to UMTS).

Intersystem handoff is a necessary feature to support the upgrade of 2G systems to UMTS as well as support the different UMTS modes. Obviously, the mobile station has to support both modes. Even though the intersystem handoff is performed after a network evaluation of resources, the mobile terminal must also support the necessary measurements to achieve it.

UMTS QUALITY OF SERVICE

Typically, QoS refers to the collective effect of service performance that determines the degree of satisfaction that end users feel about the service they are getting (3GPP 2004, "QoS"). A major goal of 3G networks is to deliver multimedia services that meet sophisticated end-to-end QoS requirements. The difficulty in providing this in 3G wireless systems results from the mobility of nodes and the unpredictable nature of the radio link. In particular, the access network is one of the most critical parts of the system because both the air interface and the terrestrial transmission resources it involves are extremely limited and the QoS constraints are tight. Hence, a 3G mobile communication network operator has to maximize the number of users while maintaining user QoS requirements. In this respect, two aspects can be clearly differentiated: (1) the network planning, which is the design of the fixed network infrastructure in terms of number of cell sites, cell site location, and number and architecture of concentration nodes; and (2) the radio resource allocation.

Multimedia traffic puts heavy bandwidth demand on cellular networks. Typically, bandwidth is the most critical resource needed by multimedia services in cellular networks. It requires that ad hoc mechanisms efficiently assign the available resources. Therefore, the need arises for sophisticated radio resources management mechanisms, which are responsible for the utilization of air-interface resources. Also, the implementation of efficient algorithms is needed to guarantee QoS requirements and provide high capacity.

UMTS Services

Because of the limitations of the air-interface capacity, the QoS classes supported in UMTS are different from those supported by fixed networks. Two types of services can be defined for 3G mobiles: *real-time services* (e.g., videoconferencing) and *non–real-time services* (e.g., database applications). In this context, the 3GPP, which is the body responsible for UMTS specifications, defined four distinct traffic classes for UMTS (3GPP 2004, "QoS"): conversational, streaming, interactive, and background.

1. The *conversational class* is intended to carry extremely delay-sensitive applications. The best-known application of this class is the voice service.
2. Within the *streaming class,* a client browser can start displaying streaming data before an entire file has been transmitted. Streaming is a one-way transport mechanism and requires the delay variation of the end-to-end flow to be limited.
3. The most important characteristic of the *interactive class* is that the content of packets be preserved and transparently transferred with low BER. The known applications for this class are Web browsing and network games.
4. The *background class* contains services that are most delay nonsensitive traffic. The known applications of this class are services that allow file downloading (e.g., FTP), e-mail, and SMS.

Resources Management

Another significant feature introduced by UMTS is the provision of QoS on an end-to-end basis. The UMTS QoS idea is based on the goal of efficient use of resources in a packet-switched network (Heier and Malkowski 2002). The main factors that affect the QoS as perceived by the user are the *new call blocking probability* and the *hand-off blocking probability.* The lack of network resources can cause unsuccessful calls. The blocking probability can occur at the radio link, at the interworking unit between the mobile and the fixed networks, or at the transmitting network. To reduce the blocking probability values, it is necessary to improve resource allocation and reserve resources for handoffs (3GPP 2004, "Radio").

Call Admission

Within the CDMA technique, all users share the bandwidth and each new connection increases the interference level of the other connections, affecting their quality of service. To keep the interference below a tolerable level, the number of users is limited to a certain threshold. The *call admission control* has to avoid overload situations when admitting or denying new users (Corbett and Everit 2003). Admission control principles make use of the load factors and an estimation of the load increase that the establishment of a new call would cause on the radio network.

Congestion Control

Congestion occurs when the admitted users cannot be satisfied with the normal services agreed for a given percentage of time because of an overload occurrence (Kasera et al. 2005). The congestion state then has to invoke some procedure—a *congestion control*—that could prevent some users from getting the normal quality-of-service margin beyond the contracted percentage of time.

Power Control

Power control mechanisms are used to reduce mobile's transmission power. In WCDMA, this is a closed-loop power command, which is a combination of outer and inner closed-loop control. The inner closed-loop power control adjusts the transmitted power in order to keep the received SIR equal to a given target. This SIR target is fixed according to the received BLER or BER. The setting of the SIR target is done by the outer loop power control, which is part the RRC layer, in order to match the required BLER (3GPP 2001, "Physical layer").

The UMTS system has three main schemes of power control (3GPP undated, "Power control"). In the first scheme, the transmitted power is updated at each time slot. It is increased or decreased by a fixed value (ΔdB):

- If $SIR_{estimated}$ is greater than SIR_{target}, then the transmitted power control command to transmit is 0, meaning that a transmit power decrease is requested; and
- if $SIR_{estimated}$ is less than SIR_{target}, then the transmitted power control command to transmit is 1, or a transmit power increase is requested.

The second scheme consists of performing a hard decision based on values read from five time slots. If all of the time slots yield a command to increase or decrease power, then it will be done for the next five time slots. If any of the commands in a group of five time slots differs from the other commands in the same group, then the power shall remain at the same level for the next five time slots.

The third scheme consists of a soft decision based on the measurements in three time slots, yielding an increase or decrease in power according to the overall weighed decision of the three time slots.

Both uplink and downlink have two different types of power control. For uplink, schemes 1 and 2 are used. The Δdb for type 1 is either 1 dB or 2 dB, whereas the ΔdB used for type 2 is 1 dB. For downlink, schemes 1 and 3 are used. The ΔdB in downlink can be 0.5 dB, 1 dB, 1.5 dB, or 2 dB; it is mandatory that the UTRAN support at least the value of 1 dB.

Resource Allocation

Because of increasing traffic asymmetry in mobile communications, there is a significant need to improve resource allocation in UMTS. Two methods of allocation are available on medium access control: *fixed channel allocation* (FCA) and *dynamic channel allocation* (DCA) (Wie and Cho 2001; Corbett and Everit 2003).

Fixed Channel Allocation. With the FCA method, the numbers of uplink and downlink channels are statically defined. There are two scenarios to implement FCA: (1) symmetric fixed channel allocation and (2) asymmetric fixed channel allocation. The symmetric case uses only one more slot for the downlink than the uplink. The asymmetric case uses more slots for the downlink than the uplink.

Dynamic Channel Allocation. DCA enables a cellular system to adapt flexibly to different load situations, thereby increasing bandwidth utilization and decreasing new call blocking. The numbers of uplink and downlink channels were dynamically defined. DCA provides an efficient allocation of the available resources by shifting the switching point within a transmission frame to accommodate the varying traffic in each direction. Thus, DCA is a better access method than FCA in a TDD-CDMA system.

Resources Reservation

In cellular networks, each mobile maintains connectivity via an *active set* (this is defined as the set of nodes B that the MS is simultaneously connected to) of cells, which are involved with the mobile during handoff. To support applications and protocols used on wired networks, the handoff processing must not significantly affect the end-to-end loss or delay of any communication. Handoff requests compete with new call requests to gain admission into a target cell. The call admission control protocol should give prioritized admission to handoff requests because, from the user's point of view, disruptions during handoffs are considered more objectionable than new call blocking.

In Bartolini (2001), a nonpreemptive prioritization scheme for call admission control in cellular networks was presented and analyzed. Two kinds of users can compete for the access to the limited number of frequency channels that are available on each cell: High-priority users represent handoff requests, whereas low-priority users correspond to initial access requests originated within the same cell. Queuing of handoff requests can be also considered.

UMTS SECURITY

The GSM lacked mutual authentication and did not provide any protection in the core network of the cellular system. The integration of security mechanisms in UMTS makes use of the experiences, which were made especially in connection with the GSM and GPRS and their weaknesses (European Telecommunications Standards Institute 2000). In fact, the UMTS security is based on second-generation security procedures with different enhancements and extensions. UMTS comprises a complete security infrastructure that contains two levels: access control and network security (3GPP 2001, "3G security"; 3GPP 2002, "3G security").

Access Control

The access control deals with security issues concerning the air interface and the UTRA network. Network access security features can be further classified into the categories of mutual authentication, confidentiality, and data integrity.

Authentication and Key Agreement

In GSM systems, the network requires an authentication of mobile users, but the network does not have to authenticate itself to the user. Therefore, eavesdropping techniques such as the use of so-called IMSI catcher devices may identify a single user and deactivate the encryption functionality. UMTS introduces a new protocol for *authentication and key agreement* (AKA), which should solve these problems and be secure against man-in-the-middle attacks (3GPP 2002, "Third Generation"). The AKA is the combination of terminal authentication and session key exchange. Its goal has twofold actions: (1) The user and the network authenticate each other and (2) the user and network agree on *cypher* (or *encryption*) and *integrity keys* (CK and IK, respectively).

The mechanism AKA is based on a challenge–response authentication protocol conceived in such a way as to achieve maximum compatibility with GSM's subscriber authentication and key establishment protocol; this makes the transition from GSM to UMTS easier. A challenge–response protocol is a security measure that is intended for an entity to verify the identity of another entity without revealing a secret password shared by the two entities. The key concept with this scheme is related to the fact that each entity must prove to the other that it knows the appropriate password without actually revealing or transmitting it.

The UMTS AKA process is invoked by a serving network after (1) first registration of a user, (2) a service request, (3) a location update request, (4) an attached request, or (5) a disconnect request or a connection reestablishment request.

To clarify the description of the generation of authentication vectors, the following symbols and notations are used:

- K for the authentication secret key;
- f1, f1*, f2 for the authentication functions defined by the UMTS standard (the functions with * are used in the resynchronization event);
- f3, f4, f5 for the key generation functions;
- SQN for sequence number; and
- ||, $\oplus$ for concatenation and exclusive OR.

Generation of Authentication Vectors at AuC

Upon receipt of an authentication data request, the AuC starts generating a fresh sequence number SQN and an unpredictable challenge RAND. Then it sends the authentication vector to the VLR. The authentication vector contains a RAND, a network *authentication token* (AUTN), an *expected result* (XRES), a temporary IK, and a temporary CK, where:

- MAC = $f1_K$(SQN || RAND || AMF) is the message authentication code;
- XRES = $f2_K$(RAND) is the expected response;
- CK = $f3_K$(RAND) is the cipher key;
- IK = $f4_K$(RAND) is the integrity key; and
- AK = $f5_K$(RAND) is the anonymity key.

Figure 10 depicts the generation actions used to create an authentication vector AV by the AuC.

The *authentication management field* (AMF) is used to define operator-specific options in the authentication process—for example, the use of multiple authentication algorithms or limits on key lifetime.

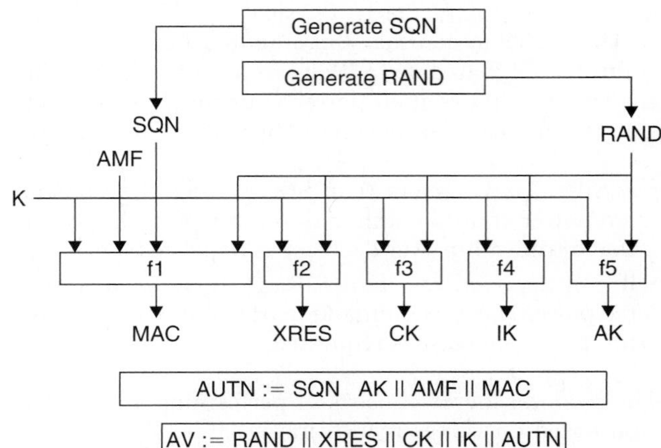

Figure 10: Generation of authentication vectors at AuC

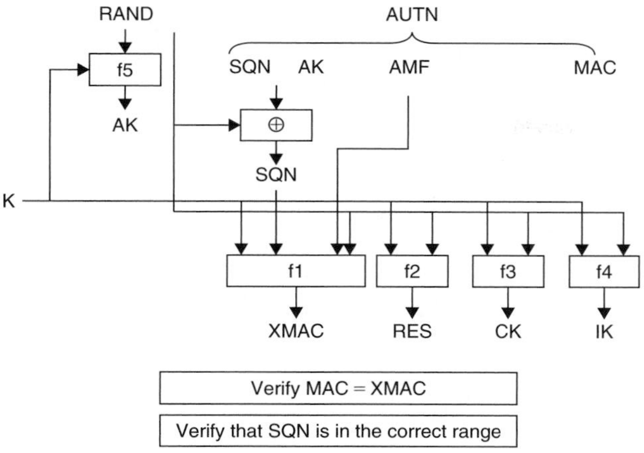

Figure 11: Generation of authentication vectors at USIM

Generation of Authentication Vectors at USIM

The universal subscriber identity module first computes the *anonymity key* [AK = $f5_K$ (RAND)] and retrieves the sequence number SQN = (SQN ⊕ AK) ⊕ AK. Next the USIM computes XMAC = $f1_K$ (SQN || RAND || AMF) and compares this with MAC, which is included in AUTN. If they are different, the user sends a user authentication reject back to the VLR or SGSN with an indication of the cause, and the user abandons the procedure. If the MAC verification was successful, the USIM verifies that the received sequence number SQN is in the correct range. If the sequence number is considered to be in the correct range, the USIM then computes RES = $f2_K$(RAND); otherwise, it sends a synchronization failure message back to the VLR or SGSN, including information about an acceptable sequence number, and abandons the procedure. Figure 11 summarizes the authentication-vector generation at the USIM.

Authentication Procedures

UMTS provides a set of procedures for authentication. These procedures work as follows.

- The mobile station discovers a VLR or SGSN. It sends its current temporary identity TMSI to the network. If the network cannot resolve the TMSI, then it requests the mobile station to send its permanent identity; the mobile stations answers the request with the IMSI:

  MS → VLR or SGSN (TMSI or IMSI)

- Once it has identified the MS, the VLR or SGSN requests authentication data from the home network of the mobile station:

  VLR or SGSN → AuC (IMSI)

- Upon receipt of a request from the VLR or SGSN, the AuC sends an ordered array of *n* authentication vectors to the VLR or SGSN. Each authentication vector contains a random challenge RAND, the corresponding AUTN, an XRES, an IK, and the CK:

  AuC → VLR or SGSN (RAND, AUTN, XRES, IK, CK)

- Once it has received the authentication vector, the VLR or SGSN selects the one authentication vector from the ordered array ($i \in [1, n]$) and sends the parameters $RAND_i$ and $AUTN_i$ to the mobile station:

  VLR or SGSN → MS ($RAND_i$, $AUTN_i$)

- The mobile station verifies $AUTN_i$ and computes the response (RES_i) to the challenge, the cipher key (CK_i), the integrity key (IK_i), and the authentication key (AK_i). If $AUTN_i$ is not correct, then the mobile station discards the message. Then the mobile station sends its authentication response (RES_i) to the visited network.

  MS → VLR or SGSN (RES_i)

- The VLR or SGSN checks whether $RES_i = XRES_i$ and decides which security algorithms the radio subsystem is allowed to use.
- The VLR or SGSN sends the allowed algorithms to the radio subsystem.
- The radio access network decides which (of the allowed) algorithms to use.
- The radio access network informs the mobile station of its choice in the security mode command message. The message also includes the security capabilities the network received from the mobile station in step 1. This message is integrity protected with the integrity key IK_i.
- The MS validates the integrity protection and checks the correctness of the security capabilities.

Finally, let us note that for compatibility with the GSM security architecture, the handoff between UMTS and GSM will be needed frequently. The UMTS AKA has been designed in such a way that roaming and handoff between GSM and UMTS works as smoothly as possible as far as security is concerned. This is facilitated by the similarity between UMTS quintets and GSM triplets. Conversion functions are specified to convert quintets into triplets and vice versa.

Provision Temporary Identities

UMTS provides user identity confidentiality through the use of temporary identities. After initial registration, users are not identified via their permanent identity IMSIs but instead use TMSIs. To avoid user traceability, which may lead to compromises of user identity confidentiality, temporary identities are changed regularly. The steps of TMSI allocation are as follows:

VLR → MS	(IMSI request)
MS → VLR	(IMSI)
VLR → MS	(TMSI allocation)
MS → VLR	(TMSI acknowledgement)

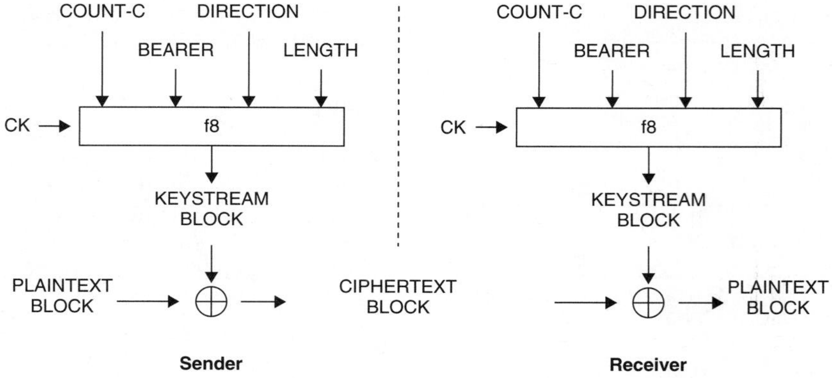

Figure 12: UTRAN encryption

UTRAN Encryption

Figure 12 shows the encryption process. It is meant to occur only between the MS and RNC. The encryption algorithm is a proprietary stream cipher called f8, which is a special mode of operation built around the KASUMI block cipher. The UTRA network encryption is based on the CK transported from the AuC to the VLR or SGSN and computed in the USIM. The keys are never transported in the clear over the radio interface. This enables interconnection of RNCs with CN nodes. The confidentiality of both user and signaling data are protected.

In addition to CK, encryption process takes a few more inputs. These are:

- the LENGTH parameter, which specifies how long the keystream shall be, with a maximum allowed length for the keystream of 20,000 bits;
- the DIRECTION and BEARER identities, which are taken into account to avoid reusing the same keystream for both directions or on different radio bearers; and
- the COUNTER, which in turn ensures that the same keystream is never used twice on the same bearer for a single direction.

The confidentiality feature is the same as in GSM, but the entities between which protection is afforded are different. In UMTS, the protection extends to the radio network controller so that microwave links between the base stations and the RNC are also covered.

Integrity Protection

The integrity protection is limited to happen only between the MS and the RNC, as depicted in Figure 13. The integrity key is derived during the AKA procedure. The UMTS integrity algorithm is implemented in the MS and in the RNC. Integrity protection is applied on a per-message basis at the RRC layer. The 128-bit IK is generated during the AKA procedure and is never transported over the radio interface. Several integrity algorithms can be supported, and a four-bit algorithm identifier is defined to indicate which algorithms are supported. This security feature has no equivalent in GSM.

Network Security

The network security comprises security features in the core network. It covers security of the communications between network elements. In particular, the mobile station is not affected by network domain security. Many different security mechanisms have been standardized by the Internet Engineering Task Force for IP-based networks.

Signaling System

A major part of the 3GPP release 99 specifications was devoted to the introduction of a completely new radio access technology while the core network part was an extension of the existing GSM specification set. This is the main reason why the protection mechanisms for core

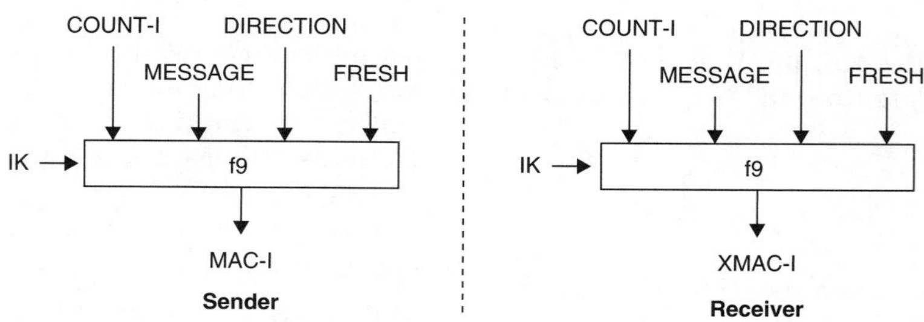

Figure 13: Integrity check

network signaling were not introduced in release 99. The security has been based on the fact that the SS7 network has been accessible only to a relatively small number of well-established organizations and institutions. It has been extremely difficult for attackers to insert or manipulate SS7 messages.

MAPsec

Starting from release 4, the situation is changing because the number of different operators and service providers that need to communicate with each other is increasing and there is a trend to replace SS7 networks with IP networks.

MAPsec's purpose is to protect confidentiality and integrity of *mobile application part* (MAP) operations (Kaaranen et al. 2001). The security services provided by MAPsec are data integrity, data origin authentication, antireplay protection, and confidentiality (optional).

MAPsec protection operates in three different modes. In the first mode, no security is guaranteed. In the second mode, only integrity is protected. In the third, both confidentiality and integrity are provided.

- For confidentiality, the header of the MAC operation is encrypted. A security header is added to indicate how decryption should be done.
- For integrity, again a MAC is calculated over the payload of the original MAP operation and the security header. A time-variant parameter is also used to prevent replay attacks (Kaaranen et al. 2001).

The MAPsec security model has a few important limitations. It was perceived by some experts to be too expensive to protect all MAP messages, and therefore a scheme to specify subsets of the MAP messages to be protected had to be invented. The protection profile scheme was developed to achieve this while also constraining the interdomain negotiations in order to reduce complexity.

IPsec

The most significant feature that is used for the protection of network domain traffic is the IPsec protocol (Kaaranen et al. 2001). It provides confidentiality and integrity of communication in the IP layer. Communicating parties can also authenticate each other using IPsec (Kaaranen et al. 2001). The main parts of IPSec are the *authentication header* (AH), the *encapsulation security payload* (ESP), and the *Internet key exchange* (IKE) (Internet Engineering Task Force 1998). The AH only provides integrity and message authentication, whereas ESP can provide both integrity and message authentication and confidentiality. In 3GPP release 5, the IKE is based on pre-shared secrets.

One serious problem with IPSec is that the protocol does not support network address translation, a technology that is used to increase the public address space. Also, the use of IPsec together with mobile IP will lead to substantial performance degradation related to extensive protocol overhead. Another serious shortcoming of IPsec is its lack of session resume functionality. In fact, without session resume, the user will have to log on every time a connection is lost, including user authentication and key exchange.

FUTURE WIRELESS NETWORKS

UMTS is a third-generation solution that promises faster communications services—including voice, fax, and Internet—anytime and anywhere with seamless global roaming. Future wireless networks will be built by a combination of many access networks that bring together mobility not only without geographical constraints but also without being tied to one particular backbone network. They will be able to provide a wide variety of new services, mobile multimedia, and global mobility support. In fact, users who have been receiving services in an urban area with access to the Internet will still be able to access services from different geographical sites. Each access network of future wireless networks will have its attributes, requirements, and mechanisms (signal quality, data rate, handoff decision, coverage discovery, security services, authentication models, etc.). This will require more research and development of architectures and protocols to interconnect those heterogeneous networks in a seamless fashion. In this context, many technical challenges need to be faced such as those associated with heterogeneous architectures, seamless handoff, and secure heterogeneous mobility.

Typically, future research must mainly focus on the following.

- Definition of future wireless network architecture that is flexible and open to existing standards: The integration of WLAN increases the capacity and extends the coverage.
- Definition of a scheme for global mobility: Future wireless networks will implement terminal mobility, personal mobility, and service provider portability.
- Development of new methods to guarantee the service continuity in roaming between different access networks.
- Provide a high level of security: Future wireless networks should maintain the same level of security services for mobile users when they roam across different access networks.
- Deployment with software defined radios: Allowing the equipment to be upgraded to new protocols and services, and supporting roaming across diverse network technologies via software upgrades.

Future wireless networks will generally be characterized by multiple radio access technologies, where different access technologies such as cellular networks (GSM, GPRS, UMTS, etc.), satellite-based networks, wireless local area networks, and wired networks should be combined on a common platform to complement each other. This platform may be called *open wireless architecture* (Zarai and Boudriga 2005), and it should address vertical handoff, translation QoS requirements, and resource allocation.

To achieve global mobility, future wireless networks should provide IP mobility. The mobile users are connecting to the unified wireless network and are free to move around the network coverage area. Global mobility should implement the following:

- *terminal mobility,* or the ability of the network to route calls and services to the terminal regardless of its point of attachment to the network and the access technology it implements;

- *personal mobility,* or the ability of user to access their personal services independent of their terminal attachment points (providing privacy, integrity, and confidentiality may be required with personal mobility); and
- *service provider portability,* which allows users or terminals to move beyond regional mobile networks and be connected to the same service regardless of the service provided, an issue that may need the implementation of such mechanisms as renegotiation and rerouting.

Within a future wireless networks framework, a mobile terminal may transition from a wired network to a cellular network, from a WLAN to a cellular network, or from a cellular network to a satellite connection. Such movement induces packet loss and latency, which can severely damage the quality of data communications. Thus, appropriate handoff mechanisms must be implemented to minimize these parameters and maintain good levels of network performances while attempting to prevent disruption. Issues involved with this objective include:

- predicting, reducing, and estimating low latency;
- reducing signaling messages overhead and processing time; and
- estimating near-zero handoff and call blocking probabilities.

Finally, it is worth mentioning that providing access for every type of network under various mobile environments and the resulting complexity of the future wireless networks systems leave mobility related procedures highly vulnerable. In addition, because location information about mobile users will be extensively used, the providers of services with unlimited access to information must analyze their security procedures to maintain overall privacy and confidentiality. Technical strategies must be developed to achieve reliable authentication and provide significant untraceability for roaming subscribers (even against attacks internal to service providers).

CONCLUSION

This chapter has presented an overview of the development of mobile systems and UMTS. Researchers have considered other types of technologies that could be utilized to extend 3G UMTS network services in dense areas. A WLAN network provides high-speed data communication in restricted coverage areas at a relatively low cost. It allows users to move around in a confined area while still connected to the network. The distinctive advantages of the UMTS and WLAN networks can be combined to provide seamless connectivity when a user moves across heterogeneous access networks.

GLOSSARY

Authentication: Establishing the validity of a claimed identity.

Cell: The smallest geographic area defined for mobile communications systems.

Code Division Multiple Access (CDMA): CDMA is a digital cellular technology that uses spread spectrum techniques that, instead of separating users by frequency, separates them through the use of digital frequency codes across the full available spectrum.

Confidentiality: The assurance that information is not disclosed to inappropriate entities or processes.

Encryption: The cryptographic transformation of data called *plaintext* into a form called *cipher text* that conceals the data's original meaning to prevent them from being known or used.

Fourth Generation (4G): A future wireless network that will enable users to dynamically switch between various wireless access technologies to the IP-based core network.

General Packet Radio Service (GPRS): GPRS is considered a 2.5G wireless technology. It enables high-speed wireless Internet and other communications such as e-mail, games, and applications.

Global System for Mobile (GSM) Communications: GSM is a digital cellular system based on TDMA narrowband technology, which gives users access to time slots on the same frequency bands. It represents a major popular 2G system.

Handoff: A process by which a mobile station changes its point of attachment from one cell to another without interruption in service or loss in connectivity.

Handoff Management: A process of initiating, executing, and controlling handoff of a mobile to ensure the best possible connectivity.

Integrity: The prevention of the unauthorized modification of information.

Location Management: Concerned with the procedures that enable the system to discover the current attachment point (or current location) of the mobile user for call delivery.

Mobility Management (MM): The essential technology that enables networks to support mobile users, allowing them to move, while simultaneously offering them incoming calls, data packets, and other services. It is concerned with location procedures and handoff management.

Quality of Service (QoS): A measure of network performance that reflects the network's transmission quality and service availability.

Roaming: The movement of a mobile station from one wireless network location to another without interruption in service or loss in connectivity.

Seamless Handoff: A handoff that is not perceptible to the user—that is, a smooth transition so that the user does not perceive any delay or interruption of service.

Second Generation (2G): Digital wireless systems that replace analog wireless systems.

Third Generation (3G): Digital wireless systems that will offer wireless Internet services on a worldwide scale, extending the scope of 2G wireless networks from simple voice telephony to complex data applications including voice over IP, video conferencing over IP, Web browsing, and multimedia services. The most prevalent 3G system is UMTS, which is based on W-CDMA.

Time Division Multiple Access (TDMA): Divides a radio frequency available to a network into time slots and then allocates slots to multiple calls. It is used in digital cellular telephone communication.

Two and a Half Generation (2.5G): A standard that appeared to enhance the 2G wireless networks with best-effort packet-switched data services.

Universal Mobile Telecommunications System (UMTS): UMTS is approved by the International Telecommunications Union and is intended for advanced wireless communications. It represents a major 3G system.

Wideband Code Division Multiple Access (W-CDMA): A 3G wireless technology derived from CDMA that transmits digitized data over a wide range of frequencies to boost speed. It uses wide 5-MHz channels and is associated with UMTS and GSM, where it boosts speed by substituting TDMA technology with CDMA.

Wireless Local Area Networks (WLANs): WLANs use radio waves instead of a cable to connect a user device, such as a laptop computer to a local area network (LAN). They provide Ethernet connections over the air and operate under the 802.11 family of specifications developed by the IEEE.

CROSS REFERENCES

See *Cellular Communications Channels*; *Code Division Multiple Access (CDMA)*; *General Packet Radio Service (GPRS)*; *Global System for Mobile Communications (GSM)*.

REFERENCES

3GPP. 2001. 3G security: Security architecture. TS 33.102 (retrieved from www.3gpp.org/ftp/Specs/html-info/33102.htm).

———. 2001. Physical layer procedures (FDD) (release 4). TS 25.214 version 4.1.0.

———. 2002. 3G security: Security architecture. TS 33.102 (retrieved from www.3gpp.org/ftp/Specs/html-info/33102.htm).

———. 2002. Third Generation Partnership Project: 3G security, security threats and requirements. TS 21.133 (retrieved from www.3gpp.org/ftp/Specs/html-info/21133.htm).

———. 2002. UTRAN general overview. TS 25.401 (retrieved from www.3gpp.org/ftp/Specs/html-info/25401.htm.

———. 2004. General UMTS architecture. TS 23.101, version 3.0.1 (retrieved from www.3gpp.org/ftp/Specs/html-info/23101.htm).

———. 2004. QoS concept and architecture. TS 23.107 (retrieved from www.3gpp.org/ftp/tsg_sa/TSG_SA/TSGS_23/Docs/PDF/SP-040033.pdf).

———. 2004. Radio resource management strategies. TR 25.922, version 6.0.1 (retrieved from www.3gpp.org/ftp/Specs/html-info/25922.htm).

———. 2005. Universal Mobile Telecommunications System UMTS: Radio interface protocol architecture. TS 125.301.

———. Undated. Power control. TS 25.101, V5.4.0.

———. Undated. UTRAN Iur interface layer 1. TS 25.421 (retrieved from www.3gpp.org/ftp/Specs/html-info/25421.htm).

———. Undated. UTRAN Iub interface layer 1. TS 25.431 (retrieved from www.3gpp.org/ftp/Specs/html-info/25431.htm).

Bartolini, N. 2001. Handoff and optimal channel assignment in wireless networks. *Mobile Networks and Applications*, 6(6): 511–4.

Corbett, D. J., and D. Everitt. 2003. Adaptive bandwidth allocation in TDD-CDMA systems. In *Proceedings of the Australian Telecommunications, Networks and Applications Conference* (ATNAC 2003), Dec. 8–10, Melbourne.

European Telecommunications Standards Institute. 2000. Digital cellular telecommunications system (phase 2+) (GSM); security related network functions. Technical Specification 100.929, V8.0.02000 (retrieved from www.etsi.org).

Heier, S., and M. Malkowski. 2002. UMTS radio resource management by transport format assignment and selection. In *Proceedings of the Fifth International Symposium on Wireless Personal Multimedia Communications*, May, London, pp. 1187–91.

Internet Engineering Task Force. 1998. The Internet key exchange (IKE). RFC 2409, November.

Kaaranen, H., S. Naghian, L. Laitinen, A. Ahtiainen, and V. Niemi. 2001. *UMTS networks: Architecture, mobility and services*. New York: John Wiley & Sons.

Kasera, S. K., R. Ramjee, S. R. Thuel, and X. Wang. 2005. Congestion control policies for IP-Based CDMA radio access networks. *IEEE Transactions on Mobile Computing*, 4(4): 349–62.

Nicopolitidis, P., M. S. Obaidat, G. I. Papadimitriou, and A. S. Pomportsis. 2003. *Wireless networks*. New York: John Wiley & Sons.

Pedersen, G. F., J. Ø. Nielsen, K. Olesen, and I. Z. Kovacs. 1999. Antenna diversity on a UMTS handheld phone. In *Proceedings of the Personal, Indoor, and Mobile Radio Communications Conference* (PIMRC), September, Osaka, Japan. Vol. 1: 152–56.

Wie, S. H., and D. H. Cho. 2001. Time slot allocation based on a region division in CDMA/TDD systems. In *Proceedings of the Fifty-Third IEEE Vehicular Technology Conference* (VTC Spring 2001). Vol. 4: 2445–9.

Zarai, F., and N. Boudriga. 2005. Provision of quality of service in open wireless architecture. In *Proceedings of the Twelfth IEEE International Conference on Electronic Circuits and Systems* (ICECS), Dec. 11–14, Gammarth, Tunisia, pp. 127–131.

International Mobile Telecommunications-2000 and 3G Wireless Systems

Mustafa M. Matalgah and Omar M. Hammouri, *University of Mississippi*

INTRODUCTION

The International Mobile Telecommunications-2000 (IMT-2000) provides the outline for worldwide wireless access by internetworking the diverse systems of terrestrial and/or satellite-based networks. In fact, this International Telecommunications Union (ITU) initiative has led to a set of recommendations in various areas of new services. Those areas include: band allocation, user bandwidth, flexibility, and richness of classes of service. Although those recommendations aggregated into a set of requirements, the IMT-2000 did not tackle technical specifications on how to achieve those requirements (Collins and Smith 2001). In this chapter, the IMT-2000 requirements, as well as specifications and radio interface technologies proposed by standards forums to meet these requirements, will be discussed. Introductory material for third-generation (3G) systems will be formulated, with special emphasis on wideband code division multiple access (W-CDMA) and code division multiple access 2000 (cdma2000) being the most widely accepted air interfaces in the major parts of the world.

The organization of the chapter is as follows. The first section describes the key specifications and objectives of 3G as well as the motivation behind it. The second section starts with a brief description of the major worldwide standardization bodies and their harmonization efforts. A basic description of the targeted 3G systems is also discussed in this section, both in Europe and North America. Evolution from second-generation (2G)–based systems to 3G is the topic of the third section, which starts with an overview of the cellular concept. The differences between the three systems—first generation (1G) through 3G—are then presented. The major wireless systems are described, as well as the strategies and evolution paths between the various systems. In the fourth section, the universal mobile telecommunications system (UMTS) is detailed, with descriptions of the different releases. Various aspects are tackled, including architecture, layering, channels, spreading, coding, and modulation. The main focuses of the fifth section are structure and layering, forward and reverse links, and channel coding of cdma2000. Finally, a conclusion summarizes the chapter, and a glossary containing the main wireless communication terms is included to help clarify the associated concepts.

OVERVIEW OF IMT-2000 AND 3G SYSTEMS

3G Systems Evolved from IMT-2000

IMT-2000 was developed to smooth the progress of standards that lay the way for a wireless infrastructure encompassing terrestrial and satellite systems that consider both fixed and mobile access for public and private networks. IMT-2000 is a radio and network access specification that defines the technology and methodology of achieving the following goals:

- Global standards
- Compatibility of service within IMT-2000 and with the fixed networks

- High quality
- Small terminals for worldwide use
- Worldwide roaming capability
- Capability for multimedia applications and a wide range of services and terminals
- Improved spectrum efficiency
- Flexibility for evolution to the next generation of wireless systems
- High-speed packet-switched data-rates:
  - Fixed: 2 Mbps
  - Pedestrian speed: 384 kbps
  - Vehicular speed: 144 kbps

ITU originally aimed to unify and standardize 3G technologies on a worldwide scope. Unfortunately, no consensus was reached because the IMT-2000 left the technical specifications behind its requirements open for proposals from interested organizations. Each organization submitted its proposals, and, in 1999, ITU approved five technologies for terrestrial air interfaces (Collins and Smith 2001). The 3G air interface to be implemented depends on the previously deployed mobile system infrastructure (i.e., the 2G network). Accordingly, the air interface to be used will depend on where in the world 3G is to be deployed. The three main 3G air interfaces are based on code division multiple access (CDMA) technologies: cdma2000, UMTS, and universal wireless communication-136 (UWC-136).

Needs for 3G Systems

Why 3G Systems

Imagine the following scenarios, taken from a technical specifications document of the 3rd-Generation Partnership Project (3GPP; 2005), which 3G technologies made possible. (Please refer to the original document for the complete list of scenarios.) Although this list is neither complete nor exhaustive, it helps to explain the motivation to port to 3G technologies.

- Increasing user expectations of:
  - Accessibility anytime and anywhere
  - Faster multimedia and data access
- Phenomenal growth in:
  - Mobile communications
  - Internet/intranet access
  - Use of laptops, palm tops, and personal digital assistants (PDAs)
  - Electronic commerce
- Future capabilities of 3G wireless:
  - Life in the twenty-first century
  - The need for outstanding applications
  - The need for mobile multimedia services
  - Economy growth
  - The need for high data rates services
  - Open and near global standards

Enhanced User Convenience

1. The user is in a voice communication and receives an incoming IP video communication. The user decides not to accept the communication but diverts the incoming video to a messaging system. The user is given an indication that there is a video message in his mailbox.
2. The user is in a voice communication and receives an incoming video communication. The user decides to accept the communication but wishes to switch between the two communications.
3. The user is idle in a network and not involved in a communication. The user modifies his user profile to divert all voice communications other than those from high-priority, pre-identified callers (e.g., his boss). In this scenario, all e-mails and text messages continue to be received regardless of the sender.
4. On receiving a communication, the calling party's identity is displayed (if not restricted), and the user shall be able to decide whether to accept the communication or divert to a messaging system. The user shall be able to request media handling of the communication (e.g., media splitting to different destinations, media conversion).
5. The user is in a communication when he receives an incoming communication; he responds to the originating party that he will respond later. The user may request that the originating party's details (if not restricted) be stored with a reminder in user's profile.

Emergency Location with Voice Conversation, Navigation, and Picture Transfer

Person(s): Ma Beth, her children, and the pet dog Bobby

Situation: The family is out driving in the countryside, and they take a turn on the slippery country road a bit too fast. They slide down into the ditch. Bobby the dog, sitting in the back of the van, is hit by a heavy box of books on top of his left paw. It may be broken, and you can tell it certainly hurts from the loud yelps that come out in a rushed stream. The rest of the family is OK; they were all buckled up.

Solution: Ma Beth reaches for her communicator as soon as she has recovered from the initial shock. She calls 112 (911 or similar). The answer comes after 23 seconds, and the operator immediately confirms the identity and the location of the van. Ma Beth is a bit taken aback by this quick information and has to think for a while, then confirms the location as possibly correct. She then states the problem and gets connected to a vet that asks a few pertinent questions. She can show a close-up picture of the dog's left paw, and the vet confirms a possible (95 percent) broken leg just above the paw. He gives a few quick instructions and sends her a map of the closest emergency animal hospital. The map shows her current position and soon displays the quickest way to get to the hospital. When they arrive there, Bobby is taken care of and things begin to look up. Even the kids are smiling now that the dog is calm and free from pain, and he looks so funny with his little cast.

Benefit(s): The initial call transfers emergency information to the operator automatically. This ensures minimum delay to correct action. The communicator transfers the picture that gives enough information to make a very accurate and fast assessment of the situation. Then the map transfer and display on the terminal, together with the current position, gives clear information and directions for Ma Beth to drive and make the right turns at every corner. In her half-shocked state, she can drive to the hospital without hesitation about where to go. This is very reassuring for all parties, including the dog who gets the fastest possible help.

Comments: The call is initially just a voice call but evolves with the best of positioning in emergency situations and navigational aid, together with picture and graphics transfer.

Application Sharing with Voice Commentary

Person(s): Marketing manager Rita and media expert Jones

Situation: The launch of a new campaign for some customers in London. Last-minute feedback indicates that one of the customers is expecting the latest gadget to be included, even if it is only a prototype. Rita knows it's not included in the presentation, and she has no information with her.

Solution: Rita calls Jones, the media guru they employed for design of their important presentations. He has the information and some pictorials. He sends them over into Rita's PowerPoint application, and they edit the new slide together as they discuss the textual information to be included.

Benefit(s): The process is extremely interactive and the session takes only five minutes, thanks to the broadband connection and the fact that they don't need to ping-pong the pictures and the text back and forth. (Emphasize mobile or fixed access as required.) The customer is happy, and a letter of intent is signed.

Comments: By adding voice and pictures to an interactive session, we achieve effectiveness and interaction, two desired components.

Global Wireline/Wireless Market Trends

Over the last few decades, telecommunication has proven to be the fastest developing industry in the market. This should be noticeable because of the increasing revenues of major telecommunications carriers and the huge number of new entrants to this market. According to Rappaport (2002), wireless communications did not have substantial market penetration until thirty-five years after its introduction. This delay could be attributed to the high costs of deployment and the technological challenges during the first decades of mobile telephone introduction.

The wireless market has experienced sharp growth during the last ten years. For instance, from 1999 to 2004, there was an explosion in the number of subscribers and the amount of sales. This growth is expected to continue, and the number of wireless subscribers is expected to augment in the coming years. In fact, it is expected that by 2010, global wireless subscribers will exceed wireline subscribers. Figure 1 shows the number of worldwide mobile telephony subscribers in billions, as well as the percentage increase in subscriber population from 1991 to 2007. The corresponding information was taken from UMTS World (2006) and is summarized in the figure.

This growth is attributed to the fact that the consumer is more and more in need of mobile services and becoming more and more adapted to wireless technologies. These continuously increasing needs have driven an important change in the mobile sector: a shift toward the convergence of all networks and devices in mobile systems to an integrated architecture that supports multimedia

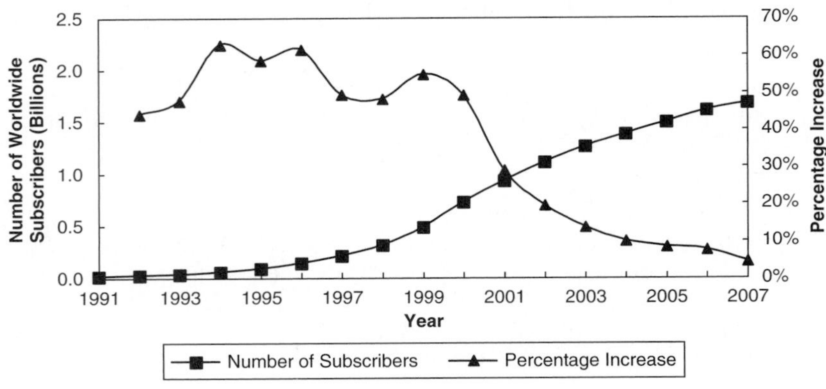

Figure 1: Population growth of worldwide subscribers

services (voice, image, video, and data). This refers to the ability to securely access any service on the network from any communicating device, any time and anywhere, with support for real-time transmission. Fortunately, this growth in the deployment of 3G wireless services has been accompanied by the fast development of low-cost and highly sophisticated mobile devices. According to the statistical handbook of the Wireless World Forum (2006), U.S. operator revenues will grow by another $20 billion in 2007. The three main trends that drive revenue growth are:

- A 44 percent rise in the number of senior (fifty- to sixty-year-old) mobile owners by 2007, to 23.29 million
- A 28.2 percent rise in the number of young (ten- to fifteen-year-old) mobile owners by 2007, to 13.36 million
- A 68 percent increase in data revenues to $17.5 billion by 2007, stimulated by rising short message service (SMS) usage.

Key Regulatory Issues and Standardization

The standardization of IMT-2000 platforms and technologies is not the activity of one single organization but of many standardization and research groups and committees (ITU 1998), including:

- Telecommunication Industry Association (TIA), United States
- Wireless Technologies and Systems Committee (WTSC), United States
- European Telecommunications Standards Institute-Special Mobile Group (ETSI-SMG)
- Association of Radio Industries and Businesses (ARIB), Japan
- Telecommunication Technology Committee (TTC), Japan
- Telecommunication Technologies Association (TTA), Korea
- Research Institute for Telecommunications Transmission (RITT), China

When the ITU communication standardization sector task group (TG) 8/1 called for radio transmission technology (RTT) proposals, various bodies submitted their proposals and those accepted were later organized into the IMT-2000 set of platforms (see Figure 2). For Europe, the ETSI-SMG proposed universal terrestrial radio access (UTRA) with versions frequency division duplexing (FDD; W-CDMA) and time division duplexing (TDD; time division synchronous code division multiple access [TD-SCDMA]). In China, the RITT proposed the TD-SCDMA. UTRA FDD (W-CDMA) was proposed by the Japanese ARIB and the Korean TTA, which also proposed cdma2000. Several proposals were presented to the ITU-R in the United States. The TIA proposed cdma2000 (evolution of CDMAOne), UWC-136 (evolution of IS-136), and wireless multimedia and messaging services (WIMS), based on W-CDMA. The WTSC presented the W-CDMA-North America (W-CDMA-NA), which was later merged with WIMS to form the wideband packet CDMA (WP-CDMA).

After the approval of ITU-R on the proposals above, two worldwide projects were established and given the names 3GPP (Europe) and 3GPP2 (North America); their purpose is to harmonize the activities between the different regions and standard bodies. This harmonization and consensus building is considered to be for the public good and benefits the manufacturer, operator, and customer. The first body, 3GPP, is responsible for the harmonization and standardization of the ETSI, ARIB, TTC, TTA, WTSC FDD, and WTSC TDD proposals. The other body, 3rd-Generation Partnership Project 2 (3GPP2), is responsible for those proposals of TTA and TIA that are cdma2000 based.

IMT-2000 Specifications

Within the IMT-2000 framework, five air-interface standards are defined for 3G systems. In fact, IMT-2000 can be thought of as a reference for different technologies

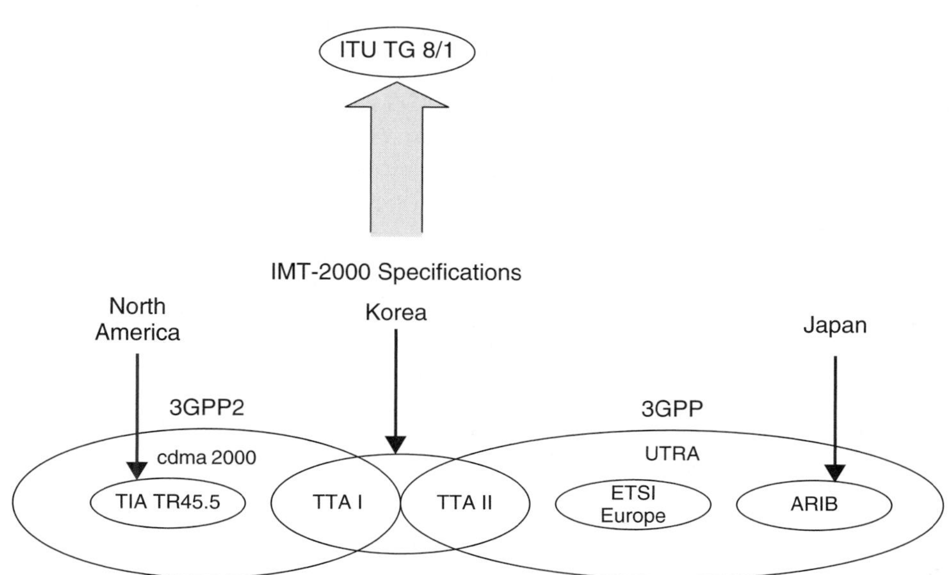

Figure 2: RTT proposals

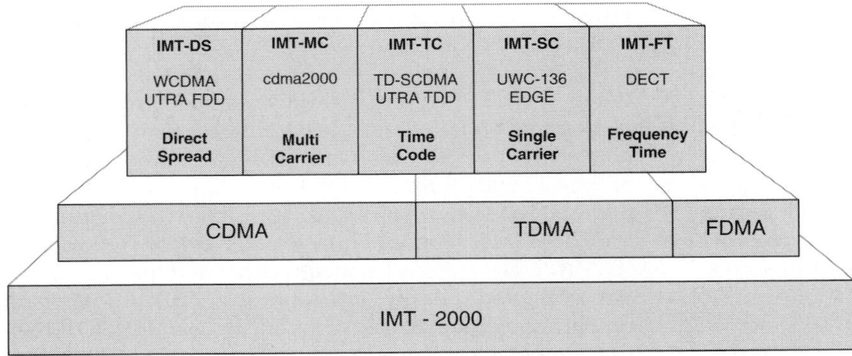

Figure 3: IMT-2000 standard platforms for 3G air interfaces

covering many frequency bands, channel bandwidths, and modulation techniques. The development of these standards and specifications is distributed via a number of international organizations and forums. Figure 3 shows the structure of the various platforms recommended by the IMT-2000 specifications. As seen in the figure, these competing radio access platforms are based on different technologies, which makes the harmonization process a difficult task. The five main standards are as follows:

UMTS (W-CDMA FDD): This is an IMT direct-spread (IMT-DS), CDMA-based technology. UMTS is also known as W-CDMA and is generally managed by the 3GPP organization (2006). This technology requires a pair of frequency bands (paired spectrum).

cdma2000: cdma2000 is an extension of the current 2G CDMA standard IS-95. It is managed by 3GPP2 (2006), a separate organization from 3GPP. This technology also requires a pair of frequency bands (paired spectrum). cdma2000 comes in a single carrier (1X) or multi-carriers (MX).

TD-SCDMA (UTRA TDD 1.28 Mcps option): This is an IMT time code (IMT-TC), also known as TD-SCDMA or the UTRA TDD 1.28Mcps option (which differs from the 3.84 Mcps option). This technology requires a single unpaired frequency band (unpaired spectrum).

UWC-136: UWC-136, also called time division multiple access single carrier (TDMA SC), is a standard proposal based on TDMA technology. UWC-136 is the extension to the current 2G TIA/EIA-136 technologies. This technology requires a pair of frequency bands (paired spectrum).

DECT: Digital enhanced cordless telecommunications (DECT) is a digital wireless technology that originated in Europe but is increasingly being adopted worldwide for cordless telephones, wireless offices, and even wireless telephone lines to the home. This technology requires a single unpaired frequency band (unpaired spectrum).

The key to the success of a standard is the availability of spectrum. WARC-92 specified the spectrum allocation for 3G systems. Figure 4 shows spectrum allocation in the major regions of the world according to IMT-2000. Europe and Asia use the frequency bands that WARC-92 allocated for IMT-2000 3G systems around 2 GHz. On the other hand, in the United States and Canada, the 2 GHz spectrum is unavailable for IMT-2000 because it was auctioned for operators using 2G mobile systems. This problem persists in other countries as well, following the U.S. personal communication system (PCS) spectrum allocation. Accordingly, those countries will employ 3G services within the existing bands.

PROPOSED 3G SYSTEM

ITU and ETSI 3G Activities

ITU is an intergovernmental organization and a specialized agency of the United Nations with headquarters in Geneva, Switzerland. ETSI is a nonprofit association with headquarters at Valbonne, France. These two bodies signed an agreement in June 2002 for mutual cooperation and exchange of documentation (ITU/ETSI 2002). Although this cooperation is built on the basis of reciprocity, the ultimate advantage is the reduction of duplication in global efforts and the development of appropriate standards responsive to global market needs.

According to this agreement, each party has its own responsibilities. The ITU Radiocommunication Sector (ITU-R) is responsible, inter alia, for studying and issuing recommendations on radiocommunication questions. The ETSI undertakes prestandardization and standardization activities in areas common to telecommunications, information technology, and sound and television broadcasting, and is responsible for standardization in the whole field of telecommunications, including radio, broadcasting, and private telecommunications.

3G Harmonization Efforts

The IMT-2000 specification defines more than one technology. In addition, it asks for harmonization and compatibility among the different technologies. This interoperability, which would provide service to users over a seamless worldwide network, is one of the major objectives for IMT-2000. Accordingly, the various technology platforms shall be able to interact completely with one another. Moreover, user handsets will be universal—in other words, usable with the various technologies. Figure 5 shows the efforts toward this harmonization. In the figure, 3GPP and 3GPP2 are two different entities. However, they are now united and work cooperatively on standard development. At the time of this writing, 3G harmonization has not been achieved but hopefully will be forthcoming soon.

China: CDMA ANSI-95 | Fixed FDD | Fixed TDD | CDMA ANSI-95 | Fixed FDD — 1865 1880 1900 1945 1960 1980 2110 2170 2200

Japan: PHS | PS => BS 3G System FDD | MSS | TDD | BS => PS 3G System FDD | MSS — 1885 1895 1918 1920 1980 2010 2025 2110 2170 2200

Europe: DECT | UMTS | MSS | UMTS | UMTS | MSS | UMTS — 1880 1900 1980 2010 2040 2110 2170 2200 2230

USA: PCS Ps => BS | PCS | PCS BS => PS | MSS | PM BA | ET | MSS — 1850 1910 1930 1990 2025 2110 2130 2160 2200

Canada: PCS Ps => BS | PCS | PCS BS => PS | MSS | FIXED | MSS — 1850 1910 1930 1990 2025 2110 2160 2200

Acronyms

BA	Broadcast Auxiliary	**BS**	Base Station	**ET**	Emerging Technology
FDD	Frequency Division Duplex	**MSS**	Mobile Satellite Systems	**PM**	Public Mobile
PS	Personal Station	**TDD**	Time Division Duplex	**UMTS**	Universal Mobile Telecommunications System

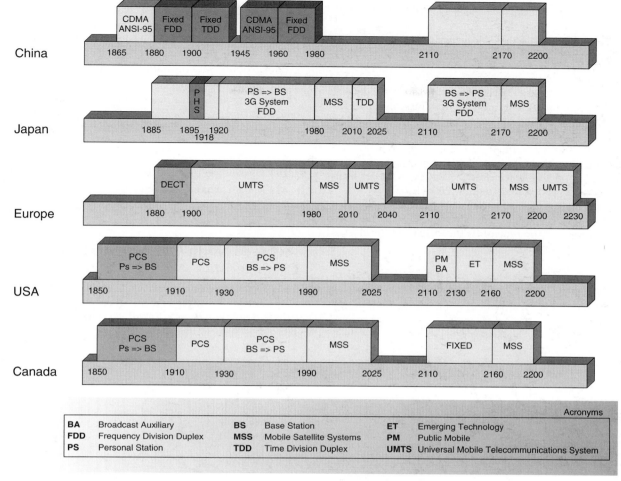

Figure 4: IMT-2000 RF allocation

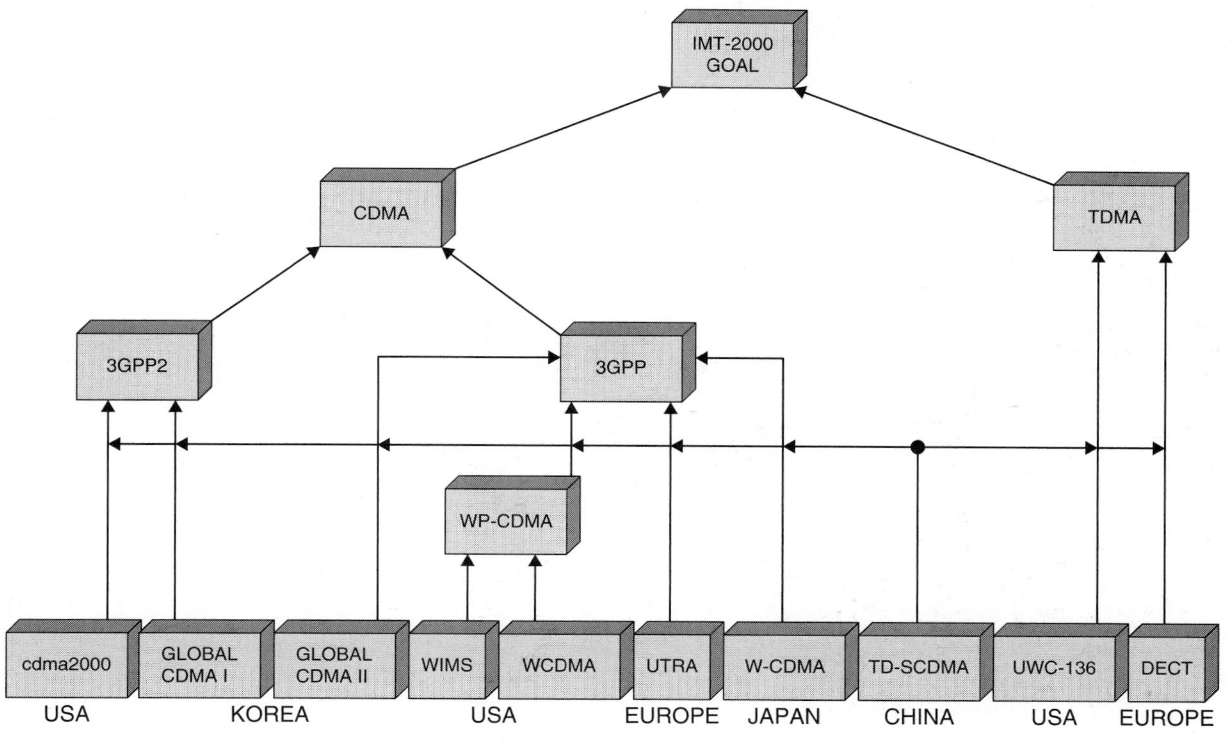

Figure 5: 3G harmonization

Proposed European 3G Systems Characteristics

The European activities toward 3G are piloted by the 3GPP. The proposed 3G system network architecture is IP based, a simplified version of which is shown in Figure 6. This IP-based architecture would have to support both stream and best-effort services. 3GPP essentially started with general packet radio service (GPRS) as the core packet network and overlaid it with call-control and gateway functions required for supporting voice over IP (VoIP) and other multimedia services (Patel and Dennett 2000).

The network offers different classes of services with varying quality of service (QoS) parameters. The divisions are based on the type of traffic, and the four classes are defined as follows:

- Conversational class (voice, video telephony, video-gaming)
- Streaming class (multimedia, video on demand, Webcast)
- Interactive class (Web browsing, network gaming, database access)
- Background class (e-mail, SMS, downloading)

The varying QoS parameters for all of these classes include bit error rate (BER), maximum transfer delay, and delay variation. The offered data rate depends on the environment:

- 144 kbits/s satellite and rural outdoor
- 384 kbits/s urban outdoor
- 2048 kbits/s indoor and low-range outdoor

Proposed North American 3G Systems Characteristics

The North American activities toward 3G are piloted by the 3GPP2. The proposed 3G system network architecture is a single network for all services, and a simplified

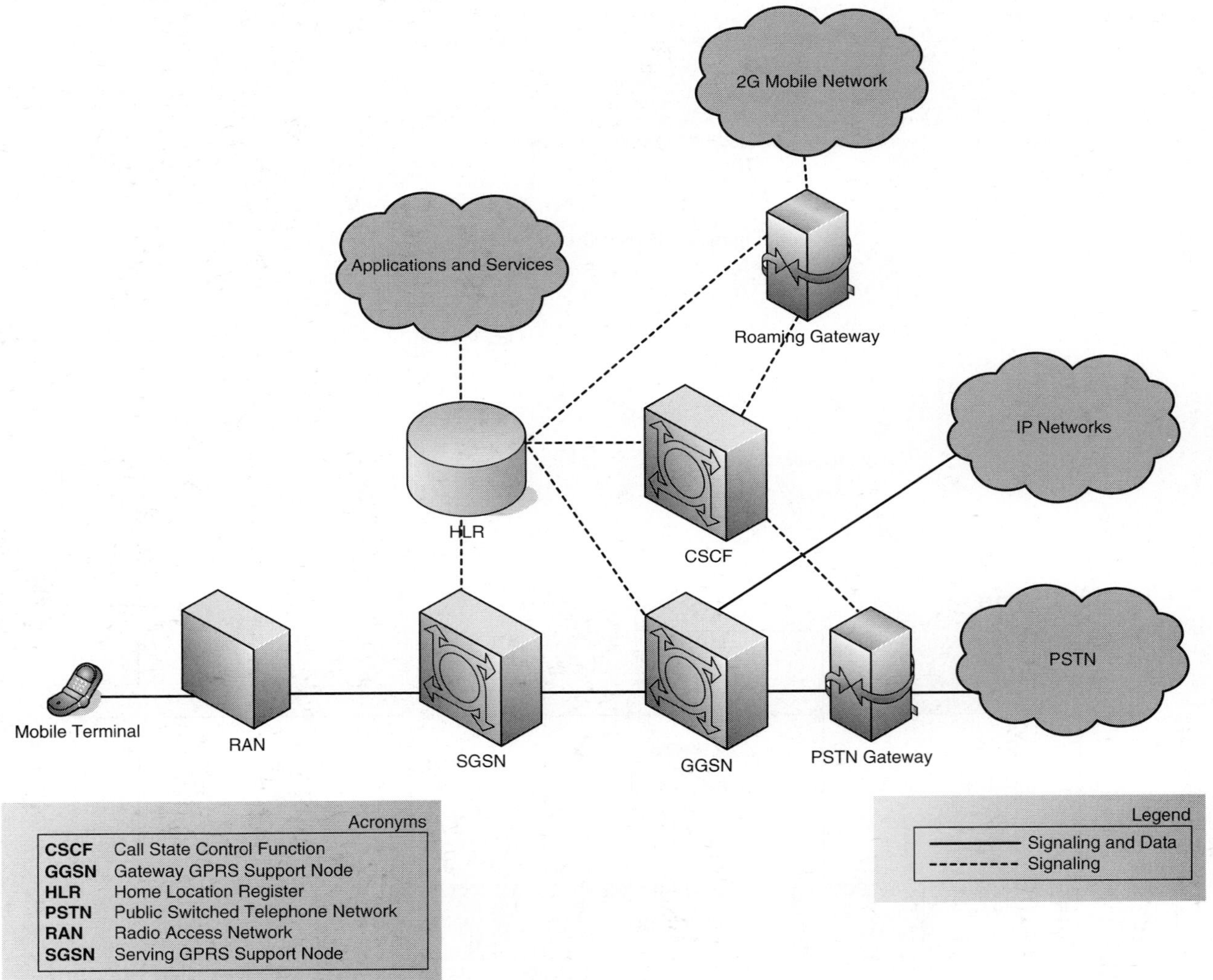

Figure 6: 3GPP proposed network

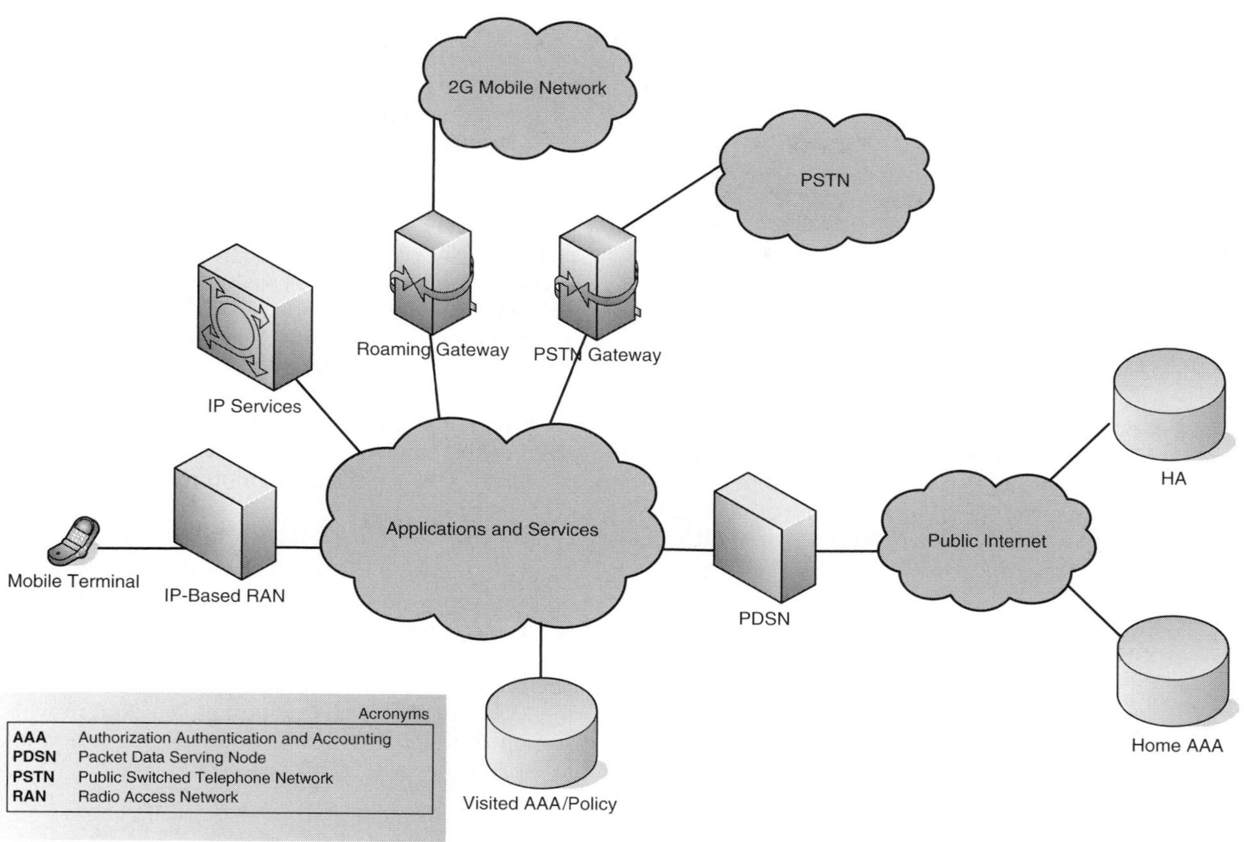

Figure 7: 3GPP2 proposed network

version is shown in Figure 7. This network offers end-to-end IP connectivity, distributed control and services, and gateways to legacy networks. 3GPP2 has created a new packet data architecture that builds on the CDMA 2G and 3G air-interface data services (Patel and Dennett 2000).

Proposed 3G Network Features

As mentioned in a 3G standard document (3GPP 2005), this new generation of mobile communications technology will create a world in which personal communications services should allow person-to-person calling, independent of location, the terminal used, the means of transmission (wired or wireless), or the choice of technology. Personal communication services should be based on a combination of fixed and wireless/mobile services to form seamless end-to-end service for the user.

The prime objectives of this new technology are:

1. To provide a single integrated system in which the user can access services in an easy-to-use and uniform way in all environments.
2. To allow differentiation among service offerings of various networks and home environments.
3. To provide a wide range of telecommunications services including those provided by fixed networks and requiring user bit rates of up to 2 Mbps, as well as services special to mobile communications. These services are supported in residential, public, and office environments, as well as in areas of diverse population densities. These services are provided with a quality comparable to that provided by fixed networks, such as integrated services digital network (ISDN).
4. To provide services via handheld, portable, vehicular-mounted, movable, and fixed terminals (including those that normally operate connected to fixed networks) in all environments (e.g., residential, private domestic, and different radio environments), provided that the terminal has the necessary capabilities.
5. To provide support of roaming users by enabling users to access services provided by their home environments even when roaming.
6. To provide audio, data, video, and particularly multimedia services.
7. To provide for the flexible introduction of telecommunication services.
8. To provide the capability to support universal personal telecommunications (UPT).
9. To provide within the residential environment the capability to enable a pedestrian user to access all services normally provided by fixed networks.
10. To provide within the office environment the capability to enable a pedestrian user to access all services normally provided by private branch exchanges (PBXs) and local area networks (LANs).

11. To provide a substitute for fixed networks in areas of diverse population densities, under conditions approved by the appropriate national or regional regulatory authority.
12. To provide support for interfaces that allow the use of terminals normally connected to fixed networks.

EVOLUTION FROM 2G-BASED SYSTEMS TO 3G

An Overview of Cellular Communications

The term *cellular* follows from the fact that a geographic coverage area is partitioned into hexagonal cells. The main reason behind this partitioning is frequency reuse. Co-channel cells—those using the same channels for voice or control—are always safely spaced to avoid interference. Figure 8 shows an example cell partitioning in which the cluster size is three—the number of cells over which no frequency reuse occurs. This increases the system capacity (i.e., the number of subscribers) without risking the quality of service.

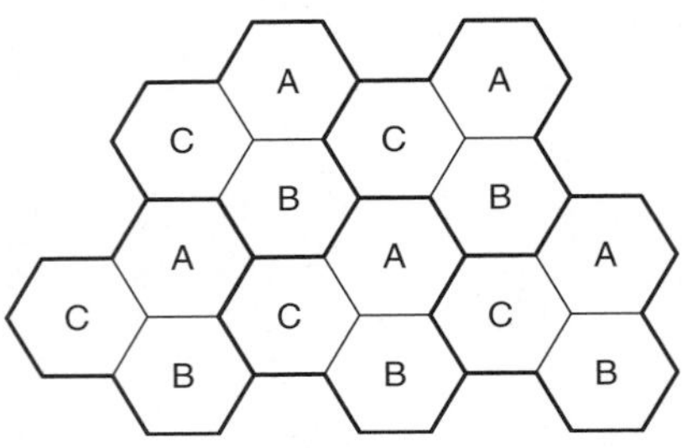

Figure 8: Clusters and cells in a cellular coverage area

The major components in a cellular system are the mobile station (MS), which is the subscriber unit, the base station (BS), which is the transmission/reception antennae tower, and the mobile switching center (MSC), which manages call establishment and teardown. These components are shown in Figure 9. The BS communicates with many MSs at a time, whereas the MS communicates with only one BS. Each MS transmits data to the BS over the reverse channel (uplink), and receives data from the BS over the forward channel (downlink). The data could be voice or control, and the channel allocation is temporary. For more information on cellular system architecture, please refer to the chapters entitled "Cellular Communications Channels" and "Cellular Telephony" in this handbook.

Handoff

Figure 9 shows an MS, a car in this case, crossing the boundaries of one cell into another. If the MS is doing the crossing during a call, this means that the call should be dropped, or that the MS gets on a new channel in the new cell. Whenever a BS detects a weak signal from the MS it automatically requests a handoff, in which the system, without user intervention, assigns a new channel to the MS in the new cell.

Power Control

Prolonging battery life has always been a main concern of mobile telephony. Power control schemes target

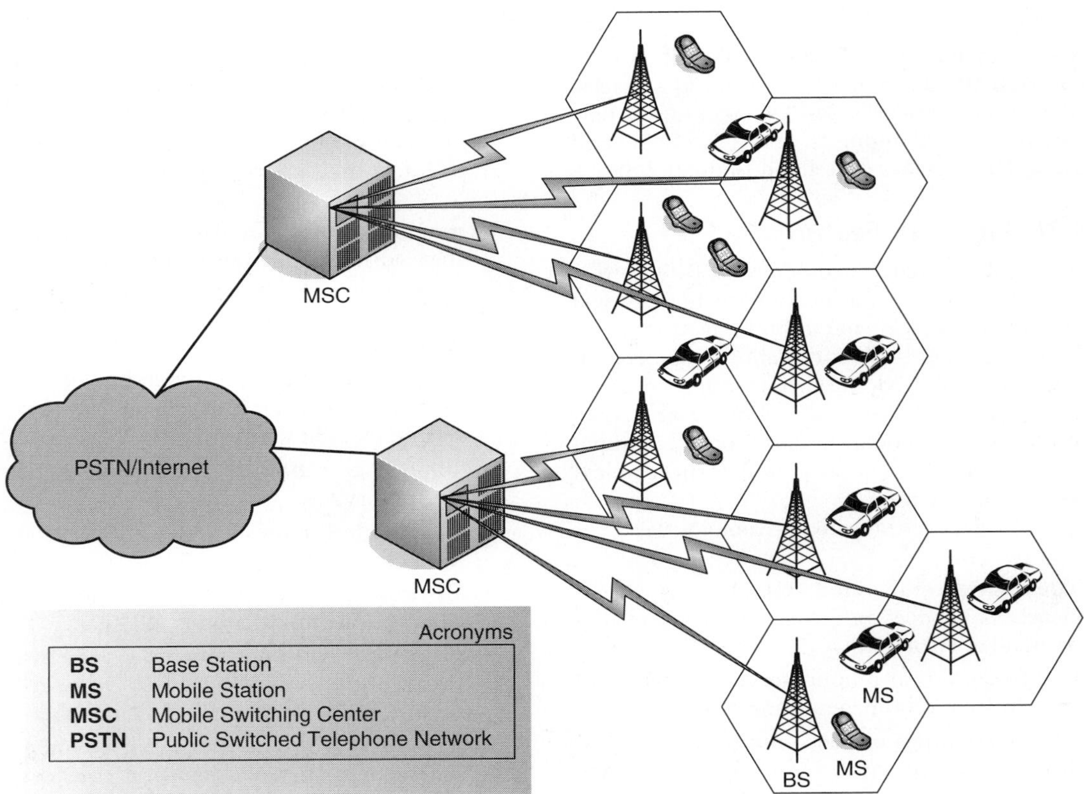

Figure 9: Cellular system architecture

this issue. In fact, base stations continually control the amount of power transmitted from mobile stations while maintaining a good quality signal. This not only extends battery life but also decreases interference caused by the transmissions of mobile stations.

Access Technologies

In any wireless communication system, the air interface needs to be accessed by multiple users simultaneously. Accordingly, the radio spectrum needs to be shared in some scheme to allow multiple subscribers to send and receive data at the same time. The major access techniques are:

Time division multiple access (TDMA): TDMA is a digital access technology that allows multiple users to access a single radio frequency channel simultaneously without interference through time sharing. Each user is assigned a specific time slot for transmission.

Frequency Division Multiple Access (FDMA): FDMA is an access technique in which the radio frequency bandwidth is divided into chunks, and the user is allocated one single channel at a time. FDMA has the advantage of controlling interference by assigning nonadjacent channels to adjacent users. Figure 10 compares FDMA and TDMA by showing how time and frequency are partitioned to allow multiple user access.

Code Division Multiple Access (CDMA): CDMA permits multiple users to occupy the same frequency spectrum or medium simultaneously. Accordingly, different users can be active all the time because each user has a uniquely different code than other users (Figure 11). The codes are shared by both the mobile station and

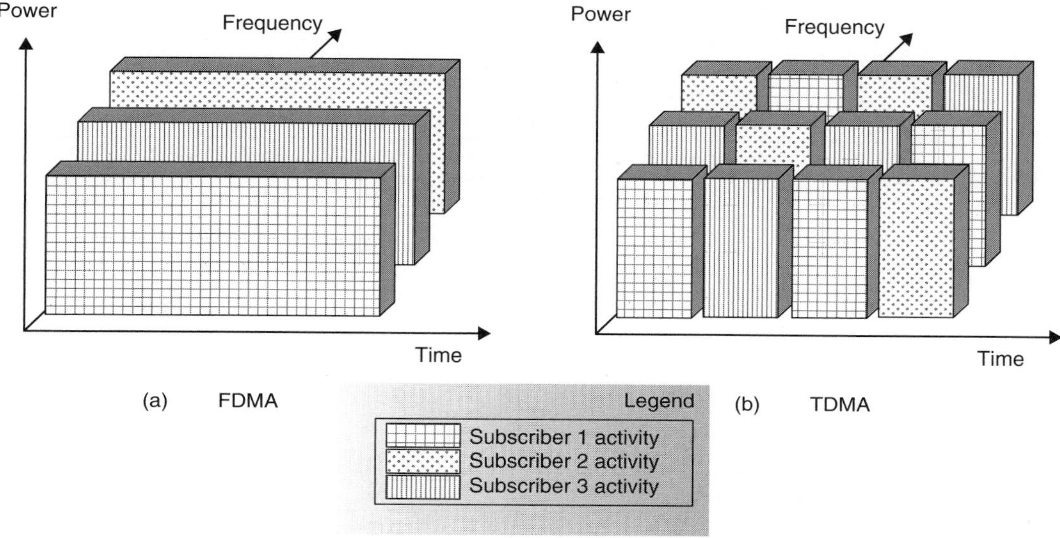

Figure 10: FDMA and TDMA compared

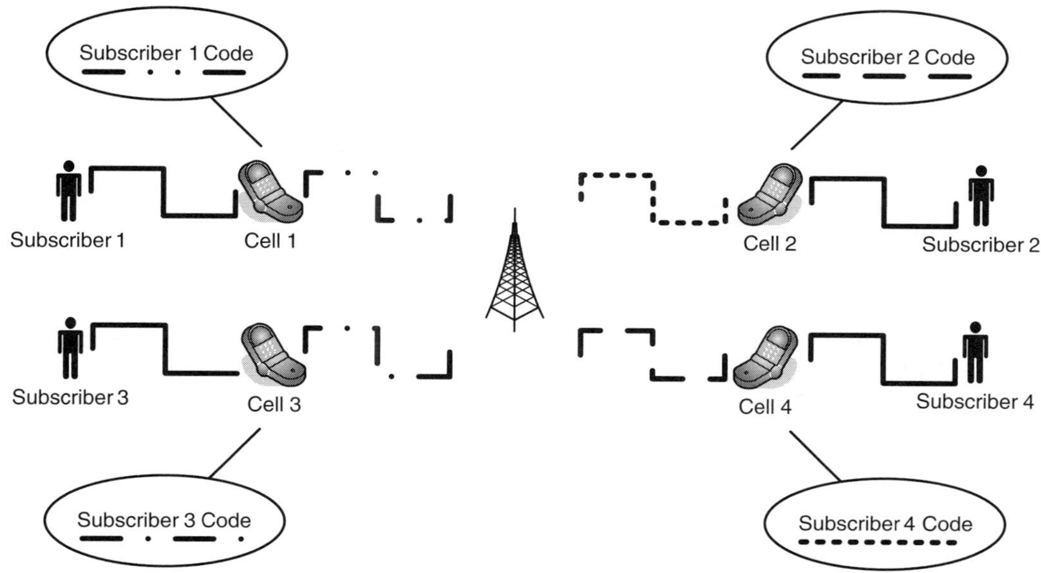

Figure 11: CDMA concept

the base station, and are called pseudo-random code sequences. Base stations in the system distinguish themselves from one another by transmitting different portions of the code at a given time. Besides this concurrent access capability, CDMA has the advantage of enhanced immunity to interference and multipath effects.

Differences between 1G, 2G, and 3G Systems

Many wireless communications exist, and many are being developed. Tables 1 through 3 summarize the most common paging, cordless, cellular, and PCS standards used in North America, Europe, and Japan.

Mobile communications in the form of analog cellular networks, or what were later called *1G systems,* started to appear in the late 1970s and early 1980s, although radio telephone systems existed before then. The first technology to be tested was the advanced mobile phone service (AMPS) technology, which was deployed in the largest U.S. cities. At the same time, AMPS was being deployed in Japan, and another technology called Nordic mobile telephone (NMT) was also being implemented in a number of European countries. A few years later, the British total access communications system (TACS) was launched. TACS was based on AMPS but featured minor variations.

The various 1G systems worked fine during the initial years of deployment. Unfortunately, a few years later, a couple of critical weaknesses started to demand the attention of operators as well as users. The mobile networks were quickly flooded with an unexpectedly huge number of subscribers. This growth abnormality was accompanied by critical security holes.

Table 1: Major Mobile Radio Standards in North America

Standard	Type	Year of Introduction	Multiple Access	Frequency Band	Modulation	Channel Bandwidth
AMPS	Cellular	1983	FDMA	824–894 MHz	FM	30
NAMPS	Cellular	1992	FDMA	824–894 MHz	FM	10
USDC	Cellular	1991	TDMA	824–894 MHz	π/4 DQPSK	30
CDPD	Cellular	1993	FH/Packet	824–894 MHz	GMSK	30
IS-95	Cellular/PCS	1993	CDMA	824–894 MHz 1.8–2.0 GHz	QPSK/ BPSK	1.25 MHz
GSC	Paging	1970s	Simplex	Several	FSK	12.5
POCSAG	Paging	1970s	Simplex	Several	FSK	12.5
FLEX	Paging	1993	Simplex	Several	4-FSK	15
DSC-1900 (GSM)	PCS	1994	TDMA	1.85–1.99 GHz	GMSK	200
PACS	Cordless/PCS	1994	TDMA/FDMA	1.85–1.99 GHz	π/4 DQPSK	300
MIRS	SMR/PCS	1994	TDMA	Several	16-QAM	25
iDEN	SMR/PCS	1995	TDMA	Several	16-QAM	25

Source: Rappaport (2002).

Table 2: Major Mobile Radio Standards in Europe

Standard	Type	Year of Introduction	Multiple Access	Frequency Band	Modulation	Channel Bandwidth
ETACS	Cellular	1985	FDMA	900 MHz	FM	25
NMT-450	Cellular	1981	FDMA	450–470 MHz	FM	25
NMT-900	Cellular	1986	FDMA	890–960 MHz	FM	12.5
GSM	Cellular/PCS	1990	TDMA	890–960 MHz	GMSK	200
C-450	Cellular	1985	FDMA	450–465 MHz	FM	20/10
ERMES	Paging	1993	FDMA	Several	4-FSK	25
CT2	Cordless	1989	FDMA	864–868 MHz	GFSK	100
DECT	Cordless	1993	TDMA	1880–1900 MHz	GFSK	1.728 MHz
DCS-1800	Cordless/PCS	1993	TDMA	1710–1880 MHz	GMSK	200

Source: Rappaport (2002).

Table 3: Major Mobile Radio Standards in Japan

Standard	Type	Year of Introduction	Multiple Access	Frequency Band	Modulation	Channel Bandwidth
JTACS	Cellular	1988	FDMA	860–925 MHz	FM	25
PDC	Cellular	1993	TDMA	810–1501 MHz	π/4 DQPSK	25
NTT	Cellular	1979	FDMA	400/800 MHz	FM	25
NTACS	Cellular	1993	FDMA	843–925 MHz	FM	12.5
NTT	Paging	1979	FDMA	280 MHz	FSK	12.5
NEC	Paging	1979	FDMA	Several	FSK	10
PHS	Cordless	1993	TDMA	1895–1907 MHz	π/4 DQPSK	300

Source: Rappaport (2002).

Research soon focused on the development of a new system that solved the security and capacity pitfalls: the 2G systems that appeared first in the market in the early 1990s. 2G systems were the first digital cellular networks. Many technologies were recommended and even deployed, all of which targeted the support of more sophisticated services coupled with the guarantee of high immunity against fraud as well as the support of more users. Moreover, 2G introduced the capability of short message service and text delivery.

2G systems varied in band usage (800, 900, 1800, and 1900 MHz bands) and offered data rates in the range of 9.6 kbps to 14.4 kbps. The three leading technologies of 2G are the global system for mobile communications (GSM), interim standard 95 (IS-95) CDMA, and IS-136 TDMA.

Approaching the year 2000, wireless voice services had almost reached their peak (Collins and Smith 2001). The goal of wireless operators soon became the application of carrier-grade services on wireless networks. With the efforts of the ITU and its IMT-2000, 3G systems were introduced, the main features of which are packet-switched network, always-on connectivity, value-added services, and global roaming. These 3G systems followed the 2G systems, such as GSM, cdmaOne, and TDMA, while enhancing the data rates to 384 kbps and more with the potential to support 2 Mbps data rates. In addition to this high throughput, 3G offered advanced converged services (multimedia services) with performance enhancements to the current quality of service (higher speech quality). Moreover, this platform became global in two scopes: (1) in terms of connecting terrestrial and satellite networks together with fixed networks, and (2) in terms of service consistency and commonality around world operators (e.g., *virtual home environment* [VHE] roaming). The main differences among the three generations can be summarized as follows:

1. First generation was analog based and, in addition to suffering from security problems, had efficiency and functionality shortcomings.
2. Second generation was a low bit-rate digital technology and was based mainly on circuit-switched voice transmission.
3. Third generation is an evolutionary step up to a fully packet-switched system that supports higher bit rates as well as a collection of multimedia and data services.

European and North American Wireless Systems

IS-95 (or CDMAOne)

IS-95, also known as TIA-EIA-95 and J-STD-008, is a 2G CDMA-based, digital, cellular standard pioneered by Qualcomm; cdmaOne is its brand name. It is a direct sequence (DS) wideband spread-spectrum technology platform that enables multiple users to access the same radio channel—hence the term *multiple access* in CDMA. IS-95 uses CDMA technology to send voice, data, and signaling data (such as a dialed telephone number) between mobile telephones and cell sites. This technology has grown quickly and has been employed widely in the United States and Asia.

Figure 12 shows the network architecture of the IS-95 platform. This is a simplified view of the network to fit both versions: IS-95/A and IS-95/B. The first element seen is the base transceiver station (BTS), with which the user communicates. There is one BTS in each cell of the network. This tower contains radio transceivers and antennas, a processor, channel cards, and other equipment necessary for providing service in the cell. The next unit is a special type of switch called the *base station controller* (BSC), which groups and controls BTSs. Several BSCs are then grouped with an MSC. This is a higher level of switching but one that includes interfacing and interworking functions (connections to the public switched telephone network [PSTN]). Besides providing routing and switching services, this unit is important because it provides many functions, including subscriber and device management and registration, location updating and call handoff, signaling, and billing information collection. The MSC is interfaced with a database called the home location register (HLR). This database stores and maintains subscriber information—mainly, as the name implies, it stores the user location.

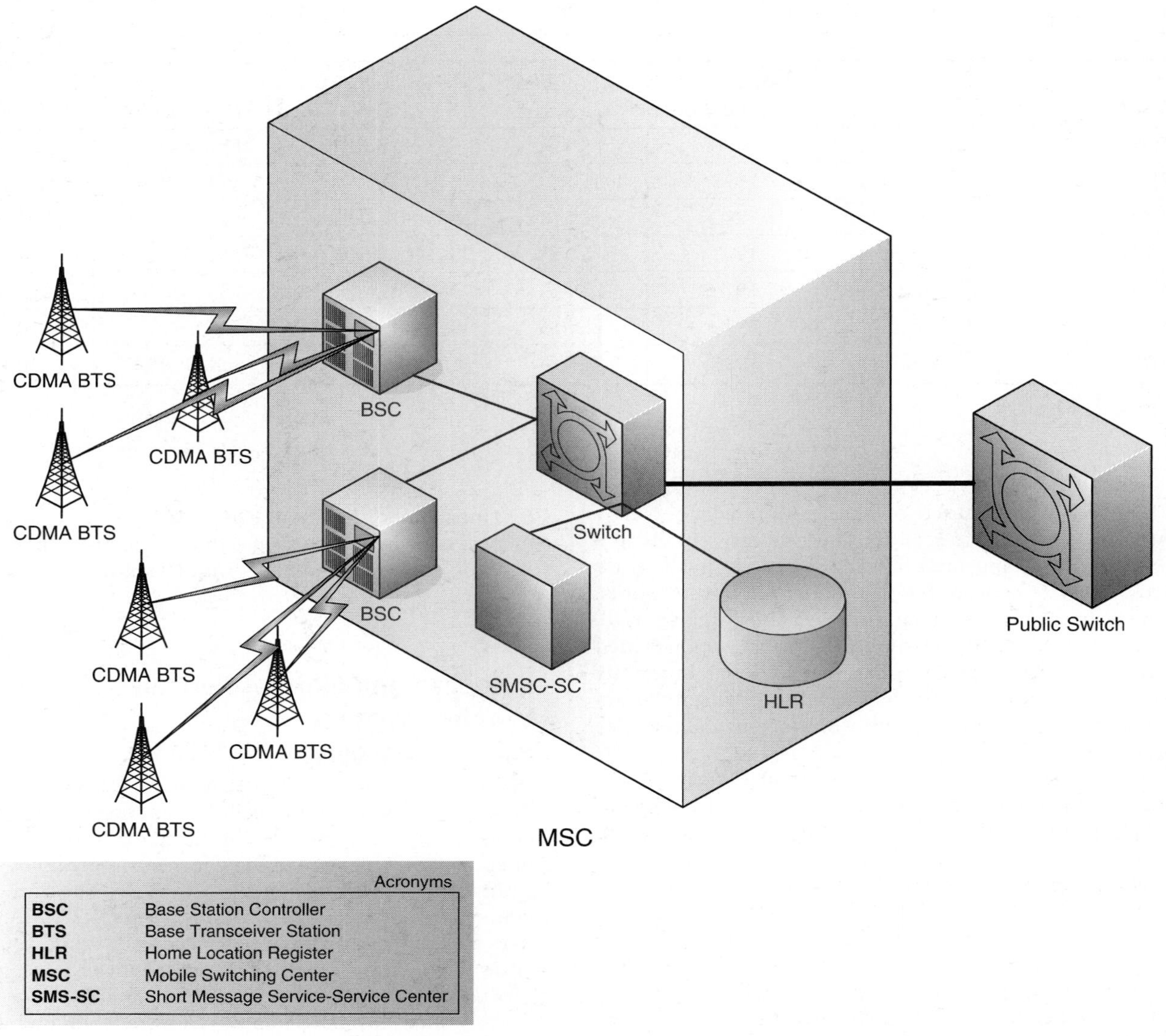

Figure 12: IS-95 network architecture

GSM

GSM is a 2G platform for mobile communications and is significant for being the basis of more advanced systems like GPRS, enhanced data rates for GSM evolution (EDGE), and UMTS. Moreover, it is the most widely accepted radio communication around the world. GSM is the European standard for digital cellular communications. Originally designed to operate in the 900 MHz frequency band, and later deployed in this spectrum, it is also deployed in the 1800 and 1900 bands. The GSM radio channel is 200 kHz wide, and it is a TDMA system (mobile users share the medium on a time division basis) with FDD (separate uplink and downlink frequency bands). GSM's major functional blocks are the switching system (SS), the base station subsystem (BSS), and the operations and support system (OSS). These will be explored shortly.

Figure 13 shows the architecture of the GSM BSS. The system is composed of the BTS and the BSC, and the interface between those two subsystems is known as the Abis interface. The BTS contains the equipment for transmitting and receiving radio signals (which provide the interface with the mobile station), antennas, and equipment for encrypting and decrypting communication with the BSC. The other part is the BSC, which is the subsystem with the intelligence and processing power. It provides a number of management, operation, and maintenance functions for mobile stations in the coverage area of the BTSs and for the overall network. The handset, in GSM jargon, is called the mobile station (MS). This station is composed of two parts: the mobile equipment (ME), which is the electronic mobile device, and the subscriber identity module (SIM). The latter is a small electronic card that maintains the key to identifying a mobile phone service subscriber's identity, as well as subscription and authentication information, preferences, and text messages. The equivalent of an SIM in UMTS is the universal subscriber identity module (USIM).

The network architecture of the GSM system is shown in Figure 14. Beginning from the BSC previously discussed, the next node is the transcoder and rate adaptation unit

Abis
Abis
Abis
BSC
BTS
BTS
BTS
MS
MS
MS
SIM
ME
MS
Acronyms
BSC Base Station Controller
BTS Base Transceiver Station
ME Mobile Equipment
MS Mobile Station
SIM Subscriber Identity Module

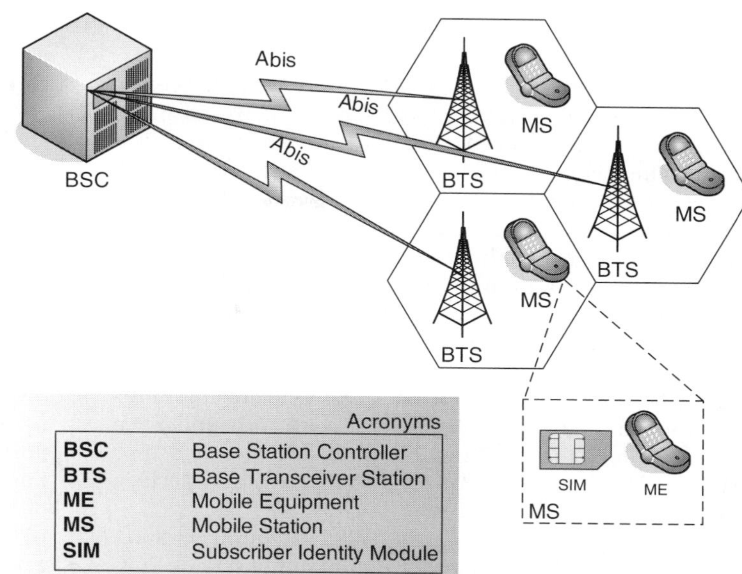

Figure 13: GSM base station subsystem (BSS)

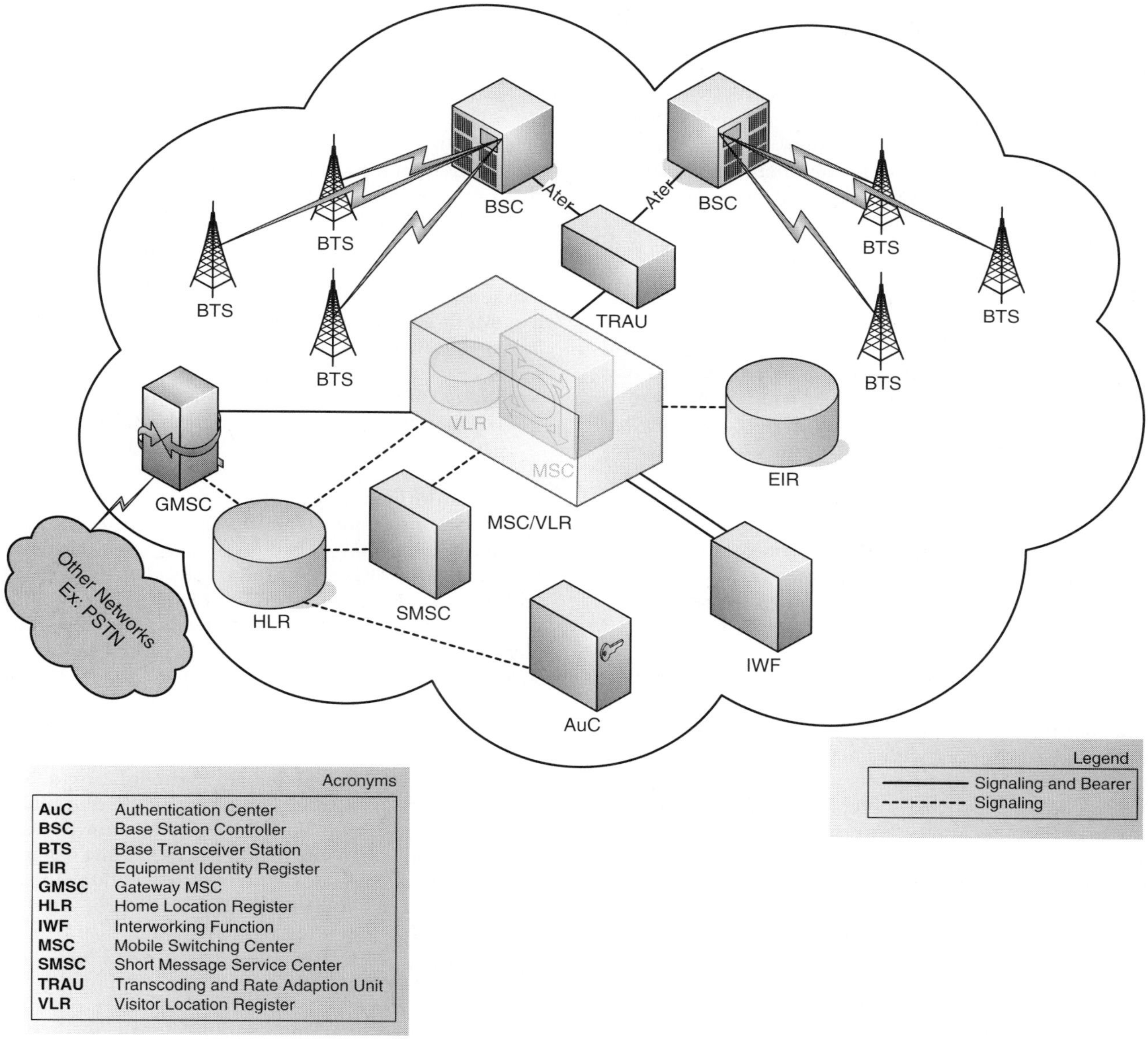

BSC
BSC
Ater
Ater
TRAU
BTS
BTS
BTS
BTS
BTS
BTS
VLR
MSC
MSC/VLR
EIR
GMSC
HLR
SMSC
AuC
IWF
Other Networks
Ex: PSTN
Acronyms
AuC Authentication Center
BSC Base Station Controller
BTS Base Transceiver Station
EIR Equipment Identity Register
GMSC Gateway MSC
HLR Home Location Register
IWF Interworking Function
MSC Mobile Switching Center
SMSC Short Message Service Center
TRAU Transcoding and Rate Adaption Unit
VLR Visitor Location Register
Legend
Signaling and Bearer
Signaling

Figure 14: GSM network architecture

(TRAU). It is the role of TRAU to convert the coded speech from GSM standard (12.2 or 13 kbps) to pulse coded modulation (PCM) standard (64 kbps), and vice versa. This helps to interface with the PSTN, which uses the PCM for speech coding. As shown in the figure, the interface between the TRAU and the BSC is known as Ater interface. A switch called the MSC then groups one or more BSCs. Call initiation, routing, and teardown functions, as well as many other important functions of the whole network, are the responsibilities of this switch. A database node called the visitor location register (VLR) helps the MSC achieve its functionality by storing information about all the mobiles that are currently under the jurisdiction of the MSC to which they are attached. The MSC node is connected to the BSC through an interface called the A-interface.

Figure 14 also shows a node called the home location register (HLR). This is another database for storing subscriber information—primarily information about services for which the subscriber has subscriptions. Furthermore, this database receives queries about the location of a certain subscriber. Two subsystems send such queries. The first one is the gateway mobile switching center (GMSC), which interfaces the GSM network to the PSTN network. The second is the short message service center (SMSC), which stores and forwards short data messages to and from subscribers. We can also see another node called the authentication center (AuC), which is also a database but stores subscriber-specific authentication information—primarily the subscriber authentication key (Ki)—as well as different authentication algorithms. For the user to be authenticated, the information stored in the AuC should match the information stored on the user's SIM card.

The figure also shows a unit known as the equipment identity register (EIR), which contains white, grey, and black lists of international mobile equipment identity (IMEI) numbers. This number uniquely identifies mobile equipment, and thus the GSM operator can grant access to specific equipment (white list) or block its access (black list). Equipment listed in the grey list may or may not be barred. Besides the GMSC, there is another unit that is important and noteworthy in the interworking context: the interworking function (IWF), which is a modem bank that helps support circuit-switched and fax services.

GPRS

Although GSM enhanced wireless communications through data services, the data rate was as slow as 9.6 kbps. It was not until general packet radio service that packet-switched data services with data rates around 64 kbps were introduced to the wireless world. In addition to increased data rates, packet switching itself is an enhancement in availability and better resource utilization. GPRS uses the same channel width of 200 kHz, like GSM divided into eight time slots; therefore, they share the same radio frequency (RF) resources. The difference is that the total number of slots that a subscriber's mobile equipment can gain access to varies. Furthermore, there are various channel coding schemes for each channel. Accordingly, the user can have access to variable data rates, given that the packet-switched paradigm itself introduces diversity to the data rate. Figure 15 shows the network architecture of the GPRS standard. It looks similar to the GSM network, except for some new nodes and interfaces as shown in the figure.

The first new node seen is the packet control unit (PCU), which helps the BSS to support packet-switching functionality through packet assembly, reassembly, and scheduling. This could be considered the air-interface access part of the packet-switching services of GPRS. The other part is packet routing, which is achieved through the serving GPRS support node (SGSN). The SGSN acts as a routing switch like the circuit-switched MSC but in the packet-switched domain. The interface of the GPRS network with the other packet-switched networks is supported through the gateway GPRS support node (GGSN). For instance, for a transmission of data from GPRS to the public Internet, GPRS data packets are tunneled inside IP packets from the SGSN to the GGSN. The charging gateway function (CGF), together with the billing system, interacts to accomplish the billing operations and maintain the user-billing data. As shown in the figure, many interface standards are imposed by the GPRS standard for links between different node types. For instance, the Gb interface defines the interaction between an SGSN and a BSC.

EDGE

Enhanced data rates for GSM evolution, or EDGE, is the step in the evolutionary path to 3G from GSM platforms and IS-136 TDMA. As mentioned previously, EDGE is considered to be a 2.75G system, or a pseudo-3G system, since it almost fulfills the 3G requirements but is not marketed as such. In fact, proponents of EDGE consider it more favorable than proposed 3G standards; it is sufficient in terms of the throughput the current user needs, much less costly than the 2 GHz 3G since no new spectrum allocation is required, and there is no need for the 5 MHz channel, having compressed the 200 kHz.

EDGE, like GSM and GPRS, uses the same channel width of 200 kHz divided into eight time slots, but with data throughput exceeding that of GSM and GPRS. The key improvement is in the air-interface modulation scheme, whereas the network core is almost the same as that of GPRS. EDGE uses 8-phase shift keying (8-PSK) in addition to the Gaussian minimum shift keying (GMSK) used in GPRS. In 8-PSK, the bandwidth is better utilized, with a tradeoff of less immunity to noise. Accordingly, there is always a variation in the EDGE network throughput, and the user may sense the difference. Depending on the location of the user and the BTS, as well as the RF conditions, the appropriate modulation and channel-coding schemes are chosen. A change in modulation scheme, intended to utilize the available bandwidth and increase throughput, results in less immunity to noise. On the other hand, using a strict coding scheme gives high immunity to noise but adds more overhead and, hence, decreases the overall throughput.

3G Systems

UWC-136

Universal wireless communication-136 was the first proposal submitted by the United States in response to the

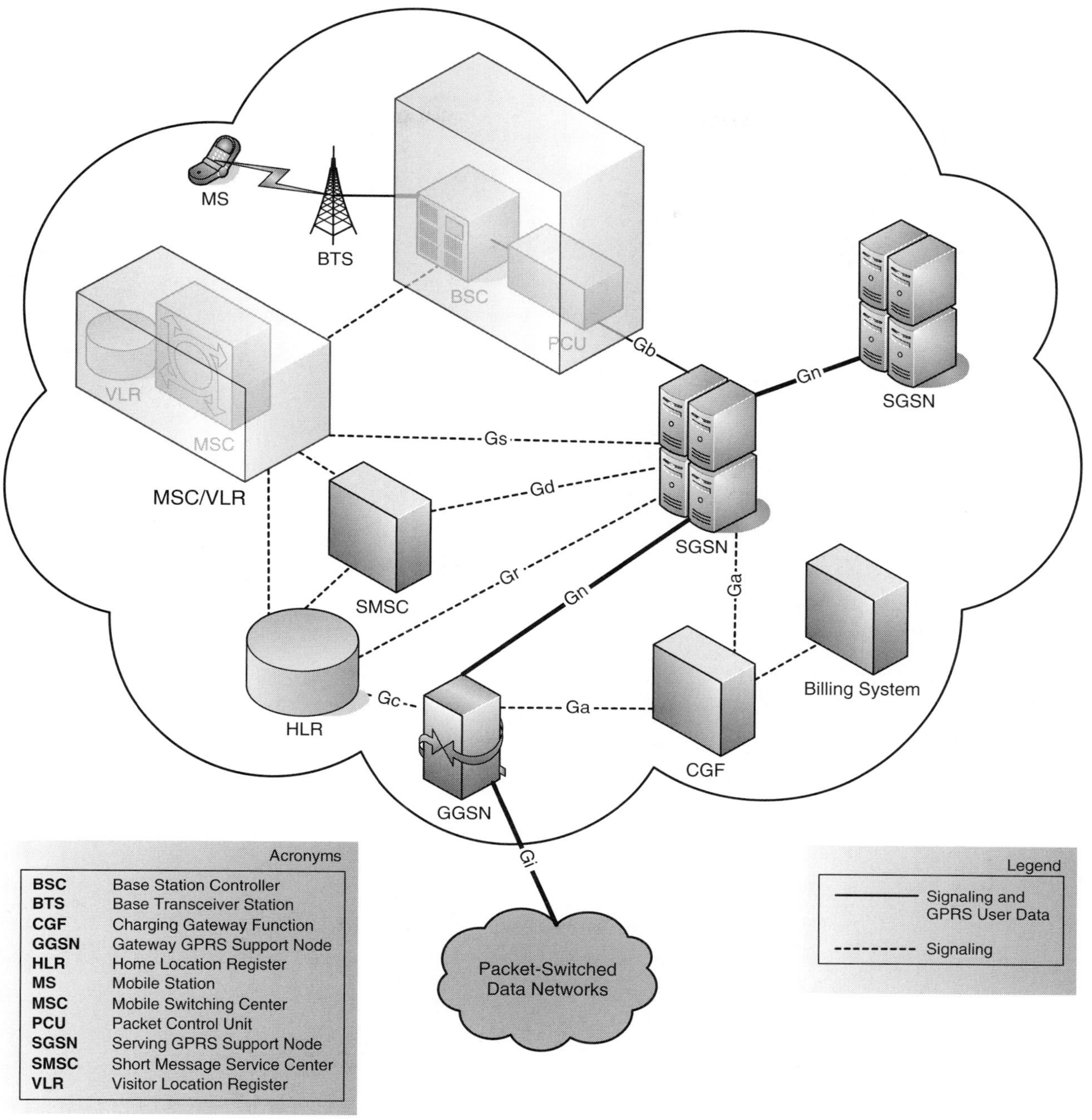

Figure 15: GPRS network architecture

IMT-2000 initiative. It was developed by the Universal Wireless Communications Consortium (UWCC) as a 3G wireless standard based on (TDMA) technology that offers backward compatibility with 2G TDMA-based IS-136 as well as GSM systems. In terms of evolutionary paths, UWC-136 is the proposed 3G destination for the 2G TIA/EIA-136 technologies. Furthermore, it is also the 3G destination platform appropriate for the 1G AMPS. The technology allows a wide range of frequencies—from 500 MHz to 2.5 GHz. The platform's radio transmission technology proposes a low-cost incremental and evolutionary deployment path for both AMPS and TIA/EIA operators.

cdma2000

Code division multiple access 2000 is the proposed evolution for cdmaOne 2G platforms and makes up a substantial part of the IMT-2000 specifications. Because the main objective of 3G systems is the support of multimedia services for fixed and mobile users, the key improvement on cdmaOne is the addition of data services to the voice service. Accordingly, this raises the need for various upgrades to existing components as well as the introduction of new ones. The major component that needs to be added is the packet data server—the packet data serving node (PDSN), shown in Figure 16. This figure shows a

Acronyms

AAA	Authentication, Authorization, Accounting
BSC	Base Station Controller
BTS	Base Transceiver Station
HLR	Home Location Register
MSC	Mobile Switching Center
PDSN	Packet Data Serving Node
SMS-SC	Short Message Service-Service Center

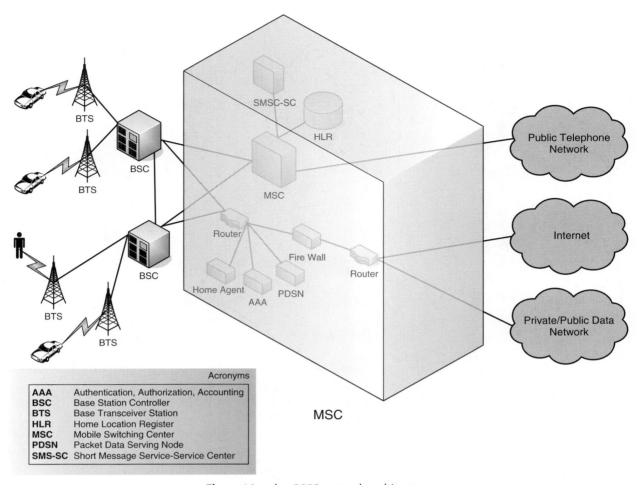

Figure 16: cdma2000 network architecture

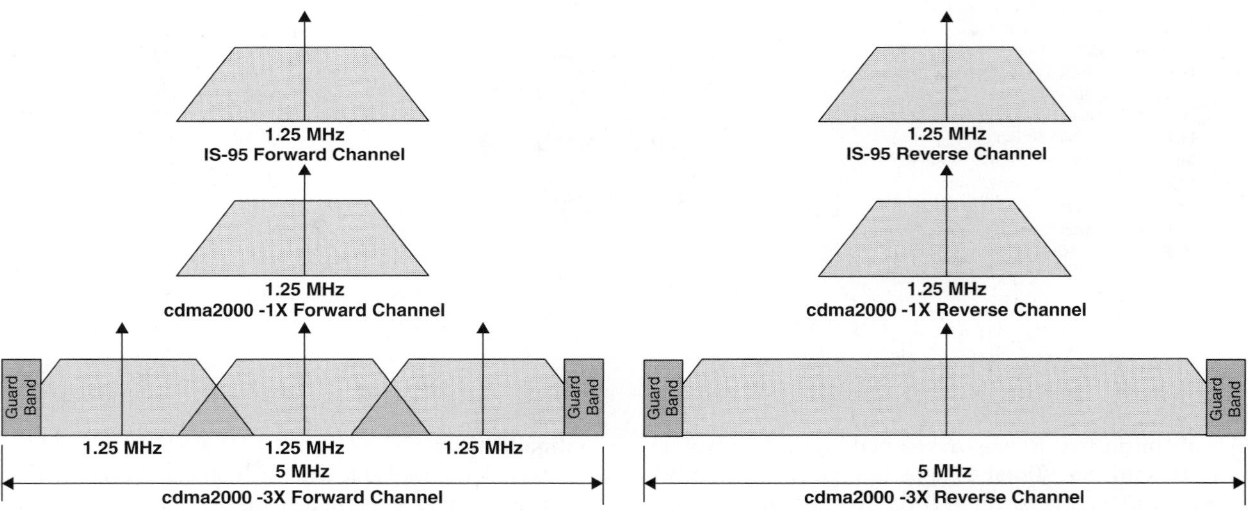

Figure 17: cdma2000 IX and 3X

simplified version of the cdma2000 network architecture. In fact, the cdma2000 network comes in two flavors, centralized and distributed, depending on the system characteristics sought.

Many times the name cdma2000 is accompanied by 1X or 3X (cdma2000-1X or cdma2000-3X). Figure 17 shows the spectrum specifications for cdma2000. The basic idea is this: cdmaOne is built over a bandwidth of 1.25 MHz, and cdma2000 is an enhancement of either the same bandwidth (1X) or multiples of it (3X). Hence, the operator makes the choice of either using the designated spectrum of 5 MHz or the existing 1.25 MHz.

cdma2000 1xRTT: The first version of cdma2000 provides data rates for a maximum of 144 kbps. This is known as cdma2000 1xRTT (RTT stands for radio transmission technology). This version uses a single 1.25 MHz channel—hence, the 1x in the name.

The next version is cdma2000 1xEV (1xEV-DO and 1xEV-DV), which is completely backward compatible with cdma2000 1xRTT. It is a two-phase evolution.

cdma2000 1xEV-DO: The first phase is cdma2000 evolution-data optimized (1xEV-DO), originally evolution-data only. The first company to deploy cdma-2000 1xEV-DO was SK Telecom in Korea, in January 2002. It is now deployed in many places around the world. This standard, as the name implies, is data only; to support voice, cdma2000 1x channels have to be used. It is defined by IS-856 and is similar to cdma2000 1x but with high data rate (HDR) capability. The first revision, Rev. 0, supports data rates up to 2.5 Mbps in the downlink and 153 kbps in the uplink. Rev. A supports data rates up to 3.1 Mbps in the downlink and 1.2 Mbps in the uplink. Besides boosting data rates, this revision also supports IP packets. The latest revision, Rev. B, supports downlink data rates up to 4.9xN Mbps and uplink data rates up to 1.8xN Mbps, where N is the number of 1.25 MHz carriers occupied by the system.

cdma2000 1xEV-DV: The second phase is cdma2000 evolution-data voice (1xEV-DV), which integrates voice and data on the same carrier with data rates up to 3.1 Mbps on the downlink and 1.8 Mbps on the uplink. Even though it followed cdma2000 1xEV-DO, many carriers have chosen to deploy the 1xEV-DO.

cdma2000 3xRTT: After the cdma2000 1xEV versions comes the cdma2000 3xRTT. This version uses three 1.25 MHz CDMA channels. It is currently under development, and no carrier has deployed it yet.

UMTS/W-CDMA

W-CDMA is a wideband direct-sequence code division multiple access (DS-CDMA). This means that the user data is spread over a wider bandwidth through multiplication by quasi-random bits called *chips*. These chips are bits derived from the CDMA spreading codes. Through the use of the appropriate chip rate, the carrier bandwidth of 5 MHz is achieved. Moreover, the operator is able to combine multiples of this 5 MHz with appropriate spacing (guard bands). This gives the channel an increased multipath diversity. W-CDMA comes in two flavors: FDD and TDD. In the former, FDD, separate carriers are used for uplink and downlink. TDD, however, is based on the use of one carrier but with time sharing between uplink and downlink channels. An added feature of W-CDMA is its adaptable user data rates; each user is allocated a time frame, and those frames differ in their data rate capabilities in order to meet the utmost packet data service.

TD-SCDMA

As a contribution to the IMT-2000, the TD-SCDMA RTT proposed by China Wireless Telecommunication Standards group (CWTS) was approved by the ITU in 1999, and technology is being developed by the Chinese Academy of Telecommunications Technology (CATT) and Siemens. TD-SCDMA uses TDD. That means that the uplink and downlink spectrum is assigned flexibly, depending on the type of information being transmitted. When asymmetrical data like e-mail and the Internet are transmitted from the base station, more time slots are used for downlink than for uplink. A symmetrical split in the uplink and downlink takes place with symmetrical services like telephony (TD-SCDMA Forum 2006).

TD-SCDMA adopts high-edged technologies such as smart antenna, software radio, joint detection, baton handover (handover that occurs without interruptions, as in soft handover but with more capabilities; see 3GPP Technical Specification Group Radio Access Network Working Group 2 [1999] for more information), and high-speed transmission technology for downlink packet data. Compared with other mobile systems, TD-SCDMA boasts outstanding technological benefits:

- High spectrum efficiency: TD-SCDMA, with the highest spectrum efficiency (given the low chip rate compared to other standards; 3GPP Technical Specification Group Radio Access Network Working Group 2 [1999]), better supports dense services in populated areas. It is capable of making full use of a fragmented spectrum, and it effectively alleviates spectrum resource shortage and limitations for the carriers.
- High capacity: The adoption of high-edged technologies dramatically lowers interference and increases system capacities.
- Highly suitable for operators' asymmetrical data services: Because TD-SCDMA is competent for dynamically adjusting data transmission rates with uplink and downlink, it suits the handling of asymmetrical IP data services.
- Low costs: The adoption of smart antenna technology decreases transmission power in the TD-SCDMA system and dramatically lowers the cost of the system products (Datang Mobile 2005).

Evolution Paths for 2G Systems to 3G Systems

Beginning in the early 1980s, the first generation of mobile communication 1G dominated with its main variants:

1G Standards

1. AMPS (800)
2. TACS (900)
3. NMT (900)
4. SMR (800 and 900)

The specialized mobile radio (SMR) system is a "walkie-talkie" type service used by taxis and delivery trucks. The numbers between brackets—for instance, the 900 in NMT (900)—denotes the frequency band used in MHz. In the early 1990s, a shift in technology from analog to digital systems was proposed, and the 2G system was introduced. Soon afterward, there arose the need for a migration path from 1G to 2G. Operators using the TACS and NMT (900) systems chose to migrate to GSM (900) systems; portion of the operators using AMPS migrated to IS-136 TDMA (800), and the rest moved to IS-95 CDMA (800). SMR operators migrated to the integrated digital enhanced network (iDEN) system that was proposed by Motorola. As shown in Figure 18, which shows the proposed evolution paths from 1G to 3G systems, the second generation featured four main systems, each one implemented in varying frequency bands.

2G Standards

1. IS-136 TDMA system in the 800 and 1900 MHz bands
2. IS-95 CDMA system in the 800 and 1900 MHz bands
3. GSM system in the 900, 1800 and 1900 MHz bands
4. iDEN system in the 800 and 1500 MHz bands

3G systems were proposed around the year 2000, together with an interim generation called 2.5G, or the evolution generation, which built up to 3G and involved an overlay of higher-capacity data transmission capability to existing 2G digital wireless networks. The major 2.5G systems are:

2.5G Standards

1. GPRS
2. EDGE
3. cdma2000 1X-RTT

It is worth noting here that a subset of these standards is referred to as 2.75G systems. The term 2.75G—which was never officially specified—is used to describe systems that fall between 2.5G and 3G systems. Those systems either do not meet the 3G requirements but are marketed as if they do (e.g., the non-multi-carrier cdma2000), or they do meet the requirements but are not marketed as such (e.g., the EDGE system that provides 3G packet data services on GSM networks). As shown in Figure 18, GSM and TDMA operators migrated to GPRS and EDGE systems, and CDMA operators migrated to cdma2000 1X-RTT.

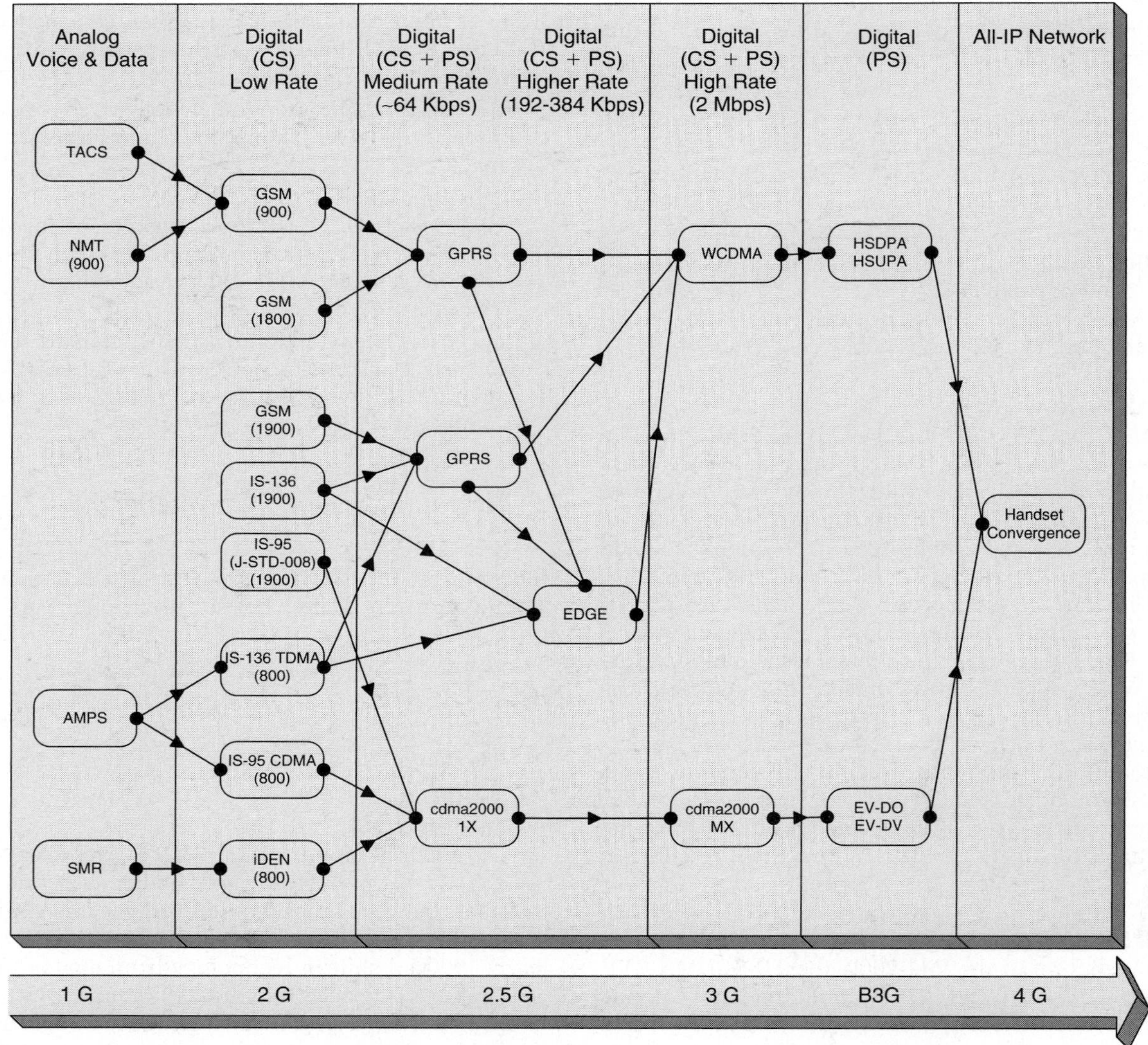

Figure 18: Proposed evolution paths (B3G: beyond 3G; CS: circuit switched; PS: packet switched)

When it comes to the migration from 2G—or even from 1G—to the 3G systems through the evolution generation 2.5G, the operator has to make the decision about which path to use. Regardless of the platform targeted, the operator has to face major issues: capacity, clarity, coverage, compatibility, and cost. The operator also has to decide on a strategy for the migration process, and those strategies typically involve either an overlay approach (no new spectrum allocation required, given an existing 2G platform) or a spectrum segmentation approach (separate radio frequency spectrum allocation needed). The fundamental enhancement of 2.5G over 2G systems was the introduction of the packet-switched data services coupled with increased speeds up to 384 kbps.

Figure 18 shows the two dominant 3G technologies: W-CDMA and cdma2000. One may wonder why only two platforms are discussed and given attention here, when we mentioned earlier that there are five standards proposed by IMT-2000. The fact is that the majority of wireless operators are targeting one of these two platforms as their future 3G platform. W-CDMA encapsulates the UTRA FDD and UTRA TDD discussed previously and is considered the choice for GPRS/EDGE (GSM-based) operators. On the other hand, cdma2000 is considered the choice for the 2G IS-95 (cdmaOne) operators and the 2.5G cdma2000 1X-RTT operators, both of which are CDMA based.

UMTS LAYERS AND CHANNEL STRUCTURES

Universal mobile telecommunications service is a category of 3G systems that groups all W-CDMA-based 3G air interfaces evolving from GSM platforms. The radio access for UMTS, known as universal terrestrial radio access (UTRA), comes in two flavors: UTRA FDD and UTRA TDD. UMTS, which is the European initiative, provides advanced communications capabilities integrated with personal and terminal mobility to meet the user and service requirements of the twenty-first century.

UMTS offers support to multimedia services, which is the capability of delivering two or more media components within one call. The standard also enables the user of a single terminal to establish and maintain several connections simultaneously. UMTS also supports universal personal telecommunications, which is a feature that enables the user to access services via any terminal, irrespective of geographic location and networks utilized. To enable number portability, an international mobile user number (IMUN) is allocated to each new user at the start of a UMTS subscription. Moreover, users should be able to move a subscription from one home environment to another without changing the IMUN provided that the new home environment offers service in the same geographic domain (3GPP UMTS 1999).

UMTS Architecture and Interfaces

Figure 19 shows the network architecture of UMTS, or what is called the core network (CN). The various components of the CN are shown together with the defined interfaces between these components. The system comprises interconnected networks, both circuit-switched and packet-switched for voice and data services. Figure 19 shows the higher-level paradigm. Basically, the circuit-switched network contains the MSC and the gateway MSC; the packet-switched network contains mainly the SGSN, the GGSN, the domain name server (DNS), the dynamic host configuration protocol (DHCP) server, the packet charging gateway, and firewalls. In summary, there are components that carry the circuit-switched (CS) roles (e.g., MSC and VLR), components that carry the packet-switched (PS) roles (e.g., SGSN and GGSN), and

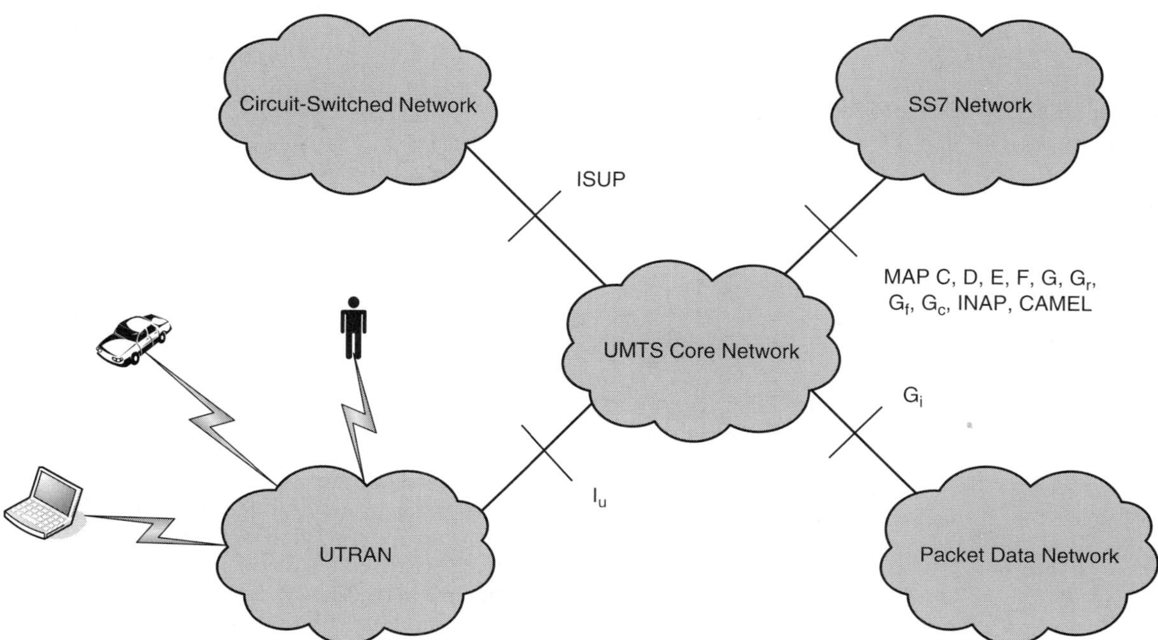

Figure 19: UMTS architecture

components that serve both parts (e.g., HLR.) In addition, several other subsystems are crucial to the operation of the CN; one example is the network management system, which applies to billing and general management.

UMTS Releases

The first release was Release 99 (R99), which was mainly an enhancement to the circuit-switched voice network and GPRS data network with the UMTS radio access network (UTRAN) (3GPP 2006). This resulted in achieving higher bandwidth, macrodiversity in handover, and support for QoS classes. The next release was Release 4 (R4), in which the circuit-switched voice network was replaced with either an ATM or an IP core network. Moreover, network-assisted location services and broadcast services were covered by R4. Release 5 (R5) was characterized by the addition of IP multimedia services (IMS), more flexible radio access network (RAN), and the high-speed downlink packet access (HSDPA). This improved throughput (end users are offered up to 14.4 Mbps in the downlink), latency (round-trip delay as low as 60ms), and capacity (data capacity is increased by a factor of 5). Major advantages of HSDPA are:

- High-speed downlink shared channel (HS-DSCH)
- Transmission time interval (TTI) of 2 ms
- Fast data traffic scheduling
- Adaptive modulation and coding (AMC)
- Fast hybrid automatic response request (HARQ) techniques (UMTS Forum 2006).

As for Release 6 (R6), improved uplink performance is achieved through high-speed uplink packet access (HSUPA), which mainly enhances coverage and throughput and reduces delay. More capabilities were added to the network in R6, including:

- Network resource sharing
- More IMS services
- Multimedia broadcast and multicast service (MBMS)—many users in parallel
- WLAN interworking
- Multiple-input multiple-output (MIMO)—multiple antennas used

Following high-speed packet access (HSPA)—which is a major improvement in performance—are HSPA+ and long-term evolution (LTE). These collectively will offer new services, including: voice over IP, multi-user gaming, and high-resolution video (UMTS Forum 2006). In order for the 3GPP system to cope with the rapid growth in IP data traffic, the packet-switched technology utilized within 3G mobile networks requires further enhancements. The high-level objectives of the move to an all-IP network (AIPN) and the drivers that are forcing this change are as follows:

- Universal seamless access: An AIPN should allow users to connect to services from a variety of device types and access systems. This should come about through the use of common protocols, addressing schemes, and mobility management mechanisms. The users may not need to know the access system used. Access systems may be selected and changed according to service needs and availability.
- Improved user experience: An AIPN should provide users with better quality. This should include rapid network selection, rapid call or session setup times, low voice-call delay, and fast data transmission.
- Reduction of cost: An AIPN should deliver a cost reduction for AIPN operators in relation to the cost of existing networks.
- Flexibility of deployment: AIPN operators should be able to build and dimension their network according to the needs of their users. The AIPN design should be scalable and should not preclude the option to use and interwork with 3GPP-defined circuit-switched domains and legacy handsets as appropriate. The AIPN design should also provide an evolution path from previous releases of the 3GPP system. This will ensure that AIPN operators can introduce an AIPN and continue to make the best use of existing network elements (3GPP AIPN 2005).

Layer Structures and Functions in UTRA

Figure 20 shows the logical layers and structure of the UTRA network. The lowest layer is the physical layer. Among the various functions of this layer are:

- RF processing, spreading, scrambling, and modulation
- Coding and decoding for error correction
- Power control
- Timing advance
- Soft handover execution

The interface of higher layers with the physical layer is the medium access control (MAC) layer. The role of this layer is to interface upper and lower layers through the mapping of logical to physical channels. The next level up is the radio link control (RLC) layer, which has different roles that include:

- RLC connection establishment and release
- Error detection
- Ensuring error-free delivery through acknowledgments
- In-sequence delivery
- Unique delivery
- QoS management

This layer offers the higher layer of both acknowledged and transparent transport services. The former means that erroneous packets are automatically retransmitted, and the latter means that they are discarded. The layer above RLC is the packet data convergence protocol (PDCP), which provides the interface between the user data and lower layers. In other words, it operates on the user data to render it in the format expected by the lower layers; this satisfies the encapsulation of lower layers. Another subtle function above the RLC is the broadcast/multicast control (BMC), which refers to message broadcasting within the

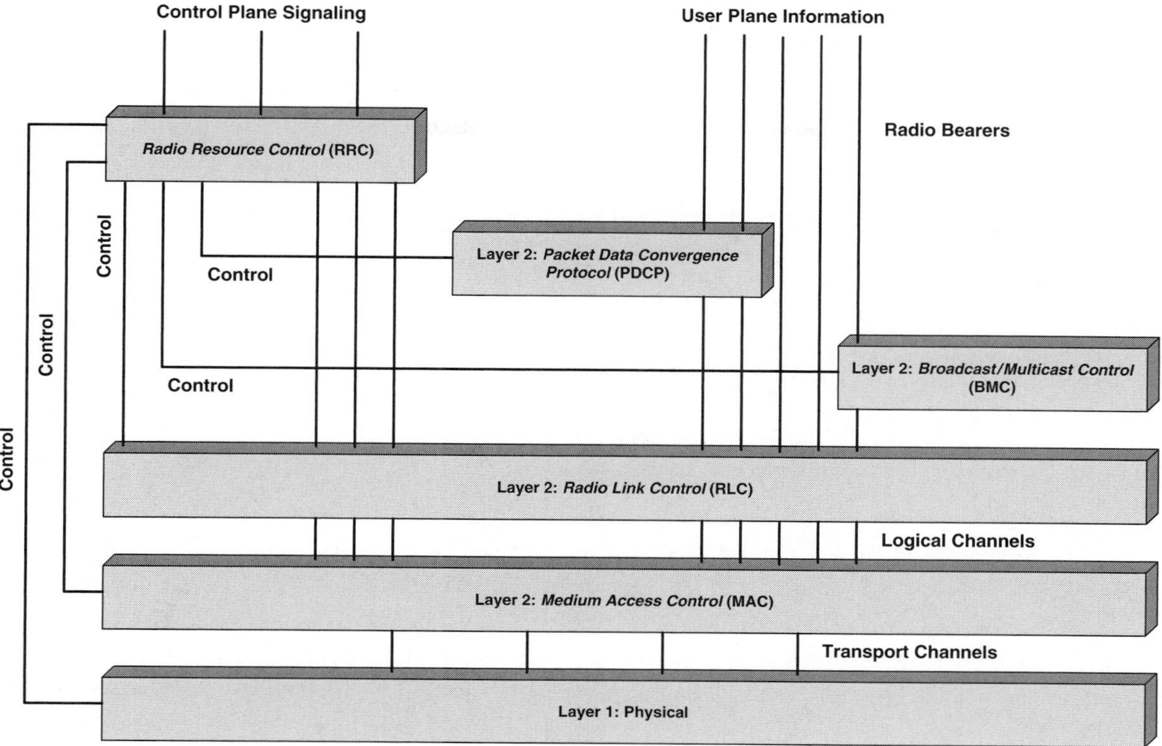

Figure 20: UMTS layers

cell, as in news or warnings. The last component—and the most important—is the radio resource control (RRC), which acts as the brain of the whole system. It comprises the processing power of the system and does the control and management jobs while connected to all layers with control lines. The RF resource allocation decisions are made at the RRC, but it has many other roles, including:

- Broadcasting of system information
- Signaling for connection initiation
- Allocation of bearers
- Measurement reporting
- Mobility management
- QoS management

Transport, Physical, and Logical Channel Identification and Mapping in UTRA

The layers already discussed collectively form an organized set of channels: logical, transport, and physical. As can be inferred from the name, physical channels are inherent in the physical layer. The MAC layer has multitransport channels, whereas the logical channels are the only way to get to the RLC layer. Furthermore, these different channels are connected through mappings of successive channel levels: logical-transport mapping and transport-physical mapping.

Transport Channels

There are two types of transport channels: common and dedicated. The common channel is shared among all users, but it can be used to transfer data to all users (broadcast) or to a single user (unicast). All channels are common except for one: the dedicated channel (DCH). Table 4 summarizes the various UTRA transport channels and their functionalities.

Physical Channels

There are two sets of physical channels: channels that are mapped with upper-layer channels for interfacing and channels that are not mapped and are functional only in the physical layer. The physical layer itself is identified by different parameters: frequency, scrambling code, channelization code, duration, and phase. The different defined physical channels are described in Table 5.

Besides the paging indicator channel (PICH), indicator channels include the acquisition indicator channel (AICH), the access preamble acquisition indicator channel (AP-AICH), and the collision detection/channel assignment indication channel (CD/CA-ICH). UMTS physical channels also include the dedicated physical data channel (DPDCH), the dedicated physical control channel (DPCCH), and the CPCH status indication channel (CSICH). Figure 21 shows the mapping between physical and transport channels.

Logical Channels

Table 6 displays the logical channels, which are the communication channels between the RLC and the MAC layer. These channels have to do with the data transmitted rather than how it is transmitted. There are two types of logical channels: control and traffic channels.

Table 4: UTRA Transport Channels

Name	Description	Type	Functionality
DCH	Dedicated Channel	Dedicated	Used to send large amounts of data in long sessions
RACH	Random Access Channel	Common	Used for signaling; small amounts of data are sent through the uplink
BCH	Broadcast Channel	Common	Data are sent from the cell to all users in the cell through the downlink
PCH	Paging Channel	Common	Used to page a given UE through the downlink
FACH	Forward Access Channel	Common	Used to send control data to the user through the downlink
CPCH	Uplink Common Packet Channel	Common	Similar to RACH but supports the sending of more data
DSCH	Downlink Shared Channel	Common	Similar to FACH but with higher data rate and the support of unicast or multicast

Table 5: UTRA Physical Channels

Name	Description	Functionality
SCH	Synchronization Channel	The base station transmits on this channel, and the UE detects the signal for correct synchronization
CPCH	Common Pilot Channel	Always transmitted by the base station for the terminal to make measurements for handover or cell reselection
Primary CCPCH	Primary Common Control Physical Channel	Used on the downlink to create the BCH channel
Secondary CCPCH	Secondary Common Control Physical Channel	Used on the downlink to carry the FACH and PCH channels
PRACH	Physical Random Access Channel	Used in the uplink to carry the RACH channel
PCPCH	Physical Common Packet Channel	Used in the uplink to carry the CPCH channel
PDSCH	Physical Downlink Shared Channel	Used on the downlink to carry the DSCH channels
PICH	Paging Indicator Channel	Used to carry the paging indicators

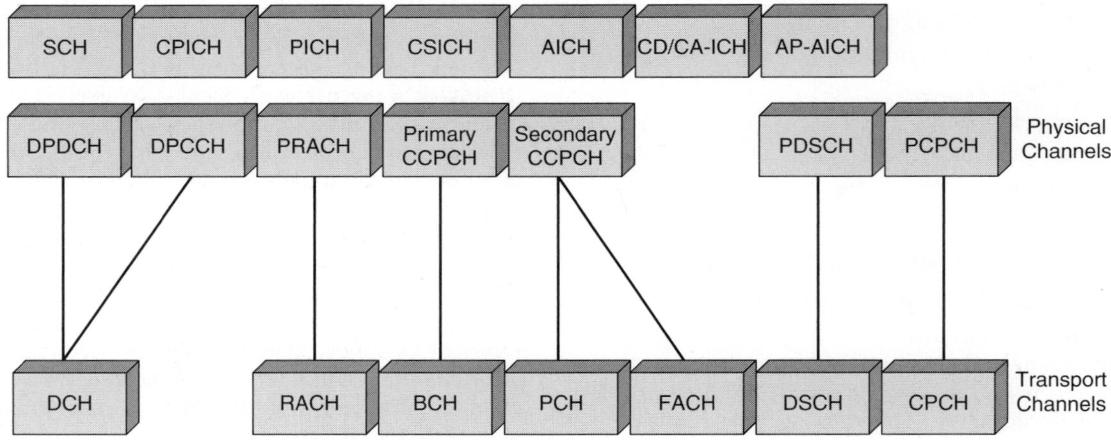

Figure 21: Physical-transport channel mapping

Figure 22 shows the mapping between logical and transport channels.

Channel Spreading and Modulation in UTRA

Three important steps take place before transmission from user equipment (UE) occurs. The data undergo spreading, also called channelization, followed by scrambling and modulation. First, different data streams from the same user are distinguished by applying the spreading code. Then, data streams from different UEs are distinguished by applying the scrambling code. Finally, the data resulting from this two-stage coding are modulated

Table 6: UTRA Logical Channels

Name	Description	Type*	Functionality
BCCH	Broadcast Control Channel	CCH	Used for downlink transmission of system information
PCCH	Paging Control Channel	CCH	Used for the paging of an MS across one or more cells
DCCH	Dedicated Control Channel	CCH	Used in the uplink by terminals to access the network without connection
CCCH	Common Control Channel	CCH	Bidirectional point-to-point control channel between the MS and the network for sending control information
DTCH	Dedicated Traffic Channel	TCH	Point-to-point channel dedicated to the UE for the transfer of user data
CTCH	Common Traffic Channel	TCH	Point-to-multipoint unidirectional channel for the transfer of user data to all UEs or a single UE

*CCH = control channel; TCH = traffic channel.

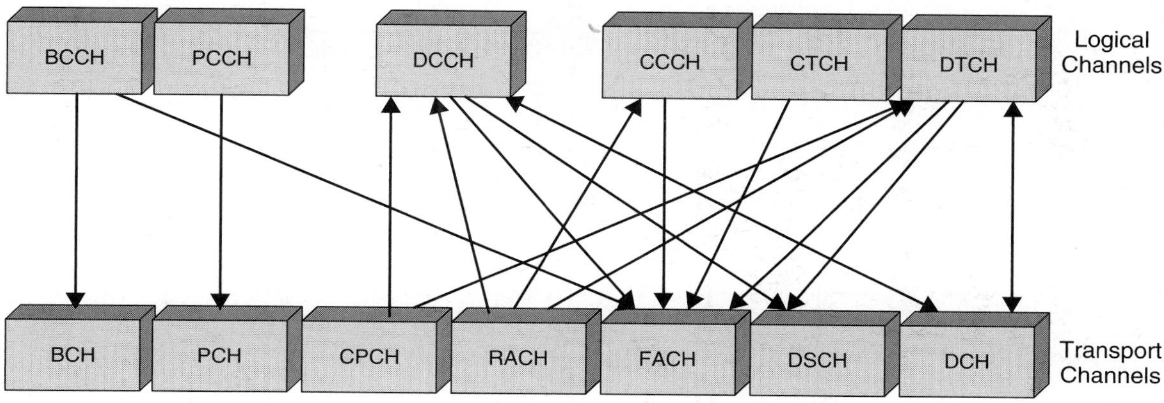

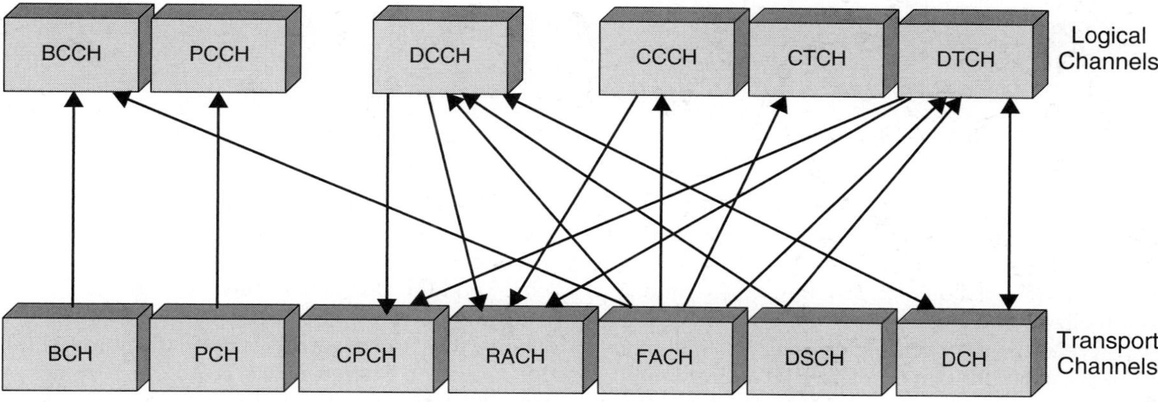

Figure 22: Logical-transport channel mapping

before being transmitted. Figure 23 shows this process for the uplink, and Figure 24 shows it for the downlink. Both codes applied to the data stream are at the chip rate of 3.84 Mcps. At the receiving end, the signal is first descrambled to separate different UEs, and then the channelization code is applied to recover the original stream.

As mentioned previously, the physical layer has multiple physical channels. These channels are distinguished during transmission by the application of the appropriate channelization codes. For instance, if the UE is transmitting data and control information, then the two channels can be easily multiplexed and demultiplexed. Figure 23

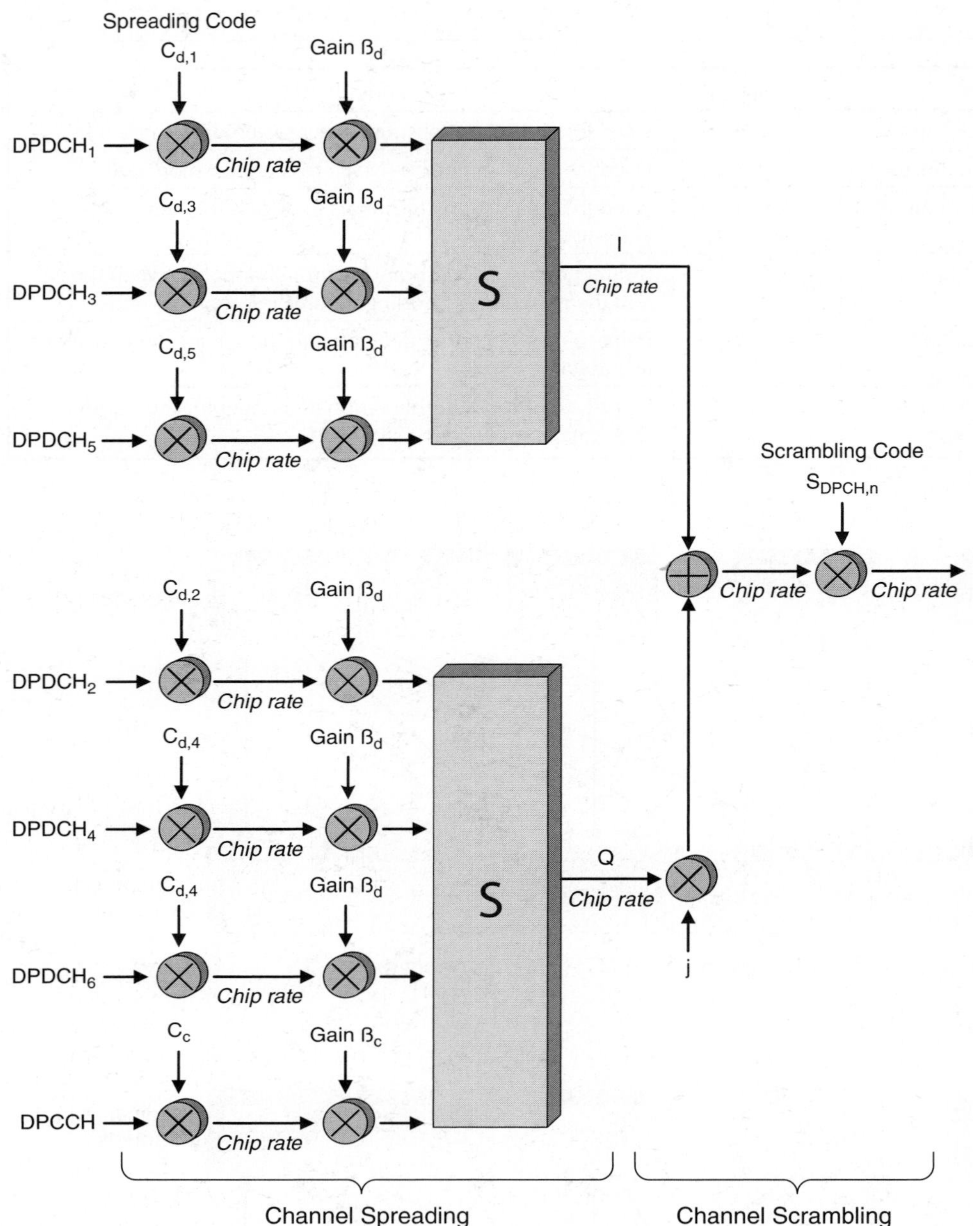

Figure 23: Uplink spreading and scrambling

shows a sample scenario; the UE is transmitting, in the uplink, data on the DPDCH as well as control information on the DPCCH. The user can use up to six DPDCHs depending on the required data rate. $C_{d,1}$, $C_{d,2}$, ..., $C_{d,6}$, and C_c are the channelization codes applied to the various channels, which spread the data at the chip rate. The odd data channels are spread (with $C_{d,1}$, $C_{d,3}$, and $C_{d,5}$) and weighted (with a gain factor of B_d), creating the stream of real bits (In-phase, or I). The even data channels are spread (with $C_{d,2}$, $C_{d,4}$, and $C_{d,6}$) and weighted (with a gain factor of B_d), then added to the control channel, which is spread (with C_c) and weighted (with a gain factor of B_c), creating the stream of imaginary bits (Quadrature phase, or Q). The real bits are added to the imaginary bits multiplied by j (where $j = \sqrt{-1}$), creating a stream of complex-valued chips at the chip rate. This resulting stream is then subjected to the complex-valued scrambling codes. There are two types of scrambling codes—long and short—with 2^{24} possibilities for each type. The two types of scrambling code are pseudo-random; the long codes have a length of 38,400 chips and the short codes have a length of 256 chips.

Figure 24 shows what happens on downlink channels. The stream to be spread is split using a serial-to-parallel converter. The even bits go to the I branch, whereas the odd bits go to the Q branch. The same channelization code is used to spread the two branches. A complex-valued stream is created when the I branch (real bits) is added to the jQ branch (imaginary bits) and is then subjected to a complex pseudo-random scrambling code. The scrambling codes used in the downlink are similar to the uplink codes but are of different lengths. In the case of downlink, the purpose of the scrambling codes is to differentiate the streams originating from different base stations (or different cells). The number of scrambling codes

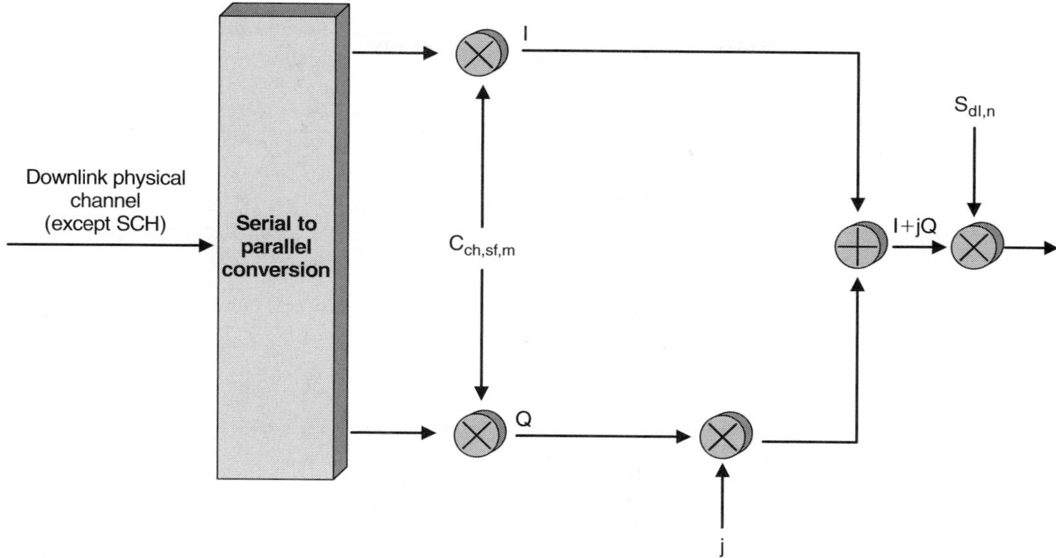

Figure 24: Downlink spreading and scrambling

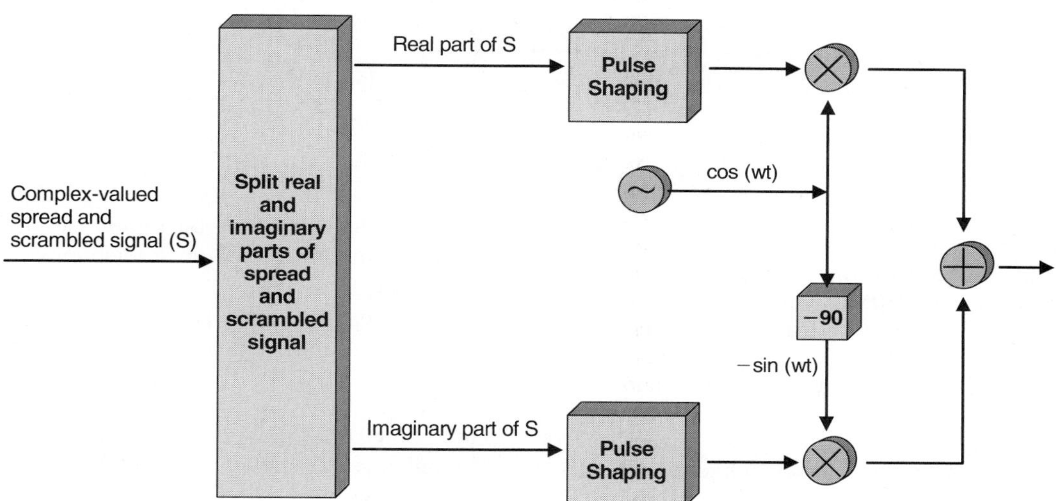

Figure 25: UTRA modulation

is $2^{18}-1$ (262,143), but only a subset of them (7,680) is used, which is further divided into primary and secondary codes in order to enhance the speed of the process.

The modulation scheme used in both uplink and downlink is quadrature phase shift keying (QPSK); Figure 25 shows the process. The stream of complex-valued chips is split into two parts: the real and imaginary bit streams. The two branches (real and imaginary) of the scrambled signal are applied to the modulator branches (I and Q).

Channel Coding and Code Allocation in UTRA

The channelization coding scheme used is called orthogonal variable spreading factor (OVSF) and is represented by the tree in Figure 26. The channel is spread by one of the spreading factors in the following set: 4, 8, 16, 32, 64, 128, and 256. The spreading factor, which affects the bandwidth used, is chosen depending on the data rate required. In general, the smaller the factor used, the larger the data rate. For instance, if a factor of 8 is to be chosen to spread data for the DPDCH, this gives a data rate of 480 kbps ($3.84 \times 10^6/8 = 480 \times 10^3$). For instance, if multiple DPDCHs are to be transmitted, the following are the codes applied:

- $C_{ch,4,1}$ spreads $DPDCH_1$ and $DPDCH_2$
- $C_{ch,4,2}$ spreads $DPDCH_3$ and $DPDCH_4$
- $C_{ch,4,3}$ spreads $DPDCH_5$ and $DPDCH_6$

In general, codes are chosen carefully. Basically, codes of the same user should be orthogonal. Also, as in the example above, codes of adjacent channels can be similar (1 and 2, 3 and 4, or 5 and 6) but codes for two even or two odd channels cannot. This is because adjacent channels are separated by the I and Q separation.

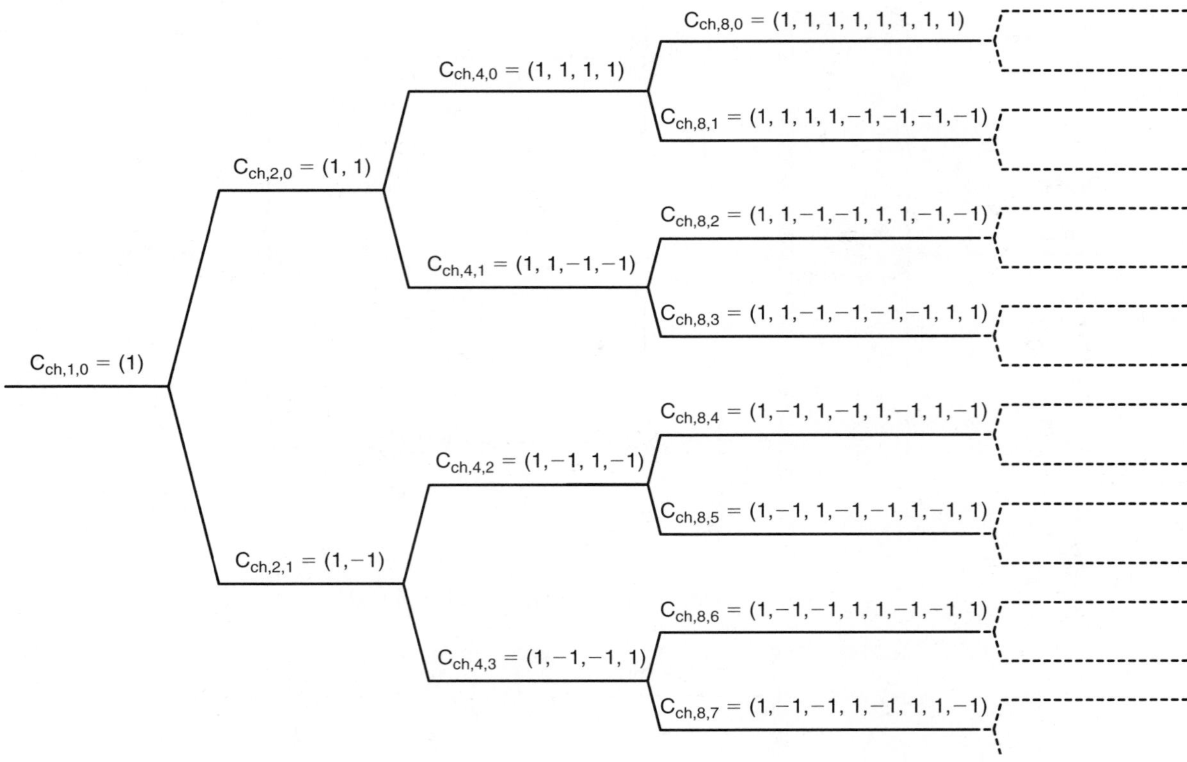

Figure 26: Spreading code tree—OVSF

Rate Matching in UTRA

Rate matching means that bits on a transport channel are repeated or punctured. Higher layers assign a rate-matching attribute for each transport channel. This attribute is semi-static and can only be changed through higher layer signaling. The rate-matching attribute is used when the number of bits to be repeated or punctured is calculated.

The number of bits on a transport channel can vary between different transmission time intervals. In the downlink, the transmission is interrupted if the number of bits is below maximum. When the number of bits between different transmission time intervals in the uplink channel is changed, bits are repeated or punctured to ensure that the total bit rate after transport channel (TrCH) multiplexing is identical to the total channel bit rate of the allocated dedicated physical channels.

If no bits are input to the rate matching for all TrCHs within a coded composite transport channel (CCTrCH), the rate matching will output no bits for all TrCHs within the CCTrCH and no uplink DPDCH will be selected in the case of uplink rate matching (3GPP 2006).

CDMA2000 LAYERS AND PHYSICAL CHANNEL STRUCTURES

cdma2000 Layering Structure

Upper-Layer Functions

Figure 27 shows the cdma2000 layering structure. In terms of each layer's services, the upper-layer functions can be summarized as follows:

- Voice services: voice telephony service, in all its flavors—mobile, PSTN, or IP telephony
- End user, data-bearing services: data services initiated by the user, including packet data, circuit data, and SMS
- Signaling: services that control the operation of the mobile

Link Layer Functions

The link layer, as shown in Figure 27, can be divided into two sublayers: MAC and LAC. Collectively, the link layer translates reliability and QoS requirements of higher layers to the physical layer. Specifically, the LAC sublayer provides point-to-point communication channels between peer upper layers as well as end-to-end reliable link layer services. The MAC layer, on the other hand, provides three important functions:

- Media access control state: controls the access of higher-layer data services to the physical layer
- Best-effort delivery: provides a best-effort level of reliability in transmission
- Multiplexing and QoS control: enforces the claimed QoS levels through prioritizing services' access

Quality of Service

The MAC sublayer has the following subdivisions:

- Physical layer independent convergence function (PLICF)
- Physical layer dependent convergence function (PLDCF)

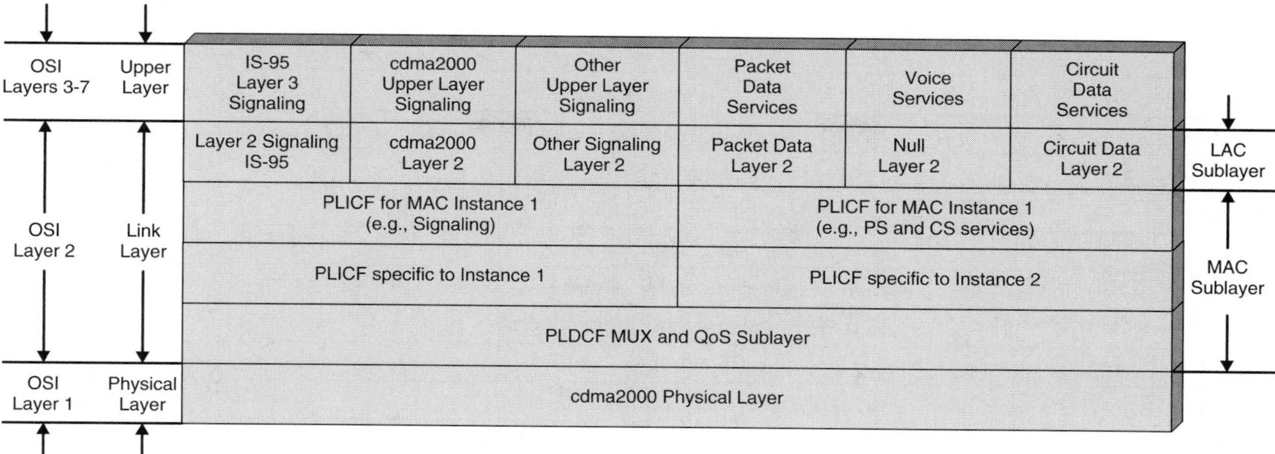

Figure 27: cdma2000 layers

- PLDCF MUX and QoS
- Instance-specific PLDCF

With this structure, the MAC sublayer provides the LAC sublayer with different QoS levels. The role of the PLICF is to provide those operations and functions that are independent of the physical layer to the MAC sublayer. Furthermore, the PLICF data service maintains state information about all of its services. The PLICF accomplishes its actual operations through the use of PLDCF functions. In other words, the PLDCF provides the interfacing between PLICF logical channels and the logical channels supported by the physical layer. PLDCF also enforces QoS levels in various ways, including the automatic retransmission request (ARQ) and the resolution of competing PLICF data services requests. Finally, the LDCF MUX and QoS sublayer coordinates the multiplexing/demultiplexing of code channels from multiple PLICF instances while ensuring requested QoS levels.

Physical Layer Functions

The physical layer mainly provides coding and modulation services for the LDCF MUX and QoS sublayers. The physical channels fall in two categories:

- Forward/reverse dedicated physical channels (F/R-DPHCH): channels used for the unicast transmission (point-to-point) from the base station to the mobile station
- Forward/reverse common physical channels (F/R-CPHCH): channels used for the broadcast or multicast transmission (point-to-multipoint) from the base station to the multiple mobile stations.

New Channels in the Physical Layer

The new channels in the physical layer of cdma2000 are shown in Table 7.

cdma2000 Reverse Link

Reverse Link Features

The key features of the reverse link are:

- Channels are primarily code-multiplexed
- Separate channels are used for different QoS and physical layer characteristics
- Transmission is continuous to avoid electromagnetic interference
- Channels are orthogonalized by Walsh functions and I/Q split so that performance is equivalent to binary phase shift keying (BPSK)
- Hybrid combination of QPSK and BPSK
- Coherent reverse link with continuous pilot
- Forward power control information is time-multiplexed with the pilot
- By restricting alternate phase changes of the complex scrambling, power peaking is reduced and side lobes are narrowed
- Independent fundamental and supplemental channels with different transmit power and frame error rate (FER) target (Garg 2001)
- Forward error correction
- Fast reverse power control
- Frame lengths

Physical Channels Structures

The various physical channels in the reverse link are listed in Table 8. R-FCH, R-SCH, and R-SCCH are known collectively as reverse traffic channels. Figure 28 shows the structure of the reverse link channel in cdma2000.

Physical Channel Spreading

The reverse link in cdma2000 uses orthogonal spreading to distinguish user channels. Code channels are associated

Table 7: New Channels in the cdma2000 Physical Layer

Name	Description	Type
F-DAPICH	Forward Dedicated Auxiliary Pilot Channel	Dedicated
F-DCCH	Forward Dedicated Control Channel	Dedicated
F-SCH1	Forward Supplemental Channel 1	Dedicated
F-SCH2	Forward Supplemental Channel 2	Dedicated
R-SCH1	Reverse Supplemental Channel 1	Dedicated
R-SCH2	Reverse Supplemental Channel 2	Dedicated
R-PICH	Reverse Pilot ChannelDedicated	
R-DCCH	Reverse Dedicated Control Channel	Dedicated
F-TDPICH	Forward Transmit Delivery Pilot Channel	Common
F-ATDPICH	Forward Auxiliary Transmit Delivery Pilot Channel	Common
F-QPCH	Quick Paging ChannelCommon	
F-BCH	Forward Broadcast Channel	Common
F-CCCH	Forward Common Control Channel	Common
F-CPCCH	Forward Common Power Control Channel	Common
F-CACH	Forward Common Assignment Channel	Common
R-CCCH	Reverse Common Control Channel	Common
R-EACH	Reverse Enhanced Access Channel	Common

Table 8: cdma2000 Reverse Physical Channels

Name	Description	Type
F-ACH	Reverse Access Channel	Common
F-EACH	Reverse Enhanced Access Channel	Common
R-CCCH	Reverse Common Control Channel	Common
R-PICH	Reverse Pilot Channel	Dedicated
R-DCCH	Reverse Dedicated Control Channel	Dedicated
R-FCH	Reverse Fundamental Channel	Dedicated
R-SCH	Reverse Supplemental Channel	Dedicated
R-SCCH	Reverse Supplemental Code Channel	Dedicated

with a Walsh function (see Figure 32) W_n^N of length 2^N Walsh chips, where N = 1, 2, ..., 6. BPSK symbols are multiplied by the Walsh function at a fixed chip rate (1.2288 Mcps).

Enhanced Access Channel

The enhanced access channel (EACH) is used for the communication from the mobile station to the base station (reverse link), to initiate communication, or to respond to a mobile-directed message. It has three modes:

- Basic access mode: The enhanced access probe contains the enhanced access channel preamble and the enhanced access data.
- Powered controlled access mode: The enhanced access probe contains the enhanced access channel preamble, the enhanced access header, and the enhanced access data.
- Reservation access mode: The enhanced access probe contains the enhanced access channel preamble and the enhanced access header. The enhanced access data is sent on the R-CCCH upon receiving the permission from the base station.

Power Control Subchannel

The mobile station inserts a reverse power control subchannel (PCCH) on the reverse pilot channel (R-PICH) when operating on the reverse traffic channel (R-TCH) with RC3 through RC6. The mobile station supports both the inner power control loop and the outer power control loop for the forward channel power control loop.

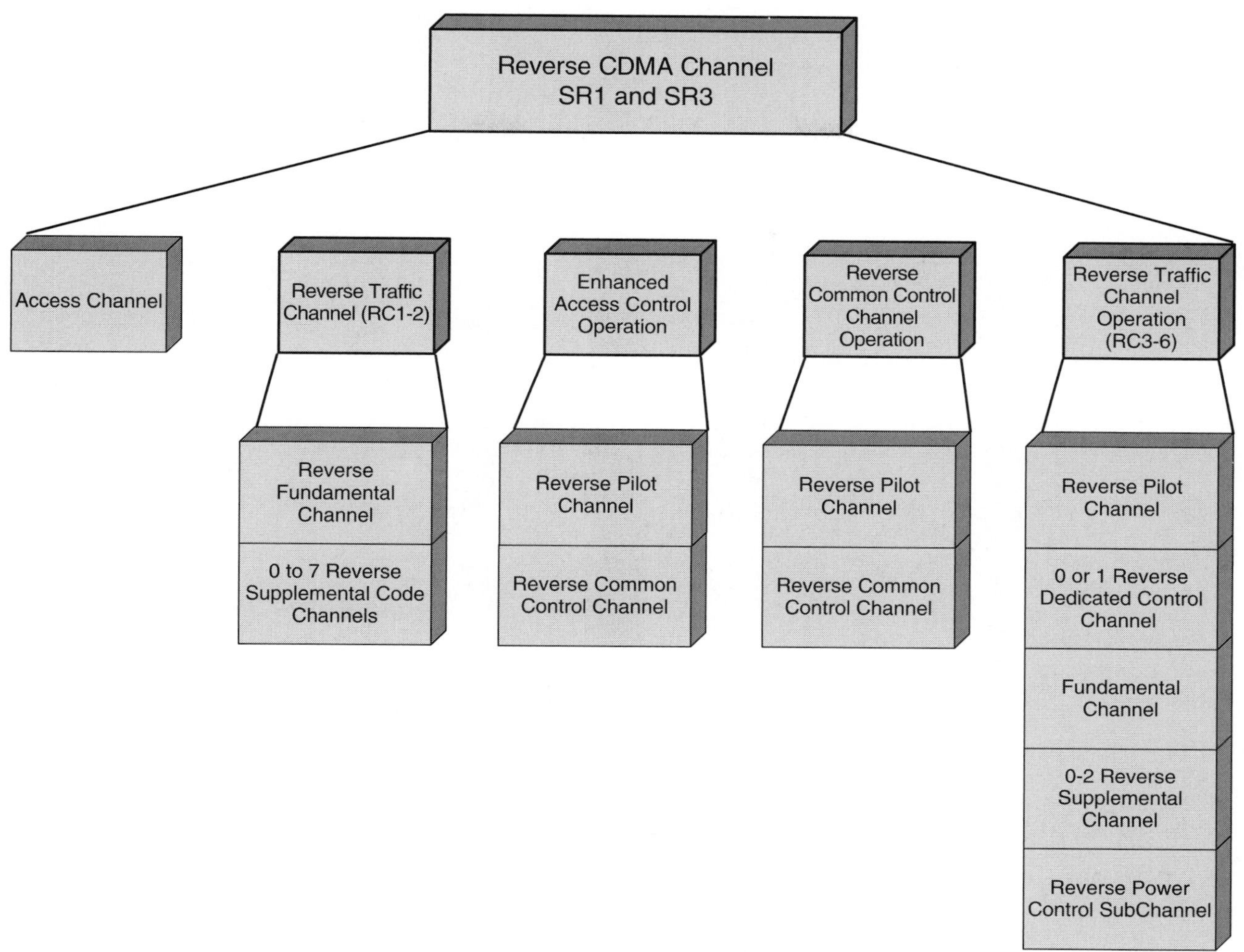

Figure 28: cdma2000 reverse link channel structure

I and Q Mapping

Figure 29 shows the I and Q mapping process that takes place after the application of the Walsh function. Coded channels are mapped to either the I or the Q branch of the complex multiplier that follows, depending on the type of channel being mapped. The mapping is predetermined, and the important thing is that channels in the same branch are chosen to be orthogonal, because they will be added together in the branch (for both I and Q branches).

cdma2000 Forward Link

Forward Link Features

As Figure 30 shows, the forward link can support multiples of the 1.2288 Mcps. This gives what is called the cdma2000 multicarrier NX, when the chip rate is $N \times 1.2288$ Mcps (where $N = 1, 3, 6, 9, 12$). The simplest case is when $N = 1$, which is the case in IS-95B but with QPSK and fast closed-loop power control. On the other hand, for $N > 1$, modulation symbols are multiplexed on N separate 1.25 MHz carriers, where each carrier is spread at a rate of 1.2288 Mcps.

Physical Channels Structures

The various physical channels in the forward link are shown in Table 9. F-FCH, F-SCH, and F-SCCH are known collectively as forward traffic channels. Figure 31 shows the structure of the forward link channel in cdma2000.

Physical Channel Spreading

The forward link in cdma2000 also uses orthogonal spreading to distinguish user channels. Code channels are associated with a Walsh function (see Figure 32) W_n^N of length 2^N Walsh chips, where $N = 1, 2, \ldots, 7$. The I and Q values of the complex modulation are multiplied by the Walsh function at a fixed chip rate (1.2288 Mcps).

Modulation and Spreading for Single- and Multi-Carrier Systems

The common modulator used with the forward link of cdma2000 is QPSK. The sole purpose of using the QPSK is to increase bandwidth.

Channel Coding and Interleaving in cdma2000

Error Correction in cdma2000

cdma2000 incorporates a forward error correction (FEC) mechanism that reduces the required signal-to-interference-noise ratio (SINR) for the required FER performance. There are two types of FEC: convolutional

Reverse Supplemental Channel 2
C
Relative Gain
Walsh Cover W_2^4 or W_6^8
Reverse Pilot Channel
A
I
Σ
Walsh Cover W_{16}^{64}
Reverse Channel Quality Indicator Channel
E
Relative Gain
Walsh Cover W_{12}^{16}
Reverse Dedicated Control Channel
B
Relative Gain
Walsh Cover W_8^{16}
Reverse Fundamental Channel
C
Relative Gain
Walsh Cover W_4^{16}
Reverse Acknowledgment Channel
D
Relative Gain
Q
Σ
Walsh Cover W_{16}^{64}
Reverse Channel Quality Indicator Channel
E
Relative Gain
Walsh Cover W_{12}^{16}
Reverse Supplemental Channel 1, Reverse Control Channel, or Reverse Enhanced Access Channel
C
Relative Gain
Walsh Cover W_1^2 or W_2^4 for R-SCH 1 or Walsh Cover W_2^8 for R-CCCH and R-EACH

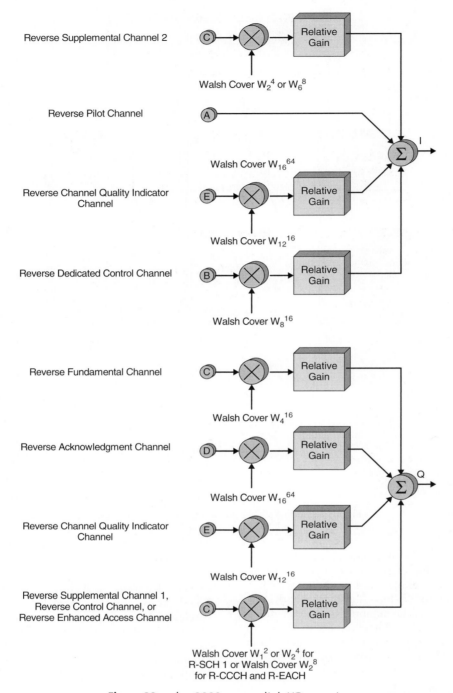

Figure 29: cdma2000 reverse link I/Q mapping

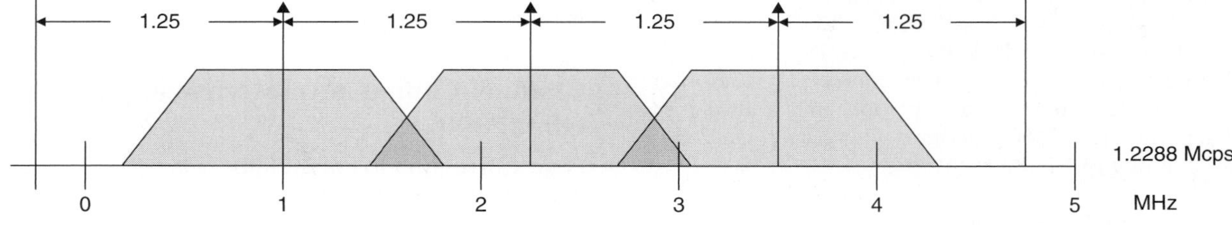

Figure 30: cdma2000 multicarrier

Table 9: cdma2000 Forward Physical Channels

Name	Description	Type
F-PICH	Forward Pilot Channel	Common
F-PCH	Forward Paging Channel	Common
F-SCH	Forward Sync Channel	Common
F-CCCH	Forward Common Control Channel	Common
F-QPCH	(Forward) Quick Paging Channel	Common
F-TDPICH	(Forward) Transmit Delivery Pilot Channel	Common
F-ATDPICH	(Forward) Auxiliary Transmit Delivery Pilot Channel	Common
F-CPCCH	Forward Common Power Control Channel	Common
F-CACH	Forward Common Assignment Channel	Common
F-BCH	Forward Broadcast Channel	Common
F-DAPICH	Forward Dedicated Auxiliary Pilot Channel	Dedicated
F-DCCH	Forward Dedicated Control Channel	Dedicated
F-FCH	Forward Fundamental Channel	Dedicated
F-SCH	Forward Supplemental Channel	Dedicated
F-SCCH	Forward Supplemental Code Channel	Dedicated

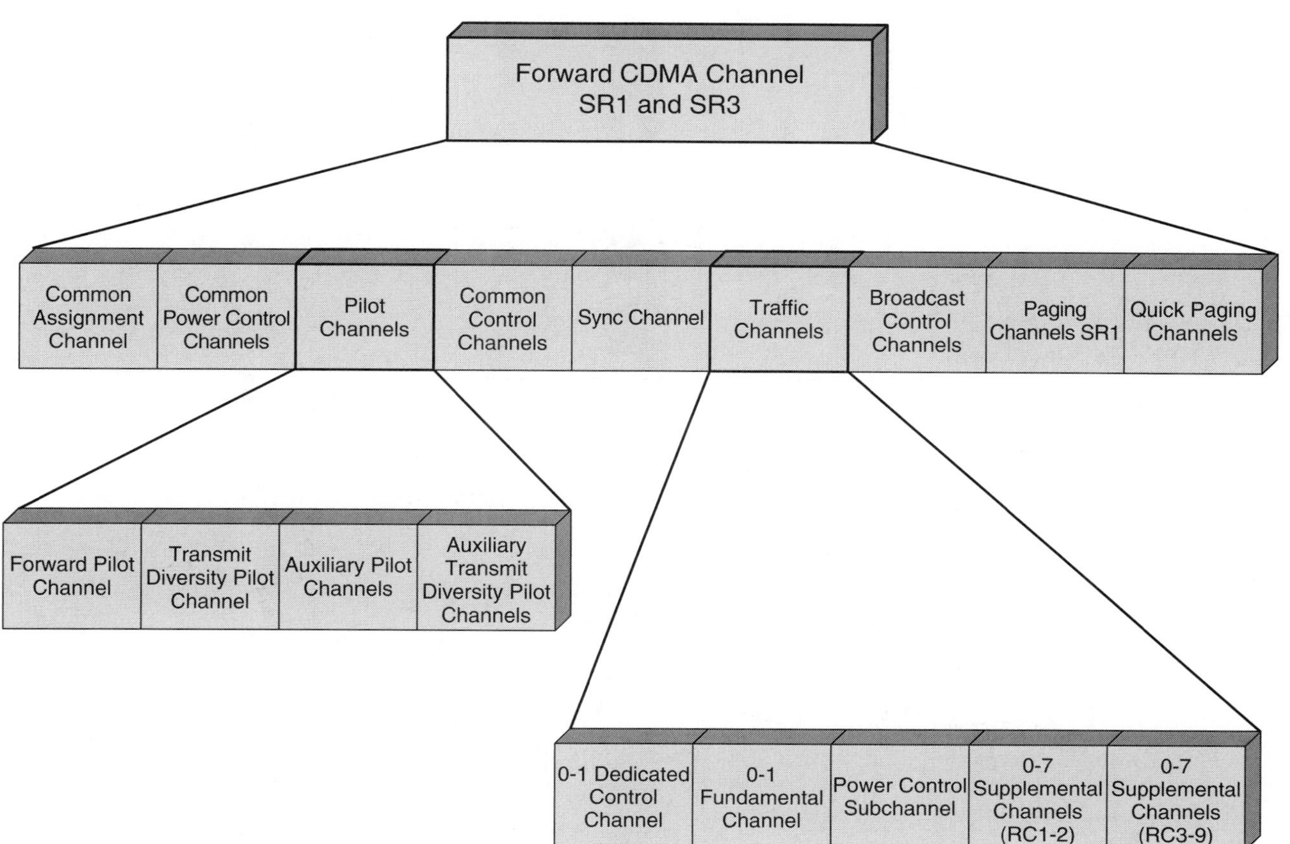

Figure 31: cdma2000 forward link channel structure

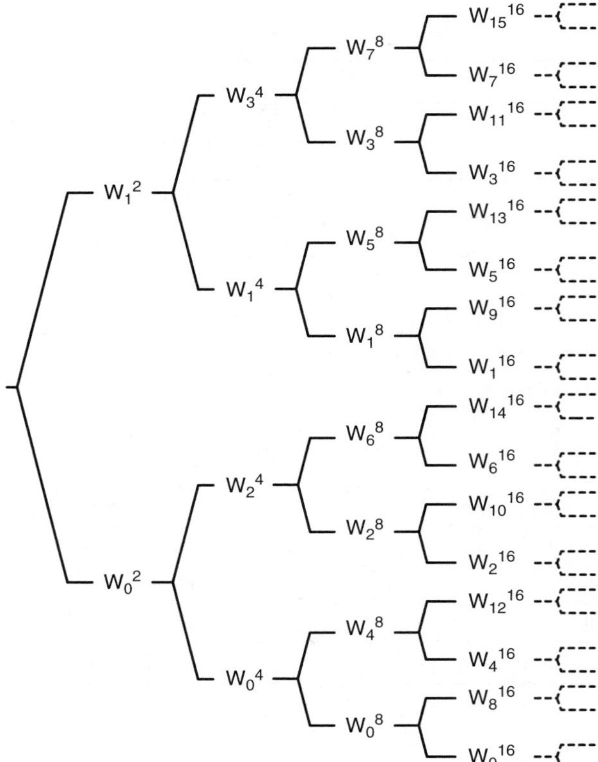

Figure 32: Walsh code

and turbo coding. The convolutional coding is suitable for short payloads, and the turbo coding is more effective in longer payloads. In general, the coding gain (gain calculated by the enhancement on the SINR in coded systems from systems absent coding) for turbo coding is proportional to the turbo interleaver size. Accordingly, turbo coding performs better with higher payloads (huge data services); otherwise, convolutional coding performs better.

Code Puncturing

After coding and before modulation, the rate of the coded symbols should be matched to one of the allowable data rates. This rate matching is similar to that in UTRA and should take place because of the differences in data rates and frame sizes of traffic channels. Repetition occurs when traffic channel-coded symbols are transmitted with a rate less than or equal to the full rate. These patterns are repeated as appropriate. But when traffic channel-coded symbols are transmitted with a rate that is a multiple of the full rate, the symbol pattern is punctured. The process of puncturing eliminates specific coded symbols and maintains others depending on the radio configuration (RC).

Turbo Coding

Turbo coding was originally presented in Berrou, Glavieux, and Thitimajshima (1993). Its performance is superior to other coding techniques, mainly because its bit

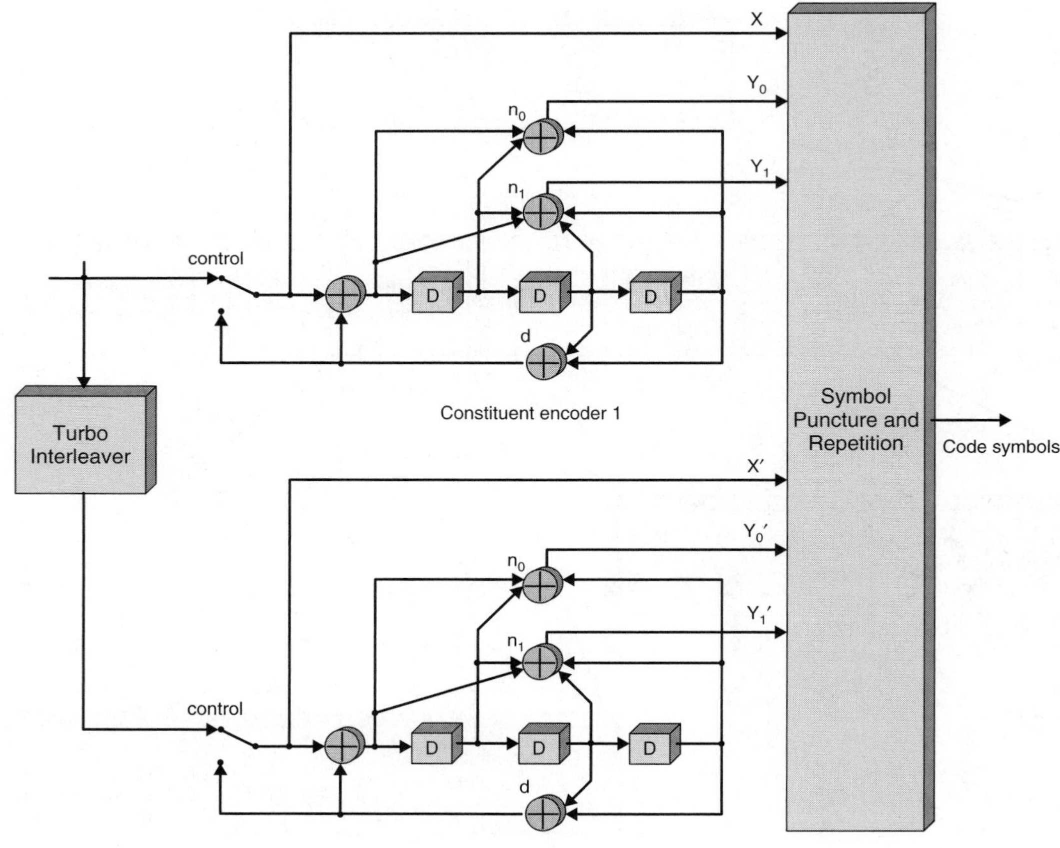

Figure 33: cdma2000 turbo coding

error rate (BER) is within a decibel or so from the Shannon capacity limit, especially when coupled with large interleavers (Vanghi, Damnjanovic, and Vojcic 2004). As shown in Figure 33, the turbo code encoder for cdma2000 is made up of two recursive convolutional encoders of length 4. The D boxes are registers that form a shift register. In convolutional coding, output bits depend on the current input bit and previous input bits. If, during each clock interval, two output bits are generated for a single input bit, we say the code rate is ½. Similarly, if three output bits are generated, the code rate is ⅓, and so on. Inherent in the turbo coder is the interleaved bit sequence, which highly affects the FER performance.

Forward Link Interleaving

Channel interleaving takes place after the FEC process on the transmitting side and before the FEC on the receiving side. The whole purpose is to immunize the transmitted data against fading. There are two types of interleavers: the bit-reversal-order interleaver and the forward-backward bit-reversal interleaver. Both techniques tend to arrange the input bit stream into a matrix while writing in columns and reading in rows.

CONCLUSION

The IMT-2000 specification was illustrated throughout the whole chapter, and the various 3G wireless technologies were discussed with broader interest in W-CDMA and cdma2000—those being the major market trends. In this chapter, network architecture and service characteristics were the two mainly tackled issues of mobile wireless systems. This fact makes the text easy to follow; it allows beginners to get a broad introductory view of the subject yet proves informative for specialists interested in enriching their knowledge.

GLOSSARY

Analog: A method of modulating radio signals so that they can transmit voice or data information.

Antenna: A physical device that enhances or facilitates the transmission and reception of radio signals.

Authentication: A feature that decreases fraud by creating a unique set of variables to identify the phone's identity.

Bandwidth: The range of frequencies a signal can be transmitted without distortion over a transmission medium.

Base Station: A fixed station in a mobile radio system used for radio communications with mobile stations. Base stations are located at the center or on the edge of a coverage region, and consist of radio channels and transmitter and receiver antennas mounted on a tower.

Broadband: A communications medium that uses a wide-bandwidth channel for transmitting large amounts of voice, data, or video information.

Carrier: A company that provides wireless telecommunications services.

CDMA (code division multiple access): The transmission of messages from a large number of transmitters over a single channel by assigning each transmitter a pseudo-random noise code (typically more than 2,000 symbols long for each bit of information) so that the codes are mathematically independent of one another.

Cell: The geographic area in which an individual cell station handles a particular call.

Cellular: The most familiar type of wireless communication. Originally called "cellular" because each service area was divided into cells.

Coding: The altering of the characteristics of a signal to make the signal more suitable for an intended application, such as optimizing the signal for transmission, improving transmission quality and fidelity, modifying the signal spectrum, increasing the information content, providing error detection and/or correction, and providing data security.

Digital: An encoding method using the binary code of 1s and 0s.

Downlink: The transmission link from the fixed part (base station) to the portable part (mobile station).

Duplex: The ability to receive and send a signal at the same time.

Encryption: A method of encoding plain text for security purposes.

FCC (Federal Communications Commission): A U.S. governing agency that regulates the communications industry.

FDMA (frequency division multiple access): The technology used in the analog cellular telephone network that divides the spectrum into thirty channels.

Handoff: Transferring a call from one site to another without losing the connection.

ISO (International Standards Organization): The body responsible for setting world technical standards. It is based in Geneva, Switzerland.

Landline: Traditionally wired telephone service.

MMS (multimedia messaging service): Similar to SMS, but, in addition to plain text, MMS messages may include multimedia elements such as pictures, video, and audio. These multimedia elements are included in the message, not as attachments (as with e-mail).

Modulation: The addition of information (or the signal) to an electronic or optical signal carrier. Modulation can be applied to direct current (mainly by turning it on and off), to alternating current, and to optical signals.

Paging: A wireless device feature that allows one to receive an alphanumeric message.

PCS (personal communication system): A wireless communications technology that operates at 1900 MHz.

PSTN (public switched telephone network): A formal name for the worldwide telephone network.

Roaming: Using your wireless phone in an area outside its home coverage area. There is usually an additional charge for roaming.

RF (radio frequency): A radio signal.

SMS (short messaging service): A PCS phone feature that permits users to receive and transmit short text messages.

Spectrum: The entire range of electromagnetic frequencies.

TDMA (time division multiple access): A satellite and cellular phone technology that interleaves multiple digital signals onto a single high-speed channel. For cellular, TDMA triples the capacity of the original analog method (FDMA). It divides each channel into three subchannels, providing service to three users instead of one. The GSM cellular system is also based on TDMA, but GSM defines the entire network, not just the air interface.

Uplink: The transmission link from the portable part (mobile station) to the fixed part (base station).

CROSS REFERENCES

See *Code Division Multiple Access (CDMA)*; *General Packet Radio Service (GPRS)*; *Global System for Mobile Communications (GSM)*; *Universal Mobile Telecommunications System (UMTS)*.

REFERENCES

3rd-Generation Partnership Project (3GPP). 2005. Service requirements for the IP multimedia (3GPP TS 22.228).

———. 2006. TS 25.212 V7.0.0. Technical specification group radio access network; Multiplexing and channel coding (FDD).

———. 2005. All-IP network (AIPN) feasibility study (3GPP TR 22.978).

———. April 2006. www.3gpp.org.

3rd-Generation Partnership Project 2 (3GPP2). April 2006. www.3gpp2.org.

3GPP Technical Specification Group Radio Access Network Working Group 2. 1999. Overview of the TDD harmonization and the key features of TD-SCDMA TSGR2#6(99)782. http://www.3gpp.org/ftp/tsg_ran/WG2_RL2/TSGR2_06/Docs/Pdfs/r2-99782.pdf.

3GPP Universal Mobile Telecommunications System (UMTS). 1999. Service aspects; Service principles (UMTS 22.01 version 3.3.0).

Berrou, C., A. Glavieux, and P. Thitimajshima. 1993. Near Shannon limit error-correcting coding and decoding: Turbo codes. In *Proceedings from IEEE International Communication Conference (ICC)*, Geneva, Switzerland, May, pp. 1064–70.

Collins, D., and C. Smith. 2001. *3G wireless networks*. New York: McGraw-Hill Professional.

Datang Mobile. 2005. http://www.datangmobile.cn/en/TD-SCDMA/standard.htm.

Garg, V. K. 2001. *Wireless network evolution: 2G to 3G*. Upper Saddle River, NJ: Prentice Hall.

Holma, H., and A. Toskala. 2000. *WCDMA for UMTS: Radio access for third-generation mobile communications*. Chippenham, England: John Wiley Sons Ltd.

International Telecommunications Union (ITU). 1998. Circular letter 8/LCCE/64. Harmonization activities related to IMT-2000 radio transmission technologies.

———. 2006. ITU activities on IMT-2000. www.itu.int/home/imt.html (accessed April 2006).

International Telecommunications Union (ITU)/European Telecommunications Standard Institute (ETSI). 2002. Agreement for mutual cooperation and exchange of documentation between ITU and ETSI. http://www.itu.int/ITU-R/study-groups/docs/rsg6-etsi/docs/itu-etsi-agreement.pdf (accessed June 1, 2006).

Patel, G., and S. Dennett, 2000. The 3GPP and 3GPP2 movements toward an all-IP mobile network. *IEEE Personal Communications*, August, pp. 62–64.

Rappaport, T. 2002. *Wireless communication principles and standards*. 2nd ed. Upper Saddle River, NJ: Prentice Hall.

Time Division Synchronous Code Division Multiple Access (TD-SCDMA) Forum. April 2006. http://www.tdscdma-forum.org/EN/index.asp.

Universal Mobile Telecommunications System (UMTS) Forum. 2006. *3G/UMTS evolution: Toward a new generation of broadband mobile services*. White paper, http://www.umts-forum.org/servlet/dycon/ztumts/umts/Live/en/umts/MultiMedia_PDFs_Papers_3G-UMTS-Evolution-white-paper-Dec-2006.

Universal Mobile Telecommunications System (UMTS) World. April 2006. http://www.umtsworld.com/industry/Subscribers.htm.

Vanghi V., A. Damnjanovic, and B. Vojcic. 2004. *The cdma2000 system for mobile communications*. Upper Saddle River, NJ: Prentice Hall.

Wireless World Forum. 2006. *USA mobile market 2006 statistical handbook*, August.

Code Division Multiple Access (CDMA)

Frank H. P. Fitzek and Marcos Katz, *Aalborg University, Denmark*

CDMA CONCEPT

Code Division Multiple Access (CDMA) is based on a technology known as spread spectrum. While CDMA focuses on the multiple access, spread spectrum has a lot more to offer. Therefore we start by giving a short historical background on the invention and principles of spread spectrum systems.

Historical Background

The story of the invention of spread spectrum technology is one of the most interesting ones in the world of communication engineering. Spread spectrum, particularly the frequency-hopping technique, was invented by the actress Hedy Lamarr, who was born in Austria in 1914 under the name Hedwig Eva Maria Kiesler. In Europe she started her career as an actress and married the multi-millionaire Friedrich Mandl, who was in the defence manufacturing business. During World War II, she attended many of her husband's business meetings and learned about the problems of remote controlled torpedoes used by the marines. Those torpedoes were controlled wirelessly by the English and Americans to direct them against German ships. Because the accuracy of the torpedo was not high enough, manual fine tuning was needed. For the wireless control, a narrow band signal was used. Once the Germans discovered the control signal transmitted by a narrow-band carrier, they could easily jam that signal to avoid the torpedo hitting its target. Hedy Lamarr came up with the idea of using multiple frequencies. The communication should take place on one frequency at a time and then jump to another channel (e.g., frequency) fast enough so as not to give, the enemy enough time to tune in the new frequency to jam it. Certainly, the change in frequency should not be predictable to the enemy. Lamarr's problem was that the change in frequency (or frequency hopping pattern) had to be synchronized between the sender on the boat and the receiver in the torpedo. After some time, Lamarr's friend George Antheil came up with a solution. Antheil had a bar in Paris with automatic pianos that were played by a piano roll. The roll had perforations in it which told the piano which keys had to be played and for how long. Eighty-eight perforations were possible in parallel (one perforation for each key on the piano).

A so-called tracker bar was used to sense the holes and give the commands to the piano. The same mechanism was envisioned for the torpedo to keep synchronization. In 1942 Lamarr and Antheil filed U.S. patent number 2,292,387 entitled *Secret Communication System* (see Figure 1). After the filling process, they offered the invention to the American military. The application of the described invention was questioned with the reasoning that *torpedoes are not large enough to place a piano in them*. In 1962, spread spectrum was used by the militaries for the first time in the Cuba crisis. Hedy Lamarr died in 2000.

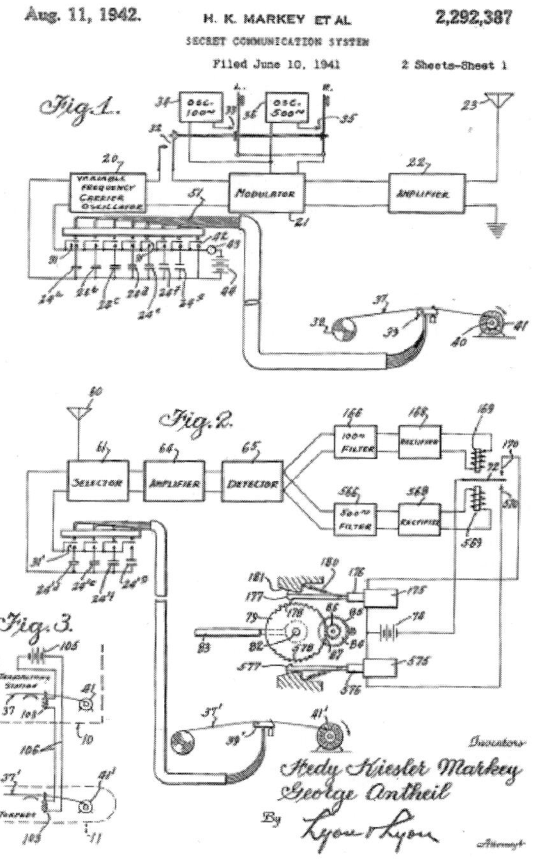

Figure 1: Patent of Lamarr and Antheil

Basic Principles of Spread Spectrum

Spread-spectrum techniques gained popularity through the needs of military communications. In contrast to narrow-band communication, spread-spectrum techniques were more resistant to hostile jammers and more difficult to intercept, two fundamental conditions for tactical communications. For a communication system to be considered a spread-spectrum system, the following criteria have to satisfied, as given in Cooper and McGillem (1986):

- The bandwidth of the transmitted spread signal has to be greater than the information bandwidth. Note that this criterion is also satisfied by frequency modulation, pulse code modulation, and delta modulation.
- The spread signal is composed of the information signal and the spreading sequence. The spreading sequence has to be independent (in the statistical sense) from the information.

The ratio of spreading bandwidth B_s to information bandwidth B_i is denoted as the processing gain $G_{Spreading} = B_s/B_i$ of a spread-spectrum system.

The processing gain does not combat white noise with frequency modulation and pulse code modulation, because the spread signal is independent of the information signal. However, spread-spectrum signals offer the following advantages for a wireless communication system:

- Spread-spectrum modulation is capable of dealing with the multi-path signals resulting from the radio channel. These signals can be considered as interference and therefore be suppressed, or the multi-path signals can be effectively exploited by collecting them, as in a rake receiver. In the section titled "Rake Receiver" we will discuss enhanced techniques developed to suppress multi-path interference even further. The multi-path interference rejection gain depends on the used spread-spectrum scheme and modulation methods.
- The receiver of a spread-spectrum system is able to distinguish between different transmitted signals using the spreading sequence. Spreading sequence design is very important for multiple access capability. The spreading sequence is actually the identification for a transmitter-receiver pair.
- Other advantages such as low probability of interception, privacy, and anti-jam capability are more relevant for military needs.

Different spreading techniques are possible. Figure 2 provides a classification of spread spectrum techniques. The diagram shows techniques such as **D**irect **S**equence *(DS)*, **F**requency **H**opping *(FH)*, and **T**ime **H**opping *(TH)*, along with their sub-classications. These techniques can be combined to combat their disadvantages and combine their benefits. Such systems are referred to as hybrid spread-spectrum systems. These systems consist of combinations of two or more basic spread-spectrum systems. There are four possible hybrid systems, namely DS/FH, DS/TH, FH/TH, and DS/FH/TH, as shown in Figure 2.

The following section gives a short introduction to the different spreading techniques and discusses their benefits.

Direct Sequence

In a **D**irect **S**equence **S**pread **S**pectrum *(DSSS)* transmitter, the information signal is directly modulated by a spreading sequence. The spreading sequence consists of a number of spreading chips with time duration τ_{chip}. The information signal consists of a number of information bits with time duration τ_{bit}. Spreading is achieved if multiple chips represent one bit.

In Figure 3, a DSSS transmitter and receiver are depicted. At the sender side the information signal $i(t)$, with data rate R_i and bandwidth B_i, is spread by a spreading sequence $c(t)$. The spreading sequence has the code symbol rate R_c, also called the chip rate. If τ_{bit} is a multiple of τ_{chip} the processing gain G_{DS} can be easily calculated by:

$$G_{DS} = \frac{\tau_{\text{bit}}}{\tau_{\text{chip}}} \tag{1}$$

Figure 4 shows a possible DSSS transmission and reception process. It can be seen how the original information signal $i(t)$ is spread before the transmission over the wireless link and how it will be despread at the receiver side. Furthermore, the influence of the jammer is also considered. If the data rate R_i is very small in comparison to the chip rate R_c, then the spread signal $s(t) = i(t) \cdot c(t)$ will have approximately the bandwidth of the spreading signal ($B_c \simeq B_s$). At the receiver end the received signal $r(t)$ will be multiplied once again with the same spreading sequence $c(t)$, which results in a despreading of the original signal $i(t)$, if the autocorrelation $\varphi_{cc}^{E}(\tau)$ is nearly zero for all $\tau \neq 0$. After the despreading, the signal will be filtered with bandwidth W_i to remove high frequencies.

The generation of DSSS signals can be achieved by a simple multiplication of the information and spreading sequences. Figure 5 shows the principle used for

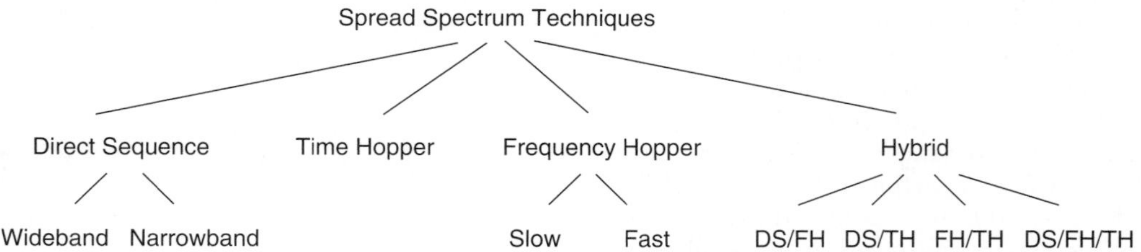

Figure 2: Classification of different spread spectrum systems

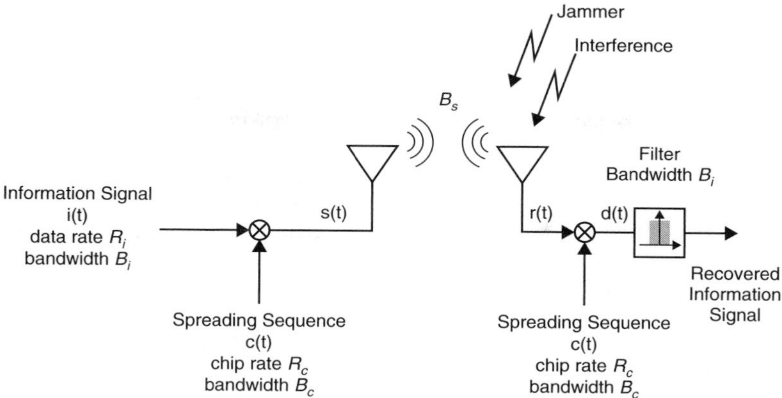

Figure 3: System model for spread spectrum transmission

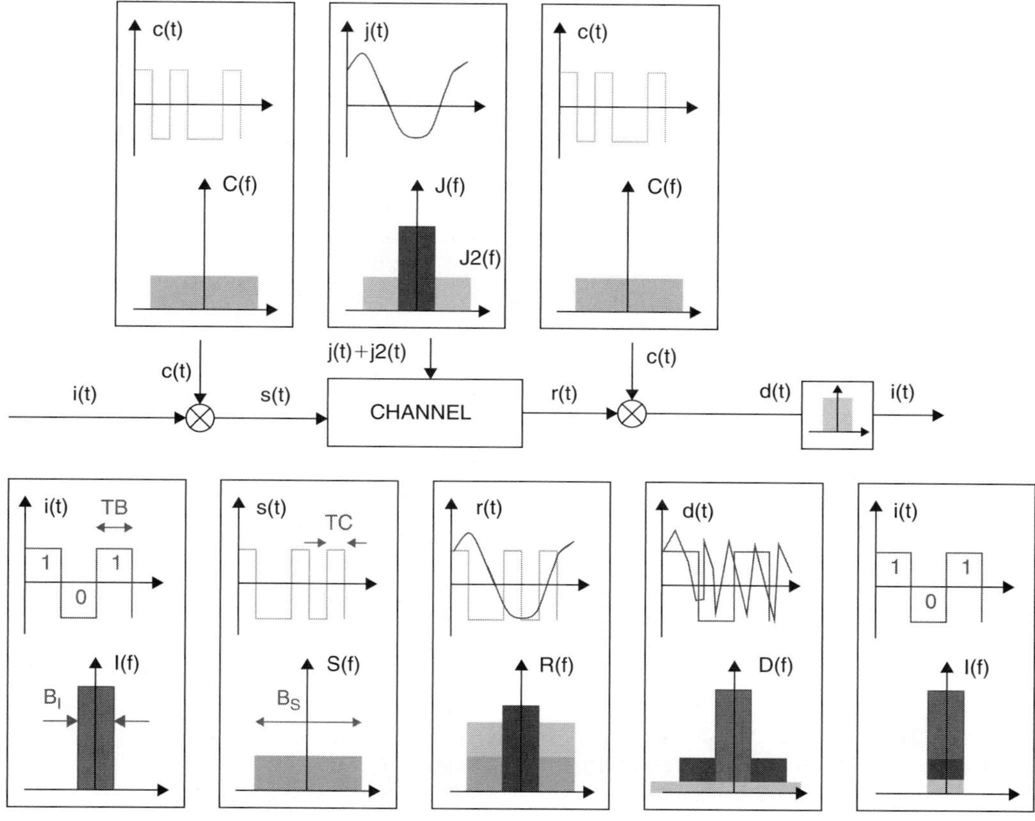

Figure 4: Transmission and reception process in a direct sequence spread-spectrum system

generating a DSSS signal for $G_{DS} = 10$. A key feature of DSSS is that multiple access capability can be achieved without synchronization between different transmitters. Multi-path interference is combated if delayed signals differ by only one chip duration. In this case all delay signals are treated as interference. On the other side the transmitter-receiver pair has to be fully chip-synchronized, as will be explained later in more detail. As explained in the section titled "Power Control Mechanism," the near-far effect has to be taken under consideration, because DSSS systems use the full bandwidth and therefore a transmitter closer to the receiver will constantly interfere and eventually destroy signals from transmitters that are far away.

Frequency Hopping

Frequency **H**opping **S**pread **S**pectrum *(FHSS)* systems periodically change the carrier frequency of the modulated information signal in a random fashion. During a time interval τ_{hop} the frequency is constant. Afterwards both the sender and receiver *hop* to another frequency. The whole bandwidth B_s is divided into frequency slices

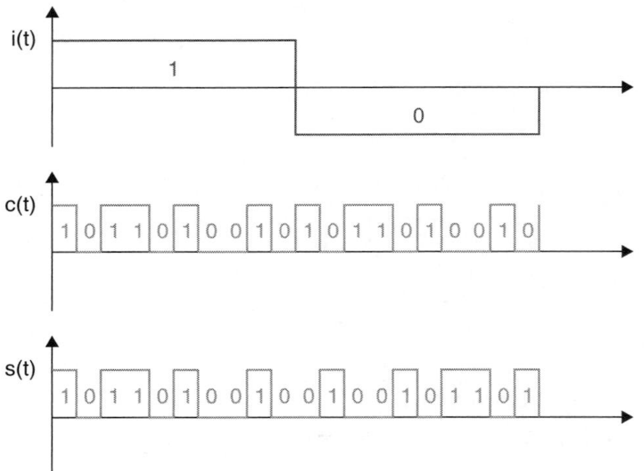

Figure 5: Direct sequence spread-spectrum signal generation, $G_{DS} = 10$

of B_{s^*}. The set of available frequencies is called a hop-set with N frequency slices. FHSS systems differ radically from DSSS systems in terms of frequency occupancy. While DSSS systems occupy the whole bandwidth all the time, FHSS systems use only one frequency slice at any point in time. FHSS systems are usually classified into *slow* and *fast* frequency hoppers, as depicted in Figure 2. If one information bit is transmitted over several frequency slices ($\tau_{\text{hop}} \leq \tau_{\text{bit}}$) the frequency hopper is referred to as *fast*. Otherwise if several bits are transmitted over one frequency slice, it is referred to as a *slow* hopper. The relation of hop duration τ_{hop} to information bit duration τ_{bit} depends upon the number of hops per information bits. If τ_{bit} is an integer multiple of τ_{hop}, then we denote $\tau_{\text{bit}} = k \cdot \tau_{\text{hop}}$. This leads to the processing gain G_{FH} (see Cooper and McGillem 1986).

$$G_{FH} = \frac{B_s}{B_i} = N \cdot k \cdot B_{s^*} \cdot \tau_{hop} \tag{2}$$

The advantage of FHSS systems in contrast to DSSS systems is the less strict synchronization requirement. FHSS allows synchronization errors of the size of τ_{hop}, DSSS only of the size of τ_{chip} (Prasad 1996).

Time Hopper

Within a **T**ime **H**opping **S**pread **S**pectrum *(THSS)*, system the time axis is divided into frames of the duration τ_{frame}. As depicted in Figure 6, each frame is divided again into N slots with time duration τ_{slot}.

A single wireless terminal (WT) will only use one slot out of k possible slots within one frame. Within this slot, the WT sends with a k times higher data rate, in contrast to the situations in which the WT would transmit within the whole frame. Interference among simultaneous wireless terminals can be minimized if coordination between terminals can be achieved. This also avoids the near-far effect. In the absence of coordination, situations occur in which more than one terminal uses a time slot. The receiver will not be able to detect either of the signals correctly. Both terminals *collide* on the wireless link. For such, cases error correction schemes are required. Time hoppers have nearly the same acquisition time as that of discrete-sequence systems, but their implementation is much simpler than that of a frequency-hopper.

Hybrid Systems

Hybrid spread spectrum systems consist of combinations of two or more basic SS systems. Therefore, there are four possible hybrid systems by combining such systems, namely DS/FH, DS/TH, FH/TH, and DS/FH/TH. The combination of different SS schemes leads to increased complexity of the transmitter and receiver, but also offers a combination of their advantages. For instance, if DSSS and FHSS schemes are combined, the hybrid SS system offers the multi-path interference rejection of the DSSS system and the immunity of the FHSS system. Table 1 briefly lists the advantages and disadvantages of different SS schemes in terms of multiple access capability, multi-path interference rejection, synchronization, and hardware complexity.

CDMA Basics

Provision of multiple access capability is indispensable in wireless communication systems, and this can be carried out in different ways. The classical approach is **F**requency **D**ivision **M**ultiple **A**ccess (FDMA), where users are separated in the frequency domain. A more recent technique is **T**ime **D**ivision **M**ultiple **A**ccess (TDMA), where users separation takes place in the time domain. Basically, FDMA and TDMA assign particular frequency or time slices to different wireless terminals. When all slices are

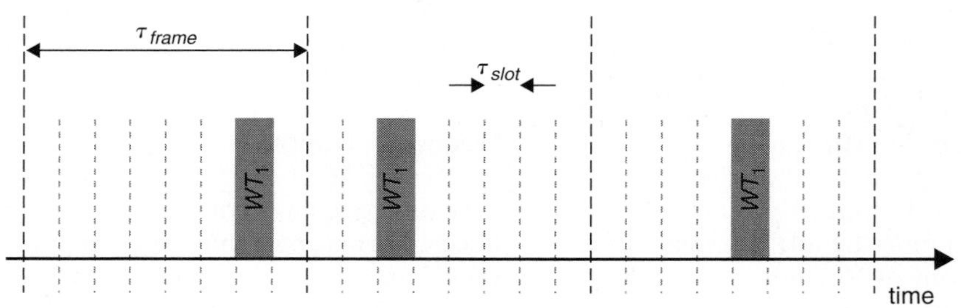

Figure 6: Time axis for a THSS system

Table 1: Comparison of Different Spread-Spectrum Techniques with Their Advantages and Disadvantages

SS Scheme	Advantages	Disadvantages
Direct-Sequence	• Best behavior for multi-path-rejection (Cooper and McGillem 1986) • Best anti-jam rejection (Cooper and McGillem 1986, Ploydoros 1994) • Best interference rejection (Cooper and McGillem 1986, Ploydoros 1994) • No synchronization among terminals (Prasad 1996, Ojanpera and Prasad 1998) • Simple implementation (Prasad 1996, Ojanpera and Prasad 1998) • Most difficult to detect (Cooper and McGillem 1986, Ploydoros 1994)	• Near-far problem (Cooper and McGillem 1986, Prasad 1996, Ojanpera and Prasad 1998, Rappaport 2001) • Require coherent bandwidth (Cooper and McGillem 1986) • Long acquisition time (Cooper and McGillem 1986, Ploydoros 1994) • Synchronization of code signal within fraction of chip time (Prasad 1996, Ojanpera and Prasad 1998)
Frequency-Hopping	• Great amount of spreading (Cooper and McGillem 1986, Ploydoros 1994) • No need for coherent bandwidth (Cooper and McGillem 1986, Prasad 1996, and Ploydoros 1994) • Short acquisition time (Cooper and McGillem 1986, Prasad 1996, Ojanpera and Prasad 1998, Ploydoros 1994) • Inherent security (Rappaport 2001) • Less affected by the near-far effect (Cooper and McGillem 1986, Prasad 1996, Ojanpera and Prasad 1998, Ploydoros 1994)	• Complex hardware (Cooper and McGillem 1986, Prasad 1996, Ojanpera and Prasad 1998, Ploydoros 1994) • Error correction is needed (Cooper and McGillem 1986, Ploydoros 1994)
Time-Hopping	• High bandwidth efficiency (Cooper and McGillem 1986, Ploydoros 1994) • Less complex hardware (Cooper and McGillem 1986, Prasad 1996, Ojanpera and Prasad 1998, Ploydoros 1994) • Less affected by the near-far effect (Cooper and McGillem 1986, Prasad 1996, Ojanpera and Prasad 1998, Ploydoros 1994)	• Error correction is needed (Cooper and McGillem 1986, Prasad 1996, Ojanpera and Prasad 1998, Ploydoros 1994) • Long acquisition time (Cooper and McGillem 1986, Prasad 1996, Ojanpera and Prasad 1998, Ploydoros 1994)

occupied in the system, no additional wireless terminal can be accommodated. Multiple access capability is also provided by **C**ode **D**ivision **M**ultiple **A**ccess (CDMA). The most common techniques of CDMA are frequency-hopped CDMA or direct-sequence CDMA. CDMA allows multiple users to simultaneously use a common channel for transmission of information (Proakis 1995). A CDMA transmitter will *code* its information signal with a code or spreading sequence particularly allocated for that user. Afterwards, the transmitter sends the coded signal to the receiver. Using the same code sequence as the transmitter, the receiver is able to decode the received signal. Also, in case the receiver receives more than one coded signal, it will be able to decode the information from the desired transmitter, if the code sequences satisfy certain cross-correlation and auto-correlation requirements (see section titled "Spreading Sequences"). The bandwidth of the coded signal is much larger than the information bandwidth. One may say that the information signal was *spread*, where spread refers to the broadening of the signal spectrum in the frequency domain. The coding process is therefore also called a spread-spectrum modulation, while the coded signal is called a spread-spectrum signal. The spreading of the information signal gives the CDMA its multiple access capability. Figures 7, 8, and 9 show the underlying principles by which subscribers can be separated in the frequency, time, or code domain, respectively.

A key-feature of CDMA systems using **P**seudo-**N**oise (*PN*) sequences is that they can tolerate *overload*, in terms of number of simultaneous supported users. Indeed, in contrast with FDMA and TDMA systems where system capacity is fixed, CDMA systems are characterized by soft capacity, a concept used to denote the fact that capacity is not a fixed figure but it actually can be traded with system performance. For instance, if we can tolerate a certain degradation in the performance of the connected wireless terminals of a given cell, we can further accommodate more users. Thus CDMA systems using PN sequences do not have any sharply defined system

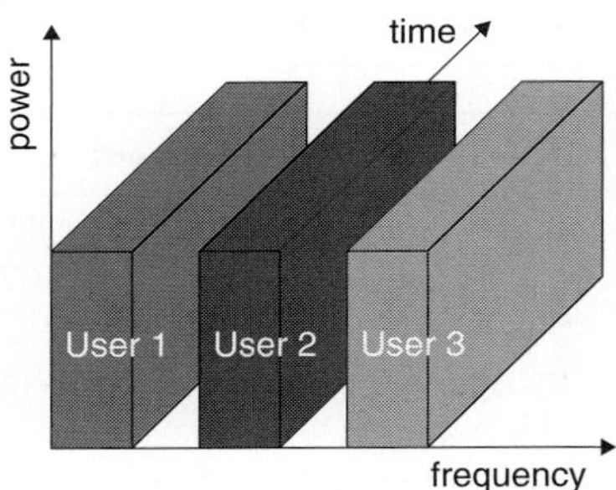

Figure 7: FDMA

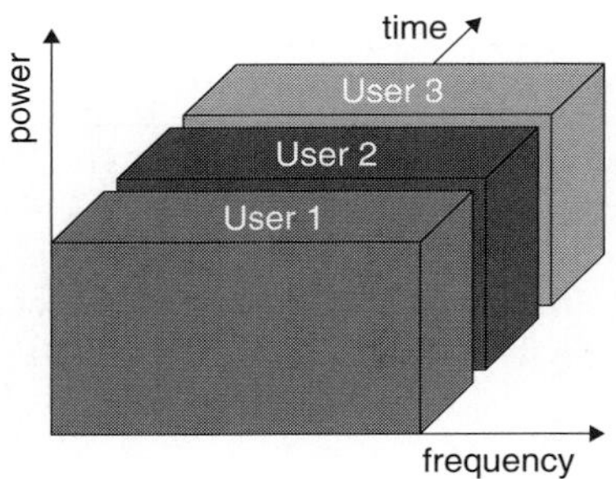

Figure 8: TDMA different multiple access techniques

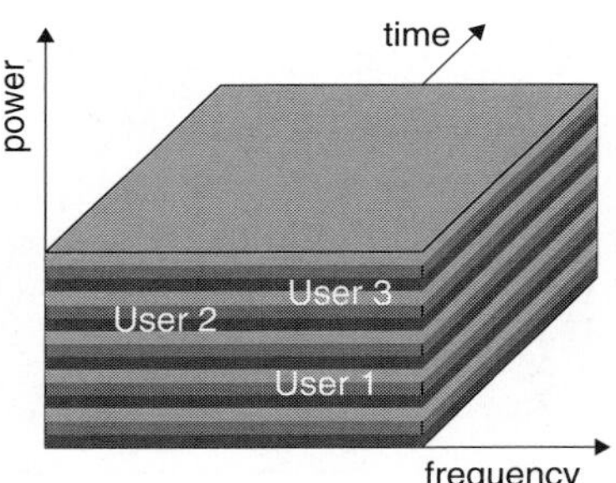

Figure 9: CDMA

capacity, like TDMA or FDMA systems. But for CDMA systems using PN sequences the **B**it **E**rror **P**robability (*BEP*) increases with the number of active terminals. To illuminate this property, we take a frequency hopping system as an example. In Figure 10 the transmission process of two wireless terminals is given. Each terminal, following the principle of frequency hopping, *hops* to another frequency slice at the beginning of a new slot. Under certain conditions depending on the hopping strategy, both terminals might use the same frequency slice. It is obvious that in the same way as the number of wireless terminals within one cell increase, the number of collisions increase as well. In general, for a spread-spectrum based system supporting access of multiple users, having more users means increasing the so-called Multiple Access Interference (MAI) and hence degrading system performance. Similarly, in a CDMA system, the more users, the higher the multiple access interference and hence the worse the performance. This is basically caused by the non-ideal cross-correlation functions (e.g., non-zero values) of the used spreading sequences which result in added interference.

The following two sections provide a short introduction to CDMA key features. The first of these two, entitled "Rake Receiver," introduces that topic. The section titled "Power Control Mechanism" gives a more detailed view of the power control entity. As already mentioned above, the design of spreading sequences plays a major role for a CDMA system. Therefore we introduce two different families of spreading sequences in the section with that title. Later, in the section titled "Classification of Enhanced CDMA Systems" we classify the different CDMA systems.

Rake Receiver

Multi-path degrades the system performance. CDMA receivers resolve multi-path interference if signals arrive more than one chip apart from each other. The direct LoS (Line of Sight) signal is typically the strongest one. For this strongest signal, the other multi-path signals are regarded as interference and therefore they can be

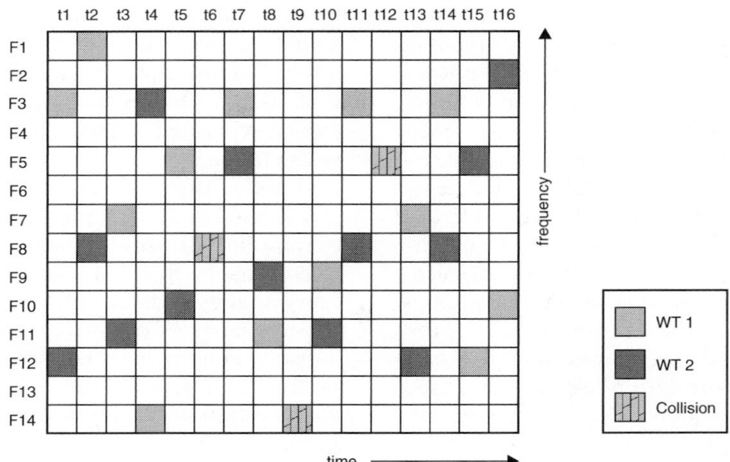

Figure 10: FHSS multiple access interference

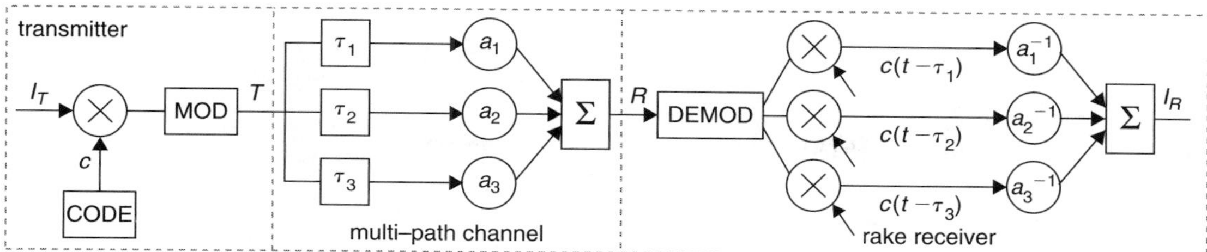

Figure 11: Rake receiver structure with three fingers and multi-path channel

suppressed with the processing gain. However, a better receiver performance is achieved by exploiting the concept of rake receivers, which aim to collect as much as possible of the received signal replicas. The example depicted in Figure 11 illustrates the basic principle of a rake receiver. After spreading and modulation of the information signal on the transmitter side the signal suffers from the multi-path channel. Different delay entities ($\tau_{i,}$ i = 1,2,3) and attenuation factors (a_i, i = 1,2,3) in Figure 11 model obstacles at different distances and with different propagation properties. The multi-path signal (coming from different propagation paths) is demodulated and passed to the rake receiver. The ideal rake receiver contains a receiver *finger* for each multi-path component. In practice the number of fingers is limited by the receiver's hardware complexity or costs. For instance, in a typical case only the strongest signals with a delay of less than $\tau_{\max}$ are taken into account. In each finger, the signals are despread and time aligned with one of the multi-path channels. After the despreading process the signals are weighted and combined. The weight of a signal corresponds in the best case to its attenuation factor. Roughly speaking, the rake receiver can be seen as the inverse of the multi-path channel. If the conditions on the multi-path channel change, the parameters of the rake receiver have to be adapted. In Barretto and Fettweis (2000), the performance gain achieved with rake receivers in DS-CDMA systems is shown. Recently, rake transmitters (also called Pre-rake, while the rake receiver is also called Post-rake) have been proposed. If the the multi-path channel is known at the transmitter, a rake transmitter produces weighted signals such that there will be only one signal at the receiver. Barreto and Fettweiss (2000) have shown that a substantial performance improvement can be achieved by applying Pre- and Post-rakes. Note that in order to apply the Pre-rake concept, the transmitter needs to know the channel state information. As always, in these cases the trade off between performance improvements and hardware/system complexity needs to be considered.

Power Control Mechanism

In a DS-CDMA system, all transmitters use the same bandwidth at the same time to send their information to the receiver. If we consider multiple transmitters connected to one receiver, the signals are received with different power levels, because wireless terminals are located at different distances from the base station. In practice, the signal strength can differ in the range of 100dB (Shapira 1999). Due to the attenuation effect, the (received) signals from transmitters closer to the receiver have higher power levels than those from transmitters that are far away. This phenomenon is called the *near-far effect*. The near-far effect plays an essential role if multi-user interference is considered. For free-space propagation, the received power falls off proportional to the square of the distance from the wireless terminal to the base station. In addition to the near-far effect, the signal strength differs dramatically due to the changing propagation conditions (moving obstacles, traffic characteristics, hand over). To overcome the changing signal strength, power control entities are implemented in the transmitters. These entities are called **T**ransmitter **P**ower **C**ontrol (TPC). The TPC adjusts the transmission power P_{trx} at the sender-side to ensure that all signals arrive at the receiver with the same power level P_{rcv}. Without such a functionality, weak signals are being masked by strong signals, making it difficult or impossible to detect the former.

For cellular CDMA mobile communications systems, the TPC plays a major role, particularly in the up-link. TPC for the down-link are only implemented to adjust a required **S**ignal to **I**nterference plus **N**oise **R**atio (*SINR*). Recall that the CDMA capacity is interference limited. Thus, the lower the power level of one terminal, the higher is the number of supported terminals. The TPC for the down-link is only implemented to adjust a required SINR. In contrast to the up-link, the conditions on the down-link change more slowly. Most TPCs consist of two types of power control, namely open-loop and closed-loop. Some wireless CDMA communication systems also have an outer loop power control, such as IS-95 (EIA/TIA 1997). The open-loop power control measures the SINR of the incoming signals and adjusts the transmission power to meet the desired SINR. Unfortunately, the conditions for up-link and down-link can differ dramatically, e.g., due to the use of frequency division multiplexing, and therefore the open-loop power control provides only a first estimation for the TPC. The closed-loop power control measures the signal power at the receiver and controls the transmitter's power. IS-95 receivers send only one bit of information to change the transmitting power in the range of 1db/1:25ms at the transmitter side. The outer loop power control gets information about the **P**acket **E**rror **P**robability (*PEP*) and compares it with the required PEP. In case of deviations, the transmitter power is adjusted. A block diagram of the power control loops of IS-95 is shown in Figure 12.

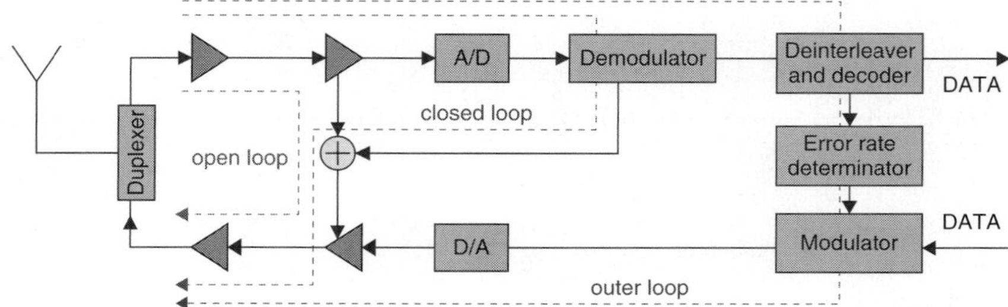

Figure 12: Power control loops for IS-95

In Jansen and Prasad (1995) it is shown that the **p**robability **d**ensity **f**unction (*pdf*) of the received power depends on the TPC algorithm, speed of the **A**daptive **P**ower **C**ontrol (*APC*) system, dynamical range of the transmitter, spatial distribution of the wireless terminals, and propagation statistics. In Jansen, Prasad and Kegal (1993), it is shown that the pdf-function can be assumed to be log normal. The pdf was given as

$$f\left(P_{rcv}\right) = \frac{1}{\sqrt{2\pi}\ \sigma P_{rcv}} \cdot exp\left[\frac{ln^2\left(P_{rcv}\right)}{2\sigma^2}\right] \qquad (3)$$

where σ is the imperfection in the TPC entity. In Jansen and Prasad 1995 it is shown that the performance degradation of a DS CDMA system with $\sigma = 1$ dB was about 60%. Therefore the system performance of a CDMA systems depends particularly on the system parameter σ. The smaller σ the better the performance. Notice that not only the variance of the used energy within one cell has to be taken into consideration, but also the inter-cell interference plays an important role in CDMA systems. In Figure 13 the interference produced/received by the center cell for/from neighboring cells is given. In Gibson (1996) it is claimed that each cell in the first tier (see Figure 13) contributes/receives about 6% of the interference. Outer tiers do not have a great impact (second tier about 0:2% of the interference). Independent of the exact amount of interference, this example shows that the overall energy used within the cell has to be limited. Power control for voice-oriented continuous traffic has dominated the work of most of the researchers for decades. However, the next generation of wireless networks are designed to support packet-oriented data traffic in addition to the *old-fashioned* voice-oriented traffic. Packet oriented traffic brings up new problems for the TPC which are quite different from voice traffic.

In Bambos and Kandukuri (2000) it is shown that packetized data without delay constraints can be sent in dependency of the channel state. If the wireless terminal has to invest too much power to transmit the packet successfully, it could also wait and send this packet later when channel conditions are good. This situation is referred to as *back off*. In the back-off case the delay of the packet will increase—a situation which is not allowed for voice oriented services (only small buffering can be tolerated in real time systems). In a nutshell, data communication introduces a new degree of freedom; the *trade-off between power consumption and delay constraints*. In consideration of this new degree of freedom, Bambos and Kandukuri (2000) presented a new protocol approach for adaptive power control, which also takes delay constraints of packets into account. We will refer to this protocol in the section entitled "Classification of Enhanced CDMA Systems."

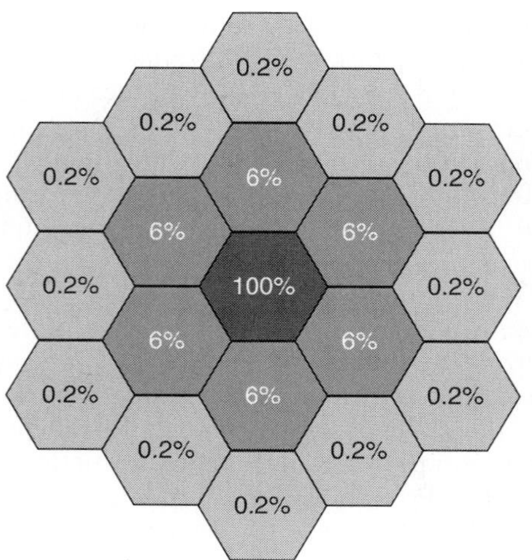

Figure 13: Inter-cell interference for adjacent cells

Spreading Sequences

The proper choice of spreading sequences enables multiple access capability for spread-spectrum based wireless communication systems. As already discussed, a sequence is a non-ambiguous identification for a transmitter-receiver pair. As practical sequences are not ideal, their election will have a great impact on the performance of a CDMA network. Spreading sequences can be divided into *orthogonal* and pseudo-noise spreading sequences. This section gives a comprehensive overview of spreading sequences of CDMA systems. The differences between pseudo-noise and orthogonal spreading sequences in terms of auto- and cross-correlation functions are then discussed. The properties of spreading sequences to accomplish multiple access capability are also investigated. Furthermore, the sets of spreading sequences for multi-code CDMA are finally discussed.

As already mentioned, in a spread-spectrum communication system the original information signal with bandwidth W_I is *spread* to a much larger transmission bandwidth W_{SS} using spreading sequences. At the receiver side, the replica of this spreading sequence is used to recover the original information. In cellular radio communication, multiple access capability is achieved by taking advantage of the autocorrelation and cross-correlation properties of the spreading sequences. Good autocorrelation and cross-correlation properties are instrumental for allowing reliable identification and detection of particular users as well as enabling user separation in a mutiple access environment. Such systems are referred to as code division multiple access (therefore, the spreading sequences are also called code sequences in the literature). A spreading sequence consists of C units called *chips*. The chips are two-valued (e.g., bipolar). The autocorrelation function of a spreading sequence reflects the similarity of this sequences with a replica of itself delayed by a time gap τ_{gap}. For a given time gap $\tau_{gap} = 0$, the autocorrelation value is one, indicating that the sequences are aligned. In any other case $\tau_{gap} \neq 0$ the autocorrelation value should be small (ideally zero) to minimize the interference among copies of the original signal that are generated and delayed by multi-path propagation. The out-of-phase characteristics of the auto-correlation function has a direct impact on how multi-path replicas affect performance. In fact, when the auto-correlation function is not strictly zero in any out-of-phase position, paths interfere with each other, causing performance degradation. This phenomenon is sometimes referred to as Interpath Interference (IPI). The cross-correlation value of two different spreading sequences represents the interference level for two signals from different wireless terminals with delay τ_{gap}. This value should be as small as possible for all τ_{gap} such that a maximum number of subscribers are allowed in the cell. As a matter of fact, the optimization of the autocorrelation and the cross-correlation cannot be done separately. They depend on each other and typically, the optimization of one side leads to a degradation of the other side.

Orthogonal Sequences. Orthogonal sequences offer zero cross-correlation for $\tau_{gap} = 0$. If all transmitters are synchronized and no multi-path is considered, the multiple access interference can then be neglected. For any other value of τ_{gap} orthogonal sequences have large cross-correlation values. Therefore, orthogonal sequences are only applied if perfect synchronization can be guaranteed within the system. The autocorrelation properties of orthogonal sequences are also poor if $\tau_{gap} \neq 0$. This happens if we consider multi-path interference. In such a situation, equalization is applied to recover the original signal.

Several methods to generate orthogonal sequences are presented in Proakis (1995) and Rappaport (2001). As representatives of the orthogonal code family, *Walsh and orthogonal Gold sequences* are presented in this section. Walsh sequences can be easily obtained by applying the Hadamard transformation (⊗ defines the Kronecker product), which is given by

$$H_0 = [1], H_2 = \begin{bmatrix} +1 & +1 \\ +1 & -1 \end{bmatrix}, H_{n+1} = H_n \otimes H_n \quad (4)$$

Each row of the Hadamard matrix represents one valid sequence with length N. This leads to an overall number of sequences $N_S = N$. Note that the overall number for PN sequences is much larger. In general the number of achievable codes N_S is limited for orthogonal spreading sequences. Another representative of the family of orthogonal spreading sequences are the orthogonal Gold sequences. Figure 14 shows that orthogonal Gold sequences have reasonable cross-correlation and autocorrelation values. These values are much better than for sequences of the Walsh family.

Pseudo Noise Sequences. PN sequences are binary sequences, which exhibit random properties similar to noise. Within the class of PN sequences, the most popular representatives are *Maximal Length* sequences, *Gold* sequences, and *Kasami* (Proakis 1995) sequences. All sequences can be generated using a **L**inear **F**eedback **S**hift **R**egister (*LFSR*), which is built by f feedback-taps (Golomb 1992). Sequences generated with a LFSR having the maximum possible period length for an f-stage shift register are called *maximal length* or simply *m-sequences*. The length of an m-sequence can be proven to be $2^f - 1$. The number of possible codes depends on the number of possible sets (also called *primitive* irreducible generators) of feedback-taps. Golomb (1992) showed that the overall number of sequences generated by a LFSR of degree f equals

$$N_S(f) = \frac{2^f - 1}{f} \prod_{i=1}^{k} \frac{P_i - 1}{P_i}, \quad (5)$$

where P_i equals the prime decomposition of $2^f - 1$. Table 2 provides the sequence length of a given degree f and the resulting number of achievable code sequences (see Stahnke 1978 for higher values of f). m-sequences have three important properties: (1) the balance property (the number of ones and the number of zeros differ by at most one), (2) the run length property (half the runs of ones and zeros have length 1, and $1/2^k$ length k for $k < n$) and (3) the shift-and-add property (combining two shifted replicas of an m-sequence yields another valid m-sequence). The periodic autocorrelation function of an m-sequence is only two-valued:

$$\Phi_{CC,mseq} = \begin{cases} 1 & k = l \cdot N \\ -\frac{1}{N} & k \neq l \cdot N \end{cases} \quad (6)$$

m-sequences have good autocorrelation properties, while the cross-correlation properties are very poor compared to Gold sequences. Gold sequences can be achieved by combining two *preferred* m-sequences. Different Gold sequences are achieved by combining one m-sequence with a delayed replica of another m-sequence. This gives an overall number of Gold sequences of $2^f + 1$ (considering two m-sequences and the possibilities of combination $2^f - 1$). The cross-correlation function $\Phi_{CC,gold}$ is three-valued $\{-t(f); -1; t(f) - 2\}$ with

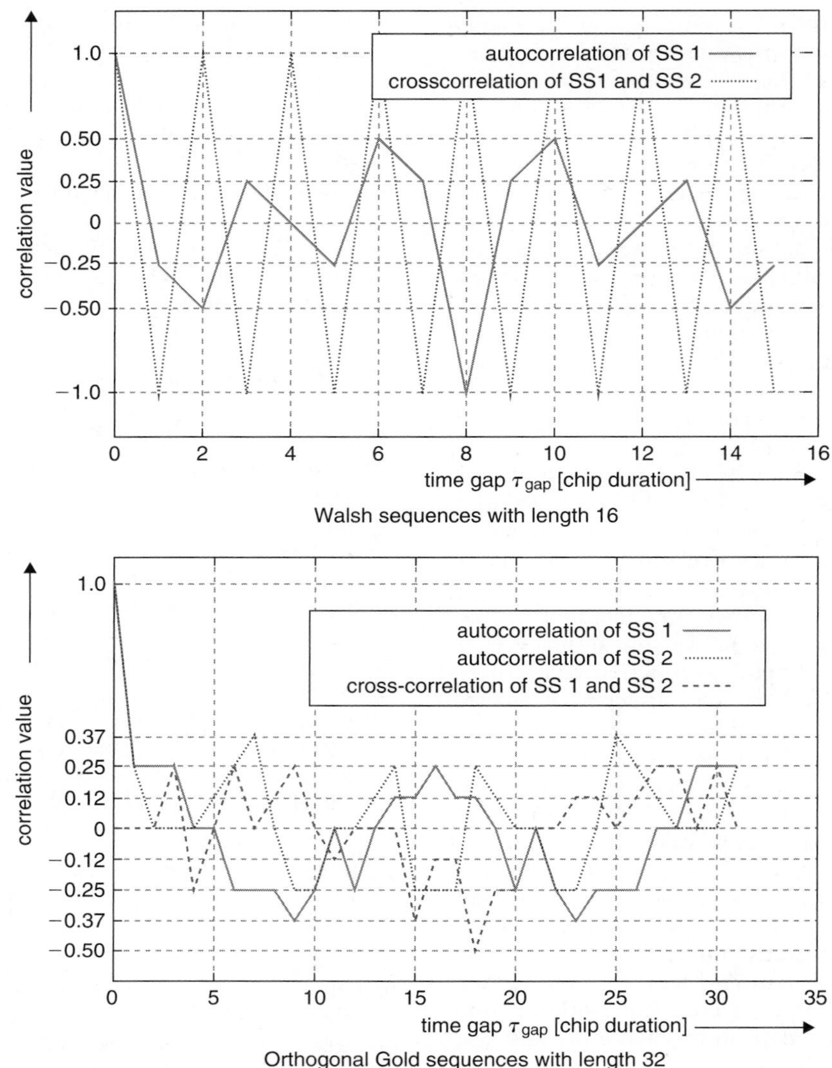

Figure 14: Auto- and cross-correlation function for Walsh and orthogonal Gold sequences

Table 2: Spreading Sequence Length with Related Number of Maximal LFSR (degree f) Spreading Sequences

f	2	4	6	8	10	12	14	16	18	20
P_i	3	15	63	255	1023	4095	16383	65535	262143	1048575
N_S	1	2	6	16	60	144	756	2048	8064	24000

$$t(f) = \begin{cases} (1 + 2^{\frac{f+1}{2}}) \cdot 2^{-f} & \text{if f odd} \\ (1 + 2^{\frac{f+2}{2}}) \cdot 2^{-f} & \text{if f even} \end{cases} \quad (7)$$

Gold (1967) showed that the cross-correlation between these sequences is uniform and bounded. Combinations of Gold sequences are used to produce the so-called *Kasami* sequences. Kasami sequences have optimal cross-correlation values achieving the Welsh lower bound (Kasami 1996). Therefore, Kasami sequences are promising candidates for spreading in W-CDMA. The scaled cross-correlation function $\Phi_{CC,\ kasami}$ is also three-valued $\{-1;\ -2^{f/2} -1; 2^{f/2} -1\}$. The auto- and the cross-correlation function for m-sequences, Gold sequences and Kasami sequences are depicted in Figure 15. For these specific examples it is shown that cross-correlation for m-sequences equals (−1/16; 1), while Gold and Kasami sequences, which are three-valued, give (−9/35; −1/35; 7/35) and (−9/63; −1/63; 7/63) respectively. Moreover, the figure gives a first qualitative estimate for auto- and cross-correlation.

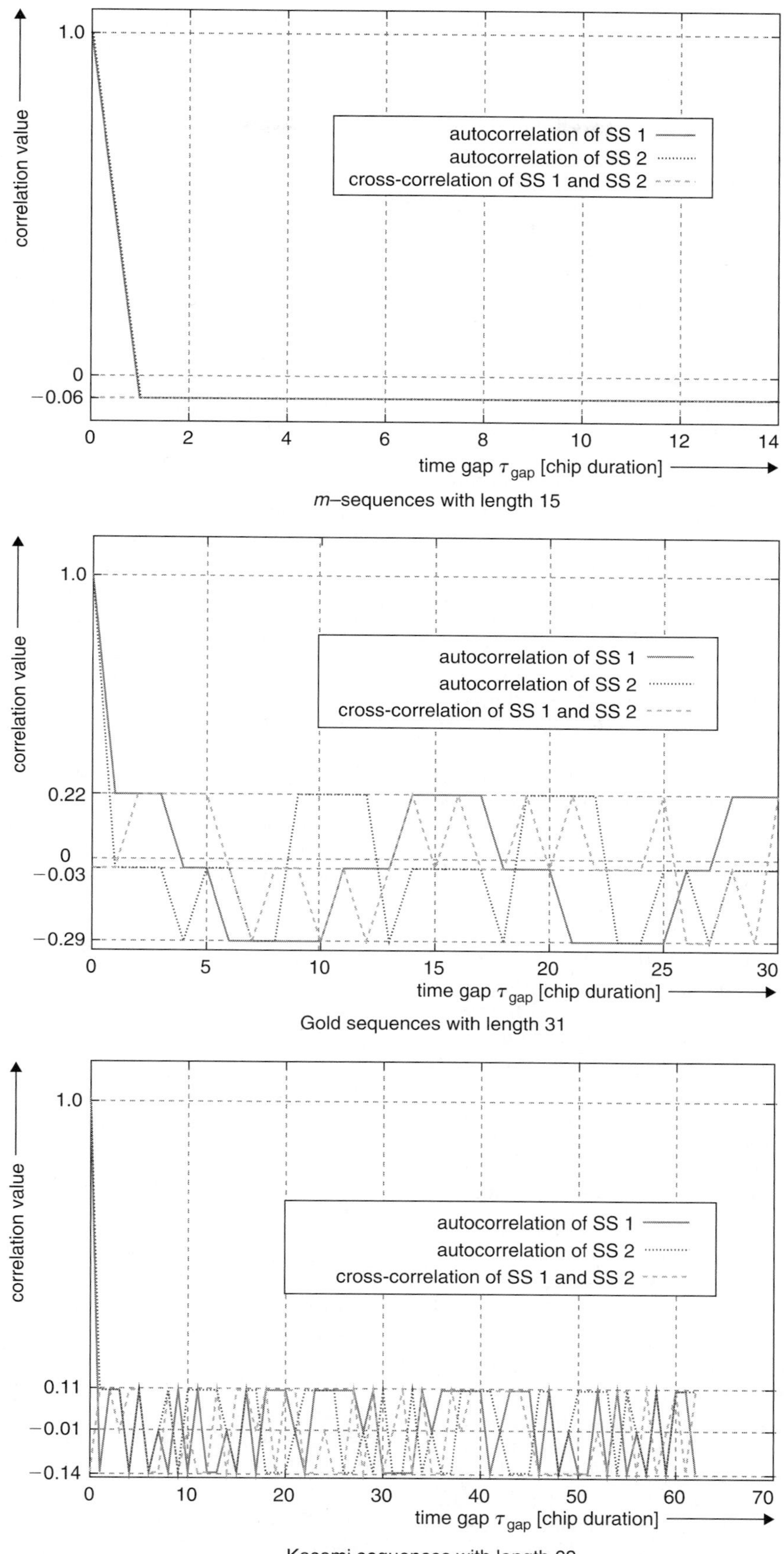

Figure 15: Auto- and cross-correlation function for m-sequences, Gold sequences, and Kasami sequences

Whenever network synchronism can *not* be achieved, PN sequences should be employed. These sequences are easy to generate and offer reasonable cross-correlation and autocorrelation values. For synchronous systems, orthogonal codes should be used. In cellular wireless communication, orthogonal codes should be used for the down-link and PN sequences should be used for the up-link.

Classification of Enhanced CDMA Systems

*A*daptive *P*ower *C*ontrol (*APC*) in CDMA systems is one way to obtain heterogenous QoS support. In contrast to recent power control mechanisms, which were designed to assign equal power to the wireless terminals, adaptive power control assigns power related to the QoS requirements. Another subgroup of the enhanced CDMA systems are **M**ulti-**R**ate CDMA systems. These are the only systems that are allowed to change their rates instantaneously and offer variable bit rates. The specific schemes of this sub-group are **F**ixed **S**preading **G**ain (*FSG*), **V**ariable **S**preading **G**ain (*VSG*), and **M**ulti-**C**ode CDMA. In contrast to Single-Code CDMA systems, Multi-Code systems support multiple times the basic bit rate. A more detailed description is given later in this section.

Adaptive Power Control. As outlined above, the power control is designed to overcome the near-far effect and tries to control the received power at the WTs. Furthermore, another goal of the power control is to increase the system capacity. Under the assumption that all wireless terminals require the same QoS (e.g., data rate, error probability, etc.), the power for each of the terminals is controlled such that sender's signals are received at the base station with the same power. This is the power control algorithm for voice-oriented services.

To support time-variable QoS, the power level of each terminal was identified in Yan and Messerschmitt (1994), Wu and Kohno (1996), Morikawa et al. (1997), and Yan and Messerschmitt (1995) as a controllable parameter. The proposed approaches dynamically adapt the QoS requirements with power control schemes. As an example, we assume k wireless terminals. Suppose that terminal $i = 1$ has the highest QoS requirements QoS_1 with power level P_1. All other terminals adjust their power level P_i according to the TPC's commands. The power level for WT i is given by

$$P_i = P_1 \cdot \frac{QoS_i}{QoS_1}. \tag{8}$$

During the transmission process, the power is adjusted depending on the channel state to achieve a required SINR; e.g., if the channel becomes worse (higher interference) the power level is increased to stabilize the SINR. The advantage of such a system is that it can be easily integrated into existing CDMA systems. Adaptive power control is a strong candidate for time-variable QoS support. In contrast to the VSG and Multi-Code approaches, adaptive power control support does not include variable bandwidth.

Fixed Spreading Gain. In the **F**ixed **S**preading **G**ain (*FSG*) approach (Immaneni and Capone 2000), the spreading gain of each bit stream is maintained constant. The chip duration is also maintained constant. The users vary the transmission time to adapt the variable bit rate requirements. The low rate users transmit for a shorter time as opposed to the higher rate users. It can be seen that the lower rate users suffer from more multi-access interference from the higher rate users, because the higher rate users transmit for longer time. However, the higher rate users suffer from multi-access interference for a shorter time. Hence, the performance for higher rate users is better than for lower rate users. To compensate for this degradation in performance, the lower rate users transmit with more power to increase their signal to interference ratio.

Variable Spreading Gain. The **V**ariable **S**preading **G**ain (*VSG*) approach (I and Sabnani 1995) offers the possibility to achieve flexible data rates. Under the assumption that the bandwidth for transmission is fixed, the spreading gain is reduced as the information bit rate increases, and vice versa. Changing the spreading gain has an impact on the energy per bit ratio. If the transmission power is fixed, an increased data rate leads to a smaller energy per bit ratio (leading to a higher bit error probability). Therefore, the VSG approach is coupled with a variable power control entity to satisfy the same SINR for wireless terminals with different bit rates. In case the transmission power is adapted to the transmission rate, high data rate terminals will influence low data rate terminals. Note that different terminals with the same SINR requirement can be accommodated by allocating power proportional to the terminals' data rates.

$$P_i = P_1 \cdot \frac{R_i}{R_1} \tag{9}$$

Whenever the transmitter changes the spreading gain, the receiver has to be informed about this change. This results in an increased signaling overhead. Because the power level varies according to the chosen data rate, the TPC will also add some more signaling overhead. In the case of short spreading sequences, VSG-CDMA systems suffer from multi-path interference, because of **I**nter **S**ymbol **I**nterference (*ISI*). If we consider a constant delay spread for the wireless link, the same number of chips are influenced, but the number of influenced symbols depends only on the spreading gain. In Ojanpera and Prasad (1998), it is shown that with VSG the high power terminals degrade the performance of low power terminals. In addition, high power terminals are using shorter spreading codes and therefore the spreading sequences have a significant impact on the system performance. Thus it might be useful to implement higher bit rates with Multi-Code CDMA systems (Ojanpera and Prasad 1998).

Multi-Code Code Division Multiple Access. In this section, the capability of WTs to transmit and receive on multiple CDMA channels by means of Multi-Code-CDMA is discussed. We consider different families of spreading

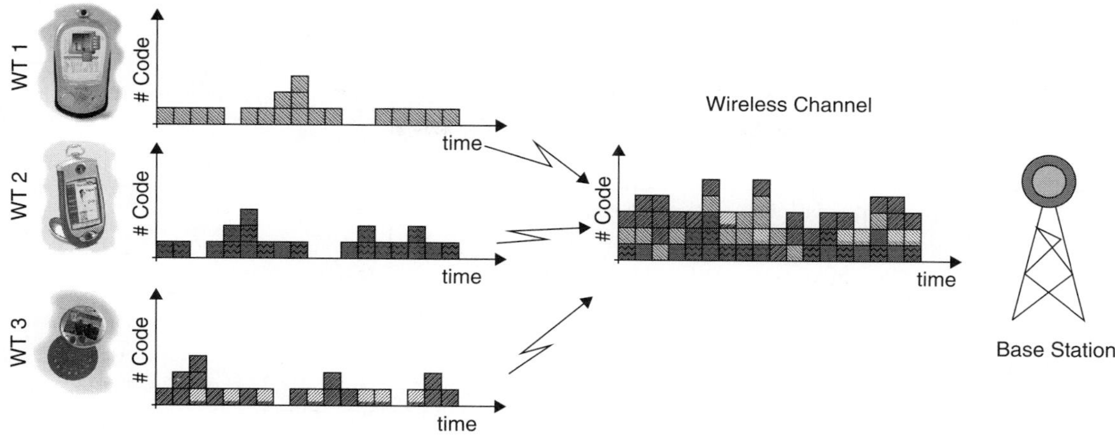

Figure 16: Statistical multiplex effect on the air interface of CDMA

sequences with their need for signaling for Multi-Code-CDMA. We then compare the Multi-Code-CDMA approach with the enhanced power control and the variable spreading gain approach. In Figure 16 the statistical multiplex effect of the air interface is depicted. For illustrative purposes we choose three WTs which transmit packets over the wireless link to the BS. For this example we assume that WTs are able to transmit also on multiple channels. This example shows how the three different *streams* of each WT with highly variable load are multiplexed on the air interface.

Multi-Code-CDMA (Lin and Gitlin 1995) can support a basic bit rate as well as integer multiples of the basic bit rate. In Multi-Code-CDMA, a high data rate is split into smaller data rates. Each small data rate is then spread by a different code sequence over the entire coherent bandwidth. All spread signals are modulated and transmitted over the wireless link. Figure 17 depicts a Multi-Code-CDMA transmitter.

The choice of spreading codes is very important to keep self-interference as low as possible. Because orthogonal sequences are used, the number of overall sequences within the cell is limited. In case one terminal wants to transmit on more channels, it has to request these channels from a centralized code depository. Thus, delay-sensitive services are hard to support. Orthogonal code sequences do benefit from the fact that self-interference does not exist as long as the system is synchronous. Synchronism exists only within the down-link and between channels of one wireless terminal in the up-link. In asynchronous systems, orthogonal codes lead to poor system performance.

The other choice of codes are PN code sequences. The number of these codes is large; however, the interference among the channels is high. Lin and Gitlin (1995) proposed to use pseudo random sequences to distinguish between the asynchronous up-link transmissions of the different wireless terminals. Additionally, they proposed to use orthogonal sequences to distinguish between synchronous up-link transmissions of a given wireless terminal. This approach gives a large total number of codes in conjunction with low self-interference between the parallel channels of a given wireless terminal. Further improvements are achieved when a central entity assigns the terminal specific pseudo random sequences (Stahnke, Boche, Fitzek and Wolisz 2000). Note that this does not require additional overhead for bit rate changes because the total number of codes is large and the codes are assigned to the terminals during link establishment. The hardware complexity, however, is higher as rake receivers are required for each channel to suppress multi-path interference. It is noted in Ojanpera and Prasad (1998) that the Multi-Code-CDMA approach is slightly more promising for multi-rate CDMA than the Variable Spreading Gain approach. It is argued that the former has a smaller signaling overhead and lower multi-path interference.

A brief overview of benefits and drawbacks of the three approaches for supporting time-variable QoS is given

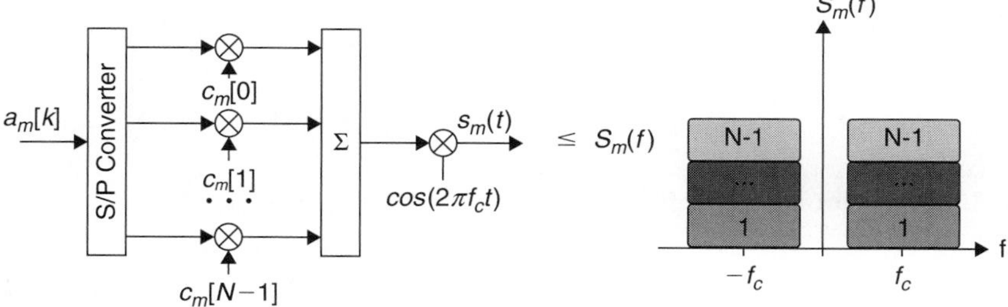

Figure 17: Multi-Code CDMA sender with the carrier frequency f_c, the spreading sequence c_m, the discrete input $a_m[k]$, and the analog output $s_m(t)$

Table 3: Enabling CDMA Technologies with Their Benefits and Drawbacks for Time-Variable QoS Support

	Enhanced Power Control	**Variable Spreading Gain**	**Multi-Code CDMA**
multi–path interference	no further impact	high rate → high ISI	no further impact
multiple access interference	→ power level	→ bit rate	→ number of channels
hardware complexity	TPC already exist	further oscillator	rake receiver for each channel
	high performance power control		
signaling overhead	TPC message	TPC message change in SG	not necessarily only for WBE sequences (Section titled "Bit Error Probability in CDMA")
enable higher data rates	no	yes	yes
granularity	—	high degree depends on spreading codes	multiple of CDMA channels
applied in	—	UMTS FDD [1]	UMTS TDD [1]

in Table 3. Note that combinations are possible to better exploit their benefits. In Ramakrishna and Holtzman (1998), the performance in terms of SINR and BEP of VSG and the Multi-Code-CDMA systems is compared. Authors in Ramakrishna and Holtzman (1998) summarize that whether a wireless terminal uses one of these approaches, it has an identical effect on both the SINR and the BEP of the other wireless terminals in the system. Furthermore the authors remark that multi-code systems have the disadvantage of instantaneous amplitude variations (for VSG they exhibit a constant instantaneous amplitude) and additional hardware complexity. In Webb, Huang, and Brink (1997) methods are introduced which reduce the hardware complexity of Multi-Code-CDMA systems significantly. Nevertheless in Ojanpera and Prasad (1998) it is claimed that multi-rate can be implemented with Multi-Code-CDMA in a slightly better way than with VSG, because of higher signaling overhead and lower multi-path interference rejection of the latter. Adaptive power control approaches have no multi-rate capability. For all approaches a high performance power control entity has to be implemented. Henceforth we use the Multi-Code-CDMA approach.

Wireless CDMA Channels

In the following, we investigate the characteristics of the CDMA uplink wireless channel. We concentrate on the usage of **P**seudo-**N**oise *(PN)* sequences. In particular the CDMA based bit error probability for non-orthogonal spreading sequences depends on the overall number of active channels in one cell. Therefore, we give a detailed overview of the major bit error probability models and the impact on throughput and capacity.

Bit Error Probability in CDMA

Direct **S**equence *(DS)* CDMA communications systems achieve their multiple access capability by assigning each WT a unique spreading sequence (see Section 1.3.3). Because of different distances between WT and BS the transmitted signals arrive at the BS with random delays τ, carrier phases ϕ and power levels P. The *exact* error probability depends on the particular spreading sequences used by the WT, random amplitude, delay and carrier phase. The calculation of the exact **B**it **E**rror **P**robability (*BEP*) for a CDMA system with **P**seudo-**N**oise (*PN*) sequences is difficult to evaluate. Therefore a variety of different error models based on Gaussian approximations can be found in Rappaport (2001). The design of the spreading sequences is not taken under consideration with the Gaussian approximations.

As given in Figure 18, we assume that J WTs simultaneously access the wireless channel. We further assume that each bit is spread by $G_{Spreading}$ chips. The transmitted signal $s(k)$ is assumed to be a sequence of two independent, identically distributed random variables (chips), where the probability of each variable is given by 1/2. Therefore we use the classical expression for uncoded BPSK modulation considering additive

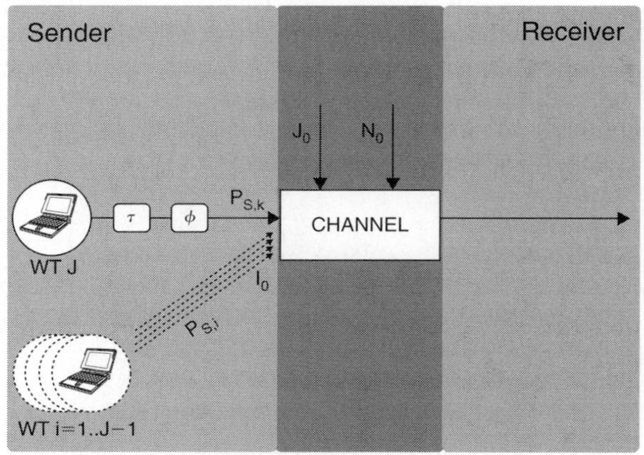

Figure 18: General CDMA channel

white Gaussian noise with power spectral density I_0 and energy per bit E_b (given in Equation 10) to calculate the bit error probability of a DS CDMA system. Assuming that all WTs arrive chip synchronously but phase asynchronously at the receiver side, the bit error probability $p_{biterror}^{BPSK}$ results in

$$p_{biterror}^{BPSK} = Q\left(\sqrt{2 \cdot SINR}\right) = Q\left(\sqrt{\frac{2 \cdot E_b}{I_0}}\right). \quad (10)$$

where $Q(x)$ is related to the complementary error function and is defined as

$$Q(x) = \frac{1}{\sqrt{2\pi}} \int_x^{\infty} e^{-t^2/2} dt. \quad (11)$$

The energy per bit E_b can be calculated by dividing the received signal power P_S by the data rate R_i.

$$E_b = \frac{P_S}{R_i}. \quad (12)$$

To calculate the power spectral density I_0, we assume perfect power control for all WTs. Perfect power control implies that all signals arrive at the receiver with the same power level. Moreover, multi-path interference is not considered in this model. Thus the noise power spectral density I_0 is influenced by three different terms as depicted in Figure 18. The additive white Gaussian noise power spectral density N_0 is characterized by the communication system, while the jammer density J_0 depends only on the jammer's hardware and his jamming technique (broadband or band limited). For simplicity we assume only broadband jamming. The last factor is made up of other active WTs which are using the channel simultaneously. The sum over the energy of all other WTs will be spread over the whole spreading bandwidth W_{SS}. The inter-chip interference was not taken into account within our assumptions. Because of the perfect power control assumption each signal will arrive with the same power level, which results in a very simply equation for the noise power spectral density I_0

$$I_0 = \frac{I}{W_{SS}} = \frac{P_S \cdot (k-1)}{W_{SS}} + N_0 + J_0, \quad (13)$$

where I is the overall noise power by all other WTs and k denotes the number of active channels within the cell. According to a Single-Code CDMA *(SC-CDMA)* system we assume one channel per WT, and if α_i represents the activity of WT i, k is generally given by $k = \sum_{j=1}^{J} \alpha_j$. Using Equations (10), (12), and (13) we obtain:

$$p_{biterror} = Q\left(\sqrt{\frac{2 \cdot \frac{P_S}{R}}{\frac{P_S \cdot (k-1)}{W_{SS}} + N_0 + J_0}}\right). \quad (14)$$

$$G_{Spreading} = \frac{T_B}{T_C} = \frac{\frac{1}{T_C}}{\frac{1}{T_B}} = \frac{W_{SS}}{R_i}. \quad (15)$$

The spreading gain has been defined as the number of chips per bit for a DS CDMA system. Thus it can be calculated by the ratio of T_B and T_C. This is equivalent to the ratio of W_{SS} and R_i.

$$p_{biterror} = Q\left(\sqrt{\frac{2 \cdot G_{Spreading}}{k - 1 + \frac{N_0 \cdot W_{SS}}{P_S} + \frac{J_0 \cdot W_{SS}}{P_S}}}\right). \quad (16)$$

The complementary error function Q function can be transformed in the *er fc* function

$$erfc(\alpha) = 2 \cdot Q\left(\sqrt{2} \cdot \alpha\right). \quad (17)$$

We model both the background noise and the jamming (in a friendly environment the jammers can also be neglected) as b wireless terminals that transmit all the time, resulting in a decreased SINR. This simplification leads to the simplified Equation (18), which can be found in Noll (1999)

$$p_{biterror}(k) = Q\left(\sqrt{\frac{2 \cdot G_{Spreading}}{k - 1 + b}}\right). \quad (18)$$

An improved Gaussian approximation has been derived by Holtzman (1992) and applied in Buehrer and Woerner (1996). The bit error probability for the improved Gaussian approximation is given in Equation (19). The calculations for the bit error probability are still simple enough but lead to quite accurate results. In Rappaport (2001) it is claimed that the improved Gaussian approximation should be used, if the number of WT is small or the spreading gain $G_{Spreading}$ is large.

$$p_{biterror}^{IMP}(k) = \frac{2}{3} Q\left(\sqrt{\frac{3 \cdot G_{Spreading}}{k-1+b}}\right) + \frac{1}{6} Q\left(\frac{G_{Spreading}}{\sqrt{\frac{(k-1+b)N}{3} + \sqrt{3}\sigma}}\right) + \frac{1}{6} Q\left(\frac{G_{Spreading}}{\sqrt{\frac{(k-1+b)N}{3} - \sqrt{3}\sigma}}\right)$$

$$\sigma^2 = (k-1+b) \times \left(\frac{23}{360} \cdot G^2_{Spreading} + \left(\frac{1}{20} + \frac{k-2+b}{36} \right) \left(G_{Spreading} - 1 \right) \right). \tag{19}$$

Packet Error Probability in CDMA

Considering the bit error probabilities in (18) we give the **P**acket **E**rror **P**robability (*PEP*) for a packet data unit of the length L_{PDU} [bit] in Equation (20) under the assumption that the bit errors occur without correlations.

$$p_{pkterror}(L_{PDU}, k) = 1 - \left(1 - p_{biterror}(k)\right)^{L_{PDU}} \tag{20}$$

If we assume a coding scheme that allows us to correct e bit errors, the packet error probability becomes smaller and is given in Equation (21) (Gu and Olafson 2000, Ploydoros 1994, Chang and Lin 1999).

$$p_{pkterror}(e, L_{PDU}, k) = 1 - \sum_{i-0}^{e} \binom{L_{PDU}}{i} \times \left(1 - p_{biterror}(k)\right)^{L_{PDU}-i} \left(p_{biterror}(k)\right)^{i} \tag{21}$$

More advanced coding schemes can be found as given by Viterbi in Viterbi 1990.

Synchronization

In any spread-spectrum system, there exists a fundamental operation that needs to be carried out in order for the receiver to demodulate and decode the target signal. This operation is *synchronization* and it needs to be done in all systems mentioned (e.g., DS, FH, TH, and hybrid combinations of them). Throughout this chapter, we have assumed that the receiver was synchronized to the incoming signal through this vital operation is sometimes difficult to achieve in practice. We briefly referred to the problem of synchronization in frequency-hopping systems in the initial example of Hedy Lamarr's invention. It is clear that in any frequency-hopping spread-spectrum system, the receiver needs to synchronously follow the hopping pattern used by the transmitter. Because this chapter deals with CDMA systems, we will here concentrate mainly on synchronization of direct sequence spread spectrum systems. Synchronization of DS systems is normally done in two stages, namely *initial synchronization*, also known as *code acquisition*, and *code tracking*. The former refers to the task of bringing the locally generated spreading sequence into phase with the received one within the accuracy of one chip, while the latter refers to the task of bringing and keeping the remaining difference to a null value.

Code Acquisition

This operation can be seen as an initial procedure for coarse alignment of the local and received sequences. The alignment of sequences is essential to allow despreading of the received signal. The receiver can be seen as a correlating unit which computes the autocorrelation function of the spreading sequence. There are several strategies for the initial code acquisition. The most common approach to code acquisition is based on a *serial search*. The receiver can control the phase of the locally generated spreading sequence in quantized steps. Typically the step size is one chip, though some fractional values are sometimes used (e.g., ¼, ½). The serial search procedure starts by correlating the sequences at a arbitrary phase position and gradually advancing the local sequence phase by one unit step. Such a procedure is repeated until the correlating unit outputs a high value, indicating that the received and local sequences are in phase. Note that mathematically the receiver is computing the auto-correlation function of the spreading sequence. Every possible relative position between these sequences is denominated a cell and the total number of cells to be searched forms the so-called *uncertainty region*. If the spreading sequence has Q chips and we search in steps of one chip, then the length of the uncertainty region is also Q. In principle we would need to test the Q cells sequentially and then select the cell with highest correlation result as that corresponding to the synchronized position. In order to expedite the process, we usually use a *threshold* to compare it with the correlation result, and whenever the threshold is exceeded we declare the signals synchronized. Of course, we would like to achieve the synchronization state as quickly as possible. This is important because users switching on their WTs would like to be wirelessly connected as soon as possible. In some occasions, very fast acquisition times are required, as in the case of packet communications. For such cases the use of *matched filters* is common where the filters are matched to the spreading sequences. Due to reasons of implementation complexity, matched filter solutions are typically used with short spreading sequences. Code acquisition is a stochastic process because it is influenced by noise and interference; hence, it cannot be deterministically modelled. In the above example, and considering a single path channel, there is a single cell where the code sequences are in line, and it referred to as the *synchro cell*. The rest of the $(Q-1)$ cells are called *nonsynchro cells*. At the synchro cell, synchronization would be declared with a given probability of detection P_D, a figure that which typically will be close to unity. P_D represents the probability that the auto-correlation result exceeds the threshold value. However, due to noise and interference we may miss the synchro cell, with a probability $1-P_D$. In such a case the serial search will move on until we again are in the synchro cell position and we have a new chance to detect synchronization. In each of the $(Q-1)$ nonsynchro cells, we may erroneously detect synchronization (due to the effects of noise and interference) with a probability P_{FA} (probability of false alarm) or we may recognize each of them as non synchronized cells with a probability $(1-P_{FA})$. The probabilities P_D, P_{FA}, the integration time (the time needed to correlate the sequences) and the threshold value are very much dependent on each other, and together with the step size and length of the uncertainty region, determine the statistics of the code acquisition process. The typical performance measures of code acquisition are the mean acquisition time and its variance. In general, code acquisition is a very difficult and critical task that needs to be done in adverse noise and interference conditions as the processing gain advantages are only available once the system is synchronized.

Code Tracking

Code tracking, also known as fine code synchronization, is a operation subsequent to code acquisition which aims to reduce and maintain the possible resulting fractional misalignment to zero. Code tracking is usually performed by a delay lock loop (DLL) which virtually tracks the temporal variations of the radio channel. The most common approach to code tracking is the early-late DLL, which correlates the received signal in two parallel *early* and *late* branches, with advanced and retarded phase delay offsets, respectively. A fractional timing offset between the local and received sequences will result in different correlation values at the early and late correlator outputs. These signals are compared and then used to control the phase of the local sequence generator in the direction of reducing the phase delay offset between sequences to zero. In other words, the timing offset between the sequences is estimated from the energy difference between the early and late correlator outputs. The code phase error has a symmetric characteristic with respect to the phase detector output, and it is usually referred to as the s-curve. The performance of code tracking can be seriously degraded by the presence of closely spaced multi-path components and (multiple access) interference.

Synchronization in CDMA Networks

In CDMA networks, interference plays an essential role in system performance, and also in synchronization performance. In particular, it is interesting to notice that every time the receiver correlates the local and received sequences, it also computes the sum of cross-correlations between the local sequence and each of the sequences corresponding to other users. Every time that the phase of the local sequence is advanced, this cross-correlation sum will take on a different value and eventually it may exceed the threshold value in non-synchronized cell positions. Multiple access interference could be very large in some cases resulting in situations with very long mean acquisition times, or even worse, sequences that could not be synchronized at all in some extreme cases. Practical CDMA systems exploit rake receivers to resolve several paths, and such a bank of receivers could be utilized already at the initial synchronization stage to acquire a number of strong paths. Once that first path is detected, the receiver can reduce its uncertainty region around that path because the remaining paths are very likely to be in close proximity to the first detected path.

CONCLUSION

In this chapter we reviewed the most relevant aspects of CDMA technology. CDMA is important because it is the underlying technology of the third generation mobile communication systems (3G), currently being deployed and starting to gain market share. Moreover, though future wireless communications are widely assumed to be based on multi-carrier systems, CDMA is tacitly present there too, either used in combination with OFDM systems or on systems based on multi-carrier CDMA (MC-CDMA) techniques. CDMA is a well understood and practically mature technology with a bright future.

GLOSSARY

CDMA: Code Division Multiple Access (CDMA) allows multiple users to access the same spectrum at the same time. The users are unambiguously distinguished by their unique associated spreading code.

DS: In case of direct sequence (DS) spreading, the spreading code is combined with the information signal by a modulo-2 operation.

FDMA: Frequency Division Multiple Access (FDMA) separates users in frequency.

FH: The information signal hops over different frequency bands in case of the Frequency Hopper (FH).

MAI: Multiple Access Interference (MAI) is a composite signal resulting from multiple users accessing the same spectrum at the same time in CDMA networks.

PN: Pseudo Noise (PN) sequences are one family of spreading sequences for CDMA.

Power Control: Power control is a functionality to adjust the transmit power to an optimal value. It is applied on both mobile and base stations.

TDMA: Time Division Multiple Access (TDMA) separates users in time.

CROSS REFERENCES

See *Spread Spectrum; Wireless Channels*.

REFERENCES

3rd Generation Partnership Project (3GPP). Universal Mobile Telecommunications System (UMTS); Selection Procedures for the Choice of Radio Transmission Technologies of the UMTS.

Bambos, N., and S. Kandukuri. 2000. Power Controlled Multiple Access (PCMA) in wireless communication networks. In *Proceedings INFOCOM* 2000, pp. 386–95.

Barretto, A. N., and G. Fettweis. 2000. Performance improvement in DS– spread spectrum CDMA systems using a PRE- and a POST–RAKE. In *International Zurich Seminar on Communications* 2000, pp. 39–46. ETH Zurich, Febr.

Buehrer, R., and B. Woerner. 1996. Analysis of adaptive multistage interference cancellation for CDMA using an improved Gaussian approximation. *IEEE Transaction on Communication*, 44 (October): 1308–21.

Chang, P. R., and C. F. Lin. 1999. Wireless ATM-based multicode CDMA transport architecture for MPEG-2 video transmission. *Special Issue on Video Transmission for Mobile Multimedia Applications*, 87(10): 1807–24.

Chih-Lin, I., and R. D. Gitlin. 1995. Multi-code (CDMA) wireless personal communications networks. In *IEEE International Conference on Communications* '95, Seattle, Washington, June 1995, pp. 1060–64.

Cooper, G. R., and C. D. McGillem. 1986. *Modern communications and spread spectrum*. Electrical and Electronic Engineering Series. New York, NY: McGraw-Hill Series in Electrical Engineering.

Telecommunications Industry Association *Mobile station-base station compatibility standard for dual–mode wide-band spread spectrum cellular systems* 1999. *EIA/TIA-95 Rev. B,* 1999. http://electronics.ihs.com/document/abstract/OQZHGBAAAAAAAAAA

Gibson, J. D. 1996. *Mobile communications—Handbook*, vol. 2. IEEE Press, 1996.

Gold, R. 1967. Optimal binary sequences for spread spectrum multiplexing. *IEEE Transaction on Information Theory*, IT-B (October): 619–21.

Golomb, S. W. 1992. *Shift register sequences*. Laguna Hills, CA: Aegean Park Press.

Gu, X., and Olafsson S. 2000. A simplified and accurate method to analyse a code division multiple-access performance. In *UCL and IEE London Communications Symposium*, http://www.ee.ucl.ac.uk/lcs/prog00.html (accessed September 28, 2007).

Holtzman, J. 1992. A simple, accurate method to calculate spread spectrum multiple access error probabilities. *IEEE Transaction on Communication*, 40 (3) March: 461–64.

I, C. L., and K. K. Sabnani. 1995. Variable spreading gain CDMA with adaptive control for true packet switching wireless networks. In *Proceedings of the ICC, 1995*. June 725–30.

Immaneni, P. and J. M. Capone. 2000. A framework for analysis of VBR traffic over CDMA. In *Proceedings of 2000 IEEE Wireless Communications and Networking Conference*, Chicago, IL, September 2000. 1096–1100.

Jansen, M. G., and R. Prasad. 1995. Capacity, throughput, and delay analysis of a cellular DS CDMA system with imperfect power control and imperfect sectorization. *IEEE Transaction on Vehicular Technology*, 44(1) February: 67–75.

Jansen, M. G., R. Prasad, and A. Kegel.1993. Capacity analysis of a cellular direct sequence code division multiple access system with imperfect power control. *IEEE Transaction on Communication*, E67-B(8): 894–905.

Kasami, T. 1996. Weight distribution formula for some class of cyclic codes. Technical Report R-285, Coordinated Science Lab., Univ. IL, Urbana.

Morikawa, H., T. Kajiya, T. Aoyama, and A. Campbell. 1997. Distributed power control for various QoS in a CDMA wireless system. *IEICE Transaction on Fundamentals*, E80-A(12):2429–36.

Noll, P. 1999. *Nachrichten Übertragung II*, vol. 2. FT. http://www-ft.ee.tu-berlin.de.

Ojanperä, T. and R. Prasad. 1998. *Wideband for third generation mobile communications*. Norwood, MA: ArTech House Publisher, universal personal communications edition, 1998.

Ploydoros, A. 1994. *An integrated physical/link–access layer model of packet radio architectures*. Technical report, Communication Sciences Institute—University of Southern California.

Prasad, R. 1996. *CDMA for Wireless Personal Communications*. Mobile Communications Series. Norwood, MA: Artech House Publishers.

Proakis, J. G. 1995. *Digital communications* 3rd ed. New York: McGraw-Hill International Edition.

Ramakrishna, S., and J. Holtzman. 1998. A comparison between single code and multiple code transmission schemes in a CDMA system. In *Proceeding IEEE Vehicular Technology Conference*—VTC 98, pp. 791–95.

Rappaport, T. S. 2001. *Wireless Communications: Principles and Practice*, vol. 1. Upper Saddle River, NJ: Prentice Hall.

Shapira, J. 1999. *Advanced CDMA workshop*. Wireless Institute of Technology, San Jose, CA, July 1999.

Stahnke, W. 1973. *Primitive binary polynomials*. Math. Comp. 27 (Oct.): 977–80.

Stanczak, S., H. Boche, F. H.P. Fitzek, and A. Wolisz. 2000. Design of spreading sequences for SMPT–based CDMA systems. In *Proceeding 34th ASILOMAR Conference on Signals Systems and Computers*, Oct, pp. 1622–26.

Viterbi, A. 1990. Very low rate convolutional codes for maximum theoretical performance of spread-spectrum multiple-access channels. *IEEE Journal on Sel Areas in Communication*, 8 (May): 641–9.

Webb, C., H. Huang, and S. Brink. 1997. Rake receiver architectures for multi–code CDMA. In *Proceedings of the Sixth WINLAB Workshop on Third Generation Wireless Information Networks*, (March), pp. 229–38.

Wu, J., and R. Kohno. 1996. A wireless multimedia CDMA system based on transmission power control. *IEEE Journal Select. Areas Communication*, 14(4) (May): 683–91.

Yun, L., and D. Messerschmitt. 1994. Power control for variable QOS on a CDMA channel. In *Proc. IEEE Milcom Conference*, (Oct): 178–82.

Yun, L., and D. Messerschmitt. 1995. Variable quality of service in CDMA systems by statistical power control. In *Proceedings IEEE International Conference Communication (ICC '95)*, (June): 713–19.

Time-Division Multiple Access

Tom S. Chan, *Southern New Hampshire University*

INTRODUCTION

Time-division multiple access (TDMA) is a technology for shared medium networks that allows several users to share the same frequency by dividing into different time slots. The users transmit in rapid succession, one after the other, each using their own time slot. The technique allows multiple users to share the same transmission medium using only the required bandwidth (Wikipedia 2005).

TDMA is also a specific second-generation (2G) mobile phone standard—interim standard 136 (IS-136) or digital advanced mobile phone service (D-AMPS)—that uses the same time-share bandwidth technique. In radio systems, TDMA is usually used alongside other multiplexing techniques, such as frequency division multiple access (FDMA) and code division multiple access (CDMA). This can be very confusing because competing 2G standards such as global system for mobile communication (GSM), personal digital cellular (PDC), and integrated digital enhanced network (iDEN) also use the TDMA technique in airwave management and signal processing. Besides cellular applications, TDMA is also used extensively in satellites, local area networks (LANs), physical security systems, and combat-net radios.

TDMA: THE MULTIPLEXING TECHNIQUE

Communication is defined as sending messages using electricity, light, or radio signals from one point to another. Multiplexing is the technique in which two or more independent messages are carried by a single medium. Although the focus is on TDMA, there are two other multiplex accessing techniques: FDMA and CDMA. FDMA is the oldest and is used widely in analog systems. It divides a carrier spectrum into frequency slots, assigning each to a different message. CDMA is the latest technique; each message is assigned and tagged with a unique identifying code, such that the relevant message can be separated out by the intended receiver.

TDMA is a multiplexing technique that allows multiple users to access a common channel without interference by allocating unique time slots to each user. The user has the entire channel, but only for a brief moment. Time-sharing is far from a novelty. Multitask operating systems apply the same principle by rotating jobs in and out of execution. TDMA divides time into slices and restricts job execution to only one slice at a time. At the completion of each slice, the current job is set aside and another is allowed to execute. Time division can either be performed equally or on demand. Synchronous TDMA gives each incoming signal an opportunity to transmit, proceeding in a round-robin fashion. However, this approach can waste bandwidth because a slot is assigned even if users have nothing to transmit. Synchronous TDMA is the most common technique in wired channels. Statistical TDMA, on the other hand, assigns time slices only to active users. With transmission no longer round-robin, addresses must be included to identify the sender and receiver. Statistical TDMA may be more efficient in bandwidth utilization but requires overhead in address processing. In wireless communication in which bandwidth is limited, statistical TDMA tends to be a more popular technique.

BRIEF HISTORY OF CELLULAR WIRELESS SYSTEMS

The advanced mobile phone system (AMPS) is an analog mobile phone system standard, developed and introduced in the United States during the early 1980s. With exponential growth, cellular systems were already running into capacity limits by the early 1990s. The need to serve more customers simultaneously with the same amount of radio spectrum was considered essential for continued growth and industry survival. Capacity was increased through the development of interim standard 54 (IS-54), a dual-mode digital cellular standard that utilized digitization, compression, and TDMA (Noll 1999). IS-54 was designated by the Telecommunications Industry Association (TIA) and became the leading technology in the United States; meanwhile, GSM was developed by the European Telecommunications Standards Institute (ETSI) and became the dominant standard in Europe and many other countries.

Japan took a different path by adopting the PDC designated by the Association of Radio Industries and Businesses (ARIB) for use exclusively in Japan. Although all of these systems used the TDMA technique, their implementations were different, and, more importantly, they are incompatible with each other.

Qualcomm proposed a cellular system, interim standard 95 (IS-95), based on spread-spectrum technology and CDMA in 1994. Even though the advertised increase in bandwidth utilization had yet to be realized, IS-95 dominated about half of the U.S. licenses. In 1995, the Federal Communications Commission (FCC) licensed the personal communication system (PCS) frequency spectrum to the public. PCS was built upon existing standards but operated between frequency bands 1800 and 1900 MHz. The evolution of IS-54 to IS-136 came shortly after the spectrum was opened up. All PCSs are digital, using either TDMA or CDMA. Hence, IS-136 is also known as PCS TDMA, and IS-95 is known as PCS CDMA. The European GSM is sometimes dubbed PCS 1900. Together, these are the most popular 2G cellular standards.

The future demand for mobile cellular services appears to be nearly unlimited, especially with the mobile Internet upon us. The third-generation (3G) technologies operating at 2 Mbps can turn phones into multimedia players, making it routine to download music and video. Currently, there are several competing 3G standards. The International Telecommunication Union (ITU) is working on the International Mobile Telecommunications-2000 (IMT-2000) initiative, into which all 3G standards will eventually merge. Direct migration to 3G networks is costly and challenging. Most wireless operators are taking an interim stage called 2.5G to achieve data rates up to 114 kbps, as compare to the 9.6 kbps in traditional 2G (see Figure 1). As we explore various TDMA wireless standards in this chapter, network architecture, topology, and cell structure issues will not be covered because they are generic and similar in most cellular technologies. For those interested in these subjects, tutorials are available from the International Engineering Consortium on IS-136 (IEC 2005a) and GSM (IEC 2005b).

IS-136 TDMA STANDARD

TDMA is an important part of the evolution from 1G analog to 2G digital systems. Although IS-136 is not the most advanced of the 2G systems, it is the first digital TDMA and provides an excellent framework for the illustration of a TDMA wireless cellular system. In fact, TDMA and IS-136 are usually synonymous with each other. Regardless of standards, wireless systems are constantly confronted with two capacity issues: voice/data and control. Similar to AMPS (TIA 1999), IS-54 (TIA 1989) uses frequency ranges at 800 MHz with 30 KHz channels to achieve multiple access by applying TDMA on an FDMA structure. The channels are divided into three time slots carrying digitized voice signals. The addition of the time slots automatically triples the voice capacity available.

IS-136 (TIA 1995) was an enhancement to IS-54 and represented the next-generation TDMA-based PCS system. The analog portion of AMPS was incorporated into the new specification to provide a smooth migration path for analog/digital dual-mode operation. IS-136 was also designed to work dual band on both the 800 MHz and the PCS 1900 MHz frequencies. Whereas IS-54 uses the three time-division channels for voice data only, IS-136 added the digital control channels (DCCHs), which enable support for new advanced features such as paging and messaging.

Digitization, Encoding, and Modulation

The basis for all digital communication involves digitization, encoding, and modulation. Digitization is the conversion of analog acoustic voice signal into digital data. As we speak into a microphone, analog audio signals are created. Since the bandwidth for phone systems is limited to 3000 Hz, frequencies below 400 Hz and above 3400 Hz in the audio signal are filtered off. The signal is converted subsequently into a digital value at a rate of 8000 samples per second with 8-bit resolution, resulting in 64 kbps digital data representing the analog voice information using the pulse code modulation (PCM) technique.

After digitization, IS-136 applies data compression with a speech coder to efficiently transmit the signal. A speech coder delineates the digitized signal and filter off patterns that are not characteristic of the human voice. The resulting signal is an approximation of the voice content that can be recreated by the receiving speech decoder. The speech coder characterizes the input signal by looking up a codebook table and selecting the code that most accurately represents the input signal.

PCM, invented decades ago, is not efficient enough for wireless network application. IS-136 uses the vector sum

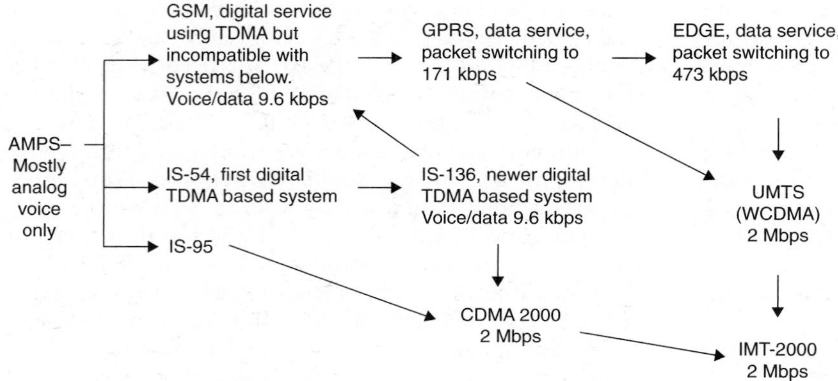

Figure 1: Common cellular wireless system and its migration path

excited linear predictive (VSELP) speech coder, which compresses voice down to 7.95 kbps and achieves an 8:1 compression. VSELP produces a speech frame containing 159 bits every 20 ms. It digitizes the voice's essential elements using digital signal processing (DSP) along with proprietary algorithms to crunch down speech and conserve bandwidth. If a speech segment is lost over the channel, the VSELP decoder can also repair the effect through speech extrapolation.

As data compression technologies develop, improved speech coders have become available. The newest version of IS-136 introduces the enhanced full rate (EFR) algebraic code-excited linear prediction (ACELP) speech coder, which supports "over the air" activation, calling name ID, enhanced handoffs, and priority access to control channels. The coder has an output of 7.40 kbps with 148 bits in a speech frame. The ACELP coder also has a higher sampling rate and offers cleaner, crisper audio quality comparable to landlines under normal channel conditions.

A modulation scheme for the mobile environment must use transmitted power and frequency bandwidth very efficiently because the mobile station is both power- and bandwidth-limited. IS-136 uses Pi/4 differential quadrature phase shift keying (DQPSK) for signal modulation, which is a technique that alternates between two quadrature constellations. The constellations are offset by Pi/4 radians, or 45 degrees, with successive symbols taken from the two constellations every other period. Phase shift is reduced from a maximum of 180 degrees to 135 degrees. DQPSK can be detected using a coherent detector, a differential detector, or a discriminator that reduces the complexity of receiver structures. DQPSK also has a high tolerance to dispersion and nonlinearities, as well as a narrow spectrum that enables close channel spacing.

Frame Structure, Slot, and Traffic Channel

A channel is simply a communication path between two devices. Typically, two radio frequencies make a cellular channel—one is needed to transmit and the other to receive. Sound waves are converted and transmitted as digital numbers or bits, but we also need to define the data structure of the channel: frame and slot. A frame is the complete unit of data transmitted between network points, which can be long or short. Apart from data, a frame also carries information about itself such as address, length, and status. In time-division multiplexing, a frame is a complete cycle of events within the time-division period. Frames hold slots, which in turn hold channels.

Slots hold individual conversation as well as signaling and controlling information within the frame. TDMA places several calls on a single frequency, separating the conversations in time. Each caller occupies a predetermined amount of time in an assigned time slot on an assigned radio frequency. Calls are combined into a digital stream, and then assigned and delivered into the right time slots on the right frequency at the right time. Radio channels in IS-136 are 30 KHz wide and identical to AMPS. Each frame is 40 ms, divided into six slots. IS-136 traffic is always full-rate, using two slots for one call. Half-rate traffic can be implemented using one slot, but this is not popular due to low quality and is unnecessary given the available capacity. A frame is divided into two blocks, with each block carrying three slots. Data rate is 48.6 kbps, with each slot transmitting 324 bits one way in 6.67 ms (see Figure 2).

The mobile station (MS) must have the transmission power off except for the assigned time slot following an assigned transmit power profile. The base station (BS)—the beacon carrier—must transmit on all six time slots at the same power level. When there is no traffic at a particular time slot, BS uses a dummy burst to fill in on the unassigned traffic. The base transmitter may adjust the transmit power level separately in each time slot, except on the beacon frequency. Thus, a higher power may be used in a time slot that is transmitting to an MS in the outer part of the cell, while a lower power may be used in a slot transmitting to an MS that is close by, improving

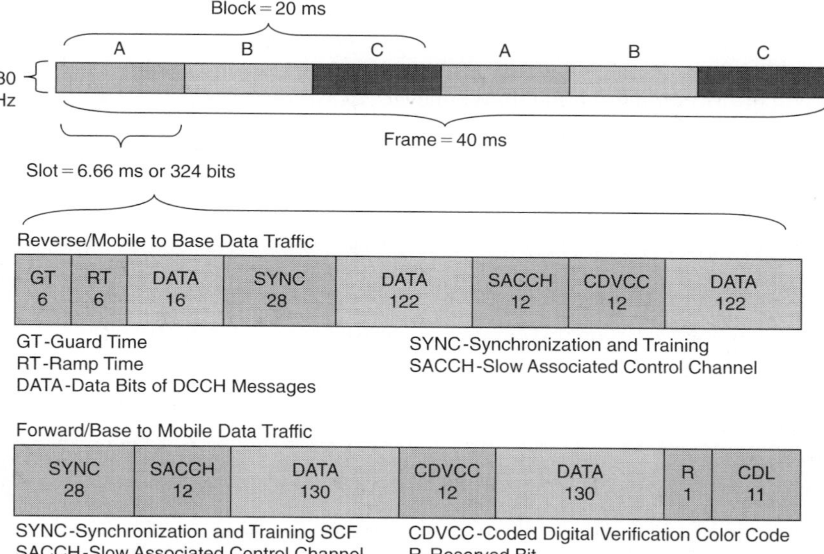

Figure 2: IS-136 frame, slot, and digital traffic channel structure

the overall interference level with other cells in the system.

Voice conversation is carried in a slot's data field. Six slots make up one frame, and two slots form a voice circuit or digital traffic channel (DTC). Bandwidth is used only partially for data—260 out of the 324 bits—because control is needed for proper DTC operation (the numerical values in Figure 2 refer to bits). Forward and reverse DTC have different structures. Definitions of the subchannels are as follows:

- Guard time (GT): period between time slots; keeps data bursts separated
- Ramp time (RT): period during which transmitter goes from a quiet state to full power
- DATA: the data bits of the actual voice conversation in digitized form
- Synchronization (SYNC): slot must synchronize with all others and the master clock
- Coded digital verification color code (CDVCC): a unique 8-bit code that simulates a marker to ensure that the correct MS is communicating with the proper BS (because frequencies are reused in the cellular system)
- Slow associated control channel (SACCH): used to pass control information (e.g., signal strength)
- Coded digital control channel locator (CDL): indicates the range of frequencies in which DCCH can be found in forward DTC only
- R: reserved

The IS-136 standard has several methods of transferring control information for the DTC, including in-band signaling using fast associated control channel (FACCH) and out-of-band signaling using SACCH. Whereas in-band signaling replaces voice data, out-of-band signaling is sent with the data. SACCH is a continuous stream of information sent using dedicated bits in each slot that coincide with the slot's voice traffic and do not affect data transmission. However, the transmission rate for SACCH is slow. For rapid or urgent delivery, control is sent via FACCH. FACCH runs in a blank-and-burst mode; the voice traffic in a slot is "blanked," and a "burst" of data is sent instead. FACCH is used during handoff or when the SACCH cannot send information fast enough. Whenever FACCH overrides the voice signal, speech quality is degraded. However, IS-136 does run more efficiently because the MS does not need to return to the control channel. The SACCH and FACCH designs optimize bandwidth utilization for continuous speech and control signaling.

Control, Logical Channels, and Superframe

The ability to use DCCH is an important enhancement for IS-136. DCCH increases paging capacity and allows the sharing of traffic and control on the same channel. Whereas SACCH and FACCH in DTC perform call association, DCCH is used for administration and services. Thus, DCCH forms the platform for a new generation of wireless features such as message services, sleep mode, private systems, and enhanced security.

In contrast to AMPS and IS-54, IS-136 has no preassigned frequency for control channels. The system can choose any frequency in each cell for this purpose, or it may change the frequency dynamically. When an IS-136 mobile phone enters a cell, carriers are scanned until a sufficiently strong signal is received such that the proper frequency for DCCH from the forward DTC CDL subchannel can be located. IS-136 does not need to exhaustively scan all the frequencies in that cell to find the proper setup channels.

IS-136 DTC and DCCH both use the same frame/slot structure (see Figure 3). In general, only one slot pair, slots 1 and 4, is required for DCCH in each cell. The numerical values in Figure 3 refer to bits, and forward and reverse DCCH have different structures. Definitions of individual subchannels are as follows:

- Guard time (GT): see DTC definition
- Ramp time (RT): see DTC definition
- DATA: data bits for DCCH messages
- Synchronization (SYNC): see DTC definition
- Preamble (PREAM): used for timing, and by the BS to set the received amplifier to avoid signal distortion
- Additional synchronization (SYNC+): additional bit pattern that provides additional synchronization information

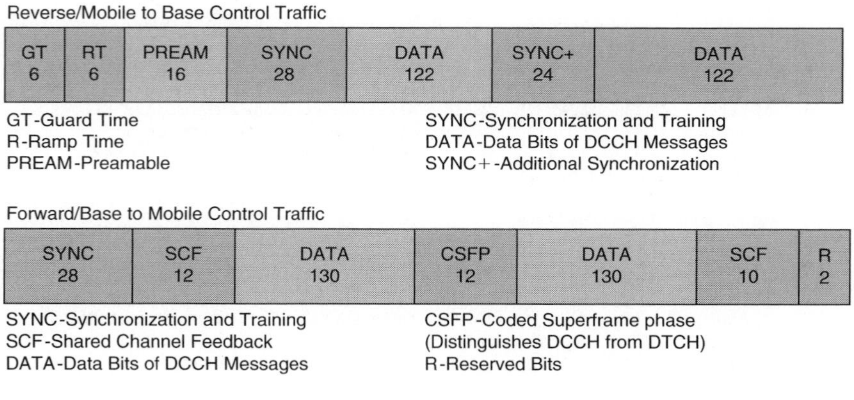

Reverse/Mobile to Base Control Traffic

GT	RT	PREAM	SYNC	DATA	SYNC+	DATA
6	6	16	28	122	24	122

GT-Guard Time
R-Ramp Time
PREAM-Preamable
SYNC-Synchronization and Training
DATA-Data Bits of DCCH Messages
SYNC+-Additional Synchronization

Forward/Base to Mobile Control Traffic

SYNC	SCF	DATA	CSFP	DATA	SCF	R
28	12	130	12	130	10	2

SYNC-Synchronization and Training
SCF-Shared Channel Feedback
DATA-Data Bits of DCCH Messages
CSFP-Coded Superframe phase (Distinguishes DCCH from DTCH)
R-Reserved Bits

Figure 3: IS-136 digital control channel structure

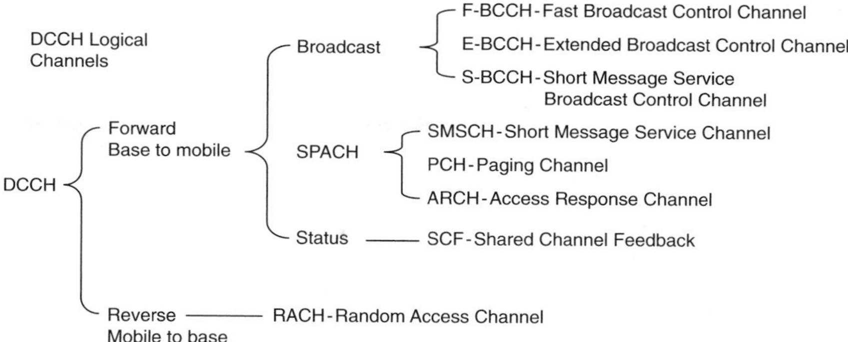

Figure 4: IS-136 DCCH logical channels

- Shared channel feedback (SCF): a collection of flags used as a method of control and to acknowledge send from MS to BS
- Coded superframe phase (SCFP): indicates to the MS which frame in the superframe is currently being transmitted

In order to organize and facilitate information flow across the cellular interface, logical channels are defined in the IS–136 DCCH to perform, sort, and prioritize signaling functions (see Figure 4). A logical channel is formed by a given slot in the sequence of frames and may be formed by the same slot number in successive frames. However, the same slot in successive frames does not necessarily belong to the same logical channel.

The multiplexed broadcast (BCCH) channel is designed to carry system configuration and rules information that the MS must follow for system access. BCCHs are multiplexed onto the DCCH forward channel and divided into the following three channels:

- Fast broadcast channel (F–BCCH): used for mandatory and time-critical information such as the system ID registration and access information; F-BCCH has a fixed repetitive cycle
- Extended broadcast channel (E–BCCH): used to carry supplementary information that is not time critical (e.g., neighbor cell lists)
- Short message service broadcast channel (S-BCCH): used to broadcast messaging service

The multiplexed point-to-point short message service messaging, paging, and access-response (SPACH) channel is used to communicate with a specific phone with logical channels as follows:

- Short message service channel (SMSCH): carries teleservice data to and from the MS
- Paging channel (PCH): carries system pages to the MS
- Access response channel (ARCH): provides system response to phone queries and administration information from the base to the MS

The random access channel (RACH) is a shared channel and the only reverse DCCH. It can be used, for example, to respond to an authentication request. RACH is controlled and acknowledged by shared channel feedback (SCF) on the forward DCCH. SCF provides status on all reverse time slots and informs all MSs of the usage at any particular time.

Superframe and hyperframe are used to multiplex logical groups of information together and provide a known repetitive, ordered sequence on the cellular interface that enables an MS to retrieve information quickly and develop a sleep mode. The mobile phone only needs to wake up at predefined instances to receive messaging. A superframe is made up of sixteen sequential frames, and a hyperframe is made up of a primary and secondary superframe. Since only slots 1 and 4 on each frame are assigned to DCCH, superframe creates a sequence of thirty-two bursts, or superframe phases (SFP), designated for either broadcast, paging, short message service, or access response information (see Figure 5). The superframe structures are flexible and broadcast to the MS when a DCCH is first acquired.

Call Operations

In PCS networks, the MS must register with the network during the initial daily power-up. Registration is accomplished by identifying the MS via a radio transmission on the reverse DCCH. Registration messages are sent from the MS to the BS on the RACH. Once the MS is authenticated, the acceptance message is returned from the BS to the MS on the ARCH. The authentication process involves encryption techniques. A random challenge number is transmitted from the BS to the MS. The MS performs a calculation using the challenge number with an internal secret number (shared secret data, part A [SSD-A]), then returns the result to BS. The SSD-A is derived from a second internal number (A-Key), which is preset at the factory or entered by the user via keyboard of the mobile set. If the BS suspects that the SSD-A has been compromised, the BS can change SSD-A via DCCH to a new value, and only the BS has knowledge of the proper A-Key value for these operations.

A call from the MS begins with an access to the BS on DCCH. The BS verifies several parameters and ensures the availability of resources for the call before selecting an idle DTC. The BS also synchronizes each MS with a master clock when a service is initiated. An MS being called is more complicated because it must first be paged

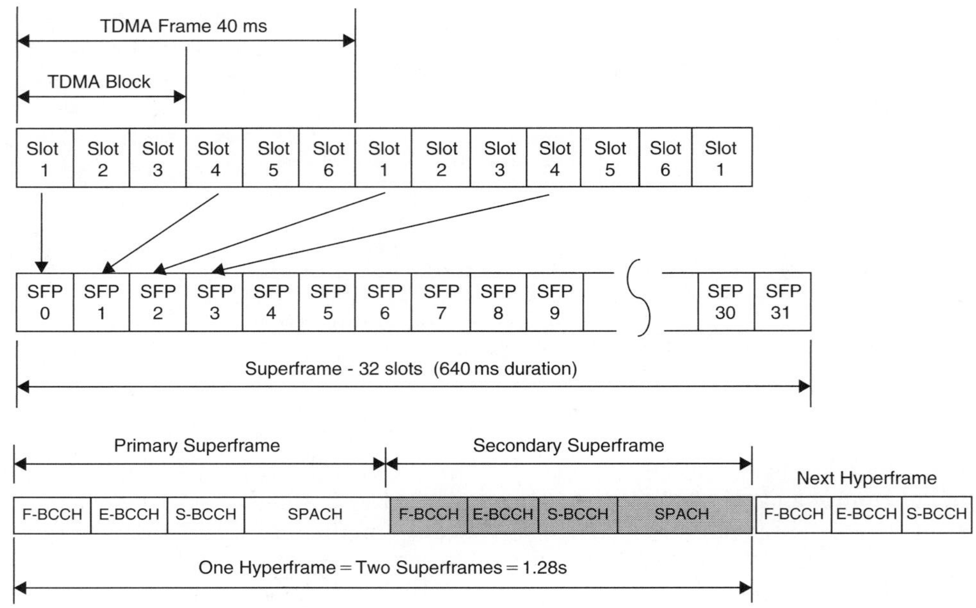

Figure 5: IS-136 frame, superframe, and hyperframe structure

before responding. In this event, the BS in the last known location area must page the MS. The MS may "sleep" in a low-powered state until a paging window appears, to conserve the battery charge. Following the receipt of a paging message, the MS must make radio access to the BS, where an exchange of messages via DCCH leads the MS to the correct DTC.

Mobile assisted handoff (MAHO) is a system in which the MS assists in the handoff decisions. IS-136 uses two types of channel quality information to determine handoff: signal strength of neighbor channels and an estimated bit error rate of the current channel. MS participation allows for reverse channel measurements that are not capable from the BS. The BS sends the MS a MAHO message containing a list of channels from up to twenty-four neighbor cells. During idle time slots, the MS measures the signal strength of these channels and continuously sends a channel strength report back to the BS. Since adjacent cells are approximately the same size, transmission delay and time adjustment can usually be avoided; a seamless handoff can typically be accomplished without losing coded speech. In reality, there is a brief interruption of the coded speech data in order to process handoff, about 0.2 s, but the missing data is interpolated by the speech coder.

THE OTHER 2G TDMA STANDARDS

2G technologies can be categorized into TDMA- and CDMA-based standards depending on the type of multiplexing used. In addition to IS-136, the main TDMA-based 2G standards are:

- GSM: originally from Europe but used worldwide
- PDC: used exclusively in Japan
- iDEN: used exclusively by Nextel in the United States

The GSM Standard

The GSM standard does not support dual-mode handset and backward compatibility. As a result, GSM has a much simpler design. Predating PCS in the United States, GSM has a version—digital cellular system 1800 (DCS 1800)—that operates at 1800 MHz, which uses less power and has greater capacity because more frequencies are available. Similar to IS-136, GSM uses a mix of FDMA and TDMA. Instead of 30 KHz, GSM divides frequency to 200 KHz channel spacing, forming 124 carriers in GSM 900 and 374 carriers in DCS 1800. Each carrier frequency is then further divided into eight slots using TDMA, with each burst lasting 0.58 ms and carrying 114 data bits, forming a 4.6ms frame with a 270 kbps gross bit rate per channel (ETSI 1989).

GSM uses Gaussian minimum shift keying (GMSK) for signal modulation. GMSK is a continuous phase modulation scheme with a constant envelope and narrow band. GMSK avoids linearity and frequency amplification requirements common in linear modulation schemes, such as Pi/4 DQPSK in IS-136. However, the DQPSK carries two bits in a symbol, making it twice as efficient as GMSK. Nevertheless, lower power efficiency in IS-136 is an important issue for mobile device regarding battery life. The GSM speech coder is based on the residually excited linear predictive (RELP) scheme, which is enhanced by including a long-term predictor. The coder provides 260 bits for a 20 ms block of speech at 13 kbps. Although the ACELP coder in IS-136 has better speech quality, RELP operates at a lower speech rate and has a lower delay (Garg and Sneed 1997).

Similar to IS-136, GSM has two types of channels: traffic channels (TCH) that transport speech and data, and control channels (CCH) that manage and administrate. Slot format for TCH is identical forward or reverse, and the time difference between transmit and receive must be

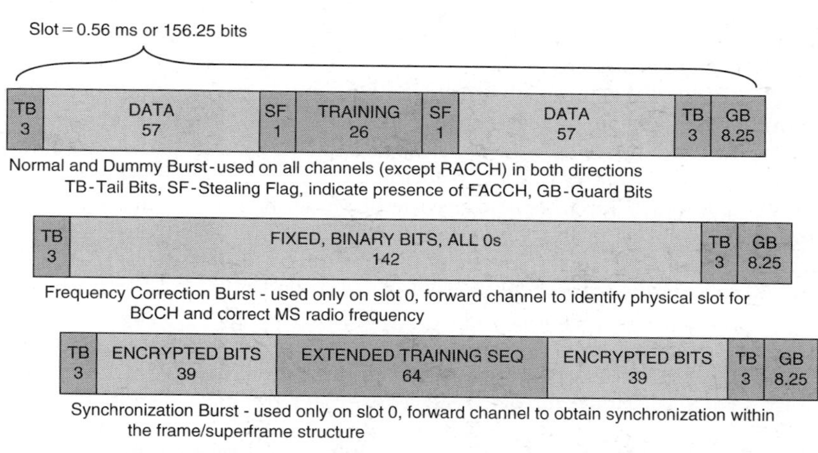

Figure 6: GSM channel structure

three time slots, which greatly simplifies its transceiver. GSM also uses frequency hopping to reduce the effects of co-channel interference, multipath, and fading. TCH are organized into a twenty-six–frame multiframe, with twenty-four used for traffic, one for SACCH, and one in reserve, with duration of exactly 120 ms (see Figure 6; numerical values refer to bits). Definitions of subchannels are as follows:

- Tail bits: used to help equalize data bits toward either end of the data stream
- Stealing flag: used to indicate a stolen data stream for control information
- Training sequence: used for equalization; eight different training sequences are used with low mutual cross-correlation, and the operator assigns a different one to neighboring cells for identification purposes
- Guard bits: bits between each time slot that keep data bursts separated

GSM logical channel definitions are as follows:

- Broadcast control channel (BCCH): continuous broadcasting to the MS
- Frequency correction channel (FCCH): used by the MS to synchronize the carrier
- Synchronization channel (SCH): used by the MS to synchronize time slot structure
- Paging channel (PCH): alerts the MS of incoming call
- Random access channel (RACH): SDCCH allocation requests from the MS
- Access grant channel (AGCH): allocates an SDCCH to the MS upon a RACH request
- Stand-alone dedicated control channel (SDCCH): negotiates services requested
- Fast associated control channel (FACCH): handover and frequency reassignments

There are four different types of transmission bursts in GSM: the normal burst, F burst for FCCH, S burst for SCH, and access burst for RACH. F burst and S burst have the same length but different structures than a normal burst. Access burst is shorter than the normal burst, with only seventy-seven data bits. The broadcast and common control channels are used for synchronization, exchange of system information, and setting up calls. These channels occupy slot 0 in a frame and cycle through every fifty-one frame times. If more control capacity is needed, slots 2, 4, and 6 can be used in the same carrier. Similar to the IS-136 hyperframe, GSM also organizes in multiframe structures. TCH and SACCHs are grouped into a twenty-six–frame multiframe, and CCHs are defined as a fifty-one–frame multiframe structure with duration of approximately 235 ms. The fifty-one frames are grouped into five sets of ten frames each, with one idle frame. Each set starts with a FCCH followed by a SCH. The remaining eight frames form two block of four. The first block of the first set is for BCCH, and the remaining nine blocks are for PCH and AGCH.

The steps involved in setting up calls are similar in all PCS systems. However, in IS-54/136, there was no original plan regarding mobile network switching; specific features are designed and added as required. In contrast, GSM was designed from the beginning with all of its network features prespecified.

The PDC Standard

PDC is a 2G cellular standard used exclusively in Japan; it is implemented in the 800 and 1500 MHz frequency bands. PDC uses a 25 KHz carrier with a variation of TDMA to implement three time slots, Pi/4-DQPSK modulation, achieving a bit rate of 11.2 kbps (ARIB 2003). PDC is the most spectrally efficient of the TDMA technologies, with six half-rate (or three full-rate) slots possible in a 25 KHz channel spacing, compared to three in 30 KHz for IS-136 and eight in 200 KHz for GSM. PDC has weak broadcast strength; this standard allows small, portable phones with light batteries at the expense of substandard voice quality. PDC also has problems maintaining the connection, particularly in enclosed spaces like elevators.

Along with the other cellular wireless standards, PDC can be developed along a gradual evolutionary path to the IMT-2000 standard. Japan is actually the first country to introduce 3G on a large commercial scale. NTT DoCoMo, Japan's dominant cellular operator with 45.4 million total customers and a 56 percent market share, rolled out its universal mobile telephone service (UMTS) network in late 2001. Japan now has nearly 14 million 3G users, compared with just a few hundred thousand in European countries such as Britain and Italy. Surveys projected that about 40 percent of Japanese subscribers would use 3G-only networks by 2005, and that 2G, PDC included, would be phased out in Japan by 2006 (Kane 2004).

The iDEN Standard

iDEN is another 2G wireless standard that uses TDMA, dividing the 25 KHz channel spacing into six 15 ms time slots. iDEN operates in 800, 900, and 1500 MHz bands and is based on GSM architecture. iDEN uses VSELP coders for voice compression and quadrature amplitude modulation (QAM) to deliver a 64 kbps data rate. QAM was chosen, in part, because it does not require adaptive equalization or other relatively expensive methods to correct for transmission path delays and rapidly changing signal strength that are common in mobile radio environments.

iDEN is a high-capacity digital trunked radio system. Conventional trunking systems define a control or traffic channel by specifying a set of inbound and outbound frequencies to a user. In iDEN, a single inbound/outbound frequency pair is shared among six users through TDMA. Each user transmits and receives only during its assigned time slot, such that the transmission from any given MS is a pulsed signal with a 1/6 duty cycle. The BS is able to transmit and receive during any of the six time slots. Each MS is assigned a unique channel designation, which is defined by a carrier number, which specifies the inbound/outbound frequency pair and a time-slot definition.

iDEN is a proprietary Motorola technology. Only Motorola makes iDEN phones, and only Motorola makes iDEN infrastructure equipment (Motorola 2000). Nextel is the largest U.S. operator of iDEN services. To provide high data rates for packet data, Nextel started to develop a 2.5G technology called WiDEN, but it is a technology with no clear path for 3G migration. Although Nextel has stated they will support iDEN through 2010, their merger with Sprint, which uses CDMA, has cast serious doubt over iDEN's future (Ankeny 2005).

TDMA AND THE MARCH TO 3G

As mobile application migrates from voice to data, technology for "continuous" packet switching is critical for 3G development. Currently, there are two 2.5G standards: general packet radio services (GPRS) for IS-136 and GSM, and CDMA/IS-95. GPRS enhances GSM by overlaying packet-switching architecture onto the current circuit-switched framework, while infrastructures such as channel structure and radio interface are preserved. Data is transmitted in the same 0.58ms burst, and modulation and encoding remain the same. Four consecutive GSM frames are aggregated to allow for higher-speed packet data transfers. In theory, GPRS enables mobile devices to connect to the Internet via a packet-switching network at speeds up to 171.2 kbps using eight time slots simultaneously (Buckingham 2000). GPRS also has a version for IS-136 that is structured similarly by aggregating IS-136 frames. However, the technology has not been widely adopted (Balachandran et al. 1999).

GPRS is considered the first step in the transition to 3G, positioned to be complementary to enhanced data rate for global evolution (EDGE). EDGE enhances the radio interface to GSM with 3*Pi/8 8-PSK modulation, enabling three bits per symbol. However, 8-PSK is more susceptible to noise and attenuation. Using eight time slots and a better filtering design, a data rate of 473.6 kbps can be acquired. EDGE and GSM signals can be transmitted on the same frequency, occupying different time slots, and both can use existing GSM equipment.

There are several competing 3G standards: UMTS as an upgrade for GSM, CDMA2000 as an upgrade for IS-95 PCS CDMA, and time-division synchronous code division multiple access (TD-SCDMA), as proposed in China (Chen, Fan, and Lu 2002). The ITU arbitrates between competing standards. It has developed a series of recommendations that define the key characteristics, which envision a worldwide common 3G interface and network. Although it does not dictate a channel or spectrum standard, ITU specifies that 3G should deliver data rates of 144 kbps in a mobile environment, 384 kbps in a pedestrian environment, and 2 Mbps in a fixed environment; both UMTS and CDMA2000 can meet these criteria (Passerini 2003).

UMTS requires paired 5 MHz frequency channels, four times as wide as the paired 1.25 MHz channels required for CDMA2000; thus, UMTS is also known as wideband CDMA (W-CDMA). It uses a combination of TDMA and CDMA technology. Similar to CDMA2000, UMTS uses variable-length spreading code with puncturing (Stallings 2002). Time-slot aggregation is also used with each frame 10 ms long, divided into sixteen time slots. By migrating to UMTS, operators will gain access to additional spectrums as well as greater capacity and expanded functionality of the new technology. Unfortunately, UMTS is currently deployed using the 1900 and 2100 MHz frequency band, and the 3G frequency auction in the United States is not scheduled until June 2006 (TechWeb 2004).

CONCLUSION

The standard 3G migration path for GSM is anticipated initially through GPRS and then UMTS. Operators may or may not deploy EDGE as an intermediary step. With regard to CDMA, whether using 800 MHz, 1900 MHz, or both, one can evolve to CDMA2000 using the current spectrum; all CDMA2000 handsets will be backward compatible. Although 3G migration path for GSM and CDMA operators are clear, the path is less certain for IS-136 because AT&T abandoned it in favor of GSM in November 2000. Currently, in the United States, Cingular/AT&T and TMobile use GSM/GPRS; Verizon and Sprint use CDMA.

Although CDMA offers better performance than GSM, there are 1.4 billion GSM subscribers—or 75 percent of cellular phone users—worldwide. With massive research and development efforts devoted to the GSM transition path and the expected economies of manufacturing scale over time, this premise alone may be a strong rationale for IS-136 operators to choose the GSM migration path.

The argument over whether CDMA or TDMA is a better technology may not be relevant. Similar to FDMA incorporating with TDMA in the IS-136 standard, newer technologies, like W-CDMA, will use CDMA, TDMA, and FDMA together to create standards built for high-speed data. Likewise, the news of TDMA IS-136's demise may also be premature. Some industry estimates assert that TDMA subscribers numbered 150 million by 2005, and TDMA technology is expected to survive another ten years. Whereas some TDMA operators are taking advantage of the changing global dynamics to offer higher wireless data rates through a GSM/GPRS overlay, TDMA will continue to prove its worth by bringing to operators large revenue streams that are critical to the funding of 3G deployment (Pearson 2001).

GLOSSARY

Authentication: The process of determining whether someone or something is, in fact, who or what it is declared to be

Base station (BS): A station in the mobile service that houses the transceiver. It defines a cell and handles the radio links with the mobile station.

Digital signal processing (DSP): Various techniques for improving the accuracy and reliability of digital communications.

Digitization: The process of converting information into a digital format, in which information is organized into discrete units of data called *bits*.

Encoding: The process of putting a sequence of characters into a specialized format for efficient transmission or storage. Decoding is the opposite process of converting an encoded format back into the original characters.

Encryption: The conversion of data into a form that cannot be easily understood by unauthorized people. *Decryption* is the process of converting encrypted data back into its original or clear form.

Frame: A complete unit of data transmitted between network points, usually containing a header and a trailer field that "frame" the data.

Handoff: In a mobile network, the radio links required are not permanently allocated for the duration of a call. Handoff is the switching of an ongoing call to a different channel or cell.

Mobile station (MS): A station in the mobile service intended to be used while in motion or during halts at unspecified points.

Modulation: The process of adding information to an electronic or optical signal carrier so that it can be sent over long distances.

Sleep mode: An energy-saving mode of operation in which all unnecessary components are shut down; common in many battery-operated devices.

Speech coder: A device that compresses digital representations of speech signals for the purpose of efficient transmission or storage.

CROSS REFERENCES

See *General Packet Radio Service (GPRS)*; *Global System for Mobile Communications (GSM)*.

REFERENCES

Ankeny, J. 2005. Sprint/Nextel merger casts doubt over iDEN's future. *Telephony Online*. http://telephonyonline.com/wireless/news/sprint_nextel_iden_021105/index.html (accessed November 15, 2005).

Association of Radio Industries and Businesses (ARIB). 2003. Personal digital cellular telecommunication system, RCR STD-27–1. http://www.arib.or.jp/english/html/overview/img/rcr_std-27_e.pdf (accessed November 15, 2005).

Balachandran, K., R. Ejzak, S. Nanda, S. Vitebskiy, and S. Seth. 1999. GPRS-136: High-rate packet data service for North American TDMA digital cellular systems. *IEEE Personal Communications*, June, pp. 35–47.

Buckingham, S. 2000. What is general packet radio service? *GSM World*. http://www.gsmworld.com/technology/gprs/intro.shtml (accessed November 15, 2005).

Chen, H., C. Fan, and W. Lu. 2002. China's perspectives on 3G mobile communications and beyond TD-SCDMA technology. *IEEE Personal Communications*, April, pp. 48–59.

European Telecommunications Standards Institute (ETSI). 1989. GSM specification. Global System for Mobile Communications, Series 01–12.

Federal Communications Commission (FCC). 1995. PCS auction update. News release. http://www.fcc.gov/Bureaus/Wireless/News_Releases/nrwl5010.txt (accessed November 8, 2005).

Garg, V., and E. Sneed. 1997. TDMA for North American PCS systems. *Bell Labs Technical Journal* (Summer): 209–20.

International Engineering Consortium (IEC). 2005a. Personal communication services: Web ProForum tutorials. http://www.iec.org/online/tutorials/pcs/.

———. 2005b. Global system for mobile communication: Web ProForum tutorials. http://www.iec.org/online/tutorials/gsm/.

Kane, Y. I. 2004. Analysis—Japan cell phone industry ready for banner 3G year. Forbes.com. http://www.forbes.com/technology/newswire/2004/01/16/rtr1213940.html (accessed November 15, 2005).

Motorola. 2000. iDEN technical overview. Release 9.1, Document #68P81095E55-E. Schaumburg, IL: Motorola, Inc.

Noll, M. 1999. *Introduction to telephones and telephone systems*. Norwood, MA: Artech House.

Passerini, R. 2003. International Mobile Telecommunications-2000 (IMT-2000). In *Proceedings of ITU-BDT Seminar on Network Evolution*, Sofia, Bulgaria, January.

Pearson, C. 2001. The power of TDMA-based technologies and the 3G evolution. Universal Wireless Communication Consortium, 3G Americas. http://www.3gsma.org/

pdfs/editorial_commentary_06_13_01.pdf (accessed November 15, 2005).

Stallings, W. 2002. *Wireless communications and networking*. Upper Saddle River, NJ: Prentice Hall.

TechWeb News. 2004. FCC plans auction of 3G spectrum. http://crn.com/sections/breakingnews/breakingnews.jhtml?articleId=56800120 (accessed November 15, 2005).

Telecommunications Industry Association (TIA). 1989. TIA/EIA/IS-54B cellular system dual-mode mobile station/base station compatibility standard.

———. 1995. TIA/EIA/IS-136 TDMA cellular/radio interface/mobile station/base station compatibility standard.

———. 1999. TIA/EIA-553 mobile station/base station compatibility specification.

Wikipedia. 2005. Time-division multiple access. http://en.wikipedia.org/wiki/Time_division_multiple_access 11/08/2005 (accessed November 15, 2005).

Carrier Sense Multiple Access Protocols

Wei Ye, *University of Southern California*

INTRODUCTION

Based on the characteristics of the physical layer and the communication medium, computer networks can be divided into two types: point-to-point connections and broadcast. In a broadcast network, *terminals* or *nodes,* share a common medium or channel. A key issue in such a network is *collision,* which results from two or more nodes sending packets at the same time in the common channel. The process of determining which node has the right to transmit in the channel at a given time is called *medium* (or *multiple*) *access control* (MAC). Therefore, the major task of MAC protocols is to avoid collisions so that nodes can efficiently share the channel. The MAC layer is normally considered as a sublayer of the data-link layer in the network protocol stack. A MAC or link layer packet is also referred to as a *frame.* Thus, we will use both these terms interchangeably throughout this chapter.

A common approach to collision avoidance is to divide the common channel into multiple distinct subchannels and assign or schedule interfering nodes to different subchannels. We refer to protocols using this approach as *scheduled protocols.* They are also referred to as *allocation-based protocols* in the literature. Common examples include *time division multiple access* (TDMA), frequency division multiple access, and code division multiple access, which divide the channel by time, frequency, and orthogonal codes, respectively. These protocols are widely used in cellular communication systems (Rappaport 1996). For example, in traditional TDMA, time is divided into frames, and each frame consists of a fixed number of slots. Each slot is assigned to a node, so that different nodes transmit at different time slots. Such a fixed pre-allocation scheme is efficient in channel utilization when all nodes have packets to send. However, it becomes wasteful when only a few nodes actually have data. To improve channel utilization in such cases, advanced schemes are required to dynamically allocate slots.

Another class of MAC protocols is based on *contention.* Rather than pre-allocating transmissions, nodes compete for a single and shared channel, thereby resulting in probabilistic coordination. Collision may happen during the contention procedure in such systems. The first class of contention-based MAC protocols is ALOHA (Abramson 1970, 1985), which has two basic variants: pure ALOHA and slotted ALOHA. In pure ALOHA (Abramson 1970), a node simply transmits a packet when the packet is generated. Packets that collide are discarded and would be retransmitted later. Pure ALOHA has a low throughput because nodes essentially make no effort to avoid collision when they initiate new transmissions. Slotted ALOHA improves the throughput by dividing time into slots and only allowing new transmissions at the beginning of each slot. The duration of each slot is exactly the packet transmission time, assuming all packets have the same length. Collision probability is reduced because new packets generated in the current slot will be transmitted in the next slot and thus will not collide with an ongoing transmission in the current slot.

Carrier sense multiple access (CSMA) (Kleinrock and Tobagi 1975) is another family of contention-based protocols. The basic idea of CSMA is listening before transmitting. The purpose of listening is to detect whether the medium is busy, an ability also known as *carrier sense.* Before a node starts a new transmission, it listens to the channel to detect possible ongoing transmissions. If a busy channel is detected, then the node delays channel access (also known as *backoff*) for a random duration, after which it again repeats the above procedure. However, if the channel is idle, the node then transmits the packet. Because of this conservative collision avoidance procedure, CSMA is able to achieve much better throughput than ALOHA. In the next section we will discuss several basic CSMA protocols and give detailed performance comparison with ALOHA protocols.

Today, CSMA is one of the most widely used MAC protocols in modern computer networks, and significant improvements have been made to make CSMA more efficient and robust. The first example is Ethernet (IEEE Computer Society 2000). Almost all desktop and laptop computers are equipped with Ethernet today. The first improvement that Ethernet made to CSMA was collision detection, allowing nodes to quickly discover collisions while transmitting. To reduce the probability of persistent collisions, Ethernet also introduced the binary exponential backoff algorithm that dynamically increases the backoff window size on repeated collisions. We will discuss these improvements below under "CSMA in Ethernet."

CSMA is also the most popular medium access mechanism employed in wireless networks. Similar to Ethernet, WiFi or IEEE 802.11 (IEEE Computer Society 1999) devices can be seen on almost every laptop or handheld computer. Because of the complexity of wireless communication, more enhancements have been made beyond Ethernet. For example, as we will discuss in the section titled "Radio Communication and Related Issues," the hidden terminal problem is a major issue in wireless networks. In IEEE 802.11, the collision avoidance technique is developed to handle the hidden terminal problem. In "CSMA Enhancements for Wireless Networks," we will discuss major CSMA enhancements for wireless networks.

Recently, CSMA has gained strong attention in wireless sensor networks. A *sensor network* is a network of embedded computers equipped with sensors and short-range radios. There are numerous potential applications for sensor networks, such as habitat monitoring, distributed tracking, and smart space. Most sensor nodes operate on batteries, so energy becomes a critical resource for these nodes. CSMA is widely used in sensor networks mainly because of its flexibility and robustness to node density and topology changes. However, pure CSMA-based protocols are not energy efficient. For example, they require nodes to always listen to the channel, which is intensely energy-consuming. A lot of recent work has focused on improving the energy efficiency in CSMA protocols. We will discuss these new techniques as well as other CSMA improvement in the section titled "CSMA in Sensor Networks."

BASIC CSMA PROTOCOLS

This section describes several basic CSMA protocols that were first presented by Kleinrock and Tobagi (1975). These protocols help us understand the basic concepts in CSMA and constitute the foundation of various advanced CSMA protocols that are widely used in practical data networks today.

These basic CSMA protocols were developed for the packet radio system. The radio channel is shared by a group of nodes, where all of them can hear each other. When a node starts transmitting, another node is able to detect the carrier after the signal propagates from the sender to the receiver. Assume the propagation delay, denoted by τ, is miniscule compared to the packet transmission time.

The first basic CSMA, called *nonpersistent CSMA*, works as follows:

1. Sense the carrier.
2. If the channel is idle, transmit the packet immediately.
3. If the channel is busy, reschedule transmission at a later time according to a randomly distributed delay function.

When scheduled retransmission time arrives, the node repeats the above process.

Compared to the nonpersistent CSMA, another variant named *1-persistent CSMA* is more aggressive in transmission. It works as follows:

1. Sense the carrier.
2. If the channel is idle, transmit the packet immediately.
3. If the channel is busy, wait and monitor the channel until it becomes idle, and then transmit the packet (with probability 1).

Because of the aggressive retransmission scheme, a collision will occur with probability 1 when two or more nodes have packets to send at the end of the current transmission.

A more general scheme is to replace the retransmission probability one with a parameter p, therefore named as *p-persistent CSMA,* via the following process:

1. Sense the carrier.
2. If the channel is idle, transmit the packet with probability p, or delay for τ seconds (the propagation delay) with probability $1 - p$. If the packet is delayed, repeat from step 1 at the end of the delay.
3. If the channel is busy, reschedule transmission to a later time according to a randomly distributed delay function.

We can see that all the above CSMA protocols require that a node first performs carrier sense when starting a new transmission. They differ in how they act after the channel is detected idle or busy. When we describe the above protocols, we assume that a node can start the CSMA process at any time. There is also a "slotted" version of these protocols in which the time axis is divided into slots with the size of τ seconds for each slot. In the slotted CSMA, all nodes are synchronized and are forced to start their CSMA process at the beginning of a slot.

To gain a better understanding of these basic CSMA approaches, we next present some performance comparison of the above protocols and the ALOHA protocol. These results were obtained by Kleinrock and Tobagi (1975). For detailed performance analysis, readers are referred to that paper.

The following assumptions are made to simplify analysis. There is no channel noise and all corrupted packets are the result of collisions. All packets are of constant length, and the packet transmission time is T. The propagation delay τ is identical for all transmitter-receiver pairs, and τ is much smaller than T. The ratio of τ and T is denoted by $a = \tau/T$. In slotted ALOHA, the slot size is T, whereas in slotted CSMA, the slot size is τ. The time needed for the node to detect the carrier is negligible. The network traffic consists of an infinite number of nodes that collectively form an independent Poisson source.

We are primarily interested in the *throughput,* which measures how many data units (bits or packets) can be transmitted in a unit time. If we can magically schedule all transmissions with no gaps and collisions, then the channel will be fully utilized and the throughput (in terms of bits per second) will be the same as the channel bandwidth. The realized throughput normalized to the channel

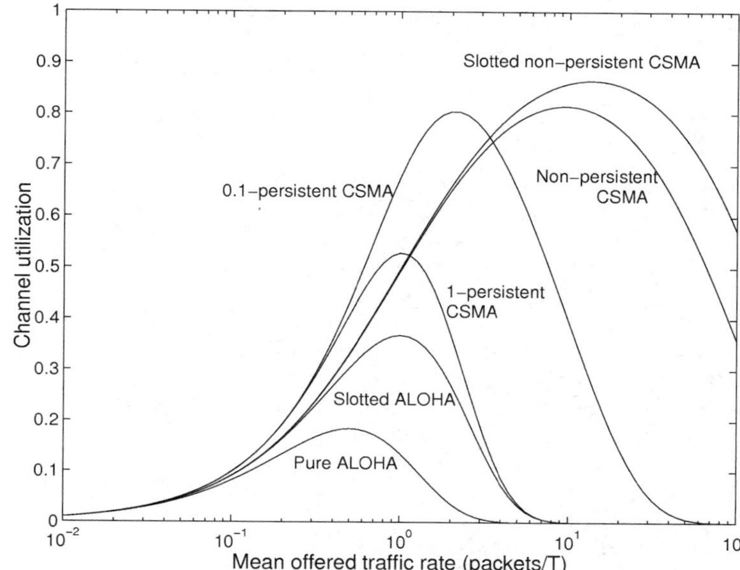

Figure 1: Channel utilization of ALOHA and basic CSMA protocols when the propagation delay is extremely small (a = 0.01) (Kleinrock and Tobagi 1975)

bandwidth is called *channel utilization*. The throughput usually changes as the offered load changes. The maximum achievable throughput of a MAC protocol is called the *capacity* of the channel under that protocol.

Figure 1 shows the channel utilization, or normalized throughput, of the ALOHA and basic CSMA protocols, with the varying offered traffic load when $a = 0.01$. We can see that the pure ALOHA has the lowest channel utilization because of its most aggressive transmission scheme. Slotted ALOHA is better than the pure ALOHA because it reduces the vulnerable interval (i.e., the maximum interval that two packets can overlap) from $2T$ to T. CSMA protocols are in general much better than ALOHA. The conservative approach of listening before transmitting is able to avoid many possible collisions. Finally, as a quantitative comparison, let us look at the maximum channel utilization—that is, the capacity of each protocol. Among the basic CSMA protocols, the slotted nonpersistent CSMA achieves the highest capacity of 0.857. In comparison, the pure and slotted ALOHA can only achieve the capacities of 0.184 and 0.368, respectively.

It should be noted that the above results are obtained when the propagation delay is extremely small—that is, $a = \tau/T = 0.01$. The performance of CSMA protocols will decrease when the propagation delay increases because it takes a longer time (τ) to perform carrier sense. When $\tau = T$, even the pure ALOHA achieves higher capacity than the nonpersistent CSMA. For a detailed comparison, the readers can refer to Kleinrock and Tobagi (1975).

CSMA IN ETHERNET

Ethernet is the most widely used *local area network* (LAN) technology today. It was developed by Xerox's Palo Alto Research Center and standardized by the Institute of Electrical and Electronics Engineers (IEEE) through its 802.3 standard (IEEE Computer Society 2000). Ethernet employs an extended version of the CSMA protocol, named *CSMA with collision detection* (CSMA/CD).

The original Ethernet (Metcalfe and Boggs 1976) uses a coaxial cable to connect all computers, as shown in Figure 2. It forms a *bus topology* in which all nodes (computers) directly share the same transmission cable or medium. Any packet that is sent by one node can be received by all nodes on the network. In other words, the transmission medium is a broadcast or shared medium.

Another type of Ethernet connection uses unshielded twisted pair cables with hubs or switches. This Ethernet implementation is most widely used today. In such a case, the hubs or switches form a *tree topology* in which computers are attached at the leaves of the tree. With the help of hubs or switches, computers attached to the network

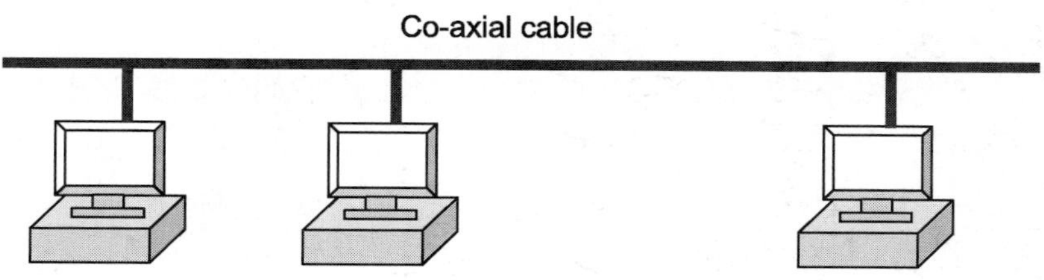

Figure 2: An Ethernet uses a coaxial cable to connect all computers

can still directly talk to each other. For example, hubs retransmit received packets to all of the attached ports so that any packet will propagate to the whole network.

Collision Detection

As described in the previous section, collision happens in the shared medium when two or more nodes transmit at the same time. In Ethernet, transmitting a packet will generate a current in the cable with a modulated signal that reflects the bits in the packet. When two nodes transmit simultaneously, they drive the cable in different ways, resulting in a mixed signal that is indistinguishable.

Ethernet employs CSMA as its basic MAC protocol and adds the enhancement on collision detection. CSMA requires nodes to listen before transmit. The process of listening detects whether there is a signal (carrier) in the cable (medium) and is therefore called *carrier sense.* When the carrier is detected, a node defers its transmission until the medium becomes idle.

Although the basic CSMA avoids many collisions, it is not able to eliminate all of them. Figure 3 shows an example of collision between nodes A and C. In the example, both nodes started carrier sense at about the same time. However, node A finished its carrier sense a little earlier than C, and it started transmitting because the channel was idle. As a result of the propagation delay, it takes a little time for A's signal to reach C. Unfortunately, just before A's signal reaches C, C has finished its carrier sense and started sending its own packet. Therefore, collision occurs when two nodes happen to start their transmission at about the same time—that is, the difference of their transmission start times is smaller than the propagation delay between the two nodes.

In Ethernet, it is possible for a node—for example, node A in Figure 3—to detect the collision while it is transmitting. To do so, a node needs to listen to the medium while transmitting. It compares what it sends to what it receives. If the two versions do not match, then collision is detected. Figure 3 shows that node A potentially has to wait for the round-trip time between A and C before it can detect the collision. To reliably detect collisions, Ethernet requires a minimum packet length that has a transmission time that corresponds to the round-trip time between two nodes with the largest allowed distance on the network. When a node detects a collision, it does not terminate its transmission immediately. Instead, it keeps sending additional bits as a jam signal, allowing all transmitting nodes to detect the collision. When all nodes detect the collision, they can prepare for the next round of contention by adjusting their backoff time, as detailed in the next section.

Binary Exponential Backoff

Now we describe the complete CSMA/CD procedure for a node to transmit a packet on Ethernet. All nodes on the Ethernet keep monitoring the physical medium for traffic. They cannot transmit when the medium is busy. When the medium becomes idle, nodes continue to defer for a proper interframe (interpacket) space. The deferral is performed by using a timer.

When a node initiates a new transmission, it checks the current carrier sense result and the deferral timer. If the medium is idle and the deferral timer is not started, the node will send immediately. If the medium is busy or the deferral timer is started, the node defers its transmission. It will send when the deferral timer fires. During transmission, it performs collision detection. If collision occurs, it will try to resend the packet after a backoff period.

The length of the backoff period increases as the number of retransmission attempts increases according to an algorithm called *binary exponential backoff* (BEB). BEB was first described by Metcalfe and Boggs (1976) and later standardized by IEEE 802.3 (IEEE Computer Society 2000). Let us consider the nth retransmission attempt. First, a backoff window is determined as 2^k, where $k = min(n, 10)$. The backoff window consists of 2^k time slots. Then a time slot r is chosen as a uniformly distributed random integer within $(0, 2^k)$. The actual backoff time is $r \times slotTime$, where *slotTime* is the duration of each slot. The value of n starts with a minimum number. Every time the transmission attempt fails, the node increments n by 1, which effectively doubles the backoff window. Therefore, the backoff window size will exponentially increase on repeated collisions until n reaches 10. The backoff algorithm effectively avoids persistent collisions on retransmissions. However, because it gives higher priority to new transmissions than retries, fairness may become an issue in some applications.

In summary, Ethernet is the most widely used LAN technology. It employs CSMA/CD as its basic MAC protocol. The major extensions of CSMA/CD to the basic CSMA are the collision detection and binary exponential backoff. Although the importance of CSMA is first exemplified by the widely adopted Ethernet technology, the collision problem is largely reduced in the later Ethernet that utilizes switches. Compared to hubs, a switch "learns" about destination hosts from the packets it relays and thus can reduce the range of flooding. In contrast to wired networks, research on CSMA has been significantly boosted in wireless networks, largely because of the complexity of the wireless medium. We next review CSMA in wireless networks.

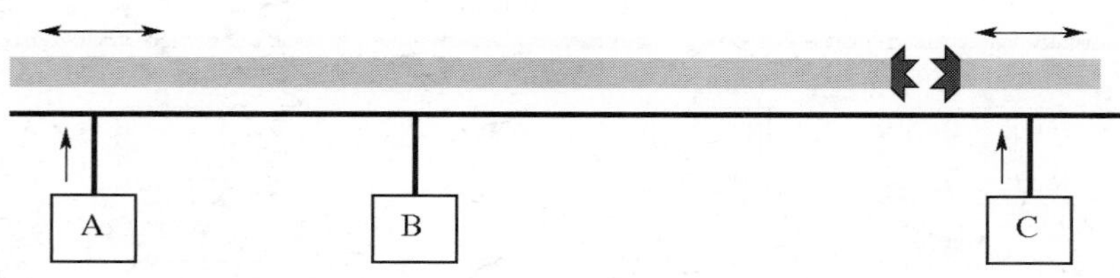

Figure 3: A collision example on Ethernet; node A sends first, but node C starts sending before it detects A's transmission

CSMA IN WIRELESS NETWORKS

Wireless networking is widely used today, mainly because of its easy deployment and convenient mobility. Popular examples include WiFi, Bluetooth, and ZigBee networks. A WiFi network is also known as a *wireless local area network*, standardized as IEEE 802.11 (IEEE Computer Society 1999). Bluetooth is designed for wireless personal area networks, and its specification is the foundation of the IEEE 802.15.1 standard (Bluetooth, undated; IEEE Computer Society 2002). ZigBee mainly targets low-rate, low-power sensor networks, and its MAC and physical layer are standardized in IEEE 802.15.4 (ZigBee Alliance, undated; IEEE Computer Society 2003). Many wireless networks adopt CSMA as their basic MAC protocol. However, different extensions have been proposed to enhance the basic CSMA protocol. Before we describe these extensions, we first look at the characteristics of radio communication and related issues to MAC protocols.

Radio Communication and Related Issues

Wireless networks have some characteristics that are different than wired networks. Understanding these characteristics helps us understand various enhancements to the basic CSMA for wireless networks. First, radio devices normally work in the half-duplex mode because the transmitter and receiver share the same radio frequency front end. If a radio turns on both of its transmitter and receiver, what enters the receiver is the signal from its own transmitter. For this reason, the transmitter and receiver do not work at the same time. When a radio is turned into transmit mode, it is not able to receive signals from other nodes. As a result, a normal radio does not have the collision detection capability as the node in Ethernet.

The second characteristic of wireless networks is that each node only has a limited transmission range. In Ethernet, packets can reach the whole network either directly or with the help of repeaters, hubs, or switches. The actual transmission range of a radio is determined by its transmission power, channel noise, and interference level as well as by the receiver's sensitivity. The limited radio range implies that CSMA will fail if two nodes cannot hear each other.

Third, collisions happen on receivers when two or more packets with comparable strength arrive at the receiver simultaneously. In this case, the receiver is not able to correctly receive any of these packets. It may completely miss both packets or receive one with errors. If two nodes cannot directly hear each other, then their concurrent transmissions may still cause collisions on some nodes that can hear both of them. Another implication is that collision depends not only on when the two nodes transmit but also on their propagation delays to reach a receiver. A third factor is the signal strength. If two packets arrive at the receiver with largely different strengths, they may not necessarily cause collision. The stronger signal can *capture* the receiver and make it treat the weaker signal as noise. The effect of channel capturing by strong signals may affect the performance of CSMA protocols (Ware et al. 2000) but can also be exploited to reduce collisions (Nadeem 2005; Whitehouse et al. 2005).

Finally, the link quality (in terms of packet error rate) varies largely between nodes at different distances and actual locations (Woo, Tong, and Culler 2003). In general, link quality decreases as the distance between nodes increases. However, there is a large area after a certain distance that a receiver cannot reliably receive packets from a transmitter, but the transmitter's signal is strong enough to collide with other transmissions. This area is known as the *gray area* (Zhao and Govindan 2003) primarily because of multipath effects and interfering signals. The gray area indicates that the radio's interference range can be much larger than the actual packet reception range.

The above characteristics imply that CSMA faces more challenges in wireless networks than in wired networks. A major problem in wireless networks is the *hidden terminal* problem (Tobagi and Kleinrock 1975), which arises in multihop networks. Figure 4 illustrates the problem on a two-hop network with three nodes. Suppose nodes A, B, and C can only hear from their immediate neighbors. When node A is sending to B, node C is not aware of this transmission, even if it keeps listening to the channel. Because its carrier sense still indicates that the medium is idle, node C can start transmitting now. Unfortunately, such transmission will collide with A's transmission at the receiving node B. Node A and C are said to be *hidden* to each other; their concurrent transmissions will cause collisions at nodes that can hear both of them. The basic CSMA is not capable of solving the hidden terminal problem because each node only has limited transmission range.

Another related problem is called the *exposed terminal problem*, as shown in Figure 5. In the example, node B

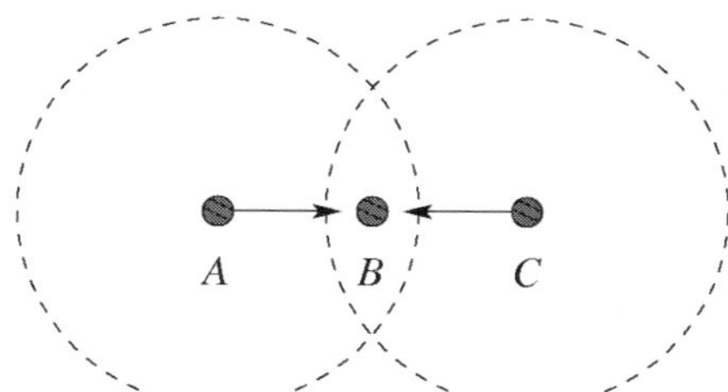

Figure 4: The hidden terminal problem: nodes A and C are hidden to each other. Dotted circles represent their transmission range. When they send at the same time, their packets collide at node B.

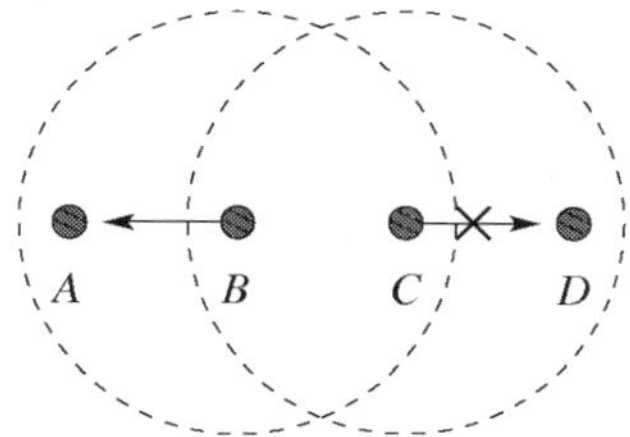

Figure 5: The exposed terminal problem. When node B sends to node A, C is exposed to the transmission. C's carrier sense does not allow it to send to D, even though such transmission does not interfere with A's reception.

is sending data to A. Again, we assume that each node can only hear its immediate neighbors. During B's transmission, node C's carrier sense will always detect a busy medium. Therefore, node C is said to be *exposed* to B's transmission, and it cannot send any packets because of the busy medium. However, if we look at node D, it is an immediate neighbor of node C but cannot hear node B. In this case, node C is actually able to send packets to D because C's transmission can be correctly received by D. More important, C's transmission will not interfere with B's current transmission because node A is too far to receive C's packets. The major problem of the exposed terminal is not collision, but reduced channel utilization.

Note that in Figures 4 and 5 we have adopted an idealized propagation model, which represents the transmission range as a circle. If a node is within the circle, it is able to receive all or most packets from the sender. If a node is outside the circle, it basically cannot receive anything. In reality, the radio propagation is much more complicated, and the transmission range is largely irregular. Moreover, the interference range is much larger than the range that packets can be correctly received (Zhao and Govindan 2003). As a result, two-hop neighbors, such as nodes A and C in Figure 5, may still have enough interference to each other when they transmit. Therefore, it is difficult to say whether node C can send during B's transmission in a real-world network. To be conservative, node C should keep silent. Another reason for node C not to send to D is that any reply message from D, such as an *acknowledgment* (ACK) message, will surely collide at node C with B's transmission. In brief, real-world protocols are less concerned about the exposed terminal problem but deal more with the hidden terminal problem.

CSMA Enhancements for Wireless Networks

This section describes some important enhancements to CSMA for wireless networks. The first one is *CSMA with collision avoidance* (CSMA/CA). Karn first described CSMA/CA to address the hidden terminal problem, and mentioned its use in the Apple Localtalk network (Karn 1990). CSMA/CA was later adopted by the wireless LAN standard, IEEE 802.11 (IEEE Computer Society 1999). The basic mechanism in CSMA/CA is to establish a brief handshake between a sender and a receiver before the sender transmits data. The handshake starts from the sender by sending a short *request-to-send* (RTS) packet to the intended receiver. The receiver then replies with a *clear-to-send* (CTS) packet. The sender starts sending data after it receives the CTS packet. The purpose of RTS-CTS handshake is to announce the following transmission to the neighboring nodes so that they will delay their potential transmissions. In the example of Figure 4, although node C cannot hear the RTS from A, it can hear the CTS from B. If a node overhears an RTS or CTS destined to other nodes, it delays its own transmission. CSMA/CA does not completely eliminate the hidden terminal problem, but now the collisions are mainly on RTS/CTS packets. Because these packets are normally much shorter than data packets, the cost of collisions can be largely reduced.

In his paper, Karn also proposed an enhancement to CSMA/CA, naming his protocol *multiple access with collision avoidance* (MACA) (Karn 1990). MACA added a duration field in both RTS and CTS packets to indicate the duration of the following data transmission so that other nodes know how long they should back off.

Multiple access with collision avoidance for wireless (MACAW) (Bharghavan et al. 1994) proposed further improvements over MACA. It added an ACK packet after each data packet. If a sender fails to receive an ACK after sending data, it will restart the CSMA process and try to resend the data. The ACK-retry process allows rapid error recovery at the link layer. Otherwise, such recovery has to be handled by the transport or application layer, which can be much slower. MACAW also demonstrated the unfairness of the BEB algorithm using two nodes generating heavy traffic. It shows that eventually only one node transmits at the channel capacity, and the other one is completely backed off. A major reason is that nodes do not share the information about the current contention level. Another reason results from the rapid change of contention window size. To rectify this problem, MACAW proposes a scheme to exchange backoff counter values in transmitted packets, as well as a gentle window adjustment algorithm with *multiplicative increase and linear decrease* (MILD).

The wireless LAN standard, IEEE 802.11, has adopted most of these features in CSMA/CA, MACA, and MACAW (except backoff value exchange and MILD) in its *distributed coordination function* (DCF). The standard has also made various other enhancements, such as virtual carrier sense, binary exponential backoff, and fragmentation support (IEEE Computer Society 1999). Virtual carrier sense is also referred to as the *network allocation vector* (NAV) in the standard. The NAV is a timer that keeps track of current channel states according to the duration information in the RTS and CTS packets. Whenever a node receives a new RTS or CTS, if the duration value is larger than the NAV timer, the node updates the NAV timer to reflect the new state of channel usage. *Virtual carrier sense* means that a node checks the NAV value to determine if the medium is busy. The medium is determined as idle only when both virtual and physical carrier sense results indicate idle.

Figure 6 illustrates the basic DCF procedure in IEEE 802.11. When a node has a new packet to send, it performs both virtual and physical carrier sense. If the medium is busy, as shown in the figure, the node defers its access until the end of the transmission (suppose the node gets a correct packet) plus an additional time called *DCF interframe space* (DIFS). During the deferral, the node keeps monitoring the channel. If the channel is still idle at the end of the DIFS, the node starts a random backoff procedure by randomly selecting a time slot in the contention window. The same BEB algorithm in Ethernet (see "Binary Exponential Backoff") is adopted to adjust the contention window size, despite its well-known fairness issue (Bharghavan et al. 1994). During backoff, the node keeps sensing the channel. If the medium keeps idle until the end of the backoff time, the node starts transmitting. If the medium becomes busy at any time during the deferral and random backoff,

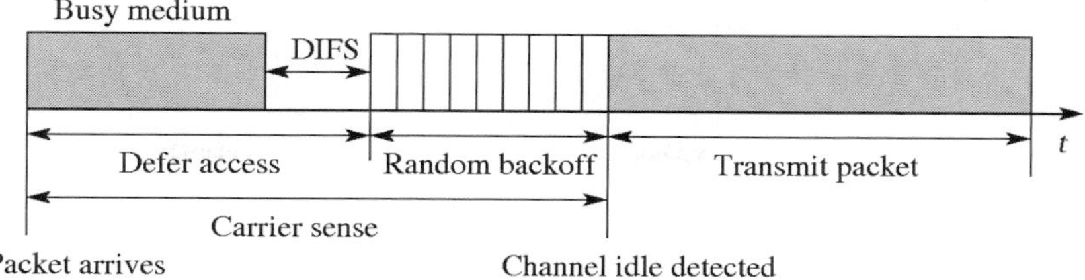

Figure 6: Packet transmission procedure in IEEE 802.11 DCF (DIFS = DCF interframe space)

the node suspends its backoff timer until the channel is sensed idle again.

DCF is the fundamental medium access method in IEEE 802.11, and it can be used with or without an access point. An ad hoc network (without access point) only runs DCF. An infrastructure network (with an access point) can optionally implement the *point coordination function* (PCF), which is a contention-free MAC with a polling mechanism that the access point uses to interrogate each node for possible transmissions. PCF and DCF normally coexist in an infrastructure network.

CSMA IN SENSOR NETWORKS

Sensor networks are a special class of wireless networks in which most nodes are equipped with embedded processors, short-range radios, and various sensors (Hill et al. 2000). A sensor network normally consists of a large number of such nodes that organize themselves into a multihop wireless network. The nodes collaborate to perform a common sensing and data-collection task. A major difference of a sensor network to a wireless LAN is that sensor nodes are highly resource constrained. They have extremely limited computing power, memory size, and energy source (usually batteries).

CSMA protocols are widely adopted in ad hoc and sensor networks, largely because of their robustness and flexibility to the changes of topology and node density. Various protocols have been proposed to improve the performance of CSMA used in traditional data networks. We next review these new approaches. We will start with energy efficiency, which is the most active area in recent CSMA research.

Improving Energy Efficiency

Traditional MAC protocols, including CSMA, usually focus on throughput or fairness. In sensor networks, energy is a critical resource, so improving energy efficiency in MAC protocols becomes a primary concern. The major reason is that the energy consumed in communication is usually much higher than that in computing. There are four major sources of energy waste in MAC protocols (Ye, Heidemann, and Estrin 2002): collision, control overhead, overhearing, and idle listening.

Collision wastes energy because all senders and the receiver spend energy on a corrupted, useless packet. *Control packets* are the overhead of energy consumption because they do not directly convey data. A third source of energy waste is *overhearing* packets that are destined to other nodes. The basic approach to avoid overhearing is to put a node into sleep when its neighbors are transmitting unrelated packets. *Power-aware multiaccess protocol with signaling* (Singh and Raghavendra 1998) does this with a separate control channel. *Sensor-MAC* (S-MAC) (Ye, Heidemann, and Estrin 2002) achieves the same goal in a single channel by utilizing RTS and CTS packets. *Idle listening* is the last major source of energy waste. It happens when the radio is listening to the channel to receive possible data or monitoring the channel activity. Reducing idle listening has been a major research topic in recent CSMA-based protocols. The rest of this subsection is devoted to this important new CSMA improvement.

Most traditional CSMA protocols keep the radio in idle state to listen to the channel when a node has no data to send. In many short-range radios, idle state consumes about the same power as it is actually receiving data. For example, on the Mica2 Mote (Crossbow Technology, undated), the idle:receive:send ratios for radio power draw are 1:1:1.4. Idle listening can dominate the energy cost in networks with infrequent data transmission and long idle time.

The basic technique to reduce idle listening is to put the radio into low duty cycles. In doing so, a node sleeps for a relatively long time and only wakes up periodically to listen for possible traffic. As an example, the Chipcon radio used on a Mica2 Mote only consumes 3μW in sleep mode (Chipcon, undated), three orders of magnitude less than that in idle or receive mode. Low duty cycle MAC protocols can significantly reduce idle listening while still providing the abstraction that the network is always available. The major trade-off is to conserve energy at the cost of increased latency (or reduced throughput).

There are two major approaches for low duty cycle operations: scheduled and asynchronous listening. In the scheduled scheme, neighboring nodes exchange their sleep and listen schedules and try to maintain synchronization. An example is the IEEE 802.11 *power-save* (PS) mode, where nodes sleep if they have no data to send, but need to wake up periodically to receive beacons. Following each beacon, there is an *ad hoc traffic indication message* (ATIM) window in which all nodes remain awake. If a node has a packet to send, it first sends an ATIM packet to notify the receiver and then sends data. This PS mode is designed for a single-hop network in which all nodes can hear each other. Directly applying it to a multihop network may lead to problems such as clock synchronization, neighbor discovery, and network partitioning (Tseng, Hsu, and Hsieh 2002).

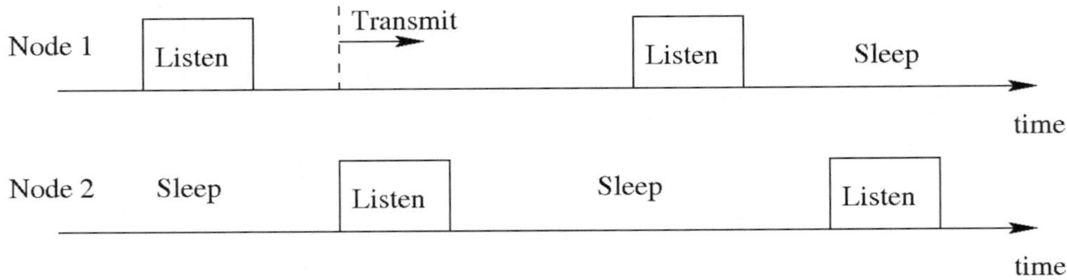

Figure 7: S-MAC allows multiple schedules for multihop networks

S-MAC is the first CSMA protocol with sleep and listen schedules designed for multihop sensor networks (Ye, Heidemann, and Estrin 2002; Ye, Heidemann, and Estrin 2004). S-MAC allows nodes to select different schedules but encourages them to follow a common one (possibly using the global schedule algorithm—see Li, Ye, and Heidemann 2005). Neighboring nodes share their schedule information, no matter whether they follow the same or a different schedule. Therefore, when a node has a packet to send, it is able to schedule its transmission at the exact moment when the receiver is listening, as shown in Figure 7. To keep schedule synchronization, each node periodically broadcasts its schedule as a synchronization (SYNC) packet. *Timeout MAC* (T-MAC) (Van Dam and Langendoen 2003) adopts the same scheduling mechanism but improves S-MAC by reducing the wakeup duration controlled by an adaptive timer.

The major advantage of scheduled listening is the efficient transmission. Its potential drawback is the overhead of schedule synchronization. However, as shown in Ye, Silva, and Heidemann (2006), such overhead can be especially small if optimal parameters are used.

In asynchronous MACs, nodes sleep and wake up on their own without explicit coordination. A promising asynchronous technique is *low-power listening* (LPL) presented in *WiseMAC* (El-Hoiydi et al. 2003) and *Berkeley media access control* (B-MAC) (Polastre, Hill, and Culler 2004). In LPL, nodes wake up briefly to check channel activity without actually receiving data. We call this action *channel sampling* or *channel polling*. If the channel is idle, the node immediately goes back to sleep. Otherwise it stays awake to receive data. Although nodes regularly poll the channel with a predefined polling period, they still wake up asynchronously. To wake up a receiver, a sender uses a long *preamble* (as long as the polling period) before each message, which is guaranteed to intersect with the receiver's polling time, as illustrated in Figure 8.

Channel polling minimizes the cost on listening because checking channel activity uses the minimum time when a node is active. Compared to S-MAC and T-MAC, channel polling is more than ten times shorter than their listening windows. Therefore, LPL consumes much less energy than S-MAC or T-MAC in lightly loaded networks. However, with asynchronous wakeup, polling efficiency is gained at the much greater cost of transmissions. Such cost can become prohibitive for some event-triggered applications.

Several approaches have been proposed to improve LPL. WiseMAC (El-Hoiydi et al. 2003) can reduce the preamble length after an initial unicast packet with a long preamble. The receiver piggybacks its next polling time in the ACK packet, allowing the sender to send the next packet with a short preamble. A similar optimization is possible in B-MAC (Polastre, Hill, and Culler 2004) for messages consisting of a sequence of packets. *Uncertainty-driven B-MAC* (UB-MAC) (Ganeriwal et al. 2005) reduces the long preambles by precisely estimating the clock drift between packet transmissions. UB-MAC requires high-precision time synchronization, which is CPU intensive. *X-MAC* (Buettner et al. 2006) embeds the destination address in the preamble, so that a node can quickly determine whether it is the intended receiver without waiting for the whole preamble. The receiver can further interrupt the sender's preamble transmission by sending back a brief ACK message. It should be noted that all the above improvement schemes are limited to unicast packets. Because nodes asynchronously poll the channel, broadcast packets have to use long preambles in order to be captured by all nodes.

Scheduled channel polling MAC (SCP-MAC) (Ye, Silva, and Heidemann 2006) takes a different approach by combining the strengths of scheduling and channel polling. SCP synchronizes the polling times of neighboring nodes, as shown in Figure 9. When sending data, a node

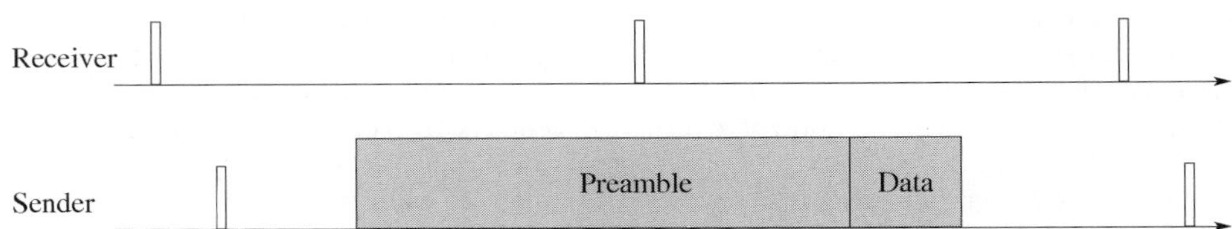

Figure 8: In LPL, nodes poll channel asynchronously. When transmitting, a node sends a long preamble to wake up the receiver(s).

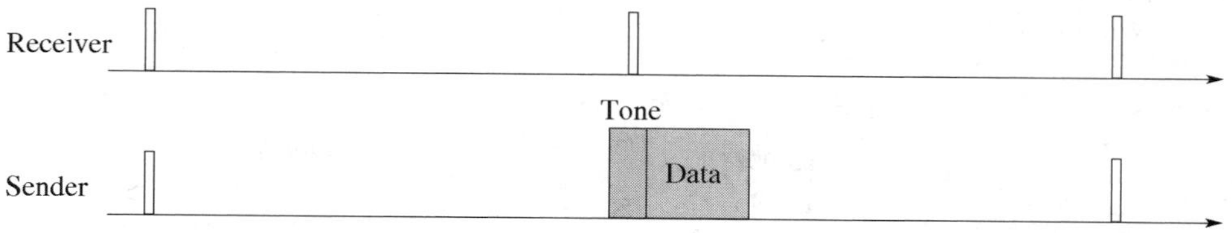

Figure 9: SCP-MAC synchronizes neighboring nodes on common schedules. When transmitting, a node sends a short tone to wake up the receiver(s).

first sends a short tone to wake up the receiver and then sends the data. The wakeup tone is much shorter than the LPL preamble, and the synchronized polling schedules enable the same efficient transmission for both broadcast and unicast packets. The major cost in SCP-MAC is maintaining schedule synchronization. However, by quantifying the cost and finding optimal parameters, SCP-MAC shows that such cost can be quite small. Analysis and experiments show that SCP-MAC can improve energy efficiency over LPL by a factor of 3 to 6 (Ye, Silva, and Heidemann 2006).

Other CSMA Improvements

In this subsection, we look at a few other schemes to improve CSMA for wireless sensor networks, the major goals of which do not include energy efficiency. These protocols focus on performance aspects such as latency, throughput, and fairness.

A side effect of the listen and sleep schedule introduced by S-MAC is the increased latency because a sender has to wait for a receiver's listening time. This delay is termed as the *sleep delay* (Ye, Heidemann, and Estrin 2004). There has been work on reducing multihop latency caused by the sleep delay. S-MAC uses RTS and CTS to inform the next-hop node of possible transmission, reducing latency at every two hops. T-MAC further adds future RTS packets so that data can keep moving over every three hops. *D-MAC* (Lu, Krishnamachari, and Raghavendra 2004) and the fast path algorithm (Li, Ye, and Heidemann 2005) try to explicitly stagger the wakeup times along a transmission path. They require the help from the routing layer to obtain path information. *Dynamic sensor MAC* (DS-MAC) (Lin, Qiao, and Wang 2004) doubles the duty cycle for reducing sleep-delay based on the queued data and average one-hop latency value computed by nodes. *Latency and energy aware MAC* (LE-MAC) (Suh, Shrestha, and Ko 2006) makes the RTS and CTS scheme used in S-MAC more effective over multiple hops by exploiting the longer physical carrier sense range for waking up relay nodes. SCP-MAC proposes adaptive channel polling, which dynamically increases the channel polling frequency of nodes driven by data traffic, and it requires no explicit signaling.

Woo and Culler proposed a MAC protocol for wireless sensor networks that combined CSMA with an adaptive rate-control mechanism (Woo and Culler 2001). Many sensor networks face the funneling problem, in which the nodes that are closer to the base station carry more traffic. The MAC protocol aims to fairly allocate bandwidth to all nodes in the network. Each node dynamically adjusts its rate of injecting its original packets to the network. The paper also suggests the use of implicit ACKs to reduce control overhead. An *implicit* ACK is the same packet that a parent node rebroadcasts after it receives from its child. To capture the implicit ACK, the child node has to keep listening, which may be inefficient because of overhearing unrelated traffic.

Tay, Jamieson, and Balakrishnan (2004) studied how to minimize collision in a fixed contention window when there are a large number of contenders. In traditional slotted CSMA, a node randomly selects a slot with uniform distribution in the contention window to perform carrier sense. Tay, Jamieson, and Balakrishnan developed CSMA/p^*, in which p^* is the optimal distribution that minimizes the collision probability given the fixed number of slots and the known number of contending nodes. The distribution p^* is nonuniform, which has extremely small values for the beginning slots and increases rapidly for the last few slots. Such a distribution is highly effective in selecting one transmitter among a large number of contenders. The authors also derives a distribution, named *Sift* (Tay, Jamieson, and Balakrishnan 2004; Jamieson, Balakrishnan, and Tay 2006), that approximates p^* without knowing the exact number of contenders.

Rhee et al. (2005) proposed a hybrid protocol to combine TDMA with CSMA, called *zebra MAC* (Z-MAC). Z-MAC assigns each node a slot, but other nodes can borrow the slot (with contention) if its owner has no data to send. Z-MAC takes advantages of both CSMA and TDMA according to the changes in traffic load. When traffic load is light, Z-MAC works like CSMA (based on B-MAC) because all nodes are allowed to access the slots whose owners do not have data. Z-MAC works like TDMA at heavy load because slot owners have higher priority than other nodes. Z-MAC significantly improves the throughput of B-MAC, but its energy efficiency remains similar to B-MAC. The major overhead of Z-MAC is the distributed slot assignment algorithm and potential periodic synchronization. Based on the same idea of combining TDMA with CSMA, the *funneling MAC* (Ahn et al. 2006) proposes to only apply the hybrid scheme around the sink, which is normally the most congested area. This scheme achieves better time synchronization than Z-MAC over long duration by adopting a centralized control on the sink node, therefore further improving performance.

CONCLUSION

In this chapter, we have reviewed CSMA protocols in modern computer networks. First, we have discussed ALOHA and basic variants of CSMA protocols. Using the conservative approach of listening before transmitting,

CSMA performs much better than ALOHA. Then we have discussed CSMA in Ethernet, which is the most widely used LAN technology today. The ability to detect collision and the use of binary exponential backoff helps CSMA maintain throughput with heavy traffic. CSMA has gained more attention with the widespread popularity of wireless technologies. We have discussed the complexity of wireless networking compared to Ethernet. Collision avoidance is the major enhancement to CSMA for the wireless LAN. Finally, CSMA has attracted strong attention in the new area of wireless sensor networks because of its robustness and flexibility. Various approaches have been proposed to improve the energy efficiency of CSMA protocols.

GLOSSARY

Backoff: The process of deferring access to the channel when a busy medium is detected.

Carrier Sense: The method that determines whether the medium is idle or busy. A busy medium indicates that a nearby node is transmitting.

Channel Polling (or Channel Sampling): The process a node uses to briefly turn on its radio to measure the channel activity.

Collision: When two concurrent transmissions corrupt each other; happens when two transmitted packets arrive at a receiver with overlapping durations and comparable signal strengths.

Contention: A probabilistic procedure that each node follows to access the shared medium.

Duty Cycle: The percentage of time that a node keeps its radio on. Nodes operate at low duty cycles to conserve energy.

Ethernet: A cable-connected LAN that is based on the shared medium and broadcasting. Ethernet is one of the most widely used LAN technologies.

Hidden Terminals: Refers to nodes that are outside the transmission range of each other but whose concurrent transmissions can collide on a receiver between them.

Idle Listening: Refers to the state that a node is listening to the channel in order to receive possible data.

Local Area Network (LAN): A computer network that spans a small area, such as within a building or a few buildings. A LAN is normally owned by a single organization.

Medium (or Multiple) Access Control (MAC): The process that determines which node has the right to transmit in a channel, or medium, at a given time. *Multiple access control* emphasizes enabling multiple users, or nodes, to access the channel.

Sensor Network: A network of embedded computers equipped with sensors and wireless communication devices. Most sensor nodes are powered by batteries and have limited computing resources.

Wireless LAN: A widely used LAN technology based on wireless communications; the current wireless LAN standard is the IEEE 802.11.

CROSS REFERENCES

See *Ethernet LANs; Principles and Applications of Ad Hoc and Sensor Networks; Wireless LANs (WLANs).*

REFERENCES

Abramson, N. 1970. The ALOHA system. In *Proceedings of AFIPS 1970 Fall Joint Computer Conference*, 37: 281–5.

———. 1985. Development of the ALOHANET. *IEEE Transactions on Information Theory,* 31(2):119–23.

Ahn, G.-S., E. Miluzzo, A. T. Campbell, S. G. Hong, and F. Cuomo. 2006. Funneling-MAC: A localized, sink-oriented MAC for boosting fidelity in sensor networks. In *Proceedings of the Fourth ACM International Conference on Embedded Networked Sensor Systems* (SenSys), November, Boulder, CO, USA. pp. 293–306.

Bharghavan, V., A. Demers, S. Shenker, and L. Zhang. 1994. MACAW: A media access protocol for wireless LANs. In *Proceedings of the ACM SIGCOMM Conference*, September, London. pp. 212–25.

Bluetooth. Undated. Online at www.bluetooth.org/.

Buettner, M., G. V. Yee, E. Anderson, and R. Han. 2006. X-MAC: a short preamble MAC protocol for duty-cycled wireless sensor networks. In *Proceedings of the Fourth ACM International Conference on Embedded Networked Sensor Systems* (SenSys), November, Boulder, CO, USA. pp. 307–20.

Chipcon. Undated. Chipcon CC1000 data sheet (retrieved from www.chipcon.com/).

Crossbow Technology. Undated. Online at www.xbow .com/.

El-Hoiydi, A., J.-D. Decotignie, C. Enz, and E. Le Roux. 2003. WiseMAC: An ultra low power MAC protocol for the WiseNet wireless sensor networks (poster abstract). In *Proceedings of the First ACM International Conference on Embedded Networked Sensor Systems* (SenSys), November, Los Angeles. pp. 302–3.

Ganeriwal, S., D. Ganesan, H. Shim, V. Tsiatsis, and M. B. Srivastava. 2005. Estimating clock uncertainty for efficient duty-cycling in sensor networks. In *Proceedings of the Third ACM International Conference on Embedded Networked Sensor Systems* (SenSys), November, San Diego, CA, USA. pp. 130–41.

Hill, J., R. Szewczyk, A. Woo, S. Hollar, D. Culler, and K. Pister. 2000. System architecture directions for networked sensors. In *Proceedings of the Ninth International Conference on Architectural Support for Programming Languages and Operating Systems*, November, Cambridge, MA, USA. pp. 93–104.

IEEE Computer Society. 1999. *Wireless LAN medium access control (MAC) and physical layer (PHY) specification*. IEEE Std. 802.11-1999. New York: LAN MAN Standards Committee.

IEEE Computer Society. 2000. *Carrier sense multiple access with collision detection (CSMA/CD) access method and physical layer specifications*. IEEE Std, 802.3-2000. New York: LAN MAN Standards Committee.

IEEE Computer Society. 2002. *Wireless LAN medium access control (MAC) and physical layer (PHY) specifications for wireless personal area networks (WPANs)*. IEEE Std. 802.15.1-2002. New York: Author

IEEE Computer Society. 2003. *Wireless LAN medium access control (MAC) and physical layer (PHY) specifications for low-rate wireless personal area networks (LR-WPANs)*. IEEE Std. 802.15.4-2003. New York: Author.

Jamieson, K., H. Balakrishnan, and Y. C. Tay. 2006. Sift: A MAC protocol for event-driven wireless sensor networks. In *Proceedings of the Third European Workshop on Wireless Sensor Networks*, February, Zurich, Switzerland. pp. 260–75.

Karn, P. 1990. MACA: A new channel access method for packet radio. In *Proceedings of the Ninth ARRL Computer Networking Conference*, September, London, Ontario, Canada. pp. 134–140.

Kleinrock, L., and F. Tobagi. 1975. Packet switching in radio channels: Part I—Carrier sense multiple access modes and their throughput delay characteristics. *IEEE Transactions on Communications,* 23(12):1400–16.

Li, Y., W. Ye, and J. Heidemann. 2005. Energy and latency control in low duty cycle MAC protocols. In *Proceedings of the IEEE Wireless Communications and Networking Conference*, March, New Orleans. pp. 676–82.

Lin, P., C. Qiao, and X. Wang. 2004. Medium access control with a dynamic duty cycle for sensor networks. In *Proceedings of the IEEE Wireless Communications and Networking Conference*, March, Atlanta, GA, USA. pp. 1534–9.

Lu, G., B. Krishnamachari, and C. Raghavendra. 2004. An adaptive energy-efficient and low latency MAC for data gathering in sensor networks. In *Fourth International Workshop on Wireless, Mobile, and Ad Hoc Networks* (WMAN), held in conjunction with the 18th IEEE International Parallel and Distributed Processing Symposium (IPDPS), April, Santa Fe, NM, USA.

Metcalfe, R., and D. Boggs. 1976. Ethernet: Distributed packet switching for local computer networks. *Communications of the ACM,* 19(5): 395–404.

Nadeem, T., L. Jiy, A. Agrawala, and J. Agrez. 2005. Location enhancement to IEEE 802.11 dcf. In *Proceedings of the IEEE INFOCOM*, March, Miami. Pp. 651–63.

Polastre, J., J. Hill, and D. Culler. 2004. Versatile low power media access for wireless sensor networks. In *Proceedings of the ACM International Conference on Embedded Networked Sensor Systems* (SenSys), November, Baltimore, MD, USA. pp. 95–107.

Rappaport, T. S. 1996. *Wireless communications, principles and practice*. Upper Saddle River, NJ: Prentice Hall.

Rhee, I., A. Warrier, M. Aia, and J. Min. 2005. Z-MAC: A hybrid MAC for wireless sensor networks. In *Proceedings of the Third ACM International Conference on Embedded Networked Sensor Systems* (SenSys), November, San Diego. pp. 90–101.

Singh, S., and C.S. Raghavendra. 1998. PAMAS: Power aware multi-access protocol with signalling for ad hoc networks. *ACM Computer Communication Review,* 28(3): 5–26.

Suh, C., D. M. Shrestha, and Y.-B. Ko. 2006. An energy-efficient MAC protocol for delay-sensitive wireless sensor networks. In *The 2nd International Workshop on RFID and Ubiquitous Sensor Networks (USN), held in conjunction with the 2006 International Conference on Embedded and Ubiquitous Computing (EUC), August, Seoul.*

Tay, Y. C., K. Jamieson, and H. Balakrishnan. 2004. Collision-minimizing CSMA and its applications to wireless sensor networks. *IEEE Journal on Selected Areas in Communications,* 22(6): 1048–57.

Tobagi, F., and L. Kleinrock. 1975. Packet switching in radio channels: Part II—The hidden terminal problem in carrier sense multiple access and the busy tone solution. *IEEE Transactions on Communications,* 23(12): 1417–33.

Tseng, Y.-C., C.-S. Hsu, and T.-Y. Hsieh. 2002. Power-saving protocols for IEEE 802.11-based multi-hop ad hoc networks. In *Proceedings of the IEEE INFOCOM*, June, New York. pp. 200–9.

Van Dam, T., and K. Langendoen. 2003. An adaptive energy-efficient MAC protocol for wireless sensor networks. In *Proceedings of the First ACM International Conference on Embedded Networked Sensor Systems* (SenSys), November, Los Angeles. pp. 171–80.

Ware, C., J. Judge, J. Chicharo, and E. Dutkiewicz. 2000. Unfairness and capture behaviour in 802.11 ad hoc networks. In *Proceedings of the IEEE International Conference on Communications*, June, New Orleans. pp. 159–63.

Whitehouse, K., A. Woo, F. Jiang, J. Polastre, and D. Culler. 2005. Exploiting the capture effect for collision detection and recovery. In *Proceedings of the Second IEEE Workshop on Embedded Networked Sensors* (EmNetS), May, Sydney, Australia.

Woo, A., and D. Culler. 2001. A transmission control scheme for media access in sensor networks. In *Proceedings of the ACM/IEEE International Conference on Mobile Computing and Networking*, July, Rome. pp. 221–35.

Woo, A., T. Tong, and D. Culler. 2003. Taming the underlying challenges of reliable multihop routing in sensor networks. In *Proceedings of the First ACM International Conference on Embedded Networked Sensor Systems* (SenSys), November, Los Angeles. pp. 14–27.

Ye, W., J. Heidemann, and D. Estrin. 2002. An energy-efficient MAC protocol for wireless sensor networks. In *Proceedings of the IEEE INFOCOM*, June, New York. pp. 1567–76.

———. 2004. Medium access control with coordinated adaptive sleeping for wireless sensor networks. *IEEE/ACM Transactions on Networking,* 12(3): 493–506.

Ye, W., F. Silva, and J. Heidemann. 2006. Ultra-low duty cycle MAC with scheduled channel polling. In *Proceedings of the Fourth ACM International Conference on Embedded Networked Sensor Systems* (SenSys), November, Boulder, CO, USA. pp. 321–34.

Zhao, J., and R. Govindan. 2003. Understanding packet delivery performance in dense wireless sensor networks. In *Proceedings of the ACM International Conference on Embedded Networked Sensor Systems* (SenSys), November, Los Angeles. pp. 1–13.

ZigBee Alliance. Undated. Online at www.zigbee.org/.

Bluetooth Technology

Brent A. Miller, *IBM Corporation*

INTRODUCTION

Launched in May 1998, Bluetooth wireless technology rapidly has become one of the most well-known means of communication in the information technology industry. The unusual name *Bluetooth* itself has garnered much attention (I discuss the origins of this name later), but the main reason for the focus that the technology receives from so many companies and individuals is the capabilities that it brings to mobile computing and communication.

This chapter discusses many facets of Bluetooth wireless technology—its origins; the associated Bluetooth Special Interest Group; its applications, especially in personal area networks; how it works; and how it addresses security issues. I also present numerous references where more information can be found about this exciting way to form wireless personal area networks (WPANs) that allow mobile devices to communicate with one another.

BLUETOOTH WIRELESS TECHNOLOGY

Bluetooth wireless technology uses radio frequency (RF) to accomplish wireless communication. It operates in the 2.4 GHz frequency spectrum; the use of this frequency range allows Bluetooth devices to be used virtually worldwide without requiring a license for operation. Bluetooth communication is intended to operate over short distances (up to approximately 100 m, although the nominal range used by most Bluetooth devices is about 10 m). Restricting communication to short ranges allows for low-power operation, so Bluetooth technology is particularly well suited for use with battery-powered personal devices that can be used to form a WPAN. Both voice and data can be carried over Bluetooth communication links, making the technology suitable for connecting both computing and communication devices, such as mobile phones, personal digital assistants (PDAs), pagers, and notebook computers. Table 1 summarizes these key attributes of Bluetooth wireless technology.

Bluetooth wireless technology originally was designed for cable replacement applications, intended to remove the need for a cable between any two devices to allow them to communicate. For example, a cable might be used to connect two computers to transfer files, to connect a PDA cradle to a computer to synchronize data, or to connect a headset to a telephone for hands-free voice calls. This sort of wired operation can often be cumbersome, because the cables used are frequently special-purpose wires intended to connect two specific devices; hence, they are likely to have special connectors that make them unsuitable for general-purpose use. This can lead to "cable clutter"—the need for many cables to interconnect various devices. Mobile users may find this especially burdensome because they need to carry their device cables with them to

Table 1: Key Bluetooth Technology Characteristics

Characteristic	Bluetooth Technology Attributes
Medium	Radio frequency in the 2.4 GHz globally unlicensed spectrum
Range	Nominally 10 m; optionally up to 100 m
Power	Low-power operation, suitable for battery-powered portable devices
Packet types	Voice and data
Types of applications	Cable replacement, wireless personal area networks
Example applications	Network access, wireless headsets, wireless data transfer, cordless telephony, retail and mobile e-commerce, travel and mobility, and many other applications

connect the devices when they are away from home, and, even with a large collection of cables, it is unlikely that all of the devices can be plugged together. Nonmobile environments, too, can suffer from cable clutter. In a home or office, wires used to connect, say, computer peripherals or stereo speakers limit the placement of these items, and the cables themselves become obstacles.

Bluetooth technology attempts to solve the problem of cable clutter by defining a standard communication mechanism that can allow many devices to communicate with one another without wires. The next section explores the genesis and evolution of Bluetooth wireless communication.

Origins

The genesis of Bluetooth wireless technology generally is credited to Ericsson, where engineers were searching for a method to enable wireless headsets for mobile telephones. Realizing that such a short-range RF technology could have wider applications, and further realizing that its likelihood for success would be greater as an industry standard rather than a proprietary technology, Ericsson approached other major telephone, mobile computer, and electronics companies about forming an industry group to specify and standardize a general-purpose, short-range, low-power form of wireless communication. This small group became the Bluetooth Special Interest Group (SIG), discussed later.

Of special interest to many is the name "Bluetooth." Such a name for an industry initiative is unusual. A two-part newsletter article (Kardach 2001) offers a full explanation of the name's origin; the salient points follow here. Some of the first technologists involved in early discussions about a short-range wireless technology were history buffs, and the discussion at some point turned to Scandinavian history. A key figure in Scandinavian history is tenth-century Danish king Harald Blåtand, who is credited with uniting parts of Scandinavia. It is said that a loose translation of his surname to English produces "blue tooth." Those involved in early discussions of this technology recognized that it could unite the telecommunications and information technology (IT) industries, and hence they referred to it as "Bluetooth," after King Harald. At that time, Bluetooth was considered a temporary code name for the project. When the time came to develop an official name for the technology and its associated special interest group, the name Bluetooth was chosen after considering several alternatives. Today, this is the trademarked name of the technology and the incorporated entity (the Bluetooth SIG, discussed next) that manages it. In fact, the SIG publishes rules and guidelines (Bluetooth SIG 2006a) for using the term.

The Bluetooth Special Interest Group

Formed in early 1998 and announced in May of that year, the Bluetooth SIG originally was a rather loosely knit group of five companies: Ericsson, Intel, IBM, Nokia, and Toshiba. These companies established themselves as Bluetooth SIG promoter members and formed the core of the SIG. Other companies were invited to join as adopter members, and the SIG's membership grew rapidly. The promoter companies, along with a few invited experts, developed the original versions of the Bluetooth specification (detailed later).

In December 1999, four additional companies—3Com, Lucent, Microsoft, and Motorola—were invited to join the group of promoter companies (later Lucent's promoter membership was transferred to its spin-off company, Agere Systems). By this time, the SIG's membership had grown to more than 2,000 companies. In addition to promoters and adopters, a third membership tier, called "associate member," also was defined. Companies may apply to become associate members and must pay membership fees. Adopter membership is free and open to anyone. In general, promoter and associate members develop and maintain the Bluetooth specification; adopter members may review specification updates before their public availability.

The SIG's original purpose was to develop the Bluetooth specification, but it has taken on additional responsibilities over time. In 2001, the SIG incorporated and instituted a more formal structure for the organization, including a board of directors that oversees all operations, a technical organization led by the Bluetooth Architecture Review Board (BARB), a marketing arm, and a legal group. The SIG continues to develop and maintain the specification and promote the technology, including sponsoring developers' conferences and other events. One important function of the SIG is to manage the Bluetooth qualification program, in which products are tested for conformance to the specification. All Bluetooth products must undergo qualification testing. In 2006, the SIG is going strong, with eight promoter companies and more than 4,000 members. The Bluetooth Web site (Bluetooth SIG 2006b) offers more details about the SIG, its members, and its current organization.

Wireless Personal Area Networks

A personal area network (PAN) generally is considered to be a set of communicating devices that someone carries with him or her. A wireless PAN (WPAN), of course, is a set of devices that communicates without cables, such as through the use of Bluetooth technology. One can imagine a sphere of connectivity that surrounds a person and moves with her or him, so that all of the devices in the WPAN remain in communication with one another.

WPANs need only short-range communication capability to cover the personal area, in contrast with local area networks (LANs) or wide area networks (WANs), which need to communicate across greater distances using an established infrastructure. One source (Miller 2001) contrasts PANs, LANs, and WANs, and particularly Bluetooth technology as a WPAN solution versus Institute of Electrical and Electronics Engineers (IEEE 1999) 802.11 WLAN technology.

The usefulness of a WPAN derives primarily from the ability of individual devices to communicate with one another in an ad hoc manner. Each device still can specialize in certain capabilities but can "borrow" the capabilities of other devices to accomplish certain tasks. For example, a PDA is useful for quickly accessing personal information, such as appointments and contacts. A mobile telephone can be used to contact people whose information is stored in the PDA. Hence, a user might look up the telephone number of an associate and then dial that number on the mobile phone. With a WPAN, however, this process can be automated: once the telephone number is accessed, the PDA software could include an option to dial the specified phone number automatically on the mobile telephone within the WPAN, using wireless communication links to transmit the dialing instructions to the phone. When combined with a wireless headset in the same WPAN, this could enable a more convenient device usage model for the user, who might never need to handle the mobile telephone at all (it could remain stored in a briefcase). Moreover, the user interface of the PDA is likely to be easier to use than a telephone keypad for retrieving contact information. This allows each of the devices (PDA, mobile phone, and wireless headset, in this example) to be optimized to perform the specific tasks that it does best. The capabilities of each device are accessed from other devices via the WPAN. Contrast this with an alternative usage model, the "all-in-one" device (such as a PDA that also functions as a mobile telephone). Such multifunction devices might tend to be cumbersome and are more difficult to optimize for specific functions.

Because it was developed primarily to replace cables that connect mobile devices, Bluetooth wireless communication is an ideal WPAN technology. Indeed, most of the popular usage scenarios for Bluetooth technology originate in a WPAN of some sort, connecting personal devices to one another or to other networks in proximity. The use of Bluetooth communication links in WPANs is illustrated next, in an examination of various Bluetooth applications.

Bluetooth Applications

Because Bluetooth technology primarily is about replacing cables, many of its applications involve well-known usage scenarios. The value that Bluetooth communication adds to these types of applications derives from the ability to accomplish them without wires, enhancing mobility and convenience. For example, dialup networking is a task commonly performed by many individuals, especially mobile professionals. One of the original usage scenarios used to illustrate the value of Bluetooth technology involves performing dialup networking wirelessly; with the use of a mobile computer and a mobile phone, both equipped with Bluetooth communication, dialup networking no longer is constrained by cables. This application and others are detailed next.

Basic Cable Replacement Applications

These applications comprise the original set of usage models envisioned for Bluetooth wireless technology. When the SIG was formed and the technology began to be popularized, these applications were touted as the most common ways in which Bluetooth wireless communication would be used. Although many other, perhaps more sophisticated, applications for Bluetooth technology have been discovered and specified, these original usage models formed the basis of the "starter set" of Bluetooth applications, and they offer a good basis for understanding Bluetooth wireless communication. Nearly all of these early applications involve a mobile computer or a mobile telephone, and, for the most part, they involve performing typical existing tasks wirelessly.

One such application, already mentioned, is dialup networking. In this application, a Bluetooth communication link replaces the wire (typically a serial cable) between a computer and a telephone. When the telephone is also a mobile device, the network connection can be entirely wireless; a Bluetooth wireless link exists between the computer and the telephone, and a wide-area communications link (using typical cellular technology, such as the global system for mobile communication [GSM], time division/demand multiple access [TDMA], or others) carries the network traffic, using the mobile telephone as a wireless modem. Figure 1 depicts this usage model.

A variant of this application uses direct (rather than dialup) connection to a network such as the Internet. In this case, the Bluetooth link allows a computer to connect to a network such as a LAN without using a cable. Together, these two applications (wireless dialup networking and wireless LAN access) form one of the original usage models that the SIG called the *Internet bridge*. Both applications involve access to a network, using existing protocols, with the main benefit being the ability to access the network without the cables that typically are required to connect the network client computer.

Another type of cable replacement application involves data transfer from one device to another. One of the most common such usage models is transferring files from one computer to another. This can be accomplished with removable media (CDs, memory keys), with cables (via a

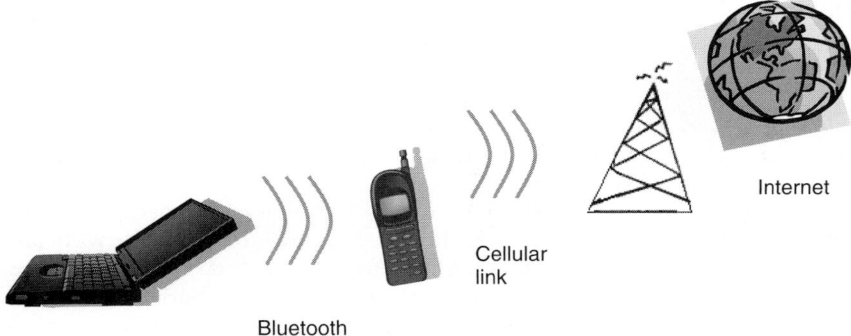

Figure 1: Dialup networking illustration

network or a direct connection), or wirelessly (using infrared or Bluetooth communication, to name two ways). Infrared file transfer is not uncommon, but it requires the two devices to have a line of sight between them. Bluetooth file transfer operates similarly to that of Infrared Data Association (IrDA) infrared file transfer (in fact, the Bluetooth protocol stack, discussed later, is designed such that the same application can be used over either transport medium). Bluetooth communication, being RF based, does not require a line of sight between the two devices, however. Moreover, through the use of standard data formats, such as *vCard* and *vCalendar* (Internet Mail Consortium 1996) and others, objects other than files can be exchanged between devices using Bluetooth links in a manner similar to that used with IrDA. So, for example, electronic business cards, calendar appointments, and contact information can be shared wirelessly among devices.

Building on this capability to exchange data objects is the application that allows these same objects to be synchronized. This means that data sets on two devices reflect the same information at the point in time when they are synchronized. Hence, in addition to simply sending a copy of contact information or a calendar appointment from one device to another, the full address book or calendar can be synchronized between the two devices so that they have the same set of contacts or appointments. This allows a user to enter information on any convenient device and then have that information reflected on other devices by synchronizing with those devices. In addition to the benefit of performing these tasks wirelessly, by using standard protocols and data formats, information can be exchanged easily among many kinds of devices. Specialized cables to connect two computers, or custom cradles to connect a PDA to a computer, are not needed once Bluetooth technology enters the picture. Instead, the same data can be exchanged and synchronized to and from notebook computers, PDAs, mobile phones, pagers, and other devices. This illustrates a hallmark of the value of Bluetooth technology: a single standard wireless link can replace many cables of various types, allowing devices that otherwise might not be able to be connected to communicate easily.

Another data transfer application is related to those just described, but it has a distinguished usage model because of the kind of data it transfers, namely, image data. The SIG called this original usage model the *instant postcard*, and it involves transferring pictures from one device to another. One reason that this application is separately described is because it involves the use of a digital camera. Today, when a camera captures new images, they typically are loaded onto a computer of some sort (or perhaps a television or similar video device) to be displayed. Through the use of Bluetooth wireless technology, this image transfer can be accomplished more easily, but, once again, this standard form of wireless link enables the same data to be transferred to other types of devices. For example, rather than uploading photos to a computer, the photos might be transferred to a mobile phone. Even if the phone's display is not suitable for viewing the photo, it still could be e-mailed to someone who could view it on his or her computer or other e-mail device.

Until now, this chapter has focused on applications involving data, but Bluetooth wireless technology is also designed to transport voice traffic (audio packets), and some of the cable replacement applications take advantage of this fact. The most notable of these is the wireless headset. Cabled headsets that connect to a mobile phone are widely used today to allow hands-free conversations. Bluetooth technology removes the cable from the headset to the telephone handset, enabling wireless operation that can allow the phone to be stowed away in a briefcase, pocket, or purse. In fact, as noted earlier, this particular application was the basis for the invention of Bluetooth technology. As with the previously discussed applications, however, once a standard wireless link is established, additional ways to connect other kinds of devices present themselves. For example, the same Bluetooth headset used with a mobile phone might also be used with a stationary telephone (again to allow hands-free operation and increased mobility) and a computer (to carry audio traffic to and from the computer). Furthermore, although Bluetooth wireless communication was not originally designed to carry more complex audio traffic (such as digital music), advances are being made that will allow it to do so. With this capability, the same wireless headset also could be used with home entertainment systems, car audio systems, and personal music players. Hence, the Bluetooth SIG dubbed this original usage model the *ultimate headset*.

A variation on the wireless headset usage model is the original usage model that the SIG called the *speaking laptop*. In this application, Bluetooth links carry audio data in the same manner as for the headset application, but in this case the audio data is routed between a telephone and a notebook computer's speaker and microphone, rather than to a headset. One usage scenario enabled with this application is that of using the notebook computer as a speakerphone: a call made to or from a mobile telephone can be transformed into a conference call ("put on the speaker") by using the speaker and microphone built into nearly all portable (and desktop) computers.

Cordless telephony is another application for Bluetooth technology. With a Bluetooth voice access point, or cordless telephone base station, a standard cellular mobile telephone also can be used as a cordless phone in a home or office. The Bluetooth link carries the voice traffic from the handset to the base station, with the call then being carried over the normal wired telephone network. This allows mobile calls to be made without incurring cellular usage charges. In addition, two handsets can function as "walkie-talkies" or an intercom system, using direct Bluetooth links between them, allowing two parties to carry on voice conversations in a home, office, or public space without any telephone network at all. Because a single mobile telephone can be used as a standard cellular phone, a cordless phone, and an intercom, the SIG called this original cordless telephony application the *three-in-one phone* usage model.

Additional Applications

Although Bluetooth wireless technology was developed especially for cable-replacement applications such as those just cited, many observers quickly realized that Bluetooth communication could be used in other ways, too. Here I describe a few of the many other applications of Bluetooth technology. For the most recent information about additional Bluetooth applications, see the Bluetooth Web site (Bluetooth SIG 2006b).

The Bluetooth SIG focused primarily on the cable-replacement applications already discussed in the original specifications that it released. The SIG has developed numerous additional profiles (detailed later) for other types of Bluetooth applications. Among these are more robust personal area proximity networking, human interface devices, printing, local positioning, multimedia, and other applications.

Bluetooth personal area networking takes advantage of the ability of Bluetooth devices to establish communication with one another based on their proximity, so that ad hoc networks can be formed. The Bluetooth network encapsulation protocol (BNEP) allows Ethernet packets to be transported via Bluetooth links, thus enabling many classic networking applications to operate in Bluetooth piconets (piconets are discussed at length in the section entitled "Bluetooth Operation"). This capability extends the Bluetooth WPAN to encompass other devices. An example is the formation of an ad hoc Bluetooth network in a conference room with multiple meeting participants. Such a network could facilitate collaborative applications such as white-boarding, instant messaging, and group scheduling. Such applications could allow group editing of documents and scheduling of follow-up meetings, all in real time. Nonetheless, it should be noted that although this scenario resembles classic intranet- or Internet-style networking in some respects, Bluetooth personal area networking is not as robust a solution for true networking solutions as is a WLAN technology, such as IEEE 802.11.

Replacing desktop computer cables with Bluetooth communication links fundamentally is a cable-replacement application (originally dubbed the *cordless computer* by the SIG). The human interface device (HID) profile describes how Bluetooth technology can be used in wireless computer peripherals such as keyboards, mice, joysticks, and so on. The Bluetooth printing profiles specify methods for wireless printing using Bluetooth communication, including "walk up and print" scenarios that allow immediate printing from any device, including mobile telephones and PDAs, as well as notebook computers, to any usable printer in the vicinity. This application of Bluetooth technology can obviate the need for specialized network print servers and their associated configuration and administration tasks.

Another application that can be realized with Bluetooth wireless technology is local positioning. Bluetooth technology can be used to augment other technologies, such as global positioning systems (GPSs), especially inside buildings, where other technologies might not work well. Using two or more Bluetooth radios, local position information can be obtained in several ways. If one Bluetooth device is stationary (say, a kiosk), it could supply its position information to other devices within range. Any device that knows its own position can provide this information to other Bluetooth devices so that they can learn their current position. Sophisticated applications might even use signal strength information to derive more granular position information. Once position information is known, it could be used with other applications, such as maps of the area, directions to target locations, or perhaps even locating lost devices. The Bluetooth local positioning working group is one of the Bluetooth working groups that develops specifications, including standard data formats and interchange methods, for applications such as local positioning.

Multimedia applications have become standard on most desktop and notebook computers, and the Bluetooth SIG has defined profiles for transporting multimedia data, such as audio and video, in Bluetooth environments.

Another emerging application area is that of automotive Bluetooth applications. Using Bluetooth communication, wireless networks can be formed in cars. Devices from the WPAN can join the automobile's built-in Bluetooth network to accomplish scenarios such as the following:

- Obtaining e-mail and other messages, using a mobile phone as a WAN access device, and transferring those messages to the car's Bluetooth network, where they might be read over the car's audio system using text-to-speech technology (and perhaps even composing responses using voice recognition technology)
- Obtaining vehicle information remotely, perhaps for informational purposes (for example, querying the car's current mileage from the office or home) or for diagnostic purposes (for example, a wireless engine diagnostic system for automobile mechanics that does not require probes and cables to be connected to the engine)
- Sending alerts and reminders from the car to a WPAN when service or maintenance is required (for example, e-mail reminders that an oil change is due or in-vehicle or remote alerts when tire pressure is low or other problems are diagnosed by the vehicle's diagnostic systems)

Several models of cars offer Bluetooth wireless technology today. This area is likely to prove to be an exciting and rapidly growing domain for the use of Bluetooth wireless technology.

These applications are only some of the potential uses for Bluetooth wireless technology. The SIG currently specifies more than thirty different profiles that describe different ways to use Bluetooth technology, and many other domains are being explored or will be invented in the future. Other noteworthy applications for Bluetooth wireless communications include mobile e-commerce, medical, and travel technologies. Bluetooth devices such as mobile phones or PDAs might be used to purchase items in stores or from vending machines; wireless biometrics and even Bluetooth drug dispensers might appear in the future (the 2.4 GHz band in which Bluetooth operates is called the industrial, scientific, and medical band); and travelers could experience enhanced convenience by using Bluetooth devices for anytime, anywhere personal data access and airline and hotel automated check-in.

The Bluetooth Protocol Stack

A complete discussion of the Bluetooth protocol stack is outside the scope of this chapter. Numerous books, including Miller and Bisdikian (2000) and Bray and Sturman (2000), offer more in-depth discussions of Bluetooth

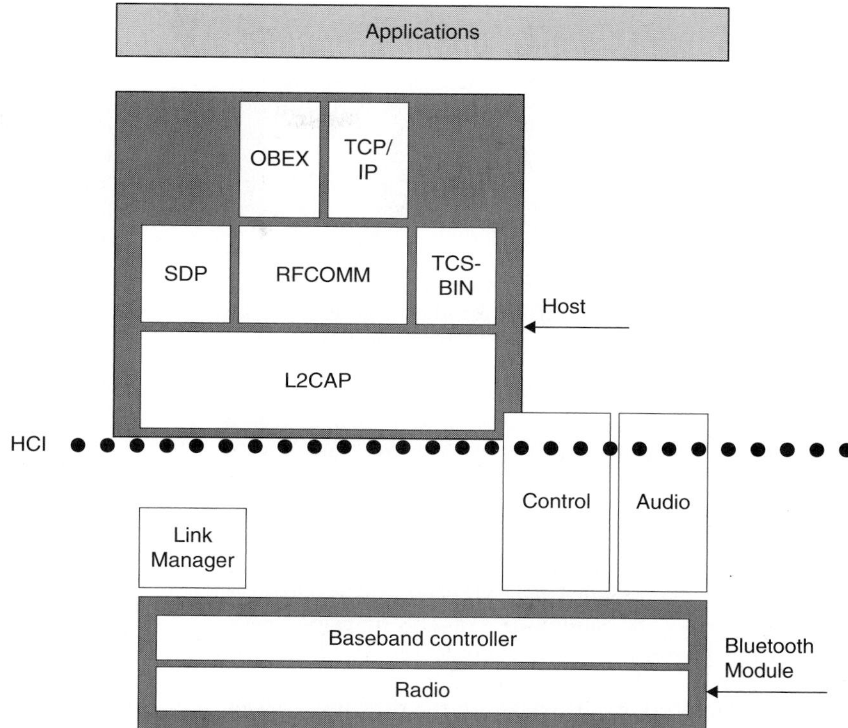

Figure 2: Bluetooth protocol stack

protocols. Here, we present an overview of Bluetooth operation and how the various protocols may be used to accomplish the applications already discussed. A typical Bluetooth stack is illustrated in Figure 2. Each layer of the stack is detailed next.

Radio, Baseband, and Link Manager

These three protocol layers constitute the Bluetooth module. Typically, this module is an electronics package containing hardware and firmware. Today, many manufacturers supply Bluetooth modules.

The radio consists of the signal-processing electronics for a transmitter and receiver (transceiver) to allow RF communication via an air interface between two Bluetooth devices. As noted earlier, the radio operates in the 2.4 GHz spectrum, specifically in the frequency range of 2.400 to 2.4835 GHz. This frequency range is divided into seventy-nine channels (along with upper and lower guard bands), with each channel having a 1 MHz separation from its neighbors. *Frequency hopping* is employed in Bluetooth wireless communication; each packet is transmitted on a different channel, with the channels being selected pseudo-randomly, based on the clock of the master device (master and slave devices are described in more detail later). The receiving device knows the frequency-hopping pattern and follows the pattern of the transmitting device, hopping to the next channel in the pattern to receive the transmitted packets.

The Bluetooth specification defines three classes of radios, based on their maximum power output:

1 mW (0 dBm)
2.5 mW (4 dBm)
100 mW (20 dBm)

Increased transmission power offers a corresponding increase in radio range; the nominal range for the 0 dBm radio is 10 m, whereas the nominal range for the 20 dBm radio is 100 m. Of course, increased transmission power also requires a corresponding increase in the energy necessary to power the system, so higher-power radios will draw more battery power. The basic cable replacement applications (indeed, most Bluetooth usage scenarios described here) envision the 0 dBm radio, which is considered the standard Bluetooth radio and is the most prevalent in devices. The 0 dBm radio is sufficient for most applications, and its low power consumption makes it suitable for use on small, portable devices.

Transmitter and receiver characteristics such as interference, tolerance, sensitivity, modulation, and spurious emissions are outside the scope of this chapter but are detailed in the Bluetooth specification (Bluetooth SIG 2004).

The baseband controller controls the radio and typically is implemented as firmware in the Bluetooth module. The controller is responsible for all of the various timing and raw data-handling aspects associated with RF communication, including the frequency hopping just mentioned, management of the time slots used for transmitting and receiving packets, generating air-interface packets (and causing the radio to transmit them), and parsing air-interface packets (when they are received by the radio). Packet generation and reception involves many considerations, including the following:

- Generating and receiving packet payload
- Generating and receiving packet headers and trailers
- Dealing with the several packet formats defined for Bluetooth communication

- Error detection and correction
- Address generation and detection
- Data whitening (a process by which the actual data bits are rearranged so that the occurrence of zero and one bits in a data stream is randomized, helping to overcome DC bias)
- Data encryption and decryption

Not all of these operations are necessarily performed on every packet; there are various options available for whether a particular transformation is applied to the data, and, in some cases (such as error detection and correction), there are several alternatives that may be employed by the baseband firmware.

The link manager, as its name implies, manages the link layer between two Bluetooth devices. Link managers in two devices communicate using the link manager protocol (LMP). LMP consists of a set of commands and responses to set up and manage a baseband link between two devices. A link manager on one device communicates with a link manager on another device. (Indeed, this is generally the case for all of the Bluetooth protocols described here; a particular protocol layer communicates with its corresponding layer in the other device, using its own defined protocol. Each protocol is passed to the next successively lower layer, where it is transformed to that layer's protocol, until it reaches the baseband, where the baseband packets that encapsulate the higher-layer packets are transmitted and received via the air interface.) LMP setup commands include those for authenticating the link with the other device; setting up encryption, if desired, between the two devices; retrieving information about the device at the other end of the link, such as its name and timing parameters; and swapping the master and slave roles (detailed later) of the two devices. LMP management commands include those for controlling the transmission power; setting special power-saving modes, called hold, park, and sniff; and managing quality-of-service (QoS) parameters for the link. Because LMP messages deal with fundamental characteristics of the communication link between devices, they are handled in an expedited manner, at a higher priority than the normal data that are transmitted and received.

Control and Audio

The control and audio blocks in Figure 2 are not actual protocols. Instead, they represent means by which the upper layers of the stack can access lower layers. The control functions can be characterized as methods for inter-protocol–layer communication. These could include requests and notifications from applications, end users, or protocol layers that require action by another protocol layer, such as setting desired QoS parameters, requests to enter or terminate power-saving modes, or requests to search for other Bluetooth devices or change the discoverability of the local device. Often, these take the form of a user-initiated action, via an application, that requires the link manager (and perhaps other layers) to take some action.

The audio block in Figure 2 represents the typical path for audio (voice) traffic. Recall that Bluetooth wireless technology supports both data and voice. Data packets traverse through the L2CAP layer (described later), but voice packets typically are routed directly to the baseband, because audio traffic is isochronous and hence time critical. Audio traffic usually is associated with telephony applications, for which data traffic is used to set up and control the call, and voice traffic serves as the content of the call. Audio data can be carried over Bluetooth links in two formats:

- Pulse code modulation (PCM), with either a-law or μ-law logarithmic compression
- Continuous variable slope delta (CVSD) modulation, which works well for audio data with relatively smooth continuity, usually the case for typical voice conversations

Host–Controller Interface

The host–controller interface (HCI) is an optional interface between the two major components of the Bluetooth stack: the *host* and the *controller*. As shown in Figure 2 and described earlier, the radio, baseband controller, and link manager constitute the module, which is often, but not necessarily, implemented in a single electronics package. Such a module can be integrated easily into many devices, with the remaining layers of the stack residing on the main processor of the device (such as a notebook computer, mobile phone, or PDA). These remaining layers, which are described next, are referred to as the host portion of the stack.

Figure 2 illustrates a typical "two-chip" solution in which the first "chip" is the Bluetooth module and the second "chip" is the processor in the device on which the host software executes. (The module itself might have multiple chips or electronic subsystems for the radio, the firmware processor, and other external logic.) In such a system, the HCI allows different Bluetooth modules to be interchanged in a device, because it defines a standard method for the host software to communicate with the controller firmware that resides on the module. So, at least in theory, one vendor's Bluetooth module could be substituted for another, so long as both faithfully implement the HCI. Although this is not the only type of partitioning that can be used when implementing a Bluetooth system, the SIG felt it was common enough that a standard interface should be defined between the two major components of the system. A Bluetooth system could be implemented in an "all-in-one" single module, where the host and controller reside together in the same physical package (often called a "single-chip" solution), although, in this case, the HCI might still be used as an internal interface. When the two-chip solution is used, the physical layer for the HCI (that is, the physical connection between the host and the controller) could be one of several types. The Bluetooth specification defines three particular physical layers for the HCI:

- Universal serial bus (USB)
- Universal asynchronous receiver/transmitter (UART)
- RS-232 serial port

Other HCI transports could be implemented; the Bluetooth specification currently contains details and considerations for these three.

Logical Link Control and Adaptation Protocol

The logical link control and adaptation protocol (L2CAP) layer serves as a "funnel" through which all data traffic flows. As discussed earlier, voice packets typically are routed directly to the baseband, whereas data packets flow to and from higher layers, such as applications, to the baseband via the L2CAP layer.

The L2CAP layer offers an abstraction of lower layers to higher-layer protocols. This allows the higher layers to operate using more natural data packet formats and protocols, without being concerned about how their data are transferred over the air interface. For example, the service discovery protocol (SDP) layer (discussed next) defines its own data formats and protocol data units. At the SDP layer, only the service discovery protocol needs to be handled; the fact that SDP data must be separated into baseband packets for transmission and aggregated from baseband packets for reception is not a concern at the SDP layer, nor are any of the other operations that occur at the baseband (such as encryption, whitening, and so on). This is accomplished because the L2CAP layer performs operations on data packets. Among these operations are segmentation and reassembly, whereby the L2CAP layer breaks higher-layer protocol data units into L2CAP packets, which in turn can be transformed into baseband packets; the L2CAP layer conversely can reassemble baseband packets into L2CAP packets that in turn can be transformed into the natural format of higher layers of the stack.

An L2CAP layer in one Bluetooth stack communicates with another, corresponding L2CAP layer in another Bluetooth stack. Each L2CAP layer can have many channels. L2CAP channels identify data streams between the L2CAP layers in two Bluetooth devices. (L2CAP channels should not be confused with baseband channels used for frequency hopping; L2CAP channels are logical identifiers between two L2CAP layers.) An L2CAP channel often is associated with a particular upper layer of the stack, handling data traffic for that layer, although there need not be a one-to-one correspondence between channels and upper-layer protocols. An L2CAP layer might use the same protocol on multiple L2CAP channels. This illustrates another data operation of the L2CAP layer: protocol multiplexing. Through the use of multiple channels and a protocol identifier (called a protocol-specific multiplexer, or PSM), L2CAP allows various protocols to be multiplexed (flow simultaneously) over the air interface. The L2CAP layer sorts out which packets are destined for which upper layers of the stack.

Service Discovery Protocol

The SDP layer provides a means by which Bluetooth devices can learn, in an ad hoc manner, which services are offered by each device. Once a connection has been established, devices use the SDP to exchange information about services. An SDP client queries an SDP server to inquire about services that are available; the SDP server responds with information about services that it offers. Any Bluetooth device can be either an SDP client or an SDP server, acting in one role or the other at different times.

SDP allows a device to inquire about specific services in which it is interested (called *service searching*) or to perform a general inquiry about any services that happen to be available (called *service browsing*). A device can perform an SDP service search to look for, say, printing services in the vicinity. Any devices that offer a printing service that matches the query can respond with a "handle" for the service; the client then uses that handle to perform additional queries to obtain more details about the service. Once a service is discovered using SDP, other protocols are used to access and invoke the service; one of the items that can be discovered using SDP is the set of protocols that is necessary to access and invoke the service.

SDP is designed to be a lightweight discovery protocol that is optimized for the dynamic nature of Bluetooth piconets. SDP can coexist with other discovery and control protocols; for example, the Bluetooth SIG has published a specification for using the Universal Plug and Play (UPnP) discovery and control technology over Bluetooth links.

RFCOMM

As its name suggests, the RFCOMM layer defines a standard serial communications protocol, specifically one that emulates serial port communication (the "RF" designates radio frequency wireless communication; the "COMM" portion suggests a serial port, commonly called a COM port in the personal computer realm). RFCOMM emulates a serial cable connection and provides the abstraction of a serial port to higher layers in the stack. This is particularly valuable for Bluetooth cable-replacement applications, because so many cable connections—modems, infrared ports, camera and mobile phone ports, printers, and others—use some form of a serial port to communicate.

RFCOMM is based on the European Telecommunications Standards Institute (ETSI) TS07.10 protocol (ETSI 1999), which defines a multiplexed serial communications channel. The Bluetooth specification adopts much of the TS07.10 protocol and adds some Bluetooth adaptation features. The presence of RFCOMM in the Bluetooth protocol stack is intended to facilitate the migration of existing wired serial communication applications to wireless Bluetooth links. By presenting higher layers of the stack with a virtual serial port, many existing applications that already use a serial port can be used in Bluetooth environments without any changes. Indeed, many of the cable-replacement applications cited earlier, including dialup networking, LAN access, headset, and file and object exchange, use RFCOMM to communicate. Because RFCOMM is a multiplexed serial channel, many serial data streams can flow over it simultaneously; each separate serial data stream is identified with a server channel, in a manner somewhat analogous to the channels used with L2CAP.

Telephony Control Specification-Binary

The telephony control specification-binary (TCS-BIN) is a protocol used for advanced telephony operations. Many of the Bluetooth usage scenarios involve a mobile telephone, and some of these use the TCS-BIN protocol. TCS-BIN is adopted from the ITU-T Q.931 standard (International Telecommunications Union 1998), and it includes functions for call control and managing wireless user groups. Typically, TCS-BIN is used to set up and manage voice calls; the voice traffic that is the content of the call is carried as audio packets, as described earlier. Applications such as the three-in-one phone usage model use TCS-BIN to enable functions such as using a mobile phone as a cordless phone or an intercom. In these cases, TCS-BIN is used to recognize the mobile phone so that it can be added to a wireless user group that consists of all the cordless telephone handsets used with a cordless telephone base station. TCS-BIN is also used to set up and control calls between the handset and the base station (cordless telephony) or between two handsets (intercom).

TCS-BIN offers several advanced telephony functions; devices that support TCS-BIN can obtain knowledge of and directly communicate with any other devices in the TCS-BIN wireless user group, essentially overcoming the master–slave relationship of the underlying Bluetooth piconet (detailed later). It should be noted that not all Bluetooth telephony applications require TCS-BIN; an alternative method for call control is the use of a modem control protocol, commonly called AT commands, via the RFCOMM serial interface. This latter method is used for the headset, dialup networking, and fax profiles.

Adopted Protocols

Although several layers of the Bluetooth protocol stack were developed specifically to support Bluetooth wireless communication, other layers are adopted from existing industry standards. I already have noted that RFCOMM and TCS-BIN are based on existing specifications. In addition to these, protocols for file and object exchange and synchronization are adopted from the IrDA, and Internet networking protocols are used in some applications.

The IrDA's object exchange (OBEX) protocol is used for the file and object transfer, object push, and synchronization usage models. OBEX originally was developed for infrared wireless communication, and it maps well to Bluetooth wireless communication. OBEX is a relatively lightweight protocol for data exchange, and several well-defined data types—including electronic business cards, e-mail, short messages, and calendar items—can be carried within the protocol. Hence, the Bluetooth SIG adopted OBEX for use in its data exchange scenarios; by doing so, existing infrared applications can be used via Bluetooth links, often with no application changes. In addition, the infrared mobile communications (IrMC) protocol is used for the synchronization usage model. Typically, infrared communication occurs via a serial port, so the adopted IrDA protocols operate via RFCOMM in the Bluetooth protocol stack.

Networking applications such as dialup networking and LAN access use standard Internet protocols, including point-to-point protocol (PPP), Internet protocol (IP), user datagram protocol (UDP), and transmission control protocol (TCP). As shown in Figure 2, these protocols operate via the RFCOMM protocol. Once a Bluetooth RFCOMM connection is established between two devices, PPP can be used as a basis for UDP–IP and TCP–IP networking packets. This enables typical networking applications, such as network dialers, e-mail programs, and browsers, to operate via Bluetooth links, often with no changes to the applications.

Bluetooth Profiles

I have presented an overview of the Bluetooth protocols, which are described in the Bluetooth core specification (Bluetooth SIG 2004). The Bluetooth SIG publishes multiple volumes of the specification, some of which define the Bluetooth profiles. Profiles offer additional guidance to developers beyond the specification of the protocols. Essentially, a profile is a formalized usage case that describes how to use the protocols (including which protocols to use, which options are available, and so on) for a particular application. Profiles were developed to foster interoperability; they provide a standard basis for all implementations to increase the likelihood that implementations from different vendors will work together, so that end users can have confidence that Bluetooth devices will interoperate with one another. In addition to the profile specifications, the SIG offers other mechanisms intended to promote interoperability; among these are the Bluetooth Qualification Program (a definition of testing that a Bluetooth device must undergo) and unplugfests (informal sessions during which many vendors can test their products with one another). Detailed discussions of these programs are outside the scope of this chapter, but more information about the profiles and other SIG programs is available on the Bluetooth Web site (Bluetooth SIG 2006b).

Our earlier discussion of Bluetooth applications presented several usage models for Bluetooth wireless communication. Many of these applications have associated profiles. For example, the dialup networking profile defines implementation considerations for the dialup networking application. Most of the applications cited here have associated profiles, and many profiles have been developed and new ones are being developed and published by the SIG; the official Bluetooth Web site (Bluetooth SIG 2006b) has a current list of available specifications. In addition, there are some fundamental profiles that describe basic Bluetooth operations that are necessary for most applications. Profiles such as the generic access profile, service discovery profile, RFCOMM profile, and others provide these core operations that enable many of the more advanced usage scenarios.

Profiles define mechanisms for file and object transfer, object push, synchronization, dialup networking, fax, headset, LAN access, cordless telephony, and intercom. The telephony (TCS-BIN) profile includes elements that are common to cordless telephony and intercom applications; similarly, the generic object exchange profile describes the common elements used for particular object exchange applications such as object transfer and synchronization, and the serial port profile defines operations used by all applications that use the RFCOMM serial cable-replacement protocol. Note that the generic object exchange profile derives from the serial port profile; this is because OBEX operates via RFCOMM in the Bluetooth protocol stack.

Other profiles describe fundamental operations for Bluetooth communication. The service discovery application profile describes how a service discovery application uses the service discovery protocol (described earlier). The generic access profile is common to all applications; it defines the basic operations that Bluetooth devices use to establish connections, including how devices become discoverable and connectable, security considerations for connections, and so on. The generic access profile also includes a common set of terminology used in other profiles; this is intended to reduce ambiguity in the specification. The generic access and service discovery application profiles are mandatory for all Bluetooth devices to implement, because they form the basis for interoperable devices.

Numerous other profiles build on the fundamental profiles to describe other applications, including basic imaging, audio and video control and transport, printing, and personal area networking. The Bluetooth Web site (Bluetooth SIG 2006b) lists all of the current profiles. Other works, including Miller and Bisdikian (2000), delve more deeply into the Bluetooth profiles.

Bluetooth Operation

Having discussed WPANs, Bluetooth applications, protocols, and profiles, I now turn our attention to some of the fundamental concepts of Bluetooth operation, illustrating an example flow for a Bluetooth connection.

At the baseband layer, Bluetooth operates on a master–slave model. In general, the *master* device is the one that initiates communication with one or more other devices. *Slaves* are the devices that respond to the master's queries. In general, any Bluetooth device can operate as either a master or a slave at any given time. The master and slave roles are meaningful only at the baseband layer; upper layers are not concerned with these roles. The master device establishes the frequency-hopping pattern for communication with its slaves, using its internal clock values to generate the frequency-hopping pattern. Slaves follow the frequency-hopping pattern of the master(s) with which they communicate.

When a master establishes a connection with one or more slaves, a *piconet* is formed. To establish the connection, a master uses processes called *inquiry* and *paging*. A master can perform an inquiry operation, which transmits a well-defined data sequence across the full spectrum of frequency-hopping channels. An inquiry effectively asks, "Are there any devices listening?" Devices that are in *inquiry scan* mode (a mode in which the device periodically listens to all of the channels for inquiries) can respond to the master's inquiry with enough information for the master device to address the responding device directly. The inquiring (master) device may then choose to page the responding (slave) device. The page is also transmitted across the full spectrum of frequency-hopping channels; the device that originally responded to the inquiry can enter a *page scan* state (a state in which it periodically listens to all of the channels for pages), and it can respond to the page with additional information that can be used to establish a baseband connection between the master and the slave. The master can repeat this process and establish connections with as many as seven slaves at a time. Hence, a piconet consists of one master and up to seven active slaves; additional slaves can be part of the piconet, but only seven slaves can be active at one time. Slaves can be "parked" (made inactive) so that other slaves can be activated. Figure 3 illustrates a typical Bluetooth piconet. Note that a device could be a slave in more than one piconet at a time, or it could be a master

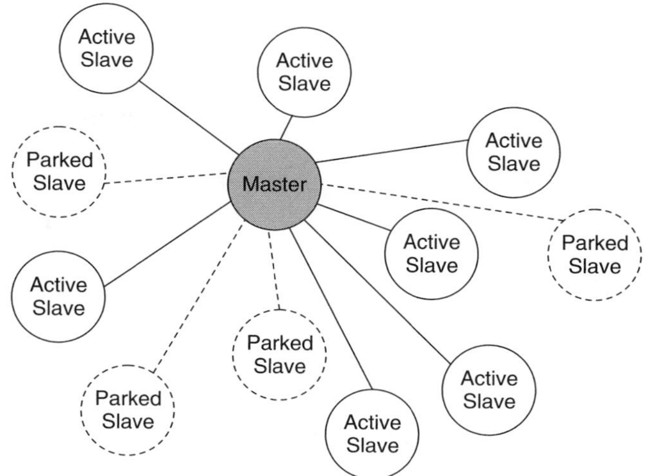

Figure 3: Example of a Bluetooth piconet

of one piconet and a slave in a second piconet. In these cases, the device participating in multiple piconets must use the appropriate frequency-hopping pattern in each piconet, so it effectively must split its time among all the piconets in which it participates. The Bluetooth specification calls such interconnected piconets *scatternets*.

Once a piconet is formed (a baseband connection exists between a master and one or more slave devices), higher-layer connections can be formed, and link manager commands and responses may be used to manage the link. At some point, it is likely that an L2CAP connection will be formed for data packets (even if the main content for a link is voice traffic, an L2CAP data connection will be needed to set up and manage the voice links). A Bluetooth device can have one data (L2CAP) connection and up to three voice connections with any other Bluetooth device at a given time (recall, however, that L2CAP connections can be multiplexed, so many different data streams can flow over the single L2CAP connection). Once an L2CAP connection is established, additional higher-layer connections can be established. If the devices are not familiar to one another already, it is likely that an SDP connection will be used to perform service discovery. RFCOMM and TCS-BIN connections also might be made, depending on the application. From here, applications can manage voice and data packets to accomplish their usage scenarios, which might be those defined by Bluetooth profiles or other ways to use Bluetooth wireless communication to accomplish a given task. Additional details about fundamental Bluetooth operations and connection establishment, including the various types of packets, master–slave communication protocols, and timing considerations, are outside the scope of this chapter but are detailed in works such as Miller and Bisdikian (2000) and Bray and Sturman (2000).

Bluetooth Security

A noteworthy aspect of Bluetooth operation is security. In the wireless world, security justifiably is a key concern for device manufacturers, device deployers, and end users.

The Bluetooth specification includes security measures such as authentication and encryption, and the Bluetooth profiles discuss which security measures should be employed in various circumstances.

At the time that a link is established, Bluetooth devices may be required to authenticate themselves to each other. This is done using a shared-secret method (other methods such as those using public keys typically require some sort of central registry, which is not appropriate for WPANs that use ad hoc networking). The first device sends a randomly generated number to the second device, which performs some computation using a link key value and returns the result to the first device. If that value is the one expected by the first device, then it considers the second device authenticated. The second device might then, in turn, authenticate the first device so that the two devices are mutually authenticated with each other. Link keys are maintained by each device; a process called *pairing* can be used to generate a link key from an initialization key the very first time two devices are introduced to each other.

Once a link has been established, the data traffic over that link may be encrypted. The encryption key is derived from the link key, so devices that exchange encrypted traffic must have been already authenticated with each other. Bluetooth links support up to 128-bit encryption; the devices mutually agree on the encryption key size.

The Bluetooth profiles provide guidance about how and when to use authentication and encryption in Bluetooth wireless communication. The generic access profile described earlier defines three different security modes (nonsecure, service-level enforced security, and link-level enforced security) and the procedures to follow to achieve those levels of security in Bluetooth communications. Other profiles specify the security measures that should be used for various applications or scenarios. For example, the file-transfer profile requires that both authentication and encryption be supported, and it recommends that they be used; the dialup networking profile requires that all data be encrypted, in addition to device authentication.

Applications are free to impose additional security restrictions beyond those that are provided in the specification. For example, applications might choose to expose data or services only to authorized users or to implement more robust user authentication schemes. Certain applications might include other security mechanisms beyond those built into the Bluetooth devices, such as the use of public key infrastructure, certificates, or other methods. More details about the operation of Bluetooth security features are included in works such as Miller and Bisdikian (2000) and Bray and Sturman (2000).

CONCLUSION

This introduction to Bluetooth wireless technology has touched on what can be done with the technology (Bluetooth applications), how it began, how it is managed (the Bluetooth SIG), and how it works (Bluetooth protocols, profiles, and operation, including security). The chapter focused on the application of Bluetooth wireless communication as a WPAN technology for connecting personal portable devices. I have also presented several references in which this topic is explored in greater detail.

With tremendous industry backing, a design to work with both voice and data, the ability to replace cumbersome cables, and many new products being deployed on a regular basis, Bluetooth wireless technology is poised to become an important way for people to communicate for the foreseeable future. From its genesis as a method to provide a wireless headset for mobile phones, this technology named for a Danish king continues to spread across the planet.

GLOSSARY

Bluetooth Special Interest Group (SIG): An industry consortium that develops, promotes, and manages Bluetooth wireless technology, including the Bluetooth qualification program and the Bluetooth brand.

Bluetooth wireless technology: Name given to a wireless communications technology used for short-range voice and data communication, especially for cable-replacement applications.

Frequency-hopping spread spectrum A method of dividing packetized information across multiple channels of a frequency spectrum that is used in Bluetooth wireless communication.

IEEE 802.11: A wireless local area network standard developed by the Institute of Electrical and Electronics Engineers that is considered complementary to Bluetooth wireless technology.

IEEE 802.15.1: A wireless personal area network standard developed by the Institute of Electrical and Electronics Engineers that is based on Bluetooth wireless technology.

Infrared Data Association (IrDA): An industry consortium that specifies the IrDA infrared communication protocols, some of which are used in the Bluetooth protocol stack.

Piconet: A Bluetooth wireless technology term for a set of interconnected devices with one master and up to seven active slave devices.

Profile: In Bluetooth wireless technology, a specification for standard methods to use when implementing a particular application, with a goal of fostering interoperability among applications and devices.

Radio frequency (RF): Used in the Bluetooth specification to describe the use of radio waves for physical layer communication.

Wireless personal area network (WPAN): A small set of interconnected devices used by one person.

CROSS REFERENCES

See *Cellular Communications Channels*; *Indoor Wireless Infrared Communications*; *Spread Spectrum*.

REFERENCES

Bluetooth Special Interest Group (SIG). 2004. Specification of the Bluetooth system, master table of contents, and compliance requirements (Version 2.0). http://bluetooth.com/Bluetooth/ Learn/Technology/Specifications/ (accessed February 26, 2006).

———. 2006a. Best practices for trademark usage. http://www.bluetooth.com/Bluetooth/SIG/Trademark/Usage/ (accessed February 26, 2006).

———. 2006b. The official Bluetooth Web site. http://www.bluetooth.com.

Bray, J., and C. Sturman. 2000. *Bluetooth: Connect without cables*. New York: Prentice Hall.

European Telecommunications Standards Institute (ETSI). 1999. Technical specification: Digital cellular telecommunications system (Phase 2+); Terminal equipment to mobile station (TE-MS) multiplexer protocol (GSM 07.10). http://webapp.etsi.org/action/PU/20020409/ts_101369v070200p.pdf (accessed February 26, 2006).

Institute of Electrical and Electronics Engineers (IEEE). 1999. Wireless standards package (802.11). http://standards.ieee.org/getieee802 (accessed February 26, 2006).

International Telecommunications Union. 1998. Recommendation Q.931—ISDN user-network interface layer 3 specification for basic call control. http://www.itu.int/rec/recommendation.asp?type=folders&lang=e&parent=T-REC-Q.931 (accessed February 26, 2006).

Internet Mail Consortium. 1996. vCard and vCalendar. http://www.imc.org/pdi (accessed February 26, 2006).

Kardach, J. 2001. The naming of a technology. *Incisor* 34: 10–12; 37: 13–15.

Miller, B. 2001. The phony conflict: IEEE 802.11 and Bluetooth wireless technology. *Informit network*. http://www.informit.com/articles/article.asp?p=24240&rl=1 (accessed February 26, 2006).

Miller, B., and C. Bisdikian. 2000. *Bluetooth revealed: The insider's guide to an open specification for global wireless communication*. New York: Prentice Hall.

FURTHER READING

Infrared Data Association. 2002. IrDA SIR data specification (and related documents). http://www.irda.org/displaycommon.cfm?an=1&subarticlenbr=7 (accessed February 26, 2006).

Institute of Electrical and Electronics Engineers. 2001. IEEE 802.15 Working Group for WPANs. http://standards.ieee.org/getieee802 (accessed February 26, 2006).

Satellite Communications Basics

Michele Luglio, *University of Rome Tor Vergata, Italy,* and Antonio Saitto, *Telespazio, Italy*

INTRODUCTION

Manmade satellites, working in orbit at significant altitude from the Earth, provide the possibility of guaranteeing visibility between points not in line of sight on the Earth due to limitations imposed by the Earth's spherical nature. Satellites actually represent an excellent, sometimes unique, means of complementing terrestrial facilities in order to complete the global information infrastructure (GII), of which every component (terrestrial cabled, terrestrial wireless, and satellite) must play the most suitable role to provide telecommunication connectivity (and hence services) anywhere and to anyone.

In this scenario, as long as the telecommunication systems assume an ever more important role in daily life (both personal and professional), satellites can represent a real added value to ensure global communications.

To introduce the basic concepts of satellite communications, a short history is presented. The rationale for using satellites is highlighted. The main characteristics of satellite systems are described, taking as a reference structure the Internet protocol stack. In addition, three standards will be presented; standardization and regulation activities will be introduced; and interoperability with terrestrial systems will be briefly addressed. Finally, conclusions are presented.

A SHORT HISTORY OF SATELLITE COMMUNICATIONS

The satellite age can be assumed to have begun in 1687 when Newton theorized his law of gravitational force. The paper "Extraterrestrial Relay" by Arthur Clarke (Clark 1945) published by *Wireless World* in October 1945, represents the first real milestone in satellite telecommunications. In that paper, Clarke designed the orbital configuration of a satellite constellation, using an orbit located at 35,800 km over the Earth's surface at the equator, coplanar with the equatorial plane, where the equilibrium between the gravitational force and the centrifugal force let a satellite appear fixed with respect to a point on the Earth's surface. The geostationary constellation was composed of three manned satellites spaced 120° apart at equal angles to get global coverage and represents the reference configuration for most of the satellite systems. A later paper by John Pierce in 1954 titled "Telecommunication Satellites" suggests the use of unmanned satellites either in geostationary (GEO) or low Earth orbit (LEO).

In 1957 the Sputnik satellite launched by the former U.S.S.R. represented the first space mission. Even though it was not designed for telecommunication, the Sputnik mission validated the mechanical possibility of putting and keeping a body in orbit around the Earth.

After that, formal acts that actually set in motion the telecommunication satellite age include the Policy Statement on Communications Satellites signed by U.S. President John F. Kennedy in 1961; the U.S. Communications Satellite Act issued in 1962 with the birth of Comsat; the intergovernmental agreement Interim Arrangements for a Global Commercial Communications Satellite System, issued in 1964 with the birth of ICSC (Interim Communications Satellite Committee); and the formation of Intelsat (International Telecommunication Satellite, with headquarters in Washington D.C.), an intergovernmental organization.

Some experimental missions using LEO, MEO (medium Earth orbit), HEO (highly elliptical orbit), or GEO constellations (*Score* in December 1958, *Courier* in October 1960, *ECHO I* in August 1960, *TELSTAR I* in July 1962, *RELAY I* in December 1962, *TELSTAR II* in May 1963, *SYNCOM II* in July 1963, *ECHO II* in January 1964, *RELAY II* in January 1964, *SYNCOM III* in August 1964, and *MOLNIYA I* in April 1965) preceded the first commercial satellite (*Early Bird*) launched in April 1965 by Intelsat to provide intercontinental fixed services utilizing a constellation in geostationary orbit. In 1976, Marisat was the first system composed of three satellites in GEO orbit to provide mobile services. It preceded the foundation of INMARSAT (International Maritime Satellite, with headquarters in London), another intergovernmental organization that aimed to provide mobile satellite services and which, in 1982, launched the first fully operational system targeted to maritime users. In the following years, INMARSAT provided service even on land masses and for aeronautical users.

In 1988, Omnitracs, the first system for land mobile services, was launched. In 1991, the Italian Italsat satellite represented the first satellite to work in the Ka band using a regenerative payload and multibeam antennas. In 1993, ACTS (Advanced Communication Technology Satellite), funded by the U.S. Congress, was launched as an experimental mission to further validate Ka-band technology, on-board processing, multibeam antennas, hopping beams, and on-board switching. In 1998, Iridium was the first satellite system designed for personal communications; it was followed a few years later by Globalstar. Both systems utilize LEO constellations. Despite limited commercial penetration, the two systems demonstrated the technical feasibility of implementing a network in space and they are currently operational.

SATELLITE SYSTEM CHARACTERISTICS

The use of satellites is justified for the following reasons:

- *Costs independent of distance (within one satellite coverage),*
- *Efficient and cost effective for collecting, broadcasting, and multicasting,*
- *Unique in areas with scarce or no infrastructures,*
- *Unique in case of disaster,*
- *Suitable for large coverage areas and long-range mobility,*
- *Relatively short deployment time,*
- *Flexible architecture,*
- *Bypass very crowded terrestrial networks,*
- *With the same terrestrial infrastructure, both fixed and mobile services,*
- *Extremely suitable for localization services worldwide.*

Assuming the Internet protocol stack as a reference, a brief description of the main characteristics of a satellite system for each layer will be presented.

Architecture

Orbits

The orbits can be classified according to eccentricity (circular or elliptical, where the Earth is located in one of the two focuses) or according to inclination with respect to the equatorial plane (equatorial, polar, or inclined) (Maral and Bousquet 2003; Lutz, Werner and Jahn 2003). Furthermore, they can be classified according to altitude: LEO, between 500 and 1,700 km; MEO, between 5,000 km and 10,000 km and at more than 20,000 km; GEO, at 35,800 km. The elliptical orbits can have the apogee between 39,000 km and 54,000 km. The altitudes below 500 km are not used to avoid atmospheric drag, whereas altitudes between LEO and MEO are not used to avoid the Van Allen belts.

The geostationary orbit theoretically allows a satellite to be in a fixed position with respect to the Earth's surface. Actually, the presence of many forces in addition to the gravitational ones induces a precession movement that may require a tracking system for the ground terminals.

Satellite systems positioned in the GEO orbit are characterized by high delay (120–135 ms one-way) and high free space losses. The elevation angle α_m decreases as the latitude increases. On the other hand, the Earth can be covered with the simplest architecture, composed of just three satellites, but excluding polar regions (above 70° latitude N and below −70° latitude S). To match user distribution requirements, the position of the satellites on the arc may not be spaced 120° apart and in some orbital positions more than one satellite can be installed. If the aim is global coverage, two coverage strategies are applicable: (a) the satellites positioned over the three ocean regions (Atlantic, Pacific, and Indian), which is the largely preferred configuration although it maximizes propagation delay and free space losses (FSL) but can implement full connectivity through double hop, or (b) the satellites positioned over land masses (Europe/Africa, Asia/Australia, and America), which minimizes delay and FSL but must be interconnected through intersatellite link (ISL) to achieve full connectivity.

LEO orbits allow better performance than GEO in terms of free space losses and propagation delay (20–40 ms), but a larger number of satellites is necessary to provide full coverage and real time interactive services (Maral and Bousquet 2003). Doppler effects and frequent handovers between spots and between satellites represent the main drawbacks. Moreover, an efficient tracking system is necessary on the ground station. The elevation angle can be very high at any latitude (even high latitude) and in general is time dependent.

Satellite systems using MEO orbits show performance in between the two previously presented. At present, they are not used for telecommunication systems but for localization and navigation systems such as GPS (global positioning system) and the forthcoming GALILEO.

Satellites in HEO orbits travel over an ellipse, inclined 63.4° with respect to the equatorial plane, in which the Earth is located in one of the two focuses (Maral and Bousquet 2003). With respect to Keplero's law, satellites on this kind of orbit span equal areas in equal time intervals. As a consequence, they go very slowly around the apogee and appear almost fixed for users located at very high latitudes. Satellite handover, the Doppler effect, and the zoom effect represent the main drawbacks but are not as critical as in the case of LEO and MEO. Delay and FSL are comparable to GEO.

The different orbital configurations need not be used alone but can be combined to create a hybrid constellation. For example, a constellation can be composed of one or more satellites in GEO orbit and one or more satellites in LEO orbits. The two components can either be interconnected to reciprocally extend coverage or can be alternative points of access to improve availability (Luglio and Pietroni 2002).

Finally, although they are not satellites in the strict sense, high altitude platform stations (HAPS) are used for telecommunication purpose. They consist of special airships (blimps or aircraft) flying at about 20 km of altitude in the stratosphere, equipped with telecommunication payload to provide service over limited spot areas (up to 200 km diameter). HAPS are conceived to operate in emergency situations (disaster or battlefield) or to provide extra capacity in hot spots from a fixed (or almost fixed) position in the space. From this point of view, they are assumed to be stationary, as GEO satellites but at any geographical position, and offering a high elevation angle (Tozer and Grace 2001; Karapantazis and Pavlidou 2005).

Space Segment

The space segment consists of the spacecraft, which contains a power section (batteries and solar panels), a stabilization and propulsion section (including propellant), a TT&C (telemetry telecommand and control) section to remotely control the spacecraft's on-board motors, and a payload section, which exploits communication functionality between two Earth stations. The payload architecture can be transparent if it acts as a bent pipe (just change the frequency and amplify signals) or it can be regenerative if it implements some on-board processing (OBP) features, which means that it must at least demodulate and remodulate signals, separating the uplink from the downlink. It can also code and decode signals, change polarization, interconnect beam to beam, route packets, and switch messages. On-board switching can be implemented at either base band or microwave frequencies.

Network Topology

The network topology concept in theory is independent of constellation characteristics but as a matter of fact applies only to geostationary systems.

Two kinds of topology are usually supported by a satellite network: star and mesh. The former consists of a central hub station and a set of user terminals, typically much smaller and less power consuming than the hub. The hub acts as the star center through which all the traffic transits; as a consequence, every pair of user terminals are physically interconnected through the hub, thus needing a double hop on the satellite, and thus maximizing delay and use of the bandwidth. In the latter topology, the user terminals can be directly interconnected among each other, needing only one hop on the satellite, thus minimizing the use of the bandwidth and delay (one hop). Hybrid configuration, with a subset of stations connected in full mesh mode and the others in star mode, is another possibility, which has trade-offs in performance.

Ground Segment

The ground segment is typically composed of Earth stations, a Network Operation Center (NOC) and a TT&C station.

The Earth terminals can be of two types: gateway and user terminals (Elbert 2000). Each terminal is equipped with a base-band section and a radio frequency (RF) section. The gateway, usually a big station, is in charge of connecting the satellite systems and the terrestrial networks. The user terminals represent the physical devices through which the users can directly access the satellite resources. They can be classified as fixed (very small aperture terminal, VSAT), transportable (VSAT-like, mounted on a vehicle but working in stationary conditions), or mobile (handheld, cellular-like). VSAT terminals suitable to the mesh topology are more complex and expensive than those used for star networks.

The NOC includes the NCC (network control center) in charge of configuration management, capacity/bandwidth management, acquisition/synchronization control, performance management, alarm management, security management, billing, and accounting. The TT&C Earth segment exchanges information with the TT&C section on-board.

Physical Layer

The physical layer concerns the capability to establish, to ensure, and to keep physical connectivity, taking into account propagation channel characteristics, and the capability to generate power on-board. In fact, the propagation channel is characterized by meaningful nonlinearity that strongly affects technical choices.

Propagation Channel

Effects of the Troposphere. In the troposphere, the most relevant impairments on the transfer characteristic of the channel are:

- attenuation;
- increase of sky noise temperature;
- depolarization;

Above 18 GHz, especially with low elevation and/or margins, there are multiple sources of atmospheric attenuation (ITU-R 2001). Total attenuation (dB) represents the combination of four factors as shown in (1):

$$A_T(p) = \sqrt{\left(A_R(p) + A_C(p)\right)^2 + A_S^2(p)} + A_G(p) \qquad (1)$$

where

- $A_R(p)$ is the attenuation due to rain for a fixed probability (dB),
- $A_C(p)$ is the attenuation due to clouds for a fixed probability (dB),
- $A_S(p)$ is the attenuation due to tropospheric scintillation for a fixed probability (dB),
- $A_G(p)$ is the gaseous attenuation due to water vapor and oxygen for a fixed probability (dB),

being p the probability of the attenuation being exceeded in the range 50% to 0.001%.

The effects due to the troposphere can be significant (in particular for example at Ka band). For a link availability of 99.9% of the time, the total attenuation (including also gaseous attenuation) is over 6.2 dB at 20 GHz and is about 12 dB at 30 GHz and over 30 dB at 40 GHz for unavailability of about 0.1% of the time. To evaluate the rain margin, a detailed procedure is presented in ITU-R (2001).

Because rain attenuation represents the main factor impacting link availability, several fade countermeasure techniques have been proposed and will be briefly presented.

Methods to Counteract Rain Fading. Considering the randomness of the phenomenon and considering that heavy rain occurs only in limited time intervals and in limited areas, it can be quite wasteful to provide high power margins all the time to all the links over a certain coverage area. Thus, many methods have been proposed to counteract rain fading. Some of these use backup resources (bandwidth, power, equipment, etc.) only in those moments and for those links for which the attenuation becomes higher than a certain threshold.

A subset of these backup resources are based on a re-route strategy that operates on a "per link" basis (site diversity, orbit diversity) (Chung and Gallois 1993; Barton and Dinwiddy 1988). Most fade countermeasure techniques are based on reallocating a shared resource (bandwidth, time slots, power, etc.) for those links where fade occurs (frequency diversity, adaptive methods). Moreover, fade countermeasures can be classified in two groups: methods for improving outage probability, and methods for improving power margin (Carassa, Tartara, and Matricciani 1988).

Site Diversity. Site diversity consists in setting up two (or more) Earth stations (and the necessary terrestrial links), used alternatively (ITU-R 2001). The distance between stations is such as to minimize the joint probability of a rain event. Figure 1 shows the site diversity concept.

The advantage gained with site diversity must be traded for the noticeable disadvantage of setting up two antennas, two stations, and providing a terrestrial link between them.

Site Diversity with Shared Resource. With a more complex approach a set of stations share a set of backup stations. The gain obtainable with such a configuration depends on the distance among the stations, on the fading probability distribution on each station, and on the ratio between the number of main stations and the number of backup stations (Luglio et al. 2002). The ratio between the number of main stations and the number of backup stations can be optimized according to desired gain and costs. Figure 2 shows a configuration with ratio equal to two.

Orbit Diversity. Orbit diversity consists in using a backup spacecraft, normally used as a spare, to protect the link

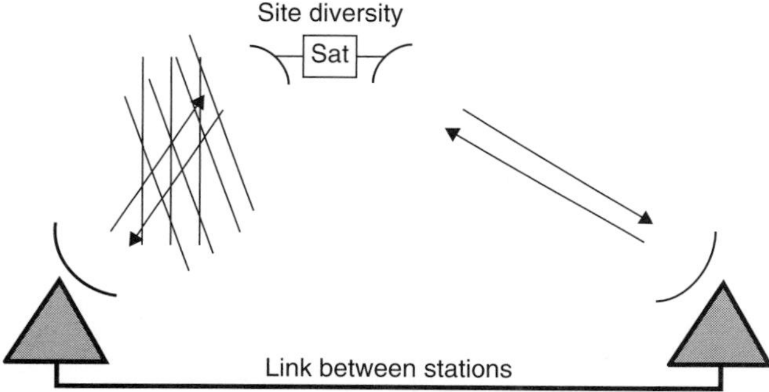

Figure 1: Site diversity concept

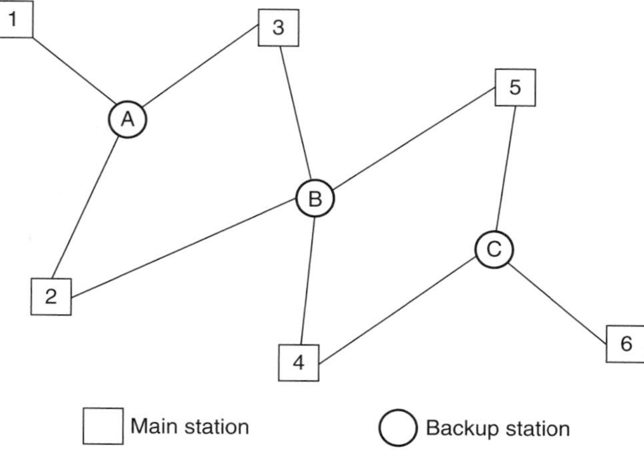

Figure 2: Configuration of multiple site diversity with shared resource

against rain outages. The measured data indicates that rain attenuations on the two converging paths are highly correlated and that the improvement factor is trivial ($\leq$1.2) (Lynn, Bergman, and Pursley 1980), unless high frequencies are used and high performance is pursued (Matricciani and Mauri 1995).

Up Path Power Control (UPPC). The negative effects due to rain fading on the uplink are compensated by increasing Earth station transmitted power, keeping the input power level of the satellite transponder constant (Chakraborty, Davarian, and Stutzman 1993). Although the Earth station would not work at maximum efficiency, the loss of downlink EIRP (Effective Isotropic Radiated Power) caused by a reduction in uplink power is eliminated (Willis and Evans 1988). The down link is weaker anyway, being unable to counteract rain fading. UPPC can easily be combined with other techniques (Chakraborty, Davarian, and Stutzman 1993).

Downlink Power Control. In case of multibeam coverage, with one station per beam and FDMA (frequency division multiple access) access, it is possible to introduce additional amplification in one (or more than one) beam in which the station requires assistance (Carassa 1987). This can be achieved with a variable gain power amplifier in each beam which allows reduction of the needed primary power.

A method similar to the one described above (variable gain on both links) that acts on power margin, is illustrated in Rautio (1980) and operates both on the uplink and on the downlink.

Repeated Transmission. In Chibisov (1987), a method based on repeated transmission of bursts, increasing signal to noise ratio, is presented. It is based on the fact that not all packages are subject to deep fading.

Burst Length Control (BLC). With Burst Length Control (applicable only in case of TDMA access), a set of time slots in the frame (shared resources) are left empty, with the aim of improving the power margin (Carassa 1987). When the power margin for a given link becomes unable to overcome rain attenuation, the emission from/to the station in difficulty is increased in time H times, obtaining a multiplication by H of its energy and the possibility of introducing a proper coding on the signal. It is very easy to implement but it offers a small power gain, especially for high frequencies (Carassa, Tartara, and Matricciani 1988).

Adaptive Modulation. The aim is to keep constant the CNR (carrier to noise ratio) and the BER (bit error rate), dynamically changing the modulation scheme. In clear sky conditions, high spectral efficiency modulation — such as 16-PSK, 64-PSK or 256-QAM, — can be used. As a countermeasure, at the onset of the fade, a more robust modulation method is introduced, such as QPSK or BPSK. Using digital signal processing (DSP) in modems to accommodate different modulation methods, can reduce the spectral efficiency as the CNR (carrier to noise ratio) decreases (Gallois 1993).

Adaptive Forward Error Correction Coding (AFEC). Methods that use adaptive coding techniques can be applied as shared resource methods (Khan, Le-Ngoc, and Bhargava 1989). These techniques provide an additional margin, coding the information streams only during periods of link degradation. The coding is possible using backup time slots, in TDMA frame, which can be assigned to any user. The decision to do so can be taken on the basis of the received signal level or the BER. If there is no rain, the reserved time slots can be used by low priority traffic.

Adaptive Coding and Rate. A combination of two of the above techniques is proposed in (Ferro 1990). It consists in varying the transmission bit rate (from 8 kbit/s up to 1 Mbit/s) and the data coding rate (1, 7/8, 2/3, 3/4, 1/2) on a sub-bursts basis. When it is necessary to compensate high attenuation, coding redundancy is first of all incremented and then data rate is reduced.

Frequency Diversity. With frequency diversity, a higher band is used to carry most of the traffic and a lower band (typically a percentage of the former) is used to assist those links in certain time intervals during which rain attenuation overcomes a certain threshold (Figure 3). The result is an increment in outage probability for high frequency links with a consequent decreasing of the power margin to take in account in dimensioning the system, considering that at high frequencies also a small variation of outage probability yields a remarkable gain for the rain margin. The main impairments are, of course, the partial duplication of RF equipment and the need for cross strapping connection on-board.

Mobility. The second very important issue regarding propagation channel concerns mobility (the use of the user terminal while moving).

Two main overlapping phenomena must be taken into account: fast fading, due to multipath, and slow fading, due to shadowing. The former is due to refraction and reflection of the main ray over the surrounding environment while the latter is due to natural (mountains, hills, trees, etc.) or man made (buildings, bridges, etc.) obstacles. Both events depend on the environment and on the relative position user satellite; thus the analytical characterization must adopt the random process theory. The received signal assumes the following expression:

$$R(t) = z(t)s(t) + n(t) \qquad (2)$$

where z(t) and n(t) are random processes. To evaluate the term z(t) different models have been proposed in literature. The most general expression is:

$$Z(t) = S_1(t)(A + x_1(t) + j \cdot y_1(t)) + S_2(t)(x_2(t) + j \cdot y_2(t)) \qquad (3)$$

where A is the (complex) LOS component, x_i, y_i ($i = 1, 2$) zero mean, independent Gaussian (fast fading) r.vs. and S_i lognormal (shadowing) r.vs. The other models can be derived from the generalized expression suppressing the factors not applying to the particular selected scenario (Corazza and Vatalaro 1993).

Satellite Diversity. Satellite diversity consists in utilizing more than one satellite to increase the number of paths between the hub and the user terminal in order to either improve E_b/N_0 or link availability, thus counteracting shadowing. The diversity order can be theoretically arbitrary (depending on constellation architecture) but in practical systems dual diversity is implemented (Loreti and Luglio 2001).

Link availability can be increased as compared to the case of a single link, being the joint probability in general lower than the single case. The advantage achieved by using diversity depends on the constellation structure and on the azimuthal correlation among links. Several propagation models applicable to diversity scenario have been developed (Loreti and Luglio 2001).

Modulation, Coding, and Interleaving

With regard to modulation, phase modulation schemes are usually adopted due to their intrinsic robustness to a non-linear channel. The most used scheme is QPSK (Quadrature Phase Shift Keying), but in particular cases even higher order modulations are used (see DVBS-2).

Channel encoding introduces redundancy to protect signals against errors. In satellite communications, concatenated coding is often adopted to counteract

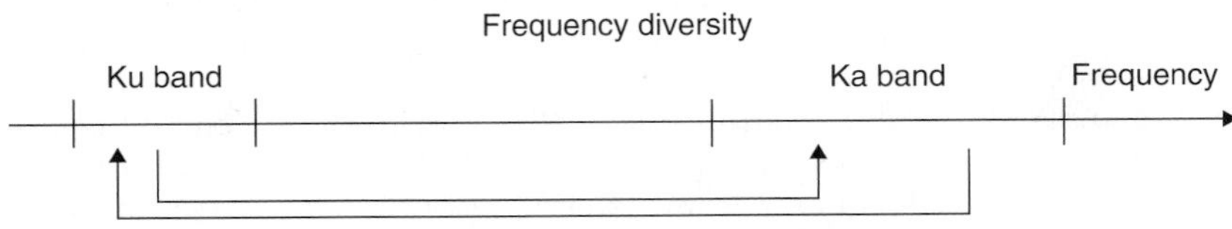

Figure 3: Frequency diversity concept

both burst errors and random errors. For example, the DVB-S (digital video broadcasting satellite) (European Telecommunication Standard Institute 1997) standard adopts Reed Solomon block coding (204,188) to combat burst errors and convolutional coding (adaptive rate from 1/2 up to 7/8) to combat random errors. Also, turbo codes have actually been used in recently launched systems (Giancristofaro et al. 2000).

Interleaving, used to combat channel fluctuations resulting from multipath, aims at randomizing bit errors to change burst errors in random errors. It consists of rearranging the order of a sequence in a deterministic way and then rebuilding the original sequence (Luglio et al. 1997). The bits can be arranged in a row of a matrix and transmitted in columns. Either block or convolutional interleaving can be implemented.

Antenna Coverage Pattern

The coverage strategy can significantly affect the physical layer. Multibeam coverage improves spatial selectivity (allowing frequency reuse) and gain, which allows less critical user terminal design and uneven power distribution at the price of increasing complexity and costs (Loreti, Luglio, and Palombini 2000).

Interference

Another impairment, mainly resulting from multibeam coverage, is the intrasystem co-channel interference (Vatalaro et al. 1995; Caini et al. 1992; Loreti and Luglio 2002). It arises from the overlapping of several side lobes of the interfering beams with the main lobe of the interfered beam. If every beam uses the same frequency (CDMA), the overlapping of two main lobes can also cause serious interference. In satellite systems, co-channel interference is more critical than in terrestrial cellular networks. In fact, for terrestrial systems, morphology and man-made buildings sometimes isolate adjacent cells and zones, allowing a more significant use of frequency reuse.

Interference Countermeasures. Some of the most effective interference reduction techniques at system level are described in Loreti and Luglio 2002 and listed below. The first two are peculiar to LEO and MEO systems, while the others can also provide meaningful results if implemented in GEO systems.

A. beam/cell turnoff;
B. intraorbital plane frequency division;
C. interorbital plane frequency division;
D. use of two orthogonal polarizations;
E. power control;
F. position dependent frequency assignment;
G. frequency hopping;
H. multi-user detection;
I. dynamic resource allocation;
J. optimum bandwidth (or code) assignment.

OBP Capabilities

OBP (on-board processing) consists of the payload's capability to at least demodulate and remodulate signals. It can greatly improve the link design because isolating uplink and downlink avoids direct transfer of noise accumulated on the uplink to the downlink. Furthermore, it achieves better performance in terms of the E_b/N_0 required, reduced power needed on both links, and reduced intermodulation.

MAC Layer

FAMA (Fixed Assignment Multiple Access) Techniques

In general, the same multiple access techniques developed and implemented on terrestrial systems are adopted. In particular, the classical orthogonal techniques are used: FDMA (frequency division multiple access), TDMA (time division multiple access), and CDMA (code division multiple access) or hybrid schemes such as MF-TDMA (multifrequency TDMA). FDMA can be implemented in different schemes: SCPL (single carrier per link), SCPS (single carrier per station), and SCPC (single carrier per channel). Each scheme performs differently in terms of efficiency and generation of intermodulation products. The use of TDMA, which is more flexible than FDMA, requires a critical synchronization system that takes into account the variance of the propagation delay, which must also be carefully considered in the design of the guard time slots (Maral and Bousquet 2003). CDMA allows full frequency reuse, satellite soft handover, satellite path diversity exploitation, and application of interference mitigation techniques such as multi-user detection (MUD) (De Gaudenzi and Giannetti 1998).

RA (Random Access) Techniques

RA (Random Access) techniques are based on the concept that each user starts transmitting when a packet is available. Because no coordination among stations is implemented, packets may collide. In the Aloha scheme, every station monitors its transmission and detects eventual collisions after an RTT or round trip time, which is ~270 ms if the management is on board or ~540 ms if the management is on the ground. Collided packets are retransmitted after a random delay. Efficiency is low. The slotted Aloha scheme improves performance in terms of efficiency, introducing the concept that packets are transmitted in time slots. Also, Selective Reject Aloha improves efficiency, taking advantage of partial collisions and allowing the retransmission of only the overlapped portion, of course, at the price of increased overhead. Finally, if packets are spread either with a PN sequence or in time, the effect of collisions is weakened.

DAMA (Demand Assignment Multiple Access) Techniques

With DAMA techniques, resources are assigned on the basis of requests. Most of these techniques share resources in the time domain. Resources can be reserved either explicitly (for a given number of time slots) or implicitly (a source occupies a certain slot until its transmission is over). Contention is limited to access times. At steady-states it virtually works as a TDMA system.

Techniques based on the PRMA (packet reservation multiple access) concept can be considered. To achieve significant efficiency, these techniques require a frame length longer than RTT (round trip time). Thus, they seem more suitable for systems in LEO orbit (Del Re et al. 1997)

DAMA protocols implemented in TDMA networks are very important and worth mentioning. In particular, in DVB RCS standard (European Telecommunication Standard Institute 2000) five different methodologies are applicable:

a) Continuous Rate Assignment (CRA)

   The resources are negotiated between RCST (return channel on satellite terminal) and NCC for all the superframes in the period. Static capacity is assigned at the beginning of the communication. No BoD (Bandwidth on Demand) delay is experienced; low efficiency is achieved.

b) Rate Based Dynamic Capacity (RBDC)

   The RCST dynamically requests capacity to NCC. Capacity is assigned after explicit request and the request expires every two superframes (by default). It aims to equal input and output transmitter buffer rate. Suitable for VBR (variable bit rate) traffic tolerating MSL (Minimum Scheduler Latency, delay introduced by the scheduler to generate the Burst Time Plan or BTP). RBDC and CRA can be jointly used (CRA ensures a fixed allocation and RBDC ensures a variable assignment for no real-time applications). It represents a trade-off solution.

c) Volume Based Dynamic Capacity (VBDC)

   The RCST dynamically requires a volume of traffic with requests being cumulative and NCC satisfies the requests. It represents a best-effort service: capacity requests aiming to empty the buffer. It is characterized by high BoD delay (RTT~1.6 s) and high efficiency.

d) Absolute Volume Based Dynamic Capacity (AVBDC)

   The requests are absolute and not cumulative as in the previous case.

e) Free Capacity Assignment (FCA)

No signaling between NCC and RCST is foreseen. Free capacity that would otherwise be wasted is automatically assigned not according to any associated traffic profile (random assignment).

Other DAMA techniques are also proposed in (Zhang 2003).

Hybrid Techniques

Hybrid techniques, combining fixed, DAMA and random assignment are also proposed in (Zhang 2003).

Network Layer

Network issues are applicable whenever routing operations are foreseen in the satellite link. Two approaches can be adopted: connection-oriented or connectionless. The latter approach is compliant with IP (Internet protocol). Moreover, the use of IP protocol well suits multicast management, and, as in a terrestrial network, connectionless networks offer some degree of fault tolerance for data delivery. Against this approach, satellite networks (referring to LEO systems) may be too dynamic for standard IP routing and Internet-style routers may require too much memory (perhaps not compatible with the limited space on-board). Among the other problems with using IP, the TTL (time-to-live) and IP packet fragmentation are emphasized because of the huge delay (Partridge and Shepard 1997).

Present satellite networks that provide multimedia wideband services offer an IP interface, managed at ground facilities. The use of regenerative payloads able to perform network-layer functionality in space can offer the opportunity to more efficiently manage satellite networks.

Transport Layer

TCP (transmission control protocol) is the layer 4 protocol which ensures reliable end-to-end communication implementing the concept of acknowledgement of received data. When the path includes a satellite link, this mechanism severely impacts performance due to the high propagation delay. To mitigate such impairments, several countermeasures can be implemented at the transport layer.

TCP Performance

Transmission Control Protocol (TCP) is based on the mechanism of the sliding window which increases exponentially during the Slow Start phase until the Slow Start Threshold is reached, and then linearly during the Congestion Avoidance phase. The high latency implies that it takes a long time to reach the optimum window size, while a high packet loss can be experienced as a consequence of the meaningful BER in particular channel conditions. Furthermore, when the satellite provides wide band access, the bandwidth x delay product becomes very large, impacting the ramping time (Stevens 1994).

TCP Performance Improvement

Several techniques have been proposed to mitigate impairments caused by delay (Allman, Glover, and Sanchez 1999; Border et al. 2001; Loreti et al. 2001; and Luglio et al. 2004). Some of them are specifically designed for satellites, while others are for more general environments. Many proposals are based on modification of the flow control (e.g., enlarging the dimension of the initial window, or reducing the number of acknowledgments) and of the recovery mechanism (dynamic estimation of the available bandwidth, etc.); others are based on modification of the architecture (e.g., splitting the path, terminating the connection at each step, and acknowledging packet reception). Among the latter type of solutions, some adopt standard algorithms or modified versions, and there are solutions typically known as accelerators, which are implemented in real systems and based on proprietary standards.

Application Layer

There is no real limitation to providing any service through a satellite network. Every kind of service and relative applications can be implemented but in some cases, performance may not be optimum. In fact, the propagation delay affects performance of real-time interactive services (e.g., voice, videoconference) but, on the other hand, the suitability to multicast operation makes satellite systems more efficient and cost effective. In particular, both real-time and store and forward services, both fixed and mobile services, both narrow band and wideband services, as well as unicast, multicast, and broadcast services are currently provided.

Payload

The payload represents the portion of the space segment in charge of exploiting telecommunications functionality in the strict sense. The payload receives the signal from the Earth stations and radiates it back after having processed it, at least in terms of converting carrier frequencies and power amplification (transparent) or implementing demodulation and remodulation, decoding and coding and several other processes (regenerative or OBP). The transmission/reception function is exploited through on-board antennas which can be either single beam or multibeam. In terms of OBP capabilities and of coverage strategy, payload architecture can be definitively classified as in Figure 4. The arrows show the possible combinations: in fact payloads can be transparent and single beam, regenerative and multiple beams, or transparent and multiple beams. In particular, from the point of view of technology, payloads evolved from transparent single beam to transparent multiple beams, thanks to the capability of accommodating larger antennas on-board that are automatically deployable and to the use of higher frequencies, then they further evolved to regenerative payloads, thanks to the capability of implementing OBP on-board.

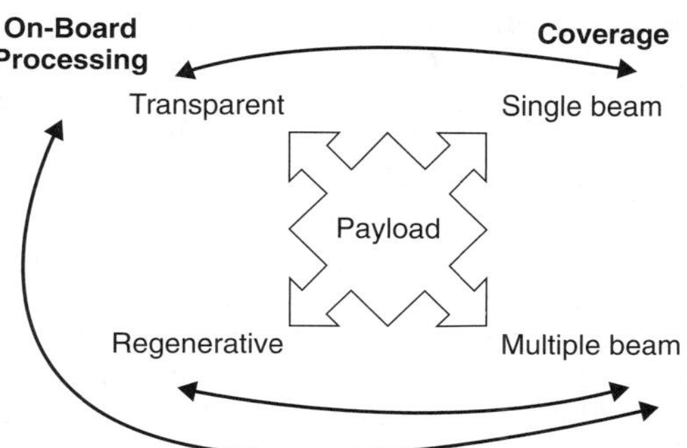

Figure 4: Payload architecture classification

The general scheme of a payload including OBP capabilities is shown in Figure 5. After the receiving antenna, a low noise amplification stage (LNA) provides the first amplification before a local oscillator (LO) down converts the signal to IF (intermediate frequency) or baseband and a demultiplexer (IMUX) disaggregates different contributions. In the eventual OBP section, the signal is demodulated, then decoded in three different stages (inner convolutional, deinterleaved and then outer Reed-Solomon) as in the case of DVB standard. Then a baseband switch matrix switches signals from beam to beam before it is again coded and modulated. Finally, after a high power amplifier (HPA) stage and an output multiplexer (OMUX) the signal is transmitted down to ground station through the transmitting antenna. The basic architecture of transparent payload can be carried out by removing the OBP chain (grey area) (Maral and Bousquet 2003). A payload can even partially implement the depicted transmission chain. Complexity and weight increase due to the presence of more hardware.

When the coverage is achieved by multibeam antennae, the connectivity between any pair of beams must be ensured. (Reduced connectivity patterns can be allowed.) The interconnection pattern is decided during the design phase on the basis of traffic forecasts. The interconnection between a pair of beams can change using switches controlled by telecommand, pre-recorded sequence, or switch matrix. Very fast reconfiguration may be required (on the order of a few hundreds of nanoseconds). To this aim, active switching elements (PIN diodes), optical switching, or a microwave switching matrix is required.

In case of MF-TDMA discipline, the switching matrix architecture can work with either the T-S-T (time-space-time) approach or the S-T-S (space-time-space) approach (*Selenia Technical Review* 1990).

Standards

Satellite systems are mostly based on proprietary standards, both in terms of hardware and services. Nevertheless, in the last years some standards have been developed for broadband services, both fixed and mobile. More emphasis will be placed on the former due to its much greater commercial impact.

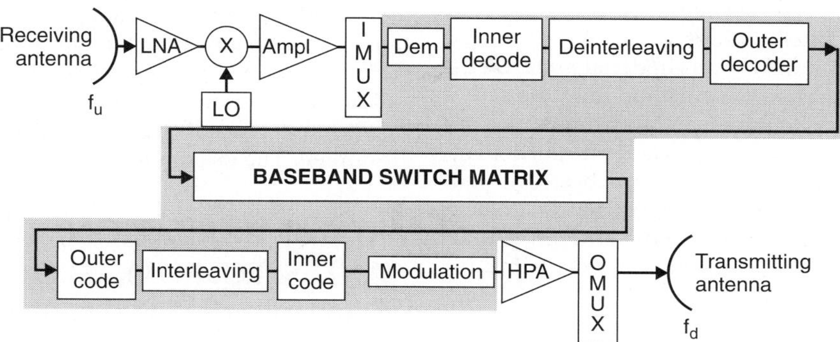

Figure 5: Payload transmission chain

DVB-S (Digital Video Broadcasting Satellite) and DVB-S2

The DVB (digital video broadcasting) standard was issued in 1997 for broadcasting services (European Telecommunication Standard Institute 1997). At present it includes standards for terrestrial fixed (DVB-T), for terrestrial mobile (DVB-H for handheld terminals), cabled (DVB-C), and satellite systems (DVB-S evolved into DVBS2 and the forthcoming DVB-SH, adaptation of DBV-H to satellite handheld terminals). The DVB-S (DVB satellite) standard regulates broadcasting of signals in digital format and how they must be processed before being transmitted. Two basic operations are regulated: base-band processing and satellite channel adaptation.

The base-band processing concerns the adoption of MPEG-2 (Moving Picture Expert Group-2) as the source coding technique on different source signals (video, audio, and data); the following (not mandatory) packetization of data of a single program into packetized elementary stream (PES); and the final multiplexing of a number of PES into the MPEG-2 transport stream (TS). The different data elements can carry independent timing information. In this way, audio information can be synchronized with video information in the receiver, even if they do not arrive aligned at the receiver, which allows the transmission of conventional television programs.

The satellite channel adaptation concerns the types of modulation and coding schemes to be adopted to meet the target quality of the signal (Bit Error Rate around 10^{-11}).

The processes involved in this adaptation are transport multiplex adaptation and randomization for energy dispersal, outer coding (i.e., Reed-Solomon), convolutional interleaving, inner coding (i.e., punctured convolutional code), base-band shaping, and modulation. The randomization is applied to make the RF spectrum approximate a white noise process. The channel coding is applied through three steps: outer code Reed-Solomon (204, 188, T = 8), convolutional interleaving with the aim of randomizing burst errors, and convolutional coding with a variable code rate (1/2, 2/3, 3/4, 5/6, and 7/8). Gray-coded QPSK modulation with absolute mapping (no differential coding) is adopted. Base-band signal is square-root-raised-cosine-filtered with a roll-off factor of 0.35.

The DVB approach offers a good degree of flexibility. A 38 Mbit/s data flux can contain eight standard definition television (SDTV) programs, four enhanced definition television programs (EDTV), or one high definition television (HDTV) program, all with associated multichannel audio and ancillary data services. The maximum data rate for a data stream is typically about 38 Mbit/s accommodated in a 33-MHz satellite transponder.

Recently, the DVB-S standard was updated in the DVB-S2 version. In the new scheme, which modifies the satellite channel adaptation block only, adaptive modulation and coding (ACM) have been introduced. In particular, low density parity check codes (LDPC) have been selected with Bose–Chaudhuri–Hochquenghem (BCH) code-block length 64,800-bit (or 16,200-bit) periodic structures that facilitate parallel decoding with about 50 decoding iterations. Available coding rates are 1/2, 3/5, 2/3, 3/4, 4/5, 5/6, 8/9, and 9/10. Moreover, five modulation formats, all optimized to operate over nonlinear transponders, have been selected: BPSK (1 bit/s/Hz), QPSK (2 bit/s/Hz), 8PSK (3 bit/s/Hz), 16APSK (4 bit/s/Hz), and 32APSK (5 bit/s/Hz). Then, three roll-off factors are allowed: 0.35, 0.25, and 0.20 (DVB-S: only 0.35). With the new standard, an optimization of spectral resources in the order of 30–40% is estimated. If confirmed, the satellite may be more competitive in terms of costs with terrestrial services such as ADSL (asymmetric digital subscriber line).

DVB RCS (DVB Return Channel on Satellite)

The success of the DVB standard due to its capability of transmitting huge quantities of data in a very flexible way, with consequent availability of low-cost technology, extends its field of applicability beyond the transmission of TV signals only. In addition, the compatibility with IP protocol allows processing of the IP packet in the DVB stream. As a consequence, first the use of DVB for one-way systems (DVB IP with return channel on terrestrial networks) has been introduced. The data are received through the same equipment (antenna and receiver) used for digital TV, but the equipment is connected to a PC with a suitable decoder. Then, a two-way standard based on DVB was recently introduced, with return channel on satellite (DVB RCS), which allows bidirectional communications up to 2 Mbit/s in the return link and shares the bandwidth on a MF-TDMA discipline (European Telecommunication Standard Institute 2000). The user terminal is very similar to the receiving equipment but with a RF front-end working at 1–4 W. The great success and market penetration of this technology is leading researchers and standardization bodies to extend the use of DVB RCS for mobile services. Specifications are expected to be issued in 2008.

S-UMTS (Satellite–Universal Mobile Telecommunication System)

Another standard that has been evaluated by ETSI concerns the satellite component of the UMTS [universal mobile telecommunication system] (Caire et al. 2002). SW-CDMA (satellite wideband CDMA) aims to ensure the maximum degree of compatibility with the W-CDMA (wideband CDMA) conceived for the terrestrial component. It is very similar to the ETSI UTRA proposal and is suited to the specific satellite environment. The main features are: wide range of bearer services (from 2.4 kbit/s up to 144 kbit/s), power and spectral efficiency achieved through path diversity exploitation, coherent demodulation on the return link, multiuser detection scheme, overhead reduction using common pilot/beam approach, and compatibility with adaptive antenna systems. Moreover, user localization capabilities are implemented. Two bit-rate options are supported: 4.096 Mbit/s (frame duration = 10 ms) and 2.048 Mbit/s (frame duration = 20 ms). QPSK and dual-BPSK (for low data rate) modulations are adopted. The use of scrambling code is optional.

STANDARDIZATION, REGULATION, AND SPECTRUM ALLOCATION

Standardization Bodies and Related Activities

Several standardization bodies are in charge of developing standards as well as related issues of interest for satellite systems. The main worldwide based institutions are listed here:

- IEEE (Institute of Electrical and Electronic Engineers) (http://www.ieee.org)
- ITU (International Telecommunication Union) (http://www.itu.int)
- ISO (International Organization for Standardization) (http://www.iso.org)

Some others are of regional interest such as:

- CEPT (European Conference of Postal and Telecommunications) (http://www.cept.org)
- ETSI (European Telecommunications Standardization Institute) (http://www.etsi.org)
- FCC (Federal Communications Commission) (http://www.fcc.gov)
- The Telecommunication Technology Committee (http://www.ttc.or.jp)

In addition to the above mentioned bodies, fora of interest are:

- IETF (Internet Engineering Task Force) (http://www.ietf.org)
- GSC (Global Standards Collaboration) (http://www.gsc.etsi.org)
- AIS (Alliance for the Information Society) (http://www.eubusiness.com)
- MMAC (Multimedia Mobile Access Communication Systems) (http://www.arib.or.jp/mmae).

ITU surely represents the most interesting, with both the Radiocommunication sector and the Telecommunication sector. As concerns the former, the most relevant study groups are:

- SG4 Fixed-Satellite Service (Systems and networks for the fixed-satellite service and inter-satellite links in the fixed-satellite service, including associated tracking, telemetry and telecommand functions).
- SG6 Broadcasting Service — terrestrial and satellite (Radiocommunication broadcasting, terrestrial and satellite, including vision, sound, multimedia and data services principally intended for delivery to the general public. Production and radiocommunication, including the international exchange of programs as well as the overall quality of service.)
- SG8 Mobile, Radiodetermination, amateur and related, Satellite Services (Systems and networks for the mobile, radiodetermination and amateur services, including related satellite services).

As concerns the telecommunication sector, the most relevant group is:

- ITU-T Study Group 13 (Next Generation Networks).

In the frame of ITU-R the WRC (World Radiocommunication Conference) is in charge to review, revise the Radio Regulations, the international treaty governing the use of the radio-frequency spectrum and the geostationary-satellite and non-geostationary-satellite orbits.

The agenda determined by the ITU Council takes into account recommendations made by previous world radiocommunication conferences. The general scope of the agenda is established four to six years in advance, and the final agenda two years in advance.

Spectrum Management and Coordination

Spectrum management is a combination of technical and administrative procedures aiming at enabling radio stations everywhere to operate on interference-free frequencies and without causing interference to other stations. It is implemented at two levels: national and international. The procedures are described in the Radio Regulations.

Coordination consists in bilateral negotiation to achieve an agreeable arrangement on the use of shared frequency bands. The procedures for coordination of space communication systems are established in the following provisions of the Radio Regulations (RR):

Article 11: Three main procedures of coordination

- Geostationary satellite network with other networks
- Earth stations with stations for terrestrial services
- Transmitting terrestrial stations with Earth stations

Resolution 46 (WRC 95):

- Non GEO systems and GEO in certain frequency bands (the difference in the determination of the need to coordinate)

Article 7 of Appendix 30:

- Fixed satellite services in the bands 11.7–012.2 GHz (Reg 2), 12.2–12.7 GHz (Reg 3) and 12.5–12.7 GHz (Reg 1) for broadcasting

The required data to be supplied at the initial coordination stage is described by a single regulatory text in the RR: Appendix S4.

Spectrum Allocation

Spectrum allocation is performed by ITU-R and in particular by the World Radiocommunication Conference. Table 1 shows, as an example, the allocated bandwidth for ITU region 2.

Different allocations can be adopted in different regions for some sub-bands. In case a global service must be provided simultaneously in more than one region (or even globally) and no common band is allocated for all the regions, a specific decision must be adopted by WRC, as in the case of Iridium and Globalstar systems.

Table 1: Spectrum Allocation for Satellite Services

	Band	Uplink	Downlink
	C	5,925–6,425 MHz 7,900–8,400 MHz	3,700–4,200 MHz 7,250–7,750 MHz 10.95–11.2 GHz
Fixed services	Ku	13.75–14.5 GHz	11.45–11.7 GHz 12.5–12.75 GHz
	Ka	27.5–30 GHz 30–31 GHz	17.7–20.2 GHz 20.2–21.2 GHz
	UHF	148–150.05 MHz	137–138 MHz
	L	1,626.5–1,660.5 MHz 1,610–1,626.5 MHz	1,525–1,559 MHz 2,483.5–2,500 MHz
Mobile services	S	2,170–2,200 MHz 2,655–2,690 MHz 7,900–8,025 MHz	1,980–2,010 MHz 2,500–2,535 MHz 7,250–7,375 MHz
	Ka	29.9–30 GHz 30–31 GHz	20.1–20.2 GHz 20.2–21.2 GHz

Table 2: Integration Levels

1	Geographical	Satellite provides service only in areas not covered by terrestrial networks; services and technologies can be different.
2	Services	Implies geographical integration and compatibility among services provided by the two networks; performance can be different.
3	Network	Same procedures and protocols allowing the same number to be dialed independently on the terminal; different carrier frequency eventually used by the two segments must be taken into account.
4	Equipment	Compatibility in terms of access, protocols, data rate; at least a part of the circuits could be shared.
5	System	Maximum level; users are not aware of what kind of connection has been established.

INTEGRATION WITH TERRESTRIAL SYSTEMS

Satellites, if used as stand-alone systems, have a limited range of application implying limited market penetrability and appeal. On the other hand, integration with terrestrial networks must be pursued both to reciprocally improve performance (satellite can complement terrestrial network and vice versa) and to gain meaningful market segments.

The use of satellite systems as an overlay network of several different terrestrial networks can represent a meaningful field of application and an interesting market segment. In fact, satellite can work as a backbone among Wi-Fi or WiMax cells, can act as a gap filler between two cells that are not contiguous, or can even extend coverage for those networks usually implemented only in hot spot areas (Luglio, Mazzenga, and Corazza 2006; Giuliano et al. 2006). In addition, satellite systems can allow ad hoc networks, usually used in very limited areas, to access very far away telecommunication networks (for example, remotely located civil protection headquarter) (Luglio et al. 2006).

In this scenario, recommendation ITU-R M.1182-1 (ITU-R 2003) identifies five levels of integration between satellite and terrestrial systems for interoperability, as shown in Table 2, where the five levels are listed and described in some detail.

CONCLUSION

Satellite systems and technology represent a valuable possibility of improving efficiency to provide telecommunication services in a computer network. Satellites can be used as stand-alone systems where terrestrial facilities are not present, when they are damaged or destroyed, or in locations where they are not economically feasible.

The basic characteristics of satellite networks have been presented, highlighting both physical aspects and network layer aspects. Interoperability with terrestrial systems has also been addressed.

GLOSSARY

Broadcast: A connection allowing information transfer from one to everybody.

Coverage Area: The area on the Earth's surface over which the signal-to-noise ratio in both up- and downlink for a user located inside is greater than the minimum required ratio.

Forward Link: The link from the hub station to the user terminal.

Gateway: The Earth station of a satellite system that ensures connection to terrestrial networks.

Global Information Infrastructure: The concept of a unique telecommunication infrastructure at planetary level to provide services everywhere to everyone.

Interference: Portion of the received power originating from unwanted source.

Multicast: A connection allowing information transfer from one to many.

Multiple Access: A regulated exploitation of a common resource by different users distributed at different locations.

Payload: Subsystem of a satellite spacecraft in charge to implement telecommunication functions.

CROSS REFERENCES

See *Geosynchronous Fixed Satellite Communications; Global Navigation Satellite Systems (GNSS); Land-Mobile Satellite Channel; Satellites in IP Networks*.

REFERENCES

AIS (Alliance for the Information Society), http://www.eubusiness.com

Allman, M., D. Glover, and L. Sanchez. 1999. Enhancing TCP over satellite channels using standard mechanism (RFC 2488, http://www.rfc-editor.org/, January).

Barton, S. K., and S. E. Dinwiddy. 1988. A Technique for Estimating the Throughput of Adaptive TDMA Fade Countermeasure Systems, *International Journal of Satellite Communications*, 6: 331–341.

Border, J. et al. 2001. Performance enhancing proxies intended to mitigate link-related degradations (RFC 3135, http://www.rfc-editor.org/).

Caini, C. et al. 1992. A spectrum- and power-efficient EHF mobile satellite system to be integrated with terrestrial cellular systems. *IEEE Journal on Selected Areas in Communications*, *10*: 1315–1325.

Caire, G. et al. 2002. Wideband-CDMA for the satellite component of UMTS/IMT-2000. *IEEE Transactions on Vehicular Technology*, *51*(2), 306–331.

Carassa, F. 1987. Methods to improve satellite systems performances in presence of rain. *Alta Frequenza*. LVI (1–2, Jan–Apr): 173, 184.

Carassa, F., G. Tartara, and E. Matricciani. 1988. Frequency diversity and its applications, *International Journal of Satellite Communications*, 6: 313–322.

Chakraborty, D., F. Davarian, and W. L. Stutzman. 1993. The JPL Ka-Band propagation measurements campaign. *SatCom Quarterly*, Jet Propulsion Laboratory, 8 Jan.: 2–9.

Chibisov, V. N. 1987. Compensation of the effects of signal fading by means of repeated transmission. *Telecommunication and Radio Engineering*, 41–42(10): 7–10.

Chung, T. K. P., and A. P. Gallois. 1993. Fade Countermeasure Intelligent System (FCMIS), IEE Colloquium on Ka Band, Nov. 15th 1993, London.

Clarke, A. C. 1945. Extra-terrestrial relays, *Wireless World*, October: 305–308.

Corazza, G. E., and F. Vatalaro. 1994. A statistical model for land mobile satellite channels and its application to non geostationary orbit systems, *IEEE Trans. Veh. Technol.*, 43 Aug.: 738–741.

Del Re, E., et al. 1997. Performance evaluation of an improved PRMA protocol for low Earth orbit mobile communication systems. *International Journal of Satellite Communications*, *15*: 281–291.

De Gaudenzi, R., and F. Giannetti. 1998. DS-CDMA satellite diversity reception for personal satellite communication: Satellite-to-mobile link performance analysis. *IEEE Transactions on Vehicular Technology*, *47*(2): 658–672.

Elbert, B. 2000. *The satellite communications ground segment and Earth station handbook*. Norwood, MA: Artech House.

ETSI (European Telecommunications Standardization Institute) http://www.etsi.org

European Telecommunication Standard Institute. 1997. Digital video broadcasting (DVB); Framing structure, channel coding and modulation for 11/12 GHz satellite services (EN 300 421 V1.1.2, Sophia-Antipolis Cedex, France).

European Telecommunication Standard Institute. 2000. Digital video broadcasting (DVB); Interaction channel for satellite distribution systems (TM2267r2 DVB-RCS001rev11, Sophia-Antipolis Cedex, France).

FCC (Federal Communications Commission), http://www.fcc.gov

Ferro, E. 1990. A satellite network for good weather conditions and for high rain attenuation., *SBT/IEEE International Telecommunications Symposium*, ITS '90, Rio de Janeiro, Brazil, Sept. 3–6 1990: 393–398.

Gallois, A. P. 1993. Fade countermeasure techniques for satellite communication links. *Int. Symp. on Communications, Theory and Applications*, July 1993.

Giancristofaro, D., et al. 2000. Performances of novel DVB-RCS standard turbo code and its applications in on-board processing satellites. Paper presented at IEEE European Mobile Personal Satcoms: Personal, Indoor and Mobile Radio Communications (Sept. 17–21 2000), London.

Giuliano, R., et al. 2006. Feasibility assessment of WIMAX and geostationary satellite integration, Third Advanced Satellite Mobile Systems Conference, May 29–31, 2006, Herrsching am Ammersee, Germany.

GSC (Global Standards Collaboration), http://www.gsc.etsi.org

IEEE (Institute of Electrical and Electronic Engineers), (http://www.ieee.org)

IETF (Internet Engineering Task Force), http://www.ietf.org

ISO (International Organization for Standardization), http://www.iso.org

ITU (International Telecommunication Union), http://www.itu.int

ITU-R. 2001. Propagation data and prediction methods required for the design of Earth-space telecommunication systems, Rec ITU P.618-7, 2001.

ITU-R. 2003. Integration of terrestrial and satellite mobile communication systems, Recommendation ITU-R M.1182-1.

Jamalipour, A. 1997. *Low Earth orbital satellites for personal communication networks*. Norwood, MA: Artech House Publishers..

Karapantazis, S., and N. F. Pavlidou. 2005. Broadband communications via high-altitude platforms: A survey, *IEEE Communications Surveys & Tutorials*, 7(1): 2–31.

Khan, M. H., T. Le-Ngoc, and V. K. Bhargava. 1989. Further studies on efficient AFEC schemes for Ka-band satellite systems. *IEEE Transactions on Aerospace and Electronic Systems*, AES-25 (1): 9–20.

Lin, S. H., H. J. Bergmann, and M. V. Pursley. 1980. Attenuation on Earth-satellite paths—Summary of 10 years experiments and studies. *Bell System Technical Journal, 59*(2): 183–228.

Loreti, P., et al. 2001. LEO satellite systems' performance with TCP-IP applications. *Proceedings of Milcom 2001,* 2: 811–815.

Loreti, P., M. Luglio, and L. Palombini. 2000. Impact of multibeam antenna design on interference for LEO constellations, 11th IEEE International Symposium on Personal, Indoor and Mobile Radio Communications, PIRMC 2000, 18–21 Sept, London: 913–917.

Loreti, P., and M. Luglio. 2001. Satellite diversity: A technique to improve link performance and availability for multicoverage constellations, in *Third Generation Mobile Communication Systems, UMTS and IMT-2000* (P. Stavroulakis, ed.), Berlin: Springer Verlag.

Loreti, P., and M. Luglio. 2002. Interference evaluations and simulations for multisatellite multispot systems. *International Journal of Satellite Communications*, 20(4): 261–281.

Luglio, M., et al. 1997. *Link design and fade countermeasures for multimedia satellite services in the frame of the SECOMS Project, ACTS Mobile Communication Summit '97*, Aalborg, Denmark, 7–10 October 1997: 37–42.

Luglio, M., et al. 2002. Large scale site diversity for satellite communication networks, *International Journal of Satellite Communications*, 20(4) July–August: 251–260.

Luglio, M., et al. 2004. On-board satellite "split TCP" proxy. *IEEE Journal on Selected Areas in Communications, 22*(2) Feb.: 362–370.

Luglio, M., et al. 2006. Interfacing satellite systems and ad hoc networks for emergency applications, Third Advanced Satellite Mobile Systems Conference, May 29–31, 2006. Herrsching am Ammersee, Germany.

Luglio, M., F. Mazzenga, and G. E. Corazza. 2006. WiMax and satellite systems interoperability scenarios identification, Third Advanced Satellite Mobile Systems Conference, May 29–31, 2006, Herrsching am Ammersee, Germany.

Luglio, M., and W. Pietroni. 2002. Optimisation of double link transmission in case of hybrid orbit satellite constellations. *AIAA Journal on Spacecrafts and Rockets*, 39(5).

Lutz, E., M. Werner, and A. Jahn. 2000. *Satellite systems for personal and broadband communications*. Berlin: Springer.

Maral, G., and M. Bousquet. 2003. *Satellite communications systems: Systems techniques and technology* (4th ed.) Chichester: Wiley.

Matricciani, E., and M. Mauri. 1995. Italsat-Olympus 20 GHz Orbital Diversity Experiment at Spino d'Adda, *IEEE Transactions on Antennas and Propagation*, 43 (1) Jan: 105–108.

MMAC (Multimedia Mobile Access Communication Systems), http://www.arib.or.jp/mmac

Partridge, C., and T. J. Shepard. 1997. TCP/IP performance over satellite links. *IEEE Network*: 44–49.

Rautio, J. C. 1980. Adaptive rain fade compensation. International Telemetry Conference Proceedings (ITC-USA '80, San Diego, CA, Oct. 14–16) 16: 35–46.

Selenia Technical Review. 1990. Special issue on Italsat. 3(4).

Stevens, W. R. 1994. *TCP/IP Illustrated*, Vol. 1, Upper Saddle River, NJ: Addison-Wesley Professional Computing Series.

The Telecommunication Technology Committee, http://www.ttc.or.jp

Tozer, T. C., and D. Grace. 2001. High-altitude platforms for wireless communications, *Electronics & Communication Engineering Journal*, 13(3): 127–137.

Vatalaro, F., et al. 1995. Analysis of LEO, MEO, and GEO global mobile satellite systems in the presence of interference and fading. *IEEE Journal on Selected Areas in Communications*, 13(2): 291–300.

Willis, M. J., and B. G. Evans. 1988. Fade countermeasures at Ka Band for Olympus, *International Journal of Satellite Communications*, 6: 301–311.

Zhang, Y. (Ed.), *Internetworking and computing over satellite networks*, Norwell, MA: Kluwer Academic Publishers, 2003.

Land-Mobile Satellite Channel

Emilio Matricciani, *Dipartimento di Elettronica e Informazione Politecnico di Milano, Italy*

THE LAND-MOBILE SATELLITE CHANNEL

Mobile satellite systems provide many services to aeronautical, maritime, vehicular (automobiles, trucks, trains), and pedestrian communications (handheld telephones). Land-mobile satellite communication usually refers to vehicular and pedestrian communications only and, as such, is a very important field of application, development, and research. Land-mobile satellite systems, however, need to be integrated with terrestrial mobile and fixed networks to optimize the overall benefits for both users and network operators (Pattan 1998).

Land-mobile satellite channels can be degraded much more seriously than fixed-satellite channels because electromagnetic waves propagate in a high hostile environment, together with the necessity of using small, simple, and low-cost antennas and receivers. The antennas are broad beam with low gain, resulting in a low sensitivity receiver. The physical environment may consist of obstructions, such as buildings and trees, that can cause multipath and severe signal attenuation and make the reception of signals of tolerable quality very difficult.

Land-mobile satellite links need to operate in the greatest variety of radio propagation conditions. At one extreme, there are open stretches of road with direct visibility to the satellite, and, at the other, there are the heavily shadowing environments of cities. At frequencies above 10 GHz, the channel may also be affected by large tropospheric fading.

Land-mobile satellite channels, as terrestrial mobile channels, are affected by multipath fading and shadowing. These phenomena are extremely important because they determine the distribution of the received power as long as tropospheric effects are not yet important. Moreover, compared to terrestrial outdoor mobile receivers, a mobile satellite receiver can receive a strong direct or specular component (if the receiving antenna is not very directive), which is essential to the line-of-sight link power budget but modifies significantly the channel statistics. Another characteristic of land-mobile satellite channels is the dependence of the propagation characteristics on the satellite orbit (Loo and Butterworth 1998; Lutz et al. 1991; Wu et al. 1994).

Satellite orbits can be geostationary (GEO), orbits in the equatorial plane at an altitude of 36,000 km, or nongeostationary (Pattan 1998). The orbit of nongeostationary satellites can occur in planes with arbitrary inclination and altitude, although the most used are low-altitude Earth orbits (LEOs; 500 to 1700 km), medium-altitude Earth orbits (MEOs; 5000 to 10,400 km), or highly elliptical orbits (HEOs; apogee around 40,000 to 50,000 km, e.g., Molniya and Tundra orbits; Pratt, Bostian, and Allnutt 2003; Maral and Bousquet 1998). Nongeostationary satellites are never seen, of course, as stationary by a mobile (or fixed) user because the satellite changes its elevation angle and slant range continuously as it crosses the sky. Therefore, the propagation channel conditions vary largely, and a strong Doppler frequency shift can appear. This is the apparent change in frequency of the transmitted signal (both in carrier frequency and symbol rate) due to the relative motion of the mobile and transmitter.

The frequency bands allocated to land-mobile satellite communications are contiguous to those allocated to the terrestrial networks so that no major differences are observed in the nature of the physical phenomena affecting radiowave propagation, but only in their intensity and time dependence. The frequency bands of the actual land-mobile satellite communications are L band (1.5 GHz) or S band (3 GHz), for example, the Globalstar system (satellites orbiting at about 1400 km; Dietrich, Metzen, and Monte 1998). At these frequencies the interaction of electromagnetic waves with the troposphere (tropospheric effects) is negligible, compared to the interaction with orography, buildings, trees, and other obstacles.

The large bandwidths allocated at K_u (12/14 GHz) and K_a (20/30 GHz) bands and the availability, today, of a mature technology for these frequency bands have made them more attractive for broadband multimedia services. However, when compared to mobile channels working at the lower frequency bands, K_u and K_a band land-mobile satellite channels face a much more hostile propagation environment and show their own unique propagation characteristics. Besides suffering the same propagation impairments of L and S bands, new impairments are measured because of the troposphere constituents—mainly rain, although rain attenuation can be statistically less severe for a vehicle than for a fixed receiver if the vehicle is driven in a straight line.

K_u and K_a band land-mobile channels suffer from more severe shadowing and faster multipath fading. The time variation of the multipath fading is directly related to Doppler effects, described by the Doppler power spectrum of the channel or by its reciprocal (coherence time of the channel), and these effects are more serious at K_a band because the electromagnetic wavelength is shorter than that at L, S, and K_u bands, so that constructive and destructive interference-producing multipath fading is much faster and the channel correlation time is much shorter.

Land-mobile satellite channels are usually required to use adaptive power control between the mobiles and the satellite. In the cases of time or frequency orthogonal systems, such as time-division multiple access (TDMA) or frequency division multiple access (FDMA), the main purpose of power control is to maintain a constant average quality for all users and to minimize the required transmit power. In a direct-sequence code division multiple access (CDMA) system, accurate adaptive power control is critical for a good overall system performance because the multiple-access users act as interferers to each other (Maral and Bousquet 1998; Pratt, Bostian, and Allnutt 2003).

The traffic flow through the terminal can be low but it has to pay for the full connection regardless. To be competitive, the size, cost, and power consumption of a land-mobile channel should approach those of the terrestrial mobile (cellular) channels, and it should be possible to connect it with the terrestrial system. The transmitted power should conform to radiation safety standards.

The signal-to-noise ratio of a land-mobile satellite channel fluctuates rapidly because of multipath fading (small-scale fading). The fading on the uplink is usually uncorrelated with that on the downlink, since the uplink and downlink frequency bands are separated by more than the coherence bandwidth of the channel. The signal may also suffer large-scale and more slowly varying shadowing losses due to blockage by buildings, hills, and trees, which are usually assumed identical on the uplink and downlink.

There are severe and practical constraints imposed on the design of a mobile terminal. The limited mounting space on vehicles largely restricts the antenna size, so that the achievable gain is low. The antennas used for the land-mobile satellite communications are similar to those used for terrestrial mobile communications in the same frequency bands, but with more demanding features and higher costs. Whether geostationary satellites are employed or not, the mobile Earth terminal may need a directional antenna, and this component can be critical because the directional beam must be dynamically oriented toward the satellite in a very rapidly changing environment.

One of the benefits of the K_a band is higher antenna gain and a substantial reduction of its physical size compared to the antennas of the lower-frequency bands. To achieve these benefits it is necessary, however, to overcome higher component losses and design a more accurate and demanding satellite-tracking system to take care of the narrower antenna beam. Both parabolic (Densmore and Jamnejad 1993) and microstrip antennas (Telikepalli et al. 1995) can be used, the latter more suited to conform to vehicle surface. The antenna system has to be rugged enough to withstand the shock and vibration of the mobile vehicle; it has to complete a full azimuth search and acquire the satellite signal within a few seconds; it has to track the satellite by compensating for vehicle yaw, pitch, and roll-up; and the tracking system should not lose track of the satellite direction during signal outages (it must rely on inertial pointing during such periods).

Whenever user terminals are mobile, it is necessary, of course, to manage their mobility so that calls can be established efficiently. To minimize call setup time and network signaling requirements, and to improve the call setup success rate, the terminal or the network must estimate the user's position. Furthermore, in a LEO or MEO satellite system the signal level may deteriorate when a connecting satellite moves out of range or is temporarily not visible because of an obstruction. Handover increases the complexity of a network, and, in general, the number of handovers decreases as the satellite orbit altitude increases because the orbit period increases too. For a LEO system, the satellite visibility is of the order of few minutes; for a MEO system, it is of the order of an hour; and for a GEO system, it is exactly twenty-four hours and no handover is needed.

The modulation schemes most often used in mobile communications are the classical binary phase shift keying (BPSK) and quadrature phase shift keying (QPSK). The carrier (BPSK) or the two orthogonal carriers (QPSK) are modulated in amplitude, double side bands, by positive and negative pulses. The carrier is suppressed to save power, and, as a consequence, the receiver has to use coherent demodulators that need to recover both the frequency and phase of the carriers in a hostile environment with significant Doppler frequency shift, especially in LEO systems. Other modulation schemes used in terrestrial mobile communications are also considered for the land-mobile satellite communications (Pattan 1998).

Depolarization must be considered whenever two orthogonal electromagnetic waves are used to increase channel capacity without increasing the bandwidth requirements, a technique known as *frequency reuse* and already applied to satellite television broadcasting at K_u band. As depolarization alters the polarization properties of the incident wave, linear and circular polarizations are transformed into elliptical polarization, and the polarization axes themselves may be rotated. As a consequence, depolarization produces interference between the two orthogonal channels and degrades system performance by reducing the effectiveness of frequency-reuse techniques.

Forward error correcting (FEC) codes are used for channel coding, as they are for mobile terrestrial communications (Hagenauer and Lutz 1987; Pratt, Bostian, and Allnutt 2003). The satellite land-mobile channel may experience error bursts due to multipath reflections and shadowing, or to rain attenuation, so that Reed-Solomon codes, concatenated with convolutional codes, are preferred because they can correct these kinds of errors. Very efficient codes are the so-called "turbo" codes that represent the most significant advance in concatenated coding, with performance approaching the Shannon limit. Turbo codes combined with a channel interleaver can combat fast multipath fading and can also be combined with techniques that combat severe slow fading due to shadowing, rain, or other atmosphere constituents. Other important codes are the low-density parity check (LDPC) codes (Gallager 1963), rediscovered ten years ago (MacKay and Neal 1996) and now likely to become the standard in error correction for applications from cell phones to interplanetary communication.

The diversity schemes used for terrestrial mobile communications can also be applied, in general, to land-mobile communications, but they have to be adapted to the highly variable propagation characteristics and to the terminal receiver.

Diversity schemes can be more effective in clear-sky conditions than in the presence of precipitation because distortions change largely only in few wavelengths (fast fading due to multipath). Antenna (and polarization) diversity can combat the fast fading due to multipath by placing two antennas at a distance of several wavelengths—an architecture that can be, of course, implemented on a vehicle.

However, when rain attenuation affects the land-mobile channel, as rain attenuation is significantly correlated over several minutes and hundreds of meters, the only diversity scheme that may be used (disregarding the trivial method of largely reducing the bit rate and thus the information rate), both in the uplink and in the downlink, is time diversity, with time delays of few minutes to combat deep fades (Ismail and Watson 2000). By transmitting the same data at least twice, with a delay of a few minutes (this delay is a function of rain attenuation; see Matricciani 2006), the receiver could recover the original data by replacing the portion corrupted by many errors with a version much less corrupted. This method, of course, can be applied only to non-real-time data communication and requires more capacity because at least two identical digital streams must be transmitted. In conclusion, it seems hard to devise real-time diversity countermeasures to rain attenuation for land-mobile channels and real-time communications.

PROPAGATION CHARACTERISTICS OF THE LAND-MOBILE SATELLITE CHANNEL

Several impairments affect the propagation of electromagnetic waves in a land-mobile satellite channel. With regard to terrestrial mobile communications, multipath and shadowing affect the received signal at any frequency band (the so-called "clear-sky" conditions); however, at frequencies above approximately 10 GHz, tropospheric effects also become very important. At these higher frequencies, the attenuation of the electromagnetic wave is due to hydrometeors (rain, snow, ice crystals, clouds) and atmospheric gases (oxygen, water vapor), and strongly depends on frequency, elevation angle, locality, and weather conditions (Crane 2003). In any mobile communication system it is fundamental to understand and model the characteristics of the electromagnetic wave propagation because link margins must be specified according to the type of environment and weather conditions.

Clear-Sky Channel

A clear-sky channel refers to a channel in which the propagation of electromagnetic wave is not affected by rain or heavy clouds. In this case, the received signal can be modeled as the sum of the direct and ground-reflected waves (coherent components) and the diffuse wave (incoherent component) because rays propagate as light (ray optics; Jakes 1994).

The *direct component* is received through a line-of-sight path. It is subject to free-space attenuation when the first Fresnel ellipsoid is cleared (Friis transmission formula applies; see Friis 1946), to attenuation due to shadowing, and to scintillation and depolarization caused by a turbulent troposphere or the ionosphere.

The main effects of the ionosphere are *depolarization* (or Faraday effect) and *scintillation* (Richharia 1999). Depolarization of linear polarized electromagnetic waves occurs because the ionosphere is birefringent in the presence of Earth's magnetic field; it is usually predictable (except under unusual atmospheric conditions such as a magnetic storm) and can be compensated by adjusting the polarization of the receive antenna. Its impairments can be minimized by using circular polarization at those frequencies (less than approximately 10 GHz) for which the effect can be significant.

Rapid fluctuation of signal amplitude, phase, polarization, or angle of arrival is known as *scintillation*. Ionospheric scintillation occurs because of small-scale variations of the ionosphere refractive index and is mainly experienced below ~4 GHz; however, in extreme conditions (e.g., during a magnetic storm or near the equator), scintillation can degrade a signal up to 7 GHz. Near the geomagnetic equator (the imaginary great circle on the Earth's surface formed by the intersection of a plane passing through the Earth's center perpendicular to the axis connecting the north and south magnetic poles), ionospheric scintillation is typically the most severe impairment experienced by land-mobile satellite systems at L, S, and C bands.

Shadowing is the attenuation of the direct component caused by any type of obstacle: trees, buildings, hills, or mountains. Measurements have shown that shadowing causes the main distortion of the received signal and determines the power margins necessary to provide a tolerable link budget to the user. The intensity and statistical frequency of shadowing depends on the elevation angle, the carrier frequency, the type of obstacle, the path length through the obstacle, and the direction of vehicle travel with respect to the satellite.

The *specular component* reflects from the ground. The reflected power depends on the roughness of the terrain and is larger for a terrain that, at a given wavelength, appears smooth (i.e., the standard deviation of the terrain roughness is small compared to the electromagnetic wavelength; Beckmann and Spizzichino 1987). As a consequence, the reflected power can largely vary in urban, suburban, and rural environments at high microwave frequencies. This component, however, usually reaches the receiver at a large angle relative the direct path, so that its contribution to the overall received signal in the satellite link can be ignored when a directive (high-gain) antenna is used. It is usually neglected in modeling the land-mobile satellite channel.

The *diffuse component* is due to multipath caused by the reflections and scattering from the space around the receiver, more specifically from outside the first Fresnel ellipsoid (which determines the line-of-sight path). This component is responsible for the small-scale variations of the signal amplitude and phase. Its power depends, at any time, on the distribution of the scattering objects surrounding the receiver. Scintillation due to the troposphere is described in the following section.

If directive antennas and carrier frequencies at L and S bands are used, then shadowing and multipath are the phenomena that dominate the land-mobile satellite channel because tropospheric effects are still negligible. This is why most studies consider only these two phenomena without even mentioning tropospheric effects.

Tropospheric Channel

Besides the clear-sky phenomena mentioned previously, at frequencies $f > 10$ GHz tropospheric phenomena cannot be ignored whenever high channel availability is required. If shadowing, obstruction, and multipath are avoided or taken care of, tropospheric phenomena remain the irreducible cause of fading and system outage, and determine the link budget (Ippolito 1989).

The main atmospheric factors affecting the propagation of electromagnetic waves in fixed or mobile satellite communication systems are due to the lower part of the atmosphere in which meteorological phenomena develop, the troposphere:

1. Attenuation (absorption) caused by atmospheric gases
2. Attenuation (scattering and absorption) and depolarization (a fraction of energy from the incident polarization is coupled to the orthogonal polarization) caused by hydrometeors (mainly rain but also hail, wet snow, ice, clouds, and fog)
3. Scintillation due to the rapid variations of amplitude and phase caused by refractive index irregularities (turbulence)

Any time there is energy absorption, there is also an increase of the system noise temperature, so that tropospheric phenomena affect the carrier-to-noise ratio in two ways: the carrier power is reduced (attenuation) and the noise power is increased, but the latter phenomenon must be considered only if the antenna is directive. Otherwise, the noise temperature entering the antenna is maximized at about 293 K.

Many gaseous constituents of the atmosphere can interact with electromagnetic waves. However, at frequencies up to approximately 300 GHz, only *oxygen* and *water vapor* produce significant absorption. The first three absorption bands are centered at about 22.2 GHz (H_2O), 50–70 GHz (O_2), and 119 GHz (O_2; Ippolito 1986). The attenuation is due to the permanent magnetic moment of the oxygen molecule that interacts with the magnetic field of the electromagnetic wave, and to the electric dipole of water vapor molecule that interacts with the electric field of the electromagnetic wave. These interactions cause a change in the rotational energy of the molecules that absorb in this way energy from the electromagnetic wave. The attenuation due to water vapor exhibits noticeable daily, seasonal, and geographical variations. In the absorption bands, satellite communication is either very demanding or impossible (Matricciani and Riva 1998a).

Hydrometeor is the general term that refers to the products of condensed water vapor in the atmosphere and observed as rain, hail, snow, ice, fog, and clouds. The presence of hydrometeors in the radiowave path, particularly rain, can produce major impairments to space communications that rapidly increase with frequency. Raindrops both absorb and scatter electromagnetic wave energy. They also depolarize the wave, thus reducing the benefits of frequency reuse, and induce rapid amplitude and phase fluctuations, antenna gain degradation, and bandwidth coherence reduction. However, even for the relatively large bandwidths needed for multimedia communication, only absorption, scattering, and depolarization are important. Because these latter phenomena are the main causes that reduce the energy of the electromagnetic wave directed to a polarization-matched antenna, their overall effect on the link budget is twofold: fading (i.e., what is termed *rain attenuation*) and the increase of the thermal noise in the receiver. The noise temperature of this additive white Gaussian noise can be approximately calculated by considering rain as a passive two-port circuit at the physical temperature of rain, with the same attenuation. A conservative estimate of this noise temperature is approximately 293 K.

Rain attenuation becomes significant when the wavelength of the electromagnetic wave in water, $\lambda_o/\sqrt{\varepsilon_r}$ (λ_o, wavelength in vacuum; $\varepsilon_r \approx 80$, relative dielectric constant of water) is comparable to the hydrometeor diameter (Oguchi 1983). Because the largest diameter of a raindrop can be 9–10 mm for high rain intensity (rain rate), it turns out that rain attenuation is significant only for frequencies higher than approximately 9–10 GHz, and that at L, S and C bands can be neglected.

The classical development to determine rain attenuation assumes that the intensity of the electromagnetic wave decays exponentially as it propagates in the rainy path. The raindrops are usually assumed to be ellipsoids (and, as such, they cause depolarization of the electromagnetic wave), and the contribution of each drop is additive and independent of that of other drops. Rainfall, is in fact, built up by many drops of different diameter and shape, synthetically described by a raindrop size distribution.

In contrast to clear-sky effects, rain attenuation, A, is always measured and calculated in decibels. The rain attenuation of an electromagnetic wave propagating in a slant path of rain of extent L km (rainy path length) in the direction of wave propagation can be expressed as:

$$A = \int_0^L Y(x)dx \text{ (dB)} \tag{1}$$

where Y is the specific attenuation (dB/km). For practical applications, the relationship between specific attenuation Y (dB/km) and rain rate R (mm/h) can be expressed as a nonlinear function of a physical quantity, the rain rate R (mm/h), which can be measured on site with a rain gauge, a robust and reliable device. The relationship between R and Y can be approximated by the power law

$$Y(x) = kR^{\alpha}(x) \text{ (dB/km)} \quad (2)$$

where k and α are assumed to be constants along the path but dependent on frequency, polarization, and temperature. Values of k and α have been calculated for many frequencies (Olsen, Rogers, and Hodge 1978; Maggiori 1981). The values given by Maggiori (1981) are those recommended by the International Telecommunication Union-Radio Communication Sector (ITU-R 1992a).

Hail and snow can also be present in a satellite path and can induce significant fades. Ice can produce significant depolarization with very little attenuation (Cox and Arnold 1984). Wet snow or rainfall, if not quickly removed from an antenna dish, can produce significant attenuation (Crane 2002).

Rain attenuation varies statistically from year to year, from season to season, from hour to hour of the day, being usually larger in summer (huge rain storms) than in winter, and larger in the afternoon and evening hours than in the morning and evening hours, at least for localities with temperate climates (Lin, Bergmann, and Pursley 1980; Goldhirsh 1980; Fukuchi et al. 1981; Cox and Arnold 1982; Matricciani 1998, 2000b, 2004).

Rain attenuation is a slow phenomenon both for fixed and mobile receivers, and is independent of antenna directivity. The average power spectrum of time series of fading during rain rapidly sampled (50 samples/s) in a fixed satellite link shows that significant power due only to rain attenuation can be found up to about 0.01–0.03 Hz. The spectrum at higher frequencies is dominated by the tropospheric turbulence, whose effects are statistically dependent on the simultaneous rain attenuation (Matricciani, Mauri, and Riva 1996; Matricciani and Riva 2005a).

Figure 1, for instance, shows the experimental average power spectrum obtained from many time series of fade at 18.7 GHz collected during rain in a 37.7 degree slant path to satellite Italsat, with a 3.5 m receiving antenna (Matricciani and Riva 2005a). It shows the typical shape predicted for a turbulent atmosphere with a complex refractive index, with two frequency intervals of different and definite slopes, separated by a frequency interval with a flatter spectrum. Up to frequencies of few hundredths of hertz we can observe the "classical" −20 dB/decade slope due only to rain attenuation (Matricciani 1994). The slope starts to change its magnitude at about 0.02 – 0.03 Hz. For frequencies larger than about 0.3 Hz, the classical −80/3 dB/decade slope due only to scintillation (i.e., −8/3 in natural units; Tatarski 1961) clearly appears.

As for frequency scaling, for not too large a range at microwaves, rain attenuation A_2 (dB) at a carrier frequency f_2 can be empirically related to rain attenuation A_1 (dB) exceeded for the same probability at a carrier frequency f_1, in the same slant path, by the power law:

$$A_2 = A_1(f_2/f_1)^a \quad (3)$$

where a is an empirical parameter ranging from 1.7 (Drufuca 1974) to approximately 2.2 (OPEX 1994).

As for elevation angle scaling, the following formula, derived by assuming a direct proportionality between A and slant rainy path length and valid for $\theta > 5$ degrees approximately, can be used to obtain a first approximation:

$$A(\theta) = A(\theta_o) \sin\theta_o / \sin\theta \quad \text{(dB)} \quad (4)$$

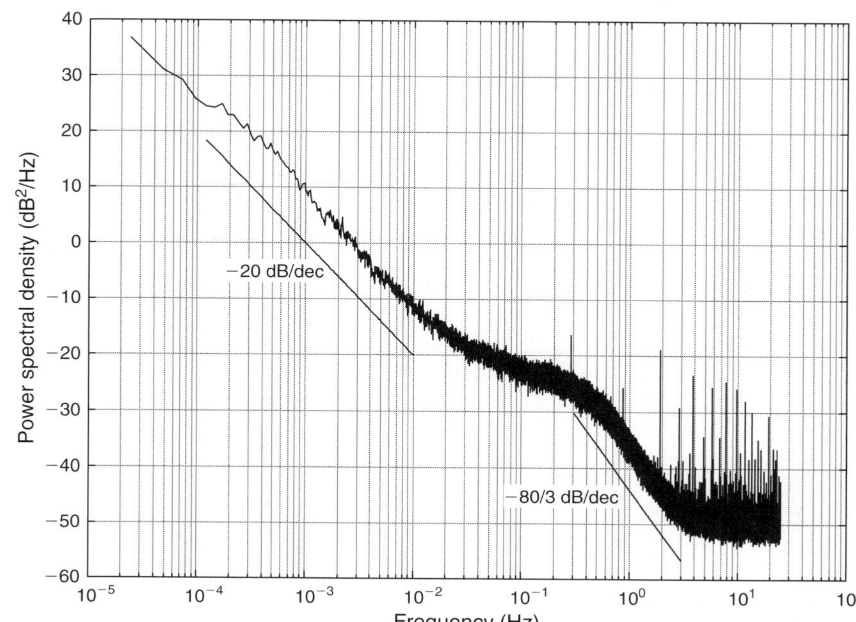

Figure 1: Average power spectrum of fade time series at 18.7 GHz during rain (using a 3.5 m diameter antenna, with sampling rate 50 Hz, up to the Nyquist frequency 25 hz)

Note: Notice the −20 dB/dec slope due to rain (rain absorption and scattering) and the −80/3 dB/dec slope due to troposphere turbulence (scintillation). Receiver noise, given by the flat portion above approximately 3 Hz, limits the range of the measurements. The "spikes" observed are due to the satellite, but they can be neglected because most of their power can be filtered out together with the receiver noise above 3 Hz.

where θ and $A(\theta)$ are, respectively, the new elevation angle and rain attenuation, and θ_o and $A(\theta_o)$ are the reference values.

Depolarization in precipitation is caused by the differential attenuation and phase shifts induced between orthogonal components of an electromagnetic wave by anisotropic hydrometeors (Chu 1971; DiFonzo, Tracchtman, and Williams 1976; Cox 1981; Capsoni et al. 1981; Allnutt 1989; Cox and Arnold 1984). For a frequency-reuse system the importance of depolarization depends on frequency, path geometry (elevation angle and tilt angle of the received polarization) and climatological factors (severity of the rainfall), and sensitivity to the interference coming from the cross-polarized signal. In systems that are operating with one polarization only, depolarization causes a small apparent increase in the path attenuation.

Although rain is the most significant constituent affecting electromagnetic wave propagation, *clouds* (Dissanayake, Allnut, and Haidara 1997) and *fog* can also be present in a satellite path and attenuate the signal. The attenuation due to suspended water droplets contained in clouds can be determined with great accuracy up to approximately 100 GHz, using the Rayleigh model of electromagnetic wave scattering. This physical approach requires the assessment of the cloud vertical profile, information that can be derived from radiosonde measurements (Vasseur and Vanhoenacker 1998). Clouds attenuation is proportional to the liquid water content rather than to the drop size distribution, as in the case of rain attenuation, and is highly variable. Cloud and fog attenuation can become significant at millimeter waves (>30 GHz).

Short-term fluctuations in radiowave amplitude and phase, referred to as *scintillation* (as for the visible optical frequencies) are generated by small-scale refractive index inhomogeneities. Tropospheric scintillations are faster than rain attenuation, with a distinct spectrum appearing at frequencies above approximately 0.1 Hz (Figure 1). Both fades and enhancements around the average signal level are observed (multiplicative effect in natural units, additive in decibels) that can be interpreted as alternate destructive and constructive interference among multiple rays. Since scintillation is not caused by an energy-loss mechanism, turbulence does not increase the system noise.

Tropospheric scintillation is usually significant only at low elevation angles or with antennas of small size, although noticeable cloud scintillations occur at much higher elevation angles. There is a distinct seasonal dependence, with frequency of occurrence approaching a maximum in summer and a minimum in winter. The magnitude of tropospheric scintillation increases moderately with frequency because its standard deviation, in decibels, increases as $f^{7/12}$. The intensity of scintillation increases with path length through the turbulent medium and decreases as the antenna beam width decreases, because of antenna aperture averaging (Tatarski 1961). Measurements at two different polarizations show that scintillation is independent of polarization (Cox 1981; Matricciani and Riva 1998b).

Scintillations are unlikely to produce serious fading in space communication systems below approximately 10 GHz and in slant paths of elevation angles above 10 degrees. Below 10 degrees and above 10 GHz, tropospheric scintillation can be a source of significant outages in satellite systems with very low power margins. Scintillation is found also during rain attenuation, to which it is correlated (Matricciani, Mauri, and Riva 1996; Matricciani and Riva 2005a), and may produce short outages (~1 s).

FREQUENCY AND TIME SELECTIVITY

Regardless of satellite type of orbit, the motion of the receiver induces time-varying channel characteristics. When the environment changes significantly (e.g., moving from urban to suburban or rural areas), clear-sky fading becomes nonstationary and more difficult to model. A simple way to model this phenomenon was introduced by Bello (1963), who proposed the notion of a wide-sense stationary channel with uncorrelated scattering, with a single state or multiple states. A single-state model describes the propagation channel only with a single, spatially invariant, statistical distribution. A multistate model describes the propagation channel with a collection of single-state models and accounts for macro-variations of the channel through probabilistic state transitions.

Large-scale fading and large-power variations are experienced when the mobile terminal travels several hundred wavelengths. Small-scale fading and possibly large-power variations are experienced when the mobile terminal travels few wavelengths because the signal amplitude changes due to constructive and destructive interference in the sum of multiple rays (multipath), mainly caused by reflections from the surrounding surfaces. In this case, power fluctuations are measurable over distances comparable to the wavelength, as small as a half wavelength.

The Fourier transform of the transfer function of the channel is modeled according to a wide-sense stationary uncorrelated random process both in frequency f and time t (Bello 1963; Durgin 2003; Parsons 2000). From the transfer function, the first- and second-order fading statistics can be estimated. First-order statistics provide the probability density function (Pdf) and the cumulative density function (Cdf, the integral of Pdf) of the received signal envelope and phase for each distinct path. Second-order statistics provide the autocorrelation properties of the fading both in the time domain (Doppler spectrum, level crossing rate and fade duration) and in the frequency domain (multipath intensity profile, delay spread; Jakes 1994).

In detail, considering a couple of frequencies (f_1, f_2) and times (t_1, t_2), the autocorrelation function $\Re(f_1, f_2; t_1, t_2)$ satisfies the condition

$$\Re(f_1, f_2; t_1, t_2) = \Re(\Delta f; \Delta t) \tag{5}$$

with $\Delta f = f_2 - f_1$ and $\Delta t = t_2 - t_1$.

The radiofrequency bandwidth that produces the function $\Re(B_c) \cong \Re(B_c; 0)$ is known as the channel *coherence bandwidth* B_C and measures the channel memory in the frequency domain. In this bandwidth all spectral components of the transmitted signal pass through the channel with equal gain and linear phase (i.e., the channel remains invariant).

Similarly, the time interval that produces the function $\Re(T_c) \cong \Re(0; T_c)$ is known as the channel *coherence time* T_c, which measures the channel memory in the time domain. This is the time interval during which the channel impulse response remains invariant.

These two memory indicators are inversely related to a pair of fundamental parameters. The coherence bandwidth B_c is related to the time delay spread T_s, according to:

$$T_s \approx \frac{1}{B_c} \tag{6}$$

The coherence time T_c is related to the Doppler frequency spread B_d (due to multipath) according to:

$$B_d \approx \frac{1}{T_c} \tag{7}$$

A useful concept is the selectivity in time and frequency. Let $R_s = 1/T$ (symbols/s) be the symbol rate of the transmitted signal. Then the fading is not selective in frequency; in other words, it is "flat" if $T >> T_s$ (i.e., the delay spread produces negligible time dispersion on the signal). However, flat-fade channels may cause deep fades. Assuming that the signal radiofrequency bandwidth B_{RF} is the order of $1/T$ (i.e., $B_{RF} \approx 1/T$), nonselectivity in frequency means $B_{RF} << B_c$. In this case, the channel is termed *narrowband*. On the other hand, if $B_{RF} >> B_c$, the channel has a constant gain and linear phase response only in a bandwidth much smaller than the radiofrequency bandwidth, and *frequency-selective* fading is experienced.

For instance, a QPSK modulation scheme delivering a total data rate R_b (bit/s) would need a radiofrequency bandwidth $B_{RF} = (1 + \delta)R_b/2$ (in this case, considering the equivalent baseband channel, the symbol rate and the bit rate coincide $R_b = R_s$), with $0 < \delta \leq 1$being the roll-off factor of the raised cosine pulses sent to the receiver sampler.

In conclusion, the fading is flat when the signal bandwidth is much less than the coherence bandwidth, $B_{RF} << B_c$ (*narrowband* channel). In this case, fading is also multiplicative; in other words, it is additive in decibels, or all frequency components undergo the same attenuation and phase shift. The fading is selective in frequency and introduces significant time dispersion and frequency distortion if $B_{RF} >> B_c$ (*wideband* channel).

Depending on frequency flatness or selectivity, statistical models are classified as narrowband or wideband, respectively. Most land-mobile satellite models are narrowband, because they have been devised for the actual data rate and satellite environments in which the direct component is generally strong, and multipath power is relatively low and can be neglected.

Fading is nonselective in time if $T << T_c$ (i.e., if the symbol period T is significantly smaller than the coherence time T_c). This means that the Doppler spread B_d is much smaller than the radiofrequency bandwidth, $B_d << B_{RF}$. The channel is then affected by *slow fading* because the channel impulse response changes slowly within the symbol duration. If this condition is not verified, the fading is selective in time, and deep fading can be experienced at particular times because of destructive interference. The channel is then affected by *fast fading* because the channel impulse response changes rapidly within the symbol duration. Tables 1 and 2 summarize the various cases just discussed.

In addition to the multipath Doppler spectrum, in land-mobile satellite communications there is an additional frequency shift—the conventional Doppler offset due to the satellite relative motion—that is very important when satellites are not in the geostationary orbit (MEO and especially LEO systems).

The mobile terminal moves in an environment whose space characteristics can be described by a coherence distance for small- and large-scale fading events. The *shadowing* (or *large-scale*) *coherence distance* is the distance that the receiver must travel to experience uncorrelated (zero correlation coefficient) large-scale fading events. The *small-scale coherence distance* is the distance that the receiver must travel to experience uncorrelated small-scale fading events. Obviously, the shadowing coherence distance is much larger than the small-scale coherence distance. Given a specific receiver speed, this means that small-scale fading events are much faster (a larger number

Table 1: Types of Fading Dependent on *Time Delay Spread* T_s and Its Characteristics

Characteristic of the Channel	Frequency-Flat Fading	Frequency-Selective Fading
Symbol period of the signal, T	Greater than channel delay spread, $T >> T_s$	Smaller than channel time delay spread, $T << T_s$
Coherence bandwidth of the channel, B_c	Greater than the radiofrequency bandwidth (narrowband channels), $B_c >> B_{RF}$	Smaller than the radiofrequency bandwidth (wideband channels), $B_c << B_{RF}$
Type of fade	Deep fade requiring more transmitter power to achieve the tolerable probability of bit error	Selective fade causing intersymbol interference; more transmitter power will not reduce it
Modeling difficulty	Relatively easier than modeling frequency-selective fading	Relatively more difficult than modeling frequency-flat fading

Table 2: Types of Fading Dependent on *Doppler Frequency Spread* B_d and Its Characteristics

Characteristic of the Channel	Slow Fading	Fast Fading
Coherence time of the channel, T_c	Greater than the symbol period of the signal, $T_c >> T$; the channel is static over one or several symbol periods	Smaller than the symbol period of the signal (time-selective fading), $T_c << T$
Doppler frequency spread of the channel, B_d	Smaller than the radiofrequency bandwidth, $B_d << B_{RF}$	Greater than the radiofrequency bandwidth, $B_d >> B_{RF}$
Type of fade	Channel changes slower than the baseband signal variations	Channel changes faster than the baseband signal variations In *fast flat-fading channels,* the amplitude of the received signal changes faster than the rate of change of the baseband signal In *fast frequency-selective fading* channels, the amplitude, phases and time delays of the multipath components change faster than the rate of change of the baseband signal
Modeling difficulty	Relatively easier than modeling fast fading	Relatively more difficult than modeling slow fading

of very short fades per unit of time) than large-scale fading events.

With regard to time, frequency, and space correlation, the *angular coherence* is the angle separation needed to experience uncorrelated fading events. The angular coherence measures the channel memory in the angular domain. Again, a distinction between small- and large-scale fading can be useful. The angular coherence is useful in the design of antenna arrays and beam-forming networks, and for angle diversity analysis.

With regard to rain attenuation, since absorption and scattering are not frequency selective up to approximately 100 GHz, even for bandwidths of a few hundred megahertz, a channel affected only by rain attenuation is flat in frequency; in other words, it is always $B_{RF} << B_c$, or the channel is always narrowband. With regard to selectivity in time, deep fades are measured when intense rainfall cells are along the satellite slant path. Deep fades may last a few minutes and are statistically described by fade duration statistics. Rain attenuation coherence distance is of the order of several hundreds of meters; hints can be obtained perhaps by considering a satellite site-diversity gain with station separation of 500–750 m (Matricciani 2003). With regard to the angular coherence of rain attenuation, hints can be derived via an angle- (orbital-) diversity gain at K_u band (Matricciani 1987).

CLEAR-SKY MODELING

The purpose of channel modeling is to understand the propagation phenomena that dominate the land-mobile satellite channel and to derive rules and expressions that can describe, statistically, the dependence of the received signal as a function of frequency, elevation angle, antenna type, and directivity (antenna gain); relative velocity between receiver and satellite; locality; type of environment (urban, suburban, rural); and weather conditions (clear sky, rain, etc.).

Accurate propagation modeling is fundamental to calculate link budgets and perform realistic quality-of-service predictions. A large number of proposed models exists for both clear-sky and rainy conditions, most of which have been obtained by a best fit to the available experimental data. Therefore, the selection of a particular model should be tightly linked to its use in performance predictions.

Extensive measurements, at UHF and especially at L and S bands, conducted in clear-sky conditions all over the world (e.g., see Goldhirsh and Vogel 1998) have provided data useful to model the land-mobile satellite channel and have produced several models, mainly empirical, for narrowband channels. Multimedia services, however, may require larger bandwidths, if they must compete and coordinate with the fixed and mobile terrestrial communication networks, so that wideband modeling is also necessary.

Narrowband Models

The narrowband models can be classified as empirical, statistical, or analytical (Karaliopoulos and Pavlidou 1999). The empirical and statistical models are the most developed and tested, whereas the analytical models are mainly concerned with the terrestrial mobile channel (as a result, we will not cover them here).

Empirical Models

Empirical models provide a mathematical function obtained by a best fit (regression) on the measured data, and, as such, they may not provide insight to understand the physical phenomena that cause attenuation. Their main advantage is the simplicity of the final mathematical expressions and easy application, but their disadvantage is that they are related to data measured at a particular site and may not be reliably applicable to other sites.

These models predict either the average attenuation caused by vegetation (mainly trees) or the link margin needed to compensate for propagation line-of-sight loss and other fades. The modeling concerns various parameters such as elevation angle, carrier frequency, path length through the vegetation, and other parameters related to the specific environment in which the measurements were made (Goldhirsh and Vogel 1998). These parameters are nearly always computed by a best fit to the measured data. Kanatas and Konstantinou (1996) provide a classification and comparison of the several empirical models proposed.

Statistical Models

Statistical models offer insight into the physical phenomena that affect the propagation of electromagnetic waves, but their application usually requires methods of numerical analysis. These models define first-order statistics (i.e., the probability density function and the cumulative probability density function of the envelope, and sometimes of the phase, of the received signal). The knowledge of these statistics is fundamental to predict adequate fade margins. Fewer studies have considered the modeling of second-order statistics, such as statistics of fade duration and level crossing rate, useful for selecting modulation and coding techniques.

There are two modeling approaches to derive *first-order* statistics: global and state-oriented. The *global* approach models the shadowing and multipath phenomena with a single probability distribution. The *state-oriented* approach models the shadowing and multipath phenomena in more detail, because it describes with a single distribution each of the several discrete states that the channel can have.

The usual, although not precise, classification of environments for global channel modeling is *urban, suburban*, or *rural*. There seems to be no distinction for the different architectural styles and street dimensions of the cities of the world, although, for instance, European cities are quite different from North American cities. A rural environment implies the existence of a line-of-sight path, in which a significant part of the electromagnetic wave reaches the receiver without being reflected or scattered. An urban environment, on the other hand, usually excludes the existence of a line-of-sight path, and the receiver is surrounded by a large number of scattering objects. Therefore, multipath is the main propagation mechanism. The suburban environment is intermediate and combines the characteristics of both urban and rural environments.

Let the baseband equivalent received signal sample in the presence of nonselective fading be defined as:

$$y = gx + n \tag{8}$$

where x is the complex transmitted signal, g is the multiplicative complex fading channel coefficient, and n is a complex additive white Gaussian noise with zero average and one-sided power spectral density N_o. In particular

$$g = re^{j\theta} \tag{9}$$

where r is the fading envelope and θ is the phase rotation introduced by the channel. The average power associated with the fading envelope is given by $E[r^2] = P$, usually normalized to unity, a value that represents the average power that would equal received propagation in free-space conditions.

Variations of the signal amplitude, r, due to attenuation caused by any type of obstacle impeding the line-of-sight path (large-scale fading) is well modeled by the log-normal distribution (Cox, Murray, and Norris 1984). The distribution used to model the variations of signal amplitude due to multipath (small-scale fading) depends on the scattering environment and on the assumption made about the components of the received wave. In urban environments, multipath is well described by a Rayleigh distribution. Now, the Rayleigh Pdf implies that an infinite number of scattering elements contribute to the resultant electromagnetic wave amplitude and phase, but this is a sufficient and not necessary condition, so that it is also experimentally found when a finite number of rays contribute to the received signal. In rural and suburban environments, in which a line-of-sight component exists for most of the time, Raleigh fading turns into Ricean fading (Lee 1995; Pattan 1998).

Large-scale shadowing can be described by a Gaussian distribution in decibels that in linear scale turns into the *log-normal distribution*, given by

$$f(r) = \frac{1}{\sqrt{2\pi}r\delta}\exp\left[-\frac{(\ln r - \mu)^2}{2\delta^2}\right] \tag{10}$$

where δ (neper) is the standard deviation and μ (neper) is the average of the normal (i.e., Gaussian) random variable $\ln r$.

The *Raleigh distribution* (applicable to urban areas) is derived by assuming that no direct component is present (i.e., that none of the multipath components prevails) and by applying the central limit theorem to the two orthogonal components of the received envelope r, which thus result in Gaussian random variables with zero average and standard deviation σ (Sklar 1997a, 1997b). The channel coefficient g becomes a zero-mean complex Gaussian variable with uniform phase distribution in $[0, 2\pi]$, and the envelope r is distributed according to the Rayleigh Pdf, given by

$$f(r) = \frac{r}{\sigma^2}\exp\left[-\frac{r^2}{2\sigma^2}\right] \tag{11}$$

where $2\sigma^2 = P$.

There is a direct component in rural and suburban environments, and fading can be modeled according to the *Rice distribution* (Lee 1995). This Pdf assumes a constant power for both direct and diffuse components and is given by

$$f(r) = \frac{r}{\sigma^2}\exp\left[-\frac{r^2 + s^2}{2\sigma^2}\right] I_0\left(\frac{rs}{\sigma^2}\right) \tag{12}$$

where σ^2 has the same meaning as for the Rayleigh distribution, s is the magnitude of the direct component, and $I_0(\cdot)$ is the zero-order modified Bessel function of the first kind. Now $P = s^2 + 2\sigma^2$.

To jointly describe large- and small-scale fading, a composite Pdf is used. The *Suzuki distribution* (Suzuki 1977) combines Rayleigh and log-normal statistics as follows:

$$f_r(r) = \frac{r}{\sqrt{2\pi}\delta}\int_0^\infty \frac{1}{\sigma^3}\exp\left[-\frac{r^2}{2\sigma^2} - \frac{(\ln\sigma - \mu)^2}{2\delta^2}\right]d\sigma \quad (13)$$

where $2\sigma^2$ is the average received power for the Rayleigh process, and δ and μ, respectively, are the standard deviation and the average value of the log-normal distribution.

The *state-oriented* approach models the long-term variations of the channel and its transitions to different states as a Markov process. A Markov process is a stochastic process that can model a system that exists only in discrete states. Short-term variations, corresponding to each individual discrete state, are described by one of the Pdfs mentioned earlier, with appropriate parameters. The probability of being in one of these states depends only on a finite number of previous states (one, two, etc.). Two matrices must be computed to define the process completely: (a) the $1 \times M$ state probability array $\boldsymbol{S}$ whose elements, S_i, express the probability of the system being in state $i = 1, 2, ..., M$; (b) the $M \times M$ transition probability matrix $\boldsymbol{P}$, whose elements P_{ij} give the probability of transition from state i to state j. Models considering one, two (Lutz et al. 1991), or three states (Karasawa, Kimura, and Minamisono 1997; Perez-Fontan et al. 1997a, 1997b) have been fitted to experimental data. In this case, state 1 describes the line-of-site condition, state 2 the moderate fading conditions, and state 3 the deep fading conditions.

The *second-order* statistics are the level crossing rate and the average fade duration (Lee 1995; Loo 1985; Hasey, Goldhirsh, and Vogel 1991). They are useful channel parameters to design interleaver and forward-error correcting codes for mitigating fading effects.

The level crossing rate, N_R, at a specific level $r = R$, is the expected rate at which the envelope crosses that level in a positive-going direction, and is given by

$$N_R = \int r' f(R, r')dr' \quad (14)$$

where "′" indicates a time derivative and $f(R, r')$ is the joint probability density function of the envelope r and its derivative r' at $r = R$.

The average fade duration under a specified level $r = R$ is the average duration of the intervals during which the envelope falls below that level. If τ_i is the duration of the i-th fade interval, the probability that $r \le R$ during a time interval T can be written as

$$P(r \le R) = \frac{1}{T}\sum_i \tau_i \quad (15)$$

and the average fade duration, $\bar{\tau}$, is given by

$$\bar{\tau} = \frac{1}{TN_R}\sum_i \tau_i = \frac{1}{N_R}P(r \le R) \quad (16)$$

Sometimes these data are obtained by a best fit on directly measured time series of fading.

Wideband Models

For both terrestrial and mobile satellite channels, wideband effects are mainly modeled by considering the impulse response of the channel in the presence of a finite number of scatterers surrounding the receiver. Geometrical (ray) optics applies. As a consequence, the time-varying impulse response, $h(t, \tau)$, of the channel is written as (Rappaport 2001):

$$h(t,\tau) = \sum_{i=0}^{N-1} A_i(t)\delta(t - \tau_i(t))\, e^{j\theta_i(t)} \quad (17)$$

where $A_i(t)$, $\tau_i(t)$, and $\theta_i(t)$ are the random time-varying amplitude, arrival time, and phase sequences, respectively; δ is the delta function; and $N - 1$ is the number of scattered wave components considered. The term for $i = 0$ represents the direct component, if there is one, and the other $N - 1$ terms represent the echoes due to multipath.

The expression for the channel impulse response suggests that it can be modeled by a tapped delay line (Rappaport 2001). This approach has been widely accepted and employed by most investigators of the terrestrial mobile channel. The several models proposed aim at defining suitable distributions for the amplitudes $A_i(t)$ (the tap gains), the delay times $\tau_i(t)$, and the Doppler spectrum of each tap or the time correlation of each discrete path (tap) gain. The same approach is followed in the few studies dedicated to the land-mobile satellite channel. The choice of the relative distributions for each model and the number of path taps is based on statistical analysis of measurements.

TROPOSPHERIC CHANNEL MODELING AT HIGH FREQUENCIES (>10 GHZ)

At frequencies between 10 and 300 GHz, electromagnetic waves can be faded because of the presence of hydrometeors (rain, snow, ice crystals, clouds) in the lower part of the atmosphere, the troposphere, and atmospheric gases (oxygen, water vapor). The characteristics of this fade strongly depend on frequency, elevation angle, locality, and climatological conditions. In the following we consider only rain attenuation because at K_u band (12–14 GHz) and K_a band (20–30 GHz), the bands to be used next for multimedia communications with fixed and mobile terminals, rain is the most important physical phenomenon to be considered (Matricciani and Riva 1998a).

There are no real measurements of rain attenuation experienced by a moving terminal—only reliable simulations (Matricciani 1995, 2000a; Matricciani and Moretti 1998; Matricciani and Selva 2002). Both first-order and second-order long-term statistics of rain attenuation likely to be experienced by a moving terminal can be, however, estimated from knowing:

1. Rain attenuation statistics experienced by fixed-system terminals
2. Type of motion of vehicles

In the following sections, we first discuss rain attenuation statistics experienced in fixed systems (which directly apply to gateway stations) and then extend them to mobile receivers.

Rain Attenuation Statistics for Fixed-System Satellite Communications

Contrary to the statistical models developed for clear-sky conditions, most statistical models of rain attenuation are empirical, and, as such, they seldom offer physical insight into the complex phenomena that cause rain. Physical models, on the contrary, are based more on the physical-mathematical relationship between rain rate along the slant path and rain attenuation. The most reliable and accurate physical model is the synthetic storm technique (SST), discussed in more detail later in the chapter.

Statistical Models

Rain attenuation can be assessed accurately by measuring, in a very narrow bandwidth close to the communication signal bandwidth, the received power of an unmodulated sinusoidal carrier (a satellite beacon). Propagation experiments, however, are very expensive and lengthy, if they are to be statistically reliable, so that they are carried out only in a few places in the world and for a limited number of years, frequencies, and link geometry. As a consequence, their results cannot be easily and directly applied to any site in the world. For this reason, many statistical models of the long-term complementary probability distribution function (cPdf) of rain attenuation (this is the cumulative probability that a given rain attenuation A [dB] is exceeded in a slant path) have been developed in the last three decades (Riva 2002) to predict this *first-order* statistic. Because rain attenuation is not frequency selective, even for bandwidths of tens of megahertz, there is no need to distinguish between narrowband and wideband models.

For a slant path to a satellite, all statistical models give the long-term rain attenuation cPdf using as physical input the rain rate cPdf measured on site or estimated from climatological global statistical maps of rain rate, and of the rain height, often approximated by the altitude of the 0 degree Celsius isotherm above mean sea level. Most models, however, have derived their parameters by a best fit on the experimental data available at the time of their development, and, as such, they do not provide a significant physical insight. Very few models have based their theory and modeling on some approximate physical features that describe, on the average, the complex meteorological phenomena (e.g., radar measurements or arrays of rain gauges). When these statistical models (approximately fifteen) are tested against concurrent satellite beacon measurements, they show, however, very similar large errors (Riva 2002). Although the ITU-R (2003a) recommends a particular prediction method—see Riva (2002)—a reliable assessment of the predicting power of most models seems hard because the data bank used to test them may be inaccurate and far from controlled "laboratory" conditions necessary for any reliable test (Matricciani and Riva 2005b).

Models of *second-order* statistics of fade (fade durations and rate of change of fade) during rain are in a similar stage of development but with worse accuracy. These statistics are useful and necessary because they directly influence some aspects of satellite system design and fade countermeasures—such as the use of common shared resources onboard the satellite, uplink power control, adaptive coding, frequency, and space and time diversity—and determine channel availability statistics.

The statistical models of duration and rate of change of rain attenuation are largely empirical because they rely on a best fit on experimental distributions conditioned to a given rain attenuation. Fade durations measured during rain can vary from a few seconds to hours, a range of about five orders of magnitude, and across this range they are not caused by the same phenomena; however, short fades ($\sim$1 s) are likely due to scintillation caused by atmosphere turbulence, whereas long fades are caused by the space-time structure of rain (rain attenuation; Matricciani 1981a, 1982a; Matricciani, Mauri, and Paraboni 1987). Therefore, it is difficult to describe the whole distribution using a single mathematical function. In general, the distribution of long fade durations ($>$1min) is modeled by a log-normal Pdf, and the distribution of short fade durations ($\leq$1 min) is modeled by a power law or another log-normal Pdf (Paraboni and Riva 1994; ITU-R 2003b).

The rate of change of rain attenuation is estimated after removing most of the signal fluctuations arising from tropospheric scintillations (Figure 1). Positive and negative rates of change (expressed in dB/s) are similar, and their absolute values can be statistically modeled by just one single log-normal Pdf (Lin, Bergmann, and Pursley 1980; Matricciani 1981b, 1982b; Dissanayake et al. 1990; Poiares-Baptista and Davies 1994). They are correlated with the attenuation itself and increase with it. They also depend on receiver filter bandwidth and time lag (period of time over which fade slope is calculated; ITU-R 2003b).

Physical Models: The Synthetic Storm Technique

A physical model based not on a best fit on radio electrical data but on independent meteorological data, such as the rain rate measured by a rain gauge, is the synthetic storm technique. The method of employing rain gauge records to generate attenuation statistics is based on the concept originally used by Hamilton and Marshall (1961) to calculate the effects of rain attenuation on data obtained by a weather radar, according to the "frozen flow" hypothesis (Taylor 1938). Drufuca (1973, 1974) applied the concept to terrestrial microwave links, Matricciani (1994, 1996) to satellite links.

As a rain pattern moves over a rain gauge, the measured rain rate $R(t)$, measured in mm/h, varies with time because of two effects: the horizontal motion (advection) of the spatial pattern of rain and the changes that occur within the time required to pass over the rain gauge. These two effects are both present in rain gauge records and are not easily separated. A "synthetic storm" is obtained by converting a rain rate time series recorded at a rain gauge to a rain rate space series by using an estimate of the storm translation speed to transform time to distance (this transformation is Taylor's "frozen flow" hypothesis applied to rain rate). Of course, this description assumes that only advection is present, and it will not give an exact description of the distribution of rain rate with distance. It is true, however, that the statistical properties of rain rate of a large number of synthetic storms are approximately the same as those of real storms. Evidence of the validity of this hypothesis can be found in the special case of convective storms in Montreal up to time lags of 40 minutes (Zawadzki 1973). As the measured average storm speed was about 50 km/h, 40 minutes correspond to a space lag of about 30 km, a length larger than that of most slant paths in Earth-satellite links or horizontal paths (terrestrial links). Zawadzki (1973) showed that there is also a marked isotropy in the patterns, indicating that statistics obtained along the direction of motion of the storm can be extended to the entire precipitation pattern, though the SST is directly applicable to storms with a major component of velocity parallel to the radio path. For widespread rain, the hypothesis of isotropy should hold even more because of the great uniformity in time and in space of this type of rain (Drufuca and Zawadzki 1975). As a consequence of this supposed statistical isotropy, there is no distinction between the direction of the storm motion and the direction of the radio path.

After Matricciani (1996) formulated the theoretical physical-mathematical foundations, established useful theorems, and devised an effective vertical profile of the precipitation that takes the melting layer into account (1991), the SST was developed to a mature stage of insight, understanding, and reliability so that it is now a powerful and accurate tool for predicting rain effects at frequency greater than 10 GHz. It can predict reliable first-order (cPdf of A; Matricciani 1996; Matricciani and Riva 2005b) and second-order (fade duration and rate of change) statistics (Matricciani 1997, 1998, 2000b, 2004) of rain attenuation that characterizes a slant path for fixed and land-mobile satellite systems (Matricciani and Moretti 1998), because it provides direct rain attenuation time series that could very likely be measured, at any frequency and polarization, for any slant path above approximately 10 degrees. The SST can be used at tropical sites as well (Emiliani, Castanet, and Feral 2005).

The predictions are significantly insensitive to the value of v, and the simulations can use the average value of v, a random variable that can be accurately described by a log-normal probability density function (Binaghi and Pawlina Bonati 1992), independent of site (Matricciani 1996; Matricciani and Moretti 1998). Statistics of v can be obtained from meteorological services. In practice, the average value of v can range from 4–5 m/s to 13–14 m/s.

The vertical structure of rain is modeled using two layers of precipitation of different depths. Starting from the ground, there is rain (hydrometeors in the form of raindrops, water temperature of 20 degrees Celsius, layer A) followed by a melting layer (layer B)—in other words, melting hydrometeors at 0 degrees Celsius. The rain intensity R (mm/h), with one minute of integration time (i.e., time series with one sample/min), in the lower layer is assumed to be uniform and given by that measured at the ground (i.e., by the rain gauge). Calculations also show that the precipitation rate in the melting layer, termed "apparent rain rate." can be supposed to be uniform and given by $R_B = 3.134R$ (Matricciani 1991).

For a site in the Northern Hemisphere at latitude $\phi°$, the height of the precipitation (rain and melting layer) above sea level is given by ITU-R (1992b) as

$$\begin{aligned} H_B &= 5 & \phi &\le 23° \\ H_B &= 5 - 0.075(\phi - 23) & \phi &> 23° \end{aligned} \tag{18}$$

For a site in the Southern Hemisphere at (negative) latitude $\phi°$, the height of the precipitation (rain and melting layer) above sea level is given by

$$\begin{aligned} H_B &= 5 & \phi &\ge -21° \\ H_B &= 5 + 0.1(\phi + 21) & -71 \le \phi &< -21° \end{aligned} \tag{19}$$

ITU-R (2001b) provides a more precise global map of the altitude of the 0 degree Celsius isotherm height above mean seal level.

The height (depth) of the melting layer is $h = 0.4$km, regardless of the latitude (Matricciani 1991).

Let us first consider a *terrestrial* radio link (parallel to the Earth's surface) of length L (km) along the horizontal axis x; let the rain rate R and the specific attenuation Y (dB/km) be linked by equation 2; and assume that k and α (layer A, 20 degrees Celsius) do not change with space or time. Let us consider a reference point x_0 (origin) at the midpoint of L. The attenuation is then given by equation 1, written as

$$A(x_0) = k \int_{x_0 - L/2}^{x_0 + L/2} R^{\alpha}(x)dx \tag{20}$$

Now, according to Taylor's hypothesis applied to rain rate, the variation of attenuation with time can be simulated by changing x_0 at a rate equal to the speed v of the storm motion, that is, at a rate

$$x_0 = vt \tag{21}$$

This process can be mathematically described by the convolution between a function of rectangular shape of unit amplitude and width L centered at the origin x_0, rect(x/L), and $Y(x)$:

$$\begin{aligned} A(x_0) &= k \int_{-\infty}^{+\infty} R^{\alpha}(x_0 + x)\,\mathrm{rect}(x/L)dx \\ &= k \int_{-\infty}^{+\infty} R^{\alpha}(x)\,\mathrm{rect}[(x_0 - x)/L]dx \end{aligned} \tag{22}$$

From equation 22 we can obtain the Fourier transform of $A(x_0)$, in the domain of space frequency $f_s = x^{-1}$ km^{-1}, as

$$S_A(f_s) = S_Y(f_s)L\,\mathrm{sinc}(f_sL) \tag{23}$$

where

$$S_A(f_s) = F[A(x_0)] \tag{24a}$$

and

$$S_Y(f_s) = F[kR^{\alpha}(x)] \tag{24b}$$

are the Fourier transforms of $A(x_0)$ and $Y(x)$, respectively, and $\mathrm{sinc}(f_sL) = \sin(\pi f_sL)/(\pi f_sL)$. Using linear-systems terminology, we can refer to $S_Y(f_s)$ as the "input spectrum" and to $L\mathrm{sinc}(f_sL)$ as the "path transfer function."

Now, by converting space to time with equation 21, and noticing that $f(\mathrm{Hz}) = vf_s$, if v is expressed in km/s, the space spectrum $S_A(f_s)$ is transformed into the temporal spectrum $\check{S}_A(f)$:

$$\check{S}_A(f) = \check{S}_Y(f)L\,\mathrm{sinc}(fL/v) \tag{25}$$

Using equation 25, by inverse Fourier transform, we finally get:

$$A(t) = F^{-1}\left[\check{S}_A(f)\right] \tag{26}$$

Equations 25 and 26 model the time evolution of rain attenuation described by the SST.

Let us recall some useful theorems (Matricciani 1996) and calculate equation 25 at $f = 0$. From Fourier transform theory, we get

$$\check{S}_A(0) = L\check{S}_Y(0) = L\int_0^{T_R} kR^{\alpha}(t)dt \tag{27}$$

where T_R is the duration of the rain rate event measured at the rain gauge. Equation 27 states that $\check{S}_A(0)$ is independent of v, and that for a rain event it is a constant. This property is just a consequence of the conservation of the quantity of water Q (mm) collected by the rain gauge during the rain event:

$$Q = \int_0^{T_R} R(t)dt \tag{28}$$

Now $\check{S}_A(0)$, by Fourier transform theory, is also given by

$$\check{S}_A(0) = \int_0^{T_A} A(t)dt = \text{constant} \tag{29}$$

In equation 29, T_A is the duration of the rain attenuation event as measured by the radio link. Notice that this conservation law (equation 29) holds in the time domain but not in the space domain, because in this latter case the linear extension of the rainy area, $R(x)$, along the direction of the horizontal path (and storm motion, because of the assumed statistical isotropy), depends on v and is given by

$$D_R = vT_R \tag{30}$$

Therefore, T_A must be given by

$$T_A = \frac{D_R + L_R}{v} = T_R + \frac{L}{v} \tag{31}$$

where L/v is the time during which the path is partially under rain but the rain gauge is not.

Notice that, when $v \rightarrow \infty$, the duration of the attenuation event coincides with the duration of the rain event; hence, in general the probability that it rains at a site as measured by a rain gauge is smaller than that measured by the radio link, and the two become approximately equal only for high storm speeds.

If, for a given rain rate pattern, v increases, then according to equation 31 the duration of the attenuation event decreases, and vice versa. In both cases, and regardless of v, according to equation 29 the area under $A(t)$ is always a constant; as a consequence, if the duration of the attenuation event is shorter than that relative to a reference speed, on average its attenuation must increase to hold the area constant, and vice versa. Hence, the same rain rate pattern can give attenuation events of different durations and peak attenuations, both functions of v of the rainstorm, although the long-term probability distributions of rain attenuation are not very sensitive to the average value of v (Matricciani 1996; Matricciani and Moretti 1998).

It is interesting and useful, though not physical, to find $A(t)$ when v approaches infinity. From equations 25 and 26 we get

$$\lim_{v \to \infty} A(t) = kR^{\alpha}(t)L \tag{32}$$

This expression yields a uniform rain rate pattern along the path. When $v \rightarrow \infty$, the transfer function in equation 25 becomes the constant L—that is, an all-pass ideal transfer function and $D_R \rightarrow \infty$. Equation 32, of course, satisfies the conservation law in equations 28 and 29.

Let us now apply the theory to a *satellite* radio link (i.e., to a slant path). Let θ be the path elevation angle and ξ the slant coordinate (see Figure 2). Then, according to the two-layer vertical structure of precipitation, equation 1 becomes

$$A(x_0) = k_A\int_0^{L_A} R^{\alpha_A}(x_0 + \Delta x_0, \xi)d\xi + k_Br^{\alpha_B}\int_{L_A}^{L_B} R^{\alpha_B}(x_0, \xi)d\xi \tag{33}$$

Table 3 reports the values of k and α for selected frequencies, available from ITU-R (1992a) or Maggiori (1981).

Notice that, in the first term of the right-hand side of equation 33, we must introduce a shift Δx_0, because the path enters layer A at $x_0+\Delta x_0$ (see Figure 2).

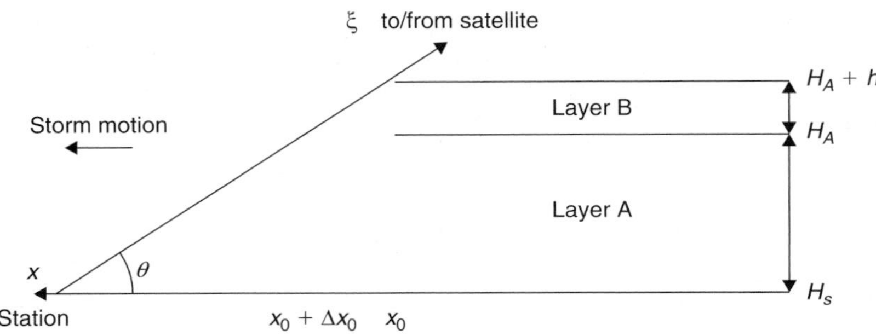

Figure 2: A slant path to a satellite
Note: The storm moves from right to left with constant speed v. The slant path first encounters layer B at abscissa x_0 and height $H_A + h$, then layer A at abscissa $x_0 + \Delta x_0$ and height H_A

Table 3: Values of k and α for Circular Polarization and Selected Carrier Frequencies

f (GHz)	Layer B (0°C)		Layer A (20°C)	
	k	α	k	α
12	0.0186	1.161	0.0178	1.221
20	0.0643	1.102	0.0722	1.083
30	0.1701	1.027	0.1780	1.007

The rainy paths in equation 33 are given by:

$$L = \frac{H - H_S}{\sin\theta} \tag{34}$$

Equation 34 yields L_B when $H = H_B$ and L_A when $H = H_A$ · H_S is the altitude of the station above sea level, and

$$\Delta x_0 = \Delta L \cos\theta = h / \tan\theta \tag{35}$$

$$\Delta L = L_B - L_A = h / \sin\theta \tag{36}$$

Fourier transform of equation 33 gives:

$$\begin{aligned} S_A(f_s) = \; & S_{Y,A}(f_s)L_A \,\mathrm{sinc}(f_s L_A)\exp(-j2\pi f_s \Delta x_0) \\ & + r^{\alpha_B} S_{Y,B}(f_s)\Delta L \,\mathrm{sinc}(f_s \Delta L) \end{aligned} \tag{37}$$

$$S_{Y,A}(f_s) = F[k_A R^{\alpha_A}(x)] \tag{38a}$$

$$S_{Y,B}(f_s) = F[k_B R^{\alpha_B}(x)] \tag{38b}$$

Now, since the speed along the slant path is given by $v(\theta) = v/\cos\theta$, the space spectrum is transformed into the conventional temporal spectrum with $f = vf_s/\cos\theta$ (Hz) as:

$$\begin{aligned} \check{S}_A(f) = \; & \check{S}_{Y,A}(f)L_A \,\mathrm{sinc}(fL_A/v(\theta))\exp(-j2\pi f\Delta x_0/v(\theta) \\ & + r^{\alpha_B} \check{S}_{Y,B}(f)\Delta L \,\mathrm{sinc}(f\Delta L/v(\theta)) \end{aligned} \tag{39}$$

$$\check{S}_{Y,A}(f) = F\{Y_A(t)\} \tag{40a}$$

$$\check{S}_{Y,B}(f) = FY_B(t) \tag{40b}$$

Finally, $A(t)$ is given by equation 26. Equation 39 satisfies, of course, the conservation law (equations 28 and 29); equation 31 holds also for slant paths (in this case, L represents the path length projected at ground).

Notice that, if $\theta = 90°$ (vertical path), then $v(\theta)\to\infty$, and, from equations 39, 36, and 26, $A(t)$ is given by

$$A(t) = k_A R^{\alpha_A}(t)(H_A - H_S) + r^{\alpha_B} k_B R^{\alpha_B}(t)h \tag{41}$$

For $\theta \neq 90°$ and $v\to\infty$ from equations 39 and 36 we get again the all-pass model (equation 32):

$$\lim_{v\to\infty} A(t) = k_A R^{\alpha_A}(t)L_A + r^{\alpha_B} k_B R^{\alpha_B}(t)(L_B - L_A) \tag{42}$$

Notice that, from equation 42 or 41, we can calculate a rain attenuation probability distribution without any simulation, by just inserting the values of rain rate exceeded with a given probability: the computed attenuation is predicted to be exceeded with the same probability. In this case, it suffices to know the cPdf of rain rate R to obtain the cPdf of A, as the latter, calculated from equation 41 or 42, is exceeded with the same probability. An estimate of the cPdf of rain rate R is provided by global maps of rain rate exceeded for several annual probabilities by the ITU-R (2001a).

Equation 42 can be used to calculate, with good confidence, rain attenuation for low values of rain rate (up to about 10 mm/h). At higher values, equation 42 gives pessimistic values. A better estimate of the SST predictions without the necessity of running the SST can be estimated by the relationship

$$A_v = aA_\infty^b \tag{43}$$

which links the value A_∞ (dB), estimated by equation 42, with the value A_v (dB); calculated with the SST, both

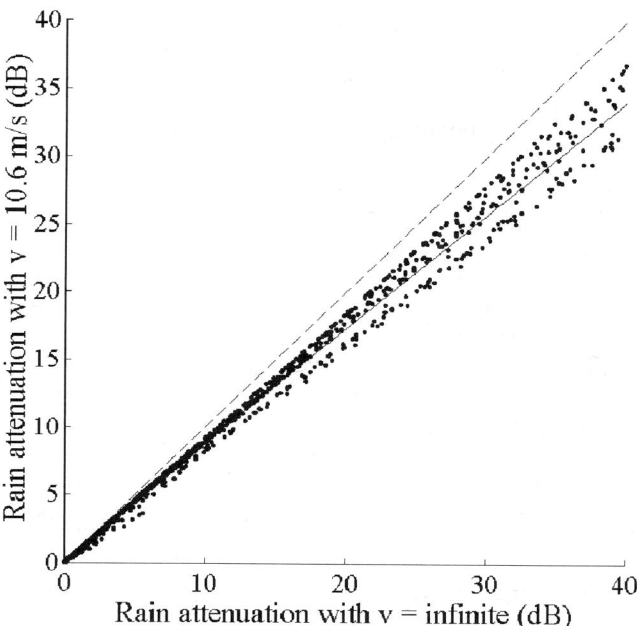

Figure 3: Scattergram of rain attenuation A_{SST} (dB) calculated with the SST (equations 39 and 26), with $v = 10.6$ m/s, as a function of rain attenuation, A_∞ (dB), calculated by assuming $v = \infty$ m/s (equation 42), for frequencies in the range of 10–30 GHz, in a 37.8 degree slant path to Italsat at Spino d'Adda (Northern Italy). The continuous line gives the best fit (equation 43); the dashed line is 45 degrees.

exceeded with the same probability. Let A_{SST} be the exact value estimated by equations 39 and 26. If we define the percentage error committed in using equation 43 as

$$\varepsilon = 100 \times \frac{A_{SST} - A_v}{A_v} \tag{44}$$

then the power law (equation 43) is reliable and tight enough (Figure 3), with small errors in large frequency ranges, as it is shown in Table 4, which also reports the values of the constants a and b. In other words, we can apply equation 43 to get the long-term cPdf of rain attenuation without the need to know the rain rate time series, which may not be available. Although equation 43 refers to a particular set of radio electrical and geographical parameters (Figure 3), its validity should be more global because it links rain attenuation calculated with rain rate data of a site to that obtainable with the SST at the same site.

Rain Attenuation Statistics for Mobile-System Satellite Communications

Rain attenuation statistics applicable to mobile satellite communication systems can be very different from those applicable to fixed terminals, linked to the same satellite, because of the relative motion of rainstorms and vehicles (Matricciani 1995, 2000a; Matricciani and Moretti 1998; Matricciani and Selva 2002). Mobile satellite communication is not affected, of course, only by rain but also by shadowing and multipath. These disturbances can plague the channel for such a long time that they establish system performance for a large range of outage probabilities, including the very low ones when rain attenuation contributes to the outage. Notice, however, that at the end of a future technological breakthrough in *smart* antennas (phased arrays with much signal processing), which may largely reduce the impact of multipath by ad hoc processing, rain will remain the irreducible cause of fading and system outage, if obstruction and shadowing are not present.

Models of Vehicle Speed

To obtain realistic values of the rain attenuation measured by a mobile terminal, we must know a reliable estimate of the probability distribution of the speed of vehicles, v_M, in different traffic and route conditions. Curiously, most literature reports more data on vehicular traffic (e.g., the number of vehicles running through a check point in a given interval of time) than vehicular speed.

The long-term Pdf of vehicular speed can be modeled by a log-normal distribution, at least for European traffic and for the three types of traffic and roads considered by Matricciani and Moretti (1998):

1. Urban routes with low-speed traffic (Model I)
2. Urban and suburban routes with high-speed traffic (Model II)
3. Freeway routes with very high-speed traffic (Model III)

For all three models, the standard deviation of ln v_M is the same—$\sigma = 0.221$—and the median values (obtained from the averages of ln v_M) are 30.1 km/h (Model I), 56.0 km/h (Model II), and 117.1 km/h (Model III).

Scaling Rain Attenuation Statistics from Fixed Systems

When a site and the cPdf of exceeding a given rain attenuation A(dB) in a fixed satellite system, $P_F(A)$, are considered (see the section entitled "Rain Attenuation Statistics for Fixed-System Satellite Communications"), it is implicitly assumed that $P_F(A)$ is applicable to sites belonging to

Table 4: Values of a and b to Be Inserted in Equation 43 for Two Wide-Frequency Ranges and Percentage Errors

Frequency Range (GHz)	a	b	Average Error $<\varepsilon>$ (%)	Standard Deviation σ (%)
10–30	0.958	0.960	0.08	9.6
10–100	0.973	0.938	0.13	7.8

a more-or-less large homogeneous geographical area centered at this site (neglecting possible orographic effects). Now, vehicles driven within this same area (and started inside or outside the area) are affected by the same rain attenuation of the fixed terminals located at the same point, but for different intervals of time, so that they measure a cPdf, $P_M(A)$, that may not coincide with $P_F(A)$, as well as different statistics of fade duration and rate of change of fade compared to a fixed terminal (Matricciani 1995).

A designer needs to know how the first-order statistic $P_F(A)$ is transformed into that applicable to a GEO or MEO satellite system for any mobile terminal, $P_M(A)$, working in the same geographical area, at the same carrier frequency, and in the same weather conditions. Matricciani (1995) has shown that $P_M(A)$ can be scaled from $P_F(A)$ according to the simple expression

$$P_M(A) = \xi(A) P_F(A) \tag{45}$$

Note that, to a first approximation, the dependence on the attenuation in the scaling factor ξ can be safely ignored because of equation 3. In other words, for a given vehicle pattern, we can scale $P_F(A)$ (e.g., estimated with the SST) to $P_M(A)$ by applying a constant value ξ (see following text).

Now, in a definite geographical area, at any given time a fraction q_{in} of the total number of vehicles moving in it may be started from inside the area (and eventually leave it, as is here assumed, by entering a contiguous area), and a fraction $q_{out} = 1 - q_{in}$ may be driven into the area from its perimeter. Realistic values of q_{in} must be estimated from traffic measurements or models. These two mutually exclusive cases can yield two quite different distributions, $P_{M,in}(A)$ and $P_{M,out}(A)$, respectively, which can be estimated separately and, once known, are necessary to design satellite communication systems for *any* vehicle driven within the area.

If $P_{M,in}(A)$ and $P_{M,out}(A)$ are known for a given pattern, then the land-mobile satellite system for that pattern can be designed, regardless of the origin of the user, just by weighting the two distributions according to the value of q_{in} to obtain the overall cPdf, $P_M(A)$, as

$$P_M(A) = q_{in} P_{M,in}(A) + (1 - q_{in}) P_{M,out}(A) \tag{46}$$

Equation 46 can be generalized to determine the cPdf of rain attenuation in a larger area made up of smaller areas with homogeneous rain rate statistics, or an area made up of cPdfs relative to different values of a parameter (e.g., pattern, elevation angle, speed model, etc.) by adding many terms weighted accordingly.

In conclusion, from equation 45 and by assuming constant values of ξ_{in} and ξ_{out}, equation 46 can be written as

$$P_M(A) = [q_{in}\xi_{in} + (1 - q_{in})\xi_{out}]\, P_F(A) \tag{47}$$

Equation 47 is very useful because it directly yields $P_M(A)$ as a function of $P_F(A)$ for any vehicle started inside or outside the area.

The results summarized as follows refer to a GEO satellite receiver at 19.77 GHz with elevation angle $\theta = 30.6°$ (Matricciani 2000a), and to a MEO satellite receiver with minimum elevation angle $\theta \geq \theta_{\min} = 30.6°$ (Matricciani and Selva 2002) located in the Po Valley (Northern Italy). The GEO satellite receiver is affected, on the average, by a larger attenuation than the MEO satellite receiver as a result of a smaller elevation angle. Although the results refer to specific systems and locations, the findings are of general applicability.

To obtain the empirical rules to transform $P_F(A)$ into $P_M(A)$ for the same rain attenuation $A_F = A_M = A$ (dB), we can consider three likely patterns, according to how vehicles are driven: (a) *zigzag* routes; (b) *ring-roads*, to simulate city patterns; and (c) *straight routes* to simulate freeways. The simulations consider a very large number of rain rate circular maps of 80 km in diameter, measured by a meteorological radar located in Spino d'Adda (45.5 degrees north, 9.5 degrees east, 84 m above sea level), in a flat countryside near Milan (Italy), collected during rainstorms randomly observed in 1989, 1991, and 1992 (Matricciani 2000a; Matricciani and Selva 2002). The rain rate maps were sampled every ninety seconds. On these maps a grid of square cells was superposed to represent city blocks and streets in cases (a) and (b), and straight lines in case (c). Now, since meteorological radars provide a reliable estimate of the horizontal structure of rain, the results can stand as experimental for both fixed and mobile satellite systems.

Similar results could also be derived by applying a bidimensional version of SST (Matricciani and Moretti 1998) instead of using radar maps. The SST simulations are very useful because they can be applied to any site and its surroundings for which only rain rate time series are available.

The results have shown that in zigzag routes, for both GEO and MEO satellite systems, it is always $P_M(A) < P_F(A)$. The detailed results depend on vehicle speed modeling and starting conditions (i.e., inside or outside the observed area). In ring roads, there is no improvement compared to the fixed system, $P_M(A) \approx P_F(A)$. In straight freeways, vehicles are always started outside and cross the entire area (i.e., $q_{in} = 0$). In this case, the results show that $P_M(A) << P_F(A)$ · $P_M(A)$, however, can change significantly in different routes and in opposite directions (anisotropy and asymmetry) for medium–large attenuation. Only at low attenuation are different directions and routes indistinguishable (isotropy and symmetry). When compared to zigzag routes or ring roads, the performance of vehicles driven in freeways is the most optimistic.

Figure 4 shows the cumulative time that rain attenuation A(dB) in abscissa is exceeded in the GEO and MEO satellite systems for fixed terminals and for vehicles running in straight freeways with speed values according to Model III (fast traffic) or Model I (low traffic, simulating a slower traffic in freeways). The results are averaged over all directions. As expected, for the same cumulative time exceeded (or probability: the corresponding cPdfs can be obtained by dividing the cumulative time by the same observation time without changing the comparison), the GEO satellite system is affected by a larger attenuation than the MEO satellite system with the same minimum elevation angle, $\theta \geq \theta_{min} = 30.6°$.

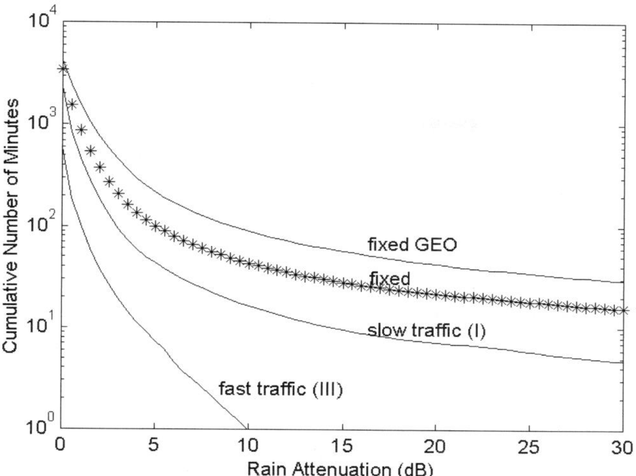

Figure 4: Cumulative time (minutes) that rain attenuation A(dB), at 19.77 GHz, in abscissa is exceeded in the GEO fixed system (curve label "fixed GEO") and MEO satellite systems for fixed terminals (curve labeled "fixed"), as well as for vehicles running in straight freeways with vehicle speed values according to Model III (fast traffic) or Model I (simulating slow traffic). The latter distributions must be compared to the curve labeled "fixed."

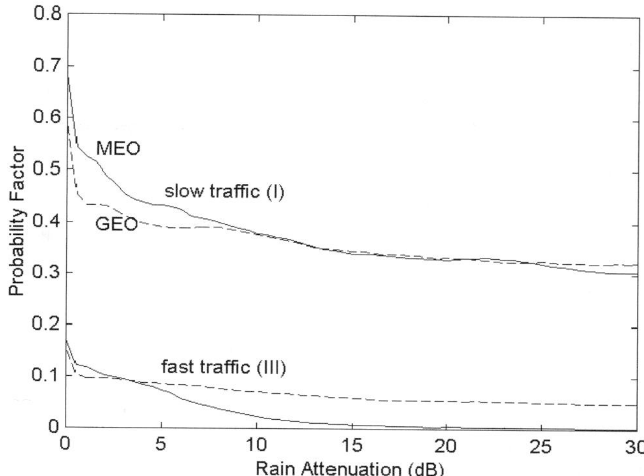

Figure 5: Probability factor $\xi(A)$ as a function of rain attenuation A(dB) at 19.77 GHz for comparable GEO (dashed lines) and MEO (continuous lines) satellite systems in the same geographical area for vehicle speed Model I (slow traffic) and Model II (fast traffic).

From Figure 4 we can obtain the probability scaling factor $\xi(A)$ for the MEO system shown in Figure 5. This figure also shows the scaling factors obtained for a GEO satellite system (Matricciani 2000b). Notice that for both MEO and GEO systems, $\xi(A)$ is not significantly different for the same patterns; for most of the attenuation range, it is practically independent of attenuation (and carrier frequency), so that a single value can be used (similar to the zigzag routes). For low attenuation, $\xi(A)$ approaches a higher value because in this range vehicles encounter low rain rates that are likely to cover large parts of the circular area, as opposed to more intense rain rates. Figure 4 shows that $\xi(A) < 0.1$ for the fast traffic (for freeways, fast traffic $\xi = \xi_{out}$ because $q_{in} = 0$), and $\xi(A) < 0.4$ for the slower traffic.

As for zigzag routes in urban or suburban traffic, Table 5 reports the constant values of ξ_{out} and ξ_{in} for speed Models I and II, respectively. For GEO and MEO mobile systems, the values of ξ are still not significantly different for the same patterns.

Second-order statistics of the fixed system are scaled to the mobile system accordingly. A fade duration must be multiplied by $\xi(A)$, and a rate of change must be divided by $\xi(A)$, for a given rain attenuation A (Matricciani 1995). For the most optimistic case (i.e., vehicles or trains) running fast in straight freeways (speed Model III), fade duration measured by a fixed receiver may be largely "shrunk" because $\xi(A) \leq 0.1$. This is a benign effect because it reduces, for a given system power margin, the duration of outages. On the other hand, the rate of change measured by a fixed receiver is now emphasized because it is multiplied by $1/\xi(A) \geq 10$, and this fact can have a significant impact on the methods that dynamically adjust some system parameters according to the instantaneous rate of change of attenuation (e.g., power margin, adaptive coding, satellite tracking, etc.), in the past designed to cope with the fixed system rates of change. Table 6 summarizes the main findings.

Table 5: Average Value of the Probability Factor ξ_{out} and ξ_{in} Zigzag Routes as a Function of p_s, ξ_{out}, and ξ_{in} (in the Range of $1 \leq A \leq 30$ dB at 19.77 GHz)

Probability of Going Straight p_s	ξ_{out} (Vehicles Started from the Perimeter of the Useful Area)				ξ_{in} (Vehicles Started Inside the Useful Area)			
	Urban Traffic (Model I)		Suburban Traffic (Model II)		Urban Traffic (Model I)		Suburban Traffic (Model II)	
	GEO	MEO	GEO	MEO	GEO	MEO	GEO	MEO
0.5	0.18	0.10	0.14	0.09	0.72	0.77	0.59	0.66
0.8	0.21	0.20	0.16	0.13	0.50	0.56	0.42	0.42
1	0.27	0.24	0.11	0.09	0.16	0.13	0.07	0.03

Table 6: First- and Second-Order Statistics of Rain Attenuation for Land-Mobile Satellite Communication as a Function of Those Measured (or Estimated) in Fixed-System Satellite Communication

Rain Attenuation Statistic for Land-Mobile Communication	Ring Roads	Zigzag Routes (see Table 4)	Freeways (see Figure 5)
Probability distribution $P_M(A)$	$P_M(A) \approx P_F(A)$	$P_M(A) = [q_{in}\xi_{in} + (1 - q_{in})\xi_{out}]P_F(A)$	$P_M(A) = \xi\, P_F(A)$
Fade duration $D_M(A)$ (min)	$D_M(A) \approx D_F(A)$	$D_M(A) = [q_{in}\xi_{in} + (1 - q_{in})\xi_{out}]D_F(A)$	$D_M(A) = \xi\, D_F(A)$
Rate of change of fade $R_M(A)$ (dB/s)	$R_M(A) \approx R_F(A)$	$R_M(A) = \dfrac{R_F(A)}{[q_{in}\xi_{in} + (1 - q_{in})\xi_{out}]}$	$R_M(A) = \dfrac{R_F(A)}{\xi}$

CONCLUSION

Land-mobile satellite communication can be degraded much more seriously than fixed-satellite channels because electromagnetic waves propagate in a high hostile environment made of obstructions, shadowing, multipath, hydrometeors, and other constituents of the atmosphere. The frequency bands now used are L band (1.5 GHz) and S band (3 GHz), but the large bandwidths allocated at K_u (12/14 GHz) band and K_a band (20/30 GHz), and the availability of a mature technology for these frequency bands, have made them more attractive for satellite broadband multimedia services. However, besides suffering the same propagation impairments of L and S bands, these bands are also affected by large fading due to the troposphere—mainly rain attenuation. We have recalled the most important radio electrical aspects (modulation, coding, multiple access, and orbits) applicable to a land-mobile satellite channel, and we have summarized in more detail the modeling of the physical channel in clear-sky and rainy conditions.

For clear-sky conditions there are so many models, especially for the more common and simple case of narrowband channels, that it is very difficult to design a system without knowing the type of environment the mobile terminal will find on route. Most of the models are empirical, and, as such, they do not allow insight into the physical causes that cause fading; therefore, deeper understanding and extrapolation to other sites and environments are not straight. Other models are theoretical and characterized by well-known probability distributions, often used jointly to describe more complex situations but always conditioned to a given "known" environment, which is hard to set in real time.

Although channel modeling concerning rain attenuation is, in principle, easier because the cause of fading can be well identified (rainfall), it may be difficult to know, for an area, the representative rain rate time series and to apply the synthetic storm technique—a physical, reliable, and powerful prediction tool—to obtain first- and second-order statistics of rain attenuation applicable to fixed systems first and to land-mobile systems second by scaling them according to the appropriate scaling factor, ξ.

The need to know the rain rate time series for a given locality is overcome when only a first-order statistic (i.e., the long-term probability distribution of rain attenuation) is required because this can be obtained by equations 42 and 43, and ITU-R global maps of rain rate as a function of probability. These predictions are approximately as reliable and accurate as those provided directly by the synthetic storm technique.

In conclusion, for both clear-sky and rainy conditions, ad hoc modeling and propagation expertise are as much of a necessity for land-mobile satellite communications as for their terrestrial counterparts, especially at frequencies greater than 10 GHz.

GLOSSARY

BPSK: Binary phase shift keying.
C band: Channels at approximately 4/6 GHz (downlink/uplink).
CDMA: Direct-sequence code division multiple access.
FDMA: Frequency division multiple access.
FEC codes: Forward error correcting codes.
GEO: Geostationary Earth orbit.
K_a band: Channels at approximately at 20/30 GHz (downlink/uplink).
K_u band: Channels at approximately 12/14 GHz (downlink/uplink).
L band: Channels at approximately 1.5 GHz.
LDPC codes: Low-density parity check codes.
LEO: Low-altitude Earth orbit.
MEO: Medium-altitude Earth orbit.
QPSK: Quadrature phase shift keying.
S band: Channels at approximately 3 GHz.
SST: Synthetic storm technique.
TDMA: Time-division multiple access.

CROSS REFERENCES

See *Geosynchronous Fixed Satellite Communications*; *Global Navigation Satellite Systems (GNSS)*; *Satellite Communications Basics*; *Satellites in IP Networks*.

REFERENCES

Allnutt, J. E. 1989. *Satellite-to-ground radiowave propagation*. London: Peter Peregrinus.

Beckmann P., and A. Spizzichino. 1987. *The scattering of electromagnetic waves from rough surfaces*. Norwood, MA: Artech House.

Bello, P. A. 1963. Characterization of randomly time-variant linear channels. *IEEE Transactions on Communication Systems* CS-11, 360–93.

Binaghi M., and A. Pawlina Bonati. 1992. Modeling of multiple site statistical dependence function through integration of dynamic features of radar rain patterns. Proceedings of *URSI Commission F Open Symposium*, Ravenscar, UK, June, pp. 2.1.1–2.1.6.

Capsoni C., D. Maggiori, E. Matricciani, and A. Paraboni. 1981. Rain anisotropy prediction: Theory and experiment. *Radio Science* 16: 909–16.

Chu, T. S. 1971. Restoring the orthogonality of two polarizations in radio communication systems, I. *Bell System Technical Journal* 50: 3063–69.

Cox, D. C. 1981. Depolarization of radio waves by atmospheric hydrometeors in Earth-space paths: A review. *Radio Science* 16: 781–812.

Cox, D. C., and H. W. Arnold. 1982. Results from the 19- and 28-GHz COMSTAR satellite propagation measurements at Crawford Hill. *Proceedings of IEEE* 7: 458–88.

———. 1984. Comparison of measured cross-polarization isolation and discrimination for rain and ice on a 19-GHz space-Earth path. *Radio Science* 19: 617–28.

Cox D. C., R. Murray, and A. Norris. 1984. 800 MHz attenuation measured in and around suburban houses. *AT&T Laboratory Technical Journal* 673 (July/August): pp. 921–54.

Crane, R. K. 1996. *Electromagnetic wave propagation through rain*. Hoboken, NJ: Wiley-Interscience.

———. 2002. Analysis of the effects of water on the ACTS propagation terminal antenna. *IEEE Transactions on Antennas and Propagation* 50: 954–65.

———. 2003. *Propagation handbook for wireless communication system design*. Boca Raton, FL: CRC.

Densmore, A. C., and V. Jamnejad. 1993. A satellite-tracking K-and K_a-band mobile vehicle antenna system. *IEEE Transactions on Vehicular Technology* 42: 502–13.

Dietrich, F. J., P. Metzen, and P. Monte. 1998. The Globalstar cellular satellite system. *IEEE Transactions on Antennas and Propagation* 46: 935–42.

DiFonzo, D. F., W. S. Tracchtman, and A. W. Williams. 1976. Adaptive polarization control for satellite frequency reuse systems. *COMSAT Technical Review* 6: 253–83.

Dissanayake, A., J. Allnutt, and F. Haidara. 1997. A prediction model that combines rain attenuation and other propagation impairments along earth-satellite paths. *IEEE Transactions on Antennas and Propagation* 45: 1546–58.

Dissanayake, A.W., D. K. McCarthy, J. E. Allnutt, R. Shepherd, and B. Arbesser-Rastburg. 1990. 11.6 GHz rain attenuation measurements in Peru. *International Journal on Satellite Communications* 8: 229–38.

Drufuca, G. 1973. Rain attenuation studies. Internal report MW-77 of the Stormy Weather Group, McGill University, Montreal, Canada.

———. 1974. Rain attenuation statistics for frequencies above 10 GHz from raingauge observations. *Journal de Recherches Atmospheriques* 1/2: 399–411.

Drufuca, G., and I. I. Zawadzki. 1975. Statistics of raingauge data. *Journal of Applied Meteorology* 14: 1419–29.

Durgin, G. 2003. *Space-time wireless channels*. Cambridge, UK: Cambridge University Press.

Emiliani, L. D., L. Castanet, and L. Feral. 2005. Review and testing analysis of rain rate and rain attenuation prediction models for satellite application in the Aburrá Valley in the country of Colombia. *Eleventh Ka-Band Conference*, Rome, 25–28 September.

Friis, H. T. 1946. A note on a simple transmission formula. Proceedings of the *I.R.E and Waves and Electrons*, July, pp. 254–56.

Fukuchi, H., M. Fujita, K. Nakamura, Y. Furuhama, and Y. Otsu. 1981. Rain attenuation characteristics on quasi-millimeter waves using Japanese geostationary satellites CS and BSE. *International Conference on Antennas and Propagation*, York, England, p. 195.

Gallager, R. G. 1963. *Low-density parity check codes*. Cambridge, MA: MIT Press.

Goldhirsh, J. 1980. Multiyear slant-path rain fade statistics at 28.56 GHz for Wallops Island, VA. *IEEE Transaction on Antennas and Propagation* 28: 934–41.

Goldhirsh, J., and W. J. Vogel. 1998. Handbook of propagation effects for vehicular and personal mobile satellite systems: Overview of experimental and modeling results. *NASA Reference Publication* 1274, 2nd ed.

Hagenauer, J., and E. Lutz. 1987. Forward error correction coding for fading compensation in mobile satellite channel. *IEEE Journal on Selected Areas in Communications* SAC-5: 215–25.

Hamilton, P. M., and J. S. Marshall. 1961. Weather-radar attenuation estimates from raingauge statistics. Internal report MW-32 of the Stormy Weather Group, McGill University, Montreal, Canada.

Hasey, Y., J. Goldhirsh, and W. J. Vogel. 1991. Fade-durations derived from land mobile satellite measurements in Australia. *IEEE Transactions on Communications* 39: 664–68.

International Telecommunication Union-Radio Communication Sector (ITU-R). 1992a. Specific attenuation model for rain for use in prediction methods. *Propagation in Non-Ionized Media*, Rec. 838, Geneva.

———. 1992b. Rain height model for prediction methods: ITU-R recommendations. *Propagation in Non-Ionized Media*, Rec. 839, Geneva.

———. 2001a. P.837-3. Characteristics of precipitation for propagation modeling. ITU-R P Series Recommendations—Radiowave Propagation.

———. 2001b. P.839-3. Rain height model for prediction methods. ITU-R P Series Recommendations—Radiowave Propagation.

———. 2003a. P.618-8. Propagation data and prediction methods required for the design of earth-space telecommunication systems. ITU-R P Series Recommendations—Radiowave Propagation.

———. 2003b. P.162-3. Prediction method of fade-dynamics on Earth-space paths. ITU-R P Series Recommendations—Radiowave Propagation.

Ippolito, L. J. 1986. *Radiowave propagation in satellite communications*. New York: Van Nostrand Reinhold.

———. 1989. Propagation effects handbook for satellite systems design. *NASA Reference Publication* 1082, no. 4.

Ismail, A. F., and P. A. Watson. 2000. Characteristics of fading and fade countermeasures on a satellite-Earth link operating in an equatorial climate, with reference to broadcast applications. *IEE Proceedings—Microwaves, Antennas, and Propagation* 147: 370–73.

Jakes, W. C. 1994. *Microwave mobile communication*. 2nd ed. Hoboken, NJ: Wiley-IEEE Press.

Kanatas, G., and P. Konstantinou. 1996. Narrow-band characterization of the land mobile satellite channel: A comparison of the empirical models. *European Transactions on Telecommunications* 7: 315–21.

Karaliopoulos, M. S., and F. N. Pavlidou. 1999. Modeling the land mobile satellite channel: A review. *Electronics & Communication Engineering Journal,* 11 (5): 235–48.

Karasawa, Y., K. Kimura, and K. Minamisono. 1997. Analysis of availability improvement in 1MSS by means of satellite diversity based on three-state propagation channel model. *IEEE Transactions on Vehicular Technology* 46: 1047–56.

Lee, C. Y. 1995. *Mobile cellular telecommunications: Analog and digital systems*. 2nd ed. New York: McGraw-Hill.

Lin, S. H., H. J. Bergmann, and M. V. Pursley. 1980. Rain attenuation on Earth-satellite paths: Summary of 10-year experiments and studies. *Bell System Technical Journal* 59: 183–228.

Loo, C. 1985. A statistical model for a land mobile satellite link. *IEEE Transactions on Vehicular Technology* 34: 122–27.

Loo, C., and J. S. Butterworth. 1998. Land mobile satellite channel measurements and modeling. *Proceedings of IEEE* 86: 1442–62.

Lutz, E., D. Cygan, M. Dippold, F. Dolainsky, and W. Papke. 1991. The land mobile satellite communication channel: Recording, statistics, and channel model. *IEEE Transactions on Vehicular Technology* 40: 375–86.

MacKay, D. J. C., and R. M. Neal. 1996. Near Shannon limit performance of low-density parity check codes. *Electronics Letters* 32: 1645–55.

Maggiori, D. 1981. Computed transmission through rain in the 1–400 GHz frequency range for spherical and elliptical drops and any polarization. *Alta Frequenza* 50: 262–73.

Maral, G., and M. Bousquet. 1998. *Satellite communications systems*. 3rd ed. Hoboken, NJ: John Wiley & Sons.

Matricciani, E. 1981a. Duration of rain-induced fades of signal from SIRIO at 11.6 GHz. *Electronics Letters* 17: 29–30.

———. 1981b. Rate of change of signal attenuation from SIRIO at 11.6 GHz. *Electronics Letters* 17: 139–41.

———. 1982a. Effects of filtering on statistics of rain-induced fade durations. *Electronics Letters* 18: 253–55.

———. 1982b. Effects of filtering on rate of change of rain-induced attenuation. *Electronics Letters* 18: 477–78.

———. 1987. Orbital diversity in resource-shared satellite communication systems above 10 GHz. *IEEE Journal on Selected Areas in Communications* 5: 714–23.

———. 1991. Rain attenuation predicted with a two-layer rain model. *European Transactions on Telecommunications* 2: 715–27.

———. 1994. Physical-mathematical model of dynamics of rain attenuation with application to power spectrum. *Electronics Letters* 30: 522–24.

———. 1995. Transformation of rain attenuation statistics from fixed to mobile satellite communication systems. *IEEE Transactions on Vehicular Technology* 44: 565–69.

———. 1996. Physical-mathematical model of the dynamics of rain attenuation based on rain rate time series and two layer vertical structure of precipitation. *Radio Science* 31: 281–95.

———. 1997. Prediction of fade duration due to rain in satellite communication systems. *Radio Science* 22: 935–41.

———. 1998. Diurnal distribution of rain attenuation in communication and broadcasting satellite systems at 11.6 GHz. *IEEE Transactions on Broadcasting* 44: 250–58.

———. 2000a. Experimental rain attenuation statistics estimated from radar measurements useful to design satellite communication systems for mobile terminals. *IEEE Transactions on Vehicular Technology* 49: 1534–46.

———. 2000b. An assessment of rain attenuation impact on satellite communication: Matching service quality and system design to the time of the day. *Space Communications* 16: 195–205.

———. 2003. Microscale site diversity in satellite and troposphere communication systems affected by rain attenuation. *Space Communications* 19: 83–90.

———. 2004. Service-oriented statistics of interruption time due to rainfall in Earth-space communication systems. *IEEE Transactions on Antennas and Propagation* 52: 2083–90.

———. 2006. Time diversity as a rain attenuation countermeasure in satellite links at K_a band. Paper presented to the First European Conference on Antennas and Propagation (EuCAP 2006), 6–10 November, Nice, France.

Matricciani, E., M. Mauri, and A. Paraboni. 1987. Dynamic characteristics of rain attenuation: Duration and rate of change of fades. *Alta Frequenza* 56: 33–45.

Matricciani, E., M. Mauri, and C. Riva. 1996. Relationship between scintillation and rain attenuation at 19.77 GHz. *Radio Science* 31: 273–79.

Matricciani, E., and S. Moretti. 1998. Rain attenuation statistics useful for the design of mobile satellite communication systems. *IEEE Transactions on Vehicular Technology* 47: 637–48.

Matricciani, E., and C. Riva. 1998a. Evaluation of the feasibility of satellite systems design in the 10–100 GHz frequency range. *International Journal of Satellite Communications* 16: 237–47.

———. 1998b. Polarization independence of tropospheric scintillation in clear sky: Results from Olympus experiment at Spino d'Adda. *IEEE Transaction on Antennas and Propagation* 46: 1400–1402.

———. 2005a. Correlation between scintillation and rain attenuation in a slant path at 18.7 GHz from Italsat high resolution measurements at Spino d'Adda. *Fifth Edition of the Mediterranean Microwave Symposium MMS'2005*, Athens, Greece, September.

———. 2005b. The search for the most reliable long-term rain attenuation Pdf of a slant path and the impact on prediction models. *IEEE Transactions on Antennas and Propagation* 53: 3075–79.

Matricciani, E., and S. P. Selva. 2002. Attenuation statistics estimated from radar measurements in MEO satellite communication systems for mobile terminals. *International Journal of Satellite Communication* 20: 167–85.

Oguchi, T. 1983. Electromagnetic wave propagation and scattering in rain and other hydrometeors. *Proceedings of the IEEE* 71: 1029–79.

Olsen, R. L., D. V. Rogers, and D. B. Hodge. 1978. The aR^b relation in the calculation of rain attenuation. *IEEE Transactions on Antennas and Propagation* 26: 318–29.

OPEX. 1994. Reference book on attenuation. Second Workshop of the Olympus Propagation Experimenters (ESA-ESTEC-WPP-083, 2), Noordwijk, the Netherlands.

Paraboni, A., and C. Riva. 1994. A new method for the prediction of fade duration statistics in satellite links above 10 GHz. *International Journal on Satellite Communications* 12: 387–94.

Parsons, J. D. 2000. *The mobile radio propagation channel*. 2nd ed. Hoboken, NJ: John Wiley & Sons.

Pattan, B. 1998. *Satellite-based cellular communications*. New York: McGraw-Hill.

Perez-Fontan, P., S. Buonomo, J. P. Poiares-Baptista, and B. Arbesser-Rastburg. 1997a. S-band LMS propagation channel behavior for different environments, degrees of shadowing and elevation angles. *IEEE Transactions on Broadcasting* 44: 40–76.

Perez-Fontan, P., J. P. Gonzalez, M. A. Vazquez-Castro, S. Buonomo, and J. P. Poiares-Baptista. 1997b. Complex envelope three state Markov model based simulator for the narrow-band LMS channel. *International Journal of Satellite Communications* 15: 1–15.

Poiares-Baptista, J. P., and P. G. Davies, eds. 1994. Reference book on attenuation measurement and prediction. OPEX Second Workshop of the Olympus Propagation Experiments, European Space Agency (ESA), WPP-083.

Pratt, T., C. W. Bostian, and J. E. Allnutt. 2003. *Satellite communications*. Hoboken, NJ: John Wiley & Sons.

Rappaport, T. S. 2001. *Wireless communications: Principles and practice*. 2nd ed. Upper Saddle River, NJ: Prentice Hall.

Richharia, M. 1999. *Satellite communication systems*. 2nd ed. New York: McGraw-Hill.

Riva, C., ed. 2002. Testing of prediction models. In *Radiowave Propagation Modeling for SatCom Services at K_u-Band and Above*, COST 255, ESA, SP-1252, 2.6-1-2.6–39.

Sklar, B. 1997a. Rayleigh fading channels in mobile digital communication systems part I: Characterization. *IEEE Communications Magazine*, July, pp. 90–100.

———. 1997b. Rayleigh fading channels in mobile digital communication systems part II: Mitigation. *IEEE Communications Magazine*, July, pp. 102–9.

Suzuki, H. 1977. A statistical model for urban radio propagation. *IEEE Transactions on Communications* 25: 673–80.

Tatarski, V. I. 1961. *Wave propagation in a turbulent medium*. New York: McGraw-Hill.

Taylor, G. I. 1938. The spectrum of turbulence. *Proceedings of the Royal Society of London* 164: 476–90.

Telikepalli, R., P. C. Strickland, K. R. McKay, and J. S. Wight. 1995. Wideband microstrip phased array for mobile satellite communications. *IEEE Transactions on Microwave Theory and Techniques* 43: 1758–63.

Vasseur, H., and D. Vanhoenacker. 1998. Characterization of tropospheric turbulent layers from the radiosonde data. *Electronics Letters* 34: 318–19.

Wu, W. W., E. F. Miller, W. L. Pritchard, and R. L. Pickholtz. 1994. Mobile satellite communications. *Proceedings of the IEEE* 82: 1431–47.

Zawadzki, I. I. 1973. Statistical properties of precipitation patterns. *Journal of Applied Meteorology* 12: 459–72.

Geosynchronous Fixed Satellite Communications

Michele Luglio, *University of Rome Tor Vergata, Italy*
Antonio Saitto, *Telespazio, Italy*

INTRODUCTION

Among human-made satellites working in orbit at significant altitudes above the Earth, geostationary (GEO) satellites are the most common. They have been the first commercial application to guarantee visibility between points on the Earth that are not in direct line of sight because of the Earth's spherical nature. For a long time, they have been the best and most economical way to allow international communications across the oceans. Currently, geostationary satellites represent also a useful complement to terrestrial facilities in order to complete the global information infrastructure in which every component (terrestrial cabled, terrestrial wireless, and satellite) must play the most suitable role to provide telecommunication connectivity (and hence services) anywhere and to anyone.

Geostationary satellites complement the terrestrial network infrastructure to complete the geographical coverage, to guarantee the *quality of service* (QoS) as a backup infrastructure (for example, in case of emergency), to supply fundamental overlay functionalities, and to deliver high-quality broadcasting and multicasting services at competitive prices.

This chapter provides general considerations on geostationary satellites and services; describes satellite system characteristics in terms of architecture, physical layer, security, and standards; deals with interoperability with terrestrial systems; describes two milestone systems; gives an overview of the major commercial systems; and finally draws conclusions.

USE OF GEOSYNCHRONOUS SATELLITES FOR FIXED SERVICES

A geosynchronous or geostationary satellite acts as a radio relay in the sky. It receives signals such as voice, data, facsimile, and video from stations located on the Earth, amplifies these signals, and sends them back to other Earth stations.

These satellites are placed in *geostationary* or *geosynchronous* orbits at an altitude of 35,786 km (22,282 miles) (Maral and Bousquet 2003). They appear to be stationary with respect to a point on the Earth because they travel around the Earth in exactly its rotation time. In principle, only three satellites in geostationary orbit above the equator are sufficient to cover the entire Earth except for uninhabited polar regions.

If one hop on the satellite is not sufficient to reach the final destination, for a pure satellite global network, signals must be relayed through a second satellite, thus requiring either a double hop or an intersatellite link.

SOME CONSIDERATIONS ON SATELLITE SERVICES

Fixed satellite services are related to all of the links with stations, with either bidirectional or one-way capability, in stationary conditions (thus including transportable stations). Nevertheless, this concept is somehow flexible because the same satellite infrastructure can deliver both fixed and mobile services (e.g., the Omnitracks service for truck localization working at 11–14 GHz). Moreover, the growing use of data and multimedia communications makes the difference even more thinly. In any case, thanks to the limited dimensions of current satellite traffic stations, they are strongly utilized for fixed, nomadic, and, thanks to the steering capability of modern antennae, mobile communications (not handheld terminals).

During the last ten years, the traditional use of satellite communications strongly evolved from trunk services across the oceans to more innovative systems based on the TCP-IP protocol and multimedia applications in those areas where satellite technology remains highly competitive. In particular, satellite networks and architectures are highly competitive and cost-effective, in addition to classical broadcast and remote area communications, in the emergency operations (including telemedicine, operating team support, etc.), for providing backup infrastructures and overlay network and supporting interoperability with different terrestrial subnetworks. The need for more capacity and bandwidth is satisfied by the use of high frequencies (as high as 30 GHz and more), allowing the use of small antennae that are available at low cost and acceptable reliability.

In recent years, dual use applications for telecommunications satellites are becoming popular (e.g., military and civilian, commercial and governmental). Satellites are essential for security, safety, and defense, but exclusive use of the capacity for institutional markets needs an extremely long time for the investment to break even, whereas the combination of high-quality commercial (typically, business to business) and institutional applications can make investment in satellites more attractive.

All of the major satellite operators and service providers offer satellite capacity to both institutional and commercial customers. The possibility of delivering secure and robust communications peer to peer is the key characteristic of the service.

SATELLITE SYSTEM RATIONALE

The use of satellites is appropriate to meet the following objectives: cost effectiveness, emergency management, quick setup, large coverage, flexibility, and enhanced connectivity.

- Costs: The advantage in terms of cost is that it is independent of distance (with one-satellite coverage) and is efficient and effective for collecting, broadcasting, and multicasting.
- Emergency: In case of emergencies or disasters, when terrestrial infrastructures can be out of order, satellites offer a unique service.
- Setup: Satellite networks are characterized by relatively short deployment time and easy setup activities.
- Coverage: Satellites offer coverage for large areas and ensure long-range mobility, and they can bypass highly crowded terrestrial networks.
- Flexibility: Satellites can offer a high degree of flexibility in terms of both architecture and resource management.
- Connectivity: Satellites can constitute both a backup network and an overlay network, and they guarantee service in areas with scarce or no infrastructure.

Architecture

Orbit and Orbit Control

In celestial mechanics, the term *orbit* defines the motion of a satellite in the presence of gravity. This orbit cannot be modified from its spontaneous evolution, which depends on the initial conditions and the presence of nongravitational forces and fields. In the case of astrodynamics, the dynamic behavior of satellites can be driven and commanded toward a defined state. The control of the trajectory phase is fundamental in space flight.

Trajectories are controlled by means of propulsive devices (thrusts) in order to achieve the final orbit objective, starting from an initial state. This control respects a set of constraints between the initial and the final state, matching defined flight performance objectives. The overall trajectory is composed of sequences of arcs with thrust switched on and sequences of arcs with thrust switched off (known as the *thrusting* and *coasting arcs,* respectively).

The orbit is characterized by the *orbit elements,* a set of independent variables that completely define the orbital motion of a satellite schematized as a test particle (Tirrò 1993). Six variables are needed to define the orbit completely, and the motion can be described via the motion of the *mass center* of the satellite. The state equations (a set of nonlinear ordinary differential equations) are used to describe the orbit element time evolution. To explicitly obtain the satellite motion, the state equations must be numerically integrated; the choice of the initial set of independent variables depends on the class of flight considered. The most common orbital sets are the Keplerian element, spherical coordinates, the equinotional set, and Cartesian variables. Keplerian coordinates are preferred for elliptical orbits.

Two variables define the ellipse form: (1) the semimajor axis and (2) eccentricity (e), the ratio between the focal distance and the major axis. When $e = 0$, the orbit is circular.

Three variables define the orientation of the ellipse in the space:

1. the *inclination angle* (i), which is the angle between the plane containing the orbit and a reference plane such as the equatorial one in the case of Earth;
2. the *ascending node right ascension* (Ω), which is the counterclockwise angle between the vertical equinox direction and the line defined by the orbital plane with the reference plane on the side of the motion of the satellite from below; and
3. the *perifocus argument* (ω), which is the counterclockwise angle along the orbit between the ascending node and the perifocus point of minimum distance from the dynamical focus of the ellipse.

The last variable is the position of the material point on the orbit at the given epoch. This is usually called the *true anomaly* (η), and it measures the counterclockwise angular distance between the perifocus and the position of the material point on the orbit.

The geostationary and geosynchronous orbits are ideally those circular orbits for which the motion period of the satellite around the Earth is equal to its rotation period. When the inclination angle is equal to 0 degrees, the orbit is called *geostationary,* and the satellite looks fixed with respect to the Earth. Otherwise, the orbit is called *geosynchronous,* and the satellite is moving essentially up and down the equatorial plane on a narrow eight. The radius of a geostationary orbit is 42,164 km, and the period is 86,164 s.

In practical cases, the following factors contribute to making the geostationary orbit unstable without control:

- the nonspherical shape of the Earth,
- radiation pressure (resulting from solar light), and
- attraction on the satellite resulting from the gravitational fields of the sun, moon, and other celestial bodies.

The satellite motion, when it has reached the final orbital position as shown in Figure 1 (which also shows all of the intermediate phases), is controlled using the suitable frequency communication band by a telemetry, ranging, and command center that keeps the satellite in place with an accuracy given by an angular box (typical sizes are within 0.05–0.1 degree for the three angles of roll, pitch, and yaw), keeping it pointed on Earth and thus minimizing propellant consumption.

A satellite system can be divided into two main segments: the space segment and the Earth segment. The general architecture is presented in Figure 2.

Space Segment

The space segment (Figure 3) can be roughly divided in the following subsystems: the structure; a power section (batteries and solar panels); a stabilization and propulsion section (including propellant); a *telemetry, telecommand, and control* (TT&C) section to remotely control the spacecraft's on-board motors; the thermal control; the on-board data handling; and a payload section that exploits communication between two Earth stations.

The payload architecture can be transparent if it acts as a bent pipe (just change the frequency and amplify signals), or it can be regenerative if it implements some *on-board processing* (OBP) features, which means that it

1. Transfer orbit
2. Solar panel partial aperture
3. First apogee boost to an intermediate orbit
4. Second apogee boost to the circular orbit
5. Solar panel total aperture
6. Communications antenna opening
7. Adjustment to the final slot on the geostationary orbit

Figure 1: Orbital transfer phases to the geostationary final position (courtesy of Telespazio)

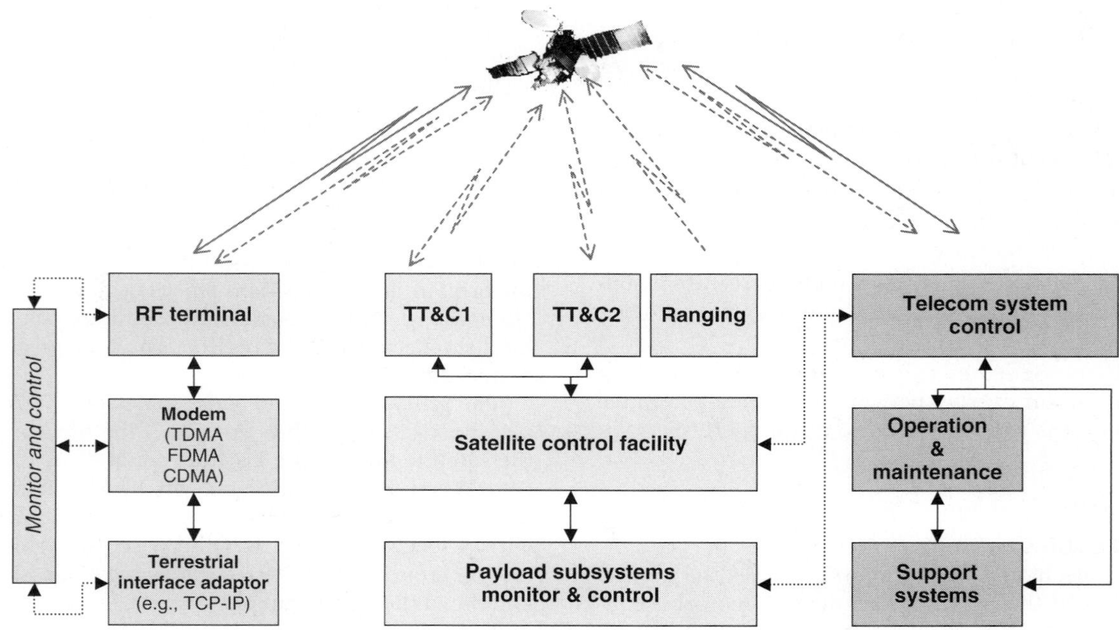

Figure 2: Satellite system general architecture

Figure 3: Space segment—Artemis (courtesy of Telespazio)

must at least demodulate and remodulate signals separating the uplink from the downlink. It can also decode signals, change polarization, interconnect beam to beam, route packets, and switch messages. On-board switching can be implemented at either baseband or microwave frequencies.

Currently, three types of on-board processing operate in the geostationary orbit:

1. *on-board processing* with full termination of the uplink at the baseband level;
2. *SkyPlex technology* in which the uplink is oversampled at the baseband level without analysis of the connectivity information and the downlink is a pseudo-*time division multiplexing* (TDM); and
3. *trans-lucid technology* in which the uplink is oversampled at the baseband level and the downlink consists of separate channel for each transmitted circuit.

An important part of the payload is the antenna subsystem. GEO satellites need large antennae to concentrate the radiated field on the coverage areas of interest on the Earth. On-board antenna size ranges from 15 meters for modern mobile communication satellites operating at L band, to 4–5 meters for those working in C band, and to 2 meter or less for those working at K_u and K_a bands.

To increase satellite capacity, antennae with multibeam capability (either fixed or steerable) are adopted. In such a configuration, frequency and polarization reuse and contoured beams limit the radiation on the area of interest, oversizing the antenna diameter and using a feed cluster to illuminate the reflector.

Frequency Bands and Coverage

The fixed satellite services have dedicated frequency bands according to the geographical region of coverage as established by the International Telecommunications Union (ITU) (Figure 4).

Because of the limitations of the geostationary orbit (which is unique), each bandwidth allotment at the national level implies several characteristics, such as the nominal orbital position and the flexibility of this position defined by the predetermined arc, the bandwidth, the service coverage, the *equivalent isotropic radiated power* (EIRP), the density of the satellites over the arc, the power spectral density, and the Earth station position. Practical difficulties with existing systems, however, have created several exceptions to a fully regulated system. For the purpose of frequency allocation, the world is divided into three regions as shown in Figure 4. The frequency allocation in the three regions is presented in Figure 5.

Efficient Use of the Geostationary Orbit and Spectrum Resource

Because of its unicity, the geostationary orbit can be overcrowded. As a consequence, it must be considered a natural resource and its shared utilization must be

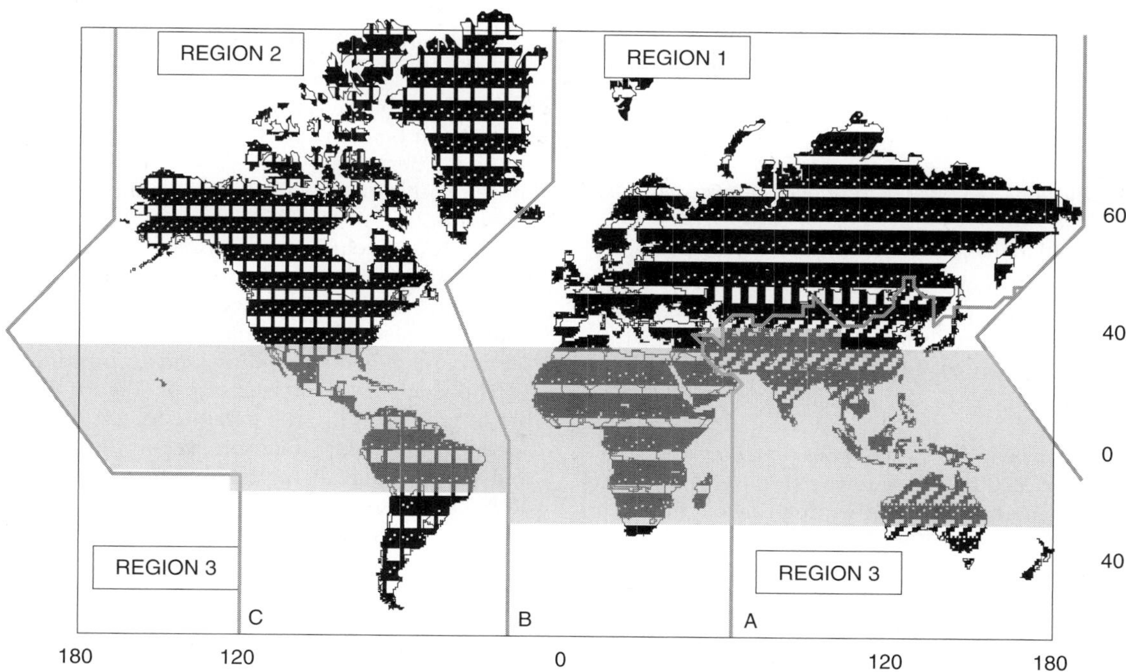

Figure 4: World frequency zones

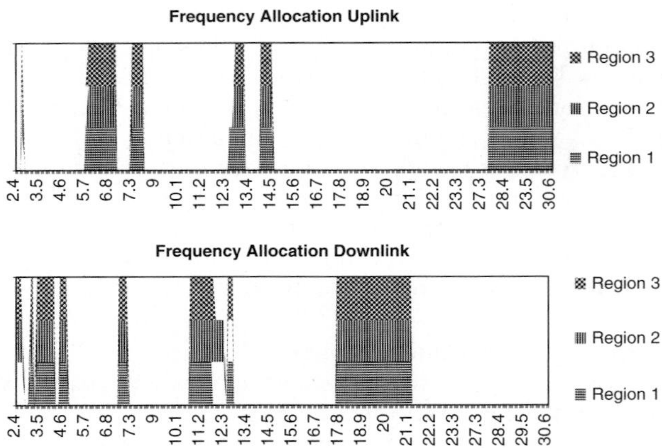

Figure 5: Uplink and downlink frequency allocation for the three world ITU regions

carefully optimized, and it is regulated by international bodies. In this respect, two problems in particular must be considered: the probability of two satellites colliding (considering the number of active and abandoned satellites) and the presence of damaging space debris. The probability of such catastrophic events has been evaluated as approximately 1 in 1 million.

Another problem concerns *radio frequency* (RF) blockage resulting from the transition of lower orbiting satellites with respect to the GEO ones. The probability of these events is some 1000 times larger than collision, but of course the impact in terms of loss of transmitted data is limited. Nevertheless, the main limitation is related to the available frequency spectrum and the total available orbital arc (360 degrees). There are many methodologies to optimize the use of the geostationary orbit, optimizing the frequency reuse, the satellite control box (station keeping), and the interference level to and from other satellites and ground stations. In this respect, coordination procedures have been set up by the ITU, as mentioned in Luglio and Saitto (2006).

Ground Segment

The ground segment is typically composed of two sections:

1. The first, which is related to payload utilization, is composed of Earth stations and the *network operation center* (NOC); and
2. the satellite operation control, which comprises the monitoring and control center, the TT&C station, and ranging stations.

The Earth stations can be of two types: gateway and user terminals (Elbert 2000). The gateway (Figure 6), usually a big station, is in charge of connecting the satellite systems with the terrestrial networks.

The user terminals (Figure 7) represent the physical devices through which users can access the satellite resources. They can be classified as *fixed* (*very small aperture terminals,* or VSATs), *transportable* (VSAT-like and mounted on a vehicle but working in stationary conditions), or *mobile* (handheld and cellular-like). Each terminal is equipped

Figure 6: A large Intelsat and a small GW (courtesy of Telespazio)

Figure 7: VSAT station (courtesy of Telespazio)

with a base-band section and an RF section. VSAT terminals can be connected in full mesh topology or in star topology. Terminals suitable to the mesh topology are more complex and expensive than those utilized for star networks.

The NOC includes the network control center, which is in charge of configuration management, capacity and bandwidth management, acquisition and synchronization control, performance management, alarm management, security management, billing, and accounting.

The satellite operation control (Figure 8) is responsible for maintaining the satellite in the orbital slot with specified accuracy (station keeping) and controlling and configuring all of the satellite subsystems via the TT&C Earth segment, which exchanges information with the TT&C section on-board and the ranging station (see Figure 9), which is used to accurately measure satellite position.

Network Topology and Connectivity

Two topologies are usually supported by a satellite network: star and mesh. The star topology (Figure 10) consists of a central hub station and a set of user terminals, typically much smaller and consuming less power than the hub. The hub acts as the star center through which all of the traffic transits; as a consequence, every pair of user terminals is physically interconnected through the hub, thus needing a double hop on the satellite, increasing delay and use of the bandwidth. In this configuration, the network is characterized by two streams: the forward stream from the hub to the terminals and the return stream from the terminals to the hub.

Figure 8: Satellite operation center

ADDITIONAL SUPPORT PROVIDED
VIA A SECOND RANGING STATION
LOCATED AT AN APPROPRIATE
LONGITUDE

Figure 9: Ranging station (courtesy of Telespazio)

In the mesh topology (Figure 11), the user terminals can be directly interconnected among one another, needing only one hop on the satellite, and thus minimizing the use of the bandwidth and the delay. In recent years, in order to allow mesh topologies without using large antennae, satellites have payloads that integrate on-board processing and nontransparent architectures. Also hybrid topologies are allowed, although they have trade-offs in performance.

The Physical Layer

The physical layer concerns the capability to establish, to ensure, and to keep physical connectivity, taking into account propagation channel characteristics and the capability to produce power on-board. In fact, the propagation channel is characterized by meaningful nonlinearity that strongly affects technical choices. Physical layer issues are more extensively presented in Luglio and Saitto (2006), but three aspects—antennae, link budgets, and synchronization—are dealt with here, particularly those aspects related to geostationary satellites.

Antennae

Satellite on-board antennae have the major task of radiating and receiving energy to and from the areas of interest. The antennae on the first missions provided global coverage of the Earth region visible from a satellite (approximately a cone of 8 degrees aperture angle). The new satellite antennae can be designed to have contoured

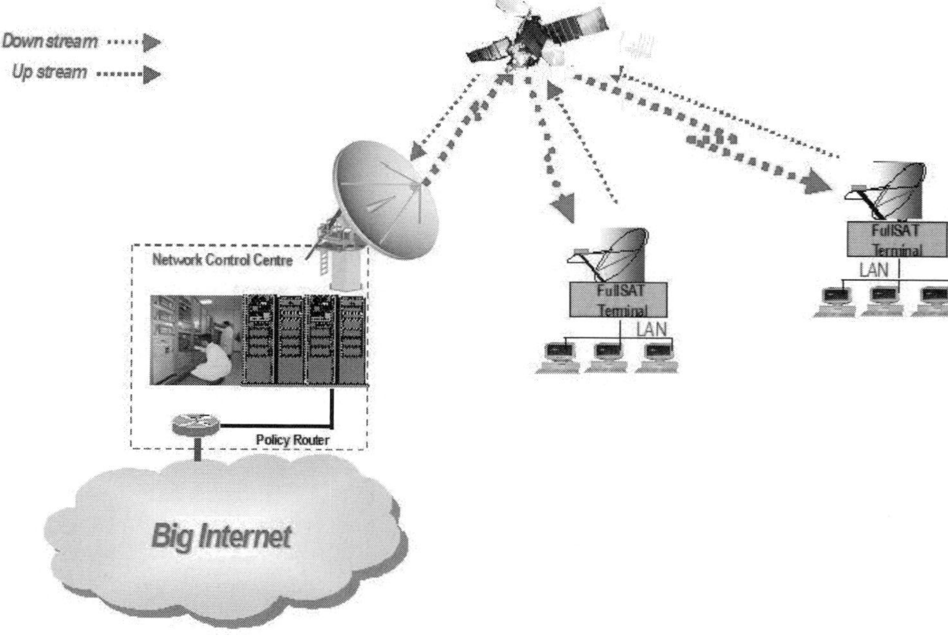

Figure 10: Typical star topology (courtesy of Telespazio)

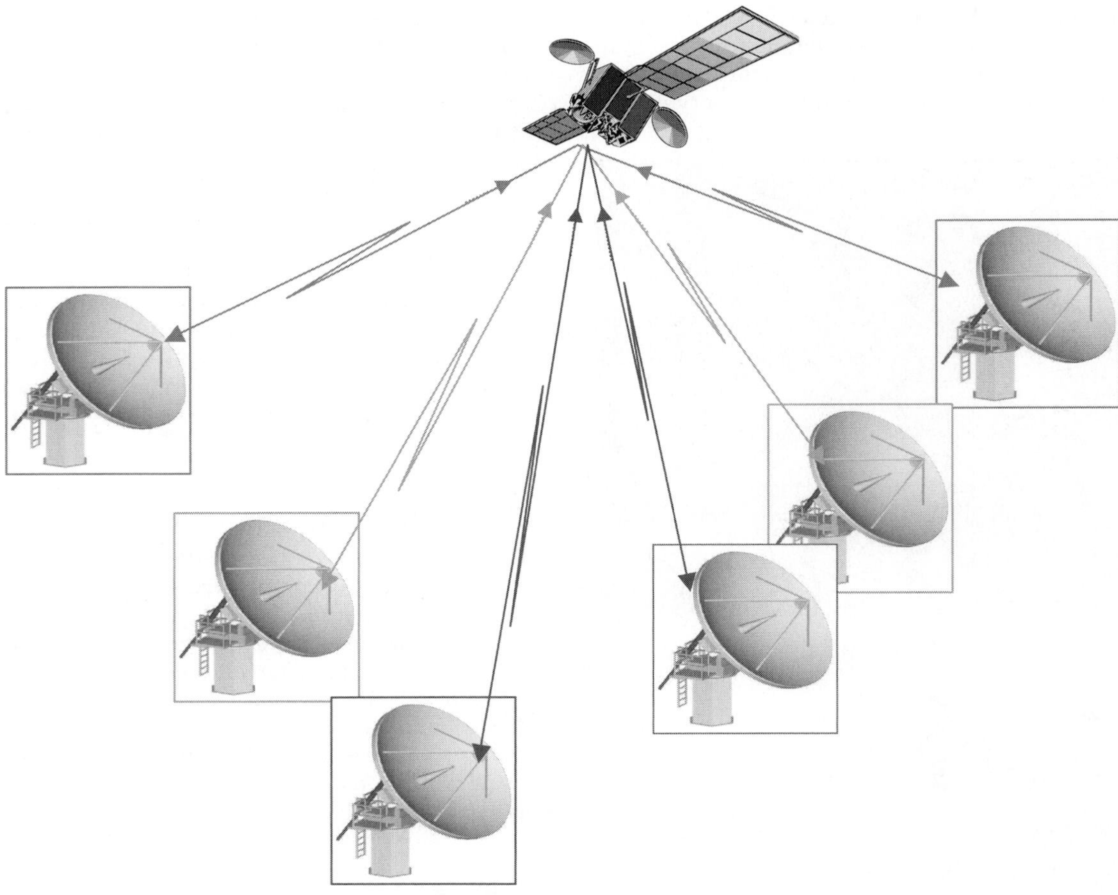

Figure 11: Typical mesh topology

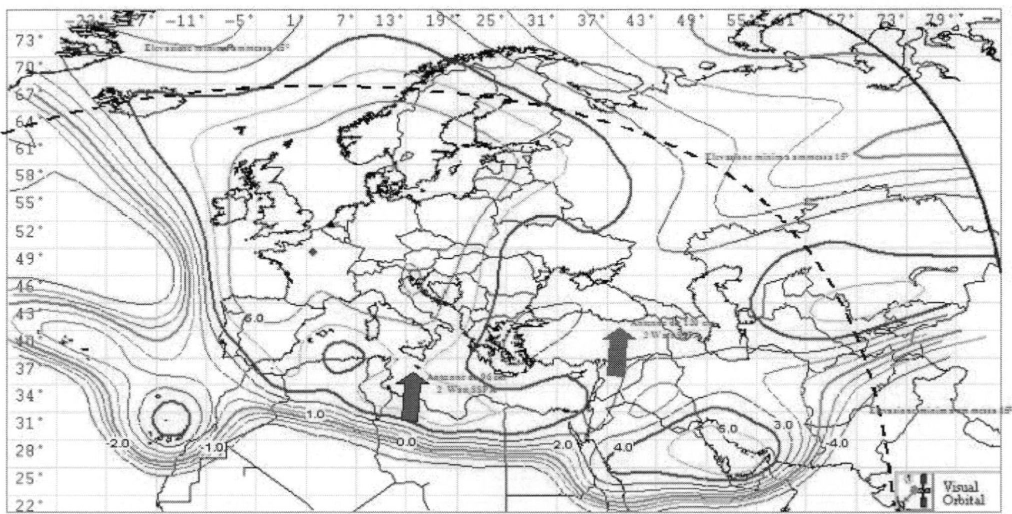

Figure 12: W3A Eutelsat at 7° east contoured beam coverage (courtesy of Telespazio)

or multiple beams to cover as far as possible strictly the region of interest with the best transmitted EIRP on the downlink and the best gain over noise temperature ratio on the uplink (Figure 12).

Earth antennae have two main functions. They provide gain (essentially the capability to concentrate the radiated energy in a cone with respect to omnidirectional radiation) and also limit the radiation into confined regions of space delimited by the antenna beam. These properties are largely dependent on the antenna size, used frequencies, and technology (reflector, array, single beam, multiple beam, etc.).

For a circular, dish antenna, the gain G is related to the antenna area A by the formula:

$$G = \eta 4\pi A/\lambda^2$$

where η is the antenna efficiency (typical values between 0.6 and 0.7 for parabolic aperture dishes) and λ is the wavelength ($\lambda = c/f$, f being the frequency and c the light speed). The half-power beam width is given by the approximate relationship

$$\theta_{3dB} \approx 70\lambda/D \text{ (degrees)}$$

being θ_{3dB} the half-power beamwidth and D the antenna diameter. Therefore, high gain and narrow beams are strongly correlated. For $\eta = 0.5$:

$$G \approx 24000/\theta_{3dB}{}^2$$

The cost of an antenna is strongly dependent on its diameter. The diameter and the accuracy have a meaningful effect not only on the gain, but also on the near and far side lobes, which are the main cause of interference among different satellites and with terrestrial systems. The trend toward using higher frequencies is also justified with increased directivity with the same antenna size.

Link Budgets

The design of a satellite network is based on the results of the relevant link budget The link budget will determine the main characteristics of the system such as size of the antennae to use, power requirements, link availability, *bit error rate* (BER), and eventually overall customer satisfaction. The parameters of a link budget and the involved mathematics are relatively simple to support preliminary estimation of end-to-end system performance.

The modeling of each component of the link budget—such as the uplink power amplifier gain and noise factors, transmit antenna gain, slant paths and corresponding atmospheric loss over distance, satellite transponder noise levels and power gains, receive antenna and amplifier gains and noise factors, cable losses, adjacent satellite interference levels, and attenuation caused by the troposphere—must be carefully evaluated, increasing the accuracy as far as the design is running and optimizing the overall performance via optimization procedures. In particular, attenuation, because of the presence of the troposphere, is mainly determined by rain, gas, clouds, and scintillation; as such, it can be characterized only statistically (Luglio and Saitto 2006). Rain represents the most significant factor; its contribution mainly depends on frequency and terminal location. In fact, the absorption of rain drops depends on the former, whereas the latter is correlated to rain intensity, which is statistically uneven in geographic distribution, and determines the slant path length inside the troposphere.

In general terms, the link budget can be considered for two classes of transponders:

1. *transparent* transponders in which the uplink *carrier-to-noise ratio* (CNR) is directly related to the down link CNR; and
2. *regenerative* transponders in which the uplink CNR and the downlink CNR are independent.

In the first case, the overall CNR $(N_0/C)_{tot}$ is given by

$$(N_0/C)_{tot} = (N_0/C)_{up} + (N_0/C)_{dw} + (N_0/C)_i + (N_0/C)_{in}$$

where N_0 is the noise power density, C is the carrier power, and *up, dw, i,* and *in* are the respective ratios for the uplink, downlink, co-channel interference, and transponder intermodulation.

In the case of the regenerative transponder, the contributions are independent and the overall performance is evaluated by the bit error rate, $(\text{BER})_{tot}$:

$$(\text{BER})_{tot} = (\text{BER})_{up} + (\text{BER})_{dw} + (\text{BER})_{in} + (\text{BER})_{iup} + (\text{BER})_{idw}$$

Synchronization Issues for TDMA Access

Synchronization is an essential aspect of digital satellite communications. Because *time-division multiple access* (TDMA) is the most utilized multiple access scheme in satellite fixed communications, synchronization issues are presented only for TDMA.

The choice of synchronization system is a function of the satellite system architecture. In general terms, synchronization is a complex estimation process that allows the general characteristics of the transmitted signal (e.g., frequency and phase of the transmitted carrier, clock and frame synchronization of the transmitted sequence) to be recovered at the receiving side. TDMA and on-board processing TDMA require highly sophisticated synchronization procedures, which may include satellite position and ranging measurement in the case of multiple beam operations, when a transmitting station cannot receive a burst transmitted by itself. In addition to carrier and bit synchronizations, which are similar to other communication systems, satellite TDMA systems require the transmission of a synchronization sequence, the correlation at the receiving station with itself, and the implementation of an acquisition and synchronization procedure, which allows the shortest and best performing bit sequence to maximize the efficiency of the TDMA burst.

The satellite movements around its nominal position imply periodic fluctuations of the clock and the need for suitable buffers of the Earth stations at the interface with the terrestrial networks to avoid losses of information. In addition to this orbital effect, satellite communications need synchronization among different stations positioned in wide areas of coverage, with or without the possibility of the transmitting reference station seeing its own transmitted signal (Figure 13) (Wu 1989).

In case the reference station can receive its signal, the synchronization of the frame and bursts can be determined by only one reference station; when the reference station cannot receive its signal, a second station in the receiving spot coverage is necessary to complete the synchronization loop. The clock and frame synchronizations are therefore peculiar to the satellite system. For TDMA systems, the RF channel is utilized by only one of the stations sharing the channel. Each station is allowed to periodically transmit limited duration bursts into the channel,

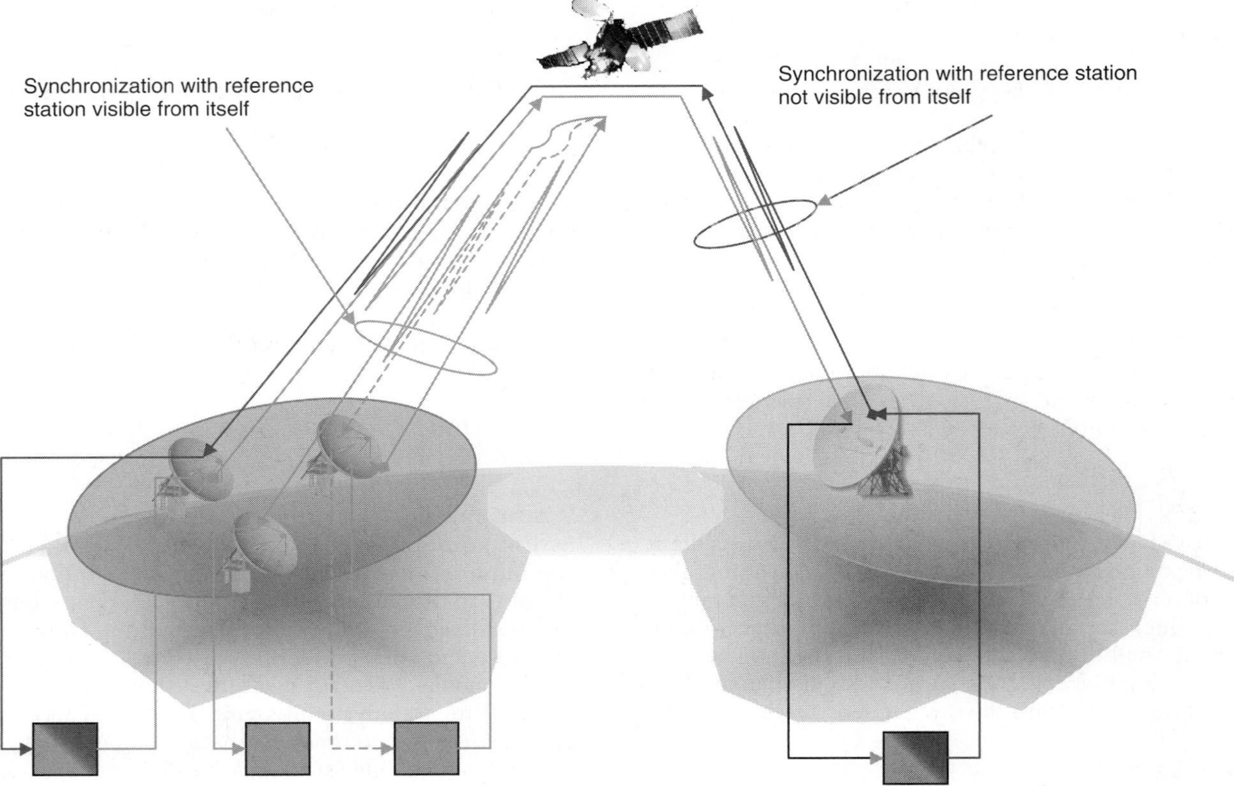

Figure 13: Synchronization schemes for transmission station visible or not visible by itself

leaving the rest of the frame to the other stations. Thus, it is mandatory to schedule the time for all of the stations on the same time and frame reference. To this aim, the reference station distributes the *start of frame* (SOF) burst to all stations included in the system. Each station is permitted to transmit in a specific frame window that includes time allowance for avoiding collision between adjacent bursts. The SOF contains a portion dedicated to carrier and bit timing recovery and is marked by a *reference unique word* (RUW). Received by all stations, the RUW is used to evaluate the reference time for all of the traffic bursts transmissions from each transmission station.

Traffic bursts are characterized by a structure similar to the reference burst called the *preamble* that carries the user information part (traffic data). The traffic data are typically of variable length, whereas the preamble is composed of four sections:

1. The first section is dedicated to carrier and bit timing recovery synchronization.
2. The second section is the *unique word* (UW) necessary for phasing the position of the burst and solving potential ambiguities of the sequence (the UW and the RUW are often derived from the same bit sequence to simplify the receiver HW configuration).
3. and 4. The third and the fourth sections are related to service channels for signaling transportation and orderwire, which is used by service providers to test QoS.

Figure 14 shows the general architecture of the TDMA burst format, including synchronization.

Security Issues

Satellite networks have an intrinsic security level supplied by the need to synchronize access (TDMA and CDMA techniques), which is a function managed by a complex hub. In addition, satellite networks can include cryptography devices for public and private keys.

It is important to briefly analyze the impact of encryption on satellite transmissions. Cryptography is based on the application of an algorithm to the transmission, which is based on the knowledge of the activation keys. This knowledge is limited to the end nodes of the encryption process. The strength of the encryption algorithm is a function of its complexity and is evaluated on: (1) the basis of the number of operations necessary to break it and (2) the not yet discovered set of rules to break it.

Complexity plays a negative role for real time encryption of high data rate stream. The encryption key can be

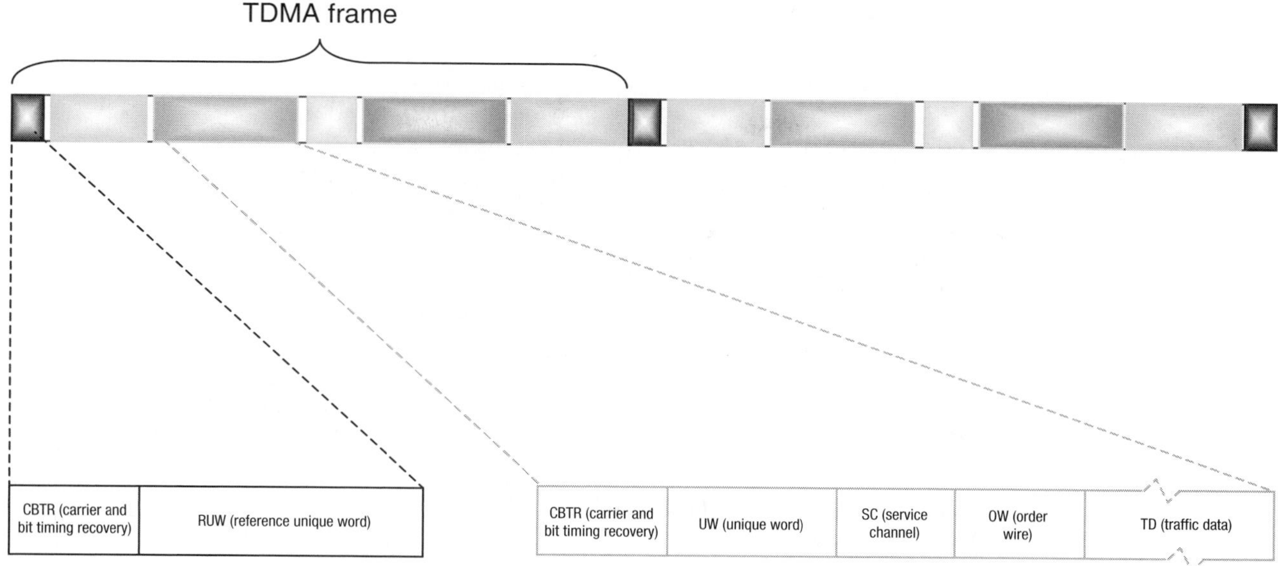

Figure 14: TDMA frame architecture and synchronization RUW and UW

private or public. In the former case, the key is distributed to the authorized correspondents. The key information, updated periodically, is an extremely delicate phase of the overall encryption process. In the latter case, from the generation of two random numbers a public modulus is generated and a procedure is available to the correspondents to have access to the clear information.

The network system security should be guaranteed at both information and communication levels. The encryption can be introduced as a service at three different levels: (1) link by link, (2) node by node, and (3) end to end.

In the link-by-link case, security is managed from the user to the control center at each level of the network. In the node-by-node case, routers and switches are included in the protection level (secure communications are managed at the routing level). In the end-to-end case, the encryption protection is solved only at the final user destination, offering the maximum level of protection. When end-to-end encryption is not viable, the critical network nodes, where encryption algorithms are applied, shall be adequately protected.

One particular satellite encryption process is the point-to-multipoint transmission, which is popular for protecting TV broadcasting from potential intrusions. A list of the main encryption processes for TV satellites includes the following.

- VideoCrypt, originally English, works on *phase alternating line* (PAL) channels with two options: the original VideoCrypt, which should be used inside the United Kingdom and Ireland; and VideoCrypt II, which is meant for continental Europe.
- EuroCrypt was developed with MAC. Almost all MAC receivers have an integrated EuroCrypt decoder.
- Nagravision, also known as Syster, is mainly used in France for SECAM (séquential colour avec mémoire) channels, but is also used with PAL in Germany and Spain. In France, it is used primarily by channels owned by the Canal+ network.
- Luxcrypt, which is used by the Dutch RTL4/V network, does not need a smart card.

Note that studies and investigation are ongoing to allow the combined use of low-orbit satellites (such as Globalstar and Iridium) and geostationary satellites to have an additional service channel with virtually no latency time to improve the overall performance of encrypted satellite channels. Security issues for satellite systems are more extensively dealt with in Luglio and Saitto (2005).

Examples of Standards

An overview on open standards is given in Luglio and Saitto (2006). In this chapter, two important proprietary standards—one for direct-to-users services and one for trunk services—are proposed: SkyPlexNet and Intelsat TDMA.

SkyPlexNet

SkyplexNet is a digital platform for broadband telecommunications that offers direct access to the satellite for interactive multimedia services: from distance learning to telemedicine, from Webcasting to videoconferencing and data transfer, from company intranet to thematic multicasting, and from the small office and home office (SOHO) to municipal networks for public services, including emergency management. The SkyplexNet network (see Figure 15) is based on SkyPlex, a digital processor that implements *digital video broadcasting over satellite* (DVB-S) baseband processing and channel adaptation on board the satellite instead of on the ground as in traditional systems. The payload may be considered somehow regenerative (in a broad sense) because it demodulates the upstream signal before entering the SkyPlex processor, in this way

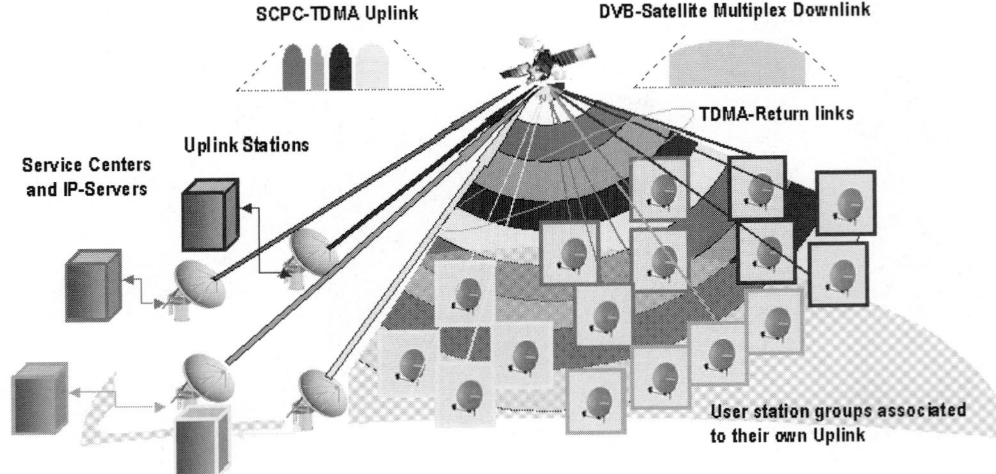

Figure 15: SkyPlexNet system architecture

providing larger flexibility with respect to traditional architectures. The new turbo SkyPlex is an improvement of the transponder carried on Hot Bird 5 in 1988 and is able to provide large flexibility in bandwidth assignment.

The main characteristics of SkyPlexNet are:

- bandwidth on demand,
- available bit rates from 512 kbit/s to 6000 kbit/s,
- connectivity on request,
- customized fare profile,
- compatibility with DVB-S (MPEG-2/-4), and
- uplink station diameter from 1.2 m to 2.2 m.

The available services are:

- digital broadcasting TV,
- business TV,
- video portals for business-to-business and business-to-consumer applications,
- audio and video streaming,
- audio and video streaming with terrestrial Internet,
- tele-education,
- multimedia content distribution on program mode and on request,
- asynchronous services for data delivery, and
- synchronous service delivery (video, audio and video, with Internet protocol, or IP, interactivity).

The main elements of the Earth segment are:

- the network operation center, which monitors and controls services, interfaces with the satellite operator, assigns capacities to users, and provides customer support;
- the customer service center, which manages contents and customer terminal interactions;
- the uplink station, which is in charge of connecting all of the network terminals of a specific customer and which transmits the uplink DVB MPEG to the satellite;
- the user terminal, which is composed of a small satellite station using a standard DVB receiver board and a SkyPlex transmission modem connected to a personal computer via an IP interface or to a satellite router if the interface is with a local network;
- the IP DVB gateway, which is the interface between the uplink station and the service center; and
- the service center, which manages the functionalities necessary to interface all of the elements of the network—in particular, user information gathering and billing, acquisition and elaboration of multimedia contents, data broadcasting and multicasting, session scheduling, bandwidth management, final user interfacing, access control, and uplink interface.

Intelsat TDMA

TDMA has been and is currently the multiple access scheme most utilized in satellite telecommunications. As a significant and general example, we will consider Intelsat TDMA.

The Intelsat TDMA transmission system has been active for more than thirty years. The system has endorsed continuous improvement and upgrading and has been the reference and the benchmark for several satellite TDMA systems (Freeman 1985). The introduction of the Hemi coverage with Intelsat VI has required the use of four reference stations (two for each area of Hemi coverage) because the reference station cannot receive its signal on the downlink channel. The general scheme of the operation of the reference stations for the two Hemi zones is shown in Figure 16.

Reference stations have the following main functionalities:

- determine satellite position for acquisition;
- provide open loop acquisition to traffic terminals;
- monitor TDMA;
- manage network;
- provide common synchronization among different Intelsat satellites;

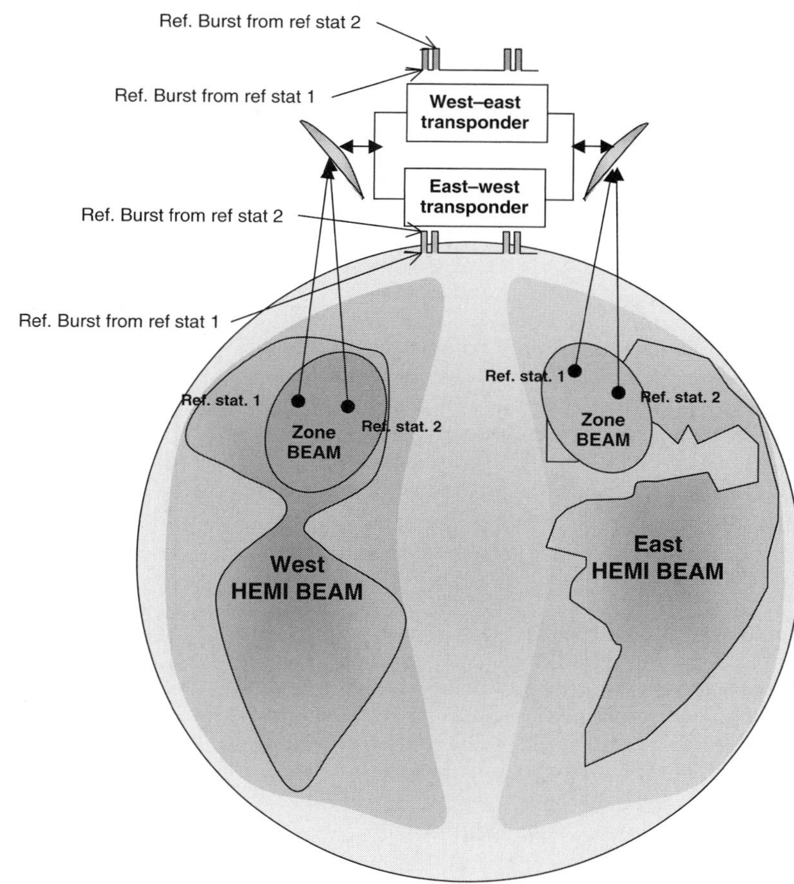

Figure 16: INTELSAT TDMA general reference stations and bursts architecture from INTELSAT VI

- provide voice, orderwire, and so on;
- provide access to the Intelsat operation center;
- generate and receive bursts with housekeeping information; and
- perform transponder hopping when necessary and possible.

The presence of one reference station for each Hemi is needed for visibility reasons (the signal from each station is directed to the other beam so that each station does not receive its own signal), whereas the presence of two reference stations for each Hemi is for redundancy. Even if both reference stations are active for each spot, the traffic terminals respond only to the primary station; the secondary station replaces the primary only in cases of failure.

The nominal time guards between the primary and the secondary reference bursts are of sixty-four symbols. The reference burst consists of a preamble and a *control and delay channel* (CDC). The traffic burst is composed of a preamble and a traffic section, consisting of at least one digital speech interpolator, and one section called DNI (Digital No Speech Interpolator) sub-bursts.

The unique words are composed of twenty-four symbols divided into two patterns of twelve that define position with respect to the start of the frame. Twelve symbols are used to solve the fourfold phase ambiguity because of the *quadrature phase shift keying* (QPSK) modulation scheme. The other twelve symbols define whether the UW is relative to the reference or the traffic burst.

The service channel is transmitted over the TDMA multiframe (consisting of sixteen frames) with a strong redundancy (one bit is repeated eight times in each burst). The CDC assigns the transmission time to the traffic stations. Transponder hopping is the ability of the traffic stations to hop across a maximum of four satellite transponders to increase the system efficiency.

The Intelsat TDMA characteristics are summarized below:

- frame period of 2 ms;
- burst transmission bit rate of 120 Mbit/s;
- nominal clear sky BER of 1×10^{-10} with FEC BCH 7/8 applied to the payload;
- QPSK with coherent demodulation phase-locked to the TDMA system clock;
- operates in any satellite beam coverage type (assignments set by Intelsat); and
- performance monitoring of uplink and downlink data displayed with time-indexed BER graphs and G.826 charts.

INTEROPERABILITY WITH TERRESTRIAL SYSTEMS

Satellite systems can play a fundamental role as an overlay network, interoperating with terrestrial infrastructures, working as a backup or backbone connection, complementing coverage, and ensuring service continuity and long-range mobility. We briefly introduce this concept with particular regard to two scenarios: the WiMAX standard and MANETs.

Interoperability with WiMAX

The *worldwide interoperability for microwave access* (WiMAX) standard, also identified as IEEE 802.16, is proposed to offer broadband wireless access to telecommunication networks. The cellular-like architecture allows interconnection of different base stations in both point-to-point mode and mesh modes, providing as much as 70 Mbit/s capacity per station.

WiMAX will provide fast Internet access and voice and video distribution services even for *no line of sight* (NLOS) environments and mobile users. These target characteristics make the system highly attractive for different market segments (both residential and business users) and geographical areas (developing countries, rural areas, and densely populated areas). Both the characteristics and the potential markets suggest that WiMAX will provide the best performance and ensure business continuity when implemented with an integrated infrastructure to interoperate with satellite systems, which assume a critically important role in such scenarios and for such applications.

In fact, satellite systems offer the technological element that can assist the WiMAX network in providing high QoS. In particular, satellites can be used to interconnect a set of base stations where no or poor terrestrial infrastructures are deployed, to guarantee coverage contiguity and service continuity for long-range mobility, or to ensure backup in case of either temporary failure or overflow of terrestrial networks. Moreover, because satellites assume a critical role in cases of emergency when terrestrial infrastructures can be seriously damaged (e.g., earthquakes, storms, terrorist attacks), it can guarantee service continuity and connectivity with remote networks or remote locations to a WiMAX network, which is likewise suitable to such scenarios. Furthermore, the two systems can reciprocally fill one another's service gaps: WiMAX as an in-building or shadowing areas gap filler for satellite and satellite as a coverage gap filler for WiMAX in uncovered areas. Finally, the integration of the two systems can help to guarantee security and safety services for monitoring and surveillance. Studies addressing feasibility assessment of an integrated infrastructure have obtained meaningful although preliminary results (Luglio, Mazzenga, and Corazza 2006a, 2006b).

Interoperability with MANETs

Mobile ad hoc networks (MANETs) are characterized by their intrinsic ability to be set up without needing any kind of infrastructure, which allows a high degree of flexibility at both the technological level and the application and service level. For this reason, they are particularly useful in environments where no fixed network infrastructure is available. For this reason, this technology is suitable for emergency application, for example, when fixed telecommunications infrastructures are seriously damaged or destroyed.

Also, satellite networks work without terrestrial infrastructure, excluding one gateway localized inside the footprint, and they are easy to set up. For the same reasons, satellites can be fruitfully utilized in case of emergency.

Nevertheless, these two technologies are not in competition, as they might appear, but are absolutely complementary. In fact, MANETs are characterized by low consumption, limited capacity user terminals, and, most important, their ability to work in an extremely limited coverage range. On the contrary, satellite systems work with medium and large dimensions, with medium- and high-power user terminals, and over extremely wide areas of coverage. Moreover, MANETs are suitable for indoor environments, whereas satellite systems cannot work in NLOS environments.

Investigation has been performed on how to implement an integrated system composed of a satellite segment and a MANET, in which each segment plays a complementary role with respect to the other, with the aim of improving the degree of service (Luglio et al. 2006).

Interoperability with Data Networks

As already mentioned, geostationary satellite systems can play a fundamental and sometimes irreplaceable role in providing connectivity, especially in specific scenarios. As concerns the use of such systems for data transfer, pursuing interoperability with terrestrial data networks is particularly meaningful. In fact, data networks are characterized by peculiar requirements such as high capacity to allow fast transfer of huge amount of data, as well as the use of specific protocols (e.g., TCP/IP) to ensure reliability. To achieve easy interoperability, the satellite component must be compliant with such requirements.

For capacity requirements, at the physical and MAC layers geostationary satellite systems are quite compliant for network-oriented solutions (up to some hundreds Mbit/s using big stations); with user-oriented solutions, they can reach either some tens of Mbit/s with proprietary standards based on full mesh or star topology and the use of VSAT stations (up to 2.4 m of diameter) or 45 Mbit/s in the forward link and typically up to 2 Mbit/s in the return link with the *digital video broadcasting return channel via satellite* (DVB-RCS) standard. The use of DVB-S can apply only to the forward link in case of one-way (over satellite link) systems such as DVB IP, being the return link implemented via terrestrial fixed networks (PSTN, ISDN, etc.).

As for network layer requirements, the use of typical reliable transport protocols (e.g., TCP/IP) means significant performance degradation because of the conspicuous latency derived from the great distance between the Earth and the satellite. Nevertheless, performance degradation can be mitigated adopting technical solutions specifically designed for satellite systems, acting either at the flow control or the architectural level. Both aspects (the physical aspects related to the use of DVB-RCS and transport protocol adaptation) are addressed in Luglio and Saitto (2006).

MILESTONE SYSTEMS IN THE K_a BAND

Several steps in satellite communications history have been meaningful milestones either in terms of technology innovation or service evolution, as briefly highlighted in Luglio and Saitto (2006). The available room in this chapter prevents us from providing details on each of these systems. Thus, we have selected two systems that represent the last real milestone in terms of both technology (use of the K_a band, OBP, multibeam antennae, steerable antennae, and switching on board) and services (direct to user, VSAT, mobile services, emergency).

ITALSAT

ITALSAT was a satellite-based telecommunication system developed by Agenzia Spaziale Italiana (ASI), the Italian space agency. The satellite was successfully launched in January 1991 (Marconicchio, Morelli, and Valdoni 1992; Dinaro et al. 1998; Martinino et al. 1992).

On board there were two payloads for point-to-point and point-to-multipoint communications in the K_a band (20/30 GHz) with Italian coverage. The most important of these two payloads, having 0.9 Gbit/s capacity, provided a multispot (six spot) coverage, as shown in Figure 17, utilizing multibeam antennae with automatic pointing control, onboard coherent QPSK demodulation, and baseband switching with emitter-coupled logic gate array technology.

The other K_a band communication payload had three (36-MHz) transparent transponders and a global coverage antenna (Figure 18). The satellite embarked also another payload in the EHF band (40–50 GHz) with European coverage for propagation experiments (Figure 19).

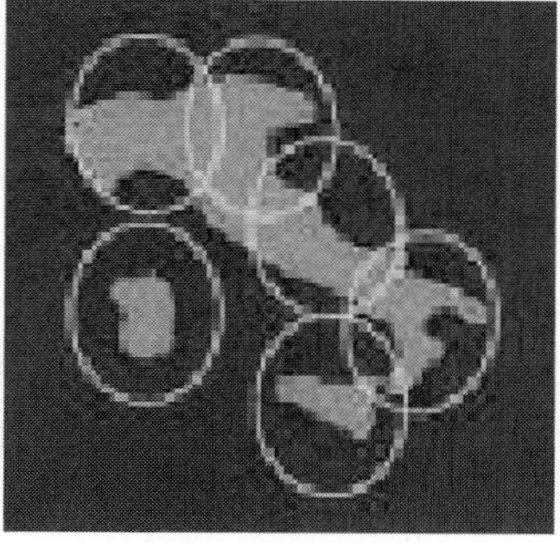

Figure 17: Multibeam coverage example (IT ALSAT F1 and F2) (courtesy of Telespazio)

Figure 18: ITALSAT "global coverage" at 20–30 GHz

Figure 19: Propagation coverage at 20–40 and 50 GHz

With the multibeam payload, the coverage was obtained with six spots (two groups of three) utilizing two independent antennae pointed toward the desired direction with a tracking system that ensured an overall error less than 0.003 degree. Each spot had the same number of carriers on both links. The total capacity was 12,000 32-kbit/s circuits (2000 for each spot). The carriers were QPSK-modulated at 147 Mbit/s. Each spot was served onboard by a single regenerative repeater, and the interspot connectivity was provided by a synchronous baseband space-switch matrix.

The main services offered were voice and data communication and television dissemination. The multibeam system was designed to be "network-oriented": Its Earth terminals were conceived to interface the terrestrial public network at its lowest hierarchical level, providing flexibility by offering its capacity in both semipermanent (i.e., changeable within a few minutes) and on-demand modes.

The ITALSAT system was conceived to perform different levels of network functions. In addition to the transmission and traffic arrangement functions, these functions allowed different types of traffic concentration. The ITALSAT network interfaced the terrestrial network by means of three kinds of stream: (1) 2 Mbit/s (trunk), (2) 2 Mbit/s stream split into individual four channels groups (split), and (3) streams with channels assigned on demand (*demand assigned multiple access*, or DAMA). Each of the six spots was designed to accept as many as sixteen but no more than sixty-four terminals (a traffic station is shown in Figure 20).

The access to the satellite was *TDMA satellite switched* (SS-TDMA) with a 32-ms frame. The six signals received on board were coherently demodulated and synchronously regenerated. Thus, the system was a *baseband SS-TDMA* (BB-SS-TDMA) type in the uplink and TDM in downlink.

The global national coverage payload had access to all points of the national territory, also offering emergency connections with disaster-hit areas and TV signal broadcasting. The coverage of the Italian territory (including islands) was obtained by means of a single antenna with a beamwidth of 1.06 degrees × 1.55 degrees.

The payload included three transparent transponders, each with a 36-MHz bandwidth. Each transponder was compatible with the following types of access and modulation: QPSK-modulated digital signals with continuous access to the satellite at 24.576 Mbit/s; analogue signals such as standard TV signals, frequency modulated

Figure 20: ITALSAT 5-m traffic station (courtesy of Telespazio)

(FM-TV) with a 27-MHz bandwidth; and signals with multicarrier digital modulation (single channel per carrier, frequency division multiple access).

ACTS

Advanced Communications Technology Satellite (ACTS) was an experimental system developed by NASA for verifying advanced technology in the K_a band (Gedney, Schertler, and Gargione 2000; Gedney et al. 1992). The satellite weight was approximately 1500 kg and measured 14.1 m from tip to tip along the solar arrays and 9.1 m from one antenna to another. Separate K_a-band antennae were provided for transmitting and receiving signals.

The multispot coverage was obtained with two hopping beams (east and west) and three fixed beams. East and west spot beams were discriminated by polarization (vertical and horizontal). Hopping beams were able to hop to many locations, dwelling long enough at each to pick up the offered traffic, even in case of nonuniform demand for traffic, at the price of greater technological complexity than the fixed beams. ACTS also had a mechanically steerable antenna that was able to be pointed anywhere, even outside the continental United States (Alaska and Hawaii). All of the beams are interconnected on board. The access technique is DAMA–TDMA.

The ground segment included the NASA ground station, a spacecraft control center, and different kind of experimenters' terminals. The interconnection on board was performed either by a baseband processor or by an IF switch matrix. The baseband processor, dynamically programmable, interconnected the two hopping beams and operated on on-board stored baseband switched TDMA. In this case (low burst rate), the received signals were demodulated, decoded, routed on a circuit-switched basis, remodulated, encoded, and transmitted in the downlink beams. The microwave switch matrix interconnected the three fixed beams and operated in SS-TDMA. In this case (high burst rate), the matrix provided dynamic interconnection among the three beams.

OVERVIEW OF THE MAJOR COMMERCIAL SYSTEMS

Intelsat

Established in 1964 as the first commercial satellite services provider, Intelsat has more than forty years of experience in satellite communications (Intelsat, undated).

The Intelsat communications network is based on fifty-one (including the acquired Panamsat network) satellites in combination with terrestrial connectivity technology to allow enterprises, governments, and service providers deliver content around the world securely and reliably to residential and business users, also ensuring mobility (see Figure 21).

The main services delivered by Intelsat are the following.

- Capacity services: Flexible, diverse satellite coverage and capacity options for quality point-to-point or point-to-multipoint services.
- Global Connex managed services: Global, integrated satellite, and terrestrial network-managed services to meet broadband, trunking, and media requirements worldwide.

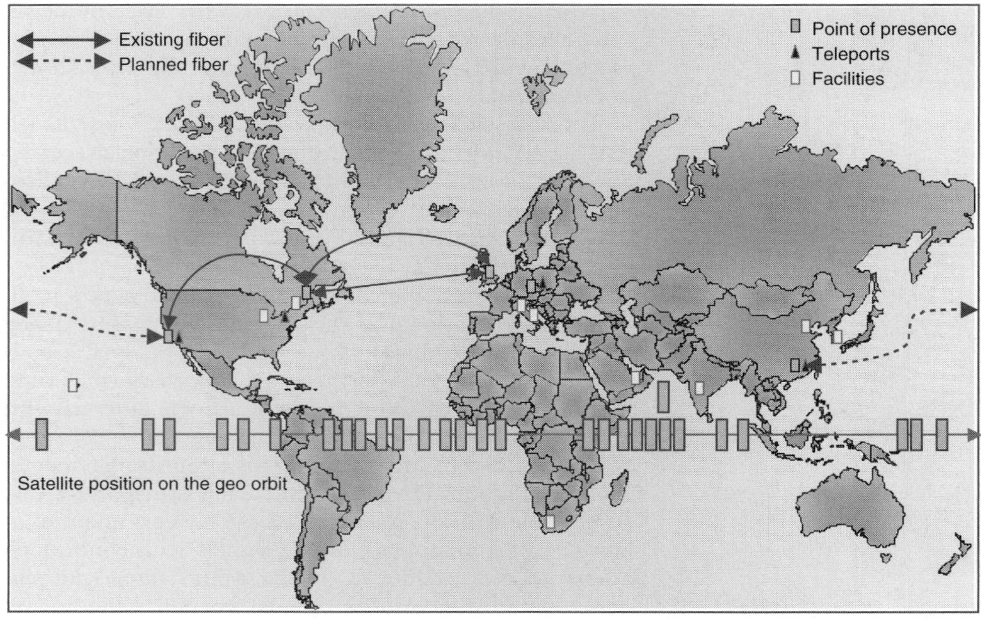

Figure 21: Intelsat satellite and terrestrial communication network map

Figure 22: The Fucino facility (courtesy of Telespazio)

- Specialized services: Value-added and specialized services, including disaster recovery, customer premises equipment programs, co-location services, and consulting and technical management, including support to satellite companies, organizations, and governments.

The twenty-eight geostationary-satellite global network is associated with ground stations, teleports, point of presence, and facilities. One of the largest stations is positioned at Fucino (Italy) which is shown in Figure 22. When satellites are operational, they are controlled from the control center in Washington, D.C., twenty-four hours a day.

Intelsat serves more than 700 customers around the world, including the world's largest Internet service providers, telecommunications companies, broadcasters, and corporate network service providers. Intelsat has offices in Brazil, China (Hong Kong), France, Germany, India, Singapore, South Africa, the United Arab Emirates, the United Kingdom, and the United States.

Intelsat provides solutions for access to or development of domestic and international networks. Satellites are also used for such diverse purposes as wide area network communication, cellular backhaul, Internet trunking, television broadcasting, and rural telephony. Intelsat is supplying systems everywhere with typical satellite performance.

The main milestones of Intelsat history are as follow:

1964 Launched the world's first commercial communications satellite

1969 First live global television broadcast of the Apollo 11 lunar landing

1974 Created the first international digital satellite voice communications service

1987 Linked 50,000 people in seventy cities for world's largest teleconference

1998 Established high-speed Internet backbone links around the world

2000 Compressed 40,000 hours of programming into two weeks for the Olympics Games in Sydney, Australia

2004 Intelsat becomes a private company after thirty-seven years as an intergovernmental organization

2006 Intelsat Ltd. acquires PanAmSat, controlling fifty-one satellites in geostationary orbit

Eutelsat

Eutelsat is another big satellite service and infrastructure provider (Eutelsat, undated). It commercializes capacity through twenty-four satellites that provide coverage over much of the world: from Europe to North Africa and the Middle East and from the United States to the Pacific Ocean and parts of Asia and Oceania. It serves more than 150 countries and more than 90 percent of the world's population. Eutelsat satellites offer a wide range of services: television and radio for public consumers, professional video services, networks for corporations, Internet services, and mobile communications. Eutelsat also has developed a set of broadband services for local, individual, and business communities, and in Italy it has opened an auxiliary point called Skylogic Italy to support services to wideband through multimedia platforms. Mainly from the orbital position of its Hot Bird satellites (13° east), Eutelsat transmits more than 1400 television channels to some 110 million of customers connected to a cable network or equipped for direct home reception.

Satellite and Services

Eutelsat satellites are positioned over the geostationary arc from the orbital position of 15 degrees west to 70.5 degrees east. The constellation is based on twenty-four satellites, twenty of which are managed completely by the company.

The Hot Bird family of satellites provides total coverage to Europe, part of Africa, and the entire Middle East. Approximately 100 million home customers are equipped to receive channels from Hot Bird satellites through the direct reception or via cable. The system provides more than 560 radio and multimedia services in the same area of coverage.

Eurobird satellites provide broadcasting and telecommunications services mainly to Central and Western Europe from the orbital positions of 28.5 degrees and 25.5 degrees east. Eurobird 1 provides continuity for telecommunication services (previously guaranteed from satellite Eutelsat II-F4), including business services, news distribution, and television and radio programs. The W series satellites serve a wide set of business users, including telecommunication companies, radio and television service providers, agencies of international news, industries, and multimedia services distributor. The W series is also the backbone network of the Eurovision and Euroradio networks for the exchange of television and radio programs at international level.

SESAT satellites (Siberia and Europe) provide a wide set of telecommunication services over a vast geographic area: from the Atlantic Ocean to eastern Russia, including a great part of Siberia. The satellites offer also military services in the Indian subcontinent through directional beams. Besides helping to develop new markets in Eastern Europe and in South Asia for all the types of telecommunication and business services, SESAT satellites guarantee also the inter-connection with Central and Western Europe. SESAT 1, at 36 degrees east (along with the satellite W4), contributes to the development of international, national, and regional services such as telephony and data services. SESAT 2, at 53 degrees east, distributes telecommunication, broadband, and broadcasting services to Europe, Africa, Middle East, and Central Asia.

Eutelsat has placed a set of three Atlantic Bird satellites, named the "Atlantic Gate": Atlantic Bird 1 (K_u band, 12.5° west), Atlantic Bird 2 (K_u band, 8° west), and Atlantic Bird 3 (K_u and C bands, 5° west). Their main purpose is to offer a wireless connection between the Americas, Europe, Africa, and Western Asia. With twenty channels, Atlantic Bird 1 offers telecommunication services between Europe and America, connecting the two continents and providing a common virtual coverage. Like Atlantic Bird 1, Atlantic Bird 2 guarantees coverage with high power in the American and European areas, allowing the eastern coasts of the Americas to reach, directly across the Atlantic, Central and Western Europe and then the Persian Gulf. Atlantic Bird 3 satisfies the entire African area and market in the C band with ten transponders. The Atlantic Gate is suitable for video applications, IP, and data.

Eutelsat II satellites in inclined orbit offer solutions to the need for low-cost, short-term professional applications (e.g., news distribution) as well as Internet services. They are mainly used for the distribution of television and telecommunication services. Initially placed in orbits at 7 degrees, 10 degrees, and 16 degrees east, these satellites now occupy other orbital positions after being replaced by the newest W satellites. The services provided are public telephony, business applications, news distribution, and exchange of radio and television programs.

The e-BIRD satellite was launched in September 2003 at 33 degrees east to provide coverage to Europe and Turkey through four beams with high power and twenty-two transponders in the K_u band. The e-BIRD was the first satellite designed for broadband, two-way Internet services. Moreover, thanks to its position, it is able to offer broadband services also through small antennae.

SES Global

SES Global is a network of satellite operators providing service in every continent (SES, undated). They operate through SES Astra in Europe; SES NEWSKIES in the Middle East, part of Asia, South America, and Africa; and SES Americom in North America. They also participate with satellite operators AsiaSat, SES Sirius, Nahuelsat, and Star One. They offer global coverage with a satellite fleet of forty satellites that reach 95 percent of the world's population.

SES Global mainly provides the following services: media broadcasting, enterprise solutions, mobile broadband solutions, government services, and global solutions.

SES Astra Products and Services

The main services offered by SES Astra are as follow.

- Broadcast services: The analogue direct-to-home platform is one of the largest in the world. It provides more than 102 million home customers with access to 1600 radio and TV channels.
- Broadband services: Astra offers a large set of broadband products and services, including end-to-end solutions directly to users.
- Services with direct cable: This set of services allows cable operators to offer broadband Internet services, high speed, and low cost to customers in all of Europe.
- Governmental services: Astra provides satellite-based specialized telecommunications solutions (bandwidth, infrastructures, and network solutions) to governmental agencies, public administrators, and their contractors.
- Technical solutions: Astra is a partner for a large set of technical solutions to manufacturers in the satellite field, operators, and other types of customers involved in the engineering field.
- Customer support: Astra has created a series of individual packages for its customers, according to their individual needs.
- Total solutions: SES Global's companies and partners offer solutions for global access. Broadcast audiovisual or broadband IP content can be transmitted all over the world without cable through the Astra European hub.

SES Astra Constellation

Astra has a constellation of thirteen satellites. Seven are placed at the orbital position of 19.2 degrees east, three at 28.2 degrees east, and three more at 5.2 degrees, 23.5 degrees, and 24.2 degrees (see Table 1).

Satellites Astra 1KR, 1E, 1F, 1G, 1H, and 2C provide capacity mainly for the transmission of broadcast and broadband multimedia services. The main customers are those situated on continental Europe in correspondence with the orbital position of 19.2 degrees east.

Astra 3A and 1D are localized at 23.5 degrees east. Their main functions include supplying capacity for directed cable and improving multimedia services in wired

Table 1: SES Astra Satellites

Satellites at 19.2° east	Satellites at 23.5° east	Satellites at 28.2° east	Satellites at 37.5° east
Astra 1KR	Astra 3A	Astra 2A	Astra 4A
Astra 1E	Astra 1D	Astra 2B	
Astra 1F		Astra 2D	
Astra 1G			
Astra 1H			
Astra 2C			

Table 2: SES Americom Constellation Characteristics

Launch date	Satellite name	Location	Payload	Satellite bus	Launch vehicle	Coverage/service area
2005	AMC-12	37.5 W.L.	C-band	Spacebus 4000C3	Proton M/Briz M	North and South America, Europe, Africa
2000	AMC-6	72 W.L.	C/K_u	A2100AX	Proton K/ Blok DM	North America
1998	AMC-5	79 W.L.	K_u	Spacebus 2000	Ariane 44L	Continental U.S.
2003	AMC-9	83 W.L.	C/K_u	Spacebus 3000B3	Proton K/ Briz M	North America
2004	AMC-16	85 W.L.	K_u/K_a	A2100AX	Atlas V	North America; 50 states
1997	AMC-3	87 W.L.	C/K_u	A2100A	Atlas 2AS	North America; 50 states
1999	AMC-4	101 W.L.	C/K_u	A2100AX	Ariane 44LP	North and South America; 50 states
1996	AMC-1	103 W.L.	C/K_u	A2100A	Atlas 2A	North America; 50 states
2004	AMC-15	105 W.L.	K_u/K_a	A2100AX	Proton M/Briz M	North America; 50 states
1997	AMC-2	85 W.L.	C/K_u	A2100A	Ariane 44L	North America; 50 states
2004	AMC-11	131 W.L.	C-band	A2100A	Atlas 2AS	North America; 50 states
2004	AMC-10	135 W.L.	C-band	A2100A	Atlas 2AS	North America; 50 states
2000	AMC-7	137 W.L	C-band	A2100A	Ariane 5G	North America; 50 states
2000	AMC-8	139 W.L.	C-band	A2100A	Ariane 5G	North America; 50 states
2000	AAP-1	108.2 E.L.	K_u	A2100AX	Proton K/Blok DM	China, Northeast Asia, South Asia

networks for corporative networks, occasional users, and business services.

The satellites Astra 2A, 2B, and 2D are placed at 28.2 degrees east and offer coverage for the United Kingdom and Ireland. These are used for direct-to-home services and mainly provide transmission capacity for broadcast and broadband multimedia services.

SES Americom Constellation

SES Americom has a constellation of twenty satellites. Table 2 shows the main characteristics of the constellation.

Hispasat

Hispasat is a Spanish company operating global satellite communications not only in the Spanish and Portuguese markets but also in the Americas, Europe, and North Africa (Hispasat, undated). Hispasat manages two orbital positions over the Atlantic region (30° west and 61° west) and operates with a constellation of three satellites (1C, 1D, and Amazonas), with one more in development (1E). It has a satellite control center near Madrid and two payload centers. The transponders of the Hispasat systems are mainly transparent (there is also an OBP Amheris payload), allowing the operators of satellite communications to transmit their different services using both analogue and digital connections.

Satellites

The Hispasat constellation is composed of four satellites. Hispasat 1C has a payload with twenty-four transponders with an operational capacity that covers both Europe and the Americas. This capacity supplies an operational level able to provide direct analogue or digital broadcasting services.

Satellite Hispasat 1D was designed to provide the following services: broadcasting satellite services, fixed satellite services, television (U.S. market), and tactical and strategic networks for the Spanish Defense Ministry. Hispasat 1D is located at orbital position 30 degrees west uses twenty-eight transponders in the K_u band. Its scope is to guarantee continuity to the services provided from satellites 1A and 1B. Hispasat 1D also has a new spot on Central Europe improve the global connectivity.

Amazonas provides coverage of the Americas, Europe, and North Africa. At the same time, it complements the coverage of the Hispasat system over the western United States, including California. Amazonas will have a life of at least fifteen years. Its sixty-three transponders will operate in the K_u and C bands.

Satellite Hispasat 1E will provide multimedia services in the K_a band and will be able to exploit additional capacity in the K_u band to have a backup in orbit, which will be useful to strategic customers.

The Hispasat operator offers the following services and applications: television (direct to home broadcasting, distribution, and contribution) and Internet, multimedia, and broadband (Internet backbone, high-speed Internet, and data and multicast broadcasting).

CONCLUSION

Fixed services that utilize geostationary satellite systems represent the major part of satellite operators' business: 95 percent or more. The utilization of satellites to provide telecommunication services represents a tiny niche market with respect to the entire telecommunication business but this niche is critically important for connectivity in remote areas and for communications in emergencies.

An overview of satellite systems characteristics, technology, services, and major operators was provided. More detail is available in the annex at the end of this chapter.

GLOSSARY

Dual Use: The use of facilities for both military and civil use.

Geostationary: Orbit around the Earth characterized by a revolution period equal to the Earth's rotation period.

Ground Segment: Component of a satellite system located on the Earth (wide sense).

Multispot Coverage: Capability of an antenna to produce more than one beam.

Payload: Component of a satellite that exploits telecommunications (in the strict sense).

Space Segment: Component of a satellite system located in orbit.

Transportable Stations: Earth stations that are easily transportable and lined up with the relevant geostationary satellite and operate as fixed stations.

Trunk Services: Telecommunication services characterized by high capacity.

CROSS REFERENCES

See *Global Navigation Satellite Systems (GNSS)*; *Land-Mobile Satellite Channel*; *Satellite Communications Basics*; *Satellites in IP Networks*.

REFERENCES

Dinaro, M., F. Marconicchio, A. Morris, A. Saitto, E. Saggese, and F. Valdoni. 1998. ITALSAT: The first preoperational SS-TDMA system. In *Proceedings of the IEEE Global Telecommunications Conference* (GLOBECOM '88), Nov. 28–Dec. 1. Vol. 3: 1774–8.

Elbert, B. 2000. *The satellite communications ground segment and Earth station handbook*. Norwood, MA: Artech House.

Eutelsat. Accessed September 10, 2007. Online at www.eutelsat.com.

Freeman, R. 1985. *Reference manual for telecommunication engineering*. New York: John Wiley & Sons.

Gedney, R. T., R. Schertler, and F. Gargione. 2000. *The advanced communications technology satellite*. Mendham, NJ: SciTech Publishing.

Gedney, R. T., D. L. Wright, J. L. Balombin, P. Y. Sohn, W. F. Cashman, and A. L. Stern. 1992. Advanced communications technology satellite (ACTS). *Acta Astronautica*, 26(11): 813–25.

Hispasat. Accessed September 10, 2007. Online at www.hispasat.com.

Intelsat. Accessed September 10, 2007. Online at www.intelsat.com.

Luglio, M., F. Mazzenga, and G. E. Corazza. 2006a. Feasibility assessment of WIMAX and geostationary satellite integration, Third Advanced Satellite Mobile Systems Conference, May 29–31. Herrsching am Ammersee, Germany.

———. 2006b. WiMax and satellite systems interoperability scenarios identification. Third Advanced Satellite Mobile Systems Conference, May 29–31. Herrsching am Ammersee, Germany.

Luglio, M., C. Monti, A. Saitto, and M. Segal. 2006. Interfacing satellite systems and ad hoc networks for emergency applications. Third Advanced Satellite Mobile Systems Conference, May 29–31. Herrsching am Ammersee, Germany.

Luglio, M., and A. Saitto. 2005. Security for satellite networks. *The handbook of information security*, edited by H. Bidgoli. New York: John Wiley & Sons.

———. 2008. Satellite communications basics. *The handbook of computer networks*, edited by H. Bidgoli. New York: John Wiley & Sons.

Maral, G., and Bousquet, M. 2003. *Satellite communications systems: Systems techniques and technology*. 4th ed. Chichester, UK: Wiley.

Marconicchio, F., G. Morelli, and F. Valdoni. 1992. *Italsat: An advanced on board processing satellite communication system*, 832–41. Washington, DC: AIAA.

Martinino, F., A. Saitto, E. Salvatori, and G. Soccodato. 1992. The ITALSAT system: Current applications and future trends. *Space Communications*, 10(2–3): 67–82.

SES. Accessed September 10, 2007. Online at www.ses-global.com.

Tirrò, S. 1993. *Satellite communications system design*. New York: Plenum Press.

Wu, W. W. 1989. *Element of digital satellite communication*. Rockville, MD: Computer Science Press.

Annex: Satellite Companies

Industry	2003 sales ($ million)	Headquarters	Space business
Boeing Co.	9358	U.S.	Satellite manufacturing, space and rocket components, launch services, launch vehicle manufacturing, ground systems, and space and engineering services and software
Lockheed Martin Corp.	8700	U.S.	Satellite manufacturing, space and rocket components, launch services, launch vehicle manufacturing, ground systems, and space and engineering services and software
EADS	3013	Netherlands	Satellite manufacturing, space and rocket components, launch services, launch vehicle manufacturing, ground systems, and space and engineering services and software
Raytheon	2978	U.S.	Space and rocket components, ground systems, and space and engineering services and software
Northrop Grumman Corp.	2800	U.S.	Satellite manufacturing, space and rocket components, ground systems, and space and engineering services and software
Alcatel Finmeccanica	2500	France-Italy	Satellite manufacturing, space and rocket components, ground systems, and space and engineering services and software
Science Applications International Corp.	1750	U.S.	Space and engineering services and software
United Space Alliance	1684	U.S.	Launch services and space and engineering services and software
DirecTV Group	1322	U.S.	Ground systems
ATK	1134	U.S.	Space and rocket components
Mitsubishi Electric Corp.	1018	Japan	Satellite manufacturing, space and rocket components, and ground systems
Honeywell Inc. 5	775	U.S.	Space and rocket components, ground systems, and space and engineering services and software
Arianespace SA	702	France	Launch services
L-3 Communications	619	U.S.	Space and rocket components, ground systems, and space and engineering services and software
Orbital Sciences Corp.	582	U.S.	Satellite manufacturing, space and rocket components, launch services, and launch vehicle manufacturing
Trimble Navigation Ltd.	541	U.S.	Ground systems
Computer Sciences Corp.	500	U.S.	Space and engineering services and software
Ball Aerospace & Technologies Corp.	476	U.S.	Satellite manufacturing, space and rocket components, and ground systems
Loral Space & Communications	474	U.S.	Satellite manufacturing and space and rocket components
General Dynamics	474	U.S.	Satellite manufacturing, space and rocket components, ground systems, and space and engineering services and software
Harris Corp.	428	U.S.	Space and rocket components, ground systems, and space and engineering services and software
Snecma	421	France	Space and rocket components

(*Continued*)

Annex: (Continued)

Industry	2003 sales ($ million)	Headquarters	Space business
United Technologies Corp.	415	U.S.	Space and rocket components
Eastman Kodak Co.	383	U.S.	Space and rocket components, ground systems, and space and engineering services and software
ITT Industries Inc.	378	U.S.	Space and rocket components, ground systems, and space and engineering services and software
EchoStar Communications Corp. 7	244	U.S.	Ground systems
ViaSat Inc.	239	U.S.	Ground systems
Mitsubishi Heavy Industries Ltd.	216	Japan	Space and rocket components, launch services, launch vehicle manufacturing, and space and engineering services and software
Aerojet	213	U.S.	Space and rocket components
Ishikawajima-Harima Heavy Industries Co. Ltd.	190	Japan	Space and rocket components, launch vehicle manufacturing, and ground systems
Gilat Satellite Networks Ltd.	190	Israel	Ground systems
MacDonald Dettwiler and Associates Ltd.	190	Canada	Space and rocket components, ground systems, and space and engineering services and software
Swales	162	U.S.	Satellite manufacturing, space and rocket components, and space and engineering services and software
EMS Technologies	126	U.S.	Space and rocket components and ground systems
MAN Technologie AG	121	Germany	Space and rocket components, ground systems, and space and engineering services and software
OHB-System AG	121	Germany	Satellite manufacturing, space and rocket components, and space and engineering services and software
Jacobs Sverdrup	118	U.S.	Space and engineering services and software
Goodrich Corp.	114	U.S.	Space and rocket components
Spacehab Inc.	95	U.S.	Space and rocket components and space and engineering services and software
ND SatCom AG	92	Germany	Ground systems
Saab Ericsson Space AB	86	Sweden	Space and rocket components
Contraves Space AG	83	Switzerland	Space and rocket components
Integral Systems Inc.	83	U.S.	Ground systems and space and engineering services and software
Dutch Space B.V.	82	Netherlands	Space and rocket components
Com Dev International Ltd.	70	Canada	Space and rocket components and ground systems
PSI Group	70	U.S.	Space and rocket components
QinetiQ	44	U.K.	Space and rocket components and ground systems
Analytical Graphics	38	U.S.	Space and engineering services and software
Vega Group PLC	36	U.K.	Ground systems and space and engineering services and software

Annex: Satellite Agencies

Agencies	Mission
Austrian Space Agency (ASA)	
Belgian Federal Science Policy	The missions of the Belgian Federal Science Policy office are exercised on three levels: scientific activities, technical activities, and cultural activities. The Department of Space Research and Applications of the Belgian Federal Science Policy office is in charge of managing the Belgian (public) participation in R&D activities carried out by industry and Belgian scientists in space-related matters. These activities are conducted primarily within the framework of the international organizations to which Belgium belongs (e.g., the European Space Agency and the European Organization for the Exploitation of Meteorological Satellites) or within the framework of bilateral agreements (e.g., with France on SPOT).
Brasil National Institute for Space Research (INPE)	
British National Space Centre (BNSC)	The BNSC is a voluntary partnership formed from ten government departments and research councils to coordinate UK civil space activity.
Canadian Space Agency/Agence Spatiale Canadienne (CSA/ASC)	
Centre National d'Etudes Spatiales (CNES)	French space agency
Comisión Nacional de Actividades Espaciales (CONAE) (Argentina)	Information on the Centro Regional de Datos Satelitales (CREDAS) and on Argentina's national space plan
Danish Space Research Institute (DSRI) (Denmark)	
Destination Earth (NASA)	The official Web site for NASA's Earth Science Enterprise
Deutsches Zentrum für Luft und Raumfahrt (DLR)	Germany's national aerospace center as well as the national space agency
European Space Agency (ESA)	
ESA Centre for Earth Observation (ESRIN)	One of four ESA establishments. Main activities: acquisition, archiving, and dissemination of data from Earth observation missions—in particular, ERS-1, for which it operates needed ground infrastructure. Main function: ESA data handling and dissemination center, being at the forefront of technologically advanced information systems.
European Space Operations Centre (ESOC)	ESA's satellite control center; responsible for the operations of all satellites and related ground stations and communications network.
European Space Technology Centre (ESTEC)	Noordwijk, the Netherlands; one of the three centers of the European Space Operations Centre
Finland National Technology Agency (Tekes)	National technology agency and main public financing organization for research and development in Finland. Coordinates and finances Finland's participation in ESA programs.
Indian Space Research Organisation (ISRO)	
International Space University (ISU)	Interdisciplinary, intercultural, and international institution preparing individuals to respond to current needs and increasing and evolving demands of space sector through multidisciplinary education and research programs
Italian Space Agency (ASI)	
National Academies of Science and Engineering (NASE) and National Research Council (NRC) Space Studies Board (SSB)	Advisory board within NRC, which is the NASE joint operational. Operates a number of standing committees and task groups that perform studies in space science and policy for the federal government.
National Aeronautics and Space Administration (NASA)	Ames Research Center (ARC)

(Continued)

Annex: (Continued)

Agencies	Mission
	Dryden Flight Research Center (DFRC) John H. Glenn Research Center at Lewis Field (formerly Lewis Research Center) Goddard Space Flight Center (GSFC), Greenbelt, MD Jet Propulsion Laboratory (JPL) Johnson Space Center (JSC) Kennedy Space Center (KSC)
National Academy of Sciences, Board on Physics and Astronomy (National Research Council)	
Netherlands Agency for Aerospace Programs (NIVR)	
Netherlands Space Research Organization (Stichting Ruimte Onderzoek Nederland, SRON)	Foundation within framework of the Netherlands Organization for Scientific Research (NWO). Initiates, develops, builds, and uses instruments for scientific research in and from space.
Norsk Romsenter (Norwegian Space Center)	Foundation cooperating closely with Ministry of Trade and Industry. Guides ESA contracts strategically. Public funds support development of industry, development and demonstration of space applications, and optimal conditions for national space research.
Romanian Space Agency (ROSA)	National public institution that coordinates and represents Romanian space program, mainly R&D components.
Space Research Institute (IKI)	As the leading organization of the Russian Academy of Sciences in the field of investigations of Outer Space, Solar System planets and other objects of the Universe, Space Research Institute (IKI) is primarily in charge of long-range planning and elaboration of space research programs of which a considerable part is performed within the framework of international space research cooperation.
Spanish Center for Development of Industrial Technology	Centro para el Desarrollo Tecnológico Industrial (CDTI) acts as Spanish delegation to ESA. Is responsible for follow-up participation of Spanish industry in European space programs.
Spanish National Institute of Aerospace Techniques	Instituto Nacional de Tecnica Aerospacial (INTA): national space agency
Swedish Space Corporation (SSC)	
Swiss Space Office (SSO)	Swiss government unit in interior ministry dealing with space affairs. Mission is to propose and implement Swiss space policy after approval by federal council. Coordinates tasks and works closely with national scientists and industries.

Annex: Satellite Operators

Operator	Country	2001 revenue ($million)	Satellites	Satellites on order
Intelsat	U.S.	1100	22	4
PanAmSat	U.S.	870.1	21	5
SES Astra (SES Global)	Luxembourg	655.5	13	1
Eutelsat	France	593.5	18	6
SES-Americom (GE Americom)	U.S.	506.7	16	6
Loral Skynet	U.S.	388.9	7	3
JSAT	Japan	298.2	8	1
New Skies Satellites	Netherlands	209	6	2
Telesat Canada	Canada	201.6	5	2
Space Communications Corp.	Japan	170.8	4	1
Arabsat	Saudi Arabia	155	3	0
Star One	Brazil	130.5	5	1
Satmex	Mexico	128	2	1
AsiaSat	Hong Kong	124.3	3	1
Telenor	Norway	121.6	3	0
Shin Satellite	Thailand	116.8	3	1
Hispasat	Spain	94.9	3	2
SingTel/Optus	Australia	85.9	5	1
Korea Telecom	South Korea	76.3	3	1
Russian Satellite Communications	Russia	61	11	5
Europestar	France	–	2	
Hellasat	Greece	–	1	

Satellites in IP Networks

Fatih Alagöz, *Bogazici University, Turkey*
Abbas Jamalipour, *University of Sydney, Australia*

AN OVERVIEW OF SATELLITE COMMUNICATIONS

For almost half a century, satellite networks have provided long-distance communications services to the public switched telephone network (PSTN) as well as television broadcasting. These services are particularly justified by the large footprint coverage of the satellite; to date, there is no substitute for satellites, especially with regard to services such as broadcasting. For these types of services, a satellite acts as a communications repeater or relay (according to whether the transmitted signal is digital or analog, respectively) that communicates with ground stations and solves the problem of transmission of electromagnetic waves between different parts of the world that are not within line of sight of one another. A noteworthy achievement in satellite communications is the formation of the International Telecommunications Satellite Organization (INTELSAT), which in 1964 established systems and standards initially for fixed-satellite service and subsequently for broadcast services among nations (Jamalipour 1998).

In the 1980s, satellites were deployed for the first time in mobile telecommunications by providing direct communications to maritime vessels and subsequently aircraft. The first major development in this area was the International Maritime Telecommunication Satellite (INMARSAT) satellite system. INMARSAT started a new era of satellite communications, called mobile satellite services (MSS), in 1982. This organization used a geostationary satellite system using L band (1.5–1.6 GHz) to provide telecommunication services mainly to ships. In the first generation of MSS, INMARSAT defined five standards: Standard A (1982), Standard B (1993), Standard C (1991), Standard M (1992/93), and Aeronautical Standard (1992). Different worldwide telecommunications services including voice, facsimile, and data were considered in these standards. INMARSAT continues its worldwide services as one of the most reliable satellite communications systems.

Although INMARSAT remains the most distinguishable satellite system of its kind, there were other MSSs developed during the first generation (1G) mobile satellite systems, such as services offered by QUALCOMM in North America (1989), ALCATEL QUALCOMM in Europe (1991), and the Japanese NASDA system (1987).

Reduction in size and cost of user terminals was the motive for second-generation (2G) MSS, which was started around 1985. In this generation, the interconnection of satellite systems with terrestrial wireless systems was also considered. INMARSAT defined its mini-M standard in 1995 with worldwide voice, data, facsimile, and telex service at 2.4 Kbps. American Mobile Satellite Corporation (AMSC), NSTAR of Japan, European mobile satellite (EMS), and several others are included in the second-generation MSS.

Geostationary orbit (GEO) satellite systems face unavoidably long propagation delay and large transmission power requirements. Consideration of small-size user terminals and direct radio communications between users and satellites (i.e., without using a ground station) led to the idea of using satellites in lower-altitude orbits than the geostationary orbit. Among possible orbit selections, low Earth orbit (LEO) satellites with altitudes between 500 and 1500 km and medium Earth orbit (MEO) satellites with altitudes between 5000 and 13000 km were considered (Jamalipour 1998). The altitude selection assures that the satellites reside outside the two Van Allen belts to avoid the radiation damage to electronic components installed in satellites. The use of these non-geostationary satellite orbit (NGSO) systems for commercial purposes started a new era in mobile satellite communications. Use of spot beam antennas in these satellites produces a cellular type structure within coverage areas; hence, a frequency reuse scheme could be applied, making the system a high-capacity, cellular-like network on the ground with satellites acting as the base stations in space.

NGSO satellite systems solved the problem of long propagation delay and high power consumption, but they introduced new challenges to the communications industry. Although it is possible to cover the world (excluding polar regions) with three GEO satellites, NGSO satellites are closer to the Earth; thus, a constellation consisting of tens of satellites is required. This means increased system complexity and, of course, higher cost to the satellite system, which eventually must be passed to the users. Many NGSO satellite systems were proposed in the early 1990s in North America and around the world and obtained frequency spectrum licenses. Only a few of these systems were completed and became operational, including IRIDIUM (1998) with sixty-six satellites and GLOBALSTAR (2000) with forty-eight satellites. However, financial problems associated with the high cost of LEO systems forced both systems to file for bankruptcy. Consequently, LEO satellite systems have changed their goal of ubiquitous market penetration and services, and continue to serve for various specialized applications such as defense and emergency. Beside higher network complexity and more expensive control management requirements of NGSO satellite systems, a LEO or MEO satellite generally has a shorter lifetime than those in geostationary systems. This results in more frequent satellite launch requirements and higher maintenance costs to the satellite system.

The financial failure of the advanced but complex IRIDIUM satellite system revealed that although the technology for implementing a mobile satellite phone system is available, it is not possible with the system then designed to compete with the fast-growing terrestrial cellular systems and new Internet services using LEO satellites. The roaming capabilities between 2G networks in different countries and those considered in 3G wireless networks are quite adequate to provide telecommunications services to the majority of the world population at lower cost and better quality (e.g., lower delay) than those that can be achieved through such satellite systems. The new trends in the telecommunications industry with regard to transmitting data and Internet traffic at high speed over wireless channels could not be matched by these satellite systems. The IRIDIUM system, for example, was able to provide short data services at the very low data rate of 2.4 kbps. However, later systems such as the geomobile THURAYA have had better success.

Satellite systems do, however, maintain their unique feature of broadcasting. *Satellite broadcasting* has been successful for a long time and continues its dominance for long-distance coverage and service to highly populated areas. Broadband satellite systems are now being incorporated into the new trends in the telecommunications industry toward high-speed Internet access.

Broadband satellites are systems that can provide high data-rate transmission in the order of one Mbps and above (Jamalipour 2001). Digital video broadcasting (DVB) systems such as Eutelsat, SES, and INTELSAT; proprietary systems such as Spaceway and iPSTAR; and proposed but undeployed systems such as Teledesic and Astrolink are among such broadband satellite systems. Standardizations of these satellite systems are ongoing to reduce cost, increase applicability, and support multicasting. GEO satellite systems are of significant interest to these services. Figure 1 depicts a simple architecture for supporting high-speed Internet access. Recently, uplink over satellite has become the preferred architecture as opposed to uplink through terrestrial link via dialup (illustrated as the dashed connection to the dialup server in Figure 1).

Broadband satellite systems can be categorized according to their specifications and capabilities. This could be based on the frequency bands of operation (C band 4–8 GHz, K_u band 10–18 GHz, K_a band 22.5–40 GHz, and higher bands Q/V 37–100 GHz), the orbit altitude and hence the satellite lifetime, power requirements and antenna size, usage of bent pipe or on-board processing (OBP) technologies, global or regional coverage of the system, satellite total capacity and user capacity, use of inter-satellite links (ISL), number of supported terminals and required gateways, protocol used in the satellite system (e.g., TCP/IP, DVB, ATM, etc.), use of open or proprietary standards, total number of satellites in the system, and total cost. Most new designs of satellite systems include OBP and on-board switching (OBS) facilities so that the satellite node changes its simple role of relaying into being an active element in the network. OBP is a general term that refers to signal

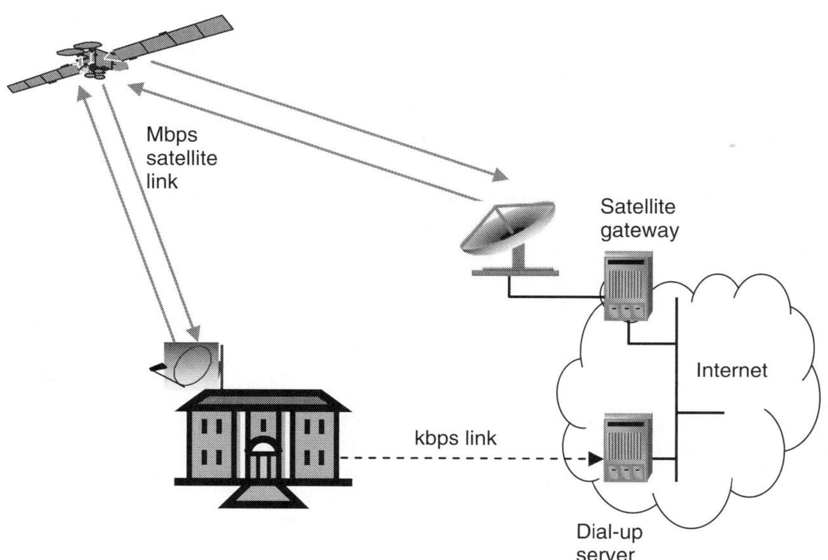

Figure 1: An architecture for satellite high-speed Internet access

processing and routing functions implemented on-board the satellite that go beyond the amplification and frequency conversion performed in conventional, transparent satellite systems. Switches in the satellites provide short latency and thus improve the QoS with regard to systems using hub stations on the ground. By using a sophisticated constellation with ISLs, connectivity in space without any terrestrial resource is possible. This feature enables far more autonomous satellite networks, which may be imperative especially for military purposes and post-disaster communications situations, where ground facilities may become potential targets or be damaged. These benefits, however, demand payloads with higher complexity.

There are many regulatory and standard bodies currently involved in development of issues related to the satellite communications industry. Regulatory bodies include the World Radio Conference (WRC), the Federal Communications Commission (FCC), the International Telecommunications Union (ITU), the European Radiocommunications Office (ERO), and many national and regional regulatory organizations. Standards are mainly developed by the Internet Engineering Task Force (IETF), the European Telecommunications Standards Institute (ETSI), the Telecommunications Industry Association (TIA), and the ITU.

Satellite systems have longer development cycles compared to terrestrial systems, and less funding and fewer engineers are usually involved in their development. Moreover, they compete over a more limited market than cellular systems. Most satellite systems are still proprietary and interfaces are not public, which in turn prevents competition. The standards for satellites will ensure interoperability and real competition and will be required for a broader consumer market. Therefore, in order to see further development in broadband satellite systems, a widely acceptable standardization is vital.

SATELLITE IP NETWORKING

Satellites in IP Networks

New multimedia and Internet services demand more cost-effective, high-quality, and high-speed telecommunications technologies and architectures. The primary issue is how to expand the current global Internet infrastructure so that the QoS can be improved from current best-effort service so that high-speed access can be economically provided. In this context, satellites can play an important role in expanding the Internet infrastructure using the large coverage area feature and providing high-speed data transmission through a high-bandwidth capacity channel. Satellites, however, would not perform this task as an isolated network but rather use an efficient integration with current terrestrial networks. So, instead of having an IP network in the sky, as suggested in earlier proposals on some satellite IP networks, a combination of terrestrial and satellite networks would be a solution to the future high-speed Internet (Marchese and Jamalipour 2005).

In a global Internet infrastructure, satellites can be used for many purposes. They can be used to connect geographically distant segments of the network or to interconnect heterogeneous networks. Satellites can provide direct telecommunications service to aircraft, ships, fast trains, and isolated local networks on the ground, or even to individual users. Flexible and quick deployment of bandwidth by satellite systems make them easily approachable by densely wired networks when required, as a good backup and support network.

Figure 2 shows two different options for the satellite payload that can be used in satellite-based Internet architectures. In Figure 2(a), the satellite is used as a reflector in space connecting separate network segments through ground gateways. In Figure 2(b), however, the satellite acts as an active component of the network that can utilize routing and switching processing. The satellites used in Figure 2 can be on any of the altitudes explained earlier—GEO, NGSO, or a combination of different altitudes. The satellites shown in Figure 2(b), in addition to having connection to the ground gateways, are also employed in intersatellite links so that network connectivity can be created in space independently. This method should be considered an important option in a future satellite-based Internet architecture. The method requires higher costs for the system and more complicated routing management. If special facilities are included in the mobile stations on the Earth, both methods can provide direct Internet connectivity to remote users without any other alternative terrestrial telecommunications infrastructure. A summary of this satellite-based Internet architecture and current proposals of this kind can be found in Kota, Pahlavan, and Leppanen 2003, and Marchese and Jamalipour 2005; Hu and Li 2001.

A satellite node can also be used as a high-speed downlink for home Internet access. Using this method, a home or office user with a satellite receiver, usually used for satellite television, can download the Internet contents at a very high data rate through the satellite downlink channel. A simple architecture of such a satellite–ground high-speed Internet was shown in Figure 1. In the architecture shown in this figure, the user first connects to his or her Internet service provider (ISP) using a normal dialup connection. The dialup connection forms a low-speed data communication (e.g., a usual 56 kbps or integrated services digital network [ISDN] connection) mainly in order to send requests to the Internet servers at the local ISP site. All Internet contents can then be forwarded to the customer through the high-speed satellite downlink upon receiving the request. The downlink can send the data to the user at speeds of one to a few Mbps using DVB satellites or other types of satellites. This method is especially appropriate for video-on-demand and real-time Internet applications in which many users located in the same region want to retrieve the same contents over the Internet. The asymmetry in the Internet traffic that usually results in up to ten times more data traffic on a typical Internet downlink connection compared to the uplink makes this method of special interest and application. Currently this method is competing with other high-speed Internet access for home users including cable modems and asymmetric digital subscriber line (ADSL) technologies. Some prototypes of these satellite Internet systems for home users have been already developed and demonstrated in Europe and other parts of the world. With some modifications addressing mobility and safety, it is possible to

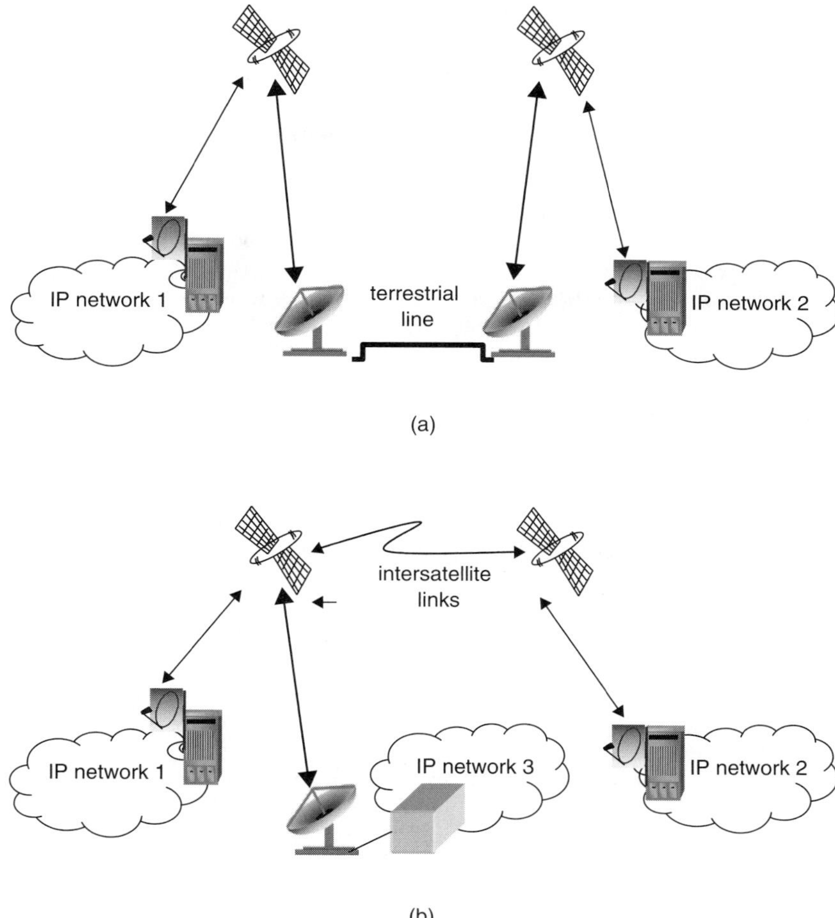

Figure 2: Two different payload options for satellite-based IP architectures: (a) bent-pipe architecture and (b) on-board processing satellites

extend the coverage of this type of Internet access to mobile users on the ground and also to long-distance flights and ships. For instance, Connexion service by Boeing began delivering real-time, high-speed Internet connectivity to airline passengers in 2004.

Satellites in 3G and B3G Networks

With the increasing popularity of portable computers and the expanding Internet capabilities of mobile phone handsets, a large demand for mobile computing has been generated in the past few years. Thus, instead of restricting data connections to be maintained always at a fixed position in the network, mobile users will be provided with equivalent multimedia and IP services. There is no doubt that the trend is toward a global mobile networking environment. In such a network, broadband satellites can be considered an integral part of the network, interconnecting the fast-growing terrestrial cellular and wired networks (Marchese and Jamalipour 2005).

Broadband satellite networks for Internet access are the new generation of satellite networks in which Internet-based applications and services will be provided to users regardless of their degree of geographical mobility. Asynchronous transfer mode (ATM) is a potential candidate for the switching mode for future broadband satellites due to its support of a variety of traffic, such as constant and variable bit rate and QoS support (Jamalipour 1998). Nevertheless, IP routing is considered the primary alternative for these satellites due to lower cost and friendliness to Internet traffic.

In the sphere of terrestrial networks, there are at present two possible approaches for establishing the task of mobile computing: cellular-based and IP-based solutions (Jamalipour 2001; Marchese and Jamalipour 2005). Intuitively, whereas a cellular-based solution enhances the current mobile communications by extending capacity for data and multimedia transmissions, an IP-based solution allows for user mobility by maintaining all ongoing Internet connections even in the presence of frequent handoffs or changes in the network points of attachment. In the forefront of these technologies, 3G and B3G wireless systems are being considered. These systems evolved by orienting the integration of three essential domains: broadband, mobile, and Internet. In such a milieu, the increasing feasibility of virtual connections allows mobile users not only to roam freely between heterogeneous networks but to remain engaged in various forms of multimedia communications. Whether this involves geographical coverage, bandwidth, or delay, it would then be up to the users to decide when and how to switch from one access network to another depending upon the availability and appropriate cost/performance considerations, advancing toward an era of all-IP based communications.

Consequently, it will be necessary to implement the 3G system as a universal solution that prompts transparent user roaming (among different wireless networks) while delivering the widest possible range of cost-effective services.

International Mobile Telecommunications-2000 (IMT-2000) is a unified 3G mobile system that supports both packet-switched and circuit-switched data transmissions with high spectrum efficiency, making the vision of anywhere, anytime communications a reality. Basically, this is a collection of standards that provides direct mobile access to a range of fixed and wireless networks. The three most significant developments are universal mobile telecommunications system (UMTS), code division multiple access 2000 (CDMA2000), and universal wireless communication-136 (UWC-136), which are the 3G successors to the main 2G technologies of global system for mobile communications (GSM), interim standard 95 (IS-95), and advanced mobile phone service (AMPS), respectively (Steele, Lee, and Gould 2001). The general idea was to make the development of 3G wireless technologies a gradual process from circuit-switched to packet-switched. Take GSM, for example: in order to have the system enhanced with improved services (by means of increased capacity, coverage, quality, and data rates), the evolution to 3G was made possible through the incorporation of an intermediate stage called general packet radio services (GPRS).

Based on the enhanced core network of GPRS, UMTS is designed to be the backward-compatible 3G standard for GSM. UMTS is the European proposal for a 3G mobile system aiming to support multimedia services with extended intelligent network features and functions. As a first step of the integration, the UMTS terrestrial radio access network (UTRAN) will coexist with GSM access networks. The idea was to develop the UMTS core network by gradually incorporating the desired UMTS features to the GSM/GPRS core network. At this stage, UTRA supports time-division duplex (WCDMA-DS TDD) and frequency division duplex (WCDMA-DS FDD) modes with the combined operation offering an optimized solution to coverage areas of all sizes. A further multi-carrier (MC-FDD) mode is to be established at a later date intended mainly for the use in CDMAOne/CDMA2000 evolutions (Steele, Lee and Gould 2001).

For satellite systems, the situation is different. The most apparent variation is that the market for satellite systems is much more limited than for their cellular counterparts. Therefore, it would be difficult to assume the same approaches for satellite systems. Instead, satellite systems can incorporate their global coverage feature for enhancement of the 3G terrestrial networks. Satellites can establish a high-speed backbone network to support the terrestrial networks and also to use their broadcast nature to deliver Internet content at high speeds directly to a group a users.

Satellite UMTS (S-UMTS), for example, is considered as a component of 3G networks (Priscoli 1999). The satellite segment of the network connects through appropriate interworking units (IWU) to the ground segments. IWU for the satellite has similar functionality as the gateways used to interconnect 2G and 3G networks for interoperation of these networks during the transition period from 2G to 3G, as well as the gateways used for interconnection of different operator networks of the same kind (e.g., GSM). For example, Figure 3 illustrates a new hybrid architecture consisting of a GEO satellite and some terrestrial 3G segments that is proposed as part of a European Satellite Communications Network of Excellence (SATNEX) project (Giambene 2005). A service center acquires information from diverse content providers on the Internet. The server distributes contents in regional caches. From local caches, information is sent to mobile users through GEO bent-pipe satellite links. Upstream transmissions from the Earth station to the MT employ a DVB-S-like air interface operated in K_a band. Downstream transmissions (acknowledgment packet [ACK] of layer 2 and layer 4) from mobile terminals move through a 3G terrestrial cellular system. The terrestrial return channel provides adequate capacity for small ACK packets, requires low transmission power, and allows for the reduction of round trip time (RTT) values.

Another similar integrated approach is hybrid terrestrial/satellite broadband services based on the ancillary terrestrial component (ATC). These hybrid services use a ground tower network of ATCs operating in L band

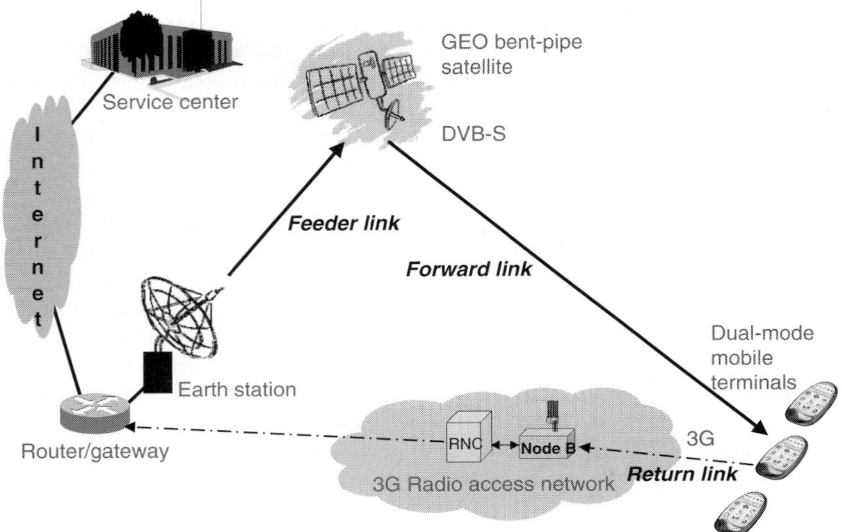

Figure 3: A hybrid architecture consisting of GEO satellites and terrestrial 3G segments

to boost the signal in dense urban environments, eliminating signal fading and interference issues common to all-satellite, first-generation MSS networks. The ATC approach was introduced into the MSS world in 2001 when the FCC authorized its use on a new system to be built by U.S.–Canadian operator Mobile Satellite Ventures. ATC supports seamless availability of service within an entire region, and the infrastructure for this MSS/ATC network can be acquired from wireless vendors using 3G/4G configurations. This allows ATC operators to offer low-cost user devices, as in the case of terrestrial operators. Moreover, with the use of L band by ATCs, the same spectrum operating over the satellite can be reused terrestrially.

Multilayered Satellites in IP Networks

Multilayered satellite architectures with interorbital links (IOLs) between layers of satellite constellations are of much interest because they may yield better performance than individual layers. Figure 4 depicts a layered satellite architecture with some Internet-based applications. For example, Dash, Durresi, and Jain (2003) consider a three-layered architecture consisting of GEOs, LEOs, and high-altitude platforms (HAPs) for VoIP application. GEOs act as backbone routers, LEOs as the second layer, and HAPs to cover special areas with high and sensitive traffic, such as battlefields and disaster areas.

CHALLENGES FOR SATELLITES IN IP NETWORKS

In this section we look at some challenging issues with regard to supporting satellite IP networks.

Physical Layer Challenges

Satellite IP networks require advanced communications technologies to increase link capacity and utilize

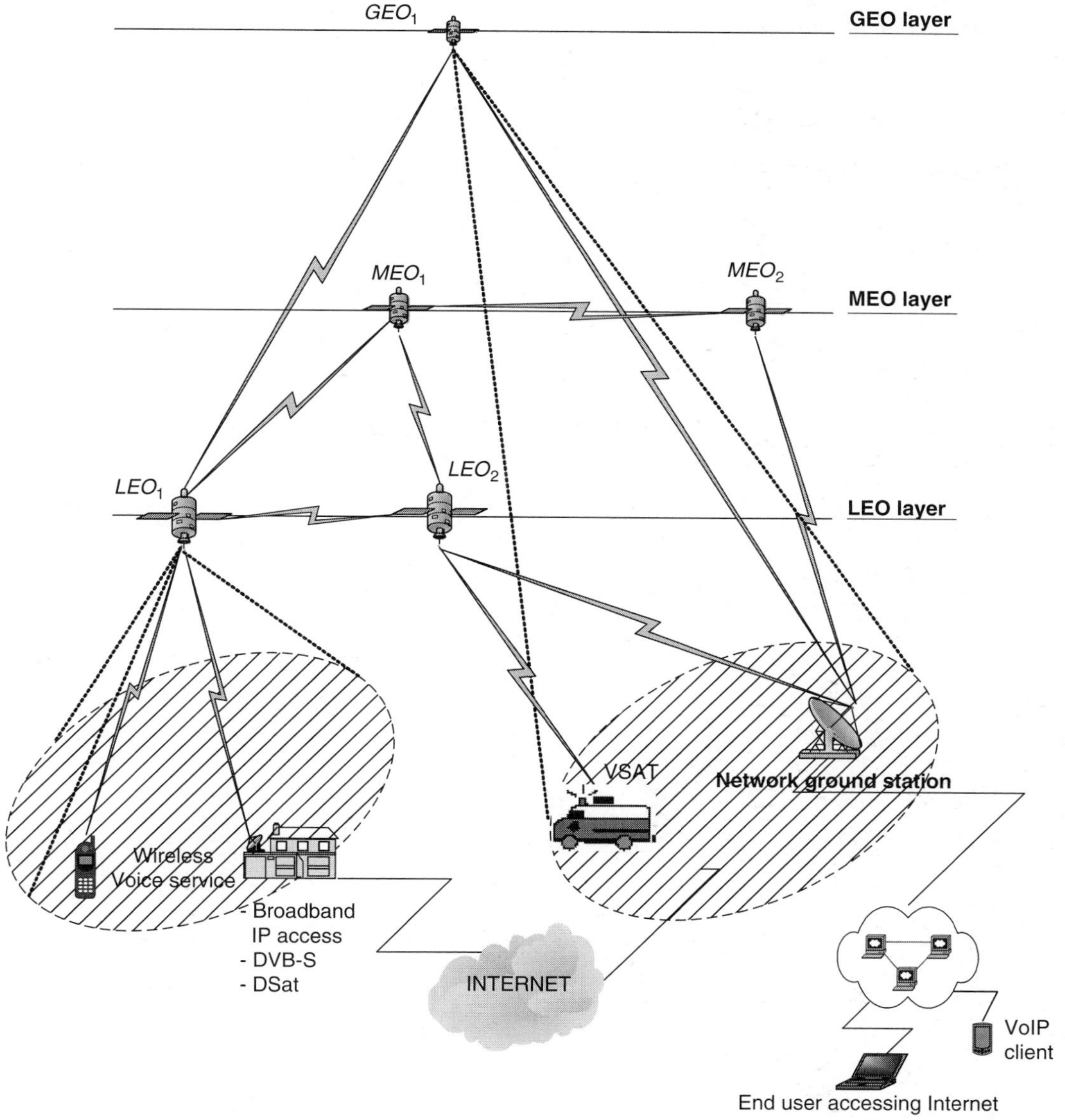

Figure 4: Layered satellite architecture with some applications

power performance and bandwidth efficiency. To achieve these aims, research on multiple fronts is under way at the physical layer. The research includes, but is not limited to, adaptive and higher-order modulation, adaptive coding, link budget analysis, adaptive power control, channel modeling, and integrated access control mechanisms. For example, instead of conventionally used quadrature phase shift keying (QPSK) modulation, 8-PSK or 16-quadrature amplitude modulation (QAM) are shown to be more efficient. Another example of research results at the physical layer is the standardization Turbo code for DVB-RCS. Although this section will not describe all of these topics, we will provide some important challenges at the physical layer for satellite IP networks. Figure 5 shows the architecture of a satellite IP network with return channel systems subject to channel problems. As seen in Figure 5, the following three system architectures for multimedia satellite networks may be distinguished: one-way communication, two-way communication with telephony return channel, and two-way communication with a transmitter at the user location. The last architecture includes different options: return link via a high-speed GEO satellite, or a lower-speed MEO or LEO (Alagöz et al. 2004). Moreover, in multimedia satellite networks, a return link may follow Link 1, Link 2, and Link 3 in Figure 5. Although any backhaul network would work, the LEO constellation enables the user to set up a GEO digital field terminal (DFT)—in which there is no terrestrial backhaul—and have immediate interconnection to a remote backhaul network. For example, a control mechanism system may be utilized to handle the physical channel problems (Alagöz et al. 2004).

Performance over satellite channels may suffer because of the variation in the channel quality due to fading, propagation anomalies, jamming, and so forth. As a consequence of these variations, the channel bit error rate may range from having almost no impact on performance to dramatically degrading performance depending on the channel conditions. Among the channel error recovery techniques used in wireless environments are automatic repeat request (ARQ) and forward error correction (FEC) techniques, or their combinations. However, in a satellite application, the ARQ techniques may not be suitable due to latency constraints, especially for real-time applications. On the other hand, there is a trade-off when employing the FEC mechanism; although the FEC may enable the system to recover erroneous packets in adverse channel conditions, processing delay due to the FEC overhead may cause further congestion and more packet loss in the network (Alagöz et al. 2004). Satellite extension of terrestrial networks is a viable capacity and coverage improvement solution. Extensive works are also being carried out in terrestrial- and satellite-UMTS (T/SUMTS) interworking. T-UMTS applies a well-configured wideband code division multiple access (W-CDMA) air interface described by 3rd-Generation Partnership Project (3GPP) standards, whereas the S-UMTS radio access network is still under standardization. The main concept of T/S-UMTS interworking is to employ the same air interface requiring only minor modifications of the terminals and aided with adaptive radio resource management (Karaliopoulos et al. 2004).

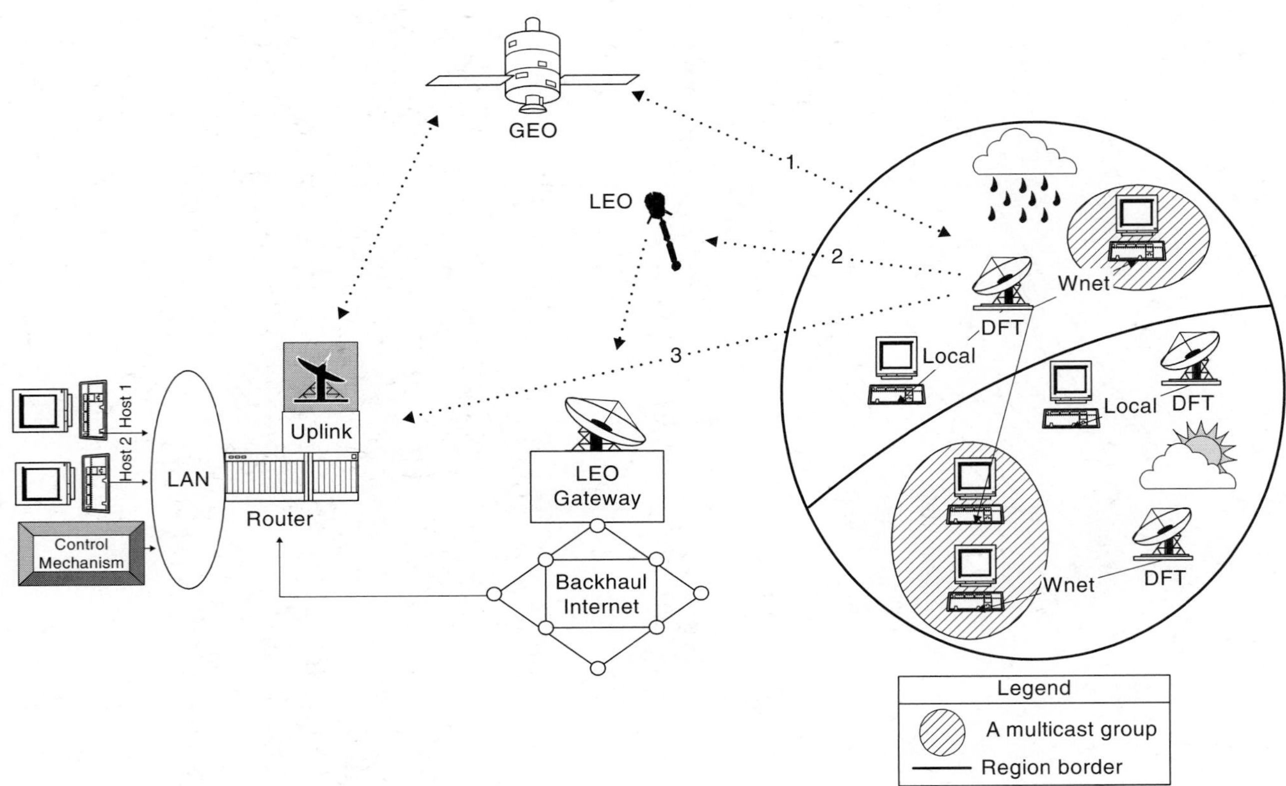

Figure 5: Architecture of a satellite IP network with return channel systems faced with channel problems

Through the use of communication satellites, networks can be interconnected on a global scale, even in geographic regions with poor terrestrial backbone infrastructure. As for the transport of data over satellite networks, protocol stacks can be optimized for the given physical characteristics. However, as IP has become the dominant networking protocol, satellite-dependent protocols have been reduced to physical layer and medium access control (MAC). The resulting protocol stack is summarized by the ETSI broadband satellite multimedia (BSM) scheme (ETSI-TR-985 2002). That scheme has been presented by the satellite standardization community as the reference architecture that allows IP over satellite. A special function is under investigation for allowing the interworking of TCP/IP protocol and satellite MAC. Matching the applications that use TCP/IP with the advantages offered by satellites, it is natural to think of TCP/IP-based applications over satellite networks; however, the general characteristics (e.g., fading) of the links heavily affect the performance of the communication (Bisio and Marchese 2004).

Medium Access Control

Recently many MAC protocols have been proposed for supporting link layer attributes of satellite networks with different user requirements and channel characteristics (Marchese and Jamalipour 2005; Barsocchi et al. 2005). Fundamental issues in designing multiple-access schemes are also summarized for next-generation mobile networks (Jamalipour, Wada, and Yamazato 2005). MAC protocols may be classified based on their functionality and characteristics as fixed assignment (FAMA), random access, demand assignment (DAMA), reservation, adaptive, and hybrid combination protocols.

In FAMA protocols, MAC can be employed to control user access to a shared satellite channel based on frequency division (FDMA), time division (TDMA) or code division (CDMA). Unfortunately, for FAMA-based protocols, the inherent nature of traffic burstiness in satellite channels may cause inefficient utilization of channel resources. Both TDMA- and CDMA-based return channel protocols are also under investigation for DVB-RCS systems. In random access protocols, users access the channel in an uncontrolled and uncoordinated fashion. Unfortunately, the resulting collisions can be minimized only at the expense of low utilization and throughput. This scheme maybe used in bursty traffic conditions with non-guaranteed successful transmission. In order to improve the performance of conventional random access techniques, other techniques including pure ALOHA, slotted ALOHA, selective reject ALOHA, capture ALOHA, adaptive spread ALOHA, and more were proposed. ALOHA was one of the first protocols introduced for packet satellite networks with throughput of 18 percent. Subsequently, slotted ALOHA and contention–resolution-based ALOHA variants were proposed, achieving throughputs of 37 percent and 43 percent, respectively (Kota, Pahlavan, and Leppanen 2003). Although random access may support larger number of terminals with bursty traffic, QoS is not guaranteed. The demand assignment multiple access (DAMA) technique addresses this issue, utilizing dynamic allocation of the system bandwidth in response to users' bandwidth requests. A resource request must be granted (reserved), given that a certain level of QoS will be maintained during transmission. DAMA-based protocols include reservation ALOHA, priority-oriented demand assignment (PODA), fixed priority-oriented demand assignment (FPODA), and round-robin reservation techniques, combined free demand assignment multiple access (CFDAMA). For example, CFDAMA may support different QoS requirements for busty traffic (Mitchell 2003). Some of their extensions and hybrid combinations are also adopted for satellite networks. These include predictive DAMA (PRDAMA), bursty targeted DAMA (BTDAMA), combined random/reservation multiple access (CRRMA), transmit before assignment using collision request (TBACR), movable boundary random/DAMA, and a few other protocols along with their performance analysis in satellite networks as given in Mitchell (2003). Unfortunately, there is no unified protocol that is superior to others for different traffic scenarios and applications. Some protocols with certain characteristics may be more suitable for particular satellite networks. The fact is that large bursts require extra buffers and higher processing capabilities to support reliable communications and guaranteed QoS. Both FAMA and DAMA are inefficient for bursty traffic. At the expense of increased design complexities, dynamic allocation strategies with random/reservation algorithms may be used to improve the throughput while keeping the delay parameters random but at an acceptable level.

Integrated layered approaches are needed to increase performance of MAC protocols. For example, with regard to physical layer attributes, TCP and/or application-layer characteristics may have a potential impact on the performance of a MAC protocol. Consider that TCP incorporates a window-based flow control algorithm with an associated TCP window size (W) control. If TCP enters congestion avoidance, W will be reduced significantly and will start a slow incremental process based on successful ACKs. That is, TCP will have the flow control of packets across a network from end-to-end and will change the packet arrival process at the satellite access point from that of an uncontrolled source (Mitchell 2003). In addition, traffic burstiness is an important characteristic that strongly influences the design or selection of a MAC protocol for satellite networks. Unfortunately, comparative studies in the literature are based on a few limited-arrival distributions with limited burst nature and message length distribution. This problem should be clarified as part of the sensitivity analysis of designed protocols.

Mobility and Handover Management

Due to higher-speed movement, the mobility management in LEO systems is more challenging than in MEO systems. Clearly, mobility is managed largely through the process of location management. In this section, we describe handover types in LEO satellite networks and location management issues.

Link Layer Handover

Inter-satellite handover occurs when the end user's communication point is changed from one satellite to another.

The research in this area focuses on algorithms for the dynamic rerouting of a connection and the admission control of handover calls to ensure QoS requirements, because the change of satellite will affect the routing of the ongoing session and the resource allocation of the satellites. The spot beam handover occurs when the mobile user switches between the spot beams of a satellite. Spot beam handovers occur very frequently (e.g., every one to two minutes) due to the small coverage area of a specific spot beam. Admission control algorithms and schemes for reducing the blocking rate for handover connection and new connections is the main concern of the research conducted in this area (Cho et al. 2002). Link handover may occur when a satellite passes over the polar area. The aim in this handover type is to reduce the signaling overhead and blocking probability caused by link handovers. Link layer handovers cause the change of one or more links between the two communicating end points. Link layer handovers may result in a change of the IP address for the end points in such a way that a network layer handover is required after a link layer handover.

Network Layer Handover

If either satellite or user terminal changes its IP address due to the movement of the satellite or the mobile user, a network layer handover is required to transfer the connection of higher-level protocol (e.g., TCP, UDP) to the new IP address. Two events that cause network layer handover in a satellite environment can be defined as follows.

Satellite as a router: When a satellite is used only for routing and does not generate or consume data, the satellite acts as a router to the Internet. Mobile users are handed over from one satellite's footprint to another as they come under the footprint of different satellites going around the earth. The mobile node (MN) needs to maintain a continuous transport layer connection with the correspondent node (CN) while their attachment point changes from satellite A to satellite B. Different satellites or even different spot beams within a satellite may be assigned different IP network addresses (Tuysuz and Alagöz 2006). Therefore, IP address changes that occur during an inter-satellite handover require a network layer handover. Routing management will be described later in the chapter.

Satellite as a mobile host: When a satellite has on-board equipment to generate data that are transmitted to workstations on the earth, or it receives control signals from the control center, the satellite acts as the end point of the communication. Although the satellite's footprint moves from ground station A to B, the satellite should maintain continuous transport layer connection with its CN. If the IP address of the satellite has to be changed when it is handed over to ground station B, a network layer handover has to be performed.

Mobile IP (MIP) is the standard proposed by the IETF to handle mobility of Internet hosts for mobile data communications. Some projects conducted by the National Aeronautics and Space Administration (NASA) consider IP in satellite networks and Mobile IP. Some of these projects also involve handovers in satellite networks. Such projects include the Operating Missions as Nodes on the Internet (OMNI) project and the Global Participations Measurement (GPM) project (Rash, Casasanta, and Hogie 2002). In addition, an analytic study of Doppler-based handover management for LEO satellites is provided in (Papapetrou and Pavlidou 2005).

Location Management

Obviously, mobility is managed largely through the process of location management. This action involves not only storing and/or retrieving information from the location database but sending paging signals whenever necessary to locate a roaming user. Although the need to notify the home network of mobile users' current locations is always present, it is questionable whether accurate location information is essential for mobile nodes that are not committed to any data transmissions. New research results for location management are crucial for improving the overall performance of satellite networks.

Mobility Management in Mobile Satellites

Mobile satellite systems using NGSO have very similar characteristics to cellular networks; thus, issues are common between these networks. The main similarity is that most of these systems use the cellular concept of increasing the total system capacity through a cellular-like coverage area arrangement, introducing similar handoff issues to those involved in cellular systems. There is, however, a major difference between the proposed scheme in satellite systems and what exists in the sphere of cellular networks. The key operational concept that differentiates the specific operations of mobility management in the two systems is the "entity" being considered as the moving object. Whereas the former encounters *mobile* movements within the fixed network architecture, the latter incurs *satellite* movements in reference to fixed mobile nodes. Essentially, this suggests that the mobility management technique will be different.

It is crucial to more closely identify the differences (or similarities) between the operations of handoff and location management in mobile satellites. Clearly, handoff management is significant only when the mobile is active; specifically, it is about the appropriate reservation of resources (e.g., bandwidth) along the roaming path of a mobile user engaging in a call connection. Its efficient operation is important to ensure that the various aspects of the QoS requirements (e.g., throughput versus forced call termination) are satisfactorily complied with. Location management, on the other hand, is mainly for users who are currently idle but are expected to receive calls (or become active) while they frequently change their point of attachment to the network. In essence, only sufficient location information (about the mobile) is maintained so that the network can loosely track the mobile's movement and subsequently incur a minimal paging (or searching) load when the precise residency is required. Consequently, it would be correct to conclude that the predicted information for handoff needs to be more reliable than the information desired for efficient location management. Based on this observation, it seems potentially viable to combine (at least to some extent) the operations of the two management processes of handoff and location.

Routing Management

In the context of NGSO systems with ISLs, one of the major challenges is employing an efficient routing protocol that yields effective use of satellites and ISLs to improve the performance of the satellite system. Specifically, due to dynamic topology with respect to satellite movement, it is hard to adopt well-known terrestrial, connection-oriented IP routing protocols like open shortest path first (OSPF) and routing information protocol (RIP) to satellites. These protocols rely on the exchange of topology information, which quickly becomes obsolete and must constantly be refreshed with new information. However, although topology of a satellite network rapidly changes, it is periodic and predictable because of the strict orbital movements of satellites. Therefore, it is reasonable to use this periodicity feature when calculating routes.

Dynamic virtual topology routing (DVTR) and virtual node (VN) protocols are common routing methods that use the periodicity of the topology changes (Werner 1997). DVTR divides the system period into a set of time intervals, so that topology remains constant during each interval. Time intervals are chosen to be short enough to assume that the traversal costs of ISLs are fixed. Therefore, optimal and alternate paths can be established using a shortest path algorithm (Werner 1997). The DVTR approach decreases the online computational complexity but adds the expense of large storage requirements. Using the VN technique, a fixed virtual topology consisting of virtual nodes is superimposed over the physical topology in order to hide the mobility of satellites from routing protocols. Each satellite corresponds to a VN at any given time. As a satellite disappears over the horizon, its corresponding VN becomes represented by the next satellite passing overhead, and the state information (such as routing table entries) is transferred to it. Routing is performed in the fixed virtual topology by the use of a common routing protocol. This scheme can directly integrate the space network with the terrestrial IP network and may provide good support for IP-multicast and IP-QoS. However, this approach has some challenging problems such as scalability of routing tables and high computational complexity in space devices.

In a satellite network, routing decisions can be made offline or on-board. In the former case, the routing algorithm could use information about predictable topology changes (e.g., changes in the ISL lengths and connections), but it would not be adaptive to traffic load changes. Therefore, on-board routing algorithms yield better efficiency for dynamic traffic cases at the expense of increased complexity.

There are various adaptive routing protocols that take the traffic characteristics into account. In the simpler case, the routing protocol is isolated, which means it uses only the information (e.g., outgoing link loads) local to the node where the routing is performed. Priority-based adaptive routing (PAR; Korçak and Alagöz 2005) is an example of isolated adaptive routing algorithms, in which each ISL is assigned a priority depending on its past utilization and buffering information. When selecting an outgoing link among reasonable ones, the priorities may be utilized to evenly distribute the traffic. Non-isolated adaptive routing algorithms, on the other hand, take into account all the other nodes and ISLs in the network. These algorithms rely on a signaling protocol in order to transport state information between nodes in the network. Therefore, non-isolated algorithms may cause high signaling overhead, as well as additional complexity in the satellite nodes (Korçak and Alagöz 2005).

Some routing protocols are designed for layered satellite architectures. For example, in the satellite grouping and routing protocol (SGRP), LEO satellites are divided into groups according to the footprint area of the MEO satellites (Chen and Ekici 2005). Each LEO group is managed by a MEO. Depending on the state information arriving from the LEOs, a MEO satellite computes the minimum delay paths for its LEO members. The hierarchical approach aims to reduce computational complexity on satellites and the communication load on the network compared with the non-isolated algorithms.

IP Multicast over Satellites

Because of the nature of satellite broadcasting capability, IP multicast over satellites may need special treatment, especially for maintaining QoS and security constraints. Traditionally, multicast allows significantly reduced load at the transport network by a source node to send data simultaneously to all the intended multicast members. In order to employ a successful and reliable multicast IP over satellites, the design requirements include efficient link utilization, dynamic joining and leaving of a multicast group, minimal overhead, high return channel link, and security issues. For example, Sun et al. (2003) emphasize some modifications required for multicast networking protocols (e.g., Internet group management protocol [IGMP], multicast routing, reliable multicast protocols, and required security issues). A satellite network architecture is also presented in Ronga et al. (2003) to provide QoS support for IP traffic based on the DiffServ paradigm, while minimizing the satellite resource waste. The performance has been evaluated in terms of throughput, packet jitter, TCP protection against UDP flooding, and wasted bandwidth on the satellite link. Finally, while the tailoring of terrestrial multicast routing protocols are in progress for satellites, IP multicast over satellites may need further investigations for dedicated routing protocols—especially for channels subject to fading.

VoIP over Satellites

VoIP services have become popular in the last decade because of their low cost and simultaneous voice-data transmission in a single session. The use of satellites with OBP capabilities for voice communication can increase if the parameters leading to the targeted performance are carefully designed. A satellite with OBP can process the received data and, according to the nature of the application, decide on the transmission properties. VoIP performance issues in layered satellite networks with onboard processing capabilities are also under investigation. Performance is an important issue of a system that results in the system being accepted by users or ignored. Therefore, parameters affecting the performance should be clearly stated (Nguyen et al. 2001). Users expect service quality from VoIP services similar to that of PSTN, which is a dedicated system for voice communication. Thus, the service levels that they face usually do not meet the expected service quality. Since voice applications are real-time applications; delay and delay variation are key parameters for the system performance. To achieve intelligible communication, delay must be restricted to certain values specified by the authorities (e.g., ITU and ETSI). Obviously, the significance of delay becomes more apparent for satellite networks. OBP with physical, data-link, and network layer functionalities may improve the performance of the application and ensure the desired quality. Satellites can buffer the incoming voice data and drop the damaged packets. Packet loss rate due to corruption and dropping, along with throughput values, show the efficiency of the system beyond delay and jitter, link utilization rate, or bandwidth efficiency.

Data and voice transmission over packet-based networks feature a major difference in requirements: data are loss sensitive and delay tolerant, whereas voice is loss tolerant and delay sensitive. For this reason, the transport layer in the VoIP protocol stack uses the user datagram protocol (UDP) to carry voice instead of the transmission control protocol (TCP). In addition, since most VoIP applications are real-time, the real-time transport protocol (RTP) is run on top of UDP to ensure end-to-end delivery services. These services include payload type identification, sequence numbering, time stamping, and delivery monitoring. Many parameters affect users' perceptions of quality, such as speech coding, packetization efficiency, silence suppression, error-concealment methods, and jitter buffer implementation.

The choice of VoIP coder-decoder (codec) depends on the available bandwidth and desired speech quality. There are a number of widely used ITU G-series codec standards, including G.711, G.726, G.729 and G.729a. Current VoIP systems typically use G.729a, which encodes and compresses voice down to 8 kbps using the code-excited linear predictive (CELP) algorithm.

VoIP packets have a long packet header consisting of IP/UDP/RTP—each 20, 8, and 12 bytes long, respectively. Header compression is a way to decrease the packet overhead. Header information that does not change after connection setup is not sent, and voice data of two or more call channels are multiplexed in one IP packet with a subheader identifying call channels. VoIP is inefficient for small voice packets, whereas large packets lead to longer delays and more packet errors. Silence suppression helps to save average bandwidth by eliminating silent periods of transmission. Finally, with more advanced and powerful integrated circuitry and microelectronics, OBP has been becoming more feasible and sensible, cost-wise. Thus, it has the potential to enable satellite networks to cope with the inherent propagation delay burden (Janssen et al. 2002), contribute to performance of VoIP applications over satellite networks (Dash, Durresi, and Jain 2003), and support ETSI standards for compliance/interoperability, such as VoIP over DVB-RCS with QoS and bandwith on-demand algorithm described in Marchese and Jamalipour (2005).

Security Management

One of the most critical aspects of satellite IP networks is security management. Satellite security can be implemented in the network, transport, and application levels. At the physical layer, satellite operators support securing the network access via a smart card. DVB standards employ two levels of security: DVB common scrambling and user scrambling in forward and return channel. At the application layer, many application-specific security solutions exists. Our main concern in this subsection is exploring IP security (IPsec) for satellites.

There are two main groups of investigations for resolving the security problems in satellites: tailoring the existing security solutions for satellite IP networks an designing a new security solution dedicated to satellite IP networks. IP security includes authentication, integrity, confidentiality, and key management issues for satellite IP networks. The broadcast nature of satellite links makes eavesdropping much easier than any other service on the Internet. Additionally, satellite security services should maintain IP security even in the presence of intentional security attacks.

The IPsec mechanism includes an authentication header and an encapsulation security payload header. Satellite communication takes different approaches regarding the dynamics of the different topologies within the network. Implementing IPsec for satellites is a major challenge (Howarth et al. 2004), and the performance of satellite IP networks may be adversely affected by some security solutions. For example, as we will see later in the chapter, utilizing performance enhancing proxies (PEPs) reduces the latency problem, but it increases the security gap at the network layer. Unless modifications are made, end-to-end IPsec with PEP cannot be trusted. One promising modification may be to employ multilayer IPsec in which TCP headers are layer one and TCP payload makes up the other layer, such that the latter can be separately encrypted. Because PEP itself must be protected from denial-of-service type attacks, traditional IP solutions such as firewall protection should be considered as well. Various IPsec implementations for satellites remain a major challenge (Marchese and Jamalipour 2005).

SATELLITE TRANSPORT OF INTERNET TRAFFIC

Broadband satellite networks are being developed to transport high-speed multimedia and, in particular, Internet traffic through high-capacity satellite channels to network segments as well as to individual users. As in the case of any other wireless network designed to deliver Internet traffic, broadband satellite networks need to connect to the backbone-wired Internet on the ground. TCP is the most commonly used protocol at the transport layer of the network stack in the Internet, originally developed in wired networks with low bit error rate (BER) on the order of less than 10^{-8}. In this context, any wireless network with Internet service needs to be compatible with the protocol used in the wired network (i.e., mainly the TCP/IP protocol). There are, however, some design issues in the TCP/IP protocol that make it difficult to use it efficiently over wireless and satellite links. Recently, many research activities have compared the performance of TCP in high-BER and high-latency channels and modification proposals to improve its performance in terrestrial and satellite wireless networks (Jamalipour 1998; Kota, Pahlavan, and Leppanen 2003; Marchese and Jamalipour 2005; Partridge and Shepard 1997; Henderson and Katz 1999; Hassan and Jain 2003).

TCP has been designed and tuned for networks in which segment losses and corruption of performance are mainly because of network congestion. This assumption might not be valid in many of the emerging networks, such as wireless networks. The flow control mechanism used in TCP is based on time-out and window-size adjustment, which can work with high utilization in wired networks with low BER on the order of 10^{-8}. However, when the wireless channel is used (partially or totally) as the physical layer with a BER as high as 10^{-3}, it may perform inefficiently. In the wireless channels, the main cause for packet loss is the high BER, not congestion as it is in wired networks. The low efficiency of the TCP in a wireless channel occurs because TCP misinterpreted that the packet loss that occurred because of the high error rate was a result of congestion. On the other hand, in high-latency networks such as satellite networks, adjustment of the window size could take a long time and reduce the system throughput.

TCP has the ability to probe the unused network bandwidth by a mechanism called *slow start* and also to back off the transmission rate upon detection of congestion through the *congestion avoidance* mechanism. The congestion control mechanism implemented by standard TCP is based upon a sliding window, which defines the number of packets injected in the network. At the connection start-up, TCP initializes a variable called congestion window (cwnd) to a value of one segment. This variable determines the transmission rate of TCP. The congestion control phase typically occurs after the slow start phase ends depending on the slow start phase threshold value. The window size is doubled for every round-trip period until a packet loss is experienced. At this time, the congestion avoidance phase is commenced, the window size is halved, and the lost packet is retransmitted. During this phase of TCP, the window size is increased only linearly by one segment at each round-trip period and might be halved again upon detection of another packet loss. If the retransmitted packet is lost, the time-out mechanism employed in TCP reduces the window size to one. Because all of these procedures are performed at periods equal to round-trip delay of the channel, the system throughput could be degraded significantly when high-latency channels such as geostationary satellites are involved. Therefore, the high-latency satellite channel combined with the slow increase of the TCP congestion window size results in underutilization of the high-capacity satellite channel.

A similar issue for TCP over satellite links is the natively large bandwidth-delay product. The bandwidth-delay product defines the maximum amount of data that can be in-flight (transmitted but not acknowledged) in a TCP connection. It represents the full utilization of that connection. In a connection that incorporates a satellite link, the main bottleneck in TCP performance is a result of the large delay-bandwidth product of the satellite link (Ehsan, Liu, and Ragland 2003). Over such a link, the normal TCP window dynamics result in significantly increased latency before the channel is fully utilized. This problem cannot be effectively solved simply by improving the satellite channel quality, or by using large initial window size. A connection using the satellite link typically also has a terrestrial part; thus, using large window end-to-end could affect the performance and fairness of the terrestrial part of the connection.

Satellite-Related TCP Modifications and Mechanisms

Some modifications to the basic TCP can be made so that it can perform more efficiently in high-latency satellite networks with Internet services. Most of the protocols described below can be found in detail in Jamalipour (1998); Kota, Pahlavan, and Leppanen (2003); Marchese and Jamalipour (2005); Partridge and Shepard (1997); Henderson and Katz (1999); and Hassan and Jain (2003). In this subsection, we present a brief description of such modifications and related mechanisms.

TCP Vegas

TCP Vegas includes a modified retransmission strategy that is based on fine-grained measurements of the round-trip time (RTT) as well as new mechanisms for congestion detection during slow-start and congestion avoidance. TCP Vegas's congestion detection mechanism is proactive; that is, it tries to sense incipient congestion by observing changes in the throughput rate.

TCP New Reno

TCP Reno does not generally recover well in the presence of multiple segment losses within one window's-worth of data. Only the first loss segment is recovered via the fast retransmit algorithm, and the rest normally must wait for a retransmission time-out recovery (the fast recovery phase is terminated after the first retransmission is acknowledged). The TCP New Reno proposal modifies the fast retransmit/fast recovery algorithms of TCP Reno to allow recovery from multiple segment losses (RFC 2582).

TCP Selective ACK

TCP with selective acknowledgment has been proposed to efficiently recover from multiple segment losses (RFC 2018, 2883). In selective ACK (SACK) TCP, acknowledgments contain additional information about the segments that have been received by the destination. When the destination receives out-of-order segments, it sends ACKs (SACKs) acknowledging them.

TCP for Transactions

TCP for transactions (T/TCP) attempts to reduce the connection handshaking latency for most connections from one and a half to one RTT for small transactions (RFC 1644). After the first connection between a pair of hosts is established, T/TCP is able to bypass the three-way handshake, allowing the sender to transmit data in the first segment. This reduction in latency can be significant for short Web traffic over satellite links.

Explicit Congestion Notification

Explicit congestion notification (ECN) allows routers to inform TCP senders about imminent congestion without dropping segments (RFC 3168). The ECN mechanism can be used as part of a mechanism to differentiate between congestion and error losses in satellite networks. The implementation of ECN requires the deployment of active queue management such as random early detection (RED) in routers.

Window Scaling and Large Initial Window Size

Small window size can severely limit TCP throughput over long propagation links. With the window scaling option, the amount of data that can be outstanding is significantly increased by introducing a scale factor to be applied to the window field. Consequently, TCP over a satellite connection can theoretically achieve a throughput of 15 Gbps, which is more than adequate for current satellite IP networks (Kota, Pahlavan, and Leppanen 2003). However, increased window size can also cause sequence number wraparound problems for TCP. To address the wraparound problem, TCP needs to implement two mechanisms—namely, protection against wraparound sequence (PAWS) numbers and round-trip time measurements (RTTM).

Pacing TCP Segments

Rate-based pacing (RBP) is a technique used in the absence of incoming ACKs, in which the TCP sender temporarily paces TCP segments at a given rate until the ACK clock can be restarted. As soon as the first acknowledgment is received, RBP ceases and TCP ACK resumes. Pacing data during the RTT of transfer may allow TCP to make effective use of high bandwidth-delay pipes, such as satellite links, even for the short transfer.

Header Compression

Header compression is a general bandwidth-efficiency technique and is also applicable in satellite IP networks (RFC 2507).

Performance Enhancing Proxies

PEPs are used to improve the performance of the Internet protocols on networks paths in which native performance suffers from characteristics of the links or subnetworks on the path. PEPs provide a safe mechanism to leverage the problems of TCP over satellite links, and have become the de facto solution on field (Kota, Pahlavan, and Leppanen 2003). They are typically implemented at the transport or application layer, although some cross-layer implementations exist. PEPs may be classified based on symmetry and transparency. Examples of transport layer PEPs are TCP spoofing and TCP connection-split proxies. In both PEP types, the goal is to shield high-latency or lossy satellite network segments from the rest of the network in a transparent way to the applications. Strictly speaking, *splitting* refers to breaking up a connection and *spoofing* refers to imitating the end point of the TCP connection.

TCP Spoofing

In TCP spoofing, a router (gateway) near the source sends back ACKs for TCP segments to give the source the illusion of a short delay path and therefore speed up the sender's data transmission. It then suppresses the true acknowledgment stream from the satellite host and takes responsibility for sending any missing data. However, unlike a TCP proxy, spoofing is transparent to both the sender and receiver.

TCP Splitting

Split, or cascading, TCP is a scheme in which a TCP connection is divided into multiple TCP connections, with a special connection running over the satellite link. The idea is that the TCP running over the satellite link can be modified, with the knowledge of the satellite's properties, to run faster. Because each TCP connection is terminated, cascading TCP is not vulnerable to asymmetric paths. It works well in cases where applications actively participate in TCP connection management (e.g., Web caching). In other cases, split TCP has the same problems as TCP spoofing.

PEP Mechanisms

PEP mechanisms include ACK spacing, local acknowledgments, local transmissions, tunnels to control routing of packets, header compression, payload compression, and priority-based multiplexing. Many TCP PEPs use TCP ACK manipulation.

Some other PEPs acknowledge TCP segments locally in order to mitigate the effect of long RTT, which speeds up the slow start—the main mechanism used in TCP spoofing. Local negative acknowledgments are also used to trigger local and fast error recovery. Local ACKs are used in PEPs with split connections. When local ACKs are used, and the data are dropped after being acknowledged by the PEP, it is the PEP's responsibility to recover the data. In this case, the PEP has to use local TCP retransmission to the receivers.

Recent TCP Enhancements

Satellite Transport Protocol

STP is a reliable, byte-oriented transport protocol that was designed to perform well over satellite links. The STP sender and receiver use buffer sizes that are of the order of the bandwidth-delay product of the links. STP mechanisms lead to low reverse channel bandwidth usage when losses are rare and to speedy recovery in the event of loss.

WISE

The wireless IP suite enhancer (WISE), which was developed at Lincoln Laboratory, improves the performance of TCP/IP protocol suite in a wireless environment, increasing the wireless link utilization. The WISE approach consists of software that is added to gateways at the periphery of the wireless segment of the network. These software components convert TCP to wireless link protocol (WLP) upon entering the wireless subnetwork and back to TCP upon exiting. WLP is a special transport protocol developed according to the physical characteristics of the wireless link at hand, and addresses the issues faced by TCP over wireless links.

Quick-Start TCP

Quick-start TCP introduces a new mechanism for transport protocols to determine an optional allowed initial congestion window at the start of data transmission. The source indicates its initial desired rate in packets per second by sending a quick-start request option in the IP header of the initial TCP SYN or SYN/ACK packet.

TCP-Peach and Improvements

TCP-Peach is based on the replacement of slow-start and fast recovery algorithms with sudden-start and rapid-recovery procedures, which rely on the introduction of dummy segments to probe the availability of the network resources to improve the network performance when segment losses are a result of link error instead of congestion. Subsequently, TCP-Peach has been improved to TCP-Peach+ for satellite IP networks. TCP-Peach+ includes the following new schemes: jump start and quick recovery, and two classical algorithms, congestion avoidance and fast retransmit. The TCP SACK option is also adopted in TCP-Peach+ to improve the performance when multiple segments are lost from one window of data. Recently, an enhancement to TCP-Peach+, called TCP-Peach++, has been proposed to improve the throughput performance for satellite IP networks with asymmetrical bandwidth and persistent fades. The delayed SACK scheme has been adopted to address the problems caused by bandwidth asymmetrical satellite links. A new protocol procedure, hold state, was developed to address the link outages caused by persistent fades. Performance evaluation shows that TCP-Peach++ effectively addresses these challenges and hence improves the throughput in satellite IP networks (Fang and Akan 2005).

TCP Westwood and Improvements

The key innovation of TCP Westwood (TCPW) is the use of bandwidth estimate to directly drive cwnd and slow-start threshold (ssthresh). The TCP sender continuously monitors ACKs from the receiver and computes its current eligible rate estimate (ERE). ERE is based on the rate of ACKs and their payload. Upon a packet loss indication (3DUPACKs or a time-out), the sender sets the cwnd and ssthresh based on ERE.

TCP-Friendly Congestion Control

Many real-time, less loss-sensitive services and applications that rely on transport protocols (e.g., UDP and RTP) are rapidly spreading over IP networks. This incurs a cohabitation issue: during congestion, TCP flows reduce data rates to release the congestion, but the non-TCP flows continue to send at the original rate. This leads to starvation of TCP traffic or even to a congestion collapse. To avoid such a situation, TCP rate adaptation rules are being defined to make non-TCP applications TCP friendly, thereby leading to a fair distribution of bandwidth.

TPC with Byte Counting and Improvements

This enhancement is designed to counter the effects of delayed ACKs on TCP throughput (RFC 2414, 3465). Delayed ACKs increase the time needed by the TCP sender to increment the congestion window during slow start. Byte counting proposes to increase the congestion window based on the number of transmitted bytes acknowledged by incoming ACKs rather than on the number of ACKs received. In this way, the congestion window is opened according to the amount of data transmitted, rather than the receiver's ACK interval, and throughput may be increased.

TCP for Asymmetric Channels

With asymmetric channel capabilities such as ADSL and DVB increasingly being deployed as high-speed Internet access networks, several mechanisms have been proposed to improve the efficiency of TCP over those channels. These include header compression, reducing the frequency of TCP ACKs, and traffic scheduling optimization.

Scalable TCP

Scalable TCP (S-TCP) is a recent proposal that focuses on modifying the TCP congestion control algorithm in order to improve performance in high-speed backbone networks (Miorandi and Giambene 2005). Like TCP, S-TCP is based on a sliding window mechanism for controlling the transmission rate. It is based on a multiplicative increase, multiplicative decrease (MIMD) algorithm. S-TCP gets its name from the fact that the time it takes to recover from a loss is independent of the congestion window. Similarly, high-speed TCP (HSTCP) has been proposed recently by Floyd for networks with a very large bandwidth-delay product (BDP) such as satellite networks (RFC 3649). The congestion control algorithm of HSTCP can be characterized as an aggressive AIMD behavior. Because both S–TCP and HSTCP are sender-based modification, they can exploit SACK capabilities (RFC 2018), whose use can improve the system performance in the presence of bursty losses in the same window of data.

REFWA

The recursive, explicit, and fair window adjustment (REFWA) scheme is presented as a solution to improve the efficiency and fairness of TCP in NGEO systems. An improvement to the REFWA scheme, REFWA Plus, is also used to combat link errors in satellite environments (Marchese and Jamalipour 2005).

Others

Various other TCP variants and enhancements have been proposed recently: TCP-DCR, proposed in Bhandarkar et al. (2005) introduces a set of simple modifications to the TCP protocol to improve its robustness to channel errors in wireless networks. It is based on the simple idea of allowing the link-level mechanism to recover the packets lost due to channel errors, thereby limiting the response of the transport protocol to primarily congestion losses. TCP-DCR delays responding to a packet loss indication by a small period of time (one RTT) to allow channel errors to be recovered by link-level retransmission. An interesting by-product of using TCP-DCR is the inherent robustness it provides against degradation due to packet re-ordering in the network. Another recent TCP variant proposal, addressing the long RTT issue in heterogeneous networks, is TCP-Hybla (Caini and Firrincieli 2004). In heterogeneous networks, TCP connections that incorporate a terrestrial or satellite radio link are greatly disadvantaged with respect to entirely wired connections because of their longer round-trip times. TCP-Hybla suggests the necessary modifications to remove the performance dependence on RTT. TCP-Hybla was found to be superior in all of the examined cases because it greatly reduces the severe penalization suffered by wireless and satellite connections. In addition to simulation works, Bisio and Marchese (2004) provide an analytical expression for TCP packet loss probability over GEO channels.

Ultimately, the use of basic TCP in future broadband satellite networks will impose significant problems, especially in the case of short transmissions (compared with the channel delay-bandwidth product). For GEO satellite links, the major problem with TCP is the long round-trip time, whereas in the case of NGSO satellite networks, the round-trip delay variation or jitter becomes more dominant. In both situations, the burst-error nature of the satellite channel and the high BER require more sophisticated flow and congestion-control mechanisms that can separate the segment loss because of network congestion or because of high channel error rate.

CONCLUSION

In this chapter, we summarized the satellite communications from a networking point of view in order to observe the role of satellites in future mobile and fixed IP networks. The historical summary provided in the first section of this chapter revealed that despite the high initial investment and maintenance costs of satellite systems, satellites will remain an irreplaceable component of long-distance communications and multimedia broadcasting. In recent years, as a result of the progress in optical communications and the increasing number of transoceanic cables, it may have been mistakenly thought that cable would replace the satellite for long-distance communications. However, the satellite's easy and quick deployment of additional capacity in any part of the world provides a distinct advantage over the deployment of cable systems. Improvement in cable television also could not replace satellite's broadcasting feature, especially due to the satellite's large footprint and simpler deployment.

When it comes to high-speed Internet access to the home, office, ships, aircrafts, and mobile users, again satellite systems show their unique features. The global Internet needs expansion both in the geographical domain and in data-transport capacity. Satellites are the main telecommunications component, if not the only one (in many terrain circumstances), that can promise such expansion. A satellite with huge on-board channel capacity and a large coverage area is sufficient to provide future deployment of new systems. A very handy example is the effort toward the realization of in-flight Internet access and VoIP services to passengers using satellite networks by major airlines and fast trains.

For high-speed Internet access to the home and small office users, currently ADSL and cable modems are the two leading technologies. With the advent of new digital video broadcasting satellite systems in North America and Europe, however, these technologies have had to compete with satellites. The number of subscribers to satellite high-speed Internet access is increasing and growing close to the other two technologies; this number is expected to increase even more rapidly with the introduction of inexpensive satellite receivers in the next few years.

Satellites have made an even larger contribution to IP networks than to individual access. A satellite node can be an intelligent ATM switch or IP router in the sky, interconnecting segments of the backbone networks on Earth. Similar to the conventional usage of satellites in public switched telephony networks, satellites can play important roles in future packet-switched networks, including the public Internet. 3G and B3G wireless networks consider Internet and multimedia traffic to have the dominant share of the network traffic load, and satellites have already shown their role in the completion of any terrestrial mobile network. An example of satellite UMTS was given in this chapter to outline the role of satellites in 3G wireless systems. Satellite ground stations acting as an interworking unit can solve the roaming issue between heterogeneous wired and wireless terrestrial networks, expanding the telecommunications to its ultimate universal stage.

Some important technical implementation issues concerned with a global IP network have been discussed in this chapter. Physical layer, medium access and mobility management, QoS, IP multicast, VoIP, and security issues have been have been discussed with regard to satellite IP networks. All of these issues are current research topics, both in mobile and satellite communications. For the high-latency satellite channel, as well as the error-prone wireless channel (including both satellite and terrestrial), the need for improvement in transport protocols currently employed in the Internet has been discussed, and state-of-the art research activities toward improvement of TCP protocols have been reviewed. Note that researchers are also working to improve the error probability of the wireless channel using forward error correction schemes and sophisticated coding algorithms. Although these works are of great importance to the establishment of a better-quality wireless channel, we should not forget there are always situations in which the wireless signal-to-noise ratio is too low and no coding scheme can improve it. Therefore, a better solution lies in the higher layers of the network, including the transport and network layers, where enhanced flow control algorithms speed up the data rate and the throughput of the wireless channel.

ACKNOWLEDGMENT

This work is supported by the State Planning Organization of Turkey under the Next Generation Satellite Networks Project.

GLOSSARY

2G: Second-generation wireless mobile cellular systems, mainly consisting of global system for mobile communications (GSM) and CDMAOne.

3G: Third-generation wireless mobile cellular systems, mainly consisting of universal mobile telecommunications system (UMTS) and CDMA2000.

B3G: The temporary name for systems under development that are beyond third generation wireless mobile cellular systems; sometimes referred to as fourth generation (4G).

DAB: Digital audio broadcasting; a technique used to transmit high-quality audio signals (e.g., radio) digitally, usually by satellite.

DVB: Digital video broadcasting; a technique used to transmit high-quality video signals (e.g., television) digitally, usually by satellite.

GEO Geostationary Earth orbit; a space orbit at about 36,000 km over Earth at which satellites may be seen from Earth as stationary objects.

Handover: Change that involves switching service from one base station to another one for a mobile user during movement; sometime referred to as handoff.

Heterogeneous Networks: Networks that consist of different types of systems (e.g., cellular, wireless LAN, etc.).

IP: Internet protocol; the main protocol used in the Internet at the network layer (layer 3); currently in version 4 (IPv4) but moving toward implementation of IPv6.

ISL: Intersatellite link; a link between adjacent satellites on an orbit or planes to provide inter-connectivity among satellites usually used in LEO satellite systems.

LEO: Low Earth orbit; a space orbit at about 1000 km over Earth at which a satellite can orbit Earth at high speeds and may be seen from Earth as a fast-moving object.

MAC: Medium access control; the protocol at layer 2 of the network to control and govern network access by multiple users.

MEO: Medium Earth orbit; a space orbit above LEO and below GEO at which a satellite will be seen from Earth as a moving object.

Mobility Management: A set of techniques that controls the movement of a mobile device within a network and is usually composed of two elements: location management and handoff management techniques.

QoS: Quality of service; maintaining the required service condition to a user in a network (e.g., providing a maximum delay or minimum data-rate speed).

Resource Management: A set of management techniques in a network to ensure that available resources—as required by the end terminal application—can be offered between peer end terminals, and how to make sure that resource allocation takes into consideration the current network conditions.

RSVP: Resource reservation protocol; a reservation control mechanism to provide quality of service to users by reserving resources beforehand; usually used in the Internet QoS establishment.

Satellite Communications: A network of spacecraft for providing telecommunications services.

TCP: Transmission control protocol; the vastly used transport protocol for the Internet that provides reliable data transfer among Internet terminals.

UDP: User datagram protocol; the transport protocol for the Internet that provides lower delay compared with TCP—at the expense of lower reliability—and is used for short message transfers or delay-sensitive applications.

VoIP: Voice over IP; a technique to deliver delay-sensitive voice packets over the Internet that can provide lower costs to users.

CROSS-REFERENCES

See *Geosynchronous Fixed Satellite Communications*; *Global Navigation Satellite Systems (GNSS)*; *Land-Mobile Satellite Channel*; *Satellite Communications Basics*.

REFERENCES

Alagöz, F., A. AlRustamani, B. Vojcic, R. Pickholtz, and D. Walters. 2004. Fixed versus adaptive admission control in direct broadcast satellite networks with return links. *IEEE Journal of Selected Areas in Communication* 22(2): 238–50.

Barsocchi, P., N. Celandroni, F. Davoli, E. Ferro, G. Giambene, F. Javier González Castaño, A. Gotta, J. Ignacio Moreno, and P. Todorova. 2005. Radio resource management across multiple protocol layers in satellite networks: A tutorial overview. *International Journal of Satellite Communications and Networking* 23(September/October): 265–305.

Bhandarkar, S., N. E. Sadry, A. L. N. Reddy, and N. H. Vaidya. 2005. TCP-DCR: A novel protocol for tolerating wireless channel errors. *IEEE Transactions on Mobile Computing* 4(5): 517–29.

Bisio, I., and M. Marchese. 2004. Analytical expression and performance evaluation of TCP packet loss probability over geostationary satellite channels. *IEEE Communications Letter* 8(4): 232–34.

Caini, C., and R. Firrincieli. 2004. TCP Hybla: A TCP enhancement for heterogeneous networks. *International Journal of Satellite Communications and Networking* 22(5): 547–66.

Chen, C., and E. Ekici. 2005. A routing protocol for hierarchical LEO/MEO satellite IP networks. *Wireless Networks* 11(4): 507–23.

Cho, S., I. F. Akyildiz, M. D. Bender, and H. Uzunalioglu. 2002. A new connection admission control for spotbeam handover in LEO satellite networks. *Wireless Networks* 8(4): 403–15.

Dash, D., A. Durresi, and R. Jain. 2003. Routing of VoIP traffic in multi-layered satellite networks. In *Proceedings of SPIE Performance and Control of Next-Generation Communications Networks, ITCOMM 2003*, Orlando, Florida, September, pp. 65–75.

Ehsan, N., M. Liu, and Rod Ragland. 2003. Evaluation of performance-enhancing proxies in Internet over satellite. *Wiley International Journal of Communication* 16(6): 513–34.

ETSI-TR-985. 2002. ETSI, Satellite earth stations and systems (SES); Broadband satellite multimedia; IP over satellite. ETSI Technical Report, TR 101 985 V1.1.2.

Fang, J., and Ö. B. Akan. 2005. TCP-Peach++: Enhancement of TCP-Peach+ for satellite IP networks with asymmetrical bandwidth and persistent fades. *LNCS* 3733(October): 145–49.

Giambene, G. 2005. Protocol integration and radio resource management in satellite networks. Proceedings of *IEEE ComSoc-TR Chapter Seminars*, Istanbul, Turkey, October.

Hassan, M., and R. Jain. 2003. *High performance TCP/IP networking*. Upper Saddle River, NJ: Prentice Hall.

Henderson, T. R., and R. H. Katz. 1999. Transport protocols for Internet-compatible satellite networks. *IEEE Journal on Selected Areas in Communications* 17(2): 326–44.

Howarth, M. P., S. Iyengar, Z. Sun, and H. Cruischank. 2004. Dynamics of key management in secure satellite multicast. *IEEE Journal on Selected Areas in Communications* 22(2): 308–19.

Hu, Y., and V. O. K. Li. 2001. Satellite-based Internet: A tutorial. *IEEE Communications* 39(3): 154–62.

Jamalipour, A. 1998. *Low Earth orbital satellites for personal communication networks*. Norwood, MA: Artech House.

———. 2001. Broadband satellite networks—The global IT bridge. Special issue, *Proceedings of the IEEE* 89(1): 88–104.

———. 2002. Satellites in IP networks. In *Wiley encyclopedia of telecommunications and signal processing*, vol. 4, edited by John G. Proakis, 2111–22. New York: John Wiley & Sons.

Jamalipour, A., T. Wada, and T. Yamazato. 2005. A tutorial on multiple access technologies for beyond 3G mobile networks. *IEEE Communications* 43(2): 110–17.

Janssen, J., D. D. Vleeschauwer, G. H. Petit, R. Windey, and J.-M. Leroy. 2002. Delay bounds for voice over IP calls transported over satellite access networks. *Mobile Networks and Applications* 7(1): 79–89.

Karaliopoulos, M., K. Narenthiran, B. Evans, P. Henrio, M. Mazzella, W. de Win, M. Dieudonne, P. Philippopoulos, D.I. Axiotis, I. Andrikopoulos, et al. 2004. Satellite radio interface and radio resource management strategy for the delivery of multicast/broadcast services via an integrated satellite-terrestrial system. *IEEE Communications* 42(9): 108–17.

Korçak, Ö., and F. Alagöz. 2005. Priority-based adaptive shortest path routing for IP over satellite networks. *AIAA Twenty-Third Communications Satellite Systems Conference*, Rome, Italy, September.

Kota, S. L., K. Pahlavan, and P. Leppanen. 2003. *Broadband satellite communications for Internet access*. Cambridge, MA: Springer.

Marchese, M., and A. Jamalipour. 2005. Key technologies and applications of present and future satellite communications. Special issue, *IEEE Wireless Communications* 12(5): 8–9.

Miorandi, D., and G. Giambene. 2005. Performance evaluation of scalable TCP and high-speed TCP over geostationary satellite links. In *Proceedings of IEEE VTC'05 Spring*, Stockholm, May–June 2005, 30(4): 2658–2662.

Mitchell, P. 2003. Effective medium access control for GEO satellites (Ph.D. thesis, University of York).

Nguyen, T., F. Yegenoglu, A. Sciuto, and R. Subbarayan. 2001. Voice over IP service and performance in satellite networks. *IEEE Communications* 39(3): 164–71.

Papapetrou, E., and F. Pavlidou. 2005. An analytic study of Doppler-based handover management in LEO satellite systems. *IEEE Transactions on Aerospace and Electronics* 41(3): 830 – 839.

Partridge, C., and T. J. Shepard. 1997. TCP/IP performance over satellite links. *IEEE Network* 11(5): 61–71.

Priscoli, F. 1999. UMTS architecture for integrating terrestrial and satellite systems. *IEEE Multimedia* 6(4): 38–44.

Rash, J., R. Casasanta, and K. Hogie. 2002. Internet data delivery for future space missions. NASA Earth Science Technology Conference, Pasadena, California, June.

Ronga, L. S., T. Pecorella, E. Del Re, R. Fantacci. 2003. A gateway architecture for IP satellite networks with dynamic resource management and DiffServ QoS provision. *International Journal of Satellite Communications and Networking* 21(4/5): 351–66.

Steele, R., C. C. Lee, and P. Gould. 2001. *GSM, CDMAOne, and 3G systems*. Chichester, UK: John Wiley & Sons.

Sun, Z., M. P. Howarth, H. Cruickshank, S. Iyengar, and L. Claverotte. 2003. Networking issues in IP multicast over satellites. *International Journal of Satellite Communications and Networking* 21(4/5): 489–507.

Tuysuz, A., and F. Alagöz. 2006. Satellite mobility pattern-based handover management algorithm in LEO satellites. Proceedings of *IEEE International Conference on Communications (ICC 2006)*, Istanbul, June.

Werner, M. 1997. A dynamic routing concept for ATM-based satellite personal communication networks. *IEEE Journal on Selected Areas in Communications* 15(8): 1636–48.

Global Navigation Satellite Systems

Omar Al-Bayari and Balqies Sadoun, *Al-Balqa' Applied University, Jordan*

INTRODUCTION

Satellite navigation systems have become an integral part of all applications in which mobility plays an important role (Heinrichs et al. 2005). These functions will be at the heart of the mobile phone third-generation (3G) networks such as the Universal Mobile Telecommunications System (UMTS). In transportation systems, the presence of receivers will become as common as seat belts or airbags, with all car manufacturers equipping their entry-level vehicles with these devices.

As for past developments, GPS launched a variety of techniques, products and, consequently, applications and services. The milestone of satellite navigation is the real-time positioning and time synchronization. For that reason the implementation of wide-area augmentation systems should be highlighted, because they allow significant improvement in accuracy and integrity performance. WAAS, EGNOS, and MSAS provide—over the United States, Europe, and Japan respectively—a useful augmentation to GPS, GLONASS, and Galileo services (Mulassano et al. 2004).

GNSS development has an interesting aspect due to its sensitive nature. Considerable events or developments are always subject to a couple of differentiators: technological developments and political decisions. In all stages of improvements, GPS and GLONASS are strictly related to those differentiators. The approval and startup of the European Galileo program is considered by far the most real innovation. It is intended that the Galileo satellite navigation system will offer improved accuracy, availability, continuity, integrity, and general robustness over the existing GPS system (GALILEO 2003; Feng 2003). Consequently, much rests on current design and development efforts to ensure the intended performance of Galileo and its value added services, particularly for the certified safety services. Technological and political decisions in Galileo substantiate that interoperability and compatibility must be achieved in forthcoming years. Such issues are true GNSS improvement for the benefit of institutions and organizations.

GNSS applications in all fields will play a key role, moving its use from the transportation domain to multimodal use, outdoors and indoors. It is expected that GNSS will increase significantly the precision in position domain (Lachapelle et al. 2002). For the wider community, the combined (and competitive) benefits of GPS and Galileo will result in major improvements in navigation, timing and related applications, and services.

To realize these benefits, a range of Galileo receivers (based on flexible system design principles and equally flexible implementation) must be made available, in time to enable the commercial exploitation and market penetration of the Galileo system and services.

The concept of a reference system for navigation is essential because GNSS and all its applications are related to the coordinate system used. The main application of GNSS is the determination of position in the global reference system any where, any time on the globe in a simple, fast, and cost-effective manner.

The integration of GNSS and other related technologies such as telecommunications (GSM, GPRS, and UMTS), the Geographic Information Systems (GIS), and Inertial Navigation System (INS) has created numerous applications that need more time to be discussed in detail. Many research efforts have been exerted in order to find new applications to promote the quality of our lives through the benefits of GNSS (Lohnert et al. 2001; Al-Bayari and Sadoun 2005).

GNSS COMPONENTS

GNSS consists of three main satellite technologies: GPS, GLONASS, and GALILEO. Each of them consists mainly of three segments: (a) space segment, (b) control segment, and (c) user segment.

These segments are almost identical in the three satellite technologies, which together make up the GNSS. As of today, the complete satellite technology is basically GPS technology and most of the existing worldwide applications are related to GPS technology. The GNSS technology will become clearer after the operation of GALILEO and the reconstruction of GLONASS by the end of 2008.

Global Positioning System

The United States Department of Defense (DoD) has developed the GPS, which is an all-weather, space-based navigation system to meet the needs of U.S. military forces and accurately determine their position, velocity, and time in a common reference system, any where on or near the Earth on a continuous basis (Wooden 1985).

GPS has made a considerable impact on almost all positioning, navigation, timing, and monitoring applications. It provides particularly coded satellite signals that can be processed in a GPS receiver, allowing the receiver to estimate position, velocity, and time (Hofmann-Wellenhof et al. 2001). There are a minimum of four GPS satellite signals that are used to compute positions in three dimensions and the time offset in the receiver clock. GPS comprises three main components:

- Space segment: The space segment of the system consists of the GPS satellites; see Figure 1 below. Space vehicles (SVs) send radio signals from space as shown in Figure 2.
- Control segment: The control segment consists of a system of tracking stations located around the world. The Master Control facility is located at Schriever Air Force Base (formerly Falcon AFB) in Colorado.
- User segment: The GPS user segment consists of the GPS receivers and the user community. GPS receivers convert space vehicle (SV) signals into position, velocity, and time estimates.

The satellites are dispersed in six orbital planes on almost circular orbits with an altitude of about 20,200 km above the surface of the Earth, inclined by 55 degree with respect to the equator and with orbital periods of approximately 11 hours 58 minutes (half a sidereal day).

GPS CONSTELLATION

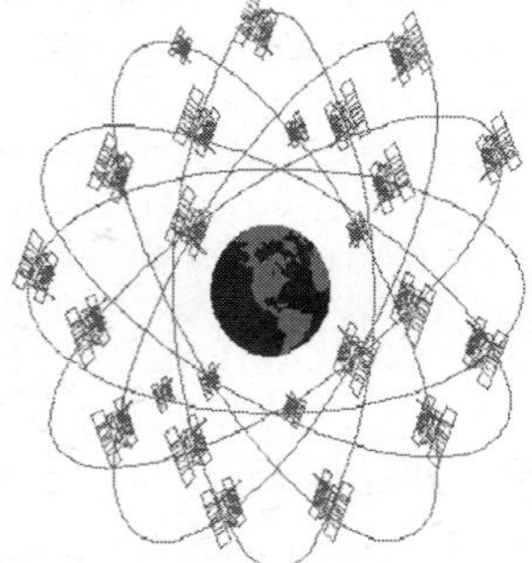

21 SATELLITES WITH 3 OPERATIONAL SPARES
6 ORBITAL PLANES, 55 DEGREE INCLINATIONS
20,200 KILOMETER, 12 HOUR ORBITS

Figure 1: Nominal GPS constellation

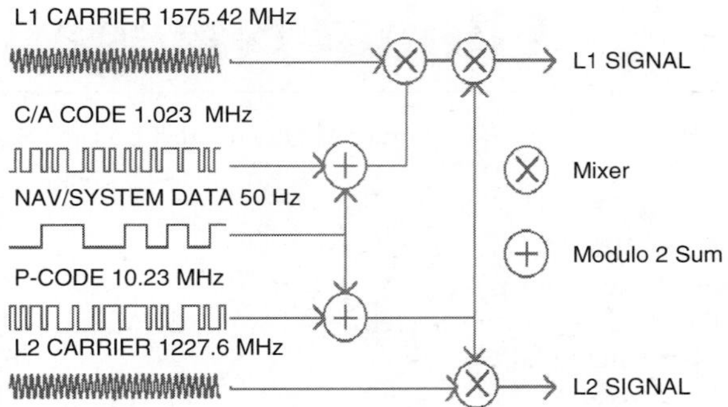

GPS SATELLITE SIGNALS

Figure 2: GPS satellite signals

The categories are Block I, Block II, Block IIR (R for replenishment), and Block IIA (A for advanced) and a further follow-up category Block IIF has also been planned (ICD-GPS, 2003). Figure 3 shows the main GPS segments.

GPS Signals

The generated signals on board the satellites are based on or derived from generation of a fundamental frequency f_o=10.23 MHz (Hofmann-Wellenhof et al. 2001). The signal is controlled by atomic clock and has stability in the range of 10^{-13} over one day. Two carrier signals in the L-band, denoted L1 and L2, are generated by integer multiplications of f_o. The carriers L1 and L2 are biphase modulated by codes to provide satellite clock readings to the receiver and transmit information such as the orbital parameters. The codes consist of a sequence with the states +1 or −1, corresponding to the binary values 0 or 1. The biphase modulation is performed by a 180° shift in the carrier phase whenever a change in the code state occurs; see Figure 4. The clear/access code (C/A-code) and precision code (P-code) are used for the satellite clock reading, both characterized by a pseudorandom noise (PRN) sequence. The W-code is employed to encrypt the P-code to the Y-code when Anti Spoofing (A-S) is applied. The navigation message is modulated using the two carriers (L1 and L2) at a chipping rate of 50 bps.

It contains information about the satellite orbits, orbit perturbations, GPS time, satellite clock, ionospheric parameters, and system status messages (Leick 2003). The modulation of L1 by P-code, C/A-code, and navigation message (D) is done using the quadrature phase shift keying (QPSK) scheme. The C/A-code is placed on the LI carrier with 90° offset from the P-code because they have the same bit transition epochs. For the L1 and L2 we have:

$$L1(t) = a_1P(t)W(t)\cos(2\pi f_1 t) + a_1C/A(t)D(t)\sin(2\pi f_1 t)$$
$$L2(t) = a_2P(t)W(t)\cos(2\pi f_2 t) \tag{1}$$

The signal broadcast by the satellite is a spread spectrum signal, which makes it less prone to jamming. The basic concept of the spread spectrum technique is that the information waveform with small bandwidth is converted by modulating it with a large-bandwidth waveform (Hofmann-Wellenhof et al. 2001).

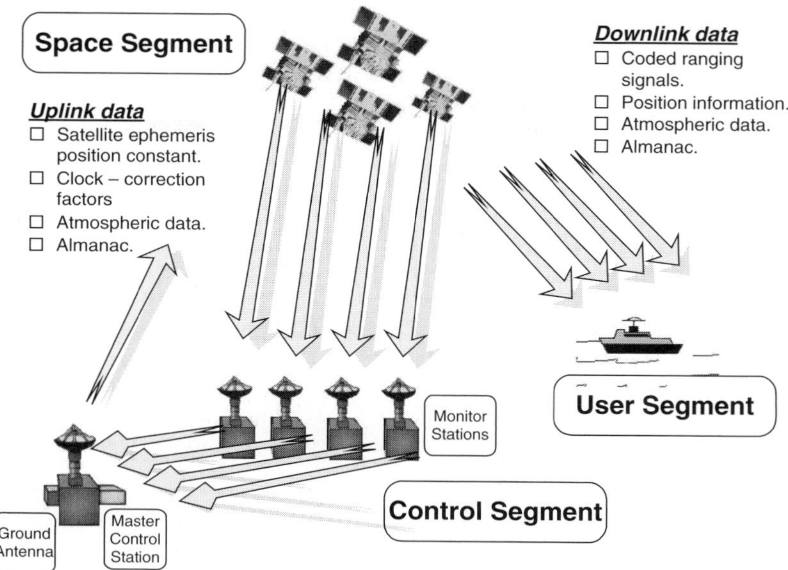

Figure 3: GPS segments (Aerospace Corporation, 2003)

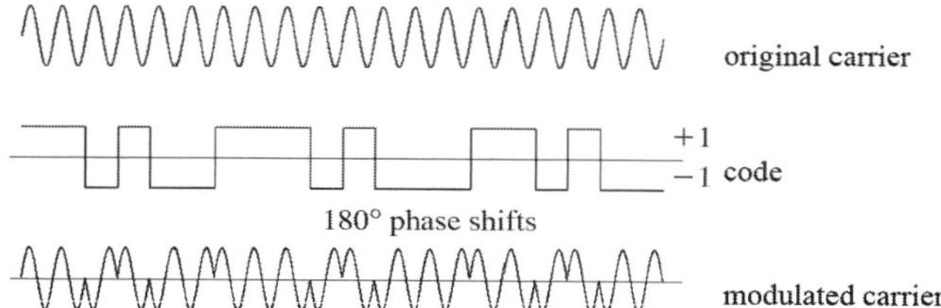

Figure 4: Biphase modulation of carrier

The generation of pseudo random sequence (PRN) in the code is based on the use of an electronic hardware device called tapped feedback shift register (FBSR). This device can generate a large variety of pseudo random codes, but in this way the generated code repeats itself after a very long time. The receiver can distinguish the signals coming from different satellites because the receiving C/A code (the Gold code), has low cross-correlation and is unique for each satellite (Leick 2003). The navigation message consists of 25 frames, with each frame containing 1,500 bit, and each frame is subdivided into 5 sub-frames with 300 bit. The information transmitted by the navigation message is periodically updated by the control segment.

Modernized GPS

Due to the vast civil applications of GPS technology during the past decade or so and due to the new technologies used in satellites and receivers, the U.S. government has decided to extend the capabilities of GPS to provide more benefits to the civil community. In addition to the existing GPS signals, new signals will be transmitted by GPS satellite; see Figure 5. Moreover, this will increase the robustness of the signals and improve resistance to signal interference. This will definitely lead to better quality of service (QoS). The new signals added to the GPS (Fontana et al. 2001), are: (i) a new L5 frequency in an aeronautical radio navigation service (ARNS) band with a signal structure designed to improve aviation applications, (ii) C/A code to L2C carrier (L2 civil signal) and (iii) a new military (M) code on L1 and L2 frequency for DoD applications. It has the potential to track signal even in poor conditions where the C/A code tracking on L1 would not be possible. The new military code will be transmitted from the Block IIR-M and IIF satellites (Betz 2002).

It is well known that the presence of dual frequency measurements (L1 and L2) has good advantages for eliminating the effect of the ionosphere and enhancing the ambiguity resolution, especially for the high-precision measurements (Liu and Lachapelle 2002). High-end civil dual frequency systems will be based on L1 CA-code and the newly designed L2 C-code. In the coming few years, the receivers will become more complex in order to allow tracking the new civil code on L2 and tracking the encrypted P on L2 (A-S).

The frequency of L5 is 1,176.45MHz, with a chipping rate of 10.23 MHz similar to P- code. The high chipping rate

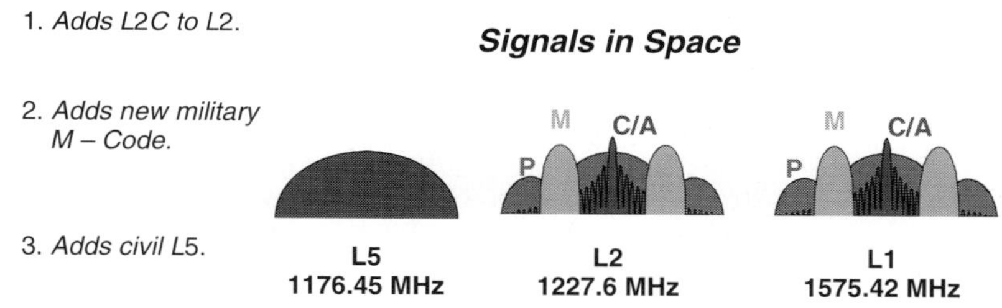

Figure 5: Modernized GPS signals

of L5 code will provide high performance ranging capabilities and better code measurement than L1 C/A code measurements (Dierendonck and Hegarty 2000).

L2 has better correlation protection with respect to L1 because it has a long code. This will be useful in severe conditions where the GPS signals are weak, such as navigation in urban, indoor, and forested areas.

The old codes and the new codes (military and civil), on the L1, L2, and L5 need more advanced modulation so as to better share existing frequency allocations with all signals by increasing spectral separation, and hence conserve the spectrum. Consequently, the binary offset carrier (BOC) is used for the military code modulations (Betz 2002).

GLONASS

The GLONASS (GLObal NAvigation Satellite System or "GLObalnaya NAvigatsionnaya Sputnikovaya Sistema") is nearly identical to GPS. The GLONASS satellite-based radio-navigation system provides positioning and timing information to users. It is operated by the Ministry of Defense of the Russian Federation (GLONASS-ICD, 2002).

The GLONASS space segment consists of 24 satellites, equally distributed in 3 orbits separated by 120° in the equatorial plane. Satellite orbital altitude is about 19,130 km above the ground surface. This results in an orbital period of 11:15:44, corresponding to 8/17 of a sidereal day.

The future of GLONASS seems uncertain due to economic problems facing the Russian Federation. The number of operational satellites was steadily decreasing over the past few years. The launch of three new GLONASS satellites in December 1998 was the first launch after a lapse of 3 years.

The Signals of the GLONASS Satellites

GLONASS satellites transmit C/A-code on L1, and P-code on L1 and L2. GLONASS observables (code and phase) are similar to GPS. The main difference between GPS and GLONASS is that GLONASS uses Frequency Division Multiple Access (FDMA) technology to discriminate among the signals of different satellites, but GPS and GALILEO use Code Division Multiple Access (CDMA) to distinguish among the satellites. All GLONASS satellites transmit the same C/A- and P-codes, but each satellite has slightly different carrier frequencies.

The nominal carrier frequencies for the L1and L2 signals may be written as shown below (Leick 2003):

$$f_1^n = 1602 + 0.5625\,.\,n \text{ MHz}$$
$$f_2^n = 1246 + 0.4375\,.\,n \text{ MHz}$$
with
$$\frac{f_1^n}{f_2^n} = \frac{9}{7}$$

where n is the frequency channel number $1 \leq n \leq 24$, covering a frequency range in L1 from 1602.5625MHz to 1615.5MHz. Because some of the GLONASS frequencies interfere with frequencies used for radio-astronomy, some changes in the frequency plan are expected after 2005 (GLONASS-ICD 2002). The navigation message is contained in the so-called sub frames, which have duration of 2.5 minutes. Each sub frame consists of five frames with a duration of 30 seconds. The navigation message contains information, similar to GPS navigation message, about the satellite orbits and their clocks, among others.

In contrast to GPS, where the broadcast ephemeredes are defined by modified Keplerian elements, the broadcast ephemeredes of GLONASS satellites are defined by positions and velocities referred to as Earth-centered and Earth-fixed systems (PZ-90). The broadcast ephemeredes of the GLONASS satellites are updated every 30 minutes.

Modernized GLONASS

According to Russian officials, the GLONASS system will be restored by 2008. The second generation GLONASS-M was launched at the end of 2004, and launch of the third generation GLONASS-K satellites is planned for 2007/2008.

As of April 2006, a total of 12 GLONASS satellites are operational with 2 GLONASS-M.

The important advantage of GLONASS-M is the ability to broadcast the civil L2 signal that can be treated as an analog of L2C GPS signal. The structure of the new signal is the same as the structure of GLONASS C/A L1 signal. Unlike GPS, GLONASS does not encrypt its P-code signals; thus, today civil receivers can use GLONASS P-code "free of charge."

GLONASS-K will have extended lifetime of 10 years, and will be capable of broadcasting L3 civil signal, on which integrity information for safety-of-life applications is available.

GALILEO

GALILEO is Europe's initiative for a state-of-the-art global navigation satellite system, providing a highly accurate, guaranteed global positioning service under civilian control. GALILEO will not be too different from the other GNSS parts, modernized GPS, and GLONASS (Salgado et al. 2001). GALILEO will provide autonomous navigation and positioning services, but at the same time will be interoperable with the two other global satellite navigation systems; the GPS and GLONASS. A user will be able to take a position with the same receiver from any of the satellites in any combination. By providing dual frequencies as standard, however, GALILEO will deliver real-time positioning accuracy down to the meter range. It will guarantee availability of the service under all but the most extreme circumstances, and will inform users within seconds of the failure of any satellite. This will make it appropriate for applications where safety is vital, such as running trains, guiding cars, and landing aircraft. The combined use of GALILEO and other GNSS systems can offer much-improved performance for all kinds of users worldwide. GALILEO is expected to be in operation by the year 2008. The first satellite of the GALILEO system (GIOVE A) was launched on December 27, 2005.

GALILEO segments

GALILEO segments are similar to GPS, but with some modification. The main extension of GALILEO, compared to GPS, is the implementation of a global/regional segment for integrity monitoring. The objective is to improve the safety of critical aircraft navigation, as well as locate and guide railway trains (GALILEO 2003).

Space Segment. The space segment or the constellation features consists of 30 Medium Earth Orbiting (MEO) satellites (27 and 3 active spare satellite), distributed evenly and regularly over three orbit planes. The projected altitude is slightly larger than for GPS 23,616 km and the inclination is 56 degrees (Benedicto and Ludwig 2002).

Ground Segment. The GALILEO ground segment is responsible for managing the constellation of navigation satellites, controlling core functions of the navigation mission such as orbit determination of satellites and clock synchronization, and determining and disseminating (via the MEO satellites) integrity information, such as the warning alerts within time-to-alarm requirements, at global level. The global ground segment will also provide interfaces with service centers. The Ground Control Segment will consist of about 12 to 15 reference stations, 5 up-link stations, and 2 control centers. The ground segment also will include 16 to 20 monitor stations, 3 up-link stations for integrity data, and 2 central stations for integrity computations.

User Segment. The user segment consists of different types of user receivers, with various capabilities related to the different GALILEO signals, in order to fulfill the various GALILEO services; see Figure 6.

GALILEO Signals

The GALILEO frequency should respect and adhere to the radio-regulations discussed and agreed upon at the International Telecommunications Union (ITU) forums, such as the World Radio-Communication Conference (WRC). Various studies were conducted before determination of the Galileo signal allocations in order to avoid interference with GPS and Glonass systems, which operate in the same portion of the RF spectrum (Hein et al. 2003).

Galileo will provide several navigation signals in right-hand circular polarization (RHCP) in the frequency ranges of 1164–1215 MHz (E5a and E5b), 1260–1300 MHz (E6) and 1559–1592 MHz (E2-L1-E1) that are part of the Radio Navigation Satellite Service (RNSS) allocation (Hein et al. 2003, GALILEO-ICD 2006). All GALILEO satellites will share the same nominal frequency, making use of code division multiple access (CDMA) techniques. GALILEO will use a different modulation scheme for its signals, the binary offset carrier (BOC), alternate BOC (AltBOC) and quadrature phase shift keying (QPSK). AltBOC modulation scheme is based on the standard BOC modulation.

Definition of Services

The GALILEO constellation offers the capability of globally broadcasting a set of six signals supporting the open, commercial, safety-of-life, and public regulated services (Hein et al. 2003). Each navigation signal is composed of one or two ranging codes and navigation data as well as, depending on the signal, integrity, commercial, and search and rescue (SAR) data. Satellite-to-user distance measurements based on ranging codes and data are used in the GALILEO user receivers to fulfill the different GALILEO services (GALILEO 2003). The main services are:

1. Open service (OS) data: These are transmitted on the E5a, E5b, and E2-L1-E1 carrier frequencies. OS data are available to all users and consist mainly of the navigation and SAR data. Open service offers positioning,

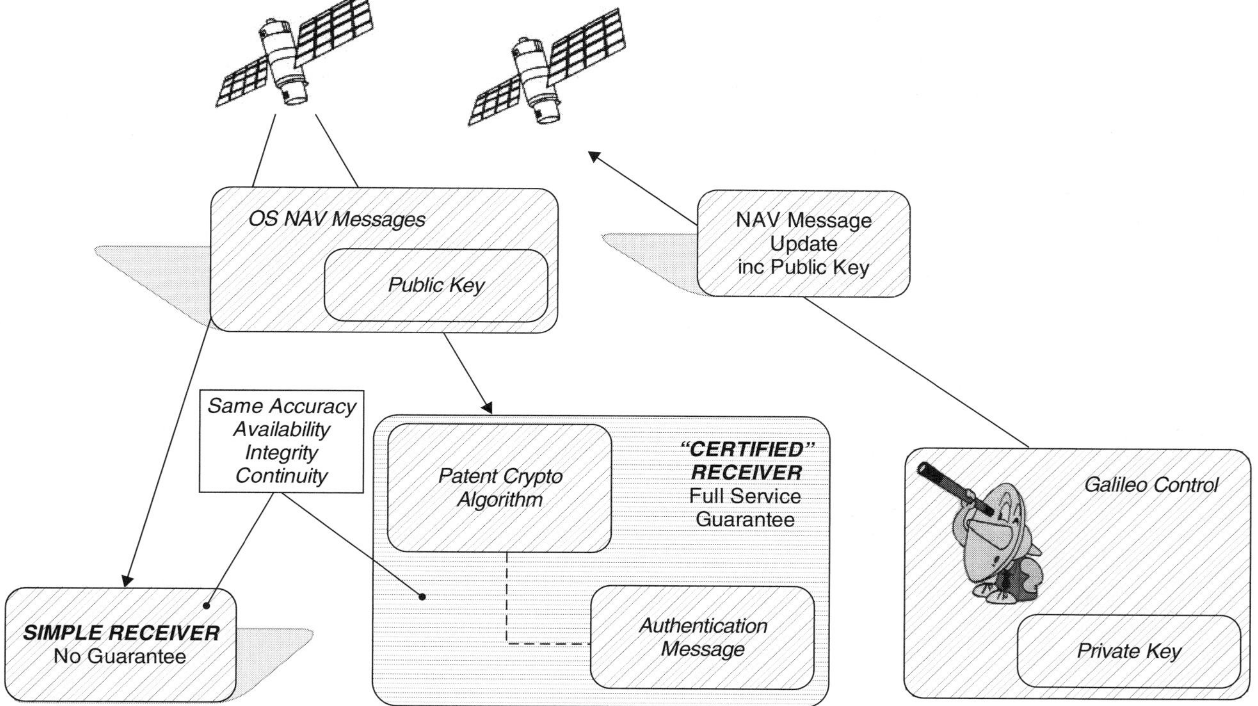

Figure 6: GALILEO system architecture (GALILEO 2003)

navigation and timing signals, which can be accessed free of charge.

2. Commercial Service (CS), data: These are transmitted on the E5b, E6, and E2-L1-E1 carriers. All CS data are encrypted and provided by service providers that interface with the Galileo Control Centre. Access to those commercial data is provided directly to the users by the service providers. The signal is designed to support very precise local differential applications (Sub-meter accuracy) using the open (option encrypted) signal overlaid with the Public Regulated Service (PRS) signal on E6, as well as to support the integration of GALILEO positioning applications and wireless communications networks.
3. Safety-of-life Services (SOL) data: These include mainly integrity and Signal in Space Accuracy (SISA) data. Combination of this Galileo services either with the current GPS as augmented by EGNOS corrections, or the future improved GPS and EGNOS integrity-only. Particularly, SOL is based on the satellite navigation signals without using added elements such as WAAS, and EGNOS. The accuracy required is about 4 meters over the globe. This could be possible by introducing the ionospheric model based on multiple frequency measurements and modeling the other GNSS errors.
4. Public Regulated Service (PRS) data: These are transmitted on E6 and L1 carrier frequencies. The Public Regulated Service is provided on dedicated frequencies to provide the capability for greater continuity of service placed under EU Governments' control for Public applications devoted to European and/or National Security, such as police, civil protection, law enforcement, civil protection (such as some emergency services) as well as other governmental activities. The PRS is robust in order to be resistant to interference, jamming, and other accidental or malicious aggressions.

GNSS SIGNALS

The signals of Modernized GPS, GALILEO, and GLONASS systems make up the GNSS signals (Table 1). Each satellite system has specific signal characteristics, but each system attempts to be compatible with the others in order to prevent the interferences and attenuation between the signals. It is important to consider that the processing of all signals should be performed using the same receiver; thus a complex receiver design is supposed to be designed and built. As mentioned above, the GNSS frequency plan will respect the radio-regulations as they are discussed and agreed upon on at ITU forums. The available spectrum which can be used for the development of Radio-Navigation Satellite Systems (RNSS) is shown in Figure 7.

On the 20th to 22nd of March 2006, (Galileo-ICD 2006), the GPS-Galileo Working Group on Radio Frequency

Table 1: GNSS Signals

System	Signal	Modulation type	Chip rate Mcps	Frequency MHz
GPS	L1	BPSK	1.023	1575.42
	L2	BPSK	1.023	1227.6
	L5	QPSK	10.23	1176.45
GLONASS	L1	BPSK	0.511	1602.5625 – 1615.5
	L2	BPSK	5.110	1246.4375 – 1256.5
GALILEO	E1	BOC	1.023	1575.42
	E5	AltBOC	10.23	1191.795
	E6	BPSK	5.115	1278.75

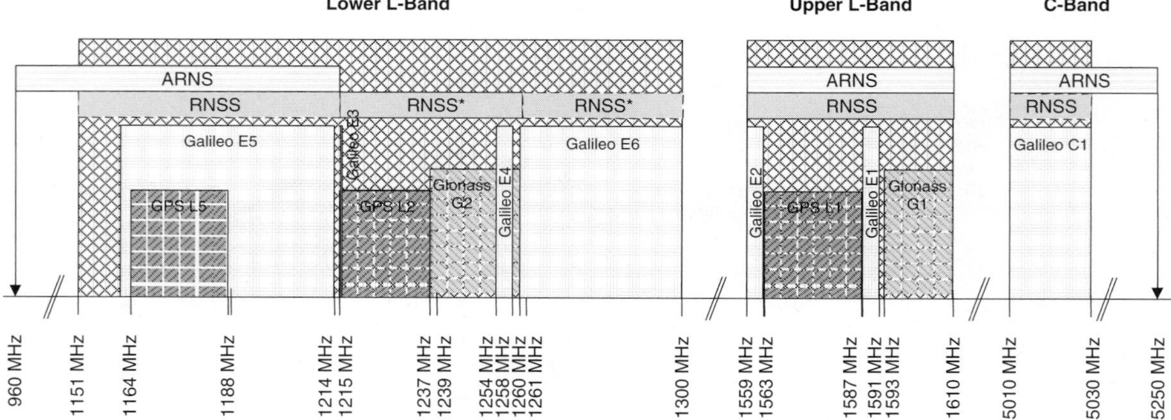

Figure 7: Radio-Navigation Satellite Systems (RNSS) frequency spectrum defined for GNSS signals (GALILEO 2005)

Compatibility and Interoperability successfully proposed a jointly-optimized common Power Spectral Density for Galileo Open Service (OS) and GPS L1C signals in L1 band, denoted as Modified Binary Offset Carrier (MBOC) in Stockholm, Sweden.

SIGNAL PROCESSING AND RECEIVER DESIGN

The main function of the signal processor in the receiver is the reconstruction of the carriers and extraction of codes and navigation messages. After this stage, the receiver performs the Doppler shift measurement by comparing the received signal to a reference signal generated by the receiver. Due to the motion of the satellite, the received signal is Doppler shifted.

The code ranges are determined in the delay lock loop (DLL) by using code correlation. The correlation technique provides all components of bimodulated signals. The correlation technique is performed between the generated reference signal and the received one (Hofmann-Wellenhof et al. 2001). The signals are shifted with respect to time so that they are optimally matched based on mathematical correlation.

Currently some geodetic type receivers are available on the market that track GPS and Glonass satellites simultaneously on both frequencies, in particular the Ashtech Z18 receiver and the TPS (Topcon Positioning Systems) Legacy receivers. The future GNSS receiver could be designed to track the different GNSS signals and could be of many types including:

- The first type could process all GNSS signals GPS L1, L2, L5, and GALILEO OS, CS using L1, E5, and E6 as well as GLONASS L1 and L2.
- The second type uses free signal and codes, GPS L1 and L2C and GALILEO OS, on L1 and E5.
- The third type uses L1 and E5.
- The fourth type uses GPS L1 and L2, which are already on the market (Ries et al. 2002).
- The fifth type uses GPS and GLONASS signals, which already exist (Leick 2003).

The most common receiver types are Intermediate Frequency receiver (IF) and the software defined radio receiver (SDR). In the RF front-end receiver, the signal is down converted to an intermediate frequency and then sampled, but SDR uses direct digitization, or bandpass sampling. (Details on GNSS receiver design can be found in Schmid et al. 2004, and in Julien et al. 2004a).

The main components of the RF-FE combined GNSS receiver are shown in Figure 8. After sampling and analog-to-digital conversion (ADC) of the received signal, the receiver performs parallel de-spreading. The received base-band signal is multiplied in parallel with the spreading codes of all visible satellites. The received signal of each satellite is multiplied in parallel with different code delay offsets. These products are then accumulated to compute the cross-correlation function.

Because BOC signals are used in GALILEO, supplementary measures are necessary due to the multiple correlation peaks of the auto-correlation function. Carrier tracking is performed using a phase-locked or frequency-locked loop (PLL or FLL). Coherent correlation combined with differential or non-coherent correlation can be done for the pilot and the data channel (Schmid et al. 2004). Multiple signals will be available at L1 within the next few years (Hein et al. 2004). Galileo will use a different modulation scheme, such as BOC and QPSK, for its signals, while GPS uses binary phase shift keying (BPSK) modulation for the open signals at L1 and L2. The L5 signal that will appear with the Block IIF satellites in 2006 will have quadrature phase shift keying (QPSK).

The binary offset carrier (BOC) modulation scheme of Galileo provides better multipath and receiver noise performance compared to the GPS binary phase shift keying (BPSK) modulation. More complex techniques are already developed for tracking BOC signal, such as bump jump and BPSK-like.

SYSTEMS COMPARISONS

Precise positioning using GNSS technology is limited by the availability of satellite signals in specific locations. With GALILEO satellites added to the current GPS and GLONASS systems, users will have the possibility of tracking a large number of the total of 75 available satellites. This will give users the ability to access instantaneous precise positioning potentially everywhere in the world on a 24/7 basis, provided their receiver units can track all the GPS-GLONASS-GALILEO signals. Table 2 summarizes the characteristics of three GNSS systems.

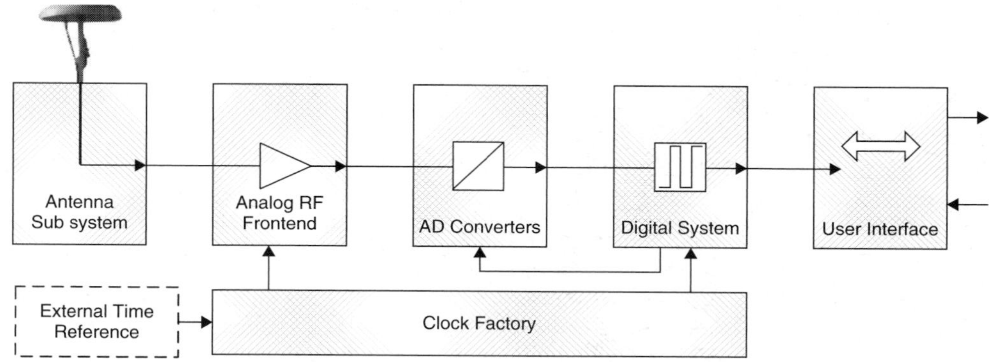

Figure 8: Hybrid GALILEO/GPS receiver concept

Table 2: Comparison of the GLONASS, GPS and GALILEO GNSS Systems

System	GLONASS	GPS	GALILEO
Nominal number of satellites	24	24	30
Design and operated by	Ministry of Defense of the Russian Federation (Military control)	DoD, USA (Military control)	ESA, (civil control) Multi-national (EU, China, India, etc.)
Operational satellites (April 2006)	12	30	1
Modernized and updated (expected full operation)	2008-2010	2004-2012	2008-2010
Orbital planes	3 (separated by120°)	6 (separated by 60°)	3 (separated by120°)
Satellites per orbital plane	8 (equally spaced)	4 (unequally spaced)	10 (equally spaced)
Orbital radius	25510 km	26560 km	29601km
Inclination of orbital planes	64.8	55	56
Revolution period	11 h 16 min	11 h 58min	14 h 5min
Satellite Laser Ranging (SLR) reflectors	All satellites	Two satellites	All satellites
Signal separation technique	FDMA	CDMA	CDMA
Reference system	PZ-90	WGS-84	GTRF
Time reference	UTC (SU)	UTC (USNO)	GST

Systems Combination

The combined use of GPS and GLONASS were not taken into account in the original design of both systems. During the first few years of the 1990s, it had become clear that the GPS+GLONASS receiver might provide advantages over a solo (GPS-only or GLONASS-only) receiver provided interoperability issues could be resolved. However, GALILEO is in a more advantageous position with respect to GPS and GLONASS because many issues related to interoperability with existing navigation systems have been taken into consideration in initial design by forming *the GPS-Galileo Working Group*. The most important issues related to using the three systems in one GNSS receiver are:

- determination of transformation parameters among the three reference coordinate systems WGS-84, PZ-90, and GTRF;
- computing the time offset between GPS, GLONASS, and GALILEO system times;
- leap seconds in GLONASS and GALILEO;
- hardware biases among GPS, GALILEO, and GLONASS channels;

At present (2007), we can say that all of those issues have been resolved to a sufficient degree for practical needs for GPS+GLONASS and have already been taken into consideration for GPS+GLONASS+GALILEO.

The advantages of the combined GPS/GLONASS/GALILEO (GNSS) in the GNSS system are summarized in the following points:

- ability to work under environments with limited visibility of satellites;
- fast OTF ambiguity resolution;
- through GNSS receivers, elimination of periods of time when total number of current GPS satellites may not be sufficient for reliable positioning at a given location;
- more robust detection and exclusion of anomalies;
- improved estimation of tropospheric and ionospheric parameters;
- reduction of time required for collecting static data.

The use of GLONASS and GALILEO can provide additional advantages when working in high latitudes (Alaska, Canada, Scandinavia, etc.) because of the higher inclination of GLONASS orbits in comparison with GPS orbits. Due to the work at different frequencies, GLONASS is also more resistant to interference and jamming.

GALILEO and Military Systems

GALILEO is specifically designed for civil and commercial purposes, and it has some differences from the other two military systems GPS and GLONASS:

- increased accuracy, service guarantees, certification, and liability of the service operator and guaranteed accuracy to one meter for some applications

- traceability of past performance and operation transparency
- increased availability of signals in demanding environments.
- superior reliability because it has an integrity message which immediately informs the user of errors that may occur.
- Coverage of difficult areas such as Northern Europe.

Integrity Problems

Integrity is defined as "the ability of a system to provide timely warnings to users when the system should not be used for navigation." GPS and GLONASS cannot provide such warnings. This can only be accomplished by augmentation systems such as DGPS reference networks. GALILEO, on the other hand, will be able to provide integrity information to its users, provided they are willing to pay for it. But integrity and availability requirements of GNSS have some limitations due to physics. The two major problems are power budget and masking. The power budget issue is due to economic and strategic reasons; the satellite signals are weak and consequently vulnerable to interference (Willigen 2003). The masking problem issue is due to use of 1-1.50GHz frequencies for navigation satellites, which cause buildings, foliage, and mountains to easily shield the signals.

REFERENCE SYSTEMS

Coordinate System

The definition of a reference coordinate system is crucial for the description of satellite motion, the modeling of observable and the interpretation of results. The reference coordinate system in satellite geodesy is global and geocentric by nature because satellite motion refers to the center of mass of the Earth (Seeber 2003; Hofmann-Wellenhof et al. 2001).

In satellite geodesy, two reference systems are required: (a) space-fixed, inertial reference system for the description of satellite motion and (b) Earth-fixed, terrestrial reference system for the positions of the observation stations and for the description of results from satellite geodesy.

Positioning using GNSS depends mainly on knowing the satellite coordinates. The position of the receiver is calculated with respect to the position of the satellite. If the range vector relation between satellite and receiver is considered, the coordinates of the satellite and receiver should be expressed in the same coordinate system.

In satellite geodesy, the two systems are used and the transformation parameters between the space-fixed and Earth-fixed coordinate systems are well known and used directly in the GNSS receiver and post-processing software to compute the position of the receivers in the Earth-fixed system.

The terrestrial reference system is defined by convention with three axes, where Z-axis coincides with the Earth's rotation axis as defined by the Conventional International Origin (CIO). The X-axis is associated with the mean Greenwich meridian, and the Y-axis is orthogonal to both Z and X axes and it completes the right-handed coordinate system; see Figure 9. An example of the terrestrial reference system is the WGS84. GPS has used the WGS84 as a reference system (Leick 2003), and with WGS84, associated a geocentric equipotential ellipsoid of revolution. The basic idea in geodesy behind using the reference ellipsoids is that they fit the real shape of the Earth.

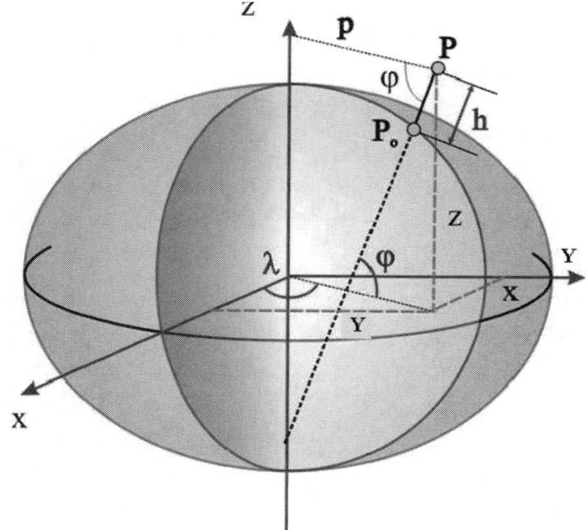

Figure 9: ECEF coordinate system and ellipsoidal coordinates

Another example of use of the terrestrial reference frame is the International Terrestrial Reference Frame (ITRF), which is established by Central Bureau of the International Earth Rotation Service (IERS). The ITRF is regularly updated and is more accurate than WGS84, but the difference between WGS84 and ITRF is now on the order of a few centimeters. This difference is mainly due to the difference between the reference stations used by each system when it is realized. Both systems are geocentric and the transformation parameters between them are regularly published by IERS.

The representation of position in geocentric Cartesian coordinates (X, Y, and Z) has less significance in navigation. Hence, the ellipsoidal representation (longitude, latitude, and height above the ellipsoid) are more commonly used for coordinate representation.

The relation between Cartesian coordinate (X, Y, Z) and ellipsoidal coordinates (φ, λ, *and* h) is expressed using the following formulas:

$$\begin{aligned} X &= (N+h)\cos\varphi\cos\lambda \\ Y &= (N+h)\cos\varphi\sin\lambda \\ Z &= (\frac{b^2}{a^2}N+h)\sin\varphi \end{aligned} \tag{2}$$

where N is the radius of curvature in prime vertical and is obtained by the following expression:

$$N = \frac{a^2}{\sqrt{a^2\cos^2\varphi + b^2\sin^2\varphi}}, \tag{3}$$

Here, *a and b* are the semi axes of the ellipsoid. The Cartesian coordinate of WGS84 is also called the ECEF (Earth Centered Earth-Fixed) coordinate system.

As mentioned above, the realization of the reference frame depends on the coordinates of ground reference stations. The Galileo Terrestrial Reference Frame (GTRF) is expected to be similar to ITRF, but will be based on the coordinates of the GALILEO ground stations. The differences between WGS84, ITRF, and the GTRF are expected to be on the order of a few centimeters. The two coordinate systems are compatible, and the accuracy obtained is good enough for most of the applications, including navigation. For highly precise measurements and for centimetric accuracy among the various systems, the transformation parameters are expected to be published by geodetic service providers such as IERS. GLONASS uses the PZ90 as a reference coordinate system, which is basically an ECEF system. The transformation parameters between PZ90 and WGS84 are published by IERS (Leick 2003).

It is interesting to note that there are many local best fitting (non-geocentric) ellipsoids used in the world. These ellipsoids are oriented and constrained by some astronomical measurements to be used as a local datum for better fitting a particular portion of the Earth. Examples of these include European datum 1950 (ED-50), which is the international ellipsoid 1924, and North American Datum 1927 (NAD-27), which is a Clarke ellipsoid. The center of the local ellipsoid doesn't coincide with true center of the Earth. Generally the distances or the vectors between the geocentric ellipsoid such as WGS84 and the local ellipsoids are well known to be used in the transformation between the local datum and the global geocentric one.

Time Reference Frame

There are many time reference systems used and they are based on various periodic processes, such as the Earth's rotation. The major types of these systems are shown in Table 3. The conversion between time systems is accomplished with well-known formulas. In GNSS (e.g., GPS), the atomic time system serves as a reference instead of the dynamic time system itself.

The GLONASS satellite clock is moved according to UTC (SU). The Galileo System Time (GST) will be a continuous coordinate time scale steered toward the International Atomic Time (ITA) with an offset of less then 33 nanoseconds. The GST limits, expressed as a time offset relative to ITA, should be 50 nanoseconds for 95 percent of the time over any yearly time interval. The difference between GST and ITA, and between GST and UTC, shall be broadcast to the users using the signal-in-space of each GALILEO service. The GALILEO ground segment will monitor the offset of the GST with respect to the GPS system time and eventually broadcast the offset to users.

OBSERVATION TECHNIQUES

The basic concept of GNSS is to measure the signal traveling time between artificial satellite and receiver. By multiplying this time by the light velocity (c), we get the range between the satellite and the receiver (Hofmann-Wellenhof et al. 2001; Leick 2003); see Figure 10:

$$Range = c.(t_R - t^S) = \Delta t_R^S \cdot c \qquad (4)$$

The time or phase measurement performed by the receiver is based on comparison between the signal received by the receiver's antenna and the reference signal generated by the receiver. The two signals are affected by the clock's errors. Therefore, the range measured is not true and it is called pseudorange. Because the signal travels through the atmospheric layers, further noise should be modeled in order to compute the precise range.

Table 3: Time Systems (Hofmann-Wellenhof et al. 2001)

Periodic process	Time system	Abbreviation
Earth rotation	Universal Time	UT
Earth revolution	Terrestrial Dynamic Time	TDT
Atomic oscillation	International Atomic Time	ITA
	UT coordinated	UTC
	GPS Time	

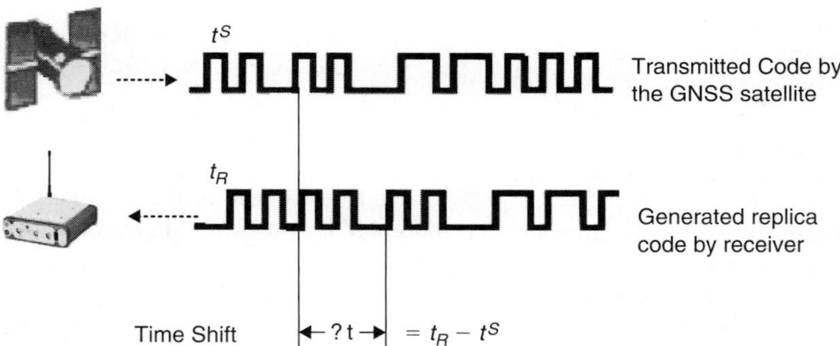

Figure 10: Basic concept of range measurement

Code Pseudorange Measurements

Code correlation technique is used to measure the time difference between the received and generated replica code. The range can be formulated as follows:

$$R_R^S = c \cdot \left[(t_{R(GNSS)} - \delta_R) - (t^{S(GNSS)} - \delta^S) \right] \quad (5)$$

where δ^S is the satellite clock offset δ^S and δ_R is the receiver clock offset δ_R. A high stability atomic clock is generally used on board the satellite, so δ^S is small and could be modeled by a polynomial with the coefficients being transmitted in the navigation message. However, the receiver clock offset δ_R is large and is treated as an unknown to be estimated in the function:

$$R_R^S = c \cdot \Delta t_{GNSS} + c \cdot (\delta^S - \delta_R) = \rho + c \cdot \Delta\delta \quad (6)$$

where ρ is the true distance between satellite and receiver and its expressed by the vector in a reference geocentric coordinate system:

$$\rho = \sqrt{(X^S - X_R)^2 + (Y^S - Y_R)^2 + (Z^S - Z_R)^2} \quad (7)$$

Phase Pseudorange Measurements

Phase pseudo range is based on the measurements of phase difference between the received and generated signal $\Delta\varphi_R^S$ at the receiver. The received carrier is Doppler shifted due to the motion of satellite (Hofmann-Wellenhof et al. 2001).

In order to calculate the range using phase measurement, we have to add to $\Delta\varphi_R^S$ the number of cycles between the satellite and the receiver, which is an ambiguous value and is often called ambiguity (N). With consideration of the initial phase errors of the satellite and receiver due to their clocks, the mathematical model of phase pseudo range can be expressed by:

$$\Delta\varphi_R^S + N = -\frac{f}{c} \cdot \rho - f\delta^S + f\delta_R \quad (8)$$

If we rearrange the above equation and use $\Phi = -\Delta\varphi_R^S$ and $\Delta\delta = \delta^S - \delta_R$, it becomes similar to the code pseudorange equation, but with the additional the ambiguity value (N):

$$\lambda \cdot \Phi = \rho + c \cdot \Delta\delta + \lambda \cdot N \quad (9)$$

where λ is the wave length.

GNSS Observable Errors

The code and phase measurements are affected by noise and errors due to the propagation of signals through atmospheric layers and due to the noise measurements. These errors can described briefly as below:

1. Satellite clock error: This can be modeled by the polynomial coefficients transmitted in the navigation message with respect to a reference time (e.g., GPS).

$$\delta^S = a_0 + a_1(t - t_0) + a_2(t - t_0)^2 \quad (10)$$

2. Orbital error: This can be eliminated by differential positioning. Precise orbits could be obtained in near real time via Internet from services centers such as International GNSS Service (IGS).
3. Ionospheric error: This error is modeled or eliminated by using the linear combination of two or multiple frequencies (Julien et al. 2004b). The relation between the ionospheric refraction has an effect on the future GNSS (L5, L2, and L1 for GPS; E5a, E5b, and E1 for GALILEO). We can write:

$$\begin{aligned} \lambda_1 \cdot \Phi_1 &= \rho + c \cdot \Delta\delta + \lambda_1 \cdot N - I_{L1} \\ \lambda_2 \cdot \Phi_2 &= \rho + c \cdot \Delta\delta + \lambda_2 \cdot N - \frac{f_1^2}{f_2^2} I_{L1} \\ \lambda_3 \cdot \Phi_3 &= \rho + c \cdot \Delta\delta + \lambda_3 \cdot N - \frac{f_1^2}{f_3^2} I_{L1} \\ &\textit{where, Ionosphere} = I_{L1} \end{aligned} \quad (11)$$

The effect of ionosphere on GNSS measurement is of special interest in solving the ambiguity number N (Liu and Lachapelle 2002). Having multiple frequencies can give more advantages for ionosphere models to estimate the first and second order effect of the ionosphere. Moreover, it allows more possibilities in the ambiguity-resolution process (Zhang et al. 2003). The ionosphere could also be modeled using the ionospheric coefficient transmitted by the navigation message.
4. The troposphere: This consists of two layers: the wet layer (up to 10 km above the surface of ground), and the dry layer from 10 to 40 km above the ground. The troposphere causes a delay in both the code and carrier observations. Because the troposphere is not frequency dependent, it cannot be canceled out by using dual frequency measurements, but it can, however, be successfully modeled. Tropospheric models depend on empirical models that consider all values of temperature, pressure, relative humidity, and mapping function. Examples of such models are the Hopfield and Saastamoninen models.
5. Receiver clock error: This is due to using a non-precise clock in the receiver (e.g., a quartz clock), which causes offset and drift in the receiver clock and GNSS reference time. This error is treated as unknown in the pseudorange computations. The clock receiver error could be eliminated in double difference equations as shown in the following section.
6. Multipath: This is caused by multiple reflections of the signals at the receiver or at the satellite due to multiple paths taken by the signal to arrive at the destination. The best way to reduce the multipath phenomenon is to choose a site away from a reflection surface (such as buildings, cars, trees, etc.), and by appropriate antenna design. Carrier phases are less affected by multipath propagation than code ranges, because multipath is frequency dependent. The multipath error could reach to a one meter level. The elimination of multipath is

possible by selecting an antenna that takes advantages of the signal polarization.

GNSS Positioning Techniques

There are two main types of positioning techniques in GNSS measurements: single-point positioning and differential positioning.

Single-Point Positioning

The basic concept of point position depends on the trilateration between the receiver and satellite. Range measurements from four satellites are needed to determine the four unknowns, X, Y, Z, and receiver clock offset ($\Delta\delta$). The analytical solution for receiver A and four satellites could be written as below:

$$\begin{aligned}
R_A^1(t) &= \sqrt{\left(X^1(t)-X_A\right)^2+\left(Y^1(t)-Y_A\right)^2+\left(Z^1(t)-Z_A\right)^2}+c\cdot\Delta\delta \\
R_A^2(t) &= \sqrt{\left(X^2(t)-X_A\right)^2+\left(Y^2(t)-Y_A\right)^2+\left(Z^2(t)-Z_A\right)^2}+c\cdot\Delta\delta \\
R_A^2(t) &= \sqrt{\left(X^3(t)-X_A\right)^2+\left(Y^3(t)-Y_A\right)^2+\left(Z^3(t)-Z_A\right)^2}+c\cdot\Delta\delta \\
R_A^4(t) &= \sqrt{\left(X^4(t)-X_A\right)^4+\left(Y^4(t)-Y_A\right)^2+\left(Z^4(t)-Z_A\right)^2}+c\cdot\Delta\delta
\end{aligned} \tag{12}$$

Generally, linearization in respect to the approximate position of the receiver is needed to resolve such a model, where the range R is measured by the receiver and the coordinate of the satellite is extracted from the navigation message. The unknowns in the above equation are X, Y, Z, and the clock error $\Delta\delta$. In the case of observing more than four satellites, the least square adjustment is performed to estimate the unknowns.

Hence, coordinates of the receiver and time offset could be obtained directly in real time with one epoch measurement. Geometric information could be obtained from the equation model as PDOP, which indicates the quality of the solution with respect to satellite geometry. Bad satellite distribution gives a large PDOP. Due to unmodeled errors in pseudo range such as ionosphere, troposphere, and orbital errors, the accuracy level of absolute positioning is within 10 meters.

Observable Difference

By considering all the systematic and random errors on the observation, we can write the math model for observable difference for code and phase measurements, respectively, as below:

$$R_A^1(t_0)=\rho_A^1(t_0)+\Delta\rho_A^1(t_0)+c\delta^1(t_0)-c\delta_A(t_0)+I_A+T_A+\varepsilon \tag{13}$$

$$\begin{aligned}\lambda\phi_A^1(t_0)=\rho_A^1(t_0)+\Delta\rho_A^1(t_0)+\lambda N_A^1+c\delta^1(t_0)\\ -c\delta_A(t_0)-I_A+T_A+\varepsilon\end{aligned} \tag{14}$$

Where $\Delta\rho_R^S$ is the orbital error, I is the ionosphere error, T is the troposphere error, and ε is the other types of noise and errors such as the ones due to multipath propagation.

Using two receivers A and B and satellite (1), we can perform Single Differences (SD). In SD the orbital error and satellite clock error are cancelled. By using two receivers and two satellites (1, 2), we can perform Double Differences (DD). In DD the clock receiver error is cancelled. By using two receivers, two satellites, and two consequent epochs, we can perform Triple Differences (TD). In TD the ambiguity is cancelled.

$$\begin{aligned}
SD &= \lambda\phi_{AB}^1(t)=\lambda\phi_B^1(t)-\lambda\phi_A^1(t)=\rho_{AB}^1(t)+\lambda N_{AB}^1-c\delta_{AB}(t_0)\\
DD &= \phi_{AB}^{12}(t)=\frac{1}{\lambda}\rho_{AB}^{12}(t)+N_{AB}^{12}\\
TD &= \phi_{AB}^{12}(t_{12})=\frac{1}{\lambda}\rho_{AB}^{12}(t_{12})
\end{aligned} \tag{15}$$

As we see, most of systematic errors are cancelled or reduced by using the observable differences. Consequently, the accuracy of position computation will be improved after eliminating or reducing these biases. The solution obtained in DD with ambiguity can provide precision to the centimetric level.

Differential Position

There is increased interest in differential positioning due to the numerous advantages of wireless communications and networks. Most of errors that affect GNSS are common between the receivers, which observe the same set of satellites (Leick 2003; Hofmann-Wellenhof et al. 2001). Thus, making differential measurement between two or more receivers could cause most of these errors to be cancelled.

The basic concept of differential position is the calculation of position correction or range correction at the reference receiver and then sending this correction to the other receiver via radio link. In this way, most of the errors are cancelled; see Figure 11. The transmitted correction could be of several types: the position or pseudo range correction, the carrier smoothed pseudo range correction, and the carrier phase correction. The mathematical model of

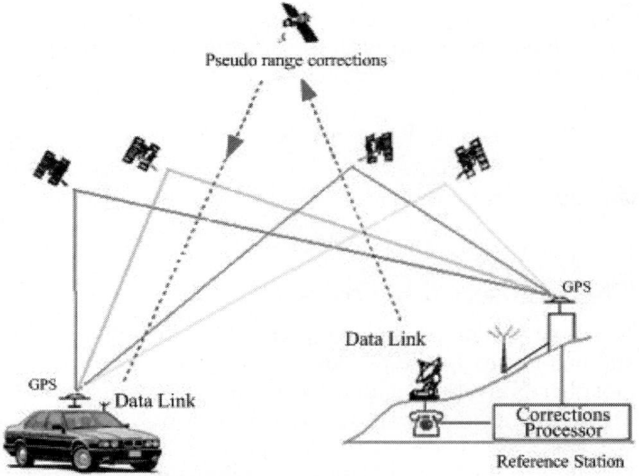

Figure 11: Differential correction

DGNSS could be written as shown below. Two receivers are used, where receiver A is installed at known reference station and B is rover/moving receiver. Pseudo range at A is given by:

$$R_A^1(t_0) = \rho_A^1(t_0) + \Delta\rho_A^1(t_0) + c\delta^1(t_0) - c\delta_A(t_0) \quad (16)$$

$$\begin{aligned} PRC^1(t_0) &= -R_A^1(t_0) + \rho_A^1(t_0) \\ &= -\Delta\rho_A^1(t_0) - c\delta^1(t_0) + c\delta_A(t_0) \end{aligned} \quad (17)$$

We have to add the range rate correction for an arbitrary epoch (t).

$$PRC^1(t) = PRC^1(t_0) + RRC^1(t_0)(t - t_0) \quad (18)$$

where $(t - t_0)$, is called the latency due to transmission time between the reference and the rover receiver. The pseudo range at receiver B can be written as:

$$R_B^1(t) = \rho_B^1(t) + \Delta\rho_B^1(t) + c\delta^1(t) - c\delta_B(t) \quad (19)$$

By adding the pseudo range from reference station, we obtain:

$$\begin{aligned} R_B^1(t)_{corr} &= R_B^1(t) + PRC^1(t) \\ &= \rho_B^1(t) + (\Delta\rho_B^1(t) - \Delta\rho_A^1(t)) - (c\delta_B(t) - c\delta_A(t)) \end{aligned} \quad (20)$$

$$R_B^1(t)_{corr} = \rho_B^1(t) - c\Delta\delta_{AB}(t) \quad (21)$$

As we see, the orbital error is cancelled and the satellite clock error is eliminated. We can also transmit the phase correction to the rover receiver. In this case, we have to add another unknown; the ambiguity N, to the equations. If the same procedure as above is applied, the phase range correction between the reference and the rover receiver will be given by:

$$\lambda\phi_B^1(t)_{corr} = \rho_B^1(t) + \lambda\Delta N_{AB}^1 - c\Delta\delta_{AB}(t) \quad (22)$$

DGNSS with phase range correction is used for most precision Real-Time Kinematics (RTK). But the ambiguity should be resolved or fixed by using the On The Fly (OTF) techniques. In phase measurement technique, the precision obtained will be at the centimeter level. Modeling the ionosphere and troposphere will eliminate or reduce the errors in DGNSS. This method gives more possibilities of obtaining high accuracy in point positioning using one receiver.

Wide Area Differential GNSS (WADGNSS)

WADGNSS is a scheme that would allow the user to perform differential positioning and obtain reliable position with high accuracy in real time over a sizeable region. WADGNSS consists of a master control station and a number of local or global monitor stations and communication links. The monitor stations gather the data from GNSS satellite, and then send them to the master control station. The master control estimates the ionosphere parameter, troposphere parameters, satellite ephemeredes, and clock errors. All these corrections are transmitted to the user via the Internet, wireless communications, or satellite communications.

Depending on the distribution of the reference monitor stations and the accuracy of error modeling and communication capabilities, the accuracy of the rover receiver could be in the range of 1 to 3m. Centimeteric accuracy could be achieved by receiving phase correction and ambiguity fixing such as the RTK and Virtual Reference Station (VRS). Programs are already developed to send the GNSS corrections to the user to obtain higher accuracy. As mentioned above, transmitting a phase correction with error models for ambiguity fixing will give centimetric precision for the rover receiver. Wireless communications and the Internet have offered us new possibilities to apply real-time positioning to obtain centimetric precision using one receiver (Leick 2003).

The mathematical model of WADGNSS can be written by adding all the errors affecting the satellite signals as follows:

$$\begin{aligned} \lambda\phi_A^1(t_0) = \rho_A^1(t_0) + \Delta\rho_A^1(t_0) + \lambda N_A^1 + c\delta^1(t_0) \\ -c\delta_A(t_0) - I_A + T_A \end{aligned} \quad (23)$$

The most common Satellite-Based Augmentation System (SBAS) programs used in WADGNSS are WAAS, EGNOS, and MSAS (WAAS 2002; GALILEO 2003)

Wide Area Augmentation System (*WAAS*)

Wide Area Augmentation System (WAAS) is a new augmentation to the United States Department of Defense's (DoD) Global Positioning System (GPS) that is designed to enhance the integrity and accuracy of the basic GPS capability.

The WAAS uses geo-stationary satellites to receive data measured from many ground stations, and it sends information to GPS users for position correction. Because WAAS satellites are of the geo-stationary type, the Doppler frequency caused by their motion is very small. Thus, the signal transmitted by the WAAS can be used to calibrate the sampling frequency in a GPS receiver. The WAAS signal frequency is 1575.42 MHz. The WAAS services will be available on both L1 and L5.

GNSS-1: EGNOS

The European Geostationary Navigation Overlay Service (EGNOS) is being developed by European Space Agency (ESA) for the Safety of Air Navigation (Eurocontrol). EGNOS will complement the GNSS systems. It consists of three transponders installed in geostationary satellites and a ground network of 34 positioning stations and four control centers, all interconnected. EGNOS, like WAAS, broadcasts the differential corrections to the GNSS users through geo-stationary satellites in the European region and beyond.

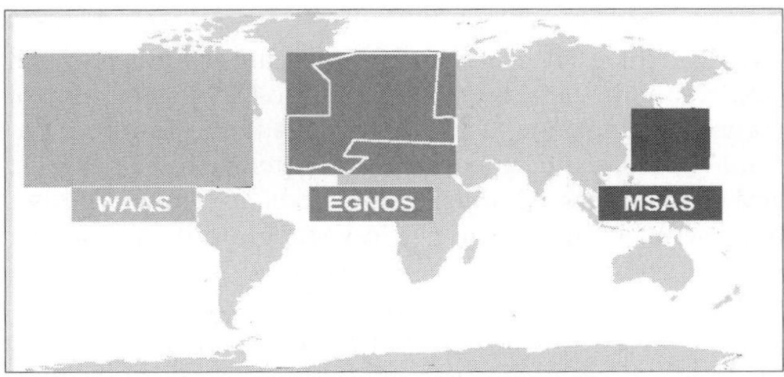

Figure 12: Footprint of global deferential corrections services of GNSS: U.S. (WAAS), E. U. (EGNOS), and the Japanese (MSAS)

MSAS

Like the WAAS and EGNOS, the Japanese MTSAT Satellite-Based Augmentation System (MSAS) is used to send the differential correction for GNSS users; see Figure 12.

WIRELESS SYSTEMS AND GNSS APPLICATIONS

Wireless communication and network systems offer a new line of GNSS applications by sending the differential position corrections to the GNSS users. Other applications forced GNSS to be integrated with wireless communications, such as the third generation (3G) wireless mobile networks for RTK network (VRS). Other applications are also integrated with GIS and wireless communications such as LBS applications (emergency call and AVL).

On the other hand, GNSS is used in digital communication networks to meet the requirement for precision timing synchronization and position information. Increased timing accuracy provides overall improvement in system performance in terms of quality and efficiency. The telecommunications infrastructure uses the GNSS signal as an integral and basic part of the system.

GNSS could improve the communication capacity of networks, especially for the UMTS third-generation using Code Division Multiple Access (CDMA) techniques. A precise time-synchronization of the different base stations (the UMTS emitter-antennas) can significantly increase the traffic capability of the system.

Timing and Synchronization

Characteristics of good telecommunications service include being continuous and transmitting information (transmission packet) with a low error rate and noise. Such a good performance can be accomplished by using precise timing and efficient synchronization mechanisms. GNSS technology is frequently used for this purpose because the GNSS chip (actually GPS chip), has a low cost and the timing information can be obtained easily from one satellite with high stability characteristics. All the clocks installed in the nodes of wireless networks should match or trace the Synchronization Standard established by The American National Standards Institute (ANSI) for performance of a primary reference source as $1x10^{-11}$. The GNSS chip is relatively inexpensive. Naturally interference or jamming of GNSS signal could affect the timing synchronization in the telecommunications network, which consequently degrades telecommunications services (Omar and Rizos 2003).

GNSS and Wireless Networks

There are many types of wireless networks, cellular networks, Wireless Local Area Networks (WLAN), and multi-hop wireless networks for providing Internet services and control systems (Nicopolitidis et al. 2003). GNSS technology is not widely used in wireless networks for positioning of information because most protocols and algorithms in wireless networks do not use position information in their operations, even though it is very advantageous for many applications such as providing Internet services for mobile users (cars, trains., etc.) (Jain et al. 2001).

Geographical Routing Algorithm (GRA) is generally used in wireless networks for packet destinations between nodes when good knowledge of network topology is not available. Using GNSS for location information and time synchronization will help to optimize packets' routes to the destination between the nodes in the ad hoc wireless network and increase the efficiency of services by selecting the closest nodes (shortest path).

RTK Networks

The RTK network concept is similar to the Wide Area DGNSS, but the reference stations are generally distributed over a regional area and the network control center is responsible for transmitting the phase measurement correction to the GNSS user (rover receiver). Mobile wireless networks (GSM, GPRS, EDGE, CDMA2000, and UMTS) are generally used in this type of application due to the need for duplex communication where the rover receiver should initially send the approximate position to the network processing center. The network processing center computes VRS observations and sends them to the user (Euler 2005); see Figure 13. This scheme is commonly used in many systems worldwide due to its economic and precision advantages. The number of reference stations in the single RTK approach is 30 stations in 10,000 km^2; however, through the use of the RTK network, the reference stations could be reduced to five stations in the 10,000 km^2 area.

Location Based Service (LBS)

Location Based Services (LBSs) provide personalized services to subscribers based on their current positions. LBSs employ accurate, real-time positioning to connect users to nearby points of interest. LBS advises them of current conditions such as traffic and weather, or provides routing and tracking information, all via wireless devices.

The location of the caller is generally determined by various position determination techniques. These include Cell-ID, Enhanced Observed Time Difference (E-OTD), Observed Timed Difference of Arrival (OTDOA), Wireless Assisted GNSS (A-GNSS) and hybrid technologies (combining A-GNSS with other standard technologies).

Positioning techniques based on the use of a GNSS or cellular network infrastructure itself is growing rapidly

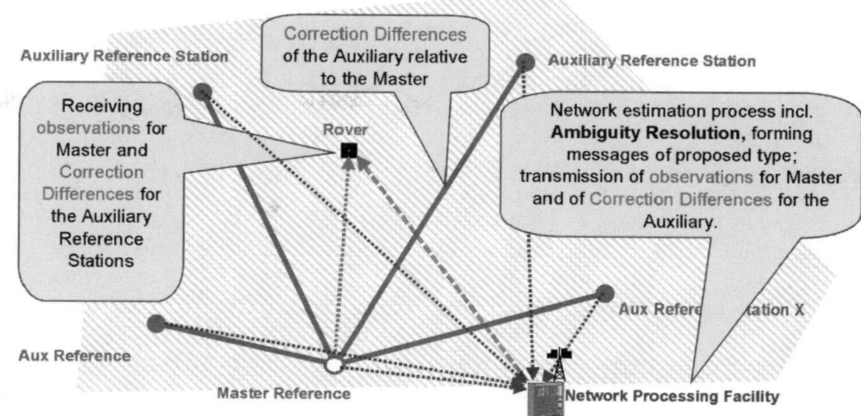

Figure 13: RTK network (Euler 2005)

in the mobile-telephone community. There are many LBS projects that already based on the combination of wireless communications (e.g., GMTS), satellite navigation (GNSS), and geographic information systems (GIS). Some of these projects are based on the Mobile Client / Server architecture (Lohnert et al., 2001).

GNSS receiver is mainly responsible for position determination, and precise time and velocity in the coordinate reference system, and then saving these data in the National Marine Electronics Association (NMEA) format to be transmitted to the control center via wireless communication or downloaded directly via serial ports such as RS-232, USB 2.0, etc.

LBS Applications

The LBS applications and needs can be divided into four main areas:

1. **Information and navigation services:** These services provide data directly to end-users, in particular destination location and criteria for trip optimization. Automobile manufacturers are offering moving map displays guided by navigation GNSS (currently GPS) receivers as an option on new vehicles. In some cases, the displays can be removed and taken into the home to plan a trip. Many rental car companies have GPS-equipped vehicles that give directions to drivers on display screens and through synthesized voice instructions. Also, some companies (such as Navtique and Tele Atlas) are specialized in preparing the maps and voice guidance for navigation systems used in vehicles.
2. **Emergency assistance:** This type of service provides the location of mobile users in case of distress and need for assistance such as: E-911 in the United States and E-112 in Europe. GIS capabilities are essential in such services.
3. **Tracking services:** In general, an AVL system consists of a GNSS receiver integrated with a GSM/GPRS module mounted on the vehicle, a communication link between the vehicle and the dispatcher, and PC-based tracking software for dispatching (Figure 14) (Al-Bayari and Sadoun 2005). Vehicle tracking is one of the fastest-growing GNSS applications today. GPS-equipped fleet vehicles, public transportation systems,

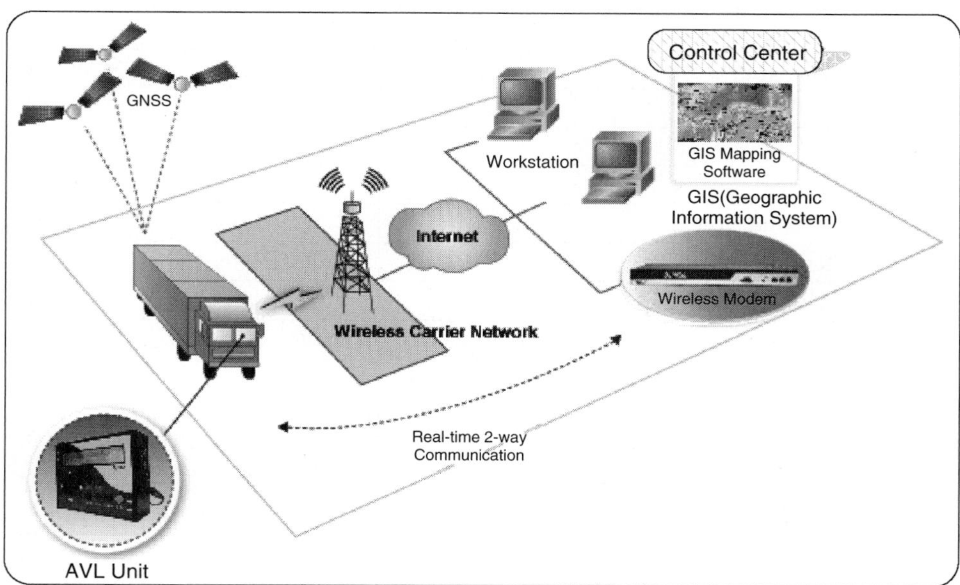

Figure 14: AVL system components

delivery trucks, and courier services use GNSS receivers to monitor their locations at all times. The principal benefit of AVL system in fleet management is the opportunity for increasing and improving the efficiency use of human and environmental resources in effective manners. Transportation infrastructure represents one of the largest and most critical investments by any country. Movement of people and goods is vital to every aspect of the country's economy. GIS- and AVL-based asset management for road and railway transportation systems can greatly improve the efficiency of operations (optimizing services, costs, and fleet usage), while at the same time, can make significant contributions to safety, including responses to natural and man-made disasters.

4. **Network related services:** Here knowledge of user's position improves communication services. Location can be achieved by integrating a GNSS receiver in the mobile phone (handheld solution) or by using the communication network itself.

LBS techniques based on GSM, GPRS, and WCDMA (Wideband Code Division Multiple Access) networks alone don't offer high accuracy. Moreover, GNSS alone is insufficient to maintain continuous positioning due to the inevitable difficulties caused by obstacles. When GNSS signals are blocked or lost, the precision of positioning will be minimized to unacceptable level. Hence, it is necessary to improve the accuracy and reliability of GNSS position.

The accuracy of position determination could be improved by Differential GNSS (DGNSS), Dead Reckoning (DR), indoor GNSS, or integrating GNSS with the above mentioned schemes such as Cell-ID (Hybrid location technology).

NMEA Format

The National Marine Electronics Association is a U.S. standards body that defines message structure, content, and protocols to allow electronic equipment installed in ships and boats to communicate with each other. GPS receivers can be configured to output various types of messages in the "NMEA format." Most computer programs that provide real-time position information understand and expect data to be in NMEA format. This data includes the complete PVT (position, velocity, time) solution computed by the GPS receiver. The idea of NMEA is to send a line of data called a sentence that is totally self-contained and independent from other sentences. There are standard sentences for each device category and there is also the ability to define proprietary sentences for use by the individual company. All of the standard sentences have a two-letter prefix that defines the device that uses that sentence type. For GPS receivers the prefix is GP), which is followed by a three-letter sequence that defines the sentence contents such as GP-RMC (GPS- Recommended Minimum Specific GPS Data). In addition, NMEA permits hardware manufacturers to define their own proprietary sentences for whatever purpose they see fit. All proprietary sentences begin with the letter P and are followed with three letters that identify the manufacturer controlling that sentence. For example a Garmin sentence would start with PGRM and Magellan would begin with PMGN. There are various versions of NMEA format (NMEA 0180, 0182, 0183).

There are many sentences in the NMEA-0183 Standard Input/Output messages protocol for all kinds of devices that may be used in a marine environment (Baddeley 2003). Some of the ones with applicability to GPS receivers are listed below: (all message start with GP.) The most important NMEA sentences include the GGA, which

Table 4: GPRMC Description

Name	Example	Units	Description
Message ID	$GPRMC		RMC protocol header
UTC (time)	101841	hhmmss.sss	Universal Time Coordinate
Status	A		A=data valid or V data not valid
Latitude	3216.4838	ddmm.mmmm	
N/S Indicator	N		N=north or S=south
Longitude	03613.9412	dddmm.mmmm	
E/W	E		E=east or W=west
Speed Over Ground	001.1	knots	
Course Over Ground	015.7	degrees	True
Date	070203	ddmmyy	
Magnetic Variation		degrees	E=east or W=west
Checksum	*10		
			End of message termination

provides the current Fix data; the RMC, which provides the minimum GPS sentences information; and the GSA, which provides the Satellite status data.

- GGA Global positioning system fixed data
- GLL Geographic position – latitude/longitude
- GSA GNSS DOP and active satellites
- GSV GNSS satellites in view
- RMC Recommended minimum specific GNSS data
- VTG Course over ground and ground speed

Each sentence has a specific record description; see Table 4. The following format is a RMC data (*RMC – **Recommended Minimum Specific GNSS Data***):

```
GPRMC,101841,A,3216.4838,N,03613.9412,E,001
.1,015.7,070203,003.5,E,A*1D,33843
```

CONCLUSION

Global Navigation Satellite Systems (GNSS) technology has become vital to many applications that range from city planning, engineering and zoning, to military applications. It has been widely accepted by all governments and organizations worldwide. That is why very soon we expect to have at least three GNSS systems: the USA GPS, European GALILEO, and the Russian GLONASS systems. There is a multibillion dollar investment in this field and intensive worldwide research activities. The impressive progress in wireless communications and networks has played a great role in increasing interest in GNSS and providing enabling methodologies and mechanisms. It is expected that all 3G and future generations of cellular phones will be equipped with GNSS chips.

GNSS technology dominates outdoor navigation, which provides accuracy to from the range of few meters to 10 m in single point positioning technique or from submeter to a few meter level in differential GNSS technique (DGNSS). Various techniques have recently been developed for indoor positioning. They offer either absolute or relative positioning capabilities with acceptable precision (Hightower and Borriello 2001). Combining these technologies with GNSS allows us to provide a more reliable and robust location solution. The most common implementation of hybrid technology for GSM, GPRS, and WCDMA is to combine A-GNSS with Cell-ID.

GLOSSARY

Ambiguity: Integer bias term; the initial bias in a carrier-phase observation of an arbitrary number of cycles. The unknown number of whole wavelengths of the carrier signal between a satellite and receiver at the beginning of tracking.

Antispoofing (AS): This is the mechanism of encrypting the P-code by W-code to produce a new Y-code, to prevent replication by potentially hostile forces.

Automatic Vehicle Location (AVL): This is the scheme that uses a navigation system, such as GPS, to find out a vehicle's position.

Differential GPS (DGPS): A technique to minimize error in GPS-derived positions by using extra data from a reference GPS receiver at a known location, to enhance the accuracy of measurements made by other GPS receivers within the same general geographic area.

Doppler Shift: The phenomenon caused when the signal transmitter and receiver are moving relative to one another. In such a situation, the frequency of the received signal will not be the same as that of the source. When the signal transmitter and receiver are moving toward each other, the frequency of the received signal is higher than that of the source, and when they are moving away form each other, the frequency becomes lower.

Earth Centered, Earth Fixed (ECEF): This is a Cartesian coordinate system that starts at the Earth's center of mass. The Z-axis is associated with the Earth's mean spin axis. The X-axis is aligned with the zero Meridian. The Y-axis is 90 degrees west of the X-axis, making up a right-handed coordinate system.

Ellipsoid: A mathematical demonstration of the Earth as an ellipse that is turned around its minor axis. This is usually used as a reference surface for geodetic surveying and navigation applications.

Geostationary Satellites: Types of popular satellite systems that are usually launched at an orbit of about 35,863 km from the surface of the Earth at the equator. At such orbit the rotational period of the Earth is equal to that of the satellite.

GNSS (Global Navigation Satellite System): A global navigation satellite system, which is made up a network of satellites that transmit ranging signals used for positioning and navigation anywhere around the globe as well as in the air or at sea. Examples of such systems include the famous and oldest U.S. Global Positioning System (GPS), the Russian GLObal NAvigation Satellite System (GLONASS), and the upcoming European GALILEO system.

Location Based Services (LBS): A term used for the technique that establishes the location of caller by using various positioning schemes.

Ionosphere: The portion of the Earth's external atmosphere where ionization caused by incoming solar radiation changes the propagation of radio waves. The ionosphere extends from about 70 kilometers to 1000 kilometers above the Earth's surface.

On-the-Fly (OTF): A term used to characterize a scheme that resolves differential carrier-phase integer ambiguities without the need to have a GPS receiver stationary at any time

Pseudorange: This refers to the calculated range from the GNSS receiver to the satellite found by taking the difference between the measured satellite transmit time and the receiver time of measurement, and multiplying by the speed of light.

Real-Time Kinematic (RTK): This refers to a DGNSS process in which carrier-phase corrections are sent in real-time from a reference receiver at a known location to one or more remote rover/mobile receivers.

Satellite-Based Augmentation System (SBAS): A geo-stationary satellite system that enhances the accuracy, integrity, and availability of the basic GNSS signals. Examples of such systems include WAAS, EGNOS, and MSAS.

CROSS REFERENCES

See *Geosynchronous Fixed Satellite Communications*; *Land-Mobile Satellite Channel*; *Satellite Communications Basics*; *Satellites in IP Networks*.

REFERENCES

Al-Bayari, O. and B. Sadoun. 2005. New centralized automatic vehicle location communications software system under GIS environment. *International Journal of Communication Systems*, 18(9): 833–46.

Aerospace Corporation. 2003. GPS primer: A student guide to the Global Positioning System. Los Angeles. Available at: http://www.aero.org/education/primers/gps/GPS-Primer.pdf (access date 12/2005).

Baddeley G. 2003. http://home.pacific.net.au/~gnb/gps/nmea.html, http://www.nmea.org

Benedicto J., and D. Ludwig. 2002. GALILEO system architecture and services. Available at http://www.estec.esa.nl/conferences/01C14/papers/3.1.doc.

Betz, J. W. 2002. Binary offset carrier modulation for radio navigation. *Navigation*, 48(4): 227–46.

Dierendonck, A. J. and C. Hegarty. 2000. The new L5 Civil GPS Signal. *GPS World*, 11: 64–71.

Euler, H. J. 2005. Reference station network information distribution, IAG Working Group 4.5.1: Network RTK. Available at http://www.network-rtk.info/euler/euler.html.

Feng, Y. 2003. Combined Galileo and GPS: A technical perspective. *Journal of Global Positioning Systems*, 2(1): 67–72.

Fontana, R., W. Cheung, P. Novak, and T. Stansell. 2001. The new L2 Civil Signal, *Proceedings of U.S. Institute of Navigation* (Salt Lake City, UT, Sept. 11–14), pp. 617–31.

GALILEO (2003). Mission Requirement Document (MRD), *European Commission*, Issue 5– Rev. 1.1, 27. March 2003. Available at http://www.galileoju.com.

GALILEO (2005). Mission High Level Definition (HLD) (2002), European Commission Communication Document, W. Doc. 2002/05 - Version 3, 23. September 2002 http://www.galileoju.com, http://www.esa.int/esaNA/index.html.

GALILEO-ICD, 2006 GAL OS SIS ICD/D.0. Available at GLONASS-ICD (2002). GLONASS Interface Control Document. Version 5, 2002, available from http://www.glonass-center.ru/ICD02_e.pdf.

Hein, G., J. Godet, J. L. Issler, J. C. Martin. P. Erhard, R. Lucas-Rodriguez, and T. Pratt. 2003. Galileo frequency and signal design. *GPS World*, June: 30–37.

Hein G.W., M. Irsigler M., J. A. Avila-Rodriguez, and T. Pany. 2004. Performance of Galileo L1 signal candidates. *Proc. ENC-GNSS* 2004, Rotterdam, The Netherlands, May 2004. Available at http://forschung.unibwmuenchen.de/papers/ktmzvhb7tqqpis3sr-pl7anp3bk6izl.pdf.

Heinrichs, G., G. Germany, J. Winkel, C. Drewes, L. Maurer, A. Springer, R. Stuhlberger, and C. Wicpalek. 2005. A hybrid Galileo/UMTS receiver architecture for mass-market applications, GNSS 2005, available at: http://www.gawain-receivers.com/publications/IfEN_Paper_GAWAIN_GNSS2005.pdf.

Hightower, J., and G. Borriello. 2001. Location systems for ubiquitous computing. Computer, *IEEE Computer Society Press*, 34(8): 57–66.

Hofmann-Wellenhof, B., H. Lichtenegger, and J. Collins. 2001. *Global positioning system: Theory and practice*, 5th ed. New York: Springer Verlag Wien.

ICD-GPS-200C (2003). Interface Control Document: Navstar GPS Space Segment/ Navigation User Interfaces. U.S. Department of Defense, IRN-200C-005R1, 14 Jan 2003. Available at http://www.navcen.uscg.gov/pubs/gps/icd200/default.htm.

Jain, R, A. Puri, and R. Sengupta. 2001. Geographical routing using partial information for wireless ad hoc networks, *IEEE Journal of Personal Communications*, 8(1) February: 48–57.

Julien, O., B, Zheng, L. Dong, and G. Lachapelle. 2004a. A complete software- based IF GNSS signal generator for software receiver development, ION GNSS 2004, Sept. 21–24, Long Beach, CA pp. 1–12.

Julien, O., P. Alves, M.E. Cannon, and G. Lachapelle. 2004b. Improved triple-frequency GPS/GALILEO carrier phase ambiguity resolution using a stochastic ionosphere modeling, *Proceedings of ION NTM* 2004 January, San Diego, CA.

Lachapelle, G., M.E. Cannon, K. O'Keefe, and P. Alves. 2002. How will Galileo improve positioning performance? *GPS World*, 13(9): 38–48.

Leick, A.. 2003. *GPS satellite surveying*, 3rd ed. New York: John Wiley.

Liu G., and G. Lachapelle. 2002. Ionosphere weighted GPS cycle ambiguity resolution, *Proceedings of the U.S. Institute of Navigation National Technical Meeting*, (San Diego, CA, January 2002), pp. 889–99.

Lohnert, E., E. Wittmann, J. Pielmeier, and F. Sayda., 2001. PARAMOUNT public safety & commercial infomobility applications & services in the mountains. *Institute of Navigation* GPS 2001, 11–14 September 2001, Salt Lake City, UT, pp. 319–25.

Mulassano P., Dovis F., and Collomb F. 2004. European projects for innovative GNSS-related applications. *GPS Solutions*, 7: 268–70.

Nicopolitidis, P., M. S. Obaidat, G. I. Papadimitriou, and A.S. Pomportsis. 2003.*Wireless networks*, New York: John Wiley.

Omar, S. and Rizos, C. (2003). Incorporating GPS into wireless networks: Issues and challenges. Presented at SatNav 2003: The 6th International Symposium on Satellite Navigation Technology Including Mobile Positioning & Location Services, Melbourne, Australia 22–25 July 2003. Available at: http://www.gmat.unsw.edu.au/snap/publications/omar_etal2003a.pdf.

Ries, L. C. Macabiau, O. Nouvel, Q. Jeandel, W. Vigneau, V. Calmettes and J.L. Issler. 2002. A software receiver for GPS-IIF L5 signal. *Proceedings of the U.S. Institute of Navigation—GPS* 2002, Sept.: 1540–53.

Salgado, S, S. Abbondanza, R. Blondel, and S. Lannelongue. 2001. Constellation availability concepts for Galileo. *Proceedings of ION NTM 2001*, Long Beach, CA, 22–24 January 2001, pp. 778–86.

Schmid, A., A. Neubaur, H. Ehm, R. Weigel, N. Lemke, G. Heinrichs, J. Winkel, J. A. Avila-Rodriguez, R. Kaniuth, T. Pany, B. Eissfeller, G. Rohmer, B. Niemann, and M. Overbeck. (2004). Combined Galileo/GPS architecture for enhanced sensitivity reception. *AEU International Journal of Electronics and Communications* 51(1): 1–8.

Seeber G. 2003. *Satellite geodesy: foundation, methods, and applications*. Berlin, New York: Walter de Gruyter.

WAAS 2002. http://www.*gps.faa.gov/Programs/WAAS/waas.htm*.

Willigen, D. van. 2003. Challenging GNSS Vulnerability, Hydro International, April 2003, 7(3), available at http://www.hydro-international.com/issues/articles/id80-Challenging_GNSS_Vulnerability.html.

Wooden, W.H. 1985. Navstar Global Positioning System. *Proceedings of the first International Symposium on Precise Positioning with Global Positioning System*, Rockville, Maryland, April 15–19, 1: 23–32.

Zhang, W., M.E. Cannon, O. Julien, and P. Alves. 2003. Investigation of combined GPS/GALILEO cascading ambiguity resolution schemes, *Proceedings of U.S. Institute of Navigation GPS/GNSS* (Portland, OR, Sept. 9–12), pp. 2599–2610.

Wireless LANs

M.S. Obaidat, *Monmouth University*
G. I. Papadimitriou, *Aristotle University, Greece*
S. Obeidat, *Arizona State University*

INTRODUCTION

Overview

During the last few years, wireless technology has permeated every aspect of our lives. The fob on a keychain (to open the car remotely), wireless mice/keyboards, and personal digital assistants (PDAs) synching with workstations are just a few examples. This proliferation of wireless devices was the result of the Federal Communications Commission (FCC) decision to open the industrial, scientific, and medical (ISM) band to the public. Wireless local area networks (WLANs) were among the domains that benefited from this release. The release from licensing motivated many companies and research labs to develop and implement wireless local area network (LAN) solutions.

This disorganized and parallel effort resulted in the emergence of proprietary solutions that do not interoperate among one another. Lack of interoperability results in limited scope of acceptance because buyers of the technology from one vendor will have to either remain with that vendor or go through the pains of trying to work out a solution using different technologies. The IEEE 802.11 Working Group was formed to create a universal standard that can be followed by different vendors.

The first standard was released in 1997 and supported data rates up to 2 Mbps (IEEE 1997); the specification defined both the physical and the medium access control layers. Other standards followed that addressed different requirements and provided higher data rates. These included the 802.11b, 802.11a, and 802.11g with higher data rates; the 802.11e for quality of service (QoS) support; the 802.11i for security, and others.

Parallel to the 802.11 effort, the European Telecommunications Standards Institute (ETSI) was working on the high performance radio LAN (HIPERLAN) project. Unlike the 802.11, which tried to use available technology, the HIPERLAN was built from scratch; the development of HIPERLAN was not driven by existing technologies and regulations. Rather, it was developed only to meet a defined set of goals. The HIPERLAN type 1 supports data rates up to 25 Mbps. HIPERLAN types 2, 3, and 4 specify standards for wireless asynchronous transfer mode (ATM) supporting data as well as QoS applications.

Applications of WLANs

Like their wired counterparts, wireless LANs can be used to provide connectivity within a limited geographic area. Mobility—the ability to move around while remaining connected—is a great feature of wireless LANs. In a working environment in which staff members need to be mobile yet constantly connected to the network, WLANs are inevitable. Doctors and nurses accessing patients' data instantly, work coordination among members at different locations of the premises, and students' access to their accounts and class information around the campus are just a few examples of how easy and convenient life can be with mobility support. An implication of mobility is outdoors connectivity. A wired network stops where your sockets and phone lines stop. A wireless LAN, on the other hand, can provide you with connectivity while you are drinking coffee at a street corner café.

A less obvious advantage of WLANs is their ability to address feasibility of running wires. Wireless LANs can be used to connect two wired LANs in different buildings. This might be the only way to provide connectivity, because accessing a public property (e.g., across the street) is not always possible. In this scenario, two bridges or switches can communicate wirelessly with each other in order to connect the two LAN segments. Even within the same building, a wired network may be unfeasible or impossible. In addition, the infrastructure-less ad hoc topology of WLANs can be used in places where fast deployment is needed (e.g., for relief and recovery teams in disaster areas). Ad hoc networks allow a group of nodes to communicate with one another in a distributed, peer-to-peer manner, without prior arrangement. They can also be used for settings in which temporary connectivity is needed (e.g., a meeting of people who need to exchange files and presentations).

Yet another advantage of wireless LANs is their cost-effectiveness. A major part of a traditional wired LAN's installation is a result of cabling, the implications of running conduits around, and so forth. Getting rid of cabling entails the seamless additions, deletions, and modifications of the topology at no cost whatsoever. Additionally, costs needed to run and maintain wires are eliminated in a WLAN.

Chapter Organization

The remainder of the chapter is organized as follows. The following section, "802.11 MAC," discusses the possible topologies of 802.11 MAC as well as the MAC protocol description. The possible physical layers, along with needed background information, are provided in the section entitled "802.11 Physical Layer." The section entitled "HIPERLANS" discusses HIPERLAN types 1 and 2. Security and QoS support in 802.11 are described in the next two sections, "WLANs Security" and "QoS Support: 802.11e." The chapter concludes with a brief description of some advanced topics in wireless networks.

802.11 MAC

Possible Topologies

Wireless LANs can be either infrastructure based or ad hoc. The latter LANs have no pre-existing infrastructure or centralized management to support the mobile nodes. They consist of wireless nodes that can freely and dynamically self-organize into arbitrary and temporary network topologies. On the other hand, an infrastructure WLAN is based on central control (e.g., by using an access point). This section will describe both schemes. The following classification of the different organizations of a wireless LAN is based on the concept of a service set. A service set is nothing but a logical grouping of nodes. A node belongs to only one service set. In this context, *belongs* means that it listens only to transmissions from a particular service set.

Basic Service Set

The basic service set (BSS) resembles the basic building block in the 802.11 architecture. Nodes in a BSS communicate with one another through an access point (AP). An access point is responsible for coordinating communication among the nodes by receiving a node's transmission and forwarding it to the respective receiver. The access point is analogous to a base station in a cellular network, and a BSS is analogous to a cell in a cellular network. The coverage area of a BSS is called a basic service area (BSA). Figure 1 illustrates the concept of a BSS (Crow et al. 1997a).

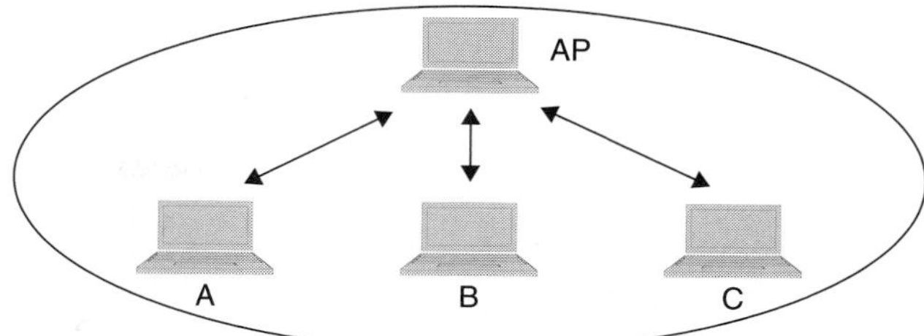

Figure 1: A BSS organization of a wireless LAN

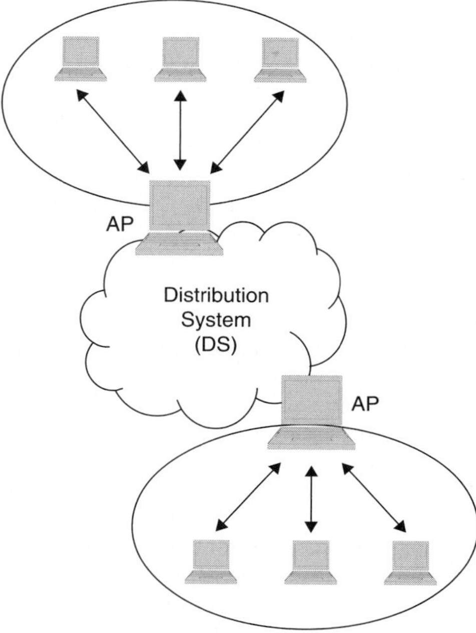

Figure 2: The ESS organization of a wireless LAN

Extended Service Set

Figure 2 shows how multiple BSSs can be connected to one another by connecting their APs to a distribution system (DS), thereby forming what is called an extended service set (ESS). Although the APs can connect to the DS via a wired or wireless connection, the connection usually is wired. The DS resembles the backbone of the ESS and is responsible for communicating MAC segments from one BSS to another or from one BSS to an external wired network (Crow et al. 1997a).

Independent Basic Service Set

The BSS and its extension (through an ESS) both resemble an infrastructure-based organization. The independent basic service set (IBSS), on the other hand, resembles the infrastructure-less ad hoc arrangement (see Figure 3). In an IBSS, stations communicate in a peer-to-peer fashion in which no AP or any other intermediary is needed. At least two stations are needed to form an IBSS.

Access Modes: DCF

The distributed coordination function (DCF) is the basic access mode of the 802.11 standard. It is based on

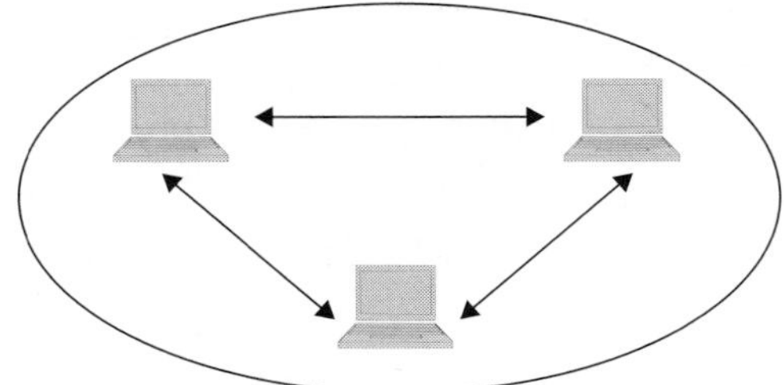

Figure 3: The IBSS (ad hoc) organization of a wireless LAN

the carrier sense multiple access with collision avoidance (CSMA/CA) scheme. The DCF is a contention-based protocol: stations have to compete every time they want to access the channel. Before delving into the details of the protocol, an important question that comes to mind is why a specialized MAC is needed. Why can't we simply adopt a wired MAC protocol? This section begins with an answer to this question, including the issues that arise in a wireless communication context.

Why Wired-Network Channel Access Does Not Work

Carrier sense multiple access with collision detection (CSMA/CD) is used in the IEEE 802.3 Ethernet standard. The basic idea is that the sender senses the medium (a cable to which all the nodes in the Ethernet segment are attached); if the medium is busy, the sender backs off and tries again later. If the channel is idle, on the other hand, the sender sends and keeps listening to the channel. If it hears a collision at any point during its transmission, the sender stops transmitting and sends a jamming signal.

The basic assumption in the CSMA/CD protocol is that a collision taking place at the receiver can be detected at the sender. This is true because the signal strength is basically the same throughout the medium. However, this assumption does not hold anymore for the wireless medium because the signal strength decreases with the square of the distance from the transmitter. Thus, an event may take place and not be detected by the transmitter. The hidden and exposed terminal problems discussed next stem from this fact. In addition, a wireless node does not have the ability to transmit and receive at the same time because its own transmission would swamp any other signal in the vicinity (Nicopolitidis et al. 2003; Schiller 2002).

Figure 4 shows three stations: A, B, and C. The transmission range of A reaches B but not C. Similarly, the transmission range of C reaches B but not A. A's detection range (the range within which A can sense the medium) does not include C. C's detection range does not include A either.

A, willing to transmit to B, senses the channel and finds it idle. As a result, it starts transmitting. Meanwhile, C becomes interested in sending data to B. Sensing an idle channel, C does not detect the ongoing transmission between A and B because it is out of its range. C also starts transmitting to B, which results in a collision at B that is not detected by either A or C. This problem, in which two nodes are out of reach of each other but within the reach of a third node, is referred to as the hidden terminal problem (or hidden node problem).

Another problem associated with the inability to detect collisions is the exposed terminal problem, which is illustrated in Figure 5. In this case, B is transmitting to A. C, willing to send to D, senses the channel and finds it busy. If C transmits, its transmission will not interfere with the ongoing transmission between B and A, because A is outside its range. C's transmission, even though it would collide with B, would not collide with A because the signal would be too weak to cause a collision. Thus, C postpones its transmission even though it should not. In this case, C is *exposed* to B.

Consider the situation in which node A is closer to node C than it is to node B, as shown in Figure 6. In this case, even though both A and B can reach C, the signal power of A's transmission is much higher than that of B's transmission. As a result, C cannot hear B's transmission.

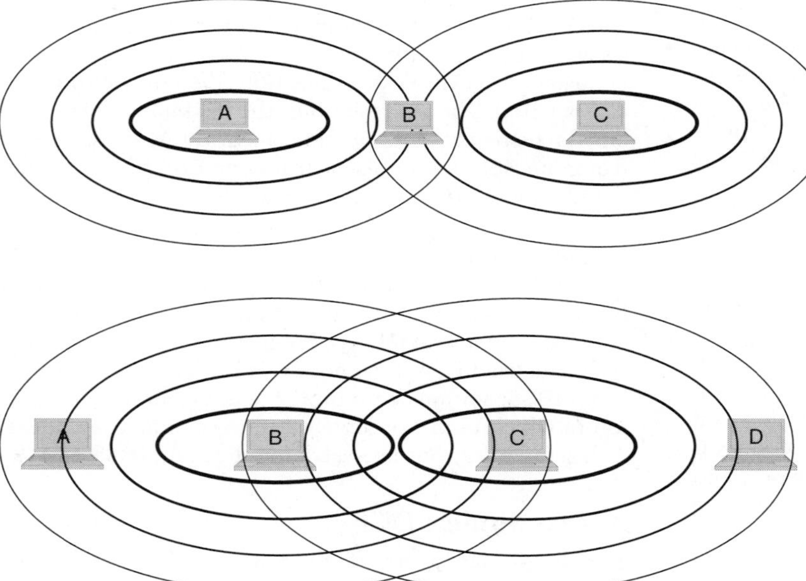

Figure 4: The hidden terminal problem
Note: C is outside the transmission and detection range of A; similarly, A is outside the transmission and detection range of C

Figure 5: The exposed terminal problem
Note: C is out of A's range but is within B's range. Hence, C postpones transmitting to D even though it should not. Although it would collide with B, it would not collide with A

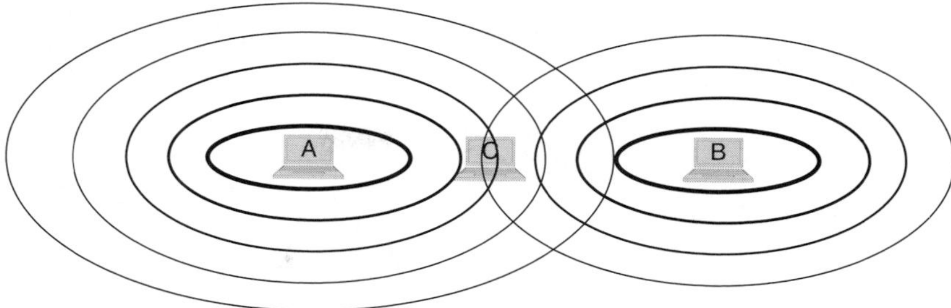

Figure 6: The near-far effect

To circumvent this problem, B has to compensate for the difference in distance by transmitting at higher signal strength. This is the near-far effect, and it contrasts with wired networks, in which nodes generally receive the same signal strength.

Carrier Sense Multiple Access with Collision Avoidance

The wireless medium imposes its own requirements on the design of a MAC protocol. The main issue to be dealt with is the inability to detect collisions; therefore, collisions have to be eliminated or at least minimized. The carrier sense multiple access with collision avoidance was created for just this purpose. Using CSMA/CA, nodes perform two types of carrier sensing: physical carrier sensing and virtual carrier sensing, which refer to sensing at the physical and MAC layers, respectively. The channel is considered busy if either the physical or the virtual carrier sensing results in a busy channel indication. Physical carrier sensing is done by monitoring the medium for any ongoing transmissions, which involves looking at the strength of any received signal. Virtual carrier sensing can be explored by reviewing how the hidden terminal problem is being handled.

In Figure 7, which has the same scenario as Figure 4, when node A decides to send to node B, it first sends a request-to-send (RTS) control packet. All nodes within the range of A overhear the RTS packet and postpone their attempt to transmit. When B receives the RTS packet, it sends back a clear-to-send (CTS) packet. All nodes in the range of B will defer any attempt to transmit. Node C is not going to transmit to B because it hears the CTS packet. This procedure is also known as the four-way handshake.

Even though the RTS/CTS exchange mitigates the hidden terminal problem, it does not solve it entirely. For example, A and C may both transmit an RTS packet at the same time. Another possibility is that when B sends the CTS, C sends an RTS resulting in a collision of both control packets at C. Node C, not hearing the CTS sent to A nor a CTS for its own RTS, retransmits the RTS, which collides with A's packet.

Collisions involving the RTS/CTS control packets carry small penalties when compared with data packets' collisions. This is readily apparent from the sizes of the RTC and CTS packets (20 bytes and 16 bytes, respectively) in contrast to the maximum data packet size, which is 2346 bytes. Thus, the RTS/CTS exchange provides better overall performance.

The basic idea behind virtual carrier sensing involves announcing for how long a node will occupy the channel so that all nodes hearing the announcement will defer their transmissions. To achieve this, every packet (be it a data packet, RTS, or CTS) carries a duration field that indicates the amount of time the channel will be needed after the current packet transmission is done. This period includes the time to transmit the RTS, CTS, data packet, and returning acknowledgment (ACK). Every node maintains what is called a network allocation vector (NAV). Nodes adjust the values of their vectors as they overhear packet transmissions. A node attempts to check the channel status (whether idle or not) only when the duration in the NAV elapses.

Priority in accessing the wireless channel is provided through the use of inter-frame spacing (IFS), which is the duration of time that has to pass before an attempt is made to access the channel. Three IFSs are defined in the protocol; in increasing order of importance, these are the distributed coordination function IFS (DIFS), point coordination function IFS (PIFS), and short IFS (SIFS). The SIFS is the shortest amount of time and hence the highest priority, followed by the PIFS (used by the PCF), and the DIFS (the time delay used by DCF frames).

Figure 8 shows how a frame transmission takes place along with the NAV table's adjustments at other nodes (those that are not involved in the current transmission). Prior to sensing the channel, a node has to wait the length of a DIFS duration. After that, if the channel is idle, the node sends an RTS. The duration field is set to include the time for the CTS, the data packet, the ACK, and

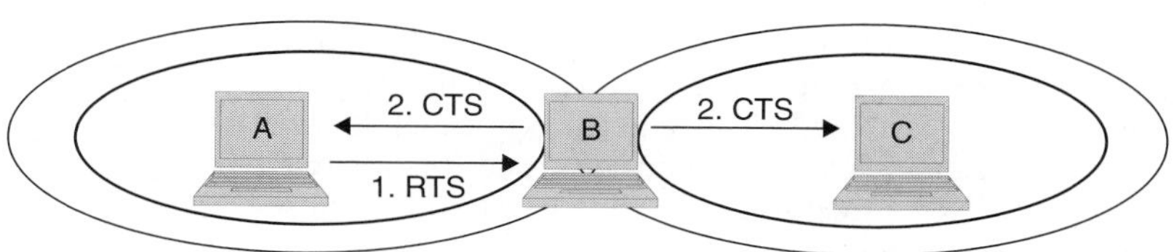

Figure 7: The RTS/CTS control packet exchange

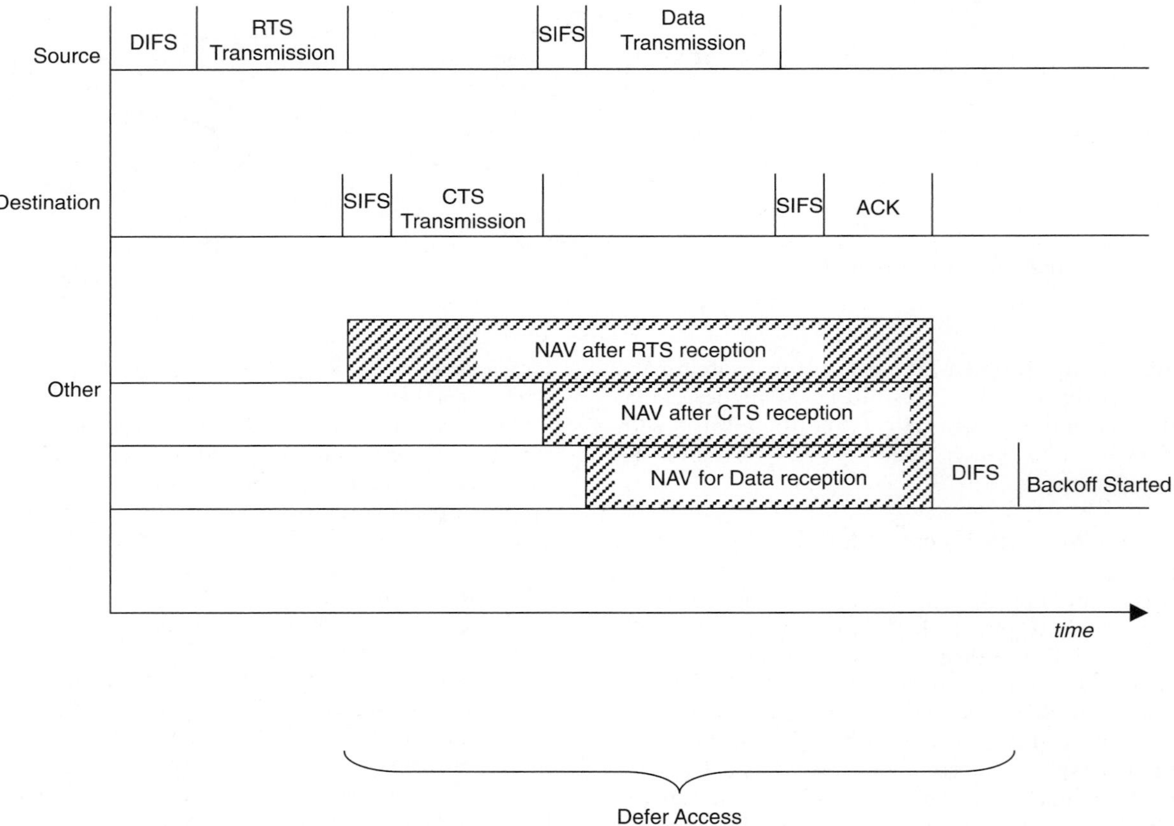

Figure 8: Frame transmission along with the changes in the NAV as time progresses

the SIFS durations that separate each one of these. When the receiver gets the RTS, it waits the length of a SIFS duration and sends back a CTS. Upon receiving the CTS, the sender waits the length of another SIFS and transmits the data packet, which is followed by another SIFS and an ACK. The success of these steps marks a successful packet transmission. Nodes wait the length of a DIFS duration and contend for the channel again.

Following a busy channel, the probability of more than one node trying to access the channel is high. The idle period following a DIFS interval is referred to as the contention window. To prevent collisions and enhance the performance, nodes enter into a back-off period so that channel access demands are spread across time. Nodes calculate a random back-off interval. A station calculates the amount of backoff to be between 0 and the minimum size of the contention window (CWmin). A station transmits only when its backoff reaches 0 and the channel is idle. In case the transmission results in a collision, the station calculates a new contention window size equal to $2^{2+i}-1$ time slots, in which i equals the number of consecutive collisions the station experienced. For every transmission failure, the station calculates a contention window until it reaches a maximum window size (CWmax). When the retry counter, i, exceeds a specific (user-defined) value, the packet is dropped. The countdown timer freezes when the channel is sensed to be busy, and it is resumed once the wireless medium is detected to be idle, subsequently for DIFS time.

Access Modes: PCF

Unlike DCF, which is a contention-based protocol used for data traffic, the point coordination function (PCF) provides a contention-free protocol that can be used for connection-oriented real-time traffic (e.g., voice). This is done by polling the stations one at a time. PCF needs an element called a point coordinator (PC), which decides when (and which) nodes can transmit according to a polling list (normally in round-robin fashion). The PC is recommended to be integrated with the AP. Given the centralized approach of PCF, which depends on the AP for polling, PCF works only for the infrastructure-based topologies and not for the ad hoc one. In addition, PCF has not yet been implemented and is not available in any WLAN card. The protocol works by dividing time into contention-free periods (CFPs). The length of the CFP is manageable and determines how often the PCF runs. Each CFP consists of a contention-free portion followed by contention-based period (i.e., for DCF traffic). Each CFP must allow for at least one DCF packet to be transmitted (so that DCF traffic does not starve). The portion allotted to PCF traffic is dynamic, and the AP can change it as the traffic requirements change. For example, if a small number of nodes is interested in the PCF service, more time is allotted to the DCF function. The AP announces the beginning of a CFP by sending a beacon frame. Stations update their NAV to the maximum length of CFP, which is a defined parameter, *CFP_Max_Duration*. Periodically, the AP sends a beacon frame that contains the remaining time of the CFP, *CFPDurationRemaining*.

To initiate the beginning of a CFP, the AP waits a PCF inter-frame space (PIFS), which is shorter than a DIFS. Thus, the AP gains access to the channel before any DCF station does. It then sends a beacon frame, which is used for synchronization and parameter information announcement. At this point, all stations have updated their NAV, and no one will access the channel unless requested by the AP. The AP can send a poll frame, a data frame (i.e., forwarding from one station to another), a combination of data and poll, or a CFP end frame.

802.11 PHYSICAL LAYER

This section explains basic concepts related to the physical layer, followed by a discussion of the main problems associated with wireless channels. Afterwards, the different radio layers of the 802.11 standard are described. The section closes with a brief look at some of the physical layer standards.

Concepts

Channel Coding and Modulation

Modulation is the process of changing the data stream to a form suitable for transmission over a physical medium. Two categories of modulation exist: analog modulation and digital modulation. Analog modulation works by impressing the analog signal containing the data on a carrier wave, with this impression aiming to change a property of the carrier wave. Digital modulation refers to the mapping of one or more bits to a symbol; the symbol is the basic unit communicated between transmitter and receiver. This works by converting a bit string (digital data) to a suitable continuous time waveform. This conversion involves modifying one of the signal characteristics amplitude, frequency, or phase), giving rise to amplitude modulation, frequency modulation, or phase modulation (see Figure 9). Amplitude refers to the signal strength; frequency refers to the number of times per second the signal repeats its pattern (measured in Hz or cycles/sec); and phase is the relative position in time.

In digital modulation, the higher the number of bits mapped to a symbol, the denser the modulation scheme. The denser the modulation scheme, the more spectrally efficient it is. The number of bits per symbol depends on the modulation scheme used. For example, if the channel bandwidth is 1 MHz, the wave frequency is fixed and equal to the frequency of the carrier wave; if every bit is mapped into a symbol, the channel capacity is 1 Mbps. This holds because 1 million wave transitions per second are supported. On the other hand, if every two bits are mapped into one symbol, the channel capacity will be double to 2 Mbps. Nonetheless, the increase in the number of bits per symbol is not arbitrary. The higher the number of bits per symbol, the higher the chances of error in recovering the bits at the receiving end.

Coding allows for maximizing the benefit of transmission over noisy wireless channels by introducing redundancies in the bits transmitted, so that the receiver can still recover a reasonably distorted packet. To be able to recover more errors, more overhead bits have to be sent. Coding efficiency refers to the ratio between data to total bits in the stream. For example, a coding efficiency of ½ means that, for every bit in the data stream, two bits have to be sent. One important issue with regard to coding schemes is the computational complexity of implementing

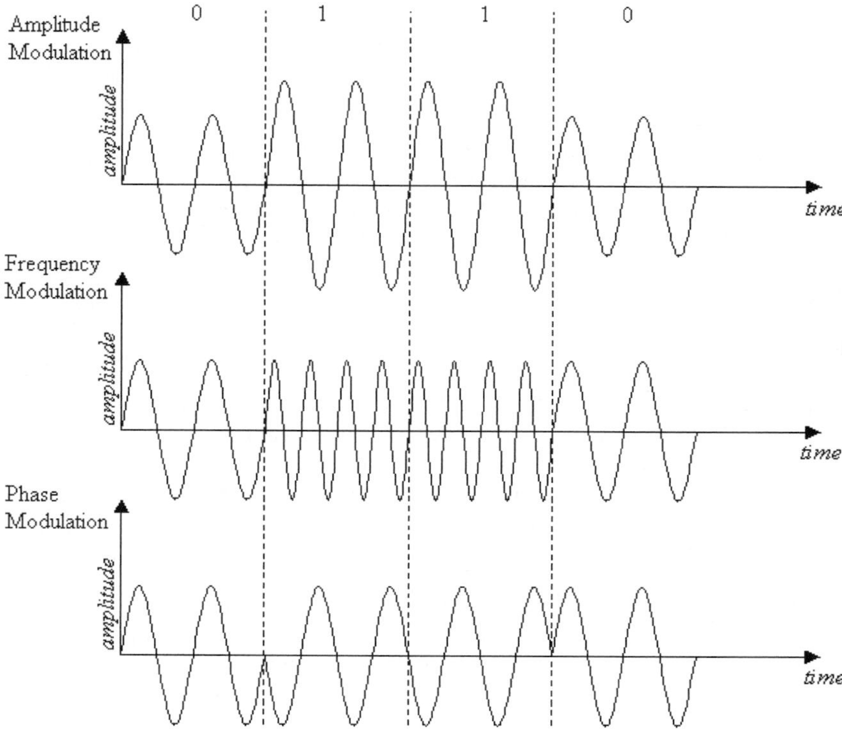

Figure 9: Illustration of amplitude, frequency, and phase modulations (bit sequence: 0110)

the code. This is especially important for portable wireless devices, which try to use their energy efficiently.

Antennas

An antenna is a device responsible for emitting or collecting electromagnetic waves for the purposes of transmission and reception. In other words, it is the interface between the transmitter/receiver and the air. An antenna takes electrical signals from the transmitter and converts them into radio (i.e., electromagnetic) signals sent on the air, and captures radio signals from the air and converts them into electrical signals at the receiver. Antennas are characterized by many parameters, including directivity/gain, polarity, and efficiency, among others (Antenova, Ltd. n.d.).

Before explaining directivity, isotropic antennas need to be defined. An isotropic antenna is an idealistic antenna, which radiates the same power in all directions. In other words, if we create a sphere around it and measure the power intensity at any point on the surface, the same value is achieved. Realistic antennas radiate more in some directions than others. Gain is the amount of power *gained* in one direction at the expense of other directions.

Electromagnetic waves consist of coupled electric and magnetic fields. Polarization refers to the position and direction of the electric field with reference to the earth's surface. An antenna can be horizontally or vertically polarized. The transmitting and receiving antennas have to have the same polarization; otherwise, a great amount of loss will occur. Efficiency of an antenna is defined as the ratio between the radiated power and the input power. An isotropic antenna has a gain of one.

Antennas can be omnidirectional, providing a 360-degree radiation pattern; directional, in which they focus their radiation in one direction to provide greater coverage distance; and diversity antennas, which actually use more than one antenna for signal reception and, when transmitting, send through the antenna with the best received signal.

Wireless Problems

Unlike wired transmissions, the wireless channel is characterized by much impairment, which—along with the scarce spectral bandwidth—makes achieving wired medium quality extremely difficult. In this subsection, the problems faced by wireless communications are briefly noted.

Path loss. As a signal propagates from the transmitter to the receiver, it attenuates (i.e., loses its energy) with distance. Thus, the longer the distance, the weaker the signal received. The free space model refers to the signal strength when the path between the transmitter and the receiver is clear of obstacles and resembles a line of sight. In the free space model, the signal attenuates with the square of the distance (i.e., d^2, where d is the distance; Nicopolitidis et al. 2003). Realistic modeling of path loss, however, depends on many other factors, including the reflecting objects and big obstructions in the path between the transmitter and the receiver. Depending on the model at hand, the signal strength decreases with distance with an exponent ranging from 3 to 6.

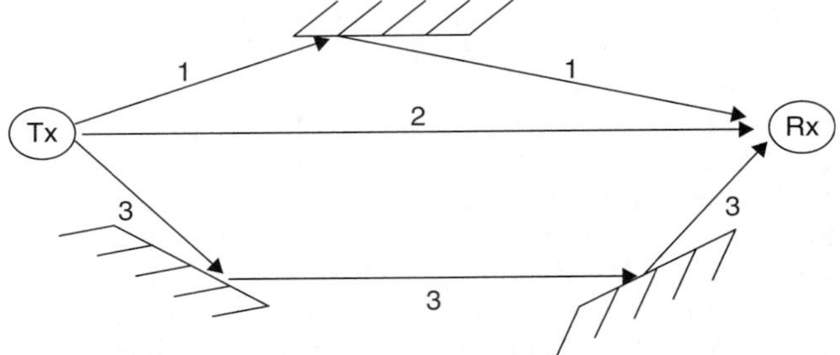

Figure 10: Illustration of a multipath propagation (numbers on the rays refer to path numbers)

Multipath fading and shadowing. When a signal is transmitted, multiple versions of the same signal take different paths in arriving to the receiver (see Figure 10). The first to arrive at the receiver is the one going through the line of sight (LOS), which is the path that does not have any obstacles between the transmitter and the receiver (Path 2 in Figure 10). Other, delayed versions follow other paths resulting from impingements on obstacles in the path. When these delayed copies arrive at the receiver, they either add constructively or destructively. Notice that the obstacles in the path are not fixed in number or position. Mobility of the transmitter, receiver, or the objects in between, changes the paths between the transmitter and the receiver. Thus, the signal quality varies with time. This phenomenon, in which the signal quality depends on the multipath propagation, is referred to as multipath fading. Another type of fading is shadow fading. When the signal encounters a large obstacle in its way, such as a building, it is attenuated severely. The amount of absorption depends on the characteristics and size of the obstacle.

Interference. Interference refers to extraneous, unwanted signals that affect the proper system operation. Not only does interference affect the quality of the signal communicated from the transmitter to the receiver, but it can also affect the functionality of the protocol. For example, the existence of another 802.11 network in the vicinity could make sources sense the channel as busy even though it is not.

Since wireless LANs work in the ISM band, which does not require any licensing, they are especially susceptible to interference. Microwave ovens, photocopying machines, medical equipments, Bluetooth-enabled devices (e.g., PDAs or laptops), and wireless phones are examples of possible sources of interference. Obviously, the existence of another WLAN segment cannot be ruled out, especially as WLANs gain more acceptance in the marketplace.

Many things can be done to deal with interference. Conducting site surveys to understand the geographic area in which the WLAN will work, maintaining strong coverage by transmitting high-power signals, and shutting down other devices that can interfere are examples of procedures that can help. As will be discussed later, wireless LANs circumvent this problem by using spread spectrum techniques (Geier 2002b).

The Radio Link

The IEEE 802.11 WLANs use either radio or infrared electromagnetic waves for data transmission. This

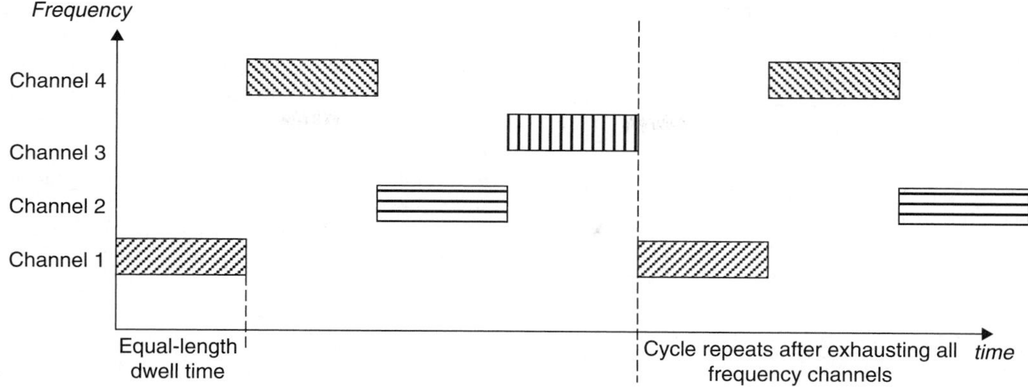

Figure 11: A four-channel FHSS system

section and the next will discuss both of these interfaces. Radio-based WLANs, which are more common than IR-based WLANs, operate at the ISM band because this band does not require any licensing from the FCC. The standard defines two physical layer methods: frequency hopping spread spectrum (FHSS) and direct sequence spread spectrum (DSSS). The basic idea of spread spectrum (whether FHSS or DSSS) involves using a very wide bandwidth to communicate data. By increasing the bandwidth used, communication will be more resilient to interference and fading because only a small portion of the bandwidth will be affected.

Frequency Hopping Spread Spectrum Physical Layer

In FHSS, the signal is spread by sending one frequency for a short period of time and then switching (hopping) to another frequency in a seemingly random fashion (see Figure 11). The hopping sequence and rate are predefined and known to both the sender and the receiver. Two types of FHSS systems exist, depending on the hopping rate. If multiple bits are transmitted over the same frequency channel, the system is called slow frequency hopping. On the other hand, if the hopping rate is greater than or equal to the bit rate—that is, if one bit or less is transmitted over a channel—the system is considered fast frequency hopping. Because wireless LANs operate on the ISM band, many sources of interference may exist. If a source of interference happens to be in the vicinity of a slow frequency hopping transmission and is operating at a frequency that is also used by the slow FH system, it will corrupt all packets sent at that frequency channel. In a fast frequency hopping system, on the other hand, very few noise spikes will take place, and the receiver will still be able to recover the data. Thus, fast hopping systems have better interference resilience (Bing 2000).

The time spent in every frequency, known as the dwell time, is limited by the FCC to a maximum of 400 ms. This means that the FHSS system hops at least 2.5 times per second. In addition, the number of frequency channels used in the hopping sequence cannot go below six channels (i.e., 6 MHz; Roshan and Leary 2004). The 802.11 standard splits the available bandwidth into seventy-nine channels, each 1 MHz wide.

The 802.11 physical layer supports two data rates: 1 Mbps and 2 Mbps. It consists of two sublayers: the physical layer convergence protocol (PLCP) and the physical medium dependent (PMD). PLCP is responsible for adding necessary headers for the purposes of synchronization, timing, and error control. The PMD is responsible for the raw transmission of bits over the air; it mainly performs modulation of the data stream.

The PLCP adds a 128-bit header to frames arriving from the MAC layer (called PLCP service data units, or PSDU). The header contains the following fields:

- A preamble, which has two subfields (96 bits):
  - Synch: An 80-bit sequence of alternating 0s and 1s starting with a 0. It is used at the receiver for time synchronization. In addition, if the receiver is using any antenna diversity technique, it uses these bits to choose the best antenna. The transmitter and the receiver must be synchronized so that they switch from one frequency to another at the same time.
  - SFD (start of frame delimiter): A specific bit string (0000 1100 1011 1101) used at the receiver for frame timing.
- PSDU length word (PLW): A 12-bit field that indicates the size of the MAC frame.
- PLCP signaling field (PSF): A 4-bit field used to specify the data rate at which the frame was transmitted. Data rates range from 1 Mbps to 4.5 Mbps in increments of 0.5 Mbps. Table 1 shows the possible values along with the data rates they indicate (Nicopolitidis et al. 2003).
- Header error control (HEC): An ITU-T cyclic redundancy check, CRC16 used for error detection.

After receiving a bit stream from the PLCP sublayer, the PMD modulates it using Gaussian frequency shift keying (GFSK). Depending on the data rate supported (whether 1 Mbps or 2 Mbps), GFSK or 4GFSK is used. 4GFSK translates every two bits into one signal element, doubling the rate. Frequency shift keying schemes, in general, convey the information by changing the frequency of the signal. Thus, the amplitude of the signal does not carry any information. This provides the flexibility of changing the

Table 1: PSF Field Value with the Data Rate Supported

Field Value	Data Rate (Mbps)
000	1
001	1.5
010	2
011	2.5
100	3
101	3.5
110	4
111	4.5

transmission power as needed. In addition, the design of the transmitter and the receiver is simple. An important drawback of FSK-based schemes is that they are not spectrally efficient. That is, the amount of information conveyed per signal element is small when compared with other modulation schemes. Figure 12 shows a block diagram of an FHSS transmitter. The input bits are fed into a GFSK modulator, which produces an analog signal from the data. A spreader that takes a pseudo-random number as an index for table look-up uses the table entry's frequency as the carrier frequency to be modulated by the output of the GFSK modulator. The resultant signal is the one transmitted in the air. The opposite process takes place at the receiving end to demodulate the received signal (Roshan and Leary 2004).

Direct Sequence Spread Spectrum Physical Layer

The main idea of DSSS is to spread the signal energy across a large bandwidth. To other unintended receivers, the signal can be treated as noise that can be easily rejected. As a result, the same frequency band can be used by multiple DSSS signals, allowing for better bandwidth usage while minimizing interference effects.

To achieve this spreading, DSSS systems map every bit in the data stream to an m-bit pattern called the pseudonoise code, or chipping code. The number of bits in the code determines the spreading factor. The higher the spreading factor, the more resilient the signal to interference. However, this is at the expense of bandwidth requirement, which shoots up. The FCC specifies a minimum spreading factor of 10. That is, a maximum data rate of 10 percent of the available channel bandwidth can be provided. The IEEE 802.11 uses an 11-chip spreading factor; every bit in the data stream is replaced by 11 bits (chip sequence) to be transmitted over the channel. Even though this may seem very expensive, the fact that it minimizes interference effects results in enhancing channel quality, which translates into fewer corrupted packets, better overall throughput performance, and decreased transmission delay as the need for retransmissions is reduced.

The receiver of a DSSS signal has to know the chipping code mappings and has to be synchronized to the correct phase of the code. That is why every packet is prefixed with a preamble for synchronization purposes.

An important difference between code division multiple access (CDMA) systems and the DSSS system used by the 802.11 is that CDMA is based on code multiplexing. That is, multiple transmissions can take place at the same time as long as different communication pairs are tuned to different codes. This requires the availability of a code pool to choose from, the logic to choose a code, and complex receivers synchronized for a specific code. In contrast, DSSS wireless LANs use the one code allowing for broadcast communication (Bing 2000).

The 802.11 DSSS physical layer supports two rates: 1 Mbps and 2 Mbps. A subsequent standard—the 802.11b—supports data rates of 5.5 Mbps and 11 Mbps. Like the FHSS physical layer, the DSSS physical layer consists of two sublayers: the PLCP and the PMD. The PLCP of DSSS is very similar to that of FHSS and serves the same purpose. The PMD modulates the data stream for transmission over the channel. The channel bandwidth supported by the 802.11 standard is 11 MHz; given that the spreading factor is 11, the data rate that can be supported is either 1 Mbps or 2 Mbps. The rate depends on the modulation scheme used. The DSSS physical layer uses differential binary phase shift keying (DBPSK), in which every symbol carries one bit, allowing for a data rate of 1 Mbps. To support the 2 Mbps rate, differential quadrature phase shift keying (DQPSK) is used, in which every symbol carries two bits from the data stream. Thus, in both cases, 1 mega symbols are being communicated. The difference lies in how many bits a symbol maps to.

Infrared

This chapter has already discussed the radio-based flavor of wireless LANs. Unlike radio-based WLANs, infrared is not regulated; hence, plenty of bandwidth is available. In addition, infrared does not suffer from the electromagnetic

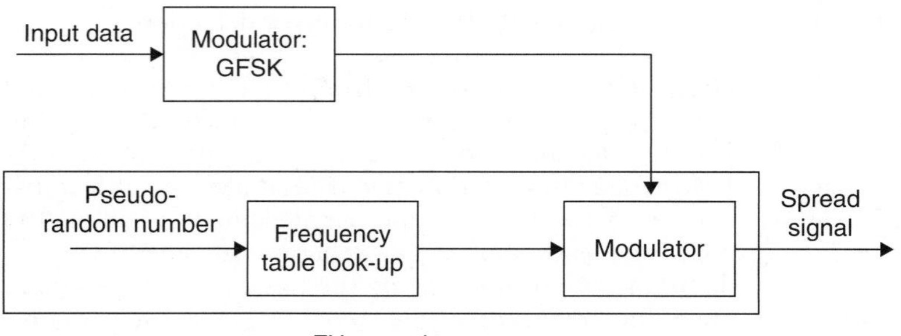

Figure 12: FHSS transmitter

interference that is a limiting factor for radio-based WLANs. However, infrared has its own sources of interference (e.g., sunlight, fluorescent light, etc.), which can substantially degrade network performance. Like visible light, infrared does not penetrate opaque objects (e.g., walls), which entails the need for an access point in every room. Even though this may seem to be a disadvantage, especially because an AP can provide large coverage in radio LANs, it actually has great advantages. First, it promises secure communication, because eavesdropping (or any security attack for that matter; e.g., denial of service) is very difficult from the outside. Second it provides interference immunity, allowing each room a separate deployment; thus, large IR LANs can be built (Stallings 2002). Finally, infrared wireless LANs are simpler to implement and hence are less expensive. This is attributed to their use of intensity modulation for data transmission, which only involves detecting the signal's amplitude—unlike radio systems, in which the frequency and/or phase needs to be detected.

One main issue of infrared LANs is the absence of products in conformance with the standard. This limits deployment of infrared LANs to small-scale usage under one management domain. Two main types of IR LANs exist: directed and omnidirectional. A directed IR LAN is used to create point-to-point connections. The transmitter and the receiver have to be placed so that a line of sight exists between them. Depending on the transmission power used, directed transmissions produce high performance in terms of transmission distance, bandwidth, and throughput achieved. Data rates ranging from 1 to 155 Mbps over a distance of 1 to 5 km can be provided (Bing 2000).

Directed IR can be used in a campus-sized network in which different segments need to be connected to one another. To do so, directed links across buildings are created to connect bridges or routers. Indoors, directed IR can also be used to connect different segments in any suitable arrangement (e.g., to connect Ethernet or token ring segments; Stallings 2002). Omnidirectional IR can be used for scenarios similar to radio LANs. A ceiling-mounted transceiver broadcasts to all nodes within a line of sight (e.g., in a room). Omnidirectional IR can be used only in an indoor environment because it relies on reflections off of objects (e.g., walls, ceilings, desks, etc.) to propagate in all directions. Even though these reflected copies allow for the freedom of aligning the transmitter and receiver, a substantial amount of the energy is lost, limiting the data rate and range of communication. Indoor omnidirectional IR LANs operate at a rate limited to 4 Mbps within a range of 10 to 20 m (Bing 2000).

Physical Layer Standards

New standards have been approved that achieve higher data rates. This section briefly discusses the main differences between the 802.11 standards a, b, and g, and how these higher rates are achieved.

IEEE 802.11b

The 802.11b defines the high rate DSSS (HR-DSSS), which allows data rates as high as 5.5 Mbps and 11 Mbps (IEEE 802.11b Working Group 1999). The PLCP of the HR-DSSS defines two types of frames: long and short. The long frame format is basically the same as in DSSS. A few fields have been added, mainly to define the data rate communicated (whether 5.5 Mbps or 11 Mbps) and the modulation scheme used. The preamble and header are always communicated at a rate of 1 Mbps to ensure backward compatibility with DSSS. The short frame has the same format as the long one, except that fewer bits are used for a field to minimize overhead. For example, as opposed to 128 bits for synchronization in the long frame, only 56 are used in the short one. The other difference is that the short frame's preamble and header are communicated at a rate of 2 Mbps (as opposed to 1 Mbps in the long frame). As before, the PMD is basically responsible for modulating the bit stream that it receives from the PLCP (Roshan and Leary 2004).

Two modulation schemes are used: complimentary code keying (CCK) and packet binary convolutional coding (PBCC). Higher data rates are achieved in the following manner. As before, an 11 MHz bandwidth is used. However, the spreading code is 8 chips long rather than 11 chips in the 1 Mbps and 2 Mbps cases. In addition, the number of bits in an 8-chip code is different. Using the CCK modulation, every 4 bits from the data stream are encoded in an 8-chip code, thus allowing for a data rate equal to

$$11 \times 10^6 \times \frac{4bits}{8chips} = 5.5\,Mbps \qquad (1)$$

Similarly, the PBCC modulation scheme codes 8 bits in an 8-chip code, allowing for a data rate of 11 Mbps.

IEEE 802.11a

Unlike the 802.11b, which works in the 2.4 GHz ISM band, the 802.11a works in the Unlicensed National Information Infrastructure (UNII) 5 GHz band (IEEE 802.11a Working Group 1999). It supports data rates up to 24 Mbps and optionally up to 54 Mbps. Three hundred MHz are used in 802.11a, which are then divided into three 100 MHz bands—each with different maximum power output. The three bands used are 5.15–5.25 GHz, 5.25–5.35 GHz, and 5.725–5.825 GHz. Devices operating at these bands produce a power equal to 50 mW, 250 mW, and 1 W, respectively. The high power output allowed in the high band makes it more suitable for building-to-building devices (e.g., bridges connecting two LAN segments). The other two bands are suitable for indoor environments. Data is modulated using the orthogonal frequency division multiplexing (OFDM) scheme. The basic premise of OR idea behind OFDM is to minimize the inter-symbol interference (ISI) problem, which occurs when a symbol takes longer to reach the receiver. This delay, called delay spread, results from multipath propagation (discussed earlier). Because of this delay, a symbol may arrive at the same time as another subsequent symbol. This can be dealt with by decreasing the number of symbols per second, thus ensuring that a symbol has an ample amount of time to reach the receiver before a subsequent symbol is sent. Obviously, this decreases the data rate achieved. Hence, OFDM breaks the channel bandwidth into subchannels.

Table 2: Supported Data Rates and the Modulation Schemes Used

Data Rate (Mbps)	Modulation Scheme
6	BPSK
9	BPSK
12	QPSK
18	QPSK
24	16-QAM
36	16-QAM
48	64-QAM
54	64-QAM

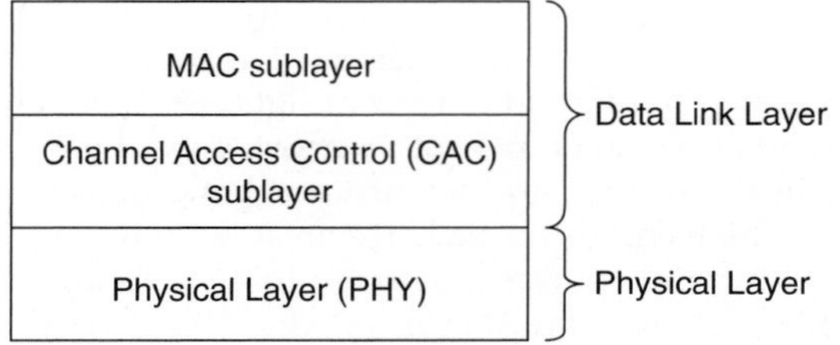

Figure 13: HIPERLAN/1 reference model

Each subchannel has a low symbol rate and thus a low ISI. The subchannels are chosen to be orthogonal; as a result, low co-channel interference occurs. A receiver tuned at a given frequency sees all other signals as zero. Table 2 shows the data rates supported by the 802.11a standard along with the modulation scheme used.

IEEE 802.11g

The 802.11g standard is very recent. It was approved in 2003 and supports data rates up to 54 Mbps (IEEE 802.11g Working Group 2003). Unlike the 802.11a, the 802.11g operates in the ISM 2.4 GHz and has backward compatibility with the 802.11b. If all the devices in the network talk 802.11g, the high data rates of 802.11g can be used. However, if any of the devices in the network talks 802.11b, all other devices have to switch to the low data rates supported by the 802.11b. The mandatory data rates are 6, 12, and 24 Mbps; the rest are optional. To ensure backward compatibility, the packet header and preamble are sent using CCK modulation, which is also used by the 802.11b, and the payload is sent using OFDM.

HIPERLANs

HIPERLAN Type 1

The high performance radio LAN (HIPERLAN) type 1, developed by the European Telecommunications Standards Institute, is the European counterpart of the IEEE 802.11. The protocol provides data rates up to 23.5 Mbps and supports low mobility conditions (1.4 m/s). Like its counterpart, its reference model (shown in Figure 13) covers both the physical (PHY) and the MAC layers. The physical layer is responsible for transmission/reception of raw data over the wireless channel. The channel access control (CAC) sublayer determines how nodes will access the channel and which nodes have the right to access by allowing access priority to be specified. The MAC defines the different protocols responsible for power conservation, multihop forwarding, security, and data transfer to upper layers (Broadband Radio Access Network [BRAN] 1998; Jain 2007; Papadimitriou et al. 2003).

Unlike the 802.11, HIPERLAN/1 has a single physical layer that is not based on spread-spectrum techniques. It uses a narrowband modulation in the 5.15–5.30 GHz range. It is important to note that HIPERLAN does not provide an infrared physical interface. Two data rates are supported: a lower rate of 1.47 Mbps, which uses FSK modulation, and a high rate of 23.5 Mbps, which employs GMSK as a modulation scheme. Thus, every packet contains a low-rate header (sent at 1.47 Mbps) followed by a high rate header plus payload (sent at 23.5 Mbps; see Figure 14). By merely looking at the low-rate header, a node can decide whether it needs to listen to the rest of the packet. This way, an over-hearing node can save power by turning off its error correction, equalization, and other functionalities as soon as it realizes it is not the intended destination of a packet. Note that Figure 14 will be clearer after the next paragraph (Bing 2000).

As the data rate transmitted over a wireless channel increases, the effect of intersymbol interference (ISI) increases. Symbol duration becomes smaller, and, as a result, delay spread effect grows. To circumvent this problem, decision feedback equalization is employed. An equalizer eliminates the effect of ISI without enhancing the noise. Equalization involves a training sequence, which is known to the receiver to be transmitted by the sender. Upon receiving this sequence, the receiver compares it with the already known sequence and adjusts its filter coefficients. At this moment, the receiver is ready to receive user data. Periodically, the receiver will need retraining to ensure effective ISI cancellation. The HIPERLAN standard does not specify what equalization technique should be used, leaving this decision to protocol implementers. GMSK has excellent power efficiency and spectral efficiency. It is a constant envelope scheme, which means that the amplitude of the signal is constant. Hence, highly efficient power amplifiers can be used (no information

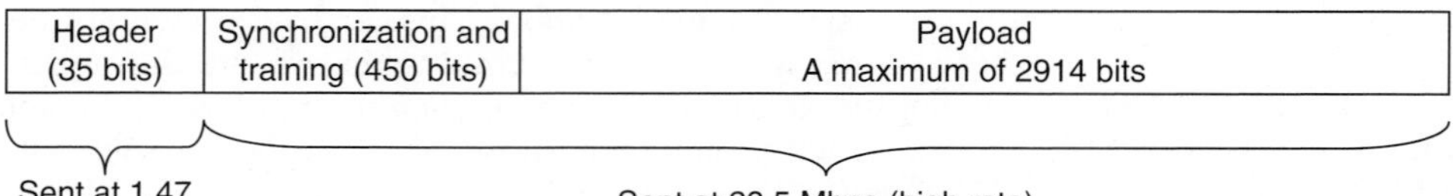

Figure 14: HIPERLAN/1 packet format (Bing 2000)

loss will occur from nonlinear amplification because the signal amplitude is not carrying any information; Rappaport 1996). In addition, forward error correction (FEC) is used to increase the throughput by minimizing the need for retransmissions of bad packets. The broadcast channel (BCH) is used where every 26 bits are coded to 31 bits (Nicopolitidis et al. 2003).

The MAC protocol of HIPERLAN/1 supports both asynchronous (data) and isochronous (audio and video) applications. The protocol does not reserve bandwidth for different users or application classes. However, it provides QoS by means of the supported priority-scheduling scheme, favoring higher-priority packets and taking into account their lifetime. The HIPERLAN/1 MAC protocol is distributed, allowing for both infrastructure and ad hoc, multi-hop topologies. A node that senses the channel idle for 1700 bit times (in the high data rate) can transmit its packet with no overhead involved. However, the chances of the channel being idle for 1700 bit times are extremely low, even for moderate load conditions. Thus, another mechanism can also grant channel access, which involves the use of the elimination yield–non-preemptive multiple access (EY-NPMA). A station that senses a busy channel first waits until the channel becomes idle, then waits for 256 bit times (called the synchronization slot), and finally runs the EY-NPMA. In an EY-NPMA scheme, channel access involves going through three phases (listed as follows), each of which can be thought of as a screening phase. In every phase, some nodes will drop from the competition, and the rest will continue on to contend in the next phase. The third phase, however, does not guarantee a single winner; thus, collisions—although unlikely—are still possible.

1. The prioritization phase consists of five slots, allowing for five priority levels. A station with priority r transmits a burst in slot r+1, indicating a busy channel if and only if it does not sense a higher-priority burst. The higher the node's priority, the faster it can get hold of the channel. At the end of this phase, one or more nodes (all with the same priority) will move on to the next phase. All others will have to wait until the next synchronization slot.
2. The elimination phase is thirteen slots long. In this phase, stations that survived the previous phase transmit a burst for a number of slots geometrically distributed with a parameter $P = 0.5$. Thus, the burst length is 1 slot with probability ½, 2 slots with probability 0.25, and so on. Each station, at the end of its burst, senses the channel to see if a longer burst has been transmitted by other stations. If yes, the station stops contending for the channel. If no, the station continues to the next phase. Obviously, the chances of having more than one winner in this phase grow with the increase in the number of nodes that make it from the previous phase.
3. The yield phase is fifteen slots long. All of the stations that made it to this phase back off for s slots, where s is geometrically distributed with a parameter $P = 0.1$. A station that senses an idle channel at the end of its back-off interval can transmit its packet.

An overview of the EY-NPMA protocol is shown in Figure 15.

HIPERLAN/1 supports ad hoc topologies using a process called interforwarding. In simple terms, nodes can communicate with nodes out of their reach by transmitting to their neighbors, who forward the communication to their neighbors, and so on until the communication reaches its intended destination. For this to work properly, nonforwarding nodes need to know their direct neighbors, and forwarding nodes need to know routing information (i.e., the next hop to get to a particular destination and the path length). The forwarding function is optional, and a node may choose not to forward traffic. A node can forward packets in two modes: point-to-point and broadcast. In broadcast mode, the forwarding node, called a multipoint relay, forwards the packet to all neighbors. Nonmultipoint relays do not forward packets they receive. The set of multipoint relays is chosen as the minimum set that covers all nodes within two hops from the node, thus minimizing the number of forwarding nodes.

Like other ad hoc networks, the multihop mode of HIPERLAN has many problems. The dynamic nature of a network in which nodes come and go makes maintaining correct information about the topology very difficult. In addition, the overhead involved in maintaining this information is very costly, especially in terms of energy because mobile nodes are battery operated. Another problem that is aggravated in a multihop network is the wireless channel conditions. Dual Doppler effect (both sender and receiver are mobile), interference caused by parallel transmissions, and fading all make the chances of a packet successfully reaching its destination very small.

HIPERLAN Type 2

Upon completion of the HIPERLAN/1 standard, the ETSI decided to merge wireless LANs and wireless local loop, the communication between the end user and the service

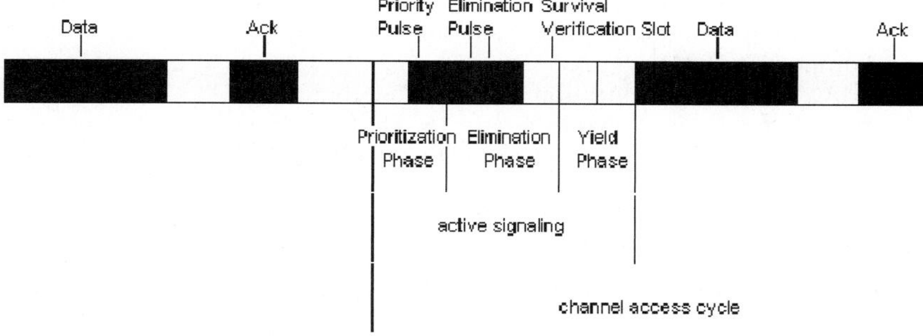

Figure 15: The EY-NPMA protocol

provider, into one protocol called the broadband radio access network (BRAN). The BRAN project standardizes wireless ATM protocols, includes HIPERLAN types 2, 3, and 4.

HIPERLAN/2 is very different from HIPERLAN/1 and has many salient features as follows (BRAN 2001; Johnsson 1999; Nicopolitidis et al. 2003):

- High data rates: HIPERLAN/2 supports data rates up to 54 Mbps.
- Connection-oriented: Communication between stations and the AP is connection oriented. A connection is established prior to any data transmission.
- QoS support: Connection orientation and the provision of high data rates enable HIPERLAN/2 to provide QoS support.
- Automatic frequency allocation: Unlike cellular networks in which static radio frequency planning is performed, the AP in HIPERLAN/2 performs dynamic frequency channel selection that is not in use by other APs, which minimizes co-channel interference.
- Power saving: A mobile station can communicate to the AP its desire to schedule sleep periods in order to minimize power consumption. At the end of every sleep period, the station wakes up to see if the AP has sent any wake-up indication. If not, the station can go back to sleep for another period.

The physical layer of HIPERLAN/2 is very similar to the physical layer of the 802.11a. They both operate in the 5 GHz band and use OFDM. In addition, both offer data rates as high as 54 Mbps. To a certain extent, the same modulation and coding schemes are used. However, their synchronization and training sequences differ.

Differences between the two protocols appear in the MAC layer. The 802.11 is based on the CSMA/CA protocol. One problem with CSMA/CA is that it is probabilistic: a station does not have any guarantee that within a given time period it will be granted the channel to transmit. These delays render the support of any real-time application very difficult, even under moderate load conditions. HIPERLAN/2 is based on dynamic time division multiple access (TDMA) with time division duplexing (TDD). In a TDMA scheme, stations are dynamically assigned time slots according to their needs. Time slots are dynamically allocated depending on transmission needs. TDD means that part of the frame is used for the uplink (communication between the stations and the AP), and part for the downlink (from the AP to the stations). Once assigned a time slot, a station can transmit on a regular basis during its slot. The AP notifies the stations when it is their time to transmit (Doufexi et al. 2002; Papadimitriou, Lagkas, and Pomportsis 2003).

A MAC frame has a duration of 2 ms and consists of different channels, as shown in Figure 16. The broadcast channel is a downlink channel through which the AP sends control information to all nodes in the network. This includes transmission power level, wake-up indicator, and identifier of the AP and the network, among other things. The frame control channel (FCH) is also a downlink channel that is used to announce how the rest of the current MAC frame has been allocated (i.e., how much for the uplink, for the downlink, and for contention). The access feedback channel (ACH), also a downlink channel, conveys information regarding previous random access attempts that took place in the RCH. The downlink and uplink phases consist of a number of packets to be communicated from and to the AP, respectively. The number of slots and how many per station is based on the AP announcements during the FCH channel. The random access channel (RCH) is an uplink channel used to compete for slots in subsequent MAC frames. Results of contention are reported back to stations in subsequent frames' ACH channels (Johnsson 1999).

WLANs SECURITY

Wireless networks are more vulnerable to security threats than wired networks because of the broadcast nature of the wireless channel. Any node within the transmission range of a wireless LAN can access it, thus enforcing security measures is of high importance in a wireless LAN. Two mechanisms are generally used to minimize security threats: authentication and encryption. Authentication ensures that only authorized nodes can access the network, and encryption ensures that confidentiality is maintained (Obaidat and Boudriga 2007).

Encryption in 802.11

Encryption is the process of transforming human-readable data (the plain text) into an unreadable form (the cipher text). Encryption and decryption typically involve the use of a common secret between the sender and the receiver (the encryption key). Figure 17 illustrates the idea of encryption. Two types of encryption exist: block cipher and stream cipher. They both involve generating a key (the stream key) from a basic secret key. In block cipher, the plain text is divided into blocks, and each block is encrypted using a fixed-size stream key. In a stream cipher, on the other hand, the data stream is processed continuously (e.g., taking one byte at a time). In addition, the stream key size is not fixed. Block ciphers provide higher levels of security than stream ciphers, but they are more computationally demanding.

The 802.11 standard uses the wired equivalent privacy (WEP) protocol, which is based on the RC4 encryption algorithm. RC4 is a stream cipher that uses symmetrical keys; if the sender uses a key K_1 to encrypt the data, the receiver uses the same key (i.e., K_1) to decrypt it. Symmetrical key encryption is simple and requires very trivial amounts of computation. The protocol tries to minimize the computation penalty introduced by encryption using

BCH	FCH	ACH	Downlink Phase		Uplink Phase	RCH

Figure 16: Format of the MAC frame in HIPERLAN/2

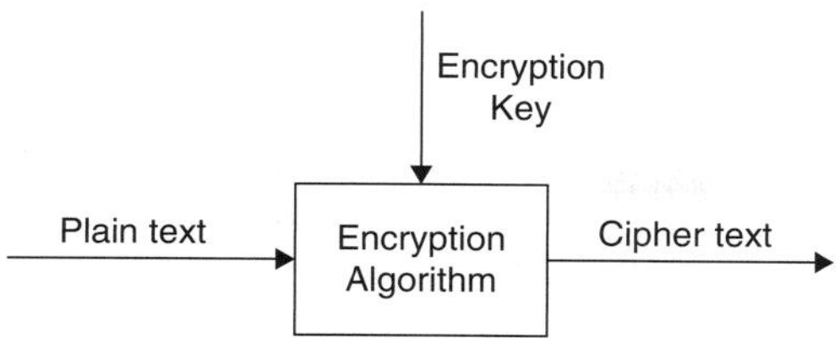

Figure 17: Block diagram of the encryption process

stream, symmetric algorithm. The protocol does not provide any key distribution mechanism and thus assumes the keys to be manually configured in the client stations as well as the access point. Two key lengths are supported: 40 bits and 104 bits. The longer the key, the more difficult it is for an attacker to conduct a brute force attack in which all possible keys are tried.

If every time an encryption algorithm is fed a plain text P and generates the same cipher text C, then that algorithm is described as an electronic code book (ECB). An attacker can do cryptanalysis to find patterns in the cipher text that can help him break the encryption. To provide higher security, WEP circumvents this problem using a concept called initialization vectors (IVs). The goal is to change the encryption algorithm's output even if fed the same plain text. Thus, the encryption of a string P results in a cipher text C_1; if the algorithm is run again, using the same string P, it will produce a cipher text C_2, and so on.

An IV is nothing but a number to be added to the key, which results in a new key. To ensure high randomness in the cipher text, the IV should be changed for every frame sent. For the receiver to be able to decrypt the message, it needs access to the IV value used at the sender, which is why every frame sent carries with it the IV used. The encryption process involves the following steps (Roshan and Leary 2004):

1. For every arriving frame, generate a 24-bit IV and append it to the secret key K_1, resulting in a stream key K_2.
2. Calculate the integrity check value (ICV) of the arriving frame. The ICV is a CRC-32 that is used to ensure that the frame has not been tampered with or corrupted in transmission.
3. Encrypt both the frame payload and the ICV using K_2.
4. Create a frame that contains the encrypted payload, the encrypted ICV, and the IV used for the encryption.

The opposite process takes place at the receiving end. The receiver extracts the IV value, constructs the stream key, uses it to decrypt the payload and the ICV, and finally compares the decrypted ICV with an ICV it calculates for the arriving payload. If both match, the frame is good (Obaidat and Boudriga 2007).

Authentication in 802.11

The 802.11 supports two authentication mechanisms: open system authentication and shared key authentication. Open system authentication is a two-way authentication that is used when a high security level is not required. A station requesting authentication sends a request to the access point. The access point responds with a frame indicating either approval or disapproval. The shared key algorithm is based on WEP and requires the station and the access point to have a shared key. A four-way authentication process takes place, which can be described as follows:

1. Client sends authentication request to the AP.
2. AP sends back a challenge.
3. Client sends back the challenge, encrypted.
4. The AP decrypts what is received and compares it with the challenge. A match results in successful authentication.

Another authentication method that is not part of the 802.11 standard yet is implemented by many vendors is the MAC address authentication. Here, the client's MAC address is compared against a list of MAC addresses that are authorized to access the network. This process is vulnerable to device theft; thus, it should be used in combination with the other two approaches to allow for more security. The MAC address list is stored in a separate server called the RADIUS server. During the authentication process, the AP communicates with the RADIUS server to see if the latter has the MAC address in question (Obaidat and Boudriga 2007).

Vulnerabilities

It is well known that the 802.11 security mechanisms are vulnerable to all sorts of attacks. As an example, consider the shared key authentication process. The AP sends the challenge in clear text format, which exposes the authentication procedure to clear text attacks. An eavesdropper can get the challenge and the response, and from these two extract the stream key. This is easy because the encryption is a simple exclusive OR (XOR) operation between the plain text and the stream key; XORing the cipher text and the clear text gives the stream key. Using the stream key, the hacker can be authenticated easily because he/she can encrypt any challenge the AP sends. Listening to the channel and obtaining all of the information sent back and forth is very simple. All a hacker needs is a sniffing software tool, which can log all of the communications taking place on the channel.

An easier way to get the key is to make an educated guess. Remember that the keys have to be manually set up. In many cases, users do not change the key when it comes from the manufacturer, which makes guessing a simple matter of knowing the default key/keys that come from different vendors.

The IV length (24 bits) presents another security threat. Given a highly loaded network or a patient hacker, the AP will exhaust all IVs and start reusing them. The hacker can thus collect enough frames with the same IV and extract the common parts between them. This would expose the secret key along with the whole wireless LAN.

The lack of AP authentication (having the AP authenticate itself to the station) is yet another vulnerability.

A hacker passively listening on the channel for an ample amount of time can collect useful information that enables him to set up an AP. Nodes closer to this (rogue) AP will connect to it. This way, the attacker will collect valid users' information and use it to access the network. This would not be possible if the AP had to authenticate itself to the stations (Geier 2002a). Even more vulnerability has been pointed out in the research community; Geier (2002a) contains a list of such sources.

QoS SUPPORT: IEEE 802.11e

As users grow accustomed to wireless LANs, their expectations rise. Users want wireless LANs to provide the same functionality as wired counterpart. In addition, the emergence of new applications of wireless LANs—including home-office networking and wireless local loop—that require delay- and loss-sensitive multimedia communication makes QoS support an inevitable extension. Corporate wireless networks are expected to provide voice over IP (VoIP) services that can reduce or even replace the need to use cell phones in the work environment. Home networks, in which a wireless network can eliminate all the wires in a home and connect the different devices together, are another foreseeable domain. Service providers would benefit from a wireless local loop for their services; this would provide a cost-effective solution and a competitive edge.

Challenges in Providing QoS over Wireless

The wireless channel is highly dynamic. The signal strength and quality are affected by fading, self-interference, co-channel interference, and noise, among other things. In addition, nodes move in random patterns and change their access points as they do so. At the same time, energy consumption has to be minimized because the devices used (laptops, PDAs, etc.) are battery operated. These and other issues make supporting QoS over wireless a very challenging task.

As we have seen, the hidden terminal problem imposes difficulties on sensing the channel and thus represents a limiting factor of the performance of the MAC protocol. The DCF of the 802.11 uses a CSMA-based protocol, which involves back-off periods of random length. Therefore, by definition the DCF is not suitable for QoS support. The PCF, even though it was proposed to address delay-sensitive applications, was found to provide poor performance for even a small number of voice communications. This is readily apparent because the increase in the number of PCF nodes results in an increase in the polling list. Hence, nodes end up waiting for longer periods for their chance to transmit. Another problem with the PCF is its lack of different priority levels. In addition, the PCF works only in the infrastructure mode and not in the ad hoc mode. As a result, the 802.11e has been developed (IEEE 802.11e Working Group 2005).

QoS Mechanisms

The 802.11e provides QoS support using two coordination functions: the hybrid coordination function (HCF) with contention avoidance, and the HCF with polled access operation. The first is more commonly referred to as the enhanced DCF (EDCF).

Table 3: ACs and Applications Addressed

AC	Applications Targeted
0	Low priority/best effort traffic
1	Video probe
2	High-rate real time (e.g., video)
3	Low-rate real time (e.g., voice)

Enhanced DCF

The 802.11e (both EDCF and HCF) supports four traffic classes known as access categories (AC) in the 802.11e terminology. Table 3 shows the different ACs and what applications they address. The protocol assumes the existence of a mechanism to classify the traffic. In other words, the protocol works with packets already marked with one of the four ACs.

The protocol supports the different priorities by mainly changing two parameters: the inter-frame spacing and the limits of the contention window. The traditional DCF supports priority in gaining the channel, by introducing different IFSs for ACKs, PCF, and DCF. Similarly, the EDCF uses different IFSs for different ACs (called arbitration IFSs, or AIFSs). Thus, higher-priority packets can acquire the channel before others. In addition, the size of the contention window is smaller for higher-priority packets. The smaller the contention window size, the faster a node can gain the channel. The smaller the CW_{min}, the shorter the back-off time. Furthermore, the faster a station reaches the CW_{max}, the faster it increments its retry counter, which results in faster channel gain.

In traditional DCF, a station has to contend for the channel for every packet it needs to transmit. EDCF, in contrast, allows transmission of more than one packet. The transmit opportunity (TXOP) is a parameter that defines the duration of time a station can seize the channel once access is gained.

If you have ever tried to make a phone call and heard the "all circuits are busy" message, you know what admission control is. Given the limited amount of resources available, a network can support a defined volume of traffic for every AC. If the input traffic of a particular AC exceeds its defined limit, all sources belonging to that AC will suffer. To prevent such behavior, admission control is applied. The goal of admission control is to deny access to any source attempting to use the channel once the predefined limit has been reached. The distributed admission control (DAC) scheme of the EDCF monitors channel utilization and announces that information to all stations in its beacon message. When the available resources approach zero, sources stop initiating new stream sessions.

HCF with Polled Access Operation

The HCF operation is very similar to the PCF function; it relies on polling to meet different nodes' requirements.

A logical entity called the hybrid coordinator (HC) that runs in the AP is responsible for scheduling and other processing related to the polling operation. Unlike the EDCF, in which the TXOP is predefined, the HCF provides a mechanism for stations to request a TXOP with specific characteristics. The HCF can operate in one of two modes: contention-free HCF and coexistence with the EDCF.

In the contention-free HCF, the AP polls the stations. In its poll message, the AP specifies the TXOP. A station with some traffic to send replies to the poll within a SIFS period. If the station does not have traffic or if the length of the TXOP is not sufficient, it replies with a null frame.

The HCF function can operate with both the EDCF and the DCF at the same time. To poll the stations, the AP waits for the duration of a PIFS time, which is shorter than what a DCF or EDCF station needs to wait for. Thus, the AP can gain the channel. Similarly, a polled station has to wait only for the duration of a SIFS time to respond to a poll. Therefore, the HCF function can work smoothly during the contention period of EDCF or DCF.

Although the EDCF has the logic to indicate whether new traffic should be initiated, it does not enforce any type of behavior on the nodes. The AP simply announces the available capacity. Honoring this information (or not) is completely up to the stations. The HCF, on the other hand, has a strict admission control mechanism. A station willing to initiate a stream has to consult with the AP, which determines whether the stream can be supported without affecting other streams. Stations communicate to the AP the QoS parameters they desire using the transmission specification (TSPEC). In the TSPEC, a station specifies the priority, data rate, delay, and frame size, among other parameters. The AP checks these requirements against the current network conditions and decides accordingly whether to honor the request, reject it, or provide the station with TSPEC that it can afford to support (i.e., renegotiate the requirements). The station may accept the offer or turn it down. A station is removed from the pollable list either when it explicitly deletes the TSPEC or when the TSPEC timer expires. The timer expires when the station sends a null frame for a number of poll requests within a defined time interval defined by the TSPEC timer.

ADVANCED TOPICS

Bluetooth

Bluetooth is a low-power (1 mW), short-range (within 10 m) technology. It was initially proposed by Ericsson as a way to use laptops for making phone calls over a cell phone. The technology has been adopted by many companies and for different applications, primarily with regard to cable replacement and ad hoc networking (intercommunication between Bluetooth-enabled devices). Like WLANs, Bluetooth works in the ISM band, which is the reason it uses the high rate frequency-hopping scheme.

A Bluetooth network is organized into piconets and scatternets. A piconet is a small network consisting of a master node and a number of slaves (between one and seven). The master node is responsible for choosing the communication channel, including frequencies and the hopping sequence used. Nodes in a piconet communicate through the master node and not directly. A node may belong to one or more piconets. This overlapping creates what is called a scatternet. The latter allows for multihop communication in which overlapping nodes serve as forwarders from one piconet to another.

The protocol consists of the following five layers, which are responsible for link establishment and maintenance, security and error control, service discovery, and communication with higher-layer protocols (Stallings 2002; Nicopolitidis et al. 2003):

1. Radio layer: This layer deals with the specifications of the air interface. Frequency bandwidth, modulation, transmission power, and channel access are specified. The standard specifies the use of GFSK for modulation. It also specifies the use of FHSS operating in a 78 MHz bandwidth with each channel occupying 1 MHz. The hopping rate is equal to 1600 hops/sec and a maximum data rate of 1 Mbps.
2. Baseband layer: This layer specifies how FHSS with TDD/TDMA is to be used for communication between nodes in a piconet. To prevent interference, nodes in different piconets use CDMA (i.e., different piconets use different hopping sequences). Two types of communication can be used. The synchronous connection-oriented (SCO) type is used for communication between a slave and a master and involves the allocation of fixed bandwidth. The asynchronous connectionless (ACL) type is a point-to-multipoint communication between the master and all of the slaves in a piconet.
3. Link manager protocol (LMP): As its name implies, this protocol specifies link setup and management between two Bluetooth devices. Issues include clock synchronization, authentication and key distribution for security purposes, the protocol version used, the nodes' mode (master or slave), and so forth.
4. Logical link control and adaptation protocol (L2CAP): This protocol defines connection-less as well as connection-oriented services. It also allows for QoS support by letting a transmitter and a receiver negotiate QoS flow parameters such as delay and delay variation.
5. Service discovery protocol (SDP): This protocol specifies how Bluetooth devices search for other Bluetooth devices and establish communication with them.

One domain in which Bluetooth is envisaged to serve greatly is home networking. Connectivity between different devices at home that serves both coordination and cable freedom will provide more user-friendly technology.

Voice over 802.11

Although wireless LANs were initially thought of as wireless versions of a wired LAN, which implies that they are solely for data communications, the fact that they are wireless introduces higher expectations. Voice over WLAN provides one such example. Even though cellular networks allow voice communications while users are on the move, a common network used for both voice and data costs less than operating two separate networks—one for data and one for voice.

As we have seen, 802.11 DCF is the fundamental access method of the 802.11 and is used for data communications. It uses CSMA/CA for channel access with a back-off algorithm to reduce the possibility of collisions. Although DCF was meant for data communications, studies have shown that it can be used for voice. However, the performance is relatively low (Prasad 1999). Because it is a random assignment scheme, DCF provides unbounded delays for high loads. Randomness means that the network cannot provide deterministic guarantees regarding delay. It is important to mention that delay and delay variation (jitter) are the key impairments for voice communications (Obaidat and Obeidat 2002; McDysan and Spohn 1999).

The inability of CSMA protocols to support real-time traffic has been studied in the context of voice/data integration over the Ethernet. It has been shown that the Ethernet can provide good performance at low loads. Moreover, it has been argued that the need for priority in WLANs is more pressing than in Ethernet for the following reasons:

1. WLANs provide lower rate than the Ethernet, which results in high queuing and transmission delays.
2. CSMA/CA has worse throughput/delay characteristics than CSMA/CD.

The PCF is used for real-time traffic that has delay bounds. However, it can operate only under the centralized scheme where there is a base station, because PCF uses polling to grant stations channel access. A lot of research has addressed the performance of voice and data over the PCF function of the IEEE 802.11. The performance of voice and data over the PCF function was studied with the assumption that voice communication takes place between stations that are in different basic service sets. The conclusion reached was that the performance of the PCF function was poor and only a few voice conversations could be supported. No echo cancellation was used; therefore, a small superframe size of 20 ms, which limits how many conversations can be in the polling list, was considered.

Crow et al. (1997b) propose the use of echo cancellation for voice communication. However, they use a 420 ms superframe size that consumes most of the delay budget of voice. This implies that if voice goes though an IEEE 802.11 link, it has to be the only link. In other words, the wireless link cannot be the last hop in the path between the source and the destination of the call. The authors suggest that when a voice station does not have any data to transmit or receive, it should be dropped from the polling list immediately. This way, the remaining bandwidth can be used by other stations. Nonetheless, leaving the list every time a station's silence period starts (i.e., the voice source is in the OFF state) will result in more delay at the beginning of every talk spurt, which will not be acceptable.

The performance of noncompressed voice (64 kbps) and data over IEEE 802.11 has been studied using an analytic approach. The conclusion is that the performance is low; with the introduction of echo cancellation, more voice conversations can be achieved, but this will affect the bandwidth available to the data stations. One recommendation for dealing with voice traffic is not to drop a voice station from the polling list, even when it is silent. Although this will limit the number of voice communications, it will control delays and delay variations, resulting in a reasonable number of voice conversations.

All of the aforementioned studies use the same PCF parameters that trade one thing for another. The key parameters here are the superframe size and the packet size. However, all of the studies concluded that voice performance over PCF is poor. A comparison between the performance of DCF and EDCF for voice, video, and data is provided in Choi et al. (2003). It is shown that EDCF provides better performance in terms of frame loss and delay for voice. However, PCF is not considered in the comparison.

CONCLUSION

This chapter introduces the reader to WLANs. It begins by providing the motivation and applications of WLANs. The most well-known WLAN standards, IEEE 802.11 and ETSI HIPERLAN, are explored. The main coordination functions (DCF and PCF) are defined, and their pros and cons are explained. Moving to the physical layer, FHSS, DSSS, and IR transmission schemes are presented, as are the a, b, and g versions of the IEEE 802.11 physical layer standard. Following the basic information, we explore issues of QoS and security in 802.11 context. We conclude the chapter by presenting some advanced related topics, such as the Bluetooth networks and the voice over 802.11 systems.

GLOSSARY

AC: Access categories; supported by the IEEE 802.11e standard in order to provide quality of service.

ACH: Access feedback channel; a time channel used in the MAC protocol of the HIPERLAN 2 standard. This is a downlink channel used by the AP to inform stations of previous random access attempts.

ACK: Acknowledgement packet transmitted by the destination node to the source node in order to acknowledge the successful reception of a data packet.

ACL: Asynchronous connectionless; in a Bluetooth network, this is a point-to-multipoint communication between the master and all of the slaves in a piconet.

Ad hoc network: A network topology in which there is no central control (base station or access point) and the stations are able to communicate directly.

AP: Access point; a station responsible for providing central control in a network cell.

ATM: Asynchronous transfer mode; a network technology based on transferring data in cells or packets of a fixed size.

Authentication: The process of identifying an individual, usually based on a username and password.

Band: A contiguous range of frequencies.

BCH: Broadcast channel; a downlink channel through which the AP sends control information to all nodes in a HIPERLAN 2 network.

Block Ciphers: An encryption type in which the plain text is divided into blocks, and each block is encrypted using a fixed-size stream key.

Bluetooth: A low-power (1 mW), short-range (within 10 m) wireless network technology.

BRAN: Broadband radio access network; an ETSI project that standardizes the wireless ATM protocols, including HIPERLAN types 2, 3, and 4.

BSA: Basic service area; the coverage area of a BSS.

BSS: Basic service set; resembles the basic building block in the 802.11 architecture. This is analogous to a cell in a cellular network.

Carrier: A waveform in a communications channel modulated to carry analog or digital signal information.

CCK: Complimentary code keying; a modulation technique used in the IEEE 802.11b standard. Using the CCK modulation, every 4 bits from the data stream are encoded in an 8-chip code, thus allowing for a data rate equal to 5.5 Mbps.

CDMA: Code division multiple access; a technique used to prevent interference among different nodes that transmit simultaneously along the same frequency band.

CFP: Contention-free period; a time interval defined by the PCF access mode.

Chip: A chip sequence is used to replace a data bit in the IEEE 802.11 standard.

Coding Techniques: Allow for maximizing the benefit of transmission over noisy wireless channels by introducing redundancies in the bits transmitted so that the receiver can still recover a reasonably distorted packet.

Collision: The situation that occurs when two or more nodes attempt to send a signal along the same channel at the same time. The result of a collision is generally a garbled message. All computer networks require some sort of mechanism to either prevent collisions altogether or recover from collisions when they do occur.

Contention-based Protocol: A MAC protocol type, in which nodes contend to gain access to the channel.

Contention-free Protocol: A MAC protocol type, usually used in infrastructure network topology, which states that the nodes do not contend for medium access; instead, there is a central control that decides which node can transmit.

CSMA/CA: Carrier sense multiple access with collision avoidance; a MAC protocol used by the IEEE 802.11 standard.

CSMA/CD: Carrier sense multiple access with collision detection; a MAC protocol used by the IEEE 802.3 (Ethernet) networks.

CTS: A clear-to-send packet is transmitted to the source node by the destination node in a IEEE 802.11 WLAN to show that it ready to receive data.

CW: Contention window; a time interval that defines the range of the back-off time in an IEEE 802.11 WLAN.

DBPSK: Differential binary phase shift keying; in an IEEE 802.11 WLAN, the DSSS physical layer uses this modulation technique in which every symbol carries one bit, allowing for a data rate of 1 Mbps.

DCF: Distributed coordination function; a contention-based protocol that resembles the basic access mode of the 802.11 standard. It is based on the CSMA/CA scheme and assumes an ad hoc network topology.

DIFS: Distributed coordination function IFS; the time delay used by DCF frames.

Directional Antennas: Focus their radiation in one direction to provide greater coverage distance.

Diversity Antennas: Receive on more than one element; when transmitting, they send through the element with the best received signal.

DQPSK: Differential quadrature phase shift keying; in order to support data rate of 2 Mbps in an IEEE 802.11 WLAN, this modulation technique is used in which every symbol carries two bits from the data stream.

DSSS: Direct sequence spread spectrum; a physical layer protocol used by IEEE 802.11. The main idea of DSSS is to spread the signal energy over a large bandwidth so that the signal can be treated as noise that can be easily rejected by unintended receivers.

ECD: Electronic codebook; any encryption algorithm that generates the same cipher text every time it is fed the same plain text.

EDCF: Enhanced DCF; this protocol is used by the IEEE 802.11e standard. It uses traffic categories to support QoS.

ESS: Extended service set; multiple BSSs can be connected to one another by connecting their APs to a distribution system, forming this service set.

ETSI: European Telecommunications Standards Institute.

Exposed Terminal: This problem can appear in an ad hoc WLAN topology. Specifically, a node postpones its transmission because it wrongly estimates that its data will collide.

EY-NPMA: Elimination yield–non-preemptive multiple access; this protocol is a contention-based MAC protocol used by the HIPERLAN 1 standard.

FCC: Federal Communications Commission; main duty is to regulate public airwaves in the United States.

FCH: Frame control channel; a downlink channel that is used by the AP to announce how the rest of the current MAC frame has been allocated. This is used by the HIPERLAN 2 WLAN standard.

FEC: Forward error control; increases the throughput by minimizing the need for retransmissions of bad packets (used by HIPERLAN).

FHSS: Frequency hopping spread spectrum; a signal is spread by sending at one frequency for a short period of time and then switching (hopping) to another frequency in a seemingly random fashion. This is a physical layer protocol used by the IEEE 802.11 standard.

GFSK: Gaussian frequency shift keying; according to the IEEE 802.11 standard, the PMD sublayer modulates data using this technique. Depending on the data rate supported (1 Mbps or 2 Mbps), either GFSK or 4 GFSK is used. 4GFSK translates every 2 bits into one signal element, allowing for double the rate.

GMSK: Gaussian minimum shift keying; this modulation scheme is used by the HIPERLAN/1 standard.

HCF: Hybrid coordination function; a QoS supportive protocol used by the IEEE 802.11e standard.

HEC: Header error control; an ITU-T cyclic redundancy check, CRC16 used for error detection by the IEEE 802.11 standard.

Hidden Terminal: This problem can appear in an ad hoc WLAN topology using carrier sense. Specifically, a node's transmission collides because it is not able to detect the transmission of another node.

HIPERLAN: High performance local area network; a WLAN standard defined by ETSI.

HR-DSSS: High-rate DSSS; defined by 802.11b, this service set allows data rates as high as 5.5 Mbps and 11 Mbps.

IBSS: Independent basic service set; resembles the infrastructure-less ad hoc arrangement. In an IBSS, stations communicate in a peer-to-peer fashion in which no AP or other intermediary is needed. At least two stations are needed to form an IBSS.

IFS: Inter-frame spacing; in an IEEE 802.11 WLAN, access priority to the wireless channel is provided by this spacing, which is the duration of time that has to pass before an attempt is made to access the channel.

Infrastructure Topology: A network topology in which the medium access is controlled centrally (using a base station or access point).

Interference: Refers to the extraneous, unwanted signals that affect the proper system operation. Not only does interference affect the quality of the signal communicated from the transmitter to the receiver, it can also affect the functionality of the protocol.

IR: Infrared.

ISI: Intersymbol interference; this problem results when a symbol takes too long to reach the receiver. This delay, called delay spread, results from multipath propagation. Because of this delay, a symbol may arrive at the same time as another subsequent symbol.

ISM: Industrial, scientific, and medical band; a frequency band that does not require any licensing; thus, it is used by many wireless applications.

L2CAP: Logical link control and adaptation protocol; used by the Bluetooth standard and defines connectionless and connection-oriented services. It also allows for QoS support by letting a transmitter and a receiver negotiate QoS flow parameters such as delay and delay variation, among other things.

LMP: Link manager protocol; specifies link setup and management between two Bluetooth devices. Issues include clock synchronization, authentication and key distribution for security purposes, the protocol version used, the nodes' mode (master or slave), and so forth.

MAC: Medium access control.

Modulation Techniques: Techniques used to modulate the data stream into a form suitable for physical transmission.

Multipath Fading and Shadowing: When a signal is transmitted, multiple versions of the same signal take different paths to reach the receiver. The first to arrive at the receiver is the one that goes through the line of sight (LOS), which is the path that does not have any obstacles between the transmitter and the receiver. Other, delayed versions follow other paths that result from impinges on obstacles in the path. When these delayed copies arrive, they either add constructively or destructively to the receiver. This phenomenon, in which the signal quality depends on the multipath propagation, is referred to as multipath fading.

NAV: Network allocation vector; in an IEEE 802.11 network, every node maintains this vector. Nodes adjust the values of their vectors as they overhear packet transmissions. A node attempts to check the channel status (whether idle or not) only when the duration in the NAV elapses.

OFDM: Orthogonal frequency division multiplexing; according to the IEEE 802.11a standard, the data are modulated using this scheme. OFDM breaks the channel bandwidth into subchannels. Each subchannel has a low symbol rate and thus low ISI. The subchannels are chosen to be orthogonal; as a result, low co-channel interference occurs.

Omnidirectional Antennas: Provide a 360-degree radiation pattern.

Path Loss: As a signal propagates from the transmitter to the receiver, it attenuates (i.e., loses its energy) with distance. This phenomenon is called path loss. It depends on many other factors as well, including the reflecting objects and big obstructions in the path between the transmitter and the receiver.

PBCC: Packet binary convolutional coding; a modulation technique used in the IEEE 802.11b standard. Using this modulation, every 8 bits from the data stream are encoded in an 8-chip code, thus allowing for a data rate equal to 11 Mbps.

PCF: Point coordination function; provides a contention-free protocol that can be used for connection-oriented real-time traffic such as voice in an IEEE 802.11 network. This is done by polling the stations one at a time using the access point.

PIFS: PCF inter-frame space; in an IEEE 802.11 network, this is the short time interval that the AP has to wait in order to gain access to the channel before any other node.

PLCP: Physical layer convergence protocol; an 802.11 sublayer protocol responsible for adding necessary headers for the purposes of synchronization, timing, and error control.

PLW: PSDU length word; a 12-bit field that indicates the size of the MAC frame used by the physical layer of the IEEE 802.11 standard.

PMD: Physical medium dependent; this sublayer is responsible for raw transmission of bits over the air; mainly performs modulation of the data stream. It is defined by the IEEE 802.11 standard.

PSF: PLCP signaling field; a 4-bit field used to specify the data rate at which a frame was transmitted. Data rates range from 1 Mbps to 4.5 Mbps in increments of 0.5 Mbps. This is defined by the IEEE 802.11 standard.

QoS: Quality of service.

RC4: A stream cipher encryption algorithm that uses symmetrical keys.

RCH: Random access channel; an uplink channel used by the nodes to compete for slots in subsequent MAC frames. This is used by the HIPERLAN/2 MAC protocol.

RTS: Request to send; in an IEEE 802.11 WLAN, this control packet is initially transmitted by the source node to the destination node to obtain permission to transmit data.

SCO: Synchronous connection oriented; in a Bluetooth network, this is a communication between a slave and a master that involves the allocation of fixed bandwidth.

SDP: Service discovery protocol; specifies how Bluetooth devices search for other Bluetooth devices and establish communication with them.

SIFS: Short IFS; according to the IEEE 802.11 MAC protocol, this is the shortest amount of time and hence the highest priority, followed by the PIFS and the DIFS.

Stream Ciphers: In a stream cipher encryption algorithm, the data stream is processed continuously (e.g., one byte at a time).

TDD: Time division duplexing; the main idea of this protocol is that part of the frame is used for the uplink and part is used for the downlink.

TDMA: Time division multiple access; in this scheme, stations are dynamically assigned time slots according to their needs.

TSPEC: Transmission specification; in an IEEE 802.11e network, stations communicate the QoS parameters they desire to the AP using this method. In the TSPEC, a station specifies the priority, data rate, delay, and frame size, among other things.

UNII: Unlicensed National Information Infrastructure; a 5GHz frequency band used by IEEE 802.11a and the HIPERLAN networks.

WEP: Wired equivalent privacy; the 802.11 standard uses this protocol, which is based on the RC4 encryption algorithm. A better and more secure protocol—called Wi-Fi protected access (WPA)—was released recently.

WLAN: Wireless local area network.

CROSS REFERENCES

See *Bluetooth Technology*; *Network QoS*; *Wireless LAN Standards*.

REFERENCES

Antenova, Ltd. Undated. http://www.gigaant.com/ (accessed April 1, 2004).

Bing B. 2000. *High-speed wireless ATM and LANs*. Norwood, MA: Artech House.

Broadband Radio Access Network (BRAN). 1998. High performance radio local area network (HIPERLAN), type 1, functional specification V1.2.1.

———. 2001. High performance radio local area network (HIPERLAN), type 2, specification V1.1.1.

Choi, S., J. DelPrado, S. Shankar, and S. Mangold. 2003. IEEE 802.11e contention-based channel access (EDCF) performance evaluation. In *Proceedings of the ICC 2003*, Vol. 2, 1151–56.

Crow, B. P., I. Widjaja, J. G. Kim, and P. Sakai. 1997a. Investigation of the IEEE 802.11 medium access control (MAC) sublayer functions. In *Proceedings of Infocom'97*, Vol. 1, 126–33.

———. 1997b. IEEE 802.11 wireless local area networks. *IEEE Communications* 35, no. 9: 116–26.

Doufexi, A., S. Armour, A. Nix, and D. Bull. 2002. A comparison of HIPERLAN/2 and IEEE 802.11a Wireless LAN Standards. *IEEE Communications Magazine* 40(5): 172–80.

Geier, J. 2002a. Minimizing 802.11 interference issues. *Wi-Fi Planet*. http://www.wi-fiplanet.com/tutorials/article.php/953511 (accessed April 1, 2004).

———. 2002b. Minimizing WLAN security threats. *Wi-Fi Planet*. http://www.wi-fiplanet.com/tutorials/article.php/1457211 (accessed April 1, 2004).

Institute of Electrical and Electronics Engineers (IEEE). 1997. Wireless LAN medium access control (MAC) and physical layer (PHY) specification. IEEE Std. 802.11.

Institute of Electrical and Electronics Engineers (IEEE) 802.11a Working Group. 1999. Supplement to IEEE standard for information technology—Telecommunications and information exchange between systems; Local and metropolitan area networks; Specific requirements—Part II: Wireless LAN medium access control (MAC) and physical layer (PHY) specifications, high-speed physical layer in the 5GHz band.

Institute of Electrical and Electronics Engineers (IEEE) 802.11b Working Group. 1999. Supplement to IEEE standard for information technology—Telecommunications and information exchange between systems; Local and metropolitan area networks; Specific requirements—Part II: Wireless LAN medium access control (MAC) and physical layer (PHY) specifications, higher-speed physical layer extension in the 2.4 GHz band.

Institute of Electrical and Electronics Engineers (IEEE) 802.11e Working Group. 2005. P802.11e: Draft amendment to standard [for] for information technology—Telecommunications and information exchange between systems; LAN/MAN specific requirements—Part II: Wireless medium access control (MAC) and physical layer (PHY) specifications, Amendment 7: Medium access control (MAC) quality of service (QoS) enhancements. Draft version D13.

Institute of Electrical and Electronics Engineers (IEEE) 802.11g Working Group. 2003. International standard for information technology—Telecommunications and information exchange between systems; Local and metropolitan area networks; Specific requirements—Part II:Wireless LAN medium access control (MAC) and physical layer (PHY) specifications, Amendment 4: Further higher data rate extension in the 2.4GHz band.

Jain, R. 2007. http://rajjain.com/cis788-99/ftp/wireless_lans/ (accessed August 10, 2007).

Johnsson, M. 1999. HiperLAN/2: The broadband radio transmission technology operating in the 5 GHz frequency band. *HiperLAN/2 Global Forum*, Version 1.0.

McDysan, D. E., and D. Spohn. 1999. *ATM theory and applications*. New York: McGraw-Hill.

Nicopolitidis, P., M. S. Obaidat, G. I. Papadimitriou, and A. S. Pomportsis. 2003. *Wireless networks*. Chichester, UK: John Wiley & Sons.

Obaidat, M. S., and N. Boudriga. 2007. *Security of e-systems and computer networks*. New York: Cambridge University Press.

Obaidat, M., and S. Obeidat. 2002. Modeling and simulation of adaptive ABR voice over ATM networks. *Simulation: Transactions of the Society for Modeling and Simulation Internationa*l (SCS) 78, no. 3: 139–49.

Papadimitriou, G., T. Lagkas, M. S. Obaidat, and A. S. Pomportsis. 2003. A new approach to the simulation of HIPERLAN wireless networks. Proceedings of *2003 European Simulation Symposium*, Delft, the Netherlands, October, pp. 459–68.

Papadimitriou, G., T. D. Lagkas, and A. S. Pomportsis. 2003. HIPERSIM: A sense range distinctive simulation environment for HIPERLAN systems. *Journal of Simulation* 79, no. 8: 462–81.

Prasad, A. R. 1999. Performance comparison of voice over IEEE 802.11 schemes. *IEEE Vehicular Technology Conference, VTC'99*, Vol. 5, pp. 2636–40.

Rappaport, T. S. 1996. *Wireless communications*. Upper Saddle River, NJ: Prentice Hall.

Roshan P., and J. Leary. 2004. *802.11 wireless LAN fundamentals*. Indianapolis, IN: Cisco Press.

Schiller, J. 2002. *Mobile communications*. Boston: Addison Wesley.

Stallings, W. 2002. *Wireless communications and networks*. Upper Saddle River, NJ: Prentice Hall.

Wireless LAN Standards

Prashant Krishnamurthy, *University of Pittsburgh*

INTRODUCTION

Wireless networks can be classified in many ways based on mobility, topology, application, or coverage. For example, using mobility, we may classify wireless networks as fixed, stationary, portable, or mobile. If we consider applications, we may look at wireless data networks and cellular voice networks. The topology of a wireless network may be based on a fixed infrastructure that enables a *mobile station* (MS) to connect to the rest of the network or the topology may be ad hoc where MSs connect to one another in a peer-to-peer manner without assistance from a fixed infrastructure. Typically in the former case, a wired distribution system that connects points of access (e.g., base stations or access points) to the fixed network is assumed. If the points of access can connect to one another using an air interface, then a mesh topology is also possible. The most popular classification is based on coverage: whether the wireless network provides service over a local area or a larger geographical region. *Wireless local area networks* (WLANs) typically cover areas ranging anywhere between parts of a building to the campus of an organization. *Wireless wide area networks* (WWANs) cover entire cities and even parts of a nation. Usually, WWANs provide lower data rates compared to WLANs and are more complex in architecture. The spectrum allocated to WWANs is typically licensed spectrum and there needs to be careful planning and deployment of WWANs. WLANs mostly form extensions to existing *local area network* (LAN) segments in organizations. They typically use unlicensed spectrum and as long as the interference is reasonable, they can be deployed by anyone, anywhere. Currently, WLANs are also being used to provide broadband Internet access in hot spots such as airports, cafes, and hotels.

There are several standards for WWANs and WLANs, and they are primarily dependent on geography. The European Telecommunications Standards Institute (ETSI) based in France is responsible for the standards activities in the European Union although these standards have been sometimes adopted in other parts of the world. In the United States, standards activities are less centralized. There are many organizations involved in standards activities such as the Institute for Electrical and Electronic Engineers (IEEE), American National Standards Institute, the Telecommunications Industry Association, and so on. Typically, a standard is created based on input from several industry groups; once such standards are approved, the International Standards Organization often adopts these standards (see Box 1 for a list of URLs for standards bodies). Many of the details in this article are derived from the IEEE 802.11 standards and information available on the IEEE 802.11 Web site.

Standards for wireless technologies must deal with a gamut of different issues, starting from the spectra that can be used by this technology and going up to defining entities in the system and the detailed protocols between them. In this chapter, we will briefly look at wireless local area network standards in general and focus on one particular WLAN standard—namely, the IEEE 802.11 standard.

WLAN Standards

Standards activities for WLANs have evolved geographically with ETSI's broadband radio access network working on *high-performance radio LAN* (HIPERLAN) standards in Europe and the IEEE on the 802.11 series in the United States. In Japan, the Multimedia Mobile Access

URLs of Standards Bodies

- American National Standards Institute: www.ansi .org
- Enhanced Wireless Consortium: www.enhancedwirelessconsortium.org/home
- European Telecommunications Standards Institute: www.etsi.org
- Institute of Electrical and Electronics Engineers: http://grouper.ieee.org/groups/ (IEEE 802.11 Working Group: http://grouper.ieee.org/groups/802/11)
- International Standards Organization: www.iso.org/
- Multimedia Mobile Access Communications: www .arib.or.jp/mmac/e/index.htm
- Telecommunications Industry Association: www.tiaonline.com
- Third Generation Partnership Project: http://www.3gpp .org
- Third Generation Partnership Project 2: www.3gpp2 .org

Communications Promotion Council working group under the Association of Radio Industries and Businesses works on WLAN standards. The spectra used by WLANs is mostly unlicensed, although some systems use licensed spectra as well (e.g., HIPERLAN in some licensed bands). The only commercially successful WLAN standard has been the IEEE 802.11. HIPERLAN/1 was standardized in the mid 1990s and supported complex multihop ad hoc networking. The medium access mechanism in HIPERLAN/1 (Wilkinson, Phipps, and Barton 1995) was based on a form of carrier sense multiple access called *elimination-yield nonpreemptive multiple access* (EY-NPMA). HIPERLAN/2 has adopted a physical layer that is very similar to IEEE 802.11a and a medium access mechanism based on reservation and TDMA. However, both these standards have not been adopted successfully in commercial products. The MMAC activities include a variety of wireless access networks (some compatible with the IEEE 802.11 standards) ranging from wireless personal area networks to outdoor fixed public networks. Recently, there have been efforts to harmonize the standards activities of ETSI, IEEE 802.11, and MMAC. Table 1 summarizes some of the 802.11, HIPERLAN, and MMAC standards. In the rest of this chapter, we will consider primarily the IEEE 802.11 standard in some detail.

INTRODUCTION TO THE IEEE 802.11 STANDARD

Within the IEEE, several standards activities are carried on by different groups. The IEEE 802 LAN/MAN standards committee is responsible for local area network standards and *metropolitan area network* (MAN) standards. Individual working groups are in charge of a variety of LAN/MAN standards, of which the 802.11 working group is responsible for WLAN standards.

Like most LAN standards, the 802.11 standard (Crow et al. 1997) is concerned only with the lower two layers of the open system interconnection OSI stack—namely, the physical (PHY) and MAC layers. The MAC and PHY layers operate under the IEEE 802.2 logical link control layer, which supports many other LAN protocols. In the case of wired LAN standards such as 802.3, several physical layers correspond to the same MAC specifications. A good example is IEEE 802.3, which was originally designed for thick coaxial cable but was subsequently revised to include thin coaxial cable, a variety of twisted pair cables, and even fiber-optic links. In the same way, the IEEE 802.11 standard specifies a common MAC protocol that is used over many different PHY standards. The PHY standards are the "base" IEEE 802.11 standard, the 802.11b and g standards, and the 802.11a standard. A new 802.11n physical layer is under consideration by the 802.11 working group. The MAC protocol is based on *carrier sense multiple access with collision avoidance* (CSMA/CA). An optional polling mechanism called *point coordination*

Table 1: Summary of Some WLAN Standards

Standard	Standards Body	Spectrum	Data Rate	Primary Medium Access	Primary Region
IEEE 802.11,b, g	IEEE	2.4-GHz ISM bands	1, 2, 5.5, 11, up to Mbps	CSMA/CA[1]	North America
IEEE 802.11a	IEEE	5-GHz UNII and ISM bands	Up to 54 Mbps	CSMA/CA	North America
IEEE 802.11n[2]	IEEE	2.4-GHz ISM bands	> 100 Mbps	CSMA/CA	North America
HIPERLAN/1	ETSI	5-GHz bands	23 Mbps	EY-NPMA[3]	Europe
HIPERLAN/2	ETSI	5-GHz bands	Up to 54 Mbps	TDMA reservation	Europe
Wireless access and WLAN	MMAC	3–60 GHz bands	20–25 Mbps	Various	Japan

[1]CSMA/CA
[2]The IEEE 802.11n standard is yet to be finalized
[3]Elimination yield nonpreemptive multiple access

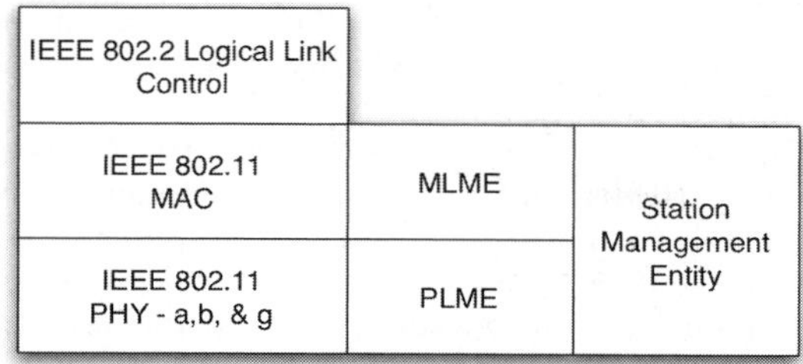

Figure 1: Protocol stack of IEEE 802.11

function (PCF) is also specified. In addition to the MAC and PHY layers, the IEEE 802.11 standard also specifies a management plane that transmits management messages over the medium and can be used by an administrator to tune the MAC and PHY layers. The *MAC layer management entity* (MLME) deals with management issues such as roaming and power conservation. The *PHY layer management entity* (PLME) assists in channel selection and interacts with the MLME. A *station management entity* handles the interaction between these management layers. Figure 1 shows the protocol stack associated with IEEE 802.11.

The base IEEE 802.11 standard specifies three different PHY layers: Two use *radio-frequency* (RF), and one uses *infrared* (IR) communications. The RF PHY layers are based on *spread spectrum* (SS): either *direct sequence* (DS) or *frequency hopping* (FH). The IR PHY layer is based on *pulse position modulation* (PPM). Two different data rates are specified: 1 and 2 Mbps for each of the three PHY layers. The RF physical layers are specified in the 2.4-GHz *industrial, scientific, and medical* (ISM) unlicensed frequency bands.

The IEEE 802.11b standard specifies the physical layer at 2.4 GHz for higher data rates: 5.5 Mbps and 11 Mbps. The PHY layer makes use of a modulation scheme called *complementary code keying* (CCK). The transmission rate depends on the quality of the signal, and it is backward-compatible with the base 802.11 standard, which is based on the *direct sequence spread spectrum* (DSSS). Depending on the signal quality, the transmission rates could fall back to lower values. The 802.11g standard further increases the data rates to as much as 54 Mbps in the 2.4-GHz ISM bands using *orthogonal frequency division multiplexing* (OFDM). The IEEE 802.11a standard (Kapp 2002) deals with the PHY layer in the 5-GHz *unlicensed national information infrastructure* (UNII) bands. Once again, data rates as high as 54 Mbps are specified in these bands with OFDM as the modulation technique. Depending on the PHY layer alternative, the frequency band is divided into several channels. Each channel supports the maximum data rate allowed by that PHY layer alternative. The proposal for an especially high rate PHY layer (>100 Mbps) called *802.11n* employs multiple input and output antennae at the transceivers. The technology is popularly called *multiple-input multiple-output* (MIMO) and also uses OFDM as the modulation scheme.

In the next few sections, the IEEE 802.11 standard is discussed in a top-down manner. First, the different topologies possible in IEEE 802.11 are considered with the focus on understanding some of the management functions. Then detailed discussions of the MAC layer of 802.11 and different PHY layer alternatives are presented. Once the basic operation of the 802.11 WLAN has been considered, security issues in IEEE 802.11 will be discussed, as will recent ongoing activities to extend the standard further.

IEEE 802.11 WLAN OPERATIONS

The topology of an IEEE 802.11 WLAN can be one of two types: infrastructure or ad hoc (see Figure 2). In the infrastructure topology, an *access point* (AP) covers a particular area called the *basic service area* (BSA), and mobile stations communicate with each other or with the Internet through the AP (Crow et al. 1997). The AP is connected to a LAN segment and forms the point of access to the network. All communications go through the AP. So an MS that wants to communicate with another MS first sends the message to the AP. The AP looks at the destination address and sends it to the second MS. The AP, along with all of the MSs associated with it, is called a *basic service set* (BSS). In the ad hoc topology (also called *independent BSS* or IBSS), MSs that are in range of each other can communicate directly without a wired infrastructure. However, it is not possible for an MS to forward packets meant for another MS that is not in the range of the source MS. Figure 2 shows schematics of both topologies. MSs and APs are identified by a 48-bit MAC address that is similar to other MAC addresses at the link layer. In an infrastructure topology, the MAC address of the AP also forms the *BSSID,* a unique identifier of the BSS.

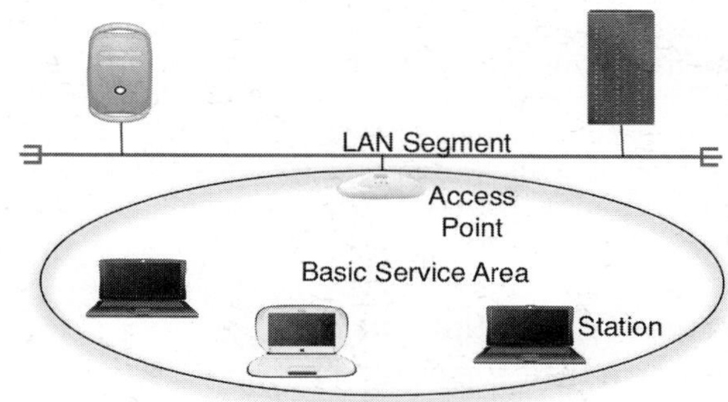

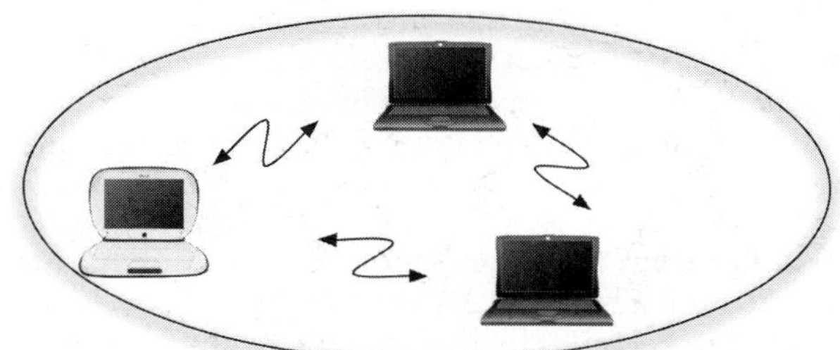

Independent Basic Service Area

Figure 2: Topologies in IEEE 802.11

If we assume that the range of communication of any WLAN device—be it an MS or an AP—is a region of radius R, then we can look at the comparative advantages of the two topologies. An MS can communicate with another MS that is as far as $2R$ away using an AP, provided both MSs are within a distance R of the AP. The cost here is the additional transmission from the AP to the destination. In the ad hoc topology, a destination MS cannot be more than a distance R from the source MS. The advantage is that the information can be received in one hop.

Extending the Coverage in Infrastructure Topology

Depending on the environment in which it is deployed and the transmit powers that are used, an AP can cover a region with a radius anywhere between 30 feet and 250 feet. The coverage depends on radio propagation characteristics in the environment and the antenna features (Pahlavan and Krishnamurthy 2002). The presence of obstacles such as walls, floors, equipment, and so on can reduce the coverage. Many new 802.11-equipped devices have integrated antennae that additionally reduce coverage. To cover a building or a campus, it often becomes necessary to deploy multiple APs that are connected to the same LAN. A group of such APs and the member mobile stations is called an *extended service set* (ESS). The coverage area is called the extended service area. The wired backbone that connects the different APs along with services that enable the ESS is called the *distribution system*. The distribution system, for example, supports roaming between APs so that MSs can access the network over a wider coverage area than before. This is similar to cellular telephone systems in which multiple base stations provide coverage to a region, each base station covering only a cell. Note, however, that cellular telephone systems have a far more complex infrastructure to handle roaming and handoff. In 802.11 WLANs, it is easy to roam within a single LAN but it requires support from higher layers (such as mobile IP) to roam across different LANs.

Network Operations in an Infrastructure Topology

When an MS is powered up and configured to operate in an infrastructure topology, it can perform a passive scan or an active scan. In the case of a passive scan, the MS simply scans the different channels to detect the existence of a BSS. The existence of a BSS can be detected through beacon frames that are broadcast by APs pseudo-periodically. The reason why it is called *pseudo-periodic* is that the beacon is supposed to be transmitted regularly at certain intervals. However, the AP cannot preempt an ongoing transmission to transmit a beacon. When we discuss the MAC layer, we will see that any device has to wait for the medium to be free before transmitting a frame. If the medium is busy, the AP will transmit the beacon after the medium becomes free, in which case the beacon may not be precisely periodic. The beacon is a management frame that announces the existence of a network. It contains information about the network: the BSSID and the capabilities of the network (the PHY alternatives it supports, if security is mandatory, whether the MAC layer supports polling, the interval at which beacons are transmitted, timing parameters, and so on). The beacon is similar to certain control channels in cellular telephone systems: for instance, the broadcast control channel (BCCH in GSM). The MS also performs signal strength measurements on the beacon frame. In the case of an active scan, the MS already knows the ID of the network that it wants to connect to. In this case, the MS sends a probe request frame on each channel. APs that hear the probe request respond with a probe response frame that is similar in nature to the beacon. In either case, the MS can create a scan report that provides it with information about the available BSSs, their capabilities, their channels, timing parameters, and other information. The MS makes use of this information to determine a compatible network that it can associate itself with.

To associate itself with an AP, the MS must authenticate itself if this is part of the capability of the network (we will look at this in a later section). Otherwise, as long as the MS satisfies the announced capabilities of the network, it can send an association request frame to the AP. The association request informs the AP of the intention of the MS to join the network; it also provides additional information about the MS such as its MAC address, how often it will listen to the beacon (called the *listen interval*), the supported data rates, and so on. If the AP is satisfied with the capabilities of the MS, then it will reply with an association response frame. In this message, the MS is given an association ID, and this frame confirms that the MS is now able to access the network. During this association phase, the MS can be authenticated by the network and vice versa. Unlike the ad hoc mode of operation, administrators can control access to the network in the infrastructure mode of operation.

If a mobile station moves across BSSs or out of coverage and returns to the BSA of an AP, then it will have to reassociate itself with the AP. For this purpose, it will use a reassociation request frame that is similar in form to the association request frame, except that the MAC address of the old AP will be included in the frame. The AP will respond with a reassociation response frame. An MS moving from one BSS to another will have to detect the drop in signal strength from the old AP and detect the beacon of the new AP before the reassociation request. It could also use a probe request message instead of detecting the beacon from the new AP. This simple handoff between two APs is MS-initiated. In cellular telephone systems, the MS is instructed by entities in the network (such as base station controllers) to perform the handoff from one base station to another. They may, however, use information supplied by the MS such as the signal strength from different base stations.

Power management is an important component of network operations in an IEEE 802.11 WLAN. When MSs have no frames to send, they can enter a sleep mode to conserve power. If an MS is sleeping when frames arrive at an AP for it, the AP will buffer such frames. A sleeping MS wakes up periodically and listens to the beacon frames. How often it wakes up is specified by the listen interval mentioned earlier. The beacon frame also contains a field called the *traffic indication map* (TIM). This field contains information about whether packets are buffered in the AP for a given MS. If an MS detects that it has frames waiting for it, it can wake up from the sleep mode and receive those frames before going back to sleep. The MS uses a power-save poll frame to indicate to the AP that it is ready to receive buffered frames.

If the MS chooses to leave the network or shut down, it will send a dissociation frame to the AP. This frame will terminate the association between the MS and the network, enabling the network to free resources that were previously reserved for the MS (such as the association ID, buffer space, etc.).

Network Operations in an Ad Hoc Topology

In an ad hoc topology, there is no fixed AP to coordinate transmissions and define the BSS. An MS that operates in ad hoc mode will power up and scan the channels to detect beacons from other MSs that may be in the vicinity and that may have set up an IBSS. If it does not detect any beacons, then it may declare its own network. If it does detect a beacon, then the MS can join the IBSS in a manner similar to the process in the infrastructure topology. MSs in an IBSS may choose to rotate the responsibility of transmitting a beacon. Power management works in a similar way except that the source MS itself has to send an *announcement traffic indication map* frame to the recipient MS.

Network Operations in Mesh Topology

Recently, wireless mesh networking has received a lot of attention because it enables the deployment of wireless networks over a large area without the need for an extensive fixed (wired) infrastructure. A wireless mesh network consists of entities that connect to each other over an air interface and relay packets in the network thus created. This eliminates the need for a wired backbone to relay packets. Some of these entities may act like APs, creating infrastructure WLANs and becoming points of access to the mesh network. Other entities will connect to the Internet and enable any device in the mesh network to access the Internet. Wireless mesh networks can use a variety of technologies such as IEEE 802.16 or WiMAX-based devices or IEEE 802.11-based devices. In 2004, a task group "S" of 802.11 was set up to investigate mesh networking with 802.11 and propose a standard for using a wireless distribution system unlike the wired distribution system in the ESS. Although the standard is not finalized, some elements of operations in a mesh network have been proposed (Lee and Zheng 2006). In a mesh network, APs (or MSs) are required to be able to relay packets to one another using the air interface so that packets may be delivered from a source MS to a destination MS through multiple wireless hops. Entities with relay capabilities are called *mesh points*. A mechanism for determining a path from one mesh point to another is also necessary, and it is expected to be implemented at the MAC layer. Mesh portals enable connectivity to other mesh networks, LANs, or the Internet. Multicast and broadcast capability at the MAC layer is also another aspect that the IEEE 802.11s standard is expected to address.

THE IEEE 802.11 MAC LAYER

Mobile stations in an IEEE 802.11 network have to share the transmission medium: air. If two MSs transmit at the same time and the transmissions are both in range of the destination, then they may collide, resulting in the frames being lost. The MAC layer is responsible for controlling access to the medium and ensuring that MSs can access the medium in a fair manner with minimal collisions. The medium access mechanism is based on carrier sense multiple access, but there is no collision detection—unlike the wired equivalent LAN standard (IEEE 802.3). Collisions are extremely hard to detect in RF because of the dynamic nature of the channel. Detecting collisions also incurs difficulties in hardware implementation because an MS has to be transmitting and receiving at the same time. Instead, the strategy adopted is to avoid collisions to the extent possible. In IEEE 802.11, there are two types of carrier sensing: (1) physical sensing of energy in the medium and (2) virtual sensing. *Virtual sensing* is implemented by decoding a duration field in the 802.11 frame that allows an MS to know the time for which a frame will last. This time is stored in a *network allocation vector* (NAV) that counts down to zero to indicate when the medium is free again. To illustrate the IEEE 802.11 MAC layer, we will use the ad hoc topology as an example. However, the procedures are identical in an infrastructure topology as well.

The Distributed Coordination Function

We will first describe the basic medium access process in IEEE 802.11 called the *distributed coordination function* (DCF). Consider Figure 3 that shows the basic method for accessing the medium in IEEE 802.11. A MS will initially sense the channel before transmission. If the medium is free, the MS will continuously monitor the medium for a period of time called the *DCF interframe space* (IFS), or DIFS. If the medium is still idle after DIFS, then the MS can transmit its frame without waiting. Otherwise, the MS will enter a backoff process. The rationale is that if another MS senses the medium after the first MS, then it will also wait for DIFS. However, before a time DIFS expires, the first MS would have started its transmission. On hearing the transmission, the second MS will have to back off. The wireless medium is harsh and unreliable, hence all transmissions are acknowledged. The destination of the frame will send an *acknowledgement* (ACK) back to the source if the frame is successfully received as follows. It will wait for a time called the *short interframe space* (SIFS) and transmits the ACK. The SIFS value is smaller than the DIFS value. All IFS values depend on the physical layer alternative. Thus, any other MS that senses the channel as idle after the original frame was transmitted will still be waiting, and ACK frames have priority over their transmissions. To maintain fairness and avoid collisions, the MS that senses the medium as free for a time DIFS and transmits a frame will have to enter the backoff process if it wants to transmit another frame immediately. The exception is when it is transmitting one frame in many fragments. In such a case, the MS can indicate the number of fragments in the first frame to be transmitted and occupy the channel until the frame is completely transmitted.

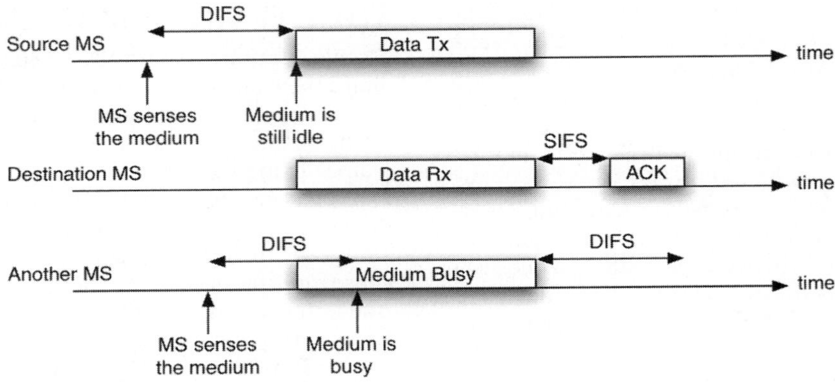

Figure 3: Basic medium access in IEEE 802.11

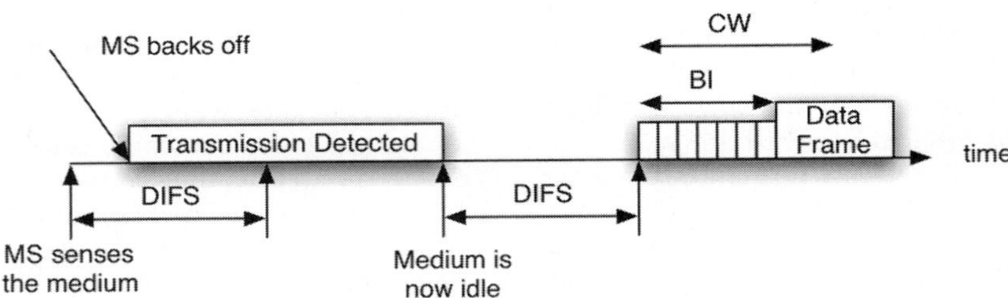

Figure 4: Backoff process in IEEE 802.11

The backoff process works as follows. Once an MS enters the backoff process, it picks a value called the *backoff interval* (BI) that is a random value uniformly distributed between zero and a number called the *contention window* (CW). The MS will then monitor the medium. When the medium is free for at least a time DIFS, the MS will start counting down from the BI value as long as the medium is free. The counter is decremented every so often (called a *slot*). If the medium is sensed as occupied before the counter goes down to zero, the MS will freeze the counter and continue to monitor the medium. As soon the counter becomes zero, the MS can transmit its frame. This process is shown in Figure 4.

The IEEE 802.11 MAC supports *binary exponential backoff* like IEEE 802.3. Initially, the CW is maintained at a value called CW_{min}, which is typically $2^5 - 1 = 31$ slots. So the BI will be uniformly distributed between 0 and 31 slots. The slot time varies, depending on the physical layer alternative. For example, it is 20 μs in the IEEE 802.11b standard and 9 μs in the 802.11a standard. If a packet is not successfully transmitted (this could be the result of collisions or a channel error), the value of CW is essentially doubled. The MS will now pick a BI value that is uniformly distributed between 0 and $2^6 - 1 = 63$ slots. This process can be continued till CW reaches a value that is CW_{max} (usually 1023 slots). The rationale behind this approach is as follows. If there are many MSs contending for the medium, then it is likely that one or more may pick the same BI value. Their transmissions will then collide. By increasing the value of CW, it is likely that this probability will go down, thereby reducing collisions.

Frames may be lost because of channel errors or collisions. A positive ACK from the destination is necessary to ensure that the frame has been successfully received. In IEEE 802.11, each MS maintains retry counters that are incremented if no ACKs are received. After a retry threshold is reached, the frame is discarded as being undeliverable.

The Hidden Terminal Problem and Optional Mechanism

In wireless networks that use carrier sensing, there is a unique problem called the *hidden terminal problem*. Suppose all MSs are identical and have a transmission and reception range of *R* as shown in Figure 5.

The transmission from MS-A can be heard by MS-C but not by MS-B. So when MS-A is transmitting a frame to MS-C, MS-B will not sense the channel as busy: MS-A is *hidden* from MS-B. If both MS-A and MS-B transmit frames to MS-C at the same time, then the frames will collide. This is the hidden terminal problem. There is a dual problem called the *exposed terminal problem*. In this case, MS-A is transmitting a frame to MS-D. This transmission is heard by MS-C, which then backs off. However, MS-C could have transmitted a frame to MS-B, and the two transmissions would not interfere or collide. In this case, MS-A is called an *exposed terminal*. Both hidden and exposed terminals cause a loss of throughput.

To reduce the possibility of collisions because of the hidden terminal problem, the IEEE 802.11 MAC has an optional mechanism at the MAC layer as shown

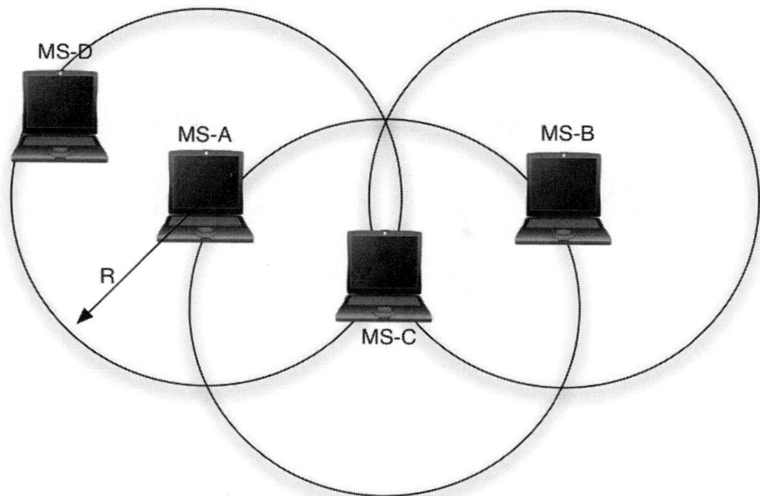

Figure 5: Illustrating the hidden and exposed terminal problems

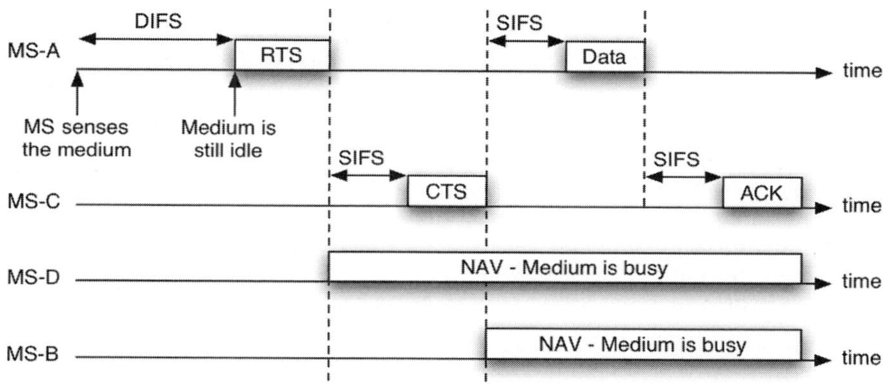

Figure 6: Operation of the RTS-CTS mechanism

in Figure 6. Suppose MS-A wants to transmit a frame to MS-C. It will first transmit a short frame called the *request-to-send* (RTS) frame. The RTS frame is heard in the transmission range of MS-A and includes MS-C and MS-D, but not MS-B. Both MS-C and MS-D are alerted to the fact that MS-A intends to transmit a frame and they will not attempt to simultaneously use the medium. This is achieved by the virtual carrier sensing process that sets the NAV to a value equal to the time it will take to successfully complete the exchange of frames. In response to the RTS frame, MS-C will send a *clear-to-send* (CTS) frame that will be heard by all MSs in its transmission range. This includes MS-B and MS-A but not MS-D. The CTS frame lets MS-A know that MS-C is ready to receive the data frame. It also alerts MS-B to the fact that there will be a transmission from some MS to MS-C. Consequently MS-B will defer any frames that it wishes to transmit in anticipation of the completion of the communication to MS-C. This way, even though MS-B is outside the transmission range of MS-A, the CTS message can be used to extend the carrier sensing range, thereby reducing the hidden terminal problem. Of course, it is quite possible that the RTS frame itself collided with a transmission from MS-B. In such a case, both MS-A and MS-B will have to enter the backoff process and retransmit their frames.

The RTS-CTS mechanism can be controlled in IEEE 802.11 by using an RTS threshold. All unicast and management frames larger than this threshold will always be transmitted using RTS-CTS. By setting this value to 0 bytes, all frames will use RTS-CTS. The default value is 2347 bytes, which disables RTS-CTS for all packets. When RTS-CTS signals are used, the CTS frame is transmitted by the destination MS after waiting simply for a time equal to SIFS. This way, the CTS frame has priority compared to all other transmissions that have to wait for at least a time DIFS and perhaps an additional waiting time in backoff. Using the RTS-CTS signals reduces the throughput of a WLAN, but it may be essential to use this in dense environments.

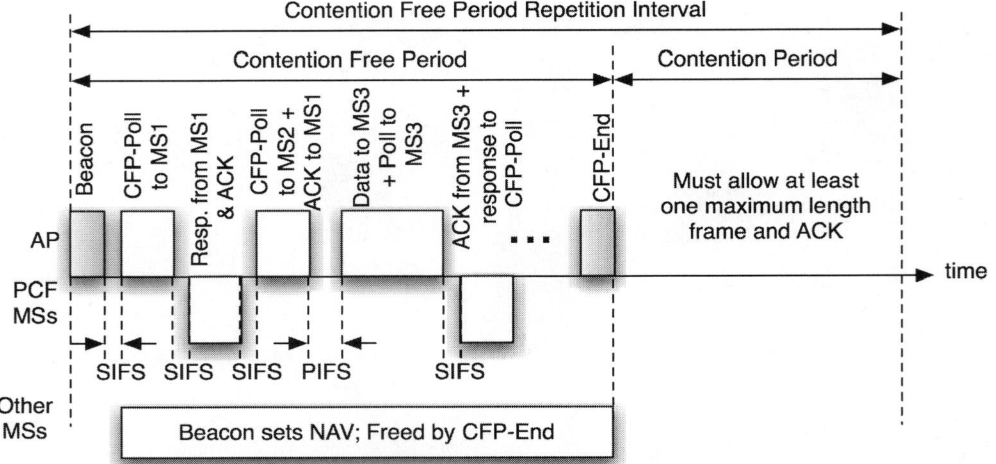

Figure 7: Operation of the PCF

The Point Coordination Function

One consequence of using CSMA/CA as described above with DCF is that it is impossible to have any bounds on the delay or jitter suffered by frames. Depending on the traffic load and the BI values that are picked, a frame may be transmitted instantaneously or it may have to be buffered until the medium becomes free. For real-time applications such as voice or multimedia, this can result in performance degradation, especially when strict delay bounds are necessary. To provide some bounds on the delay, an optional MAC mechanism—the point coordination function—is part of the IEEE 802.11 standard (Crow et al. 1997). PCF provides contention-free access to frames using a polling mechanism described below.

The process starts when the AP captures the medium by sending a beacon frame after it is idle for a time called the *PCF interframe space* (PIFS). The PIFS is smaller than the DIFS and larger than the SIFS. In the beacon frame, the AP, also called the *point coordinator,* announces a *contention-free period* (CFP) in which the usual DCF operation will be preempted. All MSs that use only DCF will set a NAV to indicate that the medium will be busy for the duration of the CFP. The AP maintains a list of MSs that need to be polled during the CFP. MSs get onto the polling list when they first associate with the AP using the association request. The AP then polls each MS on the list for data. The polls are sent after a time SIFS, and the ACKS to the poll and any associated data will be transmitted by the corresponding MS also after a time SIFS. If there is no response from a MS to a poll, the AP waits for a time PIFS before it sends the next poll frame or data. The AP can also send management frames whenever it chooses within the CFP. An example of PCF operations is shown in Figure 7.

The AP indicates the culmination of the CFP via a message called *CFP-End.* This is a broadcast frame to all MSs and frees the NAV in MSs that are only DCF-based. Following the CFP, a contention period starts. In this period, it must be possible for a MS to transmit at least one maximum length frame using DCF and to receive an ACK. The CFP can be resumed after completion of the contention period. The PCF mechanism is optional in IEEE 802.11. Most commercial systems deployed today do not support PCF, and real-time services do not have good support in WLANs today. Note that polling has a lot of overhead, especially if MSs do not have frames to send when they are polled.

MAC Frame Formats

Although this chapter will not define all of the different frame formats of an IEEE 802.11 MAC frame and discuss the fields in great detail, it will consider examples to illustrate the MAC frame formats. Figure 8 shows the general format of a MAC frame. The most significant bit is last (right-most), and the bits are transmitted from left

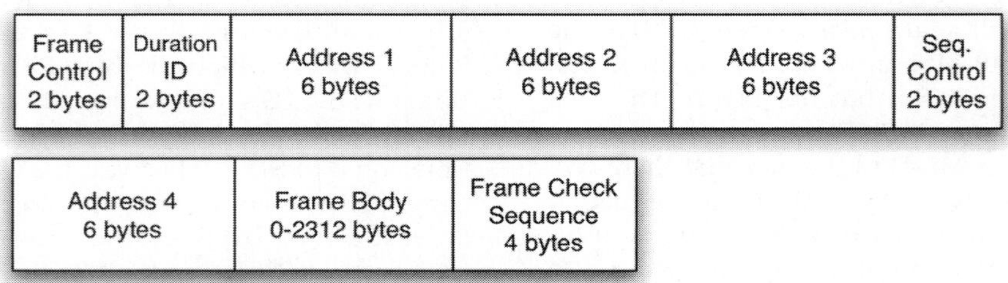

Figure 8: General format of a MAC frame

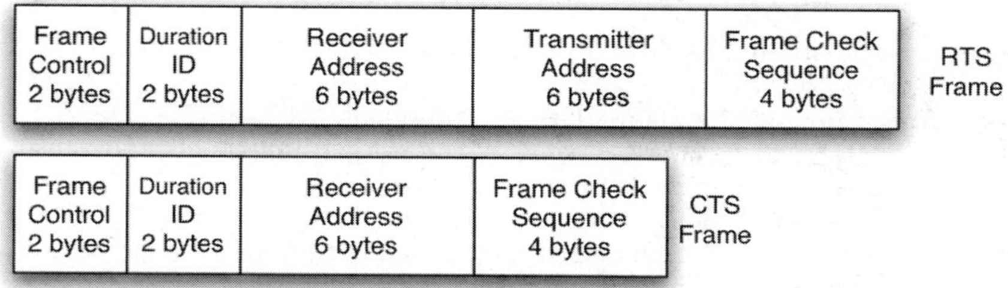

Figure 9: RTS and CTS frame formats

Time Stamp 8 bytes	Beacon Interval 2 bytes	Capab. Info. 2 bytes	SSID Variable	FH Parameter Set 7 bytes	DS Param Set 2 bytes	CF Parameter Set 8 bytes	IBSS Parameter Set 4 bytes	TIM Var.

Figure 10: Frame body of the beacon frame

to right. The frame control field has two bytes and comprises many fields. It carries information such as:

- the protocol version;
- the type of frame, including
  - management (probe request, association, authentication, and so on),
  - control (RTS, CTS, and so on, or data),
  - pure data(CFP poll and data, and null);
- the number of retries; and
- whether the frame is encrypted (discussed later).

The duration field is important to set the NAV during virtual carrier sensing.

There can be as many as four address fields in the frame (Gast 2002). The addresses can be different, depending on the type of frame. Common addresses used are the source and destination addresses, the receiver address if the destination is different from the receiver (e.g., the receiver is the AP, but the destination is a wired node on the LAN segment), the transmitter address (once again if the transmitter is different from the source, it is the AP), and the BSSID. The sequence control field is used in case there is fragmentation of frames. The frame body carries the payload from upper layers and the frame check sequence is a 32-bit cyclic redundancy check used to verify the integrity of the frame at the receiver. The frame format in Figure 8 is used in an infrastructure topology. In an IBSS, only three address fields are used.

The RTS and CTS frames are short frames: twenty and fourteen bytes, respectively (see Figure 9). The ACK frames are similar to the CTS frame.

Figure 10 illustrates the frame body of the beacon frame. The time stamp allows MSs to synchronize to a BSS. The beacon interval says how often the beacon can be expected to be heard. It is typically 100 milliseconds but could be changed by an administrator. The capability information (two bytes) provides information about the topology (whether infrastructure or ad hoc), whether encryption is mandatory, and whether additional features are supported. One such feature is *channel agility* by which the AP hops to different channels after a predetermined amount of time.

We have not discussed PHY layer alternatives yet. The parameter sets in the beacon provide information about the PHY layer parameters that are necessary to join the network. For instance, if frequency hopping is used, the FH parameter set will specify the hopping pattern. The TIM field is used to support MSs that may be sleeping as described earlier.

THE IEEE 802.11 PHYSICAL LAYER ALTERNATIVES

The IEEE 802.11 standards body has standardized several different PHY layer alternatives. When it was first standardized in 1997, there were three PHY layer options. We will call these options as the "base" IEEE 802.11 PHY layer alternatives. The IEEE 802.11b supports as much as 11 Mbps in the 2.4-GHz ISM bands, the IEEE 802.11g standard supports as much as 54 Mbps in the 2.4-GHz ISM bands, and the IEEE 802.11a standard supports as much as 54 Mbps in the 5-GHz UNII bands. Before we discuss these alternatives, let us look at the PHY layer in IEEE 802.11.

The PHY layer in IEEE 802.11 is broken into two sublayers: the *physical layer convergence protocol* (PLCP) and the *physical medium dependent* (PMD) layers. The PLCP includes a function that adapts the underlying medium dependent capabilities to the MAC-level requirements. The PLCP would, for instance, add additional fields to the frame to enable synchronization at the physical layer. The PMD actually determines how information bits are transmitted over the medium.

The Base IEEE 802.11 Standard

The base IEEE 802.11 standard specifies three different PHY layer alternatives. Two of these use RF transmissions in the 2.4 GHz ISM bands and one uses IR.

The FH Option

The first option for transmission in the 2.4-GHz ISM bands makes use of *frequency hopping spread spectrum* (FHSS) (Pahlavan and Krishnamurthy 2002). The entire band is divided into 1-MHz wide channels, and the specification makes it important to confine 99 percent of the energy to one such channel during transmission to reduce interference to the other channels. These restrictions are also due to the rules imposed by the Federal Communications Commission (FCC) in the United States. The standard specifies ninety-five such 1-MHz wide channels, and they are numbered accordingly. In the United States, only seventy-nine of these channels are allowed. Devices that use the FH option hop between these channels when transmitting frames. The dwell time in each channel is approximately 0.4 s. The hop sequences (the channel hopping pattern) depends on mathematical functions. An example hopping pattern is {3, 26, 65, 11, 46, 19, 74, . . . }. In the United States, each set of hopping patterns can have twenty-six different channels at most. This means that it is possible to create three orthogonal hopping sets (because there are seventy-nine channels in the United States). If three APs use these three orthogonal hopping sets, then there will be no interference between these networks. The modulation scheme used with FHSS is called *Gaussian frequency shift keying* (GFSK). This modulation scheme makes use of the frequency information to encode data. It is possible to use either (1) two frequencies within the channel or (2) four frequencies within the channel. In the former case, the data rate will be 1 Mbps; in the latter case, the data rate will be 2 Mbps. The advantage of the FHSS system is that the receivers are less complex to implement. The PLCP for the FHSS PMD introduces an eighty-bit field for synchronization, a frame delimiter, and fields to indicate the data rate. Depending on this field, the data rate can be modified in steps of 500 kbps from 1 Mbps to 4.5 Mbps. However, the standard only supports 1 and 2 Mbps. The values of SIFS and the slot for backoff in this option are 28 μs and 50 μs, respectively.

The DS Option

The direct sequence spread spectrum modulation technique has been the most popular commercial implementation of IEEE 802.11. DSSS has inherent advantages in multipath channels and can increase the coverage of an AP for this reason (Tuch 1991). We will briefly discuss the features of this PMD layer.

In a DSSS system, the data stream is "chipped" into several narrower pulses (chips), thereby increasing the occupied spectrum of the transmitted signal. One common way of doing this is to multiply the data stream (typically a series of positive and negative rectangular pulses) by a spreading signal (typically another series of positive and negative rectangular pulses but with much narrower pulses than the data stream). Although the data stream is random and depends on what needs to be transmitted, the spreading signal is deterministic. Figure 11a shows an example where the data stream $d(t)$ is multiplied by a spreading signal $a(t)$ to produce a signal $s(t)$ that is then modulated over an RF carrier. In this figure, eleven narrow pulses are contained within one broad data pulse. The pulses could have a positive (+) or negative (−) amplitude. This results in the bandwidth expanding by a factor of 11; this is also called the *processing gain*. A specific pattern of pulses in the spreading signal is used. The pattern used in the IEEE 802.11 standard is a Barker sequence. The interesting property of the Barker sequence is that its autocorrelation has a sharp peak and narrow side lobes as shown in Figure 11b. Because of this property, it is possible for a receiver to reject interference from multipath signals and recover information robustly in a harsh wireless environment. The Barker sequence with *differential binary phase shift keying* (DBPSK) is used for data rates of 1 Mbps; the Barker sequence with *differential quadrature phase shift keying* (DQPSK) is used for data rates of 2 Mbps. In either case, the chip rate is 11 Mcps (mega chips per second).

Unlike FHSS, a signal carrying 2 Mbps now occupies a bandwidth that is as large as 25 MHz. In the IEEE 802.11 standard, fourteen channels are specified for the

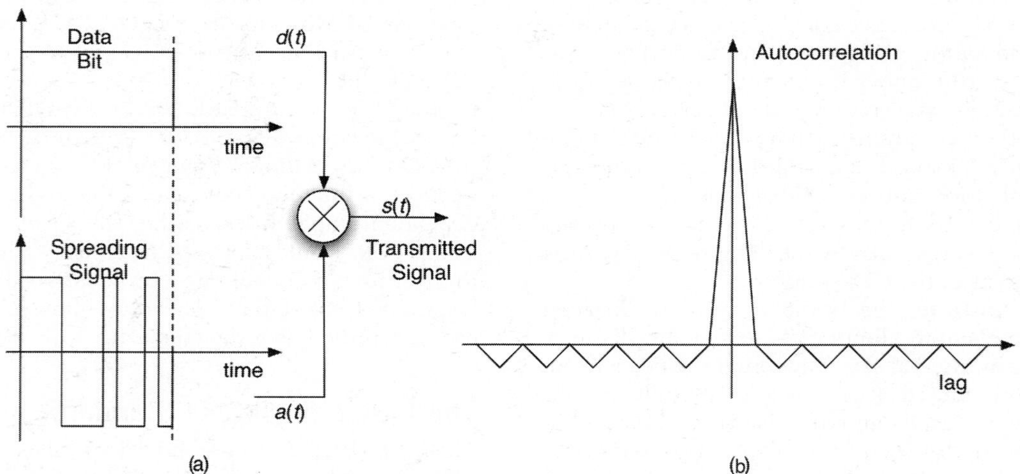

Figure 11: (a) Direct sequence spread spectrum and (b) autocorrelation of the Barker pulse

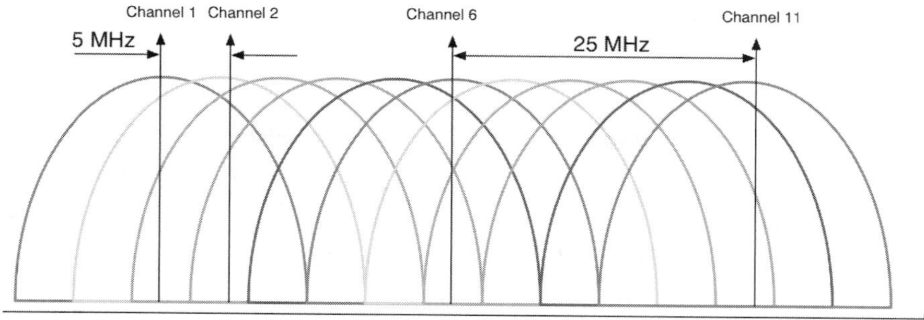

Figure 12: Channelization for IEEE 802.11 DS option

DSSS PMD. Channel 1 is at 2.412 GHz, channel 2 at 2.417 GHz, and so on. Only the first eleven channels are available for use in the United States. Figure 12 shows the channelization in the United States. Because each channel occupies roughly 25 MHz bandwidth and the channel separation is only 5 MHz, there is significant overlap between channels. If two WLANs in the same vicinity were to use adjacent channels, there would be severe interference and throughput degradation. There are three orthogonal channels—channels 1, 6, and 11—in the United States that can be deployed without interference.

The PLCP sublayer once again introduces fields for synchronization (128 bits), frame delimiting, and error checking. The PLCP header and preamble are always transmitted at 1 Mbps using DBPSK. The rest of the packet is transmitted using either DBPSK or DQPSK, depending on the data rate. The values of SIFS and the slot for backoff in this option are 10 μs and 20 μs, respectively.

The IR Option

The third option in IEEE 802.11 is to use infrared for transmission (Valadas et al. 1998). The spectrum occupied by the IR transmission is at wavelengths between 850 nm and 950 nm. The technique used for transmission is diffused infrared—that is, communications is omnidirectional. The range specified is approximately 20 m, but the transmissions cannot penetrate physical obstacles. The modulation scheme used is PPM. A data rate of 1 Mbps is supported using 16-PPM, and a data rate of 2 Mbps is supported using 4-PPM. This is in comparison with the infrared data association (IrDA) standard, which primarily allows communications at a few hundred kbps to a few Mbps between two devices (such as a laptop and a personal digital assistant) that are within a few feet of one another.

The IEEE 802.11b and g Standards

The DS option for IEEE 802.11, although successful, consumed a lot of bandwidth for the given data rate. The chip rate is 11 Mcps, but the maximum data rate is 2 Mbps. In other words, one Barker sequence of eleven chips, transmitted every microsecond, can at most carry two bits of information. To increase the data rate, the IEEE 802.11b standard adopted a slightly different method. Instead of transmitting one eleven-chip sequence every microsecond, with IEEE 802.11b the device transmits one eight-chip code word every 0.727 microseconds. Each eight-chip code word can carry as many as eight bits of information for a maximum data rate of $8/(0.727 \times 10^{-6}) = 11$ Mbps. If the code word carries only four bits of information, the data rate will be 5.5 Mbps. The code words are derived from complementary code keying (Halford et al. 1999).

Table 2: Mapping for CCK

Dibit	Phase Parameter	Dibit (d_{i+1},d_i)	Phase
(d1, d0)	φ_1	(0,0)	0
(d3, d2)	φ_2	(0,1)	π
(d5, d4)	φ_3	(1,0)	$\pi/2$
(d7, d6)	φ_4	(1,1)	$-\pi/2$

CCK works as follows for the case when eight bits are mapped into an eight-chip code word. The incoming data stream is broken into units of eight bits. Suppose the least significant bit is labeled d0, and the most significant bit is labeled d7. Then four phases are defined to correspond to the four possible values of a pair of bits as shown in the first two columns of Table 2. Depending on what the bits are, the phases then take on a value as shown in the third and fourth columns in Table 2. For example, if d5 = 0 and d4 = 1, then the phase $\varphi_3 = \pi$. Once the phases are determined, the eight-chip code word is given by the vector

$$\mathbf{C} = \begin{Bmatrix} e^{j(\varphi_1+\varphi_2+\varphi_3+\varphi_4)}, e^{j(\varphi_1+\varphi_3+\varphi_4)}, e^{j(\varphi_1+\varphi_2+\varphi_4)}, -e^{j(\varphi_1+\varphi_4)}, \\ e^{j(\varphi_1+\varphi_2+\varphi_3)}, e^{j(\varphi_1+\varphi_3)}, -e^{j(\varphi_1+\varphi_2)}, e^{j(\varphi_1)} \end{Bmatrix}$$

This vector has elements that belong to the set {+1, −1, +*j*, −*j*}, where *j* is the square root of −1. These four elements can be mapped in RF to the phase of the carrier, and the receiver can decode this phase information to recover the data bits (Pahlavan and Krishnamurthy 2002). CCK can be thought of as either a modulation scheme or a coding scheme.

The advantage of CCK is that it maintains the channelization of IEEE 802.11 while increasing the data rate by a factor of 5. CCK is also fairly robust to the degradations caused by multipath in the wireless environment. The values of SIFS and the slot for backoff in this option are 10 μs and 20 μs, respectively. IEEE 802.11b also has an optional modulation method called *packet binary convolutional coding* (PBCC) that is not widely implemented. The advantage of PBCC over CCK is the use of powerful convolutional coding for forward error correction.

The IEEE 802.11g standard (Vassis et al. 2005) maintains backward compatibility with IEEE 802.11b and IEEE 802.11 DS options by adopting minimal PHY layer frame changes and by including some mandatory and optional physical layer components. In the PLCP layer, 802.11g allows for the use of short preambles to reduce packet overhead. The four physical layers specified in this standard are prefixed by the term ERP, which stands for *extended rate physical*. The standard specifies orthogonal frequency division multiplexing and CCK as the mandatory modulation schemes with a data rate of 24 Mbps as the maximum mandatory data rate. With OFDM, IEEE 802.11g also provides for optional higher data rates of 36, 48, and 54 Mbps. OFDM is the same modulation scheme that is used in IEEE 802.11a and we discuss it below. PBCC is an optional modulation scheme in 802.11g that allows for raw data rates of 22 and 33 Mbps. We discuss OFDM in the context of 802.11a below, but the discussion could also apply to 802.11g with some modifications.

The IEEE 802.11a Standard

One primary problem for huge data rates in wireless channels is the coherence bandwidth of the wireless channel caused by multipath dispersion. The coherence bandwidth limits the maximum data rate of the channel to that which can be supported within this bandwidth (for example, if the coherence bandwidth is B Hz and the channel bandwidth is $W >> B$ Hz, a transmission bandwidth of W Hz will result in irrecoverable errors unless equalization or spread spectrum is used). To overcome this limitation, we can send data in several subchannels, each on the order of the coherence bandwidth or less, so that many of them will get through correctly. Using several subchannels and reducing the data rate on each channel increases the symbol duration in each channel. If the symbol duration in each channel is larger than the multipath dispersion, errors will be smaller and it will be possible to support larger data rates. This principle can be exploited while maintaining bandwidth efficiency using a fairly old technique: OFDM. OFDM has been used in digital subscriber lines as well to overcome the variations in attenuation with frequency over copper lines. OFDM enables spacing carriers (subchannels) as closely as possible, and implementing the system completely in digital eliminates analog components to the extent possible. OFDM (Kapp 2002) is used as the physical layer in IEEE 802.11a, HIPERLAN/2, and IEEE 802.11g.

IEEE 802.11a specifies eight 20-MHz channels (Van Nee et al. 1999). As shown in Figure 13, several subchannels are created in OFDM using orthogonal carriers in each channel. Fifty-two subchannels are specified for each channel with a bandwidth of approximately 300 kHz each. Forty-eight subchannels are used for data transmission, and four are used as pilot channels for synchronization. One OFDM symbol (consisting of the sum of the symbols on all carriers) lasts for 4 microseconds and carries anywhere between 48 and 288 coded bits. For example, at 54 Mbps, the OFDM symbol has 216 data symbols. With a code rate of 3/4, the number of coded bits/symbol will be $4 \times 216/3 = 288$. This is possible by using different modulation schemes ranging from BPSK, which has one bit per subchannel, to more complex modulation schemes such as *quadrature amplitude modulation* (QAM) that support multiple bits per subchannel. Error control coding also plays an important role in determining the data rate. Table 3 summarizes some features of the different supported data rates.

The PLCP in the case of 802.11a is a bit different in that there is no synchronization field. A rate field with four bits indicates the data rate that is being transmitted.

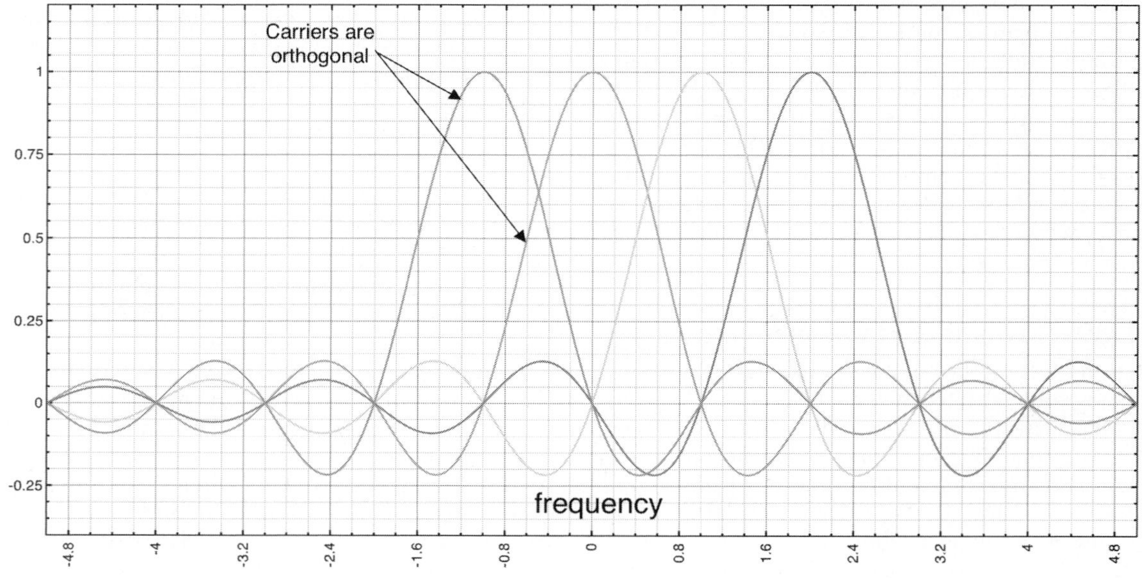

Figure 13: Orthogonal carriers in OFDM

Table 3: Data Rates and Associated Parameters in IEEE 802.11a

Data Rate (Mbps)	Modulation	Code Rate	Data Bits/Symbol	Coded Bits/ Subchannel	PLCP Rate Field
6	BPSK	1/2	24	1	1101
9	BPSK	3/4	36	1	1111
12	QPSK	1/2	48	2	0101
18	QPSK	3/4	72	2	0111
24	16-QAM	1/2	96	4	1001
36	16-QAM	3/4	144	4	1011
48	64-QAM	2/3	192	6	0001
54	64-QAM	3/4	216	6	0011

This field is shown in Table 3 for different data rates. The preamble and header are always modulated using BPSK (lower data rates). The values of SIFS and the slot for backoff in this option are 16 µs and 9 µs, respectively.

The IEEE 802.11n Standard

The current MAC and PHY layers of the IEEE 802.11 standard constrain the raw data rate to 54 Mbps and the throughput to a fraction of that depending on traffic load, channel conditions, and so on. A new task group is looking at an IEEE 802.11n standard that will look at both MAC and PHY enhancements that improve the throughput to more than 100 Mbps (as high as 600 Mbps). Note that this is not the raw data rate on the air, but the actual throughput of the network. Some of the ideas being floated to improve throughput are to use directional antennae, MIMO with OFDM, and throughput enhancements at the MAC layer. MIMO enables the spectral efficiency of links to go well above the 1 bps/Hz that is usually the order in traditional systems. This increase in spectral efficiency is possible through the use of such space-time techniques (Haykin and Moher 2005) as space-time coding, beam forming, and spatial multiplexing. These techniques either increase the reliability of the link through diversity or increase capacity by canceling interference from the simultaneous transmission of multiple data streams from multiple antennae.

The primary MAC enhancement to improve throughput in 802.11n is the use of frame aggregation to reduce overhead (Xiao 2005). At extremely high data rates, the overhead of waiting times, backoff, and frame headers can reduce throughput significantly. One method of reducing this overhead is to aggregate frames either at the MAC layer or the PHY layer. Similarly, acknowledgments can also be delayed and aggregated. Frame aggregation can be used for single destinations and multiple destinations, and it can use multiple rates for multiple destinations.

For some time, there were two competing proposals in Task Group N for the PHY and MAC layers—worldwide spectrum efficiency (WWiSE) and TGnSync—with many vendors in each group. Both proposals used MIMO at the physical layer. Products that conform to parts of these proposals were also available in the market. Neither proposal was successful in obtaining 75 percent of the vote. In January 2006, these two proposals merged with a third proposal that has been now submitted for approval. The industry consortium driving this new proposal is called the Enhanced Wireless Consortium. The organization's stated goal is to "help accelerate the IEEE 802.11n development process and promote a technology specification for interoperability of next-generation WLAN products."

Summary of PHY Layer Alternatives

Table 4 summarizes the different PHY layer alternatives in IEEE 802.11.

Table 4: Summary of PHY Alternatives in IEEE 802.11

Standard	Spectrum: United States (GHz)	Data Rates	Modulation Scheme
Base IEEE 802.11	2.402–2.479	1, 2 Mbps	GFSK, FHSS
	2.402–2.479	1, 2 Mbps	B/QPSK, DSSS
	850–950 nm	1, 2 Mbps	PPM, IR
802.11a	5.15–5.35, 5.725–5.825	6–54 Mbps	OFDM
802.11b	2.402–2.479	1, 2, 5.5, 11 Mbps	CCK
802.11g	2.402–2.479	1–54 Mbps	OFDM, CCK
802.11n	2.4 and 5 GHz	>100 Mbps	MIMO/OFDM

SECURITY ISSUES AND IMPLEMENTATION IN IEEE 802.11

Security in wireless networks is an important problem, especially because it is extremely difficult to contain radio signals within a protected perimeter (Edney and Arbaugh 2004). Anyone can listen to radio signals, and anyone can also potentially inject signals into the network. Typically, in any wireless or wired network, it is common to deploy security features or services such as confidentiality, entity authentication, data authentication, and integrity and so on to protect against security threats (Stinson 2002). The IEEE 802.11 standard has some mechanisms to provide confidentiality, integrity, and authentication at the link level. All data that leave the 802.11 link will not be protected. For instance, an MS communicating with an AP can have all its IEEE 802.11 frames that are on the air protected. Once the AP receives the frame, all protection is removed before it is transmitted on the distribution system. So additional security at the higher layers (such as IPSec or the *secure sockets layer,* SSL) may be required for some applications if the payload needs to be secure.

The original mechanism for providing confidentiality and authentication in IEEE 802.11 is called *wired equivalent privacy* (WEP) (Gast 2002). Over the last few years, several techniques for compromising WEP have been published in the literature. Tools such as AirCrack, Kismet, and WEPcrack are freely available and can be used to extract the secret key used in WEP encryption. WEP makes use of the RC4 stream cipher with forty-bit keys (although there are options to use 128-bit keys in most commercial products today). Both the implementation of WEP and the RC4 algorithm itself have vulnerabilities that have rendered WEP insecure for today's applications. WEP was initially proposed in the standard as a self-synchronizing, exportable, and efficient option. Although it does satisfy these three properties, its security has left much to be desired.

In what follows we discuss the original implementation of security in IEEE 802.11 and discuss enhancements that have been recently proposed.

Entity Authentication in IEEE 802.11

The mandatory entity authentication mechanism in IEEE 802.11 is called *open system authentication.* In this case, there is no real authentication. If one IEEE 802.11 device sends a frame to another, it is implicitly accepted. For example, an MS may simply send a frame to the AP choosing "open system" as the authentication algorithm (authentication algorithm = 0). The AP will simply accept it (if open system access is allowed) and send a response. From this transaction, the AP will obtain the MAC address of the MS for communication purposes.

A better authentication procedure is called *shared-key authentication,* in which WEP is implemented (Gast 2002). If the network is using WEP, shared-key authentication is mandatory. The assumption is that all devices in the network share a secret key. An MS will send a frame for authentication with sequence number 0, the authentication algorithm set to 1 (to indicate shared-key authentication). The AP will then send a challenge message (128 bits) in clear text to the MS along with its response. The MS will respond with an encrypted version of the challenge text. If the AP is able to verify the integrity of the reply, the MS is authenticated and it has the shared WEP key configured in it. Sometimes an MS will authenticate itself with several APs before associating itself with one of them. This process is called *preauthentication.* This authentication scheme is still not especially secure, however, and it also creates weaknesses in the protocol because of the way in which it is employed with a stream cipher.

Several commercial products also implement address filtering in which only certain MAC addresses are allowed access to the network. This is not part of the standard, and it is also possible for malicious users to spoof MAC addresses easily. However, address filtering is an additional security measure that is available for IEEE 802.11 networks.

Confidentiality and Integrity in IEEE 802.11

Confidentiality is simply provided in IEEE 802.11 by encrypting all packets using the RC4 stream cipher. Stream ciphers operate as follows. Using a secret key, a pseudo-random sequence of bits (the *key stream*) is generated. If this sequence has an especially long period and the algorithm is strong, it will be computationally impossible for someone to generate the sequence without knowing the secret key. The pseudo-random sequence thus generated will be XOR-ed with the MAC frame to make the contents of the frame secure from interception. RC4 is one algorithm to generate the pseudo-random key stream. This algorithm makes use of a secret key; in the case of WEP, it uses an *initialization vector* (IV) that is 24 bits long. Because the key is constant for all transactions, the same pseudo-random key stream is generated if the IV is not changed. An attacker could capture two streams of encrypted frames, XOR them together, eliminate the key stream, and then have an XOR of two data frames. If by some chance the attacker knows the contents of one data frame, he can get the other as well. Because the IV is only 24 bits long, it is still possible for an attacker to break the encryption scheme. One well publicized attack is the Fluhrer, Mantin, Shamir attack on RC4. In addition, there are several weak keys that could make the encryption scheme easier to break. It is also possible for an attacker to replay packets, depending on the sequence numbers that are being used. To ensure that an attacker has not modified a message, the WEP protocol uses the built-in *cyclic redundancy check* (CRC) to verify the integrity of the message. Checking the integrity of the message using the CRC has vulnerabilities that have been publicized in recent years.

Key Distribution in IEEE 802.11

The IEEE 802.11 standard does not specify how the shared keys must be distributed to devices (AP and MSs). It is usually a manual installation of keys by which a user will type the key in the device driver software. Unfortunately, this process is not scalable and has several human vulnerabilities. Users may write down the key on a piece of paper when they buy a new device and lose this paper. Some vendors have automated methods of key distribution. Cisco's light extensible authentication protocol makes use of the challenge-response mechanism to generate a key at the AP and an identical matching key locally in the MS that could then be used in a successful encrypted communication.

Security Features in 802.11i

Task Group I of the IEEE 802.11 working group has prepared an enhanced security framework for IEEE 802.11 called 802.11i that was approved as a standard in June 2004. Several vendors have already implemented elements of this standard. This framework includes what is called a *robust security network* (RSN) that is similar to WEP, but has several new capabilities in devices (Edney and Arbaugh 2004). It is possible for both WEP and RSN devices to coexist in a transitional security network.

A consortium of major WLAN manufacturers called the Wi-Fi Alliance considered options to improve security in legacy devices while 802.11i was being standardized. The proposal from this alliance is called *Wi-Fi protected access* (WPA) that introduces enhancements to WEP called *temporal key integrity protocol* (TKIP). In this protocol, RC4 is still used as the encryption algorithm. However, this protocol adds features that overcome WEP's weaknesses. A message integrity code is used instead of the CRC check. It changes the way in which IVs are generated. It changes the encryption key for every frame, increases the size of the IV, and also adds a mechanism to manage keys.

In 802.11i, RC4 is replaced by the *advanced encryption standard* (AES). In particular, the key stream and message integrity check will be generated by a *counter mode cipher block chaining MAC protocol* (CCMP). AES is a block cipher—that is, it operates on fixed blocks of data unlike a stream cipher, which generates a key stream. However, any block cipher can operate in many different standardized modes, and *cipher block chaining* (CBC) is one such mode of operation. The counter mode is another standardized mode of operation. It is expected that the counter mode will be used to generate the key stream, and the CBC will be used to generate the message integrity check. Both of these modes have been used in other systems with good security.

Both TKIP and AES-CCMP provide confidentiality and message integrity. To perform entity authentication, the IEEE 802.11 system has to still rely on challenge-response protocols. Over the years, there have been several protocols developed for dialup entity authentication and for port security in wired LANs. These include 802.1X, the *extensible authentication protocol* (EAP) and *remote authentication dial-in user service* (RADIUS). Note that all of these protocols are not equivalent. For instance, both 802.1X and RADIUS could use EAP for entity authentication and key distribution. EAP itself would use some challenge-response protocol such as challenge handshake authentication protocol (CHAP) or SSL to authenticate the devices. Both WPA and RSN mandate 802.1X and EAP as part of the access control mechanism for 802.11 networks. Note that access control is increasingly becoming an important problem with the emergence of hot spot networks in airports, cafes, and so on.

RECENT ACTIVITIES

There are some other amendments to the 802.11 standard that have been approved recently. They do not directly change the protocol on the air in the United States, but they do provide extensions to the way 802.11 systems may operate. One important issue in wireless networks is roaming between different points of access to the wired network. This is possible only if equipment from different vendors supports the same set of protocols and is interoperable. Previously, there existed a Task Group F that had proposed an *interaccess point protocol* (IAPP) to achieve multivendor interoperability. For example, when an MS moves from one AP to another and sends a reassociation request, the new AP must be able to converse with the old AP over the distribution system to inform it of the handoff and to free the resources in the old AP. This is achieved using the IAPP now standardized as 802.11f in July 2003. The 802.11f standard specifies the information and format of the information to be exchanged between access points and includes the recommended practice for multivendor access point interoperability via the IAPP across distribution systems. The competing standard for wireless LANs in Europe is the HIPERLAN/2 standard that is specified for the UNII bands. HIPERLAN/2 uses the same physical layer as IEEE 802.11a although it accommodates a few different data rates. In this standard, mechanisms are suggested for power measurement and control and radio resources management. Previously, too, there existed a Task Group H that was enhancing the current 802.11 MAC and 802.11a PHY with network management and control extensions for spectrum and transmit power management in the UNII bands with the possibility of dynamic channel selection capabilities. In this case, APs would be able to dynamically select channels based on information they can obtain about neighboring APs that may be transmitting on the same channel. This way, a laborious network planning process could be simplified. The 802.11h standard completed in October 2003 ensures that *transmit power control* and *dynamic frequency selection* satisfy the regulatory aspects in Europe.

Outside of the standards that have been specified already, there are several ongoing activities in the IEEE 802.11 working group. Several task groups are engaged in enhancing aspects of the IEEE 802.11 standard (see Table 5 for a summary). Some of these follows.

Task Group E: The 802.11 DCF considers all traffic to be the same and provides only a best effort service. This task group has developed enhancements to the MAC layer so as to provide some mechanisms for supporting *quality of service* (QoS) in wireless LANs for real-time applications such as audio, video, and media stream distribution. One technique that is being actively considered is to have different interframe space and contention window values for different classes of traffic. For example, a traffic class with higher priority would have a smaller IFS and CW range so that it waits for a smaller time compared to a traffic class with lower priority. This way, time-sensitive traffic could get access to the channel earlier. Different traffic classes have different queues in the MS,

Table 5: Summary of Task Groups and Status

Group	Group Activities	Status as of September 2006
A	5-GHz operation (high data rate extension based on OFDM)	Completed
B	2.4-GHz operation (high data rate extension as high as 11 Mbps)	Completed
E	QoS enhancements to the MAC layer	Completed (November 2005)
F	Inter Access Point Protocol	Completed (July 2003)
G	2.4-GHz operation (high data rate extension as high as 54 Mbps)	Completed
H	Spectrum and transmit power management in Europe	Completed (October 2003)
I	Security enhancements to 802.11	Completed (June 2004)
J	Operation in 4.9-GHz to 5-GHz bands in Japan	In progress
K	Radio resource management	In progress
N	High throughputs greater than 100 Mbps	Draft 1.02 in July 2006
P	Wireless access for the vehicular environment	In progress, voting on draft
R	Fast roaming between access points	In progress
S	Mesh networking of access points	In progress (started in 2004)
Y	Operation in the 3.5-GHz bands	In progress

enabling them to be treated differently. This technique is similar to service differentiation in wired networks (Pattara-atikom, Krishnamurthy, and Banerjee 2003). The MAC protocol is called *enhanced distributed channel access*. The ability to differentiate between traffic classes has become more important for *voice over IP* (VoIP) applications. The 802.11e standard was approved in November 2005.

Task Group J: This task group is considering enhancements to the current standard to provide operations in the frequency band between 4.9 GHz and 5 GHz for use in Japan. The reason for this task group is to make changes in the 802.11 standard to accommodate the regulatory demands in this spectrum in Japan. There will be expected changes to both the MAC and PHY layers to meet these regulations.

Task Group K: This task group is looking at enhanced radio resource management outside the purview of 802.11h. The primary goal of this group is to provide mechanisms to higher layers that enable radio and network measurements as necessary. Once power measurements and reporting are possible in a standardized manner, they can be exploited to make better use of the spectrum, reduce interference, and so on.

Task Group P: Future road transportation is expected to evolve into an *intelligent transportation system* (ITS). The goal of Task Group P (called *wireless access for the vehicular environment*, or WAVE) is to define enhancements to 802.11 that may be required to support ITS applications. Such definitions will include data exchange between high-speed vehicles and between these vehicles and the roadside infrastructure in the licensed ITS band (5.9 GHz).

Task Group R: In an authenticated system using 802.11i or even WEP, there is a substantial delay because of the reassociation and reauthentication procedures when an 802.11 device hands off from one BSS to another within an ESS. Such delays can be as high as 15 s and are unacceptable for real-time traffic. As VoIP becomes more important and its use over wireless LANs increases, these delays must be reduced to acceptable levels without compromising security. Such enhancements to the current 802.11 standard to provide fast handoffs between different BSSs is the responsibility of Task Group R.

Task Group S: As previously discussed, the idea of this task group is to develop enhancements to the current IEEE 802.11 standard to provide a method to configure the distribution system using the four MAC addresses, thereby enabling some form of mesh networking between access points. This could be a wired or wireless mesh network that allows for automatic topology learning and dynamic path configuration over self-configuring multihop topologies. Some proprietary protocols already perform this task to extend coverage within homes, but the standard will allow for different scenarios with different requirements (e.g., quick setup and teardown, maximizing throughput).

Task Group Y: This newly formed task group is looking at operation in the 3.5-GHz bands that were recently opened by the FCC for WLAN operation. One objective of this protocol is to develop a fair contention protocol for access to the medium.

Although not directly changing or adding to the standards, there are task groups that are involved in maintenance and other issues related to 802.11. Task Group M is performing the maintenance of the 802.11 standard. A Task Group D is looking at regulatory domain updates. There are also new proposed activities that are pending approval at various levels as of the time of the writing: for example, an 802.11t that aims to recommend practices for wireless performance prediction, an 802.11u that is considering interworking with external networks, an 802.11v for network management of mobile stations, and an 802.11w that provides protection (data integrity and authentication) of management frames. In addition, several study groups are looking at harmonizing the 802.11 and the European ETSI standards, and some are investigating the possibility of improvements to the 802.11 standard to provide higher throughput.

Other IEEE and Industry-Based Wireless Standards

The IEEE and other industry consortiums also have developed other wireless standards that are related to WLANs, but not as local area networking standards. The IEEE 802.15 standard looks at *personal area networks* (PANs), or networks related to an operating space around one person. Examples of PANs are Bluetooth networks (Haartsen and Mattisson 2000). In fact, 802.15 is based on Bluetooth. Like 802.11, there are many subcategories of standards in 802.15. One subcategory called 802.15.4 is also commercially popular with some higher layer implementation as the ZigBee standard. The 802.15.3 standard is considering high-speed physical layers that use ultrawideband. The HomeRF standard employs a protocol called *shared wireless access protocol,* which has many similarities with the 802.11 MAC and PHY layers. HomeRF is often considered a PAN standard like Bluetooth. Another IEEE wireless standard is the 802.16 standard (WiMAX) that looks at fixed wireless access. In this case, the goal is to provide fixed broadband wireless links to organizations and residences. These broadband links would replace the last-hop copper or coaxial cable and provide Internet access, video, and telephone services to the customer.

CONCLUSION

In this chapter, an overview of worldwide wireless local area networking standards was provided with a detailed consideration of the IEEE 802.11 standard and its many extensions. A top-down approach was used to describe how networks based on IEEE 802.11 operate. Details of many of the frames at the medium access control layer and the various standard physical layer alternatives were presented. A discussion of the security aspects included in the IEEE 802.11 standard followed by a summary of the many working groups involved in the standardization of IEEE 802.11 completed the chapter.

GLOSSARY

Advanced Encryption Standard (AES): The encryption algorithm used in the latest security standard for 802.11.

Advanced Mobile Phone System (AMPS): The very first cellular telephone service in the United States.

Clear to Send (CTS): Command used by an 802.11 mobile station to indicate to all other mobile stations in its receiving range about a pending transmission; helps reduce the hidden terminal problem and acknowledge an RTS packet.

Complementary Code Keying (CCK): A modulation and encoding scheme used in the 802.11b standard to increase the data rate from 2 Mbps to 11 Mbps while maintaining the original chip rate of 11 Mcps.

Counter Mode Cipher Block Chaining MAC Protocol (CCMP): Message authentication method for ensuring confidentiality and authentication in 802.11i that uses the advanced encryption standard.

Direct Sequence Spread Spectrum (DSSS): A modulation technique used in the original 802.11 standard that spreads the spectrum and provides robustness against multipath.

Distributed Coordination Function (DCF): The basic medium access method in all 802.11 networks; uses carrier sense multiple access with collision avoidance.

Interframe Space (IFS): The waiting time of 802.11 mobile stations to assist in collision avoidance. Different values are used for acknowledgements, regular frames, and polling frames.

Multiple-Input Multiple-Output (MIMO): A method of increasing the capacity of wireless links by using multiple antennae at both transmitter and receiver.

Network Allocation Vector (NAV): A number used by mobile stations to back off (stop sensing the medium) based on information about the length of current transmissions.

Orthogonal Frequency Division Multiplexing (OFDM): The modulation scheme used in 802.11a and 802.11g standards. It splits the channel into many narrow subcarriers, thereby avoiding problems related to the coherence bandwidth of the radio channel.

Point Coordination Function (PCF): An optional polling medium access mechanism that is not widely deployed in 802.11 systems.

Request to Send (RTS): Frames used by an 802.11 mobile station to indicate to all other mobile stations in its receiving range about a pending transmission and reduce the hidden terminal problem.

Wired Equivalent Privacy (WEP): The weak security protocol used in legacy 802.11 systems that made use of the RC4 stream cipher to provide confidentiality and authentication in ways that did not make the system secure.

CROSS REFERENCES

See *Local Area Networks; Wireless LANs (WLANs).*

REFERENCES

Crow, B. P., I. Widjaja, L. G. Kim, and P. T. Sakai. 1997. IEEE 802.11 wireless local area networks. *IEEE Communications Magazine*, 35(9): 116–26.

Edney, J., and W. A. Arbaugh. 2004. *Real 802.11 security: Wi-Fi protected access and 802.11i*. New York: Pearson Education.

Gast, M. S. 2002. *802.11 wireless networks: The definitive guide*. Sebastopol, CA: O'Reilly & Associates, 2002.

Haartsen, J. C., and S. Mattisson. 2000. Bluetooth—A new low-power radio interface providing short-range connectivity. In *Proceedings of the IEEE*, 88(10): 1651–61.

Halford, K., S. Halford, M. Webster, and C. Ander. 1999. Complementary code keying for RAKE-based indoor wireless communication. *IEEE International Symposium on Circuits and Systems*. Orlando, FL, USA. Vol. 4: 427–30.

Haykin, S., and M. Moher. 2005. *Modern wireless communications*. Upper Saddle River, NJ: Prentice Hall.

Kapp, S. 2002. 802.11a. More bandwidth without the wires. *IEEE Internet Computing*, 6(4): 75–79.

Lee, M. J., and J. Zheng. 2006. Emerging standards for wireless mesh technology. *IEEE Wireless Communications*, April, pp. 56–63.

Pahlavan, K., and P. Krishnamurthy. 2002. *Principles of wireless networks: A unified approach*. Upper Saddle River, NJ: Prentice Hall.

Pattara-atikom, W., P. Krishnamurthy and S. Banerjee. 2003. Distributed mechanisms for quality of service in wireless LANs. *IEEE Wireless Communications*: Special issue, *QoS in next-generation wireless multimedia communications systems,* Vol. 10: 26–34.

Stinson, D. 2002. *Cryptography: Theory and practice*. Orlando, FL: CRC Press.

Tuch, B. 1991. An ISM band spread spectrum local area network: WaveLAN. In *Proceedings of First IEEE Workshop on WLANs*, Worcester, MA, pp. 103–11.

Valadas, R. T., A. R. Tavares, A. M. D. Duarte, A. C. Moreira, and C. T. Lomba. 1998. The infrared physical layer of the IEEE 802.11 standard for wireless local area networks. *IEEE Communications Magazine*, 36(12): 107–12.

Van Nee, R., et al. 1999. New high-rate wireless LAN standards. *IEEE Communications Magazine*, 37(12): 82–8.

Vassis, D., G. Kormentzas, A. Rouskas, and I. Maglogiannis. 2005. The IEEE 802.11g standard for high data rate WLANs. *IEEE Network,* May–June, pp. 21–6.

Wilkinson, T. A., T. Phipps, and S. K. Barton. 1995. A report on HIPERLAN standardization. *International Journal on Wireless Information Networks*, 2: 99–120.

Xiao, Y. 2005. IEEE 802.11n: Enhancements for higher throughput in wireless LANs. *IEEE Wireless Communications*, December, pp. 82–91.

Bit-Interleaved Coded Modulation

Yuheng Huang, *QUALCOMM Incorporated*
James A. Ritcey, *University of Washington*

DIGITAL COMMUNICATIONS OVER FADING CHANNELS

Digital communications is an integral part of modern society, encompassing point-to-point communications, broadcast, and storage. Because of user mobility and ease of use, wireless communications is increasing at a rapid pace. This is fueled by new algorithms, new devices, and new applications. Costs are decreasing and the available content grows richer. Today we can envision digital video over wireless links received on handheld devices.

Digital communications has its modern origins in information theory, developed by Claude Shannon of Bell Labs in the late 1940s. Shannon thought of communications geometrically and spawned the advent of coding for reliable communications over noisy channels. His fundamental insight was the existence of the channel capacity, which represents the ultimate limit of data communications over the channel. The capacity depends on the signal-to-noise ratio, the available bandwidth, and the noise and fading characteristics of the channel. Early work focused on the additive white Gaussian noise (AWGN) channel and was later extended to cover wireless situations. Subsequent to the discovery of information theory, many researchers began the search for codes that could realize Shannon's ideal of reliable communications. Early block codes included those developed by Richard Hamming, Irving Reed, and Gus Solomon. These are still used in some applications today. Convolutional codes were introduced by Peter Elias. Much of these advanced signal processing techniques were ahead of their time and awaited the digital revolution in integrated circuits. At the same time and place as Shannon, John Bardeen, William Shockley, and Walter Brattain, fellow scientists at the Bell Telephone Laboratories in Murray Hill developed the transistor—later extended to the basic integrated circuit, the building block of all current digital communications technology.

A digital communication system, in the abstract, is measured by several metrics. These measure the data efficiency, the bandwidth efficiency, and the energy efficiency, and are measured by the data rate (R_b in bits/sec), bandwidth (W in Hz), and required energy-to-noise ratio (E/N_o in dB), to meet a prescribed bit error rate (BER).

The data rate measures the amount of information that flows to the receiver per unit time. For wireless systems, this is constrained by available bandwidth, and so is better quantified in terms of spectral efficiency. This is a normalized bit rate by the occupied bandwidth. In work that focuses on the physical layer, all the transmitted data is assumed to have been compressed so that the bit rate represents the information rate.

These bits may not arrive without errors; this is quantified by the BER, or probability of bit error, the major performance metric used in evaluating systems. The key dependence is a measure of energy efficiency, or effective signal-to-noise ratio. In digital communications, this is more correctly written as an energy ratio, E/N_o. This is the required energy-to-noise ratio to achieve a target BER.

Communication systems have two fundamental approaches to increase data rate. They can either transmit signal with higher bandwidth, or use a larger constellation to transmit multiple bits per symbol. Both methods are used in practice. However, an improved data rate comes at a price, a required increase in E/N_o. Coding, as predicted by Shannon, counteracts this trend by combining or encoding large groups of data in blocks. Although this allows for increased efficiency, it drives the complexity of the decoder. It also imposes delay or latency on the receiver, because bits are not put out until the entire block is decoded. Finally, the computational complexity of the system, especially at the receiver, is critical and has to meet implementation constraints. As we examine bit-interleaved coded modulation (BICM) for communications over fading channels, we will encounter all of these trade-offs.

The basic block diagram for digital communications, at its simplest level, involves three parts: the transmitter that carries out the encoding, the channel that forwards the message introducing noise and other impairments, and the receiver that reads the signal and attempts to decode the transmitted data. Outside of this framework, or further up the protocol stack, are the many networking functions that coordinate the messaging from an application viewpoint. Here we are concerned only with the physical transmission across the channel; the PHY layer, in networking terminology. Flow control, routing, acknowledgement receipts, and even data compression are outside the scope of this chapter but are discussed in many other chapters of this handbook.

The digital communications transmitter we will consider consists of several stages. First, the incoming (compressed) bit stream is encoded using a convolutional encoder. Codes of different strengths can be employed, but nominally a rate 1/2 code is used. This encoder puts out two encoded bits for each input bit. The definition of the encoder can be found in many textbooks on digital communications (Proakis 2000). The output bits are interleaved, or permuted, over a large block, usually on the order of thousands of bits. The bit interleaver is the novel item in the BICM transmitter. It serves to break the channel correlation as well as spread the coded bits in the block to facilitate decoding. Following the bit interleaver, the bits are grouped and mapped to complex symbols to prepare for transmission. We focus on 16-quadrature amplitude modulation (QAM) and 8-phase shift keying (PSK) constellations in our review of BICM, although it is indeed possible to go to larger alphabets. Increasing the alphabet size, 16-QAM being determined by a labeling of four coded bits to each symbol, generally increases the data rate. The energy efficiency decreases, and the susceptibility to system imperfections increases. A more complete discussion of the BICM code properties will follow this system overview. Finally, the transmitter pulse shapes and modulates the symbols to the appropriate carrier frequency and bandwidth. These latter components are standard to any digital pulse amplitude modulator and are discussed by Proakis (2000). This description holds for a single-carrier modulation scheme, but can be extended to multi-carrier approaches using orthogonal frequency division multiplexing (OFDM). OFDM is used in some flavors of wireless fidelity (WiFi) (802.11,11a,11g,11n) and Worldwide Interoperability for Microwave Access (WiMAX) (802.16,16a,16d). Since OFDM can compensate for delay-spread multipath and eliminate intersymbol interference, we will assume this structure in order to focus on design and performance of the coded modulation.

An overall block diagram of a generic digital communication system is shown in Figure 1. This shows the basic functionality required in the transmitter and receiver, and lists some basic impairments introduced by the channel. A complete system design is beyond the scope of our discussion here.

The primary issues will include the design of:

1. The encoder. A convolutional code is used.
2. The bit interleaver. Not shown, but pseudo-randomly permutes a large block of ($\approx 10^4$) coded bits.
3. The digital modulator. M-ary PSK or QAM is used. Space-time coding is also considered. The mapping of bits to symbols is critical.
4. The channel. A slow, flat fading channel.
5. The receiver. Primary emphasis is on design and performance of the iterative decoder. Synchronization, limited to the extraction of channel state information (CSI), is also considered.

Ultimately, the system is evaluated against the metrics listed. However, many functions are neglected in our discussion. These items would include mostly the analog interfaces such as pulse shaping, radio frequency (RF) transmitter and receiver, and synchronization beyond CSI extraction (timing, frequency, phase, etc.). They are critical to real-world performance but beyond the scope of our discussion.

We illustrate the coherent modulation formats that we will employ in Figure 2. Three constellations are shown in each row, corresponding to a member of the PSK (top) or QAM (bottom) family. The leftmost member is always the binary antipodal constellation in which 1 bit of information is conveyed per transmitted symbol. As we progress across the family, the bit rate increases, but the symbol rate remains fixed. The main examples we will present in this chapter are the last family members: 8-PSK (three bits/symbol) and 16-QAM (four bits/symbol). The QAM family has better performance but is more difficult to implement due to increased sensitivity to nonlinear distortions. The actual transmitted waveform is a mapping from the selected constellation point to an analog waveform. The details are important in system design but not critical for an assessment of BICM.

BICM employs coded modulation in which the transmitted symbol is a mapping of coded bits. The encoder is shown in our block diagram and will actually consist of two sequential operations—a convolutional encoder followed by a bit interleaver. The convolutional encoder is one technique to introduce redundancy into the information bit stream. Information theory shows that this is required to allow for error correction and reliable communications. Many codes are employable, and this is an active research area. We will discuss convolutional codes in more detail, but it is possible to replace this with more powerful turbo or low-density parity check (LDPC) codes. These more powerful codes substantially increase the complexity and change the design rules; they are beyond the scope of this chapter. Convolutional codes are widely used in commercial systems, and chipset encoders and decoders are readily available. As we will see, these are not suitable for the best performance obtainable with iterative decoding using soft feedback. They are suitable for lower performance hard-decision decoding.

The convolutional code is described by its code rate and encoder structure. The code rate $R_c = k_c/n_c$ is the ratio of

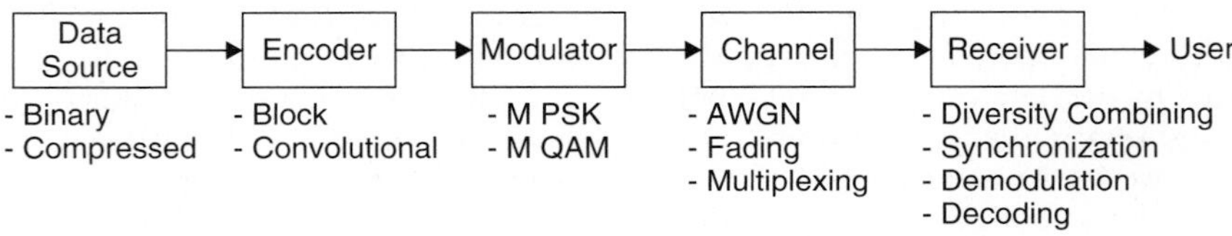

Figure 1: Block diagram for a generic digital communication system

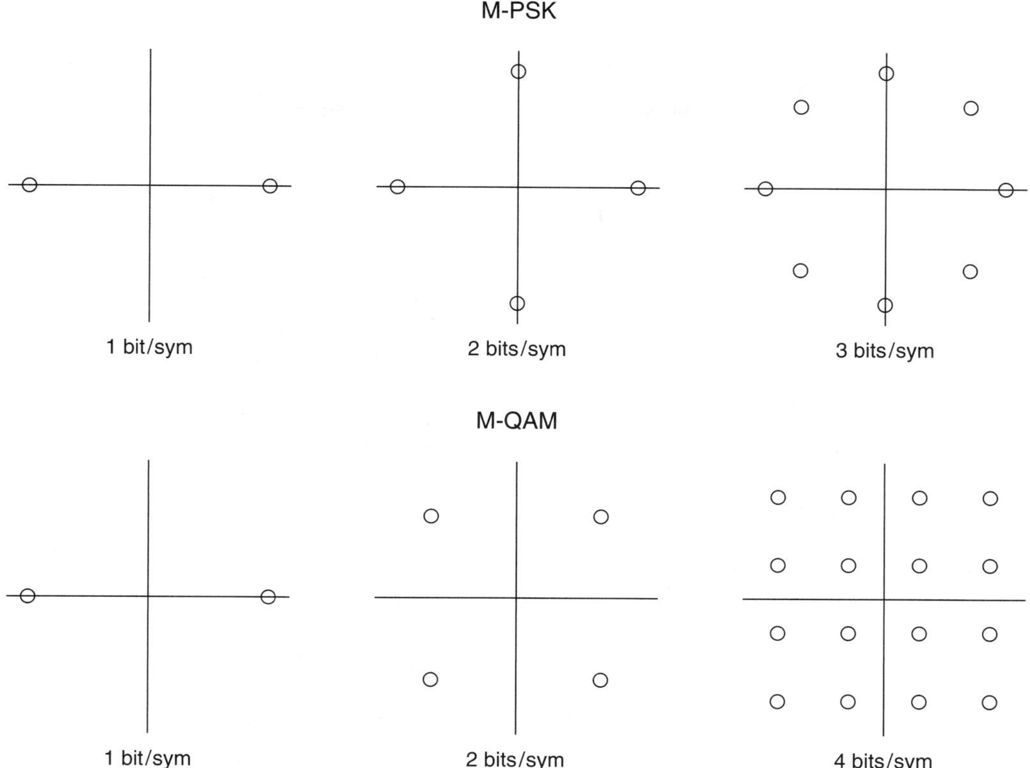

Figure 2: *M*-PSK (top) and *M*-QAM (bottom) constellations

the number of information bits put in, k_c, to the number of coded bits put out, n_c. A typical value is 1/2, which puts out two coded bits for every input information bit. This redundancy allows for error-correcting capability if the code is properly designed. However, the two output bits would need to be sent in the time period of the single input bit. This can be accomplished in one of the two ways: either by increasing the required bandwidth by signaling faster at the same information rate or by decreasing the information rate to accommodate the redundancy. This fundamental trade-off can be circumvented in our coded modulation structure. The two coded bits can be mapped to a single complex constellation point drawn from, say, 4-QAM. This holds both the bandwidth and information rate fixed. The design of these coded modulation systems, called trellis-coded modulation or TCM, was completed in the late 1980s and was critical to the design of high-rate voice-band modems. Today, these are still employed on specific channels. In BICM, the best convolutional codes of a given constraint length are employed. The constraint length can be viewed as a measure of complexity. One key difference between BICM and TCM is that, in TCM, the coding and modulation are jointly designed. In fact, the bits that are used to make up a constellation symbol can be grouped into two segments: those that are coded and those that are not. In contrast, BICM, through the random interleaving, separates coding and modulation. Capacity analysis has shown that BICM is nearly optimal over perfectly interleaved Rayleigh channels and performs very well over AWGN channels as well. This robustness is an important practical advantage for BICM, because realistic wireless channels can vary over time and exhibit more or less fading for fairly long periods. We also mention multilevel coding with multistage decoding, which is an alternative design to both TCM and BICM. This appears slightly superior in performance, at the cost of some complexity. BICM-ID with very high performance turbo or LDPC codes appears to offer the best performance at a reasonable cost at present.

The channel introduces noise and distortion onto the received signal. The noise is commonly modeled as additive, uncorrelated, and Gaussian, and arises from several sources. All receivers introduce front-end thermal noise from the electronics, and this suffices to motivate AWGN. The transmitted signal is heavily attenuated during propagation, the signal loss going as the inverse square of the transmitted distance. This transmission loss is increased at higher frequencies and can be further shadowed by non–line-of-sight (NLOS) propagation. As the wireless signal propagates in real-world scenarios, fading occurs. Fading is the destructive interference that results from the reflection of several electromagnetic ray paths from scattering objects. The variation in received signal level fluctuates, so that a statistical model is often used to design and evaluate digital communication systems. For various reasons beyond the scope of this chapter, we can assume slow, flat fading, which models the fluctuating attenuation as a random variable, constant over the duration of any symbol, while changing abruptly from symbol to symbol. The degree to which the attenuation changes, the temporal correlation, is determined by the relative velocity of the transmitter, receiver, and scatterers themselves.

A commonly accepted model is the Rayleigh fading model, in which the signal phase is completely randomized while the amplitude suffers a random attenuation modeled as a sample from the Rayleigh distribution. It models diffuse propagation in which no single propagation path dominates the totality of all paths. A more complex model, which we will illustrate, is the Ricean fading model, named after Stephen O. Rice, another Bell Lab researcher who developed much of modern noise theory in a significant paper published in the *Bell Systems Technical Journal*. Ricean fading can be described as a dominant path in the presence of a diffuse set of paths. The distribution is parameterized by the ratio of the energy in the dominant to diffuse paths, the K factor. The Ricean distribution for various values of K is shown in Figure 3. Many additional statistical models for fading have been developed for wireless channels. The correct model depends heavily on the terrain (urban/suburban/rural), the frequency band, and the mobility. The system designer is faced with developing an effective system that works in spite of the channel and does not rely on any particular assumptions. The Rayleigh model is the most conservative choice.

In the case of Ricean fading, the fading intensity per channel ν_ℓ has probability density function

$$f(\nu_\ell) = (K+1)e^{-K-(K+1)\nu_\ell} I_o\left(2\sqrt{K(K+1)\nu_\ell}\right) \tag{1}$$

where I_0 is a special mathematical function called the modified Bessel function of order 0. This probability density function is scaled to unit mean and parameterized in terms of the Ricean factor K, the ratio of specular to diffuse power.

The impact of fading on digital communications can be illustrated for binary phase shift keying (BPSK) over a Rayleigh fading channel. Assume a discrete time model of the received matched filter output at symbol t is given by

$$r_t = \alpha_t \sqrt{E} s_t + n_t \tag{2}$$

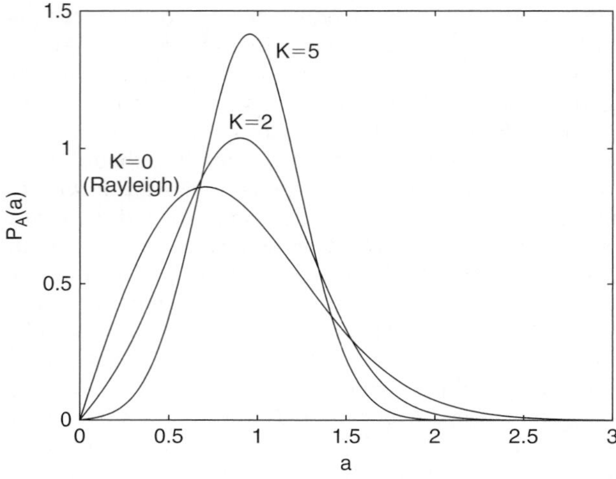

Figure 3: Ricean fading probability density functions

where s_t is the symbol, E is the energy per symbol, and n_t is a white Gaussian noise (WGN) sample of variance $N_o/2$ per dimension. The remaining factor α represents the channel attenuation. It will model the complex Rayleigh fading. Assuming perfect phase compensation, the BER is given by

$$P_e = Q(\sqrt{2S|\alpha|^2}),\ S = E/N_o. \tag{3}$$

The Q-function is the right tail of the normal distribution and is often approximated in digital communications by $Q(\sqrt{2S\,|\alpha|^2}) \approx \exp(-S\,|\alpha|^2)$. Note that the BER decays exponentially fast in $S = E/N_o$.

Next, consider the fading situation. Now the $|\alpha|$ is Rayleigh distributed and the earlier result is only conditional, and must be further averaged over the fading distribution. Carrying out the integration defines a new average probability of error given by

$$\overline{P}_e = \int Q\left(\sqrt{2S\nu}\right) f(\nu) d\nu \sim 1/4S. \tag{4}$$

The key feature is the behavior of the BER curve, in particular, how rapidly it decays for large values of signal-to-noise ratio (SNR). The decay rate is exponential in the SNR . What is the effect of the fading upon this error-rate characteristic? It is to change this rapid exponential decay into a slow algebraic decay so that, in Rayleigh fading, the BER decays only as the inverse of the SNR. Without fading mitigation, this causes losses on the order of about 30 dB.

The mitigation takes the form of diversity combining, in which multiple symbols are sent over independent channel realizations and coherently combined to average out the fading. The multiple symbols can be obtained in many ways: multiple antennas, repeated symbols, or frequency slots. These are generally less efficient than interleaving the coded symbols and sending them across effectively independent fading channels. The independence is achieved because the symbols are spread far apart in time, relative to the fading rate. The end result is that the slope of the log-BER characteristic changes from 1 to the "diversity order"L. More precisely (Proakis 2000),

$$\overline{P}_e \sim C_f(4S)^{-L},\ C_f = \binom{2L-1}{L}. \tag{5}$$

Here L is the number of independent symbols used in the combining, and C_f is a multiplicative constant. The actual value of the diversity order in more complicated scenarios depends on the fading correlation and signalling scheme.

BIT-INTERLEAVED CODED MODULATION

Next, we apply these general principles to conventional BICM. We will model BICM as the serial concatenation of the convolutional encoder, pseudo-random bit interleaver, and memoryless modulator (Caire, Taricco, and Biglieri 1998), as shown in Figure 4.

As we have discussed, the information sequence is encoded by a convolutional encoder before being bitwise

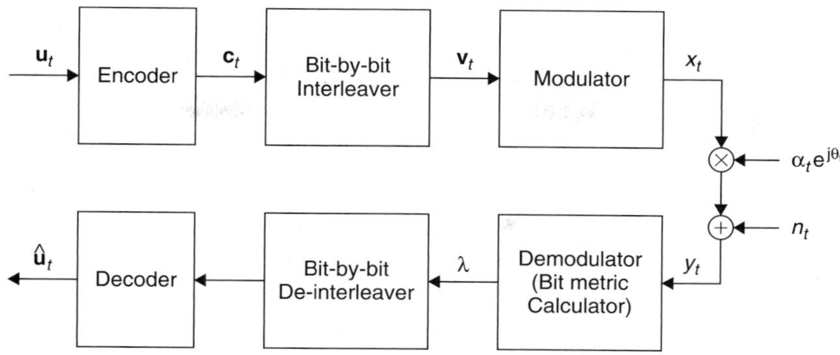

Figure 4: BICM block diagram

interleaved. The purpose of this bit interleaver (π) is to break the fading correlation and increase the diversity order from the minimum symbol distance to the minimum Hamming (bit) distance of a code, as illustrated by Zehavi (1992) and Caire et al. (1998). Then m consecutive bits of the interleaved coded sequence are grouped to form $\mathbf{v}_t$, a channel symbol at the t-th signaling interval. The modulator maps each $\mathbf{v}_t$ to a complex transmitted signal $\mathbf{x}_t = \mu(\mathbf{v}_t)$ chosen from M-ary constellation χ, where μ is the labeling map and $M = 2^m$. These labeling maps are critical to performance.

As discussed, with an OFDM system, it is reasonable to assume a flat Rayleigh (Ricean with $K = 0$) fading channel with coherent demodulation. The baseband signal at the receiver is

$$\mathbf{y}_t = \alpha_t \mathbf{x}_t + \mathbf{n}_t, \tag{6}$$

where α_t is the Rayleigh-distributed fading coefficient with $E(\alpha_t^2) = 1$, and $\mathbf{n}_t$ is a complex white Gaussian noise sample with the variance of $N_o/2$ per dimension. For the AWGN channel, $\alpha_t = 1$. Throughout this section, we will assume perfect CSI so that α_t is perfectly estimated and available to the receiver. We assume perfect knowledge of the phase and that this has been compensated in the receiver model. In practice, this CSI must be estimated from pilot symbols or tones. Later we relax this assumption.

One approach to demodulating conventional BICM is to use the Viterbi algorithm (VA) originally designed for decoding convolutional codes over AWGN channels. This requires a metric for each transmitted symbol, which is built up from metrics for each interleaved bit.

Suboptimal maximum log-likelihood bit metrics (Caire et al. 1998) can be obtained as follows:

$$\begin{aligned}\lambda(\mathbf{v}_t^i = b) &= \log \sum_{\mathbf{x}_t \in \chi_b^i} P(\mathbf{y}_t | \mathbf{x}_t) \\ &\approx \max_{\mathbf{x}_t \in \chi_b^i} \log P(\mathbf{y}_t | \mathbf{x}_t) \\ &= -\min_{\mathbf{x}_t \in \chi_b^i} \left\| \mathbf{y}_t - \alpha_t \mathbf{x}_t \right\|^2,\end{aligned} \tag{7}$$

where χ_b^i is the subset of χ whose labels have the binary value b at the i-th bit position. Each bit metric is calculated by selecting the constellation point with the minimum distance over the subset χ_b^i. These branch metrics can be obtained by adding the de-interleaved bit metrics before the Viterbi decoder.

The performance of BICM can be dramatically improved with iterative decoding.

BIT-INTERLEAVED CODED MODULATION WITH ITERATIVE DECODING

The iterative decoding receiver is based on the advances made in the design of turbo decoding algorithms.

We review the soft-decision bit metric calculation for iterative decoding (Li, Chindapol, and Ritcey 2002). Our receiver uses a suboptimal, iterative method through individually optimal but separate demodulation and convolutional decoding steps as shown in Figure 5. The Viterbi decoder is replaced by the soft-input soft-output

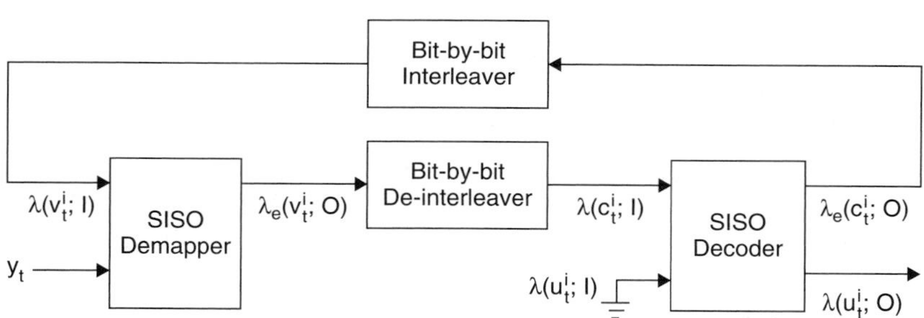

Figure 5: BICM-ID receiver with soft feedback

(SISO) decoder (Benedetto et al. 1997), and the output of the SISO decoder is fed back to the demodulator for bit metric recalculation. At the demodulator, the maximum a posteriori probability bit metrics are calculated as

$$\begin{aligned}\lambda(\mathbf{v}_t^i = b) &= \log P(\mathbf{v}_t^i = b|\mathbf{y}_t) \\ &= \log \sum_{\mathbf{x}_t \in \chi_b^i} P(\mathbf{x}_t|\mathbf{y}_t) \\ &\propto \log \sum_{\mathbf{x}_t \in \chi_b^i} P(\mathbf{y}_t|\mathbf{x}_t)P(\mathbf{x}_t). \end{aligned} \quad (8)$$

The a priori probability $P(\mathbf{x}_t)$ is unavailable on the first pass of demodulation. Therefore, an equally likely assumption is made and equation 7 is used as the input to the SISO decoder, which then generates the a posteriori probabilities for both information and coded bits. Note that the metric shown in equation 7 is just a simplification of equation 8.

Let $\mathbf{c}_t$ denote the de-interleaved version of $\mathbf{v}_t$ and $\mathbf{u}_t$ denote the input symbol corresponding to $\mathbf{c}_t$. Following the notation of Benedetto et al. (1997), we denote $P(q; I)$ as the a priori probability for a variable q. $P(q; O)$ is the a posteriori probability. Note that $P(\mathbf{u}_t; I)$ is never available because it requires knowledge of the information sequence at the receiver.

On the second pass, the extrinsic, a posteriori probabilities $P(\mathbf{c}_t^i;O)$ put out by the SISO module are interleaved and fed back as the a priori probabilities $P(\mathbf{v}_t^i;I)$ to the demodulator. Therefore, a priori probabilities for equation 8 can be computed by

$$\begin{aligned}P(\mathbf{x}_t) &= P(\mu(\mathbf{v}_t;I)) \\ &= \prod_{i=1}^{m} P(\mathbf{v}_t^i = \tilde{\mathbf{v}}_t^i(\mathbf{x}_t);I),\end{aligned} \quad (9)$$

where $\tilde{\mathbf{v}}_t^i(\mathbf{x}_t)$ is the value of the i-th bit of the label corresponding to $\mathbf{x}_t = \mu(\tilde{\mathbf{v}}_t)$. Using equation 8 and equation 9, the extrinsic a posteriori bit probabilities for the second pass demodulation can be written as

$$\begin{aligned}P(\mathbf{v}_t^i = b;O) &= P(\mathbf{v}_t^i = b|\mathbf{y}_t)/P(\mathbf{v}_t^i = b;I) \\ &= \sum_{\mathbf{x}_t \in \chi_b^i} P(\mathbf{y}_t|\mathbf{x}_t)\prod_{\substack{j\neq i\\ j=1}}^{m} P(\mathbf{v}_t^j = \tilde{\mathbf{v}}_t^j(\mathbf{x}_t);I).\end{aligned} \quad (10)$$

Equation 10 shows that we need only the a priori probabilities $P(\mathbf{v}_t^j;I)$ of the other bits ($j \neq i$) on the same channel symbol $\mathbf{v}_t$ when recalculating the bit metrics. The receiver then uses (10) to *regenerate* the bit metrics and iterates demodulation and decoding. After the last pass, the final decoded outputs are the hard decisions based on the extrinsic bit probabilities $P(\mathbf{u}_t^i;O)$. This is the total a posteriori because $P(\mathbf{u}_t^i;I)$ is unused.

Signal labeling is the crucial part of conventional BICM and BICM-ID design. It is shown by Caire et al. (1998) that Gray labeling yields the best performance for BICM. They also show that the asymptotic performance of BICM over Rayleigh fading can be approximated by

$$\log_{10} P_b \simeq \frac{-d_2(C)}{10}\left[\left(Rd_h^2(\mu)\right)_{dB} + \left(\frac{E_b}{N_0}\right)_{dB}\right] + const, \quad (11)$$

where P_b is the probability of bit error, $d_2(C)$ is the minimum Hamming distance of the code, R is the information rate, and $d_h^2(\mu)$ is the *harmonic mean* of the minimum squared Euclidean distance. For any M-ary constellation with a labeling map μ, $d_h^2(\mu)$ can be calculated by

$$d_h^2(\mu) = \left(\frac{1}{m2^m}\sum_{i=1}^{m}\sum_{b=0}^{1}\sum_{\mathbf{x}\in\chi_b^i}\frac{1}{\|\mathbf{x}-\hat{\mathbf{z}}\|^2}\right)^{-1}, \quad (12)$$

where $m = \log_2(M)$. Here $\hat{\mathbf{z}} \in \chi_{\bar{b}}^i$ is the nearest constellation point to $\mathbf{x}$.

Therefore, it is obvious that the asymptotic BICM performance over Rayleigh fading depends primarily on the minimum Hamming distance of a convolutional code $d_2(C)$ and the harmonic mean of the minimum squared Euclidean distance $d_h^2(\mu)$. Specifically, $d_2(C)$ controls the slope of the BER curve, and $d_h^2(\mu)$ gives the horizontal offset. Intuitively, the diversity order can further be increased by concatenating the larger signal constellation with a lower-rate code; however, it may not provide a lower P_b in the range of interest due to reduction in the minimum intersignal Euclidean distance among signal constellation points (Caire et al. 1998). Note that a labeling map μ is independent of a convolutional code C due to bit interleaving; therefore, it can be separately optimized in our iterative decoding algorithm without altering the code diversity. This is carried out to maximize the harmonic mean of the minimum Euclidean distance as seen with error-free feedback.

Next we repeat the analysis for BICM-ID. The reader will notice that, through feedback, information about other bits in the symbol can be used to reduce the error possibilities during decoding, as compared with BICM. As shown by Chindapol and Ritcey (2001), the asymptotic performance of the error floor of BICM-ID is obtained by

$$\log_{10} P_b \simeq \frac{-d_2(C)}{10}\left[\left(R\tilde{d}_h^2(\mu)\right)_{dB} + \left(\frac{E_b}{N_0}\right)_{dB}\right] + const, \quad (13)$$

where

$$\tilde{d}_h^2(\mu) = \left(\frac{1}{m2^m}\sum_{i=1}^{m}\sum_{b=0}^{1}\sum_{\mathbf{x}\in\chi_b^i}\frac{1}{\|\mathbf{x}-\tilde{\mathbf{z}}\|^2}\right)^{-1}. \quad (14)$$

Note that $\tilde{\mathbf{z}}$ is the only member in $\chi_{\bar{b}}^i$, so the opportunities for errors are greatly reduced as compared with BICM, which suffers from "random modulation." Because there is no change in the coding structure or constellation size, all terms on the right hand side of equation 11 and equation 13 are the same except that $\tilde{d}_h^2(\mu)$ substitutes for $d_h^2(\mu)$. Therefore, from equation 12 and equation 14 the labeling map μ should be designed such that $\|\mathbf{x}-\tilde{\mathbf{z}}\|$ is larger than $\|\mathbf{x}-\hat{\mathbf{z}}\|$ for all $\mathbf{x}$ (if possible) in order to achieve the iterative decoding gain. In other words, iterative decoding feeds back information about the other bits that can be used to reduce the error probability.

Figure 6 shows the subset partitioning for each of the four bit positions of the 16-QAM constellation. Define χ_b^i

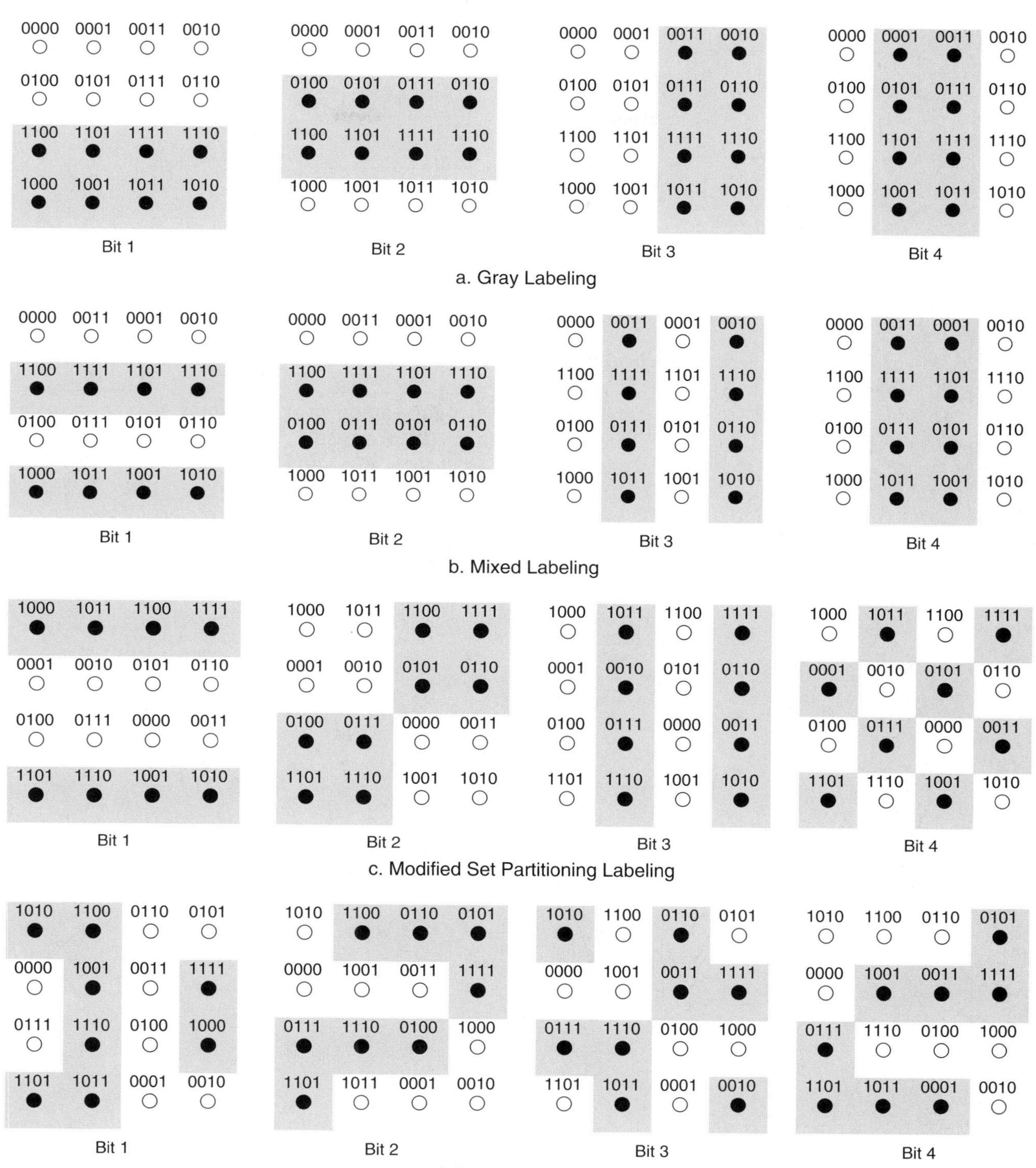

Figure 6: Subset partitions of 16-QAM for four labeling schemes

to be the subset of the constellation points for which bit i takes on value b. For example, χ_1^1 is the subset for which bit $i = 1$ takes on value $b = 1$. The shaded regions (only shown inside the unit square) correspond to the decision regions for each bit in χ_1^i, and the unshaded to χ_0^i. It is obvious that all labeling methods have the same minimum Euclidean distance between subsets of χ_1^i and χ_0^i but a different number of nearest neighbors.

Given ideal feedback of all other bits, a 16-QAM constellation is translated to a binary signaling selected from eight possible pairs. Figure 7 illustrates the increase in the minimum Euclidean distance between subsets.

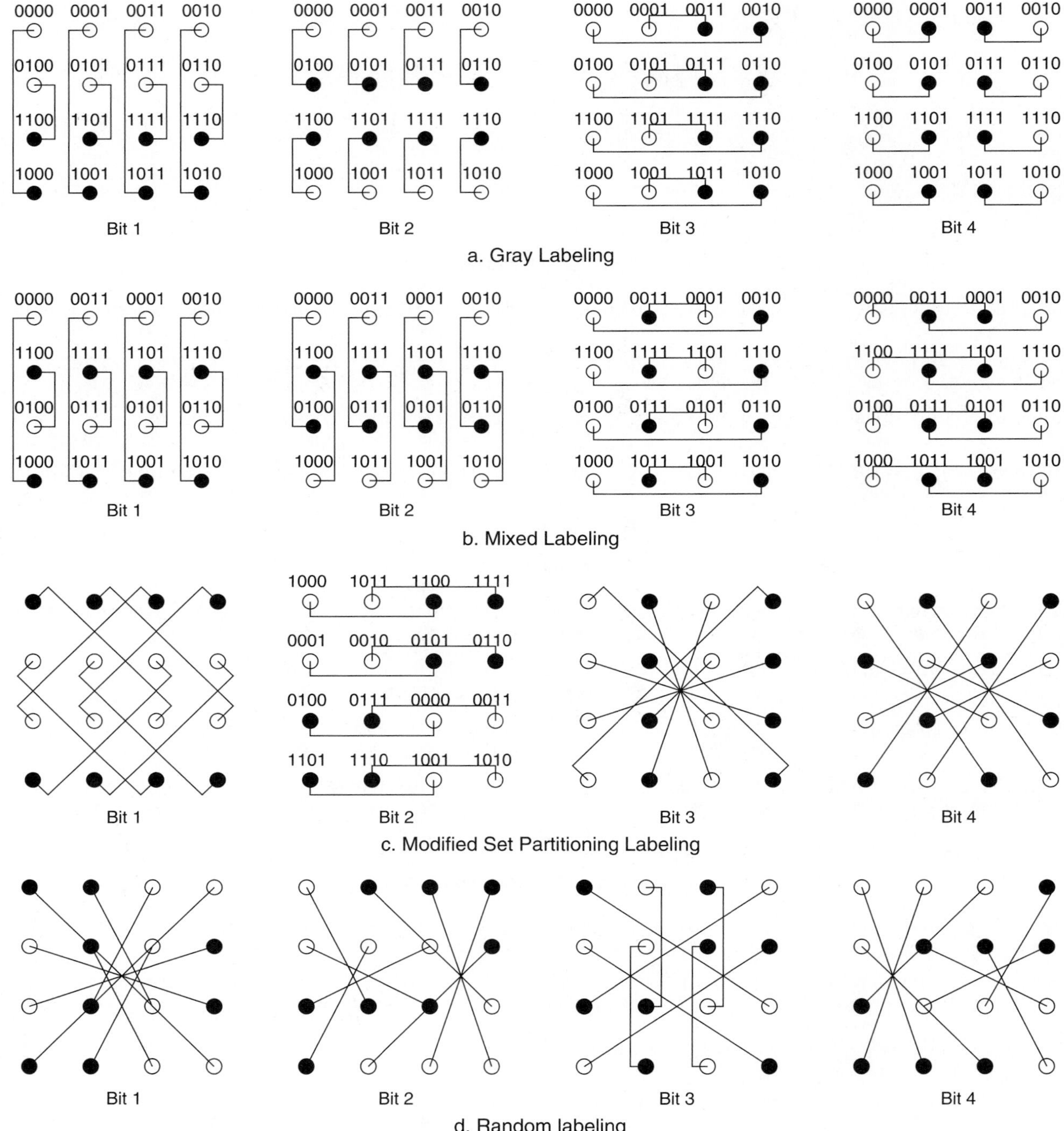

Figure 7: 16-QAM channel is converted to eight binary channels, each selected by the other three ideal feedback bits

Gray labeling is not the preferred choice because most binary signal sets resulting from ideal feedback have the same intersignal Euclidean distance as the original 16-QAM constellation.

Numerical results from calculating the *harmonic* mean of the minimum Euclidean distance before feedback, d_h^2, and after feedback, $\tilde{d}_h^2$, are shown in Table 1. We call the difference in $(\tilde{d}_h^2)_{dB}$ and $(d_h^2)_{dB}$ of conventional BICM with Gray labeling the *offset gain*.

This gives a quick comparison between various labeling schemes with iterative decoding and conventional BICM. In addition, optimization of $d_h^2(\mu)$ is done separately from our decoding algorithm; therefore, the *offset gain* is the asymptotic performance improvement regardless of the code structure. It is preferable to have a labeling map that maximizes $\tilde{d}_h^2(\mu)$ while having sufficiently large original $d_h^2(\mu)$ such that the feedback decoder can reach its ideal performance within a few passes.

Table 1: Comparison of the Harmonic Mean of the Minimum Euclidean Distance before (d_h^2) and after Ideal Feedback ($\tilde{d}_h^2$), and Differences in the Values of $(\tilde{d}_h^2)_{dB}$ and $(d_h^2)_{dB}$ of Gray Labeling

Labeling	d_h^2	$\tilde{d}_h^2$	Offset Gain (dB)
Gray	0.492	0.514	0.19
Random	0.413	2.602	7.23
Modified SP	0.420	2.279	6.65
Mixed	0.400	0.993	3.05
SP	0.441	1.119	3.56

Consider the impact of signal labeling on the offset gain. For BICM-ID with the same convolutional code, Table 1 shows that Gray labeling yields the best performance without feedback due to the largest d_h^2; however, the performance gain with feedback is very small. Random labeling gives the largest $\tilde{d}_h^2$ and thus the largest asymptotic offset gain at the cost of having the poorest first-round performance. Modified set partitioning (MSP) labeling shows a good compromise between the first-round performance and the asymptotic iterative decoding performance. Although mixed labeling does not show large feedback gain, Figure 7 shows that only one bit from the feedback affects the decoding result; therefore, mixed labeling is robust to feedback error when hard-decision feedback is used. The weaker performance improvement obtained by using Ungerboeck's set partitioning (SP) labeling (1982) over fading channels is also shown for comparison.

BICM WITH JOINT ITERATIVE CHANNEL ESTIMATION AND DECODING

So far we have studied BICM and BICM-ID over fading channels with perfect CSI at the receiver. For mobile communication systems with time-varying channel response, CSI is crucial in achieving the expected decoding performance of a channel code. To obtain CSI, pilot symbol assisted modulation (PSAM) has been proposed and proven to be effective for Rayleigh and Ricean fading channels (Cavers 1991). The transmitter periodically inserts known symbols, from which the receiver estimates channel amplitude and phase reference.

Because BICM-ID is a high-performance coded modulation that ideally operates in a very low SNR region, traditional channel estimation techniques, such as PSAM, can induce large estimation error. As an example, we consider a mobile communication system that employs BICM-ID and PSAM over Rayleigh fading channels. The symbol rate is 16k symbols/s and the Doppler is 100 Hz, which gives the normalized Doppler spread $f_d T_s = 6.25 \times 10^{-3}$. The speed of the mobile station (MS) is about 120 km/h (75 MPH) with carrier frequency 900 MHz, or 60 km/h (37.5 MPH) with carrier frequency 1.8 GHz. The BICM-ID

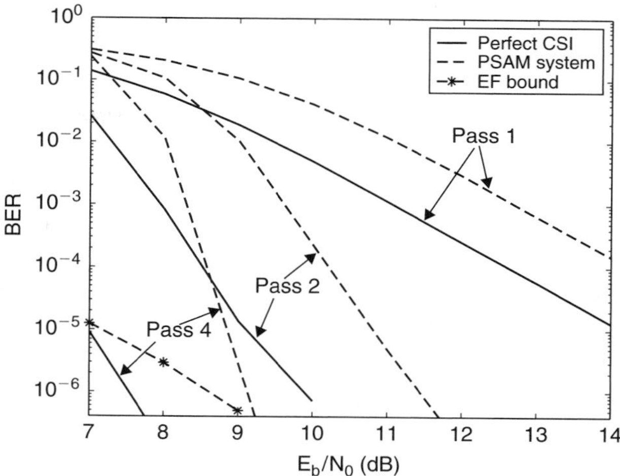

Figure 8: Performance of 16-QAM BICM-ID with perfect CSI and PSAM over Rayleigh fading. The low-pass sinc interpolator is used for PSAM. The best 16-state rate 1/2 convolutional code and MSP labeling with soft feedback are used

scheme uses 16-QAM MSP labeling (Chindapol and Ritcey 2001) with the best 16-state rate 1/2 convolutional code (Lin and Costello, Jr. 1983). The low-pass sinc interpolator is used in the PSAM channel estimation. Figure 8 compares the BER performance of this system using PSAM channel estimation with that of an ideal system with perfect CSI, in which about 1.6 dB degradation for each iteration is observed. The star-marked dashed curve shows the asymptotic BER performance predicted by the error-free feedback (EF) bound of BICM-ID with imperfect CSI (Huang and Ritcey 2003). For a given interleaving depth, the quality of channel estimation becomes the limiting item in system performance of BICM-ID (Huang and Ritcey 2003).

A similar problem also exists in turbo coding (Berrou and Glavieux 1996). As a promising solution, joint channel estimation and decoding has been explored, and iteratively filtered PSAM (IF-PSAM) is proposed and studied by Valenti and Woerner (2001) and Su and Geraniotis (2002) for turbo codes with BPSK modulation. Figure 9(a) illustrates the basic schedule for IF-PSAM, which alternates channel reestimation and decoding. The pilot symbol filter (PSF) performs initial channel estimation based on the received pilot sequence, and, after each turbo decoder iteration, the tentatively decoded data symbols are also fed back into the all symbol filter (ASF) to produce refined channel estimates.

As analyzed by Huang and Ritcey (2005c), IF-PSAM algorithm can introduce severe error propagation problems when directly applied to BICM-ID. In early decoding passes of BICM-ID, channel reestimation can be degraded because there are too many errors in the tentative decoding results. The decoder will be locked in a local minimum and never converge to the zero-error state. In such cases, channel reestimation after *each* iteration is neither beneficial nor efficient.

To solve the error propagation problem, a multistage algorithm, named sparsely interleaved estimation and decoding (SIED), was developed by Huang and Ritcey (2005c).

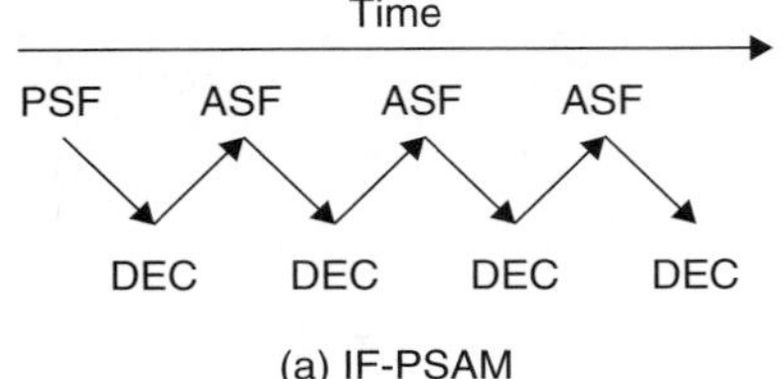

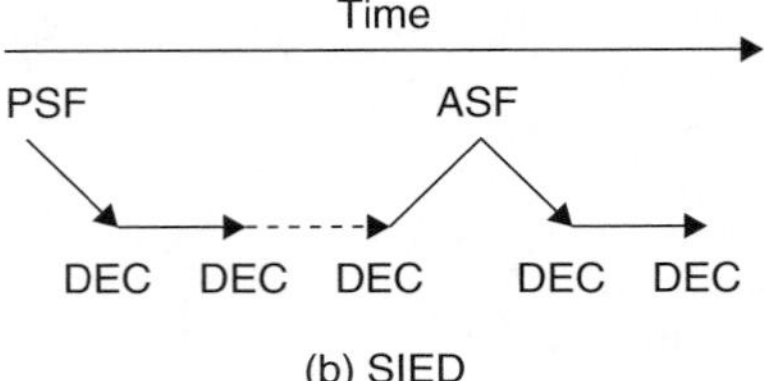

Figure 9: Illustration of the classical IF-PSAM algorithm and the recently proposed SIED algorithm for joint iterative channel estimation and decoding, showing the pilot symbol filter (PSF) and all symbol filter (ASF) alternating with the decoder (DEC)

In SIED, as shown in Figure 9 (b), decoding proceeds until the current decoder stage converges so that the decoding potential is *fully* exploited, and only then the decoder feeds back the best achievable decoding results for reestimation. Decoder convergence can be detected by keeping track of the soft decoding metrics (SDMs) proposed by Wang and Parhi (2002). Compared to IF-PSAM, the SIED algorithm improves performance with increased efficiency because unnecessary channel reestimation is avoided.

As a numerical example, Figure 10 compares the simulated BER of SIED algorithm and the classical IF-PSAM algorithm over correlated Rayleigh fading channel with normalized Doppler $f_dT_s = 0.05$. The results shown for IF-PSAM is at the fifteenth iteration; the results for SIED are from the last iteration (less than fifteen iterations) because early termination is also implemented. The solid lines are for the case with 10^5 information bits per block, and the dashed lines are for a shorter block size of 10^4 information bits. For both cases, we can clearly see that SIED outperforms the other algorithm by extensively exploiting the soft decoding output and a much-improved reestimation schedule that avoids error propagation. The SIED algorithm has about 0.5 dB improvement in E_b/N_0 over IF-PSAM.

To analyze the asymptotic BER of BICM-ID, the error-free feedback bound (EF bound) with imperfect CSI (Huang and Ritcey 2003) is also shown as reference. This bound is computed based on the assumption that the data symbols are perfectly decoded and fed back to the ASF for channel reestimation (Huang and Ritcey 2005c). As we observe, when E_b/N_0 is large enough, the BER curves for both the SIED and IF-PSAM algorithms can approach the EF bound very closely. However, the SIED algorithm requires a much lower E_b/N_0 than IF-PSAM to break the barrier of the initial channel estimation error and trigger the convergence to the ideal asymptotic performance.

BIT-INTERLEAVED SPACE-TIME CODED MODULATION WITH ITERATIVE DECODING

High–data-rate applications are considered one of the most important future breakthroughs in wireless communications, and also a very challenging goal, particularly for systems that are power, bandwidth, and complexity limited. Motivated by the need for high spectral efficiency, the use of multiple transmit and receive antennas has been extensively exploited to significantly increase channel capacity. Pioneering works by Telatar (1995) and Foschini (1996) predict remarkable spectral efficiencies

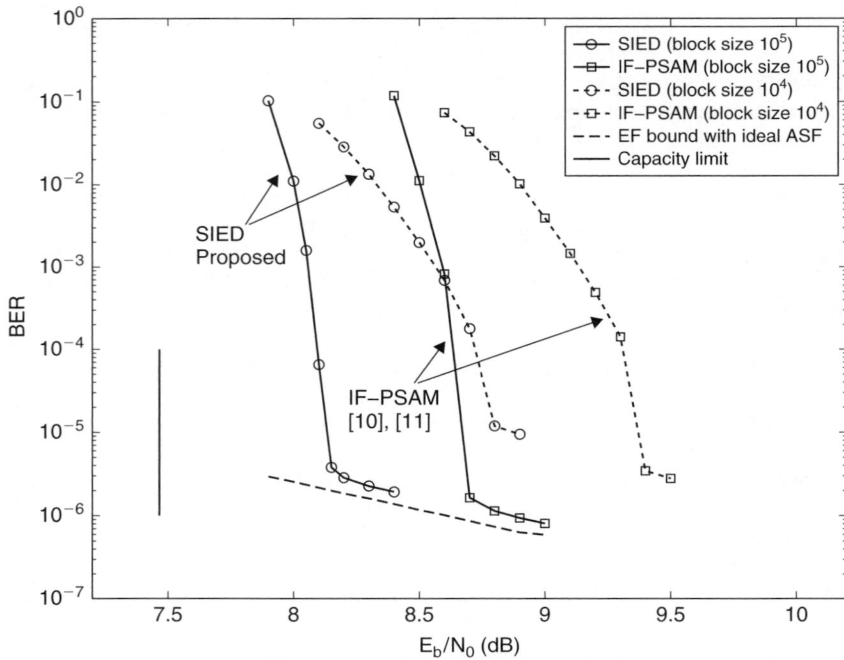

Figure 10: Comparison of the BER performance of SIED and IF-PSAM with different block sizes, over correlated Rayleigh fading channel with $f_dT_s = 0.05$. The asymptotic BER is predicted by the EF bound for the ASF with ideal feedback. The SNR limit is obtained from the BICM capacity results with imperfect CSI over uncorrelated Rayleigh fading channels

for multiple-input multiple-output (MIMO) systems. It has been shown by Telatar (1995) that the theoretical capacity increases linearly with the minimum number of the transmit and receive antennas when there is rich scattering and the channel variation can be accurately tracked.

On the other hand, the use of multiple transmit and receive antennas provides higher diversity order that can be exploited to combat severe attenuation in a multipath wireless environment. The designs of space-time codes for achieving these advantages include the Bell Laboratories layered space-time (BLAST) architecture (Foschini 1996), the trellis codes (Tarokh, Seshadri, and Calderbank 1998), and the orthogonal designs (Tarokh, Jafarkhani, and Calderbank 1999b). Bit-interleaved space-time coded modulation (BI-STCM) was proposed by Hong and Hughes (2001) as an effective approach to capture both space and time diversity.

In light of the conventional BICM-ID (Chindapol and Ritcey 2001; Li et al. 2002), in this section we consider BI-STCM with iterative decoding (BI-STCM-ID) over fast Rayleigh fading MIMO channels. A general, tight, and efficient error-free feedback bound (EF bound) is developed to analyze the asymptotic BER of BI-STCM-ID (Huang and Ritcey 2004). The design criterion is also proposed to achieve the largest asymptotic coding gain inherited in the constellation labeling (Huang and Ritcey 2005b). For orthogonal space-time block codes (STBCs), Huang and Ritcey (2005b) showed that the labeling optimization problem can be solved as a quadratic assignment problem (QAP). Numerical results show that the optimal labeling maps achieve significant improvements in the asymptotic coding gain for both the 16-QAM and 64-QAM constellations.

Figure 11(a) shows the block diagram of the BI-STCM transmitter, which is a serial concatenation of the conventional BICM (Caire et al. 1998) and an STBC $\mathcal{G}$ whose entries are linear combinations of the variables $s_1, \ldots, s_q$ and their conjugates (Tarokh et al. 1999b). The information bit sequence is first encoded by a convolutional code of rate $R_c = k_c/n_c$. Then the encoder output is bit-interleaved (B-ITL) and each $K = mq$ bits of the interleaved sequence are grouped as a channel symbol $\mathbf{v}_t = [v_t^1, \ldots, v_t^k, \ldots, v_t^K] = [\mathbf{v}_t^1, \ldots, \mathbf{v}_t^n, \ldots, \mathbf{v}_t^q]$, where $v_t^k \in \{0,1\}, 1 \le k \le K$, and $\mathbf{v}_t^n = [v_t^{(n-1)m+1}, \cdots, v_t^{nm}], 1 \le n \le q$. The modulator maps each $\mathbf{v}_t^n$ to a complex valued signal $s_t^n = \mu(\mathbf{v}_t^n)$ chosen from a 2^m-ary constellation χ according to the labeling map μ. The space-time block encoder takes the q constellation signals $(s_t^1, \ldots, s_t^q)$ to form an $L \times N_t$ space-time code word matrix $X_t = [x_l^i]$, where N_t is the number of the transmit antennas, and L is the number of the time slots for transmitting one space-time code word, and $x_l^i, 1 \le i \le N_t, 1 \le l \le L$ is the transmitted signal from the i-th antenna at time l.

Let χ be the set of space-time code word matrices. The modulator (μ, χ) and the STBC $\mathcal{G}$ jointly define the overall one-to-one mapping rule $\mathcal{M}: \{0,1\}^K \to \chi$. $\forall \mathrm{X} \in \chi$, we denote the corresponding K-tuple binary label as $\mathcal{M}^{-1}(\mathbf{X})$. Note that, for a fair comparison, we fix the total radiated power $E_s = 1$ independent of N_t. Define the rate of the STBC as $R_{ST} = q/L$ (Tarokh et al. 1999a). Thus the overall information rate of the system is $R = mR_cR_{ST}$, and the average energy per information bit is $E_b = E_s/R = 1/R$.

Consider the receiver that is equipped with N_r receive antennas. The received signal is represented by an $L \times N_r$ matrix $\mathbf{Y}_t = [y_l^j]$, where $y_l^j, 1 \le j \le N_r, 1 \le l \le L$ is the received signal by the j-th receive antenna at time l.

The channel is described by an $N_t \times N_r$ matrix $\mathbf{H}_t = [h_{i,j}]$, where $h_{i,j}$, $1 \le i \le N_t, 1 \le j \le N_r$ is the path gain from transmit antenna i to receive antenna j. For Rayleigh fading channels, the coefficients $h_{i,j}$ are modeled as independent and identically distributed (i.i.d.) complex Gaussian random variables (RVs) with zero mean and variance 0.5 per dimension. For fast-fading MIMO channels, we assume that $\mathbf{H}_t$ remains constant during the transmission of one single code word $\mathbf{X}_t$, and varies to new independent realizations in every L symbol period. This fast-fading channel model is an accurate representation of BI-STCM with sufficient interleaving depth.

The $L \times N_r$ received signal is given by

$$\mathbf{Y}_t = \mathbf{X}_t\mathbf{H}_t + \mathbf{W}_t \tag{15}$$

where $\mathbf{W}_t$ is an $L \times N_r$ noise matrix whose entries are modeled as i.i.d. complex Gaussian RVs with zero mean and variance $N_0/2$ per dimension.

The BI-STCM receiver is shown in Figure 11(b). We assume that the CSI is perfectly known at the receiver.

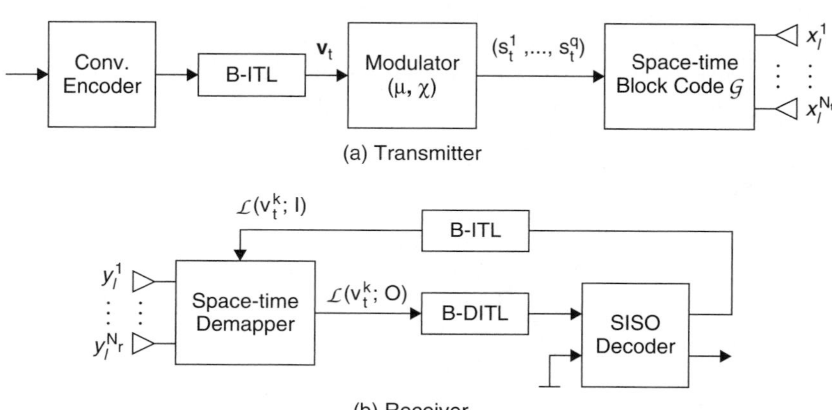

Figure 11: Bit-interleaved space-time coded modulation with iterative decoding

The metric associated with each received signal $\mathbf{Y}_t$ is the log conditional probability density function (pdf)

$$\begin{aligned}\Lambda(\mathbf{Y}_t|\mathbf{X}_t) &= \log p(\mathbf{Y}_t|\mathbf{X}_t)\\ &= N_r L \cdot \log\frac{1}{\pi N_0} - \frac{1}{N_0}\left\|\mathbf{Y}_t - \mathbf{X}_t\mathbf{H}_t\right\|^2\end{aligned} \quad (16)$$

The space-time demapper uses the maximum a posteriori (MAP) decoding algorithm, and the extrinsic log-likelihood ratio (LLR) for the unmapped bit v_t^k can be computed as

$$L_e(v_t^k;O) = \log\frac{\sum_{\mathbf{X}_t\in\chi_1^k}\exp\{\Lambda(\mathbf{Y}_t|\mathbf{X}_t) + \sum_{k'=1,\,k'\neq k}^{K}\tilde{v}_t^{k'}(\mathbf{X}_t)\,L(v_t^{k'};I)\}}{\sum_{\mathbf{X}_t\in\chi_0^k}\exp\{\Lambda(\mathbf{Y}_t|\mathbf{X}_t) + \sum_{k'=1,\,k'\neq k}^{K}\tilde{v}_t^{k'}(\mathbf{X}_t)\,L(v_t^{k'};I)\}} \quad (17)$$

where χ_1^k (or χ_0^k) is the subset of the space-time code χ in which the labels have the binary value 1 (or 0) at the k-th bit position, and $\tilde{v}_t^{k'}(\mathbf{X}_t)$ is the value of the k'-th bit of the label corresponding to $\mathbf{X}_t$.

The SISO decoder (Benedetto et al. 1997) takes the bit-deinterleaved (B-DITL) version of $\{L_e(v_t^k;O)\}$ to compute the extrinsic LLR of each coded bit, which is fed back to the demapper as the updated a priori information $L(v_t^k;I)$ on the next iteration.

Due to the large coding gain produced by iterative decoding, one is most interested in the asymptotic performance to which the iterative process converges. The most successful analysis of the BER uses the EF bound introduced by Chindapol and Ritcey (2001) for BICM-ID in a single-antenna system. In the work by Huang and Ritcey (2004), the concept of the EF bound is extended to analyze the asymptotic BER of BI-STCM-ID, and the convergence to the bound and the accuracy of the prediction are verified by simulation. The EF bound is computationally efficient and can be applied to any BI-STCM system configuration.

As shown by Caire et al. (1998), the BICM union bound of the probability of bit error is given by

$$P_b \leq \frac{1}{k_c}\sum_{d=d_f}^{\infty} W_I(d) f(d,\mathcal{M},\chi) \quad (18)$$

where d_f is the minimum Hamming distance of the convolutional code and $W_I(d)$ is the total input weight of error events at Hamming distance d. Note that $f(d,\mathcal{M},\chi)$ denotes the pairwise error probability (PEP) and depends only on the Hamming distance d, the overall mapping rule $\mathcal{M}$, and the space-time code χ.

To analyze the asymptotic BER of BI-STCM-ID, the PEP is bounded by

$$f(d,\mathcal{M},\chi) \leq \frac{1}{2\pi j}\int_{c-j\infty}^{c+j\infty}\left[\psi_{\text{ef}}(s)\right]^d \frac{ds}{s} \quad (19)$$

and

$$\psi_{\text{ef}}(s) = \frac{1}{K2^K}\sum_{k=1}^{K}\sum_{b=0}^{1}\sum_{\mathbf{X}\in\chi_b^k}\Phi_{\Delta(\mathbf{X},\mathbf{Z})}(s). \quad (20)$$

$\Phi_{\Delta(\mathbf{X},\mathbf{Z})}(s)$ is the Laplace transform of the Pdf of the metric difference $\Delta(\mathbf{X}, \mathbf{Z})$. Note that $\mathbf{X}$ is the transmitted signal, and, due to the assumption of error-free feedback, $\mathbf{Z} = \mathbf{Z}(\mathbf{X}, k)$ is the corresponding erroneously decoded signal having the same binary bit values as those of $\mathbf{X}$ except at the k-th bit position.

It is shown by Huang and Ritcey (2004) that

$$\Phi_{\Delta(\mathbf{X},\mathbf{Z})}(s) = \left(\prod_{i=1}^{N_t}\frac{1}{1-\lambda_i(-s+s^2N_0)}\right)^{N_r} \quad (21)$$

where λ_i, $i = 1, 2, \ldots, N_t$ are the eigenvalues of the $N_t \times N_t$ Hermitian matrix $\mathbf{A} = (\mathbf{X}-\mathbf{Z})^*(\mathbf{X}-\mathbf{Z})$ counting multiplicities.

With equation 21 and equation 20, we apply the Gauss-Chebyshev quadrature (Caire et al. 1998) to compute the PEP (equation 19) and hence the EF bound (equation 18) for BI-STCM-ID. Note that the summation in (equation 18) is truncated at 20 terms, which are enough to ensure the computation accuracy.

As an example, we consider a BI-STCM system equipped with $N_t = 2$ transmit antennas and $N_r = 1$ or 2 receive antennas. We use the best four-state rate 1/2 convolutional code, the 16-QAM MSP labeling (Chindapol and Ritcey 2001), and the Alamouti's space-time block code (Tarokh et al. 1999b).

Figure 12 and Figure 13 compare the simulated BER performance with the EF bounds when 1 and 2 receive antennas are used, respectively. There are ten decoding iterations performed. Each data block contains 10^4 information bits, and a total number of 5×10^8 information bits are simulated for each value of E_b/N_0 considered. The simulation results converge to the EF bounds at low BER. The theoretical EF bounds for BI-STCM-ID are very tight and accurate enough to predict the asymptotic BER performance.

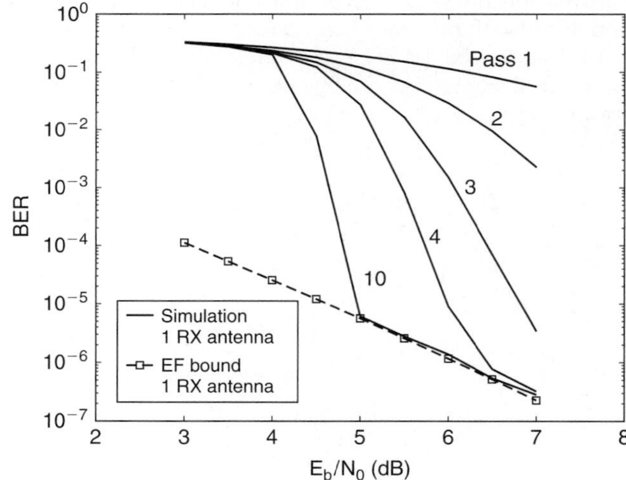

Figure 12: Comparison of the simulated BER performance with the EF bound for a BI-STCM system with two transmit antennas and one receive antenna; 16-QAM MSP labeling, four-state rate 1/2 convolutional code, and Alamouti's space-time block code

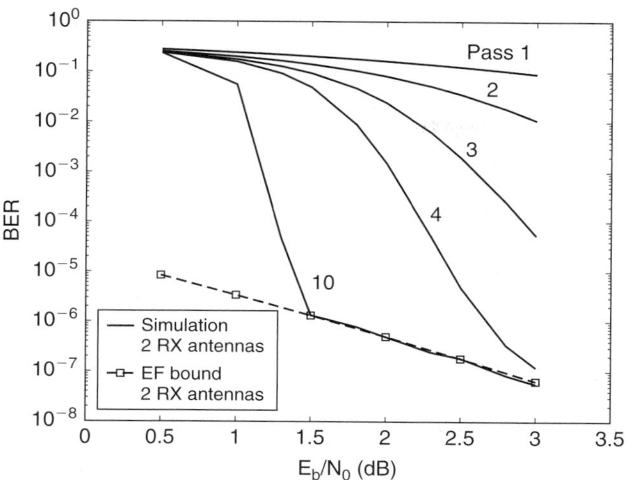

Figure 13: Comparison of the simulated BER performance with the EF bound for a BI-STCM system with two transmit antennas and two receive antennas; 16-QAM MSP labeling, four-state rate 1/2 convolutional code, and Alamouti's space-time block code

Note that computing the EF bound is much easier than the intensive BER simulation of the whole system. Also, the analytical bound is very general and can be applied for any BI-STCM configuration: convolutional (or turbo) code, constellation labeling map, and space-time block code.

Now, we consider the design of BI-STCM-ID over fast Rayleigh fading MIMO channels with N_t transmit and N_r receive antennas. The design criterion is to achieve the largest asymptotic coding gain inherited in the constellation labeling. In particular, for orthogonal STBCs designed by Tarokh et al. (1999b), the labeling design criterion reduces to maximizing the $(-N_tN_r)$-th power mean of the complete set of squared Euclidean distances associated with all error-free feedback events in the constellation (Huang and Ritcey 2005b). This power mean criterion for orthogonal STBCs can be viewed as the generalized version of the harmonic mean criterion (Caire et al. 1998) for BICM-ID in single-antenna systems.

For conventional BICM-ID, good labeling maps were proposed by Chindapol and Ritcey (2001) for 16-QAM and by Li et al. (2002) for 8-PSK constellation. These results were obtained through random computer search; recently, the binary switching algorithm has been applied to solve this labeling optimization problem (Schreckenbach et al. 2003). Basically, all these labeling maps are designed only for single-antenna systems and thus do not necessarily hold their performance in MIMO channels. For BI-STCM-ID, the effects of different labelings were studied by Zhao, Lampe, and Huber (2003). However, the labelings therein are only based on hand-crafted design, and their optimality (in the sense of asymptotic coding gain) is not guaranteed. On the other hand, adaptive labeling was proposed by Samra, Ding, and Hahn (2003) to exploit the diversity gain from multiple packet transmissions, in which the optimal schemes were obtained by solving a well-known QAP (see Cela [1998] and references therein).

For BI-STCM-ID, based on the power mean criterion, it is shown by Huang and Ritcey (2005b) that the labeling optimization problem for BI-STCM-ID also falls into the category of a QAP, and can be conveniently solved via the generic solutions to the QAP for constellations of any shape and with an arbitrary number of transmit and receive antennas. For a set of practical values of N_t and N_r, we present the optimal labeling maps for 8-PSK, 16-QAM, and 64-QAM constellations along with the maximum asymptotic coding gains.

Recalling the BICM union bound of the probability of bit error (Caire et al. 1998)

$$P_b \le \frac{1}{k_c} \sum_{d=d_f}^{\infty} W_I(d) f(d, \mathcal{M}, \chi). \tag{22}$$

For BI-STCM, the union bound of the PEP $f(d, \mathcal{M}, \chi)$ can be upper-bounded using the Chernoff technique (Hong and Hughes 2001)

$$f_{\mathrm{ub}}(d, \mathcal{M}, \chi) \le \left[\frac{1}{K2^K} \sum_{k=1}^{K} \sum_{b=0}^{1} \sum_{\mathbf{X}\in\chi_b^k} \sum_{\mathbf{Z}\in\chi_{\bar{b}}^k} \min_s \Phi_{\Delta(\mathbf{X},\mathbf{Z})}(s) \right]^d \tag{23}$$

where $\mathbf{X}$ and $\mathbf{Z}$ are the transmitted and erroneously decoded signals, respectively, and $\bar{b}$ is the complement of b. Here $\Phi_{\Delta(\mathbf{X},\mathbf{Z})}(s)$ is the Laplace transform of the pdf of the metric difference $\Delta(\mathbf{X}, \mathbf{Z}) = \|\mathbf{Y}-\mathbf{ZH}\|^2 - \|\mathbf{Y}-\mathbf{XH}\|^2$. It is shown by Tarokh et al. (1998) that

$$\min_s \Phi_{\Delta(\mathbf{X},\mathbf{Z})}(s) = \left[\prod_{i=1}^{r} \left(1 + \frac{\lambda_i}{4N_0} \right) \right]^{-N_r} \tag{24}$$

where λ_i are the nonzero eigenvalues of the matrix $\mathbf{A} = (\mathbf{X}-\mathbf{Z})^*(\mathbf{X}-\mathbf{Z})$, and r is the rank of $\mathbf{A}$.

We focus on the asymptotic performance of BI-STCM-ID (i.e., the BER floor to which the iterative decoding process converges). In such cases, irrelevant error items in equation 23 can be effectively expurgated to approach the error-free feedback performance (Huang and Ritcey 2004)

$$f_{\mathrm{ef}}(d, \mathcal{M}, \chi) \le \left[\frac{1}{K2^K} \sum_{k=1}^{K} \sum_{b=0}^{1} \sum_{\mathbf{X}\in\chi_b^k} \min_s \Phi_{\Delta(\mathbf{X},\tilde{\mathbf{Z}})}(s) \right]^d \tag{25}$$

where the labels $\mathcal{M}^{-1}(\mathbf{X})$ and $\mathcal{M}^{-1}(\tilde{\mathbf{Z}})$ differ only in the k-th bit position. As $N_0 \to 0$, using equation 24 and equation 25, we find

$$\begin{aligned} f_{\mathrm{ef}}(d, \mathcal{M}, \chi) &\sim \left[\frac{1}{K2^K} \sum_{k=1}^{K} \sum_{b=0}^{1} \sum_{\mathbf{X}\in\chi_b^k} \left(\prod_{i=1}^{\tilde{r}} \frac{\tilde{\lambda}_i}{4N_0} \right)^{-N_r} \right]^d \\ &= \left[\frac{4}{\Omega^2/N_0} \right]^{\tilde{r}N_r d} \end{aligned} \tag{26}$$

where we define

$$\Omega^2(\chi, \mathcal{M}, N_r) = \left[\frac{1}{K2^K} \sum_{k=1}^{K} \sum_{b=0}^{1} \sum_{\mathbf{X}\in\chi_b^k} \left(\prod_{i=1}^{\tilde{r}} \tilde{\lambda}_i \right)^{-N_r} \right]^{-1/(\tilde{r}N_r)}, \tag{27}$$

and $\tilde{\lambda}_i$ are the nonzero eigenvalues of the matrix $\tilde{\mathbf{A}} = (\mathbf{X}-\tilde{\mathbf{Z}})^*(\mathbf{X}-\tilde{\mathbf{Z}})$, and $\tilde{r}$ is the rank of $\tilde{\mathbf{A}}$. Using equation 26 and only including the dominant error event associated with d_f in (22) as $N_0 \to 0$, we can write

$$P_b \approx \frac{1}{k_c} W_I(d_f) f_{\text{ef}}(d_f, \mathcal{M}, \chi) = \frac{1}{k_c} W_I(d_f) \left[\frac{4}{\Omega^2 / N_0} \right]^{\tilde{r} N_r d_f}. \tag{28}$$

Recalling the definition of the overall information rate R and $E_b = 1/R$, the asymptotic BER performance of BI-STCM-ID can be represented as

$$\log_{10} P_b \approx -\frac{\tilde{r} N_r d_f}{10} \left[(R\Omega^2)_{\text{dB}} + \left(\frac{E_b}{N_0} \right)_{\text{dB}} \right] + \text{const}, \tag{29}$$

which is similar to that of conventional BICM derived by Caire et al. (1998). Thus, for large values of E_b/N_0, the BER curve on a logarithmic scale approximates a straight line with slope proportional to the overall diversity order $\tilde{r}N_r d_f$, shifted horizontally by the offset $(R\Omega^2)_{\text{dB}}$. Apparently, to achieve the best BER performance, full-diversity STBCs should be used to obtain the largest diversity gain $N_t N_r d_f$; for maximizing the coding gain Ω^2, as we will show next, constellation labeling optimization is involved.

To maximize the coding gain Ω^2 defined in equation 27 optimization of the overall mapping rule $\mathcal{M}$ is required. We focus on orthogonal STBCs, which offer full transmit diversity and the advantage of low-complexity linear processing in the decoding scheme (Tarokh et al. 1999a). For orthogonal STBCs, we will see that this optimization problem reduces to the constellation labeling design.

Definition 1 *For any constellation χ with labeling map μ, the(−p)-th error-free feedback power mean is*

$$\omega^2(\chi, \mu, p) = \left[\frac{1}{m 2^m} \sum_{k=1}^{m} \sum_{b=0}^{1} \sum_{s \in \chi_b^k} (|s - \tilde{s}|^2)^{-p} \right]^{-\frac{1}{p}} \tag{30}$$

where the labels $\mu^{-1}(s)$ and $\mu^{-1}(\tilde{s})$ differ only in the k-th bit position.

Theorem 1 (The Power Mean Criterion for Orthogonal STBCs) *For any generalized orthogonal design $\mathcal{G}$ in variables $\pm s_1$, $\pm s_1^*$ $\pm s_2$, $\pm s_2^*$, . . . , $\pm s_q$, $\pm s_q^*$, that satisfies $\mathcal{G}^*\mathcal{G} = \alpha\left(\sum_{n=1}^{q} |s_n|^2\right)\mathbf{I}_N$*

$$\max_{\mathcal{M}} \Omega^2(\chi, \mathcal{M}, N_r) = \alpha \max_{\mu} \omega^2(\chi, \mu, N_t N_r). \tag{31}$$

Proof: First, consider $k = 1, \ldots, m$. For any $\mathbf{X} = \mathcal{G}(s_1, s_2, \ldots, s_q)$, recalling the definition of $\tilde{\mathbf{Z}}$ and $\tilde{s}$, we have $\tilde{\mathbf{Z}} = \mathcal{G}(\tilde{s}_1, s_2, \ldots, s_q)$. Thus $(\mathbf{X} - \tilde{\mathbf{Z}}) = \mathcal{G}(s_1 - \tilde{s}_1, 0 \ldots, 0)$, and $(\mathbf{X} - \tilde{\mathbf{Z}})^* (\mathbf{X} - \tilde{\mathbf{Z}}) = \alpha |s_1 - \tilde{s}_1|^2 \mathbf{I}_{N_t}$. Then it follows that

$$\Omega^2(\chi, \mathcal{M}, N_r) = \left[\frac{q}{K 2^K} \sum_{k=1}^{m} \sum_{b=0}^{1} \sum_{\mathbf{X} \in \chi_b^k} (\alpha |s_1 - \tilde{s}_1|^2)^{-N_t N_r} \right]^{-\frac{1}{N_t N_r}}$$

$$= \left[\frac{q 2^{(q-1)m}}{K 2^K} \sum_{k=1}^{m} \sum_{b=0}^{1} \sum_{s \in \chi_b^k} (\alpha |s - \tilde{s}|^2)^{-N_t N_r} \right]^{-\frac{1}{N_t N_r}}$$

$$= \alpha \omega^2(\chi, \mu, N_t N_r).$$

Hence, maximizing the asymptotic coding gain $\Omega^2(\chi, \mathcal{M}, N_r)$ over $\mathcal{M}$ reduces to maximizing the power mean $\omega^2(\chi, \mu, N_t N_r)$ over all labeling maps μ of the constellation.

Remark 1 *The power mean criterion for orthogonal STBCs can be viewed as the generalized version of the harmonic mean criterion (Caire et al. 1998) for BICM-ID in single-antenna systems.*

Corollary 1 (The Power Mean Criterion for Parallel Transmission) *For the "parallel transmission" scheme $\mathcal{G}(s_1, \ldots, s_q) = [s_1 \ldots s_q]$ (with no space-time coding, e.g., Hochwald and ten Brink* [2003]),

$$\max_{\mathcal{M}} \Omega^2(\chi, \mathcal{M}, N_r) = \max_{\mu} \omega^2(\chi, \mu, N_r). \tag{32}$$

Proof: For $k = (n-1)m + 1, \ldots, nm$, $1 \le n \le q$, $(\mathbf{X} - \tilde{\mathbf{Z}}) = [0 \ldots (s_n - \tilde{s}_n) \ldots 0]$, and $(\mathbf{X} - \tilde{\mathbf{Z}})^*(\mathbf{X} - \tilde{\mathbf{Z}}) = \text{diag}(0, \cdots, |s_n - \tilde{s}_n|^2, \cdots, 0)$. The proof immediately follows Theorem 1.

Corollary 2 *For BI-STCM-ID with either orthogonal STBCs or parallel transmission, the maximum asymptotic coding gain is a nonincreasing function of the diversity order.*

Proof: Consider the BI-STCM-ID system with diversity order p ($p = N_t N_r$ for orthogonal STBCs and $p = N_r$ for parallel transmission). Let $\mu_1 = \arg\max_\mu \omega^2(\chi, \mu, p_1)$ and $\mu_2 = \arg\max_\mu \omega^2(\chi, \mu, p_2)$. Then, for $p_1 < p_2$, it follows that

$$\omega^2(\chi, \mu_1, p_1) \ge \omega^2(\chi, \mu_2, p_1) \ge \omega^2(\chi, \mu_2, p_2)$$

where the last inequality is the immediate result from the well-known power mean inequality (Bullen 2003).

Remark 2 *Corollary 2 reveals the basic trade-off between the spatial diversity gain and the maximum asymptotic coding gain in a BI-STCM-ID system.*

When orthogonal STBCs are used for BI-STCM-ID, according to Theorem 1, the optimization problem becomes $\max_\mu \omega^2(\chi, \mu, N_t N_r)$. Even for a medium-sized constellation, this becomes a formidable combinatorial optimization problem whose solution space contains $(2^m)!$ items. For example, for 16-QAM, $16! \approx 2.1 \times 10^{13}$, and for 64-QAM, $64! \approx 1.3 \times 10^{89}$. However, as we show next, by careful construction, this problem falls into the category of a classical quadratic assignment problem (QAP; see, e.g., Cela [1998] and references therein), and can be solved conveniently by applying the generic solutions to the QAP.

The QAP is one of the most difficult but extensively studied problems in optimization. We provide the general definition of the QAP (Cela 1998) for the completeness of presentation.

Definition 2 *Consider a set $\mathcal{N} = \{1, 2, \ldots, n\}$ and two $n \times n$ matrices $\mathbf{F} = (f_{i,j})$ and $\mathbf{D} = (d_{k,l})$. The quadratic assignment problem with coefficient matrices* **F** *and* **D**, *shortly denoted by QAP(***F**,**D***), can be stated as follows*

$$\min_{\pi \in \Pi_{\mathcal{N}}} \sum_{i=1}^{n} \sum_{j=1}^{n} f_{i,j} d_{\pi(i), \pi(j)} \tag{33}$$

where $\Pi_{\mathcal{N}}$ is the set of all permutations of $\mathcal{N}$.

One of the major applications of the QAP is in location theory (Cela 1998), where $f_{i,j}$ is the flow of materials from facility i to facility j, and $d_{k,l}$ is the distance from location k to location l. The objective is to find an assignment of all facilities to all locations (i.e., a permutation $\pi \in \Pi_{\mathcal{N}}$) such that the total cost of the assignment is minimized.

Proposition 1 *Maximization of the power mean $\omega^2(\chi, \mu, N_tN_r)$ over all labeling maps μ is a QAP.*

Proof: Since $N_tN_r > 0$, $\max_\mu \omega^2(\chi, \mu, N_tN_r)$ is equivalent to

$$\min_\mu \sum_{k=1}^{m}\sum_{b=0}^{1}\sum_{s\in\chi_b^k}(|s-\tilde{s}|^2)^{-N_tN_r} \quad (34)$$

Using the facility-location analogy, let the constellation points $\{s_k | k = 0, \ldots, 2^m - 1\}$ be the locations, and the labels $\{\beta(i) | i = 0, \ldots, 2^m - 1\}$ the facilities, where $\beta(i)$ denotes the m-tuple binary label corresponding to integer i. By construction, we define the "distance" (as in Definition 2) between s_k and s_l as

$$d_{k,l} = d_{s_k,s_l} = \begin{cases}(|s_k - s_l|^2)^{-N_tN_r} & k \neq l \\ 0 & k = l\end{cases}, \quad (35)$$

and define the "flow" between labels $\beta(i)$ and $\beta(j)$ as

$$f_{i,j} = \begin{cases}1, & \beta(i) \text{ and } \beta(j) \text{ differ only in one bit position} \\ 0, & \text{otherwise}\end{cases}. \quad (36)$$

Thus, equation 34 becomes

$$\min_\mu \sum_{i=0}^{2^m-1}\sum_{j=0}^{2^m-1} f_{i,j}\, d_{\mu(\beta(i)),\mu(\beta(j))}. \quad (37)$$

Since the mapping rule μ: $s_k = \mu(\beta(i))$ is essentially a permutation (of the indices) π: $k = \pi(i)$, equation 37 can be written as

$$\min_\pi \sum_{i=0}^{2^m-1}\sum_{j=0}^{2^m-1} f_{i,j}\, d_{\pi(i),\pi(j)}, \quad (38)$$

which is a QAP as in Definition **2**.

Now we show the best labeling maps for 8-PSK, 16-QAM, and 64-QAM constellations. Each labeling map is optimized in order to achieve $\max \omega^2(\chi, \mu, p)$ for a given diversity order p. The values of p under consideration and the corresponding space-time transmission schemes are listed in Table 2.

For 8-PSK constellation, since there are only $8! = 40320$ candidates, the optimal labeling can be obtained by an exhaustive computer search. Figure 14 shows the semiset partitioning (SSP) labeling (Li et al. 2002), which is optimized for conventional BICM-ID. The SSP labeling is found to be the universal optimal labeling for any diversity order p in Table 2. Note that the optimal labeling is not unique, (e.g., any rotated or reflected version of the SSP labeling is also optimal).

Table 2: The Diversity Order p and the Corresponding Space-Time Block Codes.

Diversity Order	Examples of STBCs
$p=1$	Conventional BICM-ID (single-antenna system)
$p=2$	Alamouti's $\mathcal{G}_2$ (Tarokh *et al.* 1999b), 2×1 channel; Parallel transmission (Hochwald and ten Brink 2003), 2×2 channel
$p=4$	Alamouti's $\mathcal{G}_2$, 2×2 channel; Parallel transmission, 4×4 channel
$p=8$	Parallel transmission, 8×8 channel
$p=9$	G_3 and H_3 (Tarokh et al. 1999a), 3×3 channel
$p=16$	G_4 and H_4 (Tarokh et al. 1999a), 4×4 channel

For 16-QAM and 64-QAM constellations, the optimal labeling maps can be obtained by applying the reactive tabu search (RTS) algorithm (Battiti and Tecchiolli 1994) for the QAP. In the RTS, an explicit check for the repetition of assignment configurations is performed, and the appropriate size of the list of forbidden moves is automatically determined by reacting to the occurrence of cycles. Moreover, if the search appears to be repeating in an excessive frequency, the search is diversified by a random number of moves that is proportional to the average of the cycle length (Battiti and Tecchiolli 1994).

In the labeling map search, for each diversity order considered, the RTS algorithm (Battiti and Tecchiolli 1994) performs thirty trials, each with 10^5 iterations, which are sufficiently large to guarantee convergence to the optimal results. The run time (on a Sun Ultra-10 workstation) with such a configuration is less than six minutes for 16-QAM and only about one and a half hours for 64-QAM. Table 3 lists the optimal labeling results (with the labels in decimal format) for 16-QAM. The constellation points are labeled (A, B, . . . , P) from left to right and from top to bottom (see Figure 15). Table 4 through Table 6 list the optimal labeling maps for 64-QAM for the diversity order $p = 1, 2, 4$. The labels are arranged row by row, showing their locations in the constellation.

In Table 7, we compare the asymptotic coding gain for 16-QAM with Gray labeling, MSP labeling (Chindapol

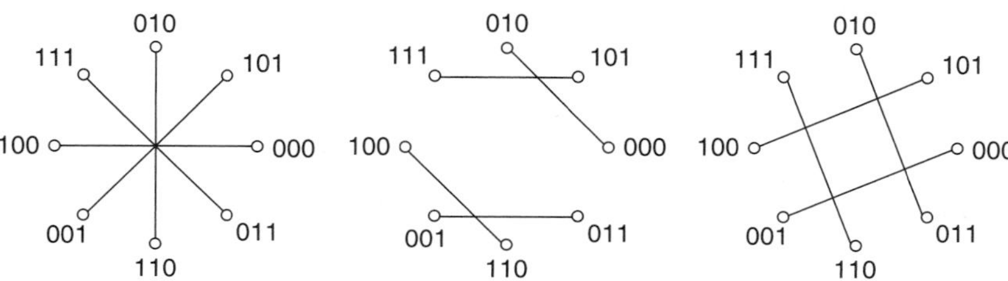

Figure 14: 8-PSK semiset partitioning labeling

Table 3: Optimal Labeling Maps for 16-QAM Constellation with Different Diversity Orders*

	A	B	C	D	E	F	G	H	I	J	K	L	M	N	O	P
$p = 1$	4	1	14	13	8	2	11	7	15	5	12	0	3	6	9	10
$p = 2$	7	14	1	11	13	4	8	2	10	3	15	5	0	9	6	12
$p = 4$	12	10	5	6	15	9	3	0	2	4	14	13	1	7	8	11
$p = 8$	12	5	11	2	15	6	8	1	0	3	13	14	9	10	4	7
$p = 9$	3	6	13	8	5	0	11	14	10	12	7	1	15	9	2	4
$p = 16$	6	12	11	7	9	5	2	1	0	15	8	13	10	3	4	14

*The labels are in decimal format (e.g., $11 = 1011_2$).

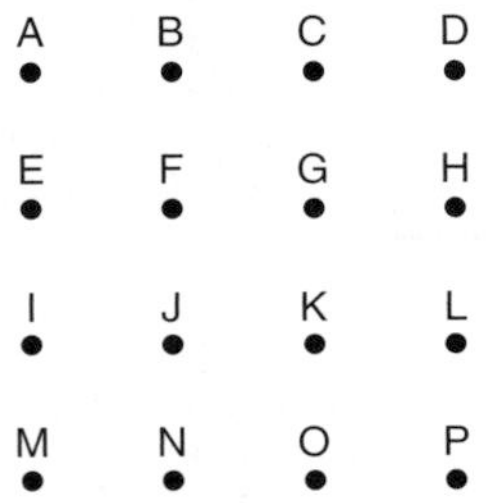

A B C D

E F G H

I J K L

M N O P

Figure 15: 16-QAM constellation

Table 4: The Optimal Labeling Map for 64-QAM Constellation with Diversity Order $p = 1$*

48	60	36	40	19	31	7	11
57	24	45	12	55	22	35	2
33	0	9	46	21	50	59	26
58	34	43	10	49	16	25	1
5	30	6	15	52	61	37	62
29	39	27	3	56	32	28	38
20	63	18	23	44	41	4	47
53	54	17	51	8	42	13	14

*The labels are in decimal format (e.g., $11 = 001011_2$).

and Ritcey 2001), and the labeling maps optimized for each specific value of p. As expected, the Gray labeling yields the smallest asymptotic coding gain for all cases. The MSP labeling, which is designed for BICM-ID in single-antenna systems, quickly loses its large coding gain as the diversity order p increases. The optimal labeling maps are about 7 dB superior to Gray labeling and 3 dB to the MSP labeling for $p > 4$. For 64-QAM constellation, Table 8 shows even more significant gains (around 13 dB) achieved by the optimal labeling maps over Gray labeling. As seen from both tables, the optimal asymptotic coding gain decreases as the diversity order p increases, which confirms Corollary 2.

Table 5: The Optimal Labeling Map for 64-QAM Constellation with Diversity Order $p = 2$*

63	53	60	45	2	19	16	1
46	29	43	57	50	7	26	11
36	12	33	40	22	38	14	4
15	5	24	9	55	31	21	35
58	27	17	0	62	52	28	42
39	48	10	3	61	47	59	49
30	20	34	18	44	37	56	32
54	51	23	6	41	13	25	8

*The labels are in decimal format (e.g., $11 = 001011_2$).

Table 6: The Optimal Labeling Map for 64-QAM Constellation with Diversity Order $p = 4$*

15	3	46	34	33	23	45	39
63	51	40	30	12	54	53	5
43	58	29	18	0	60	36	6
10	9	24	17	48	20	59	25
27	57	37	7	47	11	42	26
52	4	38	55	35	31	41	19
32	22	44	62	14	13	8	1
16	21	50	28	2	61	56	49

*The labels are in decimal format (e.g., $11 = 001011_2$).

It is well known that constellation labeling has significant impact on decoder convergence of BICM-ID, and this is clearly illustrated by the extrinsic information transfer (EXIT) chart (ten Brink 2000). Similarly, we can apply the EXIT chart technique to investigate the convergence behavior of different labeling maps for BI-STCM-ID. As an

Table 7: Comparison of the Asymptotic Coding Gain $\omega^2(\chi, \mu, p)$ for 16-QAM with Different Labeling Maps

	Gray	MSP	Optimal	Gain over Gray (dB)	Gain over MSP (dB)
$p = 1$	0.5143	2.2780	2.7190	7.2319	0.7686
$p = 2$	0.4609	1.9438	2.5460	7.4225	1.1721
$p = 4$	0.4298	1.4921	2.3414	7.3621	1.9568
$p = 8$	0.4147	1.1288	2.1791	7.2054	2.8566
$p = 9$	0.4130	1.0874	2.1591	7.1832	2.9788
$p = 16$	0.4073	0.9512	1.8418	6.5533	2.8697

Table 8: Comparison of the Asymptotic Coding Gain $\omega^2(\chi, \mu, p)$ for 64-QAM with Different Labeling Maps

	Gray	Optimal	Gain (dB)
$p = 1$	0.1546	2.8742	12.6931
$p = 2$	0.1243	2.7236	13.4067
$p = 4$	0.1090	2.4903	13.5883

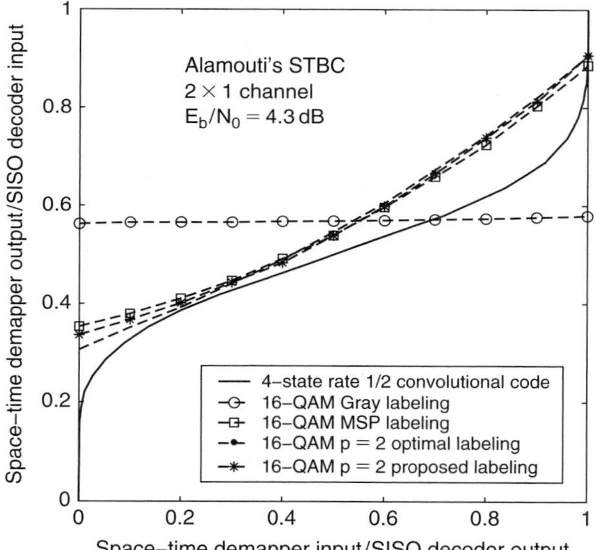

Figure 16: Comparison of space-time demapper transfer functions with 16-QAM Gray labeling, MSP labeling, and $p = 2$ optimal and proposed labeling; Alamouti's space-time block code, 2×1 fast Rayleigh fading channels.

example, Figure 16 shows the EXIT chart of a BI-STCM-ID system that uses a four-state rate 1/2 convolutional code, 16-QAM modulation, and the Alamouti's STBC (Tarokh et al. 1999b) over a 2×1 channel at $E_b/N_0 = 4.3$ dB. We compare space-time demapper transfer functions for several labelings: Gray, MSP, and the one optimized for $p = 2$. As seen from the EXIT chart, when there is perfect a priori information, the transfer function of the optimal labeling achieves the largest value, indicating its optimality in the sense of the lowest asymptotic BER floor. When there is little a priori information, the optimal labeling has the lowest transfer function, which implies a larger *pinch-off* limit (ten Brink 2000) in SNR to achieve decoder convergence. Similar results can be found in Figure 17, in which the Alamouti's STBC is used over a 2×2 channel at $E_b/N_0 = 1.0$ dB.

To obtain the constellation labeling with large asymptotic coding gain and good convergence property, we use the RTS software to produce a list of candidate labeling maps, ordered by the asymptotic coding gain $\omega^2(\chi, \mu, p)$. We examine the space-time demapper transfer functions for several top labeling maps, and select the one with the fastest convergence. As an example, Figure 18 (a) and Figure 18(b) show the recently proposed 16-QAM

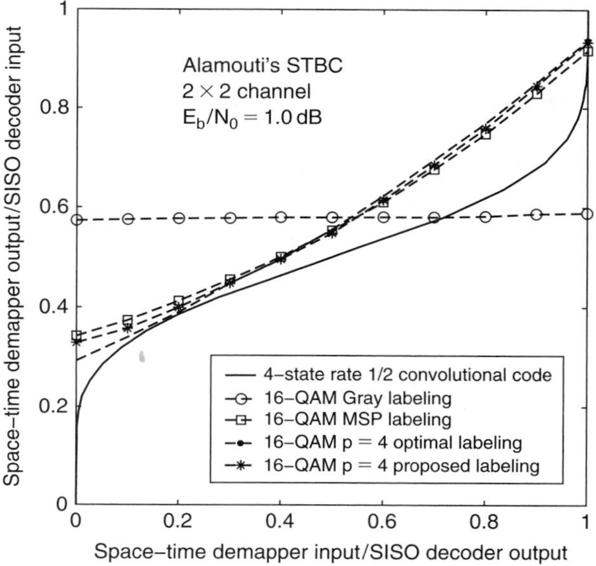

Figure 17: Comparison of space-time demapper transfer functions with 16-QAM Gray labeling, MSP labeling, and $p = 4$ optimal and proposed labeling; Alamouti's space-time block code, 2×2 fast Rayleigh fading channels

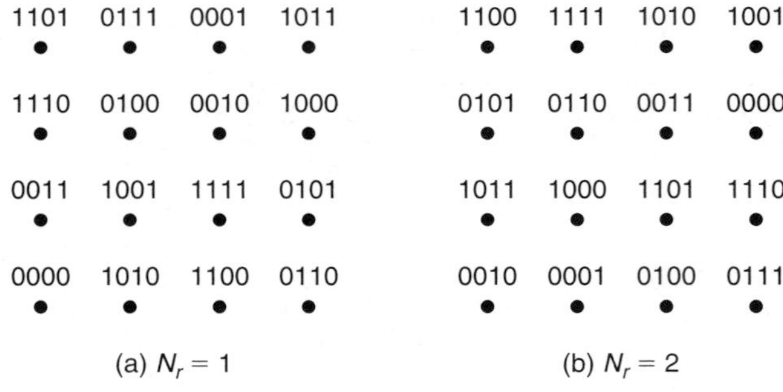

Figure 18: Recently proposed 16-QAM constellation labeling maps with improved convergence property for the BI-STCM system with the Alamouti scheme and (a) $N_r = 1$ or (b) $N_r = 2$ receive antennas

labeling maps (Huang and Ritcey 2005a) for the Alamouti's scheme with one and two receive antennas, respectively. Their improved convergence property can be clearly observed in Figure 16 and Figure 17 with higher demapper transfer functions (the star-marked dashed curves) than those of the optimal labelings in the low a priori information region. On the other hand, the asymptotic coding gains achieved by the two proposed labeling maps have negligible differences (less than 0.1 dB) from those optimized for $p = 2$ and $p = 4$ in Table 3.

Figure 19 compares the simulated BER performance for the proposed labeling maps and the 16-QAM MSP labeling with one or two receive antennas. Fifteen decoding iterations are performed. Each data block contains 10^5 information bits and 5×10^8 information bits are simulated for each value of E_b/N_0 considered. For both $N_r = 1$ and $N_r = 2$, the proposed labeling maps outperform the MSP labeling by about 1 dB coding gain around the BER of 10^{-6}. The tight EF bounds developed by Huang and Ritcey (2004) are also shown for reference.

CONCLUSION

In this chapter, we present a comprehensive review of recent research developments on bit-interleaved coded modulation over fading channels that represent the majority of those used for wireless data networks. After a short introduction to digital communications over fading channels, we addressed an important subclass of coded modulations—BICM. For a single-antenna communications system, we present design principles for BICM and BICM with iterative decoding. Regarding the more practical issues in the real system design, we discussed the impact of imperfect channel state information on the performance of BICM-ID, and reviewed recently proposed algorithms for joint iterative channel estimation and decoding. Imperfect channel knowledge is a critical aspect for real-world channels. For multiple-antenna communications systems, we present recent research on bit-interleaved space-time coded modulation with iterative decoding. This extends conventional BICM-ID to multiple-input multiple-output systems. MIMO is used in many wireless systems, and can currently be found even in inexpensive 802.11 home network products. We introduce a very tight theoretical bound to accurately predict the asymptotic bit error rate. Based on the asymptotic BER analysis, a design criterion is developed to achieve the largest asymptotic coding gain inherited from the underlying constellation labeling. BI-STCM-ID is considered a promising candidate for the next generation high–data-rate, high-performance wireless networks. BICM remains an important antecedent for many modern coded modulations. We expect to see its impact on many future generation wireless systems.

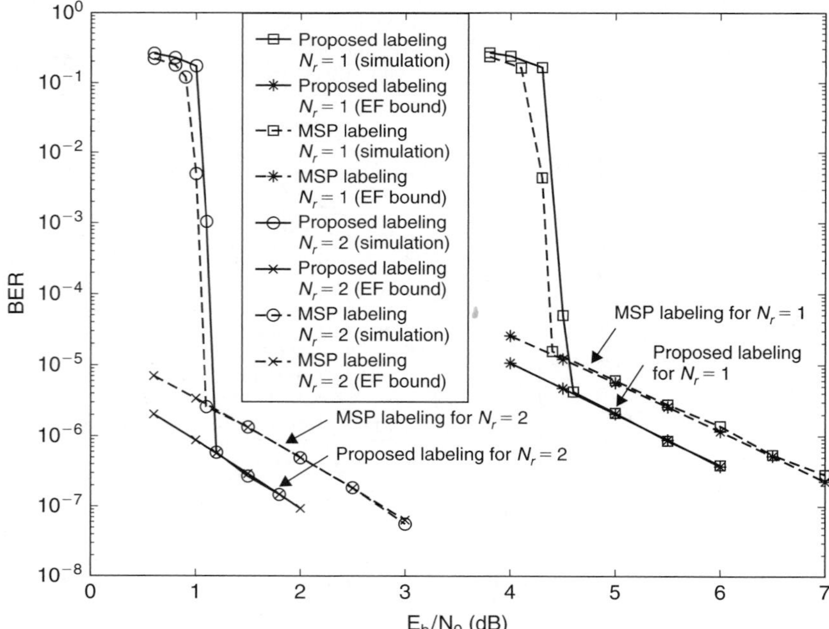

Figure 19: BER performance of the proposed labeling maps and the MSP labeling for a BI-STCM system with 16-QAM modulation, the Alamouti scheme, and one or two receive antennas

GLOSSARY

Asymptotic Bounds: The use of large signal-to-noise ratio (SNR) approximations to simplify or upper-bound a mathematical expression.

Bandwidth: A measure of frequency spread required for transmission. This is usually set by a regulatory authority, such as the FCC in the United States.

Bit Error Rate: The fraction of bits that one expects to erroneously decode. For digital communication systems to be useful, this must be extremely small—roughly one part in a million, or less.

Bit Interleaving: The system component that pseudo-randomly reorders the coded data bits for transmission. A complementary bit deinterleaver is used at the receiver.

Channel Capacity: A limit or bound on the amount of information that can be sent across a channel with negligibly small bit error rate. Generally, this increases with SNR and bandwidth.

Channel State Information: Auxiliary information about the channel, beyond the values of the transmitted bit stream. Typically this includes the carrier frequency and phase, time of arrival, and amplitude levels in a fading channel.

Coded Modulation: A digital communication system that encodes a bit stream using a convolutional, block, or other channel encoder and maps groups of bits to channel symbols.

Coherent Digital Communications: A digital communication system is coherent if it is modulated onto a frequency carrier in such a way that the frequency and phase of the carrier remain stable over the transmission. This is the standard high-performance approach to modern communication systems over channels that do not change radically over a time period much longer than the inverse of the bandwidth. In other words, the receiver must be able to carry out frequency and phase estimation.

Constellation Labeling: In a coherent modulation, a constellation of transmitted symbols is used. Each symbol must be labeled with the group of bits that selects the symbol value. For example, four bits can select one of $2^4 = 16$ symbols.

Data Rate: The rate, in bits per second, of transmitting information across the channel. One must distinguish between the bit rate and the symbol, or baud, rate by the choice of units of information.

Detection: Signal processing at the receiver to detect or decode the unknown values of the transmitted symbols. Because these symbols are drawn from a discrete finite alphabet, there is only a finite number of possible symbol values. This is in contrast to analog communications in which the transmitted waveform can take on an infinite number of values. Because of this fundamental fact, detection is easier than estimation.

Digital Communications: A communication system that transmits discrete levels, or bits of information, in contrast to continuous or analog levels.

Diversity: A measure of the number of statistically independent looks at the channel. Diversity can be increased through encoding information so that each bit is effectively transmitted over many different and independent channel realizations. It can be obtained as temporal diversity, spatial diversity, and frequency diversity, among others, and depends heavily on the particular application.

Estimation: Signal processing at the receiver to estimate the unknown values of the channel state information, such as the fading amplitude and phase. This requires either sounding the channel with pilot symbols of known value, or iterative estimation and decoding.

Fading Channel: A communication channel that introduces amplitude and phase variations along with additive Gaussian noise.

Gaussian Noise: The ever-present noise in any electronic system due to the thermal motion of electrons in resistors. It is also a good model of other external noise sources outside of the receiver.

Iterative Decoding: A decoding process that makes multiple passes over the data, utilizing constraints among bits introduced by the channel coding to aid the detection of unknown bit values. Bits that can be easily decoded, due to random chance, are used to aid the decoding of other bits that are related through the constraints. Given sufficient SNR to bootstrap this process, iteration can be used to reach a very low level of resultant bit errors.

Orthogonal Frequency Division Multiplexing (OFDM): A recent digital-signal–processing based communication system in which the channel bandwidth is partitioned into orthogonal sub-carriers, each with its own transmission. The advantage stems from transformation of frequency-selective to flat or frequency-nonselective fading, which is more easily handled at the receiver. OFDM will be widely deployed in WiMAX and fourth generation (4G) cellular systems.

Signal-to-noise Ratio: A fundamental metric that describes the channel conditions. In digital communications, this is actually an energy ratio E_b/N_o at the detector. In signal processing, a power ratio S/N at the system input is often implied. These can be related through the data rate and bandwidth:

$$\frac{S}{N} = \frac{E_b}{N_o}\frac{R_b}{W}$$

Space-time Coding: A coded modulation system that uses multiple antenna elements at the transmitter in conjunction with multi-symbol modulation to increase the diversity at the receiver. This is very important for handheld receivers for which multiple receive antennas are impractical.

Trellis-coded Modulation: A coded modulation communication system with a jointly designed convolutional encoder followed by a memoryless mapper for a higher-order constellation. One advantage is that the bandwidth expansion, normally introduced by the encoder redundancy, is eliminated.

CROSS REFERENCES

See *Digital Communications Basics; Wireless LANs (WLANs).*

REFERENCES

Battiti, R., and G. Tecchiolli. 1994. The reactive tabu search. *ORSA Journal on Computing* 6(2): 126–40.

Benedetto, S., D. Divsalar, G. Montorsi, and F. Pollara. 1997. A soft-input soft-output APP module for iterative decoding of concatenated codes. *IEEE Communications Letters* 1 (January): 22–24.

Berrou, C., and A. Glavieux. 1996. Near optimum error correcting coding and decoding: Turbo-codes. *IEEE Transactions on Communications* 44 (October): 1261–71.

Bullen, P. S. 2003. *Handbook of means and their inequalities*. Boston, MA: Kluwer Academic.

Caire, G., G. Taricco, and E. Biglieri. 1998. Bit-interleaved coded modulation. *IEEE Transactions on Information Theory* 44 (May): 927–45.

Cavers, J. K. 1991. An analysis of pilot symbol assisted modulation for Rayleigh fading channels. *IEEE Transactions on Vehicular Technology* 40 (November): 686–93.

Chindapol, A., and J. A. Ritcey. 2001. Design, analysis and performance evaluation for BICM-ID with square QAM constellations in Rayleigh fading channels. *IEEE Journal on Selected Areas in Communications* 19 (May): 944–57.

Cela, E. 1998. *The quadratic assignment problem: Theory and algorithms*. Norwell, MA: Kluwer Academic.

Foschini, G. J. 1996. Layered space-time architecture for wireless communication in a fading environment when using multiple antennas. *Bell Labs Technical Journal* 1 (Autumn) pp. 41–59.

Hochwald, B. M., and S. ten Brink. 2003. Achieving near-capacity on a multiple-antenna channel. *IEEE Transactions on Communications* 51(March): 389–99.

Hong, Z., and B. L. Hughes. 2001. Robust space-time trellis codes based on bit-interleaved coded modulation. In *Proceedings of CISS '01*, Baltimore, Maryland, March, pp. 665–70.

Huang, Y., and J. A. Ritcey. 2003. 16-QAM BICM-ID in fading channels with imperfect channel state information. *IEEE Transactions on Wireless Communications* (September): 1000–1007.

———. 2004. Tight BER bounds for iteratively decoded bit-interleaved space-time coded modulation. *IEEE Communications Letters* 8 (March): 153–55.

———. 2005a. Improved 16-QAM constellation labeling for BI-STCM-ID with the Alamouti scheme. *IEEE Communications Letters* 9 (February): 157–59.

———. 2005b. Optimal constellation labeling for iteratively decoded bit-interleaved space-time coded modulation. *IEEE Transactions on Information Theory* 51 (May): 1865–71.

———. 2005c. Joint iterative channel estimation and decoding for bit-interleaved coded modulation over correlated fading channels. *IEEE Transactions on Wireless Communications* 4 (September): 2549–58.

Li, X., A. Chindapol, and J. A. Ritcey. 2002. Bit-interleaved coded modulation with iterative decoding and 8PSK modulation. *IEEE Transactions on Communications* 50 (August): 1250–57.

Lin, S., and D. J. Costello, Jr. 1983. *Error control coding: Fundamentals and applications*. Englewood Cliffs, NJ: Prentice-Hall.

Proakis, J. G. 2000. *Digital communications*. 4th ed. New York: McGraw-Hill.

Samra, H., Z. Ding, and P. M. Hahn. 2003. Symbol mapping diversity design for packet retransmissions through fading channels. In *Proceedings of IEEE GLOBECOM'03*, San Francisco, December, pp. 1989–93.

Schreckenbach, F., N. Görtz, J. Hagenauer, and G. Bauch. 2003. Optimization of symbol mapping for bit-interleaved coded modulation with iterative decoding. *IEEE Communications Letters* 7 (December): 593–95.

Su, H.-J., and E. Geraniotis. 2002. Low-complexity joint channel estimation and decoding for pilot symbol-assisted modulation and multiple differential detection systems with correlated Rayleigh fading. *IEEE Transactions on Communications* 50 (February): 249–61.

Tarokh, V., H. Jafarkhani, and A. R. Calderbank. 1999a. Space-time block coding for wireless communications: Performance results. *IEEE Journal on Selected Areas in Communications* 17 (March): 451–60.

———. 1999b. Space-time block codes from orthogonal designs. *IEEE Transactions on Information Theory* 45 (July): 1456–67.

Tarokh, V., N. Seshadri, and A. R. Calderbank. 1998. Space-time codes for high data rate wireless communication: Performance criterion and code construction. *IEEE Transactions on Information Theory* 44 (March): 744–65.

Telatar, I. E. 1995. Capacity of multi-antenna Gaussian channels. Technical Report, AT&T Bell Labs.

ten Brink, S. 2000. Designing iterative decoding schemes with the extrinsic information transfer chart. *AEÜ International Journal of Electronics and Communications* 54 (December): 389–98.

Ungerboeck, G. 1982. Channel coding with multilevel/phase signals. *IEEE Transactions on Information Theory* 28 (January): 55–67.

Valenti, M. C., and B. D. Woerner. 2001. Iterative channel estimation and decoding of pilot symbol assisted turbo codes over flat-fading channels. *IEEE Journal on Selected Areas in Communications* 19 (September): 1697–1705.

Wang, Z., and K. K. Parhi. 2002. On-line extraction of soft decoding information and applications in VLSI turbo decoding. *IEEE Transactions on Circuits and Systems II* 49 (December): 760–69.

Zehavi, E. 1992. 8-PSK trellis codes for a Rayleigh channel. *IEEE Transactions on Communications* 40 (May): 873–84.

Zhao, L., L. Lampe, and J. Huber. 2003. Study of bit-interleaved coded space-time modulation with different labeling. In *Proceedings of IEEE Information Theory Workshop*, Paris, March, pp. 199–202.

The Wireless Application Protocol

Lillian N. Cassel and Arun Srinivasa Murthy, *Villanova University*

INTRODUCTION

The Wireless Application Protocol (WAP) is a set of standards or protocols that help bring the contents of the Internet to a mobile device. Before WAP was introduced, the users of mobile devices had very limited interactive data services. A variety of interactive services including emailing by mobile device, stock market quotes, news headlines, etc. are now available thanks to WAP.

This chapter presents the essential WAP concepts. It contains a description of the WAP2.0 specification which offers greater flexibility by accommodating better bandwidth, quick data speeds, and improved technology. The chapter can act both as a resource for developers and an introductory guide to a reader who is new to WAP.

After a brief history of WAP, the chapter is broadly divided into four sections: the overall architecture specification of WAP with details of the associated technologies including the security aspect; a description of some WAP applications and the architectures involved; an introduction to XHTMLMP—a scripting language for scripting WAP applications; and the design considerations needed when developing WAP applications. The chapter concludes with a summary and look ahead to where WAP may be heading.

A Brief History of WAP

The Wireless Application Protocol is a global standard for getting Internet content to mobile devices. In the 1990s several vendors were working on the mobile Internet and, as a result, several technologies emerged. Some of the popular ones include Nokia's Narrow Band Sockets (NBS) and Tagged Text Markup Language (TTML), Ericsson's Intelligent Terminal Transfer Protocol (ITTP), and Unwired Planets Handheld Device Markup Language (HDML). Each technology had its own purpose and some overlapped. This led to the fragmentation of the industry based on the providers. The WAP Forum was founded to aid communication among the various organizations and to provide a common set of protocols and technologies.

The WAP standards are regulated by this consortium (WAP Forum), which is now consolidated with the Open Mobile Alliance. Founded by Ericsson, Motorola, Nokia, and Open Wave in June 1997, the Open Mobile Alliance includes numerous members who are the service and content providers. An important goal of the WAP Forum is to ensure that access to the Internet by cell phones is not limited by the underlying network. WAP addresses problems like device limitations, protocol mismatch, and usability.

The Wireless Application Protocol

The Wireless Application Protocol (WAP) is a collection of protocol standards whose purpose is to enable communication between handheld wireless devices and Internet-based service providers. These service providers include Web servers providing general Web content formatted especially for small wireless devices and other service providers who target wireless devices exclusively. WAP brings the content from the Internet and other digital services to wireless handheld terminals.

The original technology built for the Internet was meant for desktops and larger computers. The advent of smaller handheld devices places constraints on the system infrastructure and design paradigms. Compared to desktop or portable computers, the particular limitations of handheld wireless devices include greatly restricted bandwidth, nonrobust connections, signal security limitations, small screens on most devices, limited battery life, restricted input options, more latency, and processor power and memory constraints (WAP Architecture 2001).

In addition to delivering Web content, WAP also provides useful services like personalization of data delivered and options for secure transmission. WAP provides a flexible security infrastructure for communications between a server and client.

The WAP layered architecture is extensible and it enables other services and applications to access the features of the protocols through a set of interfaces. Some popular applications include electronic mail, calendar, phone book, notepad and electronic commerce related applications.

The WAP Model of Web Content Access

The basic World Wide Web (WWW) model has applications and formatted data residing on a server as illustrated in Figure 1. The contents or the data can be browsed using a Web browser. A URL or the address location of the data is specified to the browser resulting in the data being displayed. The Web browser is an example of a networked application. The browser sends a request to a particular object on the server and the server responds by encoding the contents according the to standard data formats. All the content on the server is named using the standard Uniform Resource Locator (URL). The Hyper Text Transport Protocol (HTTP) is a network protocol that defines communication between a client and Web server on the Internet (WAP Architecture 2001). This is the *pull* model of WWW service interaction, so called because it is initiated by the client device which pulls the data from the server.

As shown in Figure 2, the WAP model also works on this request-response mechanism. Content stored on the Web server can be pulled by the WAP device using a WAP browser. The WAP browser on the WAP device requests for a resource using a URL. The response sent by the HTTP server is the requested content. A popular service provided by WAP is the *push* service. A push initiator on the application server can push the content to a WAP device. The contents are transmitted using the protocols of the web. The browser on the hand held devices is similar to a standard Web browser used for browsing the Internet on desktops. Both the push and the pull mechanism can be housed on the same application server as shown in Figure 2 (WAP Architecture 2001).

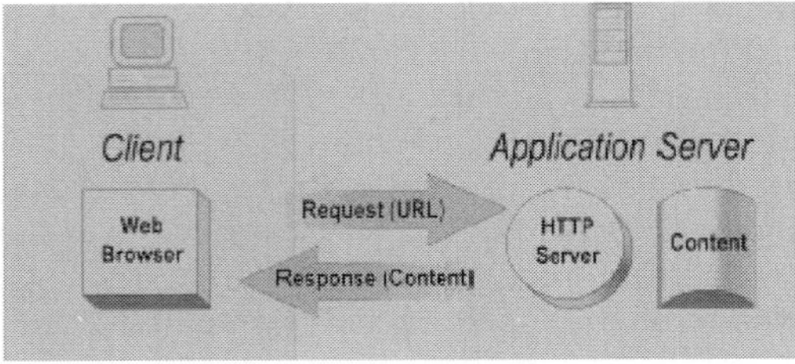

Figure 1: World Wide Web programming model (WAP Architecture 2001)

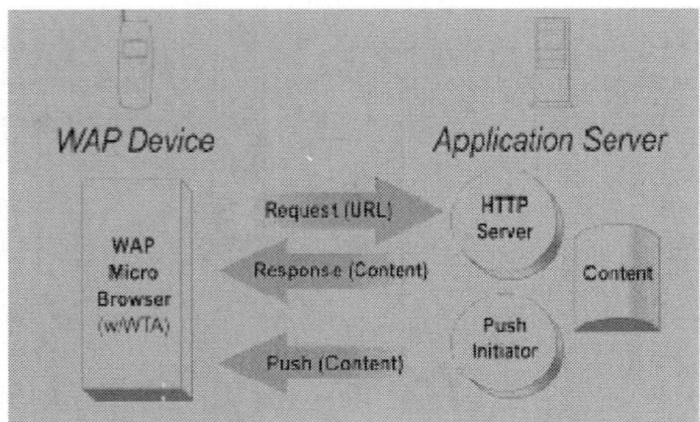

Figure 2: WAP programming model (WAP Architecture 2001)

Figure 2 shows the close relationship between the interactions of a WAP device and an ordinary client in interacting with an application server. The base WWW model is extended in the significant use of the push interaction. Thus the two technologies are very closely related and interdependent.

Performance-Enhancing Proxies

Because information organized for regular Web clients may not be well suited to handheld wireless devices, an additional component is used to bridge the gap in expectations between the Web server and its clients. Figure 3 shows the insertion of a proxy to translate between the features expected by the application server and those available on the WAP-enabled device. Proxies speed up and optimize the connection between the wireless domain and the Web. A Protocol Gateway translates the request from the wireless device to the Web. Content encoders and decoders convert the WAP content to a format that the underlying architecture can use efficiently. An advantage of having proxies is that applications can be developed on standard Web servers using proven Web technologies. Because the proxy performs the conversion between the Web and WAP formats, the existing content on a Web server can be retained. Another advantage of a proxy is that it efficiently uses the limited bandwidth between the handheld devices and the Webserver.

Standards

WAP must deal with two sets of constraints: limitations of wireless data networks and limitations of the handheld devices used to send and receive data. WAP has been designed with these restrictions in mind. Compared with wired or stationary wireless networks, network support for mobile devices include the following constraints:

less bandwidth,
more latency,
less connection stability, and
inconsistent availability.

Compared with a full featured computer, the format of the typical handheld device adds the following constraints:

less powerful CPU,
less memory (ROM and RAM),
restricted power consumption,
smaller displays,
limited input devices.

General network architecture is often described with the International Organization for Standardization (ISO) Open Systems Interconnection (OSI) Reference Model. As seen in Figure 4, the WAP protocol stack is similar to this familiar model.

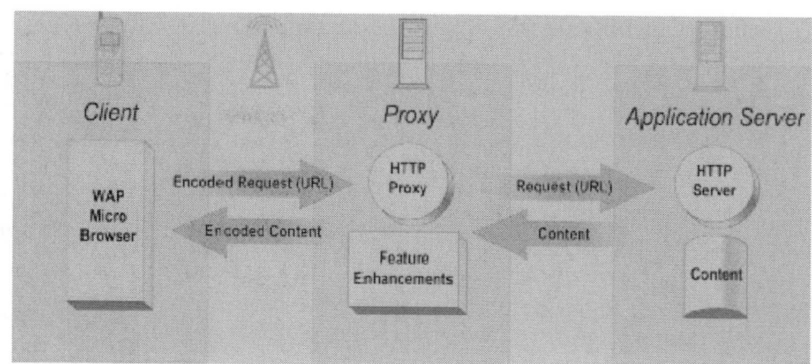

Figure 3: Performance enhancing proxy (WAP Architecture 2001)

Application	WAE
Session	WSP
Transport	WTP
(Security)	WTLS
Network	WDP

TDMA	GSM	CDMA	SMS	Other

Figure 4: WAP STACK for WAP2.0

Architecture

The WAP architecture is designed to minimize bandwidth consumption. As a result, WAP can work on both low bandwidth and broadband networks. Thus, WAP can operate over networks such as time-division multiple access (TDMA) global system for mobile communications (GSM), code division multiple access (CDMA), and short messaging service (SMS). As shown in Figure 5, the layers of the WAP stack include Wireless Application Environment (WAE), the WAP Session Protocol (WSP), the Wireless Transaction Protocol (WTP), the wireless transport layer security (WTLS) (for which there is no corresponding OSI reference layer), and WAP Datagram Protocol (WDP). A brief summary for each layer in the stack follows:

Wireless Application Environment: The WAE consists of the Wireless Markup Language (WML), XHTML Mobile Profile (XHTMLMP), and WMLScript. A detailed explanation of the WAE follows.

WAP Session Protocol: The WSP is a layer meant for the efficient exchange of data between the applications. A WSP session performs a series of request/response actions with the WTP Layer.

WAP Transaction Protocol: WTP is a layer that provides Transaction services. A sequence of request/response transactions supports both reliable and unreliable datagram deliverance.

Wireless Transport Layer Security: The WTLS is analogous to the HTTPS protocol of the Internet which provides an internet security layer. The WTLS provides the transmission of data using encryption.

WAP Datagram Protocol: The network layer is represented by this protocol in WAP. This layer is accountable for interfacing with the bearer networks like TDMA, GSM, CDMA, SMS, and the smooth transmission of data.

Comparing WAP with Internet Protocols

Using the wired environment, applications can be built using strategies like HTML, scripting languages, and SSL for secure data transport. The WAP standards are completely different from the Internet protocols. The WAP

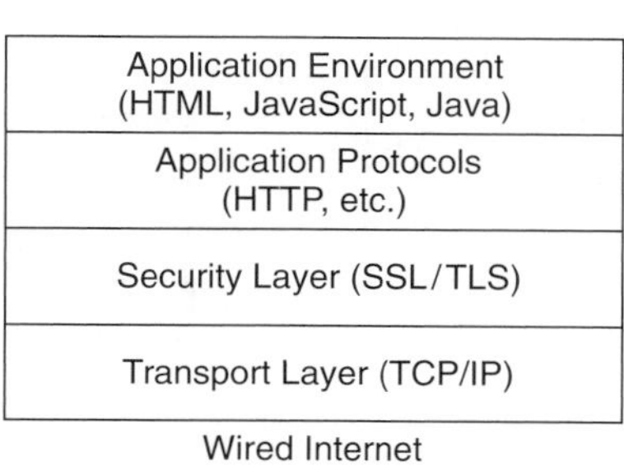

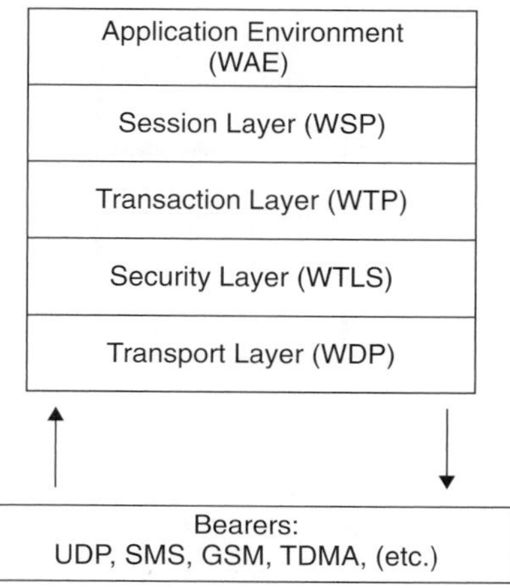

Figure 5: Wired and WAP architectures

protocols are different, the way the data is delivered is different, and the content and scripting languages are also different. The only point where both the standards meet are the security models, which also have minute differences.

Wireless Application Environment

The Wireless Application Environment (WAE) is a framework for the development of applications that can be accessed from many types of wireless devices from a variety of manufacturers. The goal is a structure in which the operators and service providers can build their products with confidence. The framework also uses other WAP technologies including the Wireless Transaction Protocol (WTP) and other Internet related technologies such as XML, URLs, scripting, and various media types. This helps the developers to build applications in a fast and flexible manner. The WAE specification is extensible in the sense that it can accommodate new technologies as they are developed. A study of WAE can be very useful for the developers.

Figure 6 is a Unified Modeling Language (UML) class diagram, which describes each component in the Wireless Application Environment structure in terms of a class. Each box represents one component, with the class name in the first compartment and the attributes in the second compartment of the box. The Wireless Markup Language (WML) script has the class libraries, which are indicated by the diamond suggesting a whole/part relationship. All the WML entities are associated with the WML2 specification, which in turn is associated with XHTML MP, the current markup language for WAP.

WAE Components

The components of WAE include XHTML Mobile Profile [XHTMLMP], WML, WCSS, WMLScript, WBXML, vCARD, and vCalendar, briefly described below:

XHTML Mobile Profile: W3C's HTML [HTML4] has evolved into XHTML and has been modularized [XHTMLMod], thus allowing operators or service providers to build their applications based on the modules necessary for the target platforms or users.

WML: The wireless markup language, an XML-based markup language designed for use on devices characterized by low bandwidth connections, limited memory and restricted CPU capacity, small screen, and limited user input interfaces.

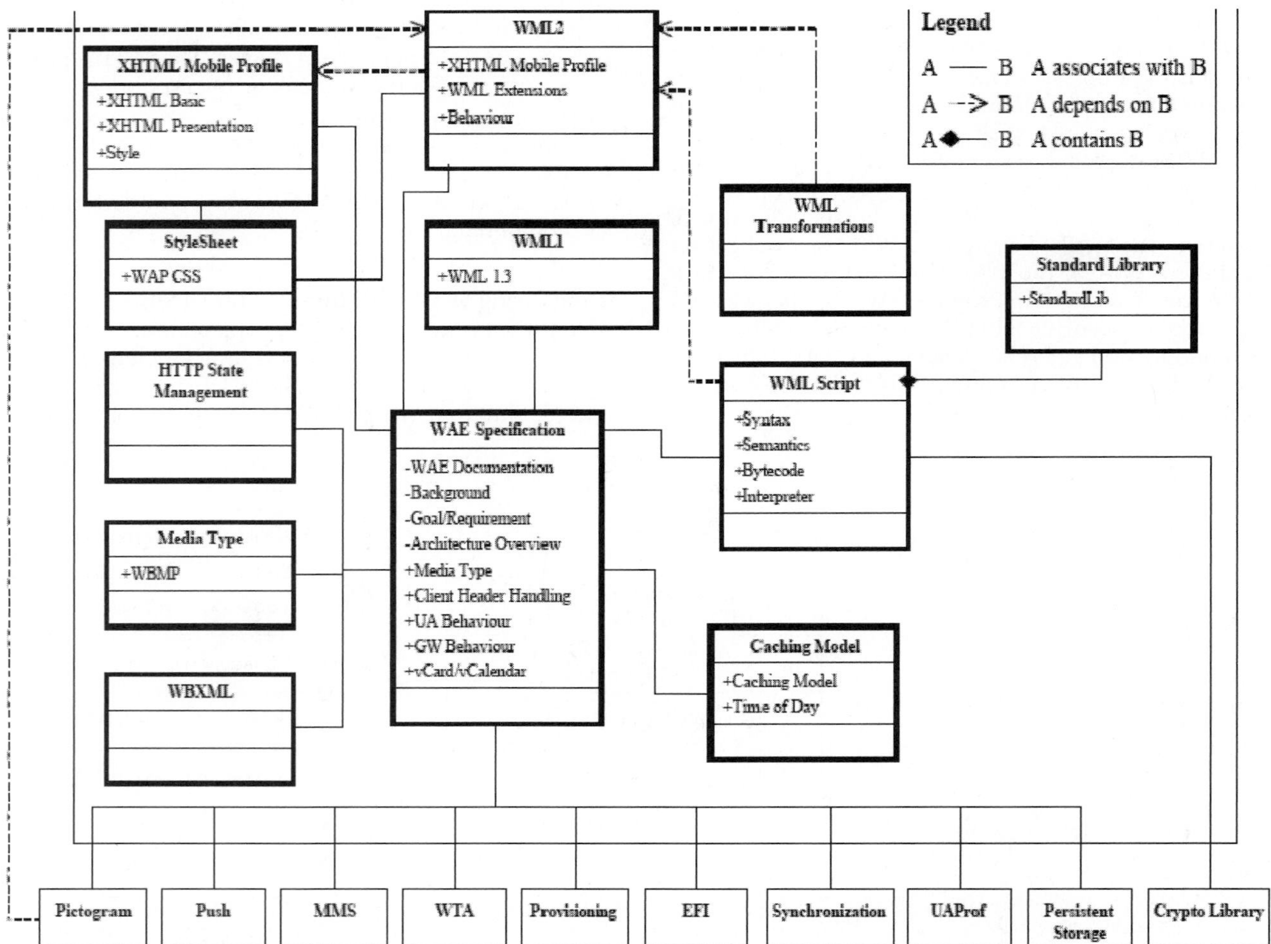

Figure 6: Wireless Application Environment 2 structure (Wireless Application Protocol 2002)

WCSS: Wireless cascading sheets are used in Web development to control display without sacrificing device-independence. WCSS is specified for the features of small mobile devices.

WMLScript: WMLScript is a lightweight scripting language similar to JavaScript, designed to run on small mobile devices.

WBXML: A compact binary representation of XML documents intended to reduce the size of the files for transmission without losing semantic information.

VCard and vCalendar: Industry standards for sharing address and calendar information.

Push and Pull Information Delivery

The normal client server model has a client requesting a service from the server. The server responds by sending the requested data back to the client. This can be thought of as the client pulling data from the server and is called pull technology. In contrast, push technology requires no explicit request from the client. In pull technology, the client initiates the transfer and the server responds. In push technology, the server initiates the transfer and the client accepts the unsought information. Figure 4 summarizes the interaction.

In WAP, a Push Initiator (PI) carries out the push operation by transmitting the content to a Push Proxy Gateway (PPG). The PPG in turn transmits the data to the WAP client. Figure 7 diagrams the components of the Push Framework. The PI is resident on an ordinary Web server. It communicates with the PPG using the Push Access Protocol (PAP). The PPG communicates with the WAP client using the Push Over the Air (OTA) Protocol. (WAP Push Architectural Overview 2001)

The PPG acts between the network of mobile devices and the servers who might push information to them. The PAP allows the PI to communicate with the PPG. PPG provides access control, including identification and authentication of the PI. The PPG gateway also parses the content to detect errors in control information and, in some cases, errors in content. The PPG provides client discovery for the push initiators, including discovery of the capabilities of a potential recipient of the pushed information. Address resolution and binary encoding permit transmission of the pushed information to a client. Protocol conversion provided by the PPG allows the disparate partners in the communication to interact. The Push OTA Protocol connects the WAP client to the PPG. Multicasting and broadcasting allow the same information to be pushed to multiple recipients (WAP Push Architectural Overview 2001).

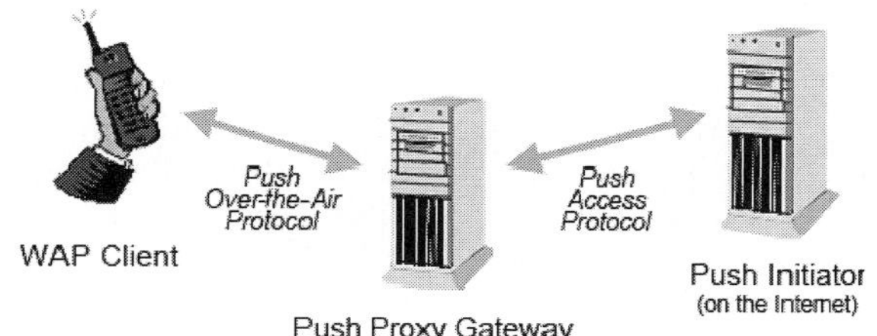

Figure 7: Push framework (WAP Push Architectural Overview 2001)

Security

There are four aspects to security in general network communications:

Privacy. Content is visible only to the intended recipient and both parties have confidence that privacy is protected. This is addressed with various levels of encryption. The degree of confidence required will be weighed against processing costs to determine the appropriate level of encryption to use.

Integrity. Content is not modified between leaving the sender and arriving at the recipient's device. Digital signatures allow a document to be verified as being the same as was transmitted. A hash code is computed over the document and sent as part of the signature. If the hash code check on the recipient side does not produce the correct results, the document has been modified.

Authentication. The sender's identity can be verified with very high degree of confidence. Passwords, authentication, and digital signatures identify the originator.

Nonrepudiation. The sender cannot later deny having sent the information. Digital signatures are the primary tools for binding the sender to the document or resource as sent.

The WAP architecture includes a Wireless Transport Layer security specification, which includes a view of the wireless network access environment as shown in Figure 8. The figure shows both pull and push proxies. Network access is achieved in one of two modes: push or pull. Some examples of push technology are familiar: pagers, Short Message Service, and e-mail notification when a user has signed up for the notification service. The user chooses this form of intrusion in order to remain aware of new activities or special offers. Additional push services are anticipated as the wireless Web develops.

End-to-end security is accomplished in the wired Web through secure socket layer (SSL) encoding. In that approach, a secure link is created end-to-end, between the sender and the receiver. Intermediate processing units, such as routers, do not see the content of the message and only participate in routing the message from source to destination.

In the wireless Web, things are more complex. The client and server usually do not communicate directly, but they rely on proxy or gateway machines to provide necessary translation and retransmission services. The proxy intervenes between the WAP enabled wireless device and the TCP/IP and HTTP process-enabled server. Thus, security questions must include the degree of trust between the content provider and the gateway and between the client and the gateway, as well as between the client and the content provider.

WAP includes WTLS, the Wireless Transport Layer Security. WTLS is used to provide secure service between the client device and its pull gateway. WTLS is used for server authentication. Client authentication, when

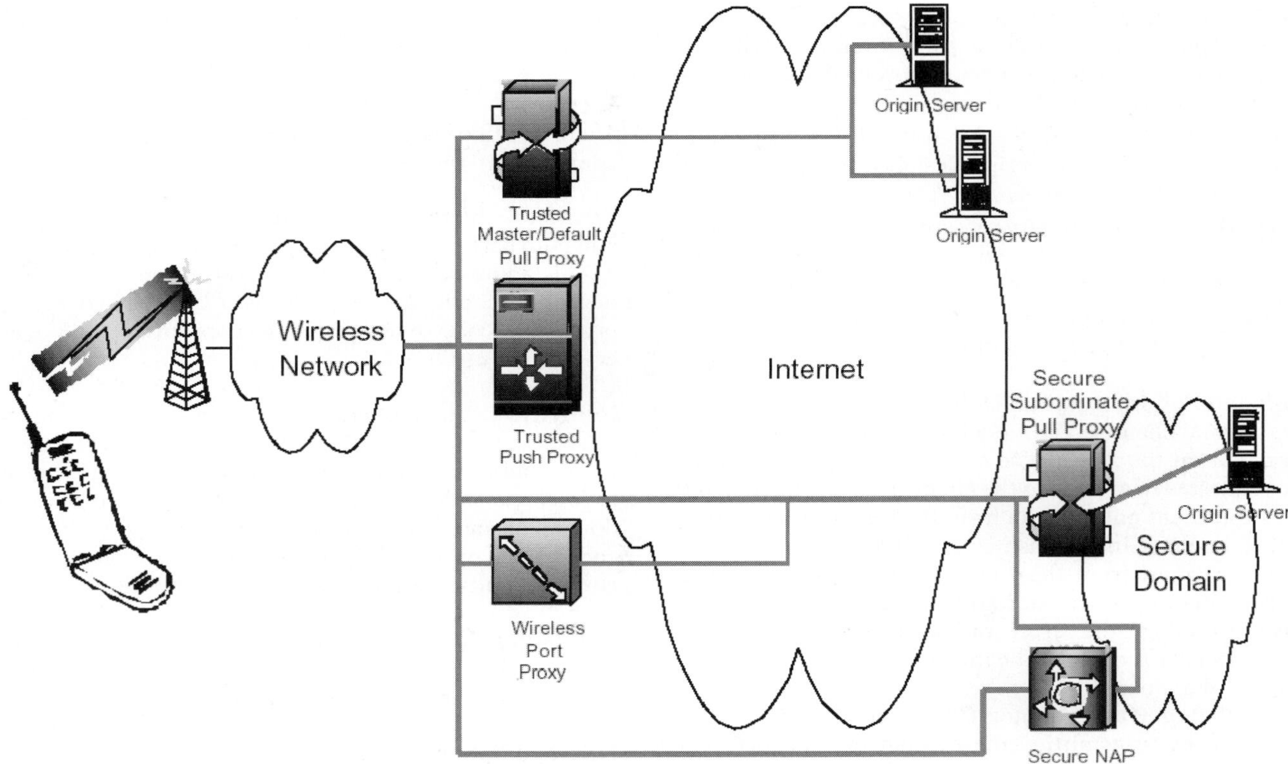

Figure 8: Wireless Network Access Environment (application Protocol 2000)

required, is left to existing mechanisms. Nonrepudiation is left to the application and can rely on existing techniques. Control in the push environment requires establishing trust between the client and the push proxy. The push proxy uses existing techniques to assure security with data providing servers.

The extra step involved is the use of a gateway between the client and the information provider. This introduces another factor into consideration of overall security. WTLS addresses security between the device and this pull gateway. Existing Web security mechanisms are used to provide security between the gateway and the service and/or data provider.

SSL is used essentially to provide secure services over the wired internet and WTLS (WAP 1.x) is a layer meant for the wireless applications using WAP. WTLS has been replaced by Transport Layer Security (TLS) as part of WAP 2.0 specifications. It provides an end-to-end encryption between the client and the server.

Mobile Access to Information Resources

The Web has a wealth of information and is taken for granted as an information and communication resource. Similarly, mobile devices have become part of daily life. Access to existing Web pages is one of the goals for handheld/mobile devices. But most of the information a mobile user may need will be dynamic. A mobile user might want to know what the traffic is just ahead or how to get from here to there. In combination with other features like Geographic Positioning Systems (GPS), an application can address the questions. When mobile users query their bank balances before making a purchase, strong encryption must protect the data transferred without unduly impacting the amount of time required to get the answer. Mobile users can also query stock quotes, credit bills, and can browse the Internet for other querying activities.

WAP Access to Databases—An Example Using the BioWAP Protocol

BioWAP is a service for handheld devices using WAP providing access to major bioinformatics database and analysis programs. For example, BioWAP provides instant access to a protein sequence database.

Large projects often generate a vast amount of data that must be stored, analyzed, and organized. The data can be stored in Internet databases and data analysis can be made here. Usually WML is used for information exchange and to provide access to the data and services from the Internet. The BioWAP protocol and database access diagram shown in Figure 9 illustrate the concepts that apply in general.

In the example, the service requests are compiled by a WAP gateway and are then sent to a WAP terminal. The Web server is very essential in the BioWAP service. It handles user's requests, then analyzes and transmits the results to the user through the WAP gateway. The Web server in BioWAP provides tools for analysis and search. The response from the server is sent back to the gateway using WML, which then compiles the WML response and delivers it to the user.

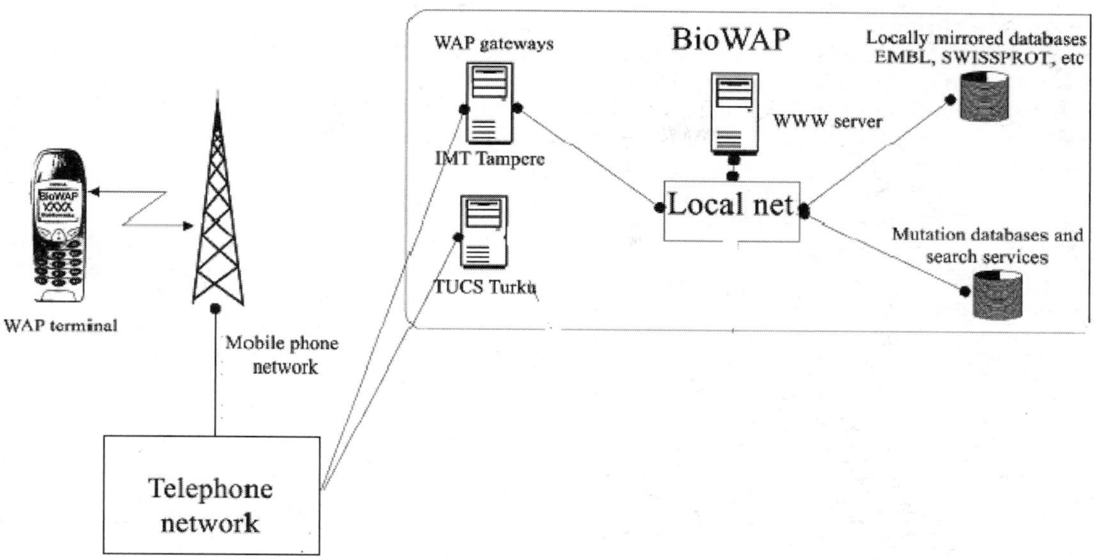

Figure 9: Mobile access to a database: the BioWAP example (Riikonen et al. 2002)

Example Applications

WAP offers the opportunity for a wide spectrum of applications in contexts ranging from automobiles to healthcare. At present, WAP enabled phones can be used to request information on personal bank accounts, stock quotes, and user specific details from various organizations. Also WAP can play an important role in health care by providing necessary patient records to visiting nurses/doctors through handheld devices. A few example applications are described below.

Automobiles—Information Related to Location, Weather, and Traffic Conditions

Current traffic, weather, and location can be sent to the system in a car by a broadcaster. WAP, which was developed especially for the use in mobile and wireless networks, is well suited to use in the area of traffic monitoring. Cars can be information centers as opposed to being only transportation entities. When the driver enters a car, the current road and weather conditions are cached in a Personal Digital Assistant (PDA). The digital audio broadcast sends data to the systems in the car about the weather and traffic conditions prevalent at the moment. The Personal Travel Assistant (PTA) helps the driver to navigate. The PTA and the PDA then calculate the shortest route for the trip and set the route accordingly for the PTA. (Bechler & Schiller 2000)

Home Health Care—Connecting the Visiting Nurse to the Hospital Information System

WAP devices can serve as a mobile access terminal for general inquiry and patient monitoring services (Hung 2000, 2003). With this system, a nurse can view the patients' monitored physiological parameters on WAP devices. The system will provide acquisition, transmission, and deposit of the physical information of the home care patient into a database. If the nurse sees a need for adding more information to the database based on current situations, he or she can do it by keying it through the WAP device. A relational database stores the patient's records. Operation cost is low due to the availability of WAP phones. A WAP-based health care system can have the following applications: ECG browsing, blood pressure browsing, patient record browsing, clinical and hospital information inquiry, and doctor's appointment browsing. Third generation mobile phones have improved the feasibility of such systems by providing greatly increased data transfer rates.

E-mail: Filtering, Notification, and Supporting Input and Output Requirements

Handheld devices provide easy access to e-mail accounts without the bulk of full laptop computers. Although cell phones and PDAs support the necessary POP and SMTP protocols, they are limited by the characteristics of these devices. Currently users can read, compose, delete, and forward messages from their mobile phones (Milasinovic 2003, Rao 2003).

Because the touch pads and the keypads on the cell phones are clumsy to use, most of the e-mail services do not ask the user to key in the login details. During the notification procedure, users are provided with a WAP link that contains a unique identifier (UID) which can be used for a one-time login procedure. The user just has to follow the provided link and it will connect the user to the mailbox.

Because of limited storage space and bandwidth, wireless handheld devices benefit from filtering of incoming mail. When the mail application downloads the e-mail headers, it scans the headers and applies the e-mail filters. The users can choose among several built-in filters or can create their own filter list. Based on the user's filter options, mail filtering eliminates unnecessary mails sent to a wireless handheld device. Some mail client applications notify the user about a piece of mail being delivered.

Location-Aware Advertising

Location-aware applications are those in which the location of a person or an object is used to focus on an application or service (Hakkila and Isomursu 2005). A mobile commerce application can make use of location aware services. Consider this example wherein a consumer has previously received a digital coupon from a shopping mall on her handheld device or a PDA. So once she has this coupon, the push initiator on the server can push data to the mobile device. The consumer, if interested, may ask for driving directions from her current location to the nearest mall. Upon arriving at the mall, the shopper is given more details regarding the store location. Once she is in the store, further information about the products and offers is sent to the PDA. Also the aisle and shelf where the product is situated can be sent to the PDA. Within each store, the handheld device may read a store guide which gives information about special offers and also has customized information about specific individuals. All of these can be accomplished using WAP.

Mobile Banking Transactions

A user with a WAP-enabled mobile phone can connect to the bank via the device. The proxy or the gateway in the structure converts the WAP protocols into the protocols suitable for the Internet. The user interface is similar to what a user sees online, but can be browsed using a mini browser. The most important aspect of an online banking structure is security. General security requirements include confidentiality, entity authentication, data authentication, and non-repudiation.

A WAP-based banking application allows users on the move to access accounts and make transactions. The transactions are recorded in a database, similar to what might happen when users access accounts from any online system. Using the WAP Push feature, a daily bank statement or alert can be sent out to a particular WAP device. Most of the leading banks have WAP-enabled services in use. TLS can provide end-to-end encryption between the client and server. TLS is part of the WAP 2.0 specification (Claessens et al. 2002).

Course Registration System

Course registration is usually done by the students either online through the Web or by filling out forms in the registrar's office. Using a WAP-based course registration system, a student can register using a handheld device and can also check all the related matter about the course like grades, assignments, and so on (Qadah and Al-Zouabi 2005).

A server database holds the information about the courses and the students. Additionally a course delivery system is present on a Web server. This course delivery system has the code/intelligence required to interact with the user as well as the database system. The student can initially start making queries to the server by keying in related text for course names. When a match is found by the Web server, it sends it to the Gateway which in turn formats it using the WAP protocol before delivering it to the user. If the student is aware of the course number, a simpler retrieval takes place. Also the server is programmed with all the prerequisites for a given course. The server makes sure the students have completed a prerequisite before assigning them to the requested course. The course registration system can be extended to a grade delivery system as well. At present only a limited number of universities have implemented this system.

Java and WAP

Currently Java is being used to develop WAP applications. Java 2 Micro Edition (J2ME) is a specification used to develop Wireless Applications. Mobile Information Device Profile (MIDP) is also an open specification which combines Java and other Web technologies. Java Servlets and Java Server Pages (JSP) are used to develop dynamic WAP content on the server side.

MIDP programming is used to develop Java applications for WAP. It is a combination of the Java programming model and the Web programming model. It is analogous to applets in Java. MIDIP files are also called MIDlets and they run using preinstalled MIDlet management software. Applets are destroyed once they are run but MIDlets stay on the device after running. The MIDlets basically serve the purpose of displaying objects on the screen of the handheld device. A sample program is given below.

```
import javax.microedition.midlet.*;
import javax.microedition.lcdui.*;

public class VillanovaMIDlet extends MIDlet
{
   TextBox box;

   public VillanovaMIDlet() {
   }
   public void startApp() {
       display = Display.getDisplay(this);
       box = new TextBox("Villanova
University", "Department of Computer
Science ", 20, 0);
       display.setCurrent(box);
   }
       public void pauseApp() {
}
       public void destroyApp(boolean
unconditional) {
   }
}
```

The program displays the contents as shown in Figure 10. The program creates a MIDlet and displays the text encapsulated by the box object.

Messaging Services and WAP

Short Messaging Service (SMS) is a Global System for Mobile Communication (GSM) service which allows users to send text messages from one wireless device to another. Messages are sent using a store and forward mechanism. The messages are forwarded to a Short Message Service Center (SMSC) which tries to send the message to the recipient. If the recipient is not available the message is stored in the SMSC. When the user becomes available, an attempt to send the message is again made, but the

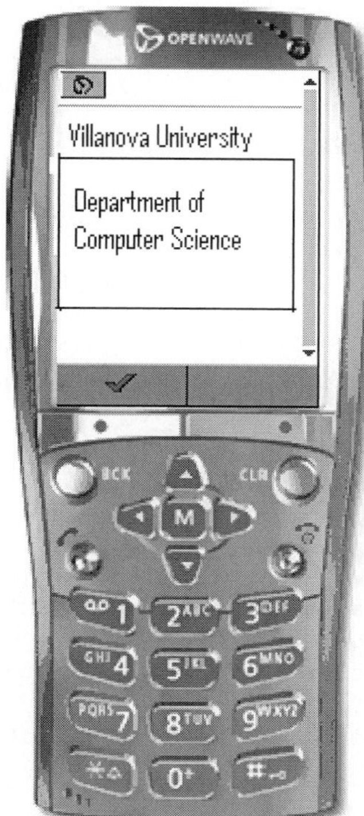

Figure 10: A sample MIDlet display

message delivery cannot be relied upon. The messages may be lost at times and may never reach the destination. A best possible delivery effort is agreed upon before the SMS is originated. Transmission between the SMSC and phone can be done using TCP/IP or using other protocols. Different languages must be encoded using the Unicode format. News alerts, financial information, and other information are the content commonly sent using SMS.

An extension to SMS is the Multimedia Messaging Service (MMS) which is a standard used for sending messages which include audio, image, video, etc. The Open Mobile Alliance (OMA) is responsible for its standardization. The initial transfer of content from the client device to the Multimedia Messaging Service Center (MMSC) is done using HTTP. Then a notification is sent to the recipient's device using a WAP push. Either an immediate or delayed delivery is performed based on the user's requirements. With the convergence of WAP and SMS, powerful applications are being built that enables communication between devices.

SMS or MMS can act as a carrier for information transfer. Data can be sent between devices that are WAP compliant using SMS or MMS. For certain applications using SMS, interactive interfaces are not that appealing when compared to the interfaces generated with WAP. Both SMS and WAP have a role in building applications that are efficient and visually appealing.

XHTML MP and Wireless Markup Languages

WML and XHTML MP are the popular scripting languages for scripting WAP applications. WML, though not the current standard (WAP 1.x) for authoring, is used on some client applications. The content below describes the basics of WML and introduces the card format for information delivered to handheld devices. Further sections introduce the use of XHTML MP, the current standard (WAP 2.0) and its syntax. Because the newer standards are based on the older WML, we begin with a brief description of WML basics.

WML Basics

As we have seen, normal HTML specified Web pages are seldom suitable for display on handheld wireless devices. The WAP protocol suite includes an XML language designed to specify items for display on these devices. The Wireless Markup Language (WML) borrows heavily from HTML, but eliminates features not suitable for these devices and adds functions that address the screen size and user input options.

The first difference to notice is the paradigm of presentation. Where the Web metaphor is a page, the WML metaphor is a card. A single application display is a deck of cards, much as people sometimes use in gathering research data in a library. Each card contains a small amount of content and may contain links to other cards in the same deck, cards in other decks, or even to conventional Web pages.

An example application is the best way to illustrate and introduce WML. The example is developed using the Open wave SDK, available free from http://www.openwave.com. The simulated displays for a mobile phone are part of the SDK. The appearance of output from a WML specification will vary according to the nature of the device on which it is displayed. The example allows a client to obtain information about a particular city. The first screen identifies the application. The WML code for this initial card is shown in Figure 11.

```
<?xml version="1.0"?>
<!DOCTYPE wml PUBLIC "-//PHONE.COM//DTD WML
1.3//EN" "http://www.phone.com/dtd/wml13.dtd">
<!-- WML file created by Openwave SDK -->
<wml>
  <card id ="Start">
   <p align="center"> <b> City information</b>

   </p>

  </card>

</wml>
```

Figure 11: First WML card specification

The first two lines of this WML file reflect the XML connection. This identifies the XML version and allows valid compilation of the file. The actual WML specification begins with <wml></wml> and ends with </wml>. Like other XML applications, each WML element has both an open and close component. Notice that the <p> (paragraph) tag must be closed by </p> unlike ordinary HTML. The <wml> . . . </wml> tags mark the beginning and end of this deck. The deck may contain as many cards as the application requires. Each card is specified by <card> . . . </card>. The <card> tag shows an id for this card that can be used to reference it from other cards. The title of this card has been centered by an option in the <p> tag and made bold by the usual <b> . . . </b>. Figure 12 shows the simulated output for this first WML example.

Next, the example adds options to the display. Each option will consist of a link to another card with further information on the chosen topic. This requires a list. The list in this application will allow the user to choose weather information, restaurants, museums, or information about public transportation. Each option in the list specifies the next card to visit if that option is selected. The entire select list goes inside a <p> . . . </p> tag element. The list code follows:

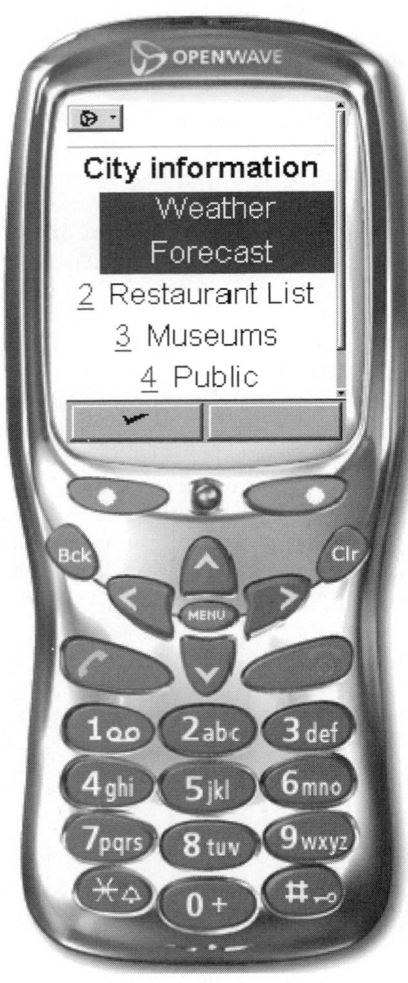

Figure 12: Simulated display of first WML code

```
<select name="listname">
  <option event = "link"> Label </option>
  </select>
```

The syntax for the list in which each option links to another card in the current deck is

```
<?xml version="1.0"?>
<!DOCTYPE wml PUBLIC "-//PHONE.COM//DTD WML
1.3//EN" "http://www.phone.com/dtd/wml13
.dtd">
<!-- WML file created by Openwave SDK -->
<wml>
    <card id ="Start">
    <p align="center"> <b>City information
</b> </p>
    <p align="center">
    <select name="categories">
        <option onpick = "#weather"> Weather
Forecast </option>
        <option onpick = "#restaurants">
Restaurant List </option>
        <option onpick = "#museums"> Museums
</option>
        <option onpick = "#trans"> Public
Transportation </option>
    </select>
    </card>
</wml>
```

The listname joins this set of options with a common title. "Label" is displayed on the user screen. The *event* is the occurrence that causes this item to be selected from among the options available. The *link* identifies the card to be displayed next. The following code includes a list of options for city information. Each link is relative, in fact is a reference to a card in the same deck. The syntax for that reference repeats the HTML syntax for a jump to a location in the same page.

Figure 12 shows the simulated output for this first list. Immediately, the constraints of the small screen become apparent. The wordy descriptions are too much for this device to display well. In Figure 13, the descriptive text is shorter and the list fits comfortably on the screen.

The user selects a list option by means of the arrow keys or by pressing the number corresponding to the chosen list entry. In Figure 13, the *Museums* entry is chosen. Pressing the button under the check mark will make the selection. To continue the application development, the additional cards are added to the deck. The empty cards are shown below:

```
<?xml version="1.0"?>
<!DOCTYPE wml PUBLIC "-//PHONE.COM//DTD WML
1.3//EN" "http://www.phone.com/dtd/wml13.
dtd">
<!-- WML file created by Openwave SDK -->
<wml>
            <card id ="Start">
<p align="center">  <b>City information</b>
</p>
      <p align="center">
```

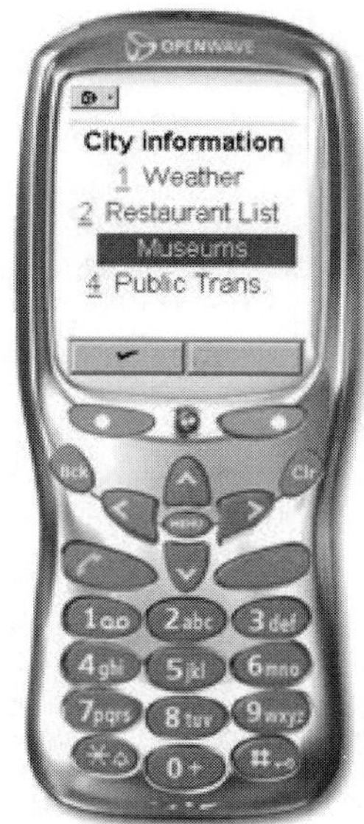

Figure 13: First list attempt

```
      <select name="categories">
      <option onpick = "#weather"> Weather
</option>
      <option onpick = "#restaurants">
Restaurant List </option>
      <option onpick = "#museums"> Museums
</option>
      <option onpick = "#trans"> Public
Trans. </option>
        </select>
        </p>
      </card>
   <card id="weather">
      <card>
   <card id="restaurants">
      </card>
   <card id = "museums">
      </card>
   <card id = "trans">
      </card>
      </wml>
```

The initial display looks no different, but now there is a card corresponding to each choice. The cards are empty currently, ready to be filled in with relevant information for this application.

Basics of XHTML Mobile Profile (XHTML MP)

XHTML (Extensible Hypertext Markup Language) MP is a language designed for Web clients having resource constraints. This is the current client scripting language used for developing client applications. XHTML MP is targeted at devices such as mobile phones, handheld devices, PDAs and pagers. It is an authoring language meant specifically for handheld mobile devices. XHTML Mobile Profile is based on the modules defined by modularization of XHTML. It can be considered as a subset of XHTML 1.1, which is based upon XHTML Basic. XHTML MP adds support for a scripting environment and helps in binding scripts to events. It also includes XHTML forms. (Passani) XHTML supports the use of style sheets which allow authors the control while presenting contents. The second part of this section describes this feature more fully. The subsection below has the tags listed with the families to which they belong.

Families of Tags

Table 1 has XHTML MP Tags organized based on the XHTML modules. The table represents the XHTML basics modules and the tags and attributes that belong to the particular modules. Table 2 shows tags that were not part of XHTML Basic but were introduced in XHTML MP.

Style Sheet

Style information can be specified for a document in one of the following three ways:

External Style Sheet
Internal Style Sheet
Inline Style Information.

External Style Sheet. The external style sheet is always associated with the link element, a special XML processing instruction. The example below associates the external style sheet "mobile.css."

Table 1: XHTML Tags Organized by XHTML Modules

Module	Element
Structure	body, head, html, title
Text	dfn, div, em, h1, h2, h3, h4, h5, h6, kbd, p, pre, q, samp, span, strong, var
Hypertext	A
List	dl, dt, dd, ol, ul, li
Basic forms	Form, input, label, select, option, textarea
Basic tables	caption, table, td, th, tr
Image	Img
Object	object, param
Meta information	Meta
Link	Link
Base	Base

Table 2: XHTML Tags Introduced in XHTML MP

Module	Element/Attributes
Forms	Fieldset, optgroup
Legacy	start attribute on ol, value attribute on li
Presentation	b, big, hr, i, small
Style sheet	style element
Style attribute	style attribute

```
<?xml-stylesheet href="mobile.css" media=
"handheld" type="text/css"?>
```

When an external document uses the link element, certain values for the rel attribute are specified. When rel="stylesheet" or rel="alternate stylesheet", the type attribute specifies the style sheet language. In the example below, a link element is used to relate the external style sheet "mystyle.css"

```
<html>
   <head>
      <link href="mystyle.css" type="text/
css" rel="stylesheet"/>
      . . .
   </head>
      . . .
<html>
```

Internal Style Sheet. The style information can be part of a document internally. The style element has an attribute called `style` which specifies the style sheet language. The following shows an example of an internal style sheet.

```
<html>
<head>
      <style type="text/css">
      P { text-align: center; }
      </style>
   . . .
   </head>
   . . ..
</html>
```

Inline Style. Style information for a single element can be set using the style attribute. This is called inline style. The style attribute is part of the core attribute set and is therefore available on every element in XHTML Mobile Profile. The default style language is the Wireless CSS [WCSS]. In the example, inline styling information is applied to a paragraph element:

```
<p style="text align: center">. . .</p>
```

Building Menus

Menus are used for interaction in all wireless applications. A menu denotes a list of navigating choices through an interface. Choosing a menu item leads to a new page being loaded and displayed to the end user. Menus can also be associated with numbers and the user can choose a number to select the particular menu choice.

```
<?xml version="1.0" encoding="UTF-8"?>
<!DOCTYPE html PUBLIC "-//WAPFORUM//DTD
XHTML Mobile 1.0//EN"
      "http://www.wapforum.org/DTD/xhtml-
mobile10.dtd">
<html xmlns="http://www.w3.org/1999/xhtml"
xml:lang="en">
<head>
   <title>Contacts - R</title>
   <link href="style.css" rel="stylesheet"
type="text/css"/>
</head>
<body>
Pick contact:
<ol>
   <li><a href="contact.jsp?id=32" accesskey=
"1">Dr.Cassel</a></li>
   <li><a href="contact.jsp?id=45" accesskey=
"2">Dr.Beck</a></li>
   <li><a href="contact.jsp?id=21" accesskey=
"3">Dr.Goelman</a></li>
   <li><a href="contact.jsp?id=17" accesskey=
"4">Dr.Perry </a></li>
</ol>
</p>
</body>
</html>
```

This list builds a numbered menu. The `<xml>` tag defines the version of XML, the encoding format, and the document standards that are followed. The `<link>` tag links to an external style sheet `style.css`. The `<ol>` tag encloses the options, which are listed individually wrapped by the `<li>` tags. The access key attribute of the `<a>` tag numbers the options. The above list displays a list of contact names that are displayed in the form of a menu in the image (Figure 14) below.

The above display has each name displayed as a link. When clicked, each takes the user to the corresponding JSP page as scripted in the XHTML listing previously.

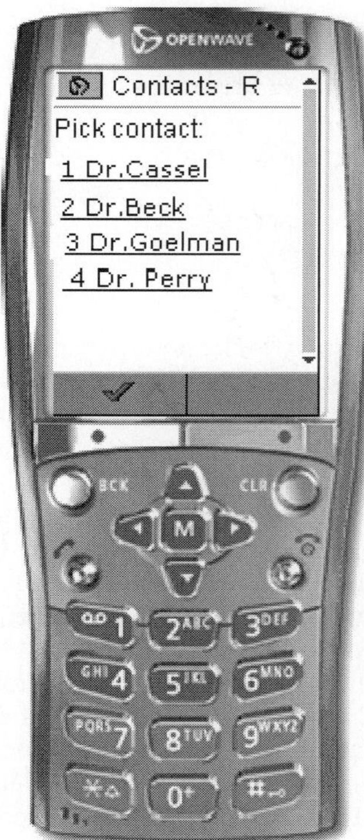

Figure 14: Menu display

Text Flow Using XHTML MP

Web browsers are used for displaying data to a user. XHTML MP provides the needed functionality. The following listing shows how text can be displayed on a browser. The image (Figure 15) following the listing displays the user defined text included in the listing. The text can be enclosed between the <body> and the <p> paragraph tags.

```
<?xml version="1.0" encoding="UTF-8"?>
<!DOCTYPE html PUBLIC "-//WAPFORUM//DTD XHTML
Mobile 1.0//EN"
"http://www.wapforum.org/DTD/xhtml-mobile10
.dtd">
<html xmlns="http://www.w3.org/1999/xhtml"
xml:lang="en">
<head>
      <title>Plain Text</title>
</head>
<body>
<p>
This is a tutorial on WML, XHTML MP and WAP.
So now is the time to learn WAP
  <div style="text-align:right"><i>Openwave
</i></div>
</p>
</body>
</html>
```

The <pre> tag is used to display preformatted text. Most of the tags collapse the white spaces in and around the text. But when it is desirable to keep the existing text formatting intact, the <pre> tag is used. The text below wrapped around the <pre> tag is displayed in Figure 16.

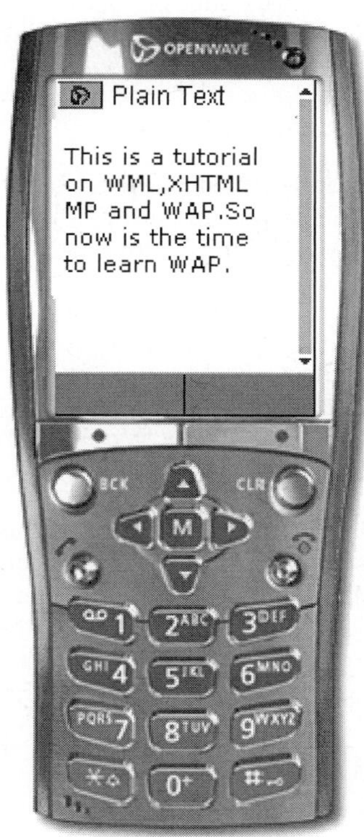

Figure 15: Text display

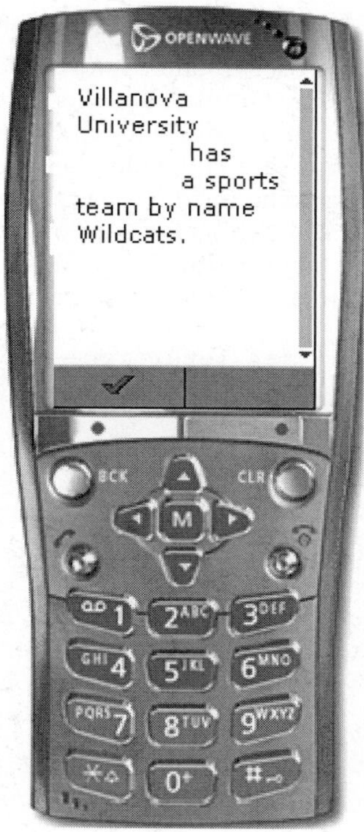

Figure 16: Display using <pre> tag

```
      <body>
      <pre>
      Villanova
      University

                has
              a sports
      team by name
      Wildcats.
   </pre>
      </body>
```

Apart from these tags, the following tags have important functionality when formatting text.

Headers: The header tags can be used to hierarchically arrange data at different levels. Also they can be used to enlarge characters to make them appear as a heading. The heading tags have the same name and function as in standard HTML. Below are the different header formats.

Emphasis Tags: Tags commonly found in HTML are used here as well. Some of the important text formatting tags are: <b> for bold, <q> for quote, <strong> for bold, <em> for emphasis, <i> for italics.

Links: The anchor tag is the most important of all the tags in XHTML MP. Text can be enclosed between the tags and the href attribute of the tag has the URL as in standard HTML.

Developing Forms Using XHTML MP

A form allows the user to enter information like names, addresses, and phone numbers and then select items using drop down boxes and radio buttons. The different tags involved with forms are embedded between the `<form>` and `</form>` tags. The form tag has the name and path of an external script, which helps in processing the data collected by the form. Below is a listing that shows the various form elements displayed in image (Figure 17).

```
<form action="/servlets/processform"
method="get">
<p>
<select name="category">
      <option value="blended" selected="
selected">Product:</option>
      <option value="books">Books</option>
      <option value="music">Music</option>
      <option value="dvd">DVD</option>
      <option value="vhs">VHS</option>
      <option value="vhs">Ringtones
</option>
</select>

<br/>

Keyword:<br/>
     <input type="text" name="key" value=""
format="" /><br/>

Are you a ACME Co. Member?<br/>
      <input type="radio" name="member"
value="yes" checked="checked" />
      Yes<br/>
      <input type="radio" name="member"
value="no" />
      No<br/>

Zip code:<br/>
      <input type="text" name="minutes"
value="" format="NNNNN" />
<br/>

Do you accept ACME conditions?<br/>
      <input type="checkbox" name="accept"
checked="checked" /><br/>
</p>

<div class="centered">
      <input type="submit" value="Submit"/>
</div>
</form>
```

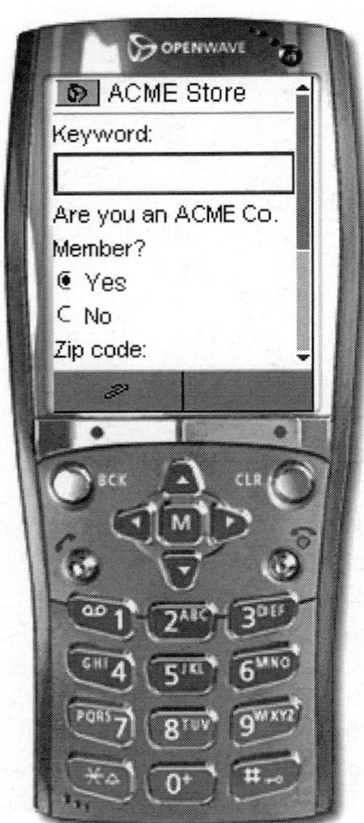

Figure 17: Form created using XHTML MP

The `<select>` tag presents a list of items to be displayed in a drop-down box. The `<input>` tag with the attribute type set to `text` displays the text box below the label "Keyword." When the type is set to `radio`, radio buttons appear instead of text boxes. Only one of the radio buttons can be selected from a range of buttons. The form can be submitted by clicking on the `submit` button. The submit button can be displayed using the `<input type="submit">` tag. When the submit button is clicked, the action attribute of the form tag is executed. Images can be embedded inside forms and Web pages in general using the `<img>` tag.

Images and Objects

The `<img>` tag is used to place pictures on WAP pages. The syntax and attributes are very straight-forward.

```
<img alt="great shot" src="greatshot.jpg"
height="88" width="120"/>
```

The `alt` attribute provides a label for the image. The `src` attribute mentions the path from which the image is to be fetched. Height and width tags specify the height and width of the image in pixels.

Using the `<object>` tag , the media type can be played or viewed within the WAP Browser.

```
<object data="music.wav" height="20"
width="20" title="Play" type="audio/x-wav"
standby="loading"/>
```

The above tag has a "wav" file, which is to be played in WAP Browser. The remaining attributes, height and width, specify the height and width of the control on the screen. The title attribute controls how the soft key label appears on the device. Figure 18 shows the effect.

DESIGN CONSIDERATIONS

Design considerations have figured in several parts of this article. The following points summarize the major issues.

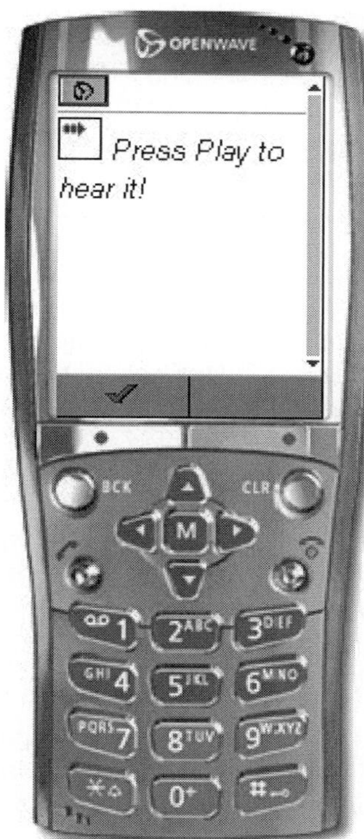

Figure 18: Display of an object on a WAP browser

Considering Speed

Bandwidth is still much lower for handheld wireless devices than for wired Web connections. As a result, bits that do not contribute to the user achieving a desired result will not be well regarded. Recent advances in the design of engaging and entertaining Web pages will not serve this population. The application developer must focus on getting the message across in as few words, symbols, and images as possible.

There is another consideration related to speed besides the limitation of bandwidth. It is important to consider where and how these devices are likely to be used. Often device users walking or taking time out from a meeting or other activity. They are not seated comfortably at their desks or in their living rooms. The other constraints on these systems mean they are not generally the first choice for casual browsing. The user wants some information and wants it now. This is not the environment for enticing the visitor to explore the wonders of the site. A prompt and pointed response to a request will suit the users' needs and bring those users back another time.

The Small Screen

The small screen has been mentioned a number of times and an example was shown in the illustrations. While bandwidth and resolution on the screen will improve, the screen will not get larger. That is because smallness is a prized feature of many of the WAP enabled devices. Some devices, such as PDAs have larger screens than others. However, application developers must assume that the screen is small and may be viewed in difficult lighting environments. Interaction must be designed for ease of use under these circumstances.

Navigation

Because of the small screen, the basic model of a "document" becomes a deck of cards. Each card contains a small amount of information and usually contains an opportunity to link to another card in the same deck or in a different deck. WAP provides all the power of the Web to reach sites and to initiate processes on remote services. However, the results of those server processes and the information on the Web pages will be constrained by the presentation environment. Each WAP client must have a way to interact with a specified set of events triggered by user actions. The way these are made available and the ease of user access will vary. An accept button and a button that goes back to the previous card are the most dependable constants. This can be designed using a scripting language like XHTML MP and WML. Presenting navigation options as links in a list allows the user to scroll through the choices and accept the most appropriate one.

CONCLUSION: SUMMARY AND LOOK AHEAD

WAP technology could bring about the convergence of mobile communications and the Internet. With new technology come risks and opportunities. The expectations for WAP have been high and the results have not always kept up.

Today, the vast majority of microprocessors go into embedded systems, many of which only support standalone applications. While the technology is there to make these appliances communicate wirelessly with each other or with humans, progress has been limited. At same time, WAP and XHTMLMP offer a general purpose, interoperable presentation platform for user interfaces.

WAP has had seen huge success in Japan. Korea is also leading the world in providing advanced WAP services. WAP on top of the Code Division Multiple Access (CDMA 2000) network has been proven to be the state of the art wireless data infrastructure. Other technologies like Multi Media Messaging and Short Message Servicing (SMS) have combined with WAP to further drive the protocol. Since 2003 and 2004, mobile service providers including Vodafone and T-Mobile have used WAP to provide wireless services, resulting in a resurgence of the protocol.

WAP is sometimes considered to have failed to live up expectations and hype. It was earlier touted to be the Web on the phone. One contributor to the difficulties of developing WAP applications is the lack of good authoring tools. Despite the investment that companies have started to make in WAP, there are concerns about the technology's usefulness and appeal. There are challenges on both the side of the devices and the side of the protocols. However, the potential use of these devices is of increasing interest, providing motivation for work in developing an increasingly sophisticated set of resources.

A complicating issue in the deployment WAP applications is the protocol itself. The protocol was initially designed to support a range of different protocols like SMS, MMS, and IP. This has led to the development of a very complex protocol. The design was ambitious and the full realization of the expectations remains a challenge. WAP provides a mechanism for bringing the Web to small portable devices that have characteristics that make them unsuitable for interfacing to regular Web pages. There remains a great opportunity to realize this potential.

GLOSSARY

BioWAP: An illustration of the use of WAP protocols to access database resources. BioWAP provides access to bioinformatics databases and analysis programs.

ISO OSI Reference Model: The standard seven layer model of communication between computers over a network. The base model is often modified for specific purposes but serves as a well-known base reference.

Location Aware Advertising: Integration of global positioning services and WAP protocols to allow broadcast of information specific to a physical location. Examples might include warnings about road conditions or traffic problems or offers of special discounts on merchandize at a nearby business.

Mobile Information Device Profile (MIDP): A specification that combines Java and other web technologies to produce MIDlets. These are run using special software on the handheld device. They are similar to applets, but they remain on the device after an initial run.

Performance Enhancing Proxies: An intermediate process provider that serves to translate between the Web materials designed for standard desktop or laptop computers and the limitations of handheld devices.

Pull Information Delivery: The delivery of content initiated by a request from the receiver.

Push Information Delivery: The delivery of content initiated by the sender without an explicit request from the receiver.

Wireless Application Environment (WAE): The part of WAP corresponding to the Application Layer of the ISO OSI Reference Model. It consists of the Wireless Markup Language (WML), XHTML Mobile Profile, Wireless Cascading Style Sheets (WCSS), WBXML, WMLScript, vCard and vCalendar.

Wireless Application Protocol (WAP): A collection of protocol standards for communication between web servers and handheld mobile devices.

WBXML: A compact, binary representation of XML documents for efficient transmission without loss of semantic content.

Wireless Transport Layer Security: A protocol element used to provide secure service between a client and a pull gateway. WTLS provides server authentication.

CROSS REFERENCES

See *Wireless Channels; Wireless Internet*.

REFERENCES

Bechler, M., and J. Schiller. 2000. The need for the wireless application protocol (WAP) in cars, *Proceedings of the 7th World Congress on Intelligent Transport Systems*, Turin, November 2000.

Bennett, C. 2001. Wireless Application Protocol 2.0, http://www.samspublishing.com/articles/article.asp?p=23999 (accessed January 4, 2006).

Cassel, L. N. 2004. Wireless Application Protocol, *The Internet encyclopedia*. NY: John Wiley.

Claessens, J., V. Dem, D. De Cock, and B. Preneel. 2002. On the security of today's on-line Electronic Banking Systems, *Computers & Security* 2002, http://joris.claessens.ws/ (accessed January 20, 2006).

Device Manager IBM 2004, http://publib.boulder.ibm.com/infocenter/iwedhelp/v6r0/index.jsp?topic=/com.ibm.websphere.dms.doc/dm/jobs_firmware_oma.html (accessed January 7, 2006).

Enterprise Java Beans Technology, http://java.sun.com/products/ejb/ (accessed May 22, 2006).

Hakkila, J., and M. Isomursu. 2005. User experiences on location-aware mobile services, November 2005, *Proceedings of the 19th Conference of the Computer-Human Interaction Special Interest Group (CHISIG) of Australia on Computer-Human Interaction: Citizens Online: considerations for today and the future OZCHI' 05*.

Held, G. 2001. *Data over Wireless Networks Bluetooth, WAP and Wireless LAN's*. New York, NY: McGraw-Hill.

How long will WAP last?, http://www.thewirelessfaq.com/how_long_will_wap_last (accessed August 27, 2006).

Hung, K., and Y. T. Zhang. 2000. Information technology applications in biomedicine, *Proceedings, 2000 IEEE EMBS International Conference* on 9–10 Nov. 2000, 28–31, Digital Object Identifier 10.1109/ITAB.2000.892343.

Hung, K., and Y. T. Zhang. 2003. Implementation of a WAP-based telemedicine system for patient monitoring, *IEEE Transactions on Information Technology in Biomedicine,* 7 (2), June: 101–07.

Kim, J. K., S. J. Ahn, and J. W. Chung. 2003. Design and implementation of WAP-based LAN segment management system using RMON, *MIB, International Journal of Network Management* 13: 187–202 (DOI: 10.1002/nem.471).

Mahmoud, Q. K. H. 2003. J2ME MIDP and WAP complementary technologies, http://developers.sun.com/techtopics/mobility/midp/articles/midpwap/.

Milasinovic, B., and K. Fertalj. 2003. An e-mail connectivity solution for WAP-enabled mobile phone. *Proceedings of the 25th International Conference on Information Technology Interfaces* (16–19) June: 587–92.

Multimedia Messaging Service, GNU Free Documentation, http://en.wikipedia.org/wiki/Multimedia_Messaging_Service (accessed September 12, 2006).

Passani, L. XHTML MP Style Guide, http://developer.openwave.com/dvl/support/documentation/guides_and_references/xhtml-mp_style_guide/index.htm (accessed May 25, 2006).

Patil, A. WAP builds Java applications, http://www.128.ibm.com/developerworks/wireless/library/wi-entwap/ (accessed January 20, 2006).

Qadah, G. Z., and W. Al-Zouabi. 2005. An XML-based system for fixed and mobile delivery of electronic services. *Proceedings of the Second International Conference on Innovations in Information Technology (IIT'05)* http://www.it-innovations.ae/iit005/proceedings/.

Rao, H., et al. 2003. iMail: A WAP mail retrieving system *Information Sciences—Informatics and Computer Science, An International Journal*, 151, May, pp. 71–91.

Riikonen, P. et al. 2002. Mobile access to biological databases on the Internet, *IEEE Transactions on Biomedical Engineering* 49, (12): 1477–79.

Schafer, S. 2002. *Learning WML-WAP basics*, http://www.developer.com/ws/proto/article.php/1377381 (accessed January 4, 2006).

Short Message Service, GNU Free Documentation, http://en.wikipedia.org/wiki/Short_message_service.

SMS versus WAP, http://www.activexperts.com/activsms/sms/wap/ (accessed September 11, 2006).

WAP Architecture, Version 12-July-2001, Wireless Application Protocol Architecture Specification, WAP-210-WAPArch-2001071, http://www.wapforum.org/.

WAP publishing, in WAP Tutor. http://www.waptutor.org.uk/publishing.html (accessed May 29, 2006).

WAP Push Architectural Overview, Version 03-Jul-2001, http://www.wapforum.org/ (accessed January 10, 2006).

Wicher, D. D., and K. Getgen. Securing the Internet without wires, http://www-128.ibm.com/developerworks/wireless/library/wi-sectrends/ (accessed September 3, 2006).

Wireless Application Protocol, 2007. http://en.wikipedia.org/wiki/WAP (accessed May 20, 2006).

Wireless Application Protocol Environment, Version 7-Feb-2002. WAP-236-WAE Spec-20020207-a http://www.openmobilealliance.org/tech/affiliates/wap/wapindex.html (accessed January 11, 2006).

Wireless ATM

Amel Meddeb and Noureddine Boudriga, *University of the 7th of November at Carthage, Tunisia*

INTRODUCTION

The ATM technology is being intensively deployed to public and private communication networks. ATM is attractive because of its potential capability to support a variety of services and the development of applications (e.g., multimedia) that require constraining quality of service (QoS). ATM was designed for transmission over fiber-optic links characterized by extremely low error rate (of the order of 10^{-12}). As wireless services become popular, wireless extension to ATM will be needed to adapt the ATM technology to a wireless environment that will allow mobile users access to the network resources. The main advantage of wireless ATM (WATM) technology will be the seamless radio extension of ATM to mobile users and the support of multimedia communications. To deploy WATM, many issues first have to be addressed. Some of the major problems are related to: (a) the QoS provision in the presence of high bit error rate at the radio links; (b) the mobility management of mobile users; and (c) the provision of handoff services.

With respect to deploying ATM on wireless links, two different approaches are observed: the first approach, which is supported mainly by the ATM Forum, involves foreseeing the presence of ATM connections toward the wireless end user. This approach is discussed in this chapter. The second approach, which is preferred for International Mobile Telecommunications-2000 (IMT-2000) and Universal Mobile Telecommunication System (UMTS), involves foreseeing the use of ATM only in the core transport network and avoids the transport of ATM on the air interface.

WATM consists of three main components: a) the ATM switches, which integrate user-to-network interfaces (UNI) and network-to-network interfaces (NNI) with additional mobility support; b) the control and switching units, which provide mobility-related signaling (e.g., registration, de-registration, location, and handoff), handle data routing, and incorporate typical ATM switches; and c) the base stations (BSs), or access points (APs), which are attached to the control service unit (CSU) ports by means of high bandwidth links. The APs are responsible for the adaptation of ATM cells to radio packets (and vice versa) and their transmission over the radio link. Mobility management has two distinct components: a) location management, which translates user names to their current location, and b) handoff, which is a handover control for dynamic rerouting of connections when the terminal crosses cell boundaries. Figure 1 depicts a graphical overview of the WATM architecture.

A mobile terminal (MT) can move within the coverage area of the base station and communicate with other MTs, in the case of MT-to-MT calls, or with traditional ATM terminals, in the case of MT-to-fixed-terminal calls. The operation of the CSU component is supported by a database (DB), which is designed to keep track of the current location and status of MTs. The CSU also can be used for security services such as terminal authentication. Finally, the CSU is in charge of processing the MT-originated signaling messages related to mobility and the standard signaling messages for the setup and release of connections. On the other hand, the BSs work as traffic concentrators on the uplink and as splitters on the downlink.

To provide integrated broadband services to a variety of mobile users and applications, WATM supports the full range of ATM services, including the constant bit rate (CBR) service and the variable bit rate (VBR) service.

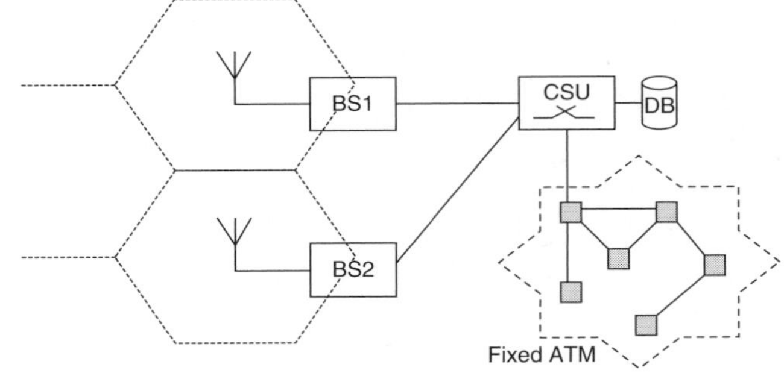

Figure 1: WATM architecture

Although the QoS of these services should be identical to those provided by a wired ATM, its provision may be constrained by the radio link access and the degree of terminal mobility. However, the benefits of WATM access technology should be observed by mobile users as a service and accessibility improvement. By providing the essential characteristics of ATM transmission, WATM can improve the performance of the QoS provision that is not achieved by other wireless networks.

The objective of this chapter is to discuss the major issues in WATM networking. The chapter is organized as follows: the first section introduces the foundations of WATM, followed by the requirements of WATM to fulfill its objectives. Next, we discuss the architecture and components of WATM. The following section introduces the protocol stack of WATM, followed by the extension of QoS in wireless systems using characteristics of ATM. We discuss the mechanisms applied to the wireless environment and adapted to WATM (e.g., handover and location management), and present the standards and implementation of products such as the wireless ATM network demonstrator (WAND) and rapidly deployable radio network (RDRN) before concluding the chapter.

FOUNDATIONS OF WATM

To make WATM easy to understand, we discuss in this section the major concepts and features of ATM and wireless technologies.

ATM Technology

ATM offers a high-speed network that integrates all types of information transfer, including real-time and non–real-time traffic. ATM represents one of the most important technologies for the wide area interconnection of heterogeneous systems. Its network is composed of a large number of switches that are connected to one another via network-to-network interface. This networking technology provides high bandwidth at low costs compared to traditional approaches that support different services by building separate dedicated networks. However, implementing ATM networks is not necessarily cheap because it requires optical backbone networks and high-speed ATM switches. The information transferred between network nodes is packaged into fixed-sized cells of 53 bytes, in which 5 bytes are reserved for the header, which contains the control information. Figure 2 depicts the structure of an ATM cell header, including six major fields. Field GFC represents the generic flow control, which is used to provide local functions such as identifying multiple stations that share a single ATM interface. The GFC field is typically not used and is set to a default value. The fields VPI and VCI identify the virtual path and the virtual channel, respectively, that the cell takes to reach its destination by passing through a series of switches. The PTI field represents the type of payload contained in the cell. The first bit of the PTI field indicates whether the cell contains user or control data. If the cell contains user data, the second bit of the PTI field indicates congestion, and the third indicates whether the cell is the last in a series of cells that represent a single AAL5 frame.

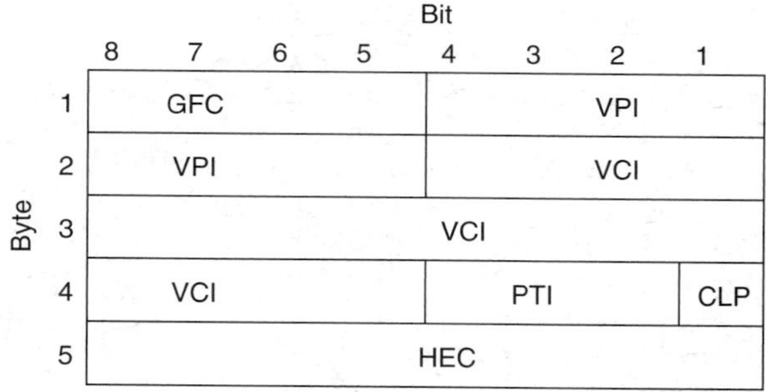

Figure 2: ATM cell header format for the UNI interface

The CLP field is a bit that is used to distinguish between high- and low-priority cells. It indicates whether the cell should be discarded when it encounters extreme congestion as it moves through the network. Finally, the HEC field indicates a checksum over the header.

ATM provides connection-oriented communication, meaning that before cells are transmitted, a connection is established between the source and destination. When the connection is set up, all cells are sent along the same route to the destination. Therefore, routing decisions take place only at the connection setup. Cells travel along virtual channels (VCs) and virtual paths (VPs); virtual paths contain a large number of virtual channels. Cells are switched according to the VP/VC identifier values contained in the incoming data. A routing table at each switch indicates the outgoing VPI/VCI for each incoming virtual channel (or incoming VPI/VCI). Hence, the VPI and VCI fields (present in the cell header) are altered as the cell goes through the switches. The typical routing protocol in ATM is the private network-to-network interface (PNNI), which divides the nodes into collections of nodes called peer groups. Peer group leaders represent their peer group members to the rest of ATM network. PNNI provides a mechanism for building hierarchies of peer groups and reduces the routing process to the construction of a route between peer group leaders and the delivery inside a peer group.

ATM signaling is the process used to establish and release ATM connections. PNNI signaling is used by an edge switch to set up the virtual channel in each switch along the path of that connection. When an end user submits a request for connection setup, the request is sent to the switch to which the end user is connected. The switch then acknowledges the request reception by sending back a call proceeding message. Between the switches along the path to destination, a PNNI setup message and a call proceeding message are sent until the destination switch is reached. If the destination agrees to set up a connection, it sends back a connect message. The connection is then set up and data can be sent.

Traffic Classes

ATM networks can be deployed to provide the transport of different data types. Five classes of services are defined in ATM:

- **Constant bit rate (CBR):** This service aims to transport CBR traffic with a fixed timing separation between data units. This service is appropriate for conventional digital voice and CBR video traffic.

- **Variable bit rate–real-time (VBR-rt):** This service is intended to transport VBR traffic combined with rigorous real-time requirements, such as video conferencing. The traffic is known to have a transmission rate that varies in time; however, ATM cannot introduce a delay variation between cells. This means that ATM tightly controls the average cell delay and the delay variation so that they do not exceed a certain value. However, occasional cell loss can be tolerated.
- **Variable bit rate–non–real-time (VBR-nrt):** This service does not provide a guaranteed delay bound. It provides a guaranteed average, but a certain amount of jitter can be tolerated. Nrt-VBR would be appropriate for data traffic, which has less strict delay requirements but still needs throughput guarantees like a local area network (LAN) interconnection.
- **Available bit rate (ABR):** This is a best effort service; neither rate nor delay can be guaranteed. The network will allocate a connection as much bandwidth as possible to meet the minimum values of the traffic contract. This service allows an ATM system to fill its channels to the maximum capacity when CBR or VBR traffics are low.
- **Unspecified bit rate (UBR):** This service does not offer any service guarantee. UBR is similar to ABR, but it does not guarantee minimum rate and bound on the cell loss rate. Typical use of UBR is best suited for IP packet transfer, file transfer, backup traffic, and e-mail delivery because they do not make any constraint on delivery.

To implement the aforementioned services, ATM uses a layer called the *ATM* adaptation layer (AAL), which adapts the incoming traffic to the ATM layers (including the physical support). As shown in Table 1, AAL is divided into two sublayers: the segmentation and reassembly (SAR) sublayer and the convergence sublayer (CS). Whereas the former sublayer transforms traffic into cells and classifies them, the latter provides traffic synchronization and error detection (Deane 1996). Four types of adaptation can be distinguished: AAL1, AAL2 (Makké et al. 2002; Villasenor-Gonzalez et al. 2002), AAL3/4, and AAL5. Table 1 discusses the major functions provided by the AAL for each type.

QoS Parameters

When a virtual channel is set up, the desired QoS is specified to make up a traffic contract between the end user and the network, which is guaranteed as long as the transmitted traffic on a connection conforms to the traffic descriptors specified in the traffic contract. To make a traffic contract well specified and to allow the negotiation of service parameters by the end user and the network, a set of QoS parameters is normalized for ATM. The QoS is specified by the following parameters:

Minimum cell rate (MCR): This parameter represents the minimum cell rate that the customer can accept.

Peak cell rate (PCR): This is the maximum rate at which the sender is expecting to send cells.

Sustained cell rate (SCR): This measures the required cell rate averaged over a long time interval.

Table 1: Major Functions of AAL Types

AAL Type	Targeted service	Details
1	Emulation of circuit	• The SAR uses the first byte of each cell to define a field of sequence in it protected by CRC.
2	Variable bit-rate video	• The SAR allows the support of low-speed data or voice. • CS provides for error correction and transports the timing information from source to destination. This is achieved by inserting time stamps or timing information into the convergence sublayer-protocol data unit.
3/4	Variable bit-rate data service	• The SAR uses four bytes per cell (sequence, priority, CRC, multiplexing). • CS adds information about delimitation of the data.
5	ABR data service	• CS generates a CRC and other identifiers (for the message). • SAR uses the bit PTI of the heading cell to identify the last cell of a message.

Cell delay variation (CDV): This parameter describes how uniformly the cells are delivered.

Cell delay variation tolerance (CDVT): This parameter describes the maximum acceptable difference in arrival time deviation from the expected cell rate.

Cell transfer delay (CTD): This parameter is the average interval of time (or average end-to-end delay) that a cell needs to travel from source to destination.

Cell loss rate (CLR): This parameter measures the fraction of sent cells that are lost or arrive so late at their destination that they are considered ineffective.

Cell error rate (CER): This represents the fraction of cells that arrive at the destination with one or more errored bits.

Cell misinsertion rate (CMR): This measures the fraction of cells that are delivered to the wrong address due to errors in the header of the received cell with respect to the number of all received cells by the destination.

Severely errored cell block ratio (SECBR): This is the ratio of N-cell blocks of which M cells contain errors.

Wireless Networking

Two categories of wireless systems can be distinguished in the literature. The first category uses point-to-point links with different bit rates and varying operational frequencies. The second category uses wireless data transmission with cellular architecture implemented with various techniques including code division multiple access (CDMA), space division multiple access (SDMA), time division multiple access (TDMA), and frequency division multiple access (FDMA). The wireless transmission systems that offer a roaming service include cellular data systems. Table 2 presents the data rates that correspond to different network and wireless techniques (Bertoni et al. 1994; Correia and Prasad 1997).

Low bit rates are offered by mobile networks that allow mobility and roaming possibilities. For example, the GSM data services offer limited QoS with respect to the QoS required by multimedia applications. Many improvements have been provided to GSM to improve its data transmission services (e.g., GPRS and HSCSD). On the other hand, the UMTS was developed to provide better QoS and security. It achieves bit rates up to 2Mb/s locally, and lower bit rates in wide area coverage. UMTS represents one of the significant improvements for the second-generation (2G) wireless systems (Raychaudhuri 1996).

Wireless Provision of QoS

QoS provisioning in wireless networks cannot use the paradigm defined for fixed networks unless it is enhanced. This is mainly because of the severe variation in the network resources availability in a wireless connection. This variation is induced by two natural factors: wireless link and mobility. In contrast to links of conventional wired networks, wireless links suffer from a high bit error rate (BER), which results in a packet loss on the wireless medium. It also induces packet delay and jitter, if error recovery mechanisms are utilized. Typically, the BER of a wireless link can be improved by designing better transmission and reception wireless subsystems. However, it is commonly agreed that there is a limit to the level of improvement because there is trade-off between BER and bandwidth in a wireless link.

On the other hand, mobility effects occur through fading and handoff. The fading characteristics of a wireless channel vary greatly based on time and spatial dependencies.

Table 2: Wireless Data Rates

Wireless Data Access	Achieved Data Rates	Mode
Digital European cordless telephone (DECT)	<1Mbits/s	per user
GSM data (general packet radio service [GPRS], high-speed circuit-switched data [HSCSD], cellular digital packet data [CDPD])	<144 kbits/s	per user
UMTS	>5 Mbits/s	shared
Industrial, scientific, and medical (ISM)-band WLANs	>54 Mbits/s	shared
High performance local area network (HIPERLAN)	<20 Mbits/s	shared
Wireless fidelity (WiFi)	>100 Mbits/s	shared
Worldwide Interoperability for Microwave Access (WiMax)	>2 Gbits/s	shared

Added to interference, fading will force the transmission link to vary its bandwidth. Moreover, as a mobile terminal roams in a wireless network and hands off from one BS to another, the wireless (e.g., the bandwidth in the new radio cell) and wired resources (if needed) would change. This can result in a major change in the availability of the network resources. Additionally, depending on the overhead of the signaling system and the rerouting protocol, the QoS-level degradation due to the connection moves during handoff. Therefore, the major issue in wireless and mobile networks with respect to QoS provisioning is to deal with the variation in resource availability. A solution to this depends on the type and level of QoS that a mobile terminal wants. For example, in a video connection, the quality of video received at the mobile terminal is closely dependent on packet loss and jitter. A solution for this is to require the mobile network to match the QoS guarantees of a fixed network, regardless of the variation. This means that the service providers have to increase the degree of pre-provisioning in the network to a high degree to mitigate packet delays and losses. This solution is unacceptable because it does not accept varying degrees of QoS guarantees and generates a great number of packet losses. A better solution would be to change the fixed service guarantee contract between the application (or mobile terminal) and the network, and to design applications so that they can accept varying degrees of QoS guarantees and generate packet flows consisting of subflows, each with a different level of loss and delay sensitivity.

Finally, the large differences between wired and wireless links in terms of BER and bandwidth result in the statement that BSs are essential for the provision of high levels of QoS. The interface between the wired part and the wireless link at a BS must make certain that the packet-level QoS of a subflow is met according to its predefined quality requirements requested by the aforementioned application. One of the mechanisms that may be needed for this is a multiple-access control protocol that maintains a minimum level of availability for the shared wireless resources. The provided availability has to offer better protection for the transmission of packets over the wireless link by implementing the required QoS of the subflow, because a unified error-control scheme would not be suitable for all subflows.

Routing is another source of QoS dissatisfaction in wireless and mobile network. Routing protocols must take into consideration the required QoS. First, every handoff operation will induce a period of time, during which the rerouting process is executed (it lasts from the time the handoff is initiated until its completion). During this period, packets cannot be transmitted and may be delayed or lost. The length of this period is dependent on the rerouting protocol. Second, the newly established route (after the handoff is performed) might not provide the same level of QoS as the one that was left.

Benefits and Problems of WATM

Because ATM provides end-to-end considerations of traffic performance, it reduces the network complexity and improves its flexibility; this is why WATM deploys a cell-relay paradigm developed for ATM. It has been adapted as the next generation of wireless architectures (Tomar and Singh 2005; Raychaudhuri 1996). WATM was intensively studied in the 1990s because it offered certain benefits. Some of these benefits are as follows:

WATM benefits. ATM technique can combine multiple media transmissions into wired networks while scaling well with different network types such as LAN, metropolitan area network (MAN), and wide area network (WAN). The motivation for integrating ATM into the wireless environment is the fact that wired communication networks can be dominated by ATM networks and the QoS can be managed via ATM-like contact. Therefore, the packet transmission, in which the packet processing time can be minimal, is generally used by WATM. One fundamental characteristic of ATM networking is the provision of bandwidth on demand. This proves that, until WATM, application development was constrained by the fact that data transmission schemes could not support various QoS parameters; in addition, the maximum data transmission bandwidth with which the applications have to be interfaced is relatively small. ATM has removed these constraints, and bandwidth has become less expensive as a result. Additionally, ATM provides good support for various traffic classes (Raychaudhuri 1996).

WATM access aims to improve service and accessibility to mobile terminals. To preserve the characteristics of ATM transmission, WATM improves performance and QoS in the ways discussed earlier. The enhancement is not attainable by conventional communication systems like cellular systems, cordless networks, or wireless LANs. Integrating ATM in a wireless environment has many technical benefits over the wireless networks that are not offered by any other networking technology.

WATM problems. The current WATM approaches impose some limits on the development of wireless solutions based on ATM. Even still, ATM shows great promise as the infrastructure technology of choice for wireless networks. There are, however, different areas in which ATM developments have been less important. One of the major issues is that ATM presents a highly complex technology. As explained previously, ATM was developed to be used with virtually unlimited bandwidth, low bit error rates, and point-to-point connections. The radio medium, used in mobile networks, features an inherently limited bandwidth, a high bit error rate, and a contending nature. Using small cells and radio access in the Gigahertz band can overcome the limited bandwidth; this provides very high bandwidth per radio cell and mobile terminal. Advanced channel coding and ARQ schemes in a logical link control (LLC) protocol can handle the high error rates, whereas a medium access control (MAC) protocol can monitor the use of the broadcast medium (Wasi 1995).

The ATM payload is relatively small. Therefore, the addition of any single byte in the header will greatly affect wireless channel throughput efficiency. The ATM header in the wireless medium may be compressed for the purpose of reducing the packet overhead. However, this compression will generate additional complexity at the wireless/wired interface (where the compression/decompression process takes place) and will increase the total data transmission time (Tomar and Singh 2005).

WATM REQUIREMENTS

The typical objective of most WATM proposals is to design a wireless network of integrated services and provide extensions of ATM-based service capabilities in a relatively transparent, seamless, and efficient manner. This means that the proposed WATM systems should support a reasonable range of services, bit rates, and QoS scenarios. Two classes of requirements are of note: system requirements and user/operator requirements.

System Requirements

As shown in Figure 3, the minimal set of the requirements that WATM should comply with can be divided into four different classes: a) the network access requirement; b) the system functions and signaling requirements; c) the requirements of offered services; and d) the requirements imposed by the supported environments. This section discusses the major requirements in these classes that make WATM special (Jabbari et al. 1995).

Network Access Requirements

The set of requirements imposed by the network access capabilities generates different issues. The first issue imposes the need to extend ATM signaling to the wireless end. The second issue necessitates mobility management by the WATM network. To resolve these issues and allow for the establishment of WATM connections, two approaches have been considered. The first approach is called *ATM over the air*, and the second is called the *interconnecting of wireless and wired parts*. For both of these approaches, it is possible to preserve the transmission characteristics of ATM to the customer access node.

One of the reasons not to use ATM in a wireless environment is that it is far too expensive to extend ATM to the user terminal compared to the advantages this can provide. To reduce the extension cost, existing installations can be used with the upgrade of the switched connections with wireless interfaces to obtain more bandwidth for terminals. A second reason is the amount of modifications needed for the standard broadband integrated services digital network (B-ISDN) signaling to properly handle the terminal mobility, because mobile users have to be able to move within the coverage area provided by the BS. The problem is that the current signaling standards do not support mobility of terminals.

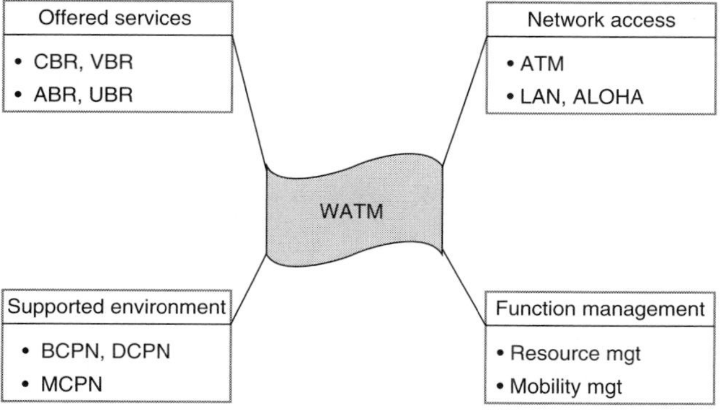

Figure 3: WATM requirements

System Functions and Signaling

ATM control processing is based on three functions: the call admission control, the call control, and the traffic policing. These functions have to be implemented within the WATM network in order to consider the wireless and mobility effects. In addition, other functions have to be added because of the wireless link and user mobility. The following aspects should be considered when implementing these functions:

- *Mobility*: This is an important aspect for the mobile terminals. WATM should be able to offer mobility services by allowing handoffs of acceptable speeds within the mobile customer access network. It is the responsibility of the host network (public ATM network) to offer roaming service between radio domains, because this service has been implemented by mobile telecommunication systems. There are many ways to implement mobility management, including a large spectrum of the existing implementations. Global system for mobile communications (GSM), for instance, solves the problem using special registers (home location register and visitor location register). Another way to implement mobility on WATM is to base it on the advanced intelligent network technologies. UMTS selects one technology to perform mobility management. Both the register and intelligent network approaches would be interesting solutions for WATM.
- *Security and privacy*: Security needs are important for transmission protection and end-to-end application security. Wireless transmission imposes new constraints on security compared to other transmissions because specific attacks can be performed on the wireless medium (e.g., replay attacks, spoofing, etc.). In WATM, packets are transmitted via the wireless interface so that the protection level is hard to determine because of the complexity and power requirements of security algorithms. However, a minimal service needs to be provided: the authentication of mobile terminals and BS.
- *Traffic and resource management (RM)*: These aspects are necessary when wireless access is used. As explained in the previous section, resource availability may vary because of the mobility (handoff), fading, and bit errors. Although ATM has included some traffic and congestion management functions, it is important to extend these to the wireless part. The customer resource management may need to be considered in the planning phase of the network access system. The improvement of the radio resource operation has to be considered by the network.
- *Call admission control (CAC)*: The CAC is a mechanism that decides whether a new call can be accepted or rejected. CAC may have to consider more than one virtual path at the same time and should depend on the architecture of the wireless access system. This introduces a certain level of complexity because wireless systems

contain multiple radio transceivers. Moreover, the traffic policing units have to ensure that all calls correspond to the traffic. The *discarded cells* are a metric that can be used to measure the QoS over the wireless links. However, these may not show the real loss of frames at the AAL5, for example, because if one of the cells in a frame is discarded by the AP, whole frames may be discarded on the AAL5 level.

Offered Services

WATM systems have the possibility to achieve high rates (exceeding 20 Mbits/s each), and they can provide support for multimedia services. The wired part of the WATM is the ATM network, which provides services that cope well—ATM networks offer flexible platforms to applications by supporting different service classes. In order to be able to offer an attractive wireless platform to multimedia applications, all of the service classes defined for the fixed ATM network should also be supported over the wireless link.

ABR is attractive for the WATM access system, especially for data communications, because it offers a way to control the cell flow using resource management cells. If the radio link is congested, the source can be notified to decrease the generated traffic. In the case of interference or fading, the minimum requirement for ABR traffic is the data loss or the impossibility of congestion signaling. On the other hand, the UBR service does not suffer from this phenomenon because QoS is not guaranteed for UBR traffic contract.

Supported Environment

There are several kinds of environments in wireless technologies that can be designed to support a mixture of bit rates and QoS parameters. The following categories of environments are maintained by the Resource Assessment and Conservation Engineering (RACE) research program (Raychaudhuri 1996):

- The Domestic Customer Premises Network (DCPN). This environment is characterized by the incapacity to update the location. In this case, the system is reduced to a radio extension of the network. The WATM service is provided only in small, isolated areas, perhaps individual cells. No mobility is provided in this environment.
- The Business Customer Premises Network (BCPN). BCPN defines a private environment, which is characterized by a private network covering the buildings of a (large) company. BCPN offers PABX-like functions within the radio-covered area. Therefore, functions like handoff and paging are implemented in this multicell environment. However, the mobility management functions are reduced to location update and handoff (fading, for example does not have to be taken into consideration).
- The Mobile Customer Premises Network (MCPN). The MCPN environment provides coverage within a mobile unit. MCPN provides the functions of DCPN and BCPN and adds the interface that is required to provide the access to the fixed network.
- The Public Network (PN): The PN has similar characteristics to a public mobile network such as the GSM network. It also provides functions for paging, location updating, roaming, and handoffs.

User/Operator Requirements

Communication services are becoming more common and are today used by people in both their work and daily lives. The basic requirement for the mobile user is easy to define: users require *ubiquitous access* to advanced communication services, regardless of location and mobility. There should be no significant difference in the type of services accessed by a user in any of the locations the mobile user can visit. On the other hand, communication services offer more and more advanced multimedia characteristics to enhance their ease-of-use and efficiency. The content of these services is not usually offered by the network operator but by an external service (or content) provider; regardless of who is the service provider, the service should be presented to users with the appropriate QoS.

The degree of mobility that must be supported by WATM is a concern. WATM focuses on the needs of mobile users. For that reason, it is necessary that it not only provide a wireless link to ATM but also support a high level of user mobility, so that communication is possible wherever the user is located. When moving between remote locations, the user mobile terminal might be powered off and thus may be restarted in various locations. This means that mobile users expect the WATM to support roaming and handoff support. In fact, the user needs to be able to move around in every location while maintaining active communication. To achieve seamless roaming capabilities for a user, WATM needs to support a number of radio interfaces.

Seen from the operator point of view, integrating mobile and fixed communication serves one the major concerns of the operator, which is the cost-effective service provision. The growth in mobile communication varies from one network to another and can be difficult to predict. Thus, an operator may need the increase to be made using progressive and cost-effective measures. This means that the initial investment to enhance the fixed infrastructure for mobile communication might be acceptable and that following investments can be done in a progressive way. This allows small companies to effectively employ wireless technology and allows large networks to increase coverage as demand grows. Therefore, the main operator requirement for WATM is to facilitate maximal sharing and reuse of fixed ATM resources and functions. In private networks, this will be a significant way to reduce the cost of advanced networking solutions for integrating wireless technologies. In the public networks, this constitutes a key requirement for the operator to stay alive.

Finally, WATM needs to support the full multimedia, multiservice semantics of fixed ATM. This is required to maintain the basic service requirements on WATM to support multimedia. Moreover, mobility should be transparent to the parties involved in communication. Communication between a fixed and a mobile terminal should be possible even if the fixed terminal has no special knowledge of the other user's mobility. In addition, WATM needs to support a number of radio interfaces to achieve seamless roaming capabilities for a user.

WIRELESS ATM ARCHITECTURES

Most of the literature on this subject discusses different solutions, models, and architectures for WATM; this section presents the major developed architectures. Several architectural components—including the fixed wireless components, mobile end users, and mobile switches—are also discussed in this section for the sake of clarity.

Wireless Integration

Integrating mobility with the existing set of ATM standards requires a compatibility of the wireless protocols with the fixed ATM architecture. To integrate wireless, a solution has to maintain the fixed ATM architecture as a subset of the WATM architecture. From a user perspective, the concept of integration means that a network appears as a seamless and coherent entity. When accessing a service, a WATM user should not need to be aware of whether access is by way of optical cables or radio links. From a network design perspective, integration handles a number of network issues. Integration includes using the same network functions and protocols for common operations, sharing network infrastructure, and providing the same set of services.

Based on the reason that integration of mobility into fixed ATM is the core concept of WATM, the integration of mobility can be reflected in the architectures defining WATM through the identification of three main alternatives: a) reuse of the fixed ATM architecture; b) added mobility to the ATM architecture; and c) enhanced ATM architecture. The first alternative assumes that the WATM can, without loss of efficiency, reuse the fixed ATM architecture. Using this approach, the WATM architecture will basically be equal to the fixed ATM architecture. This approach is generally infeasible when mobility is required, because this would mean that wireless operation does not introduce any functional changes to the ATM fixed network architecture.

Using the second alternative, WATM simply introduces additional functions into the network architecture in such a way that authorizes these functions to remain clearly separated from the fixed network aspects. If the features are isolated from the fixed ATM, WATM could be introduced by simply adding a separate, parallel architecture for it. This alternative has one desirable feature: it allows WATM to be introduced as a modular addition to fixed ATM. In its simplest form, this alternative is to a certain extent implausible, because the wireless operations and ATM functions interoperate to achieve mobility objectives, which does not cope with the simplicity of the interface that the wireless architecture should have with fixed ATM.

The third alternative appears to be the most likely way for wireless system architectures to integrate with fixed ATM network—it aims at modifying the already existing architecture. For some aspects of WATM related to mobility management and QoS provision, this approach is unavoidable. In cases in which modifications are necessary, it is commonly agreed that the amount of modifications can be kept very limited and that enhancing the fixed architectures is achievable. Unfortunately, a couple of problems are inherent in extending the ATM architecture: a) equipment built based on earlier standards might not be able to use the new architecture; and b) equipment conforming to the enhanced architecture might suffer from performance penalty, if used only to support fixed communication.

Besides the aforementioned alternative architectures, it is likely that WATM will develop through an evolutionary process in which many of the aforementioned alternatives can be used for a given architecture at different times. A typical evolutionary scenario to build the architecture could start with a WATM simply reduced to the fixed ATM architecture. In the next evolutionary step, wireless functions should be considered. At this point, wireless specific solutions could be considered and developed; however, a solution could potentially be acquired from the shelf. This might lead to the definition of a separate architecture for WATM according to the second alternative. Finally, as wireless systems become more widely used, the next step could allow fixed users to make special provisions for communication with wireless users. In this step, provision would be made for the fixed users who need access to some of the functions and capabilities of the WATM architecture.

Architectures and Components

User requirements of WATM are captured in the *service architecture*, and the operator requirements are captured in the *network architecture*. The requirement that WATM should provide the same service paradigm as a fixed ATM network is taken as the starting point to discuss the relevance of the ATM service architecture and modifications required to adapt it to mobile systems.

The purpose of service architecture is twofold: first, the service architecture must be defined in terms of a sufficiently small set of points or regions within the continuum formed by all possible user requirements. If a modular definition of the services combines simplicity with flexibility and power of expression, the network designer's task is made easier without compromising the initial user requirements. Second, service architecture provides a simple model of the capabilities of a network to potential network users. End users can benefit from this, because they need a clear view of network capabilities in order to subscribe to a network. Therefore, the service architecture typically performs a descriptive function. On the other hand, the service architecture has more central importance to the application developers and network operators, because end users are protected from the details of network use and operation. The network architecture can be defined as a set of constraints on the implementation architectures. It must be feasible to incorporate the set of functions defined by the implementation architectures into the nodes defined by the network architecture. Five architectural components can be considered in the following, including the fixed wireless components, mobile end-user devices, and mobile switches. The mobile end-user devices communicate directly with the fixed network switching devices via wired or wireless channels. Mobile switches can be connected either directly or via another mobile switch to the fixed network switches (Cong 1997).

- *Fixed wireless components*: In fixed wireless LANs, there are fixed end-user devices and switching devices, which are used to establish connections via wireless channels. In these kinds of situations, the data transmissions are made on the wireless medium, assuming that no mobility management is provided.
- *Mobile terminals*: In the digital cellular and wireless LANs, the mobile end user devices communicate directly with the fixed switching devices using wireless channels. To support the ATM connections, it is essential that the end-user devices have a wireless terminal adaptor, which communicates with the wireless access point (WAP) in the fixed switches.
- *Mobile switches with fixed end users*: Wireless channels connect end-user devices with switches. In this case, the end-user device and the switch are considered mobile equipment. There can be more than one end-user device attached to one switch. The switch has to establish connections with the fixed components using wired or wireless channels. To this end, WAP and wireless terminal adapters are used to enhance fixed and mobile switches.
- *Mobile switches with mobile users*: When the end user wants to establish a connection, it first requests it from a mobile switch, which then sets up a connection with the fixed network switches either directly or via another mobile switch. WAPs and wireless terminal adapters are also needed to support mobility. This scenario also considers end-user devices as mobile.

REFERENCE MODEL

To add mobility to the ATM network, extensions to the ATM protocol can be made. Moreover, the key functionalities of the planes and layers in the ATM protocol architecture have to be adapted to the WATM context.

WATM Protocol Architecture

WATM protocol architecture is based on the integration of radio access and mobility features within the standard ATM protocol stack. The general philosophy for adding mobility and broadband radio access to ATM is outlined in Raychaudhuri (1996), as depicted in Figure 4, which shows that a WATM system may be partitioned into two relatively independent parts: a mobile ATM infrastructure and a radio access segment, each of which can be designed and specified separately. This facilitates standardization by multiple organizations and allows for a progressive evolution of radio access technologies without having to modify the core mobile ATM network specification.

The protocol architecture defines what protocols are used at the different interfaces of a system. Since the first design of the open system interconnection (OSI) protocol reference model, every protocol definition has followed the layered approach. Therefore, the protocol architecture describes the different interfaces of the network in terms of layered stacks. To achieve integration of wireless with fixed ATM, the layered stacks of wireless and fixed ATM should coincide for those interfaces that are common. Two domains of interest can be identified in the protocol architecture: the user and control planes of the ATM network. The protocols in the user plane transport data, whereas the control plane protocols are used for signaling. Typically, the control and user planes converge at some layers (e.g., the ATM layer, in the case of ATM) so that the lowest layers of the planes are common. In ATM, the ATM and upper-layer protocols are handled in an end-to-end manner.

To be well matched with ATM, WATM should therefore embrace these key ATM protocols. The protocol architecture for WATM must allow fixed systems to communicate with mobile wireless nodes using the ATM protocol suite. In the protocol architecture for ATM, the control plane architecture is rather complicated. A distinction between the UNI and the NNI must be made for the control plane. In the UNI control plane, the connection control protocol—generally referred to as ITU Q.2931—is used to control connection setup and release. The integrated layer management interface (ILMI) protocol, defined by the ATM Forum, is used for interface management and functions such as address assignment. At the NNI in private networks, the PNNI protocol replaces the Q.2931 per ATM Forum recommendations. For public networks based on the ITU signaling standards, a protocol architecture exists for the NNI. The architecture is based on the Signalling System 7 and uses four layers.

To extend the protocol architecture of ATM to support wireless users, two objectives have been considered: a) any modifications to the user plane protocol stack should occur below the ATM layer in order to achieve end-to-end transparency; and b) signaling should remain compatible with fixed ATM where common functions exist but be implemented as a modular extension for mobile-specific aspects. In the case of protocol architectures at the UNI, significant convergence can be seen. Especially with regard to the user plane, most existing proposals are rather similar. In these proposals, the major modification

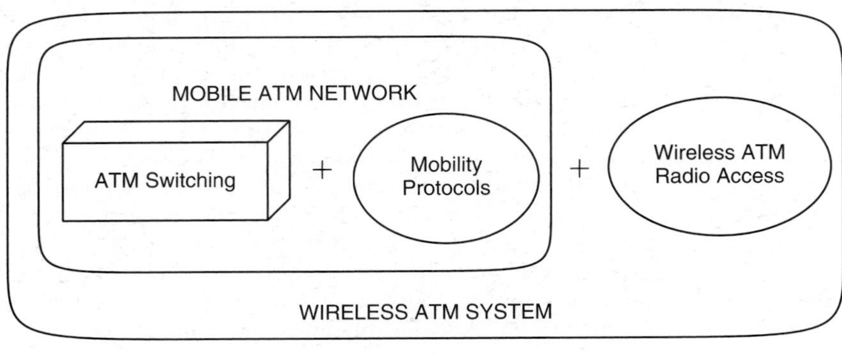

Figure 4: Modular protocol architecture of WATM system

has been to substitute the physical layer at the radio interface with three radio protocol layers, as illustrated by Figure 4. The three layers replacing the physical layer aim to provide a sufficiently constant QoS over the radio interface in order to ensure a radio link performance that maintains end-to-end QoS.

In Figure 4, the radio physical layer (PHY) is in charge of the radio transmission operations, including modulation and power control. This layer is rather dependent on the targeted frequency range and cell size. Schemes for physical layer and implementations exist in a number of frequency ranges, including the 2.5 GHz ISM band, 5 GHz, and 40/60 GHz. The PHY layer is split into two sub-layers: the physical layer convergence procedure (PLCP) and the physical medium dependent (Hyon 2001). Many types of modulations can be used such as equalized quadrature phase shift keying (QPSK), quadrature amplitude modulation (QAM), multi-carrier orthogonal frequency division multiplexing (OFDM), and spread-spectrum CDMA. Some researches focus on the use of CDMA because it can offer multiple advantages, including a good capacity and better-quality signal. Selection of modulation method and bit rate for the WATM PHY is an important standardization for both ETSI and the ATM Forum (Deane 1996).

The medium access control layer permits the radio interface to be shared by managing multiple access and contention (Sfikas, Apostolas, and Tafozolli 1998; Yuan and Motoyama 2002). In WATM, an important feature of the MAC is to allow each ATM virtual channel to be separately processed at the radio interface, so that the virtual channels can be provided with the requested QoS also at the radio interface. Distributed MAC protocols, used in existing wireless LANs (WLANs), do not provide adequate performance for WATM. This is partially a result of: a) the fact that the LAN protocols assume a much bigger payload to work efficiently; and b) the current LAN protocols cannot provide performance guarantees as required by the ATM QoS model. Subsequently, a number of new MAC protocols addressing the above issues have been proposed for this purpose. A large set of these protocols control resources by means of a single entity. If this entity is attentive to the QoS requirements of the different active connections, it can provide QoS guarantees.

The following features have to be considered to design a MAC protocol (Cong 1997):

- *Access mode*: In general TDMA, FDMA, CDMA, or a hybrid combination of these schemes can be used for accessing WATM. Because of the use of the statistical TDMA in ATM networks and because of the high bandwidth observed on the physical channel, a hybrid TDMA/FDMA scheme has been proposed in WATM systems.
- *Duplex schemes*: Two duplex schemes are considered for WATM systems: time division duplex (TDD) and frequency division duplex (FDD). TDD presents the disadvantage of generating additional overhead. However, it has the advantage of efficiency gained from the statistical multiplexing of the uplink and downlink.
- *Signaling of slot assignments*: Once the capacity allocation is determined, the slot assignments have to be signaled to the wireless terminals. This is done by grouping the reservation messages for a specific time interval into a signaling burst.
- *Transmission of capacity requests*: To guarantee the correct execution of a service strategy, the scheduler has to be informed (often, as frequently as possible) about the status of the queues inside the wireless terminals, which is performed by the transmission capacity request messages over the uplink.

The wireless data link control (DLC) layer is naturally used to enhance the error performance of the lower layers within the QoS requirements of the connections (e.g., delay bounds). For that, error-detection and retransmission protocols and forward error correction methods have to be used (Zhong et al. 2001). Mechanisms such as selective retransmission are used in different DLC proposals. Considering the control plane, the proposal views are divergent to some extent. The main theme appears to be that the fixed ATM connection control protocol is reused for the connection management. Mobility is embedded into the connection control protocol in some proposals, but most proposals use a separate protocol for mobility specific functions (see Figure 5).

To specify wireless functions, a wireless header and trailer are added over the radio link. In a wireless environment, it is necessary to use a wireless frame over the radio link encapsulating several ATM cells. This allows necessary overhead over a larger data payload. Figure 6 depicts the functions supported by the DLC layer. In the unified model language (UML) diagram, arrows show

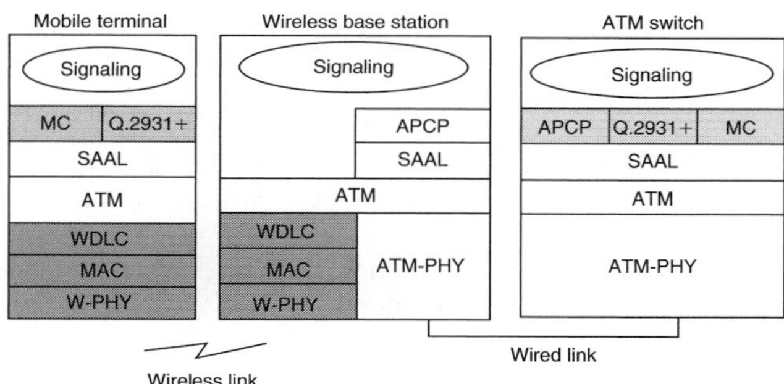

Figure 5: Control plane protocol architecture at the WATM switch UNI

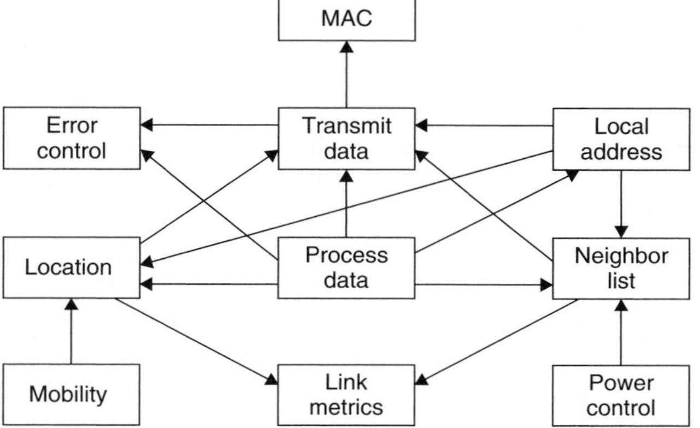

Figure 6: DLC layer architecture

the dependency among functions. For example, the data transmission function depends on MAC functions to obtain the transmission time and the used channel.

Major Functions

Figure 6 depicts the major functions implemented in different WATM architecture proposals; in the following section, we summarize the main features of these functions.

Protocol Q.2931+ refers to a generic, improved version of the fixed ATM connection management protocol (ITU Q.2931, or ATM Forum 4.0). The basic enhancements of this protocol have considered the support to handover. This enhancement only comprises two additional signaling messages. It is therefore feasible to include these messages in the basic connection management protocol. In addition, some modifications to parameters and information elements of the existing Q.2931 messages can be handled. This is required mainly to support mobile specific QoS aspects according to the service architecture. With these modifications, protocol Q.2931+ can be used for both fixed and mobile communication without significant overhead.

An access point control protocol (ACPC) is used for the interaction between the switch and the radio access system. This protocol allows the switch to control the radio access system during connection setup and handoff. The MAC protocol refers to the protocol(s) used to implement mobility control. Using a separate protocol for mobile-specific features makes the UNI protocol architecture modular. This feature is important to provide because it is in accordance with the architecture principles found in ATM, in which a number of additional protocols were proposed to achieve a high degree of modularity in the protocol architecture.

The key issues of the WATM architecture model, illustrated in Figure 6, relate to the signaling activity. The signaling ATM adaptation layer (SAAL) protocol is used to transfer the connection control protocol. Because SAAL protocol is connection oriented, it is relatively badly suited for a mobile network in which the communicating parties move between UNIs, as can happen during a handoff. This can be solved by introducing an additional network layer protocol to the WATM control plane that is capable of high-speed routing. This would allow the mobile to maintain a virtual link with the switch despite handoffs. However, a major problem occurs as a result of using a routing protocol WATM: the protocol architecture for fixed and WATM differ as far as the lower layers in the control plane stacks are concerned.

Finally, a radio resource control (RRC) is needed to support the control plane functions related to the radio access layer (RAL). The RAL should support radio resource control and management functions for the PHY, MAC, and DLC layers. The design issues of RAL include: a) control/management syntax for PHY, MAC, and DLC layers; b) meta-signaling support for mobile ATM; and c) interface to the ATM control plane (Hakan 1995). The management and control of radio resources are operated in parallel with communication control procedures. The basic management of radio resources is inherent to the radio resources control plane, whereas the overall carrier and connection control (including radio channel activation and handover execution) is managed by the communication control plane.

QUALITY OF SERVICE IN WATM

ATM provides five QoS classes of services: CBR, ABR, VBR-rt, VBR-nrt, and UBR. Functions related to the implementation of QoS in ATM are usage parameter control (UPC) and connection admission control (CAC). Typically, UPC function is implemented at the network edges and ensures that the traffic generated over a connection conforms to the declared traffic parameters. Traffic in excess may be dropped or transported on a best effort basis. The CAC function is performed by all switches and determines whether the QoS requirements of a connection can be satisfied by the available resources.

Existing implementations of WATM have chosen to maintain the existing QoS model and allow transparent extension of fixed ATM applications to the domain of wireless access. The problem with QoS provision in WATM is that it is hard to change dynamic QoS parameters for an active connection. When a new connection is requested, a set of QoS requirements is attempted. If the specified QoS cannot be satisfied by the wireless link, the connection is rejected. QoS in WATM requires a set of cooperating mechanisms at three levels:

- *At the network*: In addition to the ATM QoS mechanisms that are assumed available on the wired network, a mechanism for QoS renegotiation is useful. This authorizes the network and the mobile terminals to renegotiate a new-connection QoS when the existing QoS requirements can be maintained during a handoff.
- *At the radio interface*: A QoS-capable MAC layer is required. The mechanisms needed are resource reservation and allocation for ATM virtual circuits for various classes of QoS, and scheduling to meet delay requirements. In addition, a mechanism for error control is needed to cope with radio link nature. Finally a CAC mechanism is required to limit access to the multiple access radio link in order to maintain QoS for the serviced connections.
- *At the mobile terminal*: Mobile terminals implement several mechanisms related to QoS provisioning. These mechanisms take place at the MAC and network layers. In addition, some mechanisms at the application layer may be needed to cope with variations in the available QoS as a result of radio link degradation and terminal mobility.

The control of the QoS is handled by a controller associated with a sender and a receiver and using a control channel. For AAL5, the used connections accept an additional QoS by passing a QoS structure. To do so, a control of the QoS parameters is independently specified by the network level; this requires good knowledge of network behavior. Because this alternative provides maximum performance from the network, it is used by WATM (Hakan 1995). With regard to the ABR service category, a flow control scheme is specified by ATM forum in the traffic management (TM) specification 4.0. The source

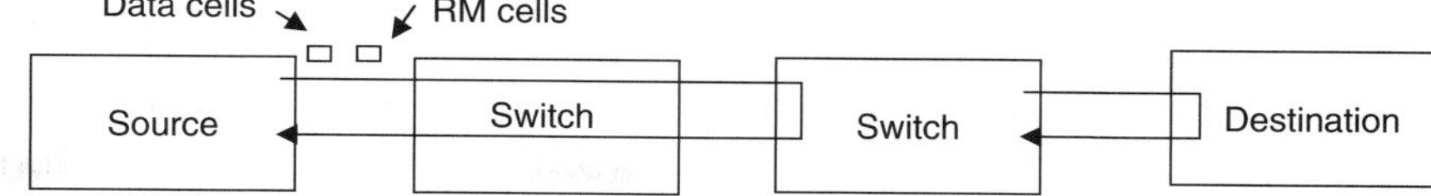

Figure 7: Explicit ABR flow control

periodically sends user and management cells downward to the destination, to inform a source of an ABR connection about the available bandwidth. As shown in Figure 7, the destination evaluates the congestion status and the supported cell rate of the connection at each switch and returns the resource management cells to the source.

The following two sections consider in more detail the major QoS mechanisms used at the MAC and the network layers.

MAC Mechanisms

The radio link in WATM is typically a multiple-access channel shared by various mobile terminals. Different multiple-access technologies can be implemented with multiple access channels, as described earlier; these include a combination of FDMA and TDMA. Each radio port operates on a certain frequency band. The mechanisms include the resource reservation, the allocation mechanism, and the scheduling function (Sfikas, Apostolas, and Tafozolli 1998; Yuan and Motoyama 2002; Porter et al. 1996).

Resource Reservation and Allocation Mechanism

WATM can use a TDMA/TDD scheme for medium access. This scheme allows the flexibility to partition the frame dynamically for downlink and uplink traffic, depending on the traffic load in each direction. Typical features of this scheme include the following:

- An important part of each slot is used for forward error control (FEC).
- A separate contention region in the frame is used for mobile terminals.
- Control packets are used for bandwidth requests and allocation announcements.
- WATM cells are modified ATM cells with added data link control and cyclic redundancy information.

In the downlink direction, the WATM is transported by various ATM connections termination using different mobile terminals. After the cells arrive at the fixed network, the allocation of TDMA slots for specific connections is based on the connection traffic and QoS parameters. In the uplink, the allocation is based on requests from the mobile terminals. The transaction of cells from multiple active connections at a mobile terminal is again subject to the scheduling scheme. Both the request for uplink slot allocation request sent by the terminal and the response are carried in control packets whose format are depicted in Figure 7, in which the sequence number is used to recover from transmission losses. Request and allocation types indicate one of four classes: CBR, ABR, VBR, and UBR. The allocation packet has a start slot field, which indicates where in the frame the mobile terminal should begin transmission. The number of allocated slots is also indicated.

The data link control can be used to reduce the impact of errors that cannot be corrected using the FEC. The DLC is responsible for selective retransmission of cells with uncorrected errors or lost cells.

Scheduling Function

The objective of a scheduler is to regulate the traffic over the radio interface with respect to the declared ATM traffic parameters of the active connections. It also ensures that the delay constraints (if any) are met over the radio interface. The selection of cells for transmission is based on the service categories of active connections as well as their traffic characteristics. A connection is also serviced based on its service category. Thus, CBR connections are serviced first, followed by VBR-rt, VBR-nrt, and ABR. In addition, for each active connection that is not of type UBR, a token-based policy can be implemented. Tokens for a connection are generated, accumulated, and removed appropriately. For example, when a cell belonging to a connection is selected for transmission, a token can be removed from the related pool (Reininger, Raychaudhuri, and Hui 1996).

Scheduling can operate a selection of the cells to service on a two-pass process. At the end of a first pass, either all of the slots in the downlink portion of the frame have been used some slots are still available. In the latter case, a second pass is started, inducing a potential excess of traffic in VBR-rt, VBR-nrt, ABR, and UBR classes. To avoid overloading the scheduler, the CAC must have some knowledge of the expected load induced by handoffs so that it can limit connection admission to preserve the QoS for active connections, while not degrading existing connections at the radio interface.

At the end of the selection phase, the scheduler has determined the number of cells to be transmitted from each active connection. Some of these cells are to be transmitted uplink while the others are to be transmitted downlink. The scheduler attempts to place the cells for transmission within the frame such that the cells take place in the appropriate part of the frame (uplink or downlink) based on the delay constraint of the corresponding connection to meet. To do this, the delay allowed over the radio segment can be determined for each connection (this value can be obtained during the connection routing phase by decomposing the path delay into delays for each hop). Then, the arrival time for the cell from the fixed network is marked for downlink cells; for uplink cells, the arrival time is estimated based on the time at which the request was received from the MT.

Network and Application Functions

In this subsection, two major classes of QoS control functions are examined: the dynamic framework control and the soft control. Whereas soft control is used to support terminal mobility and maintain acceptable application performances, the QoS framework provides mechanisms that should be able to handle the mobility and dynamic bandwidth needs (Raychaudhuri 1996).

Dynamic QoS Control

Bit rate-based metrics of multimedia applications vary significantly because of user interaction, among other things. Contributing factors for this variation include the heterogeneity of media compression schemes, the presentation quality of requirements, and the session interactivity. For this to be addressed, mechanisms that react on the dynamic variation are very helpful. A suitable QoS control mechanism would support bandwidth renegotiation to achieve high resource utilization and maintain acceptable performance. This mechanism is a key tool for supporting QoS of adaptive applications. Renegotiation may be required during handoff and when resource allocation changes are necessary as a result of instantaneous needs. An example of renegotiation mechanisms is given by VBR+, which allows multimedia applications to request bandwidth on demand (Reininger, Raychaudhuri, and Hui 1996).

Soft QoS Control

The soft QoS control service is suited for adaptive applications, which are capable of adapting their performance to available network resources. Soft QoS service consists of two parts: a usage profile, which specifies the target regime of operation, and a service contract, which quantifies the soft QoS service to be provided by the network. A usage profile might describe the media type, the interactivity model, and the mobility model. The service contract quantifies the probability that the satisfaction of a connection will fall outside an acceptable interval. While a connection is active, a dynamic resource allocation is performed. When congestion occurs, the soft QoS control mechanism reallocates resources among connections to maintain contract satisfaction. However, it is clear that such a mechanism would succeed if an appropriate cost model were set up with it. Otherwise, users would request the maximum possible QoS.

In WATM, soft QoS control allows effective support of mobile applications with high network capacity utilization. When congestion occurs in WATM, the soft QoS mechanism can allocate bandwidth to connections based on their profiles. The ITU-TQ 2963 allows three parameters—PCR, SCR, and MBS—to be modified during a call; the modifications allowed are *increase all* or *decrease all*. In addition, traffic parameter modification is done to point-to-point connections and may be requested only by the terminals that initiated the connection setup. An example of a soft QoS control mechanism is implemented by WATMnet, which uses the following modification to the Q2963 signaling mechanism:

- *Bandwidth change indication*: this message is generated by the network or called user to initiate a modification procedure.
- *Modify request*: this message allows the specification of softness profile and associated minimum acceptable satisfaction level.
- *Modify reject*: this message allows the specification of available bandwidth fraction (ABF) for each traffic descriptor parameter (PCR, SCR, and MBS); ABF is defined as the ratio of the available to requested traffic descriptor parameter (ABF- PCR, ABF-SCR, and ABF-MBS).

MOBILITY MANAGEMENT

The ATM standards are designed to support users at fixed locations and do not provide any support for location search and registration transactions that are required by mobile users. They also do not support handoff and rerouting functions that are used to keep the mobile user connected to the network during mobility.

Location Management

Location management is a two-step process that enables the WATM network to discover the current AP of the mobile user for call delivery. The first step is the location registration (or location update). During this step, the mobile terminal periodically notifies the network of its new AP, allowing the network to authenticate the user and revise the user location profile. The second step is the call delivery, during which the network is queried for the user location, and the current position of the mobile host is retrieved. Current techniques for location management involve database architecture design and the transmission of signaling messages among various components of the signaling network. As the number of mobile terminals increases, improved schemes are needed to efficiently support updates, querying delays, and paging methods. Many of the issues involved in the location management are not protocol dependent and can be relevant to different networks.

Mobility management in WATM deals with transitioning from ATM cell transport based upon widely available resources over wireline to cell transport based upon the limited and relatively unreliable resources over the wireless. Therefore, it requires the investigation of important issues such as latency, message delivery, connection routing, and QoS provision. Through the WATM Working Group, the ATM Forum has focused its efforts on developing basic mechanisms and protocol extensions for location management that address these issues. It mainly specified that new procedures must be compatible with the current ATM standards in order to be implemented with relative ease.

Major proposed protocols for WATM implement location management using two classes of techniques: a) location servers, which refer to the use of databases to store and retrieve records of the current positions (AP) of the mobile terminals within the network; and b) location advertisement, which avoids the use of databases by passing location information throughout the network via broadcast messages.

Location Servers

Location servers use two major techniques: the two-tier database and the location registers.

Two-tier database (TTD). The architecture for the TTD scheme uses bi-level databases that are distributed to zones through the network. Each mobile terminal is assumed to belong to a zone called its *home zone*. Each zone is maintained by a zone maintainer, who is in charge of controlling the zone's location update procedures. The home tier (or HLR) of the zone's database stores location information related to the mobile terminals that are permanently registered within that zone, while the second tier (or VLR) stores location information related to the mobile terminals that are visiting the zone. Upon entering a new zone, the mobile terminal detects the new zone identity broadcast from the BSs. The major steps for registration in the new zone are as follows (Akyol and Cox 1996):

1. The MT transmits a registration request message to the new MSCP that contains its user identification number, authentication data, and the identity of the previous zone.
2. The current MSCP determines the home zone of the MT from the previous zone.
3. The current and home MSCPs authenticate the user and update the home user profile with the new location information.
4. The home zone sends a copy of the profile to the current zone, which stores the profile in the VLR tier of its database.
5. The current MSCP sends a purge message to the previous zone to delete the user's profile from the previous zone's VLR tier.

Call delivery is achieved by routing the call to the last zone first. If the mobile terminal has moved and has been deleted, the call is immediately forwarded to the home zone. The home zone's HLR is queried for the current location of the mobile terminal, which is forwarded back to the calling switch; the connection can be set up to the current serving switch of the mobile terminal.

Location registers hierarchy (LRH). The LRH scheme distributes location servers throughout a hierarchical PNNI architecture. The PNNI procedure is based on a hierarchy of peer groups, each consisting of a collection of ATM switches. Each collection has a special switch called *peer leader group*, which is connected to all of the switches in its peer group. The peer group leader is also connected to a higher-ranking leader in the parent peer group. Each peer group has its own database (or location register) to store location information on every mobile terminal serviced by the peer group (Veeraraghavan and Dommetry 1997). The PNNI hierarchy allows the WATM to route connections to the mobile terminal without requiring the parent nodes to have exact locations—only the lowest referenced peer must record the location. When a mobile terminal executes a location update by sending a registration notification message to the new BS, this message is relayed to the serving switch. The registration procedure is performed as follows:

1. The new switch stores the MT new location information in the peer group's location register (LR).
2. The peer group then relays the new location information to the higher-level LRs for routing needs, stopping at the first common ancestor (or S-level) of the former and current peer groups.
3. The MT's home LR is then notified of the new S-level location of the MT.
4. After the updates are completed, the new switch sends a message to the previous switch so that the former location can be deleted from the LRs.

For call delivery, an incoming call request can be routed to the last known peer group or switch via the S-level LR. If the mobile has been removed, the last known switch propagates a location request, querying the upstream LRs until the mobile end point's address is recognized by an LR that has a pointer to the mobile current position. Then the request is sent appropriately and the location information is sent back to the calling switch.

The TTD scheme has an advantage over the LRH in that it keeps the number of queries relatively low, requiring at most two look-ups for each incoming call to find the called MT. However, the use of centralized home LR may cause increased signaling traffic and unnecessary connection setup delays if the MT is highly mobile. On the other hand, LRH has the advantage of providing information that conforms to the routing protocol in the wireline part of the network. Finally, although the two methods provide the advantage of simplicity and flexibility, they require a considerable signaling and database querying load.

Location Advertisement

Location advertisement aims to reduce the signaling and database querying load. WATM advertisement refers to the notification of appropriate network nodes of the current location of mobile terminals. Three methods can be used for location advertisement: a) the mobile PNNI, which uses the PNNI architecture by taking advantage of the internal broadcast mechanism; b) the destination-routed virtual connection trees, which advertise location information via provisioned virtual paths; and c) the integrated location resolution, which extends the signaling framework of ATM with location information elements (Akyildiz et al. 1999).

Mobile PNNI. This method uses the status notification procedures of the PNNI network to achieve automatic registration, tracing, and location of mobile terminals. The PNNI protocol calls for the exchange of PNNI topology state packets (PTSPs) between the ATM switches. The PTSPs are generated by the peer group leaders and contain information about the topology of the group, the load of each peer switch, and reachability information (i.e., address and parent peer group). By using PNNI, location information for each mobile terminal can be propagated through the WATM network. The registration procedure takes place without the use of a database and simply includes the location information in these PTSP packets. A mobile is assigned to a home switch, which is in charge of storing the route to the mobile's current switch location. The routing table is updated whenever the mobile accesses the network, leaves it, or moves to a new switch (Veeraraghavan and Dommetry 1997).

The registration procedures can be implemented via two steps: 1) the MT sends a registration message to the home switch; and 2) the home switch and the current peer group leader propagate the new location information using the PTSPs. The extended mobile PNNI algorithm includes a scheme to flood the exact location of the mobile terminal through a region of the network called a *neighborhood*. If the mobile moves to a new switch in the neighborhood of its home switch, the exact location will be flooded to the home switch, and switches outside the neighborhood will only receive the default information. When the mobile moves to a new switch, located out of the home neighborhood, the mobile must register its new location with the home switch. In both cases, the previous switch must be notified.

The call delivery can be immediately routed to the correct switch when the call is generated from inside the same neighborhood or from the home neighborhood. In all other situations, the home switch has to route the call to the current switch. However, if the latest reachability update has not been propagated completely, the last known switch has the responsibility to forward the call to the current switch.

Destination-routed virtual connection trees. This method considers that the network architecture is a collection of portable BSs connected via provisioned virtual paths that constitute a connection tree. The portable BSs are equipped with switching and buffering capabilities. Each portable BS maintains a running list of resident mobiles in its coverage. When the mobile registers or deregisters, it sends a message to its current portable BS, which adds the mobile to (or deletes the mobile from) the service list. In addition, when the mobile moves into the portable BS's region, the new portable BS must send a deregistration message to the old portable BS on behalf of the mobile and stores the mobile's identity information in its list.

Call delivery is performed by advertising the mobile terminal's identity using a broadcast message from the portable BS of the calling mobile entity. The current portable BS responds to the broadcast and starts the connection procedure. If there is no response, the connection is rejected.

Integrated location resolution (ILR). This method modifies the signaling related to the ATM call setup process to add indications of the called mobile terminal's current location. In ILR, the mobile terminal is allocated to a switch that manages information related to mobile location. When the mobile terminal moves to a new switch, it registers its presence with the new switch. The new switch is in charge of notifying the mobile's home switch of the mobile's new foreign address.

Initial call requests are routed immediately to the called mobile terminal's home switch along with a connection setup message. The call delivery for a mobile terminal that is currently away from its home switch is implemented as follows:

1. The calling terminal issues a connection setup message to the MT's home switch, which first determines that the mobile is away from home.
2. The MT's home switch sends a release message to the originating switch. This message indicates the MT's current foreign address and identifies the connection as mobile.
3. A switch in the original setup path establishes a new path for the connection to the MT and sends a new setup message to the MT's foreign address, which includes the MT's home address.

Handover Management

WATM is responsible for routing traffic through the wireless network to the wireless access point, which is currently in charge of the radio communication with the mobile terminal under its coverage. When the mobile terminal moves to a new cell covered by another AP, the WATM system must reroute traffic to the new AP for delivery. To provide communication continuity, the network must apply mechanisms responsible for handoff management, which enables WATM to maintain a user's connection at a certain level of QoS as the mobile terminal moves and changes its access point to WATM.

Typically, a handoff involves a three-step process: 1) the initiation step, during which an entity (the user or the operator) identifies the need for handoff; 2) the new connection generation, during which the network has to assign resources for the handoff connection and perform any additional routing operations; and 3) the data flow control, in which the delivery of data from the old connection path to the new connection path is maintained. In general, a handoff is one of two types: intracell handoff or intercell handoff. Intracell handoff occurs when the user moves within a cell and experiences signal strength deterioration below an acceptable threshold that results in the transfer of the user's calls to new radio channels of appropriate strength at the same base station. Intercell handoff occurs when the user moves to an adjacent cell and all its connections must be transferred to the new AP.

The main issue during handover in a WATM environment is to reduce disconnection and preserve connection quality. The requirements for the handover procedure are expanded and detailed in ATM Forum/97-0153 (Porter et al. 1996). The major requirements can be defined as follows:

- The handover procedure should be global, in the sense that it must support handover between: 1) APs within a private network; 2) APs occurring in different private networks connected by a public network; and 3) APs belonging to public networks (ATM core).
- The switching of the active virtual channels from the old routing path to the new routing path should be efficiently performed in order to minimize the interruption to cell transport.
- The handover process should be performed sufficiently fast, so that the handover decision is still valid for the new position of the mobile terminal after the handover process is complete. In fact, ensuring the completion of handover with very low delay is of primary importance in WATM.
- The handover procedure should preserve the contracted QoS of all virtual channels affected by the handover.

When this cannot be satisfied, a renegotiation process or a selective dropping process should be implemented (the dropping can be made on a priority based, if needed).

- The handover procedure should minimize the probability of cell loss while avoiding cell duplication and reordering.

The function of the handover procedure is to guarantee user mobility among the access points of the mobile ATM with no degradation of the QoS requirements. Four categories of protocols for handoff can be considered: 1) Route augmentation, which extends the original connection via a hop to the mobile's next location; 2) full connection rerouting, which maintains the connection by establishing a new route for each handoff as if it is a new call; 3) partial connection rerouting, which reestablishes some segments of the original connection while preserving the remaining ones; and 4) multicast connection rerouting, which combines the first three techniques and includes the maintenance of handoff connection routes to support the original connection.

Route Augmentation

This scheme provides a level of speed and simplicity that can potentially reduce the handoff latency and signaling complexity. It aims to extend the route of a connection from the old AP of a mobile terminal—for example, AP1—to its current switch, denoted by AP2. The key issue behind this scheme is that, following handover, the new connection consists of the existing connection from the source to AP1 followed by an additional subpath (referred to as an "extension") from AP1 to AP2. The first clear advantage of this scheme is that it makes it easier to implement handoff without affecting cell order during the handover procedure. However, the path extension simply increases the end-to-end delay and reduces network utilization because it increases the average number of paths. It also may create loops (because the new path may traverse the old path). A simple optimization of this scheme can be used to detect and eliminate loops.

Full Connection Rerouting

This scheme is the most optimal and simplest rerouting technique. It involves changing all of the segments in the connection path from the source to the previous switch. Then new channels are established from the source to the new switch, which is done by considering the connection a newly admitted call. The procedure involved in the full connection reroute handoff is outlined as follows: after registration, the mobile terminal informs the target switch of the identity of the original connection. Then the target switch forwards the handoff request to the calling switch. The calling switch and the target switch set up a new connection to the mobile terminal. Finally, to clear the original path, the calling switch sends a clear message along the old path toward the old switch.

Partial Connection Rerouting

This scheme attempts to route a connection by preserving some segments of the original route for resource management and simplicity. Two algorithms can be used for this scheme: the nearest common node rerouting (NCNR) algorithm and the hybrid connection algorithm (HCA). The NCNR routes connections according to the concept of zone. Handoff within a zone constitutes a VC update, whereas handoff between zones is based on an attempt of the algorithm to bridge the connection at the nearest WATM network node that is common to both of the zones involved in the handoff transaction. The common node can be defined as follows: in a tree topology, the common node refers to the lowest node (in the tree) that is an ancestor of the two zones. In a hierarchy structure, the common node is a higher switch that uses separate paths to the zones.

An HCA protocol starts with the mobile terminal moving to an overlapping cluster, which is a collection of BSs connected to a common cluster switch. The target BS should determine whether the handoff is intracluster or intercluster. If the handoff is intracluster, the cluster switch can perform as a crossover switch (COS); otherwise, a COS discovery process must be executed. By the time the mobile terminal fully enters the new cluster, the new path is established and the mobile terminal can send a message to the target, which can send a redirect to the COS to become part of the new connection path. Finally, the COS informs the old BS to disconnect the old path.

Multicast Connection Rerouting

This scheme combines the different paradigms presented in the preceding handoff protocols and introduces the concept of maintaining potential handoff connections in addition to the original connection. During a handoff, little network time is spent selecting a new route because several routes are already available. Two algorithms typically are used for multicast rerouting: the virtual connection tree (VCT) algorithm and the homing algorithm (HA). The VCT algorithm is based on a hierarchical collection of switching nodes connected to an ATM network in which the root is a fixed switch. Each mobile connection is assigned a set of virtual connection numbers (VCNs) that are used to identify a set of paths from the root to a leaf on the tree. The algorithm assumes that only one path is operational at a time, and that a call can be generated by a mobile terminal attached to a leaf and then sent through the root.

Handover QoS

A key issue that must be taken into account during the handover process is that of minimizing the effects of QoS disruption; handover blocking as a result of limited resources at target APs, cell loss during handover, or the speed of the whole handover process are some of the critical factors for QoS. One way to minimize QoS disruption during handover is to ensure a lossless handover. In a network consisting of very small radio cells, the number of handovers may be high—if even a single ATM cell is lost at each handover, the overall effect of cell loss on the system throughput could be significant (with the experience of delay as well). Therefore, a key design aim of handover is to be lossless.

To ensure a lossless handover, all cells in transit during the handover procedure are buffered within the network in order to maintain in-sequence cell delivery, without loss, to the wireless mobile terminal. However, ensuring lossless operation is typically done at the expense of introducing additional buffering and, therefore, a delay. This delay needs to be minimized. Hence, an issue to be further investigated is the planning of a lossless handover mechanism that also features low delay and delay variation.

An important issue in WATM that needs further investigation is the planning of an optimal handover procedure that provides the network a guaranteed level of QoS that is protected against cell loss, cell duplication, and loss of cell sequence. An optimal design of handover should offer a lossless mechanism with low delay and delay variation. It is important, in the design of handover, to have in mind some critical factors that influence handover QoS; these include handover blocking due to limited resources at target APs, cell loss during handover, and the speed of the whole handover process.

Implementing handover by choosing the right scheme and type must ensure enhanced QoS for the connection as well as handover reliability. The main consideration during handover is to maintain connection quality. Ensuring the completion of the handover procedure by preventing any cell loss and avoiding cell duplication or cell reordering with very low delay is of primary importance. Hence, a major subject for WATM research is the development of solutions ensuring that QoS resources keep pace with continually changing network states (resulting from user mobility) without consuming large amounts of overhead in the process.

WATM STANDARDS AND IMPLEMENTATIONS

WATM standards have been described by the ATM Forum (Bautz 1997; Deane 1996). The benefits that ATM provides to transport networking standards will need to be extended to support wireless networking. This extension will be developed in private wireless networks as well as public networks. The WATM-WG was specified to facilitate the integration of ATM technology to wireless networks, including cellular, fixed wireless, ad hoc networking, and satellite networks.

First, the ATM form has developed a specification for micro cellular-based systems. This specification includes mobile ATM extensions to support mobility within an ATM network. The WATM specifications are used in networks involving terminal mobility or radio access and are designed for compatibility with standard ATM equipment. These specification concern the radio access protocols, which include radio physical layer MAC for wireless channels, DLC for wireless channels errors, and wireless control protocol for radio resource management protocol extension. They also include control of location management for mobile terminals, routing for mobile connections traffic/QoS control for mobile connections, and wireless network management. The radio access specifications are dependent on the radio access technology and frequency.

The enterprises NEC, ORL, NTT, and Lucent Technologies have developed many experimental mobile ATM testbeds. A prototype called the seamless WATM network (SWAN) is an experimental indoor WATM network based on off-the-shelf 2.4 GHz ISM band radios that operate at 625 Kbps between the base and mobile terminal; it investigates the combination of wireless access and multimedia networked computing. SWAN uses room-sized pico cells and mobile multimedia end points. It enables users carrying multimedia end points such as personal digital assistants (PDAs), laptops, and portable multimedia terminals to seamlessly roam while accessing multimedia data resident in a backbone wired network. The network model of SWAN consists of BSs connected by a wired ATM backbone network, and WATM last hops to the mobile hosts (Agrawal et al. 1996).

A first-generation (1G) radio ATM testbed (Porter et al. 1996) from Olivetti and Oracle Research (ORL) Laboratories operates at 10 Mbps using a QPSK radio at 2.45 GHz and mobile-capable ORL ATM switches. Slotted ALOHA with exponential backoff is employed at the MAC layer using header compression and support for CRC and ARQ for error control. The next version of this testbed will have a data rate of 25 Mbps (Porter et al. 1996), operate in the 5 GHz bands, and have a range up to 30 m instead of the current 10 m (Sfikas, Apostolas, and Tafozolli 1998; Yuan and Motoyama 2002).

The radio ATM prototype is presented as a solution to the problem of connectivity of portables to an ATM wired network in the in-building environment. It is based on a picocellular system with a large number of BSs designed to be deployed in large numbers, each covering a short range with partially overlapping coverages. This increases the aggregate throughput and reduces some of the problems specific to a radio physical layer. Using this approach, the MAC layer is optimized to provide efficient use of bandwidth and support guarantees for ATM traffic classes.

Magic WAND is one of the largest research areas of the European Advanced Communication Technologies and Services (ACTS), working in the field of wireless broadband access networks. The main objective of the project is to design and implement a high-speed indoor WATM network. WAND is a program that is specified for the entire network, from the radio modem to the application layer. Its output is a complete system specification and a technology demonstrator. Furthermore, a set of applications—including video conference and multimedia software—is developed for the system verification. The usability and performance of the WAND system has been evaluated during the public user trials conducted in Finland and in Germany in 1998. The evaluation demonstrated the technical feasibility and business viability of a wireless media for the distribution of advanced multimedia products.

CONCLUSION

ATM is currently used in private LANs, cable TV, data networks, backbones for long-distance services, and digital subscriber line (DSL) systems for broadband residential and business services. Wireless ATM equipment and mobile products still are provisional and unproven. There are no industry-wide standards in place for implementations in either fixed or mobile environments. Solutions that do exist are proprietary, and numerous critics say that ATM's validity remains questionable in the mobile environment (Bautz 1997). However, according to some industry observers, the integration of ATM in wireless environments is promising because wireless networks already tend toward more speed and diversity.

Moreover, ATM allows the QoS provision of diverse types of applications and presents a successful way to manage delay in a wireless broadband network. This protocol has become a common option among fixed wireless service providers. On the carrier level, ATM has established itself and should continue to consolidate its position as the protocol of choice for high-capacity fiber pipes. However, whether ATM will successfully extend its reach into last-mile applications remains doubtful (Bautz 1997).

Some believe that the high multipath resistance and soft handovers associated with CDMA would provide an attractive environment for integrating ATM to wireless environments, but other research has suggested that the combination would not be efficient. Rather, ATM is best suited to TDMA schemes in which cell length and time slots can coincide, and each cell can occupy a single time slot. It is perhaps for this reason that companies have looked more favorably on third-generation implementations of ATM. In any case, high data losses appear to be a given in wireless ATM mobile networks, and powerful error correction combined with dynamic negotiation schemes may be the only way to make mobile ATM work (Hakan 1995). Despite the advantages and promises of WATM, its implementation seems to be expensive for operators compared with other candidates.

GLOSSARY

AAL (ATM Adaptation Layer): Used to adapt the protocol data units (PDUs) passed down from the higher layer to ATM cells. As the higher-level PDUs may have, in general, an arbitrary size, two functions are provided by the AAL: a) the segmentation and reassembly, and b) the convergence, which is responsible for packaging the higher-layer PDU with any additional information required for adaptation.

ATM (Asynchronous Transfer Mode): A dedicated-connection switching technology that organizes digital data into 53-byte cell units and transmits them over a physical medium using digital signal technology.

ATM Cell: The basic unit of information transfer in the ATM communication. The cell has a length of 53 bytes: five of the bytes make up the header field and the remaining 48 bytes form the user information field.

ATM QoS: The measurement, improvement, and guarantee in advance of transmission cells, error rates, and other characteristics controlled by ATM. QoS is of particular concern for the continuous transmission of high-bandwidth services. QoS is handled by ATM on the basis of service contract.

ATM Services: Four basic services are provided by the ATM. They are: 1) the constant bit rate (CBR), which specifies a fixed bit rate so that data are sent in a stream; 2) the variable bit rate (VBR), which provides a specified throughput capacity, though data are not sent evenly (this is a popular choice for voice and videoconferencing data); 3) the available bit rate (ABR), which provides a guaranteed minimum capacity but allows data to be bursted at higher capacities when the network is free; and 4) the unspecified bit rate (UBR), which does not guarantee any throughput levels (this is used for applications, such as file transfer, that can tolerate delays).

Handover: In a cellular telephone network, the transition of any given user of signal transmission from one base station to a geographically adjacent base station as the user moves around.

Q.2931+: An ITU signaling protocol that specifies the procedures for the establishment, maintenance, and clearing of network connections at the user network interface. The procedures are defined in terms of messages exchanged.

WAND: Magic WAND is a joint European project to develop a demonstration of mobile terminals for multimedia information access using a fast and wireless ATM network. Communication between the mobiles is based on portable computers, and the access points serviced by an ATM switch take place in the 5 GHz range.

CROSS REFERENCES

See *ATM (Asynchronous Transfer Mode)*; *Location Management in Personal Communication Systems*; *Network QoS*.

REFERENCES

Agrawal, P., E. Hyden, P. Krzyzanowski, P. Mishra, M. B. Srivastava, and J. A. Trotter. 1996. SWAN: A mobile multimedia wireless network. *IEEE Personal Communications,* April. http://nesl.ee.ucla.edu/pw/NESL/papers/1996/J08_1996_pc_PA.pdf (accessed October 21, 2002).

Akyilidz, I. F., J. McNair, J. Ho, H. Uzunalioglu, and W. Wang. 1999. Mobility management in next generation wireless systems. *Proceedings of the IEEE* 87(8): 1347–84.

Akyol, B., and D. Cox. 1996. Handling mobility in a wireless ATM network. *Proceedings of the IEEE Infocom '06* 3(8): 1405–13.

Bautz, G. 1997. Addressing in wireless ATM networks. ATM Forum/97-0322, April.

Bertoni, H. L., W. Honcharenko, L. R. Maciel, and H. H. Xia. 1994. UHF propagation prediction for wireless personal communications. *Proceedings of IEEE* 82(September): 1333–59.

Cong, X. 1997. Wireless ATM: An overview. http://www.cse.wustl.edu/~jain/cis788-97/wireless_atm/index.htm (accessed August 13, 1997).

Correia, L. M., and R. Prasad. 1997. An overview of wireless broadband communications. *IEEE Communications Magazine*, January, pp. 28–33.

Deane, J. 1996. WATM PHY requirements. ATM Forum/96-0785, June.

Hakan, M. 1995. Architectures of wireless ATM (thesis, Technical Research Centre of Finland).

Hyon T.-I. 2001. Wireless ATM medium access control with adaptive parallel multiple substream CDMA air-interface (thesis, Virginia Polytechnic Institute and State University). http://scholar.lib.vt.edu/theses/available/etd-06302001225755/unrestricted/final_dissertation.pdf (accessed June 19, 2001).

Jabbari, B., G. Colombo, A. Nakajima, and J. Kulkarni. 1995. Network issues for wireless communications. *IEEE Communications Magazine*, January, pp. 88–98.

Makké, R., S. Tohmé, J.-Y. Cochennec, and S. Pautonnier. 2002. Performance of the AAL2 protocol within the UTRAN. In *Proceedings of the 2nd European Conference on Universal Multiservice Networks (ECUMN 2002)*, Paris, April, pp. 92–100.

Porter, J., A. Hopper, D. Gilmurray, O. Mason, J. Naylon, and A. Jones. 1996. The ORL radio ATM system, architecture, and implementation. *ORL Radio ATM Project*. http://www.cl.cam.ac.uk/research/dtg/publications/public/files/tr.96.5.ps.Z (accessed August 30, 2007).

Raychaudhuri, D. 1996. Wireless ATM networks: Architecture, system design, and prototype. *IEEE Personal Communications* 3(4): 42–49.

Reininger, D., D. Raychaudhuri, and J. Hui. 1996. Dynamic bandwidth allocation for VBR video over ATM networks. *IEEE Journal on Selected Areas in Communications* 14(6): 1076–86.

Sfikas, G., C. Apostolas, and R. Tafozolli. 1998. Power saving mode of operation in the WATM MAC protocol. In *Proceedings of the International Conference on ATM (ICATM'98)*, Colmar, France, June, pp. 25–30.

Tomar, P., and R. Singh. 2005. Wireless communication through WATM: Technology status and challenges. In *Proceedings of RAFIT-2005*, Patiala, March, pp. 34–40.

Veeraraghavan, M., and G. Dommetry. 1997. Mobile location management in ATM networks. *IEEE Journal on Selected Areas in Communications* 15(18): 1437–54.

Villasenor-Gonzalez, L., S. Tsakiridou, L. O. Barbosa, and L. Lamont. 2002. Performance analysis of wireless ATM/AAL2 over a burst error channel. *Computer Communications* 25(1): 1–8.

Wasi, A. S. 1995. Wireless ATM overview. http://www.cse.wustl.edu/~jain/cis788-95/wireless_atm/index.html (accessed August 26, 1996).

Yuan, W. S., and S. Motoyama. 2002. Performance analysis of an MAC scheme for WATM. In *Proceedings (381) of Communications and Computer Networks*.

Zhong, L. C., J. Rabaey, C. Guo, and R. Shah. 2001. Data link layer design for wireless sensor networks. In *Proceedings of IEEE MILCOM* 2001, Washington, DC, October. http://bwrc.eecs.berkeley.edu/People/Grad_Students/czhong/documents/milcom_2001_final.pdf (accessed August 6, 2002).

Wireless IP Telephony

Manish Marwah and Shivakant Mishra, *University of Colorado, Boulder*

INTRODUCTION

Internet protocol (IP) telephony or *voice over IP* (VoIP) has seen tremendous growth in the past few years and is predicted to grow rapidly in the coming years. For instance, according to the Web site ZDNet, total VoIP equipment revenue will rise some threefold to $11.9 billion by 2010 from $3.95 billion in 2005. Both business and residential customers are switching to IP telephony. The main attractions of IP telephony are (1) cost savings, (2) better resource utilization, (3) numerous compelling services and applications arising from wireless IP telephony and its integration with Internet-based applications, and (4) reduced network administration and management.

Similarly, *wireless local area network* (WLAN) technologies, mainly *wireless fidelity* (WiFi), have grown rapidly and are becoming ubiquitous. Considering the popularity of these two important technologies (namely, IP telephony and wireless LAN), wireless IP telephony has emerged as an attractive combination that reduces costs, increases access, and provides greater control over enhanced enterprise communications tools. Current literature shows that significant savings are realized with VoIP using WiFi: Cellular phone roaming at $1.25 per minute, for instance, can be reduced to $0.02 per minute using wireless IP telephony. In fact, "dual-mode" phones such as Nokia N80 and Motorola A910 that support both cellular and wireless IP telephony are available now. This allows organizations to save on cellular phone expenses as employees use IP telephony over wireless LAN when located on company premises. Furthermore, cellular networks and WiFi complement each other in their data-transfer rates and coverage areas. Although WiFi can support high data rates (currently, as high as 54 Mbps), cellular networks support only a maximum data rate of a few Mbps. However, cellular networks have especially good geographical coverage unlike WiFi, which is only available in limited areas (sometimes referred to as *hot spots*). In addition, cellular networks typically do not have good coverage inside buildings, and in such cases wireless IP telephony can provide better connectivity and voice quality.

There are a number of technological challenges associated with transporting real-time data such as voice and video over wireless. In this chapter, we will discuss the state of the art of wireless IP telephony. In particular, we will discuss issues related to (1) mobility management; (2) *quality of service* (QoS), including mechanisms for call admission control; (3) security and privacy; and (4) *enhanced 911* (E911). Because 802.11 (IEEE 1999) (or WiFi) is the most popular WLAN technology, we discuss most of these issues in the context of 802.11-based standards, which are briefly described below.

802.11 Standards

The most commonly used WLAN technology is based on the 802.11 (or WiFi) standards (IEEE 1999). This umbrella encompasses various formalized standards that define different aspects of the WiFi technology. The WiFi physical layer is defined by standards such as 802.11b (11 Mbps) and 802.11g (54 Mbps). The forthcoming 802.11n standard, which is now in the draft stage, aims to increase data throughputs to as much as 600 Mbps.

In addition to letter standards that specify data rates, other 802.11 standards relevant to wireless IP telephony are:

- 802.11i, which defines security mechanism such as authentication, encryption, and access control;
- 802.11e, which provides QoS support for real-time applications such as voice and video; and
- 802.11r (not approved yet), which aims to reduce handoff latency during transitions between access points such that time-sensitive applications such as IP telephony are not disrupted.

For a more detailed description of 802.11 standards, see the chapter "Wireless LANs (WLANs)."

Devices using 802.11 have two modes of operation: (1) ad hoc, in which the devices directly communicate with each other, and (2) infrastructure, in which the 802.11 devices communicate through an access point.

In the infrastructure mode, an 802.11 system consists of *stations* (STAs) and *access points* (APs) as shown in

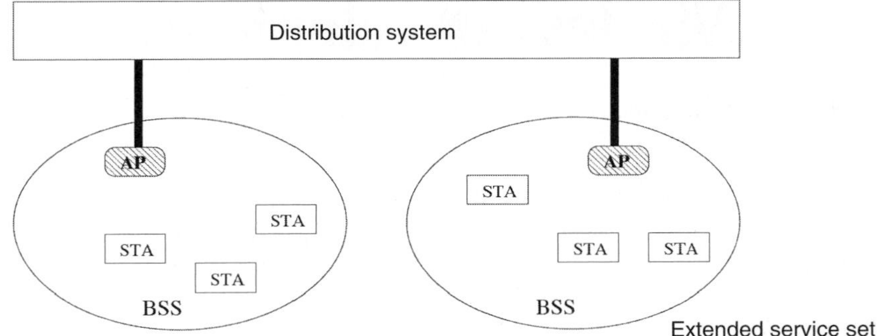

Figure 1: 802.11 infrastructure-mode architecture

Figure 1. One AP and multiple STAs that receive service from that AP constitute a *basic service set* (BSS). Multiple BSSs connected through a wired network, such as a LAN, are referred to as an *extended service set*.

Because most 802.11 installations use infrastructure mode, in the rest of this chapter, we will assume that a 802.11 network operates in this mode (unless stated otherwise).

WiMAX and IP Telephony

WiMAX (802.16) is an upcoming standard for broadband wireless wide area network access. It has a range of approximately 6 miles radius and speeds of as high as 40 Mbps per channel. The initial version of WiMAX (also called *fixed WiMAX*) is aimed at stationary or nonmobile applications, which are not sensitive to longer handoff times; a later version (802.16e or *mobile WiMAX*) aims to provide support for mobility and real-time applications such as IP telephony. For further information on WiMAX, see the chapter "Wireless Wide Area Networks (WWANs)."

Organization

The rest of this chapter is organized into five sections: mobility management; quality of service issues; security and privacy; enhanced 911; and, lastly, a conclusion.

MOBILITY MANAGEMENT

For IP telephony over wireless, mobility management has to be addressed at various levels. Standards set forth by the International Telecommunications Union (ITU) (see ITU-T 2003) recommend that for real-time voice communication, the one-way delay should be less than 150 ms. Latencies greater than this value result in poor voice quality and are discernible by a user. Handoffs between wireless APs must be done in a fast and seamless manner so that existing calls are not disrupted. In addition to L2 (layer 2, the data link layer) mobility, L3 (layer 3, the network layer) mobility is also important because the user could move to a different wireless subnet or network. Again, this must be done without any service disruption. Various mobility management techniques are discussed in Sharma, Zhu, and Chiueh 2004; Dutta et al. 2002; Ramani and Savage 2005; Mishra, Shin, and Arbaugh 2004; Park et al. 2004; Pack and Choi 2002.

Layer 2 Mobility

WiFi clients receive service through APs that typically provide coverage to distances up to 100 meters from an AP. Thus, a person using a WiFi-enabled device for a VoIP call could traverse the coverage area of several APs while walking from one area of a building to another. Furthermore, at any time, a WiFi device can only be associated with one AP (this limitation, which is part of the WiFi standards, enables packets to be efficiently routed to a WiFi device).

The process involved in changing the association from one AP to another is called a *handoff* or *handover*. A handoff usually occurs when a device moves out of the range of its current AP, causing its signal strength or signal-to-noise ratio to become unacceptable. Handoffs can be *hard* or *soft*. In a soft handoff, also referred to as a *make-before-break* handoff, the device first establishes connection with the new point of attachment before breaking the existing connection. This results in a more seamless handoff as compared to a hard handoff, also called a *break-before-make* handoff, in which the connection with the existing attachment point is broken before the new one is established.

Handoffs routinely happen during a call in cellular networks. There are two main reasons why handoffs in a cellular network are much smoother as compared to WiFi (Ramani and Savage 2005). First, in 802.11, the clients manage a handoff autonomously and independently without any knowledge of the network topology or other network characteristics. In cellular networks, by contrast, a *base station controller* or a *mobile switching center* initiates a handoff with full knowledge of the local topology and conditions such as the number of clients in the area. Furthermore, in cellular networks such as *code division multiple access* (CDMA) (Viterbi 1995), the phones perform a soft handoff in which the phone simultaneously communicates with multiple *base transceiver stations* (BTSs) before the handoff is executed to one of them. In 802.11, a handoff is hard.

Second, in cellular networks, a client continuously measures its connectivity with all the BTSs within its range and assists the network in choosing the best alternative. However, in 802.11, a client only measures the quality of its current channel because it can only send and receive on a single channel at a time. When this quality goes below a threshold, the client switches to other channels to explore the possibility of a handoff to an AP with acceptable quality. (Note that while this switchover is in progress, frames on the current channel are dropped.) There is a trade-off involved in setting this voice quality threshold value. If it is too high, it is possible that the client does not find any other AP with better quality and thus unnecessarily causes a "gap" in the service because of the search for other APs. On the other hand, if the threshold is too low, the client may continue to be attached to an AP with poor signal quality even when a better quality AP is available. Unlike the cellular network, the time taken to perform handoffs in 802.11 networks is high, ranging from several hundred milliseconds to a second, which is unsuitable for real-time traffic such as voice.

The 802.11 standard provides excellent support for "portable" entities—that is, entities that migrate frequently but do not have strict connectivity requirements while they are in motion. However, because of the handoff mechanism used and the high handoff latency, 802.11 does not provide much support for "mobile" entities—that is, entities that have tight latency and response time requirements while they are in motion. We now provide a brief description of the L2 handoff process. This is followed by a discussion of the recent research aimed at improving the L2 handoff latency.

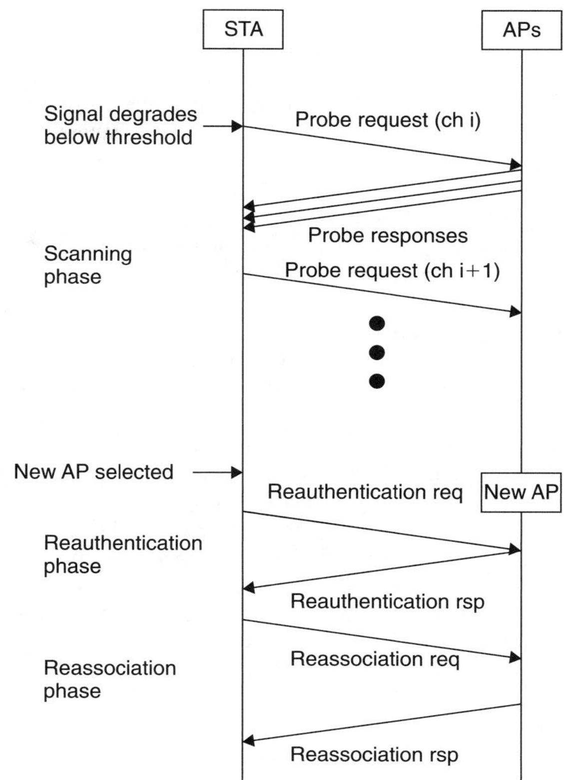

Figure 2: 802.11 handoff phases

L2 Handoff

A handoff is required as a station moves from one BSS to another. It is critical that the time taken for a handoff, or, the handoff latency, is minimal. As mentioned earlier, this latency should ideally be less than 150 ms. For seamless service, it is important that the handoff is done at the right time and to the right AP.

The steps involved in a handoff are described below and shown in Figure 2. It consists of three main phases: (1) discovery, (2) reauthentication, and, (3) reassociation.

Discovery. The discovery phase is entered when the signal quality on the current channel has degraded below a threshold level. The goal of this phase is to find another AP with acceptable signal quality. Depending on the version of 802.11 that the client is running, it switches to the corresponding channel frequencies one at a time. For each channel, the client either (1) waits for the periodic beacon (which is usually sent by an AP every 100 ms) in order to measure the quality of the corresponding AP's channel (*passive probing*) or (2) actively broadcasts a probe on the channel so that an AP operating in that channel replies back (*active probing*). Normally, active probing is much faster than passive probing.

The time taken by active probing is as follows (Ramani and Savage 2005):

$$\sum_{c=1}^{c=NumChannels} (1 - P(c)).MinChannelTime + P(c).MaxChannelTime$$

where $P(c)$ is the probability that an AP operates in channel c, MinChannelTime is the time the client waits if there is no AP operating in channel c (in other words, if it receives no response at all), and MaxChannelTime is the time the client waits if it receives at least one response (in order to allow other APs operating in that channel to respond). Suggested values of MinChannelTime vary from 1 ms (Velayos and Karlsson 2004) to 7 ms (Mishra, Shin, and Arbaugh 2003), whereas those of MaxChannelTime are approximately 11 ms (Velayos and Karlsson 2004; Mishra, Shin, and Arbaugh 2003). Using an average value of 4 ms for MinChannelTime and 11 ms for MaxChannelTime, and assuming eleven total channels (as is the case in 802.11b/g) gives the probing latency of from 40 ms (if no other AP is found) to 110 ms (if at least one AP is found on each channel). In addition, *channel switching delay* is incurred whenever a channel is changed. This can add a substantial amount of delay to the probing process. Ramani and Savage (2005) find that the probing delay using active probing for a popular 802.11b network interface card to be between 350 ms and 400 ms.

Reauthentication. After a new AP is selected, the client exchanges authentication messages with it. These establish the client's identity and its permission to use that particular AP. The reauthentication delay is approximately 20 ms (Mishra, Shin, and Arbaugh 2004).

Reassociation. After authentication, the client sends a reassociation request to the new AP, expecting a reassociation response in return to finalize the handoff. When an

AP receives a reassociation request, it exchanges station context information with the client's earlier AP. Interaccess point protocol or 802.11f is used for this exchange. The reassociation delay is on the order of approximately 20 ms.

The total time taken by the handoff process, which is the sum of the three phases, is approximately 500 ms to 1 sec (Ramani and Savage 2005). Furthermore, the probing delay is roughly 90 percent of the total time taken (Mishra, Shin, and Arbaugh 2003).

Improving L2 Handoff Latency

An extensive body of research exists on enabling faster layer 2 handoffs in order to make WLANs more suitable for IP telephony (Ramani and Savage 2005; Brik, Mishra, and Banerjee 2005; Velayos and Karlsson 2004; Mishra, Shin, and Arbaugh 2004; Park et al. 2004; Shin et al. 2004; Pack and Choi 2002). Research aimed at reducing the time taken for each of the three phases of the handoff is presented in these papers. However, because the discovery phase takes almost 90 percent of the total handoff time, a number of researchers have suggested techniques to reduce the time taken for this phase.

In SyncScan (Ramani and Savage 2005), the authors propose synchronizing the clocks on the APs and the mobile devices so that the devices can predict the exact time when the periodic beacon from an AP will be sent. This would allow a device to continuously monitor the signals from all of the APs within its range. A concern with this technique is that the device will not be able to send or receive frames on its current channel while it reads beacons on the other channels. In other words, the frames sent or received on the current channel will be dropped during these times. This problem is addressed by using send and receive buffers. Whenever the device is tuned to other channels, the frames are buffered and later processed when the device returns to its current channel. Park et al. (2004) construct a neighbor graph using network topology to narrow the list of channels, and only a few selected channels are probed. Furthermore, the authors propose algorithms that can be used to automatically generate a neighbor graph. Shin et al. (2004) use a combination of selective scanning and caching. In the selective scanning algorithm, the client remembers the channels on which replies were received on previous occasions. This reduces the handoff latency by 30 percent to 60 percent. The caching algorithm maintains a record of previous handoffs. Each entry in the cache table, keyed by an AP, stores as many as two other APs (and their corresponding channels) to which a handoff was performed from that AP. If a handoff needs to be performed, the cache table is checked first. If there is a cache hit and at least one of the two APs is still available, then the client does not need to perform scanning. However, if there is a cache miss, the selective scanning algorithm is used.

In Multiscan (Brik, Mishra, and Banerjee 2005), the authors propose to eliminate handoff latencies through use of additional client hardware. They suggest using two wireless interfaces, one of which is dedicated to looking for alternate APs. This continuous monitoring of the available APs allows the client to seamlessly handoff ongoing connections. Unlike SyncScan, Multiscan only requires changes to the clients; no changes are required to the AP infrastructure. Furthermore, unlike some techniques, Multiscan does not require any knowledge of the network topology.

In Mishra, Shin, and Arbaugh (2004), the authors aim to reduce the reassociation delay of the handoff process. Network topology information, stored as "neighbor graphs," is used to send the station context information ahead of time to APs adjacent to the client's current AP such that the context information is transferred to an AP before a client performs a handoff to it. Using this technique, the reassociation delay is reduced to 1.69 ms from 15.37 ms in the experiments performed by the authors. Although this is an order of magnitude improvement, it should be noted that the reassociation delay constitutes only a small part of the total handoff delay, and therefore the improvement made to the total handoff latency by this technique is not especially significant.

Pack and Choi (2002) examine ways to reduce the reauthentication delay. They propose to minimize this delay by having a client perform authentication (preauthentication) with multiple APs and not just its current AP.

Layer 3 Mobility

Layer 3 (or network layer) mobility is provided by the use of Mobile IP (Perkins 2002), which is an extension of IP to support mobile applications. It allows an Internet end point to retain its IP address (home address) irrespective of its point of attachment to the Internet. In other words, a host can roam across IP subnets or networks and still is contactable via its home address. This is accomplished by maintaining a home agent, whose location is fixed, and a foreign agent that registers on behalf of a mobile host. When the host is roaming, it additionally acquires a care-of address that is registered with the home agent. The host always uses its home address as the source address in any packet it sends out. The far end responds back to the host home address, which is received by the home agent. The home agent then tunnels it to the host's care-of address (located on the foreign agent). The foreign agent detunnels packets and delivers them to the mobile host. In some situations, to avoid issues with egress filters, the packets sent out by a mobile host may first be tunneled to the home agent and then sent to its intended destination. It should be noted that here the home agent acts much like a proxy for the mobile host.

For wireless IP telephony, Mobile IP allows greater mobility to end-point devices that can seamlessly move between different wireless IP subnets or networks without any disruption to ongoing calls.

Although support for network layer mobility as provided by Mobile IP is necessary for wireless IP telephony to work, it is not sufficient. Because of the strict latency requirements for voice, network layer handoff must be executed fast enough so that ongoing calls are not disrupted. In the context of Mobile IP, network layer handoff would be necessary whenever a mobile host moves to a different subnet or network. This would involve (1) tearing down the old tunnel, (2) acquiring a new care-of address, (3) registering this address with the home agent, and (4) establishing a new tunnel. Sharma, Zhu, and Chiueh (2004) discuss optimization of each of the phases involved in the handoff and achieve a reduction in the network handoff latency by a factor of 5.

In some extensions of Mobile IP, several care-of addresses can be registered simultaneously. The home agent tunnels the packets to all these addresses. This is particularly useful in a wireless environment in which the host is rapidly changing its point of attachment to the Internet. Mobile IP is supported in IPv6 (Johnson, Perkins, and Arkko 2004) with some enhancements and better integration in the TCP/IP stack as compared to IPv4. Among other advantages (Johnson, Perkins, and Arkko 2004), this obviates the need for a foreign agent. Even after a successful handoff, Mobile IP has drawbacks such as tunneling overhead and triangular routing, which is inefficient especially for delay-sensitive real-time traffic such as voice and video. To address this, Mobile IPv6 supports route optimization that allows a peer to send traffic directly to the care-of address, instead of the home address, of the mobile host (Johnson, Perkins, and Arkko 2004).

Application Layer Mobility

An alternative to supporting mobility management at the network layer is to handle it at the application layer, particularly in view of the inefficiencies incurred by network layer mechanisms such as Mobile IP. *Session initiation protocol* (SIP) can be used for performing a handoff at the application layer. SIP, described in the chapter "Voice over IP (VoIP)" is the most popular and industry accepted protocol for call control in IP telephony.

Each mobile host belongs to a home region where a SIP proxy server provides registrar service. Whenever a host moves to another region, it communicates with the local SIP proxy. Before providing service, the local (visited) proxy authenticates and registers the host with the host's home registrar. When a mobile host on an active call moves from one network to another, the following steps are involved in the handoff:

1. The host acquires a new IP address (e.g., by use of DHCP).
2. The host exchanges a set of messages with the visited SIP proxy for authentication and registration (note that the address of the SIP proxy server is included in the DHCP response).
3. After successful registration, the host sends a re-INVITE SIP message to the peer host using the call identifier of the original call to reestablish the call session. This is also referred to as *midcall mobility*, compared to *precall mobility* in which the host moves when there is no active call.

Because a number of messages need to be exchanged during handoff, the handoff delay can easily exceed 1 sec and thus is not suitable for real-time traffic (Nakajima et al. 2003). Several solutions based on SIP that minimize this delay have been proposed (Wang, Abu-Rgheff, and Akram 2004; Vali et al. 2003; Banerjee, Das, and Acharya 2006; Kwon, Gerla, and Das 2002). In Kwon, Gerla, and Das (2002), the authors propose using *shadow registration*. The key idea is that the host's current region a priori transfers authentication information related to that host to all of the neighboring regions in anticipation of the host moving to one of them. When the host does move to one of the neighboring regions, the registration step is much faster because the visited SIP registrar does not have to communicate to the host's home registrar. In Banerjee, Das, and Acharya (2006), the authors propose a soft handoff for SIP clients which have multiple network interfaces.

Vertical Handoff

A *vertical handoff* is one between heterogeneous networks—for example, between a cellular network and a WLAN. With the emergence of multimode phones (i.e., with multiple network interfaces), mobile users expect seamless operation and connectivity while moving from one network to another. For example, an employee using cellular service expects her call to seamlessly switch to wireless IP telephony once she is within the range of a WiFi service available on her company premises. A vertical handoff cannot be performed without application-level support. In Wu et al. (2005), a case study is performed of the delay incurred during vertical handoff in a WLAN–*universal mobile telephone service* (UMTS) internetwork using SIP as the mobility management protocol. The results show that a WLAN-to-UMTS handoff incurs a much larger delay (because of error-prone and bandwidth-limited wireless links) than a UMTS-to-WLAN handoff. It is suggested that soft handoff techniques be used to bring the handoff delay within acceptable limits.

QUALITY-OF-SERVICE ISSUES

Wireless IP telephony must provide same or better call quality as traditional telephony systems. Traditionally, IP (and wireless IP) has been a best effort service with each packet treated equally irrespective of its content. Although this works well for non–real-time applications such as file transfers and e-mail, real-time applications such as voice and video require strict performance guarantees from the network. If packet latency or delay, jitter, and loss exceed acceptable limits, then it has real user impact in terms of poor voice quality and dropped calls.

As real-time applications have become more prevalent on the TCP/IP networks, various QoS mechanisms have emerged. These mechanisms apply to various layers in the network stack. For the wired Ethernet MAC layer, the Institute of Electrical and Electronics Engineers' (IEEE's) 802.1p provides priority tagging. For the network layer, integrated services (Braden 1997) and differentiated services (Nichols 1998) provide QoS support. However, a QoS mechanism for 802.11 MAC had been lacking until 802.11e was approved in 2005.

The original 802.11 MAC defines two coordination functions for accessing the shared media: *distributed coordination function* (DCF) and *point coordination function* (PCF). DCF essentially uses carrier sense and collision avoidance (through use of the 802.11 RTS-CTS mechanism) for coordinating access. PCF provides channel access through polling by a centralized coordinator that usually resides at the AP. It is optional and only available in the infrastructure mode of operation (that is, when all communication to and from a device goes through an AP). Neither DCF nor PCF provides any QoS mechanisms, and all traffic has the same priority. More detailed descriptions of DCF and PCF are presented elsewhere in this handbook.

Standard 802.11e

To overcome the lack of QoS support in 802.11, 802.11e was proposed. It provides QoS in two ways.

1. *Prioritized* QoS. 802.11e enhances the DCF channel access mechanism to support different priorities for different traffic categories (similar to DiffServ—see Nichols 1998). This enhanced MAC mechanism is called *enhanced DCF*. Before a frame is transmitted, a 802.11e station listens on a channel to determine if it is busy. This channel-sensing interval depends on the priority of the frame to be transmitted. In other words, the lower the priority of the frame, the larger the sensing time. This increases the probability of transmission of higher-priority frames compared to lower-priority frames.
2. *Parameterized* QoS. 802.11e also allows parameterized QoS where an 802.11e station can effectively request a certain bandwidth to be reserved (similar to RSVP—see Braden 1997). This is provided through *enhanced PCF*. It requires a coordinator (called *hybrid coordinator*, HC) that is usually located at the AP. A station may send a *reservation request* to a HC and be allocated a *transmission opportunity* that indicates the duration for which it can transmit (once it gets a chance to transmit).

A detailed description of 802.11e is presented in Mangold et al. (2002). For wireless IP telephony, 802.11e provides two important services. First, it allows voice frames to be treated at a higher priority as compared to non–real-time data frames. Second, it provides a mechanism for implementing call admission control—that is, it allows restrictions (depending on the capacity of the 802.11 network) to be imposed on the total number of voice calls active at any time.

SECURITY AND PRIVACY

Security and privacy are important requirements of any communication network. These requirements become mandatory if the communication network is used for transferring personal or confidential information. Currently, such traditional telephone networks as the *public switched telephone network* (PSTN) provide an acceptable level of security and privacy. This security and privacy support has been achieved from a number of years of use and experience. IP telephony–based networks have introduced several new security and privacy concerns that have not been fully addressed yet (Ransome and Rittinghouse 2005). Combining wireless communications with IP telephony further introduces new caveats and security concerns that do not occur in PSTN or IP telephony-based networks. It is critical that these security and privacy issues are adequately addressed before implementing a widespread deployment of wireless IP telephony.

Unfortunately, as with IP telephony–based networks, the security and privacy concerns of wireless IP telephony have been overshadowed by the increased convenience, flexibility, cost effectiveness, and other advantages that it provides. Wireless IP telephony faces greater security and privacy risks because of a combination of several factors. These include the use of TCP/IP, the inherent characteristics of the wireless communications medium, and the relatively new protocols that have yet to be fully developed and tested.

Because wireless IP telephony uses IP as the underlying communication protocol, it inherits all of the known and unknown security weaknesses of IP. The issues of security and privacy were not considered when IP was first designed. As a result, many vulnerabilities are well known. For example, by spoofing source IP addresses, an attacker can impersonate a legitimate user and make phone calls disguised as that user. IP networks are common and easily accessible to the attackers. Furthermore, different parts of IP networks are controlled by different entities—for example, different service providers. Enforcing a common set of security protocols over these different parts of the networks is an extremely challenging task.

The wireless communications medium exacerbates the security and privacy challenges of IP telephony. We identify five sources of increased vulnerability resulting from the introduction of the wireless communications medium. First, the wireless communications medium increases the risk of eavesdropping by someone snooping packets over the air. It is relatively straightforward for an attacker to eavesdrop on a wireless communications medium using commonly available, off-the-shelf, and inexpensive equipment. In fact, it is significantly simpler for an attacker to eavesdrop over a wireless communications medium than over a wired communications medium. Thus, the privacy of telephone conversation is greatly jeopardized by incorporating wireless communication.

Second, it is relatively straightforward to launch denial-of-service attacks in the wireless communications medium. It is relatively easy to tap into a wireless communications medium; in the simplest case, an attacker can jam a wireless communications medium by injecting junk information. Of course, this simple attack requires an attacker to expend a large amount of energy. However, several intelligent denial-of-service attacks are well known that exploit specific communication patterns of network- and transport-level protocols. These attacks selectively jam specific control packets of TCP/IP protocols resulting in large number of retransmissions, or they jam for just long enough to interfere with the tail end of an IP packet. Such intelligent attacks require an attacker to expend little energy, and they cause significant damage in service availability.

Third, an attacker can take advantage of the vulnerabilities of the wireless communications medium to inject legitimate packets. This can enable the attacker to make unauthorized telephone calls, impersonate a legitimate telephone user, or even modify the contents of an ongoing telephone conversation. It is difficult to launch such an attack in traditional PSTN networks, but the wireless communications medium makes launching such attacks simpler.

Fourth, the existence of the wireless communications medium makes it easier for an attacker to compromise telephone user databases. Once again, the main reason for this simplicity is the wide pervasiveness of the wireless communications medium and the ease with which one can tap into this network. This can allow an attacker not only to steal important private information of a telephone user (including name, address, and social security and credit card numbers) but also to modify this information in insidious ways.

Finally, some parts of the radio spectrum are licensed while others are unlicensed. Cellular telephone service uses licensed radio spectrum, whereas WiFi uses unlicensed radio spectrum. As a result of this and because of high Gaussian (white) noise generated by numerous RF-emitting systems (such as APs that may have been placed in close proximity), chances of interference in WiFi are significantly high, thus making the problem of providing security and privacy more difficult.

These security and privacy vulnerabilities associated with the wireless communications medium are quite well known, and in fact have been addressed to some extent in other applications that use the wireless communications medium. As a result, solutions to address the problems of eavesdropping, tampering, and denial-of-service attacks have been developed. The key problem is that these solutions are typically not suitable for wireless IP telephony. This is because either the proposed solutions do not work well in resource-constrained mobile devices that users of wireless IP telephony tend to use or the quality of service issues such as latency, jitter, and packet loss are adversely affected.

Cryptographic algorithms, particularly asymmetric key algorithms, are highly computation-intensive. They require large amounts of memory and consume lots of power. Mobile wireless users typically tend to use relatively small, resource-constrained devices that run on low power. As a result, traditional cryptographic solutions do not work well in such devices. Furthermore, traditional solutions such as firewalls can delay or even block call setups, while computation-intensive encryption and decryption can cause unacceptable latency and jitter.

It is clear that wireless IP telephony brings in significantly higher security and privacy risks that are more than a mere nuisance. It is critical that these security and privacy concerns be addressed adequately before this promising technology is widely used.

ENHANCED 911

As people depend more on IP telephony (in many cases for all of their telephony service needs), it is vital that emergency services can accurately determine the location of a caller in an emergency in a timely manner. In PSTN systems, when a person makes a 911 call, the call is routed to the nearest *public safety answering point* (PSAP). The PSAP receives the caller's phone number and the exact location of the phone from which the call was made. The Federal Communications Commission (FCC) introduced enhanced 911 to allow mobile or cellular phone users to make 911 emergency calls and enable emergency services to locate the geographic position of the caller. This is typically implemented in current cellular telephone networks by using some form of radio location from the cellular network or a *global positioning system* (GPS) device built into the phone itself.

The packet-switched technology of IP telephony allows a caller to place a call from anywhere, unlike the PSTN in which a phone's physical location is fixed or a cellular network in which a phone's physical location is tied to the radio tower of the cell in which the phone is currently located. IP telephony severely complicates the provision of E911 service. In fact, earlier IP telephones were not integrated with the 911 system at all. However, the FCC has now mandated all IP telephony service providers to provide 911 service, including the E911 feature. There are several complicated technological problems with integrating E911 with IP telephony, and currently most IP telephony service providers only provide an ad hoc solution. For example, some service providers have encouraged their customers to register their locations from which their 911 calls should be routed to the local PSAP. Other service providers are attempting to connect customers to E911 services through the PSTN. The problem here is that the PSTN is controlled by telecom carriers who are their economic competitors.

The key problem associated with providing E911 service in IP telephony is that it is hard for an IP device to figure out its actual geographic location in a dynamic manner. This problem becomes more complicated in the case of wireless IP telephony because not only is a 911 call using a packet-switched network but also the user is mobile. It can be argued that a user is more likely to be within a short distance from a wireless access point with a fixed location. This provides a simple, though not highly accurate, solution for most situations. However, with the advent of wireless broadband services such as WiMAX or newer ad hoc wireless networks that allow an IP device that is several hops away from a wireless access point to be connected, a user can be significantly far away from a wireless access point. Another solution—although a bit expensive—is to install a GPS chip, which periodically transmits location information, in all handsets. This will enable accurate, near real-time user location information to be determined.

Determining the location of a WiFi client only from the RF signal (that is, without using other technologies such as GPS) is being actively researched. Several WLAN localization techniques have been proposed (e.g., Youssef and Agrawala 2005). Many of these use machine learning techniques to model the location of a WiFi client as a function of the properties of the signal (such as signal strength) that it receives. However, they are not always accurate and reliable. In fact, some commercial WLAN localization solutions (e.g., from Ekahau Inc.) have also emerged in the recent years.

CONCLUSION

In this chapter, we have provided a survey of the current state of the art in wireless IP telephony. We discussed key technical challenges that face wireless telephony related to mobility management, quality of service, security, privacy, and E911. Another challenge is seamless vertical handoff that would allow mobility between a WLAN and a cellular network. To be universally accepted, wireless

IP telephony must provide telephony services with the same degree of quality, high availability, and security as traditional circuit-switched telephony systems. To this end, substantial progress has been made in the past few years, and research solutions exist for most technical issues. However, it remains to be seen how fast these will be adopted and realized by industry.

GLOSSARY

802.11 Ad Hoc Mode: In this mode of operation, 802.11 wireless devices can directly communicate with each other without a need for an AP; also referred to as *peer-to-peer mode*.

802.11 Infrastructure Mode: In this mode of operation, 802.11 wireless devices communicate with each other through an AP, which also provides the connectivity of wireless devices to the wired network.

802.11 Standards: 802.11 (or WiFi) is a set of IEEE specifications that define various aspects of a wireless local area network. It consists of standards such as 802.11a and 802.11g (which define PHY and MAC layer of the WLAN), 802.11e (which defines QoS enhancements), and so on.

Access Point (AP): An AP is a layer 2 device that allows hosts in a wireless LAN to communicate with each other. It usually also provides the wireless devices with connectivity to the wired network.

Distributed Coordination Function (DCF): DCF is a MAC mechanism for providing channel access to 802.11 devices. Unlike PCF, it does not require a central coordinator.

Enhanced 911 (E911): A location technology mandated by FCC that would allow telephony service providers to locate callers in case of emergency calls. This is also required for emergency calls made using wireless IP telephony or IP telephony when it is harder to implement because of its mobile nature.

Handoff: In general, a handoff is passing an association from one entity to another. In the context of 802.11, a handoff is a transfer of association from one AP to another. A handoff is required when the current AP's signal quality becomes poor and another AP with a better signal quality is available.

IP Telephony: Use of the packet-based IP network for transporting voice calls instead of the traditional circuit-switched networks.

Jitter: In the context of IP telephony, jitter is the variation in the arrival rate of voice packets. A high jitter value leads to poor voice quality as perceived by a user.

Media Access Control (MAC): A mechanism for mediating access to each of the contending devices sharing a common resource for communication, such as a cable in case of Ethernet or the electromagnetic spectrum in case of 802.11.

Mobile IP: An IP extension for facilitating seamless operation of mobile applications. It allows hosts to roam—that is, change their point of attachment to the IP network while keeping the same IP address.

Mobility Management: In the context of wireless IP telephony, refers to mechanisms (at various layers of the network stack) to enable seamless communication (for ongoing as well as new calls) for a user who is mobile.

Packet Latency: In the context of IP telephony, refers to the delay in transporting a voice packet from a sender to a receiver. A high packet latency leads to poor voice quality.

Point Coordination Function (PCF): A MAC technique for providing channel access to 802.11 devices that uses a coordinator (unlike DCF) that is usually located at an AP.

Public Switched Telephone Network (PSTN): The publicly available, circuit-switched traditional telephony network.

Quality of Service (QoS): Refers to a mechanism for providing performance guarantees in the transportation of packets over a network. In the context of IP telephony, it refers to providing guarantees for transportation of voice packets on the IP network, which has traditionally only provided a best effort service in terms of packet loss, jitter, and latency.

Vertical Handoff: A handoff between heterogeneous access technologies—for example, between WLAN and 3G (cellular).

Voice over Internet Protocol (VoIP): Transmission of voice over an IP network as packets.

Wireless Fidelity (WiFi): WLAN based on 802.11 standards.

Wireless IP Telephony: Use of IP telephony over a wireless IP network, such as that based on the 802.11 standards (WiFi).

CROSS REFERENCES

See *Network QoS*; *Voice over IP (VoIP)*; *Wireless LAN Standards*; *Wireless LANs (WLANs)*.

REFERENCES

Banerjee, N., S. Das, and A. Acharya. 2006. Seamless sip-based mobility for multimedia applications. *IEEE Network*, 20(2): 6–13.

Braden, R. 1997. *Resource reservation protocol (RSVP)*. RFC 2205, September.

Brik, V., A. Mishra, and S. Banerjee. 2005. Eliminating handoff latencies in 802.11 WLANs using multiple radios: Applications, experience, and evaluation. In *Proceedings of the Fifth Conference on Internet Measurement 2005* (USENIX IMC), Oct. 19–21, Berkeley, CA, USA. pp. 299–304.

Dutta, A., O. Altintas, W. Chen, and H. Schulzrinne. 2002. Mobility approaches for all IP wireless networks. In *Sixth World Multiconference on Systemics, Cybernetics, and Informatics,* July 14–8, Orlando, FL, USA.

IEEE. 1999. Standard 802.11. Part 11: Wireless LAN medium access control (MAC) and physical layer (PHY) specifications, July.

ITU-T. 2003. Recommendation G.114. *One way transmission time*, May.

Johnson, D., C. Perkins, and J. Arkko. 2004. *Mobility support in IPv6*. RFC 3775, June.

Kwon, T., M. Gerla, and S. Das. 2002. Mobility management for VoIP service: Mobile IP vs. SIP. *IEEE Wireless Communications*, 9(5): 66–75.

Mangold, S., S. Choi, P. May, O. Klein, G. Hiertz, and L. Stibor. 2002. IEEE 802.11e wireless LAN for quality of service. In *Proceedings of European Wireless '02*. pp. 32–9.

Mishra, A., M. Shin, and W. A. Arbaugh. 2003. An empirical analysis of the IEEE 802.11 MAC layer handoff process. *Computer Communication Review*, 33(2): 93–102.

Mishra, A., M. Shin, and W. A. Arbaugh. 2004. Context caching using neighbor graphs for fast handoffs in a wireless network. In *Proceedings of the Twenty-Third Conference of the IEEE Communications Society* (INFOCOM), March 7–11, Hong Kong. pp. 351–61.

Nakajima, N., A. Dutta, S. Das, and H. Schulzrinne. 2003. Handoff delay analysis and measurement for sip-based mobility in IPv6. In *IEEE International Conference on Communications* (ICC). Vol. 2: 1085–89.

Nichols, K. 1998. *Definition of the differentiated services field (DS field) in the IPv4 and IPv6 headers*. RFC 2474, December.

Pack, S., and Y. Choi. 2002. Fast inter-ap handoff using predictive authentication scheme in a public wireless LAN. *Networks: The Proceedings of the Joint International Conference on Wireless LANs and Home Networks (ICWLHN 2002) and Networking (ICN 2002)*, Aug. 26–9, Atlanta. pp. 15–26.

Park, S.-H., H.-S. Kim, C.-S. Park, J.-W. Kim, and S.-J. Ko. 2004. Selective channel scanning for fast handoff in wireless LAN using neighbor graph. In *Proceedings of the Ninth International Conference on Personal Wireless Communications*, Sept. 21–23, Delft, the Netherlands. pp. 194–203.

Perkins, C. 2002. *IP mobility support for IPv4*. RFC 3344, August.

Ramani, I., and S. Savage. 2005. SyncScan: Practical fast handoff for 802.11 infrastructure networks. In *Proceedings of the IEEE Conference on Computer Communications* (INFOCOM), March, Miami. pp. 675–84.

Ransome, J. F., and J. W. Rittinghouse. 2005. *VoIP security*. New York: Elsevier.

Sharma, S., N. Zhu, and T. Chiueh. 2004. Low-latency mobile IP handoff for infrastructure-mode wireless LANS. *IEEE Journal of Selected Areas in Communications*, 22(4): 643–52.

Shin, S., A. G. Forte, A. S. Rawat, and H. Schulzrinne. 2004. Reducing MAC layer handoff latency in IEEE 802.11 wireless LANs. In *Proceedings of the Second International Workshop on Mobility Management and Wireless Access Protocols*, edited by A. Boukerche, K.M. Sivalingam, and S. E. Nikoletseas, pp. 19–26. Philadelphia: ACM.

Szabó, I. On call admission control for IP telephony in best effort networks. *Computer Communications*, 26(4): 304–313, 2003.

Vali, D., S. Paskalis, A. Kaloxylos, and L. Merakos. 2003. An efficient micromobility solution for sip networks. In *IEEE GLOBECOM*, 2003. Vol. 6: 3088–92.

Velayos, H., and G. Karlsson. 2004. Techniques to reduce IEEE 802.11b handoff time. In *IEEE International Conference on Communications*, June, Paris.

Viterbi, A. J. 1995. *CDMA: Principles of spread spectrum communication*. Redwood City, CA: Addison Wesley Longman.

Wang, Q., M. Abu-Rgheff, and A. Akram. 2004. Design and evaluation of an integrated mobile IP and SIP framework for advanced handoff management. In *IEEE International conference on Communications* (ICC), June, Paris. pp. 3921–5.

Wu, W., N. Banerjee, K. Basu, and S. K. Das. 2005. SIP-based vertical handoff between WWANs and WLANs. *IEEE Wireless Communications*, 12(3): 66–72.

Youssef, M., and A. Agrawala. 2005. The Horus WLAN location determination system. In ACM MobiSys '05, June (retrieved from www.usenix.org/publications/library/proceedings/mobisys05/tech/full_papers/youssef/youssef_html/).

Wireless Internet

Abbas Jamalipour, *University of Sydney, Australia*

INTRODUCTION

Wireless mobile Internet has been an important topic of research within academia and industry in the past few years due to the popularity and dominance of the Internet services in our daily lives and the corresponding desire to have such services ubiquitously, regardless of location and time. The wireless Internet therefore will have a much broader meaning than a simple extension of the Internet into the mobile environment. Wireless Internet is really about the integration of the conventional global Internet platform with other advanced telecommunications technologies, so that all communications services of human beings, including Internet protocol (IP) services, could be covered anytime, anywhere, and through the best available access technology. The wireless mobile Internet, which was a dream just few years ago, is now progressing so fast that it could revolutionize the whole framework of the telecommunication industry. Because of the extensive progress achieved during the last decade in the design of wireless access technology, switching and routing in the Internet, and sophisticated hardware and software, such a comprehensive Internet technology is no longer a dream but a practical reality. Whereas the first cellular-based mobile Internet services provided users with flavors of an actual wireless mobile Internet system, more research is needed to achieve the systematic goals of this network (Jamalipour 2003). Figure 1 illustrates some assumptions of a mobile Internet system.

Mobile and wireless Internet, as the name specifies, should provide a seamless transition from geographically fixed domain to a mobile environment. In this case, *seamless transition*, means that there should be no sensible change for a user who is connected to the Internet while moving from a fixed domain to a mobile domain. In a broad sense, this could even be the case when a user moves from a wireless network domain to another

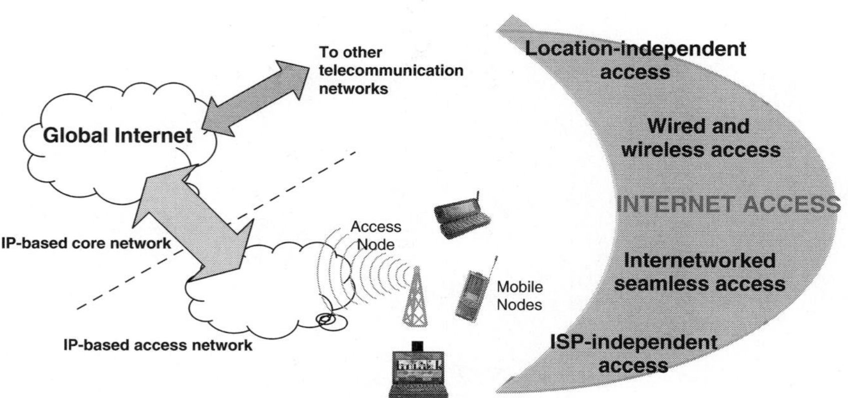

Figure 1: Internet access in a mobile environment

wireless network. The Internet access for the user should be independent of the access technology used for the Internet services.

The current network architectures used in either the wired Internet or the cellular networks would be neither appropriate nor efficient for future wireless mobile Internet, even if we assume that the cellular networks will provide the major infrastructure of the mobile Internet. Cellular networks simply cannot offer sufficient bandwidth and data rate for the mobile multimedia and Internet. The wired Internet, on the other hand, faces serious difficulties in providing service to mobile Internet users. Much of the literature in recent years has discussed this issue and how it is possible to change the network architecture to be utilized for mobile Internet (Umehira et al. 1999; Macker, Park, and Corson 2001; Oliphant 1998; Noerenberg II 2001; McCann and Hiller 2000; Ramjee et al. 2000; Mobile Wireless Internet Forum n.d.). One major issue is making the core network independent of the underlying access technology.

Currently there exist several access networks, such as second- and third-generation (2G and 3G) wireless cellular, wireless local area network (WLAN), and satellite, that offer a broad range of services. Access-specific end terminals are required for subscribers to enjoy seamless services across these networks. At present, there is no single system available that can effectively replace all of these technologies and offer all services using the same terminal. As a result, research is under way to develop the next-generation network (4G or beyond 3G [B3G]) that will facilitate seamless mobility across heterogeneous technologies by means of a single handheld terminal. This envisaged network will be a fabric of inter networked existing and future access technologies (both wired and wireless) integrated together through an IP version 6 (IPv6) transport protocol (Jamalipour, Mirchandani, and Kibria 2005; Mirchandani, Kibria, and Jamalipour 2005).

At the same time, extensive research is under way toward systems based on Institute of Electrical and Electronics Engineers (IEEE) standards for a wide coverage area from personal area networks (PANs) of the IEEE 802.15, local area networks (LANs) of the IEEE 802.11, metropolitan area networks (MANs) of the IEEE 802.16, and finally the wide area networks (WANs) of the IEEE 802.20, a serious competitor of the cellular wide area networks such as 3G systems. In addition, there are activities toward the generation of standards for handoff and roaming among those IEEE families under the IEEE 802.21 standard. Because of the closeness of WLAN to the traditional wired Internet, these new standards can open new doors to the implementation of wireless and mobile Internet in the future. Figure 2 summarizes the cellular and IEEE standards for different coverage areas.

Chapter Outline

This chapter introduces the concept and architectural requirements of the future wireless Internet from cellular and IEEE standards points of view. The vast infrastructure already deployed for cellular 2G and 3G systems, together with the current research and development on next-generation networks (NGNs) and 4G and the integrated architecture of cellular and WLAN systems, constitutes necessary knowledge for future wireless Internet. These areas are covered in this chapter.

In the following section the concepts and fundamental topics of the wireless Internet are discussed. This section includes discussions on changes in future Internet services, changes required for the dominant Internet protocol suite, evolutions in telecommunications technologies (for voice and data communications), potential mobile Internet applications that must be supported in future networks, the concept of the future telecommunications networks working in heterogeneous and cooperative ways, and a summary.

Then the next-generation networks and the heterogeneity involved are further investigated. Next-generation network motivations and features, the problems with the conventional Internet protocol suite (and possible solutions), and a summary are provided. The following section looks at the new trends in integration of wireless LAN standards with the cellular networks to provide faster data communications where possible. In this section, major interconnecting architecture proposed in the literature is discussed. Next we look at IEEE standards and how they can provide a major role in future broadband wireless Internet services. The main IEEE standards, including

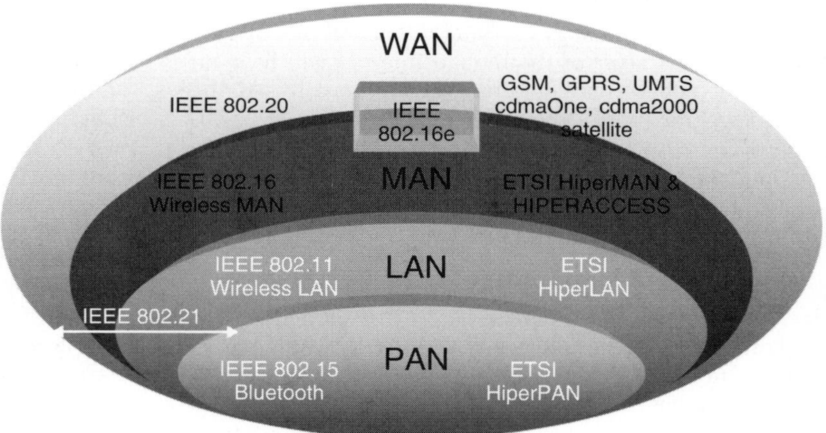

Figure 2: Coverage of IEEE standards and cellular systems

IEEE 802.11, 802.15, 802.16, 802.20, and 802.21, are reviewed and move the reader toward the realization of broadband wireless access and the Internet using these standards. The chapter closes with a conclusion.

CONCEPTS AND FUNDAMENTAL ISSUES IN WIRELESS INTERNET

The wireless mobile Internet will be different from its wired counterpart in the sense that the online service will be provided to a user regardless of the user's geographical location and the communications access network. The motives behind wireless Internet are the great success and popularity of the traditional wired Internet and the need to offer the service anytime and anywhere. This expansion of Internet service to a wide geographical area is not feasible unless several telecommunications technologies work cooperatively with one another. The mobility of a user among networks of the same types or different types, and ways to assure quality of service and handover management need to be solved before the complete wireless mobile Internet can be established.

In this section, we look at the changes that have taken place in the Internet world from a service point of view, and how these changes need to be handled by future networks. How the modular Internet protocol suite can establish the quality and security requirements of the mobile Internet of the future will be of primary importance.

Changes in Internet Service

The traditional Internet services were introduced based on the assumption of fixed networks with personal computers and servers connected through cables and located at fixed physical locations. Mobile Internet will change the types of service because the network devices and computers can be moved to different locations freely while maintaining their network connections. Services in the modern mobile Internet can transition from fixed domain to mobile domain, and vice versa. Services can also be transported from a mobile network (e.g., as a 3G system) to another mobile network (e.g., WLAN). An ideal mobile Internet will experience no noticeable change of service quality for a user moving from one domain (fixed or mobile) to another domain. This will be the main challenge of future mobile Internet design.

The access technology carrying the actual bits of data at the physical layer of the mobile Internet will have an important effect on maintaining service quality. At the same time, the mobile Internet should provide service independent of the access technology. No dramatic change in the quality of service (QoS) parameters—particularly those that can be sensed by users, such as data rate and delay—should be felt during roaming from one network to another network.

Because the current protocol stack model has a modular structure, such as one seen in TCP/IP, achieving the real multi-access technology mobile Internet would be difficult, if not impossible. Throughout this chapter we will introduce other methods to remedy such shortfalls. In the following subsection, we first summarize some changes based on the assumption that the current protocol stack model is used.

Changes in Layer Protocols

During transition from the traditional wired Internet to the wireless Internet, network protocols and architecture change dramatically. In a mobile Internet system, the user should not feel a dramatic change in quality of service (QoS) for the application currently being used. The most noticeable quality measure is the connection speed or data bit rate, which is logically followed by the delay requirements. Changes in protocol affect all layers of the network protocol stack. At the physical layer (layer 1), mobile devices have to be equipped with multiple interfaces to different access networks, including wired examples such as Ethernet cable and dialup modem and wireless examples such as wireless LAN, infrared, and cellular modems. The physical layer has to include several interfaces to layer 2 in order to manage the best connection to higher layers, and if one connection cannot provide the required quality to the application, a combination of two access networks can be granted. Consequently, link layer (layer 2) has to be modified in order to simultaneously establish and maintain two or more connections via different access networks that are provided by the physical layer. This change in the link layer protocol can be incorporated, for example, in the design of the computer operating system (OS) functions. The multi-access inclusion in layers 1 and 2 is the start of a heterogeneous system configuration.

At the network layer (layer 3), Internet protocol needs major changes so that it can handle the routing and other usual tasks of the network layer in wired and wireless environments. Mobility of the IP address should be accommodated in the future mobile Internet. Signaling requirement of the IP layer protocol has to be simplified to provide more spectrum efficiency in future wireless access networks. IP addressing and global address translation among heterogeneous networks must be performed in protocol changes at layer 3.

The transport layer on top of the IP layer may be considered the main area of modification for future mobile Internet networks. The legacy design of this layer for wired networks avoids efficient use of the radio channel capacity; thus, major modifications and extensions are required at the transport layer with dominant transmission control protocol (TCP) and user datagram protocol (UDP).

In a mobile Internet, the mobile user does not see any difference between the currently available service providers at a given time and location, and it is assumed that a user may access the Internet regardless of his or her point of attachment to the network and the supporting access and core networks. Therefore, a system for authentication and authorization of users when moving across different networks must be established. Authentication provides the proof of identity of a user to the network that the user is going to access. This process is usually performed through an authentication function procedure. Authorization certifies what type of services may be provided to an authenticated user. Therefore, it is not sufficient

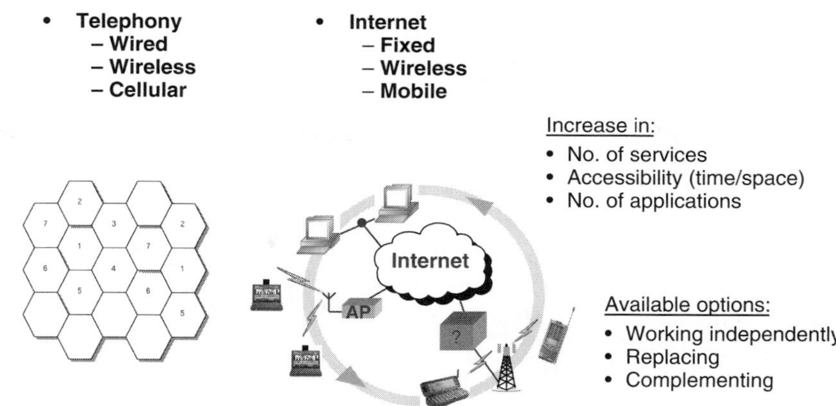

Figure 3: Evolution in telephony system and the Internet

that a user is in a capacity to connect to a network; the user has to be subscribed for a list of services that he or she will receive from the subscribed network. Accounting (the third A in the network AAA—authentication, authorization, and accounting) provides a database of what and when a user accessed while connected to a network. Accounting also provides the pricing and tariff calculation of different types of services received by the user from multiple network providers.

Mobile Internet will be shared among different telecommunication technologies and hence needs to share its limited resources. A sophisticated resource management is vitally necessary to share those resources among all coexisting technologies. Resource management schemes such as bandwidth management, admission control, congestion control, and so on will guarantee reliable performance of the network as well as a fair allocation of resources to all eligible users.

Evolution of the Telecommunications Technologies

The telephony system and the Internet have developed by very similar trends. Telephony was has started with wired connections and switching and later evolved into wireless and cordless systems. As a result of the requirement to support more users, the cellular telephony concept (i.e., spatial and frequency reuse) and various multiple-access technologies were invented. Although at this time a large number of users are on mobile telephony networks, fixed telephony still plays a major role in telecommunications, both as an end-user service provider and as the backbone of the cellular telephony system. During the advancement of the telephony network, new services and applications were generated, and the accessibility of phone communications has greatly increased in time and space.

The global Internet infrastructure has also been initiated and greatly extended within the wired network. The Internet backbone includes a large number of high-capacity digital trucks, some supported by the public telephony system and even satellite channels, and wired switches and routers forming the global Internet infrastructure. The Internet services and applications have increased significantly, at a much quicker pace than their telephony counterparts, and in a much wider range. Figure 3 summarizes the similarities between the two dominant telecommunications technologies.

The network traffic in both systems has evolved as well. The telephony system started with voice communications service and then found its way to data communications. The switches evolved to change the circuit-switched architecture into more data-friendly packet-switched networks. Soon, other multimedia traffic such as video was added to the list of traffic types. The Internet, on the other hand, began with lower rates for data communications and then increased its capacity toward high-speed data communications. Eventually it moved toward voice types of real-time traffic that require lower delay as used in voice over IP (VoIP) and videoconferencing over the Internet. Thus, it seems that there are many common points in the evolution of the two networks, which could offer different options for their cooperation in the future telecommunications infrastructure.

Fixed an Mobile Internet Applications

The next generation of the Internet should support a variety of services and applications, some via the conventional wired Internet, some via short-range mobility provided by the WLAN, some as a result of developments in cellular data communications such as short message service (SMS) and multimedia message service (MMS), and eventually others when wider mobility and Internet connectivity can be provided. Figure 4 shows some of these applications.

The mobile Internet applications are endless, and many new services are created everyday. The following list shows some examples of the applications that should be supported by the mobile Internet. Some of these applications require access to a different access technology (wired or wireless) depending on time and the users' location. Understanding these applications and services could be useful in the design process of future mobile Internet systems.

- Vehicles
  - Transmission of news, road conditions, weather, music via digital audio broadcasting (DAB)

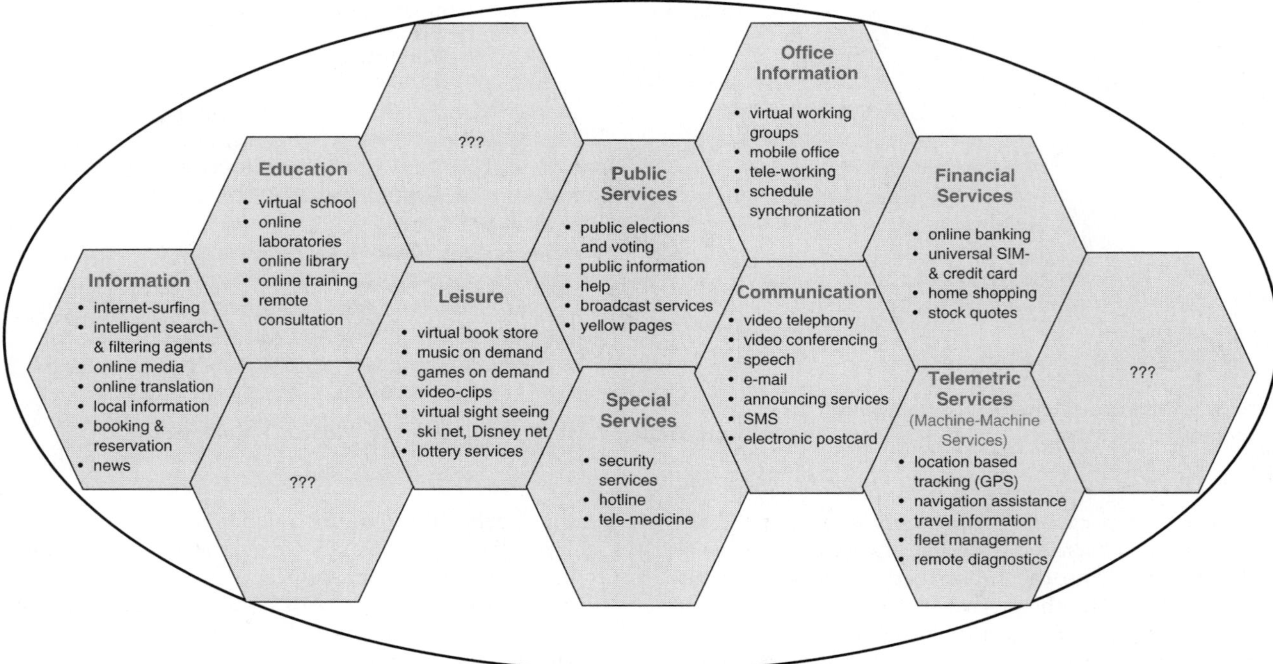

Figure 4: Fixed and mobile Internet applications

- Personal communication using cellular phones
- Position via global positioning system (GPS)
- Local ad hoc network with vehicles close by to prevent accidents, guidance system, redundancy
- Vehicle data (e.g., from buses, high-speed trains) can be transmitted in advance for maintenance

- Emergencies
  - Early transmission of patient data to the hospital, current status, first diagnosis
  - Replacement of a fixed infrastructure in case of earthquakes, hurricanes, fire, and so forth
  - Crisis, war, and so on
- Traveling salesmen
  - Direct access to customer files stored in a central location
  - Consistent databases for all agents
  - Mobile office
- Replacement of fixed networks
  - Remote sensors (e.g., weather, earth activities)
  - Flexibility for trade shows
  - LANs in historic buildings
- Entertainment, education, and so forth
  - Outdoor Internet access
  - Intelligent travel guide with up-to-date, location-dependent information
  - Ad hoc networks for multi-user games

Telecommunications Network of the Future

In order to support the future mobile and wireless Internet with all its services and applications, including those traditionally supported by the telephony systems, it is vitally important to move toward a cooperative system that consists of all advanced telecommunications technologies held together by a reliable and efficient core network. This system will be the basic structure of the future mobile Internet. Figure 5 illustrates such a system, which will be discussed in more detail in this chapter.

The telecommunication system of the future will require horizontal and vertical communications among different access technologies such as cellular, cordless, WLAN, short-range connectivity network such as Bluetooth, satellites, and wired networks. Vertical communications refer to the communication interfaces between systems of different generations or with different coverage, whereas the horizontal communications applies to the systems and networks of the same generation or type. Such two-dimensional communications will provide an efficient use of advantages of each network to provide the ultimate service to users. Appropriate roaming and handover techniques among these networks for seamless mobility will be the key to the future mobile data networks and the Internet. Figure 6 represents a simplified model for such two-dimensional internetworking.

An advanced media access technology connects the core network to the heterogeneous systems. This core network will provide seamless and transparent service negotiations including mobility, security, and quality (such as data rate, delay, packet dropping probability, etc.).

Summary

Applications have been and will be the driving forces in the evolution of all telecommunications technologies, and this will be the case for the mobile Internet too.

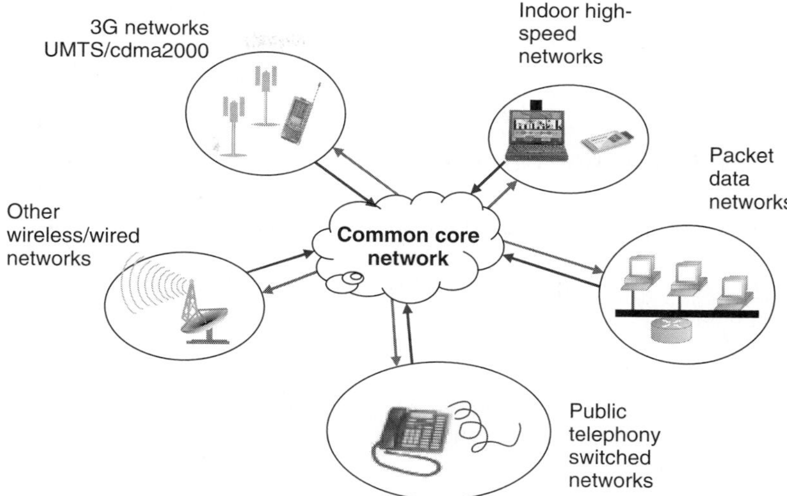

Figure 5: Interoperated telecommunications architecture

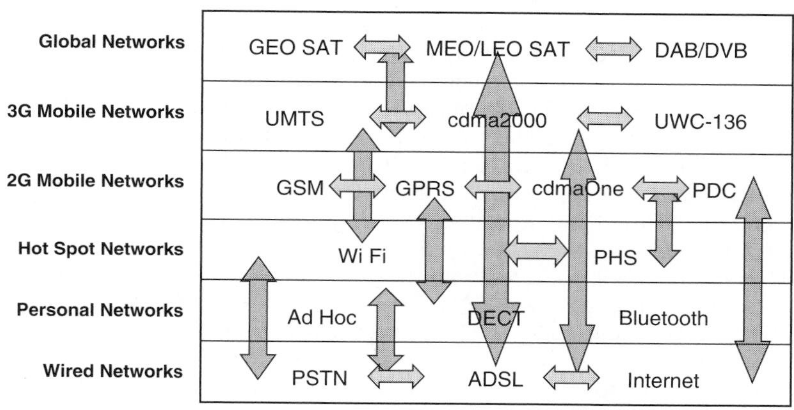

Figure 6: Two-dimensional internetworking

The success of the global Internet was mainly due to its accessibility and the usage of an open architecture, which has yielded to more affordable costs and higher popularity. Mobility will be the most recognizable feature of future telecommunications, and the wireless Internet has to find the best solutions to support mobility in heterogeneous access technology environments. Multimedia mobile applications will force future networks to be united under a common platform and to cooperate efficiently to complement the services of one another. The success of the mobile Internet will depend on the appropriate use of different technologies at proper times and in proper domains.

For the mobile Internet of the future, efficient heterogeneous traffic flow management and QoS management techniques are required. These techniques should be capable of delivering a variety of QoS and security on an end-to-end basis within the heterogeneous networks of wired and wireless segments. Traffic flow volume must be controlled by discriminatory preferences given to individual users and applications as a result of limited available spectrum. Yet, in order to keep the popularity of the Internet as it is now, best effort services should be continued for those users who want it. Best effort services are also necessary when providing the QoS is not possible due to physical channel restrictions and/or network resource availability.

NEXT-GENERATION NETWORKS AND HETEROGENEITY

The emergence of several access technologies has resulted in a multitude of heterogeneous systems targeting different service types, data rates, and users. Whereas the migration from first- to second-generation cellular systems involved the transition from analog to digital technology, the evolution from second- to third-generation cellular systems is driven by the popularity of the Internet and the need for higher data transmission availability on the move. Different available access technologies—such as second-generation global system for mobile communications (GSM) and IS-95 (CDMAOne), the enhanced higher data rate third-generation packet-switched universal mobile telecommunications system (UMTS) and CDMA2000, the high-capacity/high-bandwidth WLANs (IEEE 802.11, HIPERLAN, HIPERLAN2), high-speed digital broadcast systems such as digital audio broadcast (DAB), digital video broadcast (DVB), and so forth—with their own distinct characteristics, complement one another (see Figure 6).

However, the absence of a single architecture to integrate all existing and future systems prevents the subscribers from enjoying reliable and global end-to-end connectivity through a single subscription.

NGN: Motivations and Features

The main motivation for the research in next-generation network architecture is based on factors such as:

- Demand for better availability of services and applications
- Global connectivity all types of services anytime, anywhere, and anyhow
- Rapid increase in the number of wireless subscribers who want to make use of the same handheld terminal while roaming
- Support for bandwidth-intensive applications such as real-time multimedia, online games and videoconferencing, and traditional voice service (VoIP)

The scalable and distributed next generation (or 4G) network architecture is expected to offer services in diverse setting such as indoor, outdoor, pedestrian, and vehicular. The services will be offered over a large range of overlapping access networks (e.g., WLAN, 2G, 3G, xDSL, DVB, DAB, etc.) that offer different data rates, coverage, bandwidth, delay and loss, QoS requirements, and so forth (Jamalipour, Mirchandani, and Kibria 2005; Mirchandani, Kibria, and Jamalipour 2005; Berezdivin et al. 2002; Frodigh et al. 2001; Gustafsson and Jonsson 2003; Kellerer and Vogel 2002). Figure 7 shows a general view of this type of next-generation system with overlapping heterogeneous access networks.

The key features visible to the user in such a network (per example in Figure 7) are:

- Mobile terminals will be able to auto-configure to the specific access technology at the location of the terminal.
- Subscribers will have access to the various services on offer and enjoy a wired LAN equivalent quality of service, cost, and security, even while running real-time applications.
- Ubiquitous and seamless connectivity will be provided through effective mobility, resource, and QoS management schemes.
- The investments made by the subscriber will be respected by limiting the changes required in the multi-access mobile terminal in terms of hardware or software.

The key research objectives for such a harmonized heterogeneous 4G network architecture are:

- Integration of all existing and future communication access systems through a common IPv6 gluing mechanism.
- Development of a modular and scalable architecture with well-defined distributed network functionalities.
- Development of effective mobility, resource, and QoS management schemes to offer seamless connectivity and end-to-end QoS between peer end terminals.
- Development of physical architecture of a QoS-enabled mobile terminal capable of accessing the Internet and real-time services over a multitude of access technologies.
- Offering similar services (subject to network capacity and service policy) in both home and visited networks based on preferences and service agreements in the subscription.

IP Architecture Shortfalls and Improvements for NGN

It is widely agreed that IP will be the main component the next-generation mobile systems and therefore the future wireless Internet. With this assumption in mind, the traditional protocol stack used for IP shows some inadequacies for such an important role.

The Internet protocol stack is designed as a modular structure with a limited number of layers and their

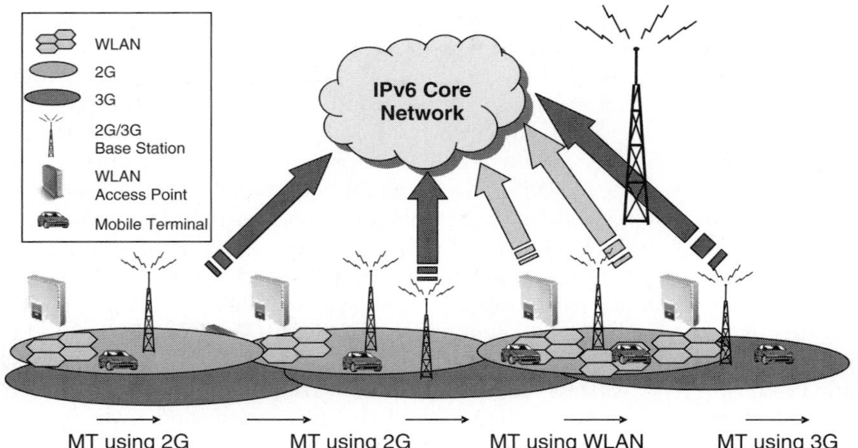

Figure 7: General view of the next-generation system showing overlapping heterogeneous access networks

associated protocols. Each layer uses services provided by its next lower layer and then provides new services to its next upper layer. In such a modular and layered architecture, communication is only possible between the adjacent layers. Figure 8 shows the conventional TCP/IP modular protocol stack. Numerous texts provide more information on the fundamentals of the TCP/IP protocol suite, including (Forouzan 2003; Stallings 2000; Comer 1999).

In the TCP/IP protocol stack, each layer is responsible for particular tasks. More specifically, the link layer (e.g., the Ethernet) provides connectivity to other network segments—that is, not to the hosts in different networks. The network layer (e.g., IP) delivers datagrams across multiple networks. Thus, a packet sent on one network can be transported to a host in a different network using IP routing mechanisms. The transport layer may be one of the two main protocols, TCP or UDP. TCP provides connection-oriented communications services, makes the communication reliable, and avoids network congestion, using its own flow and congestion control algorithms. UDP, on the other hand, provides a simple but unreliable transport mechanism for quicker communications required in some applications such as real-time and voice traffic.

Looking at this modular structure and defined tasks for layer protocols, the question is where to put the main elements necessary for NGN. In particular, for the QoS it becomes an important issue that the protocol stack can support voice, video, and other multimedia real-time services that require low delay performance. Also, the mobility among networks of the same technology (i.e., micromobility) and across networks of different technologies (i.e., macromobility) are unsolvable with the current structure.

In order to solve the problem to some degrees, extended structures for the TCP/IP protocol stack have been researched for many years. Figure 9 shows one example of the extended TCP/IP stack. In order to increase the IP address space and to ease the routing at the IP layer, new network protocols such as IPv6 have been introduced. Additionally, in order to improve the performance of TCP in the error-prone wireless channel, modified versions of the TCP have been widely introduced (Xin and Jamalipour 2005; Akyildiz et al. 2004). Additional sublayers for adaptive selection of networks and their associated media access control (MAC) protocols were also created. Note that in the extended protocol stack, the modularity of the protocol suite remains.

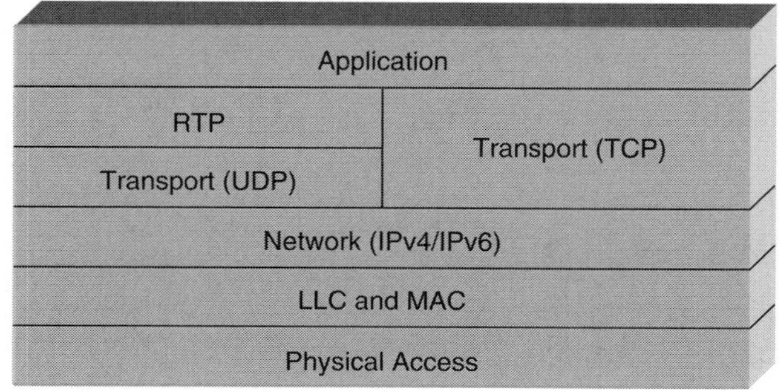

Figure 8: Conventional TCP/IP protocol stack

In Akyildiz et al. (2004), modifications of individual layer protocols are discussed that would allow the overall architecture to handle the heterogeneity in the NGN. In this paper, all changes have been made at the mobile host end, keeping the network side unchanged. In the proposed architecture called AdaptNet (Akyildiz et al. 2004), the link, transport, and application layers have been modified. At the application layer, in order to handle the fluctuations in bit rate and error rate of the wireless channel, adaptive source and channel coding techniques are employed. At the transport layer, an adaptive mobile-host–centric transport protocol is introduced—radial reception control protocol—which controls the connection congestion at the mobile host and changes the number of simultaneous transport interfaces when more bandwidth is required. At the link layer, an adaptive MAC protocol for seamless access control over heterogeneous networks is proposed. An adaptive error-correction scheme that changes the coding rate in accordance with the channel condition is also proposed.

Keeping the protocol suite in its conventional modular structure has produced many benefits in the past three decades, most notably the ability of independent people to design protocols for individual layers. However, as mentioned earlier, this modularity leaves QoS, security, and other requirements of the NGN out of scope or hard to achieve. Recently, an alternative protocol suite that includes cross-layer coordination among layers has been introduced (Carneiro, Ruela, and Ricardo 2004), as shown in Figure 10. The cross-layer architecture provides easier and quicker interactions among individual layers and changes the modularity structure of the conventional protocol suite. This, of course, may cause new problems in the independent design of protocols for layers, as more interfaces among layers than the usual interfaces to upper and lower layers must be considered.

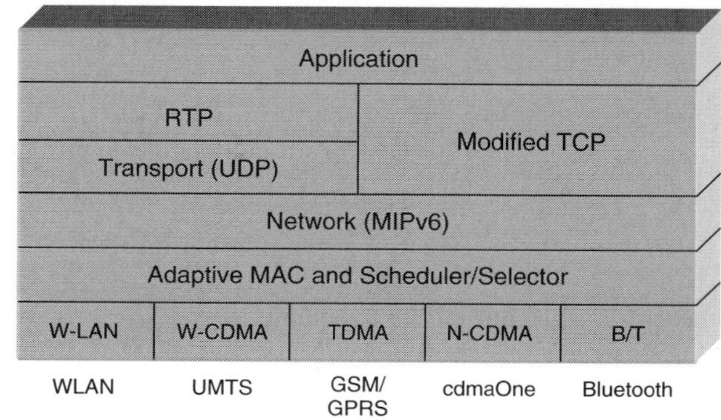

Figure 9: Extended TCP/IP protocol stack

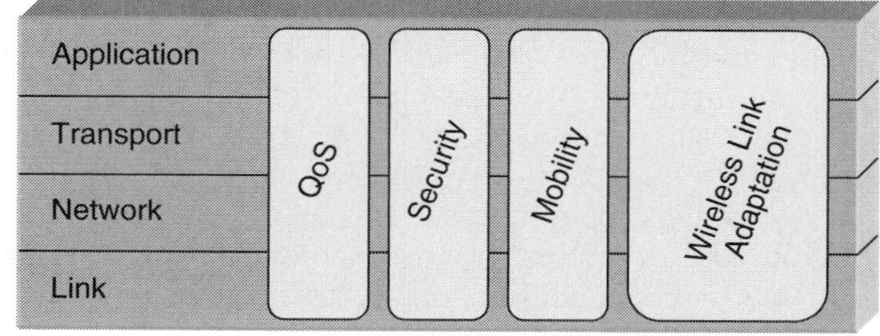

Figure 10: Cross-layer architecture design for NGN

The cross-layer architecture design modifies the overall protocol stack, removes the modularity characteristic from it, and allows the interaction of protocol layers with layers other than adjacent ones.

Four separate vertical coordination planes are considered in the cross-layer architecture of Figure 10. These planes coordinate the information exchange and actions to be carried out by individual layers. The four planes are QoS, security, mobility, and wireless link adaptation.

In order to distribute QoS requirements (at the application level) and constraints (usually at the physical level) and the coordination of the efforts by layers to achieve an acceptable QoS level, the QoS plane is used. As an example of the need for such coordination, consider the change in error rate sensed at the physical and MAC layers. In the conventional modular structure, it takes a long time for the application to find any problem at the physical channel, as it has to be passed over several layers with their individual protocol processing delays. If the information for the physical layer bit rate or error rate can be passed directly to the application layer, the application can reduce the data-generation rate. This also reduces the network congestion (due to packet loss and retransmissions by the transport and link layer protocols) and provides a better QoS to the user application.

Coordination for the security also provides a much more efficient control compared with the traditional networks. The security plane in the cross-layer architecture coordinates the security arrangements usually performed at individual layers, which sometime require unnecessary redundancy and delay in supporting the service to the user.

The mobility plane in this architecture will solve the problem of the nonmobile structure of the conventional protocol suite. The information about the change in the access technology in a heterogeneous environment can easily and quickly be directed to the upper layers in vertical and horizontal handoff events.

The wireless link adaptation in the cross-layer architecture helps avoid harmful automatic repeat request (ARQ) reactions at the link layer and the transport layer, for example. When the channel encounters high bit error rate (e.g., wireless), link layer protocol tries to correct the error, which could take a long time before the TCP flow control mechanism acts. The wireless link adaptation plane can provide a direct way of transmitting this and similar information to the higher-layer protocols, so that such unnecessary actions are not taken by the individual layers.

New open and modular architecture specifically designed for NGN and the wireless Internet has been also proposed by the author, which can be further explored in Jamalipour, Mirchandani, and Kibria 2005; Mirchandani, Kibria, and Jamalipour 2005. The proposed architecture is open, hierarchical, layered, and modular, with cross-layer coordination and distributed network functionalities. Well-defined message interfaces enable the layers within the architecture to support the cross-layer coordination under dynamic network conditions. Novel augmentations in mobility and resource management schemes are proposed that result in the consolidation of the corresponding salient areas of B3G architectures discussed in the literature. Seamless services in the network can be accessed through the reconfigurable multi-antenna end terminal. A common mechanism for control and signaling across heterogeneous networks is adopted to facilitate wireless system discovery and paging. The proposed architecture provides easier QoS and mobility management control in future heterogeneous systems. The proposed layered architecture for NGN is shown in Figure 11. The architecture includes advanced technologies such as software-defined radio (SDR) for different radio access networks (RANs). SDR would be an important element of the future NGN in which several access networks are available to the user and the best one should be used for particular applications.

Summary

The heterogeneity involved in the next-generation mobile networks and the wireless Internet requires modification of the TCP/IP protocol stack, which has been in place successfully for many years. This will be done either through an adaptive protocol design at individual layers with minimum layer interactions or through a cross-layer architecture redesign. Modification of the individual protocols to cope with the highly variable and unreliable wireless channel conditions could cure the problem for the short term. A good example of such activity is the numerous research efforts that have been carried out to improve the performance of the TCP over the wireless channel. Therefore, it is the authors opinion that for a longer-term solution the cross-layer architecture would be a better alternative because it can provide more effective solutions to the problems of QoS provisioning and security management in future wireless and mobile networks.

CELLULAR NETWORK INTEGRATION WITH WIRELESS LAN

Modern cellular networks are capable of providing high mobility, whereas a WLAN is known to have relatively high bandwidth. Ubiquitous data services and very high data rates across heterogeneous networks may be achieved by the use of a WLAN as a complementary technology to cellular data networks. Hence there is a strong need for efficient internetworking mechanisms between WLANs and cellular data networks. Such internetworking mechanisms are expected to be equipped with integrated authentication, integrated billing, roaming, terminal mobility, and service mobility (Salkintzis, Fors, and Pazhyannur 2002). A variety of internetworking architectures have been proposed by numerous researchers and groups. By and large, these proposed integration architectures may be categorized as tight coupling, loose coupling, and peer-to-peer networking (also referred as no-coupling; Wong et al. 2003; Varma et al. 2003). The definitions for these coupling mechanisms are as follows (Varma et al. 2003). (In the following, although reference is usually given to the IEEE 802.11 WLAN standard, similar discussions can be considered for other WLAN standards including the ETSI high performance local area network (HIPERLAN) and HIPERLAN2.)

In a tight coupling scenario, an IEEE 802.11 WLAN is connected to the 3G cellular core network (CN) via

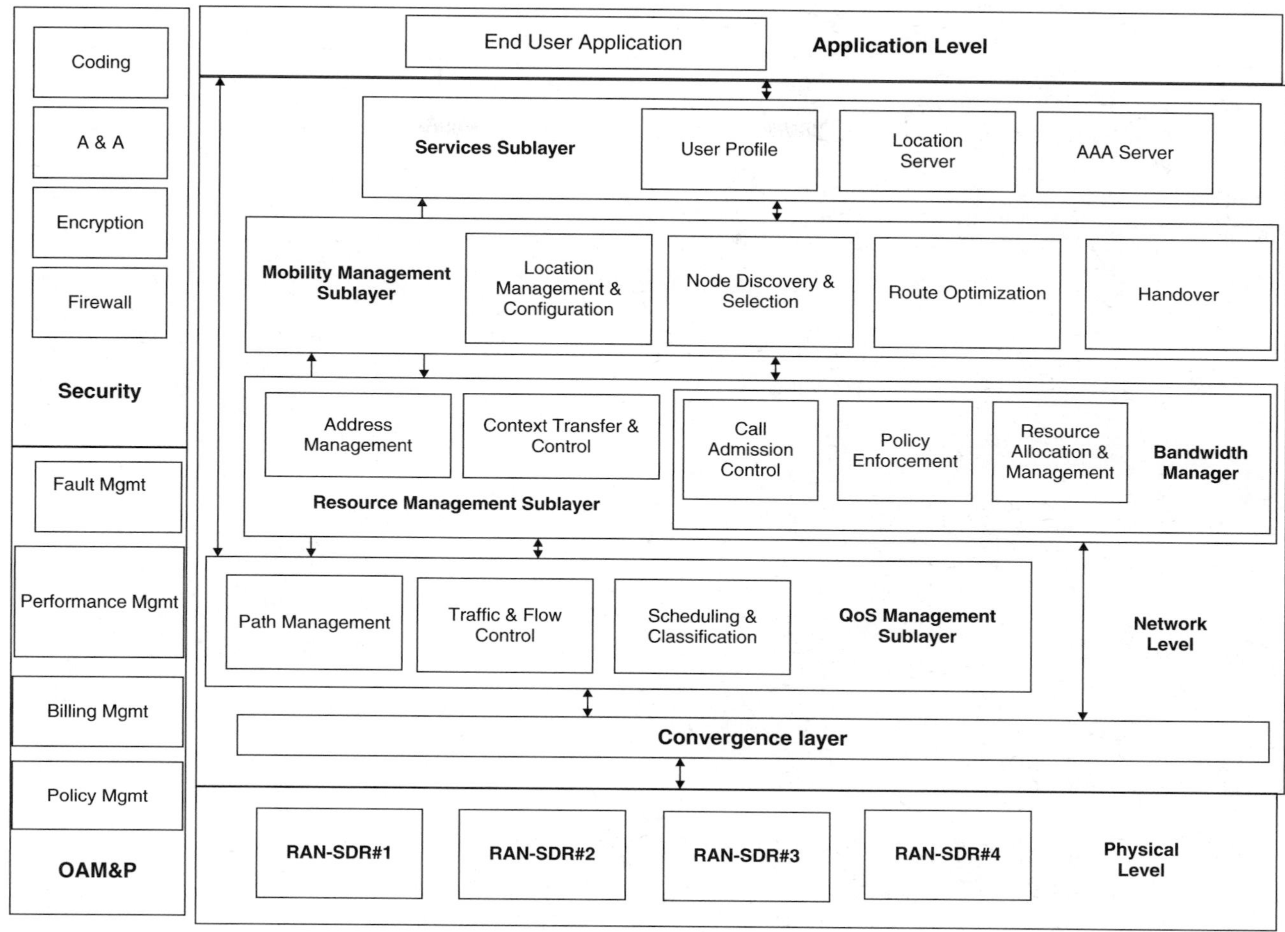

Figure 11: Layered and modular 4G network architecture

a serving general packet radio service (GPRS) support node (SGSN) emulator. Both data and UMTS signaling are transported by the IEEE 802.11 WLAN to the 3G CN via an SGSN emulator. Thus, the IEEE 802.11 basic service set (BSS) acts as another SGSN coverage area to the UMTS CN. On the other hand, a loosely coupled architecture transports UMTS signaling over IEEE 802.11 WLAN to the 3G CN, while data flows directly to the IP-based network. Figure 12 is a reference diagram that shows the tight and loose coupling points.

In tight and loose coupling methods, GPRS/UMTS signaling is carried over WLAN so that the two networks look like one from the network layer and above. In both of these cases, the 3G CN acts as the "master" network and the IEEE 802.11 WLAN behaves as the "slave" network. Although the last coupling mechanism, peer-to-peer networking, can be seen as an extension to the loose coupling architecture, it treats the two networks as peers (Wong et al. 2003). Mobile IP is used to provide a framework for mobility among these peers. The following sections provide a detailed discussion on various internetworking architectures, their advantages, and their disadvantages.

Tight Coupling Architecture

In tight coupling, the WLAN is directly connected to the 3G core network. Thus, the WLAN data traffic passes through the GPRS core network before reaching the external packet data networks (PDNs). The key functional element in the system is the GPRS interworking function (GIF), which interconnects an IEEE 802.11 extended service set (ESS) to an SGSN via the standard Gb interface (Salkintzis, Fors, and Pazhyannur 2002). This is also referred to as an SGSN emulator (Varma et al. 2003). The GIF is the function that makes the SGSN consider the WLAN a typical GPRS routing area (RA) composed of only one cell. Therefore, the handover between WLAN and GPRS can be considered handover between two individual cells. It is also worth noting that the GIF and all interconnected WLAN terminals use a 48-bit IEEE 802 MAC address.

The WLAN adaptation function (WAF) is the main component that helps the mobile station (MS) to identify the MAC address of the GIF. Hence, there is a WAF implemented in every dual-mode MS as well as the GIF for 3G signaling and data exchange over IEEE 802.11 WLAN. WAF also provides the following functions: signaling the activation of WLAN interface as the MS enters a WLAN area, discovery of the MAC address of the GIF, helping the SGSN page a mobile station over the Gb interface, transferring LLC PDUs from the mobile station to the GIF and vice-versa, and supporting QoS by implementing transmission scheduling in the GIF and the MS. A typical architecture of the WLAN in its extended service

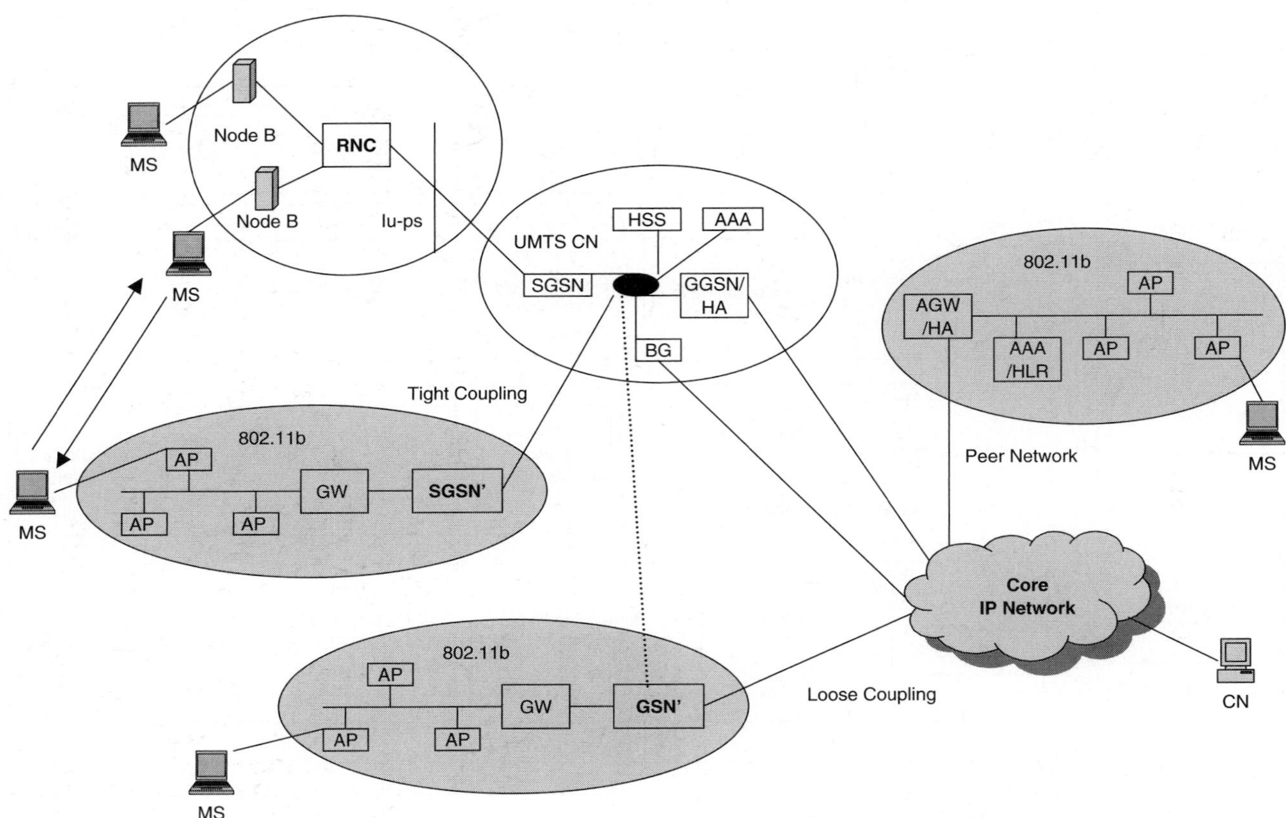

Figure 12: Alternative intergration architectures between WLAN and UMTS

set mode and its required components are shown in Figure 13.

Because the WLAN and GPRS networks connect to the same Gateway GPRS support node (GGSN), IP addresses will be assigned by the same pool. Hence, mobility across the two networks does not require a change of IP address to the MS (Varma et al. 2003). Lastly, the proposed tight coupling architecture is expected to have the following benefits (Salkintzis, Fors, and Pazhyannur 2002).

1. Seamless service continuation across WLAN and 3G networks
2. Less complicated mobility management because it follows GPRS/UMTS mobility management mechanisms.
3. Reuse of GPRS/UMTS AAA
4. Reuse of GPRS/UMTS infrastructure (e.g., core network resources, subscriber database, billing systems)
5. Increased security (GPRS/UMTS security can be applied on top of WLAN security)
6. Common provisioning and customer care
7. Access to core GPRS/UMTS services (SMS, location-based service, MMS, etc.)

Nevertheless, tight coupling can primarily be implemented in WLANs, which are owned by cellular operators. Thus, it lacks implementation capability in third-party WLANs. Furthermore there are cost and capacity concerns associated with the connection of a WLAN to an SGSN.

Loose Coupling Architecture

Similar to the previous coupling method, loose coupling architecture is also a master/slave framework. The GPRS network acts as a master, and the IEEE 802.11 WLAN acts as a slave network (or a visiting network). In order to merely provide an IP connection through a WLAN, only the AAA traffic needs to be routed to the 3G CN and not the user data traffic (Salkintzis 2004a). In this scenario, only AAA signaling is exchanged between the WLAN and the 3G home PLMN (via the 3G visited PLMN) to provide authentication, authorization, and accounting (charging). Two alternative authentication models (or flavors) for loose coupling have been identified, which are described as the "IETF flavor" and the "UMTS flavor" (Findlay et al. 2002; ETSI 2001). The primary difference between the two is essentially the authentication server itself (ETSI 2001).

During the authorization phase, the 3G AAA server can establish polices for the user data traffic. It can also serve as a proxy to route AAA signaling to and from other 3G PLMNs. Thus the 3G AAA server is an important component introduced for the loosely coupled internetworking architectures. However, more advanced types of internetworking scenarios may also require the user data traffic to be routed to the UMTS CN (Salkintzis 2004a, 2004b).

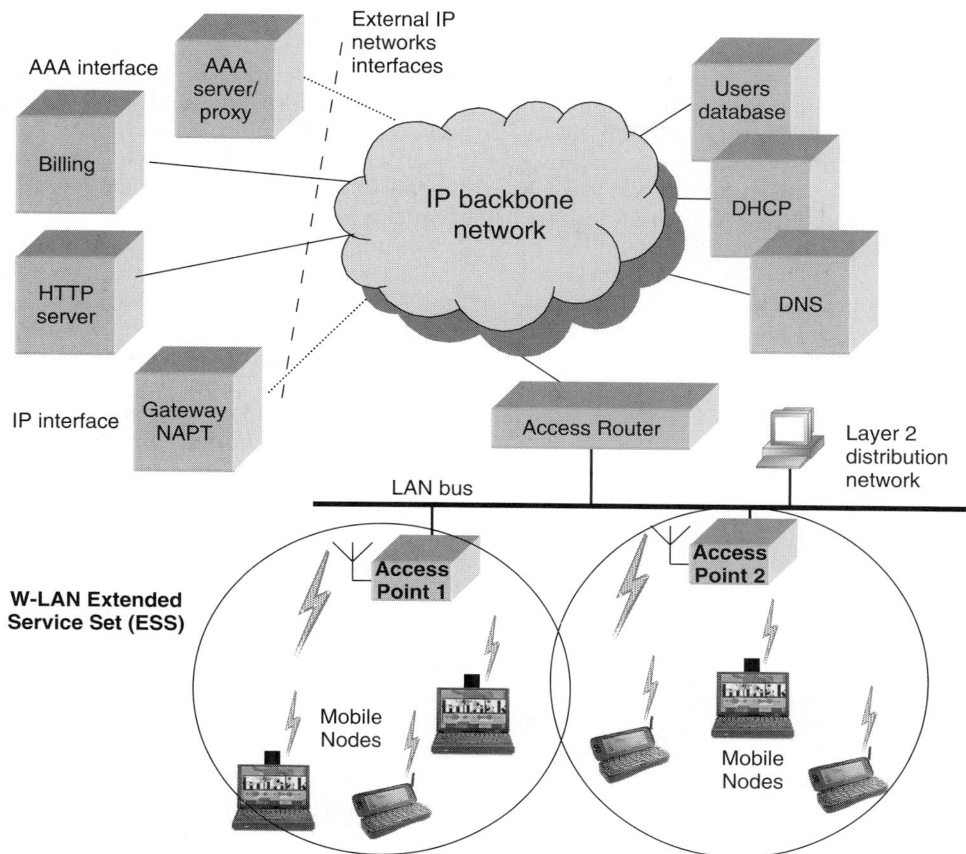

Figure 13: WLAN ESS architecture and its components in an integrated scenario

A clear advantage of the aforementioned method is that, because the data traffic is routed directly to and from the IP network (i.e., Internet) without having to route through the 3G network, a potential traffic bottleneck may be avoided. Since the 3G network and the WLAN are likely to be in different IP address domains, the MH will be allocated an IP address from the pool of addresses of the connected network. The changing of IP addresses may result in loss of connectivity. Therefore, for the loose coupling architecture, handoffs are less efficient and mobility can be considered only when the user is not in an active session (Varma et al. 2003).

Peer-to-Peer Networking Architecture

Unlike the previously discussed master/slave coupling methods, this approach treats the two networks as peers. In a peer-to-peer network architecture, 3G access and WLAN access may be provided by the same or different operators. Mobile IP (MIP) and AAA servers are used to provide a framework for mobility (Pahlavan et al. 2000). MIP is used to restructure connections when an MH roams from one peer network to another, and AAA servers provide AAA functionality.

The MIP framework consists of an MIP client (MH), a foreign agent (FA), and a home agent (HA). Outside of the home network the mobile host is identified by a care-of address associated with its point of attachment. The MH registers its care-of address with its home agent (HA). The HA resides in the home network of the MH and is responsible for intercepting the datagrams addressed to the MH's home address and tunneling them to the associated care-of address.

When a 3G network and a WLAN are accessing a public IP network, MIP can be used in the following manner (Min-hua, Yu, and Hui-min 2003). The HA function may be implemented in the GGSN and the 3G network. As the MH (whose home network is, for example, 3G) moves to a foreign network (e.g., WLAN), it registers to HA (GGSN) its current care-of address through the FA at the foreign network. When the GGSN (HA) receives packets whose destination is the MH, it tunnels these IP packets to the FA and eventually reaches the MH. Likewise, the FA functionality may be implemented at the GGSN or SGSN of the 3G network.

Nevertheless, implementation of the HA does not necessarily have to be at the GGSN. The HA could also be implemented at an external IP network (Salkintzis, Fors, and Pazhyannur 2002). This architecture implements the FA functionality at the 3G and WLAN networks, which integrates with the HA located on an external IP network. However, both 3G and WLAN networks may need to subscribe to this IP network. Although peer-to-peer networking architecture is identified as a separate internetworking architecture, some literature merely considers it a variation of the previously discussed loose coupling mechanism (Wong et al. 2003).

However, during the time frame between the MH leaving its current subnet to a new subnet, associating with a new FA, and updating the HA with the new care-of address, a packet loss (or disruption of service) can be noticed. This is because during this time interval the HA is still tunneling packets to the old FA's care-of address. Furthermore, as the distance between the MH and HA increases the service, the latency and packet loss increase. Thus, MIP framework may not be the best solution for frequently roaming users between two networks (Min-hua, Yu, and Hui-min 2003; Tsao and Lin 2002).

Summary

In this section, various architectures and levels for the 3G–WLAN internetworking were presented. The main mechanisms include tight coupling, loose coupling, and peer-to-peer coupling. Specific challenges encountered, advantages, and disadvantages of each of these architectures have been explored. Despite the fact that there is a vast range of proposed internetworking architectures, exist many open issues still exist issue is session mobility across WLAN and 3G cellular networks. For instance, when an MH with an active IP-based session (e.g., FTP or HTTP) moves from a WLAN to a 3G cellular network (or vice versa), the session must be seamlessly handed over from one network to another. Possible research questions that may arise from such a situation include how to detect the entering and leaving from a hotspot, which part of the network to handoff, and mechanisms to perform authenticated handoff. Thus, how to provide/enable seamless continuity of service across WLAN and 3G cellular networks can be ranked as a top issue.

Another important issue is to define a mechanism for user data routing via heterogeneous networks. How an optimal routing path can be decided is still an open issue (currently investigated by the 3rd-Generation Partnership Project [3GPP]. Nevertheless, matching the QoS requirements and service provisioning between WLAN and the 3G cellular networks can be considered a related issue. Provisioning of unified and integrated mechanisms for AAA and security in general is another high-priority concern. Amongst the related work done by the 3GPP in this area is to eventually adopt the IEEE 802.11i standard (per 3GPP's technical specification TS 33.234). Another related question is whether the AAA should be managed at WLAN, 3G CN, or independently. Furthermore, charging options such as postpaid, prepaid, and IP-flow–based charging must also be considered. Last but not least, terminal capabilities that support high data-rate applications, screen size, computational power, and network selection mechanisms must also be addressed.

IEEE STANDARDS TOWARD BROADBAND WIRELESS INTERNET

As previously mentioned (see Figure 2), IEEE has started a series of standards to provide a wide range of coverage for wireless and mobile data communications. Among these, the most popular standards are the IEEE 802.11 WLAN. The WLAN has already become part of cellular networks, realization of the wireless Internet, through integration with UMTS and other 3G systems to provide broadband Internet access to indoor and high-population environment. This will definitely supplement the cellular 3G networks with much higher data rates than a cellular system can provide, particularly in areas such as buildings and shopping malls where it is primarily needed.

The success of the IEEE 802.11 was more or less a result of the fact that it could integrate itself in microprocessor chips and other computer hardware quickly due to its standardization and resolved compatibility issues. IEEE is going to follow the same approach for its new standards of 802.15, 802.16, and the proposed 802.20 and 802.21. In this section, we briefly review these standards and discuss their role in future broadband wireless Internet infrastructure.

IEEE 802.11 WLAN

One of the extensions to the wired Ethernet is the wireless LAN, defined in the IEEE 802.11 standards (Crow et al. 1997; IEEE 802.11 n.d.). Wireless LAN has become very popular for providing mobile Internet access to office and campus buildings due to the ease in movement of users connected to the Internet. IEEE 802.11 standards define a set of media access protocols to extend the wired Ethernet into the wireless domain. In 1985, the Federal Communications Commission (FCC) modified the radio spectrum regulations for unlicensed devices so that wireless LAN could operate within the industrial, scientific, and medical (ISM) bands if the equipment operates under 1 watt of power. The 902 MHz and 5.725 GHz bands can be used only in the United States, whereas the 2.4 GHz band is available globally (Forouzan 2003). The usage of unlicensed ISM frequency spectrums simplifies deployment of a new wireless LAN with very little, low-cost equipment. Nomadic Internet access, portable computing, multihopping, and ad hoc networking are some of the applications of wireless LAN technology. Depending on the standard, wireless LAN can achieve a speed of 2 (IEEE 802.11), 11 (IEEE 802.11b), or 54 (IEEE 802.11a/g) Mbps, in an ideal situation and with good wireless channel conditions.

In principle, a wireless LAN domain can be provided easily through an access point (AP) cabled to the usual wired Ethernet in a LAN system. Therefore, the access point can be seen as a router or a hub connecting several end hosts to the LAN system. The only difference is that the end host will access the AP through wireless radio channels, rather than cables. Because each AP gives access to several end machines, some type of multiple-access control has to be established by the AP to share the wireless channel among all end users. Spread-spectrum technologies (e.g., direct sequence and frequency hopping) are used for this purpose in the standard. In newer version of the standard, orthogonal frequency division multiple access (OFDMA) is used.

Each AP in a wireless LAN system can provide coverage to mobile Internet users in an area up to a maximum of 500 meters in radius. Therefore, with several APs it is possible to establish a cellular-like wireless LAN. In such a case, cellular-type issues such as handoff and maximum capacity will become apparent. The users of a wireless LAN system can obtain an IP address through a dynamic host configuration protocol (DHCP), similar to a dialup connection, or by having a fixed IP address provided by their network administrator, similar to a desktop user (see Figure 13).

The technology provided by the IEEE 802.11 also allows users to dynamically form a private network without the need for an access point (Toh 2002). Therefore, it is possible to make a temporary network of computers (e.g., during a meeting) in which no single computer is the central server. All users will be on the same level of the network hierarchy. The computers in this network can exchange their data files through the wireless LAN network, which could be isolated from other local wired and wireless networks. This is a very basic implementation of a mobile ad hoc network, which clearly does not have any infrastructure behind it. The Internet Engineering Task Force (IETF) has a working group called the mobile ad hoc network (MANET) that develops the RFCs and standards for this emerging technology.

The IEEE 802.11 standard defines two types of services for the wireless LAN: the BSS and the ESS. In the basic service set, a network of computers is established either with a central base station (access point) that can connect the users of wireless LAN networks to the other parts of the wired network, or without a central base station, which provides an ad hoc network between several users without any access to other parts of the network.

Two or more wireless LANs that are using the basic service set can be connected through any of the IEEE LAN standards such as Ethernet (IEEE 802.3) to make an infrastructure of wireless LANs, so that the system covers a larger geographical area, similar to the concept of cellular networks. This configuration is the extended service set for the IEEE 802.11 standard. The wireless LAN illustration shown in Figure 13 is based on an extended service set configuration.

Two types of MAC are defined by IEEE 802.11: distributed coordination function (DCF) and point coordination function (PCF). DCF is the basic MAC protocol for wireless LAN and is the only access for ad hoc networking types of configuration. DCF is a contention access technique, which means that wireless LAN users need to compete to get a channel for data transmission. DCF is based on the fundamental Internet MAC protocol carrier sense multiple access (CSMA) with additional collision avoidance (CA), which makes it CSMA/CA (Forouzan 2003; Stallings 2000). One reason for using CSMA/CA in wireless LAN and not the usual CSMA with collision detection (CSMA/CD) used in wired LANs is that detecting a collision is not as easy for wireless media as it is for wired systems. In addition, in the case of wireless channels there is always the possibility of becoming involved with the *hidden-terminal problem*.

On the wired network, detection of another signal from a user can be performed by measuring the current signal power on the wire. However, in a wireless environment, it is possible that a user is in range of the base station and thus visible by it, but outside the range of another user, who is also seen by the base station. This phenomenon is called the hidden-terminal problem. Therefore, when a user wants to transmit a packet over the radio channel, detecting the radio signal power would show only other users in his range and not the hidden terminals. If the user transmits a packet at the same time another hidden-terminal transmits his packet, both packets will be lost. The hidden-terminal problem is illustrated in Figure 14.

To avoid the hidden-terminal effect the wireless MAC needs to add extra packet exchange before a transmission to make sure that no one else transmits at the same time. Therefore, the base station in the wireless LAN acts as a server that allows a user to transmit (or not) after a request proposal. This can be done through the use of two short control frames called request to send (RTS) and clear to send (CTS). An RTS frame is sent by a sender and includes the duration of the data packet and the acknowledgement packet. The intended receiver can reply with a CTS frame, which gives an explicit permission to send to the sender. Because all other terminals in the wireless LAN network can listen to this frame exchange, they will know about the future data transmission and can avoid interfering with the transmission. The RTS and CTS frames are short; therefore, there is less probability of being involved in a collision with other packets. In addition following successful exchange of these frames, subsequent (long) data transmission between the two terminals should be collision free.

The point coordination function is implemented on top of DCF for time-sensitive transmissions in an infrastructure wireless LAN architecture. PCF uses centralized, contention-less polling access by utilizing a software package called point coordinator (PC) (IEEE 802.11 n.d.). PC software is located at the base station and polls users, one after another, to avoid any contention for their transmissions. As the PCF runs over the DCF, the sensing process of DCF, is performed at the beginning of the PCF polling cycle only once.

The IEEE 802.11 defines three types of specifications for the physical layer, based on frequency-hopping spread spectrum (FH-SS), direct-sequence spread spectrum (DS-SS) and infrared communications. Binary phase shift keying (BPSK) and quadrature phase shift keying (QPSK) were used as the modulation schemes in DS-SS

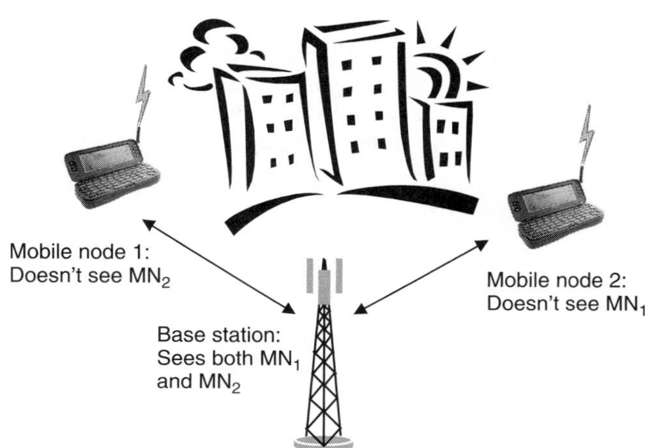

Figure 14: The hidden-terminal problem

specifications of wireless LAN for its early standard, for a bit rate of 1 and 2 Mbps, respectively. Other modulation schemes were added later in IEEE 802.11b and IEEE 802.11a standards to allow higher bit rates of 5.5 and 11 Mbps in IEEE 802.11b and 54 Mbps in IEEE 802.11a. In IEEE 802.11b, the MAC and logical link control (LLC) layer protocols are kept the same as in the original IEEE 802.11 and only the physical layer has been modified. For IEEE 802.11b, DS-SS is utilized. Dynamic rate shifting is also allowed in IEEE 802.11b so that in a noisy environment bit rate can be decreased from its highest 11 Mbps dynamically to 5.5, 2, or 1 Mbps.

IEEE has recently added new members to the 802.11 family in order to provide QoS, security, and higher speed. The IEEE 802.11e adds new QoS features to the originally non-QoS WLAN and supports multimedia and other applications that require delay limits such as VoIP, video on demand, and audio on demand. These are essential for the WLAN to reach markets in the emerging area of home networking. The IEEE 802.11i adds security features to the weak security protocol embedded in the original 802.11 called wired equivalent privacy (WEP). The new advanced encryption standard (ESA) provides greater levels of security compared to the WEP and even to the Wi Fi protected access (WPA) security standard. Security was a weak point in the IEEE 802.11 standard because as it was originally designed for working in a closed area with simple architecture. After it gained popularity in small business and open areas, WLAN had to save itself from malicious attacks. In response to this need, the new IEEE 802.11i has been developed, which includes major security upgrades compared to the original standard. In addition, IEEE 802.11n provides much higher data-rate speed at levels of 100 Mbps and above. There are many new working groups in IEEE 802.11 created for specific purposes and tasks. IEEE 802.11r, for example, specifies fast BSS transitions that will permit connectivity for fast handoffs from one base station to another (e.g., for vehicular application) in a seamless manner. With regard to real-time applications such as voice, the the normal 802.11 handoff procedure requires excessive delays, which makes it impractical for such uses. Therefore, a main application for IEE802.11r will be voice over wireless LAN networks. IEEE 802.11k is another proposed standard for how a wireless LAN should perform channel selection, roaming, and transmitting power control to optimize network performance. The IEEE 802.11k aims to redefine and improve the way traffic is distributed and managed within the network. These protocols will not be further discussed here because they are outside the scope of this chapter.

IEEE 802.15 WPAN

Whereas the IEEE 802.11 was designed to provide high-speed data transmission to local area network users, the IEEE 802.15 (n.d.) targeted short-range connectivity at very high speeds of hundreds of Kbps. Such connections can be used to connect peripheral devices to computers, headsets to mobile phones, mobile phones to computers, and so on.

The IEEE 802.15.1 was adopted from Bluetooth specifications, originally designed for use with PAN. This version is fully compatible with Bluetooth version 1.1. Two technical groups (TGs) work on different data rates; TG4 works on low data rates to provide data speeds of 20 Kbps or 250 Kbps, and TG3 works on high data rates to support data speeds of 11 Mbps to 55 Mbps.

Using this standard, up to 254 network devices can be supported with dynamic device addressing. It also supports devices in which the latency is critical, and it consists of full handshaking, security provisioning, and power management. There are sixteen channels in the 2.4 GHz band (similar to the IEEE 802.11b/g), ten channels in the 915 MHz band, and one channel in the 868 MHz band.

There are also plans to redefine the IEEE 802.15 specifications to work with the specification and description language (SDL), particularly SDL-88, SDL-92, and SDL-2000 updates of the International Telecommunications Union (ITU) recommendation Z.100.

The IEEE 802.15 will provide the lower connectivity level to the IEEE 802.11 WLAN standard and therefore complete the path between the personal and area networks.

IEEE 802.16 WMAN

The IEEE standard 802.16 was originally published in December 2001, for fixed point-to-multipoint broadband wireless systems operating in the 10–66 GHz licensed spectrum (IEEE 802.16 n.d.). Because this band requires line of sight (LOS) between the transmitter and the receiver, an amendment called IEEE 802.16a was approved in January 2003 to provide non-LOS communications in the 2–11 GHz spectrum, delivering up to 70 Mbps at distances up to 30 miles.

The main purpose of the standard was bridging the critical connection that links homes and businesses with their Internet service providers. Data slowdown in the last mile of networking path can impact the entire Web browsing experience and limit the performance of the promising services such as video on demand (VOD) and multimedia-filled Web connections. In that sense, the IEEE 802.16, which subsequently took the name Worldwide Interoperability for Microwave Access (WiMAX) set its vision on blanketing sections of cities and rural areas that are not wired for broadband, or providing an alternative to wired connections in places that are connected. Therefore, with such a vision, WiMax will compete directly with local phone and cable companies that offer wired Internet access such as asynchronous digital subscriber line (ADSL), cable modems, and leased lines.

Using the original concept of the IEEE 802.16, in which point-to-multipoint data communications were considered, a service provider sets the transceiver antenna on top of a tall building. The signal reaches the clients on a LOS basis or, in some cases, through multipath bounces from other buildings. The received signal is decoded and unencrypted, and the payload is extracted. Inside the client's building the WiMax signal can be shared via other standards such as the IEEE 802.11 WLAN access points.

WiMax was not the first attempt at broadband wireless access (BWA) on an MAN range. Much work was done and some testbeds were implemented in different locations with good results. The major change in the WiMax design was to make it standard so that it can utilize inexpensive hardware, as happened with the WLAN WiFi standard. To achieve this goal, a WiMax Forum has been established to create the standardizations and fix the compatibility issues among products, similar to the development stream previously followed for WiFi by the WiFi Alliances. The Forum began in January 2003 and currently includes major partners working on BWA products.

The later version of IEEE 802.16a for non-LOS applications, started in January 2003, operates in licensed and unlicensed bands of 2.4 and 5 GHz using OFDM similar to the IEEE 802.11a and IEEE 802.11g WLAN standards. Another standard 802.16b is also under development by IEEE for use in the licensed spectrum 11–66 GHz band. More recently, IEEE 802.16d has begun to take the place of its 802.16a counterpart with regard to better performance.

In the IEEE 802.16, different from the WLAN family, every base station dynamically distributes information about the uplink and downlink bandwidth to subscribers' stations using time division multiple access (TDMA). The MAC protocol does not use the carrier sense multiple access (CSMA) used in WLAN. Instead every station needs to get the permission and allocated bandwidth for data transmission. Therefore, since no packet contention is involved (as it is in the 802.11), the IEEE 802.16 can provide QoS to the clients. With the new efforts to bring the WiMax inside the processor chips in laptop computers, it is expected that the WiMax will be available soon for personal users. Although WiMAX's role as a MAN provider can be misunderstood by its LAN counterparts, specific differences in design of the IEEE 802.11 and 802.16 allow these two to work with each other rather than compete. In summary, the IEEE 802.16 is particularly designed for outdoor environments and optimized for those channel conditions in contrast to the IEEE 802.11, which is mainly designed for indoor channel conditions. 802.16e is the latest standard version in which mobility is being considered. 802.16e will add mobility to the 2 to 6 GHz licensed bands.

IEEE 802.20 WWAN and IEEE 802.21

The IEEE 802.20 (n.d.) is the proposal of the IEEE for mobile broadband wireless access networks (WAN) in wide geographical areas, something that is currently supported by cellular networks only. In this standard, a packet-based air interface is developed that is optimized for the transport of the IP-based services for mobile broadband wireless access (BWA). Potentially, the system will work in the licensed spectrum below 3.5 GHz. The IEEE 802.20 targets data rates over 1 Mbps per user at vehicular speeds up to 250 km/h. The application and targets of the IEEE 802.20 will be different from those considered by the IEEE 802.16e.

In order to roam from one IEEE standard to another (e.g., from a smaller area to a larger one, or vice versa), IEEE has proposed the new standard IEEE 802.21 (n.d.). In this Working Group, standards will be developed to enable handover and interoperability issues between heterogeneous networks, including both 802 and non-802 networks.

The IEEE 802.20, if completed, will provide a broadband high-speed mobile data network that will surpass the current deficiencies of cellular 3G networks and provide real broadband access to mobile users.

Summary

This section introduced some of the members of the IEEE standard family for providing broadband wireless Internet services at different ranges. Because all of these standards belong to the same family and are created from the same organization, they should be able to work easily and freely with one another. The complete set should provide a good environment for data communications in a wide geographical coverage area and at compatible data rates. The future of the wireless and mobile Internet will depend on how these new activities compete or complement the services of the previous cellular networks.

CONCLUSION

The development trend of the wireless Internet and next-generation mobile networks has now taken two distinct paths. One follows the path of cellular mobile systems and their long-standing and vastly deployed infrastructure all over the world. The evolution of the mobile cellular systems from the second-generation systems to third generation could revolutionize the amount and variety of data that can be transmitted over cellular phones. However, it won't be fast enough to equal the increase in speed of other Internet connections, mainly wired and wireless LAN systems. To supplement and help the cellular systems achieve better performance for bandwidth-demanding mobile applications, WLAN has become a partner in the integrated WLAN/cellular networks.

The second direction in broadband wireless Internet is the development of a series of IEEE standards for personal, local, metropolitan, and wide area networks, falling under the IEEE 802.1x and IEEE 802.2x standards. With the huge success and popularity of the IEEE 802.11 WLAN standard, the focus is now on other means of broadband wireless access standards, under the IEEE standard, which can provide an IP-friendly high-speed wireless network.

No matter how these rather exclusive directions develop during the next few years, the future of the mobile data and wireless Internet will depend on a heterogeneous solution that includes both approaches. From a security point of view, new security techniques should be developed that aim at higher layers of the network protocol suite in order to align with the heterogeneous nature of the physical access network. Bandwidth and resource management of large numbers of network users will eventually push the WLAN and WMAN standards to licensed spectrum, which could complicate the way these networks are used for daily wireless Internet services.

GLOSSARY

2G: Second-generation wireless mobile cellular systems, mainly consisting of global system for mobile communications (GSM) and CDMAOne.

3G: Third-generation wireless mobile cellular systems, mainly consisting of universal mobile telecommunications system (UMTS) and CDMA2000.

AAA (Authentication, Authorization, and Accounting): The mechanism or architecture used in cellular network to authenticate users, authorize their services, and bill charges.

AP: Access point; the base station of a wireless LAN or other types of networks.

B3G: The temporary system name for those under development beyond 3G wireless mobile cellular systems; sometimes referred to as 4G and also known as next-generation networks.

BSS: Basic service set; the usual form of a wireless LAN network with just one access point and several mobile devices.

Coupling: The mechanisms or architectures to integrate the wireless LAN with the cellular networks using tight or loose coupling methods.

CSMA/CA: Carrier sense multiple access with collision avoidance; the media access control protocol used in wireless LAN to avoid too many packet collisions.

DAB: Digital audio broadcasting; a technique to digitally transmit high-quality audio signals such as radio, usually by satellite.

DVB: Digital video broadcasting; a technique to digitally transmit high-quality video signals such as television, usually by satellite.

ESS: Extended service set: the cellular topology network of a wireless LAN with more than one access point.

Handover: Change of service from one base station to another one for a mobile user during movement; sometime referred to as handoff.

Heterogeneous Networks: Networks that consist of different types of systems (e.g., cellular, wireless LAN, etc).

IEEE 802.11: The main wireless LAN standard developed by IEEE; has several versions including the popular 802.11b usually referred to as WiFi.

IP: Internet protocol; the main protocol used in the Internet at the network layer (layer 3), currently is in its version 4 (IPv4) but moving toward implementation of IPv6.

MAC: Media access control: the protocol at layer 2 of the network to control and govern the network access by multiple users.

MANET: Mobile ad hoc networks; networks that are prepared and maintained temporarily for a particular purpose such as establishment of a network among computers of people attending a meeting, or among mobile terminals in a battlefield.

Mobility Management: A set of techniques that controls the movement of a mobile device within a network and is usually composed of two elements: location management and handoff management techniques.

QoS: Quality of service; maintaining the required service condition to a user in a network, such as providing a maximum delay or minimum data rate speed.

Resource Management: A set of management techniques in a network to ensure that available resources, as required by the end terminal application, can be offered between peer end terminals, and to make sure that resource allocation takes into consideration the current network conditions.

RSVP: Resource reservation protocol; a reservation control mechanism to provide quality of service to users by reserving resources beforehand; usually used in the Internet QoS establishment.

TCP: Transmission control protocol; the vastly used transport protocol in the Internet that provides a reliable data transfer among Internet terminals.

UDP: User datagram protocol; the unreliable transport protocol for the Internet that provides lower delay compared to TCP, as well as lower reliability, and is used for short message transfers or delay-sensitive applications.

VoIP: Voice over IP; a technique to deliver delay-sensitive voice packets over the Internet, which can provide lower costs to users.

WLAN: Wireless local area network; an extension of the traditional LAN systems in which the physical layer is changed from a cable or twisted pair into GHz radio frequency for easier scalability and mobility within a building or campus.

Wireless MAN: Wireless metropolitan area network; used to provide high-speed data access on a large scale outdoors. The main technology for this is the IEEE 802.16, also known as WiMax.

CROSS REFERENCES

See *Mobility Management in Heterogeneous Networks*; *Network QoS*; *Voice over IP (VoIP)*; *Wireless LAN Standards*; *Wireless LANs (WLANs)*.

REFERENCES

Akyildiz, I., Y. Altunbasak, F. Fekri, and R. Sivakumar. 2004. AdaptNet: An adaptive protocol suite for the next-generation wireless Internet. *IEEE Communications Magazine* 42(3): 128–36.

Berezdivin, R., R. Breinig, and R. Topp. 2002. Next-generation wireless communications concepts and technologies. *IEEE Communications Magazine* 40(3): 108–16.

Carneiro, G., J. Ruela, and M. Ricardo. 2004. Cross-layer design in 4G wireless terminals. *IEEE Wireless Communications Magazine* 11(2): 7–13.

Comer, D. E. 1999. *Computer networks and Internets*. 2nd ed. Upper Saddle River, NJ: Prentice Hall.

Crow, B. P., I. Widjaja, L. G. Kim, and P. T. Sakai. 1997. IEEE 802.11 wireless local area networks. *IEEE Communications Magazine* 35 (3): 116–26.

European Telecommunications Standards Institute (ETSI). 2001. Requirements and architectures for interworking between HIPERLAN/2 and 3rd generation cellular systems. ETSI TR 101 957, Version 1.1.1.

Findlay, D., H. Flygare, R. Hancock, T. Haslestad, E. Hepworth, D. Higgins, and S. McCann. 2002. 3G interworking with wireless LANs. In *Proceedings of the Third International Conference on 3G Mobile Communication Technologies*.

Forouzan, B. 2003. *Local area networks*. Boston, MA: McGraw-Hill Higher Education.

Frodigh, M., S. Parkvall, C. Roobol, P. Johansson, and P. Larsson. 2001. Future-generation wireless networks. *IEEE Personal Communications* 8(5): 10–17.

Gustafsson, E., and A. Jonsson. 2003. Always best connected. *IEEE Wireless Communications* 10(1): 49–55.

IEEE 802.11. Undated. http://www.ieee802.org/11.

IEEE 802.15. Undated. http://www.ieee802.org/15.

IEEE 802.16. Undated. http://www.ieee802.org/16.

IEEE 802.20. Undated. http://www.ieee802.org/20.

IEEE 802.21. Undated. http://www.ieee802.org/21.

Jamalipour, A. 2003. *The wireless mobile Internet—Architecture, protocols and services*. Chichester, UK: Wiley.

Jamalipour, A., V. Mirchandani, and M. R. Kibria. 2005. QoS-aware mobility support architecture for next generation mobile networks. Special issue, *Wiley Journal of Wireless Communications and Mobile Computing* 5(8): 887–98.

Kellerer, W., and H.-J. Vogel. 2002. A communication gateway for infrastructure-independent 4G wireless access. *IEEE Communications Magazine* 40(3): 126–31.

Macker, J. P., V. D. Park, and M. S. Corson. 2001. Mobile and wireless Internet services: Putting the pieces together. *IEEE Communications Magazine* 39(6): 148–55.

McCann, P. J., and T. Hiller, 2000. An Internet infrastructure for cellular CDMA networks using Mobile IP. *IEEE Personal Communications* 7(4): 6–12.

Min-hua, Y., L. Yu, and Z. Hui-min. 2003. The mobile IP handoff between hybrid networks. In *Proceedings of the Fourteenth IEEE International Symposium on Personal, Indoor and Mobile Radio Communications*, Vol. 1, pp. 265–69.

Mirchandani, V., M. R. Kibria, and A. Jamalipour. 2005. An open-system 4G/B3G network architecture. In *Proceedings of IEEE International Conference on Communications (ICC2005), Symposium on Next Generation Networks for Universal Services*, Seoul, Korea, May, pp. 1357–61.

Mobile Wireless Internet Forum (MWIF). Undated. http://www.mwif.org.

Noerenberg, J. W. II. 2001. Bridging wireless protocols. *IEEE Communications Magazine* 39(11): 90–97.

Oliphant, M. W. 1998. The mobile phone meets the Internet. *IEEE Spectrum* 8(August): 20–8.

Pahlavan, K., P. Krishnamurthy, A. Hatami, M. Ylianttila, J. P. Makela, R. Pichna, and J. Vallstron. 2000. Handoff in hybrid mobile data networks. *IEEE Personal Communications* 7(2): 34–47.

Ramjee, R., T. F. La Porta, S. Thuel, and K. Varadhan. 2000. IP-based access network architecture for next-generation wireless data networks. *IEEE Personal Communications* 7(4): 34–41.

Salkintzis, A. K. 2004a. Interworking techniques and architectures for WLAN/3G integration toward 4G mobile data networks. *IEEE Wireless Communications* 11(3): 50–61.

Salkintzis, A. K. 2004b. WLAN/3G interworking architectures for next generation hybrid data networks. In *Proceedings of the IEEE International Conference on Communications*, Paris, June, pp. 3984–88.

Salkintzis, A. K., C. Fors, and R. Pazhyannur. 2002. WLAN-GPRS integration for next-generation mobile data networks. *IEEE Wireless Communications* 9(5): 112–24.

Stallings, W. 2000. *Data and computer communications*. 6th ed. Upper Saddle River, NJ: Prentice Hall.

Toh, C.-K. 2002. *Ad hoc mobile wireless networks: Protocols and systems*. Upper Saddle River, NJ: Prentice Hall.

Tsao, S.-L., and C.-C. Lin. 2002. VGSN: A gateway approach to interconnect UMTS/WLAN networks. In *Proceedings of the Thirteenth IEEE International Symposium on Personal, Indoor and Mobile Radio Communications*, Vol. 1, pp. 275–79.

Umehira, M., M. Nakura, M. Umeuchi, J. Murayama, T. Murai, and H. Hara. 1999. Wireless and IP integrated system architectures for broadband mobile multimedia services. In *Proceedings of IEEE Wireless Communications and Networking Conference (WCNC '99)*, New Orleans, pp. 593–97.

Varma, V. K., S. Ramesh, K. D. Wong, M. Barton, G. Hayward, and J. A. Friedhoffer. 2003. Mobility management in integrated UMTS/WLAN networks. In *Proceedings of the IEEE International Conference on Communications*, Anchorage, Alaska, May, pp. 1048–53.

Wong, K. D., M. Barton, B. Kim, V. K. Varma, S. Ramesh, G. Hayward, and J. A. Friedhoffer. 2003. UMTS signaling over 802.11 wireless LAN. In *Proceedings of the Fifty-Eighth IEEE Vehicular Technology Conference*, Vol. 3, pp. 1798–1802.

Xin, F., and A. Jamalipour. 2005. TCP throughput and fairness performance in presence of delay spikes in wireless networks. *Wiley International Journal of Communication Systems (Wiley InterScience)* 18(4): 395–407.

Internetworking of Heterogeneous Wireless Networks

S. Zeadally, *University of the District of Columbia*
F. Siddiqui, *Wayne State University*

INTRODUCTION

Over the last few decades, the explosive growth of networks has had a drastic impact on the way people interact, live, work, conduct businesses, study, etc. In the past, although networking technologies such as radio and satellite have been used, most networks deployed have been predominantly wired. In recent years, we have experienced an explosive growth in wireless communication technologies. As a result, many different types of wireless networks have emerged on the market, each of which has been designed with specific purposes in mind. Wireless networks do not need wired connectivity and provide convenience to users particularly for those who are mobile. The wired Internet infrastructure is continuously being extended to connect to various types of wireless networking technologies (especially for the last mile access) that will provide wireless access to the Internet to mobile users. One of the important issues that has arisen with the rapid proliferation of a whole range of communication technologies is *heterogeneity*. To provide seamless connectivity across heterogeneous network systems remains a significant challenge. Heterogeneous networks can either refer to different types of wired, wireless, or wired-wireless (i.e., wired networks connected to wireless networks) networks. In this work, we focus on *heterogeneous wireless systems* and internetworking designs and strategies that can be deployed to enable users to exploit each wireless networking technology best suited for the purpose the wireless network was originally designed (for example, factors such as coverage area, bandwidth). An additional challenge associated with the deployment of various wireless communication systems is the ability to seamlessly roam across different types of wireless access technologies. Doing so will minimize disruption to ongoing services while a wireless user is on the move. Integration and internetworking the various wireless networks are being achieved though the Internet Protocol (IP) technology. IP is compatible with, and independent of, any actual radio access technology. By exploiting IP as the core networking protocol, various wireless access technologies can be integrated together with high flexibility (see Figure 1). IP acts as an adhesive for providing global connectivity and mobility among heterogeneous access technologies.

Currently, no single wireless network technology is capable of simultaneously providing a low latency, high bandwidth, and wide area data service to a large number of mobile users. *Wireless Overlay Networks* (Stemm and Katz, 1998), a hierarchical structure of room-size, building-size, and wide area data networks solve the problem of providing network connectivity to a large number of mobile users in an efficient and scalable way. In an overlay network, lower levels are comprised of high bandwidth wireless cells that provide a small coverage area. Higher levels in the hierarchy provide a lower bandwidth but a much wider access network. A mobile device with multiple wireless network interfaces can access these networks as it moves between different network environments. Next generation wireless systems typically constitute different types of access technologies. The heterogeneity that will characterize future wireless systems instigates the development of intelligent and efficient handoff management mechanisms that can provide seamless roaming capability to end-users moving between several different access networks.

Table 1 show some of wireless technologies which will be part of future heterogeneous wireless systems, along with their characteristics.

Some key features of next generation heterogeneous access networks include (Suk, Kai, and Hau 2003):

- High usability with anytime, anywhere connectivity.
- Support for multimedia services with low transmission cost.
- Integrated access networks with a common IP-based core.
- Use of multimodal devices, capable of supporting various types of network access technologies.
- Support for telecommunication, data, and multimedia services.
- Support for personalized services.
- Support for integrated service access from various service providers.

Overview of Wireless LANs

Wireless Local Area Networks (WLANs) are designed to support mobile computing in small areas such as buildings, parks, airports, or office complexes. The main attraction of WLANs is their flexibility. They can extend access to local area networks, such as corporate intranets, as well as support broadband access to the Internet, particularly at "hot spots," public venues where people tend to gather (Varshney 2003).

WLAN Standards

The two most popular WLAN standards are:

- The European Telecommunications Standardization Institute (ETSI) has a standardized WLAN called HiperLAN2.
- The IEEE has created standards called 802.11b [IEEE 802.11b, 1999], 802.11a and recently 802.11g. The current 802.11b standard, commonly known as Wi-Fi, supports an 11Mbits/sec maximum rate as long as the users are located within a relatively short range (typically 30–50 meters indoors and 100–500 meters outdoors) of a WLAN base station. The deployment of 802.11a and 802.11g standards which allow bit rates of up to 54 Mbits/sec will pave the way for new types of mobile applications. The 802.11b and 802.11g operate in the 2.4GHz band, together with many other devices,

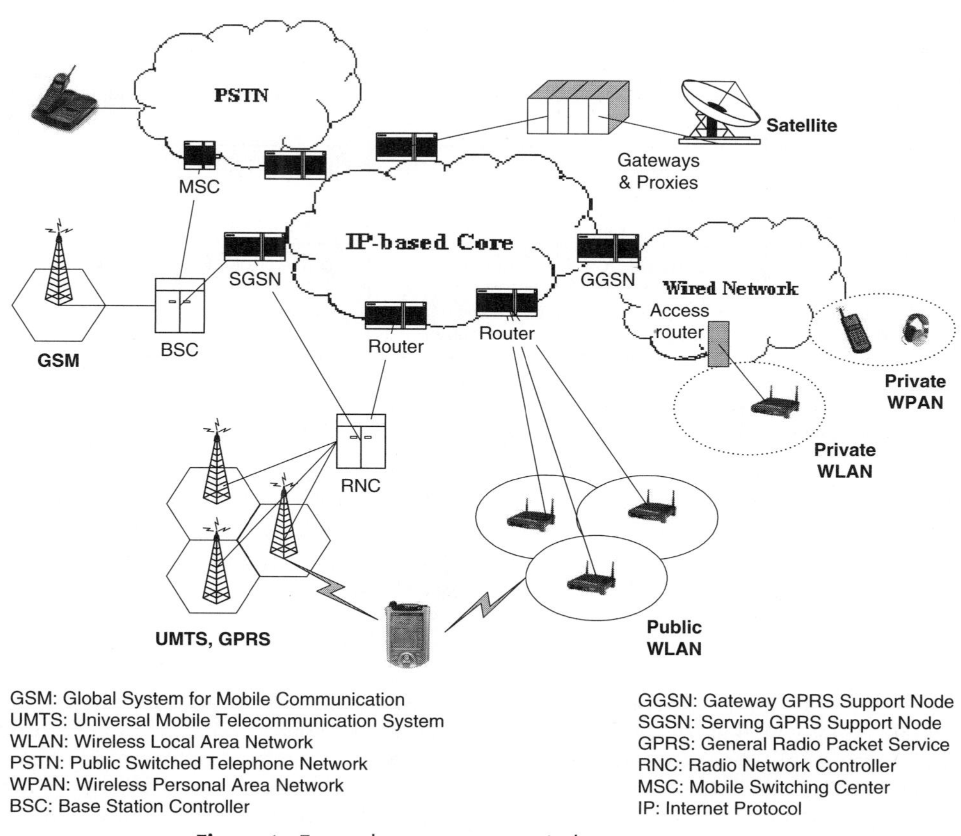

Figure 1: Future heterogeneous wireless access systems

Table 1: Characteristics of Heterogeneous Wireless Access Systems

	Access Network Type	Frequency	Data Rate	Coverage	Cost	Technology
Wireless Technologies	Bluetooth	2.4 GHz ISM Band	Max. 721 kbits/s	0.1–10 m	Low	DSSS, FHSS
	IEEE 802.11g	2.4 GHz	54 Mbits/s	50–300 m (outdoors)	Low	OFDM
	IEEE 802.11b	2.4 GHz	11 Mbits/s	50–300 m (outdoors)	Low	DSSS/CCK
	IEEE 802.11a	5 GHz	54 Mbits/s	50–300 m (outdoors)	Low	OFDM, TDD
	HiperLAN2	5 GHz	54 Mbits/s	Up to 150 m	Low	OFDM
	IMT2000, UMTS	2 GHz	Max. 2 Mbits/s	30 m–20 Km	High	FDD, TDD, W-CDMA
	IEEE 802.20	Below 3.5 GHz	Up to 9 Mbits/s	20 Km	High	OFDM
	WiMax (based on IEEE 802.16-2004)	10–66 GHz/ 2–11 GHz	Up to 75 Mbits/s (with LOS) Up to 40 Mbits/s (with NLOS)	Up to 50 Km Up to 10 Km	Medium	OFDM
	IEEE 802.16d (fixed)	2–11GHz	Up to 75 Mbits/s	Up to 50 Km	Medium	OFDM
	IEEE 802.16e (mobile)	2–6 GHz	Up to 30 Mbits/s	50 Km	Medium	OFDMA
	GSM, GPRS, HSCSD, EDGE	900,1800,1900 0 MHz	9.6 Kbits/s–384 Kbits/s	Up to 35 Km	High	TDMA, FDD
	Satellite	Up to 14 GHz	Max 144 Kbits/s	Several Kms	High	
	DAB	176–230 MHz 1452–1467.5 MHz	1.5 Mbits/s	Up to 100 Km	Low	OFDM
	DVB-T	< 860 MHz	5–31 Mbits/s	Up to 100 Km	Low	OFDM
	DECT/DECT Link	1880–1900 MHz	Up to 2 Mbits/s	Up to 50 m	Low	TDMA/TDD

IMT: International Mobile Telecommunications
UMTS: Universal Mobile Telecommunication System
GSM: Global Systems for mobile Commmunication
EDGE: Enhanced Data Rates for GSM Evolution
DECT: Digital Enhanced Cordless Telecommunications
HiperLAN: High Performance Radio Local Area Network
TDMA: Time Division Multiple Access
DASS: Direct Sequence Spread Spectrum
QAM: Quadrature Amplitude Modulation
FHSS: Frequency Hopping Spread Spectrum
HSCSD: High-Speed Circuit-Switched Data
DAB: Digital Audio Broadcasting
DVB: Digital Video Broadcasting
ADSL: Assymmetric Digital Subscriber Line
GPRS: General Radio Packet Service
OFDM: Orthogonal Frequency Division Multiplexing
FDD: Frequency Division Multiplexing
TDD: Time Division Duplex
QPSK: Quadri-Phase Shift keying
DMT: Discrete Multitone

including Bluetooth and cordless telephones. 802.11a operates in the 5 GHz band, which at this point is relatively free of interference from other electrical devices operating in this band. Although all these standards are designed for similar environments, they differ in frequency, bit rates, power requirements, and coverage.

The WLANs standardized in the IEEE 802.11 standards [IEEE 802.11b, 1999] support two modes of operation: infrastructure mode and ad-hoc mode. Of these two modes, infrastructure mode network architecture resembles the wide-area cellular networks and is of most interest to wireless Internet service providers

(WISPs). It consists of an Access Point (AP) that performs three functions:

- It implements one or more 802.11 radio interface protocols, Frequency Hopping Spread-Spectrum (FHSS), Direct Sequence Spread-Spectrum (DSSS), or Orthogonal Frequency-Division Multiplexing (OFDM).
- It implements the Carrier Sense Multiple Access with Collision Avoidance (CSMA/CA) Medium Access Control (MAC) protocol and performs packet store-and-forward to coordinate communications of Mobile Nodes (MNs) in the cell characterized by a Basic Service Set IDentifier (BSSID).
- It interfaces a cell to a packet-switched network such as Ethernet, and therefore implements layer 2 packet forwarding functions such as bridging (Xu, Papavassiliou, and Narayanan 2004).

802.11b WLAN has been widely deployed in offices, homes and public hotspots such as those in airports and hotels. Any wireless data devices with a Wi-Fi certified WLAN card can potentially be connected to the Internet (or intranet) through these WLAN at a high speed, up to 11Mbits/sec. Applications for WLAN technology include wireless data access within the home and business environments.

In addition to high speed, the other advantages of WLANs include low operation cost because of operation on unlicensed spectrum, ease of deployment, and low equipment cost. However, a serious disadvantage of WLAN is the small coverage area. An 802.11b Access Point (AP) can only communicate with WLAN stations within 100–300 feet (Luo et al. 2002).

CELLULAR TECHNOLOGY EVOLUTION

The earliest wireless systems were based on analogue technology and operated in the 800 MHz range. They used the basic cellular structure of mobile communication. However, many of these systems were limited in range and required the other party to have a similar radio. These early wireless systems gave way to the *first generation systems (1G)* in the 1980s. 1G technology limited the number of users, as each channel could only carry one conversation. The first generation technology lasted through the 1980s, when digital technology emerged, including digital signal processing techniques. *Second generation (2G)* systems were based on digital signal processing techniques and were regarded as a revolution from analogue to digital technology, and gained tremendous success during the 1990s (Jun-Zhao, Sauvola, and Howie 2001).

When the World Wide Web exploded onto the scene, it introduced the Internet to millions of people, which led to the realization that cell phones could incorporate Internet access. However, the technology of the time did not support that level of data communications, which spurred the industry into finding ways to increase the capability for data transmission. There were two products of this search—*2.5G (representing second generation telephones maximized for data communications)* and the *3G (third generation) standard* (see Figure 2).

Introduced in 2001, 2.5G telephones used a technology called digital packet switching technology. This means that each signal is broken into digital packets and each packet is sent separately. The 2.5 G extended the 2G with data switching and packet switching methods and led to hybrid communications.

The 3G (also known as *third generation*) technology involves the deployment of a new system with new services. In addition to using the digital packet switching technology, the 3G standard allows both universal access and portability across different device types. The communication speed is up to ten times faster than the speed of 2G systems and provides a multitude of services including voice, fax, Internet access, etc., with a wide range of seamless roaming.

Table 2 presents a short history of mobile telephone technology developments over the last few decades.

Researchers have already begun work on developing fourth generation (4G) wireless technologies that would support global roaming across multiple wireless and

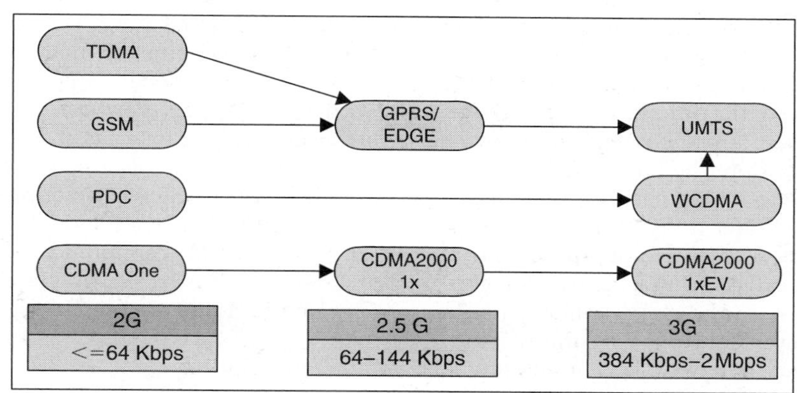

TDMA: Time division multiple access
GSM: Global system for mobile communications
CDMA: Code division multiple access
PDC: Personal digital cellular
GPRS: General packet radio service
UMTS: Universal system for mobile communications

Figure 2: Evolution of wireless communication standards

Table 2: History and Evolution of Cellular Technologies

Technology	**1G**	**2G**	**2.5G**	**3G**	**4G**
Design started	1970	1980	1985	1990	2000
Implementation	1984	1991	1999	2002	2010?
Service	Analogue voice, Synchronous data to 9.6 Kbits/s	Digital voice, Short messages	Higher capacity, packetized data	Higher capacity, broadband data up to 2 Mbits/s	Higher capacity, completely IP-oriented, multimedia, data to 100 Mbits/s
Standards	AMPS, TACS, NMT	TDMA, CDMA, GSM, PDC	GPRS, EDGE, 1XRTT	WCDMA, cdma2000	Single standard
Bandwidth	1.9 Kbits/s	14.4 Kbits/s	384 Kbits/s	2 Mbits/s	200 Mbits/s
Multiplexing	FDMA	TDMA, CDMA	TDMA, CDMA	CDMA	CDMA?
Core Network	PSTN	PSTN	PSTN, packet network	Packet Network	Internet

1XRTT CDMA data service up to 384 Kbits/s
CDMA Code Division Multiple Access
FDMA Frequency Division Multiple Access
WCDMA Wideband CDMA
TACS Total Access Communications System
GSM Global System for Mobile Communication
AMPS Advanced Mobile Phone Service
EDGE Enhanced Data for Global Evolution
GPRS General Packet Radio System
NMT Nordic Mobile Telephone
PSTN Public Switched Telephone Network
TDMA Time Division Multiple Access

mobile networks, such as from a cellular network to a satellite-based network to a high-bandwidth wireless LAN (Varshney and Jain 2001).

Wireless Overlay Networks

Figure 3 shows a typical structure (Inayat, Aibara, and Nishimura 2004) of wireless overlay networks. First, the networks' service areas are overlapped. For example, the General Packet Radio Service (GPRS) network acts as an umbrella network to the Wireless Local Area Network (WLAN) network. Even the different cells of the same network overlap. This overlapping can be used to reduce service disruption by simultaneously connecting to different subnets of the same access technology during transition from one network to another. Second, the networks support different data rates and cell sizes. For instance, IEEE 802.11b WLAN supports a data rate of 11 Mbits/s and GPRS a much lower data rate of about 9.6 Kbits/s. Third, because of the different characteristics of the networks involved, it is not possible to compare the signal powers received from the base stations of different networks to decide to which network to connect. Fourth, each network may offer a different level of reliability, security, quality of service, etc. As mobile hosts move across different networks, a mechanism for conveying the new IP address to the correspondent nodes is required. Also, the power consumed by the network interfaces is different for each network technology and is directly proportional to the transmitted power. For example, the Code Division Multiple Access (CDMA) transmitted power is much higher as compared to WLANs.

Currently, several wireless technologies and networks exist that capture different needs and requirements of mobile users. For high-data-rate local-area access, WLANs are satisfactory solutions. For wide-area communications, traditional cellular networks may provide voice and data services. For worldwide coverage, satellite networks have been used extensively in military and commercial applications. Because different wireless networks are complementary to each other, their integration will empower mobile users to be connected to the system using the *"best available"* access network that suits their needs. Next generation wireless systems are envisaged to combine a plethora of networking technologies (see Figure 4).

Overview of 3G Mobile Networks

The name 3G, standing for third generation, is a collective term for the new communication procedures, standards and devices that will improve the speed and quality of services available on the move. The 3G takes the form of handsets that can combine the functionality of a mobile phone with that of a personal computer and a PDA. Generally, 3G devices have greater transmission abilities than their predecessors, both in terms of speed and capacity. The ITU defines 3G as any device that can transmit or receive data at 144Kbits/s or better. In practice, 3G devices can transfer data at up to 384 Kbits/s. As a comparison, Global System for Mobile (GSM) communications is up to 14.4 Kbits/s and General Packet Radio Service (GPRS) is around 53.6 Kbits/s. These are used in 2G and 2.5G respectively.

3G Standards

Two main proposed systems for 3G as recognized by the International Telecommunication Union (ITU) are as follows (Vriendt et al. 2002):

- *CDMA 2000 (Code Division Multiple Access)*: CDMA was first introduced in 1995. CDMA phones also have

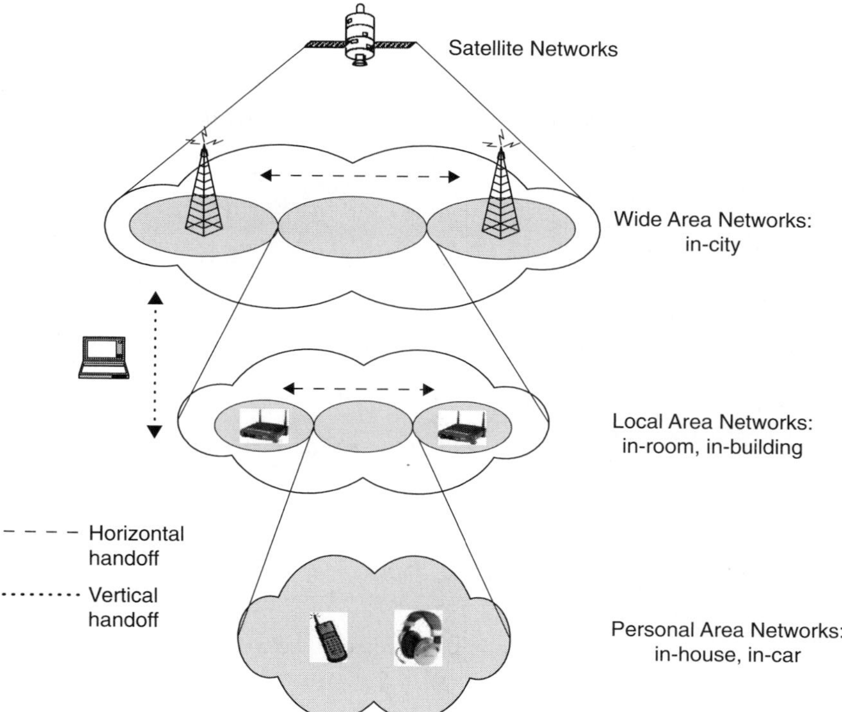

Figure 3: Wireless overlay networks

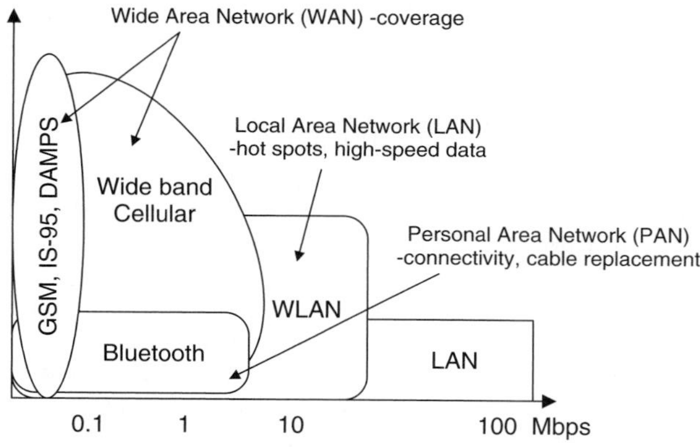

Figure 4: Link bandwidth of cellular technologies

longer standby times and also built-in reverse compatibility with earlier CDMA technology.

- *cdma2000 1x* is an evolution of cdmaOne, and supports packet data service up to 144 Kbits/sec.
- *CDMA 2000 1xEV-DO* introduces a new air interface and supports high-data-rate service on downlink. It is also known as High Rate Packet Data (HRPD). It requires a separate 1.25 MHz carrier for data only. 1xEV-DO provides up to 2.4 Mbits/sec on the downlink (from base station to terminal), but only 153 Kbits/sec on the uplink.
  - cdma2000 1xEV-DV: When deployed, this will introduce new radio techniques and an all-IP architecture for radio access and core networks. It promises data rates up to 3 Mbits/sec.
- *Universal Mobile Telecommunication System (UMTS)*: UMTS is composed of two different but related modes:
  - CDMA-direct Spread: Wideband CDMA also called Frequency Division Duplex (FDD).
  - CDMA-Time Division Duplex (TDD).

FDD mode is considered the main technology for UMTS. FDD mode is derived from CDMA and uses pseudo-random codes. Separate 5 MHz carrier frequencies are used for the uplink and downlink, respectively, allowing an end-user data rate of up to 384 Kbits/sec. FDD allows the operation of asynchronous base stations. The TDD mode is Time-Division-Synchronous Code-Division Multiple-Access (TD-SCDMA). TD-SCDMA operates on low-chip-rate carriers and allows end-user data rates of up to 2 Mbits/sec.

The 3G Network Architecture

A 3G network consists of three interacting domains: a Core Network (CN), a Radio Access Network (RAN), and the User Equipment (UE). A 3G operation uses two standard suites: UMTS and cdma2000, which have minor differences with respect to the components they have in the RAN and the CN (see Figure 5).

The main function of the 3G core network is to provide switching, routing, and transit for user traffic. It also contains the databases and the network management functions.

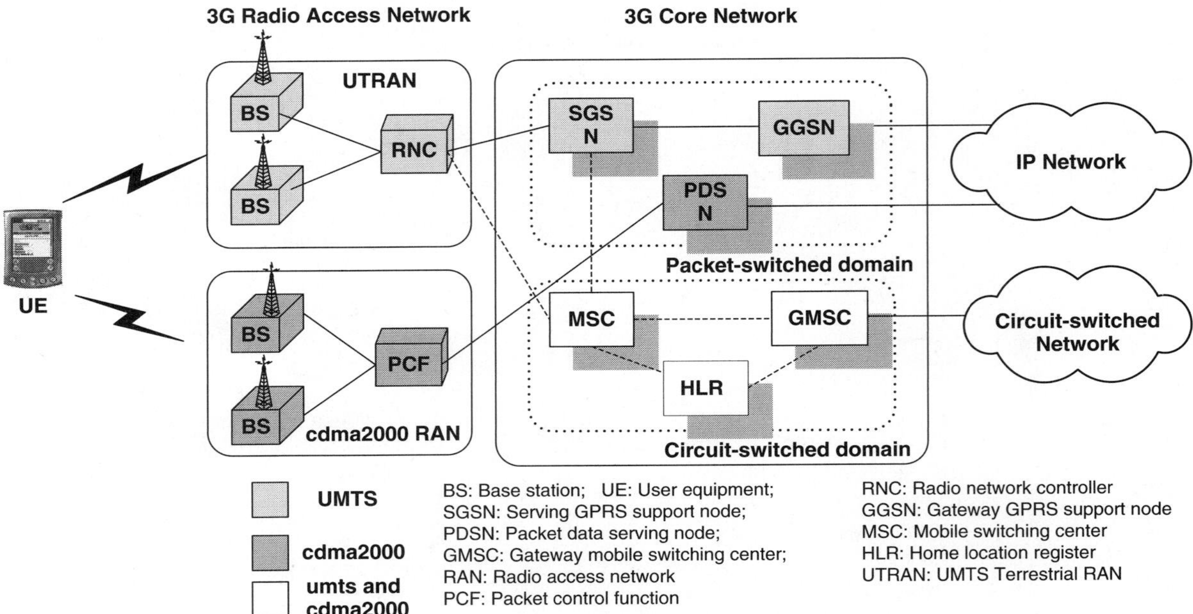

Figure 5: Components of a 3G network

The core network is divided into Circuit-Switched (CS) and Packet-Switched (PS) domains. Circuit-switched elements include Mobile Services Switching Center (MSC), Visitor Location Register (VLR), and gateway MSC. These entities are common to both the UMTS as well as the cdma2000 standards. The differences in the CN with respect to the two standards are in the PS domain. Packet-switched elements in UMTS include Serving GPRS Support Node (SGSN) and Gateway GPRS Support Node (GGSN). The cdma2000 packet-switched component is primarily the Packet Data Serving Node (PDSN). Some network elements like EIR, Home Location Register (HLR) are shared by both domains.

The main function of the MSC server is to handle call-control for circuit-based services, including bearer services, etc. The MSC server also provides mobility management, connection management, and capabilities for mobile multimedia, as well as generation of charging information. It can also be co-located with the VLR.

GGSN is the gateway to external data networks. It supports control signaling toward external IP networks for authentication and IP-address allocation, and mobility within the mobile network. GGSN provides functions for forwarding and handling user information (IP packets) to and from external networks (Internet / intranets). It also supports generation of charging information.

SGSN provides session management, i.e., mechanisms for establishment, maintenance, and release of end-user Packet Data Protocol (PDP) contexts. It also provides mobility management and supports inter-system handover within and roaming between mobile networks. SGSN also supports generation of charging information.

The PDSN incorporates numerous functions within one node. Routing packets to the IP network, assignment of dynamic IP addresses and maintaining Point-to-Point Protocol (PPP) sessions are some of its main functions. It also initiates the Authentication, Authorization and Accounting (AAA) for the mobile station.

The radio access network provides the air interface access method for the user equipment. An UMTS RAN (UTRAN) consists of Radio Network Controllers (RNC) and Base Stations (BS) or Node-B. The RNCs manage several concurrent Radio Link Protocol (RLP) sessions with the UEs and per-link bandwidth management. It administers the Node-B for congestion control and loading. It also executes admission control and channel code allocation for new radio links to be established by the Node-B.

A cdma2000 RAN consists of a base station and two logical components: the Packet Control Function (PCF) and the Radio Resources Control (RRC). The primary function of the PCF is to establish, maintain and terminate connection to the PDSN. It also communicates with the RRC to request and manage radio resources in order to relay packets to and from the mobile station. It also collects accounting information and forwards it to the PDSN.

RRC supports authentication and authorization of the mobile station for radio access. It also supports air interface encryption to the mobile station.

User equipment refers to a 3G Mobile Station (MS). It can generally operate in one of the three modes of operation:

PS/CS mode: The MS is attached to both the PS domain and the CS domain, and is capable of simultaneously operating PS and CS services.

PS mode: The MS is attached to the PS domain only and may only operate services of the PS domain.

CS mode: The MS is attached to the CS domain and may only operate services of the CS domain.

The 3G architecture also includes two general interfaces: the Iu interface between the RAN and the CN, and the Uu interface between the RAN and the UE. The Radio Access Network Application Protocol (RANAP) is implemented over this interface. The user data part of the Iu interface carries end user IP traffic encapsulated in GPRS tunnelling protocol-user plane (GTP-U) packets between the core network and the RAN (Miah and Tan, 2002).

MOBILE WIRELESS TECHNOLOGICAL TRENDS

Two areas of wireless technology that have experienced dramatic growth include cellular and wireless local area network technologies. In this section, we present some of the latest trends in the rate of increase of 3G subscribers, worldwide distribution of mobile subscribers, forecast of cellular subscribers, and world mobile subscribers, as shown in Figure 6, Table 3, Figure 7, and Table 4, respectively.

Cellular Subscribers

The first 3G WCDMA commercial network was NTT DoCoMo. It had 5000 test subscribers in the Tokyo area in September 2001. In March 2004, NTT DoCoMo subscribers had increased to three million (NTT Docomo 2006).

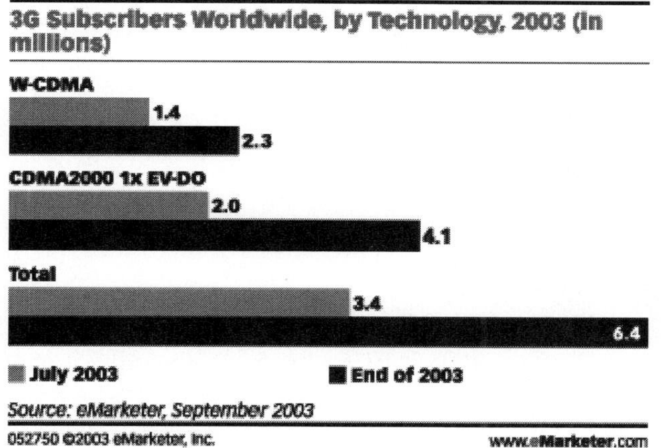

Figure 6. 3G subscribers worldwide in mid/late 2003

Table 3: Distribution of Mobile Subscribers Worldwide (Sept. 2002)

Technology	Subscribers
GSM	69.32%
CDMA	12.39%
TDMA	9.66%
Analogue	3.13%
PDC	5.49%
WCDMA	0.01%

Source: EMC via Northstream

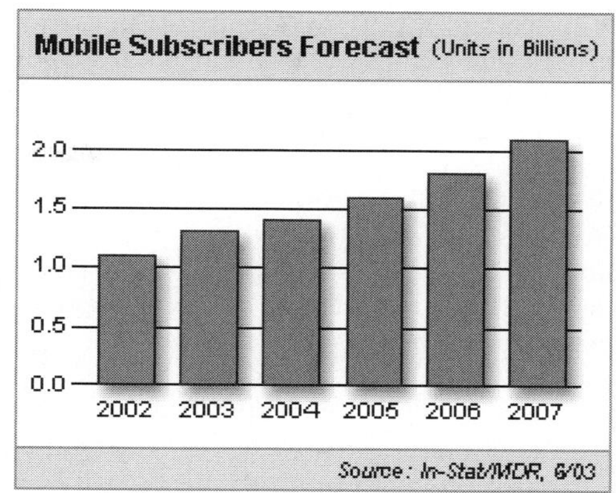

Figure 7: Cellular subscribers: 1991–2007 forecast (*source:* www.theresearchroom.com)

Table 4: World mobile subscribers, 2003–2004

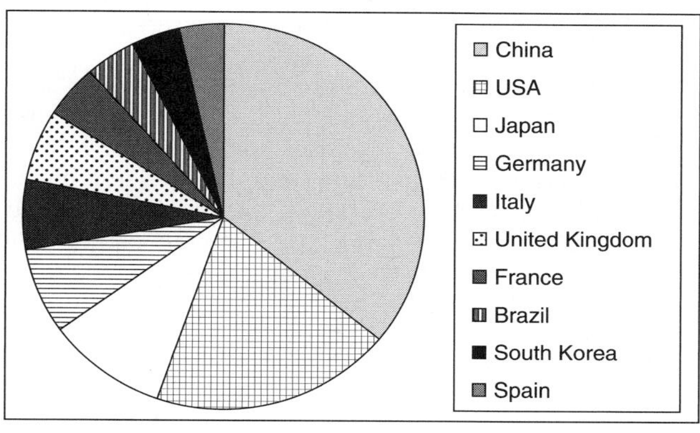

It is expected that the worldwide wireless market will grow to more than 2.3 billion subscribers by 2009. By 2009, WCDMA networks will be providing service for over 40% of the world's CDMA users. The total number of new subscribers in 2004–2009 is expected to be 777.7 million worldwide.

Wireless LAN (WLAN) Subscribers

In the United States, we expect that more than 21 million Americans will be using public Wireless Local Area Networks (WLANs) by the year 2007 (ClickZ 2002). This is mainly because users are attracted by the cheap and super fast remote Internet access provided in airports, shopping malls, coffee bars, and hotels. Public WLAN services enable users to hook up their laptops and PDAs to their Internet Service Providers (ISPs) or company intranet at speeds of up to 11 Mbits/s. The number of hot-spot locations in the U.S. is expected to grow from 3,700 this year to 41,000 by 2007. This, in turn is expected to generate over $3 billion in service revenues (ClickZ 2002).

The development of the WLAN market has been spurred on by the industry-wide adoption of a common technical platform based on the IEEE 802.11 standard. There is a rapid increase in the number of devices such as PDAs and laptops (forecast to top 91 million in the next five years), that are now being shipped with cards already installed that can make use of public WLAN networks (see Figure 8). According to recent research, the most notable issue to be resolved is the ability of public WLAN operators to provide wide coverage for potential users. These operators need to pursue roaming agreements with each other to minimize the cost of deploying access gateways in every possible hot-spot location. The distribution of WLAN hot-spot locations worldwide in recent years is shown in Table 5.

For the WLAN market to accelerate, it is imperative for service providers to offer better location information and network detection software as part of well-presented service propositions with appropriate security and pricing. The impact WLAN services will have on the cellular phone market remains unclear. Analysis predicts that by 2007 the public WLAN market will equate to about 25 percent of mobile data service revenues and could cannibalize up to 7 percent of cellular data operator revenues in the United States (ClickZ 2002).

Some of the most popular Wi-Fi Hot Spot operators and their associated number of wireless access points are given in Table 6.

The IEEE 802.16 (Chung, Chang, and Lin 2005) family of standards and its associated industry consortium, WiMax (WiMax 2004), promises to deliver high data rates over large areas to a large number of users in the near future. This exciting addition to current broadband options such as Digital Subscriber Line (DSL), cable, and Wi-Fi, promises to rapidly provide broadband access to locations in the world's rural and developing areas where broadband is currently unavailable, as well as competing for urban market share [3G UK] (see Figure 9).

It is expected that by the end of 2009, there will be more than 7 million subscribers worldwide using broadband wireless services based on 802.16REd technology, the fixed flavor of WiMax (WiMax 2004). Future wireless networks are envisioned to support different wireless communication technologies such as WPANs, WLANs, WMANs, 3GPPP, and sensor networks (Weber 2000). Today, it would be very rare to expect a single device to operate in all wireless environments. Even in situations in which a single device can establish basic connectivity in multiple wireless networks, users are faced with multiple and incompatible technologies for access control, signalling, and data transport.

INTERNETWORKING ARCHITECTURES FOR WLANS AND CELLULAR NETWORKS

A 3G wireless system such as UMTS can provide mobility over a large coverage area, but with relatively low speeds of about 144 Kbits/sec. WLANs provide high speed data services (up to 11 Mbits/sec with 802.11b and 54 Mbits/

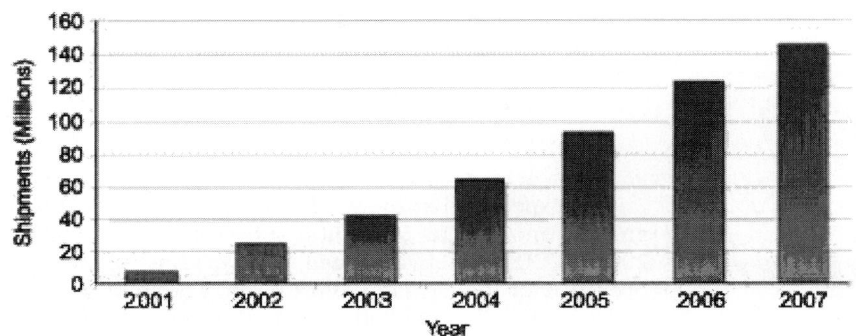

Figure 8: 802.11-based WLAN IC shipments: 2001–2007 (*Source:* Allied Business Intelligence Inc.)

Table 5: Public WLAN Hot Spot Locations Worldwide, by Type

Location	2001	2002	2003	2004	2005
Airports	85	152	292	378	423
Hotels	569	2,274	11,687	22,021	23,663
Retail Outlets	474	11,109	50,287	82,149	85,567
Enterprise Guest Areas	84	624	1,762	3,708	5,413
Stations and Ports	—	88	623	2,143	3,887
Community Hot Spots	2	266	5,637	20,561	30,659
Others	—	240	790	1,526	2,156
Total Market	**1,214**	**14,752**	**71,079**	**132,486**	**151,768**

Source: Dataquest (DataQuest 2006).

Table 6: Top Ten Wi-Fi Hotspot Operators

Headquarters	Wi-Fi Hotspot Operator	Wireless Access Points
El Segundo, CA	Infonet Services Company	12,000
Chicago, IL	Hyatt International	11,000
Bellevue, WA	T-Mobile	4,200
France	Orange	4,028
Waltham, MA	Airpath	3,504
Austin, TX	Wayport	3,000
Netherlands	Trustive	2,500
San Antonio, TX	SBC Freedom Link	2,300
Japan	DoCoMo	747
New Plymouth, ID	Truckstop.net	429

Source: www.bbwexchange.com (Broadband 2006).

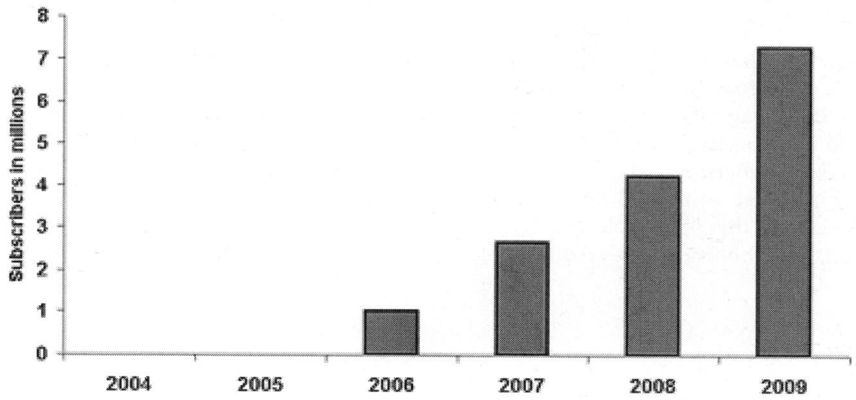

Figure 9: Worldwide forecast of 802.16REVd-based broadband wireless subscribers (2004–2009). (*Source:* Untethering Broadband WiMax, 2004)

sec with 802.11a) over a geographically smaller area. An integrated network combines the strengths of each, resulting in a wide-area system capable of providing users with ubiquitous data service ranging from low to high speed in strategic locations. Thus, 3G/WLAN integration provides users with a high-speed wireless connection as well as anytime anywhere connectivity. The integration of the two technologies implies that a seamless roaming mechanism between these heterogeneous networks needs to be present. For example, a mobile node has an ongoing session through a WLAN network. As the node moves out of the coverage of the WLAN, it should seamlessly switch to the 3G network without requiring any user-intervention or affecting the ongoing session. This handover should not be perceived by the end user. Similarly, session flow should continue through the WLAN on acquiring the WLAN coverage again. This transparent mobility between the two access networks provides users with continuous service as well as with high-speed coverage in certain areas.

Hence, WLANs are generally used to supplement the available bandwidth and capacity of a 3G network in hotspot area such as railways and airports with high-traffic densities, without sacrificing the capacity provided to cellular users. It provides support for data-intensive applications and enables smooth online access to corporate data services, while still allowing users to roam from the private pico-cell network to the wide area 3G network.

We briefly present a comparison of UMTS and WLAN technologies in Table 7.

To reap the benefits of both cellular and WLAN technologies, a standardized mechanism for internetworking between these access technologies is required to enable seamless mobility while a user roams across different networks. Several approaches have been proposed for internetworking between WLANs and cellular 3G networks.

Tightly Coupled Internetworking

In the case of the tight-coupling architecture (Hongyang Chen and Jiang 2003), the WLAN network is deployed as an alternative Radio Access Network (RAN) and connects to the 3G Core Network (CN). From the CN's point of view, the WLAN is considered like any other 3G Routing Area

Table 7: UMTS-WLAN Comparison

UMTS (3G)	WLAN
Maximum data rate only 384 Kbits/sec while moving and up to 2 Mbits/sec stationary	Maximum data rates of 11Mbits/sec, 20 Mbits/sec, or 54 Mbits/sec.
Mature mobility management handling including handover and roaming (based on GSM)	Many unresolved issues regarding mobility management
500-meter radius in urban areas	50-meter radius in urban areas

(RA) in the system. In other words, the 3G CN does not really identify the difference between an RA with WLAN technology and one with 3G technology.

The main element in the tight coupling approach (Salkintzis 2003) is a gateway that is connected inbetween the WLAN and the 3G core network's Packet Data Serving Node (PDSN). The PDSN aggregates the data traffic from multiple RNCs and interfaces the RAN to the packet-switched network. The main function of the gateway is to provide a standardized interface to the 3G core network and hide the WLAN details. In this approach, the 3G protocols for signaling, transport, billing, authentication, etc. are fully reused (see Figure 10).

When a Mobile Station (MS) is outside the WLAN area, its WLAN interface is in passive scan mode; that means, it scans a specific frequency band and searches for a beacon signal. When a beacon is received, the Service Set IDentifier (SSID) may be checked and compared against a preconfigured SSID. The SSID serves as a WLAN identifier that can help the MS to attach to the WLAN to which they have subscription.

The MSs are considered to be dual mode; i.e., they have two radio interfaces, one for 3G access and another for WLAN access. Seamless mobility is achieved by means of an RA Update (RAU) procedure which is a core mobility management function. When an MS enters a WLAN, a RAU procedure takes place and subsequent signaling and user data are carried over the WLAN interface. Similarly, when an MS exits a WLAN, another RAU procedure occurs and the 3G interface is enabled to carry further data and signaling.

The WLAN Adaptation Function (WAF) is a key component present in the MS which identifies when the WLAN radio subsystem is enabled and informs the LLC layer, which subsequently redirects signaling and data through the WLAN. The WAF provides switching between the two interfaces. Whenever, the MS is outside the WLAN area, the LLC Packet Data Units (PDUs) are transported over the 3G interface. However, when the MSs enter the WLAN coverage, the LLC PDUs are transmitted over the WLAN interface. The switching as performed by the WAF is completely transparent to the user.

Some of the benefits associated with tight coupling include: faster handoff speed, service continuity with almost no disruption while changing access networks, and

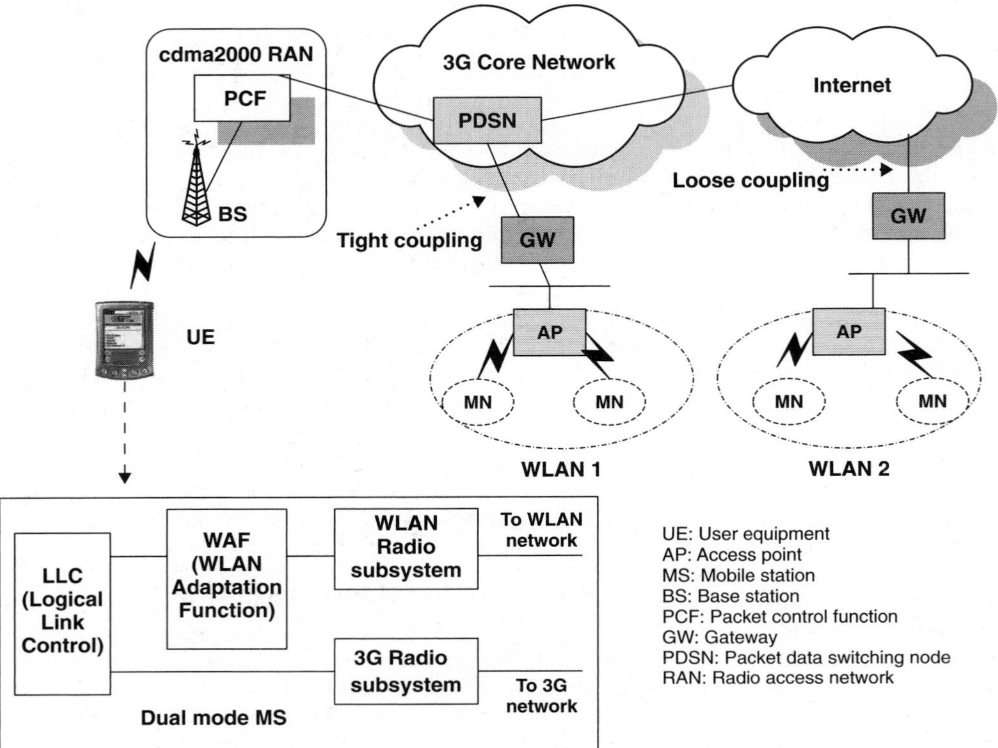

UE: User equipment
AP: Access point
MS: Mobile station
BS: Base station
PCF: Packet control function
GW: Gateway
PDSN: Packet data switching node
RAN: Radio access network

Figure 10: Tightly coupled versus loosely coupled internetworking

high security provided through the reuse of 3G security mechanisms. Drawbacks of the tight coupling approach include:

- It requires the same operator to own both the WLAN network, as well as the 3G network, because the 3G core network directly exposes its interfaces to the WLAN network.
- It does not make feasible the integration of independently operated WLANs and 3G networks without explicit connectivity to the 3G core network.
- It requires complex and expensive reconfiguration of the 3G core network and WLAN gateways.
- It makes it mandatory to use 3G-specific authentication mechanisms for authentication on WLANs, forcing WLAN providers to interconnect to 3G carriers' SS7 network to perform authentication procedures.

Loosely Coupled Internetworking

In the case of the loose-coupling approach (Buddhikot et al. 2003), the WLAN gateway connects to the Internet and does not have any direct link to 3G network elements such as the PDSNs, etc. The approach is referred to as "loosely coupled" because it completely separates the data paths in 3G and WLAN networks. In other words, in contrast to tight coupling, the WLAN data traffic does not pass through the 3G core network but goes directly to the IP network (Internet). In this approach, different mechanisms and protocols can handle authentication, billing, and mobility management in the 3G and WLAN portions of the network. However, for seamless operation to be possible, these mechanisms and protocols have to interoperate. One way of achieving this is for the WLAN gateway to support mobile IP functionalities (Perkins, 2002) to handle mobility across networks as well as Authentication, Authorization, and Accounting (AAA) services to internetwork with the 3G's home network AAA servers. There are several benefits associated with loose coupling:

- It permits independent deployment and traffic engineering of WLAN and 3G networks.
- It does not require extensive capital investments because the 3G providers can benefit from other providers' WLAN deployments.
- It provides widespread coverage through roaming agreements with many partners.
- It allows a wireless Internet service provider to provide its own public WLAN hotspot, interoperate through roaming agreements with public WLAN and 3G service providers, or manage a privately installed enterprise WLAN.

However, the loose coupling approach also suffers from various drawbacks, including higher handoff delays compared to tight coupling and the possibility of session interruption during handoff (see Table 8).

Gateway Approach for UMTS/WLAN Internetworking

The gateway approach for WLAN/3G internetworking provides seamless roaming between UMTS and WLAN networks (Tsao and Lin 2002). The two networks operate independently but offer roaming services to their customers. A new logical node, called Virtual GPRS Support Node (VGSN) is designed to connect UMTS and WLAN core networks. The node exchanges necessary information between networks, converts signals, and forwards the packets for roaming users (see Figure 11).

When a Mobile Station (MS) moves from a 3G network to a WLAN, it performs certain handover procedures. The MS first tries to obtain the VGSN address. It does so by sending a Dynamic Host Configuration Protocol (DHCP)_ DISCOVER message in the WLAN network. The VGSN responds to the MS with its IP address. After the MS receives the VGSN address, it sends a Routing Area Update (RAU) to the VGSN, using its original IP address on the 3G network. Then the VGSN sends another update request to the Gateway GPRS Support Node (GGSN) of the 3G network asking it to change its Serving GPRS Support Node (SGSN) address. The SGSN and GGSN are components of the 3G network that provide session management and interfacing to external packet data networks respectively. Then the VGSN simulates an SGSN of the 3G network.

Table 8: A Comparison of Loose Coupling and Tight Coupling

	Loose Coupling	Tight Coupling
Handoff latency	High	Low
Connectivity	Chance of service disruption during handoff	Seamless connectivity during all times
Network ownership	Independent ownership of 3G and WLAN networks permitted	Single ownership of 3G and WLAN networks
Security	Medium security	High security through the reuse of 3G security mechanisms
Deployment cost	Cheap	Expensive

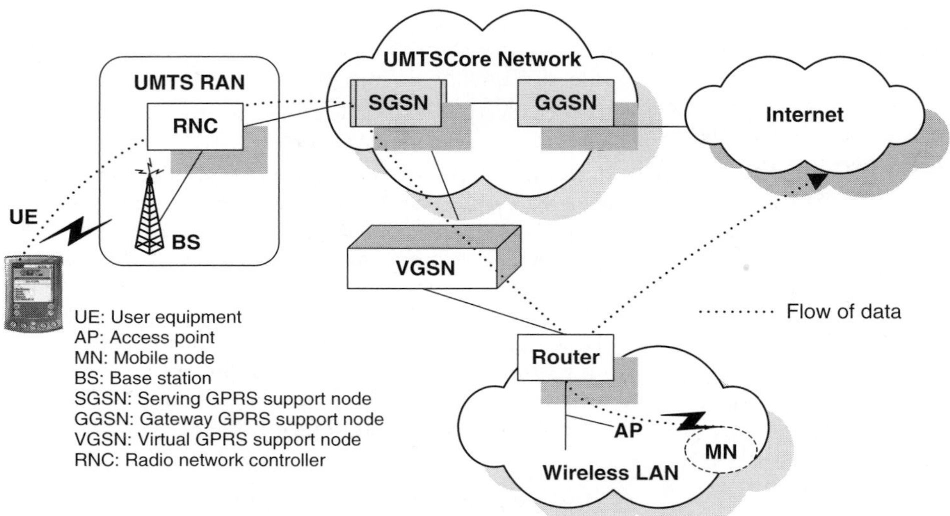

Figure 11: The gateway Internetworking approach

On receiving an update from the VGSN, the GGSN becomes aware that the MS has moved to a WLAN. The VGSN now temporarily plays the role of an SGSN. All packets destined for the MS now go through the VGSN instead of the old SGSN. The packets from the MS to the Internet can be sent out using the old IP address of the 3G network if the WLAN does not perform filtering of non-WLAN IP addresses. If the WLAN applies the filtering procedure, then the packets need to go through the VSGN to the Internet. Some benefits of the gateway approach include: the two networks are allowed to operate independently, packets for roaming users go through the VGSNs to Internet and experience low packet loss and delay, and the approach does not need to use Mobile IP.

UMTS-WLAN Internetworking with Mobile IP

The Mobile IP internetworking architecture (Tsao and Lin 2002) considers 3G and WLANs as *peer-to-peer* networks. If User Equipment (UE) decides to move from a 3G network to a WLAN network, it needs to disable its 3G protocols and use the IP stack. In order for the UE to use the same IP address that it used in the 3G network, i.e., be accessed via the old IP address, then mobile IP is used. Foreign agents and home agents are installed in the WLAN Access Router (AR) and the GGSN of the 3G network routers can tunnel and forward the data packets.

When a UE moves from the 3G network to the WLAN network, the 3G network detaches the UE as it fails to receive the periodical Route Area (RA) update message from the UE. The UE then sends a *standby* message to the SGSN, which helps the UE to reattach to the 3G network after it moves back. Once in the WLAN, the UE can send an *Agent Solicitation* message to locate the local FA. Once the UE receives a reply from the local FA, it then sends a *Registration Request* to the HA. After the Care-of-Address (CoA) in the HA is updated, the packets sent to the home network (3G) will be forwarded to the visited network (WLAN) (see Figure 12).

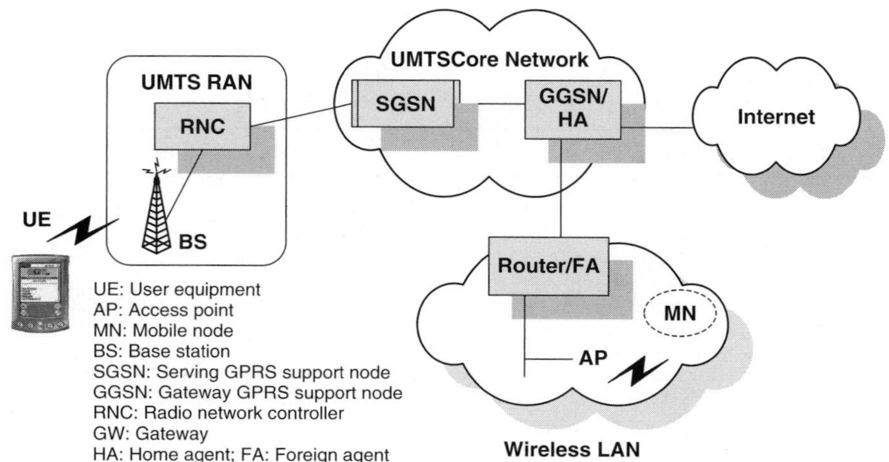

Figure 12: Architecture for mobile IP approach

Although the mobile IP approach allows easy deployment strategies, it suffers from long handover latency (Akyildiz et al. 2004) and might not be able to offer real-time services and applications.

Enterprise-oriented Integration of Cellular Networks with WLANs

The objective of an enterprise-oriented solution is to provide a secure mobile networking method for corporate users to connect their computers to office networks through cellular networks and various WLANs, including office WLAN, home WLAN, and public WLAN, where the connection is expected to remain alive when a user moves between WLAN and a cellular network.

Luo et al. propose an enterprise-oriented WLAN/3G integration solution called the Internet Roaming system (Luo et al. 2002). It is an IP-based corporate network architecture that provides seamless internetworking across office WLAN, home WLAN, public WLAN, and 3G cellular network for corporate wireless data users. The architecture consists of four components, namely, the Internet Roaming Agent (IRC), the Secure Mobile Gateway (SMG), the Secure IP Access Gateway (SIA), and the Virtual Single Account Server (VSA). The IRC is a special client tool installed on a user's computer equipped with a WLAN adapter and a cellular data modem. It provides a secure mobile IP connection from the user's computer to the corporate network, transparent to the operating system of the user's computer. The SMG is a mobile IPsec gateway installed on the corporate core network facing the Internet. It works with the IRC to maintain a secure mobile IP connection when the user's computer is connected on the Internet through a home WLAN, a public WLAN, or a cellular network. The SIA server is a special security gateway installed on the corporate intranet where the office WLAN is installed. It works with the IRC to assure the security of the office WLAN while keeping compatibility with firewalls for user computers. The VSA server manages the IRC, SMG, and SIA servers.

PERFORMANCE EVALUATION OF UMTS-WLAN INTEGRATION AT SGSN AND GGSN NODES

Via simulations using OPNET, we evaluated two internetworking architectures to interoperate the 3G (UMTS) and WLAN networks by connecting them at two strategic points: the SGSN node and the GGSN node as shown in Figure 13.

UMTS-WLAN Integration at the SGSN Node

When the UMTS and WLAN networks are connected through the SGSN node, the WLAN network does not appear to the UMTS core network as an external packet data network. Instead, it simply appears as another radio access network. The WLAN AP in this case needs to have the capability of processing UMTS messages. Thus, whenever a Mobile Node (MN) in the WLAN network wants to exchange data with the UMTS UE, it first needs to undergo the GPRS Mobility Management (GMM) attach procedure to notify the SGSN of the location on the communicating node and also to establish a packet-switched signaling connection. The WLAN AP is responsible for sending these request messages to the SGSN on behalf of the WLAN MN. The GMM attach procedure is a three-way handshake between the MN, RNC, and the SGSN. Upon completion of this procedure, the WLAN MN is authenticated into the UMTS network.

UMTS-WLAN Integration at the GGSN Node

In this type of integration, whenever an MN in a WLAN network wants to communicate with a UE in the UMTS network, it does so through the GGSN node. The UE in the UMTS network first activates the Packet Data Protocol (PDP) context that it wants to use. This operation makes the UE known to its GGSN and to the external data networks, in this case, the WLAN network. User data is transferred transparently between the UE and the WLAN network with a method known as encapsulation and

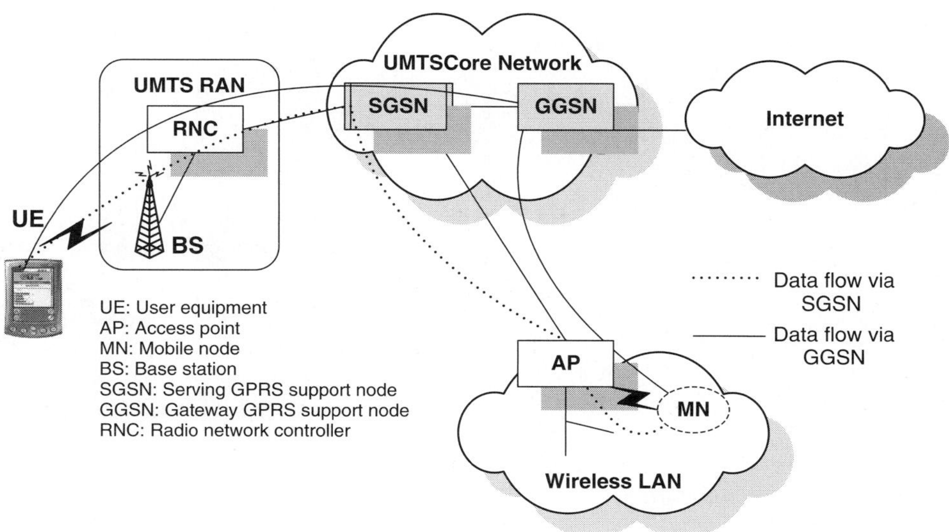

Figure 13: 3G-WLAN integration a) SGSN b) GGSN

tunneling. The protocol that takes care of this is the GPRS Tunneling Protocol (GTP). For this kind of internetworking configuration, the WLAN AP is a simple 802.11b access point and does not need to process UMTS messages.

Simulation Testbed

A network simulation model was constructed using OPNET 10.0.A (OPNET 2006). OPNET is a discrete event simulator with a sophisticated software package capable of supporting simulation and performance evaluation of communication networks and distributed systems.

The simulation environment we used had a UMTS network connected to a WLAN network. The UMTS network was composed of the RAN and a packet-based CN with SGSN and GGSN nodes. The WLAN network is composed of 802.11b wireless MNs configured in Infrastructure Basic Service Set mode. In the GGSN integration case, a simple WLAN access point was used, while in the SGSN integration case, a different access point with additional capability of processing UMTS messages was employed. The goal of the simulations was to compare the delays involved when user data is exchanged between the UMTS and WLAN networks connected via two methods, namely GGSN and SGSN. Different types of traffic were generated using three different applications, including Voice over IP (VoIP), FTP, and HTTP (web browsing) as shown in Table 9. These applications correspond to the various UMTS QoS classes—conversational class for real time flows such as VoIP, interactive, and background classes for FTP and HTTP respectively. Packet delay, jitter, upload, and download response times were measured. Other parameters associated with each application are summarized in Table 9.

Simulation Results and Discussion

Simulations performed for both UDP and TCP flows are presented. For the UDP flow (VoIP traffic), end-to-end packet delays and jitter were measured. For TCP flows (FTP, HTTP) the upload/download response times were measured.

Figure 14a shows the simulation run-times corresponding to the average file upload times experienced when transferring files of various sizes between the UE and the WLAN MN under two different integration scenarios. In Figures 14b and 15a, the average delay and jitter for voice are presented. It is observed that both delay and jitter values are much lower in the GGSN case. Similarly, Figure 15b shows the response time to access a web page of the size of 3000 bytes. As Figure 15b illustrates, the page response time is initially high and then decreases as

Table 9: Descriptions of Various Applications Tested

Application	QoS Class	Measurement (seconds)	Size	Protocol
FTP	Background	File download time	100–1000 Kilobytes	TCP
FTP	Background	File upload time	100–1000 Kilobytes	TCP
GSM encoded voice	Conversational	End-to-end delay	33 Bytes	UDP
GSM encoded voice	Conversational	Jitter	33 Bytes	UDP
HTTP Web browsing	Interactive	Page response time	3000 Bytes	TCP

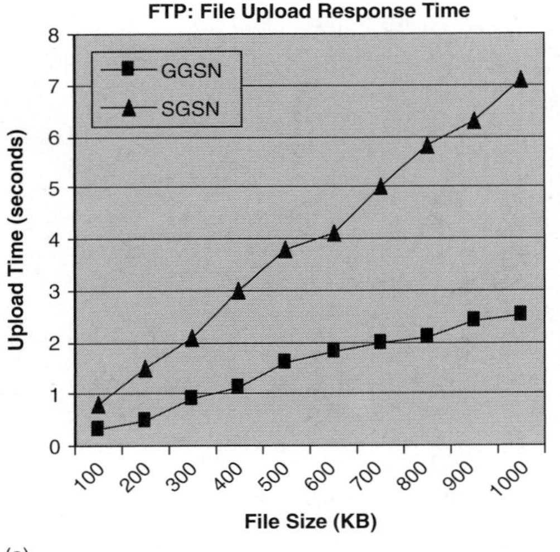

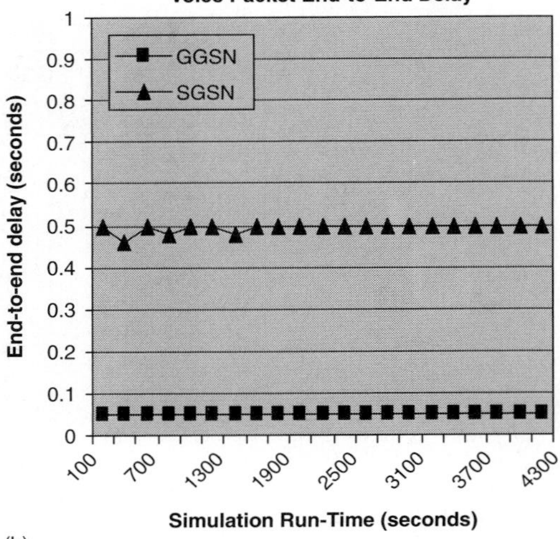

Figure 14: Application response times: a) FTP upload b) VoIP delay

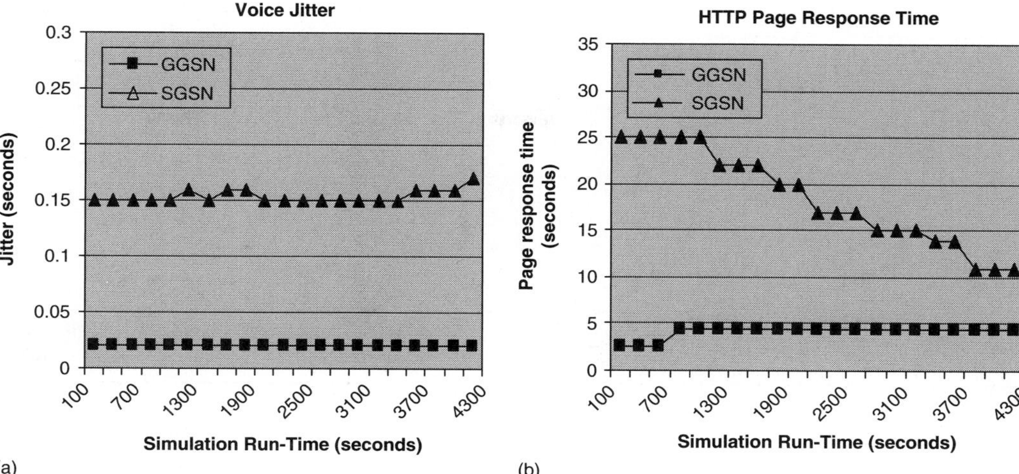

Figure 15: Application response times: a) VoIP jitter b) HTTP page response time

the simulation progresses. We speculate that this reduction in the page response time may be because the Web server's cache is initially empty and the first few page requests cause the page to be fetched from the disk, resulting in a high response time. As more requests are generated with time, the cache is being filled, increasing probability that one or more requests can be satisfied by the cache, thereby reducing the overall page response time.

The simulation results reveal that the application response time (delay) is consistently higher in the case in which the UMTS and WLAN networks are connected through the SGSN node, as compared to the case in which the two networks are connected at the GGSN. This higher response time can be attributed to the additional processing time required at the WLAN access point in the first case. When the two networks are connected at the SGSN node, the WLAN access point performs the functions of an RNC as well as a WLAN AP. Therefore, it has to perform the additional initialization steps to authenticate the WLAN MN to the UMTS network (GMM attach procedure and PDP context activations). When integration is done at the GGSN node, the WLAN AP is a simple 802.11b access point and does not require any special capabilities to process UMTS messages. Data packets are transferred between the UE and the WLAN network using encapsulation by the GPRS tunneling protocol. This reduces the packet latency because there is no additional delay due to UMTS initialization procedures or packet conversions.

The advantages of using the SGSN integration scheme include the reuse of UMTS authentication, authorization, and accounting (AAA) mechanisms; usage of common subscriber databases and billing systems; increased security features (because the UMTS security mechanisms are reused); and the possibility of having continuous sessions as users move across the two networks. The handoff in this case is very similar to an intra-UMTS handoff because the WLAN AP appears as another RNC to the SGSN node. In the case of GGSN integration, because the WLAN is considered to be an external network, different billing and security mechanisms are needed. Service disruption is also possible during a handoff from one network to another.

VERTICAL HANDOFF MANAGEMENT TECHNIQUES FOR HETEROGENEOUS WIRELESS NETWORKS

Several techniques have been proposed to perform handoffs during roaming across heterogeneous wireless access networks and most of these techniques operate at different layers of the protocol stack. In addition, most of the proposed handoff approaches are based on modification of the Mobile IP protocol and are implemented at the network layer (McNair and Fang 2004; Fan, Ni, and Esfahanian 2002; Badis and Khaldoun 2004; and Sharma et al. 2004). Other handoff strategies include SIP-based handoff (operating at the application layer) (Banerjee et al. 2004), and Stream Control Transmission Protocol-based (SCTP-based) handoff (operating at the transport layer) (Li et al. 2004). These are also other schemes for handoff management that have recently been proposed to achieve seamless mobility for TCP connections (Kim and Copeland 2003; Vidales et al. 2004). Other types of handoff schemes are based on efficient energy consumption of network interfaces (Wen-Tsuen, Jen-Chu, and Hsieh-Kuan 2004; and Minji et al. 2004). An in-depth discussion on the detailed operations of each of these protocols is beyond the scope of this paper. However, we briefly outline the purpose of each of the mobility protocols in Table 10.

We present a review (as shown in Table 11) of the various vertical handoff approaches that have been proposed over the last few years, based on features such as the type of handoff (mobile-controlled or user-controlled) basis (Inayat, Aibara, and Nishimura 2004) for handoff decision, and handoff latency. We found that most of the approaches proposed exploit handoff schemes that are mobile-controlled (i.e., handoff decision is made by the mobile node independently). Moreover, most of the handoff techniques use a simple handoff decision method (usually based on one or two factors only) and lack support for intelligent handoff decision strategies based on multiple factors such as cost, security, user preferences, and application requirements, all of which have been important factors affecting service delivery while moving over hybrid wireless networks.

Table 10: Mobility Protocols for Seamless Roaming Across Heterogeneous Wireless Access Networks

Technology	Main Function
Mobile IP	Enables mobile devices to maintain their IP addresses while moving between different networks
Mobile IPv6 (Johnson 2004)	Provides enhanced features to Mobile IP for optimizing the mobility process
Mobile Stream Control Transmission Protocol (mSCTP)	Transport layer solution that provides seamless roaming capability across different networks
Session Initiation Protocol (SIP)	Application layer solution that provides both personal and terminal mobility across different networks

Table 11: A Comparison of Vertical Handoff Approaches

Handoff Approach	Type of Handoff	Handoff Latency	Basis for Handoff Decision	Description
HOPOVER (Fan, Ni, and Esfahanian 2002)	Mobile-controlled	Moderate	Reception of WLAN signal	Addresses the problem of high handoff frequency that cannot be handled by traditional Mobile IP
WISE (Minji et al. 2004)	Mobile-assisted	Low	Energy consumption of interfaces, network load	An energy-efficient interface selection method for vertical handoffs in tightly integrated systems
Hierarchical method (Badis and Khaldoun 2004)	Mobile-controlled	Low	Reception of WLAN signal	A fast handoff scheme that reduces upward vertical handoff latency, packet loss and disruption
OMNICON (Sharma et al. 2004)	Mobile-controlled	Moderate	Reception of a strong WLAN signal	Improves Mobile IP handoff by supporting packet scheduling and buffering
TCP-based method (Kim and Copeland 2003)	Mobile-controlled	Low	Reception of WLAN signal strength and velocity	Improves performance of TCP connections during vertical handoffs
SCTP-based (Li et al. 2004)	Mobile-controlled	Moderate	Reception of WLAN signal	Improves handoff delay and throughput using the multihoming capability and dynamic address configuration of SCTP
SIP-based (Banerjee et al. 2004)	Mobile-controlled	High	Reception of WLAN signal	An application-layer solution for vertical handoffs in heterogeneous networks
Adaptive method (Wen-Tsuen, Jen-Chu, and Hsieh-Kuan 2004)	Mobile-controlled	Low	Energy consumption of interfaces, and QoS offered by networks	An effective system discovery method to reduce power consumption during vertical handoffs

END-USER TERMINAL SUPPORT FOR HETEROGENEOUS WIRELESS NETWORKS

To support the ever-increasing heterogeneity of current and future wireless access networks, we need to design and develop end-user terminals that will provide the capability to access diverse networking technologies. Current multimode devices are of two different types:

- The first type includes those devices capable of supporting multiple wireless access systems by incorporating several network interface cards and the appropriate software for switching between these network interfaces. These devices are often referred to as "multimode terminals."
- The second type includes those devices which use adaptable software modules operating on a generic, reconfigurable hardware platform consisting of Digital Signal Processors (DSPs) and general purpose microprocessors, used to implement radio functions such as generation of transmitted signal (modulation) at the transmitter and tuning/detection of received radio signals (demodulation) at the receiver. Such devices are referred to as Software-Defined Radios (SDRs) (Dillinger, Madani and Alonistioti 2003).

Multimode Wireless Terminals

Multimode wireless terminals (McCann et al. 2006) are devices that can support multiple radio access technologies and allow the reception of data over multiple system bearers with different characteristics. An intelligent multimode terminal should be able to decide *autonomously* the active interface that is "best" for an application session and to select the appropriate radio interface as the user moves in and out of the vicinity of a particular technology. The decision regarding the switching of the interface and the handoff of the active sessions to the newly active interface may be decided based on user preference setup (which may also be referred to as 'user policy') on the multimode terminal regarding the interface usage. For example, if the user has set up some preference to indicate that the PDA should default to using the fastest and cheapest interface available, the terminal will switch to the WLAN interface (assuming this is the cheapest interface available at that moment) whenever the PDA enters into the WLAN coverage area. However, the multimode terminal must also take into account other factors such as the QoS requirements of applications, cost, and other factors in selecting the most appropriate wireless network. It is worth pointing out some of the characteristics that future multimode terminal designs will be expected to support:

1. The terminal should operate with minimal inputs from the user. From a user perspective, it is preferable to carry out these decisions in an automated way rather than having to query the user every time a new interface becomes available, or an old interface disappears.
2. The terminal should be able to handle session handoffs from one interface to the other based on user policy.
3. Radio access interfaces selection should be based on user policy and other factors, including application QoS requirements and information about the network.
4. The requirements of applications need to be determined to help decide whether applications would benefit from a switch of interfaces.
5. Traffic should be smoothly transferred while the active interface is changed in a way that is transparent to the user (i.e., as seamlessly as possible).

Deployment Issues for Multimode Terminals

1. **Network Detection:** A multimode terminal must be able to detect the availability of a new network (example WLAN connectivity). For some interface technologies, resources are not exhausted even if the interface is permanently on and scanning for network access coverage continues for a long period of time. In the case of IEEE 802.11 WLANs, continuous scanning for the presence of other networks is not feasible because of the amount of power needed to keep the interface actively scanning for access points. So the issue that arises is how to activate the WLAN interface only when in the vicinity of a hotspot. Currently, this activation of the interface is left to users who manually enable their WLAN card when in a hotspot. However, because one of the multimode terminal requirements is to minimize user interaction, a desirable goal in this case would be to automate this process. One solution that would achieve this result would be to advertise the presence of nearby services (or coverage of other technologies) via the currently active interface. For example, the presence of a hotspot could be sent via GSM, which would then activate the WLAN interface automatically.
2. **Network Information:** Finding out information about networks to support interface selection decisions is another relevant issue. For example, if a user has specified that the mobile terminal should default to using the cheapest connection, then for the terminal to be able to decide on the cheapest connection, some charging information must be made available by the network. Service providers may choose to advertise certain pricing information, allowing the prices of the different networks to be compared. This information also needs to be formatted or standardized between operators so that it is easy to compare. Other information may also be advertised, such as authentication methods which allow the terminal to determine in advance if switching access networks is required. We need to investigate how to make this information available to mobile users.

To support access to different types of network technologies, it is essential to develop multimode terminals' versatile capabilities that can dynamically adapt to various wireless technologies that differ in their operating frequencies, data rate, and access technology. In addition, such multimode devices should be 'smart' enough to shift the responsibility of network selection from the user to the terminal.

INTERNETWORKING CHALLENGES OF FUTURE HETEROGENEOUS WIRELESS NETWORKS

Significant challenges need to be addressed before true internetworking and seamless integration among heterogeneous wireless access systems become a reality. The strong convergence on IP technology is a step forward towards those goals and makes IP the core networking protocol that effectively bridges various wireless communication technologies with high flexibility. However, with user requirements such as mobility, bandwidth, and access range, more research is needed on internetworking design architectures and protocols.

Several outstanding issues (Suk, Kai, and Hau 2003) still need to be resolved to deploy and implement a complete internetworking solution for transparent, seamless, secure roaming across future heterogeneous wireless networks. However, current technologies such as handoff management techniques do not yet provide adequate support. As a result, mobile users of hybrid wireless networks are often required to restart applications to connect to a new point of attachments. In a wireless environment, it is common to go out of range or coverage (for a few seconds or up to a minute) and handoff between subnets takes a finite amount of time (while handling mobility).; it is necessary to ensure that the application session state be maintained. Mobile users want fast Internet access and seamless roaming capability without the complexities of configuring devices, inputting authentication parameters, entering and changing user preferences, updating parameters, and receiving bills from multiple service operators (Kim and Copeland 2003). User demand for new services featuring seamless roaming, hassle-free authentication, and configuration requires the support of new designs and protocols that will simplify device configuration and authentication in order to make seamless roaming possible.

To summarize, we briefly discuss some of the main research issues that are expected to play a fundamental role in the design and implementation of future architectures and protocols in the future:

- **Multimodality:** To enable access to different types of wireless network technologies, we need to develop multimode terminals that are capable of to adapting to various technologies with different characteristics such as frequency of operation and data rates. In addition, these devices should be "smart" enough to make intelligent decisions on interface selection in a way that is transparent to the mobile user during roaming across different wireless networks.
- **Efficient and Seamless Roaming:**
  - **Detection of Network Coverage**: Mobile devices must be able to easily and efficiently detect the presence of a new network coverage area through processing signals sent from different wireless systems, which differ in access protocols and are incompatible with each other.
  - **Selection of the Most Appropriate Access Network**: Wireless networks differ in terms of various factors, and the task of selecting the most appropriate network is complex with respect to the needs and services of an end-user.
  - **Handoffs:** Moving across various network technologies presents the need to design intelligent and efficient handoff techniques with minimum latency and packet losses. Handoff management techniques should allow mobile users to roam among multiple wireless networks in a manner that is completely transparent to applications and disrupts connectivity as little as possible. In addition, in hierarchically structured wireless systems, the choice of the best wireless network for location and handoff management poses a significant challenge because different overlay levels might have widely varying characteristics. Moreover, in traditional mobile systems, only horizontal handoff has to be performed whereas in next generation wireless-access systems, both horizontal and vertical handoff should be performed.
- **Quality of Service (QoS) Requirements:** Next generation wireless systems will consist of various access technologies with differing parameters interconnected with a common IP-backbone. Mobile terminals will typically host various types of multimedia applications. These applications have varying requirements, which may not be satisfied by the underlying best-effort IP framework. Providing adequate QoS support including bandwidth, delay, reliability, perceived quality, and costs in a heterogeneous mobile computing environment remains a significant challenge. Mobility management in such environments also introduces new issues such as timely service delivery and QoS negotiation during inter-system handoff. The main problem in providing QoS in a mobile environment is the integration of QoS and mobility management—the ability to provide the same level of quality to the packet flow during and after the handoff. To the best of the authors' knowledge, none of the available technologies today allow full seamless IP mobility with full end-to-end QoS support. This end-to-end QoS issue (spanning over different wireless networks) becomes even more challenging given the broad range of QoS mechanisms available for each individual network. As a result, it becomes almost impossible for an application designer to select a single QoS framework that is supported across different types of networks. We need to investigate novel QoS approaches that will efficiently support end-to-end QoS over hybrid wireless networks.
- **Security:** The existence of heterogeneous wireless access systems makes end-to-end security support challenging during host mobility. This requires the development of novel, adaptive security mechanisms and protocols.
- **Billing and Pricing**: The existence of multiple networks gives rise to the presence of several network operators. To eliminate the need for separate bills associate with

specific wireless provider, we need to investigate and deploy new billing (Globalbilling 2004) and accounting procedures and mechanisms for end-users accessing various types of networks during typical sessions.

- **Context Information Transfer:**
  - **Context Transfer:** Handoff in heterogeneous environments requires the transfer of contextual information (Kempf 2002) for information flow between the mobile node and the network. Context transfer is designed to allow access routers to exchange state information regarding a mobile node's packet treatment. A context transfer protocol aims to minimize the impact of transport/routing/security-related services on the handoff performance. When a mobile node moves to a new subnet, it needs to continue services that have already been established at the previous subnet. Such services are called "context-transfer candidate services" (Georgiades and Tafazolli 2004) and include information such as Authentication, Authorization and Accounting (AAA) profiles, IP Security (IPSec) states, QoS policy, and others. A context-transfer protocol needs to be developed to allow fast re-establishment of context-transfer candidate services when a new network is encountered, to enable seamless operation of application streams during user mobility.
  - **Security of Context Transfer:** Sensitive context information must be protected to preserve user privacy and maintain security. The security context shared between different domains represents a level of trust between them. If context is transferred to another intermediate device, whether in the same domain or different domains, ideally, the same level of trust must be in place as between the intermediate device and the authentication server. Network mobility management can be optimized if contexts are transferred securely from one entity to another.
- **Inter-service Provider Compliance:** An effective handoff scheme is required on existing network infrastructures consisting of different networks owned by different service providers and should not require major modifications to the underlying networks.

CONCLUSION

Wireless technology has had a tremendous impact on our society. Wireless networks continue to be deployed at a high rate in different fields of life. Different types of wireless networks are being deployed for different purposes, depending primarily on their coverage capabilities (for example, wireless local area networks provide short coverage while cellular networks provide wide range network access) and there may be other factors such as cost and bandwidth. IP is playing a fundamental role in the convergence of heterogeneous wireless networks. However, to reap the full benefits associated with each of the underlying wireless networks being connected to each other, we need to design, implement, and deploy internetworking wireless solutions that can provide seamless connectivity and mobility in cost-effective and efficient ways. In this work, we presented and discussed some of the solutions and architectures that can support efficient internetworking and integration of heterogeneous wireless-access systems. Current roaming techniques among different wireless networks are inadequate in supporting continuity of application sessions in heterogeneous mobile environments. Innovative designs, architectures, and protocols are needed in several areas (for example, mobility management, end-to-end QoS, multimodal devices) to achieve full internetworking among heterogeneous wireless access systems.

ACKNOWLEDGMENT

This work was supported by grants from Sun Microsystems (Palo Alto) (EDUD-7824-000145-US), Microsoft Corporation (Seattle), and Ixia Corporation (Calabasas). We thank the anonymous reviewers for their candid remarks and suggestions which helped to improve the quality and presentation of this chapter. We would also like to express our sincere gratitude to the editor-in-chief, Hossein Bidgoli, for his patience, encouragement, and kind support throughout the preparation of this chapter.

GLOSSARY

Access Point (AP): An access point is a station that transmits and receives data. It connects users within a network and acts as a connection point between a wireless LAN and a wired network.

Bluetooth: Bluetooth evolved from the need to replace wires in short-range communications (e.g., serial cable between computers and peripherals) with short-range wireless links.

Global System for Mobile (GSM) Communications: GSM is a digital mobile telephone system that uses a variation of Time Division Multiple Access (TDMA).

Handoff: The process by which a mobile terminal keeps its connection active when it migrates from the coverage of one network access point to another.

HiperLAN: A set of wireless LAN standards. There are two specifications, namely, HiperLAN/1 and HiperLAN/2 which can provide link rates of 20 Mbits/s and 54 Mbits/s respectively in the 5 GHz range.

Horizontal Handoff: Handoffs that occur between access points of the same network technology.

Hot Spot: A wireless LAN node that can provide connectivity to the Internet from some specific location.

Internet Protocol (IP): A connectionless protocol that enables data transfer between computers on the Internet.

Internetworking: A term that describes software and hardware technologies and devices that enable users and their computers to interact through different types of networking technologies.

Local Area Network (LAN): A group of computers and devices sharing a wired/wireless link within a small geographic area.

Mobile IP: An Internet Engineering Task Force (IETF) standard protocol designed to allow a mobile device to move across different networks while maintaining its permanent IP address.

Personal Area Network (PAN): A computer network used for communication among computer devices close to a person. (Usually such networks span over a distance of up to 10 meters).

Session Initiation Protocol: An Internet Engineering Task Force (IETF) standard protocol to initiate interactive user sessions that involve multimedia elements such as video, voice, chat, gaming, and virtual reality.

Vertical Handoff: A handoff that occurs between access points belonging to different networking technologies.

Wide Area Network: A network that spans large distances, usually connecting many other networks together.

Wireless: A term that describes communications in which electromagnetic waves carry the signal over the communication path.

CROSS REFERENCES

See *Evolution of Mobile Cellular Networks*; *TCP/IP Suite; Universal Mobile Telecommunications System (UMTS); Wireless Broadband Access.*

REFERENCES

3G UK. 2003. 3G, http://www.3g.co.uk/PR/April2003/5211.htm. (accessed June 22, 2006).

Akyildiz, I., X. Jiang., and Mohanty, S. 2004. A survey of mobility management in next-generation all-IP-based wireless systems. *IEEE Wireless Communications*, 11(4 Aug.): 16–28.

Badis, H., and A. Khaldoun A. 2004. Fast and efficient vertical handoffs in wireless overlay networks. *Proceedings of the 15th IEEE International Symposium on Personal, Indoor and Mobile Radio Communications*, 3: 1968–1972.

Banerjee, N., et al. 2004. Analysis of SIP-based mobility management in 4G wireless networks, *Computer Communications*, 27(8): 697–707.

Broadband. 2006.WiMAX, wireless ISPs, Wi-Fi hotspots and broadband wireless technology, *Broadband Wireless Exchange Magazine*. http://www.bbwexchange.com (accessed June 22, 2006).

Buddhikot, M., et al. 2003. Design and implementation of a WLAN/cdma2000 internetworking architecture, *IEEE Communications Magazine* (Nov.): 90–100.

Chung, N., L. Chang, and C. Lin. 2005. Voice over Wireless LAN via IEEE 802.16 Wireless MAN and IEEE 802.11 wireless distribution system, *International Conference on Wireless Networks, Communications, and Mobile Computing*, 1 (June): 504–509.

ClickZ Inc. 2002. Big years ahead for WLAN market, http://www.clickz.com/stats/sectors/wireless/article.php/974711, February 2002. (accessed June 22, 2006).

DataQuest. 2006. Wireless LAN statistics. http://www.dataquest.com/press_gartner/quickstats/wireless_lan.html. (accessed June 22, 2006).

Dillinger, M., K. Madani, and N. Alonistioti. 2003. *Software defined radio: Architectures, systems, and functions.* Wiley Series in Software Radio, New York, NY: Wiley.

Fan, D., L. Ni, and A. Esfahanian. 2002. HOPOVER: a new handoff protocol for overlay networks." *Proceedings of the IEEE International Conference on Communications*, 5: 3234–39.

Georgiades, M., and R. Tafazolli, R. 2004. Security of context transfer in future wireless communications, Wireless World Research Forum 12, BELL, Nortel Networks IEEE Communications Society, Toronto, Canada, November 2004.

Globalbilling, 2004. Real-time revenue management of mobile content & entertainment. *Inside Billing*, Oct. 2004, http://www.portal.com/news_events/articles_reports/inside_billing_1004.pdf (accessed June 22, 2006).

Hongyang, B., H. Chen, and L. Jiang. 2003. Performance analysis of vertical handoff in a UMTS-WLAN integrated network. *Proceedings of 14th IEEE Conference on Personal, Indoor, and Mobile Radio Communications* Sept. 2003, 1: 187–91.

IEEE 802.11b. 1999. Part 11: Wireless LAN Medium Access Control (MAC) and Physical Layer (PHY) specifications: Higher-speed physical layer extension in the 2.4 GHz Band, IEEE 802.11b. 1999.

Inayat, R., R. Aibara, and K. Nishimura. 2004. A seamless handoff for dual-interfaced mobile devices in hybrid wireless access networks. *Proceedings of 18th IEEE International Conference on Advanced Information Networking and Applications*, 1: 373–78.

Johnson, D. 2004. Mobile Support in IPv6, RFC 3775, June.

Jun-Zhao, S., J. Sauvola, and D. Howie. 2001. Features in future: 4G visions from a technical perspective. *Proceedings of IEEE GLOBECOM* (Nov.): 25–29.

Kempf, J. 2002. Reasons for performing context transfers between nodes in an IP access network, RFC 3374, Sept. 2002.

Kim, S., and J. Copeland, 2003. TCP for seamless vertical handoff. *Proceedings of the IEEE Global Telecommunications Conference*, 2: 661–65.

Li, M., et al. 2004. A new method to support UMTS/WLAN vertical handover using SCTP, *IEEE Wireless Communications*, 11 (4): 44–51.

Luo, H., et al. 2002 Internet roaming: A WLAN/3G integration system for enterprises., *Proceedings of Asia-Pacific Optical and Wireless Communications - Wireless and Mobile Communications II*, Shanghai, China, Oct. 2002: 154–64.

McCann, S., et al. 2006, Next generation multimode terminals. http://www.roke.co.uk/download/papers/next_generation_multimode_terminals.pdf (accessed June 22, 2006).

McNair, J., and Z. Fang. 2004. Vertical handoffs in fourth generation multinetwork environments, *IEEE Wireless Communications*, 11(3): 8–15.

Miah, A., and K. Tan. 2002. An overview of 3G mobile network infrastructure, *IEEE Student Conference on Research and Development*, July 2002: 228–32.

Minji, N., et al. 2004. WISE: Energy-efficient interface selection on vertical handoff between 3G networks and WLANs. *Proceedings of the 15th IEEE International Symposium on Personal, Indoor and Mobile Radio Communications*, 1 (Sept. 2004): 692–98.

NTT DoCoMo. 2006. http://www.nttdocomo.com (accessed June 22, 2006).

OPNET, 2006. OPNET Technologies. http://www.opnet.com (accessed June 22, 2006).

Perkins, C. 2002. IP mobility support for Ipv4. RFC 3344, August 2002.

Salkintzis, A. 2003. Interworking between WLANs and third-generation cellular data networks. *Proceedings of the 57th IEEE Semi-annual Vehicular Technology Conference*, 3: 1802–1806.

Sharma, S., et. al. 2004. Omnicon: A mobile IP-based vertical handoff system for wireless LAN and GPRS links. in *Proceedings of the Second IEEE Annual Conference on Pervasive Computing and Communications*: 155–164.

Stemm, M., and Katz, R. 1998. Vertical handoffs in wireless overlay networks. *ACM Mobile Networking (MONET)*, Special Issue on Mobile Networking in the Internet, 3(4): 335–50.

Suk, Y., H. Kai, and Y. Hau. 2003. Challenges in migration to 4g mobile systems. *IEEE Communications Magazine* 41(12): 54–59.

Tsao, S. and C. Lin, C. 2002. Design and evaluation of UMTS-WLAN internetworking strategies, Volume 2. *Proceedings of IEEE Vehicular Technology Conference*: 777–81.

Varshney, U., and Jain, R. 2001. Issues in emerging 4G wireless networks. *IEEE Computer*, 34 (6): 94–96.

Varshney, U. 2003. The status and future of 802.11- based WLANs. *IEEE Computer Society Press*, 36 (6)June: 102–105.

Vidales, P., et al. 2004. Experiences with heterogeneous wireless networks: Unveiling the challenges. http://www.cl.cam.ac.uk/Research/DTG/~pav25/publications/HetNets04-Vidales.pdf (accessed June 22, 2006).

Vriendt, J., et al. 2002. Mobile network evolution: A revolution on the move, *IEEE Communications Magazine*, 40(4): 104–111.

Weber, Inc. 2000. Seamless integration of heterogeneous wireless network technologies and services. http://www.iam.unibe.ch/~rvs/research/aswn_2003/presentations/weber.pdf (accessed June 22, 2006).

Wen-Tsuen, C., L. Jen-Chu, and H. Hsieh-Kuan. 2004. An adaptive scheme for vertical handoffs in wireless overlay networks. *Proceedings of the First Annual International Conference on Mobile and Ubiquitous Systems: Networking and Services*, 2004: 111–112.

WiMax. 2004. “WiMax.” http://www.wimax.co.uk/PR2004/July2004/2063.htm, July 2004. (accessed June 22, 2006).

Xu, S., S. Papavassiliou, and S. Narayanan. 2004. Layer-2 multi-hop IEEE 802.11 architecture: Design and performance analysis. *IEE Proceedings-Communications*, 151(5) October: 460–66.

Principles and Applications of Ad Hoc and Sensor Networks

Marco Conti, *Institute of Informatics and Telematics (IIT), Italian National Research Council (CNR), Italy*

INTRODUCTION

The hardware and software progress of the last ten years has provided the basic elements (wearable computers, several wireless network technologies, devices for sensing and remote control, etc.) for the realization of pervasive computing and communication systems (Cook and Das 2004). We can envisage a physical world with pervasive, sensor-rich, network-interconnected devices embedded in the environment (Estrin et al. 2002). In these systems the environment is saturated with computing and communication capabilities that interact among them, and with the users. In this environment, virtually everything (from key chains to computers) is connected to the network and can originate and respond to appropriate communications. The nature of ubiquitous devices makes wireless networks the easiest solution for their interconnection. Furthermore, in a pervasive computing environment, the infrastructure-based wireless communication model is often not adequate: it takes time to set up the infrastructure network, and the costs associated with installing infrastructure can be quite high. These costs and delays may not be acceptable for dynamic environments in which people and/or vehicles need to be temporarily interconnected in areas without a preexisting communication infrastructure (e.g., inter-vehicular and disaster networks), or where the infrastructure cost is not justified (e.g., in-building networks, specific residential communities networks, etc.). In these cases, ad hoc networks provide a more efficient solution (Conti 2004).

In the ad hoc networking paradigm, mobile devices self-organize to create a network by exploiting their wireless network interfaces, without the need for any predeployed infrastructure. The simplest ad hoc network is a peer-to-peer network formed by a set of stations within range of one another that dynamically configure themselves to set up a temporary single-hop ad hoc network. Bluetooth piconet is probably the most widespread example of a single-hop ad hoc network (Bisdikian 2001). 802.11 wireless local area networks (WLANs) can also be implemented according to this paradigm, thus enabling communications among laptops without the need for an access point. Several emerging wireless network standards support the ad hoc networking paradigm, including IEEE 802.15.4 (also known as Zigbee) for short-range low data rate (< 250 kbps) networks, Bluetooth (IEEE 802.15.1) for personal area networks, and the 802.11 standards family for high-speed medium-range ad hoc networks (Conti 2004).

Single-hop ad hoc networks interconnect devices that are within the same transmission range. This limitation can be overcome by exploiting the multihop ad hoc paradigm. In a multihop network the network nodes (e.g., the users' mobile devices) must cooperatively provide the functionalities usually provided by the network infrastructure (e.g., routers, switches, servers). Nearby nodes can communicate directly by exploiting a single-hop wireless technology (e.g., Zigbee, Bluetooth, 802.11, etc.), whereas devices that are not directly connected communicate by forwarding their traffic via a sequence of intermediate devices (Chlamtac, Conti, and Liu 2003; Basagni et al. 2004). A multihop ad hoc network is often referred to as a *mobile ad hoc network* (MANET). MANET is not a new concept; in fact, it has been around for over twenty years, mainly used with tactical battlefield networks (Chlamtac, Conti, and Liu 2003). Recently, emerging wireless networking technologies for consumer electronics are pushing multihop networks outside the military domain. Pure multihop mobile ad hoc networks are attractive for specialized scenarios like disaster recovery, vehicle-to-vehicle communications, and home networking but currently have a very limited mass-market deployment. To turn mobile ad hoc networks in to a commodity, we should move to a more pragmatic scenario in which multihop ad hoc networks are used as a flexible and low-cost extension of the Internet. Indeed, a new class of networks is emerging from this view: the *mesh networks* (Bruno, Conti, and Gregori 2005). Unlike MANETs, in which every routing node is mobile, routing nodes in mesh networks are stationary and form the network's backbone, which has connections to the Internet. Client nodes connect to the mesh nodes and use the backbone to access the Internet. Mesh networks scenarios are moving mobile ad hoc networking from disaster-relief and battlefield scenarios to the main networking market.

Whereas mesh networks represent a short-term direction for the evolution of MANETs, *opportunistic networking* constitutes a long-term direction for the evolution of the ad hoc networking concept by opportunistically exploiting, for data delivery, nodes' mobility and contacts with other nodes/networks. In opportunistic networks the communication is still multihop, with intermediate nodes acting as routers, but in this case forwarding is not "on the fly"; intermediate nodes store the messages when no forwarding opportunity exists (e.g., no other nodes are in transmission range, or neighbors are not suitable for that communication) and exploit any contact opportunity with other mobile devices to forward the data toward the destination. In this view, sender and receiver do not need to be connected at the same time to the network via a multihop path (as in traditional MANET) to communicate. Nodes can be temporarily disconnected and/or the networks can be partitioned. It is the nodes' mobility that creates communication opportunities (Fall 2003; Li and Rus 2000; Shah et al. 2003; Zhao, Ammar, and Zegura 2004). This networking paradigm is well suited to a world of pervasive devices equipped with various wireless networking technologies (802.11 family, Bluetooth, ZigBee, etc.) that are frequently out of range from of a network but in the range of other networked devices, and sometime cross areas where some type of connectivity is available (e.g., WiFi hotspots).

Within the ad hoc networking field, wireless sensor networks have a special role. A sensor network is composed of a large number of small sensor nodes, which are typically densely (and possibly randomly) deployed inside the area in which a phenomenon is being monitored. Wireless multihop ad hoc networking techniques constitute the basis for sensor networks, too. However, the special constraints imposed by the unique characteristics of sensing devices, and by the application requirements, make the solutions designed for multihop ad hoc networks (generally) not suitable for sensor networks. Sensor networks utilize on-board batteries with limited energy that, in most application scenarios, cannot be replenished by direct human/machine intervention; therefore, power management is a pervasive issue in the overall design of a sensor network. In addition, sensor networks produce a shift in the networking paradigm: from node-centric to data-centric. The aim of a sensor network is to collect information about events occurring in the sensor field, rather than supporting the communications between nodes.

This chapter reviews the basic principles behind multihop ad hoc networks and sensor networks, and presents the most promising application scenarios.

MOBILE AD HOC NETWORKS

Mobile ad hoc networks are formed dynamically by a set of mobile nodes that are connected via wireless links without using any existing network infrastructure, such as a base station, for their operations (hence they are also referred to as infrastructure-less). The nodes are free to move randomly and organize themselves arbitrarily; thus, the network's wireless topology may change rapidly and unpredictably. Such networks may operate in a standalone fashion, or they may be connected to the Internet. However, the ad hoc network flexibility and convenience come at a price. Indeed, in addition to the traditional problems of wireless networking, the multihop nature and the lack of fixed infrastructure add a number of characteristics, complexities, and design constraints that are specific to these networks (Chlamtac, Conti, and Liu 2003; Corson, Maker, and Cernicione 1999).

- *Autonomous and infrastructure-less.* A MANET does not depend on any established infrastructure or centralized administration.
- *Multihop routing.* Every node acts as a router and forwards other nodes' packets to enable information sharing between mobile hosts.
- *Dynamically changing network topologies.* Nodes' mobility causes frequent and unpredictable changes in the network topology, which may produce route changes, network partitions, and packet losses.
- *Variation in link and node capabilities.* Nodes might have different software/hardware resources and configurations, thus generating a heterogeneous network that is complex to manage. For example, nodes may be equipped with heterogeneous interfaces that result in asymmetric links.

To cope with these issues, several functions and protocols need to be implemented in a MANET protocol stack. This has produced extensive research activities in academia and industry. The Internet Engineering Task Force (IETF) MANET Working Group (WG) has the main role in standardizing protocols for mobile multihop ad hoc networks (IETF Mobile Ad Hoc Networks Working Group n.d.). The IETF MANET WG proposes a view of mobile ad hoc networks as an evolution of the Internet. This mainly implies an Internet protocol (IP)-centric view of the network, as well as the use of a layered architecture. This paradigm has greatly simplified network design and made easier the interconnection to the Internet. However, as explained later in this chapter, this approach limits the development of efficient solutions that are very important in a resource-constrained environment such as MANET. For this reason, new mobile ad hoc networks organizations based on the cross-layering approach are emerging.

MANET Architecture and Protocols

This section briefly reviews the main protocols (see Figure 1) required to support distributed applications in a mobile ad hoc environment. In the presentation we follow a layered approach, moving from the enabling technologies up to the applications.

Enabling Technologies

Enabling technologies are a fundamental building block of ad hoc networks by providing wireless interfaces able to guarantee direct single-hop communications between users' devices. Currently, connectivity is provided by

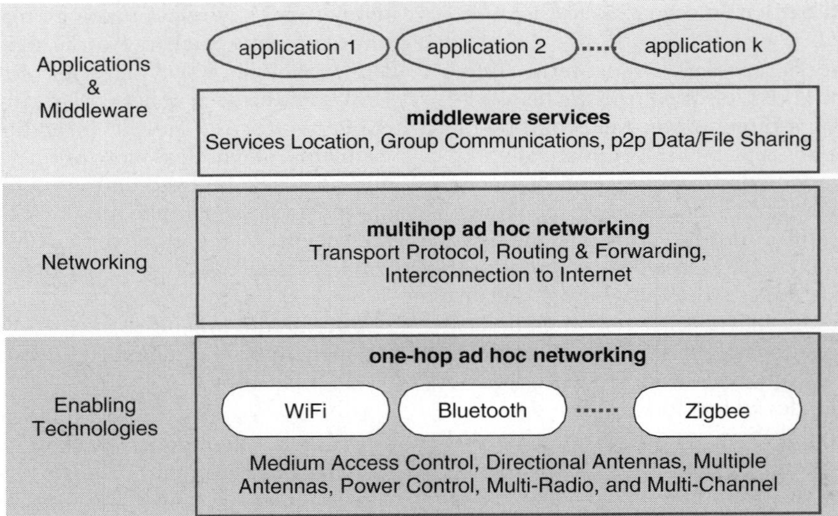

Figure 1: MANET layered architecture

wireless LANs (e.g., 802.11 WLAN standard) or somewhat smaller and less expensive Bluetooth devices. However, to provide the network connectivity to sensor nodes, technologies cheaper, simpler, lighter, and with lower power than these are necessary. These solutions should be able to support low bit rates (e.g., less than 100 Kbps), short ranges (few meters), low power requirements, and, above all, they must be extremely inexpensive. The IEEE 802.15.4 specification, also known as Zigbee, is one of the most promising solutions for short-range, low data rate (< 250 kbps), personal area networking. Specifically, 802.15.4 is designed to address wireless networking requirements for industrial control, home automation and control, inventory management, and wireless sensor networks (Callaway et al. 2002). A detailed discussion of enabling technologies for ad hoc wireless networks can be found in (Conti 2004).

The use of 802.11 technologies strongly constrains the size of multihop ad hoc networks. Indeed, both theoretical and experimental results indicate that with current technology only small-scale (i.e., 2–20 nodes) and moderate-scale (i.e., 20–100 nodes) ad hoc networks can be implemented in an efficient way. Specifically, in Gupta and Kumar (2000), it is shown that in an ad hoc network with n nodes the per-node throughput is bounded by $c/\sqrt{n}$, where c is a constant. In addition, experimental results (Gupta, Gray, and Kumar 2001) indicate that with current technologies the per-node throughput decays as $c'/n^{1.68}$, hence, only small- and moderate-scale ad hoc networks can be implemented in an efficient way. These results are confirmed by estimates reported in Gunningberg et al. (2005), which it has been pointed out that, with 802.11 technology, an ad hoc horizon exists—at two to three hops and 10 to 20 nodes—where MANET benefit virtually vanishes. The 802.11 performance limitations are strongly related to the carrier sense multiple access with collision avoidance (CSMA/CA) protocol used for controlling the access to the channel. Indeed, as pointed out in Anastasi et al. (2005), the CSMA/CA protocol induces complex relationships between the network nodes. Specifically, it is important to be aware of the impact of the transmission and physical carrier sensing ranges on the network performance. The transmission range is the zone around the sender in which the packet reception probability is high and pretty stable. Beyond the transmission range, a gray zone exists in which the packet reception probability drops toward zero in a somewhat random way (depending on the antennas' characteristics). Finally, a pretty large zone exists in which the packet reception probability is zero, but carrier sensing is active (physical carrier sensing range). As shown in Anastasi et al. (2005), the aforementioned channel model applies also to other technologies that use the CSMA/CA medium access control protocol, for example, Motes sensor networks (Motes n.d.).

A novel and promising direction for reducing the interference among stations is based on the use of directional antennas (Ramanathan 2004). 802.11 ad hoc networks typically use omnidirectional antennas. With omnidirectional antennas, while two nodes are communicating using a given channel, the MAC protocol requires that all other nodes in the vicinity (physical carrier sensing range) stay silent. With directional antennas, two pairs of nodes located in each other's vicinity may potentially simultaneously access the channel, depending on the directions of their transmissions. Directional antennas can adaptively select radio signals of interest in specific directions while filtering out unwanted interference from other directions. This can increase spatial reuse of the wireless channel. In addition, the higher power gain of directional antennas (with respect to omnidirectional antennas) extends the node transmission range (Ramanathan 2001).

Enhancements in the physical layer technologies (e.g., multi-antenna platforms, the use of orthogonal frequency division multiplexing [OFDM] as a multiple-access paradigm, improved signal processing schemes, and software defined radio) are expected to he helpful in solving performance limitations of current wireless LAN technologies (Baccarelli et al. 2005).

Networking Protocols

The aim of the networking protocols is to use the one-hop transmission services provided by the enabling technologies to construct end-to-end (reliable) delivery services, from a sender to one (or more) receiver(s) outside its transmission range by exploiting the services offered by intermediate nodes. The efforts of researchers working on MANET mainly concentrated on solving these issues (Chlamtac, Conti, and Liu 2003).

The simplest solution is based on flooding the messages through the network. Of course, flooding does not scale, and hence this approach is only suitable for limited size networks. Controlling the flooding area and/or the number of messages to flood can help to refine the technique. For example, flooding can be used when the first message has to be sent from the sender to the receiver to discover the receiver location, then successive packets can be delivered along the path discovered during delivery of the first message. Identifying the path between the sender and the receiver, and then delivering the packets along this path, is exactly the objective of routing and forwarding algorithms, respectively. Numerous routing protocols and algorithms have been proposed, and their performance under various network environments and traffic conditions have been studied and compared. Several surveys and comparative analyses of MANET routing protocols have been published (e.g., Belding-Royer 2004).

A preliminary classification of the routing protocols can be done via the type of cast property, i.e. whether they use *unicast, geocast, multicast, or broadcast* forwarding (Chlamtac, Conti, and Liu 2003). Broadcast is the basic mode of operation over a wireless channel; each message transmitted on a wireless channel is generally received by all neighbors located within one hop from the sender. The simplest implementation of the broadcast operation to all network nodes is by flooding, but this may cause the *broadcast storm problem* as a result of redundant rebroadcast (Ni et al. 1999). Schemes have been proposed to alleviate this problem by reducing redundant broadcasting (see Stojmenovic and Wu 2004).

Unicast forwarding refers to one-to-one communication in other words, one source transmits data packets to a single destination. Multicast routing protocols come into play when a node needs to send the same message, or stream of data, to multiple destinations. Geocast forwarding is a special case of multicast that is used to deliver data packets to a group of nodes situated inside a specified geographical area. From an implementation standpoint, geocasting is a form of "restricted" broadcasting: messages are delivered to all of the nodes that are inside a given region.

The analysis of routing algorithms is beyond the scope of this chapter; we refer the interested reader to Basagni et al. (2004) and Chlamtac, Conti, and Liu (2003). Hereafter, we only briefly discuss unicast routing to discover a one-to-one communication path (i.e., one source transmits data packets to a single destination), because this is the basic service for building a multihop ad hoc network.

The primary goal of unicast routing protocols is the correct and efficient route establishment and maintenance between a pair of nodes, so that messages may be delivered reliably and in a timely manner. This is the target of classical Internet link-state (e.g., open shortest path first [OSPF]) and distance-vector (e.g., routing information protocol [RIP]) routing protocols (Stevens 1994), but MANET characteristics make the direct use of these protocols infeasible. Internet protocols have been designed for networks with almost static topologies (therefore unable to keep pace with frequent link changes occurring in ad hoc environments), in which routing protocols run in specialized nodes with plentiful resources (i.e., energy, memory, processing capability, etc.). On the other hand, MANET routing protocols must operate in networks with highly dynamic topologies in which routing algorithms run on resource-constrained devices. MANET routing protocols are typically subdivided into two main categories: *proactive routing protocols* and *reactive (on-demand) routing protocols* (Belding-Royer 2004). Proactive routing protocols are derived from legacy Internet distance-vector and link-state protocols. They attempt to maintain consistent and updated routing information for every pair of network nodes by propagating, proactively, route updates at fixed time intervals. Reactive on-demand routing protocols, on the other hand, establish the route to a destination only when there is a demand for it. The source node in the route discovery process usually initiates the route request. Once a route has been established, it is maintained until either the destination becomes inaccessible or the route is no longer used (Belding-Royer 2004). Most work on routing protocols is taking place in the MANET Working Group, where four routing protocols are currently under standardization. These include two reactive routing protocols, ad hoc on-demand distance vector (AODV) and dynamic source routing (DSR), and two proactive routing protocols, optimized link state routing (OLSR) and topology broadcast based on reverse-path forwarding (TBRPF; IETF Manet Working Group n.d.). In addition to proactive and reactive protocols, another class of unicast routing protocols can be identified: *hybrid protocols*. The *zone-based hierarchical link state routing protocol* (ZRP; Samar, Pearlman, and Haas 2004) is a hybrid protocol that combines both proactive and reactive approaches, thus trying to bring together the advantages of the two approaches. ZRP defines around each node a *zone* that contains the neighbors within a given number of hops from the node. Proactive and reactive algorithms are used by the node to route packets within and outside the zone, respectively.

Location-aware routing protocols are a special case of routing protocols that use the nodes' position (i.e., geographical coordinates) for data forwarding. Specifically, a node selects the next hop for packets' forwarding by using the physical position of its one-hop neighbors and the destination node. The packets are forwarded to a neighbor in the receiver direction; for this reason, these routing protocols are also referred to as geographic routing protocols. Location-aware routing does not require routes' establishment and maintenance. No routing information is stored. The use of geo-location information avoids network-wide searches, because both control and data packets are sent toward the known geographical coordinates of the destination node. These features make location-aware routing protocols quickly adaptive to route changes and more scalable than unicast protocols such as AODV, DSR, and OLSR.

A large number of location-aware routing algorithms have been proposed in the literature. A survey of location-aware routing algorithms can be found in Giordano, Stojmenovic, and Blazevic (2003) and Widmer et al. (2003).

The low reliability of wireless communications coupled with nodes' mobility and multihop forwarding make packet loss a highly probable event in multihop ad hoc networks; hence, reliable transport protocols are often required to guarantee that the receiver sees exactly the same stream of bytes delivered by the sender. This is the task of the transmission control protocol (TCP; Stevens 1994), which indeed is the solution generally adopted for MANETs as well. Unfortunately, TCP was conceived for wired networks in which nodes do not change their position over time. Furthermore, it assumes that packet losses are almost always due to congestion phenomena causing buffer overflows at intermediate routers. These assumptions do not hold in MANETs. The MANET topology may change very frequently as a result of nodes' mobility. In addition, nodes may fail because of battery exhaustion (Chlamtac, Conti, and Liu 2003). Finally, congestion phenomena as intended in the Internet are rare events in MANETs, because packet losses due to link-layer contentions are largely predominant (Fu et al. 2003). To improve the performance of the TCP protocol in multihop ad hoc networks, several proposals have been presented (see, e.g., Wang and Zhang 2002; Liu and Singh 2001; Sundaresan et al. 2003). Almost all of these proposals are modified versions of the legacy TCP protocol used in the Internet. However, TCP-based solutions might not be the best approach when operating in MANET environments. Identifying a reliable and robust transport protocol for multihop ad hoc networks is still an open research issue. The interested reader is redirected to Chlamtac, Conti, and Liu (2003) and Anastasi et al. (2005), for an analysis of the TCP problems and new transport protocol proposals.

Middleware and Applications

Currently, in MANET the applications run directly on top of the transport layer by exploiting (via the legacy socket interface) the services offered by the TCP and UDP protocols. No middleware services are generally implemented, but each application has to implement all the services it needs. This constitutes a major complexity/inefficiency in the applications development, which can be fixed with the development of middleware platforms tuned on the unique MANET features. Currently, research on middleware for mobile ad hoc networks is still in its infancy and only recently did middleware proposals for mobile ad hoc environments appear (e.g., see Bellavista, Corradi, and Magistretti 2005, and references herein). Because ad hoc networks share many concepts with the peer-to-peer (p2p) computing system, exploiting the p2p paradigm for designing MANET middleware platforms is emerging as a very promising direction (Conti, Delmastro, and Turi 2006). In Borgia et al. (2005) and Conti, Gregori, and Turi (2005), the authors investigate the efficiency of p2p middleware platforms when implemented on mobile ad hoc networks.

In spite of the massive research efforts, multihop ad hoc networks still have limited usage scenarios. More precisely, multihop ad hoc networks are generally used either for implementing tactical networks (e.g., military communications and automated battlefields) or for supporting communications in specialized civilian scenarios (e.g., disaster recovery, planetary exploration, vehicular networks, etc.). On the other hand, general-purpose civilian applications able to push a mass-market deployment of these networks have not yet been identified. A first step in this direction is reported in MobileMAN Project Deliverable D10 (n.d.), in which new application scenarios (city cabs, mobile games, and shopping malls) have been identified that can leverage the ad hoc technology to provide valuable services to the users. Specifically, the analysis of the city cab scenario (i.e., the use of 802.11 ad hoc networks to replace the currently used taxi radio dispatch systems) has shown that such a system is viable both economically and technically (Huang et al. 2005).

Cross-Layering Functions

The network functions presented in the previous section are implemented by protocols organized according to a layered architecture. However, in a mobile ad hoc network, a set of functionalities exists that may affect (almost) all layers and require interactions among different layers for their efficient implementation. These functionalities include, among others, energy management, security, and quality of service (Chlamtac, Conti, and Liu 2003).

Energy Management

In legacy wireless networks, the objective of power management policies (hereafter, we use energy and power management interchangeably) is to minimize the battery consumption of the users' devices (Anastasi, Conti, and Passarella 2005). This is achieved by maintaining the users' devices in a low battery consumption state (e.g., doze mode). These policies are not useful in a MANET. In multihop ad hoc networks, the devices spend a significant amount of their energy to act as routers contributing to routing and forwarding the network traffic. A selfish mobile device that remains most of the time in the doze mode, without contributing to routing and forwarding, maximizes its battery lifetime but jeopardizes the network. Therefore, in multihop ad hoc networks, the objective of power management policies is to maximize the network lifetime rather than minimize the mobile-device power consumption (Ephremides 2002). Two main techniques are used (often in conjunction) to achieve this objective: i) controlling the number of active nodes, and ii) controlling the nodes' transmission power (Feeney 2004). In the first case, the basic idea is that, when a region is dense in terms of mobile devices, only a small number of them need to be turned on in order to forward the traffic. To achieve this, a set of mobile devices is identified that must guarantee network connectivity (to participate in packet forwarding), and the remaining mobile devices can spend most of the time in doze mode to minimize power consumption. Periodically, the set of active mobile devices is recomputed by selecting alternative paths in a way that maximizes the overall network lifetime.

Controlling the mobile-device transmission power is the other main direction for power management in ad hoc networks. Transmission power is highly correlated with power consumption. It determines both the amount of energy drained from the battery for each transmission and the number of feasible links. By increasing the transmission power we increase the per-packet transmission cost (negative effect), but we decrease the number of hops to reach the destination (positive effect) because more and longer links become available. Finding the balance is not simple. On one hand, we have to consider that the signal strength has an exponential decay; hence, from the transmission standpoint, to cover the sender-to-receiver distance a multihop path generally requires less power. On the other hand, on a multihop path the delay (due to the multiple hops) as well as the processing energy (to receive and locally process a packet) increase. Sterbenz et al. (2002) discuss the transmission-power impact on the network connectivity.

Security Issues in Ad Hoc Networks

The wireless, mobile, and self-organizing nature of ad hoc networks brings new security challenges to the network design. Mobile wireless networks are generally more vulnerable to information and physical security threats than fixed wired networks. Vulnerability of channels and nodes, absence of infrastructure, and dynamically changing topology make ad hoc network security a difficult task (Buttyan and Hubaux 2002). Broadcast wireless channels allow message eavesdropping and injection (vulnerability of channels). Nodes do not reside in physically protected places and therefore can easily fall under the attackers' control (node vulnerability). The absence of infrastructure makes the classical security solutions based on certification authorities and online servers inapplicable. The security of routing protocols in the MANET dynamic environment is an additional challenge. Security mechanisms that solely enforce the correctness or integrity of network operations also would not be sufficient in ad hoc networks. A basic requirement for keeping the network operational is to enforce ad hoc nodes' contribution to network operations, despite the conflicting tendency (motivated by the energy scarcity) of each node toward selfishness. Therefore, mechanisms for cooperation enforcement constitute a relevant part of ad hoc network research on security (Conti, Gregori, and Maselli 2004).

Quality of Service

A network's ability to provide quality of service (QoS) depends on the intrinsic characteristics of all the network components, from transmission links to the media access control (MAC) and network layers. MANET characteristics indicate that this type of network may provide weak support to QoS. Wireless links have a (relatively) low and highly variable capacity, as well as high loss rates. Topologies are highly dynamic and have frequent link breakages. Random access MAC protocols, which are commonly used in this environment (e.g., 802.11b), have no QoS support. Furthermore, MANET link layers typically run in unlicensed spectrums, making it more difficult to provide QoS guarantees (Macker and Corson 2004). This scenario indicates not only that QoS guarantees will be difficult to achieve in a MANET but that if nodes are *highly mobile,* even statistical QoS guarantees may be impossible to attain. Providing QoS in mobile ad hoc networks is a very complex and challenging problem (Macker and Corson 2004), and this generates a great deal of research activities at different layers of the protocol stack, including QoS MAC, QoS routing, and resource-reservation signaling (Chlamtac, Conti, and Liu 2003).

Cross-Layering in Mobile Ad Hoc Networks Design

An efficient implementation of the cross-layer functions can be achieved by avoiding a strict layering approach in which the protocols at each layer are developed in isolation, and instead taking advantage of the interdependencies among different layers. For example, from the energy management standpoint, power control and multiple antennas at the link layer are coupled with scheduling at the MAC layer, and with energy-constrained and delay-constrained routing at the network layer.

To effectively exploit interdependencies among different layers, researchers have investigated new organizations of the MANET protocol stack based on *cross-layering* (Conti et al. 2004). The basic idea behind cross-layering is to make information produced/collected by a protocol available to the whole protocol stack, so as to enable optimizations and improve network performance. Indeed, the studies on cross-layering pointed out that functionalities usually pertaining to a single layer also can improve their performance via cross-layer interactions with other network functionalities. For example, the performance of routing and forwarding protocols can significantly improve by exploiting the information available in the MAC and physical layer. However, some researchers (Kawadia and Kumar 2005) have pointed out that the layer separation principle, by guaranteeing a modular design of the protocol stack, is a value to be maintained. An "unbridled" cross-layer design can produce a spaghetti-like code that is impossible to maintain in an efficient way, because every modification needs to be propagated to all protocols.

Relaxing the Internet layered architecture by enabling cross-layer interactions among protocols but still maintaining a layered organization and the layer separation principle, represents a good compromise between the two positions (layering and cross-layering). This is made possible by introducing a vertical module, called *network status* (NeSt), which controls all cross-layer interactions through data sharing (see Conti et al. (2004) and MobileMAN Project Deliverable D13 (n.d.) for details). Specifically, the NeSt supports vertical communications among the layers by acting as a repository for information collected by network protocols (see Figure 2). Each protocol can access the network status to share its data with other protocols and interact with them. By standardizing the NeSt interface (which defines how protocols can

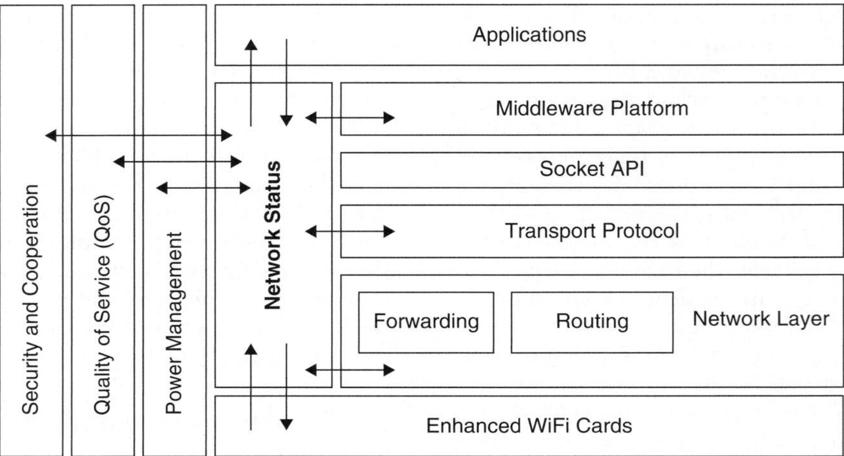

Figure 2: NeSt architecture

access/modify shared data), the layer separation principle is preserved. Indeed, in this way, cross-layer interactions do not directly take place between the interested protocols but are implemented using the abstractions exported by the NeSt, without modifying the interfaces between adjacent layers. Protocols have to implement the NeSt interface to exploit cross-layer optimizations, but no constraint exists on protocols, internal implementation. As long as the NeSt interface is implemented, a protocol can be replaced with a new release (or even with a brand-new protocol) without affecting the other protocols of the stack. In addition, using legacy protocols (i.e., no network-status enabled) is still possible although with degraded performance (i.e., without cross-layer optimizations). For example, using the legacy TCP protocol implies that cross-layer optimizations will not occur at this layer and that the transport protocol will not provide any information to the network status component. However, the overall protocol stack still operates correctly.

The design of a NeSt module from both a functional and an implementation standpoint is discussed in (Conti, Maselli, and Turi 2006). The effectiveness of the NeSt-based approach has been extensively evaluated by simulation in Conti, Gregori, and Turi (2005) and Conti, Gregori, and Maselli (2005) whereas Borgia et al. (2005) and Borgia, Conti, and Delmastro (2006) present experimental results obtained by implementing the NeSt in a multihop ad hoc network prototype.

FROM MANET TO MESH NETWORKS

As discussed earlier, currently mobile multihop ad hoc networks are tailored to very specialized missions (e.g., large-scale military applications with thousands of ad hoc nodes) or specialized civilian applications (e.g., disaster recovery, planetary exploration, etc.), and they have a very limited impact on the wireless market. By relaxing one of the main constraints of mobile ad hoc networks (the network is made of user devices only and no infrastructure exists), we move to a scenario in which multihop ad hoc networks are not isolated but emerge as a flexible and low-cost extension of the Internet. Indeed, a new class of networks is emerging from this view: the *mesh networks* (Bruno, Conti, and Gregori 2005). Mesh networks are built upon a combination of fixed and mobile nodes interconnected via wireless links to form a multihop ad hoc network (Bruno, Conti, and Gregori 2005). Different from *pure* multihop ad hoc networks, a mesh network introduces a *hierarchy* in the network architecture by introducing dedicated nodes (called *mesh routers*) communicating wirelessly to construct a *wireless backbone*. The wireless backbone has a (limited) number of connections with the wired Internet. Mobile/nomadic users obtain a multihop connectivity to the Internet by connecting to the closest mesh router (Akyildiz, Wang, and Wang 2005; Bruno, Conti, and Gregori 2005). Figure 3 illustrates the mesh network architecture, highlighting the different components and the system layers.

It is worth noting that, even though mesh networks require the existence of a wireless infrastructure (wireless mesh routers), the cost of this infrastructure is significantly lower than the cost of a traditional wired infrastructure. Indeed, broadband wired access to the Internet (e.g., via T1 or T3 access lines) is very expensive. In a mesh network, we need to provide only a limited number of *wired* ingress/egress points toward the Internet, whereas the mesh routers are in charge of routing the traffic through the wireless backbone toward these access points.

Even though mesh networks are a recent technology, they have already shown potential in the wireless market. Indeed, interesting wireless–mesh-network civilian applications have been recently deployed (Bruno, Conti, and Gregori 2005), for example:

- *Intelligent transportation systems*. The Portsmouth Real-Time Travel Information System (PORTAL) is an effective example of a mesh-network system aimed at providing real-time travel information to bus passengers in the city of Portsmouth (e.g., where the bus is and its scheduled arrival time).
- *Public safety*. The San Mateo Police Department in the Bay Area exploited a mesh network for broadband communications among all its vehicles (patrol cars, motorbikes, and bicycles).

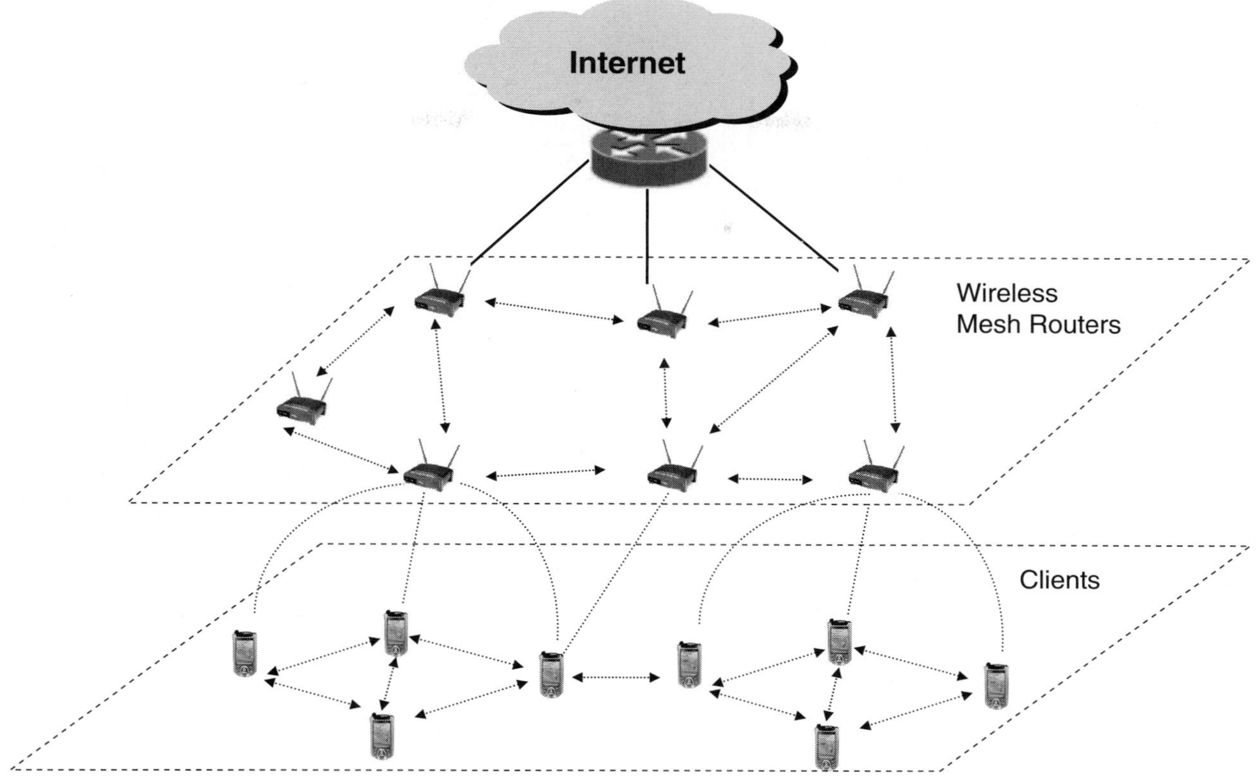

Figure 3: A wireless mesh network

- *Public Internet access*. The wireless mesh networks are the ideal solution to provide both indoor and outdoor broadband wireless connectivity in urban, suburban, and rural environments; see, for example, the metro-scale broadband city network in the City of Cerritos, California.
- *Community networks*. These networks, usually built using off-the-shelf technology (mainly 802.11), provide Internet access to a community of users that can share the same Internet access link. Several examples of this are: Seattle Wireless, Champaign-Urbana Community Wireless Network (CUWiN), the San Francisco BAWUG, and the Roofnet system at MIT.

FROM MANET TO OPPORTUNISTIC NETWORKING

MANET applications and services rely on the end-to-end principle (i.e., a path must continuously exist between the sender and a receiver for successful communications). In reality, end-to-end connectivity is a strong requirement only for interactive services such as voice over IP (VoIP), gaming, and video streaming; many other applications can still correctly operate relaxing the end-to-end constraint. For example, data applications like messaging, e-mails, data sharing, and so forth can tolerate sender-receiver disconnections. In principle, they can operate even if a sender-receiver path never exists (Fall 2003). This is a key point to overcome some of the main limitations of mobile multihop ad hoc networks in which network partitioning causes the failure of ongoing communications, and/or nodes that are temporarily disconnected from the network cannot communicate. Indeed, in opportunistic networks, a node stores the messages in its local memory until a forwarding opportunity does not exist. In this way, packets are not discarded during network disconnections but are locally stored. Specifically, in opportunistic networks the communication is still multihop with intermediate nodes acting as routers that forward the messages addressed to other nodes; however, in this case, forwarding is not "on the fly" because intermediate nodes store the messages when no forwarding opportunity exists (e.g., no other nodes are in the transmission range, or neighboring nodes are not considered useful for that communication) and exploit any contact opportunity with other mobile devices to forward information. For example, as shown in Figure 4, the man at the desktop opportunistically transfers, via a WiFi link, a message for his wife to a car crossing its area, hoping that the car will carry the information closer to its destination. Following the same approach, the car uses its Bluetooth radio to forward the message to the mobile phone of a woman who is going to the airport to catch a plane to a city close to the receiver's expected location. Proceeding the same way, the message arrives at the receiver. As is clearly shown in this example, a network connection between the man and his wife never exists, but, by opportunistically exploiting the contacts among heterogeneous devices, a message is delivered hop by hop (hopefully) closer to the destination and eventually is delivered to the receiver.

Figure 4: Opportunistic networking

Opportunistic networking is the evolution of the ad hoc networking concepts to opportunistically exploit users' mobility, which is "hostile" for legacy multihop ad hoc networks. Indeed, whereas mobility is one of the main MANET problems because it causes (due to node movement) route breakages, network disconnections, and partitions, in opportunistic networks nodes' mobility creates opportunities for communicating. The network can be partitioned and/or the receiver disconnected by the network. The mobility of nodes creates the communication opportunities. This behavior is well suited for a world of pervasive devices equipped with various wireless networking technologies (802.11 family, Bluetooth, ZigBee, etc.) that are frequently out of range of a network but are in range of other devices and sometimes cross areas in which some type of Internet connectivity is available (e.g., WiFi hotspots).

The concept of opportunistic networking can be further extended to mean that we exploit opportunistically any available communication technology (e.g., cellular, WiFi, Internet, etc.). In current pervasive systems in which nodes often have multiple network interfaces, at any time the communication paradigm would opportunistically choose for data forwarding the interface that is considered the most suitable for the given context (Haggle n.d.).

The Internet Research Task Force (IRTF) *Delay-tolerant networking* (DTN) Research Group is working to standardize architecture and protocols for enabling communications in networks with intermittent connectivity in which continuous end-to-end connectivity cannot be assumed (DTN n.d.). The basic idea is to construct an overlay, a *bundle layer*, on top of existing networks. The bundle layer exploits storing and forwarding of the information to support asynchronous data transfer between nodes in *challenged networks* with extreme communication delays and intermittent connectivity, such as interplanetary networks, military/tactical networks, disaster/emergency networks, underwater networks, and some forms of ad hoc sensor/actuator networks.

SENSOR NETWORKS

Sensor nodes constitute basic elements of pervasive environments. Recent advances in computing technology have led to the production of a new class of wireless, battery-powered, smart sensor nodes. These nodes are active devices with computing and communication capabilities that not only sample real-world phenomena but can also filter, share, combine, and operate on the data they sense (Raghunathan et al. 2002).

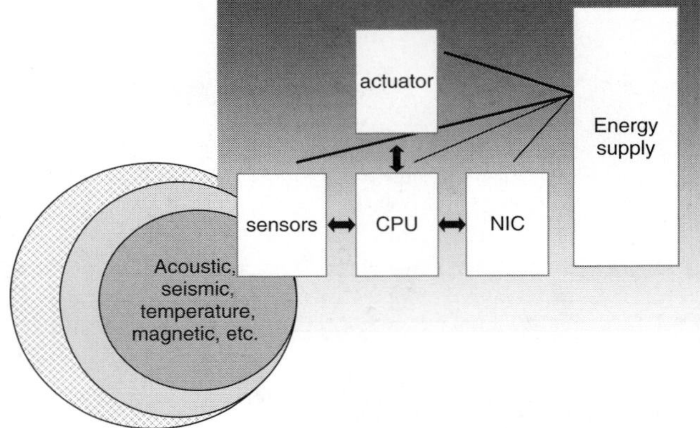

Figure 5: A simplified sensor node

Figure 5 presents a simplified scheme of a sensor node. The basic units of a sensor node are: the sensing unit (made up of a set of sensors, e.g., acoustic, magnetic, temperature, light, sound, etc.), the processing unit, a network interface (typically a radio), and the energy-supply unit (typically, a limited energy battery; Anastasi, Conti, and Passarella 2005). In addition, depending on the type of application it may have other components as well (e.g., an actuator).

Different kinds of infrastructures can be deployed to deliver the information from the sensing field to the collecting place (sink). The advances in simple, low-power, and efficient wireless communication equipment made wireless sensor networks the most interesting way to deliver the sensed data to the mobile device(s) to collect/elaborate them. The simplest way is to use single-hop wireless communications: the sensor nodes directly communicate the sensed data to a data-collection center, often referred to as a sink (see Figure 6.a).

This communication model can be efficiently applied only when the distance between the sensor nodes and the sink is limited (30 meters). In other cases, the sensor-node technology constraints (limited transmission range of wireless communication interface and/or the excessive energy drained by the wireless interface for long-distance communications) and the characteristics of the environment in which the sensor network is deployed (e.g., natural barriers) make direct communications not feasible or

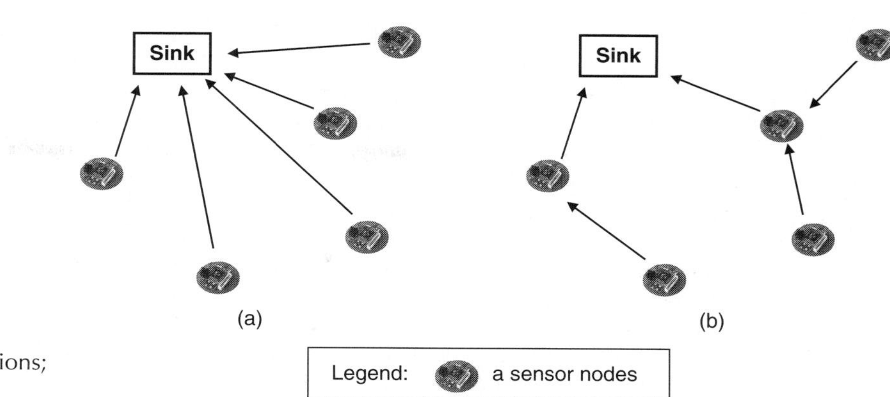

Figure 6: (a) Single-hop communications; (b) Multihops communications

effective. Therefore, as shown in Figure 6.b, each sensor node delivers the collected data to one (or more) neighbor node, one hop away. By following a multihop communication paradigm, the data are routed to the sink and through this to the user. Therefore, multihop ad hoc techniques also constitute the basis for wireless sensor networks. However, the resource constraints of the sensor nodes and the application-oriented characteristics of sensor networks make solutions designed for multihop wireless networks generally not suitable for sensor networks (Akyildiz et al. 2002). First of all, sensor nodes are limited in power, computational capacity, and memory. Sensor networks utilize on-board batteries with limited energy that cannot be replenished in most application scenarios (Starner 2003). This strongly affects the lifetime of a sensor network and makes power awareness a critical factor in the design of sensor network protocols. One possibility in these cases is *energy harvesting* from the environment; for example, energy can be obtained from light sources via solar cells. Unfortunately, at this time, energy harvesting is still in the early stages, and current technologies make available only small amounts of energy. The interested reader can find a review of energy harvesting technology in *IEEE Pervasive Computing* (2005). Sensor nodes are prone to failure and therefore are densely deployed for reliability; the number of sensor nodes in a sensor network can be several orders of magnitude higher than the nodes in an ad hoc network; although the large number of devices provides natural redundancy, correlated failures as a result of software errors could be catastrophic. Sensor nodes, once deployed, will be unattended. This makes robust operation a priority.

Sensor networks also produce a shift in the networking paradigm, from node-centric to data-centric. The aim of a sensor network is to collect information about events occurring in the sensor field rather than supporting the communications between nodes. Sensor networks are deployed to achieve a specific objective via a collaborative effort of numerous sensor nodes; the architecture, protocols, and type of sensor nodes drastically change by modifying the application scenario. Each sensor network will have a different purpose and will be customized to fit the task in an optimized way. This may imply the use of customized hardware platforms as well as applications-specific software and protocols. Therefore, before further discussing sensor networks organization, we survey possible application scenarios.

Sensor Network Applications

Sensor networks can be successfully applied in scientific research (habitat/environment monitoring), military scenarios (e.g., battlefield surveillance; reconnaissance of opposing forces; tracking of troops and equipment; nuclear, biological, and chemical attack detection, etc.), health applications (e.g., integrated patient monitoring), and commercial applications (e.g., monitoring material fatigue, structural control, managing inventory, factory process control and automation, vehicle tracking and detection, precision agriculture, etc.); see Akyildiz et al. (2002) and *IEEE Internet Computing* (2006).

Habitat and environmental monitoring include a large number of applications in which the use of sensor networks provides a very effective solution. Indeed, making regular observations of the environment is a complex and expensive task. In addition, human presence may have an impact on the monitoring of plants and animals in field conditions. For example, frequent visits can be a source of habitat modification that might bias environmental measurements. In addition, twenty-four-hour monitoring is not feasible for human beings. In this context, sensor networks represent a significant advance over traditional invasive methods of monitoring. Sensors can be deployed prior to sensitive period (e.g., breeding season, in the case of animals) or while plants are dormant or the ground is frozen (in the case of botanical studies). Several examples exist in the scientific literature of sensor network use for environment monitoring. These studies differ in the context and object to monitor; hence, different sensor networks have been adopted.

- The *Great Duck Island Habitat Monitoring* project (http://www.greatduckisland.net). This was a pilot application for monitoring migratory seabirds (Leach's Storm Petrel) on Great Duck Island, Maine. The project started in 2002 with thirty-two wireless sensor nodes to monitor the microclimates in and around nesting burrows. At the end of the field season in November 2002, over 1 million readings had been logged from the thirty-two motes deployed on the island and made available on the Internet. A second-generation network was deployed in 2003 with about 150 nodes that formed a multihop network, transferring their data to a base station. Eventually, data were transferred via satellite to the database at the University of California at Berkeley.

- *Study of Hawaii rare and endangered species of plants* (Biagioni and Bridges 2002). The PODS project (http://www.pods.hawaii.edu) developed a sensor network to study the biology of typical rare plant species and the habitats they occupy in *Hawaii Volcanoes National Park*. The aim of the study was to collect measurements of the temperature, humidity, rainfall, wind, and solar radiation in the rare species' habitat. In addition, to make inferences about factors determining the species' distribution, measurements had to be taken in nearby areas that did not have the species under study. Sensor nodes (a computer with environmental sensors and, in some cases, a high-resolution digital camera) collected data and, by exploiting a multihop paradigm, moved data toward an Internet access node.

The use of sensor networks for habitat monitoring is a very active research area. Let us also remember the use of sensor nodes proposed by Intel and the University of California at Berkeley to create a *macroscope* (sensor nodes strapped at different elevations of a redwood tree) to study the microclimate around redwoods (Tolle et al. 2005), and the habitat-sensing activities carried out by the Center for Embedded Networked Sensing (CENS) at the University of California at Los Angeles.

The next challenge is to expand monitoring to more hostile environments such as glaciers. This is indeed the objective of the *Envisense GlacsWeb project*, which focuses on monitoring the glacial environment to study subglacial bed deformations (Martinez, Hart, and Ong 2004). The system is based on probes inserted fifty to eighty meters into the glacier. The probes collect measurement samples via pressure, temperature, and orientation sensors, and deliver them to a base station located on the glacier surface, from which they are delivered to the sink. Probes use a direct wireless link to communicate with the base station.

Sensor networks for environment monitoring are also the basis for many useful civilian applications such as forest fire detection, flood detection, and precision agriculture (e.g., to monitor microclimates throughout a vineyard and add water and fertilizer when needed). Randomly and densely deployed sensor nodes are extremely useful for the early detection and localization of fires in the forest. Alarms, propagated multihop through the sensor network, enable a quick reaction before the fire becomes uncontrollable. Similarly, sensor nodes that monitor water levels and rainfall can provide early warnings of possible flooding conditions, thus helping to reduce damages. Sensor networks are ideal for studying the effects of microclimate on plant growth, thus allowing scientists to better understand the ways in which to optimize yield and quality (precision agriculture).

Health monitoring is a very promising area for the application of wireless sensor networks. In this case, sensor networks are part of a wearable system used for health monitoring. Physiological sensors (e.g., electrocardiogram, blood pressure, temperature) can be used to automatically collect physiological parameters to be delivered, via a body area network, to wearable devices for real-time processing and/or storing for future use (long-term observation). For example, the CodeBlue system (n.d.) developed at Harvard University exploits a wireless sensor network to raise an alert condition when vital signs fall outside of normal parameter values. The system, built on Mica2, MicaZ, and Telos platforms (Mica n.d.; Telos n.d.), monitors heart rate, oxygen saturation, and electrocardiogram data, and relays the data over a short-range wireless network to a set of devices, including personal digital assistants (PDAs), laptops, and ambulance-based terminals.

Tracking applications constitute another important field for sensor network applications. Instead of sensing environmental data, in this case sensor nodes are deployed to sense the presence of persons and objects. Objects can be tracked by simply tagging them with a small sensor node. The sensor node will be tracked as it moves through a field of sensor nodes that are deployed throughout the environment at known locations. The sensor nodes can be used as active tags that announce the presence of a device. Using this system, it becomes possible to ask where an object is. Tracking applications have an important role in the military field for monitoring friendly forces, equipment, and ammunition; every troop, vehicle, and piece of critical equipment can be tracked by attaching to it a sensor node that reports its status. A similar approach can be used, for example, to track and monitor doctors and patients inside a hospital.

Localization applications are among the most challenging applications that can be performed by a sensor network. For example, detecting and locating snipers is a challenging goal for armed forces and law enforcement agencies. Most successful sniper-detecting systems are based on exploiting a wireless sensor network that takes measurements of the acoustic events generated by a shot: the spherical wave (traveling at the speed of sound) produced by the muzzle blast and the shock wave generated by the supersonic projectile. By exploiting the measurements of acoustic events taken by the sensor network nodes, it is possible to determine the shooter's location and the bullet's trajectory (see, e.g., Maroti et al. 2004).

The examples above represent a set of the most promising scenarios for the utilization of sensor networks. However, sensor networks will likely be a pervasive technology that covers all aspects of life, including the arts (Burke et al. 2006).

Sensor Network Organization

The aim of a sensor network is to collect information about events that occur in the sensor field. To this end, a wireless sensor network is often organized as shown in Figure 7. Sensor nodes are densely deployed in the monitoring area, and the information collected by a sensor node is delivered to the sink by exploiting the multihop paradigm. Generally, in monitoring applications, knowledge of sensor locations is required to correctly report, for example, the origin of events generating an alarm.

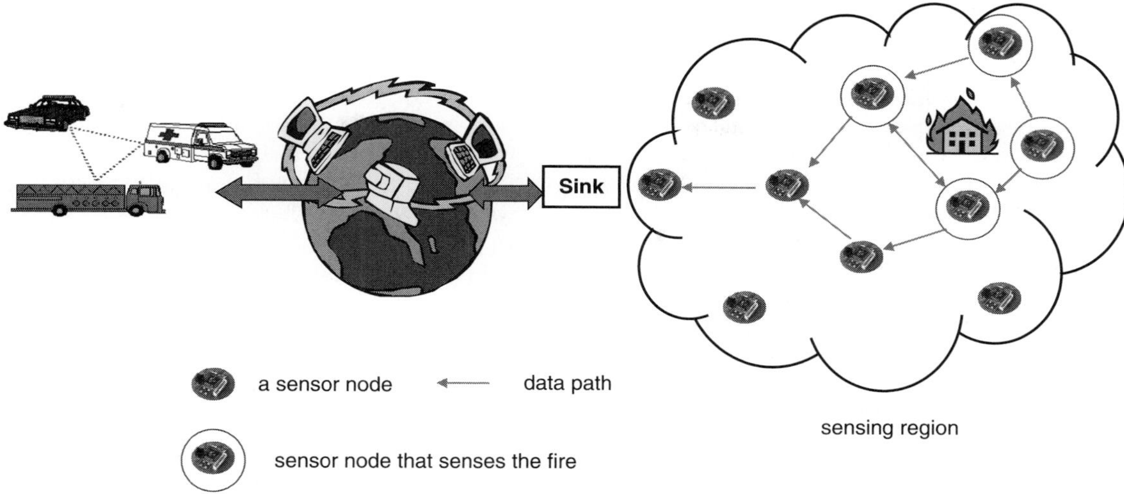

Figure 7: A wireless sensor network

Location discovery has therefore received considerable attention from the sensor network research community. Savvides and Srivastava (2004) presents an excellent review of techniques and systems for location discovery in ad hoc and sensor networks.

In monitoring applications, several sensor nodes often collect the same (or highly correlated) information (e.g., in Figure 7, all sensor nodes close to the fire sense very high temperature values); hence, not all samples need to be delivered to the sink, but only a subset or some aggregated form (e.g., in Figure 7 it is enough to report to the sink the event "temperature higher than 100°C"). This means that, because of the redundancy of the sensed information, the delivery to the sink of the information collected by a given node can tolerate some losses in many applications. The data-centric nature of sensor network applications produces a shift in the networking paradigm with respect to the node-centric view used in legacy wired and wireless networks. In sensor networks, the correct detection of an event (possibly minimizing the energy) is the aim of the networking protocol, whereas correct delivery to the sink of all information generated by the sensor nodes is not only useless but also often undesirable because of the associated energy costs and the increase in network congestion. Moreover, while in node-centric networks, the information is not manipulated inside the network (at most, packets can be discarded if resources are not available for forwarding them). In sensor networks, intermediate devices—traveling along the path from the sender (a sensor device) to the receiver (the sink)—can exploit the correlation in the observed data to reduce (via aggregation) the amount of information flowing into the network. For instance, in the Figure 7 example, a node does not forward all of the fire alarms it receives from downstream nodes but just a minimum number to guarantee that the event notification arrives at the sink. In general, each sensor node (to increase the energy efficiency of the system) aggregates the samples received by downstream nodes (e.g., combines the sampled values into a sum) before forwarding data to the sink. Indeed, in sensor networks, from the power consumption standpoint, processing is a much cheaper operation than transmitting (Doherty et al. 2001; Starner 2003). In addition, *in-network processing* contributes to a better utilization of sensor-node limited bandwidth. Therefore, whereas in mobile ad hoc networks only protocols operating at layers 1–3 of the open systems interconnection (OSI) reference model participate in the operations inside the network (higher layers are affected only in the sender and receiver devices), in a sensor network higher layers (e.g., the presentation and the application layers in which compression and aggregation of data are applied to reduce redundancy in delivered data) also contribute to power-efficient data delivery, making the sensor network protocol stack cross-layer in nature (Conti et al. 2004). TinyDB (Madden et al. 2003) represents the extreme case, in which almost all of the networking functions are implemented in the application layer. A complete analysis of research issues for designing sensor network protocols can be found in Akyildiz et al. (2002).

Sensor Networks and Data Mules

So far we have assumed that sink(s) are fixed and that measurements taken from sensor nodes far from the sink are delivered to the sink via a complex multihop process. In many applications, collecting data from the sensor nodes can be implemented in a more efficient way by adding a further level to the system hierarchy. This additional level can be implemented by introducing mobile nodes inside the network (e.g., robots) that move inside the sensors field collecting the information from neighbor nodes via single-hop ad hoc wireless communications and then move close to the sink to deliver the collected data. These nodes are often referred to in the literature as *data mules* (Shah et al. 2003; Jea, Somasundara, and Srivastava 2005). Unmanned helicopters flying over the sensor field to collect data are an example of data mules (Henkel et al. 2006).

A mule-based sensor network is useful in sparse networks in which nodes are far from one another, thus making a multihop path too expensive from the energy standpoint. In addition, this approach increases the nodes, battery lifetime, because sensor nodes are not involved in data forwarding.

The use of data mules may introduce significant energy savings in the sensor nodes because they have only to transmit their own data to the mobile nodes via short-range transmissions; on the other hand, data mules may increase the network cost, because complex mobile nodes need to be introduced and managed. One possible way to avoid this complexity is to opportunistically exploit as data mules any element that, for any reason, crosses the sensor field. For example, imagine sensor nodes spread out in an urban environment to take pollution measurements. To deliver sensor samples to a sink, we can opportunistically exploit city buses that come close to sensor nodes while moving along the streets. Via single-hop ad hoc communications, the buses collect data from the sensor nodes. The data are then delivered to the sink when the bus arrives inside the sink transmission range, or they are forwarded to other buses that have a better chance of arriving close to the sink. The effectiveness of this approach for collecting sensor data samplings in urban environments is investigated in Anastasi et al. (2006). Specifically, by exploiting simple sensor nodes (Berkeley motes), the authors show that in high-mobility scenarios as will (corresponding to vehicles moving along the city streets), the mules (vehicles) are able to collect reasonable amount of data from mote sensor nodes (Anastasi et al. 2006). A limitation of this approach is the extra delay in delivering data from the nodes to the sink, which makes this solution suitable mainly for delay-tolerant applications.

Sensor Networks and Actuators

In the previous section we introduced robots that move in the sensor fields to collect data from the sensor nodes and deliver them to the sink. In that case, the robots only collected data from the sensors; their actions did not depend on the information they collected. In a more general framework, the robots can also perform actions on the sensor field depending on the events detected by the sensors. For example, we can imagine a robot with water-sprinkling capabilities that receives fire alarms from sensor nodes and immediately operates to extinguish fire. This class of nodes, which operates on the sensor field to react to events detected by sensor nodes, is referred to in the literature as actuators or actors (Akyildiz and Kasimoglu 2004). The actors can be fixed and simple entities such as in-room water sprinklers, or resource-rich mobile robots equipped with significant processing and communication capabilities and high-capacity batteries, such as un-manned helicopters and battlefield robots. The design of sensor and actor networks presents several challenging research issues (Akyildiz and Kasimoglu 2004). Indeed, in this case we need to coordinate the sensor nodes with the actors, and coordinate the actors among themselves to select the actor(s) in charge of reacting to sensor-node detected events.

Underwater Sensor Networks

Monitoring the aquatic environment is emerging as a very interesting and challenging scenario for the use of wireless sensor networks. This scenario includes, among others (Akyildiz, Pompili, and Melodia 2005):

- Oceanographic data collection for scientific exploration, pollution control, climate monitoring, weather forecasting, and so forth
- Disaster prevention, for example, by providing tsunami warnings to exposed areas
- Undersea exploration to detect valuable minerals or help in laying cables
- Tactical surveillance by detecting underwater vehicles (e.g., submarines) (Cayirici et al. 2006)

Underwater sensor networks add to the features of legacy sensor networks (a large number of nodes, energy limitations, etc.) unique characteristics of the underwater environment that make solutions for terrestrial sensor networks not directly applicable. Novel aspects of these networks are: i) acoustic communications, ii) three-dimensional (3-D) form, and iii) high node mobility.

Acoustic Communications

Due to poor performance of radio waves in aquatic environments, underwater communications exploit acoustic wireless communications (Proakis et al. 2001). The use of acoustic signals has a major impact on the design of underwater sensor networks. First of all, the propagation speed of acoustic signals in water (0.67 s/km) is five orders lower than the radio propagation speed. Furthermore, underwater acoustic communications are negatively affected by phenomena such as noise, multipath, path loss, and Doppler spread that cause high error rates and limit the available bandwidth to few kbits/sec (Akyildiz, Pompili, and Melodia 2005).

3D Dimension

Whereas terrestrial sensor networks often have a two-dimensional design (some 3D sensor networks are used in terrestrial networks for environmental monitoring; see the section entitled "Sensor Network Applications"), underwater sensor networks are generally deployed in a 3D space.

Node Mobility

Underwater sensor nodes, unless connected to surface buoys, are subject to water current, which in a typical condition moves the objects at a speed of 3–6 km per hour. This makes the network topology very unstable and impacts message routing and forwarding.

These issues open research challenges at all layers of the protocols' stack (Cui et al. 2006). An in-depth analysis of research issues and directions for tackling them are presented in Akyildiz, Pompili, and Melodia (2005).

CONCLUSION

The number of microprocessors residing in everyday electronics is continuously increasing, and this presents new advanced forms of interaction between humans, and between humans and the physical world. Wireless networks are the natural tools for these interactions because they offer mobility and avoid wiring problems. Among these networks, ad hoc networking is rapidly gaining momentum because of its flexibility and low costs. The heterogeneity of devices to be interconnected (from small sensors and actuators to multimedia PDAs) and the large spectrum of communication requirements (from a few meters of coverage and a few kilobits of bandwidth to city-wide coverage and broadband communications) produced a set of ad hoc network technologies. At one extreme, we have sensor networks for communication among small-size, low-cost, and low-energy consumption devices (sensors) for which a high data rate is not necessary. At the other end of the spectrum we have mesh networks that, by exploiting an infrastructure of wireless mesh routers, guarantee the exchange of multimedia information among devices located in an urban area. This chapter has presented an updated overview of ad hoc networks by presenting their principles and by applications, and by pointing out the open research issues. Specifically, we discussed the relationships among different ad hoc networks and their application scenarios. The chapter began with an overview of MANET protocols and a discussion of the impact of cross-layering design on MANET architecture. Specifically, we presented an architecture that guarantees cross-layer interactions among protocols while maintaining a layered organization. Next, we discussed MANET evolution toward mesh and opportunistic networks. Mesh networks represent a short-term, market-driven evolution of MANETs. In these networks, routing nodes (mesh routers) are stationary and form a wireless ad hoc backbone, which has connections to the Internet. Client nodes use the backbone to access the Internet. On the other hand, opportunistic networking represents a long-term direction for the MANET evolution. In these networks, communications are single hop, and messages are forwarded from a node to one, or more, of its neighbors. Forwarding is performed when there is a significant probability that a node will move close to the destination or will be able to forward the data to nodes closer to the destination than itself. The last part of the chapter discussed ad hoc networking in the context of sensor networks. A sensor network is composed by a (possibly large) number of small sensor nodes, which are deployed inside an area to monitor. We extensively discussed the constraints on the network organization as a result of the limited resources of sensing devices and application requirements. Based on the application scenario, we presented different models for organizing a sensor network, including a brief overview of underwater sensor networks.

ACKNOWLEDGMENT

This work was partially funded by the Information Society Technologies program of the European Commission under the MobileMAN (IST-2001-38113) and HAGGLE (027918) grants. I wish to express my thanks to the anonymous referees for helpful comments and suggestions.

GLOSSARY

Acoustic Wireless Networks: Wireless networks that use acoustic signals for communication among nodes. Typically used in underwater environments.

Actuator: Robot able to perform actions on the sensor field as a reaction to the events detected by the sensor nodes.

Ad Hoc Network: Wireless network in which mobile devices communicate directly without relying on any pre-deployed infrastructure. This type of network is also referred to as an infrastructure-less network.

Body Area Network (BAN): Short-range (wireless) network for interconnecting devices distributed on the human body.

Cross Layering: A design principle for organizing the protocol stack exploiting interlayer dependencies. Through cross-layering a protocol can use the information collected at other layers of the protocol stack.

Data Mule: A mobile element that crosses a sensor field, collects data from sensor nodes, and delivers data to a sink.

Delay-Tolerant Network (DTN): Architecture and protocols standardized by the IRTF *Delay-tolerant networking* (DTN) Research Group for enabling communications in networks with intermittent connectivity in which continuous end-to-end connectivity cannot be assumed, such as interplanetary networks, military/tactical networks, disaster/emergency networks, and some forms of ad hoc sensor/actuator networks.

Energy Harvesting/Scavenging: Methodologies and techniques to be implemented in mobile devices to make them able to collect energy from the environment without intervention of any external operator.

Geographic Routing: Routing protocols that use the nodes' location (i.e., geographical coordinates) for data forwarding. They are also known as location-aware routing protocols.

Infrastructure-Based Network/Systems: Wireless network/system with a preinstalled fixed infrastructure. Mobile devices access the fixed infrastructure through access points.

In-Network Processing: General technique used in sensor networks to reduce the amount of information flowing into the network (from sensor nodes to the sink), thus reducing energy consumption associated with data transmission.

Mesh Network: A multihop ad hoc network that uses dedicated nodes (called *mesh routers*) communicating wirelessly to construct a *wireless backbone* that has a (limited) number of connections with the wired Internet. Mobile users obtain a multihop connectivity to the Internet by connecting to the closest mesh router.

Mobile Ad Hoc Network (MANET): Ad hoc network in which the source and destination nodes are not within the transmission range of each other. Communication occurs through intermediate nodes. Nodes in a MANET thus act as nodes and router at the same time.

Opportunistic Network: Heterogeneous multihop ad hoc network that exploits any contact opportunity to forward data. Forwarding is performed by opportunistically exploiting the network interfaces (wired and wireless) that a node has. When no forwarding opportunity exists (e.g., there are no other nodes in the transmission range, or neighboring nodes are considered not useful for that communication), a node locally stores the messages. This type of network is suitable for sparse and frequently disconnected networks.

Pervasive Computing: A computing paradigm that refers to a scenario in which the environment is saturated with intelligent devices. User personal devices interact with external devices in a transparent way.

Power/Energy Management: Methodologies and tools aimed to efficiently manage the energetic resource of mobile devices.

Sensor Network: A network of sensor nodes are densely and randomly deployed inside the area in which a phenomenon is being monitored. Each sensor node delivers the collected data to one (or more) neighbor node, one hop away. By following a multihop communication paradigm, the data are routed to a special node (sink) and, through this, to the user.

Sensor Node: Tiny device with computing, wireless communication, and sensing capabilities that can be used for various purposes. Typical sensing tasks could be temperature, light, sound, and so forth.

Sink Node: A special node used in sensor networks to collect information acquired by sensor nodes.

Underwater Sensor Network: A sensor network used in underwater environments. For communication, it uses acoustic signals instead of radio signals.

Vehicular Networks: Mobile ad hoc networks used for car-to-car communication. Cars located between the source and destination cars operate as traffic relays.

WiFi Hotspot: Public place in which an access point is available that allows mobile devices to access the Internet. WiFi hotspots are typically available at airports, railway stations, hotels, malls, and so forth.

CROSS REFERENCES

See *Emerging Trends in Routing Protocols in Mobile Wireless Ad Hoc and Sensor Networks*; *Medium Access in Ad Hoc and Sensor Networks*; *Network Middleware*; *Network QoS*.

REFERENCES

Akyildiz, I. F., and I. H. Kasimoglu. 2004. Wireless sensor and actor networks: Research challenges. *Ad Hoc Networks* 2: 351–67.

Akyildiz, I. F., D. Pompili, and T. Melodia. 2005. Underwater acoustic sensor networks: Research challenges. *Ad Hoc Networks* 3: 257–79.

Akyildiz, I. F., W. Su, Y. Sankarasubramaniam, and E. Cayirci. 2002. Wireless sensor networks: A survey, *Computer Networks* 38: 393–422.

Akyildiz, I. F., X. Wang, and W. Wang. 2005. Wireless mesh networks: A survey, *Computer Networks* (4): 445–87.

Anastasi, G., E. Ancillotti, M. Conti, and A. Passarella. 2005. "TPA: A transport protocol for ad hoc networks. In *Proceedings of the Tenth IEEE Symposium on Computers and Communications*, Cartagena, Spain, June, pp. 51–56.

Anastasi, G., E. Borgia, M. Conti, E. Gregori, and A. Passarella. 2005. Understanding the real behavior of mote and 802.11 ad hoc networks: An experimental approach. *Pervasive and Mobile Computing* 1(2): 237–56.

Anastasi, G., M. Conti, E. Gregori, C. Spagoni, and G. Valente. 2006. Motes sensor networks in dynamic scenarios: An experimental study for pervasive applications in urban environments. *Journal of Ubiquitous Computing and Intelligence (JUCI)* 1(1): 9–16.

Anastasi, G., M. Conti, and A. Passarella. 2005. Power management in mobile and pervasive computing systems. Chap. 24 in *Algorithms and protocols for wireless and mobile networks*, edited by Azzedine Boukerche. Boca Raton, FL: CRC-Hall.

Baccarelli, E., M. Biagi, R. Bruno, M. Conti, and E. Gregori. 2005. Broadband wireless access networks: A roadmap on emerging trends and standards. Chap. 14 in *Broadband services to businesses communities: Business models and technologies*, edited by C. Szabo, I. Chlamtac, and A. Gumaste. New York: John Wiley and Sons.

Basagni, S., M. Conti, S. Giordano, and I. Stojmenovic, eds. 2004. *Mobile ad hoc networking*. New York: IEEE Press and John Wiley and Sons.

Bellavista, P., A. Corradi, and E. Magistretti. 2005. REDMAN: An optimistic replication middleware for read-only resources data in dense MANETs. *Pervasive and Mobile Computing*, 1(3): 279–310.

Belding-Royer, E. 2004. Routing approaches in mobile ad hoc networks. In *Mobile ad hoc networking*, edited by S. Basagni, M. Conti, S. Giordano, and I. Stojmenovic. New York: IEEE Press and John Wiley & Sons, Inc.

Biagioni, E. S., and K. W. Bridges. 2002. The application of remote sensor technology to assist the recovery of rare and endangered species. *The International Journal of High Performance Computing Applications* 16 (3): 315–24.

Bisdikian, C. An overview of the Bluetooth wireless technology. *IEEE Communications Magazine*, December, pp. 86–94

Borgia, E., M. Conti, and F. Delmastro. 2006. MobileMAN: Design, integration and experimentation of cross-layer mobile multihop ad hoc networks. *IEEE Communications Magazine*, July, pp. 80–85.

Borgia, E., M. Conti, F. Delmastro, and E. Gregori. 2005. Experimental comparison of routing and middleware solutions for mobile ad hoc networks: Legacy vs. cross-layer approach. In *Proceedings of the ACM SIGCOMM Workshop on Experimental Approaches to Wireless Network Design and Analysis (E-WIND)* Philadelphia, August, pp. 82–87.

Bruno, R., M. Conti, and E. Gregori. 2005. Mesh networks: Commodity multihop ad hoc networks. *IEEE Communications Magazine*, March, pp.123–31.

Burke, J., J. Friedman, E. Mendelowitz, H. Park, and M. B. Srivastava. 2006. Embedding expression: Pervasive computing architecture for art and entertainment. *Pervasive and Mobile Computing* 2(1): 1–36.

Buttyan, L., and J. P. Hubaux. 2002. Report on a working session on security in wireless ad hoc networks. *Mobile Computing and Communications Review* 7(1): 74–94.

Callaway, E., P. Gorday, L. Hester, J. A. Gutierrez, and M. Naeve. 2002. Home networking with IEEE 802.15.4: A developing standard for low-rate wireless personal area networks. *IEEE Communications Magazine*, August, pp. 70–77.

Cayirici, E., H. Tezcan, Y. Dogan, and V. Coskun. 2006. Wireless sensor networks for underwater survelliance systems. *Ad Hoc Networks* 4(4): 431–46.

Chlamtac, I., M. Conti, and J. Liu. 2003. Mobile ad hoc networking: Imperatives and challenges. *Ad Hoc Networks* 1(1): 13–64.

CodeBlue project. Undated. http://www.eecs.harvard.edu/~mdw/proj/codeblue/ (accessed August 29, 2007).

Conti, M. 2004. Wireless communications and pervasive technologies. Chap. 4 in *Environments: Technologies, protocols and applications*, edited by Diane Cook and Sajal K. Das. New York: John Wiley and Sons.

Conti, M., F. Delmastro, and G. Turi. 2006. Peer-to-peer computing in mobile ad hoc networks. In *Mobile middleware*, edited by A. Corradi and P. Bellavista. Boca Raton, FL: CRC Press.

Conti, M., S. Giordano, G. Maselli, and G. Turi. 2004. Cross layering in mobile ad hoc network design. *IEEE Computer*, February, pp. 48–51.

Conti, M., E. Gregori, and G. Maselli. 2004. Cooperation issues in mobile ad hoc networks. In *Proceedings of IEEE ICDCS Workshops*, Tokyo, Japan, March, pp. 803–8.

Conti, M., E. Gregori, and G. Maselli. 2005. Improving the performability of data transfer in mobile ad hoc networks. In *Proceedings of the Second IEEE International Conference on Sensor and Ad Hoc Communications and Networks (SECON)*, Santa Clara, California, September, pp. 153–63.

Conti, M., E. Gregori, and G. Turi. 2005. A cross layer optimization of Gnutella for mobile ad hoc networks. In *Proceedings of the ACM MobiHoc Symposium*, Urbana-Champain, Illinois, May, pp. 343–54.

Conti, M., G. Maselli, and G. Turi. 2006. A flexible cross-layer interface for ad hoc networks: Architectural and implementation issues. *Ad Hoc & Sensor Wireless Networks: An International Journal* 2(2): 189–204.

Cook, D., and Sajal K. Das. 2004. *Environments: Technologies, protocols and applications*. New York: John Wiley and Sons.

Corson, M. S., J. P. Maker, and J. H. Cernicione. 1999. Internet-based mobile ad hoc networking. *IEEE Internet Computing*, July August, pp. 63–70.

Cui, J.-H., J. Kong, M. Gerla and S. Zhou. 2006. Challenges: Building scalable mobile underwater wireless sensor networks for aquatic applications special issue. *IEEE Network on Wireless Sensor Networking*, 20(3): 12–18.

Delay Tolerant Networking Research Group. Undated. http://www.dtnrg.org/.

Doherty, L., B. A. Warneke, B. E. Boser, and K. S. J. Pister. 2001. Energy and performance considerations for smart dust. *International Journal of Parallel Distributed Systems and Networks*, 4(3): 121–33.

Ephremides, A. 2002. Energy concerns in wireless networks. *IEEE Wireless Communications* 9(4): 48–59.

Estrin, D., Culler, K. Pister, and G. Sukhatme. 2002. Connecting the physical world with pervasive networks. *IEEE Pervasive Computing* 1(1): 59–69.

Fall, K. 2003. A delay-tolerant network architecture for challenged internets. In *Proceeding of ACM SIGCOMM*, Karlsruhe, Germany, August, pp. 27–34.

Feeney, L. 2004. Energy efficient communication in ad hoc wireless networks. In *Mobile ad hoc networking*, edited by S. Basagni, M. Conti, S. Giordano, and I. Stojmenovic. New York: IEEE Press and John Wiley & Sons, Inc.

Fu, Z., P. Zerfos, H. Luo, S. Lu, L. Zhang, and M. Gerla. 2003. The impact of multihop wireless channel on TCP throughput and loss, In *Proceedings of IEEE INFOCOM 2003*, San Francisco, California, March/April, pp. 1744–53.

Giordano, S., I. Stojmenovic, and L. Blazevic. 2003. Position-based routing algorithms for ad hoc networks: A taxonomy. In *Ad hoc wireless networking*, edited by X. Cheng, X. Huang and D.Z. Du, 103–136. Norwell, MA: Kluwer.

Gunningberg, P., H. Lundgren, E. Nordstrom, and C. Tschudin. 2005. Lessons from experimental MANET research, Special issue, *Ad Hoc Networks* 3(2): 221–33.

Gupta, P., R. Gray, and P. R. Kumar. An experimental scaling law for ad hoc networks. http://black.csl.uiuc.edu/~prkumar/postscript_files.html, (accessed May 16, 2001).

Gupta, P., and P. R. Kumar. 2000. The capacity of wireless networks. *IEEE Transactions on Information Theory* IT-46 (2): 388–404.

Haggle project. Undated. http://www.haggleproject.org.

Henkel, D., C. Dixon, J. Elston, and T. X. Brown. 2006. A reliable sensor data collection network using unmanned aircraft. In *Proceedings of ACM REALMAN 2006*, Florence, May, pp. 125–27.

Huang, E., W. Hu, J. Crowcroft, and I. Wassell. 2005. Toward commercial mobile ad hoc network applications: A radio dispatch system. In *Proceedings of the ACM MobiHoc Symposium*, Urbana-Champain, Illinois, May, 355–65.

IEEE Internet Computing. 2006. Special issue, March/April.

IEEE Pervasive Computing. January-March 2005. Special issue on, Energy harvesting and conservation 4(1): 2–71.

Internet Engineering Task Force (IETF) Mobile Ad Hoc Networks (MANET) Working Group. Undated. http://www.ietf.org/html.charters/manet-charter.html.

Jea, D., A. A. Somasundara, and M. B. Srivastava. 2005. Multiple controlled mobile elements (data mules) for data collection in sensor networks. In *Proceedings of the IEEE International Conference on Distributed Computing in Sensor Systems (DCOSS)*, Marina del Rey, California, June/July, pp. 244–57.

Kawadia, V., and P. R. Kumar. 2005. A cautionary perspective on cross layer design. *IEEE Wireless Communications Magazine*, February, pp. 3–11.

Li, Q., and D. Rus. 2000. Sending messages to mobile users in disconnected ad-hoc wireless networks. In *Proceedings of ACM MOBICOM*, Boston, August, pp. 44–55.

Liu, J., and S. Singh. 2001. ATCP: TCP for mobile ad hoc networks. *IEEE J-SAC* 19(7): 1300–15.

Macker, J. P., S. Corson. 2004. Mobile ad hoc networks (MANET): Routing technology for dynamic, wireless networking. In *Mobile ad hoc networking*, edited by S. Basagni, M. Conti, S. Giordano, and I. Stojmenovic. New York: IEEE Press and John Wiley & Sons, Inc.

Madden, S. R., M. J. Franklin, J. M. Hellerstein, and W. Hong. 2003. The design of an acquisitional query processor for sensor networks. In *Proceedings of SIGMOD*, San Diego, June, pp. 491–502.

Maroti, M., G. Simon, A. Ledeczi, and J. Sztipanovits. 2004. Shooter localization in urban terrain. *IEEE Computer*, August, pp. 60–61.

Martinez, K., J. K. Hart, and R. Ong. 2004. Environmental sensor networks. *IEEE Computer*, August, pp. 50–56.

MobileMAN Project Deliverable D10. Undated. Online article available at http://cnd.iit.cnr.it/mobileMAN/pub-deliv.html.

MobileMAN Project Deliverable D13. Undated. Online article available at http://cd.iit.cnr.it/mobileMAN/pub-deliv.html.

Motes. Undated. http://www.xbow.com/Home/HomePage.aspx (accessed August 30, 2007).

Ni, S.-Y., Y.-C. Tseng, Y.-S. Chen, and J.-P., Sheu. 1999. The broadcast storm problem in a mobile ad hoc network. In *Proceeding of MOBICOM '99*, Seattle, August, pp. 151–162.

Proakis, J., E. Sozer, J. Rice, and M. Stojanovic. 2001. Shallow water acoustic networks. *IEEE Communications Magazine*, November, pp. 114–19.

Raghunathan, V., C. Schurgers, S. Park, M. Srivastava. 2002. Energy aware wireless microsensor networks. *IEEE Signal Processing Magazine*, March, pp. 40–50.

Ramanathan, R. 2001. On the performance of ad hoc networks with beamforming antennas. In *Proceedings of ACM MobiHoc*, Long Beach, California, October, pp. 95–105.

Ramanathan, R. 2004. Antenna beamforming and power control for ad hoc networks. 2004. In *Mobile ad hoc networking*, edited by S. Basagni, M. Conti, S. Giordano, and I. Stojmenovic. New York: IEEE Press and John Wiley & Sons, Inc.

Samar, P., M. R. Pearlman, and Z. J. Haas. 2004. Independent zone routing: An adaptive hybrid routing framework for ad hoc wireless networks. *IEEE/ACM Transactions on Networking (TON)*, 12(4): 595–608.

Savvides, A., and M. Srivastava. 2004. Location discovery. In *Mobile ad hoc networking, edited by* S. Basagni, M. Conti, S. Giordano, and I. Stojmenovic. New York: IEEE Press and John Wiley & Sons, Inc.

Shah, R. C., S. Roy, S. Jain, and W. Brunette. 2003. Data mules: Modeling and analysis of a three-tier architecture for sparse sensor networks. *Ad Hoc Networks* 1(2/3): 215–33.

Starner, T. E. 2003. Powerful change part 1: Batteries and possible alternatives for the mobile market. *IEEE Pervasive Computing*, October–December, pp. 86–88.

Sterbenz, J. P. G., R. Krishnan, R. R., Hain, A.W. Jackson, D. Levin, R. Ramanathan, and J. Zao. 2002. Survivable mobile wireless networks: Issues, challenges, and research directions. In *Proceedings of the Third ACM Workshop on Wireless Security*, Atlanta, September, pp. 31–40.

Stevens, W. R. 1994. *TCP/IP illustrated, vol. 1: The protocol*. Reading, MA: Addison-Wesley.

Sundaresan, K., V. Anantharaman, H.-Y. Hsieh, and R. Sivakumar. 2003. ATP: A reliable transport protocol for ad-hoc networks. In *Proceedings of the Fourth ACM Symposium on Mobile Ad Hoc Network and Computing (MobiHoc 2003)*, Annapolis, Maryland, June, pp. 64–75.

Stojmenovic, I., and J. Wu. 2004. Broadcasting and activity-scheduling in ad hoc networks. In *Mobile ad hoc networking*, edited by S. Basagni, M. Conti, S. Giordano, and I. Stojmenovic. New York: IEEE Press and John Wiley & Sons, Inc.

Tmote. Undated. http://www.moteiv.com/.

Tolle, G., D. Gay, W. Hong, J. Polastre, R. Szewczyk, D. Culler, N. Turner, K. Tu, S. Burgess, T. Dawson, et al. 2005. A macroscope in the redwoods. In *Proceedings of the Third Conference on Embedded Networked Sensor Systems*, San Diego, California, November, pp. 51–63.

Wang, F., and Y. Zhang. 2002. Improving TCP performance over mobile ad-hoc networks with out-of order detection and response. In *Proceedings of ACM MobiHoc* 2002, Lausanne, Switzerland, June, pp. 48–57.

Widmer, J., M. Mauve, H. Hartenstein, and H. Füβler. 2003. Position-based routing in ad-hoc wireless networks. In *The handbook of ad hoc wireless networks*, edited by M. Ilyas. Boca Raton, FL: CRC Press.

Zhao, W., M. Ammar, and E. Zegura. 2004. A message ferrying approach for data delivery in sparse mobile ad hoc networks. In *Proceedings of the Fifth ACM International Symposium on Mobile Ad Hoc Networking and Computing*, Tokyo, May, pp. 187–98.

Medium Access in Ad Hoc and Sensor Networks

Vojislav B. Mišić and Jelena Mišić, *University of Manitoba, Canada*

INTRODUCTION

Wireless ad hoc networks are a category of wireless networks that utilize multihop packet relaying yet are capable of operating without any infrastructure support (Perkins 2001; Ram Murthy and Manoj 2004; Toh 2002). Applications that necessitate ad hoc networking capabilities include mobile, collaborative, and distributed computing; mobile access to the Internet; wireless mesh networks; military applications; emergency response networks; and others. Ad hoc networks are formed by a number of devices, possibly heterogeneous, with wireless communication capabilities that connect and disconnect at will. In addition, some of these devices may be mobile and are thus able to change their location frequently. Ad hoc networks with mobile nodes are often referred to as *mobile ad hoc networks* (MANETs). Even without mobility, nodes can join or leave an ad hoc network at will, and such networks need to possess self-organizing capability in terms of media access, routing, and other networking functions. As such, the design and deployment of wireless ad hoc networks presents several challenges that do not exist, or exist in rather different forms, in traditional wired networks. Some of the most important challenges are as follows:

- *Self-organization, adaptability, and self-healing*. The trademark feature of ad hoc networks is the ability of individual nodes to attach to and detach from such networks at will and in the absence of any fixed infrastructure. Therefore, such networks need protocols that can support and facilitate the tasks of topology construction, reconfiguration, and maintenance, as well as routing, traffic monitoring, and admission control. Note that the above constraint does not mean that an infrastructure, if present, cannot or should not be used; it just means that the network ought to be able to function with or without such infrastructure. Furthermore, as sudden departures or even failures of individual nodes are to be expected in many applications, the network should possess self-healing capabilities so as to continue to function.

- *Scalability* of the network refers to its ability to retain certain performance parameters regardless of large changes in the number of nodes deployed in that network. Scalability is an important aspect of ad hoc networks, and it is closely related to the self-organizing property. Scalability is highly dependent on the amount of overhead in terms of bandwidth and power expenditure needed to exchange control packets at various layers (*medium access control*, or MAC; routing and transport, etc.) of network functionality. It is also affected by the manner in which the network is organized, as will be seen in subsequent discussion.
- *Delay* considerations are of crucial importance in certain types of applications—for example, in military applications such as battlefield communications or detection and monitoring of troop movements, or in health care applications where patients with serious and urgent medical conditions must be continuously monitored for important health variables via ECG, EEG, or other probes. Low delays can be achieved by bandwidth reservation requested by the source device through some kind of admission control that will monitor and prevent network congestion or by some kind of scheduling. In the latter two cases, control is exerted by some device that performs the role of network coordinator or base station. (Such a role can be, and often is, temporary.)

We stress that providing prescribed delay bounds is a nontrivial issue in traditional wired networks. In a network with nonstationary topology formed by mobile, resource-constrained nodes, maintaining the delays within prescribed bounds is even more complex. As a minimum, we might just try to reduce the delays—but this is not an easy task either. Delay minimization is often hampered by the instability of the network topology as well as by fluctuations in traffic characteristics. As a result, any minimum that may be achieved is likely to be of an ephemeral character, and constant monitoring and minimization of delays is necessary.

- *Throughput*. In some applications, the most important performance target is throughput rather than delay. Such is the case in several collaborative, distributed computing applications and in mobile access to the Internet, which might include significant amounts of multimedia traffic. At the physical (PHY) level, throughput may be impaired by packet errors caused by noise and interference. At the MAC level, throughput may be impaired by collisions if a contention-based medium access mechanism is used, or by unfairness if bandwidth reservation- or scheduling-based access mechanism is used. (Detailed descriptions of these mechanisms can be found below.) Cross-layer optimization that accounts for those effects—preferably, all of them—may be needed to achieve high throughput.
- *Packet and data losses*. Loss of information is not tolerated in ad hoc networks, and active measures to restore reliability of data transfers must be undertaken at both the MAC and upper layers.
- *Fairness*. In most cases where throughput is the most important performance indicator, fairness among different nodes or users is also of importance. Again, the instability of topology and the nonstationary traffic characteristics tend to make this problem much more difficult in wireless ad hoc networks than in traditional wired networks.
- *Power management*. Some of the nodes in an ad hoc network might operate on battery power, in which case power-management functions become necessary. Although energy efficiency is a desirable feature in general, it is seldom a crucial issue in ad hoc networks. The power source either has sufficient capacity (e.g., a car battery can be expected to provide ample medium access in ad hoc and sensor networks capacity to operate a laptop) or may be recharged as needed (e.g., when using a PDA device at home or in the office). Cases in which the minimization of energy consumption becomes the main limiting parameter for a wireless device are not too common.
- *Low maintenance*. Finally, all maintenance tasks in ad hoc networks should be automated or (at worst) be simple enough to be undertaken by nonspecialist human operators such as owners of laptop computers and PDAs. This requirement might be considered as an extension (or perhaps generalization) of the requirement for self-organizing capabilities mentioned above.

MAC Design Goals in Ad Hoc Networks

The MAC protocol is that part of the overall network functionality that deals with problems of achieving efficient, fair, and dependable access to the medium shared by many different devices (Stallings 2002). The role of the MAC protocol is particularly important in wireless networks that differ from their wired counterparts in many aspects. The most important among those differences stem from the very nature of the wireless communication medium, where two devices need not be explicitly connected to be able to communicate; instead, it merely suffices that they are within the radio transmission range of each other.

For example, when two or more packets are simultaneously received, the receiver may encounter problems. At best, the unwanted packets are treated as noise that impairs the reception of the packet intended to be received but can be filtered out. At worst, the correct packet may be damaged beyond repair and the receiver may be unable to make any sense out of it; this condition is referred to as a *collision*. Collisions waste both network bandwidth and power resources of individual devices, transmitters, and receivers alike, and active measures should be taken to reduce the likelihood of their occurrence.

Common approaches for collision minimization in wired networks include detection and avoidance. Collision detection is widely used in wired networks, where it involves the simple act of listening while transmitting. However, this is not feasible in wireless communication, where few devices are equipped with the required capability

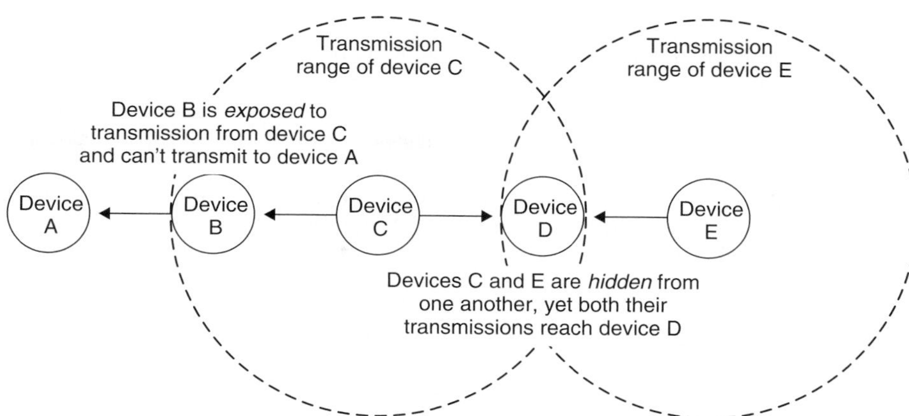

Figure 1: Hidden and exposed terminal problem

(Stallings 2002). Furthermore, packet collisions in wireless networks may occur in scenarios that cannot occur in wired ones. Two of the most common scenarios—commonly referred to as the *hidden* and *exposed terminal problems*, respectively—are depicted in Figure 1. Let us assume that the network contains five identical devices or nodes A, B, C, D, and E, and that the distances between the pairs A and B, B and C, C and D, and D and E are equal and just a bit smaller than the transmission range of each node.

- The hidden terminal problem occurs when the nodes C and E simultaneously start transmission toward node D. They cannot hear each other's transmission (they are hidden from each other), but node D can hear both of them and it senses a collision on the medium.
- The exposed terminal problem is experienced by node B, which wants to transmit a packet to node A. However, on checking the medium, node B overhears the transmission from C, even though it is not the intended recipient, and must defer its transmission for a while. At best, it has to wait until C finishes its transmission. Time and bandwidth are thus wasted because there can be no collision at A, which cannot hear transmissions from C.

The hidden and exposed terminal problems are particularly harmful because some of the offenders may be entirely unaware of them; as a result, such conditions are difficult to control and prevent. Both problems become even more complex if different nodes transmit at different power levels and thus have different transmission ranges. It should come as no surprise that these problems are addressed—with a varying degree of success—by virtually all of the MAC protocols for wireless ad hoc networks.

Because collision detection is not available, MAC protocols for wireless networks must rely on collision avoidance techniques (including explicit scheduling, bandwidth reservation, and listening to the medium) *before* attempting to transmit a packet. This last procedure is commonly known as clear *channel assessment* (O'Hara and Petrick 1999; IEEE 2003a, 2003b), although other terms may be occasionally encountered as well.

Obviously, MAC protocols in wireless networks face both traditional challenges encountered in wired networks and new ones that stem from the use of the wireless communication medium. The most important features of MACs in ad hoc wireless networks can be summarized as follows (Ram Murthy and Manoj 2004):

- The operation of the protocol should be distributed, preferably without a dedicated central controller. If the use of such a controller cannot be avoided, then the role should be only temporary, and devices with appropriate capabilities must be allowed to undertake it for a certain period of time.
- The protocol should be scalable to large networks.
- The available bandwidth must be utilized efficiently, including the minimization of packet collisions and minimization of the overhead needed to monitor and control network operation. In particular, the protocol should minimize the effects of hidden and exposed node problems.
- The protocol should ensure fair bandwidth allocation to all the nodes. Preferably, the fairness mechanism should take into account the current level of congestion in the network.
- The MAC protocol should incorporate power-management policies to minimize the power consumption of the node and of the entire network.
- The protocol should provide *quality-of-service* (QoS) support for real-time traffic wherever possible. Real-time, in this context, implies data traffic with prescribed performance bounds; these may include throughput, delay, delay jitter, and other performance indicators.

Two additional issues deserve mention. The first issue is time synchronization among the nodes, which is required for the purpose of bandwidth reservation and allocation. Time synchronization is usually achieved by having one of the nodes periodically broadcast some sort of synchronization signal (the *beacon*), which is then used by other nodes. Although the use of periodic beacon transmissions facilitates the process of placing the reservation requests and subsequent broadcasting of reservation allocations, it requires that some node is capable of, and willing to, act as the central controller—which is somewhat contrary to the distributed, self-organizing character of an ad hoc network. In particular, additional provisions must be made to replace the controller node when it departs from the network or experiences a failure; this is part of the self-healing property of ad hoc networks described above. Furthermore, the use of beacons consumes the bandwidth and affects the scalability of the MAC algorithm.

The second issue is related to the interference from neighboring nodes. As this interference is harmful, steps have to be taken to reduce it, most often through appropriate multiplexing techniques. According to Stallings (2002), multiplexing techniques are available in the following domains:

- in the frequency domain (i.e., through frequency division multiple access), wherein different frequency bands are allocated to different devices or subnetworks;
- in the code domain (i.e., through code division multiple access), wherein different devices use different code sequences;
- in the time domain (i.e., through time division multiple access), wherein different devices transmit at different time; or
- in the space domain, where the range and scope of transmissions is controlled through the use of transmitter power control and directional antennae, respectively.

Strictly speaking, all of these techniques belong to the PHY layer, and they are reviewed in greater detail in some of the earlier chapters. Although the MAC layer is completely oblivious to the first two techniques, it can utilize the latter two (multiplexing in time and space domain) or even integrate them to a certain extent. (For example, time multiplexing is a close relative of scheduling.) This cross-layer integration and optimization allows the MAC protocol to better address the requirements outlined above. We note that such integration is not too common in ad hoc networks, where the MAC layer is more likely to cooperate with the network (and possibly transport layers above it) than with the PHY layer below; still, MAC protocols exist that make use of it, as will be explained later.

CLASSIFICATION OF MAC PROTOCOLS FOR AD HOC NETWORKS

Before we present some of the important MAC protocols for wireless ad hoc networks, we will give a brief overview of possible criteria for classifying those protocols; the reader will thus be able to grasp main features of different MAC protocols and identify the important similarities as well as differences among them.

Mechanism for Accessing the Medium

Probably the most intuitive among the classification criteria is the manner of accessing the medium, which comes in the following three main flavors:

- *contention-based protocols* are those in which a potential sender node must compete with all others in order to gain access to the medium and transmit its data;
- *Bandwidth reservation-based protocols* in which provisions exist for requesting and obtaining bandwidth (or time) allocations by individual senders; and
- *scheduling-based protocols* in which the transmissions of individual senders are scheduled according to some predefined policy that aims to achieve one or more of the objectives outlined above, such as the maximization of throughput, fairness, flow priority, or QoS support.

Note that the third option requires the presence of an entity that is responsible for implementing the aforementioned policy. In most cases, this requirement translates into the requirement for a permanent or temporary central controller. Note also that the policy to be pursued should be adaptive, depending on the traffic or other conditions in the network. The presence of a central controller is also sometimes needed in protocols that use the second option.

Quite a few among the existing MAC protocols offer more than one of those mechanisms. This may be accomplished by slicing the available time into intervals of fixed or variable size, which are referred to as *cycles* or *superframes* (O'Hara and Petrick 1999; IEEE 2003a, 2003b), and assigning certain portions of those intervals to different categories of access from the list above. For example, the IEEE 802.11 *point coordinator function* (PCF) uses superframes in which the first part is reserved for (optional) contention-free access, while the second part is used for contention-based access (ANSI/IEEE 1999; O'Hara and Petrick 1999). A similar approach is adopted in the IEEE 802.15.4 protocol in its beacon-enabled, slotted *carrier sense multiple access with collision avoidance* (CSMA/CA) mode (IEEE 2003b), except that the contention access period precedes the contention-free period in the superframe.

On the other hand, some MAC protocols offer optional features that modify the manner in which the protocol operates and effectively introduce a different mechanism for medium access control. For example, the IEEE 802.11 *distributed coordinator function* (DCF) utilizes pure contention-based access in its default form but allows bandwidth reservation on a per-packet basis through the optional *request-to-send, clear-to-send* (RTS–CTS) handshake (ANSI/IEEE 1999).

Alternative Classifications on the Basis of Medium Access Mechanism

An alternative classification criterion could be devised by assuming that contention-based access will always be present and then using the presence or absence of the latter two access mechanisms as the basis for classification. This approach results in the common (and marginally more practical) classification into pure contention-based MACs, contention-based MACs with reservation mechanisms, and contention-based MACs with scheduling mechanisms (Ram Murthy and Manoj 2004). A variant of this approach distinguishes between contention-based or random access–based protocols, scheduling or partitioning ones, and polling-based ones. Yet even these classifications are neither unambiguous because the presence of optional features outlined above leads to the same protocol being attached to more than one category nor comprehensive because some of the existing protocols cannot be attached to any single category (Ram Murthy and Manoj 2004). Because of these shortcomings, it is listed as an alternative only.

Mechanism Used for Bandwidth Reservation and Its Scope

These two criteria apply only to MAC protocols that employ some form of bandwidth reservation and thus actually represent subclassifications within the previous one based on the mechanism used to access the medium. With respect to the mechanism used for bandwidth reservation, we can distinguish between the protocols that use some kind of handshake (e.g., RTS–CTS) and those that use out-of-band signaling, most notably the *busy tone approach*, which is an extension of the familiar concept from the traditional telephony systems.

With respect to the scope of bandwidth reservation, we can distinguish between the protocols that request bandwidth for a specified time (i.e., for a single packet or for a group of consecutive packets, commonly referred to as a *burst*) and those that request bandwidth allocation for an unspecified time. In both cases, time can be measured in absolute units or in data packets. In the former case, bandwidth allocation is valid for the transmission of a specified number of packets only; in the latter case, it has to be explicitly revoked by some central authority or perhaps waived by the requester itself.

Another scheme based on the concept related to bandwidth reservation is the family of the so-called multichannel MAC protocols. Most communication technologies use only one channel out of several available in the given frequency band. Multichannel MACs exploit this feature to employ channel hopping in order to improve bandwidth utilization or reduce congestion.

Presence and Scope of Synchronization

The presence or absence of time synchronization among the nodes in the network is another criterion that can be used to classify MAC protocols for wireless ad hoc networks. Synchronization, if present, may need to be extended to all of the nodes in the network (*global synchronization*); alternatively, it may apply to just a handful of nodes that are physically close to one another (*local synchronization*). In the former case, a central controller may be needed to initiate and broadcast the necessary synchronization information.

Synchronization is most often linked to scheduling and bandwidth reservation, because basic synchronization intervals are often used to apportion the available bandwidth to appropriate sender nodes. However, bandwidth reservation and allocation can be accomplished in an asynchronous manner, in particular when reservation is requested on a per-packet basis, whereas synchronous protocols can be used even with pure contention-based access. For example, the IEEE 802.15.4 protocol in its beacon-enabled, slotted CSMA/CA mode without guaranteed time slots uses pure contention-based access, yet all transmissions must be synchronized to the beacon frames periodically sent by the network coordinator (IEEE 2003b).

Synchronization is one of the most important factors that may affect scalability of the network. As the size of the network grows, synchronization becomes more difficult and more costly to establish and maintain. In particular, protocols that rely on global synchronization will suffer the most degradation; for example, it has been shown that the construction and maintenance of a globally optimal schedule in a multilevel Bluetooth network (a *scatternet*) is a nondeterministic polynomial time-complete problem (Johansson, Körner, and Tassiulas 2001).

Presence and Permanence of a Controller

Another possible classification criterion is the presence and permanence of a central network controller or coordinator. Whereas wireless ad hoc networks by default should be able to function without a permanent or dedicated central controller, quite a few protocols rely on certain monitoring and control functions that can only be provided by a local or global controller. This is the case with several of the MAC protocols that use bandwidth reservation, as well as with all of the MAC protocols that use scheduling. In fact, even some pure contention-based protocols rely on the presence of a controller for administrative tasks such as time synchronization and sometimes even node admission. Again, the presence of a controller affects the scalability of the network because the amount of work the controller has to do—most of which is administrative and control overhead—must grow with the number of nodes. Hierarchical decomposition or layering is often used to reduce this overhead, but it leads to additional problems in synchronization and delays.

Interference Reduction Mechanism

With respect to the interference reduction mechanisms mentioned above, a clear-cut classification may be hard to define. Multiplexing in the time domain (i.e., through *time-division multiple access*, or TDMA) effectively means that the MAC protocol utilizes some kind of scheduling or, at the very least, bandwidth reservation. As a result, any classification based on the use of TDMA techniques is effectively a replication of the first classification above—that is, the one based on the mechanism for medium access control.

However, the use (or absence) of techniques for space domain multiplexing can still be useful as a criterion for classifying the MAC protocols, in which case we can distinguish among:

- protocols that do not use any form of multiplexing in the space domain,
- protocols that use power control to limit the transmission range, and
- protocols that use directional antennae to limit the scope of their transmissions.

We note that the second and third categories are not mutually exclusive and MAC protocols exist that use one or the other multiplexing technique—or both at the same time.

Interdependence of Classification Criteria

As can be seen, not all of the classification criteria outlined above are entirely independent of each other; rather, they exhibit a certain overlap or redundancy. Still, they are useful in the study of MAC protocols because they tend to highlight different aspects of their design and operation. In the discussions that follow, we will look at the MAC protocols in the following order: contention-based protocols; protocols that use bandwidth reservation; protocols that use multiple channels, out-of-band signaling, and directional antennae; and protocols that use polling.

CONTENTION-BASED MAC PROTOCOLS

Basic Carrier Sense Multiple Access

Most of the MAC protocols are derived from the basic *carrier sense multiple access* (CSMA) mechanism (Bertsekas and Gallager 1991). CSMA is a pure distributed protocol without centralized control, which operates as follows. The node that wants to transmit a packet first performs the clear channel assessment procedure—that is, it listens to the medium for a prescribed time. If the medium is found to be clear (or idle) during that time, then the node can transmit its packet. Otherwise—that is, if another transmission is in progress—the node backs off by waiting for a certain time before undertaking the same procedure again.

Different MAC algorithms use different ways to calculate the time they need to listen to the channel during the clear channel assessment procedure and to calculate the time to wait (i.e., the duration of the backoff period) before the next transmission attempt.

It is possible that the transmissions from two or more nodes overlap in time, which results in a collision and loss of all packets involved. If lossless communication is desired, collisions must be detected so that the lost packets can be retransmitted. Because a collision can be detected only at the receiver side, some form of acknowledgment from the receiver may be needed; some MAC protocols provide this facility, whereas others leave it to some of the upper layers (most likely, the transport layer). The former approach is more efficient in terms of reaction time, whereas the latter allows for much simpler implementation of the MAC protocol used.

In the basic CSMA protocol, carrier sensing is performed only at the sending node. Therefore, the hidden terminal problem is still present. Moreover, the exposed terminal problem leads to deferred transmissions and thus reduces bandwidth utilization.

We note that a separate chapter is devoted to the details of the CSMA protocol.

IEEE 802.11 MAC

Strictly speaking, the IEEE 802.11 protocol (O'Hara and Petrick 1999) is intended for *wireless local area networks* (WLANs) rather than wireless ad hoc networks. However, it is interesting to examine it in some detail, mainly on account of its ubiquity, and because it uses most of the main concepts that are reused in many MAC protocols for ad hoc networks. The protocol covers the functional areas of access control, reliable data delivery, and security; in the following we will focus on the first two areas, as the last one (security) is beyond the scope of this chapter.

Reliable transfer is achieved through the use of *acknowledgment* (ACK) packets or frames, sent by the destination node upon successful data-packet reception. Medium access is regulated in two ways, the first of which is a distributed contention-based mechanism known as the *distributed coordination function*, which does not require a centralized controller. The DCF, based on the CSMA protocol described above, operates as follows. The node that wants to transmit a packet first performs the clear channel assessment procedure—that is, it listens to the medium for a time equal to the *interframe space* (IFS). If the medium is found to be clear (or idle) during that time, then the node can transmit its packet immediately; otherwise—that is, if another transmission is in progress—the node waits for another IFS period. If the medium remains idle during that period, the node backs off for a random interval and again senses the medium. During that time (referred to as the *backoff window* or *contention window*), if the medium becomes busy, the backoff counter is halted; it resumes when the medium becomes idle again. When the backoff counter expires and the medium is found to be idle, the node can transmit the packet.

A possible scenario in which this procedure is applied is schematically depicted in Figure 2. There are several points worth mentioning. First, the backoff interval is chosen as a random number from a predefined range. After each collision, the range is doubled to reduce the likelihood of a repeated collision. After each successful transmission, the range is reset to its initial value, which is typically small. This approach is known as *binary exponential backoff* (BEB) (Stallings 2002) In this manner, the protocol ensures a certain level of load smoothing in case of frequent collisions caused by heavy traffic.

Second, to enhance reliability and avoid the hidden and exposed terminal problems to a certain extent, the RTS–CTS handshake—well known from wired communications—may optionally be used. In this case, the node that wants to send a data packet first sends a request-to-send packet to the designated receiver; if ready, it responds with a clear-to-send packet. Both RTS and CTS packets contain information about the duration of the forthcoming transmission, including the optional acknowledgment. Once the sender receives the CTS packet, it may begin actual data transmission, which may optionally be followed by an ACK packet. The RTS–CTS handshake constitutes a

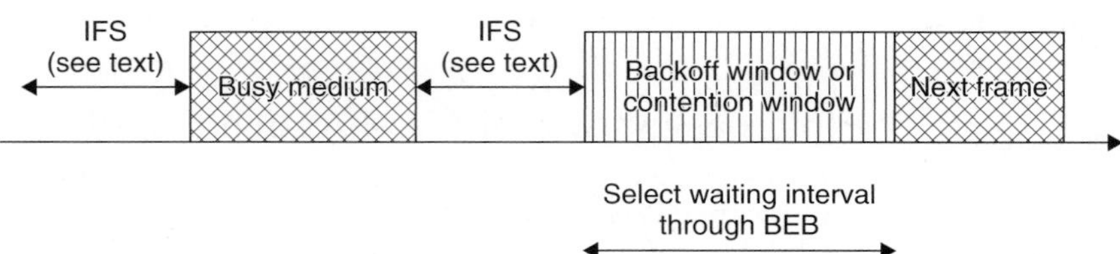

Figure 2: Basic access method in IEEE 802.11 DCF

simple form of bandwidth reservation on a per-packet or per-group basis, as will be explained below.

Reliability of transmission is enhanced because the RTS and CTS packets are generally much shorter than data packets; if they collide, the time waste is not high, but the risk that subsequent data packets will experience a collision is substantially reduced. The hidden terminal problem is avoided because other nodes within the transmission range of the receiver, on hearing the CTS packet, become aware of a forthcoming data transmission and defer their transmission for the time interval specified. On the other hand, a transmission from an exposed terminal may prevent the sender from initiating the RTS–CTS handshake. However, once the sender receives a proper CTS packet, it can assume that the receiver is not affected by the interfering transmission and can thus proceed with the data-packet transmission.

Third, to ensure the proper functioning of the protocol, three different IFS intervals are used: a *short IFS* (SIFS), a medium-duration *point coordination function IFS* (PIFS), and a long-duration *distributed coordination function IFS* (DIFS). The existence of several IFS intervals of different duration actually serves to implement different priority levels for different types of access. The DIFS interval is used for ordinary asynchronous traffic, whereas the SIFS interval, being the shortest, is used in the following cases:

- when the receiver sends an ACK packet on successful reception of a data packet (in this manner, ACK packets are safe from collisions because regular data packets wait longer);
- when the sender wants to send another data packet on receiving an ACK packet for a previous one (in this manner, a burst of packets commonly obtained by segmenting a longer packet from the upper layers can be delivered quickly and with little risk from collision, although such transmissions can result in unfairness because there is a limit on the duration of the burst that can be transmitted); and
- when the node sends a CTS packet on receiving a RTS packet from a prospective sender (again, the use of the SIFS interval minimizes the risk that the CTS packet will experience a collision).

The PIFS interval is used in an alternative access method known as the *point coordination function*, which is implemented on top of DCF. The PCF requires the presence of a central point coordinator, hence the name. The point coordinator defines an interval known as a *superframe*. In the first part of the superframe, the coordinator issues polls to all nodes configured for polling. The polls are sent using the regular CSMA algorithm outlined above. When a poll packet is sent, the polled node may respond using the SIFS interval. If the coordinator receives the response, then it issues another poll but using the PIFS interval. The polling continues in round-robin fashion (i.e., one node at a time) until all of the nodes are polled. Then the point coordinator remains idle until the end of the superframe, which allows for DCF-style contention-based access by all other nodes. The structure of the PCF superframe is schematically shown in Figure 3. The duration

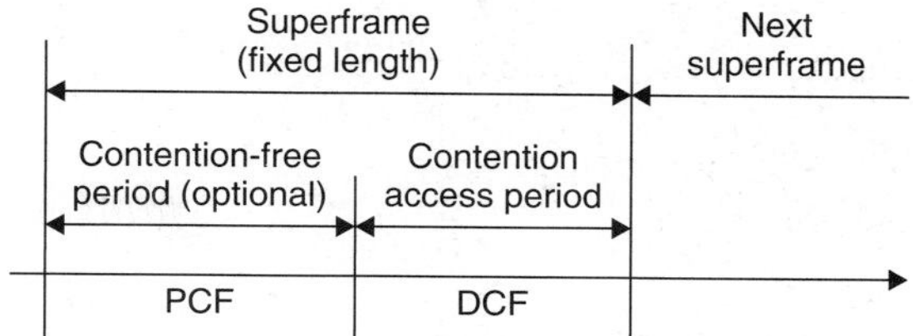

Figure 3: Superframe structure with IEEE 802.11 PCF

of the superframe is fixed, but an ongoing transmission may force the coordinator to defer the beginning of a polling cycle; in this case, the useful duration of the superframe will be reduced.

Although the IEEE 802.11 DCF is able to deal with asynchronous traffic, the presence of synchronous traffic with specified (and reasonably stable) throughput over prolonged periods of time is well served by its PCF counterpart. Still, the PCF functionality is designated as an optional facility in the 802.11 standard (ANSI/IEEE 1999), and it is rarely used in practice.

Multiple Access Collision Avoidance

One of the pioneering attempts to define a MAC protocol for ad hoc networks is the *multiple access collision avoidance* (MACA) protocol described by Karn (1990). Similar to the 802.11 DCF, the MACA protocol uses the three-way handshake with RTS and CTS packets preceding the data-packet transmission; but unlike the 802.11 protocol, MACA does not use carrier sensing. The sender initiates the handshake with a RTS packet, to which the receiver should respond with a CTS packet. Once the sender receives the CTS packet without errors, it commences the transmission of the data packet. If a packet is destroyed through a collision, the sender undertakes a backoff procedure using the BEB algorithm. Figure 4 depicts the operation of the MACA protocol. Note that explicit acknowledgments of successful data-packet transmissions are not used in this protocol.

Both RTS and CTS packets contain information about the duration of the data transmission. Nodes in the vicinity of the sender, such as node A in Figure 4, hear the RTS packet and defer the transmission of their packets so that the sender can receive the CTS packet. Nodes in the vicinity of the receiver (node B in Figure 4) hear the CTS packet and defer the transmission of their packets so that the receiver can receive the data packet. In this manner, both the hidden and exposed terminal problems are avoided—to a certain extent, because the risk of collisions is reduced but not entirely eliminated—and RTS and CTS packets can still collide. However, the exponential backoff used in the MACA protocol creates the risk of a different yet equally severe problem—namely, that of unfairness, which can quickly lead to starvation under heavy loads.

As an example, consider the network that consists of two sender and two receiver nodes, positioned in the manner schematically depicted in Figure 5. Let both senders 1 and 2 generate a high volume of traffic, and let sender 1 capture the medium first and start transmitting packets. Because of random timing of packet transmissions, a number of

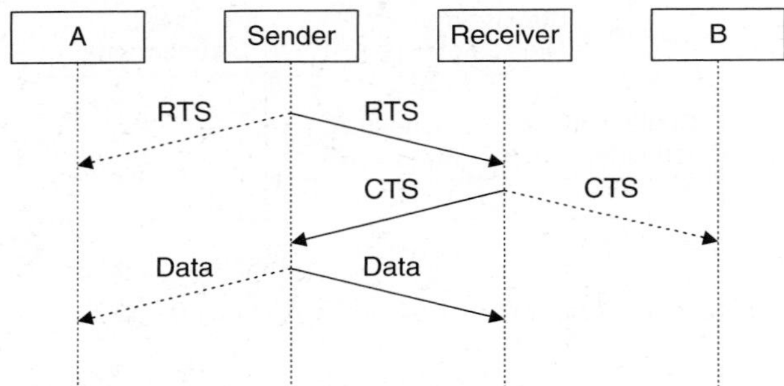

Figure 4: Timing diagram of the control handshake in the MACA protocol

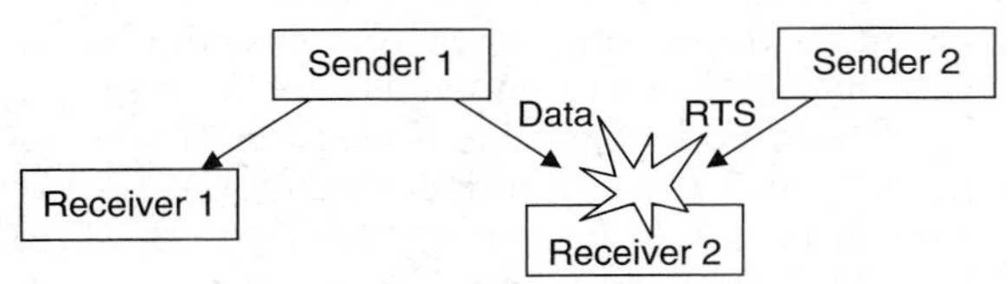

Figure 5: Collisions of data and RTS packets can cause starvation in the MACA protocol

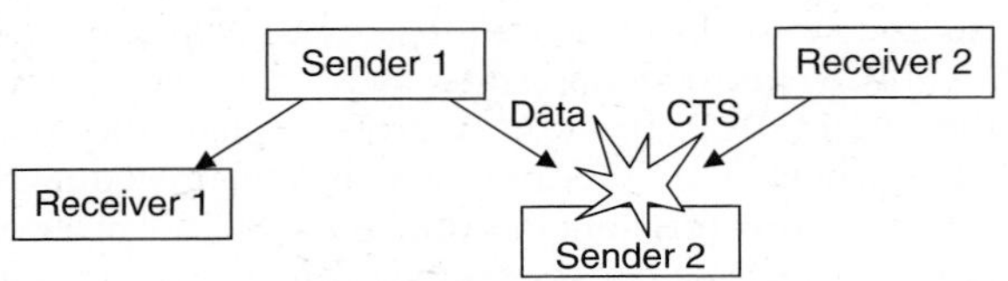

Figure 6: Collisions of data and CTS packets can cause starvation in the MACA protocol

packets from sender 2 may experience collisions. Because receiver 2 does not send proper CTS packets, sender 2 backs off repeatedly—but the backoff window keeps getting longer and longer because of the BEB algorithm. As a result, sender 2 is starved—that is, it is effectively blocked from accessing the medium.

Several variations of this problem occur in different scenarios. Consider, for example, the network with two senders and two receivers, shown in Figure 6, in which an exposed node (sender 2) is able to hear the transmissions from sender 1 but not those from receiver 1. Thus, it is free to commence its handshake while sender 1 transmits a data packet to the receiver 1. Sender 2 sends a RTS packet to receiver 2 which responds with a CTS packet, which in turn collides with the data packet from sender 1. Because the sender 2 does not receive a CTS packet, it will keep increasing its backoff window unnecessarily and effectively starve in the process.

A similar scenario is shown in Figure 7, where sender 2 is within the transmission range of receiver 2 but beyond the transmission range of sender 1. If sender 2 transmits data to receiver 2, then receiver 1 is able to hear those transmissions and unable to respond to the RTS packet sent by sender 1. Because sender 1 does not get any response (i.e., CTS packets) to its RTS packets, it concludes that there are collisions and effectively starves by continually increasing its backoff window.

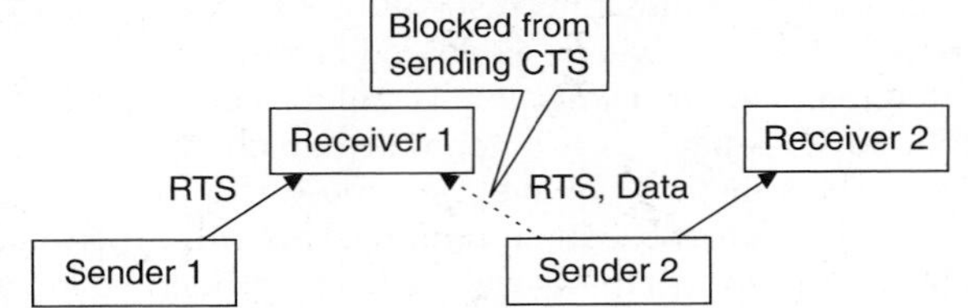

Figure 7: An exposed receiver can lead to starvation of a remote sender in the MACA protocol

Multiple Access Collision Avoidance Protocol for WLANs

To alleviate the problems of the MACA protocol, Bharghavan et al. (1994) have proposed several modifications to it; the improved protocol is known as *multiple access collision avoidance protocol for WLANs* (MACAW). The bulk of those modifications attempt to solve the starvation problems, most notably those caused by unfairness. An obvious solution is to somehow balance the backoff windows of neighboring nodes, which should result in balancing their respective probabilities to access the medium. First, modification consists of augmenting the packet header with an additional field that contains the current value of the backoff counter of the transmitting node. A node that receives the packet reads and copies it into its own backoff counter. In this manner, the backoff windows of the nodes will tend to have similar values.

Second, modification aims to avoid the rapid increase of the duration of the backoff window. The reader will recall that the original BEB algorithm prescribes that the range within which a random value is chosen for the backoff window is to be doubled after each collision and reset to the initial value after a successful transmission. As a result, the duration of the backoff window can exhibit rather large and abrupt variations. Instead, the MACAW algorithm uses the so-called multiplicative increase, linear decrease backoff mechanism. In this approach, a collision causes the backoff counter to be increased by a constant factor—for example, the value of 1.5 is typically used—whereas a successful transmission simply decrements the backoff counter by one. In this manner, the backoff counter changes much less abruptly, and long contention windows after unsuccessful transmissions are avoided.

Starvation of an exposed node is addressed through the introduction of a small control packet designated as a *data-sending* (DS) packet; this packet is sent immediately before the actual data packet. The corresponding timing diagram is shown in Figure 8, where nodes A and B defer their transmissions because of a pending data packet from sender to the receiver—although B learned about it from the CTS packet and A learned about it through the DS packet.

Another change introduces per-flow fairness instead of per node, as is the case in MACA. When several data flows originate at a single node, separate queues are maintained for each flow and the backoff procedure is performed independently for each queue. When a node has one or more packets ready for transmission, then it chooses the queue for which the backoff window is the shortest.

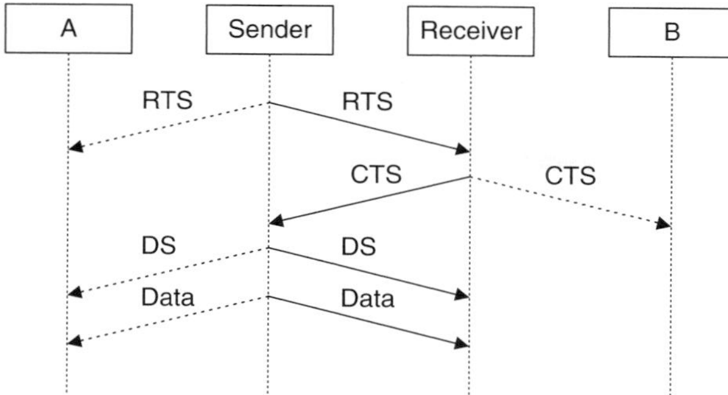

Figure 8: The role of the DS packet in the MACAW protocol

As mentioned above, the MACA protocol does not use acknowledgments, and reliable transport is the responsibility of the transport layer. However, most implementations of the TCP protocol use long time-out delays—on the order of hundreds of milliseconds—to be able to accommodate a wide range of transmission delays. Correction of erroneous or lost packets thus incurs substantial delays. To reduce those delays, the MACAW protocol introduces explicit ACK packets that are sent by the receiving node on successful reception of a data packet. If the ACK packet is missing, then the sender will attempt to retransmit the same packet, only this time with an increased value of the backoff counter. It retransmits the RTS packet for the same data packet. Now if the data packet was not correctly received the first time, the entire transmission cycle is repeated. However, if the data packet was correctly received (which means that the ACK packet was lost, most likely because of a collision), the receiver responds with the appropriate ACK packet instead. This informs the sender that the original data transmission was successful, and the sender may move on to the next data packet.

Another modification addresses the scenario depicted in Figure 7. This type of starvation is alleviated through the use of another control packet known as *request to request to send* (RRTS). In other words, when receiver 1 receives a RTS packet to which it cannot respond, it sends a RRTS packet to sender 1 in the next contention period. Neighboring nodes that hear this packet—including sender 2—are obliged to remain silent for two successive RTS–CTS cycles, which gives sender 1 sufficient time to retransmit its RTS packet and receive the corresponding CTS packet. In this manner, the remote sender is able to conclude the data-packet transmission without starvation. Figure 9 shows the corresponding timing diagram.

Floor Acquisition Multiple Access

Fullmer and Garcia-Luna-Aceves (1995) have proposed a family of protocols known as *floor acquisition multiple access* (FAMA) that generalize the approach based on CSMA access with the control packet handshake. In this sense, both the MACA and MACAW protocols belong to the FAMA family.

The basic concept behind the FAMA protocols is that the sender node has to acquire the floor before attempting to transmit its data. This is accomplished through the control packet handshake. Although control packets themselves may suffer collisions, the protocols ensure that the data-packet transmission is collision-free. The original proposal

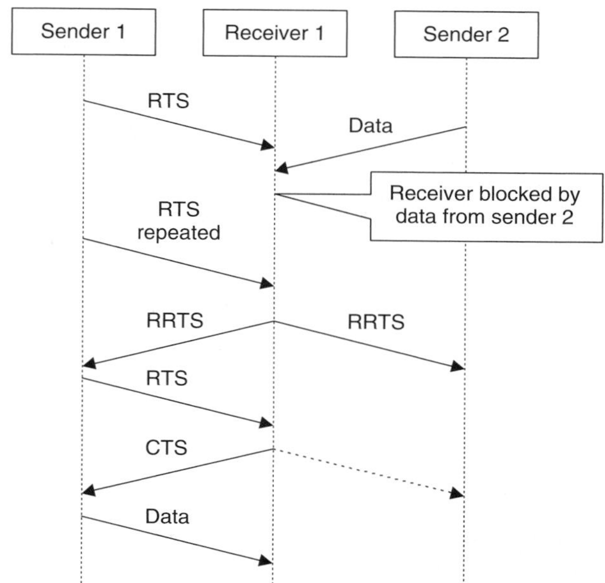

Figure 9: The role of the RRTS packet in the MACAW protocol

(Fullmer and Garcia-Luna- Aceves 1995) discusses several variants of the FAMA protocol and derives the timing relationships and constraints that allow it to achieve collision-free data transmission. In this process, the round-trip propagation time of the channel is used to derive the waiting times at particular steps in the protocol.

Another interesting feature of the FAMA protocols is that some among them allow the sender to use a single control RTS–CTS handshake before sending a packet burst, similar to the 802.11 DCF protocol. In this case, the bandwidth utilization is improved because the overhead incurred by the control handshake is shared by all of the packets in the burst.

MACA by Invitation

Talluci, Gerla, and Fratta (1997) have adopted a different approach that aims to reduce the number of control packets (and, by extension, the overhead thus incurred); this protocol is known as *MACA by invitation* (MACA-BI). The main change from the original MACA protocol is that data transmission can be initiated by the receiver, rather than the sender. The receiver sends the *ready to receive* (RTR) packet to the sender, which, if ready, simply responds with the data packet. The corresponding timing diagram is shown in Figure 10, where the receiver's hidden neighbor A hears the RTR packet and defers its transmission until the data packet is received. However, collisions are not eliminated altogether through this technique. In particular, RTR packets may collide with each other (for example, when two potential receivers request data from the same sender) or with data packets sent from a hidden terminal in the vicinity.

The main problem of the MACA-BI protocol stems from the fact that the receiver does not know in advance the moments of packet arrivals at the sender or the length of those packets. Instead, the receiver must estimate those values and embed the estimates in the RTR packet. To improve the accuracy of those estimates and thus increase

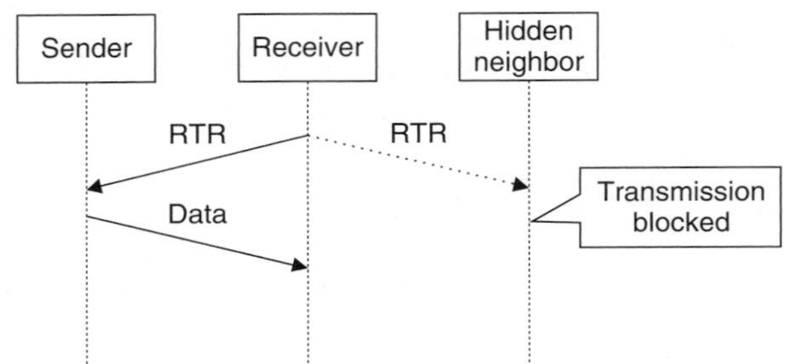

Figure 10: Receiver-initiated data-packet transmission in the MACA-BI protocol

the overall efficiency of the protocol, the format of the data packets may be modified to include control information about the data flows at the sender—for example, the number of backlogged packets queued for transmission and their individual lengths. Furthermore, the sender is allowed to initiate transmission in the usual manner—that is, by sending an RTS packet with appropriate control information.

MACA with Reduced Handshake

In many cases, the sender usually sends a burst of packets to the receiver, rather than a single packet: for example, when TCP connections are established in a wireless ad hoc network. This observation has inspired Toh et al. (2000) to devise a protocol known as *MACA with reduced handshake* (MARCH) that aims to reduce the overhead incurred by the control packet handshake. In this protocol, data-packet transmission is initiated by the sender, which sends a regular RTS packet to the receiver; the receiver responds with a CTS packet. Subsequent transmissions use only RTS packets preceding the data packets. Obviously, the more packets are transmitted in a burst, the more efficient transmission will be because the control packet overhead is shared by all of the packets in the burst.

By itself, this feature would not be worth mentioning because other protocols described above contain similar provisions. But the importance (and the main contribution) of the MARCH protocol is in its use of a reduced handshake for multihop transmissions through one or more intermediate nodes, a common scenario in wireless ad hoc networks (Toh 2002) that neither the original MACA nor its numerous variants specifically address. Consider the network with four nodes A, B, C, and D, in which data packets are sent in bursts from A to D through intermediate nodes B and C. In MACA, this transmission has to be implemented as a series of single-hop (i.e., node-to-node) transfers with the full control handshake for each hop, as shown in Figure 11. The MARCH protocol makes use of the fact that the RTS–CTS exchange between the sender and the receiver can often be heard by the next hop receiver; in our example, the control handshake between nodes A and B actually alerts the next hop receiver C to the forthcoming data transmission. Consequently, the control handshake between the nodes B and C can be simplified by omitting the RTS packets. Instead, node C can simply send the CTS packet to node B as soon as the data transmission from node A is finished. In this

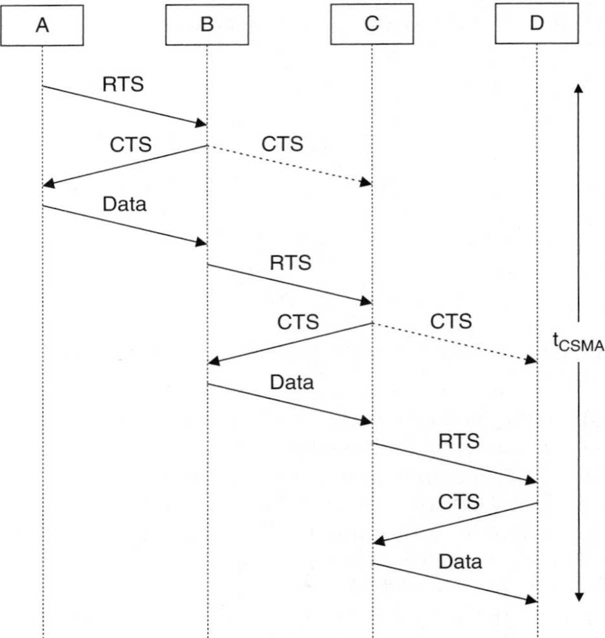

Figure 11: Multihop tramsmission of a packet burst in the original MACA protocol

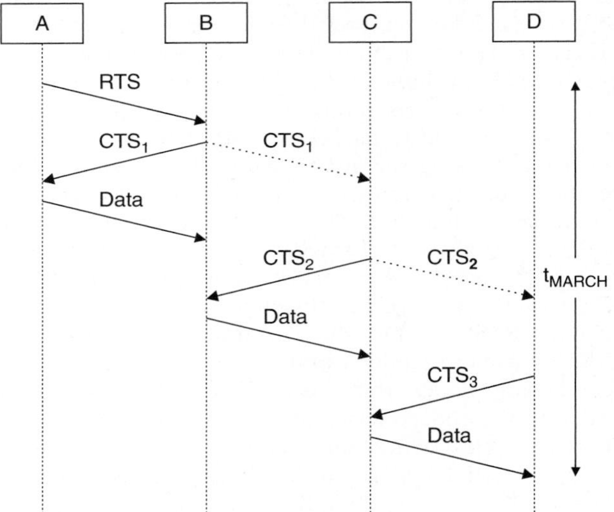

Figure 12: Multihop transmission of a packet burst in the MARCH protocl

manner, the control handshake is simplified and the associated overhead is reduced, which leads to substantial improvements in efficiency (i.e., increased throughput and reduced end-to-end delay) when compared to the original MACA or its variants described earlier. The control handshake in the MARCH protocol is shown in Figure 12.

We note that the MARCH protocol does require assistance from the routing algorithm because the CTS packets have to carry proper route identification so that the intended receiver (and only it) can issue the required CTS.

MAC PROTOCOLS THAT USE BANDWIDTH RESERVATION

Bandwidth reservation can be implemented only if some form of multiplexing in the time domain—that is, TDMA—is used. In the TDMA approach, available time is partitioned into time frames or slots that can be requested by and subsequently allocated to the nodes that have data to send. As noted above, this approach necessitates the presence of a centralized control in the form of a dedicated controller node. Time partitioning is typically done in a hierarchical manner, with smaller intervals (slots or frames) grouped into larger ones (cycles or superframes). Node transmissions are then aligned to the slot boundaries. In this manner, the controller node is able to monitor the utilization of the channel and to allocate bandwidth while taking into account QoS requirements and fairness among the nodes; bandwidth allocation also can be performed on a permanent or one-off basis.

In the area of wireless networks, the concept of bandwidth reservation was historically first exploited with satellite networks (Bertsekas and Gallager 1991) and later in wireless ATM starting with the *packet reservation multiple access* (PRMA) protocol described by Goodman et al. (1989). A nice overview of reservation techniques for wireless ATM networks can be found in the work by Sanchez, Martinez, and Marcellin (1997). We will now describe a few representative protocols that use the reservation approach in wireless ad hoc networks.

Distributed Packet Reservation Multiple Access

In the *distributed PRMA* (D-PRMA) protocol proposed by Jian et al. (2002), each frame is divided in slots, and each slot is divided into minislots, as shown in Figure 13. Each minislot can be used for data transmission or for control handshake. In the latter case, the first part of the minislot is used for the RTS packet or *busy indication* (BI) signal, while the second part is used for the CTS or BI. All nodes that have a packet for transmission must listen to the medium at the beginning of each slot. If the medium is free, they compete for access by sending the RTS packet in the RTS–BI part of the first minislot of each slot. If the node receives the CTS response in the same minislot, it can use the remaining portion of the slot (minislots 2 to m) for its transmission. If a collision occurs in the RTS–BI field, the contention process continues in subsequent minislots of the same slot until one node wins the slot.

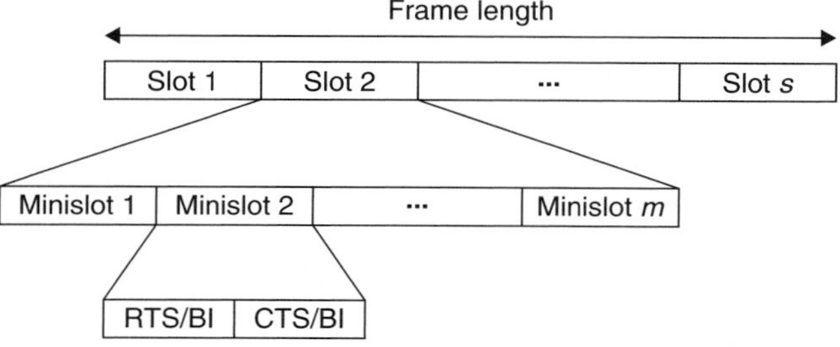

Figure 13: Frame structure in D-PRMA protocol

Once a node wins the slot, it transmits its data in the next minislot. Transmission lasts until the end of the slot or until there is no more data, whichever is shorter. Other nodes that want to transmit will find the channel busy and have to wait. Provisions are made to eliminate the risk of collision for CTS packets (the designated receiver sends a CTS packet only if it receives a RTS packet correctly—that is, without collision), the hidden terminal problem (nodes that hear the CTS packet defer their transmission until the end of the current slot) as well as the exposed terminal problem (nodes that hear the RTS but not the CTS packet are still allowed to transmit).

The D-PRMA protocol tries to cater to the fact that nodes in an ad hoc network can carry both synchronous (voice or multimedia) and asynchronous data traffic; the former is generally delay-sensitive but much less loss-sensitive than the latter. To give priority to synchronous traffic as soon as it is generated by the application, the D-PRMA protocol introduces priorities to each node. Priority is a parameter p with a value between 0 and 1; nodes will start contending for access in a free minislot with probability p or skip it and wait for the next opportunity with probability $1 - p$. Nodes with synchronous traffic are allowed two exceptions: (1) Any such node can start the contention process in minislot 1 with the probability of 1 and (2) any such node that manages to win a slot is allowed to reserve that same slot in every frame until the end of the session. (Nodes with asynchronous traffic can win a single slot only and have to contend again for each subsequent slot.)

Reserved slots are identified through a BI signal sent by the sender (the node with synchronous traffic that has won the slot in the previous frame) in the RTS–BI portion of minislot 1, and by the receiver in the CTS–BI part of that same minislot. In this manner, other nodes learn about the reservation and do not contend for that slot in the current frame. End of the data stream and the corresponding reservation is announced simply by the absence of the BI signal.

We note that the RTS packet carries the address of its one-hop destination, and only the destination node is allowed to reply with a CTS packet. Nodes that hear the CTS packet are not allowed to transmit within the same slot. Similar to the MACA protocol, any node that hears the RTS packet but not the CTS one is allowed to transmit.

Hop Reservation Multiple Access Protocol

The *hop reservation multiple access* (HRMA) protocol utilizes multiplexing in both time and frequency domain (Tang and Garcia-Luna-Aceves 1999a). In the time domain, available time is partitioned into frames, which are in turn divided in slots. In the frequency domain, different frequencies are used for different slots; in this manner, the HRMA is effectively a variant of the well know *frequency hopping spread spectrum* (FHSS) approach (Stallings 2002). The first slot in the frame is selected as the synchronization slot, which is why it always uses the same frequency. All other slots consist of two subslots that use different frequencies from the hopping sequence. The first subslot is used for transmitting hop-reservation packets, RTS packets, CTS packets, and data packets. The second subslot is used for receiving acknowledgement packets for the data transmission received during the previous subslot. The frame structure of the HRMA protocol is shown in Figure 14.

Collision Avoidance Time Allocation Protocol

The *collision avoidance time allocation* (CATA) protocol divides the frame into a number of equally sized slots (Tang and Garcia-Luna-Aceves 1999b). Each slot is divided into five minislots: The first four are control minislots, and the fifth one is the data minislot. A node that wishes to transmit data reserves the data minislot by transmitting a RTS packet in the second control minislot. The intended receiver responds with a CTS packet in the third control minislot. On receiving the CTS packet, the sending node transmits a *not-to-send* (NTS) packet in the fourth minislot; the NTS packet serves to regulate the multicast or broadcast transmission. The frame structure of the CATA protocol is shown in Figure 15.

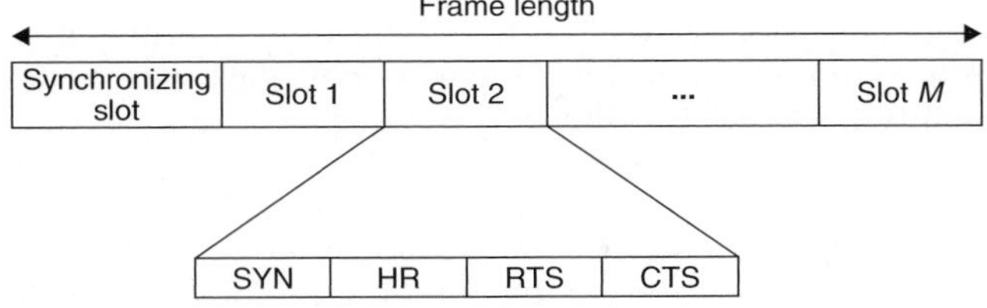

Figure 14: Frame structure in HRMA protocl

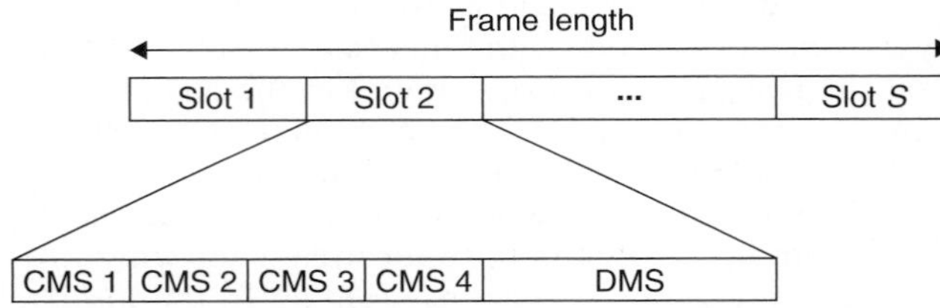

Figure 15: Frame structure in the CATA protocol

MACA with Piggybacked Reservation

The *MACA with piggybacked reservation* (MACA-PR), originally proposed by Lin and Gerla (1999), is an example of the cross layer interaction of MAC and routing layers with two priority levels: for real-time and data packets, respectively. Communications in the MACA-PR protocol are schematically shown in Figure 16. As in many other protocols, time is divided in slots. Each node maintains the *reservation table* (RT) with all reserved slots of the nodes in its transmission range. A node that has a non–real-time packet ready for transmission will first perform carrier sensing in the slot that is labeled as free in its RT. If the channel is found to be free in that slot, then the node transmits the RTS packet and receives CTS packet. Both RTS and CTS packets contain the information about the time period needed for data-packet transmission (labeled *network allocation vector*, or NAV). The CTS packet is followed by the data packet, which is in turn followed by the acknowledgement.

For real-time traffic in which data packets are sent with known periodicity, the first packet from the stream is sent as a regular non–real-time packet. However, the reservation for the next packet is piggybacked on the current data packet. This reservation contains the time period in which the next data packet is to be transmitted. All neighbors that hear the reservation will update their reservation tables accordingly. In case of transmission failure, real-time packets are not retransmitted.

The MACA-PR protocol avoids the hidden terminal problem by periodic exchange of reservation tables. Furthermore, reservation information times out if it is not refreshed during a certain time period.

Distributed Priority Scheduling

The *distributed priority scheduling* (DPS) protocol was initially proposed by Kanodia et al. (2004). The DPS protocol assumes that nodes use the 802.11 distributed

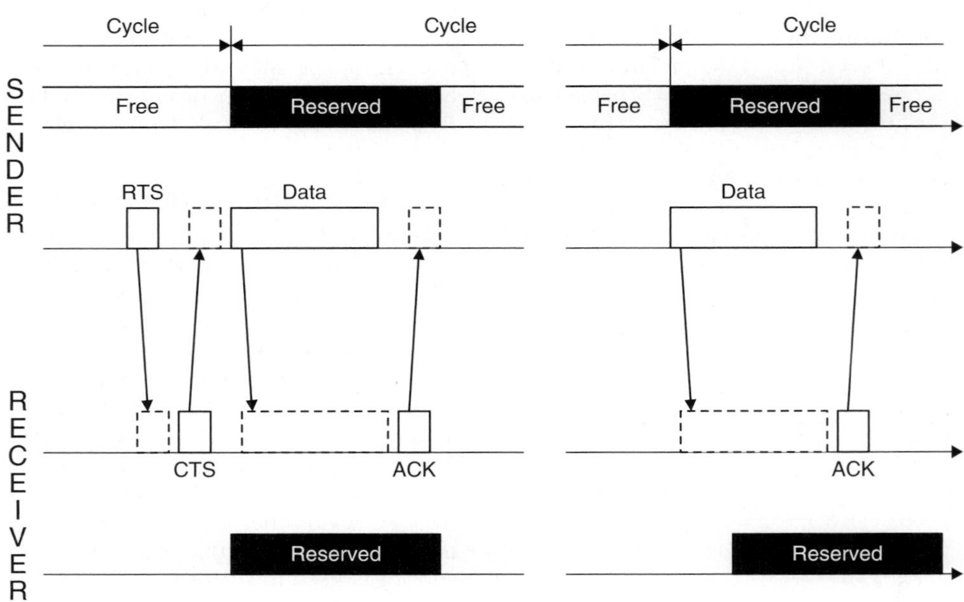

Figure 16: Communication in MACA-PR protocol

coordination function with the RTS–CTS–data–ACK handshake. Nodes send packet priority information piggybacked at the end of the RTS packet. Each node stores the information about the priority of overheard packets, and calculates its own priority relative to the nodes in the neighborhood. The receiving node will append the priority information at the CTS packet together with the sender's ID. Neighboring nodes then extract priority and node ID information from the RTS and CTS packets they have overheard and calculate their own rank relative to the neighbors. The rank is used to calculate the node backoff window according to the 802.11 DCF. For multihop communications, where end-to-end delay bounds for the packet are specified, the packet priority may change (increase) in the downstream nodes in order to meet the bound. Communication of table updates in the DPS protocol is shown in Figure 17.

MULTICHANNEL MAC PROTOCOLS

The main distinguishing feature of the protocols from the multichannel MAC protocols group is the utilization of several available channels—effectively, a form of frequency and channel multiplexing—to reduce congestion. Conceptually, this idea is not new: Many protocols apply channel partitioning—for example, 802.11 (ANSI/IEEE 1999; O'Hara and Petrick 1999) or HRMA (Tang and Garcia-Luna-Aceves 1999a)—and the FHSS variant of the CDMA approach is widely used at the physical level (Stallings 2002). But all of these protocols allocate individual channels according to a predetermined hopping sequence or a pseudo-random sequence in case of FHSS. On the contrary, multichannel MAC protocols select channels in a dynamic fashion that takes into account the current state of congestion of all of the available channels. Two main approaches are possible: (1) a dedicated channel is used for coordination and control and (2) the entire transmission (i.e., both control handshake and data) of each flow uses a different channel (Shi, Salonidis, and Knightly 2006). Although both approaches are capable of improving throughput, they suffer from different problems. In the first, some node pairs may be unable to communicate for prolonged periods; in the second, the dedicated control channel incurs some overhead, and its capacity should be carefully determined to avoid congestion in that channel. We will now present a few of the most important multichannel MAC protocols.

Multichannel CSMA with Soft Channel Reservation

This multichannel CSMA protocol was originally proposed by Nasipuri, Zhuang, and Das (1999). It assumes that the available frequency band is partitioned into N channels, and each node monitors all N channels whenever it is not transmitting. Channels in which the total received signal strength is below a predefined threshold are marked as idle, and the time instants at which this parameters drops below the threshold are marked; remaining channels are busy. When a packet arrives, the node checks its list of idle channels to see if the last channel it used is free. If so, this channel is used to transmit the packet; if not, a channel is randomly selected from the list. If there are no free channels, the node waits for the first channel to become idle. If the selected channel has remained idle during a period of long interframe space, the node initiates the transmission; otherwise, a random backoff is undertaken. An ongoing backoff is immediately cancelled if the channel becomes busy, and a new backoff is scheduled when the channel becomes idle again. *Soft reservation* refers to the fact that the scheme obviously gives preference to the last channel that was successfully used and thus tends to reserve a channel for each node (Nasipuri, Zhuang, and Das 1999). Distributed, dynamic channel allocation allows this scheme to significantly reduce the chances of collision, even in heavy traffic conditions, but it still suffers from two major problems. At the implementation level, the radio subsystem must be sophisticated enough to monitor the received signal strength on a per-channel basis for all channels; such

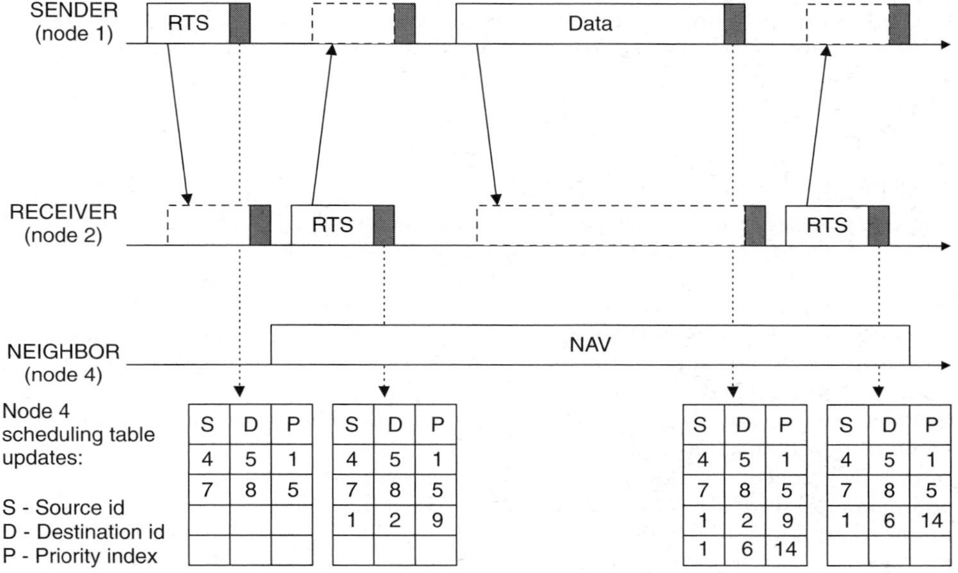

Figure 17: Packet transmission in the DPS protocol

radios are more complex and more costly. At the conceptual level, the fact that channels are selected by the transmitting node means that the scheme still suffers from the hidden terminal problem at the receiver node.

This last observation was the foundation for the improved scheme in which channel selection is performed by the receiver (Jain, Das, and Nasipuri 2001). In the improved scheme, a dedicated, shared channel is used to transmit RTS and CTS packets, which is effectively a form of out-of-band signaling (to be discussed below). A node that has a packet to send begins by sensing the state of all data channels and builds a list of free channels, much as in the original proposal. If no free channel is found, ten a backoff procedure is undertaken and the sensing is repeated. Once a free channel is found, the node then sends a RTS packet via the control channel; this packet contains the transmitter's list of free channels. The receiver then forms its own list of free channels, compares it to the one supplied by the transmitted, and selects the channel to be used for actual data transmission in the following manner. If the two lists overlap, then the receiver selects the best common channel (i.e., the one with the least received signal strength and consequently the least interference); this information is sent back to the transmitter within an RTS packet. If the two lists do not overlap, then the receiver does nothing; the transmitter eventually times out and repeats the procedure after a backoff. On receiving a valid RTS packet, the data packet is transmitted on the designated data channel. Successful transmission is acknowledged on the same data channel; failure to receive proper acknowledgment triggers another backoff and repetition of the entire procedure.

It is worth noting that nodes that overhear the RTS packet do not attempt to use the designated data channel during the entire duration of data transmission. Nodes in the vicinity of the transmitter are able to hear the RTS packet but not the CTS packet; these are required to refrain from transmitting only for the duration of the CTS transmission (in fact, until the transmitter's time out) but do not have to wait until the final ACK packet. In this manner, collisions between control handshake and data packets are avoided, the hidden terminal problem is alleviated, and throughput is improved. Again, the main problem is related to the implementation of the radio subsystem capable of monitoring the state of all channels in a given frequency band.

Slotted Seeded Channel Hopping

The *slotted seeded channel hopping* (SSCH) approach was initially proposed by Bahl, Chandra, and Dunagan (2004). SSCH is a distributed protocol for making and coordinating channel switching decisions, with the main objective of improving the throughput. Although the original paper describes the implementation in the IEEE 802.11 environment, the SSCH protocol is portable to other environments as well because it can be implemented in software without any modification of the radio subsystem. In SSCH, time is partitioned into slots of 10 ms, which suffices for approximately thirty-five transmissions of packets of maximum allowed length; this value was chosen to minimize the overhead of channel switching. Each node maintains a list of channels that will be used, as well as the times when transmissions will switch to the corresponding channels; this is referred to as the *channel schedule*. Each node also maintains, or strives to maintain, the channel schedules for all of the other nodes it is aware of. In this manner, the protocol ensures that any given pair of nodes will ultimately be able to communicate, despite the possibility of unexpected schedule changes. Channel schedules are kept in a compact form as a current channel and a rule used for updating the channel to avoid the excessive overhead needed for synchronization. The rule is actually a seed used to update the channel table, hence the name of the protocol. Data packets are kept in separate per-neighbor queues that are themselves ordered by perceived neighbor reachability. At the beginning of a slot, packet transmissions are attempted, preceded by the IEEE 802.11 RTS–CTS control handshake; the protocol visits all of the queues in a round-robin fashion. Unsuccessful transmissions cause the corresponding flow to be assigned lower priority for one-half of a slot duration, which limits the bandwidth waste incurred when transmitting on a wrong channel, or to an unreachable node. At the same time, packets are not dropped from the queue before the destination node is found unreachable during a full cycle of all channels. In this manner, the SSCH protocol is able to improve bandwidth utilization compared to other approaches.

Asynchronous Multichannel Coordination Protocol

The use of multiple channels in the *asynchronous multichannel coordination protocol* (AMCP) by Shi, Salonidis, and Knightly (2006) is guided by the goal of reducing the likelihood of starvation in CSMA-based multihop networks. In this case, the main cause of starvation is the lack of coordination between transmitters that cannot hear each other but prevent others from transmitting (even though this would not cause collisions). The AMCP protocol addresses this problem through the use of the so-called channel tables kept by each node that contain information about the scheduled availability of the data channels. In addition, each node may choose a preferred data channel for its own transmissions. When a data packet is to be transmitted, the node will check if its preferred channel is available; if not, an available channel is selected at random. The node then attempts the RTS–CTS handshake on the control channel; the RTS packet includes the information about the selected data channel. If the receiver finds it available, it responds with a so-called confirming CTS packet and immediately switches to the designated channel for data transmission. The transmitter switches to the designated channel and transmits the data packet. On successful reception, both nodes label the channel as *preferred* and switch back to the control channel. If the receiver finds that the designated channel is not available, it responds with a rejecting CTS packet that contains a list of available channels and remains on the control channel. The transmitter randomly selects another channel from those available to both transmitter and receiver and undertakes another round of control handshake.

In the AMCP protocol, coordination is accomplished as follows. A neighboring node that overhears an RTS or a confirming CTS packet updates its channel table by labeling the designated channel unavailable for the announced duration of data transmission (including the CTS and ACK packets). No action is taken when a rejecting CTS is overheard. Starvation is avoided because this node can still use other available channels for its data transmissions. Furthermore, if the neighboring node wants to transmit data to one of the nodes that have just started their control handshake, it will defer its transmission for the entire duration of the ongoing transmission but set its contention window size to the minimum value; in this manner, it can undertake the deferred transmission as soon as possible, with a high probability of success, and thus minimize the likelihood of starvation.

MAC PROTOCOLS WITH POWER MANAGEMENT

Protocols from the power-management group try to reduce contention by controlling the transmission power on a per-packet basis. The obvious but naïve solution is to transmit RTS and CTS packets at the maximum available power so that they reach the widest possible audience. On the contrary, data and ACK packets should be transmitted at the lowest power level needed to reach their target to minimize the risk of contention. Although the risk of contention is indeed reduced but not fully eliminated, the susceptibility of data and ACK packets to noise and interference is increased. In extreme cases, this approach may result in unidirectional links—that is, one node can hear the other but the opposite is not true. These cases are much more difficult to handle.

Power-Aware Multiaccess Protocol with Signaling

Singh and Raghavendra (1998) were among the first to try to combine the MAC protocol with power-conserving features. The communication protocol itself is based on the MACA protocol (Karn 1990), augmented with a separate control and signaling channel similar in concept to the *busy tone multiple access* (BTMA) approach of Tobagi and Kleinrock (1975). In *power-aware multiaccess protocol with signaling* (PAMAS), a node that wants to transmit a packet sends the RTS packet to the designated receiver. The receiver that hears the RTS packet checks the control channel first; if no transmission is heard for a specified time t (equal to the round-trip time plus the duration of the RTS–CTS packet), it responds with the CTS packet and transmits a busy tone on the control channel. Unlike some of the algorithms described earlier, the busy tone in PAMAS is shorter: It lasts twice as long as the RTS–CTS packet. The busy tone is also sent when the node receiving a packet hears a RTS packet or detects some activity on the control channel; this prevents other potential receivers from sending their own CTS and thus prevents a potentially interfering transmission (the hidden terminal problem). On receiving the CTS packet, the sender begins the data-packet transmission. If the CTS packet is not received within the specified time-out, the sender performs a binary exponential backoff and repeats the attempt. The backoff countdown may be interrupted if an RTS request is received from another node, in which case the sender switches to reception mode according to the rules outlined above.

To conserve power, any node without packets to send goes to sleep. Moreover, if an ongoing transmission is detected in the neighborhood (through the presence of a busy tone on the control channel), all unaffected nodes should go to sleep. In the latter case, the sleep should last as long as the ongoing transmission. If the node wakes up without any packets to transmit, it goes to sleep again, but if it wakes up with a packet ready to be sent, it simply sends an RTS packet. If another transmission is in progress, the node conducts a probe over the control channel to find out how long will this transmission last. The probe protocol can be simplified considerably if the control channel is always active (Singh and Raghavendra 1998); however, this defeats the purpose for which the power control mechanism was introduced in the first place.

The PAMAS protocol is important because it shows that the medium access control mechanism can be linked with the power-conservation mechanism without affecting the end-to-end packet delay (Singh and Raghavendra 1998). Its main problem stems from the separation of data and control channels because such radios are infeasible to implement in resource-constrained sensor nodes. A further problem is the implicit assumption that switching in and out of the active state is much shorter than the average packet transmission time, which simply does not hold in most real systems.

Dynamic Power-Saving Mechanism

Jung and Vaidya (2002) have described a *dynamic power-saving mechanism* (DPSM) that optimizes the power saving mechanisms available in the IEEE 802.11 DCF (ANSI/IEEE 1999). In the DPSM scheme, time is divided into beacon intervals to which all nodes should synchronize. At the beginning of each beacon interval, all nodes must be awake for the duration of the so-called *ad hoc traffic indication message* (ATIM) window. Any node that has data to transmit announces its intention using the ATIM frame, which is subsequently acknowledged by the corresponding receiver. These transmissions are performed using the regular CSMA/CA mechanism of IEEE 802.11. Nodes that are about to receive data stay awake throughout the beacon interval, and so do the transmitting nodes that have received the proper acknowledgment. Other nodes can doze off—that is, they can switch to a low power state until the next beacon. In the original 802.11 standard (ANSI/IEEE 1999), the duration of the ATIM window is fixed, which does not give optimal results. In other words, an ATIM window that is too short means that not all nodes that have data will succeed in announcing and actually performing their transmissions, which degrades throughput. On the other hand, an ATIM window that is too long leads to higher energy consumption because all nodes must remain awake throughout this time interval, which leaves too little time for actual data transmissions and thus degrades throughput at high loads.

In DPSM, this power-saving mechanism is enhanced in several ways, all of which aim to improve power efficiency. First, ATIM windows of variable duration allow the network to adjust to traffic conditions; in addition, each node can choose its own ATIM window size. Second, a single ATIM frame is to be used per destination node, thus reducing contention during the ATIM window. However, each data packet must contain information about the remaining number of packets to be sent, which allows the receiver to determine whether all packets were received or not. Third, a node that finishes a data transmission, either as the transmitter or the receiver, is allowed to doze off until the next beacon interval, which improves energy efficiency.

Dynamic adjustment of the ATIM window size uses several criteria: the number of packets pending transmission, the information overheard from other nodes' ATIM frames (each ATIM frame contains the information about the current contention window size of the transmitting node), the ATIM frames received while waiting for a previously announced data transmission, and the information on the number of retries for the current ATIM frame. In this manner, the DPSM scheme can be fine-tuned to improve energy efficiency without affecting throughput.

Power Control Mechanism

The power control mechanism of Jung and Vaidya (2005) uses the basic scheme described above but with the following change: The sender changes its power level from minimum to maximum during the transmission of a data packet, as shown in Figure 18. The duration of the maximum level transmission is chosen to be long enough for the nodes in the vicinity to sense the ongoing transmission and defer those of their own. In this manner, the risk of collisions is reduced (albeit not altogether eliminated), while the power consumption is reduced below that of the original IEEE 802.11 CDF.

MAC PROTOCOLS THAT USE DIRECTIONAL ANTENNAE

The protocols in the group use directional antennae to limit the spatial coverage of data transmissions and, consequently, reduce the risk of collisions. The underlying assumption is that the difference in received signal strength (i.e., the selection diversity) will allow the receiving subsystem to determine the approximate location of the correspondent (i.e., which antenna segment is to be used). The basic idea is simple: The sender sends a RTS packet in all directions and the receiver responds with an omnidirectional CTS, which informs all prospective neighbors about the forthcoming transmission. The sender transmits the data packet using a single antenna segment: the one that is oriented toward the receiver. In this manner, it will minimize its interference with its neighbors in all other directions. This scheme is depicted in Figure 19; it was first proposed by Nasipuri et al. (2000).

The problem with this approach is that it must be coupled with power control insofar as the directional transmissions must use reduced power levels to achieve a transmission range that is equal or close to the one obtained with omnidirectional transmission. In case the same power level is used for both types of transmissions, an increase in collisions in the coverage of the directional beam will be observed.

A similar protocol is described by Ko, Shankarkuman, and Vaidya (2000), as well as by others, the main difference being the assumption that the sender knows the location of the receiver and thus can use a directional RTS instead of the omnidirectional one.

An interesting variation of the basic protocol is described by Korakis, Jakllari, and Tassiulas (2003). In this case, the RTS packet is transmitted omnidirectionally but through a one-by-one antenna segment in a circular fashion, while the CTS packet is transmitted directionally after all directions have been covered by the RTS. The RTS packet contains the information about the duration of the forthcoming transmission and the segment it covers. Hence, the nodes that hear the RTS (but are not the designated receiver) can decide whether or not to defer their transmissions. The sender listens for the CTS omnidirectionally. The data and ACK packets are sent directionally. In this manner, the potential for interference (and resulting collisions) is reduced. A simple extension of the protocol allows the nodes to record the information about their neighbors' locations, which helps avoid certain hidden terminal scenarios that result from the use of directional antennae.

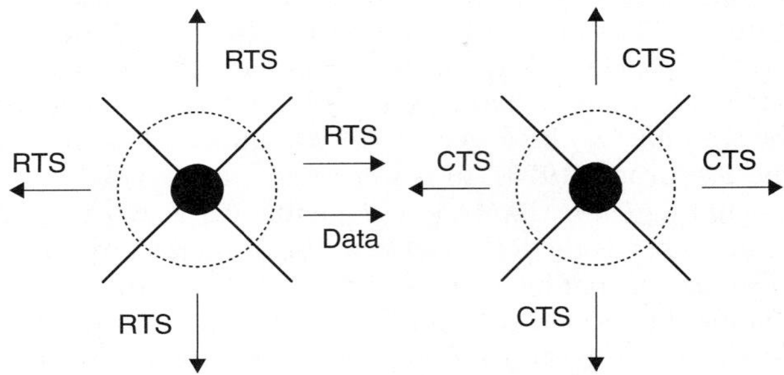

Figure 19: Packet transmission using a directional antenna with four segments

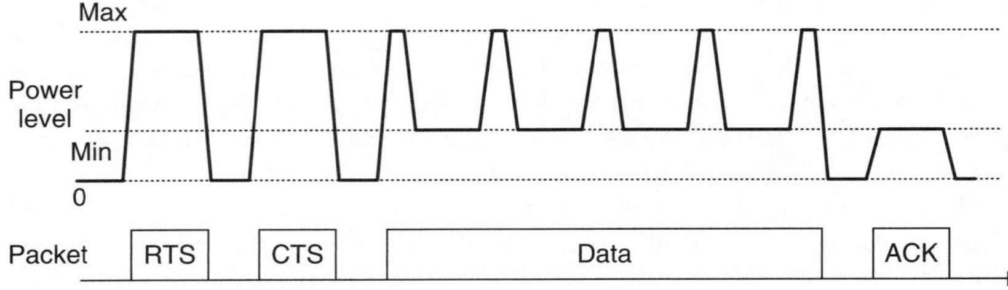

Figure 18: Power profile of a packet transmission in the PCM scheme

MAC PROTOCOLS THAT USE OUT-OF-BAND SIGNALING

Ensuring collision-free data transmissions requires that the potential interfering senders are informed about pending data transmissions in a timely fashion. The protocols described in the previous section use the control handshake before the actual transmission. Although this approach does help alleviate some of the problems that may cause collision, it is unable to completely eliminate collisions. Moreover, transmitting control packets uses bandwidth, and together with backoff windows of variable size reduces the overall bandwidth utilization of the network. The protocols described in this section adopt a different approach—namely, they use a separate channel (the control channel) to convey information that prevents collisions or to conduct the actual handshake. The idea has its origins in traditional telephony systems in which a special busy tone informs the party that wants to initiate a call about another transmission in progress.

Busy Tone Multiple Access

The busy tone multiple access protocol by Tobagi and Kleinrock (1975) noted earlier is the first reported work on the busy tone approach. In BTMA, a separate control channel is used to transmit a busy tone when the node is active. The busy tone could be as simple as a pure sine wave at a predefined frequency. Any node that wants to transmit will check the control channel first. If the busy tone is present, the transmission will be deferred for some random time; if the control channel is idle, the node starts transmitting the busy tone and simultaneously starts its data transmission. In the original proposal, the transmission power of the control channel is increased to ensure that the range of the busy tone is approximately twice that of the data transmission; a later modification uses the same transmission range for both channels but mandates that the nodes that sense the data transmission in progress forward the busy tone to other nodes in their transmission range. Either way, no other node within the two-hop transmission range is allowed to transmit. This approach is simple and effective—but perhaps too effective because many of the nodes prevented from transmitting could actually engage in communications of their own without interfering with the current transmission. Bandwidth utilization tends to be poor.

Receiver-Initiated BTMA

A derivative of the basic BTMA known as *receiver-initiated BTMA* (RI-BTMA), originally described by Wu and Li (1987), combines a time-slotted approach akin to TDMA with a much simpler handshake protocol that employs a single busy tone. In this case, the prospective sender listens to the control channel until it finds a free slot—that is, the one without a busy tone. Once such a slot is found, it sends a small preamble packet on the data channel. (The time slot on both data and control channels is equal to the duration of the preamble packet.) The designated receiver responds by activating its busy tone on the control channel. On hearing this tone, the sender may begin the data-packet transmission. Once the packet is received, the receiver turns off the busy tone.

Dual BTMA

Deng and Haas (1998) have proposed an improved version of this approach, called the *dual busy tone multiple access* (DBTMA). In this protocol, the data channel is used exclusively for data transmissions, whereas the control channel is used for the RTS-CTS handshake and for two busy tones that indicate a reception and a transmission in progress, respectively.

The DBTMA protocol operates as follows. A node that wants to transmit a packet checks the control channel for the presence of a receiving busy tone; if none is detected, the node sends the RTS packet to the receiver on the control channel. On receiving the RTS packet, the receiver checks the control channel for the presence of a transmitting busy tone, which would indicate that a transmission is already in progress in the vicinity. If none is present, the receiver responds with a CTS packet via the control channel and then activates its receiving busy tone to alert other nodes in its vicinity that it is receiving a data packet. On receiving the CTS packet, the sender activates the transmitting busy tone on the control channel and begins the data transmission on the data channel. When the data-packet transmission is finished, the sender turns off the transmitting busy tone; the receiver turns off the receiving busy tone after it has received the data packet.

The DBTMA protocol is able to achieve almost twice the value of channel utilization of the basic BTMA or some RTS- and CTS-based protocols such as MACA or MACAW, mainly because the use of two busy tones blocks only the transmissions from nodes in the vicinity of the receiver but not those in the vicinity of the sender.

The main problem with all protocols based on the busy tone approach is the need for two radios because the busy tone uses a different frequency or frequencies from the data channel. This requirement may not be simple to satisfy, in particular in conjunction with other requirements such as small physical size and limited energy source. On account of this, MAC protocols that utilize a separate control channel with busy tones have not been especially successful in practice.

MAC PROTOCOLS THAT USE POLLING

Bluetooth

Bluetooth is among the few true polling protocols used in ad hoc networks (Bluetooth SIG 2004), thus its adoption as the IEEE standard 802.15.1 (IEEE 2002). Bluetooth devices are organized in small networks known as *piconets*, with as many as 255 devices; one acts as the master and as many as seven others can be active at any given time; the remaining ones are parked. The channel time is divided into time slots of $T = 625$ µs, and all communications in the piconet are synchronized to this clock. Bluetooth uses a variant of the TDMA protocol in which all communications are performed under the control of the piconet master; in fact, all communications in the piconet must pass *through* the master. The master polls the slaves by sending them packets with appropriate identification; slaves can

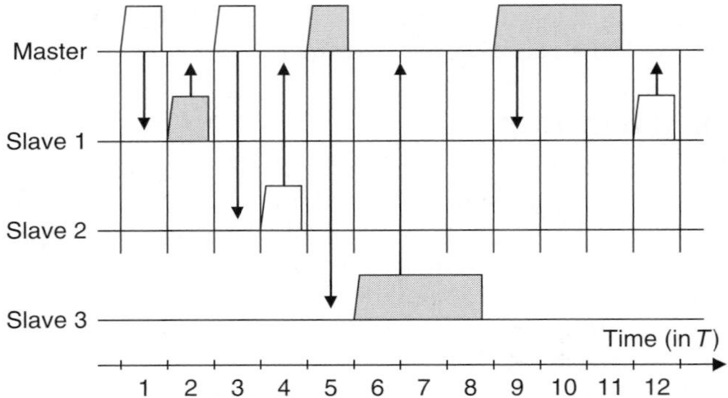

Figure 20: TDD communication in a Bluetooth piconet

talk back to the master only when addressed and only immediately after being addressed by the master. The operation of this protocol is schematically shown in Figure 20.

Master (downlink) and slave (uplink) transmissions occur in alternative slots in a scheme known as *time-division duplexing* (TDD). The Bluetooth TDD protocol requires that an addressed slave must respond to the master's poll even when it has no data to send; a similar requirement holds for the master as well (in Figure 20, white symbols denote empty packets while gray symbols denote packets that carry data). An important consequence of the TDD protocol is that both the throughput and end-to-end delays critically depend on the polling discipline—that is, the algorithm used by the master to poll active slaves in the piconet. Several such disciplines have been proposed and analyzed in recent years; a detailed overview and analysis can be found in Mišić and Mišić (2005).

The TDD protocol is collision-free and, in theory, should be more energy-efficient than the collision-based MAC protocols, but the advantage is not so noticeable in practice. The main source of inefficiency of the protocol is the fact that even empty packets use bandwidth: They last for one slot T, whereas data packets can last for one, three, or five slots T. Furthermore, all slaves must listen to master transmissions at all times and respond when polled, even when there is no data to transmit in either direction. Special modes defined by the official Bluetooth standard allow slaves to detach temporarily from the piconet to minimize energy consumption or perform other tasks (Bluetooth SIG 2004).

SENSOR NETWORKS

Sensor networks are a class of wireless networks intended for monitoring environmental phenomena in a given physical space; such networks find increasing usage in areas as diverse as military applications, object surveillance, structural health monitoring, and agriculture and forestry, among others. Monitoring may be continuous, with a prescribed data rate that may change over time; it may also be triggered by an explicit demand from a controlling node or a specific event in the environment. Environmental phenomena to be monitored include simple physical variables such as temperature, humidity, light, pressure, pH value, and the like; however, other phenomena also can be monitored, such as the presence or absence of a specific object (say, an inventory item with a radio frequency ID tag), or movements of persons and objects (e.g., cars). The spaces to be monitored include rooms, hallways, foyers, homes, backyards, streets, and larger buildings and structures (e.g., bridges) as well as open spaces such as fields or forests. Sensor nodes can be deployed in large numbers—from tens through hundreds to even thousands. Sensor networks are often expected to operate autonomously, with little or no human intervention, for prolonged periods of time. Sensor nodes are seldom mobile, and even when mobility is present, not all of the nodes are equipped with appropriate capabilities. Given such a diverse set of applications and requirements, it should come as no surprise that the constraints that guide the design and deployment of wireless sensor networks differ, sometimes substantially, from those that hold in wireless ad hoc networks (Sohrabi et al. 2000; Achir and Ouvry 2004). Let us now discuss those constraints in more detail.

Energy Efficiency

Probably the most important difference results from the fact that sensor nodes typically operate on limited battery power, which means that the maximization of network lifetime (and, consequently, minimization of power consumption) is sine qua non for sensor networks. On the contrary, power consumption is seldom the critical requirement for ad hoc networks.

The constraint of minimal energy consumption translates into two distinct yet closely related design requirements (Jones et al. 2001):

1. The communication efficiency must be maximized through the design of simple yet flexible and effective communication protocols and functions.
2. Those protocols and functions must be implemented by small chips with limited computational and memory resources. Simultaneous achievement of these objectives necessitates some kind of cross-layer protocol optimization in which the MAC layer would use the information obtained from the PHY layer to control its own operational characteristics. At the same time, optimal operation of the upper, network, and transport layers requires the knowledge of appropriate information from both the PHY and MAC layers. Again, such tight integration is not common in ad hoc networks.

An important consequence of the requirement for energy efficiency is the limited transmission range of most sensor node radio subsystems; few real devices have a transmission range of more than 100 meters (300 feet), and ranges of 10 meters (30 feet) and even less are not uncommon.

Protocol Efficiency

Regarding communication protocols, the main sources of inefficiency are packet collisions, but also overly complex handshake protocols, receiving packets destined for other nodes, and idle listening to the medium (Singh and Raghavendra 1998; Ye, Heidemann, and Estrin 2004). Actual power consumption of sensor nodes, often called *motes*, depends mostly on the radio subsystem and its operating mode. In most (but not all) cases, transmitting uses 25 percent to 100 percent more energy than receiving; idle mode in which the radio is turned on but does not transmit or receive consumes some 10 percent to 20 percent less energy than receiving (Stemm and Katz 1997; Bhardwaj and Chandrakasan 2002). However, most savings can be made by putting the node to sleep, when power consumption drops by one to two orders of magnitude, depending on the hardware (Jung and Vaidya 2002; Van Dam and Langendoen 2003).

Use of Redundant Sensors

Because nodes are small and cheap to produce and the network lifetime needs to be maximized, it is often feasible to deploy the sensors in a given physical space in much larger numbers than necessary to obtain the desired rate of information flow. If redundant sensors are used, they can be periodically sent to sleep to minimize their duty cycle, which extends the lifetime of individual sensors and of the entire network and reduces or eliminates the need for operator intervention, thus reducing the operational cost of the network (Akan and Akyildiz 2005). The use of redundant sensors has profound implications on the design of MAC protocols, as will be seen below.

Node Specialization

Another important distinction is related to the role of individual nodes. An ad hoc network allows its nodes to choose the specific role, or roles, they would like to play—data source, destination, or intermediate router—at any given time. In most cases, a node is free to switch to a different role or roles whenever it finds it appropriate or is instructed to do so by the specific application currently executing on it. On the contrary, nodes in a sensor network have specific roles that either do not change often or never change at all. Most of the nodes act as sensing nodes, some act as intermediaries that route the traffic and (possibly) performs some administrative duties, and a small number of nodes (sometimes only a single node) act as the network sink (or sinks) toward which all the sensed data ultimately flows (Akyildiz et al. 2002). A group of sensor nodes under the control of an intermediary is sometimes referred to as a *subnetwork* or *cluster*, while the intermediary itself is known as *cluster-head*. We note that the number of intermediate levels interposed between the sensing nodes and the network sinks depends on several variables such as the size of the network, the size of the physical space that the network has to monitor, the transmission range of individual nodes, and (to some extent) the actual MAC protocol used.

Traffic Characteristics

The traffic in sensor networks is rather asymmetric because the bulk of it flows from the sensing nodes toward the network sink (this is often referred to as the *uplink* direction). The traffic in the opposite direction is generally much smaller and consists of control information and possibly queries issued by the network sink on behalf of the corresponding sensing application (Intanagonwiwat, Govindan, and Estrin 2000). Furthermore, traffic patterns in sensor networks are rather different than in ad hoc networks. For example, temperature or humidity monitoring might require periodic or nearly periodic transmissions—in essence, synchronous traffic with low data rate—whereas object surveillance and other event-driven sensing applications exhibit low average traffic volume and random bursts with considerably higher peak rates.

Furthermore, data packets are often much smaller in sensor networks. Original data from sensing nodes typically consists of only a few data values reported by appropriate sensors. Intermediate nodes may choose to aggregate those values to improve energy efficiency and reduce bandwidth and energy consumption; data aggregation is more common in networks with a larger number of hierarchical levels. At the same time, the number of sensor nodes and their spatial density may be extremely large, depending on the size of the space to be monitored and the requirements of the sensing application.

Quality-of-Service Requirements

Maintaining prescribed delay bounds in a network of resource-constrained nodes with limited transmission range is a complex issue. Delay considerations are of crucial importance in certain classes of applications—for example, in military applications such as battlefield communications and detection and monitoring of troop movement, or in health care applications where patients in special care units must be monitored for important health variables (via ECG or EEG) because of a serious and urgent medical condition. Low delays can be achieved either by bandwidth reservation, as utilized in variations of the TDMA approach, or by some kind of admission control that will prevent network congestion, if the CSMA approach is used. At the same time, the requirement for maximum throughput is relaxed because of the following. First, the exact value of the throughput requirement is usually prescribed by the sensing application, unlike general networks where the goal is to obtain as much throughput as possible. Second, energy efficiency dictates the use of protocols that incorporate power control, which will strive to keep the nodes inactive for as long as possible (Akan and Akyildiz 2005). To obtain the desired throughput, it suffices to adjust the mean number of active nodes.

Even packet losses can be catered to in this manner because we do not care whether a given packet from a given node will reach the network sink—as long as the sink receives a sufficient number of packets from other nodes. Any packet loss can be compensated for (in the long term) by varying the mean number of active nodes. In a certain sense, fairness is not needed at the node and packet level as long as it is maintained at the cluster level (Callaway 2004). On the contrary, fairness at the node and packet level is important in ad hoc networks.

Differences from Ad Hoc Networks

The requirements outlined above lead to several important differences between sensor networks and ad hoc networks, most notably the following:

- Power efficiency and lifetime maximization are the foremost requirements for sensor networks.

- Self-organization is important in both ad hoc and sensor networks. In the former case, this is because of dynamicity and node mobility, which cause frequent topology changes and makes self-organization more difficult; in the latter, this is mostly caused by sensor nodes exhausting their battery power (i.e., dying), although mobile sensors are used in some applications.
- Throughput maximization is often required in ad hoc networks but is not too common in sensor networks.
- Delay minimization is typically assigned much higher priority in sensor networks than in their ad hoc siblings.
- The use of redundant sensors allows for a certain level of fault tolerance; on the contrary, packet losses are intolerable in ad hoc networks.
- Scalability is an important issue because of the potentially large number of sensors; scalability is also important in ad hoc networks, but it is limited by the available bandwidth and the desired throughput.
- Nodes in ad hoc networks are often mobile, whereas most sensor networks have no mobile nodes.

In more than one sense, wireless ad hoc networks are a class of networks with flexible topology but without infrastructure, which should cater to all kinds of networking tasks. On the other hand, sensor networks are highly specialized networks that perform a rather restricted set of tasks under severe computational and communication restrictions.

MAC PROTOCOLS FOR WIRELESS SENSOR NETWORKS

The requirements and constraints outlined above mean that the design of wireless sensor networks and their associated protocols is a rather challenging task. The discussions that follow will present several MAC protocols for wireless sensor networks and highlight the conceptual approaches in which they attempt to address those challenges. Similar overviews can be found in Akyildiz et al. (2002) and, more recently, in Demirkol, Ersoy, and Alagöz (2006). Furthermore, an interesting overview of some of the protocols (and a detailed description of others) can be found in Sohrabi et al. (2000).

In the following, we will briefly present a couple of representative MAC protocols for sensor networks. Second, we present the recently adopted IEEE 802.15.1 and IEEE 802.15.4 standards as the industry standards for *wireless personal area networks* (WPANs) that hold great potential for *wireless sensor network* (WSN) application. We agree with the opinion expressed by Callaway (2004) that "the success of wireless sensor networks as a technology rests on the success of the standardization efforts to unify the market and avoiding the proliferation of proprietary, incompatible protocols that, although, perhaps optimal in their individual market niches, will limit the size of overall wireless sensor market."

Adaptive Rate Control with CSMA

Woo and Culler (2001) have augmented the basic CSMA protocol with adaptive rate control to improve energy efficiency and so-called multihop fairness—that is, in multihop scenarios, fairness can be measured as the balance between the traffic that originates in the node itself and the traffic that the node has to relay on behalf of others (route-thru traffic). Note that the traffic generated by any given node is, in fact, the route-thru traffic for all other nodes it has to pass through.

In the ideal case—a network with symmetric traffic—the knowledge about the total number of size of the network would help the node to estimate the allowed amount of its contribution. Because this information is hard or even impossible to obtain, an adaptive mechanism with a linear increase and multiplicative decrease is used to control the transmission rate of an application. The goal for any given node is to ensure fairness among all nodes whose traffic it routes. Moreover, because dropping the route-thru traffic is a waste of resources (it will have to go through that same route again or be lost), such traffic is given preference over the locally generated one. Measures are also taken to reduce the impact of the hidden node problem for pairs of nodes that are two hops away yet able to hear one another, for which Woo and Culler (2001) use the terms *child* and *grandparent nodes*.

When used in conjunction with a random delay before transmission, the adaptive rate mechanism provides an effective control mechanism without explicit control packets, in particular in scenarios where traffic loads are low, which is common in many sensor network applications.

S-MAC

The S-MAC protocol is designed for deployment in multihop WSN, where packet destinations are uniformly distributed (Ye, Heidemann, and Estrin 2004). Each device alternates between active periods, in which it communicates with other nodes, and inactive or sleep periods that ensure energy efficiency by keeping the duty cycle low. A complete cycle that includes an active and an inactive period is referred to as a *frame*. The information about the identity of the sensor node and its next scheduled sleep time is called an *activity schedule*.

The main feature of S-MAC is the self-synchronization of activity schedules for different sensor nodes, which is achieved as follows. On returning from sleep, a node listens to the medium for a specified time to check for other nodes' schedules. If a schedule is received, it is immediately adopted and followed; if not, the node chooses a schedule of its own and starts to follow it. Either way, it will start broadcasting SYNC packets with the information about the adopted schedule. However, if a node receives a different schedule at a later time, it may drop its own schedule and adopt the new one. Alternatively, it can add the new schedule to its own, which facilitates multihop communications between nodes that cannot communicate directly because of limited transmission range. A node periodically listens to SYNC broadcasts from other nodes; this lessens the risk of neighbor nodes following completely different schedules (and missing each other's active periods) and facilitates schedule reconfiguration when the network topology changes. In this manner, nodes collect information about their neighbors and build local tables of active periods of neighbors. Each node uses its table to schedule its sleep periods with the goal of being awake simultaneously with some of its neighbors so that packet exchange can take place. In fact, *virtual clusters* are formed by the nodes that follow the same schedule; this facilitates communication among them.

During the active period, a node either listens or transmits a data packet. The listening period is organized in two phases that accommodate SYNC broadcasts and data transmissions, respectively. Packet transmission is achieved using slotted CSMA with RTS–CTS handshake. Before the node sends a SYNC or RTS packet of its own, it listens to the medium for a random period of time. After the transmission of a RTS packet, node waits for the CTS packet and then transmits the data packet. If the CTS response does not arrive during the listening period, then the node goes back to sleep and tries again in the next active period.

The delay in multihop transmissions can be extremely long if each node along the route receives the packet in one active period and transmits it in the next one. To reduce this delay, nodes in S-MAC use the so-called adaptive listening: A node that overhears the neighbor's transmission (RTS or CTS) will stay awake beyond the end of the active period. In this manner, if this node is the next destination of the packet, it can receive it immediately rather than after going through the sleep period.

To reduce transmission latency, a node that has more than one packet to send (a burst) can use only one control handshake per burst. This feature is referred to as *message passing* (Ye, Heidemann, and Estrin 2004). However, explicit acknowledgments are required after each successfully transmitted packet, which somewhat offsets the power savings obtained by spreading the cost of the handshake over all packets in the burst. If an ACK packet is not received, the sender will retry the transmission of the last packet; if the maximum number of retries is reached, the sender will abort the transmission and start over. Acknowledgments ensure reliable transmission but also inform other nodes about the transmission in progress and thus help avoid the hidden terminal problem. In other words, both data and ACK packets have a duration field that specifies the total transmission time for the burst, including the ACK packets. Therefore, nodes that hear either a data packet or an ACK packet from an ongoing burst transmission may go to sleep until its scheduled finish time.

Although simple and efficient, S-MAC suffers from scalability problems. As the size of the network increases, it becomes increasingly difficult for a node to maintain a coordinated schedule, and the power consumption of relaying nodes—which have to receive and transmit packets—increases. As a result, energy efficiency deteriorates. Decreasing the duty cycle may counter this trend, but it increases the delays and reduces the throughput.

Time-Out MAC

The main drawback of the S-MAC is the fixed duty cycle—that is, the ratio of the active period to the entire frame time, which does not depend on the traffic in the network. To reduce the power consumption even more, active periods should be as short as possible under the given traffic pattern. This is the main concept of the *time-out MAC* (T-MAC) proposed by Van Dam and Langendoen (2003).

The T-MAC borrows the concept of distributed synchronization from the S-MAC, except that nodes that hear a schedule different from their own must follow both (this is not mandatory in S-MAC). This provision ensures that neighboring nodes will always be able to communicate.

T-MAC nodes can optionally go to sleep when they hear an ongoing transmission of which they are not a party. Although this forced sleep (which is mandatory in S-MAC) may save energy, it also leads to increased collision overhead and reduced throughput (Van Dam and Langendoen 2003).

In T-MAC, a node keeps listening and (perhaps) transmitting as long as it is active. It will switch to sleep if no activation event has occurred for a specified time *TA*. Activation events include activity on the medium, including end of own transmission or acknowledgment, and the firing of an activation timer (which brings a sleeping node back to the active state). The time-out value *TA* is chosen to ensure that the node does not miss any communication directed to it. Nodes that have data packets must attempt transmission as soon as their active period starts; other nodes in its neighborhood will be awake and, hopefully, able to receive the data. A potential sender listens to the medium for a random time within a fixed contention interval and then undertakes the RTS–CTS handshake.

As noted earlier, many sensor networks exhibit asymmetric traffic patterns: The bulk of the traffic is directed toward the network sink. In this case, it is possible that some transmissions will be delayed until the next active period simply because one of the relaying nodes was unaware of it and went to sleep (the early sleeping problem) as shown in Figure 21. To overcome this problem, the node that overhears a CTS packet destined for another node can send a *future request to send* (FRTS) packet to inform the future destination node about the forthcoming data transmission. The FRTS packet contains the duration of the transmission copied from the CTS packet; the destination node can then stay awake for that long. This mechanism, shown in Figure 22, reduces the delay and increases the overall throughput of the network.

Another possible problem in multihop relaying is that an intermediate node that has a nearly full buffer with data to forward receives the RTS packet announcing a forthcoming data transmission from another sender. Accepting that data increases the risk of buffer overflow and data loss; in addition, it may increase the delay because of the early sleeping problem. The T-MAC protocol allows such a node to give priority to its own transmission by sending a RTS packet to the proper destination rather

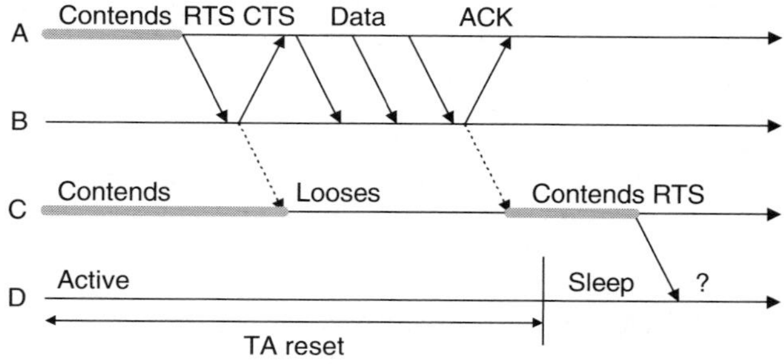

Figure 21: Early sleeping problem in multihop communication

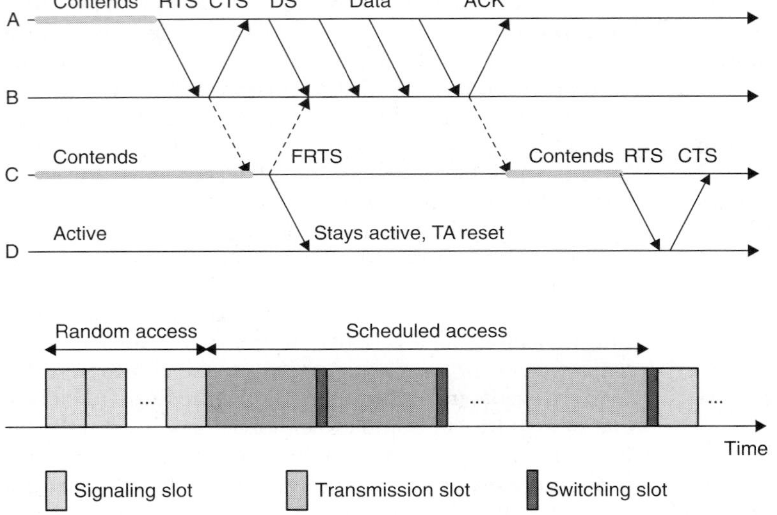

Figure 22: The use of FRTS packet avoids early sleeping

Figure 23: Time slot organization in TRAMA

that responding with the CTS packet as usual. In fact, such a node takes over the medium, which it has effectively won anyway, only for a different purpose.

Although this technique, known as *full-buffer priority*, can offer substantial improvement in performance, it may be risky to use under heavy loads: If too many nodes start taking over the medium, the risk of collisions rapidly increases. To avoid such situations, the node is allowed to use full-buffer priority only if the number of times it has lost contention exceeds the predefined threshold.

Traffic-Adaptive Medium Access

Although the T-MAC protocol is able to offer considerable power savings compared to S-MAC under variable workloads, it suffers from similar problems related to scalability, especially under heavy loads. A possible solution to keep the energy efficiency under control is to reduce the timeout value, but this increases delays and impairs the ability to react to changing network conditions. The *traffic-adaptive medium access* (TRAMA) protocol proposed by Rajendran, Obraczka, and Garcia-Luna-Aceves (2006) attempts to overcome this problem through a traffic-adaptive scheme that selects receivers according to announced transmitter schedules. It is based on an earlier protocol known as *node-activation multiple access* (Bao and Garcia-Luna-Aceves 2001) has employed a similar approach but without concern for energy efficiency.

TRAMA assumes a single, time-slotted channel for both data and control transmissions. Time is divided into periods of random access, interleaved with periods of scheduled access, as shown in Figure 23.

Three subprotocols are used to exchange neighbor information (*neighbor protocol*, or NP), exchange schedule information (schedule exchange protocol), and elect the transmitters and receivers for the current time slot (adaptive election algorithm). The network starts in random access period wherein each node transmits basic signaling information in a randomly selected slot. This period essentially serves to construct and subsequently maintain the information about the node's neighbors. Although collisions of signaling packets are possible, the duration of the random access period is chosen to guarantee consistent neighbor information with a high degree of confidence.

Each node calculates its schedule interval based on the traffic pattern of the application and the neighbor information obtained in the NP phase. In addition, it calculates the number of slots in the subsequent schedule interval for which it has the highest priority among its two-hop neighbors (the winning slots). This information, together with the designated receivers for those slots (i.e., the packets to be transmitted therein), is announced through schedule packets. Priority is determined according to node identity and the time slot in question; ideally, this process assigns unique (and globally known) priorities to each node and time slot combination. A node may give up its slot if there are no data packets to transmit; such vacant slots can be used by other nodes in the neighborhood. Some of its winning slots will go unused if the number of such slots exceeds the number necessary to transmit all the data in that node's queue. The ChangeOver slot denotes the slot after which all winning slots are unused; it is used for announcing the next schedule, and all of the nodes must listen to it. A node that has no data to send and has not been designated as the receiver may switch to low-power mode until the next ChangeOver slot.

Although the scheduling mechanism used in TRAMA ensures collision-free data transmissions and allows for longer sleep times than in other protocols such as S-MAC, some inefficiency is caused by the fixed size of the transmission slots, which imposes a lower limit on the duty cycle. Another problem is that the priority calculations must be repeated for each slot in every scheduled access period, which may cause problems in a network implemented with resource-constrained nodes.

Other MAC Protocols for Sensor Networks

In the following, we will briefly mention several other protocols for wireless sensor networks, both those that focus entirely on MAC layer issues and those that include issues related to other layers as well. The reader should note that a several subsequent chapters are devoted to issues of broadcasting, routing, data gathering, and localization in sensor networks.

Low Energy Adaptive Clustering Hierarchy

Heinzelman, Chandrakasan, and Balakrishnan (2000) have attempted to minimize energy consumption in the scenario in which the sensor networks consists of several identical, resource-constrained nodes that generate unidirectional traffic sent to a single network sink. Although this protocol, known as *low energy adaptive clustering hierarchy* (LEACH), focuses mostly on routing issues, it does integrate elements from both network and MAC layer, which is why a brief overview is included here.

The main idea of the LEACH algorithm is that the sensors should autonomously organize themselves into clusters, with one node acting as the cluster-head. Sensors elect themselves to be the cluster-heads with a certain probability, which depends on the remaining energy of the sensor and the number of sensors in the entire network. Becoming the cluster-head is a unilateral decision and no negotiation is involved. To balance the power consumption, the role of the cluster-head is randomly rotated among the sensors in the cluster.

Once elected, the cluster-head advertises its presence. All sensor nodes must listen to the advertisements. They decide which cluster they will join and inform the corresponding cluster- head. All transmissions so far use CSMA. When the cluster-head gathers sufficient knowledge about the sensors in its cluster, it creates a TDMA transmission schedule and broadcasts it. (The original proposal assumes that CDMA coding is used for intracluster communication so that collisions can be avoided.) Once a sensor knows its cluster and its transmission schedule, it may go to sleep until the time comes for its transmission, thus conserving the least amount of power.

When the cluster-head receives the data from all the sensors in the cluster, it aggregates it and sends it to the network sink. A new round of clustering then follows.

Ideally, the LEACH algorithm should result in energy levels of individual sensors being used up at about the same rate. Of course, the cluster-head must remain active throughout the entire cycle, but the rotation of the cluster-head role should ensure that the load is evenly balanced among all nodes.

Wave Scheduling

Wave scheduling, originally proposed by Trigoni et al. (2004), is an example of an integrated protocol that spans the MAC, network, and even portions of the transport layer of the traditional networking protocol stack (Stallings 2002). It partitions the network into cells such that the nodes in a cell are assumed to be able to communicate only with the nodes in their own cell and its immediate neighbors. In fact, the assumption is that the cells are near rectangular, although this is not necessary for the proper functioning of the algorithm.

Transmissions are then scheduled utilizing a sequence of activations of edges that connect two cells. Each activation period includes a contention-based period followed by a contention-free period. In the contention period, the GAF scheduling protocol (Xu, Heidemann, and Estrin 2001) is run locally in each cell: The nodes attempt to determine whether the current leader has sufficient energy to continue its leadership role. If this is not the case, then a new leader is elected and messages queued for delivery are handed over by the previous leader, together with intercell routing information. The remaining nodes send the sensed data to the leader. Ordinary nodes can then go to sleep until the next activation period. In the contention-free period, accumulated messages are transferred from one cell leader to the next one. A special message informs the receiver if there are no messages to deliver, in which case both leaders can go to sleep to conserve energy.

Two distinct wave schedules are defined. In the *simple wave* schedule, messages are coordinated in east–west and north–south directions. This allows simultaneous transmissions from the leaders when the distance between them exceeds the transmission range. North–south and east–west schedules occur in interleaved fashion. In the *pipelined wave*, the graph obtained by the cell-to-cell edges is partitioned into a collection of maximal independent sets that can then be activated simultaneously without interference. Both wave schedules avoid interference, and they can be tuned to achieve minimum energy or minimum delay routing.

Stationary MAC and Startup

The *stationary MAC and startup* (SMACS) procedure, originally proposed by Sohrabi et al. (2000), deals with the creation of a suitable TDMA-like schedule without a centralized authority. In SMACS, neighbor discovery and channel assignment phases are lumped together, and channels for node-to-node communication are assigned immediately after the two nodes involved learn about each other's existence. By the time all nodes find out about all of their neighbors, an operational network with a flat topology is formed. *Channels*, in the SMACS terminology, are in fact time slots within a superframe of sufficient duration. To reduce contention, it is advisable to assign different frequencies to different channels whenever possible.

Berkeley MAC

A rather different approach was proposed by Polastre, Hill, and Culler (2004). Instead of trying to optimize the behavior of the MAC protocol, the *Berkeley MAC* (B-MAC) protocol optimizes the low-power listening and clear channel sensing on a popular Mica2 hardware (Hill et al. 2000). Other medium access mechanisms that use these primitives can then be implemented on top of the B-MAC platform.

Zebra MAC

The *zebra MAC* or Z-MAC (Rhee et al. 2005) combines the strengths of the CSMA and TDMA approaches. A node can transmit in any time slot after successful carrier sensing, as in CSMA, but the designated owners of that particular slot take precedence. This concept reduces the risk of collision while still allowing other nodes to transmit in that slot. In addition, lightweight synchronization schemes are utilized to provide the network with some resilience to topology changes and control information loss. However, the ZMAC protocol does not consider the situation in which individual nodes go to sleep, which severely limits its usability in several sensing applications.

IEEE 802.15.4

The recent IEEE 802.15.4 standard (IEEE 2003b) is not specifically intended for use in wireless sensor networks—it was originally designed as a *low data rate WPAN* (LR-WPAN)—but its simplicity and low data rate make it an attractive choice for sensing applications as well (Callaway 2004). The IEEE 802.15.4 protocol is a full-function MAC and PHY protocol that requires other layers above it to function properly, in contrast with most other proposals, which simplify several layers into a single, integrated one.

An IEEE 802.15.4 network can operate in two modes: (1) the beacon-enabled, slotted CSMA/CA mode in which a dedicated coordinator must be present; and (2) beaconless, unslotted CSMA/CA similar to the 802.11 DCF in its basic form (without the RTS–CTS handshake). In the former case, the interval between two successive beacon frames is split between an active and inactive period, which allows the entire network to conserve energy by going to sleep. Also, a portion of the active part of the superframe can be reserved for scheduled access, which is allocated on request. However, requests to allocate such time must be made through packets that undergo contention. The performance of IEEE 802.15.4 networks at the MAC level is not fully explored yet, especially their suitability for low-power applications, although some results have recently been reported (Mišić, Shafi, and Mišić 2006).

CONCLUSION

As the discussion above shows, the area of MAC protocols for ad hoc and sensor networks does not suffer from any shortage of research results. Nonetheless, there are still many open issues that need to be addressed, mainly in the domain of sensor networks.

First, the selection of the actual protocol is still largely unsolved, even though most proposals use some variant of contention-based access derived from the ubiquitous CSMA approach. In addition, the problems of hidden and exposed terminals still plague most, if not all, of the proposed protocols.

Second, the simultaneous minimization of energy consumption and optimization of different performance metrics of the MAC protocol requires more research. Although some proposals do assume a specific structure of the sensor field and try to find the optimum solution for that particular case, more generic solutions are needed.

Third, synchronization problems are also difficult, in particular when sensor nodes sleep for prolonged intervals and wake up only to find that their clock has drifted away from that of the nodes that are active. Although several algorithms exist that tackle this problem, solutions that would be generic enough to fit most sensing applications have yet to be found.

From the practical perspective, we can expect further reductions in the physical size and consumption of sensor devices. Advances in integrated circuit technology will allow more complex protocols to be implemented. However, fundamental problems related to transmission range and power will still remain. In particular, severe resource constraints mean that tight integration and cross-layer design that encompasses the functionality of PHY, MAC, routing, and (possibly) data aggregation layers will be a practical necessity.

These and many other questions will most likely be answered with further applications of wireless sensor devices.

GLOSSARY

Backoff: Random delay introduced after a node or device that wants to transmit data has detected that the medium is not idle. Often used synonymously with binary exponential backoff.

Bandwidth Reservation: A procedure through which a portion of bandwidth is reserved for exclusive use by a link (i.e., for the transmission from one node to another) before the actual transmission takes place.

Beacon: A special packet transmitted periodically by the network coordinator in order to facilitate synchronization of other nodes and devices in the network.

Binary Exponential Backoff: Backoff procedure in which the range to choose the actual backoff duration from doubles after every unsuccessful clear channel assessment (in some protocols) or attempt to transmit data (in others).

Burst: A sequence of packets transmitted in short succession, often generated by segmenting a longer packet from a higher protocol layer.

Channel Hopping: Switching through available channels (in most cases, different frequencies in the designated radio frequency band) in a defined, often pseudorandom manner, with the goal of reducing the impact of interference and noise.

Clear Channel Assessment or Clear Channel Sensing: Listening to the channel before transmission to detect whether the medium is idle (i.e., used by another node or device).

Clear-to-Send (CTS): Control packet sent by the designated data receiver to indicate its readiness to receive the data transmission from the potential transmitter. Usually sent in response to the RTS packet sent by the potential transmitter.

Cluster: Group of nodes or devices that work together under the control of a central controller or coordinator referred to as a *cluster-head*. Commonly used for sensor networks.

Collision: Situation when two or more packet transmissions overlap in time and cannot be successfully received.

Contention: Situation in which two or more nodes or devices compete for medium access.

Coordinator: Node in the network that has special responsibilities in terms of monitoring or managing network operation.

Distributed Coordinator Function (DCF): One operational mode in an IEEE 802.11 compliant network in which contention arbitration is performed without a central controller or coordinator.

Duty Cycle: Ratio of the period in which a node is active to the period in which the node is inactive (or sometimes to the sum of active and inactive period durations).

Exposed Terminal: Node or device whose transmission may prevent a potential transmitter from sending the data even though there would be no collision at the receiver.

Fairness: Ability of the network to provide sufficient (and possibly comparable) level of service to all of its nodes.

Frame: Periodic time unit containing one or more packet transmissions and other activities by participants in a communications link; sometimes grouped to form a superframe and sometimes used to designate a packet or, more precisely, any data unit defined by a particular protocol.

Handshake: Exchange of control signals in order to make proper arrangement for subsequent data exchange.

Hidden Terminal: Node or device that is beyond the reach of the transmitter node, but whose transmissions can reach the receiving node and thus cause collision.

Interframe Spacing (IFS): Prescribed time intervals between specific transmissions in an IEEE 802.11-compliant network. Several different IFS intervals exist in the 802.11 standard.

Multihop: Communication between two nodes or devices through one or more intermediary nodes.

Out-of-Band: Separate channel or, in general, any mechanism distinctly different from the regular data channel; often used for the exchange of control information.

Piggybacking: Adding a small amount of extra information to a packet that has a well-defined purpose (e.g., data or control).

Point Coordinator Function (PCF): One operational mode in an IEEE 802.11-compliant network in which one of the nodes acts as a central controller or coordinator.

Polling: Procedure whereby a coordinator node queries other nodes in the network it controls to find out the amount of data they want to transmit and thus allocate bandwidth for those transmissions.

Request-to-Send (RTS): Control packet through which a node that wants to send data informs the designated receiver (and other nodes within its transmission range) about the intended data transmission. The receiver should respond with a CTS packet.

Round-Trip Time: Time interval from the beginning of a data packet transmission to the end of the subsequent acknowledgment packet.

Scalability: Ability of the network to operate without significant changes in performance in a wide range of network sizes.

Scheduling: General procedure of allocating resources (usually time) to different links (and corresponding nodes or devices). Also used to designate the mechanism whereby allocation is performed according to some predefined criteria, including but not limited to the volume and other characteristics of traffic.

Self-Healing: Ability of the network to operate when some of its nodes suddenly cease to function.

Signaling: Generic label for communication wherein only control information is exchanged (as opposed to data transmission).

Single-Hop: Direct communication between two nodes or devices without an intermediary.

Starvation: Situation in which a node has data to transmit but cannot gain access to the medium.

Superframe: Periodic time interval (sometimes referred to as a *cycle*) that contains several smaller units, often designated as *slots* or *slices*.

CROSS REFERENCES

See *Emerging Trends in Routing Protocols in Mobile Wireless Ad Hoc and Sensor Networks; Network Middleware; Network QoS; Principles and Applications of Ad Hoc and Sensor Networks*.

REFERENCES

Achir, M., and L. Ouvry. 2004. Power consumption prediction in wireless sensor networks. In *Proceedings of the Sixteenth ITC Specialist Seminar on Performance Evaluation of Wireless and Mobile Systems*, Aug. 31–Sept. 2, Antwerp, Belgium.

Akan, Ö. B., and I. F. Akyildiz. 2005. ESRT: Event-to-sink reliable transport in wireless sensor networks. *IEEE/ACM Transactions on Networking*, 13(5): 1003–16.

Akyildiz, I. F., W. Su, Y. Sankarasubramaniam, and E. Cayirci. 2002. Wireless sensor networks: A survey. *Computer Networks*, 38: 393–422.

ANSI/IEEE. 1999. *Standard for part 11: Wireless LAN medium access control (MAC) and physical layer (PHY) specifications*. New York: IEEE.

Bahl, P., R. Chandra, and J. Duganan. 2004. SSCH: Slotter seeded channel hopping for capacity improvement in IEEE 802.11 ad-hoc wireless networks. In *Proceedings of the Tenth Annual International Conference on Mobile Computing and Networking* (ACM MobiCom'04), Sept. 26–Oct. 1, Philadelphia, pp. 216–30.

Bao, L., and J. J. Garcia-Luna-Aceves. 2001. A new approach to channel access scheduling for ad hoc networks. In *Proceedings of the Seventh Annual International Conference on Mobile Computing and Networking* (MobiCOM'01), July 16–21, Rome, pp. 210–21.

Bertsekas, D. P., and R. Gallager. 1991. *Data networks*. 2d ed. Englewood Cliffs, NJ: Prentice-Hall.

Bhardwaj, M., and A. Chandrakasan. 2002. Bounding the lifetime of sensor networks via optimal role assignments. In *Proceedings of the Twenty-First Annual Joint Conference of the IEEE Computer and Communications Societies* (IEEE INFOCOM 2002), June 23–7, New York, Vol. 3: 1587–96.

Bharghavan, V., A. Demers, S. Shenker, and L. Zhang. 1994. MACAW: A media access protocol for wireless LANs. In *Proceedings of the Conference on Communications Architectures, Protocols, and Applications* (ACM SIGCOMM '94), Aug. 31–Sept. 2, London, pp. 212–25.

Bluetooth SIG. 2004. Draft specification of the Bluetooth system, version 2.0.

Callaway, E. H. Jr. 2004. *Wireless sensor networks, architecture and protocols*. Boca Raton, FL: Auerbach Publications.

Demirkol, I., C. Ersoy, and F. Alagöz. 2006. MAC protocols for wireless sensor networks: A survey. *IEEE Communications Magazine*, 44(4): 115–21.

Deng, J., and Z. J. Haas. 1998. Dual busy tone multiple access DBTMA: A new medium access control for packet radio networks. In *Proceedings of International Conference on Universal Personal Communications* (IEEE ICUPC 1998), Oct. 5–9, Florence, Italy, pp. 973–7.

Fullmer, C. L., and J. J. Garcia-Luna-Aceves. 1995. Floor acquisition multiple access (FAMA) for packet radio networks. In *Proceedings of the Conference on Applications, Technologies, Architectures, and Protocols for Computer Communications* (ACM SIGCOMM 1995), Aug. 22–6, Philadelphia, pp. 262–73.

Goodman, D. J., R. A. Valenzuela, K. T. Gayliard, and B. Ramamurthi. 1989. Packet reservation multiple access for local wireless communications. *IEEE Transactions on Communications*, 37(8): 885–90.

Heinzelman, W. R., A. Chandrakasan, and H. Balakrishnan. 2000. Energy-efficient communication protocol for wireless microsensor networks. In *Proceedings of the Thirty-Third Annual Hawaii International Conference on System Sciences* (CD-ROM), Jan. 4–7, Maui, HI.

Hill, J., R. Szewczyk, A. Woo, S. Hollar, D. Culler, and K. Pister. 2000. System architecture directions for networked sensors. In Proceedings of the Ninth International Conference on Architectural Support for Programming Languages and Operating Systems, Nov. 12–5, Cambridge, MA, pp. 93–104.

IEEE. 2002. *Standard for part 15.1: Wireless medium access control (MAC) and physical layer (PHY) specifications for wireless personal area networks (WPAN)*. New York: Author.

———. 2003a. *Standard for part 15.3: Wireless medium access control (MAC) and physical layer (PHY) specifications for high rate wireless personal area networks (WPAN)*. New York: Author.

———. 2003b. *Standard for part 15.4: Wireless MAC and PHY specifications for low rate WPAN*. New York: Author.

Intanagonwiwat, C., R. Govindan, and D. Estrin. 2000. Directed diffusion: A scalable and robust communication paradigm for sensor networks. In *Proceedings of the Sixth Annual International Conference on Mobile Computing and Networking* (MobiCOM '00), Aug. 6–11, Boston, pp. 56–67.

Jain, N., S. R. Das, and A. Nasipuri. 2001. A multichannel CSMA MAC protocol with receiver-based channel selection for multihop wireless networks. In *Proceedings of the Tenth International Conference on Computer Communications and Networks* (IC3N), October, Phoenix, pp. 432–9.

Jian, S., J. Rao, D. He, and C. C. Ko. 2002. A simple distributed PRMA for MANETs. *IEEE Transactions on Vehicular Technology*, 51(2): 293–305.

Johansson, N., U. Körner, and L. Tassiulas. 2001. A distributed scheduling algorithm for a Bluetooth scatternet. In *Proceedings of the Seventeenth International Teletraffic Congress* (ITC'17), Sept. 24–8, Salvador da Bahia, Brazil, pp. 61–72.

Jones, C. E., K. M. Sivalingam, P. Agrawal, and J. C. Chen. 2001. A survey of energy efficient network protocols for wireless networks. *Wireless Networks*, 7(4): 343–58.

Jung, E.-S., and N. H. Vaidya. 2005. A power control MAC protocol for ad hoc networks. *Wireless Networks*, 11 (1–2): 55–66.

Kanodia, V., C. Li, A. Sabharwal, B. Sadeghi, and E. Knightly. 2004. Distributed priority scheduling and medium access in ad hoc networks. *Wireless Networks*, 8(5): 455–66.

Karn, P. 1990. MACA: A new channel access method for packet radio. In *Proceedings of the ARRL/CRRL Amateur Radio Computer Networking Conference*, September, pp. 134–40.

Ko, Y. B., V. Shankarkumar, and N. H. Vaidya. 2000. Medium access control protocols using directional antennas in ad hoc networks. In *Proceedings of the IEEE Conference on Computer Communications* (INFOCOM 2000), March 26–7, Tel Aviv. Vol. 1: 13–21.

Korakis, T., G. Jakllari, and L. Tassiulas. 2003. A MAC protocol for full exploitation of directional antennas in ad-hoc wireless networks. In *Proceedings of the Fourth ACM International Symposium on Mobile Ad Hoc Networking and Computing* (MobiHoc'03), June 1–3, Annapolis, MD, pp. 98–107.

Lin, C. R., and M. Gerla. 1999. Real-time support in multihop wireless networks. *Wireless Networks*, 5(2): 125–35.

Mišić, J., and V. B. Mišić. 2005. *Performance modeling and analysis of Bluetooth networks: Network formation, polling, scheduling, and traffic control*. Boca Raton, FL: CRC Press.

Mišić, J., S. Shafi, and V. B. Mišić. 2006. Cross-layer activity management in a 802.15.4 sensor network. *IEEE Communications Magazine*, 44(1): 131–6.

Nasipuri, A., S. Ye, J. You, and R. E. Hiromoto. 2000. A MAC protocol for mobile ad-hoc networks using directional antennas. In *Proceedings of the IEEE Wireless Communications and Networking Conference*, Sept. 23–8, Chicago. Vol. 1: 1214–9.

Nasipuri, A., J. Zhuang, and S. R. Das. 1999. A multichannel CSMA MAC protocol for multihop wireless networks. In *Proceedings of the IEEE Wireless Communications and Networking Conference*, September, New Orleans, pp. 1402–6.

O'Hara, B., and A. Petrick. 1999. *IEEE 802.11 handbook: A designer's companion*. New York: IEEE Press.

Perkins, C. E., ed. 2001. *Ad hoc networking*. Boston: Addison-Wesley.

Polastre, J., J. Hill, and D. Culler. 2004. Versatile low power media access for wireless sensor networks. In *Proceedings of the International Conference on Embedded Networked Sensor Systems* (SenSys'04), Nov. 3–5, Baltimore, pp. 95–107.

Rajendran, V., K. Obraczka, and J. J. Garcia-Luna-Aceves. 2006. Energy-efficient, collision- free medium access control for wireless sensor networks. *Wireless Networks*, 12(1): 63–78.

Ram Murthy, C. and B. Manoj. 2004. *Ad hoc wireless networks, architecture and protocols*. Upper Saddle River, NJ: Prentice Hall.

Rhee, I., A. Warrier, M. Aia, and J. Min. 2005. Z-MAC: A hybrid MAC for wireless sensor networks. In *Proceedings of the International Conference on Embedded Networked Sensor Systems* (SenSys'05), Nov. 2–4, San Diego, pp. 90–101.

Sanchez, J., R. Martinez, R. and M. W. Marcellin. 1997. A survey of MAC protocols proposed for wireless ATM. *IEEE Network*, 11(6): 52–62.

Shi, J., T. Salonidis, and E. W. Knightly. 2006. Starvation mitigation through multi-channel coordination in CSMA multi-hop wireless networks. In *Proceedings of the Seventh ACM International Symposium on Mobile Ad Hoc Networking and Computing* (MobiHoc'06), May 22–5, Florence, Italy, pp. 214–25.

Singh, S., and Raghavendra, C. S. 1998. PAMAS: Power aware multi-access protocol with signaling for ad hoc networks. *ACM SIGCOMM Computer Communications Review*, 28(3): 5–26.

Sohrabi, K., J. Gao, V. Ailawadhi, and G. J. Pottie. 2000. Protocols for self-organization of a wireless sensor network. *IEEE Personal Communications*, 7(5): 16–27.

Stallings, W. 2002. *Wireless communications and networks.* Upper Saddle River, NJ: Prentice Hall.

Stemm, M., and R. H. Katz. 1997. Measuring and reducing energy consumption of network interfaces in hand-held devices. *IEICE Transactions on Communications: Special Issue on Mobile Computing*, E80-B(8): 1125–31.

Talluci, F., M. Gerla, and L. Fratta. 1997. MACA-BI (MACA by invitation): A wireless MAC protocol for high speed ad hoc networking. In *Proceedings of the IEEE Sixth International Conference on Universal Personal Communications* (ICUPC 1997), Oct. 12–6, San Diego, pp. 913–7.

Tang, Z., and J. J. Garcia-Luna-Aceves. 1999a. Hop-reservation multiple access (HRMA) for ad hoc networks. In *Proceedings of the Conference on Computer Communications* (IEEE INFOCOM 1999), March, New York, pp. 194–201.

———. 1999b. A protocol for topology-dependent transmission scheduling in wireless networks. In *Proceedings of the Wireless Communications and Networking Conference* (IEEE WCNC 1999), Sept. 21–4, New Orleans, pp. 1333–37.

Tobagi, F. A., and L. Kleinrock. 1975. Packet switching in radio channels: Part II—The hidden terminal problem in carrier sense multiple access and busy tone solution. *IEEE Transactions on Communications*, pp. 1417–33.

Toh, C.-K. 2002. *Ad hoc mobile wireless networks: Protocols and systems*. Upper Saddle River, NJ: Prentice-Hall PTR.

———, V. Vassiliou, G. Guichal, and C. H. Shih. 2000. MARCH: A medium access control protocol or multihop wireless ad hoc networks. In *Proceedings of the Twenty-First Century Military Communications Conference* (IEEE MILCOM 2000), October, Los Angeles. Vol. 1: 512–6.

Trigoni, N., Y. Yao, A. Demers, J. Gehrke, and R. Rajaraman. 2004. WaveScheduling: Energy-efficient data dissemination for sensor networks. In *Proceedings of the First Workshop on Data Management for Sensor Networks* (DMSN'04), Aug. 30, Toronto, pp. 48–57.

Van Dam, T., and K. Langendoen. 2003. An adaptive energy-efficient MAC protocol for wireless sensor networks. In *Proceedings of the Conference on Embedded Networked Sensor Systems* (ACM SenSys'03), Oct. 15, Los Angeles, pp. 171–80.

Woo, A., and D. Culler. 2001. A transmission control scheme for media access in sensor networks. In *Proceedings of the Seventh Annual International Conference on Mobile Computing and Networking* (MobiCOM'01), July 16–21, Rome, pp. 201–35.

Wu, C., and V. O. K. Li. 1987. Receiver initiated busy tone multiple access in packet radio networks. In *Proceedings of the ACM Workshop on Frontiers in Computer Communications Technology* (ACM SIGCOMM'87 Workshop), Aug. 11–13, Stowe, VT, Vol. 17(5): 336–42.

Ye, W., J. Heidemann, and D. Estrin. 2004. Medium access control with coordinated adaptive sleeping for wireless sensor networks. *ACM/IEEE Transactions on Networking*, 12(3): 493–506.

Xu, Y., J. Heidemann, and D. Estrin. 2001. Geography-informed energy conservation for ad hoc routing. In *Proceedings of the Seventh Annual International Conference on Mobile Computing and Networking* (MobiCOM'01), July 16–21, Rome, pp. 70–84.

Emerging Trends in Routing Protocols in Mobile Wireless Ad Hoc and Sensor Networks

Jamal N. Al-Karaki, *The Hashemite University, Jordan*

INTRODUCTION

Wireless communication and networking technology is rapidly developing and evolving. In general, a wireless network can be an infrastructured or infrastructure-less (ad hoc) network. In an infrastructured wireless network, fixed and wired gateways are used to connect mobile users. In ad hoc networks, all nodes are mobile and can be connected dynamically in an arbitrary manner. All nodes of these networks can act as routers and take part in discovery and maintenance of routes to other nodes in the network. This improves network flexibility and lowers the cost of establishing wireless networks. Mobile ad hoc networks (MANETs) and wireless sensor networks (WSNs) are two prominent classes of ad hoc networks. MANETs exhibit high mobility patterns, whereas WSNs suffer from limited and unreplenishable energy sources. A WSN is composed of a large number of sensor nodes that are densely deployed either inside the phenomenon or very close to it (Akyildiz et al. 2002). The position of the nodes need not be engineered or predetermined; hence, random deployment in inaccessible areas is possible. Applications involving MANETs and WSNs are of a wide variety, including emergency response information, energy management, medical monitoring, logistics and inventory management, battlefield management, home security, machine failure diagnosis, and chemical or biological detection (Akyildiz et al. 2002).

As a result of the mobility characteristic of MANETs, the topology of the network is continuously changing. Moreover, the link weight and capacity are not stable because of many parameters such as noise, fading, power, and interference. On the other hand, the traditional wired networks have a topology that rarely changes and has stable bandwidth and low error rates. Hence, routing in wireless environments is a challenging problem that has motivated many researchers to develop both general-purpose and problem-specific routing protocols (Royer and Toh 1999). Overall, a routing scheme for MANETs and WSNs can fall within many categories, as depicted in Figure 1(a). Note that the categories in the figure overlap one another; a set of protocols can also be divided into different categories. Another look at the classes of protocols in Figure 1(a) would result in another classification with respect to WSNs—as shown in Figure 1(b), for example.

The rest of this chapter is organized as follows. In the following section, the routing challenges in both MANETs and WSNs are discussed in detail. Next, we present a detailed classification of routing protocols in MANETs, followed by another detailed classification of routing protocols in WSNs. The final section outlines the future challenges of routing in mobile ad hoc and sensor networks.

ROUTING CHALLENGES IN MOBILE AD HOC AND SENSOR NETWORKS

Several technical challenges face the design of efficient routing protocols in MANETs. Many of these challenges are applicable to both MANETs and WSNs, especially those related to the constantly changing network topology due to node mobility in MANETs and node failure in WSNs, the limited bandwidth of a shared wireless medium, and the limited power capacity. However, there are some challenges that are specific to either MANETs or WSNs (see Akyildiz et al. [2002] for a list of differences between MANETs and WSNs). Therefore, some the routing protocols surveyed in this chapter apply to general ad hoc networks, and others are specific either to MANETs or to WSNs. The routing protocols attempt to overcome various difficulties that prevent the wide deployment of

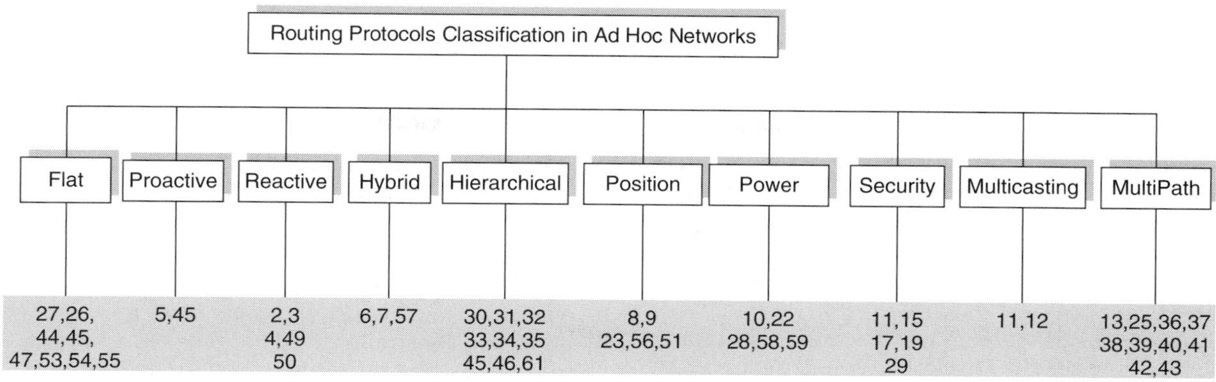

Figure 1(a): Routing protocols in MANETs and WSNs

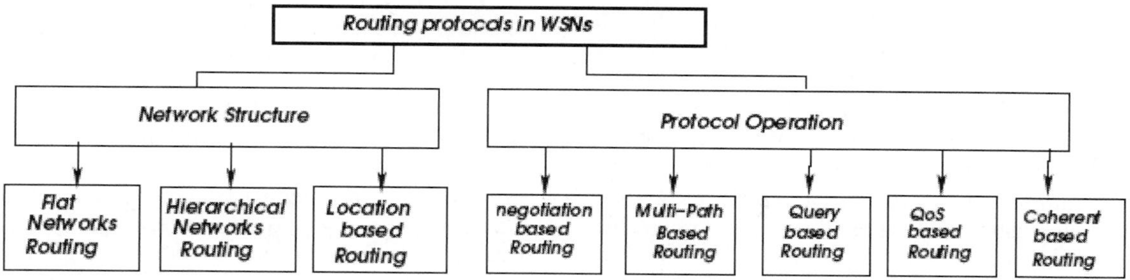

Figure 1(b): Routing protocols in WSNs—Another perspective (Al-Karaki and Kamal 2004)

MANETs and WSNs. These difficulties are a result of the following challenges:

1. *Challenges due to the dynamic topology:* The issue of mobility does not exist in fixed networks. Even in infrastructured wireless networks, the mobile nodes move from the domain of one access point to the domain of another access point. In MANETs, there is a high possibility that the topology may vary at a fast rate. The complications imposed by mobility in MANETs may severely degrade the network quality. The frequent route breakage is a natural consequence of mobility, which complicates routing. Such topological dynamics are further complicated by the natural grouping behavior in a mobile user's movement, which leads to frequent network partitioning. Network partitioning poses significant challenges to the design of routing protocols and complicates connection establishment at large. The topology in WSNs may vary as a result of node death; thus, connectivity will vary as well. That is, the malfunctioning of a few nodes can cause significant topological changes and might require rerouting of packets and reorganization of the whole network.
2. *Challenges due to the scarce resources:* The wireless spectrum is a limited resource that must be utilized efficiently. In addition, the wireless medium is a shared medium in which signal attenuation, interference, multipath propagation effects (e.g., fading), and the unguided nature of the transmitted wave all contribute to wasting the bandwidth resource. Effective management of this resource is a key factor in routing in both MANETs and WSNs.
3. *Challenges due to the absence of communication infrastructure:* Standard networks use an infrastructure. In MANETs and WSNs, there is no preexisting infrastructure or default router; every mobile node should be able to act as a router and forward packets to other nodes. Therefore, a routing protocol must consider the self-creating and self-organizing features of MANETs.
4. *Challenges due to power limitations:* The nodes in an ad hoc wireless network are typically powered by batteries with a limited energy supply. Solutions that reduce power consumption will often be favored, all other factors being equal. An important and challenging issue in ad hoc wireless networks is how to conserve energy, maximizing the lifetime of nodes and thus of the network itself. Because routing is an essential function in these networks, developing power-aware routing protocols for ad hoc wireless networks has been an intensive research area in recent years. Mobile nodes need to use their battery-limited power supply in a manner that prolongs the lifetime of the battery. If the battery power is used blindly, mobile nodes or sensor nodes will fail quickly, and this affects the network availability and functionality. Power-aware routing schemes, therefore, are designed to provide solutions for this problem.
5. *Challenges due to heterogeneous nodes and networks:* Mobile nodes can be heterogeneous, thus enabling an assortment of different types of links to be part of the same ad hoc network. MANETs are typically heterogeneous networks with various types of mobile nodes. The same issue arises when sensor nodes are equipped with batteries that have variable capabilities. Dealing with node heterogeneity is a key factor for the successful operation of routing protocols for heterogeneous MANETs.

6. *Challenges due to link quality:* The problem of link quality is particularly significant in MANETs and WSNs. The essential effect on MANETs is that the link quality can become extremely variable, often in a random manner. Although some parts of this effect can be predicted because variations in link quality impact packet delivery and trigger error-recovery procedures, many parameters such as bandwidth availability, latency, reliability, and jitter are affected. As a result, the link becomes unreliable, and this affects routing protocols.
7. *Challenges due to other layers:* Because of the direct coupling between the physical layer and the upper layers, the traditional protocol stack is not sufficient for wireless networks. Cross-layer design methodology, in which the information is exchanged between different protocol layers dynamically, is an active research area to improve wireless network performance. In a wireless network, the physical layer, media access control (MAC) layer, and routing layer all contend for the network resource. The physical layer affects MAC and routing decisions with its transmission power and rate.
8. *Challenges due to lack of centralized control:* In MANETs and WSNs, distributed algorithms are preferable because of the lack of a central entity.
9. *Transmission media:* In a multihop ad hoc network, communicating nodes are linked by a wireless medium. Each node has a limited transmission range; hence, routing is multihop in general. This imposes new requirements of node roles and the necessity of node cooperation. In a multihop ad hoc sensor network, each node plays the dual role of data originator and data router.

All of these challenges apply to both MANETs and WSNs. Certain challenges are particular to WSNs—for example, energy, computation, and communication resources. The wireless sensor node can be equipped with a limited power source that can be used to perform computations and transmit information. As such, WSN shows a strong dependence on battery lifetime. Some sensor nodes may fail or be blocked because of a lack of power, physical damage, or environmental interference. The failure of sensor nodes should not affect the overall task of the sensor network. Hence, energy-conserving forms of communication and computation are essential. Furthermore, sensors have limited computing power and therefore may not be able to run sophisticated routing protocols. The number of sensor nodes deployed in studying a phenomenon may be in the order of hundreds or thousands; depending on the application, the number of nodes can be even greater. New schemes must be able to work with this many nodes. A sensor node made up of many hardware components should be smaller than a cubic centimeter, consume extremely low power, operate unattended, operate in high volumetric densities, have low production cost, and adapt to the environment.

In the next two sections, we review the efforts that have been exerted in the area of routing in both MANETs and WSNs—in particular, fostering new routing attempts. These efforts attempt to overcome, or at least circumvent, the aforementioned challenges to provide possible solutions to the routing problems in these networks.

ROUTING PROTOCOLS IN MOBILE AD HOC NETWORKS

This section presents a survey of the recent advances in routing protocols in MANETs. In fact, the focus of the routing protocols in MANETs spans a wide variety of topics. In particular, quality of service (QoS), power efficiency, and security mechanisms are some of the important constraints in ad hoc networks. At times, many parameters are integrated together to guarantee optimum performance with minimum overhead. It is worth noting that several studies address the routing issue in ad hoc networks along certain dimensions (Wang et al. 2000; Chaudhry et al. 2005; Higaki and Umeshima 2004; Lee et al. 2005; Wang and Olariu 2004; Ducatelle, Gianni, and Maria 2005; Nanda and Gray 2004; Lu and Feng 2005; Subramanian et al. 2004; Mao et al. 2003; Guven et al. 2005; Hong, Xu, and Gerla 2002; Hollick et al. 2004). This chapter aims to modernize and encapsulate the previous studies in a comprehensive manner. Many routing protocols have been proposed in recent years for MANETs. Traditionally, these protocols have been classified as being on-demand or table-driven–based routing protocols. Many of these protocols—for example, dynamic source routing (DSR; Johnson and Maltz 1996) and ad hoc on demand vector (AODV; Perkins, Royer, and Das 1999)—commonly use minimum hop counts as metric to find routes, operating under the assumption that a link that is good for the route discovery process is still good for data packets, and that the link quality is either good or bad. In De Couto et al. (2002), experimental evidence showed that using minimum hop count as a metric often leads to less capacity than the existing best paths, because the link quality is spread out, some links are asymmetric, and link quality varies over time. Additionally, many of the proposed protocols are dependent on either the distance vector or link-state routing algorithms. However, some protocols opt to minimize processing overhead, topology maintenance, and loop prevention.

Flat Routing Protocols

In flat networks, all nodes play the same role. In flat routing, the next hop that a mobile node will take to the destination is a physical next hop of this node. In Draves, Padhye, and Zill (2004a), multi-radio link-quality source routing (MR-LQSR) routing protocol for multihop wireless network is proposed. In this protocol, most of the nodes equipped with multiple radios are either stationary or minimally mobile. MR-LQSR is a combination of the LQSR protocol (Draves, Padhye, and Zill 2004b) and a routing metric weighted cumulative expected transmission time (WCETT). The weight is used to select the radio that has the best transmission time among the available links.

However, flat routing will cause performance degradation in large ad hoc networks for several reasons. First, the route hop count will be higher in a large-scale network, causing more route breakage and end-to-end delay. Second, the overhead introduced by the routing protocol can consume more network capacity. Third, the routing information about remote nodes can be inaccurate as a result of the long transmission time.

Reactive or On-Demand Routing Protocols

On-demand routing protocols typically search for a route only when needed. They normally operate on flat as well as hierarchical architectures. Moreover, they are widely used in multipath routing protocols because they can recover from route changes more efficiently than other protocols. The multipath source routing (MSR; Wang et al. 2000) protocol provides an example of such protocols. MSR is an extension of DSR in which all of the discovered paths are stored in a route cache with a unique route index in a process called *path finding*. In this algorithm, the routing loops can be easily detected and eliminated. In MSR, the route is determined by the source and intermediate nodes only forward the packets (see Figure 2).

As a result, the computation complexity is limited in the source nodes. It has been found that the throughput and end-to-end delay are improved using the MSR instead of DSR. However, the main drawback of this protocol is the processing overload of originating the packets.

Another on-demand protocol is the ad hoc on-demand multipath distance vector (AOMDV; Chaudhry et al. 2005) protocol, which uses the traditional single path routing protocol—ad hoc on-demand distance vector (AODV) protocol—to generate multiple paths. AOMDV reduces the delay up to 20 percent and also reduces the frequencies of route discovery. AODV determines the path of the route only when the source node needs to send data. The mobile intermediate nodes keep track of neighbors by sending hello messages and determine the validity of routes by setting timers. When the link is broken, an error message is sent to the source node to delete the broken link entry. The AODV mechanism is shown in Figure 3.

Another on-demand routing protocol is multiple route AODV (MRAODV; Higaki and Umeshima 2004). MRAODV confronts the mobility nature of ad hoc networks by finding multipaths to send data between a pair of source/destination nodes. In MRAODV, separated reverse path fragments are connected to achieve additional routes. According to simulation results, more additional routes are detected in this protocol than in other protocols. Figure 3 shows the operation of the protocol in a high-level perspective in which the source node can reach the destination node using multiple paths. Note that, when a path is broken, an error message is used to notify the sender of route invalidity.

Proactive Routing Protocols

This set of protocols keeps track of route updates between different nodes at all times. It also monitors the changes in network topology and thus guarantees that the destination node will be reachable. Proactive protocols distinguish themselves from the reactive ones with

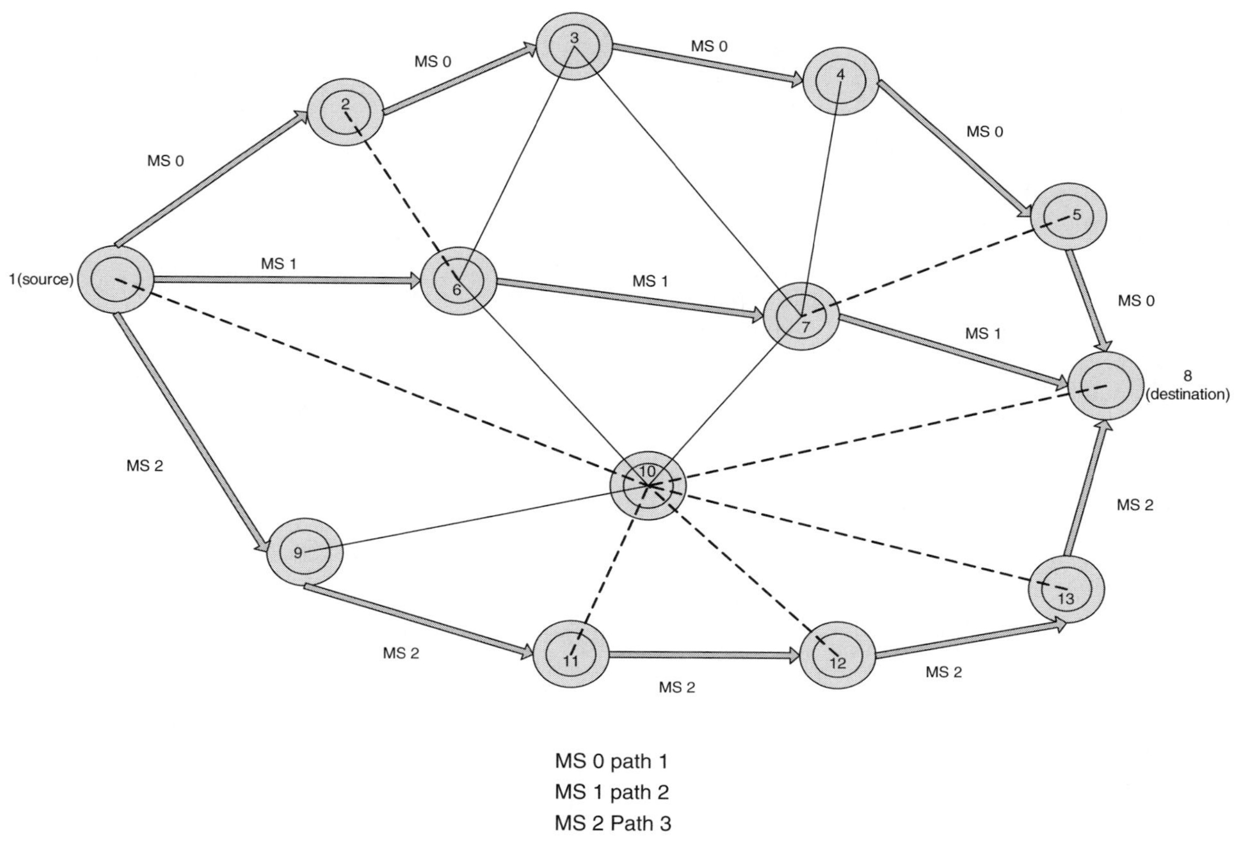

Figure 2: The MSR routing protocol operation

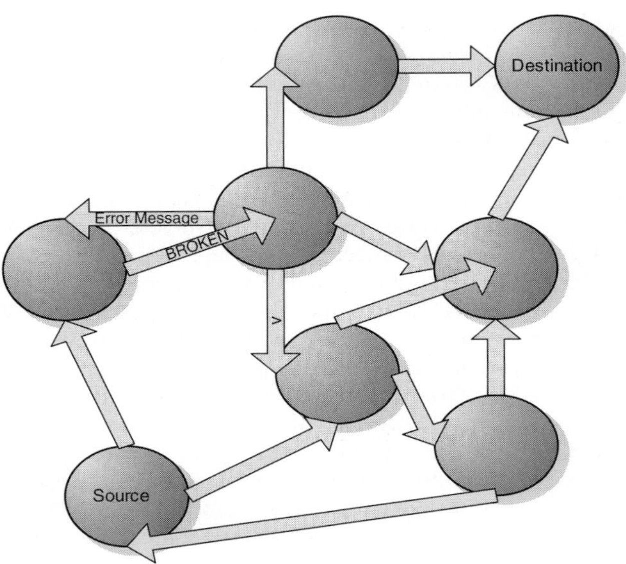

Figure 3: AODV routing mechanism

the ability to recover from broken routes in a short time by always keeping an image of network topology. However, the proactive protocols may incur high overhead in order to maintain up-to-date images of the network topology and may also result in latency in receiving valid routing information.

The traditional destination sequenced distance vector (DSDV) is an example of such protocols, in which every routing node stores a routing table to all destinations. Nodes periodically update the routing tables by sending either the full routing table or simply the new changes in the network topology. To improve the performance of the DSDV, a new routing protocol that utilizes multiple channels was proposed in Lee et al. (2005). A DSDV with multi-channels (DSDV-MC) uses multiple channels to obtain the use of alternative paths and thus increase capacity and recover from errors immediately. Moreover, the protocol uses one channel for control messages and another channel for user data to avoid the inefficiency of bandwidth utilization from routing table update messages. Results have shown that DSDV-MC enhances the traditional DSDV by lowering the packet drop rate. To avoid inefficiencies from periodic updates in the proactive routing protocol, the proposed scheme divides the network layer into control and data planes. Nodes send routing updates using the control channel and user packets using the data channel. Simulation results indicate that DSDV-MC exploits multiple channels to improve network capacity.

Hybrid Routing Protocols

This type of protocol incorporates the functionality of both the on-demand routing algorithms and the proactive ones. Hence, the performance of the protocol is expected to outperform that of the two previously mentioned protocol types. The traditional zone routing protocol (ZRP) is an example of such protocols. ZRP is locally proactive and globally reactive; each node in the architecture behaves as both a cluster head and a member of other clusters at the same time. The goal of ZRP is to minimize the sum of the proactive and reactive control overhead. The key idea of ZRP is that each node proactively advertises its link state over a fixed number of hops, called the zone radius. The nodes on the boundary of the routing zone are called *peripheral nodes* and play an important role in the reactive zone-based route discovery. One of the drawbacks of the ZRP algorithm is that more memory is required because of the hierarchal structure of the algorithm, which does not exist in the proactive or on-demand routing algorithms. An enhancement over ZRP is the two-zone routing protocol (TZRP; Wang and Olariu 2004), a hybrid routing protocol in which a single zone serves a dual purpose. Specifically, TZRP aims to decouple the protocol's ability to adapt to traffic characteristics from its ability to adapt to mobility. To do that, each node maintains two zones: a crisp zone and a fuzzy zone. By adjusting the sizes of these two zones independently, a lower total routing control overhead can be achieved.

Another hybrid routing algorithm is ant agent for hybrid multipath routing in mobile ad hoc networks (AntHocNet; Ducatelle, Gianni, and Maria 2005), in which the route setup of this scheme is performed by an on-demand algorithm and the route exploration is done via proactive scheme. This protocol is built on top of an ant colony optimization (ACO) framework. It has been observed that ants can converge to the shortest path between the nest and the food source, thereby eliminating all other paths. This was the main idea of AntHocNet. To apply the concept of ACO, each node in MANET generates ants to the desired destination. While the ants are moving, they collect information about the path such as the number of hops, connection quality, and round-trip time. When it reaches the destination food source, it returns back to the source and modifies the routing table of the intermediate nodes. The routing tables at each node contain all possible paths to the desired destination with a value that indicates the quality of the link. This value is modified periodically by the ants on their way back to the nest. The modified values are used to select multiple paths for both ants and data. Following this approach, path quality value is modified periodically, the routing decision is done locally, and data can be sent via several paths to enable load balancing. However, drawbacks include relatively large amounts of overhead as well as reduced adaptability to the network situation.

Virtual backbone routing (VBR) is proposed in Liang and Haas (2006). It combines both local proactive and global reactive routing over a variable-sized zone hierarchy. It is a scalable routing protocol that utilizes the idea of selective representation of topology details, in which each node maintains routing information about close links only, and the initiated route queries need not reach the far nodes. The VB is constructed from nodes selected dynamically during the network lifetime and is refreshed through a distributed database coverage heuristic (DDCH). Each node within the VB serves as a database that is queried by source nodes to get information about all links within the database zone. DDCH is a distributed algorithm to generate VB. Initially, nodes are not connected to any database; they are in the *panic state*. Each node that has the maximum dependency number within its zone (i.e., the maximum number of panic nodes, including the node itself) joins the current VB. VBR construct routes based on the least number of hops criteria.

Geographic Position-Assisted Protocols

This set of routing protocols uses the position information to select the best route that can minimize power, overhead, and latency (Mauve, Widmer, and Hartenstein 2001). The multipath location-aided routing (MLAR; Nanda and Gray 2004) is an example of such protocols. MLAR use 3-D positional information, particularly a hybrid extension to the well-known LAR and GRID that works in 3-D. MLAR is a hybrid algorithm that uses multipath routing (alternate path caching) in 3-D. Specifically, MLAR replaces LAR with multipath LAR in GRID. MLAR shows better efficiency and scalability than LAR, AODV, and AOMDV in both 2-D and 3-D.

Predictive mobility and location-aware routing protocol (PMLAR; Lu and Feng 2005) is another type of protocol that includes mobility behavior in the design of the protocol, as well as a prediction mechanism of the destination node. The region for packet forwarding is determined by predicting the future trajectory of the destination node. The routing performance can be effectively improved by adopting the prediction mechanism of the proposed PMLAR algorithm. The operation of PMLAR includes three phases: location service, route discovery, and route maintenance. When a source node *S* intends to transmit data packets to the destination node *D*, it needs to know the position of the destination node. Node *S* activates a location service to obtain the position information of *D*. Figure 4 demonstrates the location predication of PMLAR. As the figure shows, node *S* will initiate a flooding process to send out the request packet to obtain *D*'s position information. Following rebroadcast by the intermediate node, the destination node *D* is informed that a position request has been initiated by *S*. Node *D* will start the prediction mechanism to compute the radius of a predicted zone. Then it sends back to node S the position, time stamp, and velocity of node *D*.

After it receives the position information of node *D*, source node *S* sends a route request (RREQ) message to initiate the route discovery process. The selection of a forwarding node, denoted by node N_i in the figure, is confined within the request zone, which is a rectangular region defined by the predicted zone as shown in Figure 4. Following receipt of the RREQ packet from *S*, N_i will verify whether it is located within the request zone. If the criterion is satisfied, N_i will record itself on the routing information within the RREQ packet header and rebroadcast the packet to the next node N_i. The process continues until node *D* is reached, upon which *D* will send out the route reply (RREP) packet to the source node *S* via the reverse route. Simulation results show that the PMLAR algorithm outperforms other routing protocols under different network topologies.

The adaptive cell relay (ACR) routing protocol is presented in Du and Wu (2006). ACR targets MANETs that have a varied density. It divides the routing area into square cells in which each cell contains one node. ACR combines three techniques to get a scalable, low-delay, and energy-aware routing protocol. These techniques are: cell relay (CR) routing for dense networks, large cell (LC) routing for sparse networks, and an adaptive scheme to detect network density changes to select the suitable routing technique. CR is an on-demand protocol based on source routing in which the source records all of the cells that lie on the direct line drawn between the source and the destination cells. Next, a route request packet from the source will be flooded to the recorded cells until

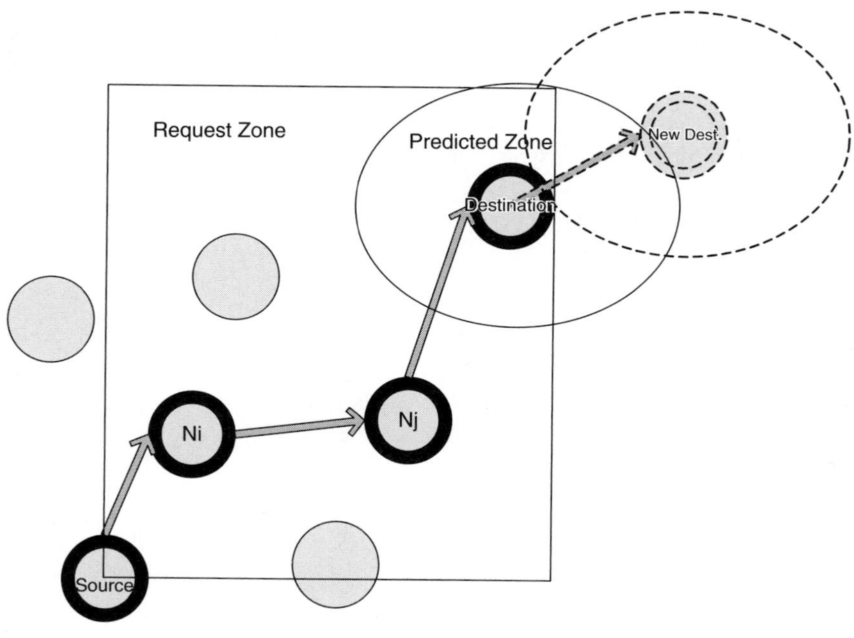

Figure 4: Location prediction in PMLAR

it reaches the destination. At that time, the destination will reply with a route reply packet so the source will know that a route exists. LC works in the same way as CR; the only exception is that the cell size is larger to reduce the probability of empty cells. To detect the density changes within the network, an adaptive head (AH) is selected. The AH stores the node count and the routing area boundary to calculate the density. The AH also receives a density change message from new nodes, nodes that have one of its neighbors die, or nodes that have moved outside of the network boundary. The AH adjusts the node count accordingly. ACR also features a technique that can detect when the network boundary shrinks. Based on the density changes, AH will flood a strategy change message to select the suitable routing technique.

Power-Aware Routing Protocols

Many power-aware routing protocols have been proposed from a variety of perspectives (Li, Cordes, and Zhang 2005). As stated earlier, although energy efficiency is important in MANETs, it is considered more important in WSNs. In general, power consumption depends on the position and the role of the node. For example, the cluster head in hierarchical protocols consumes more power than other nodes because they generate and route data continuously.

In Li, Cordes, and Zhang (2005), a survey of a number of energy-aware routing protocols in wireless ad hoc networks was performed. The routing protocols were broadly divided into five categories: active energy-saving protocols, passive energy-saving protocols, network lifetime maximizing protocols, topology control protocols, and energy-efficient multicasting and broadcasting protocols (see Figure 5). Li, Cordes, and Zhang provided a set of energy-aware protocols and comparisons between these protocols.

The multipath power-sensitive routing protocol (MPSR; Subramanian et al. 2004) is an example of power-aware routing protocols in which the objective is to improve the mean time to node failure and minimize the energy variance between different nodes. In MPSR, the routing function constructs the routing tables depending on the remaining power of the nodes. A node will forward the packet to the path that will consume the minimum power. A maximum number of paths can be stored in the node; if no path is found, the node must initiate a route discovery process in which request messages are flooded in the network. Each node adds its remaining power and address to the route request message. When the message reaches the destination node, it calculates the average power and sends a reply message back to the source node including all nodes power and addresses that passed by it. Figure 6 shows the format of the message just described, in which node A is sending through a series of nodes (i.e., B, C, etc.) to the destination node. Simulation results show that MPSR works better than DSR in high-mobility circumstances with less packet loss rate.

In MPSR, every node in the network is treated equally, and the overall network is stable for a long time. Another interesting feature of MPSR is that the end-to-end packet delay does not increase significantly. Simulation results show that the performance of MPSR protocol outperforms traditional dynamic source routing.

Multicasting Protocols

The increase in the number of multicast applications in the wireless environment is considered the main motivation for developing the ad hoc multicast protocols. Multipath multicast routing algorithm (MRPM; Mao et al. 2003) is an example of such protocols in which the algorithm chooses the next hop based on cost factors. Another multicast protocol used in real-time applications and media streaming is the multipath real-time transport protocol (MRTP; Guven et al. 2005). This protocol is based on the real-time transport protocol (RTP) and the real-time transport control protocol (RTCP), which complete each other in end-to-end data streaming applications such as video and audio conferencing. The multiobjective multipath routing algorithm for multicast flows (MMRAM) is yet another multicast protocol. Multiple paths usually exist

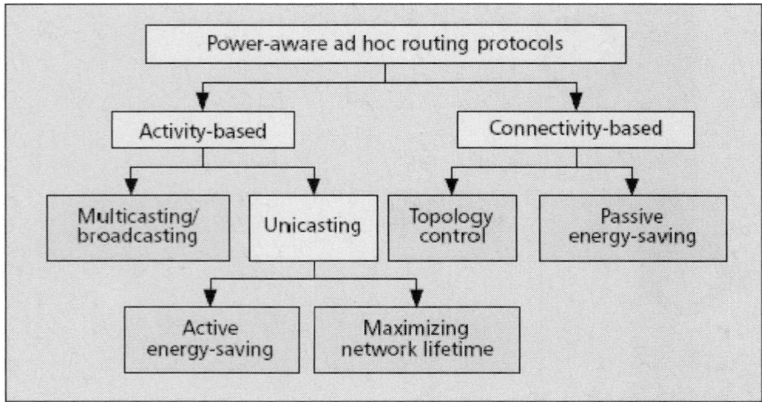

Figure 5: Categorization of power-aware ad hoc routing protocols

Addr A	P_A	Addr B	P_B	Addr C	P_C	Addr D	P_D	....

Figure 6: Remaining power request/reply message

between any source and destination nodes. Such path diversity has been demonstrated to be effective in combating congestion and link failures for improved media quality. The multipath real-time transport protocol (MRTP) provides a convenient vehicle for real-time applications to partition and transmit data using multiple flows. It has been shown that, with one additional path, MRTP outperformed single-flow RTP by a significant margin. More simulation results were presented to demonstrate multicasting capabilities of MRTP.

Security Routing Protocols

The need for a secure end-to-end connection in wireless networks is of great interest; hence, many protocols were proposed to accomplish this task (Argyroudis and O'Mahony 2005; Yih-Chun and Perrig 2004). Multipath TCP security (MTS; Mao et al. 2003) is one such protocol in which the source node adaptively chooses the available route instead of testing the stored routes one by one. Therefore, the route of the TCP session is not fixed but changes continuously. The source uses route discovery to initiate multiple paths and the destination, and at the same time sends check packets to make sure that the route path is still alive. Hence, the source node has many route options from which to select the most secure path among them (Niculescu 2005).

The route discovery process described in earlier sections sends request messages to the network in which each message includes the packet type field, source address, destination address, broadcast ID, and hop count. The broadcast ID is incremented each time by one. When the message propagates, each node stores the message, increases the hop count, inserts its own address, and forwards it to the neighboring nodes. It is possible for the intermediate node to receive several copies of the same request, so the node stores the broadcast ID to eliminate duplicate copies. When the request reaches the destination node, it stores the messages and unicasts a reply message (that includes a reply ID instead of a broadcast ID) to the source node following the same path. Figure 7(a) shows the route request mechanism and Figure 7(b) shows the route reply.

This protocol was found to offer good performance and security. However, when the node movement speed increases, MTS delay increases significantly. Another method to secure the data is by dividing it into several chunks and then forwarding it to different paths. This method will secure confidentiality and reduce the chance of eavesdropping. At the same time, this will increase the collision among the paths and hence decrease the packet delivery ratio.

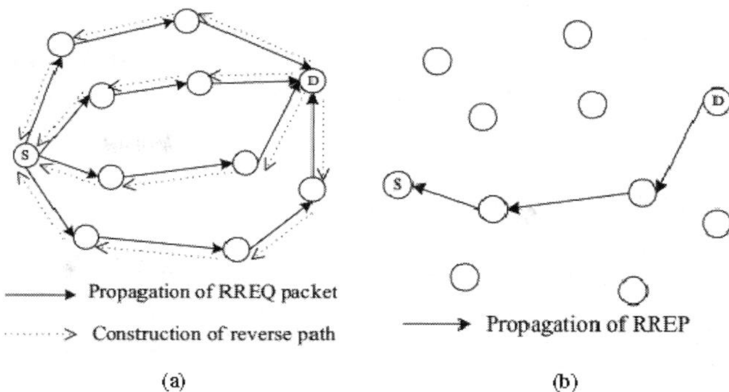

Figure 7: (a) Route request broadcast (b) Route reply unicast

Many of the routing protocols for ad hoc networks were designed with no attention to security issues. Ad hoc networks are generally vulnerable to internal and external attacks. For example, the two well-known protocols DSR and AODV suffer from nay security issues. In particular, redirection by modifying route sequence numbers or route direction is one such attack in AODV. Figure 8 presents an example in which an attacker is able to route data to himself from node B. Tunneling is another attack in which the attackers use a direct virtual channel among them as though they are adjacent to each other physically. The main idea of this attack is shown in Figure 9.

There are other attacks that generate false routing information to mislead the routing nodes. The *falsifying route errors attack* is an example in which some protocols, such as the DSR, depend heavily on the routing error messages to discover and maintain the paths between the source and destination. Table 1 summarizes the vulnerability of the DSR and AODV protocols to the previously mentioned attacks.

Solutions to the different previously mentioned attacks vary depending on the attack type and the network

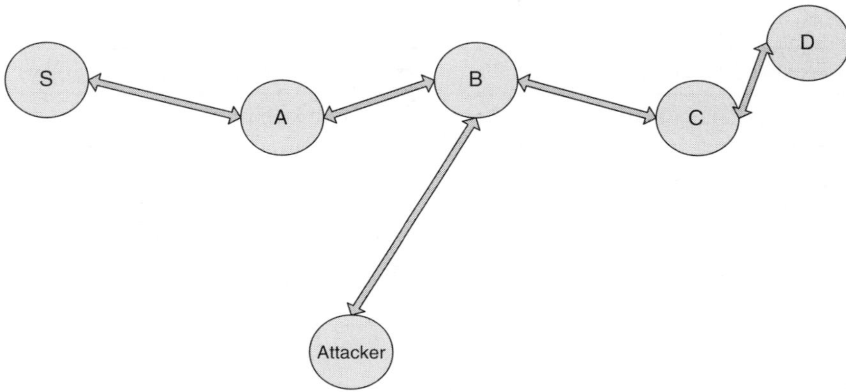

Figure 8: General network topology

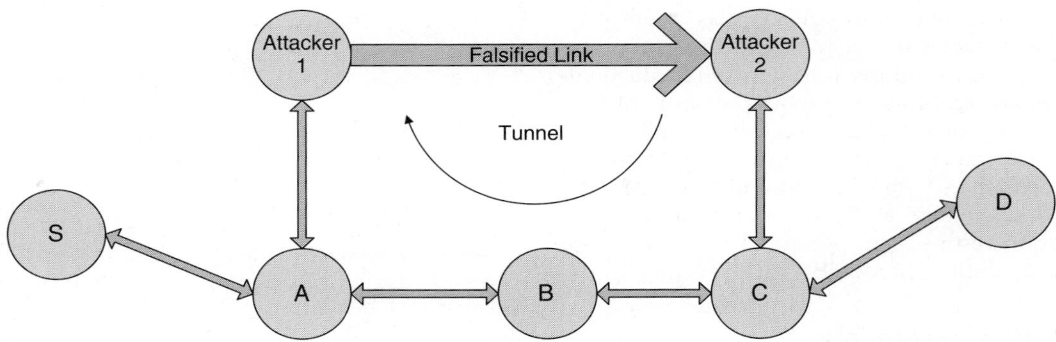

Figure 9: Tunneling attack

Table 1: Vulnerability of AODV and DSR

Type of Attack	AODV	DSR
Modify route sequence number	Yes	No
Modify hop count	Yes	No
Modify source route	No	Yes
Tunneling	Yes	Yes
Spoofing	Yes	Yes
Falsifying route errors	Yes	Yes
Broadcast falsified routes	No	Yes
Rushing attack	Yes	Yes

topology and metrics. Authentication during all routing phases is one of the proposed solutions. The trust-level metric is another proposed solution that mirrors the minimum trust value required by the sender. The trust level is embedded in the control messages, and nodes will not process the incoming packet unless it passes certain predefined trust levels. Security-aware routing (SAR), which is a modification of the AODV based on the security level described, is an example of such protocols. However, this approach better determines the trust level in hierarchal topologies and requires more support (e.g., authentication) in other topologies.

Secure neighbor verification is one of the proposed solutions to checking the identity of neighboring nodes. It consists of a three-round message exchange between two nodes; they are considered neighbors if they exchange the messages successfully. If they do not, the two nodes are not physically neighbors because of the effect of one of the previously mentioned attacks. The main drawback of this approach is the increase in overhead when mobility increases.

Randomized message forwarding is used to minimize the effect of the rushing attack described previously. In this solution, the node selects one of the incoming RREQ packets randomly instead of forwarding the first received request immediately. With this approach, the probability of forwarding the vulnerable request decreases as the number of queued requests in each node increases. However, there is a trade-off between the number of queued nodes, increasing security, and increasing the overhead in the network. Table 2 summarizes the previously mentioned solutions.

A survey of secure ad hoc routing protocols for mobile wireless networks is presented in Patroklos, Argyroudis, and O'Mahony (2005). The surveyed protocols follow the table-driven and source-initiated on-demand approaches. The protocols were classified into five categories: solutions based on asymmetric cryptography; solutions based on symmetric cryptography; hybrid solutions; reputation-based

Table 2: Proposed Solutions Comparison

Proposed Solution	Prevented Attacks	Drawbacks
Authentication in all phases	- External and internal attacks - Spoofing - Redirection by modifying sequence number	- Requires certificate authority or key sharing
Trust-level metric	- All attacks prevented by authentication - All attacks on higher trust levels nodes	- Requires certificate authority or key sharing - Requires defining trust level
Secure neighbor verification	- All attacks prevented by authentication rushing	- Requires certificate authority or key sharing - Increased overhead when mobility increases
Randomized forwarding	- Rushing	- Latency

solutions; and a category of add-on mechanisms that satisfy specific security requirements.

Multi-Level Hierarchical Routing

To address the network scalability problem, hierarchical routing protocols are normally developed. In hierarchical routing protocols, the network is divided into a number of clusters of fixed or variable size. Inside each cluster, a node will act as a cluster head; all of the nodes in the cluster are within direct transmission range of the head. Sometimes, a node that lies in the transmission range of more than one cluster head is called a gateway and can be used by cluster heads to relay packets between clusters. Numerous hierarchical routing protocols have been proposed for MANETs and WSNs; a comprehensive review can be found in Perkins (2000). Here we briefly present several protocols that have been proposed recently. In hierarchical routing, the overhead and complexity are a result of the selection and maintenance of the cluster head. There are several algorithms to select a cluster head, including low-ID algorithm (Chiang et al. 1997), weighted algorithm (Basagni 1999), and highest-connectivity algorithm (Ye et al. 2001). When one cluster change causes additional leader changes in the network, this is called the *rippling effect*. The adaptive routing using clusters (ARC) protocol (Gerla and Tsai 1995) solves this problem by limiting the leadership changes so they only occur when one cluster becomes a subset of another cluster. When the number of mobile nodes increases further, multi-hierarchical routing protocols are developed to increase scalability. In a multi-hierarchical protocol, the heads of the clusters form a higher-level cluster, and a leader of this cluster will be selected, thereby forming a tree structure. The adaptive routing using cluster hierarchies (ARCH; Belding-Royer 2003) is a multilevel hierarchical clustering protocol that extends ARC. In ARCH, mobile nodes periodically exchange hello messages between neighboring nodes to build a cluster hierarchy. Safari is another hierarchical routing protocol, which claims to provide large-scale mobile wireless network connectivity and basic network services. It consists of three basic protocols: self-organization, scalable routing, and distributed address resolution.

The hierarchical LANMAR (H-LANMAR; Saha and Johnson 2004) is another multilevel hierarchical routing protocol. The key difference of H-LANMAR is that it assumes that there are some special nodes—called *backbone nodes* (BNs)—in the ad hoc network that are equipped with several powerful, long-range radios in addition to the general radios. The higher-level links can be established to connect the BNs to become a backbone network.

Multipath Routing Protocols

As a result of the dynamic characteristics of ad hoc networks, the wireless links tend to break. A new route has to be found before the source can continue sending packets, which will take time and increase delay. In multipath routing, multiple routes may be found between the source and the destination nodes. The advantages of multipath routing include load balancing, fault tolerance, and higher aggregate bandwidth. In most MANETs, multipath protocols are needed to facilitate efficient connectivity between nodes that are not necessarily within each other's wireless range. Many routing protocols in MANETs preserve a caching mechanism by which multiple routing paths to the same destination are stored. Multipath routing is essential for load balancing and offering quality of service. Other benefits of multipath routing include: the reduction of computing time that routers' CPUs require, high resilience to path breaks, high call acceptance ratio (in voice applications), and better security. However, excessive power consumption and congestion can occur if the protocol is not designed carefully.

The disadvantages of multipath routing protocols, compared to unipath protocols, are their complexity and overhead (Mueller and Ghosal 2004). A new routing metric, the route outage probability (ROP), is proposed for channel fading environments with single and multipath routing (Park, Andrews, and Nettles 2003). ROP is defined as the probability of packet transmission failure in a route due to channel fading, and can be represented by the average received signal-to-noise ratio (SNR). In multipath routing, ROP is used with the multiroute path selection (MRPS; Souryal, Vojcic, and Pickholtz 2001) scheme to select a certain number of routes to the destination for the source and intermediate nodes. In Ye, Krishnamurthy, and Tripathi (2003), a multipath extension to AODV, called AODV-multipath (AODVM), was proposed. Multiple disjoint routes can be found using the AODVM route discovery process. A recent paper (Ganjali and Keshavarzian 2004) provides a contradictory conclusion to the widely accepted belief that multipath can significantly improve network balance by numerical analysis and simulations. When we choose the shortest path, the route is actually very close to the line that connects the source and destination in a dense ad hoc network, and the traffic in the center of the network is heavily loaded (Ganjali and Keshavarzian 2003). Unless a very large number of paths are used (e.g., 100), multipath has a similar effect on load balance as unipath.

Ducatelle, Di Caro, and Gambardella (2005) describe the hybrid algorithm AntHocNet, an ACO algorithm for routing in MANETs. The route setup of this scheme is performed by reactive algorithm; the route probing and exploration are performed by proactive scheme. The related simulation experiments show that AntHocNet can outperform AODV in terms of delivery ratio and average delay, especially in more mobile and larger networks. Scalability is also promising in this scheme. However, potential drawbacks include relatively large amounts of overhead and reduced adaptability to the network situation.

Hierarchical routing protocols tend to avoid excessive overhead by limiting the local traffic to the local management—only global movements are reported between zones and hierarchical layers. This, on the other hand, increases the complexity of the routing schemes. In Bohacek et al. (2005), a technique is proposed to reduce the computational complexity of max-flow routing, based on a hierarchical decomposition of the network (hierarchical max-flow routing, or HMFR). Max-flow routing forwards packets in such a way that the impact of failures is minimized. However, the computational complexity of max-flow routing is quite high; therefore, it is not reasonable for moderate-size networks. Other hierarchical routing protocols—such as hierarchical state routing (HSR), zone-based hierarchical link-state routing protocol (ZHLS), and clusterhead gateway switch routing (CGSR)—fall under the same category. The multipath routing algorithms used in Li and Kwok (2005) do not rely on a centralized encryption facility (e.g., a public key infrastructure [PKI] server) or complicated distributed keying protocols. The algorithm, called multipath TCP security (MTS), enhances data security by having source nodes adaptively choose the available routes rather than exhaustively testing the stored routes one by one. Simulation results show that the algorithm provides a reasonably good level of security and performance.

Table 3, adapted from Adibi and Erfani (2006), provides examples from the protocols proposed for MANETs and compares them according to the classification map shown in Figure 1. Note that this is not an exhaustive list of the protocols surveyed in this chapter.

ROUTING PROTOCOL IN WIRELESS SENSOR NETWORKS

The main task of sensor nodes in WSNs is to collect specific data from the surrounding environment and then route it to the base station (BS, also known as sink) node. Routing protocols in WSNs have tried to address many common design issues such as power conservation, data security, node positioning, and data collection and aggregation problems. Many routing and data dissemination protocols have been proposed for WSNs. In general, routing in WSNs can be broadly divided into flat-based routing, hierarchical-based routing, and adaptive-based routing depending on the network structure. Furthermore, these protocols can be classified into

Table 3: Routing Protocols for MANETs

Protocol	On Demand	Pro-active	Hybrid	Hierarchal	Geographic	Power Aware	Multi-cast	Flat	Multi-path
DSR	O							O	
MSR	O							O	O
AODMDV	O							O	
AODV	O							O	
DSDV		O						O	
TERA		O						O	
HMFR				O					
ZRP			O					O	
ANT			O					O	
HSR				O					
ZHLS				O					
CGSR				O					
MLAR					O				O
MPSR						O			
MRPM							O		O
MRTP							O		O
MMRAM							O		O
MTS									
ACR					O				
VBR			O						
TUTWSNR					O	O			
EBMR					O	O			
RCDR		O				O			
GERA					O				

multipath-based, query-based, negotiation-based, or location-based routing techniques depending on the protocol operation. Next, we provide a brief overview of the most relevant studies; a detailed survey on routing techniques in WSNs can be found in Al-Karaki and Kamal (2004) and Niculescu (2005).

One of the main aspects of sensor networks is that the solutions tend to be very application specific. Thus, three main paradigms for communication in ad hoc sensor networks have been investigated, namely, node centric, data centric, and position centric (Niculescu 2005). In the node-centric scheme, protocols perform routing among nodes based on names, and data can be routed independently from upper layers and can recover from node failures easily via route redirection.

Data-Centric Routing Protocols

In the data-centric approach, redundant data will be aggregated in order to save energy. Intanagonwiwat, Govindan, and Estrin (2000) proposed a popular data aggregation paradigm for WSNs called *directed diffusion*. Using this method, all data generated by sensor nodes are named by attribute-value pairs. The BS requests data by broadcasting interests. An interest, which describes a task required by the network, diffuses through the network hop by hop and draws gradients that satisfy the interest toward the BS. When interests fit gradients, paths of information flow are formed; some paths are reinforced to prevent further flooding according to a local rule. In order to reduce communication costs, data are aggregated on the way. The operation of directed diffusion is shown in Figure 10.

The minimum cost forwarding algorithm (MCFA; Ye et al. 2001) exploits the fact that the direction of routing is always known, that is, toward the fixed external base station. Hence, a sensor node needs only to maintain the lowest0cost route estimate from itself to the BS. Heinzelman, Chandrakasan, and Balakrishnan (2000) introduced a hierarchical clustering algorithm for WSNs called the low-energy adaptive clustering hierarchy (LEACH). LEACH is a cluster-based protocol that includes a distributed cluster formation in which the sensors elect themselves cluster heads with some probability. Cluster head nodes compress data that arrive from nodes that belong to the respective cluster and send an aggregated packet to the BS. Although data processing can take place anywhere in the network, LEACH achieves energy savings by processing data at its cluster head nodes. In Bandyopadhyay and Coyle (2003), results in stochastic geometry were used to derive solutions for the values of two parameters (the number of hops to reach a cluster head and the probability of becoming a cluster head) of a modified max-min d-clustering algorithm to minimize the total energy.

A cost-aware dynamic routing protocol, Tempere University of Technology WSN routing (TUTWSNR), is presented in Suhonen et al. (2006). TUTWSNR considers multiple cost metrics at the same time to find the optimal path. These metrics include delay, reliability, and energy. It uses the same technique that is used in directed diffusion to construct (sink-initiated) routes during the network initial setup; the only exception is that the sink does not need to refresh the interest periodically. Gradients are created from sources to destinations in which the node with the lowest cost will have a high gradient. To allow mobility, add flexibility, and recover from route failures, alternative node-initiated routes are created; this corresponds to the maintenance phase. The cost function is used to determine the next hop cost. It tends to maximize route reliability, minimize energy consumption, minimize delay, and balance node load.

Energy-balancing multipath routing (EBMR; Chen and Nasser 2006) extends the network lifetime using multipaths alternately; the BS is responsible for establishing, maintaining, and selecting the best route. The BS depends on the current energy level of the nodes that are constructing the route to select the route with the minimum energy cost. EBMR reduces the communication and routing overhead within the network. Sensor nodes need not maintain up-to-date routing information; they only need to know the current routes toward the BS. Wu and Havinga (2006) propose a reliable cost-based data-centric routing (RCDR) protocol. RCDR utilizes data aggregation and two types of gradients: local and global. Based on the local gradients, data from nodes around the event are routed toward the vent-originated node (local maxima). The local maxima node aggregates the data and sends the final report to the BS. The global gradient is used to establish routes between the local maxima and the BS. RCDR tolerates sink or BS movement without

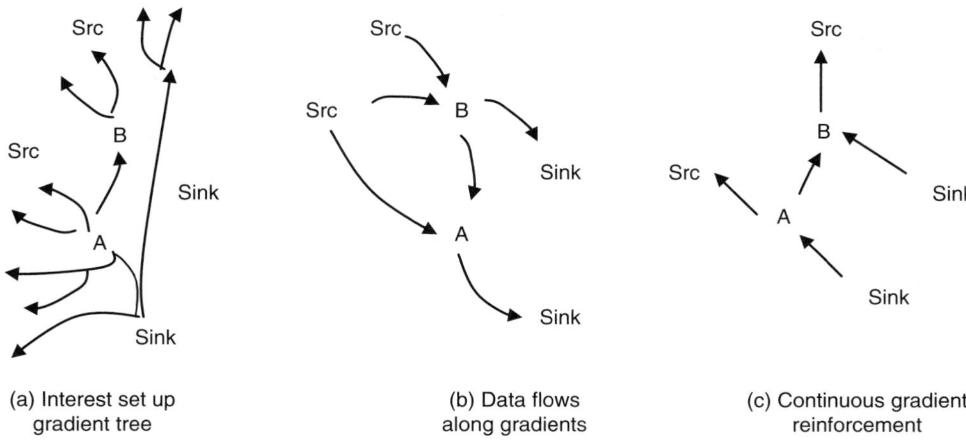

Figure 10: Directed diffusion routing approach (Intanagonwiwat, Govindan, and Estrin 2000)

the need to reset the network to restore gradients. This is done via negative gradients based on queries sent from the sink to its old local neighbors.

Position-Centric Routing Protocols

This approach uses nodes' positions to identify node and route data to the destination. This protocol introduces several problems, such as defining a positioning system and node positioning. Node positioning is related to the geography of the field and line-of-sight problems. Using a global positioning system is a power-aware challenge. Once the source knows the position of the destination node, it forwards the data to the nearest node to the destination. Routing tables are not needed in this approach, and it is also independent from mobility when the positions of intermediate nodes are known. However, the main disadvantage of position-centric routing protocols is that the source must know the position of the destination to forward the data. Position-centric protocols can combine other factors with regard to route construction in addition to the distance to the BS. For example, geographic and energy-aware routing (GEAR; Yu, Estrin, and Govindan 2001) depends on both the energy level of the next node and the distance to the BS to find the optimal route. A geographic routing algorithm (GERA) is presented in Santos et al. (2006). GERA begins its work by dividing the nodes into clusters. This is accomplished by sending hello messages that contain the node location and its power status. The cluster head is the first node that sends the hello message. Next, the source looks for the sink location and forwards the data to the closest reachable node to the BS. Table 4 summarizes the differences among different wireless sensor network paradigms.

It was concluded in Niculescu (2005) that the position-centric approach, although the oldest and best understood, is not the most appropriate for large-size, low-energy, application-specific sensor networks.

Node-Centric Routing Protocols

In node-centric routing, target nodes are explicitly addressed by source nodes. The target node can be a single node, a group of nodes, or the set of all nodes in the network. In other words, we may have unicast with one destination, multicast with several destinations belonging to one group, or broadcast when sending to all nodes.

In this type of routing, nodes play a key role in the operation of the routing protocol. In particular, the probability of node failure and environmental effects on sensor nodes receives considerable attention in the literature. One of the most well-known solutions for this problem is path redundancy; modified flooding algorithms and gradient broadcast are two examples of these methods (Koubaa and Song 2004). In flooding-based protocols, each node sends a received packet to some of its neighbors. As a result, a packet will reach the destination via many paths, which will guarantee the correct delivery of the packet. This is one advantage of flooding. Other advantages of flooding include simplicity, reliability, scalability, and system robustness. However, flooding has very poor performance because a large number of copies of a packet is disseminated throughout the network. Modified flooding algorithms have been proposed to improve flooding performance. These protocols use geographical information and reduce the number of copies of a packet distributed in the network by reducing the number of unnecessary relay nodes and equivalent relay paths. In these modified algorithms, there is a trade-off between energy consumption and network robustness.

Gradient broadcast (Koubaa and Song 2004) is another routing protocol that addresses the problem of robust data forwarding using unreliable sensor nodes with error-prone wireless channels. In this algorithm, the sink builds and maintains a cost field. Each node keeps the cost for forwarding a packet from itself to the sink. Nodes closer to the sink have smaller costs. Because multiple paths exist between a source and the sink, a source assigns a credit to each report it sends out to control the degree of path redundancy. The credit is some extra budget that enables a packet to be forwarded over multiple paths, each of which has a cost no greater than the total budget of the credit plus the cost of the source. The amount of credit determines the width of the paths, thus the degree of robustness and overhead.

Table 4: Comparisons among Three Routing Approaches in WSNs

	Node Centric	Data Centric	Position Centric	Energy Centric
Compatibility	*Yes*	*No*	*N/A*	*Yes*
Layered	*Yes*	*No*	*Yes*	*Yes*
Additional Requirements	*Yes*	*Yes*	*No*	*Yes*
Routing:				
-				*Yes*
Mobility				*Yes*
-	*No*	*No*	*Yes*	
Scalability	*No*	*Yes*	*Yes*	
Discovery	*No*	*Yes*	*(Some support)*	*(Some support)*
Querying	*No*	*Yes*	*No*	*No*

Another protocol is the node-centric load-balancing algorithm for wireless sensor networks (Dai and Han 2006). The idea is that by spreading the workload across a sensor network, load balancing reduces hot spots and increases the energy lifetime of the sensor network. In Dai and Han (2006), a node-centric algorithm was proposed to construct a load-balanced tree among sensor networks of asymmetric architecture. The algorithm achieves routing trees that are more effectively balanced than routing based on breadth-first search (BFS) and shortest path obtained by Dijkstra's algorithm.

Energy-Centric Routing Protocols

As stated earlier, saving energy consumption is one of the main challenges in WSNs. A massive number of studies in the WSN research are concerned with saving energy in all protocol stacks designed for WSN. A number of these protocols appear in Al-Karaki and Kamal (2004). However, more recent studies that tackle the same issue have also been introduced. Among these protocols is the link quality estimation-based routing protocol (LQER) (Koubaa and Song 2004), in which the link quality is estimated with (m,k)-firm. The basic idea of link quality estimation based on (m,k)- firm is that at least m out of any k consecutive deadlines in task windows must be met by the task flow. Based on this idea, (m,k)-firm–based link quality estimation can be designed (i.e., if m out of k history packets are transmitted successfully, the link quality is qualified). In application, a suitable value of k will be determined in different environments. Through simulation, it can be found that when $k = 9$, (m,k)-firm link quality can meet the requirements of minimum energy saving. LQER is designed based on a minimum hop field-based routing protocol that has an objective of high energy efficiency (Zhuchang and Yining 2004). The main idea of minimum hop field-based routing protocol (Tong and Culler 2003) is for each node to remember the node with minimum hop that is one hop smaller than itself in all one-hop–away neighboring nodes. When data are to be delivered, one node can be specified from the set of all eligible nodes to be a transmit node. As shown in Figure 11, assume that the minimum hop of node S is 7, and its transmission node set includes four nodes—D, C, E, and A—with a node hop of 6. In this way, it can be guaranteed that data are delivered through the shortest path without producing redundant information. When a node transmits data, all of its one-hop–away neighbors receive the packet, but only the node specified in the packet will actually transmit the packet. Packets are transmitted to the base station in this way via the shortest path.

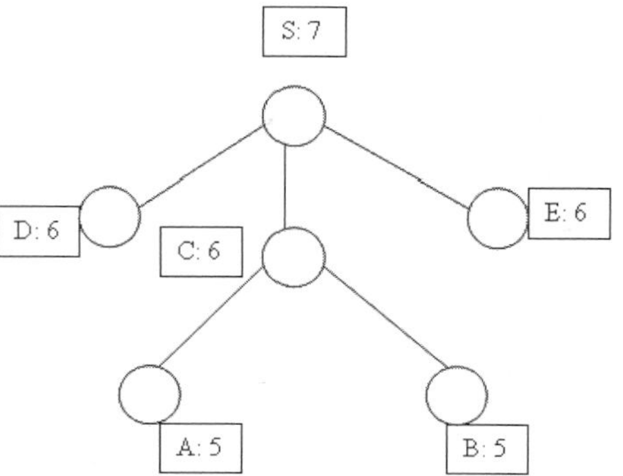

Figure 11: An example of minimum hop field-based routing protocol

A more recent study on energy-centric routing in WSNs appeared in Ye et al. (2005). The main idea is to build a tool, called an energy-centric scale (ECscale), which continuously monitors the status of energy resources following network deployment. The information on energy status can be used to early-notify both the sensors and deployers of resource depletion in some parts of the network. It can also be used to perform energy-efficient routing in WSNs. Optimal as well as approximate energy-centric routing in WSNs, with the objective of maximizing the network lifetime, was proposed. Simulation results show that this scheme is scalable and can provide many levels of energy savings when compared to conventional routing schemes.

CONCLUSION

This chapter surveyed a number of contemporary papers that explore routing protocols in wireless mobile ad hoc and sensor networks. The design of such protocols spans a wide array of parameters. This chapter tried to encapsulate the previous studies in this field and present a detailed categorization along several parameters such as underlying structure, path cardinality, and type of operation. Overall, the surveyed protocols can be divided into the following categories: proactive, reactive, position, energy, secure, flat, and hierarchical routing protocols. Designing a good energy-efficient routing protocol for ad hoc wireless networks is still a challenging task. Although extensive efforts have been exerted thus far on the routing problem, there are still some challenges facing effective solutions of the routing problem. First, there is a tight coupling to the physical world and embedded in unattended control systems. Second, sensors are characterized by a small footprint; as such, nodes present stringent energy constraints because they live with a small, finite energy source. This also differs from traditional fixed but reusable resources. Third, more work on the development of power-efficient multicasting or broadcasting protocols should be conducted, especially localized protocols. An interesting subarea is power-efficient geocasting, in which a packet is delivered to all nodes within a specific geographical region. Fourth, hierarchical routing is an old technique to enhance scalability and efficiency of the routing protocol. However, novel techniques of tiered architectures (a mix of form and energy factors) to network clustering for maximizing the network lifetime are a strong research area in WSNs. Fifth, time and location synchronization are needed, and energy-efficient techniques for associating time and spatial coordinates with data to support collaborative processing are also required. Finally, self-configuration and reconfiguration are essential to the lifetime of unattended systems in dynamic, constrained energy environments. This is important for keeping the network up and running. As nodes die and leave the network, update and reconfiguration mechanisms should take place. An important feature in every routing protocol is to adapt to topology changes very quickly and to maintain network functions.

ACKNOWLEDGMENT

The author would like to express his deep thanks and gratitude to Ashraf Ali, Fadi Shehab, and Ghada Al-Mashaqbeh for their help in preparing parts of this article. We also appreciate the feedback, comments, and advice by anonymous referees, which helped improve the article quality.

GLOSSARY

Data-Centric Routing: A routing approach in which data are collected based on specific attributes.

Energy-Centric Routing: A routing approach in which routing decisions are based on energy concentrations in network regions.

Flat Network: A network in which each node plays the same role.

Hierarchical Network: A network in which a set of nodes is selected to act as superior layer(s) and perform a set of specific functions.

Location-Based Routing: A routing protocol in which the positions of nodes are used in forwarding the packets toward the destination nodes.

Mobile Ad Hoc Networks: A collection of wireless mobile or static nodes that dynamically form a temporary network without the use of any existing network infrastructure or centralized control.

Negotiation-Based Routing: A routing approach in which nodes negotiate data attributed before data are really exchanged.

Proactive Routing: A routing protocol in which a set of routes are found and stored for current and future use.

Quality of Service: A set of primitives that govern the quality of the data exchanged between nodes (e.g., end-to-end delay).

Reactive Routing: A routing protocol in which routes are only found when needed and no state information is maintained.

Routing: Moving data between a pair or a group of nodes such that certain requirements are met.

Wireless Medium: The open air that is shared among wireless nodes; its characteristics can vary with time.

Wireless Sensor Networks: A collection of wireless sensor nodes that are deployed either randomly or in predetermined locations to sense, collect, process, and communicate raw data.

CROSS REFERENCES

See *Broadcasting in Ad Hoc and Sensor Networks; In-network Data Aggregation in Wireless Sensor Networks; Medium Access in Ad Hoc and Sensor Networks; Network Middleware; Network QoS; Principles and Applications of Ad Hoc and Sensor Networks.*

REFERENCES

Adibi, S., and S. Erfani. 2006. A multipath routing survey for mobile ad-hoc networks. *IEEE CCNC*.

Argyroudis, P. G, and D. O'Mahony. 2005. Secure routing for mobile ad hoc networks. *IEEE Communications Surveys* 7(3): 2–21.

Ahmed, A., H. Shi, and Y. Shang. 2003. A survey on network protocols for wireless sensor network. In *Proceedings of the International Conference on Information Technology: Research and Education*, pp. 301–5.

Akyildiz, I. F., W. Su, Y. Sankarasubramaniam, and E. Cyirci. 2002. Wireless sensor networks: A survey. *Computer Networks* 38(4): 393–422.

Al-Karaki, J. N., and G. Al-Mashagbeh. 2006. Energy-centric routing in wireless sensor networks. In *Proceedings of IEEE ISCC06*, Sardinia, Italy, June, pp. 948–54.

Al-Karaki, J. N., and A. E. Kamal. 2004. Routing techniques in wireless sensor networks: A survey. *IEEE Wireless Communications* 11(6): 6–28.

Argyroudis, P. G., and D. O'Mahony. 2005. Secure routing for mobile ad hoc networks. *IEEE Communications Surveys and Tutorials*, pp. 2–21.

Bandyopadhyay, S., and E. Coyle. 2003. An energy-efficient hierarchical clustering algorithm for wireless sensor networks. In *Proceedings of INFOCOM 2003*, San Francisco, April, pp. 1713–23.

Basagni, S. 1999. Distributed clustering for ad hoc networks. In *Proceedings of the International Symposium on Parallel Architectures, Algorithms, and Networks, Fremantle, Australia*, June, pp. 310–15.

Belding-Royer, E. M. 2003. Multi-level hierarchies for scalable ad hoc routing. *Wireless Networking (WINET)* 9(5): 461–78.

Bohacek, S., J. P. Hespanha, C. Lim, and K. Obraczka. 2005. Hierarchical max-flow routing. *IEEE GLOBECOM*.

Chaudhry, S. R., A. Al-Khwildi, Y. Casey, H. Aldelou, and H. S. Al-Raweshidy. 2005. A performance comparison of multi on-demand routing in wireless ad hoc networks. In *Proceedings of IEEE International Conference on Wireless And Mobile Computing (WiMob'2005)*, Montreal, August, pp. 9–16.

Chen, Y., and N. Nasser. 2006. Energy-balancing multipath routing protocol for wireless sensor networks. In *Proceedings of ACM Third International Conference on Quality of Service in Heterogeneous Wired/Wireless Networks (QShine '06)*, Waterloo, Ontario, Canada, August.

Chiang, C., H. Wu, W. Liu, and M. Gerla. 1997. Routing in cluster multi-hop, mobile wireless networks with fading channel. In *Proceedings of IEEE Singapore International Conference on Network (SICON)*, April, pp. 197–211.

Dai, H., and R. Han. 2006. A node-centric load balancing algorithm for wireless sensor networks. Technical report, Department of Computer Science, University of Colorado at Boulder.

De Couto, D. S. J., D. Aguayo, B. A. Chambers, and R. Morris. 2002. Performance of multihop wireless networks: Shortest path is not enough. In *Proceedings of the First Workshop on Hot Topics in Networking (HotNets-I)*, Princeton, New Jersey, October, pp. 83–88.

Djenouri, D., and L. Khelladi. 2005. A survey of security issues in mobile ad hoc and sensor networks. Cerist Center of Research, Algiers Nadjib Badache, University of Science and Technology, Algiers.

Draves, R., J. Padhye, and B. Zill. 2004a. Comparison of routing metrics for static multi-hop wireless networks. In *Proceedings of the ACM Special Interest Group on*

Data Communications (SIGCOMM), Portland, Oregon, August, pp. 133–144.

Draves, R., J. Padhye, and B. Zill. 2004b. Routing in multi-radio, multi-hop wireless mesh networks. In *Proceedings of the ACM International Conference on Mobile Computing and Networking (MobiCom)*, Philadelphia, September/October, pp. 114–128.

Du, X., and D. Wu. 2006. Adaptive cell relay routing protocol for mobile ad hoc networks. *IEEE Transactions on Vehicular Technology* 55(1): 278–85.

Ducatelle, F., G. Di Caro, and L. M. Gambardella. 2005. Ant agents for hybrid multipath routing in mobile ad hoc networks. *Wireless On-Demand Network Systems and Services (WONS)*.

Ducatelle, F., D. Gianni, and L. Maria. 2005. Ant agents for hybrid multipath routing in mobile ad hoc networks. *Wireless On-Demand Network Systems and Services*, pp. 44–53.

Ganjali, Y., and A. Keshavarzian. 2003. Performance analysis of reactive shortest single-path and multi-path routing mechanism with load balance. *IEEE Computer and Communications Societies (INFOCOM)*.

Ganjali, Y., and A. Keshavarzian. 2004. Load balancing in ad hoc networks: single-path routing vs. multi-path routing. In *Proceedings of the Twenty-Third Conference of the IEEE Communications Society (Infocom2004)*.

Gerla, M., and J. T. Tsai. 1995. Multicluster, mobile, multimedia radio network. *ACM-Baltzer Journal of Wireless Networks* 1(3): 255–65.

Guven, T., R. La, M. Shayman, and B. Bhattacharjee. 2005. Measurement-based multipath multicast. In *Proceedings of INFOCOM 2005*, Miami, Florida, March, pp. 2803–8.

Heinzelman, W. R., A. Chandrakasan, and H. Balakrishnan. 2000. Energy-efficient communication protocol for wireless microsensor networks. In *Proceedings of HICSS'00*, Hawaii, January, pp. 8–20.

Higaki and S. Umeshima. 2004. Multiple-route ad hoc on-demand distance vector (MRAODV) routing protocol. In *Proceedings of Parallel and Distributed Processing Symposium*, Santa Fe, New Mexico, April, p. 237.

Hollick, M., I. Martinovic, T. Krop, and I. Rimac. 2004. A survey on dependable routing in sensor networks, ad hoc networks, and cellular networks. In *Proceedings of Euromicro Conference*, Rennes, France, August/September, pp. 495–502.

Hong, X., K. Xu, and M. Gerla. 2002. Scalable routing protocols for mobile ad hoc networks. *IEEE Network* 16(4): 11–21.

Intanagonwiwat, C., R. Govindan, and D. Estrin. 2000. Directed diffusion: A scalable and robust communication paradigm for sensor networks. In *Proceedings of ACM MobiCom'00*, Boston, August, pp. 56–67.

Johnson, D. B., and D. A. Maltz. 1996. Dynamic source routing in ad hoc networks. In *Mobile computing*, edited by T. Imielinski and H. Korth, 152–81. Norwell, MA: Kluwer Academic Publishers.

Koubaa, A., and Y. Q. Song. 2004. Loss-tolerant QoS using firm constraints in guaranteed rate networks. In *Proceedings of Tenth IEEE Real-Time and Embedded Technology and Applications (RTAS'04)*, Toronto, Canada, May, pp. 526–33.

Lee, U., S. F. Midkiff, and J. S. P. Bradley. 2005. A proactive routing protocol for multi-channel wireless ad-hoc networks (DSDV-MC). In *Proceedings of IEEE Conference on Information Technology: Coding and Computing*, April, pp. 710–15.

Li, J., D. Cordes, and J. Zhang. 2005. Power-aware routing protocols in ad hoc wireless networks. *IEEE Wireless Communications* 12(6): 69–81.

Li, Z., and Y.-K. Kwok. 2005. A new multipath routing approach to enhancing TCP security in ad hoc wireless networks. In *Proceedings of the International Conference on Parallel Processing*, Oslo, Norway, June, pp. 372–79.

Liang, B., and Z. J. Haas. 2006. Hybrid routing in ad hoc networks with a dynamic virtual backbone. *IEEE Transactions on Wireless Communications* 5(6): 1392–1405.

Lu, T.-E., and K.-T. Feng. 2005. Predictive mobility and location-aware routing protocol in mobile ad hoc networks. In *Proceedings of Global Telecommunications Conference (GLOBECOM)*, St. Louis, Missouri, November/December. p. 5.

Mao, S., D. Bushmitch, S. Narayanan, and S. Panwar. 2003. MRTP: A multiflow real-time transport protocol for ad hoc networks. In *Proceedings of IEEE Vehicular Technology Conference*, Orlando, Florida, October, pp. 2629–34.

Mauve, M., A. Widmer, and H. Hartenstein. 2001. A survey on position-based routing in mobile ad hoc networks. *IEEE Network* 15(6): 30–39.

Mueller, S., and D. Ghosal. 2004. Multipath routing in mobile ad hoc networks: Issues and challenges. Paper in *Lecture notes in computer science*, ed. by M. C. Calzarossa and E. Gelenbe.

Nanda, S., and R. S. Gray. 2004. Spatial multipath location aided ad hoc routing. In *Proceedings of Thirteenth International Conference on Computer Communications and Networks (ICCCN)*, Chicago, October, p. 544.

Niculescu, D. 2005. Communication paradigms for sensor networks. *IEEE Communications Magazine*, March, pp. 116–22.

Park, M., J. G. Andrews, and S. Nettles. 2003. Wireless channel-aware ad hoc cross-layer protocol with multiroute path selection diversity. In *Proceedings of IEEE Vehicular Technology Conference*, Orlando, Florida, October, pp. 2197–2201.

Perkins, C. 2000. *Ad hoc networking*. Reading, MA: Addison-Wesley.

Perkins, C. E., E. M. Royer, and S. R. Das. 1999. Ad hoc on-demand distance vector routing. IETF draft, http://www.ietf.org/ internet-drafts/draft-ietf-manet-aodv-04.txt.

Royer, E. M., and C. -K. Toh. 1999. A review of current routing protocols for ad hoc mobile wireless networks. *IEEE Personal Communications* 6(2): 46–55.

Saha, A. K., and D. B. Johnson. 2004. Self-organizing hierarchical routing for scalablead hoc networking (slides). *Mesh Networking Summit 2004*, Washington, June.

Santos, R. A., A. Edwards, O. Alvarez, A. Gonzalez, and A. Verduzco. 2006. A geographic routing algorithm for wireless sensor networks. In *Proceedings of CERMA 2006*, Cuernavaca, Mexico, September, pp. 64–69.

Souryal, M., B. Vojcic, and R. Pickholtz. 2001. Ad hoc, multihop CDMA networks with route diversity in a Rayleigh fading channel. *IEEE Milcom*, vol. 2.

Subramanian, A., A. Anto, J. Vasudevan, and P. Narayanasamy. 2004. Multipath power-sensitive routing protocol for mobile ad hoc networks. In *Proceedings of the First Working Conference on Wireless On-Demand Network Systems (WONS2004)*.

Suhonen, J., M. Kuorilehto, M. Hannikainen, and T. D. Hamalainen. 2006. Cost-aware dynamic routing protocol for wireless sensor networks: Design and prototype experiments. In *Proceedings of PIMRC 2006*, Helsinki, Finland, September, pp. 1–5.

Wang, L., and A. Olariu. 2004. A two-zone hybrid routing protocol for mobile ad hoc networks. *IEEE Transactions on Parallel and Distributed Systems* 15(12): 1105–16.

Wang, L., L. Zhang, Y. Shu, and M. Dong. 2000. Multipath source routing in wireless ad hoc networks. *CCECE 2000*, March.

Woo, A., T. Tong, and D. Culler. 2003. Taming the underlying challenges of reliable multihop routing in sensor networks. In *Proceedings of SenSys03*, Los Angeles, November, pp. 14–27.

Wu, J., and P. Havinga. 2006. Reliable cost-based data-centric routing protocol for wireless sensor networks. In *Proceedings of SNPD 2006*, Las Vegas, Nevada, June, pp. 267–72.

Ye, F., A. Chen, S. Liu, and L. Zhang. 2001. A scalable solution to minimum cost forwarding in large sensor networks. In *Proceedings of the Tenth International Conference on Computer Communications and Networks (ICCCN)*, Phoenix, Arizona, October, pp. 304–9.

Ye, F., G. Zhong, S. Lu, and L. Zhang. 2005. Gradient broadcast: A robust data delivery protocol for large-scale sensor networks. *WINET* 11(2): 285–298.

Ye, Z., S. Krishnamurthy, and S. Tripathi. 2003. A framework for reliable routing in mobile ad hoc network. In *Proceedings of IEEE INFOCOM 2003*.

Yih-Chun, H., and A. Perrig. 2004. A survey of secure wireless ad hoc routing. *IEEE Security and Privacy Magazine*, May/June, pp. 28–39.

Yu, Y., D. Estrin, and R. Govindan. 2001. Geographical and energy-aware routing: A recursive data dissemination protocol for wireless sensor networks. UCLA Computer Science Department technical report, UCLA-CSD TR-01-0023, May.

Zhuchang, M., and S. Yining. 2004. Research on routing protocol of a large wireless sensors network. *Computer Engineering and Applications*, pp. 165–67.

Broadcasting in Ad Hoc and Sensor Networks

François Ingelrest, *IRCICA/LIFL University, Switzerland*, David Simplot-Ryl, *Université de Lille, France*
Hong Guo, *LRC, Ontario Public Service, Canada*, and
Ivan Stojmenović, *University of Birmingham, UK, and University of Ottawa, Canada*

INTRODUCTION

We consider dynamic wireless networks in which each node has the same and fixed transmission range. Ad hoc wireless networks are considered in conference, rescue, and military scenarios, while small size battery powered sensor networks are envisioned for monitoring the environment, with individual sensors reporting observed events (movement, temperature, chemicals, etc.) to a base station. The physical layer is approximated by assuming that a message sent by one of nodes is received correctly by all neighbors located within the transmission range (*one-to-all* communication). Among the common problems found in ad hoc and sensor networks is *broadcasting*, where a message is to be sent from one node to all hosts of the network. Applications of this broadcasting communication include route discovery, information dissemination, and synchronization.

Because of limited range of radio waves, a host is normally unable to directly communicate with all the recipient nodes. To fulfill a broadcasting task, many hosts thus have to act as routers by relaying the message to their physical neighbors. The simplest procedure is to have each node relay the message (exactly once) to its neighbors. This straightforward solution is known as *blind flooding* and is part of the IETF standardized *dynamic source routing* (DSR) protocol, described by Johnson et al. 2004. However, in non-sparse networks, this solution generates a lot of redundancy and collisions that could possibly prevent the broadcasting from being correctly performed. This issue, studied by Ni et al. 1999, is known as the *broadcast storm problem*. Moreover, significant energy is consumed by the redundant messages, which is an important consideration in low power sensor nodes.

A number of other broadcast protocols, more energy-efficient, have been proposed to replace blind flooding. Some of them are *centralized*, where nodes need to know the global topology of the network. In ad hoc or sensor networks, this causes a huge and unacceptable overhead for information exchange. Moreover, this information generally has a low lifetime due to frequent topology modifications which occur because of mobility and changes in activity status from active to sleeping and vice versa.

Ad hoc and sensor networks require protocols, called *localized*, that rely only on local information that can be easily and quickly acquired. Methods covered here require each node to know the position of all its neighbors (1-hop positional knowledge), or the list of all its direct neighbors and their neighbors (2-hop topological knowledge). These protocols also need to be *reliable*. The reliability of a broadcast protocol refers to its capability of reaching all nodes connected to the source, assuming an ideal MAC layer. A high or even perfect delivery ratio is required for most applications.

Localized broadcast protocols covered in this chapter provide reliable broadcasting. They can be divided into two categories:

- *Self-pruning* schemes: each node locally decides whether to forward the packet. We describe several existing definitions, including a general definition by Wu and Dai, 2003 for k-hop neighborhood information, and L-hop forwarding history.
- *Neighbor-designating* schemes: each node is told by the upstream sender whether it needs to forward the packet. This can be done either via the data packet or via a previously sent control packet.

Williams and Camp (2002), comprehensively compared existing broadcast methods. Neighbor knowledge algorithms were claimed to be better suited to ad hoc networks than other approaches. Their comparison, however, did not include dominating set-based broadcast protocols, and did not consider any neighbor elimination scheme. Therefore, we believe that the best existing methods were overlooked in that paper, which motivated as to perform the comparison in this chapter.

We simulated the best existing localized schemes, and present here major comparative data. Among all the examined schemes, an enhanced definition for computing connected dominating sets seems to give the overall best results.

PRELIMINARIES

It is assumed that nodes all have the same transmission radius R. Two nodes are neighbors, and can communicate, if the distance between them is no more than R. This assumption is referred to as the *unit disk graph* model. The set of nodes is noted as V and the set of neighbors of a node u is noted as $N(u)$. The set of k-hop neighbors of node u, including u itself, is noted as $N^k(u)$. The degree of u is its number of neighbors and the density of the network is the average degree of nodes. Each node u is assigned a unique identifier id(u), which may be an IP or a MAC address. Finally, the distance between two nodes u and v is measured in number of hops, which is equal to the minimum number of edges to cross from u to v. In Figure 1, the distance between nodes a and h is 3 hops. The degree of node a is 3. The set of 1-hop neighbors of a is $\{b, c, e\}$, and the set of its 2-hop neighbors is $\{d, f, g\}$.

Nodes have a k-hop knowledge if they know each neighboring node within a distance of k hops. This knowledge is acquired using regular HELLO messages. The two selected protocols use either $k = 1$ or $k = 2$, mainly depending on whether or not positional (geographic) information is available. Geographic position and distances between neighbors may be obtained by using a location system such as the *global positioning system* (GPS) and by including locations in HELLO messages.

In the graph representing the 2-hop knowledge at each node, there is a difference between topological and positional information that may be used. If position information is available, each node may conclude, based on their locations, whether two of its 2-hop neighbors are neighbors themselves. Such a conclusion cannot be made without position information (that is, based solely on topological information), and therefore, no edge between such neighbors is assumed. Figure 2 illustrates the difference between these two assumptions, considering node a. With topological information, in Figure 2(a), the 2-hop neighbors $\{c, e, f, g\}$ are assumed to not be directly connected. This is not the case with positional information in Figure 2(b). Note that node c is always known to be a common neighbor of nodes b and d because it appears in both neighborhood lists.

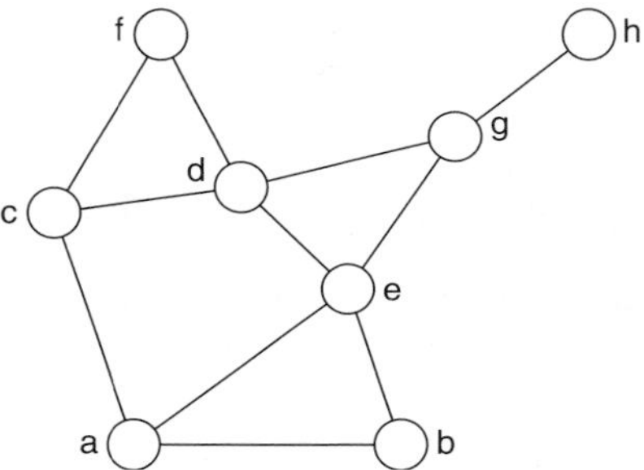

Figure 1: A sample network

BROADCASTING PROTOCOLS

Multipoint Relay Protocol

The *multipoint relay* (MPR) protocol was proposed by Qayyum et al. (2002) and belongs to the family of neighbor-designating methods. In this algorithm, it is assumed that nodes have a 2-hop topological knowledge. Each node u that has to forward the message first selects a subset of relays among its 1-hop neighbors that covers the same 2-hop nodes as the complete set of 1-hop neighbors does. Such a set is called a multipoint relay set. Here, node a covers node b if a and b are 1-hop (direct) neighbors. For example, nodes c and e (1-hop neighbors of a) in Figure 1 cover nodes d, f, g (2-hop neighbors of a). The selection is then forwarded within the packet so that receivers can determine whether they have been selected. Each node that receives the message for the first time checks if it is designated as a relay node by the sender. In this case, the message is forwarded after the selection of a new relaying set of neighbors. A variant exists in which nodes select their relays before having to broadcast a packet, in a *proactive* manner, and selection is sent within HELLO messages.

Obviously, it is important to select small sets of relays. Finding such a set of minimal size is known as the *minimum set cover* problem and is described by Garey and Johns (1979) as a NP-complete problem. A greedy heuristics was proposed by Quayyum et al. (2002) and was first described by Lovasz (1975). Considering a node u, it can be described as follows:

1. Place all 2-hop neighbors of u in a set MPR′(u) of uncovered 2-hop neighbors.

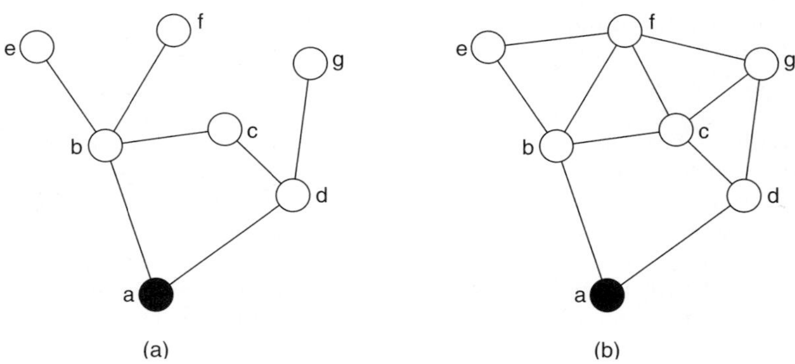

Figure 2: Topological information vs. positional information

2. First select all 1-hop neighbors of u that are the only possible relays for some 2-hop neighbors. Relays are placed in MPR(u), and covered 2-hop neighbors are removed from MPR′(u).
3. While the set MPR′(u) is not empty, repeatedly select the 1-hop neighbor not already selected that covers the greatest number of nodes in MPR′(u). Each time a new node is added to MPR(u), remove its neighbors from MPR′(u). In case of a tie, choose the node with the highest degree.

An example of this heuristics is given in Figure 3, where f is the source node. The algorithm starts with MPR(f) = ϕ and MPR′(f) = $\{a, b, e, i\}$. The node c is the only one able to reach a, so it is added to MPR(f), and nodes a and b are removed from MPR′(f). No other mandatory 1-hop neighbor of f exists, so other relays are selected according to the number of nodes in MPR′(f) that they cover. Nodes d and h each cover only one node in MPR′(f), while node g covers both e and i at the same time. Therefore, g is chosen and added to MPR(f). The set MPR′(f) being empty, no other nodes are selected.

Connected Dominating Sets

In Figure 4(a), a sample network is given in which each white node has a black neighbor in its 1-hop neighborhood. The set of these black nodes $\{c, g\}$ is called a *dominating set*, and these nodes are said to be *dominant*. More formally, a subset $V_D \subseteq V$ is said to be dominating if each node either belongs to V_D, or has at least one neighboring node that belongs to V_D. A *connected dominating set* (CDS), illustrated in Figure 4(b), may be used for broadcasting. In CDS based broadcasting, each node, receiving the packet, will retransmit it if and only if it belongs to selected CDS. Let us suppose that node e wants to broadcast a message. It sends the message to nodes a and g. Node g is dominant and therefore forwards the message to nodes f, h, and i. Node h forwards the message to c and d, and node c forwards it to node b.

A centralized heuristics by Guha and Khuller (1998), can be described as follows. Each node is initially colored white. The densest node in the graph is then colored black, and all its neighbors grey. Then, while there are some white nodes, the grey node with the largest number of white neighbors is selected, colored as black node, and all its white neighbors as grey nodes. Ties can be resolved by using some keys (identifiers). At the end, the set of black nodes is a CDS. This algorithm provides low numbers of nodes in CDS but it cannot be efficiently applied in a decentralized network. However, the size of the resulting set provides a good estimate of the limits one can reach with localized heuristics.

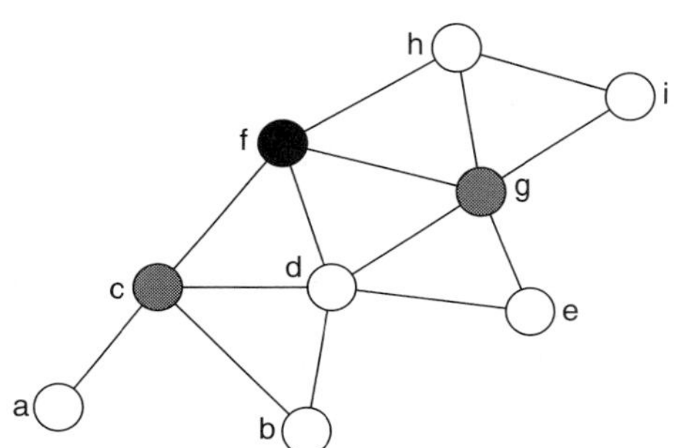

Figure 3: Applying MPR at node f: MPR (f) = $\{c, g\}$

Coverage by 1-Hop Neighbors

Wu and Li (1999) proposed an algorithm that has been later improved in terms of message overhead by Stojmenović et al. (2001) and Stojmenović (2004). A node is referred to as *intermediate* if it has at least two 1-hop neighbors not directly connected. A node u is covered by a neighbor v if any other neighbor of u is a neighbor of v, and if v has a higher key than u. Nodes that are not covered by any neighbor are called *inter-gateway* nodes. A node u is covered by two directly connected neighbors v and w if any other neighbor of u is a neighbor of either v or w, and if v and w have higher keys than u. Inter-gateway nodes that are not covered by any pair of connected 1-hop neighbors become *gateway* nodes. As proven in Stojmenović et al. (2001) and Stojmenović (2004) each node can decide whether or not it is an inter-gateway or a gateway node without exchanging any message with its neighbor (assuming 1-hop positional or 2-hop topological information is available via HELLO messages), and the obtained set is indeed a CDS.

This rule has been further improved in terms of number of dominating nodes by Dai and Wu (2003). They proposed

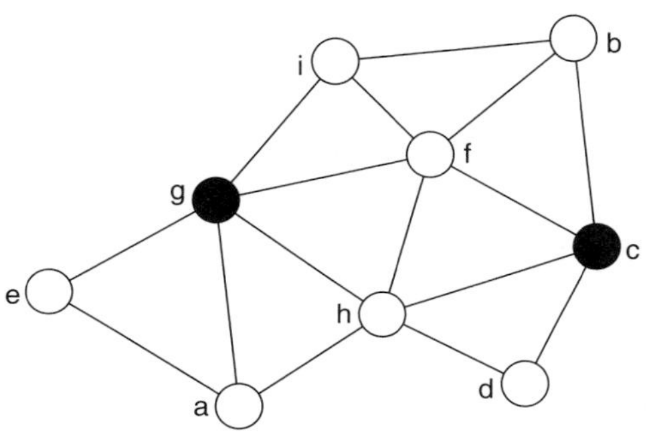

(a) A dominating set $\{c, g\}$

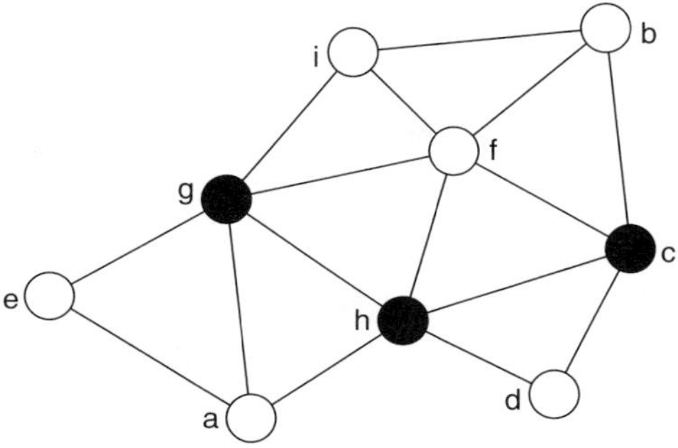

(b) A connected dominating set $\{c, g, h\}$

Figure 4: Two dominating sets

a more general rule where by coverage may be provided by an arbitrary number of connected 1-hop neighbors. A modification of this *generalized self-pruning rule* has been proposed by Stojmenović and Wu (2004) in order to avoid similar message exchanges between neighbors.

Generalized Self-Pruning Rule. A node u is covered by a set of 1-hop neighbors A_u if A_u is connected, any other neighbor of u is also a neighbor of a node in A_u and any node in A_u has a higher key than u.

A simple algorithm for verifying this condition is proposed in Carle and Simplot-Ryl (2004), as follows. First, each node checks if it is intermediate. Then each intermediate node u constructs a subgraph G_h of its 1-hop neighbors with higher keys. In the graph composed of $N(u)$, each node which has a lower key than u is removed, as well as the corresponding edges. The resulting subgraph is denoted by G_h. If the latter is empty or disconnected, then u is in the dominating set. If G_h is connected but there is a neighbor of u which is not a neighbor of any node from G_h, then u is in the dominating set. Otherwise u is covered and is not in the dominating set. Dijkstra's shortest path algorithm may be used to test the connectivity. (It is performed locally at each node). Non-intermediate nodes are never dominant. This rule is illustrated in Figure 5, where identifiers of nodes are used as keys using lexicographical order for comparisons. Nodes $\{d, e\}$ are not intermediate because they do not have unconnected neighbors. The graphs G_h for nodes a ($\{e, g, h\}$), b ($\{c, f, i\}$), c ($\{d, f, h\}$), and f ($\{g, h, i\}$) are all connected, and cover neighbors with lower keys. (Graphs G_h are indicated by their vertices only, respectively.) Thus, nodes a, b, c and f are not dominant. Only nodes g, h, and i decide to mark themselves as dominant. For instance, graph G_h for node g has vertices $\{i, h\}$ which are not connected, while this graph for nodes i and h is empty.

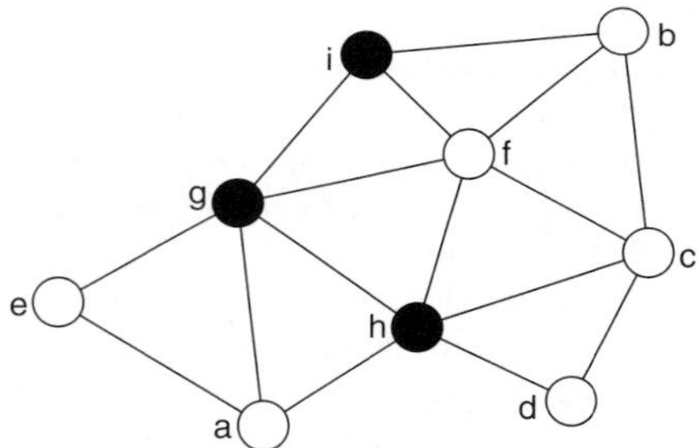

Figure 5: Applying Dai and Wu's algorithm

The key of a node may simply be its identifier, as used by Wu and Li (1999), or a pair (degree, id), as proposed in Stojmenović et al. (2001). For example, Wu et al. (2003) proposed this key for a node u:

$$\text{key}(u) = \{\text{energy}(u), \text{degree}(u), \text{id}(u)\}.$$

This means that nodes with higher energy levels have a higher probability of being elected as dominant. If the energy levels for two nodes are equal, then the second key, degree, is used for comparison. Finally, if there is a tie with the degree as well, the identifier is used. Figure 6 illustrates different sort of keys. In Figure 6(a), the key of a node is its identifier. In Figure 6(b) the degree is used as the primary key and the identifier as the secondary one. Some other keys were later proposed and studied by Shaikh et al. (2003).

Coverage by 2-Hop Neighbors

If positional information is not available, the described methods for covering neighbors by 1-hop neighbors all require 2-hop topological knowledge, because nodes need to know their neighbors and the neighbors of their neighbors. This knowledge, once available, could be better used by applying some enhanced concepts. To illustrate this, let us consider Figure 7(a) where the generalized self-pruning rule has been applied with identifiers as keys. The node a has been marked as dominant because it has two neighbors $\{b, f\}$, not directly connected, which are not covered by any set of neighbors with higher priority. In fact, a is itself covered by $\{b, e, f\}$ although e is not a 1-hop neighbor, and a could be marked as passive. While e is not a direct neighbor of a, this does not prevent the latter from verifying whether any of its neighbors are neighbors of e, or whether $\{b, e, f\}$ are connected, because e appears in the list of neighbors sent to a by its 1-hop neighbors, and therefore such a conclusion can be made. Similarly in 7(b), node b concludes that it is not dominant because

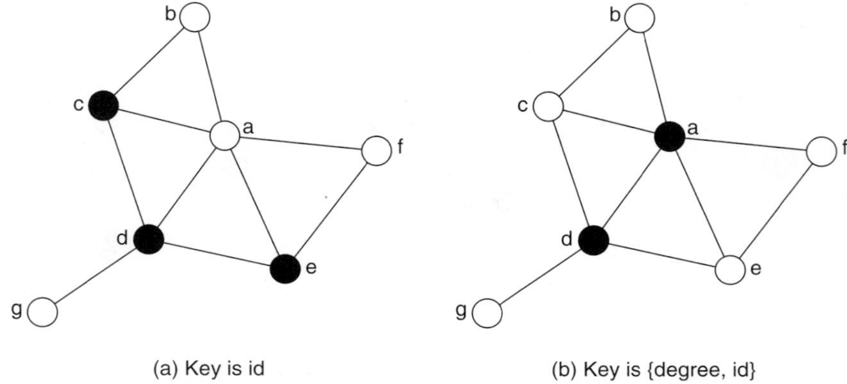

Figure 6: Applying Dai and Wu's algorithm with different keys

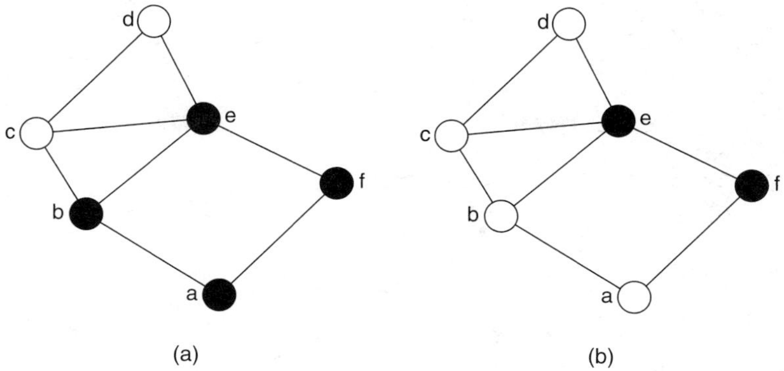

Figure 7: The enhanced definition of Dai and Wu's algorithm

all its neighbors $\{a, c, e\}$ as well as itself are covered by its connected higher key 2-hop neighbors $\{e, f\}$.

Therefore, we give an enhanced definition for computing a dominating set V_D, in general form (Wu and Dai 2003). We will later only discuss and implement the case $k = 2$, believing that the control overhead for $k > 2$ is prohibitive for use in practice.

Enhanced Dominating Sets. An intermediate node u is not dominant if there exists in its k-hop neighborhood a connected set A_u of nodes with either higher priorities or visited status, such that each neighbor of u either belongs to A_u or is a neighbor of a node in A_u.

Visited node status will be discussed in the next section, and, for now (in all definitions in this sub-section), we assume that u is not aware of any visited node.

Node u, if not dominant, must itself also be a neighbor of a node in A_u. To show that, assume that u has no neighbor in A_u, and consider its neighbor w with the highest key. Node w must be in the dominating set, because there does not exist another neighbor of u with higher key than the key of w, to cover u, which is a contradiction.

Note that when topological information is used, u is not aware of possible links between its 2-hop neighbors. It may therefore declare the set disconnected, although in reality it may not be (refer to Figure 2). This can be avoided by using positional information.

We now prove that this enhanced definition produces subset of nodes with respect to previous definition, and that it indeed produces a CDS.

Theorem 1. *The dominating set V_D obtained with the enhanced definition is a subset of the one obtained with the generalized self-pruning rule.*

Proof. In the generalized self-pruning rule, a node u is marked as not dominant if the subset of higher priority neighbors is connected and covers the neighborhood of u. As $N(u) \subseteq \dot{N}^2(u)\setminus\{u\}$, if there exists such a set in $N(u)$, then it also exists in $\dot{N}^2(u)\setminus\{u\}$. It can be derived that nodes marked as not dominant by the generalized self-pruning rule are also marked as not dominant by the enhanced definition. Only dominant nodes may be unmarked by the new definition.

Theorem 2. *For any given graph on which the enhanced definition is applied, each node u either belongs to V_D or is a neighbor of a node in V_D.*

Proof. Assume that the set V_D is not dominating. Let u be a non-dominant node with no dominant neighbor. Node u is covered by A_u, the set of 2-hop neighbors with higher key values than u. Let v be the node with the highest key value in $N(u)$. Node v has higher priority than u because of the existence of A_u and the need for at least one node from A_u to be 1-hop neighbor of u. Node v is not dominant because u is not covered by V_D. It is thus covered by a set A_v. Therefore, u is neighbor of a node w from A_v. Node w is therefore neighbor of u and has higher key value than v, which is a contradiction with respect to the choice of v.

Theorem 3. *For any given connected graph, there exists a path between any two nodes in the dominating set produced by the enhanced definition.*

Proof. We may assume that nodes are removed one by one in ascending order of priority instead of being removed simultaneously and will show that the removal of any node u preserves the connectivity. Let vuw be a path via node u. Node u is removed because of the set A_u, which is connected and covers its neighbors. Moreover, no nodes of A_u have already been removed since A_u contains nodes with higher priority than u. This means that there are two nodes v' and w' from A_u so that v is neighbor of v', w is neighbor of w', and v' and w' are connected in A_u. This means that nodes v and w remain connected after removal of node u. We can thus deduce that a node u will never remove itself from the dominating graph if there does not exist another path between any two components that are 'glued' together thanks to u.

These proofs are similar to the general proofs given by Wu and Dai (2003). All three proofs do not depend on the possible links between 2-hop neighbors. They are therefore valid for both topological and positional information. This does not mean that they will result in the same CDS. On the contrary, they can differ, because these additional links may be used to make connected a set of neighbors with higher priorities.

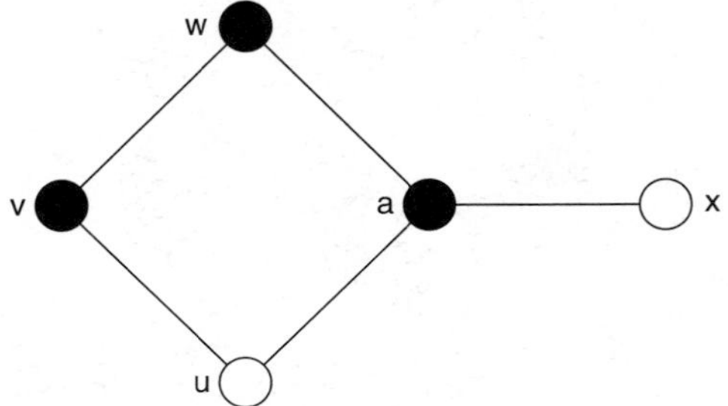

Figure 8: A new algorithm must be used for the enhanced definition

The algorithm described earlier for the general coverage by 1-hop neighbors is not applicable for this enhanced definition. Indeed, computing the graph G_h of neighbors with higher priority within the 2-hop neighborhood leads to nodes falsely marked as dominant, as illustrated by Figure 8. Node u is not dominant because there exists a connected set $\{v, w\}$ which covers $\{a, u\}$. However, the set G_h within the 2-hop neighborhood, $\{v, w, x\}$, is not connected. Using the original algorithm, u would have been marked as dominant. We therefore describe here a different algorithm from that presented in Wu and Dai (2003) for testing whether a node u will declare itself dominant, as follows. The algorithm takes $O(k^2d^2)$ time, where d is the average density.

1. Create a graph G_h composed from the nodes of higher priority than u (possibly including visited nodes) within the k-hop neighborhood of u.
2. Find the connected components in G_h; this can be done by repeated application of Dijkstra's shortest path algorithm, starting each time from an unseen node. Alternately, depth first search or breath first search protocols may be repeatedly applied to find all components.
3. If there is a connected component which covers all 1-hop neighbors of u, then mark u as not dominant.

Other approaches exist for computing CDS. Wan et al. (2004) thus compute a very small (non-connected) dominating set and then compute a spanning tree to connect it. Because such methods have huge time and communication costs, we did not consider them in our evaluation. An extensive performance comparison of CDS construction algorithms, including such methods, has been done by Basagni et al. (2006). They focused on pure CDS algorithms, and did not consider additional mechanisms like the NES.

Neighbor Elimination Scheme

The *neighbor elimination scheme* (NES, or *wait and see*) described by Stojmenović and Seddigh (2000) and by Peng and Lu (2000) provides a simple way to eliminate redundant messages. In this method, when a node receives a message to broadcast, it sets a *timeout* period before transmitting. That is, nodes do not retransmit immediately, but wait for *timeout* duration while monitoring their neighborhood. If all neighbors become covered during the monitoring time, then the node does not transmit. Otherwise, if the node's timeout expires and there are still uncovered neighbors, the node transmits. The timeout may be randomly chosen, or it may be computed based on several parameters. One solution is to let nodes with more neighbors rebroadcast earlier, so that more nodes can be covered by one transmission. We thus may define the timeout as *timeout* = *C*/*numberUncovered*, where C is a constant and *numberUncovered* is the number of neighbors that have not received the packet, based on node's knowledge. (Some neighbors could have received the packet from 2-hop neighbors that are not 1-hop neighbors; thus the node may not be aware of these transmissions). Ties can be resolved by using identifiers of nodes.

Figure 9(a) illustrates this scheme: node s sends a broadcast message to its neighbors b, d, and g. Each of these three nodes chooses a *timeout* duration inversely proportional to the number of its uncovered neighbors. For the sake of simplicity, let $C = 1$. Node b thus chooses to wait 1/2 time units (TU), d chooses 1/3 TU, and g chooses 1/2 TU. At step 2 in Figure 9(b), node d transmits next and forwards the message to its neighbors a, b, c, h, and s. Node c sets up a timeout of 1/2 TU and node a a timeout of 1 TU (because of g). Node h has no uncovered neighbors, so it does nothing. Note that a could also cancel the retransmission, but it is not aware that g already got the message from s. Node g now only has to wait 1/6 TU, because 1/3 time units have elapsed since it chose a timeout of 1/2 TU. Node b now has only one uncovered neighbor, so it changes its original timeout to 1 TU, reduced by already elapsed time 1/3, so its waiting time is 2/3. At step 3 in Figure 9(c), node g forwards the message to a, f, and s, allowing a to cancel its retransmission. The remaining timeouts are 1/2 for b and 1/3 for c. Finally at step 4 in Figure 9(d), c forwards the message to b, d, e, and i. Node b thus cancels its retransmission.

We call a *relay candidate* a node which is in a multipoint relay set or in a connected dominating set. This scheme may be used as an added feature to improve the performance of existing broadcasting protocols. Regardless of the underlying algorithm, the NES can indeed be added to decrease the number of transmissions while still preserving the reliability, as follows. When a node receives the broadcasting message for the first time, two cases are possible. Either the node is not a relay candidate, in which case the packet is simply dropped, or it is a relay candidate, and then an NES is started, as described. During the NES, each 1-hop neighbor covered by other transmissions of the broadcast packet is removed from an internal list, which at first contains all the 1-hop neighbors, and timeout is adjusted. When the timeout expires, the forwarding is done only if the node still has uncovered 1-hop neighbors. Obviously, if all neighbors are covered by very first received message, the retransmission is canceled immediately without invoking NES.

We will now revisit the general definition of enhanced dominating sets, completing the notion of *visited nodes* already mentioned there. The case when NES is not applied will be referred to as the case of empty set of visited nodes, or the case with 0-hop forwarding history, according to the definition used in Wu and Dai (2003).

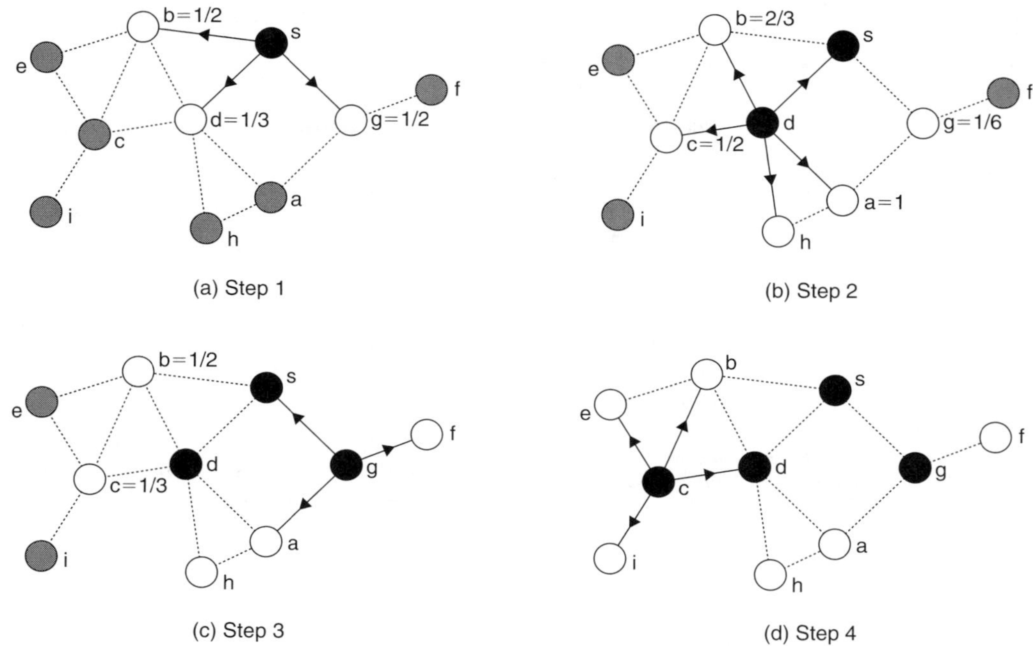

Figure 9: NES example

The application of NES to any of the methods will be referred to as the case of broadcasting with 1-hop forwarding history. In this case, the set of visited nodes is equal to the set to neighbors from which the message has been received. That is, visited nodes are exactly the nodes that have already retransmitted the packet. All neighbors of visited nodes are then eliminated by NES strategy. The node then applies coverage criterion to determine whether or not to retransmit. This means that the node waits for more information that would allow for a potential cancellation. If at the end of the timeout, there is still not enough information to allow the cancellation, then the transmission is performed. If the decision is to retransmit, then the node applies an additional *timeout* waiting period for possible enlargement of the set of visited nodes and hoping for subsequent cancellation of retransmission. Note that Wu and Dai (2003) did not discuss any analogous *wait and see* strategy.

The general case of L-hop forwarding history is also discussed and experimented with by Wu and Dai (2003). The case $L = 2$ corresponds to including, in the retransmitted packet, the identifiers of all neighbors from which this packet has been already received. The receiving node will then learn about all 2-hop neighbors which have so far retransmitted the message, and consider them as *visited* nodes in the general definition. While this method reduces the number of retransmissions, it also increases message length, adding to energy and bandwidth consumption. We therefore did not consider the case $L > 1$ in our experiments.

Connected Dominating Sets Based on MPR

Adjih et al. (2005) proposed a CDS election scheme based on MPR, later improved by Wu (2003). In this algorithm, each node computes its multipoint relays and transmits the forward list to its neighbors. To do this, it requires a third round of HELLO messages after 2-hop neighborhood topology is gained. Each intermediate node decides to belong to CDS if it has either the smallest id in its neighborhood, or it is the multipoint relay of the neighbor with the smallest id. When MPR's are being selected, free neighbors are added first to the set of relays. A node u is a free neighbor of v if v is not the smallest id neighbor of u.

Figure 10 illustrates this algorithm. Nodes d and e are not intermediate, and thus are not dominant. Nodes a and b are intermediate and have the smallest id in their neighborhood; thus, they are dominant. Using the greedy heuristics by Qayyum et al. (2002) nodes g and h are the multipoint relays of a, and nodes c and f are the multipoint relays of b. Because they are MPR's of their neighbor with smallest id, they are thus dominant. The particular example given here does not reflect the real performance of the algorithm in most cases.

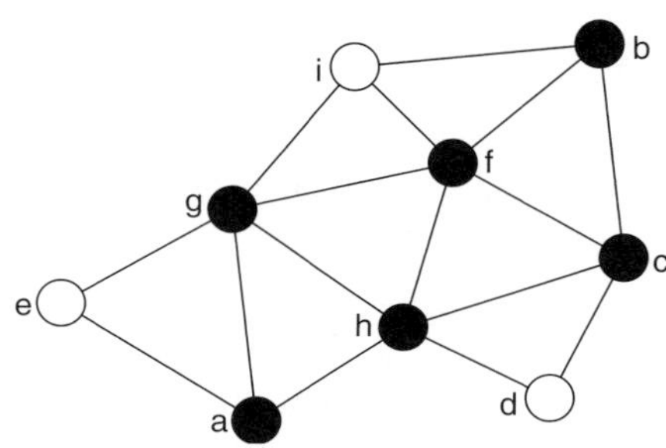

Figure 10: CDS obtained using the MPR-based definition

Broadcasting for Mobile Ad Hoc Networks

The techniques described so far assumed that the topology did not change since the last round of HELLO messages, and that topology does not change while broadcasting is in progress. To address moderate and high mobility scenarios that could violate this assumption, Stojmenović (2006) described the following broadcasting protocol. It adapts itself to all mobility scenarios, without tuning any parameter to change between static, moderate, and high mobility modes. This is important because other existing threshold-based approaches, switching between different protocols, may result in different protocols running at different nodes simultaneously, in addition to the incurred cost for gathering possibly suboptimal thresholds.

Nodes periodically exchange HELLO messages to update local knowledge up to two hops. The source node transmits the message. Upon receiving the message for the first time, each node initializes two lists: the receiver list (RL) of all nodes (up to a 2-hop distance) believed to have received the packet, and a list of neighbors in need of message (NN). The retransmission is cancelled if it is not in a selected connected dominating set. Otherwise a timeout waiting period is set. For each further message received, and its own message sent, every node updates RL, NN, and timeout. At the end of timeout, the node transmits if NN is non-empty. The message is memorized until T HELLO messages are received. The nodes add one bit to their HELLO message, indicating whether or not their list NN is empty, which is used in dominating set decisions. For each HELLO message received, NN is updated. Nodes that are no longer 1-hop neighbors are eliminated from the list, while new neighbors, not present in RL, are added. Regardless of previous decisions, all nodes that so far received the broadcast packet check whether new NN is non-empty. If so, they start fresh timeout.

EVALUATION OF PERFORMANCES

In this section, we provide experimental results about the performances of the selected protocols. The experiments were carried out in two phases. In the first phase, the performance of the basic schemes was evaluated. In the second phase, we added a neighbor elimination scheme to these algorithms and evaluated the performance of the resulting methods.

We use the commonly adopted random unit disk graphs, described earlier in this chapter, to model ad hoc networks. They are generated as follows: the network is always composed of 600 nodes randomly (and uniformly) placed in a square area which is scaled to obtain a given average degree. The radius R is set to be equal to 200 meters. For each measure, 500 broadcasts are launched and for each broadcast, a new *connected* network is generated. In connected graphs, the broadcast packet always reaches all hosts of the network because the broadcasting protocols are reliable.

We adopt certain assumptions to appropriately define the scope of our study. An ideal MAC layer is used, which provides for collision-free broadcasting. The hosts are static while broadcasting is in progress. Thus, any effect that mobility may have on the protocols is avoided. Because of localized algorithms being applied, it is assumed that relative positions of nodes do not change sufficiently to impact the performance while broadcasting is in progress. Only one broadcasting task at a time is in the network and there is no other message traffic while broadcasting is in progress: thus, we avoid the impact of collisions in our experimental data. A protocol with a lower overhead on one broadcasting task is expected to maintain better performance relative to other protocols when collisions are considered. Each node retransmits packets (if it has to retransmit according to the protocol) only once. All its 1-hop neighbors receive this packet correctly. While a node transmits, none of its neighbors up to 2 hops are transmitting. This assumption was used to eliminate the problem of interference when a node receives two radio transmissions at the same time from two of its neighbors, which are not neighbors themselves.

The acronyms used are as follows:

- MPR: The multipoint relays protocol. The heuristics used is the original one proposed by Qayyum et al. (2002) and 2-hop neighbors already covered (and known as covered by the node) are not considered when computing multipoint relays for a given node.
- CH: Connected dominating sets using the centralized heuristics by Guha and Khuller (1998). This one thus has *global* information on the network.
- DW: Connected dominating sets using the definition by Dai and Wu (2003). The key of a node is equal to the record {degree, id}.
- EDW: Connected dominating sets using the enhanced definition of DW, with topological information.
- EDWPOS: EDW with positional information.
- MPR-DS: Connected dominating sets based on MPR.

We first give the percentage of retransmitting nodes (noted PRN) in Figure 11. Figure 11(a) indicates that the MPR has a higher ratio compared to the other localized schemes. Moreover, each message in the MPR is longer. DW and MPR-DS behave equally well, this observation being consistent with results by Adjih et al. (2005). The enhanced definition EDW of DW gives better results than the latter as expected, and even better with positional information.

In Figure 11(b) we observe that the neighbor elimination scheme has significantly improved all localized schemes. It is interesting to note that all localized schemes obtain approximately same results after the addition of an NES. Not surprisingly, CH, as a centralized heuristics, always obtains very good results, and applying NES on top of it does not bring improvements. This is explained by the very low number of retransmitting nodes, and by the high distance between them, as will be shown later on. However, other schemes, while being localized, obtain close performance. When NES is applied, the number of relays in localized schemes is less than 1.5 times the one in CH. For the density of 30, the PRN of CH is equal to 7.8%, while the PRN of EDW is equal to11.5%. This proves that localized schemes can be as good as centralized ones.

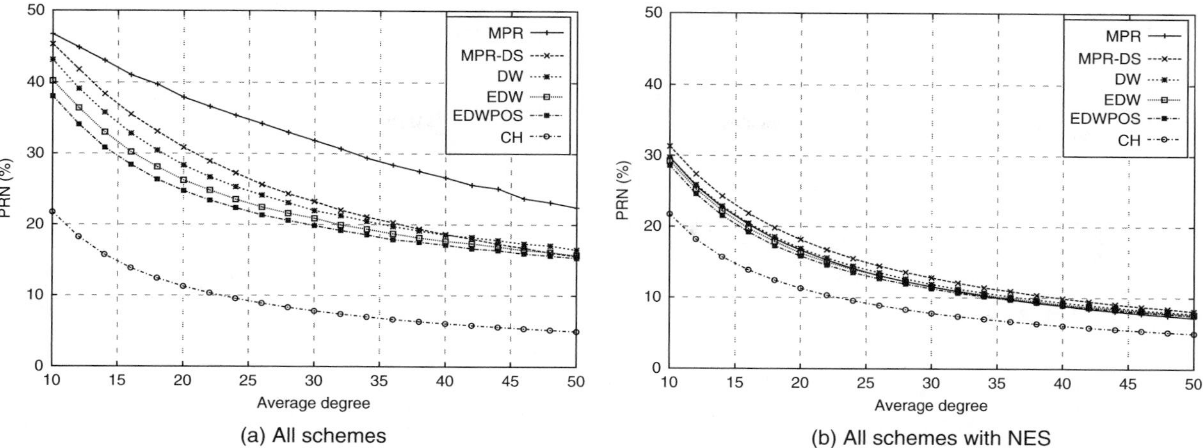

Figure 11: PRN versus average degree

We now give results about the number of times each non-transmitting node receives the message (NTN). CH has the best performance and the NTN values are relatively stable for all d values, while NES does not have a significant impact on it. In Figure 12, it is shown that MPR has the worst performance on this metric because as it seems to generate more redundancy, while other localized schemes obtain very similar results. We also observe that the number of received copies increases with the degree d, and that the neighbor elimination scheme is able to effectively reduce this redundancy. Indeed, as illustrated by Figure 12(b), nodes receive fewer copies of the same message, and traffic in the network is thus also greatly reduced. This improvement is obvious for all the localized schemes.

As with NTN, we measure the number of times each transmitting node receives the message (NTT). An observation similar to NTN can be obtained for NTT from Figure 13. That is, there is less redundancy in sparse networks than in dense ones. Recall that when the average degree d increases, fewer nodes retransmit the message. However, the number of times each node, transmitting or not, receives the same message increases. This can be explained by the increased coverage of each transmission. According to our observations, it appears that the transmitting nodes receive more copies of the same message than non-transmitting nodes. Once again, we notice that the neighbor elimination scheme greatly improves the localized schemes, while CH does not benefit from it. It is interesting to note that, in the latter, each node receives approximately the same number of copies of the message, whether or not it is a transmitting node.

Finally, in Figure 14, we give a comparison of the CDS schemes in terms of the dominant graphs they produce. Figure 14(a) gives the average degree of the CDS; this is the average number of dominant neighbors per dominant node. Not surprisingly, this value is dependent on the average size of the CDSs: the smallest is the set, and the smallest is the average degree, so CH obtains the best results while other algorithms are somewhat equivalent, with a smaller degree for MPR-DS. An interesting remark is that the degree of the CDSs produced by the centralized heuristics is constant for every density and is always around the value of 2. We also consider in Figure 14(b) the average length of the edges between two dominant neighbors divided by R. This value seems relatively

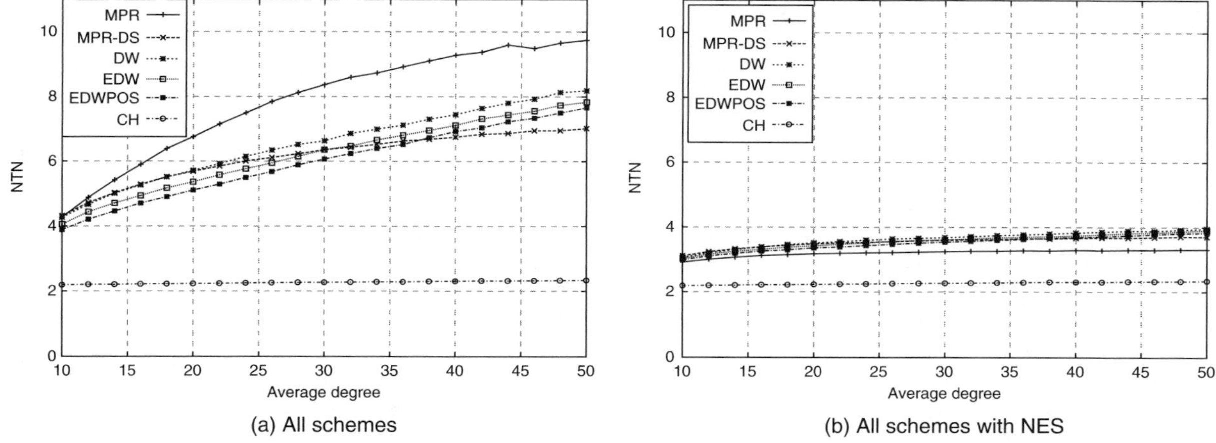

Figure 12: NTN versus average degree

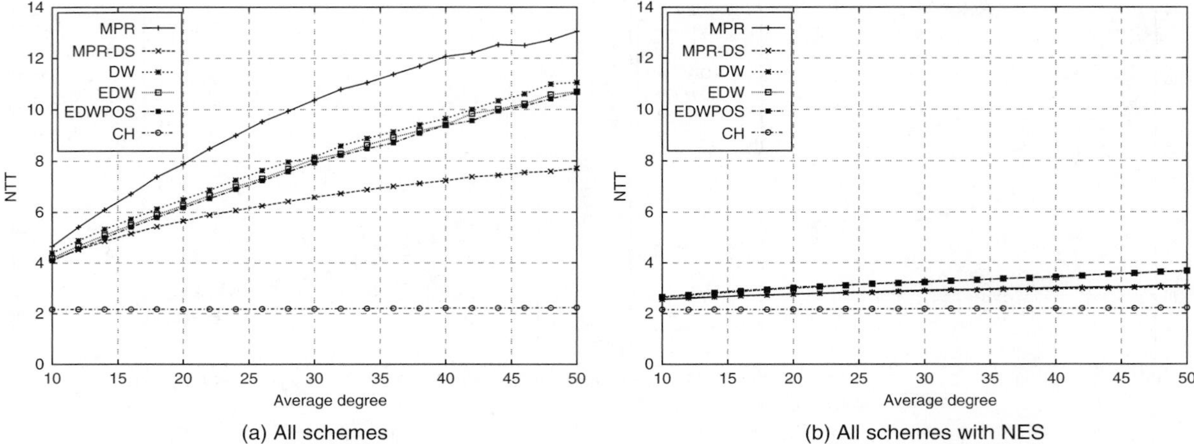

(a) All schemes (b) All schemes with NES

Figure 13: NTT versus average degree

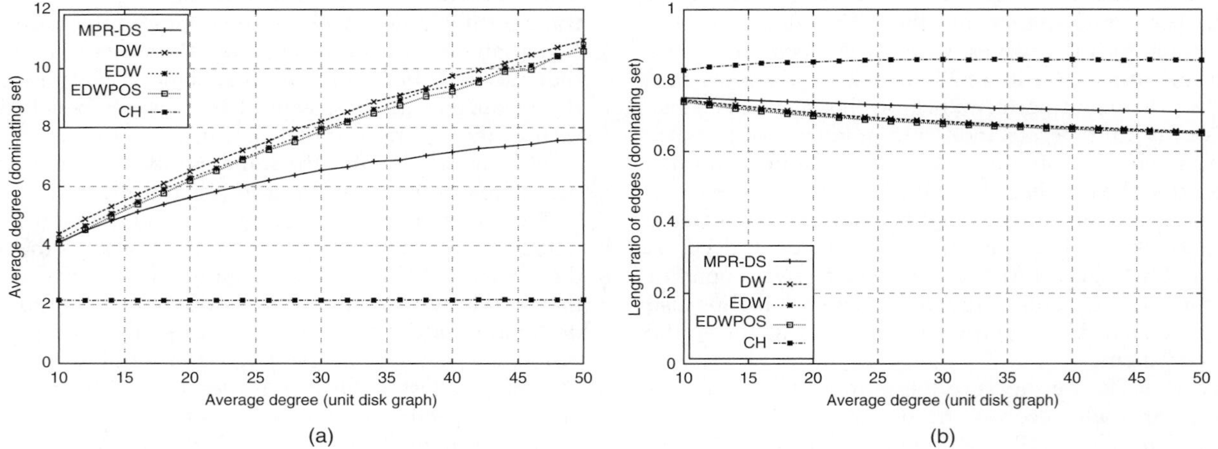

(a) (b)

Figure 14: Comparison of the produced CDSs

stable and does not really depend on the degree of the unit disk graph. The four localized schemes obtain nearly the same results, while CH has higher values. This can be easily explained: in this heuristics; at each step, the node with the highest number of 'non-covered' neighbors is chosen, and we can expect this value to increase with the distance between the nodes.

CONCLUSION

From the variety of simulations studied, we can draw a number of conclusions. The first, and most important one, is about the neighbor elimination scheme. It enhances the performance of all the protocols as an added feature. In our simulation studies, it reduces the number of instances of re-broadcasting, as well as message redundancy of both transmitting and non-transmitting nodes, and provides more enhancements in dense networks. Even in sparse networks, enhancements are sufficiently high to be noticeable. The MPR protocol seems to benefit the most from the addition of the NES.

Among all the examined localized schemes, EDWPOS + NES appears to require the fewest number of retransmissions. If we restrict consideration to topological information, the enhanced definition EDW + NES still is the one with the lower retransmission count, but the advantage over the two other NES based schemes is not major. The MPR-DS + NES scheme seems equivalent to other CDS schemes, but requires a third round of HELLO messages, and therefore is inferior in dynamic networks. It thus appears that pure dominating set-based approaches are winning methods overall, remaining competitive in all network scenarios.

All algorithms depend on the density of the network. In sparse networks, more nodes need to rebroadcast to reach all the nodes in the network. As the density increases, proportionally fewer nodes need to rebroadcast. As the density of the network increases, so does the number of times each node, transmitting or non-transmitting, receives the same message. The transmitting nodes receive more copies of the same message than non-transmitting nodes for all *d* values.

For future research related to this chapter, a more realistic environment could be considered. Indeed, we evaluated the performance of the selected schemes and the constructive effect of adding an NES, and we assumed an ideal MAC layer. But in real networks, as the network density increases, heavier contention and collision increase the probability of packet loss. Future study could thus evaluate the performance of the broadcasting protocols under contention, collision, and other network conditions.

Another issue in wireless ad hoc and sensor networks is the presence of node mobility and different transmission radii. Maintenance of connected dominating structure in the presence of moving nodes is a significant operation that may involve a significant amount of message traffic. Different transmission ranges of the mobile nodes or a hidden terminal problem might cause unidirectional links. The performance evaluation of the broadcasting protocols may provide new insights by considering the influence of these factors.

More work still needs to be done about the evaluation of energy consumption when energy spent upon reception of packets is taken into account. Indeed, it has been pointed out very recently that the reception of a message can be more expensive than its transmission (Lu et al. 2005). In this case, the number of receiving nodes becomes a factor of prime importance, even more than the number of transmitting nodes: as the density increases, there are fewer transmissions but more receptions, and thus the energy consumption also increases until a threshold is reached, where the number of transmissions is sufficiently low to counterbalance the high number of receptions. This is different from what has been considered in previous studies and quite a new problem to solve.

GLOSSARY

Broadcasting: Sending a packet from a source node to all other nodes.

Dominating Set: A set of nodes such that every node either belongs to this set, or is a neighbor of a node that belongs to this set.

Positional Knowledge: The term used when a node knows the exact location of its neighbors.

Reliable Broadcasting Protocol: A broadcasting protocol that ensures delivery of the packet to every node connected to the source node, under ideal conditions.

Topological Knowledge: A term used when a node is only aware of links between its neighbors, but does not know their location.

CROSS REFERENCES

See *Emerging Trends in Routing Protocols in Mobile Wireless Ad Hoc and Sensor Networks; Medium Access in Ad Hoc and Sensor Networks; Network Middleware; Network QoS; Principles and Applications of Ad Hoc and Sensor Networks*.

REFERENCES

Adjih, C., P. Jacquet, and L. Viennot. 2005. Computing connected dominated sets with multipoint relays. *Ad Hoc & Sensor Wireless Networks*, 1(12):27–39.

Basagni, S., M. Mastrogiovanni, A. Panconesi, and C. Petrioli. 2006. Localized protocols for ad hoc clustering and backbone formation: A performance comparison. *IEEE Transactions on Parallel and Distributed Systems*, 17(4):292–306.

Carle, J., and C. Simplot-Ryl. 2004. Energy efficient area monitoring by sensor networks. *IEEE Computer Magazine*, 37(2):40–46.

Dai, F., and J. Wu. 2003. Distributed dominant pruning in ad hoc networks. In *Proceedings of the IEEE International Conference on Communications (ICC'03)*, Anchorage, Alaska.

Garey, M., and D. Johnson. 1979. *Computers and Intractability: A Guide to the Theory of NP-Completeness*. San Francisco: W.H. Freeman.

Guha, S., and S. Khuller. 1998. Approximation algorithms for connected dominating sets. *Algorithmica*, 20(4):374–87.

Johnson, D., D. Maltz, and Y. Hu. 2004. The dynamic source routing protocol for mobile ad hoc networks (DSR). Internet Draft, draft-ietf-manet-dsr-10.txt.

Lovasz, L. 1975. On the ratio of optimal integral and fractional covers. *Discrete Mathematics*, 13:383–90.

Lu, J., F. Vallois, and D. Barthel. 2005. Range adjustement for broadcast protocols with a realistic radio transceiver energy model in short-range wireless networks. In *Proceedings of the International Conference on Mobile Ad Hoc and Sensor Networks (MSN'05)*, Wuhan, China.

Ni, S., Y. Tseng, Y. Chen, and J. Sheu. 1999. The broadcast storm problem in a mobile ad hoc network. In *Proceedings of the International Conference on Mobile Computing and Networking (MobiCom'99)*, Seattle, WA.

Peng, W., and X. Lu. 2000. On the reduction of broadcast redundancy in mobile ad hoc networks. In *Proceedings of the ACM International Symposium on Mobile Ad Hoc Networking and Computing (ACM MobiHoc)*, Boston, MA.

Qayyum, A., L. Viennot, and A. Laouiti. 2002. Multipoint relaying for flooding broadcast messages in mobile wireless networks. In *Proceedings of the Hawaii International Conference on System Sciences (HICSS'02)*, Big Island, Hawaii.

Shaikh, J., I. Stojmenović, and J. Wu. 2003. New metrics for dominating set based energy efficient activity scheduling in ad hoc networks. In *Proceedings of the International Workshop on Wireless Local Networks (WLN 2003)*, Bonn, Germany.

Stojmenović, I. 2004. Comments and corrections to 'dominating sets and neighbor elimination-based broadcasting algorithms in wireless networks'. *IEEE Transactions on Parallel and Distributed Systems (IEEE TPDS)*, 15(11):1054–55.

———. 2006. Adaptive parameterless broadcasting for static, mobile, and highly mobile ad hoc networks. University of Ottawa, unpublished manuscript.

Stojmenović, I., and M. Seddigh. 2000. Broadcasting algorithms in wireless networks. In *Proceedings of the SSGRR, International Conference on Advances in Infrastructure for Electronic Business, Science, and Education on the Internet*, L'Aquila, Italy.

Stojmenović, I., M. Seddigh, and J. Zunic. 2001. Dominating sets and neighbor elimination-based broadcasting algorithms in wireless networks. *IEEE Transactions on Parallel and Distributed Systems*, 13(1):14–25.

Stojmenović, I., and J. Wu. 2004. Broadcasting and activity scheduling in ad hoc networks. *Mobile Ad Hoc Networking*, (S. Basagni et al., eds.): 205–229. IEEE Press.

Wan, P., K. Alzoubi, and O. Frieder. 2004. Distributed construction of connected dominating sets in wireless ad hoc networks. *ACM/Kluwer Mobile Networks and Applications (MONET)*, 9(2):141–49.

Williams, B., and T. Camp. 2002. Comparison of broadcasting techniques for mobile ad hoc networks. In *Proceedings of the ACM International Symposium on Mobile Ad Hoc Networking and Computing (MOBIHOC'02)*, Lausanne, Switzerland.

Wu, J. 2003. An enhanced approach to determine a small forward node set based on multipoint relays. In *Proceedings of the IEEE Vehicular Technology Conference (VCT 2003)*, Orlando, FL.

Wu, J., and F. Dai. 2003. Broadcasting in ad hoc networks based on self-pruning. *International Journal of Foundations of Computer Science (IJFCS)*, 14(2):201–221.

Wu, J., and H. Li. 1999. On calculating connected dominating sets for efficient routing in ad hoc wireless networks. In *Proceedings of the ACM International Workshop on Discrete Algorithms and Methods for Mobile Computing and Communications (DIALM 1999)*, Seattle, WA.

Wu, J., B. Wu, and I. Stojmenović. 2003. Power-aware broadcasting and activity scheduling in ad hoc wireless networks using connected dominating sets. *Wireless Communications and Mobile Computing*, 4(1): 425–38.

Data Monitoring and Gathering in Sensor Networks

Symeon Papavassiliou and Stella Kafetzoglou, *National Technical University of Athens, Greece*
Jin Zhu, *University of Northern Iowa*

INTRODUCTION

The recent advances in micro sensor technology and low-power analog/digital electronics have led to the development of distributed, wireless networks of sensor devices. Sensor networks of the future are envisioned to consist of hundreds of inexpensive nodes that can be readily deployed in physical environments to collect useful information (e.g., seismic, acoustic, medical, and surveillance data) in a robust and autonomous manner. A distributed sensor network is usually a self-organized system composed of a large number of sensor nodes that collaborate with one another to measure different parameters that may vary with time and space, and to send the corresponding data to a collector center for further processing.

Application domains are diverse and can encompass a variety of data types including acoustic, image, and various chemical and physical properties. These sensor nodes will perform significant signal processing, computation, and network self-configuration to achieve scalable, robust, and long-lived networks. Furthermore, because of power and transmission range limitations, data dissemination in sensor networks is typically carried out as a collective operation, in which sensors collaborate to get data from different parts of the sensor network to the information sinks (Akyildiz et al. 2002). The collaboration among different sensor nodes is mostly realized through multihop network architectures because of their energy-efficiency and scalability features (Shen, Srisathapornphat, and Jaikaeo 2001).

A major energy consumer in wireless sensor networks is radio communication. A comparison of the cost of computation to communication presented by Pottie and Kaiser (2000) reveals that 3000 instructions can be executed for the same cost as the transmission of one bit over 100 m. Energy conservation in such networks involves two dominant approaches to minimize communication overhead. The first is at the medium access control (MAC) and network layers, where nodes turn off their radios when they are not required for multihop communication. The second is data reduction through in-network processing (also called data aggregation), where correlations in data are exploited to reduce the size of collected and transmitted data, and correspondingly communication cost. Because local computation is much cheaper than radio communication, supporting some in-network processing to reduce data within the network, and thus shifting the computation into the network, can provide significant energy savings.

Toward this direction several research works in the literature have discussed the problems of developing efficient joint routing and data management techniques, as well as application-specific data aggregation processes, to support efficient data monitoring and gathering approaches in sensor networks. Furthermore, several issues associated with the data aggregation process with the specific objective of meeting the task requirements (i.e., quality of service [QoS] constrained data monitoring and gathering) have also been recognized and considered recently. The rest of this chapter is structured as follows. We first present some performance metrics of interest for the design of efficient data monitoring and gathering methods, followed by a discussion of the related traffic and data correlation models. We then discuss several issues associated with the sensor node deployment patterns for the implementation of effective data monitoring. We also describe several data gathering approaches by classifying them into many diverse categories according to different features and design dimensions of the wireless sensor networks, and present some indicative associated protocols. Finally, we present a relative qualitative comparison of the different data gathering approaches, highlighting their respective merits, drawbacks, and performance.

PERFORMANCE METRICS

Before we describe and discuss the various data gathering and dissemination approaches, we first present some performance metrics of interest and their impacts on the design of efficient and effective data monitoring and gathering methods. The sensor network should dynamically adapt to the system and topology changes; at the same time, it needs to balance the trade-offs among the various performance metrics. Following is a summary of the main performance metrics that need to be considered by the data monitoring and gathering approaches in sensor networks.

Delay/latency: For time-crucial applications, the sensor nodes are required to complete the data monitoring and gathering task within a predefined and strict latency; any data received out-of-date is considered useless. The definition of *delay* is application dependent; the *latency* might be defined as the time interval from the point when a query is sent out until proper information is received by an end user. Alternatively, it may be defined as the time required for some collected data to be transmitted back to the collection sites. In most cases, of practical interest are some statistics with respect to the delay (e.g., average delay, probability that delay is less than some given threshold), rather than single delay values.

Energy efficiency and network lifetime: The parameters used to evaluate the degree of energy efficiency include the average energy used to transmit a bit to/from the source to the collection center (J/bit), the total energy consumption/dissipation over an operation time period (J/unit time), and the ratio of the energy consumed to transmit the data payload to that consumed to transmit the overhead. Closely related to the energy efficiency is network lifetime. Depending on the application under consideration, the network lifetime can be defined as the time interval from the point that the sensor network starts its operation until: 1) the first node dies; 2) the sensing coverage falls below a prespecified threshold; 3) the number of active nodes is less than a prespecified threshold; or 4) loss of communication to the collection site by all sensor nodes occurs.

Accuracy: The precise definition of the accuracy is determined by the specific application. For example, if the sensor network is used to monitor environmental variables, the observed signal specifications such as temporal resolution, spatial resolution, and range accuracy are the accuracy parameters of concern. In target detection and classification applications, the accuracy may involve the missing-detection probability, false-alarm probability, and the average classification accuracy.

Sensing coverage: According to the deployment schemes, the sensing coverage can be divided into two categories: deterministic coverage and stochastic coverage. *Deterministic coverage* means that the placement is predetermined so that each node can be deployed at a specific position. The predefined deployment patterns could be uniform in different areas of the sensor field, or can be weighted to compensate for the more critically monitored areas. The *stochastic coverage* refers to the scenario in which the sensor field is covered with sensors randomly distributed throughout the environment. The sensing coverage relies not only on the appropriate placement of the nodes but also on their sensing capabilities.

Throughput: Because the bandwidth in sensor networks is limited and high node density may produce large amounts of data, the end-to-end transmission throughput needs to be maximized, besides providing fairness and low complexity of implementation. In some applications such as forest fire or nuclear power plant monitoring (Mladineo and Knezic 2000; Lin, Wang, and Sun 2004), the information disseminated may increase abruptly when an emergency event occurs, and as a result peak throughput provided should satisfy the requirements under this scenario.

Additional parameters: Some additional simplified and specific metrics, such as bit-hop metric (Pattem, Krishnamachari, and Govindan 2004), the ratio of payload data to overhead of packets, and the probability of buffer overflow have also been used to indicate the degree of energy efficiency. Lindsey, Raghavendra, and Sivalingam (2002) proposed and used the product of the energy and delay (i.e., energy*delay) as a potential metric to capture the system performance on balancing the energy and delay cost for data gathering in sensor networks. Alternatively, weighted cost functions can be used to balance the trade-offs of the various performance metrics. The cost function can be defined as the sum of products of the weights and the corresponding performance elements (e.g., delay, energy efficiency, accuracy, Zhu, Papavassiliou, and Yang 2006), where the weights can be adjusted according to the end-user demands and requirements.

TRAFFIC MODELING AND DATA CORRELATION

Sensor networks are typically more application specific than traditional communication networks that are designed to accommodate various types of traffic and applications. As a result, closely related to the data monitoring and gathering process for different applications and scenarios are the corresponding traffic models and data correlation models.

Traffic Models

Depending on the patterns of the measurement and information to be monitored and transmitted, the traffic can generally be divided into three main categories: deterministic traffic, event-driven or threshold-sensitive traffic, and response-to-inquiry traffic. For the first type, there is a steady traffic flow between the source node and the sink. In such cases, sensors usually generate deterministic and/or periodic traffic, in which each node transmits its data once every specific time interval. The event-driven or threshold-based mode corresponds to cases where transmission of information is triggered by an event (e.g., a monitored variable exceeds some threshold; the change of an attribute value exceeds some predefined threshold, etc.). The sensor networks that aim at object detection or system monitoring (e.g., road traffic monitoring, forest fire monitoring, etc.) usually present this type of traffic. The third class, response-to-inquiry traffic, corresponds to cases where the sensors respond to inquiries dispensed by an end user or observer, which may be targeted to a specific set of sensors and/or for a specific time interval.

In general, various applications may involve more than one traffic modes. For example, in a seismic monitoring sensor network, the observation value will be periodically sent back to the collection site to record and accumulate data at the normal operation state for further analysis and processing; however, when the seismic intensity (vibration amplitude) measured exceeds a specific threshold, the observation will be transmitted to the sink immediately and the end users may further issue inquiry-based traffic. The different traffic and load conditions in the network may impact the performance of the data gathering approach. For instance, the ad hoc response-to-inquiry traffic results in two-way communication that involves the dissemination of both the inquiries and the collected data, whereas the other two modes mainly generate one-way communication flows. The data dissemination and gathering strategies should be selected taking into account the different traffic models. For deterministic traffic, the data gathering strategy can be optimized based on certain known patterns, whereas in principle the data gathering strategy should be able to adapt to the burst change of the traffic, in order to accommodate other traffic modes as well.

Data Correlation Modeling

Unlike traditional wireless cellular networks, in which the communication is person-to-person and the contents of conversations are irrelative to one another, in sensor networks the data in the neighboring nodes are considered highly correlated because the observed objects in the same geographical location are usually strongly correlated. Under this assumption, the data processing and aggregation might utilize the spatial correlation of local nodes and dramatically decrease the amount of information to be transmitted. Estimation of the data correlation properties based on the previous and current collected data can be used to locally optimize the data compression and aggregation in the subsequent data gathering phases. Furthermore, utilizing the appropriate spatial correlation models to generate synthetic data based on the availability of only a small amount of experimental data inputs allows for efficient and accurate testing and evaluation of the corresponding data monitoring and gathering approaches (Jindal and Psounis 2004).

With respect to the signals emitted from certain sources, it is usually assumed that the signal magnitude of the event's effect at a distance *d* from the source is proportional to $1/d^{\alpha}$, where α is the propagation parameter. The value of α depends on the type of sensing event (e.g., seismic vibration, sound, light, infrared signal, etc.) and the medium in which the signals travel/propagate (e.g., ground, air, water). If the observation has multiple sources, the signal event arriving at a node is usually obtained as some function of the multiple events' effect.

In principle, the readings at each sensor can be regarded as samples of a random variable. Therefore, statistical joint moments of two random variables can be used to summarize the corresponding correlation properties. Assuming that the observations at two nodes are represented by random variables X and Y, respectively, then the ij-th joint moment of X and Y is represented by $E(X^iY^j)$. For $i = j = 1$, the resulting moment E(XY) is called the correlation of X and Y, whereas the covariance of X and Y is defined as: $COV(X,Y) = E[(X - E(X))(Y - E(Y))]$, where E[X] and E[Y] denote the expected values of random variables X and Y, respectively . Both of these statistics are among the most commonly used to characterize the correlation between two observation sets. For sensors using n-bit A/D converters, based on the fact that a reading can be represented as one of the 2^n possible values whereas the difference of the readings among nearby nodes may be represented by fewer than n bits, Chou, Petrovic, and Ramchandran (2003) proposed a differential encoding method that allows nodes to transmit fewer bits for each reading. A linear model is used to estimate the correlation between two sample data of two nodes and to further determine the number of bits with which to ask the sensors to encode their values. According to this model, the optimal scaling factor that can provide best estimation between two known reading sets X and Y was found to be $E[XY]/E[Y^2]$.

In a more information-theoretic based approach, the correlation among observations at different sensors can also be characterized by the joint entropy of multiple sources (Pattem, Krishnamachari, and Govindan 2004). Given knowledge of some data from other sensors, the conditional entropy of the quantized data of one sensor can be computed. It is expected that the conditional entropy decreases when nodes get closer. Thus, using entropy coding, sensors can compress their data and transmit at a rate equal to the corresponding conditional entropy.

SENSOR DEPLOYMENT FOR DATA MONITORING AND GATHERING

The overall purpose of an efficient data monitoring and gathering methodology is to provide accurate and timely information, and at the same time extend the network operation lifetime for as long as possible. The optimal data gathering strategy depends on the density of nodes, position of sink, task requirements, and amount of correlation among the sources of the data. Therefore, to develop effective data monitoring and gathering strategies, we first need to develop an appropriate deployment scheme, which includes determining the number of nodes, density, types of sensor nodes, and how to deploy the nodes (e.g., deterministic or random), to achieve the required objectives, such as sensing coverage, fault tolerance, measurement accuracy, and so forth.

The placement of sensors has significant effects on many factors associated with the data monitoring and gathering in sensor networks, such as the desired accuracy, temporal and spatial resolution, evolution of the information to be gathered and disseminated, connectivity, efficient routing, and fault tolerance. The deployment planning process involves a detailed analysis of the environmental map and related data to determine the most appropriate placement of sensor nodes and maximize the sensor field coverage. In general, the sensing coverage reflects how well an area is monitored or tracked by sensors. Because of the inherent uncertainty associated with the processes of monitoring and sensing, probabilistic modeling of sensor coverage is desired. After the sensors are deployed according to a predetermined pattern, the locations of the nodes can be adjusted or additional sensor nodes may be placed to

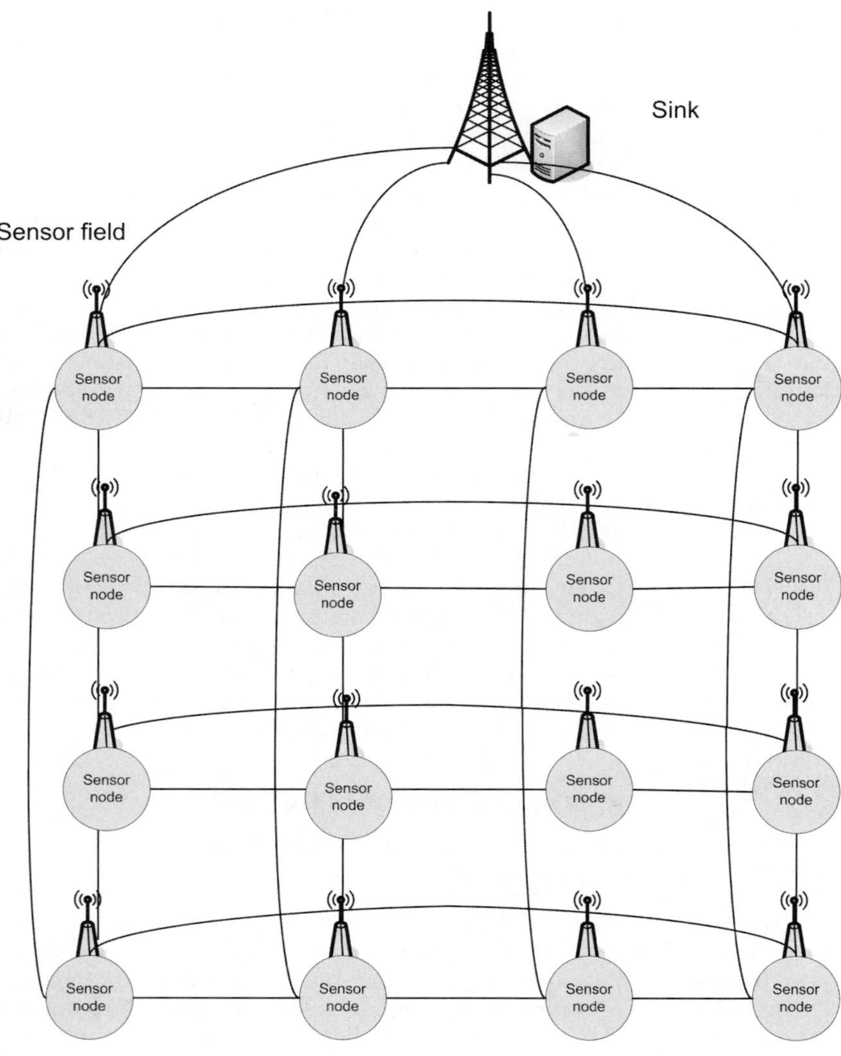

Figure 1: Predetermined mesh topology sensor network

maintain the required sensor coverage and/or the desired network connectivity as the sensor network evolves.

Various deployment approaches that may range from deterministic to random have been considered by taking into account different constraints and situations. In Figure 1, a predetermined mesh topology is presented; Figure 2 depicts the topology of a randomly deployed network. Specifically, for deterministic deployment, each node is placed at a specific position (manually or using robots) to maximize the sensor coverage. This method is suitable for cases where the sensors are static or fixed and sufficient knowledge of the environment is available for precalculation of the optimal sensor positions. This case is similar to the art gallery problem (AGP; O'Rourke 1987), and usually the suboptimum solution can be obtained by heuristics methods. For example, Chakrabarty et al. (2002) have developed approaches for deployment in two- and three-dimensional grids by formulating the node placement problem as combinatorial optimization and coding theory problems, and solving them using integer linear programming.

Although this kind of well-controlled node placement can provide good coverage for a given scenario, it is infeasible in many situations because the sensors may be deployed in unfriendly areas or the associated cost could be quite high for deterministic placement of a large number of nodes. Therefore, the alternative option—random deployment of sensor nodes, such as throwing sensor nodes from air vehicles into the target area—is often more practical and desirable. In this case, the sensor field is covered with sensors randomly distributed in the environment, the aforementioned stochastic coverage; Meguerdichian et al. (2001) proposed a centralized polynomial time algorithm for the computation of worst-case and best-case coverage for random deployment using Voronoi diagram and graph search algorithms. In order to achieve energy efficiency, several algorithms have been proposed to address how to adaptively place sensors into the sleep mode while still maintaining full coverage of the sensing fields (see, e.g., Cerpa and Estrin 2002; Huang and Tseng 2003).

In some situations, it is expected that only very limited prior knowledge of the possible targets—or even no knowledge of the corresponding terrain—would be available. In this case, the single-step deployment may produce inferior coverage because of the lack of environmental information. One alternative method is to deploy sensors

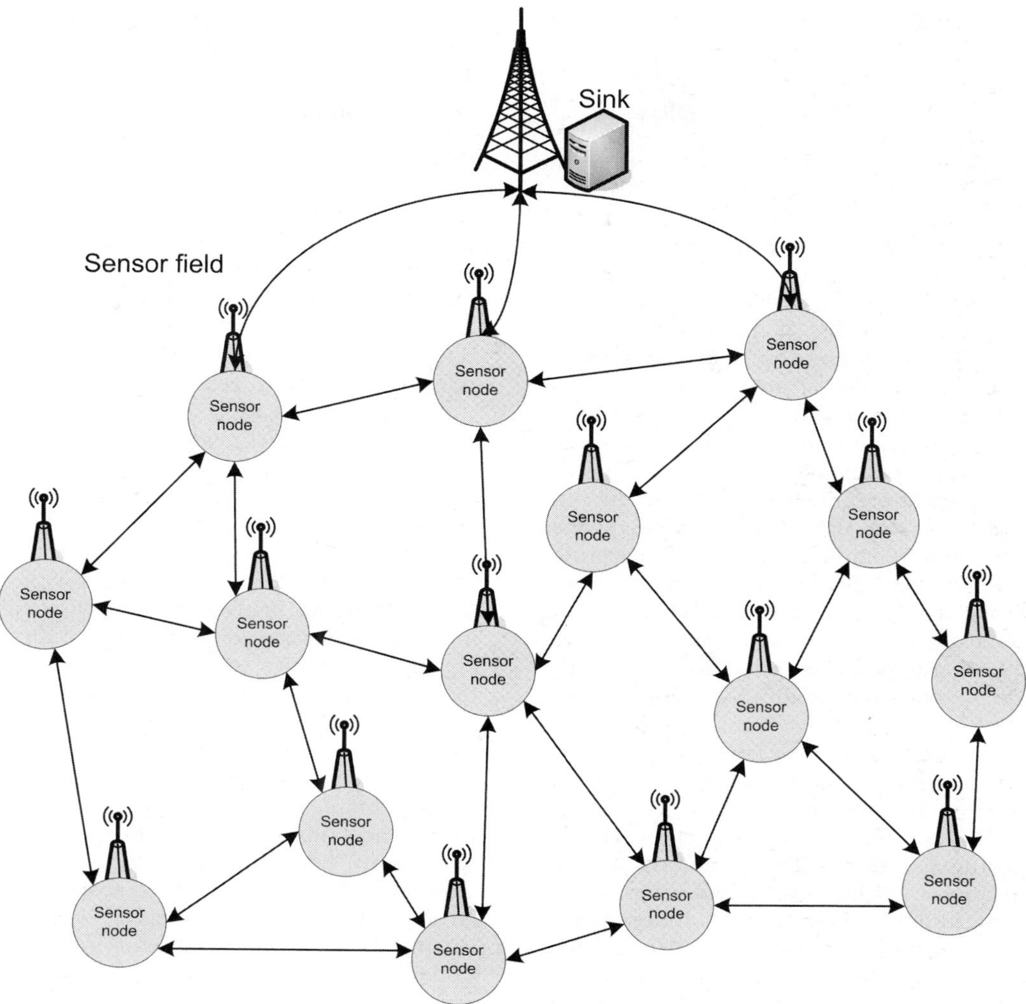

Figure 2: Randomly deployed sensor network

sequentially (i.e., to scatter a subset of the sensors at each step) and the information cumulated from previous deployed sensor nodes will be used to determine the further deployment steps. Clouqueur et al. (2002) developed an incremental deployment approach of sensor nodes for target detection purposes. Only subsets of the available nodes are deployed in each step until the minimum exposure or probability of target detection is achieved. Additional methods have been proposed to determine the insufficiently covered regions based on different criteria. For instance, Huang and Tseng (2003) proposed polynomial-time algorithms, in terms of the number of sensors, to determine whether every point in the sensor field is covered by at least k sensors.

It should be noted here that a large number of uncertainties may occur in the sensor deployment process. For instance, when dispensing sensors from air vehicles, the actual landing position is affected by many elements, including the trace of air vehicles, the wind, the terrain conditions, and other obstacles such as trees and buildings. Recently, Zou and Chakrabarty (2004) proposed a new approach to address the uncertainty problem. The proposed approach aims at optimizing the number of sensors and determining their placement in order to maximize the average desired coverage, as well as the coverage of the most vulnerable regions in the sensor field. Even for deterministic deployment, the expected sensor coverage and the actual results may differ because of the change of environment as the network evolves. Therefore, as previously mentioned, further adjustment may be required after the initial deterministic or random deployment. This could be achieved either by moving the deployed nodes to their desired location or by placing supplementary sensor nodes to cover the blind spots. Because the position of mobile nodes is easy to adjust, they are usually used to implement self-deployment or to provide enhanced flexibility. Toward this direction, Wang, Cao, and La Porta (2004) have designed distributed movement-assisted self-deployment protocols for mobile sensors, based on the principle of moving sensors from densely deployed areas to sparsely deployed areas.

Another important design challenge of a sensor network is the issue of self-organization, which refers to the ability of the system to achieve the necessary organizational structures without requiring human intervention. Self-organization is a critical attribute needed to achieve the wide use and applicability of distributed sensor networks. Consequently, once the sensors are deployed, they have to form networks in an autonomous matter, using self-organizing procedures to discover their neighbors and acquire their location. In addition, because of the dynamic nature of the network and the energy constraints of the sensors, fault tolerance and self-healing are required for an operation that will be left unattended for an extended time to be feasible. Sensors may get disconnected from the network because of their battery depletion, and new sensors may be deployed to maintain the connectivity and the environmental coverage of the network. Therefore, self-organization procedures (e.g., self-management, self-healing) must be provided so that the network can work in a robust and autonomous manner. For instance, Sohrabi et al. (2000) have presented a series of protocols for establishing and maintaining connectivity in wireless sensor networks: the self-organizing medium access control for sensor networks (SMACS), eavesdrop and register (EAR), and sequential assignment routing (SAR) protocols. Gupta, Das, and Gu (2003) also addressed the self-organization issue and developed protocols for sensor networks for efficient query execution. Moreover, most of the data gathering approaches presented later in the chapter include methods for handling sensor node failures and insertions.

As mentioned earlier, one of the key features of self-organization is localization. Location awareness of the sensors is crucial for the operation of a large-scale network, enabling the intelligent selection of appropriate devices and supporting useful coordination among them. In addition, localization can offer a complementary way to reduce energy consumption in multihop wireless sensor networks (e.g., by improving routing; Bulusu, Heidemann, and Estrin 2000). In many cases, sensors are assumed to have knowledge of their location based on global positioning system (GPS) coordinates. In reality, however, this solution may be not applicable to all sensors because of cost, antenna size, and power consumption constraints; therefore, several localization techniques have been proposed in the literature. Most of these consider the case where a few sensor nodes (known as beacon or anchor nodes) of the network have a priori knowledge of their positions, either from a GPS device or by manual configuration, whereas the rest of the network sensors acquire their location by calculating their distance from the anchor nodes based on the packets received and the signal strength (Langendoen and Reijers 2003). Depending on the number of beacons used, as well as the algorithms deployed for the calculation of the distance and the angle/direction, a different grade of location accuracy can be achieved.

Experimental Sensor Network Deployment

Sensor networks can greatly improve environment monitoring for many civil and military applications, such as target detection and classification, precision agriculture, habitat monitoring, or patient monitoring. One of the experimental wireless sensor network pioneers is the Great Duck Island project (http://www.greatduckisland.net). In August 2002, researchers from UC-Berkeley/Intel Research Laboratory deployed a mote-based tiered sensor network on Great Duck Island, Maine, to monitor the behavior of storm petrel. Furthermore, in December 2004, the OSU DARPA-NEST team completed the first demonstrations and experiments of ExScal (www.cast.cse.ohio-state.edu/exscal/). The ExScal project deploys about 1000 sensor nodes and 200 backbone nodes, making it the largest wireless network assembled to date. The purpose of the development of ExScal is for the detection and classification of multiple intruders types over an extended perimeter. Other habitat-monitoring examples include the PODS Project (http://www.pods.hawaii.edu/), which is used to remotely monitor the rare species of plants in Hawaii for long-term study, and ZebraNet (http://www.princeton.edu/~mrm/zebranet.html), which is used to study zebra behaviors such as long-range migration, interspecies interactions, and nocturnal behavior. The Sensor Web (http://sensorwebs.jpl.nasa.gov/) measures light levels, air temperature, humidity, soil temperature, and soil moisture, and the collected data are used to study the effects of microclimate on plant growth. Recently, Intel also deployed a sensor network with sixty-five nodes at a vineyard in British Columbia, Canada (http://www.intel.com/research/vert_agri_vineyard.htm). Wine grapes are highly sensitive to temperature; therefore, real-time temperature; data from the motes (sensor nodes developed by UC-Berkeley) can identify which vines are most likely to need frost-control measures, whereas the cumulative temperature data can help the grower choose the best moment to pick the grapes. Finally, with regard to patient monitoring, several experimental sensor networks have been deployed. Researchers from Harvard University have developed a scalable software infrastructure for wireless medical devices, called CodeBlue (http://www.eecs.harvard.edu/~mdw/proj/codeblue/). CodeBlue is designed to provide routing, naming, discovery, and security for wireless medical sensors, personal digital assistants (PDAs), personal computers (PCs) and other devices that may be used to monitor and treat patients in a range of medical settings. The sensor nodes that are used are called VitalDust (Vital Sign Sensors) and collect heart rate, oxygen saturation, and EKG data, and relay it over a short-range (100m) wireless network to any number of receiving devices, including PDAs, laptops, or ambulance-based terminals. Moreover, the ubiquitous monitoring environment for wearable and implantable sensors (UbiMon) project aims at addressing general issues related to using wearable and implantable sensors for distributed mobile monitoring (http://www.ubimon.org/).The aforementioned experimental sensor networks can provide empirical data sets for further study and optimization of the data sensor networks.

DATA GATHERING STRATEGIES

The simplest possible strategy to send data from the sensor nodes to a base station is called *raw data gathering* and consists of direct transmission of the information from all sensors to the sink (Heinzelman, Chandrakasan, and Balakrishnan 2000). If the base station is far away from the sensors, a huge amount of transmit power is required, which would lead to a quick depletion of the energy recourses of every sensor and consequently reduce the network's lifetime. Although the raw data gathering approach could in principle provide a nearly optimal solution in cases where the sink is close to the nodes, in most cases, even for moderate-sized sensor networks, this approach is considered energy inefficient. To prolong the network's lifetime, data reduction is necessary; this is achieved mainly through in-network processing. Because the observed objects in the physical world are usually highly correlated, sensors that are deployed close to one another are expected to collect similar information about their environment, and thus data aggregation methods can be utilized to improve the overall data gathering operation.

Data gathering approaches can be classified into many diverse categories according to different features and design dimensions of the wireless sensor networks and associated protocols. More specifically, given the network's structure and organization, data gathering approaches can be divided into two main categories: hierarchical and nonhierarchical protocols. The hierarchical approaches are further divided into the cluster-based, chain-based, and aggregation tree constructive protocols. Clustering is the partitioning of a data set into subsets, so that the data in each subset share some common trait. In the case of wireless sensor networks, nodes are organized into groups, called *clusters*, and a node is elected to act as the group leader (called the *cluster head*). Clusters can also be used to form different layers of a hierarchy. The member nodes of each cluster send their data to the cluster head, which is responsible for sending the collected data either to a higher layer cluster head or directly to the sink. Chain-based protocols construct a chain connecting all nodes, thus reducing the total distance of data transmission. Nodes send their data to their neighbor node in the chain, and each node is responsible for forwarding its neighbor's data, possibly along with its own data. At each round, only one sensor transmits the total data packet to the sink. The third category of the hierarchical approaches includes protocols that construct trees rooted at the sink and spanning the whole network. In these schemes, each node sends its data to its parent in the tree, and the parent node fuses it with its own readings and passes it to its parent one layer above until the aggregated packets reach the final destination node. On the other hand, the nonhierarchical approaches disseminate the data throughout the whole network in a flat manner, without involving any physical or logical hierarchical structure (e.g., through flooding).

One of the basic and critical operational processes in sensor networks, that is closely related to the data gathering is the routing process. Therefore, a large number of strategies that have been proposed in the literature perform the gathering of data generated in the network along with the corresponding routing decisions made, in order to optimize the overall process. On the other hand, there is a class of protocols for data gathering that aims to be routing independent. The objective of this class of protocols is to provide a more generalized and flexible data aggregation and gathering framework that achieves energy efficiency in a way that is independent of and complementary to the routing protocol.

An additional dimension encountered in wireless sensor networks—different from most of other wireless and personal networks—refers to the nature and the different kinds of data that are transmitted. Although a large number of approaches send the collected data in their genuine form, it is possible that alternative approaches can be used to send encoded data to reduce the amount of data transmitted in every gathering round. This approach also constitutes a form of aggregation or, more precisely, fusion, and the corresponding techniques are known as distributed data compression techniques. They mainly reduce the amount of data transmitted by exploiting the spatial correlations that exist among different data packets.

A separate class of data aggregation methods can be created by several approaches that take advantage of the spatial correlations between the sensors' readings, in a rather different way than the ones mentioned above, by selecting only a subset of sensors to perform data gathering. More precisely, these approaches do not perform actual data aggregation but instead at each gathering round select subsets of nodes to report their readings. Neighborhood nodes are expected to collect analogous information; therefore, only one is active at each round and sends its gathered data to the sink. The other nodes move into idle or sleep mode to save their energy resources. These methods are comparable to the MAC approaches in which sensor nodes turn off their radios to achieve energy efficiency.

Furthermore, it should be noted that in most common scenarios in sensor networks, individual sensors are deployed in an area and are usually immobile, forming a wireless fixed network. However, there are some cases (e.g., for tracking applications) where the sensors can move either by outside force or by their corresponding mobility component. Therefore, for these cases, mobility presents an additional challenge that may affect the operation and effectiveness of the data monitoring and gathering process.

In wireless sensor networks, the sensors either continuously sense their environment and send their data to the sink in a periodic manner or gather data in an event-driven way, in which sensors report their readings only if an event has occurred (e.g., a value threshold has been exceeded). However, in some cases, users or applications may request data on demand by posing different types of queries to the sink. Therefore, the methodology and frequency of the data collection process also pose different and interesting design challenges in wireless sensor networks.

The aforementioned categorizations and classes of data monitoring and gathering approaches do not constitute mutually exclusive groups, and, as a result, one methodology may belong to more than one class. Naturally hybrid solutions are required to consider and balance the corresponding trade-offs, depending on the overall objective of the developed strategy. In the following section, we present a more detailed description of each one of these classes, by providing representative protocols and describing the operation and functionality of these approaches.

Hierarchical Protocols

Cluster-Based Protocols

As mentioned before, in cluster-based approaches clusters are formed with one leader (cluster head) at each cluster. The cluster head is engaged in collecting all the

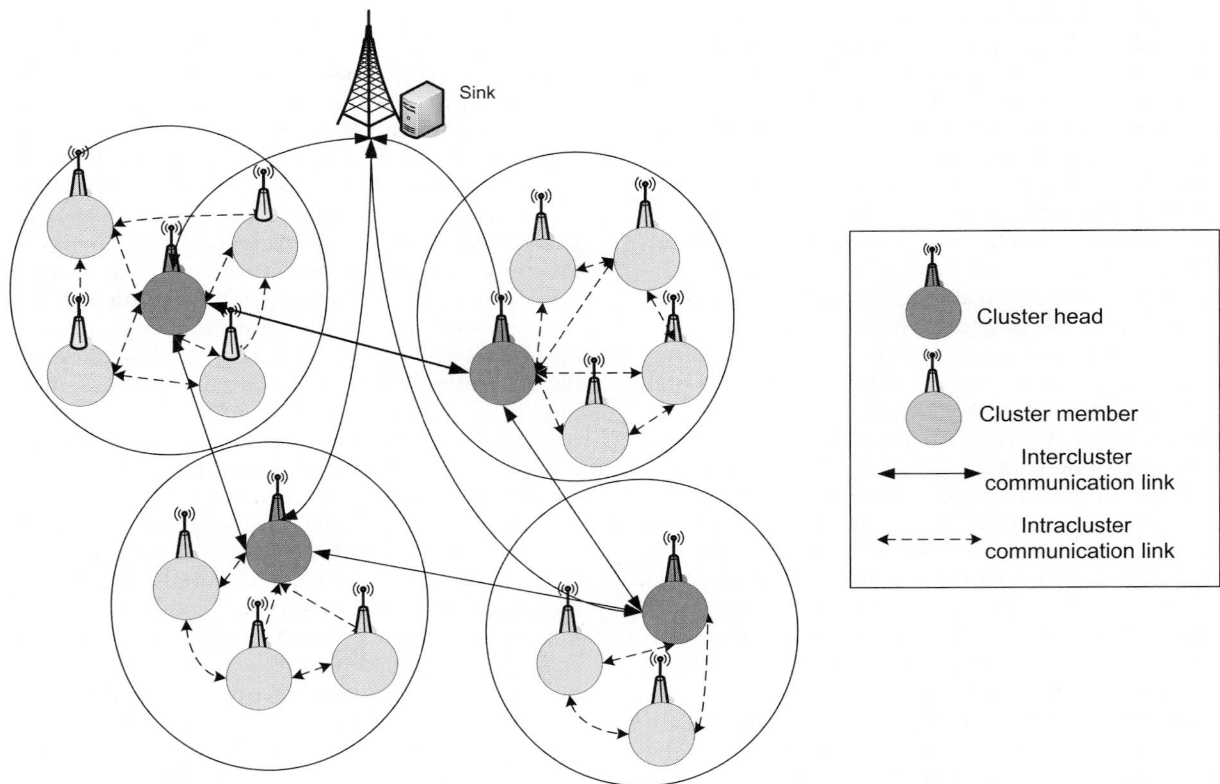

Figure 3: Cluster-based data gathering approach

data from the members of its cluster, performing some sort of data aggregation in order to reduce the data size, and forwarding it either to a higher-layer cluster head or directly to the sink. The corresponding cluster-based formation is illustrated in Figure 3.

Heinzelman, Chandrakasan, and Balakrishnan (2000) presented the low-energy adaptive clustering hierarchy (LEACH) protocol, which is considered one of the most representative cluster-based protocols. In the implementation of LEACH, sensors are organized into clusters with one node acting as leader at each round. The member nodes of each cluster send their data to their cluster head, which in turn performs local data fusion to compress the amount of data to be sent, and at the end of each round sends the corresponding data to the sink. The cluster head sensors, which at each round transmit to the sink, consume significantly larger amount of energy, especially when compared to the other types of nodes. In order not to drain the batteries of these sensors, randomized rotation of the high-energy cluster-head role is utilized. The clusters are reconstructed every round and every time a new sensor is elected cluster head in a random way. In a centralized version of LEACH, called LEACH–C (Heinzelman 2000), the cluster formation is done at the beginning of each round using a centralized algorithm initiated by the base station. Although this version of the protocol performs better than LEACH, the associated energy cost for the cluster formation is higher and knowledge of the network topology is required for the cluster formation phase.

Another approach suggests an enhanced version of the LEACH algorithm, namely E-LEACH (Pham, Kim, and Moh 2004). This implementation contains four phases: a) advertisement, b) cluster setup, c) schedule creation, and d) data transmission. The first three phases are identical to the original LEACH algorithm, whereas in the last phase all cluster heads, after receiving the data from their cluster members, form a chain using a greedy algorithm starting from the cluster head that is farthest from the sink and transmit their data along the chain.

Choi, Shah, and Das (2004) proposed a two-phase clustering scheme to improve energy efficiency. In the first phase, the sensor network is partitioned into clusters, each with a cluster head, and sensors join the nearest cluster head by forming a direct link to it. During the second phase, cluster members are required to search for a cluster member neighbor who is closer than the cluster head, and form a data relay link to it. Each time a member node has data to transmit, it either uses the direct link or the data relay link to send its data, depending on the delay constraint to be met. The data relay point aggregates its sensed data and received ones, and then forwards the aggregated data to its data relay point or the cluster head. When all data have been collected at the cluster head, it is forwarded to the sink. In this way, further improvements in energy savings and distribution of the cluster head's workloads can be achieved.

Dasgupta, Kalpakis, and Namjoshi (2003) proposed an alternative cluster-based approach for data gathering. The network is partitioned into clusters, called *super sensors*, which make use of a greedy clustering algorithm that selects the farthest sensor node i from the sink and forms a cluster that includes node i and its $(c-1)$ nearest neighbors, where c is a constant. The process continues until all sensors have become members of a cluster. For every super sensor, a maximum data gathering lifetime schedule is computed using a greedy clustering-based maximum lifetime data aggregation (CMLDA) heuristic. A data gathering schedule specifies how the data packets from all the sensors are collected and transmitted to the sink. Based on each schedule computed, aggregation trees are constructed for the sensors.

Chain-Based Protocols

Another class of hierarchical protocols for data gathering is the chain-based protocols. Chain-based protocols construct a chain that connects all nodes, thereby reducing the distance of total data transmission and decreasing the energy dissipation per round. A representative chain-based topology is shown in Figure 4. Among the simplest chain-based protocols presented in the literature is the linear-chain scheme. A linear chain connects all nodes within the network and data is transmitted from one end of the chain to the other. Each node attaches its own data to the received data to form a larger packet and sends it to the next node. To conserve energy, each node maintains the same size of header.

Among the most representative examples of a linear-chain protocol is the power-efficient gathering in sensor information systems (PEGASIS) protocol (Lindsey, Raghavendra, and Sivalingam 2002), in which each node communicates only with its closer neighbor and takes turns transmitting to the sink. The nodes are organized to form a chain, which can either be computed in a centralized manner by the sink and broadcast to all nodes or accomplished by the sensor nodes themselves using a greedy algorithm. At each round, a node receives a data packet from its neighbor in the chain, fuses it with its own data (thus generating a single packet of the same length) and transmits it to its other neighbor in the chain. At each round, only one node is assigned to transmit the total data packet to the sink. Each time a different node is selected in order to increase the network's lifetime. The drawback to the linear-chain schemes is the large delay from data sensing to data transmission to the base station, and therefore enhanced chain-based schemes for data gathering have been proposed.

A chain-based protocol for data broadcasting and data gathering was also the subject of a similar study presented by Du, Wu, and Zhou (2003), which is suitable especially in cases of sparse sensor networks. The authors divided the network into regions based on a center node. At each region, the linear-chain scheme is employed to gather the data of the sensors within the region at the center node. The center node can either combine the collected data using an aggregation function or simply relay the separate packets to the sink. The multichain scheme proposed constructs the subchains through a sequence of insertions.

Lindsey, Raghavendra, and Sivalingam (2002) also presented a binary combining scheme using code division multiple access (CDMA) in which it is possible for node pairs to communicate using different codes, thereby avoiding radio interference. Data are combined using pairs of nodes at each level, which results in a hierarchy of $\lceil \log N \rceil$ levels, where N is the total number of sensors in the network and $\lceil \log N \rceil$ represents the least integer greater than $\log N$. For data gathering, each node at a given level transmits to its neighbor. However, nodes that receive at each level, are the only ones that are active in the next level.

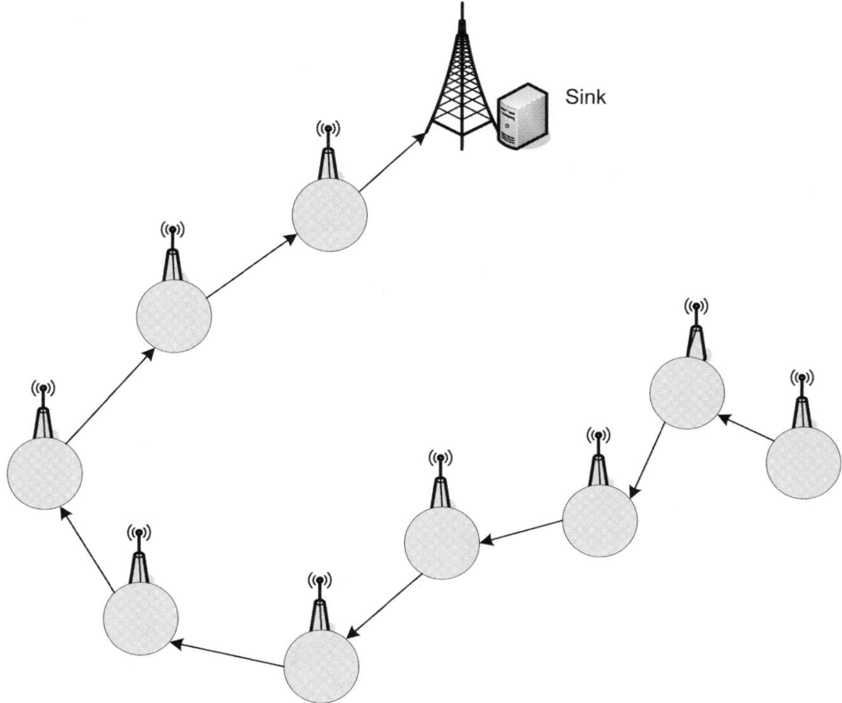

Figure 4: Chain-based data gathering approach

At the top level only one node is active and is responsible for transmitting the total packet to the base station. The nodes perform data fusion at each level, except for the end nodes. By allowing nodes to transmit simultaneously, the delay cost is reduced in comparison with the simple linear-chain scheme. However, using different codes for the communication of the sensors may not be applicable, because the CDMA-capable nodes are expensive. Thus, Lindsey, Raghavendra, and Sivalingam (2002) presented a chain-based three-level scheme without using CDMA. To allow simultaneous transmissions with minimum interference, the sensors of the network are divided in G groups (where G is a random integer and G = 10 is considered a near optimal choice). Within each group, the linear-chain scheme is used for G simultaneous transmissions.

Tree-Constructive Protocols

In these schemes, a rooting tree is constructed that spans the whole network. The sink initiates the process, and, at each step, new sensors join the tree until all nodes become members of the tree, either as internal nodes or leaves. The data gathering is performed along with the rooting; each node sends its data to its parent in the tree until the packets reach the destination node (i.e., the sink). Packets can also be aggregated in their way up to the root to conserve energy. Figure 5 presents the resulting topology of a typical aggregation tree-based protocol.

Thepvilojanapong, Tobe, and Sezaki (2005) suggested the efficient data gathering (EDGE) protocol, which is basically a tree-constructing algorithm for data gathering. The tree is constructed as follows: the root initiates the tree construction by broadcasting a child request (CRQ) packet. Each node that is not a member of the tree collects a number of parent candidates, which are saved at a parent candidate (PC) table, and chooses one according to some metrics (e.g., the response time that signifies their distance). Then it sends a child reply (CPR) packet to the selected parent, and the parent responds by sending a child acceptance (CAC) packet. Specific joining and leaving procedures are provided by the protocol to handle the dynamic nature of sensor networks. If there is node failure, the tree is reconstructed. When the sink requests data or the nodes have data to send, the data gathering is performed using the gathering tree. Each node forwards its own data and all of the received data to its parent, until all the data are collected at the sink. If a node is not attached to the tree, it buffers the data and sends it later.

In a similar study, Tan and Körpeo (2003) proposed another tree-constructive algorithm, namely the power-efficient data gathering and aggregation protocol (PEDAP). The PEDAP computes a minimum spanning tree over the sensor network where the costs of the edges are proportional to the transmission costs. Each sensor node belonging to the tree aggregates (or fuses) the data provided by its children with its own, and transmits one single packet to its parent until it reaches the root of the tree (i.e., the sink). Prim's algorithm is used to compute the minimum spanning tree, and it is initiated

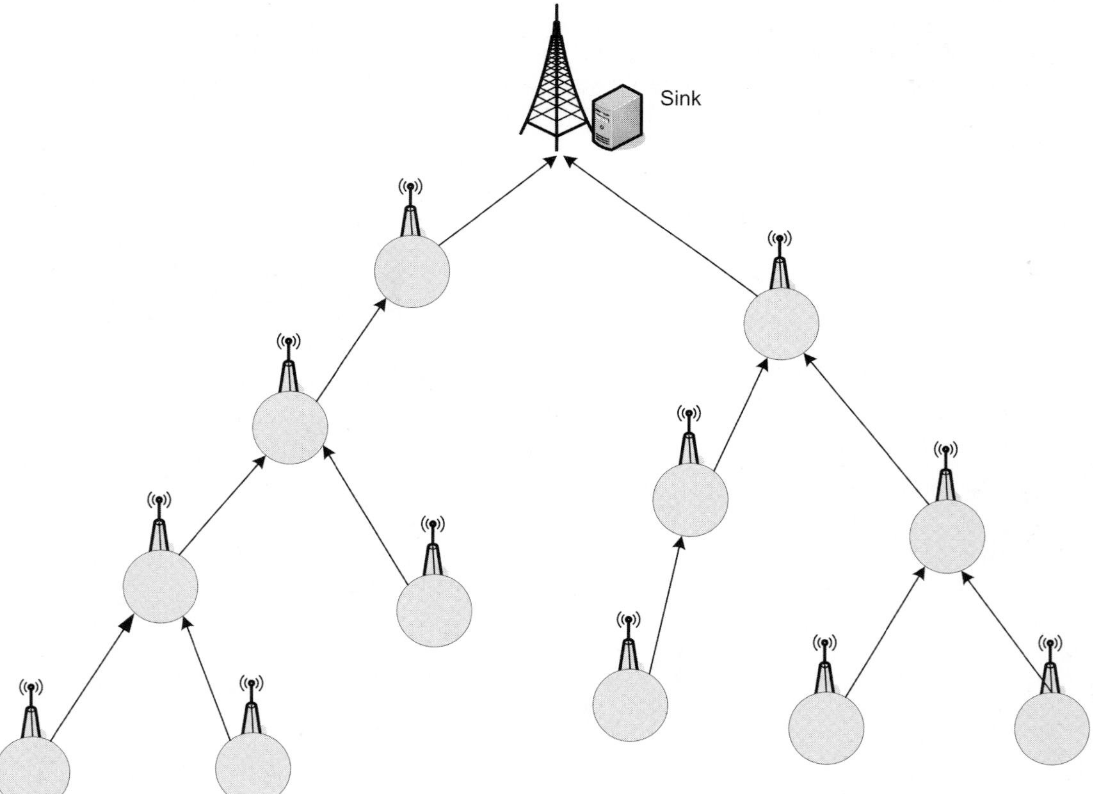

Figure 5: Tree-constructive data gathering approach

every k rounds to adapt to the given state of the network. Parameter k is configurable and presents a trade-off between complexity and accuracy.

Non-Hierarchical Protocols

Flooding is considered one of the most well-known non-hierarchical protocols in which the information is disseminated to the entire sensor network. Whenever a node has data to send, a copy is sent to all its neighbors. Likewise, whenever a node receives a data packet, it makes a copy and forwards it to its neighbors, except the neighbor from which it originally received the data. The use of flooding for data gathering is considered energy inefficient because a significantly large number of redundant data packets inundate the network and sensors consume their energy to handle these packets. Therefore, this approach is rarely used for data gathering and is useful only for very specific applications. Gossiping, (Heinzelman, Kulik, and Balakrishnan et al. 1999) is an enhancement of the flooding approach used to partially overcome the associated energy inefficiency problem. In gossiping, sensors do not forward the data packet to all of their neighbors but randomly select one to send the packet to. In that way, fewer copies of data packets are made and less traffic is generated in the network; as a result, less energy is depleted in every node.

The non-hierarchical approaches also include the directed diffusion proposed by Intanagonwiwat, Govindan, and Estrin (2000). This scheme is data centric—as data generated by a sensor node are named by attribute value pairs. The base station or any other node requests named data by sending interests, and data matching the interest are then drawn down toward that node. Each time a node senses data, the data are disseminated throughout the sensor network. This dissemination sets up gradients within the network, and, if interests fit gradients, paths of information flow from the nodes to the one that requested the data (usually the sink). The sensor network, in particular the sink, reinforces a small number of these paths in order to "draw down" higher quality data. To reduce the communication costs and the energy that is dissipated, data are aggregated on the way to the sink.

Routing-Independent and Probabilistic Methods

The data gathering approaches discussed in the preceding subsection are to a large extent dependent on the routing decision. In this section, different approaches that are routing independent and use probabilistic methods for performing data aggregation are presented. The corresponding aggregation strategies can be implemented at every individual node in a distributed fashion and are in principle complementary to the respective routing protocol used.

Zhu, Papavassiliou, and Yang (2006) presented a novel approach called QoS-constrained data aggregation and processing (Q-DAP), in which the application QoS requirements are taken into account to determine when and where to perform the aggregation function. Each intermediate sensor node determines independently whether or not to perform data aggregation randomly with some specific probability that is precalculated according to the resource conditions and the specific task requirements. One of the main principles of the proposed scheme is that the network does not need to be formed into clusters to perform the data aggregation, whereas the task QoS requirements are taken into account to determine when and where to perform the aggregation in a distributed fashion, based on the availability of local information only. Upon receiving the data packets, the intermediate nodes determine whether or not to perform aggregation or simply forward the packet. One of the following may happen: a) If the delay constraint provided by the application can be met with probability γ, the node waits (i.e., the packet is deferred) for a certain time interval τ for other packets to arrive and aggregate the data received, forming one single packet. When the time interval expires, it forwards the data to the next sensor node where the same procedure is followed until the data reaches the sink. With probability $(1-\gamma)$, the node simply forwards the data. b) The node checks (determines) whether the delay constraint can be met only if the packet is not deferred, and forwards it to the next hop. c) The node determines whether the delay constraint cannot be satisfied in any case and discards the packet. Both the probability γ and the deferred time interval τ can be defined by the application or the user. The proposed scheme has been shown to offer significant energy savings, mainly because of the traffic reduction that is achieved by the data aggregation. In Figure 6, an example of this approach is illustrated in which three packets are combined in one packet during the deferred period τ.

Another probabilistic application-independent data aggregation scheme has been presented by He et al. (2004), in which the authors proposed an adaptive mechanism that reduces the energy consumed by sending a smaller amount of data at the MAC layer. The aggregation function is performed at a completely different layer employed between the data-link control layer and the network layer. Packets to be transmitted are passed from the network layer to the data aggregation layer, where they are concatenated in one aggregated packet, and afterwards the packet is passed to the MAC layer for transmission. The number of packets to be concatenated is determined by a control unit that makes decisions according to the current network conditions. When the aggregated packet reaches the next node, the reverse procedure is followed: the packet is de-aggregated and passed to the network layer where only packets that are destined for that node are maintained, and the others are sent for rerouting.

As previously mentioned, the decision of how many packets should be concatenated into a single one is made by a control unit based on various network and traffic conditions. Thus, when the delay at the MAC layer is high, the number of packets to be concatenated is large. On the other hand, when there is light traffic in the network, packets may not wait for others to form a concatenated packet but will be transmitted as soon as they are received. There should be an upper bound on how much time the packets are going to stay in the aggregation layer and wait for others to form a single packet, because usually there is an associated delay threshold for the delivery of the data to the final destination.

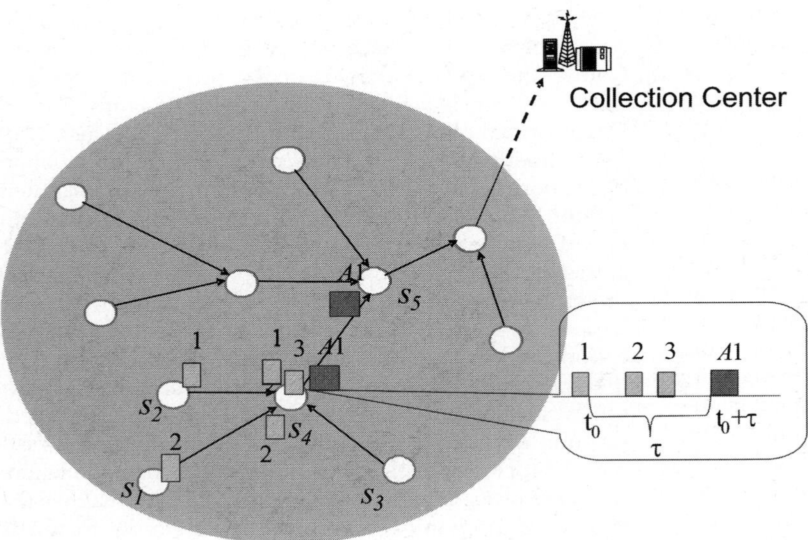

Figure 6: Data aggregation in the Q-DAP approach

Data Gathering Based on the Nature of Data

The data gathering approaches in sensor networks can be described and classified based on the nature of the data to be transmitted. Distributed data compression schemes are widely used for sending out the data collected at each gathering round. The nature of data in this case is encoded. Other techniques are based on the dissemination of metadata before sending their actual data.

Distributed Data Compression Techniques

One of the basic principles behind the minimization of the energy consumption in a wireless sensor network is to reduce the number of bits transmitted at each data gathering round. Another approach for achieving efficient data gathering is based on the source coding principle. There exist several distributed data compression techniques in the literature that compress the data generated at each node while exploiting the spatial correlations among them. However, any approach used for data coding and compression has to take into account the associated overhead cost for processing (i.e., coding and decoding). The processing cost should not be very high; otherwise, the energy savings from the information communication reduction would not improve the overall energy cost.

In general, in data compression approaches, a sensor node uses an aggregation function to encode the data available at a node before forwarding it to the sink. These schemes can be classified into multi-input and single-input coding strategies. In the first case, aggregation is performed at a node only if all input information from multiple nodes is available to explore the correlation properties among several nodes, whereas in the latter case the encoding of a node's information depends only on the information of another node (Rickenbach and Wattenhofer 2004). Moreover, the single-input coding strategies are further divided into the self-coding and foreign-coding techniques. In the self-coding strategies, data are only allowed to be encoded at the producing node and only in the presence of side information from at least one other node. In the foreign-coding techniques, a node is only available to encode raw data originating at another node as it is routed toward the sink using its own data. In their work, the authors introduced two algorithms to solve the minimum-energy gathering problem, which is the minimization of the total energy consumption in the network for every round of data gathering. Specifically, in the case of foreign coding the minimum-energy gathering algorithm (MEGA) was proposed, which first computes a shortest path tree rooted at the sink using Dijkstra's algorithm. Consecutively, the algorithm computes for each sensor node u_i a corresponding node u_j that encodes the packet p_i using its own data, and this procedure results in a coding tree. For the computation of a coding tree, an algorithm solving the directed minimum spanning tree problem is used. Once a packet is encoded, it is routed at the sink following the shortest path, because recoding and further coding are not possible. MEGA yields a minimum-energy data gathering topology of $O(n^3)$, where n is the number of sensors in the network. Furthermore, the authors also proposed an approximation algorithm, namely the low-energy gathering algorithm (LEGA), for the case of self-coding in order to solve the problem of finding a minimum-energy data gathering tree, which is known to be NP-complete.

Another approach that makes use of the side information presence in one node is described by Chou, Petrovic, and Ramchandran (2003), where the removal of the inherent correlation in the sensors is achieved through a distributed compression algorithm. Simple lightweight encoders exist in every sensor node, and a more complex decoder exists at the gathering node (i.e., the sink). The nodes do not need to know the correlation structure in order to encode their data; they only need to have knowledge of the total number of bits that will be used for encoding. This kind of information is provided by the sink, which has global knowledge of the correlations that exist among the sensors of the network. This approach can be combined with other energy-saving techniques, such as aggregation of data, resulting in a more energy-efficient strategy for data gathering. Furthermore, Tang, Raghavendra, and Prasanna (2003), proposed an energy-efficient distributed coding scheme called energy-efficient distributed source coding (EEADSC) that exploits the spatial correlation in data collected from nodes forming a cluster, based on the use of a Lagrangian cost function. This approach aims to compensate for the high energy cost incurred by the coding and decoding processing, by not allowing the decoder to directly communicate with the encoder. The EEADSC coding scheme uses trellis-coded quantization (TCQ), which results in the reduction of the bits transmitted and can be also combined with other data aggregation techniques to achieve greater energy savings.

Dissemination of Metadata

Sensor protocols for information via negotiation (SPIN) protocols belong to a family of adaptive negotiation-based information dissemination methodologies suitable for wireless sensor networks, suggested by Heinzelman, Kulik, and Balakrishnan (1999). According to this paradigm, sensors use metadata to describe their sensing data, whose size is small compared to data's size. Every time a sensor has data to send, it advertises it to its neighbors by sending an Advertisement (ADV) message packet containing only the metadata. Then, the nodes that have received the ADV packet and are interested in the data advertised send back a request for data (REQ) message. Finally, the node sends its actual sensed data. In an enhanced energy-aware implementation of the protocol, a low-energy threshold is defined for each sensor. When a sensor node observes that its energy is approaching this threshold, it reduces its participation in the whole procedure of the protocol, meaning that it will not initiate the three stage handshake if it does not have sufficient energy to complete all of the three stages. In this way, data are gathered to the base station in each round and result in an energy-aware gathering paradigm.

Inquiry-Based Data Gathering

In wireless sensor networks, usually the sensor nodes collect information about their environment (e.g., measuring the temperature for a given region) and send their readings to the sink either continuously, periodically, or whenever an event occurs that triggers such data dissemination (e.g., a value threshold has been exceeded). The majority of the protocols previously described have assumed this type of data collection process. However, in some cases on-demand data gathering may be required. This happens when a user outside the sensor network desires to collect data for a specific task by sending a declarative query to the sink. The sink proceeds in transmitting the query to all the nodes that are responsible for providing an answer to the query. The nodes send their readings back to the sink through a multihop route, and the intermediate nodes might perform some sort of aggregation to the data.

The Cougar approach (Yao and Gehrke 2002), treats the sensor network as a huge distributed database system in which each sensor node holds part of the data. In the proposed architecture, there is a query proxy layer on each node that interacts with both the routing and the application layer. There also exists a query optimizer that, after receiving queries from the outside world, generates a query processing plan that results in an efficient way of computing the query. It also elects a leader node in which the in-network aggregation will take place, or, alternatively, partial aggregation can be executed at the intermediate nodes to reduce the data size. One drawback of this approach is that the in-network computation requires synchronization among sensor nodes along the communication path, because nodes have to wait for their neighbors' results for the aggregation.

A similar approach is presented by Madd et al. (2002), in which a generic aggregation service, namely, the tiny agregation (TAG), is developed for ad hoc networks. Within the context of this scheme, a user from outside the network poses queries to the sink that are forwarded to all nodes. Sensors that respond to the query send their data back to the sink following a routing tree rooted at the sink. As data flow to the sink, they are aggregated to the intermediate nodes according to a defined aggregation function. The TAG approach consists of two phases: a distribution phase in which aggregate queries are pushed into the network, and a collection phase in which the aggregate values are routed up from children to parents until they reach the root. As in the Cougar approach, synchronization is required in order for parents to wait for their children's readings to perform the aggregation function and reduce data size.

Based on the previous two approaches that implement data gathering by posing queries to the network, a variety of other methods have been proposed that use similar Techniques and, in some cases, suggest enhancements. temporal coherency-aware in-network aggregation (TiNA; Sharaf et al. 2004), for example, provides a further improvement in terms of energy savings with some reduction in the quality of the data. A routing tree rooted at the sink is used for the propagation of the query and the collection of the results. Another unique feature of this approach is that it introduces a tolerance clause (tct) into the query, which represents the maximum change that can occur in the overall quality of data (and is defined by the user). For example, a tct of 5 percent signifies that values with changes lower than 5 percent will not be reported and calculated for the final result of the query. Consequently, energy reduction is achieved because fewer data are transmitted with the loss of the corresponding quality of data. Depending on the desired accuracy of the results, different levels of energy reduction can be provided.

Finally, the adaptive periodic threshold-sensitive energy-efficient sensor network (APTEEN) protocol (Manjeshwar, Zeng, and Agrawal 2002), also makes use of queries posed by users to gather the data generated in the network. This scheme categorizes the queries into three types, depending on the type of data—historical, on-time, and persistent queries—all of which are answered by the sink. The clustering algorithm used in Heinzelman (2000) is used to partition the network into clusters, and cluster heads are charged with the aggregation of data. Furthermore, adjacent nodes that sense similar data form pairs. The APTEEN protocol achieves lower energy consumption by allowing only one sensor of every pair to send data at each round, letting the other go into sleep mode.

Selecting Subsets of Sensors for Data Gathering

Data gathering in sensor networks has been proven to be a costly operation, because sensors consume a great amount of energy when receiving and transmitting data. All the approaches presented above used different methodologies and aggregation functions to reduce data size. However, another important category of data gathering protocols exploits the data correlation provided from sensor readings that are placed close to each other, but from a different perspective. At each round, not all sensors need to send their data to the sink, and thus only a subset of nodes should be selected to transmit.

Following this paradigm, Gupta et al. (2005) investigated the problem of selecting a connected correlation-dominating set that can be used for data gathering. The connected correlation-dominating set forms a connected graph, and its signal values are sufficient to derive the signal values of all the sensors of the network with sufficient accuracy. The approach first finds the correlation existing among the sensors and afterward enforces an algorithm for finding the connected correlated subset of nodes. Similar to this approach, Choi and Das (2005) proposed the use of data reporters for transmitting data to the sink at each round. The idea is to allow only a set of k sensors, named data reporters, to send data to the sink while the remaining cache their readings and send them during the following rounds, thus saving energy. Every node takes turns being selected as a data reporter. The number k of data reporters is selected to be sufficient for a desired sensing coverage defined by the users or the applications. The coverage is inversely proportional to the energy savings; the lower the desired coverage, the longer the data reporting latency in each sensor. For the selection of the k data reporters in each round, three schemes were developed: the non-fixed randomized selection (NRS) as well as the non-fixed and fixed disjoint randomized selection (N-DRS and F-DRS, respectively). In the first case, the selected k sensors in one round may not be different in the next round, whereas in the latter case, the set of k data reporters in a given round is completely different from the set selected in the next rounds.

Chen, Guan, and Pooch (2004) attempted to minimize the energy dissipated by reducing the dissemination of redundant data. The proposed approach provides services for data retrieval at different levels of details, depending on the application. Nodes that cover the same sensing area collect correlated data; therefore, not all nodes need to transmit their readings. Again, during each gathering round, a subset of nodes is selected whose readings provide the desired resolution data level. Less detail is acceptable depending on the user's specifications. Therefore, different levels of energy savings are achieved.

A completely different approach for data gathering is explored by Qi, Xu, and Wang (2003). The authors do not exploit the correlation of data as in the above approaches; instead they propose a mobile-agent–based collaborative signal and information processing scheme. Nodes do not send their raw data to the sink, but mobile agents are deployed that can migrate from node to node, gather the data, perform processing, and return to the sink. Although this approach improves energy consumption, it requires additional overhead costs for the generation and migration of the mobile agents.

Data Gathering in Mobile Environments

All of the approaches for data gathering in wireless sensor networks presented earlier in this chapter have considered cases in which the sensor nodes are mainly static and have little or no ability to move. Indeed, this is the most common scenarios in sensor networks, where sensors are deployed in an area and are usually immobile, thereby forming a wireless fixed network. However, protocols have been proposed in the literature for efficient data gathering on mobile sensor networks, where the sensors can move either by outside force or by their corresponding mobility component. For example, a sensor may be attached to a moving device especially designed for tracking purposes. In these cases, because of the mobility of the sensor nodes, the network topology changes quickly and continuously; therefore, many of the aforementioned protocols may not be effective or adequate for data gathering and monitoring under these circumstances.

Liu and Lee (2004) proposed a cluster-based protocol for power-efficient data gathering in mobile sensor networks based on the LEACH protocol introduced by Heinzelman, Chandrakasan, and Balakrishnan (2000). Similarly to the original LEACH protocol, the network is partitioned into clusters and a different sensor may act as cluster head in each gathering round for sending all the gathered data of its members to the sink. The cluster formation, however, is different from the case where the nodes are static, because the sensors move around within a prespecified region. At each round, the sensors may decide to become members of a different cluster and move away from their previous cluster head. In this case, the cluster formation procedure may be called more often, resulting in increased energy consumption.

The formation can be performed by first electing the cluster heads and having these nodes broadcast advertisement messages to all the nodes, including their position, speed, and direction. Sensors in turn calculate the distance between themselves and all cluster heads and, taking into consideration their relative direction, decide which cluster to join. After the formation of the clusters has been completed, the cluster heads collect the data from their members, perform some sort of aggregation, and send the data to the final destination (i.e., the sink). Because of the high power consumption and to reduce the probability that the energy of a few sensors get depleted quickly and unfairly, various algorithms for cluster head selection that will minimize the total amount of energy consumed at each round have been proposed in the literature. Experiments have demonstrated that this approach provides a power-efficient data gathering strategy for mobile sensor networks.

Another approach, which also constructs clusters for data aggregation in sensor networks that have two kinds of nodes that can be either mobile or stationary—relay and sensor nodes—has been described in the work of Chae et al., (2004). The members of a cluster perform their tasks (e.g., sensing, data dissemination, etc.) at specific intervals and during their idle time can be put into sleep mode to save energy. Each relay node broadcasts a message Relay node ID (RID) with lifetime to all of the sensor nodes in a cluster. If there are no sensors that operate for the real-time monitoring, the relay node and the cluster members are put into power-saving mode. Slightly before the lifetime expires, they wake up and perform their tasks until another RID with larger lifetime broadcast occurs.

RELATIVE PERFORMANCE COMPARISON

In the following section, we present a relative qualitative comparison of the different data gathering approaches and highlight their respective merits, drawbacks, and performance. Specifically, we summarize the functionality and outline the basic operational characteristics of each category, and then we present a table that provides a comprehensive comparison of the various approaches against different performance metrics of interest that have been described in this chapter. The various data gathering and monitoring approaches that have been presented take into account different design objectives and principles, and therefore aim to optimize different performance parameters and metrics (e.g., energy consumption, delay/latency, accuracy/loss of data, etc.).

More specifically, with respect to the hierarchical and nonhierarchical strategies, the protocols that belong to the first category present in principle better energy efficiency. As a result, in all the methods that belong to the hierarchical approaches (i.e., cluster-based, chain-based, and tree-constructive protocols), the network lifetime is increased at the cost of the delay. Furthermore, associated with the hierarchical approaches is an initialization phase that is required for the definition of the different layers of hierarchy, as well as maintenance costs required for the management and reconstruction of the hierarchical approach during the data gathering operation. It has been also demonstrated that the energy cost introduced by data aggregation is negligible compared to the corresponding communication and data transmission cost. Depending on the data aggregation function used at each sensor node (e.g., average, sum, discard of duplicate packets), the final data delivered to the collection center may be different from the original data, resulting in some level of loss in the data accuracy.

On the other hand, the nonhierarchical approaches (e.g., flooding, gossiping, etc.) do not need to go through any initialization phase and in general present lower implementation complexity and maintenance costs. All of the sensor nodes that are involved in the data gathering operation send their data to all of their neighbors without performing any in-network processing (e.g., data aggregation). As a result, all of the sensors consume larger amount of energy and the corresponding network lifetime is decreased. With regard to consideration of the delay constraints, the nonhierarchical protocols deliver data in a more timely manner during their first periods of operation or when they operate under low traffic load. However, as the traffic load increases and the data packets that travel through the network increase, severe delays are observed from collisions and bottlenecks; this also has a significant negative impact on the achievable network throughput.

With respect to the probabilistic and routing independent approaches, in addition to their distributed nature and demonstrated energy efficiency, one of their key principles is that they can be combined with any other energy-aware routing protocol to attain even higher energy gains. Furthermore, because of their distributed, probabilistic behavior, they can decide independently whether or not to perform in-network processing to reduce the amount of data transmitted, thus succeeding in satisfying the delay constraints posed by the application.

The data gathering approaches that are based on the nature of data mainly aim to accomplish the data gathering operation in an energy-efficient manner. More specifically, the protocols that perform data compression in the presence of correlated data transmit fewer amounts of data with the trade-off of the occurrence of some information loss (provided that the compression is not lossless), while the use of encoders and decoders increases the processing cost and latency. If metadata is transmitted, there is no additional processing cost and the total amount of data packets traversing the network is reduced. With reference to the inquiry-based data gathering protocols, the collection center poses different queries to the network that are addressed only by a subset of nodes, thus reducing the total amount of information collected at the center. The accuracy of the collected data depends on whether or not the nodes perform some kind of aggregation as well as the type of the aggregation function utilized. Moreover, in certain protocols, sensor nodes do not transmit their reading if there is a small variation from the previous transmission, thus resulting in greater information loss in some cases.

Finally, the last class of protocols considered here does not perform in-network processing but explores the correlation of the sensor readings by not allowing some sensors to transmit in specified communication rounds. The main characteristic of these approaches is that the energy consumption can be controlled (i.e., reduced) by adjusting the subset of sensors to transmit at each cycle, at the cost of reducing the corresponding achievable network sensing coverage. Table 1 presents a qualitative relative comparison of the aforementioned methods against a common set of parameters.

CONCLUSION

Remote sensing is expected to become an integral part of our lives as we strive to use sensor technologies to monitor our surrounding space for a variety of applications such as security, health, education, comfort, environment, traffic, safety, and so forth. These applications require tight coupling with the physical world, as opposed to the personal communication focus of conventional wireless networks; therefore, the wireless sensor networks pose significantly different design, implementation, and deployment challenges. Sensors should be networked to facilitate the transmission and dissemination of the measured/monitored parameters to some collector sites where the information is further processed for decision-making purposes. Multiple sensors offer fault tolerance and better monitoring capabilities of parameters that present both

Table 1: Comparison of Data Gathering Strategies

Categorization		Metrics			
		Delay	**Energy consumption**	**Data loss**	**Implementation complexity**
Based on the structure of the network	• Hierarchical				
	- cluster based				
	- chain based				
	- tree constructive				
	• Nonhierarchical				
Routing independent—probabilistic					
Based on the nature of data	• Compression techniques				
	• Dissemination of metadata				
Inquiry based					
Selection of subset of sensors					

spatial and temporal variances, and can provide valuable inferences about the physical world to the end user.

In this chapter, we focused on the problem of energy-efficient data monitoring and gathering in sensor networks. The sensor networks should dynamically adapt to the system and topology changes, and at the same time they need to balance the trade-offs among various performance metrics. Therefore, we first identified the major performance metrics of interest for the data monitoring and gathering process, and we discussed the related traffic and data correlation models. We then identified and reviewed various issues associated with the sensor node deployment patterns, which are closely related to the effective data monitoring. Furthermore, we described several data gathering approaches by classifying them into diverse categories according to the different features and design dimensions of the wireless sensor networks, and we presented some indicative associated protocols. Finally, we provided a relative comparison of all of the different approaches—outlining their major merits and drawbacks, highlighting their differences, and evaluating their relative behavior based on a common set of parameters.

GLOSSARY

Chain-Based Protocol: A network protocol that constructs chains of nodes for the performance of a specific task.

Cluster: A group of similar objects that are grouped together to perform a specific task.

Cluster-Based Protocol: A network protocol that constructs clusters of nodes for the performance of a specific task.

Data Aggregation: Any process in which information is gathered and redefined into a summary form based on some rules or criteria.

Data Compression: The process of reducing data size without significant loss of information, usually by encoding information using fewer bits than the ones used by an unencoded representation.

Data Correlation: A measure of the degree of dependency between two or more variables that represent data.

Data Fusion: The process of combining data from different sources to eliminate redundant transmissions and provide a rich, multidimensional view of the environment being monitored.

Data Gathering: The process of collecting the data of multiple sources to, usually, a single collection center.

Data Monitoring: The process of periodic or continuous measurement of the data transmitted and received in a network.

Hierarchical Protocol: A network protocol that assigns/recognizes different roles and functionalities within the components of a network. Components are classified according to various criteria into successive levels or layers.

Non-Hierarchical Protocol: A network protocol in which every component can perform similar roles and functionalities.

Self-Organization: A process in which the internal organization of a system is formed and maintained automatically without being guided or managed by an outside source.

Tree-Constructive Protocol: A network protocol that constructs trees that span the network, in which the nodes can either be leaves or internal nodes, for the performance of a specific task.

CROSS REFERENCES

See *Broadcasting in Ad Hoc and Sensor Networks*; *Emerging Trends in Routing Protocols in Mobile Wireless Ad Hoc and Sensor Networks*; *Medium Access in Ad Hoc and Sensor Networks*; *Network Middleware*; *Network QoS*; *Principles and Applications of Ad Hoc and Sensor Networks*.

REFERENCES

Akyildiz, I. F., W. Su, Y. Sankarasubramanian, and E. Cayirci. 2002. A survey on sensor networks. *IEEE Communications Magazine*, 40, pp. 102–14.

Bulusu, N., J. Heidemann, and D. Estrin. 2000. GPS-less low cost outdoor localization for very small devices. *IEEE Personal Communications Magazine*, 7, pp. 28–34.

Cerpa, A., and D. Estrin. 2002. ASCENT: Adaptive self-configuring sensor networks topologies. In *Proceedings of the Twenty-First Annual Conference of IEEE Computer and Communications Societies,* New York, June, pp. 1278–2002.

Chae, D. H, K. H. Han, K. S. Lim, K. H. Seo, and K. H. Won. 2004. Power saving mobility protocol for sensor network. In *Proceedings of the Second IEEE Workshop on Software Technologies for Future Embedded and Ubiquitous Systems*, Vienna, Austria, May, pp. 122–26.

Chakrabarty, K., S. S. Iyengar, H. Qi, and E. Cho. 2002. Grid coverage for surveillance and target location in distributed sensor networks. *IEEE Transactions on Computers* 51: 1448–53.

Chen, J., V. Guan, and U. Pooch. 2004. An efficient data dissemination method in wireless sensor networks. In *Proceedings of the IEEE Global Telecommunications Conference*, Dallas, Texas, November, pp. 3200–4.

Choi, W., and S. K. Das. 2005. A novel framework for energy-conserving data gathering in wireless sensor networks. In *Proceedings of the Twenty-Fourth Annual Conference of IEEE Computer and Communications Societies*, Miami, Florida, March, pp. 1985–96.

Choi, W., P. Shah, and S. K. Das. 2004. A framework for energy-saving data gathering using two-phase clustering in wireless sensor networks. In *Proceedings of the IEEE First Annual International Conference on Mobile and Ubiquitous Systems: Networking and Services*, pp. 203–12.

Chou, J., D. Petrovic, and K. Ramchandran. 2003. A distributed and adaptive signal processing approach to reducing energy consumption in sensor networks. In *Proceedings of the IEEE Communications Society*, San Francisco, April, pp. 1054–62.

Clouqueur, T., V. Phipatanasuphorn, P. Ramanathan, and K. K. Saluja. 2002. Sensor deployment strategy for target detection. In *Proceedings of First ACM International Workshop on Wireless Sensor Networks and Applications*, Atlanta, Georgia, September, pp. 42–48.

Dasgupta, K., K. Kalpakis, and P. Namjoshi. 2003. An efficient clustering–based heuristic for data gathering and aggregation in sensor networks. In *Proceedings of IEEE Wireless Communications and Networking*, New Orleans, Louisiana, March, pp. 1948–53.

Du, K., J. Wu, and D. Zhou. 2003. Chain-based protocols for data broadcasting and data gathering in the sensor networks. In *Proceedings of the International Parallel and Distributed Processing Symposium*, Nice, France, April, pp. 260–67.

Gupta, H., S. R. Das, and Q. Gu. 2003. Connected sensor cover: Self-organization of sensor networks for efficient query execution. In *Proceedings of the Fourth ACM International Symposium on Mobile Ad Hoc Networking and Computing*, Annapolis, Maryland, June, pp. 189–200.

Gupta, H., V. Navda, S. R. Das, and V. Chowdhary. 2005. Efficient gathering of correlated data in sensor networks. In *Proceedings of the Sixth ACM International Symposium on Mobile Ad Hoc Networking and Computing*, Urbana-Champaign, Illinois, May, pp. 402–13.

He, T., B. Blum, J. Stankovic, and T. Abdelzaher. 2004. AIDA: Adaptive application independent data aggregation in wireless sensor networks. *ACM Transactions on Embedded Computing Systems* 3: 426–57.

Heinzelman, W. 2000. Application-specific protocol architectures for wireless sensor networks (PhD thesis, Massachusetts Institute of Technology).

Heinzelman, W. R, A. Chandrakasan, and H. Balakrishnan. 2000. Energy efficient communication protocol for wireless microsensor networks. In *Proceedings of the Thirty-Third Annual Hawaii International Conference on System Sciences*, Maui, January, p. 10.

Heinzelman, W. R., J. Kulik, and H. Balakrishnan. 1999. Adaptive protocols for information dissemination in wireless sensor networks. In *Proceedings of the Fifth Annual ACM/IEEE International Conference on Mobile Computing and Networking*, Seattle, Washington, August, pp.174–85.

Huang, C. F., and Y. C. Tseng. 2003. The coverage problem in a wireless sensor network. In *Proceedings of ACM International Workshop on Wireless Sensor Networks and Applications*, San Diego, California, September, pp. 115–21.

Intanagonwiwat, C., R. Govindan, and D. Estrin. 2000. Directed diffusion: A scalable and robust communication paradigm for sensor networks. In *Proceedings of the Sixth Annual International Conference on Mobile Computing and Networking*, pp. 56–67.

Jindal, A., and K. Psounis. 2004. Modeling spatially-correlated sensor network data. In *Proceedings of First Annual IEEE Communications Society Conference on Sensor and Ad Hoc Communications and Networks*, Santa Clara, California, October, pp. 162–71.

Langendoen, K., and N. Reijers. 2003. Distributed localization in wireless sensor networks: A quantitative comparison. *Computer Network* 43(4): 499–518.

Lin, R., Z. Wang, and Y. Sun. 2004. Wireless sensor networks solutions for real time monitoring of nuclear power plants. In *Proceedings of Fifth World Congress on Intelligent Control and Automation*, Hangzhou, China, June, pp. 3663–67.

Lindsey, S., C. Raghavendra, and K.M. Sivalingam. 2002. Data gathering algorithms in sensor networks using energy metrics. *IEEE Transactions on Parallel and Distributed Systems* 13: 924–35.

Liu, C. M., and C.H. Lee. 2004. Power efficient algorithms protocols for data gathering on mobile sensor networks. In *Proceedings of the First ACM International Workshop on Performance Evaluation of Wireless Ad Hoc, Sensor, and Ubiquitous Networks*, Venice, Italy, October, pp. 121–22.

Madden, S. R., M. J. Franklin, J. M. Hellerstein, and W. Hong. 2002. TAG: A tiny aggregation service for ad-hoc sensor networks. In *Proceedings of the Fifth Symposium on Operating Systems Design and Implementation*, Boston, December, pp. 131–46.

Manjeshwar, A., Q. A. Zeng, and D. P. Agrawal. 2002. An analytical model for information retrieval in wireless sensor networks using enhanced APTEEN protocol. *IEEE Transactions on Parallel and Distributed Systems* 13: 1290–1302.

Meguerdichian, S., F. Koushanfar, M. Potkonjak, and M. B. Srivastava. 2001. Coverage problems in wireless ad-hoc sensor networks. In *Proceedings of Twentieth Annual Joint Conference of IEEE Computer and Communication Societies*, Anchorage, Alaska, April, pp.1380–87.

Mladineo, N., and S. Knezic. 2000. Optimization of forest fire sensor network using GIS technology. In *Proceedings of the Twenty-Second International Conference on Information Technology Interfaces*, Pula, Croatia, June, pp. 391–96.

O'Rourke, J. 1987. *Art gallery theorems and algorithms*. New York: Oxford University Press.

Pattem, S., B. Krishnamachari, and R. Govindan. 2004. The impact of spatical correlation on routing with compression in wireless sensor networks. In *ACM Proceedings of the Third International Symposium on Information Processing in Sensor Networks*, Berkeley, California, April, pp. 28–35.

Pham, T., E. J. Kim, and M. Moh. 2004. On data aggregation quality and energy efficiency of wireless sensor network protocols—Extended summary. In *Proceeding of the First International Conference on Broadband Networks*, San Jose, California, October, pp. 730–32.

Pottie, G. J., and W.J. Kaiser. 2000. Wireless integrated network sensors. *Communications of the ACM* 43: 51–58.

Qi, H., Y. Xu, and X. Wang. 2003. Mobile-agent–based collaborative signal and information processing in sensor network. *Proceedings of the IEEE* 91: 1172–83.

Rickenbach, P., and R. Wattenhofer. 2004. Gathering correlated data in sensor networks. In *Proceedings of the 2004 Joint Workshop on Foundations of Mobile Computing*, Philadelphia, October, pp. 60–66.

Sharaf, M. A., J. Beaver, A. Labrinidis, and P. K. Chrysanthis. 2004. *Balancing energy efficiency and quality of aggregate data in sensor networks. The International Journal on Very Large Data Bases* 13: 384–403.

Shen, C. C, C. Srisathapornphat, and C. Jaikaeo. 2001. Sensor information networking architecture and applications. *IEEE Personal Communications* 8: 52–59.

Sohrabi, K., J. Gao, V. Ailawadhi, and G. J. Pottie. 2000. Protocols for self-organization of a wireless sensor network. *IEEE Personal Communications* 7(5): 16–27.

Tan, H. Ö., and I. Körpeo. 2003. Power efficient data gathering and aggregation in wireless sensor networks. *ACM SIGMOD Record* 32: 66–71.

Tang, C., C. S. Raghavendra, and V. K. Prasanna. 2003. An energy efficient adaptive distributed source coding scheme in wireless sensor networks. In *Proceedings of IEEE International Conference on Communications*, Seattle, Washington, May, pp. 732–37.

Thepvilojanapong, N., Y. Tobe, and K. Sezaki. 2005. On the construction of efficient data gathering tree in wireless sensor networks. In *Proceedings of IEEE International Symposium on Circuits and Systems*, Kobe, Japan, May, pp. 648–51.

Wang, G., G. Cao, and T. La Porta. 2004. Movement-assisted sensor deployment. In *Proceedings of the Twenty-Third Annual Joint Conference of the IEEE Computer and Communications Societies*, Hong Kong, March, pp. 2469–79.

Yao, Y., and J. Gehrke. 2002. The Cougar approach to in-network query processing in sensor networks. *ACM SIGMOD Record* 31: 9–18.

Zhu, J., S. Papavassiliou, and J. Yang. 2006. Adaptive localized QoS-constrained data aggregation and processing in distributed sensor networks. *IEEE Transactions on Parallel and Distributed Systems* 17(9): 923–33.

Zou, Y., and K. Chakrabarty. 2004. Uncertainty-aware and coverage-oriented deployment for sensor networks. *Journal of Parallel and Distributed Computing* 64: 788–98.

FURTHER READING

CodeBlue project. http://www.eecs.harvard.edu/~mdw/proj/codeblue/.

ExScal project. http://www.cast.cse.ohio-state.edu/exscal/.

Habitat monitoring on Great Duck Island. http://www.greatduckisland.net.

The James Reserve. http://www.jamesreserve.edu/.

PODS. http://www.pods.hawaii.edu/.

Sensor Web. http://sensorwebs.jpl.nasa.gov/.

UbiMon project. http://www.ubimon.org/.

Wireless vineyard smart agriculture. http://www.intel.com/research/vert_agri_vineyard.htm.

ZebraNet. http://www.princeton.edu/~mrm/zebranet html.

In-Network Data Aggregation in Wireless Sensor Networks

Kemal Akkaya, *Southern Illinois University, Carbondale*
Ismail Ari, *Hewlett-Packard Laboratories, Palo Alto, CA*

INTRODUCTION

Advances in microelectronics have enabled the development of exceptionally tiny sensor nodes that have the ability of measuring ambient conditions such as temperature, pressure, humidity, light intensity, and motion (Akyildiz et al. 2002). The sensed data can then be transmitted through an on-board radio transmitter to single or multiple *base stations* (BSs) where it can be further processed. The tiny size and inexpensive cost of such emerging sensor nodes has encouraged practitioners to explore using them collaboratively in a network formed in ad hoc manner. Such a networked sensor system not only is cost-effective but also can provide fast and accurate information gathering in remote and risky areas. Figure 1 depicts a typical sensor network architecture. The BS acts as a gateway for linking the sensors to multiple command nodes.

The past few years have witnessed increased interest in the potential use of *wireless sensor networks* (WSNs) in applications such as disaster management, combat field reconnaissance, border protection, and security surveillance (Mainwaring et al. 2002; Burrell, Brooke, and Beckwith 2004; Agora et al. 2004, 2005).

It is envisioned that WSNs will be part of the future Internet where real-time information will be queried through sensors deployed almost everywhere in our living environments. This direction suggests that gathering and processing large volumes of data from WSNs will continue to be one of the most important problems for researchers in coming years.

However, because sensors have severe resource constraints in terms of power, processing capability, memory, and storage, it is challenging to provide efficient solutions to the data-gathering problem. Energy limitations have been an especially pressing issue that affects the design of WSNs at all layers of the protocol stack (Akyildiz et al. 2002; Akkaya and Younis 2005). Many researchers have investigated various mechanisms such as shutting down the radio, eliminating control packets, and using topology-management algorithms (Xu and Heideman 2001; Cerpa and Estrin 2002) to reduce energy consumption in WSNs.

Data aggregation is also among those mechanisms utilized to save energy and achieve energy efficiency. It is the process of combining multiple data packets into one by looking at their contents. For instance, WSNs may have a lot of redundant data because multiple sensors can sense similar information when they are close to each other. Therefore, there is no need to send the same information to the BS more than once when a summary of the readings from those sensors can be sent. Thus, data aggregation will decrease the number of transmissions in the network, eventually reducing the bandwidth usage and eliminating unnecessary energy consumption in both transmissions and receptions.

Although data aggregation may help reduce the number of transmissions and hence energy consumption (Krishnamachari, Estrin, and Wicker 2002; Heidemann et al. 2001), it may adversely affect other performance metrics such as delay, accuracy, and security. For instance, data aggregation may cause the nodes to wait for their children to send their data in a tree topology, increasing the delay that the packets face (Erramilli, Malta, and Bestavros 2004; Akkaya, Younis, and Youssef 2005; Yu, Krishnamachari, and Prasanna 2004). In addition, it can decrease the accuracy of the result received at the

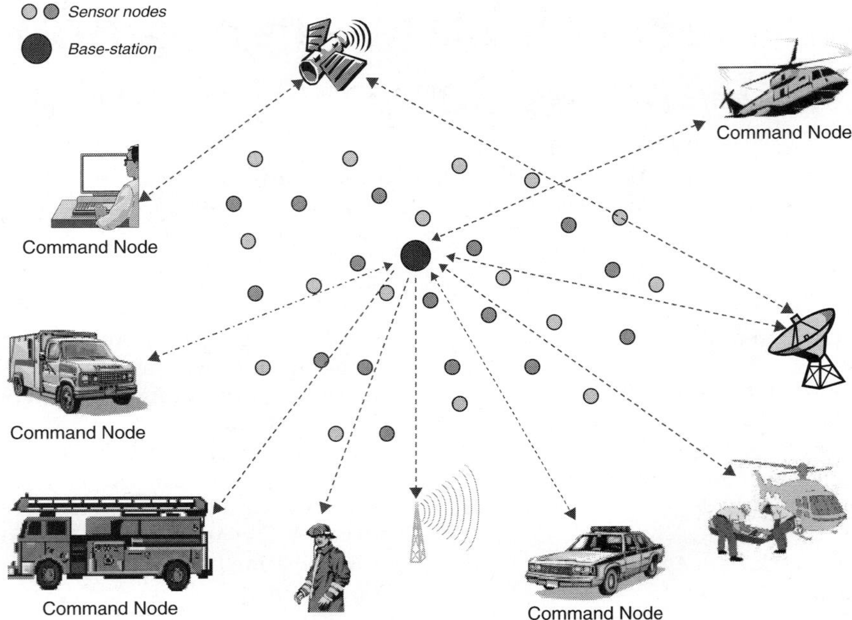

Figure 1: A typical sensor network architecture

BS because many readings from different sources are eliminated through data aggregation when the packets are en route (Solis and Obraczka 2004). Finally, security is another concern because authentication and encryption are required before packets can be safely combined (Hu and Evans 2003; Castelluccia, Mykletun, and Tsudik 2005; Girao, Westho, and Schneider 2004).

In this chapter, we will describe how data-aggregation issues are tackled in WSNs for optimal performance in terms of energy and bandwidth. In addition, we will discuss several trade-offs arising as a consequence of data aggregation in terms of latency, accuracy, and security and summarize solutions in the literature that address these issues.

The chapter is organized as follows. In the balance of this section, we will describe and motivate data aggregation and differentiate it from other in-network data-processing techniques. The second section discusses modeling of the in-network data-aggregation problem. The third section covers the impact of data aggregation on data latency. Aggregation and accuracy trade-offs are discussed in the fourth section. In the fifth section, secure data aggregation is explained in detail. Finally, the chapter's conclusion points out problems that may be subject to future research.

Motivation and Description of Data Aggregation

Given that sensor nodes are severely constrained in terms of battery lifetime, the aim is to always come up with techniques to increase such lifetime. Battery power is needed by a sensor node to perform computations with its CPU and, most importantly, to transmit and receive packets through its radio. Thus, an obvious solution would be to reduce the CPU usage and the number of transmission and receptions. Today, we know that energy consumed for communication (i.e., transmission and reception) is much higher than computation. For instance, with the energy consumed to transmit 1 Kb of data a distance of 100 meters, it is possible to execute 3 million instructions (Sohrabi et al. 2000). Therefore, it is wise to focus on reducing the communication costs and promote more computation than communication. Note that such a reduction in the number of transmissions and receptions will also increase the available bandwidth, which is also a scarce source for WSNs.

There are many opportunities in WSNs to reduce the number of transmission and receptions because WSNs are characterized by huge numbers of nodes with considerable redundant data because of the similarity of reports sensed by sensor nodes at nearby locations as seen in Figure 2. In this example, node C does not need to transmit the same data it received from A and B on overlapping

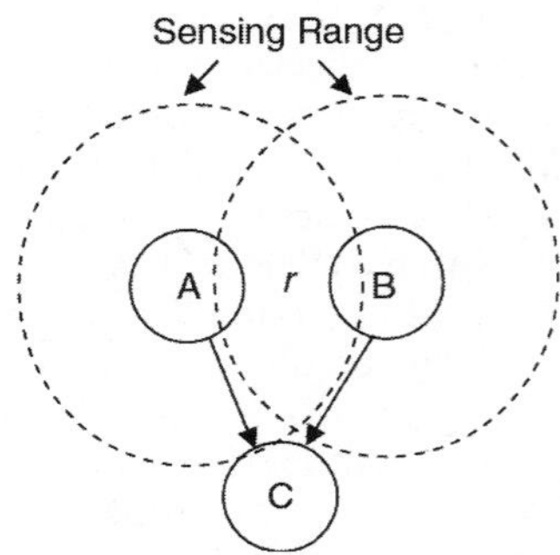

Figure 2: Two sensors (A and B) cover an overlapping geographic region, and C may get copies of data from these sensors

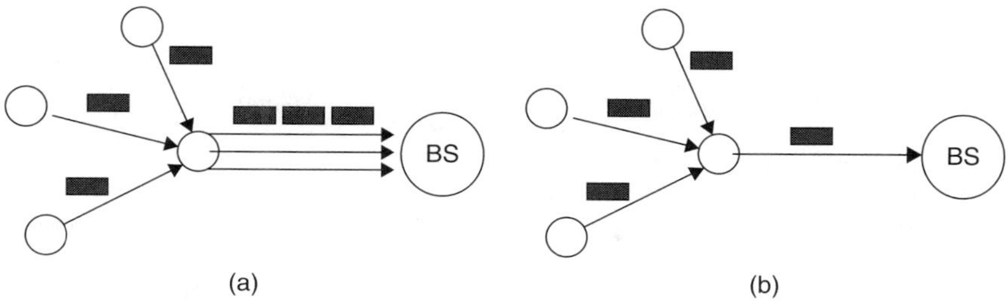

Figure 3: (a) No data aggregation and three transmissions to the BS; (b) data aggregation with one transmission to the BS

region *r*. Instead, it can send just one copy of that data and hence save one transmission and reception.

Other cases in which the number of communications can be reduced are *aggregate queries*. These are queries where the result is computed based on the data received from every node. For example, if a query is asking for the average temperature in a region, then each sensor's value should be received at the BS and averaged. However, there is no need for the BS to receive all of the values. Instead, the average can be calculated within the network while the packets are traveling through the BS. A node can get the values from its neighbors, compute the average (i.e., create one packet out of n), and send the average to the upper nodes. This definitely reduces the number of transmissions significantly as seen in Figure 3.

Because data aggregation in WSNs is done by the intermediate nodes en route to the BS incrementally, it is usually referred as *in-network* data aggregation. Typically, an aggregation tree rooted at the BS is created with the source sensors as leaf nodes. When data are flowing toward a single BS, this aggregation tree is called *convergecast tree,* which is the inverse of a broadcast tree. A typical convergecast tree is depicted in Figure 4. In such a tree, an intermediate node can combine multiple packets, suppress them, and help calculate part of some aggregation function such as average, count, maximum, or minimum. Each intermediate node in a convergecast tree may have multiple child nodes to receive data and a parent node to transmit data.

There are several applications in which data aggregation can be employed. As mentioned, in sensor databases, data aggregation is a crucial technique for performing aggregate queries. For instance, if the sensors

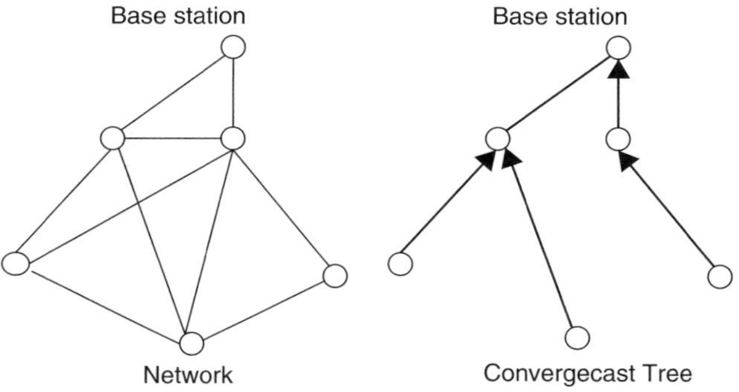

Figure 4: A sensor network and its corresponding data-aggregation tree

are employed in an inventory-control application, the number of objects can be summed and transmitted along with the region's information to the BS. The goal is to perform the computation near the sources and then send an aggregated report (Lin and Huang 2005). Similarly, data aggregation can be used to monitor the average available energy in different parts of a region where an event is taking place (Zhao, Govindan, and Estrin 2002). Finally, it can be embedded in any WSN protocol to eliminate redundant data.

Although it is possible to reduce data transmissions and save energy through data aggregation, we note that it is not by itself adequate to extend the lifetime of the WSNs. For instance, data aggregation cannot be applied to control packets for routing or for time synchronization. Therefore, for applications that send a lot of control packets, data aggregation may not provide the desired energy savings. In addition, data aggregation may require sensor nodes to be active most of the time, which is by itself an energy-consuming task. Keeping the radio on most of the time can eliminate some of the energy gain through data aggregation, depending on the application and the network architecture.

Other Types of In-Network Processing

In addition to the data aggregation considered in this chapter, there are many other forms of in-network processing that can help reduce the size of data to be transmitted and hence help save energy. These in-network processing techniques include data fusion, data compression, data filtering, and data elimination. In this section, we will briefly describe these techniques so that the scope of data aggregation we consider in this chapter can be better distinguished from them.

Data Fusion

In-network data aggregation is often confused with data fusion. Most people assume that they mean the same thing. In fact, they are interrelated and often used interchangeably in WSN research. However, there is a slight distinction between these two techniques. Data fusion is a broader technique that includes data aggregation as a subprocess and focuses on information rather than data with the use of several interdisciplinary techniques such as signal processing, statistical analysis, machine learning, and probability. Whereas data aggregation is introduced with the need to reduce data redundancy and the number of transmissions in WSNs, data fusion has already been used in the past extensively for different systems, including wired multisensor systems (Hall and Llinas 2001; Musick and Malhotra 1994). Data fusion takes multiple sources and forms of data and uses all of these data in a way such that a better picture of the observed phenomena is formed. In this way, the phenomena can be better predicted and understood and in turn controlled. Note that, as a consequence of the data fusion, the resulting information is often abstract, generalized, or summarized, and hence the amount of data is reduced. The popular and widely accepted process model for data fusion identifies five levels in a data fusion process (Hall and Llinas 2001): Level 0 is the subobject assessment, level 1 is the object assessment, level 2 is the situation assessment, level 3 is the impact assessment, and level 4 is the process refinement. In this hierarchy, data aggregation is employed in level 0, where some signal processing is performed.

Data Compression

Compression is one of the most effective methods to reduce data size. However, there is a trade-off between the compression and the size of the data to be transmitted. The larger the data, the more energy will be consumed in performing the compression. Thus, the main issue is to identify the ratio of the energy that needs to be utilized for both compression and transmission. Obviously, the advantage of compression is the possibility of data generation close to the original. Recent research has focused on proposing energy-efficient encoding and decoding functions for historical sensor data (Lin et al. 2005; Scaglione 2003). Most research has concentrated on JPEG formats for images and MPEG formats for video.* The motion-compensated encoding may be employed to reduce the bit rate (Obraczka, Manduchi, and Garcia-Luna-Aceves 2002). The discrete cosine transform, which is widely used in JPEG and MPEG, is computationally intensive; it is doubtful that energy-limited sensors can handle it. The alternate approach is to use the discrete wavelet transform, which can be used in both the JPEG-2000 and MPEG-4 standards.

Data Elimination

The easiest way to eliminate some of the packets is to perform temporal aggregation or decrease the data-sampling rate of the sensor nodes. In temporal aggregation, a node caches the reading and compares it with the next reading. If there is not a significant difference between the readings, it might not make sense to send it again. A threshold for the difference of consecutive readings can be defined in order to make the sending decision as done in Cougar (Yao and Gehrke 2002) and TEEN (Manjeshwar and Agrawal 2001). In this way, the number of transmissions from a sensor can be significantly reduced. Similarly, depending on the application level interest, the period for collecting a reading from a sensor node can be increased. This especially makes a significant difference if the sent data are image or video data.

* The acronyms are derived from Joint Photographic Experts Group and Moving Picture Experts Group, respectively.

Data Filtering

Data filtering refers to the elimination of incorrect, invalid, or unknown noisy sensor data. It is a part of data fusion in WSNs and has been extensively used to eliminate redundancy and noise, clean the data, and make predictions based on spatio-temporal characteristics (Faradjian, Gehrke, and Bonnet 2002; Cheng and Prabhakar 2003; Elnahrawy 2003; Wen, Agogine, and Kai 2004). The goal in most of these approaches is to model the sensor data by using statistical techniques such as Bayesian-based approximation and Gaussian distribution to handle the imprecision. Handling imprecision and modeling sensor data enables future estimations, eliminates outliers, and hence reduces the number of transmissions.

In this chapter, we will mainly focus on spatial data aggregation and its networking aspects in WSNs. The other forms of in-network processing mentioned above are beyond the scope of this chapter.

MODELING IN-NETWORK DATA AGGREGATION IN WSNS

Given that in-network data aggregation reduces energy consumption, the main research problem is how to create a convergecast tree to maximize the lifetime of the WSN. Specifically, the main problems to consider are how to create the convergecast tree, how to select the routes, and where to do the aggregation in this tree. In this section, we will describe the protocols that modeled the data-aggregation problem using different approaches.

Tree-Based In-Network Data Aggregation

Finding the optimal convergecast tree in a WSN can be can be modeled as a *minimum Steiner tree* (MST) problem, which is known to be NP-hard (Krishnamachari, Estrin, and Wicker 2002). MST is, in fact, a multicast tree with minimum number of edges. Because a convergecast tree is the reverse of a multicast tree, it can be used in modeling a convergecast tree. Then an MST can be defined as follows: Given a complete graph $G = (V, E)$ and a subset $S < V$ of required vertices, a Steiner tree is a subtree of G that includes all of the vertices in S. Assuming that each source node transmits only once in a convergecast tree, an MST should have the minimum number of edges. For example, Figure 5 shows three convergecast trees with different numbers of edges. However, the third one (i.e., MST) is better in terms of energy savings because it provides the minimum number of transmissions to the BS.

Because the optimum solution to the MST problem is NP-hard, several suboptimal schemes have been proposed. We now describe three different heuristics for this problem: center at the nearest source, shortest path trees, and greedy incremental trees.

Center at the Nearest Source

In the *center at the nearest source* (CNS) heuristic, the idea is to determine the node that is closest to the BS and have all of the other sensor sources send their data to this particular node. This node receives all of the data, aggregates them, and sends the aggregation to the BS. Therefore, it

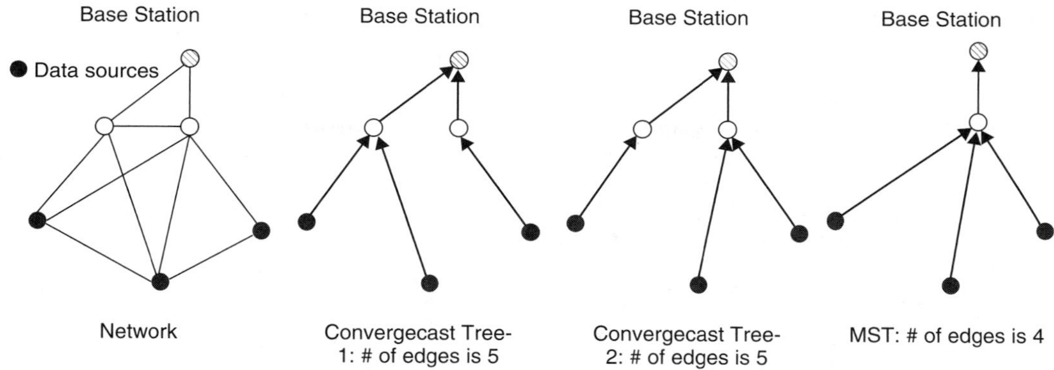

Figure 5: Possible convergecast trees for a network with three data sources. MST gives the optimal cost in terms of number of transmissions to the BS.

is named the *center.* It is more likely that this center node would be on the path of most of the sensors and thus will help reduce the number of transmissions significantly. Note that with this method, the MST of the WSN is optimized the longest trunk (i.e., with the maximum number of nodes at the last level of the tree).

Shortest Path Trees

The *shortest path trees* (SPTs) heuristic proposes to determine the shortest path from each sensor to the BS. Data are then aggregated at each common intermediate hop of these shortest paths through the BS.

Greedy Incremental Trees

In the case of *greedy incremental trees* (GITs), the convergecast tree is built sequentially to merge paths and provide more aggregation. First, the shortest path from the closest source to the BS is found. Then the other sources start connecting to this shortest path, forming a convergecast tree. This heuristic has been shown to provide an approximation ratio of 2 (Takahashi and Matsuyama 1980).

All of these heuristics have been implemented by Krishnamachari, Estrin, and Wicker (2002), and a comparison in terms of energy gain is made by trying different number of sources, transmission ranges, and distances to the BS. The results have shown that in all cases 50 percent to 80 percent energy savings are achieved with respect to the case where no data aggregation is performed. In addition, the energy saving through SPTs and GITs are more significant because they provide aggregation at all levels of the tree. However, this type of aggregation will increase the latency of packets, which will be discussed later.

Cluster-Based, In-Network Data Aggregation

Given the resource constraints of sensor nodes, some researchers considered partitioning the network into clusters and deploying cluster-heads to perform data aggregation (Chen, Liestman, and Liu 2005; Kumar et al. 2003; Heinzelman, Chandrakasan, and Balakrishnan 2000; Lindsey and Raghavendra 2002; Çam et al. 2006). The job of these cluster-heads is specifically aggregating the data received from the sensors and transmitting them to the BS. In most scenarios, they do not perform any sensing. In addition, these aggregator nodes can be more resource-rich than the sensors (Chen, Liestman, and Liu 2005; Kumar et al. 2003; Lee and Wong 2006). Such a resource-rich node can significantly alleviate the load of data aggregation and transmission from the sensor nodes, which eventually increases the lifetime of the WSN. Note that depending on the availability of these resource rich nodes, they can also be employed for data aggregation at any level of the convergecast tree. Thus, MST-based heuristics can also be applied to these kinds of heterogeneous WSNs where powerful nodes exist.

Low-energy adaptive clustering hierarchy (LEACH) (Heinzelman, Chandrakasan, and Balakrishnan 2000), *energy-efficient and secure pattern-based data aggregation* (ESPDA) (Çam et al. 2006) and *power-efficient gathering in sensor information systems* (PEGASIS) (Lindsey and Raghavendra 2002), however, do not consider such powerful nodes and thus elect a cluster-head among the sensor nodes that performs the data aggregation. Although LEACH considers clusters where each sensor can reach the cluster-head within one hop, PEGASIS creates chains of sensor nodes in which a leader is designated as the aggregator. ESPDA, on the other hand, considers clusters with multihop routes. In all of these approaches, sensor nodes take turns to be elected as the cluster-head so that the load of being cluster-head is distributed evenly among the sensor nodes in the network.

Application-Specific, In-Network Data Aggregation

Because data aggregation mostly focuses on eliminating redundant data, in most cases application information is useful to reduce such redundancy. This idea is initially utilized in directed diffusion (Intanagonwiwat, Govindan, and Estrin 2000) which is one of the famous and widely used routing paradigms for WSNs. Directed diffusion suggests the use of attribute-value pairs for the data, and queries are created in an on-demand basis by using those pairs. Attribute-value pairs such as name of objects, interval, duration, and geographical area are used to name the data. This naming is then exploited to perform in-network aggregation. Once the data are known through low-level naming, intermediate nodes receiving the data can cache, filter, and suppress the data before transmitting to the parent node. With this method, each sensor can perform in-network data aggregation, and redundancy can be eliminated significantly.

An improvement to directed diffusion's application-specific, in-network data aggregation is to both utilize application information and minimize the number of edges in the convergecast tree. Specifically, this solution applies application-specific aggregation in a MST. A sample implementation of this approach is done in Heidemann et al. (2001) by performing the aggregation as close to the data sources as possible as in the case of the CNS heuristic proposed in Krishnamachari, Estrin, and Wicker (2002). Not only can the approach provide a 42 percent traffic reduction with respect to nonaggregation, but also it can handle nested queries (e.g., group by queries) perfectly with CNS heuristic.

Application-specific, in-network data aggregation is promising for future large-scale sensor databases in which a lot of complex queries are submitted frequently. One obvious disadvantage of these approaches is the need to reprogram the sensors for each different application. The used naming schemes are application-dependent, and each scheme should be defined a priori. Moreover, the matching process for data and queries might require some extra overhead at the sensors.

Structure-Free, In-Network Data Aggregation

The above described in-network aggregation approaches focus on the creation of a convergecast tree and the clusters and determination of aggregation points that need to be done upfront when the WSN is deployed for an application. This requires a lot of signaling overhead in creating, maintaining, and updating the proposed structures. Therefore, recently researchers have started to investigate the potential of using structure-free data aggregation (Enachescu et al. 2004; Fan, Liu, and Sinha 2005). For instance, in Enachescu et al. (2004), a randomized algorithm is proposed to provide a constant time approximation to the problem of determining optimal convergecast tree that is NP-complete. The authors claim that the approach will eliminate the need for special data-routing structures for some aggregation functions. Similarly, in Fan, Liu, and Sinha (2005), data aggregation is performed without using a predefined convergecast tree. The idea of spatial aggregation is based on *data-aware anycast* (DAA), which is performed at the *medium access control* (MAC) level. Rather than transmitting a data packet to a particular node, the goal is to determine the nodes that have packets ready to transmit and then send the packets to them. This increases the chance for spatial aggregation without referring to any convergecast tree. Furthermore, to get packets from multiple nodes ready at a certain node, that node delays its own transmission for a random amount of time. Simulation results have shown that the proposed approach based on DAA and randomized delay can decrease the number of transmissions by 77 percent when compared to opportunistic aggregation in which packets are aggregated whenever there is an opportunity.

THE IMPACT OF DATA AGGREGATION ON DATA LATENCY

Although data aggregation is confirmed to save significant energy in WSNs, there is a price for it: an inherent trade-off between energy and latency. Data aggregation may increase the end-to-end latency for the data packets and hence may not be applicable for the applications where end-to-end latency is critical. This is an important problem for large-scale sensor databases, where users submit frequent aggregation queries and would like to get the results within a certain amount of time. Such a typical query can be specified as "Report the average (maximum, minimum, etc.) measurement (temperature, pressure, radiation, etc.) in a certain region within D time units every T time units," where $D < T$.

The increase in the end-to-end latency results from increased wait times for the intermediate nodes when performing data aggregation. Each intermediate node may have multiple children, and the data-gathering process from these children may not always be synchronized because of the unbalanced structure of data-aggregation trees, node failures, congestion, and packet losses. Therefore, the increased latency for the aggregated packets becomes an issue when convergecast trees are in use. In this section, we first provide information about time-synchronization issues for performing data aggregation and then we summarize the aggregation approaches in WSNs for minimizing the latency while at the same time achieving the desired level of aggregation.

Time Synchronization for In-Network Data Aggregation

To eliminate redundant packets at an aggregating node, the node should make sure that these packets were generated at similar times. Therefore, the packets should be time-stamped with a precision on the same order as the event frequency when they are generated. This is more stringent than in traditional wired networks as far as the data-aggregation process is considered. An imprecise time-synchronization method will not only cause the sensor to fail to recognize the duplicate packets but also affect the waiting time of a packet in a node. In addition, to perform data aggregation, the scope of the time-synchronization algorithm should cover a wide area because the packet is traveling via multihops to the BS and being cached at some intermediate nodes.

Given the criticality of a precise and persistent time-synchronization algorithm, many new algorithms were proposed specifically for WSNs (Elson, Girod, and Estrin 2002; Sichitiu and Veerarittiphan 2003; Elson and Römer 2002). These algorithms updated the current synchronization algorithms such as network time protocol by considering the energy and communication constraints of the sensors in the design.

Modeling the Delay-Constrained Data-Aggregation Problem

When latency is the concern, the data-aggregation problem can be modeled as a constrained MST problem that is also an NP-hard problem (Kompella, Pasquale, and Polyzos 1993). In that case, the problem should ensure two things:

1. For all paths from source sensors to the BS, the end-to-end latency should be less than the desired deadline.
2. The final convergecast tree should provide the minimum possible energy consumption.

It is a nontrivial problem to both determine a convergecast tree that will minimize the energy consumption and ensure that each path will meet the timing constraints. Therefore, there exist no heuristics to the constrained MST problem in WSNs. However, there are different approaches with different assumptions.

One approach that deals exactly with the constrained MST problem is based on utilizing some special packet-scheduling techniques such as *weighted fair queuing* (WFQ) (Erramilli, Malta, and Bestavros 2004). This approach initially forms a convergecast tree that suits contemporary best-effort traffic. It then utilizes WFQ to support on-time delivery of delay-constrained (real-time) data. The idea is to identify the longest path in terms of hop counts on the initial convergecast tree for which the end-to-end delay is acceptable. A work-around mechanism is presented to ensure timeliness of packets on unfeasible paths (i.e., paths that cannot meet the desired deadline) by modifying the tree so that the packets are aggregated at another relay node that is closer to the BS. It is proved in this work that when a feasible path is found for the longest path in terms of hop counts among the real-time sources, the other sources connecting to this longest path can meet the end-to-end delay bounds. Simulation results have shown that the approach provides significant increase in timeliness at the price of a slight increase in energy consumption when compared to non–WFQ-based aggregation. The approach maintains the same level of timeliness for low traffic rates and slightly increases deadline misses for reasonably higher rates.

Another solution that considered a slightly different version of the same problem is proposed in He et al. (2003). In this case, the aim is to reduce the end-to-end delay rather than to provide certain guarantees. The proposed protocol is an *application-independent data aggregation* (AIDA) that does not depend on the type of the application. However, this solution works between the MAC and the network layers, which is the difference from Erramilli, Malta, and Bestavros (2004). The main idea is to concatenate a number of packets at the MAC layer at once, called *degree of aggregation,* to minimize the number of transmissions and packet overhead for accessing the channel. The concatenated packets are decomposed when reached to the destination. This is an adjustable parameter, and a feedback-based mechanism is used to adjust it based on the changing traffic conditions. Queuing delay is the factor used as feedback. By eliminating the need for accessing the channel and transmission for packets, the energy is saved and end-to-end delay is not affected and even decreases in high loads. However, the approach just considers aggregation at the MAC layer, and there is no optimization at the network layer. Therefore, the proposed approach is not suitable for implementing typical aggregation functions such as sum and average. Furthermore, one main disadvantage of their approach is that when the concatenated packet is dropped or lost for any reason, the recovery process will be extremely expensive, reducing the energy and latency gains.

The constrained MST problem may become simpler when the convergecast tree is known a priori. In this case, the problem reduces to scheduling the transmissions or adjusting the transmission time on each link so that for each path the end-to-end deadline is met. This problem is studied in Yu, Krishnamachari, and Prasanna (2004) under a nonmonotonic energy model—namely, *quadrature amplitude modulation* (QAM). Using this model, the bit rates on each link can be adjusted for a desired latency. The more power used for transmitting a bit, the faster it travels and hence the delay is reduced. Therefore, the aim is to minimize the total energy consumption on a path (and hence on the whole convergecast tree) while keeping the latency in check. A distributed online dynamic programming-based approach is proposed to minimize the energy usage (Yu, Krishnamachari, and Prasanna 2004). However, the solution assumes minimal interference among the nodes at the MAC layer, which is a difficult task to achieve in practice.

A possible and simple solution when the convergecast tree is known is to divide the given deadline into the number of nodes on a particular path and allow each node this amount of time to perform the data aggregation (Roedig, Barroso, and Sreenan 2004). In this case, each sensor node knows the maximum amount of time it can wait before aggregating the packets it has and transmitting to the parent node. However, this waiting time may greatly affect the accuracy of the data received at the BS as will be discussed later. Depending on the latency constraint, the accuracy performance will differ. For instance, if the latency is especially small, then the waiting time for a sensor will be especially short and hence the accuracy of the data at the BS will be reduced because the number of children contributing the aggregated data will be smaller. Therefore, this factor should also be included when formulating the solution.

Aggregation Delay and Network Topology

The end-to-end delay in data aggregation can also be affected by the network connectivity. The network connectivity is an issue in WSNs because most of the time the radios of sensors are shut down to save energy. Therefore, not all of the sensor nodes are always available for performing data aggregation. An interesting research problem at this point is to look at the delay performance of data aggregation under the influence of topology control. This problem is studied in Erramilli, Malta, and Bestavros (2004), where the possible effects of the network topology on the performance of data aggregation in terms of energy, delay, and fidelity is investigated. The aim is to maintain network connectivity with the minimum possible number of active sensor nodes and maximizing in-network data aggregation.

The simulation results have shown that topology management can have a detrimental effect on the network in terms of increased delays: Because connectivity strives to maintain minimum possible number of active nodes for energy considerations, the aggregation process is delayed until some of the nodes wake up. The increase in delay resulting from topology control may reduce the savings in energy from aggregation. Hence, in the presence of in-network data aggregation, careful coordination between routing and topology control is needed. In addition, shorter and fatter (i.e., dense) aggregation trees should be employed for best energy-delay trade-off results.

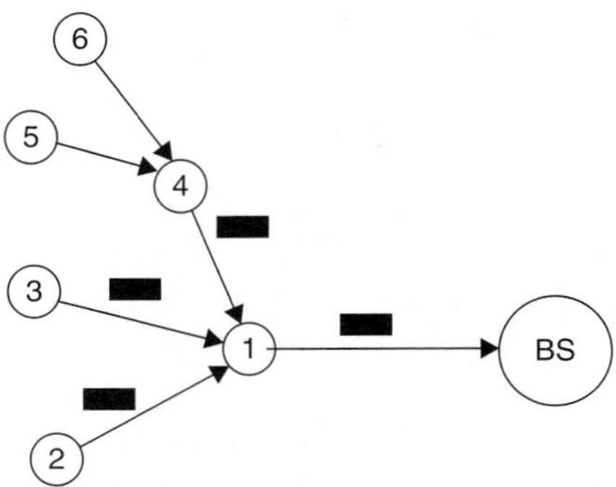

Figure 6: The question is, how long should node 1 wait before it performs the aggregation and forwards the packet to the BS? Note that in this case the packet coming from node 4 can be delayed more than the packets coming from nodes 2 and 3.

THE IMPACT OF DATA AGGREGATION ON DATA ACCURACY

In WSNs, it is critical to decide how long a sensor node will wait for its children to forward the aggregated data to the upper nodes in a convergecast tree in order to decide the level of accuracy of the data at the BS. Accuracy is measured by the number of nodes contributing to the result received at the BS. For example, if the average temperature is computed in a specific region, picking two sensor readings is less reliable and accurate than picking twenty readings. The more nodes contribute, the more accurate the data will be. Given that sensors are employed in sheer numbers, the accuracy of the received data at the BS can be adjusted based on the utilized aggregation and routing mechanism.

However, determining the number of sensors nodes contributing to the result is a difficult problem because such a decision can also affect energy and latency performance. Although an increased number of readings means increased accuracy of the result, collecting those readings from the sensors may increase the waiting times at the intermediate nodes. In addition, the increase in the number of contributions will mean an increased number of transmissions, which eventually increases the energy consumption of the sensor nodes. This section covers the description of approaches that explore the trade-off among accuracy and other metrics such as energy and latency when performing in-network data aggregation. We focus especially on mechanisms pursued in sensor databases by the data management research community to decide the waiting time of a parent node before data aggregation is performed.

Determination of Waiting Times

Different mechanisms have been proposed to set the waiting time duration for a particular node before aggregating the messages from its children and forwarding the aggregation to the upstream node as seen in Figure 6. The used timing model has a strong effect on the accuracy of the received data at the BS. Three widely used timing models that have been described in Solis and Obraczka (2004) are periodic simple, periodic per-hop, and periodic per-hop adjusted.

In the *periodic simple* approach, each node is assigned a predefined and fixed amount of waiting time. The *periodic per-hop* approach, on the other hand, requires each node to wait for all of its children so that all of them send their data and aggregation can be performed. In the *periodic per-hop adjusted* approach, the time durations are assigned based on the position of the nodes in the convergecast tree. This is also called the *cascading time-out* approach in which a node's time-out happens right before its parents. Simulation results have shown that the cascading time-out approach can provide six times more energy savings with respect to the periodic simple and periodic per-hop approaches (Solis and Obraczka 2004). Furthermore it provides exactly the same accuracy with the case when there is no data aggregation, whereas periodic simple and periodic per-hop approaches significantly decrease the accuracy (by approximately 50 percent).

The third approach is similar to epoch division approach in *tiny aggregation* (TAG) (Madden et al. 2002a) which is proposed to define a *structured query language* (SQL)-like declarative query language for expressing aggregation queries over streaming sensor data. This query language is applied as an abstraction between the user and the network protocol. Because TAG deals with aggregation queries, it does not provide any technique for eliminating redundancy. Rather, partial results for the aggregate queries are computed at the intermediate nodes, which reduces the number of transmissions.

TAG has two phases for data collection: *distribution* and *collection*. It introduces an epoch clause that represents the time to wait for getting the next answer for the query. The synchronization of the nodes in the tree to receive and transmit data is maintained through the subdivision of the epoch value into shorter intervals called *slots*. At each slot there is one level of nodes (in the convergecast tree) that are transmitting and another level of nodes that are receiving. This continues similarly up to the level of the BS as can be observed in Figure 7. Note that this is similar to the cascading time-out approach defined in Solis and Obraczka (2004).

In TAG, when the child does not have data that conform to the defined predicate, it does not send the data but rather notifies the parent node that it will not be sending data so that the parent will not wait for that node for performing aggregation. The idea in TAG is to do aggregation whenever possible in the tree through the BS.

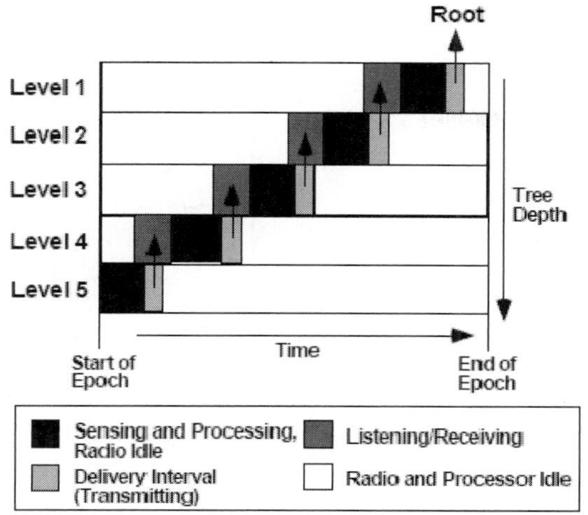

Figure 7: Epoch-based aggregation in TAG (Wen et al. 2004)

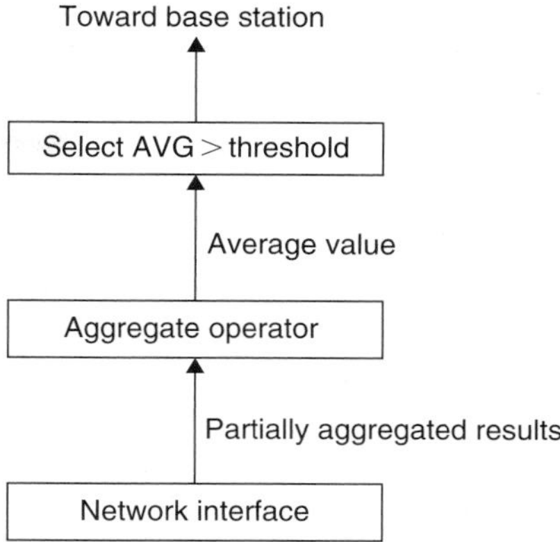

Figure 8: Query handling in Cougar: The leader node gets all of the readings, calculates the average, and, if greater than a threshold, sends it to the BS (Yao and Gehrke 2002)

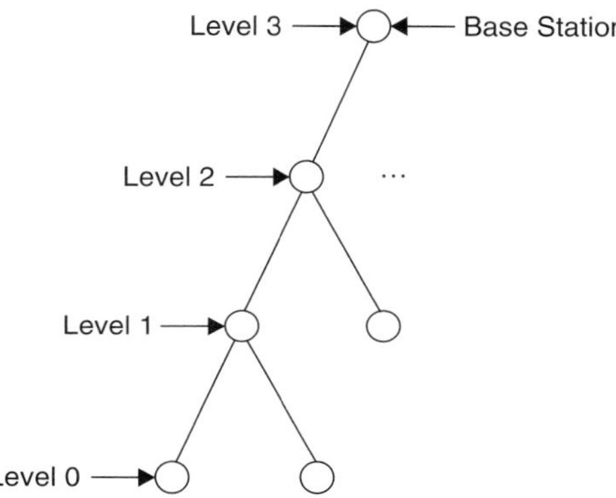

Figure 9: Multiple levels in a convergecast tree (Yuan, Krishnamurthy, and Tripathi 2003)

TAG separates data aggregation and routing functions, emphasizing that data aggregation should consider what data will be collected rather than how they are collected. Note that this is a different interpretation when compared to Solis and Obraczka (2004). The main idea here is to allow the expression of aggregation logic in a separate layer than the routing layer so that the system can dynamically adjust the routing decisions based on the used aggregation function. This also gives the user the opportunity to modify the system's behavior on the fly.

The periodic per-hop approach (i.e., waiting for all the children) defined in Solis and Obraczka (2004) is also employed in Cougar (Yao and Gehrke 2002). Cougar is similar to TAG: Declarative queries are used to abstract query processing from the network layer functions such as selection of relevant sensors and to utilize in-network data aggregation to save energy. The abstraction is ensured through a new query layer that is between the network and application layers. Cougar proposes an architecture for the sensor database system in which sensor nodes select a leader node to perform the aggregation and transmit the data to the BS. The BS is responsible for generating a query plan that specifies the necessary information about the data flow and in-network computation for the incoming query and sending it to the relevant nodes. The architecture provides in-network computation ability for all of the sensor nodes as seen in Figure 8, which is redrawn from Yao and Gehrke (2002).

Although waiting for all of the child nodes can increase the accuracy of the result at the BS, it will definitely worsen the delay because not all of the child nodes send their data at the same time to the parent node. One solution to eliminate this problem is to have a perfectly balanced convergecast tree so that two nodes at the same level will face the same delay because they will have the same number of nodes under their subtrees. However, it is clear that creating a perfectly balanced tree is not always possible because of large number of sensors, random deployments of sensors, and complex tree creation operations. Thus, a mechanism that is independent from the structure of the tree and assigns waiting times to intermediate nodes based on their proximity to the BS is proposed in Yuan, Krishnamurthy, and Tripathi (2003) (see Figure 9). In this case, a node extremely close to the BS should wait more than the node that is far away from the BS. The presented mechanism broadcasts to all sensors the level of desired data accuracy and their hop distances to the BS. The sensors using this information compute their waiting times for data aggregation. The simulation results have confirmed that the proposed synchronization protocol can achieve the desired accuracy irrespective of the convergecast tree structure.

This approach is similar to the epoch-based approach of TAG (Madden et al. 2002a) and periodic per hop in Solis and Obraczka (2004). The only difference is that, in this case, the BS decides a level of accuracy depending on the application and sends a parameter to all of the nodes accordingly. The nodes receiving this parameter compute their waiting times for data aggregation. Therefore, the level of accuracy is adjustable.

Another approach to get different accuracy levels is used in Fjords (Madden et al. 2002b), which presents data aggregation mechanisms using query languages similar to SQL. To speed up the result of aggregated queries, Fjords

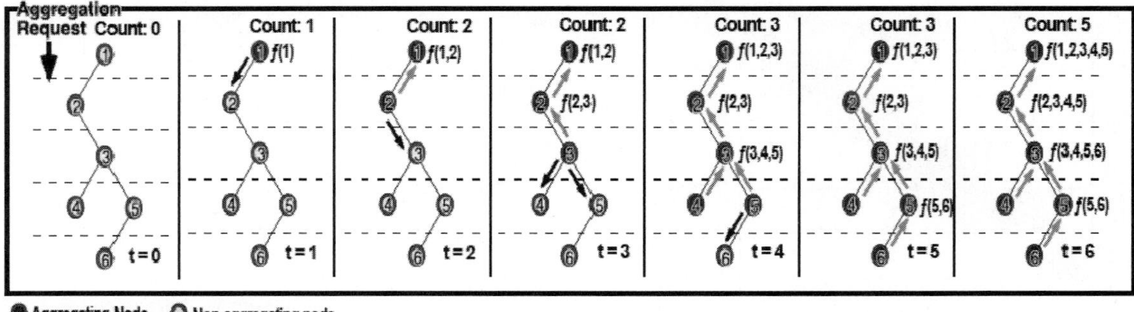

Figure 10: Pipelined aggregation in Fjords (Madden et al. 2002b). The time is divided into slots. At slot 1, the nodes at level 1 of the convergecast tree send their readings; at slot 2, nodes at levels 1 and 2 send their readings and so on. Thus, at each slot, an aggregated reading is received at node 1. The accuracy of the reading increases with the time.

suggests using a pipelined aggregation approach that continuously updates the aggregation result. The approach creates a convergecast tree initially by using broadcasting. The tree consists of multiple levels, and each level has sensors. When an aggregate query for periodic information retrieval is submitted, the nodes on the first level reply to the BS in a predefined time slot. In the next slot, the nodes on both the second and first levels reply. This continues until reaching the leaf nodes (see Figure 10, redrawn from Madden et al. 2002b). When a leaf node is reached, the BS will have replies from all of the nodes at all levels, leading to a robust and accurate result. This pipelined approach in Fjords provides multilevel accuracy, which is not the case in both TAG and Cougar.

Accuracy at the Link Layer

An interesting solution to improve the accuracy can be pursued at the link layer. Because this layer is responsible for improving reliability of the packet delivery, it can be exploited to improve the transmission reliability of the aggregated packets (Karl, Löbbers, and Nieberg 2003). This is especially important because aggregated packets have a lot of information and have required significant effort to create. If they are not recovered well enough, this may cause a significant degradation in the accuracy of the received information at the BS.

Therefore, the approach in Karl, Löbbers, and Nieberg (2003) is to try to assess how much effort to expend in deciding on different options of error correction at the link layer, depending on the capacity of information carried out by the data packet. For instance, if it is an aggregated packet, more sophisticated techniques such as *forward error correction* (FEC) or *automatic repeat request* (ARQ) can be employed before the transmission of the packet at the link layer. Although this sophisticated mechanism can increase data accuracy at the BS, it can also increase energy consumption of the sensor nodes. Therefore, depending on the application and the amount of information that an aggregated packet carries, a decision about how to reliably transmit the packet to the BS should be made. This is an interesting research challenge that creates a trade-off between energy and accuracy. Note that this problem is independent from the problem of adjusting waiting times, which also affect the accuracy. The solution to this problem will be complementary to that problem.

SECURITY-AWARE DATA AGGREGATION

Most of the research on data aggregation in WSNs has assumed that all of the participating sensors and base stations are honest and trustable. However, sensors and other powerful nodes within WSNs can easily be compromised by physical tampering and other mechanisms. In such cases, the aggregation mechanisms should be resilient enough to handle the attacks initiated by those compromised nodes. Although the type of these attacks may differ, a typical attack related to data aggregation is to send false reports to the BS so that it will infer wrong results. Most of the protocols that will be described in this section deal with this problem. We discuss and compare the different solutions.

We also discuss the approaches that propose aggregation mechanisms for data that are encrypted or signed. This is extremely important because confidentiality in sensor communications will be a standard in future protocols. However, no aggregation is possible with encrypted data unless decryption is performed. Obviously, this offsets the energy gain through aggregation, so solutions are needed to perform data aggregation under confidential communications.

Data Aggregation under Compromised Sensors

To achieve secure and reliable data aggregation, security mechanisms that prevent the user from making false decisions at the BS are needed. *Secure information aggregation* (SIA) (Przydatek, Song, and Perrig 2004) is known to be the first work that considers security in data aggregation for WSNs. The work provides a security framework for developing algorithms for computing several aggregation functions such as, max, min, median, and sum, even though the aggregator or a fraction of sensor nodes are corrupted. The framework labeled *aggregate-commit-prove* has three steps. First, an aggregator node (other than the BS) collects the data from the sensors

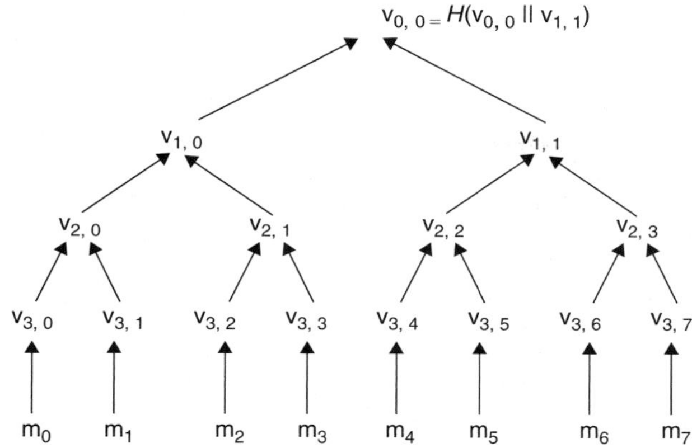

Figure 11: Merkle hash tree creation (Przydatek et al. 2004). A hash is computed by concatenating two hashes from the children of a node.

that are authenticated. Second, the aggregator computes the result based on the received and authenticated data. Finally, it transmits the result along with a correctness proof to the BS.

The proofs are created through *Merkle hash trees* in which a hash is computed by concatenating two hashes from the children of a node as seen in Figure 11, which is redrawn from Przydatek, Song, and Perrig (2004). By checking the correctness of the proof, the BS can conclude whether or not the aggregator is cheating. This work provides an algorithm for the computation of each aggregation function, including median, average, count, maximum, and minimum.

In this Merkle-based tree approach, the formed tree is a binary tree in which only the leaf nodes generate data. Recently, a similar but more flexible *secure hop-by-hop data aggregation approach* (SDAP) was proposed by Yang et al. (2006). SDAP logically determines groups of sensors within a convergecast tree and applies the idea of the Merkle hash tree on these groups through the BS. Thus, the tree can be arbitrary, allowing the intermediate nodes to aggregate their own results. For each group, a leader performs the aggregation and sends the result to the BS along with the proofs obtained through message authentication codes. The BS collects results from all of the groups and then evaluates their authenticity. Once this is done, the BS employs an outlier detection algorithm to eliminate the outliers from the received data. Based on the outcome of the outlier-detection algorithm, any suspicious groups are identified. In that case, those groups are asked to attest to the validity of their aggregates. If a group under attestation fails to support its earlier aggregate, the BS will discard this aggregate. SDAP calculates the final aggregate over all of the group aggregates that are either normal or passed the attestation procedure.

The same problem has also been studied in Du et al. (2003), who named it *witness-based aggregation* (WBA). The proposed approach selects some witness nodes to monitor the aggregation process. In addition to witness nodes, a data aggregator node is assumed that transmits the result to the BS. Each witness node is responsible for computing the aggregated result, getting a message authentication code of the result and forwarding it to the aggregator node. The aggregator node along with the result it has received from the sensors should transmit the proofs (i.e., message authentication codes from witnesses) to the BS. The BS can check the proofs and determine whether the aggregated results are correct as seen in Figure 12 (redrawn from Du et al. 2003). If there are

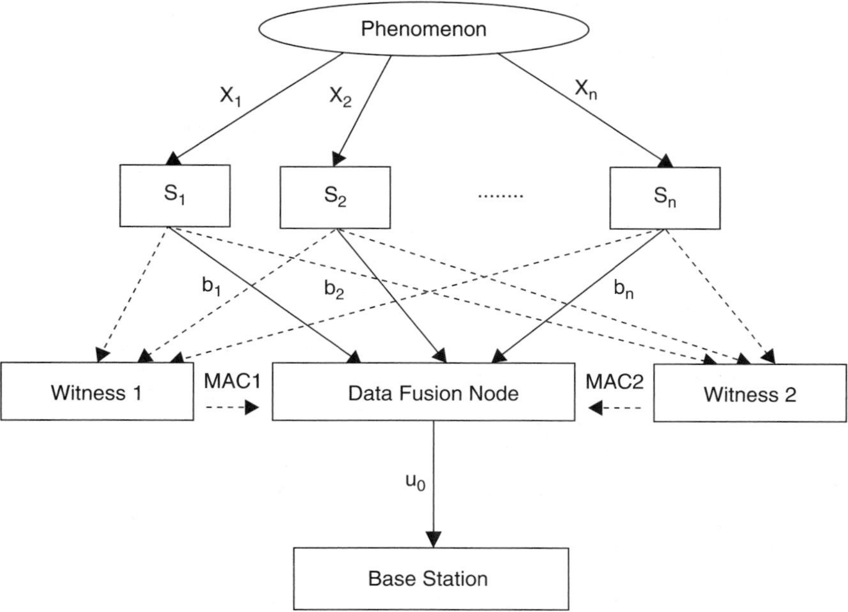

Figure 12: Verification by two witnesses and an aggregator (Du et al. 2003). Witnesses 1 and 2 also perform the aggregation from nodes S_1 to S_n, creating a message authentication code of the result and sending it to the data fusion node. All of the results are then sent to the BS by the data fusion node.

incorrect results, the BS can contact one of the witness nodes to receive the correct result.

Note that the approach summarized here is similar to SIA. The only difference is that WBA additionally employs witness nodes to double perform the result computation. In fact, both approaches utilize the same idea of using one-way hash functions in sensor nodes to relay the results to the BS. Although MAC computation is used to create proofs in WBA, Merkle-based hash trees are used in SIA to verify whether the aggregators are cheating.

Yet another approach called *secure aggregation* (SA) to the same problem is discussed in Hu and Evans (2003). In this case, however, there are neither aggregators nor witness nodes as opposed to SIA and WBA. Rather, the proposed solution in SA involves something called *delayed aggregation and authentication* in order to prevent intruders or compromised nodes from changing the result at the BS. Delayed aggregation suggests that the aggregation of data at a parent node will not be performed but forwarded to the grandparent as is. The grandparent will, however, perform data aggregation and authentication. The main idea of aggregation at the grandparent is to be able to detect the bogus data coming from the possibly compromised nodes that are close neighbors (i.e., child and parent). For example, in Figure 13, nodes A and B send their IDs, data R_A, R_B, to node E with a message authentication code of the data. E then forwards this information along with the message authentication code of the aggregated data (R_A, R_B) to its parent G. G finally performs aggregation of R_A and R_B, and hence can verify its correctness by computing its message authentication code and comparing it with the one it has.

In fact, SA uses MAC computation as done in WBA for performing authentication, but it is not performed at each level of the tree. Therefore, it is not clear whether it is as secure as WBA unless an experimental evaluation is made. Although this is lacking in SA, an analytical cost of the proposed protocol is computed to show that the protocol significantly reduces energy and introduces little overhead when compared to insecure aggregation.

In all of these approaches, all of the sensed data are sent from the source sensor to upper-level nodes and data aggregation is performed at the upper levels. To further eliminate unnecessary redundant transmissions from the source sensors, ESPDA (Çam et al. 2006) has been proposed to transmit the representatives of the data called *pattern codes.* A pattern code is defined to represent the characteristics and summary of the sensed data. This is especially useful for the sensors with multiple sensing units. To generate the pattern codes, the cluster-head of the sensors generates a pattern seed that is a random number and broadcasts in encrypted format. Note that the paper considers a clustered architecture in which a sensor is randomly picked as the cluster-head for a period of time. Each cluster-head aggregates the data and sends it to the BS. Therefore, initially asymmetric keys are distributed to sensors and the cluster-head to perform encryption and decryption using the blowfish algorithm.

The idea is to detect redundancy by just looking at the transmitted pattern codes at the cluster-head. In addition, before sending the pattern codes, each sensor exchanges its sensing region information with other sensors within its neighborhood. During this process, if there are overlapping regions, some of the sensors are forced to go to sleep because their data would be redundant. Once the redundant pattern codes are detected at the cluster-head, only distinct sensors are picked to send data in encrypted form to the BS through the cluster-head. Performance evaluations have shown that ESPDA can reduce the bandwidth usage by 50 percent when compared to a conventional data aggregation algorithm without compromising the security of the system.

Aggregation of Encrypted Data

An extremely interesting security problem is the aggregation of encrypted data without decrypting it (Castelluccia, Mykletun, and Tsudik 2005; Girao, Westho, and Schneider 2004). In fact, the research on this problem is quite necessary because most of the communication among the sensor nodes is envisioned to be encrypted and authenticated in future applications. In such deployments, decrypting the data, performing the aggregation, and reencrypting the data for transmission will not only be highly inefficient in terms of energy consumption but

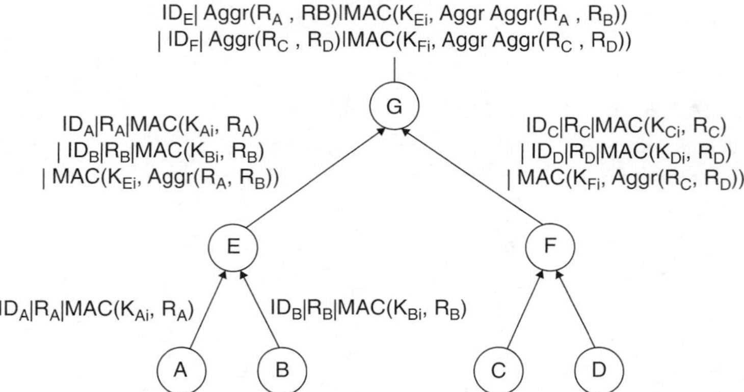

Figure 13: Delayed aggregation in a sample tree (Hu and Evans 2003). G performs aggregation of A, B and C, D and compares the results with the MACs of aggregated data coming from E and F to verify the correctness.

will also generate unnecessary traffic, decreasing the available bandwidth.

If the aggregation function is known a priori, one solution to this problem is to be able to perform the aggregation with encrypted data; this process is called *homomorphic encryption*. Using this approach, a different scheme is needed for each aggregation function—for instance, performing encrypted addition and average require different algorithms. Castelluccia, Mykletun, and Tsudik (2005) study these kind of algorithms, including schemes for addition, average, and variance. Girao, Westho, and Schneider (2004) present a different algorithm for computing the average. The main issue in this research is to come up with light-weight schemes that will not bring a computationally expensive load to the sensor nodes. However, this type of aggregation may not work for all functions. For example, it is not possible to eliminate data redundancy by just looking at the encrypted data.

CONCLUSION

In-network data aggregation in WSNs has attracted a lot of attention from the research community because of its potential for reducing the energy consumption of severely constrained sensor nodes. In this chapter, we described how in-network data aggregation is performed and summarized how it impacts energy, latency, accuracy, and security by discussing several approaches.

Although the summarized approaches solved many interesting problems and contributed to the development of WSNs, there are still many open issues. The following are possible future research issues to be investigated.

- We envision that the design of query languages for WSNs in order to handle aggregate queries will attract more research in the future. This is especially critical for the design of high-level programming languages for WSNs—that is, *macroprogramming*. Providing acceptable latency and accuracy along with energy efficiency should be included in query language designs. New query languages that can support specification of these metrics in the queries for sensor databases are also needed. This definitely necessitates collaboration between the networking and data management communities.
- Delay-constrained data aggregation has not been given enough consideration. Therefore, efficient heuristics for solving the *delay-constrained MST problem* are needed to provide delay guarantees for data aggregation. Another concern that will affect the heuristic is the type of aggregation function used. For complex aggregation functions such as median and histogram, there will be additional delays for computation that may affect the end-to-end data latency received at the BS.
- The problem of link layer recovery for aggregated packets mentioned in Karl, Löbbers, and Nieberg (2003) can be another interesting future challenge that may promote research into error control and correction with energy trade-offs. Because aggregated packets carry more information, it may be wise to handle their link layer transmissions with more sophisticated error-correction algorithms. This can be adjusted based on the location of the packet in the convergecast tree.
- An interesting technique to improve accuracy without affecting energy usage can be using adaptive sampling (Willett, Martin, and Nowak 2004). In this case, a small representative subset of sensors is picked to respond to a query. In such cases, performing data aggregation will require careful treatment because not all of the sensors are involved. Thus, investigating the relation between in-network data aggregation and adaptive sampling is an interesting research direction.
- Some performance comparison studies are needed to assess the best approach for secure data aggregation (such as SIA, WBA, and SA) in terms of energy, delay, and accuracy when compromised nodes or aggregators falsely contribute to the aggregated results.
- The data aggregation for multimedia data in wireless image and video sensors is a completely new area that requires considerable research (Kumar et al. 2003). Multimedia data aggregation is challenging because of the limited power the sensors have. Currently, the aggregation is performed only on images by eliminating temporal redundant objects. Video data aggregation has not yet been accomplished because of the additional challenges presented by delay and jitter (i.e., delay variation) requirements.
- In heterogeneous WSNs, data aggregation and computationally expensive operations are planned to be performed in special nodes that are assumed to be more powerful than sensors. Therefore, an interesting research problem for heterogeneous WSNs is to determine the number of aggregators and optimal locations for such nodes for best performance in terms of energy, delay, and accuracy.
- All of the discussed approaches in this chapter assume a single BS. In some setups, multiple BSs are employed. In this case, a research challenge is determining how to perform data aggregation in multiple-source, multiple BS WSNs. Xue, Cui, and Nahrstedt (2005) is an initial attempt to consider this problem; it proposes an algorithm to combine multiple convergecast trees into a data structure named *aggregation forest*. However, this solution is based on an updated Dijkstra's shortest-path algorithm that does not provide a lot of opportunities for data aggregation. New approaches are needed that will consider other heuristics such as CNS for aggregation forests.
- Finally, it would be interesting to quantify and compare the affects of data aggregation with data caching on delay, accuracy, and so on in WSNs. Nodes could cache and reuse previously retrieved data from neighboring nodes to quickly respond to repeated queries, thus reducing delay and saving network bandwidth. They could also save the results of queries or computations for additional energy savings and reduced delay. However, accuracy of the results could decrease as a trade-off, therefore it would be an interesting future work to investigate the applicability of these techniques to different scenarios.

GLOSSARY

Automatic Repeat Request (ARQ): Mechanism for handling errors at the link layer.

Base Station: Node that collects data from the sensors.

Convergecast Tree: The reverse of a multicast tree in which a node receives data from multiple nodes.

Heuristics: An algorithm that tries to get solutions close to optimal in a reasonable amount of time.

In-Network Processing: The operations performed when data packets are traveling in the network.

Message Authentication Code: A tag that is computed by applying a function with a key to a message for authentication purposes.

Network Topology: The graph created with sensors as the vertices and the links among them as the edges.

Query Language: Computer language to create queries for databases (e.g., sensor databases).

Weighted Fair Queuing (WFQ): A packet-scheduling mechanism that uses multiple queues to serve to different classes of packets in a weighted round-robin fashion.

CROSS REFERENCES

See *Broadcasting in Ad Hoc and Sensor Networks; Data Gathering and Monitoring in Sensor Networks; Emerging Trends in Routing Protocols in Mobile Wireless Ad Hoc and Sensor Networks; Medium Access in Ad Hoc and Sensor Networks; Network Middleware; Network QoS; Principles and Applications of Ad Hoc and Sensor Networks*.

REFERENCES

Agora, A., P. Dutta, S. Bapat, V. Kulathumani, H. Zhang, V. Naik, V. Mittal, H. Cao, M. Demirbas, M. Gouda, Y. Choi, T. Herman, S. Kulkarni, U. Arumugam, M. Nesterenko, A. Vora, and M. Miyashita. 2004. A line in the sand: A WSN for target detection, classification, and tracking, In *Computer Networks: The International Journal of Computer and Telecommunications Networking*, 46(5): 605–34.

Agora, A., R. Ramnath, E. Ertin, et al. 2005. Exscal: Elements of an extreme scale wireless sensor network. In *Proceedings of the Eleventh IEEE International Conference on Embedded and Real-Time Computing Systems and Applications*, Ohio State University, Columbus, OH, pp. 102–8.

Akkaya, K., and M. Younis. 2005. A survey of routing protocols in wireless sensor networks. *Elsevier Ad Hoc Network Journal*, 3(3): 325–49.

Akkaya, K., M. Younis, and M. Youssef. 2005. Efficient aggregation of delay-constrained data in wireless sensor networks. In *Proceedings of Internet Compatible QoS in Ad Hoc Wireless Networks* (IC-QAWN), Jan. 3–6, Cairo, pp. 904–9.

Akyildiz, I. F., W. Su, Y. Sankarasubramaniam, and E. Cayirci. 2002. Wireless sensor networks: A survey. *Computer Networks*, 38: 393–422.

Burrell, J., T. Brooke, and R. Beckwith. 2004. Vineyard computing: Sensor networks in agricultural production. *IEEE Pervasive Computing*, 3(1): 38–45.

Çam, H., S. Ozdemir, P. Nair, D. Muthuavinashiappan, and H. O. Sanli. 2006. Energy-efficient secure pattern based data aggregation for wireless sensor networks. *Computer Communications*, February, pp. 446–55.

Castelluccia, C., E. Mykletun, and G. Tsudik. 2005. Efficient aggregation of encrypted data in wireless sensor networks. In *Proceedings of the Second Annual International Conference on Mobile and Ubiquitous Systems* (ACM/IEEE MobiQuitous), July 17–21, San Diego, pp. 109–17.

Cerpa, A., and D. Estrin. 2002. ASCENT: Adaptive self-configuring sensor networks topologies. In *Proceedings of the Twenty-First Annual Joint Conference of the IEEE Computer and Communications Societies* (INFOCOM 2002), June 23–7, New York, pp. 1278–87.

Chen, Y. P., A. L. Liestman, and J. Liu. 2005. Energy-efficient data aggregation hierarchy for wireless sensor networks. In *Proceedings of the International Conference on Quality of Service in Heterogeneous Wired/Wireless Networks* (QShine'05), August, Orlando, FL, pp. 7.

Cheng, R., and S. Prabhakar. 2003. Managing uncertainty in sensor databases, in Special Section on Sensor Network Technology and Sensor Data Management. *SIGMOD Record*, 32(4): 41–6.

Du, W., J. Deng, S. H. Yunghsiang, and P. K. Varshney. 2003. A witness-based approach for data fusion assurance in wireless sensor networks. In *Proceedings of IEEE GLOBECOM*, Dec. 1–5, San Francisco, pp. 1435–9.

Elnahrawy, E. 2003. *Research directions in sensor data streams: Solutions and challenges*. DCIS Technical Report DCIS-TR-527, Rutgers University, May.

Elson, J., L. Girod, and D. Estrin. 2002. Fine-grained network time synchronization using reference broadcasts. In *Proceedings of the Fifth Symposium on Operating Systems Design and Implementation*, December, Boston, pp. 147–63.

Elson, J., and K. Römer. 2002. Wireless sensor networks: A new regime for time synchronization. In *Proceedings of the First Workshop on Hot Topics in Networks* (HotNets-I), Oct., 28–9, Princeton, NJ, pp. 149–54.

Enachescu, M., A. Goel, R. Govindan, and R. Motwani. 2004. Scale-free aggregation in sensor networks. In *Proceedings of the First International Workshop on Algorithmic Aspects of Wireless Sensor Networks* (Algosensors), July 16, Turku, Finland, pp. 71–84.

Erramilli, V., I. Malta, and A. Bestavros. 2004. On the interaction between data aggregation and topology control in wireless sensor networks. In *Proceedings of the First IEEE Communications Society Conference on Sensor and Ad Hoc Communications and Networks* (IEEE SECON 2004), Oct. 4–7, Santa Clara, CA, pp. 557–65.

Fan, K., S. Liu, and P. Sinha. 2005. On the potential of structure-free data aggregation in sensor networks. In *Proceedings of IEEE INFOCOM 2006*, April 23–9, Barcelona, pp. 1–12.

Faradjian, A., J. E. Gehrke, and P. Bonnet. 2002. Gadt: A probability space adt for representing and querying the physical world. In *Proceedings of the Eighteenth*

International Conference on Data Engineering (ICDE 2002), Feb. 26–March 1, San Jose, CA, pp. 201–11.

Girao, J., D. Westho, and M. Schneider. 2004. CDA: Concealed data aggregation in wireless sensor networks. In *Proceedings of the ACM Workshop on Wireless Security* (ACM WiSe), Oct. 1, Philadelphia.

Hall, D. L., and J. Llinas. 2001. *Handbook of multisensor data fusion*. Boca Raton, FL: CRC Press.

He, T., B. M. Blum, J. A. Stankovic, and T. Abdelzaher. 2003. AIDA: Adaptive application independent aggregation in sensor networks. *ACM Transactions on Embedded Computing System*, 3(2): 426–57.

Heidemann, J., F. Silva, C. Intanagonwiwat, R. Govindan, D. Estrin, and D. Ganesan. 2001. Building efficient wireless sensor networks with low-level naming. In *Proceedings of the 18th ACM Symposium on Operating Systems Principles*, Oct. 21–4, Banff, Alberta, Canada, pp. 146–59.

Heinzelman, W., A. Chandrakasan, and H. Balakrishnan. 2000. Energy-efficient communication protocol for wireless microsensor networks. In *Proceedings of the Thirty-Third Annual Hawaii International Conference on System Sciences*, Jan. 4–7, Maui, HI, vol. 2: 1–10.

Hu, L., and D. Evans. 2003. Secure aggregation for wireless networks. In *Proceedings of Workshop on Security and Assurance in Ad Hoc Networks*, Jan. 28, Orlando, FL, pp. 384.

Intanagonwiwat, C., R. Govindan, and D. Estrin. 2000. Directed diffusion: A scalable and robust communication paradigm for sensor networks. In *Proceedings of the International Conference on Mobile Computing and Networking* (MobiCom'00), August, Boston, pp. 56–67.

Karl, H., M. Löbbers, and T. Nieberg. 2003. A data aggregation framework for wireless sensor networks. In *Proceedings of 11th Annual Workshop on Circuits, Systems and Signal Processing* (ProRISC), Nov. 26–7, Utrecht, Netherlands.

Kompella, V. P., J. C. Pasquale, and G. C. Polyzos. 1993. Multicast routing for multimedia communication. *IEEE/ACM Transactions on Networking*, pp. 286–92.

Krishnamachari, B., D. Estrin, and S. Wicker. 2002. The impact of data aggregation in wireless sensor networks. In *Proceedings of International Workshop on Distributed Event-Based Systems*, July 2–3, Vienna, pp. 575–8.

Kumar, R., M. Wolenetz, B. Agarwalla, J. Shin, P. Hutto, A. Paul, and U. Ramachandran. 2003. DFuse: A framework for distributed data fusion. In *Proceedings of the First International Conference on Embedded Networked Sensor Systems*, Nov. 5–7, Los Angeles, pp. 114–25.

Lee, W. M., and V. W. S. Wong. 2006. E-span and LPT for data aggregation in wireless sensor networks. in *Elsevier Computer Communications Journal* (special issue on wireless sensor networks), 29(13–14): 2506–20.

Lin, S., D. Gunopulos, V. Kalogeraki, and S. Lonardi. 2005. A data compression technique for sensor networks with dynamic bandwidth allocation. In *Proceedings of Twelfth International Symposium on Temporal Representation and Reasoning*. Burlington, VT, pp. 186.

Lin, T.-H., and P. Huang. 2005. Sensor data aggregation for resource inventory applications. In *Proceedings of the IEEE Wireless Communications and Networking Conference* (WCNC), March, New Orleans, vol. 4: 2369–74.

Lindsey, S., and C. Raghavendra. 2002. PEGASIS: Power-efficient gathering in sensor information systems. In *Proceedings of IEEE Aerospace Conference*, March 9–16, Big Sky, MT, vol. 3: 1125–30.

Madden, S., M. J. Franklin, J. Hellerstein, and W. Hong. 2002a. TAG: A tiny aggregation service for ad hoc sensor networks. In *Proceedings of the Fifth Symposium on Operating Systems Design and Implementation* (OSDI '02) Dec. 9–11, Boston, pp. 131–46.

Madden, S., R. Szewczyk, M. J. Franklin, and D. Culler. 2002b. Supporting aggregate queries over ad-hoc wireless sensor networks. In *Proceedings of the Sixth IEEE Workshop on Mobile Computing Systems and Applications* (WMCSA 2002), June 19–20, Callicoon, NY, pp. 49–58.

Mainwaring, A., J. Polastre, R. Szewczyk, D. Culler, and J. Andersen. 2002. Wireless sensor networks for habitat monitoring. In *Proceedings of ACM Workshop on Wireless Sensor Networks and Applications*, September, Atlanta, pp. 88–97.

Manjeshwar, A., and D. P. Agrawal. 2001. TEEN: A protocol for enhanced efficiency in wireless sensor networks. In *Proceedings of the First International Workshop on Parallel and Distributed Computing Issues in Wireless Networks and Mobile Computing*, April, San Francisco.

Musick, S., and R. Malhotra. 1994. Chasing the elusive sensor manager. In *Proceedings of IEEE National Conference on Aerospace and Electronics*, May 23–27, Dayton, OH, pp. 606–13.

Obraczka, K., R. Manduchi, and J. J. Garcia-Luna-Aceves. 2002. Managing the information flow in visual sensor networks. In *Proceedings of the Fifth International Symposium on Wireless Personal Multimedia Communication* (WPMC 2002), October, Honolulu, pp. 1177–81.

Przydatek, B., D. Song, and A. Perrig. 2004. SIA: Secure information aggregation in sensor networks. In *Proceedings of the ACM Conference on Embedded Networked Sensor Systems* (SenSys 2004), Nov. 5–7, Los Angeles, pp. 255–65.

Roedig, U., A. Barroso, and C. J. Sreenan. 2004. Determination of aggregation points in wireless sensor networks. In *Proceedings of the Thirtieth Euromicro Conference*, Sept. 1–3, Rennes, France, pp. 503–10.

Scaglione, A. 2003. Routing and data compression in sensor networks: Stochastic models for sensor data that guarantee scalability. In *Proceedings of the International Symposium on Information Theory* (ISIT2003), June 29–July 4, Yokohama, Japan, pp. 174.

Sichitiu, M. L., and C. Veerarittiphan. 2003. Simple, accurate time synchronization for wireless sensor networks. In *Proceedings of IEEE Wireless Communications and Networking Conference* (WCNC 2003), March 16–20, New Orleans, pp. 1266–73.

Sohrabi, K., et al. 2000. Protocols for self-organization of a wireless sensor network. *IEEE Personal Communications*, 7(5): 16–27.

Solis, I., and K. Obraczka. 2004. The impact of timing in data aggregation for sensor networks. In *Proceedings of the International Conference on Communications*, June, Paris, vol. 6: 3640–5.

Takahashi, H., and A. Matsuyama. 1980. An approximate solution for the Steiner problem in graphs. *Mathematica Japonica*, 24(6): 573–7.

Wen, Y.-J., M. A. Agogine, and G. Kai. 2004. Fuzzy validation and fusion for wireless sensor networks. In *Proceedings of IMECE2004 2004 ASME International Mechanical Engineering Congress and RD&D Expo*, Nov. 13–19, Anaheim, CA, USA.

Willett, R., A. Martin, and R. Nowak. 2004. Backcasting: Adaptive sampling for sensor networks. In *Proceedings of the Third International Symposium on Information Processing in Sensor Networks* (IPSN'04), April 26–27, Berkeley, CA, pp. 124–33.

Xu, Y., and J. Heideman. 2001. Geography-informed energy conservation for ad hoc routing. In *Proceedings of the Seventh ACM Mobile Computing and Communication*, July 16–21, Rome, pp. 70–84.

Xue, Y., Y. Cui, and K. Nahrstedt. 2005. Maximizing lifetime for data aggregation in wireless sensor networks. In *Mobile Networks and Applications* (MONET), Special Issue on Energy Constraints and Lifetime Performance in Wireless Sensor Networks, 10(6): 853–64.

Yang, Y., X. Wang, S. Zhu, and G. Cao. 2006. SDAP: A secure hop-by-hop data aggregation protocol for sensor networks. In *Proceedings of the Seventh ACM International Symposium on Mobile Ad Hoc Networking and Computing* (MobiHoc), May 22–5, Florence, Italy, pp. 356–67.

Yu, Y., B. Krishnamachari, and V. K. Prasanna. 2004. Energy-latency trade-offs for data gathering in wireless sensor networks. In *Proceedings of the Conference on Computer Communications* (IEEE Infocom 2004) March 7–11, Hong Kong, pp. 244–55.

Yuan W., S. V. Krishnamurthy, and S. K. Tripathi. 2003. Synchronization of multiple levels of data fusion in wireless sensor networks. In the *Proceedings of IEEE GLOBECOM*, San Francisco, CA, December. Vol. 1, pp. 221–25.

Zhao, Y. J., R. Govindan, and D. Estrin. 2002. Residual energy scan for monitoring sensor networks. In the *Proceedings of the IEEE Wireless Communications and Networking Conference* (WCNC'02), March 17–21, Orlando, FL, pp. 356–62.

Cognitive and Software Defined Radios for Dynamic Spectrum Access

Troy Weingart and Douglas C. Sicker, *University of Colorado, Boulder*

INTRODUCTION

A convergence of technology trends is changing the operational and design characteristics of radio devices. The first of these technology trends is software-defined radio (SDR). SDRs allow much of what was previously done with application-specific hardware, such as signal processing, to be accomplished in software, whereas traditional radios have fixed designs and are often implemented solely in hardware (e.g., application-specific integrated circuit [ASIC] technology; see Figure 1). Next is cognitive radio (CR) technology, wherein the device can autonomously make decisions about its operation in response to environmental changes (e.g., interference) or changes in the required capability of the device (e.g., application requirements). Such capabilities will enable future radios to vary waveforms and frequencies within their hardware constraints, as well as reconfigure how their network protocols operate. It should be mentioned that the distinctions among these technologies might appear blurry. For example, although it is possible to build a CR on top of an SDR—a cognitive/software-defined radio (C/SDR)—it is certainly not necessary. In other words, one could develop a CR that is not built on top of a software-defined radio. One should also understand that any of the technologies (SDR, CR, or C/SDR) could be the basis of a platform that offers frequency agility. Frequency agile devices can change how and where they operate within the radio spectrum by moving among a set of frequency bands.

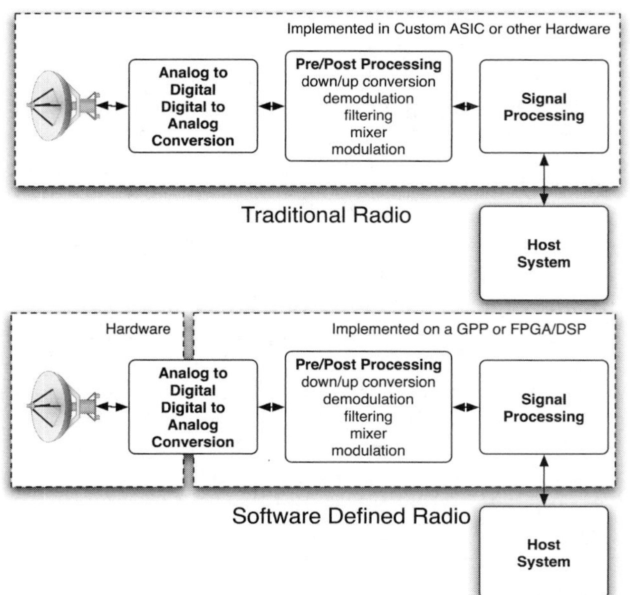

Figure 1: Traditional versus software-defined radio

An SDR can be described as a transceiver in which much of the physical layer is programmable, allowing the device to be reconfigured to meet changing needs. Integral to this ability to reconfigure is the support for various modulation schemes, frequency adaptation, and portable waveforms. The International Telecommunications Union–Radiocommunications (ITU-R) defines an SDR as "A radio in which the RF operating parameters of frequency range, modulation type, and/or output power can be set or altered by software, or the technique by which this is achieved" (ITU-R 2004). Higher up the network protocol stack is the ability to adapt the medium access control (MAC) and routing capabilities, although this higher-layer functionality is generally not considered part of an SDR. The foundations of SDR are rooted in a collection of hardware and software, with the objective to move a significant part of the radio's processing from the analog to the digital domain and from the hardware to the software domain, thus affording the flexibility, interoperability, and efficiency required. The ideal SDR is one that allows all

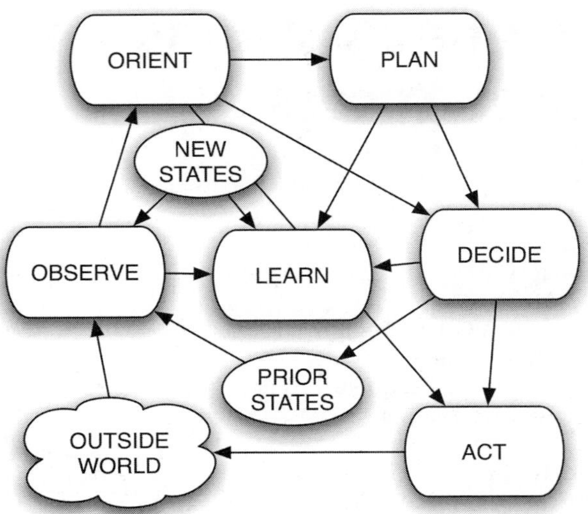

Figure 2: Simplified cognition cycle (Mitola 2000)

signal processing to be done digitally in software (Bose 1999), although this might not be a reasonable approach given the limitations of input/output and computing bottlenecks.

In 1999, Mitola (2000) coined the term *cognitive radio* to represent a device that is aware of its environment and can adapt its operation in complex ways. At its core, a CR can sense, adapt, and learn from its surroundings. Mitola developed a comprehensive cycle of cognition for a CR, a simplified version of which is shown in Figure 2. In the chart, he describes the possible steps that a CR might take in assessing its environment; these include observe, orient, plan, learn, decide, and act. Various complex relationships can be defined among these steps.

Software-defined and cognitive radio can combine into a highly flexible device, one that is aware of its radio frequency environment. These C/SDRs are ideally suited for the creation of frequency agile radios, in which the device can autonomously select operating parameters in a way that improves access to available spectrum and thereby could contribute to improvements in spectrum utilization (we refer to this as *dynamic spectrum utilization*). One can envision an advanced wireless network that dynamically allocates and reallocates spectrum or dynamically reconfigures itself in response to changes in policy and environmental conditions. This type of flexible spectrum usage raises interesting issues regarding the role of primary users (i.e., incumbent spectrum users) and secondary users (i.e., new users of the spectrum). For example, to what extent is a secondary user allowed to interfere with primary users, and how do we even define such interference? This level of flexibility in a wireless platform not only allows us to reexamine the problem of spectrum utilization, it also offers the ability for devices to cooperatively configure themselves to support the quality-of-service demands of applications running across the network.

One might appropriately ask whether frequency agile radios represent anything new. In some ways, they do not—there are many systems and devices that incorporate some subset of this technology. Current second-generation cellular technology incorporates sophisticated transmit power control. Even a typical 802.11 card supports many of the requirements of a frequency agile device: they rely heavily on software to operate (although not at the physical layer); they can sense their environment (through listen-before-talk [LBT] and channel sounding); and they can alter their frequency parameters (within a set of channels). However, they do all of these things in a rather rudimentary manner. One could also argue that even conventional hardware radios have some of these characteristics, although, they are much more limited in terms of their ability to dynamically alter their operation and have certain physical limits in terms of their potential for reconfiguration (simply because of the physical and cost constraints of adding hardware to support additional features). The configurations of such conventional devices are generally set during the design phase, and there is little to no ability to alter this configuration after development. Finally, conventional hardware radios are developed through baseband design methods, whereas SDRs overlay a software architecture on top of this model. This ability to alter the design of the device is powerful in that it offers the ability for upgrading, patching, and altering a device that has already been deployed.

Taxonomy

In this section, a taxonomy for defining future radio technology is presented. At one end of the taxonomy there is the traditional radio, in which specific functionalities are determined during initial design and are generally implemented in hardware. Next in the taxonomy are SDRs, which are functionally equivalent to their analog predecessors; however, these devices are implemented on field-programmable gate arrays (FPGA), digital signal processors (DSP), general-purpose processors (GPP), and/or other programmable processors. Such devices shift hardware-based functionality and control to software. The rise of SDR began alongside the transition from radios that used highly specialized DSP hardware to those that use GPP and software (Tennenhouse and Bose 1995). In addition to the GPP, SDR has driven parallel advancements in other radio components, including new antenna, amplifier, and filter technology. Advancements in this area also fueled a need for analog-to-digital converters that were cheaper, faster, and more power efficient. There are a host of problems in specifying computer architectures that are able to meet the demands of an SDR. Furthermore, cost, power, size, and weight limitations might initially influence the capacity and design of SDR technology.

At the other end of the taxonomy are radios that incorporate computational intelligence. These *cognitive* radios will be able to sense, learn, and act in response to changes in their environment. The ultimate cognitive radio will be able to autonomously negotiate and propose entirely new optimized protocols for use in the networking environment. In other words, this technology would allow devices to dynamically reconfigure their operational parameters to enhance performance metrics such as throughput, bit error rate, or delay. It is important to note that a cognitive radio could be built on top of either a traditional radio or a software-defined radio. Table 1 presents this taxonomy.

Table 1: Taxonomy of Traditional, Software-Defined, and Cognitive Radios

Traditional Radio	• Specific functionalities determined during initial design (limited upgradeability) • Design based on traditional design models • Implemented in hardware (e.g., ASIC-based technology)
Software-Defined Radio	• New functionality can be added through software updates (enhanced upgradeability) • Design largely based on software design models • Implemented on programmable processors
Cognitive Radio	• Required functionality can be determined and negotiated (intelligent upgradeability) • Combines software design with reasoning techniques • Implemented in flexible hardware and/or software

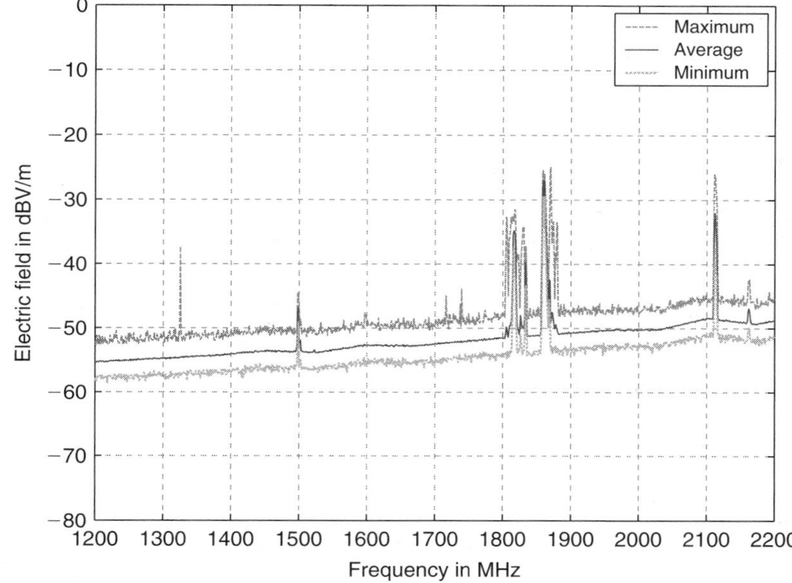

Figure 3: Mid-high band spectrum sample from a large city in Europe, 1,200 MHz to 2,200 MHz (Courtesy of Patrick Ryan)

Motivation

Among the many reasons for developing frequency agile radios, the two strongest motivations are (1) for purposes of efficiently accessing spectrum, which is perceived as a scarce resource, and (2) for improving interoperability of wireless devices. Around the world, various government agencies and industry players have realized that current radio technology will not adequately meet the demands of the future. A large amount of funding has been directed at solving the interoperability problems between military components. Changes in funding and grant solicitations also mark a shift in research focus from one centered on achieving interoperable radios to one focused on highly adaptable, flexible, and reconfigurable communication devices and algorithms.

A common thread in both the research and funding shift is increased efficiency in our use of the available radio frequency (RF) spectrum. A 2005 study undertaken in the Atlanta metropolitan area reported that less than 7 percent of the available spectrum was being utilized during the several months that the study was conducted. Additionally, 77 percent of the spectrum in this area was completely unused (Petrin and Steffes 2005). However, observed availability does not mean that the spectrum is not "owned" by some agency or corporate body. Indeed, it doesn't even mean that it is not being used (e.g., radio astronomy bands, where earth stations simply listen for RF signals from outer space).

The scarcity of spectrum is influenced by both technical and regulatory practices. However, ownership issues aside, it is clear that there is a vast amount of unused and underutilized spectrum. Figure 3 presents a graph of spectrum occupancy from 1.2 GHz to 2.2 GHz in a large European city. Universal mobile telecommunications system (UMTS) and global system for mobile communications (GMS) services in the 1.8–1.9 GHz range are the major occupants of the band; note the low occupancy in the remainder of the band. The area between 1.2 and 1.8 GHz, with the proper technical and regulatory support, would be ideally suited for operating a frequency agile device. Initial findings show that even simple noncooperative sharing techniques can offer significant improvements, with cooperative protocols offering an order of magnitude increase in available spectrum (Horne 2003).

Much of the resistance to adopting emerging wireless technologies stems from the huge cost involved when removing and replacing existing infrastructure with technology that can support the new standards (Bose 1999).

On the other hand, a C/SDR platform may be able to adapt to new standards by downloading and installing new software. The flexibility inherent in the C/SDR also allows it to adapt to changes in policy. The recent focus on homeland security, in light of the ineffective use of the emergency bands, has given impetus to many of the scenarios that illustrate the promise of C/SDR. One could imagine a government agency implementing a change to local spectrum policy in response to a disaster. Updates to policy, when acted on by a C/SDR network, could affect reallocation of spectrum to support increased demand during the emergency. Work in the C/SDR space has also been directed at improving interoperability among radio devices. The pressure for this interoperability is significant within the U.S. military (where each service uses different and incompatible radio technology) and by public safety entities such as police, fire, and ambulance.

PRIOR WORK IN SOFTWARE-DEFINED RADIO

This section is focused on providing an overview of the research in software-defined radio. The work encompasses Department of Defense (DoD) efforts, which are focused on waveform portability and radio interoperability, as well as work done in the private sector, which focuses on solving input/output (I/O) and computation problems associated with moving traditionally analog or custom ASIC components and processes to a general-purpose processor. Figure 4 provides a timeline of some of the major SDR and CR developments, and the following sections provide an overview of prior work within this space.

SPEAKeasy

SPEAKeasy was a joint program of the U.S. Air Force, Army, Navy, and Defense Advanced Research Projects Agency (DARPA) that arose from interoperability problems that were experienced during the Grenada conflict (Lackey and Upmal 1995). SPEAKeasy was to develop a radio that would allow multiple waveforms at multiple frequencies to coexist in the same physical unit. Additionally, it would provide the ability to communicate with legacy radios. Along with basic research and development, the production schedule included prototype demonstrations. The initial prototype, shown in 1995, demonstrated multiband operation, programmability, and bridging. Development and prototype demonstrations continued until late 1998. Many key ideas and concepts for SDRs arose from the development of this system. There was a need for a software architecture that would decouple the radio hardware from the software framework. This would allow hardware to advance independently of the software architecture. Additionally, there was a need to capitalize on commercially available products because the DoD could no longer afford to fund proprietary solutions. To ease maintenance of the radio, the developers saw a need for over-the-air updating of the radio software. SPEAKeasy was nominally one of the first software radios in operation.

Joint Tactical Radio System

The SPEAKeasy project was transformed into a fully funded DoD project soon after its last demonstration in 1998. The Joint Tactical Radio System (JTRS; n.d.) was founded on concepts that were a part of the SPEAKeasy project and a vision document within the military (Joint Vision 2010/2020). The program funds the production of a host of radios ranging from inexpensive terminals with reduced waveform support to multiband/mode/channel radios that support advanced narrowband and wideband capabilities. These high-end devices will also include integrated computer networking features. The primary goal of JTRS is to develop a family of radios that is able to meet expanding bandwidth requirements and is interoperable, affordable, and scalable. The program managers felt that the only way to meet these objectives was to require that the radios conform to open physical and software architectures. JTRS has experienced significant difficulties in meeting program goals and cost constraints.

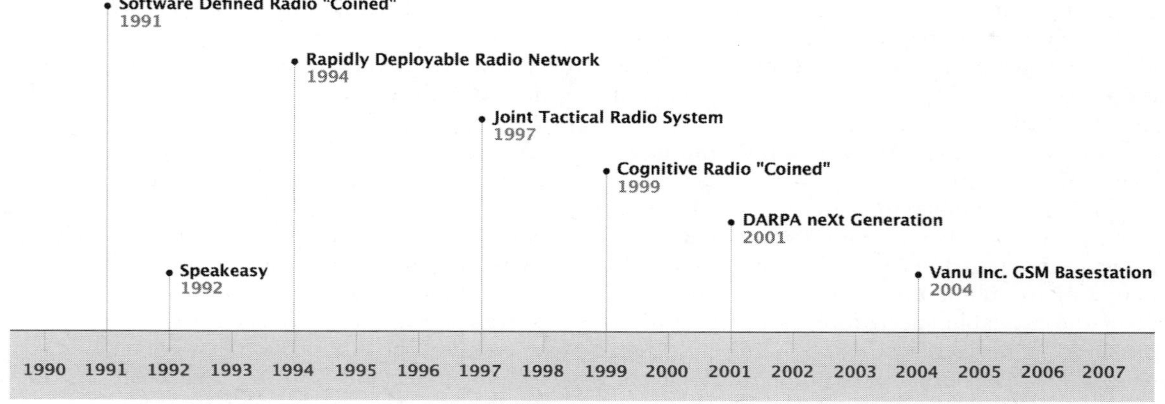

Figure 4: Timeline of software-defined and cognitive radio developments

A key component of the JTRS is the Software Communications Architecture (SCA). The SCA is an open architecture framework that utilizes the Common Object Request Broker Architecture (CORBA) to dictate the structure and operation of the radio. Critical components of the architecture are standards for loading waveforms, running applications, and system integration. The SCA Hardware Framework (SCA/HW) dictates minimum specifications for hardware devices. These two frameworks ensure that software written to the SCA will work on compliant hardware. Although this approach has some backing, there are shortcomings. First, it has grown into a complex and heavy design. Second, it does not offer any capabilities for the emerging needs of a dynamic system such as a CR. Finally, it is not well oriented toward lightweight implementations. The SCA is currently at version 3.0 and has been adopted as a standard by the Object Management Group (OMG).

Rapidly Deployable Radio Network

The Rapidly Deployable Radio Network (RDRN) was another early SDR (1994–1999) that was specifically designed to address problems when implementing mobile, rapidly deployable, and adaptive wireless communications (Evans et al. 1999). Researchers created a high-speed asynchronous transfer mode (ATM)-based wireless communication system that was adaptive at both the link and network layers, allowing rapid deployment and response in a changing environment. Their concept of operation was to deploy a backbone of switches that would automatically configure into an appropriate topology, enabling users to access the backbone via a cellular-like architecture. The RDRN project incorporated digitally controlled antenna beams, programmable radios, adaptive link layer protocols, and mobile node management. The combination of the network layer routing protocol and directional phase array antenna was the basis for the adaptive point-to-point topology algorithm. Additionally, at the data-link layer they were able to change modulation, frame lengths, and enable and disable forward error correction; however, project literature states that these are set at device program time. They concede that the next steps for the project would be to develop an algorithm that would run in the radio processor, enabling dynamic adjustments to power level, coding depth, antenna pointing, modulation type, and data rate.

Vanu

During the mid-1990s, effort was directed at realizing the transition from specialized hardware to GPP. Vanu Bose set out to demonstrate that it was possible to implement a high-data rate, computationally intensive, real-time signal-processing application on a GPP. This effort formed the basis of his thesis and later launched his company, Vanu Inc. (n.d.). His doctoral work produced an SDR that was able to run on a general-purpose processor. In this work, he acknowledged that there are huge opportunities to improve wireless networking using SDR technology. He recognized that a radio that could adapt and change its operating characteristics in real time could significantly impact wireless communication. In November 2004, Vanu's software radio global system for mobile communications (GSM) base station became the first device to successfully complete the Federal Communications Commission (FCC)'s certification process governing SDR devices. Mid Tex Cellular operates the first commercial deployment of this system. Vanu's Anywave GSM base station is capable of remote software updates, allows multiple standards to coexist on one network, and has the potential to decrease cellular maintenance budgets by as much as 20 percent (Whickham 2005).

End-to-End Reconfigurability

The end-to-end reconfigurability (E2R; n.d.) project is among a host of international efforts to realize the potential of SDR. The E2R project aspires to develop designs and prototype systems that focus on the end-to-end perspective. The project, now in its second phase, is focusing on producing platforms that are accessible across the device and user spectrum, ranging from advanced cellular handsets for the consumer to advanced spectrum management tools for the regulator.

Summary

This early research is important because of the progress made in the realization of the SDR. The research provides valuable insight into the design and implementation of future platforms. Additionally, the systems and research covered in this section provide historical perspective and bolster the case for intelligent processing on a software radio. Much of this early work in SDR set the foundation for, and in some cases directly called for, research to begin in creating intelligent radio systems. Generally, the research and development in software-defined radio has been characterized by the building of systems to solve specific problems. The DoD efforts are focused on waveform portability and radio interoperability. The RDRN project was centered on mobile and rapidly deployable disaster response communication. The work done by Vanu Bose focused on solving I/O and computation problems associated with moving traditionally analog or custom ASIC components and processes to a general-purpose processor.

PRIOR WORK IN COGNITIVE RADIOS

Scientific and commercial interest in cognitive radio stems from its goals: to increase access to available spectrum, and improve interoperability and reliability through adaptive and efficient use of spectrum. In terms of spectrum policy (or the rules that govern spectrum usage), CR offers the ability to intelligently manage access to the spectrum. The popularity of CR in the research community is being fueled, in part, by this goal. Other research focuses on the development of algorithms to exploit more general networking goals. Research has only begun to tackle the issues raised when a system of these highly reconfigurable SDR platforms is acting in concert.

Genesis

Mitola described how a cognitive radio could enhance the flexibility of personal wireless services through a new language called the Radio Knowledge Representation

Language (RKRL; Mitola 2000). RKRL was a language for describing the features and capabilities of a radio. Mitola describes it as a set-theoretic ontology of radio knowledge. Mitola's doctoral dissertation was presented in May 2000, and his research resulted in the development of an architecture for CR and the formulation of a set of use cases for computationally intelligent radios. Additionally, he developed a simulation environment in order to test the viability of RKRL. The simulation focused on natural language processing in a CR. The experience he gained while conducting this simulation led to the formulation of his architecture for CR. This work set the stage for future research in the area by providing a description of what it means for a radio to incorporate computational intelligence. Mitola also described nine levels of operations that relate to the functionality of a cognitive device (Mitola 2000). These levels ranged from basic preprogrammed devices (Level 0) to devices that could dynamically create new protocols based on the environmental conditions and communication requirements (Level 8).

Algorithms for Cognitive Radio

Often the word *algorithm* causes one to envision a complex and involved solution to a problem. However, there are whole classes of algorithms that are simple, elegant, and applicable to C/SDR. Algorithms of this sort are members of a class of direct methods for tackling problems associated with the design and implementation of a C/SDR. Some of the more well-known approaches are the LBT algorithms, all variants on the notion that the sender should sense (listen) to the medium before attempting to access it (Metcalf and Boggs 1976; IEEE Standard 802.11 1997). Another technique, transmit power control, seeks to minimize the transmit power used in communication among nodes to decrease the overall interference. Dynamic frequency selection (DFS) algorithms have seen a corresponding rise in interest in the literature coincident with the increase in popularity of C/SDR. Horne (2003) details four common approaches:

1. Channel availability check. Before starting a transmission, the sender must monitor the channel for a defined period of time to determine whether a signal is present (LBT).
2. In-service monitoring. The radio device must continually listen on the channel by searching for signals between transmissions.
3. Channel abdication. On detection of a signal, the device must stop transmitting and move to another channel.
4. Channel non-occupancy. If a channel is occupied, the sending device will not utilize the channel for a set time period.

These techniques are present in common everyday devices like many cordless 900 MHz phones. These phones sense interference on a channel and switch to another to obtain a clear signal.

Game theory relies on a mathematical model of an interactive decision process. In C/SDR, the network of radios is bounded by actions wrapped in a mathematical model. The game theorist uses the analytical power of game theory to guide his or her algorithmic decisions. There has been some research done in applying game theory to C/SDR; this work is concerned with bounding and qualifying potential algorithms according to a game that approximates the function of a CR (Neel, Reed, and Gilles 2004). The authors contend that game models will give insight into algorithmic complexity. This approach to bounding potential algorithms in a defined game space is interesting; however, it does not appear to offer direct insight into what the underlying algorithm should be. Other work in this area includes the application of machine learning or similar techniques to the problem of decision making within CR networks. For example, Rieser (2004) describes a biologically inspired cognitive engine that employs a genetic algorithm to optimize the robustness of the radio network. He developed a cognitive model and architecture that was able to operate in unforeseen communication environments and recall past successful configurations via memory.

A broad range of potential algorithms exists for controlling CRs. LBT and DFS algorithms are important because they are simple algorithmic examples that afford huge returns. Nevertheless, they suffer from one-dimensionality in that they focus on interference-free channel access alone. Investigation of simple algorithms like LBT across multiple dimensions could yield promising results. A collection of simple algorithms acting in concert could drastically outperform individual component solutions. The game theoretic approach is useful if one is interested in characterizing potential algorithms in a game space; however, the algorithm behind this characterization remains a black box. The work in genetic algorithms demonstrates that cognitive processes can successfully reconfigure in response to changing channel conditions with success in achieving the CR's goal (Rieser 2004).

Beyond these described methods, numerous other techniques—such as Markov models, neural nets, expert systems, and fuzzy logic—could be used to implement a CR. The question remains as to which of these will actually be applied in a real system.

DARPA XG

The DARPA Next Generation (XG) Communications (n.d.) Advanced Technology Office (ATO) is the project management arm of a DoD project whose objective was to develop and demonstrate a prototype spectrum agile radio. They set a performance target of increasing spectrum utilization tenfold without causing harmful interference to primary/noncooperative radios. The project is addressing spectrum management difficulties associated with deployment and spectrum scarcity issues through development of devices and protocols for opportunistic spectrum access. In this scenario, a primary user should not experience interference when a secondary user attempts to access a band. One method for mitigating inference by the secondary user is to require the secondary to vacate the band and continually check for primary users. Much of the work in this area is dependent upon the development of highly sensitive detectors and the combination of individual and group sensing to determine the RF environment. This data will be combined with a variety of additional information to assist the device in making scheduling decisions about how best to operate. Other sources of data could be derived from location, time of day, and databases containing pertinent data and policies on primary users. A Web Ontology Language (OWL)-based policy description will assist the decision process by providing rules and behaviors in machine-readable form. Combined, this information will indicate the spectrum "holes" that are available for the user.

A secondary objective of the program was to leverage and develop technologies that enable dynamic access to spectrum within constraints provided by machine-readable policies. Technology central to this goal includes adaptive MAC protocols, hardware-independent policy-based reasoning, and new waveforms. The policy engine operates by obtaining a set of policy conditions that might associate with a certain device, in a certain location, attempting to make use of a certain band. The policies will be expressed in extensible markup language (XML), and the engine will parse these policies to determine a limited set of possible operational conditions for the device. The device then determines how these might best be used to meet communication requirements. Each of these policies is authenticated, and its operation will be traceable. Ultimately, the goal is to provide a framework that describes the policy boundary for a device; then the device will be able to operate within these boundaries in a variety of ways. The architecture supporting this policy-driven operation is depicted in Figure 5.

Additionally, XG is pursing the creation of a waveform that combines noncontiguous narrowband channels. These waveforms will respond to and capitalize on spectral vacancies in both time and frequency. As we move higher in the protocol stack, the system is able to adapt to future MAC layer protocols and algorithms. Here the difficulty lies in being able to maximize spectrum utilization while still allowing short-duration transient reallocations

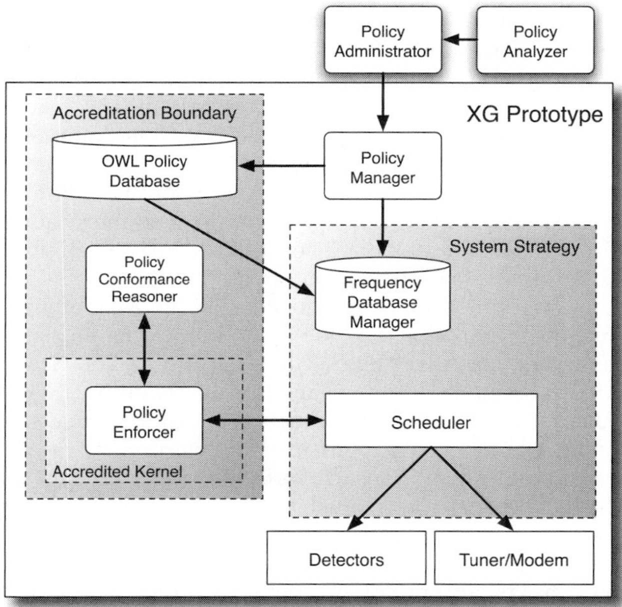

Figure 5: The DARPA XG architecture

without saturating the network with protocol overhead. The XG project's objectives are addressed through theoretical work, simulation, and platform development.

Recent Work in Cognitive Radio Networking

Haykin (2005) provides a thorough overview of cognitive radios and describes the basic capabilities that a "smart" wireless device might offer. Others describe techniques for applying CRs to improve the coordinated use of spectrum (Berlemann, Mangold, and Walke 2005; Buddhikot et al. 2005). Sahai, Hoven, and Tandra (2004) describe some of the physical layer limits and limitations of cognitive radios, including the difficulties associated with determining whether or not a radio frequency band is occupied. Nishra et al. (2005) have implemented a testbed for evaluating the physical and data link layers of such networks. Additionally, Thomas, DaSilva, and MacKenzie (2005) describe the basic concept of a CR network and provide a case study to illustrate how such a network might operate. Weingart (2006) and Weingart, Sicker, and Grunwald (2006) looked at using statistical analysis of variance (ANOVA) as part of a technique called design of experiments (DOE), to inform algorithmic decisions about the most effective configuration of the C/SDR. This approach produces an analytical model for the CR, which can either predict radio performance given a configuration and/or identify those parameters that have the greatest effect on performance. It is also worth noting that the standards communities are actively focusing on cognitive radio (these efforts will be discussed later in the chapter).

CHALLENGES FOR FREQUENCY AGILE COGNITIVE RADIOS

The ability of frequency agile radios to sense radio frequencies and alter operational parameters such as frequency, power, modulation, beam direction, and link access protocol creates an opportunity whereby devices could autonomously decide how best to operate to improve their access to the radio frequency environment. However, assessing the radio environment is a difficult task—one that will require the development of new hardware and software, complex propagation assessment techniques, and complex information integration. It also will require the radio community to rethink what defines harmful interference. New certification and assurance techniques will have to be developed to assure that frequency agile devices won't misbehave. To understand the need for certification, consider the problems that might arise if secondary user devices interfere with public safety and aeronautical users.

The hope is that such adaptive devices will (1) allow for open radio architectures, (2) take advantage of price declines in computing devices, (3) support novel methods for accessing the spectrum, and (4) reduce the custom nature of radio chip design. However, it is uncertain whether these devices might intentionally or inadvertently operate outside of their expected RF parameters. Reliability, security, and design issues also remain unresolved.

Among the most significant technical challenges for frequency agile cognitive radios (FACR) is the ability to detect whether a band is occupied and guarantee that secondary users will not interfere with primary users in that band. The development of high sensitivity detectors combined with supplemental information concerning the potential RF usage in a particular area (i.e., geo-location data, detection data from other local nodes, or possibly information contained in a database) will allow the cognitive part of the radio to determine whether a particular band is available for use. One unresolved issue is the development of appropriate measures for interference. Regulatory agencies and standards bodies are presently examining the issue of interference measurements. One proposed concept is that of an *interference temperature*. As described in the FCC Spectrum Policy Task Force Report (n.d.), an interference temperature offers a method for measuring and controlling the potential noise generation. A maximum interference level could be set for a particular RF band; if a secondary user can operate under that interference level, it would be considered as not causing interference in that band. The difficult issue is measuring and ensuring that the level is maintained.

Researchers tend to overlook some of the more esoteric concerns, such as those presented by regulators. A key component in the success of FACR is its acceptance as a fundamentally sound technology by those who regulate and control the radio spectrum. The technology that is proposed by researchers needs to be visible and understandable. That is, the regulators and the incumbents, those who have "ownership" of the radio spectrum, must be able to understand the mechanisms by which the radio operates and believe that it will perform as intended. Clearly, FACRs offer a new way of allocating spectrum to users. These advanced allocation techniques could allow national regulatory organizations to move from a rigid spectrum allocation mechanism to an interference-avoiding, open access model. Furthermore, the flexibility of such devices could facilitate the introduction of secondary spectrum markets. Such radios could (1) improve network performance, (2) improve spectrum utilization and availability, and (3) support novel interoperability designs. However, it is unclear just how the devices will be controlled and how interference might be determined in some of the potential operating environments.

As previously described, DARPA is funding an effort to create a human understandable radio policy language and associated computational engine. Additionally, regulators and incumbents must be comfortable with FACR technology before they will allow it to operate. This will likely involve certification of the algorithms and mechanisms that drive the device. For incumbent RF license holders, certification gives assurance that the FACR will not interfere in their transmission and that the devices operating in their RF space will relinquish their spectrum when required. There is also a large effort within the FCC to rework the current command-and-control model of spectrum allotment, assignment, and allocation. A transition to a legal structure that is more suited to advancements in radio technology, such as FACR and ultra-wideband, is under way.

Various national regulatory agencies are working on improving spectrum policy; notably the Office of Communications (Ofcom) in the United Kingdom, the Ministry of Internal Affairs and Communications (MIC) in Japan, and the FCC in the United States. Ofcom (n.d.) recently released an in-depth analysis of C/SDRs and has been active in promoting novel approaches to spectrum management. In the United States, the FCC is actively seeking to improve the efficiency of spectrum management and is considering new regulatory models, including: (1) the development of secondary markets for spectrum, (2) the specification of receiver standards, (3) the consideration of FACRs, (4) exemptions for operation in TV bands, and (5) the development of an interference temperature (see www.fcc.gov, specifically FCC n.d., 2005; FCC Spectrum Policy Task Force Report n.d.). Together, these developments represent a fundamental shift in thinking about the potential to use spectrum in very new and exciting ways.

The significance of this type of regulatory reform must also be considered in the context of how regulatory agencies typically evolve, which tends to be slowly. The potential for change and the potential for new technology are quite substantial. This potential could be lost or delayed if the regulators find that the technology is not up to supporting these types of new spectrum models. Of concern to the policy makers are whether interference can be avoided and whether the device will operate as it should. The potential to interfere with primary spectrum users must be considered particularly because these incumbent spectrum holders have substantial lobbying influence. Furthermore, current national borders do not deal with the issue of spectrum sharing in their laws and enforcement methods; therefore, such efforts must consider international agreements.

Many of the software challenges in FACR are driven by Mitola's (2000) vision of the ultimate cognitive radio. He envisioned a system that was capable of reasoning about its environment. The system would draw upon past experience and current environmental conditions to make intelligent decisions about how it should reconfigure. Key components of realizing his vision were the radio's ability to sense, remember, learn, and act. In developing such technology, it will be important to understand how an FACR should sense the environment, determine what environmental inputs should be processed and when, and determine how environmental information is communicated to other systems in the network. Additionally, there are a host of problems that must be overcome in distributed systems, operating systems, and interaction with base hardware components. Research about how FACRs synchronize configurations, maintain communication during reconfiguration, and accomplish over-the-air software updates securely is also critical.

Another important area to consider is that of how trade-offs are balanced by the FACR in meeting its goals. The radio's cognitive engine will be driven by knowledge of its operating environment and its goals; additionally, the radio must cope with environmental information that will change over time. These changes in environment, goals, or networking conditions will force the radio to change its current operating mode, much in the way an operating system must respond to interrupts. For example, if a wireless link is riddled with interference, an FACR could react by changing its current default route to bypass the interference or enable forward error correction on the noisy link. It will be important to define and evaluate how the FACR is affected by interrupts to its current operating mode. This analysis may reveal which interrupts require immediate, delayed, or no action.

Beyond physical layer adaptation, an FACR will allow for dynamic cross-layer adaptation. Work in the area of cross-layer optimization has typically focused on enhancing throughput, quality of service (QoS), and energy consumption (Goldsmith and Wicker 2002). However, these types of cross-layer optimizations tend to be limited in their application. In fact, most of the work in this area tends to focus narrowly on two layers, precluding unique solutions. In other words, they do not consider a broadly adaptive solution nor do they consider user-level requirements. Kawadia and Kumar (2005) have presented an interesting critique of cross-layer design; they warn that cross-layer optimization offers both advantages and disadvantages to the system designer. The dangers they discuss include the potential for (1) spaghetti design (i.e., complex, seemingly unstructured design), (2) proliferation problems, and (3) dependency issues. When dealing with complex systems—in which there are hundreds, if not thousands, of potential configurations—one will find that there is not a simple set of rules that can be universally applied. FACRs with a large number of configurations will require online evaluative methods to account for unintended interactions between the FACR's settings and the radio frequency environment (Weingart 2006).

The adaptive and dynamic natures of these systems lead to other interesting questions. It will be important to quantify the amount of time that a cognitive process can devote to computing a radio configuration, thus allowing characterization of the types of processing that can be done without negatively affecting communication. This line of research should also provide insight into what processing should be done in real time, off-line, or in the background. Another challenge is devising a set of metrics that can be used to evaluate and guide the design of the FACR's computational engine. The following metrics may be considered: goodput, latency, bit error rate, medium access delay, fairness, power consumption, spectrum utilization, and reconfiguration time. Also of interest is how a cognitive system will manage trade-offs in optimizing network performance and reliability.

For readers interested in working within the open source community on SDR, there is the GNU Radio Project (n.d.). This work particularly is focused on the development of software-defined waveforms. Work described in Weingart et al. (2005) and Doerr et al. (2005) focuses on the development of low-cost, adaptive MAC systems. By making these products reasonably priced, one lowers the threshold for engaging in experimental efforts as opposed to theoretical work.

Although they are not the focus of this chapter, there are numerous interesting problems at the physical layer to consider. Various physical layer issues are equally important to achieve flexible radios (e.g., the RF front end, the signal processing implemented in software, the analog-to-digital converters and processors, and the control mechanisms that put requirements on the network). One of the problems in creating a flexible SDR is that of developing a flexible RF front end. Interesting work is under way in developing a microelectromechanical system (MEMS)-based antenna. Developing analog-to-digital converters that are appropriate for SDR systems will require changes to the sampling capability and the range of existing systems. Significant work is under way in the area of FPGA-based SDRs. Together, advances in these areas will have a significant impact on the realization of more flexible SDR platforms and therefore more flexible frequency agile radios.

STANDARDS

Before closing this chapter, it is worth mentioning the newly formed standards efforts that have responded to the development of frequency agile devices. Although a number of groups are working on standards relating to FACRs, this section briefly describes recent efforts undertaken by the IEEE Project 1900 Next Generation Radio and Spectrum Management Committee and the 802.22 Working Group on Wireless Regional Area Networks.

The P1900 (n.d.) group is broken into four subgroups; 1900.1 Definitions, 1900.2 Interference and coexistence analysis, 1900.3 Software Assurance, and 1900.4 Certification. P.1900.1 (n.d.) is working to develop standards terms and concepts for spectrum management, policy-defined radio, adaptive radio, and software-defined radio. According to their documents

> This standard will provide technically precise definitions and explanations of key concepts in the fields of spectrum management, policy defined radio, adaptive radio, software-defined radio, and related technologies. . . . The document will also describe how these technologies interrelate and can be use in a wide variety of communication service environments to achieve new capabilities while at the same time providing mechanisms supportive of new spectrum management paradigms and spectrum access.

P1900.2 (n.d.) will "provide technical guidelines for analyzing the potential for coexistence or in contrast interference between radio systems operating in the same frequency band or between different frequency bands." The goal is to guide the analysis of interference modeling and thereby improve the efficient use of the spectrum. P.1900.3 is seeking to develop conformance evaluation for SDR software modules. The purpose is to provide recommendations for the practices that will lead to compliance for adaptive devices. Much of this work will focus on the development of formal methods for evaluating a specific software design before the device is actually created.

IEEE 802.22 (n.d.) is looking at wireless regional area networks (WRANs) that could operate in the unused TV broadcast channels. 802.11h is looking at ways of improving the sharing of spectrum among 802.11 users. There are two basic ways that this is operating: dynamic frequency selection and transmission power control (TPC). DFS provides a means for selecting and using a certain spectral band to avoid interference. TPC allows for the reduction of interference and the saving of power by managing power on access points and devices in a network.

The International Telecommunications Union is actively looking at standards efforts in the CR and SDR space. Other standards efforts, including 802.11k, 802.11y, 802.16h, are also addressing aspects related to cognitive radios.

CONCLUSION

New radio technologies promise to redefine how we design and build radio platforms. The combination of SDRs with cognitive functionality will enable the introduction of frequency agile devices and bring about radically different mechanisms for managing and accessing radio frequency resources. This technology promises increased efficiency in spectrum use, flexible device design, and device interoperability. However, there are still a number of technical problems to resolve before this technology is ready to market. Among these difficult issues are signal detection, interference avoidance, and device assurance. Some of the more interesting and uncertain influences in this area have nothing to do with technology; rather, they depend on decisions from within the public policy and regulation communities. Additional research directions in the area of frequency agile technology can be found at Dynamic Spectrum Access Networks (DySpan; n.d.), the Workshop on Technology and Policy for Accessing Spectrum (TAPAS; n.d.), and the SDR Forum (n.d.).

GLOSSARY

Cognitive Radio: A transceiver that can sense and autonomously reason about its environment.

Cooperative Protocol: A protocol wherein the communicating elements act to jointly enhance operation.

Cross-layer Optimization: A mechanism in which information from multiple layers of a protocol stack is jointly used to improve system performance.

Dynamic Frequency Selection: A mechanism that allows a transceiver to detect available spectrum, access and use that spectrum, and abdicate its use when necessary.

Dynamic Spectrum Utilization: A process of adaptively selecting frequency-operating parameters to optimize a desired utilization measure.

Frequency Agile Radio: A transceiver that can change the frequency bands in which it operates.

Hardware Radio: A radio that defines and possibly changes its capabilities through its hardware.

Policy-based Reasoning: A mechanism that relies on a set of rules to inform decision processes.

Policy Engine: An algorithm that includes policy-based reasoning as an input for selecting sets of viable operating conditions.

Software-defined Radio: According to the ITU-R (2004), "A radio in which the RF operating parameters of frequency range, modulation type, and/or output power can be set or altered by software, or the technique by which this is achieved."

Spectrum Policy: A subset of regulatory policy and one that defines the valid use of the spectrum or the intended direction for the use of the spectrum.

Transmit Power Control: The mechanism that allows for the adaptation of transmit power of a transceiver.

CROSS REFERENCES

See *Cellular Communications Channels*; *Spread Spectrum*.

REFERENCES

Berlemann, L., S. Mangold, and B. H. Walke. 2005. Policy-based reasoning for spectrum sharing in cognitive radio networks. In *Proceedings of IEEE DySPAN 2005*, Baltimore, November, pp. 1–10.

Bose, V. 1999. Design and implementation of software radios using a general-purpose processor (PhD thesis, Massachusetts Institute of Technology).

Buddhikot, M., P. Kolody, S. Miller, K. Ryan, and J. Evans. 2005. Dimsumnet: New directions in wireless networking using coordinated dynamic spectrum access. In *Proceedings of IEEE WoWMoM 2005*, Taormina, June, pp.78–85.

Defense Advanced Research Projects Agency (DARPA) Next Generation (XG) Communications. Undated. http://www.darpa.mil/ato/programs/xg.

Doerr C., T. Weingart, D. Sicker, and D. Grunwald. 2005. MultiMAC: An adaptive MAC framework for dynamic radio networking. In *Dynamic Spectrum Access Networks (DySPAN)*, pp. 548–55.

End-to-End Reconfigurability. Undated. www.e2r2.motlabs.com.

Evans, J., G. Minden, K. Shanmugan, V. Frost, B. Ewy, R. Sanchez, C. Sparks, M. Kambhammetty, J. Roberts, R. Plumb, and D. Petr. 1999. The rapidly deployable radio network. *IEEE Journal on Selected Areas in Communications* 17(4): 689–703.

Federal Communications Commission (FCC). Undated. FCC rulemaking in the area of SDR/CR, secondary markets, and related spectrum issues. www.fcc.gov/spectrum.

———. 2005. Facilitating opportunities for flexible, efficient, and reliable spectrum use employing cognitive radio technologies. FCC 05–57. Available at fromhraunfoss.fcc.gov/edocs_public/attachmatch/FCC-05–57A1.pdf.

FCC Spectrum Policy Task Force Report. Undated. www.fcc.gov/sptf.

GNU Radio Project. Undated. Philosophy of the GNU project. www.gnu.org/philosophy/philosophy.html.

Goldsmith, A., and S. Wicker. 2002. Design challenges for energy-constrained ad hoc wireless networks. *IEEE Wireless Communications* 9: 8–27.

Haykin, S. 2005. Cognitive radio: Brain-empowered wireless communications. *IEEE Journal on Selected Areas in Communications* 23(2): 201–20.

Horne, W. D. 2003. Adaptive spectrum access: Using the full spectrum space. In *Proceedings of the Telecommunications Policy Research Conference*, Arlington, Virginia, September, pp. 1–11.

IEEE Standard 802.11. 1997. IEEE standard for wireless LAN medium access control (MAC) and physical layer (PHY) specification, June.

IEEE 802.22. Undated. www.ieee802.org/22/.

ITU-R. 2004. WP8A draft report on SDR, September.

Joint Tactical Radio System. Undated. http://jtrs.army.mil.

Kawadia, V., and P. R. Kumar. 2005. A cautionary perspective on cross-layer design. *IEEE Wireless Communications Magazine* 12: 3–11.

Lackey, R. J., and D. W. Upmal. 1995. Speakeasy: The military software radio. *IEEE Communications Magazine* 33(5): 56–61.

Metcalf, R. M., and D. R. Boggs. 1976. Ethernet: Distributed packet switching for local computer networks. *Communications of the ACM* 19(7): 395–404.

Mitola, J., III. 2000. Cognitive radio: An integrated agent architecture for software-defined radio (PhD thesis, Royal Institute of Technology).

Neel, J. O., J. H. Reed, and R. P. Gilles. 2004. Game models for cognitive radio algorithm analysis. In *Proceedings of the Software-Defined Radio Forum Technical Conference*, Phoenix, Arizona, June, pp. 27–32.

Nishra, S., D. Cabric, C. Chang, D. Willkomm, B. Schewick, A. Wolisz, and R. Brodersen. 2005. A real-time cognitive radio testbed for physical and link layer experiments. In *Proceedings of IEEE DySPAN 2005*, Baltimore, November, pp. 562–67.

Office of Communications (Ofcom). Undated. Cognitive radio. www.ofcom.org.uk/research/technology/overview/emer_tech/cograd/.

———. Undated. Software defined radio. www.ofcom.org.uk/research/technology/overview/emer_tech/sdr/.

P1900. Undated. http://grouper.ieee.org/groups/emc/emc/ieee_emcs_-_sdcom/P1900-X_Stds/ieee_emcs_-_p1900-x_main.htm.

Petrin, A., and P. G. Steffes. 2005. Analysis and comparison of spectrum measurements performed in urban and rural areas to determine the total amount of spectrum usage. In *Proceedings of the International Symposium on Advanced Radio Technologies*, Boulder, Colorado, March, pp. 9–12.

Rieser, C. 2004. Biologically inspired cognitive radio engine model utilizing distributed genetic algorithms for secure and robust wireless communications and networking (PhD thesis, Virginia Polytechnic Institute and State University).

Sahai, A., N. Hoven, and R. Tandra. 2004. Some fundamental limits in cognitive radio. In *Proceedings of the Allerton Conference on Communications Control and Computing*, Monticello, Illinois, October.

Software Defined Radio (SDR) Forum. Undated. www.sdrforum.org.

Tennenhouse, D. L., and V. G. Bose. 1995. Spectrumware: A software oriented approach to wireless signal processing. In *Proceedings of the First Annual International Conference on Mobile Computing and Networking (MobiCom '95)*, Berkeley, California, November, pp. 37–47.

Thomas, R., L. DaSilva, and A. MacKenzie. 2005. Cognitive networks. In *Proceedings of IEEE DySPAN 2005*, Baltimore, November, pp. 352–60.

Vanu, Inc. Undated. www.vanu.com.

Weingart, T. 2006. A method for dynamic reconfiguration of a cognitive radio system (PhD thesis, University of Colorado at Boulder).

Weingart, T., D. Sicker, and D. Grunwald. 2006. A predictive model for cognitive radio. In *Proceedings of the Military Communications Conference (MILCOM 2006)*, Washington, DC, October, pp. 1–7.

Weingart, T., D. Sicker, D. Grunwald, and M. Neufeld. 2005. Adverbs and adjectives: An abstraction for software defined radio. In *Proceedings of the International Symposium on Advanced Radio Technologies*, Boulder, Colorado, March, pp. 183–92.

Whickham, R. 2005. Long-awaited SDR becomes commercial reality. *Wireless Week*, March, p. 62.

Workshop on Technology and Policy for Accessing Spectrum (TAPAS). Undated. www.wtapas.org.

Localization in Wireless Networks

Slim Rekhis and Noureddine Boudriga, *University of the 7th of November, Tunisia*
Mohammad S. Obaidat, *Monmouth University*

NEED FOR WIRELESS LOCALIZATION

In the face of the increased numbers of mobile computing devices, the emergence of wireless networking technologies, and the provision of high connectivity for mobile devices, a great interest in localization has arisen. Localization is actually a requirement that an agent under mobility or interacting with mobile components has to accomplish no matter whether the agent has wireless communication capabilities or not. Localization is the determination of the location of any wireless component based on some techniques of measurement. Localization applies to three objects: (a) the user as a whole entity, (b) the services as software resources on mobile computing platforms, and (c) the entities acting on behalf of users. Applications needing to track a mobile user may require the position of a user at different periods of time, while a user needing to access a service (e.g., a bank's ATM) may require the service of an application providing the location of the nearest access point. A Mobile Service Switching center in GSM systems may act on behalf of a mobile user who has roamed under its coverage (Nicopolitidis et al. 2003).

It is obvious that compared to fixed networks, wireless networks may suffer from a high bit-error rate, inconsistent quality of service, and inefficient bandwidth utilization. These drawbacks are more important when nodes are on the move. They make wireless localization a challenging task to achieve. On the other hand, because mobile nodes are expected to support different types of applications and services that may run in continuous time or in real-time, and provide different qualities of services to various types of traffic, wireless localization helps considerably, in mitigating these drawbacks. A clear illustration of this duality can be stated through the three following facts:

The first important impact of wireless localization is on resource utilization, because it can facilitate the allocation, control, and effective use of the resource. In cellular networks, for instance, where a node can find itself under the radio coverage of more than one base station, localization may help it locate and choose the nearest base station. This helps three objectives: (a) the signal degradation can be avoided or reduced; (b) the radio frequencies can be allocated effectively; and (c) the node can preserve the life duration of its battery as it decreases its transmission power. Localization may also contribute to the enforcement of equitable sharing of resources within a network. An example of localization sharing is represented by the distribution of printing jobs, required by n mobile nodes. For this, a printing request issued by a node can be sent to a printer selected based on the geographical location and positions of the network nodes. More generally, if in a network, a set of resources is shared among a set of n nodes, localization could significantly enforce equitable sharing of the set of resources. In addition, localization allows better enforcement of security policy, which is a set of rules and requirements defining how to protect and manage an information system to achieve some specific security objectives. The whole idea is to appropriately place control of the resources. For instance, a user, can be prohibited access to sensitive files from a given building when he or she is located in a special area. Other users may not be allowed to carry laptop computers outside the company's building. This can be achieved by having an application manage the location of all laptops (Obaidat and Boudriga 2007).

Another use for localization is in the routing process, where a node location can be used as a routing criterion. In the context of wireless mesh networks, a node sends a message (to be routed to a destination) to the node closest to the destination, among those nodes that provide the highest data throughput or the minimal failing rate in order to guarantee efficient message delivery. In addition, location-aware services can be accessed, offered, and managed based on location-based information. For example, in a replicated multimedia service, the server can be selected (or reselected when the user moves) based on the user location. Another example is seen in the emergence of location-based services. Recently, the need for wireless localization became concretely materialized as a safety requirement for cellular mobile callers. For instance, the wireless enhanced 911 requirements (E911), mandated by the U.S. Federal Communication Commission (FCC), seek to improve the effectiveness and reliability of wireless 911 service by providing additional information on wireless 911 calls.

The wireless E911 program is divided into two parts called Phase I and Phase II. Phase I requires carriers, upon valid request by a local Public Safety Answering Point (PSAP), to report the telephone number of a wireless 911 caller as well as the location of the antenna that received the call. Phase II requires wireless carriers to provide more precise location information, including the caller location (within 50 to 300 meters in most cases). Such requirements have motivated the development of novel location-sensing positioning techniques for an accurate estimation of caller's location in indoor and outdoor surroundings.

Nowadays, the widespread use of wireless networking technology including Wi-Fi, Bluetooth, and cellular phone networks, has led to the need to have wireless devices be available through indoor and outdoor environments. Because these devices are equipped with radio frequency components that can be used to sense location, and because these devices represent a computing platform able to run location-based applications, localization services in wireless networks are going to become a part of everyday life. Localization will not be imposed only for emergency and safety purposes. On the contrary, localization will be driven by commercial services and applications able to exploit such valuable information (i.e., the user's position) to enhance their scope. These applications range from fleet management and asset tracking to security access and mobile advertising. To further emphasize the need for wireless localization, we provide below some specific examples of future services and applications that can be enhanced by the use of location information:

1. Fleet management is currently the main domain covered by commercial wireless localization services for clients such as taxi services, shuttles, and emergency vehicles which are constrained to act efficiently in a timely manner. Locating vehicle position is of high importance for the management of the fleet and the efficiency of the service the fleet provides. In this context, the Global Positioning System (GPS) is widely used. It computes users' locations based on signal reception from at least four satellites in a network composed of 24 running geo-orbital GPS satellites.
2. Asset tracking has also demonstrated an important need for wireless location-based applications. Tracking covers a large spectrum of services that are required to cover large geographic areas, provide good estimates of the asset location, and guarantee the privacy of related information (such as location, asset identity, etc). Examples of tracking services include: a) vehicle localization; b) car protection against theft; and c) safety and emergency applications, including the location of individuals. Wireless localization may also serve for advertising purposes. For instance, an application can use mobile devices to advertise goods in the mobile area. The content of the advertisement may need to be changed from one area to another to attract users more successfully.
3. The proliferation of mobile cellular phones has encouraged people to carry mobile devices wherever they are walking, driving, or working. The availability of mobile devices, combined with localization techniques, will ameliorate daily life of citizens, because those devices may be transformed into real-time contextual information sources that can be used to monitor daily services such as road traffic, making it possible to avoid traffic jams or find the nearest point of access. In addition, wireless localization technology can be efficiently used to monitor users' interaction with their environment; and thus opening up new opportunities for location-aware applications. For example, profiling customers based on temporal location information can open the door for applications that can better cope with customer behavior and needs.
4. Currently, a great deal of interest in security is attracting research work in wireless communication. Location information may be used to enforce some security measures, such as filtering users' traffic based on their location, or controlling access to shared resources based on location-based security policies. The need and importance of wireless localization continue to attract many efforts to detect intrusion and anomalies in localization platforms and to protect communication related to location information.

LOCALIZATION ISSUES

Wireless networks (such as the GSM, UMTS, 802.11, and 802.16) differ in terms of technology, topology, and infrastructure. Each one of these networks provides different technical challenges to implementing a fast, accurate, and robust positioning system. Therefore, it is not feasible to choose one positioning system as a universal solution to enable roaming among these networks, (to locate users and use existing wireless devices including laptops, PDAs, and cell phones) without any need to install or acquire additional hardware or modify the existing infrastructure. A wide spectrum of works has provided interesting discussion about current localization technologies and applications, and has addressed technical challenges and limitations (see list of references).

A position may be referred to by using an *absolute* reference or *relative* reference. An absolute reference places an object (a mobile station, in general) within a common frame of reference. For example, the GPS navigation system gives an object's position in terms of latitude and longitude and possibly altitude. On the other hand, a relative reference is described on a local frame of reference relative to some particular object of interest (such as a base station in GSM). Localization aims to make available two varieties of information, a *physical location* and a *symbolic location*. A physical position is typically defined by a set of coordinates in either two or three dimensions that identify a particular point, in space or on a surface such as a map or the plan of a building. A symbolic position is a more theoretical concept that is basically defined in relation to other objects or places. It may be said that a location is in a particular room, or under the coverage of a particular radio cell. Physical location is accurate in comparison with symbolic location because each position is unique.

In a localized computation system, the responsibility of computing a location is placed on the mobile terminal of the object being located. The Global Positioning System (GPS) system is an example of a localized computation system, in which a satellite system provides the reference from which positions can be calculated, but knows nothing about the location of a particular device. Alternatively, an infrastructure-based system assumes that the location is calculated by the system for its use or for transmission to a device. Localized computation may be required if privacy is an issue, while an infrastructure-based system may be appropriate to reduce power consumption and computational power required at the mobile device.

Four key features of location systems can be distinguished: *accuracy, precision, scale,* and *identity recognition*. While accuracy refers to the granularity of the measurement used to locate the object, precision is a measure of how often the system is expected to achieve a defined level of accuracy. These two features are strongly related and should be addressed together. A system may be described as reaching an accuracy of 1 meter with a precision of 95 percent, meaning that positions within 1 meter of the true position will be reported 95 percent of the time. On the other hand, scale refers to the range of a system and the number of mobile devices it can service. A system may provide locations within a room, throughout a building, across a city, or worldwide (as in the case of GPS). The number of clients a system can support may be limited by the computation power or the network bandwidth. It may be unlimited if mobile devices determine their own positions. Finally, identity recognition is the ability of a system to determine the identity of the mobile devices that it locates. Identity information may be useful in cases in which mobile clients require service implementing authentication.

The localization problem has received considerable attention in the past, because many applications need to have the location in which objects or individuals can be found. Therefore, various location services have been developed. No doubt, the GPS is the most well used location service in use today. The approach taken by GPS, however, is inappropriate for low-cost networks (such as ad-hoc networks and wireless sensor networks) because the GPS is based on an extensive infrastructure. Therefore, cost is an important requirement to consider for the deployment of any location system. Cost may be measured in terms of capital expenditure, time, and other factors such as bandwidth and network resource use. It is also necessary to be aware of the environmental *limitations* of the location system to be used. For example, GPS systems do not work effectively indoors.

There is always a trade-off between cost and location accuracy. In fact, providing a high degree of accuracy typically requires expensive acquisition and installation of sensors, deploying dedicated infrastructure, and using sophisticated signal propagation models. For instance, Cambridge's Active Bat system (Addlesee et al. 2001), which can locate users with a maximal deviation of 9 centimeters of their true position, requires that each user to be identified wear a special badge. It also needs a large infrastructure of fixed sensors and requires accurate placement of sensors. On the other hand, the use of location methods such as the OTD (Observed Time Difference (Sun et al. 2005) scheme, which is based on observing the time difference feature of existing GSM cellular network systems to locate users, represents an inexpensive solution. It does not require acquisition of any additional hardware or software on the existing handsets. However, it only provides accuracy between fifteen to a hundred meters.

Wireless cell networks represent promising candidates for location services. Nowadays, these networks are covering a large part of the world and allow phone service companies to provide the location of users based on the observation of phones by cell towers. However, the position accuracy provided is too weak (on the order of hundreds of meters), and heavily depends on the cell size, in addition to the wireless environment characteristics, channel fading, interference, and multipath conditions. While the Enhanced 911 requirements have driven providers to supply handsets with GPS, the accuracy did recently become very close to hundred of meters. While such a value may be sufficient for emergency purposes, it may be too inaccurate for many other localization-based indoor services. Although GPS was widely used in navigation, it cannot be considered an essential location solution due to many limitations related to signal weakness. Indeed, GPS reliability is lost when used in indoor environments or in highly dense areas.

Wireless IEEE 802.11 represents an interesting networking technology for providing accurate positioning systems. Based on this technology, several localization systems were proposed. For example, the RADAR system (Hightower and Borriello 2001) was developed by Microsoft to locate users in the proximity of base stations with an accuracy of 3 meters. However, such a system requires extensive calibration by taking readings on a 1 meter grid, and its enhancement to three-dimensional areas is difficult. In addition, RADAR suffers from the environment sensitivity issue. Actually, weather variation may alter signal strength, and thus degrades the localization process.

Positioning in sensor networks is of particular interest due to its challenging issues. Wireless sensor networks are used in many applications, including environmental and industrial ones. They are composed of mobile nodes equipped with sensing capabilities. Sensor nodes are typically deployed in high numbers, and are very often assumed to operate autonomously. Consequently, the final position of these nodes cannot be determined at deployment; that is why localization awareness is essential in sensor networks. A wireless positioning system for sensor networks should be designed with consideration of the fact that sensor nodes are constrained to be inexpensive, of small physical size, limited power, and reduced memory and computation capabilities. For instance, equipping a sensor node with a GPS receiver is typically inappropriate because it increases the cost and energy consumption in sensor networks.

Security presents a critical issue for wireless localization. Unlike mobile-based location technology, network-based technology, such as cellular network or WLAN, does not involve the mobile station in the computation of its position, (Sayed, Tarighat, and Khajehnouri 2005). Position is usually computed by the network infrastructure, and is sent back to the mobile station. While in network-based technology, no modification is required to be implemented in the mobile node; users need to trust the provider, to be sure that the provider protects the information related to their position, and that transmission is done in a secure manner. In mobile-based location technology such as GPS, the mobile station listens to satellites and estimates its own position locally. Security of position information becomes a major issue only if the mobile device needs to send it to the network core.

A final interesting issue is related to position representation, which should take into consideration the set of constraints that are imposed by communication, interpretation, and storage of such information. Broadly speaking, no single representation is useful in all circumstances. Where in general cases sensors provide numerical coordinates in the form of (x, y, z), some applications based on sensors require more semantic information, such as a building, floor, room, and desk; or more specific numerical detail such as probability or uncertainty. In other circumstances, such as fleet management, both coordinates and additional information are required, such as weather, terrain characteristics, and traffic pattern.

SIGNAL PROPAGATION AND LOCALIZATION

Phenomena such as signal attenuation, reflection, scattering, and diffraction have important roles in location estimation. Their effect is more significant in non-satellite systems that have to operate in complex propagation environments, such as urban or mountainous areas. This section gives the most important issues in radio propagation related to localization.

Principles

The power density flow, F, is given by $F = P_T G_T / 4\pi d^2$, where P_T is the transmitted power, G_T is a factor characterizing the transmitting antenna, and d is the distance. The received power P_R, which is given in decibels, can be shown to be equal to:

$$P_R = P_T + 10\log(G_T) + 10\log(G_R) + 20\log(\lambda) - 20\log(d) - 22 \quad (1)$$

where λ is the wavelength and G_R is the gain of the receiving antenna. This equation is valid in free-space environment, where there are no reflections, no absorption, no diffraction, and no distortions. If the line-of-sight between transmitter and receiver is obstructed, the received signal power PR is significantly smaller than the

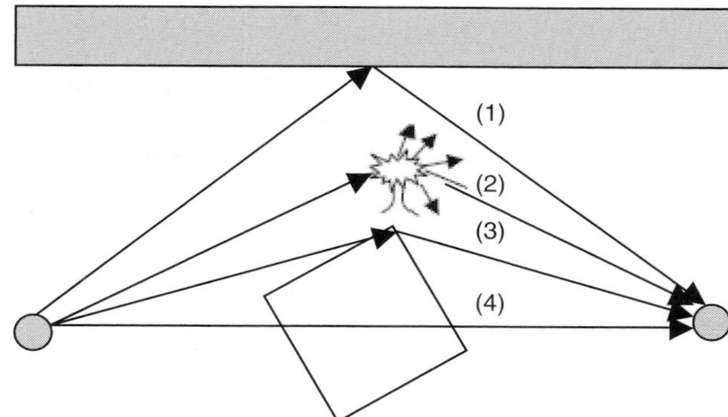

Figure 1: Propagation mechanisms (reflection (1), scattering (2), diffraction (3), and (4) line-of-sight)

value provided by Equation (1). Because the medium is mainly the atmosphere and, to a lesser degree, materials such as glass, concrete, and wood, the signal loses a certain proportion of its energy due to interactions with the medium on every unit of distance it propagates. In fact, absorption causes the power density flow to decrease proportionally to γ^{-d}, where γ is a parameter that depends on the medium and signal frequency. This means that the curve representing the loss in terms of distance s linear. Absorption loss is particularly great in the upper microwave band, where frequencies are higher than 10 GHz. Absorption caused by media other than air is basically high.

In addition to absorption, obstructions cause the wave to be reflected, which further decreases the amount of energy passing through the wave. Reflection occurs when a wave meets an obstacle with of a size larger than the used wavelength. The component of the wave reflected back usually loses part of its energy by absorption to the material; the remaining part passes through the reflecting object. The received signal consists of the line-of-sight ray and the reflected ray. The two rays arriving at a receiver can have different phases and, in the worst case, they can cancel each other out. The magnitude of the reflected signal depends on the properties of the reflecting surface, the frequency of the wave, and the angle of incidence (Figure 1).

On the other hand, when a wave passes an edge (such as a corner of a building), the wave curves around the edge and continues to propagate. This effect is called diffraction. The more the wave has to curve around a corner, the more it loses its energy. However, in practice the diffracted waves can be neglected if there is a line-of-sight between the transmitter and the receiver.

Finally, scattering is another source of energy loss. Scattering occurs when the propagation path contains obstacles whose dimensions are comparable to the wavelength of the incident wave. The radio wave is scattered in a number of directions. Scattering is the most difficult event to predict, compared to reflection and diffraction.

Propagation Models

Prediction of radio wave propagation is useful in location estimation. Propagation models are used to predict the properties of the propagation waves, the received signal and its variability. They also can help predict many other parameters that affect communication systems. A propagation model can be defined by a set of mathematical expressions, diagrams, and algorithms to represent the radio characteristics of an environment. Various levels of abstraction can be used for construction of the propagation models, depending on the amount of available information about the environment and the required accuracy of the predictions. For example, in planning a satellite communication system, sufficient accuracy is generally reached by taking into consideration free-space attenuation, absorption, and ground reflection. In addition, in urban areas, reflections and diffractions caused by buildings and scattering caused by trees have a strong influence on wave propagation. Based on this, propagation models can be divided into three categories: general models, geographic models, and empirical models.

General models typically describe the received power as a function of the distance between the transmitter and the receiver. One of the most interesting general models one can consider is the *log-loss model*, which is an extension of the free-space attenuation of Equation (1). The received power is given by:

$$P_R = P_T + a + bx\log(d) + c \qquad (2)$$

where a and b are parameters indicating how the signal strength decreases as a function of the distance, and c is an error term. If the value of b is –20, the attenuation corresponds to the free space model. If geographic information such as earth topography and land use maps are available, geographical models can be used to predict propagation. Such models can be established before a location system is implemented. The so-called ray-optical models use reflection and diffraction equations to model the paths of signal using two approaches: ray launching and ray tracing. In the first approach, several rays are sent in all directions from the transmitter. The rays proceed straight on until they hit an obstacle, creating one or several reflected or diffracted rays. A prediction of the resulting field is estimated by considering at each point all the rays that have passed through that point. In the second approach, one can start from some point in the prediction area, and considers potential rays arriving to that point from all directions. Figure 2 depicts ray launching (a) and ray tracing (b).

Empirical models use data collected in the same location where the model is used. In contrast to the aforementioned models, empirical models can be used only when the system is in operation. The data are used in a way similar to inference to obtain information on the parameters of the signal in different parts of the area. Empirical models are potentially accurate, because their predictions correspond to the actual propagation phenomena, even when no information is available about the environment. However, the major disadvantage of empirical models is the need to reconstruct them every time the environment changes.

Location Estimation Models

Location estimation is the act of obtaining the location of a mobile entity. Several location estimation techniques have been developed. A large set of applications of location estimation use the GPS satellite system, which provides location estimates with an accuracy of a couple of meters. They also use techniques that use signals between the mobile entity (to locate) and terrestrial transmitters, which can be dedicated for this purpose or be apart of a communication system (such as a cellular telephone system). Accurate estimates require measuring the strength, time delay, angle of arrival, or other properties of the signals transmitted between the mobile entity and the base stations. In the geometric approach to location estimation, the measurements are transformed into distance and angle estimates.

Several ways can be considered to distribute the estimation location between the mobile entity and the other components of the system. The observed signals can be sent or received by the mobile entity. The component performing the actual location estimation can be different from the component observing the signals. In mobile-based estimation, the mobile entity performs the necessary measurements of the downlink signals to deduce its own location without any uplink communication. For this to be achieved, the network has to broadcast some additional data, such as the locations of the base stations. Therefore, the approach is called the network-assisted technique. On the other hand, if the mobile entity performs the measurements and transmits the results to the network to be processed, the approach is called the mobile-assisted technique.

Location estimation can be performed using various measurements. When the approach is geometric, the

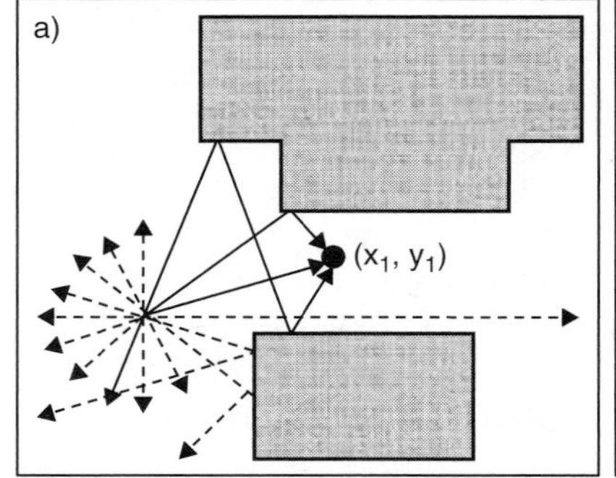

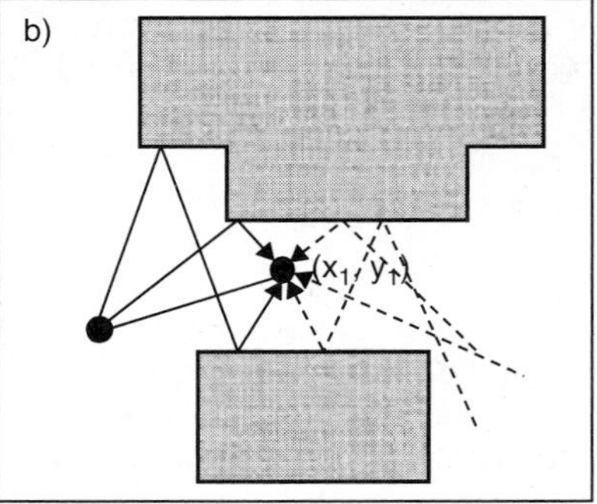

Figure 2: Ray-optical models

measurements are transformed into distances or angles with respect to a set of reference points (base stations, for example). In the angle-arrival location estimation method, the direction of the signal arriving from the mobile system to two base stations is measured. If the locations of the base stations are known, one can use triangulation to deduce the location of the mobile system. Angle measurements require additional hardware to be installed, such as antenna arrays.

If the time delay between transmission and reception of the signal is known, one can estimate the distance by multiplying the time delay by the speed of the light. Various distance estimates can be used to estimate location with the time of arrival method. However, it is clear that even a small error in the clock at the transmitter or the receiver can generate a major error in distance estimation. One way to alleviate the synchronization problem is to use differences in the delays of several base stations instead of absolute times. Time differences are used in the time difference of arrival method, which computes the difference in time delays, $r_{i,j}$, between the mobile system and base stations i and j using the following equation:

$$r_{i,j} = \sqrt{(x_i - x)^2 + (y_i - y)^2} - \sqrt{(x_j - x)^2 + (y_j - y)^2}$$

where (x_i, y_i), (x_j, y_j), and (x, y) represent the coordinates of base station i, base station j, and the mobile station, respectively.

Finally if the signal strength is known, the distance can be estimated in a way similar to the one used in the time of arrival method. Unfortunately, it has been noticed that signal strength is not sufficient for an accurate location estimation.

BASIC LOCATION TECHNIQUES

This section divides location techniques into three classes: a) triangulation-based, which exploit the geometric properties of a triangle to compute location; b) proximity-based, which determine whether or not the object is near a known location; and c) fingerprinting-based, which estimates the observer location or mobile position based on the signature of sensor data. For each class, the section describes the basic concept of the used techniques and provides an example of a localization system.

Triangulation

Triangulation is the method that exploits the geometric properties of triangles. It computes the node position using measured distances from at least three non-collinear points in a two-dimensional plane, and at least four non-collinear points in a three-dimensional plane. The measured distance basically be obtained using three possible methods: direct measure, time of flight (ToF), and signal attenuation. Direct measure is a method that lets the mobile entity automatically coordinate its physical movements (Hightower and Borriello 2001). The method is very complicated to implement, despite the simplicity of the underlying concept. The mathematical notions relative to techniques described hereinafter are written based on Sayed, Tarighat, and Khajehnouri (2005). These notions include: the time of arrival (ToA), the time difference of arrival (TDoA), and the Angle of Arrival (AoA).

ToA: The ToA method is based on computing the time that a signal takes to move from a mobile node to a reference point. Suppose, for instance, that a wireless signal pulse emitted by a mobile entity takes 10 microseconds to reach a receptor at a point P. As the signal has a velocity equal to the speed of light, the distance is for about 3 kilometers around the central point P with respect to $(n-1)$ fixed points denoted by $(x_2, y_2), \ldots, (x_n, y_n)$. We now explain how to estimate the node position in a Cartesian coordinate system. We denote by (x_m, y_m) the coordinates of the mobile in such two dimensional system. The coordinates can be computed by solving the following equations:

$$d_1 = x_m^2 + y_m^2 \text{ and } d_s = (x_s - x_m)^2 + (y_s - y_m)^2, \quad \text{for } 2 \le s \le n \tag{3}$$

where the unknown position is denoted by (x_m, y_m) and (x_s, y_s), which denotes the coordinate of a given fixed point s. The system can be linearized by subtracting the last equation from the first $(n-1)$ equations. Reordering the terms gives a proper system of linear equations. This called multilateration.

Figure 3 depicts such a situation where n is equal to three distances, d1, d2, and d3, that separate the mobile node from the three points BS1, BS2, and BS3, respectively. It can be seen that the two solutions (x_m, y_m) can be obtained by solving the first two equations. The third equation will help resolve ambiguity by choosing the solution that results in the shortest distance. To improve this, measurements need to be able to efficiently combine more than three sources, mitigating potential errors (mainly due to noise and inaccuracy) that could affect the set of measurements d_i. To provide a solution to this issue, techniques such as the maximum likelihood estimator MLE, (McGuire, Plataniotis, and Venetsanopoulos 2003) or the least square solution (Sayed, Tarighat, and Khajehnouri 2005) can be used.

TDoA: One important issue that related to the use of the ToF technique is synchronization between the sender and receiver so that d_i is the actual distance. In this context, the higher the velocity of the signal, the higher the

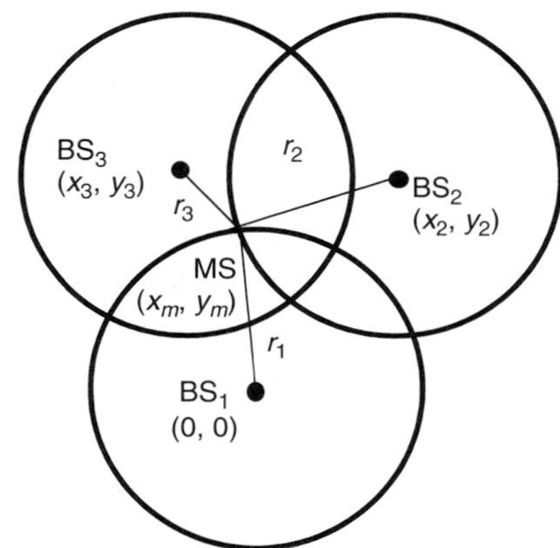

Figure 3: Time of arrival localization technique

resolution of the sender and receiver clocks should be. For instance, using light pulses requires a clock, which is of six times the magnitude of the one used with a sound wave (314 meters per second). To avoid generating errors in the location estimation using the ToA technique, the TDoA is introduced. A difference between time of arrival of the mobile signal at point P_i and P_1 is defined by $(t_i - t_1)$. Consequently the related distance difference can be written by the following relation:

$$d_{i1} = d_i - d_1 = (t_i - t^0)c - (t_1 - t^0)c = (t_i - t_1)c$$

Now, it can be seen that such a difference is independent of the mobile clock time. The set of the aforementioned equations can be rewritten under the form:

$$-x_i x_m - y_i y_m = d_{i1} d_1 + \frac{1}{2}(d_{i1}^2 - K_i^2), \text{ for } 1 < i < n. \quad (4)$$

The obtained equations can be rewritten in a matrix form as follows:

$$H_x = d_1 c = e \quad (5)$$

where:

$$H = \begin{bmatrix} x_2 & y_2 \\ x_3 & y_3 \\ \cdots & \cdots \\ x_n & y_n \end{bmatrix}, \quad c = \begin{bmatrix} -d_{21} \\ -d_{31} \\ \cdots \\ -d_{n1} \end{bmatrix}, \quad e = \frac{1}{2}\begin{bmatrix} K_2^2 - d_{21}^2 \\ K_3^2 - d_{31}^2 \\ \cdots \\ K_3^2 - d_{n1}^2 \end{bmatrix}$$

This can be easily solved.

AoA: The AoA localization method is based on measuring the angle of the incoming signal from at least two fixed points, and estimating the mobile position using triangulation. To do so, directional antenna arrays should be used, and the angle of arrival can be computed by measuring the phase difference or the power spectral density between or across the antennas array. Briefly speaking, let us consider n fixed points $P_i = (x_i, y_i)$. For every, Pi, let i denotes the angle of arrival of the incoming signal from the mobile M whose coordinates are (x_m, y_m). The latter can be described under the relation:

$$\begin{bmatrix} x_m \\ y_m \end{bmatrix} = \begin{bmatrix} x_i \\ y_i \end{bmatrix} + \begin{bmatrix} r_i \cos\alpha_i \\ r_i \sin\alpha_i \end{bmatrix}$$

More generally, we have: $Hx = b$ with:

$$H = \begin{bmatrix} 1 & 0 \\ 0 & 1 \\ \hline 1 & 0 \\ 0 & 1 \\ \vdots & \vdots \\ \hline 1 & 0 \\ 0 & 1 \end{bmatrix}, \quad x = \begin{bmatrix} x_m \\ y_m \end{bmatrix}, \quad b = \begin{bmatrix} d_1 \cos\alpha_1 \\ d_1 \sin\alpha_1 \\ \hline x_2 + d_2 \cos\alpha_2 \\ y_2 + d_2 \sin\alpha_2 \\ \vdots \\ \hline x_n + d_n \cos\alpha_n \\ y_n + d_n \sin\alpha_n \end{bmatrix}$$

which yields the least square solution of x.

The last method presents several advantages when compared to ToA and TDoA. These include the following; a) the number of fixed point are less than those of ToAs and TDoAs; and b) no synchronization of the fixed points clocks is required. However, because AoA requires the use of directional antennas, the angle of arrival is very difficult to compute at the phone level for 2G networks unless an overlay of AoA sensors is appended to the infrastructure, which makes the solution expensive. On the other hand, the AoA localization technique is not well suited to the urban environment, because the accuracy of the estimated position is subject to degradation due to multipath propagation and reflection (see Figure 4).

Signal Strength

In cellular networks, base stations are constantly transmitting signal on the control channels while a mobile listens on the air interface and making measurements for handover decision. These measurements, which contain the signal strength from the serving and the neighboring base stations, can be used to compute the distance that separates the mobile from the base stations. Using signals from at least three different base stations, a triangulation can be performed to compute the location of the mobile station. In the case where location computation is executed at the mobile level, the base station should send its coordinates. If the computation is to be performed at the network level, modifications need to be introduced to the mobile in order to enable it sending these measurements in idle mode.

On the other hand, in reality propagation conditions are far from free-space propagation and the use of such a technique faces many challenges. In fact, in urban areas, signal degradations due to multipath fading and shadowing are very important. Moreover, the signal level decreases more rapidly than in rural areas. Thus, an efficient environment-dependent propagation model needs to be considered to estimate the mobile position based on the received signal strength.

Because the transmitted signal power at the base station, the received signal power at the mobile station, and the antenna gain are known to the system, the pathloss can be computed as:

$$\text{Pathloss} = \text{Power at MS} - \text{Power at BS} - \text{BS Antenna Gain} - \text{MS Antenna Gain}$$

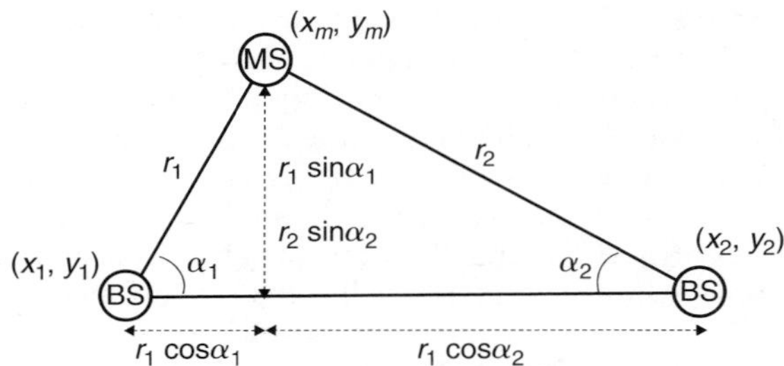

Figure 4: Angle of arrival localization technique

Several mathematical models have been proposed that enable estimation of the mobile position based on the signal pathloss. The Hata-Okumura mathematical model (Hata 1980), which is solely dependent on the mobile position, can be used for location estimation. The Hata-Okumura model consists of the free-space loss and a correlation between the distance and the frequency of the signal. Okumura presented the functions graphically as curves. Different curves exist for open, urban and suburban areas.

Fingerprinting

One approach to overcoming the problem of signal irregularity is to let the system learn the signal characteristics. Theoretically, any signal information that depends on the environment in the neighborhood of the mobile can be collected and used to estimate the location of the mobile. This information may include the received signal strength, the multipath pattern of the transmitted signal, TDOA and AOA measurements, signal time delay, and channel impulse response. This information can be measured at different known locations and recorded. When a new point needs to be localized, these quantities can be compared to the ones encountered before. The new location can then be assumed to be close to the previously collected points that have similar signal characteristics. This technique is called *fingerprinting* and the collected characteristics are called *fingerprints*. Thus, to localize a mobile node using fingerprinting, the collected fingerprint has to be compared to the fingerprints collected during a training period, whose positions are known.

Fingerprint-based localization takes advantage of two factors: a) characteristics of signals collected by mobile terminals show considerable spatial variability, because a radio source may be observed differently from two positions a few meters apart; and b) the signal characteristics are consistent in time, because a signal at a given location is likely to be the same at similar moments. In addition, fingerprinting-based localization systems present the advantage of allowing very accurate estimation of the location. Such a localization technique can be used with various technologies and different types of signal characteristics. However, the system is highly reliable in the face of changes in the environment, such as construction of new buildings, weather conditions, and mobility of objects (e.g., cars and persons) in the environment.

Informally speaking, a fingerprinting-based technique operates as a 2-phase process. In the first phase (called the *training phase*), fingerprints are computed at a set of *Reference Points* (RPs) that are appropriately distributed over the coverage area. After visiting all the RPs, a database of location fingerprints is built. The fingerprints can be recomputed several times to cope with the time variation and the degradation that occurs in signal propagation for several reasons, including shadowing. The fingerprints also may need some processing before they are stored (e.g., averaging all the taken measures). Theoretically, one can consider that the more RPs are considered in the training phase, the better the position accuracy will be. However, if the RF number is too high, the training phase may become laborious.

In the second phase (called the *positioning phase*), the available signal fingerprint is retrieved at the mobile position. Then, it is computed, and the mobile location is estimated by comparing the latter with the RP's fingerprints that are stored in the database, using different possible searching/matching algorithms, which are classified as deterministic and probabilistic (Li et al. 2005). In the deterministic approach, an algorithm (e.g., nearest neighbor) can be used to calculate the distance between the measured signal parameters vector and the vectors in the database. The mobile position will be associated with the RP that represents the shortest distance. In the probabilistic approach (Kaemarungsi 2005), a model of signal propagation using a probability distribution may be required. Once the signal parameter distribution is detected at a given position, the conditional probability theory is used to determine the probability of the mobile location.

The fingerprinting approach can be used with different wireless technologies such as GSM and WLAN. It also works with different types of input data, but the most common fingerprints are signal strength and time of arrival.

CELLULAR/WIRELESS/AD-HOC NETWORK LOCALIZATION

The aim of this section is to provide an overview of the localization techniques and solution designs in cellular, wireless, and ad-hoc networks. For each one of these networks, we address frequently used technologies.

Localization in Cellular Networks

This subsection gives an idea of the set of solutions provided in the literature and the positioning algorithms used in 2G, 2.5G, and 3G cellular networks. Finally, this section briefly discusses some standardization issues.

Localization in GSM

Introduced in the early 1990s, the Global System for Mobile Communication (GSM) is today one of the leading digital cellular systems. The architecture of this network is hierarchical and consists of cells. A cell is of variable size. It represents the smallest unit which is covered by the radio signal and frequency of a single transmitter. As radio frequencies are limited, the cellular concept allows using the same frequency within cells away from each other. A GSM network can be seen as the union of a set of Base Station Systems (BSS) and a set of Switching Systems (SS). While a BSS is responsible for the radio tasks, the SS processes calls and performs subscriber-related functions.

Cell-ID. To set a call within a GSM network, it is necessary to know in which cells the communicating users are located. The identification of a cell is made by a *Cell Global Identity* (CGI). A CGI is structured into four parts: country code, network code, location area, and cell identity. The identity of the cell is located within two components. The first component is the *Home Location Register* (HLR), which is a database that permanently stores and manages the operator subscribers. For every subscribed mobile, it includes the last serving cell location. The second place is the *Visitor Location Register* (VLR), which holds, for every local and roaming subscriber, some information including the Cell-ID. Because cells represent a fixed infrastructure, their identity can be translated to into coordinates and used for localization.

Such a technique is inexpensive and requires easy calculations to determine the position of the mobile. Moreover, it only requires minimal changes to the existing network infrastructure. In fact, a dedicated control channel needs to be used in order to transmit cell coordinates. However, this technique has a major drawback: level of accuracy. The accuracy is a function of the cell size, which varies from 1 to 3 km in urban areas and from 2 to 20 km in suburban and rural areas.

The Cell-ID positioning method was also proposed by the 3rd Generation Partnership Project (3GPP). Different from 2G cellular networks, a 3G mobile phone may perform a soft handover. In this case, it may be associated with different cell IDs; that is why all the returned cell IDs need to be combined in order to determine the proper Cell-ID.

E-OTD. The Enhanced Observed Time Difference (E-OTD) is a TDoA positioning method based on an already existing feature in the GSM system, the Observed Time Difference (OTD). The theoretical principle of the method is based on taking three measures: 1) the Observed Time Difference (OTD); 2) the Real Time Difference (RTD); and 3) the Geometric Time Difference (GTD). The first measure represents the time difference between the reception of bursts from two different Base Transceiver Stations (BTS). It requires the mobile to use technically advanced signal processing algorithms to discover the earliest arriving signal, rejecting multipath, for instance. The second measure is the synchronization interval in the network between two BTSs. It is equal to the time difference between the two moments at which the two BTS send the same burst. Because the network is not synchronized, the RTD is typically different from zero. Unlike OTD, RTD requires installing an additional component, called the Location Measurement Unit (LMU), in the infrastructure. Note that the LMU can be also installed at the BTS level. The third measure is the actual time interval between the reception of two bursts from two BTSs due to geometry. The measures discussed are related by: GTD = OTD - RTD. The GTD value defines a constant as a time difference between two BTS, and thus it produces a hyperbola. Because the mobile position can be estimated as the intersection of two hyperbolas, at least three BTS are required in The E-OTD method.

The advantage of the E-OTD lies in its accuracy. However, weak signal, multipath fading, and interference phenomena highly degrade the produced results. The drawbacks are obvious. Both network and mobile handset modifications are required, and a slow response time results.

Localization in 3G Cellular Networks

For the sake of simplicity and clarity, we discuss here a special case of 3G networks, the UTRAN (3GPP 2005) (UMTS Terrestrial Radio Access Networks). In UTRAN, the Base Station is referred to as *Node B*, while the mobile terminal is denoted by *User Equipment* (UE). Two methods are used in 3G networks: the *Observed Time Difference of Arrival* and the *hybrid positioning* methods.

OTDoA. The Observed Time Difference of Arrival (OTDoA) method is considered as the E-OTD version in 3G cellular networks (Zhao 2002). The mobile position is computed based on TDoA technique and at least three fixed neighbors (Nodes B) are required. Inheriting the same weaknesses of the E-OTD in 2G cellular networks, the method's accuracy depends on the geographic position of the base stations, is subject to degradation due to multipath radio propagation, and is dependent on the precision of the timing measurements.

In addition to weaknesses common to the E-OTD method, in WCDMA networks where the same the frequency is used by all the base stations, in-band interference may affect the accuracy of the location estimation. In fact, when a mobile is near its serving site, reception of the signal of other base stations using the same frequency may be blocked. This is a bit problematic because at least three measurements from three different base stations are required. To mitigate the problem, another variant of OTDoA, called OTDoA-IPDL, was proposed. It makes every base station pseudo-randomly cease to transmit for an idle period on the downlink, during which time the mobile can measure other neighbor signals. In the case in which the transmitters are not synchronized, the Relative Time Difference (RTD) must be provided.

Hybrid Positioning Methods. To increase the accuracy, reliability, and coverage of the estimated positions, several hybrid-positioning methods have been proposed. Cell-ID, for instance, can be combined with the Timing Advance (TA) method, or the Round-Trip Time (RTT) for a hybrid positioning in GSM and UMTS networks, respectively (Borkowski, Niemelä, and Lempiäinen 2005). In rural and sub-rural areas where a line of sight may be available between the mobile and the base station, an AOA-RTT hybrid position technique has been provided as an UMTS location technique. A single Node B that is equipped with an array antenna may be enough to estimate the mobile location. The RTT resolution, the beam width of the antenna array, and the increase of location error with the growth of the distance separating the mobile and the base station, represent the potential limitations of this technique.

To increase the accuracy of hybrid positioning methods such as EOTD/AGPS, Cell-ID/AGPS have been proposed. OTDoA-AoA is another hybrid positioning technique provided for the 3G UMTS cellular networks. In fact, as in these networks, where the AOA and the OTDoA measurements will be available without additional costs, combination of these two techniques will be useful for enhancing accuracy of the estimated position. The accuracy thus obtained is better than that obtained when either of these two methods is used alone (Thomas, Cruickshank, and Laurenson 2001). The errors in AoA measurements (due to the lack of availability of a line-of-sight condition) will be correlated with the errors in OTDoA measurements (due to timing measurement errors involving the serving base stations).The position estimation becomes possible using only two base stations simultaneously in the presence of a Non-Line of Sight Problem (NLoS).

Localization in Wireless LAN

Recently, great emphasis has been placed on development of WLAN-based indoor positioning systems, including Bluetooth and WiFi. The decrease in cost of WLAN networks made them interesting for use as positioning systems. Two main approaches have been proposed in the literature for WLAN indoor positioning solutions: client-based systems and client-assisted systems. The first approach assumes that a client performs location estimation based on scene analysis or signal strength characteristics. With the latter, no supplementary hardware is needed because signal strength characteristics are part of the operating mode of the wireless hardware.

Two major localization solutions are based on signal strength: the propagation model and the empirical model. The propagation model is based on the fact that as a signal crosses an environment, it loses its strength, depending on the distance and the properties of the environment. Using a theoretical model to describe distance in terms of signal strength parameters, the node location can be computed. The use of such a method provides accuracy that is somehow proportional to the complexity of the model used. The localization is fairly accurate when the mobile is in the proximity of the access point, and decreases as the distance between the mobile and the access point increases.

The empirical model is based on the use of pre-recorded information on signal strength for a set of locations. It operates in offline and online phases. In the offline phase, an RF map is created. In that case, a number of points are selected and traversed, and the received signal strength from all audible access points' measurements are collected and stored in a database. Later, in the online phase, when a mobile entity wants to estimate its location, signal strength from all the access points is assessed and the database is queried for the closest match. The match obtained will be considered the location.

One drawback of such a solution is the effort to be spent in the offline phase. In fact, the radio wave properties may vary depending on the number of people in the monitored area, the temperature and the humidity. Moreover, because the solution is based on the variation of the signal strength, which becomes unnoticeable below some variation, by which the location accuracy is bounded. Nonetheless, despite these drawbacks, the empirical model is more accurate than the propagation model.

Localization in Ad-Hoc Networks

Ad-hoc networks represent a growing area in wireless networks. They represent a group of nodes linked via a wireless medium. A particular and important example of ad-hoc networks is the ad-hoc sensor network, whose nodes are expected to perform distributed sensing. Sensor ad-hoc networks have been widely used in many attractive applications including intrusion detection, health care, and wildlife monitoring. They are designed with constraints related to low cost, moderate use of computational and memory resources, and power limitation.

Types of Localization Solutions. Localization solutions in ad-hoc networks can be classified into three categories: localization with beacons, localization with moving beacons, and beacon-free localization. The first category of localization solutions in ad-hoc networks assumes that a fraction of nodes, called *beacons or anchors nodes,* have a priori knowledge of their positions. Nodes with an unknown initial position are called *unknowns*. To define their location, the nodes start by estimating their 2D position using a proximity-based model (at least three beacons are available in its coverage) or ranging-based methods (e.g., RF time of flight, ultrasound, ultra wide band). After that, they refine their location to get better accuracy. Once a node has estimated its position, it becomes a beacon node and helps the remaining unknowns to estimate their positions.

Because the number of initial beacons is quite a few compared to the number of unknowns, it becomes possible to equip them with more power, sophisticated antennas, and even different hardware (e.g., hardware that uses GPS). It is even possible to use a node for the purpose of broadcasting location information (e.g., GPS satellites). The number and position of beacons have considerable influence on the accuracy of the location. For instance, in the case in which an environment is not homogenous, meaning that the computed location error may be different from one point to another, placing beacons in areas that provide the higher levels of error would be practical. Because energy consumption represents a hard constraint in sensor networks, the localization algorithms should be robust, and should use the minimum number of beacons possible.

The second category of localization solutions in ad-hoc networks uses a set of moving nodes that know their positions, called anchors, to achieve considerable savings in power consumption and cost. In fact, because the motion of the remaining nodes can be predictable, ad-hoc nodes can stay in sleep mode, and wake up only when the observers arrive in order to send data. Here, the data transfer can be initiated by the observer, which saves energy consumption. Because an observer needs a period of time t to send its data, an ad-hoc node should remain in the range of that observer during that period. Besides, it is important for the ad-hoc node to know whether it will remain within the transmission range for a sufficient amount of time, before it starts transmission. In the case where the ad-hoc node moves out of transmission range, it causes a data loss called outage. Because nodes are randomly distributed, it happens that an observer simultaneously receives different requests from ad-hoc nodes that should be sent in a limited time before they move out of transmission range. Thus, to avoid outage, it becomes crucial to use robust queuing systems that take into consideration waiting times and arrival processes.

The third category of localization solutions in ad-hoc networks operates without the use of beacons.

Motivations to design such systems are as follows: First, the use of beacons considerably increases the cost of building ad-hoc networks, especially in sensor networks. Second, depending on the environment and the ad-hoc node capability, it may not be feasible to set beacons and equip them with a localization system. (A GPS receiver, for instance, does not work in an indoor environment.) Third, even with the use of beacons, there might be some areas within the network that remain without beacons. Finally, because unknowns can act as beacons after their position is estimated, error may increase from one estimation to another. In a beacon-free localization, the position of every node is determined via node-to-node communication. At the beginning, every node starts with an unknown position. Then, they cooperate with each other to estimate their local distance. The estimated distance has a translation and orientation degrees of freedom. Simply put, the computed location is a relative position of the nodes compared to each other. In the case where an absolute position is required, conversion of the assigned orientation and coordinates should be done based on reference information (e.g., GPS).

Types of positioning algorithms: A wide spectrum of issues appears when designing positioning algorithms for Ad-hoc networks. This sub-section discusses the various possibilities related to existing positioning algorithms, including incremental versus concurrent algorithms, range-based versus range-free algorithms, centralized versus distributed algorithms, and multi-hop versus single-hop algorithms. Incremental algorithms start with a minimum number of nodes that know their position. Then, the remaining nodes recursively calculate their positions, using the relative distance separating them from nodes with known positions. Important drawbacks of this approach include: a) propagation error and cascading error may affect the accuracy of the whole positioning system; b) the nodes are vulnerable to failure, and c) the algorithms may not converge. Note that some algorithms may be applied to reduce propagation errors. On the opposite side, concurrent algorithms allow each node to calculate and refine its position in parallel with others. Thanks to the use of an iterative optimization scheme, differences between real and estimated positions can be reduced, and convergence of computation can be faster.

Range-based algorithms assume that some ad-hoc nodes can perform range-estimates by exploiting techniques such as ToA, RSSI, and AoA. However, the need for special hardware makes these nodes less portable and less cost effective. In addition, handling propagation issues—including errors, fading, and interference—is essential. In contrast, range-free algorithms assume that no node is equipped with special hardware for estimatinge its position. The location is estimated based only on the received message from neighbors. For instance, the APIT test algorithm (He et al. 2003) is used to determine whether a node is located inside or outside each triangle composed by all combinations of three possible beacons.

Centralized algorithms work by assuming that the ad-hoc nodes send estimates of their distance from their neighbors to a central node, which performs computations to determine the position of each node and then broadcasts the results. These systems suffer from communication overhead and non-scalability of the network. Moreover, a failure of the centralized node leads to the disabling of the whole localization system. The use of centralized solutions would penalize nodes close to the server. The problem can become crucial when these nodes contain less memory and reduced bandwidth. Network partitioning is another challenge that makes centralization impossible. Finally, changing topology may disturb the centralized solution. In the opposite case, distributed algorithms assume that each node communicates with the others to independently compute its own location. Thus, scalability can be enhanced and communication overhead is reduced.

Multi-hop algorithms assume that a node does not directly receive signals from beacons. A node computes its location based on the number of hops that separate it from the beacon node and the average of the node density. DV-hop (Niculescu and Nath 2000) represents an example of a method that uses such an approach. Single-hop algorithms are similar to the positioning systems in cellular networks and WLANs, in which a node collects the TDoA, RSSI, or AoA information directly from the base stations or access points to compute location. However, when large or well-spaced obstacles occupy the monitored area, the DV-hop scheme will not provide accurate estimation of the node position because it does make assumptions about the internal topology of the deployment area. In this context, the node clustering approach was provided in Chan, Luk, and Perrig (2005), and is based on a clustering sensor network in order to create a regular structure of cluster heads (nodes selected as representatives to a small portion of the nodes in the whole network). The remaining nodes, which represent the majority of the network's nodes, will be able to use to cluster heads as reference nodes. The approach provided in Medidi et al. (2006) applies complex localization algorithms to estimate cluster heads' position using hop-based algorithm. After the cluster heads' coordinates are determined, the triangulation technique is used for mobile nodes' localization. Each node will calculate the Euclidian distance to the cluster heads in its neighboring clusters and then estimate the average hop distance using three-Euclidian distance and corresponding hop length. A location message is then broadcast to mobile nodes containing its coordinates and the estimated hop distance to x nodes (x will be chosen as a tradeoff between message overhead and accuracy of the estimated location). After receiving at least three location messages from different cluster heads, a node will be able to estimate its coordinates using triangulation techniques. The key power of the protocol lies in the possibility of using classical hardware without introducing any assumptions about the node's hardware.

Ecolocation (Yedavalli et al. 2005) is another recent approach which is dedicated specifically for wireless sensor networks. This approach is based the fact that the location of some nodes (called *reference* nodes) are known. Any one of the remaining nodes (called *unknowns*) which wants to compute its position broadcasts a localization packet. The technique does not convert signal strength values into distance estimates. The reference nodes will collect some RSS measurements on that packet and send them to an entity responsible for estimating the location. The collected RSS measurements will be used to determine an ordered sequence of reference nodes. Because for every possible grid-point in the monitored area, the ideal distance-based ordering sequence of reference nodes is supposed to be determined from the outset, the two ordering sequences are compared. The best location estimate to the *unknown* node will be the one that maximizes the number of satisfied constraints, or the centroid of these locations in the case in which there is more than one location. Experimental results have shown that the echolocation technique provides better accuracy than that provided by Maximum Likelihood Estimator and Centroid localization techniques. Some other approaches such as the one reported in Ramadurai and Sichitiu (2003) consider the use of distributed localization algorithms using a probabilistic approach. They take into account range measurement inaccuracies. These approaches assume that nodes in a sensor network can belong to two different classes, namely beacons and unknowns. The key idea of such approaches lies in the fact that the probability distribution of each signal strength, as well as the mean and standard deviation, can be calculated and tabulated as a function of distance.

Localization in Wireless Sensor Networks (WSNs)

Because the main function expected from a WSN is event reporting, a significant and precise interpretation of such an event cannot be guaranteed unless its accurate location is determined. Localization in sensor networks is challenged by the limited capability of sensor nodes and the need for energy conservation. This is a conflicting-objective-based problem because: a) collaborative communication and computation among network sensor nodes becomes a requirement, b) communication among network sensor nodes should be minimized to reduce energy requirements; and c) power capability of sensor nodes is limited so that complex signal processing algorithms should not be used. To cope with these challenges, theories and models are needed to provide optimal coverage of the supervised area in preparation for tracking of target mobility (Hamdi, Boudriga, and Obaidat 2006).

The coverage approach is important in the sense that the optimal number of sensor nodes should be determined for a certain detection accuracy and quality, and the optimal positioning strategy of sensors should be determined. Many coverage optimality concepts were proposed in the literature, including: blanket coverage, barrier coverage, and sweep coverage (Hamdi, Boudriga, and Obaidat 2006). The first concept (blanket coverage) aims to maximize the rate of detection in the covered sensing area, while the second (barrier coverage) aims to minimize the probability of undetected penetration of nodes through the sensing area barrier. The last (sweep coverage) is a trade-off between the two quoted objectives, blanket coverage objective and barrier coverage objective). Developing an optimal node positioning strategy should be performed with awareness that other properties such as routing complexity and congestion rate may be affected. In fact, because sensor nodes should forward gathered events to an analysis center, deploying a network with a high density will guarantee better coverage, but on the other hand, it may increase the likelihood of congestion. Four main deployment strategies were mentioned in the literature: *k-coverage*, *(K, R_t) coverage*, *k-connectivity coverage*, and *path observability*. In k-coverage (Kumar et al. 2004; Zhou, Das, and Gupta 2004), every point which is within the region A can be sensed by K sensors. Such a strategy allows reception of detection messages within the region even in the presence of packet loss, which is a very common phenomenon in multi-hop wireless sensor networks. In *(K, R_t)* coverage, K sensors are within a region A to track a target t having a radius R_t. In *k-connectivity*, the network is k-connected, meaning that there are k-nodes disjoint communication paths between every pair of nodes. Such a strategy is mainly used when the transmission and forwarding capability of the networks need to be enhanced. In path observability strategy, the focus is on exposure of the moving object to the sensing field, because the main objective behind the use of such a strategy is mobile target tracking in the monitored field. It becomes more important to address the problem of node placement strategy when the mobility or the dynamic activation of sensor nodes is taken into consideration. In fact, nodes may switch between "sleep" and "activate" for the purpose of energy control, and may also change their positions by time. In this context, more importance should be given by the literature on studying the impact of mobility and energy control on coverage.

To guarantee efficient use of the sensor network for tracking, node placement should done in an optimal manner, covering the entire surveillance zone. In this context, the number of required sensor nodes is highly dependant on the localization technique that will be used to determine the node position. For instance, if the sensor network is modeled as a two- or a three-dimensional grid, the location of the target will be determined by pinpointing it at a grid point. With the granularity of a single grid point, it is generally difficult to locate a target using the location of one sensor. If sensors are positioned in such a way that a subset of them should cover every grid point, the precision of the trajectory of moving targets and their positions will be enhanced and easily determined.

To locate a target and track its path during mobility, several methodologies were proposed. While the traditional method could be based on the use of a centralized database or computing facility, the latter becomes a bottleneck in terms of requested resource and induced network traffic directed toward it. Therefore, such an approach is not adequate due to lack of scalability and absence of fault-tolerance. To avoid flooding, some approaches suggested not using all the nodes for tracking. Only a selection of nodes that have the best data collaboration can be used to save power and bandwidth cost. Several metrics can be used as the basis of selection, such as: a) detection quality (including detection resolution), sensitivity, and false alarms; b) track quality including tacking error and tracking length; c) scalability including network size, number of events, and number of active queries; d) solvability including fault tolerance; and e) resource usage in terms of power/bandwidth consumption. With the use of such a concept, only the leader node will generate an estimate of the object state and will hand off the state information to the next selected leader. The latter could make a combination of the estimated information and derive a new state, and then select the next leader itself. The current leader will periodically return the information to the unexpected node via the shortest path. Some other distributed tracking schemes try to improve accuracy by combining information retrieved from several nodes instead of relying on one neighbor (Wang et al. 2003).

A SURVEY OF WELL-KNOWN LOCALIZATION SYSTEMS

This section describes three well-known, widely used, and accurate wireless localization systems. The first is one of the well-known Global Navigation Satellite Systems (GNSS) that was introduced by the United States and called GPS (Global Navigation Satellite) system, which represents the most familiar example of a location system and provides wide-area coverage. It is used extensively in military and commercial applications, such as vehicle tracking. The second system is the APS system, which was designed for localization in wireless ad-hoc networks. The third is the RADAR system, which provides localization in indoor environments based on the 802.11 wireless networking technology.

Global Positioning System

The Global Positioning System (GPS) is a worldwide localization system that covers almost the entire earth and provides real-time three-dimensional position (longitude, latitude, and altitude). The system was developed by the U.S. Department of Defense and was officially called NAVSTAR (Navigation Signal Timing And Ranging). The GPS system can be considered a combination of three main segments: the *space segment*, the *system controller segment*, and the *user segment*.

The Space Segment. This segment is composed of 29 orbiting satellites containing a minimum of 24 operating satellites. It is designed to maintain full operational capability even if two satellites are in failure state. The satellites are positioned in six earth-centered orbital planes; each one of them is inclined by 55 degrees with respect to the equator and is located at a distance of 12,000 nautical miles above the earth. Each GPS satellite takes 12 hours to orbit the earth and is primarily powered by sun-seeking solar panels while using Ni-Cad batteries as a secondary power. Every GPS satellite continually broadcasts its position and timing data via two UHF (Ultra High Frequency) radio bands, frequency designated as L1 and L2, respectively. The first frequency is designed for civilian use while the second is reserved only for military use. Two codes are broadcast on the L1 frequency: C/A code and P code. The C/A code, which stands for Coarse Acquisition, is available for civilian use and provides Standard Positioning Service achieving horizontal accuracy of 15 meters, approximately. The second code, which stands for Precise Code, is broadcast on both L1 and L2 frequencies and is only available for military use.

Each transmitted signal is 1023 bits long and is transmitted using CDMA (Code Division Multiple Access) multiplexing method, which lets all the satellites share the same frequency. A GPS signal is composed of three different types of information. The first type is a *Pseudorandom code* that identifies which satellite is transmitting the information. The second type, which is called the *Ephemeris data*, is transmitted by every satellite to show orbital information relative to itself and to every other satellite in the system. It mentions where each satellite is located at any time. The third type, which is called the *Almanac data*, carries information about the status of the satellite and the current date and time.

The **control segment** is composed of a set of five monitor stations, three ground antennas, and a Master Control Station (MCS). The monitor stations track all satellites in view; accumulating ranging data. This information is processed at the MCS to determine satellite orbits and update each satellite's navigation message. Updated information is transmitted to each satellite via the ground antennas.

The user segment, which is composed of GPS receivers, uses the process of trilateration to estimate position, requiring that at least four satellites are within the line-of-sight of the receiver. Note that readers should be reminded that the satellite position is known by the receiver because it is transmitted as part of the message it sends. To measure its distance from every satellite, the receiver has to compute the time delay between satellite transmission and terminal reception and then multiply the time delay by the speed of light. As a GPS receiver is synchronized with a satellite, it generates the same pseudo-random sequence (the receiver is able to calculate the same identical sequence starting from a known seed number) at the same time. Upon receiving the sequence from the satellite, the receiver looks back in its memory to determine when the same sequence was emitted, and therefore infers the time delay. After computing its distance from four satellites, it computes its distance as the intersection of four imaginary spheres. Such a sphere is centered around a satellite and has a radius equal to the distance that separates the receiver from the satellite. In practice, the fourth measurement is required to correct the clock error.

Many sources of error may affect GPS measurements, including atmospheric effects, satellite orbit errors, receiver noise, multipath ambiguities, and satellite clock errors. As the GPS signal goes through the ionosphere and troposphere, it may be refracted and its speed can be changed unpredictably. This effect becomes more apparent when the satellite moves toward the horizon because the angle of inclination increases and the signal has to cross a thicker atmosphere layer. Depending on their frequencies, changes in speed are different from one signal to another. GPS receivers may exploit the received phase difference between L1 and L2 signals frequencies to infer the atmospheric effects and proceed with correction. Errors may also occur due to sunspot activity that creates interference with the GPS signal, measurement noise, signal distortion caused by electrical interference, or even errors inherent in the GPS receiver itself.

Multipath reflections means that a signal is received by different paths, due mainly to reflection and refraction from the ground and surrounding terrestrial objects. Multipath reflections may also considerably affect position accuracy. For the case of long delay multipath signals, GPS receivers can proceed with filtering out using techniques such as Narrow Correlator Spacing (Cannon et al. 1994). As for short delay multipath, it may considerably reduce precision because the reflected signal can be very close to the real one. Special antenna features such as a ground plane, or a choke ring antenna can be used (Rao, Sarma, and Kumar 2006). Accuracy of the GPS positioning can also be affected by the *Geometric Dilution of Precision* (GDOP), which is a measure of the quality of the satellite configuration. This parameter value is computed from geometric relationships between the receiver position and the positions of the satellites that the receiver is using for navigation. A high GDOP value results when angles from receiver to satellites are similar, whereas a low GDOP value occurs when those angles are different. The higher the GDOP value, the lower the probability of precision.

To increase the accuracy of GPS receivers, several solutions have been proposed. Among these solutions, one can distinguish *Differential GPS* (DGPS), which uses a set of fixed ground based reference stations (also called GPS base station) with known location to reduce the effect of atmospheric errors during position computation (multipath errors are not resolved, however). Because its location is known, a GPS base station can compute errors (e.g., the timing errors) in its position calculation and broadcast this information to mobile GPS receivers in the same surrounding area. The receivers will correct their position estimation and reach an accuracy of 1 to 3 meters.

There are two modes of differential corrections: a) real-time differential GPS and b) post-processed differential correction. In the first mode, the location error is transmitted as a local signal and a mobile receiver directly provides the corrected position. However, this mode requires having a mobile GPS receiver equipped with correction software and able to interpret the base station signal. In the second mode, raw location values from mobile GPS receivers are combined together with data from base stations and a differential correction software is used to apply error correction. However, this solution requires that both mobile receivers and base stations be provided with storage capabilities. In the case in which the mobile GPS receiver and the base stations are produced by different manufacturers and experience compatibility problems, *Receiver Independent Exchange* (RINEX) format, for instance, may be used to guarantee compatibility (Cooksey 2006).

Several other techniques were proposed, similar to GPS (Wikipedia 2006). The major techniques include WAAS (Wide Area Augmentation System), EGNOS (Euro Geostationary Navigation Overlay Service), and MSAS (the Multi-Functional Satellite Augmentation System) which uses a series of ground reference stations to calculate location errors and then uploads such values to a series of additional satellites. Additionally, an alternative to GPS was proposed by the European Union to be operational by 2010. The positioning system is called GALILEO and is intended to provide greater precision than that provided by GPS. The system will be composed of three orbital planes located at 23,222 km above the earth and inclined 56 degrees with respect to the equator. Each orbital plane will be composed of nine operational satellites and one active spare per orbital plane. The GALILEO system improves coverage notably in northern regions such as Scandinavia. The signal transmission is performed with more power in comparison with the GPS signal, and over wide frequency bands. This makes reception possible in indoor environments and improves robustness against multipath effects. GALILEO is not expected to replace GPS, but rather is expected to be combined with it for maximum coverage.

Four different navigation services will be provided by the GALILEO positioning system. The first, called Open Service (OS), will be available for free access and be broadcast in two bands at 1164–1214 MHz and at 1563–1591 MHz. In the case in which a receiver uses the two signals, it can achieve an accuracy of less than 4 meters horizontally and less than 8 meters vertically. The second provided service, called *Commercial Service* (CS), will offer accuracy of less than one meter for an additional fee. The system uses encryption to facilitate charging and introduces a third signal band (1260–1300 MHZ) in addition to the two bands used in the OS service. The accuracy of location estimation may go down 10 centimeters if the system is used with ground stations. The third service is called *Safety of Life Service* (SoL). It provides accuracy comparable to OS service and is intended for safety-critical transport applications. The last service, called *Public Regulated Service* (PRS), is encrypted to control access and is available for security authorities.

RADAR

RADAR System is a Microsoft tool for user location and system tracking that uses ambient IEEE 802.11 signals to estimate position. This system's strong point is that it does not require any transformation or modification of the existing wireless infrastructure. RADAR assumes that a few access points (or base stations) are deployed in a manner that provides overlapping coverage. The basic version of the RADAR system allows computing of 2D positions of mobile devices, by taking measurements relative to Signal Strength and Signal to Noise Ratio at the base station when it receives a signal (Bahl and Padmanabhan 2000). However, providing localization in three dimensions such as in a multi-floored building remains a considerable challenge. Moreover, any mobile device to be tracked should support WLAN networking. Such a requirement becomes restrictive in the case in which devices are equipped with low computational and power capabilities.

To estimate the user's position, the system starts working in an offline phase by creating a radio map of the area under which it operates. This map represents a set of recorded information about the received radio signal from the access points as a function of the user's locations in the building. An entry in the database is in the form of $(x, y, z; ss_i)$ where (x, y, z) represents the physical coordinates of the mobile where it takes the signal measurements and ss_i represents the signal strength that propagates from the access point number i. The basic version of the system uses three access points, in such a case; a database entry will take the form (x, y, ss_1, ss_2, ss_3). Because the offline phase requires an important effort of deployment, two approaches were proposed for the creation of the radio map. The first approach is an empirical method that involves a mobile user that moves within the building and manually records its location and the associated received signal strength from access points that are within its range. The second method aims at creating a radio propagation model relative to indoor RF propagation in order to reduce dependence on empirical data. The model supports different building layouts, takes into consideration large-scale path loss, and attenuation due to obstacles (e.g., walls) between access points and receivers.

Later, in the online phase, the mobile takes a real-time measurement of the signal strength of each access point within its range and searches through the database for the entry producing the best match. The location associated with such an entry will be taken as the best matching location. To search through the database, the system uses a search technique called NNSS (or Nearest Neighbor(s) in Signal Space). The algorithm bases its search on computing the *Euclidian distance* (in the signal space) between the real-time computed set of measurements ($ss1$, $ss2$, $ss3$) and each recorded set (ss'1, ss'2, ss'3) in the radio map database. The estimated user location will be relative to the physical coordinates of the entry that minimizes the distance. Another variant of the algorithm proposes to take a particular interest when there are more than one matching entry in the database. In that case, the algorithm averages the physical location of closely matching entries and provides that average as the location estimation.

Two major drawbacks of the RADAR system can be mentioned: a) RADAR is dependent on changes in the environment such as weather, moved objects, and variation in hardware; b) RADAR does not scale over large areas mainly due to the necessity of extensive calibration. On the other hand, the system has shown good accuracy with the empirical model. In fact, the error distance, which is defined as the Euclidian distance between the real position and the estimated one, is shown to be lower than 3 meters, (this is typically comparable to the size of a room within a building). Additionally, the RADAR system was adopted in many commercial products including *Ekahau*, *Pinpoint*, and *WhereNet*, due to its effectiveness in terms of cost and accuracy. In comparison with other well-known systems, the RADAR location system provides less accuracy than indoor location systems (e.g., Cricket [Hightower and Borriello 2001]) but on the other hand, it does not require specialized infrastructure. Compared to GPS, RADAR provides better accuracy, but less coverage

The RADAR system has experienced several enhancements: a) the support of continuous user tracking, taking information from the past into account to better estimate the user's location; b) the use of an environment profiling technique that takes into account changes in the environment conditions; and c) the extension of the NNSS algorithm to support three-dimensional environments (Bahl, Balachandran, and Padmanabhan 2000). This enables the RADAR system to use multiple radio maps dynamically and improves its accuracy.

APS

The Ad-hoc Positioning System (APS) is a range-free localization system. We demonstrate hereinafter how the APS system brings a solution to computation and power constraint challenges in ad-hoc networks and how it provides localization.

APS is a distributed hop-by-hop positioning algorithm that extends the Distance Vector routing (DV) and the GPS system. Starting with a set of nodes called landmarks (a concept inherited from GPS), which are highly powered nodes capable of performing self-location computation and which have good line-of-sight conditions. The APS system propagates position estimation capability to regular nodes using a hop-by-hop method (a concept inherited from DV routing). Note that the number of landmarks is supposed to be reduced and that regular nodes may not be in contact with enough landmarks. The key ideas behind the design of APS can be summarized by the following facts: a) distribution of positioning algorithms that face the challenges related to low memory and bandwidth, partitioning, and changing topology; b) minimization of node-to-node communication to preserve energy, c) tolerance to network disconnection; and d) absolute position providing in the GPS coordinate system. APS proposes a set of positioning schemes that depend on the node capabilities. The major schemes are the DV-hop, DV-distance, Euclidean, DV-coordinate, DV-bearing, and DV-position (Niculescu and Nath 2004).

DV-Hop. The Distance Vector-Hop (DV-Hop) scheme consists of three phases. In the first phase, nodes start using distance vector exchange to obtain the shortest path to landmarks in terms of hops. Every node will maintain a table $\{X_i, Y_i, h_i\}$ where X_i and Y_i represent the unknown coordinates of landmark i, and h_i is the number of hops that separate the current node from landmark i. The aim of the second phase is to let a landmark estimate the average size in meters for one hop and distribute it as a correction value c_i. In fact, given the distance (in hops) to other landmarks that it estimated in the first phase and the known coordinates of these landmarks, we can compute c_i as:

$$c_i = \frac{\sum \sqrt{(X_i - X_j)^2 + (Y_i - Y_j)^2}}{\sum h_i}, i \neq j, \text{all landmarks } j$$

Such correction is distributed to the neighbors using a controlled flooding mechanism. In the third phase and after receiving the correction value, a node will be able to transform distances to landmarks in hops to distances in meters. The output will be used to perform trilateration and estimate the node's position in the entire network. The main advantage of the DV-hop method is characterized by its independency to the range or angle measurement errors. However, it assumes that the network is isotropic (i.e., properties are the same in all directions) for a reasonable deployment.

DV-Distance. The DV-distance scheme introduces a little improvement in the distance-vector algorithm metric, compared to DV-hop scheme. In fact, the distance between nodes is measured using radio signal strength and is propagated in meters rather than in hops. Unfortunately, propagated errors in measurements weaken the method's accuracy.

Euclidean Propagation Model. This method is based on propagation of the estimated Euclidean distance to landmarks. As shown in Figure 5, the problem can be stated as follows: Given a landmark L and two nodes B and C that have already estimated their Euclidian distance ($r1$ and $r2$) to L, the aim is to help node A, which is in communication with B and C to estimate its distance d to L. The problem can be solved by considering the quadrilateral ABCL because A already has estimated knowledge of the values of all the sides and one diagonal of the quadrilateral ABCL. Solving this problem yields to two possible values for the distance from node A to L. The *Neighbor vote method* can be applied to decide which value is acceptable, if there is a third node (D) that can be used. Replacing node C by D will lead to a pair of distance estimates. The correct distance is part of both pairs.

DV-Bearing. Given that the two neighbor nodes B and C know their bearings (the angle with respect to a fixed direction) to landmark L, a node A in the proximity of B and C can compute its bearing to B and C. After receiving their bearings from C and B, node A will be able to compute all the angles in the triangle ABC and BCL and therefore infer the bearing of A with respect to L. After computing its bearing with respect to three landmarks, node A can infer its position using the AoA technique.

DV-Coordinate Propagation Method: To use the method, a pre-processing phase is required. This phase aims at allowing every node in the network to establish its own coordinate system centered at itself. An assumption is made, stating that second hop information is available. As depicted by Figure 6, a node A, after estimating its range to node E and G and the range between them, chooses

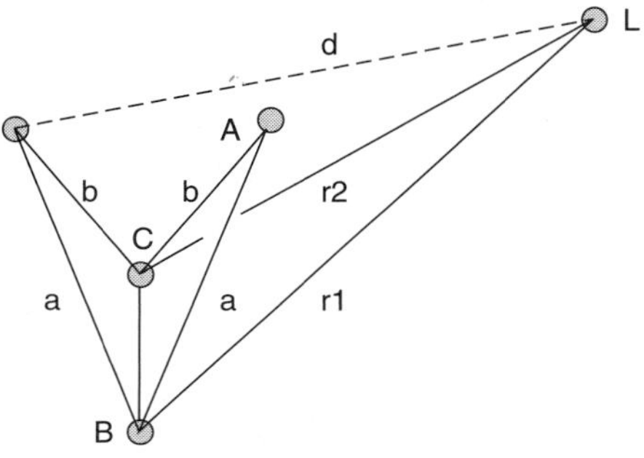

Figure 5: Euclidean propagation model

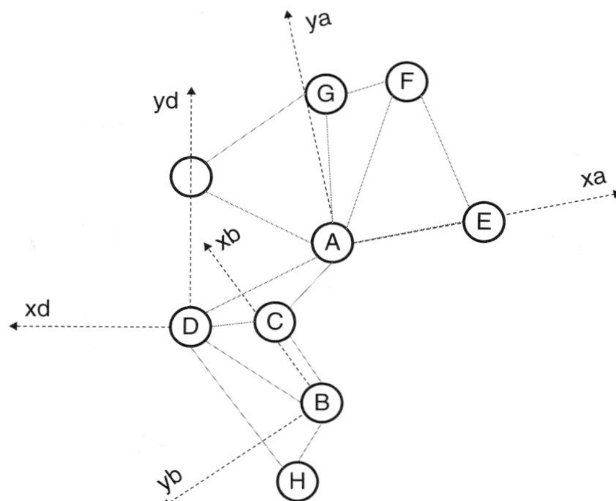

Figure 6: DV-coordinate propagation

axes x_a and y_a as a local coordinate system. After that, it computes the coordinates of all immediate neighbors.

The second phase is registration with neighbors, which intends to let a node compute a transformation matrix with respect to its neighbors. Consequently, a node X, which receives from node Y the local coordinates of node Z, will be able to translate such coordinates to its own system. Later, at the DV propagation phase, only the coordinates of a landmark are forwarded from one node to another. When a node X receives the coordinates of a landmark, it immediately transforms them into its local system using the appropriate computed transformation matrix. To estimate its position, a node can choose between two methods that showed the same performance. In the first scheme, the node transforms all the received coordinates of landmarks and then solves the trilateration problem. In the second scheme, because the node has the coordinates of the landmarks in the global and local system, it computes a global transformation matrix and uses it to estimate its global coordinates.

One drawback of the method is error propagation. In fact, uncertainty in locally computed coordinates is amplified by the uncertainty that occurs due to application of the transformation matrix (uncertainty that comes from the registration phase) and then is propagated to neighbor nodes.

ADVANCED ISSUES IN LOCALIZATION

Several advanced issues related to localization in wireless networks are under investigation. The major issues include: a) indoor localization; b) the sensing of mobile resources and c) positioning security

Indoor Localization. Accurate indoor localization has been a constant objective of the wireless communication research community. Most research activities on indoor localization have been based on short-range signals such as 802.11, Bluetooth, and Infrared. However, a very few works have shown that indoor localization using wide-area cellular networks can reach high accuracy. Indoor cellular network-based localization has several advantages including:

1. A cellular network operates in a licensed band of frequencies, and thus does not suffer from interference from nearby devices.
2. A cellular network presents a stable environment that allows a localization system to operate properly for a long period before needing calibration.
3. The wide acceptance of cellular networks (e.g., GSM, UMTS) makes them appropriate channels for the delivery of localization-based value-added services.

Research in cellular network based localization would have to face several challenges including: a) achieving an accuracy that can compete with 802.11 localization solutions (by using diversity, for instance); and b) providing efficient localization in three-dimensional environments. The first accurate GSM-based localization solution has used the concept of fingerprinting to achieve an accuracy as low as 2.5 meters (Otason et al. 2005).

Mobile Sensing. The localization of individual mobile sensor nodes and mobile targets without relying on external infrastructure is receiving considerable attention because a wide spectrum of applications need to know the location of objects and individuals they are involved with. Recently, a number of localization systems have been proposed for wireless sensor networks (Langendoen and Reijiers 2003). However, truly distributed localization algorithms should satisfy the following requirements:

- The localization algorithm should be self-organizing in the sense that it does not depend on global infrastructures. This implies that there is no fine control over placement of the sensor nodes when the network is deployed.
- It should be robust, meaning that it is tolerant to security intrusions and node failures. The nodes are also assumed to continue sensing even when they get out of coverage and report events when they return to radio coverage.
- It should be energy efficient in the sense that it requires little computation and communication, especially when security protection is required for the need of privacy and alert confidentiality.

The aforementioned requirements immediately eliminate almost all proposed localization for wireless sensor networks.

Secure Positioning. So far, the problem of positioning in wireless networks has been addressed basically in a non-adversarial environment. Nowadays, we observe two types of attacks on localization systems: internal and external. Typically, an attacker can perform timely attacks by delaying or speeding up the signal used for localization, or can perform power level modification attacks by replaying signals between nodes and base stations. Attacks are targeting all localization systems, propagation techniques, and estimation methods.

Examples of attacks have addressed the GPS system, because current GPS receivers can be completely fooled by GPS satellite simulators that produce fake satellite radio signals that are stronger than the real signal. Civilian GPS devices were not designed for secure positioning. A few simple changes to GPS receivers would allow them to detect relatively unsophisticated attacks; but sophisticated attacks would remain very hard to detect. On the other hand, the techniques based on the received signal characteristics to compute the location can be mislead by an internal attacker reporting a false power level to a trusted node or modifying the measured distance between two trusted nodes by jamming the communication between the two nodes or replaying their messages with higher power.

Several research works have addressed the secure positioning problem. In Brands and Chaum (1994), the authors propose an RF distance bounding technique that allows the nodes to "upper bound" their distances to other nodes and prevent internal attackers from reducing the measured distance. In Capkun and Hubeaux (2006), the authors analyzed the resistance of positioning techniques against position and distance spoofing attacks. They also proposed a mechanism, *called verifiable multilateration*, for secure positioning of wireless devices.

CONCLUSION

Recently, location-based services have gained considerable attention. Several kinds of services and applications need to be aware of their positions, including environment monitoring, target tracking, and intrusion detection. In this article, we stressed the need for localization in the wireless environment, and presented the various issues surrounding localization techniques. We also described the most important issues in radio propagation that are related to localization, particularly in non-satellite systems operating in complex environments. Moreover, several techniques for position calculation were described, and localization solutions for cellular, wireless, and ad-hoc networks were illustrated. For every one of these networks, a well-known, widely used, and accurate wireless localization system was described. This article has given special attention to advanced issues related to indoor localization, mobile resources sensing and positioning security.

The future outlook in wireless localization should address techniques for position estimation in ad-hoc and sensor networks in which the nodes' computational resources are limited, infrastructure is absent, coverage problems may occur, environment is subject to intrusions, and a tradeoff between traffic overhead reduction and position accuracy is a concern. In general, indoor localization continues to require dedicated hardware and signal propagation schemes. Enhancing existing localization techniques used by cellular networks, for instance, to provide a global localization (for both indoor and outdoor) will be of high importance in terms of coverage, cost, and practicality. Finally and due to the increase and sophistication of security attacks, interest in digital investigation of security incidents continues to gain significant importance. In this context, providing new techniques of investigation that benefit from localization information will be of the utmost importance.

GLOSSARY

APS: Ad-hoc Positioning System. A positioning system that copes with the characteristics of ad-hoc networks (changing topology, low power constraints). It uses a distributed, hop-by-hop positioning algorithm that extends distance vector routing and GPS positioning. The algorithm assumes that only a small number of nodes are able to compute their absolute position themselves (called anchor nodes), and allows all the remaining nodes (called unknowns) to compute their positions based on their distance estimation to anchor nodes.

Bluetooth: A wireless personal area network technology, known as IEEE 802.15, which provides communication between digital devices, including PDAs, and mobile phones. The devices communicate when they are in range, using a radio communication system that induces low power consumption and requires unlicensed short-range radio frequency.

CDMA: Code Division Multiple Access. A technique that spreads a signal over a frequency band that is larger than the signal, allowing numerous signals to occupy a single transmission channel. Each signal is encoded using a pseudo-random sequence. Only the receiver, which knows the right code, can suitably decode the received signal.

Euclidian Distance: Represents the ordinary distance between two points. It is equal to the root square difference between coordinates of these points.

Free Space Loss: The loss of signal strength when ideal propagation condition are assumed: radio waves emanate from the source of radio energy and travel in all directions in a straight line (i.e., the effects of diffraction, reflection, and scattering are removed). The loss only depends on frequency and distance.

GPS: Global Positioning System. Represents the most known worldwide satellite navigation system. It consists of a network of 24 orbiting satellites that send radio signal, enabling GPS receivers to compute their three-dimensional position, velocity, and time.

GSM: Global System for Mobile Communications. Represents the most popular standard for cellular mobile phones in Europe. GSM is a second generation mobile phone system which operates in 450 MHz, 900 MHz, 1800 MHz, or 1900 MHz frequency band (some countries, such as the USA, use the 850 MHz and 1900 MHz bands because the 900 and 1800 MHz frequency bands were already allocated) and use variation of time division multiple access (TDMA).

Indoor Propagation Channel: A wireless channel characterized by a high attenuation of the transmitted signal due to internal walls and furniture, a short delay of echo, and a low delay spread. Typically, the distance between transmitter and receiver is short (e.g., both are located in the same building). The temporal variations of the channel are slow compared with outdoor propagation, where a mobile antenna may be mounted on a car.

Localization: Broadly speaking, localization means determining the locality or the position of a given object. The wireless localization is the assignment of coordinates (consistent with physical location) to nodes in a wireless network.

Mobile Ad-Hoc NETworks: (MANET). It is a network of mobile routers (some of them may simply act as a host) that move randomly, communicate by wireless links, and forming an arbitrary topology that can change rapidly, randomly, and unpredictably.

Multilateration: A process by which an object's position is computed based on the time difference of arrival (TDOA) of at least three signals emitted by synchronous transmitters. Not to be confused with with lateration, which uses absolute measurements of time-of-arrival (TOA).

RADAR: A location and tracking system devised by Microsoft, which allows mobile devices equipped with IEEE 802.11 networking technology to use ambient signals to estimate their position. The position is computed either using empirical methods that compare the signal fingerprint with previous measured locations mapped on a radio map, or using a mathematical models of indoor signal propagation.

RSSI: Received Signal Strength Indication. A measurement of the received signal strength (energy integral) by the antenna. The signal strength indicator on a cell phone display is a common example. The higher the RSSI, the stronger the signal.

Signal Fingerprint: Information computed from a received signal that identifies its dependency on the wireless environment. Such information could include received signal strength, multipath pattern of the transmitted signal, TDOA and AOA measurements, signal time delay, or even channel impulse response.

Signal Propagation: The means by which a radio signal flows from a place to another, typically from a transmitting antenna to a receiver antenna.

Spoofing: The process by which an entity (e.g., a program) forges data to impersonate another and gain an illegitimate access or privilege.

UHF: Ultrahigh Frequency. Electromagnetic waves whose frequency ranges from 300 MHz to 3 GHz. Consequently, the UHF wavelengths ranges are between 10 centimeters and 1 meter. The UHF band is widely used by satellites, communication and broadcasting, and cellular phone networks.

UMTS: Universal Mobile Telecommunications Service. The European standard for third-generation mobile telephony. It is envisioned as the successor to Global System for Mobile Communications (GSM) in Europe. Theoretically, UMTS increases the transmission speed to 2 Mbps per mobile, establishes a global roaming standard, and provides simultaneous support for a wide range of services including digitized voice and video, and packet transmission of data.

WCDMA: Wideband Code Division Multiple Access is a third generation (3G) cellular network that uses CDMA technique for multiplexing.

Wireless Mobile Sensor: A device that represents a basic component of a Wireless Sensor Network (WSN). It senses signals to monitor physical conditions (e.g., location, temperature, pressure) at different locations. Typically, it is equipped with a small microcontroller, a source of energy, and a radio transceiver. It should be of small size and price, so that it can be deployed in large numbers.

CROSS REFERENCES

See *Principles and Applications of Ad Hoc and Sensor Networks; Wireless Channels*.

REFERENCES

3GPP. 2005. Stage 2 functional specification of User Equipment (UE) positioning in *UTRAN.* TS 25.305.

Addlesee , M., et. al. 2001. Implementing a sentient computing system. *Computer,* 34(8): 50–56. IEEE Computer Society Press. Los Alamitos, CA.

Bahl, P., A. Balachandran, and V. N. Padmanabhan. 2000. Enhancements to the RADAR user location and tracking system. Technical Report. Microsoft Research. MSR-TR-2000-12.

Bahl, P., and V. N. Padmanabhan. 2000. RADAR: An in-building RF-based user location and tracking system. *IEEE Infocom* (Tel-Aviv, Israel, Mar. 2000): 775–84.

Borkowski, J., J. Niemelä, and J. Lempiäinen. 2005. Enhanced performance of cell ID+RTT by implementing forced soft handover algorithm. IEEE Vehicular Technology Conference, Sept. 2005.

Borriello, G., et al. 2005. Delivering REAL-WORLD ubiquitous location systems. *Communications of the ACM,* 48(3): 36–41.

Brands, S., and D. Chaum. 1994. Distance-bounding protocols. *Proceedings of workshop on the theory and applications of cryptographic techniques*, 1994: 344–59.

Cannon, M. E., et al. 1994. Performance analysis of a narrow correlator spacing receiver for precise static GPS positioning. *Position Location and Navigation Symposium* (Las Vegas, NV. Apr. 11–15, 1994).

Capkun, S., and J. P. Hubeaux. 2006. Secure positioning in wireless networks. *IEEE Journal on Selected Areas in Communications*, 24(2): 221–32.

Chakrabarty, K., et al. 2002. Grid coverage for surveillance and target location in distributed sensor networks. *IEEE Transactions on Computers*. 51(12): 1609–14.

Chan, H., M. Luk, and A. Perrig. 2005. Using clustering information for sensor network localization. *The International Conference on Distributed Computing in Sensor Systems* (DCOSS 2005).

Cooksey, D. 2006. Understanding the Global Positioning System (GPS). http://www.montana.edu/places/gps/understd.html (accessed Apr. 26, 2006).

COST Action 231. 1999. Digital mobile radio towards future generation systems, final report. Tech. Rep., European Communities, EUR 18957, 1999.

Hamdi, M., N. Boudriga, and M. S. Obaidat. 2006. Designing a wireless sensor network for mobile target localization and tracking. *Proceedings of IEEE Globcom 2006 Conference* (San Francisco, CA, Nov. 2006).

Hata, M. 1980. Empirical formula for propagation loss in land mobile radio services. *IEEE Transactions on Vehicular Technology* 29(3):317–25.

He, T., et al. 2003. Range-free localization scheme for large scale sensor networks. *The 9th International Conference on Mobile Computing and Networking (MOBICOM)* (San Diego, CA. Sept. 14–19, 2003).

Hightower, J., and G. Borriello. 2001. Location systems for ubiquitous computing. *IEEE Computer Magazine* August: 57–66.

Hightower, J., and G. Borriello. 2001. A survey and taxonomy of location systems for ubiquitous computing. Technical Report UW-CSE 01-08-03. University of Washington, Computer Science and Engineering.

Kaemarungsi, K. 2005. Design of indoor positioning systems based on location fingerprinting technique. University of Pittsburg. School of Information Science. PhD thesis.

Kumar, S., et al. 2004. On k-coverage in a mostly sleeping sensor network. *International Conference on Mobile Computing and Networking* (2004): 144–58.

Langendoen, K., and N. Reijiers. 2003. Distributed localization in wireless sensor networks: A quantitative comparison. *Computer Networks* 43: 499–518.

Li, B. et al. 2005. Probabilistic algorithm to support the fingerprinting method for CDMA location. *GNSS 2005* (Hong Kong, Dec 8–10, 2005).

Medidi, M., et al. 2006. Scalable localization in wireless sensor networks. *High Performance Computing (HiPC)*, December 2006, Bangalore, India.

McGuire, M., K. N. Plataniotis, and A. N. Venetsanopoulos. 2003. Location of mobile terminals using time measurements and survey points. *IEEE Transactions on Vehicular Technology.* 52(4): 999–1011.

Nicopolitidis, P., et al. 2003. *Wireless Networks*. New York: Wiley.

Niculescu, D., and B. Nath. 2003. Ad hoc positioning system (APS) using AOA. *IEEE Infocom* (San Francisco, CA, Apr. 2003):1734–43.

Niculescu, D., and B. Nath. 2004. Position and orientation in ad hoc networks. *Elsevier Ad hoc Networks, 2* (2004):133–51.

Obaidat, M., and N. Boudriga. 2007. *Security of e-systems and computer networks*. Cambridge University Press, 2007.

Otason, V., et al. 2005. Accurate GSM indoor localization. *Ubicom 2005*, M. Beigl et al. (eds.), *Lecture Notes on Computer Science* 3660 Springer, 2005: 141–58.

Patwari, N., et. al. 2005. Locating the nodes. *IEEE Signal Processing Magazine*, 22(4): 54–69.

Ramadurai, V., and M. Sichitiu. 2003. Localization in wireless sensor networks: A probabilistic approach. *2003 International Conference on Wireless Networks (ICWN 2003)* (Las Vegas, NV, June 2003): 275–80.

Rao, B. R. K., A. D. Sarma , and Y. R. Kumar. 2006. Technique to reduce multipath GPS signals. *Current Science*. P. Balaram (ed.). *90*(2):207–11.

Sayed, A., A. Tarighat, and N. Khajehnouri. 2005. Network-based wireless location: Challenges faced in developing techniques for accurate wireless location information. *IEEE Signal Processing Magazine* 22(4): 24–40.

Srinivasan, A., and J. Wu. 2007. A survey on secure localization in wireless sensor networks. (forthcoming). *Encyclopedia of Wireless and Mobile Communications*, B. Furht (ed.). London: CRC Press, Taylor and Francis Group.

Sun, G., et al. 2005. Signal processing techniques in network-aided positioning. *IEEE Signal Processing Magazine* 22(4):12–23.

Thomas, N. J., D. G. M. Cruickshank , and D. I. Laurenson. 2001. Performance of a TDOA-AOA hybrid mobile location system. Second International Conference on 3G Mobile Communication Technologies, pp. 216–220.

Wang, X., et al. 2003. Integrated coverage and connectivity configuration in wireless sensor networks. First ACM Conference on Embedded Networked Sensor Systems. (SenSys03), Nov. 2003, pp. 2839.

Wikipedia. Global Positioning System. http://en.wikipedia.org/wiki/GPS (accessed April, 26, 2006).

Yedavalli, K., et al. 2005. Ecolocation: A sequence-based technique for RF localization in wireless sensor networks. *Fourth International Symposium on Information Processing in Sensor Networks,* pp. 285–92.

Zhao, Y. 2002. Standardization of mobile phone positioning for 3G systems. *IEEE Communications Magazine* 40 (7): 108–16.

Zhou, Z., S. Das, and H. Gupta. 2004. Connected k-coverage problem in sensor networks. *Thirteenth International Conference on Computer Communications and Networks* (ICCCN 2004, Chicago, IL), pp. 373–78.

Interference Management in Wireless Networks

Keivan Navaie, *Tarbiat Modares University, Iran*
Shahrokh Valaee, *University of Toronto, Canada*

INTRODUCTION

In wireless communication, information is carried by electromagnetic waves that propagate in space and can be received by all terminals located within the radio coverage area of the transmitter. This characteristic of wireless communication is often referred to as *broadcast effect*, in which the signal destined to a particular terminal is also received by other terminals and may interfere with their own reception. Such an environment is usually called a *shared medium*, in which a transmitted signal can be overheard by many terminals. Each receiver in a shared medium receives a superposition of the signals transmitted from multiple terminals and destined to distinct receivers. An elaborate multiple-access scheme should be designed to separate the compound signal into its individual components, and extract the signal of interest.

A direct solution to this problem is to modulate the information on a set of orthonormal bases, $\{\mathbf{v}_1, \mathbf{v}_2, \ldots, \mathbf{v}_n\}$, where $\mathbf{v}_i$ is the ith basis vector and n is the dimensionality of the space. Examples of basis vectors include the time slot in *time division multiplexing* (TDM), a frequency band in *frequency division multiplexing* (FDM), a set of orthogonal spreading codes in *code division multiplexing* (CDM), and a cell site in *space division multiplexing* (SDM). In all of these examples, the signal subspace is represented by a set of orthonormal bases,

$$\left\langle \mathbf{v}_i, \mathbf{v}_j \right\rangle = \delta_{ij} \tag{1}$$

where $\langle.,.\rangle$ is the scalar product operator, and δ_{ij} is the Kronecker delta function defined as

$$\delta_{ij} = \begin{cases} 1 & \text{if } i = j \\ 0 & \text{if } i \neq j. \end{cases} \tag{2}$$

Using this representation of the signal subspace, the modulation can be defined as an invertible mapping from the set of source alphabet to the signal subspace. Here, for brevity of discussion, we assume that modulation is performed by multiplying the basis vector by the input data. Therefore, the received signal $\mathbf{r}$ can be represented by

$$\mathbf{r} = \sum_{i=1}^{n} b_i v_i \tag{3}$$

where b_i is the data of the ith user. The receiver isolates the signal of interest by computing the scalar product between the compound signal $\mathbf{r}$ and the corresponding basis vector:

$$\left\langle \mathbf{r}, \mathbf{v}_j \right\rangle = b_j \tag{4}$$

where we have used equation 1

Unfortunately, in practice it is very difficult to maintain orthogonality among the basic vectors; we usually have

$$\left\langle \mathbf{r}, \mathbf{v}_j \right\rangle = b_j + \sum_{i=1, i\neq j}^{n} b_i \left\langle \mathbf{v}_i, \mathbf{v}_j \right\rangle + \mathbf{n} \tag{5}$$

where $\mathbf{n}$ is the background noise. The summation $\sum_{i=1,i\neq j}^{n} b_i \langle \mathbf{v}_i, \mathbf{v}_j \rangle$ in equation 5 is referred to as the *interference*.

As noticed in equation 5, in multiuser wireless communications, the main sources of error are background noise and interference. The error is pronounced if the noise or interference components in equation 5 are strong. The strength of these components, relative to the signal strength, is usually measured with the *signal-to-interference plus noise ratio* (SINR), defined as

$$\text{SINR} = \frac{S}{I + N} \tag{6}$$

where S is the power of signal, I is the power of interference, and N is the power of noise. If $I \ll N$, the system is noise limited and the interference has minimal or no impact on the performance of the system. On the other hand, if $I \gg N$, the system is interference limited and noise has a small impact on the performance and can be safely ignored. A major challenge in an interference-limited system is that, unlike noise, which can be overcome by increasing signal power, interference cannot be combated by increasing the signal power. Indeed, increasing signal power will increase interference to other users and will reduce their throughput. In this chapter, we will focus on interference management techniques in interference limited networks.

DS-CDMA Networks

It is well known that *direct-sequence code division multiple access* (DS-CDMA) systems have some desirable features such as dynamic channel sharing, a wide range of operating environments, graceful degradation of the quality of service (QoS), and ease of cell planning. DS-CDMA systems can also support a multiservice mix of services with a broad range of bursty traffic characteristics and QoS requirements.

DS-CDMA systems are interference limited (Viterbi 1995); therefore, multiple-access interference plays an important role in the performance analysis of such systems. Consequently, managing the total interference for all services is a major challenge in multiservice wireless networks (Viterbi 1995). As a result of high bandwidth and simple receivers in user equipments, downlink interference has a more destructive effect than uplink interference. Therefore, in this chapter we will only focus on downlink interference.

Proper utilization of more accurate information on the temporal behavior of the downlink interference can lead to the development of effective resource control mechanisms. However, the conventional approaches for modeling interference in wireless DS-CDMA networks only use the marginal distribution of the total interference (Viterbi 1995; Verdu 1998; Chung and Hanly 2001), and do not consider its temporal behavior. In contrast, here we consider such temporal behavior in multiservice wireless DS-CDMA networks.

Temporal behavior of interference in long timescales for packet data services in a cellular network has been studied in Zhang, Hu, and Shroff (2002) and Zhang and Konstantopoulos (2005), where interference is modeled as a continuous-time process, graceful degradation of the QoS for limited interferences is assumed, and the effects of the call admission procedure are ignored. In Taqqu, Willinger, and Sherman (1997), an ON-OFF process is assumed for user traffic, and the basic concept of heavy-tail processes is utilized to explain the self-similarity of total interference. An ON-OFF process typically refers to the mutually independent, alternating ON periods (during which packets are emitted at a constant rate) and OFF periods (during which no packets are sent). Obviously, this method is not applicable to heterogeneous DS-CDMA cellular networks that support both packet-based and connection-oriented services. In addition to using an ON-OFF traffic model, Zhang and Konstantopoulos (2005), make the following assumptions: the total bandwidth (and as a consequence the number of users) is infinity; the allocated power to each user is the inverse of the slow-fading channel gain; and a specific wireless channel model is assumed in which the auto-correlation function of channel variations and the transmit power process are of the order of $O(k^{-\alpha+1})$ for $k \to \infty$, where α is the minimum decay exponent of the tail of the ON and OFF processes. Under these conditions, Zhang and Konstantopoulos (2005), show that the total downlink (and also uplink) interference has asymptotic second-order self-similarity. We will show that, although the heavy-tail assumption of channel auto-correlation function and the infinite bandwidth are relaxed, the total interference depicts asymptotic second-order self-similarity in heterogeneous DS-CDMA networks.

We propose a model for the downlink interference over long time scales and show that it provides significant insight and considerable intuition for designing efficient radio resource control mechanisms. In these time scales, the QoS must be considered over the lifetime of a call/session. For this reason, and for clarity of presentation, we will ignore many physical layer effects because they are pertinent only to much shorter time scales. Rather, we take a simplified model of the lower layers that captures enough of the physical layer characteristics for our purposes, and which has already been successfully used in Viterbi (1005), Chung and Hanly (2001), and Evans and Everitt (1999).

Several system parameters—such as the total number of active users (interferers), their call durations, the allocated power to each call in the corresponding base station, channel variations, and user mobility—cause temporal fluctuation of interference. To model these effects, we take a cross-layer approach in which the traffic characteristics at the application layer and the information on the wireless channels are combined to model the downlink interference.

This chapter focuses on the asymptotic temporal behavior of downlink interference for long time lags, which is essential for efficient predictive/adaptive radio resource control. We show that, for long time lags, the auto-covariance of the downlink interference in a DS-CDMA cellular network with a mix of Poisson and heavy-tail traffics decays subexponentially. This observation indicates that the downlink interference has long-range dependence, and therefore is an asymptotically self-similar process. The predictive nature of the self-similar interference is then utilized to develop a novel cross-layer adaptive-predictive radio resource controller. We use this adaptive-predictive algorithm to estimate the interference fluctuations and then exploit the multi-user diversity (Viswanath, Tse, and Larioa 2002) through the utility-based optimal scheduling.

TOTAL DOWNLINK INTERFERENCE

In this chapter we consider a cellular DS-CDMA network with heterogeneous services. Within this network, the total downlink interference measured at the receiver of a given user is represented by a discrete time process $I(n)$, where n is the time index. For a user in the network coverage area, $I(n)$ represents the average interference over a window of length T_w seconds (the modeling time scale), with $T_w \gg T_c$, where $1/T_c$ is the spreading bandwidth of the cellular DS-CDMA network. Therefore, $I(n)$ is the sum of the transmitted powers by all base stations, multiplied by the corresponding channel gain from each of those base stations to the user under study, as follows

$$I(n)=\sum_{c=1}^{C}\xi^c(n)P^c(n)g^c(n) \quad (7)$$

where C is the number of cells in the network, $P^c(n)$ is the total transmit power of the base station in cell c, $g^c(n)$ is the channel gain from the base station in cell c to the user, and $\xi^c(n)$ is the cross-correlation between the spreading sequences of the user of interest and other users. Note that, in equation 7 the power allocated to the user under study is not included in $P^1(n)$. For convenience, we assume that the user is located in cell $c=1$ and that $\xi^c(n)=1$. A nonzero $\xi^c(n)$ in equation 7 indicates that the basis vectors at the receiver are nonorthogonal (c.f. equation 5). To obtain the total interference in equation 7, we first study $P^c(n)$ and $g^c(n)$ separately.

Base Station Transmit Power

In time slot n, each base station serves a set of active users (calls) in its cell coverage area. For simplicity, we assume that each call is served by only one base station. We further assume that each call starts at the beginning of a time slot and that its duration is an integer multiple of T_w. The transmit power of the base station is the sum of allocated powers to all calls in the corresponding cell c. Therefore, $P^c(n)$ is

$$P^c(n)=\sum_{j=1}^{J}\sum_{i=1}^{N_j^c(n)} p_{ji}^c(n) \quad (8)$$

where J is the number of services provided by the network, $N_j^c(n)$ is the number of calls of service j in cell c at time n, and $p_{ji}^c(.)$ is the allocated power to call i of service j in cell c. For the ith call of service j in cell c, $p_{ji}^c(.)$ has a real value equal to the allocated power over its call duration, and is equal to zero otherwise.

The two random variables at time instant n in equation 8 are $N_j^c(n)$ and $p_{ji}^c(n)$. The number of active calls $N_j^c(n)$ can be uniquely identified by $\mu_j^c(n)\in\mathbb{Z}_+, \mathbb{Z}_+=\{0,1,2,\ldots\}$, the number of new call arrivals for service j in cell c at time n, and $\{\tau_{ji}^c, i\in\mathbb{N}\}, \mathbb{N}=\{1,2,\ldots\}$, the call duration sequence process. We assume that for each given cell c and service j, the call duration sequence process, τ_{ji}^c, the arrival rates sequence process, $\mu_{ji}^c(.)$, and the allocated power sequence process, $p_{ji}^c(.)$, are independent random processes, with each being an independent identically distributed (i.i.d.) random process. In the sequel, we denote $\tau_{ji}^c, \mu_{ji}^c(n)$, and $p_{ji}^c(n)$ by the generic random variables $\tau_j^c, \mu_j^c(n)$, and $p_j^c(n)$, respectively. It is straightforward to show that the downlink interference can be completely specified by $p_j^c(n)$, $g^c(n)$, $\mu_j^c(n)$ and τ_j^c, for all j and c (Navaie et al. 2006).

To obtain the characteristics of $P^c(n)$, we need to have the number of active calls for different service types and their corresponding call durations in equation 8 as well as the allocated power over their activity time.

1. *New call arrivals:* In DS-CDMA cellular networks, it has been assumed that no new call arrivals are blocked and no calls are terminated prematurely (Viterbi 1995; Evans and Everitt 1999). This can be justified to some extent by soft blocking of calls in DS-CDMA cellular networks, meaning that there is no hard limit on the number of available channels, and all users suffer from a gradual performance degradation as the load is increased. Here, we assume that $\mu_j^c(n)$ has a Poisson distribution with parameter λ_j^c. Therefore, $\lambda_j^c=E[\mu_j^c(n)]$.
2. *Call durations:* We denote both packet duration and call duration as *call duration* in this chapter. Assume that the call duration is a random variable with a known distribution. Call durations of different service types are assumed to be independent from one another. For voice-only wireless and wireline networks, it is invariably assumed that call durations are exponentially distributed (Viterbi 1995; Kelly 1991). Distribution of call durations in future wireless systems are expected to be similar to the ones in current wireline networks, for which extensive statistical analysis and measurements have established that the distribution of call durations for data and multimedia services are heavy tailed (see, e.g., Erramilli et al. 2002). For a heavy-tailed distribution, the rate of decay of its probability density function is much slower than that of the Poisson distribution. Pareto distribution has been used to model call durations in Erramilli et al. (2002).
3. *Allocated power to each call:* To obtain $p_j^c(n)$, we note that, for a given channel, the allocated power to a given user at time slot n is generally a concave function of its bit rate. Here, for simplicity, we assume that the allocated power is a linear function of the bit rate. We also assume that the system can support any arbitrary bit rate.

Wireless Channel Gain

In equation 7, the transmitted power by each base station is multiplied by the corresponding channel gain $g^c(n)$. To obtain the channel gain, we assume a deterministic distance-dependent path loss and two fading effects: *fast fading* and *shadowing*. Note that fast fading (e.g., Rayleigh or Rician), which is partly canceled out by fast power control, affects $P^c(n)$ in equation 7 in smaller time scales than does the shadowing. Moreover, the short-range effect of fast fading is averaged out in longer time scales such as T_w. Therefore, the channel gain $g^c(n)$ is

$$g^c(n)=L_c d_c^{-\gamma_c}\theta^c(n) \quad (9)$$

where d_c is the distance between the base station c and the user for which the downlink interference is measured; γ_c is the path loss exponent, which is a function of the antenna height and the signal propagation environment; L_c is an environmental constant; and $\theta^c(n)$ is the slow-fading process. Parameter γ_c may vary from slightly less than 1 for hallways within buildings, to larger than 2.5 in dense urban environments and hard-partitioned office buildings (Stuber 1996). The slow-fading process $\theta^c(n)$ has a log-normal distribution with standard deviation σ_c.

The Gudmundson correlation model (Stuber 1996) is used for log-normal shadowing as

$$\Theta^c(n+1) = \rho^c \Theta^c(n) + (1-\rho^c)\nu^c(n) \quad (10)$$

where the time scale is T_f (fading period), $T_f \geq T_w$, $\Theta^c(n) = \log \theta^c(n)$ is the log-normal fading in dB, $\nu^c(n)$ is a zero-mean white Gaussian noise with variance $\sigma_c^2(1+\rho^c)/(1-\rho^c)$, and $0 < \rho^c < 1$ is the channel correlation coefficient.

TEMPORAL BEHAVIOR OF DOWNLINK INTERFERENCE

In this section, we derive the asymptotic temporal behavior of the auto-covariance function of the downlink interference $C(k)$. Using the assumptions of the previous section, it is straightforward to show that the auto-covariance function of $I(n)$ is

$$C(k) = \sum_{c=1}^{C} \left[C_P^c(k) C_g^c(k) + C_g^c(k)(m_P^c)^2 + C_P^c(k)(m_g^c)^2 \right] \quad (11)$$

where m_P^c and $C_P^c(k)$ are, respectively, the mean and the covariance function of the process $P^c(n)$, and m_g^c and $C_g^c(k)$ are the mean and the covariance function of the channel process $g^c(n)$. Note that here we assume a fast power control mechanism to deal with the undesirable effects of fast fading. Fast-fading and shadowing processes are also assumed to be independent. Therefore, we assume that $P^c(n)$ and $g^c(m)$ are also independent for all n and m.

Before examining the effects of traffic characteristics on the auto-covariance of the downlink interference in equation 11, we need to define regular and slow-varying functions.

Definition 1: A function $f(x) > 0$, $x \in \mathbb{R}$ is called a *regular varying function* (rvf) if there exists an $\alpha \in \mathbb{R}$ (such that for all $u \in \mathbb{R}_+$, $\frac{f(ux)}{f(x)} \to u^\alpha$, as $x \to \infty$. The value of α is the *regularity index* of $f(x)$. If $\alpha = 0$, then f is called a *slow-varying function* (svf). We denote $\mathcal{RV}_\alpha$ as the set of regular varying functions such that if $f(x) \in \mathcal{RV}_\alpha$, then $f(x) = L(x)x^\alpha$, where $L(x)$ is an svf (Bingham, Goldie, and Teugels 1987).

A random variable X is said to be heavy tailed with infinite variance if $P(|X| \geq x) \in \mathcal{RV}_\alpha$ for $0 < \alpha < 2$.

Example: *Downlink asymptotic temporal behavior (single-cell case)*: Assume a single-cell system (i.e., $C = 1$) with constant channel gain $g^c(n) = g_0$. For brevity, we drop the cell index in the sequel. Suppose that there are two services (i.e., $J = 2$), both with Poisson distributions for call arrivals with rates of λ_1 and λ_2. Service $j = 1$ has an exponentially distributed call duration, and service $j = 2$ has a heavy-tail distribution of call durations. Assume further that the call duration of service $j = 2$ has a discrete Pareto-type distribution,

$$\Pr\{\tau_2 = l\} = L_2(l) l^{-\alpha-1}, \quad 1 < \alpha < 2, \quad (12)$$

where $L_2(l)$ is a slow-varying function, and α is the shape parameter of the distribution. A small value for parameter α results in a distribution with a heavier tail. Intuitively, equation 12 implies that there is no typical distribution of call durations (i.e., call durations are highly variable, exhibit infinite variance, and fluctuate over a wide range of values). With these assumptions, it is possible to show that (Navaie et al. 2006)

$$\sum_{k=-\infty}^{+\infty} \left| C_P(k) \right| = \infty. \quad (13)$$

This equation indicates that, in case of constant channel gains with heavy-tail distribution of call duration, the downlink interference exhibits extended temporal correlations.

A process whose auto-covariance function satisfies equation 13 is called a *long-range dependent* (LRD) process (Beran 1994). For an LRD process, the correlation between its two samples decreases very slowly with an increase in the temporal distance between those samples. In general, the auto-covariance function of an LRD process for $k \to \infty$ is $C(k) \sim L(k)k^{-\beta}$, where $L(k)$ is a slow-varying function, symbol '~' means *behaves asymptotically as*, and $0 < \beta < 1$. In the preceding example, if the distributions of call durations are exponential for both services, their auto-covariance functions are absolutely summable; therefore, the resulting auto-correlation function decays exponentially and creates a *short-range dependent* (SRD) process. The auto-correlation of an SRD process does not have a heavy tail. Note that, for most standard time series, such as auto regressive moving average (ARMA) and Markovian models, the auto-covariance function decays exponentially (Brockwell and Davis 1991), and thus $\sum_{k=-\infty}^{+\infty} |C(k)| < \infty$.

In the preceding example, it is shown that for a constant channel, the heavy-tailed distribution of call durations results in LRD downlink interference. We now extend this observation to more general channel conditions. Assume that the auto-covariance function of the channel process is

$$C_g^c(k) \sim L_g^c(k) k^{-\beta_g^c}, \quad k \to \infty \quad (14)$$

where k denotes time with a temporal resolution T_w, $L_g^c(k)$ is a slow-varying function, and $\beta_b^c > 0$ is the channel auto-covariance decay exponent. For $\beta_g^c < 1$, the channel process is LRD, and for $\beta_g^c > 1$, the channel process is SRD. In the time scales of interest, this model is consistent with the Gudmundson (1991) correlation model for fading channels.

Proposition 1: For the finite-mean total transmit power process $P^c(n)$, the channel gain $g^c(n)$, and for $k \to \infty, C_P^c(k) \sim L_P^c(k)k^{-\beta_P^c}$ and $C_g^c(k) \sim L_g^c(k)k^{-\beta_g^c}$, the auto-covariance function of the total interference, $C(k)$, satisfies

$$C(k) \sim L^*(k)\, k^{-\beta^*}, \quad k \to \infty \quad (15)$$

where $L_P^c(k)$, $L_g^c(k)$, and $L^*(k)$ are svf, and $\beta^* = \min_c \min\{\beta_g^c, \beta_P^c\}$.

Proof: See Navaie et al. (2006).

SELF-SIMILARITY OF DOWNLINK INTERFERENCE

We now propose an asymptotically self-similar (as-s) model for the downlink interference that extracts the values of its LRD parameters. Let $I(.)$ be a second-order stationary process with a finite mean. We define the aggregate process $I^m(.)$ of $I(.)$ at the aggregation level $m > 1$ by

$$I^m(n) = \frac{1}{m}(I(nm - m + 1) + \ldots + I(nm)). \tag{16}$$

The process $I^m(.)$ is obtained from $I(.)$ by partitioning the observation interval into nonoverlapping blocks of size m and averaging $I(.)$ in each block. For each $m > 1$, $I^m(.)$ defines a new second-order finite-mean stationary process. The family $\{I^m(.) : m \geq 1\}$ of aggregate processes is useful for studying the temporal behavior of the total interference at different time scales corresponding to different resource control mechanisms.

A process $I(.)$ is as-s if the correlation coefficients of the average process of block length m as $m \to \infty$ are identical to those of a self-similar process (Tsybakov and Georganas 1999). A sufficient condition for a second-order stationary process $I(.)$ to be asymptotically self-similar is that for $k \in \mathbb{Z}_+$, $k \to \infty$, the auto-covariance function of $I(.)$, in other words $C(k) \sim L(k)k^{-\beta}$, in which $0 < \beta < 1$, and $L(k)$ is an svf (Tsybakov and Georganas 1999). Note that an as-s process is also LRD.

Asymptotically Self-Similar Model for the Downlink Interference

We will now develop an as-s model for the downlink interference. Suppose that the total interference is a finite-mean, finite-variance second-order stationary process. We assume that the auto-covariance function of the channel process $g^c(n)$ is as it was in equation 14 for $c = 1, \ldots, C$, and $0 \leq \beta_g^c \leq 1$, in which for $\beta_g^c = 1$ the channel process is SRD. In the following proposition, we derive the necessary conditions on traffic and channel characteristics under which the downlink interference is an as-s process.

Proposition 2: Consider the downlink interference process, $I(.)$, and for $c = 1, \ldots, C$, let β_P^c satisfy

$$\sum_{j=1}^{J} \lambda_j^c \Pr\{\tau_j^c = k\} r_j^c(k) \sim L_P^c(k) k^{-\beta_P^c - 2}, \quad k \to \infty, \forall_c \tag{17}$$

where $r_j^c(k)$ is the auto-covariance function of $p_j^c(n)$ and $L_P^c(k)$ is an svf. Now, $I(.)$ is an as-s process with self-similarity index $H = 1 - \beta^*/2$ if there exists at least one c such that $0 < \beta_P^c < 1$ or $0 < \beta_g^c < 1$, and where $\beta^* = \min_c \min\{\beta_P^c, \beta_g^c\}$.

Proof: See Navaie et al. (2006).

Proposition 2 gives the sufficient conditions for asymptotic self-similarity in the total downlink interference. It combines the service call arrival rate, λ_j, the service call duration distribution, $\Pr\{\tau_j = k\}$, and the correlation function of the allocated power, $r_j^c(k)$, to give the sufficient conditions.

In equation 17, note that if the call duration process of service j^* is heavy tail, then for $k \to \infty$,

$$\sum_{j=1}^{J} \lambda_j \Pr\{\tau_j^c = k\} r_j^c(k) \sim \lambda_{j^*} \Pr\{\tau_{j^*}^c = k\} r_{j^*}^c(k). \tag{18}$$

Therefore, we can conclude that the asymptotic behavior of the auto-covariance function of the total downlink interference in a mixed voice and multimedia or packet data, with regular channel variations and regular power transmission, is influenced by providing service to users with heavy-tailed call durations.

MODEL-BASED OPTIMAL DOWNLINK INTERFERENCE PREDICTION

Because the self-similar processes have long-range dependence (Beran 1994), the samples of data in such processes are correlated over long periods. Therefore, a predictor can use a sequence of measured interference samples to precisely estimate the level of interference in future time slots. In this section, we model the total downlink interference with *fractional Gaussian noise* (fGn) and utilize this model to devise an optimal downlink radio resource management scheme (Navaie, Valaee, and Sousa 2005).

If the variance and the self-similarity index, H, of a zero-mean self-similar process are known—subject to assuming an idealized Gaussian setting—the process can be modeled by the fGn.

Definition 2: *Fractional Gaussian noise* (fGn; Beran 1994) is a self-similar Gaussian process with the auto-covariance function

$$\gamma(k) = \frac{\sigma_0^2}{2}(|k+1|^{2H} - 2|k|^{2H} + |k-1|^{2H}), k \in \mathbb{Z}, \tag{19}$$

where σ_0^2 is the variance and H is the self-similarity index.

We assume a large number of users in the coverage area of the network. We also select an appropriate time scale and assume that the resource control mechanism does not alter the total downlink interference model. The interference is then modeled using a fGn process as

$$I(n) = m_I(n) + z(n), \tag{20}$$

where $m_I(n)$ is the average of $I(n)$ measured over the window $(n - L, n - 1)$, and $z(n)$ is fGn.

We use the correlation structure of the total received interference and the auto-covariance of fGn, equation 19, to propose the following optimal linear predictor for the total interference (Brockwell and Davis 1991):

$$\hat{I}(n+1) = m_I(n) + (\Gamma^{-1}\underline{\gamma})^T(\mathbf{I}(n) - m_I(n)\mathbf{1}_M), \tag{21}$$

where $\hat{I}(n+1)$ is the predictor of $I(n+1)$, $\mathrm{I}(n) \triangleq [I(n), I(n-1), \ldots, I(n-M+1)]^T$ is the $M \times 1$ vector of stored interference measurements, M is the memory length of the predictor, Γ is the covariance matrix with entities $\Gamma_{ij} \triangleq \gamma(i-j)$, $\underline{\gamma} \triangleq [\gamma(1), \ldots, \gamma(M)]^T$, where $\gamma(n)$ is given in equation 19, and $\mathbf{1}_M$ is the $M \times 1$ identity vector; the superscript T denotes vector transposition. At a given instant n, the mobile terminal of each user measures the level of interference and adjusts the values of parameters $m_I(n)$, $\sigma_0(n)$, and H. A simple weighted summation of

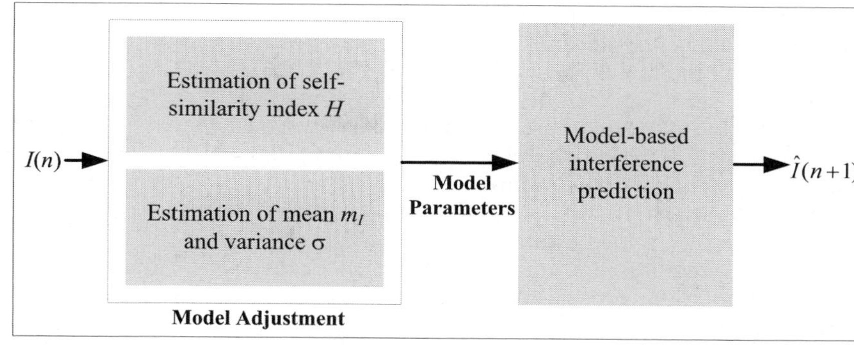

Model-based optimal linear interference predictor for each user
(a)

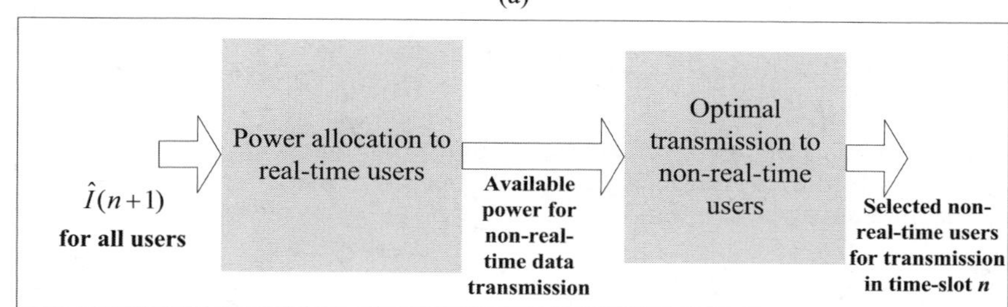

Optimal non-real-time data transmission
(b)

Figure 1: Model-based adaptive-predictive throughput maximization of non-real-time data in the downlink: (a) user module, (b) network

measured values of total interference is used for mean estimation as follows

$$m_I(n) = \frac{1}{M} \sum_{k=n-M}^{n-1} I(k). \tag{22}$$

The interference variance is also estimated by

$$\sigma_0(n) = \frac{1}{M-1} \sum_{k=n-m}^{n-1} (I(k) - m_I(n))^2. \tag{23}$$

To estimate the self-similarity index, H, we use an on-line version of the Abry-Veitch wavelet-based estimator in Roughan, Abry, and Veitch 2000). This method uses wavelet transformation to perform a weighted least squares fitting for the different octaves, in a multi-resolution platform. The computational complexity for this method is in the order of $O(M)$. The confidence interval of the estimated self-similarity index, $\widehat{H}$, by the Abry-Veitch method is given by

$$\widehat{H} - \sigma_{\widehat{H}} z_\beta \le H \le \widehat{H} + \sigma_{\widehat{H}} z_\beta, \tag{24}$$

where z_β is the $(1-\beta)$ quantile of the standard Gaussian distribution—in other words, $P(z \ge z_\beta) = \beta$—and

$$\sigma_{\widehat{H}} = \left(\frac{2}{(\ln 2)^2 2^{-j_1} M}\right)\left(\frac{1-2^J}{1-2^{-(J+1)}(J^2+4)+2^{-2J}}\right), \tag{25}$$

where $J = j_2 - j_1$, and j_2 and j_1 are two different octaves with $j_2 > j_1$.

Once $m_I(n)$, $\sigma_0(n)$, and H are estimated, they are used in equation 21 to predict the level of interference in the subsequent control window. In view of simplicity of mobile terminals, it would be possible to simply measure the interference at the mobile terminal, communicate the result back to the base station, adjust the model parameters, and predict the interference in the base station. The base station uses the predicted downlink interference to allocate the available power to non-real-time users.

The variance of the prediction error is: $\epsilon = \gamma(0) - \gamma_1^T \Gamma^{-1} \gamma_1$. It can be shown that the variance of error is not sensitive to the value of M for $M \ge 5$; therefore, the optimal linear predictor can be implemented using a small number of measured interference samples.

The proposed radio resource management procedure is shown as a two-step process in Figure 1. In part a of the figure, an estimate of the interference is obtained. Figure 1b illustrates the hierarchical power allocation process at the base station, where the power is first allocated to real-time users and then the remaining power is distributed among non-real-time users. Note that, in our proposed scheme, the interference predictor in Figure 1a is implemented for all users, including real-time and non-real-time users. This interference predictor can be implemented at the mobile station, at the base station, or at the radio network controller. In each case, the measured interference level, $I_i(n)$, where i is the user index, should be provided to the predictor in appropriate time scales. The base station or the radio network controller then uses the predicted interference levels, $\hat{I}_i(n+1)$, to allocate the transmit power in the next control window.

PERFORMANCE OPTIMIZATION FOR NON-REAL-TIME DATA TRANSMISSION

In this section, we propose two techniques to allocate power to backlogged best-effort traffic. In the first technique, the available power is allocated to users with the best channel conditions. In such an approach, the users with bad channel conditions may experience excessive delay; hence, the system may have poor delay performance. In the second technique, we use a utility-based approach (Kelly 1997) and propose an optimal utility-based scheduling algorithm to maximize the base-station utility for a given available transmit power.

In the control window n, let $\mathcal{G}(n)$ be the set of real-time users (e.g., voice and multimedia) served with a *guaranteed* delay requirement and $\mathcal{B}(n)$ be the set of delay-tolerant users waiting in the queue to be served under the *best-effort* service category. Because we consider in this section the power allocation in a given cell, hereafter we drop the cell index for brevity.

Power Allocation to Guaranteed Service Users

For a user i in $\mathcal{G}(n)$, with bit rate $R_i(n)$, and the required bit energy to the interference plus noise spectral density, ρ_i, the allocated power should be

$$P_i(n) = \frac{\rho_i R_i(n)}{W g_i(n)}(\hat{I}_i(n) + P_N(n)), i \in \mathcal{G} \quad (26)$$

where $g_i(n)$ is the channel gain between the base station and user i and $P_N(n)$ is the background noise power at the receiver of user i.

We assume that the total transmit power of the base station at instant n is $P_{max}(n)$. This value may be set either permanently at the network dimensioning phase or adaptively by the radio network controller. Therefore, the available power for non-real-time users in the control window n, $P_A(n)$, is

$$P_A(n) = P_{max}(n) - \sum_{i \in \mathcal{G}(n)} p_i(n). \quad (27)$$

Next, we distribute $P_A(n)$ among backlogged non-real-time traffic.

Power Allocation to Delay-Tolerant Non-Real-Time Users

Our objective is to find a set of users in $B(n)$—namely, $S(n)$—to maximize the total throughput of non-real-time traffic for a given value of the available transmit power $P_A(n)$ in the n th control window with length T_w. Let $p_i(t)$ denote the allocated power to the i th non-real-time user at time t. The signal-to-interference and noise ratio of non-real-time user i can be written as

$$\text{SINR}_i(t) \triangleq \frac{g_i(t)p_i(t)}{\sum_{j \in s(t), j \neq i} \xi_{ij} p_j(t) g_j(t) + I_i(t) + P_N(t)} \quad (28)$$

where $t \in [(n-1)T_w, nT_w]$, $g_i(t)$ is the channel gain between the base station and user i, and $I_i(t)$ is the total interference received from the adjacent stations and from the signal transmitted to other real-time users in the same cell. The coefficient $0 < \mu_{ij} \leq 1$ is the effective fraction of the received signal power from transmitter j that contributes to the interference experienced by user i.

Define the average rate of user i over control window n by

$$R_i(n) \triangleq \frac{1}{T_w} \int_{nT_w}^{(n+1)T_w} r_i(t)dt \quad (29)$$

where $r_i(t)$ is the instantaneous bit rate defined as

$$r_i(t) = \frac{W}{\rho_i} \text{SINR}_i(t), \quad i \in S(n) \quad (30)$$

where ρ_i is the required E_b/I_0 for user i, and $W = 1/T_c$ is the spreading bandwidth.

The maximum throughput of the non-real-time traffic for a given value of the available transmit power $P_A(n)$ is found from

$$\max_{S(n)} \max_{p_i(t), i \in S(n)} T_w \sum_{i \in S(n)} R_i(n) \quad (31)$$

$$\text{s.t.} \ \frac{1}{T_w} \int_{nT_w}^{(n+1)T_w} r_i(t)dt = R_i(n), i \in S(n) \quad (32)$$

$$r_i(t) = \frac{W}{\rho_i} \text{SINR}_i(t), \quad i \in S(n) \quad (33)$$

$$\sum_{i \in S(n)} p_i(t) \leq P_A(n), \quad nT_w \leq t \leq (n+1)T_w. \quad (34)$$

Note that, for maximizing the throughput, it is beneficial to allocate the maximum available power over the window $[0,T_w]$. Therefore, equation 34 holds with equality.

It is straightforward to show that the solution to the optimization problem (equations 31 through 34) belongs to the set of *time domain schedulers* (Viswanath, Tse, and Larioa 2002; Berggren et al. 2001; Bender et al. 2000). Generally speaking, time domain scheduling is a scheme in which the total power is allocated to a single user over a fraction of T_w. During this period, the base station transmits only to one user, and the rest of the users are kept inactive. Using time domain scheduling, in equations 31 through 34, a portion of T_w is allocated to a selected user and the base station transmits to that user with transmission power $P_A(n)$. Therefore, in each control window, $S(n)$ includes the users with the best channel condition and backlogged traffic at the base station. Transmission to such users maximizes the total network throughput for a given value of P_A(n). The order of transmission for the users in $S(n)$ during the control window n is not specified by the optimization problem in equation 31.

Delay Fair Resource Scheduling

We assume that each control window of length T_w seconds contains N_F frames of T_f seconds (see Figure 2). Data traffic is packetized into fixed F-bit packets and transmitted

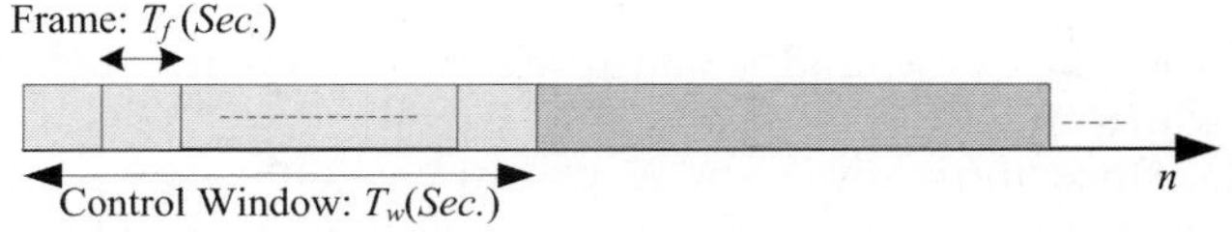

Figure 2: Multi–time-scale system; each control window contains M frames.

in an integer number of frames. At control window n, a number of packets destined to the users in the coverage area are waiting in the base station to be served. The available transmit power, to be allocated to the best-effort service, is $P_A(n)$.

Let $\ell_i(n)$ be the number of required frames for transmission of packet i in control window n,

$$\ell_i(n) = \left\lceil \frac{F}{R_i(n)T_f} \right\rceil, \tag{35}$$

where $\lceil . \rceil$ gives the upper nearest integer and $R_i(n)$ is the bit rate of the channel to the corresponding destined user. Note that $R_i(n)$ obtained from equation 29 depends on the predicted interference and the channel gain. In practice, variable bit rates are implemented by using the orthogonal variable spreading factor technique (see, e.g., Holma and Toskala 2000). Therefore, only a limited number of choices for $R_i(n)$ would be available.

For packet i, we associate the utility function, $u_i(n)$, which shows the benefit that network earns if the packet is served in control window n. Utility function serves as an optimization objective for packet transmission. It can be used to optimize radio resource allocation to build a bridge among different service and network parameters in different layers. The earned benefit modeled by the utility function provides a priority metric for a packet served by a base station; the larger the value of the utility function, the higher the priority of transmitting the corresponding packet.

The utility function $u_i(n)$ is a function of allocated network resources to that packet as well as its experienced delay. For non-real-time traffic, it is a function of $R_i(n)$ and $d_i(n)$, where $d_i(n)$ denotes the amount of time that the packet has spent in the system. The benefit earned by the base station is an increasing function of the wireless link quality. In addition, for two users with the same channel quality and backlogged packets at time n, it would be more beneficial—from the network point of view—to serve the packet with a larger experienced delay.

For a packet i, transmitted in control window n, we define the following utility function,

$$u_i(n) \triangleq \frac{1}{l_i(n)} \exp\left(d_i(n) - \bar{d}(n)\right), \tag{36}$$

where $\bar{d}(n) = \frac{1}{N(n)} \sum_{i \in B(n)} d_i(n)$ is the average delay and $N(n)$ is the number of backlogged packets. Note that in equation 36, a packet is given a large utility either when the corresponding user experiences a "good" channel condition or when it experiences a relatively "bad" delay. The utility function in equation 36 is similar to that given in Shakkottai and Stolyar (2002), which attempts to provide fairness in delay. Different utility functions can be designed to satisfy various design objectives. Generally, a utility function is defined by the service provider to quantify the trade-off between the performance (e.g., throughput) and fairness.

We define the total network utility at each control window n as the network performance indicator. Our objective is to maximize the total system utility as

$$\max_{S(n) | P_A(n)} \sum_{i \in S(n)} u_i(n) \tag{37}$$

$$\text{s.t.} \sum_{i \in S(n)} \ell_i(n) \leq N_F. \tag{38}$$

The inequality in equation 38 enforces the system downlink resource constraint. The output of the maximization problem, equation 37, is $S(n)$. Maximization (equation 37) selects the packets that result in the highest total utility, subject to constraint (equation 38). Therefore, at each control window, the solution to equation 37 gives the packets that are scheduled for transmission. Because we solve this optimization problem for each control window, hereafter we drop the time index n for brevity.

Scheduling Algorithm

It is straightforward to show that the optimization problem in equations 37 and 38 is indeed a classical combinatorial problem: the 0–1 Knapsack problem (0–1 KP; Keller, Pferschy, and Pisinger 2004). We note that 0–1 KP is NP-Hard; thus, the exhaustive search solution for KP would be to try all $2^{N(n)}$ cases, where $N(n)$ is the number of backlogged packets at time n. Obviously, such algorithms are not suitable for practical purposes. Instead, we use dynamic programming to solve equations 37 and 38.

Dynamic programming decomposes the optimization problem into smaller problems and then recursively obtains the value of the maximum utility in terms of the solutions to smaller problems (Bertsimas and Demir 2002). Consider the array $U(i : 1, \ldots, N, m : 0, \ldots, M)$, where N is the number of packets in the base station in the corresponding control window. The entry $U(i, m)$ contains the maximum achieved utility of any subset of packets $\{1, \ldots, i\}$ of the total allocated frames m

$$U(i,m) \triangleq \max_{S_i} \left\{ \sum_{j \in S_i} u_j \middle| \sum_{j \in S_i} m_j \leq m \right\}, \tag{39}$$

where $S_i \epsilon \{1, 2, \ldots, i\}$. The maximum achieved utility is $U(N, M)$. Now, $U(i, m)$ can be defined in terms of the solution to the smaller problems,

$$U(i,m) = \max\left\{U(i-1,m), u_i + U(i-1, M - m_i)\right\}. \tag{40}$$

The pseudo-code of the proposed algorithm is illustrated in Figure 3. In the proposed algorithm, we compute the values of $U(i, m)$ from the bottom up, using equation 40 with the initial condition $U(0, m) = 0$. To keep track of the selected packets for transmission, in Figure 3 we have considered the auxiliary boolean array $s(i, m)$, which is equal to 1 if the decision is to take the ith file in $U(i, m)$, and 0 otherwise. The set of the selected packets for transmission is then constructed using the array $s(., .)$ by the procedure in the second part of the algorithm in Figure 3.

SIMULATION RESULTS

To study the system performance, we consider a two-tier hexagonal cell configuration with a wrap-around technique (Harada and Prasad 2002). A universal mobile

```
Calculating the maximum achieved utility
for (m = 0 to M)
    U(0,m) ← 0;
for (i = 1 to N) {
    for (m = 0 to M) {
        if ((m_i ≤ M) and (u_i + U(i − 1, m − m_i))
> U(i − 1, m))) {
            U(i, m) ← u_i + U(i − 1, m − m_i);
            s(i, m) ← 1;
        }
        else {
            U(i, m) ← U(i − 1, m);
            s(i, m) ← 0;
        }
    }
}
Constructing the answer set
K=M;
for (i = N to 1) {
    if (s(i, K) == 1) {
        output i;
        K ← K − m_i;
    }
}
```

Figure 3: A dynamic programming approach for optimal downlink resource allocation

telecommunications system (UMTS; Holma and Toskala 2000) cellular network, with a fast power controller running at 1500 updates per second, is simulated. Cross-correlation between the codes is assumed to be 0.5. Three traffic types are used: 12.2 kbps voice (with the required $E_b/I_0 = 5$ dB), 32 kbps data (with the required $E_b/I_0 = 3$ dB), and 64 kbps data (with the required $E_b/I_0 = 2$ dB). We assume a steady 5 Erlangs of voice traffic. For data traffic, we assume Pareto call duration. The control window is $T_w = 10$ ms.

We assume that the channel gain $g^c(n)$ is given by equation 9. The Gudmundson correlation model (Stuber 1996) with $\sigma_c = 8$ dB and $T_f = 100$ ms is used for log-normal shadowing. Users are distributed uniformly in the cell coverage area and have different service types. The details of the simulation setting are given in Table 1.

Table 1: Simulation Parameters

Parameter	Value
Number of BSs	19
Cell Radius	100 m
Base Station Transmit Power	10 W
Physical Layer	Based on UMTS
Power Control	Fast Power Control 1500/s
T_w	10 ms
Standard Deviation of Fading	8 dB
Loss Exponent	−4
Thermal Noise Density	−174.0 dBm/Hz
T_f	100 ms
$E\xi^1$	0.5
Services	12.2 kbps voice, 32 and 64 kbps data
12.2 kbps voice	$E_b/I_0 = 5$ dB, 5 Erlangs
32 kbps data	$E_b/I_0 = 3$ dB, Pareto Dist. Pareto Dist., $\alpha_1 = 1.5$, $E\tau_1 = 2$ s
64 kbps data	$E_b/I_0 = 2$ dB, Pareto Dist. Pareto Dist., $\alpha_2 = 1.8$, $E\tau_2 = 1.5$ s
Bit Rates (non-real-time traffic)	16, 32, 64, 144, 384 kb/s

Model Validation

In the aforementioned configuration, we studied the time trace of the received downlink interference measured at different locations. Figure 4 illustrates segments of the received interference time trace (shifted to time 0) in the time scales of $t_s = 100$ ms, 250 ms, 500 ms, and 1s. Measurements were taken at an arbitrary location in cell $c = 1$. High variations are seen in traces of different time scales. A bursty behavior, which is the same for all time scales, is observed. As predicted earlier, the figure shows that the total interference is a self-similar process.

We also estimate the values of the self-similarity index H using the Whittle estimator (Paxson 1995). The Whittle estimator gives $H = 0.65$. Extensive simulations on the self-similarity in the total downlink interference under different channel and service combinations are also presented in Navaie et al. (2006).

We will now show that fGn is an appropriate model for $I(n)$. We use the quantile-quantile (Q-Q) plot (Beran 1994) to show that the total interference is a Gaussian process. The Q-Q plot is a graphical technique that determines whether two data sets have the same probability distribution. A Q-Q plot is a plot of the quantiles of the first data set against the quantiles of the second data set. A quantile is the fraction of points whose values are smaller than the given value; that is, the x percent quantile is a point at which x percent of the points in the data set have values smaller than the given value and $(1 - x)$ percent have values larger than that value. If the two sets come from a population with the same distribution, the points should fall approximately along the 45-degree reference line. The received total interference values are the first data set, and the values generated by a Gaussian distribution with the same mean and variance are in the second data set. In Figure 5, the Q-Q plot shows that the received total interference for the aforementioned configuration can be closely approximated by the Gaussian distribution.

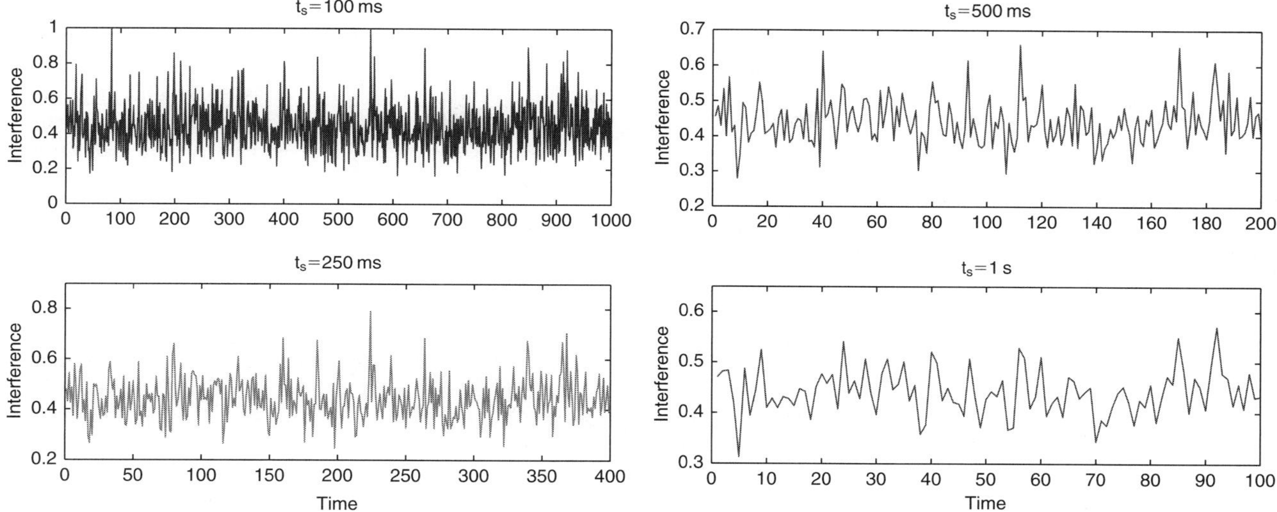

Figure 4: The total interference versus time for a multiservice DS-CDMA network with a mixture of voice and long-range dependent data services

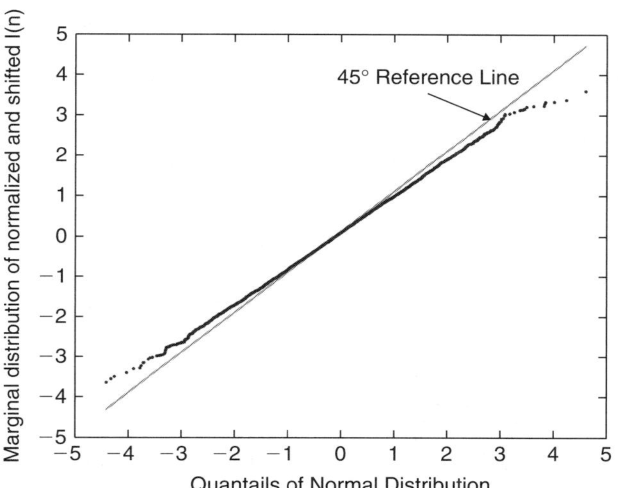

Figure 5: The Q-Q plot for the marginal distribution of total interference

Performance of the Adaptive-Predictive Method

To study the performance of the proposed method, we add a fourth non-real-time traffic. This traffic constitutes fixed-size packets with Poisson arrival with rate λ. We use a linear predictor with $M = 5$ taps to predict the interference level; we have found that the predictor error is not sensitive to the value of M for $M \geq 5$.

We have run fifty independent simulation trials with users uniformly dispersed in the cell coverage area. In the sequel, we report the average values in these runs for two systems. The first system (System A) uses the proposed method in this chapter for interference prediction. A confidence interval of 95 percent for the estimate of the self-similarity index, H, is considered. For non-real-time traffic, we first consider System A using the throughput-optimal time domain scheduling (System A-TDS-Th) in equations 31 through 34, and the utility-maximized time domain scheduling in equations 37 and 38 (System A-TDS-U). The second system (System B) uses the average values of the last five samples of the measured interference as the predicted value. We consider System B using the throughput-optimal time domain scheduling (System B-TDS-Th) in equations 31 through 34, and without it (System B-CDMA).

We compare the cell throughput for the non-real-time data service of the systems A and B for different values of the interference self-similarity index H. We consider System B-CDMA as the benchmark and normalize the cell throughput in each case to the corresponding value of the throughput in System B-CDMA. The results are illustrated in Figure 6. A significant improvement in the average cell throughput is seen in Figure 6 where our proposed adaptive-predictive method for interference

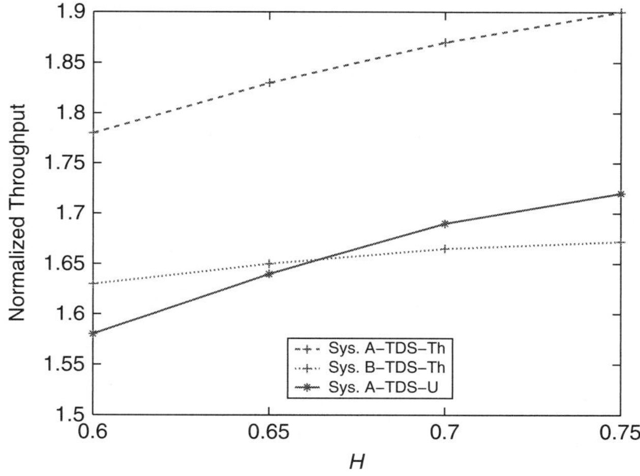

Figure 6: The normalized average cell throughput versus H

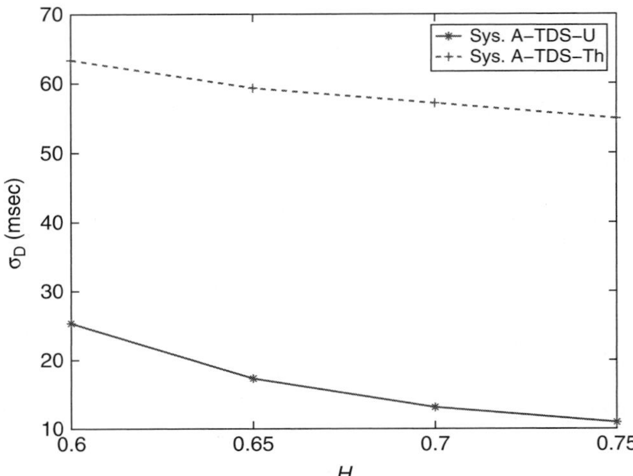

Figure 7: The standard deviation of the packet delay versus H

prediction is used. As expected, the cell throughput of System A-TDS-U is smaller than that of System A-TDS-Th because we trade the throughput for the delay fairness.

In Figure 6, it is also interesting to note that even for larger values of H, System A-TDS-U outperforms System B-TDS-Th. This is a result of the more accurate interference predication using our proposed predictive-adaptive method.

We have also found the standard deviation of the actual packet delay for systems A-TDS-U and A-TDS-Th. A small value for the standard deviation indicates fairness in delay. As can be seen in Figure 7, by using the utility-based optimization, the fairness in delay is significantly improved.

An important question to ask is: "What is the impact of applying our proposed method on the self-similarity of interference?" Because the self-similarity of downlink interference emanates from user traffic characteristics, the application of the proposed scheme—and possibly other radio resource control mechanisms—would not alter the self-similarity of the downlink interference; however, it may alter the model parameters. Table 2 illustrates the estimated values of H for the cellular network with the parameters given in Table 1 and with a 95 percent confidence interval after our proposed method is applied. In this table, $\hat{H}$ of five independent simulation runs with different non-real-time packet arrival rates for the given throughput $R = 5000$ bps are presented. The results in Table 2 confirm the following two points: first, the interference in the downlink is self-similar, as its self-similarity index is greater than 0.5; and second, the self-similarity index does not depend on the arrival rates of non-real-time traffic. This is because the self-similarity in the downlink interference emanates from the traffic characteristics of the real-time calls, which have heavy-tail call durations.

Table 2: Estimated H for Different Simulation Runs

	$\hat{H}$ for Different Runs of Simulation				
$\lambda = 5$	0.6431	0.6357	0.6201	0.6520	0.6461
$\lambda = 10$	0.6373	0.6480	0.6542	0.6516	0.6391
$\lambda = 15$	0.6512	0.6439	0.6448	0.6484	0.6435
$\lambda = 20$	0.6405	0.6534	0.6350	0.6282	0.6431

CONCLUSION

In this chapter, we formulated the total downlink interference in a multiservice cellular DS-CDMA network as a stochastic process that depends on the traffic characteristics of users, the transmit power, and the channel variations. We have shown that, under certain conditions, the auto-correlation function of the total interference is a regularly varying function. We further proposed an as-s model for the total interference and derived the conditions for the channel and traffic characteristics under which the as-s model for the total downlink interference is valid. We then used the predictive structure of the total downlink interference to maximize non-real-time data throughput in a multiservice DS-CDMA cellular network. We proposed a model-based linear adaptive-predictive method to estimate the level of interference. The estimated downlink interference of all users is then used in a resource manager to increase the system throughput and minimize the delay for non-real-time data transmission. The simulation studies also confirm that the interference model is valid for a broad range of arrival rates of non-real-time traffic. The self-similarity of downlink interference persists even after the time domain scheduler is applied.

GLOSSARY

Base Station: A physical network element in the radio access network that is responsible for radio transmission and reception to or from the user terminal.

Cross-layer Modeling: *Cross-layer design* refers to a design done by actively exploiting the dependence between different network layers to obtain performance gains. This is in sharp contrast with the layered design, in which functionalities located at different isolated layers are designed independently based on a standard set of outputs provided by lower layers.

Inter System Interference: The received interference originated as a result of the operation of other wireless systems in the same area that share the same set (or part of that set) of radio resources.

Intra System Interference: The received interference originated as a result of the communication to/from other users in that system.

Multi-user Diversity: A potential form of diversity inherent in a wireless network with multipleusers, provided by independent time-varying channels across the different users. Multi-user diversity gain is achieved via exploiting delay tolerance of non-real-time traffic to opportunistically schedule the transmission when corresponding time-varying channel capacity happens to be at (or near) its peak.

Network Capacity: The number of users in the coverage area that can be supported concurrently by the network with a certain level of QoS. The network capacity is related to different parameters, including radio access network technology, radio transmission characteristics of the network area, users' traffic profiles, and their spatial distribution.

Network Coverage Area: A geometrical area in which radio transmission and reception to or from the user terminal with certain signal quality is achievable.

Radio Resource: In wireless communication, different approaches are utilized to share the scarce wireless medium among multiple users. In most of these approaches, the wireless medium is modeled as a quantity called *radio resource*. Examples of radio resource include the allocated transmit power in DS-CDMA, the number of time slots in time division multiple access (TDMA), and the number of subchannels in frequency division multiple access (FDMA).

Radio Resource Management: A general term for to a set of functions that manage efficient access to the shared radio resource in a multiple-user wireless network. Usually, different functionalities in different network layers are utilized to tackle various dynamics in the corresponding time scales.

Wireless Packet Scheduling: A functionality that manages transmission scheduling to (or from) corresponding users subject to resource and service constraints.

CROSS REFERENCES

See *Code Division Multiple Access (CDMA); Wireless Channels.*

REFERENCES

Bender, P., P. Black, M. Grob, R. Padovani, N. Sindhushayana, and A. Viterbi. 2000. CDMA HDR: A bandwidth-efficient high-speed wireless data service for nomadic users. *IEEE Communications Magazine*, July, pp. 70–77.

Beran, J. 1994. *Statistics for long-memory processes*. New York: Chapman & Hall.

Berggren, F., S. L. Kim, R. Jäntti, and J. Zander. 2001. Joint power control and intra-cell scheduling of DS-CDMA non-real-time data. *IEEE Journal on Selected Areas in Communications* 19(10): 1860–70.

Bertsimas, D., and R. Demir. 2002. An approximate dynamic programming approach to multidimensional knapsack problems. *Management Science* 48(4): 550–65.

Bingham, N. H., C. M. Goldie, and J. L. Teugels. 1987. *Regular variation*. Cambridge, UK: Cambridge University Press.

Brockwell, P., and R. Davis. 1991. *Time series: Theory and methods*. 2nd ed. New York: Springer-Verlag.

Chung, C. C., and S. V. Hanly. 2001. Calculating the outage probability in CDMA network with spatial poisson traffic. *IEEE Transactions on Vehicular Technology* 50(1): 183–204.

Erramilli, A., M. Roughan, D. Veitch, and W. Willinger. 2002. Self-similar traffic and network dynamics. In *Proceedings of the IEEE* 90(5): 800–19.

Evans, J., and D. Everitt. 1999. On the teletraffic capacity of CDMA cellular networks. *IEEE Transactions on Vehicular Technology* 48(1): 153–65.

Gudmundson, M. 1991. Correlation model for shadow fading in mobile radio systems. *Electronics Letters* 27(33): 2145–46.

Harada, H., and R. Prasad. 2002. *Simulation and software radio for mobile communications*. Norwood, MA: Artech House.

Holma, H., and A. Toskala. 2000. *WCDMA for UMTS: Radio access for third-generation mobile communications*. New York: John Wiley & Sons.

Keller, H., U. Pferschy, and D. Pisinger. 2004. *Knapsack problems*. Berlin: Springer-Verlag.

Kelly, F. P. 1991. Loss networks. *Annals of Applied Probability 1:* 319–78. Online article available at http://www.statslab.cam.ac.uk/~frank/PAPERS/loss.html.

Kelly, F. P. 1997. Charging and rate control for elastic traffic. *European Transactions on Telecommunications* 8: 33–37. Online article available at http://www.statslab.cam.ac.uk/~frank/elastic.ps.

Navaie, K., S. Valaee, A. R. Sharafat, and E. S. Sousa. 2006. On the downlink interference in heterogeneous wireless DS-CDMA networks. *IEEE Transactions on Wireless Communications* 5(2): 384–93.

Navaie, K., S. Valaee, and E. S. Sousa. 2005. Cross-layer modelling for efficient transmission of non-real-time data traffic over downlink DS-CDMA heterogeneous networks. In *Proceedings of IEEE International Conference on Wireless and Mobile Computing, Networking and Communications (WiMob2005)*, Montreal, Canada, August, pp. 92–99.

Paxson, V. 1995. Fast approximation of self-similar network traffic. University of California at Berkeley, technical report LBL-36750/UC-405, April. Online article available at http://citeseer.ist.psu.edu/paxson95fast.html.

Roughan, M., P. Abry, and D. Veitch. 2000. Real-time estimation of the parameters of long-range dependence. *IEEE/ACM Transactions on Networking* 8: 467–76.

Shakkottai, S., and A. Stolyar. 2002. Scheduling for multiple flows sharing a time-varying channel: The exponential rule. Online article available at http://citeseer.ist.psu.edu/shakkottai00scheduling.html.

Stuber, G. L. 1996. *Principles of mobile communication*. Norwell, MA: Kluwer Academic.

Taqqu, M. S., W. Willinger, and R. Sherman. 1997. Proof of fundamental result in self-similar traffic modelling. *Computer Communication Review* 27(2): 5–23.

Tsybakov, B., and N. D. Georganas. 1999. Self-similar processes in communications networks. *IEEE Transactions on Information Theory* 44(5): 1713–25.

Verdu, S. 1998. *Multiuser detection*. New York: Cambridge University Press.

Viswanath, P., D. Tse, and R. Larioa. 2002. Opportunistic beamforming using dumb antennas. *IEEE Transactions on Information Theory* 48(6): 1277–94.

Viterbi, A. J. 1995. *CDMA: Principles of spread spectrum communication*. Reading, MA: Addison-Wesley.

Zhang, J., M. Hu, and N. B. Shroff. 2002. Bursty data over CDMA: MAI self-similarity rate control and admission control. In *Proceedings of INFOCOM'02*, New York, June pp. 391–99.

Zhang, J., and T. Konstantopoulos. 2005. Multi-access interference processes are self-similar in multimedia CDMA cellular networks. *IEEE Transactions on Information Theory* 51(3): 1024–38.

Wireless Wide Area Networks

Anthony H. Smith and Raymond A. Hansen, *Purdue University*

INTRODUCTION

As organizations continue to expand their wide area networks to provide high-availability data access, many are turning to wireless technologies to resolve these issues. However, there is still a general lack of knowledge about the technologies and their associated capabilities. This chapter addresses issues important to identifying appropriate wireless technologies for implementation in enterprise wide area networks.

A *wireless wide area network* (WWAN) is a network that covers a vast area, usually measured in miles or kilometers, and uses the propagation of radio signals to transmit data. At a minimum, it consists of one *access point* (AP) and one client, or subscriber unit, at a remote site. The AP is usually deployed with a connection to a traditional wired network at a company's main office or service provider's central office. The connection is considered broadband with throughput rates greater than 200 Kbps. When microwave transmissions and advanced modulation techniques are utilized, throughput rates can reach 100 Mbps or higher (Wayne and Safran 2000).

Explosive growth in the numbers of network users and their corresponding traffic has resulted in the laying of thousands of miles of fiber-optic cable. However, the vast majority of *Internet service providers* (ISPs) and businesses still use T1's, *digital subscriber lines* (DSLs), or *integrated services digital network* (ISDN) connections to transition from *local area networks* (LANs) to *wide area networks* (WANs). WWAN hardware and its applications offer many benefits with little or no increased cost to the consumer. Companies that have implemented WWAN solutions have reported higher initial costs, although the cost of WWAN usage is usually lower over time, with a relatively short return-on-investment period. The main reason for these lower costs is that, once in place, a WWAN usually has no recurring monthly service fees, unlike traditional wireline implementations (such as a T1).

WWAN technologies and implementations have successfully replicated throughputs greater than a T1's 1.544 Mbps and are often ten times this rate or greater. As stated in "Understanding Wireless WAN Communications" (undated), nearly 97 percent of companies in large commercial buildings have no direct fiber access. A WWAN can often bridge the gap between the building and the high-speed fiber connection. As a result, WWANs have been increasingly integrated into the corporate world. WWANs can provide many new services, which will help drive down broadband connection prices for most consumers (Mehta 2004).

As demonstrated by Table 1, a comparative look at existing wireline WAN technologies compared to wireless WAN will reveal the reasons for the explosive growth in WWANs.

Table 1: WWAN Technology Summary

	PSTN	ISDN	T1	DSL	Cable	Fiber	WWAN
Availability	High	Low	High	Growing	Growing	Poor	As needed
Throughput	Poor	Low	Medium	Medium	Medium	Very high	High
Recurring costs	Very low	Medium	High	Medium	Medium	Very high	No: capital only
Right of way required	Yes	Yes	Yes	Yes	Yes	Yes	No
Distance from POP	N/A	5 miles	20 miles	15,000 ft	10 miles	100 miles	30 miles
Voice	Yes	Yes	Yes	Marginal	Marginal	Yes	Yes
Video	No	No	Marginal	Marginal	Marginal	Yes	Yes
Time to market	N/A	Slow	Medium	Medium	Medium	Slow	Fast

WWAN INFRASTRUCTURE

Generally, WWAN implementations fall into one of the following three categories (Intel 2005).

1. Backhauls: Point-to-point antennae provide high bandwidth requirements to a single location (similar to a T1 connection). This bandwidth may then be distributed via one of the next two categories of WWANs.
2. Last mile connections: Point-to-multipoint antennae connect residential and business subscribers (similar to xDSL or cable).
3. Large-area coverage access: Base stations are used to allow mobility and large user counts, often with limited bandwidth (similar to current mobile phone connectivity).

Although using the unlicensed frequency spectrum has obvious benefits (e.g., no licensing fees and lower equipment costs based on the economies of scale), there are times when using licensed bands may be beneficial. Currently, nine bands are set aside for licensed wireless network use (3.7, 6, 7, 8, 11, 13, 18, 23, and 38 GHz), providing significantly more available spectrum than those available within the unlicensed bands. Other benefits of using licensed spectrum include control by the Federal Communications Commission (FCC) to minimize interference in a given geographical area, higher power allotment, and better reliability because of reduced interference. In addition, there is an inherently higher level of security because of the limited-access nature of the licensed spectrum. This makes equipment for the licensed spectrums less readily available, which reduces the chances of "casual" attacks.

The disadvantages of licensed frequency use include paying registration fees to the FCC, higher equipment cost, and the limited availability of frequencies and channels. Typically, equipment based on licensed frequencies is more difficult to install and configure correctly. Table 2 shows typical performance and use of various spectra.

Delivering bandwidth wirelessly between two points is typically done one of two ways: (1) by dedicated backhauls or (2) through the use of distributed mesh topologies. *Dedicated backhauls* are point-to-point links that use high-bandwidth, low-latency equipment and are commonly configured in a star topology. This application is best suited for areas with clear line of sight between elevated locations such as towers. As more sites are added to increase distances from the location of the wireline central network (or Internet) feed, the cost of implementing dedicated backhaul units and the risk of one outage affecting multiple sites increase exponentially.

An alternative means of providing bandwidth to a distant location is to implement a *mesh topology*. In this configuration, each site can communicate directly with neighboring sites and provide dynamic bandwidth allocation to all sites. This provides additional redundant links between towers and minimizes the risk of a widespread outage. However, this comes at the cost of potential reductions in network bandwidth available to each site. Mesh topology is best suited for areas where line of sight is not available to the main bandwidth distribution points or where high levels of redundancy are essential.

WWAN TECHNOLOGIES

Cellular Providers

The telecommunications industry has changed dramatically since the first telephone company was started in 1877. AT&T, formerly the leading U.S. communications organization since the nineteenth century, no longer provides full service and support to all U.S. users. The industry's focus has shifted from simple connectivity and basic voice conversations to the transmission of voice, data, and information. As technology progresses, new facets of telecommunications are being forged. Light and fiber optics, rather than electricity and copper wires, are the new backbone structures (AT&T 2005). Industry forerunners are pursuing systems that provide mobility, accessibility, reliability, high data rates, and security.

Consumers, both residential and business, seek smaller, more portable, and more versatile devices that increase productivity (AT&T 2005). Mobile wireless devices include *personal digital assistants* (PDAs), new smart cell phones, and laptops that give the user the ability to have data access from anywhere. As a result, telecommunications companies scramble to implement new wireless network technologies to meet consumers' needs.

Table 2: Typical Performance and Uses of Selected Spectrums

Frequency	Bandwidth	Range and Coverage	Flexibility	Typical Uses
900 MHz	Low	High	High	Cordless phones, wireless speakers, wireless remotes, baby monitors, some remote control systems, traffic control systems, supervisory control and data acquisition systems
2.4 GHz	High	Medium	Low	Cordless phones, WiFis, wireless speakers, wireless remotes, Bluetooth, closed-circuit TV, microwaves
5.2 GHz	High	Low	Medium	WiFi, audiovisual repeaters
5.8 GHz	High	Low	Medium	Cordless phones, WiFis, audiovisual repeaters, wireless remotes, baby monitors

The goal of these new mobile wireless technologies is to present voice and high-speed data access anytime and anywhere. The new mobile networks require smart computers and radios, encoding and security, routers and switches, and, most importantly, packet-switched traffic. Packet-switched mobile networks allow all forms of information to be converted and compressed or condensed and then sent to an end user or back to a server. To efficiently and accurately send voice and data, the mobile wireless network must be able to meet the following important criteria (SPG Media Group 2004):

- widespread radio frequency coverage for digital transmission;
- the ability to hand off from location to location, tower to tower;
- high-speed transfers for mobility and accessibility;
- secure, guarded transmission to prevent overlap and bleeding; and
- a variety of terminals (cell phones, PDAs, laptops) that can access high-speed services.

The mobile wireless network technology that is capable of providing all of these features is known as *third generation* (3G). 3G networks can provide voice and data services for public, personal, and business applications (FCC 2005).

The protocol for all 3G communications was defined by the International Mobile Telecommunications-2000 (IMT-2000), a sanctioned standardization development by the International Telecommunications Union (ITU). IMT-2000 was attended by leading technological nations, including the United States, the United Kingdom, Japan, China, and Korea. Together, these nations defined the IMT-2000 as "a framework for worldwide wireless access by linking the diverse systems of terrestrial and/or satellite based networks. It will exploit the potential synergy between digital mobile telecommunications technologies and systems for fixed and mobile wireless access systems" (ITU-R 2005). The three mostly widely distributed 3G architectures presented in IMT-2000 include:

1. *wideband code division multiple access* (W-CDMA), also called *universal mobile telecommunications system* (UMTS), which uses wide direct spread spectrum;
2. *CDMA multicarrier* (CDMA2000); and
3. *time-division multiple access* (TDMA) single carrier (*enhanced data rates for GSM evolution,* or EDGE).

Of the three 3G architectures being implemented, UMTS and CDMA2000 are the most common. These provide for a transition from existing 2 and 2.5G (a step toward 3G that did not provide for the data rates required by 3G). The 3G architecture increases the available data rates, security, and capabilities of all mobile wireless devices that utilize its features.

UMTS is based on the existing GSM and *general packet radio service* (GPRS) architecture. Its features include:

- transfer rates of 144 kbps mobile to 2Mbps fixed (indoor),
- uplink frequencies of 1885–2025 MHz and downlink frequencies of 2110–2200 MHz,
- the W-CDMA protocol for uplink and downlink communications,
- GSM backward compatibility, and
- *subscriber identity module* (SIM) card interoperability from network to network and device to device.

As the 2G technology GSM was being upgraded to UMTS, more innovation was needed to maximize connectivity (UMTS Forum undated). The European Union and the European Telecommunication Standards Institute (ETSI) were already collaborating on development and deployment issues. The partnership had unified companies, including Vodafone, T-Mobile, Mobitel, TIM/Teleset, Belgacom, 3, Tele2, O2, Orange, and Swisscom. With the European providers already embracing fiber-optic networks, a plan was devised to implement the next generation in network addressing: *Internet Protocol version 6* (IPv6) (Cisco Systems undated). Because of the limited number of unique addresses that could be generated by the current *Internet Protocol version 4* (IPv4), only a small number of mobile wireless users would have access to the new packetized data network. IPv6 utilizes hexadecimal numbering (0–9, A–F) to provide an IP address for every network device in the world because of its increased (128-bit) address space. Each new mobile device or user could be issued an IP to be used with mobile terminals. The technology provided maximum access to all networks and users with the ability to swap SIM cards and to port and store terminal information for multiple devices (Vodafone Group 2005).

The mobile wireless initiative in East Asia is particularly expansive, with the three largest users of 3G networks being China, Japan, and Korea. Korea has the greatest concentration of mobile users of any nation in the world. Mobile consumers in these markets have made wireless devices an essential part of their lives. Users manipulate advanced PDAs, smart cell phones, and laptops to access e-mail, online resources, and business applications. The wireless mobile terminals are more than a means of network connectivity, they are tools and instruments.

The landscape of the mobile wireless in Asia is truly 3G. The industry in China and Korea is primarily regulated by the government and several national companies. To compete effectively in the international economic realm, East Asian governments recognized the need to attract more corporate investment and innovation. To make this a reality, the decision to deploy fiber optics throughout these nations was made (Flynn 2005). With a largely rural, agricultural population, China already had a cellular phone base working on the 2G GSM platform. China's Research Institute of Telecommunications developed a partnership with TekTronix to implement that nation's first GPRS network, an interim technology between 2G and 3G. Korea's Telecommunications Technologies Association chose to use CDMA (Telecommunications Technology Association 2001).

In Japan, fiber optics had long been expected to replace copper and wire networks by the mid-1990s. NTT DoCoMo, the leading telecommunications provider in the country, began its research into 3G in the 1990s (SPG Media Group 2004). The Association of Radio Industry and Business (ARIB) and Telecommunication Technology Committee (TTC), Japan's version of the U.S. FCC and the American National Standards Institute, jointly decided that the 2G CDMA standard would be the framework for its move to 3G. There is speculation that CDMA can also evolve into 3.5G and 4G technologies (with much higher data rates and better mobility). With Vodafone Japan (a subsidiary of the European telecommunications giant Vodafone), DoCoMo began to import 3G innovations for its main testing grounds. Vodafone Japan's implementation used GSM and UMTS technologies. To meet the standard that was set by the TTC and ARIB, Vodafone added cross functionality with CDMA-based networks. NTT DoCoMo introduced the first 2.5G technology, i-Mode, in February 1999. By 2001, DoCoMo and its vendors had worked out most of the problems with i-Mode and began to deploy full 3G to its customer base. The new service, renamed FOMA, was an instant success. By late 2001, DoCoMo's FOMA service had coverage to 90 percent of its customers (nearly 40 million subscribers). As of 2005, 98 percent of the Japan population was covered by DoCoMo's FOMA service, and it continues to grow.

Unlike the European and Asian networks, the American mobile wireless vendors and suppliers lack the unification that aided the European GSM and UMTS movement. There are four major American wireless providers: AT&T Wireless, Sprint Communications Corporation (with Nextel Communications), T-Mobile, and Verizon Wireless (with 45 percent of its financing from a Vodafone Group division). There are also smaller regional providers that pay fees to use the networks of these nationwide mobile wireless carriers. Within these corporations, each has its own private practices, proprietary standards, and, most importantly, 2G technologies (GSM Association 2005). See Table 3.

Although all of these providers are members of the same wireless consortiums, receive terminals from the same vendors, and are regulated by the Federal Communications Commission, these Fortune 500 companies do not generally share research, advancements, or breakthroughs. Although the EU–ETSI partnership actually defined a local, nationwide, and continentwide standards for use and development, there is no such agreement among these four providers and the FCC.

Table 3: Major U.S. Cellular Providers

Carrier	2G Technology (Current)	3G Technology (Future)	International Access
Cingular	GSM	UMTS	Roaming in 170 countries
T-Mobile	GSM	UMTS	Roaming in 140 countries
Sprint	CDMA / iDEN	EvDO / WCDMA	Roaming in 35 countries
Verizon	CDMA	EvDO / WCDMA	Roaming in 11 countries

The four primary carriers have harnessed 2G technologies and are researching and slowly implementing 3G. Cingular has released its GPRS technology, claiming that it has features of 3G but is based on GSM 2G technology. GPRS is often referred to as 2.5G because it is not fully 3G (Wireless Internet Institute 2004). Its features include the following:

- use of GSM (both *time* and *frequency division multiple access*, or TDMA and FDMA) and TDMA technologies to increase data throughput;
- use of four time slots for downlink and one slot for uplink;
- theoretical throughput of 20–200 Kbps;
- division into classes (classes 4, 6, 8, 10, etc.) that use more time slots for downlink and uplink; and
- attempted incorporation of Internet Protocol, point-to-point protocol, and X.25 protocol suite into its connections.

Over time, 2.5G GPRS evolved into EDGE technology (sometimes called 2.75G). EDGE improved on GSM and GPRS techniques, raising speed to 384 kbps. Features of EDGE include:

- 8 PSK (phase shift keying) as modulation for advanced line coding;
- video and multimedia applications and connectivity;
- minimum compliance to the ITU definition of 3G;
- packet-switched, IP connection–based network connectivity; and
- 3G implementation via UMTS.

To counter the GPRS–EDGE technology, Verizon and Sprint independently deployed their 2.5G technology, CDMA2000 $1 \times$ Radio Transmission Technology ($1 \times$ RTT). The $1 \times$ RTT technology is based on the 2G CDMA, which uses a unique code to allow multifrequency transmission, and $1 \times$ RTT features:

- transmission speeds near 144 kbps;
- growth possibilities to 3.5 and 4G implementations;
- combinations of CDMA 2G frequencies;
- multiple time slots (like GPRS) to manipulate several frequencies and increase downlink and uplink capacities;
- improved quality of voice transmissions and security; and
- 3G implementation of *Evolution Data Optimized* (EvDO).

As of mid-September 2005, the progress of U.S. 3G deployment was as shown in Table 4 (Patterson 2005).

IEEE 802.16: Broadband Wireless Access

Originally, *broadband wireless access* (BWA) was designed to overcome the distance and load limitations of current DSL and cable networks. Customers outside of the

Table 4: Cellular Providers' Migration Plans and Time Frames

Technology	Provider	3G Migration Plan	Current Availability	Monthly Rates	Nationwide Rollout
GSM	Cingular	UMTS	13 major markets	~$80/mo	End of 2006
	T-Mobile	UMTS	No	N/A	2007
CDMA	Verizon	1 × EvDO	Most metropolitan markets	~$60/mo	End of 2006
	Sprint	1 × EvDO	No	N/A	Begin in early 2006

distance and load limitations are unable to use these networks. The high cost associated with running copper or fiber-optic cable to each subscriber location was the driving force behind the initial BWA technologies. As early as 2002, there were an estimated 2400 *wireless ISPs* (WISPs) in the United States using mostly proprietary equipment. The use of this proprietary equipment has limited the cost effectiveness of using BWA technologies (Johnston and LaBrecque 2003).

In mid-1999, the IEEE recognized the need for a broadband wireless access standard. According to the WirelessMAN Working Group (2002), BWA was suffering from a limited reach because of the lack of a universal standard. Seeking to expand the availability of BWA, the IEEE started development of the 802.16 standard, which was approved for publication in December 2001. Since its approval, the 802.16 standard has undergone several amendments and revisions, including 802.16a, 802.16-2004, and 802.16e.

In essence, WiMAX (an acronym for Worldwide Interoperability for Microwave Access) is the practical implementation of the IEEE 802.16 standard. The WiMAX Forum is the nonprofit organization that developed the WiMAX compatibility standards and is responsible for testing and validating the products that are being developed with the WiMAX name. According to the WiMAX Forum (2005) the 10 GHz to 66 GHz specifications are complete and have been submitted to the WirelessMAN Working Group. The 2 GHz to 11 GHz specifications are nearing completion and will be submitted to the working group on completion.

Many of the world's largest telecommunications companies are betting that WiMAX holds the potential to combine the benefits of DSL, 3G, and Wi-Fi networking technologies into one platform and push broadband access into new regions and devices (Hines 2005). Although this may be true, it will be several years before such an infrastructure is in place (Singer 2005). Many public safety and utility applications for WiMAX are also anticipated, including meter-reading tools, traffic monitoring, and video surveillance systems.

According to Fujitsu (2004), the WiMAX Forum has chosen to use the 802.16 mandatory 256 OFDM PHY (i.e., *orthogonal frequency division multiplexing* and *physical layer*) interface as the required technology to receive WiMAX certification. This choice was made to increase interoperability with the European HiperMAN specification, which uses the same 256 OFDM PHY. Fujitsu (2004) stated that the WiMAX Forum is also currently evaluating the encryption options specified by 802.16-2004. Specifically, they are determining whether to adopt the *advanced encryption standard* (AES) specification as an alternative to the mandatory *data encryption standard* (DES) encryption.

In theory, a single WiMAX base station will be capable of covering a thirty-mile area with speeds as high as 75 Mbps to non–line-of-sight users. This will provide enough bandwidth to support hundreds of simultaneous users from a single base station (Intel 2005). WiMAX has several robust *quality-of-service* (QoS) features built into the protocol. With WiMAX, traffic can be managed based on subscriber's service agreement. The QoS provisioning offers a grant-request mechanism that allocates a portion of each transmitted frame as a contention slot. The contention slot is used to request and uplink a slot from the base station. This method is used to avoid the collisions that are normally seen in a *carrier sense multiple access with collision avoidance* (CSMA/CA) or *collision detection* (CSMA/CD) network with a large number of users (Fujitsu 2004).

The initial design for 802.16 was for last mile communications, providing high-speed data to people in rural areas or in countries with developing infrastructures. According to the WirelessMAN Working Group (2002), the initial 802.16 standard was designed to efficiently use the 10 GHz to 66 GHz bandwidth. The medium access control layer for the standard was designed to support multiple physical layer specifications. Using licensed frequencies in the 10 GHz to 66 GHz range two-way communications with varying levels of traffic can be achieved. The initial standard for 802.16 is restricted to line of sight between the transmitter and receiver, making it useful as a standardized wireless backhaul but not entirely useful for actual subscriber connections (WirelessMAN Working Group 2002).

The 802.16a standard was approved in January 2003. The 802.16a amendment covers medium access control modifications and additional physical layer specifications for 2 GHz to 11 GHz. This amendment includes both licensed and unlicensed bands in the 2-GHz to 11-GHz spectrum (Intel 2005).

The 802.16-2004 revision was ratified in June 2004 and replaces the previous 802.16a standard. As stated in a white paper from Fujitsu (2004), the 802.16-2004 standard specifies three PHY options. A mandatory PHY mode of 256-point OFDM is specified. In addition to the mandatory OFDM PHY layer, single carrier and 2048 *orthogonal frequency division multiple access* (OFDMA) modes are also specified. It should also be noted that the European Standard HiperMAN uses the same OFDM specification.

The 802.16-2004 standard uses duplexing to create bidirectional uplink and downlink channels for data transmission. The standard supports both *time division duplexing* (TDD) and *frequency division duplexing* (FDD). The licensed band solutions use FDD, while license-exempt band solutions use TDD (Intel 2005). Frequency division duplexing requires two channel pairs to reduce interference. One channel is used to transmit, while the other receives. FDD is well suited for voice because of its minimal delay. However, FDD does increase equipment costs because of equipment complexity. Time division duplexing, in contrast, uses a single channel for uplink and downlink. The uplink and downlink time slots can be dynamically allocated, depending on traffic load.

The 802.16-2004 standard also defines specific encryption schemes to be used. The data encryption standard is specified as the mandatory encryption scheme for data, and triple DES is specified for key encryption. The following encryption suites have been specified for use with 802.16-2004 (Fujitsu 2004):

- CBC-mode 56-bit DES, no data authentication, and two-key 3-DES;
- CBC-Mode 56-bit DES, no data authentication, and RSA-1024; and
- CCM-Mode AES, no data authentication, and 128-bit AES.

The 802.16-2004 standard uses spectrum in the 2 GHz to 11 GHz band for both licensed and license-exempt transmission. Table 5 shows the spectra that have been allocated around the world for 802.16-2004 use.

According to Intel's 2005 white paper on deploying license-exempt systems, the 2.5 GHz and 3.5 GHz bands have been selected for licensed use as shown in Table 5, whereas the 5.8-GHz band has been selected for worldwide license-exempt usage. The 802.16-2004 standard supports channel sizes between 1.5 MHz and 20 MHz within these allocated bands.

The WirelessMAN Working Group is currently developing the 802.16e amendment, which will cover physical and medium access control layers for combined fixed and mobile operation in licensed bands. In short, this amendment will add mobile clients to the 802.16 infrastructure. Mobile clients will be able to hand off between base stations, allowing roaming between service areas. For instance, a city could have several base stations servicing fixed and mobile clients. As a mobile client moves out of the range of one base station and into the range of another, a handoff between the base stations would occur, providing seamless roaming for the mobile client. Figure 1 below shows various WiMAX deployments (Intel 2005).

Table 5: Spectrum Assigned for 802.16 Deployments

Geographic Region	Spectrum Assigned for 802.16 (GHz)
North America	2.5, 5.8
Asia (Pacific)	3.5, 5.8
Europe	3.5, 5.8
Central and South America	2.5, 3.5, 5.8
Africa and Middle East	3.5, 5.8

IEEE 802.20: Mobile Broadband Wireless Access

The 802.20 standard, also known as mobile broadband wireless access, was created to fill in the mobility gaps that 802.16e left behind and to provide global mobility to its users (Table 6). Although the 802.20 standard is still a work in progress, it boasts the ability to have a range as far as 15 km (9 miles). According to Lipset (2003), a user can travel at a staggering 250 km/hr (150 miles per hour) and still maintain a constant connection through its handoff process! This is partially because of the fact

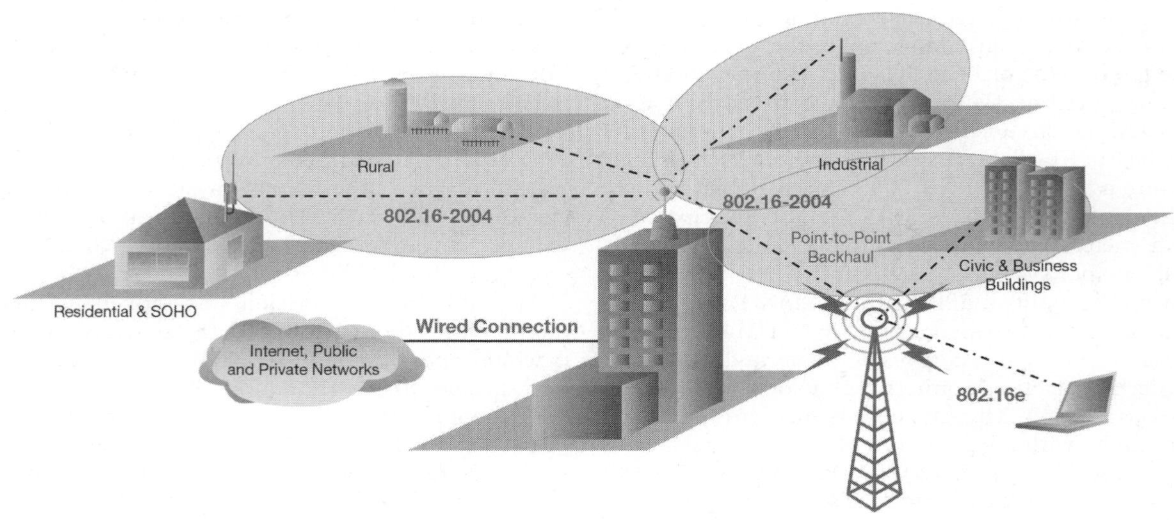

Figure 1: WiMAX deployments

Table 6: Comparison of 802.16e and 802.20

	802.16e	802.20
Type of mobility	Local	Global*
Physical range	1–3 miles	~10 miles*
Maximum velocity for handoff	75 mph	150 mph*
Maximum data rate	~70 Mbps*	16 Mbps
Specified frequencies for use	2–11 GHz*	3–3.5 GHz
Spectral efficiency	5 bps/Hz*	3.2 bps/Hz
Products to market (predicted)	Mid-2007*	2008

*Indicates higher-performing technology.

that the handoff process for 802.20 will have a latency of less than 20 milliseconds. As a result of this, the user will be able to maintain the connection while driving on the interstates or riding bullet trains. The standard will utilize the 3-GHz to 3.5-GHz frequency ranges and will be able to transmit data at 16 Mbps, which is the equivalent of more than ten households or businesses having dedicated T1 connections. According to IEEE 802.20 (IEEE 2005), the connection will be able to utilize four to six different channels and will have a spectral efficiency of 3.2 bps/Hz.

Clearly, 802.16e has many advantages over 802.20, as the WiMAX Forum will agree. In fact, lacking the backing and support of the WiMAX Forum alone may prove to be the end of the 802.20 standard, especially when one considers the dwindling support for 802.20 and the infighting and special interests within the standard's working group. Another advantage that 802.16e has is that the standard-based equipment will most likely enter the market long before the 802.20 standard because many companies such as Intel and CyberTAN have already announced product launches in 2006 and 2007. In contrast to this, Intel announced in 2005 that it would no longer fund research for 802.20 and would most likely not produce chip sets supporting 802.20. This earlier release may be enough to get much wider acceptance and infrastructure in place for 802.16e, thus leaving companies and users doubtful about upgrading to 802.20 equipment when it is finally available several years in the future.

Another advantage for 802.16e is that the standard will be backward-compatible with previous 802.16a infrastructure. On the other hand, 802.20 is not backward-compatible with any previous infrastructure, and all equipment for 802.20 will have to be purchased new at the time of installation. Also, the higher bandwidth that 802.16e provides (70 Mbps) as opposed to 802.20's 16 Mbps is a huge advantage for 802.16e. Many in the United States will say that the high-speed handoffs provided by 802.20 are irrelevant because the United States currently has few high speed trains in place, and most people who drive would not have passengers in their cars to utilize the uninterrupted high-speed connection that 802.20 provides to its users.

WIFI Use as a WWAN

Although originally conceived as an indoor *wireless local area network* (WLAN) technology, it quickly became apparent that 802.11 (WiFi) could be used to cover large outdoor areas or campuses for mobile users and for backhaul and last mile use. In most campus implementations, simply utilizing a high-gain, omnidirectional antenna will provide the necessary coverage area for mobility within that environment. By providing multiple overlapping cells in this way, ubiquitous coverage of a campus can be achieved. Generally, the same access points that are used for a WLAN can be used as the bridge to the wireline network infrastructure (resulting in access to local resources or Internet connectivity), the major difference being the type of antennae used between the two points (Cisco Systems 2005). When used in a wireless backhaul situation, each link end point typically has a high-gain directional antenna installed. The type of antenna used usually depends on the link distance. A Yagi antenna can be used in relatively short link distances of one to two miles, whereas a parabolic dish or grid antenna can be used to establish a link distance of as many as ten miles with clear line of sight. This backhaul configuration could allow the extension of an existing LAN by functioning as a layer 2 bridge, or the backhaul could connect two existing LANs by providing the connection between two layer 2 routers.

Many WISPs have used WiFi as a low-cost method of providing last mile connectivity. Unfortunately, poor network design ("underengineering") has led to many problems with 802.11 WISP successes. Utilizing WiFi as a last mile technology requires line of sight between the two link points. This configuration typically utilizes a high-gain sector antenna (or set of antennae to provide 360-degree coverage) at a centralized locale, and each customer location employs a high-gain antenna. The sector antenna at the centralized locale allows multiple connections from a client device within the coverage area. The customer's parabolic dish or grid antenna allows for a connection directly to one sector antenna. The antennae in this configuration provide a link distance of approximately one mile.

In addition to conventional wireless star topologies, many 802.11 vendors are now offering wireless mesh-based products. As described earlier in this chapter, mesh has many advantages in WWANs. Mesh networks are proving to be extremely useful for municipalities and other providers who wish to cover large areas with increased redundancy and multiple data paths. Each mesh AP, which includes traffic routing functionality, usually uses two different radios operating in two different frequencies. One radio provides coverage for wireless clients, while the other establishes and manages connections to other wireless mesh devices. In this way, the two separate functions are segregated from interfering with one another. Each radio interface on the mesh AP uses an omnidirectional antenna to provide the greatest coverage for connectivity to clients while also maintaining a connection to an adjacent mesh device or set of devices. These wireless mesh access points run a proprietary dynamic routing algorithm that determines the best path through the wireless mesh to an upstream wired network device.

In addition, because each wireless mesh access point does not require a connection to an expensive distribution system, cost savings can be realized versus a traditional wireless access point and wired infrastructure implementation.

CONVERGENCE

Key factors that warrant consideration on the best wireless technology include coverage area, bandwidth requirements, backhaul availability, security needs, and types of end-user devices. By converging multiple technologies, it should be possible to roam from one network to another. For example, because 802.11 currently offers the best indoor data rates and is the most cost-effective to implement in that environment, it only makes sense to use those existing networks for voice and data transport in that environment. As a user leaves the coverage area of the WiFi network, the ideal solution would be to access the next most appropriate (i.e., concerning throughput and coverage) and available wireless network. As 802.16 (WiMAX) becomes more readily available, it would be the next logical network to access with a roaming wireless device. If a WiMAX connection is not available, then transparently accessing one of the cellular providers' 3G networks would be the next logical step. Instead of one wireless technology that provides a constant connection no matter where users are located, using a mix of available technologies (whichever has the best connectivity and throughput at a location) seems to be the next logical step in wireless connectivity.

Security is an important consideration that has demanded attention in recent years. Integration of different wireless network technologies may pose challenging security scenarios. Although cellular networks such as 2.5 and 3G have built-in security features, integrating security with WiFi and WiMAX connections presents a significant and ongoing challenge.

Finally, the end-user device itself has unique requirements in order to function on a heterogeneous network. Although single devices that access multiple different wireless technologies are being introduced, the issues of maintaining a constant session between different networks has not been fully realized. Although protocols such as Mobile IP allow a user to roam across various networks, it will take a significant amount of work to fully implement. In addition, each WiFi network will need to be configured correctly, which is difficult to imagine based on the number of privately owned WiFi networks. Such integration depends on certain business and technical considerations. Business considerations such as service-level agreements and integrated billing systems will need to be implemented. Technical considerations such as interoperability between systems, design, and maintenance will need to be considered as well.

The number of mobile subscribers has increased at a rate that has far exceeded expectations. In 2000, there were 400 million subscribers worldwide; by 2010, worldwide subscribers are projected to reach 2.1 billion users. Wireless traffic continues to shift from traditional voice to multimedia communications. Future services are going to require increasingly larger bandwidth requirements. The convergence of wireless technologies is critical in managing this increasing demand. The convergence between 3G with WiFi and WiMAX will provide various advantages to both network operators and subscribers. Future mobile systems will provide high quality of service; easy access to high-speed Internet, voice, and video communication; and access to the global positioning system via a single converged device. Several leading companies—including Motorola, Sony Ericsson, T-Mobile, Cingular, AT&T Wireless, and Alcatel—are lobbying the WiFi-Cellular Convergence Alliance to provide standards with respect to billing, roaming, and handoffs. This convergence could be a step toward the promise of 4G wireless systems.

CONCLUSION

Wide area wireless networks can be effectively used to provide high data bandwidth to end users over a large geographic area. WWAN infrastructure can be as simple as a pair of transceivers (such as a single access point and client radio), or it can consist of hundreds of interconnected access points serving thousands of mobile clients. Numerous technologies can be used to construct a wireless wide area network, providing point-to-point and point-to-multipoint connections. WWANs can be used by individuals, companies, municipalities, or service providers as a wire line replacement technology, providing a high level of mobility for high-speed networks. Many WWAN technologies can provide throughput over 100Mbps using radios in the microwave frequencies along with advanced modulation techniques.

The many different types of WWAN technologies will continue to see explosive growth in coming years. The proliferation of cellular 3G networks by wireless service providers will offer users low-cost mobile access to data from many divergent devices, including PDAs, laptop computers, and smartphones. Broadband wireless access, including WiMAX, will increasingly be a viable, cost-effective alternative to wireline network access for residential, business, and municipal use. In many instances, WWANs will be used as a complementary technology to traditional wide area networks, giving network engineers a cost-effective means of providing network connectivity wherever needed.

GLOSSARY

Broadband Wireless Access (BWA): The group of wireless technologies that provide high throughput access to data networks.

CDMA2000: The third-generation (3G) cellular telecommunications standard for voice and data transmission that utilizes CDMA and a pair of 1.25-MHz channels to support peak download rates of 1.5 Mbps.

Code Division Multiple Access (CDMA): A spread spectrum multiplexing technology that utilizes all of the available spectrum and assigns each device a unique pseudo-random code to encode data for transmission.

European Telecommunication Standards Institute ETSI): A European nonprofit organization that is responsible for creating standards and documentation in telecommunications, broadcasting, and related areas.

Federal Communications Commission (FCC): The U.S. government agency that is responsible for regulating interstate radio, TV, wire, satellite, and cable communications.

Global System for Mobile (GSM): Formerly titled *Groupe Spécial Mobile,* the 2G cellular telecommunications standard that was created in 1990 to provide quality voice communication and data transfers as high as 9600 bps. GSM and its successors are the most widely deployed cellular systems in the world.

Orthogonal Frequency Division Multiplexing (OFDM): A modulation technique used in 802.11a, 802.11g, and WiMAX in which the digital carrier signal is divided into multiple subcarrier signals that are transmitted simultaneously, reducing channel cross talk.

Universal Mobile Telecommunications System (UMTS): The 3G cellular telecommunications standard developed by ETSI that is capable of providing high-quality voice communications with data transfer rates as high as 2Mbps.

WiMAX Forum: The nonprofit consortium of organizations that define compliance standards and testing and validation methods for device certification.

Wireless Fidelity (WiFi): The industry term for the IEEE802.11 standards, typically 802.11b/g.

Wireless Wide Area Network (WWAN): The use of digital radio equipment to provide a dedicated point-to-point connection or point-to-multipoint connections that typically span distances greater than 400 meters.

Worldwide Interoperability for Microwave Access (WiMAX): The industry implementation of the IEEE802.16 standards.

CROSS REFERENCES

See *Code Division Multiple Access (CDMA); IMT-2000 (International Mobile Telecommunications-2000) and 3G Wireless Systems; Time Division Multiple Access (TDMA); Wireless Broadband Access.*

REFERENCES

AT&T Corporation. 2005. The history of AT&T (retrieved from www.att.com/history/#).

Cisco Systems. 2005. Cisco Aironet antenna reference guide (retrieved from www.cisco.com/en/US/products/hw/wireless/ps469/products_data_sheet09186a008008883b.html#wp1005702).

———. Undated. Implementing Mobile IPv6 (retrieved from www.cisco.com/univercd/cc/td/doc/product/software/ios123/123cgcr/ipv6_c/sa_mobv6.pdf).

Federal Communications Commission (FCC). 2005. 3G (retrieved from www.fcc.gov/3G/).

Flynn, K. (2005). Partners for innovation: Global standardization collaboration intensifies. (retrieved from www.etsi.org/pressroom/Previous/2005/2005_09_gsc.htm).

Fujitsu. 2004. WiMAX technology and deployment for last-mile wireless broadband and backhaul applications (retrieved from www.fujitsu.com/downloads/MICRO/fma/formpdf/FMA_Whitepaper_WiMAX_8_04.pdf).

GSM Association. 2005. GSM: The wireless evolution (retrieved from www.gsmworld.com/technology/index.shtml).

Hines, M. 2005. WiMAX watchers admit it's unfit for mainstream (retrieved from www.extremewimax.com/article/WiMax+Watchers+Admit+its+Unfit+for+Mainstream/163765_1.aspx).

IEEE. 2005. Standard 802.20: Channel models document for IEEE 802.20 (retrieved from http://www.ieee802.org/20/).

Intel. 2005. Deploying license-exempt WiMAX solutions (retrieved from www.intel.com/netcomms/technologies/wimax/306013.pdf).

ITU-R. 2005. Radio technologies (retrieved from www.itu.int/ITU-R/).

Johnston, D. J., and M. LaBrecque. 2003. IEEE 802.16 WirelessMAN specification accelerates wireless broadband access. *Technology@Intel Magazine* (online at www.intel.com/technology/magazine/standards/st08031.pdf).

Lipset, V. 2003. 802.16e vs. 802.20 (online at www.wifiplanet.com/columns/article.php/3072471).

Mehta, S. N. 2004. Finding the reward in telecom's risk. *Fortune*, 150: 331–3.

Patterson, B. 2005. 3G cell phone service (online at: http://reviews.cnet.com/4520-3504_7-5664933-1.html?tag=more).

Singer, M. 2005. Intel pushes WiMAX around the globe. CNET News (retrieved from http://news.zdnet.com/2100-1035_22-5944874.html).

SPG Media Group. 2004. NTT DoCoMo FOMA 3G mobile phone service, Japan (retrieved from www.mobilecomms-technology.com/projects/foma/).

Telecommunications Technology Association. 2001. Specification for mobile wireless platform (retrieved from www.tta.or.kr/English/new/main/index.htm).

UMTS Forum. Undated. 3G/UMTS commercial deployments (retrieved from www.umts-forum.org/servlet/dycon/ztumts/umts/Live/en/umts/Resources_Deployment_index).

Vodafone Group. 2005. Mobile future (retrieved from http://online.vodafone.co.uk/dispatch/Portal/appmanager/vodafone/wrp?_nfpb=true&_pageLabel=Page_BOS_MainContent&pageID=AV_0517).

Wayne, R., and E. Safran. 2000. Digital microwave's wireless backbone. *InternetWeek*, 802: 35–6.

WiMAX Forum. 2005. Technical information (retrieved from www.wimaxforum.org/technology).

Wireless Internet Institute. 2004. Wi-Fi or 3G: Who's winning the duel over wireless data delivery? (retrieved from www.w2i.org/pages/oped/2004/0609.html).

WirelessMAN Working Group. 2002. IEEE 802.16 backgrounder (retrieved from www.wirelessman.org/pub/backgrounder.html).

Wireless Broadband Access

Hsiao-Hwa Chen, *National Sun Yat-Sen University, Taiwan*
Mohsen Guizani, *Western Michigan University*

INTRODUCTION

Recently, wireless broadband access (WBA) has emerged as a very active research area in the wireless communications community. As its name implies, a broad definition for wireless broadband access is "accessing broadband services wirelessly." Using this definition, WBA technologies bear two important characteristics features. First, they have to be able to operate wirelessly, such that the services can be provided without the need for wired connections. Second, they should be able to offer wireless services at a sufficiently wide bandwidth, over which many content-rich services can be included. In this sense, many wireless services available now can in general be viewed as WBA applications, which may differ from one another in terms of the size of their coverage areas and their capabilities to support mobility, as long as they can provide sufficient bandwidth. For instance, different third-generation (3G) mobile cellular systems, based on either CDMA2000 (1xEV-DV) or W-CDMA (high-speed downlink packet access [HSDPA]), can provide a bit rate of at least 2 Mbps, which is enough to support many data communication applications, such as Internet browsing, file upload and download, video conferencing, and so forth. The 3G infrastructure can be viewed as a type of WBA technology that supports mobility and covers a relatively large area. On the other hand, recently emerging ultra-wideband (UWB) can offer wireless connections to various stationary or portable terminals in a small area with a typical radius less than twenty meters. The data transmission rate of a UWB system can reach 500 Mbps or higher, making it an ideal means to provide wireless broadband access for personal digital assistants (PDAs) external data storage units, and other equipment that requires high-speed data transfer with little mobility support. Therefore, the UWB is also a WBA technology in a broad sense. Similarly, we can find many other currently available wireless services that can also be classified as wireless broadband access technologies.

On the other hand, the WBA technology can also be defined in a narrow sense, such that it is usually referred to as a particular kind of wireless networking technology that should cover a relatively large area (at least a few kilometers in radius) and is able to provide point-to-multipoint or point-to-point wireless access. Using this narrow definition, the WBA technology works like a wireless version of x digital subscriber line (xDSL) technologies to provide wideband access to houses, buildings, and other premises as an alternative "last-mile" or "first-mile" solution. Some WBA technology (such as that specified in the Institute of Electrical and Electronics Engineers (IEEE) 802.16e standard) can support mobile terminals at a vehicular speed. A typical example of WBA technology using this narrow definition is IEEE 802.16 standards, also commonly called wireless metropolitan area networks (WMANs) or Worldwide Interoperability for Microwave Access (WiMAX) technology. A similar technology called wireless broadband (WiBro) has also been developed in Korea.

In this chapter, we try to follow the broad definition to discuss the issues of wireless broadband access technology in general. However, some emphasis will be given to the introduction of WiMAX technology. The content covered in this chapter aims to offer readers both a global view of wireless broadband access and sufficient coverage of WiMAX technology.

While discussing WBA technology broadly, we will review the different wireless networks and standards currently available. IEEE 802.11, wireless local area networks (WLANs) and wireless fidelity (WiFi) are ideal for isolated "islands" of wireless connectivity; WiMAX (WMANs) and 3G (wireless wide area networks [WWANs]) are needed for long-distance wireless coverage. Meanwhile, some people believe that WiMAX and 3G are both required because their optimum platforms differ: WiMAX works best for computing platforms, such as laptops and notebook

Table 1: Different Wireless Networking Technologies for Different Applications

Technology	Standard	Use	Data Rate	Range	Frequency
UWB	802.15.3a*	WPAN	110–480 Mbps	<30 feet	7.5 GHz
WiFi	802.11a	WLAN	<54 Mbps	<300 feet	5 GHz
WiFi	802.11b	WLAN	<11 Mbps	<300 feet	2.4 GHz
WiFi	802.11g	WLAN	<54 Mbps	<300 feet	2.4 GHz
WiMAX	802.16d	WiMAX	<75 Mbps (20 MHz bandwidth)	Typically 4–6 miles	Sub 11 GHz
WiMAX	802.16e	Mobile WiMAX	<30 Mbps (10 MHz bandwidth)	Typically 1–3 miles	2–6 GHz
W-CDMA	3G	WWAN	<2 Mbps (<10 Mbps in HSDPA)	Typically 1–5 miles	1.8, 1.9, 2.1 GHz
CDMA2000 1xEv-DO	3G	WWAN	<2.4 Mbps	Typically 1–5 miles	400, 800, 900, 1700, 1800, 1900, 2100 MHz
EDGE	2.5G	WWAN	<348 Kbps	Typically 1–5 miles	1.9 GHz

*The IEEE 802.15.3a group was disbanded very recently, after the completion of the draft of this book chapter.

computers, whereas 3G is best for mobile devices like PDAs and cell phones. On the other hand, the UWB offers very short-range wireless connectivity, perfect for home entertainment environments, wireless USB, or IEEE 1394. Therefore, each technology is important for different reasons with regard to providing general wireless broadband access, as shown in Table 1.

This chapter is outlined as follows. In the next section we will briefly introduce the history of wireless broadband access technologies, focusing on the standardization process of IEEE 802 Task Groups in making various wireless networking standards. The following five sections will discuss WLANs, wireless personal area networks (WPANs), WMANs, WWANs, and wireless regional area networks (WRANs), respectively. Although this chapter covers different wireless data networks, we spend more time discussing WMANs (or WiMAX) to acknowledge the important role WMANs a play in wireless broadband access technology. The chapter concludes with a brief summary.

THE ROAD TO WBA

The development of wireless broadband access technologies is closely related to the historical background of wireless data networks in general. In this section, we will discuss the history of the first data network and concentrate on the role played by the standardization processes of various IEEE 802 standards.

Pioneer Wireless Network: ALOHANET

The history of wireless data networks can be traced back at least to the early 1970s, when a pioneer wireless data network project, called ALOHANET, was carried out at the University of Hawaii. The research project on ALOHANET acted like a testbed to develop a wireless packet radio network, which formed a basis for today's all-Internet protocol (IP) wireless networks. The objective for the ALOHANET project was to offer a wireless data-link connection among different campuses located on the different islands of Hawaii, to facilitate the data communications needed to exchange information, and to connect different remote data terminals with the mainframe computers situated in the central campus.

In ALOHANET, a very basic medium access control (MAC) protocol was used, which works in a random multiple-access scheme to allow all users to share the common communication resources in both time and frequency domains. Therefore, it works in a way that is similar to code division multiple access (CDMA) in terms of their capability to share resources in both time and frequency. However, the difference between the two is that ALOHANET usually will not guarantee successful simultaneous transmissions (due to collision) even if the number of active users is less than the system capacity; in CDMA, all simultaneous transmissions will be successful as long as the number of active users is limited to the system capacity. The most important feature of random multiple-access techniques is its suitability for supporting burst-type traffic (i.e., all traffic will be delivered in short packets, whose transmissions do not need an end-to-end circuit connection, to realize the connectionless information delivery). This in particular is well suited for IP-based wired and wireless networking applications. All random multiple-access–based networks offer services to users on a best effort basis, in which not all traffic will always be successful, but a relatively high resource-sharing efficiency can be achieved working in a packet-switched operation mode.

The random multiple-access scheme is one of the most widely used MAC protocol designs in today's all-wireless data networks. The simplest random multiple-access scheme is pure ALOHA, which originated from ALOHANET. It works in a very simple manner: when a packet is coming to a transmitter in the ALOHA system, it will just send it into the channel. The fate of the sent packet will depend on the status of the receiver, which should be located within effective radio coverage of the transmitter. If the receiver is busy (either busy transmitting or busy receiving from another transmitter), the sent packet will be ignored and the transmitter will realize the failure of the transmission after a fixed delay, which should be made longer than any possible turnaround time of the channel (which should be more than twice as long as the one-way propagation delay between the transmitter and the receiver). Then, the transmitter should resend the same packet after a random delay called back-off time, which is used to avoid a series of collisions due to possible transmissions from two or more transmitters that retransmit at the same time. The transmitter will continue the same process until it succeeds in sending this packet. The packet transmissions in a pure ALOHA system are illustrated in Figure 1. On the other hand, if the intended receiver does receive the packet from the transmitter successfully, the receiver should send back an acknowledgment, which will be used as a token of successful transmission by the transmitter.

Network Standardization by IEEE

The wide proliferation of wireless data networks can be facilitated by standardization of the technologies; otherwise, the compatibility would be a serious problem when end-user terminals move from one network to another, which may be designed by different vendors. Many international organizations have been actively pushing for the standardization of wireless data networks, including WBA technologies. Because of space limitations, in this chapter we concentrate on the discussion of various IEEE 802 standards for wireless data networks in general, although many other organizations are also working hard to make numerous standards for wireless networking, such as the European Telecommunications Standard Institute (ETSI), and others.

The IEEE is a nonprofit, transnational, technical professional organization with over 350,000 members. IEEE supports many activities, including conferences, publications, and local chapter functions. In addition, IEEE carries out an active program in standardization through the IEEE Standards Association (IEEE-SA). Although many IEEE-SA activities are global in scope, its efforts are accredited by the American National Standards Institute (ANSI). ANSI's oversight ensures that its guiding principles of consensus, due process, and openness are followed. IEEE-SA standards are openly developed with consensus in mind. Participation in their development and use is entirely voluntary. However, history has shown that standards developed in an open forum can produce high-quality, broadly accepted results that can focus companies and forge industries. The IEEE-SA oversees the standardization process through the IEEE-SA Standards Board. Project development is delegated to individual standard sponsors that are generally units of the IEEE's technical societies.

In fact, the IEEE develops and maintains technological standards based on the recommendations of individuals, with their expertise in the technology being standardized. Scientists, manufacturers, and end users provide input to the institute, which comes to a consensus about the standards suitable for a particular technology. Use of an IEEE standard is wholly voluntary, and the existence of an IEEE standard does not imply that there are no other ways to produce, test, measure, purchase, market, or provide goods and services related to the scope of the IEEE standard (IEEE 802.11 1999). Research scientists, manufacturers, and end users all benefit from the shared specifications contained in the standards. When everyone uses the standard, customers can use equipment from different manufacturers with no incompatibilities.

Here, we are interested in particular in the set of IEEE 802 standards that have a lot to do with the physical (PHY) and data-link layers of local and metropolitan area networks. These are the bottom two layers in the International Organization for Standardization (ISO)/open system interconnection (OSI) networking model, which are far from the application layer and are concerned with data transmission (and reception) between computers in LANs and MANs. The IEEE has split the data-link layer into two different sublayers: logical link control (LLC) and media access control, as shown in Figure 2. The IEEE

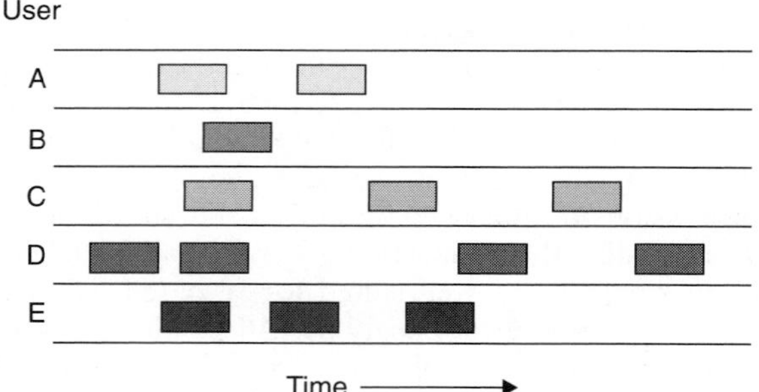

Figure 1: Illustration of random or uncoordinated transmissions of packets in ALOHANET in Hawaii in the early 1970s; five users (A, B, C, D, and E) exist, and any packets overlapped in time are collided

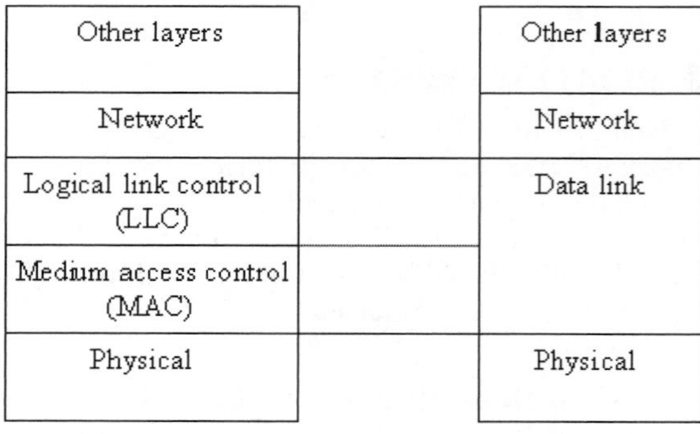

Figure 2: MAC sublayer and LLC sublayer split in IEEE 802 standards (Forouzan 2001)

Table 2: IEEE 802 Standards List

802.1	Higher-layer LAN protocols
802.2	Logical link control
802.3	Ethernet (wired)
802.4	Token bus
802.5	Token ring
802.6	Metropolitan area networks (MANs)
802.7	Broadband
802.8	Fiber optic
802.9	Isochronous LAN
802.10	LAN/MAN security
802.11	Wireless LAN: 2.4 GHz or 5 GHz band
802.12	Demand priority
802.13	Not used
802.14	Cable modem
802.15	Wireless PAN
802.16	Wireless broadband access (WBA)
802.17	Resilient packet ring
802.18	Radio regulations
802.19	Coexistence
802.20	Mobile wireless broadband access
802.21	Handover and interoperability in heterogeneous networks
802.22	Wireless regional area networks (WRANs) in TV bands

LLC protocol concerns the logical address, control information, and data portions of a high-level data-link control (HDLC) frame, whereas the MAC protocols deal with synchronization, error control, and physical addresses. The MAC protocols, such as the random multiple-access protocol discussed in the previous section, are specific to the LAN using them (e.g., Ethernet, token ring, token bus, etc.; Forouzan 2001).

Various IEEE 802 series standards were developed to offer technical standard references, which all people can follow on a volunteer basis. All widely quoted IEEE 802.x (where x can be equal to 1 to 22) standards are listed in Table 2. Not all IEEE 802.x standards were developed inclusively for wireless data networks, let alone for wireless broadband access networks. For instance, the IEEE 802.3 standards are concerned with Ethernet (often wired) communications. Originally, they supported 10 Mbps data rates, but as network terminals became faster and thus capable of running multimedia applications, and as the need to share high-speed servers among LANs became widespread, faster data rates were included in the standards. They were updated in the mid-1990s to include "fast Ethernet" transmission rates of 100 Mbps, and in the late 1990s the Gigabit Ethernet was standardized under 802.3 (Pahlavan and Krishnamurthy 2002). Experts attest that the two major drives of this industry have always been the ease of installation and the increase in data rate, the two important characteristics of Fast Ethernet and Gigabit Ethernet. Thus, Ethernet dominated other 802.3 LAN IEEE standards (the token ring and token bus).

Here, we are obviously interested in the IEEE 802.11, which specifies a series of standards on WLANs; the IEEE 802.15, which specifies a series of standards for WPANs; the IEEE 802.16, which specifies a series of standards for WMANs; the IEEE 802.22, which is a newly established standard project under the IEEE 802 group aimed at providing WRAN; and WWANs, which are usually implemented by cellular mobile networks. In the subsequent sections, we will discuss the context of wireless broadband access technology.

WIRELESS LOCAL AREA NETWORKS (WLANs)

Of all IEEE 802 standards, those for WLANs specified in IEEE 802.11 standards are by far the most widely seen in the literature concerning wireless networks. The main reason is that the applications of WLANs have been flourishing, and business related to WLANs has been going extremely well, as can be seen from the great number of hot spots that exist on the streets of any major city in the United States, Japan, and Europe.

The IEEE 802.11 technology comprises a series of standards, ranging from IEEE 802.11a to IEEE 802.11w,

Table 3: IEEE 802.11 Wireless Local Area Networks (WLANs)

802.11a	Wireless LAN: 5 GHz band
802.11b	Wireless LAN: 2.4 GHz band
802.11c	Wireless LAN: Higher layers
802.11d	Wireless LAN: MAC
802.11e	Wireless LAN: MAC, QoS, including packet bursting
802.11f	Higher layers
802.11g	Wireless LAN: Higher-rate 2.4 GHz band
802.11h	Wireless LAN: MAC based on cognitive radio
802.11i	Wireless LAN: MAC
802.11j	Wireless LAN: Japanese spectrum 4.9 and 5 GHz
802.11k	Wireless LAN: With radio resource measurement
802.11l	(Reserved, typologically unsound)
802.11m	Wireless LAN: Maintenance of the standard
802.11n	Wireless LAN: Higher throughput improvements
802.11o	(Reserved, typologically unsound)
802.11p	WAVE (DSRC) — Vehicular wireless access
802.11q	(Reserved, typologically unsound)
802.11r	Fast roaming
802.11s	ESS mesh networking
802.11t	Wireless performance prediction (WPP) — test methods and metrics
802.11u	Interworking with non-802 networks
802.11v	Wireless network management
802.11w	Protected management frames

as shown in Table 3. There are approximately twenty different IEEE 802.11 standards, each representing a specific wireless local area network technology/architecture. With a typical data rate between 11 Mbps and 54 Mbps, WLANs can also be considered a wireless broadband access technology that can provide many diverse data services, including Internet applications, video conferencing, and other multimedia options. Therefore, it is justified to discuss WLANs under the context of WBA technology, which is the focus of this chapter.

When developing the standards for wireless networks, the IEEE observed the radio frequency regulations of the U.S. Federal Communications Commission (FCC), because radio waves were the transmission medium of choice for wireless networking. In 1985, the FCC designated certain portions of the radio frequency spectrum for industrial, scientific, and medical (ISM) use, and these became known as the ISM bands, which include (1) 902 MHz–928 MHz, a bandwidth of 26 MHz; (2) 2.4 GHz–2.4835 GHz, a bandwidth of 83.5 MHz, commonly called the 2.4 GHz band; and (3) 5.725 GHz - 5.850 GHz, a bandwidth of 125 MHz, commonly called the 5 GHz band. Within certain guidelines, the FCC's regulations allow users to operate radios inside these bands without an FCC license, an obvious boon for the developers of wireless network technology (and for the users who do not have to obtain a license to operate their cell phones).

The 802.11 standards have evolved over time, and presently six methods for wireless data transmission are defined in the 802.11 standards. Each means of transmission represents its own physical layer design within a certain 802.11 standard. The first IEEE 802.11 standards were completed in 1997 and defined three of these physical layers for 1 and 2 Mbps data rates. An overview of these PHY layers is provided in Table 4 and also explained as follows.

1. The direct sequence spread spectrum (DSSS) physical layer uses the 2.4 GHz band and can transmit data at 1 or 2 Mbps. The DSSS technique was first used for military communications. To prevent jamming and, to a lesser extent, eavesdropping, radios that use DSSS transmit their signals across the entire available ISM band at very low power. This prevents interference from narrowband signals (jammers or others) and lessens the likelihood of transmission errors. Eavesdroppers may interpret these signals as background noise (IEEE 802.11 1999).
2. The frequency hopping spread spectrum (FHSS) physical layer also uses the 2.4 GHz band for transmission

Table 4: IEEE 802.11 Physical Layers

DSSS	2.4 GHz	1 or 2 Mbps
FHSS	2.4 GHz	1 or 2 Mbps
DFIR	850 to 950 nm (infrared)	None implemented
COFDM	5 GHz	54 Mbps
HR/DSSS	2.4 GHz	5.5 or 11 Mbps
OFDM	2.4 GHz	54 Mbps

Table 5: IEEE 802.15 Wireless Personal Area Networks (WPANs)

802.15.1	WPAN: Bluetooth
802.15.2	WPAN: Coexist with WLANs
802.15.3	WPAN: Ultra-wideband (UWB) technology
802.15.4	WPAN: ZigBee and low-speed WPANs
802.15.5	WPAN: Mesh networking (not finalized)
802.15.6	WPAN: Ultra-fast WPANs (not finalized)

at 1 or 2 Mbps, and also originated in military applications. Two communicating radios using FHSS change frequencies according to a predetermined pseudorandom pattern, and only remain on a given frequency for a split second (FCC regulations require the frequency hops to take place every 400 milliseconds or less). This technique minimizes the chances that more than one radio device will be transmitting on the same frequency at the same time. If a sender happens to detect interference from another radio at a particular frequency, it retransmits its data after the next hop to a different frequency. FHSS was phased out of 802.11 in the 802.11b standards.

3. The diffused infrared (DFIR) physical layer uses near-visible light in the 850 nm to 950 nm range for signaling (IEEE 802.11 1999). However, unlike infrared TV remote controls that need a line of sight to work, devices that follow the 802.11 DFIR standards do not need to be aimed at one another, permitting the construction of a true LAN (IEEE 802.11 1999). But, there are no wireless networking products currently available that implement this physical layer [17]. One potential source of interference when using this technology, for example, is a human being walking between a personal computer (PC) and its printer when they were trying to communicate.
4. The fourth 802.11 physical layer is defined by IEEE's 802.11a standards: the coded orthogonal frequency division multiplexing (COFDM) layer is capable of transmitting data at 54 Mbps by using the broader 5 GHz band. However, FCC regulations limit the transmission power used at these higher frequencies and thus reduce the distance higher-frequency transmissions can travel. For these reasons, radios that use COFDM technology must be closer together than those using the other physical layers introduced earlier. The obvious benefit of COFDM is speed. Cognitive radio technology has been introduced to allow IEEE 802.11a networks to operate even under potential mutual interference. This led to a new standard, called IEEE 802.11h, which applies two important elements of cognitive radio technology—dynamic frequency selection (DFS) and transmit power control (TPC)—to constantly monitor the environment to avoid possible interference to the primary users.
5. The IEEE 802.11b standards cover the fifth physical layer, the high-rate direct sequence spread spectrum (HR/DSSS) layer. Using this layer, data can be transmitted at 5.5 or 11 Mbps, rivaling the standard Ethernet rate of 10 Mbps; as a result, this has become the most widely used IEEE 802.11 physical layer despite only entering the scene in 1999. HR/DSSS technology is an extension of DSSS technology and is designed to be backward compatible with its predecessor (both operate in the 2.4 MHz band).
6. The sixth 802.11 physical layer is detailed in the IEEE 802.11g standards and is backward compatible with 802.11b. The orthogonal frequency division multiplexing (OFDM) physical layer allows 54 Mbps data rates in the 2.4 MHz band. The speed of transmission under OFDM and COFDM is sufficient to carry voice and image data fast enough for most users, and thus to provide wireless broadband access to end users.

WIRELESS PERSONAL AREA NETWORKS

The WPAN technologies can also be considered one of the ways to provide wireless broadband access, depending on the real bandwidth a WPAN can work with. The specifications of WPANs are given under the IEEE 802.15 standard series, and the different WPANs standards are listed in Table 5.

IEEE 802.15.1 Standard

The 802.15.1 standards define the PHY and MAC layers for small, short-distance wireless networks. The core technology specified in IEEE 802.15.1 is largely based on Bluetooth technology. The term *personal operating space (POS)* is introduced in the standard to refer to the small area covered by a WPAN. Defined by IEEE terms, a POS is the space around a person or object that typically extends up to 10 m in all directions and envelops the person, whether stationary or in motion. The IEEE 802.15.1 standards have been developed to ensure coexistence with all IEEE 802.11 networks (IEEE Part 15.3 2003). The 802.15.1 WPANs may operate in the 2.4 GHz ISM band (IEEE Part 15.3 2002), which is the same as that in which the IEEE 802.11 networks operate. Therefore, the IEEE 802.15.1 standards put forth a lot of effort to avoid possible mutual interference between the WPANs and other networks operating in the same unlicensed ISM band.

Much of this standard is derived from Bluetooth core, profiles, and test specifications (IEEE Part 15.3 2003). The objective is to make the 802.15.1 WPANs capable of employing Bluetooth devices, if desired. The terms *Bluetooth WPAN* and *IEEE 802.15.1 WPAN* refer to the specific and single example of a WPAN presented in this standard series (IEEE Part 15.3 2003). According to the standards, an IEEE 802.15.1 WPAN can be viewed as a personal communications bubble around a person. Within this bubble, which moves as a person moves around, personal devices can connect with one another. These devices may be under the control of a single individual or several people's devices that may interact with one another (IEEE PArt 15.3 2003).

Unlike the traditional devices used in WLANs, 802.15.1 WPAN devices often include digital cameras, PDAs, and global positioning system (GPS) units—the devices that run on batteries—which are generally more mobile than the servers, client computers, and printers found on a WLAN. Therefore, the 802.15.1 standards define smaller power levels and area coverage for WPANs (around 10 m) than for WLANs (around 100m). In addition, whereas WLANs generally have an unending life span, the life span of a WPAN is for as long as a master device participates in the WPAN (IEEE Part 15.3 2003). The 802.15.1 standards permit the WPANs to connect to 802.11 WLANs or 802 (wired) LANs, if desired (IEEE Part 15.3 2003).

802.15.1 WPAN uses fast frequency-hopping (F-FH) CDMA for its multiple-access technology, which implies that the hopping rate is much greater than the symbol rate. The Bluetooth standard employs frequency hops fixed at 2402+k MHz, where k = 0,1, ..., 78, with a nominal hop rate of 1600 hops per second. This results in a single hop slot of 625 microseconds. The modulation scheme used in IEEE 802.15.1 is Gaussian prefiltered binary frequency shift keying (FSK).

The Bluetooth specification has a raw data rate of 1 Mbps. However, because of the overhead reserved for the various Bluetooth protocols, the available net data rate is approximately 723 kbps. Bluetooth can support an asynchronous data channel, up to three simultaneous synchronous voice channels, or a channel that simultaneously supports asynchronous data and synchronous voice. Each voice channel is a synchronous link allowing 64 kbps in each direction. The asynchronous channel can support an asymmetric link of up to 723.2 kbps in either direction while permitting 57.6 kbps in the return direction, or a 433.9 kbps symmetric link. The actual data rates depend on the kind of error-correction capability employed, which is a characteristic of the type of packets being transferred ("Short Description of Bluetooth" n.d.).

IEEE 802.15.3a Standard

If IEEE 802.15.1 is not viewed as a fully qualified wireless broadband access technology because of its limitation of the highest data transmission rate, the IEEE 802.15.3a standard can be considered a WBA technology, at least in its broad definition, with its highest data rate being able to reach 500 Mbps.

The IEEE 802.15.3 standard defines low-cost and low–power-use protocols for high-speed (up to 500 Mbps) WPANs. UWB technology is supported, including ad hoc piconet formation and disassembly. The speed is meant to satisfy user multimedia needs (IEEE Wireless MAC and PHY Specifications n.d.). Low power use is ensured with protocols that either allow the WPAN to establish a (low) power setting for its devices, or allow communicating devices with a good connection to lower their power as long as the connection remains strong (IEEE Wireless MAC and PHY Specifications n.d.).

The core of the IEEE 802.15.3a standard is the UWB technology, which can be viewed as a derivative of spreading spectrum technology, in particular the time-hopping spread-spectrum (THSS) technique, which is also considered a multiple-access technology, being particularly suited for extremely narrow pulse transmissions. Before discussing the technical details of the UWB technologies, we would like to review briefly the history of the UWB technologies as well as the recent research activities carried out in this area.

Since the introduction of UWB technology to commercial applications in the early 1990s (Fullerton 1991), much of its initial research has focused on the applications of THSS (Win and Scholtz 2000), in which several pulses in each symbol duration are sent with a particular time offset pattern that is predetermined by a unique signature code for multiple access. The implementation of a THSS UWB system requires a precise network-wise synchronization clock. This inevitably increases overall hardware complexity at a transceiver, which used to be a major concern with regard to realizing a feasible UWB system at its early stage. On the other hand, direct sequence (DS) techniques can also work jointly with UWB systems to provide multiple access among different users within the same WPAN. The operation of a DS-UWB system does not need an accurate synchronization clock. The use of antipodal pulses in DS modulation can boost effective transmission power, which is very important to improve detection efficiency of a UWB receiver because of to the severe emission constraints imposed on power spectral masks specified in the FCC Part 15.209, in which the maximal transmitting power for a UWB transmitter should be lower than −41.3 dBm within the bandwidth from 3.1 GHz to 10.6 GHz.

In September 1998, the FCC issued a notice of inquiry (NOI), and, within a year, the Time Domain Corporation, U.S. Radar, and Zircon Corporation had received waivers from the FCC to allow limited deployment of a small number of UWB devices to support continued development of the technology. In addition, the University of Southern California (USC) UltRa Lab received an experimental license to study UWB radio transmissions. In May 2000, a notice of proposed rule making (NPRM) was issued by the FCC. In April 2002, after extensive commentary from the industry, the FCC issued its first report and order on UWB technology, thereby providing regulations to support deployment of UWB radio systems. This FCC action was a major change in the approach to the regulation of radio frequency (RF) emissions, allowing a significant portion of the radio frequency (RF) spectrum, originally allocated in many smaller bands exclusively for specific uses, to be effectively shared with low-power UWB radios.

The FCC regulations classify UWB applications into several categories with different emission regulations in each case. Maximum emissions in the prescribed bands are at an effective isotropic radiated power (EIRP) of −41.3 dBm per MHz, and the −10 dB level of the emissions must

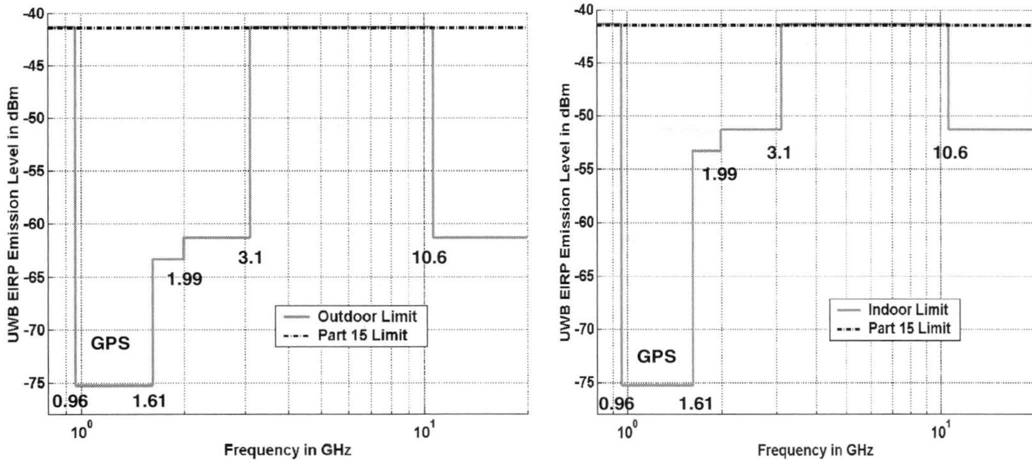

Figure 3: FCC regulated spectral masks regarding the indoor and outdoor UWB communications applications

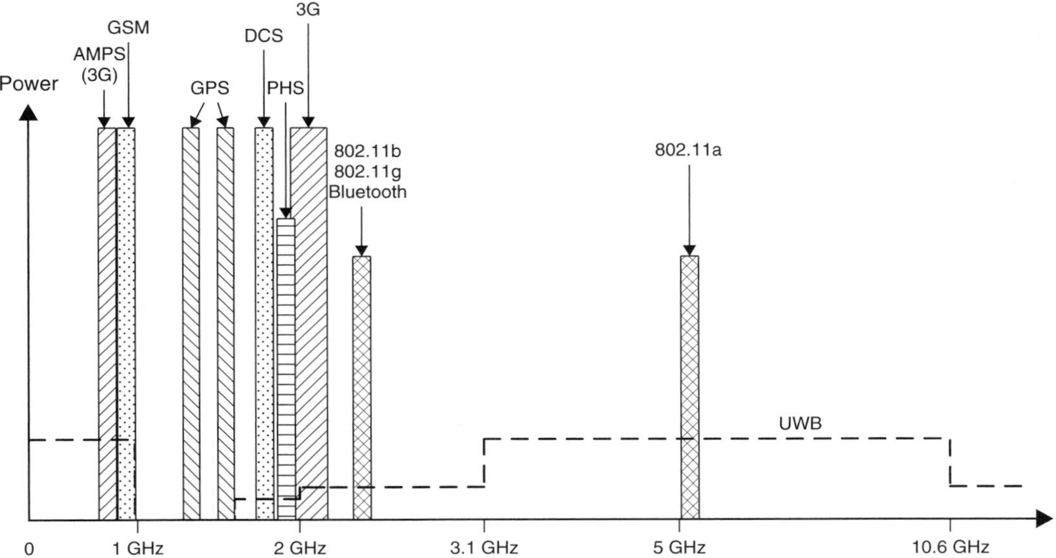

Figure 4: Other communications applications in the vicinity of UWB operating bands

fall within the prescribed band, as shown in Figure 3, which should be compared with Figure 4 to recognize other communication applications in the vicinity of the UWB operating bands.

It will be very interesting to summarize different types of UWB technologies suggested so far under the context of the IEEE 802.15.3a standard. There are four major UWB technologies that have been proposed. The first type is time-hopped (TH) or time-modulated (TM) UWB, which is a traditional UWB scheme that is often called impulse radio (IR) UWB. The TH-UWB is by far the earliest version of UWB technology and remains an important solution even today. The traditional impulse radio technology can be called as either time-hopped or time-modulated UWB; both names are widely used. The TH-UWB can be further divided into two subcategories, analog impulse radio multiple access (AIRMA) and digital impulse radio multiple access (DIRMA), which were suggested in Win and Scholtz (1998a, 1998b, 2000). The second UWB technology is direct-sequence CDMA-based UWB, as discussed earlier, and can be implemented with a multi-carrier CDMA architecture. Another UWB scheme that has gained much popularity is based on OFDM technology, namely OFDM-UWB, which can be implemented on a multiband (MB) OFDM scheme. The MB-OFDM UWB technology is particularly useful when cognitive radio technology will be used. In addition, some people also proposed frequency-modulation (FM)–based UWB systems, which can be implemented by swept frequency technology. Figure 5 shows a family tree for all possible UWB technologies that have been proposed so far. Depending on the techniques a UWB uses, the IEEE 802.15.3a standard can offer a data rate from 20 Mbps up to 500 Mbps. Without a doubt, IEEE 802.15.3a can be considered a WBA technology under its broad definition.

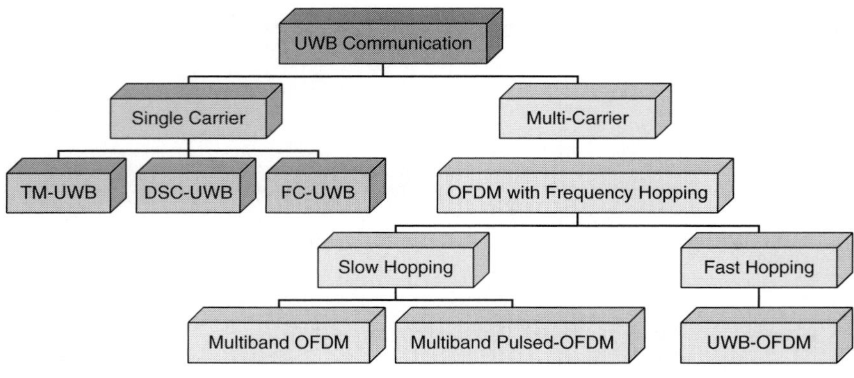

Figure 5: Family tree for various UWB technologies

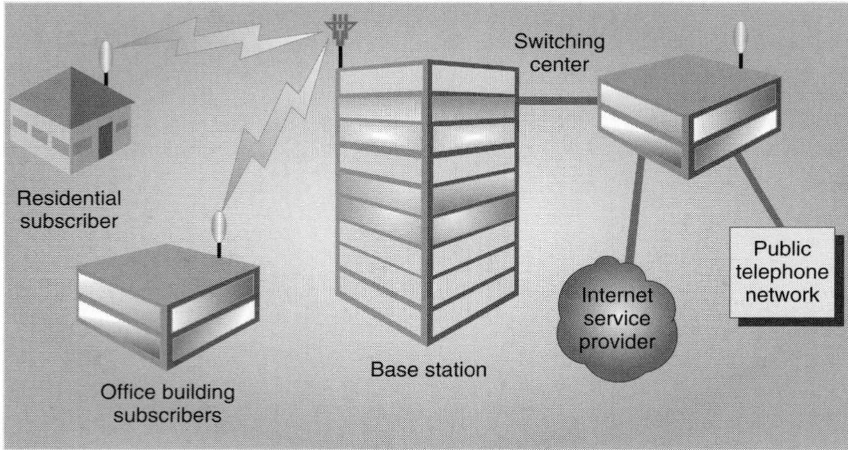

Figure 6: Conceptual view of an IEEE 802.16-based WMAN

WIRELESS METROPOLITAN AREA NETWORKS

WMANs are always considered as a means to provide wireless broadband access to houses, buildings, and other premises as an alternative last-mile solution to wired xDSL technology. IEEE 802.16 is the most important WMAN standard developed to address wireless broadband access applications to link commercial and residential buildings to high-speed core networks and thereby provide access to those networks. IEEE 802.16's work has primarily aimed at a point-to-multipoint topology with a cellular deployment of base stations, each tied into public networks and in contact with fixed wireless subscriber stations. The subscriber stations typically include rooftop-mounted antenna/radio units connected to indoor network interface units, although in some cases both units could be indoors or both outdoors. Initial work has aimed at businesses, with much of the market focus on small- to medium-sized enterprises. Attention has increasingly turned toward residential opportunities, particularly as the lower frequencies have become available for two-way service. Additionally, potential applications for IEEE 802.16 WMANs include deployment in vast rural areas in both developed and developing countries.

A conceptual view of an IEEE 802.16-based WMAN is shown in Figure 6, in which a WMAN base station is mounted on top of the higher building to service several lower buildings/houses through wireless broadband access air-link. The base station is usually connected to fixed wideband networks. IEEE 802.16 series standards give technical specifications for WMANs, also commonly called WiMAX technologies.

History of IEEE 802.16 Standard

The activities of IEEE 802.16 standardization were initiated by activity of the National Wireless Electronics Systems Testbed (N-WEST) at the U.S. National Institute of Standards and Technology (NIST). The N-WEST organized a kickoff meeting at the 1998 IEEE Radio and Wireless Conference (RAWCON). Altogether, forty-five delegates accepted an invitation to meet with the IEEE 802 Working Group in November 1998, and IEEE 802 then approved the formation of a study group. That group met twice and wrote the Task Group 1 project authorization request (PAR). The Working Group's first session took place in July 1999. At that meeting, the Task Group 2 PAR was approved by IEEE 802. In November 1999, IEEE 802.16 created the study group that developed the Task Group 3 PAR, which was subsequently approved in March 2000. At that time, a study group for the license-exempt bands was set up and developed the acronym WirelessHUMAN (wireless high-speed unlicensed metropolitan area network) to describe the standard effort. The Task Group 3 PAR was approved in December 2000. Currently, IEEE 802.16 has 137 members, 74 potential members, and 59 official observers. Its work has been closely followed; for example, the IEEE

802.16 Web site received over 2.8 million file requests in the year 2000. IEEE 802.16 maintains close working relationships with standards bodies in the International Telecommunications Union (ITU) and ETSI, particularly with the high performance radio access (HIPERACCESS) and high performance radio metropolitan area network (HIPERMAN) programs of ETSI's Broadband Radio Access Networks (BRAN) project and with ETSI Working Group TM4. Several publications provide additional detail about those activities (Foerster and Sater 2000; Petry 2001).

The standardization of IEEE 802.16 technology took a progressive path, which is continuing even today. The process for IEEE 802.16 standardization learned a lesson from the IEEE 802.11 standards before it. Some consider the original IEEE 802.11 (WiFi) specifications a dismal failure. Initially, in order to grab the early market share, all of the vendors interpreted the specifications differently. A great deal of wireless LAN equipment was on the market well before there were IEEE 802.11 standards. However, it was very expensive, and there was no interoperability. With that in mind, WiMAX is already far ahead of the game. WiMAX has a standard, and the IEEE 802.16 Task Group has worked to figure out how to support WiMAX and make it grow on a long-term basis. The IEEE 802.16 Task Group helps bring all the information together that vendors and carriers can work with. Therefore, the standardization process for IEEE 802.16 is really a success story, especially when compared to IEEE 802.11.

The IEEE 802.16a was approved by the IEEE in January 2003 and is basically an amendment to the more general 802.16 core standard developed in December 2001 by IEEE Task Group 1. The core 802.16 specification was an air-interface standard for wireless broadband access systems using point-to-multipoint infrastructure designs, and operating at radio frequencies between 10 GHz and 66 GHz. It targeted an average bandwidth performance of 70 Mbps and peak rates up to 268 Mbps. However, that standard was not complete in many peoples' minds. It applied only to line-of-sight deployment in licensed spectrum, neglecting to offer any conformance guidelines and ignoring ongoing development of the similar European HIPERMAN standard. The IEEE was working quickly, as it typically does, and with 802.16a it built more functionality into that original draft. The 802.16a collection of amendments took into account the emergence of licensed and license-exempt broadband wireless networks operating between 2 GHz and 11 GHz, with support for non-line-of-sight (NLOS) architectures that could not be supported in higher frequency ranges. Support for NLOS performance was one of the primary physical layer differences in 802.16a, which was developed with the requirements of lower frequencies.

In 802.16a, there were actually three new PHY-layer specifications: a single-carrier layer, a 256-point FFT OFDM layer, and a 2048-point FFT OFDMA layer. The 256-point waveform is the one that is employed in both WiMAX and the ETSI's HIPERMAN standard, ensuring worldwide interoperability. The amended standard also allowed for WiMAX deployment in varying channel capacities to address the different amounts of spectrum carriers own from market to market, and in different parts of the world. The inclusion of TDD and FDD duplexing schemes was yet another positive move for the technology's international potential. Beyond the additions at the PHY layer, the 802.16a version made further enhancements to the MAC layer, which uses a slotted TDMA uplink/downlink protocol between the WiMAX base station and the subscriber terminal. This type of intelligent scheduling of user access to the network improves latency, affecting the network capability to support voice and video services, and overall service reliability. Other quality of service (QoS) features include automatic retransmission request (ARQ), per-connection QOS, and automatic power control. IEEE 802.16a offers a better set of MAC and PHY profiles to work with compared to IEEE 802.16 standard.

Although 802.16a does much to improve on the original standard, the core standard has had enough amendments attached to it that the IEEE redrafted the specification. The new standard, referred to as 802.16 Revision D, was ready in the third quarter of 2004. The new core specifications included everything that changed about the standard after the 802.16 standard was issued. However, the evolution of the WiMAX standard would not be complete with 802.16 RevD. In December 2005, the IEEE proposed IEEE 802.16e, another new amendment that introduced mobility into what WiMAX proponents hope will be a thriving market for broadband wireless.

The standardization process for IEEE 802.16-based WiMAX continues even today. An important step for the latest WiMAX technology is its introduction of cognitive radio technology to address the needs to operate in some licensed bands with incumbent users, which are the primary users of the bands. This version of WiMAX will be included in IEEE 802.16h, which is still on its way to becoming new standard.

Why WiMAX?

The initial motivation to propose WiMAX technology was to overcome the deployment difficulties of broadband wired access for Internet and other data-centric applications. The demands for broadband data access are driven by wide applications of Internet services. As shown in Table 6, worldwide Internet users constitute approximately 14.6 percent of the total population, meaning that almost one-sixth of the world's total population are Internet users. From this data, we can see how important the Internet is in today's world.

To deliver the Internet services to every household, the broadband data access capability is a must. Currently, there are three common ways to provide fixed-line broadband data access. One is to use fixed wideband optical fiber cables, also called *fiber to home*. This approach has been used in many new buildings and is relatively expensive to carry out. Another common way to provide the fixed broadband data access is to use relatively cheap and already-existing telephone lines with the help of xDSL technology to provide every household with broadband data access. The xDSL has in fact become a default standard technology for offering broadband data access in many countries throughout the world because of fixed-line infrastructure and relatively low cost to implement in virtually every home. The third method to implement fixed-line broadband data access is to use existing cable TV transmission systems via

Table 6: Top Twenty Countries with the Most Internet Subscribers (2005)

Country	No. of Subscribers	Population in 2005	Penetration Rate	World Percentage
United States	202,888,307	296,208,476	68.5 %	21.6 %
China	103,000,000	1,282,198,289	7.9 %	11.0 %
Japan	78,050,000	128,137,485	60.9 %	8.3 %
Germany	47,127,725	82,726,188	57.0 %	5.0 %
India	39,200,000	1,094,870,677	3.6 %	4.2 %
United Kingdom	35,807,929	59,889,407	59.8 %	3.8 %
South Korea	31,600,000	49,929,293	63.3 %	3.4 %
Italy	28,610,000	58,608,565	48.8 %	3.0 %
France	25,614,899	60,619,718	42.3 %	2.7 %
Brazil	22,320,000	181,823,645	12.3 %	2.4 %
Russia	22,300,000	144,003,901	15.5 %	2.4 %
Canada	20,450,000	32,050,369	63.8 %	2.2 %
Spain	15,565,138	43,435,136	35.8 %	1.7 %
Indonesia	15,300,000	219,307,147	7.0 %	1.6 %
Mexico	14,901,687	103,872,328	14.3 %	1.6 %
Taiwan	13,800,000	22,794,795	60.5 %	1.5 %
Australia	13,784,966	20,507,264	67.2 %	1.5 %
Netherlands	10,806,328	16,316,019	66.2 %	1.2 %
Poland	10,600,000	38,133,891	27.8 %	1.1 %
Malaysia	9,513,100	26,500,699	37.9 %	1.1 %
Rest of the World	176,943,950	2,444,250,712	7.2 %	18.8 %
World Total	938,710,929	6,420,102,722	14.6 %	100.0 %

a set-top box, also called a *cable modem*, to connect to Internet services. Obviously, all aforementioned broadband data access technologies have serious limitations in the sense that they all rely on fixed-line infrastructure, without which the broadband data access would not be possible.

On the other hand, wireless broadband access does not require any forms of fixed-line infrastructure; it can work as long as a WBA subscriber station connected with fixed public wideband lines is installed (a couple miles away from the point at which the WBA services are required) and a set-top box transceiver is available at home. Therefore, the WBA technology has clear advantages in terms of operational readiness and implementation flexibility to provide point-to-multipoint and point-to-point wireless broadband access services, which can range from normal voice calls to multimedia applications such as real-time video conferences and so on. This unique characteristic of the WBA makes it a must for all natural disaster rescue missions and other emergency operations. The recent Hurricane Katrina rescue operations in New Orleans have shown its usefulness and effectiveness.

General Features of WBA

WiMAX is a certification mark for products that pass conformity and interoperability tests for the IEEE 802.16 standards. Products that pass the conformity tests for WiMAX are capable of forming wireless connections between them to permit the carrying of Internet packet data. WiMAX is similar to WiFi in concept but includes certain improvements that are aimed at enhancing performance and should permit usage over much greater distances. IEEE 802.16 is Working Group number 16 of IEEE 802, specializing in point-to-multipoint WBA.

Before we address the general features of wireless broadband access, we would like to take a closer look at WiMAX. WiMAX is a broadband wireless point-to-multipoint (although it can also be used for point-to-point applications in general) specification from the IEEE 802.16 Working Group. Unlike wireless LAN technologies such as WiFi (IEEE 802.11), WiMAX is designed to operate as a wireless MAN. This places WiMAX in the same class as the earlier 802.16 standards, multichannel multipoint distribution service (MMDS) and local multipoint distribution service (LMDS). As WiMAX technology matures, both MMDS and LMDS will be replaced by much more advanced WiMAX systems, which can deliver the same services in a much more cost-effective way. WiMAX can operate in both FCC-licensed and non-licensed bands. Licensed WiMAX operates in the 10 to 66 GHz range; unlicensed WiMAX operates in the 2 to 11 Ghz range.

Table 7: IEEE 802.16 WBA Technologies (WMANs or WIMAX)

802.16a	WBA: For 2–11 GHz band, up to 70 Mbps, NLOS
802.16b	WBA: Quality of Service (5–6 GHz)
802.16c	WBA: Interoperability (10–66 GHz)
802.16d	WBA: Builds on 802.16c (2–66 GHz)
802.16e	WBA: Mobility support (2–6 GHz)
802.16f	WBA: Builds on 802.16e to improve multihop functionality
802.16g	WBA: Efficient handover and improved QoS
802.16h	WBA: Cognitive radio technology

Under the umbrella of IEEE 802.16 standards, there are eight different standards, as shown in Table 7, from IEEE 802.16a to IEEE 802.16h (where every letter represents a different amended WMAN standard).

What Makes WiMAX Different from WLAN

Although WLANs can also provide wireless broadband data access to users with a respectful data throughput (from 11 Mbps to 54 Mbps), WMANs usually cover a much larger area, which can be as large as thirty kilometers in radius, depending on the traffic models and data-transmission rate requirements. Therefore, WBA covers not only a local area but a metropolitan area, just as its name suggests in WMAN. To understand this point is a clear distinction must be made between a WLAN and a WMAN, which can be rather confusing. As previously mentioned, we would like to consider WBA technology a general networking technology that provides wireless data access to end users.

There is another important distinction between IEEE 802.16 WMANs (WiMAX) and other wireless networking technologies, such as WLANs. WiMAX allows multiple frequency bands operation to send payload data to the end users, such that it can effectively avoid possible interference to the other existing wireless applications and thus can enhance the communication quality. This important feature has been implemented specifically in IEEE 801.16h, which works based on cognitive radio technology and uses intelligence to understand the operating environment, such that it can shift to another frequency band when it knows that existing primary users are in the same band.

In addition, WiMAX offers a scalable data transmission throughput management scheme to adjust the use of available frequency spectrum depending on the data-rate requirements from different users. For instance, if a user demands a relatively high transmission rate, the use of OFDM technique can to increase the data throughput by dividing a relatively wide service band into many narrow subcarrier channels for parallel transmission. Based on current standard specifications, a WiMAX system can fully support many different transmission modes, such as IPv4, IPv6, Ethernet protocol, asynchronous transmission mode, and so on. Its effective coverage area can reach as far as thirty miles with its uplink and downlink transmission speed of 75 Mbps, which is great enough to carry any multimedia contents in its wireless bit pipe.

WIMAX Major Operational Advantages

The major operational advantages for WiMAX technology can be summarized as follows.

1. WiMAX offers a flexible architecture.

   WiMAX supports several system architectures, including point-to-point, point-to-multipoint, and ubiquitous coverage. The WiMAX MAC supports point-to-multipoint and ubiquitous service by scheduling a time slot for each subscriber station (SS). If there is only one SS in the network, the WiMAX base station (BS) will communicate with the SS on a point-to-point basis. A BS in a point-to-point configuration may use a narrower-beam antenna to cover longer distances.
2. WiMAX can work in a very high security level.

   WiMAX supports advanced encryption standard (AES) and triple data encryption standard (3DES). By encrypting the links between the BS and the SS, WiMAX provides subscribers with privacy (against eavesdropping) and security across the broadband wireless interface. Security also provides operators with strong protection against theft of service. In addition, WiMAX has built-in VLAN support, which provides protection for data that are being transmitted by different users on the same BS.
3. WiMAX provides scalable QoS requirements.

   WiMAX can be dynamically optimized for the mixture of traffic that is being carried. Four types of service are supported: (a) unsolicited grant service (UGS), which is designed to support real-time data streams consisting of fixed-size data packets issued at periodic intervals, such as T1/E1 and voice over IP; (b) real-time polling service (rtPS), which is designed to support real-time data streams consisting of variable-sized data packets that are issued at periodic intervals, such as MPEG video; (c) non–real-time polling service (nrtPS), which is designed to support delay-tolerant data streams consisting of variable-sized data packets for which a minimum data rate is required, such as FTP; and (d) best effort (BE), which is designed to support data streams for which no minimum service level is required and that can be handled on a space-available basis.
4. WiMAX is suitable for quick deployment.

   Compared with the deployment of wired solutions, WiMAX requires little or no external plant construction. For example, excavation to support the trenching of cables is not required. Operators that have obtained licenses to use one of the licensed bands, or that plan to use one of the unlicensed bands, do not need to submit additional applications to the government (in particular the case in the US). Once the antenna and equipment are installed and powered, WiMAX is ready for service. In most cases, deployment of WiMAX can be completed in a matter of hours, compared with months for other solutions.
5. Multilevel service is available in WiMAX.

   The manner in which QoS is delivered is generally based on the service-level agreement (SLA) between the service provider and the enduser. Further more one service provider can offer different SLAs to different subscribers, or even to different users on the same SS.

6. Interoperability is another important advantage of WiMAX.

   WiMAX is based on international, vendor-neutral standards, which make it easier for endusers to transport and use their SS at different locations, or with different service providers. Interoperability protects the early investment of an operator because it can select equipment from different equipment vendors, and it will continue to drive the costs of equipment down as a result of mass adoption. WiBro technology developed by Korea will eventually be harmonized with WiMAX to make them fully compatible with each other.

7. WiMAX is a technology with great portability.

   As with current cellular systems, once the WiMAX SS is powered up, it identifies itself, determines the characteristics of the link with the BS (as long as the SS is registered in the system database), and then negotiates its transmission characteristics accordingly.

8. Mobility is supported in WiMAX.

   The IEEE 802.16e amendment has added key features in support of mobility. Improvements have been made to the OFDM and OFDMA physical layers to support devices and services in a mobile environment. These improvements, which include scalable OFDMA, MIMO, and support for idle/sleep mode and handoff, will allow full mobility at speeds up to 160 km/hr. The WiMAX Forum-supported standard has inherited OFDM's superior NLOS performance and multipath-resistant operation, making it highly suitable for the mobile environment.

9. WiMAX can operate in a cost-effective way.

   WiMAX is based on an open, international standard. Mass adoption of the standard, and the use of low-cost, mass-produced chipsets and handsets, will drive costs down dramatically, and the resultant competitive pricing will provide considerable cost savings for service providers and endusers.

10. WiMAX offers wider coverage.

    WiMAX dynamically supports multiple modulation levels, including BPSK, QPSK, 16-QAM, and 64-QAM. When equipped with a high-power amplifier and operating with a low-level modulation (e.g., BPSK or QPSK), WiMAX systems are able to cover a large geographic area when the path between the BS and the SS is unobstructed.

11. Non–line-of-sight operation is allowed in WiMAX.

    NLOS usually refers to a radio path with its first Fresnel zone completely blocked. WiMAX is based on OFDM technology, which has the inherent capability of handling NLOS environments. This capability helps WiMAX products deliver broad bandwidth in a NLOS environment, which other wireless product cannot do.

12. WiMAX has a high capacity.

    Using multilevel modulation schemes (e.g., 64-QAM) and channel bandwidth (currently 7 MHz, with planned evolution toward the full bandwidth specified in the associated IEEE and ETSI standards), WiMAX systems can provide significant bandwidth to endusers.

Family of IEEE 802.16 Standards

The operation frequency bands allocated for IEEE 802.16 are between 2 and 66 GHz, which is a very wide range compared to the spectrum on which other wireless networks (e.g., WLANs, mobile cellular networks, etc.) operate. The IEEE 802.16 operation band can be further divided into two portions, one being the bandwidth between 10 to 66 GHz, which is dedicated to line-of-sight (LOS) WiMAX applications. In this band, the services are targeted for a relatively large coverage area of up to thirty miles in radius. On the other hand, the WiMAX services within a relatively small area will be given in a band between 2 and 11 GHz, in which radio wave propagation properties are better suited for NLOS applications.

As shown in Table 7, IEEE 802.16a standard services WiMAX applications in 2–11 GHz band, in which both licensed and nonlicensed radio spectra are covered. The wireless broadband access applications are offered in a point-to-point or point-to-multipoint scheme, possibly under NLOS propagation scenarios. Under the IEEE 802.16a standard, multiple receivers can be interconnected for data transmissions, and thus the total coverage areas can be extended effectively. In the IEEE 802.16b standard, the radio spectrum band in 5–6 GHz will be used. It was designed to support in particular the WiMAX services with very high requirements for QoS to provide different data applications, such as voice, data, video, and other multimedia applications (e.g., voice over IP services, etc.). On the other hand, IEEE 802.16c was proposed to provide wireless broadband data access in a relatively high band between 10 and 66 GHz, which is especially useful to deliver WiMAX services in a relatively large area. In this scheme, the LOS operation model is preferred. IEEE 802.16d (also called the IEEE 802.16-2004 standard) is an enhanced version of the IEEE 802.16a and IEEE 802.16c standards. It can operate under both 2–11 GHZ and 10–66 GHZ bands. The scheme offers very flexible operation modes.

All aforementioned WiMAX standards, from IEEE 802.16a to IEEE 802.16d, support only fixed or at most portable wireless broadband access; they cannot provide services to terminals with a vehicular speed mobility. Therefore, IEEE 802.16e was proposed in particular for mobility support, and its services are provided within a 2–6 GHz band. Another important feature of IEEE 802.16e is its downward compatibility to IEEE 802.16d.

We should note that there is an overlapped range in the spectral band allocation for the WiMAX applications: 2–11 GHz and 10–66 GHz. The overlapping happens in the 10–11 GHz band and will help the backward compatibility for future WiMAX applications developed for both lower and higher band operations.

Technical Aspects of IEEE 802.16

WiMAX based on the IEEE 802.16 standard has a theoretical maximum bandwidth of 75 Mbps. This bandwidth can be achieved using 64-QAM 3/4 modulation. 64-QAM can only be utilized under optimal transmission conditions. WiMAX supports the use of a wide range of modulation algorithms to enable the most bandwidth to be realized under all conditions. WiMAX has a theoretical maximum range of thirty-one miles with a direct line of sight. However, non–line-of-sight conditions will seriously limit the potential range. In addition, some of the frequencies utilized by WiMAX are subject to interference from rain fade. The unlicensed WiMAX frequencies are subject to RF interference from competing technologies and competing WiMAX networks.

Next, we will discuss in more detail on the technical accomplishments of IEEE 802.16 standards.

MAC Layer of IEEE 802.16

The IEEE 802.16 Working Group follows the traditional IEEE 802 approach of developing multiple physical layer options supported by a common MAC layer, which was developed by Task Group 1 along with the original 10–66 GHz physical layer. Although the service requirements of the other air-interface projects differ, the original MAC layer design is flexible enough to support, with some necessary extensions, all three physical layer designs.

The IEEE 802.16 MAC layer, as shown in Figure 7, draws from the data-over-cable standard (Radio Frequency Interface Specification n.d.) that has been successfully deployed in hybrid-fiber coaxial (HFC) cable systems, which have a similar point-to-multipoint architecture. However, the MAC protocol engine uses a different design. It is a connection-oriented MAC layer architecture that is able to tunnel any protocol across the air interface with full QoS support. Asynchronous transfer mode (ATM) and packet-based convergence layers provide the interface to higher protocols. Although extensive bandwidth allocation and QoS mechanisms are provided, the details of scheduling and reservation management are left unstandardized and provide an important mechanism for vendors to differentiate their equipment, according to some specific tailor-made requirements from the end users.

An important MAC feature in IEEE 802.16 standards is the option of granting bandwidth to a subscriber station rather than to the individual connections it supports. This provides the option of allowing a smart subscriber station to manage its bandwidth allocation among its users. This can make for more efficient allocation.

The IEEE 802.16 MAC layer is designed to be versatile and flexible. For example, it supports several multiplexing and duplexing schemes; some possibilities are described in the following subsections. In general, the point-to-multipoint architecture is implemented with a controlling base station interacting with many subscriber stations, as mentioned in the previous sections. The downlink from the base station may be channelized and sectorized, but, within a channel and sector, all subscriber stations receive the same signal and retain only messages addressed to them. The uplink from the subscriber stations is shared, with access assigned by the base station.

10–66 GHz Physical Layer of IEEE 802.16

The 10–66 GHz physical layer in IEEE 802.16 standards assumes line-of-sight propagation with no significant concern over multipath propagation. Either of two basic modes may be used. The continuous mode uses frequency division duplexing (FDD), with simultaneous uplink and downlink on separate frequencies. A continuous time-division multiplexed downstream allows a powerful concatenated coding scheme with interleaving. The burst mode allows time-division duplexing (TDD), with the uplink and downlink sharing a channel but not transmitting simultaneously. This allows dynamic reassignment of the uplink and downlink capacity. This mode also allows

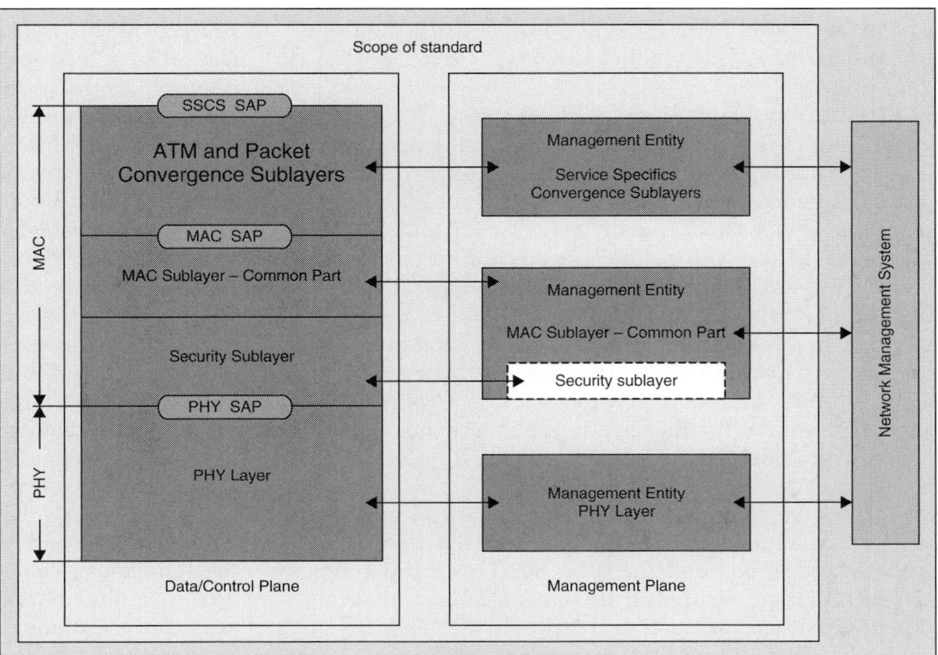

Figure 7: IEEE 802.16 reference layered model and protocol stack

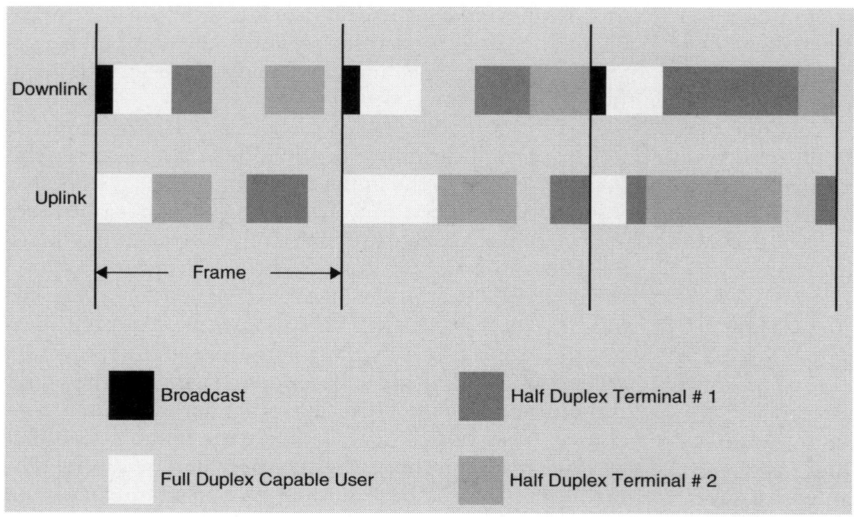

Figure 8: Example of burst FDD bandwidth allocation in IEEE 802.16 standards

burst FDD, which supports half-duplex FDD subscriber stations that do not simultaneously transmit and receive, as shown in Figure 8, and may therefore be less expensive. Both TDD and burst FDD support adaptive burst profiles in which different modulation (QPSK, 16-QAM, or 64-QAM) and coding schemes may be dynamically assigned on a burst-by-burst basis. This real-time trade-off of capacity versus robustness again offers opportunities to vendors to implement sophisticated algorithms to differentiate their approach while retaining interoperability.

The choice of continuous or burst operation mode may depend on the available channel bandwidth allocations and other regulatory issues. Because the IEEE 802.16 standards are intended for worldwide use, the channelization is left flexible, although the recommendations are included. These suggest symbols rates as high as 43.4 MBd in a 50 MHz channel, which, assuming the use of 64-QAM modulation scheme, translates to a data rate as high as 260 Mbps in that channel.

2–11 GHz Physical Layer of IEEE 802.16

Task Group 3 was responsible for developing a standard for 2–11 GHz WBA. In the United States, the primary targeted frequencies are in the multichannel multipoint distribution service bands, mostly between 2.5 and 2.7 GHz, compared to the worldwide 3.5 and 10.5 GHz that are likely allocated for the applications. Because non–line-of-sight operation is practical and because of the lower component costs, these bands are seen as good prospects for residential and small-business services. The spectrum availability is suitable to these uses. Task Group 1 considered a number of physical layer approaches and selected a baseline draft in spring 2001. At the same time, the MAC enhancements were developed.

To provide for rapid development, Task Group 4 is working under a narrow charter. It is tasked with developing a PHY layer based on the IEEE 802.11a OFDM and/or HIPERLAN/2 physical layer architecture and is developing MAC enhancements. It works closely with Task Group 3 to ensure harmony. Coordination of base stations under independent operators in unlicensed spectrum is an important issue facing this group. One proposal is to consider an optional mesh networking architecture in addition to a point-to-multipoint topology. Some participants have proposed the MAC enhancement schemes to support the mesh networking; this is clearly a testimony to the flexibility of the IEEE 802.16 MAC. Different major IEEE 802.16 standards are compared in Table 8.

Applications of WiMAX Technology

Because of its unique features, WiMAX technology is capable of providing wireless broadband access to many important applications.

The WiMAX, as a wireless MAN technology, can connect several IEEE 802.11(WiFi) WLAN hotspots with one another and other parts of the global Internet and can provide a wireless alternative to cable and xDSL for last-mile (or first-mile) broadband access. IEEE 802.16 offers up to thirty-one miles of linear service area range and allows connectivity between users without a direct line of sight. This should not be taken to mean that users from thirty-one miles away without line of sight will have connectivity; practical limits from real-world tests seem to be around three to five miles. The technology has been claimed to provide shared data rates up to 70 Mbps, which, according to WiMAX proponents, provides enough bandwidth to simultaneously support more than sixty business users with T1-type connectivity, which is well over a thousand homes at 1Mbps xDSL-level connectivity. Real-world tests, however, show practical maximum data rates between 500 kbps and 2 Mbps, depending on conditions at a given site.

There is also some interesting potential for interoperability of WiMAX with legacy cellular networks. WiMAX antennas can share a cell tower without compromising the function of cellular arrays already in place. Companies that already lease cell sites in widespread service areas have a unique opportunity to diversify, and often already have the necessary spectrum available to them

Table 8: Comparison of Different Major IEEE 802.16 Standards

	802.16	802.16a/REVd	802.16e
Completed time	December 2001	802.16a: January 2003 802.16 REVd: Q3 2004	December 2005
Spectrum (GHz)	10–66	<11	<6
Channel condition	LOS only	NLOS	NLOS
Data rate/channelization	32–134 Mbps/28 MHz	<75 Mbps/20 MHz	<15 Mbps/5 MHz
Modulation	QPSK, 16 QAM, 64 QAM	256OFDM, OFDMA, 64 QAM, 16 QAM, QPSK, BPSK	Same as REVd
Mobility	Fixed	Fixed and portable	Mobile, regional roaming
Channel bandwidth	20, 25, 28 MHz	Selected bandwidth between 1.25 and 20 MHz, up to 16 subchannels	Same as REVd
Typical cell radius	1–3 miles	3–5 (<30 miles)	1–3 miles

(i.e., they own the licenses for radio frequencies important to increased speed and/or range of a WiMAX connection). WiMAX antennae may even be connected to an Internet backbone via either a light fiber optics cable or a directional microwave link. Some cellular companies are evaluating WiMax as a means of increasing bandwidth for a variety of data-intensive applications. In line with these possible applications is the technology's ability to serve as a very high bandwidth "backhaul" for Internet or cellular phone traffic from remote areas to a backbone. Although the cost-effectiveness of WiMAX in a remote application will be higher, it is definitely not limited to such applications, and may in fact be an answer to expensive urban deployments of T1 backhauls as well. Given developing countries' (such as those in Africa) limited wired infrastructure, the costs to install a WiMax station in conjunction with an existing cellular tower or even as a solitary hub will be diminutive compared to developing a wired solution. The wide, flat expanses and low population density of such an area lends itself well to WiMAX and its current diametrical range of thirty miles. For countries that have skipped wired infrastructure because of of inhibitive costs and unsympathetic geography, WiMAX can enhance wireless infrastructure in an inexpensive, decentralized, deployment-friendly, and effective manner.

WiMAX technology provides an important means to establish emergency telecommunication links to the outside world, such as natural disaster rescue missions, where the wired or cellular network infrastructure may be totally destroyed by earthquake, tsunami, hurricane, and so forth. The usefulness of WiMAX in disaster relief operations is due mainly to its operation readiness and deployment flexibility. You need only to mount a WiMAX base station on top of a master from which a secure connection (also via microwave links) with outside networks is available, and then you can establish the voice, data, and video communications. Some companies have started to design WiMAX products for emergency telecommunication applications. A good example of the effectiveness of WiMAX was the aftermath of the devastating Hurricane Katrina. The FCC allowed an isolated temporary shelter in rural Louisiana to use the still-experimental technology WiMAX as a powerful, high-speed wireless link to the nearest functioning Internet connection point, fifteen miles away. WiMAX worked flawlessly and now discussions are under way to make wireless access a big part of New Orleans' reconstructed communications infrastructure.

Because of its deployment agility, military operations are yet another possible application for WiMAX technology, which can be deployed and torn down very quickly for battlefield telecommunication and commanding applications. WiMAX-based ad hoc or mesh wireless networks can provide a vital communication solution for future military operations.

Public safety services and private networks are another potential application of WiMAX technology. Support for nomadic services and the ability to provide ubiquitous coverage in a metropolitan area provide a tool for law enforcement, fire protection, and other public safety organizations, enabling them to maintain critical communications under a variety of adverse conditions. Private networks for industrial complexes, universities, and other campus type environments also represent a potential business opportunity for WiMAX.

Another interesting application of WiMAX under consideration is gaming. Sony and Microsoft are closely considering the addition of WiMax as a feature in their next generation of game consoles. This will allow gamers to create ad hoc networks with other players. This may prove to be one of the "killer applications" driving WiMax adoption: WiFi-like functionality with vastly improved range, greatly reduced network latency, and the capability to create ad hoc mesh networks.

WiMAX technology can also provide an important means for offshore communications. Oil and gas producers can use WiMAX equipment to provide communication links from land-based facilities to oil rigs and platforms, to support remote operations, security, and basic communications. Remote operations include remote troubleshooting of complex equipment problems, site monitoring, and database access. For example, video clips of malfunctioning components or subassemblies can be transmitted to a land-based team of experts for analysis. Security includes alarm monitoring and video surveillance. Basic communications includes voice telephony, e-mail, Internet access, and video conferencing. WiMAX networks are quickly and easily deployed. The network can be set up or redeployed in a matter of hours, if not minutes, even when oil rigs and platforms are moved to other locations. Wired solutions are not appropriate for this scenario because the facilities are offshore, and because oil rigs are temporarily located and moved regularly within the oil or gas field. In the event of having to temporarily abandon an offshore facility, communications for monitoring the status of the asset can continue to be maintained if using battery-backed WiMAX terminals.

Government agencies, large enterprises, industrial campuses, transportation hubs, universities, and colleges, can use WiMAX networks to connect multiple locations, sites, and offices within their campus. Campus communication systems require high data capacity, low latency, a large coverage footprint, and high security: like other usage scenarios, campus networks carry a mixture of voice, data, and video, which the WiMAX QoS helps prioritize and optimize. It takes less time and fewer resources to interconnect a campus through a WiMAX network, because excavation and external construction are not required. Some campuses have been in place for a long time, and digging trenches for cable may not be permitted. In such cases, WiMAX solutions may be one of the most cost-effective ways to interconnect campus buildings. Even if wired installations are permitted, the lead time to deploy a wired solution is much longer than the lead time to deploy a WiMAX solution, without offering any accompanying benefits.

Obviously, WiMAX technology can also be a vital solution to provide rural connectivity. Service providers use WiMAX networks to deliver service to underserved markets in rural areas and the suburban outskirts of cities. The delivery of rural connectivity is critical in many developing countries and underserved areas of developed countries, where little or no infrastructure is available. Rural connectivity delivers much-needed voice telephony and Internet service. Because the WiMAX solution provides extended coverage, it is a much more cost-effective solution than wired technology in areas with lower population densities. WiMAX solutions can be deployed quickly, providing communication links to these underserved areas, thereby offering a more secure environment, and helping to improve their local economies.

Released WiMAX Services/Products

Many WiMAX products have been announced since the second quarter of 2005. For example, major cities such as Los Angeles, New York, Chicago, Boston, Providence (Rhode Island), and San Francisco/Oakland will be served by TowerStream, as of 2005. TowerStream claims to offer a complete Internet and VoIP phone solution, which charges a very reasonable price for T1 Internet Access plus VoIP phone lines. TowerStream uses the latest fixed-wireless technology that is the basis of WiMAX.

On the other hand, Seattle is served by Sprint and Speakeasy net, which can service T1 Internet access and VoIP lines. It can also offer a private WAN service that delivers private point-to-multipoint connections for the small to medium-sized business based on fixed WiMAX technology.

In China, Dalian and Chengdu are implementing pre-WiMAX networks that will be upgradeable when certification testing begins. Current Towerstream, Speakeasy, and other deployments are of proprietary systems that include Airspan Networks, Aperto, Alvarion VL OFDM, and Dragonwave. Trial deployments have been mostly outside of the United States because of limited spectrum availability. Sprint has announced that it will begin trials of precertified WiMAX systems. TowerStream will also introduce WiMAX systems to follow their highly successful pre-WiMAX network servicing businesses, educational facilities, and government entities.

At the July 2005 WiMAX Forum meeting in Vancouver, British Columbia, Canada, WiMAX systems began certification testing. Disney took part in the proof of concept (POC) display, which showed real simultaneous multimedia capabilities possible through the WiMAX technology.

In addition to the aforementioned urban area rollouts, WiMAX is like WiFi in that you can "roll your own." Several vendors already had some form of products in 2004, usually in a pre-standards-compliance stage so that multivendor interoperability within a single network segment could not be reasonably expected. Several companies have been planning rollouts of compliant chipsets in FPGAs in 2005 and ASICs the following year, which will shrink the digital electronics suitable for PCMCIA and MiniPCI type of form factors. Intel is expected to be a major driver toward price reduction. Taken at face value, Intel claims to be able to drive the price per user to zero over the next three to four years, as a result of embedding WiMAX function into the system processors and board architectures for notebook PCs, PDAs, and other devices. Of course, the price will not be zero exactly because premium features drive acceptance of premium "Intel Inside"-driven designs. But as a competitive positioning strategy, the ability to embed multimode WiMAX/WiFi/cellular into consumer and IT products should create a compelling argument for WiMAX's acceptance.

WiBro Technology

When talking about WiMAX services, we have to take a look at WiBro technology, which was a wireless broadband access standard created independently by the South Korean government, showing that Korea will aim for WBA even without the blessing of the international community. However, the development of the WiBro technology proceeded under the shadow of the IEEE 802.16 WIMAX standard with regard to its technical specifications and architecture for both the physical and upper layers.

The WiBro supports mobile terminals up to 120 km/h, and its base station can cover an area of 1–5 km in radius.

Table 9: The Comparison of WiBro Technology with Other Wireless Networking Technologies

	WiBro	TD-CDMA	HSDPA	EV-DO	WLAN
Peak data rate	DL: 18.4 Mbps	DL: 3.1 Mbps	DL: 14 Mbps	DL: 3.1 Mbps	802.11b: 11 Mbps
	UL: 6.1 Mbps	UL: 900 Kbps	UL: 2 Mbps	UL: 1.2 Mbps	802.11a/g: 54 Mbps
Bandwidth	9 MHz	5 MHz(10 MHz)	5 MHz	1.25 MHz	20 MHz
Air link	OFDMA	TDMA, CDMA	TDMA, CDMA	CDMA	CSMA/CA
Duplex	TDD	TDD	FDD	FDD	TDD
Mobility	Mid	High	High	High	Low
Coverage	Mid	Mid	Large	Large	Small
Standard	TTA &802.16e	3GPP	3GPP	3GPP2	802.11

The Korean government has allocated 100 MHz bandwidth at 2.3 GH_Z band in particular for WiBro services. The Phase 1 standardization for WiBro technology was finalized in June 2004, and WiBro technology was put into trial service in 2005 at the Pusan APEC meeting, which showed its impressive performance to all delegates in attendance Another importance chance for Korean to demonstrate their WiBro technology is the Winter Olympic Games to be held in Turin, Italy, February 2006. Sumsung will provide the WiBro-based wireless broadband access technology to the organizer of the Turin 2006 Winter Olympic Games. The next-generation WiBro technology will provide a downlink data rate up to 20 Mbps and uplink data rate up to 6 Mbps, which will be 1.4 to 3 times faster than what HSDPA (an enhanced W-CDMA) can do. Therefore, the kind of impact WiBro technology exerts on the WWANs still needs to be watched closely. The comparison between WiBro and other different wireless networking technologies is shown in Table 9.

Therefore, we have to say that, until now, perhaps the most telling deployments for WiMAX will be for the WiBro mobile derivative: WiBro has the South Korean government's support with the requirement for each carrier to spend over one billion U.S. dollars for deployments. The Koreans sought to develop WiBro as a regional and potentially international alternative to 3.5–4G systems. But given the lack of self-developed momentum as a standard, WiBro has joined WiMAX and agreed to harmonize with the similar OFDMA-based 802.16e version of the standard. What makes WiBro rollout, which will start in April of 2006, a good test case for the overall WiMAX effort, is that it is mobile and well thought-out for delivery of WBA services, and the fact that the deployment is taking place in a highly sophisticated, broadband-saturated market. WiBro will go up against 3G and very high-bandwidth wire line services rather than as gap filler or rural underserved market deployments. WiBro will be in direct competition with 3G and high-bandwidth wired services, which pose tough competition.

In a very interesting move, WiMAX heavyweight supporter, Intel, and WiBro technology proponent, LG Electronics, announced in November 2005 that they would work together to speed up the harmonization of worldwide WMAN technologies, including WiMAX and WiBro technologies. Intel will support the merging of WiMAX

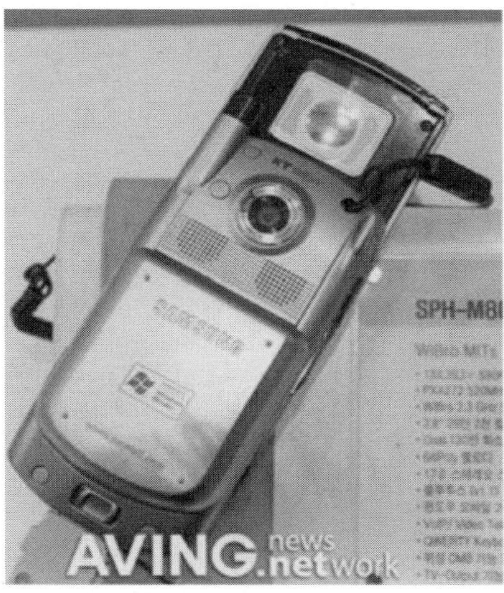

Figure 9: Samsung SPH-M8000 WiBro smart phone

and WiBro standards to reduce the redundant investment on the similar WMAN technologies throughout the world. This move, according to many is positive for all parties as it will eventually benefit the end users and equipment vendors as well. At the moment, the Korean government is about to issue three WiBro licenses. Many people believe that three Korean companies, KT, SK Telecom, and Hanaro Telecom, will most likely be the winners.

Samsung Electronics recently demonstrated its first WiBro smart phone, SPH-M8000 (see Figure 9), at the Second Communication and Broadcasting Convergence Exhibition & Conference. This model of a WiBro phone uses a slide-up front cover design with a QWERTY full-functional keyboard under the front cover. It operates on the platform of Windows Mobile 2003 Second Edition for Pocket PC Phone with Intel PXA272 CPU, which can run up to a 520 MHz clock. Its screen uses 2.8 inch QVGA (240×320) TFT touch panel with 260,000 colors. The SPH-M8000 is equipped with two cameras, the front one using 300,000 resolution and the back one using 3 million resolution. It also supports Bluetooth v1.1 for earphone and other short-range communications. The weight of SPH-M8000 is only 184 g, which is very light to carry around.

WIRELESS WIDE AREA NETWORKS (WWANs)

Wireless wide area networks encompass a fairly large group of wireless technology, or mobile cellular technologies, which have experienced three generations until now. The first generation (1G), including AMPS, NMT, TACS, and so forth, was based on analog technology and very large cell size. The average capacity of the 1G WWAN was very low and international roaming was not possible. The 2G WWAN technology was based on digital technology; examples include GSM, IS-95, JDC, and so on. Similar to the 1G cellular systems, 2G WWANs were still voice centric, and they had limited capability to support slow data services. The 3G WWANs include CDMA2000, W-CDMA, and TD-SCDMA standards, proposed respectively by the United States, Europe/Japan, and China, to respond to the call from the ITU for IMT-2000 global mobile telecommunication initiatives. Today, 3G cellular networks have been deployed in many countries throughout the world.

Because our objective here is to discuss WBA, we will not discuss any of the details of the 3G cellular standards, although they also belong to WBA technology in a broad sense. However, we will need to know the difference between the major 3G standards and WiMAX technology in this section so that we can understand more about the possible future developmental trends of the two technologies. A recent move made by WiMAX is the standardization of IEEE 802.16e, which is able to support vehicular-speed mobility and regional roaming (handoffs); thus, the boundary between the mobile cellular and WiMAX technologies becomes very blurred. This necessitates a clearer definition of the roles WiMAX plays in the midst of cellular mobile system evolution from 3G to B3G. The question now is whether WiMAX will be a gap filler of different wireless services (as claimed now by Intel and many other WiMAX proponents), including mobile cellular and WLANs, or will it be a strong competitor for the future mobile communication market with 3G and B3G cellular technologies? This is not an easy question to answer at the moment.

If we look at the air-link technologies adopted by 3G WWANs and WiMAX systems, we find that the 3G is dominated by CDMA multiple access technology without exception: all 3G standards including CDMA2000, W-CDMA, TD-SCDMA, and so forth use CDMA for their air-link technology. On the other hand, WiMAX promotes strongly OFDMA technology as its primary multiple-access physical layer architecture. There have been many serious debates in symposia and conferences around the world about which form of multiple-access technology should be selected as B3G's core air-link design: CDMA or OFDMA? It is, again, a difficult question to answer. At the moment, it seems that the OFDMA has the upper hand, and more people tend to support the use of OFDMA, than CDMA, which is now considered a legacy technology that should be replaced by something new (e.g., OFDMA). Therefore, the comparison of the 3G WWANs versus WiMAX seems to be equal to the comparison of CDMA versus OFDMA. For this reason, we offer some discussions on the issue as follows.

Multipath Mitigation in 3G and WiMAX

Multipath interference occurs when multiple reflected signals arrive at a same wireless receiver. These signals may have been reflected off of buildings, walls, trees, hills, or other solid objects. When the mobile user is indoors (and the base station is located outside), there is no line-of-sight signal at all. Because each of the signals is reflected from different objects, each has traveled a different distance, causing some signals to arrive earlier than others. This results in the signals arriving at random phase offsets of one another. The signals then experience fading through destructive (and constructive) interference when the signals become superimposed on one another. This interference is often referred to as Intersymbol interference (ISI). The amount of fading depends on the delay spread of the signal as well as the power level of each signal (some multipath returns may have weaker signals due to attenuation, possibly caused by an object such as a tree).

Technologies using CDMA (e.g., 802.11b and 3G) and other wideband technologies are very susceptible to multipath fading, because the delay time can easily exceed the symbol duration, which causes the symbols to completely overlap (ISI). The use of several parallel subcarriers in OFDMA enables much longer symbol duration, which makes the signal more robust to multipath time dispersion. For example, if we want to send information at a rate of 1000 bps, we could do this serially where each bit would take 1/1000th of a second. Any delays longer than 1/1000th of a second would overlap the next bit. On the other hand, by sending 1000 bits in 1000 parallel streams, each bit would take one second to transmit and a 1/1000th second delay would only overlap by 1/1000th of the transmission interval for any given bit, basically eliminating any interference. By adding a small guard time, the ISI can effectively be mitigated in OFDMA.

Multipath fading affects certain frequencies of a transmission and can result in deep fading at certain frequencies, resulting in frequency selective fading. One reason this occurs is because of the wideband nature of the signals. When a signal is reflected off of a surface, different frequencies reflect in different ways. In Figure 10, both CDMA (left) and OFDMA (right) experience selective fading near the center of the band. With optimal channel coding and interleaving, these errors can be corrected (the coded BER does not increase at all). CDMA tries to overcome this by spreading the signal out and then equalizing the whole signal (the coded BER increases proportionally to the increase in the raw BER). OFDMA is therefore more resilient to frequency selective fading than CDMA.

Adaptive Modulation and Coding in 3G and WiMAX

Both W-CDMA (HSDPA) and OFDMA utilize QPSK and QAM. For W-CDMA, adaptive modulation and coding (AMC) is only used on the downlink (HSDPA), because the uplink still relies on W-CDMA 3rd-Generation Partnership Project (3GPP) release 99, which uses QPSK but not QAM. Modulation and coding rates can be changed to achieve higher throughput, but higher-order modulation will require better channel conditions (i.e., signal-to-noise

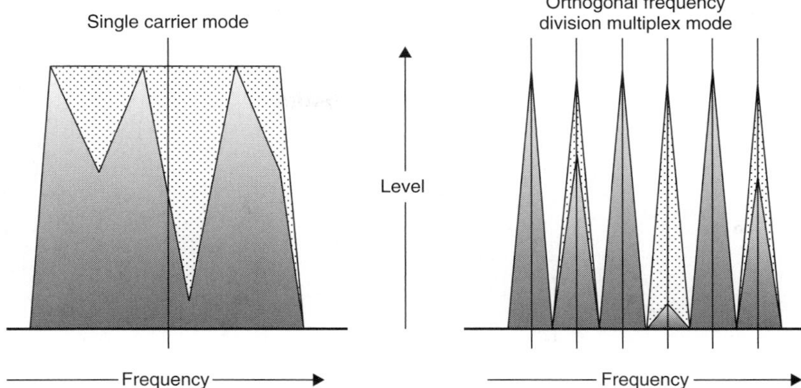

Figure 10: Comparison of CDMA and OFDMA under frequency selective fading channel, where the dotted area represents the transmitted spectrum and the solid area is the receiver input

Table 10: System-Level Performance Results for FTP Traffic with Maximum Throughput Scheduling

	OFDMA	W-CDMA(MMSE)	W-CDMA(RAKE)
Users per sector	40	40	40
Average OTA throughput (Mbps)	4.45	3.83	3.03
Average packet call throughput (kbps)	1802	1170	490
Average residual BLER	0.002	0.002	0.000
Average packet delay (s)	2.33	3.56	8.54

ratio). WiMAX uses higher-order modulations like QAM 64 to the areas closer to the base station, whereas lower-order modulations like QPSK are used to extend the range of the base station.

Performance results, conducted for one of the 3GPP Working Groups (R1-040571 2004), showed that although OFDMA is able to achieve the maximum throughput of 9.6 Mbps (16-QAM), W-CDMA (HSDPA) does not exceed 3 Mbps. From these results, it appears that an even higher discrepancy may be found when utilizing higher modulation and code rates to yield even higher throughput for OFDMA. Table 10 shows some system-level performance results comparing WiMAX and W-CDMA (HSDPA) (3GPP 2004). Even with more advanced receivers (MMSE), OFDMA is found to perform better in this environment. Furthermore, these results were obtained using OFDMA up to 16-QAM. Using more advanced OFDMA and modulation techniques (such as those included in 802.16e), the gap would likely widen. WiMAX (802.16e) in fact supports a higher-order modulation of 64-QAM (optional 256-QAM). It is important to note that although both of these technologies offer higher throughput, it appears that OFDMA may provide a greater range of higher throughput when compared to HSDPA (where the highest speeds, using 16-QAM, may only be provided within hot-spot size coverage). It should also be noted that, although AMC can be utilized in both the downlink and uplink for WiMAX, AMC has only been defined for the downlink portion of W-CDMA (HSDPA).

AMC in a multipath environment may offer OFDMA further advantages because the flexibility to change the modulation for specific subchannels allows WiMAX to be optimized at the frequency level. Another alternative would be to assign those subchannels to a different user who may have better channel conditions for that particular subchannel. This could allow users to concentrate transmit power on specific subchannels, resulting in improvements to the uplink budget and greater range. This technique is known as space division multiple access (SDMA). Figure 11 shows how subchannels could be chosen depending on the received signal strength. The subchannels on which the user is experiencing significant fading are avoided, and power is concentrated on channels with better channel conditions. With OFDMA, the client device could choose subchannels based on geographical locations with the potential of eliminating the impact of deep fades. CDMA-based technologies utilize the same frequency band regardless of where the user is. Of course, the assistance from smart antenna can give a CDMA a similar capability, but at a high implementation cost.

Spectral Efficiency of 3G and WiMAX

Spectral efficiency is another serious concern to an operator because of the limited spectrum availability and the cost of a spectrum license. It is also important to consider frequency reuse to understand deployment of multiple cells. OFDMA typically requires a frequency reuse factor of one to three, implying that the available spectrum must be split up into a three-cell formation. For example, if a carrier has 5 MHz of available spectrum, it needs to divide it into three channels of 1.75 MHz each, so that adjacent cells utilize different frequencies to avoid interference. For WiMAX, this results in a maximum of

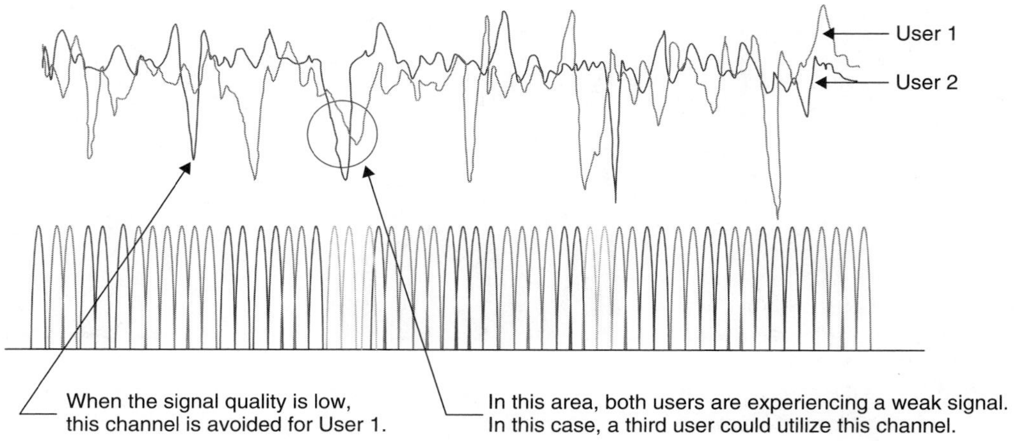
User 1
User 2
When the signal quality is low,
this channel is avoided for User 1.
In this area, both users are experiencing a weak signal.
In this case, a third user could utilize this channel.

Figure 11: OFDMA avoids subchannels with deep fade; the signals on the top indicate the received signal strength, and the bottom part of the figure indicates which subcarriers are then chosen for each signalbillions. Source: U.S. Census Bureau, 2004

approximately 6 Mbps per cell compared to 14.4 Mbps achievable by HSDPA. However, although the maximal throughput may be lower for WiMAX, it must be remembered that the 14.4 Mbps achievable by HSDPA would be very limited in coverage. WiMAX also supports larger channel sizes up to 20 MHz. To overcome this limitation, OFDMA systems can maintain a frequency reuse near one if there are location-sensitive transmissions near the edge of the cell that use a subset of the carriers, and/or if using advanced antenna systems (AAS), although AAS may be too expensive.

In CDMA-based 3G WWANs, the coverage of the cell expands and shrinks depending on the number of users. This is known as *cell breathing* and occurs because, with CDMA, users transmit at the same time (and are identified by their unique codes). The interference is averaged among the other users so that, as users are added to the cell, the coverage shrinks, and as users leave the cell, the coverage expands. A user downloading data can significantly reduce the coverage and force voice users to "soft" handoff to another cell. Such an increase in handoff rates would require that more cells be added to ensure coverage and eliminate any dead spots. This problem could be worsened with the deployment of HSDPA as a result of more bursty data and higher data rates. Another possible solution would be to deploy HSDPA on a separate 5 MHz channel.

HSDPA aggregates up to fifteen shared codes for highest capacity. Each user of the HSDPA channel requires a unique code for control access to the data channel. This limitation in code availability could lead to blocked voice calls. Because of this limitation and client complexity, most clients will initially be limited to five codes. Furthermore, because each user will require at least one code or carrier set allocated to him or her this can have a great impact on the number of users supported by each system. CDMA systems must also provide one code for each voice call, which implies that, in order to support a broadband data pipe, service providers will need to deploy HSDPA on a separate 5 MHz channel.

Before ending this section, we would like to look back at the issue raised at the beginning of this section. CDMA technology was "invented" by Qualcomm Inc., which, without a doubt, was the first company to introduce the CDMA into commercial (or civilian) applications in a large scale, making interim standard 95 (IS-95) for cellular mobile systems one of the major 2G technologies. It should also be noted that Qualcomm is still holding the majority of CDMA-related patents or IPRs, which have given the company a great deal of benefit in terms of the loyalty returns, license fees, and so on, making the company one of a very few perpetual gainers in the U.S. stock market. The sky-rocketed share price of the company today is proof of this. Therefore, Qualcomm obviously enjoys the current status quo of dominance of CDMA technology in the global 3G cellular market. Nobody knows what Qualcomm will do if B3G abandons CDMA and use another multiple-access technology, such as OFDMA. As mentioned earlier, Qualcomm recently secured the acquisition of Flarion, a small company that developed a coded OFDMA scheme to potentially replace CDMA as a prime multiple-access technology for B3G wireless, including WiMAX. The reposturing of their systems and OFDM patent portfolios as being central to OFDMA-based IEEE 802.16e developments has broadened the level of interest in the emerging field of OFDMA wireless. Some questioned the motivation of Qualcomm's move: is this an attempt to stall adoption of WiMAX? Or is this recognition by Qualcomm that OFDMA will likely become a predominant core multiple-access technology for 4G and beyond wireless systems? The answer to these questions will not be known for some time.

WIRELESS REGIONAL AREA NETWORKS

This section covers a new IEEE 802 standard, or IEEE 802.22, which is targeted at VHF/UHF analog TV bands to be released from U.S. TV companies that will upgrade their traditional analog TV to digital TV broadcasting services. The wireless data networks based on the IEEE 802.22 standard (2004) will be called wireless regional area networks or simply Wi-TV technology.

Initially, the FCC was looking at means by which the 6 MHz wide licensed spectrum in the UHF band (FCC 2004) currently assigned to TV broadcasters, can be reused in secondary markets as a path to last-mile data access (for this reason, we can also refer to WRANs as a useful means of providing WBA services). This proposal would set power levels up to 8 dB higher than those currently allowed in those bands, thereby greatly increasing range and coverage area. In addition, the propagation characteristics at the lower UHF frequencies are particularly attractive, offering the possibility of longer distance, lower power, and fewer base stations.

It is interesting to note that many technologies could use this TV spectrum, although the WiMAX community is keen to claim it for its own. In March 2004, when the IEEE 802.22 group was set up, the powerful IEEE 802.16 Working Group was angered when its proposal that the cognitive radio work should be kept under its auspices, rather than in a separate group, was defeated. However, this has not halted its supporters, led by Intel, in their quest to turn the IEEE 802.22 efforts to their advantage.

The story behind the conflict between IEEE 802.16 and IEEE 802.22 groups highlights the importance of cognitive radio technology and its applications in either WMANs or WRANs operating in underused VHF/UHF TV bands. The cognitive radio technology used for IEEE 802.22 will act as its core to scan the bands, select those unoccupied for its communications purpose, and stop immediately when it detects the signals sent from incumbent users.

The IEEE 802.22 Working Group insisted when the group began work that Wi-TV would work with existing IEEE 802 architectures, serving as a regional area network complementing both the WiFi WLANs and the WiMAX WMANs. The IEEE 802.22 group also pointed out that WiMAX is not suitable for TV spectrum because it does not include cognitive radio functions. On the other hand, the IEEE 802.16 group denounced that claim, noting that WiMAX does in fact have a provision for cognitive radios (which will be included in its new amendment, standard IEEE 802.16h) to avoid interference with other WiMAX devices at higher frequencies, and that it could easily be adapted for UHF frequencies.

In December 2004, the IEEE 802.22 group accused the 802.16 group of overstepping its scope and developing its cognitive radios for "coexistence with primary users," not just WiMAX users, and asked the WiMAX committee to reaffirm the limits of its scope. The WiMAX group declined and received support from another IEEE task group, 802.19, which saw no reason why both groups could not work on the problem separately. The fight is still going on about which group will be allowed to use the VHF/UHF bands for wireless broadband access, even with the help of cognitive radio technology. At the time of the writing of this chapter, the 802.22 group appears to have been given permission to move forward, while the 802.16 group has to stay on its original 2–66 GHz bands.

CONCLUSION

This chapter begins with the definition of wireless broadband access technology, and then, by following its broad definition, reviews almost all possible candidates for the WBA applications: WLANs, WPANs, WWANs, WRANs, and, of course, WMANs. The chapter can serve as an information source for wireless data networking in general, although we focus on WMAN, or simply WiMAX.

This chapter is written in a way that is suitable for everyone, from a communications engineer with background knowledge on wireless communications and networks, to a student who is just beginning his or her third year of study in an undergraduate program. The introduction of different wireless networking technologies proceeds in a very descriptive way, with little mathematics. Many illustrations have been used to give vivid pictures of the complex concepts behind each wireless technology. Therefore, we hope that this chapter will be found useful to people who are working to achieve their goals in related professions.

ACKNOWLEDGMENT

We would like to take this unique opportunity to express our sincere thanks to all of the people who helped us in the entire course of preparation of the chapter. Specifically, we want to thank Professor Hossein Bidgoli for his kind invitation to make the writing of this chapter possible. At the same time, both Hsiao-Hwa Chen and Mohsen Guizani would like also to thank many of their students for their assistance during this project as well as their families for their patience and encouragement.

GLOSSARY

ALOHANET: A packet radio data network developed at the University of Hawaii in the early 1970s to provide wireless data access to different campuses in the university.

IEEE 802.11: A series of standards made by IEEE to specify the operation of wireless local area networks.

IEEE 802.11a: A WLAN standard that operates in the 5 GHz band and offers a data transmission rate up to 54 Mbps.

IEEE 802.11b: A WLAN standard that operates in the 2.4 GHz band and offers a data transmission rate up with 11 Mbps.

IEEE 802.11g: A WLAN standard that operates in the 2.4 GHz band and offers a data transmission rate up to 54 Mbps. IEEE 802.11g is backward compatible with IEEE 802.11b.

IEEE 802.11p: A new wireless networking standard that is dedicated to vehicular wireless access. It is also called *dedicated short-range communications* or simply *WAVE technology*.

IEEE 802.15: A series of standards for wireless personal area networks (WPANs).

IEEE 802.15.1: A WPAN standard based on Bluetooth technology.

IEEE 802.15.3a: A WPAN standard based on ultra-wideband (UWB) technology.

IEEE 802.16: A series of standards for wireless metropolitan area networks (WMANs).

IEEE 802.16e: Specifies the standard for WMANs operating in the 2–6 GHz band. It can also support vehicular mobility.

IEEE 802.22: Specifies a new wireless networking standard targeted at VHF/UHF analog TV bands to be released from those U.S. TV companies that will upgrade their traditional analog TV to digital TV broadcasting services.

WBA: Wireless broadband access.

WiBro: A technology to support wireless metropolitan area networks developed by the Korean government. It can support mobile terminals up to 120 km/h and its base station can cover an area of approximately 1–5 km in radius. It will be made compatible with WiMAX eventually, although currently it is not.

WiMAX: Worldwide Interoperability for Microwave Access, a certification mark for products that pass conformity and interoperability tests for the IEEE 802.16 standards.

WLAN: Wireless local area network.

WMAN: Wireless metropolitan area network.

WPAN: Wireless personal area network.

WRAN: Wireless regional area network.

CROSS REFERENCES

See *Metropolitan Area Networks*; *Wireless LANs (WLANs)*; *Wireless Wide Area Networks (WWANs)*.

REFERENCES

Federal Communications Commission (FCC). 2004. Unlicensed operation in the TV broadcast bands. ET Docket No. 04–186.

Foerster, J., and G. Sater. 2000. LMDS standards architectural issues. In *Proceedings of the 2000 IEEE Wireless Communications and Networking Conference*, Chicago, September, 3: 1590–1594.

Fullerton, L. 1991. UWB waveforms and coding for communications and radar. In *Proceedings of Telesystems Conference*, Atlanta, Georgia, March pp. 139–41.

Forouzan, B. 2001. *Data communications and networking*. New York: McGraw-Hill.

http://www.comsoc.org/pubs/surveys/4q98issue/prasad.html

http://www.ee.iitb.ernet.in/uma/~aman/bluetooth/

http://www.swedetrack.com/usblue1.htm.

IEEE 802.11. 1999. http://standards.ieee.org/getieee802/802.11.html, (accessed September 13, 2007).

IEEE 802.15.4. 2003. Wireless medium access control (MAC) and physical layer (PHY) specifications for high rate wireless personal area networks (WPANs). https://www-inst.eecs.berkeley.edu/~cs150/ProtectedDocs/ieee-802.15.4-2003.pdf (accessed September 13, 2007).

IEEE 802.22. 2004. Standard for wireless regional area networks (WRAN)-specific requirements—Part 22: Cognitive wireless RAN medium access control (MAC) and physical layer (PHY) specifications: Policies and procedures for operation in the TV bands.

IEEE Part 15.3. 2003. Wireless medium access control (MAC) and physical layer (PHY) specifications for wireless personal area networks (WPANs), September 29, 2003.

Pahlavan, K., and P. Krishnamurthy. 2002. *Principles of wireless networks: A unified approach*. Upper Saddle River, NJ: Prentice Hall.

Petry, B. 2001. Wireless broadband access: High rate, point to multipoint, fixed antenna systems. In *The RF and microwave handbook*, edited by Mike Golio. Boca Raton, FL: CRC.

R1-040571. 2004. Further results on link-level comparisons of WCDMA and OFDM transmission. Alcatel, May.

Radio Frequency Interface Specification. Undated. Version 1.1: Data-over-cable service interface specifications, Cable Television Laboratories, Inc.

TSG-RAN-1. TR 25.892: Feasibility study for OFDM for UTRAN enhancement version 2.0.0, June.

Win, M. Z., and R. A. Scholtz. 2000. Ultra-wide bandwidth time-hopping spread-spectrum impulse radio for wireless multiple-access communications. *IEEE Transactions on Communications* 48(4): 679–91.

Win, M. Z., and R. A. Scholtz. 1998a. Impulse radio: How it works. *IEEE Communications Letters* 2: 36–38.

Win, M. Z., and R. A. Scholtz. 1998b. On the robustness of ultra-wide bandwidth signals in dense multipath environments. *IEEE Communications Letters* 2: 10–12.

Indoor Wireless Infrared Communications

Z. Ghassemlooy, *Northumbria University, UK*

INTRODUCTION

The fourth generation (4G) wireless communication systems will include a number of different complementary access technologies rather than a single technology, with the ultimate goal of providing omnipresent connectivity, ranging from high-mobility cellular systems to fixed and low-mobility indoor environments. Today's RF based networks may be able to support one or perhaps two high-capacity users per cell, which is highly wasteful with cell sizes of ~100 meters accommodating ten's of users. Multiple high-capacity users could only be serviced by deploying a similar number of systems, all within the same locale. This would create a situation where the multiple cells almost completely overlap, which then raises concerns with regards to interference, carrier re-use, etc. In contrast, IR could deliver the necessary capacity to each user through multiple user-sized cells, and because of the intrinsically abrupt boundary of these cells, interference would be negligible and carrier re-use would not be an issue. Indeed, IR (or OW) is a future proofed solution because additional capacity far beyond the capabilities of radio could be delivered to users as their needs increase with time. Figure 1 shows the mobility of RF and OW systems for a range of bit rates. Perhaps the largest installed short-range stationary wireless communications links are optical, rather than RF. It is argued that IR has a part to play in the wider 4G vision. In large open environments such as railway station, exhibition halls, etc., where individual users require 100 Mbps or more, IR with tracking capabilities could be the most sensible solution because of its improved wavelength re-use within the same location, security, and high data rates.

First proposed as a medium for short-range wireless communication more than two decades ago, IR wireless offers a number of advantages over its RF counterpart, such as abundance of unregulated bandwidth (200 THz in the 700–1500 nm range), no multipath fading when intensity modulation and direct detection is used, high security connectivity, higher capacity per unit volume (bps/m^3) due to neighboring cells sharing the same frequency, cost effectiveness at rates near 100 Mbps, small cell size and minimal absorption effects at 800–890 nm and 1550 nm wavelengths. The comparison between RF and IR for indoor wireless communications is shown in Table 1. Optical wireless LAN has been used in large scale in a number of applications such as telemedicine, laptops, PDAs, museums, etc (Kahn and Barry 1997). According to the IEEE 802.11 specifications, the OW physical layer can support data rate up to 2 Mbps with a potential to migration to higher data rates (IEEE Standard 802.11 1997). The operating wavelength is between 850 nm and 950 nm and the link span could be as long as 10–12 m. The Infrared Data Association (IrDA) has standardised low cost and short range (1–8 m) infrared data links supporting data rates ranging from 2.5 kbps to 16 Mbps (for a short range line-of-sight) at wavelength between 850 nm and 900 nm (IrDA 2006). To an extent, RF and IR may be viewed as complementary rather than competitive media. For example, if a wireless LAN is required to cover a large area in which users can roam freely and remain connected to the network at all times, then RF is the only cost-effective medium that can achieve this. If, however, a wireless LAN is required to cover a more modest area but deliver advanced bandwidth-hungry multimedia network services such as video conferencing and video on demand, then IR is the only medium that truly has the bandwidth available to deliver this.

This chapter provides a general introduction to the indoor optical wireless links, discussing their unique properties and the constraints imposed on the system. Also discussed are the various link configurations and their advantages and disadvantages, the channel characteristics, ambient light interference, and modulation schemes.

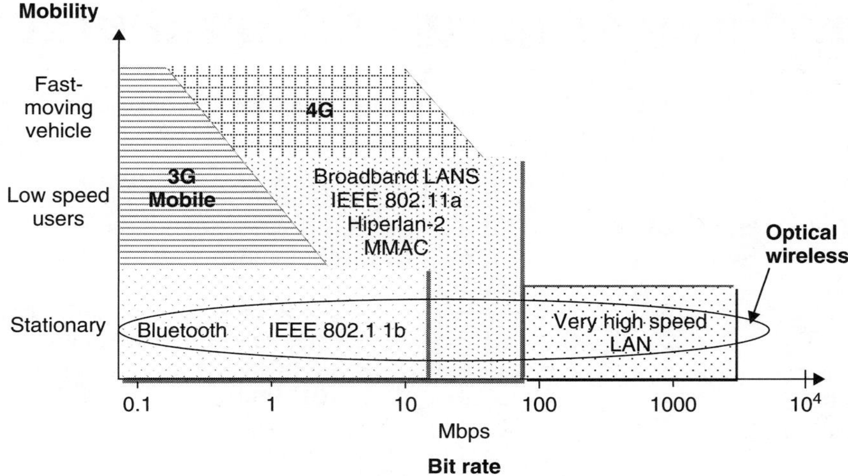

Figure 1: Mobility of RF and optical wireless (IR) systems versus bit rate

Table 1: Properties of Radio and Infrared Wireless

Property	Radio	Infrared	Implication for Infrared
Bandwidth regulated	Yes	No	Approval not required World-wide compatibility
Passes through walls	Yes	No	Inherently secure Carrier reuse in adjacent rooms
Multipath fading	Yes	No	Simple link design
Multipath dispersion	Yes	Yes	Problematic at high data rates
Path loss	High	High	
Dominant noise	Other users	Background light	Short range
Average power is proportional to	$\int \|f(1)\|^2 dt$, $f(t)$ is the input signal	$\int f(t)\, dt$	High peak-average ratio

PROPERTIES OF INDOOR OPTICAL WIRELESS LINKS

For low-cost IR wireless communications, intensity modulation with direct detection (IM/DD) is the only feasible method of communication (Barry 1994). In this mode of operation, the intensity or power of the optical source $x(t)$ is directly modulated by varying the drive current. At the receiver, a photodetector is used to generate a photocurrent $y(t)$, which is proportional to the instantaneous optical power incident upon it. As with RF systems, indoor OW links are also subject to multipath propagation, which is most pronounced in links using non-directional transmitters and receivers. Multipath propagation causes the received electric field to undergo severe amplitude fades on the scale of a wavelength, and consequently, a detector smaller than one wavelength would experience multipath fading. However, in IR the total photocurrent generated is proportional to the integral of the optical power over the entire photodetector surface, which is typically millions of square wavelengths, thus providing an inherent spatial diversity to prevent multipath fading (Barry 1994). However, multipath propagation does lead to dispersion, thus resulting in pulse spreading. Here the channel is modelled as a linear baseband channel with an impulse response $h(t)$ as shown in Figure 2, where R is the photodetector responsivity.

Optical wireless transceivers usually operate in environments containing an intense amount of ambient light emanating from both natural (solar) and artificial sources (incandescent and fluorescent). The average combined power of this background radiation generates a DC photocurrent I_B in the photodetector, giving rise to shot noise $n(t)$, which has a single-sided power spectral density N_o, given as (Moreira et al. 1995):

$$N_O = 2qI_B, \tag{1}$$

where q is the electron charge. Even when optical filtering is used to reject out of band light sources, the received signal power is much lower than the power from ambient light sources, typically 25 dB lower (Barry 1994).

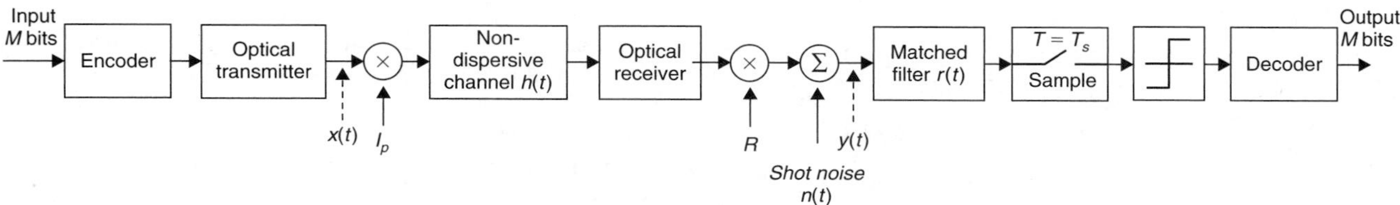

Figure 2: A typical IM/DD optical wireless system block showing transmitter, channel, receiver

Consequently, I_B is much larger than the maximum photocurrent generated by the signal, and hence, the shot noise may be regarded as white, Gaussian, and independent of the received signal (Lee and Messerschmitt 1994). In the presence of intense ambient light, which is usually the case, shot noise is the dominant noise source in a typical diffuse receiver (Barry 1994). Note that if little or no ambient light is present, the dominant noise source is receiver preamplifier noise, which is also signal independent and Gaussian. Additionally, artificial ambient light sources also generate a periodic interference signal, which must be added to $n(t)$. The equivalent baseband model of an optical wireless link (see Figure 2), can be summarised by (Kahn and Barry 1997):

$$y(t) = Rx(t) \otimes h(t) = n(t), \tag{2}$$

where the symbol "⊗" denotes convolution. $x(t)$ defined in terms of information data sequence $\{s_n\}$ and symbol time T_s is given as:

$$x(t) = \sum f_{s_n}(t - nT_s). \tag{3}$$

While (2) is simply a linear filter channel with additive noise, IR systems differ from conventional electrical or RF systems because $x(t)$ represents power rather than amplitude. This places two constraints on the transmitted signal. Firstly, $x(t) \geqslant 0$, and secondly, eye safety requirements limit the maximum optical transmit power which may be employed. Generally, it is the average power P_t requirement which is the most restrictive and hence, the average value of $x(t)$ must not exceed a specified value of P_t defined as (Barry 1994):

$$P_t \geq \lim_{T\to\infty} \frac{1}{2T} \int_{-T}^{T} x(t)\, dt. \tag{4}$$

This is in contrast to the time-averaged value of $|x(t)|^2$, which is the case on conventional channels when $x(t)$ represents amplitude. The average received optical power is given by $P_r = H(0)P_t$, where $H(0) = \int_{-\infty}^{\infty} h(t)\, dt$ is the channel DC gain.

LINK CONFIGURATION

Indoor optical wireless links may be configured in a variety of ways to support a multitude of applications. Street et al. (1997) grouped these into four generic system configurations: directed LOS, non-directed LOS, diffuse, and tracked, as illustrated in Figure 3.

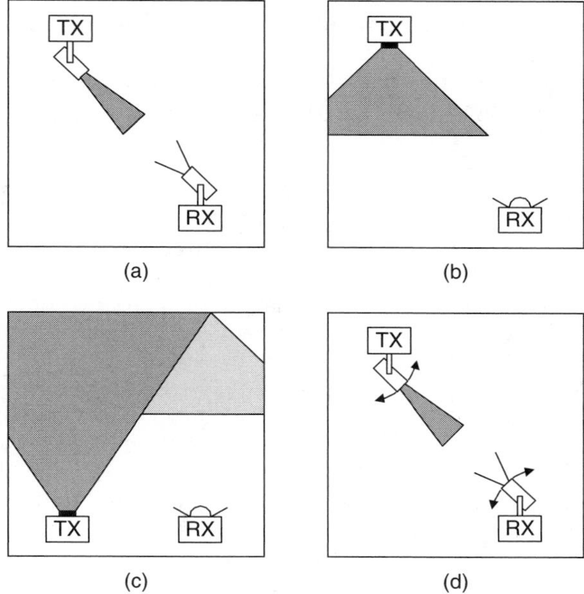

Figure 3: Link configurations: (a) directed LOS, (b) non-directed LOS, (c) diffuse, and (d) tracked

Directed LOS

Direct LOS as shown in Figure 3(a), offers excellent transmission capacity up to a few Gbps and high power efficiency by using narrow beam transmitters and narrow field of view (FOV) receivers. The use of narrow FOV receivers allows optical concentrators to be employed along with thin film optical filters, because the angular dependence of the filter response does not pose a problem. Furthermore, directed LOS systems do not suffer from multipath propagation, and ambient background light is largely rejected. Thus, the potential data rate is limited only by the available power budget rather than multipath dispersion (Smyth et al. 1995). However, directed LOS links must be pointed prior to use, and require an uninterrupted line-sight path between the transmitter and the receiver, thus making them susceptible to blocking. In addition to this, by their very nature, they are more suited to point-to-point links rather than point-to-multipoint broadcast type links, thus reducing their flexibility. Directed LOS is the chosen configuration for IrDA links (IrDA 2001), which offer simple peer-to-peer networking between portable electronic devices such as laptops, palmtops, PDAs, and digital cameras. These devices are specified to operate over a maximum range of 1 m, and offer data rates from 9.6 kbps to 4 Mbps (IrDA 2001).

Non-directed LOS

The non-directed LOS configuration, Figure 3(b), uses wide beam transmitters and wide FOV receivers to achieve an increased coverage area and alleviate the need for pointing. In comparison with the directed LOS, these benefits are achieved at the expense of a reduced irradiance for a given range and transmit power. The use of wide-angle transmitters and receivers means that a portion of the received signal may have undergone one or more reflections from walls and room objects, thus giving rise to multipath propagation. Additionally, because the majority of power incidents on the photodetector are due to the LOS path, non-directed LOS links are still prone to blocking. Non-directed LOS links are well suited to point-to-multipoint broadcast type applications. A typical scenario for this link topology would be an OW access point located on the ceiling of a room, providing connectivity to the portable devices within its coverage area. Computer generated holograms have been proposed as a means of accurately defining the coverage area of non-directed LOS links (Smyth et al. 1995). Through control of the coverage area, large rooms may be divided into "optical cells", each serviced by a different infrared access port. Such architecture has been used in experimental systems (McCullagh and Wisely 1994) and proposed for a number of practical applications including telepoints (Nicholls, Greaves and Unwin 1996), trading desks, and desk area networks (Heatley and Neild 1999). Compared with the LOS, non-directed LOS systems are more susceptible to large dynamic variations of signal-to-noise ratio, leading to link failures. To overcome this problem, rate-adaptive transmission systems have been proposed that use repeated and punctured convolutional codes (Ohtsuki 2003) and angle diversity together with rate-adaptive transmission schemes (Tavares et al. 2003).

Diffuse

Exhibiting a similar behavior to that of visible light, infrared signals are absorbed by dark objects, diffusely reflected by light-coloured objects, and directionally reflected from shiny surfaces (Kahn and Barry 1997). Such characteristics have given rise to another link configuration referred to as the diffuse, see Figure 3(c), in which reflections from room boundaries are relied upon to provide coverage. This was first proposed in 1979 by Gfeller and Bapst. Typically, a diffuse transmitter points vertically upwards towards the ceiling, emitting a wide beam of infrared energy with an angular distribution given by the generalized Lambertian law as:

$$P(\theta) = \frac{n+1}{2\pi} P_t \cos^n \theta, \tag{5}$$

where, n is the Lambertian exponent, P_t is transmitted power, θ is the angle between the initial direction of light and the direction of maximum power. The receiver has a wide FOV, and collects the signal after it has undergone one or more reflections from the ceiling, walls, and objects in the room. Typical values for reflection coefficients are from 0.4 to 0.9 for white plaster walls, varying between 0.7 and 0.85 depending on surface texture and angle of incidence (Gfeller and Bapst 1979). From a user's point of view, the diffuse link topology is the most convenient because it does not require any pointing of the transmitter or receiver, nor does it require an LOS path to be maintained. In addition to this, the configuration is also extremely flexible, and can be used for both infrastructure and ad hoc networks (Street et al. 1997). However, along with non-directed LOS links, diffuse links requires relatively high optical power (~0.5 W) to illuminate the room. It also incurs a high optical path loss, which is typically in the range of 50–70 dB for a horizontal separation distance of up to 5 m (Kahn, Krause, and Carruthers 1995). The path loss is increased further if a person is standing next to the receiver such that the main signal path is obstructed, a situation referred to as shadowing. In addition to this, diffuse links must also contend with severe multipath propagation. Intersymbol interference (ISI) limits the maximum unequalized bit rate to ~260 Mbps (Gfeller and Bapst 1979). Thus, for a coverage volume of $10 \times 10 \times 3$ m, the unequalized bit rate would be limited to ~16 Mbps or higher (Smyth et al. 1995). Nevertheless, to date the diffuse configuration has received the greatest interest from the research community, and the number of experimental diffuse links has been reported covering bit rates up to 50 Mbps. Diffuse is also the chosen link configuration for the IEEE 802.11 infrared physical layer standard (IEEE Standard 802.11 1997), and diffuse systems are now commercially available (Spectrix 2000).

LOS with Tracking

Although diffuse links offer bit rates up to several tens of megabits per second, this is not adequate to support broadband applications such as video conferencing. For multi-user applications, there are basically two major schemes that can support very high bit rates. These are LOS links with tracking (Jungnickel et al. 2001), and the multiple-spot diffusing (MSD) scheme (Kavehrad and Jivkova 2003). The former, see Figure 3(d), offers high power efficiency and potentially high bit rates ($>$ 100 Mbps) of directed LOS links, with the increased coverage enjoyed by non-directed LOS systems. In an early experimental tracked system developed by B.T. Labs, which achieved a bit rate of 1 Gbps, the tracking was performed using mechanical steerable optics (Wisely 1996). However, mechanical steerable optics are prohibitively expensive and difficult to miniaturize. Consequently, in the same paper, Wisely et al. proposed a solid state tracked system, using multi-element transmitter and receiver arrays along with a lens arrangement. Using this arrangement, steering is merely a matter of selecting the appropriate array element. Note that along with diffuse links using multi-beam transmitters and angle-diversity receivers, tracked systems offer the potential to implement space-division multiplexing, whereby multiple users can communicate without suffering a loss of per-user capacity, because each user is located in a different cell.

Kavehrad and Jivkova (2003) have shown that the use of MSD with a multi-beam transmitter and angle diversity receiver (see Figure 4), results in a significant improvement in system performance and higher data rates

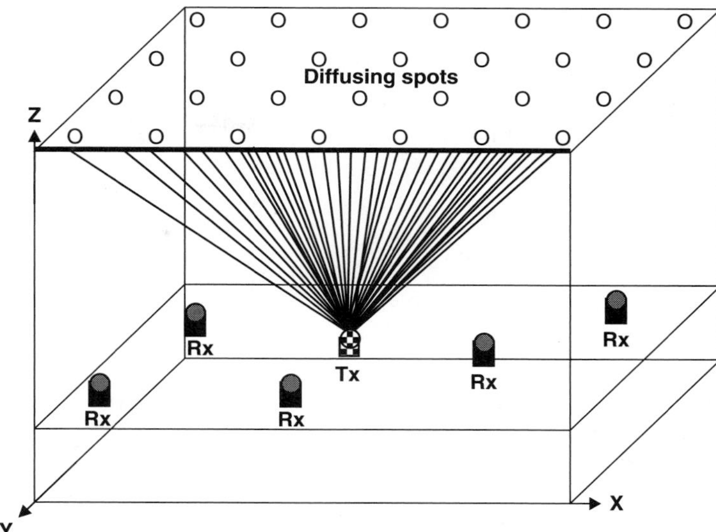

Figure 4: Multi-spot diffusing configuration

can be achieved by covering the entire ceiling of a room with a regular grid of diffusing spots to ensure uniform distribution of optical power as well as roaming capability. Each diffusing spot can be created using a separate laser source and a lens; however it is rather complex to create a large number of diffusing spots. Alternatively, diffusing spots can be created using the holographic technique with a single laser source (Pakravan, Simova and Kavehrad 1997). However, the technique results in nonhomogeneous distribution of optical power. This problem could be overcome by employing computer-generated holograms, where wavefronts produced will have prescribed amplitude and phase distributions. The hologram cell patterns, lattice spacing is given as (Kavehrad and Jivkova 2003):

$$\Delta S = \lambda ht - r/\Lambda, \tag{6}$$

where, Λ is the cell size and $ht-r$ is the height between transmitter and reflecting surface.

For non-directed LOS and diffuse links, significant performance improvements can be achieved using an angle-diversity receiver rather than a single element detector. This may be implemented in one of two ways. A non-imaging angle-diversity implementation consists of multiple receiving elements that are oriented in different directions, each element having its own non-imaging concentrator. The main drawback of this approach is that it can lead to an excessively bulky and costly receiver. A more elegant implementation is the imaging angle-diversity receiver, the so-called "fly-eye receiver," first proposed by Yun and Kavehrad (1992), which consists of an imaging optical concentrator (e.g., a lens) with a segmented photodetector array placed at its focal plane. Regardless of the implementation method, the photocurrent generated by each element is amplified separately and may then be processed in a variety of ways, which vary in terms of performance and complexity. Angle-diversity receivers can simultaneously achieve a high optical gain and a wide field of view. By exploiting the fact that unwanted signals are generally received from different directions than that of the desired signal, they can significantly reduce the effects of ambient light noise, co-channel interference, and multipath distortion. A further improvement in the power efficiency of diffuse links can be achieved by replacing the single wide-beam diffuse transmitter with a multi-beam transmitter, sometimes referred to as a quasi-diffuse transmitter, which consists of multiple narrow beams pointing in different directions (Yun and Kavehrad 1992).

Hybrid configuration based on diffuse and tracked links exploits the advantages of both schemes. In this configuration the tracked system is used all the time, provided a direct path exists between transmitter and receiver. When the path is blocked, the system switches to the diffuse back-up link until the direct path is established once more (see Figure 5). In order to ensure a distortion-free communication link, a receiver with direction diversity narrow FOV should be used. Narrow FOV results in significantly

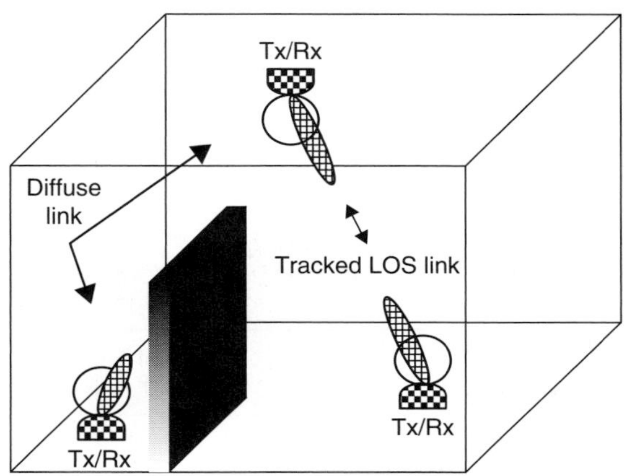

Figure 5: Hybrid diffuse and tracked LOS links

reduced received optical power at the receiver compared with the ambient light.

Therefore, to improve the signal-to-noise ratio (SNR), an optical filter together with an optical concentrator should be used prior to detection. The total SNR is defined by:

$$SNR_T = \sum_{i=1}^{N} SNR_i, \quad SNR_T = \frac{[P_t R H_i(0)]^2}{N_{0i} R_b}, \tag{7}$$

where, N is the number of receiver branches, P_t is the optical signal power, $H_i(0)$ is the path loss at the ith receiver branch, and N_{0i} and R_b are the noise variance and data rate, respectively. It is shown that with the use of a holographic receiver front-end, the path loss is 6 dB lower and the SNR is 11 dB larger than with a bare receiver. Note that in contrast to conventional channels, where the SNR is proportional to the first power of the received average power, in optical systems the SNR is proportional to the square of the received optical average power, implying that for IM/DD optical links P_t must be relatively high and it can tolerate only a limited path loss.

STANDARDS AND EYE SAFETY

There are several "Infrared Data Association" IrDA (IrDA 2006) standards in existence today, covering a wide range of bit rates from 9.6 kbps to 4 Mbps. However, all links require an LOS and are only specified to work over a one meter range. For OW LANs, the IEEE 802.11 standard specifies three physical layers, two using radio with spread spectrum modulation and one using IR in the 780–950 nm wavelength range, and bit rates of 1 or 2 Mbps using diffuse propagation (IEEE 1997). However, radiation in this wavelength can be focussed onto the retina, causing thermal damage. The eye safety limit is a function of the viewing time, wavelength, and apparent size of the optical source. The standard makes a distinction between point sources (on which the eye can focus) and large area sources, which form an extended image on the retina. The standard treats laser and LED sources equally. For modulated optical sources, generally, the average power level limits the transmitted optical power. In general, the average power for a pulse train of duration 100s must not exceed the power of a single pulse of duration 100s. Table 2 shows the Class 1 power limits for both point and extended sources for a number of important wavelengths (Street et al. 1997). Here α is the angle subtended by the source at measurement point and MPE is equal to power captured by a 50 mm diameter aperture 100 mm from the optical detector.

CHANNEL CHARACTERISTICS

The power penalties directly associated with the channel may be separated into two factors, these being optical path loss and multipath dispersion (Carruthers and Kahn 1996). For directed LOS and tracked configurations, reflections do not need to be taken into consideration, and consequently the path loss is easily calculated from knowledge of the transmitter beam divergence, receiver size, and separation distance. For non-directed LOS and diffuse links, the optical path loss is more complex to predict because, it is dependent on a multitude of factors such as room dimensions, the reflectivity of the ceiling, walls, and objects within the room, as well as the position and orientation of the transmitter and receiver, to name but a few. In order to predict the path loss for non-directed LOS and diffuse links, it is necessary to analyse the distribution of optical power for a given setup. Gfeller and Bapst (1979) studied the power distribution for diffuse links, basing their model on single reflections only. The authors showed that by using an optical source consisting of multiple elements oriented in different directions, a more uniform coverage can be obtained over a larger area, compared with a single wide-beam optical source. Light is emitted with Lambertian characteristics and at the receiver, light collected from all directions is summed. Barry et al. (1993) adopted a recursive algorithm to allow higher order reflections to be taken into account. Lomba, Valadas and Duarte (1993) addressed the optimization of the optical power distribution for diffuse and non-directed LOS links. Pakravan and Kavehrad (1995) also analysed the optical power distribution for a typical conference room using various link configurations.

While determining the distribution of optical power throughout a room is adequate for basic power budget calculations, it does not allow the power penalty due to multipath propagation to be accurately predicted, because multiple reflections are not taken into consideration. Although the optical power associated with two or more reflections is relatively small, the signal arrives at the receiver much later than that undergoing only one reflection, and hence, cannot be ignored when considering high-speed non-directed LOS and diffuse links. In

Table 2: Class 1 Source Maximum Permissible Exposure (MPE) Power Limits

Wavelength	Point Source MPE ($\alpha < \alpha_{min} = 0.011$ rad, exposure time > 1 s)	Extended Source MPE ($\alpha > \alpha_{max} = 0.1$ rad, exposure time > 1 s)
850 nm	0.44 mW	$0.8(\alpha_{max}/\alpha_{min})$ mW
980 nm	0.8 mW	$0.8(\alpha_{max}/\alpha_{min})$ mW

order to generate an impulse response which includes higher order reflections, Barry et al. (1993) developed a ray-tracing algorithm in which the path loss and time delay are calculated for every path containing a given number of reflections. The algorithm then sums together all contributions to give an overall impulse response. Abtahi and Hashemi (1995) modified this work to consider the effects of furniture and people within the room, and also rooms of irregular shape. Pakravan and Kavehrad (1995) used a neural network to speed up the algorithm developed by Barry, whereby only a fraction of the total number of points need to be calculated, from which the neural network learns the rest. Lomba, Valadas, and Duarte (2000) developed a computationally efficient ray-tracing algorithm which uses look-up tables and progressively decreased resolution to speed up the simulation. Lopez-Hernandez, Perez-Jimenez, and Santamaria (1998) also developed a computationally efficient algorithm based on Monte Carlo analysis, where a path of a single photon is tracked during a random flight in a room until it is detected by the receiver. Although ray tracing is a reliable technique, it is not as efficient as the Gfeller and Bapst. A different approach was taken by Carruthers and Kahn (1996), who developed the ceiling bounce model, based on the claim that realistic multipath infrared channels can be characterised by only two parameters, these being optical path loss $H(0)$ and root mean square (RMS) delay spread D_{rms}. The authors adopt a two stage modeling approach: first assuming an infinitely large room, i.e., considering only a single reflection from the ceiling, and then making a correction which takes into account the position of the transmitter and receiver within the room. Multipath delay spread occurs due to reflection from different surfaces and local scattering, giving rise to intersymbol interference. Multipath leads to pulse dispersion, and it can also occur in the LOS point-to-point configuration due to movement of people within the vicinity of the communication links. The channel impulse response defined in terms of a unit step function $u(t)$ is given as:

$$h(t,a) = H(0)\frac{6a^6}{(t+a)^7}u(t), \tag{8}$$

where, a depends on the room size and the locations of the transmitter and receiver. For co-located transmitter and receiver, $a = 2H/c$ where H is the height of the ceiling above the transmitter and receiver and c is the speed of light. The delay spread is also related to as:

$$D_{rms} = \frac{a}{12}\left(\frac{13}{11}\right)^{0.5}. \tag{9}$$

For a given channel characteristics, H_0, P_e and R_b, and a modulation scheme the power and D_{rms} are normally defined in terms of their normalised values. For power it is defined as $P_t/P_{\text{OOK-ideal}}$ and the normalised D_{rms} is defined as $D_T = D_{rms}R_b$. Here, $P_{\text{OOK-ideal}}$ is the power of the system using on-and-off keying (OOK) on ideal channel. In indoor OW systems, because the room configuration is fixed, the link with IM/DD could be considered as a linear time variant, and linear equalisation schemes, spread spectrum techniques, coding, antenna diversity and directivity, and polarization techniques could be employed to compensate for any multipath dispersion.

OPTICAL COMPONENTS

Optical Sources

From a commercial point of view, the wavelength band between 780 and 950 nm is currently the best choice for most infrared applications due to the availability of low cost light-emitting diodes (LEDs) and laser diodes (LDs), and because it coincides with the peak responsivity of inexpensive silicon photodetectors. However, electromagnetic radiation in this band can cause damage to the human eye, and is therefore subject to eye safety regulations. The standard on laser safety contains a number of classifications, the lowest power of which is Class 1, implying that a device is safe under all foreseeable circumstances of use. The classification limits are dependent on a number of parameters, these being wavelength, apparent source size, pulse duty factor, and exposure duration. The standard treats LD and LED sources equally, the only difference being that LDs are generally categorised as point sources, which can be focussed to a small area on the retina, whilst LEDs usually fall under the extended source category, and form a larger image on the retina. From a power budget point of view, the wavelength band around 1.5 μm would be a much better choice, because the safety standard permits larger optical transmit powers to be used, and as shown in Figure 6, ambient light sources emit less power at these wavelengths. However, the major drawback to operating at such wavelengths is the lack of low cost optoelectronic devices available at present. The choice of optical source is largely dependent on the cost and performance. LEDs benefit from low cost and simple drive circuitry, but suffer from poor electrical-to-optical conversion efficiency, limited bandwidth, and broad spectral width (typically 40 nm), which prevents the use of narrow-band optical filters at the receiver. In contrast, LDs are more costly and require more complicated drive circuitry, but offer a number of advantages such as improved conversion efficiency, wide modulation bandwidth, and narrow spectral width, thus making them the obvious choice for high speed links. In terms of eye safety, LEDs are generally supplied in a lensed package and do not require any additional components to make them eye safe. Laser diodes, on the other hand, are essentially point source devices and must be diffused using computer generated holograms and/or integrating sphere diffusers in order to be classified as eye safe.

Photodetectors

The photodetector used in an IR system must have high responsivity to maximise the system power margin and wide bandwidth to allow for high data rates. There are two types of photodetectors: the positive-intrinsic-negative (PIN) photodiode and the avalanche photodiode (APD). The APDs achieve a very good performance when the

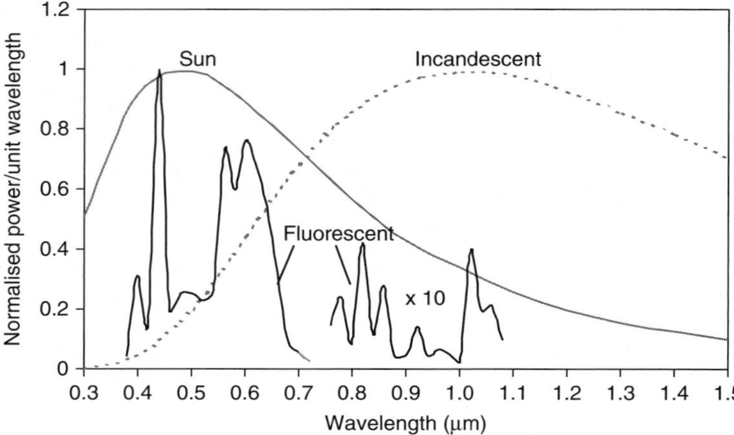

Figure 6: Optical power spectra of common ambient light sources

ambient light is very low, i.e., for LOS systems. However, in non-directed links, particularly diffuse links, where shot noise due to ambient light is dominant, the gain achieved by APDs decreases the SNR because the random nature of the APD's internal gain increases the variance of the shot noise by a factor greater than the signal gain (Kahn and Barry 1997). PIN photodiodes are preferable to APDs for use in non-directed links (Kahn and Barry 1997), offering low-cost, and large surface area, which results in improved signal-to-noise ratio (SNR) because the received signal power increases linearly with the area, while the noise power increases with its square root.

Optical Concentrators and Filters

Optical wireless receivers generally employ some form of optical concentrator in order to increase the effective area of the detector. High gains can be achieved using compound parabolic concentrators, but these devices have a narrow FOV and are therefore limited to use in directed links. Non-directed links generally make use of a hemispherical lens, which achieves a wide FOV and an omni-directional gain (Kahn and Barry 1997; Street et al. 1997). Optical filtering is also generally used to attenuate the out-of-band background radiation. Two basic types of optical filters exist; these being long-pass filter (LPF) and band-pass filter (BPF). LPFs are generally constructed of colored glass, and pass all wavelengths longer than a specified cut-on wavelength (Kahn and Barry 1997). In conjunction with a silicon PIN photodiode, which typically has a sensitivity range from 400 nm to 1.1 μm, LPFs result in a band-pass response with a spectral width on the order of several hundred nanometers. In contrast, BPFs, also referred to as interference filters, are constructed of multiple layers, and can achieve extremely narrow bandwidths. Such filters can be extremely effective when used in conjunction with LDs. However, one of the characteristics of BPF is that the pass band shifts as the angle of incidence changes. Therefore, this can result in a narrowing of the FOV, which may be unacceptable in non-directed links. This problem can be solved by bonding the band pass filter to the curved surface of a hemispherical lens (Spectrix 2000).

Preamplifier

A transimpedance amplifier is the best choice as a preamplifier stage at the receiver because it achieves a wide bandwidth and large dynamic range without the need for equalisation (Kahn and Barry 1997; Street et al. 1997; Phang and Johns 1999). The large dynamic range is important to accommodate variable link distances. The choice between employing a field-effect transistor (FET) or a bipolar-junction transistor (BJT) in the preamplifier depends on many factors. For example, FETs achieve low noise at high bit rates but suffer from relatively low transconductance, while BJTs achieve higher transconductances leading to better power conception (Kahn and Barry 1997; Street et al. 1997).

Ambient Light Sources

Artificial sources of ambient light introduce a periodic interference signal in optical wireless receivers which, if ignored, has the potential to degrade link performance. The three main sources of ambient light are sunlight, incandescent lamps, and fluorescent lamps and their optical power spectra are shown in Figure 6. Note that the spectra have been scaled to have equal maximum value, and the longer wavelength region of the fluorescent lamp spectrum has been amplified by a factor of 10 in order to make it clearly visible. When present, direct sunlight is typically much stronger than the other two sources, and represents an unmodulated source of ambient light with a very wide spectral width and a maximum power spectral density located at ~500 nm. All artificial ambient light sources are modulated, either by the mains frequency or, in the case of some fluorescent lamps, by a high-frequency switching signal.

Incandescent Lamp. Incandescent lamps have a maximum power spectral density around 1 μm, and produce an interference signal which is a near-perfect sinusoid with a frequency of 100 Hz. With this source, only harmonics up to 400 Hz carry a significant amount of power, and beyond that, all harmonics are more than 60 dB below the fundamental. The average received photocurrent I_B and

Table 3: I_B and $I_{pk\text{-}pk}$ for Incandescent Bulb with and without Optical Filtering

	Without Optical Filter	With Optical Filter	Reduction
I_B	100 μA	20.5 μA	79.5 %
I_{pk-pk}	65.2 μA	12 μA	81.6 %
I_B/I_{pk-pk}	1.53	1.71	

Table 4: I_B and $I_{pk\text{-}pk}$ for Low and Frequencies Fluorescent Lamp with and without Optical Filtering

	Without Optical Filter		With Optical Filter		Reduction	
	Low Frequency	High Frequency	Low Frequency	High Frequency	Low Frequency	High Frequency
I_B	100 μA	100 μA	5.4 μA	3.9 μA	94.6 %	96.1 %
I_{pk-pk}	67.7 μA	33.6 μA	9.6 μA	4.9 μA	85.8 %	85.4 %
I_B/I_{pk-pk}	1.48	2.98	0.56	0.80		

peak-to-peak interference signal photocurrent I_{pk-pk} for a 60 W incandescent bulb are given in Table 3. With optical filtering, I_B is reduced by 79.5 %, and the peak-to-peak amplitude of the interference signal is reduced by 81.6 %. The ratio of I_B/I_{pk-pk} is fairly similar both with and without optical filtering.

Fluorescent Lamp Driven by Conventional Ballast. Low frequency fluorescent lamps are driven by the mains frequency. For the low-frequency fluorescent lamps (Ballast – Crompton C237 1 × 75W and tube – Osram L 70W/23), the average received photocurrent and peak-to-peak interference signal photocurrent are given in Table 4. Optical filtering gives a significant reduction in both the average background photocurrent and the peak-to-peak interference amplitude. Because the reduction in I_B is greater than the reduction in I_{pk-pk}, with the optical filter in place, the peak-to-peak variation of the photocurrent is actually greater than the average background photocurrent.

Fluorescent Lamp Driven by Electronic Ballast. Fluorescent lamps driven by high-frequency electronic ballasts have a number of advantages over their low frequency counterparts, such as reduced electrical power consumption for a given level of illumination and increased life-expectancy of the tubes. The actual switching frequency used varies from one manufacturer to another, but is typically in the range 20–40 kHz. Its spectrum contains harmonics of the switching frequency and also harmonics of the mains frequency, similar to low frequency fluorescent lamps. Harmonics of the switching frequency can extend into the MHz range, and therefore present a much more serious impairment to optical wireless receivers. The average received photocurrent and the peak-to-peak interference signal photocurrent are given in Table 4. Without optical filtering, for a given background photocurrent, the interference amplitude produced by the high-frequency fluorescent lamp is only about half that produced by the low-frequency fluorescent lamp. Optical filtering gives a similar reduction in I_B and I_{pk-pk} as it did for the low-frequency fluorescent lamp.

MODULATION SCHEMES

Selecting a modulation technique is one of the key technical decisions in the design of any communication system. Before selection can take place, it is necessary to define the criteria on which the various modulation techniques are to be assessed. For the indoor OW channel, the main criteria are power efficiency and bandwidth efficiency, which will be discussed here.

Power Efficiency. In order to comply with eye safety regulations, the average optical power emitted by an optical wireless transceiver is limited, as expressed in (4). Furthermore, in portable battery powered equipment, it is desirable to keep the electrical power consumption to a minimum, which also places limitations on the optical transmit power. Consequently, power efficiency is the most important criterion when evaluating modulation techniques suitable for indoor optical wireless communication systems. Thus, different schemes are usually compared in terms of the average optical power required to achieve a desired bit error rate (BER) at a given data rate.

Bandwidth Efficiency. When shot noise is dominant, generally the received SNR is proportional to the photodetector area. Consequently, single element receivers favor the use of large area photodetectors. However, the high capacitance associated with large area photodetectors has a limiting effect on receiver bandwidth. In addition to this, for non-directed LOS and diffuse link configurations, the channel bandwidth is limited by multipath propagation. Therefore, it follows that modulation schemes which have a high bandwidth requirement are more susceptible to intersymbol interference, and consequently incur a greater power penalty. Thus, bandwidth efficiency is the second most important criterion when evaluating modulation techniques.

There are other considerations, such as cost and complexity for mass-market applications. Achieving excellent power efficiency and/or bandwidth efficiency is of little use if the scheme is so complex to implement that cost renders it unfeasible. Another consideration when evaluating modulation techniques is the ability to reject the interference emanating from artificial sources of ambient light. The simplest method to achieve this for the baseband schemes is to use electrical high-pass filtering. Consequently, it is desirable that the chosen modulation technique does not have a significant amount of its power located at DC and low frequencies, thereby reducing the effect of baseline wander and thus permitting the use of higher cut-on frequencies. In addition to this, if the chosen modulation technique is required to operate at medium to high data rates over non-directed LOS or diffuse links, then multipath dispersion becomes an issue. Thus, it is also desirable that the scheme be resistant to ISI resulting from multipath propagation.

For the IM/DD indoor OW channel, candidate modulation techniques can be grouped into two general categories, these being the baseband and sub-carrier modulation (SCM) (also known as multiple-subcarrier modulation) schemes. In SCM, multiple digital streams are multiplexed in the RF domain and modulated onto a single wavelength optical carrier signal using intensity, phase, or frequency modulation. The IM/DD is the simplest and the cheapest option. SCM is more bandwidth efficient than its counter part the single-carrier modulation and it allows transmission with minimal ISI on frequency selective and multipath channels, thus offering realization of high-speed communications (Ohtsuki 2003). A particularly attractive scheme that uses multiple carriers overlapped in the frequency domain is known as the orthogonal frequency division multiplexing (OFDM), capable of supporting high data rates without the need for channel equalisers (Gonzalez et al. 2006). But SCM schemes are less power efficient than pulse modulation techniques because of inclusion of a DC offset in order to satisfy the requirement that $x(t)$ cannot be negative, as expressed in (4).

There is a range of modulation schemes such as analogue, digital, and baseband modulation techniques that are used in OW communications. Here the latter, which includes OOK and the family of pulse time modulation techniques, will be highlighted. There are many different types of modulation schemes, each with its particular advantages and disadvantages, and experimental and analytical performance of these modulation schemes have been extensively studied by a number of researchers (Barry 1994; Kahn and Barry 1997; McCullagh and Wisely 1994; Wong, O'Farrell, and Kiatweerasakul 2000; and Ghassemlooy, Hayes, and Wilson 2003). Because the average optical power emitted by an IR transceiver is limited, the performance of modulation techniques is compared in terms of the average received optical power required to achieve a desired BER at a given data rate.

OOK

Of all the various modulation schemes for IM/DD, OOK is the simplest and the most commonly used, where a zero and a one are represented by zero intensity and some positive intensity, respectively as shown in Figure 7. OOK can use either non-return-to-zero (NRZ) or return-to-zero (RZ) pulse formats. OOK-RZ (with reduced pulse duration) is more power efficient than OOK-NRZ but requires more transmission bandwidth. The detailed performance analysis of OOK on AWGN channel can be found in (Barry 1994; and Kahn and Barry 1997). The OOK with return-to-zero-inverted (RZI) signalling format has been used in commercial IrDA based devices operating below 4 Mbps.

Pulse Position Modulation (PPM)

PPM is a good alternative to OOK to provide better power efficiency at the cost of reduced bandwidth efficiency. In PPM, M bits input data are mapped to one of L possible symbols, where $L = 2^M$; see Figure 7. Each symbol consists of a pulse occupying one slot and $L-1$ empty slots. The information is encoded by the position of the pulse within the symbol. By increasing the number of bits per symbol, the power efficiency of the code is improved at the expense of the bandwidth efficiency. PPM has been used widely in OW systems and is also adopted for the IEEE 802.11 infrared physical layer standard and IrDA serial data links operating at 4 Mbps. There are several types of PPM, such as differential PPM (Shiu and Kahn 1999), multiple PPM (Parker and Barry 1996), and differential amplitude PPM (Sethakaset and Gulliver 2004). In addition to these, coded schemes such as convolutional-coded PPM and trellis-coded overlapping PPM also exist, each with its own advantages and disadvantages. Compared with OOK, PPM does increase system complexity because both slot and symbol synchronizations are required in the receiver. Table 7 compares OOK-NRZ, OOK-RZ, and PPM in terms of both power and bandwidth efficiencies. The power efficiency is defined by the required transmitted power to achieve a target BER, and the bandwidth efficiency is defined as zero-crossing bandwidth ($R_b = 1$/pulse width). Modulation schemes with a much wider pulse width (e.g., OOK-NRZ) are the least power efficient, but are bandwidth efficient. Bandwidth efficient modulation schemes offer advantages such as resilience to multipath distortion and less complex system implementation. For a given bandwidth efficiency, the PPM is the more power efficient; however, it is more susceptible to multipath-induced intersymbol interference. Uncoded PPM employing optimal maximum-likelihood sequence detection (MSLD) and sub-optimum equalization still suffers from larger ISI penalties than OOK. However, coding (e.g., Trellis) could be used to effectively mitigate the effects of ISI.

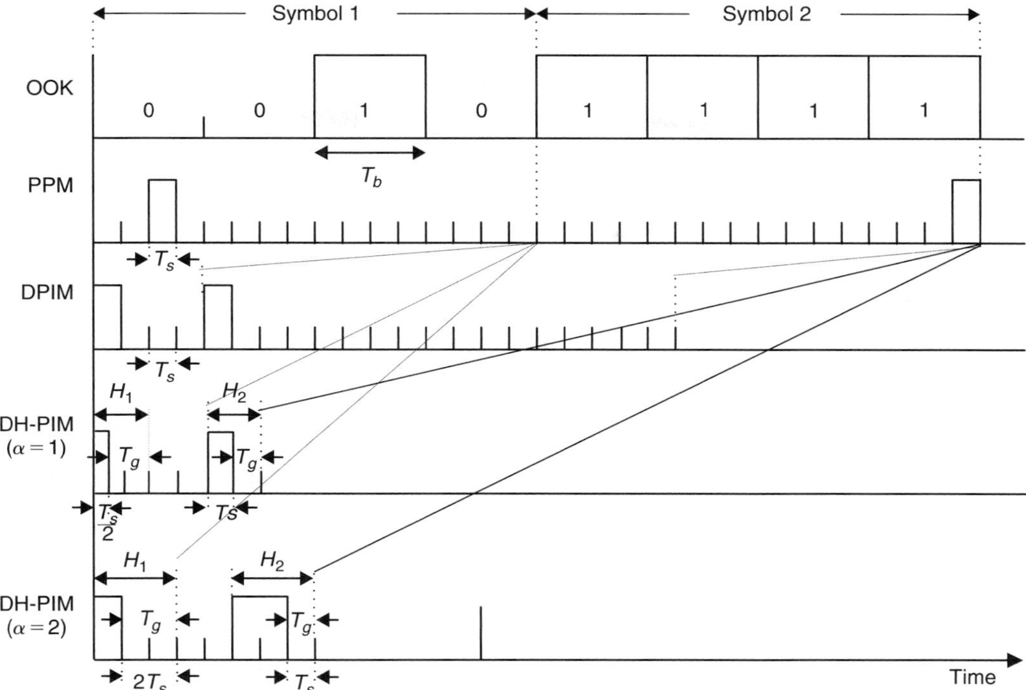

Figure 7: OOK, PPM, DPIM, and DH-PIM symbol structure

Digital Pulse Interval Modulation (DPIM)

In each PPM symbol with a fixed length, the empty slots following a pulse are essentially redundant, and with the removal of these redundant slots the symbol length thus becomes variable, thus leading to digital pulse interval modulation (DPIM). In DPIM, information is encoded by varying the number of empty slots between adjacent pulses (Ghassemlooy and Hayes 2000). As with L-PPM, L-DPIM maps each block of $M = \log_2 L$ input bits to one of L possible symbols (see Figure 7). Unlike L-PPM, however, symbol durations are variable and determined by the information content of each particular symbol. In order to avoid symbols, which have no slots between adjacent pulses, guard slots may be added to each symbol immediately following the pulse. Thus, each symbol consists of a pulse of constant power with duration less than one slot T_s, followed by k empty slots, where $1 \leqslant k \leqslant L$. The minimum and maximum symbol durations are $2T_s$ and $(L + 1)T_s$, respectively. In L-PPM, each symbol has a fixed duty cycle of $1/L$, whereas in L-DPIM symbols have a variable duty cycle with the average length higher than $1/L$. Consequently, for a fixed value of L, DPIM has a higher average power requirement compared with PPM. In L-PPM, the slot rate is given as $R_S = LR_b/M$, where R_b is the OOK bit rate. In L-DPIM, there are two options for the slot rate, as discussed in the following sections.

Dual Header Pulse Interval Modulation (DH-PIM)

The characteristics of OW systems can be further exploited by modifying the DPIM into the DH-PIM, which has a shocter symbol length, thus resulting in increased transmission capacity and improved bandwidth at the cost of slightly reduced power efficiency (Aldibbiat, Ghassemlooy, and McLaughlin 2001). Also DH-PIM offers built-in symbol synchronization, relatively straightforward slot synchronization, and improved immunity to the multipath dispersion at high dispersive medium compared with DPIM. DH-PIM is anisochronous scheme with a symbol composed of a header followed by a number of blank time slots signifying the signal information; see Figure 7. The header can take one of two different states (H_1 or H_2), depending on the pulse duration. In H_1 and H_2, the pulse durations are $\alpha T_s/2$ and αT_s, respectively. The number of information slots $d_n \in \{0,1,\ldots, 2^{M-1}-1\}$ is variable and depends on the binary value of the input data (M-bit). If the most significant bit of the input data is 0, then d_n is equal to the decimal value of the input data; otherwise it is equal to the decimal value of the 1's complement of the input data.

Performance

The performance of the optical wireless system defined in terms of SNR is given as:

$$SNR = \frac{(P_t H(0)R)^2}{N_0 R_b}. \tag{10}$$

where, N_0 and R_b are the noise variance and data rate, respectively. Note that the SNR is a function of the square power; thus OW systems will naturally require high transmitted power and limited path loss compared to the

Table 5: Energy Per Pulse and Bandwidth Requirements for OOK, PPM, DPIM, DH-PIM

Modulation Type	Energy Requirement/Pulse	Bandwidth Requirement B_{req}
OOK-NRZ	$(RP_{ave})^2/R_b$	R_b
OOK-RZ$_\alpha$	$(RP_{ave})^2/\alpha R_b$	R_b/α
PPM	$LM(RP_{ave})^2/R_b$	$2^M R_b/M$
DPIM	$L_{ave}M(RP_{ave})^2/R_b$	$(2^M+3)R_b/2M$
DH-PIM	$16ML_{ave}(RP_{ave})^2/9\alpha R_b$	$(2M^{-1}+2\alpha+1)R_b/\alpha M$

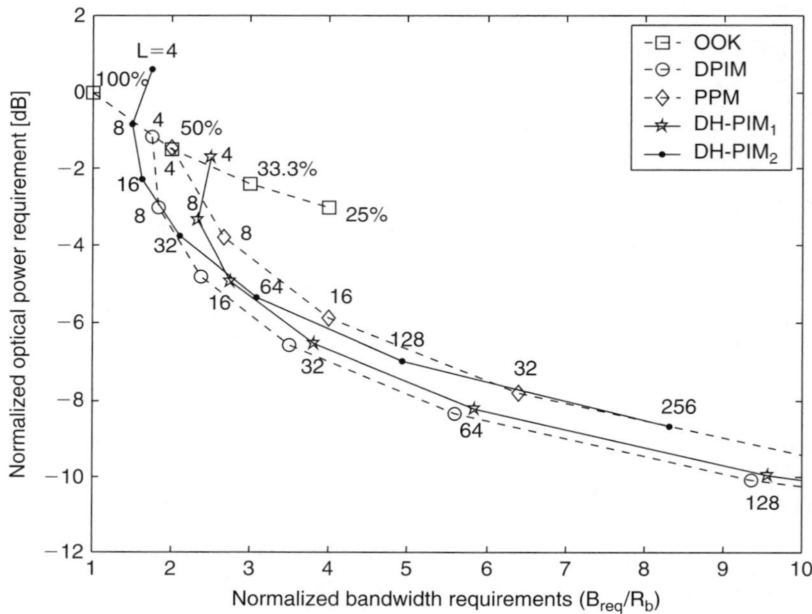

Figure 8: Optical power requirements for OOK, PPM, DPIM, DH PIM1, and DH PIM2 normalized to OOK-NRZ against bandwidth requirement normalized to the bit rate for different bit resolution (i.e., $M = \log_2 L$)

electrical systems. These differences have a profound effect on system design. On conventional channels, the SNR is proportional to the average received power, whereas on optical wireless links, it is proportional to the square of the average received optical signal power; thus implying that relatively high optical transmit powers are required, and only a limited path loss can be tolerated. The fact that the average optical transmit power is limited suggests that modulation techniques possessing a high peak-to-mean power ratio are favorable. This is generally achieved by trading off power efficiency against bandwidth efficiency. When the shot noise is dominant, the SNR is also proportional to the photodetector area. Thus, single element receivers favour the use of large area detectors. However, as the detector area increases so does its capacitance, which has a limiting effect on receiver bandwidth. This is in direct conflict with the increased bandwidth requirement associated with power efficient modulation techniques, and hence, a trade off exists between these two factors.

Table 5 shows the energy and bandwidth requirement for a number of modulation schemes. The bandwidth requirement, defined as the span from DC to the first null in the power spectral density (PSD) of the transmitted waveform, is also normalized to OOK. The average optical power requirement versus bandwidth requirement for OOK, PPM, DPIM and DH-PIM are shown in Figure 8.

CONCLUSION

The combination of a need for effective short-range indoor OW connectivity, ample unlicensed bandwidth, relative security, and a high transmission rate at a low cost makes an OW link preferable to the RF link in many applications. In this chapter, an overview of OW for indoor application was introduced. A number of IR wireless link configurations were introduced, each suitable for different applications. In terms of system design, the limitations directly imposed by the channel, such as the path loss and dispersion, are largely dependent on the chosen link configuration. For example, LOS links have a small path loss and do not suffer from multipath propagation. However, in order to achieve a degree of mobility, it is necessary to use a tracked configuration, but that greatly increases cost and complexity of the system. In contrast, non-directed links offer some mobility without increasing system complexity, but ought to overcome high path loss and multipath propagation. Indoor IR links are required to operate in the presence of intense ambient light. Along with contributing to the generation of shot noise, artificial ambient light also introduces a periodic interference signal in optical receivers. Of all the artificial ambient light sources, the fluorescent lamps driven by electronic ballasts are potentially the most detrimental to system performance because their detected electrical spectrum can contain harmonics into the MHz region. The extent to which ambient light sources affect link performance is also dependent, to a degree, on the chosen link configuration. Due to the directional nature of their transmitters and receivers, directed links can reject much of the background radiation, while non-directed links are more susceptible to it. Irrespective of the chosen link configuration, the indoor optical wireless channel is unique, combining the filtered Gaussian noise characteristics of conventional wire-based channels with the IM/DD constraints of fiber-optic systems. From a system design point of view, the diffuse configuration suffers the most severe channel parameters and consequently presents the greatest challenge to achieving robust, high-speed communication. As for the modulation techniques, there are a number of options, each offering its own advantages and disadvantages in terms of power and bandwidth efficiencies, and system complexity.

GLOSSARY

Ambient Light: In an optical wireless system, it is the light (due to sun, and man-made sources) that illuminates a room or a detector.

Average Power: The power averaged over a cycle of an electromagnetic signal.

Channel: A path for conveying electromagnetic signals (electrical or optical) from a source to a destination.

Diffuse Reflection: Reflection from a surface which may not maintain the integrity of the incident wavefront.

Dispersion: Any process by which an electromagnetic signal (electrical or optical) propagating through a physical channel is corrupted because different frequencies/wavelengths of the signal have different propagation velocities within the physical channel.

Fading: The variation (with time) of the amplitude or relative phase, or both, of one or more of the frequency components of the received signal.

Field of View (FOV): The angular size of an optical source being viewed by a photodetector.

Intensity Modulation: The intensity (amplitude) of light being directly modulated by the input data.

Intersymbol Interference: The distortion manifested in the temporal spreading and consequent overlap of individual pulses, to the degree that the receiver cannot reliably distinguish between individual signal elements.

Lambertian Source: An optical source with an intensity directly proportional to the cosine of the angle from which it is viewed.

Modulation: The process of varying a characteristic of a high frequency carrier signal in accordance with a low frequency information signal.

Multipath: The propagation phenomenon that results in electromagnetic signals' reaching the receiver by two or more paths.

Optic Filter: Transmits or blocks a range of wavelengths, polarizations, etc., or selectively displaces an optical beam.

Path Loss: The attenuation undergone by an electromagnetic signal when propagating through a communication channel (or medium). Attenuation usually expressed in dB.

Photocurrent: The current that flows through a photodiode, as the result of exposure to optical radiant power.

Photodetector: A semiconductor device that converts an optical power into an equivalent electrical signal containing the same information.

Pulse Interval Modulation (PIM): Modulation in which the temporal intervals of the pulses are varied in accordance with some characteristic of the modulating data.

Pulse-Position Modulation (PPM): Modulation in which the temporal positions of the pulses are varied in accordance with some characteristic of the modulating data.

Responsivity: In a photodetector, the ratio of the electrical output to the optical input (usually expressed in A/W).

Shot Noise: The noise caused by random fluctuations in the motion of charge carriers, also defined as the fluctuation in the number of photons, which results in a random photo-current.

Signal-to-Noise Ratio (SNR): The ratio of the amplitude or power of the desired signal to the amplitude or power of noise signals at a given point in time.

CROSS REFERENCES

See *Bluetooth Technology; Free-Space Optics; Frequency and Phase Modulation; Optical Sources; Wireless Channels.*

REFERENCES

Abtahi, M., and H. Hashemi. 1995. Simulation of indoor propagation channel at infrared frequencies in furnished office environments, *Proceedings of the 6th IEEE International Symposium on Personal, Indoor and Mobile Radio Communications*, Toronto, Canada, (1): 306–10.

Aldibbiat, N. M., Z. Ghassemlooy, and R. McLaughlin. 2001. Error performance of dual header pulse interval modulation (DH-PIM) in optical wireless communications, *IEEE Proceedings Optoelectronics*, 148(2): 91–96.

Barry, J. R. 1994. *Wireless Infrared Communications*, Boston: Kluwer Academic Publishers.

Barry, J. R., et al. 1993. Simulation of multipath impulse response for indoor wireless optical channels, *IEEE Journal on Selected Areas in Communications,* 11(3): 367–79.

Carruthers, J. B., and J. M. Kahn. 1996. Modeling of non-directed wireless infrared channels, *Proceedings of IEEE International Conference on Communications.* Dallas, (2): 1227–31.

Gfeller F. R., and U. H. Bapst. 1979. Wireless in-house data communication via diffuse infrared radiation, *Proceedings of the IEEE.* (Nov. 1979) 67(11): 1474–86.

Ghassemlooy, Z., and A. R. Hayes. 2000. Pulse interval modulation for IR communications, *International Journal of Communication Systems — special issue on Optical Wireless Communication Systems*, (13): 519–36.

Ghassemlooy, Z., A. R. Hayes, and B. Wilson. 2003. Reducing the effects of intersymbol interference in diffuse DPIM optical wireless communication, *IEE Proceedings on Optoelectronics,* 150(5): 445–52.

Gonzalez, O., et al. 2006. Adaptive ODFM system for communications over the indoor wireless optical channels, *IEE Proceedings On Optoelectronics*, 153(4): 139–44.

Heatley, D. J. T., and J. Neild. 1999. Optical wireless - the promise and the reality, *Proceedings of IEE Colloquium on Optical Wireless Communications*, London, 1/1–1/6.

IEEE. 1997. Standard No. 802.11–1997.

Infrared Data Association (IrDA). 2006. URL: http://www.irda.org/ (Date of access: April 2006).

Infrared Data Association (IrDA). 2001. *Serial Infrared Physical Layer Specification, Version 1.4,* http://www.irda.org/displaycommon.cfm?an=1&subarticlenbr=7, (accessed April 2006).

Jungnickel V., et al. 2001. 155 Mb/s wireless transmission with imaging infrared receiver, *IEE Electronic Letters,* 37(5): 314–15.

Kahn, J. M., and J. R. Barry. 1997. Wireless infrared communications. *Proceedings of the IEEE,* 85(2): 265–98.

Kahn, J. M., W. J. Krause, and J. B. Carruthers. 1995. Experimental characterization of non-directed indoor infrared channels. *IEEE Transactions on Communications*, 43(2,3,4): 1613–23.

Kavehrad, M., and S. Jivkova. 2003. Indoor broadband optical wireless communications: optical subsystem designs and their impact on channel characteristics. *IEEE Wireless Communications*: 30–35.

Lee, E. A., and D. G. Messerschmitt. 1994. *Digital Communication*, 2nd Edition. Boston: Kluwer Academic Publishers.

Lomba, C., R. T. Valadas, and A. M. de Oliveira Duarte, 1993. Propagation losses and impulse response of the indoor optical channel: a simulation package, IEEE Document No. IEEE P802.11–93/78.

Lomba, C., R. T. Valadas, and A. M. de Oliveira Duarte, 2000. Efficient simulation of the impulse response of the indoor wireless optical channel. *International Journal of Communication Systems*, 13(7, 8): 537–50.

Lopez-Hernandez, F. J., R. Perez-Jimenez, and A. Santamaria. 1998. Monte Carlo calculation of impulse response on diffuse IR wireless indoor channels. *IEE Electronics Letters*, 34(12): 1260–62.

McCullagh, M. J., and D. R. Wisely. 1994. 155 Mbit/s optical wireless link using a bootstrapped silicon APD receiver, *Electronics Letters*, 30(5): 430–32.

Moreira, A. J. C., R. T. Valadas, and A. M. De Oliveira Duarte. 1995. Characterisation and modelling of artificial light interference in optical wireless communication systems. In *Proceedings of the 6th IEEE International Symposium on Personal, Indoor and Mobile Radio Communications.* September 27–29, pp. 326–31.

Nicholls, P., S. D. Greaves, and R.T. Unwin. 1996. Optical wireless telepoint. In *Proceedings of the IEE Colloquium on Optical Free Space Communication Links.* February 19, pp. 4/1–4/6.

Ohtsuki, T. 2003. Multiple-subcarrier modulation in optical wireless communications, *IEEE Communications Magazine*. 41(3): 74–79.

Pakravan, M. R, E. Simova, and M. Kavehrad. 1997. Holographic diffusers for indoor infrared communication system, *International Journal of Wireless Information Networks*, 4(4): 259–74.

Pakravan, M. R., and M. Kavehrad. 1995. Design considerations for broadband indoor infrared wireless communication systems. *International Journal of Wireless Information Networks,* 2(4): 223–38.

Parker, H., and J. R. Barry. 1996. Performance analysis and channel capacity for multiple-pulse position modulation on multipath channels, *Proceedings of the* 7th *IEEE International Symposium on Personal, Indoor and Mobile Radio Communications*, October 1996, 1: 247–51.

Phang, K., and D. A. Johns. 1999. A CMOS optical preamplifier for wireless infrared communications. *IEEE Transactions on Circuits and Systems II: Analog and Digital Signal Processing,* 46(7): 852–59.

Sethakaset, U., and T. A. Gulliver. 2004. Differential amplitude pulse-position modulation for indoor wireless optical channels, *IEEE Globecom*: 1867–71.

Shiu, D., and J. M. Kahn. 1999. Differential pulse-position modulation for power-efficient optical communication. *IEEE Transactions on Communications*. 47(8): 1201–10.

Smyth, P., et al. 1995. Optical wireless: A prognosis. *Proceedings of SPIE Conference on Wireless Data Transmission*, Philadelphia. October, 2601: 212–25.

Spectrix Corporation 2000. Spectrix Wireless Network-TechnicalOverview,Availableat:http://www.spectrixcorp.com/techoverview.pdf. (accessed: April 15, 2006).

Street, A. M., et al. 1997. Indoor optical wireless systems — A review. *Optical and Quantum Electronics*, 29: 349–78.

Tavares, A., et al. 2003. Angle diversity and rate-adaptive transmission for indoor wireless optical communications. *IEEE Communications Magazine*, 41(3): 64–73.

Wisely, D. R. 1996. A 1Gbit/s optical wireless tracked architecture for ATM delivery. *Proceedings of IEE Colloquium on Optical Free Space Communication Links*. February, 14/1–14/7.

Wong, K. K., T. O'Farrell, and M. Kiatweerasakul. 2000. Infrared wireless communication using spread spectrum techniques. In *IEE Proceedings—Optoelectronics.* August, 147(4): 308–14.

Yun, G., and M. Kavehrad. 1992. Spot diffusing and fly-eye receivers for indoor infrared wireless communications. *Proceedings of the 1992 IEEE Conference on Selected Topics in Wireless Communications*, (June 1992): 286–92.

Reviewers List

Abaza, Mahmoud, Athabasca University, Canada
Abbas, Kaja, University of California, Irvine
Abdel Hamid, Ayman Adel, Arab Academy for Science, Technology, and Maritime Transport, Egypt
Abdeljabbar, Wael, Mission College
Abdel-Wahab, Hussein, Old Dominion University
Abdu, Hasina, The University of Michigan, Dearborn
Ablowitz, Mark J., University of Colorado, Boulder
Abolmaesumi, Purang, Queen's University, Canada
Adams, Chris, University of Colorado, Boulder
Agathoklis, Pan, University of Victoria, Canada
Agrawal, Gopal, Texas A&M University, Texarkana
Akkaya, Kemal, Southern Illinois University
Akl, Robert, University of North Texas
Albright, Richard, Goldey-Beacom College
Ali, Sanwar, Indiana University of Pennsylvania
Aliyazicioglu, Zekeriya, California State Polytechnic University, Pomona
Al-Jaroodi, Jameela, University of Bahrain, Kingdom of Bahrain
Allan, Robert J., Daresbury Laboratory, UK
Allen, James M., University of North Dakota
AlRegib, Ghassan, Georgia Institute of Technology
Al-Shaer, Ehab, DePaul University
Altay, Gökmen, Bahcesehir University, Turkey
Altintas, Ayhan, Bilkent University, Turkey
Amin, Mohammad, National University
Amjad Umar, Fordham University
Anderson, Anne H., Sun Microsystems, Inc.
André, Paulo Sérgio de Brito, Universidade de Aveiro, Portugal
Andreozzi, Sergio, Istituto Nazionale di Fisica Nucleare (INFN), Italy
Ankiewicz, Adrian, Australian National University, Australia
Antonio, Patricia San, University of Maryland, Baltimore County
Anwar, Zahid, Intel Corporation
Ardakani, Masoud, University of Alberta, Canada
Argles, David, University of Southampton, UK
Argüello, Francisco, University of Santiago de Compostela, Spain
Arifler, Dogu, Eastern Mediterranean University, North Cyprus
Astani, Marzie, Winona State University
Atai, Javid, University of Sydney, Australia
Atti, Venkatraman, Arizona State University
Avoine, Gildas, Massachusetts Institute of Technology
Awan, Asad, Purdue University
Azad, Abul K. M., Northern Illinois University

Baaren-Hopper, Joanna van, University of Connecticut
Babula, Eduard, Universidad Carlos III de Madrid, Spain
Babulak, Eduard, University of Pardubice, Czech Republic
Badia, Leonardo, Università degli Studi di Padova, Italy
Baehr, Craig, Texas Tech University
Baeza-Yates, Ricardo, Yahoo! Research, Spain
Baggag, Abdelkader, McGill University, Canada
Bakos, Jason D., University of South Carolina
Baldwin, Rusty O., Air Force Institute of Technology
Barnes, Frank, University of Colorado, Boulder
Barnes, Stuart J., University of East Anglia, UK
Barnhart, Billy S., Webster University and AT&T
Bartolacci, Michael R., Penn State University, Berks
Basu, Kalyan, University of Texas, Arlington
Baudoin, Geneviève, ESIEE, France
Baumgartner, Robert, Vienna University of Technology, Austria
Beavers, Gordon, University of Arkansas
Bedell, Paul, Independent Consultant
Bellardo, John M., California Polytechnic State University
Bellavista, Paolo, DEIS—Università degli Studi di Bologna, Italy
Ben Slimane, Slimane, The Royal Institute of Technlogy (KTH), Sweden
Benhaddou, Driss, University of Houston
Benkabou, Fatima Zohr, Université de Moncton, Canada
Bennette, Daniel, University of Maryland University College Europe
Benvenuto, Nevio, University of Padova, Italy
Berg, George, University at Albany, SUNY
Berkes, Jem E., University of Waterloo, Canada
Berlemann, Lars, Swisscom Innovations, Switzerland
Berman, David J., DBM Technology Consulting
Bernstein, Larry, Stevens Institute of Technology
Bertoss, Alan A., University of Bologna, Italy
Biagioni, Edoardo S., University of Hawaii, Mānoa
Bianc, Andrea, Politecnico di Torino, Italy
Binsted, Kim, University of Hawaii, Manoa
Birant, Derya, Dokuz Eylul University, Turkey
Birru, Dagnachew (Dan), Philips Research North America
Biswas, Abhijit, Jet Propulsion Laboratory, California Institute of Technology
Biswas, Anjan, Delaware State University
Bjerke, Bjorn A., Qualcomm, Inc.
Bocchino Jr., Robert L., University of Illinois
Bocquet, Wladimir, France Telecom R&D, Japan
Bode, Arndt, Technische Universität München, Germany
Bodnar, Bohdan L., Motorola, Inc.
Bohn, Jürgen, Wernher von Braun Center for Advanced Research, Brazil
Bollen, Johan, Los Alamos National Laboratory
Bolyard, John W., University of West Florida
Bonnel, Wanda, University of Kansas
Boppana, Rajendra V., University of Texas, San Antonio
Border, Charles, Rochester Institute of Technology
Boroson, Don M., MIT Lincoln Laboratory
Bose, Sanjay K., Nanyang Technological University, Singapore
Bostian, Charles W., Virginia Tech
Bouras, Christos, University of Patras, Greece
Brännström, Robert, Luleå University of Technology, Sweden
Braun, Mark J., Gustavus Adolphus College

Braun, Torsten, University of Bern, Switzerland
Brewster, Gregory, DePaul University
Briscoe, Bob, BT, UK
Broughton, S. Allen, Rose-Hulman Institute of Technology
Brown, Andrew, University of Southampton, UK
Brown, Eric Paul, Canyon College
Brown, Stuart M., New York University
Bryan, David A., College of William and Mary and SIPeerior Technologies, Inc.
Buchholz, Dale, DePaul University
Bucy, Erik P., Indiana University
Buhari, M. I. Seyed Mohamed, University Brunei Darussalam, Brunei
Burn, David R., Southern Illinois University, Carbondale
Burpee III, Howard A., Southern Maine Community College
Butler, Donald, University of Texas, Arlington
Byrd, Gregory T., North Carolina State University

Cabri, Danijela, University of California, Berkeley
Cai, Qingbo, Case Western Reserve University
Cai, Yu, Michigan Technological University
Caini, Carlo, Università di Bologna, Italy
Calabresi, Leonello, Univerity of Maryland, University College
Ćalić, Janko, University of Bristol, UK
Callahan, Dale, University of Alabama, Birmingham
Camarillo, Gonzalo, Ericsson
Can Vuran, Mehmet, Georgia Institute of Technology
Candan, K. Selcuk, Arizona State University
Cannistra, Robert M., Marist College
Cantrell, Cyrus D., The University of Texas, Dallas
Cao, Lei, The University of Mississippi
Cao, Xiaojun, Rochester Institute of Technology
Cardei, Ionut, Florida Atlantic University
Cardell-Oliver, Rachel, The University of Western Australia, Australia
Careglio, Davide, Universitat Politècnica de Catalunya, Spain
Carlson, David E., University of Florida
Carroll, Bill D., The University of Texas, Arlington
Castane, Laurent, Onera, France
Castillo, Carlos, Yahoo! Research, Spain
Cernocky, Jan "Honza," Brno University of Technology, Czech Republic
Chaffin, Dorothea S., Park University
Chambers, Robert, Lightspeed Systems
Champion, Jean-Luc, UN/CEFACT Forum, Belgium
Chan, Sammy, City University of Hong Kong, Hong Kong
Chan, Tom S., Southern New Hampshire University
Chandra, Vigs, Eastern Kentucky University
Chandrashekhara, K., University of Missouri, Rolla
Chaudet, Claude, GET/ENST, France
Che, Hao, University of Texas, Arlington
Chen, Chien-Chung, National Taiwan University, Taiwan
Chen, Jim Q., University of Maryland, University College
Chen, Ju-Ya, National Sun Yat-Sen University, Taiwan
Chen, Li-Wei, Vanu Inc.
Chen, Runhua, The University of Texas, Austin
Chen, Whai-En, National Chiao Tung University, Taiwan
Chen, Yu-Che, Northern Illinois University
Cheng, Tee Hiang, Nanyang Technological University, Singapore
Chepkevich, Richard A., "Sam," Hawaii Pacific University
Chess, David M., IBM Watson Research Center
Chiani, Marco, DEIS, University of Bologna, Italy
Chiao, J. C., The University of Texas, Arlington
Cho, Pak S., CeLight, Inc.
Choi, Byung K., Michigan Technological University
Choi, Young B., James Madison University
Choksy, Carol E. B., Indiana University, Bloomington
Christensen, Ken, University of South Florida
Chuah, Chen-Nee, University of California, Davis
Chuah, Teong-Chee, Multimedia University, Malaysia
Chudoba, Katherine M., Florida State University
Chung, Chia-Jung, California State University, Sacramento
Chung, Sam, University of Washington, Tacoma
Clarke, Roger, Xamax Consultancy Pty Ltd, Australia, and University of Hong Kong
Cohen, Daniel, George Mason University
Cohen, David J., University of Maryland, University College
Collings, Neil, University of Cambridge, UK
Collins, J. Stephanie, Southern New Hampshire University
Colonna, Danilo, ENEA C. R. Frascati, Italy
Comellas, Jaume, Universitat Politècnica de Catalunya, Spain
Connel, Mark, State University of New York, Cortland
Conti, Claudio, Research Center Enrico Fermi, Italy
Coopman, Ted M., University of Washington
Corazza, Giovanni E., University of Bologna, Italy
Cordeiro, Carlos, Philips Research North America
Craenen, B. G. W., Napier University, UK
Craig, Richard, San Jose State University
Crawford, George W., Penn State McKeesport
Crnkovic, Jakov, University at Albany (SUNY)
Cronin, Eric, University of Pennsylvania
Crowcroft, Jon, University of Cambridge, UK
Cui, Dongzhe, Bell Labs—Lucent Technologies
Cui, Yi, Vanderbilt University

Dai, Huaiyu, North Carolina State University
Dai, Yuan-Shun, Indiana University Purdue University Indianapolis
Daniels, Robert C., The University of Texas, Austin
Danielson, David R., Stanford University
Daoud, Moh, Las Positas College
Daskalopulu, Aspassia, University of Thessaly, Greece
David, John J., Wake Forest University
De Leenheer, Marc, Ghent University, Germany
Debbah, Merouane, Eurecom Institute, France
Debrunne, Christian H., Colorado School of Mines
DeJoie, Anthony, Telcordia Technologies
Dellacca, David, Indiana University-Purdue University Indianapolis (IUPUI)
Desai, Uday B., Indian Institute of Technology, India
Deters, Ralph, University of Saskatchewan, Canada
Develi, Ibrahim, Engineering Erciyes University, Turkey
Dhadwal, Harbans S., State University of New York, Stony Brook
Di Cecca, Angelo, Alcatel Alenia Space
Diaz, Michel, LAAS-CNRS, France
Dick, Steven J., Southern Illinois University, Carbondale
Dietrich, Sven, CERT
Ding, Hao, Norwegian University of Science and Technology, Norway
Ding, Qin, Pennsylvania State University, Harrisburg
Ding, Wei, The University of Houston, Clear Lake

Dor, Jean-Baptiste, France Telecom, France
Doran, K. Brewer, Salem State College
Dorsz, Jeff, Saddleback College
Downing, Rob, IP Infusion
Drábek, Vladimír, Brno University of Technology, Czech Republic
Dringus, Laurie P., Nova Southeastern University
Drummond, Lúcia Maria de A., Universidade Federal Fluminense, Brazil
Durbano, James P., EM Photonics, Inc.
Dyo, Vladimir, University College London, UK

Edd, Wesley M., Verizon Federal Network Systems / NASA Glenn Research Center
Eddie Rabinovitch, ECI Technology
Edirisinghe, Ruwini Kodikara, Monash University, Australia
Edwards, Paul N., University of Michigan, Ann Arbor
Efstathiou, Elias C., Athens University of Economics and Business, Greece
Egbert, Brian G., Sprint Nextel
Egedigwe, Eges, Eastfield College of Dallas County Community College System
Ehrensberger, Juergen, HEIG-VD, Switzerland
Ehrich, Thomas A., Golden Gate University
Ekbia, Hamid R., Indiana University
El Fatmi, Sihem Guemara, High School of Communications, Tunisia
Elin, Larry, Syracuse University
Elliot, Stephen John, Purdue University
Elmusrati, Mohammed Salem, University of Vaasa, Finland
Enck, William, The Pennsylvania State University
Erbacher, Robert F., Utah State University
Erenshteyn, Roman, Goldey-Beacom College
Erol, Ali, University of Nevada, Reno
Esmahi, Larbi, Athabasca University, Canada
Evans, Gary, Southern Methodist University
Ewert, Craig, University of Maryland University College (UMUC)

Faber, Brenton, Clarkson University
Falconer, David, Carleton University, Canada
Fallah, M. Hosein, Stevens Institute of Technology
Fan, Guangbin, Intel Research, China
Farahat, Nader, Polytechnic University of Puerto Rico
Farhang-Boroujeny, Behrouz, University of Utah
Farley, Toni, Arizona State University
Farren, Margaret, Dublin City University, Ireland
Faruque, Abdullah, Southern Polytechnic State University
Fazel, Khaled, Ericsson GmbH, Germany
Feiler, Michael, Merritt College
Feng, Jack, Bradley University
Fernandes, Stenio F. L., Federal Center for Education in Technology (CEFET), Brazil
Fernback, Jan, Temple University
Ferner, Clayton, University of North Carolina, Wilmington
Ficek, Zbigniew, The University of Queensland, Australia
Figg, William C., Dakota State University
Fitkov-Norris, Elena, Kingston University, UK
Fitzek, Frank H. P., Aalborg University, Denmark
Fitzgibbons, Patrick W., SUNY Institute of Technology
Fitzpatrick, John, University College Dublin, Ireland
Fleisc, Brett D., University of California, Riverside
Fleischmann, Kenneth R., Florida State University, and Drexel University
Fonseka, John P., University of Texas, Dallas
Ford, Davis, Zeno Consulting, Inc.
Ford, Steve, Northeastern State University
Foschini, Luca, DEIS—Università degli Studi di Bologna, Italy
Fowler, Thomas B., Mitretek Systems
Fox, Geoffrey, Indiana University
Fox, Louis, University of Washington
Frank, Michael P., FAMU-FSU College of Engineering
Frantti, Tapio, Technical Research Centre, Finland
Freed, Shirley Ann, Andrews University
Freelan, Joseph Curtis, University of Notre Dame
Fricke, Justus Ch., University of Kiel, Germany
Friesen, Norm, Simon Fraser University, Canada
Fritts, Jason E., Saint Louis University
Frolik, Jeff, University of Vermont
Fu, Xiang, Georgia Southwestern State University
Fukami, Cynthia V., University of Denver
Fuller, Dorothy P., Black Hills State University

Gallagher, Helen, Computer Clarity, Glenview, Illinois
Gao, Jie, State University of New York, Stony Brook
Gao, Liang, Huazhong University of Science and Technology, China
Garcia-Armada, Ana, University Carlos III de Madrid, Spain
Gauch, John M., The University of Kansas
Gavrilenko, Vladimir, Norfolk State University
Gebali, Fayez, University of Victoria, Canada
Gentzsch, Wolfgang, University of North Carolina, Chapel Hill
Ghafouri-Shiraz, H., University of Birmingham, UK
Giambene, Giovanni, University of Siena, Italy
Giangarra, Paul P., IBM
Glick, Madeleine, Intel Research Cambridge, UK
Glushko, Robert J., University of California, Berkeley
Goffe, William L., State University of New York, Oswego
Gong, Yili, Chinese Academy of Sciences, China
Gonzalez Benitez, Ruben A., Universidad Veracruzana, Mexico
Goodarzy, Hormoz, Cambridge College
Goodsell, David S., The Scripps Research Institute
Gordon, Jr., Horace C., University of South Florida
Govindavajhala, Sudhakar, Princeton University
Grandy, Holger, University of Augsburg, Germany
Graupner, Sven, Hewlett-Packard Laboratories, Palo Alto
Gray, Charles G., Oklahoma State University
Greaves, David, University of Cambridge, UK
Grimaud, Gilles, INRIA/CNRS/ University, France
Groth, Dennis P., Indiana University
Guan, Yong Liang, Nanyang Technological University, Singapore
Guenach, Mamoun, Department of Telecommunication and Information Processing
Gunther, Jake, Utah State University
Guo, Jinhua, University of Michigan, Dearborn
Guo, Li-Qiang, University of Limerick, Ireland
Guo, Yile, Nokia
Gurses, Eren, The Norwegian University of Science and Technology, Norway
Gurusamy, Mohan, National University of Singapore, Singapore

Haddadi, Hamed, University College London, UK
Hadidi, Rassule, University of Illinois, Springfield
Hadjicostis, Christoforos, University of Illinois, Urbana-Champaign
Haenggi, Martin, University of Notre Dame

Haghverdi, Esfandiar, Indiana University, Bloomington
Hague, Rob, Independent Consultant, UK
Hammell II, Robert J., Towson University
Hammer, Florian, Telecommunications Research Center Vienna (ftw.), Austria
Han, Youngnam, Information and Communications University, Korea
Hanchey, Cindy Meyer, Oklahoma Baptist University
Hansse, Øyvind, University of Tromsø, Norway
Haque, Saira N., Syracuse University
Härmä, Aki, Philips Research Laboratories
Harper, Christopher, Temple University
Harris, Jr., Frederick C., University of Nevada, Reno
Hartel, Pieter, University of Twente, The Netherlands
Hasan, Aamir, University of Texas, Austin
Hasan, Mohammad Masud, University of Texas, Dallas
Hasina Abdu, The University of Michigan, Dearborn
Havill, Jessen T., Denison University
Hawkin, Joseph, University of Alaska, Fairbanks
Hayden, Patrick, McGill University, Canada
Hayee, M. Imran, University of Minnesota, Duluth
He, Dan, University of Surrey, UK
Heckenberg, Norman, The University of Queensland, Australia
Heidari, Sam, Ikanos Communications, Inc.
Heijenk, Geert, Uniiversity of Twente, The Netherlands
Heim, Gregory R., Boston College
Heintzelman, Matthew Z., Saint John's University
Helfers, Eric C., University of Maryland, University College, and Johns Hopkins University
Helm, Pamela C., Radford University
Henkel, Werner, International University Bremen (IUB), Germany
Henry, Joel, University of Montana, Missoula
Hershey, John E., GE, Research
Hesselbach-Serra, Xavier, Universitat Politècnica de Catalunya, Spain
Hettak, Khelifa, Industry Canada, Canada
Higgs, Bryan J., Rivier College
Hiwasaki, Yusuke, NTT Corp., Japan
Hizlan, Murad, Cleveland State University
Ho, Chen-Shie, National Taiwan University, Taiwan
Hoag, John C., Ohio University
Hoffmeyer, Jim, Western Telecom Consultants, Inc.
Hogrefe, Dieter, Georg-August-Universitaet Goettingen, Germany
Hole, Kjell Jørgen, University of Bergen, Norway
Holzer, Richard, University of Passau, Germany
Hong, Edwin, University of Washington, Tacoma
Horan, Stephen, New Mexico State University
Horikis, Theodoros P., University of Colorado, Boulder
Hostetler, Michael, Park University
Howenstine, Erick, Northeastern Illinois University
Hu, Yuh-Jong, National Chengchi University, Taiwan
Huang, Chin-Tser, University of South Carolina
Huang, Freeman Yufei, Queen's University, Canada
Hudson, James M., Georgia Institute of Technology
Huemer, Mario, University of Erlangen-Nuremberg, Germany
Hunsinger, Jeremy, Virginia Polytechnic Institute and State University
Hurley, Stephen, Cardiff University, UK
Hussmann, Heinrich, University of Munich, Germany
Huston, Geoff, Asia Pacific Network Information Center (APNIC)

Ibrahim, Hassan, University of Maryland
Iftode, Liviu, Rutgers University
Ilk, H. Gokhan, Ankara University, Turkey
Ingram, Mary Ann, Georgia Institute of Technology
Ionescu, Dan, University of Ottawa, Canada
Iraqi, Youssef, Dhofar University, Oman
Ishaq, A. Faiz M., The University of Lahore, Pakistan
Iskander, Cyril-Daniel, The MathWorks Inc.
Islam, M. Saif, University of California, Davis
Iversen, Jakob Holden, University of Wisconsin, Oshkosh

Jablonski, Dan, John Hopkins University
Jackson, Henry L. "Jack," Austin Community College
Jacobs, Raymond A., Ashland University
Jajszczyk, Andrzej, AGH University of Science and Technology, Poland
Jank, Wolfgang, University of Maryland
Jayakar, Krishna, The Pennsylvania State University
Jenkins, David, University of Plymouth, UK
Jenq, Yih-Chyun, Portland State University
Ji, Ping, City University of New York
Jia, Weijia, City University of Hong Kong, Hong Kong
Jiang, Tao, University of Michigan, Dearborn
Jiang, Yuming, Norwegian University of Science and Technology, Norway
Jin, Hai, Huazhong University of Science and Technology, China
Joadat, Reza, Richmond University, UK
Johnson, J. T., Institute for Analytic Journalism
Johnson, Michael P., Carnegie Mellon Universitiy
Jones III, Creed, Seattle Pacific University
Jones, James G., University of North Texas
Jordan, Kurt, Calumet College of St. Joseph
Jun, Jaeyeon, Mazu Networks

Kabara, Joseph, University of Pittsburgh
Kan, Min-Yen, National University of Singapore, Singapore
Kandus, Gorazd, Jozef Stefan Institute, Slovenia
Kang, Jaewon, Rutgers University
Kang, Joonhyuk, Information & Communications University, Korea
Kapfhammer, Gregory M., Allegheny College
Karandikar, Abhay, Indian Institute of Technology, India
Karapetyan, Aram, Yerevan State University, Armenia
Karp, Tanja, Texas Tech University
Karush, Gerald, Southern New Hampshire University
Kato, Nei, Tohoku University, Japan
Katos, Vasilios, University of Portsmouth, UK
Katzy, Bernhard R., University Bw Munich (D) and Leiden University (NL), Germany
Kawanish, Tetsuya, National Institute of Information and Communications Technology, Japan
Kayssi, Ayman, American University of Beirut, Lebanon
Keenan, Susan M., University of Northern Colorado
Keliher, Liam, Mount Allison University, Canada
Kent, M. Allen, Montana State University
Kerrigan, John E., University of Medicine and Dentistry of New Jersey
Kesden, Gregory, Carnegie Mellon University
Keselman, Yakov, Microsoft Corporation
Kesidis, George, Pennsylvania State University
Keys, Anthony C., University of Wisconsin, Eau Claire

Khatri, Farzana I., MIT Lincoln Laboratory
Kholodovych, Vladyslav, University of Medicine & Dentistry of New Jersey
Khosla, Raj, Colorado State University
Khunboa, Chatchai, Khon Kaen University, Thailand
Kim, Jinoh, University of Minnesota
Kim, JongWon, Gwangju Institute of Science & Technology, Korea
Kim, Su Myeon, Samsung Advanced Institute of Technology
Kimmel, Howard, New Jersey Institute of Technology
Kivshar, Yuri, Australian National University, Australia
Kleist, Virginia Franke, West Virginia University
Knolle, Jonathan W., California State University, Chico
Kobtsev, Sergey, Novosibirsk State University, Russia
Kocyigit, Altan, Middle East Technical University, Turkey
Kodi, Avinash, University of Arizona
Kolias, Christos, University of Southern California
Kolumban, Geza, Budapest University of Technology and Economics, Hungary
Kong, Albert, The University of the West Indies, Trinidad & Tobago
Koppler, Alois, Kukla Electronics, Austria
Kornhauser, Alain L., Princeton University
Korpeoglu, Ibrahim, Bilkent University, Turkey
Koucheryavy, Yevgeni, Tampere University of Technology, Finland
Kretschmer, Tobias, London School of Economics, UK
Kriehn, Gregory R., California State University, Fresno
Krishnamurthy, Prashant, University of Pittsburgh
Krishnan, Iyengar N., Johns Hopkins University
Kritzinger, Pieter S., University of Cape Town, South Africa
Krotov, Vlad, University of Houston
Kruger, Anton, The University of Iowa
Kruger, Lennard G., Library of Congress
Kuhn, Marc, Institut für Kommunikationstechnik, Switzerland
Kumar, Aarti, Motorola Inc.
Kumar, Chiranjeev, Indian School of Mines University (ISM), India
Kumar, Santosh, University of Memphis
Kumar, Saurabh, University of Southern California
Kummerfeld, Sarah, Stanford University
Kumwilaisak, Wuttipong, King Mongkut's University of Technology, Thailand
Kurkovsky, Stan, Central Connecticut State University
Kurkowski, Stuart, Colorado School of Mines
Kursh, Steven R., Northeastern University
Kut, Alp, Dokuz Eylul University, Turkey
Kwok, Yu-Kwong Ricky, The University of Hong Kong, Hong Kong
Kwon, James Minseok, Rochester Institute of Technology
Kyperountas, Spyros, Motorola Labs
Kyprianou, Andreas, University of Cyprus, Cyprus

Lacity, Mary C., University of Missouri
Lagerstrom, Eric J. "Rick," Golden Gate University
Lamblin, Claude, France Telecom R&D, France
Land, Martin, Hadassah College, Israel
Landfeldt, Bjorn, University of Sydney, Australia
Langar, Rami, University of Waterloo, Canada
Langendoen, Koen, Delft University of Technology, The Netherlands
Larson, Robert E., University of Washington
Lassous, Isabelle Guerin, INRIA ARES/CITI, France
Law, K. L. Eddie, Ryerson University, Canada
Lawrence, Ramon, University of British Columbia Okanagan, Canada
Leangsuksun, Chokchai, Louisiana Tech University
LeBlanc, Cathie, Plymouth State University
Lee, Gyungho, University of Illinois, Chicago
Lee, Jung Woo, Stanford University
Lehman, Ann C., University of Illinois, Urbana-Champaign
Lehr, William, Massachusetts Institute of Technology
Leitgeb, Erich, Graz University of Technology, Austria
Leonardo Badia, IMT Lucca, taly
Li, Chih-Peng, National Sun Yat-Sen University, Taiwan
Li, Frank Y., University of Oslo, Norway
Li, Honglin, North Dakota State University
Li, Jun, University of Oregon
Li, Tongtong, Michigan State University
Li, Zexian, Nokia
Liang, Chuck C., Hofstra University
Liang, Jie, Simon Fraser University, Canada
Liebenau, Jonathan, London School of Economics, UK
Light, Jennifer S., Northwestern University
LiKamWa, Patrick, University of Central Florida
Lin, Bin, Northwestern University
Lin, Xiaojun, Purdue University
Lineman, Jeffrey P., Northwest Nazarene University
Liszka, Kathy J., The University of Akron
Liu, Boan, Tsinghua University, China
Liu, Chang, Northern Illinois University
Liu, Fenghai, Mintera Corporation
Liu, Huaping, Oregon State University
Liu, Xiang, Bell Labs, Lucent Technologies
Liu, Xiangqian, University of Louisville
Llewellyn, Mark, University of Central Florida
Lo, Shou-Chih, National Dong Hwa University, Taiwan
Lodwig, Sunita, University of South Florida
Löh, Hermann, CeTIM, Germany
Lorenz, Pascal, University of Haute Alsace, France
Losada, David E., University of Santiago de Compostela, Spain
Love, John, Australian National University, Australia
Lozano-Nieto, Albert, The Pennsylvania State University
Lu, Guo-Wei, The Chinese University of Hong Kong, Hong Kong
Lu, Yuanqiu, New Jersey Institute of Technology
Lugmayr, Artur R., Tampere University of Technology
Luo, Jun, Ecole Polytechnique Fédérale de Lausanne (EPFL), Switzerland

Ma, Maode, Nanyang Technological University, Singapore
Mabry, Edward A., University of Wisconsin, Milwaukee
Mache, Jens Mache, Lewis & Clark College, Oregon
Magistretti, Eugenio, DEIS—Università degli Studi di Bologna, Italy
Maguire, Paul, Dublin City University (DCU), Ireland
Mahanti, Anirban, University of Calgary, Canada
Mai, Bin, Northwestern State University, Louisiana
Mailaender, Laurence, Lucent Technologies, Bell Labs
Majumdar, Abhik, University of California, Berkeley
Makani, Joyline, Dalhousie University, Canada
Malkevitch, Joseph, York College (CUNY)
Mambretti, Joe, Northwestern University
Mandujano, Salvador, Intel Corporation
Mann, Catherine L., Brandeis University and Peterson Institute for International Economics
Mano, Chad D., University of Notre Dame
Mao, Shiwen, Auburn University

Mapp, Glenford, Middlesex University, UK
Markman, Kris M., Bridgewater State College
Marks, Gregory A., University of Michigan and Merit Network
Marsic, Ivan, Rutgers University
Marsteller, Matthew R., Carnegie Mellon University
Martel, Normand M., Medical Technology Research Corp.
Martin, Jim, Clemson University
Martin, Richard K., The Air Force Institute of Technology (AFIT)
Martins, Luis L., Georgia Institute of Technology
Mashburn, Ronald, West Texas A & M University
Mason, Sharon P., Rochester Institute of Technology
Mateti, Prabhaker, Wright State University
McConn, Charlotte Eudy, Penn State University
McFadden, Anna C., The University of Alabama
McFarland, Daniel J., Rowan University
McKeever, Susan, Dublin Institute of Technology, Ireland
Mehlenbacher, Brad, North Carilina State
Menif, Mourad, Ecole Supérieure des Communications (SupCom), Tunisia
Menth, Michael, University of Wuerzburg, Germany
Mertins, Alfred, University of Oldenburg, Germany
Metesh, Ed, Montana Tech
Miers, Judson, University of Kansas
Mihaila, George Andrei, IBM Research
Milenkovic, Aleksandar, The University of Alabama, Huntsville
Millard, Bruce R., Arizona State University
Miller, Holmes E., Muhlenberg College
Miller, Joseph B., University of Kentucky
Milosevic, Milos, Schlumberger Technology Corporation
Minoli, Daniel, Stevens Institute of Technology
Mirchandani, Vinod, The University of Sydney, Australia
Miscetti, Stefano, Laboratori Nazionali di Frascati dell' INFN, Italy
Mishra, Piyush, Michigan Technological University
Misra, Christopher, University of Massachusetts, Amherst
Mitchell, John, University College London, UK
Mitchell, Joseph N., Southwest Research Institute, San Antonio
Moerman, Ingrid, Ghent University, Belgium
Mohanty, Saraju P., University of North Texas
Moision, Bruce, Jet Propulsion Laboratory (JPL), California Institute of Technology
Mokhtar, Simohamed Lotfy, Ecole Militaire Polytechnique, Algeria
Monberg, John, University of Kansas
Montante, Robert, Bloomsburg University of Pennsylvania
Montpetit, Marie-Jose, Motorola Connected Home Solutions
Morgan, Brian M., Marshall University
Moser, Allen W., Everett Community College
Mostafa, Javed, Indiana University, Bloomington
Motlagh, Bahman S., University of Central Florida
Mucchi, Lorenzo, University of Florence, Italy
Mueller, Milton L., Syracuse University
Murata, Masayuki, Osaka University, Japan
Murphy, John, University College Dublin, Ireland
Murphy, Richard, Southwest Research Institute, San Antonio, Texas
Murray, Alan, Ohio State University

Naimi, Linda L., Purdue University
Nair, Suku, Southern Methodist Unversity
Natarajan, Preethi, University of Delaware
Nelson, David Allen, University of Central Oklahoma
Nesbary, Dale, Oakland University
Neufeld, Derrick J., The University of Western Ontario, Canada
Neuman, Clifford, University of Southern California
Ngom, Alioune, University of Windsor, Canada
Ni, Jun, University of Iowa
Niar, Smail, University of Valenciennes, France
Nickerson, Matthew, Southern Utah University
Nithiyanandam, N., Sri Venkateswara College of Engineering, India
Noble, Bradley L., Southern Illinois University, Edwardsville
Nohlberg, Marcus, University of Skövde, Sweden
Noll, John, Santa Clara University
Nolle, Daniel E., United States Treasury Department
Noonan, Liam, Tipperary Institute, Ireland
Nuaymi, Loutfi, ENST Bretagne, France

Okazaki, Shintaro, Autonomous University of Madrid, Spain
Olan, Michael J., Richard Stockton College
Oldham, Joseph D., Centre College
Ole Bernsen, Niels, University of Southern Denmark, Denmark
Oliver Jr., Walter E., Howard University
Olsen, Torodd, Telenor Research and Innovation
Ong, Hong, Oak Ridge National Laboratory (ORNL)
Ortiz, Therezita K., St Petersburg College
Östling, Per-Erik, Aalborg University, Denmark
Ostrowski, John W., California State University, Long Beach
Ozmen, Andy, University of Cambridge, UK

Pagli, Linda, Dipartimento di Informatica, Pisa, Italy
Pak Shing, Cho, CeLight, Inc.
Palazzo, Sergio, Università di Catania, Italy
Paliwal, Kuldip K., Griffith University, Australia
Panetta, Karen, Tufts University
Pang, Qixiang, The University of British Columbia, Canada
Pangburn, Michael S., University of Oregon
Pantos, George, National Technical University of Athens, Greece
Paolo, Bellavista, DEIS—Università degli Studi di Bologna, Italy
Paprzycki, Marcin, Polish Academy of Science, Poland
Paragas, Fernando, University of the Philippines, Philippines
Parks, Lance Michael, Cosumnes River College
Parlos, Alexander G., Texas A&M University
Parssian, Amir, Instituto de Empresa
Passarella, Andrea, University of Cambridge, UK
Patel, Nilesh, University of Michigan, Dearborn
Patel, Ram Bahadur, M. M. Engineering College, India
Patrick, Eric, Northwestern University
Pelish, Matthew D., University at Albany, SUNY
Pérez, Jorge, Kennesaw State University
Perkis, Andrew, The Norwegian University of Science and Technology, Norway
Perlot, Nicolas, German Aerospace Center (DLR), Germany
Peroni, Isidoro, Università degli Studi di Roma, Italy
Perrig, Adrian, Carnegie Mellon University
Phanse, Kaustubh S., Luleå University of Technology, Sweden
Phifer, Lisa, Core Competence Inc.
Phillips, W. Greg, Royal Military College of Canada, Canada
Piotrowski, Victor, University of Wisconsin, Superior
Place, Jerry P., University of Missouri, Kansas City

Podell, Harold J., Johns Hopkins University
Polajnar, Andrej, University of Maribor, Slovenia
Poland, Ron A., Clinton Community College
Polycarpou, Andreas H., University of Denver
Ponterio, Robert, SUNY College, Cortland
Pontes, Marlene, WiNGS Telecom, Brazil
Poole, Melissa J., University of Missouri, Columbia
Porter, J. David, Oregon State University
Porter, Jr., Lon A., Wabash College
Potkonjak, Miodrag, University of California, Los Angeles
Poutrina, Ekaterina, University of Rochester
Pratter, Frederick E., Eastern Oregon University
Preece, Alun, University of Aberdeen, UK
Preston, Jon A., Clayton State University
Pritsky, N. Todd, Hill Associates, Inc., and Champlain College
Prunier, James (Tom), Southwestern College
Pucella, Riccardo, Northeastern University
Puliafito, Antonio, Università di Messina, Italy

Qad, Ala, University of Nebraska, Lincoln

Ra, Ikyeun, University of Colorado, Denver and Health Sciences Center
Raatikainen, Pertti, VTT Telecommunications, Finland
Rachidi, Tajje-eddine, Al Akhawayn Univertsity, Morocco
Radu, Mihaela E., Rose-Hulman Institute of Technology
Raghuwanshi, Pravin M., DeVry University
Raja, M. Yasin Akhtar, University of North Carolina, Charlotte
Rajput, Saeed, Think-Sync, Inc.
Rakocevic, Veselin, City University, UK
Rao, Soma Venugopal, Indian Institute of Technology, India
Rapeli, Juha, University of Oulu, Finland
Rasmussen, Jeremy, Sypris Electronics, LLC
Raynal, Michel, Irisa Université de Rennes 1, France
Razaghi, Peyman, University of Toronto, Canada
Razavi, Mohsen, Massachusetts Institute of Technology
Razmov, Valentin, University of Washington
Recor, Jeff, CTG, Inc.
Redi, Jason K., BBN Technologies
Reed, Lisa J., University of Portland
Refai, Hakki H., The University of Oklahoma, Tulsa
Rehrl, Karl, Salzburg Research, Austria
Reichinger, Kurt, Vienna University of Technology, Austria
Reichl, Peter, Telecommunications Research Center Vienna (ftw.), Austria
Reiher, Peter, University of California, Los Angles
Reinschmidt, Kenneth F., Texas A&M University
Reiter, Joshua J., Johns Hopkins University
Ren, Jian, Michigan State University
Requicha, Aristides A. G., University of Southern California
Riabov, Vladimir V., Rivier College
Richard A. Stanley, Worcester Polytechnic Institute
Robila, Stefan A., Montclair State University
Rogers, David V., Communications Research Centre, Canada
Rollins, Sami, Mount Holyoke College
Romero, Alfonso E., University of Granada, Spain
Rose, Chris, Erudio College
Roset, Cesare, University of Rome "Tor Vergata," Italy
Rosu, Marcel C., IBM T. J. Watson Research Center
Rovati, Luigi, University of Modena and Reggio Emilia, Italy
Rupf, John A., Southern Polytechnic State University
Ryan, Kevin, Stevens Institute of Technology
Ryoo, Jungwoo, Pennsylvania State University, Altoona

Sabelli, Nora H., SRI International
Sachdev, D. K., SpaceTel Consultancy LLC and George Mason University
Saengudomlert, Poompat, Asian Institute of Technology, Thailand
Safaai Jazi, Ahmad, Vigina Tech
Salane, Douglas E., John Jay College of Criminal Justice
Saliba, Anthony, Charles Sturt University, Australia
Saligheh Rad, Hamidreza, Harvard University
Sampei, Seiichi, Osaka University, Japan
Sandy, Mary F., DePaul University
Sankar, Ravi, University of South Florida
Sarac, Kamil, University of Texas, Dallas
Satterlee, Brian, Liberty University
Savoie, Michael J., The University of Texas, Dallas
Schaumont, Patrick, Virginia Tech
Scheets, George, Oklahoma State University
Schlager, Mark, SRI International
Schmidt, Dieter S., University of Cincinnati
Schmitz, Corby, Loyola University Chicago
Schneider, Gerardo, University of Oslo, Norway
Schoute, Frits C., Delft University of Technology, The Netherlands
Schreiner, Wolfgang, Johannes Kepler University, Austria
Schubin, Mark, Technological Consultant
Schultz, E. Eugene, High Tower Software
Schwaig, Kathy S., Kennesaw State University
Schwarz, Thomas, S. J., Santa Clara University
Schwebel, Joseph P., University of St. Thomas
Scornavacc, Eusebio, Victoria University of Wellington, New Zealand
Seltzer, Wendy, Berkman Center for Internet & Society, Harvard Law
Selviah, David R., University College London, UK
Semrau, Penelope, California State University, Los Angeles
Servetti, Antonio, Politecnico di Torino, Italy
Sessions, Chad, Essex Corporation
Sethi, Adarshpal, University of Delaware
Shah, Dinesh S., Portland State University
Shah, Rahul, Intel Corporation
Shalunov, Stanislav, Internet2
Shamsi, Mehrdad, University of Toronto, Canada
Shand, Brian, University of Cambridge, UK
Shank, Patti, Learning Peaks LLC
Shao, Zili, The Hong Kong Polytechnic University, Hong Kong
Sharma, Vimal, Cardiff University, UK
Shay, William, University of Wisconsin, Green Bay
Shedletsky, Leonard J., University of Southern Maine
Shen, Dou, Hong Kong University of Science and Technology, Hong Kong
Shepard, Scott, University of Central Florida
Sherman, Richard C., Miami University
Shi, Qicai, Motorola Labs
Shimeall, Timothy J., Carnegie Mellon University
Shin, Dongwan, New Mexico Tech
Shokrani, Arash, Carlton University, Canada
Shrestha, Deepesh Man, Ajou University, South Korea
Shumba, Rose, Indiana University of Pennsylvania
Siekkinen, Matti, University of Oslo, Norvay

Simco, Greg, Nova Southeastern University
Simmons, Ken, Augusta Technical College
Simpson, Jr., Charles Robert (Robby), Georgia Institute of Technology
Singh, Manpreet, Cornell University and Google
Singh, Nirvikar, University of California, Santa Cruz
Singh, Vijay P., University of Kentucky
Sisalem, Dorgham, Tekelec Inc.
Sivrikaya, Fikret, Rensselaer Polytechnic Institute
Skoglund, Mikael, Royal Institute of Technology, Sweden
Slay, Jill, University of South Australia, Australia
Slimani, Yahya, Sciences of Tunis, Tunisia
Sloan, Joseph H., Webster University
Smith, Alan, BT Group
Smit, Anthony H., Purdue University
Smith II, Raife F., Southern University
Smith, Garry, University of Edinburgh, UK
Smith, Lloyd M., University of Wisconsin, Madison
Smith, Richard E., University of St. Thomas
Snow, Charles, George Mason University
Somasundaram, Siva, Stevens Institute of Technology
Song, Hongjun, University of Memphis
Song, Xiaoyu, Portland State University
Sopitkamol, Monchai, Kasetsart University, Thailand
Spegel, Marjan, J. Stefan Institute, Slovenia
Speidel, Joachim, University of Stuttgart, Germany
Spon, Kenneth, Federal Reserve Bank of Kansas City
Srinivasan, Bhaskar, Robert Bosch Corporation
Stachursk, Dale, University of Maryland, University College
Stackpole, Bill R., Rochester Institute of Technology
Stahl, Bernd Carsten, De Montfort University, UK
Stamp, Mark, San Jose State University
Stan, Sorin G., Philips Consumer Electronics, The Netherlands
Stastny, Richard, OeFEG Telekom, Austria
Stavrou, Angelos, Columbia University
Stavrou, Stavros, University of Surrey, UK
Steckler, Brian D., Naval Postgraduate School
Stefanov, Andrej, Polytechnic University
Stefanovic, Darko, University of New Mexico
Stern, Harold P. E., University of Alabama
Stevens, J. Richard, Southern Methodist University
Stiber, Michael, University of Washington, Bothell
Stiemerling, Oliver, ecambria systems GmbH, Germany
Stolfo, Salvatore J., Columbia University
Stork, Milan, University of West Bohemia, Czech Republic
Stout, Glenn Allan, Colorado Technical University
Striegel, Aaron, University of Notre Dame
Stylianos Drakatos, Florida International University
Sud, Seema, George Mason University
Suh, Changsu, Hanback Electronic, Republic of Korea
Sullivan, Richard J., Federal Reserve Bank of Kansas City
Sun, Chen, ATR Wave Engineering Laboratories, Japan
Sun, Hongxia, University of Calgary, Canada
Sun, Zhili, University of Surrey, UK
Sunda, S. Shyam, Penn State University
Sung, Dan Keun, Korea Advanced Institute of Science and Technology, Korea
Sur, Sayantan, The Ohio State University
Swedin, Eric G., Weber State University

Tabak, Leon, Cornell College
Tang, Zaiyong, Louisiana Tech University
Tangsangiumvisai, Nisachon, Chulalongkorn University, Thailand
Tarhuni, Naser G., Helsinki University of Technology, Finland
Tayahi, Moncef Benjamin, University of Nevada, Reno
Taylor, Nolan J., Indiana University, Indianapolis
Teitelbaum, Ben, Internet2 and BitTorrent
Tel, Gerard, University of Utrecht, The Netherlands
Temelkuran, Burak, Omniguide, Inc.
Terrell, Thomas F., University of South Florida
Tewari, Hitesh, Trinity College, Ireland
Teyeb, Oumer M., Aalborg University, Denmark
Thiruvathukal, George K., Loyola University, Chicago
Thomas, George, University of Louisiana, Lafayette
Thomas, Joseph R., University of Maryland
Thompson, Charles, Univeristy of Massachusetts, Lowell
Thompson, Dale R., University of Arkansas
Thompson, Steve C., University of California, San Diego
Thorne, Steven L., The Pennsylvania State University
Tirkel, Andrew, Monash University, Australia
Todd, Byron, Tallahassee Community College
Tomasin, Stefano, University of Padova, Italy
Tomažič, Sačo, University of Ljubljana, Slovenia
Tomlin, Chas, University of Southampton, UK
Toniatti, Tiziana, Siemens Networks
Toppin, Ian N., Clayton State University
Toumpis, Stavros, University of Cyprus, Cyprus
Trabelsi, Chokri, Lucent Technologies
Tran, Duc A., University of Dayton
Traynor, Patrick, Penn State University
Trigon, Niki, University of London, UK
Trostmann, Manfred F., University of Maryland, University College, Europe
Troxel, Ian, University of Florida
Tucker, Catherine, Massachusetts Institute of Technology
Turner, Stephen W., The University of Michigan, Flint
Tweedy, Edward, Rockingham Community College
Tyrer, Harry W., University of Missouri, Columbia

Ugur, Ahmet, Central Michigan University
Ugweje, Okechukwu, The University of Akron
Ulusoy, Özgür, Bilkent University, Turkey
Umar, Amjad, University of Pennsylvania
Uyar, Ahmet, At Mersin University, Mersin, Turkey

Valcourt, Scott A., University of New Hampshire
Van Camp, Julie C., California State University, Long Beach
Van den Boom, Henrie, Eindhoven University of Technology, The Netherlands
Van Engelen, Robert, Florida State University
Van Hook, Pamela, DeVry University
VanDeGrift, Tammy, University of Portland
Vanderster, Daniel C., University of Victoria, Canada
Vanelli-Coralli, Alessandro, University of Bologna, Italy
Varela, Martin, VTT Electronics, Finland
Vartiainen, Matti, Helsinki University of Technology, Finland
Vasconcelos, Wamberto Weber, University of Aberdeen, UK
Vaughan, Norman Vaughan, The University of Calgary, Canada

Venables, Phil, Independent Consultant
Verdurmen, E. J. M., Eindhoven University of Technology, The Netherlands
Verticale, Giacomo, Politecnico di Milano, Italy
Vidács, Attila, Budapest University of Technology and Economics, Hungary
Viehland, Dennis, Massey University, New Zealand
Villanti, Marco, DEIS—University of Bologna, Italy
Vishnevsky, Vladimir M., Russian Academy of Sciences, Russia
Viswanathan, Harish, Bell Labs, Alcatel-Lucent
Vivekanandan, Vijayanth, The University of British Columbia, Canada
Vogel, Christine, University of Texas, Austin
Vyavahare, Prakash, SGSITS, India

Wahl, Mark, University of Texas, Austin
Walden, Eric, Texas Tech University
Wall, Kevin W., Qwest Information Technologies, Inc.
Wallace, Layne, University of North Florida
Wan, Tat-Chee, Universiti Sains Malaysia, Malaysia
Wang, David C., Verizon Communications
Wang, Haomin, Dakota State University
Wang, Lan, University of Memphis
Wang, Minhua, State University of New York, Canton
Wang, Qian, Dublin Institute of Technology, Ireland
Wang, Suosheng, Indiana University
Wang, Yongge, University of North Carolina, Charlotte
Wang, Yu, University of North Carolina, Charlotte
Wang, Zhicheng, Clark Atlanta University
Warfield, Andrew, University of Cambridge, UK
Weatherspoon, Hakim, University of California, Berkeley
Webb, William, Ofcom, UK
Weinig, Shelly, Colombia University
Wellens, Matthias, RWTH Aachen University, Germany
Werstein, Paul, University of Otago, New Zealand
Whitaker, Roger, Cardiff University, UK
White, Curt M., DePaul University
White, Gregory B., The University of Texas, San Antonio
White, Stephanie, Long Island University
Wietfeld, Christian, University of Dortmund, Germany
Wijesekera, Duminda, George Mason University
Wilkerson, Trena Lashley, Baylor University
Wilkinson, Anthony Barry, University of North Carolina, Charlotte
Wilkinson, Timothy D., University of Cambridge, UK
Williams, Kevin, University of Cambridge, UK
Williamson, Carey, University of Calgary, Canada
Wilson, C. Diane, Central Missouri State University
Wing, William R., Oak Ridge National Labs
Witschnig, Harald, Philips Semiconductors, Austria
Wolff, Richard S., Montana State University
Wong, Yue-Ling, Wake Forest University
Wood, David, MITRE Corporation
Woolley, Sandra I., University of Birmingham, UK
Wu, Jingxian, Sonoma State University
Wu, Ke-Li, The Chinese University of Hong Kong, Hong Kong
Wu, Kui, University of Victoria, Canada
Wu, Ningning, University of Arkansas, Little Rock
Wu, Zhiqiang (John), Wright State University
Wulich, Dov, Ben-Gurion University, Israel
Wykle, Helen H., University of North Carolina, Asheville

Xiao, Yang, The University of Memphis
Xie, Shizhong, Tsinghua University, China
Xu, Kaixin, Scalable Network Technologies, Inc.
Xu, Xizhen, New Jersey Institute of Technology
Xue, Fei, University of California, Davis

Yagami, Raymond, University of Maryland
Yam, Scott S-H., Queen's University, Canada
Yamagiwa, Shinichi, INESC-ID/IST, Portugal
Yang, Cheer-Sun, West Chester University
Yang, Laurence T., St. Francis Xavier University, Canada
Yang, Lie-Liang, University of Southampton, UK
Yang, Shanchieh Jay, Rochester Institute of Technology
Yang, Xiuge, Ansoft Corporation
Yang, Y. R., Yale University
Yao, JingTao, University of Regina, Canada
Yao, Wenbing, Brunel University, UK
Yaprak, Ece, Wayne State University
Yedavalli, Kiran, University of Southern California
Yee, Wai Gen, Illinois Institute of Technology
Yi, Kwan, University of Kentucky
Yi, Yunjung, Honeywell Inc.
Yildiz, Melda N., William Paterson University
Yin, Lijun, State University of New York, Binghamton
Yin, Si, New Jersey Institute of Technology
Yoneki, Eiko, University of Cambridge, UK
Yoon, Jaewan, Old Dominion University
Youssef, Mahmoud, Rutgers University
Yu, Ming, State University of New York
Yu, William Emmanuel S., Ateneo de Manila University, Philippines
Yu, Chansu, Cleveland State University
Yuksel, Murat, Rensselaer Polytechnic Institute

Zaharov, Viktor, Polytechnic University of Puerto Rico
Zakhidov, Erkin, Uzbekistan Academy of Sciences, Uzbekistan
Zaki, Mohammed J., Rensselaer Polytechnic Institute
Zaman, Muhammad H., The University of Texas, Austin
Zawacki-Richter, Olaf, HfB—Business School of Finance & Management, Germany
Zehm, Brenda, Axia College of Western International University
Zekavat, Seyed Alireza (Reza), Michigan Technological University
Zeng, Qing-An, University of Cincinnati
Zerfos, Petros, Deutsche Telekom Laboratories, Germany
Zghal, Mourad, Sup'Com, Tunisie
Zhang, Chi, Florida International University
Zhang, Jinye, University of Victoria, Canada
Zhang, Liqiang, Indiana University, South Bend
Zhang, Zhao, Iowa State University
Zhao, Jiying, University of Ottawa, Canada
Zhao, Julie Yuhua, Miami University
Zho, Bo, University of Surrey, UK
Zhou, Luying, Institute for Infocomm Research, Singapore
Zhou, Zhaoxian, University of Southern Mississippi
Zhu Liu, AT&T Labs, Research
Zhu, Yifeng, University of Maine
Zimermann, Alfred E., Hawai'i Pacific University
Zou, Hanli, Broadcom Corporation
Zubairi, Junaid Ahmed, State University of New York, Fredonia
Zuo, Yongrong, Qualcomm Incorporated
Zuuring, Hans, University of Montana
Zvonar, Zoran, Analog Devices

Index

Page numbers followed by an *f* indicate that the entry is included in a figure.
Page numbers followed by a *t* indicate that the entry is included in a table.